Teacher's Edition

Prentice Hall EARTH SCIENCE

New York
Physical Setting/Earth Science

Contents in Brief

See Program Component List on page NY 2

Teacher's Edition

Prentice Hall EARTH SCIENCE

Physical Setting/Earth Science

Tarbuck ◆ Lutgens

Illustrated by **Dennis Tasa**

PEARSON
Prentice Hall

Needham, Massachusetts
Upper Saddle River, New Jersey

Dear New York Earth Science Teacher

This first edition of *Prentice Hall Earth Science* follows the tradition, philosophy, and pedagogy of our introductory college text, *Earth Science,* that is in its Tenth Edition. *Prentice Hall Earth Science* is intended to provide a thorough survey of the Earth Sciences for students with limited backgrounds in the subject. In creating this high school edition, every part of the book was examined to update content and improve the clarity of the narrative. We have attempted to provide clear, readable discussions of topics in a format that helps students identify key concepts with frequent headings to guide the way. Chapters are broken down into topic clusters followed by section assessments to monitor students' understanding. The important theme, *Earth as a System,* is introduced in Chapter 1 and then carried throughout the book to help students develop an awareness and appreciation of the important interdependencies among Earth's spheres.

The outstanding illustration program that has been the hallmark of our college titles is also an important feature of this program. Dennis Tasa, a gifted artist and award winning Earth Science illustrator, has once again brought the subject to life with outstanding instructional illustrations and maps. MapMaster activities have been created to support geographical literacy in the context of Earth Science concepts.

This book was also designed and written with the New York Physical Setting/Earth Science course in mind. The Core Curriculum is woven into every chapter, as you will see in the correlations on the pages that follow. In addition, a special profile of New York was included to ensure that state-specific standards have been thoroughly addressed. Students are given the tools they need to understand the Core Curriculum for Earth Science with ample Regents practice found throughout the text. The program components address the variety of instructional needs you face daily in dealing with a diverse student population. Careful attention has been paid to providing the media and technology components that help students recognize that today's Earth is a continuous work in progress. When students actively work with these materials they are better able to comprehend the time frames over which Earth's dynamic processes occur.

Your Teacher's Edition is a new endeavor designed to keep you current in the subject matter and provides useful instructional tools. Welcome to *Prentice Hall Earth Science.* We hope you and your students enjoy the experience.

Sincerely,
Ed Tarbuck
Fred Lutgens

Credits begin on page 802, which constitutes an extension of this copyright page.

ISBN 0-13-126034-0

1 2 3 4 5 6 7 8 9 10   10 09 08 07 06 05 04

Integrated Professional Development

Your New York Teacher's Edition can help you manage and improve your daily instruction. Features herein will help you meet the demands of standards mastery, classroom diversity, and hand-on science instruction.

Standards-Based Instruction

The Regents Earth Science Core Curriculum is organized to use as a guide for how you will structure your teaching, and how much time you will spend on any given concept.

Year at a Glance

Use this chart for a long-range view of where the Core Curriculum Standards for Physical Setting/Earth Science are covered in *Prentice Hall Earth Science.*

Section-by-Section Correlation and Pacing

Use this chart for long- and short-term planning to ensure coverage of all the Core Curriculum Objectives are covered in your Earth Science course for full-year periods or half-year blocks and with students working above and below grade level.

Professional Development

Explore educational research and its application to various aspects of instruction and find out how *Prentice Hall Earth Science* incorporates this research to aid your growth and development as a teacher. The topics included are:

- **Research**
- **Inquiry**
- **Reading**
- **Geographic Literacy**
- **Earth System Science**
- **Differentiated Instruction**
- **Science, Technology, and Society**
- **Internet Literacy**
- **Assessment**

Master Materials List

Find a complete listing of all the materials you need for the Student Edition activities.

Physical Setting/Earth Science Content Progression

Use the charts on the following pages for an overview of where the Mathematics, Science, and Technology Learning Standards and the Core Curriculm are covered in *Prentice Hall Earth Science*. Standard 4 which contains the Earth Science Content Standards is listed last. The complete text for all of the Learning Standards can be found on the New York State Department of Education website.

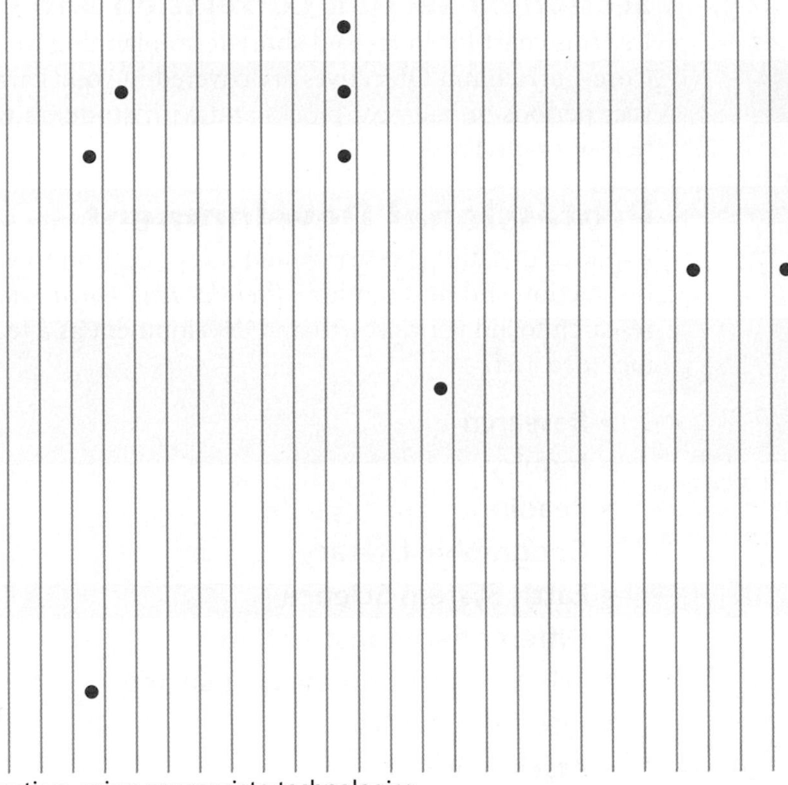

Physical Setting/Earth Science	EARTH SCIENCE CHAPTERS																									
	1	2	3	4	5	6	7	8	9	10	11	11A	12	13	14	15	16	17	18	19	20	21	22	23	24	25
STANDARD 1 Analysis, Inquiry, and Design use mathematical analysis, scientific inquiry, and engineering design, as appropriate, to pose questions, seek answers, and develop solutions.																										
MATHEMATICAL ANALYSIS																										
KEY IDEA 1 Abstraction and symbolic representation are used to communicate mathematically.												●														
KEY IDEA 2 Deductive and inductive reasoning are used to reach mathematical conclusions.					●							●														
KEY IDEA 3 Critical thinking skills are used in the solution of mathematical problems.				●								●														
SCIENTIFIC INQUIRY																										
KEY IDEA 1 The central purpose of scientific inquiry is to develop explanations of natural phenomena in a continuing, creative process.																							●			●
KEY IDEA 2 Beyond the use of reasoning and consensus, scientific inquiry involves the testing of proposed explanations involving the use of conventional techniques and procedures and usually requiring considerable ingenuity.															●											
KEY IDEA 3 The observations made while testing proposed explanations, when analyzed using conventional and invented methods, provide new insights into phenomena.																										
ENGINEERING DESIGN																										
KEY IDEA 1 Engineering design is an iterative process involving modeling and optimization (finding the best solution within given constraints); this process is used to develop technological solutions to problems within given constraints.				●																						
STANDARD 2 Access, generate, process, and transfer information, using appropriate technologies.																										
INFORMATION SYSTEMS																										
KEY IDEA 1 Information technology is used to retrieve, process, and communicate information as a tool to enhance learning.												●	●		●										●	
KEY IDEA 2 Knowledge of the impacts and limitations of information systems is essential to its effective and ethical use.												●														
KEY IDEA 3 Information technology can have positive and negative impacts on society, depending upon how it is used.					▲		●		●			●		●						●						

Physical Setting/Earth Science	EARTH SCIENCE CHAPTERS																								
	1	2	3	4	5	6	7	8	9	10	11	11A	12	13	14	15	16	17	18	19	20	21	22	23	24	25
STANDARD 6 Interconnectedness: Common Themes understand the relationships and common themes that connect mathematics, science, and technology and apply the themes to these and other areas of learning.																										
SYSTEMS THINKING KEY IDEA 1 Through systems thinking, people can recognize the commonalities that exist among all systems and how parts of a system interrelate and combine to perform specific functions.						●						●														
MODELS KEY IDEA 2 Models are simplified representations of objects, structures, or systems used in analysis, explanation, interpretation, or design.		●	●				●	●			●				●											
MAGNITUDE AND SCALE KEY IDEA 3 The grouping of magnitudes of size, time, frequency, and pressures or other units of measurement into a series of relative order provides a useful way to deal with the immense range and the changes in scale that affect the behavior and design of systems.	●											●	●	●										●		
EQUILIBRIUM AND STABILITY KEY IDEA 4 Equilibrium is a state of stability due either to a lack of change (static equilibrium) or a balance between opposing forces (dynamic equilibrium).																								●		
PATTERNS OF CHANGE KEY IDEA 5 Identifying patterns of change is necessary for making predictions about future behavior and conditions.		●						●			●	●	●			●		●	●	●				●		
OPTIMIZATION KEY IDEA 6 In order to arrive at the best solution that meets criteria within constraints, it is often necessary to make trade-offs				●								●							●			●				
STANDARD 7 Interdisciplinary Problem Solving apply the knowledge and thinking skills of mathematics, science, and technology to address real-life problems and make informed decisions.																										
CONNECTIONS KEY IDEA 1 The knowledge and skills of mathematics, science, and technology are used together to make informed decisions and solve problems, especially those relating to issues of science/technology/society, consumer decision making, design, and inquiry into phenomena.			●	●								●	●									●				
STRATEGIES KEY IDEA 2 Solving interdisciplinary problems involves a variety of skills and strategies, including effective work habits; gathering and processing information; generating and analyzing ideas; realizing ideas; making connections among the common themes of mathematics, science, and technology; and presenting results.	●							●		●	●	●		●							●			●		
STANDARD 4 Understand and apply scientific concepts, principles, and theories pertaining to the physical setting and living environment and recognize the historical development of ideas in science.																										
KEY IDEA 1 The Earth and celestial phenomena can be described by principles of relative motion and perspective. INDICATOR 1 Explain complex phenomena, such as tides, variations in day length, solar insolation, apparent motion of the planets, and annual traverse of the constellations.																●									●	

Physical Setting/Earth Science	EARTH SCIENCE CHAPTERS																									
	1	2	3	4	5	6	7	8	9	10	11	11A	12	13	14	15	16	17	18	19	20	21	22	23	24	25
1.1.a. Most objects in the solar system are in regular and predictable motion.																	●						●	●		●
1.1.b. Nine planets move around the Sun in nearly circular orbits.																							●	●	●	●
1.1.c. Earth's coordinate system of latitude and longitude, with the equator and prime meridian as reference lines, is based upon Earth's rotation and our observation of the Sun and stars.	●																						●			●
1.1.d. Earth rotates on an imaginary axis at a rate of 15 degrees per hour. To people on Earth, this turning of the planet makes it seem as though the Sun, the moon, and the stars are moving around Earth once a day. Rotation provides a basis for our system of local time; meridians of longitude are the basis for time zones.	●																						●	●		
1.1.e. The Foucault pendulum and the Coriolis effect provide evidence of Earth's rotation.																				●			●			
1.1.f. Earth's changing position with regard to the Sun and the moon has noticeable effects.																	●	●					●			
1.1.g. Seasonal changes in the apparent positions of constellations provide evidence of Earth's revolution.																							●			
1.1.h. The Suns apparent path through the sky varies with latitude and season.																										
1.1.i. Approximately 70 percent of Earth's surface is covered by a relatively thin layer of water, which responds to the gravitational attraction of the moon and the Sun with a daily cycle of high and low tides.																	●						●			
INDICATOR 2 Describe current theories about the origin of the universe and solar system.	●																									
2.a. The universe is vast and estimated to be over ten billion years old. The current theory is that the universe was created from an explosion called the Big Bang.	●																						●		●	●
2.b. Stars form when gravity causes clouds of molecules to contract until nuclear fusion of light elements into heavier ones occurs. Fusion releases great amounts of energy over millions of years.	●																								●	●
2.c. Our solar system formed about five billion years ago from a giant cloud of gas and debris. Gravity caused Earth and the other planets to become layered according to density differences in their materials.	●																						●	●	●	●
2.d. Asteroids, comets, and meteors are components of our solar system.													●								●	●	●	●		
2.e. Earth's early atmosphere formed as a result of the outgassing of water vapor, carbon dioxide, nitrogen, and lesser amounts of other gases from its interior.	●		●											●												
2.f. Earth's oceans formed as a result of precipitation over millions of years. The presence of an early ocean is indicated by sedimentary rocks of marine origin, dating back about four billion years.			●										●		●	●	●		●							
2.g. Earth has continuously been recycling water since the outgassing of water early in its history. This constant recirculation of water at and near Earth's surface is described by the hydrologic (water) cycle.	●			●	●	●						●		●					●							

Physical Setting/Earth Science	EARTH SCIENCE CHAPTERS																									
	1	2	3	4	5	6	7	8	9	10	11	11A	12	13	14	15	16	17	18	19	20	21	22	23	24	25
2.h. The evolution of life caused dramatic changes in the composition of Earth's atmosphere. Free oxygen did not form in the atmosphere until oxygen-producing organisms evolved.														●												
2.i. The pattern of evolution of life-forms on Earth is at least partially preserved in the rock record.													●	●										●		
2.j. Geologic history can be reconstructed by observing sequences of rock types and fossils to correlate bedrock at various locations.	●		●								●	●	●	●												
KEY IDEA 2 Many of the phenomena that we observe on Earth involve interactions among components of air, water, and land.																										
INDICATOR 2.1 Use the concepts of density and heat energy to explain observations of weather patterns, seasonal changes, and the movements of Earth's plates.																		●	●	●						
2.1.a. Earth systems have internal and external sources of energy, both of which create heat.	●			●														●								
2.1.b. The transfer of heat energy within the atmosphere, the hydrosphere, and Earth's interior results in the formation of regions of different densities. These density differences result in motion.	●															●		●		●						
2.1.c. Weather patterns become evident when weather variables are observed, measured, and recorded. These variables include air temperature, air pressure, moisture (relative humidity and dewpoint), precipitation (rain, snow, hail, sleet, etc.), wind speed and direction, and cloud cover.					●		●					●						●	●	●	●					
2.1.d. Weather variables are measured using instruments such as thermometers, barometers, psychrometers, precipitation gauges, anemometers, and wind vanes.																			●	●	●					
2.1.e. Weather variables are interrelated.					●		●												●	●	●					
2.1.f. Air temperature, dewpoint, cloud formation, and precipitation are affected by the expansion and contraction of air due to vertical atmospheric movement.				●	●													●	●	●	●					
2.1.g. Weather variables can be represented in a variety of formats including radar and satellite images, weather maps (including station models, isobars, and fronts), atmospheric cross-sections, and computer models.	●											●						●	●	●	●					
2.1.h. Atmospheric moisture, temperature and pressure distributions; jet streams, wind; air masses and frontal boundaries; and the movement of cyclonic systems and associated tornadoes, thunderstorms, and hurricanes occur in observable patterns. Loss of property, personal injury, and loss of life can be reduced by effective emergency preparedness.										●		●						●	●	●	●					
2.1.i. Seasonal changes can be explained using concepts of density and heat energy. These changes include the shifting of global temperature zones, the shifting of planetary wind and ocean current patterns, the occurrence of monsoons, hurricanes, flooding, and severe weather.												●			●	●	●	●	●	●	●					
2.1.j. Properties of Earth's internal structure (crust, mantle, inner core, and outer core) can be inferred from the analysis of the behavior of seismic waves (including velocity and refraction).	●							●	●		●															

Content Progression

NEW YORK

Physical Setting/Earth Science

Physical Setting/Earth Science	EARTH SCIENCE CHAPTERS																									
	1	2	3	4	5	6	7	8	9	10	11	11A	12	13	14	15	16	17	18	19	20	21	22	23	24	25
2.1.k. The outward transfer of Earth's internal heat drives convective circulation in the mantle that moves the lithospheric plates comprising Earth's surface.	●							●	●	●					●			●		●						
2.1.l. The lithosphere consists of separate plates that ride on the more fluid asthenosphere and move slowly in relationship to one another, creating convergent, divergent, and transform plate boundaries. These motions indicate Earth is a dynamic geologic system.	●							●	●	●	●	●			●											
2.1.m. Many processes of the rock cycle are consequences of plate dynamics. These include the production of magma (and subsequent igneous rock formation and contact metamorphism) at both subduction and rifting regions, regional metamorphism within subduction zones, and the creation of major depositional basins through down-warping of the crust.			●						●	●	●	●		●	●											
2.1.n. Many of Earth's surface features such as mid-ocean ridges / rifts, trenches / subduction zones/island arcs, mountain ranges (folded, faulted, and volcanic), hot spots, and the magnetic and age patterns in surface bedrock are a consequence of forces associated with plate motion and interaction.	●								●	●	●	●			●											
2.1.o. Plate motions have resulted in global changes in geography, climate, and the patterns of organic evolution.	●								●	●	●	●			●							●				
2.1.p. Landforms are the result of the interaction of tectonic forces and the processes of weathering, erosion, and deposition.	●				●				●	●	●	●		●	●											
2.1.q. Topographic maps represent landforms through the use of contour lines that are isolines connecting points of equal elevation. Gradients and profiles can be determined from changes in elevation over a given distance.	●					●	●					●														
2.1.r. Climate variations, structure, and characteristics of bedrock influence the development of landscape features including mountains, plateaus, plains, valleys, ridges, escarpments, and stream drainage patterns.						●					●	●			●							●				
2.1.s. Weathering is the physical and chemical breakdown of rocks at or near Earth's surface. Soils are the result of weathering and biological activity over long periods of time.	●		●		●		●					●	●	●												
2.1.t. Natural agents of erosion, generally driven by gravity, remove, transport, and deposit weathered rock particles. Each agent of erosion produces distinctive changes in the material that it transports and creates characteristic surface features and landscapes. In certain erosional situations, loss of property, personal injury, and loss of life can be reduced by effective emergency preparedness.		●		●	●	●				●		●														
2.1.u. The natural agents of erosion include: Streams, glaciers, wave action, wind, masss movement.					●	●	●					●			●	●	●									

Physical Setting/Earth Science	EARTH SCIENCE CHAPTERS																									
	1	2	3	4	5	6	7	8	9	10	11	11A	12	13	14	15	16	17	18	19	20	21	22	23	24	25
2.1.v. Patterns of deposition result from a loss of energy within the transporting system and are influenced by the size, shape, and density of the transported particles. Sediment deposits may be sorted or unsorted.						●						●				●										
2.1.w. Sediments of inorganic and organic origin often accumulate in depositional environments. Sedimentary rocks form when sediments are compacted and/or cemented after burial or as the result of chemical precipitation from seawater.			●									●		●		●		●								
INDICATOR 2.2 Explain how incoming solar radiation, ocean currents, and land masses affect weather and climate.												●			●		●		●	●	●	●				
2.2.a. Insolation (solar radiation) heats Earth's surface and atmosphere unequally due to variations in:														●	●			●	●	●	●					
2.2.b. The transfer of heat energy within the atmosphere, the hydrosphere, and Earth's surface occurs as the result of radiation, convection, and conduction.	●													●	●	●	●	●	●	●	●	●			●	
2.2.c. A locations climate is influenced by latitude, proximity to large bodies of water, ocean currents, prevailing winds, vegetative cover, elevation, and mountain ranges.												●			●	●	●	●	●	●	●	●				
2.2.d. Temperature and precipitation patterns are altered by: natural events such as El Niño and volcanic eruptions, or human influences.			●	●						●		●					●	●	●	●	●	●				
KEY IDEA 3 Matter is made up of particles whose properties determine the observable characteristics of matter and its reactivity.																										
INDICATOR 3.1 Explain the properties of materials in terms of the arrangement and properties of the atoms that compose them.		●																								
3.1.a. Minerals have physical properties determined by their chemical composition and crystal structure.		●	●	●								●														
3.1.b. Minerals are formed inorganically by the process of crystallization as a result of specific environmental conditions.		●		●						●					●				●	●						
3.1.c. Rocks are usually composed of one or more minerals.		●	●	●							●	●														

Section-by-Section Correlation and Pacing Guide

Use this organization for long- and short-term planning to ensure coverage of the Core Curriculum in your Earth Science course. The Pacing Guide reflects general times in single periods and blocks, and can be modified to best meet the needs of your students.

Chapter 1: Introduction to Earth Science	Core Curriculum	Pacing Guide	
1.1 What Is Earth Science?	4.1.2., 4.1.2.a., 4.1.2.b., 4.1.2.c., 4.1.2.e., 4.2.1.b., 4.2.2.b.	6.5 periods	3.25 blocks
Earth's Place in the Universe	4.1.2.a., 4.1.2.b., 4.1.2.c.		
1.2 A View of Earth	4.1.2.e., 4.1.2.g., 4.2.1.b., 4.2.1.k., 4.2.1.l., 4.2.1.n., 4.2.1.o., 4.2.1.p., 4.2.2.b.		
1.3 Representing Earth's Surface	4.1.1.c., 4.2.1.q., 6.3., 7.2.		
1.4 Earth System Science	4.1.2.g., 4.2.1.a., 4.2.1.b., 4.2.2.b.		
1.5 What Is Scientific Inquiry?			
Studying Earth from Space	4.1.1.c., 4.1.1.d.		
Determining Latitude and Longitude	4.1.1.c., 4.1.1.d.		

Chapter 2: Minerals	Core Curriculum	Pacing Guide	
2.1 Matter	4.3.1., 4.3.1.a., 4.3.1.b., 4.3.1.c.	7 periods	3.5 blocks
2.2 Minerals	4.3.1.a., 4.3.1.b., 4.3.1.c.		
2.3 Properties of Minerals	4.3.1.a., 4.3.1.b., 4.3.1.c.		
Gemstones	4.3.1.a., 4.3.1.c.		
Mineral Identification	4.3.1.a., 4.3.1.b., 4.3.1.c., 6.2.		

Chapter 3: Rocks	Core Curriculum	Pacing Guide	
3.1 The Rock Cycle	4.1.2.j., 4.2.1.m., 4.2.1.w., 4.3.1.c.	7 periods	3.5 blocks
3.2 Igneous Rocks	4.1.2.j., 4.2.1.m., 4.3.1.c.		
3.3 Sedimentary Rocks	4.1.2.f., 4.1.2.j., 4.2.1.m., 4.2.1.w., 4.3.1.c.		
3.4 Metamorphic Rocks	4.1.2.j., 4.2.1.m., 4.3.1.c., 6.2.		
The Carbon Cycle	4.1.2.e., 4.2.2.d., 6.5., 7.1.		
Rock Identification	4.1.2.j., 4.2.1.m., 4.3.1.a., 4.3.1.c., 6.2.		

Chapter 4: Earth's Resources	Core Curriculum	Pacing Guide	
4.1 Energy and Mineral Resources	4.3.1.a., 4.3.1.b., 4.3.1.c., 6.6., 7.1.	8 periods	4 blocks
4.2 Alternate Energy Sources	6.6., 7.1.		
4.3 Water, Air, and Land Resources	4.1.2.g., 4.2.1.f., 4.2.2.d., 6.6.		
4.4 Protecting Resources	4.2.2.d., 6.6.		
Bingham Canyon, Utah: The Largest Open-Pit Mine	7.1.		
Finding the Product that Best Conserves Resources	1.1., 1.3., 6.6., 7.1.		

Chapter 5: Weather, Soil, and Mass Movements	Core Curriculum	Pacing Guide	
5.1 Weathering	4.2.1.s., 4.2.1.u.	5 periods	2.5 blocks
5.2 Soil	4.1.2.g., 4.2.1.p., 4.2.1.t., 4.2.1.u.		
5.3 Mass Movements	4.1.2.g., 4.2.1.t., 4.2.1.u.		
Effect of Temperature on Chemical Weathering	4.2.1.c., 4.2.1.e., 4.2.1.f., 4.2.1.s.		

*These entries comprise the core course for student working below grade level.

Chapter 6: Running Water and Groundwater	Core Curriculum	Pacing Guide	
6.1 Running Water	1.2., 4.1.2.g., 4.2.1.t., 4.2.1.u.	6 periods	3 blocks
6.2 The Work of Streams	1.2., 4.2.1.r., 4.2.1.u., 4.2.1.v., 6.1.		
6.3 Water Beneath the Surface	4.1.2.g., 4.2.1.q.		
The Ogallala Aquifer: How Long Will the Water Last?	4.1.2.g.		
Investigating the Permeability of Soils	4.1.2.g., 4.2.1.u.		

Chapter 7: Glaciers, Deserts, and Wind	Core Curriculum	Pacing Guide	
7.1 Glaciers	4.2.1.u.	6 periods	3 blocks
7.2 Deserts	4.2.1.c., 4.2.1.e., 4.2.1.s.		
7.3 Landscapes Shaped by Wind	4.2.1.t., 4.2.1.u		
Interpreting a Glacial Landscape	4.2.1.q., 4.2.1.t., 4.2.1.u., 6.2.		

Chapter 8: Earthquakes and Earth's. Interior	Core Curriculum	Pacing Guide	
8.1 What Is an Earthquake?	2.3., 4.2.1.j., 4.2.1.l., 7.2.	6 periods	3 blocks
8.2 Measuring Earthquakes	2.3., 4.2.1.j., 4.2.1.l., 7.2.		
8.3 Destruction from Earthquakes	2.3., 4.2.1.j., 4.2.1.l., 7.2.		
8.4 Earth's Layered Structure	4.2.1.j., 4.2.1.k., 4.2.1.l.		
Locating an Earthquake	4.2.1.j., 4.2.1.l., 6.2., 7.2.		

Chapter 9: Plate Tectonics	Core Curriculum	Pacing Guide	
9.1 Continental Drift	4.2.1.j., 4.2.1.k., 4.2.1.l.	8 periods	4 blocks
9.2 Plate Tectonics	4.2.1.k., 4.2.1.l., 4.2.1.n., 4.2.1.o., 4.2.1.p.		
9.3 Actions at Plate Boundaries	4.2.1.l., 4.2.1.m., 4.2.1.n.		
9.4 Testing Plate Tectonics	4.2.1.k., 4.2.1.l., 4.2.1.n., 4.2.1.o., 4.2.1.p.		
9.5 Mechanisms of Plate Tectonics	4.2.1.j., 4.2.1.k., 4.2.1.l., 4.2.1.n., 4.2.1.o.		
Plate Tectonics into the Future	4.2.1.l., 4.2.1.n., 4.2.1.o., 4.2.1.p., 6.5.		
Paleomagnetism and the Ocean Floor	4.1.2.f., 4.2.1.l., 4.2.1.n.		

Chapter 10: Volcanoes and Other Igneous Activity	Core Curriculum	Pacing Guide	
10.1 The Nature of Volcanic Eruptions	4.2.1.l., 4.2.1.n., 4.2.2.d., 4.3.1.b., 7.2.	3 periods	2.5 blocks
10.2 Intrusive Igneous Activity	4.2.1.m., 4.3.1.b.		
10.3 Plate Tectonics and Igneous Activity	4.2.1.h., 4.2.1.k., 4.2.1.l., 4.2.1.m., 4.2.1.n., 4.2.1.o., 4.2.1.p., 4.2.2.d.		
Melting Temperature of Rocks	4.1.2.j., 4.2.1.k., 4.2.1.l., 4.2.1.m., 4.3.1.c.		

Chapter 11: Mountain Building	Core Curriculum	Pacing Guide	
11.1 Rock Deformation	4.1.2.j., 4.2.1.m., 4.2.1.n., 4.3.1.c.	3 periods	2.5 blocks
11.2 Types of Mountains	4.2.1.l., 4.2.1.n., 4.2.1.r.2		
11.3 Mountain Formation	4.2.1.l., 4.2.1.m., 4.2.1.n., 4.2.1.o., 4.2.1.p., 4.2.1.r.		
The San Andreas Fault System	4.2.1.j., 4.2.1.l., 4.2.1.n.		
Investigating Anticlines and Synclines	4.1.2.j., 4.2.1.j., 4.2.1.m., 4.3.1.c.		
Mountain Building away from Plate Margins	4.2.1.l., 4.2.1.m., 4.2.1.n., 4.2.1.r., 4.2.1.t., 6.2.		
Damaging Earthquakes East of the Rockies	4.2.1.j., 4.2.1.l., 4.2.1.n., 7.2.		

Chapter 12: Geologic Time	Core Curriculum	Pacing Guide	
12.1 Discovering Earth's. History	4.1.2.i., 4.1.2.j., 4.3.1.c.	7 periods	3.5 blocks
12.2 Fossils: Evidence of Past Life	4.1.2.i., 4.1.2.j., 7.1.		
12.3 Dating with Radioactivity	4.1.2.f., 4.1.2.j.		
12.4 The Geologic Time Scale	4.1.2.j., 4.2.1.s., 6.3.		
Using Tree Rings to Date and Study the Recent Past	2.1., 6.5.		
Fossil Occurrence and the Age of Rocks	4.1.2.i., 4.1.2.j., 6.3., 7.1.		

Chapter 13: Earth's. History	Core Curriculum	Pacing Guide	
13.1 Precambrian Time: Vast and Puzzling	4.1.2.e., 4.1.2.g., 4.1.2.h., 4.1.2.j., 4.2.2.a., 4.2.2.b., 6.5.	6 periods	3 blocks
13.2 Paleozoic Era: Life Explodes	4.1.2.e., 4.1.2.h., 4.1.2.i., 4.2.1.p.		
13.3 Mesozoic Era: Age of Reptiles	4.1.2.d. 4.1.2.h., 4.1.2.i., 6.5.		
13.4 Cenozoic Era: Age of Mammals	4.1.2.i., 4.1.2.j., 4.2.1.m., 4.2.1.s., 6.5.		
Demise of the Dinosaurs	4.1.2.d., 4.1.2.i., 4.1.2.j., 7.2.		
Modeling the Geologic Time Scale	4.1.2.i., 4.1.2.j., 6.3.		

Chapter 14: The Ocean Floor	Core Curriculum	Pacing Guide	
14.1 The Vast World Ocean	2.1., 2.3., 4.1.2.f., 4.2.1.l., 4.2.2.b., 4.2.2.c.	5 periods	3 blocks
14.2 Ocean Floor Features	4.1.2.f., 4.2.1.l., 4.2.1.m., 4.2.1.n., 4.2.1.r., 4.2.2.b.		
Explaining Coral Atolls—Darwin's. Hypothesis	4.2.1.l., 4.2.1.n., 4.2.1.p.		
14.3 Seafloor Sediments	1.2., 4.2.1.u., 4.2.1.v., 4.2.1.w.		
14.4 Resources from the Seafloor	4.1.2.f., 4.2.1.i., 4.2.2., 4.2.2.a., 4.2.2.b.		
Modeling Seafloor Depth Transects	4.2.1.l., 4.2.1.n., 6.2.		

Chapter 15: Ocean Water and Ocean Life	Core Curriculum	Pacing Guide	
15.1 The Composition of Sea Water		4 periods	3.5 blocks
15.2 The Diversity of Ocean Life			
15.3 Oceanic Productivity	4.2.1.b., 4.2.2.b.		
How Does Temperature Affect Water Density?	4.2.1.b., 4.2.1.i.		

Chapter 16: The Dynamic Ocean	Core Curriculum	Pacing Guide	
16.1 Ocean Circulation	4.2.1.i., 4.2.2., 4.2.2.b., 4.2.2.c.	6 periods	3 blocks
Shoes and Toys as Drift Meters	4.2.2.b., 4.2.2.c., 4.2.2.d.		
16.2 Waves and Tides	4.1.1., 4.1.1.f., 4.1.1.i., 4.2.1.u., 4.2.2.b.		
16.3 Shoreline Processes and Features	4.2.1.u., 4.2.1.w.		
Graphing Tidal Cycles	4.1.1.a., 4.1.1.i., 6.5.		

Chapter 17: The Atmosphere: Structure and Temperature	Core Curriculum	Pacing Guide	
17.1 Atmosphere Characteristics	4.2.1., 4.2.1.b., 4.2.1.c., 4.2.1.f., 4.2.1.g., 4.2.1.i., 4.2.2.a., 4.2.2.b., 4.2.2.c.	7 periods	3.5 blocks
17.2 Heating the Atmosphere	4.2.1.b., 4.2.1.k., 4.2.2.a., 4.2.2.b.		
17.3 Temperature Controls	4.2.1.c., 4.2.1.f., 4.2.1.h., 4.2.1.k., 4.2.2.a., 4.2.2.b., 4.2.2.c., 4.2.2.d.		
Heating Land and Water	4.2.1.a., 4.2.2.a., 4.2.2.b.		

Chapter 18: Moisture, Clouds, and Precipitation	Core Curriculum	Pacing Guide	
18.1 Water in the Atmosphere	4.1.2.f., 4.1.2.g., 4.2.1., 4.2.1.c., 4.2.1.d., 4.2.1.e., 4.2.1.f., 4.2.2.b., 4.2.2.d., 4.3.1.b.	7 periods	3.5 blocks
18.2 Cloud Formation	4.2.1.c., 4.2.1.e., 4.2.1.f., 4.2.1.g., 4.2.1.h., 4.2.1.i., 4.2.2., 4.2.2.c., 4.2.2.d., 6.5.		
18.3 Cloud Types and Precipitation	4.1.2.g., 4.2.1.c., 4.2.1.e., 4.2.1.f., 4.2.2.a., 4.2.2.b., 4.2.2.d., 4.3.1.b.		
Atmospheric Stability and Air Pollution	4.2.1.c., 4.2.1.e., 4.2.1.f., 4.2.1.h., 4.2.2.b., 6.6.		
Measuring Humidity	4.2.1.c., 4.2.1.d., 4.2.1.e., 4.2.1.f.		

Chapter 19: Air Pressure and Wind	Core Curriculum	Pacing Guide	
19.1 Understanding Air Pressure	4.2.1., 4.2.1.b., 4.2.1.c., 4.2.1.d., 4.2.1.e., 4.2.1.f., 4.2.1.h., 4.2.1.k., 4.2.2.b.	6 periods	3 blocks
19.2 Pressure Centers and Winds	4.2.1.b., 4.2.1.c., 4.2.1.e., 4.2.1.h., 4.2.1.i., 4.2.1.k., 4.2.2.a., 4.2.2.b.		
19.3 Regional Wind Systems	4.2.1.c., 4.2.1.e., 4.2.1.f., 4.2.1.h., 4.2.1.i., 4.2.2., 4.2.2.b., 4.2.2.c., 4.2.2.d.		
Tracking El Niño from Space	4.2.1.g., 4.2.2.c., 4.2.2.d., 4.3.1.b.		
Observing Wind Patterns	4.2.1.c., 4.2.1.d., 4.2.1.e., 4.2.1.f., 4.2.1.g.		

Chapter 20: Weather Patterns and Severe Storms	Core Curriculum	Pacing Guide	
20.1 Air Masses	4.2.1.e., 4.2.1.f., 4.2.1.g., 4.2.1.h., 4.2.2., 4.2.2.a., 4.2.2.b., 4.2.2.c., 4.2.2.d., 6.5.	6 periods	3 blocks
20.2 Fronts	4.2.1.c., 4.2.1.f., 4.2.1.g., 4.2.1.h., 6.5.		
20.3 Severe Storms	2.3., 4.2.1.h., 7.2.		
Middle-Latitude Cyclones	4.2.1.c., 4.2.1.d., 4.2.1.e., 4.2.1.f., 4.2.1.g., 4.2.1.h., 4.2.1.i., 4.2.2.c.		

Chapter 21: Climate	Core Curriculum	Pacing Guide	
21.1 Factors That Affect Climate	4.2.1.r., 4.2.2., 4.2.2.c., 4.2.2.d.	7 periods	3.5 blocks
21.2 World Climates	4.1.2.d., 4.2.1.r., 4.2.2., 4.2.2.c.		
21.3 Climate Changes	4.1.2.d., 4.2.2.d., 6.6., 7.1.		
Human Impact on Climate and Weather	4.2.2.b., 4.2.2.d.		

Chapter 22: Origin of Modern Astronomy	Core Curriculum	Pacing Guide	
22.1 Early Astronomy	1.1., 4.1.1.a., 4.1.1.b., 4.1.2.c., 4.1.2.d.	7 periods	3.5 blocks
22.2 The Earth-Moon-Sun System	4.1.1.a., 4.1.1.b., 4.1.1.d., 4.1.1.f.		
22.3 Earth's. Moon	4.1.1.b., 4.1.1.d., 4.1.1.f.		
Foucault Experiment	4.1.1.c., 4.1.1.d., 4.1.1.e., 4.1.1.f.		
Modeling Synodic and Sidereal Months	4.1.1.a., 4.1.1.b., 4.1.1.d., 4.1.1.f., 4.1.1.g., 4.1.1.i.		

Chapter 23: Touring Our Solar System	Core Curriculum	Pacing Guide	
23.1 The Solar System	4.1.1.a., 4.1.1.b., 4.1.2.c.	7 periods	3.5 blocks
23.2 The Terrestrial Planets	4.1.1.a., 4.1.1.b., 4.1.1.d., 4.1.2.c.		
23.3 The Outer Planets	4.1.1.a., 4.1.1.b., 4.1.1.d., 4.1.2.c.		
23.4 Minor Members of the Solar System	4.1.2.d.		
Is Earth on a Collision Course	4.1.2.d., 4.1.2.i., 7.2.		
Modeling the Solar System	4.1.1.a., 4.1.1.b., 4.1.1.d., 4.1.2.c., 4.1.2.d., 6.3.		

Chapter 24: Studying the Sun	Core Curriculum	Pacing Guide	
24.1 The Study of Light	4.1.2.a.	6 periods	3 blocks
24.2 Tools for Studying Space	2.1.		
24.3 The Sun	4.1.1.b., 4.1.1.f., 4.1.2.b., 4.1.2.c.		
Solar Activity and Climatic Change	4.2.2.b., 6.5.		
Tracking Sunspots	6.5.		

Chapter 25: Beyond Our Solar System	Core Curriculum	Pacing Guide	
25.1 Properties of Stars	1.1., 4.1.1.a., 4.1.1.b., 4.1.2.b.	7 periods	3.5 blocks
25.2 Stellar Evolution	4.1.2.b.		
25.3 The Universe	4.1.2.a., 4.1.2.b., 4.1.2.c.		
Astrology, Forerunner of Astronomy	4.1.1., 4.1.1.a., 4.1.1.b.		
Observing Stars	1.1., 4.1.1.c., 4.1.2.b.		

Chapter 11A: Earth System Profile	Core Curriculum	Pacing Guide	
Growth and Economic Development	1.2., 1.3., 7.1.	5 periods	2.5 blocks
Geological History	4.2.1.l., 4.2.1.m., 4.2.1.n., 4.2.1.o., 4.2.1.p., 4.2.1.u., 4.2.1.w., 6.5		
Physiographic Regions	4.2.1.p., 4.2.1.r., 4.2.1.s., 4.2.1.u.,		
Geology of Landforms	1.2., 4.1.2.j., 4.2.1.p., 4.2.1.q., 4.2.1.r., 4.2.1.t., 4.2.1.u., 4.2.1.v., 4.2.1.w., 4.3.1.a., 4.3.1.c., 6.1., 6.3.		
Natural Resources	4.3.1.a., 4.3.1.c., 6.6., 7.1.		
Ecosystems	4.1.2.g., 4.2.1.c., 4.2.2.d., 6.1., 6.6., 7.1.		
Soil	4.2.1.m., 4.2.1.p., 4.2.1.s., 4.2.1.t., 4.2.1.u., 4.2.1.v., 4.2.1.w.		
Fresh Water	4.1.2.g., 6.1., 6.6.		
Coastal Regions	4.2.1.u., 6.6., 7.1.		
Climate	1.2., 2.1., 4.2.1.c., 4.2.1.g., 4.2.1.h., 4.2.2., 4.2.2.c.		
Weather Patterns	1.1., 1.2., 4.2.1.c., 4.2.1.h., 4.2.1.i., 4.2.2., 4.2.2.c., 6.5.		
Using the Internet to Research Disaster Safety	1.2., 1.3., 2.1., 2.2., 2.3., 4.2.1.h, 7.1., 7.2.		
How Could Global Warming Impact New York?	2.1., 4.2.1.c., 4.2.1.g., 4.2.1.h., 4.2.1.i., 4.2.1.u., 4.2.2., 4.2.2.c., 4.2.2.d., 6.1., 6.6., 7.1.		

National Science Education Standards

Correlation to National Science Education Standards

Content Standard	Chapter/Section
CONTENT STANDARD A • Science as Inquiry	
A-1 Abilities necessary to do scientific inquiry	Inquiry Activity: Chapters 1–25, Exploration Lab: Chapters 1, 2, 3, 5, 6, 7, 8, 9, 10, 11, 12, 14, 15, 16, 17, 18, 19, 22, 23, 24, 25, Quick Lab: Chapters 3, 8, 9, 10, 13, 14, 21, Application Lab: Chapters 4, 13, 20
A-2 Understandings about scientific inquiry	Sections 1.3, 1.5, 2.3, 8.2, 8.3, 8.4, 9.1, 9.5, 11.1, 12.3, 13.1, 14.1, 14.2, 19.1, 19.3, 22.1, 22.3, 23.2, 23.3, 23.4, 24.1, 25.1, 25.2, 25.3, Inquiry Activity: Chapter 21, Exploration Lab: Chapters 1, 2, 3, 6, 7, 8, 9, 10, 11, 12, 14, 15, 16, 17, 18, 19, 21, 22, 23, 24, 25, Application Lab: Chapters 4, 13, 20, Quick Lab: Chapters 9, 13, 14, 21
CONTENT STANDARD B • Physical Science	
B-1 Structure of atoms	Sections 2.1, 4.2, 5.1, 24.3, 25.2
B-2 Structure and properties of matter	Sections 2.1, 2.2, 2.3, 3.2, 7.1, 12.3, 18.1, 18.3
B-3 Chemical reactions	Sections 2.1, 3.4, 4.1, 4.3, 5.2, 7.2, 8.4, 14.2, 21.3, 25.2
B-4 Motions and forces	Sections 16.2, 19.1, 19.2, 22.1, 22.3, 23.1, 25.2, Exploration Lab: Chapter 16
B-5 Conservation of energy and increase in disorder	Sections 17.2, 17.3, 18.1, 18.2, 20.2, 24.3, 25.1
B-6 Interactions of energy and matter	Sections 8.1, 8.2, 8.3, 8.4, 16.2, 16.3, 17.2, 24.1, 24.2, 24.3, 25.2
CONTENT STANDARD C • Life Science	
C-1 The cell	Section 15.3
C-2 Molecular basis of heredity	
C-3 Biological evolution	Sections 13.2, 13.3, 13.4
C-4 Interdependence of organisms	Sections 1.2, 1.4, 4.1, 4.2, 4.3, 4.4, 5.2, 6.1, 15.2, 15.3, 16.1, 16.3, 17.1, 21.3
C-5 Matter, energy, and organization in living systems	Sections 4.1, 15.1, 15.2, 15.3
C-6 Behavior of organisms	Section 15.2

Correlation to National Science Education Standards

Content Standard	Chapter/Section
CONTENT STANDARD D • Earth and Space Science	
D-1 Energy in the earth system	Sections 1.1, 1.2, 1.4, 3.1, 4.2, 4.3, 5.1, 6.1, 6.3, 9.2, 9.3, 9.5, 10.3, 13.2, 15.1, 16.1, 16.2, 16.3, 17.1, 17.2, 17.3, 18.2, 18.3, 19.1, 19.2, 19.3, 20.1, 21.1, 21.2, 21.3, 23.2, 24.3, Exploration Lab: Chapter 12
D-2 Geochemical cycles	Sections 1.4, 2.2, 3.1, 3.3, 3.4, 4.1, 4.3, 5.1, 5.2, 6.1, 7.1, 7.2, 7.3, 8.4, 10.1, 10.2, 10.3, 12.2, 12.3, 14.2, 14.3, 14.4, 15.1, 16.1, 17.2, 18.1
D-3 Origin and evolution of the earth system	Sections 1.1, 1.2, 1.4, 2.1, 3.3, 4.1, 7.1, 8.1, 8.2, 8.3, 9.1, 9.2, 9.3, 9.4, 10.1, 11.1, 11.2, 11.3, 12.1, 12.2, 12.3, 12.4, 13.1, 13.2, 13.3, 13.4, 16.3, 17.1, 21.3, 22.1, 22.2, 22.3, 23.1, 24.3, Application Lab: Chapter 13
D-4 Origin and evolution of the universe	Section 24.3, 25.1, 25.2, 25.3
CONTENT STANDARD E • Science and Technology	
E-1 Abilities of technological design	Inquiry Activity: Chapter 8
E-2 Understandings about science and technology	Sections 1.3, 4.1, 4.2, 6.2, 8.2, 8.3, 8.4, 9.1, 9.4, 14.1, 14.4, 22.1, 22.3, 23.2, 23.3, 23.4, 24.1, 24.2, 24.3, 25.3, Exploration Lab: Chapter 21, Inquiry Activity: Chapter 8
CONTENT STANDARD F • Science in Personal and Social Perspectives	
F-1 Personal and community health	Sections 1.4, 4.3
F-2 Population growth	Sections 1.4, 4.1, 4.2, 4.4
F-3 Natural resources	Sections 1.4, 4.1, 4.2, 4.3, 4.4, 5.2, 6.3, 14.2, 14.4, Inquiry Activity: Chapter 6
F-4 Environmental quality	Sections 1.4, 4.1, 4.2, 4.3, 4.4, 5.1, 5.2, 6.3, 17.1
F-5 Natural and human-induced hazards	Sections 1.4, 4.1, 4.2, 4.3, 4.4, 5.1, 5.2, 5.3, 6.1, 6.2, 6.3, 7.2, 7.3, 8.1, 8.2, 8.3, 10.1, 20.1, 20.3, 21.3
F-6 Science and technology in local, national, and global challenges	Sections 1.4, 4.1, 4.2, 4.3, 4.4, 5.2, 6.2, 6.3, 8.2, 8.3, 16.3, 20.3, 21.3, Application Lab: Chapter 4
CONTENT STANDARD G • History and Nature of Science	
G-1 Science as a human endeavor	Sections 8.3, 9.1, 9.4, 9.5, 12.1, 12.2, 12.4, 13.2, 14.1, 14.2, 19.3, 22.1, 24.1, 24.2, 25.1, Exploration Lab: Chapters 21, 25
G-2 Nature of scientific knowledge	Sections 1.1, 1.5, 2.3, 5.3, 8.3, 9.1, 9.4, 10.2, 11.3, 12.1, 12.2, 12.4, 13.4, 22.1, 24.1, 25.2, Exploration Lab: Chapter 11, Quick Lab: Chapter 13
G-3 Historical perspectives	Sections 1.1, 1.2, 1.3, 1.5, 7.1, 9.1, 9.2, 9.4, 10.3, 11.3, 12.1, 12.2, 12.4, 16.2, 22.1, 24.1, 24.2, 24.3, 25.1, 25.2, 25.3

Research and *Prentice Hall Earth Science*

In developing *Prentice Hall Earth Science,* the development team used research studies as a central, guiding element. Research on high school science programs indicated key elements of a textbook program that ensure students' success: support for reading and mathematics in science, consistent opportunities for inquiry, and on-going assessment opportunities. This research was conducted in phases and still continues today.

Prentice Hall Research Cycle

1. Exploratory: Needs Assessment

Periodic surveys conducted with high school science teachers and supervisors track trends and the impact of state and national standards as well as curriculum issues and challenges. Specific product development research includes personal interviews with teachers, discussions with advisory panels, focus groups, and quantitative surveys. Prentice Hall explored the specific needs of teachers, students, and other educators as we developed *Prentice Hall Earth Science.*

2. Formative: Prototype Development and Field-Testing

During this phase of research, Prentice Hall develops prototype materials that are tested with users and nonusers to critique the lesson structure, design, and presentation. Qualitative and quantitative surveys provide extensive feedback on specific elements that aid concept mastery as well as support teacher instructional methodology. Ongoing reviews are channeled back into the program development for continuous improvement.

3. Summative: Validation Research

Finally, Prentice Hall continues to conduct long-term research based on scientific, experimental designs under actual classroom conditions. This research identifies what works and what can be improved in subsequent revisions of *Prentice Hall Earth Science.* We also continue to monitor the program in the market. We talk to our users about what works, and then we begin the cycle over again.

In preparation for No Child Left Behind (NCLB) mandates for science anticipated by 2007, Pearson Prentice Hall is committed to providing scientific research to support the efficacy of our science programs in the classroom. Our study designs will follow closely the criteria of NCLB. Since NCLB specifies a minimum level of improvement that students much achieve each year, actual adequate yearly progress (AYP) will be reflected in the research used to validate the program.

Foundational Research: Inquiry in the Science Classroom

"How do I know if my students are inquiring?" "If students are busy doing lots of hands-on activities, are they using inquiry?" "What is inquiry, anyway?" If you're confused, you are not alone. Inquiry is the heart and soul of science education, with most of us in continuous pursuit of achieving it with our students!

Defining Science Inquiry

What is it? Simply put, inquiry is the intellectual side of science. It is thinking like a scientist—being inquisitive, asking why, and searching for answers. The National Science Education Content Standards define inquiry as the process in which students begin with a question, design an investigation, gather evidence, formulate an answer to the original question, and communicate the investigative process and results.

Understanding Inquiry

The National Research Council in Inquiry and the National Science Education Standards (2000) identified several "essential features" of classroom inquiry. We have modified these essential features into questions to guide you in your quest for enhanced and more thoughtful student inquiry.

1. ***Who asks the question?*** In most curricula, these focusing questions are an element given in the materials. As a teacher you can look for labs that, at least on a periodic basis, allow students to pursue their own questions.
2. ***Who designs the procedures?*** To gain experience with the logic underlying experimentation, students need continuous practice with designing procedures. Some labs in which the primary target is content acquisition designate procedures. But others should ask students to do so.
3. ***Who decides what data to collect?*** Students need practice in determining the data to collect.
4. ***Who formulates explanations based upon the data?*** Students should be challenged to think—to analyze and draw conclusions based on their data, not just copy answers from the text materials.
5. ***Who communicates and justifies the results?*** Activities should push students to not only communicate but justify their answers. Activities also should be thoughtfully designed and interesting so that students want to share their results and argue about conclusions.

Making Time for Inquiry

One last question—Must each and every activity have students do all of this? The answer is an obvious and emphatic No. Some activities focus on content acquisition, and thus they specify the question and most of the procedures. But many others stress in-depth inquiry from start to finish.

Michael J. Padilla, Ph.D.
President NSTA, 2004–2005
Professor of Science Education
University of Georgia
Athens, Georgia

"Because inquiry is an intellectual pursuit, it cannot merely be characterized by keeping students busy and active."

Evaluator's Checklist

Does your science program promote inquiry by—

- ✔ Enabling students to pursue their own questions
- ✔ Allowing students to design their own procedures
- ✔ Letting students determine what data are best to collect
- ✔ Challenging students to think critically
- ✔ Pushing students to justify their answers

Inquiry in the Student Edition

Prentice Hall Earth Science offers the most opportunities to get students to think like scientists. By providing inquiry activities throughout the program, *Prentice Hall Earth Science* enables students to enhance their understanding of Earth Science concepts by participating in discovery.

Flexible lab options are included in every chapter, with options from directed to open-ended, thereby providing you with the flexibility to address all types of learners, deal with limited lab time, and provide effective experiences using easily accessible equipment. As Michael Padilla notes, some activities focus on content acquisition, and thus the exploratory question and most of the procedures are specified. But many other stress in-depth inquiry from start to finish.

Prentice Hall Earth Science encourages students to develop inquiry skills across the spectrum from teacher-guided to open-ended. Even more opportunities for real-life applications of inquiry are included in **Earth as a System, People and the Environment,** and **Understanding Earth** features. In addition, the GEODe CD-ROM provides many opportunities for students to analyze data and draw conclusions.

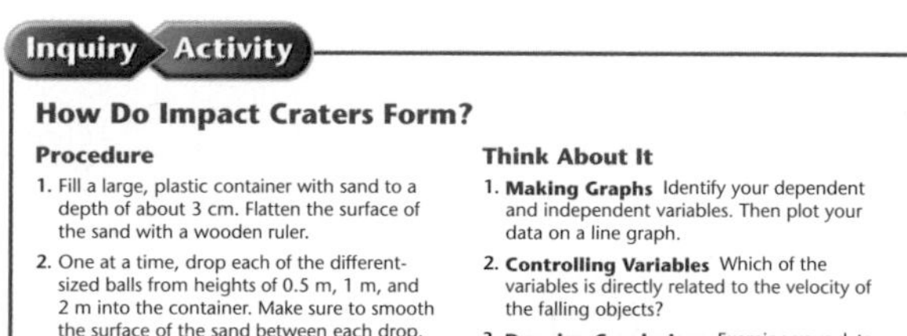

Inquiry Activity

How Do Impact Craters Form?

Procedure

1. Fill a large, plastic container with sand to a depth of about 3 cm. Flatten the surface of the sand with a wooden ruler.
2. One at a time, drop each of the different-sized balls from heights of 0.5 m, 1 m, and 2 m into the container. Make sure to smooth the surface of the sand between each drop.
3. Measure the diameter and height of the crater produced each time. Record your measurements in a data table.

Think About It

1. **Making Graphs** Identify your dependent and independent variables. Then plot your data on a line graph.
2. **Controlling Variables** Which of the variables is directly related to the velocity of the falling objects?
3. **Drawing Conclusions** Examine your data closely. What can you conclude about the general relationships between crater size and the size, mass, and velocity of the object that produced the crater?

An **Inquiry Activity** at the start of every chapter enables students to explore and discover concepts before reading about them in the chapter.

Set a Purpose

Quick Labs help students apply Earth Science concepts and skills. These activities often take less than one class period.

Quick, Effective, and Hands-On

Quick Lab

Observing Some of the Effects of Pressure on Mineral Grains

Materials

soft modeling clay; 2 pieces of waxed paper (each 20 cm × 20 cm); 20–30 small, round, elongated plastic beads; small plastic knife

Procedure

1. Use the clay to form a ball about the size of a golf ball. Randomly place all of the beads into this model rock.
2. Make a sketch of the rock. Label the sketch *Before.*
3. Sandwich the model rock between the two pieces of waxed paper. Use your weight to apply pressure to the model rock.
4. Remove the waxed paper and observe your "metamorphosed" rock.
5. Draw a top view of your rock and label it *After.* Include arrows to show the directions from which you applied pressure.
6. Make a cut through your model rock. Sketch this view of the rock.

Analyze and Conclude

1. **Comparing and Contrasting** How did the *Before* sketch compare with the *After* sketch of your model rock?
2. **Drawing Conclusions** How does pressure affect the mineral grains in a rock?
3. **Inferring** Was pressure the only agent of change that affected your rock? Explain.

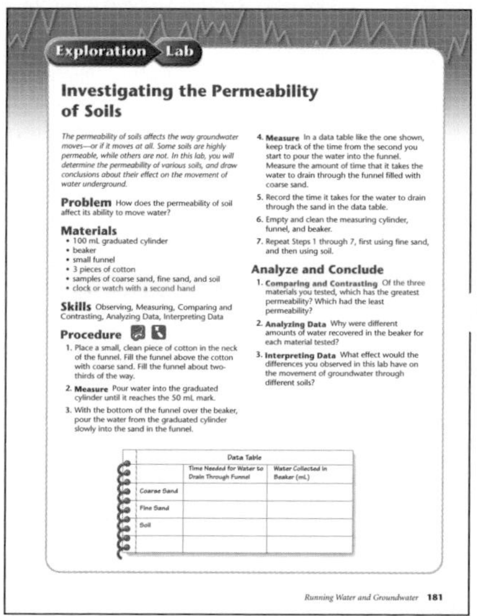

Exploration Lab

Investigating the Permeability of Soils

The permeability of soils affects the way groundwater moves—or if it moves at all. Some soils are highly permeable, while others are not. In this lab, you will determine the permeability of various soils, and draw conclusions about their effect on the movement of water underground.

Problem How does the permeability of soil affect its ability to move water?

Materials

- 100 mL graduated cylinder
- beaker
- small funnel
- 3 pieces of cotton
- samples of coarse sand, fine sand, and soil
- clock or watch with a second hand

Skills Observing, Measuring, Comparing and Contrasting, Analyzing Data, Interpreting Data

Procedure

1. Place a small, clean piece of cotton in the neck of the funnel. Fill the funnel above the cotton with coarse sand. Fill the funnel about two-thirds of the way.
2. **Measure** Pour water into the graduated cylinder until it reaches the 50 mL mark.
3. With the bottom of the funnel over the beaker, pour the water from the graduated cylinder slowly into the sand in the funnel.
4. **Measure** In a data table like the one shown, keep track of the time from the second you start to pour the water into the funnel. Measure the amount of time that it takes the water to drain through the funnel filled with coarse sand.
5. Record the time it takes for the water to drain through the sand in the data table.
6. Empty and clean the measuring cylinder, funnel, and beaker.
7. Repeat Steps 1 through 7, first using fine sand, and then using soil.

Analyze and Conclude

1. **Comparing and Contrasting** Of the three materials you tested, which has the greatest permeability? Which had the least permeability?
2. **Analyzing Data** Why were different amounts of water recovered in the beaker for each material tested?
3. **Interpreting Data** What effect would the differences you observed in this lab have on the movement of groundwater through different soils?

Data Table

	Time Needed for Water to Drain Through Funnel	Water Collected in Beaker (mL)
Coarse Sand		
Fine Sand		
Soil		

Running Water and Groundwater 181

Explore and Develop Key Concepts

An **Exploration Lab** or **Application Lab** in every chapter enables students to explore Earth Science concepts in depth and develop key science skills.

Inquiry Skills Chart

The *Prentice Hall Earth Science* program provides comprehensive practice and assessment of science skills, with an emphasis on the process skills necessary for inquiry. Use this chart to track skill coverage in the Student and Teacher Editions.

Science Process Skills

	Labs and Activities
Observing	Inquiry Activity: Chapters 1, 2, 4, 5, 8, 9, 10, 11, 12, 13, 17, 18, 19, 20, 23, 24, 25 Quick Lab: Chapters 10, 13 Exploration Lab: Chapters 2, 3, 6, 7, 11, 15, 17, 18, 19, 22, 23, 24, 25 Application Lab: Chapters 4, 20
Inferring	Inquiry Activity: Chapters 1, 6, 10, 11, 12, 13, 16, 18 Quick Lab: Chapters 3, 8, 9, 10, 13 Exploration Lab: Chapters 1, 5, 9, 12, 14, 15, 16, 21 Application Lab: Chapters 13, 20
Predicting	Inquiry Activity: Chapters 5, 7, 10, 14, 24, 25 Quick Lab: Chapters 8, 14 Exploration Lab: Chapters 5, 21 Application Lab: Chapter 20
Measuring	Exploration Lab: Chapters 1, 2, 3, 5, 6, 8, 9, 11, 14, 17, 18, 21 Application Lab: Chapters 4, 13
Calculating	Inquiry Activity: Chapter 15 Quick Lab: Chapter 9 Exploration Lab: Chapters 8, 9, 10, 16, 18, 19, 21, 23 Application Lab: Chapters 4, 13
Classifying	Inquiry Activity: Chapter 6 Exploration Lab: Chapters 2, 11
Using Tables and Graphs	Inquiry Activity: Chapter 22 Quick Lab: Chapter 8 Exploration Lab: Chapters 5, 7, 8, 10, 12, 14, 15, 16, 17, 21, 24
Using Models	Inquiry Activity: Chapters 17, 20 Exploration Lab: Chapters 17, 22, 23
Designing Experiments	Inquiry Activity: Chapters 1, 4, 12 Exploration Lab: Chapter 5
Formulating Hypotheses	Inquiry Activity: Chapters 2, 3, 9, 12, 20 Exploration Lab: Chapters 5, 12
Controlling Variables	Inquiry Activity: Chapter 22

Science Process Skills (continued)

	Labs and Activities
Analyzing Data	Exploration Lab: Chapters 5, 6, 9, 10, 14, 17, 18, 19, 21, 22, 23, 24, 25 Application Lab: Chapter 13
Drawing Conclusions	Inquiry Activity: Chapters 6, 7, 11, 14, 15, 16, 22 Quick Lab: Chapters 3, 14, 21 Exploration Lab: Chapters 5, 7, 8, 9, 10, 11, 14, 15, 16, 22 Application Lab: Chapter 4
Communicating Results	Inquiry Activity: Chapters 11, 15, 18, 19 Quick Lab: Chapters 3, 9, 10, 14, 21 Exploration Lab: Chapter 15 Application Lab: Chapters 4, 5, 6
Evaluating and Revising	Inquiry Activity: Chapter 4

Critical Thinking Skills

	Text and Teacher's Edition Features/Labs and Activities
Comparing and Contrasting	Inquiry Activity: Chapters 3, 8, 23 Quick Lab: Chapters 3, 14, 21 Exploration Lab: Chapters 1, 2, 3, 6, 14, 17, 18, 19 Application Lab: Chapters 4, 20 Assessment: Chapters 1, 2, 3, 4, 5, 7, 8, 9, 10, 11, 12, 13, 20
Applying Concepts	Inquiry Activity: Chapters 18, 19 Quick Lab: Chapter 13 Exploration Lab: Chapters 1, 3, 11, 12, 16, 17, 18, 19 Assessment: Chapters 1, 2, 3, 4, 5, 6, 8, 9, 10, 11, 12, 15, 16, 17, 18, 19, 21, 22, 23
Interpreting Diagrams/Photographs	Exploration Lab: Chapters 1, 8, 9, 11, 12, 15, 19 Application Lab: Chapter 13 Assessment: Chapter 13, 14
Making Judgments	Assessment: Chapter 5
Problem Solving	Inquiry Activity: Chapters 4, 15 Quick Lab: Chapter 14 Exploration Lab: Chapters 14, 15, 16, 18, 21, 23
Relating Cause and Effect	Application Lab: Chapter 4 Assessment: Chapters 4, 6, 7, 10, 13, 15, 16, 18, 20, 24
Making Generalizations	Assessment: Chapters 13, 14, 22, 23

Reading Strategies

	Text and Teacher's Edition Features
Using Prior Knowledge	Reading Strategy: Sections 17.2, 23.2 Build Reading Literacy/Teacher's Edition: Chapter 13 Review Science Concepts/Teacher's Edition: Chapters 1, 2, 3, 4, 5, 6, 7, 8, 9, 10, 11, 12, 13, 14, 15, 16, 17, 18, 19, 20, 21, 22, 23, 24, 25 Chapter Pretest/Teacher's Edition: Chapters 1, 2, 3, 4, 5, 6, 7, 8, 9, 10, 11, 12, 13, 14, 15, 16, 17, 18, 19, 20, 21, 22, 23, 24, 25
Previewing	Reading Strategy: Sections 2.2, 4.2, 5.3, 6.3, 10.1, 11.2, 15.1, 17.3, 19.3, 25.1 Build Reading Literacy/Teacher's Edition: Chapters 2, 14
Predicting	Reading Strategy: Sections 1.2, 9.4, 24.1 Build Reading Literacy/Teacher's Edition: Chapter 15
Building Vocabulary	Reading Strategy: Sections 3.1, 4.3, 5.1, 6.1, 7.1, 8.1, 13.1, 14.1, 15.2, 16.2, 18.3, 20.1, 23.4
Identifying the Main Idea	Reading Strategy: Sections 9.5, 12.1, 15.3, 16.1, 18.2, 19.1 Build Reading Literacy/Teacher's Edition: Chapter 10
Identifying Cause and Effect	Reading Strategy: Sections 20.3, 21.3 Build Reading Literacy/Teacher's Edition: Chapter 9
Comparing and Contrasting	Reading Strategy: Sections 1.5, 2.1, 5.2, 9.2, 10.2, 11.1, 17.1, 19.2, 22.1, 24.2 Build Reading Literacy/Teacher's Edition: Chapters 8, 23
Sequencing	Reading Strategy: Sections 8.4, 22.3, 25.2 Build Reading Literacy/Teacher's Edition: Chapters 16, 25
Relating Text and Figures	Reading Strategy: Section 23.1 Build Reading Literacy/Teacher's Edition: Chapter 7
Summarizing	Reading Strategy: Sections 4.4, 7.2, 9.1, 13.3, 14.3, 16.3, 21.1, 23.3 Build Reading Literacy/Teacher's Edition: Chapters 5, 24
Outlining	Reading Strategy: Sections 1.4, 2.3, 3.2, 3.3, 3.4, 7.3, 8.2, 9.3, 10.3, 11.3, 12.4, 14.2, 20.2, 21.1, 25.3 Build Reading Literacy/Teacher's Edition: Chapter 12
Monitoring Your Understanding	Reading Strategy: Sections 1.3, 4.1, 6.2, 8.3, 12.2, 12.3, 18.1, 22.2, 24.3 Build Reading Literacy/Teacher's Edition: Chapter 17

Graphic Organizers

	Text and Teacher's Edition Features
Concept Maps and Web Diagrams	Reading Strategy: Sections 2.2, 4.2, 4.4, 14.4, 16.3, 23.2 Thinking Visually: Chapters 10, 11, 15, 17, 18, 19, 20, 22, 24, 25 Build Reading Literacy/Teacher's Edition: Chapter 10 Build Vocabulary/Teacher's Edition: Sections 2.1, 7.1, 7.3, 9.2, 11.2, 13.2, 14.2, 15.2, 16.2, 17.2, 18.3, 19.2, 20.2, 21.2, 23.4, 24.2, 25.2
Compare-and-Contrast Tables	Reading Strategy: Sections 2.1, 5.2, 9.2, 10.2, 11.1, 13.4, 19.2, 22.1, 24.2 Thinking Visually: Chapter 23 Build Reading Literacy/Teacher's Edition: Chapters 8, 23 Build Vocabulary/Teacher's Edition: Section 20.2
Venn Diagrams	Reading Strategy: Sections 1.5, 17.1 Build Reading Literacy/Teacher's Edition: Chapter 23 Build Vocabulary/Teacher's Edition: Sections 5.3, 20.3
Flowcharts	Reading Strategy: Sections 8.4, 22.2, 22.3, 23.1, 25.2 Build Reading Literacy/Teacher's Edition: Chapters 9, 16, 25 Build Vocabulary/Teacher's Edition: Sections 13.2, 13.4
Cycle Diagrams	Build Reading Literacy/Teacher's Edition: Chapter 25 Build Vocabulary/Teacher's Edition: Sections 3.1, 6.1
Outlines	Reading Strategy: Sections 1.4, 2.3, 3.2, 3.3, 3.4, 7.3, 8.2, 9.3, 10.3, 11.3, 12.4, 14.2, 20.2, 21.2, 25.3 Build Reading Literacy/Teacher's Edition: Chapter 12
Tables	Reading Strategy: Sections 1.1, 1.2, 1.3, 3.1, 4.1, 4.3, 5.1, 5.3, 6.1, 6.2, 6.3, 7.1, 8.1, 8.3, 9.1, 9.4, 9.5, 10.1, 11.2, 12.1, 12.2, 12.3, 13.2, 14.1, 14.3, 15.1, 15.2, 15.3, 16.1, 16.2, 17.2, 17.3, 18.1, 18.2, 18.3, 19.1, 19.3, 20.1, 20.2, 21.1, 21.3, 23.3, 23.4, 24.1, 24.3, 25.1 Thinking Visually: Chapter 21 Build Reading Literacy/Teacher's Edition: Chapters 2, 11, 14 Build Vocabulary/Teacher's Edition: Sections 5.1, 12.3, 22.3, 23.3, 24.1

Reading Comprehension in the Science Classroom

Q&A

Q: Why are science texts often difficult for students to read and comprehend?

A: In general, science texts make complex literacy and knowledge demands on learners. They have a more technical vocabulary, a more demanding syntax, and place a greater emphasis on inferential reasoning.

Q: What does research say about facilitating comprehension?

A: Studies comparing novices and experts show that the conceptual organization of experts' knowledge is very different from that of novices. For example, experts emphasize core concepts when organizing knowledge, while novices focus on superficial details. To facilitate comprehension, effective teaching strategies should support and scaffold students as they build an understanding of the key concepts and concept relationships within a text unit.

Q: What strategies can teachers use to facilitate comprehension?

A: Three complementary strategies are very important in facilitating student comprehension of science texts. First, guide student interaction with the text using the built-in strategies. Second, organize the curriculum in terms of core concepts (e.g., the **Key Concepts** in each section). Third, develop visual representations of the relationships among the key concepts and vocabulary that can be referred to during instruction.

Nancy Romance, Ph.D.
Professor of Science Education
Florida Atlantic University
Fort Lauderdale, Florida

"Effective teaching strategies should support and scaffold students as they build an understanding of the key concepts and concept relationships within a text unit."

Evaluator's Checklist

Does your science program promote reading comprehension with—

- ✔ Text structured in an outline format and key concepts highlighted in boldface type
- ✔ Real-world applications to activate prior knowledge
- ✔ Key concepts, critical vocabulary, and a reading skill for every section
- ✔ Relevant photos and carefully constructed graphics with questions
- ✔ Reading checkpoints that appear in each section

Reading Support in the Student Edition

During the section—

- Reading Strategy sections provide tools to reinforce core skills.
- Boldface sentences identify each key concept and encourage students to focus on the big ideas of science.
- Reading Checkpoints reinforce students' understanding by slowing them down to review after concepts are discussed.
- Caption questions help students interpret the art and photos and connect them to the text.

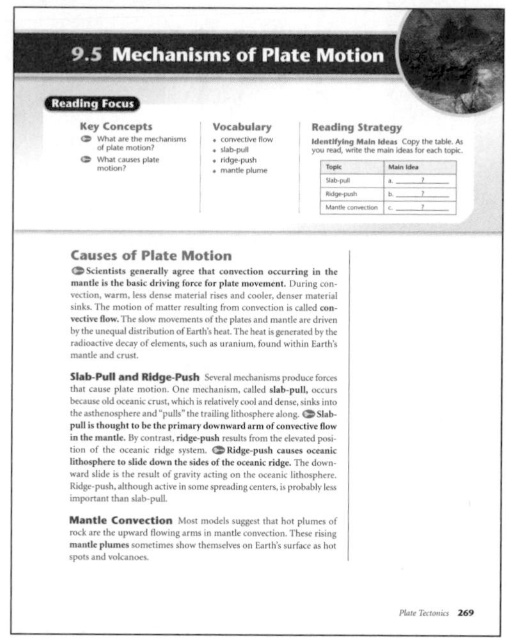

9.5 Mechanisms of Plate Motion

Reading Focus

Key Concepts
- What are the mechanisms of plate motion?
- What causes plate motion?

Vocabulary
- convective flow
- slab-pull
- ridge-push
- mantle plume

Reading Strategy

Identifying Main Ideas Copy the table. As you read, write the main ideas for each topic.

Topic	Main Idea
Slab-pull	a. ?
Ridge-push	b. ?
Mantle convection	c. ?

Causes of Plate Motion

Scientists generally agree that convection occurring in the mantle is the basic driving force for plate movement. During convection, warm, less dense material rises and cooler, denser material sinks. The motion of matter resulting from convection is called **convective flow.** The slow movements of the plates and mantle are driven by the unequal distribution of Earth's heat. The heat is generated by the radioactive decay of elements, such as uranium, found within Earth's mantle and crust.

Slab-Pull and Ridge-Push Several mechanisms produce forces that cause plate motion. One mechanism, called **slab-pull,** occurs because old oceanic crust, which is relatively cool and dense, sinks into the asthenosphere and "pulls" the trailing lithosphere along. **Slab-pull is thought to be the primary downward arm of convective flow in the mantle.** By contrast, **ridge-push** results from the elevated position of the oceanic ridge system. **Ridge-push causes oceanic lithosphere to slide down the sides of the oceanic ridge.** The downward slide is the result of gravity acting on the oceanic lithosphere. Ridge-push, although active in some spreading centers, is probably less important than slab-pull.

Mantle Convection Most models suggest that hot plumes of rock are the upward flowing arms in mantle convection. These rising **mantle plumes** sometimes show themselves on Earth's surface as hot spots and volcanoes.

Plate Tectonics 269

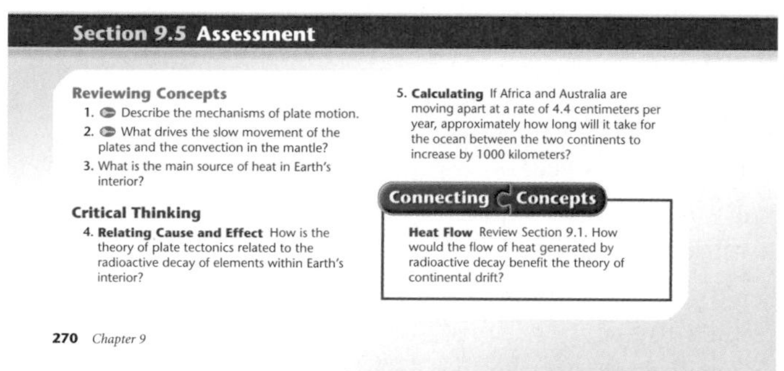

Section 9.5 Assessment

Reviewing Concepts
1. Describe the mechanisms of plate motion.
2. What drives the slow movement of the plates and the convection in the mantle?
3. What is the main source of heat in Earth's interior?

Critical Thinking

4. **Relating Cause and Effect** How is the theory of plate tectonics related to the radioactive decay of elements within Earth's interior?
5. **Calculating** If Africa and Australia are moving apart at a rate of 4.4 centimeters per year, approximately how long will it take for the ocean between the two continents to increase by 1000 kilometers?

Connecting Concepts

Heat Flow Review Section 9.1. How would the flow of heat generated by radioactive decay benefit the theory of continental drift?

270 *Chapter 9*

After students read—

- Section Assessments revisit the key concepts, use critical thinking skills, and extend learning.

Additional Reading Support

Guided Reading and Study Workbook

- The organization parallels the structure and sequence of the student text.
- Workbook format provides a convenient place for students to keep their study notes organized.
- Each section opens with the Reading Strategy activity to build comprehension skills, and gives students an arsenal of study tools based on graphic organizers.
- Lesson questions reinforce students' understanding of Key Concepts and supporting content.
- Tables, diagrams, and puzzles are also used to help students retain information.
- Teacher's Edition includes all answers in red.

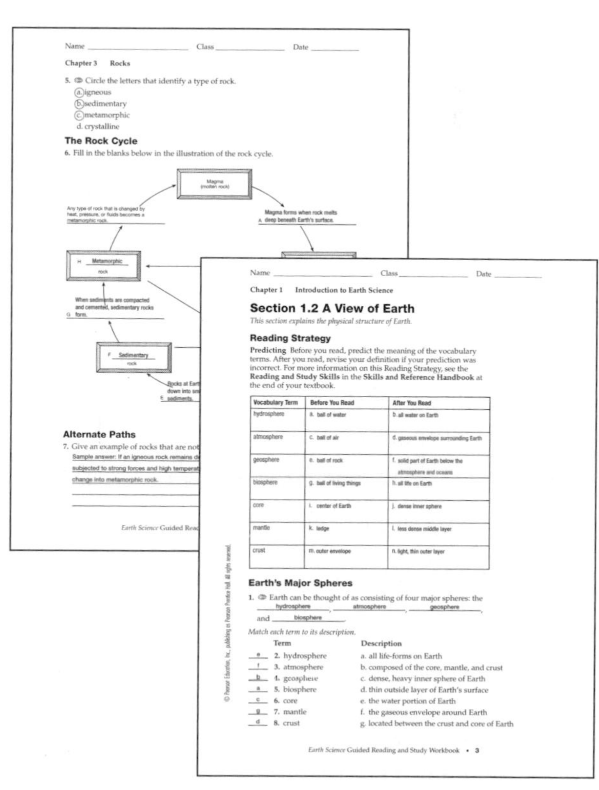

Name ______ Class ______ Date ______

Chapter 3 Rocks

5. Circle the letters that identify a type of rock.
(a) igneous
(b) sedimentary
(c) metamorphic
d. crystalline

The Rock Cycle

6. Fill in the blanks below in the illustration of the rock cycle.

Alternate Paths

7. Give an example of rocks that are not ...

Name ______ Class ______ Date ______

Chapter 1 Introduction to Earth Science

Section 1.2 A View of Earth

This section explains the physical structure of Earth.

Reading Strategy

Predicting Before you read, predict the meaning of the vocabulary terms. After you read, revise your definition if your prediction was incorrect. For more information on this Reading Strategy, see the **Reading and Study Skills** in the **Skills and Reference Handbook** at the end of your textbook.

Vocabulary Term	Before You Read	After You Read
hydrosphere	a. ball of water	b. all water on Earth
atmosphere	c. ball of air	d. gaseous envelope surrounding Earth
geosphere	e. ball of rock	f. solid part of Earth below the atmosphere and oceans
biosphere	g. ball of living things	h. all life on Earth
core	i. center of Earth	j. dense inner sphere
mantle	k. ledge	l. less dense middle layer
crust	m. outer envelope	n. light, thin outer layer

Earth's Major Spheres

1. Earth can be thought of as consisting of four major spheres: the hydrosphere, atmosphere, geosphere and biosphere.

Match each term to its description.

Term	Description
e 2. hydrosphere	a. all life-forms on Earth
f 3. atmosphere	b. composed of the core, mantle, and crust
b 4. geosphere	c. dense, heavy inner sphere of Earth
a 5. biosphere	d. thin outside layer of Earth's surface
c 6. core	e. the water portion of Earth
g 7. mantle	f. the gaseous envelope around Earth
d 8. crust	g. located between the crust and core of Earth

Earth Science Guided Reading and Study Workbook • 3

Geographic Literacy in the Science Classroom

As the *Geography for Life: National Geography Standards* (1994) state, "There is now a widespread acceptance among the people of the United states that being literate in geography is essential if students are to leave school equipped to earn a decent living, enjoy the richness of life, and participate responsibly in local, national, and international affairs." An Earth Science program can help teachers facilitate geographic literacy with a focus on map skills.

Defining Geographic Literacy

Geography skills are the ability to ask a geographic question, acquire and analyze geographic information, and answer geographic questions. To be truly literate in geography, students must be able to apply their knowledge and skills to understand the world.

Elements for Success

To help all students gain a base upon which to build geographic literacy, programs should introduce basic geography skills early in the school year. Maps must be developmentally appropriate, clear, clean, and accurate. Maps should be attractive and present subject matter in appealing ways, so the students want to use them to learn. A third element that can lead to success is the incorporation of technology into the teaching and learning of geography. Research has shown the importance of the Internet in particular, with 8th-grade students who have high Internet usage scoring higher in geography (NAEP, 2001)*.

Students will interact with the maps in *Prentice Hall Earth Science* through MapMaster Skills Activities.

Map Skill Development in the Student Edition

Maps are used extensively in *Prentice Hall Earth Science* to convey Earth Science concepts, but with an underpinning of these geographic themes. Using these themes can help set a context for learning concepts.

- **Location** helps students answer the question, "Where is it?"
- **Regions** are defined by a set of similar characteristics. For example, the state of Hawaii is in the political region of the United States, and it is also in the tropical climate region.
- **Place** identifies the natural and human features that make one place different from every other place.
- **Movement** shows how materials or characteristics that originate in one area affect another area. For example, the warm waters of the Gulf Stream moderate the climates of northern latitude countries.

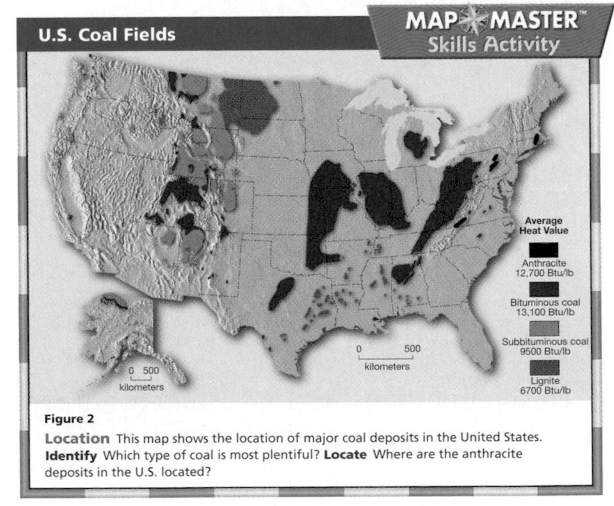

Figure 2
Location This map shows the location of major coal deposits in the United States. **Identify** Which type of coal is most plentiful? **Locate** Where are the anthracite deposits in the U.S. located?

*U.S. Department of Education, Office of Educational Research and Improvement, National Center for Education Statistics, National Assessment of Educational Progress (NAEP, 2001 Geography Assessment)

Exploring Earth System Science

Prentice Hall Earth Science helps students develop an awareness of Earth's many interacting parts. This theme is introduced in Chapter 1 as students are introduced to the four spheres: hydrosphere, geosphere, atmosphere, and biosphere. Throughout the text students see the delicate balance among the spheres and the cause-and-effect relationships that result when that balance is disrupted. **Earth as a System, People and the Environment, How the Earth Works,** and **Understanding Earth** all highlight individual systems and their inevitable and vital interactions. In addition, most Chapter Assessments contain questions that focus on the Earth System theme. These items help ensure that students are thinking about the content on a global level.

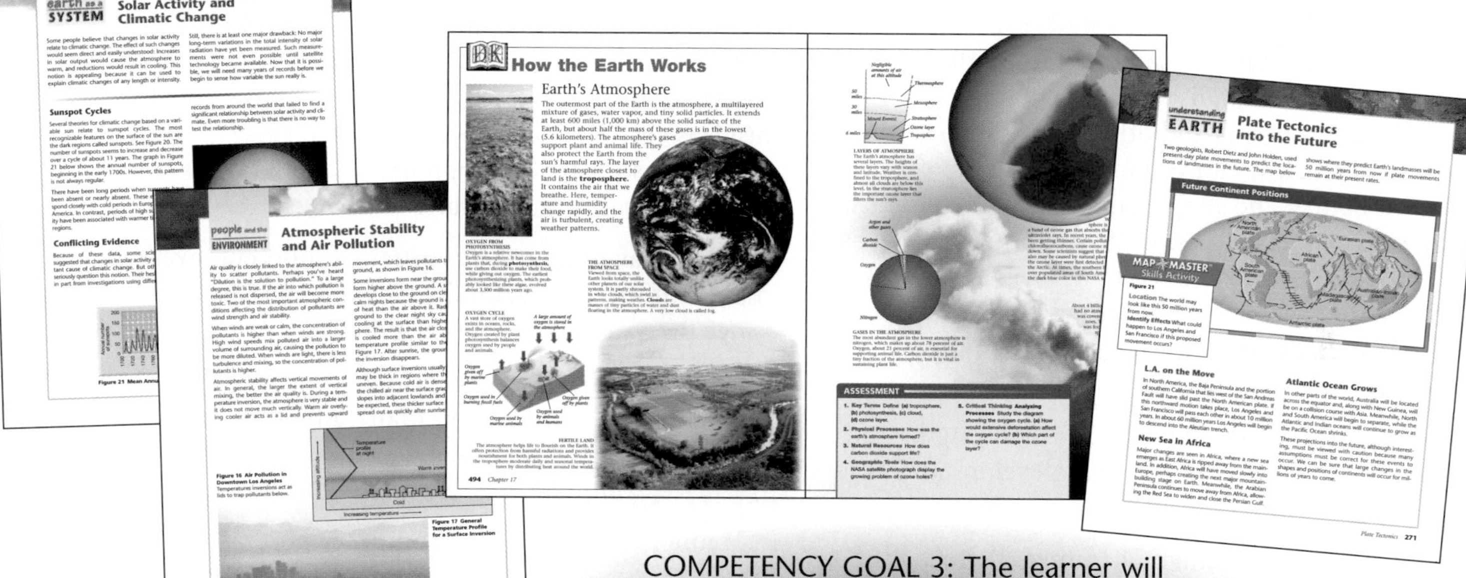

COMPETENCY GOAL 3: The learner will build an understanding of the origin and evolution of the Earth system.

Earth System Assessment Items in the Student Edition

Chapter	Item Number	Chapter	Item Number
1	25, 26, 34	13	20, 23
2	—	14	Performance Assessment
3	36	15	26, 27, 32
4	32, 33	16	24, 29
5	36, Performance Assessment	17	23, 26
6	22	18	30
7	31	19	23, 27
8	—	20	36, 37
9	26, 29	21	30, 31, 32
10	32	22	27
11	—	23	—
11A	—	24	Performance Assessment
12	25	25	—

Differentiated Instruction in the Science Classroom

What is differentiated instruction?

When you begin your school year, you quickly observe the spectrum of your students—some with limited science backgrounds and some that are very proficient in science, some with basic English skills and some that are very proficient in English, some that are independent workers and others that can't sit still for a minute. How can you meet the needs of all of these students? The simple answer is: *Differentiated Instruction*—focusing on students' individual needs and providing varied materials and grouping patterns that accommodate individual learning differences. Differentiated instruction emphasizes these principles:

1. All students are unique and their strengths and needs change as their literacy develops and as they grow in their knowledge of science.
2. Instruction that attempts to meet the needs of all students must be flexible and adaptable for each individual.
3. Assessment of students' strengths and needs must be continuous to ensure that students learn all they can.
4. Instruction must be multi-sensory with learning opportunities that rely on all of the senses, and it must be scaffolded for each student's learning level.
5. Instruction with multi-media enhances the probability of each student's learning.

What techniques help differentiate instruction?

Whenever possible, enhance learning with **one-to-one teaching episodes,** conferring individually with one student while other students are working independently. In addition, **small group instruction** for students with similar instructional needs is very effective when you are in close proximity so that your supportive interactions with the group can be immediate.

A wide array of materials written at different levels makes information accessible to students. This range of materials should include:

- **Print materials** that are written at many different reading levels and exhibit many different genres and formats (textbooks, magazines, newspaper articles, computer messages, reference materials).
- **Media** including videos, computer programs, multi-media productions, and virtual reality explorations.
- **Artifacts** or realia that make information accessible to students, e.g., pictures and videos, music and objects that can be touched and studied.

Depending upon prior content knowledge, students require **different levels of pacing.** Differentiated instruction requires that some lessons be accelerated for some students and decelerated for others, and often requires the repetition of a lesson.

Differentiated Instruction in the Earth Science Program

Differentiated instruction does not mean that the teacher offers each and every student in the class a "different" lesson but rather that multiple methods of instruction are used to maximize each student's likelihood of understanding the material. The *Prentice Hall Earth Science* program provides a variety of support and instructional materials to meet the learning needs of all students.

Support for Students

Highlights among the materials that support differentiated instruction for students are:

- **Reading support** that is provided "before, during, and after" every Student Edition section.
- Strong **visual learning strand** in the Student Edition where graphs, charts, illustrations, and photographs work hand-in-hand with the text to clarify complex topics.
- Go Online **Web resources** from NSTA SciLinks and PHSchool.com give students opportunities to master concepts outside the text.
- The **Guided Reading and Study Workbook** supports every section of the Student Edition, guiding students through the content and providing practice for reading and math skills.
- The Laboratory Manual gives students **hands-on experiences with the content** while challenging students according to their ability levels.
- **Discovery Channel Video Field Trips** make the content accessible through dynamic footage and high-impact stories.
- The **GEODe CD-ROM** provides animations and activities to show students complex, large-scale processes in a medium that makes them easier to understand.
- The **Interactive Textbook** contains the complete Student Edition online and on CD-ROM for an interactive visual experience with the content in which they get reading support, activities, and assessment feedback.

Support for Teachers

- The **customized instruction** teaching notes within each section differentiate instruction for less proficient readers, advanced readers, English Language Learners, and inclusion/special needs students.
- **Customize for English Language Learners** teaching notes within the sections give additional support for beginning and intermediate skill levels.
- **Leveling of the student resources and teaching notes** on the planning guide, at point-of-use, and in the lesson plans aids planning for all students.
- **Chapter Tests** assess students with a level of rigor appropriate to their ability levels.

Customize for English Language Learners

Tailor your presentation by speaking directly and simplifying the terms and sentence structures used to explain key concepts. For example, split a cause-and-effect sentence into two sentences labeled Cause and Effect. A sample cause sentence might be *Water expands when it freezes.* A sample effect sentence might be *The frozen water enlarges cracks in rocks.* Other techniques include using visual aids and body language when appropriate to emphasize important concepts. For example, you can clasp your hands together, then move them apart when discussing how water expands when it freezes.

Customize for Inclusion Students

Learning Disabled Visuals often simplify and clarify key concepts. Take a few moments to ensure that all students correctly interpret photographs, tables, graphs, and diagrams. For example, you can have students plot the data in Figure 10 on p. 133 in a bar graph to assess their understanding of soil composition. You can make copies of Figure 11 on p. 134 and encourage students to draw intersecting lines on the soil-texture diagram, to identify soil type. If students still have difficulty interpreting Figure 11, use transparency 3D and pick a point on the diagram to represent a soil sample, then trace a path along the relevant lines to help students identify the percentages of clay, silt, and sand in the sample.

Science, Technology, and Society

The application of science concepts to real-world problems and their solutions is one high-interest way to engage students in the study of science concepts. See how the National Science Education Standards and the AAAS Benchmarks promote this idea.

From the National Science Education Standards

In a world filled with the products of scientific inquiry, scientific literacy has become a necessity for everyone. Everyone needs to use scientific information to make choices that arise every day. Everyone needs to be able to engage intelligently in public discourse and debate about important issues that involve science and technology. And everyone deserves to share in the excitement and personal fulfillment that can come from understanding and learning about the natural world. Copyright (c) 1995 National Academy of Sciences. All Rights Reserved.

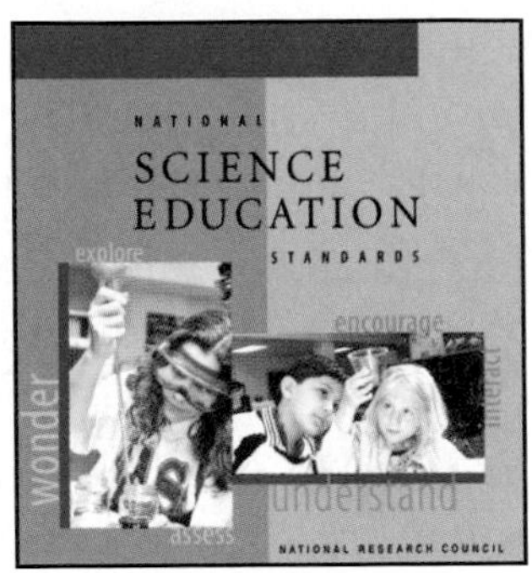

National Science Education Standards, 1995

"More and more jobs demand advanced skills, requiring that people be able to learn, reason, think creatively, make decisions, and solve problems."

From the AAAS Benchmarks

Gaining an understanding of the concept of social trade-offs may be one of the most important components of a comprehensive education. Because social problems typically involve a variety of factors and interests, it is rare that one solution to a problem will carry all the benefits and avoid all disadvantages. Because increasing some advantages is likely to decrease others, most realistic solutions involve compromise among advantages and disadvantages. If the habit of considering alternatives and their consequences is to be functional for students, they should exercise it in a rich variety of contexts. Copyright (c) 1993 by American Association for the Advancement of Science.

STS in the Student Edition

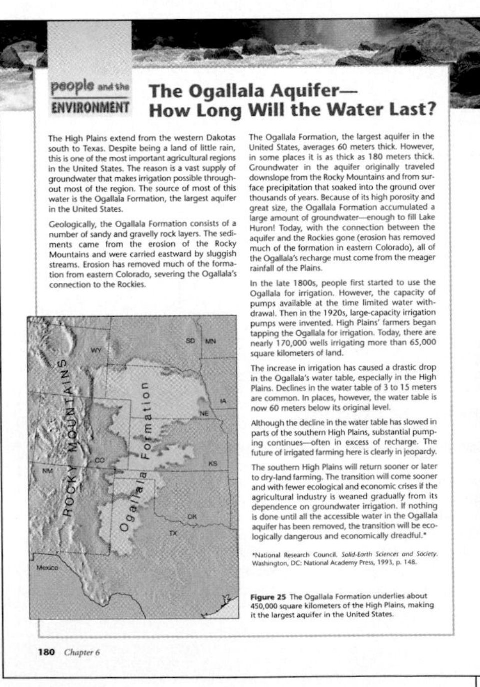

people and the ENVIRONMENT

The Ogallala Aquifer—How Long Will the Water Last?

The High Plains extend from the western Dakotas south to Texas. Despite being a land of little rain, this is one of the most important agricultural regions in the United States. The reason is a vast supply of groundwater that makes irrigation possible throughout most of the region. The source of most of this water is the Ogallala Formation, the largest aquifer in the United States.

Geologically, the Ogallala Formation consists of a number of sandy and gravelly rock layers. The sediments came from the erosion of the Rocky Mountains and were carried eastward by sluggish streams. Erosion has removed much of the formation from eastern Colorado, severing the Ogallala's connection to the Rockies.

The Ogallala Formation, the largest aquifer in the United States, averages 60 meters thick. However, in some places it is as thick as 180 meters thick. Groundwater in the aquifer originally traveled downslope from the Rocky Mountains and from surface precipitation that soaked into the ground over thousands of years. Because of its high porosity and great size, the Ogallala Formation accumulated a large amount of groundwater—enough to fill Lake Huron! Today, with the connection between the aquifer and the Rockies gone (erosion has removed much of the formation in eastern Colorado), all of the Ogallala's recharge must come from the meager rainfall of the Plains.

In the late 1800s, people first started to use the Ogallala for irrigation. However, the capacity of pumps available at the time limited water withdrawal. Then in the 1920s, large-capacity irrigation pumps were invented. High Plains' farmers began tapping the Ogallala for irrigation. Today, there are nearly 170,000 wells irrigating more than 65,000 square kilometers of land.

The increase in irrigation has caused a drastic drop in the Ogallala's water table, especially in the High Plains. Declines in the water table of 3 to 15 meters are common. In places, however, the water table is now 60 meters below its original level.

Although the decline in the water table has slowed in parts of the southern High Plains, substantial pumping continues—often in excess of recharge. The future of irrigated farming here is clearly in jeopardy.

The southern High Plains will return sooner or later to dry-land farming. The transition will come sooner and with fewer ecological and economic crises if the agricultural industry is weaned gradually from its dependence on groundwater irrigation. If nothing is done until all the accessible water in the Ogallala aquifer has been removed, the transition will be ecologically dangerous and economically dreadful.*

*National Research Council. *Solid-Earth Sciences and Society.* Washington, DC: National Academy Press, 1993, p. 148.

Figure 25 The Ogallala Formation underlies about 450,000 square kilometers of the High Plains, making it the largest aquifer in the United States.

180 *Chapter 6*

Careers in Earth and Space Science

The career opportunities available in Earth and space science are far reaching—from exploring distant galaxies to investigating deep inside Earth. Here are a few of these exciting careers.

Meteorologist
Meteorologists study how the physical characteristics, processes, and movements of the atmosphere affect the environment. They use this information to forecast the weather and study the patterns of weather change, such as droughts and global warming.
Educational requirements Four-year college degree, majoring in meteorology or atmospheric science

Seismologist
Seismologists are Earth scientists who investigate earthquakes. They determine the location and size of earthquakes, and use seismic waves to study Earth's interior. Some seismologists help the building industry design earthquake-proof structures.
Educational requirements
Four-year college degree, majoring in geology, geophysics, or mathematics

Surveying Technician
Helping to measure and map Earth's surface are the responsibilities of surveying technicians. They assist land surveyors who measure distances, directions, and contours on, above, or below Earth's surface. Surveying technicians use surveying instruments to collect data and then enter the data into computers.
Educational requirements
Two-year junior or community college program, one to three years of technical school

xviii

Internet Literacy

Over the past 5 years, real-time access to data from current scientific research has grown, virtual science explorations have been posted online, and access to scientists' conceptual understandings has increased. Teachers who make wise use of Web resources can extend the breadth and depth of classroom learning and prepare students for academic and technical futures.

While there is a wealth of information on the Internet, "scaffolding" Web experiences for students can reduce the chances for misdirection and wasted time and increase the educational value of the activity. Successful scaffolding strategies used by teachers include:

- **Pointing students to educational Web sites or portals rather than general search engines as starting points**
- **Providing links to pre-selected Web resources for assignments or embedding pre-selected links in student assignments**
- **Selecting or designing projects and research questions that require synthesis and analysis of gathered information**

Central to use of Internet resources in standards-based education is the need for critical evaluation of information sources. Because the Web is an open-publishing, unmoderated medium, students often find misleading and sometimes blatantly false information. Both teachers and students must be able to critically evaluate sources of information so that learners focus on materials that develop conceptual understanding rather than misleading material. To this end learners must be able to discriminate between valid, reputable sources and those that are not.

Cathy Dickerson
Curriculum Specialist for Technology
Humbolt County Office of Education
Eureka, California

"Our challenge is to focus on using Web resources to enhance educational experiences for our students."

Internet Literacy in the Student Edition

- **Point-of-use learning links vetted by NSTA**
- **Student Worksheets with every learning link**

PHSchool.com

- **Self-assessments**
- **Interactivities**
- **Learning links**

- **Current science articles linked by topic**

Internet Literacy

NEW YORK

Assessment in the Science Curriculum

No Child Left Behind clearly challenges school districts across the nation to raise expectations for all students with testing of student achievement in science beginning in 2007–2008.

A primary goal of NCLB is to provide classroom teachers with better data from scientifically valid assessments in order to inform instructional planning and to identify students who are at risk and require intervention. It has been a common practice to teach a science lesson, administer a test, grade it, and move on. This practice is a thing of the past. With the spotlight now on improving student performance, it is essential to use assessment results as a way to identify student strengths and challenges. Providing student feedback and obtaining student input is a valuable, essential part of the assessment process.

Assessment is a never-ending cycle, as is shown in the following diagram. Although you may begin at any point in the assessment cycle, the basic process is the same.

Use a variety of assessment tools to gain information and strengthen student understanding.
ASSESS
Analyze assessment results to create a picture of student strengths and challenges.
ANALYZE
Choose a target to create a focused path on which to proceed.
TARGET
Identify strategies to achieve the target, create a plan for implementation, and choose assessments tools.
STRATEGIZE
Implement the plan with a focus on gathering and using assessment information throughout.
IMPLEMENT

An important assessment strategy is to ensure that students have ample opportunities to check their understanding of skills and concepts before moving on to the next topic. Checking for understanding also includes asking appropriate, probing questions with each example presented. This enables students and teachers to know whether the skills or concepts being introduced are actually understood.

Eileen Depka
Supervisor of Standards and Assessment
Waukesha, Wisconsin

"Meeting the NCLB challenge will necessitate an integrated approach to assessment with a variety of assessment tools."

Evaluator's Checklist

Does your science program include assessments that—

- ✔ Are embedded before, during, and after lesson instruction
- ✔ Align to standards and to the instructional program
- ✔ Assess both skill acquisition and understanding
- ✔ Mirror the various formats of standardized tests

Assessment in *Prentice Hall Earth Science*

The range of strategies in *Prentice Hall Earth Science* for monitoring progress will help you find the right opportunity for reaching all your students. The assessment strategies in *Prentice Hall Earth Science* ensure student success in content mastery as well as high-stakes test performance.

In the Student Edition

Caption Questions enhance critical thinking skills and maximize the effectiveness of art, graphics, and narrative.

Reading Checkpoints reinforce students' understanding of the material just covered.

Section Assessment Questions model the way students think, and reviews and assesses their understanding of the Key Concepts.

Comprehensive Chapter Reviews and ***Assessment*** provide opportunities for students to check their own understanding and practice valuable high-stakes test-taking skills.

In the Program Resources

ExamView®, Computer Test Bank CD-ROM provides teachers access to thousands of modifiable test questions.

Progress Monitoring Assessments with Student Test Prep Workbook include diagnostic and prescription tools, progress-monitoring aids, and practice tests that help teachers focus on improving test scores.

Interactive Textbook provides a wealth of assessment tools. Students can monitor their progress at point of use with ongoing assessment, help tutorials, and instant feedback.

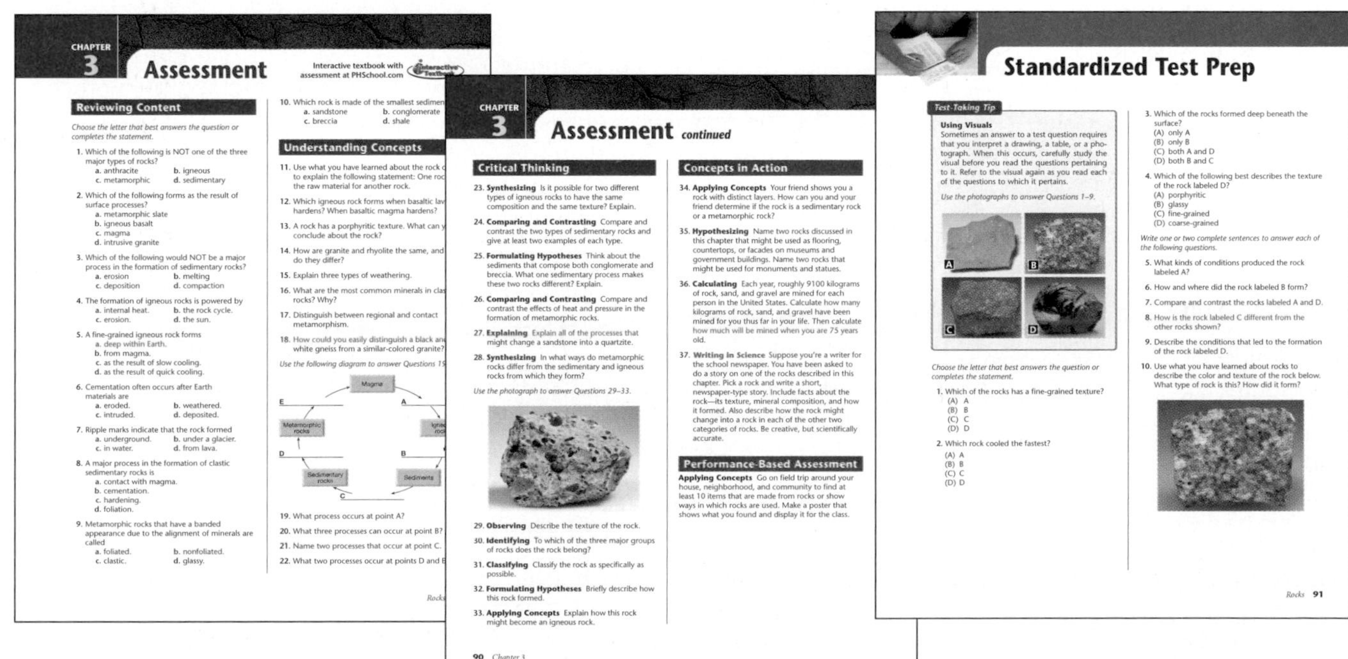

Master Materials List

Item	*Quantity	Chapter
Air Movement in Pressure Cells, p. 550	1 copy	19 Lab
Aluminum foil	1 sheet	14 Lab
Antacid tablet	5	5 Lab
Anthracite sample	1	3 Lab
Apple	1	12.1 IA
Augite sample	1	2 Lab
Balance	1	2 Lab, 14.4 QL
Ball, different-sized	3	22.1 IA
Ball, small rubber	1	15.1 IA
Basketball	1	22 Lab
Basalt sample	1	3.1 IA, 3 Lab
Beaker, 100-mL	1	6 Lab, 15 Lab
Beaker, 250-mL	1 2	5 Lab, 7.1 IA, 18.1 IA 17 Lab
Beaker, 400-mL	1	14.4 QL
Bituminous coal	1	3 Lab
Board, short	2	19.1 IA
Bone, small	1	12.1 IA
Book, large	1 2	8.1 IA 19.1 IA
Bottle, 1-L plastic	2	20.1 IA
Calcite sample	1	2.1 IA, 2 Lab
Calculator	1	9.1 QL, 9 Lab, 18 Lab, 23 Lab
Cardboard box, small	1	24 Lab
Cardboard box, large	1	24 Lab
Cardboard sheet, (20 cm × 20 cm)	1	23.1 IA
Carton, juice 1.89-L 946-mL 240-mL	 1 1 1	 4 Lab 4 Lab 4 Lab
Clay, modeling	1 piece	3.4 QL, 14 Lab
Clay sample	1	14.1 IA
Club soda	2 bottles	10.1 QL
Common Minerals, pp. 54–55	1 copy	2 Lab
Compass, drawing	1	1 Lab, 8 Lab
Conglomerate sample	1	3 Lab
Container, clear plastic	1	14.1 IA, 22.1 IA
Container, clear plastic, rectangular	1	16.1 IA
Container, identical	2	21.1 QL
Container, with lid 1-L	1	5.1 IA
Cotton ball	3	6 Lab
Fan with high/low settings	1	16.1 IA
Feldspar sample	1	2 Lab
Fluorite sample	1	2 Lab
Food coloring	1	15 Lab
Fossil sample	variety	13.1 IA
Funnel, small	1	6 Lab
Geologic Time Scale p. 357	1 copy	12 Lab
Glass jar, clear	1	5.1 IA
Glitter	1/4 tsp	20.1 IA
Globe	1	1 Lab
Gneiss sample	1	3.1 IA, 3 Lab
Goggles, safety	1	2.1 IA
Graduated cylinder, 50-mL	1	2 Lab
Graduated cylinder, 100-mL	1 2	6 Lab 15 Lab
Graduated cylinder, 500-mL	2	15.1 IA
Granite sample	1	3.1 IA, 3 Lab
Gypsum sample	1	2 Lab
Hair sample	1	12.1 IA
Halite sample	1	2.1 IA, 2 Lab
Hammer	1	2.1 IA, 2 Lab
Hand lens	1	2.1 IA, 2 Lab, 3.1 IA, 5.1 IA, 14.1 IA
Hornblende sample	1	2 Lab
Hydrochloric acid solution	4 mL	3 Lab
Hydrochloric acid solution, dilute	5 mL	2 Lab
Ice crystals	250 mL	7.1 IA
Ice cube	12	5 Lab, 15 Lab, 18.1 IA
Insect wing	1	12.1 IA
Knife, plastic	1	3.4 QL

Key: IA=Inquiry Activity **QL**=Quick Lab **Lab**=End-of-Chapter Lab *=Quantities per group

Item	*Quantity	Chapter
Knife, steel blade	1	2 Lab
Knife, table	1	7.1 IA
Lamp	1	22 Lab
Leaf sample	1	12.1 IA
Light source	1	17 Lab
Limestone sample	1	3.1 IA, 3 Lab
Magnetite sample	1	2 Lab
Magnifying glass	1	7.1 IA, 12.1 IA
Map, p. 241	1 copy	8 Lab
Map, world	1	1 Lab, 8 Lab, 9.1 IA, 10.1 IA
Marble sample	1	3.1 IA, 3 Lab
Marker, permanent	1	10.1 IA
Markers, felt-tip (water-based ink)	1 set	3 Lab, 21.1 IA
Masking tape	4 strips	21.1 QL
Meter stick	1	13 Lab, 22.1 IA, 23 Lab
Mica sample	1	2 Lab
Microscope	1	12.1 IA
Northern Hemisphere, p. 550	1 copy	19 Lab
Notebook	1	25 Lab
Obsidian sample	1	3 Lab
Olivine sample	1	2 Lab
Orange	1	12.1 IA
Paper, 5-m adding machine tape	1	13 Lab
Paper, 6-m adding machine tape	1	23 Lab
Paper, black construction	1 sheet	17.1 IA
Paper, graph	1 sheet	5 Lab, 12 Lab, 14 Lab, 15 Lab, 16 Lab, 17 Lab
Paper, tracing	1 sheet	11 Lab, 20 Lab
Paper, white	1 sheet	4.1 IA, 19 Lab, 22 Lab, 24.1 IA
	2 sheets	14.1 IA
Paper, white unlined	1 sheet	9.1 IA, 23.1 IA, 24 Lab
Paper towels	1 roll	2 Lab, 10.1 QL, 20.1 IA, 21.1 QL
Peanut	1	12.1 IA
Pen	1	21.1 IA
Pencil	1	4.1 IA, 8 Lab, 9 Lab, 11 Lab, 13 Lab, 14 Lab, 16 Lab, 17.1 IA, 19 Lab, 20 Lab, 21 Lab, 22 Lab, 23.1 IA, 24.1 IA, 24 Lab
Pencils, colored	1 set	10 Lab, 15 Lab, 17 Lab, 23 Lab
Penlight	1	25 Lab
Penny	1	2 Lab
Plastic bead, small, round	20–30	3.4 QL
Plastic putty	1 chunk	11.1 IA
Plate, glass	1	2 Lab
Protractor	1	1 Lab, 11 Lab
Psychrometer	1	18 Lab
Pushpin	2	23.1 IA
Pyrite sample	1	2 Lab
Raisin	1	12.1 IA
Resource object	5–10	4.1 IA
Ring stand	1	17 lab
Rock, small	5–10	5.1 IA
Rubber band, large, thick	1	11.1 IA
Ruler, metric (30-cm)	1	1 Lab, 4 Lab, 9 Lab, 16.1 IA, 20 Lab, 22.1 IA, 23.1 IA, 24 Lab
Sand, coarse	1	6 Lab
Sand sample	1	6 Lab, 14.1 IA, 17 Lab, 21.1 QL, 22.1 IA
Sandstone sample	1	3.1 IA, 3 Lab
Salt, non-iodized	4–5 tbsp	14.4 QL
Scalpel	1	14 Lab
Scissors	1	2 Lab, 4 Lab, 9.1 IA, 20.1 IA
Seashell	1	12.1 IA
Seismogram, p. 223	1 copy	8.2 QL
Shale sample	1	3 Lab
Shoe box	1	14 Lab
Slate sample	1	3 Lab
Soap, liquid 30-mL	1	20.1 IA
Soil sample, potting	1	6 Lab

NEW YORK

Item	*Quantity	Chapter
Softball	1	22 Lab
Southern Hemisphere, p. 551	1 copy	19 Lab
Spoon, table	1	14.4 QL
Spring scale	1	2 Lab
Star Charts (Appendix)	1 copy	25 Lab
Stick, flat wooden	2	17 Lab
Stick, small	1	12.1 IA
Stick, thin, wooden 25-cm	1	11.1 IA
Stirring rod	1	15 Lab
Stirring rod, glass	1	14.4 QL
Strainer	1	5.1 IA
Streak plate	1	2 Lab
String	20–35 cm	23.1 IA
Talc sample	1	2 Lab
Tape, duct	10-cm strip	20.1 IA
Tape, removable	4 strips	20 Lab
Tape, transparent	4 strips	23.1 IA, 24 Lab
Telescope	1	24 Lab
Temperature Curves Graph p. 301	1 copy	10 Lab

Item	*Quantity	Chapter
Tennis ball	1	19.1 IA
Test tube	2	15 Lab
Thermometer	1 2	5 Lab, 18.1 IA 17 Lab
Thermometer, laboratory	2	21.1 QL
Thread, thin	2 cm	2 Lab
Tooth, small	1	12.1 IA
Topographic Map, p. 211	1	7 Lab
Travel-time Graph p. 225	1 copy	8.2 QL
Washer, flat rubber 3/8" hole	1	20.1 IA
Watch or clock with a second hand	1	5 Lab, 6 Lab, 14.1 IA, 19.1 IA, 21.1 QL
Water, distilled	3 mL	3 Lab
Water, hot	200 mL	5 Lab
Water, noncarbonated	2 bottles	10.1 QL
Water, room temperature		18 Lab
Wax paper, 20-cm square	2	3.4 QL
Wood block	2	19.1 IA

Earth Science Media Products

In addition to the GEODe CD-ROM to accompany *Prentice Hall Earth Science,* you can order additional media products created by Dennis Tasa. Products can be ordered online at TasaGraphicArts.com or by calling the toll free number 800-293-2725. The following is a quick overview of available products. CD-ROMs run on both Macintosh and Windows operating systems. See the online catalog for system requirements.

The Theory of Plate Tectonics
CD-ROM format, written by Ed Tarbuck and Fred Lutgens

Earth's Dynamic Surface
CD-ROM format, written by Frank J. Passaglia

Tasa Portfolios
Four volumes, CD-ROM format with *JPEG* images; each volume offers 100 illustrations (with and without captions, with and without labels)

Tasa Photo CD-ROMs
Three volumes, CD-ROM format with *JPEG* images; each volume offers 100 photos

Introduction to Topographic Maps
CD-ROM format, written by Kenneth Pinske

Explore the Planets
CD-ROM format, written by G. Jeffrey Taylor

The Wonders of Rocks and Minerals
CD-ROM format, written by Ed Tarbuck, Fred Lutgens, Edward Greaney

Hands-On Mineral Identification
CD-ROM format, written by M. Darby Dyar

Illustrated Dictionary of Earth Science
CD-ROM format, written by American Geological Institute

Plate Tectonics 3-D Puzzle, Map, and Activity Kit
Includes Plexiglas puzzle, five full color maps, fifty black and white maps, and three activities with Teacher's Guide

Prentice Hall

EARTH SCIENCE

Physical Setting/Earth Science

Tarbuck ◆ Lutgens

Illustrated by **Dennis Tasa**

Needham, Massachusetts
Upper Saddle River, New Jersey

New York
Physical Setting/Earth Science

Print Components

New York Student Edition

New York Teacher's Edition

New York Progress Monitoring Assessments

New York Standardized Test Preparation Workbook

Lesson Plans
Laboratory Manual
Laboratory Manual, Annotated Teacher's Edition
Guided Reading and Study Workbook
Guided Reading and Study Workbook, Annotated Teacher's Edition
Chapter Tests

Technology

New York Earth Science Computer Test Bank CD-ROM

Prentice Hall Earth Science Teacher Express CD-ROM for New York

Earth Science Interactive Textbook
Earth Science Transparencies
Discovery Channel Earth Science Video Field Trips
Prentice Hall Earth Science Web Site
GEODe: Earth Science CD-ROM

Front matter

Page NY 5, James Randklev/Corbis; **NY 6 tr,** Dennis Tasa; **NY 6 tl,** GeoScience Resources/American Geological Institute (AGI); **NY 6 ml, NY 6 bl,** Edward J. Tarbuck; **NY 7,** Carl Purcell/Photo Researchers, Inc.; **NY 9,** Ira Block/National Geographic Image Collection; **NY 10,** Gary Bell/Seapics.com/Innerspace Visions; **NY 11,** Kent Wood/Science Source/Photo Researchers, Inc.; **NY 13,** Royal Observatory, Edinburgh/AATB/Science Photo Library/Photo Researchers, Inc.; **NY 15 t,** Bettmann/Corbis; **NY 15 m,** Ted Spiegel; **NY 15 b,** Science Photo Library; David Frazier/Photo Researchers, Inc.; **NY 17,** Art Wolfe; **NY 20,** Alan Schein/Corbis; **NY 23,** Ed Betz/AP; **NY 25,** Jeff Greenberg/ACE; **NY 26,** Syracuse Newspapers/Buffalo News/The Image Works; **NY 27,** Kevin Ferris; **NY 34 tl,** Reuters/Corbis; **NY 34 tr,** David Parker/Science Photo Library/Photo Researchers, Inc.; **NY 34 b,** David Frazier/ Photo Researchers, Inc.; **NY 35 tl,** Owen Franken/Stock Boston; **NY 35 tm,** Bill & Sally Fletcher/Tom Stack & Associates, Inc.; **NY 35 tr,** Bojan Breceli; **NY 35,** galaxy, Pat Lanza-Field/Bruce Coleman, Inc.; **NY 35 b,** James King-Holmes/Science Photo Library/Photo Researchers, Inc.

Chapter 11A

Pages ES 2–ES 3, James Randklev/Corbis; **ES 5,** David Sailors/Corbis; **ES 8 t,** Jim Wark/Peter Arnold; **ES 8 b,** Getty Images; **ES 9,** Harde Truesdale/The Image Works; **ES 10 t,** David Meunch/Corbis; **ES 10 b,** Jeffrey C. Freedman/Howe Caverns; **ES 11,** Hardie Truesdale Photography/Image State; **ES 12 t,** Lester V. Bergman/Corbis; **ES 12 m,** David Jennings/AP; **ES 12 b,** Getty Images; **ES 13,** Dave Jennings/AP/Wideworld Photos, **ES 14 t,** Kevin Ferris; **ES 14 b,** Elinor Osborn; **ES 15,** Richard Walker/Bruce Coleman; **ES 16,** Tim Roske/AP/Wideworld Photos; **ES 18 t,** Alan Schein/ Corbis; **ES 18 b,** Mark Gibson/Alamy; **ES 20 t,** Ed Betz/AP/Wideworld Photos; **ES 20 b,** B. Banaszewski/www.JonReis.com; **ES 21,** Ed Bailey/ AP/Wideworld Photos; **ES 22 t,** Jeff Greenberg/ACE; **ES 22 b,** Jeff Greenberg/ The Image Works; **ES 24,** Syracuse Newspapers/Buffalo News/The Image Works; **ES 32,** Corbis; **ES 33–48,** New York State Education Department.

Credits begin on page 802, which constitutes an extension of this copyright page.

ISBN 0-13-125955-5
1 2 3 4 5 6 7 8 9 10   10 09 08 07 06 05 04

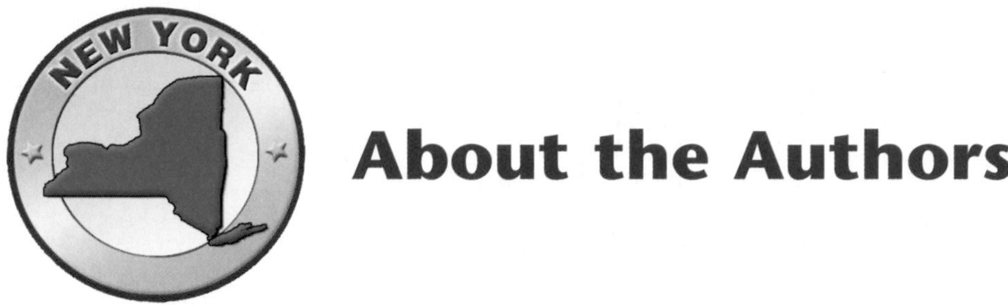

About the Authors

Edward J. Tarbuck

Edward J. Tarbuck served twenty-nine years as Professor of geosciences at Illinois Central College. During twenty of those years he was also Chair of the Math, Science and Engineering Department. Ed now holds a place as Professor Emeritus at Illinois Central College.

Frederick K. Lutgens

For thirty years, Frederick K. Lutgens served as Professor of geosciences at Illinois Central College. During his career he was awarded "The Faculty Who Make a Difference" honor in recognition of his outstanding academic performance and dedication to students. He is also Professor Emeritus at Illinois Central College.

Tarbuck and Lutgens

The term *synergistic* applies to the combined efforts of Tarbuck and Lutgens, two names widely recognized and respected in the field of geosciences. Early in their careers, they shared frustrations with the limited availability of textbooks designed for non-majors. Out of their dilemma sprang a series of textbooks that are utilized nationwide and have been published in English, Spanish, Italian and Korean. They have co-authored over forty editions of college textbooks including *Earth Science,* now in its 10th edition, *Earth: Introduction to Physical Geology,* and *The Atmosphere*. Tarbuck and Lutgens have received several publishing honors including the *Texty Award* for *Earth* and the *McGuffy Award* for *Earth Science,* both from the Text and Academic Authors Association.

With unfailing interest in exposing students to the broad world of geosciences, Tarbuck and Lutgens collaborated on the development and implementation of a field studies program that continues today at Illinois Central College.

Illustration by Dennis Tasa

Dennis Tasa has been illustrating college textbooks since 1978, specializing in the area of geology and geography. In 1993, he expanded his illustration work to develop and produce Earth Science educational CD-ROMs. Dennis has won numerous awards for his illustration and software products including EDDIE Awards by ComputEd Education Software Review for both Middle School and High School Science; Silver Awards, Summit Creative Awards; and the Children's Software and New Media Review School All Star Award.

It is with great pride that Prentice Hall brings the talents of this superb author team to the high school classroom.

High School Earth Science Consultant, Writer, and Reviewer

Michael Wysession

Michael Wysession received his Ph.D. in geophysics from Northwestern University in 1991. He is an Associate Professor in Earth and Planetary Sciences at Washington University in St. Louis, Missouri. His area of specialization is using seismic waves to explore Earth's interior. Dr. Wysession is an author on more than 50 scientific publications. For his research, he was awarded a Presidential Faculty Fellowship at the White House. He also has created educational simulations to accurately show how seismic waves propagate.

New York *Physical Setting/Earth Science* Program Advisors

The following teachers gave Prentice Hall feedback to shape this New York edition of Earth Science.

Donna Jean Bolner
Earth Science Teacher
LaGrange Middle School
LaGrangeville, New York

Robert A. Fendrick
Earth Science Teacher
Tottenville High School
Staten Island, New York

Thomas Lewis
Former Earth Science Teacher
Greece Central Schools
Rochester, New York

Glenn Dolphin
Earth Science Teacher
Union-Endicott Central Schools
Endicott, New York

JulieAnn Hugick
Earth Science Teacher
Eastchester Middle School
Eastchester, New York

Bradly A. Pendergraft
Earth Science Teacher
Salmon River Central School
Ft. Covington, New York

Teacher Reviewers

Helen A. Bastin
Bloomington High School North
Bloomington, Indiana

David R. Blakely
Arlington High School
Arlington, Massachusetts

Joseph M. Bosco Jr.
New Britain High School
New Britain, Connecticut

Jo A. Combs
Broward County Schools
Ft. Lauderdale, Florida

Scott Cordell
Earth Science Teacher
Armarillo, Texas

Elizabeth Elixman Campbell
Warren Central High School
Indianapolis, Indiana

Glen Dolphin
Union-Endicott High School
Endicott, New York

Richard P. Filson
Edison High School
Stockton, California

Greg J. Geisen
New Albany High School
New Albany, Indiana

Georgina Koch Hidalgo
Miami-Dade County Public Schools
Miami, Florida

Kristine J. Kelley
Wilkes Central High School
Wilkesboro, North Carolina

Kevin Leineweber
Tippecanoe School Corporation
Lafayette, Indiana

Marian J. Marley
Wilkes Central High School
Wilkesboro, North Carolina

Bruce A. Mellin
Brooks School
North Andover, Massachusetts

George Mumford
Dover, Massachusetts

Michael Passow
White Plains Middle School
White Plains, New York

Gregory S. Small
William Henry Harrison High School
Evansville, Indiana

Thomas J. Vaughn
Arlington High School
Arlington, Massachusetts

Donald G. Wafer
Muncie Central High School
Muncie, Indiana

Jeffrey A. Williams
New Albany High School
New Albany, Indiana

Content Reviewers

Glen C. Kroeger, Ph.D.
Associate Professor and Chair Geosciences Department
Trinity University
San Antonio, Texas

George S. Mumford, Ph.D.
Professor of Astronomy, Emeritus
Tufts University
Medford, Massachusetts

Scott M. Rochette, Ph.D.
Department of the Earth Sciences
State University of New York at Brockport
Brockport, New York

Ronald Sass
Ecology and Evolutionary Biology
Rice University
Houston, Texas

Paul R. Stoddard, Ph.D.
Department of Geology and Environmental Geosciences
Northern Illinois University
DeKalb, Illinois

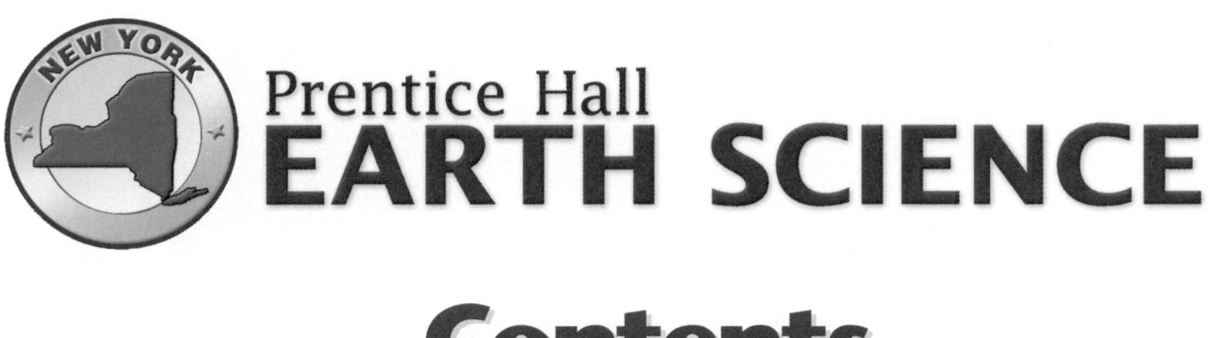
NEW YORK
Prentice Hall
EARTH SCIENCE

Contents

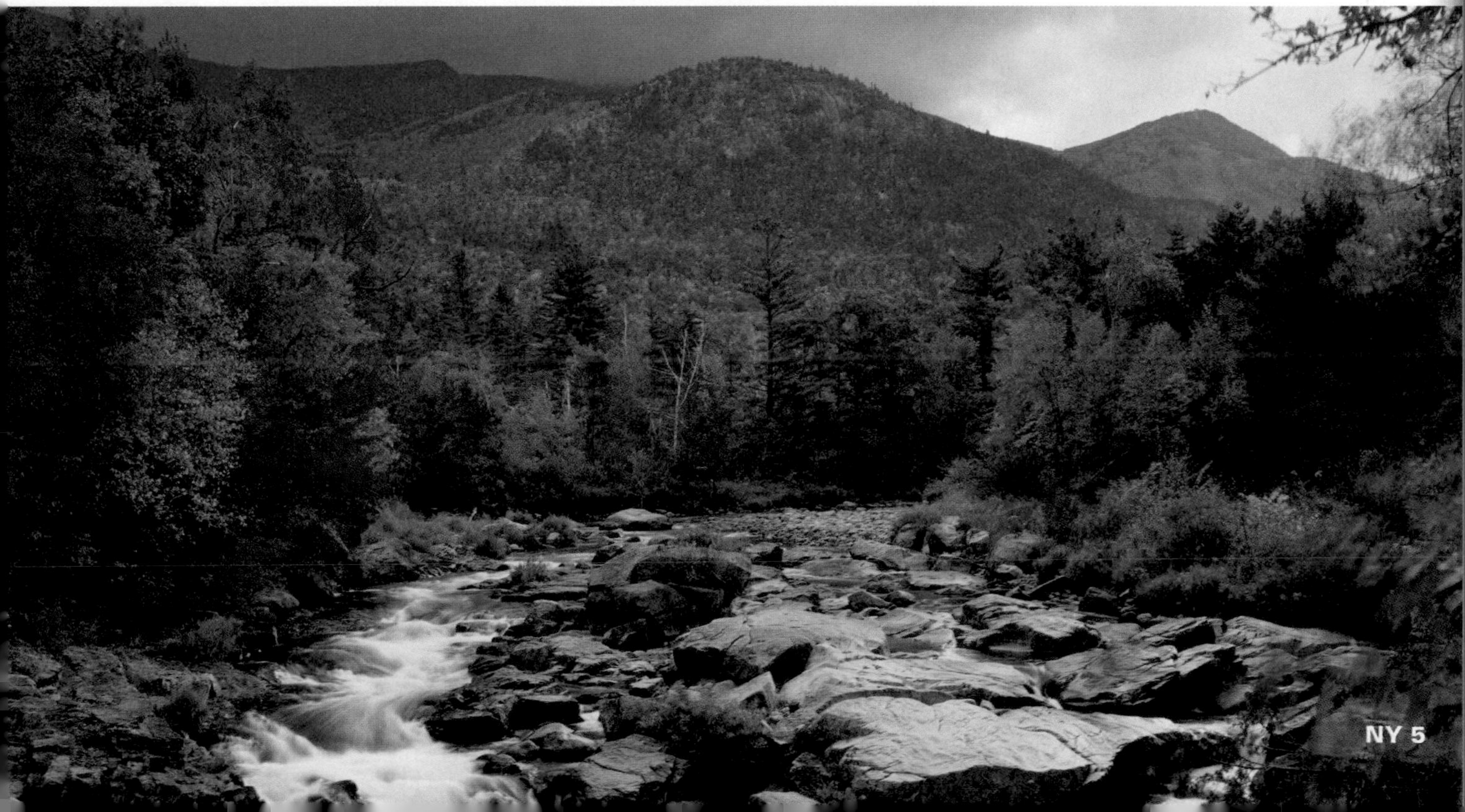

Unit 1 Earth's Materials

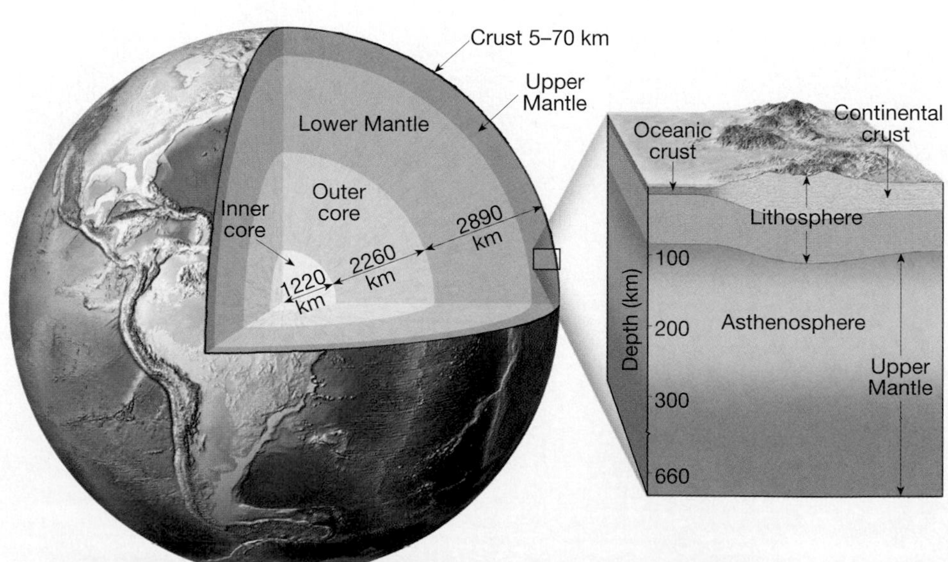

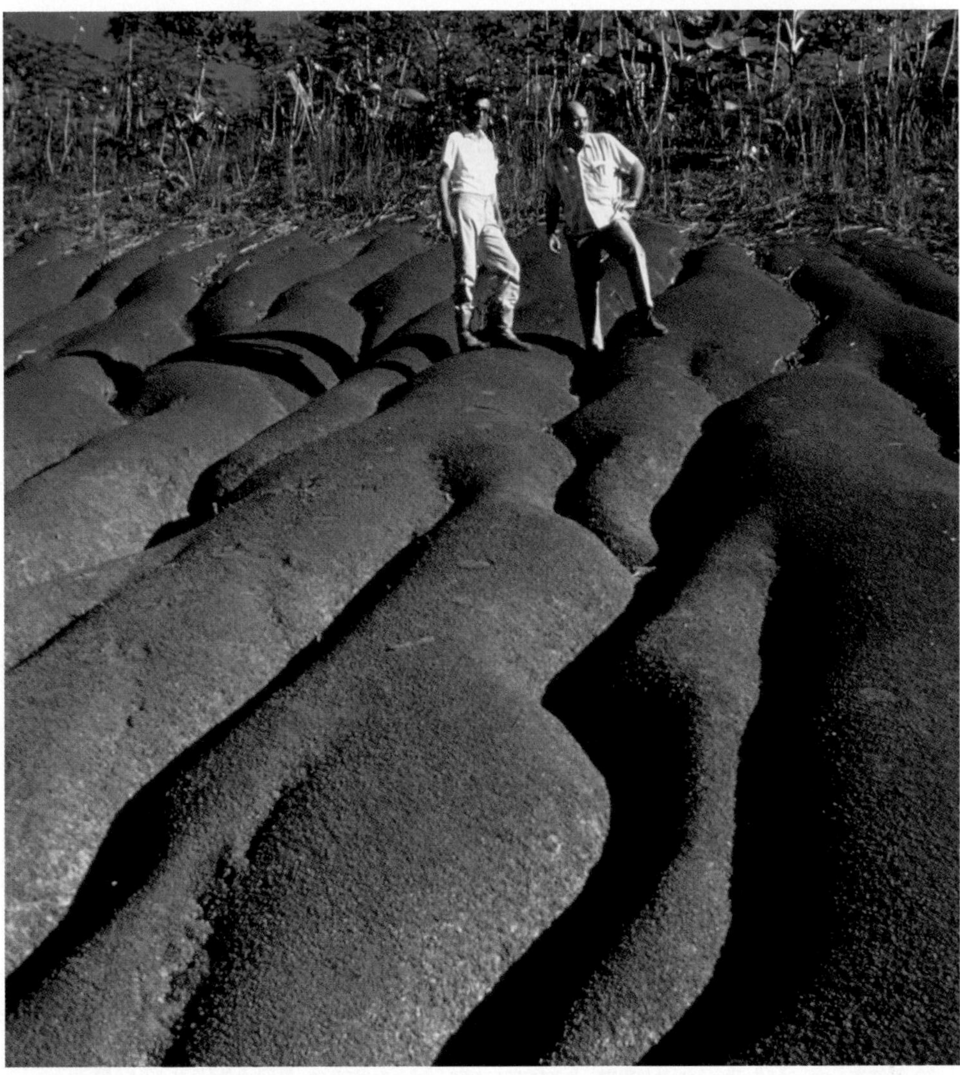

Unit 2 Sculpturing Earth's Surface

Contents

Unit 3 Forces Within

Unit 4 Historical Geology

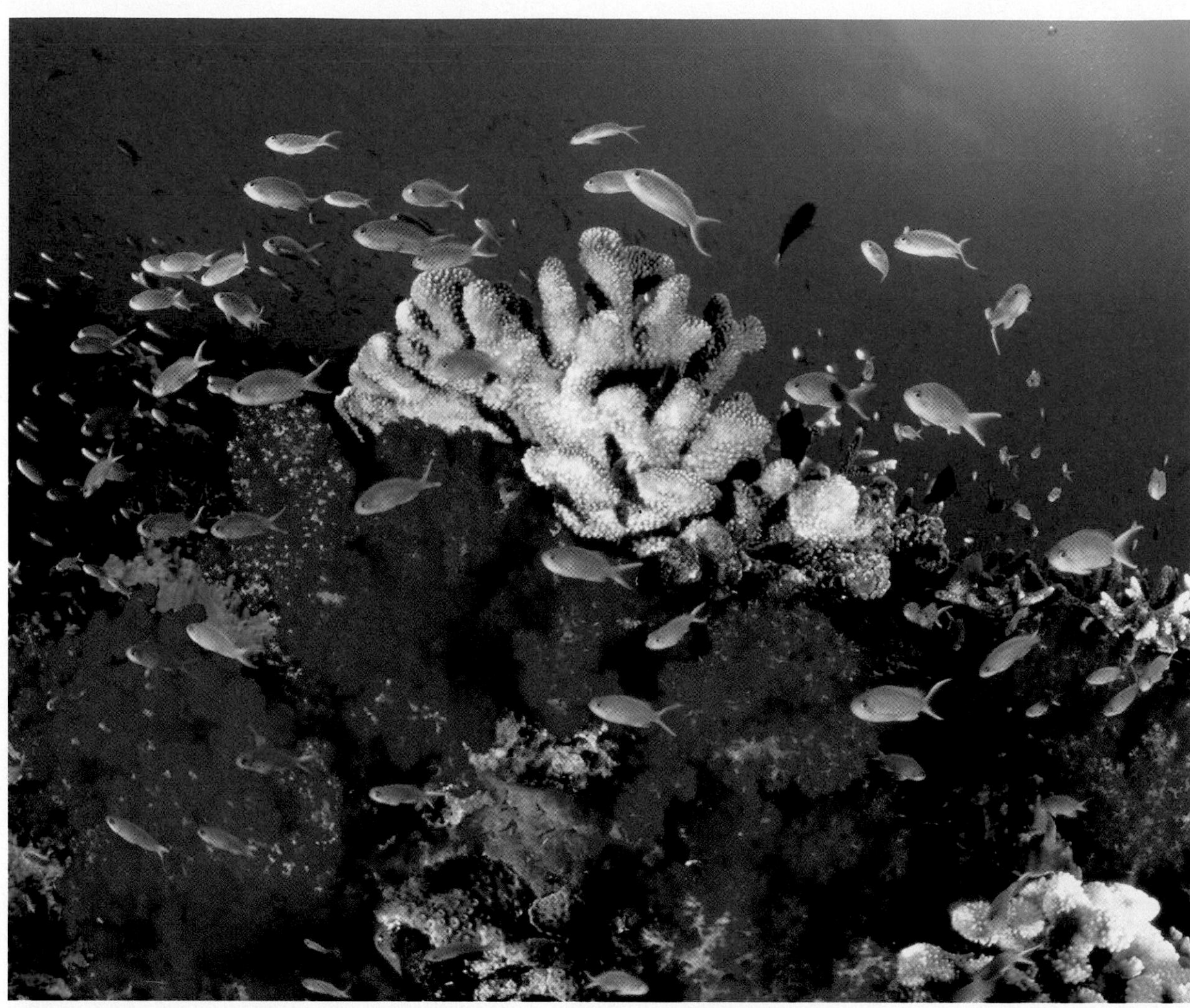

Unit 5 Oceanography

Unit 6 Meteorology

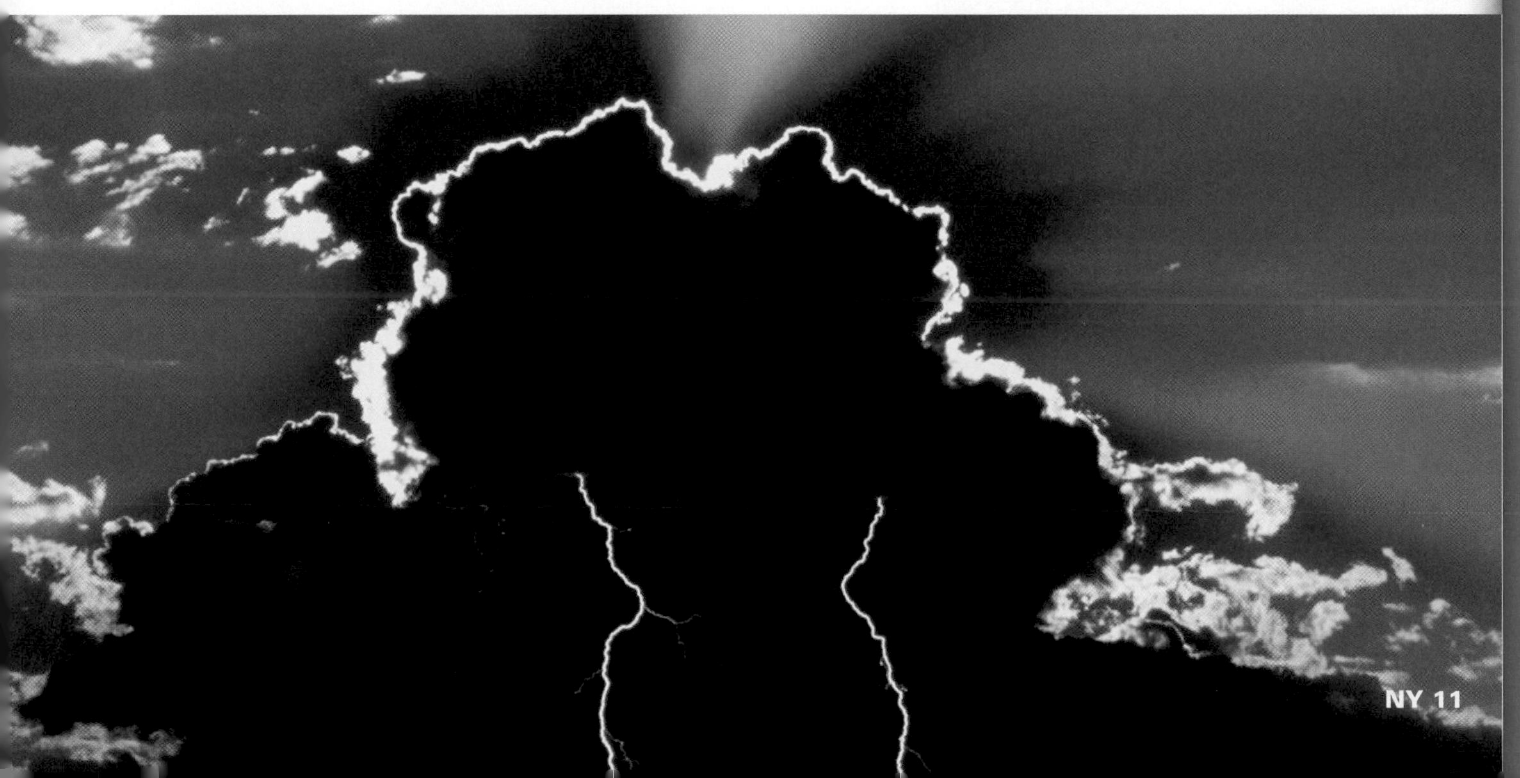

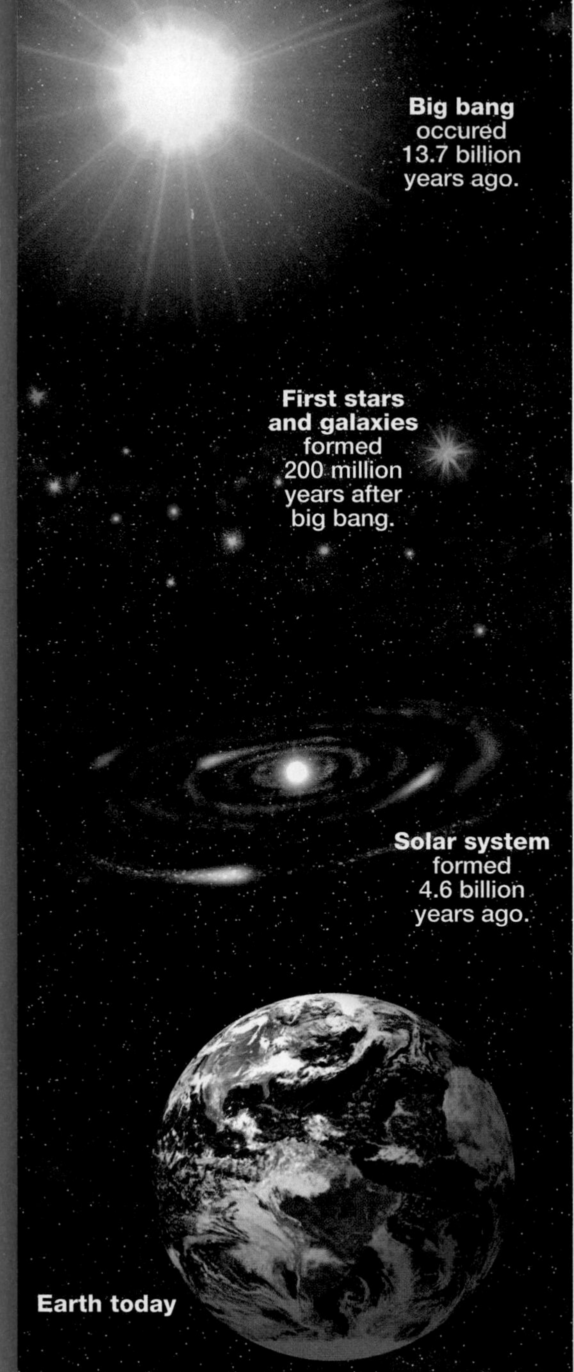
Big bang
occured
13.7 billion
years ago.
First stars
and galaxies
formed
200 million
years after
big bang.
Solar system
formed
4.6 billion
years ago.
Earth today

Unit 7 Astronomy

Skills and Reference Handbook

Labs and Activities

Inquiry Activity

Begin each chapter with an activity that sets a purpose for reading.

Quick Lab

Introduce and reinforce key lesson content using simple materials.

Exploration Lab

Practice and develop science methods.

Application Lab

Apply concepts in a real-world context.

Problem-Solving Activity

Apply science content in a new situation.

Features

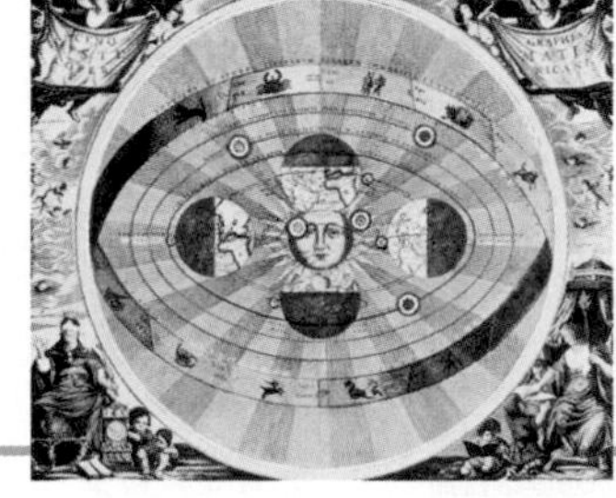

Recognize some of the important interrelationships among Earth's spheres.

people and the
ENVIRONMENT

Develop a better understanding of the effects of human activity on the natural environment.

understanding
EARTH

Examine some of the difficulties encountered by scientists as they collect reliable data about our planet.

How the Earth Works

MAP MASTER™ Skills Activity

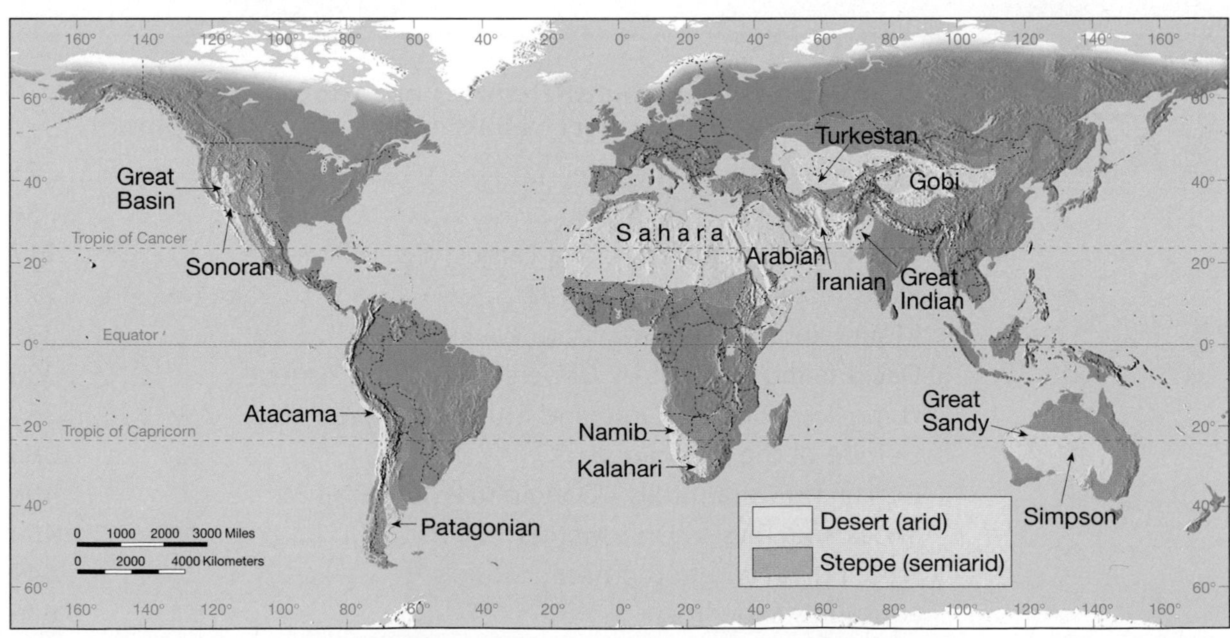

Video Field Trip

These videos will take you to places all over the world to explore some Earth Science topics that make our planet so unique in the universe.

This engaging CD-ROM takes you on an audiovisual tour of the key concepts in the text. Through the wonder of animation, you can actually see in just a few seconds the dynamic processes that occur on Earth over millions of years. To be sure that you understand what you've learned, you'll work with a number of interesting interactive exercises to test your knowledge of each topic.

Unit 1 Earth Materials

A. Minerals
   1. Introduction
   2. Major Mineral Groups
   3. Properties Used to Identify Minerals
   4. Mineral Identification

B. Rock Cycle

C. Igneous Rocks
   1. Introduction
   2. Igneous Textures
   3. Naming Igneous Rocks

D. Sedimentary Rocks
   1. Introduction
   2. Types of Sedimentary Rocks

E. Metamorphic Rocks
   1. Introduction
   2. Agents of Metamorphism
   3. Textural and Mineralogical Changes
   4. Common Metamorphic Rocks

Unit 2 Sculpturing Earth's Surface

A. Hydrologic Cycle

B. Running Water
   1. Stream Characteristics

C. Groundwater
   1. Groundwater and its Importance
   2. Springs and Wells

D. Glaciers
   1. Introduction
   2. Budget of a Glacier

E. Deserts
   1. Distribution and Causes of Dry Lands
   2. Common Misconceptions About Deserts

Unit 3 Forces Within

A. Earthquakes
   1. What is an Earthquake?
   2. Seismology: Earthquake Waves
   3. Locating an Earthquake
   4. Earth's Layered Structure

B. Plate Tectonics
   1. Introduction
   2. Plate Boundaries

C. Igneous Activity
   1. The Nature of Volcanic Eruptions
   2. Materials Extruded During an Eruption
   3. Volcanoes
   4. Intrusive Igneous Activity

Audiovisual tutorials and aerial views make large-scale concepts easier to understand.

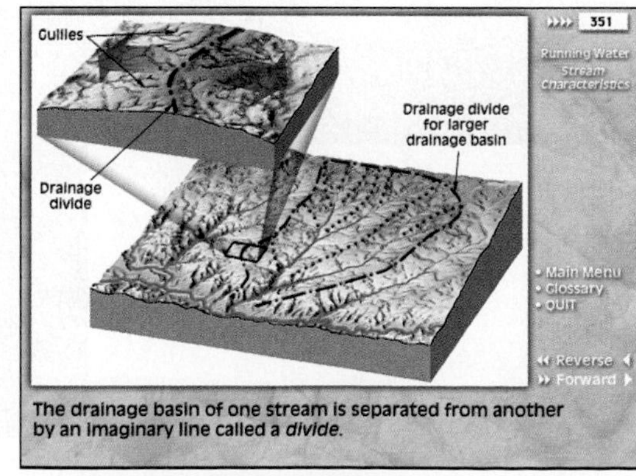

from Stream Characteristics

Animations can quickly show you changes that have occurred over thousands of years.

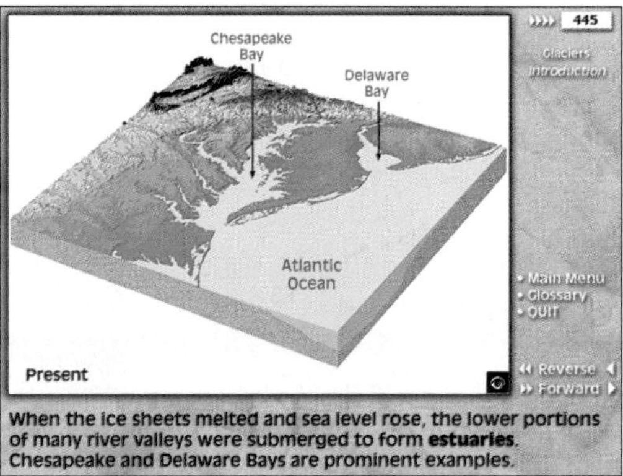

445
Glaciers Introduction
Chesapeake Bay
Delaware Bay
Atlantic Ocean
Present
• Main Menu
• Glossary
• QUIT
Reverse
Forward
When the ice sheets melted and sea level rose, the lower portions of many river valleys were submerged to form **estuaries**. Chesapeake and Delaware Bays are prominent examples.

from Introduction to Glaciers

Contents

New York Learning Standards for Mathematics, Science, and Technology

The State of New York defines seven learning standards as the foundation of instruction for math, science, and technology.

Below you will find the seven learning standards that apply to this course. Pay particular attention to Standard 4. The Core Curriculum starting on the next page further defines Standard 4. The Core Curriculum is broken down into Key Ideas and Performance Indicators. Each chapter in your textbook contains a Regents Prep quiz to practice and increase your skills throughout the year.

Standards 1, 2, 6, and 7 describe the laboratory, problem-solving, and applied topics in your curriculum. You will encounter these throughout the year, as well as on the Regents Prep pages and other exams your teacher will give to help you prepare for the Regents Examination.

Learning Standards

STANDARD 1

Students will use mathematical analysis, scientific inquiry, and engineering design, as appropriate, to pose questions, seek answers, and develop solutions.

STANDARD 2

Students will access, generate, process, and transfer information using appropriate technologies.

STANDARD 3

Students will understand mathematics and become mathematically confident by communicating and reasoning mathematically, by applying mathematics in real-world settings, and by solving problems through the integrated study of number systems, geometry, algebra, data analysis, probability, and trigonometry.

STANDARD 4

Students will understand and apply scientific concepts, principles, and theories pertaining to the physical setting and living environment and recognize the historical development of ideas in science.

STANDARD 5

Students will apply technological knowledge and skills to design, construct, use, and evaluate products and systems to satisfy human and environmental needs.

STANDARD 6

Students will understand the relationships and common themes that connect mathematics, science, and technology and apply the themes to these and other areas of learning.

STANDARD 7

Students will apply the knowledge and thinking skills of mathematics, science, and technology to address real-life problems and make informed decisions.

New York Physical Setting/Earth Science Core Curriculum

The High School Regents Examination for Physical Setting/Earth Science measures mastery of Standards 1, 2, 4, 6, and 7. Most of the exam covers Standard 4. Use this listing as the set of objectives that must be mastered prior to taking the exam. The Regents Practice Exam pages at the end of each chapter in your text address these objectives.

STANDARD 1

Students will use mathematical analysis, scientific inquiry, and engineering design, as appropriate, to pose questions, seek answers, and develop solutions.

Mathematical Analysis: Key Idea 1

Abstraction and symbolic representation are used to communicate mathematically.

- use eccentricity, rate, gradient, standard error of measurement, and density in context

Mathematical Analysis: Key Idea 2

Deductive and inductive reasoning are used to reach mathematical conclusions.

- determine the relationships among: velocity, slope, sediment size, channel shape, and volume of a stream
- understand the relationships among: the planets' distance from the Sun, gravitational force, period of revolution, and speed of revolution

Mathematical Analysis: Key Idea 3

Critical thinking skills are used in the solution of mathematical problems.

- in a field, use isolines to determine a source of pollution

Scientific Inquiry: Key Idea 1

The central purpose of scientific inquiry is to develop explanations of natural phenomena in a continuing, creative process.

- show how our observation of celestial motions supports the idea of stars moving around a stationary Earth (the geocentric model), but further investigation has led scientists to understand that most of these changes are a result of Earth's motion around the Sun (the heliocentric model)

Core Curriculum

Scientific Inquiry: Key Idea 2

Beyond the use of reasoning and consensus, scientific inquiry involves the testing of proposed explanations involving the use of conventional techniques and procedures and usually requiring considerable ingenuity.

- test sediment properties and the rate of deposition

Scientific Inquiry: Key Idea 3

The observations made while testing proposed explanations, when analyzed using conventional and invented methods, provide new insights into phenomena.

- determine the changing length of a shadow based on the motion of the Sun

Engineering Design: Key Idea 1

Engineering design is an iterative process involving modeling and optimization (finding the best solution within given constraints); this process is used to develop technological solutions to problems within given constraints.

- after experimenting with conduction of heat (using calorimeters and aluminum bars), make recommendations to create a more efficient system of heat transfer
- determine patterns of topography and drainage around your school and design solutions to effectively deal with runoff

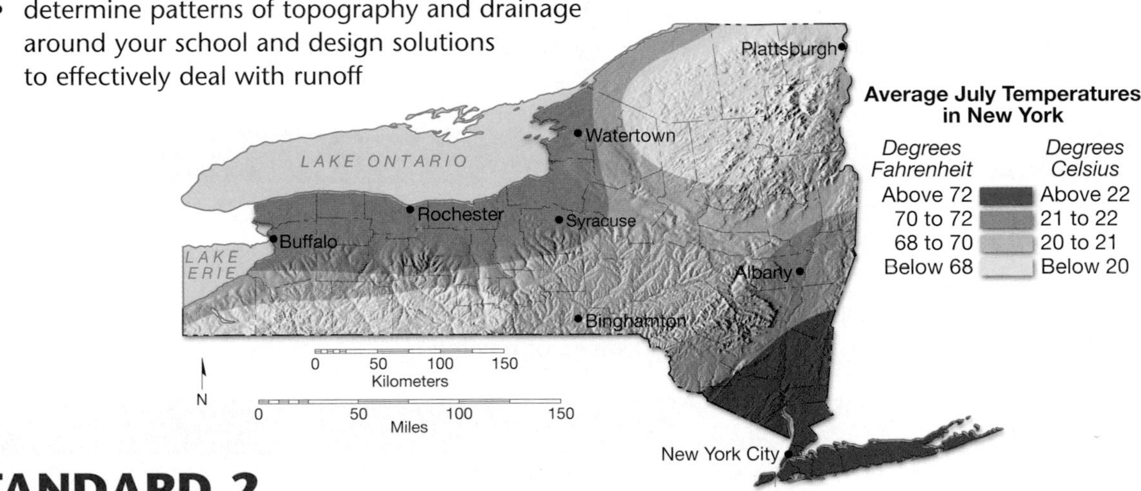

STANDARD 2

Students will access, generate, process, and transfer information using appropriate technologies.

Information Systems: Key Idea 1

Information technology is used to retrieve, process, and communicate information as a tool to enhance learning.

- analyze weather maps to predict future weather events
- use library or electronic references to obtain information to support a laboratory conclusion

Information Systems: Key Idea 2

Knowledge of the impacts and limitations of information systems is essential to its effective and ethical use.

- obtain printed or electronic materials which exemplify miscommunication and/or misconceptions of current commonly accepted scientific knowledge

Information Systems: Key Idea 3

Information technology can have positive and negative impacts on society, depending upon how it is used.

- discuss how early warning systems can protect society and the environment from natural disasters such as hurricanes, tornadoes, earthquakes, tsunamis, floods, and volcanoes

STANDARD 4

Students will understand and apply scientific concepts, principles, and theories pertaining to the physical setting and living environment and recognize the historical development of ideas in science.

Key Idea 1

The Earth and celestial phenomena can be described by principles of relative motion and perspective.

Performance Indicator 1.1

Explain complex phenomena, such as tides, variations in day length, solar insolation, apparent motion of the planets, and annual traverse of the constellations.

1.1a Most objects in the solar system are in regular and predictable motion.

1.1b Nine planets move around the Sun in nearly circular orbits.

1.1c Earth's coordinate system of latitude and longitude, with the equator and prime meridian as reference lines, is based upon Earth's rotation and our observation of the Sun and stars.

1.1d Earth rotates on an imaginary axis at a rate of 15 degrees per hour. To people on Earth, this turning of the planet makes it seem as though the Sun, the moon, and the stars are moving around Earth once a day. Rotation provides a basis for our system of local time; meridians of longitude are the basis for time zones.

1.1e The Foucault pendulum and the Coriolis effect provide evidence of Earth's rotation.

1.1f Earth's changing position with regard to the Sun and the moon has noticeable effects.

1.1g Seasonal changes in the apparent positions of constellations provide evidence of Earth's revolution.

1.1h The Sun's apparent path through the sky varies with latitude and season.

1.1i Approximately 70 percent of Earth's surface is covered by a relatively thin layer of water, which responds to the gravitational attraction of the moon and the Sun with a daily cycle of high and low tides.

Performance Indicator 1.2

Describe current theories about the origin of the universe and solar system.

1.2a The universe is vast and estimated to be over ten billion years old. The current theory is that the universe was created from an explosion called the Big Bang. Evidence for this theory includes: cosmic background radiation and a red-shift (the Doppler effect) in the light from very distant galaxies.

1.2b Stars form when gravity causes clouds of molecules to contract until nuclear fusion of light elements into heavier ones occurs. Fusion releases great amounts of energy over millions of years.

1.2c Our solar system formed about five billion years ago from a giant cloud of gas and debris. Gravity caused Earth and the other planets to become layered according to density differences in their materials.

1.2d Asteroids, comets, and meteors are components of our solar system.

1.2e Earth's early atmosphere formed as a result of the outgassing of water vapor, carbon dioxide, nitrogen, and lesser amounts of other gases from its interior.

1.2f Earth's oceans formed as a result of precipitation over millions of years. The presence of an early ocean is indicated by sedimentary rocks of marine origin, dating back about four billion years.

1.2g Earth has continuously been recycling water since the outgassing of water early in its history. This constant recirculation of water at and near Earth's surface is described by the hydrologic (water) cycle.

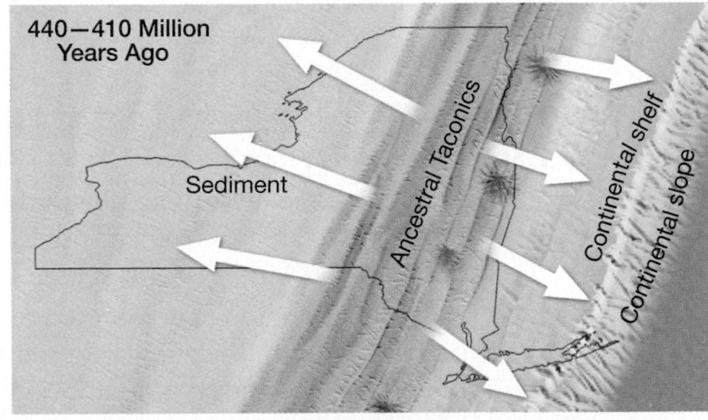

1.2h The evolution of life caused dramatic changes in the composition of Earth's atmosphere. Free oxygen did not form in the atmosphere until oxygen-producing organisms evolved.

1.2i The pattern of evolution of life-forms on Earth is at least partially preserved in the rock record.

1.2j Geologic history can be reconstructed by observing sequences of rock types and fossils to correlate bedrock at various locations.

Key Idea 2

Many of the phenomena that we observe on Earth involve interactions among components of air, water, and land.

Performance Indicator 2.1

Use the concepts of density and heat energy to explain observations of weather patterns, seasonal changes, and the movements of Earth's plates.

2.1a Earth systems have internal and external sources of energy, both of which create heat.

2.1b The transfer of heat energy within the atmosphere, the hydrosphere, and Earth's interior results in the formation of regions of different densities. These density differences result in motion.

2.1c Weather patterns become evident when weather variables are observed, measured, and recorded. These variables include air temperature, air pressure, moisture, precipitation, wind speed and direction, and cloud cover.

2.1d Weather variables are measured using instruments such as thermometers, barometers, psychrometers, precipitation gauges, anemometers, and wind vanes.

2.1e Weather variables are interrelated.

2.1f Air temperature, dewpoint, cloud formation, and precipitation are affected by the expansion and contraction of air due to vertical atmospheric movement.

2.1g Weather variables can be represented in a variety of formats including radar and satellite images, weather maps, atmospheric cross-sections, and computer models.

2.1h Atmospheric moisture, temperature and pressure distributions; jet streams, wind; air masses and frontal boundaries; and the movement of cyclonic systems and associated tornadoes, thunderstorms, and hurricanes occur in observable patterns. Loss of property, personal injury, and loss of life can be reduced by effective emergency preparedness.

2.1i Seasonal changes can be explained using concepts of density and heat energy. These changes include the shifting of global temperature zones, the shifting of planetary wind and ocean current patterns, the occurrence of monsoons, hurricanes, flooding, and severe weather.

2.1j Properties of Earth's internal structure can be inferred from the analysis of the behavior of seismic waves.

2.1k The outward transfer of Earth's internal heat drives convective circulation in the mantle that moves the lithospheric plates comprising Earth's surface.

2.1l The lithosphere consists of separate plates that ride on the more fluid asthenosphere and move slowly in relationship to one another, creating convergent, divergent, and transform plate boundaries. These motions indicate Earth is a dynamic geologic system.

2.1m Many processes of the rock cycle are consequences of plate dynamics. These include the production of magma at both subduction and rifting regions, regional metamorphism within subduction zones, and the creation of major depositional basins through down-warping of the crust.

2.1n Many of Earth's surface features such as mid-ocean ridges/rifts, trenches/subduction zones/island arcs, mountain ranges, hot spots, and the magnetic and age patterns in surface bedrock are a consequence of forces associated with plate motion and interaction.

2.1o Plate motions have resulted in global changes in geography, climate, and the patterns of organic evolution.

2.1p Landforms are the result of the interaction of tectonic forces and the processes of weathering, erosion, and deposition.

2.1q Topographic maps represent landforms through the use of contour lines that are isolines connecting points of equal elevation. Gradients and profiles can be determined from changes in elevation over a given distance.

2.1r Climate variations, structure, and characteristics of bedrock influence the development of landscape features including mountains, plateaus, plains, valleys, ridges, escarpments, and stream drainage patterns.

2.1s Weathering is the physical and chemical breakdown of rocks at or near Earth's surface. Soils are the result of weathering and biological activity over long periods of time.

2.1t Natural agents of erosion, generally driven by gravity, remove, transport, and deposit weathered rock particles. Each agent of erosion produces distinctive changes in the material that it transports and creates characteristic surface features and landscapes. In certain erosional situations, loss of property, personal injury, and loss of life can be reduced by effective emergency preparedness.

2.1u The natural agents of erosion include: streams (running water), glaciers (moving ice), wave action, wind, and mass movement.

2.1v Patterns of deposition result from a loss of energy within the transporting system and are influenced by the size, shape, and density of the transported particles. Sediment deposits may be sorted or unsorted.

2.1w Sediments of inorganic and organic origin often accumulate in depositional environments. Sedimentary rocks form when sediments are compacted and/or cemented after burial or as the result of chemical precipitation from seawater.

Performance Indicator 2.2

Explain how incoming solar radiation, ocean currents, and land masses affect weather and climate.

2.2a Insolation (solar radiation) heats Earth's surface and atmosphere unequally due to variations in:

- the intensity caused by differences in atmospheric transparency and angle of incidence which vary with time of day, latitude, and season
- characteristics of the materials absorbing the energy such as color, texture, transparency, state of matter, and specific heat
- duration, which varies with seasons and latitude.

2.2b The transfer of heat energy within the atmosphere, the hydrosphere, and Earth's surface occurs as the result of radiation, convection, and conduction.

2.2c A location's climate is influenced by latitude, proximity to large bodies of water, ocean currents, prevailing winds, vegetative cover, elevation, and mountain ranges.

2.2d Temperature and precipitation patterns are altered by: natural events such as El Niño and volcanic eruptions, or human influences including deforestation, urbanization, and the production of greenhouse gases such as carbon dioxide and methane.

Key Idea 3

Matter is made up of particles whose properties determine the observable characteristics of matter and its reactivity.

Performance Indicator 3.1

Explain the properties of materials in terms of the arrangement and properties of the atoms that compose them.

3.1a Minerals have physical properties determined by their chemical composition and crystal structure.

3.1b Minerals are formed inorganically by the process of crystallization as a result of specific environmental conditions. These include:

- cooling and solidification of magma

- precipitation from water caused by such processes as evaporation, chemical reactions, and temperature changes
- rearrangement of atoms in existing minerals subjected to conditions of high temperature and pressure.

3.1c Rocks are usually composed of one or more minerals.

STANDARD 6

Students will understand the relationships and common themes that connect mathematics, science, and technology and apply the themes to these and other areas of learning.

Systems Thinking: Key Idea 1

Through systems thinking, people can recognize the commonalities that exist among all systems and how parts of a system interrelate and combine to perform specific functions.

- analyze a depositional-erosional system of a stream

Models: Key Idea 2

Models are simplified representations of objects, structures, or systems used in analysis, explanation, interpretation, or design.

- draw a simple contour map of a model landform
- design a 3-D landscape model from a contour map
- construct and interpret a profile based on an isoline map
- use flowcharts to identify rocks and minerals

Magnitude and Scale: Key Idea 3

The grouping of magnitudes of size, time, frequency, and pressures or other units of measurement into a series of relative order provides a useful way to deal with the immense range and the changes in scale that affect the behavior and design of systems.

- develop a scale model to represent planet size and/or distance
- develop a scale model of units of geologic time
- use topographical maps to determine distances and elevations

Equilibrium and Stability: Key Idea 4

Equilibrium is a state of stability due either to a lack of change (static equilibrium) or a balance between opposing forces (dynamic equilibrium).

- analyze the interrelationship between gravity and inertia and its effects on the orbit of planets or satellites

Patterns of Change: Key Idea 5

Identifying patterns of change is necessary for making predictions about future behavior and conditions.

- graph and interpret the nature of cyclic change such as sunspots, tides, and atmospheric carbon dioxide

- based on present data of plate movement, determine past and future positions of land masses
- using given weather data, identify the interface between air masses, such as cold fronts, warm fronts, and stationary fronts

Optimization: Key Idea 6

In order to arrive at the best solution that meets criteria within constraints, it is often necessary to make trade-offs.

- debate the effect of human activities as they relate to quality of life on Earth systems (global warming, land use, preservation of natural resources, pollution)

STANDARD 7

Students will apply the knowledge and thinking skills of mathematics, science, and technology to address real-life problems and make informed decisions.

Connections: Key Idea 1

The knowledge and skills of mathematics, science, and technology are used together to make informed decisions and solve problems, especially those relating to issues of science/technology/society, consumer decision making, design, and inquiry into phenomena.

- analyze the issues related to local energy needs and develop a viable energy generation plan for the community
- investigate two similar fossils to determine if they represent a developmental change over time
- investigate the political, economic, and environmental impact of global distribution and use of mineral resources and fossil fuels
- consider environmental and social implications of various solutions to an environmental Earth resources problem

Strategies: Key Idea 2

Solving interdisciplinary problems involves a variety of skills and strategies, including effective work habits; gathering and processing information; generating and analyzing ideas; realizing ideas; making connections among the common themes of mathematics, science, and technology; and presenting results.

- collect, collate, and process data concerning potential natural disasters (tornadoes, thunderstorms, blizzards, earthquakes, tsunamis, floods, volcanic eruptions, asteroid impacts, etc.) in an area and develop an emergency action plan
- using a topographic map, determine the safest and most efficient route for rescue purposes

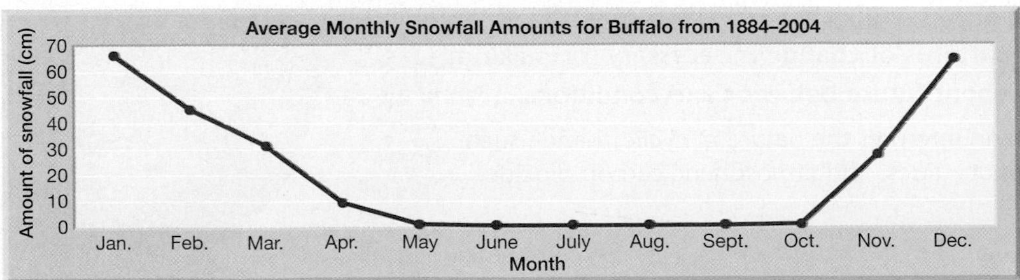

Your Guide to the Regents High School Examination for Physical Setting/Earth Science

What Is the Regents Examination Program for Science?

Regents Examinations for high school science are achievement tests designed to measure your understanding of the standards and core curriculum for that course. This is the information you'll find on pages NY 20–NY 27 of this text. The Regents Examination for Physical Setting/Earth Science is generally given in June and August. The exam is timed, and you will be given three hours to complete your work. You must attain a minimum score of 65 to receive credit towards a Regents diploma for the course. Note that there can be changes in administration policies and in the format and structure of the exam.

Earth Science Reference Tables will be made available to you for the exam. These are the same tables that you will find in Chapter 11A of this text. Many of the questions on the exam require you to interpret the tables, charts, and maps in these reference materials. All parts of the exam include questions that may require the use of the Reference Tables.

Physical Setting/Earth Science examination currently consists of the following:

> **Part A** of the exam contains about 35 multiple-choice questions. Answers for Part A questions are recorded on the answer sheet at the back of the exam.

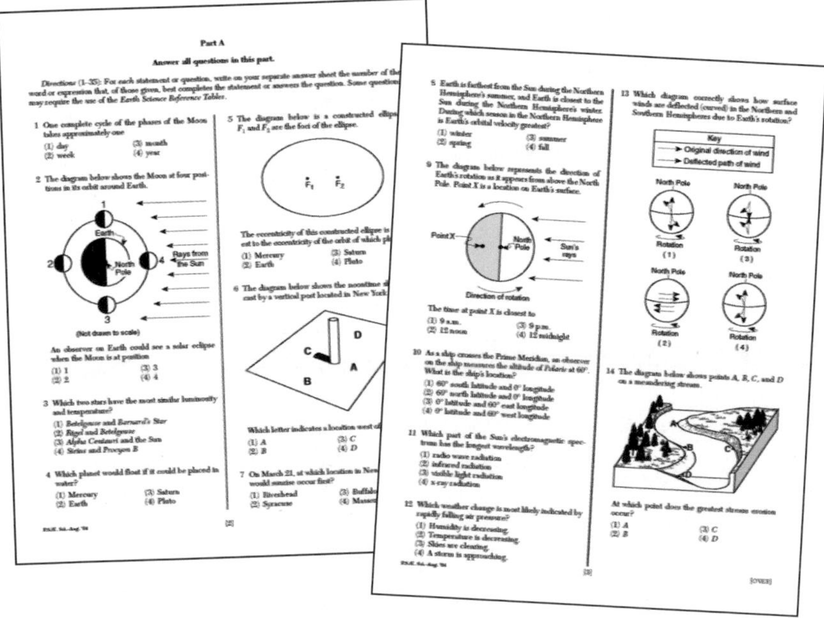
Part A

Answer all questions in this part.

Pages from Part A of a past exam

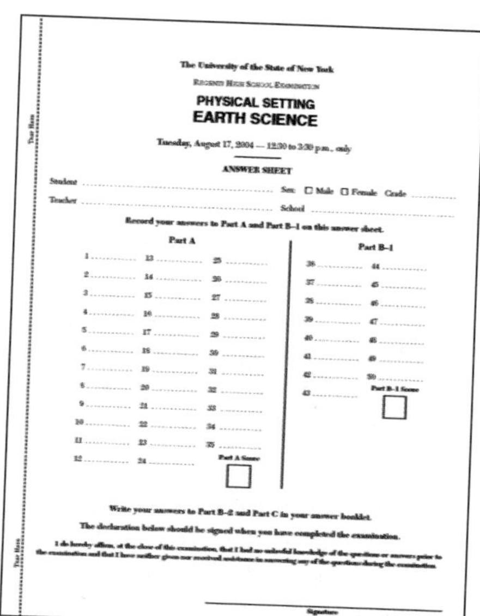
The University of the State of New York

PHYSICAL SETTING
EARTH SCIENCE

ANSWER SHEET

Part A

Part B–1

Answer sheet for Parts A and B–1

Part B–1 also contains multiple-choice questions. There are about 15 items in this section, and multiple items are linked to a single diagram or chart. Answers for these items are also recorded on the answer sheet at the back of the exam.

Part B–2 items include short answer, extended response, and items that involve completing diagrams and tables. This section of the exam can contain 8–10 items. Answers for items in Part B–2 are recorded in a separate answer booklet.

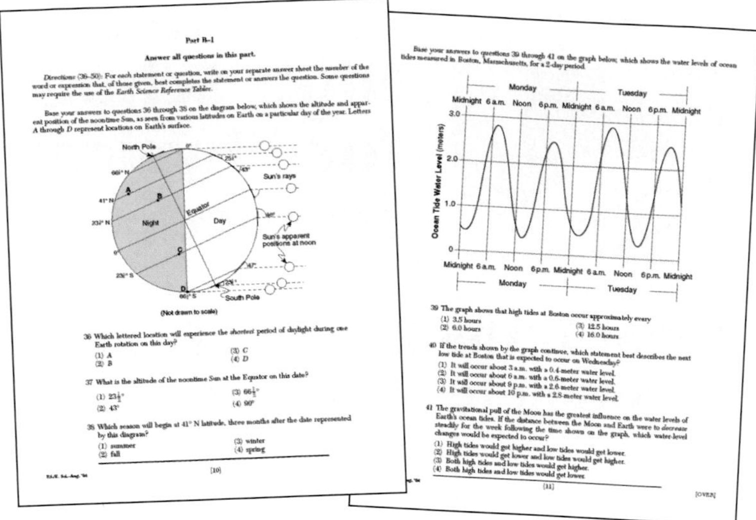

Pages from Part B–1 of a past exam

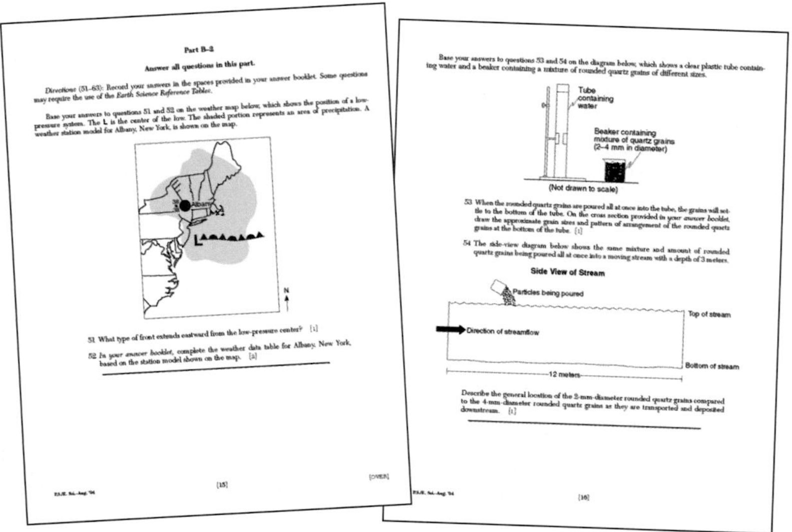

Pages from Part B–2 of a past exam

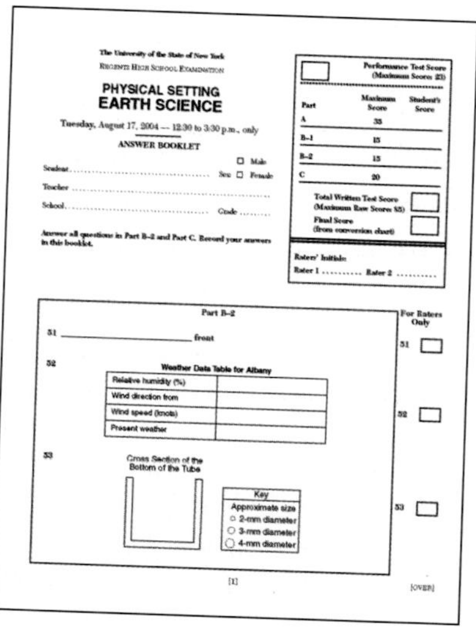

Answer sheet sample for Part B–2

Part C of the exam can contain 10–15 items. The items in this section include essays and labeling diagrams and maps. In some cases, you will be expected to read a passage of text and answer several questions related to the passage. Answers for these items are also recorded in the answer booklet.

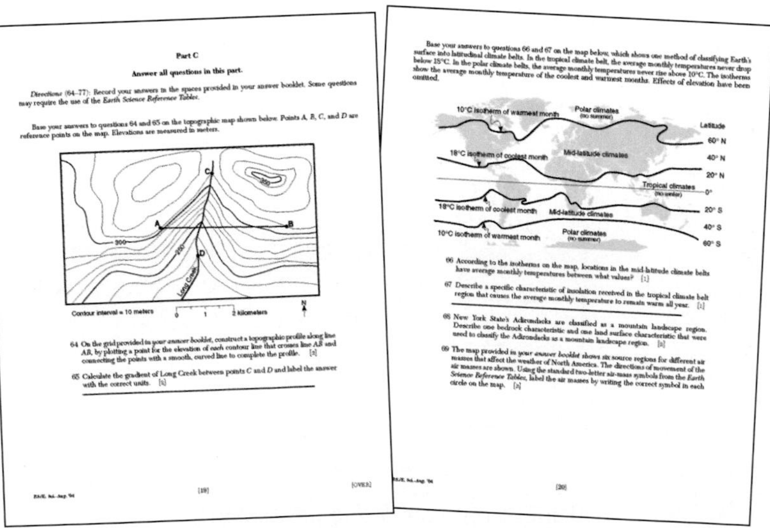

Pages from Part C of a past exam

Getting Ready for the Exam

Throughout the Year

Using the Regents Practice Exams

At the end of each chapter in your text, you'll find a Regents Practice Exam. Use these throughout the year to test your understanding of the topics that will be on the actual exam. The practice exams include the same question formats that you'll find on the Regents Examination. You may be asked to use the Earth Science Reference Tables in Chapter 11A to answer some of the items.

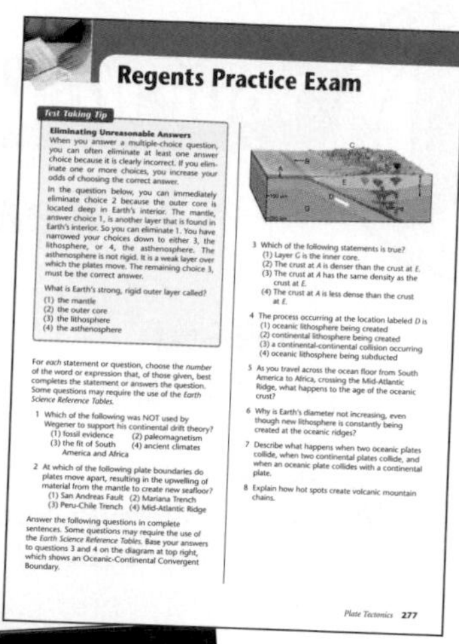
Regents Practice Exam

Test-Taking Tip

Plate Tectonics 277

Countdown to the Test

Using the New York Standardized Test Preparation Workbook

This special workbook includes two Regents Practice Tests in the same style and format as the actual exam. Your teacher will most likely want you to complete these practice exams in the two weeks prior to the actual exam date to determine what you need to review and study more carefully.

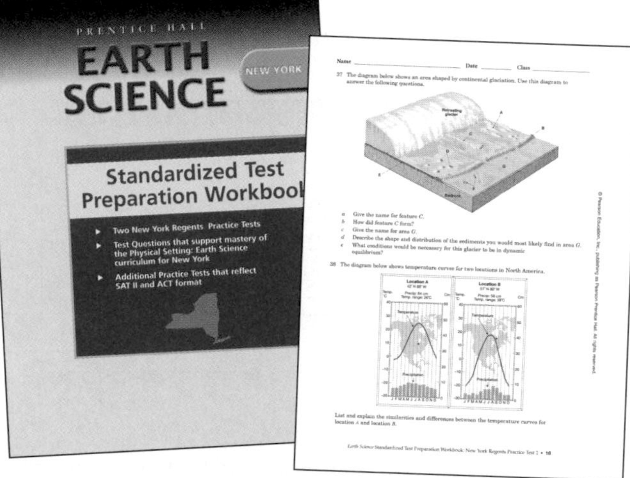

What to Expect on Exam Day

You will need your own pens, pencils, erasers, rulers, and a four-function or scientific calculator. Your calculator will be checked upon entering the exam room for pre-programmed functions.

Your school will provide any other materials that you will need, including the exam, reference tables, answer sheets, and scrap paper. You may not bring any other materials into the exam room. During the exam, you may not use any communications devices such as cell phones, digital pagers, or calculators with communications capabilities.

Tips for Success

- Get a good night's sleep before the exam.
- Relax! You will think more clearly if you are relaxed while taking the exam.
- Make it a practice to read each test question twice before answering to be sure you understand the question. Remember that you have three hours.
- Make your best attempt in answering each question. Answer all of the questions in each part of the exam.
- Write clearly and legibly. Do not use red ink or red pencil. Do not try to erase any answers written in ink. Cross out the original answer and write the new answer.
- Be sure you've filled in all the heading information on the answer sheets before turning in the exam.

Good luck!

Your Roadmap for Success!

1. Read for Meaning

Before You Read

Use the Reading Focus to preview the important concepts and vocabulary in the section. The Reading Strategy helps you practice the skills to improve comprehension.

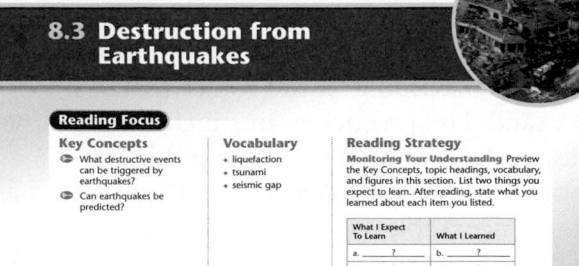

8.3 Destruction from Earthquakes

Reading Focus

Key Concepts
- What destructive events can be triggered by earthquakes?
- Can earthquakes be predicted?

Vocabulary
- liquefaction
- tsunami
- seismic gap

Reading Strategy
Monitoring Your Understanding Preview the Key Concepts, topic headings, vocabulary, and figures in this section. List two things you expect to learn. After reading, state what you learned about each item you listed.

What I Expect To Learn	What I Learned
a. ?	b. ?
c. ?	d. ?

The Good Friday Alaskan Earthquake in 1964 was the most violent earthquake to jar North America in the 20th century. The earthquake was felt throughout Alaska. It had a moment magnitude of 9.2 and lasted 3 to 4 minutes. The quake left 131 people dead and thousands homeless. The state's economy was also badly damaged because the quake affected major ports and towns. Had the schools and businesses been open on this holiday, the death toll would surely have been much higher.

Seismic Vibrations

The 1964 Alaskan earthquake gave geologists new insights into the role of ground shaking as a destructive force. **The damage to buildings and other structures from earthquake waves depends on several factors. These factors include the intensity and duration of the vibrations, the nature of the material on which the ...uilt, and the design of th...**

Figure 10 Earthquake Damage This five-story building in Anchorage, Alaska, collapsed from the great earthquake of 1964. Very little structural damage was incurred by the steel-framed building to the left.
Inferring ***Why do some buildings undergo little damage, while nearby buildings are nearly destroyed?***

As You Read

The Key Concepts highlight the important ideas you need to know. Ask for help if you don't understand these concepts.

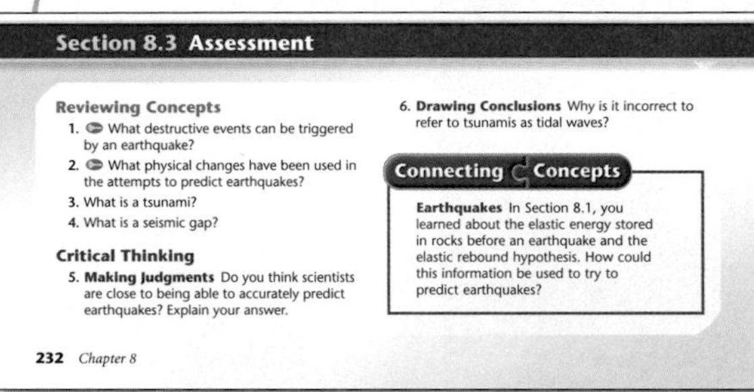

Section 8.3 Assessment

Reviewing Concepts
1. What destructive events can be triggered by an earthquake?
2. What physical changes have been used in the attempts to predict earthquakes?
3. What is a tsunami?
4. What is a seismic gap?

Critical Thinking
5. **Making Judgments** Do you think scientists are close to being able to accurately predict earthquakes? Explain your answer.
6. **Drawing Conclusions** Why is it incorrect to refer to tsunamis as tidal waves?

Connecting Concepts

Earthquakes In Section 8.1, you learned about the elastic energy stored in rocks before an earthquake and the elastic rebound hypothesis. How could this information be used to try to predict earthquakes?

232 *Chapter 8*

After You Read

The Section Assessment tests your understanding of the Key Concepts. If you can't answer these items, go back and review the section.

2. Review the Core Curriculum and the Earth Science Reference Tables

You'll find a complete overview of the Core Curriculum starting on page NY 20. Read this material carefully because it defines what you need to learn. The Earth Science Reference Tables start on page ES 33. Test items using these diagrams and tables can be found on the Regents Examination.

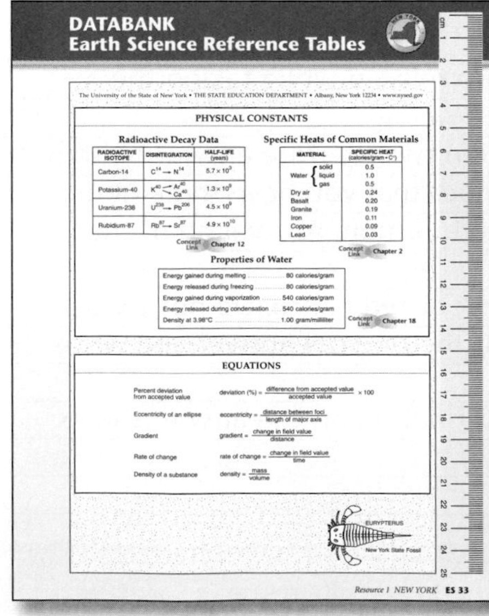

DATABANK
Earth Science Reference Tables

The University of the State of New York • THE STATE EDUCATION DEPARTMENT • Albany, New York 12234 • www.nysed.gov

PHYSICAL CONSTANTS

Radioactive Decay Data

RADIOACTIVE ISOTOPE	DISINTEGRATION	HALF-LIFE (years)
Carbon-14	$C^{14} \rightarrow N^{14}$	5.7×10^3
Potassium-40	$K^{40} \rightarrow Ar^{40}$, Ca^{40}	1.3×10^9
Uranium-238	$U^{238} \rightarrow Pb^{206}$	4.5×10^9
Rubidium-87	$Rb^{87} \rightarrow Sr^{87}$	4.9×10^{10}

Concept Link Chapter 12

Specific Heats of Common Materials

MATERIAL	SPECIFIC HEAT (calories/gram • C°)
Water, solid	0.5
Water, liquid	1.0
Water, gas	0.5
Dry air	0.24
Basalt	0.20
Granite	0.19
Iron	0.11
Copper	0.09
Lead	0.03

Concept Link Chapter 2

Properties of Water

Energy gained during melting	80 calories/gram
Energy released during freezing	80 calories/gram
Energy gained during vaporization	540 calories/gram
Energy released during condensation	540 calories/gram
Density at 3.98°C	1.00 gram/milliliter

Concept Link Chapter 18

EQUATIONS

Percent deviation from accepted value: $\text{deviation (\%)} = \frac{\text{difference from accepted value}}{\text{accepted value}} \times 100$

Eccentricity of an ellipse: $\text{eccentricity} = \frac{\text{distance between foci}}{\text{length of major axis}}$

Gradient: $\text{gradient} = \frac{\text{change in field value}}{\text{distance}}$

Rate of change: $\text{rate of change} = \frac{\text{change in field value}}{\text{time}}$

Density of a substance: $\text{density} = \frac{\text{mass}}{\text{volume}}$

EURYPTERUS
New York State Fossil

Resource 1 NEW YORK **ES 33**

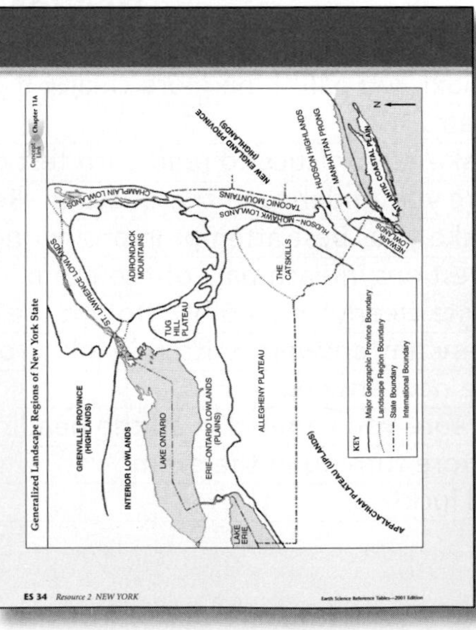

3. Pay Attention to the Art and the Photos

Illustrations and Text Work Together

As you read, look at the illustrations and read the captions. They help make the concepts clearer.

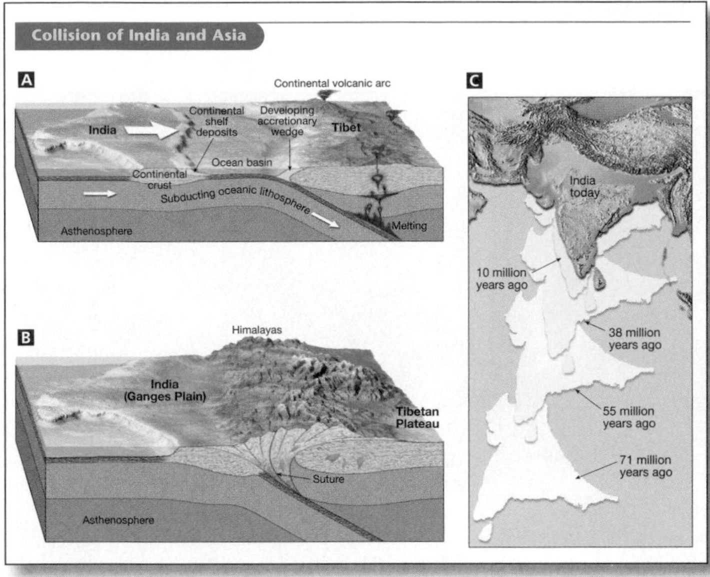

Figure 14 **A** The leading edge of the plate carrying India is subducted beneath the Eurasian plate. **B** The landmasses collide and push up the crust. **C** India's collision with Asia continues today.

Analyzing Data

Use the diagram below to answer Questions 24–26.

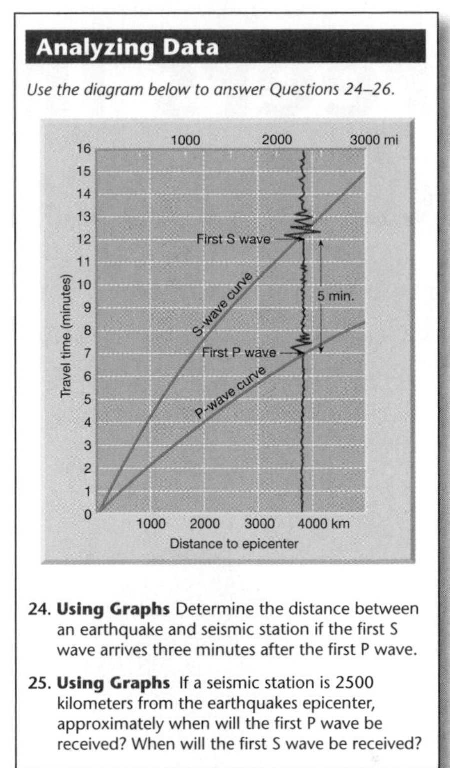

24. **Using Graphs** Determine the distance between an earthquake and seismic station if the first S wave arrives three minutes after the first P wave.
25. **Using Graphs** If a seismic station is 2500 kilometers from the earthquakes epicenter, approximately when will the first P wave be received? When will the first S wave be received?

Analyzing Data

Most science tests will include questions that require you to interpret tables, charts, and graphs. Use the practice items to build your skill in analyzing data in tables, charts, and graphs.

4. Practice for Test Success

Complete Assignments to Check Your Understanding

The Assessment pages for each chapter cover the Key Concepts. Items similar to those on the Regents Examination are highlighted for you.

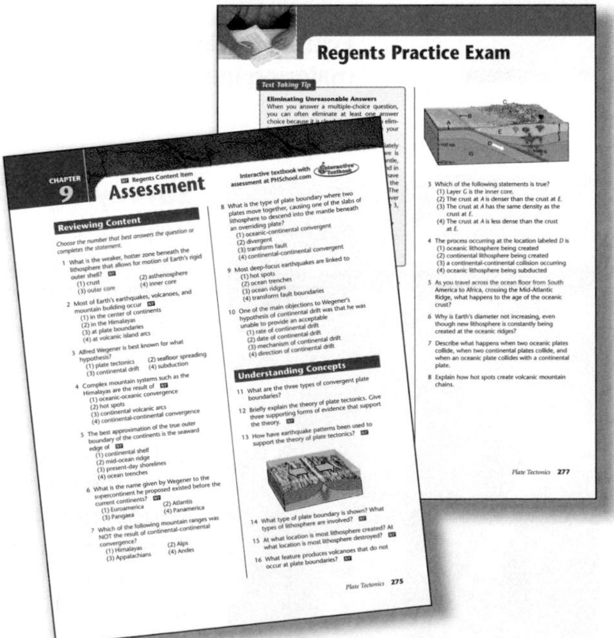
Regents Practice Exam

Chapter 9 Assessment

Reviewing Content

Understanding Concepts

The Regents Practice Exam pages are mini-tests that match the form and type of questions you'll see on the actual exam. Use these to be sure that you've mastered Core Curriculum objectives.

Roadmap

Careers in Earth and Space Science

The career opportunities available in Earth and space science are far reaching—from exploring distant galaxies to investigating deep inside Earth. Here are a few of these exciting careers.

Meteorologist

Meteorologists study how the physical characteristics, processes, and movements of the atmosphere affect the environment. They use this information to forecast the weather and study the patterns of weather change, such as droughts and global warming.

Educational requirements Four-year college degree, majoring in meteorology or atmospheric science

Seismologist

Seismologists are Earth scientists who investigate earthquakes. They determine the location and size of earthquakes, and use seismic waves to study Earth's interior. Some seismologists help the building industry design earthquake-proof structures.

Educational requirements Four-year college degree, majoring in geology, geophysics, or mathematics

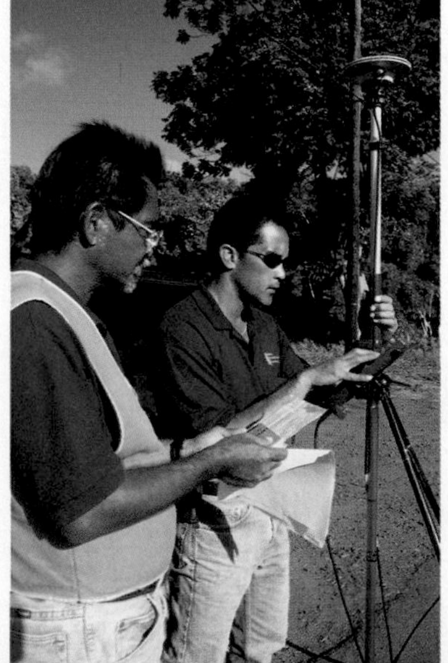

Surveying Technician

Helping to measure and map Earth's surface are the responsibilities of surveying technicians. They assist land surveyors who measure distances, directions, and contours on, above, or below Earth's surface. Surveying technicians use surveying instruments to collect data and then enter the data into computers.

Educational requirements Two-year junior or community college program, one to three years of technical school

For: Career links
Visit: PHSchool.com
Web Code: ccb-3000

Commercial Diver

Just about anywhere there is water, there is a need for commercial divers. Their work ranges from operating submersibles to helping map the ocean floor. They may perform underwater surveys or carry out underwater rescue and salvage operations.

Educational requirements High-school diploma, diving-school certification or naval training

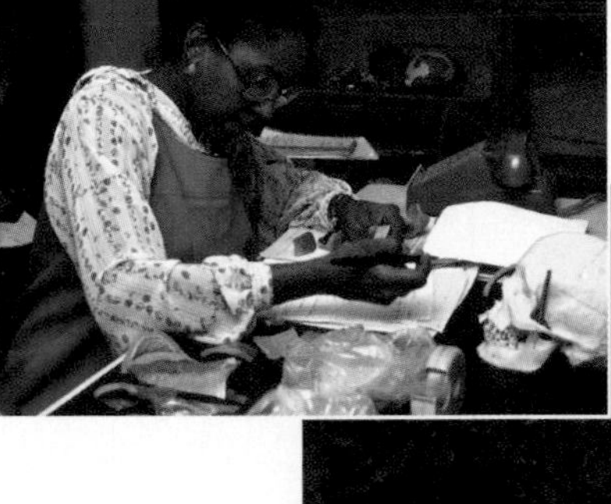

Archaeologist

Archaeologists excavate, preserve, study, and classify objects and structures from past cultures. In order to interpret what they see at a particular site, archaeologists must be able to identify different types of soil and notice the smallest of changes in soil characteristics.

Educational requirements Master's degree in anthropology or archaeology

Astronomer

Astronomers use the laws of physics and mathematics to study the universe. They may specialize to investigate the moon, sun, planets, stars, or galaxies, such as the Andromeda Galaxy shown in the photo at the left. They also may use what they know about astronomy to help develop satellites and spacecraft.

Educational requirements Doctoral degree in physics, astrophysics, or space physics

CHAPTER 1

Planning Guide

Use these planning tools
Use Teacher Express for all your planning needs

SECTION OBJECTIVES	STANDARDS NATIONAL	STANDARDS STATE	ACTIVITIES and LABS
1.1 What Is Earth Science? pp. 2–5 1 block or 2 periods 1.1 **Define** Earth science. 1.2 **Describe** the formation of Earth and the solar system.	A-1, D-1, D-3, G-2, G-3		**SE** Inquiry Activity: Developing Your Observation Skills, p. 1 L2 **TE** Teacher Demo: Separation and Density, p. 4 L2 **LM** Laboratory Skills Checkup 1,2,3,4 L1
1.2 A View of Earth, pp. 7–10 1 block or 2 periods 1.3 **Describe** Earth's four major spheres. 1.4 **Differentiate** among the three parts of the geosphere. 1.5 **State** the value of the theory of plate tectonics to Earth Science.	C-4, D-1, D-3, G-3		**TE** Teacher Demo: Earth's Layers, p. 8 L2 **TE** Teacher Demo: Convection and Plates, p. 10 L2 **LM** Evaluating Precision L1
1.3 Representing Earth's Surface, pp. 11–17 1 1/2 blocks or 3 periods 1.6 **Locate** points on Earth's surface by their latitude and longitude. 1.7 **Describe** the advantages and disadvantages of different types of maps. 1.8 **Explain** what makes topographic maps different from other maps.	A-2, E-2, G-3		**TE** Teacher Demo: Conic and Gnomonic Projections, p. 13 L2 **SE** Exploration Lab: Determining Latitude and Longitude, pp. 26–27 L2
1.4 Earth System Science, pp. 18–22 1 block or 2 periods 1.9 **Describe** the primary goal of Earth system science and **define** the term *system*. 1.10 **Describe** Earth's two major sources of energy. 1.11 **Explain** how humans affect Earth's systems. 1.12 **Distinguish** between renewable and nonrenewable resources.	C-4, D-1, D-2, D-3, F-1, F-2, F-3, F-4, F-5, F-6		**TE** Build Science Skills, p. 22 L2
1.5 What Is Scientific Inquiry? pp. 23–24 1/2 block or 1 period 1.13 **Define** the terms *hypothesis* and *theory*.	A-1, A-2, G-2, G-3		**LM** Measuring Volume and Temperature L1

Ability Levels	
L1	For students who need additional help
L2	For all students
L3	For students who need to be challenged

Components

SE	Student Edition	**GRSW**	Guided Reading & Study Workbook	**TP**	Test Prep Resources	**GEO**	Geode CD-ROM
TE	Teacher's Edition			**onT**	onlineText	**T**	Transparencies
LM	Laboratory Manual	**TEX**	Teacher Express	**DC**	Discovery Channel Videos	**GO**	Internet Resources
CUT	Chapter Tests	**CTB**	Computer Test Bank				

RESOURCES PRINT and TECHNOLOGY	SECTION ASSESSMENT
GRSW Section 1.1 **T-1** Formation of Solar System—Nebular Hypothesis **T-5** Formation of Stars and Galaxies **TEX** Lesson Planning 1.1	**SE** Section 1.1 Assessment, p. 5 **onT** Section 1.1
GRSW Section 1.2 **T-2** Earth's Layered Structure **TEX** Lesson Planning 1.2	**SE** Section 1.2 Assessment, p. 10 **onT** Section 1.2
GRSW Section 1.3 **T-371** Earth's Grid System **T-372** Locating Places Using Grid System **T-373** Longitude as Distance **DC** Mapping the World **TEX** Lesson Planning 1.3	**SE** Section 1.3 Assessment, p. 17 **onT** Section 1.3
GRSW Section 1.4 **T-3** Hydrologic Cycle **T-4** Growth of World Population **TEX** Lesson Planning 1.4	**SE** Section 1.4 Assessment, p. 22 **onT** Section 1.4
GRSW Section 1.5 **TEX** Lesson Planning 1.5	**SE** Section 1.5 Assessment, p. 24 **onT** Section 1.5

Go Online

Go online for these Internet resources.

PHSchool.com
Web Code: cjk-9999

NSTA SCILINKS
Web Code: cjn-1013
Web Code: cjn-1014
Web Code: cjn-1015

Materials for Activities and Labs

Quantities for each group

STUDENT EDITION

Exploration Lab, pp. 26–27
globe, protractor, ruler, compass or round object for tracing, world map

TEACHER'S EDITION

Teacher Demo, p. 4
2 large glass jars with lids, 100 mL sand, 100 mL rock salt, 100 mL sugar, 100 mL water, 100 mL vegetable oil, 100 mL corn syrup

Teacher Demo, p. 8
hard-boiled egg, knife

Teacher Demo, p. 10
hot plate; deep, wide glass container such as a lasagna pan; diluted tomato soup; large, thin sponges; scissors; tongs

Teacher Demo, p. 13
small globe, blank transparency sheet

Build Science Skills, p. 22
pictures of houses underwater due to a flood (natural or human-made), pictures of buildings damaged by an earthquake, pictures of a coastal home being swept out to sea due to beach erosion

Chapter Assessment

ASSESSMENT

SE Assessment, pp. 29–30
CUT Chapter 1 Test
CTB Chapter 1
onT Chapter 1

STANDARDIZED TEST PREP

SE Chapter 1, p. 31
TP Progress Monitoring Assessments

interactive textbook with assessment at PHSchool.com

CHAPTER 1

Before you teach

Michael Wysession
Washington University

Big Ideas

Earth science involves the study of Earth and its neighbors in the solar system. Earth science is very interdisciplinary, involving aspects of geology, chemistry, physics, and biology.

Space and Time Earth is located in the outer part of the Milky Way galaxy. Earth and the rest of the solar system formed about 4.56 million years ago and are about one-third the age of the universe. Gravity caused Earth to form layers based upon density. Going from the center out, Earth consists of a metal core, rocky mantle and crust, liquid ocean, and a gaseous atmosphere. The biosphere, which is an important geological agent, is found in the geosphere, hydrosphere, and atmosphere. Earth's surface is best represented on a globe, though maps are more convenient. There are many different ways of projecting the globe onto a two-dimensional map, and many different kinds of maps such as topographic and geologic maps.

Forces and Motion Plate tectonics, involving the lateral motions of pieces of Earth's surface, is ultimately responsible for the formation and structure of the continents, and provides the framework for understanding modern Earth science.

Earth as a System Earth System Science is an approach to viewing Earth as the result of many different interconnected systems. Environmental science is an aspect of Earth Science that is concerned with issues related to the human impact on our planet such as the use of natural resources and the alteration of Earth's surface.

Earth Science Refresher

Uniformitarianism vs. Catastrophism

In the 18th and 19th centuries, many debates in geology focused on how Earth formed. Scientists often took one of two polarized views. Catastrophists, often with a theological interest, envisioned a world that formed rapidly in a series of "catastrophic" events. Uniformitarians, with a more naturalist view, thought the Earth formed over an unimaginably long period of time from the slow, continual geologic processes seen today. It turned out that both were right to some degree: Earth formed relatively rapidly in a catastrophic manner 4.56 billion years ago, but has cooled slowly and relatively continuously since then.

Most processes in Earth Science occur over a spectrum of scales that can be seen as catastrophic at one end and continual at the other. There are thousands of earthquakes that occur every day, part of a continual cracking and bending of the plates, but it is the rare catastrophic ones that release the most energy and account for most of the plate motion. Small volcanic eruptions occur continuously, but it is the occasional enormous eruption that adds so much gas and dust into the atmosphere that global climates are changed. It is estimated that about three tons of cometary and meteoroid debris enters Earth's atmosphere each day, mostly in the form of tiny grains. However, separated by tens or hundreds of millions of years, impacts from large asteroids have likely caused mass extinctions and indelibly altered the course of life through their chance collisions. And, of course, in each of these examples, there is a full spectrum of activity covering all the intermediate levels as well. So be aware, when teaching all aspects of Earth Science, from streams and floods to folding and faulting, that the same process occurs at many scales, and been seen from both a Uniformitarian and a Catastrophist point of view.

Address Misconceptions

Students may think that Earth and the Milky Way are at the center of the universe. They may have inferred this from learning that almost all galaxies are moving away from the Milky Way in all directions. For a strategy that helps to overcome this misconception, see **Address Misconceptions** on **p. 6.**

Go Online PD LINKS

For: Chapter 1 Content Support
Visit: www.SciLinks.org/PDLinks
Web Code: cjn-0199

Biogeosciences

One of the most exciting new areas of research and discovery in the Earth sciences concerns the incorporation of biology. It turns out that a huge number of geochemical processes that once were thought to occur inorganically are now caused by or catalyzed by bacteria and other one-celled organisms. Bacteria have been found everywhere there is water, including within the tiny pore spaces between mineral grains of rocks deep beneath Earth's surface! Many minerals are made by biological processes, and it is now realized that Earth's geology would be very different if it were not for the presence of life. As a result, there are a rapidly growing number of biologists now working in university geology departments, and the areas of biogeology and biogeochemistry are where some of the most exciting new research is being done.

Address Misconceptions

Students may think that only human actions can seriously affect the environment. Use the example of the eruption of Mount St. Helens to emphasize that natural events can have wide-spread and negative effects on the environment. For a strategy that helps to overcome this misconception, see **Address Misconceptions** on **p. 20.**

Build Reading Literacy

Anticipation Guide

Stimulating Interest in a Topic

Strategy Engage students actively with a selection by activating prior knowledge, arousing interest, and helping establish purposes for reading. Generate a series of statements related to the topic of a passage for students to respond to and discuss before reading. Choose a passage from this chapter, such as Section 1.4, pp. 18–22, and prepare a set of statements ahead of time.

Example

1. Prior to class, read through the passage and identify major concepts and details.

2. Construct an anticipation guide as follows:

• Write 5–10 short, but thought-provoking, declarative statements about the most important concepts featured in the section.

• If students are likely to have misconceptions about the topic, be sure to include statements that address those misconceptions.

• The statements could be in either a true-false or an agree-disagree format.

• To the left of each statement, put a blank for student responses.

3. Before assigning the section to read, either display the guide on the board or on an overhead, or distribute individual worksheets. Students can respond to the statements individually or as a group.

4. Discuss students' responses, asking students to support their answers using examples from past experience or prior reading.

5. Then, have students read the section, evaluating the statements from the anticipation guide as they read.

6. After reading, revisit the guide, encouraging students to compare and contrast their current ones. Have students quote information from the passage to support their decisions.

See p. 8 for a script on how to use the anticipation guide strategy with students. For additional Build Reading Literacy strategies, see pp. 2, 3, 9, 12, 19, and 23.

ASSESS PRIOR KNOWLEDGE

Use the Chapter Pretest below to assess students' prior knowledge. As needed, review these concepts.

Review Science Concepts

Section 1.1 Review the parts of the solar system, and the concept that the solar system is just one part of the Milky Way galaxy, which is just one part of the universe. Review with students that denser objects sink while less dense objects float. This will help students understand how Earth's layers formed.

Section 1.2 Remind students that Earth's liquid water and atmosphere make it unique among the planets.

Section 1.3 Have students recall the locations of North America, the equator, the prime meridian, and the International Date Line on a world map. Review the compass rose (N-S-E-W).

Section 1.4 Review the concept of a system. Discuss living and nonliving (biotic and abiotic) factors in the environment.

Section 1.5 Encourage students to recall the idea that an observation is something you notice with your senses.

Review Math Skills

Ratio Students will need to understand ratios and how ratios can be written (as a fraction or with a colon). Direct students to the Math Skills in the Skills Handbook at the end of the student text.

CHAPTER 1 Introduction to Earth Science

CONCEPTS in Action

Exploration Lab
Determining Latitude and Longitude

Earth as a System
Earth's Place in the Universe

Understanding Earth
Studying Earth From Space

Video Field Trip

Mapping the World

Take a field trip with Discovery Channel to learn more about maps. Answer the following questions after watching the video.

1. Name and describe two types of maps.
2. What is the significance of the prime meridian, and what European city does it run through?

Go Online
PHSchool.com

For: Chapter 1 Resources
Visit: PHSchool.com
Web Code: cjk-9999

This photograph shows British Columbia's Mount Robson, the highest point in the Canadian Rockies. ▶

Chapter Pretest

1. True or False: Our solar system consists only of Earth and the sun. *(False)*
2. Object A is denser than water. If object A is dropped into a cup of water, what will happen to the object? *(c)*
   a. Object A will float on top of the water.
   b. Object A will float in the middle of the water.
   c. Object A will sink to the bottom of the cup.
3. What is Earth known to have that other planets in our solar system are not known to have? *(c)*
   a. an atmosphere b. volcanoes
   c. liquid water d. rings
4. What is the name of the imaginary horizontal line that goes around Earth's middle? *(a)*
   a. equator b. prime meridian
   c. international date line
5. Which of these imaginary lines crosses through Greenwich, England? *(b)*
   a. equator b. prime meridian
   c. international date line
6. Fill in the locations for west, east, and south on the compass rose to the right.

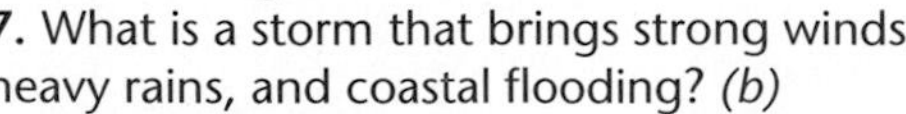

7. What is a storm that brings strong winds, heavy rains, and coastal flooding? *(b)*
   a. tornado b. hurricane c. tsunami

Chapter Preview

Inquiry Activity

Developing Your Observation Skills

Procedure
Look at the photograph on this page. Have you ever seen anything like it?

Think About It

1. **Observing** What features can you identify in the photograph?
2. **Inferring** Where do you think this photograph came from?
3. **Designing Experiments** If you were an Earth scientist, how could you use this photograph in your work?

DISCOVERY CHANNEL SCHOOL

Video Field Trip
Mapping the World

Encourage students to view the Video Field Trip "Mapping the World."

ENGAGE/EXPLORE

Developing Your Observation Skills **L2**

Purpose This eye-catching photo should intrigue your students.

Skills Focus **Observing, Inferring**

 **Prep Time** 5 minutes

Materials textbook

Class Time 10 minutes

Teaching Tip Some students may have difficulty identifying the water line that separates the land and sky from their reflection in the water. Once this line is indicated to students, they should be able to see that the bottom half of the image is a reflection.

Expected Outcome Students will observe mountains, water, clouds, and a glacier (snow and ice).

Think About It
1. Features include mountains, water, clouds, ice, snow, and a glacier.
2. The photograph was taken in British Columbia, Canada.
3. This photograph could be used to observe cloud types and predict the weather. This photograph could be used to study the shape and structure of the mountains to determine their geologic history. An Earth scientist can infer from this picture that past glaciation has shaped the mountains, and uplifting caused by tectonic plate movements built these mountains.

Section 1.1

1 FOCUS

Section Objectives

1.1 **Define** Earth science.
1.2 **Describe** the formation of Earth and the solar system.

Reading Focus

Build Vocabulary L2

Word Parts Ask students to use a dictionary to determine the meanings of the following word parts: *geo-* (Earth); *astro-* (outer space); *-ology* (study of); *-ography* (study of); *-onomy* (study of)
Based on this discussion and their prior knowledge, have students predict the meaning of this section's vocabulary words. Then, have students look up the words in the Glossary to check their predictions and make any necessary corrections. *Meteorology* will likely present a problem, with most students predicting that it is the study of meteors, rather than the study of the atmosphere.

Reading Strategy L2

a. Earth, earthquakes, mountains, volcanoes, Earth's history
b. oceanography
c. composition and movements of seawater, coastal processes, seafloor topography, marine life
d. meteorology
e. atmosphere, weather, climate
f. astronomy
g. universe, solar system

2 INSTRUCT

Overview of Earth Science

Build Reading Literacy L1

Refer to **p. 216D** in **Chapter 8**, which provides guidelines for comparing and contrasting.

Compare and Contrast Have students create a table to compare and contrast physical geology and historical geology. They should fill in their table as they read the first part of this section. Areas to consider include the focus of each area and examples of what is studied.
Visual

1.1 What Is Earth Science?

Reading Focus

Key Concepts

- What is the study of Earth science?
- How did Earth and the solar system form?

Vocabulary

- Earth science
- geology
- oceanography
- meteorology
- astronomy

Reading Strategy

Categorizing As you read about the different branches of Earth science, fill in the column with the name of each branch and list some of the things that are studied.

geology	a. ?
b. ?	c. ?
d. ?	e. ?
f. ?	g. ?

The spectacular eruption of a volcano, the magnificent scenery of a rocky coast, and the destruction created by a hurricane are all subjects for Earth science. The study of Earth science deals with many fascinating and practical questions about our environment. What forces produced the mountains shown on page 1? Why does our daily weather change? Is our climate changing? How old is Earth? How is Earth related to the other planets in the solar system? What causes ocean tides? What was the Ice Age like? Will there be another?

Understanding Earth is not an easy task because our planet is always changing. Earth is a dynamic planet with a long and complex history.

Figure 1 Scientists called paleontologists study fossils, which are signs of life in the distant past, to find out how life-forms have changed through time.
Posing Questions ***What questions do you have about this fossil?***

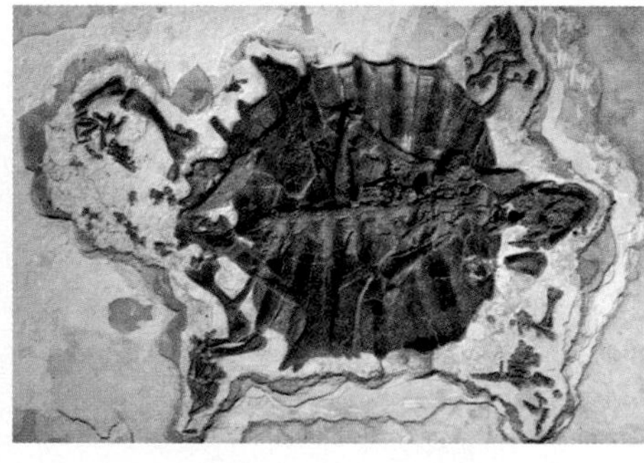

Overview of Earth Science

Earth science is the name for the group of sciences that deals with Earth and its neighbors in space. Earth science includes many subdivisions of geology such as geochemistry, geophysics, geobiology and paleontology, as well as oceanography, meteorology, and astronomy.

Units 1 through 4 focus on the science of **geology,** a word that means "study of Earth." Geology is divided into two broad areas—physical geology and historical geology.

Physical geology includes the examination of the materials that make up Earth and the possible explanations for the many processes that shape our planet. Processes below the surface create earthquakes, build mountains, and produce volcanoes. Processes at the surface break rock apart and create different landforms. Erosion by water, wind, and ice results in different landscapes. You will learn that rocks and minerals form in response to Earth's internal and external processes. Understanding the origin of rocks and minerals is an important part of understanding Earth.

In contrast to physical geology, the aim of historical geology is to understand Earth's long history. Historical geology tries to establish a timeline of the vast number of physical and biological changes that have occurred in the past. See Figure 1. We study physical geology before historical geology because we must first understand how Earth works before we try to unravel its past.

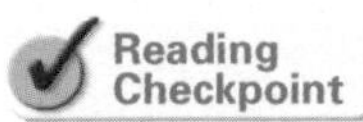

What are the two main areas of geology?

Unit 5 is devoted to **oceanography.** Oceanography integrates the sciences of chemistry, physics, geology, and biology. Oceanographers study the composition and movements of seawater, as well as coastal processes, seafloor topography, and marine life. See Figure 2.

Unit 6 examines the composition of Earth's atmosphere. The combined effects of Earth's motions and energy from the sun cause the atmosphere to produce different weather conditions. This, in turn, creates the basic pattern of global climates. **Meteorology** is the study of the atmosphere and the processes that produce weather and climate. Like oceanography, meteorology also involves other branches of science.

Unit 7 demonstrates that understanding Earth requires an understanding of Earth's position in the universe. The science of **astronomy,** the study of the universe, is useful in probing the origins of our own environment. All objects in space, including Earth, are subject to the same physical laws. Learning about the other members of our solar system and the universe beyond helps us to understand Earth.

Throughout its long existence, Earth has been changing. In fact, it is changing as you read this page and will continue to do so. Sometimes the changes are rapid and violent, such as when tornados, landslides, or volcanic eruptions occur. Many changes, however, take place so gradually that they go unnoticed during a lifetime.

Figure 2 Oceanographers study all aspects of the ocean—the chemistry of its waters, the geology of its seafloor, the physics of its interactions with the atmosphere, and the biology of its organisms.

Formation of Earth

Earth is one of nine planets that revolve around the sun. Our solar system has an orderly nature. Scientists understand that Earth and the other planets formed during the same time span and from the same material as the sun. **The nebular hypothesis suggests that the bodies of our solar system evolved from an enormous rotating cloud called the solar nebula. It was made up mostly of hydrogen and helium, with a small percentage of heavier elements.** Figure 3 on page 4 summarizes some key points of this hypothesis.

Use Community Resources L2

The USGS (United States Geological Survey) has a network of regional offices where geologists study geological phenomena at local, regional, and global levels. Their activities include monitoring earthquake activity, mapping subsurface rock formations, and providing the public with information about geologic events such as floods and landslides. Ask a USGS geologist from a local office to talk to the class about what geologists do at their jobs. Ask students to prepare questions in advance.
Interpersonal

Formation of Earth

Build Reading Literacy L1

Refer to **p. 186D** in **Chapter 7,** which provides guidelines for relating text and visuals.

Relate Text and Visuals Have students turn ahead in the text to Figure 3 on p. 4 for a visual representation of the nebular hypothesis. Have them read the figure caption, then use the figure to describe the major steps in the nebular hypothesis. *(Solar system begins as cloud of dust and gases. Cloud starts to rotate and collapse. Heated center forms the sun. Cooling creates solid particles. Collisions create asteroid-sized bodies. Asteroids form the inner planets. Lighter materials and gases form the outer planets.)*
Visual

Customize for English Language Learners

Students should use the words and word parts they just learned, along with their prior knowledge, to define the following words: *oceanographer, meteorologist, geography, geologist, geological, astronaut, astronomer.* Students should then use a dictionary to check their definitions. Review the correct meanings of these words with students when they are finished.

Answer to . . .

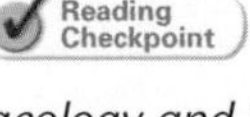

The two main areas of geology are physical geology and historical geology.

Section 1.1 (continued)

Use Visuals L1

Figure 3 Have students study the diagram illustrating the nebular hypothesis. Ask: **What do all stages of this hypothesis have in common?** *(In all stages, the system is spinning.)* **What was the first stage in the development of our solar system?** *(Our solar system began as an enormous cloud of gas and dust.)* **Challenge students to make a timeline or flowchart of the key events in the formation of our solar system.** *(Students should make a timeline or flowchart based on steps A through E given in the figure caption.)*
Visual, Logical

Teacher Demo

Separation and Density L2

Purpose Students see how substances separate based on density.

Materials 2 large glass jars with lids, 100 mL sand, 100 mL rock salt, 100 mL sugar, 100 mL water, 100 mL vegetable oil, 100 mL corn syrup

Procedure At the start of the class, place all of the solids in one jar and all the liquids in another jar. Put the lids on both jars and shake them carefully. Let the jars settle during the class. Then, have the students look at them. Ask: **Why did the liquids separate?** *(Differences in density made the liquids rise or fall and separate.)* **Why didn't the solids separate?** *(The solid particles were unable to move past each other.)* **What state was Earth most likely in when it separated into layers?** *(The materials that made up Earth must have been molten or nearly molten.)*

Expected Outcome The liquids will separate into different layers. The solids will remain mixed.
Visual, Logical

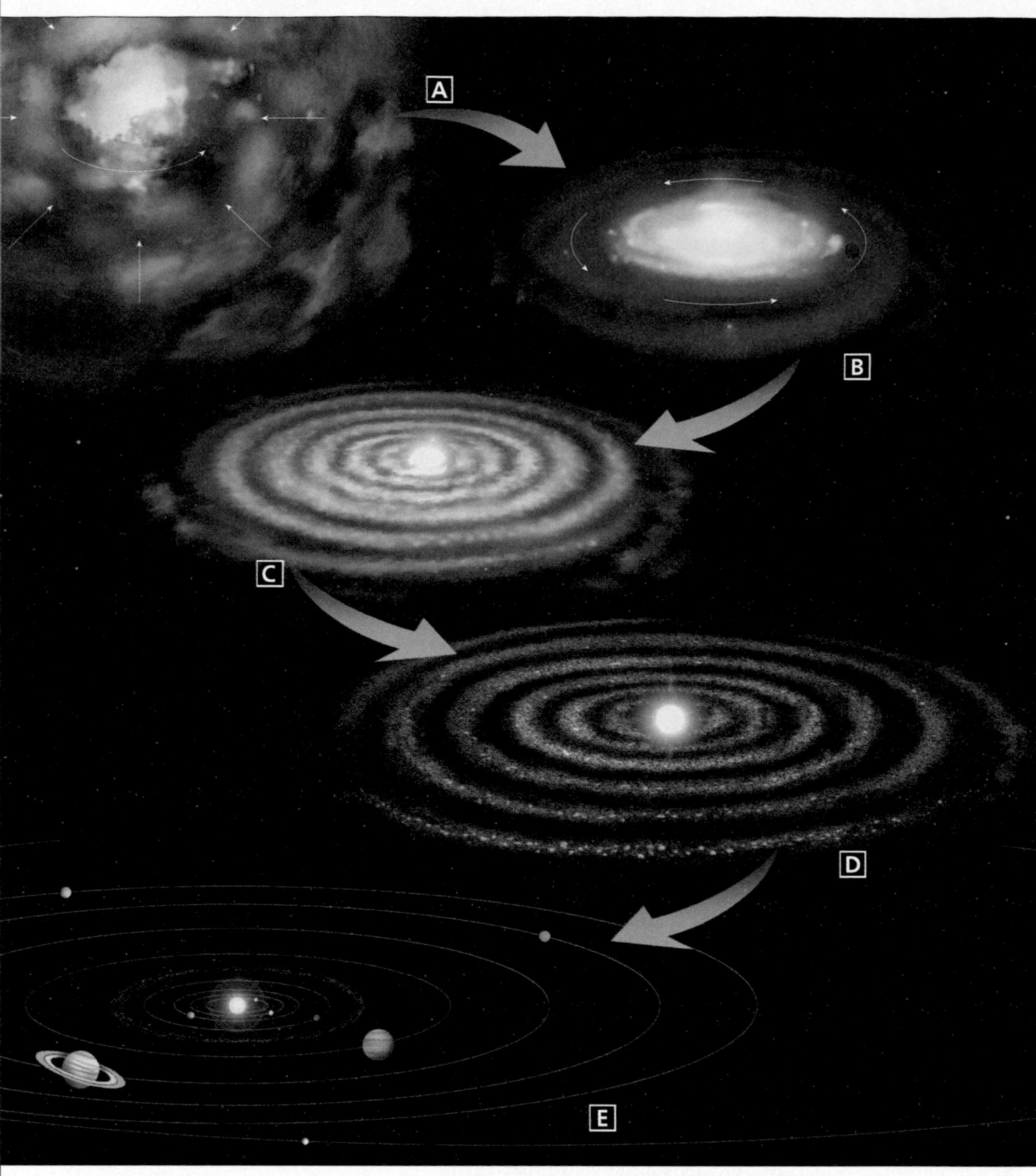

Figure 3 Formation of the Solar System According to the Nebular Hypothesis A Our solar system began as an enormous cloud of dust and gases made up mostly of hydrogen and helium with a small percentage of heavier elements. **B** This cloud, called a nebula, started to rotate and collapse toward the center of the cloud. Heat was generated at the center, which eventually formed the sun. **C** Cooling of the nebula caused rocky and metallic materials to form tiny solid particles. **D** Repeated collisions of these particles resulted in the formation of asteroid-sized bodies. **E** These asteroids eventually combined to form the four inner planets—Mercury, Venus, Earth, and Mars. The lighter materials and gases combined farther away from the center to form the four outer planets—Jupiter, Saturn, Uranus, and Neptune.

4 *Chapter 1*

Facts and Figures

As Earth was forming, density differences caused denser materials to sink to Earth's core, while less dense materials escaped to the atmosphere. Density differences continue to shape Earth today. Today's volcanic eruptions are generally caused by less dense magma and gases rising up through the mantle until they penetrate the crust, resulting in a volcanic eruption. This is an example of the principle of uniformitarianism, which is essential to the study of geology. This principle states that the processes that exist on Earth today are identical to the processes that existed on Earth in the distant past. This principle allows geologists to make useful inferences based on contemporary observations.

High temperatures and weak fields of gravity characterized the inner planets. As a result, the inner planets were not able to hold onto the lighter gases of the nebular cloud. The lightest gases, hydrogen and helium, were whisked away toward the heavier planets by the solar wind. Earth, Mars, and Venus were able to retain some heavier gases including water vapor and carbon dioxide. The materials that formed by outer planets contained high percentages of water, carbon dioxide, ammonia, and methane. The size and frigid temperatures of the outer planets provided the surface gravity to hold these heavier gases.

Layers Form on Earth Shortly after Earth formed, the decay of radioactive elements, combined with heat released by colliding particles, produced some melting of the interior. This allowed the denser elements, mostly iron and nickel, to sink to Earth's center. The lighter, rocky components floated outward, toward the surface. This sinking and floating is believed to still be occurring, but on a much smaller scale. As a result of this process, Earth's interior is not made of uniform materials. It consists of layers of materials that have different properties.

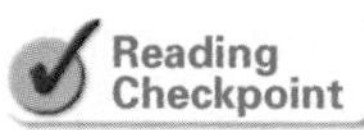

Why does Earth have layers?

An important result of this process is that gaseous materials were allowed to escape from Earth's interior, just as gases escape today during volcanic eruptions. In this way, an atmosphere gradually formed along with the ocean. It was composed mainly of gases that were released from within the planet.

Section 1.1 Assessment

Reviewing Concepts

1. What are the sciences that are included in Earth science?
2. What topics are included in the study of physical geology?
3. Explain how physical geology differs from historical geology.
4. Describe the nebular hypothesis.

Critical Thinking

5. **Forming Conclusions** Explain why Earth is called a dynamic planet.
6. **Inferring** Would meteorology be a useful science to apply to the study of planets such as Mercury and Mars? Explain.
7. **Hypothesizing** Suppose that as Earth formed, all lighter elements were released to surrounding space. How might this affect the structure of Earth today?

Connecting Concepts

Summarizing Earth science is composed of many different areas of study. Why is it important to include all of these areas in the study of Earth and the solar system?

Build Science Skills L2

Inferring Based on the information in this section, ask students to infer which of Earth's layers will be the densest. Have students turn ahead in the text to Figure 6 on p. 8 to see a diagram of Earth's layers.
Logical

3 ASSESS

Evaluate Understanding L2

To assess students' knowledge of section content, ask them to answer the Key Concepts questions at the beginning of this section.

Reteach L1

Have students use Figure 3 to explain in their own words the formation of our solar system.

Connecting Concepts

Because Earth is an ever-changing planet, all the spheres on Earth are interactive and affect one another. To understand Earth's existence and history, it is important to study all aspects of Earth together.

Answer to . . .

Earth has layers because denser elements sank to Earth's center and less dense elements floated to the surface.

Section 1.1 Assessment

1. Earth science includes many subdivisions of geology such as geochemistry, geophysics, geobiology, and paleontology, as well as meteorology, oceanography, and astronomy.
2. Physical geology includes processes that operate on and below Earth's surface such as volcanoes, mountain building, erosion, and earthquakes.
3. Historical geology's aim is to understand Earth's history. Physical geology's aim is to understand the processes that shape Earth.
4. This hypothesis suggests that the solar system began as an enormous cloud of dust and gas. The cloud began to rotate, heat was produced, and the cloud began to collapse toward the center. The sun formed at the center from this heat. Cooling of the cloud caused rocky and metallic materials to form the inner planets. The outer planets formed from lighter materials and gases.
5. The surface of Earth is continually changing due to its layered structure.
6. It would not be very useful because these two planets have only very thin atmospheres. Very few meteorological processes are occurring on them.
7. If all the lighter elements were no longer a part of Earth's structure, Earth probably would not have layers defined by their density.

Earth's Place in the Universe **L2**

Background

The Milky Way is a collection of several hundred billion stars, the oldest of which is about 10 billion years. It is one of a cluster of approximately 28 galaxies, called the Local Group, that exists in our region of the universe. Initially, the oldest stars in the Milky Way formed from nearly pure hydrogen. Later, succeeding generations of younger stars, including our Sun, would have heavier, more complex atoms available for their formation.

Teaching Tips

- As students read the feature and look at Figure 4, have them make a timeline of the events shown from the big bang to the present.
- While reading Earth's Place in the Universe feature, have students create a flowchart showing the chain of events starting with the big bang and ending with the formation of our sun and the planets of our solar system. *(Big Bang → Protons and neutrons appear → Hydrogen and helium form → Hydrogen and helium condense into clouds → Galaxies and galaxy clusters form and start spreading apart → Clouds of gas and dust collapse, forming stars → Stars become supernovas → Nebula, enriched from supernovas, contracts, rotates, and flattens → Planets and our sun form)*

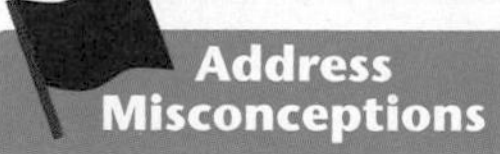

L2

Students may think that the Milky Way is at the center of the universe. They may have inferred this from learning that almost all galaxies are moving away from the Milky Way in all directions. To dispel this misconception, have students mark with a black marker a number of dots on a partially inflated balloon. Blow up the balloon and observe what happens to the dots. They all move away from each other, as do almost all galaxies. All points in the universe can be thought of as being the center of the universe, as everything else is moving away from everything else.
Visual

earth as a SYSTEM

Earth's Place in the Universe

For centuries, people who have gazed at the night sky have wondered about the nature of the universe, Earth's place within it, and whether or not we are alone. Today many exciting discoveries in astronomy are beginning to provide answers about the origin of the universe, the formation and evolution of stars, and how Earth came into existence.

The realization that the universe is immense and orderly began in the early 1900s. Edwin Hubble and other scientists demonstrated that the Milky Way galaxy is one of hundreds of billions of galaxies, each of which contains billions of stars. Evidence supports that Earth, its materials, and all living things are the result of the Big Bang theory. The universe began between 13 and 14 billion years ago as a dense, hot, massive amount of material exploded with violent force. See Figure 4. Within about one second, the temperature of the expanding universe cooled to approximately 10 billion degrees. Basic atomic particles called protons and neutrons began to appear. After a few minutes, atoms of the simplest elements—hydrogen and helium—had formed. The initial conversion of energy to matter in the young universe was completed.

During the first billion years or so, matter (essentially hydrogen and helium) in the expanding universe clumped together to form enormous clouds that eventually collapsed to become galaxies and clusters of galaxies. Inside these collapsing clouds, smaller concentrations of matter formed into stars. One of the billions of galaxies to form was the Milky Way.

During the life of most stars, energy produced as hydrogen nuclei (protons) fuses with other hydrogen nuclei to form helium. During this process, called nuclear fusion, matter is converted to energy. Stars begin to die when their nuclear fuel is used up. Massive stars often have explosive deaths. During these events, called supernovas, nuclear fusion produces atoms such as oxygen, carbon, and iron. These atoms may become the materials that make up future generations of stars. From the debris scattered during the death of a preexisting star, our sun, and the solar system formed

Our star, the sun, is at the very least a second-generation star. Along with the planets in our solar system, the sun began forming nearly 5 billion years ago from a large interstellar cloud called a nebula. This nebula consisted of dust particles and gases enriched in heavy elements from supernova explosions. Gravitational energy caused the nebula to contract, rotate, and flatten. Inside, smaller concentrations of matter began condensing to form the planets. At the center of the nebula there was sufficient pressure and heat to initiate hydrogen nuclear fusion, and our sun was born.

It has been said that all life on Earth is related to the stars. This is true because the atoms in our bodies and the atoms that make up everything on Earth, owe their origin to a supernova event that occurred billions of years ago, trillions of kilometers away.

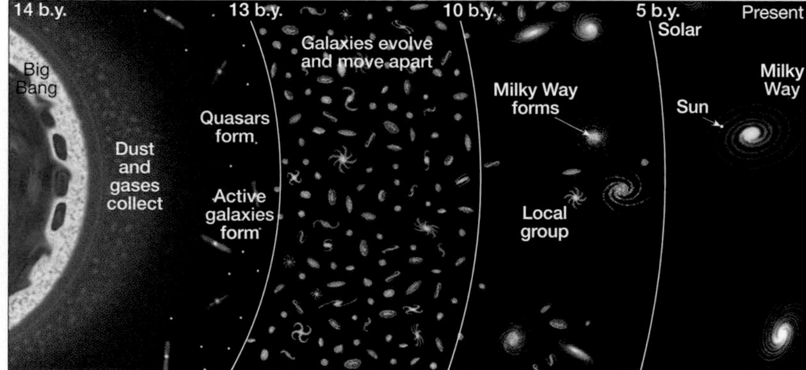

Figure 4 Big Bang Theory Between 13 and 14 billion years ago, a huge explosion sent all of the universe's matter flying outward at great speed. After a few billion years, the material cooled and condensed into the first stars and galaxies. About 5 billion years ago, our solar system began forming in a galaxy that is now called the Milky Way galaxy.

1.2 A View of Earth

Reading Focus

Key Concepts

- What are the four major spheres into which Earth is divided?
- What defines the three main parts of the solid Earth?
- Which model explains the position of continents and the occurrence of volcanoes and earthquakes?

Vocabulary

- hydrosphere
- atmosphere
- geosphere
- biosphere
- core
- mantle
- crust

Reading Strategy

Predicting Before you read, predict the meaning of the vocabulary words. After you read, revise your definition if your prediction was incorrect.

Vocabulary Term	Before You Read	After You Read
hydrosphere	a. ___?___	b. ___?___
atmosphere	c. ___?___	d. ___?___
geosphere	e. ___?___	f. ___?___
biosphere	g. ___?___	h. ___?___
core	i. ___?___	j. ___?___
mantle	k. ___?___	l. ___?___
crust	m. ___?___	n. ___?___

A view such as the one in Figure 5A provided the *Apollo 8* astronauts with a unique view of our home. Seen from space, Earth is breathtaking in its beauty. Such an image reminds us that our home is, after all, a planet—small, self-contained, and in some ways even fragile.

If you look closely at Earth from space, you may see that it is much more than rock and soil. The swirling clouds and the vast global ocean emphasize the importance of water on our planet.

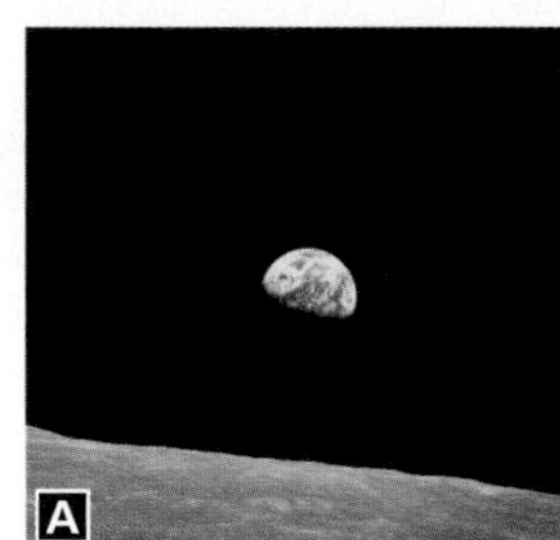

Figure 5 A View that greeted the *Apollo 8* astronauts as their spacecraft emerged from behind th Moon. **B** Africa and Arabia are prominent in this image of Earth taken from *Apollo 17.* The tan areas are desert regions. The bands of clouds over central Africa are associated with rainforests. Antarctica, which is covered by glacial ice, is visible at the south pole. The dark blue oceans and white swirling clouds remind us of the importance of oceans and the atmosphere.

Earth's Major Spheres

The view of Earth shown in Figure 5B should help you see why the physical environment is traditionally divided into three major spheres: the water portion of our planet, the **hydrosphere;** Earth's gaseous envelope, the **atmosphere;** and the **geosphere.**

Our environment is characterized by the continuous interactions of air and rock, rock and water, and water and air. The **biosphere,** which is made up of all the life-forms on Earth, interacts with all three of these physical spheres. **Earth can be thought of as consisting of four major spheres: the hydrosphere, atmosphere, geosphere, and biosphere.**

Section 1.2

1 FOCUS

Section Objectives

1.3 **Describe** Earth's four major spheres.

1.4 **Differentiate** among the three parts of the geosphere.

1.5 **State** the value of the theory of plate tectonics to Earth Science.

Reading Focus

Build Vocabulary L2

Word Parts Explain to students that *hydro-* relates to water and *atmos-* relates to air. Have them use this information, along with prior knowledge, to predict the meaning of the vocabulary words for this section.

Reading Strategy L2

Sample answer:
a. ball of water
b. all water on Earth
c. ball of air
d. gaseous envelope surrounding Earth
e. ball of rock
f. solid part of Earth below the atmosphere and oceans
g. ball of living things
h. all life on Earth
i. center of Earth
j. dense inner sphere
k. ledge
l. less dense middle layer
m. outer envelope
n. light, thin outer layer

2 INSTRUCT

Earth's Major Spheres

Use Visuals L1

Figure 5 This image of Earth was taken by astronauts in space. Ask: **Which of Earth's features are visible from space?** *(oceans, continents, clouds)* **What does the color of the land that is visible tell you about the climate in those regions?** *(Brown indicates a desert climate. Green indicates a wet climate.)* **What other Earth features do you think would be visible from space?** *(smoke from forest fires and city lights at night)* **Who might find images from space useful?** *(meteorologists, geologists, oceanographers)*
Visual, Verbal

Build Reading Literacy L1

Refer to **p. 1D**, which provides guidelines for guided anticipation.

Anticipation Guide Ask students to respond to the following questions in writing before they read this section. Have students check their answers and make changes as needed after they finish reading the section. Students should answer True or False to the following series of statements:

- The atmosphere contains all of the water on Earth. *(F)*
- Groundwater is part of Earth's hydrosphere. *(T)*
- Earth's atmosphere does nothing to protect us from the sun's radiation. *(F)*
- There is no crust under Earth's oceans. *(F)*
- Earth's crust is the same thickness under land as under water. *(F)*
- The only layer of Earth that is solid is the crust. *(F)*
- The biosphere affects all other spheres of Earth. *(T)*

Verbal

Teacher Demo

Earth's Layers L2

Purpose Provide students with a three-dimensional model of Earth's layered structure.

Materials hard-boiled egg, knife

Procedure Show students a hard-boiled egg. Crack the shell in several places so pieces of shell can slide a bit over the white of the egg. Tell students the shell of the egg represents Earth's crust, which is a thin layer, cracked and broken into plates that can move. Cut the egg in half. Show students that the white of the egg represents Earth's mantle, and the yolk of the egg represents Earth's core.

Expected Outcome Students will be able to relate the structure of the egg to the structure of Earth and can use this representation to create a mental model of what Earth's layers look like.
Visual, Logical

Hydrosphere Water is what makes Earth unique. All of the water on Earth makes up the hydrosphere. Continually on the move, water evaporates from the oceans to the atmosphere, falls back to Earth as rain, and runs back to the ocean. The oceans account for approximately 97 percent of the water on Earth. The remaining 3 percent is fresh water and is present in groundwater, streams, lakes, and glaciers.

Although these freshwater sources make up a small fraction of the total amount of water on Earth, they are quite important. Streams, glaciers, and groundwater are responsible for sustaining life and creating many of Earth's varied landforms.

Atmosphere A life-sustaining, thin, gaseous envelope called the atmosphere surrounds Earth. It reaches beyond 100 kilometers above Earth, yet 90 percent occurs within just 16 kilometers of Earth's surface. This thin blanket of air is an important part of Earth. It provides the air that we breathe. It protects us from the sun's intense heat and dangerous radiation. The energy exchanges that continually occur between space, the atmosphere, and Earth's surface produce weather and climate.

If Earth had no atmosphere, life on our planet as we know it could not exist. Many of the processes and interactions that make the surface such a dynamic place would not occur. For example, without weathering and erosion, the face of our planet might more closely resemble the moon.

Geosphere Lying beneath both the atmosphere and the ocean is the geosphere. **Because the geosphere is not uniform, it is divided into three main parts based on differences in composition—the core, the mantle, and the crust.** Figure 6A shows the dense or heavy inner sphere that is the core; the less dense mantle; and the lighter, thin crust. The crust is not uniform in thickness. It is thinnest beneath the oceans and thickest beneath the continents. Figure 6B shows that the crust and uppermost mantle make up a rigid outer layer called the lithosphere. Beneath the lithosphere, the rocks become partially molten, or melted. They are able to slowly flow because of the uneven distribution of heat deep within Earth. This region is called the asthenosphere. Beneath the asthenosphere, the rock becomes more dense. This region of Earth is called the lower mantle.

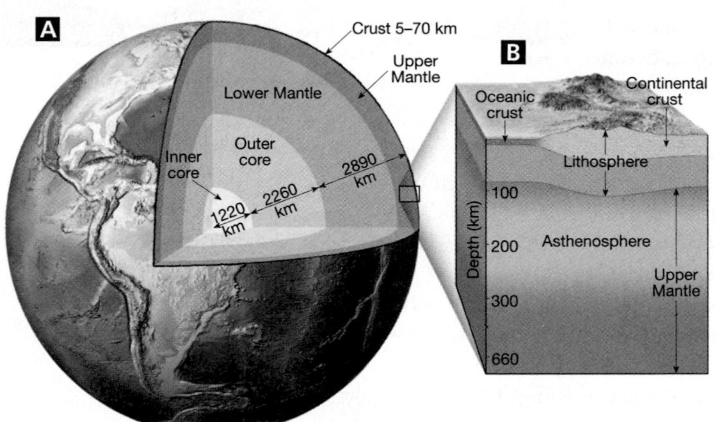

Figure 6 A On this diagram, the inner core, outer core, and mantle are drawn to scale but the thickness of the crust is exaggerated by about 5 times. **B** There are two types of crust—oceanic and continental. The lithosphere is made up of the crust and upper mantle. Below the lithosphere are the asthenosphere and the lower mantle.

Customize for Inclusion Students

Learning Disabled Have learning disabled students draw labeled pictures illustrating each of Earth's four major spheres: hydrosphere, atmosphere, geosphere, and biosphere. Be sure they include Earth's layers in their sketch of the solid Earth. They can use Figure 6 as a guide.

Biosphere The biosphere includes all life on Earth. It is concentrated in a zone that extends from the ocean floor upward for several kilometers into the atmosphere. Plants and animals depend on the physical environment for life. However, organisms do more than just respond to their physical environment. Through countless interactions, organisms help maintain and alter their physical environment. Without life, the makeup and nature of the solid Earth, hydrosphere, and atmosphere would be very different.

What are Earth's four major spheres?

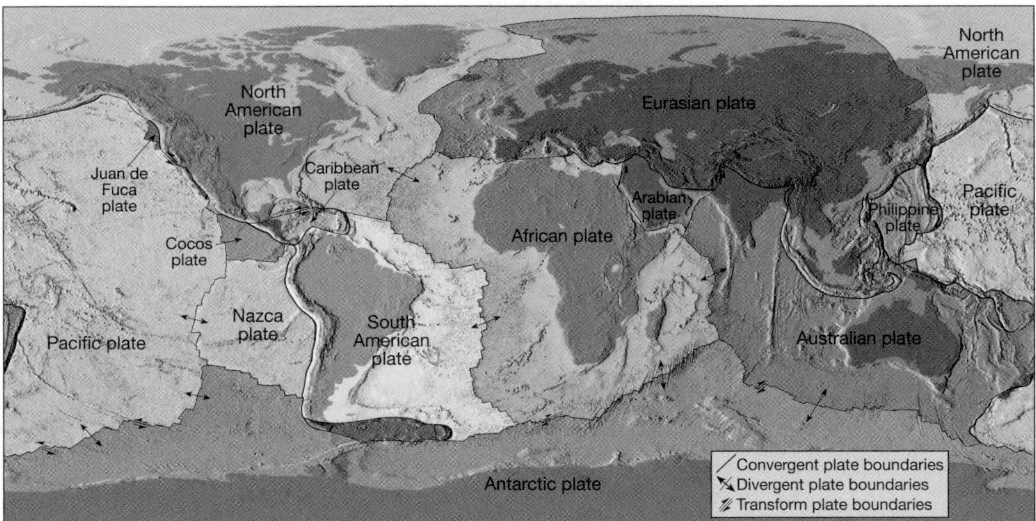

Figure 7 Plate Tectonics There are currently 7 major plates recognized and numerous smaller plates.
Relating Cause and Effect ***What is the relationship between mountain chains and plate boundaries?***

Plate Tectonics

You have read that Earth is a dynamic planet. If we could go back in time a billion years or more, we would find a planet with a surface that was dramatically different from what it is today. Such prominent features as the Grand Canyon, the Rocky Mountains, and the Appalachian Mountains did not exist. We would find that the continents had different shapes and were located in different positions from those of today.

There are two types of forces affecting Earth's surface. *Destructive forces* such as weathering and erosion work to wear away high points and flatten out the surface. *Constructive forces* such as mountain building and volcanism build up the surface by raising the land and depositing new material in the form of lava. These constructive forces depend on Earth's internal heat for their source of energy.

Facts and Figures

It is important to note that the "solid Earth" is not really all solid. The crust, mantle, and inner core are solid, but the outer core is liquid. In addition, a tiny part of Earth's mantle (in the astherosphere) is molten, which gives rise to the lava that flows out of volcanoes. Scientists have inferred the state of matter for each of Earth's layers by studying the paths that seismic waves take through Earth.

Build Science Skills

Making Judgments Present groups with the questions below. Challenge them to reach a consensus answer to each question. Once all groups have finished, have one student in each group present the results. Ask: **How does the hydrosphere, atmosphere, and geosphere affect the biosphere?** *(Flooding, tornadoes, hurricanes, volcanoes, and earthquakes have caused loss of life and habitat.)* **How do members of the biosphere affect the geosphere?** *(Humans have dug mines into the crusts. Burrowing animals also affect the solid Earth, though often in more of a temporary way.)* **How do members of the biosphere affect the hydrosphere and atmosphere?** *(Humans have polluted both water and air. Human-made dams and those built by beavers can have a dramatic effect on the flow of rivers.)* **Does the biosphere influence the other spheres more than the other spheres influence the biosphere? Explain your answer.** *(Students can answer either way as long as they have solid reasoning to support their decision. For example, when changes in the other spheres threaten the biosphere, humans usually find a way to adjust to the changes. However, the other spheres are not always able to respond to human efforts.)*
Verbal

Plate Tectonics

Build Reading Literacy

Refer to **p. 362D** in **Chapter 13,** which provides guidelines for using prior knowledge.

Use Prior Knowledge Based on their previous experiences with words such as *construction* and *destroy*, have students predict the definitions of the terms *constructive forces* and *destructive forces*. Help students see this connection and then check that they understand both terms by asking them to list some destructive forces and some constructive forces.
Verbal

Answer to . . .

Figure 7 *Mountain chains are often found along plate boundaries.*

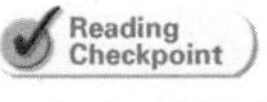

The four major spheres are the hydrosphere, atmosphere, geosphere, and biosphere.

Section 1.2 (continued)

Teacher Demo

Convection and Plates L2

Purpose Students observe how heat from within Earth can move plates.

Materials hot plate; deep, wide glass container such as a lasagna pan; diluted tomato soup; large, thin sponges; scissors; tongs

Procedure Fill the container about halfway with tomato soup, and put it on the hot plate. Slowly heat it until convection cells form (soup rising in the center and falling at the edges). While the soup is heating, cut various rough plate shapes out of the sponges. Use the tongs to place the sponges on the surface of the soup. Have students observe what happens to the sponges. (If necessary, review the concept of convection.) Ask: **Why is the soup moving?** *(Heat from below creates convection cells.)* **Why do the "plates" move?** *(The moving soup carried the plates along with it.)* **How is the actual movement of Earth's plates different from this demonstration?** *(The molten rock in the mantle is solid, and therefore slower-moving than the soup, and so the actual plates move much more slowly.)*

Safety Caution students not to touch the hot container or soup.

Expected Outcome The heat will create convection cells that move the sponges around.
Visual, Logical

Within the last several decades, a great deal has been learned about the workings of Earth. In fact, this period is called a revolution in our knowledge about Earth. This revolution began in the early part of the twentieth century with the idea that the continents had moved about the face of the Earth. This idea contradicted the accepted view that the continents and ocean basins are stationary features on the face of Earth. Few scientists believed this new idea. More than 50 years passed before enough data were gathered to transform this hypothesis into a widely accepted theory. **The theory that finally emerged, called plate tectonics, provided geologists with a model to explain how earthquakes and volcanic eruptions occur and how continents move.**

What is the difference between destructive forces and constructive forces?

According to the plate tectonics model, Earth's lithosphere is broken into several individual sections called plates. Figure 7 on page 9 shows their current position. These plates move slowly and continuously across the surface. This motion is driven by the result of an unequal distribution of heat within Earth. Ultimately, this movement of Earth's lithospheric plates generates earthquakes, volcanic activity, and the deformation of large masses of rock into mountains. You will learn more about the powerful effects of plate tectonics in Chapter 9.

Section 1.2 Assessment

Reviewing Concepts

1. Which of Earth's spheres do each of these features belong: lake, meadow, canyon, cloud?
2. What are the three main parts of the geosphere?
3. Why is the solid Earth layered?
4. The plate tectonics theory explains the existence and occurrence of what features?
5. What sort of energy allows the tectonic plates to move?
6. Describe an example of how water moves through the hydrosphere.

Critical Thinking

7. **Inferring** Using the definitions of spheres as they occur on Earth, what spheres do you think are present on Venus?
8. **Applying Concepts** Describe a situation in which two or more of Earth's spheres are interacting.
9. **Classifying** Choose an Earth science branch. List how some of its studies relate to Earth's spheres.

Connecting Concepts

Earth's Spheres You learned in Section 1.1 that Earth is a dynamic planet. Explain how features in each of Earth's spheres are changing over time.

3 ASSESS

Evaluate Understanding L2

Have students make posters showing Earth's layers and spheres. Students should label their drawings with the terms crust, mantle, core, hydrosphere, biosphere, and atmosphere.

Reteach L1

Use Figure 7 to review Earth's plates and the concept of plate tectonics.

Connecting Concepts

Students' answers could include discussions of the hydrosphere (sea level changes), atmosphere (weather and climate changes), geosphere (erosion of topsoil, earthquake occurrence), and biosphere (evolution of living things).

Section 1.2 Assessment

1. lake: hydrosphere, meadow: geosphere, canyon: geosphere, cloud: atmosphere
2. The three main parts of the geosphere are the core, mantle, and crust.
3. The layers formed because of density differences in the materials that made up early Earth.
4. Plate tectonics explains mountains, continents, ocean basins, earthquakes, and volcanoes.
5. Plate tectonics depends on Earth's internal heat.
6. Sample answer: Water in a lake evaporates into the atmosphere. The water vapor condenses and falls from the clouds into the lake as rain and the cycle begins again.
7. geosphere, atmosphere
8. Sample answer: waves (hydrosphere) crashing onto the shore (geosphere); birds (biosphere) flying in the sky (atmosphere)
9. Sample answer: meteorology: cloud cover—atmosphere; rain storms—hydrosphere and atmosphere

1.3 Representing Earth's Surface

Reading Focus

Key Concepts

- What lines on a globe are used to indicate location?
- What problems do mapmakers face when making maps?
- How do topographic maps differ from other maps?

Vocabulary

- latitude
- longitude
- topographic map
- contour line
- contour interval

Reading Strategy

Monitoring Your Understanding Preview the Key Concepts, topic headings, vocabulary, and figures in this section. List two things you expect to learn. After reading, state what you learned about each item you listed.

What I Expect to Learn	What I Learned
a. ___?___	b. ___?___
c. ___?___	d. ___?___

Determining Location

Today we use maps and computer programs to help us plan our routes. Long ago, people had to rely on maps that were made using data and information that were collected by travelers and explorers. Today computer technology is available to anyone who wants to use it. Mapmaking has changed a lot throughout recorded history.

After Christopher Columbus and others proved that Earth was not flat, mapmakers began to use a global grid to help determine location.

Global Grid Scientists use two special Earth measurements to describe location. The distance around Earth is measured in degrees. **Latitude is the distance north or south of the equator, measured in degrees. Longitude is the distance east or west of the prime meridian, measured in degrees.** Earth is 360 degrees in circumference. Lines of latitude are east-west circles around the globe. All points on the circle have the same latitude. The line of latitude around the middle of the globe, at 0 degrees (°), is the equator. Lines of longitude run north and south. The prime meridian is the line of longitude that marks ° of longitude as shown in Figure 8.

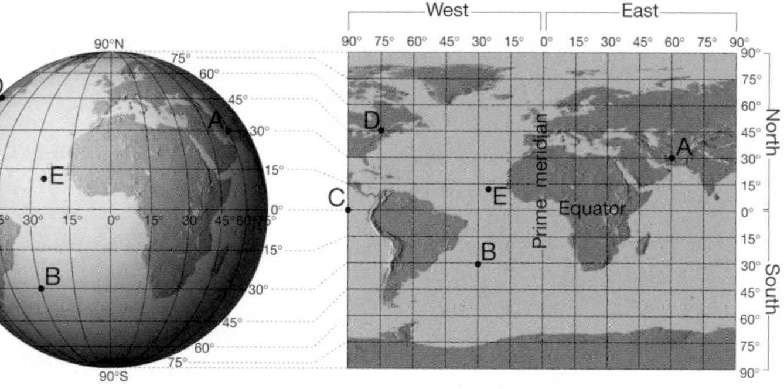

Figure 8 Global Grid

Section 1.3

1 FOCUS

Section Objectives

1.6 **Locate** points on Earth's surface by their latitude and longitude.

1.7 **Describe** the advantages and disadvantages of different types of mass.

1.8 **Explain** what makes topographic maps different from other maps.

Reading Focus

Build Vocabulary L2

Paraphrase Have students look up the vocabulary words for this section in the Glossary and then rewrite the definitions in their own words. Help students remember latitude lines run horizontally across Earth with the mnemonic "Lat lies flat." Similarly, help them see that longitude lines run the "long way" over Earth.

Reading Strategy L2

Sample answer:

a. I expect to learn about latitude and longitude.

b. Latitude lines measure degrees north and south of the equator; longitude lines measure degrees east and west of the prime meridian.

c. I expect to learn about different types of maps.

d. There are many different types of maps. Maps are hard to make accurately. Different map types have different advantages and disadvantages.

2 INSTRUCT

Determining Location

Use Visuals L1

Figure 8 Help students find point D on the global grid in this figure. Ask: **What is the latitude and longitude of point D?** *(45°N, 75°W)* **What major city is near point D?** *(Montreal, Canada)* **If an earthquake occurred near point D, are people at point A likely to feel it? Why or why not?** *(No, point D is in the Western Hemisphere and point A is in the Eastern Hemisphere.)*
Visual, Logical

Maps and Mapping

Use Visuals L1

Figure 9 Use this diagram to explain the concepts of latitude and longitude and how they are measured. Emphasize that although latitude and longitude are usually shown on Earth's surface, they are actually measured inside Earth. Ask: **From which point is latitude measured?** *(the equator)* **From which point is longitude measured?** *(the prime meridian)*
Visual, Logical

Build Reading Literacy L1

Refer to **p. 124D** in **Chapter 5,** which provides guidelines for summarizing.

Summarize Have students write a summary of this section that includes each map type and its advantages and disadvantages. This can be done as a table. Here is an example:

Map Type	Advantages	Disadvantages
Mercator projection	Rectangular; longitude lines are parallel; directions shown accurately	Sizes and distances distorted
Robinson projection	Most distances, sizes, and shapes are accurate	Distortions around the map edges
Conic projection	Great accuracy over small areas; good for road and weather maps	Lots of distortion on most of the map
Gnomonic projection	Reliably shows the shortest distance between two points	Exact distances and directions are distorted

Visual, Verbal

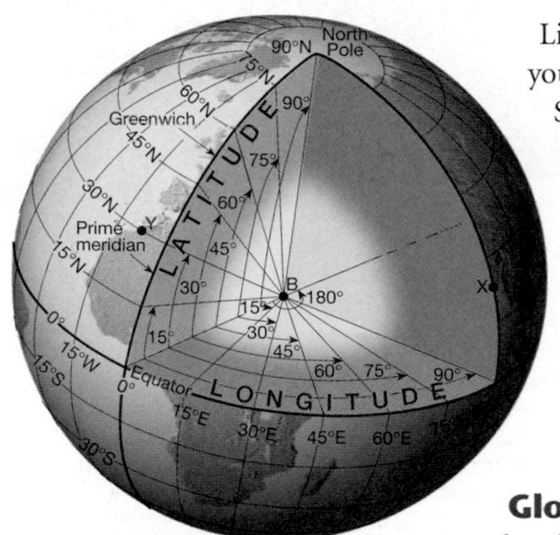

Figure 9 Measuring Latitude and Longitude

Lines of latitude and longitude form a global grid. This grid allows you to state the absolute location of any place on Earth. For example, Savannah, Georgia, is located at 32° north latitude and 81° west longitude.

The equator divides Earth in two. Each half is called a hemisphere. The equator divides Earth into northern and southern hemispheres. The prime meridian and the 180° meridian divide Earth into eastern and western hemispheres.

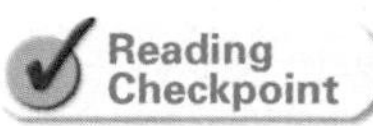

How does the global grid divide Earth?

Globes As people explored Earth, they collected information about the shapes and sizes of islands, continents, and bodies of water. Mapmakers wanted to present this information accurately. The best way was to put the information on a model, or globe, with the same round shape as Earth itself. By using an accurate shape for Earth, mapmakers could show the continents and oceans of Earth much as they really are. The only difference would be the scale, or relative size.

But there is a problem with globes. Try making a globe large enough to show the streets in your community. The globe might have to be larger than your school building! A globe can't be complete enough to be useful for finding directions and at the same time small enough to be convenient for everyday use.

Maps and Mapping

A map is a flat representation of Earth's surface. But Earth is round. Can all of Earth's features be accurately represented on a flat surface without distorting them? The answer is no. **No matter what kind of map is made, some portion of the surface will always look either too small, too big, or out of place. Mapmakers have, however, found ways to limit the distortion of shape, size, distance, and direction.**

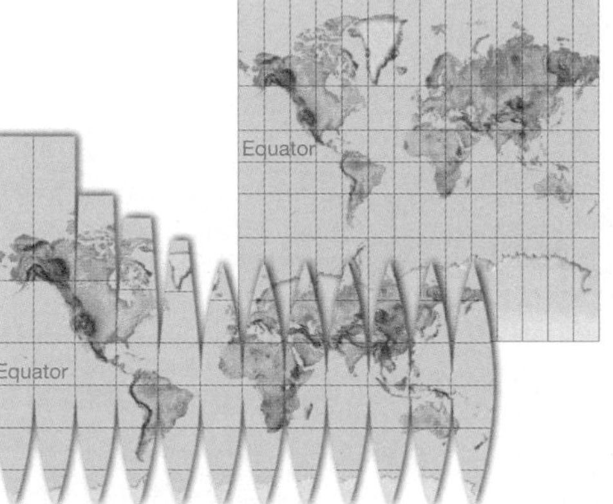

Figure 10 Mercator Map To make a Mercator map, mapmakers have to carve an image of Earth's surface into slices and then stretch the slices into rectangles. Stretching the slices enlarges parts of the map. The enlargement becomes greater toward the north and south poles. ***Observing** What areas on the map appear larger than they should?*

The Mercator Projection In 1569, a mapmaker named Gerardus Mercator created a map to help sailors navigate around Earth. On this map, the lines of longitude are parallel, making this grid rectangular, as shown on the map in Figure 10. The map was useful because, although the sizes and distances were distorted, it showed directions accurately. Today, more than 400 years later, many seagoing navigators still use the Mercator projection map.

Customize for Inclusion Students

Learning Disabled Students can more easily locate positions on a map using latitude and longitude coordinates by using the following procedure. First, help students orient themselves to the map by locating the equator and the prime meridian. Have students go over those two key points using a highlighter and extend the lines out to the edge of the paper. Next, have students write *N* in the left and right margins above the equator, and *S* in the left and right margins below the equator. Students should write *W* in the margins above and below the map west of the prime meridian, and write *E* in the margins above and below the map east of the prime meridian.

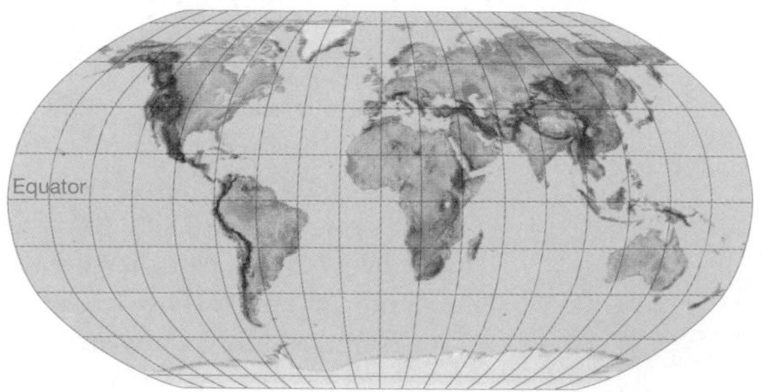

Figure 11 Robinson Projection Map Compare this map to the Mercator projection. **Comparing and Contrasting** ***How do the shapes in the continents differ between these maps? Are there any other differences?***

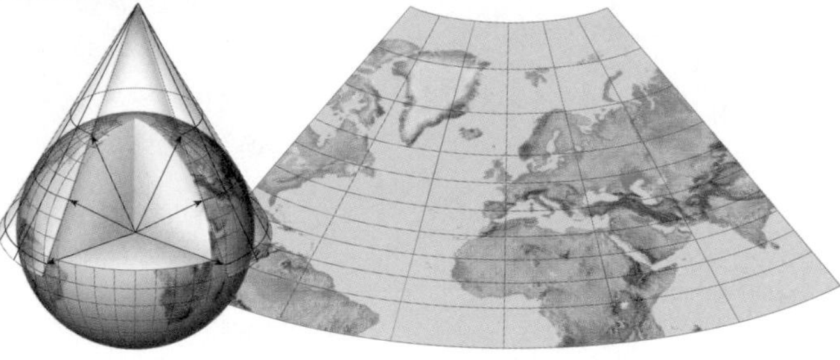

Figure 12 Conic Projection Map Because there is little distortion over small areas, conic projections are used to make road maps and weather maps.

Different Projection Maps for Different Purposes

The best projection is always determined by its intended use. The Robinson projection map is one of the most widely used. Maps that use this projection show most distances, sizes, and shapes accurately. However, even a Robinson projection has distortions, especially in areas around the edges of the map. You can see this in Figure 11. Conic projection maps are made by wrapping a cone of paper around a globe at a particular line of latitude, as shown in Figure 13. Various points and lines are projected onto the paper. There is almost no distortion along the line of latitude that's in contact with the cone, but there can be much distortion in areas away from this latitude. Because accuracy is great over a small area, these maps are used to make road maps and weather maps. Gnonomic projections, as shown in Figure 13, are made by placing a piece of paper on a globe so that it touches a single point on the globe's surface. Various points and lines are then projected onto the paper. Although distances and directions are distorted on these maps, they are useful to sailors and navigators because they show with great accuracy the shortest distance between two points.

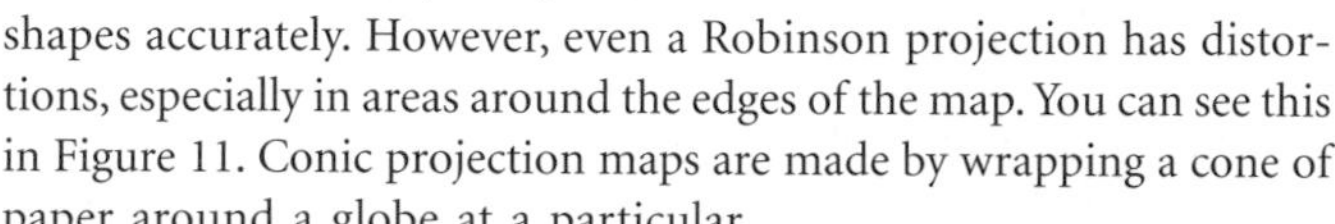

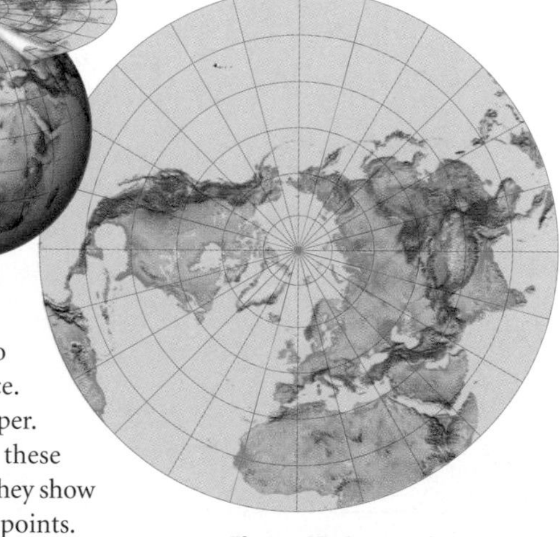

Figure 13 Gnomonic Projection Map Gnomonic projections allow sailors to accurately determine distance and direction across the oceans.

 *What major problem must mapmakers overcome?*

Teacher Demo

Conic and Gnomonic Projections **L2**

Purpose Students see how conic and gnomonic projections are made.

Materials small globe, blank transparency sheet

Procedure Use a photocopier to copy the maps in Figures 12 and 13 onto a blank transparency sheet. Make the figures as large as possible. Cut the transparency in half to separate the figures. Wrap the copy of Figure 12 around the globe in a cone shape as shown. Point out how the features of the globe line up with the projection. Hold the copy of Figure 13 flat on top of the North Pole as shown. Ask: **Where was the conic projection most accurate?** *(near the latitude where the cone touches the globe)* **Least accurate?** *(near the top and bottom)* **Where was the gnomonic projection most accurate?** *(near the North Pole)*

Expected Outcome Students will observe how the projections are related to round Earth.
Visual, Logical

Use Visuals **L1**

Figures 10–13 Advise students to look carefully at Figures 10–13 to see how each map is created and why this process results in distortion. Ask: **Based on Figure 10, how does the way a Mercator map is created cause distortion?** *(Since the Mercator map is made by slicing a globe, each section is rounded and the sections don't fit together, so each piece must be stretched into a rectangle, causing distortion.)* **Using Figure 11, explain how a conic projection map is created.** *(A cone of paper is put over a globe, and the lines of the globe are projected onto the paper.)*
Visual

Answer to . . .

Figure 10 *the areas near the poles*

Figure 11 *The continents are less distorted near the poles The longitude lines are straight, not curved.*

 *into hemispheres*

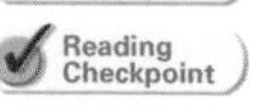 *Representing round Earth on flat paper causes distortion in shape, size, distance.*

Topographic Maps

Use Community Resources L2

A cartographer is someone who makes maps. While maps were once drawn entirely by hand based on aerial photographs, almost all modern mapmaking is done using computers. Training in GIS (geographic information systems) is usually required for the job. Ask a cartographer from a local college, university, or government office to talk to the class about how maps are made. Have students prepare questions in advance.
Interpersonal

Build Science Skills 

Applying Concepts Have students answer the following questions by using Figure 15. Ask: **Find an area with a steep slope. Name a feature in this area.** *(the southern part of the map; Sugar Loaf Mountain)* **How do you know that this area has a steep slope?** *(The contour lines are close together.)* **Find an area on the map with a gentle slope. Name a feature in this area.** *(the eastern edge of the map; Turquoise Lake)* **How can you tell that this area has a gentle slope?** *(The contour lines are far apart.)* Discuss students' answers and clarify if needed.
Visual

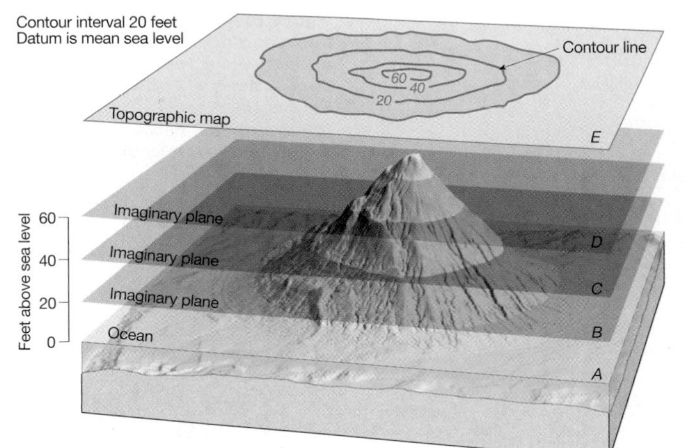

Figure 14 This illustration shows how contour lines are determined when topographic maps are constructed.

Topographic Maps

A **topographic map,** like the one shown in Figure 15, represents Earth's three-dimensional surface in two dimensions. **Topographic maps differ from the other maps discussed so far because topographic maps show elevation. Topographical maps show elevation of Earth's surface by means of contour lines.** Most also show the presence of bodies of water, roads, government and public buildings, political boundaries, and place names. These maps are important for geologists, hikers, campers and anyone else interested in the three-dimensional lay of the land.

Contour Lines The elevation of the land is indicated by using contour lines. Every position along a single contour line is the same elevation. Adjacent contour lines represent a change in elevation. Every fifth line is bold and labeled with the elevation. It is called an index contour. The **contour interval** tells you the difference in elevation between adjacent lines. The steepness of an area can be determined by examining a map. Lines that are closer together indicate a steeper slope, while lines farther apart indicate a gentler slope. You can see this relationship on the illustration in Figure 14. Contour lines that form a circle represent a hill. A depression is represented by circular contours that have hachure marks, which are small lines on the circle that point to the center. Contour lines never touch or intersect.

Figure 15 Topographic Map This is a portion of the Holy Cross, Colorado, topographic map. Contour lines are shown in brown.

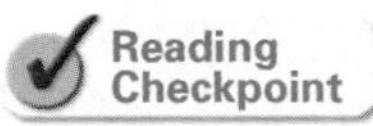

Reading Checkpoint

How do topographic maps indicate changes in elevation?

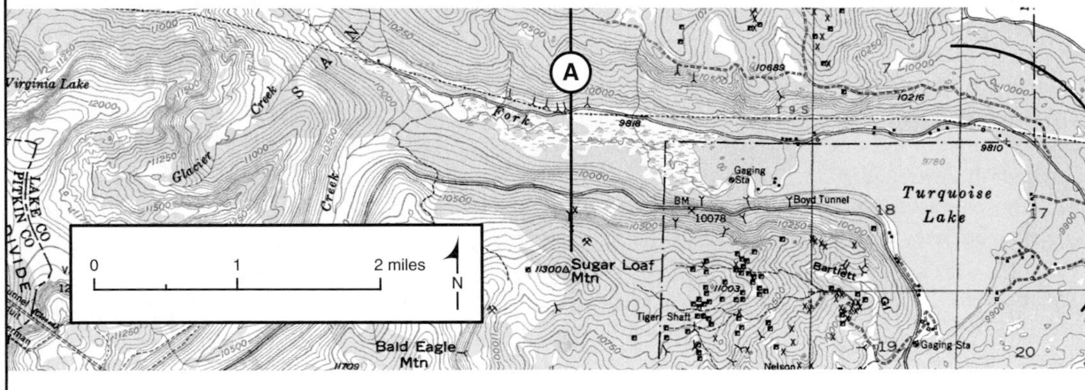

14 *Chapter 1*

Facts and Figures

Topographic maps contain a great deal of information. Each map has a legend that gives information about the map and the symbols used on it. The legend lists the title of the map (usually a major feature), the dates the map was produced and revised, and the latitude and longitude. There is a small diagram showing the map's location in the state and the names of adjacent maps. A small box contains the contour interval and the scale as a ratio and as scale bars in miles, feet, and kilometers/meters. A magnetic declination diagram shows the differences in degrees among true north, grid north, and magnetic north. A long list explains the symbols shown on the map, which can include contour lines, depressions, ocean depth lines, boundaries, survey markers, forests, fields, built-up areas, buildings, roads, and railways.

Scale A map represents a certain amount of area on Earth's surface. So it is necessary to be able to determine distances on the map and relate them to the real world. Suppose you want to build a scale model of a boat that is 20 feet long. If your model is a 1/5-scale model, then it is 4 feet long.

In a similar way, a map is drawn to scale where a certain distance on the map is equal to a certain distance at the surface. Because maps model Earth's surface, the scale must be larger than that of the model boat. Look at the scale on the map in Figure 16. The ratio reads 1:24,000. This means that 1 unit on the map is equal to 24,000 units on the ground. Because the ratio has no units, it may stand for anything. We usually use inches or centimeters for our units. If the 1 stands for 1 centimeter on the map, how many kilometers does the 24,000 stand for on the ground?

Another scale provided on a map is a bar scale. See Figure 15. This allows you to use a ruler to measure the distance on the map and then line the ruler up to the bar to determine the distance represented.

Geologic Maps It is often desirable to know the type and age of the rocks that are exposed, or crop out, at the surface. This kind of map is shown in Figure 16. **A map that shows this information is called a geologic map.** Once individual rock formations are identified, and mapped out, their distribution and extent are drawn onto the map. Each rock formation is assigned a color and sometimes a pattern. A key provides the information needed to learn what formations are present on the map. Contour lines are often included to provide a more detailed and useful map.

For: Links on mapping
Visit: www.SciLinks.org
Web Code: cjn-1013

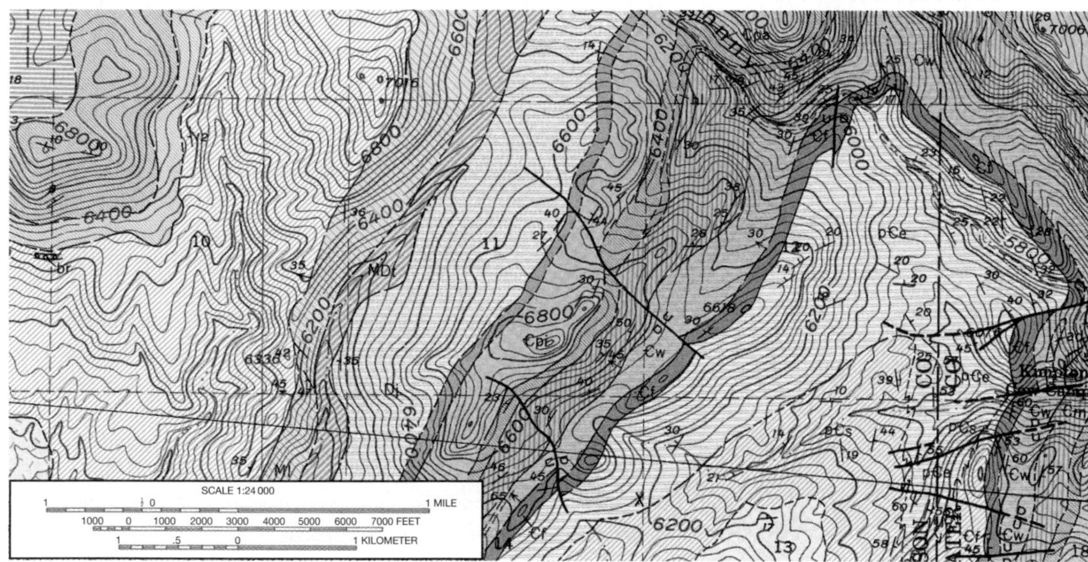

Figure 16 Geologic Map The color coding on the map represents some rock formations in Montana. Each color and pattern represents a different type of rock.

Integrate Math L2

Working With Ratios Working with a map key to determine actual distances often requires the use of ratios, a topic taught in math class. Explain the following process to your students. If a map legend has 1:24,000, this suggests that 1 unit (centimeters or inches) on the map is equal to 24,000 units (centimeters or inches) on Earth. To determine how many kilometers 1 cm on the map would equal, set up a ratio (using the conversion factor 1 km = 100,000 cm), as follows: 1 km / 100,000 cm = *x*km / 24,000 cm, then solve the ratio by cross-multiplication. The result will be that 1 cm on the map represents 0.24 km on Earth. Because 1:24,000 represents a ratio, it does not matter what unit is used as long as the map's unit matches the unit on Earth. This ratio would allow students to determine how many inches on Earth corresponded to inches on the map. **Logical**

Direct students to the **Math Skills** in the **Skills and Reference Handbook** at the end of the student text for additional help.

Use Community Resources L2

Geologic maps are used by research scientists, government agencies, and mining companies. Ask a geologist from a local college, university, mining company, or government office to talk to the class about how geologic maps are made, what information they show, and how they are used. Ask students to prepare questions in advance. **Interpersonal**

Download a worksheet on mapping for students to complete, and find additional teacher support from NSTA SciLinks.

Answer to . . .

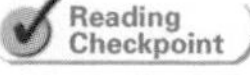

Topographic maps indicate changes in elevation with contour lines. Lines closer together indicate a steeper slope.

Advanced Technology

Use Visuals **L1**

Figure 17 Tell students that the image shown is similar to a photograph, but taken from a satellite orbiting around Earth. Ask: **What are the light blue areas?** *(moving sediment)* **Where is the sediment coming from?** *(It is carried down by the Mississippi River.)* **What is the area at the center right side of the image called and how do you think it was formed?** *(the Mississippi delta was formed from sediments deposited by the river.)*
Visual, Logical

Integrate Social Studies **L2**

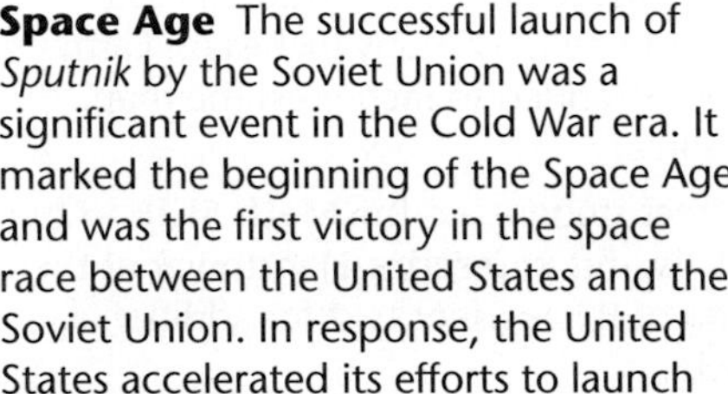

Space Age The successful launch of *Sputnik* by the Soviet Union was a significant event in the Cold War era. It marked the beginning of the Space Age and was the first victory in the space race between the United States and the Soviet Union. In response, the United States accelerated its efforts to launch its own satellite.

Figure 17 Satellite Image of the Mississippi River Delta Moving sediment (light blue) indicates current patterns. Red shows vegetation.

Advanced Technology

Advanced technology is used to make maps that are more accurate than ever before. **Today's technology provides us with the ability to more precisely analyze Earth's physical properties.** Scientists now use satellites and computers to send and receive data. These data are converted into usable forms such as pictures and numerical summaries.

The process of collecting data about Earth from a distance, such as from orbiting satellites, is called remote sensing. Satellites use remote sensing to produce views of Earth that scientists use to study rivers, oceans, fires, pollution, natural resources, and many other topics. How might a scientist use the image shown in Figure 17?

We can use this technology in our daily lives too. For example, Global Positioning Systems (GPS) can provide maps in our cars to help us reach our destinations. GPS consists of an instrument that receives signals to compute the user's latitude and longitude as well as speed, direction, and elevation. GPS is an important tool for navigation by ships and airplanes. Scientists use GPS to track wildlife, study earthquakes, measure erosion, and many other purposes. Table 1 describes some of the technology that is particularly useful in the study of Earth science.

Facts and Figures

The first satellite to orbit Earth was called *Sputnik.* The Soviet Union launched it on October 4, 1957. It was a 23-inch, 184-pound metal ball containing a thermometer, a battery, and a radio transmitter. On its exterior, four whip antennas transmitted short-wave frequencies between 20 and 40 MHz, common frequencies intended to make *Sputnik's* presence obvious to the world, and particularly to the United States. *Sputnik* orbited Earth for 92 days before burning up in Earth's atmosphere.

Type of Equipment	Capabilities
Table 1 Technology and Earth Science	
Weather Satelllites	• These monitor atmospheric temperature and humidity, ground and surface seawater temperature, cloud cover, and water-ice boundaries. • They can help locate sources of distress signals. • They are able to scan Earth's surface in one 24-hour period.
Navigation Satellites	• These assist ships and submarines to determine their exact location at any time.
Landsat Satellites	• The first Landsat satellite was launched in 1972. Landsat 7 was launched in 1999. • They provide data on Earth's landmasses, coastal boundaries, and coral reefs. • Pictures taken are transmitted to ground stations around the world. • They orbit Earth every 99 minutes and complete 14 orbits per day. • Total coverage of Earth is achieved in 16 days.
Global Positioning System (GPS)	• This system combines satellite information with computer technology to provide location information in three dimensions: latitude, longitude, and altitude. • Three satellite signals are detected by a receiver. The distance from the satellites to the receiver is calculated, and the location is determined using the triangulation method. A fourth signal is then used to mathematically determine exact position.
Very Long Baseline Interferometry (VLBI)	• VLBI utilizes a large network of antennas around the world to receive radio waves from space objects such as quasars. • In Earth science, VLBI is used in geodesy, or the measurement of the geosphere. • Using the arrival times of radio waves from quasars, the position of radio telescopes on Earth are determined to within millimeters of their position. • Small changes in the telescope positions allow scientists to study tectonic plate motions and other movements of Earth's crust with great precision and accuracy.

Section 1.3 Assessment

Reviewing Concepts

1. Describe the two sets of lines that are used on globes and some maps.
2. What happens to the images on the globe when they are transferred to a flat surface?
3. What is the purpose of contour lines on topographic maps?
4. What two lines mark zero degrees on the globe? In which directions do these lines run?
5. Why is the Mercator projection map still in use today?
6. What types of advanced technology are used in mapmaking today?

Critical Thinking

7. **Applying Concepts** Why are there so many different types of maps?
8. **Drawing Conclusions** How can data from VLBI be used in mapmaking today?
9. **Conceptualizing** An area on a topographic map has the following contour line configuration: First, the lines are fairly widely spaced. Then they are closely spaced. Finally, they are circular. Describe the topography represented by these lines.

Math Practice

Use the bar scale on Figure 15 to answer the following question.

10. Determine the distance along the shoreline of Turquoise Lake from the gaging station on the west shore to the gaging station on the south shore. Record your answer in kilometers.

Section 1.3 Assessment

1. Lines of latitude are east-west circles around the globe. Lines of longitude run north and south.
2. They become distorted.
3. Contour lines indicate elevation.
4. The lines are the equator, which runs east and west, and the prime meridian, which runs north and south.
5. It is useful to sailors because although size and shape are distorted, it shows directions accurately.
6. Sample answer: satellites, computers, high-powered telescopes, sonar, GPS, VLBI
7. Each type of map is particularly useful in some capacity. Conic projections are good for small-scale maps such as road maps. Topographic maps help geologists and hikers. Mercator projections help sailors to navigate.
8. Because small-scale changes in position can be detected by VLBI technology, movements of Earth's crust can be measured precisely.
9. The land starts out relatively flat and rises steeply to the top of a hill.

Build Science Skills L2

Posing Questions Have students select one type of equipment described in Table 1 to research. Encourage students to make a list of questions about the equipment, such as when and where it was invented and by whom. Then have them research how the technology works and close with some applications of the technology they selected. Students can present their work as a written report, an oral report, or a poster to share with the class.
Verbal, Visual

3 ASSESS

Evaluate Understanding 

Give students a topographic map that includes latitude and longitude. Have them locate specific features on the map, such as hills and depressions, based on the shapes of the contour lines. Have students determine the latitude and longitude of these features. Give students the latitude and longitude of a few sites of interest on the map and have them tell you what they find at each of those locations.

Reteach 

Have students answer the Assessment questions in small groups. Assign the lower ability students to answer the Reviewing Concepts questions and the higher ability students to answer the Critical Thinking questions. Have partners then share and discuss their answers. Once all groups are finished, have students report their answers to the class. Clarify concepts as needed.

Math Practice

Solution
10. The distance in centimeters on the map is approximately 5.5 cm. The distance on the ground is approximately 3.43 km.

Section 1.4

1 FOCUS

Section Objectives

1.9 **Describe** the primary goal of Earth system science and **define** the term *system*.

1.10 **Describe** Earth's two major sources of energy.

1.11 **Explain** how humans affect Earth's systems.

1.12 **Distinguish** between renewable and nonrenewable resources.

Reading Focus

Build Vocabulary L2

Word Forms Have students predict the meanings of *open system* and *closed system* based on their prior knowledge of the words *open*, *closed*, and *system*. Have students verify their predictions by reading the section.

Reading Strategy L2

Earth System Science

A. What is a System?
  1. System—any size group of interacting parts forming a whole
  2. Types of Systems—closed and open

B. Earth as a System
  1. Earth has two energy sources—the sun and Earth's interior.
  2. The parts of the Earth system are linked so a change in one part can cause changes in all the other parts.

2 INSTRUCT

What Is a System?

Build Science Skills L2

Using Analogies The text gives an analogy of a car's cooling system to a natural system. Challenge students to think of other analogies between human-made and natural systems. They should write a description of the analogy they choose, including diagrams if appropriate. The descriptions should explain how the analogies are similar to the actual process and different from it.
Verbal, Logical

1.4 Earth System Science

Reading Focus

Key Concepts
- How is Earth a system?
- What is a system?
- Where does the energy come from that powers Earth's systems?
- How do humans affect Earth's systems?
- What makes a resource renewable or nonrenewable?

Vocabulary
- system

Reading Strategy

Outlining As you read, make an outline of the most important ideas in this section. Begin with the section title, then list the green headings as the next step of the outline. Outline further as needed.

I. Earth System Science
  A. What is a System?
    1. ___?___
    2. ___?___
  B. ___?___

As we study Earth, we see that it is a dynamic planet with many separate but interactive parts or spheres. Earth scientists are studying how these spheres are interconnected. **This way of looking at Earth is called Earth system science. Its aim is to understand Earth as a system made up of numerous interacting parts, or subsystems.** Instead of studying only one branch of science, such as geology, chemistry, or biology, Earth system science tries to put together what we know from our study of all of these branches. Using this type of approach, we hope to eventually understand and solve many of our global environmental problems.

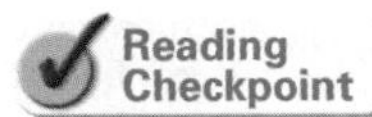

What Is Earth system science?

What Is a System?

Most of us hear and use the term system frequently. You might use your city's transportation system to get to school. A news report might inform us of an approaching weather system. We know that Earth is just a small part of the much larger solar system.

A system can be any size group of interacting parts that form a complex whole. Most natural systems are driven by sources of energy that move matter and/or energy from one place to another. A simple analogy is a car's cooling system. It contains a liquid (usually water and antifreeze) that is driven from the engine to the radiator and back again. The role of this system is to transfer the heat generated by combustion in the engine to the radiator, where moving air removes the heat from the system.

This kind of system is called a closed system. Here energy moves freely in and out of the system, but no matter enters or leaves the system. In the case of the car's cooling system, the matter is the liquid. By contrast, most natural systems are open systems. Here both energy and matter flow into and out of the system. In a river system, for example, the amount of water flowing in the channel can vary a great deal. At one time or place, the river may be fuller than it is at another time or place.

Earth as a System

The Earth system is powered by energy from two sources. **One source is the sun, which drives external processes that occur in the atmosphere, hydrosphere, and at Earth's surface.** Weather and climate, ocean circulation, and erosional processes are driven by energy from the sun. **Earth's interior is the second source of energy.** There is heat that remains from the time Earth formed. There is also heat continuously generated by the decay of radioactive elements. These sources power the internal processes that produce volcanoes, earthquakes, and mountains.

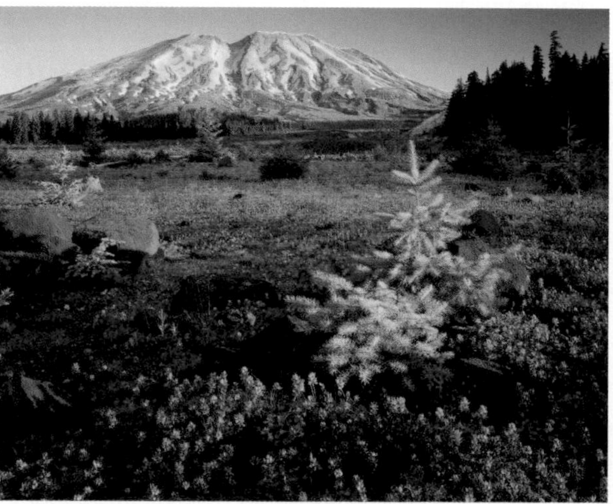

Figure 18 When Mount St. Helens erupted in May 1980, the area shown here was buried by a volcanic mudflow. Now, plants are reestablished and new soil is forming.

The parts of the Earth system are linked so that a change in one part can produce changes in any or all of the other parts. For example, when a volcano erupts, lava may flow out at the surface and block a nearby valley. This new obstruction influences the region's drainage system by creating a lake or causing streams to change course. Volcanic ash and gases that can be discharged during an eruption might be blown high into the atmosphere and influence the amount of solar energy that can reach Earth's surface. The result could be a drop in air temperatures over the entire hemisphere.

How do we know that Earth's systems are connected?

Over time, soil will develop on the lava or ash-covered surface and, as shown in Figure 18, plants and animals will reestablish themselves. This soil will reflect the interactions among many parts of the Earth system—the original volcanic material, the type and rate of weathering, and the impact of biological activity. Of course, there would also

Build Reading Literacy L1

Refer to **p. 216D** in **Chapter 8,** which provides guidelines for comparing and contrasting.

Compare and Contrast Help students understand the difference between an open system and a closed system. Have students make a comparison chart, starting with the definition of each type of system. Have students classify each system listed during the brainstorming session as either an open system or a closed system. Example:

	Open System	Closed System
Definition	Energy and matter move in and out of the system.	Energy moves in and out of the system, but matter cannot enter or leave.
Examples	weather system river system	cooling system

Have students research a list of systems. Then have students put each system in the correct column on their comparison chart.
Verbal, Logical

Earth as a System

Build Science Skills L2

Relating Cause and Effect Using this section of the textbook, have students make a concept map showing how a volcanic eruption (an event of the geosphere) can causes changes in all the other spheres (hydrosphere, atmosphere, and biosphere). Have students use the concept map to make a poster to be displayed in the classroom. Challenge students to create a product that is both visually appealing and scientifically accurate. Ask students to think of another event on Earth and predict how it would affect all the other spheres. Have students make another concept map poster on this event.
Visual, Group

Customize for English Language Learners

Review with English language learners the meanings of the words *open* and *closed.* Help students relate the meanings of *open* and *closed* to *open system* and *closed system.* Before teaching the terms *renewable resources* and *nonrenewable resources,* explain what it means to renew a library book (take it out again before you return it). Help students relate this use of the word *renew* to the terms *renewable resources* and *nonrenewable resources.* Tell students that if they are not allowed to renew a library book (nonrenewable) it is often because the library does not have enough books on that topic to meet the needs of their patrons. Explain that a renewable resource can be used as often as we like because there is always more of it being made.

Answer to . . .

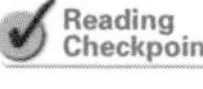

Earth system science is a way of looking at Earth as a system made up of several interacting subsystems.

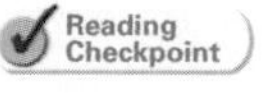

Events taking place in one part can produce changes in all the other parts.

Address Misconceptions L2

Students may think that only human actions can seriously affect the environment. Use the example of the eruption of Mount St. Helens to emphasize that natural events can have widespread and negative effects on the environment. The 1980 eruptions spread ash over much of eastern Washington. About 500 square kilometers of forest were destroyed or damaged. Most large animals in the area were killed by the blast, but some small animals survived. More than 20 years later, the area is still fairly barren. It may take at least 200 years for the forest to be restored to its previous state. Large mammals such as elk have already repopulated the area, along with birds, insects, and small mammals.

People and the Environment

Use Visuals L1

Figure 19 This flood was caused by the action of humans. Ask: **What was the actual cause of this flood?** *(building the Aswan Dam)* **What are some ways humans can cause floods or make them worse?** *(by clearing forests, building cities, and constructing dams)* **Visual, Logical**

be significant changes in the biosphere. Some organisms and their habitats would be eliminated by the lava and ash, while new settings for life, such as the lake, would be created. The potential climate change could also have an effect on some life-forms.

The Earth system is characterized by processes that occur over areas that range in size from millimeters to thousands of kilometers. Time scales for Earth's processes range from milliseconds to billions of years. Despite this great range in distance and time, many processes are connected. A change in one component can influence the entire system.

Humans are also part of the Earth system. **Our actions produce changes in all of the other parts of the Earth system.** When we burn gasoline and coal, build breakwaters along a shoreline, dispose of our wastes, and clear the land, we cause other parts of the Earth system to respond, often in unforeseen ways. Throughout this book, you will learn about many of Earth's subsystems, such as the hydrologic (water) system, the tectonic (mountain-building) system, and the climate system. Remember that these components and we humans are all part of the complex interacting whole we call the Earth system.

Figure 19 The benefit that was intended by the construction of the Aswan Dam in Egypt was not achieved.
Drawing Conclusions *How might the flooding here have been avoided?*

People and the Environment

Environment refers to everything that surrounds and influences an organism. Some of these things are biological and social. Others are nonliving such as water, air, soil and rock as well as conditions such as temperature, humidity, and sunlight. These nonliving factors make up our physical environment. Because studying the Earth sciences leads to an understanding of the physical environment, most of Earth science can be characterized as environmental science.

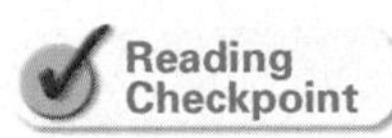

Reading Checkpoint *What are examples of nonliving factors?*

Today the term *environmental science* is usually used for things that focus on the relationships between people and the natural environment. For example, we can dramatically influence natural processes. A river flooding is natural, but the size and frequency of flooding can be changed by human activities such as clearing forests, building cities, and constructing dams. Unfortunately, natural systems do not always adjust to artificial changes in ways we can anticipate. An alteration to the environment that was intended to benefit society may have the opposite effect, as shown in Figure 19.

Resources Resources are an important focus of the Earth sciences. They include water and soil, metallic and nonmetallic minerals, and energy. Together they form the foundation of modern civilization. The Earth sciences deal not only with the formation and occurrence of

Facts and Figures

One of the reasons it is often difficult to predict how natural systems will respond to unexpected changes is the prevalence of positive and negative feedback mechanisms. Processes that feed into changes, making them more severe, are considered positive feedback. As humans put more carbon dioxide into the air, Earth may hold more of the sun's heat and begin to warm. This warming may cause snow and ice near the poles to melt. This melting may make Earth absorb more of the sun's rays, thus increasing Earth's temperature further. This is an example of positive feedback. Negative feedback mechanisms work to return the system to the way it was before the change. For example, an increase in Earth's temperature may result in an increase in evaporation, and then an increase in clouds. Clouds cause Earth to reflect more of the sun's rays back into space, cooling Earth back down.

these vital resources but also with maintaining supplies and the environmental impact of their mining and use.

Resources are commonly divided into two broad categories—renewable resources and nonrenewable resources. **Renewable resources can be replenished over relatively short time spans.** Common examples are plants and animals for food, natural fibers for clothing, and forest products for lumber and paper. Energy from flowing water, wind, and the sun are also considered renewable resources.

Important metals such as iron, aluminum, and copper plus our most important fuels of oil, natural gas, and coal are classified as nonrenewable resources. **Although these and other resources continue to form, the processes that create them are so slow that it takes millions of years for significant deposits to accumulate.** Earth contains limited quantities of these materials. Although some nonrenewable resources, such as aluminum, can be used over and over again, others, such as oil, cannot. When the present supplies are exhausted, there will be no more.

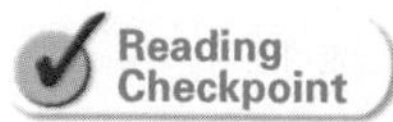

How do renewable and nonrenewable resources differ?

For: Links on environmental decision-making
Visit: www.SciLinks.org
Web Code: cjn-1014

Population Figure 20 shows that the population of Earth is growing rapidly. Although it took until the beginning of the nineteenth century for the population to reach 1 billion, just 130 years were needed for the population to double to 2 billion. Between 1930 and 1975, the figure doubled again to 4 billion, and by about 2010, as many as 7 billion people may inhabit Earth. Clearly, as population grows, so does the demand for resources. However, the rate of mineral and energy resource usage has increased more rapidly than the overall growth of the population.

How long will the remaining supplies of basic resources last? How long can we sustain the rising standard of living in today's industrialized countries and still provide for the growing needs of developing regions? How much environmental deterioration are we willing to accept to obtain basic resources? Can alternatives be found? If we are to cope with the increasing demand on resources and a growing world population, it is important that we have some understanding of our present and potential resources.

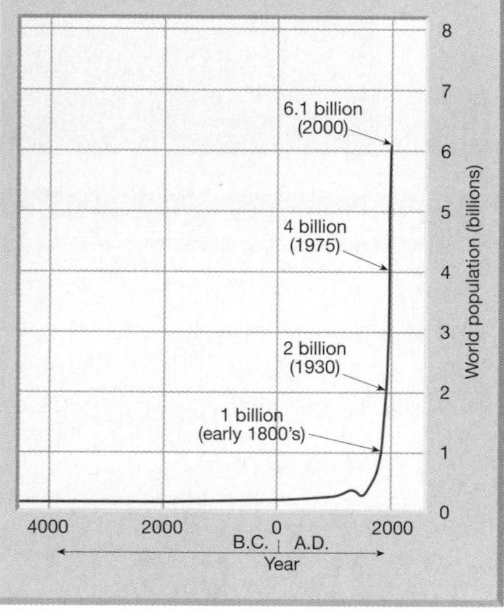

Figure 20 Growth of World Population

Environmental Problems

In addition to the search for mineral and energy resources, the Earth sciences must also deal with environmental problems. Some of these problems are local, some are regional, and still others are global. Humans can cause problems, such as the one shown in Figure 21. **Significant**

Build Science Skills

L2

Problem Solving Explain that when supplies of a nonrenewable resource start running low, it is often possible to substitute some other resource. Have students work in small groups to brainstorm and research alternatives to oil that can be used when all of our oil has been used up. If students are having trouble getting started, suggest that they focus on transportation and power generation. Areas students can investigate include natural gas, coal, biodiesel, nuclear power, wind power, and solar power. Have each group present their results to the class.
Interpersonal, Logical

L2

Students may think that the world population is expected to continue to increase indefinitely. Tell students that many demographers (scientists who study changes in human populations) expect population growth to slow down over the next 100 years. In fact, some predict that the total population may even decrease. The reason for this is that in many developed countries, people are not having enough children to replace themselves. Most current population growth is occurring in developing countries. However, as those countries develop, their birth rates are also expected to fall.

Go Online
NSTA SCiLINKS

Download a worksheet on environmental decision-making for students to complete, and find additional teacher support from NSTA SciLinks.

Answer to . . .

Figure 19 *The flooding could have been avoided by not building the dam.*

Nonliving factors include water, air, soil, rock, temperature, humidity, and sunlight.

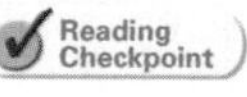

Renewable resources can be replenished over a relatively short time span. Nonrenewable resources take millions of years to accumulate.

Environmental Problems

Build Science Skills

L2

Inferring Discuss with students that events such as earthquakes, landslides, floods, hurricanes, beach erosion from coastal storms, and drought are natural processes. Help students understand that these natural processes become hazards "only when people try to live where these processes occur." Provide small groups of students with one or more pictures of damage from natural disasters. Some examples to use would be flooded homes, a coastal home about to be carried out to sea, buildings damaged by an earthquake, or urban flooding due to too much paved land. Ask: **What happened here? How could this disaster have been prevented?** *(Sample answer: This home is being carried out to sea because it was built too close to the ocean. These homes were flooded because they were built on a flood plain. This building was destroyed because it was built too close to a fault line.)* Have students infer the answers to these two questions, and then share their ideas with the class. Use this as an opportunity to introduce students to various Earth events and processes that will be studied later in the year.
Visual

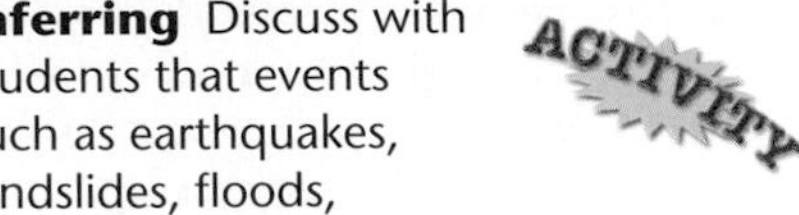

3 ASSESS

Evaluate Understanding

Ask students to write a five-question quiz on this section along with an answer key. Then have students ask one another the questions.

Reteach

Use the outlines students created for this chapter's reading strategy to review the main ideas from this section.

Connecting Concepts

Images can show scars of landslides, suggesting that the area may not be stable.

Answer to . . .

Figure 21 *Sample answer: home heating, motor vehicles, industry, power plants*

Figure 21 Air pollution in the Chinese city of Guangzhou. Air quality problems affect many cities. **Interpreting Photographs** ***What may have contributed to this air pollution problem?***

threats to the environment include air pollution, acid rain, ozone depletion, and global warming. The loss of fertile soils to erosion, the disposal of toxic wastes, and the contamination and depletion of water resources are also of considerable concern. The list continues to grow.

People must cope with the many natural hazards that exist such as the one shown in Figure 22. Earthquakes, landslides, floods, hurricanes, and drought are some of the many risks. Of course, environmental hazards are simply natural processes. They become hazards only when people try to live where these processes occur.

It is clear that as world population continues to grow, pressures on the environment will increase as well. Therefore, an understanding of Earth is essential for the location and recovery of basic resources. It is also essential for dealing with the human impact on the environment and minimizing the effects of natural hazards. Knowledge about Earth and how it works is necessary to our survival and well being. Earth is the only suitable habitat we have, and its resources are limited.

Figure 22 The damage here was caused by a landslide that was triggered by an earthquake.

Section 1.4 Assessment

Reviewing Concepts

1. Why do scientists study Earth as a system?
2. If a system is a collection of interacting parts, what happens when one of the parts is changed?
3. What are the two sources of energy that power Earth's systems?
4. List three ways that humans affect Earth's systems.
5. Large numbers of tiny ocean organisms die every day, fall to the ocean floor, are buried, and are eventually converted to oil and natural gas. Why are these two fuels considered nonrenewable?

Critical Thinking

6. **Applying Concepts** Describe the parts of a tree in terms of it being a system.
7. **Evaluating** Is it possible for humans to have no effect on any of Earth's systems? Explain.
8. **Applying Concepts** How can scientists help to prevent a natural process from becoming an environmental hazard?

Connecting Concepts

City Planning In Section 1.3, you learned about Landsat satellite imaging. How can data from Landsat help city planners determine where and where not to build?

Section 1.4 Assessment

1. Earth is a system made up of numerous interacting parts, or subsystems.
2. Other parts may also change.
3. The sources are the sun and reactions in Earth's interior.
4. Sample answer: contaminating water, polluting air, disposing of toxic waste
5. It takes too long (millions of years) for the organisms to be converted into oil.
6. Roots transport food and water up through the trunk, which holds the tree upright. The trunk transports food and serves as support for branches and leaves. Leaves help keep the tree moist and shaded and release excess water through pores.
7. No, every day you affect at least one of Earth's systems, even on the smallest scale. Simply breathing changes the atmosphere around you or stepping on the grass may affect the biosphere beneath your foot.
8. Sample answer: They can analyze an area to see if it is safe to live there. If the land is unstable or subject to flooding, they may make recommendations that people not choose to live there.

1.5 What Is Scientific Inquiry?

Reading Focus

Key Concepts

- What is a hypothesis?
- What is a theory?

Vocabulary

- hypothesis
- theory

Reading Strategy

Comparing and Contrasting Complete the Venn diagram by listing the ways hypothesis and theory are alike and how they differ.

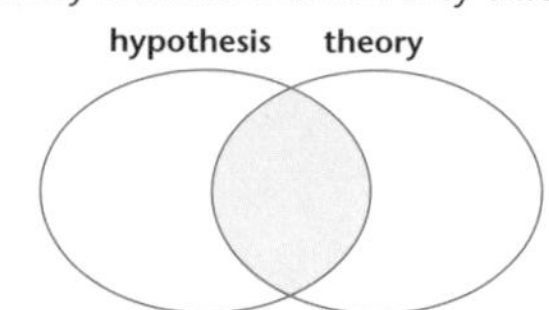

All science is based on two assumptions. First, the natural world behaves in a consistent and predictable manner. Second, through careful, systematic study, we can understand and explain the natural world's behavior. We can use this knowledge to make predictions about what should or should not be expected. For example, by knowing how oil deposits form, geologists are able to predict the most likely sites for exploration.

The development of new scientific knowledge involves some basic steps. First, scientists collect data through observation and measurement. These data are essential to science and serve as the starting point for the development of scientific theories.

Hypothesis

Once data have been gathered, scientists try to explain how or why things happen in the manner observed. Scientists do this by stating a possible explanation called a scientific hypothesis. Sometimes more than one hypothesis is developed to explain a given set of observations. Just because a hypothesis is stated doesn't mean that it is correct or that the scientific community will automatically accept it.

Before a hypothesis can become an accepted part of scientific knowledge, it must be tested and analyzed. If a hypothesis can't be tested, it is not scientifically useful, no matter how interesting it might seem. Hypotheses that fail rigorous testing are discarded. The history of science is filled with discarded hypotheses. One of the best known is the Earth-centered model of the universe. This hypothesis was based on the apparent movement of the sun, moon, and stars around Earth.

For: Links on scientific methods
Visit: www.SciLinks.org
Web Code: cjn-1015

Section 1.5

1 FOCUS

Section Objectives

1.13 **Define** the terms *hypothesis* and *theory.*

Reading Focus

Build Vocabulary 

Word Meanings Before they read the section, have students write down definitions for *hypothesis* and *theory*. As they read the section, have them note the scientific definitions of these terms and compare them to their definitions.

Reading Strategy 

Hypothesis: an idea someone wants to test; Theory: an explanation that is supported by evidence and widely accepted; Similarities: could be proven wrong, can be tested

2 INSTRUCT

Hypothesis

Build Reading Literacy 

Refer to **p. 446D** in **Chapter 16**, which provides guidelines for sequencing.

Sequence Tell students to create a flowchart showing the steps toward the development of a scientific theory. They should begin the flowchart as they are reading the introduction to this section and should end it at Scientific Methods. *(Sample response: Collect data → Develop hypotheses or models → Test hypothesis (experiment) → Accept, modify, or reject hypothesis → If well tested, the hypothesis becomes a theory.)* Have students check their flowchart against the sequence of steps provided in the Scientific Methods section of the text.
Visual, Verbal

Download a worksheet on scientific methods for students to complete, and find additional teacher support from NSTA SciLinks.

Section 1.5 (continued)

Theory

Address Misconceptions L2

Students often think that a scientific theory is an ultimate truth, and therefore can never be changed. This is not true. A theory is only accepted if a multitude of tests support the theory. However, if even one scientist finds a situation where the theory fails, that theory is again called into question and must be revised or replaced. For this reason, science is constantly changing. One example is medicines or supplements that have been promoted and used for years suddenly being pulled off the shelves after the discovery of unexpected and dangerous side effects.
Verbal

Scientific Methods

Integrate Language Arts L2

Representing Definitions There are many definitions for the word *model*. Have students use a dictionary to write down as many definitions of the word as possible. Then have them draw or cut out pictures representing these definitions. Help students determine which definition is most appropriate in this section.
Visual, Verbal

3 ASSESS

Evaluate Understanding L2

Give students the steps of the scientific method in random order, and have them put the steps in the correct order.

Reteach L1

Have students illustrate each step of the scientific method on the flowchart they created earlier. Help students understand that scientists regularly go back a few steps in the method as they attempt to arrive at a theory.
Visual

Writing in Science

Many scientists repeated the same observations and recorded similar results. These observations were made in many places around the world, yet all had the same basic principles. Advise students that they can find out more about the theory of plate tectonics in Chapter 9.

As the mathematician Jacob Bronowski stated, "Science is a great many things, but in the end they all return to this: Science is the acceptance of what works and the rejection of what does not."

Theory

When a hypothesis has survived extensive testing and when competing hypotheses have been eliminated, a hypothesis may become a scientific **theory.** **A scientific theory is well tested and widely accepted by the scientific community and best explains certain observable facts.** For example, the theory of plate tectonics provides the framework for understanding the origin of continents and ocean basins, plus the occurrence of mountains, earthquakes, and volcanoes.

Scientific Methods

The process of gathering facts through observations and formulating scientific hypotheses and theories is called the scientific method. There is no set path that scientists must follow in order to gain scientific knowledge. However, many scientific investigations involve the following steps: (1) the collection of scientific facts through observation and measurement, (2) the development of one or more working hypotheses or models to explain these facts, (3) development of observations and experiments to test the hypotheses, and (4) the acceptance, modification, or rejection of the hypothesis based on extensive testing.

Section 1.5 Assessment

Reviewing Concepts

1. You have just come up with an explanation to a question that has bothered you for some time. What must you do to have your explanation become a hypothesis?
2. Explain how a hypothesis can become a theory.
3. According to the scientific community, how does the natural world behave?
4. What happens if more than one hypothesis is put forward to explain the same observations?
5. When is a model useful in scientific investigations?

Thinking Critically

6. **Applying Concepts** Why do most scientists follow a set order of steps when carrying out a scientific investigation?
7. **Designing Experiments** While carrying out an investigation, a scientist observes some unexpected results. What are the scientist's next steps?
8. **Understanding Concepts** Why is it necessary to use careful and systematic methods when carrying out scientific investigations?

Writing in Science

Explanatory Paragraph It took a long time for the scientific community to accept the theory of plate tectonics. Write a paragraph suggesting how the use of proper scientific methods helped the theory gain acceptance.

Section 1.5 Assessment

1. Test and analyze the hypothesis.
2. A hypothesis can become a theory once it has survived extensive testing and when competing hypotheses have been eliminated.
3. in a consistent and predictable manner
4. They are all tested and analyzed.
5. A model can be used at any point in the process such as testing a hypothesis or explaining a theory.
6. If an orderly set of steps is followed, the observations and results are more reliable. The experiment can be conducted again using the same procedure.
7. Sample answer: The scientist should record his or her observations and any numerical results that can be recorded. The scientist should continue carrying out the experiment and reanalyze the hypothesis to see if it can be adjusted to accommodate the new results.
8. To be accepted by the scientific community, all experiments must be able to be conducted repeatedly with the same results obtained and with a minimal amount of error. By using systematic methods, this can be done.

understanding
EARTH
Studying Earth From Space

Scientific facts are gathered in many ways, such as laboratory studies, field observations, and field measurements. Satellite images like the one in Figure 23 are another useful source of data. Such images provide perspectives that are difficult to get from more traditional sources. The high-tech instruments aboard many satellites enable scientists to gather information from remote regions where data are otherwise scarce.

The image in Figure 23 makes use of the Advanced Spaceborne Thermal Emission and Reflection Radiometer (ASTER). Because different materials reflect and give off energy in different ways, ASTER can provide detailed information about the composition of Earth's surface. Figure 23 is a three-dimensional view looking north over Death Valley, California. The data have been computer enhanced to exaggerate the color variations that highlight differences in types of surface materials.

Figure 23 This satellite shows detailed information about the composition of surface materials in Death Valley, California. It was produced by superimposing nighttime thermal infrared data, acquired on April 7, 2000, over topographic data from the U.S. Geological survey. (Image courtesy of NASA)

Salt deposits on the floor of Death Valley appear in shades of yellow, green, purple, and pink. These indicate the presence of carbonate, sulfate, and chloride minerals. The Panamint Mountains to the west and the Black Mountains to the east are made up of sedimentary limestones, sandstones, shales, and metamorphic rocks. The bright red areas are dominated by the mineral quartz, found in sandstone; the green areas are limestone. In the lower center of the image is Badwater, the lowest point in North America.

understanding
EARTH

Studying Earth From Space L2

Background ASTER is an imaging instrument that obtains detailed maps of land surface temperature. It flies on a satellite called Terra, which was launched in 1999. ASTER is part of NASA's Earth Observing System (EOS), which is a series of satellites, a science component, and a data system. EOS will help scientists develop a deeper understanding of Earth as an integrated system—the interactions among the biosphere, hydrosphere, lithosphere, and atmosphere.

Teaching Tips

- As students read the feature and look at Figure 23, have them identify on the image the various regions described in the text.
- Explain to students that this image does not show the true colors of Death Valley as seen from space. Instead, the colors were inserted by scientists to indicate differences in surface composition. Ask: **What do you think this image would look like in true color?** *(Since Death Valley is a desert, it would be mostly tan in color.)* **Based on the information given on what the colors indicate, what is the composition of the most distant mountains in the image?** *(mostly limestone, with some sandstone and a little bit of salt)*
- Have students research ASTER and EOS on NASA's web site and prepare a report to the class.

Visual, Logical

Exploration Lab

Determining Latitude and Longitude 

Objective
In this activity, students will:

- measure angles with a protractor in order to accurately draw and label latitude and longitude lines.
- locate points on Earth's surface using their latitude and longitude.

Skills Focus **Interpreting, Measuring, Inferring**

 **Prep Time** 15 minutes

Class Time 30 minutes

Teaching Tips
Some students will not remember how to use a protractor. Provide small-group instruction for these students before starting the lab.

Expected Outcome Students will understand how the measurements for latitude and longitude lines were made by early mapmakers and will create a diagram that looks like the following:

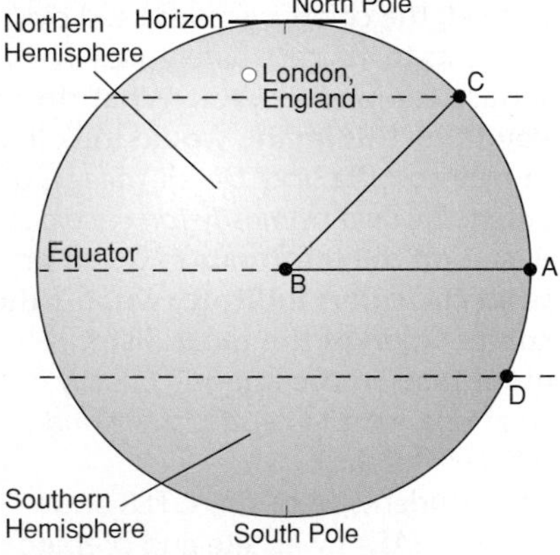

Answers to Procedure Questions
1–4 See sketch above.
3. The latitude is 45°N.
4. 25°S
5. Answers will vary depending on the globe used.
6. A: 30°N latitude, B: 5°S latitude, C: 55°N latitude, D: 35°S latitude, E: 0° latitude, F: 20°N latitude
7. A: 56°N 37°E, B: 29°S 31°E, C: Answers will vary depending on where students live.
8. Answers will vary depending on where students live.
9. See sketch above.
10. Answers will vary depending on the globe used.
11. A: 30°E, B: 20°W, C: 45°E, D: 75°W, E: 65°E, F: 68°W
12. Answers will vary depending on where students live.

Exploration Lab

Determining Latitude and Longitude

Using maps and globes to find places and features on Earth's surface is an essential skill required of all Earth scientists. The grid that is formed by lines of latitude and longitude form the basis for locating points on Earth. Latitude lines indicate north-south distance and longitude lines indicate east-west distance. Degrees are used to mark latitude and longitude distances on Earth's surface. Degrees can be divided into sixty equal parts called minutes (′) and a minute of angle can be divided into sixty parts, called seconds (″). Thus, 31°10′20″ means 31 degrees, 10 minutes, and 20 seconds. This exercise will introduce you to the systems used for determining location on Earth.

Horizon
North Pole
London, England
C
B
A
D
South Pole

Figure A

Problem
How are latitude and longitude calculated and how do they indicate a particular location's position on the globe?

Materials

- globe
- protractor
- ruler
- compass or round object for tracing
- pencil
- world map

Skills
Interpreting, Measuring, Inferring

Procedure

Part A: Determining Latitude

1. Figure A represents Earth, with point B its center. Draw this figure on a separate piece of paper. Locate the equator on the globe. Sketch and label the equator on your diagram. Label the Northern Hemisphere and Southern Hemisphere on your diagram.
2. On your diagram, make an angle by drawing a line from point A on the equator to point B (the center of Earth). Then extend the line from point B to point C in the Northern Hemisphere. The angle you have drawn (<ABC) is 45°. By definition of latitude, point C is located at 45° N latitude.
3. Draw a line on your figure through point C that is also parallel to the equator. What is the latitude at all points on this line? Record this number on the line.
4. Using a protractor, measure <ABD on your paper. Then draw a line parallel to the equator that also goes through point D. Label the line with its proper latitude.
5. How many degrees of latitude separate the latitude lines (or parallels) on the globe that you are using? Record this on your paper.
6. Refer to Figure B. Determine the latitude for each point A–F. Be sure to indicate whether it is north or south of the equator and include the word "latitude." Record these numbers on your paper.

7. Use a globe or map to locate the cities listed below. On your paper, record their latitude to the nearest degree.
   A. Moscow, Russia
   B. Durban, South Africa
   C. Your home city
8. Use the globe or map to give the name of a city or feature that is equally as far south of the equator as your home city is north.

Part B: Determining Longitude

9. Locate the prime meridian on Figure C. Sketch and label it on your diagram. Label the Eastern and Western Hemispheres.
10. How many degrees of longitude separate each meridian on your globe? Record this on your paper.
11. Refer to Figure C. Determine the longitude for each point A–F. Be sure to indicate whether it is east or west of the Prime Meridian. Record these numbers on your paper.
12. Use the globe or map to give the name of a city or feature that is equally as far east of the prime meridian as your home city is west.

Analyze and Conclude

1. **Applying Concepts** What is the maximum number of 1 degree longitude or latitude lines that can be drawn on a globe?
2. **Comparing and Contrasting** How are longitude and latitude lines the same and how are they different?
3. **Thinking Critically** Amelia Earhart, her flight engineer, and her plane are believed to have been lost somewhere over the Pacific Ocean. It is now thought that the coordinates that she was given for her fuel stop at Howley Island in the Pacific Ocean were wrong. Knowing what you do about how latitude and longitude coordinates are written, why would a wrong number have been so catastrophic for her?

Go Further Use reference books or the Internet to research the number of time zones on Earth. Find out how many there are and draw their boundaries on the figure you created for this lab. What time zone do you live in? What time zone is the location that you chose in question 12? What is the time difference between these two locations?

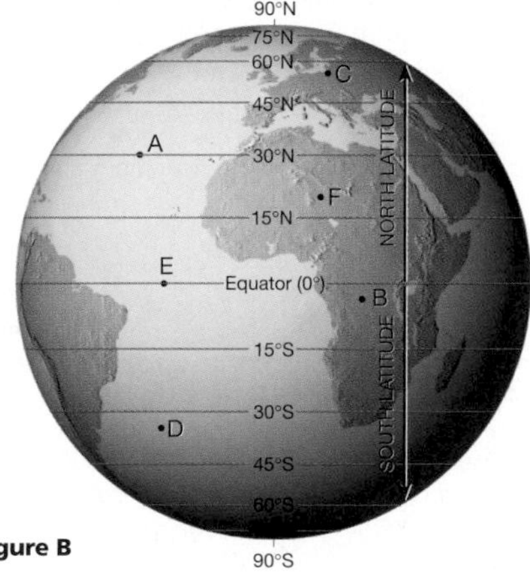

Figure B

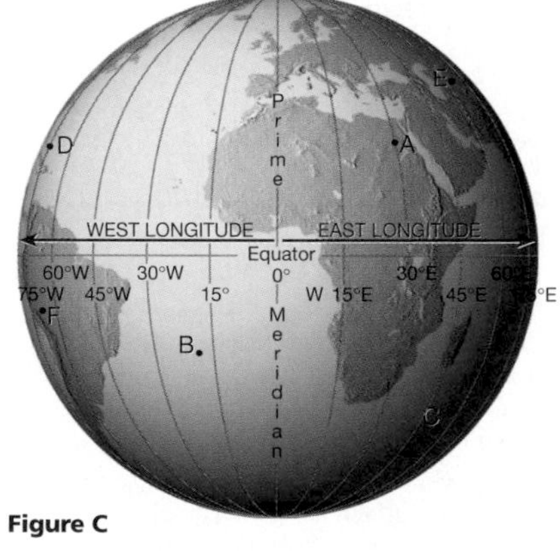

Figure C

Analyze and Conclude

1. 360 longitude lines and 180 latitude lines

2. Both latitude and longitude are measured in degrees. Latitudes are N/S measurements, longitudes are E/W measurements. Lines of latitude all run parallel to each other. Because lines of longitude run north and south, they follow the curvature of Earth and meet at the poles.

3. Earth is very large. Even a mistake of a minute or seconds of a degree may have set her in the wrong direction, unable to spot a small island in the ocean.

Go Further

Answers to the questions depend on where students live.

Visual, Logical

Study Guide

Study Tip

Study Daily
Encourage students to study their notes for a few minutes each day. Advise them to read their notes over, make sure they are complete, add color to sketches, highlight import facts, make flashcards for new vocabulary and concepts, and keep a list of questions related to things they don't understand. This will help your students to follow along in class more easily and do better on exams.

CHAPTER 1

Study Guide

1.1 What Is Earth Science?

Key Concepts

- Earth science is the name for the group of sciences that deals with Earth and its neighbors in space.
- The nebular hypothesis suggests that the bodies of our solar system eveolved from an enormous rotating cloud called the solar nebula. It was made up mostly of hydrogen and helium, with a small percentage of heavier elements.

Vocabulary

Earth science, *p. 2;* geology, *p. 2;* oceanography, *p. 3;* meteorology, *p. 3;* astronomy, *p. 3*

1.2 A View of Earth

Key Concepts

- Earth can be thought of as consisting of four major spheres: the hydrosphere, atmosphere, geosphere, and biosphere.
- Because the geosphere is not uniform, it is divided into three main parts based on differences in composition—the core, the mantle, and the crust.
- The model that explains the position of continents and the occurrence of volcanoes and earthquakes is called plate tectonics.

Vocabulary

hydrosphere, *p. 7* atmosphere, *p. 7;* geosphere, *p. 7;* biosphere, *p. 7;* core, *p. 8;* mantle, *p. 8;* crust, *p. 8*

1.3 Representing Earth's Surface

Key Concepts

- Latitude is the distance north or south of the equator, measured in degrees. Longitude is the distance east or west of the prime meridian, measured in degrees.
- No matter what kind of map is made, some portion of the surface will always look either too small, too big, or out of place. Mapmakers have, however, found ways to limit the distortaion of shape, size, distance, and direction.
- Topographic maps differ from other maps because topographic maps show elevation.
- The elevation of the land is indicated by using contour lines.
- A map that shows the type and age of exposed rock is called a geologic map.
- Today's technology provides us with the ability to more precisely analyze Earth's physical properties.

Vocabulary

latitude, *p. 11;* longitude, *p. 11;* topographic map, *p. 14;* contour line, *p. 14;* contour interval, *p. 14*

1.4 Earth System Science

Key Concepts

- Earth system science aims to study Earth as a system made up of numerous interacting parts, or subsystems.
- A system can be any size group of interacting parts that form a complex whole.
- The sun drives external processes that occur in the atmosphere, hydrosphere, and at Earth's surface. Earth's interior is also a source of energy.
- Our actions produce changes in all other parts of the Earth system.
- Renewable resources can be replenished over relatively short time spans. Nonrenewable resources form over such a long period of time that it takes millions of years for significant deposits to accumulate.
- Significant threats to the environment include air pollution, acid rain, ozone depletion, and global warming.

Vocabulary

system, *p. 18*

1.5 What Is Scientific Inquiry?

Key Concepts

- A hypothesis is a statement made by scientists to explain how or why things happen in the manner observed.
- A scientific theory is well tested and widely accepted by the scientific community and best explains certain observable facts.

Vocabulary

hypothesis, *p. 23;* theory, *p. 24*

Chapter Assessment Resources

Print
Chapter Test, Chapter 1
Test Prep Resources, Chapter 1

Technology
Computer Test Bank, Chapter 1 Test
Online Text, Chapter 1
Go Online, PHSchool.com, Chapter 1

CHAPTER 1

NY Regents Content Item

Assessment

Interactive textbook with assessment at PHSchool.com

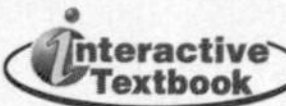

Reviewing Content

Choose the number that best answers the question or completes the statement.

1 The science that deals with the study of the atmosphere is
(1) oceanography (2) meteorology
(3) geology (4) astronomy

2 What caused Earth to develop layers as it cooled?
(1) differences in composition
(2) the magnetic field
(3) the speed of rotation
(4) escaping gases

3 What drives the process of plate tectonics, the currently accepted explanation for the movement of drifting continents? NY
(1) gravity
(2) ocean currents
(3) unequal heat distribution
(4) earthquakes

4 Lines of latitude describe position NY
(1) north or south of the equator
(2) east or west of the equator
(3) north or south of the prime meridian
(4) east or west of the prime meridian

5 The Robinson map projection is considered very useful because
(1) all of the continents are the same size
(2) most distances, sizes, and shapes are accurate
(3) it shows landmasses in three dimensions
(4) features along latitude lines are accurate

6 Which of the following maps shows the three dimensions of Earth's surface?
(1) Mercator projection
(2) topographic
(3) gnomonic
(4) conic

7 Which type of technology can scientists use to monitor coral reef development?
(1) Landsat satellites (2) VLBI
(3) computer imaging (4) weather satellites

8 What makes a hypothesis scientifically useful?
(1) Many people think it is a good idea. NY
(2) It can be tested.
(3) It contains numerical data.
(4) It applies directly to Earth science.

9 The theory that Earth's lithosphere is broken into large sections that move is called
(1) biosphere (2) global positioning
(3) nebular (4) plate tectonics

10 On a topographic map, contour lines that are closer together indicate NY
(1) forest (2) a steeper slope
(3) a mountain top (4) roads

Understanding Concepts

11 Briefly list the events that led to the formation of the solar system.

12 Identify the appropriate Earth sphere represented by the following list: mountains, lakes, ice, and snow. NY

13 List the three parts of the geosphere indicated at the letters in the figure below. NY

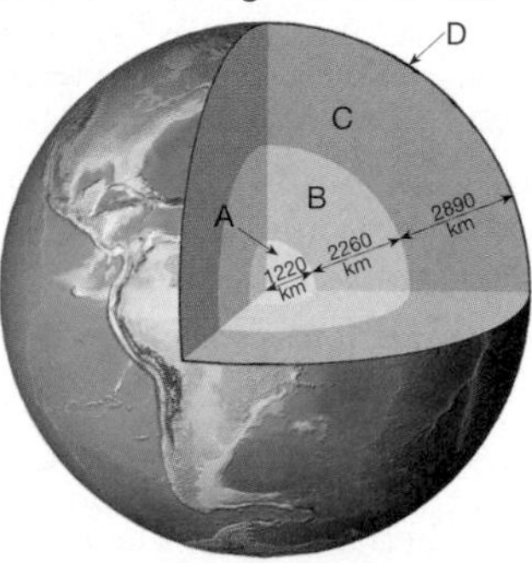

14 The Mercator projection map shows Earth's features on a grid. Why is this map useful to sailors?

15 Why is the contour interval included on a topographic map? NY

16 What type of satellite is used to monitor cloud cover and air temperature?

17 What happens to matter and energy in a closed system? NY

18 What types of factors make up our nonliving environment?

Homework Guide

Section	Questions
1	1, 2, 11
2	3, 9, 12, 13, 24–26, 34, 36, 37
3	4–7, 10, 14–16, 27–33, 35
4	17–21
5	8, 22, 23

Assessment

Reviewing Content

(1) 2 (2) 1 (3) 3
(4) 1 (5) 2 (6) 2
(7) 1 (8) 2 (9) 4
(10) 2

Understanding Concepts

(11) A large cloud of dust and gas formed, then began to rotate and collapse. Heat increased toward the center, forming the sun. As cooling progressed, the cloud condensed into rocky and metallic materials that eventually became the inner planets. The outer planets formed mainly from gases.
(12) mountains—geosphere; lakes—hydrosphere; trees—biosphere; clouds—atmosphere; ice —hydrosphere; snow—hydrosphere
(13) A—inner core; B—outer core; C—mantle; D—crust
(14) It shows directions accurately.
(15) It tells you the change in elevation from line to line.
(16) a weather satellite
(17) Matter does not enter or leave a closed system, but energy moves freely in and out.
(18) soil, air, water, rocks
(19) The sources are the sun and Earth's interior.
(20) It must be replenished over a relatively short period of time.
(21) Sample answers: earthquakes, floods, landslides, hurricanes, drought
(22) 1. collection of scientific facts,
2. development of hypotheses,
3. observation and experimentation to test hypotheses
4. acceptance, modification, or rejection of the hypothesis

Chapter 1

Critical Thinking

(23) A hypothesis is a possible explanation for how or why an observed phenomena happens. A scientific theory is formed after a hypothesis has been well tested and accepted by the scientific community as the best explanation for certain observable facts.
(24) Humans can't drink ocean water. Because only 3 percent of Earth's water is fresh water, we only have a small amount of water available to us.
(25) Most of Earth's life forms need oxygen to live. Our atmosphere contains oxygen. If Earth had no atmosphere, there would be no oxygen, and most organisms would not be able to survive.
(26) Sample answers: atmosphere —less oxygen released into the air, less carbon dioxide absorbed, less water vapor present; biosphere—fewer trees in the area, loss of habitat for tree-dwelling organisms; geosphere—increased erosion from absence of tree roots, less physical weathering from tree roots in the area; hydrosphere—less water vapor released into the air, which results in less water returning to the ground in the form of precipitation
(27) Great Plains—the contour interval would be small because the elevation changes slowly over larger distances; Colorado—the contour interval would be high because the elevation changes greatly over a short distance. If the contour interval was small, the map would have to be very large in order to correctly show the changes in elevation and the topography of the area.

Math Skills

(28) 1 km = approximately 0.6 mile
(29) 7.5 km
(30) one fourth around the globe; one third around the globe

Map Skills

(31) approximately 1.5 miles
(32) 11,300
(33) The land east of the lake is much flatter than the southwestern shore, as indicated by the proximity of the contour lines on the southwest side of the lake.

CHAPTER 1

Assessment *continued*

19 What are the two sources of energy for the Earth system?

20 What requirements must be satisfied in order for a resource to be considered renewable?

21 List at least four processes that could be regarded as natural hazards.

22 Briefly describe the four steps that most scientific investigations follow.

Critical Thinking

23 **Comparing and Contrasting** How is a scientific hypothesis different from a scientific theory?

24 **Applying Concepts** If oceans cover nearly 71 percent of Earth's surface, why is it important to conserve water? NY

25 **Inferring** Explain the following statement: If Earth had no atmosphere, our planet would be lifeless. NY

26 **Hypothesizing** Predict what the effect will be on some of Earth's systems if a forest is cut down for lumber.

27 **Comparing and Contrasting** As part of the Great Plains of the United States, the topography of the state of Kansas is relatively flat. On the other hand, portions of the state of Colorado are mountainous. Describe how the contour interval and the contour lines might vary on topographic maps of these two states. NY

Math Skills

Use the bar graph to answer questions 28 and 29.

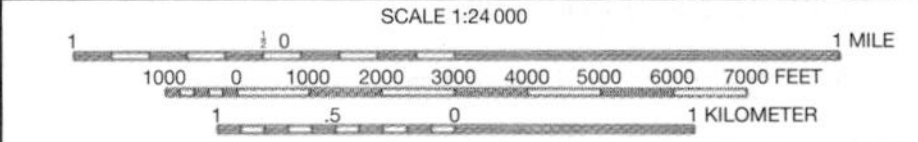

28 **Using Graphs** Approximately how many miles is 1 kilometer equal to?

29 **Calculating** If 1 kilometer is equal to 1 centimeter on the map, what is the distance in km between two cities that are 7.5 cm apart? NY

30 **Calculating** Recall that Earth is divided into 360 degrees. If you travel to a location that is 90 degrees starting from the prime meridian, what percentage of the distance around the globe have you gone? What about a location that is 120 degrees from the prime meridian? NY

Map Skills

Use the topographic map in Figure 15 on page 14 to answer questions 31–33.

31 **Reading Maps** About how wide is Turquoise Lake at its widest point from east to west? NY

32 **Reading Maps** What is the elevation of Sugar Loaf Mountain? NY

33 **Reading Maps** How does the land on the east side of Turquoise Lake differ from the land on the southwest side of the lake? How do you know? NY

Concepts in Action

34 **Applying Concepts** List at least three examples of how you can influence one or more of Earth's major spheres.

35 **Applying Concepts** A local company wants to open a new limestone quarry. Explain what type of map they should use to determine if limestone is present in your area.

36 **Classifying** The planet Mars has been in the news recently. Based on the information that has been reported, list and explain the spheres that are present or might have been present on Mars. NY

37 **Writing in Science** You are given the opportunity to address the city council about the proposed construction of a dam on the river in your community. Prepare a list of questions about the project that you would like to ask the city council and the dam engineers before deciding whether or not you would support the project. NY

Concepts in Action

(34) Sample answers: hydrosphere—You use water everyday for bathing, washing clothes, and cooking; atmosphere—driving to school burns gasoline, which emits pollutants into the air; using a clothes dryer releases hot air.
(35) The company should use a geologic map. This map will give them information on the local rock types, whether limestone is present, and the extent of the rock formations.
(36) hydrosphere, geosphere, biosphere (possibly in the past)
(37) Students should include a discussion on the impact on Earth's spheres and the interaction among the spheres and the dam.

Regents Practice Exam

Test-Taking Tip

Narrowing the Choices
If, after reading all the answer choices, you are not sure which one is correct, eliminate those answers that you know are wrong. In the question below, read the descriptions provided in I, II, and III. Eliminate any of these that you know to be wrong. Then carefully read the answer choices and choose the one that matches up with your decision above.

Which of these statements is(are) true of geologic maps?

I. They show the location and extent of different rock formations.
II. They indicate the age of each rock formation.
III. They never indicate the topography of the land.

(1) I only
(2) I and II
(3) I, II and III
(4) II only

(Answer: 2)

For *each* statement or question, choose the *number* of the word or expression that, of those given, best completes the statement or answers the question. Some questions may require the use of the *Earth Science Reference Tables.*

1 What is the primary source of energy for Earth's weather, climate, and ocean circulation?
(1) gravity
(2) the sun
(3) Earth's core
(4) Earth's rotation

2 Which of the following is primarily caused by human activity?
(1) hurricanes
(2) landslides
(3) ozone depletion
(4) earthquakes

3 Which of the following is considered a nonrenewable resource?
(1) wood
(2) solar energy
(3) livestock
(4) petroleum

Answer the following questions in complete sentences. Some questions may require the use of the *Earth Science Reference Tables.* Base your answers to questions 4 and 5 on the diagram below, which shows a Global Grid.

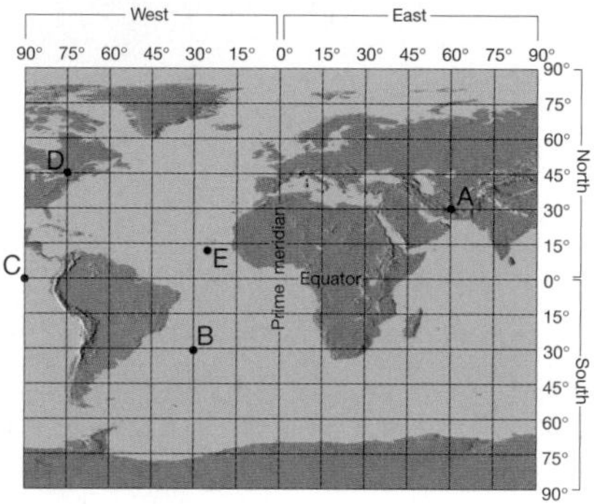

4 What is the latitude and longitude for point *A* on this map?

5 Which point on this map is located closest to New York State?

6 How can you determine the direction in which a stream on a topographic map flows?

7 State the primary cause of earthquakes and volcanoes on Earth.

Regents Practice Exam

(1) 2
(2) 3
(3) 4
(4) 30°N 60°E
(5) *D*
(6) Read the contours, streams flow downhill; or contours tend to point upstream, in the direction opposite the stream's flow
(7) movement of Earth's plates

Your students can independently test their knowledge of the chapter and print out their results.

CHAPTER 2

Planning Guide

Use these planning tools
Use Teacher Express for all your planning needs

SECTION OBJECTIVES	STANDARDS NATIONAL	STANDARDS STATE	ACTIVITIES and LABS
2.1 Matter, pp. 34–43 1 block or 2 periods **2.1** **Explain** how elements are related to minerals. **2.2** **Identify** the kinds of particles that make up atoms. **2.3** **Explain** the differences between ions and isotopes. **2.4** **Explain** what compounds are and **describe** why they form. **2.5** **Compare and contrast** the three major types of chemical bonds.	A-1, B-1, B-2, B-3, D-3		**SE** Inquiry Activity: How Are a Group of Minerals Alike and Different? p. 33 L2 **TE** Build Science Skills, p. 38 L2 **TE** Teacher Demo: Isotopes and Numbers, p. 39 L2 **TE** Teacher Demo: Comparing Bonds, p. 42 L2
2.2 Minerals, pp. 44–49 1 block or 2 periods **2.6** **List** five characteristics of minerals. **2.7** **Describe** the processes that result in mineral formation. **2.8** **Explain** how minerals can be classified. **2.9** **List** some of the major groups of minerals.	B-2, D2		**TE** Teacher Demo: Crytallization of Sulfur, p. 45 L2 **TE** Teacher Demo: Precipitation of a Mineral, p. 46 L2 **TE** Build Science Skills, p. 48 L2
2.3 Properties of Minerals, pp. 50–55 1 block or 2 periods **2.10** **Explain** why color is often not a useful property in identifying minerals. **2.11** **Define** the terms *luster, crystal form, streak,* and *Mohs scale.* **2.12** **Distinguish** between cleavage and fracture. **2.13** **Explain** density and how it can be used to identify substances. **2.14** **Describe** some other properties that can be used to identify minerals.	A-1, A-2, B-2, G-2		**TE** Build Science Skills, p. 54 L2 **TE** Evaluate Understanding, p. 55 L2 **SE** Exploration Lab: Mineral Identification, pp. 58–59 L2 **LM** Crystal Systems L3

Ability Levels

L1 For students who need additional help
L2 For all students
L3 For students who need to be challenged

Components

SE	Student Edition	**GRSW**	Guided Reading & Study Workbook	**TP**	Test Prep Resources	**GEO**	Geode CD-ROM
TE	Teacher's Edition	**TEX**	Teacher Express	**onT**	onlineText	**T**	Transparencies
LM	Laboratory Manual	**CTB**	Computer Test Bank	**DC**	Discovery Channel Videos	**GO**	Internet Resources
CUT	Chapter Tests						

RESOURCES PRINT and TECHNOLOGY	SECTION ASSESSMENT
GRSW Section 2.1 **T-6** Periodic Table of the Elements **T-7** Two Models of the Atom **T-8** Chemical Bonding of Sodium and Chlorine **TEX** Lesson Planning 2.1	**SE** Section 2.1 Assessment, p. 43 **onT** Section 2.1
GRSW Section 2.2 **T-11** Two Representations of the Silicon-Oxygen Tetrahedron **T-12** Common Silicate Minerals **T-13** Common Nonsilicate Mineral Groups **GEO** Earth Materials ↳ Rock Cycle **TEX** Lesson Planning 2.2	**SE** Section 2.2 Assessment, p. 49 **onT** Section 2.2
GRSW Section 2.2 **T-9** Mohs Scale of Mineral Hardness **T-10** Abundance of the Most Common Elements in Earth's Continental Crust **DC** Gold **TEX** Lesson Planning 2.2	**SE** Section 2.3 Assessment, p. 55 **onT** Section 2.3

Go Online

Go online for these Internet resources.

PHSchool.com
Web Code: cjk-9999

Web Code: cjn-1021
Web Code: cjn-1023

Materials for Activities and Labs

Quantities for each group

STUDENT EDITION

Inquiry Activity, p. 33
hand lenses, small hammers, safety goggles, samples of the colorless varieties of fluorite, quartz, halite, and calcite

Exploration Lab, p. 58
mineral samples, hand lens, streak plate, copper penny, steel knife blade, glass plate, piece of quartz, dilute hydrochloric acid, magnet, hammer, 50-mL graduated cylinder, tap water, balance, thin thread, scissors, paper or cloth towels, Table 2 on pp. 54–55

TEACHER'S EDITION

Build Science Skills, p. 38
materials found at home or in the classroom

Teacher Demo, p. 39
overhead projector, red and green gummy candies

Teacher Demo, p. 42
rock salt, chalk, copper wire, hammer, goggles

Teacher Demo, p. 45
two crucibles, 50-mL beaker, water, teaspoon, sulfur powder, tongs, Bunsen burner, magnifying glass

Teacher Demo, p. 46
rock salt, spoon warm water, 400-mL beaker, shallow pan or tray

Build Science Skills, p. 48
modeling clay or gumdrops, toothpicks

Build Science Skills, p. 54
small samples of calcite and dolomite, goggles, gloves, dropper bottles of dilute HCl

Evaluate Understanding, p. 55
4 or 5 mineral samples of varying hardness (unidentified)

Chapter Assessment

ASSESSMENT

SE Assessment, pp. 61–62
CUT Chapter 2 Test
CTB Chapter 2
onT Chapter 2

STANDARDIZED TEST PREP

SE Chapter 2, p. 63
TP Progress Monitoring Assessments

interactive textbook with assessment at PHSchool.com

CHAPTER 2

Before you teach

Michael Wysession
Washington University

Big Ideas

Earth is mostly made of rock (2/3 by weight, 5/6 by volume). These rocks are made of minerals. There are more than 3800 different named minerals, though most rocks are made of only a small number of these.

Matter and Energy Atoms combine naturally to form minerals. Atoms consist of a nucleus, containing protons and neutrons, surrounded by clouds of electrons. Atoms have different properties when they occur as different isotopes (varying numbers of neutrons) and ions (varying numbers of electrons).

Forces and Motion Atoms bond in several different ways, including covalent, ionic, and metallic bonding. The electrical charge of ions and their sizes determine which atoms can combine in a stable manner to form minerals. Mineral grains or crystals are the accumulation of enormous numbers of atoms or ions bonding with a particular repeating structure. The manner in which the three-dimensional crystal lattice of atoms is constructed determines the mineral's characteristics, such as crystal form, luster, color, streak, hardness, fracture, cleavage, and density.

Earth as a System Most minerals form from the crystallization of magma, which is molten rock. Minerals can also form through precipitation, or by the alteration of existing minerals through changes in temperature and pressure. Because of the high abundance of the elements oxygen and silicon, most rocks are silicates, which usually involve combinations of silicon-oxygen tetrahedra with other elements.

Earth Science Refresher

Why Are Particular Minerals Abundant?

1. Stellar Nucleosynthesis. The products of a pre-solar nebula depend upon the reactants available. While most hydrogen and helium (and a small amount of lithium) formed during the Big Bang, Earth's other elements formed much later. The oxygen, carbon, and other atoms larger than helium form within stars, and are ejected into space during a star's supernova phase. When our solar system formed, the planets were made from the remains of stars that were "dead"—had finished their fusion stages. The stellar production of these larger elements, called nucleosynthesis, does not make equal amounts of all elements. In terms of mass, Earth's principal elements are iron (35 percent), oxygen (30 percent), silicon (15 percent), magnesium (13 percent), nickel (2.4 percent), sulfur (1.9 percent), calcium (1.1 percent), and aluminum (1.1 percent). These elements are made more abundantly within stars than other elements. Most of the iron, nickel, and sulfur sank to form Earth's core. The rest are the primary elements available for minerals and rocks.

2. Earth's location in the solar system. As you will see in Chapter 23, different planets have different compositions. Planets close to the sun are metal-rich. Planets a bit farther out, such as Earth, are rock-rich. Planets farther from the sun are gas-rich and ice-rich. This is a result of the temperatures in the solar system when the planets were forming. Had Earth been closer or farther from the sun, the abundances of elements available to make minerals and rocks would have been different.

Address Misconceptions

Many students think that atoms become positively charged as a result of gaining protons. However, electrons are the only subatomic particles that can be removed from or added to an atom during a chemical reaction. For a strategy that helps to overcome this misconception, see **Address Misconceptions** on **p. 40**.

Go Online NSTA PDLINKS

For: Chapter 2 Content Support
Visit: www.SciLinks.org/PDLinks
Web Code: cjn-0299

3. Electrical charge and ion size compatibility. Chapter 2 describes how the electrical charges of compounds must add to zero for the compound to be stable. In addition, compounds that have ion sizes that fit together well tend to be more stable, and so these are the minerals that we tend to find in nature. One way to think of this is that, because atoms are always oscillating, if the ions don't fit together well, their vibrations create an unstable compound structure. Stable minerals have atoms that fit together well. When minerals are pushed to greater depths, their ions get reduced in size. Negative ions, which are usually larger, are compressed more easily than positive ions. This compression can change the relative sizes of the ions, and minerals that were stable at the surface may now become unstable. When this happens, mineral structures will fall apart and rearrange into the more compatible structures of new minerals.

Address Misconceptions

Students may think that the minerals discussed in this chapter are the same as the minerals found in vitamin pills. They are related but not the same. In earth science, a mineral is a naturally occurring inorganic crystalline solid. In contrast, minerals found in vitamin pills are inorganic compounds made in the laboratory that contain elements needed by the body. For a strategy that helps to overcome this misconception, see **Address Misconceptions** on **p. 44**.

Build Reading Literacy

Preview

Skim Ahead to Understand Text Organization

Strategy Get an advance idea of how the text is organized and activate prior knowledge. This prereading strategy involves skimming the titles, headings, visuals, and boldfaced text. Like checking a roadmap before beginning a trip, previewing helps the reader to recall familiar material and to prepare to learn new material. Before students begin to read, select a portion of Chapter 2 for them to preview, such as pp. 34–35.

Example

1. Ask students to look at the chapter title, section titles, and heads. Tell them to notice whether the terms and concepts mentioned are familiar or unfamiliar.
2. Have students look at the Reading Focus for the specific section to be previewed.
3. Ask students to compare the key concepts and the boldfaced statements in the section.
4. Have students look at the visuals in the section and (where possible) relate each to a specific heading.
5. You may wish to have students prepare a study guide using the headings, key concept questions, and vocabulary as categories in a chart showing the section organization. Have students read the selected pages in depth, filling in the chart with details as they read.

See p. 50 for a script on how to use this strategy with students. For additional strategies, see pp. 34, 42, and 45.

ASSESS PRIOR KNOWLEDGE

Use the Chapter Pretest below to assess students' prior knowledge. As needed, review these concepts.

Review Science Concepts

Section 2.1 Review the information about elements that can be derived from the periodic table. Review the basic structure of atoms.

Section 2.2 Review the naming of simple chemical compounds. Recall what a precipitate is.

Section 2.3 Review SI measurement units and density.

Review Math Skills

Line Graphs Review with students what a line graph shows and how the axes should be labeled.

Direct students to the **Math Skills** in the **Skills Handbook** at the end of the student text.

CHAPTER

2 Minerals

CONCEPTS in Action

Exploration Lab
Mineral Identification

Understanding Earth
Gemstones

Earth Materials
↳ Rock Cycle

Video Field Trip
Gold

Take a trip to Brazil with the Discovery Channel and see how gold on the Rio Medeira River is mined. Answer the following questions after watching the video.

1. In what two parts of Earth is gold found?
2. Describe what happens to gold during the "smelting" process.

Go Online
PHSchool.com

For: Chapter 2 Resources
Visit: PHSchool.com
Web Code: cjk-9999

The large reddish-orange crystals are ▶ crystals of wulfenite. Wulfenite is one of more than 3800 minerals found on Earth.

32 *Chapter 2*

Chapter Pretest

1. What are the three particles that make up atoms? *(b)*
   - **a.** protons, isotopes, and electrons
   - **b.** protons, neutrons, and electrons
   - **c.** protons, isotopes, and neutrons
   - **d.** neutrons, isotopes, and electrons
2. What are the main types of chemical bonds? *(ionic bonds, covalent bonds, metallic bonds)*
3. What elements make up NaCl? *(c)*
   - **a.** sodium and carbon
   - **b.** sodium and calcium
   - **c.** sodium and chlorine
   - **d.** nitrogen and chlorine
4. True or False: A precipitate forms from dissolved substances *(True)*
5. A 1-cubic-centimeter sample of a mineral has a mass of 2 grams. What is the density of the mineral? *(c)*
   - **a.** 1
   - **b.** 1 g/cm^3
   - **c.** 2 g/cm^3
   - **d.** 2
6. How is data shown on a line graph? *(a series of points joined by a line)*

Chapter Preview

Inquiry Activity

How Are a Group of Minerals Alike and Different?

Procedure

1. Obtain the mineral samples from your teacher. Examine them closely.
2. Make a data table to record at least three ways that the samples are alike.
3. Now record at least three ways that the samples differ.
4. Classify the minerals into two groups based on your observations. Give reasons for your classification scheme.
5. Put on safety goggles. Gently strike each sample with a hammer and observe the pieces of each sample. If necessary, use these results to reclassify the minerals into two groups.

Think About It

1. **Observing** What kinds of characteristics did you observe in all of the samples?
2. **Contrasting** How did the samples differ?
3. **Formulating Hypotheses** Each of the minerals you just observed belongs to a different group. Design a scheme for how these minerals might be classified into four different groups.

Video Field Trip

Gold

Encourage students to view the Video Field Trip "Gold."

ENGAGE/EXPLORE

How Are a Group of Minerals Alike and Different? L2

Purpose In this activity, students will classify four mineral samples by observing similarities and differences among the samples.

Skills Focus Observing, Comparing and Contrasting, Classifying

 **Prep Time** 10–15 minutes

Materials hand lenses, small hammers, safety goggles, samples of the colorless varieties of fluorite, quartz, halite, and calcite

Class Time 20–25 minutes

Safety Students need to wear safety goggles during this activity. Remind students to handle the hammers carefully and not to taste any of the minerals.

Teaching Tips

- Label the samples with permanent markers or numbered pieces of masking tape before distributing them to students.
- The breakage surfaces will vary among the minerals. Halite and calcite should break to produce three planar surfaces; fluorite will produce four. Quartz will break to form uneven surfaces that resemble broken glass.

Expected Outcome Students shouldn't have problems noting similarities and differences among the substances. Students should be able to describe at least one unique characteristic of each mineral.

Think About It

1. Similarities might include size and/or shape and possibly heft (the estimated weight of a mineral when held in the hand). Other similarities include color, transparency, and the fact that each mineral is a solid.
2. Depending on the samples used, the minerals may vary in size and shape. The way in which each mineral breaks is also unique. If students did the test for solubility, the dissolving of the halite is another difference.
3. Accept all reasonable responses. The most likely schemes will be by size, shape, color, luster, and shattering ability.

Section 2.1

1 FOCUS

Section Objectives

2.1 **Explain** how elements are related to minerals.
2.2 **Identify** the kinds of particles that make up atoms.
2.3 **Explain** the differences between ions and isotopes.
2.4 **Explain** what compounds are and **describe** why they form.
2.5 **Compare and contrast** the three major types of chemical bonds.

Reading Focus

Build Vocabulary L2

Concept Map Have students construct a concept map using the terms *chemical bond*, *ionic bond*, *covalent bond*, and *metallic bond*. The main concept (*chemical bond*) should be at the top. Tell students to place the terms in ovals and list the characteristics of each type of bond underneath the oval. For each type of bond, students should include some examples and their properties.

Reading Strategy L2

Differences: Electron is much less massive than proton and neutron; electron is negatively charged, proton is positively charged, neutron is not charged.
Similarities: All are subatomic particles.

2 INSTRUCT

Elements and the Periodic Table

Build Reading Literacy L1

Refer to **p. 392D** in **Chapter 14**, which provides guidelines for this strategy.

Preview Have students preview the section (pp. 34–43), focusing their attention on headings, visuals, and boldfaced material. Ask: **Based on your preview, which figure in the section do you think contains the most information?** *(Figure 1 on pp. 36–37)* **Based on your preview, name three classes of elements.** *(metals, nonmetals, and metalloids)*
Visual, Verbal

2.1 Matter

Reading Focus

Key Concepts

- What is an element?
- What particles make up atoms?
- What are isotopes?
- What are compounds and why do they form?
- How do chemical bonds differ?

Vocabulary

- element
- atomic number
- energy level
- isotope
- mass number
- compound
- chemical bond
- ion
- ionic bond
- covalent bond
- metallic bond

Reading Strategy

Comparing and Contrasting Copy the graphic organizer. As you read, complete the organizer to compare and contrast protons, neutrons, and electrons.

	Protons	Electrons	Neutrons
Differences			
Similarities			

You and everything else in the universe are made of matter. Matter is anything that has volume and mass. On Earth, matter usually exists in one of three states—solid, liquid, or gas. A solid is a type of matter that has a definite shape and a definite volume. Rocks and minerals are solids. A liquid is matter that has a definite volume, but not a definite shape. Earth's oceans, rivers, and lakes are liquids. A gas is matter that has neither a definite shape nor a definite volume. Most of Earth's atmosphere is composed of the gases nitrogen and oxygen. Though matter can be classified by its physical state: solid, liquid, or gas, it is more useful to look at its chemical composition and structure. Each of Earth's nearly 4000 minerals is a unique substance. The building blocks of minerals are **elements.**

Elements and the Periodic Table

The names of many elements are probably very familiar to you. Many common metals are elements, such as copper, iron, silver, and gold. **An element is a substance that cannot be broken down into simpler substances by chemical or physical means.** There are more than 112 known elements, and new elements continue to be discovered. Of these, 92 occur naturally, the others are produced in laboratories.

The elements have been organized by their properties in a document called the periodic table, which is shown in Figure 1 on pages 36 and 37. You see from the table that the name of each element is represented by a symbol consisting of one, two, or three letters. Symbols provide a shorthand way of representing an element. Each element is

Go Online SCILINKS NSTA
For: Links on the periodic table
Visit: www.SciLinks.org
Web Code: cjn-1021

Download a worksheet on the periodic table for students to complete, and find additional teacher support from NSTA SciLinks.

also known by its atomic number, which is shown above each symbol on the table. Look at the block for sulfur, element 16, and gold, element 79. Sulfur and gold are minerals made of one element. Most elements are not stable enough to exist in pure form in nature. Thus, most minerals are combinations of elements.

The rows in the periodic table are called periods. The number of elements in a period varies. Period 1, for example, contains only two elements. These elements are hydrogen (H) and helium (He). Period 2 contains the elements lithium (Li) through neon (Ne). Periods 4 and 5 each contain 18 elements while Period 6 includes 32 elements.

The columns in the periodic table are called groups. Note that there are 18 groups in the periodic table shown on pages 36 and 37. Elements within a group have similar properties.

Of the known elements, only eight make up most of Earth's continental crust. These eight elements are listed in Table 1. Notice that six of the eight elements in Table 1 are classified as metals. Metals have specific properties such as the ability to be shaped and drawn into wire. Metals are also good conductors of heat and electricity. They combine in thousands of ways to form compounds, the building blocks of most Earth materials. To understand how elements form compounds we need to review their building blocks which are atoms.

Table 1 Relative Abundance of the Most Common Elements in Earth's Continental Crust

Element	Approximate Percentage by Weight
Oxygen (O)	46.6
Silicon (Si)	27.7
Aluminum (Al)	8.1
Iron (Fe)	5.0
Calcium (Ca)	3.6
Sodium (Na)	2.8
Potassium (K)	2.6
Magnesium (Mg)	2.1
All others	1.7

Source: Data from Brian Mason.

Atoms

As you might already know, all elements are made of atoms. **An atom is the smallest particle of matter that contains the characteristics of an element.**

The central region of an atom is called the nucleus. The nucleus contains protons and neutrons. Protons are dense particles with positive electrical charges. Neutrons are equally dense particles that have no electrical charge. Electrons, which are small particles with little mass and negative electrical charges, surround an atom's nucleus.

Protons and Neutrons A proton has about the same mass as a neutron. Hydrogen atoms have only a single proton in their nuclei. Other atoms contain more than 100 protons. The number of protons in the nucleus of an atom is called the **atomic number.** All atoms with six protons, for example, are carbon atoms. The atomic number of carbon is 6. Likewise, every atom with eight protons is an oxygen atom. The atomic number of oxygen is 8.

Atoms have the same number of protons and electrons. Carbon atoms have six protons and therefore six electrons. Oxygen atoms have eight protons in their nuclei and have eight electrons surrounding the nucleus.

Customize for English Language Learners

To help students understand the idea of energy levels, have them work in pairs to think of everyday situations that involve different levels. Examples might include dresser drawers, shelves in a bookshelf, and bleachers ins a gym. Ask students how these analogies are different from energy levels in atoms. *(Energy levels are not physical objects and are not evenly spaced.)* If you have a bookshelf in the class, have students place marbles on different levels to represent electrons.

Build Math Skills L2

Using Tables and Graphs Have students convert Table 1 into a circle graph. Ask: **Why would a circle graph be a good alternative way to show the information in Table 1?** *(A circle graph shows the parts that make up a whole, just as the elements listed in the table make up a whole—100 percent of the elements in the continental crust.)* Suggest that students first estimate the size of each wedge of the circle graph and draw the graph accordingly. Then have them precisely draw the graph by first multiplying each percent by 360° to find the central angle of each wedge. They can then use a protractor to draw each central angle on a circle. Students can compare their estimates with their precise graphs. Some students may wish to create their graphs using software. Ask: **What advantage does a circle graph have over a table of percentages?** *(The sizes of the wedges of the graph often make it easier to compare different quantities.)*
Visual, Logical

Atoms

Integrate Biology L2

Cell Nucleus Students may know that most cells in living organisms also have a structure called a nucleus. Inform students that the cell's nucleus contains the cell's genetic, or hereditary, material. Ask: **How are an atom's nucleus and a cell's nucleus similar?** *(They are both central structures of a basic unit.)* **How are the two nuclei different?** *(The cell nucleus controls the activities of the cell. The atomic nucleus does not have a similar function.)*
Logical

L2

Although the text says that all matter is made of atoms, this is not strictly true everywhere in the universe. For example, the solar wind produced by the sun consists of a stream of protons and electrons. Also, in a neutron star, enormous pressure forces electrons and protons in the atoms in a star to combine with each other, leaving only a very dense ball of neutrons.
Logical

Use Visuals **L1**

Figure 1 Use this figure to discuss how information is shown on a periodic table. Ask: **What are the boldfaced single or double letters, such as *H* and *Li*?** *(symbols for each element)* **What is the number above each symbol?** *(the element's atomic number)* **What is the number below each symbol?** *(the element's atomic mass)* **What do the colors of the boxes indicate?** *(They show whether an element is a metal, transition metal, nonmetal, noble gas, lanthanide, or actinide.)*
Visual, Logical

Build Science Skills **L2**

Using Tables and Graphs Use the data in Figure 1 to show the advantage of arranging elements by atomic number instead of atomic mass. Make a large graph with atomic number on the horizontal axis and atomic mass on the vertical axis for elements 1 through 20. Draw straight lines between the points. Ask: **What does the graph show about the general relationship between atomic number and atomic mass?** *(As the atomic number increases, so does the atomic mass.)* **Are there any points on the graph that do not follow the pattern?** *(Yes, the atomic mass of element 18, argon, is greater than the atomic mass of element 19, potassium.)* Point out that arranging the elements strictly by increasing atomic mass would result in some elements with unlike properties being grouped together.
Visual, Logical

Periodic Table of the Elements

Figure 1

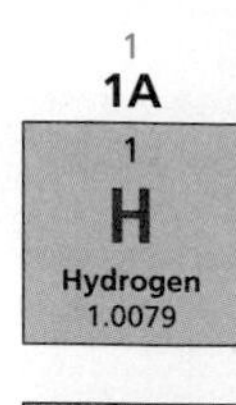

	Nonmetals	Metals	Metalloids
Solid	C	Li	B
Liquid	Br	Hg	
Gas	H		
Not found in nature		Tc	

1 1A	2 2A	3 3B	4 4B	5 5B	6 6B	7 7B	8 8B	9 8B
1 H Hydrogen 1.0079								
3 Li Lithium 6.941	4 Be Beryllium 9.0122							
11 Na Sodium 22.990	12 Mg Magnesium 24.305							
19 K Potassium 39.098	20 Ca Calcium 40.08	21 Sc Scandium 44.956	22 Ti Titanium 47.90	23 V Vanadium 50.941	24 Cr Chromium 51.996	25 Mn Manganese 54.938	26 Fe Iron 55.847	27 Co Cobalt 58.933
37 Rb Rubidium 85.468	38 Sr Strontium 87.62	39 Y Yttrium 88.906	40 Zr Zirconium 91.22	41 Nb Niobium 92.906	42 Mo Molybdenum 95.94	43 Tc Technetium (98)	44 Ru Ruthenium 101.07	45 Rh Rhodium 102.91
55 Cs Cesium 132.91	56 Ba Barium 137.33	71 Lu Lutetium 174.97	72 Hf Hafnium 178.49	73 Ta Tantalum 180.95	74 W Tungsten 183.85	75 Re Rhenium 186.21	76 Os Osmium 190.2	77 Ir Iridium 192.22
87 Fr Francium (223)	88 Ra Radium (226)	103 Lr Lawrencium (262)	104 Rf Rutherfordium (261)	105 Db Dubnium (262)	106 Sg Seaborgium (263)	107 Bh Bohrium (264)	108 Hs Hassium (265)	109 Mt Meitnerium (268)

Lanthanide Series

57 La Lanthanum 138.91	58 Ce Cerium 140.12	59 Pr Praseodymium 140.91	60 Nd Neodymium 144.24	61 Pm Promethium (145)	62 Sm Samarium 150.4

Actinide Series

89 Ac Actinium (227)	90 Th Thorium 232.04	91 Pa Protactinium 231.04	92 U Uranium 238.03	93 Np Neptunium (237)	94 Pu Plutonium (244)

Metals—elements that are good conductors of heat and electric current

Nonmetals—elements that are poor conductors of heat and electric current

Metalloids—elements with properties that are somewhat similar to metals and nonmetals

Facts and Figures

Although plutonium is classified as a synthetic element, traces of plutonium isotopes Pu-238 and Pu-239 appear at low concentrations (about one part per 1011) in pitchblende, a uranium ore. In 1971, Darlene Hoffman, a scientist at Los Alamos National Laboratory, discovered traces of Pu-244 in Precambrian rocks. Because this isotope has a half-life of about 82 million years, it probably existed when Earth formed.

Key	
Atomic number	6
Element symbol	C
Element name	Carbon
Atomic mass	12.011

10	11 1B	12 2B	13 3A	14 4A	15 5A	16 6A	17 7A	18 8A
								2 He Helium 4.0026
			5 B Boron 10.81	6 C Carbon 12.011	7 N Nitrogen 14.007	8 O Oxygen 15.999	9 F Fluorine 18.998	10 Ne Neon 20.179
			13 Al Aluminum 26.982	14 Si Silicon 28.086	15 P Phosphorus 30.974	16 S Sulfur 32.06	17 Cl Chlorine 35.453	18 Ar Argon 39.948
28 Ni Nickel 58.71	29 Cu Copper 63.546	30 Zn Zinc 65.38	31 Ga Gallium 69.72	32 Ge Germanium 72.59	33 As Arsenic 74.922	34 Se Selenium 78.96	35 Br Bromine 79.904	36 Kr Krypton 83.80
46 Pd Palladium 106.4	47 Ag Silver 107.87	48 Cd Cadmium 112.41	49 In Indium 114.82	50 Sn Tin 118.69	51 Sb Antimony 121.75	52 Te Tellurium 127.60	53 I Iodine 126.90	54 Xe Xenon 131.30
78 Pt Platinum 195.09	79 Au Gold 196.97	80 Hg Mercury 200.59	81 Tl Thallium 204.37	82 Pb Lead 207.2	83 Bi Bismuth 208.98	84 Po Polonium (209)	85 At Astatine (210)	86 Rn Radon (222)
110 *Uun Ununnilium (269)	111 *Uuu Unununium (272)	112 *Uub Ununbium (277)		114 *Uuq Ununquadium				

*Name not officially assigned.

63 Eu Europium 151.96	64 Gd Gadolinium 157.25	65 Tb Terbium 158.93	66 Dy Dysprosium 162.50	67 Ho Holmium 164.93	68 Er Erbium 167.26	69 Tm Thulium 168.93	70 Yb Ytterbium 173.04

95 Am Americium (243)	96 Cm Curium (247)	97 Bk Berkelium (247)	98 Cf Californium (251)	99 Es Einsteinium (252)	100 Fm Fermium (257)	101 Md Mendelevium (258)	102 No Nobelium (259)

Integrate Language Arts

Elements 110, 111, 112, and 114 have not been named yet. Scientists can propose names for new elements, but the International Union of Pure and Applied Chemistry has final approval. Until new elements receive official names, chemists refer to them by their Latin-based atomic numbers. For example, element 114 is called ununquadium, Latin for one-one-four. Increase students' familiarity with the periodic table by discussing some of the strategies used to name elements (scientists, geographic locations, mythological characters).
Verbal, Portfolio

Build Science Skills

Comparing and Contrasting For this activity, use a periodic table that is several years old to display or distribute to students. You might use one from an older textbook. To illustrate the dynamic nature of science, have students compare Figure 1 to the older periodic table. Ask: **What differences do you notice between the two periodic tables?** *(Depending on when the older table was printed, the number of elements may vary and some elements in Period 7 may not have assigned names. Some values for atomic mass are likely to vary.)* Make a list of responses on the board. Then ask: **How will the periodic table change in the future?** *(Unnamed elements will be assigned official names and more elements may be discovered.)*
Visual, Verbal

Use Visuals 

Figure 2 Use this diagram to show a model of the atom. Explain to students that each energy level contains a certain number of electrons.
Visual

Build Math Skills 

Calculating An electron has a mass of 9.11×10^{-28} g. Have students calculate a more exact ratio between the mass of a proton and the mass of an electron. If necessary, review the idea of a ratio: a dimensionless number used to compare two values. *(The mass of a proton is 1.674×10^{-24} g. 1.674×10^{-24} g/9.11×10^{-28} g = 1838)* The ratio is actually 1836:1. The error is due to rounding.
Logical

Build Science Skills L2

Using Models Have students build models of atoms similar to Figure 2 using materials found at home or in the classroom. Models do not have to be exactly to scale but should show the relationships among the particles clearly.
Visual, Logical

Isotopes

Build Science Skills 

Calculating Oxygen-18 has a mass number of 18 and 10 neutrons in its nucleus. Oxygen-17 has a mass number of 17 and 9 neutrons in its nucleus. Ask: **What is the atomic number of oxygen?** *(8)*
Logical

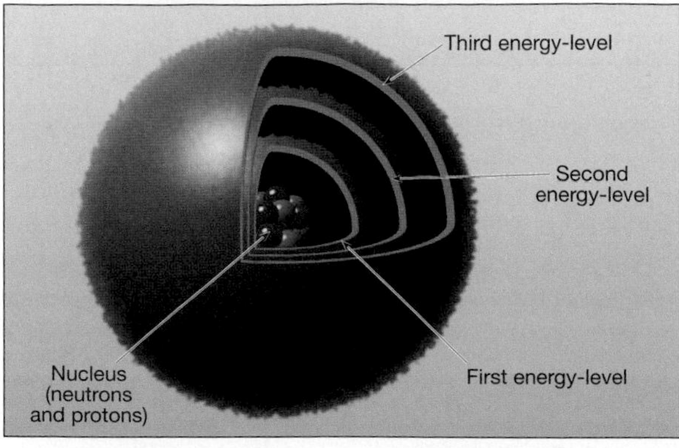

Figure 2 Model of an Atom The electrons that move about an atom's nucleus occupy distinct regions called energy levels.

Electrons An electron is the smallest of the three fundamental particles in an atom. An electron has a mass of about 1/1836 the mass of a proton or a neutron. Electrons move about the nucleus so rapidly that they create a sphere-shaped negative zone. You can picture moving electrons by imagining a cloud of negative charges surrounding the nucleus, as shown in Figure 2.

Electrons are located in regions called **energy levels.** Each energy level contains a certain number of electrons. Interactions among electrons in the outermost energy levels explains how atoms form compounds, as you will find out later in the chapter.

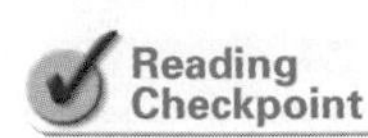
How are electrons, protons, and neutrons alike and how are they different?

Isotopes

Atoms of the same element always have the same number of protons. For example, every carbon atom has 6 protons. Carbon is element number 6 on the periodic table. But the number of neutrons for atoms of the same element can vary. **Atoms with the same number of protons but different numbers of neutrons are isotopes of an element.** Isotopes of the same element are labeled using a convention called the mass number and with the element's name or symbol. The **mass number** of an atom is the total mass of the atom (protons plus neutrons) expressed in atomic mass units. The proton and the neutron each have a mass that is slightly larger than the atomic mass unit. Recall that the mass of an electron is so small that the number of electrons has no effect on the mass number of an atom.

Carbon has 15 different isotopes. Models for three of these are shown in Figure 3. Carbon-12 makes up almost 99 percent of all carbon on Earth. Carbon-12 has 6 protons and 6 neutrons. Carbon-13 makes up much of the remaining naturally occurring carbon atoms on Earth. Carbon-13 has 6 protons and 7 neutrons.Though only traces of carbon-14 are found in nature, the presence of this isotope is often used to determine the age of once-living things. Carbon-14 has 6 protons and 8 neutrons

The nuclei of most atoms are stable. However, many elements have atoms whose nuclei are unstable. Such atoms disintegrate through a process called radioactive decay. Radioactive decay occurs because the forces that hold the nucleus together are not strong enough.

Q & A

Q *Are the minerals in this chapter the same as those in dietary supplements?*

A Not ordinarily. Most minerals found in dietary supplements are compounds made in the laboratory. These dietary minerals often contain elements that are metals, such as calcium, potassium, magnesium, and iron. From the geologist's point of view, a mineral must be a naturally occurring crystalline solid.

Facts and Figures

Carbon-14 can be used to find the ages of some objects. Carbon-14 is formed continuously by natural processes in the atmosphere. Carbon in the atmosphere reacts with oxygen to form carbon dioxide. Plants take in carbon dioxide during photosynthesis, the process by which they use energy in sunlight to make food. Initially, the ratio of carbon-14 to carbon-12 is the same in plants as it is in the atmosphere. The same is true for an animal that eats a plant. After a plant or animal dies, though, it no longer takes in carbon. The carbon-14 gradually undergoes radioactive decay to form nitrogen-14 with a half-life of 5730 years. The age of an object containing plant or animal material can be determined by comparing the ratio of carbon-14 to carbon-12 in the object to the ratio of these isotopes in the atmosphere. If the ratio of carbon-14 to carbon-12 in the object is one-quarter the ratio of carbon-14 to carbon-12 in the atmosphere, for example, then two half-lives, or 11,460 years, have passed since the plant or animal was alive.

During radioactive decay, unstable atoms radiate energy and particles. Some of this energy powers the movements of Earth's crust and upper mantle. The rates at which unstable atoms decay are measurable. Therefore certain radioactive atoms can be used to determine the ages of fossils, rocks, and minerals.

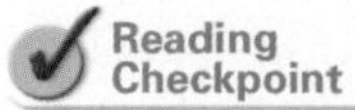
Reading Checkpoint *What are isotopes?*

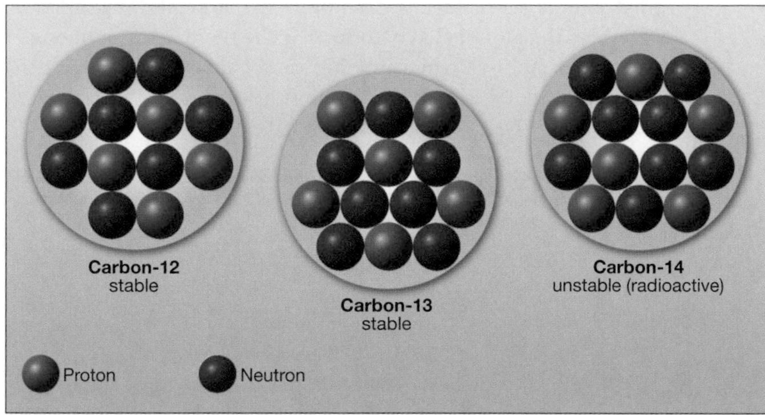

Figure 3 Nuclei of Isotopes of Carbon Carbon has many isotopes. Of these, three occur in nature.
Comparing and Contrasting ***How are the nuclei of these isotopes the same, and how do they differ?***

Why Atoms Bond

Most elements exist combined with other elements to form substances with properties that are different from the elements themselves. Sodium is often found combined with the element chlorine as the mineral halite. Lead ore is really the mineral galena, which is the element, lead, combined with the element, sulfur. Chemical combinations of the atoms of elements are called **compounds.** **A compound is a substance that consists of two or more elements that are chemically combined in specific proportions.** Compounds form when atoms are more stable (exist at a lower energy state) in a combined form. The chemical process, called bonding, centers around the electron arrangements of atoms. Thus, when atoms combine with others to form compounds, they gain, lose, or share electrons.

Scientists have discovered that the most stable elements are found on the right side of the periodic table in Group 8A (18). These elements have a very low reactivity and exist in nature as single atoms. Scientists explain why atoms form compounds by considering how an atom undergoes changes to its electron structure to be more like atoms in Group 8A.

Teacher Demo

Isotopes and Numbers L2

Purpose Students will observe the relationships among number of protons, number of neutrons, atomic number, and mass number for different isotopes.

Materials overhead projector, red and green gummy candies

Procedure Explain that the green candies represent neutrons and the red candies represent protons. Model a carbon-12 nucleus by placing a group of 6 red candies and 6 green candies on the overhead. Ask students to count the number of candies (particles) to determine the mass number of the carbon atom *(12)*. Then ask students what the atomic number is for carbon *(6)*. Then remove a red candy (proton) and ask if the atom is still carbon *(no)*. Replace the red candy and add a green candy (neutron). Ask students if the atom is still carbon *(yes)*. Then ask: **How is this atom different from the original one?** *(The atom has a different isotope, carbon-13.)* Show students the appropriate notation to represent isotopes: element name with mass number or element symbol with mass number and atomic number.

carbon-13 or $^{13}_{6}C$

Expected Outcome Students should gain a familiarity with mass numbers, atomic numbers, and isotopes.
Visual

Answer to . . .

Figure 3 *The isotopes all have the same number of protons, and thus, the same atomic number, but each has a different number of neutrons.*

Reading Checkpoint *They all are subatomic particles that make up atoms. Protons have positive electrical charges, neutrons have no charge, and electrons have negative charges. Protons and neutrons are found in an atom's nucleus. Electrons move about the nucleus.*

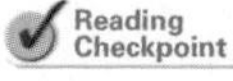
Reading Checkpoint *Isotopes are atoms of the same element with the same number of protons but different numbers of neutrons.*

Build Science Skills L2

Predicting Emphasize that, except for hydrogen and helium, the dots in an electron dot diagram do not represent all of the electrons in an atom, just the valence electrons.

Have students look at Figure 4. Ask them to predict the electron dot diagrams for rubidium, strontium, indium, tin, antimony, tellurium, iodine, and xenon. *(These elements—Rb, Sr, In, Sn, Sb, Te, I, and Xe—have the same valence electron configurations as the elements directly above them in the periodic table.)*
Logical, Visual

Types of Chemical Bonds

Many students think that atoms become positively charged as a result of gaining protons. Challenge this misconception by explaining that electrons are the only subatomic particles that can be removed from or added to an atom during a chemical reaction. Remind students that protons are bound into the nuclei of atoms and cannot be removed or added during chemical reactions.
Logical

Integrate Chemistry L2

Ionic Compounds and Conduction Why are solid ionic compounds poor conductors of electricity whereas melted ionic compounds are good conductors? Tell students that for an electric current to flow through a substance, charged particles must be able to move from one place to another. In a solid ionic crystal, the ions are fixed in a lattice. Ask: **Why can't ionic solids conduct electricity?** *(Since the ions are in fixed positions, they cannot conduct current.)* **What happens if the solid is melted?** *(The ions are freed from the lattice.)* **Why is the melted solid a good conductor of electricity?** *(The ions can move around and conduct a current.)*
Logical

Look at Figure 4. It shows the shorthand way of representing the number of electrons in the outer energy level. Recall that electrons move about the nucleus of an atom in a region called an electron cloud. Within this cloud, only a certain number of electrons can occupy each energy level. For example, a maximum of two electrons can occupy the first energy level. From Figure 4, you see that helium (He) is shown with two electrons. A maximum of eight electrons can be found in the second energy level. You also see from the figure that neon (Ne) is shown with eight electrons. **When an atom's outermost energy level does not contain the maximum number of electrons, the atom is likely to form a chemical bond with one or more other atoms. Chemical bonds** can be thought of as the forces that hold atoms together in a compound. The principal types of chemical bonds are ionic bonds, covalent bonds, or metallic bonds.

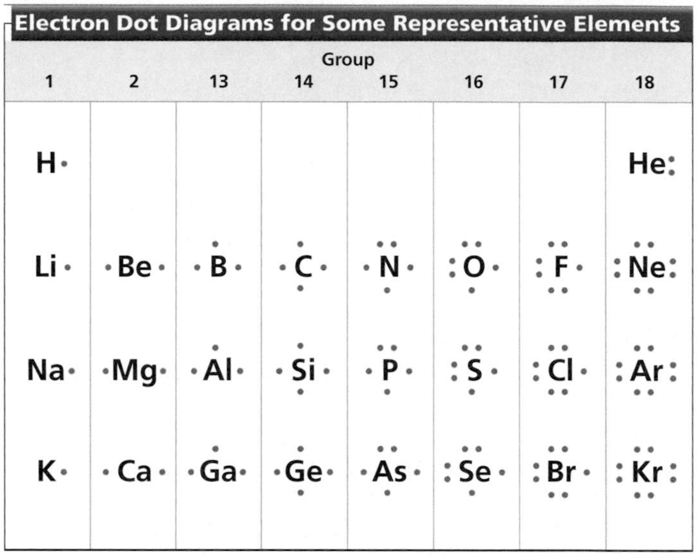

Figure 4 In an electron dot diagram, each dot represents an electron in the atom's outer energy level. These electrons are sometimes called valence electrons.
Observing ***How many electrons do sodium and chlorine have in their outer energy levels?***

Electron Dot Diagrams for Some Representative Elements

Group 1	2	13	14	15	16	17	18
H·							He:
Li·	·Be·	·B· (3 dots)	·C· (4 dots)	·N· (5 dots)	:O· (6 dots)	:F· (7 dots)	:Ne: (8 dots)
Na·	·Mg·	·Al· (3 dots)	·Si· (4 dots)	·P· (5 dots)	:S· (6 dots)	:Cl· (7 dots)	:Ar: (8 dots)
K·	·Ca·	·Ga· (3 dots)	·Ge· (4 dots)	·As· (5 dots)	:Se· (6 dots)	:Br· (7 dots)	:Kr: (8 dots)

Types of Chemical Bonds

Ionic Bonds An atom that gains electrons becomes negatively charged. This happens because the atom now has more electrons than protons. An atom that loses electrons becomes positively charged. This happens because the atom now has more protons than electrons. An atom that has an electrical charge because of a gain or loss of one or more electrons is called an **ion.** Oppositely charged ions attract each other to form crystalline compounds. **Ionic bonds form between positive and negative ions.**

Some common compounds on Earth have both a chemical name and a mineral name. For example, table salt has a chemical name, sodium chloride, and a mineral name, halite. Salt forms when sodium (Na) reacts with chlorine (Cl) as shown in Figure 5A. Sodium is very unstable and reactive. Sodium atoms lose one electron and become positive ions. Chlorine atoms gain one electron and become negative ions. These oppositely charged ions are attracted to each other and form the compound called sodium chloride.

The properties of a compound are different from the properties of the elements in the compound. Sodium is a soft, silvery metal that reacts vigorously with water. If you held it in your hand, sodium could burn your skin. Chlorine is a green poisonous gas. Chemically combined these atoms produce table salt, the familiar crystalline solid that is essential to health.

What happens when two or more atoms react?

Formation of Sodium Chloride

Figure 5 **A** When sodium metal comes in contact with chlorine gas, a violent reaction occurs. **B** Sodium atoms transfer one electron to the outer energy levels of chlorine atoms. Both ions now have filled outer energy levels **C** The positive and negative ions formed attract each other to form a crystalline solid with a rigid structure.

B

C

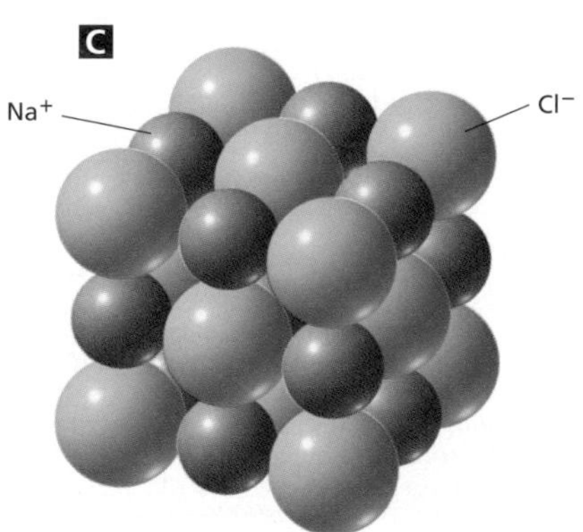

Use Visuals L1

Figure 5 Use this diagram to explain how an ionic compound forms. Ask: **What happens to the sodium atom when it loses an electron?** *(It becomes a positive ion.)* **What happens to a chlorine atom when it gains an electron?** *(It becomes a negative ion.)* **What happens to the two ions?** *(They are attracted to each other and form a compound.)*
Visual, Logical

Integrate Health L2

Sodium and Chlorine in the Body
Sodium chloride, or table salt, is an essential nutrient for human beings. Tell students that sodium and chlorine both help maintain the acid-base balance in the body. Sodium is also involved in maintaining the water balance of the body and in nerve function. Chlorine is needed for the formation of gastric juice for digestion of food. The average American gets about 20 times the required intake of sodium.
Logical

Answer to . . .

Figure 4 *Sodium has one electron in its outer energy level (valence electron) and chlorine has seven.*

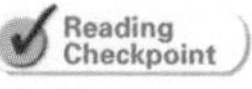

Electrons are gained, lost, or shared when two or more atoms react to form a compound.

Build Reading Literacy L1

Refer to **p. 502** in **Chapter 18,** which provides guidelines for this strategy.

Visualize Tell students that forming a mental image of concepts they are learning helps them remember new concepts. After students have read about ionic, covalent, and metallic bonds, have them visualize models for each type of bond. Then encourage students to draw diagrams that demonstrate the differences among these three types of bonds.
Visual

Comparing Bonds L2

Purpose Students observe differences in the properties of substances with different bonds.

Materials rock salt, chalk, copper wire, hammer, goggles

Procedure Take students outside to an open area. Allow them to examine the samples of rock salt, chalk, and copper wire. Have students stand back a safe distance. Put on goggles, then place each sample on a hard surface and hit it with a hammer. Invite students to observe how each sample looks after being pounded with the hammer.

Expected Outcome The rock salt and chalk shatter because they are ionic and covalent substances, respectively. The copper wire changes shape instead of shattering because metals are malleable.
Visual

L2

Many students do not differentiate among atoms, molecules, and ions in their perceptions of particles. Challenge this misconception by having students make drawings to represent an atom, a molecule, and an ion. Students should draw a single sphere for an atom, at least two spheres joined in some way for a molecule, and one sphere with either a plus or a minus sign for an ion.
Visual

A

B

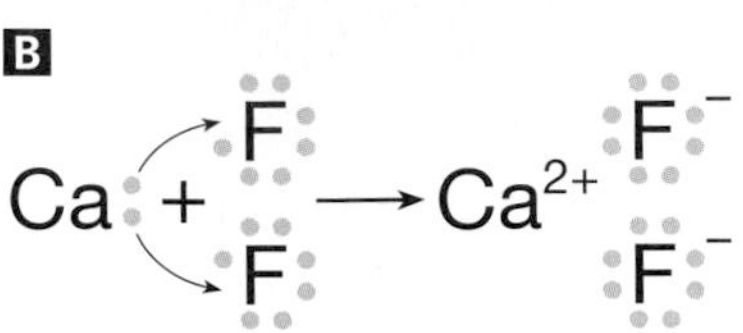

Figure 6 Ionic Compound A Fluorite is an ionic compound that forms when calcium reacts with fluorine. **B** The dots shown with the element's symbol represent the electrons in the outermost levels of the ions. **Explaining** ***Explain what happens to the electrons in calcium atoms and fluorine atoms when fluorite forms.***

Compounds that contain ionic bonds are called ionic compounds. Figure 6 shows calcium fluoride, a common ionic compound. Our model for ionic bonding suggests that one calcium atom transfers two electrons from its outermost energy level to two atoms of fluorine. This transfer gives all atoms the right numbers of electrons in their outer energy levels. The compound that forms is known as the mineral fluorite.

Ionic compounds are rigid solids with high melting and boiling points. These compounds are poor conductors of electricity in their solid states. When melted, however, many ionic compounds are good conductors of electricity. Most ionic compounds consist of elements from groups 1 and 2 on the periodic table reacting with elements from groups 16 and 17 of the table.

How do ionic bonds form, and what are some properties of ionic compounds?

Covalent Bonds **Covalent bonds form when atoms share electrons.** Compounds with covalent bonds are called covalent compounds. Figure 7 shows silicon dioxide, one of the most common covalent compounds on Earth. Silicon dioxide forms when one silicon atom and two oxygen atoms share electrons in their outermost energy levels. Silicon dioxide is also known as the mineral quartz.

The bonding in covalent compounds results in properties that differ from those of ionic compounds. Unlike ionic compounds, many covalent compounds have low melting and boiling points. For example, water, a covalent compound, boils at 100°C at standard pressure. Sodium chloride, an ionic compound, boils at 1413°C at standard pressure. Covalent compounds also are poor conductors of electricity, even when melted.

A

B

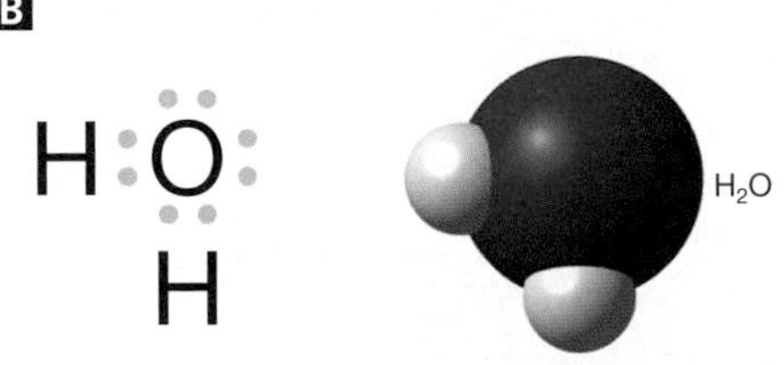

Figure 7 Covalent Compounds A Quartz is a covalent compound that forms when silicon and oxygen atoms bond. **B** Water consists of molecules formed when hydrogen and oxygen share electrons.

The smallest particle of a covalent compound that shows the properties of that compound is a molecule. A molecule is a neutral group of atoms joined by one or more covalent bonds. Water, for example, consists of molecules. These molecules are made of two hydrogen atoms covalently-bonded to one oxygen atom. The many gases that make up Earth's atmosphere, including hydrogen, oxygen, nitrogen, and carbon dioxide, also consist of molecules.

Facts and Figures

Unlike ionic and covalent compounds, metals are malleable and ductile. Instead, metal ions are held together in a "sea of electrons" referred to as the metallic bond. When a piece of metal is deformed, the ions move to new positions. The piece of metal does not break because the ions are still held attracted to the electrons.

Metallic Bonds Metals are malleable, which means that they can be easily shaped. You've observed this property when you wrapped aluminum foil around food or crushed an aluminum can. Metals are also ductile, meaning that they can be drawn into thin wires without breaking. The wiring in your school or home is probably made of the metal copper. Metals are excellent conductors of electricity.

Metallic bonds form when electrons are shared by metal ions. Figure 8 shows a model for this kind of bond. The sharing of an electron pool gives metals their characteristic properties. Using the model you can see how an electrical current is easily carried through the pool of electrons. Later in this chapter, you will learn about some metals that are classified as minerals.

A

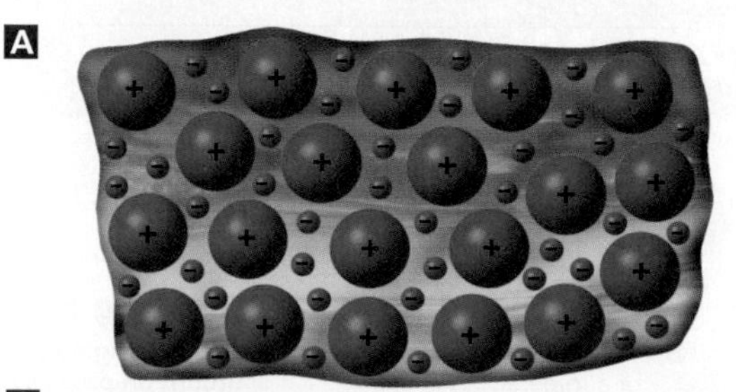

B

Figure 8 Metallic Bonds A Metals form bonds with one another by sharing electrons. **B** Such bonds give metals, such as this copper, their characteristic properties. Metals can be easily formed and shaped.

3 ASSESS

Evaluate Understanding L2

Have students describe why substances form ionic, covalent, and metallic bonds.

Reteach L1

Use Figures 5 and 6 to review the formation of ions and ionic bonds. Be sure students understand that the ionic bond is the electrostatic attraction between ions of opposite charge. Ionic compounds do not exist as discrete pairs of ions, but as aggregates of ions.

Math Practice

Solutions

10. The atomic number, which is the number of protons in an element, is the same for each isotope of carbon. The mass number varies from 8 (6 protons + 2 neutrons) to 24 (6 protons + 18 neutrons).

Section 2.1 Assessment

Reviewing Concepts

1. What is an element?
2. What kinds of particles make up atoms?
3. What are isotopes?
4. What are compounds and why do they form?
5. Contrast ionic, covalent, and metallic bonds.

Critical Thinking

6. **Comparing and Contrasting** Compare and contrast solids, liquids, and gases.
7. **Applying Concepts** What elements in Table 1 are metals?
8. **Applying Concepts** A magnesium atom needs two electrons to fill its outermost energy level. A chlorine atom needs one electron to fill its outermost shell. If magnesium reacts with chlorine, what type of bond will most likely form? Explain.
9. **Applying Concepts** Which elements in the periodic table might combine with oxygen to form compounds similar to magnesium dioxide (MgO_2)?

Math Practice

10. The isotopes of carbon have from 2 to 16 neutrons. Use this information to make a table that shows the 15 isotopes of carbon and the atomic number and mass number of each.

Answer to . . .

Figure 6 *Calcium transfers its two electrons to two fluorine atoms, forming two fluoride ions.*

Ionic bonds form when electrons are transferred from one atom to another. Ionic compounds are rigid solids with high melting and boiling points and are poor conductors of electricity in their solid states. When melted, many ionic compounds are good conductors of electricity.

Section 2.1 Assessment

1. An element is a class of matter that contains only one type of atom. An element cannot be broken down, chemically or physically, into a simpler substance with the same properties.
2. Protons and neutrons are found in an atom's nucleus, while electrons move about this central core.
3. Isotopes are atoms of the same element that have the same number of protons but different numbers of neutrons.
4. A compound is a substance that consists of two or more elements. Compounds form as the result of changes in the arrangement of electrons in the outermost shells of the bonded atoms.
5. Ionic bonds are those that form when electrons are transferred. Covalent bonds involve the sharing of electrons. Metallic bonds exist when electrons are shared by metallic ions.
6. All are forms of matter, and thus all are made of atoms. A solid has a definite shape and definite volume. A liquid has a definite volume, but not a definite shape. A gas has neither a definite volume nor a definite shape.
7. aluminum, iron, calcium, sodium, potassium, magnesium
8. An ionic bond forms because magnesium will give up or transfer its two electrons to two chlorine ions.
9. Elements in groups 1 and 2 have similar properties to those of magnesium and often combine with oxygen to form compounds.

Section 2.2

1 FOCUS

Section Objectives

2.6 **List** five characteristics of minerals.
2.7 **Describe** the processes that result in mineral formation.
2.8 **Explain** how minerals can be classified.
2.9 **List** some of the major groups of minerals.

Reading Focus

Build Vocabulary L2

Word Parts Help students understand the meaning of the word *tetrahedron* by breaking the word down into parts. The part *tetra* comes from the Greek word for "four." The part *hedron* comes from the Greek word for "face." So a tetrahedron is a shape that has four faces.

Reading Strategy L2

Silicates: made of tetrahedra; quartz; feldspar
Carbonates: contain carbon, oxygen, and one or more other metallic elements; calcite; dolomite
Oxides: contain oxygen, and one or more other elements; rutile; corundum
Sulfate and sulfides: contain sulfur; gypsum; galena
Halides: contain a halogen ion plus one or more other elements; halite; fluorite
Native elements: substances that exist as free elements; gold; silver

2 INSTRUCT

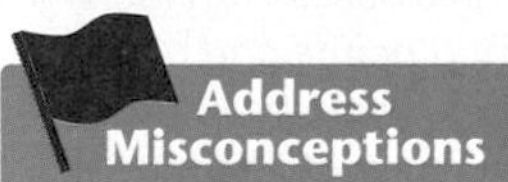

L2

Students may think that the minerals discussed in this chapter are the same as the minerals found in vitamin pills. They are related, but not the same. Remind students of the Q&A on p. 38. In earth science, a mineral is a naturally occurring inorganic crystalline solid. In contrast, minerals found in vitamin pills are inorganic compounds made in the laboratory that contain elements needed by the body. Many elements needed by the body are metals such as calcium, potassium, phosphorus, magnesium, and iron.
Logical

2.2 Minerals

Reading Focus

Key Concepts

- What are five characteristics of a mineral?
- What processes result in the formation of minerals?
- How can minerals be classified?
- What are some of the major groups of minerals?

Vocabulary

- mineral
- silicate
- silicon-oxygen tetrahedron

Reading Strategy

Previewing Copy the organizer below. Skim the material on mineral groups on pages 47 to 49. Place each group name into one of the ovals in the organizer. As you read this section, complete the organizer with characteristics and examples of each major mineral group.

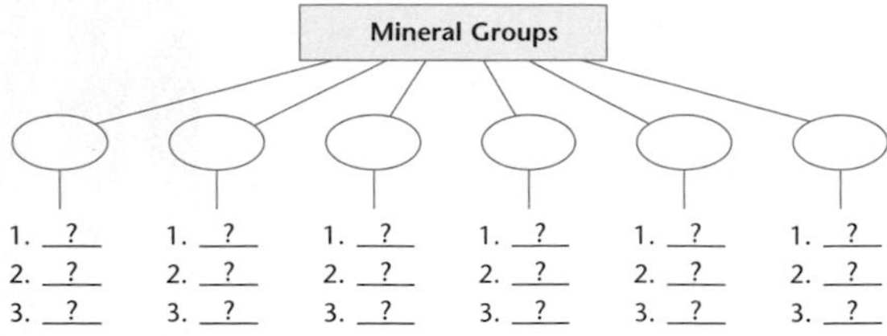

Look at the salt shaker in Figure 9B. This system is made up of the metal cap, glass container, and salt grains. Each component is made of elements or compounds that either are minerals or that are obtained from minerals. In fact, practically every manufactured product that you might use in a typical day contains materials obtained from minerals. What other minerals do you probably use regularly? The lead in your pencils actually contains a soft black mineral called graphite. Most body powders and many kinds of make-up contain finely ground bits of the mineral talc. Your dentist's drill bits contain tiny pieces of the mineral diamond. It is hard enough to drill through your tooth enamel. The mineral quartz is the main ingredient in the windows in your school and the drinking glasses in your family's kitchen. What do all of these minerals have in common? How do they differ?

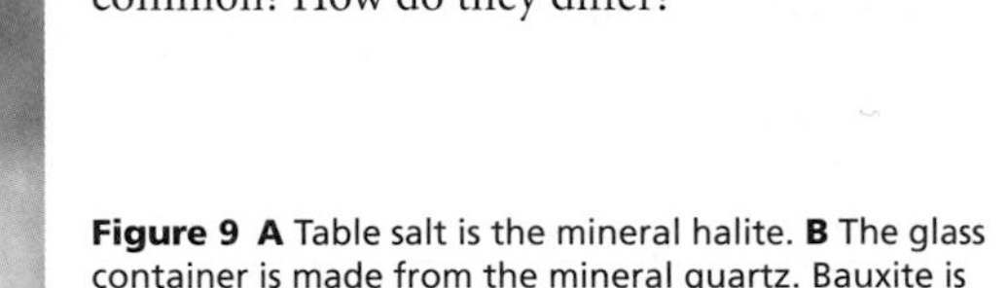

A

B

Figure 9 **A** Table salt is the mineral halite. **B** The glass container is made from the mineral quartz. Bauxite is one of the minerals that provides aluminum for the cap.

Minerals

A mineral in Earth science is different from the minerals in foods. **A mineral is a naturally occurring, inorganic solid with an orderly crystalline structure and a definite chemical composition.** For an Earth material to be considered a mineral, it must have the following characteristics:

1. **Naturally occurring** A mineral forms by natural geologic processes. Therefore, synthetic gems, such as synthetic diamonds and rubies, are not considered minerals.
2. **Solid substance** Minerals are solids within the temperature ranges that are normal for Earth's surface.
3. **Orderly crystalline structure** Minerals are crystalline substances which means that their atoms or ions are arranged in an orderly and repetitive manner. You saw this orderly type of packing in Figure 5 for halite (NaCl). The gemstone opal is not a mineral even though it contains the same elements as quartz. Opal does not have an orderly internal structure.
4. **Definite chemical composition** Most minerals are chemical compounds made of two or more elements. A few, such as gold and silver, consist of only a single element (native form). The common mineral quartz consists of two oxygen atoms for every silicon atom. Thus the chemical formula for quartz would be SiO_2.
5. **Generally considered inorganic** Most minerals are inorganic crystalline solids found in nature. Table salt (halite) is one such mineral. However, sugar, another crystalline solid is not considered a mineral because it is classified as an organic compound. Sugar comes from sugar beets or sugar cane. We say "generally inorganic" because many marine animals secrete inorganic compounds, such as calcium carbonate (calcite). This compound is found in their shells and in coral reefs. Most geologists consider this form of calcium carbonate a mineral.

How Minerals Form

Minerals form nearly everywhere on Earth under different conditions. For example, minerals called silicates often form deep in the crust or mantle where temperatures and pressures are very high. Most of the minerals known as carbonates form in warm, shallow ocean waters. Most clay minerals form at or near Earth's surface when existing minerals are exposed to weathering. Still other minerals form when rocks are subjected to changes in pressure or temperature. **There are four major processes by which minerals form: crystallization from magma, precipitation, changes in pressure and temperature, and formation from hydrothermal solutions.**

Feldspar

Quartz

Muscovite

Hornblende

Figure 10 These minerals often form as the result of crystallization from magma.

Minerals

Build Reading Literacy L1

Refer to **p. 334D** in **Chapter 12,** which provides guidelines for this strategy.

Outline Have students read the text on pp. 45–49 about how minerals form and mineral groups. Encourage students to use the headings as major divisions in an outline. Have students refer to their outlines when answering the questions in the Section 2.2 Assessment.
Verbal, Logical

How Minerals Form

Teacher Demo

Crystallization of Sulfur

Purpose Students observe how the rate of cooling of a mineral affects crystal size.

Materials two crucibles, 50-mL beaker, water, teaspoon, sulfur powder, tongs, Bunsen burner, magnifying glass

Procedure Put a teaspoon of powdered sulfur into one of the crucibles. Using tongs, hold the crucible near the burner flame until the sulfur melts. Set the crucible aside to cool. Put a teaspoon of powdered sulfur into the second crucible. Put about 200 mL of water in the beaker. Melt the sulfur in the second crucible and carefully pour the molten sulfur into the beaker. Pour off the water. As soon as the first crucible has cooled, allow students to look at both sets of crystals using the magnifying glass.

Safety Wear goggles, apron, and heat-resistant mitts while melting the sulfur. Make sure students are at a safe distance from the crucible and flame and that the room is well ventilated.

Expected Outcome The sulfur in the first crucible, which cooled slowly, will have bigger crystals than the sulfur that cooled quickly.
Visual, Logical

Customize for English Language Learners

To help students learn and understand the names of the different mineral groups, have them focus on the roots of the names and ignore the endings. The beginning of *silicates,* for example, is *silic-*. This is similar to *silicon* and indicates that silicates contain silicon. Have students go though all the other names, isolate the beginnings of the names, and figure out what the name indicates about what elements the minerals contain *(carbonates: carbon-, carbon; oxides: ox-, oxygen; sulfates and sulfides: sulf-, sulfur; halides: hal-, halogens).*

Teacher Demo

Precipitation of a Mineral

L2

Purpose Students observe how a mineral can form by precipitation.

Materials rock salt, spoon warm water, 400-mL beaker, shallow pan or tray

Procedure Out of view of students, add rock salt spoon by spoon to a beaker of warm water, stirring as you go. Stop when no more salt will dissolve. Show the beaker to students and ask them if there is a mineral in it. Most will say no. Then pour the liquid into the pan and leave it in a warm and/or sunny spot. (If you don't have a suitable warm and/or sunny spot or want to save time, pour some of the solution into an evaporation dish and heat it on a hot plate.) When the water has evaporated, show the pan to students and ask them to identify the substance in it *(halite crystals).*

Expected Outcome As the water evaporates, the salt will precipitate out of the solution and form crystals.
Visual, Logical

Build Science Skills

Inferring Sometimes rocks are buried deep under Earth's surface. When they reach the surface again they are often changed into a different type of rock. Ask students why this happens. *(The rocks are subjected to great heat and pressure deep below Earth's surface. The heat and pressure cause reactions that change the minerals and thus produces new types of rocks.)*
Logical

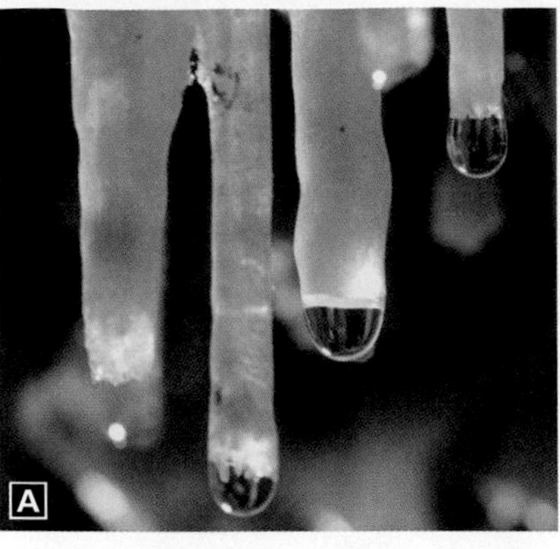

Figure 11 **A** This limestone cave formation is an obvious example of precipitation. **B** Halite and calcite are also formed by precipitation.

Crystallization from Magma Magma is molten rock. It forms deep within Earth. As magma cools, elements combine to form minerals such as those shown in Figure 10 on page 45. The first minerals to crystallize from magma are usually those rich in iron, calcium, and magnesium. As minerals continue to form, the composition of the magma changes. Minerals rich in sodium, potassium, and aluminum then form.

Precipitation The water in Earth's lakes, rivers, ponds, oceans, and beneath its surface contains many dissolved substances. If this water evaporates, some of the dissolved substances can react to form minerals. Changes in water temperature may also cause dissolved material to precipitate out of a body of water. The minerals are left behind, or precipitated, out of the water. Two common minerals that form in this way are shown in Figure 11.

Pressure and Temperature Some minerals, including talc and muscovite, form when existing minerals are subjected to changes in pressure and temperature. An increase in pressure can cause a mineral to recrystallize while still solid. The atoms are simply rearranged to form more compact minerals. Changes in temperature can also cause certain minerals to become unstable. Under these conditions, new minerals form, which are stable at the new temperature.

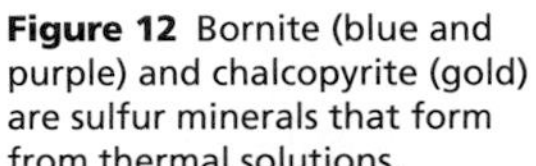

Figure 12 Bornite (blue and purple) and chalcopyrite (gold) are sulfur minerals that form from thermal solutions.

Hydrothermal Solutions A hydrothermal solution is a very hot mixture of water and dissolved substances. Hydrothermal solutions have temperatures between about 100°C and 300°C. When these solutions come into contact with existing minerals, chemical reactions take place to form new minerals. Also, when such solutions cool, some of the elements in them combine to form minerals such as quartz and pyrite. The sulfur minerals in the sample shown in Figure 12 formed from thermal solutions.

Describe what happens when a mineral is subjected to changes in pressure or temperature.

Mineral Groups

Over 3800 minerals have been named, and several new ones are identified each year. You will be studying only the most abundant minerals. **Common minerals, together with the thousands of others that form on Earth, can be classified into groups based on their composition.** Some of the more common mineral groups include the silicates, the carbonates, the oxides, the sulfates and sulfides, the halides, and the native elements. First, you will learn about the most common groups of minerals on Earth—the **silicates.**

Silicates If you look again at Table 1, you can see that the two most abundant elements in Earth's crust are silicon and oxygen. **Silicon and oxygen combine to form a structure called the silicon-oxygen tetrahedron.** This structure is shown in Figure 13. The tetrahedron, which consists of one silicon atom and four oxygen atoms, provides the framework of every silicate mineral. Except for a few silicate minerals, such as pure quartz (SiO_2), most silicates also contain one or more other elements.

Silicon-oxygen tetrahedra can join in a variety of ways, as you can see in Figure 14 on the next page. The silicon-oxygen bonds are very strong. Some minerals, such as olivine, are made of millions of single tetrahedra. In minerals such as augite, the tetrahedra join to form single chains. Double chains are formed in minerals such as hornblende. Micas are silicates in which the tetrahedra join to form sheets. Three-dimensional network structures are found in silicates such as quartz and feldspar. As you will see, the internal structure of a mineral affects its properties.

What is the silicon-oxygen tetrahedron, and in how many ways can it combine?

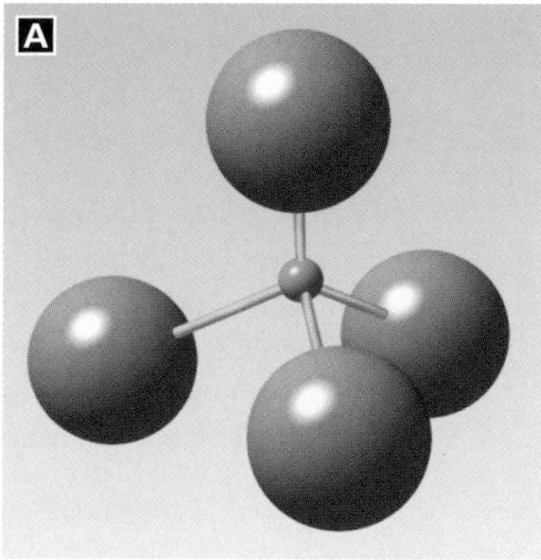

Figure 13 **A** The silicon-oxygen tetrahedron is made of one silicon atom and four oxygen atoms. The rods represent chemical bonds between silicon and the oxygen atoms. **B** Quartz is the most common silicate mineral. A typical piece of quartz like this contains millions of silicon-oxygen tetrahedra.

Mineral Groups

L2

Students may think that the silicates described in this section are the same materials as those in silicon computer chips or silicone sealant. They are different materials, although all three contain silicon. Silicon chips are made from pure silicon, which does not contain the oxygen found in silicates. Silicone is an artificially-made silicon-oxygen polymer gel that feels rubbery and is water repellent, chemically inert, and stable at extreme temperatures.
Verbal

Use Visuals **L1**

Figure 13 Use this diagram to explain the basic structure of silicates. Ask: **What is the atom at the center of the tetrahedron?** *(a silicon atom)* **What are the four atoms at the corners of the tetrahedron?** *(oxygen atoms)* **What do the rods represent?** *(chemical bonds between the atoms)* **Why is this structure called a tetrahedron?** *(it has four sides, or faces)*
Visual

Facts and Figures

Judging from the enormous number of known minerals, one might think that a large number of elements are needed to make them. Surprisingly, the bulk of these minerals are made up of only eight elements. These elements, in order of abundance, are oxygen (O), silicon (Si), aluminum (Al), iron (Fe), calcium (Ca), sodium (Na), potassium (K), and magnesium (Mg). These eight elements represent over 98 percent by weight of the continental crust. The two most abundant elements, oxygen and silicon, comprise nearly three-fourths of Earth's continental crust. These elements are the main building blocks of silicates. The most common group of silicates, the feldspars, compose over 50 percent of Earth's crust. Quartz is the second most abundant mineral in the continental crust. It is a silicate made mostly of oxygen and silicon.

Answer to . . .

The mineral often becomes unstable, and its atoms react to form a new mineral.

The silicon-oxygen tetrahedron consists of one silicon atom and four oxygen atoms and provides the framework of every silicate mineral. These tetrahedra can join to form single chains, double chains, sheets, and three-dimensional networks. In these arrangements the corner oxygen atoms are shared between silicon atoms so the ratio is not necessarily 1 to 4.

Build Science Skills

L2

Using Models Have students use Figures 13 and 14 to build models of the various silicate structures. They can use balls of modeling clay or gumdrops to represent silicon and oxygen atoms and toothpicks to represent chemical bonds. First have each student build several silicon-oxygen tetrahedra as shown in Figure 13. Then have students work in groups to combine their tetrahedra into chains and other structures as shown in Figure 14.
Kinesthetic, Visual, Logical

ACTIVITY

Use Visuals

L1

Figure 14 Use this diagram to explain the different structures that silicate tetrahedra can form. Ask: **How does a single chain form?** *(A series of tetrahedra are joined together end-to-end.)* **How are double chains formed?** *(Two single chains are joined together side-by-side.)* **How are sheets formed?** *(Many single chains are joined together side-by-side.)*
Visual

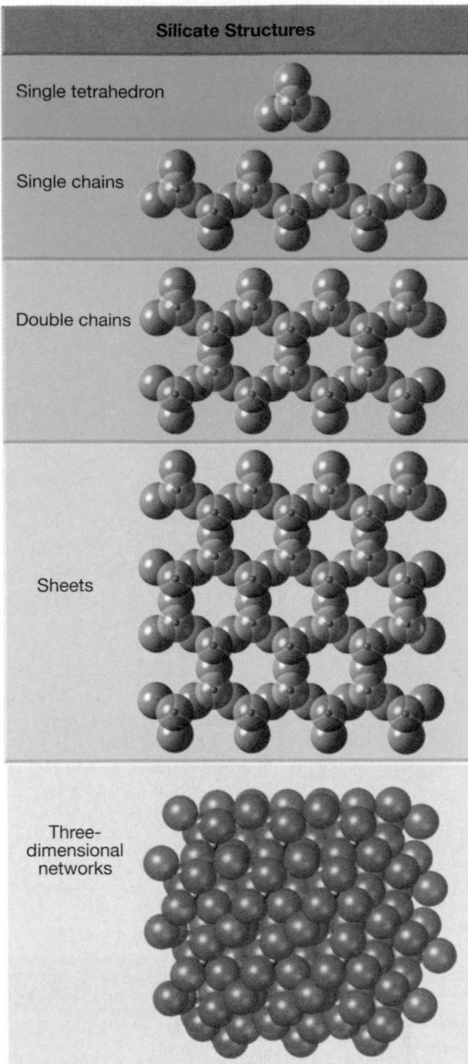

Figure 14 Silicon-oxygen tetrahedra can form chains, sheets, and three-dimensional networks.
Formulating Hypotheses ***What type of chemical bond is formed by silicon atoms in an SiO_4 tetrahedron?***

Recall that most silicate minerals crystallize from magma as it cools. This cooling can occur at or near Earth's surface, where temperatures and pressures are relatively low. The formation of silicates can also occur at great depths, where temperatures and pressures are high. The place of formation and the chemical composition of the magma determine which silicate minerals will form. For example, the silicate olivine crystallizes at temperatures of about 1200°C. Quartz crystallizes at about 700°C.

Some silicate minerals form at Earth's surface when existing minerals are exposed to weathering. Clay minerals, which are silicates, form this way. Other silicate minerals form under the extreme pressures that occur with mountain building. Therefore, silicate minerals can often provide scientists with clues about the conditions in which the minerals formed.

Carbonates Carbonates are the second most common mineral group. **Carbonates are minerals that contain the elements carbon, oxygen, and one or more other metallic elements.** Calcite ($CaCO_3$) is the most common carbonate mineral. Dolomite is another carbonate mineral that contains magnesium and calcium. Both limestone and marble are rocks composed of carbonate minerals. Both types of rock are used in building and construction.

Oxides **Oxides are minerals that contain oxygen and one or more other elements, which are usually metals.** Some oxides, including the mineral called rutile (TiO_2), form as magma cools deep beneath Earth's surface. Rutile is titanium oxide. Other oxides, such as corundum (Al_2O_3), form when existing minerals are subjected to changes in temperature and pressure. Corundum is aluminum oxide. Still other oxides, such as hematite (Fe_2O_3), form when existing minerals are exposed to liquid water or to moisture in the air. Hematite is one form of iron oxide.

Sulfates and Sulfides Sulfates and sulfides are minerals that contain the element sulfur. Sulfates, including anhydrite ($CaSO_4$) and gypsum ($CaSO_4 \cdot 2H_2O$), form when mineral-rich waters evaporate. Sulfides, which include the minerals galena (PbS), sphalerite (ZnS), and pyrite (FeS_2), often form from thermal, or hot-water, solutions. Figure 15 shows two of these sulfides.

Halides Halides are minerals that contain a halogen ion plus one or more other elements. Halogens are elements from Group 7A of the periodic table. This group includes the elements fluorine (F) and chlorine (Cl). The mineral halite (NaCl), table salt, is a common halide. Fluorite (CaF_2) is also a common halide and is used in making steel. It forms when salt water evaporates.

Native Elements Native elements are a group of minerals that exist in relatively pure form. You are probably familiar with many native elements, such as gold (Au), silver (Ag), copper (Cu), sulfur (S), and carbon (C). Native forms of carbon are diamond and graphite. Some native elements form from hydrothermal solutions.

Figure 15 Sulfides A Galena is a sulfide mineral that can be mined for its lead. **B** Pyrite is another sulfide that is often called fool's gold.
Inferring *What element do you think pyrite is generally mined for?*

Section 2.2 Assessment

Reviewing Concepts

1. What are five characteristics of a mineral?
2. Describe four processes that result in the formation of minerals.
3. How can minerals be classified?
4. Name the major groups of minerals, and give at least two examples of minerals in each group.

Critical Thinking

5. **Comparing and Contrasting** Compare and contrast sulfates and sulfides.
6. **Formulating Conclusions** When hit with a hammer, quartz shows an uneven breakage pattern. Using Figure 14, what can you suggest about its structure?
7. **Applying Concepts** To which mineral group do each of the following minerals belong: bornite (Cu_5FeS_4), cuprite (Cu_2O), magnesite ($MgCO_3$), and barite ($BaSO_4$)?

Writing in Science

Explanatory Paragraph Coal forms from ancient plant matter that has been compressed over time. Do you think coal is a mineral? Write a paragraph that explains your reasoning.

Use Community Resources L2

Invite a geologist from a local college or company to visit the classroom and discuss different groups of minerals with students. Ask the geologist to bring in samples from each group of minerals to show to students.
Visual, Interpersonal

3 ASSESS

Evaluate Understanding L2

Have students describe the four major processes by which minerals can form.

Reteach L1

Review the five characteristics that a material must have to be considered a mineral. Have students list and define all of the science terms used in the description of the five characteristics. Then review each of the five points again to be sure students understand them.

Writing in Science

Students should explain that because coal is formed from once-living things, it is not considered a mineral. Also, coal is a carbon-based material that falls into the class of organic compounds.

Answer to . . .

Figure 14 *covalent*

Figure 15 *Iron (Fe)*

Section 2.2 Assessment

1. A mineral is a natural, inorganic solid with an orderly internal structure and a definite chemical composition.
2. Crystallization occurs when minerals form as magma cools. Precipitation is a process whereby minerals form as waters rich in dissolved substances evaporate. Changes in pressure and temperature can cause the atoms in a mineral to change places to form a new mineral. Precipitation from hydrothermal solutions is another way in which minerals form.
3. Minerals can be classified according to their compositions.
4. silicates (quartz, feldspar, olivine, and mica); carbonates (calcite, dolomite); oxides (rutile, corundum, hematite); sulfates (anhydrite, gypsum); sulfides (galena, pyrite, sphalerite); halides (fluorite, halite); native elements (gold, silver, copper, iron, sulfur, diamond)
5. Both contain the element sulfur. Sulfates also contain oxygen and a metallic element. Sulfides contain only sulfur and one or more other metallic elements.
6. The tetrahedra that combine to form quartz share very strong bonds, resulting in an uneven breakage.
7. Bornite is a sulfide mineral, cuprite is an oxide, magnesite is a carbonate mineral, and barite is a sulfate.

Section 2.3

1 FOCUS

Section Objectives

2.10 **Explain** why color is often not a useful property in identifying minerals.
2.11 **Define** the terms *luster, crystal form, streak,* and Mohs scale.
2.12 **Distinguish** between cleavage and fracture.
2.13 **Explain** density and how it can be used to identify substances.
2.14 **Describe** some other properties that can be used to identify minerals.

Reading Focus

Build Vocabulary L2

Paraphrase As students read the section, have them look for the vocabulary terms that describe properties of minerals. For each term, have students write a definition in their own words. If students are having trouble, use mineral samples to demonstrate each of the properties.

Reading Strategy L2

A.1 Often not used to identify minerals
A.2 Small amounts of different elements can give the same mineral different colors.
B.1 Describes how light is reflected from surface
B.2 Metallic and nonmetallic lusters

2 INSTRUCT

Color

Build Reading Literacy L1

Refer to **p. 32D** in this chapter, which provides guidelines for this strategy.

Preview Before they read the section, have students skim the headings, visuals, and boldfaced sentences and terms to preview how the text is organized. Have students note any unfamiliar terms and concepts and make notes about these as they read the section.
Verbal

2.3 Properties of Minerals

Reading Focus

Key Concepts

- What properties can be used to identify minerals?
- What is the Mohs scale?
- What are some distinctive properties of minerals?

Vocabulary

- streak
- luster
- crystal form
- hardness
- Mohs scale
- cleavage
- fracture
- density

Reading Strategy

Outlining Before you read, make an outline of this section, following the format below. Use the green headings as the main topics. As you read, add supporting details.

I. Properties of Minerals
  A. Color
    1. ________
    2. ________
  B. Luster
    1. ________
    2. ________

As you can see from the photographs in this chapter, minerals occur in different colors and shapes. Now you will learn that minerals vary in the way they reflect light and in the way in which they break. You will also find out that some minerals are harder than others and that some minerals smell like rotten eggs. All of these characteristics, or properties, of minerals can be used to identify them.

Color

One of the first things you might notice about a mineral is its color. While color is unique to some minerals, this property is often not useful in identifying many minerals. **Small amounts of different elements can give the same mineral different colors.** You can see examples of this in Figure 16.

Figure 16 Small amounts of different elements give these sapphires their distinct colors. **Observing** ***Why is color often not a useful property in mineral identification?***

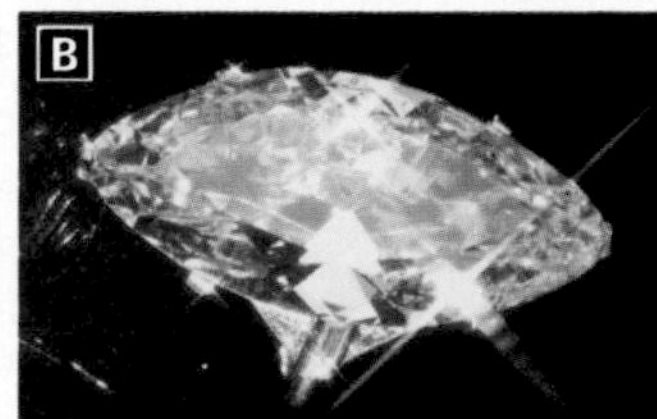

Figure 17 **A** The mineral copper has a metallic luster. **B** The brilliant luster of diamond is also known as an adamantine luster.

Streak

Streak is the color of a mineral in its powdered form. Streak is obtained by rubbing a mineral across a streak plate, a piece of unglazed porcelain. While the color of a mineral may vary from sample to sample, the streak usually doesn't. Therefore, streak can be a good indicator. Streak can also help to see the difference between minerals with metallic lusters and minerals with nonmetallic lusters. Metallic minerals generally have a dense, dark streak. Minerals with nonmetallic lusters do not have such streaks.

Luster

Luster is used to describe how light is reflected from the surface of a mineral. Minerals that have the appearance of metals, regardless of their color, are said to have a metallic luster. The piece of copper shown in Figure 17A has a metallic luster. Minerals with a nonmetallic luster are described by many adjectives. These include vitreous or glassy, like the quartz crystals in Figure 5. Other lusters include pearly, silky, and earthy. Diamond has an adamantine, or brilliant luster. Some minerals appear *somewhat* metallic and are said to have a sub-metallic luster.

Crystal Form

Crystal form is the visible expression of a mineral's internal arrangement of atoms. Every mineral has a distinct crystal form.

Usually, when a mineral forms slowly and without space restrictions, it will develop into a crystal with well-formed faces—sides, top, and bottom—as shown in Figure 18. Most of the time, however, minerals compete for space. This crowding results in an intergrown mass of small crystals. None of these crystals shows its crystal form.

What two conditions produce crystals with well-defined faces?

Figure 18 Crystal Form **A** This quartz sample shows hexagonal (six-sided) crystals. The ends of the crystals have a pyramid shape. **B** Fluorite often forms cubic crystals.

Customize for Inclusion Students

Behaviorally Disordered For students who have difficulty concentrating on reading or class lectures, have them explore mineral samples on their own to learn about the properties of minerals. Students can work on their own or in small groups to explore three to five minerals. Encourage students to take notes about each mineral's color, luster, crystal form, streak, hardness, cleavage, fracture, and density.

Streak

Integrate Chemistry **L2**

Streak Color There are several reasons why a mineral's streak color may differ from the color of the mineral itself. Some translucent minerals are colored by trace impurities of other elements. These colors are visible in a large sample because light passes through the impurities before reaching the eye. A streak will often not show this coloring effect and will appear white instead. Also, the structure and surface coatings of a sample may affect its color. Again, the streak will not show these effects and will instead show the true color of the mineral. Have students research how streak can be used to distinguish gold from iron pyrite. *(Samples of both have a gold color. Gold has a golden streak but iron pyrite has a black streak.)*
Logical

Luster

Integrate Physics **L2**

Causes of Luster The type of luster a mineral displays depends on how light interacts with the surface of the sample. If most of the light is reflected or absorbed, the mineral will have a metallic luster. A few minerals allow a small amount of light to penetrate, and have submetallic luster. Nonmetallic luster occurs when light can pass through the sample. If the mineral has a high index of refraction (the amount that light bends when it is passing through the mineral), such as diamond, the luster is described as adamantine. Minerals with lower indices of refraction have glassy or vitreous luster.
Logical, Visual

Crystal Form

Use Visuals **L1**

Figure 18 Show students a sample of granite with coarse texture. Point out the quartz crystals in the rock. Have students compare these crystals with the quartz crystals in Figure 18A. Ask: **Why do the crystals look so different if they are both quartz?** *(The crystals in the granite did not have adequate space in which to develop the full crystal form shown in the photograph.)*
Visual

Answer to . . .

Figure 16 *The same mineral can be different colors.*

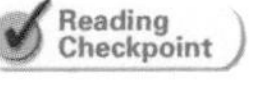

unrestricted space and a slow rate of formation

Hardness

Use Visuals

L1

Figure 19 Have students use the Mohs scale of hardness to give the hardness ranges for the following descriptions: a mineral that can be scratched by your fingernail *(less than 2.5)*, a mineral that cannot be scratched by your fingernail and cannot scratch glass *(2.5 to 5.5)*, a mineral that scratches glass *(greater than 5.5)*.
Visual

Build Science Skills

L1

Inferring Ask: **What does the use of a pencil tell you about the hardness of graphite?** *(Graphite, or pencil "lead," is a very soft mineral because it leaves a mark, or streak, when rubbed against paper or most surfaces.)* **What can you say about the hardness of chalk versus the hardness of a chalkboard?** *(Chalk is softer than the board.)* **What kind of minerals could you not test for streak when using a streak plate?** *(Minerals that are harder than the streak plate will not leave a streak; instead they will scratch the plate.)*
Logical

Cleavage

Integrate Language Arts

Origin of the Names Mica and Muscovite Tell students that the name "mica" probably came from the Latin word *micare*, which means "to shine" and refers to mica's appearance. Muscovite, a common type of mica, was named after the old Russian state of Muscovy. In the 1300s, it was common in Muscovy to use mica as a substitute for glass, so it was called muscovy glass. Biotite is another common type of mica. Have students research the origin of that name. *(It was named for J. B. Biot, a French physicist.)*
Verbal

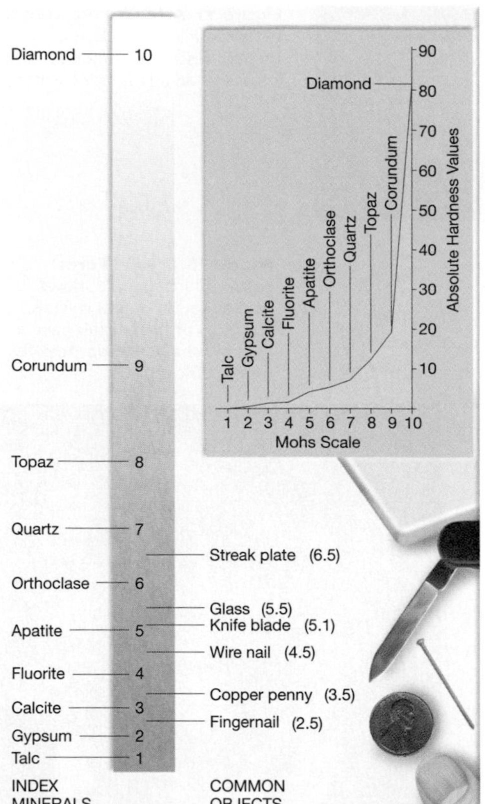

Figure 19 Mohs Scale to Hardness Common objects can be used with the Mohs scale to determine mineral hardness. **Using Tables and Graphs** ***A mineral has a hardness of 4.2. Which common items on the chart will that mineral scratch?***

Hardness

One of the most useful properties to identify a mineral is hardness. **Hardness** is a measure of the resistance of a mineral to being scratched. You can find this property by rubbing the mineral against another mineral of known hardness. One will scratch the other, unless they have the same hardness.

Geologists use a standard hardness scale called the Mohs scale. **The Mohs scale consists of 10 minerals arranged from 10 (hardest) to 1 (softest).** See Figure 19. Any mineral of unknown hardness can be rubbed against these to determine its hardness. Other objects can also be used to determine hardness. Your fingernail, for example, has a hardness of 2.5. A copper penny has a hardness of 3.5. A piece of glass has a hardness of about 5.5. Look again at Figure 19. The mineral gypsum, which has a Mohs hardness of 2, can be easily scratched by your fingernail. The mineral calcite, which resembles gypsum, has a hardness of 3. Calcite cannot be scratched by your fingernail. Calcite, which can resemble the mineral quartz, cannot scratch glass, because its hardness is less than 5.5. Quartz, the hardest of the common minerals with a Mohs hardness of 7, will scratch a glass plate. Diamond, the hardest mineral on Earth, can scratch anything.

Reading Checkpoint ***Describe three or four of the most useful properties for identifying unknown minerals.***

Cleavage

In the atomic structure of a mineral, some bonds are weaker than others. These weak bonds are places where a mineral will break when it is stressed. **Cleavage is the tendency of a mineral to cleave, or break, along flat, even surfaces.**

Minerals called micas show the simplest type of cleavage. Because the micas have weak bonds in one direction, they cleave to form thin, flat sheets, as shown in Figure 20A. Look again at Figure 14. Can you see the relationship between mica's internal structure and the cleavage it shows? Mica, and all other silicates, tend to cleave between the silicon-oxygen structures rather than across them. This is because the silicon-oxygen bonds are strong. The micas' sheet structure causes them to cleave into flat plates. Quartz has equally strong silicon-oxygen bonds in all directions. Therefore, quartz has no cleavage but fractures instead.

Some minerals have cleavage in more than one direction. Look again at Figure 11. Halite (11A) has three directions of cleavage. The cleavage planes of halite meet at 90-degree angles. Calcite (11B) also has three directions of cleavage. The cleavage planes of calcite, however, meet at 75-degree angles.

Fracture

Minerals that do not show cleavage when broken are said to fracture. Fracture is the uneven breakage of a mineral. For example, quartz shows a curvy and glassy fracture. Like cleavage, there are different kinds of fracture. Minerals that break into smooth, curved surfaces like the quartz in Figure 20B have a conchoidal fracture. Other minerals, such as asbestos, break into splinters or fibers. Many minerals have an irregular fracture.

How are cleavage and fracture different?

Figure 20 **A** Mica has cleavage in one direction and therefore cleaves into thin sheets. **B** The bonds in quartz are very strong in all directions, causing quartz to display conchoidal fracture.

Density

Density is a property of all matter that is the ratio of an object's mass to its volume. Density is a ratio and can be expressed using the following equation.

$$Density\ (D) = \frac{mass\ (m)}{Volume\ (V)}$$

Density is expressed using derived units with a unit of mass over a unit of volume. For example, the density of copper is 8.96 g/cm^3 (grams per cubic centimeter). Therefore, any sample of pure copper with a volume of one cubic centimeter will have a mass of 8.96 grams.

Many common minerals have densities between 2 and 5 g/cm^3. Some metallic minerals have densities that are often greater than rock-forming minerals. Galena, the ore of lead, has a density around 7.5 g/cm^3. The density of gold is 19.3 g/cm^3. The density of a pure mineral is a constant value. Thus, density can be used to determine the purity or identity of some minerals.

For: Links on mineral identification
Visit: www.SciLinks.org
Web Code: cjn-1023

Fracture

Use Visuals **L1**

Figure 20 Use these photographs to explain fracture and cleavage. Ask: **What is cleavage?** *(the tendency of a mineral to break along flat, even surfaces)* **Which mineral shows cleavage?** *(mica)* **What is fracture?** *(the uneven breakage of a mineral)* **Which mineral shows fracture?** *(quartz)*
Visual

Density

Integrate Chemistry **L2**

Density and Atomic Mass Specific gravity was once used to distinguish minerals. However, today geologists use density. The specific gravity of a mineral depends on its density. (Density is mass per unit of volume and is expressed in grams per cubic centimeter.) Density in turn depends mainly on the chemical composition of a mineral. Minerals made of elements with high atomic masses generally have higher densities than minerals made of atoms with low atomic masses. Tell students that the mineral galena contains large amounts of lead, which has a high atomic mass. Ask: **Would you expect the density of galena to be relatively low or high?** *(high)* Tell students that the mineral quartz is made up of silicon and oxygen, which have low atomic masses. **Would you expect the density of quartz to be relatively low or high?** *(low)*
Logical

Download a worksheet on mineral identification for students to complete, and find additional teacher support from NSTA SciLinks.

Facts and Figures

Like mica, asbestos is a sheet-forming mineral. However, unlike flat sheets of mica, sheets of asbestos roll up in a tight needle-like formation. These needles can cause serious damage to lungs if inhaled. Before people realized that asbestos caused a health risk, it was a popular insulation material. Now, many older buildings must undergo expensive asbestos removal in order to be safe.

Answer to . .

Figure 19 *copper penny and fingernail*

 *Hardness, streak, luster, and density are the most definitive properties that can be used to identify minerals*

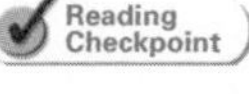 *Cleavage is the tendency for a mineral to break along flat, even surfaces. Fracture is the uneven breakage of a mineral.*

Section 2.3 (continued)

Distinctive Properties of Minerals

Use Community Resources L2

As noted on p. 49, invite a geologist from a local college or company to visit the classroom and discuss properties of minerals with students. Ask the geologist to bring in samples of unusual minerals and demonstrate their properties to students.
Visual, Interpersonal

Build Science Skills L2

ACTIVITY

Designing Experiments Give each student or group of students two mineral samples. Tell them only that one is calcite and the other is dolomite. Have students design an activity they could do without any additional materials or equipment to determine the identities of the two samples. *(Try to scratch the samples with each other. The one that is scratched is softer and is calcite.)* Then ask students how they might identify the samples using additional materials. *(Place dilute hydrochloric acid on each sample to see if it fizzes.)* Have them carry out their experiment. Be sure students wear safety goggles and gloves when using the hydrochloric acid. Dispense the acid in small dropper bottles and be sure it is diluted.
Logical

Table 2 Some Common Minerals and Their Properties

Name	Chemical Formula and Mineral Group	Common Color(s)	Density (g/cm^3)	Hardness	Comments
Quartz	SiO_2 silicates	colorless, milky white, pink, brown	2.65	7	glassy luster; conchoidal fractures
Orthoclase feldspar	$KAlSi_3O_8$ silicates	white to pink	2.57	6	cleaves in two directions at 90°
Plagioclase feldspar	$(Na,Ca)AlSi_3O_8$ silicates	white to gray	2.69*	6	cleaves in two directions at 90°; striations common
Galena	PbS sulfides	metallic silver	7.5*	2.5	cleaves in three directions at 90°; lead gray streak
Pyrite	FeS_2 sulfides	brassy yellow	5.02	6–6.5	fractures; forms cubic crystals; greenish-black streak
Sulfur	S native elements	yellow	2.07*	1.5–2.5	fractures; yellow streak smells like rotten eggs
Fluorite	CaF_2 halides	colorless, purple	3.18	4	perfect cleavage in three directions; glassy luster
Olivine	$(Mg,Fe)_2SiO_4$ silicates	green, yellowish-green	3.82*	6.5–7	fractures; glassy luster; often has granular texture
Calcite	$CaCO_3$ carbonates	colorless, gray	2.71	3	bubbles with HCl; cleaves in three directions
Talc	$Mg_3Si_4O_{10}(OH)_2$ silicates	pale green, gray, white	2.75*	1	pearly luster; feels greasy; cleaves in one direction
Gypsum	$CaSO_4 \bullet 2H_2O$ sulfates	colorless, white, gray	2.32	2	glassy or pearly luster; cleaves in three directions
Muscovite mica	$Kal_3Si_3O_{10}(OH)_2$ silicates	colorless in thin sheets to brown	2.82*	2–2.5	silky to pearly luster; cleaves in one direction to form flexible sheets

* Average density of the mineral

Figure 21 Calcite shows the property of double refraction.

Distinctive Properties of Minerals

Some minerals can be recognized by other distinctive properties. Talc and graphite, for example, both have distinctive feels. Talc feels soapy. Graphite feels greasy. Metallic minerals, such as gold, silver, and copper, are easily shaped. Some types of magnetite are magnetic and can be used to pick up paper clips and small nails. When a piece of transparent calcite is placed over printed material, the letters appear doubled as Figure 21 shows. This property is called double refraction. Streaks of a few minerals that contain sulfur smell like rotten eggs. Carbonate minerals, such as calcite, will fizz when they come into contact with hydrochloric acid.

A mineral's properties depend on the elements that compose the mineral (its composition) and its structure (how its atoms are arranged). Table 2 lists some of the more common minerals and their properties. You will use this table to identify minerals in the lab on pages 58 and 59.

54 Chapter 2

Table 2 Some Common Minerals and Their Properties, *continued*					
Name	Chemical Formula and Mineral Group	Common Color(s)	Density (g/cm^3)	Hardness	Comments
Biotite mica	$K(Mg,Fe)_3(AlSi_3O_{10})(OH)_2$ silicates	dark green to brown to black	3.0*	2.5–3	perfect cleavage in one direction to form flexible sheets
Halite	$NaCl$ halides	colorless, white	2.16	2.5	has a salty taste; dissolves in water; cleaves in three directions
Augite	$(Ca, Na)(Mg, Fe, Al)(Si, Al)_2O_6$ silicates	dark green to black	3.3*	5–6	glassy luster; cleaves in two directions; crystals have 8-sided cross section
Hornblende	$(Ca, Na)_{2\text{-}3}(MgFeAl)_5Si_6(SiAl)_2O_{22}(OH)_2$ silicates	dark green to black	3.2*	5–6	glassy luster; cleaves in two directions; crystals have 6-sided cross section
Hematite	Fe_2O_3 oxides	reddish brown to black	5.26	5.5–6.5	metallic luster in crystals; dull luster in earthy variety; dark red streak
Dolomite	$CaMg(CO_3)_2$ carbonates	pink, colorless, white, gray	2.85	3.5–4	does not react to HCl as quickly as calcite; cleaves in three directions
Magnetite	Fe_3O_4 oxides	black	5.18	6	metallic luster; black streak; strongly magnetic
Copper	Cu native elements	copper-red on fresh surface	8.9	2.5–3	metallic luster; fractures; can be easily shaped
Graphite	C native elements	black to gray	2.3	1–2	black to gray streak; marks paper; feels slippery

Section 2.3 Assessment

Reviewing Concepts

1. Describe five common properties of minerals that can be used to identify them.
2. How is the Mohs scale used?
3. What are some unique properties that can be used to identify minerals?

Critical Thinking

4. **Applying Concepts** What kind of luster do the minerals shown in Figure 15 have? Explain your choice.
5. **Applying Concepts** Hornblende is a double-chain silicate. How many planes of cleavage do you think hornblende has when it breaks? Explain your answer.
6. **Applying Concepts** A mineral scratches a piece of fluorite but cannot be scratched by a piece of glass. What is this mineral's hardness?

Connecting Concepts

Mineral Properties Choose one of the minerals pictured in this chapter. Find out to which mineral system it belongs as well as its luster, streak, hardness, specific gravity, and whether it cleaves or fractures. Also note any unique properties of the mineral.

Section 2.3 Assessment

1. Sample answers: luster, crystal form, streak, Mohs hardness, magnetism, density, odor, double refraction, cleavage, and fracture.
2. The Mohs scale is an ordering of minerals according to hardness.
3. Feel, magnetism, double refraction, odor, and reaction to HCl are a few properties unique to only some minerals.
4. Both minerals have metallic luster because they appear to shine like metals.
5. Hornblende cleaves in two directions when the two sets of bonds in the double chain structure break.
6. The mineral's hardness is greater than 4 but less than 5.5 on the Mohs hardness scale.

Integrate Social Studies L2

Mining Economics Mineral resources are Earth's storehouse of minerals that can be recovered for use. The term *ore* refers to useful metallic minerals that can be mined at a profit. For pure elements, the element must be concentrated well above the level of its average crustal abundance to be worth mining. Copper must be present at about 100 times its average concentration, whereas for aluminum the ratio is only 4. Have students research the history of the copper mine at Bingham Canyon, Utah. *(It is one of the largest open-pit mines on Earth. Mining was halted in 1985 because it was uneconomic but later restarted with new equipment that made it profitable.)* **Verbal, Logical**

3 ASSESS

Evaluate Understanding L2

Provide students with 4 or 5 unidentified minerals. Challenge students to place the minerals in order of hardness from softest to hardest. They should rub any two of the minerals together and repeat this process until they can determine the order of hardness. Remind students that a harder mineral will scratch a softer mineral and a softer mineral may leave a streak on a harder mineral. After rubbing two minerals together, students may need to rub the mark with their finger to tell if it is a scratch or a streak.

Connecting Concepts

Answers will vary. Most of the minerals pictured in this chapter are described in Table 4. Many are shown on the GEODe CD-ROM as well.

understanding
EARTH

Gemstones

L2

Background

- Why can diamond and graphite be made of the same material (carbon) but form such different minerals? You could make a diamond out of your pencil if you could squeeze it hard enough. The pressure would compress the carbon atoms of the graphite together until they eventually formed the strong covalent bonds of diamond. In fact, this is roughly how synthetic diamonds are made: by squeezing carbon very tightly. Natural diamonds are thought to form more than 150 km beneath the surface, where the pressures are very high. The diamonds that we find at the surface have been brought up from deep within Earth by geologic processes.
- Pure quartz, containing only SiO_2, is clear and colorless. However, natural quartz comes in many color varieties that form when different elements are contained in the crystal structure. If small amounts of titanium and iron are included, the result is rose quartz. The inclusion of manganese produces purple amethyst. The inclusion of aluminum produces smoky quartz.
- A precious gemstone that has gained in popularity in recent years is tanzanite. Mined only in the east-African country of Tanzania, tanzanite was discovered in 1967. Its color ranges from a light purplish blue to the more prized deep blues. The most prized stones are deep blue rimmed in a purplish hue. This hydrated calcium aluminum silicate is actually the blue variety of the gemstone called zoisite. But the jeweler Louis Comfort Tiffany, who popularized the gem after its discovery, thought that the correct name of *blue zoisite* was too reminiscent of the word *suicide*. So he suggested *tanzanite* instead.

understanding
EARTH
Gemstones

Precious stones have been prized by people since ancient times. Unfortunately, much misinformation exists about the nature of gems and the minerals of which they are composed. Part of the misinformation stems from the ancient practice of grouping precious stones by color rather than mineral makeup. For example, the more common red spinels were often passed off to royalty as rubies, which are more valuable gems. Even today, when modern techniques of mineral identification are commonplace, yellow quartz is frequently sold as topaz.

What's In a Name?

Compounding the confusion is the fact that many gems have names that are different from their mineral names. For example, diamond is composed of the mineral of the same name, whereas sapphire is a form of corundum, an aluminum oxide-rich mineral. Although pure aluminum oxide is colorless, a tiny amount of a foreign element can produce a vividly colored gemstone. Therefore, depending on the impurity, sapphires of nearly every color exist. Pure aluminum oxide with trace amounts of titanium and iron produce the most prized blue sapphires. If the mineral corundum contains enough chromium, it exhibits a brilliant red color, and the gem is called ruby. Large gem-quality rubies are much rarer than diamonds and thus command a very high price.

If the specimen is not suitable as a gem, it simply goes by the mineral name corundum. Although common corundum is not a gemstone, it does have value as an abrasive material. Whereas two gems—rubies and sapphires—are composed of the mineral corundum, quartz is the parent mineral of more than a dozen gems. Table 3 lists some well-known gemstones and their mineral names.

Precious or Semiprecious?

What makes a gem a gem instead of just another mineral? Basically, certain mineral specimens, when cut and polished, possess beauty of such quality that they can command a price that makes the process of producing the gem profitable. Gemstones can be divided into two categories: precious and semiprecious. A *precious* gem has beauty, durability, size, and rarity, whereas a *semiprecious* gem usually has only one or two of these qualities. The gems that have traditionally enjoyed the highest esteem are diamonds, rubies, sapphires, emeralds, and some varieties of opal. All other gemstones are classified as semiprecious. It should be noted, however, that large, high-quality specimens of semiprecious stones can often command a very high price.

Obviously, beauty is the most important quality that a gem can possess. Today we prefer translucent stones with evenly tinted colors. The most favored hues appear to be red, blue, green, purple, rose,

Figure 22 Emerald is the dark green variety of the mineral beryl. More common blue-green beryl is aquamarine.

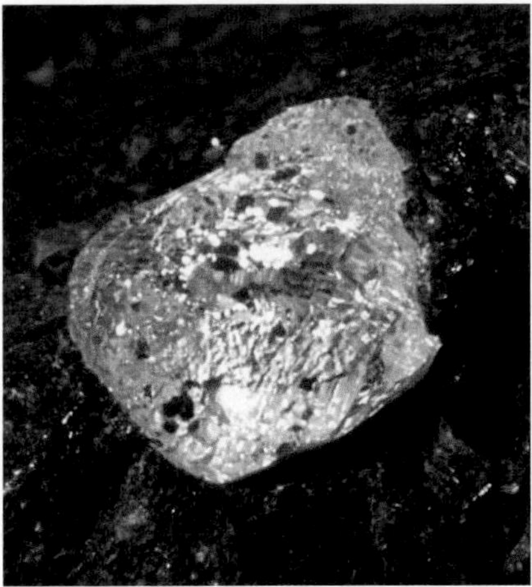

Figure 23 A diamond in the rough looks very different from the brilliant, multi-faceted gem it can become.

and yellow. The most prized stones are deep red rubies, blue sapphires, grass-green emeralds, and canary-yellow diamonds. Colorless gems are generally less than desirable except in the case of diamonds that display "flashes of color" known as brilliance.

Notice in figure 23 that gemstones in the "rough" are dull and would be passed over by most people as "just another mineral." Gemstones must be cut and polished by experienced artisans before their true beauty can be displayed.

The durability of a gem depends on its hardness—that is, its resistance to abrasion by objects normally encountered in everyday living. For good durability, gems should be as hard or harder than quartz, as defined by the Mohs scale of hardness. One notable exception is opal, which is comparatively soft (hardness 5 to 6.5) and brittle. Opal's esteem comes from its fire, which is a display of a variety of brilliant colors including greens, blues, and reds.

It seems to be human nature to treasure that which is rare. In the case of gemstones, large, high-quality specimens are much rarer than smaller stones. Thus, large rubies, diamonds, and emeralds, which are rare in addition to being beautiful and durable, command the very highest prices.

Table 3 Some Important Gemstones

Gem	Mineral Name	Prized Hues
Precious		
Diamond	Diamond	Colorless, yellows
Emerald	Beryl	Greens
Opal	Opal	Brilliant hues
Ruby	Corundum	Reds
Sapphire	Corundum	Blues
Semiprecious		
Alexandrite	Chrysoberyl	Variable
Amethyst	Quartz	Purples
Aquamarine	Beryl	Blue-greens
Cat's-eye	Chrysoberyl	Yellows
Chalcedony	Quartz (agate)	Banded
Citrine	Quartz	Yellows
Garnet	Garnet	Reds, greens
Jade	Jadeite or nephrite	Greens
Moonstone	Feldspar	Transparent blues
Peridot	Olivine	Olive greens
Smoky quartz	Quartz	Browns
Spinel	Spinel	Reds
Topaz	Topaz	Purples, reds
Tourmaline	Tourmaline	Reds, blue-greens
Turquoise	Turquoise	Blues
Zircon	Zircon	Reds

Teaching Tips

- Stories of mystery, adventure, and intrigue surround some of the more famous gemstones, such as the Hope Diamond. Invite students to research some of these stories and share them with the class. You might suggest some students create a booklet for distribution among the class.
- Invite a jeweler, gem cutter, or gemologist to the class to discuss how a rough stone is turned into a beautifully cut gem. Note how hardness, cleavage, and refraction are taken into account when cutting gems.

Verbal, Interpersonal

Exploration Lab

Mineral Identification L2

Objectives
After completing this activity, students will be able to
- explain some of the simple tests that can be used to identify minerals.
- differentiate among some of the common rock-forming minerals.

Skills Focus Observing, Comparing and Contrasting, Measuring

 **Prep Time** 20 minutes

Advance Prep Order the minerals from a scientific supply house at least one month before you plan to do this activity. Minerals should include several different varieties of quartz, calcite, magnetite, gypsum, talc, feldspar, olivine, fluorite, augite, hornblende, pyrite, halite, and mica. Make sure the mineral samples will fit into the graduated cylinders you plan to use.
- Label the samples with numbers, using a permanent marker so that you can check students' results.
- You may want to assemble mineral testing kits for students to use. These can be easily made by placing one of each testing item—acid bottle, knife, piece of quartz, magnet, streak plate, glass plate, penny, and hand lens—into small, study cardboard boxes. Students can share the minerals to be observed.
- If students do the Go Further exercise, you will need some small hand samples of the following rocks: sandstone, granite, limestone, marble, and schist.

Class Time 45 minutes

Safety Have students wear their safety goggles and aprons during the entire activity. Remind them to take care when breaking the minerals and that only a gentle blow is needed to break most of the samples they will be examining. Also remind students not to taste any of the minerals or the acid.

Teaching Tips
- If you don't want the samples destroyed, have students omit Part C. Alternatively, you can break a set of samples and have them on display for students to observe.
- Stress to students to use only a drop or two of acid to test each of the minerals and to thoroughly wash the samples after testing them with the HCl.

Exploration Lab

Mineral Identification

Most minerals can be easily identified by using the properties discussed in this chapter. In this lab, you will use what you have learned about mineral properties and the table on pages 54 and 55 to identify some common rock-forming minerals. In the next chapter, you will learn about rocks, which are mixtures of one or more minerals. Being able to identify minerals will enable you to understand more about the processes that form and change the rocks at and beneath Earth's surface.

Problem How can you use simple tests and tools to identify common minerals?

Materials
- mineral samples
- hand lens
- streak plate
- copper penny
- steel knife blade
- glass plate
- piece of quartz
- dilute hydrochloric acid
- magnet
- hammer
- 50 mL graduated cylinder
- tap water
- balance
- thin thread
- scissors
- paper or cloth towels
- Table 2 on pages 54–55

Skills Observing, Comparing and Contrasting, Measuring

Procedure    

Part A: Color and Luster

1. Examine each mineral sample with and without the hand lens. Examine both the central part of each mineral as well as the edges of the samples.
2. Record the color and luster of each sample in a data table like the one shown on the next page.

Part B: Streak and Hardness

3. To determine the streak of a mineral, gently drag it across the streak plate and observe the color of the powdered mineral. If a mineral is harder than the streak plate (H = 7), it will not produce a streak.
4. Record the streak color for each mineral in your data table.
5. Use your fingernail, the penny, the glass plate, the knife blade, and the piece of quartz to test the hardness of each mineral. Remember that if a mineral scratches an object, the mineral is harder than the object. If an object scratches a mineral, the mineral is softer than the object.
6. Record the hardness values for each sample in your data table.

Part C: Cleavage and Fracture

7. With your goggles on and everyone out of your way, gently strike one of the mineral samples with a hammer.
8. Observe the broken mineral pieces. Does the mineral cleave or fracture? Remember that cleavage is breakage along flat, even surfaces and fracture is uneven breakage. Record your observations in your data table.
9. Repeat Steps 7 and 8 for the other minerals.

Data Table										
Mineral Number	Color	Luster	Streak	Relative Hardness	Cleavage/ Fracture	Density				Other Properties
						m	V_1	V_2	d	
1										
2										
3										
4										
5										
6										
7										
8										

Part D: Density

10. Using a balance, determine the mass of your mineral sample. Record the mass in the first column under Density.
11. Cut a piece of thread about 20 cm long. Tie a small piece of your mineral sample to one end of the thread.
12. Securely tie the other end of the thread to a pencil or pen.
13. Fill the graduated cylinder about half full with water. Record the volume of the water in the second column under Density.
14. Lower the mineral into the graduated cylinder. Read the volume of the water now. Record the volume in the third column under Density.
15. Calculate the density of the mineral using the following equation:

$$\frac{\text{mass}_1}{\text{volume}_2 - \text{volume}_1}$$

Record this value in the fourth column.

Part E: Other Properties

16. Use the magnet to determine if any of the minerals are magnetic. Record your observations in the data table.
17. Place the transparent minerals over a word on this page to see if any have the property of double refraction. If a mineral has this property, you will see two sets of the word. Record your observations.
18. Compare the feel of the minerals. In the data table, note any differences.
19. Carefully place one or two drops of dilute hydrochloric acid on each mineral. Record your observations. When you are finished with this test, wash the minerals well with tap water to rinse away the acid.

Analyze and Conclude

1. **Identifying** Use your data and Table 2 to identify each of the minerals tested.
2. **Evaluating** Which of the properties did you find most useful? Least useful? Give reasons for your answers.
3. **Comparing and Contrasting** In general, how did the minerals with metallic luster differ from those with non-metallic luster?
4. **Classifying** Classify your minerals into at least three groups based on your observations. How does your classification scheme differ from those of at least two other students?

Go Further Obtain some rock samples from your teacher or collect some of your own. Use the hand lens to try to identify the minerals in each rock. Make a table in which to record your observations. Compare your table to the information presented in Chapter 3.

Questioning Strategies
Ask: **Why must you measure the volume of water before and after adding the mineral to the graduated cylinder to calculate density?** *(Density is the ratio of the mass of a mineral to its volume. The water displaced by the mineral is its volume.)*

Expected Outcome Students should be able to accurately identify at least one-half to three-fourths of the samples by using what they know about mineral properties and the information in Table 4.

Sample Data
Compare students' data and observations with the information provided in Table 4.

Analyze and Conclude
1. Most students should be able to correctly identify at least half of the minerals provided.
2. Answers will vary, but might include color and luster as the two least useful properties; and density, streak, hardness, and breakage as the most useful.
3. Minerals with metallic luster tend to have higher densities than minerals with non-metallic luster.
4. Students' classification schemes will probably differ, but might be based on similarities and differences in relative hardness, density, luster, type of breakage, or color.

Go Further
Most students will probably be able to identify some of the larger minerals in the rocks. Quartz, feldspar, and hornblende are found in many granites. Quartz is also a major component of many sandstones. Limestone and marble are often mostly calcite.
Visual, Logical

Chapter 2

Study Guide

Study Tip

Plan Ahead
Tell students to examine their schedules at least a week before the test. They should figure out how much time they will have available to study. Then students should divide up that time and plan when they are going to study each topic covered on the test. Encourage students to review the most important topics first. That way, students can cut the time allotted for reviewing less important topics if they have less time for studying than they expected.

Thinking Visually
The mineral is green, has a glassy luster, and does not appear to have cleavage.

Assessment

Reviewing Content

(1) 2 (2) 2 (3) 3 (4) 1
(5) 4 (6) 2 (7) 2 (8) 4
(9) 1

Understanding Concepts

(10) Protons, neutrons, and electrons make up all atoms. Protons are positive particles found in the nucleus of an atom. Neutrons are neutral particles in the nucleus. Electrons are negative particles that orbit an atom's nucleus.
(11) Ionic and covalent bonds are forces that hold atoms together in compounds. Ionic bonds form between ions of opposite charge. Covalent bonds form when electrons are shared.
(12) The five characteristics of a mineral are that it is naturally occurring, inorganic, solid, has definite internal structure, and has definite chemical composition.

CHAPTER 2

Study Guide

2.1 Matter

Key Concepts

- An element contains only one type of atom. Therefore, an element cannot be broken down, chemically or physically, into a simpler substance.
- An atom is a submicroscopic particle made of even smaller components called protons, neutrons, and electrons.
- Atoms with the same number of protons but different numbers of neutrons are isotopes of an element.
- A compound is a substance that consists of two or more elements. Compounds form when electrons are transferred or shared to form bonds.
- When an atom's outermost energy level does not contain the maximum number of electrons, the atom is likely to form a chemical bond with one or more other atoms.
- Ionic bonds form between positive and negative ions. Covalent bonds form when atoms share electrons. Metallic bonds form when electrons are shared by metal ions.

Vocabulary

element, *p. 34*; atomic number, *p. 35*; energy level, *p. 38*; isotope, *p. 38*; mass number, *p. 38*; compound, *p. 39*; chemical bond, *p. 40*; ion, *p. 40*; ionic bond, *p. 40*; covalent bond, *p. 42*; metallic bond, *p. 43*

2.2 Minerals

Key Concepts

- A mineral is a naturally occurring, inorganic solid with an orderly internal structure and a definite chemical composition.
- There are four major processes by which minerals form: crystallization from magma, precipitation, changes in pressure and temperature, and formation from hydrothermal solutions.
- Common minerals, together with the thousands of others that form on Earth, can be classified into groups based on their composition.
- Silicates are the most common minerals on Earth and are made of millions of silicon-oxygen tetrahedra. Carbonates contain carbon, oxygen, and one or more other elements. Oxides contain oxygen and one or more other elements, usually metals. Sulfates and sulfides are minerals that contain sulfur. Halides contain a halogen ion plus one or more other elements. Native elements are minerals that exist in relatively pure form.

Vocabulary

mineral, *p. 45*; silicate, *p. 47*; silicon-oxygen tetrahedron, *p. 47*

2.3 Properties of Minerals

Key Concepts

- Small amounts of different elements can give the same mineral many different colors.
- Streak is the color of a mineral in its powdered form.
- Luster describes how light is reflected from the surface of a mineral.
- Crystal form is the visual expression of a mineral's internal arrangement of atoms.
- The Mohs scale is a scale that can be used to determine a mineral's hardness.
- Cleavage is the tendency of a mineral to cleave, or break along flat, even surfaces; fracture is uneven breakage.
- Density is a property of all matter that is the ratio of an object's mass to its volume.
- Some minerals can be recognized by other distinctive properties.

Vocabulary

streak, *p. 51*; luster, *p. 51*; crystal form, *p. 51*; hardness, *p. 52*; Mohs scale, *p. 52*; cleavage, *p. 52*; fracture, *p. 53*; density, *p. 53*

Thinking Visually

Observing Use what you have learned about minerals and Table 2 to list as many properties as possible of the mineral below.

Chapter Assessment Resources

Print
Chapter Test, Chapter 2
Test Prep Resources, Chapter 2

Technology
Computer Test Bank, Chapter 2 Test
Online Text, Chapter 2
Go Online, PHSchool.com, Chapter 2

NY Regents Content Item

Assessment

Interactive textbook with assessment at PHSchool.com 

Reviewing Content

Choose the number that best answers the question or completes the statement.

1 Which of the following is neutrally charged?
(1) an ion (2) a compound
(3) an electron (4) a proton

2 Atoms combine when
(1) their outer electron shells are filled
(2) their electrons are shared or transferred
(3) the number of protons and neutrons is the same
(4) the number of electrons and protons is the same

3 Compounds with low boiling points have
(1) metallic bonds (2) ionic bonds
(3) covalent bonds (4) no chemical bonds

4 Minerals that form from magma form as the result of NY
(1) crystallization (2) evaporation
(3) precipitation (4) condensation

5 The mineral barite ($BaSO_4$) is a(n)
(1) oxide (2) silicate
(3) carbonate (4) sulfate

6 Color is often not a useful identification property because NY
(1) some minerals are colorless
(2) the same mineral can be different colors
(3) different minerals can be different colors
(4) some minerals are single elements

7 What is a mineral's streak? NY
(1) the resistance to being scratched
(2) the color of the mineral in powder form
(3) the way in which the mineral reflects light
(4) the way the mineral reacts to hydrochloric acid

8 A particular mineral breaks like a piece of glass does. Which of these describes the breakage? NY
(1) cleavage (2) hardness
(3) metallic luster (4) fracture

9 Mineral properties depend on composition and NY
(1) structure (2) luster
(3) cleavage (4) streak

Understanding Concepts

10 Name the three types of particles found in an atom and explain how they differ.

11 Compare and contrast ionic and covalent bonds.

12 What are five characteristics of a mineral? NY

13 Explain three ways in which new minerals can form from existing minerals. NY

14 Contrast the composition of minerals in each of the mineral groups discussed in the chapter.

15 How is cleavage related to a mineral's atomic structure? NY

16 Give examples of four minerals that can be identified by unique properties. Describe each property. NY

Use this diagram to answer questions 17–21.

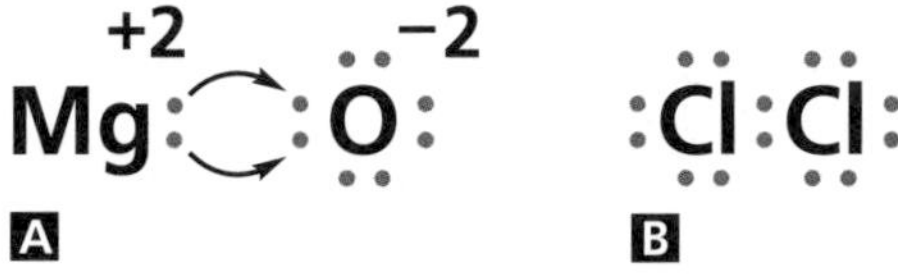

17 Briefly describe the kind of bond that is formed when two atoms shown in **A** bond.

18 Describe the kind of bond that forms when the atoms shown in **B** bond.

19 Is the atom on the left in **A** an ion? Explain your answer.

20 Use the periodic table to determine the atomic number of the atom on the left side of **A**. What group is this element in?

21 The atoms in **B** contain 17 protons. Are these atoms ions when they bond with each other? Can these atoms form ions when they react with other elements? Explain your answers.

Assessment (continued)

(13) New minerals can form from existing minerals when they are subjected to changes in temperature or changes in pressure and when the existing minerals are exposed to water at or near Earth's surface or to thermal solutions.
(14) Silicates contain silicon, oxygen, and often one or more other elements. Carbonates are made of carbon, oxygen, and one or more other elements. Oxides contain oxygen and one or more other elements, usually metals. Sulfates contain sulfur, oxygen, and one or more other elements. Sulfides also contain sulfur and one or more metallic elements. Halides are compounds that contain a halogen and one or more other elements. Native elements are minerals that exist as single elements.
(15) Some bonds in minerals are weaker than others. When a mineral is stressed, these bonds break to form flat, even surfaces.
(16) Graphite feels greasy; talc feel soapy. Magnetite is attracted to objects containing iron. Calcite has double refraction. Sulfur minerals have unique odors. Some carbonates such as calcite will fizz when exposed to HCl.
(17) Because an electron is being transferred from the magnesium to the oxygen, an ionic bond is formed.
(18) Because the chlorine atoms share electrons, a covalent bond is formed.
(19) Yes, because it contains a different number of electrons than protons.
(20) The atomic number is 12. The group is 2.
(21) No, the model shows them to be covalently bonded forming a molecule. Yes, chlorine atoms form ions when reacting with metals in Groups 1 and 2.

Homework Guide

Section	Questions
1	1–3, 10, 11, 17–24
2	4, 5, 12–14, 25–31
3	6–9, 15, 16, 32–34

Chapter 2

Critical Thinking

(22) The atoms are isotopes.
(23) KCl; potassium chloride
(24) Metals form metallic bonds with one another by sharing a pool of electrons. When a metal is pounded into a sheet or drawn into a wire, the electrons and the metallic ions merely shift their positions.
(25) Most silicates crystallize from magma as it cools. Silicates can also form as the result of changes in temperatures and pressures. Some silicate minerals form at Earth's surface when existing minerals are exposed to water. Other silicates form under the extreme pressures associated with mountain building.
(26) The mineral might form another mineral as the result of exposure to air and water, or it might react as the result of being subjected to lower pressures and temperatures at Earth's surface.
(27) a. carbonate
b. sulfide
c. chromate
d. halide
(28) The unit is the silicon-oxygen tetrahedron.
(29) They are single chains and double chains.
(30) Minerals with these structures will break along planes of weakness, that is, between the oxygen bonds, to form flat, even surfaces.
(31) The double chain structure is more complex because more tetrahedra combine to form two chains, rather than one.

Concepts in Action

(32) The mineral could be tested for hardness using either another diamond or a piece of corundum. If the mineral is a diamond, it will scratch the corundum and be as hard as the other diamond.
(33) Quartz and corundum are often used as abrasives because of their hardness. Graphite is a common lubricant because of its greasiness and softness. Mica is a common ingredient in many kinds of make-up.
(34) The volume of the brick is
30 cm × 8 cm × 4 cm = 960 cm^3
The mass would equal 960 cm^3 ×
19.3 g/cm^3 = 18,528 g or 18.5 kg
(rounded)

Assessment *continued*

Critical Thinking

22 **Comparing and Contrasting** Three atoms have the same atomic number but different mass numbers. What can you say about the atoms?

23 **Predicting** Potassium metal in group 1 of the periodic table is very reactive. When placed in chlorine gas, potassium reacts to form a halide compound. Using Figure 4 and the periodic table propose the formula and name for the compound.

24 **Formulating Hypotheses** Why do you think metals can easily be rolled into thin sheets and drawn into wires? (*Hint:* Think about the arrangement of electrons in metals.)

25 **Explaining** Explain the processes that result in the formation of silicate minerals.

26 **Formulating Hypotheses** A mineral forms deep beneath the surface. It reaches Earth's surface during mountain building. Describe two things that might happen to this mineral at the surface. NY

27 **Applying Concepts** Classify the following minerals based on their chemical formulas.

a. $NaCO_3$ *b.* PbS
c. $FeCr_2O_4$ *d.* CaF_2

Use the diagrams above to answer questions 28–31.

28 **Identifying** What is the basic structural unit in these two diagrams? NY

29 **Classifying** What are the names given to these two silicate structures?

30 **Applying Concepts** How do these two structures affect mineral breakage? NY

31 **Formulating Hypotheses** Which of the two structures is more complex? Explain your choice.

Concepts in Action

32 **Applying Concepts** Your friend shows you a crystal that he thinks is a diamond. Without asking an expert, how could you tell if the crystal is really a diamond? NY

33 **Hypothesizing** Which two minerals discussed in this chapter would be useful as abrasives? Which could be used as a lubricant? Which might be used in sparkly eye shadows?

34 **Calculating** Gold has a density of 19.3 g/cm^3. What would be the mass of a gold brick that is 30 cm long, 8 cm wide, and 4 cm tall? NY

Performance-Based Assessment

Applying Concepts Go on a scavenger hunt around your school or home to find at least 20 items that are minerals, that contain minerals, or that were obtained from minerals. Make a poster that shows what you found and display it for the class.

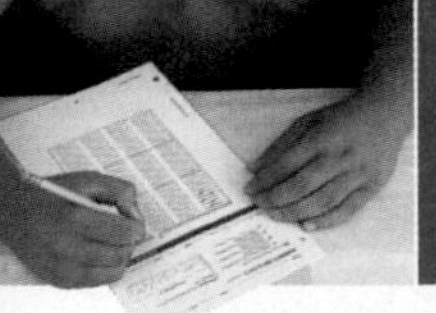

Regents Practice Exam

Test-Taking Tip

Evaluating
Sometimes an answer to a test question contains accurate information, but does not actually answer the question being asked. When this happens, follow the suggestions given below. Use this test-taking tip to answer questions 1–3 on this page.

- Reread the question several times if necessary.
- Check to see that the information in each answer choice is accurate.
- Eliminate answers you know are incorrect.
- Check to see that your answer choice answers the question being asked.

For *each* statement or question, choose the *number* of the word or expression that, of those given, best completes the statement or answers the question. Some questions may require the use of the *Earth Science Reference Tables.*

1 A hiker found a large deposit of the mineral halite. How did this deposit most likely form?
(1) evaporation of a large body of water
(2) cooling of magma
(3) geothermal activity
(4) weathering of metamorphic rocks

2 A jogger sees a clear mineral with cleavage, and a non-metallic, glassy luster that is easily scratched by a fingernail. This mineral should be identified as
(1) graphite (2) quartz
(3) fluorite (4) gypsum

3 Diamond and graphite have the same chemical composition, however their physical characteristics are very different. Which statement explains why they are different?
(1) Their colors are different.
(2) Their carbon atoms are arranged differently.
(3) They have different masses.
(4) Graphite's carbon is not radioactive.

Answer the following questions in complete sentences. Some questions may require the use of the *Earth Science Reference Tables.* Base your answers to questions 4 through 6 on the diagram below, which shows Mohs Scale of Hardness.

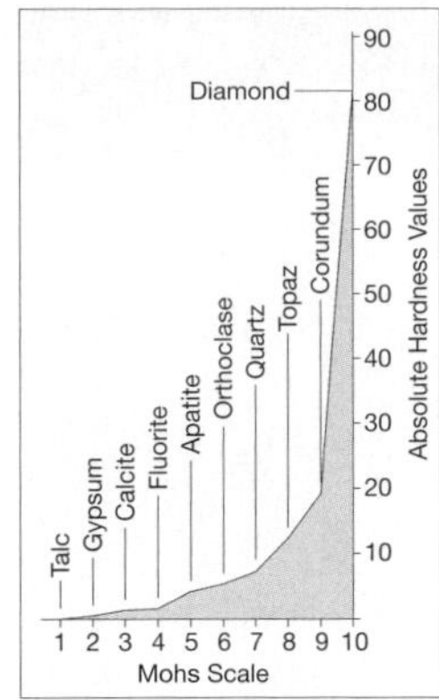

4 Which mineral could scratch calcite, but not apatite?

5 Which mineral can scratch all other minerals?

6 If your teacher gave you this graph with all the minerals listed on it (labeled *A* – *J*), explain how you could use hardness to determine the name of each sample.

7 List and explain how to perform three mineral tests useful for determining the identity of a mineral.

8 Use the definition of a mineral to explain the conditions under which H_2O could be considered a mineral.

Regents Practice Exam

(1) 1
(2) 4
(3) 2
(4) flourite
(5) diamond
(6) Answers will vary, but should show a logical process where the minerals' comparative hardnesses are determined. For example: take mineral *A* and try to scratch the others with it, put all minerals it scratched to the left, mineral *A* in the middle, and the minerals it could not scratch to the right. Repeat this process, preserving the order from softest to hardest, based on which minerals were scratched, until all minerals have been sequenced.
(7) Answers should include at least three of the following:

Luster is determined by observing how the mineral reflects light.

Cleavage and fracture are determined by hitting minerals with a hammer and observing how they break.

Density is determined by finding the mass and volume of a mineral and using the formula d=m/v.

Hardness is determined by attempting to scratch the mineral with objects of known hardness such as fingernail, penny, steel, glass, or other minerals.

Crystal form is determined by observing the shape of a mineral's crystals.

(8) When H_2O (water) is frozen (as ice) it can be considered a mineral because it is solid, inorganic, naturally occurring, has an orderly internal structure (crystal form), and a definite chemical composition.

Performance-Based Assessment

Students should be able to identify most items that are made of metals and glass. Other items that are minerals or obtained from minerals include table salt, pencil "lead," and gemstones in jewelry. Plastics would not be considered in this scavenger hunt because they are made from petroleum, which is an organic substance.

Your students can independently test their knowledge of the chapter and print out their results.

CHAPTER 3

Planning Guide

Use these planning tools
Use Teacher Express for all your planning needs

SECTION OBJECTIVES	STANDARDS NATIONAL	STANDARDS STATE	ACTIVITIES and LABS
3.1 The Rock Cycle, pp. 66–69 1 block or 2 periods 3.1 **Define** the term *rock*. 3.2 **Identify** the three major types of rocks and **explain** how they differ. 3.3 **Describe** the rock cycle. 3.4 **List** the forces that power Earth's rock cycle.	A-1, D-1, D-2		**SE** Inquiry Activity: What Are Some Similarities and Differences Among Rocks? p. 65 L2 **TE** Teacher Demo: Weathering, p. 68 L2 **TE** Build Science Skills, p. 68 L2
3.2 Igneous Rocks, pp. 70–74 1 block or 2 periods 3.5 **Compare and contrast** intrusive and extrusive igneous rocks. 3.6 **Demonstrate** how the rate of cooling affects an igneous rock's texture. 3.7 **Classify** igneous rocks according to texture and composition.	B-2		**TE** Build Science Skills, p. 70 L2 **TE** Teacher Demo: Crystal Formation, p. 72 L2
3.3 Sedimentary Rocks, pp. 75–79 1 block or 2 periods 3.8 **Describe** the major processes involved in the formation of sedimentary rocks. 3.9 **Distinguish** between clastic sedimentary rocks and chemical sedimentary rocks. 3.10 **Identify** the features that are unique to some sedimentary rocks.	D-2, D-3		**TE** Address Misconceptions, p. 76 L2 **TE** Build Science Skills, p. 76 L2 **TE** Teacher Demo: Chemical Weathering, p. 77 L2 **TE** Build Science Skills, p. 78 L2
3.4 Metamorphic Rocks, pp. 80–84 1 block or 2 periods 3.11 **Predict** where most metamorphism takes place. 3.12 **Distinguish** contact metamorphism from regional metamorphism. 3.13 **Identify** the three agents of metamorphism and **explain** what changes they cause. 3.14 **Recognize** foliated metamorphic rocks and **describe** how they form. 3.15 **Classify** metamorphic rocks.	A-1, A-2, B-3, D-2		**SE** Quick Lab: Observing Some of the Effects of Pressure on Mineral Grains, p. 82 L2 **SE** Exploration Lab: Rock Identification, pp. 86–87 L2 **LM** Classifying Rocks Using a Key L1

Ability Levels	
L1	For students who need additional help
L2	For all students
L3	For students who need to be challenged

Components

SE	Student Edition	**GRSW**	Guided Reading & Study Workbook	**TP**	Test Prep Resources	**GEO**	Geode CD-ROM
TE	Teacher's Edition			**onT**	onlineText	**T**	Transparencies
LM	Laboratory Manual	**TEX**	Teacher Express	**DC**	Discovery Channel Videos	**GO**	Internet Resources
CUT	Chapter Tests	**CTB**	Computer Test Bank				

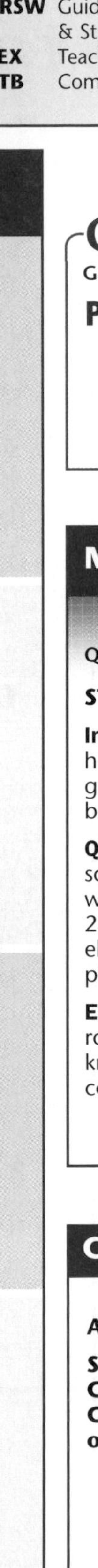

RESOURCES PRINT and TECHNOLOGY	SECTION ASSESSMENT
GRSW Section 3.1 **T-14** Rock Cycle **DC** The Rock Cycle **TEX** Lesson Planning 3.1 GEODE Earth Materials ↳ Rock Cycle	**SE** Section 3.1 Assessment, p. 69 **onT** Section 3.1
GRSW Section 3.2 **T-15** Bowen's Reaction Series **T-16** Evolution of Magma **T-17** Classification of Igneous Rocks **TEX** Lesson Planning 3.2 GEODE Earth Materials ↳ Igneous Rocks	**SE** Section 3.2 Assessment, p. 74 **onT** Section 3.2
GRSW Section 3.3 **T-18** Classification of Sedimentary Rocks **T-19** Formation of Coal **TEX** Lesson Planning 3.3 GEODE Earth Materials ↳ Sedimentary Rocks	**SE** Section 3.3 Assessment, p. 79 **onT** Section 3.3
GRSW Section 3.4 **T-20** Pressure as a Metamorphic Agent **T-21** Classification of Metamorphic Rocks **T-22** The Carbon Cycle **TEX** Lesson Planning 3.4 GEODE Earth Materials ↳ Metamorphic Rocks	**SE** Section 3.4 Assessment, p. 84 **onT** Section 3.4

Go Online

Go online for these Internet resources.

PHSchool.com
Web Code: cjk-9999

NSTA SCILINKS
Web Code: cjn-1032
Web Code: cjn-1033
Web Code: cjn-1034

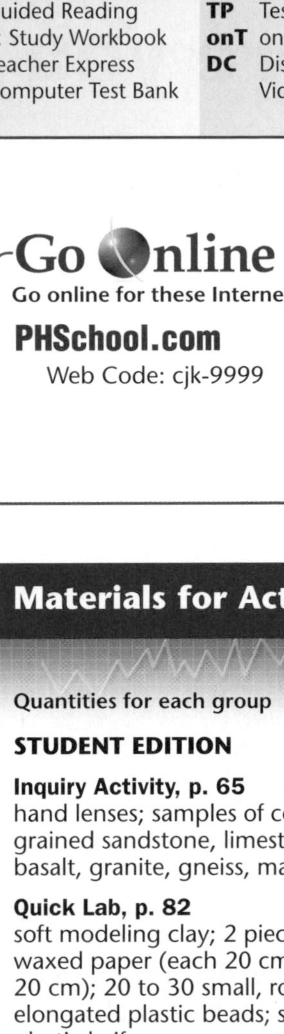

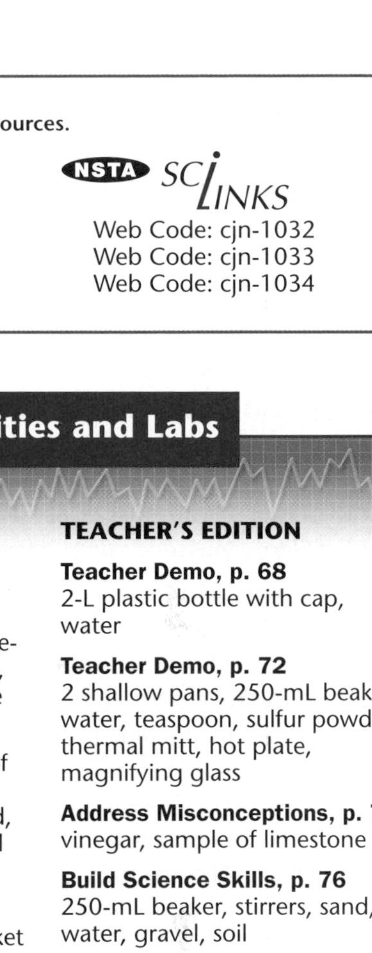

Materials for Activities and Labs

Quantities for each group

STUDENT EDITION

Inquiry Activity, p. 65
hand lenses; samples of coarse-grained sandstone, limestone, basalt, granite, gneiss, marble

Quick Lab, p. 82
soft modeling clay; 2 pieces of waxed paper (each 20 cm × 20 cm); 20 to 30 small, round, elongated plastic beads; small plastic knife

Exploration Lab, pp. 86–87
rock samples, hand lens, pocket knife, dilute hydrochloric acid, colored pencils

TEACHER'S EDITION

Teacher Demo, p. 68
2-L plastic bottle with cap, water

Teacher Demo, p. 72
2 shallow pans, 250-mL beaker, water, teaspoon, sulfur powder, thermal mitt, hot plate, magnifying glass

Address Misconceptions, p. 76
vinegar, sample of limestone

Build Science Skills, p. 76
250-mL beaker, stirrers, sand, water, gravel, soil

Teacher Demo, p. 77
calcium tablet, 250-mL beaker, vinegar

Chapter Assessment

ASSESSMENT

SE Assessment, pp. 89–90
CUT Chapter 3 Test
CTB Chapter 3
onT Chapter 3

STANDARDIZED TEST PREP

SE Chapter 3, p. 91
TP Progress Monitoring Assessments

interactive textbook with assessment at PHSchool.com

CHAPTER 3

Before you teach

Michael Wysession
Washington University

Big Ideas

Rocks are solid mixtures of one or more minerals. The study of igneous, sedimentary, and metamorphic rocks is the foundation of geology.

Space and Time Rocks occupy 5/6 of the volume of Earth and account for 2/3 of its mass (the rest consists of metal alloys in the core). The oldest rocks are meteorites, more than 4.5 billion years old, which formed at the same time as Earth.

Forces and Motion Igneous, sedimentary, and metamorphic rocks are interconnected by a set of processes called the rock cycle. A common path through the rock cycle is for igneous rock to be weathered, transported, and deposited to eventually become sedimentary rock. Then this sedimentary rock is subjected to high temperatures and pressures that turn it into metamorphic rock. Eventually the metamorphic rock melts to become new igneous rock. However, different geological histories result in different paths through the rock cycle.

Matter and Energy There are many factors that affect the appearance of a rock. For igneous rocks, these factors include the composition and the rate of cooling. For sedimentary rocks, these include the types of sediment compacted (clastic, chemical, biological). For metamorphic rocks, these include the amounts of heat, pressure, and hot fluids the rocks are exposed to.

Earth as a System Rocks are scientifically important because their characteristics are a unique result of the history of their formation. This provides geologists with a kind of time machine that lets them learn about the conditions that existed on Earth long ago.

Earth Science Refresher

Different Igneous Rocks

In addition to there being many different kinds of minerals, there are many different kinds of rocks. While this might seem reasonable for sedimentary and metamorphic rocks (after all, if you start with different kinds of sediments or bedrock, you will end up with different sedimentary or metamorphic rocks), why should this be the case for igneous rocks? The reason is that minerals crystallize and melt at different temperatures. This simple fact has given rise to a wide diversity of igneous rock types. When the initially molten Earth began to cool and crystallize, there wasn't just one kind of igneous rock formed—there was a whole range.

Bowen's Reaction Series

The process of igneous rock formation is called Bowen's reaction series. When magma begins to crystallize, there is a particular order in which the minerals solidify. There are two sets of reactions that are going on at the same time. In one set, olivine crystallizes first, then pyroxene, amphibole, and then biotite. In the other set, calcium-rich plagioclase feldspar first crystallizes, changing to being sodium-rich as the temperature lowers. The last minerals to crystallize are potassium feldspar, muscovite, and quartz. Why does this reaction series happen? Part of the reason has to do with the way the SiO_2 tetrahedra are connected in the minerals. In the olivine, individual SiO_2 tetrahedra are bonded to other ions. This is fairly easy to construct, so olivine crystallizes easily. The micas require the silica tetrahedra to form sheets, and as this is harder to do, they take longer to crystallize. Lastly, the quartz has a dense 3-D structure of interconnected silica tetrahedra. This is the hardest to form, so it crystallizes last. With minerals forming at different times, they also end up forming in different places, with the result that different kinds of rocks are created.

Students may mistakenly believe that rocks are stronger than the forces of nature. The agents of mechanical and chemical weathering can break down rocks over time. For a strategy that helps to overcome this misconception, see **Address Misconceptions** on **p. 76.**

Go Online NSTA PD LINKS

For: Chapter 3 Content Support
Visit: www.SciLinks.org/PDLinks
Web Code: cjn-0399

Example of Crystallization: The Palisades Cliffs

There are many examples of the crystallization process, such as the Palisades Cliffs of New Jersey, across the Hudson River from Manhattan. The Palisades formed as an igneous sill, up to 600 m thick, about 200 million years ago when Africa and North America rifted apart. The bottom third of the cliffs are rich in olivine, which crystallized first and settled out to the bottom of the sill. The middle third of the sill is largely made of pyroxene, which crystallized after the olivine. During these processes, the feldspar composition changed from being calcium-rich to sodium-rich, so that sodium-rich feldspar dominates the top third of the cliffs.

Example of Melting: Granite Batholiths

Did you ever wonder why the cores of many mountain ranges, such as the Appalachians or the Sierra-Nevadas, are made of granite? The reason is Bowen's reaction series in reverse. When continents collide, rock gets thrust up (to form mountains) and also down. The rock that is pushed down becomes hotter with depth, and eventually begins to melt. The first minerals to melt are the ones at the bottom of the reaction series: quartz, muscovite, and potassium feldspar, which are the main ingredients of granite. This melt is buoyant, so it rises up into the heart of the mountain range. Here, temperatures are cooler, so the magma crystallizes to form granite. If the plate collision occurs for a long time, a lot of granite can be generated. When erosion removes the mountain tops, the granite batholiths are exposed.

Build Reading Literacy

Directed Reading/Thinking Activity (DRTA)

Predict, Read, Confirm, Revise Predictions

Strategy Help students develop their own reading and thinking processes by setting their own purposes for reading. Select a section of Chapter 3 for students to read, such as Section 3.1, pp. 66–69. Before modeling the strategy with students, divide the targeted section into approximately four equal portions. Present the steps in the example below.

Example

1. **Preview** Tell students to survey the section by analyzing the titles, headings, visual elements, and boldfaced type. Have students also read the introductory and concluding paragraphs.
2. **Predict/Generate Questions** Ask students to hypothesize and predict what they will learn, and to formulate their own "teacher-type" questions to be answered; that is, of the type that a teacher might ask. List students' responses on the board.
3. **Read/Evaluate and Refine Predictions** Have students read a portion of the section. Pause afterward for students to evaluate their predictions. Discuss any answers they learned to their questions, and any prior misconceptions that were clarified. Ask students to formulate refined predictions and questions based on the new information.
4. Repeat the process for the remaining text portions.

See p. 76 for a script on how to use this strategy with students. For additional strategies, see pp. 67, 72, and 83.

ASSESS PRIOR KNOWLEDGE

Use the Chapter Pretest below to assess students' prior knowledge. As needed, review these concepts.

Review Science Concepts

Section 3.1 Encourage students to recall what they know about different states of matter. Review the structure of an atom.

Section 3.2 Review the definition of a mineral. Have students compare and contrast different types of classification systems. Also, discuss the composition of Earth's crust.

Section 3.3 and **Section 3.4** Have students explain how minerals form. Ask them to describe some tests they could perform to identify minerals.

CHAPTER 3 Rocks

CONCEPTS in Action

Quick Lab
Observing Some of the Effects of Pressure on Mineral Grains

Exploration Lab
Rock Identification

Earth as a System
The Carbon Cycle

Earth Materials
↳ Rock Cycle
Igneous Rocks
Sedimentary Rocks
Metamorphic Rocks

Discovery Channel School **Video Field Trip**
The Rock Cycle

Take a field trip through the rock cycle with Discovery Channel and learn about how rocks are constantly forming, changing, and eroding.

1. Name two natural forces that lead to rock erosion.
2. What can happen to rock that is buried beneath Earth's surface?

For: Chapter 3 Resources
Visit: PHSchool.com
Web Code: cjk-9999

Columns of rock called hoodoos dot ▶ Bryce Canyon National Park.

64 *Chapter 3*

Chapter Pretest

1. Describe the strength of bonds between atoms in a solid. *(Atoms in a solid are tightly bound together.)*
2. What is a mineral? *(A mineral is a naturally occurring, inorganic solid with a definite chemical structure and unique physical properties.)*
3. True or False: Only eight elements make up the bulk of the minerals found in Earth's crust. *(True)*
4. What is the most common mineral group? *(b)*
   a. carbonates b. silicates
   c. oxides d. halides
5. What are rock-forming minerals? *(minerals that make up most of the rocks of Earth's crust)*
6. What are some common properties of minerals? *(crystal form, luster, color, streak, hardness, cleavage, fracture, and specific gravity)*

Chapter Preview

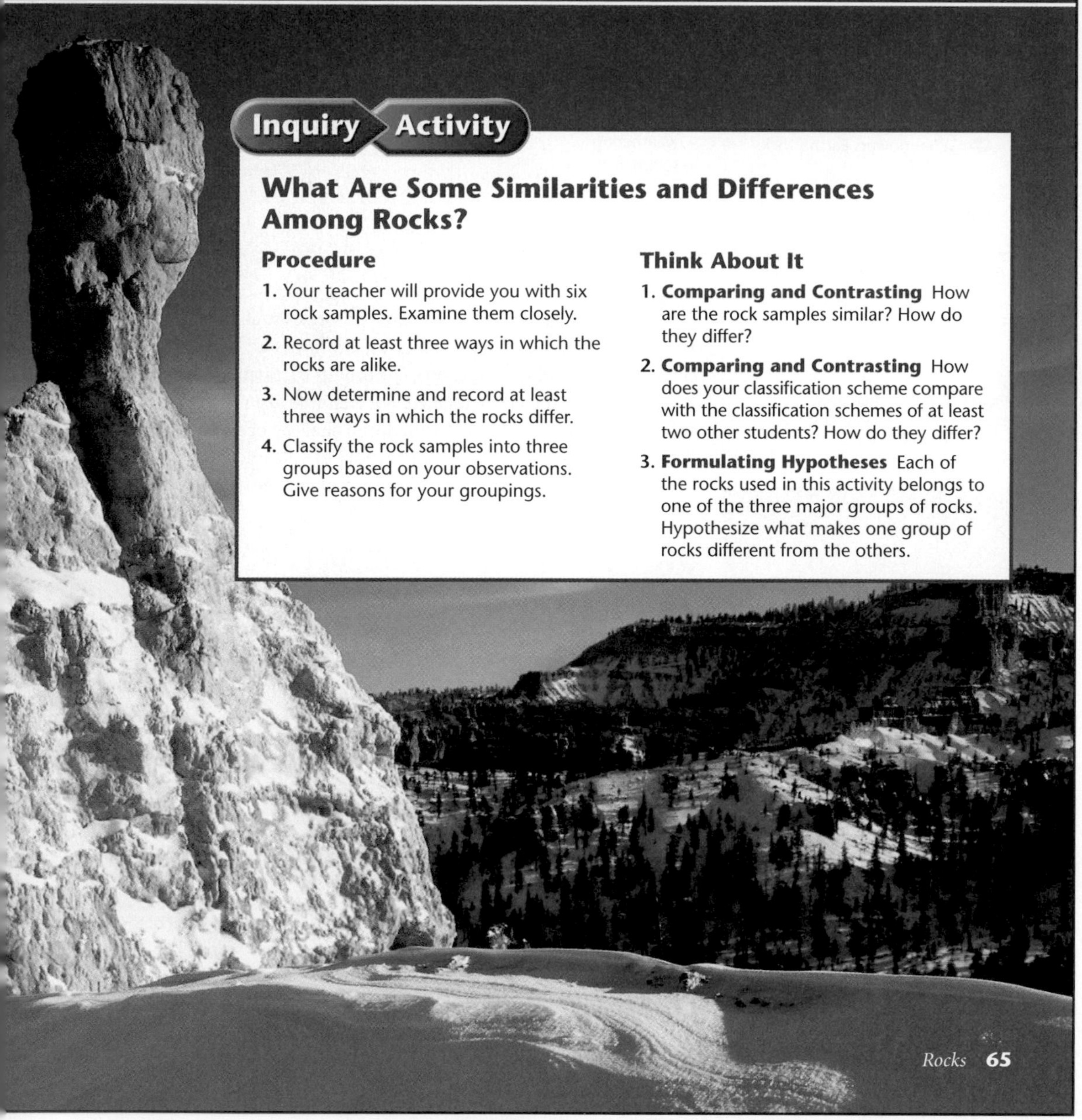

Inquiry Activity

What Are Some Similarities and Differences Among Rocks?

Procedure

1. Your teacher will provide you with six rock samples. Examine them closely.
2. Record at least three ways in which the rocks are alike.
3. Now determine and record at least three ways in which the rocks differ.
4. Classify the rock samples into three groups based on your observations. Give reasons for your groupings.

Think About It

1. **Comparing and Contrasting** How are the rock samples similar? How do they differ?
2. **Comparing and Contrasting** How does your classification scheme compare with the classification schemes of at least two other students? How do they differ?
3. **Formulating Hypotheses** Each of the rocks used in this activity belongs to one of the three major groups of rocks. Hypothesize what makes one group of rocks different from the others.

Video Field Trip

The Rock Cycle

Encourage students to view the video field trip "The Rock Cycle."

ENGAGE/EXPLORE

Inquiry Activity

What Are Some Similarities and Differences Among Rocks? L2

Purpose Students will classify six rocks into three groups using similarities and differences among the rocks.

Skills Focus Observing, Comparing and Contrasting, Classifying

 **Prep Time** 10–15 minutes

Materials hand lenses, samples of coarse-grained sandstone, limestone, basalt, granite, gneiss, and marble

Class Time 20–25 minutes

Teaching Tip Have students note differences and similarities in the way each sample feels when rubbed with the fingers (smooth or rough), the texture of each sample (the size, shape, and arrangement of the minerals in the rock), and the overall color of the rocks (light-colored or dark-colored).

Expected Outcome Students will find that size, texture, color, shape, and composition account for most differences and similarities among the rocks.

Think About It

1. Similarities might include the color, shape, size, texture, or composition of the rocks. Some students might also state that all rocks are solids or that all rocks appear to be mixtures. Differences among the samples include size, shape, composition, color, and texture.

2. Most students will probably attempt to classify the rocks based on color or texture. For example, students might group limestone and marble based on similarities in color and texture. They might use color and mineral composition to place granite and gneiss in the same group. Students might put sandstone and basalt into a group based on their unique textures. Accept any reasonable classification schemes.

3. Accept any reasonable response—color, texture, or composition. Some students might be able to infer that rocks can be classified according to the way they were formed.

1 FOCUS

Section Objectives

3.1 **Define** the term *rock*.

3.2 **Identify** the three major types of rocks and **explain** how they differ.

3.3 **Describe** the rock cycle.

3.4 **List** the forces that power Earth's rock cycle.

Reading Focus

Build Vocabulary L2

Cycle Diagram Have students construct a cycle diagram of the rock cycle. Students should use the terms *igneous rock, sedimentary rock, metamorphic rock, sediments, magma,* and *lava* to indicate the materials involved in the rock cycle. The processes of the rock cycle are shown in Figure 2 on p. 67. Tell students to place the terms in ovals and use labeled arrows to indicate how one process leads to another.

Reading Strategy L2

a. a solid mixture of one or more minerals
b. rock that forms when magma or lava cools and hardens
c. rock that forms when sediments become compacted and cemented
d. bits of earth materials

2 INSTRUCT

Rocks

Use Visuals L1

Figure 1 Ask: **How does the texture of obsidian compare with that of pumice?** *(Obsidian is smooth; pumice is rough.)* **What other differences do you see?** *(Sample answer: The color and shape of the samples are different.)* **Visual**

3.1 The Rock Cycle

Reading Focus

Key Concepts

- What is a rock?
- What are the three major types of rocks?
- How do igneous, sedimentary, and metamorphic rocks differ?
- What is the rock cycle?
- What powers Earth's rock cycle?

Vocabulary

- rock
- igneous rock
- sedimentary rock
- metamorphic rock
- rock cycle
- magma
- lava
- weathering
- sediments

Reading Strategy

Building Vocabulary Copy and expand the table to include each vocabulary term. As you read, write down the definition for each term.

Term	Definition
rock	a. ?
igneous rock	b. ?
sedimentary rock	c. ?
sediments	d. ?

Why do we study rocks? All Earth processes such as volcanic eruptions, mountain building, weathering, erosion, and even earthquakes involve rocks and minerals. Rocks contain clues about the environments in which they were formed. For example, if a rock contains shell fragments, it was probably formed in a shallow ocean environment. The locations of volcanic rocks tell a story of volcanic activity on Earth through time. Thus, you can see that a basic knowledge of rocks is essential to understanding the Earth.

Figure 1 **A** Obsidian and **B** pumice are two examples of rocks that do not have a crystalline structure.

Rocks

A rock is any solid mass of mineral or mineral-like matter that occurs naturally as part of our planet. A few rocks are composed of just one mineral. However, most rocks, like granite, occur as solid mixtures of minerals. A characteristic of rock is that each of the component minerals retains their properties in the mixture. A few rocks are composed of nonmineral matter. Coal is considered a rock even though it consists of organic material. Obsidian and pumice, shown in Figure 1, are volcanic rocks that do not have a crystalline structure.

Rocks are classified into three groups based on how they were formed. **The three major types of rocks are igneous rocks, sedimentary rocks, and metamorphic rocks.** Before examining each group, you will look at a model for the rock cycle, which is the process that shows the relationships between the rock groups.

What are the three types of rocks?

The Rock Cycle

Earth is a system. It consists of many interacting parts that form a complex whole. **Interactions among Earth's water, air, and land can cause rocks to change from one type to another. The continuous processes that cause rocks to change make up the rock cycle.** Most changes in the rock cycle take place over long periods of time.

Figure 2 shows some key events in the rock cycle. Refer to the figure throughout this section as you examine how rock might change over time. Look at Figures 2A and 2B. **Magma** is molten material that forms deep beneath Earth's surface. **When magma cools and hardens beneath the surface or as the result of a volcanic eruption, igneous rock forms.** Magma that reaches the surface is called **lava.**

Rock Cycle

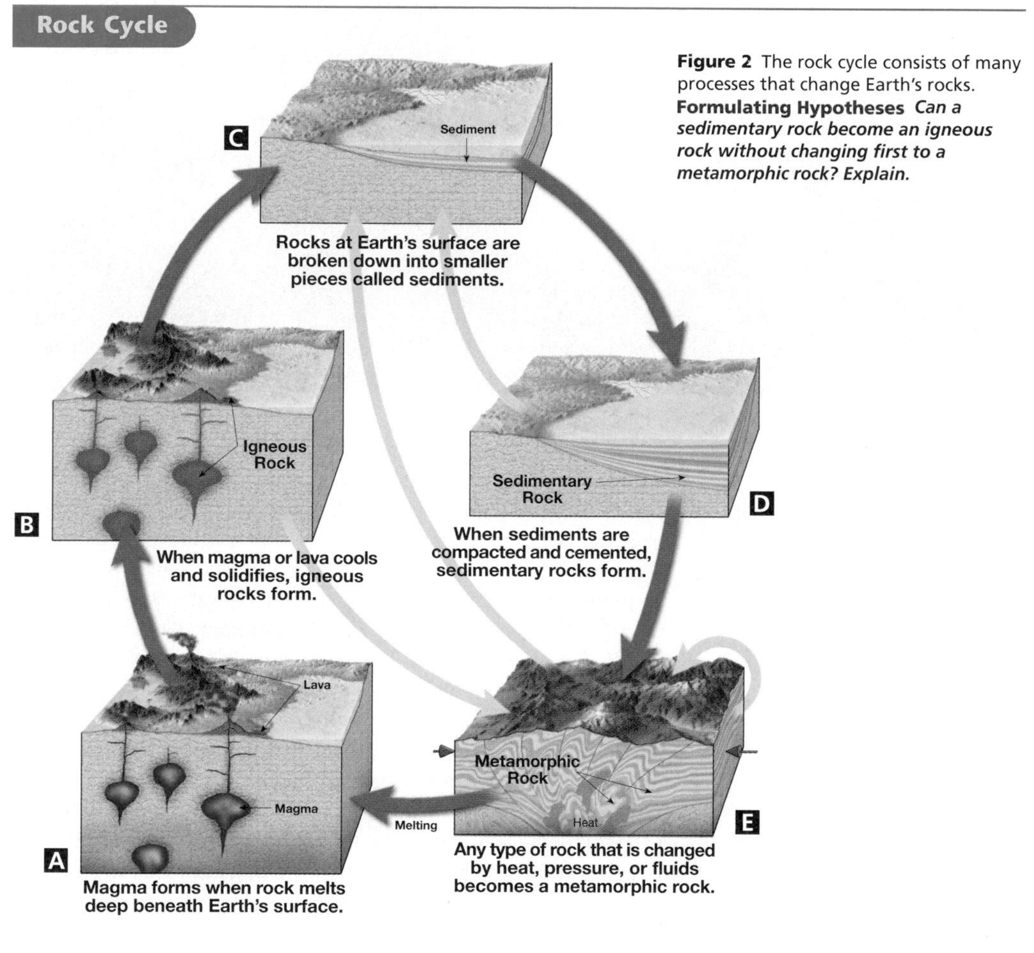
C
Sediment
Rocks at Earth's surface are broken down into smaller pieces called sediments.
Igneous Rock
B
When magma or lava cools and solidifies, igneous rocks form.
Sedimentary Rock
D
When sediments are compacted and cemented, sedimentary rocks form.
Lava
Magma
A
Magma forms when rock melts deep beneath Earth's surface.
Metamorphic Rock
Melting
Heat
E
Any type of rock that is changed by heat, pressure, or fluids becomes a metamorphic rock.

Figure 2 The rock cycle consists of many processes that change Earth's rocks. **Formulating Hypotheses** ***Can a sedimentary rock become an igneous rock without changing first to a metamorphic rock? Explain.***

Customize for English Language Learners

Encourage students to compile vocabulary terms into a science glossary. Have students consult dictionaries to obtain the pronunciation and definition of each term and then write these items in their glossaries. Model how to use the dictionary to determine the proper pronunciation of difficult words, such as *igneous* or *metamorphic*. Students may also want to draw simple diagrams next to the terms to further help them to remember each word's meaning. To reinforce language skills, have students arrange the terms in alphabetical order.

The Rock Cycle

Use Visuals L1

Figure 2 Point out that the arrows represent the processes that link each group to the others. Ask: **What processes form sedimentary rocks?** *(compaction and cementation)* **What possible changes might a sedimentary rock undergo?** *(A sedimentary rock might be broken back down into sediments. Heat and pressure could change it into a metamorphic rock.)* **What type of rock is formed by cooling magma or lava?** *(igneous rock)* **What happens to igneous rock that is weathered?** *(It is broken down into sediments.)*
Visual

Build Reading Literacy 

Refer to **p. 186D** in **Chapter 7**, which provides the guidelines for relating text and visuals.

Relate Text and Visuals Tell students to read the text on pp. 67–68. Have them list any concepts about the rock cycle that are unclear or difficult to understand. Write a few of these concepts on the board. Then have students carefully study Figure 2. Using the list on the board, have volunteers explain how the visual helped them to better understand the rock cycle.
Verbal, Visual

Answer to . . .

Figure 2 *No, because any change in temperature and/or pressure will cause the sedimentary rock to become a metamorphic rock. If the temperatures and/or pressures are great enough, the metamorphic rock will melt to form magma, which will crystallize to form an igneous rock.*

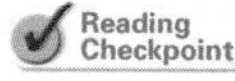
Reading Checkpoint

Igneous rocks, sedimentary rocks, and metamorphic rocks are the three major types of rocks. Igneous rocks form when magma or lava cools. Sedimentary rocks form when sediments become compacted and cemented. Metamorphic rocks form when existing rocks are changed by heat, pressure, or solutions.

Teacher Demo

Weathering L2

Purpose Students will observe how ice can be an agent of weathering.

Materials 2-L plastic bottle with cap, water

Procedure Fill the plastic bottle nearly full with water and put on the cap. Have students note the level of the water. Place the bottle in the freezer for several hours, then have students observe the frozen water.

Expected Outcome Students will observe how the ice expanded and distorted the bottle. Tell them that in a similar way, water can seep through cracks and pores in rocks, then freeze and expand to break apart the rocks.
Visual

Build Science Skills L2

Using Models Have students work with a partner to design simple models that show how pressure affects rocks. For example, students can place a heavy textbook on a sandwich or squeeze a piece of modeling clay between their hands.
Kinesthetic, Interpersonal

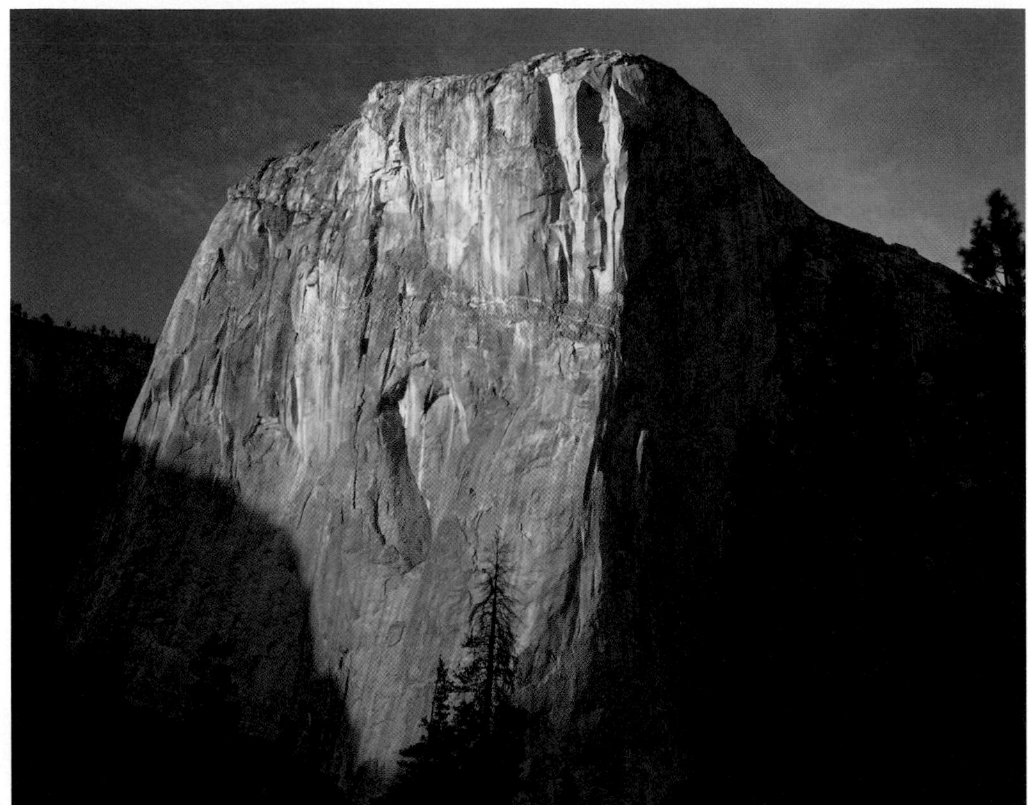

Figure 3 El Capitan in Yosemite National Park This granite was once buried deep beneath Earth's surface. Now that it is exposed, it will eventually weather and form sediments.

What will happen if an igneous rock that formed deep within Earth is exposed at the surface? Any rock at Earth's surface, including the granite shown in Figure 3, will undergo weathering. **Weathering** is a process in which rocks are physically and chemically broken down by water, air, and living things. These weathered pieces of earth materials are **sediments.** Sediments are often moved by water, gravity, glaciers, or wind. **Eventually, sediments are compacted and cemented to form sedimentary rock, as shown in Figure 2C and 2D.**

If the sedimentary rocks become buried deep within Earth, they will be subjected to increases in pressure and/or temperature. **Under extreme pressure and temperature conditions, sedimentary rock will change into metamorphic rock, as shown in Figure 2E.** If the metamorphic rocks are subjected to additional pressure changes or to still higher temperatures, they may melt to form magma. The magma will eventually crystallize to form igneous rock once again.

Facts and Figures

Some of the most important accumulations of metals, such as gold, silver, copper, mercury, lead, platinum, and nickel, are produced by igneous and metamorphic processes. For example, as a large magma body cools, the heavy minerals that crystallize early tend to settle to the lower portion of the magma chamber. This type of process is particularly active in large basaltic magmas where chromite, magnetite, and platinum are occasionally generated. Layers of chromite, an ore of chromium, are mined from such deposits in the Bushveld Complex in South Africa, which contains more than 70 percent of the world's known platinum reserves.

Alternate Paths

The purple arrows in Figure 2 show only one way in which an igneous rock might form and change. Other paths are just as likely to be taken as an igneous rock goes through the rock cycle. The blue arrows show a few of these alternate paths.

Suppose, for example, that an igneous rock remained deeply buried. Eventually, the rock could be subjected to strong forces and high temperatures such as those associated with mountain building. Then, the igneous rock could change into one or more kinds of metamorphic rock. If the temperatures and pressures were high enough, the igneous rock could melt and recrystallize to form new igneous rock.

Figure 4 The roof on this house is made of slate. Slate is a metamorphic rock that forms from the sedimentary rock shale. **Explaining** *How can shale become slate?*

Metamorphic and sedimentary rocks, as well as sediment, do not always remain buried. Often, overlying rocks are stripped away, exposing the rock that was once buried. When this happens, the rocks weather to form sediments that eventually become sedimentary rocks. However, if the sedimentary rocks become buried again, metamorphic rocks, like those used for the roof tiles in Figure 4, will form.

Where does the energy that drives Earth's rock cycle come from? **Processes driven by heat from Earth's interior are responsible for forming both igneous and metamorphic rocks. Weathering and the movement of weathered materials are external processes powered by energy from the sun. External processes produce sedimentary rocks.**

Section 3.1 Assessment

Reviewing Concepts

1. What is a rock?
2. What are the three major types of rocks?
3. How do igneous, sedimentary, and metamorphic rocks differ?
4. What is the rock cycle?
5. What powers Earth's rock cycle?

Critical Thinking

6. **Comparing and Contrasting** Compare and contrast igneous and metamorphic rocks.
7. **Applying Concepts** How might a sedimentary rock become an igneous rock?
8. **Applying Concepts** List in order the processes that could change one sedimentary rock into another sedimentary rock.

Writing in Science

Writing to Persuade Coral reefs are made of calcite that is secreted by the corals and algae that make up the reefs. Over time, this calcite accumulates to form limestone. Use what you know about minerals and rocks to write a paragraph explaining whether or not you think that this limestone is a rock.

Alternate Paths

Use Community Resources L2

Invite a construction contractor to discuss with the class how various rocks are used as building materials. Ask the contractor to bring in sample supplies for students to examine. Have students prepare by brainstorming questions to ask the contractor about the different qualities of rocks, such as durability and strength.
Verbal

3 ASSESS

Evaluate Understanding L2

Have students draw sketches illustrating the source of the energy that drives the rock cycle. For example, to represent the interior processes that form igneous rocks, a sketch might show molten material deep inside Earth.

Reteach L1

Use Figure 2 to draw a diagram of the rock cycle that does not include arrows. Make copies of the diagram and distribute it to students. Have students add arrows showing the relationships among the processes of the rock cycle.

Writing in Science

Students should recall that most limestones are made from organic sediments such as shells and the secretions of corals. This limestone is a biochemical sedimentary rock.

Answer to . . .

Figure 4 *If shale is subjected to an increase in pressure and/or temperature, it can become the metamorphic rock called slate.*

Section 3.1 Assessment

1. Most rocks are mixtures of one or more minerals. Some rocks, however, are not made of minerals.
2. igneous rocks, sedimentary rocks, and metamorphic rocks
3. Rocks differ in the way they form. Igneous rocks form when magma or lava cools and solidifies. Sedimentary rocks form when sediments become compacted and cemented. Metamorphic rocks form when existing rocks are changed by heat, pressure, or solutions.
4. interactions among Earth's water, air, and land which cause rocks to change
5. processes deep within Earth and energy from the sun
6. Both form as the result of increases in pressure or temperature. Igneous rock formation involves melting, while the formation of metamorphic rocks does not.
7. The sedimentary rock could become buried at depths where temperatures and pressures were great enough to cause melting. When the melted material (magma) cooled and hardened, an igneous rock would form.
8. weathering, transportation, deposition, compaction, and cementation

Section 3.2

1 FOCUS

Section Objectives

3.5 **Compare and contrast** intrusive and extrusive igneous rocks.

3.6 **Demonstrate** how the rate of cooling affects an igneous rock's texture.

3.7 **Classify** igneous rocks according to texture and composition.

Reading Focus

Build Vocabulary L2

Word Parts To help students distinguish between intrusive and extrusive rocks, have them look up the meanings of the prefixes *in-* and *ex-*. Students will find that both prefixes stem from Latin terms. *In-* means "within or into"; *ex-* means "out of" or "outside." Point out that by knowing the meaning of these prefixes, students can better remember which igneous rocks form "within" Earth and which form "outside," or on, Earth's surface.

Reading Strategy L2

A.1. rock that forms when magma hardens beneath Earth's surface
A.2. Common example of igneous intrusive rock is granite.
B.1. rock that forms when lava hardens
B.2. Common example of igneous extrusive rock is rhyolite.

2 INSTRUCT

Build Science Skills L2

Inferring Reiterate that magma, which occurs beneath Earth's surface, often cools more slowly than lava, which occurs at Earth's surface. Then have students examine Figure 5. Ask them to use the photograph to infer why lava often cools more quickly than magma. *(Lava is exposed to air and water, which speeds up its cooling rate.)*
Logical

3.2 Igneous Rocks

Reading Focus

Key Concepts

- How are intrusive and extrusive igneous rocks alike and different?
- How does the rate of cooling affect an igneous rock's texture?
- How are igneous rocks classified according to composition?

Vocabulary

- intrusive igneous rock
- extrusive igneous rock
- porphyritic texture
- granitic composition
- basaltic composition
- andesitic composition
- ultramafic

Reading Strategy

Outlining Copy the outline and complete it as you read. Include points about how each of these rocks form, some of the characteristics of each rock type, and some examples of each.

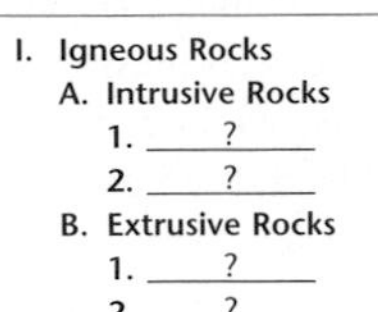
I. Igneous Rocks
A. Intrusive Rocks
1. ____?____
2. ____?____
B. Extrusive Rocks
1. ____?____
2. ____?____

Recall from the discussion of the rock cycle that igneous rocks form when magma or lava cools and hardens. When the red hot lava shown in Figure 5 cools, a dark-colored igneous rock called basalt will form. If this melted material had stayed deep beneath Earth's surface, a very different kind of igneous rock would have been produced as the material cooled. Different kinds of igneous rocks form when magma and lava cool and harden.

Figure 5 Basaltic Lava Lava from this Hawaiian volcano flows easily over Earth's surface. When this lava cools and hardens, the igneous rock called basalt will form.

Formation of Igneous Rocks

The word *igneous* comes from the Latin word *ignis,* which means "fire." Perhaps that is why people often associate igneous rock with fiery volcanic eruptions like the one shown in Figure 5. Igneous rock also forms deep beneath Earth's surface.

Figure 6 **A** Granite is an intrusive igneous rock that forms when magma cools slowly beneath Earth's surface. **B** Rhyolite is an extrusive igneous rock that forms when lava cools quickly at Earth's surface.

Intrusive Igneous Rocks **Rocks that form when magma hardens beneath Earth's surface are called intrusive igneous rocks.** That is because they *intrude* into the existing rocks. We would never see these deep rocks were it not for erosion stripping away the overlying rock.

Magma consists mainly of the elements silicon and oxygen, plus aluminum, iron, calcium, sodium, potassium, and magnesium. Magma also contains some gases, including water vapor. These gases are kept within the magma by the pressure of the surrounding rocks. Because magma is less dense than the surrounding rocks, it slowly works its way toward the surface. As magma rises, it cools, allowing elements to combine and form minerals. Gradually, the minerals grow in size, forming a solid mass of interlocking crystals. Granite, shown in Figure 6A, is a common intrusive igneous rock.

Extrusive Igneous Rocks You know that when magma reaches Earth's surface, it is called lava. Lava is similar to magma, except that in lava, most of the gases have escaped. **When lava hardens, the rocks that form are called extrusive igneous rocks.** That is because they are *extruded* onto the surface The rhyolite shown in Figure 6B is an extrusive igneous rock.

Q *How are magma and lava the same, and how are they different?*

A Magma and lava are both terms used to describe melted rock. The composition of magma and lava can be the same. However, magma is melted material beneath Earth's surface. Lava is melted material at Earth's surface.

Formation of Igneous Rocks

Use Visuals L1

Figure 6 Ask: **In what ways are the two rocks similar?** *(Sample answer: Both are solids. Both are light-colored igneous rocks.)* **In what ways are the two rocks different?** *(Sample answer: The granite is multicolored and has a rough surface. The rhyolite is more uniformly colored and has a smoother surface.)*
Visual

L2

Ask students to describe the mass of rocks in relation to other solid objects. Some may mistakenly think that all rocks are heavy. Bring a sample of pumice into class. Pass around the rock, giving all students an opportunity to feel its heft. Many pumice samples will float in water. Place your sample in a pan of water to demonstrate this. Explain that some rocks, such as pumice, form when lava cools very quickly, leaving numerous air bubbles in the rock. The air bubbles cause pumice to be light.
Kinesthetic

Customize for Inclusion Students

Learning Disabled Have samples of igneous rocks available for students to examine. As they read the section, have them arrange the samples on a posterboard and write details about the texture and composition of the rocks under each sample. For example, students can write "coarse-grained, granitic" under a sample of granite.

Classification of Igneous Rocks

Teacher Demo

Crystal Formation L2

Purpose Students will observe how the rate of cooling affects crystal size.

Materials 2 shallow pans, 250-mL beaker, water, teaspoon, sulfur powder, thermal mitt, hot plate, magnifying glass

Procedure Put a teaspoon of sulfur powder into a shallow pan. Heat the pan until the sulfur melts, then place it aside to slowly cool. Heat another teaspoon of sulfur powder in a second shallow pan. Pour the melted sulfur into a beaker half-filled with water so that the sulfur cools quickly. Allow students to view the resulting crystals from both trials with a magnifying glass.

Expected Outcome Students will observe that cooling rates affect the size of crystals—the sulfur that cooled slowly formed larger crystals than the sulfur that cooled quickly.
Visual

Build Reading Literacy 

Refer to **p. 362D** in **Chapter 13**, which provides the guidelines for using prior knowledge.

Use Prior Knowledge Ask students what they think of when they hear the word *texture*. Students will likely say that texture refers to the way an object feels to the touch. Ask them to describe some textures they have felt. *(Sample answers: rough, smooth, sticky, powdery)* Explain that the scientific meaning of *texture* in this section refers to the overall appearance of a rock based on the size, shape, and arrangement of its crystals.
Intrapersonal, Verbal

Q *Native Americans used obsidian for making arrowheads and cutting tools. Is this the only material they used?*

A No. Native Americans used whatever materials were locally available to make tools, including any hard dense rock material that could be shaped. This includes materials such as the metamorphic rocks slate and quartzite, sedimentary deposits made of silica called jasper, chert, opal, flint, and even jade. Some of these deposits occur in only a few areas. That helps anthropologists reconstruct trade routes between different Native Americans groups.

Classification of Igneous Rocks

A quick glance at the two rocks in Figure 6 tells you that they are different. The granite contains large mineral grains. Only a few of the mineral grains in the sample of rhyolite can be seen with the unaided eye. **Texture and composition are two characteristics used to classify igneous rocks.** Texture describes the appearance of an igneous rock based on its size, shape, and the arrangement of its interlocking crystals. The composition classes of igneous rocks are based on the proportions of light and dark minerals in the rock.

Coarse-Grained Texture The rate of cooling strongly affects the textures of igneous rocks. If magma cools very slowly, few centers of crystal growth develop. Slow cooling also allows charged atoms, or ions, to move large distances within the magma. **Slow cooling results in the formation of large crystals.** Igneous rocks with large crystals exhibit a coarse-grained texture.

Fine-Grained Texture If cooling of magma or lava occurs rapidly, the ions in the melted material lose their motion and quickly combine. This results in a large number of tiny crystals that all compete for the available ions. **Rapid cooling of magma or lava results in rocks with small, interconnected mineral grains.** Igneous rocks with small grains are said to have a fine-grained texture.

Glassy Texture When lava spews onto Earth's surface, there may not be enough time for the ions in the lava to arrange themselves into a network of crystals. So the solids produced this way are made of randomly distributed ions. Such rocks have a glassy texture. The obsidian and pumice shown in Figure 1 on page 66 are igneous rocks with glassy textures.

Porphyritic Texture A large body of magma located deep within Earth may take tens of thousands of years to harden. Minerals that crystallize from the magma do not form at the same rate or at the same time. It is possible for some crystals to become quite large before others even start to form. The resulting rock can have large crystals, called phenocrysts, surrounded by fine-grained minerals. Rocks with very different-size minerals experience different rates of cooling. These rocks have a **porphyritic texture.** The igneous rock shown in Figure 7 has a porphyritic texture.

Figure 7 This sample of andesite displays igneous rock with a porphyritic texture.
Describing ***Describe how this rock probably formed.***

How does the rate of cooling of magma or lava affect the texture of igneous rocks?

Granitic Composition One group of igneous rocks includes those that are made almost entirely of the light-colored silicate minerals quartz and feldspar. Igneous rocks in which these are the main minerals are said to have a **granitic composition.** In addition to quartz and feldspar, most granitic rocks contain about 10 percent dark silicate minerals. These dark minerals are often biotite mica and amphibole. Granitic rocks contain about 70 percent silica and are the major rocks of the continental crust. Rhyolite is an extrusive granitic rock. Compare granite and rhyolite again in Figure 6 on page 71.

Go Online SCILINKS NSTA

For: Links on igneous rocks
Visit: www.SciLinks.org
Web Code: cjn-1032

Basaltic Composition Rocks that contain many dark silicate minerals and plagioclase feldspar have a **basaltic composition.** Basaltic rocks are rich in the elements magnesium and iron. Because of their iron content, basaltic rocks are typically darker and denser than granitic rocks. The most common basaltic rock is basalt, shown in Figure 8. Gabbro is an intrusive igneous rock with a basaltic composition.

Figure 8 Basalt is an igneous rock made mostly of dark-colored silicate minerals.
Describing ***Describe the texture of this igneous rock.***

Other Compositional Groups
Rocks with a composition between granitic and basaltic rocks have an **andesitic composition.** This group of igneous rocks is named after the common volcanic rock andesite. Andesitic rocks contain at least 25 percent dark silicate minerals—mainly amphibole, pyroxene, and biotite mica. The other dominant mineral in andesitic rocks is plagioclase feldspar.

Another important igneous rock is peridotite. This rock contains mostly the minerals olivine and pyroxene. Because peridotite is composed almost entirely of dark silicate minerals, its chemical composition is referred to as **ultramafic.** Although ultramafic rocks are rare at Earth's surface, much of the upper mantle is thought to be made of peridotite.

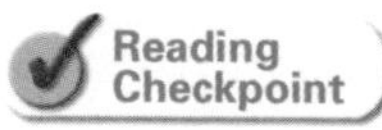

Describe the main differences between granitic and basaltic rocks.

Integrate Chemistry L2

In the early twentieth century, N. L. Bowen, a geologist, discovered that as magma cools, certain minerals crystallize first at very high temperatures. At successively lower temperatures, other minerals form. Bowen also demonstrated that if a mineral remains in the molten solution after crystallization, it will react with the remaining liquid to produce the next mineral, in a sequence known as Bowen's reaction series. Allow students to study Bowen's reaction series, Transparency 15. Tell them to compare the chart with Table 1 on p. 74. Ask: **What do you notice about the minerals that make up the rocks?** *(Each rock group consists of minerals that crystallize in the same temperature range.)*
Logical, Visual

Download a worksheet on igneous rocks for students to complete, and find additional teacher support from NSTA SciLinks.

Facts and Figures

Magma is basically a very hot, thick fluid, but it also contains solids and gases. The solids are mineral crystals. The liquid portion of the magma body is composed of ions that move about freely. However, as magma cools, the random movements of the ions slow, and the ions begin to arrange themselves into orderly patterns. This process is called crystallization. Usually not all of the molten material solidifies at the same time. Rather, as it cools, numerous small crystals develop. In a systematic fashion, ions are added to these centers of crystal growth. When the crystals grow large enough for their edges to meet, their growth ceases for lack of space, and crystallization continues elsewhere. Eventually, all of the liquid is transformed into a solid mass of interlocking crystals.

Answer to . . .

Figure 7 *The rock experienced at least two episodes of cooling. Slow cooling resulted in the larger mineral grains. Rapid cooling produced the fine-grained minerals.*

Figure 8 *The rock is a fine-grained igneous rock.*

Reading Checkpoint *A slowly cooling magma or lava will produce rocks in which the mineral grains are relatively large. Quickly cooling molten material will result in rocks with small mineral grains. Lava that is cools extremely rapidly will produce a glassy rock. Rocks that form as the result of different cooling rates will have both large and small mineral grains.*

Granitic rocks contain mostly quartz and feldspar and thus are light-colored. Basaltic rocks are rich in iron and thus are dark-colored and more dense.

Section 3.2 (continued)

Use Visuals **L1**

Table 1 Make sure all students can clearly read the table. If necessary, make enlarged copies of the table for students. Ask: **Which rocks have the highest percentage of dark minerals?** *(ultramafic rocks)* **Identify a coarse-grained basaltic rock.** *(gabbro)* **What minerals are in granite?** *(quartz, potassium feldspar, sodium-rich plagioclase feldspar)*
Visual

3 ASSESS

Evaluate Understanding **L2**

Using Table 1 as a guide, have each student make two tables. One table should show the different textures of igneous rocks. The second table should show the composition of igneous rocks.

Reteach **L1**

Use a simple graphic to help summarize the relationship between cooling rate and crystal size in igneous rocks. For example, draw an arrow pointing upward on the board. Label the arrow "Cooling rate." Ask: **As the rate of cooling increases, what happens to crystal size?** *(It decreases.)* To illustrate the answer, draw a downward-pointing arrow next to the first arrow. Label this second arrow "Crystal size."

Writing in Science

Sample answer: Obsidian likely formed when lava reached Earth's surface and cooled very rapidly. Refer to the text and Table 1 to evaluate students' answers.

To summarize, igneous rocks form when magma or lava cools and hardens. Intrusive rocks form when magma cools and hardens deep within Earth. Extrusive rocks form when lava cools and hardens on Earth's surface. Igneous rocks can be classified according to texture and composition. A general classification scheme based on texture and mineral composition is shown in Table 1.

Table 1 Classification of Major Igneous Rocks

		Granitic	Andesitic	Basaltic	Ultramafic
Chemical Composition		Granitic	Andesitic	Basaltic	Ultramafic
Dominant Minerals		Quartz Potassium feldspar Sodium-rich plagioclase feldspar	Amphibole Sodium- and calcium-rich plagioclase feldspar	Pyroxene Calcium-rich plagioclase feldspar	Olivine Pyroxene
TEXTURE	Coarse-grained	**Granite**	**Diorite**	**Gabbro**	**Peridotite**
	Fine-grained	**Rhyolite**	**Andesite**	**Basalt**	**Komatiite** (rare)
	Porphyritic	"Porphyritic" precedes any of the above names whenever there are appreciable phenocrysts.			Uncommon
	Glassy	**Obsidian** (compact glass) **Pumice** (frothy glass)			
Rock Color (based on % of dark minerals)		0% to 25%	25% to 45%	45% to 85%	85% to 100%

Section 3.2 Assessment

Reviewing Concepts

1. Compare and contrast the formation of intrusive and extrusive igneous rocks.
2. How do coarse-grained igneous rocks form?
3. How are igneous rocks classified according to composition?
4. How do fine-grained igneous rocks form?
5. How do igneous rocks with glassy textures form?

Critical Thinking

6. **Contrasting** Contrast basalt and granite in terms of how each forms, the texture of each rock, the color of each rock, and each rock's composition.
7. **Formulating Hypotheses** The extrusive igneous rock pumice contains many small holes. Hypothesize how these holes might form.

Writing in Science

Explanatory Paragraph Write a paragraph to explain how one of the igneous rocks pictured in this chapter may have formed.

Section 3.2 Assessment

1. Both types of rocks form when molten material cools and solidifies. Intrusive igneous rocks form when magma cools and solidifies within Earth. Extrusive igneous rocks form when lava cools and hardens at the surface.
2. Coarse-grained igneous rocks form when magma cools slowly within Earth.
3. Igneous rocks can be classified by composition based on the major minerals in the rocks. Light-colored rocks have granitic compositions. Dark-colored rocks have basaltic compositions. Dark-colored rocks that contain only olivine and pyroxene are ultramafic rocks.
4. Fine-grained igneous rocks form when lava cools quickly at Earth's surface.
5. Igneous rocks with glassy textures form when lava cools very quickly.
6. Granite forms as magma slowly cools below the surface. This slow rate of cooling produces large mineral grains. Most of these minerals are quartz and feldspar, thus granite is light-colored, with a granitic composition. Basalt forms when lava cools quickly at the surface. This quick cooling rate results in very small mineral grains. The major minerals in basalt are dark-colored silicates that give basalt its dark color. A basalt has a basaltic composition.
7. Lava is magma that reaches the surface. As it rises, reduced pressure on the magma causes some of its gases to come out of solution. These gases form bubbles or holes as the molten material cools.

3.3 Sedimentary Rocks

Reading Focus

Key Concepts

- Describe the major processes involved in the formation of sedimentary rocks.
- What are clastic sedimentary rocks?
- What are chemical sedimentary rocks?
- What features are unique to some sedimentary rocks?

Vocabulary

- erosion
- deposition
- compaction
- cementation
- clastic sedimentary rock
- chemical sedimentary rock

Reading Strategy

Outlining Copy this outline beneath the outline you made for Section 3.2. Complete this outline as you read. Include points about how each of these rocks form, some of the characteristics of each rock type, and some examples of each.

II. Sedimentary Rocks
A. Clastic Rocks
1. ___?___
2. ___?___
B. Chemical Rocks
1. ___?___
2. ___?___

All sedimentary rocks begin to form when existing rocks are broken down into sediments. Sediments, which consist mainly of weathered rock debris, are often transported to other places. When sediments are dropped, they eventually become compacted and cemented to form sedimentary rocks. The structures shown in Figure 9 are made of the sedimentary rock called sandstone. It is only one of many types of sedimentary rocks.

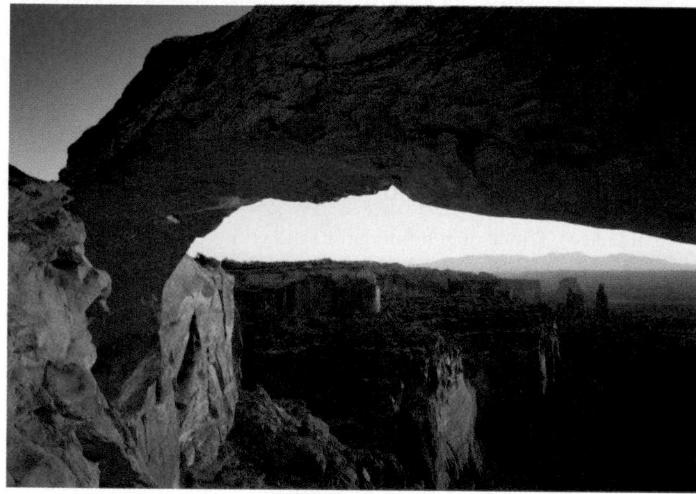

Figure 9 Sedimentary Rocks in Canyonlands National Park, Utah The rocks shown here formed when sand and other sediments were deposited and cemented. Weathering processes created this arch.

Section 3.3

1 FOCUS

Section Objectives

3.8 **Describe** the major processes involved in the formation of sedimentary rocks.

3.9 **Distinguish** between clastic sedimentary rocks and chemical sedimentary rocks.

3.10 **Identify** the features that are unique to some sedimentary rocks.

Reading Focus

Build Vocabulary L2

LINCS Have students **L**ist the parts of the vocabulary words that they know. For example, *cement* is part of *cementation.* Next, they should **I**magine a mental picture of the term's meaning and describe the image in their own words. Sediments held together by cement might be an image for cementation. Students should then make a **N**ote of a familiar "sound-alike" word. They can **C**onnect the terms by making up a short story about the meaning of the term that incorporates the sound-alike word. Lastly, students should conduct a **S**elf-test by quizzing themselves on the vocabulary terms.

Reading Strategy L2

A.1. rock made up of weathered bits of rocks and minerals
A.2. Common example of clastic sedimentary rock is shale.
B.1. rock that forms when dissolved minerals precipitate from water
B.2. Common example of chemical sedimentary rock is limestone.

2 INSTRUCT

Build Reading Literacy L1

Refer to **p. 64D** in **Chapter 3**, which provides the guidelines for directed reading/thinking activity (DRTA).

DRTA Before students read this section, have them preview the key concepts, vocabulary terms, and headings. Ask: **What do you think you will learn in this section?** *(Sample answer: about sedimentary rock formation, clastic sedimentary rocks, and chemical sedimentary rocks)* **What type of questions might a teacher ask about this topic?** *(Sample answer: How do sedimentary rocks form? How are sedimentary rocks classified?)* List these questions on the board. As students read the section, pause to discuss the answers to the questions.
Verbal

Formation of Sedimentary Rocks

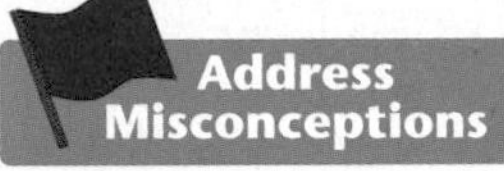

L2

Some students may think that rocks are stronger than the agents of mechanical and chemical weathering. To help dispel this misconception, place a few drops of vinegar on a sample of limestone. Have students observe the resulting chemical reaction. Ask: **What do you think would happen if the acid continued to drip on the rock over a long period?** *(The rock would eventually break down or be chemically weathered.)*
Visual, Logical

Build Science Skills

L2

ACTIVITY

Observing Provide small groups of students with 250-mL beakers, stirrers, sand, water, gravel, and soil. Tell students to half-fill the beakers with water. They should then pour about a handful of each material into the water. Have them stir the mixture, then observe what happens to the materials. Ask: **Which materials settled on the bottom? Which settled on the top?** *(The heavier materials settled on the bottom; the smaller, lighter materials settled on the top.)* **What does this activity model?** *(the settling out of sediments from a fluid, such as water or air)*
Kinesthetic, Visual

Formation of Sedimentary Rocks

The word *sedimentary* comes from the Latin word *sedimentum*, which means "settling." Sedimentary rocks form when solids settle out of a fluid such as water or air. The rocks shown in Figure 10 formed when sediments were dropped by moving water. The sediments eventually became cemented to form rocks. Several major processes contribute to the formation of sedimentary rocks.

Weathering, Erosion, and Deposition Recall that weathering is any process that breaks rocks into sediments. Weathering is often the first step in the formation of sedimentary rocks. Chemical weathering takes place when the minerals in rocks change into new substances. Weathering also takes place when physical forces break rocks into smaller pieces. Living things, too, can cause chemical and physical weathering.

Weathered sediments don't usually remain in place. Instead, water, wind, ice, or gravity carries them away. **Erosion involves weathering and the removal of rock. When an agent of erosion—water, wind, ice, or gravity—loses energy, it drops the sediments. This process is called deposition.** Sediments are deposited according to size. The largest sediments, such as the rounded pebbles in the conglomerate in Figure 10A, are deposited first. Smaller sediments, like the pieces of sand that make up the sandstone in Figure 10B, are dropped later. Some sediments are so small that they are carried great distances before being deposited.

A

B

Figure 10 Although these two rocks appear quite different, both formed when sediments were dropped by moving water. **A** Conglomerate is made of rounded pebbles cemented together. **B** Sandstone is made of sand grains cemented together.

Compaction and Cementation After sediments are deposited, they often become lithified, or turned to rock. **Compaction** and **cementation** change sediments into sedimentary rock. **Compaction is a process that squeezes, or compacts, sediments.** Compaction is caused by the weight of sediments. During compaction, much of the water in the sediments is driven out.

Cementation takes place when dissolved minerals are deposited in the tiny spaces among the sediments. Much of the cement in the conglomerate shown in Figure 10A can be seen with the unaided eye. The cement holding the sand grains together in the sandstone in Figure 10B, however, is microscopic.

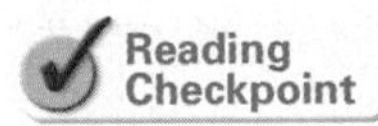

Briefly describe the five major processes involved in the formation of sedimentary rocks.

Customize for English Language Learners

Compile a classroom library using up-to-date magazines and newspaper articles. Select reading materials that correspond to chapter content. For example, try to find articles that discuss different types of rocks. Avoid academic journals and reference materials with high reading levels. Provide opportunities for ELL students to read the articles in class. This will give them a broader context in which to place this chapter's vocabulary terms and key concepts.

Classification of Sedimentary Rocks

Just like igneous rocks, sedimentary rocks can be classified into two main groups according to the way they form. The first group includes rocks that are made of weathered bits of rocks and minerals. These rocks are called **clastic sedimentary rocks.** The second group forms when dissolved minerals precipitate from water solutions. These rocks are called **chemical sedimentary rocks.**

Figure 11 **A** Shale and **B** breccia are common clastic sedimentary rocks. This sample of shale contains plant fossils. **Formulating Hypotheses** *How do you think this breccia might have formed?*

Clastic Sedimentary Rocks Many different minerals are found in clastic rocks. The most common are the clay minerals and quartz. This is because clay minerals, like those that make up much of the shale in Figure 11A, are the most abundant products of chemical weathering. Quartz, which is a major mineral in the breccia shown in Figure 11B, is a common sedimentary mineral for a different reason. It is very durable and resistant to chemical weathering.

Clastic sedimentary rocks can be grouped according to the size of the sediments in the rocks. When rounded, gravel-size or larger particles make up most of the rock, the rock is called conglomerate. If the particles are angular, the rock is called breccia. Sandstone is the name given to rocks when most of the sediments are sand-size grains. Shale, the most common sedimentary rock, is made of very fine-grained sediment. Siltstone is another fine-grained rock.

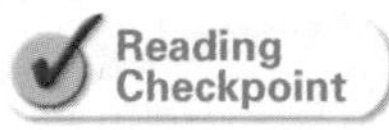

Describe the major types of clastic sedimentary rocks.

Chemical and Biochemical Sedimentary Rocks Chemical sedimentary rocks form when dissolved substances precipitate, or separate, from water solution. This precipitation generally occurs when the water evaporates or boils off leaving a solid product. Examples of this type of chemical rock are some limestones, rock salt, chert, flint, and rock gypsum.

For: Links on sedimentary rocks
Visit: www.SciLinks.org
Web Code: cjn-1034

Classification of Sedimentary Rocks

Chemical Weathering L2

Purpose Students will observe how chemical weathering can change the minerals in rocks.

Materials calcium tablet, 250-mL beaker, vinegar

Procedure Half-fill the beaker with vinegar. Place the calcium tablet into the vinegar. Allow students to observe the reaction.

Expected Outcome Students will observe that the calcium fizzes, foams, and eventually dissolves in the vinegar. Explain that chemical weathering breaks down rocks in a similar, though slower, fashion.
Visual

Download a worksheet on sedimentary rocks for students to complete, and find additional teacher support from NSTA SciLinks.

Answer to . . .

Figure 11 *Rocks were weathered. The larger fragments were deposited. Fine-grained sediments were deposited later. Little compaction occurred because of the size of the angular sediments. Dissolved minerals entered the spaces among the sediments and held them together to form the breccia.*

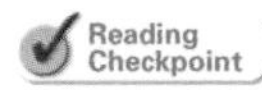

Weathering breaks existing rocks into smaller pieces. Erosion is the process whereby sediments are moved from place to place. Deposition occurs when sediments are dropped by erosional agents. Compaction is the process of squeezing sediments. Cementation is a process that "glues" sediments together to form sedimentary rocks.

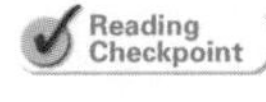

Conglomerates and breccias are made mostly of gravel-sized sediments. Sandstone is made mostly of sand-size grains. Shale and siltstone are fine-grained rocks in which clay-size or smaller particles are the major components.

Build Science Skills L2

Designing Experiments ACTIVITY
Have students work in small groups to design an experiment to show how sedimentary rocks form when dissolved minerals precipitate from water. Students should develop a hypothesis and procedure, listing controls, safety measures, and materials to be used. A sample experiment might involve placing table salt in water, then heating the water until it evaporates. If time permits, allow students to carry out their experiments.
Logical, Interpersonal

Features of Some Sedimentary Rocks

Use Visuals L1

Figure 13 Ask: **Based on its appearance, what can you infer about the rock labeled A?** *(It may have formed along a beach or stream bed.)* **What can you infer about the rock labeled B?** *(It may have formed when wet mud or clay dried and shrank.)*
Visual

Figure 12 This biochemical rock, called coquina, is a type of limestone that is made of hundreds of shell fragments.

About 90 percent of limestones are formed from biochemical sediments. Such sediments are the shells and skeletal remains of organisms that settle to the ocean floor. The coquina in Figure 12 is one obvious example. You can actually see the shells cemented together. Another biochemical rock is chalk, the material used to write on a chalkboard.

Features of Some Sedimentary Rocks

Sedimentary rocks, like other types of rocks, are used to unravel what may have happened in Earth's long history. **The many unique features of sedimentary rocks are clues to how, when, and where the rocks formed.** Each layer of a sedimentary rock, for example, records a period of sediment deposition. In undisturbed rocks, the oldest layers are found at the bottom. The youngest layers are found at the top of the rocks. Ripple marks like the ones shown in Figure 13A may indicate that the rock formed along a beach or stream bed. The mud cracks in Figure 13B formed when wet mud or clay dried and shrank, leaving a rock record of a dry environment.

Fossils, which are the traces or remains of ancient life, are unique to some sedimentary rocks. Fossils can be used to help answer many questions about the rocks that contain them. For example, did the rock form on land or in the ocean? Was the climate hot or cold, rainy or dry? Did the rock form hundreds, thousands, millions, or billions of years ago? Fossils also play a key role in matching up rocks from different places that are the same age.

To summarize, sedimentary rocks are rocks that form as the result of four major processes. *Weathering* produces particles called sediments. Wind, water, ice, and gravity *erode* and *deposit* these sediments. Over time, the sediments are *compacted and cemented* to form rocks. Sedimentary rocks can be classified according to how they form. A general classification scheme based on a rock's formation, texture, and composition is shown in Table 2.

Figure 13 **A** Ripple marks and **B** mud cracks are features of sedimentary rocks that can be used to learn about the environments in which the rocks formed.

Facts and Figures

Unlike other chemical sedimentary rocks, which are rich in calcite or silica, coal is made mostly of organic matter. When coal is viewed under a magnifying glass, chemically altered leaves, bark, and wood are visible. The materials provide evidence that coal is the end product of the burial of large amounts of plant materials over long periods of time. The initial stage of coal formation is the accumulation of large quantities of plant remains in a swampy environment. Coal then undergoes successive stages of formation. With each stage, higher temperatures and pressures drive off impurities and volatiles.

Table 2 Classification of Major Sedimentary Rocks

Clastic Sedimentary Rocks

Texture (grain size)	Sediment Name	Rock Name
Coarse (over 2 mm)	Gravel (rounded fragments)	**Conglomerate**
	Gravel (angular fragments)	**Breccia**
Medium (1/16 to 2 mm)	Sand	**Sandstone**
Fine (1/16 to 1/256 mm)	Mud	**Siltstone**
Very fine (less than 1/256 mm)	Mud	**Shale**

Chemical Sedimentary Rocks

Composition	Texture (grain size)	Rock Name	
Calcite, $CaCO_3$	Fine to coarse crystalline	**Crystalline Limestone**	
		Travertine	
	Visible shells and shell fragments loosely cemented	**Coquina**	Biochemical Limestone
	Various size shells and shell fragments cemented with calcite cement	**Fossiliferous Limestone**	Biochemical Limestone
	Microscopic shells and clay	**Chalk**	Biochemical Limestone
Quartz, SiO_2	Very fine crystalline	**Chert (light colored) Flint (dark colored)**	
Gypsum $CaSO_4 \cdot 2H_2O$	Fine to coarse crystalline	**Rock Gypsum**	
Halite, NaCl	Fine to coarse crystalline	**Rock Salt**	
Altered plant fragments	Fine-grained organic matter	**Bituminous Coal**	

Section 3.3 Assessment

Reviewing Concepts

1. Contrast weathering, erosion, and deposition.
2. Name four clastic sedimentary rocks and explain how these rocks form.
3. Name four chemical sedimentary rocks and explain how these rocks form.
4. Explain how three different features of sedimentary rocks can be used to determine how, where, or when the rocks formed.
5. What is compaction?
6. Where do the cements that hold sediments together come from?

Critical Thinking

7. **Applying Concepts** Briefly describe how the rock shown in Figure 12 may have formed.
8. **Predicting** Which type of sediments do you think would undergo more compaction—grains of sand or grains of clay? Explain your choice.
9. **Formulating Conclusions** Suppose you found a sedimentary rock in which ripple marks were pointing toward the ground. What could you conclude about the rock?

Connecting Concepts

Sedimentary Rocks Choose one of the sedimentary rocks pictured in this section. Find out how the rock is useful to people.

Use Visuals L1

Table 2 Ask: **How does the texture of gravel compare with that of sand?** *(Gravel has a coarse texture; grain size is more than 2 mm. Sand has a medium texture; grain size is 1/16 to 2 mm.)* **What type of detrital sedimentary rock has a very fine texture?** *(shale)* **What is the chemical composition of chalk?** *(calcite)* **Which chemical sedimentary rock is made up of halite?** *(rock salt)*
Visual

3 ASSESS

Evaluate Understanding L2

Give students samples of sandstone, siltstone, shale, breccia, and conglomerate. Have them use magnifying glasses to classify the rocks according to grain size.

Reteach L1

Review Table 2. As you discuss the different types of textures and chemical compositions, explain how each sedimentary rock likely formed.

Connecting Concepts

Sample answer: Shale is used in construction. Coal is used as an energy resource.

Section 3.3 Assessment

1. Weathering is any process in which rocks are broken down into smaller pieces. Erosion involves the weathering and removal of sediments. Deposition is the dropping of sediments by agents of erosion.
2. Conglomerate, breccia, sandstone, shale, and siltstone are clastic rocks. Clastic rocks form when bits of weathered materials are compacted and cemented together.
3. Most limestones, rock salt, rock gypsum, flint, and chert are chemical sedimentary rocks that form when dissolved minerals precipitate from water.
4. Each layer of a sedimentary rock records a period of deposition. Ripple marks indicate that a rock bed formed in water. Mud cracks are indicative of unusually dry periods. Fossils can be used to determine if a rock formed on land or in the ocean, if the climate was hot or cold, or rainy or dry, and when the rock containing them formed.
5. Compaction is the process that squeezes, or compacts, sediments.
6. Cements are dissolved minerals that are deposited in the tiny places among the sediments.
7. Animals with shells died. The shells accumulated and became cemented to form a sedimentary rock.
8. Because they are smaller, clay particles undergo more compaction than sand-size particles.
9. Ripple marks indicate that a rock formed in water. And, because the ripple marks were pointing down, one can infer that the rock has been overturned from its original position.

Section 3.4

1 FOCUS

Section Objectives

3.11 **Predict** where most metamorphism takes place.

3.12 **Distinguish** contact metamorphism from regional metamorphism.

3.13 **Identify** the three agents of metamorphism and **explain** what changes they cause.

3.14 **Recognize** foliated metamorphic rocks and **describe** how they form.

3.15 **Classify** metamorphic rocks.

Reading Focus

Build Vocabulary L2

Paraphrase Explain vocabulary terms using words students know. For example, *contact metamorphism* occurs when two rocks come into contact with one another. *Regional metamorphism* takes place over a large region. *Foliated metamorphic rocks* have distinct layers. *Nonfoliated metamorphic rocks* do not. Once students are able to distinguish among the vocabulary terms, focus on the processes that cause the different types of metamorphism and the different types of metamorphic rock.

Reading Strategy L2

A.1. rock that forms when minerals recrystallize at right angles to the direction of pressure
A.2. Common example of foliated metamorphic rock is slate.
B.1. rock that does not have a banded texture
B.2. Common example of nonfoliated metamorphic rock is marble.

2 INSTRUCT

Formation of Metamorphic Rocks

Use Visuals L1

Figure 14 Ask students to describe the rocks. *(Sample answer: The rocks are folded and multicolored.)* **What force could cause the rocks to fold?** *(intense pressure)*
Visual

3.4 Metamorphic Rocks

Reading Focus

Key Concepts

- Where does most metamorphism take place?
- How is contact metamorphism different from regional metamorphism?
- What are three agents of metamorphism, and what kinds of changes does each cause?
- What are foliated metamorphic rocks, and how do they form?
- How are metamorphic rocks classified?

Vocabulary

- metamorphism
- contact metamorphism
- regional metamorphism
- hydrothermal solution
- foliated metamorphic rock
- nonfoliated metamorphic rock

Reading Strategy

Outlining Copy this outline beneath the outline you made for Section 3.3. Complete it as you read. Include points about how each of these rocks form, some of the characteristics of each rock type, and some examples of each.

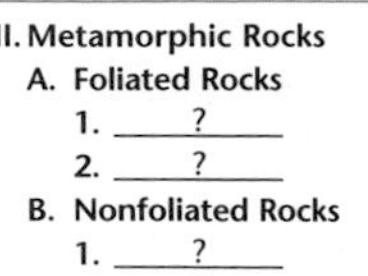
III. Metamorphic Rocks
A. Foliated Rocks
1. ___?___
2. ___?___
B. Nonfoliated Rocks
1. ___?___
2. ___?___

Figure 14 Deformed Rock Intense pressures metamorphosed these rocks by causing them to fold as well as change composition.

Recall that metamorphic rocks form when existing rocks are changed by heat and pressure. **Metamorphism** is a very appropriate name for this process because it means *to change form.* Rocks produced during metamorphism often look much different from the original rocks, or parent rocks. The folds in the rocks shown in Figure 14 formed when the parent rocks were subjected to intense forces. These highly folded metamorphic rocks may also develop a different composition than the parent rocks had.

Formation of Metamorphic Rocks

Most metamorphic changes occur at elevated temperatures and pressures. These conditions are found a few kilometers below Earth's surface and extend into the upper mantle. Most metamorphism occurs in one of two settings—contact metamorphism or regional metamorphism.

Contact Metamorphism When magma intrudes—forces its way into—rock, contact metamorphism may take place. **During contact metamorphism, hot magma moves into rock.** Contact metamorphism often produces what is described as low-grade metamorphism. Such changes in rocks are minor. Marble, like that used to make the statue in Figure 15, is a common contact metamorphic rock. Marble often forms when magma intrudes a limestone body.

Figure 15 Statue Carved from Marble Marble is a common metamorphic rock that forms as the result of contact metamorphism of limestone.

Regional Metamorphism During mountain building, large areas of rocks are subjected to extreme pressures and temperatures. The intense changes produced during this process are described as high-grade metamorphism. **Regional metamorphism results in large-scale deformation and high-grade metamorphism.** The rocks shown in Figure 14 on page 80 were changed as the result of regional metamorphism.

Agents of Metamorphism

The agents of metamorphism are heat, pressure, and hydrothermal solutions. During metamorphism, rocks are usually subjected to all three of these agents at the same time. However, the effect of each agent varies greatly from one situation to another.

Heat The most important agent of metamorphism is heat. Heat provides the energy needed to drive chemical reactions. Some of these reactions cause existing minerals to recrystallize. Other reactions cause new minerals to form. The heat for metamorphism comes mainly from two sources—magma and the change in temperature with depth. Magma essentially "bakes" any rocks that are in contact with it. Heat also comes from the gradual increase in temperature with depth. In the upper crust, this increase averages between 20°C and 30°C per kilometer.

When buried to a depth of about 8 kilometers, clay minerals are exposed to temperatures of 150°C to 200°C. These minerals become unstable and recrystallize to form new minerals that are stable at these temperatures, such as chlorite and muscovite. In contrast, silicate minerals are stable at these temperatures. Therefore, it takes higher temperatures to change silicate minerals.

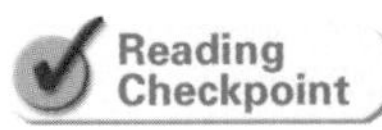

Compare and contrast contact and regional metamorphism.

Q *How hot is it deep in the crust?*

A The deeper a person goes beneath Earth's surface, the hotter it gets. The deepest mine in the world is the Western Deep Levels mine in South Africa, which is about 4 kilometers deep. Here, the temperature of the surrounding rock is so hot that it can scorch human skin. In fact, miners in this mine often work in groups of two. One miner mines the rock, and the other operates a large fan that keeps the worker cool.

Build Science Skills L2

Posing Questions Have students read the text about contact metamorphism and regional metamorphism. Then have them pose questions about the concepts that can be answered through experimentation, observation, or research.
A sample question might be: During contact metamorphism, what causes the magma to move into the rock? *(Magma is less dense than surrounding rock so pressure forces it toward the surface. As it moves, it can come into contact with and alter surrounding rock.)*
Logical

Agents of Metamorphism

Integrate Physics L2

Buried rocks are subject to a force known as *confining pressure,* wherein pressure is applied equally in all directions. In contrast, *differential stress* is unequal force applied in different directions. Differential stress, which occurs during mountain-building, acts mainly along one plane. Rocks subjected to differential stress are shortened in the direction in which pressure is applied and lengthened in the direction perpendicular to the pressure. Have students observe while you squeeze a ball of clay between your palms. Ask: **Is this an example of confining pressure or differential stress?** *(differential stress)*
Kinesthetic, Visual

Customize for Inclusion Students

Behaviorally Disordered Minimize distractions for students with behavioral disorders. For example, have students sit near the front of the class so that they are focused on you, rather than their classmates. Before conducting any activities, make sure students clear off their desks. If necessary, provide storage space in the classroom for students' books and other materials.

Answer to . . .

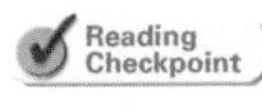

Both processes change existing rocks into metamorphic rocks. Contact metamorphism is caused by magma and often produces slight changes in rocks. Regional metamorphism is large-scale deformation that can result in drastic changes to the rocks involved.

Observing Some of the Effects of Pressure on Mineral Grains **L2**

Objective
After completing this activity, students will be able to observe the effect of pressure on the rearrangement of mineral grains in a model rock.

Skills Focus **Modeling, Observing, Inferring**

Prep Time 10 minutes to organize materials

Class Time 15 minutes

Expected Outcome Students will observe that the pressure from opposite directions—from above (their pushing down on the "rock") and below (the table's pushing up on the "rock")—will cause "minerals" to align at right angles to the direction of stress.

Analyze and Conclude
1. The model minerals were randomly distributed throughout the rock before pressure was applied. The minerals aligned themselves at right angles to the direction of stress.
2. Pressure causes the minerals to reorient themselves in the rock.
3. No, heat from the hand and contact with the table also affected the model rock.
Kinesthetic, Visual

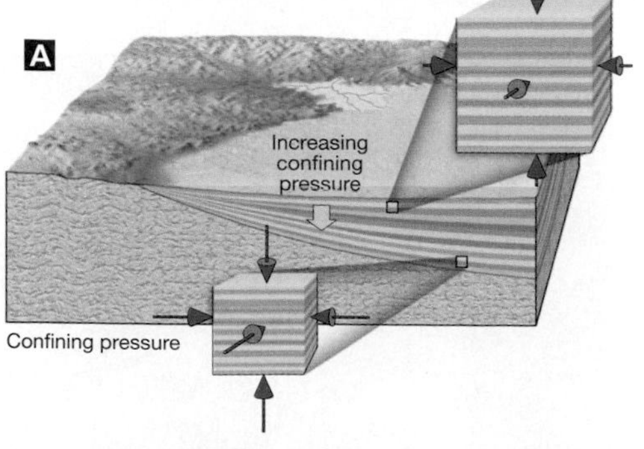

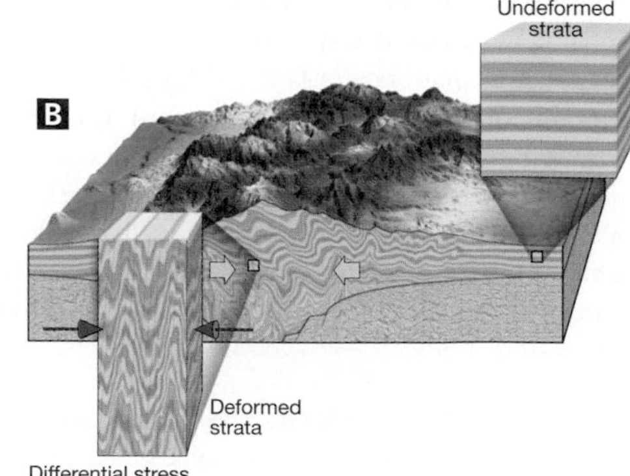

Figure 16 Pressure (Stress) As a Metamorphic Agent
A Forces in all directions are applied equally to buried rocks.
B During mountain building, rocks subjected to differential stress are shortened in the direction that pressure is applied.

Figure 17 Imagine the tremendous amounts of pressure that caused these rocks to fold.

Pressure (Stress) Pressure, like temperature, also increases with depth. Like the water pressure you might have experienced at the bottom of a swimming pool, pressure on rocks within Earth is applied in all directions. See Figure 16. Pressure on rocks causes the spaces between mineral grains to close. The result is a more compact rock with a greater density. This pressure also may cause minerals to recrystallize into new minerals.

Increases in temperature and pressure cause rocks to flow rather than fracture. Under these conditions, mineral grains tend to flatten and elongate.

Quick Lab

Observing Some of the Effects of Pressure on Mineral Grains

Materials
soft modeling clay; 2 pieces of waxed paper (each 20 cm × 20 cm); 20–30 small, round, elongated plastic beads; small plastic knife

Procedure
1. Use the clay to form a ball about the size of a golf ball. Randomly place all of the beads into this model rock.
2. Make a sketch of the rock. Label the sketch *Before*.
3. Sandwich the model rock between the two pieces of waxed paper. Use your weight to apply pressure to the model rock.
4. Remove the waxed paper and observe your "metamorphosed" rock.
5. Draw a top view of your rock and label it *After*. Include arrows to show the directions from which you applied pressure.
6. Make a cut through your model rock. Sketch this view of the rock.

Analyze and Conclude
1. **Comparing and Contrasting** How did the *Before* sketch compare with the *After* sketch of your model rock?
2. **Drawing Conclusions** How does pressure affect the mineral grains in a rock?
3. **Inferring** Was pressure the only agent of change that affected your rock? Explain.

During mountain building, horizontal forces metamorphose large segments of Earth's crust.This often produces intricately folded rocks like those shown in Figure 17.

Reactions in Solution Water solutions containing other substances that readily change to gases at the surface play an important role in some types of metamorphism. Solutions that surround mineral grains aid in recrystallization by making it easier for ions to move. When solutions increase in temperature reactions among substances can occur at a faster rate. When these hot, water-based solutions escape from a mass of magma, they are called **hydrothermal solutions.** These hot fluids also promote recrystallization by dissolving original minerals and then depositing new ones. As a result of contact with hydrothermal solutions, a change in a rock's overall composition may occur.

Figure 18 Gneiss is a foliated metamorphic rock.
***Inferring** In which directions was pressure exerted on this rock?*

Classification of Metamorphic Rocks

Like igneous rocks, metamorphic rocks can be classified by texture and composition. **The texture of metamorphic rocks can be foliated or nonfoliated.**

For: Links on metamorphic rocks
Visit: www.SciLinks.org
Web Code: cjn-1033

Foliated Metamorphic Rocks When rocks undergo contact metamorphism, they become more compact and thus more dense. A common example is the metamorphic rock slate. Slate forms when shale is subjected to temperatures and pressures only slightly greater than those at which the shale formed. The pressure on the shale causes the microscopic clay minerals to become more compact. The increase in pressure also causes the clay minerals to align in a similar direction.

Under more extreme conditions, certain minerals will recrystallize. Some minerals recrystallize with a preferred orientation, which is at right angles to the direction of the force. The resulting alignment usually gives the rock a layered or banded appearance. This rock is called a **foliated metamorphic rock.** Gneiss, the metamorphic rock shown in Figure 18, is a foliated rock. Another foliated metamorphic rock is schist.

Figure 19 Marble is a nonfoliated metamorphic rock.

Nonfoliated Metamorphic Rocks A metamorphic rock that does not have a banded texture is called a **nonfoliated metamorphic rock.** Most nonfoliated rocks contain only one mineral. Marble, for example, is a nonfoliated rock made of calcite. When its parent rock, limestone, is metamorphosed, the calcite crystals combine to form the larger interlocking crystals seen in marble. A sample of marble is shown in Figure 19. Quartzite and anthracite are other nonfoliated metamorphic rocks.

Contrast foliated and nonfoliated metamorphic rocks.

Classification of Metamorphic Rocks

Build Reading Literacy L1

Refer to **p.124D** in **Chapter 5**, which provides the guidelines for summarizing.

Summarize Have students read the text on page 83. In their own words, have them summarize how metamorphic rocks are classified. *(Sample answer: Metamorphic rocks are classified by texture. There are two kinds of textures—foliated and nonfoliated. Foliated metamorphic rocks have a layered look; nonfoliated metamorphic rocks do not have a layered appearance.)*

Verbal

Download a worksheet on metamorphic rocks for students to complete, and find additional teacher support from NSTA SciLinks.

Facts and Figures

Slate is a very fine-grained foliated rock composed of minute mica flakes. The most noteworthy characteristic of slate is its excellent rock cleavage, meaning that it splits easily into flat slabs. This property has made slate a most useful rock for roof and floor tiles, chalkboards, and billiard tables. Slate is most often generated by the low-grade metamorphism of shale, though less frequently it forms from the metamorphism of volcanic ash. Slate can be almost any color, depending on its mineral constituents. Black slate contains organic material; red slate gets it color from iron oxide; and green slate is usually composed of chlorite, a micalike mineral.

Answer to . . .

Figure 18 *Pressure was exerted from the sides.*

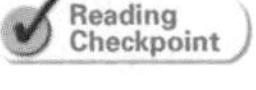

Foliated metamorphic rocks have a layered or banded appearance. Nonfoliated metamorphic rocks do not have a banded texture.

Use Visuals L1

Table 3 Ask: **What is the parent rock of schist?** *(phyllite)* **Which has undergone more intense metamorphism, slate or gneiss? Explain your answer.** *(Gneiss has undergone more intense metamorphism, as indicated by the arrow in the table.)* **Which nonfoliated rock has the finest grains?** *(anthracite)*
Visual

3 ASSESS

Evaluate Understanding L2

Have students examine Table 3. Ask: **Generally, what can you say about the relationship between texture and increasing metamorphism that results in foliated rocks?** *(The more intense the metamorphism, the courser the texture, or larger the grain size.)*

Reteach L1

Have students make tables that compare and contrast contact metamorphism and regional metamorphism.

Writing in Science

Sample answer: All are solids that form and change because of Earth processes. All can be classified according to texture and/or composition. The major difference among the three rock types is that each forms at different temperatures and pressures.

To summarize, metamorphic rocks form when existing rocks are changed by heat, pressure, or hydrothermal solution. Contact metamorphism is often caused when hot magma intrudes a body of rock. Changes during this type of metamorphism are minor. Regional metamorphism is associated with mountain building. Such metamorphic changes can be extreme. Metamorphic rocks can be classified by texture as foliated or nonfoliated, as shown in Table 3.

Table 3 Classification of Major Metamorphic Rocks

Rock Name	Texture	Grain Size	Comments	Parent Rock
Slate (Increasing Metamorphism ↓)	Foliated	Very fine	Smooth dull surfaces	Shale, mudstone, or siltstone
Phyllite	Foliated	Fine	Breaks along wavy surfaces, glossy sheen	Slate
Schist	Foliated	Medium to Coarse	Micaceous minerals dominate	Phyllite
Gneiss	Foliated	Medium to Coarse	Banding of minerals	Schist, granite, or volcanic rocks
Marble	Nonfoliated	Medium to coarse	Interlocking calcite or dolomite grains	Limestone, dolostone
Quartzite	Nonfoliated	Medium to coarse	Fused quartz grains, massive, very hard	Quartz sandstone
Anthracite	Nonfoliated	Fine	Shiny black organic rock that fractures	Bituminous coal

Section 3.4 Assessment

Reviewing Concepts

1. Where does most metamorphism take place?
2. Compare and contrast contact metamorphism and regional metamorphism?
3. Name the agents of metamorphism and explain how each changes a rock.
4. What are foliated rocks, and how do they form?
5. How are metamorphic rocks classified?

Critical Thinking

6. **Applying Concepts** What is the major difference between igneous and metamorphic rocks?
7. **Predicting** What type of metamorphism—contact or regional—would result in a schist? Explain your choice.
8. **Formulating Conclusions** Why can the composition of gneiss vary but overall texture cannot?

Writing in Science

Explanatory Paragraph Write a short paragraph that explains the major differences and similarities among the three major rock groups.

Section 3.4 Assessment

1. Most metamorphism takes place in a zone that begins several kilometers below the surface and extends into the upper mantle.
2. Contact metamorphism is a process whereby slight changes occur in rocks as the result of an increase in temperature resulting from a magma body. Regional metamorphism, which is associated with mountain-building, can result in high-grade changes in both composition and structure.
3. Heat can cause existing minerals to recrystallize or it can cause new minerals to form. Pressure produces a more compact rock with a greater density. Pressure also causes minerals to recrystallize. Fluids aid in recrystallization by making it easier for ions to move and by dissolving original minerals and depositing new ones.
4. Foliated rocks are banded metamorphic rocks that form when minerals realign as the result of pressure from opposing sides.
5. Metamorphic rocks can be classified according to composition and texture.
6. While both types of rocks form as the result of changes in temperature and pressure, metamorphism does not involve melting.
7. Schists, as indicated in Table 3, are the result of high-grade metamorphism that is generally associated with mountain-building.
8. Gneiss is a banded rock that forms as the result of pressure from opposing sides. This directional pressure results in foliation. However, because the parent rocks of gneisses can vary, so can the compositions of these metamorphic rocks.

The Carbon Cycle

To illustrate the movement of material and energy in the Earth system, we can take a brief look at the carbon cycle, shown in Figure 20. Pure carbon is rare in nature. It is found mainly as two minerals—diamond and graphite. Most carbon is bonded to other elements to form compounds. Carbon dioxide (CO_2), for example, is an important gas in Earth's atmosphere. Calcite ($CaCO_3$) is a mineral found in many sedimentary and metamorphic rocks. Hydrocarbons, such as coal, oil, and natural gas, are compounds made of carbon and hydrogen. Carbon also combines with hydrogen and oxygen to form the basic compounds that make up living things. This important element moves continually among Earth's major spheres by way of the carbon cycle.

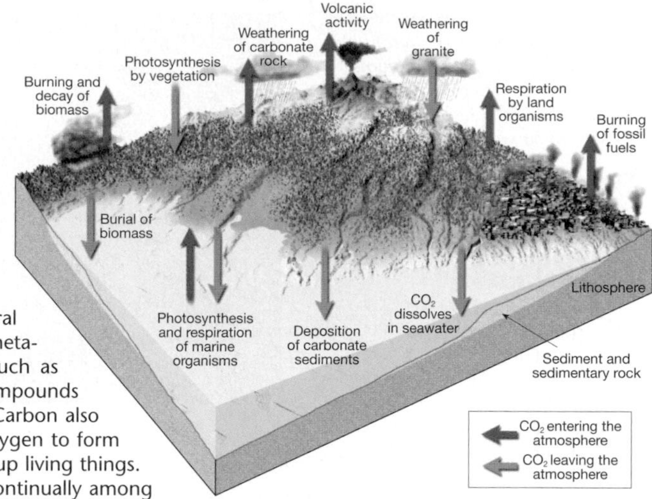

Figure 20 The Carbon Cycle

Carbon Dioxide on the Move

In the atmosphere, carbon is found mainly as carbon dioxide. This gas absorbs much of the energy given off by Earth. Therefore, carbon dioxide influences the heating of the atmosphere. Carbon dioxide constantly moves into and out of the atmosphere by way of four major processes: photosynthesis, respiration, organic decay, and combustion of organic material.

Carbon and Fossil Fuels

Some carbon from decayed organic matter is deposited as sediment. Over long periods of time, this carbon becomes buried. Under the right conditions, some of these carbon-rich deposits are changed to fossil fuels, such as coal. When fossil fuels are burned, huge quantities of carbon dioxide enter into the air.

The Role of Marine Animals

Chemical weathering of certain rocks produce bicarbonate ions that dissolve water. Groundwater, rivers, and streams carry these ions to the ocean. Here, some organisms extract this substance to produce body parts—shells, skeletons, and spines—made of calcite. When the organisms die, these hard parts settle to the ocean floor and become the sedimentary rock called limestone.

The Complete Cycle

The source of most CO_2 in the atmosphere is thought to be from volcanic activity early in Earth's history. When CO_2 combines with water, it forms carbonic acid. This substance reacts with rock through chemical weathering to form bicarbonate ions that are carried by groundwater and streams to the ocean. Here, marine organisms take over and sedimentary rock is eventually produced. If this rock is then exposed at the surface and subjected to chemical weathering, CO_2 is also produced. Use Figure 20 to trace the path of carbon from the atmosphere to the hydrosphere, the geosphere, the biosphere, and back to the atmosphere.

The Carbon Cycle L2

Background

- During photosynthesis, plants absorb carbon dioxide from the atmosphere and use it to produce the essential organic compounds—complex sugars—that they need for growth. When animals consume plants or other animals that eat plants, the animals use these organic compounds as a source of energy. Then, through the process of respiration, the animals return carbon dioxide to the atmosphere. Plants also return some carbon dioxide to the atmosphere by way of respiration.
- When plants die and decay or are burned, this biomass is oxidized and carbon dioxide is returned to the atmosphere.
- The lithosphere is by far Earth's largest depository of carbon. A variety of rocks contain carbon. The most abundant is limestone. When limestone undergoes chemical weathering, the stored carbon is released into the atmosphere.

Teaching Tips

- Have students contrast different solids that contain carbon, such as coal, diamond, graphite, calcite, and limestone. Have students explain how the carbon is released from each of these components of the lithosphere into Earth's other spheres.
- Write the chemical equations for photosynthesis and respiration on the board or on an overhead transparency to reinforce the fact that the products of one reaction are the reactants of the other reaction.
- Use a clean, empty 2-L bottle, plants, soil, and a thermometer to make a mini-greenhouse to demonstrate how gases in the air, including carbon dioxide, can absorb solar energy. Refer to the following Web site for tips on such a demonstration: http://www.bigelow.org/virtual/handson/greenhouse_make.html

Exploration Lab

Rock Identification **L2**

Objective
After completing this activity, students will be able to differentiate among some of the common rocks.

Skills Focus Observing, Comparing and Contrasting, Applying Concepts

 **Prep Time** 20 minutes

Advance Prep Order the rock specimens from a scientific supply house at least one month before conducting this activity. Rocks should include anthracite, bituminous coal, granite, gneiss, marble, limestone, basalt, obsidian, shale, slate, a coarse-grained sandstone, quartzite, and conglomerate.

Label the samples with numbers, using a permanent marker so that you can check students' results.

Diluted hydrochloric acid can be prepared using 3.65 mL of concentrated hydrochloric acid diluted to 1 L with distilled water.

Class Time 45 minutes

Safety Students should wear safety goggles and aprons. Remind students to take care when testing the rocks for calcite and to thoroughly rinse the samples with fresh tap water to remove the acid.

Teaching Tips
- Students can work in pairs or small groups to complete this investigation.
- Keys or guides to rock identification may be useful for some students.
- Remind students to use only a drop or two of acid to test the rocks for calcite and to thoroughly wash the samples after testing them with the acid.
- Review, if necessary, the properties of some of the more common minerals that students will observe in the rocks, including quartz, calcite, hornblende, mica, and feldspar.

Exploration Lab

Rock Identification

Most rocks can be easily identified by texture and composition. In this lab, you will use what you have learned about rocks as well as the information on minerals from Chapter 2 to identify some common rocks.

Problem
How can you use composition and texture to identify common rocks?

Materials
- rock samples
- hand lens
- pocket knife
- dilute hydrochloric acid
- colored pencils
- Chapter 2, Table 4 and Chapter 3, Tables 1, 2, 3

Skills
Observing, Comparing and Contrasting, Measuring

Procedure    

1. On a separate sheet of paper, make a copy of the data table shown below. Add any other columns that you think might be useful.
2. Examine each rock specimen with and without the hand lens. Determine and record the overall color of each rock.
3. Try to identify all of the minerals in each rock, using the information in Chapter 2 Table 4. Record your observations.

Data Table

Rock	Overall Color	Composition	Texture	Sketch	Rock Type	Rock Name
1.						
2.						
3.						
4.						
5.						

4. Determine and record the presence of any organic matter in any of the samples.
5. Observe the relationships among the minerals in each rock to determine texture. Refer to Chapter 3 Tables 1, 2, and 3 if necessary. Record your observations.
6. Note and record any other unique observations of the samples.
7. In your data table, make and color a detailed sketch of each sample.
8. Identify each sample as being an igneous rock, a sedimentary rock, or a metamorphic rock.
9. Name each sample. Use the photographs in this chapter and Tables 1, 2, and 3 if necessary.

Analyze and Conclude

1. **Evaluating** Which of the rock identification characteristics did you find most useful? Which of the characteristics did you find least useful? Give reasons for your answers.
2. **Comparing and Contrasting** How did identifying rocks compare with the mineral identification lab you did in Chapter 2? How is identifying rocks different from identifying the minerals that compose the rocks?
3. **Applying Concepts** Match the metamorphic rocks with their probable parent rocks.
4. **Applying Concepts** Choose two pairs of rocks used in this investigation. Write a brief description for each pair that explains how one rock can be changed into the other. Refer to the diagram of the rock cycle on page 67.

Go Further Obtain permission to collect some local rock samples from a park or nearby road. Use what you have learned about rocks and minerals to identify the rocks. Then write a brief history of each sample to explain how it formed and how it has changed since being formed.

Questioning Strategies
Ask: **How are rocks different from minerals?** *(Minerals are inorganic, natural solids with a definite chemical composition and a specific internal arrangement of atoms. Most rocks are mixtures in which the arrangement and amounts of the components vary.)*
How can all rocks be classified and identified? *(by texture and composition)*

Expected Outcome Students should be able to accurately identify at least one half to three fourths of the samples provided.

Sample Data

Compare students' data and observations with the information provided in Tables 1, 2, and 3.

Analyze and Conclude

1. Sample answer: Texture was more useful than composition—it was easier to determine texture than to determine composition.

2. Sample answer: The processes are similar because both involved determining the identity of a material using specific properties. The processes differ in that texture and composition are not standard properties used in mineral identification.

3. Bituminous coal is the parent rock of anthracite, sandstone the parent rock of quartzite, limestone the parent rock of marble, granite the parent rock of gneiss, and shale the parent rock of slate.

4. Sample answer: Pressure and heat can change shale, a sedimentary rock, into slate, a metamorphic rock. Students' answers should follow the paths described in the rock cycle shown on p. 67.

Go Further

Stress that students obtain permission before collecting rock samples. They should be accompanied by a responsible adult.
Kinesthetic, Logical

Study Guide

Study Tip

Study With a Partner

Suggest that students pair up as study partners, and spend at least one afternoon a week working together. Students can quiz each other on key concepts, compare notes, and discuss discrepancies.

CHAPTER 3

Study Guide

3.1 The Rock Cycle

Key Concepts

- A rock is any solid mass of mineral or mineral-like matter that occurs naturally.
- The three major types of rocks are igneous, sedimentary, and metamorphic.
- Interactions among Earth's water, air, and land can cause rocks to change from one type to another. The continuous processes that cause rocks to change make up the rock cycle.
- When magma cools and hardens beneath the surface or as the result of a volcanic eruption, igneous rock forms.
- Eventually sediments are compacted and cemented to form sedimentary rocks.
- Under extreme pressure and temperature conditions, sedimentary rock will change into metamorphic rock.
- Heat from Earth's interior and energy from the sun power the rock cycle.

Vocabulary

rock, *p. 66;* igneous rock, *p. 66;* sedimentary rock, *p. 66;* metamorphic rock, *p. 66;* rock cycle, *p. 67;* magma, *p. 67;* lava, *p. 67;* weathering, *p. 68;* sediments, *p. 68*

3.2 Igneous Rocks

Key Concepts

- Rocks that form when magma hardens beneath Earth's surface are called intrusive igneous rocks.
- When lava hardens, the rocks that form are called extrusive igneous rocks.
- Texture and composition are two characteristics used to classify igneous rocks.
- Slow cooling results in the formation of large crystals.
- Rapid cooling of magma or lava results in rocks with small, interconnected mineral grains.

Vocabulary

intrusive igneous rock, *p. 71;* extrusive igneous rock, *p. 71;* porphyritic texture, *p. 72;* granitic composition, *p. 73;* basaltic composition, *p. 73;* andesitic composition, *p. 73;* ultramafic, *p. 73*

3.3 Sedimentary Rocks

Key Concepts

- Erosion involves weathering and the removal of rock. When an agent of erosion—water, wind, ice, or gravity—loses energy, it drops the sediments. This process is called deposition.
- Compaction is a process that squeezes, or compacts, sediments.
- Cementation takes place when dissolved minerals are deposited in the tiny spaces among the sediments.
- Just like igneous rocks, sedimentary rocks can be classified into two main groups according to the way they form.
- The many unique features of sedimentary rocks are clues to how, when, and where the rocks formed.

Vocabulary

erosion, *p. 76;* deposition, *p. 76;* compaction, *p. 76;* cementation, *p. 76;* clastic sedimentary rock, *p. 77;* chemical sedimentary rock, *p. 77*

3.4 Metamorphic Rocks

Key Concepts

- Most metamorphic changes occur at elevated temperatures and pressures. These conditions are found a few kilometers below Earth's surface and extend into the upper mantle.
- During contact metamorphism, hot magma moves into rock.
- Regional metamorphism results in large-scale deformation and high-grade metamorphism.
- The agents of metamorphism are heat, pressure, and hydrothermal solutions.
- Metamorphic rocks can be classified by texture as foliated or nonfoliated.

Vocabulary

metamorphism, *p. 80;* contact metamorphism, *p. 81;* regional metamorphism, *p. 81;* hydrothermal solution, *p. 83;* foliated metamorphic rock, *p. 83;* nonfoliated metamorphic rock, *p. 83*

Chapter Assessment Resources

Print

Chapter Test, Chapter 3
Test Prep Resources, Chapter 3

Technology

Computer Test Bank, Chapter 3 Test
Online Text, Chapter 3
Go Online, PHSchool.com, Chapter 3

CHAPTER 3

NY Regents Content Item

Assessment

Interactive textbook with assessment at PHSchool.com 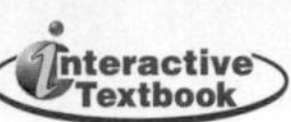

Reviewing Content

Choose the number that best answers the question or completes the statement.

1 Which of the following is NOT one of the three major types of rocks?
(1) anthracite (2) igneous
(3) metamorphic (4) sedimentary

2 Which of the following forms partly as the result of surface processes?
(1) metamorphic slate
(2) igneous basalt
(3) magma
(4) intrusive granite

3 Which of the following would NOT be a major process in the formation of sedimentary rocks?
(1) erosion (2) melting
(3) deposition (4) compaction

4 The formation of igneous rocks is powered by
(1) internal heat (2) the rock cycle
(3) erosion (4) the sun

5 A fine-grained igneous rock forms
(1) deep within Earth
(2) from magma
(3) as the result of slow cooling
(4) as the result of quick cooling

6 Cementation often occurs after Earth materials are
(1) eroded (2) weathered
(3) intruded (4) deposited

7 Ripple marks indicate that the rock formed
(1) underground (2) under a glacier
(3) in water (4) from lava

8 A major process in the formation of clastic sedimentary rocks is
(1) contact with magma
(2) cementation
(3) hardening
(4) foliation

9 Metamorphic rocks that have a banded appearance due to the alignment of minerals are called
(1) foliated (2) nonfoliated
(3) clastic (4) glassy

10 Which rock is made of the smallest sediments?
(1) shale (2) conglomerate
(3) breccia (4) sandstone

Understanding Concepts

11 Use what you have learned about the rock cycle to explain the following statement: One rock is the raw material for another rock. NY

12 Which igneous rock forms when basaltic lava hardens? When basaltic magma hardens? NY

13 A rock has a porphyritic texture. What can you conclude about the rock?

14 How are granite and rhyolite the same, and how do they differ? NY

15 Explain three types of weathering. NY

16 What are the most common minerals in clastic rocks? Why?

17 Distinguish between regional and contact metamorphism. NY

18 How could you easily distinguish a black and white gneiss from a similar-colored granite? NY

Use the following diagram to answer questions 19–22.

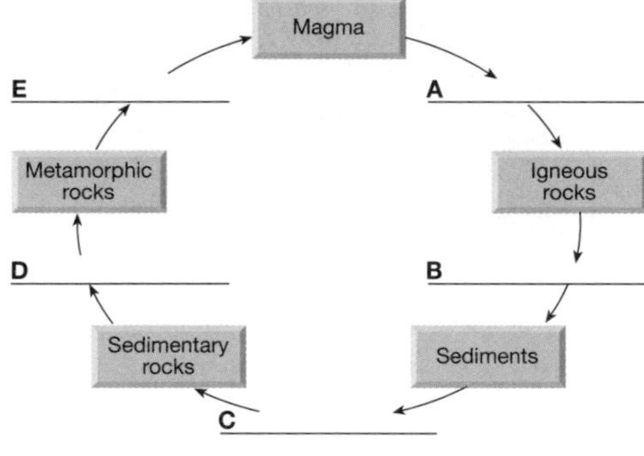

19 What process occurs at point A? NY

20 What three processes can occur at point B? NY

21 Name two processes that occur at point C. NY

22 What two processes occur at points D and E? NY

Homework Guide

Section	Questions
1	1–4, 11, 19–22, 36, 37
2	5, 12–14, 23, 35
3	6–8, 15, 16, 24, 25, 29–34
4	9, 10, 17, 18, 26–28

Assessment

Reviewing Content

(1) 1 (2) 1 (3) 2
(4) 1 (5) 4 (6) 4
(7) 3 (8) 2 (9) 1
(10) 1

Understanding Concepts

(11) Igneous rocks form from magma, which can be produced when any type of rock melts. Sedimentary rocks form as the result of changes in igneous, sedimentary, or metamorphic rocks. Likewise, metamorphic rocks form when any type of rock is changed by heat, pressure, and/or hot fluids.
(12) Basalt forms when basaltic lava hardens; gabbro, the coarse-grained (intrusive) equivalent of basalt, forms when basaltic magma hardens.
(13) A porphyritic texture indicates that the rock underwent at least two different episodes of cooling.
(14) Both are igneous rocks that have the same composition. Granite forms deep beneath the surface and therefore is coarse-grained. Rhyolite forms at much shallower depths and thus is fine-grained.
(15) Chemical weathering changes the composition of a rock. Physical weathering breaks the rock into smaller pieces. Weathering by organisms can be both physical and chemical.
(16) Clay minerals and quartz are the most common minerals in clastic rocks because clays are common products of chemical weathering and quartz is very resistant to weathering.
(17) Regional metamorphism subjects rocks to extreme changes in temperatures and pressures. As a result, the rock undergoes structural and compositional changes. During contact metamorphism, intruding magma causes a rise in temperature of the parent rock. Changes are often slight.
(18) The gneiss is foliated—bands of white minerals alternate with bands of black minerals. The color distribution of the granite is more random.
(19) Magma or lava solidifies.
(20) weathering, erosion, deposition
(21) compaction and cementation
(22) metamorphism (D) and melting (E)

Critical Thinking

(23) No, if two rocks have the same composition, then they are the intrusive and extrusive equivalents of one another. Thus, they cannot have the same textures.
(24) Both clastic and chemical sedimentary rocks form at or near Earth's surface as a result of weathering, erosion, deposition, compaction, and/or cementation. They differ in their textures and compositions. Clastic rocks include sandstone, conglomerate, breccia, siltstone, and shale. Chemical rocks include most limestones, rock salt, rock gypsum, chert, and flint.
(25) The length of time that the sediments that compose the rocks are eroded causes the sediments in a conglomerate to become rounded.
(26) Both change rocks. Heat provides the energy needed to drive chemical reactions. Some of these reactions cause existing minerals to recrystallize. Other reactions cause new minerals to form. Pressure can cause changes in composition and texture.
(27) The sandstone could become buried and thus be subjected to changes in temperature and/or pressure. If conditions are right, these changes could cause recrystallization of minerals in the sandstone and change the rock to quartzite.
(28) The metamorphic rocks often have a different composition; they can be foliated, unlike the parent rocks; the minerals might be larger than in the parent rocks; and the metamorphic rocks are often more dense than the rocks from which they formed.
(29) coarse-grained
(30) sedimentary
(31) coarse-grained clastic sedimentary rock
(32) Rocks were weathered to form sediments. The sediments were eroded, deposited, compacted, and cemented to form the rock.
(33) This rock could become an igneous rock if it were subjected to increases in temperatures and pressures high enough to cause melting.

CHAPTER 3

Assessment *continued*

Critical Thinking

23 **Synthesizing** Is it possible for two different types of igneous rocks to have the same composition and the same texture? Explain. NY

24 **Comparing and Contrasting** Compare and contrast the two types of sedimentary rocks and give at least two examples of each type. NY

25 **Formulating Hypotheses** Think about the sediments that compose both conglomerate and breccia. What one sedimentary process makes these two rocks different? Explain.

26 **Comparing and Contrasting** Compare and contrast the effects of heat and pressure in the formation of metamorphic rocks.

27 **Explaining** Explain all of the processes that might change a sandstone into a quartzite. NY

28 **Synthesizing** In what ways do metamorphic rocks differ from the sedimentary and igneous rocks from which they form? NY

Use the photograph to answer questions 29–33.

29 **Observing** Describe the texture of the rock. NY

30 **Identifying** To which of the three major groups of rocks does the rock belong? NY

31 **Classifying** Classify the rock as specifically as possible. NY

32 **Formulating Hypotheses** Briefly describe how this rock formed. NY

33 **Applying Concepts** Explain how this rock might become an igneous rock. NY

Concepts in Action

34 **Applying Concepts** Your friend shows you a rock with distinct layers. How can you and your friend determine if the rock is a sedimentary rock or a metamorphic rock? NY

35 **Applying Concepts** Name two rocks discussed in this chapter that might be used as flooring, countertops, or facades on museums and government buildings. Name two rocks that might be used for monuments and statues. NY

36 **Calculating** Each year, roughly 9100 kilograms of rock, sand, and gravel are mined for each person in the United States. Calculate how many kilograms of rock, sand, and gravel have been mined for you thus far in your life. Then calculate how much will be mined when you are 75 years old.

37 **Writing in Science** Suppose you're a writer for the school newspaper. You have been asked to do a story on one of the rocks described in this chapter. Pick a rock and write a short, newspaper-type story. Include facts about the rock—its texture, mineral composition, and how it formed. Also describe how the rock might change into a rock in each of the other two categories of rocks. Be creative, but scientifically accurate. NY

Performance-Based Assessment

Applying Concepts Go on field trip around your house, neighborhood, and community to find at least 10 items that are made from rocks or show ways in which rocks are used. Make a poster that shows what you found and display it for the class.

Concepts in Action

(34) A metamorphic rock will be denser and more compact than its sedimentary parent rock. It will also have a different composition. The layers in a sedimentary rock indicate different periods of deposition whereas the layers in a metamorphic rock are compositional layers.
(35) Polished marble, sandstone, conglomerate, and granite are often used for facades, flooring, countertops, and monuments. Marble is used to produce some statues and sculptures.
(36) Sample answer: 9,100 kg/year × 14 years = 127,400 kg; 9,100 kg/year × 75 years = 682,500 kg
(37) Use the information on the rock cycle and Tables 1, 2, and 3 to evaluate students' newspaper stories' features. Allow time for a few volunteers to read their stories to the class.

Regents Practice Exam

Test-Taking Tip

Using Visuals
Sometimes an answer to a test question requires that you interpret a drawing, a table, or a photograph. When this occurs, carefully study the visual before you read the questions pertaining to it. Refer to the visual again as you read each of the questions to which it pertains.

Use the photographs to answer questions 1–5.

For *each* statement or question, choose the *number* of the word or expression that, of those given, best completes the statement or answers the question. Some questions may require the use of the *Earth Science Reference Tables.* Base your answers to questions 1 through 4 on the diagram above, which shows different types of rocks.

1 Which of the following statements is true about the rocks shown above?
 (1) Sample *B* has a coarse-grained texture.
 (2) Sample *C* cooled very quickly on the surface.
 (3) Sample *D* cooled the slowest.
 (4) Sample *A* cooled deep underground.

2 Which rock most likely formed from the molten material that cooled and solidified at the fastest rate?
 (1) *A* (2) *B*
 (3) *C* (4) *D*

3 Which of the rocks probably formed as a result of slow cooling deep underground?
 (1) *A* (2) *B*
 (3) *C* (4) *D*

4 Which of the following terms best describes the texture of the rock labeled *D*?
 (1) porphyritic (2) glassy
 (3) fine-grained (4) coarse-grained

Answer the following questions in complete sentences. Some questions may require the use of the *Earth Science Reference Tables.* Base your answer to question 5 on the diagram to the left, which shows different types of rocks.

5 Under what conditions could a rock similar to sample *D* form?

6 Explain one similarity and one difference between sandstone and breccia.

7 A student finds a rock containing mineral crystals arranged in colored bands. Should this rock be classified as igneous, sedimentary, or metamorphic? Explain your answer.

8 If the Earth warms significantly, the Great Salt Lake in Utah will probably evaporate. Once the evaporation is complete, what rock will most likely be left behind? Explain your answer.

9 Explain the steps required to turn a deposit of sand into sandstone.

10 Describe the color and texture of the rock shown below. Describe the conditions required for this rock to form. Give the name of this rock.

Regents Practice Exam

(1) 1
(2) 4
(3) 2
(4) 2
(5) Sample *D* would form if lava cooled very quickly on the surface.
(6) Similarities: made of sediments; composed mostly of quartz, feldspar, and clay minerals; contain fragments of other rocks; may contain sand; form as a result of deposition, compaction, and cementation
Differences: sandstone's grains are smaller, 0.006 cm – 0.2 cm, and sand-sized, while breccia's grains are larger, more like the size of pebbles or cobbles
(7) This rock is metamorphic because it contains mineral crystals and is foliated.
(8) Rock salt will be left behind because as the water evaporates, the salt will be left behind, forming the mineral halite, which will then be cemented into rock salt.
(9) Sand must be compacted and cemented to become sandstone.
(10) The rock is light colored and coarse-grained; cooled slowly deep underground; is called granite

Performance-Based Assessment

Provide students with some local references, brochures, or tour guides to get them started, if necessary. As an alternative, plan a class field trip to see the ways in which rocks are an integral part of your community.

Your students can independently test their knowledge of the chapter and print out their results.

CHAPTER 4

Planning Guide

Use these planning tools
Use Teacher Express for all your planning needs

SECTION OBJECTIVES	STANDARDS		ACTIVITIES and LABS
	NATIONAL	STATE	
4.1 Energy and Mineral Resources, pp. 94–101 1 1/2 blocks or 3 periods 4.1 **Distinguish** between renewable and nonrenewable resources. 4.2 **Identify** which energy resources are fossil fuels. 4.3 **Predict** which energy resources might replace dwindling petroleum supplies in the future. 4.4 **Describe** the processes that concentrate minerals into large deposits as they form. 4.5 **Recognize** how nonmetallic mineral resources are used.	A-1, B-3, C-4, C-5, D-2, D-3, E-2, F-2, F3, F-4, F-5, F-6		**SE** Inquiry Activity: How Can You Determine the Resources You Use? p. 93 L2 **TE** Teacher Demo: Observing Coal, p. 96 L2 **TE** Build Science Skills, p. 96 L2 **TE** Teacher Demo: Varying the Size of Crystals, p. 99 L2 **TE** Build Science Skills, p. 100 L2
4.2 Alternate Energy Sources, pp. 102–107 1 block or 2 periods 4.6 **Evaluate** the advantages of solar energy. 4.7 **Explain** how nuclear power plants use nuclear fission to produce energy. 4.8 **Evaluate** wind power's potential for providing energy in the future. 4.9 **Relate** how hydroelectric power, geothermal energy, and tidal power contribute to our energy resources.	B-1, C-4, D-1, E-2, F-2, F-3 F-4, F-5, F-6		**TE** Build Science Skills, p. 103 L1 **TE** Teacher Demo: Modeling Hydroelectric Power, p. 105 L2 **TE** Teacher Demo: Making a Geyser, p. 106 L2
4.3 Water, Air, and Land Resources, pp. 108–112 1 block or 2 periods 4.10 **Explain** why fresh water is a vital resource. 4.11 **Recognize** why the chemical composition of the atmosphere is important. 4.12 **Identify** Earth's important land resources.	B-3, C-4, D-1, D-2, F-1, F-3, F-4, F-5, F-6		**TE** Teacher Demo: Motion Accelerates Erosion, p. 111 L2
4.4 Protecting Resources, pp. 113–116 1/2 block or 1 period 4.13 **Identify** the first laws passed to deal with water pollution. 4.14 **Name** the most important law passed to deal with air pollution. 4.15 **Explain** what is involved in protecting land resources.	A-1, A-2, C-4, F-2, F-3, F-4, F-5, F-6		**TE** Teacher Demo: Making an Oil Slick, p. 114 L1 **SE** Application Lab: Finding the Product that Best Conserves Resources, pp. 118–119 L2 **LM** Recovering Oil L2 **LM** Desalinization by Distillation L3

Ability Levels
L1 For students who need additional help
L2 For all students
L3 For students who need to be challenged

Components

SE	Student Edition	**GRSW**	Guided Reading & Study Workbook	**TP**	Test Prep Resources	**GEO**	Geode CD-ROM
TE	Teacher's Edition	**TEX**	Teacher Express	**onT**	onlineText	**T**	Transparencies
LM	Laboratory Manual	**CTB**	Computer Test Bank	**DC**	Discovery Channel Videos	**GO**	Internet Resources
CUT	Chapter Tests						

RESOURCES PRINT and TECHNOLOGY	SECTION ASSESSMENT
GRSW Section 4.1 **T-24** Ore Mineral of Important Metals **T-25** Uses of Nonmetalic Minerals **TEX** Lesson Planning 4.1	**SE** Section 4.1 Assessment, p. 101 **onT** Section 4.1
GRSW Section 4.2 **T-23** U.S. per Capita Use of Mineral and Energy Resources **TEX** Lesson Planning 4.2	**SE** Section 4.2 Assessment, p. 107 **onT** Section 4.2
GRSW Section 4.3 **TEX** Lesson Planning 4.3	**SE** Section 4.3 Assessment, p. 112 **onT** Section 4.3
GRSW Section 4.4 **DC** PET Clothes **TEX** Lesson Planning 4.4	**SE** Section 4.4 Assessment, p. 116 **onT** Section 4.4

Go Online

Go online for these Internet resources.

PHSchool.com
Web Code: cjk-9999

Web Code: cjn-1041
Web Code: cjn-1042
Web Code: cjn-1043
Web Code: cjn-1044

Materials for Activities and Labs

Quantities for each group

STUDENT EDITION

Inquiry Activity, p. 93
objects that contain resources

Application Lab, pp. 118–119
juice cartons (1.89-L, 946-mL, and 240-mL volumes), scissors, metric ruler

TEACHER'S EDITION

Teacher Demo, p. 96
samples of lignite, bituminous, and anthracite

Build Science Skills, p. 96
graduated cylinder or tall jar, vegetable oil, water, gravel, antacid tablet (optional)

Teacher Demo, p. 99
2 crucibles, beaker, water, teaspoon, sulfur powder, clamp, Bunsen burner, magnifying glass

Build Science Skills, p. 100
samples of limestone, cement, and concrete; dilute hydrochloric acid; dropper

Build Science Skills, p. 103
long, narrow potato chip can; scissors; long wooden skewer; tape; 20- × 30-cm piece of transparency film; hot dog

Teacher Demo, p. 105
piece of plastic or transparency film, scissors, plastic straw, straight pin, jar, water, metric ruler

Teacher Demo, p. 106
water; 250- or 500-mL Pyrex flask with tight-fitting, one-hole rubber stopper; glass tube 33–45 cm long; hot plate or Bunsen burner; ring stand; strong, small plastic bowl or container; ice pick or drill; plumber's putty

Teacher Demo, p. 111
2 identical clean 1-L jars with lids, marking pen, water, 2 identical pieces of hard candy, measuring cup

Teacher Demo, p. 114
large, clear, glass bowl; vegetable oil; water; cocoa powder

Chapter Assessment

ASSESSMENT

SE Assessment, pp. 121–122
CUT Chapter 4 Test
CTB Chapter 4
onT Chapter 4

STANDARDIZED TEST PREP

SE Chapter 4, p. 123
TP Progress Monitoring Assessments

interactive textbook with assessment at PHSchool.com

CHAPTER 4

Before you teach

Michael Wysession
Washington University

Big Ideas

Humans are dependent upon Earth for many different resources for survival. Earth science includes the discovery, extraction, and use of these resources.

Space and Time Resources can be roughly divided into renewable and nonrenewable categories. Renewable resources, such as water, food, and solar energy, are replenished over short time scales. Nonrenewable resources, such as coal, oil, and metals, have limited supplies that cannot be replenished.

Forces and Motion Mineral and metal resources become concentrated through a variety of geological processes that include igneous activity, precipitation from hydrothermal solutions, and erosionally-formed placer deposits.

Matter and Energy Humans are dependent upon clean water and air, and therefore the hydrologic cycle and atmospheric processes are vitally important. Human pollution can easily reduce these resources. Humans also rely upon and need to carefully manage land resources such as topsoil and trees. Our society relies heavily upon nonrenewable fossil fuels such as coal, petroleum, natural gas, and uranium (for nuclear power), and is beginning to use tar sands and oil shale. However, there is an increasing trend toward using renewable energy sources such as solar (both active and passive), wind, hydroelectric, geothermal, and tidal power.

Earth as a System Earth's resources will last longer if they are carefully managed, a process called conservation. There is a growing awareness of the need for conservation, including efforts to reduce consumption and to reuse and recycle resources where possible.

Earth Science Refresher

End of the Cenozoic Era

Humans have become the most powerful geologic agent of change on Earth's surface. In this context, it is impossible to investigate Earth science from a removed, objective point of view. The study of Earth science must also be a study of humans and human activity because of its remarkable effect on the atmosphere, hydrosphere, geosphere, and even biosphere. Nowhere else is this as dramatically seen as in the reduction of the number of species of life on Earth. It is hard to quantify the number of species that are currently going extinct. However, because of factors like the deforestation of rain forests and the introduction of foreign species into new environments, it has been estimated that up to 10 percent of the world's species are going extinct every 25 years. Because geologists use periods of mass extinction to define geological time periods, in a very short amount of time we may already have brought about an end to the Cenozoic Era, which has encompassed the past 65 million years. The morality of this is a topic of debate: was the asteroid impact that killed off the dinosaurs "bad"? However, with power should come responsibility, and humans need to be aware of the geological power that they now wield.

Address Misconceptions

Students may have many misconceptions about nuclear energy. They may think that a nuclear power plant may explode. Others fear that the electricity might be radioactive or that nuclear wastes release radioactivity into the air. And some think that these plants produce power through nuclear explosions. Nuclear power plants are not that different from coal-burning plants. The heat needed to boil water into steam is produced by burning fossil fuels in a coal-burning power plant. For a strategy that helps to overcome this misconception, see **Address Misconceptions** on **p. 104.**

Go Online PDLinks NSTA

For: Chapter 4 Content Support
Visit: www.SciLinks.org/PDLinks
Web Code: cjn-0499

Address Misconceptions

Students may hold the misconception that there is an actual hole in the sky that lets UV radiation through. The "hole" is actually a cyclic reduction in the concentration of ozone over Antarctica. The reason for concern is the fact that each year more ozone is being depleted and less is being repaired. For a strategy that helps to overcome this misconception, see **Address Misconceptions** on **p. 110.**

Humans are by no means the first life-forms to have shaped Earth's surface, nor have they yet had the most impact. Photosynthesizing bacteria created the oxygen in Earth's atmosphere that later allowed for the development of life on the surface of continents. Worms burrowing in ocean sediments have kept carbon dioxide from being locked away, and so have helped keep the climate stable over the past half-billion years. Land plants have covered vast portions of the continents, greatly altering the means and rates of erosion. The remains of ocean life have created the vast layers of the rock limestone. Human activity still pales in comparison. However, our release of different gases has already significantly affected global warming and the ozone layer in the atmosphere. Water pumping has removed much of the existing groundwater resources in many areas. The roads and parking lots of urbanized areas have not only reduced groundwater recharge, but greatly increased runoff into streams, worsening the effects of floods. At the same time, many river dams have prevented the occurrence of river flooding and therefore increased the buildup of sediment within the rivers. The human need for energy and mineral resources is resulting in an increasing amount of Earth's surface being stripped away to find these resources. Most significantly, with rising populations and global industrialization, all of these trends will continue to increase, so humans may yet attain the distinction of having altered Earth more than any other species.

Build Reading Literacy

Using Context Clues

Understanding the Meaning of Words

Strategy Help students determine the meaning of unfamiliar words. This strategy helps students use clues from the surrounding text to help them infer an unfamiliar word's meaning. Before students begin, assign a section in Chapter 4 for them to read, such as Alternate Energy Sources, pp. 102–107.

Example

- When students encounter a word they are unfamiliar with have them read the rest of the sentence to determine clues other words in the sentence may give as to the meaning of the unfamiliar word.
- Have students read the surrounding sentences looking for hints in the word's meaning.
- Have students synthesize the meaning from a reading of the whole passage.
- Have students scan the text for a possible definition of the word highlighted in bold or an illustration of it in a diagram.
- Once students think they have determined the word's meaning they should verify it by checking in a dictionary.

See p. 95 for a script on how to use this strategy with students. For additional strategies, see pp. 97, 103, 111, and 115.

ASSESS PRIOR KNOWLEDGE

Use the Chapter Pretest below to assess students' prior knowledge. As needed, review these concepts.

Review Science Concepts

Section 4.1 Reviewing rock types and the concept of density ensures that students will understand the structure of oil traps. A review of minerals will enhance understanding of the formation of mineral deposits.

Section 4.2 A short discussion of the structure of an atom will enhance students' understanding of nuclear energy.

Section 4.3 Reviewing the composition of Earth's atmosphere will give students a baseline for understanding air pollution and the presence of undesirable chemicals in the atmosphere.

Section 4.4 A review of minerals and their limited availability will lead students to realize the importance of conservation practices.

CHAPTER

4 Earth's Resources

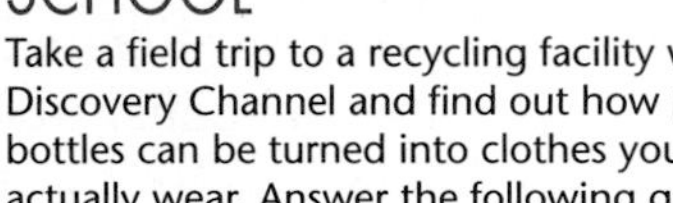

Application Lab
Finding the Product that Best Conserves Resources

Understanding Earth
Bingham Canyon, Utah: The Largest Open-Pit Copper Mine

Video Field Trip
PET Clothes

Take a field trip to a recycling facility with Discovery Channel and find out how plastic bottles can be turned into clothes you can actually wear. Answer the following questions after watching the video.

1. Approximately how many plastic bottles end up in landfills every year?
2. Name two ways that using PET bottles in manufacturing clothes can help preserve the environment.

For: Chapter 4 Resources
Visit: PHSchool.com
Web Code: cjk-9999

Once a mountain, this hole is now the world's largest open-pit mine. ▶

92 *Chapter 4*

Chapter Pretest

1. True or False: The electrons of an atom take part in radioactive decay. *(False)*
2. Which of the following is not a physical property of a mineral? *(c)*
   a. hardness
   b. luster
   c. reactivity
3. Describe briefly the two sources of material that make up sedimentary rocks. *(Sediments that make up sedimentary rocks may originate as solid particles from weathered rocks or as soluble material produced by chemical weathering.)*
4. Which gas is present in the greatest concentration in Earth's atmosphere? *(b)*
   a. carbon dioxide
   b. nitrogen
   c. oxygen
   d. ozone
5. What is the difference between a mineral and a rock? *(Minerals have an orderly internal structure and a definite chemical composition. Rocks are usually aggregates of several minerals and thus have a varied chemical composition and no orderly internal structure.)*
6. When might a mineral deposit not be considered an ore? *(when the mineral has no economic value)*

Chapter Preview

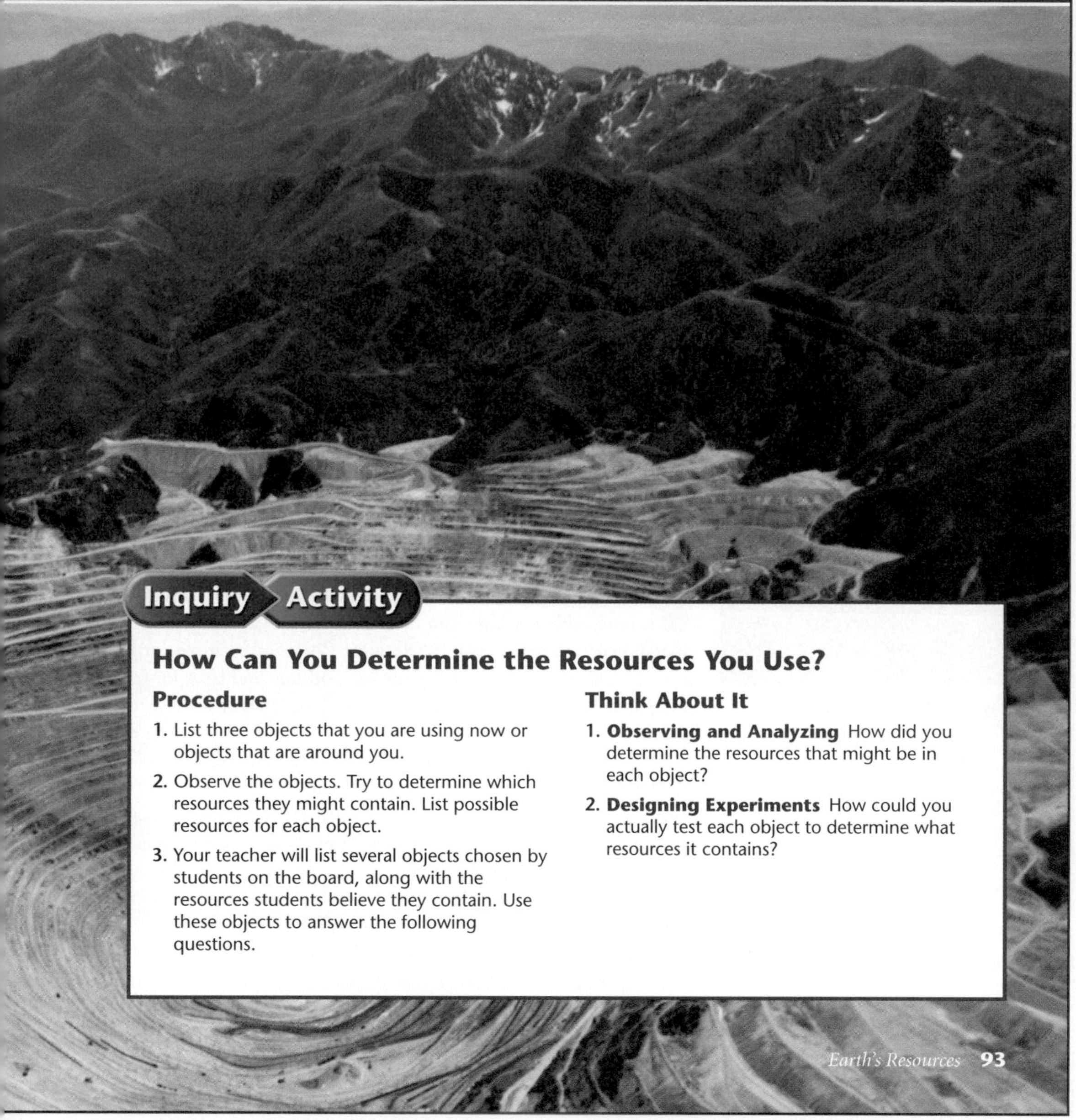

Inquiry Activity

How Can You Determine the Resources You Use?

Procedure

1. List three objects that you are using now or objects that are around you.
2. Observe the objects. Try to determine which resources they might contain. List possible resources for each object.
3. Your teacher will list several objects chosen by students on the board, along with the resources students believe they contain. Use these objects to answer the following questions.

Think About It

1. **Observing and Analyzing** How did you determine the resources that might be in each object?
2. **Designing Experiments** How could you actually test each object to determine what resources it contains?

ENGAGE/EXPLORE

Inquiry Activity

How Can You Determine the Resources You Use? L2

Address Misconceptions

Students may believe that fossil fuels are Earth's only natural resources. Explain that air, water, living things, energy sources, rocks, and minerals all are resources.

Purpose In this activity, students begin to recognize the resources found in everyday objects.

Skills Focus Observing, Designing Experiments, Analyzing, Evaluating

 **Prep Time** 5 minutes

Materials objects that contain resources

Advance Prep 10 minutes to set out objects

Class Time 10 minutes

Teaching Tip When you gather objects for students to examine, be sure to include some plastic items. This will lead to a discussion of petroleum as a source of plastics and other polymers.

Expected Outcome Students should realize that resources are found in almost all everyday objects.

Think About It

1. Answers will vary. Students will most likely use the physical characteristics of the objects to try to identify the resources.

2. Answers will vary. Students may propose burning the object, physically separating its components, or testing the object with acid or other substances.

Video Field Trip

PET Clothes

Encourage students to view the Video Field Trip "PET Clothes."

Section 4.1

1 FOCUS

Section Objectives

4.1 **Distinguish** between renewable and nonrenewable resources.

4.2 **Identify** which energy resources are fossil fuels.

4.3 **Predict** which energy resources might replace dwindling petroleum supplies in the future.

4.4 **Describe** the processes that concentrate minerals into large deposits as they form.

4.5 **Recognize** how nonmetallic mineral resources are used.

Reading Focus

Build Vocabulary L2

Word Forms Ask students to write a short paragraph explaining how a renewable library book is similar to a renewable resource. After students read the section, ask them if their paragraphs must be changed. If so, what changes would they make?

Reading Strategy L2

Answers will vary depending on students' prior knowledge and what they learn from the section.

2 INSTRUCT

Renewable and Nonrenewable Resources

Use Visuals L1

Figure 1 Point out some of the features of the New York skyline. Ask: **What mineral resources can be found in the scene in the photo?** *(stone facings on buildings, iron ore in the steel structures, petroleum in the asphalt streets)* **What energy resources probably power the lights in the photo?** *(probably coal, possibly nuclear fuel)*
Visual

4.1 Energy and Mineral Resources

Reading Focus

Key Concepts

- What is the difference between renewable and nonrenewable resources?
- Which energy resources are fossil fuels?
- Which energy resources might replace dwindling petroleum supplies in the future?
- What processes concentrate minerals into deposits sufficiently large enough to mine?
- How are nonmetallic mineral resources used?

Vocabulary

- renewable resource
- nonrenewable resource
- fossil fuel
- ore

Reading Strategy

Monitoring Your Understanding Copy this table onto a separate piece of paper before you read this section. List what you know about energy and mineral resources in the first column and what you'd like to know in the second column. After you read, list what you have learned in the last column.

Energy and Mineral Resources		
What I Know	What I Would Like to Know	What I Learned
a. ?	c. ?	e. ?
b. ?	d. ?	f. ?

Figure 1 Mineral resources went into the construction of every building in this New York skyline. Energy resources keep the lights on, too.

Mineral and energy resources are the raw materials for most of the things we use. Mineral resources are used to produce everything from cars to computers to basketballs. Energy resources warm your home, fuel the family car, and light the skyline in Figure 1.

Renewable and Nonrenewable Resources

There are two categories of resources—renewable and nonrenewable. **A renewable resource can be replenished over fairly short time spans such as months, years, or decades.** Common examples are plants and animals for food, natural fibers for clothing, and trees for lumber and paper. Energy from flowing water, wind, and the sun are also renewable resources.

By contrast, a nonrenewable resource takes millions of years to form and accumulate. When the present supply of nonrenewable resources run out, there won't be any more. Fuels such as coal, oil, and natural gas are nonrenewable. So are important metals such as iron, copper, uranium, and gold.

Earth's population is growing fast which increases the demand for resources. Because of a rising standard of living, the rate of mineral and energy resource use has climbed faster than population growth. For example, 6 percent of the world's population lives in the United States, yet we use 30 percent of the world's annual production

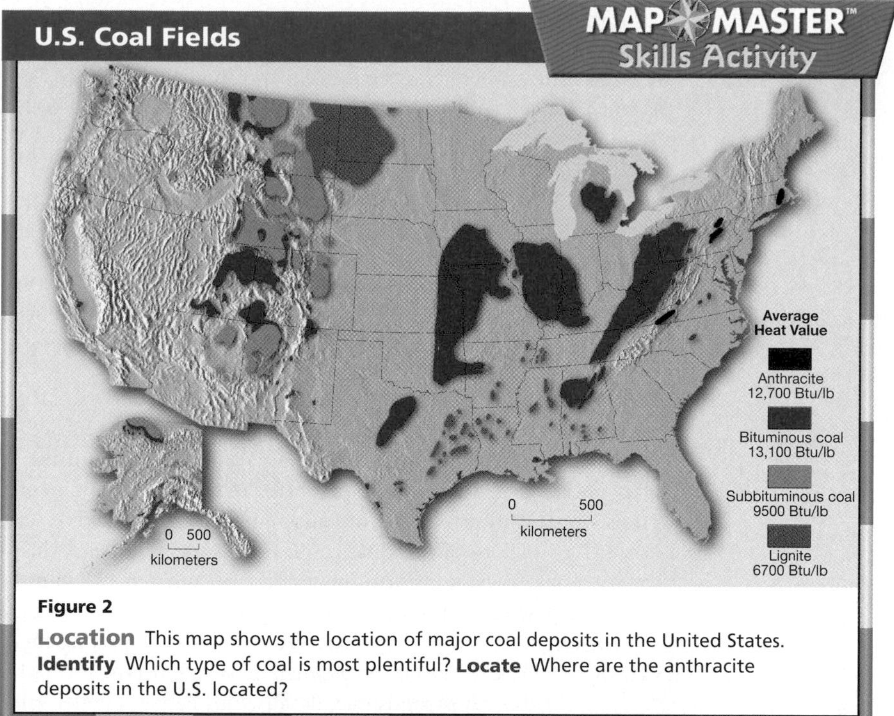

Figure 2
Location This map shows the location of major coal deposits in the United States. **Identify** Which type of coal is most plentiful? **Locate** Where are the anthracite deposits in the U.S. located?

of mineral and energy resources. How long can existing resources provide for the needs of a growing population?

Fossil Fuels

Nearly 90 percent of the energy used in the United States comes from fossil fuels. A **fossil fuel** is any hydrocarbon that may be used as a source of energy. **Fossil fuels include coal, oil, and natural gas.**

Coal Coal forms when heat and pressure transform plant material over millions of years. Coal passes through four stages of development. The first stage, peat, is partially decayed plant material that sometimes look like soil. Peat then becomes lignite, which is a sedimentary rock that is often called brown coal. Continued heat and pressure transforms lignite into bituminous coal, or soft coal. Bituminous coal is another sedimentary rock. Coal's last stage of development is a metamorphic rock called anthracite or hard coal. As coal develops from peat to bituminous, it becomes harder and releases more heat when burned.

Power plants primarily use coal to generate electricity. In fact, electric power plants use more than 70 percent of the coal mined today. The world has enormous coal reserves. Figure 2 shows coal fields in the United States.

For: Links on fossil fuels
Visit: www.SciLinks.org
Web Code: cjn-1041

Fossil Fuels

Integrate Economics L2

Resource Dependence Tell students that modern industries require many different mineral resources. Although some countries have substantial mineral deposits, no nation is self-sufficient. Because deposits are limited in number and location, all countries use trade to fulfill some of their needs. Students can research which countries are major suppliers of various resources and color a world map to show these sources of resources such as aluminum, iron, gold, and copper.
Visual, Kinesthetic

Answers
Identify bituminous coal
Locate in Pennsylvania, Virginia, Rhode Island, and Massachusetts

Build Reading Literacy

Refer to **p. 92D**, which provides the guidelines for using context clues.

Using Context Clues Have students explain the meaning of the term *fossil fuels*. The text discussion on how fossil fuels were formed should allow students to infer the meaning of the term. *(Coal, oil, and natural gas are fuels that formed from the remains, or fossils, of once-living plants and animals.)*
Verbal, Logical

Customize for Inclusion Students

Gifted Have students research the hydrocarbons that are found in petroleum. They might enjoy drawing structures or making models (using model-building kits or gumdrops and toothpicks) of straight-chain hydrocarbons and some of the simpler ring hydrocarbons. Students can also investigate the process of fractional distillation, in which crude petroleum is separated into different components or fractions according to their boiling points. The various fractions produced range from fuel gasoline to thick asphalts and lubricating grease.

Download a worksheet on fossil fuels for students to complete, and find additional teacher support from NSTA SciLinks.

Observing Coal L2

Purpose Students compare various stages of coal.

Materials samples of lignite, bituminous, and anthracite (Coal samples are often available from fuel companies, which are listed under *Coal* in the Yellow Pages of the phone book.)

Procedure Obtain samples of various coals. Pass samples around so students can compare them.

Expected Outcomes Anthracite will likely be a shiny dark grey or black. Bituminous and lignite will not be shiny, and lignite will likely be more brown in color than the other samples. Students will be able to break off pieces of lignite and possibly bituminous, but anthracite is too hard to break easily.
Visual

Use Visuals L1

Figure 3 Have students examine the diagram of an oil trap. Ask: **What prevents the gas and oil from rising to the surface and evaporating?** *(a cap rock)* **Why does the natural gas collect above the petroleum?** *(The gas is less dense than the oil.)* **What might happen if tremendous pressure builds up in the oil trap?** *(The pressure might force the petroleum up to the surface and cause a "gusher" or oil fountain.)*
Visual, Logical

Build Science Skills L2

Using Models ACTIVITY Have students make a model of an oil trap and observe the difference in densities of rock, oil, and water. In a graduated cylinder or tall jar, have students mix equal quantities of vegetable oil, gravel, and water. Let stand for 10 minutes and observe the layers that form. Students will find that the gravel sinks to the bottom of the container and the oil floats on top of the water layer. Ask: **What would happen if an antacid tablet were dropped into the graduated cylinder?** *(Bubbles of carbon dioxide would be produced. The bubbles would rise to the top and dissipate into the air.)* **What do the bubbles of carbon dioxide represent?** *(natural gas deposits)*
Kinesthetic, Visual

Although coal is plentiful, its recovery and use present problems. Surface mining scars the land. Today, all U.S. surface mines must restore the land surface when mining ends. Underground mining doesn't scar as much. However, it has been costly in terms of human life and health. Mining is safer today because of federal safety regulations. Yet, the hazards of collapsing roofs and gas explosions remain.

Burning coal—much of which is high in sulfur—also creates air pollution problems. When coal burns, the sulfur becomes sulfur oxides in the air. A series of chemical reactions turns the sulfur oxides into sulfuric acid, which falls to Earth as acid precipitation—rain or snow that is more acidic than normal. Acid precipitation can have harmful effects on forests and aquatic ecosystems, as well as metal and stone structures.

Petroleum and Natural Gas Petroleum (oil) and natural gas form from the remains of plants and animals that were buried in ancient seas. Petroleum formation begins when large quantities of plant and animal remains become buried in ocean-floor sediments. The sediment protects these organic remains from oxidation and decay. Over millions of years and continual sediment build up, chemical reactions slowly transform some of the organic remains into the liquid and gaseous hydrocarbons we call petroleum and natural gas.

These materials are gradually squeezed from the compacting, mud-rich sediment layers. The oil and gas then move into nearby permeable beds such as sandstone. Because this happens underwater, the rock layers containing the oil and gas are saturated with water. However, oil and natural gas are less dense than water, so they migrate upward through the water-filled spaces of the enclosing rocks. If nothing stops this migration, the fluids will eventually reach the surface.

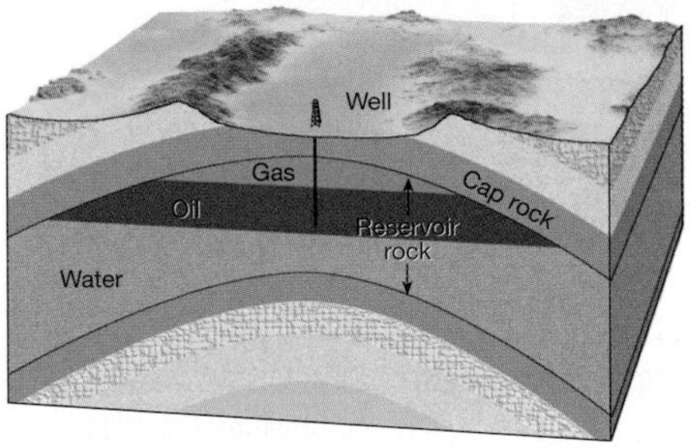

Sometimes an oil trap—a geologic structure that allows large amounts of fluids to accumulate—stops upward movement of oil and gas. Several geologic structures may act as oil traps, but all have two things in common. First, an oil trap has a permeable reservoir rock that allows oil and gas to collect in large quantities. Second, an oil trap has a cap rock that is nearly impenetrable and so keeps the oil and gas from escaping to the surface. One structure that acts as an oil trap is an anticline. An anticline is an uparched series of sedimentary rock layers, as shown in Figure 3.

When a drill punctures the cap rock, pressure is released, and the oil and gas move toward the drill hole. Then a pump lifts the petroleum out.

Figure 3 Anticlines are common oil traps. The reservoir rock contains water, oil, and gas. The fluids collect at the top of the arch with less dense oil and gas on top.
Interpreting Diagrams ***Why is the water located beneath the oil and gas?***

What two features must an oil trap have?

Facts and Figures

Different stages of coal have different moisture and heat contents. In general, the lower the moisture content of a coal, the higher the heat content will be. Lignite has a high inherent moisture content, sometimes as high as 45 percent. The heat content of lignite ranges from 9 to 17 million Btu per ton. Bituminous coal has a moisture content that is usually less then 20 percent. The heat content of bituminous coal ranges from 21 to 30 million Btu per ton. Anthracite coal has the lowest moisture content, generally less than 15 percent. The heat content of anthracite ranges from 22 to 28 million Btu per ton.

Tar Sands and Oil Shale

In the years to come, world petroleum supplies will dwindle. **Some energy experts believe that fuels derived from tar sands and oil shales could become good substitutes for dwindling petroleum supplies.**

Tar Sands Tar sands are usually mixtures of clay and sand combined with water and varying amounts of a black, thick tar called bitumen. Deposits occur in sands and sandstones, as the name suggests, but also in shales and limestones. The oil in these deposits is similar to heavy crude oils pumped from wells. The oil in tar sands, however, is much more resistant to flow and cannot be pumped out easily. The Canadian province of Alberta (Figure 4) has the largest tar sand deposits, which accounts for about 15 percent of Canada's oil production.

Currently, tar sands are mined at the surface, much like the strip mining of coal. The excavated material is then heated with pressurized steam until the bitumen softens and rises. The material is processed to remove impurities, add hydrogen, and refine into oil. However, extracting and refining tar sand requires a lot of energy—nearly half as much as the end product yields.

Obtaining oil from tar sand has significant environmental drawbacks. Mining tar sand causes substantial land disturbance. Processing also requires large amounts of water. When processing is completed, contaminated water and sediment accumulate in toxic disposal ponds.

Only about 10 percent of Alberta's tar sands can be economically recovered by surface mining. In the future, other methods may be used to obtain the more deeply buried material, reduce the environmental impacts, and make mining tar sands more economical.

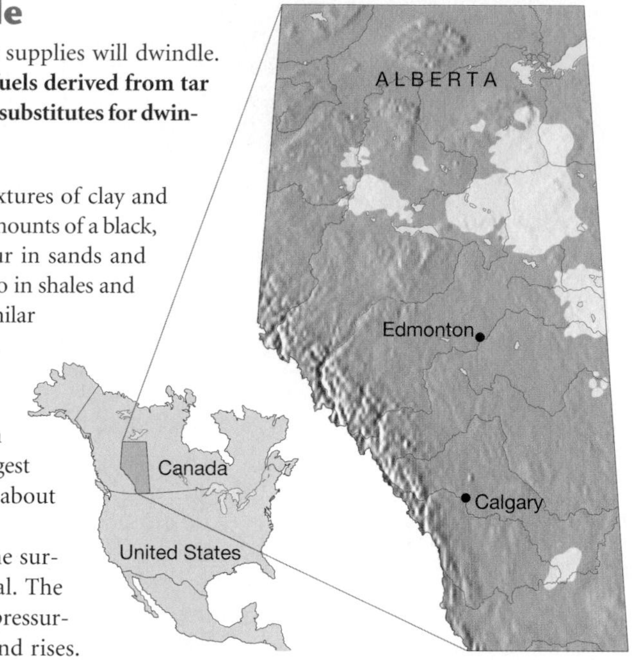

Figure 4 Tar Sand Deposits In North America, the largest tar sand deposits occur in the Canadian province of Alberta. They contain an estimated reserve of 35 billion barrels of oil.

What are some environmental drawbacks to mining tar sands?

Oil Shale Oil shale is a rock that contains a waxy mixture of hydrocarbons called kerogen. Oil shale can be mined and heated to vaporize the kerogen. The kerogen vapor is processed to remove impurities, and then refined.

Roughly half of the world's oil shale supply is in the Green River Formation of Colorado, Utah, and Wyoming. See Figure 5 on page 98. The oil shales are part of sedimentary layers that accumulated at the bottom of two extremely large, shallow lakes 57 to 36 million years ago.

Tar Sands and Oil Shale

Build Reading Literacy L1

Refer to **p. 124D** in **Chapter 5,** which provides the guidelines for summarizing.

Summarize Have students summarize the process by which tar sands are extracted from their deposits by making a flow diagram. Diagrams should have the various steps of the process labeled. Ask: **Why are tar sands so much more difficult to extract than petroleum?** *(Tar sands are so thick that they do not flow. Thus, they cannot be pumped out of the ground the way crude oil can. Hot fluids are injected into the tar sands to reduce the material's resistance to flow. The material can then be pumped out.)* **Logical**

Facts and Figures

Oil shales contain an enormous amount of oil. Worldwide, the U.S. Geological Survey estimates that there are more than 3000 billion barrels of oil in shales that could yield more than 38 liters of oil per ton of shale. However, present technology is only able to recover less than 200 billion barrels. Still, estimated U.S. resources are about 14 times greater than those of conventionally recoverable oil.

Answer to . . .

Figure 3 *The density of water is greater than the densities of oil and gas, so water is located beneath oil and gas.*

Reading Checkpoint *permeable reservoir rock to allow oil and gas to collect and a cap rock that keeps oil and gas from escaping*

Reading Checkpoint *Processing requires a lot of energy and water and causes the accumulation of contaminated water and sediment in toxic disposal ponds. Mining causes substantial land disturbance.*

Use Visuals L1

Figure 5 Have students examine the map. Ask: **Where is the Green River Formation located?** *(Northern Colorado, Wyoming, and Utah)* **Does this area have abundant water supplies?** *(No, the area is semi-arid.)*
Visual, Logical

Formation of Mineral Deposits

Build Science Skills 

Using Tables and Graphs Have students choose three ores and make a table listing the metal present in each, where in the United States each is mined, and what each is used for. Students can list other information about the chosen ores as well.
Intrapersonal, Verbal

Integrate Chemistry 

Crystal Size Tell students that the crystal size of minerals that form from magma is determined by how quickly the magma cools. If the rate of cooling is slow, the atoms of the mineral have time to arrange themselves into a large crystal lattice. If cooling is rapid, the atoms have time to arrange themselves only into small crystals. The Teacher Demo on the next page can be done as part of this discussion.
Visual, Kinesthetic

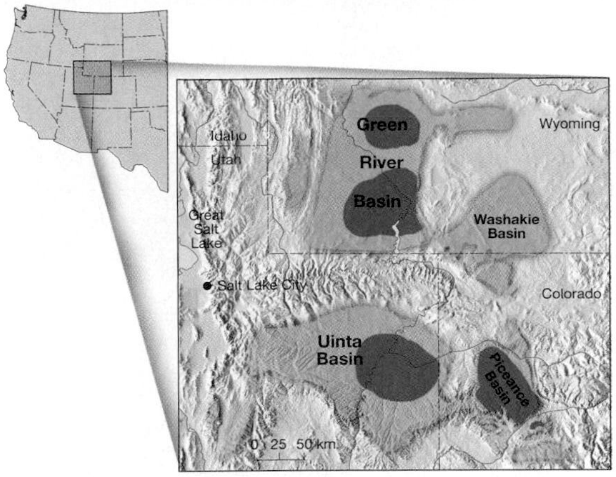

Figure 5 Distribution of Oil Shale in the Green River Formation The areas in red are the richest deposits.
Posing Questions ***How might the mining and processing of oil shale become more economically attractive?***

Some people see oil shale as a partial solution to dwindling fuel supplies. However, the heat energy in oil shale is only about one-eighth that in crude oil because oil shale contains large amounts of minerals. This mineral material adds costs to the mining, processing, and waste disposal of oil shale. The processing of it requires large amounts of water, which is scarce in the semi-arid region where the shales are found. Current technology makes mining oil shale an unprofitable solution.

Formation of Mineral Deposits

Practically every manufactured product contains substances that come from minerals. Mineral resources are deposits of useful minerals that can be extracted. Mineral reserves are deposits from which minerals can be extracted profitably. **Ore** is a useful metallic mineral that can be mined at a profit.

There are also known deposits that are not yet economically or technologically recoverable. These deposits, as well as deposits that are believed to exist, are also considered mineral resources.

The natural concentration of many minerals is rather small. A deposit containing a valuable mineral is worthless if the cost of extracting it exceeds the value of the material that is recovered. For example, copper makes up about 0.0135 percent of Earth's crust. However, for a material to be considered a copper ore, it must contain a concentration of about 50 times this amount.

Geologists have established that the occurrences of valuable mineral resources are closely related to Earth's rock cycle. The rock cycle includes the formation of igneous, sedimentary, and metamorphic rock as well as the processes of weathering and erosion. **Some of the most important mineral deposits form through igneous processes and from hydrothermal solutions.**

Mineral Resources and Igneous Processes Igneous processes produce important deposits of metallic minerals, such as gold, silver, copper, mercury, lead, platinum, and nickel. For example, as a large body of magma cools, heavy minerals crystallize early and settle to the bottom of the magma chamber. Chromite (chromium ore), magnetite, and platinum sometimes form this way. Such deposits produced layers of chromite at Montana's Stillwater Complex. Another deposit is found in the Bushveld Complex in South Africa. This deposit contains over 70 percent of the world's known platinum reserves.

Hydrothermal Solutions Hydrothermal (hot-water) solutions generate some of the best-known and most important ore deposits. Examples of hydrothermal deposits include the gold deposits of the Homestake Mine in South Dakota; the lead, zinc, and silver ores near Coeur D'Alene, Idaho; the silver deposits of the Comstock Lode in Nevada; and the copper ores of Michigan's Keweenaw Peninsula.

Most hydrothermal deposits form from hot, metal-rich fluids that are left during the late stages of the movement and cooling of magma. Figure 6 shows how these deposits form. As the magma cools and becomes solid, liquids and various metal ions collect near the top of the magma chamber. These ion-rich solutions can move great distances through the surrounding rock. Some of this fluid moves along openings such as fractures or bedding planes. The fluid cools in these openings and the metallic ions separate out of the solution to produce vein deposits, like those shown in Figure 7. Many of the most productive gold, silver, and mercury deposits occur as hydrothermal vein deposits.

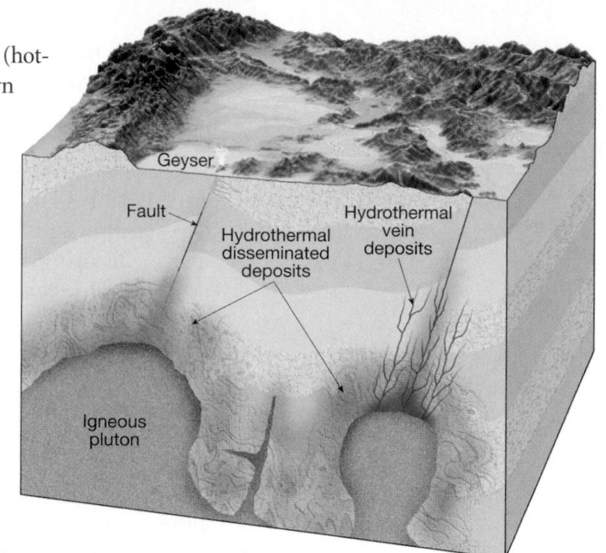

Figure 6 Mineral-rich hot water seeps into rock fractures, cools, and leaves behind vein deposits.

Placer Deposits Placer deposits are formed when eroded heavy minerals settle quickly from moving water while less dense particles remain suspended and continue to move. This settling is a means of sorting in which like-size grains are deposited together due to the density of the particles. Placer deposits usually involve minerals that are not only heavy but also durable and chemically resistant. Common sites of accumulation include point bars on the inside of bends in streams, as well as cracks, depressions, and other streambed irregularities.

Figure 7 Light veins of quartz lace a body of darker gneiss in Washington's North Cascades National Park.

Use Visuals L1

Figure 6 Have students examine the diagram of hydrothermal deposition. Ask: **Where are minerals likely to be deposited as veins?** *(in rock fractures)* **What is the source of the hot mineral-laden water in the diagram?** *(the geyser)*
Visual, Logical

Teacher Demo

Varying the Size of Crystals L2

Purpose Students observe how sulfur crystals form in relation to their rate of cooling.

CAUTION: This demonstration should be done in a fume hood or area with very good ventilation. Sulfur fumes can adversely affect students with respiratory problems.

Materials 2 crucibles, beaker, water, teaspoon, sulfur powder, clamp, Bunsen burner, magnifying glass

Procedure Place 1 teaspoon of powdered sulfur in one of the crucibles. Heat the crucible until the sulfur melts, then allow it to cool slowly. Place 1 teaspoon of sulfur in the second crucible. Melt the sulfur, and slowly pour it into a beaker that has been half-filled with water.

Expected Outcome Students should notice that the sulfur that cooled slowly developed larger crystals than the sulfur that cooled rapidly in water.
Visual, Logical

Facts and Figures

The term *placer* is probably of Spanish derivation and was used by the early Spanish miners in both North and South America as a name for gold deposits found in the sands and gravels of streams. Originally, the term seems to have meant "sand bank" or "a place in a stream where gold was deposited."

Answer to . . .

Figure 5 *Oil shale may become more economically attractive if the prices of petroleum and other competing fuels rise.*

Use Visuals L1

Figure 8 Have students think about prospecting for gold. Ask: **Why does the gold dust settle to the bottom of the pan?** *(The gold dust is heavier than the other material suspended in the water.)* **Why doesn't the gold dissolve in water?** *(Gold is not soluble in water.)* **Visual, Logical**

Nonmetallic Mineral Resources

Build Science Skills 

Designing Experiments ACTIVITY

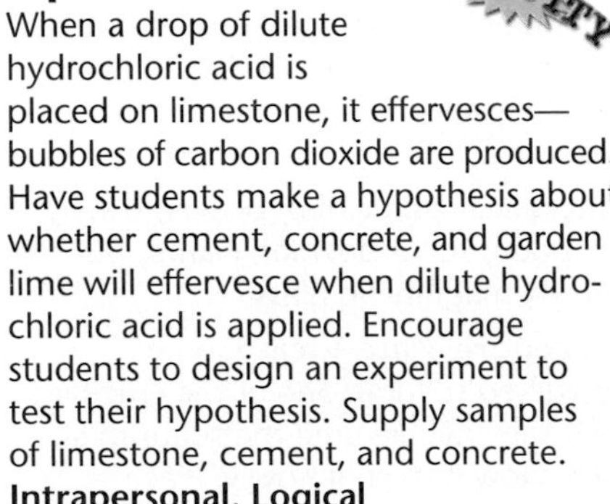

When a drop of dilute hydrochloric acid is placed on limestone, it effervesces—bubbles of carbon dioxide are produced. Have students make a hypothesis about whether cement, concrete, and garden lime will effervesce when dilute hydrochloric acid is applied. Encourage students to design an experiment to test their hypothesis. Supply samples of limestone, cement, and concrete. **Intrapersonal, Logical**

Figure 8 Placer deposits led to the California gold rush. Here, a prospector in 1850 swirls his gold pan, separating sand and mud from flecks of gold.

Q *How big was the largest gold nugget ever discovered?*

A The largest gold nugget ever discovered was the Welcome Stranger Nugget found in 1869 as a placer deposit in the gold-mining region of Victoria, Australia. It weighed a massive 2520 troy ounces (210 pounds, or 95 kilograms) and, at today's gold prices, was worth over $700,000. The largest gold nugget known to remain in existence today is the Hand of Faith Nugget, which was found in 1975 near Wedderburn, Victoria, Australia. It was found with a metal detector and weighs 875 troy ounces (73 pounds, or 33 kilograms). Sold in 1982, it is now on display in the Golden Nugget Casino in Las Vegas, Nevada.

Gold is the best-known placer deposit. In 1848, placer deposits of gold were discovered in California, sparking the famous California gold rush. Early prospectors searched rivers by using a flat pan to wash away the sand and gravel and concentrate the gold "dust" at the bottom. Figure 8 shows this common method. Years later, similar deposits created a gold rush to Alaska. Sometimes prospectors follow the placer deposits upstream. This method may lead prospectors to the original mineral deposit. Miners found the gold-bearing veins of the Mother Lode in California's Sierra Nevadas by following placer deposits.

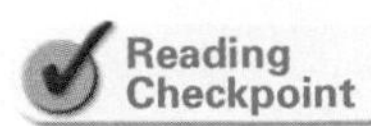

Reading Checkpoint *What are mineral resources?*

Nonmetallic Mineral Resources

Nonmetallic mineral resources are extracted and processed either for the nonmetallic elements they contain or for their physical and chemical properties. People often do not realize the importance of nonmetallic minerals because they see only the products that resulted from their use and not the minerals used to make the products.

Examples of nonmetallic minerals include the fluorite and limestone that are part of the steelmaking process and the fertilizers needed to grow food, as shown in Table 1.

Nonmetallic mineral resources are divided into two broad groups—building materials and industrial minerals. For example, natural aggregate (crushed stone, sand, and gravel), is an important material used in nearly all building construction.

Some substances, however, have many uses in both construction and industry. Limestone is a good example. As a building material, it is used as crushed rock and building stone. It is also an ingredient in cement. As an industrial mineral, limestone is an ingredient in the manufacture of steel. Farmers also use it to neutralize acidic soils.

Many nonmetallic resources are used for their specific chemical elements or compounds. These resources are important in the manufacture of chemicals and fertilizers. In other cases, their importance is related to their physical properties. Examples include abrasive minerals such as corundum and garnet.

Although industrial minerals are useful, they have drawbacks. Most industrial minerals are not nearly as abundant as building materials. Manufacturers must also transport nonmetallic minerals long distances, adding to their cost. Unlike most building materials, which need a minimum of processing before use, many industrial minerals require considerable processing to extract the desired substance at the proper degree of purity.

Facts and Figures

Our society uses enormous quantities of nonmetallic minerals each year. The per-person consumption of non-fuel resources in the United States totals more than 11 metric tons. About 94 percent of these resources are nonmetallics.

Table 1 Occurrences and Uses of Nonmetallic Minerals

Mineral	Uses	Geological Occurrences
Apatite	Phosphorus fertilizers	Sedimentary deposits
Asbestos (chrysotile)	Incombustible fibers	Metamorphic alteration
Calcite	Aggregate; steelmaking; soil conditioning; chemicals; cement; building stone	Sedimentary deposits
Clay minerals (kaolinite)	Ceramics; china	Residual product of weathering
Corundum	Gemstones; abrasives	Metamorphic deposits
Diamond	Gemstones; abrasives	Kimberlite pipes; placers
Fluorite	Steelmaking; aluminum refining; glass; chemicals	Hydrothermal deposits
Garnet	Abrasives; gemstones	Metamorphic deposits
Graphite	Pencil lead; lubricant; refractories	Metamorphic deposits
Gypsum	Plaster of Paris	Evaporite deposits
Halite	Table salt; chemicals; ice control	Evaporite deposits, salt domes
Muscovite	Insulator in electrical applications	Pegmatites
Quartz	Primary ingredient in glass	Igneous intrusions, sedimentary deposits
Sulfur	Chemicals; fertilizer manufacture	Sedimentary deposits, hydrothermal deposits
Sylvite	Potassium fertilizers	Evaporite deposits
Talc	Powder used in paints, cosmetics, etc.	Metamorphic deposits

Section 4.1 Assessment

Reviewing Concepts

1. What is the difference between a renewable and a nonrenewable resource?
2. What are the three major fossil fuels?
3. What are tar sands and oil shale?
4. How do hydrothermal deposits form?
5. What are the two broad categories of nonmetallic mineral resources?
6. Compare and contrast the formation of coal with that of petroleum and natural gas.

Critical Thinking

7. **Drawing Conclusions** Why isn't the use of tar sands more widespread in the United States?
8. **Applying Concepts** Explain how following placer deposits upstream would help prospectors find the original deposit.

Writing in Science

Compare-Contrast Paragraph Write a paragraph describing the difference in the use of nonmetallic building minerals and nonmetallic industrial minerals.

Use Visuals L1

Table 1 Have students study the table. Ask: **What is halite, and what are its uses?** *(Halite is table salt. In addition to seasoning food, it is used in chemical processes and to melt ice.)* **Which mineral listed occurs in Kimberlite pipes?** *(diamond)* **Which mineral listed occurs as hydrothermal deposits?** *(fluorite)* **Visual, Logical**

3 ASSESS

Evaluate Understanding L2

To assess students' knowledge of section content, have them list two renewable resources and two nonrenewable resources. Students should explain why each resource listed is renewable or nonrenewable.

Reteach L1

Have students make a poster diagramming the process by which coal is formed. The type of vegetation depicted should be appropriate for the time. *(Large tree ferns and other swamp vegetation were predominant in coal swamps during the Pennsylvanian and Permian periods.)*

Writing in Science

Building materials are abundant, need little processing, need not be pure, and are usually found close to where they are used. Industrial minerals are used for their chemical or physical properties, are relatively scarce, must be extracted and purified, and must be transported.

Answer to . . .

Reading Checkpoint *Mineral resources are Earth materials that are extracted and processed for either the metals or the elements they contain.*

Section 4.1 Assessment

1. Renewable resources have unlimited supplies and can be replaced; nonrenewable resources have limited supplies and cannot be replaced.
2. coal, petroleum, natural gas
3. geologic structures that contain low grade hydrocarbons mixed with clay, sand, or shale
4. Hydrothermal deposits form from hot, metal-rich fluids that are left when magma cools. The metal ions collect as mineral deposits in small openings such as rock fractures.
5. building materials and industrial minerals
6. Coal was formed from plant material that collected in swamps. Petroleum and natural gas were formed from plant and animal material that collected and were buried in ancient seas.
7. Most of the world's tar-sand deposits are in Canada. The few deposits in the United States are in California. In addition, mining tar sands has serious environmental drawbacks and is expensive.
8. Placer deposits are minerals that are carried by moving water from a source upstream. By following the deposits upstream, it is possible to find the original deposit.

Section 4.2

1 FOCUS

Section Objectives

4.6 **Evaluate** the advantages of solar energy.

4.7 **Explain** how nuclear power plants use nuclear fission to produce energy.

4.8 **Evaluate** wind power's potential for providing energy in the future.

4.9 **Relate** how hydroelectric power, geothermal energy, and tidal power contribute to our energy resources.

Reading Focus

Build Vocabulary L2

Word Parts Have students break the word *geothermal* into its parts. They should use a dictionary to find the meaning and derivation of each part. *(Geo- or ge- is a Greek combination form meaning "earth or ground." Thermal comes from the Greek word therme meaning "coming from heat." Geothermal energy is heat that comes from within Earth.)*

Reading Strategy L2

a. solar energy
b. nuclear energy
c. wind energy
d. hydroelectric power
e. geothermal energy
f. tidal power

2 INSTRUCT

Solar Energy

Use Visuals L1

Figure 9 Have students examine the photo. Tell them that the structures on the ground are tracking mirrors that reflect the solar energy onto a receiver mounted on the tower. Ask: **What do you think happens to the solar energy once it enters the receiver?** *(The solar energy is absorbed by a fluid, typically molten salt or air, and used to generate steam to power a conventional turbine.)* **Can electricity be generated at night?** *(No; energy can be stored at night, but not generated at night.)*
Visual, Logical

4.2 Alternate Energy Sources

Reading Focus

Key Concepts

- What are the advantages of using solar energy?
- How do nuclear power plants use nuclear fission to produce energy?
- What is wind power's potential for providing energy in the future?
- How do hydroelectric power, geothermal energy, and tidal power contribute to our energy resources?

Vocabulary

- hydroelectric power
- geothermal energy

Reading Strategy

Previewing Skim the section and start a concept map for the various alternate energy resources.

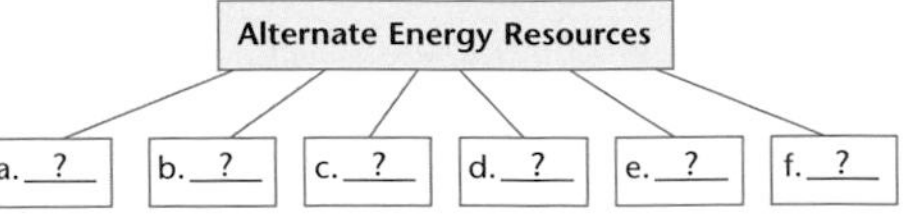

Figure 9 Solar One is a solar installation used to generate electricity in the Mojave Desert near Barstow, California.

There's no doubt that we live in the age of fossils fuels. These nonrenewable resources supply nearly 90 percent of the world's energy. But that can't last forever. At the present rates of consumption, the amount of recoverable fossil fuels may last only another 170 years. As the world population soars, the rate of consumption will climb as well. This will leave fossil fuel reserves in even shorter supply. In the meantime, the burning of huge quantities of fossil fuels will continue to damage the environment. Our growing demand for energy along with our need for a healthy environment will likely lead to a greater reliance on alternate energy sources.

Solar Energy

Solar energy is the direct use of the sun's rays to supply heat or electricity. **Solar energy has two advantages: the "fuel" is free, and it's non-polluting.** The simplest and perhaps most widely used solar energy systems are passive solar collectors such as south-facing windows. As sunlight passes through the glass, objects in the room absorb its heat. These objects radiate the heat, which warms the air.

More elaborate systems for home heating use an active solar collector. These roof-mounted devices are usually large, blackened boxes covered with glass or plastic. The heat they collect can be transferred to areas where it is needed by circulating air or liquids through piping. Solar collectors are also used to heat water for domestic and commercial needs. For example, solar collectors provide hot water for more than 80 percent of Israel's homes.

102 Chapter 4

There are a few drawbacks to solar energy. While the energy collected is free, the necessary equipment and installation is not. A supplemental heating unit is also needed when there is less solar energy—on cloudy days or in the winter—or at night when solar energy is unavailable. However, over the long term, solar energy is economical in many parts of the United States. It will become even more cost effective as the prices of other fuels increase.

Research is currently underway to improve the technologies for concentrating sunlight. Scientists are examining a way to use mirrors to track the sun and keep its rays focused on a receiving tower. Figure 9 shows a solar collection facility with 2000 mirrors that was built near Barstow, California. This facility heats water in pressurized panels to over 500°C by focusing solar energy on a central tower. The superheated water is then transferred to turbines, which turn electrical generators.

Another type of collector, shown in Figure 10, uses photovoltaic (solar) cells. They convert the sun's energy directly into electricity.

Figure 10 Solar cells convert sunlight directly into electricity. This array of solar panels is near Sacramento, California.
Applying Concepts *What characteristics would you look for if you were searching for a location for a new solar plant?*

What are the two main advantages of using solar energy?

Nuclear Energy

Nuclear power meets about 7 percent of the energy demand of the United States. The fuel for nuclear plants, like the one in Figure 11, comes from radioactive materials that release energy through nuclear fission. **In nuclear fission, the nuclei of heavy atoms such as uranium-235 are bombarded with neutrons. The uranium nuclei then split into smaller nuclei and emit neutrons and heat energy.** The neutrons that are emitted then bombard the nuclei of adjacent uranium atoms, producing a chain reaction. If there is enough fissionable material and if the reaction continues in an uncontrolled manner, fission releases an enormous amount of energy as an atomic explosion.

In a nuclear power plant, however, the fission reaction is controlled by moving neutron-absorbing rods into or out of the nuclear reactor. The result is a controlled nuclear chain reaction that releases great amounts of heat. The energy drives steam turbines that turn electrical generators. This is similar to what occurs in most conventional power plants.

Figure 11 Diablo Canyon Nuclear Plant Near San Luis Obispo, California Reactors are in the dome-shaped buildings. You can see cooling water being released to the ocean.
Analyzing *The siting of this plant was controversial because it is close to faults. Why would that be a cause for concern?*

Build Science Skills L2

Using Models ACTIVITY
Have students make a model solar oven. Each student will need a long, narrow potato chip can; scissors; a long wooden skewer; tape; a 20- × 30-cm piece of transparency film; and a hot dog. The can should be cut as follows: make two 8-cm cuts around the can connected by an 18-cm cut to form an *H*. Bend back the flaps but do not remove them from the can. They will be used to reflect solar energy onto the hot dog. Cover the opening on the inside of the can with the transparency film and tape the film into place. Make small holes in the metal end of the can and in the plastic lid. Remove the lid. Put a hot dog lengthwise onto the skewer and slide the skewer into the can, inserting the end into the hole in the metal end. Put the plastic lid on the can and insert the other end of the skewer into the hole in the lid. The hot dog will be suspended inside the can. Place the solar oven into direct sunlight and adjust the flaps so that they reflect solar energy onto the hot dog. Ask students what they can do to make the hot dog cook faster. *(Answers will vary. Students may suggest that they can insulate the can or enlarge the flaps with aluminum foil.)*
Kinesthetic, Logical

Nuclear Energy

Build Reading Literacy L1

Refer to **p. 362D** in **Chapter 13**, which provides the guidelines for using prior knowledge.

Use Prior Knowledge Have students use their knowledge of the structure of an atom to make a model of an atom having 6 protons and 6 neutrons.
Ask: **How many electrons will this atom have?** *(6)* **What element is represented by this atom?** *(carbon)* **Is this atom radioactive? Explain.** *(It is not radioactive because its nucleus is stable.)*
Kinesthetic, Logical

Customize for English Language Learners

Encourage students who are new to the United States to describe any differences in the use or production of energy they may have observed. For example, cooking and heating fuels may be different from those used in the United States. Many European and Asian countries rely more heavily on nuclear power than Americans do. For example, 75 percent of France's power comes from nuclear energy.

Answer to . . .

Figure 10 *abundant sunlight, long summers, abundant space*

Figure 11 *Faults are prone to earthquakes which could damage the reactor.*

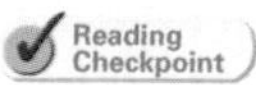

The fuel is free and it's non-polluting.

Address Misconceptions **L2**

Students may have many misconceptions about nuclear energy. They may think that a nuclear power plant may explode. Others fear that the electricity might be radioactive or that nuclear wastes release radioactivity into the air. Some students may think nuclear power plants produce power through nuclear explosions. Explain to students that nothing is exploded or burned. The uranium that is brought to Earth's surface during coal mining can have a greater effect on the environment than nuclear waste. Nuclear power plants are not that different from coal-burning plants. The heat needed to boil water into steam is produced by burning fossil fuels in a coal-burning power plant. Ask: **Where does the heat needed to produce steam come from in a nuclear power plant?** *(from splitting certain atoms of uranium)* Once the steam is produced, it turns the blades of a turbine, which causes a generator to produce electricity. Ask: **Is the process of producing electricity from steam in a nuclear plant the same or different from the process in a coal-burning plant?** *(the same; only the method of producing steam is different.)*
Logical

Wind Energy

Build Science Skills **L2**

Applying Concepts Ask: **Why are mountain passes good locations for wind farms?** *(Most mountain passes have strong, steady winds that sweep through the area.)* **What other locations would make good locations for wind farms?** *(along a seacoast)*
Intrapersonal, Logical

Download a worksheet on wind for students to complete, and find additional teacher support from NSTA SciLinks.

At one time, energy experts thought nuclear power would be the cheap, clean energy source that would replace fossil fuels. But several obstacles have slowed its development. First, the cost of building safe nuclear facilities has increased. Second, there are hazards associated with the disposal of nuclear wastes. Third, there is concern over the possibility of a serious accident that could allow radioactive materials to escape. The 1979 accident at Three Mile Island in Pennsylvania made this concern a reality. A malfunction in the equipment led the plant operators to think there was too much water in the primary system. Instead there was not enough water. This confusion allowed the reactor core to lie uncovered for hours. Although there was little danger to the public, the malfunction resulted in substantial damage to the reactor.

Unfortunately, the 1986 accident at Chernobyl in Ukraine was far more serious. In this case, the reactor went out of control. Two small explosions lifted the roof of the structure, and pieces of uranium spread over the surrounding area. A fire followed the explosion. During the 10 days that it took to put out the fire, the atmosphere carried high levels of radioactive material as far away as Norway. Eighteen people died within six weeks of the accident. Thousands more faced an increased risk of death from cancers associated with the fallout.

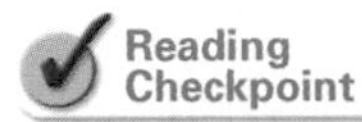

Reading Checkpoint *What is nuclear fission?*

For: Links on wind
Visit: www.SciLinks.org
Web Code: cjn-1042

Figure 12 These wind turbines are operating near Palm Springs, California.

Wind Energy

According to one estimate, if just the winds of North and South Dakota could be harnessed, they would provide 80 percent of the electrical energy used in the United States. Wind is not a new energy source. People have used it for centuries to power sailing ships and windmills for grinding grains.

Following the "energy crisis" brought about by the oil embargo of the 1970s, interest in wind power and other alternative forms of energy grew. In 1980, the federal government started a program to develop wind-power systems, such as the one shown in Figure 12. The U.S. Department of Energy set up experimental wind farms in mountain passes with strong, steady winds. One of these facilities, at Altamont Pass near San Francisco, now operates more than 7000 wind turbines. In the year 2000, wind supplied a little less than one percent of California's electricity.

Some experts estimate that in the next 50 to 60 years, wind power could meet between 5 to 10 percent of the country's demand for electricity. Islands and other isolated regions that must import fuel for generating power are major candidates for wind energy expansion.

The future for wind power looks promising, but there are difficulties. The need for technical advances, noise pollution, and the cost of large tracts of land in populated areas are obstacles to development.

Facts and Figures

Although many people think wind power is a new development, the use of multiple wind turbines to perform a task is nothing new. Dutch engineers used multiple windmills to drain water from their countryside. The Dutch called these early wind farms *gangs* of windmills, and a group can still be seen southeast of Rotterdam at Kinderdijk. Windmills may also have been the driving force of the industrial revolution in the Netherlands during the eighteenth century. Dutch millers constructed an amazing assembly of more than 700 industrial windmills in a region northwest of Amsterdam. These windmills powered Dutch industry before the use of coal became widespread in the rest of Europe.

Figure 13 Glen Canyon Dam and Lake Powell on the Colorado River As dam operators release water in the reservoir, it passes through machinery that drives turbines and produces electricity.

Hydroelectric Power

Like wind, moving water has been an energy source for centuries. The mechanical energy that waterwheels produce has powered mills and other machinery. Today, the power that falling water generates, known as **hydroelectric power,** drives turbines that produce electricity. In the United States, hydroelectric power plants produce about 5 percent of the country's electricity. Large dams, like the one in Figure 13, are responsible for most of it. The dams allow for a controlled flow of water. **The water held in a reservoir behind a dam is a form of stored energy that can be released through the dam to produce electric power.**

Although water power is a renewable resource, hydroelectric dams have finite lifetimes. Rivers deposit sediment behind the dam. Eventually, the sediment fills the reservoir. When this happens, the dam can no longer produce power. This process takes 50 to 300 years, depending on the amount of material the river carries. An example is Egypt's Aswan High Dam on the Nile River, which was completed in the 1960s. It is estimated that half the reservoir will be filled with sediment by 2025.

The availability of suitable sites is an important limiting factor in the development of hydroelectric power plants. A good site must provide a significant height for the water to fall. It also must have a high rate of flow. There are hydroelectric dams in many parts of the United States, with the greatest concentration in the Southeast and the Pacific Northwest. Most of the best U.S. sites have already been developed. This limits future expansion of hydroelectric power.

Geothermal Energy

Geothermal energy is harnessed by tapping natural underground reservoirs of steam and hot water. **Hot water is used directly for heating and to turn turbines to generate electric power.** The reservoirs of steam and hot water occur where subsurface temperatures are high due to relatively recent volcanic activity.

Hydroelectric Power

Modeling Hydroelectric Power L2

Purpose Students determine how the amount of energy from falling water increases with increasing height.

Materials piece of plastic or transparency film, scissors, plastic straw, straight pin, jar, water, metric ruler

Procedure Make a pinwheel by cutting a square piece of plastic or transparency film. Attach the pinwheel to a plastic straw by placing a straight pin through the center of the pinwheel and through the straw. Hold the pinwheel over a sink while a student pours a full jar of water on the pinwheel from a measured height. Have students count the number of turns the pinwheel makes. Repeat the procedure several times using the same amount of water and the same rate of flow. Vary only the height of the water jar above the pinwheel.

Expected Outcome The pinwheel should turn faster and make more turns as the water is poured from increasing height.
Visual, Kinesthetic

Geothermal Energy

Integrate Geography L2

Iceland Inform students that geothermal energy is one of Iceland's greatest natural resources. The capital of Iceland has enjoyed this valuable source of power for more than 60 years. Geothermal heat is used mostly to heat fresh water, which is utilized directly for central heating. Over 89 percent of all the houses in Iceland are heated this way. Geothermal water is also used in swimming pools, for melting snow, farm fishing, drying timber and wool, and heating greenhouses. Ask: **What can you tell about volcanic activity in Iceland?** *(Iceland is volcanically active.)* **Do you think Iceland's energy source is renewable or nonrenewable?** *(renewable)*
Intrapersonal, Logical

Answer to . . .

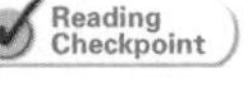

Nuclear fission is the splitting of an unstable nucleus of an atom into smaller parts, releasing large amounts of energy.

Teacher Demo

Making a Geyser

L2

Purpose Students model a geyser and observe how it works.

Materials water; 250- or 500-mL Pyrex flask with tight-fitting, one-hole rubber stopper; glass tube 33–45 cm long; hot plate or Bunsen burner; ring stand; strong, small plastic bowl or container; ice pick or drill; plumber's putty

Safety Use caution when inserting the glass tube into the stopper. Perform this demo behind a safety shield. Have everyone in the room wear goggles.

Procedure Fill the flask with water about 3/4 full. Carefully insert the glass tube in the rubber stopper. Place the stopper in the flask and adjust the tube so that it goes down into the flask about 3/4 of the way to the bottom. Place the flask on the hot plate or on a ring stand just above a Bunsen burner. Drill a hole in a strong, small plastic bowl or container. Work the top of the glass tube into the hole in the bowl and position the bowl on a ring stand above the flask. Plumber's putty can be applied to the bottom of the bowl around the glass tube to keep the bottom of the bowl from leaking. The glass tube should extend up an inch or so into the bowl. The bowl will catch the water from an eruption and also allow the water to flow back into the model. Fill the bowl until water runs down the tube into the flask. Keep adding water until the flask and tube are full. Do not fill the bowl above the top of the glass tube. Turn the hot plate on and allow the water to heat up. Observe how long it takes for an eruption to occur.

Expected Outcomes As the water in the flask turns to steam, pressure builds up inside the flask. Water erupts into the air inside the bowl. After the eruption, water from the bowl should run back down the tube into the flask.
Visual, Kinesthetic

Figure 14 The Geysers is the world's largest electricity-generating geothermal facility. Most of the steam wells are about 3,000 meters deep.

Q *Is power from ocean waves a practical alternative energy source?*

A It's being seriously explored now. In November 2000, the world's first commercial wave power station opened on the Scottish island of Islay. It provides power for the United Kingdom. The 500-kilowatt power station uses an oscillating water column, in which incoming waves push air up and down inside a concrete tube that is partly under the ocean's surface. Air rushing in and out of the top of the tube drives a turbine to produce electricity. If the facility succeeds, it could open the door for wave power to become a significant contributor of renewable energy in some coastal areas.

In the United States, areas in several western states use hot water from geothermal sources for heat. The first commercial geothermal power plant in the United States was built in 1960 at The Geysers, shown in Figure 14. The Geysers is an important source of electrical power for nearby San Francisco and Oakland. Although production in the plant has declined, it remains the world's premier geothermal field. It continues to provide electrical power with little environmental impact. Geothermal development is now also occurring in Nevada, Utah, and the Imperial Valley of California.

Geothermal power is clean but not inexhaustible. When hot fluids are pumped from volcanically heated reservoirs, the reservoir often cannot be recharged. The steam and hot water from individual wells usually lasts no more than 10 to 15 years. Engineers must drill more wells to maintain power production. Eventually, the field is depleted.

As with other alternative methods of power production, geothermal sources are not expected to provide a high percentage of the world's growing energy needs. Nevertheless, in regions where people can develop its potential, its use will no doubt grow.

In what two ways is geothermal energy used?

Tidal Power

Several methods of generating electrical energy from the oceans have been proposed, yet the ocean's energy potential still remains largely untapped. The development of tidal power is one example of energy production from the ocean.

Tides have been a power source for hundreds of years. Beginning in the 12th century, tides drove water wheels that powered gristmills

Facts and Figures

There are 600 to 700 geysers in the world today. Between 400 and 500 of these are found in Yellowstone National Park. Geysers form in areas where groundwater can circulate several thousand feet deep in Earth's crust and be heated by a volcanic heat source. Geysers exist only when certain conditions are present: a volcanic heat source, molten rock (magma) near the surface, water that can circulate near the heat source and become superheated, a "plumbing" system, and silica-rich rocks that can sustain the force that is needed for an eruption.

and sawmills. During the seventeenth and eighteenth centuries, a tidal mill produced much of Boston's flour. But today's energy demands require more sophisticated ways of using the force created by the continual rise and fall of the ocean.

Tidal power is harnessed by constructing a dam across the mouth of a bay or an estuary in coastal areas with a large tidal range. The strong in-and-out flow that results drives turbines and electric generators. An example of this type of dam is shown in Figure 15.

The largest tidal power plant ever constructed is at the mouth of France's Rance River. This tidal plant went into operation in 1966. It produces enough power to satisfy the needs of Brittany—a region of 27,000 square kilometers—and parts of other regions. Much smaller experimental facilities have been built near Murmansk in Russia, near Taliang in China, and on an arm of the Bay of Fundy in Canada.

Tidal power development isn't economical if the tidal range is less than eight meters or if a narrow, enclosed bay isn't available. Although the tides will never provide a high portion of the world's ever-increasing energy needs, it is an important source at certain sites.

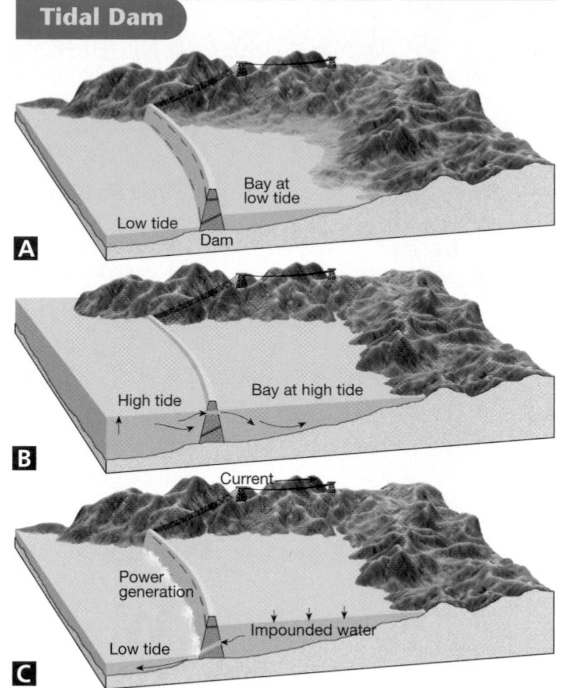

Figure 15 **A** At low tide, water is at its lowest level on either side of the dam. **B** At high tide, water flows through a high tunnel. **C** At low tide, water drives turbines as it flows back to sea through a low tunnel.
Analyzing Concepts ***Why is a large tidal range (difference in water level between high and low tide) needed to produce power?***

Section 4.2 Assessment

Reviewing Concepts

1. What are the advantages and drawbacks of using solar energy?
2. How do nuclear power plants produce energy?
3. What percentage of our energy might be met by wind power over the next 60 years?
4. What are the advantages and drawbacks of hydroelectric power, geothermal energy, and tidal power?

Critical Thinking

5. **Predicting** Why will the interest in alternate energy sources probably grow in the future?
6. **Classifying** Identify solar, nuclear, and wind power as renewable or nonrenewable energy sources. Explain your answers.

Explain a Concept Write a letter to a family member explaining how tidal power works.

Tidal Power

Use Visuals

Figure 15 Have students study the diagram. Ask: **What might be a biological disadvantage of a tidal dam?** *(The dam probably disrupts marine or coastal ecosystems.)* **Which way does water flow through the dam at high tide?** *(toward land)* **Which way does water flow through the dam at low tide?** *(toward the sea)*
Visual, Logical

3 ASSESS

Evaluate Understanding

To assess students' knowledge of section content, have each student write three review questions. Invite students to read their review questions to the class. Have the class answer the questions. Continue until everyone has had a turn to read their questions or until unique questions have all been answered.

Reteach

Have students make a table of alternate energy sources, the advantages and disadvantages of each, and whether each source is renewable or nonrenewable.

Writing in Science

Students' letters will vary but they should mention that both a large tidal range and a narrow, enclosed bay are requirements for harnessing tidal energy. Letters should also describe how a tidal dam operates and the direction of water flow at high and low tides.

Section 4.2 Assessment

1. advantages: free and unlimited supply of energy; drawbacks: expensive equipment, supplemental heating unit needed when solar energy is not available
2. Heat produced by the nuclear fission of uranium atoms is used to heat water. The steam drives a turbine that turns an electrical generator, producing electric power.
3. between 5 and 10 percent
4. Hydroelectric—advantages: renewable; drawbacks: dams have finite lifetimes, high water levels needed. Geothermal—advantages: clean; drawbacks: nonrenewable, suitable sites are rare. Tidal—advantages: renewable; drawbacks: limited sites available with enclosed bays and large tidal range
5. Fossil fuel reserves will be in very short supply due to growing demand for energy and for a healthy environment.
6. Solar and wind power are renewable energy sources because the supplies of sunlight and wind are unlimited. Nuclear energy is nonrenewable because the supply of uranium is limited.

Answer to . . .

Figure 15 *The greater the tidal range, the more potential energy the water will have. This energy is converted to mechanical energy when the turbine's blades turn, then to electrical energy by the generator.*

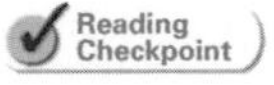

directly for heating and to turn turbines to generate electricity

1 FOCUS

Section Objectives

4.10 **Explain** why fresh water is a vital resource.

4.11 **Recognize** why the chemical composition of the atmosphere is important.

4.12 **Identify** Earth's important land resources.

Reading Focus

Build Vocabulary L2

Paraphrase Before students read the section, have them explain what they think *point source* and *nonpoint source* mean. After they have read the section, ask students to explain the meanings of the terms in their own words, noting how their definitions have changed, if at all.

Reading Strategy 

a. pollution that does not have a specific point of origin
b. runoff, water filtering through piles of waste rock
c. water that flows over the land rather than seeping into the ground
d. waste oil from streets, pesticides off farm fields
e. gases that help maintain a warm temperature near Earth's surface
f. carbon dioxide, methane, water vapor

2 INSTRUCT

The Water Planet

Use Community Resources 

Have students research the water supply in their community. They should find out where their water comes from and how it is treated to make it safe for human use. The Department of Public Works or the water department will have this information. Students may be able to tour the municipal water treatment plant.
Verbal, Interpersonal

4.3 Water, Air, and Land Resources

Reading Focus

Key Concepts

- Why is fresh water a vital resource?
- Why is the chemical composition of the atmosphere important?
- What are Earth's important land resources?

Vocabulary

- point source pollution
- nonpoint source pollution
- runoff
- acid precipitation
- global warming

Reading Strategy

Building Vocabulary Copy the table below. As you read, add definitions and examples to complete the table.

Definitions	Examples
point source pollution: Pollution that can be traced to a location	factory pipes, sewer pipes
nonpoint source pollution: a. ___?___	b. ___?___
runoff: c. ___?___	d. ___?___
greenhouse gas: e. ___?___	f. ___?___

Water, air, and land resources are essential for life. You need clean air and water every day. What's more, soil provides nutrients that allow plants—the basis of our own food supply—to grow. How do people use—and sometimes misuse—these vital resources?

The Water Planet

Figure 16 shows Earth's most prominent feature—water. Water covers nearly 71 percent of Earth's surface. However, most of this water is saltwater, not fresh water. Oceans have important functions. Their currents help regulate and moderate Earth's climate. They are also a vital part of the water cycle, and a habitat for marine organisms. Fresh water, however, is what people need in order to live. **Each day, people use fresh water for drinking, cooking, bathing, and growing food.** While fresh water is extremely important, Earth's reserves are relatively small. Less than one percent of the water on the planet is usable fresh water.

Figure 16 Oceans cover almost three fourths of Earth surface, making Earth a unique planet.

Freshwater Pollution Pollution has contaminated many freshwater supplies. In general, there are two types of water pollution sources—point sources and nonpoint sources. **Point source pollution** is pollution that comes from a known and specific location, such as the factory pipes in Figure 17. Other examples include a leaking landfill or storage tank.

Nonpoint source pollution is pollution that does not have a specific point of origin. **Runoff,** the water that flows over the land rather than seeping into the ground, often carries nonpoint source pollution. Runoff can carry waste oil from streets. It can wash sediment from construction sites or pesticides off farm fields and lawns. Water filtering through piles of waste rock from coal mines can carry sulfuric acid into rivers or lakes. This contaminated water can kill fish and other aquatic life.

As you can see in Table 2, water pollution has adverse health effects. Pollutants can damage the body's major organs and systems, cause birth defects, lead to infectious diseases, and cause certain types of cancers. Contaminated fresh water can sicken or kill aquatic organisms and disrupt ecosystems. What's more, fish and other aquatic life that live in contaminated waters often concentrate poisons in their flesh. As a result, it is dangerous to eat fish taken from some polluted waters.

What is the difference between a point and nonpoint water pollution source?

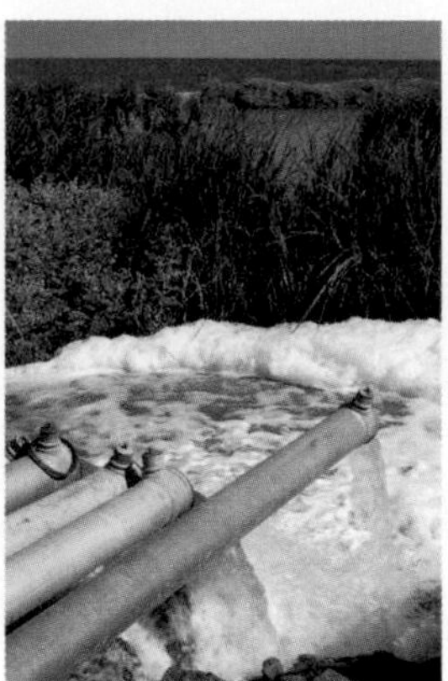

Figure 17 Pollution from point sources, such as these factory pipes, is easy to locate and control.

Table 2 Major Types of Water Pollution

Type	Examples	Sources	Effects
Disease organisms	Bacteria, viruses	Wastes from people and animals	Typhoid, cholera, dysentery, infectious hepatitis
Wastes that remove oxygen from water	Animal manure and plant debris that bacteria decompose	Sewage, animal feedlots	Great amounts of bacteria can remove oxygen from water, killing fish
Inorganic chemicals	Acids, toxic metals	Industrial effluent, urban runoff, household cleaners	Poisons fresh water and can sicken those who drink it
Organic chemicals	Oil, gasoline, plastic, pesticides, detergent	Farm and yard runoff, industrial waste, household cleaners	Some cancers, disorders of nervous and reproductive systems
Plant fertilizer	Water soluble compounds with nitrate, phosphorus ions	Sewage, manure, farm and garden runoff	Spurs rapid growth of algae that decay and deplete water's oxygen; fish die
Sediment	Soil	Erosion	Disrupts aquatic food webs, clogs lakes and reservoirs, reduces photosynthesis of aquatic plants
Radioactive substances	Radon, uranium, radioactive iodine	Nuclear power plants, uranium ore mining and processing	Some cancers, birth defects, genetic mutations

Use Visuals L1

Table 2 Have students study the table. Ask: **Why is fertilizer considered a pollutant if it is needed by plants?** *(It causes rapid growth of algae that decay and deplete water's oxygen.)* **What are some sources of water pollution from organic chemicals?** *(farm and yard runoff, industrial waste, and household cleaners)* **Where do disease organisms that pollute water come from?** *(wastes from people and animals)* **What two types of water pollution can cause cancers in humans?** *(organic chemicals and radioactive substances)*
Visual

Build Science Skills L2

Applying Concepts Have students explain how fish and other aquatic life that live in polluted water can concentrate poisons in their flesh. *(Fish and other aquatic organisms pass large amounts of water through their bodies as they extract oxygen from the water. If pollutants are also extracted from the water, they will accumulate in the fish's flesh in increasing concentration. This process is similar to that of a strainer concentrating material from the water that is poured through it.)*
Verbal

Customize for English Language Learners

Have students use a dictionary to look up the meaning of *acid precipitation.* Ask them to list the different forms that acid precipitation can take. *(acid snow, rain, fog)* Ask students why acid precipitation can take many forms. *(Precipitation occurs when water vapor condenses in the atmosphere. The form of precipitation depends on temperature, altitude, and other physical conditions.)*

Answer to . . .

Point source pollution is pollution that comes from a known and specific location. Nonpoint source pollution is pollution that does not have a specific point of origin.

Earth's Blanket of Air

Use Visuals L1

Figure 19 Have students examine the graphs. Ask: **What makes up almost half of all air pollution?** *(carbon monoxide)* **What fraction of pollution sources are industrial processes?** *(about 15 percent)* **What do you think is the source of most carbon monoxide pollution?** *(vehicle exhaust and fuel combustion)*
Visual, Logical

Ask students if there is a hole in the ozone layer high above Earth. If they say yes, they may hold the misconception that there is an actual hole in the sky that lets UV radiation through. Show students NASA satellite photos of ozone distribution so they can read the ozone concentration in the "hole." Explain that ozone is being depleted around the globe but is particularly severe in certain areas, notably above Antarctica. This depletion is actually a temporary depletion of ozone in September and October of each year. In December and January, the "hole" is repaired. The reason for concern is the fact that each year, more ozone is being depleted and less is being repaired. Ask: **What happens during periods of ozone depletion?** *(More UV radiation reaches Earth's surface.)* **Why are scientists concerned if the "hole" is repaired each year?** *(The hole is not completely repaired, and increasing amounts of ozone are being destroyed.)*
Logical

Figure 18 Cars, trucks, and buses are the biggest source of air pollution. Laws that control motor vehicle emissions have helped make the air cleaner in many areas.

Earth's Blanket of Air

Earth's atmosphere is a blanket of nitrogen, oxygen, water vapor and other gases. **The chemical composition of the atmosphere helps maintain life on Earth.** First and foremost, people and other animals could not live without the oxygen in Earth's atmosphere. But the atmosphere is also part of several other cycles, such as the carbon cycle, that make vital nutrients available to living things.

The atmosphere also makes life on land possible by shielding Earth from harmful solar radiation. There is a layer of protective ozone high in the air. Ozone is a three-atom form of oxygen that protects Earth from 95 percent of the sun's harmful ultraviolet (UV) radiation.

Certain greenhouse gases in the atmosphere—such as carbon dioxide, methane, and water vapor—help maintain a warm temperature near Earth's surface. When solar energy hits Earth, the Earth gives off some of this energy as heat. The gases absorb the heat Earth emits, keeping the atmosphere warm enough for life as we know it.

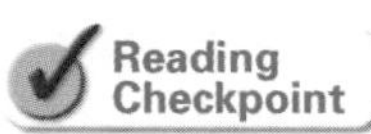

What is the role of ozone in the atmosphere?

Primary Pollutants

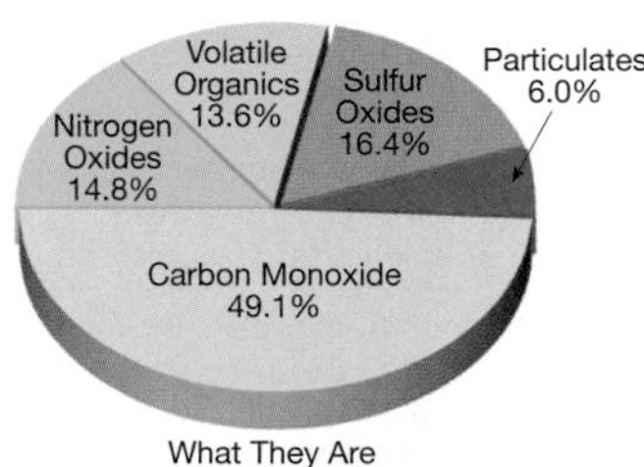

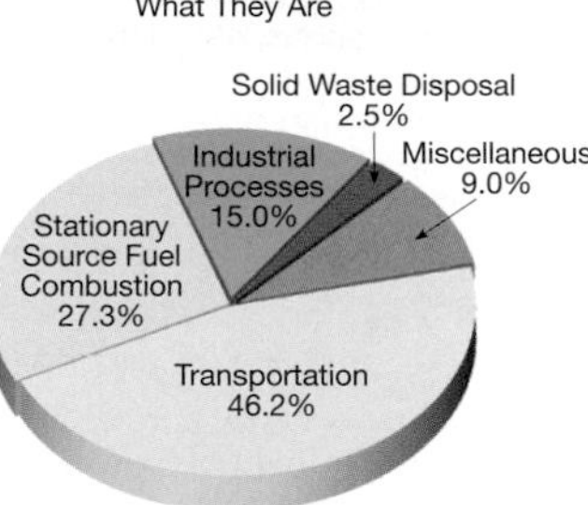

Figure 19 Major Primary Pollutants and Their Sources Percentages are calculated on the basis of weight.
***Using Graphs** What are the three major primary pollutants? What is the major source of air pollution?*

Pollution in the Air Pollution can change the chemical composition of the atmosphere and disrupt its natural cycles and functions. Fossil-fuel combustion is the major source of air pollution. Most of this pollution comes from motor vehicles and coal or oil-burning power plants. Motor vehicles, like those in Figure 18, release carbon monoxide, nitrogen oxide, soot, and other pollutants. Some of the pollutants react to form smog. Power plants release sulfur dioxide and nitrogen oxides. These pollutants combine with water vapor in the air to create acid precipitation. Figure 19 shows the primary air pollutants and the sources of those pollutants.

The burning of fossil fuels also produces carbon dioxide, an important greenhouse gas. The amount of carbon dioxide in the atmosphere has increased since industrialization began in the nineteenth century. This increase has altered the carbon cycle and contributed to the unnatural warming of the lower atmosphere, known as **global warming.** Global warming could lead to enormous changes in Earth's environment. These changes could include the melting of glaciers, which would contribute to a rise in sea level and in the flooding of coastal areas.

Chlorofluorocarbons (CFCs) once used in air conditioners and plastic foam production destroy ozone in the stratosphere layer of the atmosphere. Researchers say that a significant loss of ozone could result in an increased incidence of health problems like cataracts and skin cancers because more of the sun's UV radiation would reach Earth's surface.

Facts and Figures

Primary pollutants are those emitted by identifiable sources. They immediately pollute the air when they are emitted. Primary pollutants are also dangerous because they form secondary pollutants when chemical reactions take place among the primary pollutants. The mixture of gases and particles that make up urban smog is a good example of a secondary pollutant. Smog forms when unstable organic compounds and nitrogen oxides from vehicle exhaust react in the presence of sunlight.

Air pollution is a major public health problem. It can cause coughing, wheezing, headaches, as well as lung, eye, and throat irritation. Long-term health effects include asthma, bronchitis, emphysema, and lung cancer. The U.S. Environmental Protection Agency estimates that as many as 200,000 deaths each year are associated with outdoor air pollution.

Go Online SCI LINKS NSTA

For: Links on environmental toxins
Visit: www.SciLinks.org
Web Code: cjn-1043

Land Resources

Earth's land provides soil and forests, as well as mineral and energy resources. How do land resources impact your daily life? Soil is needed to grow the food you eat. Forests provide lumber for your home, wood for furniture, and pulp for paper. Petroleum provides energy and is in the plastic of your computer and CD boxes. Minerals such as zinc, copper, and nickel make up the coins in your pocket. Removing and using resources from Earth's crust can take a heavy environmental toll.

Damage to Land Resources There are an estimated 500,000 mines in the United States. Mines are essential because they produce many of the mineral resources we need. But mining tears up Earth's surface and destroys vegetation, as you can see in Figure 20. It can also cause soil erosion and create pollution that contaminates surrounding soil and water and destroys ecosystems.

Agriculture has many impacts on the land as well. Today, farmers can produce more food per hectare from their land. Extensive irrigation also has allowed many dry areas to be farmed for the first time. But heavy pumping for irrigation of dry areas is depleting the groundwater. And over time, irrigation causes salinization, or the build-up of salts in soil. When irrigation water on the soil evaporates, it leaves behind a salty crust. Eventually, the soil becomes useless for plant growth.

Figure 20 Surface mining destroys vegetation, soil, and the contours of Earth's surface. However, laws now require mine owners to restore the surface after mining operations cease.

Land Resources

Motion Accelerates Erosion

Purpose Students demonstrate how the motion of water increases the long-term effects of erosion.

Materials 2 identical clean 1-L jars with lids, marking pen, water, 2 identical pieces of hard candy, measuring cup

Procedure Label the jars A and B. Place a piece of candy in each jar. Pour 500 mL of water into each jar. Cover both jars. Place them in a location where both can be seen. Shake jar A once or twice a day. Do not disturb jar B.

Expected Outcome After only 2 days, students should be able to see that the disturbed candy has dissolved much more than the undisturbed candy.
Kinesthetic, Visual

Build Reading Literacy L1

Refer to **p. 246D** in **Chapter 9,** which provides the guidelines for relating cause and effect.

Relate Cause and Effect Have students think about the build-up of salts in soil. Ask: **Why can salts build up in soil used for intensive farming?** *(In order to grow large amounts of crops in an area, farmers add heavy applications of fertilizers to support the additional plants. Salts from the fertilizer eventually build up in the soil.)*
Logical

Download a worksheet on environmental toxins for students to complete, and find additional teacher support from NSTA SciLinks.

Answer to . . .

Figure 19 *The major primary pollutants are carbon monoxide, sulfur and nitrogen oxides, and volatile organics. The major source of air pollution is fossil-fuel combustion.*

Ozone absorbs harmful ultraviolet radiation from the sun, thus protecting life.

MAP MASTER™ Skills Activity

Answers

Identifying Effects The amount of virgin forest was much greater in 1620. The eastern half of the United States has lost almost all of its virgin forest. There are now more virgin forests in the western half of the country than in the eastern half.

3 ASSESS

Evaluate Understanding L2

To assess students' knowledge of section content, have them write a short paragraph explaining how ozone can be essential to life when it is in the upper stratosphere, yet a serious pollutant when it is closer to Earth's surface.

Reteach L1

Have students summarize their knowledge of water, land, and air resources by making an outline of the section. They can use the heads as a guide and add information under each head.

Connecting Concepts

Student paragraphs should suggest that wasting paper causes more trees to be cut down, resulting in a loss of species due to elimination of their habitat. When trees are clear-cut, the forest eventually will be replaced by a second-growth forest that has greater area but less diversity than the original forest.

MAP MASTER™ Skills Activity

Virgin Forests 1620–1998

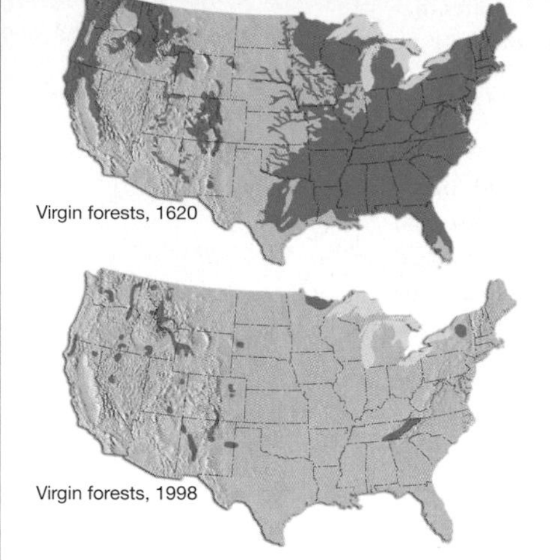

Figure 21

Location These maps compare the location of virgin forests in the contiguous 48 states of the U.S. in 1620 and in 1998. **Identifying Effects** How has the amount of virgin forest changed? How has the location of virgin forest changed?

Trees must be cut to supply our need for paper and lumber. But the removal of forests, especially through clear-cutting, can damage land. Clear-cutting is the removal of all trees in an area of forest. Cleared areas are susceptible to soil erosion. Forest removal also destroys ecosystems and wildlife habitat. The United States actually has more hectares of forest today than it did a century ago. That's because much of the virgin forest (forest that had never been cut down) that was cut long ago has regrown as second-growth forest. The forest is not as diverse as the virgin forest—it does not contain as much variety of plant species. Some forestland has also become tree plantations, with even fewer species. As you see in Figure 21, the United States has lost most of its virgin forest during the last few centuries.

Finally, land serves as a disposal site. You may have seen landfills and other waste facilities. When disposal is done correctly, there is minimal impact on land. But many old landfills leak harmful wastes that get into soil and underground water. The same is true of buried drums of chemicals, which were often disposed of illegally. Waste is inevitable. But there is a need for ways to reduce it and make the disposal safer.

Section 4.3 Assessment

Reviewing Concepts

1. Why is fresh water a vital resource?
2. Why is the chemical composition of Earth's atmosphere important?
3. What is the difference between point source pollution and nonpoint source pollution?
4. What do Earth's land resources provide?

Critical Thinking

5. **Applying Concepts** How would Earth be different if there were no greenhouse gases?
6. **Classifying** Which of the following is a nonpoint source pollution of water: rainwater pouring from an eroded bank into a river, a boat emptying a waste tank into a lake, or a sewage plant sending sewage into a river through a pipe?
7. **Relating Cause and Effect** How would the removal of sulfur from coal affect the type of air pollution in a local area? Explain your answer.

Connecting Concepts

Write a brief paragraph that connects the following: waste of paper, loss of species diversity of forests, and the increase in second-growth forest area.

Section 4.3 Assessment

1. People need fresh water for drinking, cooking, bathing, and growing food.
2. The chemical composition of Earth's atmosphere helps to maintain life on Earth.
3. Point source pollution has a known and specific location. Nonpoint source pollution does not have a specific point of origin.
4. soil, forests, mineral and energy resources
5. Earth would be too cold to sustain life.
6. rainwater pouring from an eroded bank into a river
7. Removing sulfur from coal would decrease the amount of sulfur oxides in the air. Sulfur oxides combine with water vapor to form acid precipitation, so the acidity of the precipitation both locally and in more distant areas would decrease.

4.4 Protecting Resources

Reading Focus

Key Concepts

- When were the first laws passed to deal with water pollution?
- What was the most important law passed to deal with air pollution?
- What is involved in protecting land resources?

Vocabulary

- conservation
- compost
- recycling

Reading Strategy

Summarizing After reading this section, complete the concept map below to organize what you know about the major laws that help keep water, air, and land resources clean.

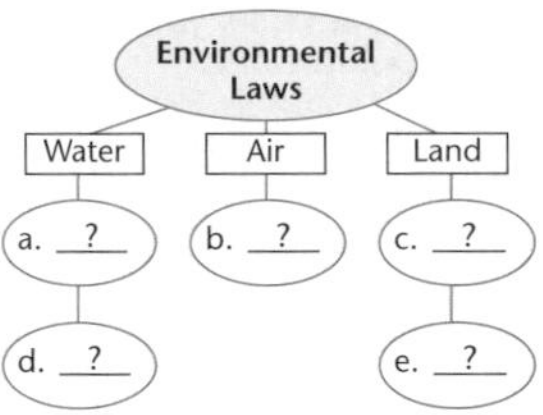

Each year, Americans throw out about 30 million cell phones, 18 million computers, 8 million TV sets, and enough tires to circle the Earth about three times. With just 6 percent of the world's population, Americans use about one third of the world's resources—and produce about one third of the world's garbage.

This high rate of consumption squanders resources, many of which are nonrenewable. The manufacture and disposal of these products uses enormous amounts of energy and creates pollution, as shown in Figure 22. Is there a way to have the products and services we want and still protect resources and create less pollution?

Many people think conservation and pollution prevention are the answer. **Conservation** is the careful use of resources. Pollution prevention means stopping pollution from entering the environment.

Between the late 1940s and 1970, a number of serious pollution problems got the public's attention. Severe air pollution events killed hundreds and sickened thousands in the United States and elsewhere. In the late 1960s, many beaches closed due to pollution. An oil spill off the California coast killed wildlife. Then in 1969, Americans watched news reports of Ohio's polluted Cuyahoga River catching fire and burning for days.

Figure 22 Strict laws have helped curb air pollution, though it remains a problem.

Section 4.4

1 FOCUS

Section Objectives

4.13 **Identify** the first laws passed to deal with water pollution.

4.14 **Name** the most important law passed to deal with air pollution.

4.15 **Explain** what is involved in protecting land resources.

Reading Focus

Build Vocabulary L2

Word Forms Have students use a dictionary to find words that are related to the vocabulary term *conservation*. Each word should be used in a sentence. Knowing the meaning of words such as *conservative* and *conserve* will help students understand the concept of conservation.

Reading Strategy L2

a. Clean Water Act
b. Clean Air Act
c. Resource Conservation and Recovery Act
d. Safe Drinking Water Act
e. Comprehensive Environmental Response, Compensation, and Liability Act

2 INSTRUCT

Integrate Biology L2

Oil Spills and Marine Life Ask students if they know why oil spills are dangerous to wildlife. Tell them that oil destroys the insulating ability of fur-bearing mammals, such as sea otters, and the water-repelling abilities of a bird's feathers, thus exposing these animals to cold water and air temperatures. Many marine birds and animals also swallow oil when they try to clean themselves, which can poison them. Ask: **What is the function of bird feathers?** *(They keep the bird warm and waterproofed, and help the bird fly.)* **What happens to feathers when they get oiled?** *(They become heavy, matted, and soggy.)*
Verbal, Logical

Keeping Water Clean and Safe

Use Visuals

Table 3 Have students read the information in the table. Ask: **How should you dispose of old batteries?** *(Use a hazardous waste site or collection to dispose of them.)* **What happens to household chemicals when they are dumped down a drain?** *(They move through sewers into rivers, lakes, or streams.)*
Visual, Logical

Teacher Demo

Making an Oil Slick

L2

Purpose Students examine the way oil reacts when it mixes with water.

Materials large, clear, glass bowl; vegetable oil; water; cocoa powder

Procedure Mix a little cocoa powder with the oil so it will resemble crude oil. This mixture will make it easier for students to observe the oil. Fill the bowl with water to about 5 cm from the top. Pour some of the oil–cocoa mixture onto the water.

Expected Outcomes Oil and water do not mix, but form two separate layers. The oil, even a little drop, will quickly spread out over the water surface and break up into many little blobs. When oil is spilled onto the ocean, it can be pushed and transported by the wind, currents, and tides because it stays on the top of the water.
Kinesthetic, Visual

Protecting the Air

Use Visuals

Table 4 Have students read the information in the table. Ask: **How can you use solar energy in your home?** *(Allow sunshine in through the windows.)* **Name one way you can use your own physical energy instead of fossil fuel energy.** *(I can walk or ride a bike instead of using a car.)*

Table 3 How You Can Prevent Water Pollution
• Never pour household chemicals (paints, thinners, cleaners, pesticides, waste oil) down the drain or into the toilet.
• Never dump toxic chemicals in the gutter or onto the ground.
• Don't put items that contain hazardous substances, such as batteries or old computer monitors, into the trash.
• Find out about hazardous waste collection sites and times from your local sanitation or public works department.
• Avoid using hazardous substances in the first place.

Keeping Water Clean and Safe

Both the public and government officials became increasingly concerned about pollution. **Starting in the 1970s, the federal government passed several laws to prevent or decrease pollution and protect resources.**

America's polluted rivers and lakes got early attention. In 1972, the U.S. Congress passed the Clean Water Act (CWA). Among other provisions, the law requires industries to reduce or eliminate point source pollution into surface waters. It also led to a huge increase in the number of sewage treatment plants, which eliminated the discharge of raw sewage into many lakes, rivers, and bays. There are still water pollution problems. But because of the CWA, the percentage of U.S. surface waters safe for fishing and swimming increased from 36 percent to 62 percent between 1972 and the end of the 1990s.

The Safe Drinking Water Act of 1974 helped protect drinking resources. It set maximum contaminant levels for a number of pollutants that could harm the health of people. Public water resources are cleaner today because of this law. See Table 3 for ways that individuals can help conserve water and keep it clean.

What did the Clean Water Act do?

Protecting the Air

As lawmakers were tackling water pollution in the 1970s, air pollution was also on the agenda. **In 1970, Congress passed the Clean Air Act, the nation's most important air pollution law.** It established National Ambient Air Quality Standards (NAAQS) for six "criteria" pollutants known to cause health problems—carbon monoxide, ozone, lead, sulfur dioxide, nitrogen oxides, and particulates (fine particles). Air monitors, such as the one in Figure 23, sample the air. If the maximum permissible level of pollutants in the air is exceeded, local authorities must come up with plans to bring these levels down. Between 1970 and 2001, the emissions of the six criteria pollutants regulated under the Clean Air Act decreased 24 percent. Over the same time span, energy consumption increased 42 percent and the U.S. population grew by 39 percent.

Today, power plants and motor vehicles use pollution control devices to reduce or eliminate certain byproducts of fossil fuel combustion. Power plants are also more likely to use low-sulfur coal. These controls cut down on emissions of sulfur and nitrogen oxides that often produce acid rain.

Figure 23 Air Sampler

Customize for Inclusion Students

Learning Disabled Have students cut out photos from magazines and newspapers that show water usage and conservation. Students can make a poster with these photos, writing a description next to each photo. If enough photos are collected, two posters can be made, one for water usage and the other for conservation methods. Posters can be hung in a school hallway during Conservation Awareness Week or as part of a conservation program.

Increased use of clean, alternate energy sources such as solar, wind, and hydroelectric power, can also help clear the air. These energy sources don't create air or water pollution, and they're based on renewable resources.

Cars with electric and hybrid (combination of electric and either natural gas, gasoline, or diesel) motors produce fewer or no tailpipe emissions. Several of these lower-emissions models are now available. Some of the hybrid models are also very efficient and get high gas mileage. When a car can go farther on a tank of gas, it uses less fuel and creates less pollution.

Energy conservation is an important air pollution control strategy. Fossil-fuel combustion produces most of the electricity in the United States. If we can use less electricity we would have to burn less fossil fuel. Less fossil-fuel combustion means less air pollution. You can see several energy conservation tips in Table 4.

Table 4 How You Can Save Energy
• Recycle when possible.
• Let the sun in on bright winter days using solar energy to warm rooms.
• Use energy-saving fluorescent bulbs instead of incandescent bulbs where you can.
• Turn off lights when you leave a room. Turn off the radio, TV, or computer when you're not using them.
• Walk or ride a bike when you can.
• When buying electric products, look for the Energy Star sticker which denotes energy-saving products.

What did the Clean Air Act do?

Caring for Land Resources

Protecting land resources involves preventing pollution and managing land resources wisely. Farmers, loggers, manufacturers, and individuals can all take steps to care for land resources.

Farmers now use many soil conservation practices to prevent the loss of topsoil and preserve soil fertility. In contour plowing, farmers plow across the contour of hillsides. This method of farming decreases water runoff that washes away topsoil. Another conservation method is strip cropping—crops with different nutrient requirements are planted in adjacent rows. Strip cropping helps preserve the fertility of soil.

Selective cutting conserves forest resources. In this method of logging, some trees in an area of a forest are cut, while other trees remain. This practice preserves topsoil as well as the forest habitat. Clear-cutting, on the other hand, removes whole areas of forest and destroys habitats and contributes to the erosion of topsoil.

Some farmers and gardeners now use less pesticides and inorganic fertilizers to decrease chemicals in soil and on crops. Natural fertilizers such as compost or animal manure have replaced inorganic commercial fertilizers on some fields. **Compost** is partly decomposed organic material that is used as fertilizer. Integrated Pest Management (IPM) uses natural predators or mechanical processes (such as vacuuming pests off leaves) to decrease the number of pests. Pesticide use is a last resort.

For: Links on emerging technologies

Visit: www.SciLinks.org

Web Code: cjn-1044

Caring for Land Resources

Build Reading Literacy L1

Refer to p. **216D** in **Chapter 8,** which provides the guidelines for comparing and contrasting.

Compare and Contrast Tell students that there are two major methods of forestry. Clear-cutting involves the complete removal of all the trees in an area. In selective logging, only certain trees are removed. Trees left standing form a buffer zone. Ask: **Compare the amount of erosion that would take place with both kinds of forestry practices.** *(Clear-cutting exposes bare soil, which is subject to erosion. Selective logging creates buffer zones of trees that slow runoff and prevent any eroded soil from being washed away.)* **Do you think forests are a renewable resource?** *(Answers will vary. The trees will grow back as a second-growth forest, but it will be less diverse than the virgin forest.)* **Logical**

Download a worksheet on emerging technologies for students to complete, and find additional teacher support from NSTA SciLinks.

Facts and Figures

Integrated Pest Management (IPM) practices began in the 1920s. Progress was slow, however, due to the abundance of inexpensive and effective synthetic pesticides and limited knowledge of their long-term effects on organisms and the environment. Rachel Carson's book, *Silent Spring,* brought the effects of chemical pesticides to the public eye in 1962, and IPM practices became more popular. There are several lines of IPM: chemical controls (the use of pheromones to attract and capture pests), cultural controls (crop rotations, sanitation, and pruning), biological controls (introducing predators, parasites, or pest disease organisms), and genetic controls (breeding pest-resistant crops and tolerant plant varieties).

Answer to . . .

The Clean Water Act led to an increase in sewage treatment plants; it requires industries to reduce or eliminate point source pollution into surface waters.

The Clean Air Act established six criteria pollutants and required communities to not exceed certain levels of pollution for these pollutants.

Section 4.4 (continued)

Use Community Resources 

Have students investigate recycling programs in their community. If none are available, students may be interested in starting a limited one. If a program exists, students may want to volunteer in some way. Alternatively, students may be interested in participating in a community-wide composting project. **Kinesthetic, Intrapersonal**

3 ASSESS

Evaluate Understanding 

To assess students' knowledge of section content, have them explain the difference between conservation and pollution prevention. *(Conservation is the careful use of resources. Pollution prevention involves ways to prevent pollution from occurring or stopping pollution from entering the environment.)*

Reteach 

Have students make a table listing the laws discussed in this section. For each law, students should write what it does and what it accomplished.

Student paragraphs should include the ideas that the recycling of aluminum soda cans conserves aluminum and produces less waste.

Figure 24 Recycling saves resources, reduces energy consumption, and prevents pollution.

Some laws reduce the possibility of toxic substances getting into the soil. Since 1977, sanitary landfills have largely replaced open dumps and old-style landfills. Sanitary landfills have plastic or clay liners that prevent wastes from leaking into the surrounding soil or groundwater. The Resource Conservation and Recovery Act (RCRA) of 1976 has decreased the illegal and unsafe dumping of hazardous waste. The law requires companies to store, transport, and dispose of hazardous waste according to strict guidelines. The 1980 Comprehensive Environmental Response, Compensation, and Liability Act (Superfund) mandates the cleaning up of abandoned hazardous waste sites that are a danger to the public or the environment.

 ***What is the RCRA and what does it do?***

Creating less waste by using fewer products and recycling products also helps preserve land resources. **Recycling** is the collecting and processing of used items so they can be made into new products, as Figure 24 shows. By conserving resources and producing less waste, everyone can contribute to a cleaner, healthier future.

Section 4.4 Assessment

Reviewing Concepts

1. When were the first laws passed to deal with water pollution?
2. Identify the most important air pollution control law.
3. What are National Ambient Air Quality Standards?
4. How does selective cutting of forests conserve topsoil?
5. How can gardeners care for land resources?

Critical Thinking

6. **Applying Concepts** How can turning off lights when you're not using them help decrease air pollution?
7. **Relating Cause and Effect** Explain how the Superfund law helps prevent pollution from entering underground water sources.

Writing in Science

Explanatory Paragraph Write a brief paragraph explaining how recycling your aluminum soda cans helps conserve resources and energy.

Answer to . . .

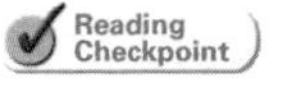 *The Resource Conservation and Recovery Act requires companies to store, transport, and dispose of hazardous waste according to strict guidelines.*

Section 4.4 Assessment

1. The first laws were passed in the 1970s. The Clean Water Act was passed in 1972.
2. The Clean Air Act, the most important air pollution law, was passed in 1970.
3. NAAQS are maximum permissible levels of six pollutants known to cause health problems.
4. The trees that are left standing keep topsoil from eroding and washing away.
5. by using less pesticides and inorganic fertilizers; by using compost and Integrated Pest Management
6. When you turn off lights, you use less electricity. Since the fuels that produce electricity cause air pollution, less electricity needed means less fuel used and less pollution produced.
7. The Superfund law mandates the cleaning up of dangerous abandoned hazardous waste sites. This prevents the toxic wastes from leaching out of the site and entering underground water sources.

understanding EARTH

Bingham Canyon, Utah: The Largest Open-Pit Mine

This huge pit was once where a mountain stood. It's Bingham Canyon copper mine, the largest open-pit mine in the world. The mine, southwest of Salt Lake City, Utah, is 4 kilometers across and covers almost 8 square kilometers. It's so deep—900 meters—that if a steel tower were built at the bottom, it would have to be five times taller than France's Eiffel Tower to reach the pit's rim.

Figure 25 Aerial view of Utah's Bingham Canyon copper mine, the largest open-pit copper mine on Earth.

The pit began in the late 1800s as an underground silver and lead mine. Miners later discovered copper. There are similar deposits at several sites in the American Southwest and in a belt from southern Alaska to northern Chile.

The ore at Bingham Canyon formed after magma was intruded to shallow depths. After this, shattering created extensive fractures in the rock. Hydrothermal solutions penetrated these cracks, and ore minerals formed from the solutions.

Although the percentage of copper in the rock is small, the total volume of copper is huge. Ever since open-pit operations started in 1906, some 5 billion tons of material have been removed, yielding more than 1.2 million tons of copper. Miners have also recovered significant amounts of gold, silver, and molybdenum.

The ore body is far from exhausted. Over the next 25 years, the mine's owners plan to remove and process an additional 3 billion tons of material. This mining operation has generated most of Utah's mineral production for more than 80 years. People have called it the "richest hole on Earth."

Like many older mines, the Bingham pit was unregulated during most of its history. Development occurred before today's awareness of the environmental impacts of mining and prior to effective environmental laws. Today, problems of groundwater and surface water contamination, air pollution, and land reclamation are receiving long overdue attention at Bingham Canyon.

understanding EARTH

Bingham Canyon, Utah: The Largest Open-Pit Mine L2

Background

For much of its hundred-year history, Bingham Canyon was owned by Kennecott Copper Corp. However, during the post-1973 oil crisis shake-out, the company was acquired by British Petroleum. It was then sold to Rio Tinto, which operates Bingham Canyon through its subsidiary, Kennecott Utah Copper Corp. The mine employs about 1,400 people and produces about 15 percent of the nation's copper.

Teaching Tips

- Have students research chalcopyrite, the major ore at Bingham Canyon. The formula for chalcopyrite is $CuFeS_2$. The ore is 0.56 percent copper. Chalcopyrite crystals have unevenly faced tetrahedrons that are striated in different directions. The mineral has a metallic luster and a brassy-gold color somewhat less yellow than pyrite.
- Have students make posters showing the processing of copper from mining to grinding and flotation to roasting and smelting to purification by electrolysis.
- Have students make lists of some of the many uses of copper.
- Discuss the importance of copper throughout history, especially in the Bronze Age (bronze is an alloy of tin and copper). Mention the use of copper in brass (an alloy of copper and zinc).
- Tell students that the mine's open pit is one of only a few human-made objects that can be seen from space.
- Have students examine a penny. The composition of the penny has changed several times through the years. During World War II, pennies looked silvery because they were made of zinc-coated steel, due to a shortage of copper. After the war, the composition went back to the traditional copper until 1982. After 1982, the composition was changed again, using cheaper zinc for the core and coating the outside with the traditional copper.

Logical

Application Lab

Finding the Product that Best Conserves Resources L2

Objectives

In this activity, students will
- measure the dimensions of three different-sized juice cartons.
- calculate the surface area of the three cartons.
- compare the amount of cardboard in the three cartons.
- evaluate the packaging as to which conserves resources the best.

Address Misconceptions

Students may think that the surface areas of the three cartons will be the same because the volumes are the same. Use this analogy. You have three identical boxes that you want to gift wrap and give to the same person. Ask: **How much wrapping paper will you need if you wrap the three boxes together compared to wrapping each box separately?** *(You will need less wrapping paper if you wrap the three boxes together.)*

Skills Focus Observing, Measuring, Calculating, Comparing and Contrasting, Relating Cause and Effect, Drawing Conclusions

Prep Time 10 minutes

Advance Prep Begin to gather juice cartons well in advance of doing this lab.

Class Time 30 minutes

Safety Be careful when using scissors.

Teaching Tips
- Have students bring juice cartons from home. You may be able to get used 240-mL cartons at a day care or preschool facility.
- To save class time, have students cut out and measure the cartons in class and do the calculations at home.
- Have students make three copies of the diagram and write the dimensions directly on the copies. This will ensure that they do not forget to include the bottom of the carton in their calculations.

Application Lab

Finding the Product that Best Conserves Resources

When you buy a product, you usually consider factors such as price, brand name, quality, and how much is in the package. But do you consider the amount of resources the package uses? Many products come in packages of different types and materials. You might buy a larger pack if you use a lot, or a tiny pack if you like the convenience of individual servings. But how much cardboard, plastic, or glass are you using—or wasting—depending on your choice? How about the trees, petroleum, and other resources needed to make those packages? In this lab, you will compare three sets of packages that hold the same amount of juice to determine how your decisions about packaging affect the use of resources.

Problem Which packaging conserves resources the best?

Materials
- 1 1.89-L (64 fl. oz) cardboard juice carton
- 1 946-mL (32 fl. oz) cardboard juice carton
- 1 240-mL (8 fl. oz) cardboard juice carton
- scissors
- metric ruler

CAUTION *Be careful when using scissors.*

Skills Observing, Measuring, Calculating, Comparing and Contrasting, Relating Cause and Effect, Drawing Conclusions

Procedure

Part A: Determine the Amount of Material in Each Package

1. Work in groups of three or four. Use scissors to cut apart the three cartons your teacher gives your group. Then spread each one out as you see here.

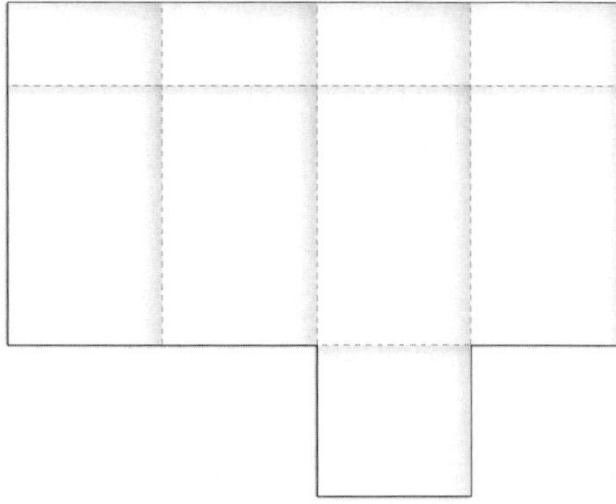

2. Measure the dimensions of the cartons with the ruler.
3. Calculate the area of each carton on a separate sheet of paper. Use these equations:
   - Area of a rectangle: $A = l \times w$ (l = length; w = width)
   - Area of a square: $A = s^2$ (s = length of a side of the square)

Data Table			
	Area of Cardboard in One Carton	Number of Cartons Needed to Hold 1.89 L	Area of Cardboard to Hold 1.89 L
1.89 L		1	
946 mL		2	
240 mL		8	

4. Copy the data table above on a separate sheet of paper. Then record the data you calculated.

Part B: Compare the Amount of Material in the Packages

5. On a separate sheet of paper, calculate how much more cardboard is used when you buy 1.89 L of juice in the two 946-mL cartons instead of one 1.89-L carton.

   Use this procedure:

   a) Subtract the area of material in the 1.89-L carton from the area of material in the two 946-mL cartons.

   b) Divide the answer you get in part a by the area of material in the 1.89-L carton.

   c) Multiply the answer you get in part b by 100. This is how much more material is in the two containers, expressed as a percentage.

6. Repeat this procedure for the material in eight small containers.

Analyze and Conclude

1. **Comparing and Contrasting** Based on your data, does buying the juice in one large carton or in an 8-pack of small individual cartons use more cardboard? How does buying the juice in two medium-size cartons compare.
2. **Relating Cause and Effect** How does buying the juice in several cartons instead of one large carton impact the use of resources?
3. **Drawing Conclusions** Suppose you have determined which set of cardboard cartons uses the least resources. Then you find out that the same size carton of juice comes in plastic and glass as well as cardboard. How would you decide which of these containers would be the best choice, in terms of saving resources?

Questioning Strategies

If you want to take 240 mL of juice in your lunch, what can you do that would conserve resources? *(The desired amount of juice can be poured from a large carton into a thermos bottle or plastic container at home.)*

Expected Outcome Students will find that as the size of the carton decreases, the percentage of cardboard to volume increases.

Analyze and Conclude

1. Buying an 8-pack of small cartons uses more cardboard. Buying two medium-size cartons uses more cardboard than one large-size carton but less than an 8-pack.
2. More trees will have to be cut down to supply the materials that make up the additional amount of cardboard.
3. Making plastic uses petroleum, a nonrenewable resource, but the plastic container may be made of recycled plastic. Likewise, a glass container may be made of recycled glass. Without knowing the source of the container material, it would be difficult to reach an informed decision. The container that can be recycled would be the best choice because recycling decreases the use of resources.

Go Further

Have students visit a local supermarket or look around their kitchens and find examples of excessive packaging. They will most likely find individual packets of food in boxes, which may be wrapped. For example, teabags are often individually wrapped and placed in a cardboard box, which is wrapped in cellophane.

Logical, Kinesthetic

Study Guide

Study Tip

Occasionally, Study With a Friend
Divide the class into small groups, and ask each group to make a list of questions that would cover all the Key Concepts in the chapter. Then, have groups exchange lists and answer the questions they receive from another group.

CHAPTER 4

Study Guide

4.1 Energy and Mineral Resources

Key Concepts

- A renewable resource can be replenished over fairly short time spans, whereas a nonrenewable resource takes millions of years to form and accumulate.
- Fossil fuels include coal, oil, and natural gas.
- Some energy experts believe that fuels derived from tar sands and oil shales could become good substitutes for dwindling petroleum supplies.
- Some of the most important mineral deposits form through igneous processes and from hydrothermal solutions.
- Nonmetallic mineral resources are extracted and processed either for the nonmetallic elements they contain or for their physical and chemical properties.

Vocabulary

renewable resources, *p. 94;* nonrenewable resource, *p. 94;* fossil fuel, *p. 95;* ore, *p. 98*

4.2 Alternate Energy Sources

Key Concepts

- Solar energy has two advantages: the "fuel" is free, and it's non-polluting.
- In nuclear fission, the nuclei of heavy atoms such as uranium-235 are bombarded with neutrons. The uranium nuclei then split into smaller nuclei and emit neutrons and heat energy.
- Some experts estimate that in the next 50 to 60 years, wind power could provide between 5 to 10 percent of the country's demand for electricity.
- The water held in a reservoir behind a dam is a form of stored energy that can be released through the dam to produce electric power.
- Hot water is used directly for heating and to turn turbines to generate electric power.
- Tidal power is harnessed by constructing a dam across the mouth of a bay or an estuary in coastal areas with a large tidal range. The strong in-and-out flow that results drives turbines and electric generators.

Vocabulary

hydroelectric power, *p. 105;* geothermal energy, *p. 105*

4.3 Water, Air, and Land Resources

Key Concepts

- Each day, people use fresh water for drinking, cooking, bathing, and growing food.
- The chemical composition of the atmosphere helps maintain life on Earth.
- Earth's land provides soil and forests, as well as mineral and energy resources.

Vocabulary

point source pollution, *p. 108;* nonpoint source pollution, *p. 109;* runoff, *p. 109;* global warming, *p. 110*

4.4 Protecting Resources

Key Concepts

- Starting in the 1970s, the federal government passed several laws to prevent or decrease pollution and protect resources.
- In 1970, Congress passed the Clean Air Act, the nation's most important air pollution law.
- Protecting land resources involves preventing pollution and managing land resources wisely.

Vocabulary

conservation, *p. 113;* compost, *p. 115;* recycling, *p. 116*

Chapter Assessment Resources

Print
Chapter Test, Chapter 4
Test Prep Resources, Chapter 4

Technology
Computer Test Bank, Chapter 4 Test
Online Text, Chapter 4
Go Online, PHSchool.com, Chapter 4

CHAPTER 4

NY Regents Content Item

Assessment

Interactive textbook with assessment at PHSchool.com 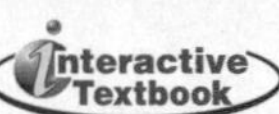

Reviewing Content

Choose the number that best answers the question or completes the statement.

1 Nonrenewable resources are those that NY
(1) will never run out
(2) take one or two decades to replace
(3) have finite supplies
(4) are contaminated by pollution

2 Which of the following is a fossil fuel? NY
(1) uranium
(2) coal
(3) wood
(4) ozone

3 Petroleum and natural gas form from NY
(1) the remains of plants and animals buried in seas long ago
(2) the decay of radioactive sediments underground
(3) plant material that collected millions of years ago in swamps
(4) heating and cooling of magma in underground chambers

4 Hydroelectric power produces electricity using
(1) the sun's rays
(2) wind
(3) moving water
(4) storms

5 Which of the following substances is a fuel used in nuclear power plants? NY
(1) sulfur dioxide
(2) uranium
(3) petroleum
(4) carbon dioxide

6 Point source pollution comes from sources that are NY
(1) basically unknown
(2) directly identifiable
(3) very small
(4) dumped illegally

7 An unnatural warming of the atmosphere near Earth's surface is called NY
(1) solar wind
(2) ozone accumulation
(3) acid precipitation
(4) global warming

8 The careful use of resources is NY
(1) conservation
(2) recycling
(3) composting
(4) deposition

9 The Clean Air Act
(1) makes all air pollution illegal
(2) limits greenhouse gases in outdoor air
(3) limits nonpoint source pollution
(4) set limits on certain pollutants in outdoor air

10 What type of pollution did the Clean Water Act succeed in limiting?
(1) carbon dioxide
(2) sewage
(3) solid waste
(4) acid precipitation

Understanding Concepts

11 What are the three major types of fossil fuels? NY

12 What is a major negative impact of the use of fossil fuels? NY

13 What is the difference between a mineral resource and an ore?

14 Briefly explain how active solar collectors work.

15 Why do hydroelectric dams have limited lifetimes?

16 Explain why fresh water is a vital resource. NY

17 How can farmers help protect land resources?

18 When were some of the earliest laws passed to deal with water pollution? Why were they passed at that time?

19 Explain why an anticline might be a good place to search for petroleum and natural gas.

20 What are three things that you can do to prevent water pollution? NY

21 What are three things that you can do to save energy? NY

Homework Guide

Section	Questions
1	1–3, 11, 13, 22, 25, 30
2	4, 5, 14, 15, 24, 26, 31
3	6, 7, 12, 16, 27–29, 32
4	8–10, 17, 18, 23, 33

Assessment

Reviewing Content

(1) 3 (2) 2 (3) 1
(4) 3 (5) 2 (6) 2
(7) 4 (8) 1 (9) 4
(10) 2

Understanding Concepts

(11) petroleum, natural gas, coal
(12) Burning fossil fuels is a major source of air pollution.
(13) A mineral resource is a deposit of useful minerals that can be extracted; an ore is a useful metallic mineral that can be mined at a profit.
(14) A collector is a blackened, glass-covered box mounted on a roof. The sun's rays shine on the box and heat the air inside it. The heat warms air or water in pipes that pass through the box. The pipes bring the heated air or water to areas of the building where they are needed.
(15) Sediment builds up behind the dams, which eventually makes them unusable for producing electric power.
(16) People need fresh water for drinking, cooking, growing food, and bathing.
(17) Farmers can use methods such as contour plowing and strip cropping to reduce soil erosion and nutrient loss. They can also cut down on chemical contamination of soil by using natural fertilizers such as manure and compost, and by using pest-control methods that rely on fewer pesticides, such as Integrated Pest Management.
(18) Some of the earliest laws were passed in the 1970s, as the result of a number of serious pollution incidents that got the attention of the public and government officials.
(19) Anticlines act as oil traps that contain petroleum and natural gas. Anticlines keep the petroleum and gas from escaping to the surface.
(20) Answers may include: Never pour household chemicals down the drain, never dump toxic chemicals onto the ground, do not put hazardous materials into the trash.
(21) Answers may include: Recycle when possible, turn off lights when you leave a room, walk or ride a bike when you can instead of using a car.

Critical Thinking

(22) Tar sands and oil shale are not a good long-term energy solution because they are nonrenewable, so they can be depleted just as the fossil fuels we use today are being depleted. Extracting and processing these resources also disturbs the land, produces harmful wastes, and requires enormous amounts of energy (tar sands) or water (oil shale).
(23) Recycling paper results in decreased need for making new paper. This means preserving forest resources by cutting down fewer trees and using less energy resources to run mills where paper is made. Manufacturing less paper also means that paper mills would produce less pollution.
(24) Increased use of alternate energy sources could result in decreased use of fossil fuels, which would make the known resources last longer. Their use also could reduce pollution.
(25) A vein deposit of ore can form when hot, metal-rich fluids that form in magma chambers move into fractures in adjacent rock. As the fluids cool, metal separates out of the solution to form metal deposits as veins in the rock.
(26) In both cases, the power source turns a turbine, which turns a generator that produces electricity. In a tidal plant, the movement of the tides drives the turbine. In a nuclear plant, the heat created by fission creates steam that drives the turbine.

Analyzing Data

(27) The graph shows the average surface temperature of the atmosphere between 1860 and 2000.
(28) The average temperature has generally been trending upward; the average temperature in 2000 was about 14.4°C.
(29) The graph would probably show a lower average surface temperature. The large-scale burning of fossil fuels that began with industrialization gradually raised the amount of the greenhouse gas carbon dioxide in the air, which likely accounts for part of the global temperature rise after that time.

Assessment *continued*

Critical Thinking

22 **Applying Concepts** Some people predict that tar sands and oil shale will one day supply much of our energy needs. Are tar sands and oil shale a good long-term energy solution? Explain. NY

23 **Relating Cause and Effect** What effect can recycling paper have on the use of resources and the creation of pollution?

24 **Inferring** How might an increased use of alternate energy sources such as wind and solar radiation affect the lifetime of fossil fuel resources? NY

25 **Summarizing** Describe how a hydrothermal solution can produce a vein deposit of ore.

26 **Comparing and Contrasting** What is the difference between how electricity is produced with tides and how it's produced in a nuclear power plant?

Analyzing Data

Use the diagram below to answer questions 27–29.

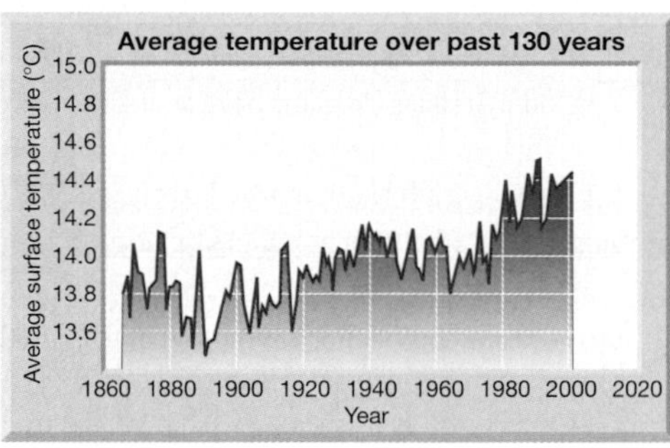

27 **Interpreting Graphs** What does this graph show? NY

28 **Using Graphs** What is the general temperature trend during the time period shown on the graph? What was the average temperature in 2000? NY

29 **Drawing Conclusions** How would you expect the graph to be different between 1700 and 1800, before the start of widespread industrialization? Explain. NY

Concepts in Action

30 **Classifying** Limestone is a nonmetallic mineral that has several uses: as a stone used for structures; as a substance used to neutralize acidic soils; as an ingredient in the manufacture of steel. Should limestone be classified as an industrial mineral or a building mineral. Explain.

31 **Analyzing Concepts** The factors in favor of the use of solar power include the fact that the fuel it uses is free, it's renewable, and it doesn't create pollution. Identify drawbacks of the use of solar power. NY

32 **Summarizing** What is the effect of the destruction of ozone on human life? NY

33 **Connecting Concepts** What is the relationship between petroleum production, the increased use of hybrid cars, and the level of air pollutants regulated by the Clean Air Act that are in the air?

Performance-Based Assessment

Drawing Conclusions Locate an electric power plant that is in or close to your community. Find out which method it uses to produce electricity. Take into consideration the way the plant produces power, its location, the pollution it produces, and the number of people it serves. Write a short essay on the plant's impact on the environment and on your community in general.

Concepts in Action

(30) Limestone can be classified as an industrial mineral and a building material. As a stone used for structures, limestone is a building material. As a soil neutralizer and an ingredient in steel, limestone is an industrial mineral.
(31) Possible answer: Facilities take up a lot of space; solar power can't produce power at night or in cloudy weather. Accept any other reasonable answers.
(32) Ozone shields Earth from most of the sun's harmful ultraviolet radiation. The loss of ozone means more UV reaches Earth's surface, resulting in a higher incidence of certain health problems such as cataracts and skin cancers.
(33) The increased use of hybrid cars would probably result in less use of fuels such as gasoline, which is made from petroleum. Lower petroleum production would probably be possible. Less burning of fuels such as gasoline would mean less production of gases in auto exhaust that are regulated by the Clean Air Act, such as carbon monoxide, nitrogen oxides, and particulates.

Regents Practice Exam

Test-Taking Tip

Make Logical Connections
A cause-and-effect statement may seem to be true when it is actually false. The statement may seem true because the stated cause and effect are both accurate. However, there may be no logical connection between the cause and the effect. In the question below, the opening phrase contains an accurate statement about fossil fuels. But only one answer provides a logical effect of the statement in the opening phrase.

Because fossil fuels are nonrenewable resources,
(1) solar energy is renewable.
(2) petroleum and natural gas often form together.
(3) supplies of coal, oil, and natural gas are finite.
(4) most power plants in the United States use fossil fuels to produce electricity.

(Answer: 3)

For *each* statement or question, choose the *number* of the word or expression that, of those given, best completes the statement or answers the question. Some questions may require the use of the *Earth Science Reference Tables.*

1 Which of the following is a nonrenewable resource?
(1) geothermal energy
(2) petroleum
(3) solar power
(4) hydroelectric power

2 Recycling is an important way to reduce resource consumption because
(1) reducing waste is better than recycling it
(2) it decreases the use of new resources to make products
(3) it is beneficial to the environment
(4) curbside pick-up makes recycling more convenient in many communities

Answer the following questions in complete sentences. Some questions may require the use of the *Earth Science Reference Tables.* Base your answers to questions 3 through 5 on the line graph below.

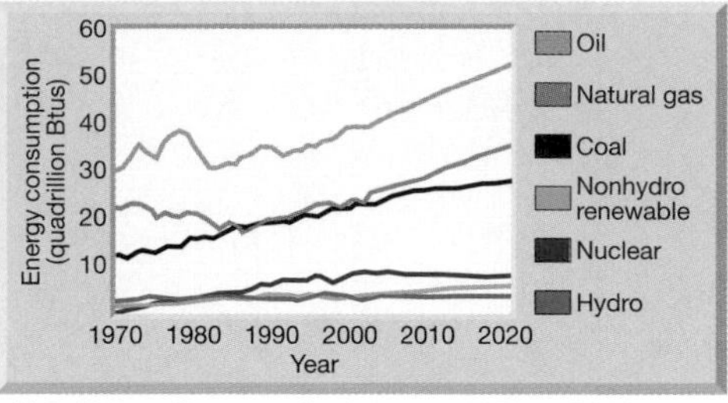

U.S. Energy Consumption between 1970 and 2000, and Projected Consumption between 2000 and 2020

3 Which fuel source had the highest rate of consumption during this period?
(1) coal (2) nuclear
(3) oil (4) hydroelectric

4 Describe how the consumption of coal has changed over time.

5 The use of which resource has changed the least over time?

6 What is the primary cause of global warming?

7 Describe the causes and effects of ozone depletion.

Regents Practice Exam

(1) 2
(2) 2
(3) 3
(4) The consumption of coal has steadily increased over time.
(5) The use of nonhyrdo (nonhydroelectric) renewable resources has changed the least.
(6) The primary cause of global warming is the burning of fossil fuels, or the release of excess carbon dioxide.
(7) Ozone depletion is caused by the release of chlorofluorocarbons (CFCs) from air conditioners and plastic foams. The effect of ozone depletion is an increased amount of ultraviolet radiation from the sun reaching Earth's surface. This may result in an increase in cataracts and skin cancer in people.

Performance-Based Assessment

Student answers will vary based on the power plants in or near your community. Answers should show students' understanding of the characteristics and impacts of the process used to produce electricity at the plant, and the plant's impact on the environment.

Your students can independently test their knowledge of the chapter and print out their results.

CHAPTER 5

Planning Guide

Use these planning tools
Use Teacher Express for all your planning needs

SECTION OBJECTIVES	STANDARDS NATIONAL	STANDARDS STATE	ACTIVITIES and LABS
5.1 Weathering, pp. 126–132 1 block or 2 periods **5.1** **Define** mechanical weathering. **5.2** **Explain** chemical weathering. **5.3** **Identify** the factors that affect the rate of weathering.	A-1, B-1, D-1, D-2, F-4, F-5		**SE** Inquiry Activity: What Causes Weathering? p. 125 L2 **TE** Build Science Skills, p. 127 L2 **TE** Teacher Demo: Modeling Exfoliation, p. 128 L2 **TE** Build Science Skills, p. 129 L2 **SE** Exploration Lab: Effect of Temperature on Chemical Weathering, pp. 150–151 L2
5.2 Soil, pp. 133–142 1 block or 2 periods **5.4** **Recognize** the major components of soil and **list** the most important factors in soil formation. **5.5** **Explain** how soil varies with depth. **5.6** **Compare and contrast** the three common types of soil. **5.7** **Demonstrate** how human activities affect the rate of soil erosion.	B-3, C-4, D-2, F-3, F-4, F-5, F-6		**TE** Teacher Demo: Water Absorption in Different Soils, p. 134 L2 **TE** Build Science Skills, p. 136 L2 **TE** Build Science Skills, p. 137 L2 **TE** Build Science Skills, p. 140 L2
5.3 Mass Movements, pp. 143–147 1 block or 2 periods **5.8** **Define** mass movement. **5.9** **Identify** the factors that trigger mass movements. **5.10** **Classify** mass movements.	A-1, F-5, G-2		**TE** Teacher Demo: Oversteepened Slopes, p. 144 L2 **LM** Some Factors That Affect Soil Erosion L2

Ability Levels

L1 For students who need additional help
L2 For all students
L3 For students who need to be challenged

Components

SE	Student Edition	**GRSW**	Guided Reading & Study Workbook	**TP**	Test Prep Resources	**GEO**	Geode CD-ROM
TE	Teacher's Edition	**TEX**	Teacher Express	**onT**	onlineText	**T**	Transparencies
LM	Laboratory Manual	**CTB**	Computer Test Bank	**DC**	Discovery Channel Videos	**GO**	Internet Resources
CUT	Chapter Tests						

RESOURCES PRINT and TECHNOLOGY	SECTION ASSESSMENT
GRSW Section 5.1 **T-26** Mechanical Weathering Increases Surface Area **T-27** Sheeting **T-28** Products of Weathering GEODe Sculpturing Earth's Surface ↳ External vs Internal Process **DC** Weathering and Erosion **TEX** Lesson Planning 5.1	**SE** Section 5.1 Assessment, p. 132 **onT** Section 5.1
GRSW Section 5.2 **T-29** Composition of Soil **T-30** Soil Texture Diagram **T-31** Idealized Soil Profile **T-32** Summary of Soil Types **T-374** World Soil Orders **T-375** Soil Distribution **T-376** Soil Distribution GEODe Earth Materials ↳ Sedimentary Rocks **TEX** Lesson Planning 5.2	**SE** Section 5.2 Assessment, p. 142 **onT** Section 5.2
GRSW Section 5.3 **T-33** Four Rapid Forms of Mass Wasting **T-34** Gros Ventre Rockslide **T-35** Process of Creep **TEX** Lesson Planning 5.3	**SE** Section 5.3 Assessment, p. 147 **onT** Section 5.3

Go Online

Go online for these Internet resources.

PHSchool.com
Web Code: cjk-9999

NSTA SCILINKS
Web Code: cjn: 2052

Materials for Activities and Labs

Quantities for each group

STUDENT EDITION

Inquiry Activity, p. 125
1-L plastic container with lid, rocks, water, strainer, clear glass jar, hand lens

Exploration Lab, pp. 150–151
250-mL beaker, thermometer, hot water (40–50°C), ice, 5 antacid tablets, stopwatch, graph paper

TEACHER'S EDITION

Build Science Skills, p. 127
water, container, other materials of students' choice

Teacher Demo, p. 128
large onion, small kitchen knife

Build Science Skills, p. 129
new nail, rusted nail

Teacher Demo, p. 134
sand, silt, clay, water, three plastic cups, nail, 250-mL beaker, paper towel

Build Science Skills, p. 136
hand lens, soil sample

Build Science Skills, p. 137
thermometer, lamp, soil samples

Build Science Skills, p. 140
soil, plastic container, spray bottle with adjustable tip, water

Teacher Demo, p. 144
bag of potting soil, water, cardboard box, plastic knife

Chapter Assessment

ASSESSMENT

SE Assessment, pp. 153–154
CUT Chapter 5 Test
CTB Chapter 5
onT Chapter 5

STANDARDIZED TEST PREP

SE Chapter 5, p. 155
TP Progress Monitoring Assessments

interactive textbook with assessment at PHSchool.com

CHAPTER 5

Before you teach

Michael Wysession
Washington University

Big Ideas

As fast as plate tectonics can create land, weathering destroys it. The ultimate energy source of weathering is the sun, though its major agent is water. It could be said that the first law of geology is that rocks fall downhill. This occurs as mass movements, which are driven by Earth's gravitational attraction.

Space and Time The entire surface of continents is slowly being destroyed through a combination of mechanical and chemical weathering. Mechanical weathering primarily occurs by frost wedging, unloading (pressure release), and the activities of plants and animals. Chemical weathering occurs though reactions involving water and materials dissolved within it. The rates of weathering are highly variable, and depend upon regional rock types and climate.

Forces and Motion Mass movements involve portions of the ground moving downhill together. They take many different forms, including rockfalls, slides, slumps, flows, and creep. Mass movements can be triggered by too much or too little water, over-steepened slopes, or the occurrence of earthquakes.

Matter and Energy Weathering of rock results in the production of soil, which is vital for human existence because it supports plant life. Soil contains a mixture of mineral matter (in differing amounts of sand, silt, and clay), organic matter, water, and air. Soil develops from the top down, and varies greatly depending upon the type of parent rock and regional climate.

Earth as a System Chemical weathering occurs more rapidly when rain water is acidic, so the formation of acid rain through human industrial activities has greatly increased weathering in some parts of the world.

Earth Science Refresher

Causes of Chemical Weathering

Chemical weathering is the result of the remarkable properties of water. Because of the polar nature of the water molecule (partial positive charge on hydrogen atoms off to one side of the molecule, the partial negative charge on the oxygen atom off to the other side), all minerals dissolve to some degree in water. This process, called dissolution, is very important in the weathering of minerals like calcite, and therefore for the formation of caves in rocks like limestone, especially if the water is acidic.

When water reacts with carbon dioxide, it creates carbonic acid. This chemical not only enhances dissolution, but performs weathering in another way. When carbonic acid and water react with minerals like feldspar, some of the feldspar's ions are removed, and minerals are formed. This process, called hydrolysis, is responsible for the weathering of feldspars into clay minerals.

Water chemically reacts with minerals that contain metals like iron in a different manner. In a process called oxidation, water and oxygen react with metal-rich minerals to form new minerals. This process is often called rusting, and the new minerals are the rust.

It is important to establish the difference between the process that occurs when a substance dissolves in water, and the process that occurs when substances react in a water solution. When describing chemical weathering in the chapter, we note that water either reacts with gases in the air to form acids or cause oxidation. Water also provides the medium for soluble ions to react.

Go Online PDLINKS NSTA
For: Chapter 5 Content Support
Visit: www.SciLinks.org/PDLinks
Web Code: cjn-0599

Chemical Weathering and Climate Change

In addition to being responsible for shaping the surface of the continents, weathering also plays an important role in controlling climate. This is because carbon dioxide plays a crucial role in both.

Carbon dioxide, which is important in weathering as carbonic acid, is also important in controlling climate because it absorbs radiation emitted by Earth's surface, the process called the greenhouse effect. If a lot of carbon dioxide is in the form of carbonic acid, then it isn't in the atmosphere, and a global cooling can occur. Interestingly, these two factors—weathering rates and the greenhouse effect—work counter to each other, and help to stabilize Earth's climate. Carbon dioxide is constantly entering the atmosphere from volcanic eruptions and from the ocean. Higher levels of carbon dioxide lead to a warmer climate, which causes higher rates of weathering. However, this weathering removes carbon dioxide from the atmosphere in the form of carbonic acid, lowering global temperatures again.

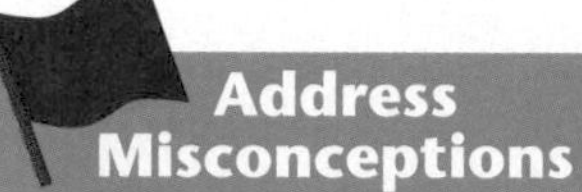

Students may believe that soil has always existed in its present form. Soil evolves over time. A fully developed soil may change in response to changes in climate, vegetation, and other factors. For a strategy that helps to overcome this misconception, see **Address Misconceptions** on **p. 135**.

An interesting result of the connection between weathering and the greenhouse effect is that plate tectonics can alter global climate. During times of active continental collisions, many new mountains are created. This causes accelerated weathering rates, and therefore the removal of carbon dioxide from the atmosphere. The result is that periods of global cooling are associated with periods of continental plate collisions. The global cooling trend that has occurred over the past 40 million years has been attributed to the collision of India with Asia and the formation of the Himalayan Mountains.

Build Reading Literacy

Summarize

Briefly Restating the Main Ideas

Strategy Help students understand a topic by restating the main ideas. Students read a section of the text and then identify main ideas and supporting details. They summarize what they have read by briefly restating the main concepts in a sentence or two. Summarizing can be employed to review brief subsections as well as entire sections and chapters. Have students read the beginning of Section 5.1, pp. 126–128.

Example

1. Ask students to carefully read the selected passage. Then, have them review the passage and identify the main ideas. Demonstrate this process by using the bold headings, Key Concept statements, and vocabulary as aids in determining what the passage is mostly about. List the main ideas on the board.
2. Direct students to write brief summaries of the passage by restating each of the main ideas in one or two sentences, using their own words. Remind students to focus on the most important concepts, omitting details and examples. Students should check to be sure that their summary covers the terms mentioned in the bold headings.
3. Assign the next passage for students to read and summarize. You may want to have students work in small groups to compare their summaries.
4. Have students read and summarize the rest of Section 5.1.

See p. 139 for a script on how to use this strategy with students. For additional strategies, see pp. 127 and 145.

ASSESS PRIOR KNOWLEDGE

Use the Chapter Pretest below to assess students' prior knowledge. As needed, review these concepts.

Review Science Concepts

Section 5.1 Review the processes of the rock cycle. In particular, focus on how weathering breaks down rocks.

Section 5.2 Reemphasize that the Earth system is made up of numerous interacting subsystems. Discuss how the biosphere interacts with the solid Earth.

Section 5.3 Review the definition of *gravity*. Make sure students understand that gravity is a universal force between all objects. Remind students that certain human activities can negatively impact the environment.

CHAPTER 5 Weathering, Soil, and Mass Movements

CONCEPTS in Action

Exploration Lab
Effect of Temperature on Chemical Weathering

How Earth Works
Soil

Sculpturing Earth's Surface
↳ External vs Internal Process

Earth Materials
↳ Sedimentary Rocks

DISCOVERY CHANNEL SCHOOL **Video Field Trip**
Weathering and Erosion

Take a rugged field trip through the great outdoors with Discovery Channel and find out the roles weathering and erosion play in the creation of Earth's most beautiful features. Answer the following questions after watching the video.

1. Describe the creative forces of erosion.
2. How is soil created?

For: Chapter 5 Resources
Visit: PHSchool.com
Web Code: cjk-9999

Weathering caused these spectacular rock formations in Arizona's Monument Valley. ▶

124 *Chapter 5*

Chapter Pretest

1. What process breaks down rock into small pieces? *(c)*
a. cementation **b.** compaction
c. weathering **d.** deposition

2. Is weathering classified as an internal or external process? Explain your answer. *(Weathering is an external process. It acts on rocks at or near Earth's surface.)*

3. True or False: The biosphere includes Earth's core, the less dense mantle, and the crust. *(False)*

4. Give one example of how living things interact with their physical environment. *(Sample answer: A beaver may build a dam across a stream and create a large aquatic environment.)*

5. Which statement best describes the force of gravity? *(d)*
a. Earth's gravity pulls objects toward the center of the planet.
b. Objects do not have to be in contact with one another to experience the force of gravity.
c. Gravity is the force that acts between any two objects.
d. All of the above

6. Describe one positive effect and one negative effect of human activities on the environment. *(Sample answer: A positive effect is creating a wildlife refuge. A negative effect is cutting down a forest.)*

SCULPTURING EARTH'S SURFACE

Chapter Preview

Inquiry Activity

What Causes Weathering?

Procedure

1. Fill a 1-L plastic container about half full of rocks. Add enough water to barely cover the rocks.
2. Place a tight-fitting lid on the container, and shake the container vigorously 100 times.
3. Hold a strainer over a clear glass jar. Pour the water and rocks into the strainer.
4. Use a hand lens to observe the bottom and sides of the empty container. Then use the hand lens to observe the water in the glass jar.

Think About It

1. **Observing** What did you see on the bottom or sides of the empty container during Step 4? How did shaking the rock-and-water mixture change the appearance of the water?
2. **Predicting** How do you think your observations would change if you put the rocks and water back in the container and repeated Steps 2 through 4 several more times?
3. **Predicting** Suppose you found a stream where water ran over a rock ledge into a pool. What would you expect to find at the bottom of the pool?

Weathering, Soil, and Mass Movements **125**

Video Field Trip

Weathering and Erosion

Encourage students to view the Video Field Trip "Weathering and Erosion."

ENGAGE/EXPLORE

What Causes Weathering? L2

Purpose Students will observe how weathering breaks down rocks.

Skills Focus **Observing, Predicting**

 **Prep Time** 10 minutes

Materials 1-L plastic container with lid, rocks, water, strainer, clear glass jar, hand lens

Class Time 15 minutes

Teaching Tip Have students work in pairs to complete the activity. One student can shake the container while the other counts the number of shakes.

Expected Outcome Shaking the container simulates weathering. Students will observe small rock fragments and other sediments in the bottom of the container and in the water.

Think About It

1. There should be small rock fragments on the bottom or sides of the empty container. The water in the jar may be slightly cloudy, and there may be grit on the bottom of the jar.
2. Sample answer: There would be more rock fragments in the empty container and more grit in the jar, and the water in the jar would become cloudier.
3. rock fragments or other sediment

Section 5.1

1 FOCUS

Section Objectives

5.1 **Define** mechanical weathering.
5.2 **Explain** chemical weathering.
5.3 **Identify** the factors that affect the rate of weathering.

Reading Focus

Build Vocabulary L2

Vocabulary Rating Chart Have each student construct a chart with four columns labeled Term, Can Define or Use It, Heard or Seen It, and Don't Know. Students should then write the vocabulary terms *mechanical weathering, frost wedging, talus, exfoliation,* and *chemical weathering* in column 1 and rate their knowledge of each term by putting a check in one of the other columns. Before reading the text, ask questions that help students anticipate the meaning of the terms based on prior knowledge. For example, ask: **What is a wedge used for?** *(to force objects apart)* After students have read the section, have them revise their charts.

Reading Strategy L2

a. process in which physical forces break rock into pieces without changing the rock's mineral composition
b. process in which water enters cracks in a rock, enlarges the cracks by freezing and expanding, and breaks the rock
c. large piles of rock fragments that usually form at the base of cliffs
d. process in which slabs of outer rock separate and break loose
e. the transformation of rock into one or more new compounds

5.1 Weathering

Reading Focus

Key Concepts

- What is mechanical weathering?
- What is chemical weathering?
- What factors affect the rate of weathering?

Vocabulary

- mechanical weathering
- frost wedging
- talus
- exfoliation
- chemical weathering

Reading Strategy

Building Vocabulary Copy the table. As you read the section, define each vocabulary term.

Vocabulary Term	Definition
Mechanical weathering	a. ?
Frost wedging	b. ?
Talus	c. ?
Exfoliation	d. ?
Chemical weathering	e. ?

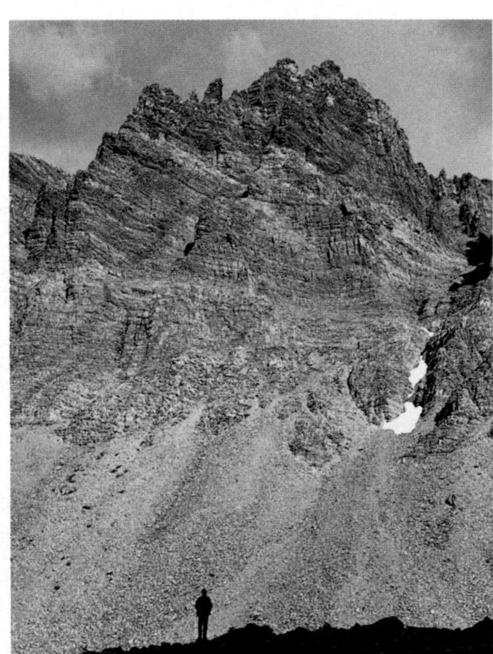

Figure 1 Weathering Ice, rain, and wind are slowly breaking down the rock in this mountain. The rock fragments accumulate in sloped deposits at the base of the mountain.

Earth's surface is constantly changing. Internal forces gradually raise some parts of the surface through mountain building and volcanic activity. At the same time, external processes continually break rock apart and move the debris to lower elevations, as shown in Figure 1. The breaking down and changing of rocks at or near Earth's surface is called weathering. Weathering is a basic part of the rock cycle and a key process in the Earth system. There are two types of weathering—mechanical and chemical. Though these processes are different, they are at work at the same time.

Mechanical Weathering

Mechanical weathering occurs when physical forces break rock into smaller and smaller pieces without changing the rock's mineral composition. Each piece has the same characteristics as the original rock. Breaking a rock into smaller pieces increases the total surface area of the rock. Look at Figure 2. When rock is broken apart, more surface area is exposed to chemical weathering. **In nature, three physical processes are especially important causes of mechanical weathering: frost wedging, unloading, and biological activity.**

Mechanical Weathering and Surface Area

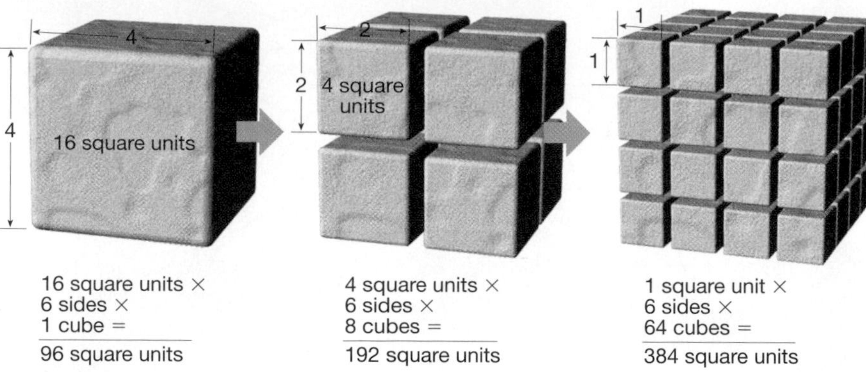

Figure 2 By breaking a rock into smaller pieces, mechanical weathering increases the rock's surface area that can be exposed to chemical weathering. **Calculating** *Calculate the total surface area if each of the 64 cubes shown in the right diagram were broken into 8 equal-sized cubes.*

Frost Wedging When liquid water freezes, it expands by about 9 percent, exerting a tremendous outward force. This force is great enough to burst water pipes during the winter. In nature, water works its way into every crack in rock. When water freezes and expands, it enlarges the cracks. After many freeze-thaw cycles, the rock breaks into pieces. This process, which is shown in Figure 3, is called **frost wedging.** Frost wedging is most common in mountainous regions in the middle latitudes. Here daily freezing and thawing often occur. Sections of rock that are wedged loose may tumble into large piles called **talus,** which typically form at the base of steep, rocky cliffs.

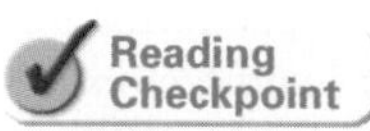

Explain how water can cause mechanical weathering.

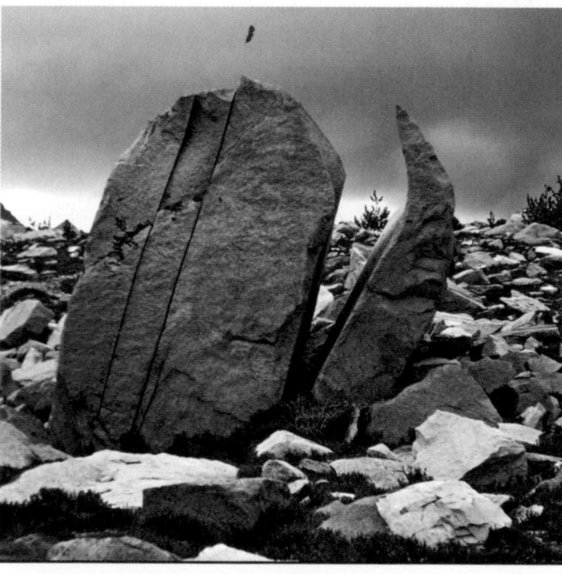

Figure 3 Frost Wedging Rainwater entered cracks in this boulder. Each time the water froze, it expanded. Eventually, the boulder split.

2 INSTRUCT

Mechanical Weathering

Build Reading Literacy L1

Refer to **p. 334D** in **Chapter 12,** which provides the guidelines for outlining.

Outline Have students create an outline of Section 5.1 (pp. 126–132). Outlines should follow the head structure used in the text. Major headings are shown in green, and subheadings are shown in blue. Ask: **Based on your outlines, what do you expect to learn about in this section?** *(mechanical weathering, chemical weathering, and rates of weathering)*
Verbal

Use Visuals L1

Figure 2 Ask: **Which of the three diagrams has the most exposed surface area?** *(the third one)* **If the diagrams were actual rocks, which one would experience the least chemical weathering?** *(the first one)*
Visual

Build Science Skills L2

Designing Experiments ACTIVITY
Have students work in small groups to design experiments showing how water expands when frozen. Students should write down each step of their procedures, listing materials used and safety measures. A sample experiment might involve pouring water into a container, placing the container in a freezer overnight, then observing the effect of the frozen water on the container. If time permits, allow students to perform their experiments. Be sure to approve all procedures beforehand.
Logical, Group

Customize for English Language Learners

Tailor your presentation by speaking directly and simplifying the terms and sentence structures used to explain key concepts. For example, split a cause-and-effect sentence into two sentences labeled Cause and Effect. A sample cause sentence might be *Water expands when it freezes.* A sample effect sentence might be *The frozen water enlarges cracks in rocks.* Other techniques include using visual aids and body language when appropriate to emphasize important concepts. For example, you can clasp your hands together, then move them apart when discussing how water expands when it freezes.

Answer to . . .

Figure 2 *64 cubes × 8 = 512 cubes; 1 square unit/side × 6 sides/cube × 512 cubes = 768 square units*

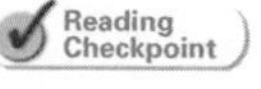

Water works its way into cracks in rock. When water freezes, it expands, enlarging the cracks. After many freeze-thaw cycles, the rock breaks.

Use Community Resources 

Arrange for students to take a walking tour of your community to look for signs of mechanical weathering. If possible, bring along a camera or camcorder to document the field trip. Have students attempt to classify each example of mechanical weathering as frost wedging, unloading, or biological activity.
Visual

Teacher Demo

Modeling Exfoliation 

Purpose Students will observe a model of the process of exfoliation.

Materials large onion, small kitchen knife

Procedure Stand before the class and hold up a large, unpeeled onion. Cut off the top of the onion and show students its inner layers. Peel the onion, layer by layer. Wash your hands afterwards.

Expected Outcomes Have students relate the activity to Figure 4, which shows an example of exfoliation. Have them point out the onionlike layers of the Half Dome in Yosemite National Park.
Visual

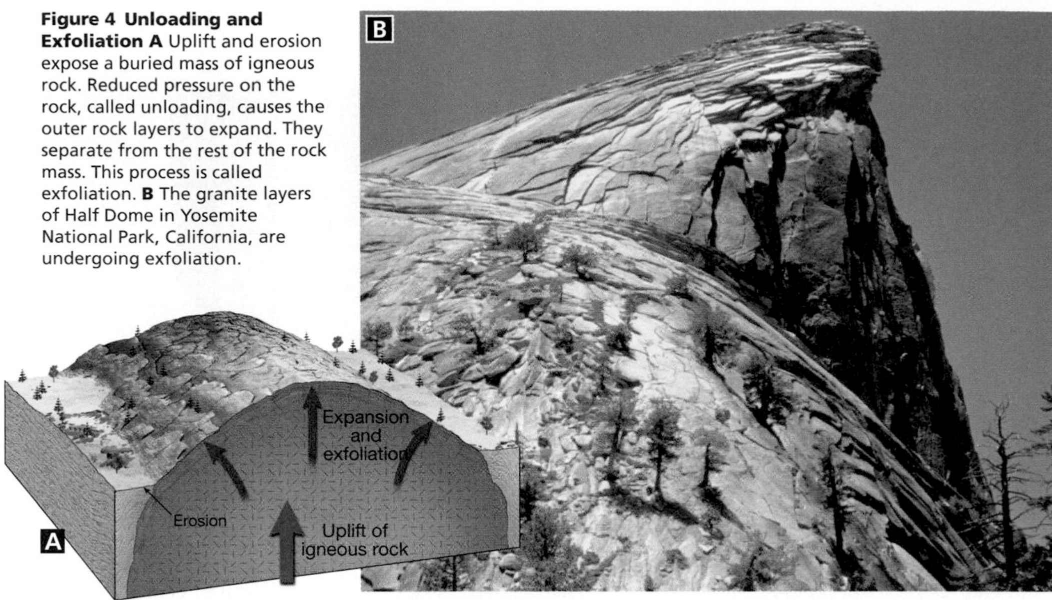

Figure 4 Unloading and Exfoliation A Uplift and erosion expose a buried mass of igneous rock. Reduced pressure on the rock, called unloading, causes the outer rock layers to expand. They separate from the rest of the rock mass. This process is called exfoliation. **B** The granite layers of Half Dome in Yosemite National Park, California, are undergoing exfoliation.

Unloading Large masses of igneous rock may be exposed through uplift and erosion of overlying rocks. When that happens, the pressure exerted on the igneous rock is reduced. This is known as unloading. As illustrated in Figure 4A, unloading causes the outer layers of the rock to expand more than the rock below. Slabs of outer rock separate like the layers of an onion and break loose in a process called **exfoliation.** Exfoliation is especially common in rock masses made of granite. It often produces large, dome-shaped rock formations. Figure 4B shows one of these formations. Other important exfoliation domes are Stone Mountain, Georgia, and Liberty Cap also in Yosemite National Park.

A striking example of the weathering effects of unloading is shown in deep underground mining. Newly cut mine tunnels suddenly reduce the pressure on the surrounding rock. As a result, large rock slabs sometimes explode off the walls of the tunnels.

Figure 5 The roots of this tree are causing mechanical weathering by widening the cracks in the rock.

Biological Activity The activities of organisms, including plants, burrowing animals, and humans, can also cause mechanical weathering. As Figure 5 shows, plant roots grow into cracks in rock, wedging the rock apart as they grow. Burrowing animals move rocks to the surface, where weathering is more rapid. Decaying organisms produce compounds called acids that cause chemical weathering.

Humans accelerate mechanical weathering through deforestation and blasting in search of minerals or in the creation of new roads.

Chemical Weathering

Chemical weathering is the transformation of rock into one or more new compounds. The new compounds remain mostly unchanged as long as the environment in which they formed does not change. You can contrast chemical weathering and mechanical weathering with a sheet of paper. Tearing the paper into small pieces is like mechanical weathering of rock. Burning the paper, which changes it into carbon dioxide and water, is like chemical weathering.

Water Water is the most important agent of chemical weathering. Water promotes chemical weathering by absorbing gases from the atmosphere and the ground. These dissolved substances then chemically react with various minerals. Oxygen dissolved in water reacts easily with certain minerals, forming oxides. For example, iron-rich minerals get a yellow to reddish-brown coating of iron oxide when they react with oxygen. Iron oxide is the rust that forms when iron-containing objects are exposed to water. Figure 6A shows this rust on barrels.

Water absorbs carbon dioxide when rain falls through the atmosphere. Water that seeps through the ground also picks up carbon dioxide from decaying organic matter. The carbon dioxide dissolved in water forms carbonic acid. This is the weak acid in carbonated soft drinks. Carbonic acid reacts with many common minerals.

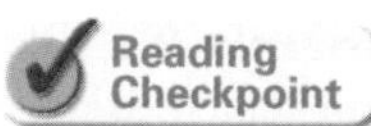

How are water, oxygen, and carbon dioxide involved in chemical weathering?

Figure 6 A Oxygen reacted with the iron in these barrels, forming iron oxide, or rust. **B** This granite gravestone, placed in 1868, shows little evidence of chemical weathering. **C** The inscription date (1872) on this marble gravestone is nearly illegible due to chemical weathering.

Chemical Weathering

Build Science Skills L2

Observing Obtain a new, unrusted nail and a thoroughly rusted nail. Allow students to carefully examine both. Break the rusted nail into two pieces to emphasize how weak it is. Ask: **How do the two nails differ?** *(They differ in strength, appearance, and color.)* Have students relate their observations to chemical weathering. Ask: **What could you infer about the minerals in a rock that had the same color as the rusted nail?** *(The minerals likely contain iron that reacted with oxygen and water.)*
Visual, Kinesthetic

ACTIVITY

Facts and Figures

Weathering creates many important mineral deposits by concentrating minor amounts of metals that are scattered throughout unweathered rock into economically valuable concentrations. Such a transformation can take place in two ways. In one situation, chemical weathering coupled with downward-percolating water removes undesired materials from decomposing rock, leaving the desired elements enriched in the upper zones of the soil. The second way is basically the reverse of the first. The desirable elements that are found in low concentrations near the surface are removed and carried to lower zones, where they are redeposited and become more concentrated.

Answer to . . .

Water dissolves some of the minerals in rock. Oxygen dissolved in water reacts with certain minerals, forming oxides. Carbon dioxide dissolved in water forms carbonic acid, which reacts with many common minerals.

Address Misconceptions L2

During a student's education, a good deal of emphasis is placed on the scientific method and proper investigation techniques. For this reason, many students mistakenly think that scientific knowledge advances mainly through experimentation. In fact, in several fields, including geology, observation is the key to understanding natural processes. This section offers an excellent opportunity to point out the role of observation in science. Challenge students to brainstorm other fields where observation is crucial to understanding natural processes. *(astronomy, biology, ecology)*
Verbal

Integrate Chemistry 

Weathering of Granite The weathering of the potassium feldspar component of granite takes place as follows:

$$2KAlSi_3O_8 + 2(H^+ + HCO_3^-) + H_2O \rightarrow Al_2Si_2O_5(OH)_4 = 2K^+ + 2HCO_3^- + 4SiO_2.$$

In this reaction, the hydrogen ions (H^+) attack and replace potassium ions (K^+) in the feldspar structure, thereby disrupting the crystalline network. Once removed, the potassium is available as a nutrient for plants or becomes the soluble salt potassium bicarbonate ($KHCO_3$), which may be incorporated into other minerals or carried to the ocean in dissolved form by streams. Have students summarize the chemical reaction in their own words. *(Potassium feldspar reacts with carbonic acid and water to produce mainly clay minerals.)*
Logical

Figure 7 One Effect of Acid Precipitation Acid precipitation contributed to the chemical weathering of this stone building facade in Leipzig, Germany.

Water in the atmosphere also absorbs sulfur oxides and nitrogen oxides. These oxides are produced by the burning of coal and petroleum. Through a series of chemical reactions, these pollutants are converted into acids that are the major cause of acid precipitation. Acid precipitation accelerates the chemical weathering of stone monuments and structures, such as the one shown in Figure 7.

Chemical Weathering of Granite To illustrate how chemical weathering can change the properties of rock, let's consider granite. Recall that granite consists mainly of the minerals feldspar and quartz. When granite is exposed to water containing carbonic acid, the feldspar is converted mostly to clay minerals. Quartz, in contrast, is much more resistant to carbonic acid and remains unchanged. As the feldspar slowly changes to clay, the quartz grains are released from the granite. Rivers transport some of this weathered debris to the sea. The tiny clay particles may be carried far from shore. The quartz grains are deposited near the shore where they become the main component of beaches and sand dunes.

Chemical Weathering of Silicate Minerals Recall that silicate minerals make up most of Earth's crust and are composed largely of just eight elements. When silicate minerals undergo chemical weathering, the sodium, calcium, potassium, and magnesium they contain dissolve and are carried away by groundwater. Iron reacts with oxygen, producing iron oxide. The three remaining elements are aluminum, silicon, and oxygen. These elements usually combine with water and produce clay minerals. See Table 1 for a list of products of weathering.

Table 1 Products of Weathering

Mineral	Residual Products	Materials in Solution
Quartz	Quartz grains	Silica
Feldspars	Clay minerals	Silica K^+, Na^+, Ca^{2+}
Amphibole (hornblende)	Clay minerals Limonite Hematite	Silica Ca^{2+}, Mg^{2+}
Olivine	Limonite Hematite	Silica Mg^{2+}

Spheroidal Weathering Chemical weathering can change the physical shape of rock as well as its chemical composition. For example, when water enters along the joints in a rock, it weathers the corners and edges most rapidly. These parts of the rock have a greater surface area than the faces have. As a result, the corners and edges become more rounded. The rock takes on a spherical shape, as shown in Figure 8A. This process is called spheroidal weathering.

Figure 8 Spheroidal Weathering A The edges of these granite rocks in California's Joshua Tree National Monument were rounded through spheroidal weathering. **B** Spheroidal weathering has caused the outer layers of this rock to loosen and separate.

As Figure 8B shows, spheroidal weathering sometimes causes the outer layers of a rock to separate from the rock's main body. This can happen when the minerals in the rock turn to clay, which swells by adding water. The swelling exerts a force that causes the layers to break loose and fall off. This allows chemical weathering to penetrate deeper into the boulder. Although the effects of this type of spheroidal weathering resemble exfoliation, the two processes are different. Spheroidal weathering is a form of chemical weathering. Exfoliation is caused by unloading. The layers that separate from the rock are not chemically changed.

Rate of Weathering

Mechanical weathering affects the rate of chemical weathering. By breaking rock into smaller pieces, mechanical weathering accelerates chemical weathering by increasing the surface area of exposed rock. **Two other factors that affect the rate of weathering are rock characteristics and climate.**

Rock Characteristics Physical characteristics of rock, such as cracks, are important in weathering because they influence the ability of water to penetrate rock. However, a rock's mineral composition also dramatically affects its rate of weathering. You can see this by visiting a cemetery and comparing old gravestones made from different rock types. Gravestones made of granite, like the one in Figure 6B on page 129, are relatively resistant to chemical weathering. You can easily read the inscriptions on a granite gravestone that is over 100 years old. In contrast, marble gravestones undergo much more rapid chemical weathering, as shown in Figure 6C on page 129. Marble is composed of calcite (calcium carbonate), which easily dissolves even in weak acids.

Use Visuals L1

Figure 8 Have students compare Figure 8 to Figure 4 on p. 128. Have them discuss the similarities and differences between spheroidal weathering and exfoliation. *(Both are types of weathering that give rock a layered appearance. Spheroidal weathering is a form of chemical weathering. Thus, the composition of the rock changes. Exfoliation is a type of mechanical weathering; the composition of the rock does not change.)*
Visual, Verbal

Rate of Weathering

Build Science Skills L2

Inferring Hold up an atlas in front of the class. Select an area and briefly describe its climate in terms of hot and wet, cold and dry, hot and dry, and so on. Have students infer rates of weathering for each location. *(In general, areas that are hot and wet have higher rates of weathering than do areas that are cooler and drier.)*
Logical, Visual

Section 5.1 (continued)

Build Science Skills L2

Communicating Results Show students a copy or transparency of Bowen's reaction series. Have them note the order of crystallization of minerals. Students can then use the series to sequence the resistance of silicates to weathering, starting with the least resistant mineral. *(olivine, pyroxene, amphibole, biotite mica, potassium feldspar, muscovite mica, and quartz)*
Verbal

3 ASSESS

Evaluate Understanding L2

Have students describe the relationship between burning coal and chemical weathering. *(Oxides produced by burning coal react with water in the atmosphere to create acid precipitation. Acid precipitation, in turn, accelerates rates of chemical weathering.)*

Reteach L1

Give students examples of different types of weathering, such as unloading and spheroidal weathering, and have them classify the examples as mechanical or chemical.

Solutions L2

7. diameter = 2 m; radius = 1 m; area of sphere = $4\pi(1\text{ m})^2 = 4\pi\text{ m}^2 = 12.57\text{ m}^2$; area of two hemispheres = area of sphere + (2 × area of circle) = $4\pi\text{ m}^2 + [2 \times \pi(1\text{ m})^2] = 4\pi\text{ m}^2 + 2\pi\text{ m}^2 = 6\pi\text{ m}^2 = 18.85\text{ m}^2$

Answer to . . .

Figure 9 *The parts where the formations are thinnest weather most rapidly.*

Figure 9 These boldly sculpted pinnacles in Bryce Canyon National Park show differential weathering. ***Drawing Conclusions*** *In which parts of these formations is weathering happening most rapidly?*

Silicates are the most abundant mineral group. Silicates weather in the same sequence as their order of crystallization. Olivine crystallizes first and weathers most rapidly. Quartz, which crystallizes last, is the most resistant to weathering.

Climate Climatic factors, especially temperature and moisture, have a strong effect on the rate of weathering. For example, these factors control the frequency of freeze-thaw cycles, which affect the amount of frost wedging. Temperature and moisture also affect the rate of chemical weathering. They influence the kind of vegetation and how much is present. Regions with lush vegetation generally have a thick layer of soil rich in decaying organic matter that releases acids into the water.

The climate most favorable for chemical weathering has high temperatures and abundant moisture. So, chemical weathering is very slow in arid regions. It is also slow in polar regions because the low temperatures there keep moisture locked up as ice.

Differential Weathering Different parts of a rock mass often weather at different rates. This process, called differential weathering, has several causes. Differences in mineral composition are one cause. More resistant rock protrudes as pinnacles, or high peaks, such as those shown in Figure 9. Another cause is the variations in the number and spacing of cracks in different parts of a rock mass.

Section 5.1 Assessment

Reviewing Concepts

1. What happens to a rock's mineral composition during mechanical weathering?
2. What is unloading? How does it contribute to weathering?
3. How does chemical weathering affect the compounds in rock?
4. Name two rock characteristics and two climatic factors that affect the rate of weathering.

Critical Thinking

5. **Using Analogies** Think about the following processes: dissolving a piece of rock salt in a pan of water and grinding a peach pit in a garbage disposal. Which process is more like mechanical weathering, and which is more like chemical weathering?
6. **Applying Concepts** The level of carbon dioxide in the atmosphere is increasing. How might this affect the rate of chemical weathering of Earth's surface rocks? Explain your reasoning.

Math Practice

7. Suppose frost wedging splits a spherical rock 2 m in diameter into two equal-sized hemispheres. Calculate the total surface area of the original rock and of the two hemispheres. (The area of a circle = πr^2, and the surface area of a sphere = $4\pi r^2$, where r is the radius.)

Section 5.1 Assessment

1. It does not change.
2. Unloading is the reduction in pressure that happens when a mass of rock is exposed. It causes the outer layers of the rock to expand, which makes slabs of outer rock separate and break loose.
3. It transforms them into one or more new compounds.
4. Rock characteristics include cracks and mineral composition; climatic factors include temperature and moisture.
5. mechanical weathering—grinding a peach pit in a garbage disposal; chemical weathering—dissolving a piece of rock in a pan of vinegar
6. An increased level of carbon dioxide should result in higher levels of carbonic acid, which reacts with many common minerals. Therefore, the rate of chemical weathering should increase.

5.2 Soil

Reading Focus

Key Concepts

- What are the major components of soil?
- What are the most important factors in soil formation?
- How does soil vary with depth?
- What are three common types of soil?
- How do human activities affect the rate of soil erosion?

Vocabulary

- regolith
- soil
- soil horizon
- soil profile
- pedalfer
- pedocal
- laterite

Reading Strategy

Comparing and Contrasting Copy the table. After you read, compare the three types of soils by completing the table.

Soil Type	Where It's Found
Pedalfer	a. ___?___
Pedocal	b. ___?___
Laterite	c. ___?___

Soil, an important product of weathering, covers most land surfaces. Along with air and water, it is one of our most important resources. All life depends on a dozen or so elements that come from Earth's crust. Once weathering and other processes create soil, plants absorb the elements and make them available to animals, including humans.

Characteristics of Soil

Weathering produces a layer of rock and mineral fragments called **regolith,** which covers nearly all of Earth's land surface. **Soil is the part of the regolith that supports the growth of plants.** Three important characteristics of soil are its composition, texture, and structure.

Soil Composition **Soil has four major components: mineral matter, or broken-down rock; organic matter, or humus, which is the decayed remains of organisms; water; and air.** The proportions of these components vary in different soils. Figure 10 shows that in a good-quality surface soil, mineral matter and organic matter make up half the total volume. The organic matter in soil, or humus, consists of the decayed remains of animal and plant life. The other half consists of pore spaces where air and water circulate.

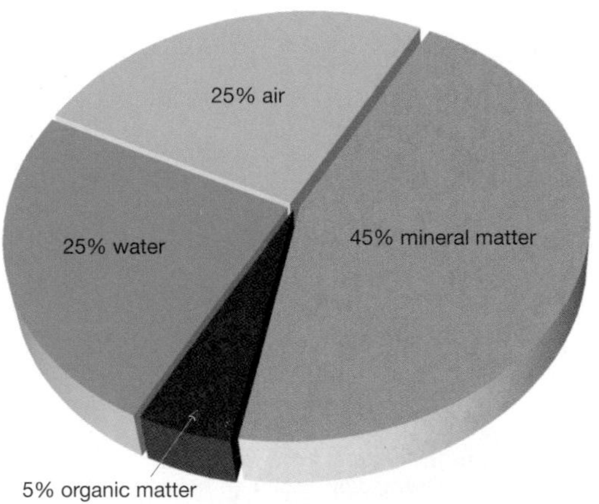

Figure 10 Composition by Volume of Good-Quality Soil
Using Graphs *What percentage of this soil consists of water and mineral matter?*

Section 5.2

1 FOCUS

Section Objectives

5.4 **Recognize** the major components of soil and **list** the most important factors in soil formation.

5.5 **Explain** how soil varies with depth.

5.6 **Compare and contrast** the three common types of soil.

5.7 **Demonstrate** how human activities affect the rate of soil erosion.

Reading Focus

Build Vocabulary L2

Paraphrase As you teach the text that pertains to a particular vocabulary word, have a volunteer read aloud the definition of the vocabulary word. Finish teaching the passage, then have students write the definition in their own words.

Reading Strategy L2

a. temperate, forested areas that receive more than 63 cm of rain each year
b. drier areas that have grasses and brush vegetation
c. hot, wet tropical areas

Answer to . . .

Figure 10 *70 percent*

2 INSTRUCT

Characteristics of Soil

Use Visuals L1

Figure 11 Give students several sample soil textures, and have them use the diagram to identify the corresponding soil type. For example, ask: **What type of soil consists of 60 percent clay, 20 percent sand, and 20 percent silt?** *(clay)*
Verbal

Water Absorption in Different Soils L2

Purpose Students will observe the ability of different soils to absorb water.

Materials sand, silt, clay, water, 3 plastic cups, nail, 250-mL beaker, paper towel

Procedure Use the nail to puncture a small hole in the bottom of each cup. Fill one cup halfway with sand. Fill another cup with silt and a third cup with clay. Place the cups on a paper towel. Ask students to predict which soil sample will absorb the most water. Then pour about 50 mL of water into each cup.

Expected Outcomes Students will correctly predict that the silt absorbs the most water. Water rapidly drains out of the sand and does not easily penetrate the clay.
Visual

Q *I've seen photos of footprints left on the lunar surface by astronauts. Does this mean the moon has soil?*

A Not exactly. The moon has no atmosphere, water, or biological activity. So, the weathering processes that occur on Earth don't take place on the moon. However, the lunar surface is covered by a layer of gray debris called lunar regolith, which was ejected by meteorite impacts over a few billion years. Changes occur so slowly on the lunar surface that the footprints left by the *Apollo* astronauts will probably look fresh for millions of years.

The percentage of organic matter in soil varies greatly. Certain bog soils are composed almost entirely of organic matter. Desert soils may contain only a tiny amount. In most soils, organic matter or humus is an essential component. It is an important source of plant nutrients and increases the soil's ability to retain water. Poor soils can be enriched with the addition of humus.

The water and air components of soil are also vital for plant growth. Soil water provides the moisture needed for chemical reactions that sustain life. Soil water provides nutrients in a form that plants can use. Air is the source of the carbon dioxide plants use to produce sugar during photosynthesis.

Soil Texture Most soils contain particles of different sizes. Soil texture refers to the proportions of different particle sizes. To classify soil texture, the U.S. Department of Agriculture has established categories based on the percentages of clay, silt, and sand in soil. The diagram in Figure 11 shows how the percentages differ for each category. For example, point A, near the left-center part of the diagram, represents a soil composed of 40 percent clay, 10 percent silt, and 50 percent sand. Such a soil is called a sandy clay. In soils called loam, which occupy the central part of the diagram, neither clay, silt, nor sand is dominant.

Texture strongly influences a soil's ability to support plant life. Sandy soils may drain and dry out too quickly, while clay-rich soils drain very slowly. Plant roots often have difficulty penetrating soils that contain a high percentage of clay and silt. Loam soils are usually best for plant growth. They retain water better and store more nutrients than do soils composed mainly of clay or sand.

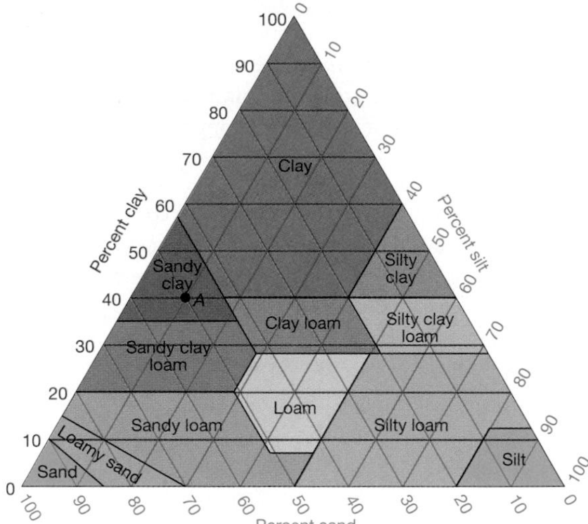

Figure 11 Soil-Texture Diagram The texture of any soil can be represented by a point on this diagram.
Interpreting Diagrams ***What type of soil consists of 10 percent clay, 60 percent silt, and 30 percent sand?***

Customize for Inclusion Students

Learning Disabled Visuals often simplify and clarify key concepts. Take a few moments to ensure that all students correctly interpret photographs, tables, graphs, and diagrams. For example, you can have students plot the data in Figure 10 on p. 133 in a bar graph to assess their understanding of soil composition. You can make copies of Figure 11 on p. 134 and encourage students to draw intersecting lines on the soil-texture diagram, to identify soil type. If students still have difficulty interpreting Figure 11, use transparency 3D and pick a point on the diagram to represent a soil sample, then trace a path along the relevant lines to help students identify the percentages of clay, silt, and sand in the sample.

Soil Structure Soil particles usually form clumps that give soils a particular structure. Soil structure determines how easily a soil can be cultivated and how susceptible it is to erosion. Soil structure also affects the ease with which water can penetrate the soil. This, in turn, influences the movement of nutrients to plant roots.

Soil Formation

Soil forms through the complex interaction of several factors. **The most important factors in soil formation are parent material, time, climate, organisms, and slope.** Although these factors all interact, we'll examine them separately.

Figure 12 Parent Materials and Soils

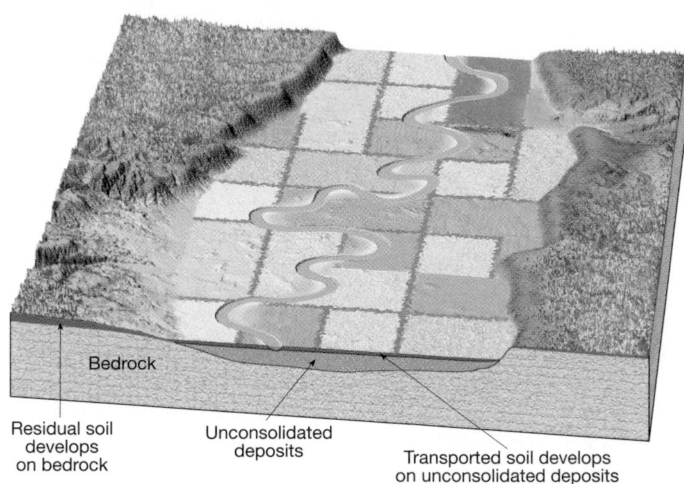

Parent Material The source of the mineral matter in soil is known as the parent material. Notice in Figure 12 that parent material may be either bedrock or unconsolidated deposits, such as those in a river valley. The soil that forms on bedrock is called residual soil. The soil that forms on unconsolidated deposits is called transported soil. Its parent material was moved from another location by gravity, water, wind, or ice.

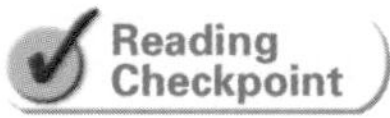
What is the difference between residual soil and transported soil?

Go Online SCiLINKS NSTA

For: Links on soil
Visit: www.SciLinks.org
Web Code: cjn-2052

Soil Formation

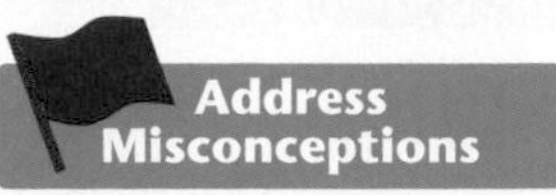
Address Misconceptions

L2

Show students a sample of soil. Ask them if they believe the soil has always existed in its present form. If they answer yes, students may have misconceptions about the formation of soil. Have them read the key concept sentence on p. 135. Point out that soil evolves over time. In addition, a mature soil may change in response to changes in climate, vegetation, and other factors. **Verbal**

Download a worksheet on soil for students to complete, and find additional teacher support from NSTA SciLinks.

Answer to . . .

Figure 11 *silty loam*

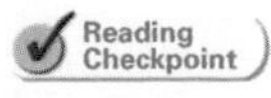
Residual soil forms on bedrock. Transported soil forms on unconsolidated deposits.

Integrate Biology L2

Organic Matter The chief function of plants and animals is to furnish organic matter to soil. Certain bog soils are composed entirely of organic matter, while desert soils may contain only a tiny percentage of organic matter. Although the quality of organic matter varies substantially among soils, it is the rare soil that completely lacks it. After students have read the text on p. 136, ask them to explain why the interactions between organisms and soil can be thought of as a continuous cycle. *(Organisms die and decay, contributing to soil fertility. Fertile soils nourish organisms, which eventually die and decay, continuing the cycle.)*
Logical

Build Science Skills L2

Observing Give small groups of students a hand lens and a different soil sample taken from your area. Try to obtain the samples from widely divergent areas, such as a garden, playground, and stream bank. Have students examine the samples and write reports describing the soils. Students should mention soil color, soil texture, and other distinguishing characteristics, such as particle size and the presence of organic matter.
Kinesthetic, Visual

The nature of the parent material influences soils in two ways. First, it affects the rate of weathering and the rate of soil formation. Because unconsolidated deposits are already partly weathered, they provide more surface area for chemical weathering. Therefore, transported soil usually develops more rapidly than residual soil develops. Second, the chemical makeup of the parent material affects the soil's fertility. Fertility influences the types of plants the soil can support.

Time The longer a soil has been forming, the thicker it becomes. The parent material largely determines the characteristics of young soils. As weathering continues, however, the influence of the parent material can be overshadowed by the other factors, especially climate.

Climate Climate has the greatest effect on soil formation. Variations in temperature and precipitation influence the rate, depth, and type of weathering. For example, a hot, wet climate may produce a thick layer of chemically weathered soil. In the same amount of time, a cold, dry climate might produce only a thin layer of mechanically weathered debris. The amount of precipitation also influences soil fertility by affecting the rate at which nutrients are removed from the soil. Finally, climate has a big effect on the types of organisms that live on and in the soil.

The influence of climate is so great that soil scientists have found that similar soils can be produced from different parent materials in the same climate. Dissimilar soils can be produced from the same parent material in different climates.

Organisms The types of organisms and how many there are in a soil have a major impact on its physical and chemical properties. In fact, scientists name some soils—such as prairie soil, forest soil, and tundra soil—based on the soils' natural vegetation.

Plants are the main source of organic matter in soil. Animals and microorganisms may also contribute. Because organic matter releases nutrients when it decays, it contributes to soil fertility. As you read in Section 5.1, the decay of organic matter also produces acids that speed up weathering.

Microorganisms, including fungi, bacteria, and single-celled protozoans, play an active role in decomposing dead plants and animals. Some bacteria also aid soil fertility by converting nitrogen gas into nitrogen compounds that plants can use.

Burrowing animals mix the mineral and organic matter in soil. Earthworms, for example, feed on organic matter as they burrow through soil. The earthworms in a single hectare (10,000 square meters) can mix thousands of kilograms of soil each year. The holes made by burrowing animals also help water and air to penetrate into soil.

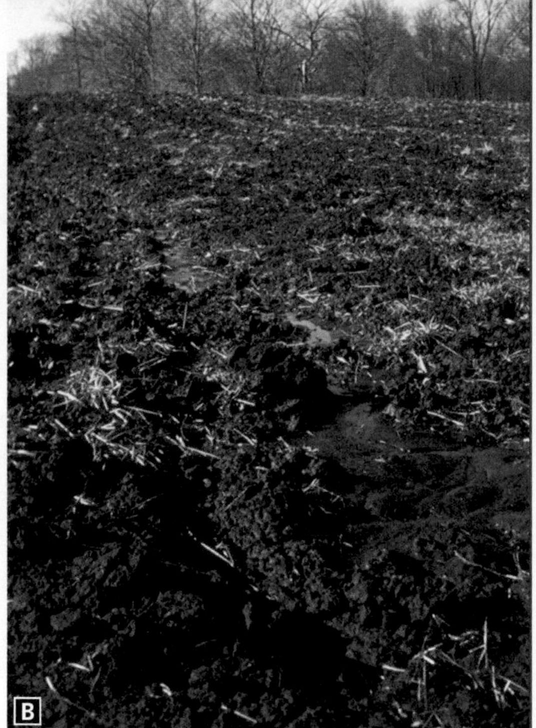

Figure 13 Slope and Soil Thickness A Little or no soil develops on steep slopes. **B** Flat areas often have very thick soil.

Slope The slope of the land can vary greatly over short distances. Such variations can result in very different soil types. Many of the differences are related to the amount of erosion and the water content of the soil.

On steep slopes, erosion is accelerated. Little water can soak in, so the soil generally holds too little moisture for vigorous plant growth. As a result, soils are usually thin or nonexistent on steep slopes, as shown in Figure 13A. In contrast, flat areas have little erosion and poor drainage. As Figure 13B shows, the waterlogged soils that form here are typically thick and dark. The dark color results from large amounts of organic matter.

The direction a slope faces also affects soil formation. In the temperate zone of the Northern Hemisphere, south-facing slopes receive much more sunlight than do north-facing slopes. Consequently, soils on south-facing slopes are usually warmer and drier. These differences may influence the types of plants that grow in the soil.

Although you have read about five separate factors that affect soil formation, remember that they all work together to form soil. No single factor is responsible for a soil's composition.

Explain how the slope of the land affects soil thickness.

Build Science Skills **L2**

Measuring On a sunny day, take students outside and have them measure the temperatures of soils in south-facing slopes and north-facing slopes. If necessary, take along a small spade to loosen the soils. You may wish to insert a thermometer into the soils yourself to avoid breakage accidents. Have students record the temperatures. Students should find that soils in south-facing slopes are warmer than soils in north-facing slopes. If it is not feasible to conduct this activity outside, have students measure the temperatures of two piles of soils. One pile should be placed under a lamp to represent a south-facing slope. The other pile should be placed in the shade to represent a north-facing slope.
Kinesthetic, Visual

Facts and Figures

When Earth is viewed as a system, soil is referred to as an interface, or common boundary where different parts of a system interact. This is an appropriate designation because soil forms where the solid Earth, the atmosphere, the hydrosphere, and the biosphere meet. Soil is a material that develops in response to complex environmental interactions among different parts of the Earth system. Over time, soil gradually evolves to a state of equilibrium or balance with the environment. Soil is dynamic and sensitive to almost every aspect of its environment. When environmental changes occur, such as climate, vegetative cover, or animal activity, the soil responds. Any such change produces a gradual alteration of soil characteristics until a new balance is reached.

Answer to . . .

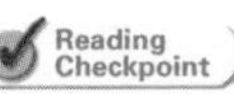

Steep slopes have more erosion, so their soil is usually thin or nonexistent. Flat areas have little erosion, so their soils are typically thick.

The Soil Profile

Use Visuals

L1

Figure 14 This diagram divides a soil profile into three general horizons. Tell students that soil scientists often use a more in-depth approach—they may divide a soil profile into five or more horizons. For example, a typical O horizon is made up of fresh and decomposing organic matter. The E horizon is the zone of leaching, where inorganic soil components are dissolved and carried into lower zones. Based on Figure 14 and the related text on p. 138, have students infer the location of the O horizon and the E horizon. *(The O horizon is the uppermost layer of soil. The E horizon is located between the A horizon and the B horizon.)*
Visual

The Soil Profile

The processes that form soil operate from the surface downward. **Soil varies in composition, texture, structure, and color at different depths.** These variations divide the soil into zones known as **soil horizons.** A vertical section through all of the soil horizons is called a **soil profile.** In some soil profiles, the soil horizons blend gradually from one to another. In others, like the one shown in Figure 14A, the soil horizons are quite distinct. Mature soils usually have three distinct soil horizons, which are identified in Figure 14B. From the surface downward, these horizons are called the A, B, and C horizons.

A Horizon The A horizon is commonly known as topsoil. Its upper part consists mostly of organic matter, including loose leaves and partly decomposed plant structures. It is teeming with insects, fungi, and microorganisms. The lower part of the A horizon is a mixture of mineral matter and organic matter.

B Horizon The B horizon, or subsoil, contains fine clay particles washed out of the A horizon by water that filters through pore spaces. In some soils, the clay that accumulates in the B horizon forms a compact, impenetrable layer called hardpan. The B horizon is the lower limit of most plant roots and burrowing animals.

C Horizon Between the B horizon and the unaltered parent material is the C horizon, which contains partially weathered parent material. While the A and B horizons barely resemble the parent material, the C horizon does.

Figure 14 Soil Profiles A The A, B, and C horizons have different characteristics. **B** Three soil horizons are visible in this soil. **Interpreting Photographs** ***Using the diagram in B as a guide, identify the soil horizons in A.***

A horizon (Topsoil)
Loose and partly decayed organic matter
Mineral matter mixed with some organic matter
B horizon (Subsoil)
Clay transported from above
C horizon
Partially weathered parent material
Unweathered parent material
A

B

Facts and Figures

In a detailed soil profile, the O horizon consists largely of organic material. Its upper portion is primarily plant litter and other recognizable organic debris. Its lower portion is made of humus. Organisms are plentiful in this horizon. The A horizon also is a zone of high biological activity and high levels of humus—up to 30 percent in some instances. Below the A horizon is the E horizon, a light-colored layer that contains little organic material. As water percolates downward through this zone, finer particles are carried away in a process known as eluviation. The moving water also dissolves soluble inorganic soil components and carries them to lower zones, a process known as leaching. Much of the material removed by eluviation is deposited in the B horizon, which is also known as the zone of accumulation. In contrast to the C horizon, which is made up of partially altered parent rock, the O, A, E, and B horizons together constitute solum, or true soil.

Soil Types

Recall that climate is the most important factor in soil formation. Climate also has a major effect on the type of soil that forms. **Three common types of soil are pedalfer, pedocal, and laterite.**

Pedalfer **Pedalfers** usually forms in temperate areas that receive more than 63 cm of rain each year. This soil type is present in much of the eastern half of the United States, most often in forested areas. The B horizon in pedalfers contains large amounts of iron oxide and aluminum-rich clays, giving it a brown to red-brown color.

Pedocal **Pedocals** are found in the drier western United States in areas that have grasses and brush vegetation. Because chemical weathering is slower in dry climates, pedocals generally contains less clay than pedalfers. Pedocals contain abundant calcite, or calcium carbonate, and are typically a light gray-brown.

Figure 15 The Temple at Angkor Wat, Cambodia This temple was constructed of laterite bricks between 1113 and 1150.

Laterite **Laterites** form in hot, wet tropical areas. Chemical weathering is intense under such conditions. So laterites are usually deeper than soils that develop over a similar period in temperate areas. The large quantity of water that filters through these soils removes most of the calcite and silica. Iron oxide and aluminum oxide are left behind. The iron oxide gives laterite a distinctive orange or red color.

When dried, laterite becomes very hard and practically waterproof. For centuries, people in portions of South and Southeast Asia have made bricks by digging up laterite, shaping it, and allowing it to harden in the sun. Ancient structures built of laterite bricks, such as the one shown in Figure 15, are well preserved even today.

Soil Types

Build Reading Literacy L1

Refer to **p. 124D,** which provides the guidelines for summarizing.

Summarize Ask students to read Soil Types on pp. 139–140. Tell them to carefully review the passage and identify main ideas. Clues to main ideas include headings, key concept statements, and vocabulary terms. List the main ideas on the board. Using the list as a guide, have students write brief summaries of the passage. Encourage students to repeat the procedure for the remainder of the section.
Verbal

Use Community Resources 

Contact a representative of your county extension agency or the local branch of the state soil conservation district. Ask the representative to discuss your area's soil types with students. He or she can bring in soil-testing kits and discuss ways to reduce soil erosion.
Verbal

Answer to . . .

Figure 14 *The dark horizon at the top is the A horizon. The lighter horizon below it is the B horizon. The horizon below that is the C horizon.*

Integrate Biology L2

Erosion and Plant Roots The clearing of a rain forest not only removes the supply of plant nutrients from laterite soils, it also leads to accelerated erosion. When vegetation is present, its roots anchor the soil while its leaves and branches provide a canopy that protects the ground from the full force of frequent heavy rains. Removal of the vegetation also exposes the ground to strong direct sunlight. When baked by the sun, laterites can harden and become nearly impenetrable to water and crop roots. Ask students to summarize how the clearing of a rain forest affects laterite soils. *(The clearing of a rain forest removes the supply of nutrients from the soil, accelerates soil erosion, and exposes laterites to strong direct sunlight.)*
Verbal

Soil Erosion

Build Science Skills L2

ACTIVITY

Observing Take students outside for the following activity. Place a large pile of soil in a plastic container. Obtain a spray bottle with an adjustable tip. Allow students to take turns using the bottle to observe how water erodes soil. Encourage students to experiment with different spray settings to simulate different types of rainfall. A fine mist, for example, would represent a light rain and cause little erosion. A full spray would represent a heavy rainfall and cause heavy erosion.
Visual, Kinesthetic

Figure 16 Clearing a Tropical Rain Forest in Borneo The laterite soil cannot support agriculture for more than a few years.

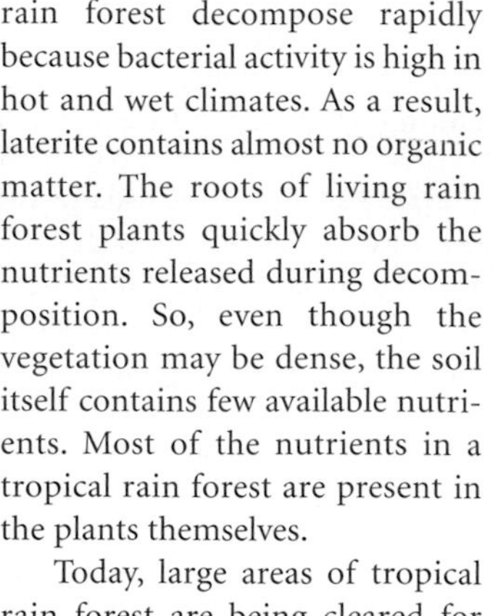

Plants that die in a tropical rain forest decompose rapidly because bacterial activity is high in hot and wet climates. As a result, laterite contains almost no organic matter. The roots of living rain forest plants quickly absorb the nutrients released during decomposition. So, even though the vegetation may be dense, the soil itself contains few available nutrients. Most of the nutrients in a tropical rain forest are present in the plants themselves.

Today, large areas of tropical rain forest are being cleared for timber and to provide land for agriculture, as shown in Figure 16. However, laterite is one of the poorest soils for agriculture. Because laterite contains little organic matter and few nutrients, it cannot nourish crops. The nutrients it does have are soon washed out by the plentiful rainwater that filters through the soil. In only a few years, the soil in a freshly cleared area may be completely useless for growing crops. Without trees or crop plants to anchor the soil and shield the ground from the full force of heavy rains, the soil erodes quickly.

Reading Checkpoint *Why is the soil in a tropical rain forest poorly suited for agriculture?*

Soil Erosion

Soils are just a tiny fraction of all Earth materials, yet they are a vital resource. Because soils are necessary for the growth of rooted plants, they are the foundation of the human life-support system. However, soils are among our most abused resources. The loss of fertile topsoil is a growing problem as human activities disturb more of Earth's surface.

How Water Erodes Soil Soil erosion is a natural part of the constant recycling of Earth materials known as the rock cycle. Water, wind, and other agents move soil from one place to another. Every time it rains, raindrops strike the soil surface with surprising force. As Figure 17 shows, each drop acts like a tiny bomb, blasting soil particles off the surface. Water flowing across the surface then carries away the dislodged particles. Because thin sheets of water move the soil particles, this process is called sheet erosion.

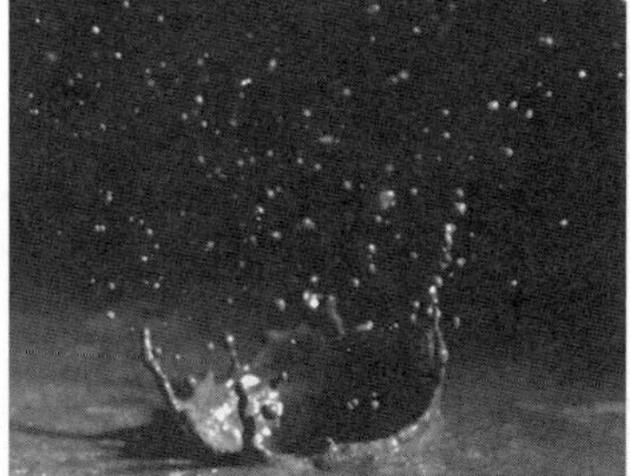

Figure 17 Soil Erosion by Raindrops A raindrop can splash soil particles more than a meter away from where it strikes the soil.

140 Chapter 5

After flowing as a thin sheet for a short distance, the water forms tiny streams called rills. As more water enters the rills, they erode the soil further, creating trenches known as gullies, like those shown in Figure 18. Although most dislodged soil particles do not move far during each rainfall, large quantities eventually make their way downslope to a stream. The stream transports these soil particles, which are now called sediment, and eventually deposits them.

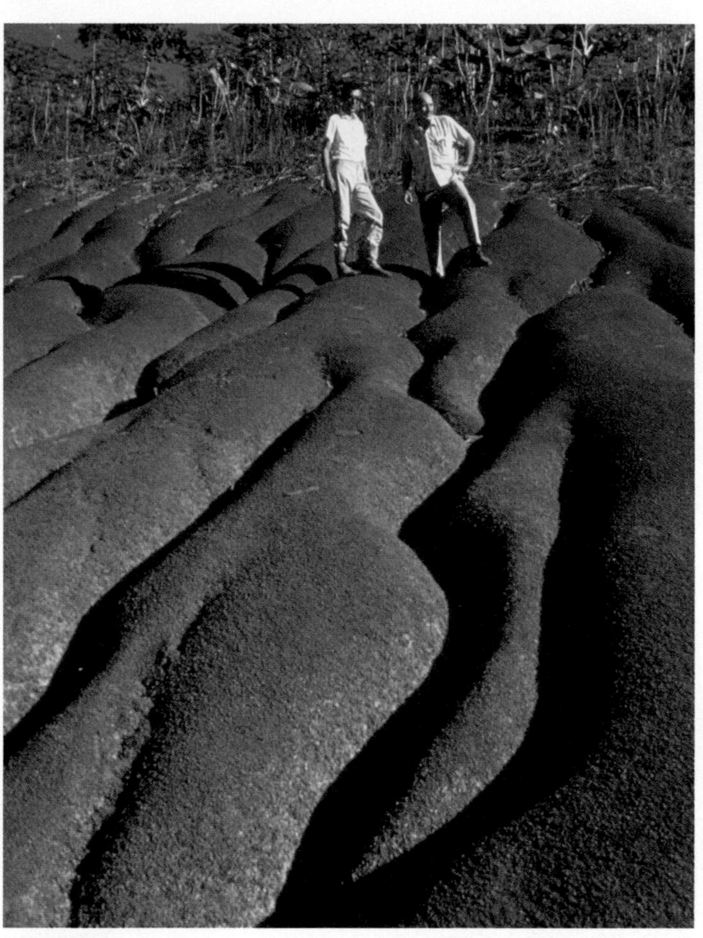

Figure 18 Gullies The unprotected soil in this field in southern Colombia is deeply eroded.

Rates of Erosion In the past, soil eroded more slowly than it does today because more land was covered by trees, grasses, and other plants. **However, human activities that remove natural vegetation, such as farming, logging, and construction, have greatly accelerated erosion.** Without plants, soil is more easily carried away by wind and water.

Scientists can estimate the rate of erosion due to water by measuring the amount of sediment in rivers. These estimates indicate that before humans appeared, rivers carried about 9 trillion kg of sediment to the oceans each year. In contrast, the amount of sediment currently transported to the sea by rivers is about 24 trillion kg per year.

Wind generally erodes soil much more slowly than water does. During a prolonged drought, however, strong winds can remove large quantities of soil from unprotected fields. That's exactly what happened during the 1930s in the part of the Great Plains that came to be known as the Dust Bowl.

The rate of soil erosion depends on soil characteristics and on factors such as climate, slope, and type of vegetation. In many regions, including about one-third of the world's croplands, soil is eroding faster than it is being formed. This results in lower productivity, poorer crop quality, and a threatened world food supply.

Reading Checkpoint *How do human activities affect rates of erosion?*

Use Visuals **L1**

Figure 18 Ask: **What caused the gullies to form?** *(water erosion)* **Based on what you have read about clearing tropical rain forests, what can be done to the Colombian field to reduce soil erosion?** *(plant vegetation)*
Visual

Answer to . . .

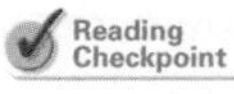

Reading Checkpoint *The soil is usually laterite, which contains little organic matter. Its few nutrients are quickly washed out by the plentiful rainwater.*

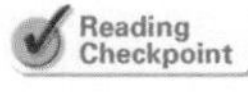

Reading Checkpoint *Human activities have greatly accelerated erosion.*

Section 5.2 (continued)

Integrate Social Studies L2

The Dust Bowl In the 1930s, the Great Plains experienced a prolonged drought which, combined with the agricultural practices of that era, led to widespread soil erosion. Numerous families were displaced from their farms and emigrated west. Have students research and report on one aspect of the Dust Bowl. For example, they might discuss how much soil was lost or how farmers responded to the crisis by implementing new agricultural techniques.
Verbal

3 ASSESS

Evaluate Understanding L2

Have students sketch and label a soil profile showing A, B, and C horizons, along with parent rock.

Reteach L1

Have students make tables summarizing the three soil types discussed in this section. Tables should include characteristics of each soil type and the climate in which it is found.

Connecting Concepts

A hot, wet climate favors chemical weathering, which hastens soil formation. Therefore, the soil that forms in this climate is usually thick. There is little chemical weathering in a cold, dry climate, so soil forms slowly and is usually thin, consisting mostly of mechanically weathered debris.

Sediment Deposition Another problem caused by excessive soil erosion is the deposition of sediment. Rivers that accumulate sediment must be dredged to remain open for shipping. As sediment settles in reservoirs, they become less useful for storing water, controlling floods, and generating electricity.

Some sediments are contaminated with agricultural pesticides. When these chemicals enter a river or lake, they endanger organisms that live in or use the water, including humans. Sediments also contain soil nutrients, which may come from natural processes and from added fertilizers. Excessive nutrient levels in lakes stimulate the growth of algae and plants. This can accelerate a process that eventually leads to the early death of the lake.

Controlling Erosion Although we cannot completely eliminate soil erosion, we can significantly slow it by using soil conservation measures. You have seen how a misunderstanding of the composition of rain forest soil has led to the destruction of millions of acres leaving only severely leached, unproductive land. Conservation measures include steps taken to preserve environments and protect the land. These measures include planting rows of trees called windbreaks, terracing hillsides, plowing along the contours of hills, and rotating crops. Preserving fertile soil is essential to feeding the world's rapidly growing population.

Section 5.2 Assessment

Reviewing Concepts

1. List the four major components of soil.
2. How does climate affect soil formation?
3. Describe the contents of the three soil horizons found in most mature soils.
4. What climates are usually associated with pedalfer, pedocal, and laterite?
5. How can an activity such as road construction affect the rate of soil erosion?

Critical Thinking

6. **Relating Cause and Effect** A gardener notices that rain showers usually produce long-lasting puddles on the soil in her garden. Is it more likely that the soil contains too much sand or too much clay? Explain.
7. **Predicting** Which activity would cause more sediment to be deposited in a river that flows through a gently sloping valley—cultivating the valley or cultivating the hills that surround the valley? Explain.

Connecting Concepts

Weathering and Soil Using what you learned about chemical weathering in Section 5.1, explain why the soils formed in a hot, wet climate and a cold, dry climate are different.

Section 5.2 Assessment

1. mineral matter; organic matter, or humus; water; air
2. Climate influences the rate, depth, and type of weathering, the rate at which nutrients are removed from the soil, and the types of organisms that live on and in the soil.
3. The A horizon, or topsoil, contains a mixture of mineral matter and organic matter, as well as many insects, fungi, and microorganisms. The B horizon, or subsoil, contains fine clay particles washed out of the A horizon. The C horizon contains partially weathered parent material.
4. pedalfer—temperate climate with more than 63 cm of rain per year; pedocal—dry climate; laterite—hot, wet tropical climate
5. Such activities may accelerate erosion by removing natural vegetation, allowing soil to be carried away more easily by wind and water.
6. too much clay, because sandy soils drain quickly, while clay-rich soils drain slowly
7. cultivating the hills that surround the valley, because erosion is accelerated on slopes, and erosion leads to sediment deposition

5.3 Mass Movements

Reading Focus

Key Concepts

- What is mass movement?
- What factors trigger mass movements?
- How do geologists classify mass movements?

Vocabulary

- mass movement
- rockfall
- rockslide
- slump
- mudflow
- earthflow
- creep

Reading Strategy

Previewing Copy the table. Before you read the section, rewrite the green topic headings as *what* questions. As you read, write an answer to each question.

Question	Answer
a. ___?___	b. ___?___
c. ___?___	d. ___?___

Earth's land surface consists of slopes, some steep and others very gradual. While most slopes appear stable, they are always changing. The force of gravity causes material to move downslope. **The transfer of rock and soil downslope due to gravity is called mass movement.** Some types of mass movement are so slow that you cannot see them. Others, such as landslides like the one illustrated in Figure 19, are very sudden.

The combined actions of weathering and mass movement produce most landforms. Once weathering weakens and breaks rock apart, mass movement moves the debris downslope. There a stream usually carries it away. Stream valleys are the most common of Earth's landforms.

Q *Are snow avalanches a type of mass movement?*

A Yes. These thundering downslope movements of snow and ice can also transport large quantities of rock, soil, and trees. About 10,000 snow avalanches occur each year in the mountainous western United States. Besides damaging buildings and roads at the bottom of slopes, they are especially dangerous to skiers. In an average year, snow avalanches claim between 15 and 25 lives in the United States and Canada. Snow avalanches are a growing problem as more people participate in winter sports and recreation.

Figure 19 Landslide This home in Pacific Palisades, California, was destroyed by a landslide triggered by the January 1994 Northridge earthquake.

Section 5.3

1 FOCUS

Section Objectives

5.8 **Define** mass movement.
5.9 **Identify** the factors that trigger mass movements.
5.10 **Classify** mass movements.

Reading Focus

Build Vocabulary L2

Venn Diagrams Have students construct Venn diagrams showing the differences and similarities between mudflows and earthflows. The diagrams should consist of two overlapping circles. One circle should be labeled Mudflow; the other should be labeled Earthflow. Similarities between the two types of mass movements should be listed in the middle, or overlapping, part of the circles. Differences should be listed in those parts of the circles that do not overlap. Students can construct other Venn diagrams to compare and contrast rockfalls and rockslides, and slump and creep.

Reading Strategy L2

a. What triggers mass movements?
b. saturation of surface materials with water, oversteepening of slopes, removal of vegetation, and earthquakes
c. What are the types of mass movements?
d. rockfalls, slides (or rockslides), slumps, flows (or mudflows and earthflows), and creep

2 INSTRUCT

Use Visuals L1

Figure 19 Tell students that in some cases, damages from earthquake-induced mass movements are greater than damages caused directly by an earthquake's ground vibrations. After students have examined the photograph, ask them to explain why the term *mass movement* is appropriate for this type of natural hazard. *(A large amount of mass in the form of rock and soil moves downslope.)*
Visual

Triggers of Mass Movements

Oversteepened Slopes L2

Purpose Students will observe how the angle of a slope contributes to mass movements.

Materials bag of potting soil, water, cardboard box, plastic knife

Procedure Use the soil to create a gently sloping hillside in the cardboard box. Add water, if necessary, to help the hill maintain its form. Gently shake the box and have students observe the effects on the soil. Recreate the hill. This time, however, use the knife to cut away a good portion of one slope so that it is sharply steepened. Again, shake the box and have students observe the effects on the soil.

Expected Outcomes Some erosion and movement will occur during both trials. However, students will note that mass movements were more severe on the steepened slope.
Visual

Figure 20 Mudflow In October 1998, heavy rains from Hurricane Mitch led to massive mudflows in Central America.
Formulating Hypotheses ***What human activities before the rains might have contributed to the mudflows?***

Triggers of Mass Movements

Gravity is the force behind mass movements. Several factors make slopes more susceptible to the pull of gravity. **Among the factors that commonly trigger mass movements are saturation of surface materials with water, oversteepening of slopes, removal of vegetation, and earthquakes.**

Water Heavy rains and rapid melting of snow can trigger mass movement by saturating surface materials with water. This was the case when torrential downpours associated with Hurricane Mitch caused devastating mudflows, as shown in Figure 20. When the pores in sediment become filled with water, the particles slide past one another more easily. You can demonstrate this effect with sand. If you add water until the sand becomes slightly moist, the sand grains will stick together. However, if you add enough water to fill all the pores between the sand grains, the sand-water mixture will ooze downhill. Clay also becomes very slick when it is wet.

Oversteepened Slopes Loose soil particles can maintain a relatively stable slope up to a certain angle. That angle ranges from about 25 to 40 degrees, depending on the size and shape of the particles. If the steepness of a slope exceeds the stable angle, mass movements become more likely. Such slopes are said to be oversteepened. An oversteepened slope can result when a stream undercuts a valley wall or waves pound against the base of a cliff. People may also create oversteepened slopes by excavating during the construction of roads and buildings.

How do oversteepened slopes trigger mass movements?

Customize for English Language Learners

Have students work in pairs to think of possible interactions among the factors that trigger mass movements. For example, students might note that slopes are sometimes steepened during road construction. The steepening of slopes often involves the removal of vegetation. Following a heavy rain, a mass movement might occur on the barren, steepened slope. Strengthen discussion skills by having students share their examples with the class. Encourage students to refer to the text on pp. 144–145 as they brainstorm ideas.

Removal of Vegetation Plants make slopes more stable because their root systems bind soil and regolith together. When plants are removed by forest fires or by human activities such as logging or farming, the likelihood of mass movement increases. An example that illustrates the stabilizing effect of plants occurred several decades ago on steep slopes near Menton, France. Farmers replaced olive trees, which have deep roots, with carnations, a more profitable but shallow-rooted crop. Planting carnations made the slopes less stable. A landslide on one of the slopes killed 11 people.

Earthquakes Earthquakes are one of the most dramatic triggers of mass movements. An earthquake and its aftershocks can dislodge enormous amounts of rock and unconsolidated material. In many areas, these mass movements cause more damage than the ground vibrations themselves. The landslide shown in Figure 19 was triggered by an earthquake.

Types of Mass Movements

Geologists classify mass movements based on the kind of material that moves, how it moves, and the speed of movement. We'll consider five basic types of mass movement: rockfalls, slides, slumps, flows, and creep.

Rockfalls A **rockfall** occurs when rocks or rock fragments fall freely through the air. This type of mass movement is common on slopes that are too steep for loose material to remain on the surface. Many rockfalls result from the mechanical weathering of rock caused by freeze-thaw cycles or plant roots. Rockfalls sometimes trigger other mass movements.

Slides In a slide, a block of material moves suddenly along a flat, inclined surface. Slides that include segments of bedrock are called **rockslides.** They often occur in high mountain areas such as the Andes, Alps, and Canadian Rockies. Rockslides are among the fastest mass movements, reaching speeds of over 200 km per hour. Some rockslides, such as the one shown in Figure 21, are triggered by rain or melting snow.

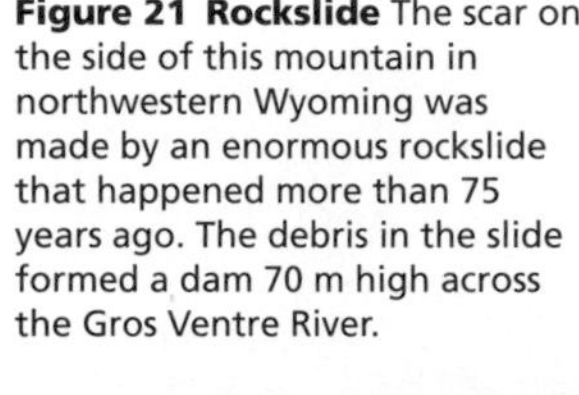

Figure 21 Rockslide The scar on the side of this mountain in northwestern Wyoming was made by an enormous rockslide that happened more than 75 years ago. The debris in the slide formed a dam 70 m high across the Gros Ventre River.

Types of Mass Movements

Build Reading Literacy L1

Refer to **p. 64D** in **Chapter 3,** which provides the guidelines for a DRTA strategy.

Directed Reading/Thinking Activity (DRTA) Have students read the first paragraph under the heading Types of Mass Movements. List the five basic types of mass movements on the board. Point out that each term is very descriptive. Based on the terms alone, have students predict the following for each mass movement: the kind of material that moves, how it moves, and the speed of the movement. For example, students will likely predict that rockfalls involve rocks, and that the rocks fall at a fast speed. Record all ideas on the board. Then, have students read each subsection under the heading. After they have finished reading a subsection, pause to review their predictions, and make any necessary modifications. Repeat until the entire passage has been read. Conclude by having students confirm which of their predictions were correct.
Verbal

Answer to . . .

Figure 20 *activities that remove natural vegetation, such as farming, logging, and construction*

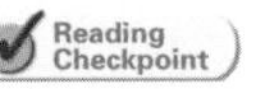

Loose soil particles can maintain a relatively stable slope up to a certain angle. If the steepness of a slope exceeds that angle, mass movements become more likely.

Build Science Skills L2

Posing Questions After students have read the text on pp. 145–147, ask if they have any questions about types of mass movements. List the questions on the board. Assign small groups a question to research. Have students present their answers to the class.
Verbal, Group

Use Visuals L1

Figure 23 Have students compare and contrast Figures 22 and 23. Ask: **How are slumps and earthflows similar? How are they different?** *(Both move at a relatively slow rate. A slump refers to a block of material that moves along a curved surface. An earthflow refers to material that moves downslope as a thick fluid.)*
Visual

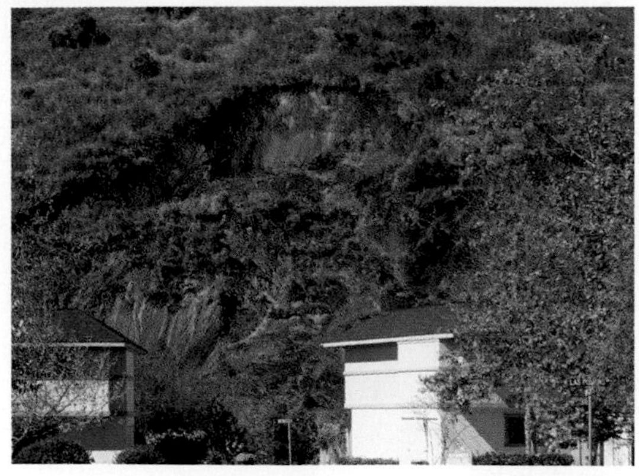

Figure 22 Slump Heavy rains triggered this slump in Santa Barbara, California. Notice the crescent-shaped cliff just above the slump.

Slumps A **slump** is the downward movement of a block of material along a curved surface. The material in a slump usually does not travel very fast or very far. As the block moves, its upper surface sometimes tilts backward. Slumps leave a crescent-shaped cliff just above the slump, which you can see in Figure 22. They are common on oversteepened slopes where the soil contains thick accumulations of clay.

Flows Flows are mass movements of material containing a large amount of water, which move downslope as a thick fluid. Flows that move quickly, called **mudflows,** are common in semiarid mountainous regions, such as parts of southern California. In these regions, protective vegetation is sparse. A heavy downpour or rapid snowmelt can flood canyons with a mixture of soil, rock, and water. The mixture may have the consistency of wet concrete. It follows the contours of the canyon, taking large boulders and trees along with it. As you saw in Figure 20, mudflows in populated areas are very dangerous and destructive. In 1988, a massive mudflow triggered by the eruption of Nevado del Ruiz, a volcano in Colombia, killed 25,000 people.

Earthflows are flows that move relatively slowly—from about a millimeter per day to several meters per day. Their movement may continue for years. Earthflows occur most often on hillsides in wet regions. When water saturates the soil and regolith on a hillside, the material breaks away, forming a tongue-shaped mass like the one shown in Figure 23. Earthflows range in size from a few meters long and less than 1 m deep to over 1 km long and more than 10 m deep.

How do mudflows differ from earthflows?

Figure 23 Earthflow This small, tongue-shaped mass movement occurred on a newly formed slope along a recently built highway. **Comparing and Contrasting** ***Which other type of mass movement looks most similar to an earthflow?***

Facts and Figures

Landslides threaten lives and property in all 50 states. To reduce the risk from active landslides, the U.S. Geologic Survey (USGS) uses real-time landslide monitoring systems. Data from a variety of sensors installed at active landslides are transmitted by radio to USGS computers. The monitoring systems focus on detecting precipitation and groundwater conditions that could destabilize a hill slope. They also record the acceleration of slide movement and ground vibrations associated with this movement.

Creep The slowest type of mass movement is **creep,** which usually travels only a few millimeters or centimeters per year. One factor that contributes to creep is alternating between freezing and thawing, as Figure 24A shows. Freezing expands the water in soil, lifting soil particles at right angles to the slope. Thawing causes contraction, which allows the particles to fall back to a slightly lower level. Each freeze-thaw cycle moves the particles a short distance downhill.

Because creep is so slow, you cannot observe it directly as it happens. However, the effects of creep are easy to recognize. As Figure 24B shows, creep causes structures that were once vertical to tilt downhill. Creep can also displace fences and crack walls and underground pipes.

Figure 24 Creep A Repeated expansion and contraction of the soil on a slope results in a gradual downhill movement of the soil. **B** Years of creep have caused these gravestones to tilt. **Inferring** ***In which direction is creep occurring in this photograph?***

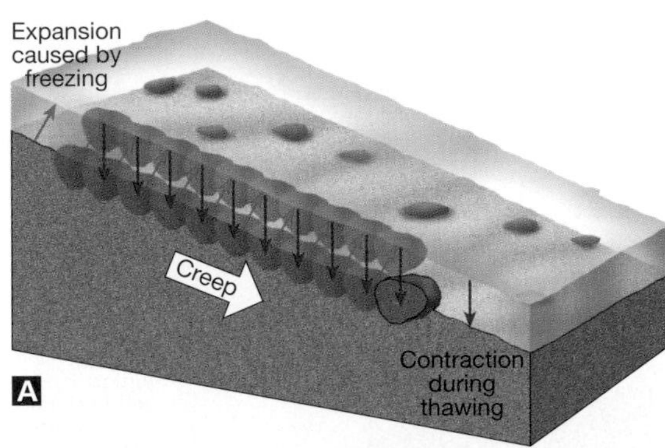

Section 5.3 Assessment

Reviewing Concepts

1. What is mass movement?
2. How does water trigger mass movements?
3. How does a rockfall differ from a rockslide?
4. What is the slowest type of mass movement?

Critical Thinking

5. **Applying Concepts** When highway engineers build a road in a mountainous area, they insert drainage pipes into the slopes alongside the road. Explain why.
6. **Making Judgments** Which mass movement—a slump, a mudflow, or an earthflow—poses the greatest risk to human life? Explain your reasoning.

Explanatory Paragraph Explain how people can make mass movements more likely. Include two examples in your explanatory paragraph.

Use Visuals **L1**

Figure 24 Ask: **Does gravity play a role in the process of creep? Explain your answer in terms of the diagram.** *(Yes, gravity plays a role in the process of creep. As shown in the diagram, gravity causes the materials to move downslope.)*
Visual

3 ASSESS

Evaluate Understanding **L2**

Based on what they have learned about mass movements, have students debate whether development should be banned on steep slopes. Encourage students to use facts from this section to support their opinions.

Reteach **L1**

Have students describe the factors that contribute to creep, the slowest type of mass movement. *(alternating periods of freezing and thawing)*

Writing in Science

One example is excavating during the construction of roads and buildings, which can produce oversteepened slopes. Another example is removing plants on slopes. Plants stabilize slopes because their root systems bind soil and regolith together.

Section 5.3 Assessment

1. the transfer of rock and soil downslope due to gravity
2. Water fills the pores in sediment, allowing the particles to slide past one another more easily.
3. In a rockfall, rocks or rock fragments fall freely through the air. In a rockslide, a block that includes segments of bedrock moves suddenly along a flat, inclined surface.
4. creep
5. The pipes allow water to drain out of the soil and regolith in the slopes, reducing the chance that a mass movement will carry slope material onto the road.
6. a mudflow, because it is the only one of the three that moves quickly

Answer to . . .

Figure 23 *a slump*

Figure 24 *from left to right*

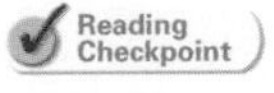 *Mudflows move quickly, while earthflows move relatively slowly.*

How the Earth Works

1 FOCUS

Objectives

In this feature, students will
- describe how soil is formed.
- identify the qualities of different kinds of soil.
- explain how soil supports various kinds of life.

Reading Focus

Build Vocabulary

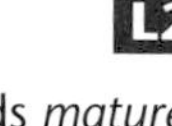

Define Terms Write the words *mature* and *immature* on the board. Have students look up the meaning of *mature* in a dictionary. Then underline the prefix *im-* and tell them that it means "not." Explain that by adding the prefix *im-*, writers turn words into their opposites. Have students practice creating opposites by adding *im-* to the following words: *possible, probable, polite.*

2 INSTRUCT

Use Visuals

Have students study the diagram that shows how soil is formed. Ask them to define *regolith. (weathered rock)* Then ask: **What is the difference between mature soil and immature soil?** *(Mature soil has more humus and supports a wide variety of plants and animals.)*
Visual

How the Earth Works

Soil

On the surface of the Earth, **soil** is the thin layer of loose material in which plants grow. Soil consists partly of mineral particles, and partly of **organic matter** derived from living plants and animals and their remains. Other key components of soil are water and air. Complex natural processes build soil over many thousands of years. The process begins when rock is broken down by weathering. Next, plants take root in the weathered rock. Then, organic material in the soil, called **humus,** is formed from decaying vegetation and animals. Different types of soil occur because of variations in climate, types of vegetation, and types of rock. In large countries like Russia, there is a wide variety of soil types.

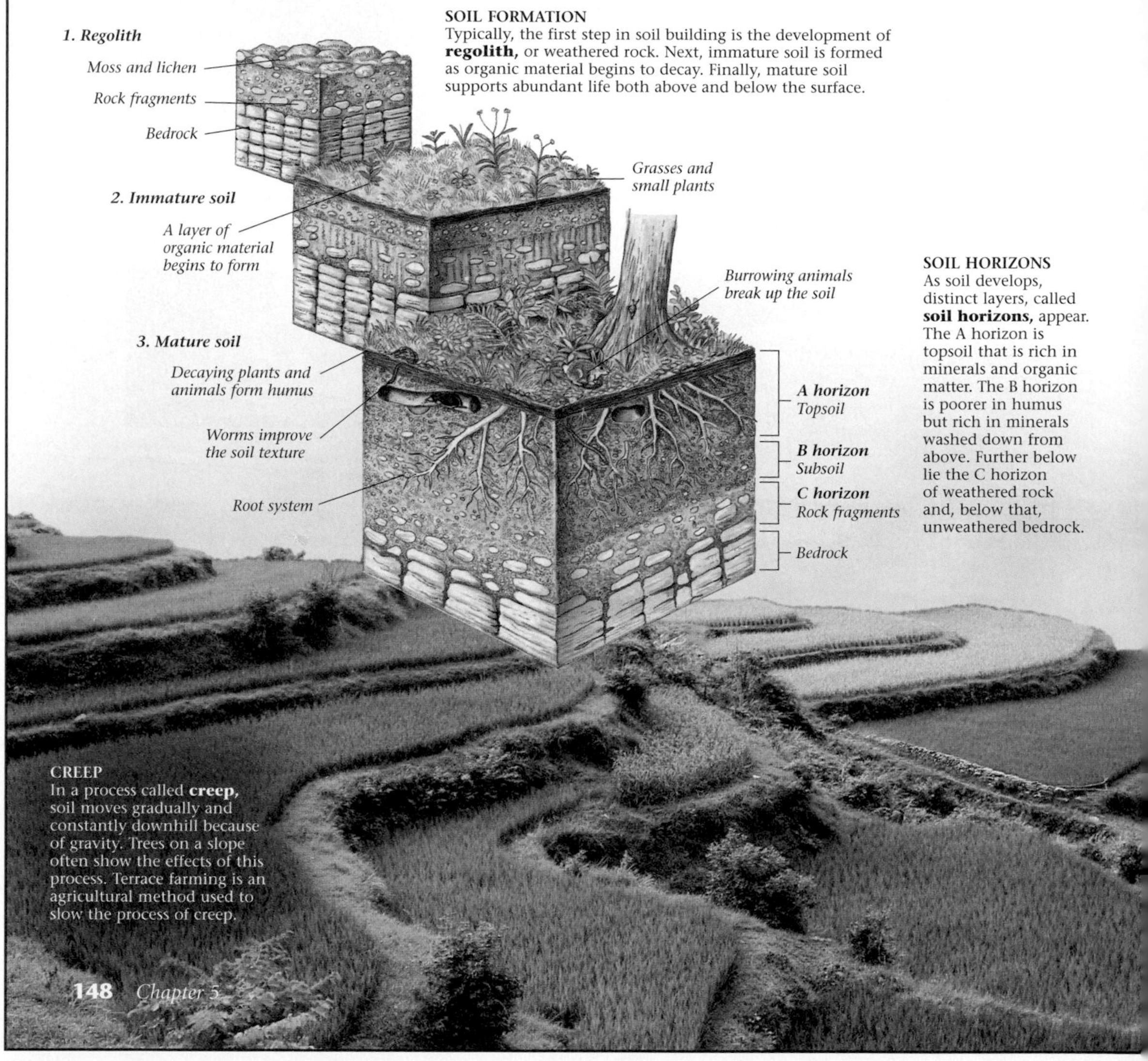

SOIL FORMATION
Typically, the first step in soil building is the development of **regolith,** or weathered rock. Next, immature soil is formed as organic material begins to decay. Finally, mature soil supports abundant life both above and below the surface.

1. Regolith
Moss and lichen
Rock fragments
Bedrock

2. Immature soil
A layer of organic material begins to form
Grasses and small plants

3. Mature soil
Decaying plants and animals form humus
Worms improve the soil texture
Root system
Burrowing animals break up the soil

A horizon *Topsoil*
B horizon *Subsoil*
C horizon *Rock fragments*
Bedrock

SOIL HORIZONS
As soil develops, distinct layers, called **soil horizons,** appear. The A horizon is topsoil that is rich in minerals and organic matter. The B horizon is poorer in humus but rich in minerals washed down from above. Further below lie the C horizon of weathered rock and, below that, unweathered bedrock.

CREEP
In a process called **creep,** soil moves gradually and constantly downhill because of gravity. Trees on a slope often show the effects of this process. Terrace farming is an agricultural method used to slow the process of creep.

Customize for Inclusion Students

Gifted Have students plan a memorial garden to honor someone. Have them decide the size and location of the garden. Then have them use the library or Internet to find out what plants grow best in their climate and what kind of soil is best for the plants. Students should present a diagram of their garden along with text to describe it.

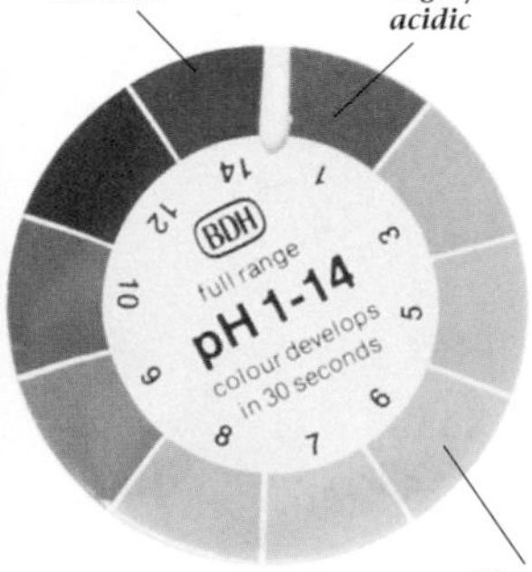

Highly alkaline

Highly acidic

Neutral

SOIL pH
The pH scale measures acidity or alkalinity on a scale of 0 to 14. When a chemical solution called an indicator is added to a soil sample, the indicator changes color, showing the soil's pH. Most plants thrive only in soils with a pH between 5 and 9.

Clay soil

Silty soil

Sandy soil

SOIL TEXTURE
Soil texture depends on the size and nature of soil particles. Clay soils have the smallest grains, silty soils have medium-sized grains, and sandy soils have the largest grains. **Loam,** a mixture of clay, silt, and sand, is the best soil for agriculture.

Wildflowers

Grass

Snail

Decomposing leaf

Slug

Roots

LIFE IN THE SOIL
Soil is home to a vast array of life, including microorganisms, ants, termites, worms, and rodents. Fungi and bacteria convert dead plant and animal matter into chemicals that enrich the soil. Burrowing creatures improve the soil by mixing it.

Spodosol is a sandy soil found in northern coniferous forests.

Aridisols, found in deserts, have high concentrations of salts

SOIL CLASSIFICATION
Some experts recognize thousands of different soil types. The U.S. Department of Agriculture has devised a comprehensive soil classification system for categorizing soils. Each type of soil can be identified by the characteristics of its horizons.

ASSESSMENT

1. **Key Terms** Define **(a)** soil, **(b)** organic matter, **(c)** humus, **(d)** regolith, **(e)** soil horizon, **(f)** creep, **(g)** loam.
2. **Physical Processes** Describe the three stages of soil formation.
3. **Physical Characteristics** How do various types of soil differ from one another?
4. **Natural Resources** What soil characteristics are most beneficial for agriculture?
5. **Critical Thinking Making Comparisons** Study the cross-sections of spodosol and aridisol. **(a)** How are they alike? **(b)** How do they differ? **(c)** Do research to learn more about their different characteristics.

Bellringer L2

Ask students to describe in as many ways as they can how the sand at the beach is different from the soil in which plants grow in a flowerpot. *(Sample answer: Sand is lighter in color; it washes away easily; it does not make things as dirty; water runs right through it.)* Tell students that as they read this lesson, they will learn some of the reasons for the differences.
Logical

3 ASSESS

Evaluate Understanding

Have students draw a circular flowchart that illustrates the mutually beneficial relationship between soil and the creatures that live in it. Then ask: **How do people rely on soil? What changes do they make to it?** Have students use information from the feature to support their answers.

Reteach

Make a two-column chart and label it *Ways Soil Can Be Different.* In the left column, write: *Soil is different at different depths.* In the right column, have students add facts from the feature to support the statement. Then have them complete the chart by showing how the texture and pH of soil can vary.

Assessment

1. **(a)** the thin layer of loose material in which plants grow; **(b)** material derived from living plants and animals and their remains; **(c)** organic material formed from decaying vegetation and animals; **(d)** weathered rock; **(e)** distinct soil layer; **(f)** the gradual and constant movement of soil downhill due to gravity; **(g)** soil made up of clay, silt, and sand

2. First is the development of weathered rock. Then organic material begins to decay and form immature soil. At last mature soil forms when more decaying plants and animals form humus.

3. Soils differ in their depth, level of acidity or alkalinity, texture or size, and nature of soil particles.

4. Loam with a pH between 5 and 9 is best for agriculture.

5. **(a)** Both have different horizons. **(b)** Spodosol is found in northern coniferous forests, while aridisol is found in deserts. Aridisol has a high salt content. **(c)** Sample answer: Spodosols are acidic with lots of humus; aridisols have salt layers with accumulations of lime or gypsum.

Exploration Lab

Effect of Temperature on Chemical Weathering L2

Objective
In this activity, students will determine the relationship between temperature and chemical weathering.

Skills Focus Analyzing Data, Drawing Conclusions, Formulating Hypotheses, Designing Experiments, Predicting, Inferring

 **Prep Time** 10 minutes

Class Time 45 minutes

Teaching Tip Have students work in small groups to complete the activity. Assign each group member a task, such as recording water temperature or calculating average temperatures.

Questioning Strategies Ask: **What two climatic factors affect rates of chemical weathering?** *(temperature and moisture)* **Which type of climate experiences the highest rates of chemical weathering?** *(hot and wet climates)*

Expected Outcome Students will observe that the antacid tablets dissolve most rapidly at high temperatures. They will recognize that rates of chemical weathering increase as temperature increases.

Exploration Lab

Effect of Temperature on Chemical Weathering

Water is the most important agent of chemical weathering. One way water promotes chemical weathering is by reacting with the minerals in rocks. In this lab, you will examine the effect of temperature on chemical weathering by measuring the rate at which antacid tablets dissolve in water at different temperatures. These tablets contain calcium carbonate, the mineral found in rocks such as limestone and marble.

Problem How does temperature affect the rate of chemical weathering?

Materials
- 250-mL beaker
- thermometer
- hot water (40–50°C)
- ice
- 5 antacid tablets
- stopwatch
- graph paper

Skills Measuring, Using Tables and Graphs, Drawing Conclusions, Inferring

Procedure  

1. On a sheet of paper, copy the data table.
2. Add a mixture of hot water and ice to the beaker. Use the thermometer to measure the temperature of the mixture. Add either more hot water or more ice until the temperature is between 0°C and 10°C. The total volume of the mixture should be about 200 mL.
3. When the temperature is within the correct range, remove any remaining ice from the beaker. Record the starting temperature of the water in your data table. Remove the thermometer from the beaker.
4. Drop an antacid tablet into the beaker. Start the stopwatch as soon as the tablet enters the water. Stop the stopwatch when the tablet has completely dissolved and no traces of the tablet are visible. (Don't wait for the bubbling to stop.) Record the time in your data table.
5. Place the thermometer in the beaker and wait for the temperature of the water to stabilize. Record the final temperature of the water in your data table.

Data Table

Starting Temperature (°C)	Dissolving Time(s)	Final Temperature (°C)	Average Temperature (°C)

6. Calculate the average temperature by adding the starting and final temperatures and dividing by 2. Record the result in your data table.
7. Repeat Steps 2 through 6 four more times, once at each of the following temperature ranges: 10–20°C, 20–30°C, 30–40°C, and 40–50°C. Adjust the relative amounts of hot water and ice to produce the correct water temperatures. The total volume of water and ice should always be about 200 mL.
8. On graph paper, make a graph with average temperature on the *x*-axis and dissolving time on the *y*-axis. Plot your data on the graph. Draw a smooth curve through the data points.

Analyze and Conclude

1. **Analyzing Data** At which temperature did the antacid tablet dissolve most rapidly?
2. **Analyzing Data** At which temperature did the antacid tablet dissolve most slowly?
3. **Drawing Conclusions** What is the relationship between temperature and the rate at which antacid tablets react with water?
4. **Formulating Hypotheses** Based on your observations, form a hypothesis about the relationship between temperature and the rate of chemical weathering.
5. **Designing Experiments** How could you test your hypothesis?
6. **Predicting** What would your results have been if you had ground each tablet into a fine powder before dropping it into the water? Would your conclusion be the same or different? Explain.
7. **Inferring** Would a limestone building weather more rapidly in Homer, Alaska, or in Honolulu, Hawaii? (Both cities receive about the same amount of precipitation in an average year.) Explain your reasoning.

Go Further Look for signs of chemical weathering on old stone buildings in your community. Consult your local library or historical society to find out when the buildings were constructed and what type of stone they are made of.

Sample Data See sample answers in the data table on the student page.

Analyze and Conclude

1. the highest temperature
2. the lowest temperature
3. Antacid tablets react more rapidly in water as the temperature increases.
4. As temperature increases, the rate of chemical weathering increases.
5. Sample answer: perform a similar experiment using rock that is sensitive to chemical weathering, such as limestone. Test the water for the presence of calcium or carbonate ions.
6. The dissolving times would have been shorter because grinding increases the surface area exposed to water. The conclusion would be the same because increasing surface area would speed the rate of reaction at each temperature.
7. Honolulu; Hawaii is much closer to the equator than Alaska is, so the average temperature in Honolulu is greater than that in Homer. The higher temperature promotes faster chemical weathering.

Go Further

Answers will vary.
Kinesthetic, Portfolio

Study Guide

Study Tip

Make a List
Suggest that students make a list of everything they need to review for a test a day or two before the test. Creating the list is a thorough review in itself. Students can study the list on their way to and from school, during lunch, and between classes.

Assessment

Reviewing Content

(1) 3 (2) 1 (3) 4
(4) 2 (5) 4 (6) 2
(7) 3 8) 1 (9) 3
(10) 2

Understanding Concepts

(11) The total surface area increases. The process represents mechanical weathering.
(12) Exfoliation is a process in which unloading causes slabs of outer rock to separate and break loose. Examples include Stone Mountain in Georgia and Half Dome in Yosemite National Park.
(13) By breaking rocks into smaller pieces, mechanical weathering increases the surface area of exposed rock.
(14) Carbonic acid forms when carbon dioxide reacts with water. It converts feldspar mostly to clay minerals.
(15) Climate has the greatest effect. It influences the rate, depth, and type of weathering, the rate at which nutrients are removed from soil, and the types of organisms that live on and in the soil.
(16) On steep slopes, erosion is accelerated, so soils are usually thin or nonexistent. In flat areas, there is little erosion, so soils are typically thick.

CHAPTER 5

Study Guide

5.1 Weathering

Key Concepts
- Mechanical weathering occurs when physical forces break rock into smaller and smaller pieces without changing the rock's mineral composition.
- In nature, three physical processes are especially important causes of mechanical weathering: frost wedging, unloading, and biological activity.
- Chemical weathering is the transformation of rock into one or more new compounds.
- Two factors that affect the rate of weathering are rock characteristics and climate.

Vocabulary
mechanical weathering, *p. 126;* frost wedging, *p. 127;* talus, *p. 127;* exfoliation, *p. 128;* chemical weathering, *p. 129*

5.2 Soil

Key Concepts
- Soil is the part of the regolith that supports the growth of plants.
- Soil has four major components: mineral matter, or broken down rock; organic matter, or humus, which is the decayed remains of organisms; water; and air.
- The most important factors in soil formation are parent material, time, climate, organisms, and slope.
- Soil varies in composition, texture, structure, and color at different depths.
- Three common types of soil are pedalfer, pedocal, and laterite.
- Human activities that remove natural vegetation, such as farming, logging, and construction, have greatly accelerated erosion.

Vocabulary
regolith, *p. 133;* soil, *p. 133;* soil horizon, *p. 138;* soil profile, *p. 138;* pedalfer, *p. 139;* pedocal, *p. 139;* laterite, *p. 139*

5.3 Mass Movements

Key Concepts
- The transfer of rock and soil downslope due to gravity is called mass movement.
- Among the factors that commonly trigger mass movements are saturation of surface materials with water, oversteepening of slopes, removal of vegetation, and earthquakes.
- Geologists classify mass movements based on the kind of material that moves, how it moves, and the speed of movement.

Vocabulary
mass movement, *p. 143;* rockfall, *p. 145;* rockslide, *p. 145;* slump, *p. 146;* mudflow, *p. 146;* earthflow, *p. 146;* creep, *p. 147*

Chapter Assessment Resources

Print
Chapter Test, Chapter 5
Test Prep Resources, Chapter 5

Technology
Computer Test Bank, Chapter 5 Test
Online Text, Chapter 5
Go Online, PHSchool.com, Chapter 5

CHAPTER 5

NY Regents Content Item

Assessment

Interactive textbook with assessment at PHSchool.com 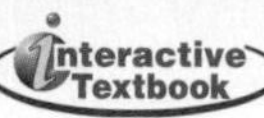

Reviewing Content

Choose the number that best answers the question or completes the statement.

1 The breaking down and changing of rocks at or near Earth's surface is called NY
(1) mass movement (2) sheet erosion
(3) weathering (4) uplift

2 Which of the following is NOT a cause of mechanical weathering? NY
(1) dissolving (2) frost wedging
(3) unloading (4) burrowing

3 In which type of climate does chemical weathering occur most rapidly? NY
(1) cold, dry (2) cold, wet
(3) warm, dry (4) warm, wet

4 Organic matter in soil is also called NY
(1) regolith (2) humus
(3) talus (4) loam

5 A soil's texture is determined by its
(1) water content
(2) mineral composition
(3) thickness
(4) particle sizes

6 In soils with distinct soil horizons, the topmost zone is the NY
(1) parent material (2) A horizon
(3) B horizon (4) C horizon

7 Compared to past rates of soil erosion, the current rate is NY
(1) lower
(2) about the same
(3) higher
(4) impossible to determine

8 Which of the following does NOT usually trigger mass movements? NY
(1) growth of native vegetation on slopes
(2) formation of oversteepened slopes
(3) saturation of surface materials with water
(4) vibration of the ground during an earthquake

9 When a block of material moves downward along a curved surface, the process is called
(1) a rockslide (2) a rockfall
(3) a slump (4) an earthflow

10 Which of the following best describes a mudflow?
(1) movement too slow to be observed directly
(2) material moving downslope as a thick fluid
(3) material falling freely through the air
(4) sudden movement along a flat, inclined surface

Understanding Concepts

11 What happens to the total surface area of the cubes in the process shown below? What type of weathering does this process represent? NY

12 What is exfoliation? Give an example of a feature produced by exfoliation. NY

13 How does mechanical weathering promote chemical weathering? NY

14 How is carbonic acid formed in nature? What happens when this acid reacts with feldspar?

15 Which factor has the greatest effect on soil formation? Explain. NY

16 How does slope affect the formation of soil? NY

17 Describe the major characteristics of A, B, and C horizons. NY

18 Distinguish between pedalfer and pedocal.

19 List three negative effects of soil erosion.

20 Explain how weathering and mass movement together produce most landforms. NY

21 What is the force behind mass movements? What other factors can trigger mass movements? NY

22 Distinguish between rockfalls and rockslides.

23 Distinguish between mudflows and earthflows.

24 How do freezing and thawing contribute to creep? NY

 Homework Guide 

Section	Questions
1	1–3, 11–14, 25–28, 33, 34
2	4–7, 15–19, 29–32, 35
3	8–10, 20–24, 36, 37

(17) The A horizon contains a mixture of mineral matter and organic matter and is teeming with insects, fungi, and microorganisms. The B horizon contains fine clay particles washed out of the A horizon; the clay sometimes forms a compact, impenetrable layer called hardpan. The B horizon is the lower limit of most plant roots and burrowing animals. The C horizon contains partially weathered parent material.
(18) Pedalfer usually forms in temperate areas with an annual rainfall greater than 63 cm. It is present in much of the eastern half of the United States, most often in forested areas. It contains large amounts of iron oxide and aluminum-rich clays and is brown to red-brown in color. Pedocal is found in the drier western United States in areas that have grasses and brush vegetation. It generally contains less clay than pedalfer does. Pedocal is rich in calcite and is typically light gray-brown in color.
(19) Possible answers include those related to loss of cropland (lowering farm productivity, reducing crop quality, and threatening the world food supply) or sediment deposition (hindering shipping on rivers, reducing the effectiveness of reservoirs, endangering organisms through pesticide contamination, and causing the early death of lakes).
(20) Once weathering weakens and breaks rock apart, mass movement moves the debris downslope, where a stream usually carries it away.
(21) Gravity is the force behind mass movements. Other factors that can trigger mass movements include saturation of surface materials with water, oversteepening of slopes, removal of vegetation, and earthquakes.
(22) A rockfall occurs when rocks or rock fragments fall freely through the air. A rockslide occurs when a block of material that includes segments of bedrock moves suddenly along a flat, inclined surface.
(23) Mudflows are flows that move quickly, typically in semiarid mountainous regions, following a heavy downpour or rapid snowmelt. Earthflows are flows that move relatively slowly, most often in wet regions when water saturates the soil and regolith.
(24) Freezing expands the water in soil, lifting soil particles at right angles to the slope. Thawing causes contraction, which allows the particles to fall back to a slightly lower level. Each freeze-thaw cycle moves the particles a short distance downhill.

Critical Thinking

(25) In northern states, there is more freezing and thawing during the winter, so frost wedging causes more severe weathering of roads.
(26) Mechanical weathering produces smaller pieces of the same rock, while chemical weathering produces new compounds from the rock.
(27) Marble will weather more rapidly. Hot, wet climates favor chemical weathering, which acts more rapidly on marble than on granite.
(28) The most important agent of chemical weathering is water, which is scarce in a desert.
(29) Soil erosion is not artificial. It is a natural part of the constant recycling of Earth materials known as the rock cycle. However, humans can accelerate erosion through activities that remove natural vegetation, such as farming, logging, and construction.

Analyzing Data

(30) A: thin or nonexistent; B: thick
(31) B: transported soil; C: residual soil
(32) The slope in area D is greater than that in area C. Because the rate of erosion is greater on steeper slopes, the soil is thinner in area D.

CHAPTER 5

Assessment *continued*

Critical Thinking

25 **Inferring** Roads in northern states such as Maine and Michigan need to be repaired more often than roads in southern states such as Florida and Louisiana. What form of mechanical weathering could account for this? NY

26 **Comparing and Contrasting** How do the effects of mechanical weathering on rock differ from the effects of chemical weathering? NY

27 **Predicting** Granite and marble are exposed at the surface in a hot, wet region. Which of the rocks will weather more rapidly? Why?

28 **Applying Concepts** Heat speeds up most chemical reactions. Why then does chemical weathering happen slowly in a hot desert? NY

29 **Making Judgments** Do you think that soil erosion is an artificial byproduct of careless land use by humans? Explain.

Analyzing Data

Use the diagram below to answer questions 30–32.

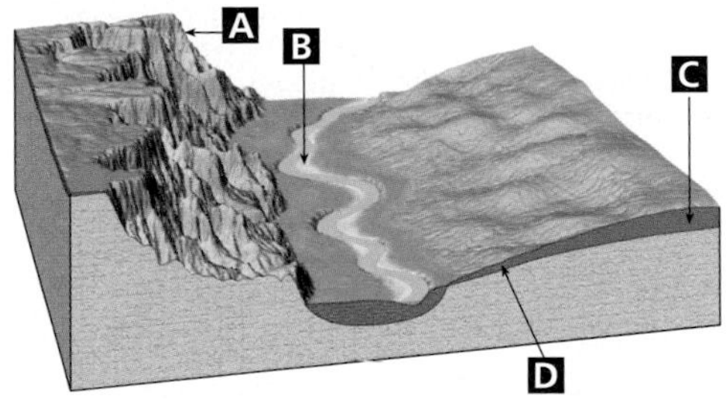

30 **Comparing and Contrasting** Compare the thickness of the soil in the areas labeled A and B.

31 **Interpreting Diagrams** What name is given to the soil that develops in the area labeled B? In the area labeled C?

32 **Inferring** Why is the soil in the area labeled D thinner than the soil in the area labeled C?

Concepts in Action

33 **Using Analogies** Explain how the following scenario is analogous to weathering: One evening you place a sealed jar full of water in a freezer. The next morning, the water has turned to ice and the jar is cracked. NY

34 **Applying Concepts** A committee has been established to design a stone memorial commemorating 100 soldiers who died in battle. The committee decides to use a large block of marble for the memorial. Considering only the memorial's durability, would it be better to use the whole block as a single memorial for all 100 soldiers or to divide it into 100 blocks of equal size, one for each soldier? NY

35 **Classifying** How would you determine the texture of the soil in your area?

36 **Making Judgments** Should a homeowner in a dry, mountainous area remove all vegetation from surrounding slopes to reduce fire danger? Explain why or why not.

37 **Writing in Science** Write a paragraph describing one type of mass movement. Include a specific example of a time when such a mass movement made the news.

Performance-Based Assessment

Observing Look for places in your community where people have taken specific actions to reduce erosion. Such places may include sites where buildings are being constructed or roads are being built or repaired. Make a list of each action and explain how it is intended to reduce erosion.

Concepts in Action

(33) The water expanded as it froze, exerting pressure on the jar and cracking the glass. A similar process occurs during the type of mechanical weathering called frost wedging, in which water enters cracks in rock, expands during freezing, and enlarges the cracks.
(34) It would be better to use the whole block as a single memorial. Smaller blocks would have a greater total surface area exposed to chemical weathering, which is accelerated in areas that have a warm, wet climate.
(35) Examine a sample of the soil to determine how much clay, silt, and sand it contains. Then use the diagram in Figure 11 to classify soil texture.
(36) No, removing all vegetation would promote erosion and increase the chance of mudflows. It would be safer to trim the vegetation, leaving it alive with its roots intact.
(37) Students should focus their paragraph on one of the mass movements discussed in Section 5.3. Encourage students to gather information for their paragraphs from library or Internet resources.

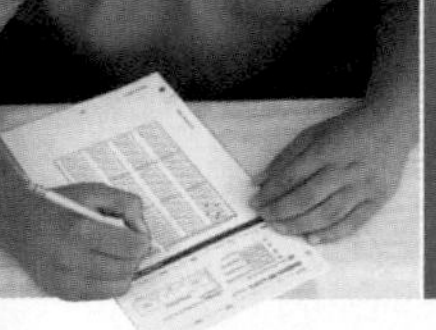

Regents Practice Exam

Test-Taking Tip

Watch for Qualifiers

The words *best* and *least* are examples of qualifiers. If a question contains a qualifier, more than one answer will contain correct information. However, only one answer will be complete and correct for the question asked. Look at the question below. Eliminate any answers that are clearly incorrect. Then choose the remaining answer that offers the best explanation for the question asked.

Which mass movement is LEAST dangerous to people walking below a slope?

(1) rockslide
(2) rockfall
(3) creep
(4) mudflow

(Answer: 3)

For *each* statement or question, choose the *number* of the word or expression that, of those given, best completes the statement or answers the question. Some questions may require the use of the *Earth Science Reference Tables.*

1 Which of the following climatic conditions would result in the most chemical weathering?
(1) high temperatures, low humidity
(2) low temperatures, high humidity
(3) low temperatures, low humidity
(4) high temperatures, high humidity

2 Which of the following is the best example of mechanical weathering?
(1) water freezing, causing rock cracks to expand
(2) oxygen causing rust
(3) carbonic acid dissolving limestone
(4) water changing feldspar into clay minerals

Answer the following questions in complete sentences. Some questions may require the use of the *Earth Science Reference Tables.* Base your answers to questions 3 and 4 on the Soil-Texture diagram at top right.

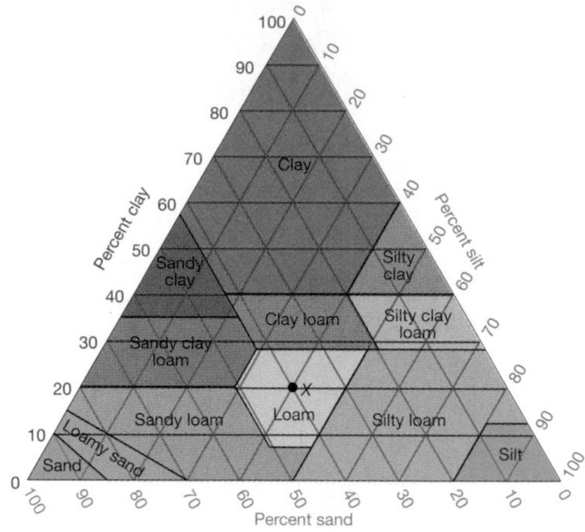

3 What are the percentages of clay, silt, and sand in the soil at the point labeled *X*?
(1) 60% clay, 80% silt, 60% sand
(2) 0% clay, 40% silt, 60% sand
(3) 20% clay, 40% silt, 40% sand
(4) 50% clay, 40% silt, 10% sand

4 The name given to soil that contains 60% clay, 20% silt, and 20% sand is
(1) clay
(2) loam
(3) silty clay loam
(4) sandy loam

5 How does the surface area of an exposed rock affect its rate of weathering?

6 Explain why water is considered the primary agent of erosion on Earth.

7 Explain what frost wedging is and why it happens.

8 State one method by which soil erosion can be reduced, and explain how this method works to reduce erosion.

Regents Practice Exam

(1) 4
(2) 1
(3) 3
(4) 1
(5) Increasing the surface area increases the rate of weathering.
(6) Water causes mechanical weathering when it freezes in rock cracks, and also causes many types of chemical weathering when it is a liquid. Water generally increases the weathering rate of all substances.
(7) When water freezes in rock cracks, causing the cracks to expand, this is called frost wedging. Frost wedging occurs because water expands when it freezes.
(8) Planting vegetation reduces erosion because roots hold the soil in place and soak up excess water. Planting trees in rows reduces wind erosion by reducing wind speeds. Using terracing or contour plowing in hilly areas reduces soil erosion by reducing the rate at which water moves over the land.

Performance-Based Assessment

Examples may include setting up soil-catching barriers around building sites, covering exposed slopes along roads with straw or netting, and terracing sloped planting areas.

Your students can independently test their knowledge of the chapter and print out their results.

CHAPTER 6

Planning Guide

Use these planning tools
Use Teacher Express for all your planning needs

SECTION OBJECTIVES	STANDARDS NATIONAL	STANDARDS STATE	ACTIVITIES and LABS
6.1 Running Water, pp. 158–163 1 block or 2 periods **6.1** **Explain** how the water cycle circulates Earth's water supply in an unending cycle. **6.2** **Explain** how the water cycle is kept in balance. **6.3** **Describe** the ability of a stream to erode and transport material. **6.4** **Compare and contrast** the changes in gradient and discharge between a stream's headwaters and mouth. **6.5** **Define** base level.	A-1, C-4, D-1, D-2, F-3, F-5		**SE** Inquiry Activity: How Do Local Bodies of Water Affect Your Community? p. 157 L2 **TE** Build Science Skills, p. 159 L2 **TE** Teacher Demo: The Ability to Erode, p. 160 L2
6.2 The Work of Streams, pp. 164–170 2 blocks or 4 periods **6.6** **Explain** how streams erode their channels and transport sediments. **6.7** **Explain** how stream deposition occurs. **6.8** **Identify** the two general types of stream valleys. **6.9** **Predict** the causes of floods and **describe** major flood control measures. **6.10** **Explain** the relationship between streams and drainage basins.	E-2, F-5, F-6		**TE** Teacher Demo: Alluvium, p. 166 L2 **TE** Build Science Skills, p. 167 L2 **SE** Exploration Lab: Investigating the Permeability of Soils, p. 181 L2 **LM** Rivers That Shape the Land L2
6.3 Water Beneath the Surface, pp. 171–179 2 blocks or 4 periods **6.11** **Describe** the location and movement of groundwater. **6.12** **Describe** the formation of a spring. **6.13** **Explain** environmental threats to water supplies. **6.14** **Describe** the formation of caverns. **6.15** **Describe** landforms in karst areas.	A-1, A-2, D-1, F-4, F-5, F-6		**TE** Teacher Demo: Water Table, p. 172 L2 **LM** Modeling Cavern Formation L1

Ability Levels

- **L1** For students who need additional help
- **L2** For all students
- **L3** For students who need to be challenged

Components

SE	Student Edition	**GRSW**	Guided Reading & Study Workbook	**TP**	Test Prep Resources	**GEO**	Geode CD-ROM
TE	Teacher's Edition	**TEX**	Teacher Express	**onT**	onlineText	**T**	Transparencies
LM	Laboratory Manual	**CTB**	Computer Test Bank	**DC**	Discovery Channel Videos	**GO**	Internet Resources
CUT	Chapter Tests						

RESOURCES PRINT and TECHNOLOGY	SECTION ASSESSMENT
GRSW Section 6.1 **T-36** Distribution of Earth's Water **T-37** Earth's Water Balance **T-38** World's Largest Rivers by Discharge **T-39** Cross Section Along the Length of a Stream **T-40** Resistant Layer of Rock as a Local (Temporary) Base Level **T-41** Increase in Stream's Base Level **GEODe** Sculpturing Earth's Surface ↳ Hydrologic Cycle **TEX** Lesson Planning 6.1	**SE** Section 6.1 Assessment, p. 163 **onT** Section 6.1
GRSW Section 6.2 **T-42** Structure and Growth of a Simple Delta **T-43** Mississippi Delta **T-44** Natural Levees **T-45** Stream Eroding Its Floodplain **T-46** Lateral Movement of Meanders **T-47** Formation of a Cutoff and Oxbow Lake **T-48** Mississippi River Drainage Basin **T-49** Drainage Patterns **GEODe** Sculpturing Earth's Surface ↳ Running Water **DC** Dams **TEX** Lesson Planning 6.2	**SE** Section 6.2 Assessment, p. 170 **onT** Section 6.2
GRSW Section 6.3 **T-50** Estimated Distribution of Water in the Hydrosphere **T-51** Features Associated with Subsurface Water **T-52** Idealized Diagrams of a Geyser **T-53** A Cone of Depression **T-54** Artesian Systems **T-55** Groundwater Contamination **T-56** Flood Lag Time—Rural vs. Urban **T-57** Map of Ogallala Formation **GEODe** Sculpturing Earth's Surface ↳ Groundwater **TEX** Lesson Planning 6.3	**SE** Section 6.3 Assessment, p. 179 **onT** Section 6.3

Go Online

Go online for these Internet resources.

PHSchool.com
Web Code: cjk-9999

NSTA SciLinks
Web Code: cjn-2062
Web Code: cjn-2064
Web Code: cjn-2065

Materials for Activities and Labs

Quantities for each group

STUDENT EDITION

Exploration Lab, p. 181
100-mL graduated cylinder; beaker; small funnel; 3 pieces of cotton; samples of coarse sand, fine sand, and soil; clock or watch with a second hand

TEACHER'S EDITION

Build Science Skills, p. 159
shoe boxes, cardboard, aluminum foil, cotton balls, clay

Teacher Demo, p. 160
stream table, soil, short length of hose, bucket, access to sink or running water

Teacher Demo, p. 166
mixed sediment (pebbles, sand, silt, and clay-sized particles), clear glass jar with lid, water

Build Science Skills, p. 167
sloped paint trays, sand, water source

Teacher Demo, p. 172
large clear plastic cup; clean, dry sand; water

Chapter Assessment

ASSESSMENT

SE	Assessment, pp. 183–184
CUT	Chapter 6 Test
CTB	Chapter 6
onT	Chapter 6

STANDARDIZED TEST PREP

SE	Chapter 6, p. 185
TP	Progress Monitoring Assessments

interactive textbook with assessment at PHSchool.com

CHAPTER 6

Before you teach

Michael Wysession
Washington University

Big Ideas

The water cycle is a defining feature of Earth's surface. The water cycle, involving the evaporation, precipitation, stream runoff, and ground infiltration of water, shapes and changes continental surfaces.

Space and Time Oceans contain 97.2 percent of Earth's surface water, with most of the rest in glaciers and groundwater. Though only a tiny amount of water exists in streams and the atmosphere, huge amounts of water pass through them. Networks of streams form drainage basins that allow rain to eventually drain back to the oceans. Groundwater, though hidden to sight, is vitally important to humans. In the United States, it supplies drinking water for 50 percent of the population and 40 percent of agriculture. Groundwater is retrieved from aquifers that have high porosity and permeability. Caverns form underground when they are below the water table, but develop familiar cave formations when they are above the water table.

Forces and Motion Streams erode or deposit sediment, depending upon their velocity and sediment load. Stream velocity depends upon discharge and slope gradient. Stream valleys tend to be narrow and V-shaped at their steep headwaters, and wider along flatter gradients, forming floodplains. Most of the erosion and transportation of sediment occurs during times of stream flooding.

Matter and Energy The surface part of the water cycle, and therefore of the rock cycle as well, is ultimately powered by the sun through evaporation and the movement of air.

Earth as a System The erosion and transportation of sediment occurs in the form of dissolved, suspended, and bed loads. Sediment is deposited whenever flowing water slows, forming deltas, alluvial fans, and levees.

Earth Science Refresher

Deep-Earth Water Cycle

We are most familiar with the surface water cycle involving evaporation, precipitation, and streams, but there is another, even larger water cycle involving the deep Earth. The rock of the mantle contains a huge amount of water, estimated to be up to five times the amount of water in the ocean. This water has a lubricating effect on the mantle rock, allowing it to flow and to melt much more easily that it would if it were dry.

This water in the deep Earth interacts with the surface through the process of plate tectonics—at subduction zones and volcanoes. When the giant sheets of the ocean seafloor subduct beneath other plates and sink into the mantle, they carry water with them. This water seeps into the ocean crust during the tens to hundreds of millions of years that that lie beneath the oceans. Most of this water leaves the subducting lithosphere and rises back to the surface within magma. Most of the gas that accompanies the eruption of subduction zone volcanoes is water vapor. Some of the water gets carried deeper into the mantle, perhaps eventually to accompany erupting magma at mid-ocean ridge volcanoes. There is more water involved with the deep Earth water cycle than the surface water cycle, but because of the very slow rates of plate tectonic motions, water moves through it at a much slower rate.

Address Misconceptions

Some students may think that a "100-year flood" only occurs every 100 years. This is not true. The probability is that it will only happen every 100 years but it could happen during any year. For a strategy that helps to overcome this misconception, see **Address Misconceptions** on **p. 169.**

For: Chapter 6 Content Support
Visit: www.SciLinks.org/PDLinks
Web Code: cjn-0699

The Changing Shapes of Streams

Streams naturally change their course. Meanders continually cross a floodplain over time, and stream deltas jump around when the stream mouth gets clogged with sediment. However, most people don't like rivers suddenly cutting through their farms, houses, and towns, so artificial levees are built to keep the rivers in their present course. The buildup of sediment in streams forces the levees to be built higher and higher. One of the world's largest engineering construction projects is the United States Army Corps of Engineers' attempt to keep the Mississippi River from changing its shape. In fact, the Mississippi River flows past New Orleans about 5 m higher than the level of the city, kept in place by high levees. People look up to see ships pass.

As can be seen in Figure 9 on p. 166, however, this situation is not stable. Notice how the Atchafalaya River presents a much shorter path to the Gulf of Mexico. The Mississippi would naturally switch to this course, as it has in the past, if it were not for the artificial levees. It almost did in 1973. During the great flood of that year, rushing waters almost undermined the concrete structures to flood gates that opened into the Atchafalaya. Had the great Mississippi River jumped course, there would have been no way of ever getting it back, and New Orleans would have been left dry. Even though the floodgates have been repaired, there is still a chance that a large enough flood could make the Mississippi jump its tracks for good.

Build Reading Literacy

Reciprocal Teaching

Modeling Strategies in Combination

Strategy Help students learn to apply the strategies of predict, question, clarify, and summarize. Teaching this strategy should take place over several days, beginning with the teacher modeling and leading students in discussion. The teacher gradually turns leadership over to students and becomes a facilitator, intervening only as needed. Prepare for the reading by choosing a passage of several paragraphs from Chapter 6. Make a copy of the paragraphs and note appropriate places to model the strategies for students.

Example

1. Read a few paragraphs aloud or have one student read aloud as other students follow along silently.

2. Discuss appropriate strategies for clarifying meaning and getting past trouble spots in the passage. Engage the group in discussing ways to apply each of the following strategies:

- Predicting what will come next in the text. Remind students to use what they already know about a topic to make connections that will help them understand what comes next.
- Asking "teacher-like questions" to check understanding and to think about what they need to find out.
- Clarifying the meaning of unfamiliar words or concepts.
- Summarizing what has been read.

3. Reread the paragraphs, modeling all four strategies.

4. Continue reading a few paragraphs at a time, discussing and modeling.

5. Repeat the process with different passages over a few days, gradually turning over the leadership role to students by having them lead the discussion of portions of the text.

6. When students are comfortable with the strategies, they can lead the entire discussion. Intervene only to get students back on track or to jump-start a discussion.

See p. 159 for a script on how to use this strategy with students. For additional strategies, see pp. 161, 162, 164, 173, and 177.

SCULPTURING EARTH'S SURFACE

Chapter 6

ASSESS PRIOR KNOWLEDGE

Use the Chapter Pretest below to assess students' prior knowledge. As needed, review these concepts.

Review Science Concepts

Section 6.1 Students would benefit from a brief discussion on cloud formation and water in the atmosphere. This would allow them to become familiar with the behavior of moisture in the atmosphere as it relates to the water cycle.

Section 6.2 Review with students the concept of velocity. This will make the discussion of streams easier for them to understand.

Section 6.3 Reviewing erosion and weathering will provide students with the background to discuss the formation of groundwater features as well as the work that a stream can do. Also, a quick look at some major rock types, especially limestone, will provide students with the background into karst regions and less resistant rock.

CHAPTER 6 Running Water and Groundwater

CONCEPTS in Action

Exploration Lab
Investigating the Permeability of Soils

People and the Environment
The Ogallala Aquifer—How Long Will the Water Last?

Sculpturing Earth's Surface
↳ Hydrologic Cycle
Running Water
Groundwater

Discovery CHANNEL SCHOOL **Video Field Trip**

Dams

Take a field trip to China with the Discovery Channel and learn about the construction of the Three Gorges dam on the Yangtze River. Answer the following questions after watching the video.

1. What led to the decision to build a dam on the Yangtze River?
2. Name two disadvantages of the Three Gorges Dam.

For: Chapter 6 Resources
Visit: PHSchool.com
Web Code: cjk-9999

This photograph shows Lost Yak Rapids ▶ on Chile's Rio Bio Bio.

156 *Chapter 6*

Chapter Pretest

1. True or False: A nonrenewable resource will be replenished within your lifetime? *(False)*
2. Briefly discuss the connection between weathering and erosion. *(Erosion is the moving of weathered material.)*
3. What type of rock reacts in weak acid? *(c)*
   a. granite
   b. shale
   c. limestone
   d. gneiss
4. True or False: There can be more moisture in warm air than in cool air. *(True)*
5. Velocity is equal to *(a)*
   a. distance/time
   b. time × length
   c. distance × distance
   d. distance × depth

SCULPTURING EARTH'S SURFACE

Chapter Preview

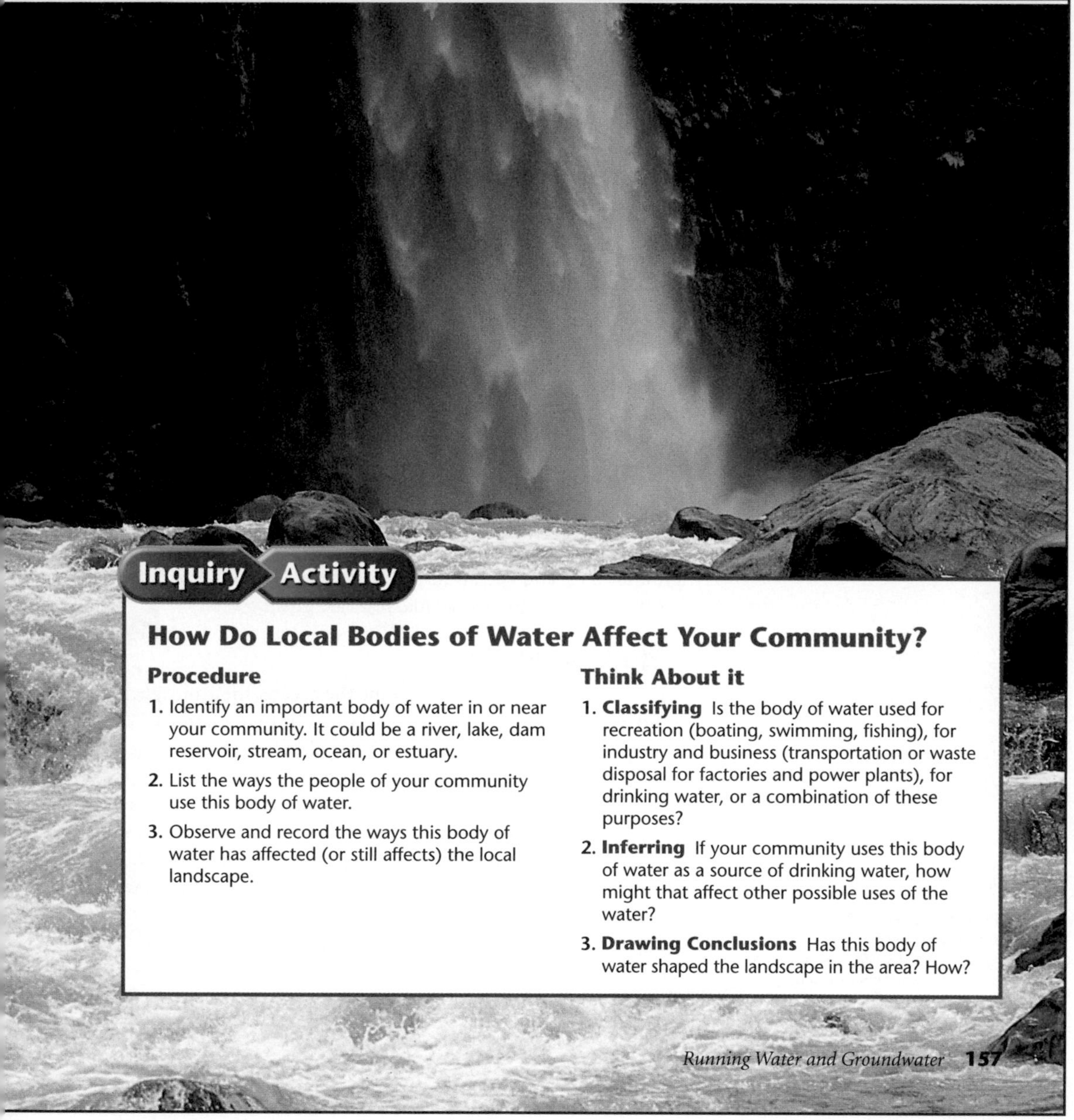

Inquiry Activity

How Do Local Bodies of Water Affect Your Community?

Procedure

1. Identify an important body of water in or near your community. It could be a river, lake, dam reservoir, stream, ocean, or estuary.
2. List the ways the people of your community use this body of water.
3. Observe and record the ways this body of water has affected (or still affects) the local landscape.

Think About it

1. **Classifying** Is the body of water used for recreation (boating, swimming, fishing), for industry and business (transportation or waste disposal for factories and power plants), for drinking water, or a combination of these purposes?
2. **Inferring** If your community uses this body of water as a source of drinking water, how might that affect other possible uses of the water?
3. **Drawing Conclusions** Has this body of water shaped the landscape in the area? How?

Video Field Trip

Dams

Encourage students to view the Video Field Trip "Dams."

ENGAGE/EXPLORE

How Do Local Bodies of Water Affect Your Community? L2

Purpose In this activity, students will identify an important body of water in their community. They will explore how people use the body of water and how it affects the community.

Skills Focus Classifying, Inferring, Drawing Conclusions

Prep Time none

Materials paper, pencil, computer and other research sources

Class Time 50 minutes

Expected Outcome Students will understand the effect an important body of water has had and continues to have on their community.

Think About It

1. Answers will vary according to the body of water chosen.
2. The body of water could only be used in ways that would carefully monitor pollutants that go into the water.
3. Answers will vary according to the body of water chosen.

Section 6.1

1 FOCUS

Section Objectives

6.1 **Explain** how the water cycle circulates Earth's water supply in an unending cycle.

6.2 **Explain** how the water cycle is kept in balance.

6.3 **Describe** the ability of a stream to erode and transport material.

6.4 **Compare and contrast** the changes in gradient and discharge between a stream's headwaters and mouth.

6.5 **Define** base level.

Reading Focus

Build Vocabulary L2

Cycle Diagram Have students create a cycle diagram of the water cycle. Instruct students to place the terms in ovals and connect the ovals with lines.

Reading Strategy L2

Water cycle—unending circulation of Earth's water supply
Infiltration—movement of surface water through cracks and pore spaces
Transpiration—release of water vapor by plants into the atmosphere

2 INSTRUCT

The Water Cycle

Use Visuals L1

Figure 1 Direct student's attention to the pie graph of the distribution of Earth's water. Ask: **What percent of Earth's water is in freshwater lakes and streams combined?** *(0.0091 percent)* **Visual**

6.1 Running Water

Reading Focus

Key Concepts

- What is the water cycle?
- What does it mean to say Earth's water cycle is balanced?
- What is the most important factor in determining the power of a stream to erode and transport material?
- How do gradient and discharge change between a stream's source and its mouth?
- What is a stream's base level?

Vocabulary

- water cycle
- infiltration
- transpiration
- gradient
- stream channel
- discharge
- tributary
- base level
- meander

Reading Strategy

Building Vocabulary Copy the table. As you read the section, define in your own words each vocabulary term listed in the table.

Vocabulary Term	Definition
Water cycle	?
Infiltration	?
Transpiration	?

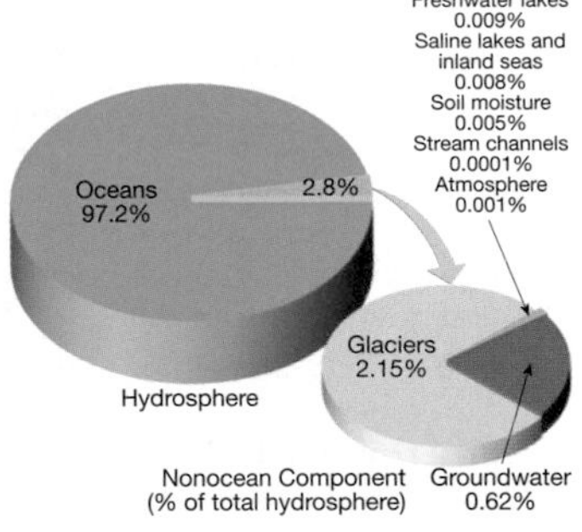

Figure 1 Distribution of Earth's Water
Using Graphs ***What percentage of Earth's water is not held in its oceans?***

Water is everywhere on Earth—oceans, glaciers, rivers, lakes, air, soil, and living tissue. All of these reservoirs make up Earth's hydrosphere. Most of it—about 97.2 percent—is stored in oceans, as Figure 1 shows. Ice sheets and glaciers account for another 2.15 percent, leaving only 0.65 percent to be divided among lakes, streams, groundwater, and the atmosphere. The water found in glaciers, ice sheets, lakes, streams, groundwater, and the atmosphere may seem like a tiny percent of Earth's water, but the actual quantities are great.

The Water Cycle

Water constantly moves among the oceans, the atmosphere, the solid Earth, and the biosphere. This unending circulation of Earth's water supply is the water cycle. This cycle is possible because water readily changes from one state of matter—solid, liquid, or gas—to another at temperatures and pressure common on Earth's surface.

The water cycle, shown in Figure 2, is a gigantic worldwide system powered by energy from the sun. The atmosphere provides the most important link between the oceans and land. Water evaporates into the atmosphere from the ocean, and to a lesser extent from the continents. Winds transport this moisture-rich air until conditions cause the moisture to condense into clouds. Precipitation—rain and snow—then falls to Earth. Precipitation that falls into oceans has completed

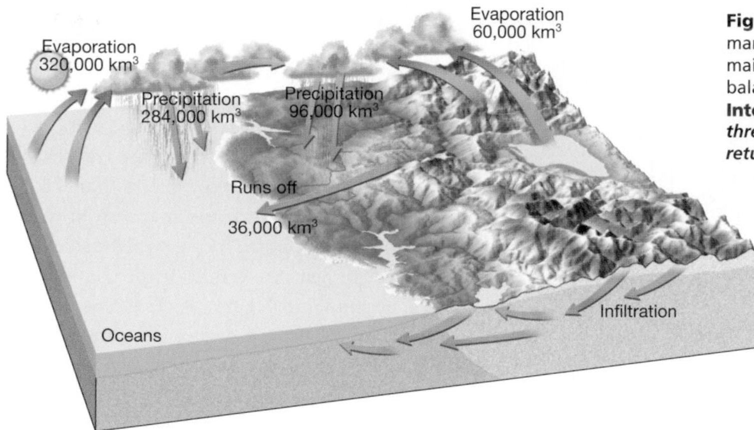

Figure 2 The Water Cycle The many processes of the water cycle maintain Earth's overall water balance.
Interpreting Diagrams *In which three ways does precipitation return to oceans?*

one full cycle and is ready to begin another. However, water that falls on land must make its way back to the ocean to complete the full cycle.

 *What is Earth's hydrosphere?*

What happens to precipitation that falls on land? Some of it slowly soaks into the ground through infiltration. **Infiltration** is the movement of surface water into rock or soil through cracks and pore spaces. The water gradually moves through the land and actually seeps into lakes, streams, or the ocean. When the rate of rainfall exceeds Earth's ability to absorb it, the excess water flows over the surface into lakes and streams in a process called runoff. Much of that runoff returns to the atmosphere because of evaporation from the soil, lakes, and streams. Plants also absorb water and release it into the atmosphere through **transpiration.**

When precipitation falls in very cold areas—at high elevations or high latitudes—the water may not immediately soak in, run off, or evaporate. Instead, it may become part of a glacier. Glaciers store large amounts of water on land. If present-day glaciers were to melt and release all their water, ocean levels would rise by several dozen meters.

Earth's Water Balance

Even with all these processes occurring, Earth's water cycle is balanced. **Balance in the water cycle means the average annual precipitation over Earth equals the amount of water that evaporates.** There are local imbalances. For example, precipitation exceeds evaporation over continents. Over oceans, evaporation exceeds precipitation. However, the fact that the level of world oceans is not changing very much indicates the system is balanced.

Build Science Skills L2

Using Models Have students create their own three-dimensional model of the water cycle. Provide them with materials to build this model, including shoe boxes, cardboard, aluminum foil, cotton balls, and clay. Their model should represent the major processes at work in the water cycle. Display the models around the classroom for other students to compare. ACTIVITY
Kinesthetic, Visual

Earth's Water Balance

Build Reading Literacy L1

Refer to **p. 156D** in this chapter, which provides the guidelines for reciprocal teaching.

Reciprocal Teaching Have students read about the water cycle with a partner. One partner reads the section out loud. The other partner draws a diagram that explains what is being read. The partners then switch roles. The second partner re-reads the section, while the other partner fills in any gaps in the water cycle diagram.
Intrapersonal

Answer to . . .

Figure 1 *2.8 percent*

Figure 2 *Precipitation returns to oceans as rain or snow, as runoff, and through infiltration.*

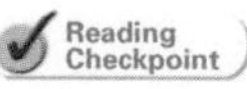 *The hydrosphere is Earth's waters—in oceans, glaciers, rivers, lakes, air, soil, and in living tissue.*

Streamflow

Teacher Demo

The Ability to Erode L2

Purpose Students are provided with a visual representation of the impact that gradient and discharge have on the ability of a stream to erode and transport material.

Materials stream table, soil, short length of hose, bucket, access to sink or running water

Procedure Fill the stream table with dry soil. Set the stream table at a slight angle (less than 45 degrees). Position the hose at one end of the stream table. Turn on the water, releasing a small but steady stream into the hose. Have students observe the resulting erosion and sediment transported into the bucket at the other end of the stream table. Turn off the water and spread the soil out again to form a continuous cover of soil. Perform the demonstration several more times, using different variables. For example, increase the discharge of the stream by turning the water up so a more forceful stream is created. Increase the gradient of the stream by raising and lowering the stream table. Have students predict what will happen in each scenario before turning on the water. Discuss the impact the variables will have on the area surrounding the stream as well as the areas downstream.

Expected Outcome Students will understand how streams can erode soil and transport materials.

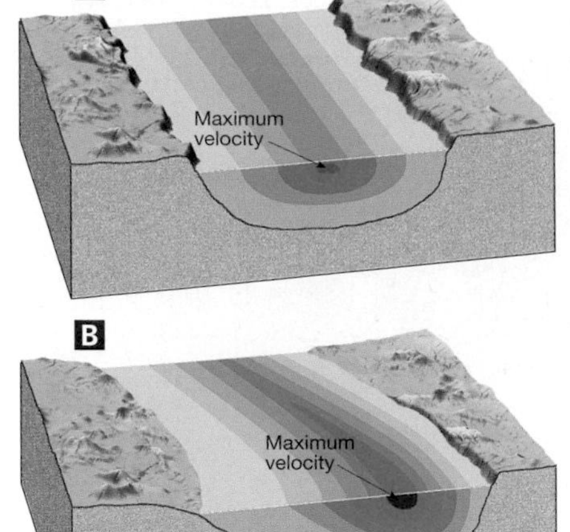

Figure 3 A Along straight stretches, stream velocity is highest at the center of the channel. **B** When a stream curves, its zone of maximum speed shifts toward the outer bank. **Interpreting Diagrams** ***How does velocity change with depth in the middle of the stream?***

Streamflow

Gravity influences the way water makes its way to the oceans. Streams and rivers carry water downhill from the land to the sea. The time this journey takes depends on the velocity of the stream. Velocity is the distance that water travels in a period of time. Some slow streams flow at less than 1 kilometer per hour, whereas a few rapid ones may flow at speeds that exceed 30 kilometers per hour. Along straight stretches, the highest velocities are near the center of the channel just below the surface, as shown in Figure 3A. The center of the channel is where friction is lowest. A stream's zone of maximum speed shifts toward its outer bank when a stream curves, as Figure 3B shows.

The ability of a stream to erode and transport materials depends largely on its velocity. Even slight changes in velocity greatly change the amount of sediment that water can transport. Several factors determine the velocity of a stream. They include its gradient; the shape, size, and roughness of its channel; and its discharge.

Gradient **Gradient** is the slope or steepness of a stream channel. Gradient is usually expressed as the vertical drop of a stream over a certain distance. Portions of the Mississippi River have very low gradients of 10 centimeters per kilometer or less. By contrast, some mountain streams tumble downhill at a rate of more than 40 meters per kilometer. This mountain stream's gradient is 400 times steeper than that of the lower Mississippi. Gradient varies over a stream's length and between streams. The steeper the gradient, the more energy the stream has as it flows downhill. Compare the steep and gentle gradients in Figure 4.

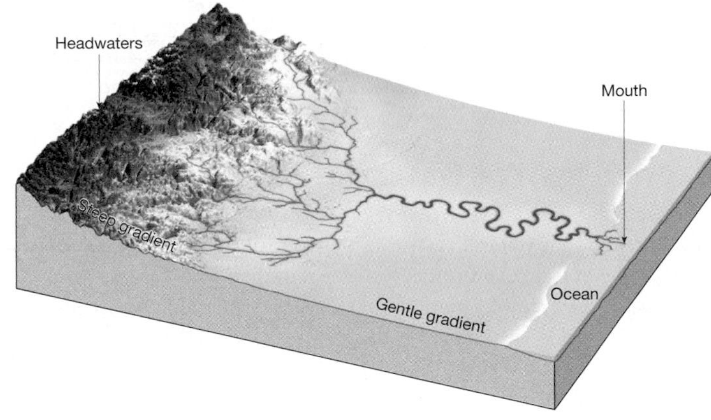

Figure 4 This cross section along the length of a stream shows a steeper gradient upstream, and a gentler gradient downstream.

160 Chapter 6

Customize for Inclusion Students

Learning Disabled Make concept maps for each section and cover them with clear contact paper. Then, cut the maps into puzzle pieces. Provide students with the pieces and have them put the puzzle together. After students complete the puzzle, have them make flashcards of concept connections and added notes. Students may have cards with the factors determining the velocity of a stream. They may also have concept cards with an important word missing. Example: **The _______ of a stream is the volume of water flowing past a specific point in a specific amount of time.** On the back of the card, the answer *discharge* is written.

Channel Characteristics A **stream channel** is the course the water in a stream follows. As the water flows, it encounters friction from the sides and the bottom of its channel. This friction slows its forward movement. The shape, size, and roughness of the channel affect the amount of friction. For example, an irregular channel filled with boulders creates enough turbulence to slow the stream significantly. Water in a smooth channel flows more easily. Larger channels also have more efficient water flow because a smaller proportion of water is in contact with the channel surfaces.

Discharge The **discharge** of a stream is the volume of water flowing past a certain point in a given unit of time. Discharge is usually measured in cubic meters per second. Table 1 lists the world's largest rivers in terms of discharge. The discharges of most rivers change with rainfall and snowmelt. The size and velocity of the stream also changes when discharge changes. The stream channel widens and deepens to handle additional water. As the size of the channel increases, there is less friction and the water flows more swiftly .

Building urban centers around a stream channel can also affect discharge. For example, the magnitude and frequency of floods can increase. The construction of streets, parking lots, and buildings covers soil that once soaked up water. Less water soaks into the ground and runoff increases, especially at times of heavy rainfall. Also, because less water soaks into the ground, the dry season flow of streams is reduced greatly. Urbanization is just one example of how humans can interfere with the normal flow of streams.

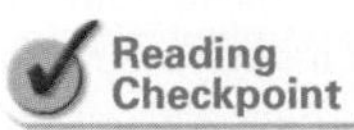

What factors determine the velocity of a stream?

Table 1 World's Largest Rivers Ranked by Discharge

Rank	River	Country	Average Discharge m^3/s
1	Amazon	Brazil	212,400
2	Congo	Zaire	39,650
3	Yangtze	China	21,800
4	Brahmaputra	Bangladesh	19,800
5	Ganges	India	18,700
6	Yenisei	Russia	17,400
7	Mississippi	United States	17,300
8	Orinoco	Venezuela	17,000
9	Lena	Russia	15,500
10	Parana	Argentina	14,900

Build Reading Literacy L1

Refer to **p. 446D** in **Chapter 16,** which provides guidelines for sequencing.

Sequence Have students create a flowchart that follows a stream from its headwaters to the mouth. Students should insert comments along the way about the gradient, slope, and material the stream is carrying.
Verbal

Integrate Math L2

Visualizing Gradient If students have difficulty understanding the expression of gradient as a vertical drop over a certain distance, tell them to visualize a right-angled triangle. The vertical side corresponds to the vertical drop, the base side represents the "certain distance," and the hypotenuse represents the gradient, or slope. With this model in mind, it should be easy for students to recognize that a gradient of 40 m/km is much steeper than one of 10 cm/km. To further illustrate this concept, divide students into groups and have them make three-dimensional models using a table top (or flat surface), a meter stick, and two objects of drastically different lengths (such as a paperclip and a textbook) to represent the different vertical drops.

You can substitute an object that is wider than the meter stick (such as a 2×4 piece of lumber) to further illustrate how larger gradients yield greater velocity by letting a marble roll down the slope(s). The greater the slope, the faster the marble will roll.
Visual, Kinesthetic

Facts and Figures

Many people, if asked what the longest river in the United States is, would probably say the Mississippi. In actuality, it is the Missouri River. The Missouri River has its headwaters in Three Forks, Montana, and flows to near St. Louis, Missouri—a distance of 4342 km. The Mississippi River is only 3757 km long.
The headwater of the Mississippi River is in Lake Itasca, Minnesota, and it flows to the Gulf of Mexico.

However, if one looks at the Mississippi and Missouri rivers together, they form the third longest river in the world. Only the Nile and the Amazon rivers are longer. The actual length of the Mississippi varies by 48 to 80 km each year and has shortened by several hundred kilometers since the 1800s. Most of the shortening is due to efforts to reduce flood damage.

Answer to . . .

Figure 3 *Velocity generally decreases with depth.*

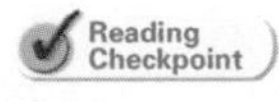

Gradient and discharge determine the velocity of a stream.

Changes from Upstream to Downstream

Use Visuals L1

Figure 5 Have students study the diagram in Figure 5. Ask: **Compare the way the stream looks on the steep gradient with the shape the stream makes on the gentle gradient.** *(The stream is branched and fairly straight on the steep gradient. It is very curvy on the gentle gradient.)*
Visual

Build Reading Literacy L1

Refer to **p. 186D** in **Chapter 7,** which provides the guidelines for this strategy.
Relate Text and Visuals Photocopy and distribute Figure 5 or ask students to sketch the picture on a sheet of paper. Ask them to label a meander, a tributary, and the mouth of the stream. They should also include an arrow indicating the direction in which the headwaters would be located.
Visual

Changes from Upstream to Downstream

One useful way to study a stream is to look at its profile. A profile is a cross-sectional view of a stream from its source, or headwaters, to its mouth—the point downstream where the river empties into another body of water. In Figures 4 and 5, you can see that the most obvious feature of a typical stream profile is a decreasing gradient or slope from its headwaters to its mouth.

While gradient decreases between a stream's headwaters and mouth, discharge increases. The amount of discharge increases because more and more tributaries enter the main channel as it moves downstream. A **tributary** is a stream that empties into another stream. In most humid regions, the groundwater supply adds even more water. As the river moves downstream, its width, depth, and velocity change with the increased volume of water it carries.

The observed increase in the average velocity of the water downstream contradicts what people may think about mountain streams. Most people believe that mountain streams are swift and lowland rivers are slow. Although a mountain stream may look like a violent, gushing flow of water, its average velocity is often less than the average velocity of a river near its mouth.

The difference in velocity is mostly due to the great efficiency of the larger downstream channel. In the headwaters area where the gradient may be steep, water often flows in a small channel over many boulders. The small channel and rough bed increase fiction. This increase in friction scatters the water in all directions and slows its movement. However, downstream the channel is usually smoother so that it offers less resistance to flow. The width and depth of the channel also increase toward the mouth to handle the greater discharge. These factors permit the water to flow more rapidly.

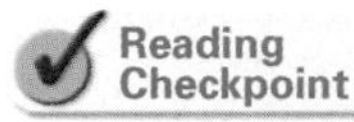

What is a stream profile?

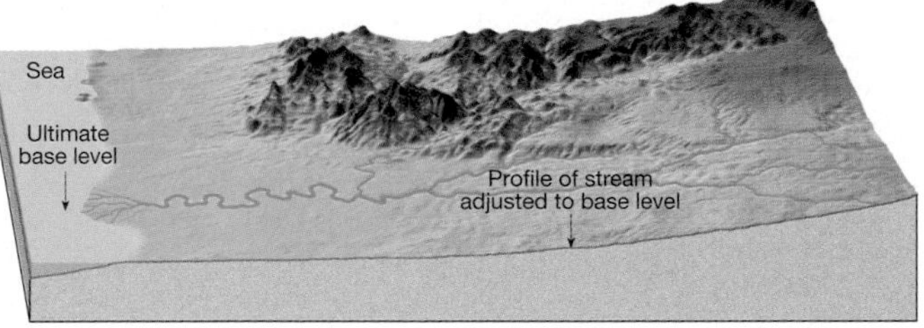

Figure 5 Sea level is the ultimate base level of any stream.

Base Level

Streams can't erode their channels endlessly. There is a lower limit to how deep a stream can erode. **Base level is the lowest point to which a stream can erode its channel.** The base level is the level at which the mouth of a stream enters the ocean, a lake, or another stream.

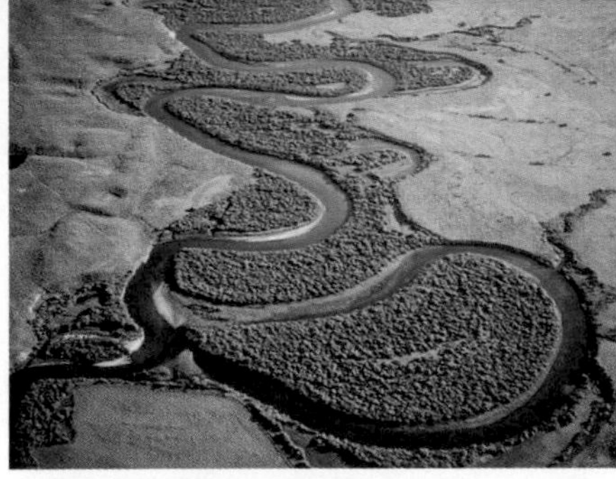

Figure 6 A river in a broad, flat-floored valley near base level often has a channel with many meanders. **Inferring** ***Is the river in this picture close to or high above its base level?***

There are two types of base level—ultimate base level and temporary base level. As Figure 5 shows, sea level is the ultimate base level because it's the lowest level that stream erosion can lower the land. Temporary base levels include lakes, resistant layers of rock, and main streams that act as base level for their tributaries. For example, when a stream enters a lake, its velocity quickly approaches zero. Its ability to erode ceases. The lake prevents the stream from eroding below its level at any point upstream from the lake. However, because the outlet of the lake can cut downward and drain the lake, the lake is only a temporary obstacle to the stream's ability to erode its channel.

A stream in a broad, flat-bottomed valley that is near its base level often develops a course with many bends called **meanders,** as shown in Figure 6. If base level dropped or the land was uplifted the river, which is now considerably above base level, would have excess energy and would downcut its channel. The result could be incised meanders—a winding river in a steep, narrow valley, as shown in Figure 7.

Figure 7 When land is gradually uplifted, a meandering river adjusts to being higher above base level by downcutting. The result can be a landscape with incised meanders, such as these in Utah's Canyonlands National Park.

For: Links on river systems
Visit: www.SciLinks.org
Web Code: cjn-2062

Section 6.1 Assessment

Reviewing Concepts

1. What is the water cycle?
2. How is Earth's water cycle balanced?
3. Where is most of Earth's water located?
4. What part does infiltration play in the water cycle?
5. What factor most influences the power of a stream to erode and transport material?
6. How do gradient and discharge change between a stream's headwaters and its mouth?
7. How might lowering base level affect stream erosion?

Critical Thinking

8. **Relating Cause and Effect** What would happen if evaporation exceeded precipitation over the continents and oceans?
9. **Comparing and Contrasting** How does the development of urban areas along streams and rivers affect discharge during periods of heavy rainfall?

Math Practice

10. A stream that is 27 kilometers long drops 90 meters in elevation from its headwaters to its mouth. What is the stream's gradient?

Section 6.1 Assessment

1. The water cycle is the unending circulation of the water supply on Earth.
2. The average annual precipitation over Earth equals the amount of water that evaporates.
3. oceans
4. Infiltration is the movement of surface water into rock or soil through cracks and pore spaces.
5. The stream's velocity is the most influencing factor.
6. While gradient decreases between a stream's headwaters and mouth, discharge increases.
7. Lowering base level could result in incised meanders.
8. The Earth's surface and oceans would start to dry up.
9. It can increase the magnitude and frequency of floods.

Base Level

Build Science Skills **L2**

Predicting Have students study the photo of a meander on the right in Figure 6. Ask them to predict what may happen to the meander if the river suddenly flooded. Have students write their answer in their notebooks. When students read the section on flooding on p. 168, allow them to return to their original answer to see if they were correct.
Verbal

3 ASSESS

Evaluate Understanding **L2**

To assess students' knowledge of section content, have them write two questions about stream flow. Review the questions for accuracy, and then have students form groups and ask each other their approved questions.

Reteach 

Use Figure 2 to summarize the main concepts about the water cycle. Use Figure 4 to review the characteristics of a stream near its headwaters and its mouth.

Solution
10. 90 meters per 27 kilometers
90 m/27 km = 3.33 m/km

Download a worksheet on river systems for students to complete, and find additional teacher support from NSTA SciLinks.

Answer to . . .

Figure 6 *The flat landscape and meanders indicate it's close to base level.*

 *A stream profile is a cross-section view of a stream from its headwaters to its mouth.*

1 FOCUS

Section Objectives

6.6 **Explain** how streams erode their channels and transport sediments.
6.7 **Explain** how stream deposition occurs.
6.8 **Identify** the two general types of stream valleys.
6.9 **Predict** the causes of floods and **describe** major flood control measures.
6.10 **Explain** the relationship between streams and drainage basins.

Reading Focus

Build Vocabulary L2

Paraphrase Ask students to write the vocabulary terms on a sheet of paper. Instruct students to write a definition, in their own words, for each term as they encounter the term while going through the chapter. After writing their own definition, encourage students to write the term in a complete sentence.

Reading Strategy L2

Answers will vary. Sample answer: What I Expect to Learn—how erosion happens and what features it can form What I Learned—streams erode by lifting loose particles and by abrasion meanders

2 INSTRUCT

Erosion

Build Reading Literacy L1

Refer to **p. 334D** in **Chapter 12**, which provides guidelines for outlining.

Outline Have students outline the section, leaving room for notes. Then have students scan through each heading and find the main idea. Allow students to refer to their outlines when answering the questions in Section 6.2 Assessment. **Logical, Verbal**

6.2 The Work of Streams

Reading Focus

Key Concepts

- How do streams erode their channels and transport sediment?
- How does stream deposition occur?
- What are the two types of stream valleys?
- What causes floods, and what are the major flood control measures?
- What is the relationship between a stream and a drainage basin?

Vocabulary

- bed load
- capacity
- alluvium
- delta
- natural levee
- floodplain
- flood
- drainage basin
- divide

Reading Strategy

Monitoring Your Understanding Preview the Key Concepts, topic headings, vocabulary, and figures in this section. List two things you expect to learn about each. After reading, state what you learned about each item you listed.

What I Expect to Learn	What I Learned

Streams are Earth's most important agents of erosion. They can downcut or erode their channels. They can also transport enormous amounts of sediment. Most of the sediment a stream carries comes from weathering. Weathering produces huge amounts of material that are delivered to the stream by sheet flow, mass movements, and groundwater. Eventually, streams drop much of this material to create many different depositional features.

Erosion

Streams generally erode their channels lifting loose particles by abrasion, grinding, and by dissolving soluble material. When the flow of water is turbulent enough, it can dislodge loose particles from the channel and lift them into the moving water. In this manner, the force of running water rapidly erodes some streambeds and banks. The stronger the current is, the more erosional power it has and the more effectively the water will pick up particles.

Sand and gravel carried in a stream can erode solid rock channels like sandpaper grinds down wood. Moreover, pebbles caught in swirling stream currents can act like cutting tools and bore circular "potholes" into the channel floor.

What are three ways that streams erode their channels?

Sediment Transport

Streams transport sediment in three ways.
1. **in solution (dissolved load)**
2. **in suspension (suspended load)**
3. **scooting or rolling along the bottom (bed load)**

Dissolved Load Most of the dissolved load enters streams through groundwater. Some of this load also enters by dissolving rock along the stream's course. The amount of material the stream carries in solution changes depending on climate and the geologic setting. Usually the dissolved load is expressed as parts of dissolved material per million parts of water (parts per million, or ppm). Some rivers may have a dissolved load of 1000 ppm or more. However, the average figure for the world's rivers is estimated at 115 to 120 ppm. Streams supply almost 4 billion metric tons of dissolved substances to the oceans each year.

Suspended Load Most streams carry the largest part of their load in suspension. The visible cloud of sediment suspended in the water is the most obvious portion of a stream's load. Streams usually carry only sand, silt, and clay this way. However, streams also transport larger particles during a flood because water velocity increases. The total amount of material a stream carries in suspension increases dramatically during floods, as shown in Figure 8.

Figure 8 During this 1997 flood, the suspended load in the muddy Ohio River is clearly visible. The greatest erosion and sediment transport occur during floods. **Applying Concepts** ***What other types of load might account for the muddiness of the river?***

Bed Load **Bed load** is that part of a stream's load of solid material that is made up of sediment too large to be carried in suspension. These larger, coarser particles move along the bottom, or bed, of the stream channel. The suspended and dissolved loads are always moving. But the bed load moves only when the force of the water is great enough to move the larger particles. The grinding action of the bed load is very important in eroding the stream channel.

Competence and Capacity The ability of streams to carry a load is determined by two factors: the stream's competence and its capacity. Competence of a stream measures the largest particles it can transport. A stream's competence increases with its velocity. In fact, the competence of a stream increases four times when the velocity doubles.

The **capacity** of a stream is the maximum load it can carry. Capacity is directly related to a stream's discharge. The greater the volume of water in a stream is, the greater its capacity is for carrying sediment.

Sediment Transport

Integrate Chemistry L2

Solutions and Suspensions Streams transport sediment in solution and in suspension. In chemistry, a solution is a homogeneous mixture of dissolved substances. A suspension is a heterogeneous mixture that separates into layers over time. Ask students to write a paragraph explaining how streams are both solutions and suspensions. *(Streams are composed, in part, of groundwater that contains dissolved substances, and in this way streams are solutions. Streams also transport fine sand, silt, and clay that are not dissolved, but rather suspended in moving water. In this way, streams are suspensions.)*
Verbal

Build Science Skills L2

Using Models Some students will have difficulty comprehending the tiny scale of one part per million. To help build number sense and awareness of how small a part per million is, ask students to imagine they have a budget of one million dollars, and have them think of the cost of their lunch in terms of parts per million. A four-dollar lunch would be equal to 4 ppm. This represents only a tiny fraction of their total budget.
Logical

Customize for English Language Learners

Students who are learning English can benefit from real-life examples that relate to science content. Encourage students to think of actual flooding events that may have occurred in your area or that they have heard about on the news. Have them discuss the type of damage done by the flood and some of the amazing pictures of rescues and houses floating downstream. Encourage students to share their knowledge and examples with the class.

Answer to . . .

Figure 8 *Dissolved load might account for the muddiness of the river.*

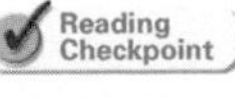 *Streams erode their channels lifting loose particles by abrasion, grinding, and by dissolving soluble material.*

Deposition

Alluvium

L2

Purpose Students learn how deposition occurs in a stream.

Materials mixed sediment (pebbles, sand, silt, and clay-sized particles), clear glass jar with lid, water

Procedure Fill the jar about one-third full with the mixed sediment. Pour water into the jar and tightly close the lid. Shake the jar and allow sediment to settle out.

Expected Outcome Sediment should settle out in layers, with pebbles on the bottom and clay-sized particles at the top. The water sorts the material as the energy from the shaking dissipates, the heavier material drops out sequentially. If this is not illustrated, try using a larger jar, which will allow more room for the materials to settle out.

MAP MASTER™ Skills Activity

Answers
Locating southeast
Locating New Orleans gets farther from the mouth as the delta is built.

MAP MASTER™ Skills Activity

Mississippi Delta Region

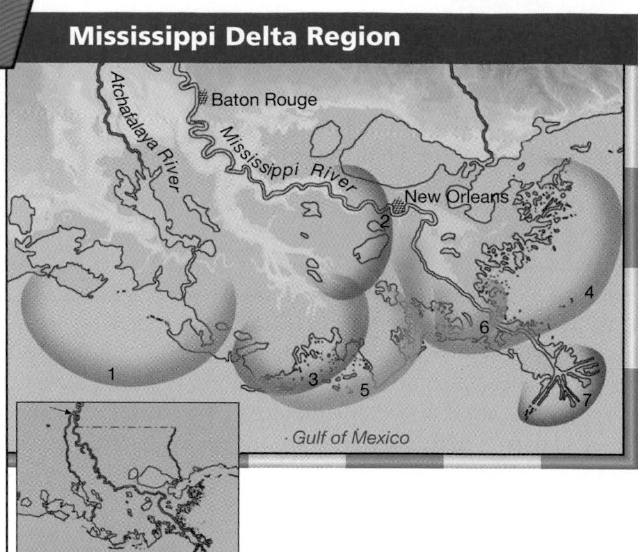

Figure 9
Movement This map shows the growth of the Mississippi River delta over the past 5,000 to 6,000 years. As you can see, the river has built a series of sub-deltas, one after the other. The numbers indicate the order in which they were deposited.
Locating In which overall direction has the Mississippi River built its delta over the past few thousand years?
Locating How has the growth of the delta changed the location of the mouth of the Mississippi River in relation to New Orleans?

Deposition

Whenever a stream slows down, the situation reverses. As a stream's velocity decreases, its competence decreases and sediment begins to drop out, largest particles first. Each particle size has a critical settling velocity. **Deposition occurs as streamflow drops below the critical settling velocity of a certain particle size. The sediment in that category begins to settle out.** Stream transport separates solid particles of various sizes, large to small. This process is called sorting. It explains why particles of similar size are deposited together.

The sorted material deposited by as stream is called **alluvium**. Many different depositional features are made of alluvium. Some occur within stream channels. Some occur on the valley floor next to the channel. And others occur at the mouth of a stream.

Deltas When a stream enters the relatively still waters of an ocean or lake, its velocity drops. As a result, the stream deposits sediment and forms a delta. A **delta** is an accumulation of sediment formed where a stream enters a lake or ocean. As a delta grows outward, the stream's gradient lessens and the water slows down. The channel becomes choked with sediment settling out of the slow-moving water. As a result, the river changes direction as it seeks a shorter route to base level. The main channel often divides into several smaller channels called distributaries as shown in sub-delta 7 in Figure 9. These shifting channels act in the opposite way of tributaries.

Facts and Figures

The city of New Orleans, Louisiana, is built on a delta at the mouth of the Mississippi River. As is expected, the water table in this area is very high due to the fact that the delta is built right into the ocean. This high water table leaves New Orleans with a troubling problem—how do they bury their dead?

Early settlers were forced to bury their dead in shallow graves due to the high water table. If they dug down only a few feet, the grave filled with water and caused the casket to float.

Finally, settlers adopted another method of burial. They built above-ground vaults. Today many of the cemeteries in New Orleans have tombs arranged in a street-like fashion. In fact, the cemeteries are often referred to as "cities of the dead."

Rather than carrying water into the main channel like tributaries, distributaries carry water away. After many shifts of the channel, a delta may grow into a triangular shape, like the Greek letter delta (Δ). However, not all deltas have this idealized shape. Differences in the shapes of shorelines and variations in the strength of waves and currents result in different shapes of deltas.

Natural Levees Some rivers occupy valleys with broad, flat floors. Successive floods over many years can build natural levees along them. A **natural levee** is a landform that parallels some streams. They form when a stream overflows its banks. When it overflows, its velocity rapidly decreases and leaves coarse sediment deposits in strips that border the channel. As the water spreads out over the valley, less sediment is deposited. This uneven distribution of material produces the gentle slope of the natural levee.

Stream Valleys

Narrow Valleys The Yellowstone River, shown in Figure 10, is an excellent example of a narrow valley. **A narrow V-shaped valley shows that the stream's primary work has been downcutting toward base level.** Rapids and waterfalls are the most prominent features of a narrow valley. Both rapids and waterfalls occur where the stream profile drops rapidly. The variations in the erosion of the underlying bedrock cause these rapid drops.

Wide Valleys Once a stream has cut its channel closer to base level, downward erosion becomes less dominant. More of the stream's energy is directed from side to side. The result is a widening of the valley as the river cuts away first at one bank and then at the other.

The side-to-side cutting of a stream eventually produces a flat valley floor, or **floodplain.** A floodplain is appropriately named because during a flood the river overflows its banks and floods the plain.

Streams that flow on floodplains move in meanders. Once a bend in a channel begins to form, it grows larger. Most of the erosion occurs on the outside of the meander—often called the cut bank—where velocity and turbulence are greatest. Much of the debris the stream removes at the cut bank moves downstream where it is deposited as point bars. Point bars form in zones of decreased velocity on the insides of meanders. In this way, meanders move side to side by eroding the outside of bends and depositing on the inside.

Figure 10 The Yellowstone River is an example of a V-shaped valley. The rapids and waterfall show that the river is vigorously downcutting the channel.

Stream Valleys

Integrate Language Arts L2

Prefixes Remind students that a tributary is a stream that empties into another stream (p. 162). The text provides a contextual definition of *distributary*, but tell students that even without this context, they could deduce that a distributary is the opposite of a tributary by knowing the prefix *dis-* means, among other things, "opposite of." Encourage students to make a list of common word parts as they read. Have them look up each one in a dictionary. Doing so will help them with new vocabulary and verbal portions of standardized tests.
Verbal

Build Science Skills L2

Designing Experiments ACTIVITY Divide students into groups and ask them to model a delta using a sloped paint tray (the type used with rollers), sand, and a constant supply of water (such as from a hose or faucet). *(First, dampen the sand. Then distribute the sand evenly in a thin layer over the sloped part of the tray. Supply a gentle but constant flow of water to the top of the slope, and observe the channel the water makes in the sand. Next, observe how some sand is eroded and transported to the mouth of the channel, where it settles into the pool of water at the flat part of the tray.)*
Kinesthetic, Visual

Build Science Skills 

Inferring Draw on the board a cross section of the river valley. *(a broad relatively flat-bottomed shape, similar to a horizontal bracket)* Then have students draw cross sections representing at least three earlier stages in the development of the valley. Tell them the first stage should be of a time when waterfalls and rapids were common along the river's course. *(Cross sections should show a narrowing valley with the earliest cross section showing a V-shaped valley.)*
Logical

Use Visuals L1

Figure 11 Have students study the streams shown in the figures. Ask: **Are other oxbow lakes shown on these diagrams?** *(Yes, the remnants of two other crescent-shaped lakes are shown.)* **What does this show you about the river?** *(The oxbow lakes indicate previous positions of the river.)* **Where might the next oxbow lake form along this section of river?** *(It will most likely form along the course at the lower part of the diagrams, where a neck is forming at the base of a meander that loops to the left. Some students might think the course of the river at the top of the diagrams represents an even narrower neck that is not shown but would pinch off the large meander to the right, forming an oxbow lake.)*
Visual, Logical

Floods and Flood Control

MAP MASTER™ Skills Activity

Answer
Interpreting Photographs The second satellite image shows the rivers during flood stage. You can tell the rivers are at flood stage because the area covered by water is much wider.

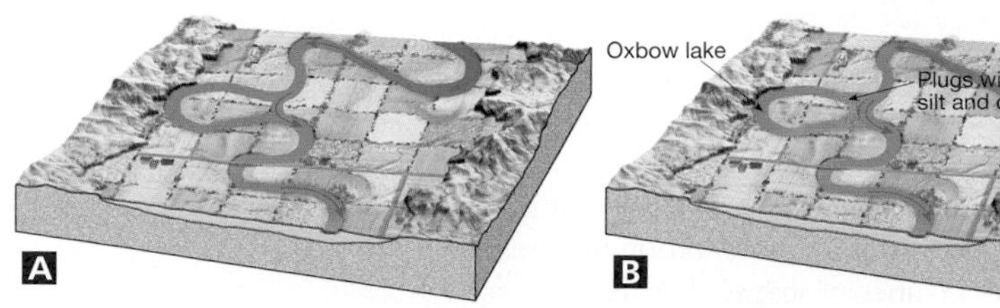

Figure 11 A One meander has overtaken the next, forming a ring of water on the floodplain. **B** After deposits of sediment cut off the ring, an oxbow lake forms.

Erosion is more effective on the downstream side of a meander because of the slope of the channel. The bends gradually travel down the valley. Sometimes the downstream movement of a meander slows when it reaches a more resistant portion of the floodplain. This resistance allows the next meander upstream to overtake it, as shown in Figure 11. Gradually the neck of land between the meanders is narrowed. Eventually the river may erode through the narrow neck of land to the next loop. The new, shorter channel segment is called a cutoff and, because of its shape, the abandoned bend is called an oxbow lake. Such a situation is shown in the bottom portion of Figure 6 on page 163.

Floods and Flood Control

A **flood** occurs when the discharge of a stream becomes so great that it exceeds the capacity of its channel and overflows its banks. Floods are the most common and most destructive of all natural geologic hazards.

Most floods are caused by rapid spring snow melt or storms that bring heavy rains over a large region. Heavy rains caused the devastating floods in the upper Mississippi River Valley during the summer of 1993, as shown in Figure 12.

Unlike far-reaching regional floods, flash floods are more limited in extent. However, flash floods occur with little warning, and they can be deadly as walls of water sweep through river valleys. Several factors

MAP MASTER™ Skills Activity

Mississippi River Flooding

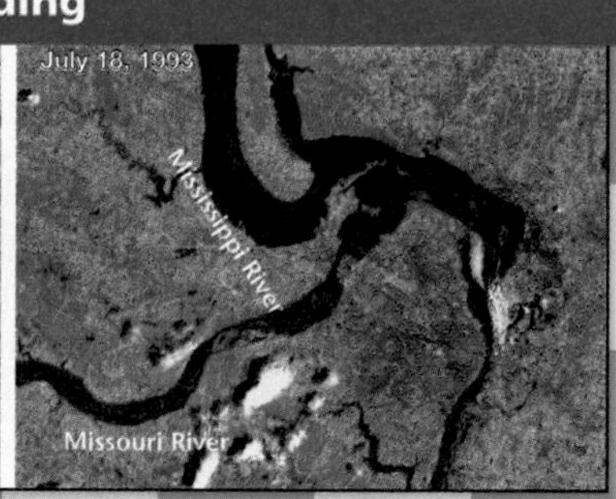

Figure 12
Region These satellite images show the confluence of the Missouri and Mississippi rivers. The first photo shows the rivers during normal flow.
Interpreting Photographs What does the second satellite image show? How do you know?

Facts and Figures

On May 31, 1889, residents of Johnstown, Pennsylvania, heard what sounded like a roar of thunder. Their worst fears were realized. The South Fork Dam, located 22.4 km upstream along the Little Conemaugh River, broke after a night of heavy rain. Twenty million tons of water crashed down the river valley made narrower by the growing community. Over 2200 people died as a result of the flood and the aftermath of fires that followed.

influence flash floods: rainfall intensity and duration, surface conditions, and topography. As you have learned, many urban areas are susceptible to flash floods. Mountainous areas are also susceptible because steep slopes can send runoff into narrow canyons.

Human interference with the stream system can worsen or even cause floods. A prime example is the failure of a dam or an artificial levee. These structures are designed to contain floods of a certain size. If that size is exceeded, water can then spill over or break through a dam or levee and rush downstream causing a disastrous flood.

There are several flood control strategies. **Measures to control flooding include artificial levees, flood control dams, and placing limits on floodplain development.**

Artificial Levees Artificial levees are earthen mounds built on the banks of a river. These levees increase the volume of water a channel can hold. When levees confine a river during periods of high water, the river often deposits material in its channel as the discharge diminishes. This discharge is sediment that would have been dropped on the floodplain. Because the stream cannot deposit material outside of its channel the bottom of the channel is gradually built up. When the channel is built up, it takes less water to overflow the levee. As a result, people may have to raise the height of the levee periodically to protect the floodplain behind it. Moreover, many artificial levees are not built to withstand periods of extreme flooding. For example, there were many levee failures in the Midwest during the summer of 1993 when the upper Mississippi experienced record flooding.

Flood-Control Dam Flood-control dams store floodwater and then let it out slowly. Since the 1920s, thousands of dams have been built on nearly every major river in the United States. Many dams have other non-flood related functions, such as providing water for irrigation and for hydroelectric power generation.

Although dams may reduce flooding and provide other benefits, building dams has consequences. For example, dams trap sediment. Deltas and floodplains downstream can erode because silt no longer replenishes them during floods. Built up sediment behind a dam means the volume of the stored water will gradually diminish. This build-up reduces the effectiveness of the dam for flood control. Large dams also cause ecological damage to river environments.

Limiting Development Today many scientists and engineers advocate sound floodplain management instead of building structures. That often means preserving floodplains in their natural state. Minimizing development on floodplains allows them to absorb floodwaters with little harm to homes and businesses.

Q *Sometimes a major flood is described as a 100-year flood. What does that mean?*

A The phrase "100-year flood" is misleading because it makes people believe that such an event happens only once every 100 years. In truth, a huge flood can happen any year. The phrase "100-year flood" is really a statistical designation. It indicates that there is a 1-in-100 chance that a flood this size will happen during any year. Perhaps a better term would be the "1-in-100 chance flood."

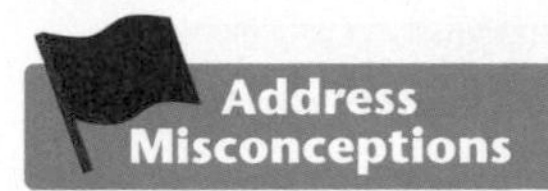

L2

Some students may have heard the term "100-year flood" and assume that this means that floods only occur in the area every 100 years. This is not true and is often misleading. A major flood can occur along a river during any year. What the term does suggest, however, is that statistically speaking there is a 1 in 100 chance that in any given year, a major flood will occur. The chances of flooding along any stream are reevaluated periodically. It has been found that the flooding likelihood changes and that major flooding may occur more frequently than every 100 years. Ask students to predict what sort of human activity may increase the likelihood of flooding. *(Urban development and the building of dams may increase the amount of serious flooding in an area.)*
Logical

Drainage Basins

Use Visuals

L1

Figure 13 Point out the Mississippi River drainage basin. Ask: **Do other drainage basins exist within this one?** *(Yes, every stream, regardless of size, has its own drainage basin. A larger river, such as the Mississippi, will have a drainage basin that includes those of all of its tributaries.)* **Where is the divide that is commonly called the Continental Divide?** *(This is the western portion of the Mississippi River drainage basin divide that runs through the Rocky Mountains.)*

Use Community Resources

Drainage Basins Invite a hydrologist to speak to the class about a drainage basin in your area. Have students trace out the drainage basin of a local stream or river and discuss their findings with the scientist.
Interpersonal

3 ASSESS

Evaluate Understanding

To assess students' knowledge of section content, have them create a visual showing a narrow and a wide stream valley.

Reteach

Have students make a chart summarizing the differences between erosion and deposition.

Student paragraphs should describe accurately researched floods and their causes and effects.

Drainage Basins

Every stream has a drainage basin. **A drainage basin is the land area that contributes water to a stream.** An imaginary line called a **divide** separates the drainage basins of one stream from another. Divides range in scale from a ridge separating two small gullies on a hillside to a continental divide, which splits continents into enormous drainage basins. The Mississippi River has the largest drainage basin in North America. See Figure 13. The river and its tributaries collect water from more than 3.2 million square kilometers of the continent.

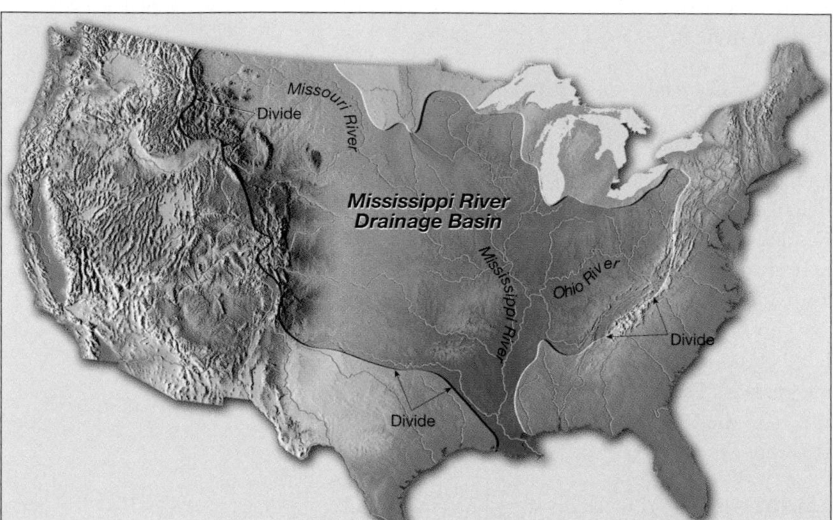

Figure 13 Mississippi River Drainage Basin Divides are the boundaries that separate drainage basins from each other.

Section 6.2 Assessment

Reviewing Concepts

1. How do streams erode their channels?
2. What causes floods?
3. What is the relationship between a stream and a drainage basin?
4. How do streams transport sediments?

Critical Thinking

5. **Analyzing Concepts** How does urban development interfere with the natural function of floodplains?
6. **Summarizing** Explain the formation of one of the landforms that streams create by deposition.

Writing in Science

Descriptive Paragraph Use library sources or the Internet to research the causes of a recent major flood. Write a paragraph that tells the name of the flood, when it happened, where it happened, and the conditions that led to the flood itself.

170 *Chapter 6*

Section 6.2 Assessment

1. Streams erode their channels by lifting loose particles by abrasion, grinding, and by dissolving soluble material.
2. Floods occur when the discharge of a stream exceeds the capacity of the channel. Most floods are caused by rapid spring snow melt and storms.
3. A drainage basin is the land area that contributes water to a stream.
4. Streams transport sediment in solution, in suspension, and by rolling along the bottom.
5. Urban development can decrease the effectiveness of floodplains by replacing water-absorbing vegetation with concrete and asphalt and increasing flooding.
6. Sample answer: Deltas are formed as accumulating sediment is deposited where a stream or river enters a lake or ocean.

6.3 Water Beneath the Surface

Reading Focus

Key Concepts

- Where is groundwater and how does it move?
- How do springs form?
- What are some environmental threats to groundwater supplies?
- How and where do most caverns form?
- What landforms are common in an area of karst topography?

Vocabulary

- zone of saturation
- groundwater
- water table
- porosity
- permeability
- aquifer
- spring
- geyser
- well
- artesian well
- cavern
- travertine
- karst topography
- sinkhole

Reading Strategy

Previewing Copy the table below. Before you read the section, rewrite the green topic headings as how, why, and what questions. As you read, write an answer to each question.

Question	Answer
How does water move underground?	

The ground beneath your feet isn't as solid as you might think. It includes countless tiny pore spaces between grains of soil and sediment. It also contains narrow joints and fractures in bedrock. Together these spaces add up to an immense volume of tiny openings where water collects underground and moves.

Underground water in wells and springs provides water for cities, crops, livestock, and industry. In the United States, it is the drinking water for more than 50 percent of the population. It also provides 40 percent of the irrigation water and more than 25 percent of industry's needs.

Distribution and Movement of Water Underground

When rain falls, some of the water runs off, some evaporates, and the rest soaks into the ground to become subsurface water. The amount of water that ends up underground in an area depends on the steepness of slopes, the nature of surface materials, the intensity of rainfall, and the type and amount of vegetation.

Distribution Some of the water soaks into the ground, but it does not travel far. Molecular attraction holds it in place as a surface film on soil particles. This near-surface zone is called the belt of soil moisture. Roots, voids left by decayed roots, and animal and worm burrows crisscross this zone. These features help rainwater seep into soil.

Section 6.3

1 FOCUS

Section Objectives

6.11 **Describe** the location and movement of groundwater.
6.12 **Describe** the formation of a spring.
6.13 **Explain** environmental threats to water supplies.
6.14 **Describe** the formation of caverns.
6.15 **Describe** landforms in karst areas.

Reading Focus

Build Vocabulary L2

Paraphrase Students may find terms such as *porosity, permeability, aquifer,* and *artesian* unfamiliar. Encourage students to create their own definitions for these terms to help them remember their meaning.

Reading Strategy L2

Sample answers

Question	Answer
How does water move underground?	by twisting and turning through interconnected small openings
How does a spring form?	when the water table intersects the ground surface
What is a well?	a hole bored into the zone of saturation
What are some environmental problems associated with groundwater?	overuse and contamination
What kind of terrain do Karst areas have?	irregular terrain with many sinkholes

2 INSTRUCT

Distribution and Movement of Water Underground

Build Science Skills L2

Inferring After students read p. 171, ask: **On sloping land, which would likely result in more groundwater: a quick thunderstorm or the same volume of water from a longer, gentle rain? Why?** *(the gentle rain because the water would have more time to soak into the ground rather than run off the land)* **Logical**

Teacher Demo

Water Table

L2

Purpose Students visually see the boundary between the zone of saturation and the zone of aeration.

Materials large clear plastic cup; clean, dry sand; water

Procedure Fill the cup about two-thirds full with the clean sand. Slowly pour the water on top of the sand and allow it to filter down to the bottom. Add enough water so that the cup is approximately half full of water.

Expected Outcome Students should be able to clearly see the separation between the sand that contains water and the sand that does not have water in its pore space. Identify this boundary for them as the water table. Students can then infer what would happen to the water table in times of drought or excessive rainfall.

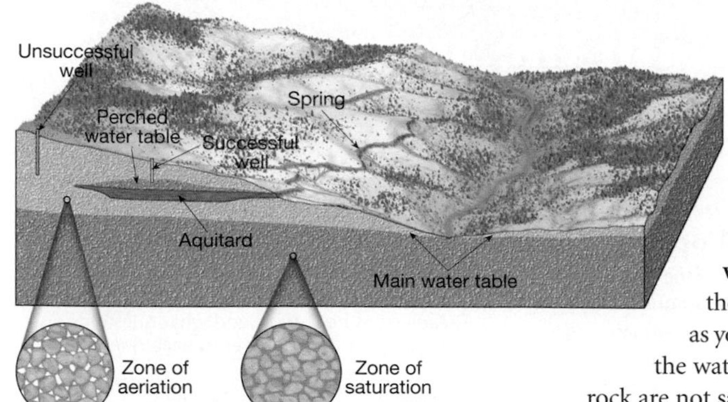

Figure 14 This diagram shows the relative positions of many features associated with subsurface water.
***Applying Concepts** What is the source of the spring in the center of the illustration?*

Much of the water in soil seeps downward until it reaches the zone of saturation. The zone of saturation is the area where water fills all of the open spaces in sediment and rock. Groundwater is the water within this zone. The upper limit of the zone of saturation is the **water table,** as you can see in Figure 14. The area above the water table where the soil, sediment, and rock are not saturated is the zone of aeration. Wells cannot pump water from this zone. The water clings too tightly to the rocks and soil. Only below the water table—where water pressure is great enough to allow water to enter wells—can water be pumped.

Movement The flow and storage of groundwater vary depending on the subsurface material. The amount of groundwater that can be stored depends on porosity. **Porosity** is the percentage of the total volume of rock or sediment that consists of pore spaces. Spaces between sedimentary particles form pore spaces. Joints, faults, and cavities also are formed by the dissolving of soluble rocks such as limestone.

Rock or sediment may be very porous and still block water's movement. The **permeability** of a material is its ability to release a fluid. **Groundwater moves by twisting and turning through interconnected small openings. The groundwater moves more slowly when the pore spaces are smaller.** If the spaces between particles are too small, water cannot move at all. For example, clay has high porosity. But clay is impermeable because its pore spaces are so small that water can't move through them.

Impermeable layers that get in the way or prevent water movement are aquitards. Larger particles, such as sand, have larger pore spaces. Water moves through them easily. Permeable rock layers or sediments that transmit groundwater freely are **aquifers.** Aquifers are important because they are the source of well water.

Figure 15 A spring flows from a valley wall into a stream.

Springs

A spring forms whenever the water table intersects the ground surface. A **spring** is a flow of groundwater that emerges naturally at the ground surface, as shown in Figure 15. Springs form when an aquitard blocks downward movement of groundwater and forces it to move laterally.

Customize for English Language Learners

Have students work in pairs to think of ways that groundwater can be conserved. Examples include shutting off the faucet when brushing your teeth, taking shorter showers, and running the dishwasher only when full. Strengthen discussion skills by having students share their examples with the class.

Hot Springs A hot spring is 6°C to 9°C warmer than the mean annual air temperature where the spring occurs. There are more than 1000 hot springs in the United States

Temperatures in deep mines and oil wells usually rise with an increase in depth at an average of 2°C per 100 meters. So when groundwater circulates at great depths, it becomes heated. If it rises to the surface, the water may emerge as a hot spring. This process heats many hot springs in the eastern United States. However, more than 95 percent of the hot springs in the United States are in the West. The source of heat for most of these hot springs is cooling igneous rock. In some places, hot acidic groundwater mixes with minerals from adjacent rock to form thick, bubbling mineral springs called mudpots.

Geysers A **geyser** is an intermittent hot spring or fountain in which a column of water shoots up with great force at various intervals. Geysers often shoot up columns of water 30 to 60 meters. After the jet of water stops, a column of steam rushes out—usually with a thundering roar. Perhaps the most famous geyser in the world is Old Faithful in Yellowstone National Park. It erupts about once each hour.

Geysers occur where extensive underground chambers exist within hot igneous rocks. Follow the formation of a geyser in Figure 16. As relatively cool groundwater enters the chambers, the surrounding rock heats it. The weight of the overlying water creates great pressure at the bottom of the chamber. This pressure prevents the water from boiling at the normal surface temperature of 100°C. However, the heat makes the water expand, and it forces some of the water out at the surface. This loss of water reduces the pressure in the chamber. The boiling point drops. Some of the water deep within the chamber then turns to steam and makes the geyser erupt. Following the eruption, cool groundwater again seeps into the chamber. Then the cycle begins again.

What is a geyser?

Geyser Eruption Cycle

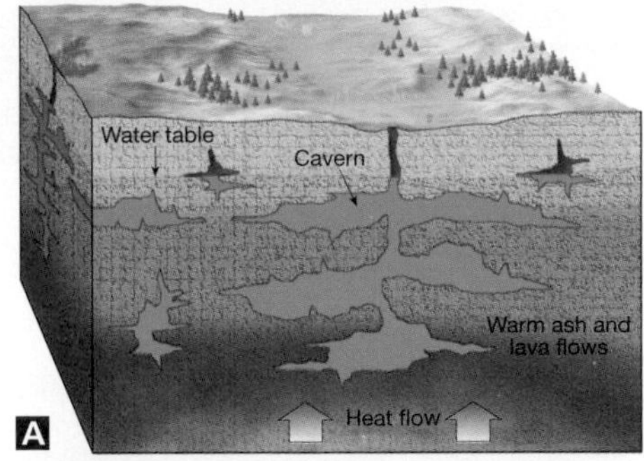

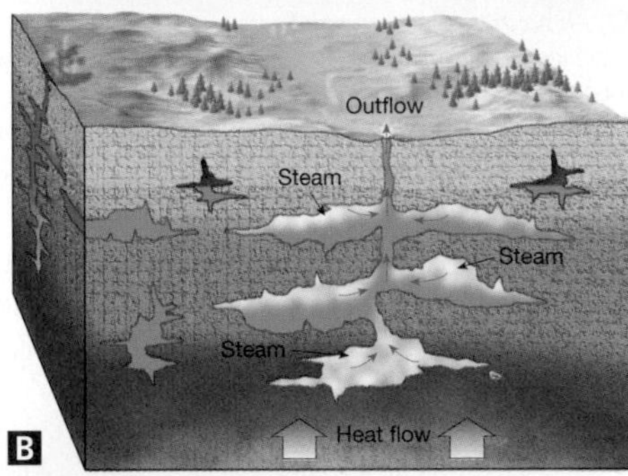

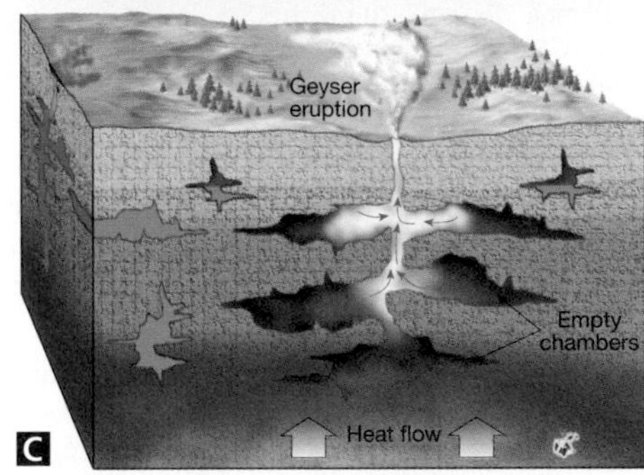

Figure 16 A Groundwater enters underground caverns and fractures in hot igneous rock where it is heated to near its boiling point. **B** Heating causes the water to expand, with some being forced out at the surface. The loss of water reduces the pressure on the remaining water, thus reducing its boiling temperature. Some of the water flashes to steam. **C** The rapidly expanding steam forces the hot water out of the chambers to produce a geyser. The empty chambers fill again, and the cycle starts anew.

Springs

Build Reading Literacy L1

Refer to **p. 502D** in **Chapter 18,** which provides the guidelines for visualizing.

Visualize Have students keep their books closed. Tell them to listen carefully while you read the section on geysers. Ask students to describe how they visualize what is occurring under ground at a geyser. Invite students to work in pairs to discuss how they visualized the process.
Visual

Use Visuals L1

Figure 16 Have the students study the diagram showing the geyser eruption cycle. Ask: **What heats the groundwater in the underground caverns?** *(hot igneous rock)* **What happens to the water when it is heated?** *(The water expands. Some water is forced to the surface; some turns to steam.)* **How is a geyser produced?** *(Expanding steam forces the hot water out of the chambers.)*
Visual, Verbal

Facts and Figures

Yellowstone National Park is home to approximately two thirds of the geysers on Earth. Included in these is one of the most famous geysers, Old Faithful. Despite its name, Old Faithful can be rather unpredictable. It usually erupts every 76 minutes but it can range from 35 minutes to 2 hours. The time between eruptions depends upon the length of the previous eruption.

Old Faithful can shoot up water to 60 m. This is not the largest geyser, however. Steamboat Geyser, also located in Yellowstone, is the largest geyser in the world. It can shoot water 90 m into the air.

Answer to . . .

Figure 14 *The source of the spring is the higher water table within the zone of aeration.*

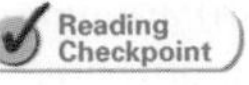

A geyser is an intermittent hot spring or fountain in which a column of water shoots up at various intervals.

Wells

Use Visuals

Figure 17 Ask students to compare the wells in both diagrams in Figure 17. Ask: **As you can see in the diagrams, two of the wells went dry as a result of heavy pumping and one well stayed productive. What rule of well digging can you deduce from this example?** *(When digging a well, be sure to sink it well below the average water table.)* **Visual, Logical**

Use Community Resources L2

Invite a hydrologist or water conservationist to speak to the class on ways to conserve the use of groundwater. The Soil and Water Conservation Society can provide a list of local chapters and resources. To prepare for the presentation, have students research current positions on water conservation. They can develop a list of questions to ask the speaker. **Interpersonal, Verbal**

Download a worksheet on aquifers for students to complete, and find additional teacher support from NSTA SciLinks.

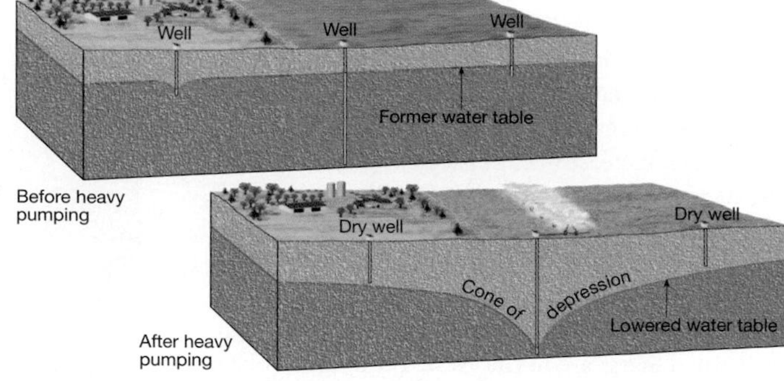

Figure 17 A cone of depression in the water table often forms around a pumping well. If heavy pumping lowers the water table, some wells may be left dry.

Q *I have heard people say that supplies of groundwater can be located using a forked stick. Can this actually be done?*

A What you describe is a practice called "water dowsing." In the classic method, a person holding a forked stick walks back and forth over an area. When water is detected, the bottom of the "Y" is supposed to be attracted downward.

Geologists and engineers are extremely doubtful, to say the least. Case histories and demonstrations may seem convincing, but when dowsing is exposed to scientific scrutiny, it fails. Most "successful" examples of water dowsing occur in places where water would be hard to miss. In a region of adequate rainfall and favorable geology, it is difficult to drill and *not* find water!

For: Links on aquifers
Visit: www.SciLinks.org
Web Code: 2064

Wells

A **well** is a hole bored into the zone of saturation. Irrigation for agriculture is by far the single greatest use of well water in the United States—more than 65 percent of groundwater used annually. Industrial uses of groundwater rank a distant second, followed by the amount used by homes.

The level of the water table may change considerably during a year. The level can drop during the dry season and rise following periods of rain. To ensure a continuous water supply, a well must penetrate far below the water table. The water table around the well drops whenever a substantial amount of water is withdrawn from a well. This effect is called drawdown, and it decreases with an increase in distance from the well. The result of a drawdown is a cone of depression in the water table. This cone of depression is shown in Figure 17. For most small domestic wells, the cone of depression is tiny. However, when wells are used for irrigation or industry, a very wide and steep cone of depression can result.

Water must be pumped out of most wells. However, water rises on its own in some wells, sometimes overflowing the surface. An **artesian well** is any formation in which groundwater rises on its own under pressure. For such a situation to occur, two conditions must exist. First, water must be in an aquifer that is tilted so that one end is exposed at the surface, where it can receive water. Second, there must be aquitards both above and below the aquifer to stop the water from escaping. The pressure created by the weight of the water above forces the water to rise when a well taps the aquifier.

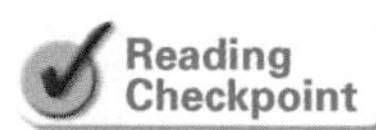

How does an artesian well differ from most wells?

Environmental Problems Associated with Groundwater

As with many valuable natural resources, groundwater is being threatened at an increasing rate. **Overuse and contamination threatens groundwater supplies in some areas.**

Treating Groundwater as a Nonrenewable Resource

Groundwater seems like an endlessly renewable resource. However, supplies are finite. In some regions, the amount of water available to recharge an aquifer is much less than the amount being withdrawn.

The High Plains provides one example of severe groundwater depletion. In some parts of the region, intense irrigation has gone on for a long time. Even if pumping were to stop now, it could take thousands of years for the groundwater to be fully replenished.

The ground may sink when water is pumped from wells faster than natural processes can replace it. As water is withdrawn, the ground subsides because the weight of the overburden packs relatively loose sediment grains more tightly together.

This type of subsidence is extreme in the San Joaquin Valley of California, as shown in Figure 18. Land subsidence due to groundwater withdrawal for irrigation began there in the mid-1920s. It exceeded eight meters by 1970. During a drought in 1976 and 1977, heavy groundwater pumping led the ground to sink even more. Land subsidence affected more than 13,400 square kilometers of irrigable land—one half the entire valley.

Groundwater Contamination The pollution of groundwater is a serious matter, particularly in areas where aquifers provide much of the water supply. Common sources of groundwater pollution are sewage from septic tanks, farm wastes, and inadequate or broken sewers.

If sewage water that is contaminated with bacteria enters the groundwater system, it may become purified through natural processes. The harmful bacteria can be mechanically filtered by the sediment through which the water passes, destroyed by chemical oxidation, and/or assimilated by other organisms. For purification to occur, however, the aquifer must be of the correct composition.

For example, extremely permeable aquifers have such large openings that contaminated groundwater may travel long distances without being cleansed. In this case, the water flows too quickly and is not in contact with the surrounding material long enough for purification to occur. This is the problem at Well 1 in Figure 19A.

What are some common sources of groundwater pollution?

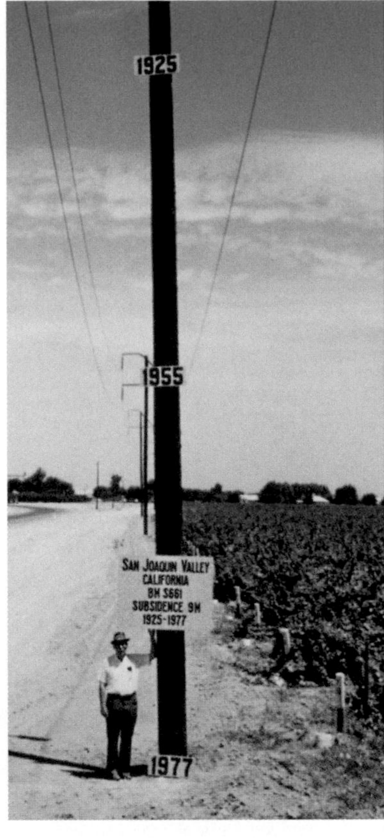

Figure 18 The marks on the utility pole indicate the level of the surrounding land in years past. Between 1925 and 1975 this part of the San Joaquin Valley sank almost 9 meters because of the withdrawal of groundwater and the resulting compaction of sediments.

Environmental Problems Associated with Groundwater

Integrate Health **L2**

Groundwater Contamination Arsenic contamination of groundwater is a common problem. Arsenic is a known carcinogen. It was once an ingredient in pesticides used on apple orchards. Many communities now are testing old apple orchards and finding that there are significant amounts of arsenic in their soil, which seeps into the groundwater. The Environmental Protection Agency (EPA) recently revised the standard for safe levels of arsenic in drinking water. Prior to January 22, 2001, the acceptable level was 50 parts per billion. Now public water systems must comply with the new acceptable level of 10 parts per billion by January 23, 2006. This will serve as a further level of protection of our groundwater resources. Ask students to research other types of groundwater contamination and steps that have been taken to prevent or eliminate it. Pairs of students can present short reports to the class.
Interpersonal, Verbal

Facts and Figures

Drilling a well can be a daunting task. Not only do you have to locate the source of water on your property and determine how much water is available, you have to estimate the amount of water that you, your family, and possibly your business will need. The following are estimates that can be used to determine the peak demand that will be placed on a well.

For a single family home, figure on 190 to 285 L of water a day per person. Maintenance of an average lawn and garden requires 190 to 3800 L per day. Farmers are faced with a more challenging estimate. For example, dairy cattle require 133 L per day per animal for drinking water. A goat requires 7.6 L per day; each pig requires 15.2 L, a horse 45.6 L per day. A flock of 100 chickens requires 19 to 38 L of drinking water per day and a flock of 100 turkeys needs 38 to 68 L per day.

Answer to . . .

In an artesian well, water rises on its own, instead of being pumped.

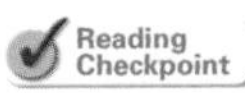

Common sources of groundwater pollution are sewage from septic tanks, farm wastes, and inadequate or broken sewers.

Build Science Skills L2

Applying Concepts After reading the section on Groundwater Contamination, present the following problem to the class. **Imagine you are an environmental scientist and have been called in to solve a groundwater contamination problem. Some people have noticed that their well water has a funny smell and taste and they think that the contamination is coming from a farmer who lives upstream. The farmer insists that he is not contaminating the water supply and suggests instead that a large chemical factory farther upstream is to blame. How can you determine where the contamination is originating?** *(Answers will vary but students may recognize a few places to start. For example, they should suggest determining the type of contamination. Is the water supply being contaminated by fertilizer, for example? Identifying the contaminant will help in pinpointing the source. They also may recognize that by testing the groundwater upstream and downstream from the farmer, they may be able to identify if the contamination is occurring upstream or downstream of the farm.)* **Logical, Intrapersonal**

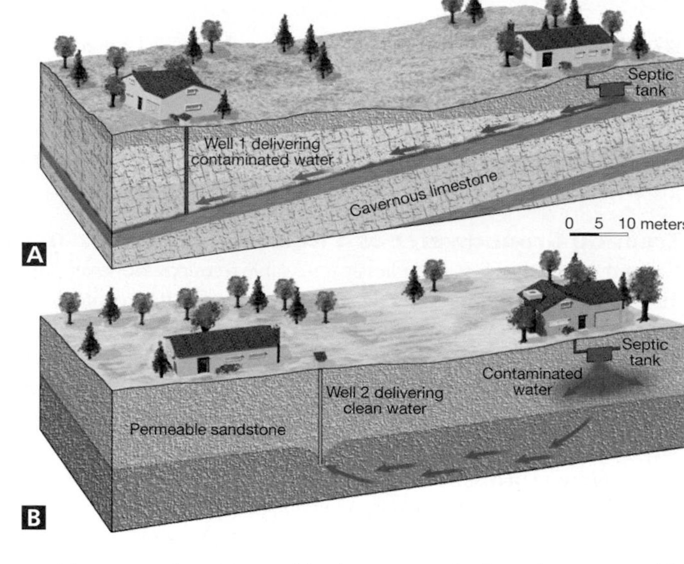

Figure 19 **A** Although the contaminated water has traveled more than 100 meters before reaching Well 1, the water moves too quickly through the cavernous limestone to be purified. **B** As the discharge from the septic tank percolates through the permeable sandstone, it is purified in a short distance.

However, when the aquifer is composed of sand or permeable sandstone, the water can sometimes be purified after traveling only a few dozen meters through it. The openings between sand grains are large enough to permit water movement, yet the movement of the water is slow enough to allow enough time for its purification. This is the case at Well 2 in Figure 19B.

Other sources and types of contamination also threaten supplies, as you can see in Figures 20 and 21. These include fertilizers that are spread across the land, pesticides, and highway salt. In addition, chemicals and industrial materials—some hazardous—may leak from pipelines, storage tanks, landfills, and holding ponds. As rainwater oozes through the refuse, it may dissolve contaminants. If this material reaches the water table, it will mix with and contaminate groundwater. In coastal areas, heavy use can deplete aquifers, causing underground saltwater to enter wells.

Once the source of the problem has been identified and eliminated, the most common practice is to abandon the water supply. Abandoning the water supply allows the pollutants to flush out gradually. It's the least costly and easiest solution, but the aquifer must stay unused for years. To speed up this process, engineers sometimes pump out and treat polluted water. The aquifer then recharges naturally, or the treated water is pumped back in. This process can be risky, because there is no way to be sure that treatment has removed all the pollution. Prevention remains the most effective solution to groundwater contamination.

Some substances in groundwater are natural. Ions of substances (from adjacent rock) such as calcium and iron make some water "hard." Hard water forms scum with soap instead of suds. It can also deposit residue that clogs pipes. But hard water is generally not a health risk.

Figure 20 Agricultural chemicals sprayed on farm fields can seep into soil and contaminate underground water supplies.

Figure 21 If landfills leak, harmful waste buried in them can escape into groundwater.

Facts and Figures

The Environmental Protection Agency (EPA) recognizes that groundwater needs to be treated as a nonrenewable resource. They have strict regulations on public water supplies but have no control over private wells and water sources. They do, however, have some suggestions for homeowners with private wells to ensure that this vital resource remains protected. They advise homeowners to

- periodically inspect exposed portions of the well for settling or damaged well casings.
- create a slope in the area around the well to drain runoff away from the well.
- have the well tested each year for bacteria and nitrates and other possible contaminants.
- avoid using pesticides, herbicides, fuels, and other contaminants near the well.
- inspect septic systems regularly.
- refrain from disposing of hazardous material in septic systems or abandoned wells.

Caverns

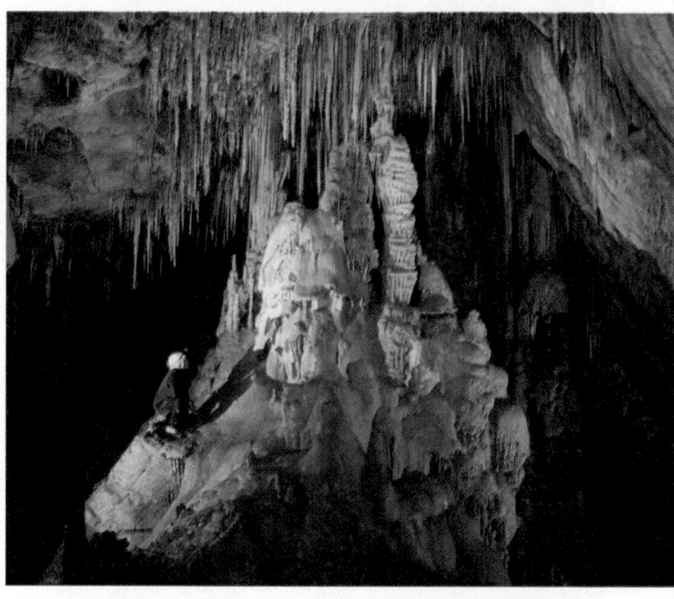

Figure 22 The dissolving action of groundwater creates caverns. These dripstone features are in Three Fingers Cave in New Mexico.

The most spectacular results of groundwater's ability to erode rock are limestone caverns. Soluble rocks, especially limestone, underlie millions of square kilometers of Earth's surface. Limestone is nearly insoluble in pure water. But water containing small quantities of carbonic acid dissolves it easily. Most natural water contains the weak acid because rainwater dissolves carbon dioxide from the air and decaying plants. Therefore, when groundwater comes in contact with limestone, the carbonic acid reacts with calcite in the rocks. Calcium bicarbonate forms. As groundwater carries away calcium carbonate in solution, it slowly erodes rock. A **cavern** is a naturally formed underground chamber, such as the one you see in Figure 22. There are thousands of caverns in the United States. Most are fairly small, but some have spectacular dimensions. Carlsbad Caverns in southeastern New Mexico is a famous example. One chamber has an area equivalent to 14 football fields, and it is high enough to fit the U.S. Capitol building inside it.

Erosion forms most caverns at or below the water table in the zone of saturation. Here, acidic groundwater follows lines of weakness in the rock, such as joints and bedding planes. As time passes, the dissolving process slowly creates cavities and enlarges them into caverns. Material the groundwater dissolves eventually flows into streams and then the ocean.

The features that produce the greatest curiosity for most cavern visitors are depositional stone formations. These formations give some caverns a wonderland appearance. They form from seemingly endless dripping of water over great spans of time. The calcium carbonate that is left behind produces the limestone we call **travertine.** These cave deposits are commonly called dripstone.

Although the formation of caverns takes place in the zone of saturation, the deposition of dripstone features is not possible until the caverns are above the water table in the zone of aeration. The formation of caverns in the zone of aeration commonly occurs as nearby streams cut their valleys deeper. As the elevation of the stream drops, the water table also lowers, leaving the caverns high and largely dry.

Caverns

Use Visuals L1

Figure 22 Challenge students to imagine themselves as the spelunker(cave explorer) in the photograph. Ask: **What temperature and overall climate would be in the Three Fingers Cave?** *(Climate would be cool and very damp.)*
Visual

Build Reading Literacy L2

Refer to **p. 474D** in **Chapter 17,** which provides guidelines for the monitor your understanding strategy.

Monitor Your Understanding Have students read the section on caverns. When students reach the end of that section, have them write the main ideas of that section. Have students ask themselves, "Did I have any trouble reading this section? If so, why?" Invite students to come up with their own strategies to improve their understanding of cavern formation and features. Have students use their own strategies as they continue reading.
Intrapersonal, Verbal

Customize for Inclusion Students

Hearing Impaired Reinforce the lesson's content by providing a variety of visual examples. Be sure to spend time on all the visual examples provided in the text. In addition, you may wish to provide a visual display of how limestone can be dissolved in a dilute acid. Place several drops of hydrochloric acid on a sample of limestone. Students will observe a bubbling action. Challenge students to imagine how this action could, over a long period of time, create an underground cavern.

Karst Topography

Build Science Skills L2

Inferring Describe for students the characteristics of "hard" water. Water containing a lot of dissolved minerals can impact the performance of soap and leave a residue behind on fixtures and shower curtains. Ask students if they think the water may be hard in a karst region, and if so, what mineral is most likely dissolved in the groundwater? *(The water is hard in a karst region due to the calcium dissolved in the water from the erosion of the limestone under ground.)*
Logical

Integrate Chemistry 

Acid Rain on Karst Topography
Explain to students that chemical and power plants release sulfur dioxide and nitrogen monoxide into the air. These chemicals combine with precipitation to become acid rain. Acid rain harms plants, animals, and soil. It also affects karst topography because limestone is vulnerable to the effects of acid. Have students research the effects of acid rain on karst topography. Ask each student to prepare a presentation that includes a graph or chart of data collected.
Verbal, Logical

Download a worksheet on sinkholes for students to complete, and find additional teacher support from NSTA SciLinks.

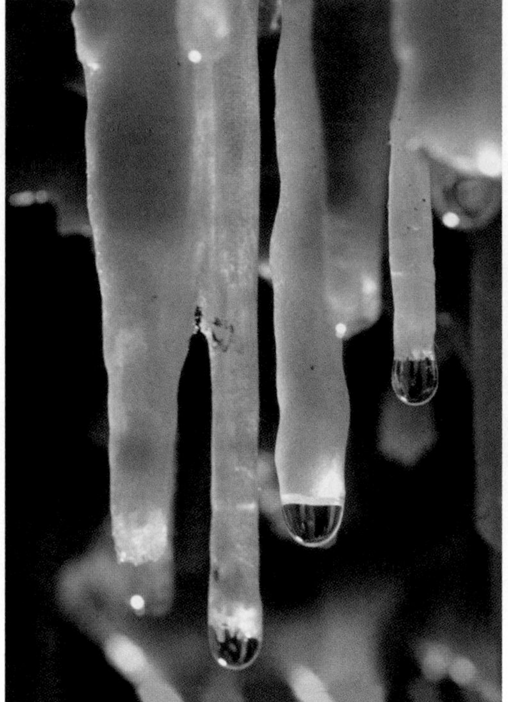

Figure 23 Soda straw stalactites in Great Basin National Park's Lehman Caves.
Relating Cause and Effect *What part do these drops of water play in the formation of the stalactites?*

Dripstone Features Perhaps the most familiar dripstone features are stalactites. Stalactites are icicle-like stone pendants that hang from the ceiling of a cavern. They form when water seeps through cracks in the cavern ceiling. When water reaches air in the cave, some of the dissolved carbon dioxide escapes from the drop and calcite begins to separate out. Deposition occurs as a ring around the edge of the water drops. As drops fall, each one leaves a tiny trace of calcite behind. This calcite creates a hollow limestone tube called a soda straw, as shown in Figure 23. Often the hollow tube becomes plugged or its supply of water increases. When a stalactite becomes plugged or the water supply increases, the water flows and deposits along the outside of the tube. As deposition continues, the stalactite takes on the more common conical shape.

Stalagmites are formations that develop on the floor of a cavern and reach up toward the ceiling. The water supplying the calcite for stalagmite growth falls from the ceiling and splatters over the surface of the cavern floor. As a result, stalagmites do not have a central tube. They are usually more massive and more rounded on their upper ends than stalactites. Given enough time, a downward-growing stalactite and an upward-growing stalagmite may join to form a column.

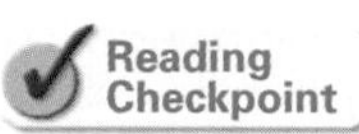

What is a dripstone deposit?

Karst Topography

Many areas of the world have landscapes that have been shaped largely by the dissolving power of groundwater. These areas are said to have **karst topography.** This term comes from the *Krs* region of Slovenia, where such topography is strikingly developed. In the United States, karst landscapes occur in many areas that are underlain by limestone. These areas include parts of Kentucky, Tennessee, Alabama, southern Indiana, and central northern Florida.

Karst areas typically have irregular terrain, with many depressions called sinkholes. A **sinkhole** is a depression produced in a region where groundwater has removed soluble rock. In the limestone areas of Florida, Kentucky, and southern Indiana, there are tens of thousands of these depressions. They vary in depth from just a meter or two to more than 50 meters.

For: Links on sinkholes
Visit: www.SciLinks.org
Web Code: cjn-2065

Sinkholes commonly form in one of two ways. Some develop gradually over many years without any physical disturbance to the rock. In these situations, downward-seeping rainwater containing carbon dioxide dissolves limestone below the soil. These depressions are fairly shallow and have gentle slopes. Sinkholes can also form suddenly when the roof of a cavern collapses. The depressions created in this way are steep-sided and deep. When they form in populated areas, they may be a serious geologic hazard, as shown in Figure 24.

In addition to a surface pockmarked by sinkholes, karst regions usually show a striking lack of surface drainage (streams). Following a rainfall, runoff is quickly funneled below ground through sinkholes. It then flows through caverns until it finally reaches the water table. Where streams do exist at the surface, their paths are usually short. The names of such streams often give a clue to their fate. In the Mammoth Cave area of Kentucky, for example, there is Sinking Creek, Little Sinking Creek, and Sinking Branch. Some sinkholes become plugged with clay and debris, creating small lakes or ponds.

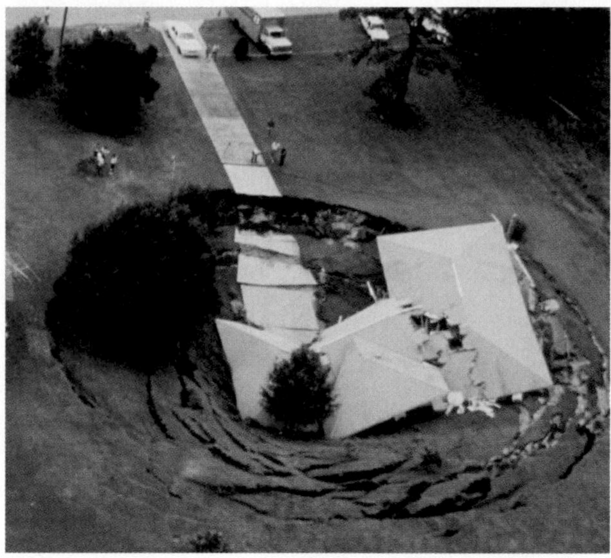

Figure 24 This small sinkhole formed suddenly in 1991 when the roof of a cavern collapsed. It destroyed this home in Frostproof, Florida.

Section 6.3 Assessment

Reviewing Concepts

1. Where is groundwater located under the surface?
2. How does water move underground?
3. What are some environmental threats to groundwater supplies?
4. How and where do most caverns form?
5. What landforms are common in an area of karst topography?

Critical Thinking

6. **Comparing and Contrasting** What is the difference between stalactites and stalagmites?
7. **Analyzing Concepts** How is groundwater a nonrenewable resource?
8. **Analyzing Concepts** Explain why caverns form in the zone of saturation, while dripstone features form in the zone of aeration?

Writing in Science

Relating Cause and Effect Write a paragraph that connects these three concepts: land subsidence, extensive farming in dry regions, and water conservation.

3 ASSESS

Evaluate Understanding

L2

To assess students' knowledge of section content, have them create a visual of the inside of a cavern. Encourage students to include as many features as possible.

Reteach

L1

Use Figure 24 to discuss the hazards of living in a region with karst topography.

Writing in Science

Student paragraphs should accurately describe cause-and-effect relationships among land subsidence, extensive farming in dry regions, and water conservation.

Section 6.3 Assessment

1. in the zone of saturation
2. Groundwater moves by twisting and turning through interconnected small openings.
3. overuse and contamination
4. Most caverns form by erosion at or below the water table in the zone of saturation.
5. depressions and sinkholes
6. Stalactites are dripstone features that cling to the ceiling of a cavern. Stalagmites are dripstone features that build upward from a cavern floor.
7. Groundwater is becoming a nonrenewable resource in some areas due to overuse and contamination.
8. The deposition of dripstone is not possible until the caverns are above the water table.

Answer to . . .

Figure 23 *The water in each drop that drips down a stalactite contains dissolved minerals. Each water drop that evaporates leaves a small deposit at the end of the stalactite.*

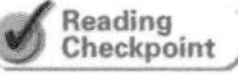

Reading Checkpoint *A dripstone deposit is a rock deposit that forms as water containing dissolved minerals drips from cavern walls, leaving the minerals behind when the water evaporates.*

people and the ENVIRONMENT

The Ogallala Aquifer—How Long Will the Water Last? L2

Background

- Dry-land farming is a system of producing crops without irrigation in semi-arid regions. These regions often receive less than 50 cm of rainfall per year. Dry-land farmers usually rebuild soil moisture by allowing the land to be unplanted or mulched in alternate years.
- In May, 2003, the United States government provided $53 million to aid Western farmers and ranchers impacted by drought. About half of this funding went to farmers and ranchers in the High Plains. The funds helped implement technologies and practices to conserve water to relieve the long-term impact of drought on the region.

Teaching Tips

- Ask students to research dry-land farming and other methods that reduce agricultural dependence upon irrigation. Have them create a presentation with visuals that would educate people about these methods and the importance of finding a solution to the decline in the High Plains water table.
- Have students find out about regions in the world where there are large supplies of groundwater. Ask students to address these questions: What is the source of the groundwater? How is groundwater used by people in the region? How are they accessing it? Is the water table in danger of becoming low? If so, what are plans to help remedy the situation?

Visual

people and the ENVIRONMENT

The Ogallala Aquifer—How Long Will the Water Last?

The High Plains extend from the western Dakotas south to Texas. Despite being a land of little rain, this is one of the most important agricultural regions in the United States. The reason is a vast supply of groundwater that makes irrigation possible throughout most of the region. The source of most of this water is the Ogallala Formation, the largest aquifer in the United States.

Geologically, the Ogallala Formation consists of a number of sandy and gravelly rock layers. The sediments came from the erosion of the Rocky Mountains and were carried eastward by sluggish streams. Erosion has removed much of the formation from eastern Colorado, severing the Ogallala's connection to the Rockies.

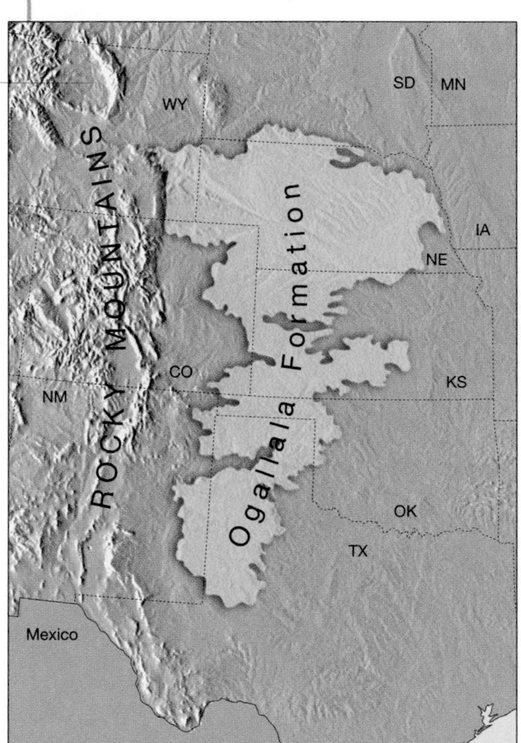

The Ogallala Formation, the largest aquifer in the United States, averages 60 meters thick. However, in some places it is as thick as 180 meters thick. Groundwater in the aquifer originally traveled downslope from the Rocky Mountains and from surface precipitation that soaked into the ground over thousands of years. Because of its high porosity and great size, the Ogallala Formation accumulated a large amount of groundwater—enough to fill Lake Huron! Today, with the connection between the aquifer and the Rockies gone (erosion has removed much of the formation in eastern Colorado), all of the Ogallala's recharge must come from the meager rainfall of the Plains.

In the late 1800s, people first started to use the Ogallala for irrigation. However, the capacity of pumps available at the time limited water withdrawal. Then in the 1920s, large-capacity irrigation pumps were invented. High Plains' farmers began tapping the Ogallala for irrigation. Today, there are nearly 170,000 wells irrigating more than 65,000 square kilometers of land.

The increase in irrigation has caused a drastic drop in the Ogallala's water table, especially in the High Plains. Declines in the water table of 3 to 15 meters are common. In places, however, the water table is now 60 meters below its original level.

Although the decline in the water table has slowed in parts of the southern High Plains, substantial pumping continues—often in excess of recharge. The future of irrigated farming here is clearly in jeopardy.

The southern High Plains will return sooner or later to dry-land farming. The transition will come sooner and with fewer ecological and economic crises if the agricultural industry is weaned gradually from its dependence on groundwater irrigation. If nothing is done until all the accessible water in the Ogallala aquifer has been removed, the transition will be ecologically dangerous and economically dreadful.*

*National Research Council. *Solid-Earth Sciences and Society.* Washington, DC: National Academy Press, 1993, p. 148.

Figure 25 The Ogallala Formation underlies about 450,000 square kilometers of the High Plains, making it the largest aquifer in the United States.

Exploration Lab

Investigating the Permeability of Soils

The permeability of soils affects the way groundwater moves—or if it moves at all. Some soils are highly permeable, while others are not. In this lab, you will determine the permeability of various soils, and draw conclusions about their effect on the movement of water underground.

Problem How does the permeability of soil affect its ability to move water?

Materials

- 100 mL graduated cylinder
- beaker
- small funnel
- 3 pieces of cotton
- samples of coarse sand, fine sand, and soil
- clock or watch with a second hand

Skills Observing, Measuring, Comparing and Contrasting, Analyzing Data, Interpreting Data

Procedure 

1. Place a small, clean piece of cotton in the neck of the funnel. Fill the funnel above the cotton with coarse sand. Fill the funnel about two-thirds of the way.
2. **Measure** Pour water into the graduated cylinder until it reaches the 50 mL mark.
3. With the bottom of the funnel over the beaker, pour the water from the graduated cylinder slowly into the sand in the funnel.
4. **Measure** In a data table like the one shown, keep track of the time from the second you start to pour the water into the funnel. Measure the amount of time that it takes the water to drain through the funnel filled with coarse sand.
5. Record the time it takes for the water to drain through the sand in the data table.
6. Empty and clean the measuring cylinder, funnel, and beaker.
7. Repeat Steps 1 through 7, first using fine sand, and then using soil.

Analyze and Conclude

1. **Comparing and Contrasting** Of the three materials you tested, which has the greatest permeability? Which had the least permeability?
2. **Analyzing Data** Why were different amounts of water recovered in the beaker for each material tested?
3. **Interpreting Data** What effect would the differences you observed in this lab have on the movement of groundwater through different soils?

Data Table

	Time Needed for Water to Drain Through Funnel	Water Collected in Beaker (mL)
Coarse Sand		
Fine Sand		
Soil		

Exploration Lab

Investigating the Permeability of Soils L2

Objective In this activity, students will explain how the permeability of soil affects its ability to move water.

Skills Focus Observing, Measuring, Comparing and Contrasting, Analyzing Data, Interpreting Data

 **Prep Time** 10 minutes

Advance Prep If time is limited, set up the apparatus for the students ahead of time.

Class Time 40 minutes

Teaching Tip If the time needed for the water to seep through the cotton proves to be too long, line the funnel with a coffee filter instead.

Expected Outcome Students should find that it takes the longest time for the water to filter through the fine sand. The length of time for the water to filter through the soil depends on the composition of the soil, but it is most likely that the quickest filtering time is through the coarse sand.

Analyze and Conclude

1. The coarse sand has the greatest permeability. The fine sand has the least permeability.
2. Some of the water was left behind in the sample. For example, the soil sample trapped water in the organic material and finer grained sediment.
3. In general, the soils with coarser grain would move water faster.
Logical

Study Guide

Study Tip

Organize New Information
This chapter contains many new words and much new information. Tell students to create outlines, charts, flashcards, timelines, and concept maps to help them visualize relationships. Have students create a vocabulary list with definitions for all of the vocabulary terms in their own words.

CHAPTER 6

Study Guide

6.1 Running Water

Key Concepts

- Water constantly moves among the oceans, the atmosphere, the solid Earth, and the biosphere. This unending circulation of Earth's water supply is the water cycle
- Balance in the water cycle means the average annual precipitation over Earth equals the amount of water that evaporates.
- The ability of a stream to erode and transport materials depends largely on its velocity.
- While gradient decreases between a stream's headwaters and mouth, discharge increases.
- Base level is the lowest point to which a stream can erode its channel.

Vocabulary

water cycle, *p. 158;* infiltration, *p. 159;* transpiration, *p. 159;* gradient, *p. 160;* stream channel, *p. 161;* discharge, *p. 161;* tributary, *p. 162;* meander, *p. 163*

6.2 The Work of Streams

Key Concepts

- Streams generally erode their channels by dissolving soluble material, by lifting loose particles, and by abrasion, or grinding.
- Streams transport their load of sediment in three ways: (1) in solution (dissolved load), (2) in suspension (suspended load), and (3) scooting or rolling along the bottom (bed load).
- Deposition occurs as streamflow drops below the critical settling velocity of a certain particle size.
- There are two general types of stream valleys: narrow V-shaped valleys and wide valleys with flat floors.
- Most floods are caused by rapid spring snow melt and storms that bring heavy rains over a large region.
- Measures to control flooding include the construction of artificial levees, building flood control dams, and placing limits on floodplain development.
- A drainage basin is the land area that contributes water to a stream.

Vocabulary

bed load, *p. 165;* capacity, *p. 165;* delta, *p. 166;* natural levee, *p. 167;* floodplain, *p. 167;* flood, *p. 168;* drainage basin, *p. 170;* divide, *p. 170*

6.3 Water Beneath the Surface

Key Concepts

- Much of the water in soil seeps downward until it reaches the zone of saturation. The zone of saturation is the area where water fills all of the open spaces in sediment and rock. Groundwater is the water within this zone.
- Groundwater moves by twisting and turning through interconnected small openings. The groundwater moves more slowly when the pore spaces are smaller.
- A spring forms whenever the water table intersects the ground surface.
- Overuse and contamination threatens groundwater supplies in some areas.
- Erosion forms most caverns at or below the water table in the zone of saturation.
- Karst areas typically have irregular terrain, with many depressions called sinkholes.

Vocabulary

zone of saturation, *p. 172;* groundwater, *p. 172;* water table, *p. 172;* porosity, *p. 172;* permeability, *p. 172;* aquifer, *p. 172;* spring, *p. 172;* geyser; *p. 173;* well, *p. 174;* artesian well; *p. 174;* cavern, *p. 177;* travertine, *p. 177;* karst topography, *p. 178;* sinkhole, *p. 178*

Chapter Assessment Resources

Print
Chapter Test, Chapter 6
Test Prep Resources, Chapter 6

Technology
Computer Test Bank, Chapter 6 Test
Online Text, Chapter 6
Go Online, PHSchool.com, Chapter 6

CHAPTER 6

NY Regents Content Item

Assessment

Interactive textbook with assessment at PHSchool.com 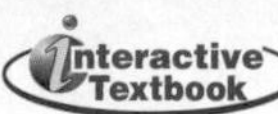

Reviewing Content

Choose the number that best answers the question or completes the statement.

1 The energy for the water cycle comes from the NY
(1) ocean
(2) sun
(3) atmosphere
(4) soil

2 How does water move from plants to the atmosphere? NY
(1) infiltration
(2) precipitation
(3) transpiration
(4) condensation

3 By what process do rivers move material? NY
(1) weathering
(2) infiltration
(3) mass wasting
(4) erosion

4 A river's discharge is generally greatest NY
(1) at its source
(2) on its floodplain
(3) at its mouth
(4) at the sides of its channel

5 When do rivers deposit sediment? NY
(1) when their velocity decreases
(2) when they are in the midst of flooding
(3) when their velocity increases
(4) when they plunge over waterfalls

6 A stream's drainage basin is water that NY
(1) flows into it
(2) infiltrates from it into the ground
(3) is removed from it for drinking water
(4) is within 100 kilometers of its channel

7 What is a stream's bed load? NY
(1) material that moves along its bottom
(2) material that is carried in solution
(3) material that floats on its surface
(4) material that is carried in suspension

8 Where is groundwater located? NY
(1) zone of aeration
(2) zone of reduction
(3) zone of saturation
(4) zone of distribution

9 Water in an artesian well
(1) dries up after a short amount of time
(2) rises on its own under pressure
(3) has been contaminated by saltwater
(4) is heated by cooling igneous rocks

10 Caverns form when rocks such as limestone are dissolved by a mixture of water and
(1) carbonic acid
(2) sulfur dioxide
(3) nitrogen
(4) ammonia

11 Which of these landforms is characteristic of an area with karst topography?
(1) mountains
(2) canyons
(3) sinkholes
(4) drumlins

Understanding Concepts

12 Write a list of numbered statements that summarize the major steps in the water cycle. NY

13 How does a stream's gradient affect is velocity? NY

14 Why does a stream's base level affect how it downcuts its channel?

15 Which type of stream valley is formed primarily by downcutting? NY

16 What are the main causes of floods?

17 What is the relationship between a spring and the water table?

18 Why are leaking landfills and septic tanks of concern to people who use groundwater? NY

19 How do stalactites form?

20 What type of rock is often associated with the formation of caverns and karst topography?

21 How do dripstone columns form?

Homework Guide

Section	Questions
1	1–4, 12, 22, 27–30
2	5–7, 13–16, 23, 24, 32–34
3	8–11, 17–21, 25, 26, 31

Assessment

Reviewing Content

(1) 2	(2) 3	(3) 4
(4) 3	(5) 1	(6) 1
(7) 1	(8) 3	(9) 2
(10) 1	(11) 3	

Understanding Concepts

(12) The constant circulation of Earth's water among the oceans, the atmosphere, the solid Earth, and the biosphere.
(13) Velocity increases as gradient increases.
(14) A stream downcuts its channel until it reaches its base level.
(15) a V-shaped valley
(16) rapid spring snowmelt and/or storms that bring heavy rain over a large region
(17) Springs can form where the water table meets the ground surface.
(18) Contaminants from leaking landfills and septic tanks can enter soil and eventually leak into and pollute groundwater supplies.
(19) Stalactites form as water containing dissolved minerals drips from the ceiling of a cavern. The water evaporates and leaves a deposit of calcite behind. Over a long period of time, these deposits lengthen into icicle-like formations that hang from the ceiling.
(20) limestone
(21) Dripstone columns form when downward-growing stalactites join with upward-growing stalagmites.

Chapter 6

Critical Thinking

(22) There must be as much water leaving Earth's surface as returning to it overall, or the system would break down. The breakdown would occur because too much water would be accumulating on Earth's surface and not enough would be evaporating, or too much would be evaporating, causing Earth's surface to become drier.
(23) The velocity would increase.
(24) The stream's capacity would increase.
(25) Some porous materials soak up liquids in their pore spaces. These pore spaces are small and not well connected. So the liquid can't easily move through the material.
(26) It is unlikely that the area has a karst landscape. Karst landscapes form in regions where water (containing acids) dissolves certain types of rock (often limestone) underground. A dry area with resistant rock doesn't have the needed characteristics.

Analyzing Data

(27) ice sheets and glaciers
(28) Add the percents for "Lakes and reservoirs" and "River water" to get 0.553 percent.
(29) Take the percentage of water not in "ice sheets and glaciers" (about 15 percent) and find what percentage that is of Earth's fresh water (3 percent), or 15 percent of 3 percent, which is 0.45 percent.
(30) Earth's freshwater supply is a small percentage of the whole—less than 1 percent. It's nonrenewable, and it's crucial for life on Earth. So Earth's fresh water is a precious resource that must be protected.

CHAPTER 6

Assessment *continued*

Critical Thinking

22 **Analyzing Concepts** Why must Earth's water cycle be balanced or conserved in order for the system to work? NY

23 **Relating Cause and Effect** How would a reduction in friction in a stream channel affect the stream's velocity? NY

24 **Applying Concepts** A stream's discharge decreases. Explain how this affects the stream's capacity?

25 **Summarizing** Briefly explain how a material can be porous but also impermeable. NY

26 **Drawing Conclusions** The bedrock under a region is primarily a very hard rock that doesn't easily erode. The area is also very arid. Is it likely that this area has a karst landscape? Explain your answer.

Analyzing Data

Use the graph below to answer questions 27–30.

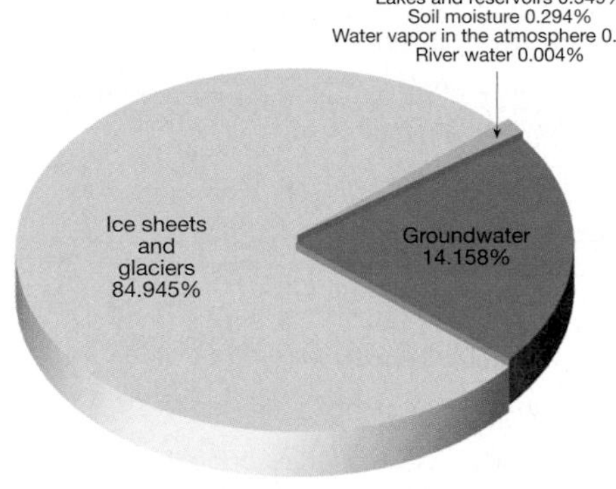

27 **Using Graphs** Where is the greatest percentage of Earth's fresh water located? NY

28 **Calculating** What percentage of Earth's fresh water is held in rivers, lakes, and reservoirs?

29 **Calculating** Oceans hold about 97 percent of Earth's water. The rest of the water is fresh. What percentage of Earth's water is freshwater that people can use for drinking, cooking, and growing crops?

30 **Drawing Conclusions** Taking into account your answer to question 29 above, explain why many people think of Earth's supply of fresh water as a resource that must be protected.

Concepts in Action

31 **Applying Concepts** A person drills a well into an area where there is a known aquifer underground. But the well doesn't produce water. What might be the cause of the problem? What does this person need to know about the water table in this area to solve the problem?

32 **Predicting** Erosion reduces the size of pebbles on the bottom of a stream channel. Which of the following would be most affected: the stream's competence, velocity, or discharge? Explain your answer.

33 **Connecting Concepts** Explain what deltas and natural levees have in common.

34 **Writing in Science** Imagine you live in a town that floods often. The people in your community want to take measures to decrease the amount of flooding and property damage. The community has identified three choices: a set of natural levees, a flood control dam, or clearing development from the river floodplain. Write a letter to the editor supporting one of these choices.

Performance-Based Assessment

Drawing Diagrams Draw a graphic organizer that shows the major steps of the water cycle. Label each step.

Concepts in Action

(31) The well isn't deep enough and is probably above the water table. The well must be dug deeper until it is beneath the water table in the zone of saturation to produce water.
(32) Velocity and competence would be most affected. Velocity would increase because there is less friction in the streambed. With increased velocity, the stream's competence, or ability to carry larger particles, would also increase. The size of the pebbles on the streambed wouldn't necessarily change its discharge.
(33) Deltas and natural levees are both depositional figures. They form when a stream's velocity decreases and it deposits sediment. However, deltas form at the mouths of streams, while natural levees form along the sides of their channels.
(34) Students can choose any method, but must demonstrate their knowledge of its benefits for flood control.

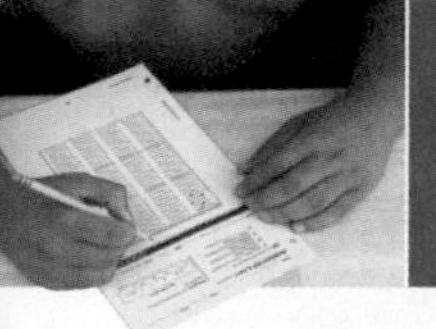

Regents Practice Exam

Test-Taking Tip

Evaluating and Revising
Frequently, a scientifically accurate answer choice may not answer the question that is being asked. Keep these tips in mind.

- Verify what the question is asking.
- Determine if an answer choice is a true statement or not.
- Determine if a true answer choice actually answers the question.
- Be cautious with inserted or deleted words that make a false statement seem accurate.

Practice using these tips in question 3.

For *each* statement or question, choose the *number* of the word or expression that, of those given, best completes the statement or answers the question. Some questions may require the use of the *Earth Science Reference Tables.*

1 Which of the following processes is the most direct result of the sun's energy?
(1) formation of clouds
(2) runoff
(3) evaporation
(4) infiltration

2 The ability of a stream to erode sediments is called carrying power. Which factor is most important in determining the carrying power of a stream?
(1) porosity
(2) stream velocity
(3) dissolved load
(4) channel width

3 As the gradient of a stream channel increases, the stream's
(1) carrying power decreases and it slows down
(2) velocity increases and deposition increases
(3) deposition decreases and it slows down
(4) velocity increases and erosion rate increases

4 When soil is impermeable, it
(1) allows water to flow freely through it
(2) has no water in it at all
(3) does not allow water to pass through it
(4) has large pore spaces

5 The "Relationship of Transported Particle Size to Water Velocity" graph found in the *Earth Science Reference Tables* illustrates the critical settling velocities for different sizes of sediments. According to this graph, the minimum rate of flow at which a stream can transport sediments the size of cobbles is closest to
(1) 200 cm/sec
(2) 300 cm/sec
(3) 400 cm/sec
(4) 500 cm/sec

Answer the following questions in complete sentences. Some questions may require the use of the *Earth Science Reference Tables.*

6 Explain how a soil could be porous but not permeable.

7 Describe the three ways that streams can transport sediments.

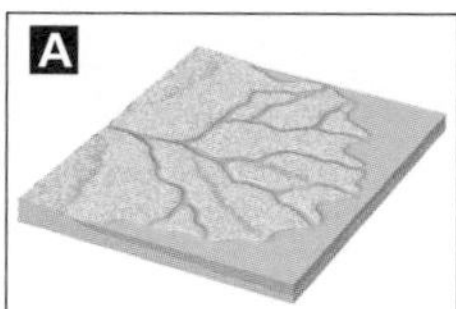

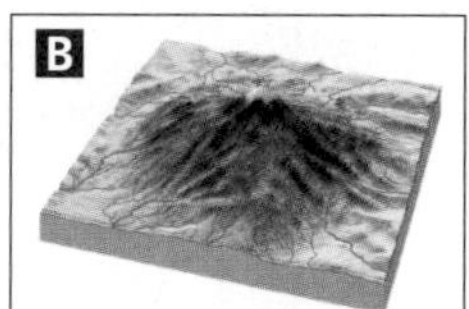

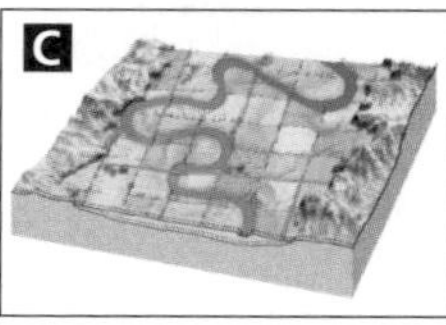

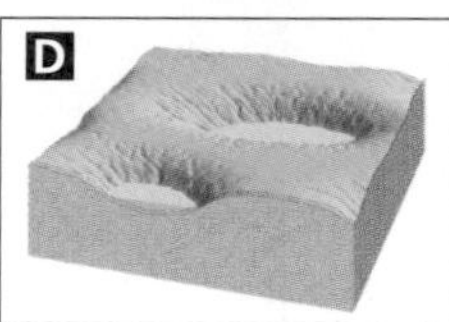

8 Which of the diagrams above shows a delta? Explain how a delta forms.

Regents Practice Exam

(1) 3
(2) 2
(3) 4
(4) 3
(5) 1
(6) If the pore spaces between particles do not connect, water cannot flow through the material.
(7) Streams can carry sediments dissolved in solution, floating on or in the water (suspension), or as bedload (rolling and bouncing along the bottom of the streambed).
(8) Diagram *A* shows a delta. Deltas form when streams slow down as they approach a larger body of standing water, and deposit large amounts of sediments.

Performance-Based Assessment

Graphic organizers should include at least these features arranged cyclically: evaporation, cloud formation, precipitation, runoff and infiltration, then back to evaporation.

Your students can independently test their knowledge of the chapter and print out their results.

CHAPTER 7

Planning Guide

Use these planning tools
Use Teacher Express for all your planning needs

SECTION OBJECTIVES	STANDARDS NATIONAL	STANDARDS STATE	ACTIVITIES and LABS
7.1 Glaciers, pp. 188–198 1 block or 2 periods **7.1** **Describe** the different types of glaciers and where each type is found. **7.2** **Explain** how glaciers move and **describe** the different types of glacial drift. **7.3** **Identify** the landscape features that glaciers form. **7.4** **Explain** the causes of the most recent ice age.	A-1, B-2, D-2, D-3, G-3		**SE** Inquiry Activity: How Does Pressure Affect Ice Crystals? p. 187 L2 **TE** Teacher Demo: Glacial Erosion, p. 192 L2 **TE** Build Science Skills, p. 195 L2 **SE** Exploration Lab: Interpreting a Glacial Landscape, pp. 210–211 L2 **LM** Continental Glaciers Change Earth's Topography L2
7.2 Deserts, pp. 199–202 1 block or 2 periods **7.5** **Describe** how running water affects deserts. **7.6** **Explain** the roles mechanical and chemical weathering play in the formation of deserts.	B-3, D-2, F-5		**TE** Teacher Demo: Desert Water Erosion, p. 201 L2
7.3 Landscapes Shaped by Wind, pp. 203–207 1 block or 2 periods **7.7** **Describe** two ways that wind can cause erosion. **7.8** **Identify** types of landforms that are deposited by the wind. **7.9** **Describe** how sand dunes differ.	A-1, A-2, D-2, F-5		**TE** Teacher Demo: Wind Erosion, p. 205 L2

Ability Levels

- **L1** For students who need additional help
- **L2** For all students
- **L3** For students who need to be challenged

Components

SE	Student Edition	**GRSW**	Guided Reading & Study Workbook	**TP**	Test Prep Resources	**GEO**	Geode CD-ROM
TE	Teacher's Edition	**TEX**	Teacher Express	**onT**	onlineText	**T**	Transparencies
LM	Laboratory Manual	**CTB**	Computer Test Bank	**DC**	Discovery Channel Videos	**GO**	Internet Resources
CUT	Chapter Tests						

RESOURCES PRINT and TECHNOLOGY	SECTION ASSESSMENT
GRSW Section 7.1 **T-58** Continental Ice Sheets **T-59** Glaciers Cause Changing Coastlines **T-60** Snowline Separation **T-61** Erosional Landforms Created by Alpine Glaciers **T-62** End Moraines **T-63** Maximum Extent of Glaciation in Northern Hemisphere **T-64** Maps Showing Preglacial and Postglacial Rivers **T-65** Pluvial Lakes of the Western United States **T-66** Supercontinent Pangaea and the Continents Today 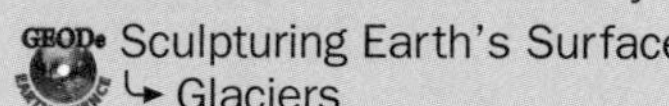 Sculpturing Earth's Surface ↳ Glaciers **DC** Glaciers **TEX** Lesson Planning 7.1	**SE** Section 7.1 Assessment, p. 198 **onT** Section 7.1
GRSW Section 7.2 **T-67** Orbital Variations **T-68** Evolution of a Mountainous Desert Landscape **T-69** Formation of Desert Pavement 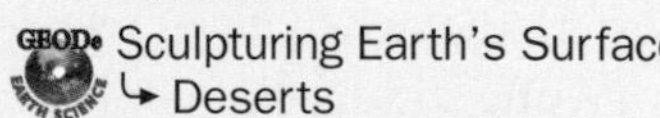 Sculpturing Earth's Surface ↳ Deserts **TEX** Lesson Planning 7.2	**SE** Section 7.2 Assessment, p. 202 **onT** Section 7.2
GRSW Section 7.3 **T-70** Cross-Bedding in Sand Dunes **T-71** Sand Dune Types **T-72** Ice Movement and Changes in the Terminus at Rhone Glacier, Switzerland **T-73** Location of Aral Sea **T-74** The Shrinking Aral Sea **TEX** Lesson Planning 7.3	**SE** Section 7.3 Assessment, p. 207 **onT** Section 7.3

Go Online

Go online for these Internet resources.

PHSchool.com
Web Code: cjk-9999

NSTA SCiLINKS
Web Code: cjn-2071
Web Code: cjn-2073

Materials for Activities and Labs

Quantities for each group

STUDENT EDITION

Inquiry Activity, p. 187
ice crystals or snow, beaker, table knife, magnifying glass

Exploration Lab, pp. 210–211
topographic map

TEACHER'S EDITION

Teacher Demo, p. 192
sand, soap, ice cube

Build Science Skills, p. 195
freezer, sand, ice cube trays, water, sloping paint tray

Teacher Demo, p. 201
sharpened pencil, paper cup, scissors, 1/2 of a drinking straw, modeling clay, cookie sheet, ruler, large beaker, water, soil, two 2" × 4" boards about 15 cm long

Teacher Demo, p. 205
sand, large piece of cardboard, water

Chapter Assessment

ASSESSMENT

- **SE** Assessment, pp. 213–214
- **CUT** Chapter 7 Test
- **CTB** Chapter 7
- **onT** Chapter 7

STANDARDIZED TEST PREP

- **SE** Chapter 7, p. 215
- **TP** Progress Monitoring Assessments

interactive textbook with assessment at PHSchool.com

CHAPTER 7

Before you teach

Michael Wysession
Washington University

Big Ideas

While flowing water is the primary agent of erosion and deposition, in certain environments ice and wind also play important roles.

Space and Time Glaciers occur in two forms: valley glaciers (cold because of altitude) and continental glaciers (cold because of latitude). Glacial ice accumulates through snowfall, and wastes through melting, calving, and sublimation. During ice ages, large portions of continents are covered with a thick sheet of ice. The major cause of ice ages is likely changes in Earth's orbital parameters, called Milankovitch cycles.

Forces and Motion Glaciers flow by plastic flow and basal slip, and erode through plucking and abrasion. Erosional features include U-shaped valleys, hanging valleys, cirques, arêtes, and horns. Depositional glacial features include moraines, kettles, drumlins, and outwash plains. In deserts, wind erodes by deflation and abrasion, forming desert pavements. Wind deposits sediments in the form of dunes and layers of loess. Different wind patterns form different kinds of dunes.

Matter and Energy In deserts mostly, weathering occurs mechanically through running water, even though most streams are intermittent.

Earth as a System No two geological environments are the same, so the relative importances of flowing water, ice, and wind as agents of the rock cycle are different in every location.

Earth Science Refresher

Ice Ages of the Past

The recent ice age created a dramatic change on Earth's surface. Present-day Chicago was under a few kilometers of ice. When the ice melted, bursting glacial lakes eroded giant valleys in a matter of days, leaving ripple marks a hundred meters apart! Mammals evolved thick coats of fur to survive, and the lowered sea level allowed many different life-forms (including humans) to settle across previously unconnected continents. But this was not the only ice age, nor was it the most severe.

About 280 million years ago, just before the mass extinction of life at the end of the Paleozoic era, there was a period of extreme glaciation. In fact, this is being considered as a factor that led to extinctions. The continents were in different places, and the existence of glaciation in places like India and Australia from this era was used as evidence of continental drift by Alfred Wegener.

There were several periods, however, of even more extreme glaciation that may have occurred during 750–550 million years ago. The possibility is currently being investigated that there were times when Earth was totally covered by ice, a scenario referred to as "Snowball Earth." The climate would have been so cold that even the surfaces of the oceans would have been frozen. Life, which was still only single-celled at this point, would have had to survive around volcanoes, at mid-ocean ridges, or cracks in the sea ice. During the periods of extreme glaciation, carbon dioxide would have built up beneath the ice to the extent that when it was released, Earth's climate would have rapidly swung to very hot conditions involving a rampant greenhouse effect. As carbon dioxide began to be removed from the atmosphere and deposited in ocean sediments, the climate would swing toward a Snowball Earth condition again.

Go Online PDLINKS NSTA

For: Chapter 7 Content Support
Visit: www.SciLinks.org/PDLinks
Web Code: cjn-0799

This never happened again after the evolution of multicellular life, and it is likely that we have worms to thank for this. Ocean worms continually churn up sediments through the construction of their burrows, and it is possible that this activity prevented too much carbon dioxide from being stored in ocean sediments, and so preventing any more extreme ice ages.

Interestingly, it is through the other life-forms that we know the history of Earth's climate. The shells of marine animals are made of calcium carbonate, which is a combination of calcium, carbon, and oxygen. Most oxygen atoms are $^{16}_{8}O$ isotopes, but a small number are $^{18}_{8}O$ isotopes. Marine shells form with either isotope indiscriminately. Water that evaporates from the ocean and falls as ice or snow, however, is almost entirely made of $^{16}_{8}O$ isotopes because the $^{18}_{8}O$ isotopes require much more energy to evaporate. That means that when there is a lot of glacial ice on land (which is all made with $^{16}_{8}O$), the ocean water is enriched in $^{18}_{8}O$. By looking at the ratio of $\frac{^{18}_{8}O}{^{16}_{8}O}$ isotopes in marine shells, geologists can determine if they formed during periods of glaciation.

Address Misconceptions

Students may have the misconception that glaciers cannot form in the tropics. Glaciers form wherever there are low temperatures and adequate supplies of snow. Because the temperatures drop with an increase altitude, glaciers can occur in the tropics at high elevations. Even near the equator, glaciers form at elevations above 5000 m. For a strategy that helps to overcome this misconception, see **Address Misconceptions** on **p. 189.**

Build Reading Literacy

Relate Text and Visuals

Use Graphic Elements to Clarify and Extend

Strategy Help students relate visuals to text, in order to clarify difficult concepts in the text or to understand information beyond that stated in the text. This strategy enables students to focus on their own thought processes as they actively make use of photos and illustrations as tools to support comprehension. Before students begin, choose a section in Chapter 7, such as Section 7.3, Types of Sand Dunes, pp. 206–207.

Example

1. Have students keep their book closed as you read a few paragraphs aloud, including text that refers to a figure. You may want to think aloud as you read, saying, for example, "I wonder what that would look like?"

2. Then, have students open their book to the passage that you read. Tell them to reread it and then study the figure and its caption carefully. Ask what parts of the passage make more sense when students look at the figure.

3. Point out that visuals also sometimes communicate information that is not in the text. Have students identify any new information that can be learned from the figure.

4. Have students work in pairs, with one reading aloud through the text reference to a figure, and then both working together to discuss how the figure helps them understand the passage or provides additional information.

See p. 189 for a script on how to use this strategy with students. For additional strategies, see pp. 200 and 204.

SCULPTURING EARTH'S SURFACE
Chapter 7

ASSESS PRIOR KNOWLEDGE

Use the Chapter Pretest below to assess students' prior knowledge. As needed, review these concepts.

Review Science Concepts

Review 7.1 Reviewing the concept of erosion ensures that students will understand the impact that glaciers have on the landscape.

Review 7.2 Reviewing chemical and mechanical weathering will help students understand the geological processes that occur in desert climates.

Review 7.3 Reviewing the concepts of soil erosion will help students understand the significance of erosion by wind.

CHAPTER 7 Glaciers, Deserts, and Wind

CONCEPTS in Action

Exploration Lab
Interpreting a Glacial Landscape

How the Earth Works
Erosion

Sculpturing Earth's Surface
↳ Glaciers
Deserts

DISCOVERY CHANNEL SCHOOL **Video Field Trip**
Glaciers

Take a field trip through cold waters with Discovery Channel and find out how glaciers helped shape Earth. Answer the following questions after watching the video.

1. What happened to the glaciers at the end of the last ice age? How did the end of the ice age affect Earth?
2. How are icebergs formed?

For: Chapter 7 Resources
Visit: PHSchool.com
Web Code: cjk-9999

This fjord at Tracy Arm, Alaska, formed as a glacier carved the valley that became submerged as sea level rose. ▶

Chapter Pretest

1. What are two types of weathering? *(chemical and mechanical)*
2. What happens to a rock during weathering? *(It is broken into smaller pieces and converted into new minerals.)*
3. What are two erosional forces that move soil from one place to another? *(wind, ice, and water)*
4. What is mechanical weathering? *(physical forces that break rock into smaller and smaller pieces without changing the rock's composition)*
5. Soil erosion is a natural process that is part of which cycle? *(c)*
   a. carbon b. phosphorus
   c. rock d. water
6. True or False: Plants stabilize soil and prevent erosion. *(True)*
7. True or False: Glaciers, groundwater, waves, and wind are insignificant causes of landform changes. *(False)*
8. What is the most important agent in chemical weathering? *(c)*
   a. erosion b. climate
   c. water d. wind

Chapter Preview

Inquiry Activity

How Does Pressure Affect Ice Crystals?

Procedure

1. Obtain a beaker full of ice crystals, either by collecting snow outside or by scraping ice crystals from the inside surfaces of a freezer. Use a magnifying glass to observe the loose crystals. Sketch their appearance in your science notebook.
2. Use your hands to mold a snowball from the crystals. Then squeeze the snowball as hard as you can, making the snowball compact.
3. Use a table knife to cut the snowball in half. Observe the compressed crystals with your magnifying glass and sketch them.

Think About It

1. **Drawing Conclusions** How did the ice crystals change after you squeezed them? Describe how pressure seems to affect ice crystals.
2. **Predicting** The raw material for glaciers is snow. Predict how snowflakes will change under the increasing pressure of overlying snow.

ENGAGE/EXPLORE

How Does Pressure Affect Ice Crystals? L2

Purpose In this activity, students will observe the effect of pressure on ice crystals.

Skills Focus Observing, Drawing Conclusions, Predicting

 **Prep Time** 20 minutes

Materials ice crystals or snow, beaker, table knife, magnifying glass

Advance Prep Fill beakers with ice crystals or snow in advance. Store the beakers in a freezer until you are ready to use them.

Class Time 20 minutes

Expected Outcome Students will observe open spaces in individual ice crystals before pressure is applied. After pressure is applied, the individual ice crystals are compacted and the open spaces are no longer visible.

Think About It

1. The ice crystals appear to fuse and grow larger. Pressure appears to cause ice crystals to fuse and transform to solid ice.
2. As snow piles up on top of snowflakes, they will be subject to increasing pressure. The pressure will cause the flakes to fuse and become ice.

Discovery Channel School

Video Field Trip

Glaciers

Encourage students to view the Video Field Trip "Glaciers."

Section 7.1

1 FOCUS

Section Objectives

7.1 **Describe** the different types of glaciers and where each type is found.

7.2 **Explain** how glaciers move and **describe** the different types of glacial drift.

7.3 **Identify** the landscape features that glaciers form.

7.4 **Explain** the causes of the most recent ice age.

Reading Focus

Build Vocabulary L2

Concept Map Have students construct a concept map using as many vocabulary terms as possible and the following landform features: hanging valleys, cirques arêtes, and horns. Students should place the main concept (Glaciers) in the center oval and use descriptive linking phrases to connect the terms. Instruct students to place the terms in ovals and connect the ovals with lines on which linking words are placed.

Reading Strategy L2

a. Glacier—a thick ice mass that forms over hundreds or thousands of years
b. Ice sheet—an enormous ice mass that flows in all directions from one or more centers and covers everything but the highest land
c. Moraine—layers or ridges of till left behind when glaciers melt
d. Till—material deposited directly by a glacier

7.1 Glaciers

Reading Focus

Key Concepts

- What types of glaciers exist, and where is each type found?
- How do glaciers move?
- What distinguishes the various types of glacial drift?
- What landscape features do glaciers form?

Vocabulary

- ice age
- glacier
- snowline
- valley glacier
- ice sheet
- glacial trough
- till
- stratified drift
- moraine

Reading Strategy

Building Vocabulary Draw a table similar to the one below that includes all the vocabulary terms listed for the section. As you read the section, define each vocabulary term in your own words.

Vocabulary Term	Definition
Glacier	a. ____?____
Ice Sheet	b. ____?____
Moraine	c. ____?____
Till	d. ____?____

Figure 1 Valley Glacier Barry Glacier, in Alaska's Chugach Mountains, slowly advances down this valley.

Earth's climate strongly influences the processes that shape its surface. In this section, you will see the strong link between climate and geology in studying how glaciers shape the land.

Types of Glaciers

As recently as 15,000 years ago—the blink of an eye in geologic history—up to 30 percent of Earth was covered by glacial ice. At that time, Earth was coming out of an **ice age**—a period of time when much of Earth's land is covered in glaciers. Sheets of ice that were thousands of meters thick shaped places like the Alps, Cape Cod, and Yosemite Valley. Long Island, the Great Lakes, and the fjords of Norway were all formed by glaciers. A **glacier** is a thick ice mass that forms over hundreds or thousands of years. Today glaciers still cover nearly 10 percent of Earth's land area. In these regions they continue to sculpt the landscape.

Customize for English Language Learners

Have students create an illustrated science glossary using the vocabulary terms and additional terms that are unfamiliar. Students should write the definition of the term in their own words. Then, students should draw a diagram illustrating the meaning of the term.

Glaciers originate on land in places where more snow falls each winter than melts each summer. The **snowline** is the lowest elevation in a particular area that remains covered in snow all year. At the poles, the snowline occurs at sea level. Closer to the equator, the snowline is near the top of tall mountains. Instead of completely melting away, snow above the snowline accumulates and compacts. The compressed snow first recrystallizes into coarse grains of ice. Further pressure from added snow above changes the coarse grains into interlocking crystals of glacial ice.

A glacier appears to be motionless, but it's not. Sit beside a glacier for an hour and you may hear a sporadic chorus of creaks, cracks, and groans as the mass of ice slowly moves downhill. Just like running water, groundwater, wind, and waves, glaciers are dynamic agents of erosion. They accumulate, transport, and deposit sediment. Thus, glaciers are an important part of the rock cycle.

For: Links on glaciers
Visit: www.SciLinks.org
Web Code: cjn-2071

Valley Glaciers Thousands of small glaciers exist in high mountains worldwide. Unlike fast-flowing mountain streams, glaciers advance only a few centimeters to meters each day. **Valley glaciers** are ice masses that slowly advance down valleys that were originally occupied by streams. **A valley glacier is a stream of ice that flows between steep rock walls from a place near the top of the mountain valley.** Like rivers, valley glaciers can be long or short, wide or narrow, single or with branching tributaries. Figure 1 shows a valley glacier in Alaska.

Ice Sheets **Ice sheets** are enormous ice masses that flow in all directions from one or more centers and cover everything but the highest land. **Ice sheets are sometimes called continental ice sheets because they cover large regions where the climate is extremely cold. They are huge compared to valley glaciers.** Ice sheets covered much of North America during the recent ice age. Figure 2 shows the two remaining ice sheets, which combined cover almost 10 percent of Earth's land area. One ice sheet covers about 80 percent of Greenland. It averages nearly 1500 meters thick, and in places it rises to 3000 meters above the island's surface.

The huge Antarctic Ice Sheet in the Southern Hemisphere is nearly 4300 meters thick in places. This glacier accounts for 80 percent of the world's ice, and it holds nearly two-thirds of Earth's fresh water. If it melted, sea level could rise 60 to 70 meters and many coastal cities would flood.

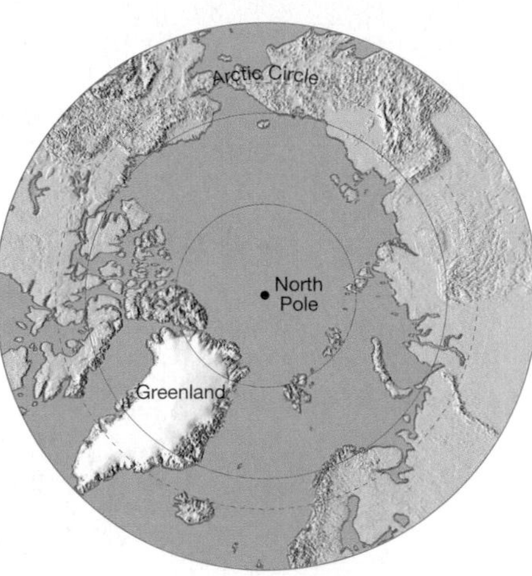

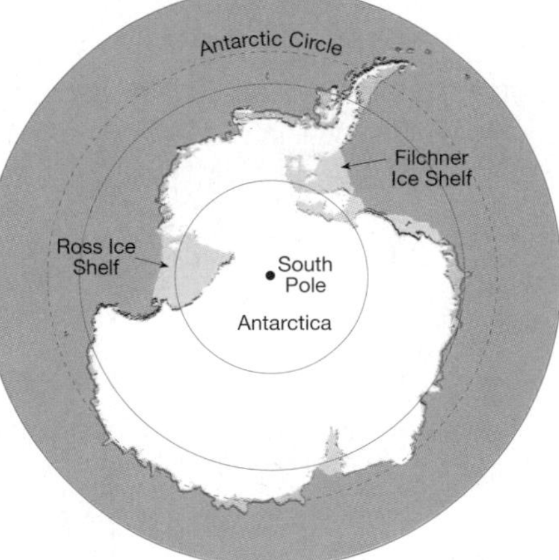

Figure 2 The only present-day ice sheets are those covering Greenland and Antarctica.

Where do ice sheets exist on Earth today?

2 INSTRUCT

Types of Glaciers

Build Reading Literacy L1

Refer to **p. 186D**, which provides the guidelines for relating text and visuals.

Relate Text and Visuals Have students read pp. 188–189. Have students use Figures 1 and 2 to distinguish between valley glaciers and ice sheets. *(Valley glaciers are ice masses that slowly advance down valleys originally occupied by streams. Ice sheets are enormous ice masses that cover large regions.)*
Visual, Logical

L2

Students may have the misconception that glaciers cannot form in the tropics. Glaciers form whenever there are low temperatures and adequate supplies of snow. Because temperatures drop with an increase in altitude, glaciers can occur in the tropics at high elevations. Even near the equator, glaciers form at elevations above 5000 m. Examples of equatorial glaciers include those atop Mt. Kenya and Mt. Kilimanjaro in East Africa. Have students use a map or an atlas to find these mountains and the distance to the equator.
Verbal, Visual

Build Science Skills L2

Comparing and Contrasting Have students read the text on valley glaciers and ice sheets. Ask: **How are these two types of glaciers similar?** *(Both types of glaciers are composed of ice.)* **How do they differ?** *(Valley glaciers are smaller and advance slowly down valleys. Ice sheets cover everything except the highest land in a large region.)*
Verbal

Go Online NSTA SCILINKS

Download a worksheet on glaciers for students to complete, and find additional teacher support from NSTA SciLinks.

Answer to . . .

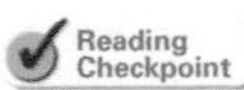

Greenland, Antarctica

How Glaciers Move

Use Visuals

L1

Figure 4 Have students look at the illustration. Ask: **What is the zone of accumulation?** *(the region of the glacier where snow accumulates and ice forms)* **What is the zone of wastage?***(the foot of the glacier where it loses ice and snow)* **What must happen for a glacier to advance?** *(The glacier must accumulate more ice and snow than is lost at the foot.)* **What must happen for a glacier to retreat?** *(The amount of accumulation must be less than the amount of waste.)*
Verbal

Integrate Physics

Most glaciers are blue, unless they contain a large amount of eroded sediment at the surface. Invite students to search the Internet or printed reference sources to find photographs of blue glaciers. Explain that glacial ice absorbs the longer red wavelengths of visible white light while reflecting and scattering shorter blue wavelengths. Ask: **What is another real-world example of something that reflects short wavelengths to cause a blue appearance?** *(the sky)*
Verbal, Logical

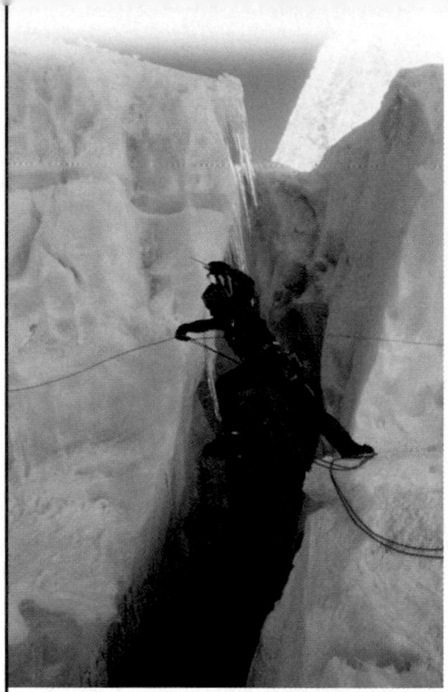

Figure 3 Crevasses like this one in Pakistan can extend 50 meters into a glacier's brittle surface ice.

How Glaciers Move

You might wonder how a glacier, which is solid, can move. **The movement of glaciers is referred to as flow. Glacial flow happens two ways: plastic flow and basal slip.** Plastic flow involves movement within the ice. Under high enough pressure, the normally brittle ice begins to distort and change shape—a property known as plasticity. The weight of overlying ice exerts this pressure on the ice below, causing it to flow. Plastic flow begins at about 50 meters below the glacier surface.

Basal slip is the second cause of glacial movement. Due to gravity, the entire ice mass actually slips and slides downhill along the ground. The upper 50 meters of a glacier is not under enough pressure to have plastic flow. The surface of the glacier behaves differently than the ice below. This uppermost zone of a glacier is brittle, and it is referred to as the zone of fracture. This brittle topmost ice piggybacks a ride on the flowing ice below. The zone of fracture experiences tension when the glacier moves over irregular terrain. This tension results in gaping cracks called crevasses. Crevasses can be 50 meters deep. They are often hidden by snow and make travel across glaciers dangerous, as shown in Figure 3.

Rates of Glacial Movement Different glaciers move at different speeds. Some flow so slowly that trees and other vegetation grow in the debris on their surface. Other glaciers can advance several meters per day. Some glaciers alternate between periods of rapid movement and periods of no movement whatsoever.

Budget of a Glacier Glaciers form where more snow falls in winter than can melt during the summer. They constantly gain and lose ice. Snow accumulates, and ice forms at the head of the glacier in the zone of accumulation, shown in Figure 4. Here new snowfall thickens the glacier and promotes movement. The area of the glacier beyond the snowline is called the zone of wastage. Here the glacier loses ice—and any new snow—to melting.

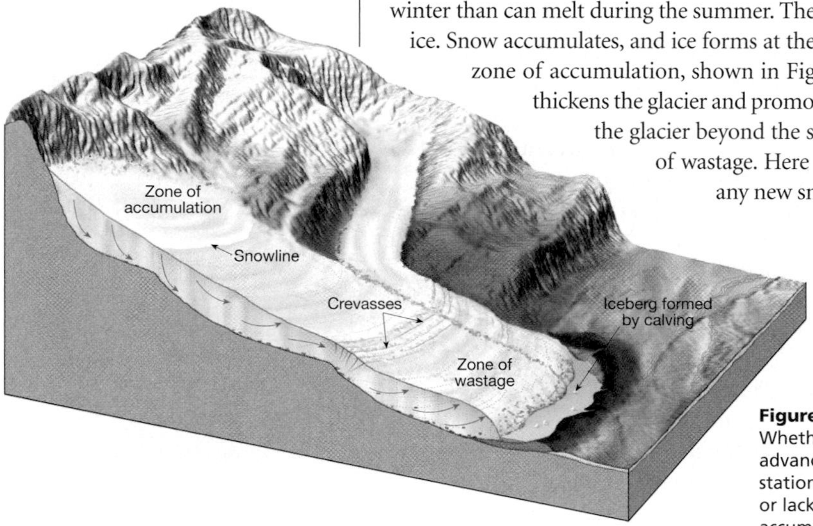

Zone of accumulation
Snowline
Crevasses
Iceberg formed by calving
Zone of wastage

Figure 4 How a Glacier Moves Whether the margin of a glacier advances, retreats, or remains stationary depends on the balance or lack of balance between accumulation and wastage.

Facts and Figures

Glaciers are a part of a fundamental cycle in the Earth system—the water cycle. Water is constantly cycled through the atmosphere, biosphere, and geosphere. Time and time again, the same water is evaporated from the oceans into the atmosphere, precipitated upon the land, and carried by rivers and underground streams back to the sea. However, when precipitation falls at high elevations or high latitudes, the water may not immediately make its way toward the sea. Instead, it may become part of a glacier. Although the ice will eventually melt and make its way to the sea, it may be stored as glacial ice for tens, hundreds, or even thousands of years.

Glaciers also lose ice when large pieces break off their fronts in a process called calving. Calving creates icebergs where glaciers meet the ocean. Because icebergs are just slightly less dense than seawater, they float low in the water. Only about 10 percent of their mass is visible above the surface, as shown in Figure 5. The Greenland Ice Sheet calves thousands of icebergs each year. Many drift southward into the North Atlantic where they are navigational hazards.

The foot of a glacier can advance, retreat, or remain in place. Which course it follows depends on the glacier's budget. **The glacial budget is the balance or lack of balance between accumulation at the upper end of a glacier and loss, or wastage, at the lower end.** If more ice accumulates at the glacier head than melts or calves at the glacier foot, then the glacier advances. The glacier retreats when it loses ice faster than it gains ice. If a glacier gains ice at the same rate as ice melts or calves off, the front or terminus of the glacier remains stationary. Whether the front of a glacier advances, retreats, or remains stationary, the ice within the glacier continues to flow forward. In the case of a receding glacier, the ice still flows forward, but not rapidly enough to offset wastage.

What causes a glacier to retreat?

Figure 5 Calving A Ice calves from the front of the Hubbard glacier in Alaska's Wrangell-St. Elias National Park. Once it lands in the water the ice is called an iceberg. Icebergs float on their sides. **B** Just 10 percent of their mass is visible above the surface.

Integrate Social Studies L2

Glaciers in North America Have students research glaciers that are or have been in North America. Have students prepare a computer presentation showing pictures of different elements of glaciers, such as types of glaciers, physical landforms left by glaciers, and glacial erosion.
Verbal, Visual

Build Science Skills L2

Applying Concepts Remind students that a glacier advances when it accumulates more ice than it loses. Tell students about Hubbard Glacier in Alaska, which is pictured in Figure 5. Several other smaller glaciers feed Hubbard Glacier, and the bulk of it is advancing at a rate of about 6 m per year (although one part is advancing at a rate of about 11 m per day and is threatening to close off the Russell Fiord from the sea). Unlike Hubbard Glacier, most glaciers have actually thinned and retreated in the last century. Instruct students to find an example of a retreating glacier. *(Sample answers: Aletsch Glacier in Switzerland, Bering Glacier in Alaska)*
Verbal

Answer to . . .

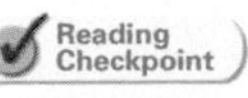

A glacier retreats when it loses ice faster than it gains ice.

Glacial Erosion

Teacher Demo

Glacial Erosion L2

Purpose Students will observe how rocks and sand incorporated into glaciers form striations.

Materials sand, soap, ice cube

Procedure Place the ice cube in the sand. Sand will stick to the ice cube. The sand represents the rocks and debris that glaciers pick up as they move. Then, scrape the ice cube across the bar of soap. The scratches in the soap represent the striations carved into the surrounding rock by a moving glacier.

Expected Outcome Students will see how easily the sand carves grooves into the soap. The same process occurs between glaciers and surfaces such as bedrock and valley walls that surround a glacier.
Visual, Logical

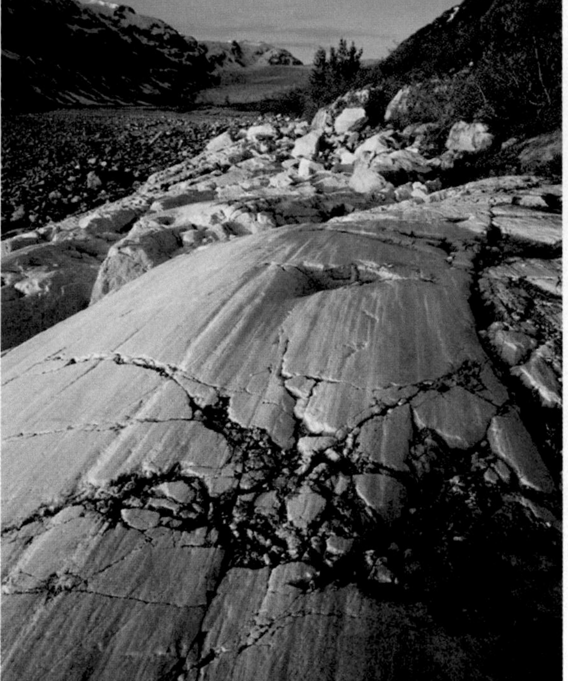

Figure 6 Glacial Abrasion A glacier smoothed and polished this rock surface in Alaska's Glacier Bay. Rock fragments embedded in the glacier carved the scratches and grooves.

Glacial Erosion

Glaciers are nature's bulldozers. Their ice scrapes, scours, and tears rock from valley floors and walls. Glaciers then carry the rocks down the valley. The rock fragments that are eroded by the glacier drop at the glacier's foot where the ice melts. Unlike streams, which drop sediments while they flow, glaciers hold everything until they melt. They can carry rocks as big as buses over long distances. **Many landscapes were changed by the widespread glaciers of the recent ice age.**

How Glaciers Erode Glaciers mainly erode the land in two ways: plucking and abrasion. Rock surfaces beneath glaciers break up as melted water from the glacier penetrates the cracks. When the water refreezes it expands and pries the rock apart. As a glacier flows over the fractured bedrock surface, it loosens and lifts blocks of rock and incorporates them into the ice. This type of glacial erosion is called plucking.

A second form of glacial erosion is called abrasion. As the glacial ice and its load of rock fragments slide over bedrock, they work like sandpaper to smooth and polish the surface below. The pulverized rock produced by this glacial gristmill is appropriately called rock flour. So much rock flour may be produced that streams of meltwater leaving the glacier often have the grayish appearance of skim milk—visible evidence of the grinding power of the ice. When the ice at the bottom of a glacier contains large rock fragments, long scratches and grooves may be gouged in the bedrock, shown in Figure 6. These glacial striations provide valuable clues to the direction of past glacial movement. By mapping the striations over large areas, geologists often can reconstruct the direction the ice flowed.

As with other agents of erosion, the rate of glacial erosion is highly variable. These differences are mainly controlled by four factors: 1) rate of glacial movement; 2) thickness of the ice; 3) shape, abundance, and hardness of the rock fragments in the ice at the base of the glacier; and 4) the type of surface below the glacier.

How do glaciers cause erosion?

Facts and Figures

In addition to valley and continental glaciers, other types of glaciers also exist. Covering some uplands and plateaus are masses of glacial ice called ice caps. Like ice sheets, ice caps completely bury the underlying landscape but are much smaller. Ice caps occur in Iceland and many other places. Another type of glacier, known as piedmont glaciers, occupies broad lowlands at the bases of steep mountains and forms when one or more valley glaciers emerge. The advancing ice spreads out to form a large sheet. The size of individual piedmont glaciers varies greatly. The largest piedmont glacier in North America is the Malaspina Glacier in southeastern Alaska.

Landforms Created by Glacial Erosion

Erosion by valley glaciers produces many spectacular features in mountainous areas. **Glaciers are responsible for a variety of erosional landscape features, such as glacial troughs, hanging valleys, cirques, arêtes, and horns.** Compare and contrast the mountain setting before, during, and after glaciation as shown is Figure 7.

Glaciated Valleys Before glaciation, alpine valleys are usually V-shaped because streams are well above base level and are downcutting. However, in mountain regions that have been glaciated, the valleys are no longer narrow. As a glacier moves down a valley once occupied by a stream, the glacier widens, deepens, and straightens the valley. The once narrow V-shaped valley is changed into a U-shaped **glacial trough.**

The amount of glacial erosion depends in part on the thickness of the ice. Main glaciers cut U-shaped valleys that are deeper than those carved by smaller side glaciers. When the ice recedes, the valleys of the smaller side glaciers are left standing higher than the main glacial trough. These higher valleys are called hanging valleys. Rivers flowing from hanging valleys sometimes produce spectacular waterfalls, such as those in Yosemite National Park, California.

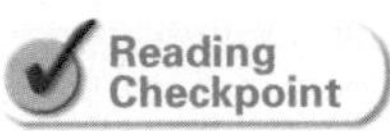

What is a glacial trough?

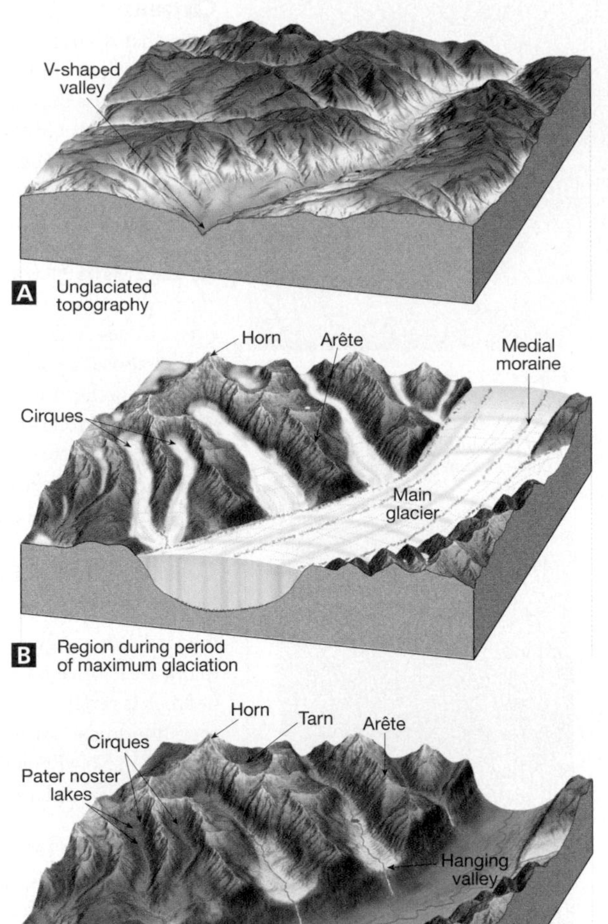

Figure 7 Erosional Landforms Caused by Valley Glaciers
A shows what the valley glaciers looked like in this mountainous region. **B** reveals the modified landscape and its features.
Inferring ***What direction did the main valley glacier flow? How do you know?***

Landforms Created by Glacial Erosion

Use Visuals **L1**

Figure 7 Have students look carefully at Figures 7A and 7B. Ask: **How would you describe a cirque?** *(a bowl-shaped depression that is surrounded on three sides by steep rock walls)* **How did the arête form?** *(The rock walls surrounding the cirques eroded, cirques on opposite sides of the divide grew and formed a sharp ridge.)* **How did the horn form?** *(Several cirques surrounded a single high mountain. As the cirques grew, a single horn emerged.)*
Visual, Verbal

Build Science Skills **L2**

Using Analogies Ask students if they have ever taken a bath when they were dirty. Ask: **What does the bottom of the tub look like if you let the water drain out?** *(All of the dirt settles to the bottom of the tub.)* Explain that this is similar to the way a glacier deposits its load of debris. As the ice melts from the glacier, the debris falls to the terrain just as the suspended dirt falls to the bottom of the tub.
Verbal

Answer to . . .

Figure 7 *from lower left to upper right; because the glacial trough forms at the beginning of the glacier*

Glaciers erode by plucking and abrasion.

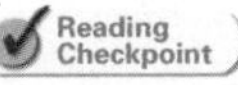

a once narrow V-shaped valley that changes into a U-shape after a glacier moves down the valley

Glacial Deposits

Use Visuals L1

Figure 9 Have students look carefully at Figure 9. Ask: **Why is glacial till an unsorted mixture of debris?** *(Glacial till is debris that drops out of the glacier as it melts. The till consists of a random assortment of whatever the glacier has picked up as it moved along.)* **What is the difference between till and stratified drift?** *(Till is material deposited directly by a glacier. Stratified drift is deposited by glacial meltwater. Till consists of random-sized objects that are picked up by the glacier. Stratified drift is deposited by size and weight.)*
Verbal

Use Community Resources 

Invite an Earth science specialist from a local college that is familiar with glaciers to speak to the class. Ask the person to bring pictures or slides that he or she can share with the class.
Interpersonal, Visual

Figure 8 Cirque Natural amphitheaters like this one in Canada's Yukon Territory result from the plucking action of ice in a glacier's zone of accumulation.

Cirques A cirque is a bowl-shaped depression at the head of a glacial valley that is surrounded on three sides by steep rock walls, as shown in Figure 8. These impressive features are the focal point of the glacier's growth because they form where snow and ice accumulate at the head of a valley glacier. Cirques begin as irregularities in the mountainside. Glaciers carve cirques by plucking rock from along the sides and the bottom. The glaciers then act as conveyor belts that carry away the debris. Sometimes the melting glacier leaves a small lake in the cirque basin.

Arêtes and Horns Other mountain landscapes carved by valley glaciers reveal more than glacial troughs and cirques. Snaking, sharp-edged ridges called arêtes and sharp pyramid-like peaks called horns project above the surroundings. You can see these features in the Alps and the northern Rockies. Horns like the Matterhorn in Switzerland form where several cirques surround a single high mountain. The converging cirques create one distinctive horn. Arêtes form where cirques occur on opposite sides of a divide. As these cirques grow, the divide separating them is reduced to a narrow, sharp ridge.

Glacial Deposits

Glaciers transport huge loads of debris as they slowly advance across the land. When a glacier melts it deposits its sediment. For example, in many areas once covered by the ice sheets of the recent ice age, the bedrock is rarely exposed because glacial deposits that are dozens—or even hundreds—of meters thick completely cover the terrain. Rocky pastures in New England, wheat fields in the Dakota plains, and rolling Midwest farmland are all landscapes resulting from glacial deposition.

Types of Glacial Drift **Glacial drift applies to all sediments of glacial origin, no matter how, where, or in what form they were deposited. There are two types of glacial drift: till and stratified drift. Till** is material deposited directly by the glacier. It is deposited as the glacier melts and drops its load of rock debris. Unlike moving water and wind, ice cannot sort the sediment it carries. Therefore, till deposits are usually unsorted mixtures made up of many particle sizes. Notice the unsorted till in Figure 9.

Stratified drift is sediment laid down by glacial meltwater. Stratified drift contains particles that are sorted according to size and weight of the debris. Some deposits of drift are made by streams coming directly from the glacier. Stratified drift often consists of sand and gravel, because the meltwater cannot move large boulders and finer sediments remain suspended and are carried far from the glacier.

Boulders found in till or lying free on the ground are glacial erratics. Their mineral content is different from the underlying bedrock, which shows they were carried there by some means. In parts of New England and other glaciated areas, glacial erratics are scattered throughout

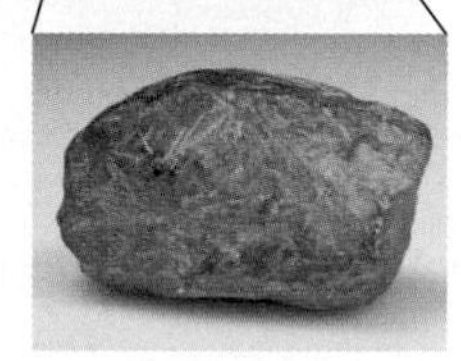

Figure 9 Glacial till is an unsorted mixture of many different sediment sizes. A close look often reveals cobbles that have been scratched as they were dragged along by the glacier.

pastures and farm fields. Early settlers cleared the smaller ones from their fields and piled them into stone fences that remain today. Geologists can sometimes determine the path of a long-gone glacier by studying the minerals in glacial erratics.

What is glacial drift?

Moraines, Outwash Plains, and Kettles

Glaciers are responsible for a variety of depositional features, including moraines, outwash plains, kettles, drumlins, and eskers.

When glaciers melt, they leave layers or ridges of till called **moraines.** These widespread glacial features come in several varieties.

Figure 10 The dark stripe running down the middle of this glacier is a medial moraine. It formed from the lateral moraines of these two merging valley glaciers.

Lateral Moraines The sides of a valley glacier gather large amounts of debris from the valley walls. Lateral moraines are ridges that form along the sides of glacial valleys when the glacier melts and leaves the material it has gathered. Medial moraines are formed when two valley glaciers join to form a single ice stream. Observe the medial and lateral moraines in Figure 10. The till that was once carried along the edges of each glacier joins to form a dark stripe of debris within the newly enlarged glacier.

End Moraines and Ground Moraines Glaciers can remain stationary for long periods of time. When a glacier is stationary it means snow and ice accumulate at the head of the glacier at the same rate snow and ice melt at the foot of the glacier. Within the glacier, the ice still flows. It acts as a conveyor belt to carry rock debris to the end of the glacier. When the ice there melts, it deposits the debris and forms a ridge called an end moraine. The longer the glacier remains stationary, the larger the end moraine grows.

Ground moraines form when glaciers begin to recede. The glacier front continues to deliver debris. The glacier deposits sediment as the ice melts away. However, instead of forming a ridge, the retreating glacier creates a rock-strewn, gently rolling plain. This ground moraine fills in low spots and clogs old stream channels. Ground moraine can thus result in poorly drained swamp lands.

Moraines, Outwash Plains, and Kettles

Build Science Skills L2

Comparing and Contrasting Have students read the text on moraines. Ask: **What do all moraines have in common?** *(All moraines are glacial deposits of till.)* Ask: **How do the various types of moraines differ?** *(Moraines are categorized by how and where the till is deposited. The till of lateral moraines forms on the side of the glacier. The till of a stationary glacier forms at the end of the glacier, forming an end moraine. Receding glaciers scatter till across the width of the glacier as it retreats. Terminal and recessional moraines form when a glacier forms an end moraine and ground moraines many times before it completely melts.)*
Verbal

Build Science Skills L2

Designing Experiments ACTIVITY Instruct students to design an experiment that models glacial deposition of till. Suggest they use a freezer and the following materials: sand, ice cube trays, water, and a pan or tray with a slope, such as the type used with painting rollers. *(Students' designs will vary, but may involve covering sand with water in the ice cube tray and using the freezer to make ice, then placing the ice cubes with sand on the sloped pan or tray to see how sand collects as the ice melts.)*
Kinesthetic, Logical

Customize for Inclusion Students

Gifted Have interested students conduct research to find out what glacial activity their area has experienced. Their research should include current activity if there are glaciers in your area, or historical activity of glaciers and ice sheets during ice ages. They should investigate whether till, stratified drift, or glacial erratics have been deposited, and whether any moraines or glacial features were created. Encourage them to contact local geologists if they can. Then have them prepare a presentation of their findings for the class. If no notable glacial activity has occurred in your area, instruct students to pick a region that was affected by glaciers, such as the Great Lakes region.

Answer to . . .

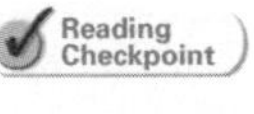

Glacial drift is all sediment that is deposited by a glacier.

Build Science Skills L2

Comparing and Contrasting Have students read the text on pp. 196–197 about outwash plains, kettles, drumlins, and eskers. Ask: **What do outwash plains, kettles, drumlins, and eskers have in common?** *(All are landscape features formed by glaciers.)* **How do they differ?** *(An outwash plain is a deposit of sediment left by the glacial meltwater. A kettle forms when blocks of stagnant ice become buried and eventually melt. This melting leaves pits in the glacial sediment. Drumlins are streamlined hills composed of till. The steep side of a drumlin once faced the direction of the advancing ice and the gentler slope points in the direction the ice moved. Eskers are snake-like ridges composed of sand and gravel that were deposited by streams once flowing in tunnels beneath the glaciers.)*
Verbal

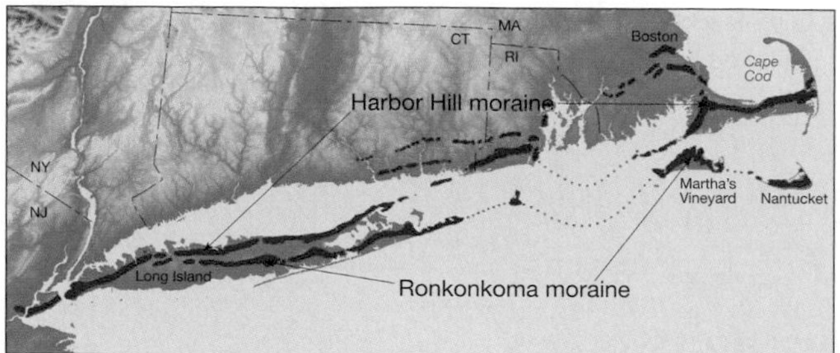

Figure 11 Long Island, Cape Cod, Martha's Vineyard, and Nantucket are remnants of an end moraine.

Terminal and Recessional Moraines Glaciers can periodically retreat, then find equilibrium again and remain stationary for some time. A glacier forms a new end moraine during the stationary period, then another ground moraine once it starts retreating again. This pattern can repeat many times before the glacier completely melts. The farthest end moraine is the terminal end moraine. The end moraines that form when the ice front occasionally becomes stationary during its retreat are recessional end moraines.

End moraines that formed in the recent ice age are prominent in the landscapes of the Midwest and Northeast. The Kettle Moraine is a scenic one that occurs in Wisconsin near Milwaukee. New York's Long Island is part of a series of end moraines stretching from eastern Pennsylvania to Cape Cod, Massachusetts. Figure 11 shows the locations of these end moraines that form part of the Northeast coast.

Outwash Plains At the same time that an end moraine is forming, streams of fast-moving meltwater emerge from the bases of glaciers. As mentioned before, this water is often so choked with fine sediment that it looks like milk. Once it leaves the glacier, the water slows and drops the sediment in a broad, ramp-like accumulation downstream from the end moraine. This type of sediment ramp resulting from an ice sheet is called an outwash plain.

Kettles You can often find depressions and small lakes called kettles within end moraines and outwash plains, as shown in Figure 12. Kettles form when blocks of stagnant ice become buried in drift and eventually melt. This melting leaves pits in the glacial sediment. A well-known example of a kettle is Walden Pond near Concord, Massachusetts. Thousands of kettles dot the landscape of the Upper Midwest in Wisconsin and Minnesota.

Drumlins and Eskers Moraines are not the only landforms deposited by glaciers. Some landscapes have many elongated parallel hills made of till. Other areas have conical hills and narrow winding ridges made mainly of stratified drift. If you know what to look for, the signs of a once-glaciated landscape are unmistakable—especially from an airplane.

Drumlins are streamlined hills composed of till. Drumlins are taller and steeper on one end, and they range in height from 15 to 60 meters and average 0.4 to 0.8 kilometer long. The steep side of the hill faces the direction the ice came from, and the gentler slope points in the direction

Customize for Inclusion Students

Learning Disabled You can revise the procedure described in "Designing Experiments" on p. 195 to help slow and visual learners understand the formation of the depositional features caused by glaciers. Use ice cubes containing pepper and various planar surfaces (one grooved, and one flat) to model these depositional features. You may alternatively choose to have students use these materials to design experiments themselves.

the ice moved. Drumlins occur in clusters called drumlin fields. Near Rochester, New York, one cluster contains nearly 10,000 drumlins. Their streamlining shows they were molded by active glaciers.

Eskers are snake-like ridges composed of sand and gravel that were deposited by streams once flowing in tunnels beneath glaciers. They can be several meters high and many kilometers long. Many eskers are mined for the sand and gravel they contain.

What depositional features do glaciers form?

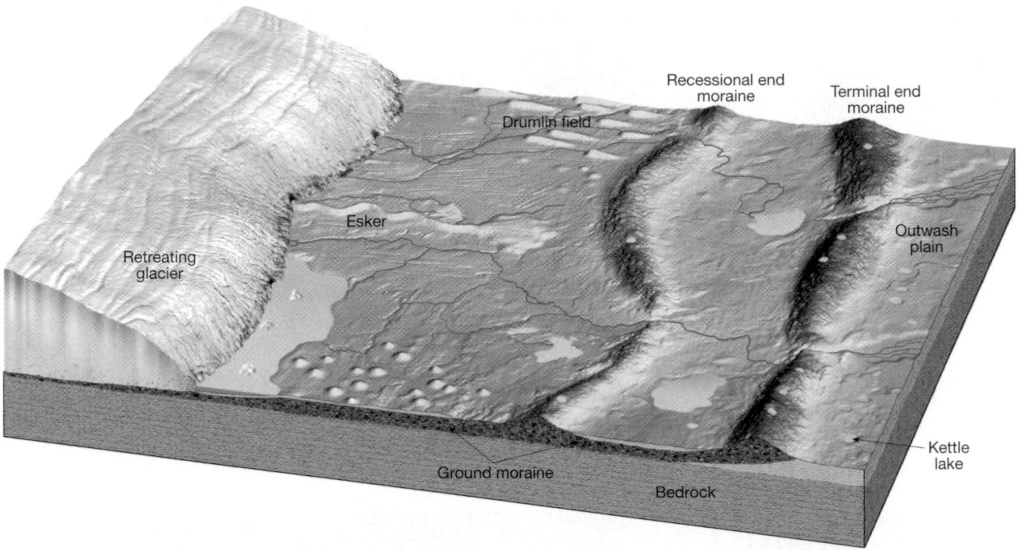

Figure 12 The landscape left by a retreating glacier includes a number of distinctive features. The terminal end moraine marks the farthest extent of the glacier. Recessional moraines occur where a retreating glacier temporarily becomes stationary.
Using Analogies *How is a glacier like a conveyor belt?*

Glaciers of the Ice Age

During the recent ice age continental ice sheets and alpine glaciers covered a lot more land than they do today. People once thought that glacial deposits had drifted in on icebergs or that they swept across the landscape in a catastrophic flood. However, scientific field investigations during the nineteenth century provided convincing evidence that an extensive ice age explained these deposits and many other features.

During the recent ice age, glaciers covered almost 30 percent of Earth's land, including large portions of North America, Europe, and Siberia, as shown in Figure 13. The Northern Hemisphere had twice the ice of the Southern Hemisphere. The Southern Hemisphere has far less land, so glaciation was mostly confined to Antarctica. By contrast, North America and Eurasia have plenty of land where the ice sheets could spread.

Glaciers of the Ice Age

Integrate Biology **L2**

Change in Sea Level A far-reaching effect of the most recent ice age was the worldwide change in sea level that accompanied each advance and retreat of the ice sheets. The snow that forms glaciers ultimately comes from moisture evaporated from the oceans. Therefore, when the ice sheets increased in size, sea level fell and the shorelines shifted seaward. Estimates suggest that sea level was as much as 100 m lower than today. Land that is presently flooded by the oceans was dry. The Atlantic Coast of the United States lay more than 100 km to the east of New York City. France and Britain were joined where the English Channel is today. Alaska and Siberia were connected across the Bering Strait. Southeast Asia was tied by dry land to the islands of Indonesia. Ask: **If Siberia and Alaska were connected by a land bridge, would biologists find evidence of this? Explain.** *(Yes, biologists should find evidence such as fossil remains of the same animals in both locations. In fact, fossil remains suggest that there was a migration of mammoths across the Bering Strait from Asia into North America.)*
Verbal, Logical

Answer to . . .

Figure 12 *It carries rock and debris along with it as it moves, just as a conveyor belt carries items along with it as it moves.*

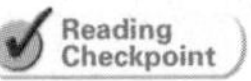

moraines, outwash plains, drumlins, eskers

Section 7.1 (continued)

3 ASSESS

Evaluate Understanding 

Divide the class into six groups. Have each group write three questions about the material covered in one of the following headings: Types of Glaciers; How Glaciers Move; Glacial Erosion; Landforms Created by Glacial Erosion; Glacial Deposits; Moraines, Outwash Plains, and Kettles; and Glaciers of the Ice Age. Invite students to take turns asking one question of the class.

Reteach 

Use Figures 4 and 7 to review information about glaciers.

Solution

7. 10 m / 1 month × 1 month / 30 days = 0.33 m/day or about 33 cm/day

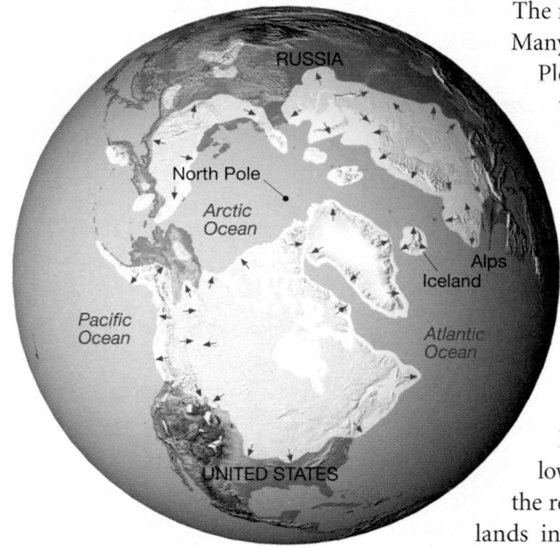

Figure 13 This map shows the extent of Northern Hemisphere ice sheets during the recent ice age.

The recent ice age began two to three million years ago. Many of the major glacial episodes occurred during the Pleistocene epoch when wooly mammoths and saber-toothed cats roamed the landscape. To some people the Pleistocene is synonymous with the recent ice age, but it actually began before this epoch on the geologic time scale.

Ice Age Effects on Drainage The ice sheets greatly affected the drainage patterns over large regions. For example, before glaciation, the Missouri River flowed northward toward Hudson Bay in Canada. The Mississippi River flowed through central Illinois. Furthermore, the Great Lakes did not exist. Their locations were marked by lowlands with rivers that flowed toward the east. During the recent ice age, glacial erosion transformed these lowlands into wide, deep basins that filled with water and eventually became the Great Lakes.

The formation and growth of ice sheets triggered changes in climates beyond the glacial margins. Regions that are arid today became cooler and wetter. This change in climate resulted in the formation of lakes in such areas as the Basin and Range region of Nevada and Utah. One of these lakes was ancient Lake Bonneville, which covered much of western Utah. The Great Salt Lake is all that remains of this glacial lake.

Section 7.1 Assessment

Reviewing Concepts

1. What are the two basic types of glaciers? Where is each type found?
2. Describe how glaciers move. Which property or properties of ice allow this movement?
3. How does glacial till differ from stratified drift? Describe one glacial feature made of each type of sediment.
4. Name three glacial features formed by erosion and three that are formed by deposition. What does each feature look like?

Critical Thinking

5. **Comparing and Contrasting** Compare and contrast advancing and retreating glaciers.
6. **Inferring** The snowline at the poles is sea level. Close to the equator, the snowline occurs high up on the tallest mountains. What is the relationship between the distance from the equator and snowline?

Math Practice

7. A glacier advances 20 meters over a period of about two months. What is its approximate rate of advance per day?

Section 7.1 Assessment

1. Valley glaciers look like streams of ice flowing between steep rock walls. They exist in high mountains. Ice sheets are enormous ice masses that cover everything but the highest land. The biggest ones are in Greenland and Antarctica.

2. Glaciers slip downhill due to gravity as well as flowing due to actual movement within the ice. The property known as plasticity allows for this.

3. Glacial till is an unsorted mixture of many different sizes. Moraines, which are ridges formed from material dropped by glaciers, are made of till. Stratified drift contains particles sorted by size and weight of the debris. Outwash plains, which are sediment ramps that extend downstream of an end moraine, are composed of stratified drift.

4. Erosion: cirque—a bowl-shaped depression at the head of a glacial valley; arête—snaking, sharp-edged ridge; horn—pyramid-shaped peak. Deposition: end moraine—debris dropped in a ridge at the face of a stationary glacier; ground moraine—a rock-strewn, gently rolling plain formed from sediments dropped by a retreating glacier; drumlins—streamlined hill made of glacial till

5. Both types flow and carry debris. Advancing glaciers accumulate ice faster than ice melts; retreating glaciers melt faster than ice accumulates.

6. The farther away from the equator you travel, the lower the snowline is.

7.2 Deserts

Reading Focus

Key Concepts

- How does running water affect deserts?
- What roles do mechanical and chemical weathering play in forming deserts?

Reading Strategy

Summarizing Write each blue heading in the section on a sheet of paper. Write a brief summary of the text for each heading.

Weathering
?
?

The Role of Water
?
?

Vocabulary

- alluvial fan
- playa lake

Desert landscapes reveal the effects of both running water and wind. As you will see, these combine in different ways in different places to result in a variety of desert landscapes.

Geologic Processes in Arid Climates

If you live in a humid region, visiting a desert might at first seem like encountering an alien planet. Rounded hills and curving slopes are typical of humid regions. By contrast, deserts have angular rocks, sheer canyon walls, and surfaces covered in pebbles or sand, shown in Figure 14. Despite their differences, the same geologic processes operate in both humid regions and deserts.

Weathering In humid regions, well-developed soils support an almost continuous cover of vegetation. In these regions, the slopes and rock edges are rounded and the landscape reflects the strong influence of chemical weathering. **By contrast, much of the weathered debris in deserts has resulted from mechanical weathering.** That debris consists of rock whose minerals remain unchanged. In dry lands, rock weathering of any type is greatly reduced because of the lack of moisture and scarcity of organic acids from decaying plants. **Chemical weathering, however, is not completely absent in deserts. Over long time spans, clays and thin soils do form.** Many iron-bearing silicate minerals oxidize, producing the rust-colored stain found tinting some desert landscapes.

Figure 14 Desert landscapes vary a great deal. This landscape is in California's Death Valley.

Section 7.2

1 FOCUS

Section Objectives

7.5 **Describe** how running water affects deserts.

7.6 **Explain** the roles mechanical and chemical weathering play in the formation of deserts.

Reading Focus

Build Vocabulary  L2

Paraphrase Have students write the definition of each vocabulary term in their own words.

Reading Strategy L2

Weathering Sample answer: Mechanical weathering is dominant in the desert. Chemical weathering does occur, but the process is very slow.

The Role of Water Sample answer: Although it doesn't rain often in the desert, the erosional effects of rain are significant.

2 INSTRUCT

Geologic Processes in Arid Climates

Build Science Skills  L2

Observing Have students look closely at Figure 14. Ask: **If someone showed you this photograph, what are three features that would lead you to conclude that this was a desert climate?** (*Sample answers: sparse vegetation; only small, shrub-like vegetation present; lots of exposed soil and gravel*)
Visual, Logical

Build Reading Literacy L1

Refer to **p. 586D** in **Chapter 21,** which provides the guidelines for SQ3R (Survey, Question, Read, Recite, Review).

SQ3R Teach this independent-study skill as a whole-class exercise. Direct students to survey the section and write headings such as Geologic Processes in Arid Climates. As they survey, ask students to write one question for each heading, such as "What type of weathering occurs in a desert climate?" Then, have students write answers to the questions as they read the section. After students finish reading, demonstrate how to recite the questions and answers, explaining that vocalizing in your own words helps you retain what you have learned. Finally, have students review their notes the next day.
Verbal

Use Visuals L1

Figure 16 Have students look carefully at Figure 16. Ask: **When rain falls at the top of these barren mountains, what will the water look like when it reaches the bottom?** *(The water will be dirty because it will contain a lot of sediment that it has picked up as it flowed down the mountainside.)* **What happens to the sediment when the water reaches the gentle slopes in the foreground of this picture?** *(The rain water loses velocity and dumps its load of sediment on the gentle slopes.)*
Verbal

A

B

Figure 15 A Most of the time stream channels in deserts remain dry. **B** This is the same stream shortly after a heavy shower. Ephemeral streams can cause a large amount of erosion in a short time.
Predicting ***How long will the water flow in this stream?***

Reading Checkpoint *Why do deserts experience less chemical weathering than humid regions?*

The Role of Water Permanent streams are normally found in humid regions. However, in the desert, you'll find bridges with no water beneath them and dips in the road where empty stream channels cross. **In the desert, most streams are ephemeral—they only carry water after it rains.** A typical ephemeral stream might flow for only a few days or just a few hours during a year. In some years, the channels may not carry any water. In the western states people call these dry creeks *washes* or *arroyos.*

Customize for Inclusion Students

Learning Disabled For students with difficulty reading and writing, customize the Writing in Science feature on p. 202 to allow students to make a multimedia presentation instead of a written report.

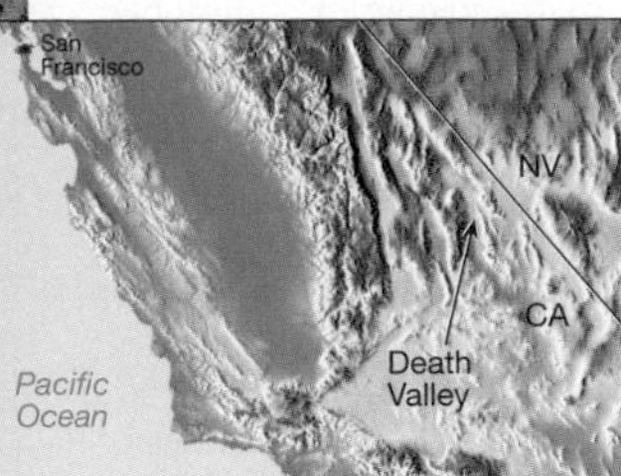

Figure 16 Alluvial Fans Over the years, alluvial fans enlarge and merge with fans from adjacent canyons to produce an apron of sediment along the mountain front.

Ephemeral streams are known for dangerous flash flooding after heavy rains. During heavy showers, so much rain falls that the soil cannot absorb it. The lack of vegetation allows water to quickly run off the land, as shown in Figure 15. The floods end as quickly as they start. Because there are fewer plants in deserts to anchor the soil, the amount of erosion caused during a single-short lived rain event is impressive. Floods in humid regions are different. A flood on a river like the Mississippi can take days to reach its crest and days to subside.

Basin and Range: A Desert Landscape

Because arid regions typically lack permanent streams, they have interior drainage. This means that they have intermittent streams that do not flow out of the desert to the ocean. In the United States, the dry Basin and Range provides an excellent example. The region includes southern Oregon, all of Nevada, western Utah, southeastern California, southern Arizona, and southern New Mexico. The name Basin and Range is an apt description for this region, because it contains more than 200 relatively small mountain ranges that rise 900 to 1500 meters above the basins that separate them.

When the occasional torrents of water produced by sporadic rains move down the mountain canyons, they are heavily loaded with sediment. Emerging from the confines of the canyon, the runoff spreads over the gentler slopes at the base of the mountains and quickly loses velocity. Consequently, most of its load is dumped within a short distance. The result is a cone of debris known as an **alluvial fan** at the mouth of a canyon, as shown in Figure 16.

Basin and Range: A Desert Landscape

Desert Water Erosion **L2**

Purpose Students will observe how water erodes a barren landscape and how alluvial fans form.

Materials sharpened pencil, paper cup, scissors, 1/2 of a drinking straw, modeling clay, cookie sheet, ruler, large beaker, water, soil, two 2" × 4" boards about 15 cm long

Procedure Use the sharpened pencil to make a hole in the side of the paper cup near the bottom. Insert one end of the straw into the hole in the cup. Seal the hole around the straw with modeling clay. Cover the cookie sheet with a thin layer of soil. Elevate the cookie sheet about 10 cm with a board. Set the cup at the top of the cookie sheet. Hold your finger over the end of the straw to keep the water from flowing. Use the beaker to fill the cup with water. Remove your finger and let the water flow. Observe what happens to the soil. Observe how far the soil flowed past the end of the cookie sheet. Elevate the cookie sheet 5 cm and repeat the experiment. Observe what happens to the soil and how far the soil flowed past the end of the cookie sheet. Note any differences in the two elevations.

Expected Outcomes Students will observe the soil flow off the cookie sheet just as the soil flows off a barren landscape. Students also should observe that soil will not flow as far when the slope is less steep. Alluvial fans form when the slope is not steep.
Visual

Facts and Figures

Many of the world's deserts are located in two belts. One belt is located along the Tropic of Cancer in the Northern Hemisphere. The deserts located in this belt are the Gobi in China, the deserts in southwestern North America, the Sahara in North Africa, and the Arabian and Iranian deserts in the Middle East. The second belt is located along the Tropic of Capricorn in the Southern Hemisphere. These deserts include the Patagonia in Argentina, the Kalahari in southern Africa, and the Great Victoria and Great Sandy deserts of Australia. These belts are formed when hot, moist air at the equator rises, cools, and loses its moisture. Then, the air descends, picking up moisture and drying out the land, creating these desert regions along the tropics.

Answer to . . .

Figure 15 *for a few hours to a few days*

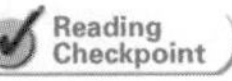 *Water is necessary for chemical weathering, so arid climates experience less chemical weathering than humid regions. Also, fewer plants exist to decay and contribute organic acids.*

Section 7.2 (continued)

3 ASSESS

Evaluate Understanding L2

Have students write three review questions for the section. Invite students to take turns asking questions to the class.

Reteach L1

Use Figures 14, 15, and 16 to review the main ideas in this section.

First the ephemeral stream will be dry. Then, a sudden rush of water will occur that builds both in volume and velocity for several hours. The flood will then subside as quickly as it started.

Q *I heard that deserts are expanding. Is that true?*

A Yes. The problem is called desertification, and it refers to the alteration of land to desert-like conditions as the result of human activities. It commonly takes place on the margins of deserts and results mostly from inappropriate land use. It is triggered when the modest natural vegetation in marginal areas is removed by plowing or grazing. When drought occurs, as it often does in these regions, and the vegetative cover has been destroyed beyond the minimum to hold the soil against erosion, the destruction becomes irreversible. Desertification is occurring in many places but is particularly serious in the region south of the Sahara Desert known as the Sahel.

On the rare occasions of abundant rainfall, or snowmelt in the mountains, streams may flow across the alluvial fans to the center of the basin, converting the basin floor into a shallow **playa lake.** Playa lakes last only a few days or weeks, before evaporation and infiltration remove the water. The dry, flat lake bed that remains is called a *playa.*

Humid regions have complex systems of rivers and streams that drain the land. Streams in dry regions lack this extensive drainage system. **Most desert streams dry up long before they ever reach the ocean. The streams are quickly depleted by evaporation and soil infiltration.**

Some permanent streams do manage to cross arid regions. The Colorado and Nile Rivers begin in well-watered mountains with huge water supplies. The rivers are full enough at the beginning to survive their desert crossings. The Nile River, for example, leaves the lakes and mountains of central Africa and covers almost 3000 kilometers of the Sahara without a single tributary adding to its flow. In humid regions, however, rivers generally gain water from both incoming tributaries and groundwater.

The point to remember about running water in the desert is this: although it is infrequent, it is an important geological force. **Most desert erosion results from running water. Although wind erosion is more significant in deserts than elsewhere, water does most of the erosional work in deserts.** Wind plays a different primary role in the desert. It transports and deposits the sediments to create dunes.

Section 7.2 Assessment

Reviewing Concepts

1. How are ephemeral streams different form streams in humid locations?
2. How do weathering processes affect deserts?
3. Why is erosion by running water important in deserts?
4. How does a river survive crossing an arid region?

Critical Thinking

5. **Comparing and Contrasting** Compare and contrast the Nile River with the Mississippi River. Which factor is most responsible for their differences?
6. **Applying Concepts** Explain how evaporation affects drainage systems in desert areas.

Writing in Science

Suppose you are standing on a bridge over an ephemeral stream in the desert. Write a paragraph describing what you might see following a sudden downpour.

Section 7.2 Assessment

1. Ephemeral streams are not permanent but have a greater propensity to produce flash floods, which cause substantial erosion.
2. Water and wind cause mechanical weathering and produce angular rocks, sheer canyon walls, and pebble-covered surfaces.
3. Because there are fewer plants in deserts to anchor the soil, there can be a great amount of erosion caused during a single short-lived rain event.
4. It must be full enough at the beginning to survive the soil infiltration and evaporation that occur in the desert.
5. Both carry water. The Nile has few tributaries. The Mississippi drainage system is highly branched. The Mississippi takes longer to crest and subside. Climate is the factor most responsible for the rivers' differences.
6. Streams in desert areas lack extensively branched drainage systems. They do not flow out of the desert to oceans, and instead have interior drainage, helping evaporation to dry up ephemeral streams.

7.3 Landscapes Shaped by Wind

Reading Focus

Key Concepts

- How does deflation cause erosion in the desert?
- How does abrasion shape desert landscapes?
- What types of landforms are deposited by wind?
- How do sand dunes differ?

Vocabulary

- deflation
- desert pavement
- loess
- dune

Reading Strategy

Outlining Before you read, make an outline of this section. Use the green headings as the main topics and the blue headings as subtopics. As you read, add supporting details.

Landscapes Shaped by Wind
I. Wind Erosion
A. Deflation
B. Abrasion
II. ____?____
A. ____?____

Wind Erosion

Compared with running water, wind does not do nearly as much erosional work on the land, even in deserts. But wind is still an important force. Humid areas can resist wind erosion because moisture binds soil particles together and plants anchor the soil. But desert soils are dry and have less vegetation to hold soil in place. Therefore, wind does its most effective erosional work in deserts.

Strong desert winds pick up, transport, and deposit great quantities of fine sediment. Farmers of the Great Plains experienced the power of wind erosion during the 1930s. After they plowed the natural vegetation from this semi-arid region, a severe drought set in. The land was left exposed to wind erosion. Vast dust storms swept away the fertile topsoil. The area became known as the Dust Bowl.

Wind erodes in the desert in two ways: deflation and abrasion. Deflation is the lifting and removal of loose particles such as clay and silt. Coarser sand particles roll or skip along the surface in a process called saltation. These large sand particles make up the bed load. In portions of the Dust Bowl, deflation lowered the land by a meter or more in only a few years, as shown in Figure 17.

Deflation also results in shallow depressions called blowouts. You can see thousands of blowouts in the Great Plains. They range from small dimples less than 1 meter deep and 3 meters wide to depressions more than 45 meters deep and several kilometers across.

Figure 17 The mounds in this photo show the level of the land before deflation removed the topsoil. The mounds are 1.2 meters tall and are anchored by vegetation. The photo was taken in July 1936 in Granville, North Dakota and reveals the extent of the damage in the Dust Bowl. **Applying Concepts** ***How did farmers contribute to ruining the land during the Dust Bowl?***

Section 7.3

1 FOCUS

Section Objectives

- **7.7** **Describe** two ways that wind can cause erosion.
- **7.8** **Identify** types of landforms that are deposited by the wind.
- **7.9** **Describe** how sand dunes differ.

Reading Focus

Build Vocabulary L2

Concept Map Have students construct a concept map using all of the vocabulary terms. Students should place the main concept (Landscapes Shaped by Wind) in the center oval and use descriptive linking phrases to connect the terms. Instruct students to place the terms in ovals and connect the ovals with lines on which linking words are placed.

Reading Strategy L2

II. Wind Deposits; **A.** Loess; **B.** Sand Dunes; **III.** Types of Sand Dunes; **A.** Barchan Dunes; **B.** Transverse Dunes; **C.** Barchanoid Dunes; **D.** Longitudinal Dunes; **E.** Parabolic Dunes; **F.** Star Dunes

2 INSTRUCT

Wind Erosion

L2

Students may think that an area shrouded in mist cannot be a desert. This is not true. Deserts shrouded in mist form along coastlines. Cold waters from the Arctic and Antarctic regions and cold water from ocean depths move toward the equator and cool the air currents above them. This cool air carries fog and mist, but little rain. These misty air currents flow across the coastal regions of southern California, Baja California, southwest Africa, and Chile.

Answer to . . .

Figure 17 *Mechanized cultivation removed prairie grass from large areas, leaving soil vulnerable to wind.*

Section 7.3 (continued)

Use Visuals

L1

Figure 18 Have students look closely at Figure 18A. Ask: **What is occurring in the first picture of Figure 18A?** *(Deflation of the desert surface begins. Fine sediment is removed from the surface of the desert floor.)* **What is occurring in the second picture of Figure 18A?** *(Deflation continues as fine sediment is removed, leaving only coarse particles.)* **What is occurring in the third picture of Figure 18A?** *(All fine particles are removed. The remaining coarse particles have been compressed into desert pavement.)*
Visual, Verbal

Wind Deposits

Build Reading Literacy

L1

Refer to **p. 392D** in **Chapter 14,** which provides the guidelines for preview.

Preview Have students read the bold subheads and examine the figures in the section. Then, ask students to list the important concepts they learned or will learn in the section. *(how landscapes are shaped by wind and what wind erosion and wind deposits can do)*
Visual, Verbal

Integrate Language Arts

Dust Bowl Literature John Steinbeck's novel *The Grapes of Wrath* is about an Oklahoma farming family who are forced to leave their home and move to California in a desperate attempt to survive during the Dust Bowl and the Depression. Select a passage from this novel to share with the class.
Verbal

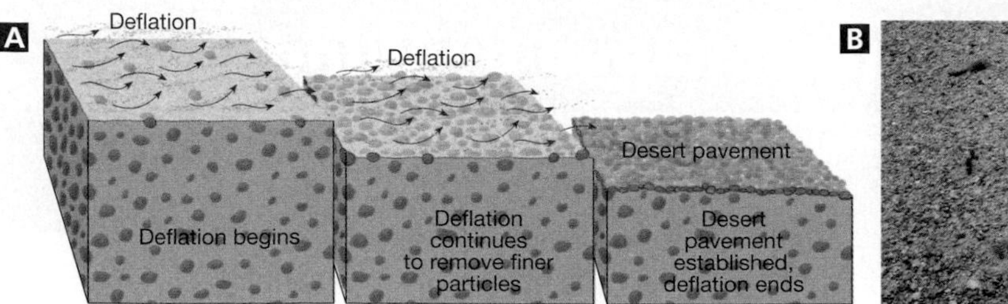

Figure 18 A These cross sections show how deflation removes the sand and silt of the desert surface until only coarser particles remain. These coarser particles concentrate into a tightly packed layer called desert pavement. **B** Desert pavement like this in Arizona's Sonoran Desert protects the surface from further deflation. **Predicting** ***What will happen if a vehicle disturbs this desert pavement?***

In portions of many deserts, the surface is characterized by a layer of course pebbles and cobbles that are too large to be moved by the wind. Deflation creates a stony surface layer called **desert pavement** when it removes all the sand and silt and leaves only coarser particles. See Figure 18. The remaining surface of coarse pebbles and cobbles is protected from further deflation—unless vehicles or animals break it up. If something does disturb the surface, the wind begins eroding once again.

Wind can erode by abrasion, too. Abrasion happens when windblown sand cuts and polishes exposed rock surfaces. Blowing sand can grind away at boulders and smaller rocks, sometimes sandblasting them into odd shapes. Abrasion is often credited for features such as balanced rocks that stand high atop narrow pedestals or the detailing on tall pinnacles. However, these features are not the results of abrasion. Sand rarely travels more than a meter above the surface, so the wind's sandblasting effect is limited in a vertical extent. However, in some areas, telephone poles have been cut through near the base.

What is deflation?

Figure 19 This loess bluff near the Mississippi River in southern Illinois is about 3 meters high.

Wind Deposits

The wind can create landforms when it deposits its sediments, especially in deserts and along coasts. Both layers of loess and sand dunes are landscape features deposited by wind. These blankets of silt and mounds of sand are striking features in some parts of the world.

Loess **Loess** is windblown silt that blankets the landscape. Dust storms over thousands of years picked up this material, transported it, and then deposited it. The thickest and most extensive deposits of loess on Earth occur in western and northern China. The silt was derived from nearby deserts. This fine, buff-colored sediment gives the Yellow River its name. You also can find loess in the United States. See Figure 19. Strong winds sweeping across glacial sediments created significant loess deposits in portions of South Dakota, Nebraska, Iowa, Missouri, Illinois, and the Columbia Plateau in the Pacific Northwest.

Customize for English Language Learners

Help beginning language learners by using a Cloze strategy to extract key information from the text about wind deposits. After reading the section Wind Deposits, have students fill in the blanks in the following sentences: **The wind can create landforms when it deposits its _______, especially in deserts and along _______. Both layers of loess and _______ are landscape features deposited by the _______. Unlike deposits of _______, which forms blanket-like layers over broad areas, winds commonly deposit _______ in mounds or ridges called _______.** *(sediments, coasts, sand dunes, wind, loess, sand, dunes)*

Figure 20 Sand slides down the steeper face of a dune in New Mexico's White Sands National Monument. Wind blows sand up the opposite, windward, face of the dune, then it drops down this sheltered side. Slippage along the steep side results in migration of the dune in the direction the wind blows.

Figure 21 These cross beds are part of the Navajo Sandstone in Zion National Park, Utah.

Sand Dunes Like running water, wind releases its load of sediment when its velocity falls and the energy available for transport diminishes. Sand begins to accumulate wherever an obstruction crosses its path and slows its movement. **Unlike deposits of loess, which form blanket-like layers over broad areas, winds commonly deposit sand in mounds or ridges called dunes.** Dunes can occur in places where the wind encounters an obstruction. The wind's velocity falls and the sand particles drop to the ground. Dunes can begin near obstructions as small as a clump of vegetation or a rock. Once the sand starts to mound up it serves as its own obstruction, and it traps more and more sand. With enough sand and long periods of steady wind, the mound of sand becomes a dune.

Dunes often are steeper on the sheltered side and more gently sloping inclined on the side facing the wind. Wind blows sand grains up the gentler windward side. Once the sand blows over the crest of the dune, the wind slows and the sand drops out. The sheltered side of the dune becomes steeper, and the sand eventually slides down the slope, as shown in Figure 20. In this way, the dune tends to migrate in the direction the wind blows.

As sand is deposited on the sheltered side of the dune, it forms layers inclined in the direction the wind is blowing. These sloping layers are called cross beds. When the dunes are eventually buried under other layers of sediment and become sedimentary rock, the cross beds remain as a record of their origin, as shown in Figure 21.

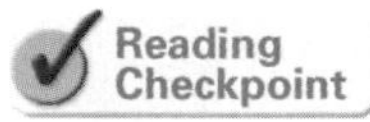

How do obstructions help to form dunes?

For: Links on wind erosion
Visit: www.SciLinks.org
Web Code: cjn-2073

Teacher Demo

Wind Erosion

Purpose Students will observe how wind erodes the landscape.

Materials sand, large piece of cardboard, water

Procedure Make two mounds of sand on the cardboard. Sprinkle water over one and leave the other one dry. Blow across the wet sand. Then, blow across the dry sand.

Expected Outcomes Students will observe the wet sand does not move. They will also observe that the dry sand is blown away by the movement of air just as wind moves the sand in a desert or in a dry region.
Visual, Logical

Download a worksheet on wind erosion for students to complete, and find additional teacher support from NSTA SciLinks.

Facts and Figures

What caused the Dust Bowl? Clearly, the fact that portions of the Great Plains experienced some of North America's strongest winds is important. However, it was the huge expansion of agriculture that set the stage for this disastrous period of soil erosion. Mechanization allowed the rapid transformation of the grass-covered prairies of this semiarid region into farms. Between 1870 and 1930, the area of cultivation in the region expanded nearly tenfold, from about 10 million acres to more than 100 million acres. As long as precipitation was adequate, the soil remained in place. However, when a prolonged drought struck in the 1930s, the unprotected fields were vulnerable to the wind. The results were severe crop loss, crop failures, and economic hardship.

Answer to . . .

Figure 18 *Further deflation will remove more sand and silt.*

Deflation occurs when wind lifts and removes loose particles such as clay and silt.

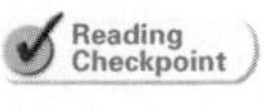

Obstructions reduce wind velocity and cause sand particles to drop to the ground.

Types of Sand Dunes

Build Science Skills L2

Interpreting Diagrams Have students study Figure 22. Ask: **Which sand dunes form from wind that blows in a single direction?** *(barchan, transverse, barchanoid, and parabolic)* **Which sand dunes form from wind that blows in multiple directions?** *(longitudinal and star)*
Verbal, Logical

Integrate Language Arts L2

Word Roots Tell students that one of the meanings of the Latin root *trans-* is "across." Ask students to discuss why *transverse* is an appropriate name for this type of dune. *(The wind blows across the dune.)*
Verbal

Types of Sand Dunes

Dunes are not just random heaps of sand. They occur in a variety of consistent forms worldwide. **What form sand dunes assume depends on the wind direction and speed, how much sand is available, and the amount of vegetation.** Figure 22 shows six different types of dunes.

Barchan Dunes Solitary sand dunes shaped like crescents are called barchan dunes. These form on flat, hard ground where supplies of sand and vegetation are limited. Barchan dunes move slowly and only reach heights of about 30 meters. If the wind direction is constant, barchan dunes remain symmetrical. One tip of the dune can grow larger than the other if the wind direction varies somewhat.

Transverse Dunes If prevailing winds are steady, sand is plentiful, and vegetation is sparse, dunes form in a series of long ridges. They are called transverse dunes because these ridges are perpendicular to the direction of the wind. Transverse dunes are typical in many coastal areas.

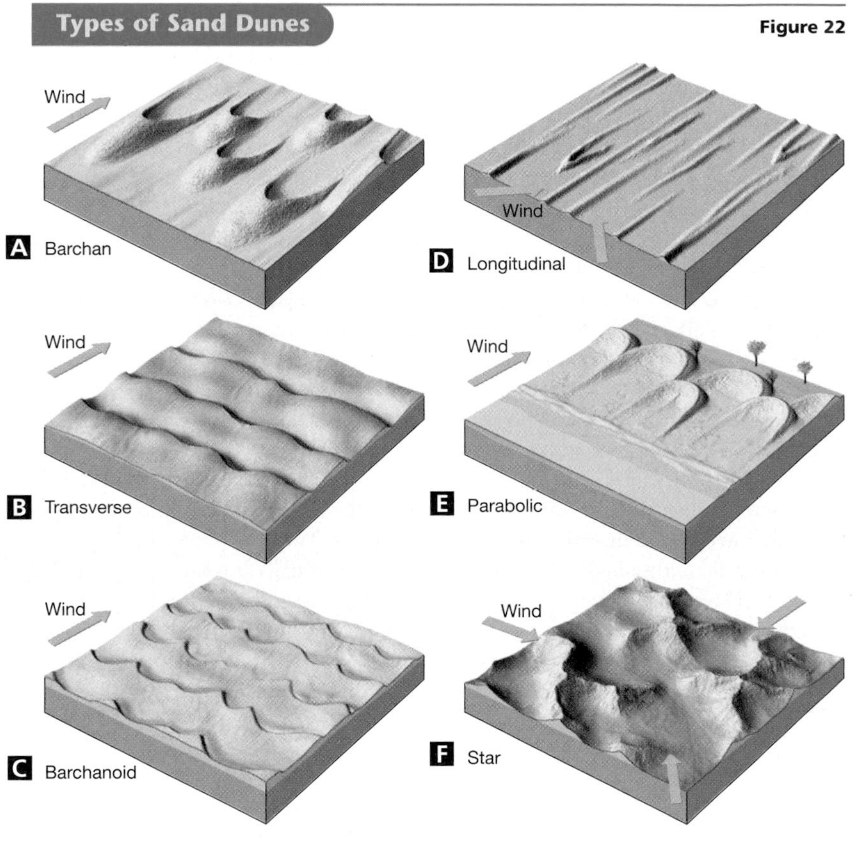

Customize for Inclusion Students

Visually Impaired Use dampened sand to create models of each type of sand dune pictured in Figure 22 for students with visual impairments.

They also comprise the "sand seas" found in parts of the Sahara and Arabian deserts. Transverse dunes in both of these deserts reach heights of 200 meters, measure 1 to 3 kilometers across, and extend for distances of 100 kilometers or more.

Barchanoid Dunes A common dune form that is intermediate between a barchan and transverse dune is the barchanoid dune. These scalloped rows of sand form at right angles to the wind. The rows resemble a series of barchans that have been positioned side by side. You can see them at White Sands National Monument in New Mexico.

Longitudinal Dunes Longitudinal dunes are long ridges of sand that form parallel to the prevailing wind. These dunes occur where sand supplies are moderate and the prevailing wind direction varies slightly. In portions of North Africa, Arabia, and central Australia, longitudinal dunes can reach nearly 100 meters high and extend for more than 100 kilometers.

Parabolic Dunes Parabolic dunes look like backward barchans. Their tips point into the wind instead of away from it. They form where some vegetation covers the sand. Parabolic dunes often form along the coast where strong onshore winds and abundant sand are available.

Star Dunes Star dunes are isolated hills of sand mostly found in parts of the Sahara and Arabian deserts. Their bases resemble stars and they usually have three or four sharp ridges that meet in the middle. Star dunes develop in areas of variable wind direction, and they sometimes reach heights of 90 meters.

Q *Aren't deserts mostly covered with sand dunes?*

A Many people think a desert is covered in drifting sand dunes. Some deserts do have striking sand dunes. But sand dunes worldwide represent only a small percentage of the total desert area. Dunes cover only one-tenth of the world's largest desert, the Sahara, and only one-third of the world's sandiest desert, the Arabian, is covered in dunes.

Section 7.3 Assessment

Reviewing Concepts

1. How does deflation lower the surface of the desert?
2. What would you expect to see in areas subject to abrasion?
3. What was the Dust Bowl, and why did it occur?
4. How does a dune help itself to grow?
5. What factors determine the shape of sand dunes?

Critical Thinking

5. **Comparing and Contrasting** Compare and contrast loess and sand dunes.
6. **Designing Experiments** Describe how you would conduct an experiment to determine the wind speed necessary to suspend sand, silt, and clay particles.

Connecting Concepts

Which dune type would you expect to travel the least? Explain your answer.

3 ASSESS

Evaluate Understanding L2

Ask students to write three quiz questions using the information in this section. Have students work in groups to quiz each other.

Reteach L1

Have students explain in their own words how the sand dunes are formed in Figure 22.

Connecting Concepts

Star dunes would travel the least, because variable winds will move the dunes back and forth rather than in a single direction.

Section 7.3 Assessment

1. Wind removes the loose clay and silt particles from the surface.
2. polished rock surfaces; oddly shaped rocks called ventifacts
3. a vast area of the Great Plains where wind erosion occurred in the 1930s; because a drought made the plowed ground vulnerable to wind erosion
4. It serves as its own wind obstruction, causing the wind to slow and sand to drop out.
5. wind direction and speed, how much sand is available, amount of vegetation
6. Both are wind-blown deposits. Loess is made of silt; dunes are made of sand.
7. Answers should include a reasonable way to alter and measure the wind speed, as well as to collect particles.

1 FOCUS

Objectives

In this feature, students will
- define erosion and identify its agents.
- describe the effects of erosion on different landforms.

Reading Focus

Build Vocabulary 

Define Terms Write the word *erosion* on the board. Have students define it. Have students brainstorm a list of places that show the effects of erosion in your region. Remind them of beaches, canyons, and other appropriate places.

2 INSTRUCT

Bellringer L2

Ask students if they have ever collected rocks from a river or ocean. Ask: **What was the texture of the rocks you collected?** *(Most of them are smooth.)* Ask: **What would account for the smoothness of these rocks?** *(The constant motion of the water on the rocks wears down rough points and makes the surface smooth.)* Discuss how running water affects hard objects and land over time.
Logical

Use Visuals 

Have students study the pictures and diagrams on this page and the next. Ask: **Are the effects of erosion obvious from year to year? Why or why not?** *(In most cases, the effects are not obvious because erosion is a gradual process. In the case of erosion due to desert storms, the effects are more immediately obvious.)*
Visual

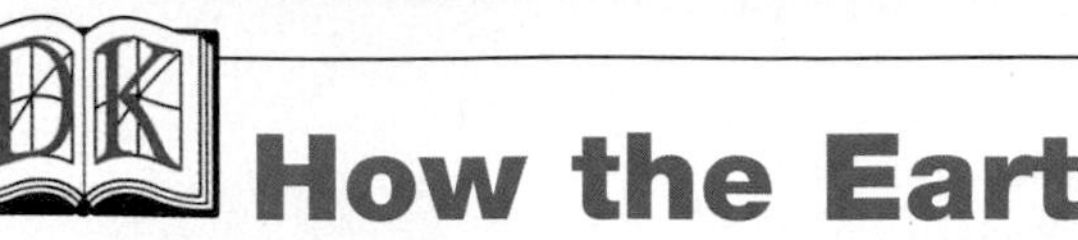

How the Earth Works

Erosion

Erosion is the process by which rocks are broken down by weathering and the loose material is carried away. Rock material can be moved by streams and rivers, by waves, by glacial ice, or by wind. The number of fragments that are moved and the distance that they travel are affected by factors such as the size and weight of the particles and the speed at which the eroding agent is moving. The eroded material is carried to another site where it is deposited as **sediment.** Erosion affects the landscapes of Central Asia, the Caucasus, and all regions of the world.

WATER FLOWING
As water flows from highlands to the sea, sharp descents result in rapids and waterfalls. Flowing water is an important agent of erosion.

SAND DUNES
A dune begins to form where a plant or other obstacle slows the wind, which drops its load of sand. As the sand piles up, it creates an ever-growing barrier to the wind, causing more sand to be dropped. Eventually the dune crest may collapse like an ocean wave.

EROSION IN ARID LANDS
When rare torrential rain comes to arid areas in Central Asia and elsewhere, entire mountainsides may be swept clean of boulders, rock fragments, sand, and clay. Flash floods wash eroded material down **wadis**—the valleys of streams that are usually dry.

SEAS OF SAND
The huge amounts of sand that comprise some deserts started out as rock that was weathered to form fine particles. The finer the particle, the farther it can be transported by agents of erosion.

Customize for Inclusion Students

Gifted Have students research ways to minimize erosion at the library or on the Internet. Ask them to create a flowchart or diagram that shows what people can do to minimize erosion. Students can present their diagrams to the class and explain them.

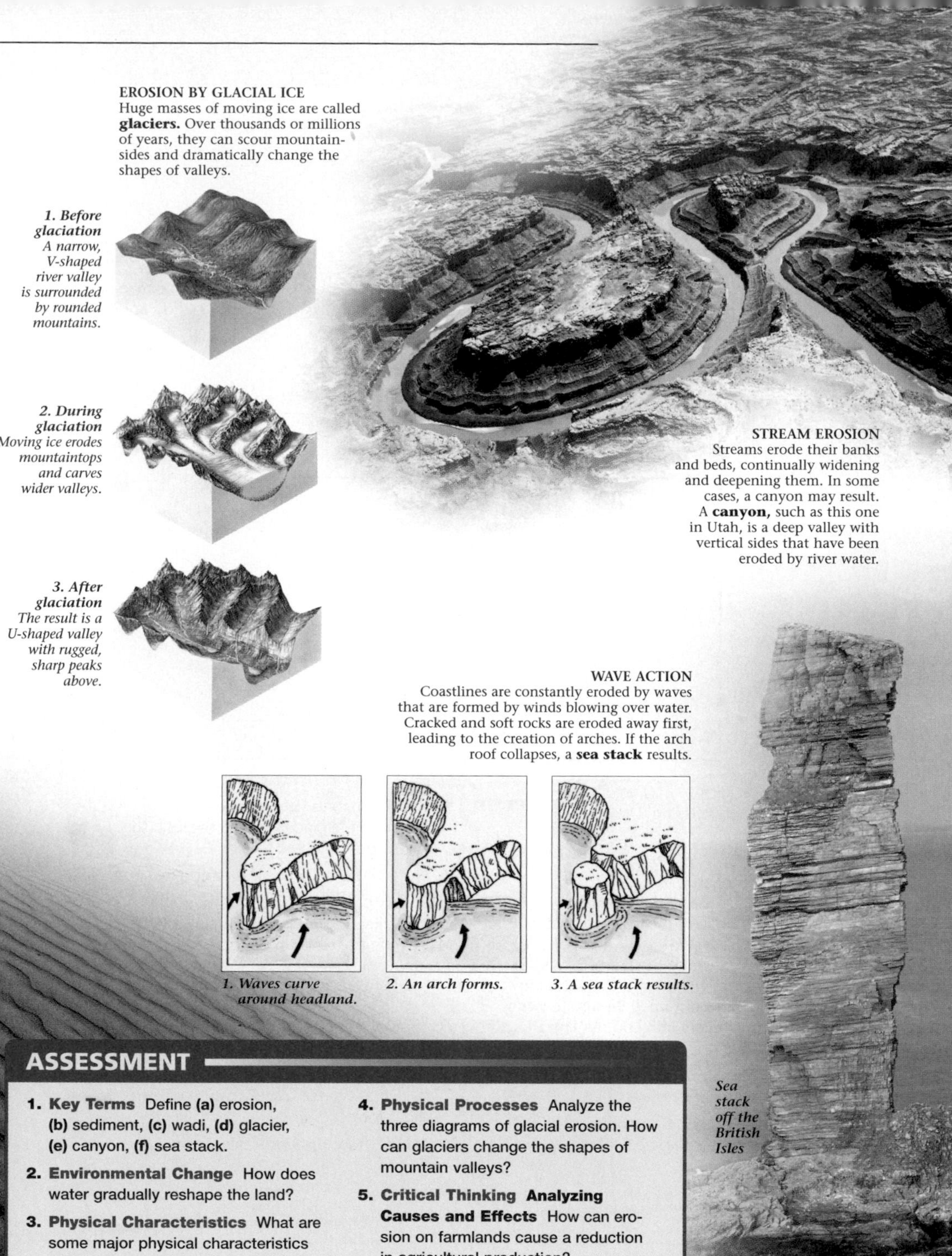

EROSION BY GLACIAL ICE
Huge masses of moving ice are called **glaciers.** Over thousands or millions of years, they can scour mountainsides and dramatically change the shapes of valleys.

1. Before glaciation *A narrow, V-shaped river valley is surrounded by rounded mountains.*

2. During glaciation *Moving ice erodes mountaintops and carves wider valleys.*

3. After glaciation *The result is a U-shaped valley with rugged, sharp peaks above.*

STREAM EROSION
Streams erode their banks and beds, continually widening and deepening them. In some cases, a canyon may result. A **canyon,** such as this one in Utah, is a deep valley with vertical sides that have been eroded by river water.

WAVE ACTION
Coastlines are constantly eroded by waves that are formed by winds blowing over water. Cracked and soft rocks are eroded away first, leading to the creation of arches. If the arch roof collapses, a **sea stack** results.

1. Waves curve around headland. *2. An arch forms.* *3. A sea stack results.*

Sea stack off the British Isles

ASSESSMENT

1. **Key Terms** Define **(a)** erosion, **(b)** sediment, **(c)** wadi, **(d)** glacier, **(e)** canyon, **(f)** sea stack.
2. **Environmental Change** How does water gradually reshape the land?
3. **Physical Characteristics** What are some major physical characteristics of an arid landscape eroded by wind and rain?
4. **Physical Processes** Analyze the three diagrams of glacial erosion. How can glaciers change the shapes of mountain valleys?
5. **Critical Thinking Analyzing Causes and Effects** How can erosion on farmlands cause a reduction in agricultural production?

209

3 ASSESS

Evaluate Understanding L2

Have students write sentences using the key terms from this feature. Remind them that the sentences should include the definition of each term. Encourage students to use more than one key term per sentence when possible.

Reteach L1

Draw a two-column chart on the board. Label the columns *Eroding Agent* and *Effects*. Have students use information from the text to describe how streams, waves, glaciers, and other eroding agents change the landscape.

Assessment

1. (a) the transport of loose material broken down by weathering; **(b)** eroded material that is deposited; **(c)** a valley of a usually dry stream; **(d)** a huge mass of moving ice; **(e)** a deep valley with vertical sides that have been eroded by river water; **(f)** a column of eroded coastline

2. Flowing water in the form of waterfalls, rivers, oceans, or rain breaks up rocks and other loose material.

3. Sample answer: sand dunes formed and unformed by wind, wadis created during flash floods, sand formed from rocks eroded by wind

4. Glaciers can change narrow, V-shaped valleys into wider, U-shaped valleys.

5. The soil's nutrients wash or blow away, making the land less productive.

Exploration Lab

Interpreting a Glacial Landscape

L2

Objectives
In this activity, students will:
- use a topographic map to identify geographic features formed by glaciers.
- infer how geographic features were formed.

Skills Focus **Graphing, Inferring, Drawing Conclusions**

 **Prep Time** 10 minutes to copy map

Class Time 45 minutes

Expected Outcome Many geographic features on a topographical map are easily identified and their origin is easily inferred.

Exploration Lab

Interpreting a Glacial Landscape

Topographic maps are valuable tools geologists use to interpret landscapes. Especially in the field—when your view can be limited—these maps not only help you determine your location, they can offer a bigger landscape picture than what is actually visible. See how well you can do at identifying glacial features on the map and interpreting them to reconstruct geologic history.

Problem How can a topographic map allow you to interpret a glacially formed landscape?

Materials
- topographic map
- piece of blank paper
- pencil

SOUTH NORTH

Sugar Loaf Mountain Bear Lake

Skills Graphing, Inferring, Drawing Conclusions

Procedure

1. Following line A on the map, sketch a topographic profile of the Lake Fork Valley onto the grid above. Place the straight edge of your blank paper along the line and mark in pencil where it meets every fifth contour line (the darker guide contours). Be sure to write the elevation of every fifth contour line along the *y*-axis of the profile grid.
2. How can you tell from your profile that the valley was formed by a glacier?
3. Was the valley shaped by a continental ice sheet or by a valley glacier? Explain how you know.
4. Use the map to help you describe the direction the glacier flowed through this valley. How can you tell?
5. Which letter arrow points to cirques? You can refer to Figure 7 in your textbook for help.
6. The lakes inside cirques are called tarns. Identify the tarns inside the cirques you just found.
7. Which letter arrows point to hanging valleys?
8. Which letter arrows point to arêtes?
9. Name a peak on the map that is a horn.
10. Feature E on the map is composed of glacial till. What type of glacial feature is E, and how did it form?
11. Explain how Turquoise Lake formed.

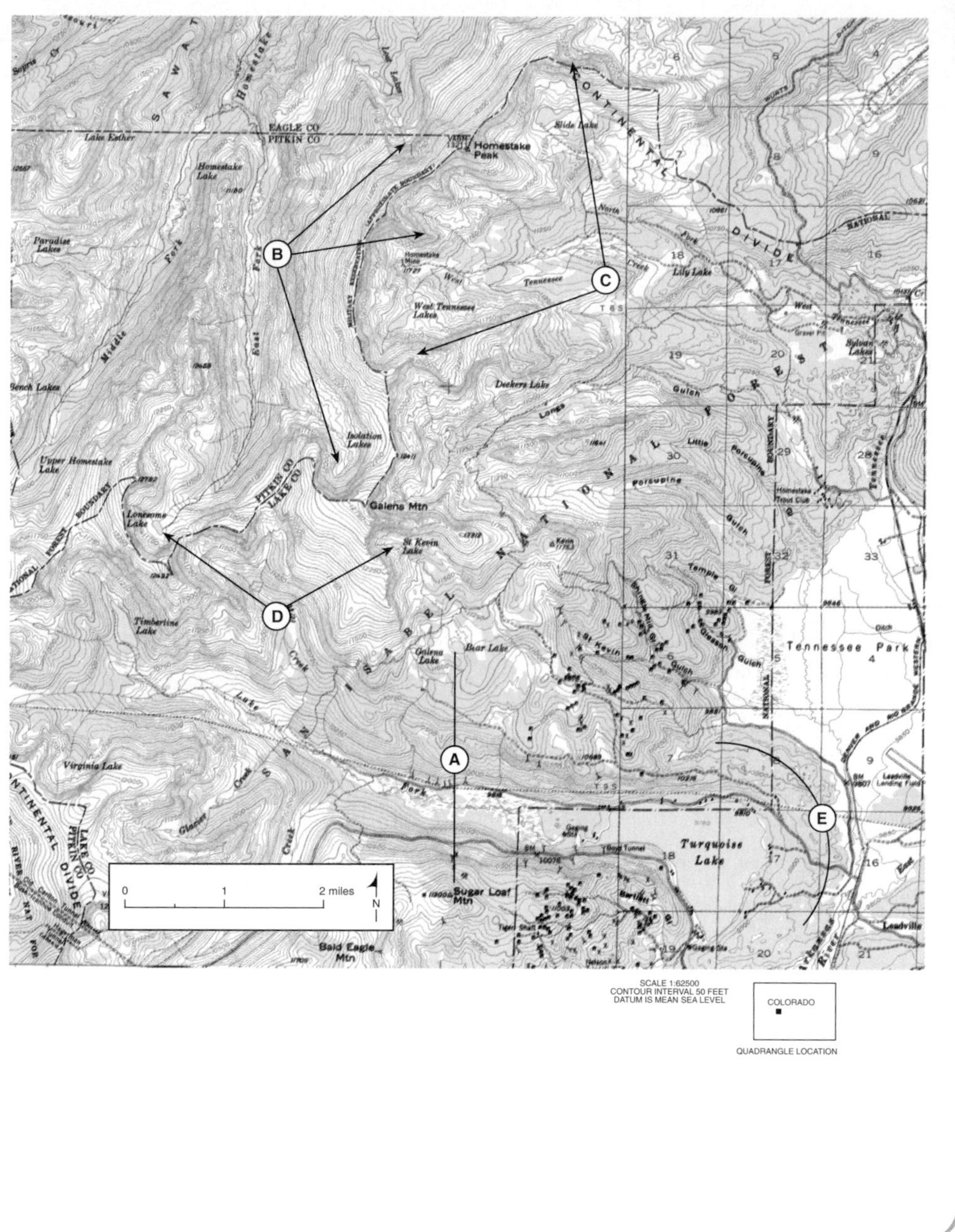

Answers to Procedure Questions

1. Student profiles should show a U-shaped valley.

2. because it is U-shaped

3. valley glacier because it occurs in an alpine region with classic valley glacier features

4. west to east because the direction is downhill

5. D

6. Lonesome, St. Kevin lakes

7. B

8. C

9. Galena Mountain

10. It is an end moraine made of debris deposited by stationary face of the valley glacier. Water backed up behind the end moraine as the glacier retreated.

11. A glacier carved out of a U-shaped valley that ran west-east between the Galena Mountain region to the north and the Sugar Loaf and Bald Eagle Mountain region to the south. The glacier moved down slope, accumulating mass where topography leveled off, carving a deep enough basin for Turquoise Lake to form from melted ice and runoff.

Visual, Logical

Glaciers, Deserts, and Wind 211

Study Guide

Study Tip

Review Daily
Encourage students to set a time each day to review their science notes and text. This is an easier, more effective, and less stressful way to prepare for quizzes and tests, as compared to cramming all of the studying in a day or two before an exam. Even spending as little time as 15–20 minutes per day reviewing information recently covered in class can help students improve performance by monitoring their understanding before the class moves on to new concepts. Encourage students to write down any questions that come up during this daily study routine and bring them to class so that you can answer them.

CHAPTER 7

Study Guide

7.1 Glaciers

Key Concepts

- Valley glaciers are found in mountains. They are streams of ice that flow between steep rock walls from a place near the top where snow accumulates.
- Ice sheets cover large regions where the climate is extremely cold. They are huge compared to valley glaciers.
- The movement of glaciers is referred to as flow. Glacial flow happens two ways: plastic flow and basal slip.
- The glacial budget is the balance or lack of balance between accumulation at the upper end of a glacier and its loss at the lower end.
- Many landscapes were changed by the widespread glaciers of the recent ice age.
- Glaciers are responsible for a variety of erosional landscape features, such as hanging valleys, cirques, arêtes, and horns.
- Glacial drift applies to all sediments of glacial origin, no matter how, where, or in what form they were deposited. There are two types of glacial drift: till and stratified drift.
- Glaciers are responsible for a variety of depositional landscape features, including moraines, outwash plains, kettles, drumlins, and eskers.

Vocabulary

ice age, *p. 188;* glacier, *p. 188;* snowline, *p. 189;* valley glacier, *p. 189;* ice sheet, *p. 189;* glacial trough, *p. 193;* till, *p. 194;* stratified drift, *p. 194;* moraine, *p. 195*

7.2 Deserts

Key Concepts

- Mechanical weathering produces most of the debris in most deserts. Chemical weathering does exist in the desert; however, the process is slow. Chemical weathering results in thin soils and the familiar rust-tinted desert landscapes.
- In the desert, most streams are ephemeral—they only carry water after it rains.
- Because there are fewer plants in deserts to anchor the soil, the amount of erosion caused during a single short-lived rain event is impressive.
- Most desert streams dry up long before they ever reach the ocean. The streams are quickly depleted by evaporation and soil infiltration.
- Most desert erosion results from running water. Although deserts experience more wind erosion than other places, water is still the foremost agent that carves arid landscapes.

Vocabulary

alluvial fan, *p. 201;* playa lake, *p. 202*

7.3 Landscapes Shaped by Wind

Key Concepts

- Wind erosion is more effective in deserts than in humid regions.
- There are two types of wind erosion: deflation and abrasion.
- The wind can create landforms when it deposits its sediments. Layers of loess and sand dunes are landscape features deposited by wind.
- A sand dune's form depends on the wind direction and speed, the amount of sand available, and the amount of vegetation.

Vocabulary

deflation, *p. 203;* desert pavement, *p. 204;* loess, *p. 204;* dune, *p. 205*

212 *Chapter 7*

Chapter Assessment Resources

Print
Chapter Test, Chapter 7
Test Prep Resources, Chapter 7

Technology
Computer Test Bank, Chapter 7 Test
Online Text, Chapter 7
Go Online, PHSchool.com, Chapter 7

CHAPTER 7

NY Regents Content Item

Assessment

Interactive textbook with assessment at PHSchool.com 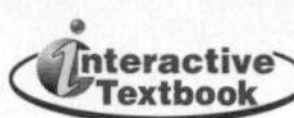

Reviewing Content

Choose the number that best answers the question or completes the statement.

1 Icebergs are produced when large pieces of ice break from the front of glacier during a process called
(1) plucking
(2) deflation
(3) calving
(4) abrasion

2 What type of dune forms at right angles to the wind when there is abundant sand, a lack of vegetation, and a constant wind direction?
(1) barchan
(2) transverse
(3) longitudinal
(4) parabolic

3 During which division of geologic time did the most recent ice age occur? NY
(1) Pliocene
(2) Paleocene
(3) Pleistocene
(4) Miocene

4 All sediments of glacial origin are NY
(1) till
(2) glacial drift
(3) stratified drift
(4) outwash

5 What term is used to describe desert streams that carry water only during periods of rainfall called?
(1) playas
(2) ephemeral
(3) episodic
(4) occasional

6 The two major ways that glaciers erode land are abrasion and NY
(1) plucking
(2) tension
(3) deflation
(4) slipping

7 The most noticeable result of deflation in some places are shallow depressions called
(1) sinkholes
(2) blowouts
(3) ventifacts
(4) kettles

8 In which of these places do extensive yellow loess deposits occur?
(1) Canada (2) Cambodia
(3) China (4) Australia

9 Which of the following is NOT a feature associated with valley glaciers? NY
(1) horn (2) cirque
(3) arête (4) arroyo

10 The broad, ramp-like surface of stratified drift built adjacent to the downstream edge of most end moraines is a (an) NY
(1) kettle
(2) drumlin
(3) outwash plain
(4) terminal moraine

Understanding Concepts

11 Why is the uppermost 50 meters of a glacier called the zone of fracture?

12 How do the erosional processes of plucking and abrasion work? NY

Use the diagram below to answer question 13.

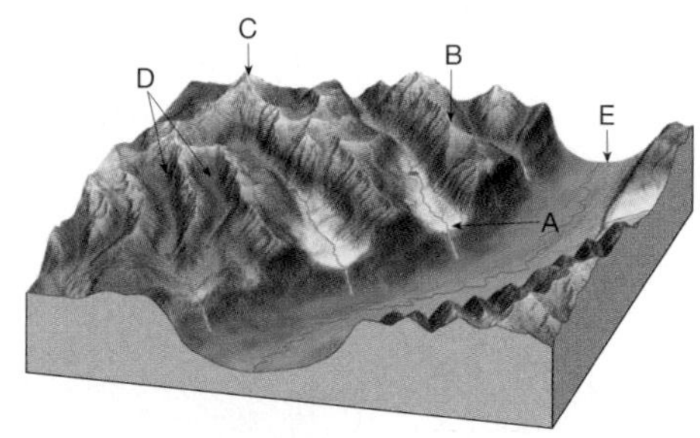

13 The area in the diagram was eroded by valley glaciers. For each feature listed below, write the letter of that feature in the diagram. NY
a cirque
b glacial trough
c hanging valley
d horn
e arête

Homework Guide

Section	Questions
1	1, 3, 4, 6, 10–15, 17, 21–28, 30, 31
2	5, 9, 18, 20, 24, 30
3	2, 7, 8, 16, 19, 24, 29–31

Assessment

Reviewing Content

(1) 3	(2) 2	(3) 1
(4) 2	(5) 2	(6) 1
(7) 2	(8) 3	(9) 4
(10) 3		

Understanding Concepts

(11) The ice is brittle, and there isn't enough pressure for plastic flow; deep cracks form as the glacier moves over rough terrain.
(12) In plucking, meltwater beneath the glacier seeps into rock cracks, refreezes, pries rock apart, and carries fragments along with the glacial ice. In abrasion, rock fragments on the underside of a glacier smooth rock beneath the moving glacier.
(13) a) D
b) E
c) A
d) C
e) B
(14) a)forms at the face of a stationary glacier
b) forms at the sides of a glacier where it scours valley walls
c) scatters glacial drift over the ground as a glacier recedes
(15) a)A
b) G
c) C
d) B
(16) Wind blows sand up the gentler slope to its crest. The sand drops down the steeper slope. Eventually, the steeper slope slides and moves the crest in the same direction as the wind blows.
(17) Glaciers hold onto their sediment over long distances until they melt. Water drops sediments once velocity decreases.
(18) Desert streams only flow in response to rainfall. They produce flash floods. They usually dry up before reaching the ocean. They usually don't have tributaries.
(19) Deflation begins again, removing sediments formerly protected by the rocks and cobbles of the pavement. Blowouts can occur.
(20) Water is the most important agent of erosion, but wind works better at eroding in the desert than in humid regions.
(21) Under the great pressure of overlying snow and ice, the normally brittle material becomes plastic, so it can deform.
(22) Cracks only form where the ice is brittle. Below 50 m, the ice exhibits plasticity due to pressure.

Critical Thinking

(23) If accumulation is greater than melting, the glacier advances. If accumulation is less than melting, the glacier retreats. If accumulation equals melting, the glacier remains stationary.
(24) All three help to break up rock and transport sediments. Wind is the weakest factor because it does a poor job at carrying sediments. Water carries and sorts sediments. Glaciers break up and remove rock and carry it over long distances, but glaciers usually deposit the debris unsorted.
(25) Rock outcroppings derive from the local bedrock. Erratics derive from bedrock that occurred some distance away, where the erratic was plucked by the glacier.

Analyzing Data

(26) just over 5000 m
(27) 75 percent
(28) The farther away from the equator you travel, the closer to sea level the snowline becomes.

Concepts in Action

(29) The fan would model the wind, and the playing cards would model the protective cover of vegetation. Students would need to vary the factors of wind direction, wind speed, amount of sand, and amount of protective cover to model each type of sand dune.
(30) erosion: arête, cirque, desert pavement, drumlin, hanging valley, horn, ventifact; deposition: alluvial fan, dune, moraine, esker, erratic, kettle, outwash plain
(31) Climate determines whether an area will be glaciated, arid, windy, dry, or wet. Glaciers, water, and wind are Earth's primary agents of erosion. Earth's glaciated areas are those most transformed by erosion, followed by those areas subject to running water, and then by those affected by wind. Deserts are more affected by wind than any other area, but are still more affected by running water.

Assessment *continued*

14 Describe each type of moraine: NY
a end moraine
b lateral moraine
c ground moraine

15 Identify the glacier features in the diagram. NY

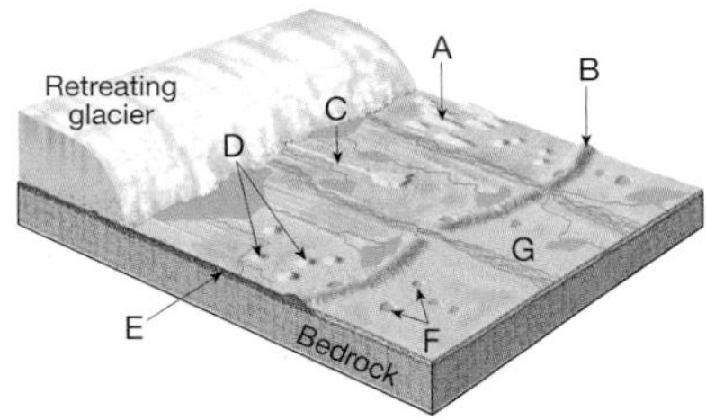

a drumlin
b outwash plain
c esker
d end moraine

16 Describe how sand dunes migrate. NY

17 How does the transport of sediment by glaciers differ from transport by water? NY

18 How do desert streams differ from those in humid regions?

19 What results when desert pavement is disturbed?

20 Describe the relative importance of wind and running water in eroding the desert landscape.

21 How is it possible for ice to flow?

22 Why do crevasses only extend 50 meters or so beneath the surface of a glacier?

Critical Thinking

23 **Relating Cause and Effect** Explain how a glacier's budget determines whether it advances, retreats, or remains stationary. NY

24 **Comparing and Contrasting** In what ways are the erosional actions of wind, water, and glaciers similar? How are they different? NY

25 **Inferring** Explain why glacial erratics will usually contain different minerals than the rock outcropping where they are found. NY

Analyzing Data

Use the graph below to answer questions 26–28.

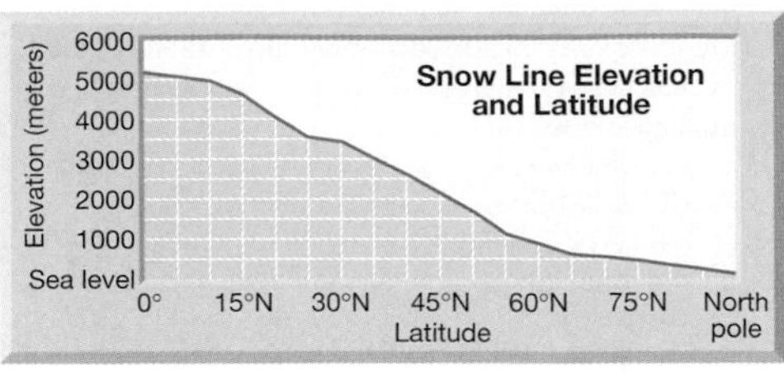

26 **Inferring** What is the minimum elevation required for year-round snow on a mountain located on the equator? NY

27 **Inferring** Suppose a 2000-meter mountain was located at 75 degrees north of the equator. What percentage of its height would have year-round snow?

28 **Drawing Conclusions** Write a statement that summarizes the information in the graph. NY

Concepts in Action

29 **Using Models** Explain how you would model each type of sand dune using a fan, a pan full of sand, and some playing cards.

30 **Classifying** Which types of landscape features described in this chapter resulted from erosion? Which types resulted from deposition? NY

31 **Writing in Science** Write a paragraph that summarizes the role of climate in the development of the landscapes discussed in this chapter. NY

Performance-Based Assessment

Researching Eskers are one glacial feature that people have transformed into a resource. Find out why glacial sediments are useful, who mines them, how they mine them, and the extent of their commercial value. Explain whether glacial deposits are considered renewable or non-renewable resources.

Regents Practice Exam

Test-Taking Tip

Avoiding Careless Mistakes
Students often make mistakes when they fail to read a test question and the possible answers carefully. Read the question carefully and underline key words that may change the meaning of the question, such as *not, except,* or *excluding.* After choosing an answer, reread the question to check your selection.

Choose the number that best answers the question or completes the statement.

1. Which of the following is NOT associated with water?
(1) ephemeral stream
(2) kettle
(3) hanging valley
(4) blowout

(Answer: 4)

For *each* statement or question, choose the *number* of the word or expression that, of those given, best completes the statement or answers the question. Some questions may require the use of the *Earth Science Reference Tables.*

1 Which of the following is NOT associated with water?
(1) ephemeral stream
(2) kettle
(3) hanging valley
(4) blowout

2 Which statement about glaciers is NOT true?
(1) They cover 30 percent of Earth's surface.
(2) They form U-shaped valleys.
(3) They can flow.
(4) They form when more snow accumulates than melts.

3 Wind erosion is NOT likely
(1) in a desert
(2) near the shore
(3) during a drought
(4) in a forest

4 A large pile of unsorted sediment has just been found in a remote area of upstate New York. This sediment was most likely deposited by
(1) glacier meltwater
(2) a stream
(3) glacial ice
(4) wind

5 When a stream emerges from a mountain canyon, the stream slope is greatly reduced. As a result the sediment is deposited within a short distance and forms a(n)
(1) sand dune
(2) alluvial fan
(3) moraine
(4) kettle lake

Answer the following question in complete sentences. Some questions may require the use of the *Earth Science Reference Tables.*

6 Explain why running water is the primary agent of erosion in deserts.

7 Compare valley glaciers and continental ice sheets with respect to their size and rate of movement.

8 What role do glaciers play in Earth's rock cycle?

Regents Practice Exam

(1) 4
(2) 1
(3) 4
(4) 3
(5) 2
(6) Since there is very little vegetation in deserts to hold soil in place, even short periods of rain result in a large amount of runoff that quickly reshapes the land.
(7) Continental ice sheets cover a larger area and move more slowly than valley glaciers.
(8) Glaciers break down rocks of all types into sediments that can deposit and cement into sedimentary rocks.

Performance-Based Assessment

Student answers will vary but should accurately reflect their research. Sample answer: Sand and gravel are used in road building and as surface aquifers for drinking water wells. Students should indicate that glacial deposits are considered nonrenewable.

Your students can independently test their knowledge of the chapter and print out their results.

CHAPTER 8

Planning Guide

Use these planning tools
Use Teacher Express for all your planning needs

SECTION OBJECTIVES	STANDARDS NATIONAL	STANDARDS STATE	ACTIVITIES and LABS
8.1 What Is an Earthquake? pp. 218–221 1 block or 2 periods **8.1** **Compare and contrast** the epicenter and focus of an earthquake. **8.2** **Identify** the cause of earthquakes. **8.3** **Compare and contrast** aftershocks and foreshocks.	A-1, B-6, D-3, E-1, E-2, F-5		**SE** Inquiry Activity: How Can Buildings Be Made Earthquake-Safe? p. 217 L1 **TE** Build Science Skills, p. 219 L2 **TE** Teacher Demo: Sweet Stress, p. 219 L2
8.2 Measuring Earthquakes, pp. 222–228 1 block or 2 periods **8.4** **Identify** the three types of seismic waves. **8.5** **Explain** how to locate the epicenter of an earthquake. **8.6** **Describe** the different ways earthquakes are measured.	A-1, A-2, B-6, D-3, E-2, F-5, F-6		**TE** Teacher Demo: Seismic Waves, p. 223 L2 **SE** Quick Lab: Measuring the Distance to Epicenters, p. 226 L2 **SE** Exploration Lab: Locating an Earthquake, pp. 240–241 L2 **LM** Modeling Liquefaction L2 **LM** Design and Build a Simple Seismograph L3
8.3 Destruction from Earthquakes, pp. 229–232 1 block or 2 periods **8.7** **Describe** the factors contributing to earthquake damage. **8.8** **Identify** other dangers associated with earthquakes. **8.9** **Explain** the potential for earthquake prediction.	A-2, B-6, D-3, E-2, F-5, F-6, G-1, G-2		**TE** Build Science Skills, p. 231 L2
8.4 Earth's Layered Structure, pp. 233–237 2 blocks or 4 periods **8.10** **List** the layers of Earth based on composition and physical properties. **8.11** **Describe** the composition of each layer of Earth.	A-1, A-2, B-3, B-6, D-2, E-2		**TE** Teacher Demo: Floating Crackers, p. 234 L2

Ability Levels	
L1	For students who need additional help
L2	For all students
L3	For students who need to be challenged

Components

SE	Student Edition	GRSW	Guided Reading & Study Workbook	TP	Test Prep Resources	GEO	Geode CD-ROM
TE	Teacher's Edition			onT	onlineText	T	Transparencies
LM	Laboratory Manual	TEX	Teacher Express	DC	Discovery Channel Videos	GO	Internet Resources
CUT	Chapter Tests	CTB	Computer Test Bank				

RESOURCES PRINT and TECHNOLOGY	SECTION ASSESSMENT
GRSW Section 8.1 **T-75** Earthquakes: Focus and Epicenter **T-76** Elastic Rebound GEODe Forces Within ↳ Earthquakes **DC** Earth in Motion **TEX** Lesson Planning 8.1	**SE** Section 8.1 Assessment, p. 221 **onT** Section 8.1
GRSW Section 8.2 **T-77** Principle of the Seismograph **T-78** Typical Seismic Record **T-79** Types of Seismic Waves **T-80** Travel-time Graph **T-81** Finding an Earthquake Epicenter **T-82** Earthquakes—Global Distribution **T-83** Modified Mercalli Intensity Scale **T-84** Determining Richter Magnitude **T-85** Earthquake Magnitudes and Expected World Incidence **T-86** Region Most Affected by the Good Friday Earthquake of 1964 **TEX** Lesson Planning 8.2	**SE** Section 8.2 Assessment, p. 228 **onT** Section 8.2
GRSW Section 8.3 **T-87** Schematic Drawing of Tsunami **T-88** Tsunami Travel Times to Honolulu **T-89** Some Notable Earthquakes **T-90** Probability of a Major Earthquake on the San Andreas Fault **T-91** Paths of Seismic Rays **TEX** Lesson Planning 8.3	**SE** Section 8.3 Assessment, p. 232 **onT** Section 8.3
GRSW Section 8.4 **T-92** Earth's Layered Structure **T-93** P and S Wave Paths **T-94** Lehmann Discontinuity **TEX** Lesson Planning 8.4	**SE** Section 8.4 Assessment, p. 237 **onT** Section 8.4

Go Online

Go online for these Internet resources.

PHSchool.com
Web Code: cjk-9999

NSTA SCILINKS
Web Code: cjn-3081
Web Code: cjn-3082

Materials for Activities and Labs

Quantities for each group

STUDENT EDITION

Inquiry Activity, p. 217
cardboard (thin), sugar cubes, peanut butter, large book, window screen (or wire meshing), scissors or wire cutters to cut screen

Quick Lab, p. 226
Figures 6 and 8A

Exploration Lab, pp. 240–241
pencil, drawing compass, world map or atlas, photocopy of map on p. 241

TEACHER'S EDITION

Build Science Skills, p. 219
flexible metric ruler

Teacher Demo, p. 219
chocolate-covered candy bar with nougat center

Teacher Demo, p. 223
coiled spring toy

Build Science Skills, p. 231
sand, potting soil, thin tray, wire netting, water, craft sticks for model house

Teacher Demo, p. 234
shallow baking pan, package of pudding, 2 cups milk,several animal crackers

Chapter Assessment

ASSESSMENT

SE	Assessment, pp. 243–244
CUT	Chapter 8 Test
CTB	Chapter 8
onT	Chapter 8

STANDARDIZED TEST PREP

SE	Chapter 8, p. 245
TP	Progress Monitoring Assessments

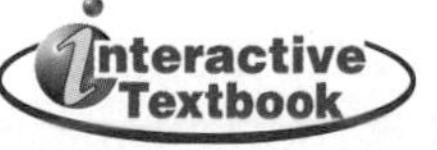

interactive textbook with assessment at PHSchool.com

CHAPTER 8

Before you teach

Michael Wysession
Washington University

Big Ideas

Earthquakes are the rupture of rock within Earth. The result of the rupture is a fault. Earthquakes are important because they are significant natural hazards, with the capability of destroying cities. They are also important because the waves they create are used to investigate the structure of Earth's interior.

Space and Time Earthquakes can occur anywhere near Earth's surface, but mostly occur in narrow bands that turn out to be the boundaries between pieces of lithosphere. About 200,000 earthquakes are located each year. An earthquake usually lasts for only seconds, and there may be a wait of years to hundreds of years between large earthquakes on a given fault. Despite a tremendous amount of research, efforts to predict earthquakes have been unsuccessful, and it may turn out that earthquakes cannot be predicted.

Forces and Motion Earthquakes occur because bending stresses within the rock exceeds the strength of the rock. The rupture causes seismic waves to propagate through Earth (P and S waves) and along its surface (surface waves).

Matter and Energy Seismic waves, as with most waves, are a propagation of energy, not matter. Seismic waves are recorded on seismographs, and the amplitudes of the waves are used to determine the magnitude of the earthquake. The biggest earthquakes release more energy than the world's entire nuclear arsenal.

Earth as a System Seismic waves are used to make images of Earth's layering, which is based on density, with the light rock of the crust overlying the heavier rock of the mantle, which overlies the dense iron/nickel core. Though high pressures keep most of Earth's interior solid, the high temperatures cause some of it to be molten.

Earth Science Refresher

The Start of Seismology

Interestingly, much of our understanding of seismology, and therefore of Earth's interior structure, is the result of politics. The seismic waves from an earthquake are similar to, but distinctly different from, those of an underground nuclear bomb. Therefore, since the early 1960s, the United States has helped to install worldwide networks of seismographs for the purpose of monitoring nuclear testing, initially in the Soviet Union, and now elsewhere. With these seismographs, we have always known of the nuclear capabilities of other countries. The seismic data, however, have also allowed us to make detailed images of Earth's interior.

How Earthquakes Are Located

In this chapter is an example of how an earthquake could be located using P and S waves from three seismographs. In actual use, however, an earthquake is located using thousands of seismographs. These seismographs record the seismic waves digitally, and in many cases broadcast out the data in real-time through the Internet or via satellite. Computer programs analyze the seismograms automatically, and determine the best location, magnitude, and fault orientation that matches the observed seismograms. In this way, information about an earthquake can be available minutes after it occurred, allowing for fast hazard assessment such as whether or not a tsunami warning should be announced.

Address Misconceptions

Many students may think that small- to medium-sized earthquakes in an area will decrease the chances of a major earthquake in the same region because the smaller earthquakes will release all of the built-up energy. Explain that this is not true. The amount of energy released in a major earthquake is much greater than can be released in a series of smaller earthquakes. For a strategy that helps to overcome this misconception, see **Address Misconceptions** on p. 227.

Go Online NSTA PD LINKS

For: Chapter 8 Content Support
Visit: www.SciLinks.org/PDLinks
Web Code: cjn-0899

Earth's Layering

Seismic waves travel at different speeds depending upon the property of the materials. Seismic waves also reflect off of boundaries between different materials. These are the main ways by which we have identified the different layers within Earth. The layers can be a result of changes in composition, stiffness, or mineral structure. The composition between the crust and mantle (and mantle and core) is different, so waves bounce off of these boundaries and can be detected. Within the mantle, however, there are other layers that are observed. The asthenosphere is a region where the temperature within Earth is very close to the melting point of mantle rock. This makes the rock relatively soft and causes seismic waves to travel more slowly through it. The stiffer mantle rock beneath the asthenosphere is often called the mesosphere, and seismic waves travel through it faster because it is *not* close to melting. There are other layers, however, that result from mineral phase changes. At a depth of about 410 km, the olivine we know at the surface becomes unstable, and its atoms rearrange into a denser structure called β-olivine. This creates a boundary seen by reflecting seismic waves. Around a depth of 520 km, this β-olivine becomes unstable, and changes to spinel. At about 660 km, the spinel becomes unstable and changes to a much denser and stiffer material called perovskite. This is a major boundary, and is used to separate the upper and lower mantles, discussed more in the next chapter. Because the lower mantle comprises most of Earth, and because most of the lower mantle is perovskite, the single most abundant material within Earth is perovskite, which is made of iron, magnesium, silicon, and oxygen.

Earthquake Hazards: Present Everywhere

The most seismically active regions of the United States are along the plate boundaries of the western coast (California, Oregon, Washington, and Alaska). However, it turns out that there are seismic hazards in all states. Our continent is old and filled with faults, and stresses within the rock can cause earthquakes anywhere. Some states not on the West Coast have had magnitude 6 (or greater) earthquakes in recorded time. There is an active field of engineering research that is working to design buildings, bridges, and other structures that can withstand the shaking from earthquakes.

Build Reading Literacy

Compare and Contrast

Identify Similarities and Differences

Strategy Help students read and understand material that discusses two or more related topics or concepts. This strategy helps students identify similarities and differences, thus enabling them to link prior knowledge with new information. Before students begin, assign a section in Chapter 8 for them to read, such as Section 8.2, pp. 222–228.

Example

1. Have students compare two or more topics or concepts under a section heading. Tell them that when they compare, they should focus on both similarities and differences. Remind them to look for these signal words:

- Similarities: *similar, similarly, also, just as, like, likewise, in the same way*
- Differences: *but, however, although, whereas, on the other hand, different, unlike*

2. Have students contrast two or more topics or concepts. Remind students that when they contrast, they should focus only on differences.

3. Have students create a chart or diagram comparing or contrasting two or more topics or concepts they read about in the section. Suggest that they create either a compare/contrast table or a Venn diagram to present their information.

See p. 221 for a script on how to use this strategy with students. For additional strategies, see pp. 224, 227, 230, 234, and 236.

ASSESS PRIOR KNOWLEDGE

Use the Chapter Pretest below to assess students' prior knowledge. As needed, review these concepts.

Review Science Concepts

Section 8.1 Reviewing the concept of potential energy will help students to understand the elastic rebound hypothesis. An overview of waves and wave propagation will allow students to visualize the movement of waves from the focus of an earthquake.

Section 8.2 Students should review different types of waves in order to better understand the movement of seismic waves through Earth. Reviewing the different types of rocks and discussing their density will help students understand the movement of seismic waves through different rock types.

Section 8.3 A review of tidal waves will emphasize that tsunamis and tidal waves are actually distinct and different types of waves. A discussion of weathering and mass wasting will refresh students' general understanding of the dangers and mechanics of landslides, in a general sense.

Section 8.4 Review with students the basic characteristics of minerals and rocks. This will make the discussion of the composition of the layers of Earth more meaningful and successful.

CHAPTER

Earthquakes and Earth's Interior

CONCEPTS in Action

Quick Lab
Measuring the Distance to Epicenters

Exploration Lab
Locating an Earthquake

How the Earth Works
Effects of Earthquakes

Forces Within
↳ Earthquakes

Video Field Trip
Earth in Motion

Take a field trip to the center of the Earth with the Discovery Channel and find out how earthquakes occur. Answer the following questions after watching the video.

1. Describe how the meeting of two tectonic plates can lead to an earthquake.
2. Where does the greatest damage occur during an earthquake?

Go Online
PHSchool.com

For: Chapter 8 Resources
Visit: PHSchool.com
Web Code: cjk-9999

Destruction caused by a major earthquake that struck northwestern Turkey on August 17, 1999. More than 17,000 people died. ▶

Chapter Pretest

1. Potential energy is *(b)*
   a. energy of motion.
   b. stored energy.
   c. used energy.
2. True or False: Granite is denser than basalt. *(False)*
3. The average continental crust is composed of ____________. *(granite)*
4. The main force driving landslides is *(a)*
   a. gravity.
   b. time.
   c. water.
5. True or False: Tidal waves are created by the pull of the moon and sun. *(True)*

Chapter Preview

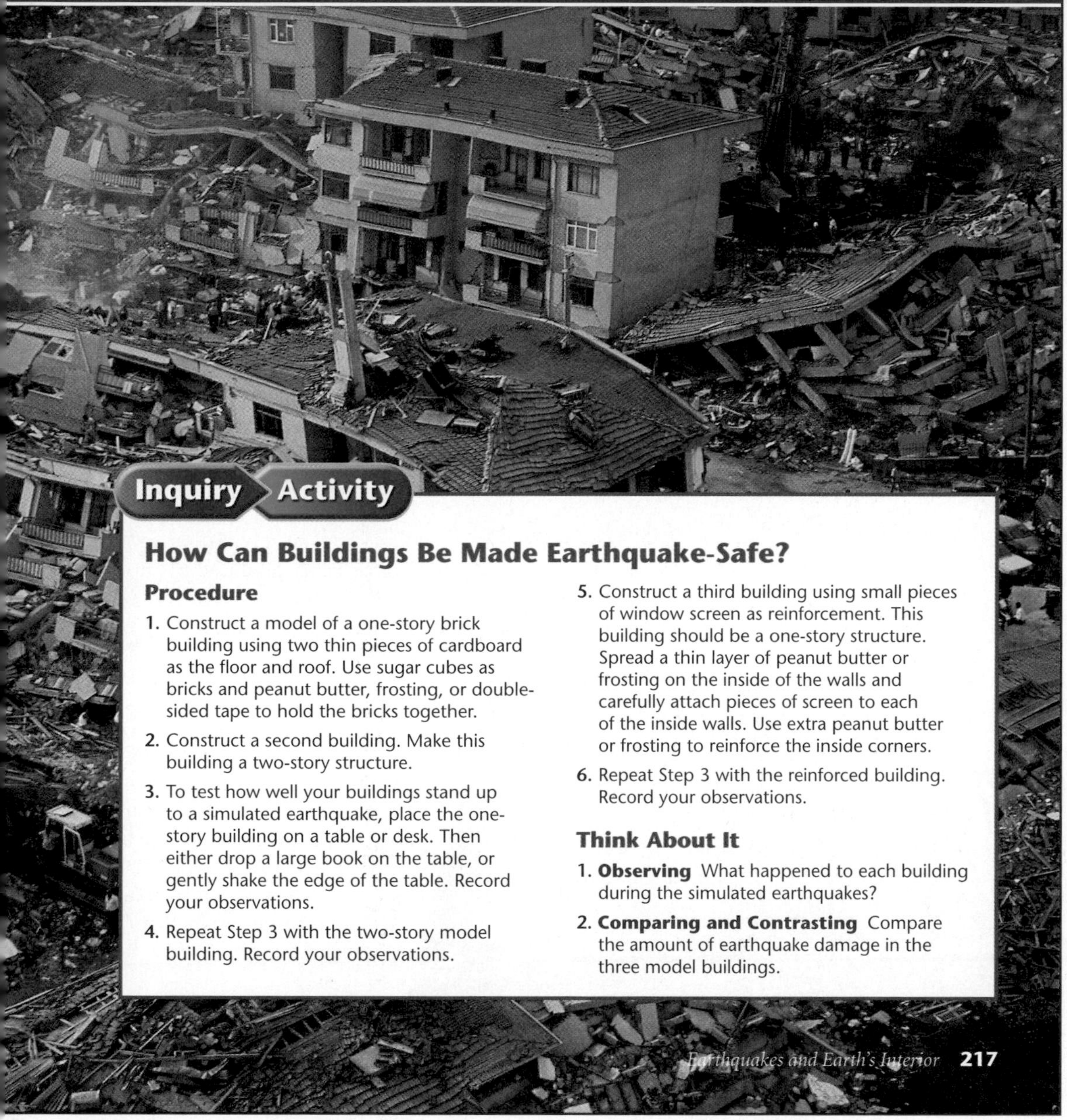

Inquiry Activity

How Can Buildings Be Made Earthquake-Safe?

Procedure

1. Construct a model of a one-story brick building using two thin pieces of cardboard as the floor and roof. Use sugar cubes as bricks and peanut butter, frosting, or double-sided tape to hold the bricks together.
2. Construct a second building. Make this building a two-story structure.
3. To test how well your buildings stand up to a simulated earthquake, place the one-story building on a table or desk. Then either drop a large book on the table, or gently shake the edge of the table. Record your observations.
4. Repeat Step 3 with the two-story model building. Record your observations.
5. Construct a third building using small pieces of window screen as reinforcement. This building should be a one-story structure. Spread a thin layer of peanut butter or frosting on the inside of the walls and carefully attach pieces of screen to each of the inside walls. Use extra peanut butter or frosting to reinforce the inside corners.
6. Repeat Step 3 with the reinforced building. Record your observations.

Think About It

1. **Observing** What happened to each building during the simulated earthquakes?
2. **Comparing and Contrasting** Compare the amount of earthquake damage in the three model buildings.

Video Field Trip

Earth in Motion

Encourage students to view the Video Field Trip "Earth in Motion."

ENGAGE/EXPLORE

Inquiry Activity

How Can Buildings Be Made Earthquake-Safe? 

Purpose Students will design, construct, and test model houses to simulate how different building designs can be used to resist earthquake damage.

Address Misconceptions

Students may not know what it means for a building to be considered "earthquake-safe." Explain that while it is impossible to completely protect buildings from earthquake damage, reinforcements and crossbars can be used to strengthen buildings, and certain construction materials, such wood or steel, are preferable over concrete because they allow for greater flexibility.

Skills Focus Modeling, Observing, Comparing and Contrasting

Prep Time 10 minutes

Materials cardboard (thin), sugar cubes, peanut butter, large book, window screen (or wire meshing), scissors or wire cutters to cut screen

Class Time 20 minutes

Safety Monitor students using scissors and/or wire cutters.

Teaching Tips To conserve materials, and keep students from using scissors, pre-cut the screens and direct students to build their walls to the correct dimensions. Also direct students to use the same force when testing their models.

Expected Outcome The two-story model should collapse, the one-story model without screening may or may not collapse, and the one-story model with screening should not collapse.

Think About It

1. Students should observe that the one-story, screen-reinforced model is the most stable. The two-story model lacking screens is the least stable.
2. Answers will vary; damage should be minimal on the one-story model with screening, and most extreme on the two-story model without screening.

Section 8.1

1 FOCUS

Section Objectives

8.1 **Compare and contrast** the epicenter and focus of an earthquake.
8.2 **Identify** the cause of earthquakes.
8.3 **Compare and contrast** aftershocks and foreshocks.

Reading Focus

Build Vocabulary L2

Word Parts Tell students that the prefix *epi-* is from the Greek word for "on" or "above." Ask them to guess what the word *epicenter* means based on this *(above the center)*. What other words can students come up with that have the same prefix? *(epidermis, epidemic)*

Reading Strategy L2

a. vibration of Earth due to release of pressure
b. focus
c. location inside Earth where energy is released in earthquake
d. epicenter
e. spot on surface of Earth directly above focus
f. fault
g. large fracture in Earth's crust and mantle

2 INSTRUCT

Earthquakes

Use Visuals L1

Figure 1 Direct student's attention to the facade of the building. Ask: **How many stories do you think this building was originally?** *(at least three)* **What happened to the other stories?** *(They were crushed in the motion of the earthquake.)*
Visual

8.1 What Is an Earthquake?

Reading Focus

Key Concepts

- What is a fault?
- What is the cause of earthquakes?

Vocabulary

- earthquake
- focus
- epicenter
- fault
- elastic rebound hypothesis
- aftershock
- foreshock

Reading Strategy

Building Vocabulary Copy the table below. Then as you read the section, write a definition for each vocabulary term in your own words.

Vocabulary	Definition
earthquake	a. ?
b. ?	c. ?
d. ?	e. ?
f. ?	g. ?

Each year, more than 30,000 earthquakes occur worldwide that are strong enough to be felt. Fortunately, most of these earthquakes are minor tremors and do very little damage. Generally, only about 75 major earthquakes take place each year. Most of these occur in remote regions. However, occasionally a large earthquake occurs near a city. Under these conditions, an earthquake is one of the most destructive natural forces on Earth, as shown in Figure 1.

Earthquakes

An **earthquake** is the vibration of Earth produced by the rapid release of energy. Earthquakes are often caused by slippage along a break in Earth's crust.

Figure 1 This damage occurred in San Francisco's Marina District from the 1989 Loma Prieta earthquake.

Focus and Epicenter The point within Earth where the earthquake starts is called the **focus.** The released energy radiates in all directions from the focus in the form of waves. These waves are similar to the waves produced when a stone is dropped into a calm pond. The impact of the stone sets water waves in motion. An earthquake is similar because it produces seismic waves that radiate throughout Earth.

The focus of an earthquake is the place within Earth where the earthquake originates. When you see a news report about an earthquake, the reporter always mentions the place on Earth's surface where the earthquake has been located. The **epicenter** is the location on the surface directly above the focus, as shown in Figure 2.

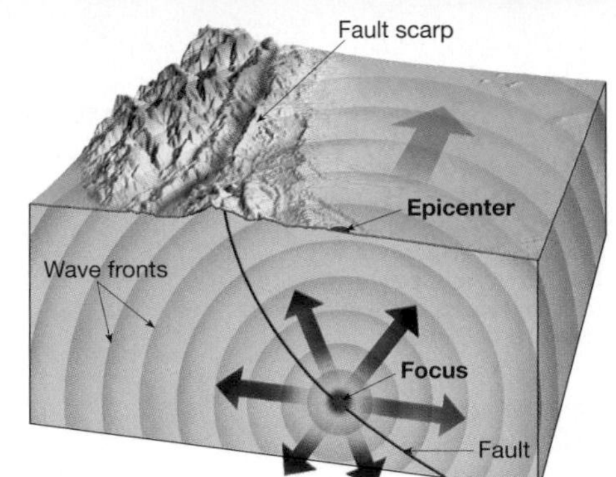

Figure 2 The focus of each earthquake is the place within Earth where the earthquake originated. The foci (plural of focus) are located along faults. The surface location directly above the focus is called the epicenter.
Predicting ***Where do you think the damage from an earthquake is usually greatest?***

Faults A lot of evidence shows that Earth is constantly changing. We know that Earth's crust has been uplifted at times. We have found many ancient wave-cut features meters above the level of the highest tides. Offsets in fence lines, roads, and other structures indicate that horizontal movements of Earth's crust are also common, as seen in Figure 3. Earthquakes are usually associated with large fractures in Earth's crust and mantle called **faults.** **Faults are fractures in Earth where movement has occurred.**

What is a fault?

Cause of Earthquakes

Before the great 1906 San Francisco earthquake, the actual causes and effects of earthquakes were not understood. The San Fransisco earthquake caused horizontal shifts in Earth's surface of several meters along the northern portion of the San Andreas Fault. The 1300-kilometer San Andreas fracture extends north and south through southern California. Studies following the 1906 quake found that during this single event, the land on the western side of the San Andreas Fault moved as much as 4.7 meters to the north compared to the land on the eastern side of the fault.

Based on these measurements and related studies, a hypothesis was developed to explain what had been observed. Figure 4 on page 220 illustrates this hypothesis. Part A shows an existing fault. In part B, forces within Earth slowly deform the crustal rocks on both sides of the fault, shown by the bent features of the rocks. These forces cause the rocks to bend and store elastic energy, just like a wooden stick does if it is bent. Elastic energy is the same kind of energy that is stored when you stretch a rubber band. Eventually, the resistance caused by internal friction that holds the rocks together is overcome. The rocks slip at the weakest point (the focus). The movement will exert forces farther along the fault, where additional slippage will occur until most of the built-up energy is released. This slippage allows the deformed rock to snap back in place. The vibrations we call an earthquake occur as the rock elastically returns to its original shape.

Figure 3 Slippage along a fault caused an offset in this orange grove east of Calexico, California. The white arrows show the direction of movement on either side of the fault.

Cause of Earthquakes

Build Science Skills L2

Using Models Have students use a plastic, flexible ruler to model the vibrations that cause earthquakes. Students should place the ruler on the edge of their desk, with approximately half of the ruler hanging off the edge. Tightly holding the other half to the desk, they should bend the ruler down. Releasing the ruler will model the release of energy along a fault. Students will be able to visualize the waves generated along the fault as the energy is released.
Kinesthetic, Visual

Teacher Demo

Sweet Stress L2

Purpose Students witness the buildup of stress and the result of the release of energy in an earthquake through the use of a candy bar as a model.

Materials chocolate-covered candy bar with nougat center (such as Three Musketeers)

Procedure Unwrap the candy bar and ask students to describe the surface of the chocolate coating. Grab both ends of the candy bar and slowly begin to bend the ends down. Ask students to observe the cracks on the surface as the stress is built up. Keep bending the candy bar until it breaks or snaps. Ask students to describe the final moments of the candy bar as well as what happened when the candy bar broke.
Visual, Logical

Customize for English Language Learners

Earthquakes only happen in certain areas of the world. These areas are called Earthquake belts. The rim or edge of the Pacific Ocean is the largest of these belts. Another belt stretches from China to Southeast Asia to Africa and Europe. A third earthquake belt lies under the Atlantic Ocean. With a partner, look at a map of the world. Identify the areas where there are earthquake belts. List on a piece of paper the names of the oceans or land masses where you think there are earthquake belts.

Answer to . . .

Figure 2 *at the epicenter*

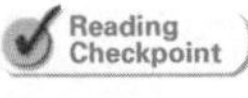

A fault is a fracture in Earth where movement has occurred.

Section 8.1 (continued)

Use Community Resources L2

Help students conduct a Web search of their town's geologic history. Compile a list of any earthquakes or notable seismic activity, and have students investigate major events further. They can consult reference and online sources, or gather firsthand knowledge by interviewing people who experienced any events. See if their research leads to any evidence of property damage or rock deformations in their area, such as a photograph like Figure 3.

If information on local geologic events is not available, have students visit the U.S. Geological Survey's Web site to search for recent earthquakes. Then have groups look at online articles from newspapers in the area of an earthquake.

Use Visuals L1

Figure 4 Ask: **What evidence of deformation is present in the fourth picture?** *(Each stream has been divided in two.)*

Integrate Physics L2

Potential and Kinetic Energy Read the first paragraph of the section on Elastic Rebound Hypothesis aloud. Ask students to identify the words that relate to energy. Explain that *stored* energy is potential energy, and *the release of energy* is kinetic energy.

Figure 4 As rock is stressed it bends, storing elastic energy. Once the rock is strained beyond its breaking point, it ruptures and releases the stored energy in the form of seismic waves. **Inferring** ***How do you think the temperature of rock would affect its ability to bend or break?***

Elastic Rebound Hypothesis The springing back of the rock into its original place is called elastic rebound. The rock behaves much like a stretched rubber band does when it is released. The explanation says that when rocks are deformed, they first bend and then break, releasing stored energy. This explanation for the release of energy stored in deformed rocks is called the **elastic rebound hypothesis.**

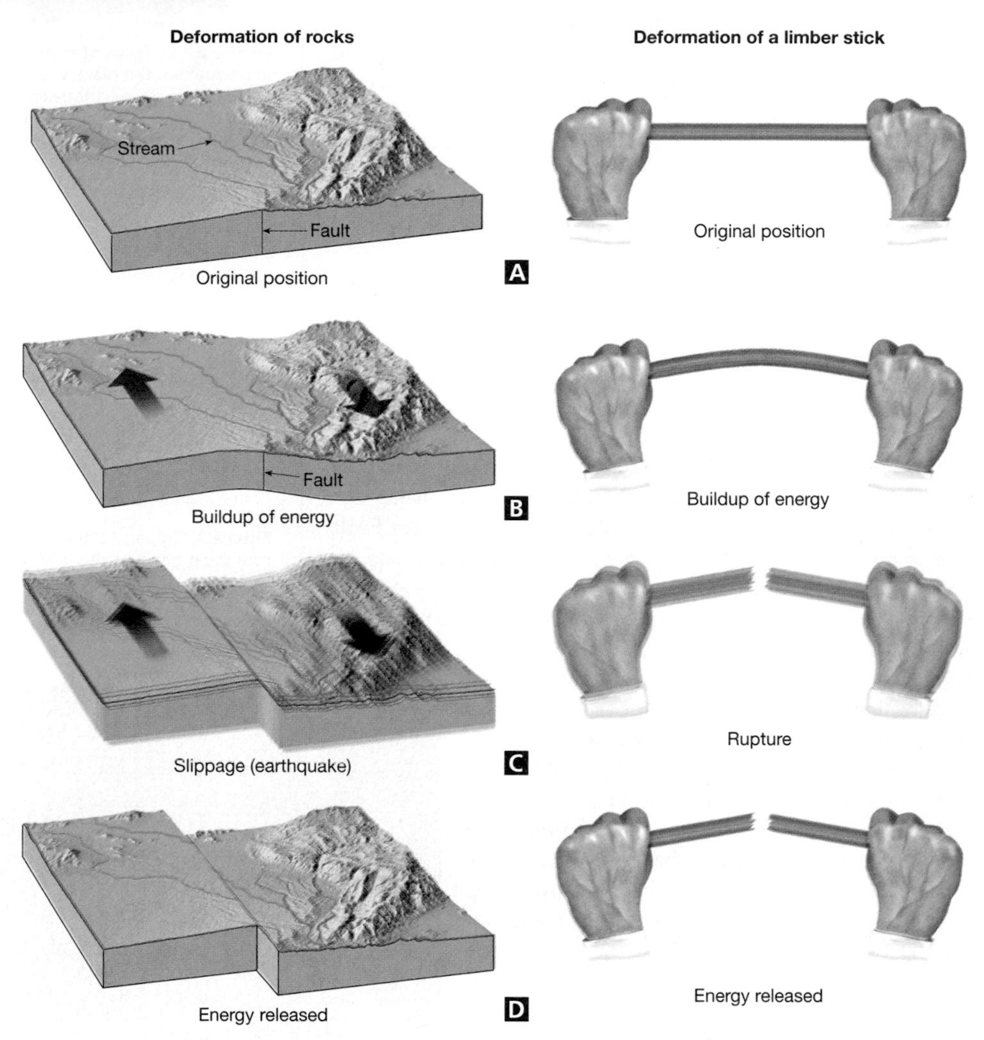

Facts and Figures

San Diego, California, and Santa Barbara, California, are on opposite sides of the San Andreas fault. They are currently approximately 562 km apart. The plates on either side of the San Andreas fault move at about the same rate as your fingernails grow, or about 45 mm/yr. At this rate, San Diego will reach Santa Barbara's current location in approximately 10 million years!

Most earthquakes are produced by the rapid release of elastic energy stored in rock that has been subjected to great forces. When the strength of the rock is exceeded, it suddenly breaks, causing the vibrations of an earthquake. Earthquakes most often happen along existing faults. They occur when the frictional forces on the fault surfaces are overcome.

Aftershocks and Foreshocks The intense shaking of the 1906 San Francisco earthquake lasted about 40 seconds. Most of the movement along the fault occurred in this short time period. However, additional movements along this and nearby faults continued for several days. The movements that follow a major earthquake often produce smaller earthquakes called **aftershocks.** These aftershocks are usually much weaker than the main earthquake, but they can sometimes destroy structures weakened by the main quake. Small earthquakes called **foreshocks** often come before a major earthquake. These foreshocks can happen days or even years before the major quake.

The San Andreas Fault is the most studied fault system in the world. Studies have shown that displacement has occurred along segments that are 100 to 200 kilometers long. Each fault segment behaves a bit differently than the other segments. Some parts of the San Andreas show a slow, gradual movement known as fault creep. This movement happens fairly smoothly. Other segments regularly slip and produce small earthquakes. However, some segments stay locked and store elastic energy for hundreds of years before they break and cause great earthquakes.

For: Links on earthquakes
Visit: www.SciLinks.org
Web Code: cjn-3081

Build Reading Literacy L1

Refer to **p. 216D**, which provides the guidelines for compare and contrast.

Compare and Contrast Have students review the section on aftershocks and foreshocks. Ask them to complete a Venn diagram.
Verbal

3 ASSESS

Evaluate Understanding 

Have students create a diagram that shows the difference between the focus and the epicenter of an earthquake.

Reteach 

Ask students to use Figure 4 to explain how deformation can occur in rocks. Provide them with a popsicle stick so they can recreate the phenomena.

Solution
9. 25 yr × 1.5 cm/yr = 37.5 cm

Section 8.1 Assessment

Reviewing Concepts

1. What is a fault?
2. Describe the cause of earthquakes.
3. What is an earthquake?
4. What is the source of an earthquake called?
5. What are foreshocks and aftershocks?

Critical Thinking

6. **Connecting Concepts** How are faults, foci, and epicenters related?
7. **Inferring** What is meant by elastic rebound?
8. **Making Judgments** Why do most earthquakes cause little damage and loss of life?

9. In 25 years, how much movement will result from a fault that slowly slips 1.5 centimeters per year?

Download a worksheet on earthquakes for students to complete, and find additional teacher support from NSTA SciLinks.

Answer to . . .

Figure 4 *Rocks at higher temperatures would bend more before breaking.*

Section 8.1 Assessment

1. A fault is a fracture in Earth where movement has occurred.
2. Earthquakes are caused by the release of elastic energy stored in rock that has been subjected to great forces. This causes the vibrations of an earthquake as the rocks elastically return to their original state.
3. An earthquake is the motion that results as rocks release elastic energy.
4. The source of an earthquake is the focus.
5. Aftershocks are smaller, weaker earthquakes that occur after the main earthquake. Foreshocks are small earthquakes that come before a major earthquake.
6. The focus of an earthquake is the place within Earth where the earthquake begins. The spot on the surface directly above the focus is the epicenter. Most earthquakes are usually associated with large fractures in the crust known as faults.
7. Elastic rebound is the process in which deformed rocks first bend and then break, releasing energy.
8. Most earthquakes do little damage because most of them occur in areas that are not populated.

Section 8.2

1 FOCUS

Section Objectives

8.4 **Identify** the three types of seismic waves.

8.5 **Explain** how to locate the epicenter of an earthquake.

8.6 **Describe** the different ways earthquakes are measured.

Reading Focus

Build Vocabulary L2

Word Parts Tell students that the prefix *seismo-* is Greek for "shaking." Ask them to infer what a seismograph and a seismogram are. Challenge them to come up with other terms that begin with the prefix *seismo- (seismology, seismologist).*

Reading Strategy L2

- B. Body Waves
- II. Locating an Earthquake
  - A. Earthquake Distance
  - B. Earthquake Direction
  - C. Earthquake Zones
- III. Measuring Earthquakes
  - A. Richter Scale
  - B. Moment Magnitude

8.2 Measuring Earthquakes

Reading Focus

Key Concepts

- What are the types of seismic waves?
- How is an earthquake epicenter located?
- How is the size of an earthquake measured?

Vocabulary

- seismograph
- seismogram
- surface wave
- P wave
- S wave
- moment magnitude

Reading Strategy

Outlining As you read, make an outline of the important ideas in this section. Use the green headings as the main topics and the blue headings as subtopics.

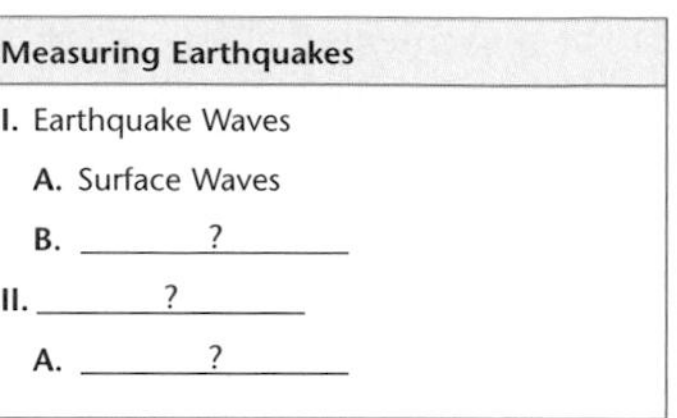

Measuring Earthquakes

- I. Earthquake Waves
  - A. Surface Waves
  - B. ____?____
- II. ____?____
  - A. ____?____

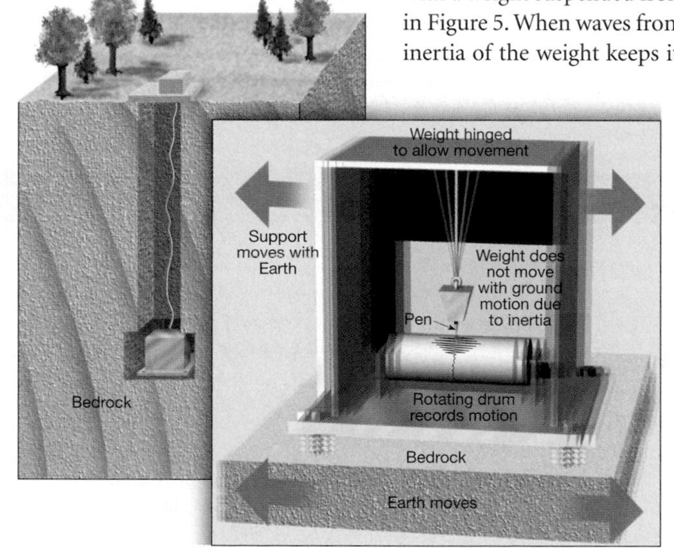

Figure 5 The seismograph (*seismos* = shake, *graph* = write) amplifies and records ground motion.

The study of earthquake waves, or seismology, dates back almost 2000 years. The first attempts to discover the direction of earthquakes were made by the Chinese. **Seismographs** are instruments that record earthquake waves. The idea behind seismographs can be demonstrated with a weight suspended from a support attached to bedrock as shown in Figure 5. When waves from an earthquake reach the instrument, the inertia of the weight keeps it stationary, while Earth and the support vibrate. Because the weight stays almost motionless, it provides a reference point to measure the amount of movement that occurs as waves pass through the ground below. The movement of Earth compared to the stationary weight can be recorded on a rotating drum, shown in Figure 5.

Modern seismographs amplify and electronically record ground motion, producing a trace, called a **seismogram.** A typical seismogram (*seismos* = shake, *gramma* = what is written) is shown in Figure 6.

Customize for Inclusion Students

Learning Disabled Place the palms of your hands together and slide one quickly against the other. This movement represents two rock surfaces slipping against each other. The fingertips of the hand that moves forward are like the rock that moves forward. This is called a "push wave" or P wave. The wave travels at about 8 km/s.

Earthquakes also send out a second kind of wave. This time put your hands together with a pencil between them. Slide one hand forward to represent the slipping rock surfaces. The pencil rotates, or twists, as you move your palm. In the same way, rocks twist between slipping surfaces. The twisting rocks send a "twist wave," or S wave, throughout Earth. A twist wave travels more slowly than a push wave, moving through Earth at about 5 km/s.

Earthquake Waves

The energy from an earthquake spreads outward as waves in all directions from the focus. Seismograms show that two main types of seismic waves are produced by an earthquake—surface waves and body waves.

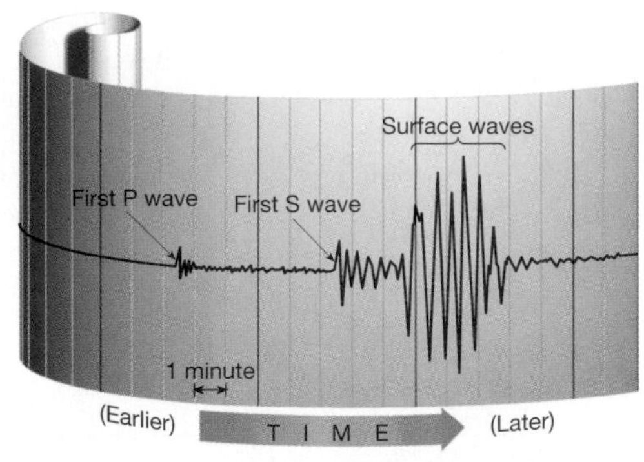

Figure 6 Typical Seismogram The first wave to arrive is the P wave, followed later by S waves. The last waves recorded are the surface waves.
Measuring ***What is the time interval in minutes between the start of the first P wave and the start of the first S wave?***

Surface Waves **Surface waves** are seismic waves that travel along Earth's outer layer. The motion of surface waves is complex. Surface waves travel along the ground and cause the ground and anything resting upon it to move. This movement is like ocean waves that toss a ship. Surface waves move in an up-and-down motion as well as a side-to-side motion, as shown in Figures 7E and 7F. The side-to-side motion is especially damaging to the foundations of buildings. These movements make surface waves the most destructive earthquake waves.

Body Waves The other waves that travel through Earth's interior are called body waves. Body waves are identified as either P waves or S waves, depending on how they travel through the materials within Earth. Figures 7B and 7D shows differences between the two kinds of waves. **P waves** are push-pull waves—they push (compress) and pull (expand) rocks in the direction the waves travel. P waves are also known as compression waves. In contrast, **S waves** shake the particles at right angles to their direction of travel. This can be shown by fastening one end of a rope and shaking the other end, as in Figure 7C. S waves are transverse waves. P waves temporarily change the volume of the material they pass through by alternately compressing and expanding it, as in Figure 7A. S waves temporarily change the shape of the material they pass through. Gases and liquids will not transmit S waves because they do not rebound elastically to their original shape.

A seismogram shows all three types of seismic waves—surface waves, P waves, and S waves. By observing a typical seismic record, as shown in Figure 8 on page 225, you can see that the first P wave arrives at the recording station, then the first S wave, and then surface waves. The waves arrive at different times because they travel at different speeds. Generally, in any solid material, P waves travel about 1.7 times faster than S waves. Surface waves travel the slowest at about 90 percent of the speed of the S waves.

Reading Checkpoint *Which seismic wave travels fastest?*

2 INSTRUCT

Earthquake Waves

Seismic Waves L2

Purpose Students will see the ways that the three different seismic waves move though substances with the use of a coiled spring toy.

Materials coiled spring toy

Procedure Have a student hold one end of the spring toy. Hold the other end of the toy and step away from the student to stretch the spring out. Gather approximately one fifth of the spring in your hand and let go. Ask students to explain what they observed as the bunch of coils moves down the extending spring. Explain to students that this is how a P wave travels through a medium. Again, with the spring stretched out, gently move the toy from side to side in a snake-like motion. Students should observe how the toy moves as a result of such motion. Explain that this is how an S wave moves. Finally, move your end of the toy in a rolling motion (like winding a fishing reel) creating waves. Students should realize they are observing the motion of surface waves.
Kinesthetic, Visual

Integrate Language Arts L2

Ancient cultures had their own ways of explaining earthquakes. For example, an ancient Indian legend explains how elephants carried Earth on their backs. When the elephants grew tired and lowered their heads, an earthquake occurred. An ancient Siberian legend says that Earth was pulled on a sled by dogs. Whenever one of the dogs stopped to scratch its fleas, an earthquake resulted. Challenge students to discover more ancient legends about earthquakes, and then to make up their own myth or legend that might serve as an explanation for earthquakes.
Verbal

Answer to . . .

Figure 6 *approximately 5 minutes*

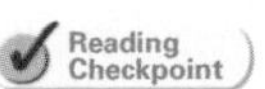
Reading Checkpoint *P waves*

Locating an Earthquake

Build Reading Literacy **L1**

Refer to **p. 156D** in **Chapter 6,** which provides the guidelines for reciprocal teaching.

Reciprocal Teaching Have students read the section with a partner. One partner reads a paragraph out loud. Then the other partner summarizes the paragraph's contents and explains the main concepts. The partners continue to switch roles with each new paragraph until they have finished the section. **Intrapersonal**

Build Reading Literacy **L1**

Refer to **p. 216D** which provides the guidelines for this reading strategy.

Compare and Contrast Ask students to use the visuals and the captions in Figure 7 to describe how the three types of waves are different. *(P waves compress and expand material in the same horizontal direction of the waves' energy. S waves are transverse waves that cause the ground to shake up and down, perpendicular to the waves' direction. Surface waves travel along the outer layer and can move in both up-and-down motions and side-to-side motions.)*

Locating an Earthquake

The difference in velocities of P and S waves provides a way to locate the epicenter. You can compare this difference to a race between two cars. The winning car is faster than the losing car. The P wave always wins the race, arriving ahead of the S wave. The longer the race, the greater will be the difference in arrival times of the P and S waves at the finish line (the seismic station). The greater the interval measured on a seismogram between the arrival of the first P wave and the first S wave, the greater the distance to the earthquake source.

Figure 7 Each type of seismic wave has characteristic motions.

Seismic Waves

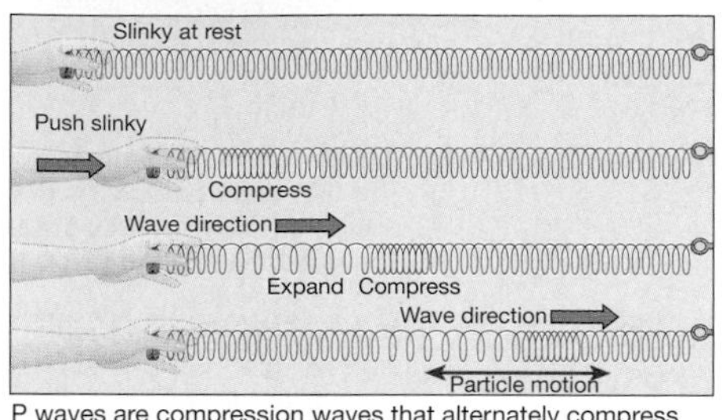

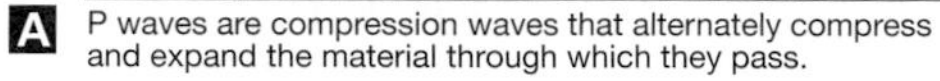

A P waves are compression waves that alternately compress and expand the material through which they pass.

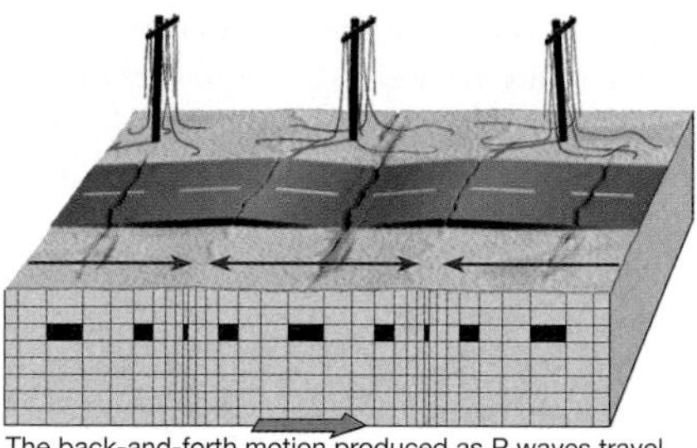

B The back-and-forth motion produced as P waves travel along the surface can cause the ground to buckle and fracture.

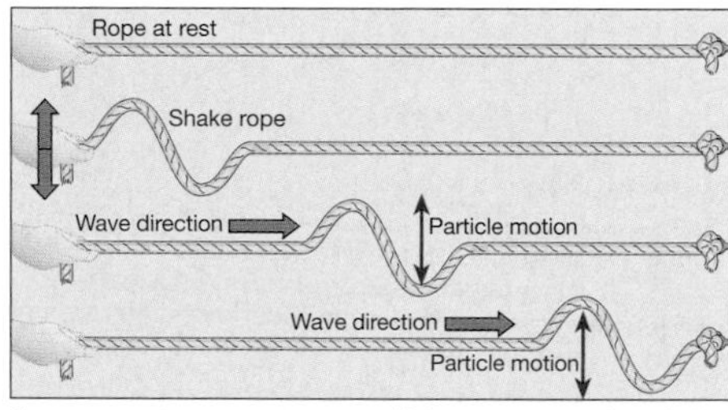

C S waves are transverse waves which cause material to shake at right angles to the direction of wave motion. The length of the red arrow is the displacement, or amplitude, of the S wave.

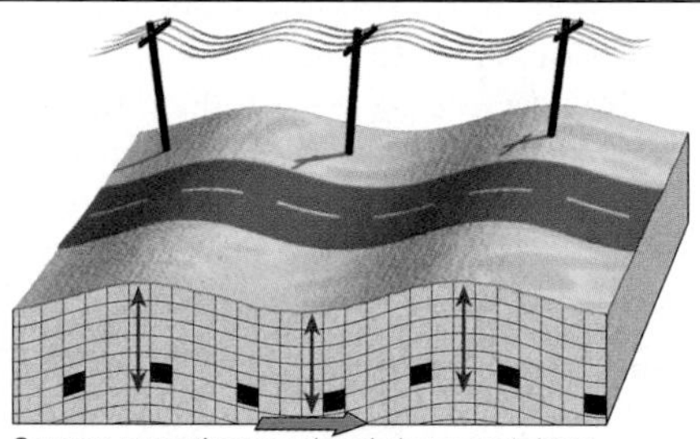

D S waves cause the ground to shake up-and-down and sideways.

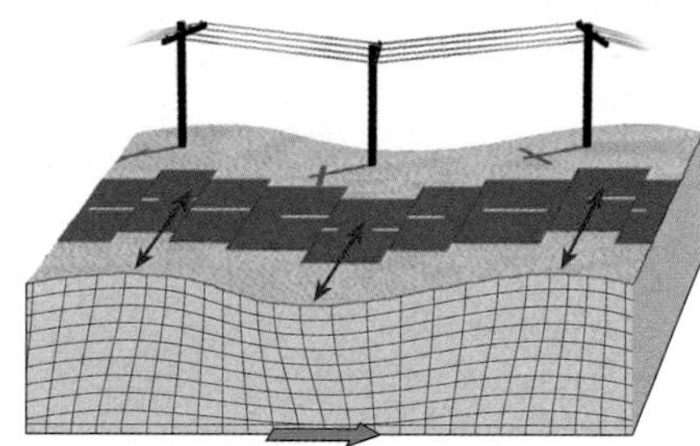

E One type of surface wave moves the ground from side to side and can damage the foundations of buildings.

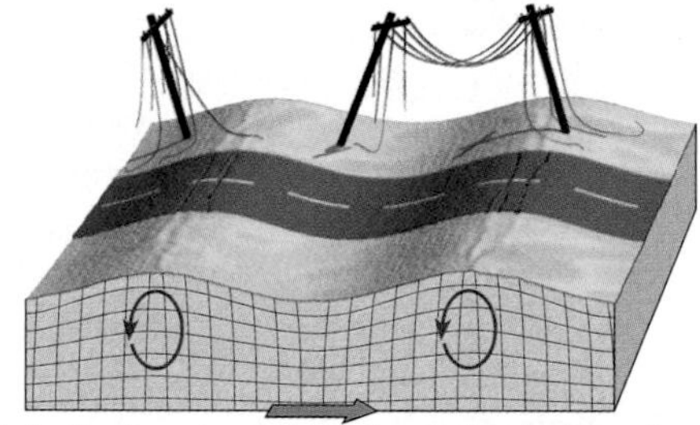

F Another type of surface wave travels along Earth's surface much like rolling ocean waves. The arrows show the movement of rock as the wave passes. The motion follows the shape of an ellipse.

Customize for Inclusion Learners

Learning Disabled Ask students to simulate P waves and S waves with a slinky and jump rope. Instruct them to recreate the scenarios pictured in Figure 7A and 7C if they require help getting started.

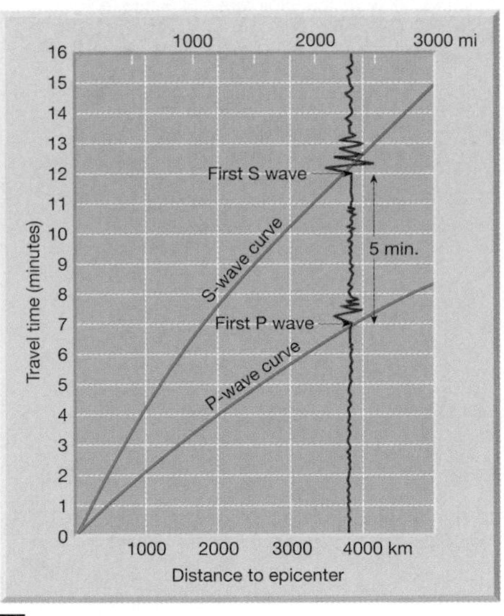

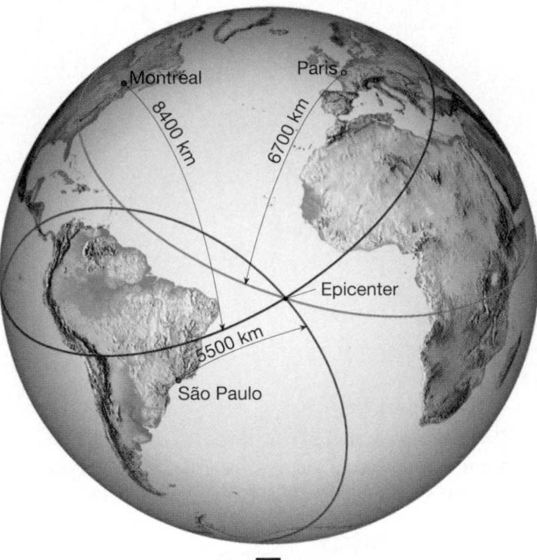

Figure 8 Locating an Earthquake A A travel-time graph is used to determine the distance to the epicenter. The difference in arrival times of the first P wave and the first S wave in the graph is 5 minutes. So the epicenter is roughly 3800 kilometers away. **B** The epicenter is located using the distance obtained from three seismic stations. The place the circles intersect is the epicenter.

Earthquake Distance A system for locating earthquake epicenters was developed by using seismograms from earthquakes whose epicenters could be easily pinpointed from physical evidence. Travel-time graphs are constructed from these seismograms, as shown in Figure 8A. Using the sample seismogram in Figure 6 and the travel-time curves in Figure 8A, we can determine the distance from the recording station to the earthquake in two steps. First, find the time interval between the arrival of the first P wave and the first S wave on the seismogram. Second, find on the travel-time graph the equivalent time spread between the P and S wave curves. From this information, you can see that this earthquake occurred 3800 kilometers from the seismograph.

Earthquake Direction Now we know the distance, but what about the direction? The epicenter could be in any direction from the seismic station. As shown in Figure 8B, the precise location can be found when the distance is known from three or more different seismic stations. On a globe, we draw a circle around each seismic station. Each circle represents the distance of the epicenter from each station. The point where the three circles intersect is the epicenter of the quake. **Travel-time graphs from three or more seismographs can be used to find the exact location of an earthquake epicenter.**

Integrate Math **L2**

The epicenter of an earthquake is located using information on the arrival times of the P and S waves at three seismograph stations. Ask: **Why must three seismograph stations be used? Why aren't two enough to locate the epicenter?** *(The intersection of three circles will yield a more exact location. If only two stations were used, these two circles would most likely intersect at two points. This would give two possible locations for the same earthquake.)* **Logical, Visual**

Use Visuals **L1**

Figure 8 Make sure students understand how to read the travel-time graph. Explain that distance is expressed in both kilometers (bottom) and miles (top), and tell them that one kilometer equals approximately 0.6 miles. Ask: **If a station records 2 minutes elapsed time between the arrival of the first P wave and the arrival of the first S wave, how far in kilometers is that station from the epicenter?** *(about 1000 km)* A good way to help students comprehend all the information compiled in a travel-time graph is to create one on the board. Plot data points to simulate how seismic recordings are used to create P and S wave curves.

Measuring Earthquakes

Measuring the Distance to Epicenters L2

Objective
After completing this activity, students should be able to use a travel-time graph and data from a seismogram to determine information about the epicenter of an earthquake.

Skills Focus **Inferring, Predicting**

 **Prep Time** 5 minutes

Class Time 20 minutes

Expected Outcome Students will successfully use the travel-time graph and seismogram to answer the questions.

Analyze and Conclude
1. 1000 km = approximately 2 minutes
2000 km = approximately 3.5 minutes
2400 km = approximately 4 minutes
3000 km = approximately 4.4 minutes
2. The farther away from the epicenter, the greater the time between the arrival of the first P wave and the first S wave.
3. The vibrations recorded on the seismogram would probably become less pronounced, with peaks that were not as high, or in some other way different, as the distance to the epicenter increases.

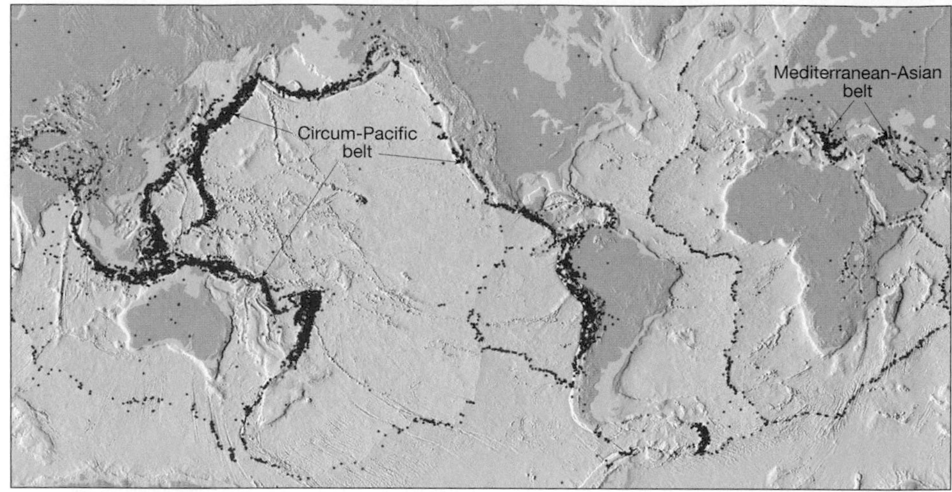

Figure 9 Distribution of the 14,229 earthquakes with magnitudes equal to or greater than 5 from 1980 to 1990.
Observing *Where do you find most of the earthquakes—in the interiors of the continents or at the edges?*

Quick Lab

Measuring the Distance to Epicenters

Procedure

1. Look at Figures 6 and 8A. Figure 6 is a seismogram and Figure 8A is a travel-time graph. Use the graph to answer the Analyze and Conclude questions.
2. Make sure to use only the bottom scale on the x-axis, measured in kilometers, to answer the questions.

Analyze and Conclude

1. **Reading Graphs** What is the difference in arrival times in minutes between the first P wave and first S wave for stations that are the following distances from an epicenter: 1000 km, 2000 km, 2400 km, and 3000 km?
2. **Inferring** How does the difference in arrival times of the first P wave and first S wave on a seismogram change? How does it change if the station is farther from the epicenter?
3. **Predicting** How do you think the vibrations recorded on a seismogram would change as the distance to the epicenter increases?

Earthquake Zones About 95 percent of the major earthquakes occur in a few narrow zones, as shown in Figure 9. Most of these earthquakes occur around the outer edge of the Pacific Ocean. This zone is known as the circum-Pacific belt. Active earthquake areas in this zone include Japan, the Philippines, Chile, and Alaska's Aleutian Islands. A second zone of earthquake activity occurs along the Mediterranean Sea. This is the Mediterranean-Asian belt. Another continuous belt extends for thousands of kilometers through the world's oceans. This zone coincides with the oceanic ridge system.

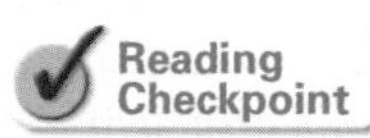 *Where do most earthquakes occur?*

Measuring Earthquakes

Historically, scientists have used two different types of measurements to describe the size of an earthquake—intensity and magnitude. Intensity is a measure of the amount of earthquake shaking at a given location based on the amount of damage. Intensity is not a quantitative measurement because it is based on uncertain personal damage estimates. Quantitative measurements, called magnitudes, were developed that rely on calculations using seismograms. Magnitudes are a measure of the size of seismic waves or the amount of energy released at the source of the earthquake.

Facts and Figures

The circum-Pacific belt, or the Ring of Fire, accounts for approximately 75 percent of the world's earthquake activity. It also contains some of the major volcanic mountains and mountain ranges on Earth. That is why it is called the Ring of Fire. The following is a list of the mountain ranges and volcanoes that are part of the Ring of Fire: the Andes Mountains and the volcanoes Cotopaxi and Azul, the Mexican volcanoes Popocatepetl and Paricutin, the Cascade Mountains and Mount Saint Helens, the Aleutian Islands, and Mount Fuji volcano in Japan.

226 Chapter 8

Richter Scale A familiar but outdated scale for measuring the magnitude of earthquakes is the Richter scale. The Richter scale is based on the amplitude of the largest seismic wave (P, S, or surface wave) recorded on a seismogram. Earthquakes vary greatly in strength, so Richter used a logarithmic scale. A tenfold increase in wave amplitude equals an increase of 1 on the magnitude scale. For example, the amount of ground shaking for a 5.0 earthquake is 10 times greater than the shaking produced by an earthquake of 4.0 on the Richter scale.

Seismic waves weaken as the distance between the earthquake focus and the seismograph increases. The Richter scale is only useful for small, shallow earthquakes within about 500 kilometers of the epicenter. Most of the earthquake measurements you hear on news reports use the Richter scale. Scientists, however, no longer use it.

Moment Magnitude In recent years, scientists have been using a more precise means of measuring earthquakes. It is called the moment magnitude scale. The **moment magnitude** is derived from the amount of displacement that occurs along a fault zone. It doesn't measure the ground motion at some distant point. The moment magnitude is calculated using several factors. These factors include the average amount of movement along the fault, the area of the surface break, and the strength of the broken rock: (surface area of fault) × (average displacement along fault) × (rigidity of rock). Together these factors provide a measure of how much energy rock can store before it suddenly slips and releases this energy during an earthquake. **Moment magnitude is the most widely used measurement for earthquakes because it is the only magnitude scale that estimates the energy released by earthquakes.**

Table 1 describes the damage and incidence of earthquakes of different magnitudes. Compare this information to the earthquakes listed in Table 2 on page 228.

Table 1 Earthquake Magnitudes and Expected World Incidence

Moment Magnitudes	Effects Near Epicenter	Estimated Number per Year
< 2.0	Generally not felt, but can be recorded	> 600,000
2.0–2.9	Potentially perceptible	> 300,000
3.0–3.9	Rarely felt	> 100,000
4.0–4.9	Can be strongly felt	13,500
5.0–5.9	Can be damaging shocks	1,400
6.0–6.9	Destructive in populous regions	110
7.0–7.9	Major earthquakes; inflict serious damage	12
8.0 and above	Great earthquakes; destroy communities near epicenter	0–1

L2

Many students may think that small- to medium-sized earthquakes in an area will reduce the chances of a major earthquake in the same region because the smaller earthquakes will release all of the built-up energy. To challenge this misconception, ask students to consider the amount of energy released in an earthquake. Ask: **How much more ground shaking does an earthquake with a measure of 8.0 on the Richter scale have compared with an earthquake with a measure of 3.0 on the Richter scale?** *(about 100,000 times more ground shaking)* **How many smaller earthquakes measuring 3.0 on the Richter scale would need to occur to equal the same amount of ground shaking of an 8.0 earthquake?** *(about 100,000 smaller earthquakes)*
Logical

Build Reading Literacy L1

Refer to **p. 474D** in **Chapter 17,** which provides guidelines for monitor your understanding.

Monitor Your Understanding
Display a world map with the names of major cities. Help students find the locations where the earthquakes listed in Table 2 occurred. Then ask students whether the earthquake's location is in any of the earthquake zones described on page 226. *(Most are in the circum-Pacific belt. Armenia—1988; Iran—1990; Latur, India—1993; and Izmit, Turkey—1999 are in the Mediterranean-Asian belt. The Charleston, SC, earthquake of 1886 is not in any of the zones described in the text.)*

Answer to . . .

Figure 9 *at the edges*

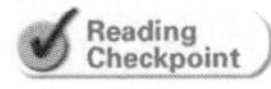

along the edge of the Pacific Ocean

3 ASSESS

Evaluate Understanding L2

Have students write three review questions for this section. Students should then break into groups of three or four and ask each other their questions.

Reteach L1

Review the types of seismic waves from earthquakes by asking students to explain what they see in Figure 7.

An earthquake measuring a moment magnitude of 6 could prove to be potentially devastating to structures not built to new earthquake standards. Poorly built structures would suffer significant damage. However, structures that were constructed with earthquake safety in mind would most likely fare well. Students should use Tables 1 and 2 from the text as a reference in looking at the damage caused by earthquakes with a moment magnitude of 6 or more.

Table 2 Some Notable Earthquakes

Year	Location	Deaths (est.)	Magnitude†	Comments
*1886	Charleston, South Carolina	60		Greatest historical earthquake in the eastern United States
*1906	San Francisco, California	1500	7.8	Fires caused extensive damage.
1923	Tokyo, Japan	143,000	7.9	Fire caused extensive destruction.
1960	Southern Chile	5700	9.6	Possibly the largest-magnitude earthquake ever recorded
*1964	Alaska	131	9.2	Greatest North American earthquake
1970	Peru	66,000	7.8	Large rockslide
*1971	San Fernando, California	65	6.5	Damages exceeded $1 billion.
1985	Mexico City	9500	8.1	Major damage occurred 400 km from epicenter.
1988	Armenia	25,000	6.9	Poor construction practices caused great damage.
*1989	Loma Prieta, California	62	6.9	Damages exceeded $6 billion.
1990	Iran	50,000	7.3	Landslides and poor construction practices caused great damage.
1993	Latur, India	10,000	6.4	Located in stable continental interior
*1994	Northridge, California	57	6.7	Damages exceeded $40 billion.
1995	Kobe, Japan	5472	6.9	Damages estimated to exceed $100 billion.
1999	Izmit, Turkey	17,127	7.4	Nearly 44,000 injured and more than 250,000 displaced.
1999	Chi Chi, Taiwan	2300	7.6	Severe destruction; 8700 injuries
2001	El Salvador	1000	7.6	Triggered many landslides
2001	Bhuj, India	20,000†	7.9	1 million or more homeless

*U.S. earthquakes
†Widely differing magnitudes have been estimated for some earthquakes. When available, moment magnitudes are used.
SOURCE: U.S. Geological Survey

Section 8.2 Assessment

Reviewing Concepts

1. List the two categories of seismic waves.
2. Briefly describe how the epicenter of an earthquake is located.
3. Describe the two different ways to measure the size of an earthquake.
4. In what order do the basic types of seismic waves reach a seismograph?

Critical Thinking

5. **Comparing and Contrasting** Describe the differences in speed and mode of travel between primary waves and secondary waves.
6. **Applying Concepts** How does a seismograph measure an earthquake?

Writing in Science

Descriptive Paragraph Write a paragraph describing in your own words what would occur in an earthquake that has been measured as a moment magnitude of 6.0.

Section 8.2 Assessment

1. The two categories of seismic waves are body waves (P and S) and surface waves.
2. The epicenter of an earthquake is located using data taken from at least three different seismograph stations. The time that the first P wave arrives at the station is then subtracted from the time that the first S wave arrives. This value can then be turned into a distance using a travel-time diagram. This distance means that the epicenter is that far from the station. A circle is drawn around each seismograph station and the circles meet where the earthquake epicenter is likely to be found.
3. Earthquakes can be measured by their intensity (or level of damage done) or by the magnitude (amplitude of seismic waves).
4. P wave, S wave, surface wave
5. P waves push and pull rocks in the direction of travel. Their velocity is greater than the velocity of S waves. S waves shake the particles of material at right angles to their direction of travel.
6. In concept, a seismograph has a weight which is suspended from a support that is attached to bedrock. When the bedrock shakes, the weight remains stationary which allows it to act as a reference point. The movement of Earth can then be compared to the weight and recorded on a stationary drum.

8.3 Destruction from Earthquakes

Reading Focus

Key Concepts

- What destructive events can be triggered by earthquakes?
- Can earthquakes be predicted?

Vocabulary

- liquefaction
- tsunami
- seismic gap

Reading Strategy

Monitoring Your Understanding Preview the Key Concepts, topic headings, vocabulary, and figures in this section. List two things you expect to learn. After reading, state what you learned about each item you listed.

What I Expect To Learn	What I Learned
a. ?	b. ?
c. ?	d. ?

The Good Friday Alaskan Earthquake in 1964 was the most violent earthquake to jar North America in the 20th century. The earthquake was felt throughout Alaska. It had a moment magnitude of 9.2 and lasted 3 to 4 minutes. The quake left 131 people dead and thousands homeless. The state's economy was also badly damaged because the quake affected major ports and towns. Had the schools and businesses been open on this holiday, the death toll would surely have been much higher.

Seismic Vibrations

The 1964 Alaskan earthquake gave geologists new insights into the role of ground shaking as a destructive force. **The damage to buildings and other structures from earthquake waves depends on several factors. These factors include the intensity and duration of the vibrations, the nature of the material on which the structure is built, and the design of the structure.**

Building Design All multistory buildings in Anchorage, Alaska, were damaged by the vibrations. However, the more flexible wood-frame buildings, such as homes, were less damaged. Figure 10 offers an example of how differences in construction can affect earthquake damage. You can see that the steel-frame building on the left withstood the vibrations. However, the poorly designed building on the right was badly damaged. Engineers have learned that unreinforced stone or brick buildings are the most serious safety threats during earthquakes.

Figure 10 Earthquake Damage This five-story building in Anchorage, Alaska, collapsed from the great earthquake of 1964. Very little structural damage was incurred by the steel-framed building to the left.
Inferring *Why do some buildings undergo little damage, while nearby buildings are nearly destroyed?*

Customize for Inclusion Students

Gifted When we consider how many earthquakes there are in one year, the number of earthquakes that cause terrible damage is actually very small. The amount of damage an earthquake causes depends on many conditions. For example, if a building is well constructed and built on solid ground, it may survive an earthquake. Most injuries and deaths during earthquakes are because of poor construction or substandard building sites. Another serious problem is not knowing how to respond to an earthquake. When people panic and rush out of buildings there is a danger of being trampled, suffocated, or injured by falling debris. Go to the Red Cross website at http://www.redcross.org/services/disaster and read about earthquake safety.

Section 8.3

1 FOCUS

Section Objectives

- **8.7** **Describe** the factors contributing to earthquake damage.
- **8.8** **Identify** other dangers associated with earthquakes.
- **8.9** **Explain** the potential for earthquake prediction.

Reading Focus

Build Vocabulary L2

Paraphrase Ask students to write the vocabulary words on a sheet of paper. Instruct students to write a definition, in their own words, for each term as they encounter the term while going through the chapter. After writing their own definition, they should also write a complete sentence with the term.

Reading Strategy L2

Sample answers:
a. how seismic vibrations can cause damage
b. Damage depends on the building design, intensity and length of time of the vibrations, and the material that the building was constructed on.
c. dangers associated with earthquakes
d. These include tsunamis, landslides, and fire.

2 INSTRUCT

Seismic Vibrations

Reading Strategy L2

Invite a structural engineer to speak to the class about the construction of earthquake-safe buildings. Have students ask about specific regulations for building codes in your area.
Interpersonal

Answer to . . .

Figure 10 *Damage to buildings often depends on the construction and design of the building. For example, buildings made of wood often are more flexible than buildings made of concrete.*

Address Misconceptions 

Many students may have heard that the safest place in a house during an earthquake is in a doorway. Challenge this misconception by pointing out that modern doorways are no stronger than other sections of a house and usually have doors that could swing and injure someone. Encourage students to come up with another plan for earthquake safety. This should involve ducking under a sturdy table or desk and staying clear of objects that could tip over, such as file cabinets and bookcases.

Build Reading Literacy L1

Refer to **p. 334D** in **Chapter 12**, for guidelines on outlining content.

Outline Have students read the section. Then have students use the headings as major divisions in an outline. Allow students to refer to their outlines when answering the questions in Section 8.3 Assessment.
Visual

Tsunamis

Build Science Skills 

Observing Have pairs of students investigate recent or historically significant tsunamis. (They may use library resources or conduct a Web search.) After students have had time to obtain information, have them compare their findings with another group.
Interpersonal, Verbal

Q *What is the largest wave triggered by an earthquake?*

A The largest wave ever recorded occurred in Lituya Bay, about 200 kilometers west of Juneau, Alaska. On July 9, 1958, an earthquake triggered an enormous rockslide that dumped 90 million tons of rock into the upper part of the bay. The rockslide created a huge splash wave that swept over the ridge facing the rockslide. The splash uprooted or snapped off trees 522 meters above the bay. Even larger splash waves may have occurred 65 million years ago when an estimated 900-meter wave is thought to have resulted from a meteorite impact in the Gulf of Mexico.

Liquefaction Where loosely consolidated sediments are saturated with water, earthquakes can cause a process known as **liquefaction.** Under these conditions, what had been stable soil turns into a liquid that is not able to support buildings or other structures. Buildings and bridges may settle and collapse. Underground storage tanks and sewer lines may float toward the surface.

When does liquefaction occur?

Tsunamis

Most deaths associated with the 1964 Alaskan quake were caused by seismic sea waves, or **tsunamis.** These destructive waves often are called tidal waves by news reporters. However, this name is incorrect because these waves are not produced by the tidal effect of the moon or sun.

Causes of Tsunamis **A tsunami triggered by an earthquake occurs where a slab of the ocean floor is displaced vertically along a fault. A tsunami also can occur when the vibration of a quake sets an underwater landslide into motion.** Once formed, a tsunami resembles the ripples created when a pebble is dropped into a pond. A tsunami travels across the ocean at speeds of 500 to 950 kilometers per hour. Despite this speed, a tsunami in the open ocean can pass without notice because its height is usually less than 1 meter, and the distance between wave crests can range from 100 to 700 kilometers. However, when the wave enters shallower coastal water, the waves are slowed and the water begins to pile up to heights that sometimes are greater than 30 meters, as shown in Figure 11.

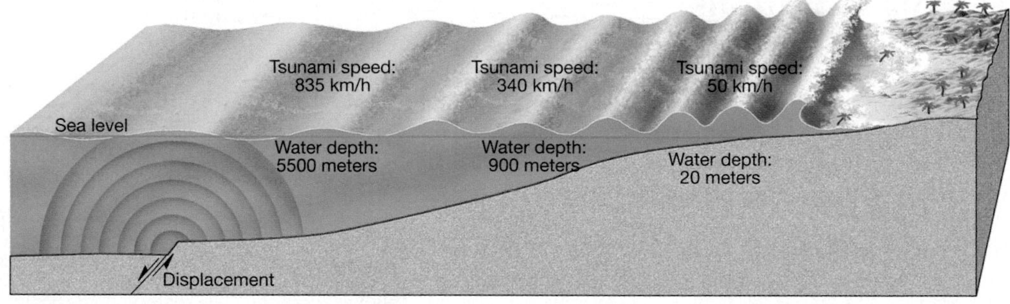

Figure 11 Movement of a Tsunami A tsunami is generated by movement of the ocean floor. The speed of a wave moving across the ocean is related to the ocean depth. Waves moving in deep water travel more than 800 kilometers per hour. Speed gradually slows to 50 kilometers per hour at depths of 20 meters. As waves slow down in shallow water, they grow in height until they topple and hit shore with tremendous force.

Tsunami Warning System The destruction from a large tsunami in the Hawaiian Islands led to the creation of a tsunami warning system for coastal areas of the Pacific. Large earthquakes are reported to the Tsunami Warning Center in Honolulu from seismic stations around the Pacific. Scientists use water levels in tidal gauges to determine whether a tsunami has formed. Within an hour of the reports, a warning is issued. Although tsunamis travel very rapidly, there is sufficient time to evacuate all but the area closest to the epicenter. Fortunately, most earthquakes do not generate tsunamis. On the average, only one or two destructive tsunamis are generated worldwide every year. Only about one tsunami in every 10 years causes major damage and loss of life.

What areas are protected by the tsunami warning system?

Other Dangers

The vibrations from earthquakes cause other dangers, including landslides, ground subsidence, and fires.

Landslides **With many earthquakes, the greatest damage to structures is from landslides and ground subsidence, or the sinking of the ground triggered by the vibrations.** The violent shaking of an earthquake can cause the soil and rock on slopes to fail, resulting in landslides. Figure 12 shows some of the damage landslides can cause. Earthquake vibration can also cause large sections of the ground to collapse, liquefy, or subside. Ground subsidence can cause foundations to collapse, as shown in Figure 12. It can also rupture gas and water pipelines.

Figure 12 This landslide caused by the 1964 Alaskan earthquake destroyed many homes. More than 200 acres of land slid toward the ocean.
Interpreting Photos ***Assuming the land was originally horizontal, to what angle have the trees on the left side of the photo been tilted?***

Fire The 1906 San Francisco earthquake reminds us of the major threat of fire. The city contained mostly large wooden structures and brick buildings. The greatest destruction was caused by fires that started when gas and electrical lines were cut. Many of the city's water lines had also been broken by the quake, which meant that the fires couldn't be stopped. A 1923 earthquake in Japan caused an estimated 250 fires. They devastated the city of Yokohama and destroyed more than half the homes in Tokyo. The fires spread quickly due to unusually high winds. More than 100,000 people died in the fires.

Other Dangers

Build Science Skills L2

Using Models ACTIVITY
Students should create a model of a house on a small hill using sand, potting soil, and thin wire netting. The model should be no more than 30 cm high. Then, students will shake their model in such a way that mimics an earthquake. They will then observe what happens to the hill and the buildings placed on it. Ask: **What happens to the buildings on the slope?** *(Answers will vary but students should see that the buildings slid down the slope.)* **What impact could water have on the model earthquake?** *(The damage would probably be worse if the hillside was saturated with water.)*
Kinesthetic

Use Community Resources L2

Instruct students to ask their village or city officials about local tsunamis, landslides, or fires that resulted from an earthquake. Some sources to contact might be fire departments, city halls, and newspaper or media archives. Ask them to brainstorm appropriate questions and ask the official they hope to interview.

Facts and Figures

The 1906 earthquake in San Francisco was one of the most devastating in the United States. The earthquake and resulting fires caused an estimated 3,000 deaths and $524 million in property loss. Damage in San Francisco alone was estimated at $20 million; outside the city, it was estimated at $4 million. The duration of the shaking in San Francisco was about 1 minute.

The earthquake damaged buildings and structures in all parts of the city and county of San Francisco. On the San Andreas fault, buildings were completely destroyed or torn apart; trees fell to the ground. The surface of the ground was torn and heaved into furrow-like ridges. Roads crossing the fault line were impassable. Pipelines were broken, shutting off the water supply to the city. The fires that ignited soon after the earthquake quickly raged through the city because of the lack of water to control them.

Answer to . . .

Figure 12 *45°*

Liquefaction occurs when loosely consolidated soils saturated with water are shaken by earthquake waves.

coastal areas of the Pacific

Predicting Earthquakes

Integrate Biology L2

Can Animals Predict Earthquakes? There is much speculation as to the ability of animals to predict earthquakes. Documented cases have shown snakes and bees rapidly leaving their homes, excessive dog barking, and erratic behavior in domesticated and wild animals prior to major earthquakes. The US Geological Survey, however, is more skeptical. They acknowledge the abundance of cases of reported behavioral changes prior to an earthquake but there aren't enough reproducible connections to conclusively state that animals are predicting the earthquakes. Have students research specific cases of odd animal behavior prior to earthquakes and present their findings in a newspaper article.
Verbal

3 ASSESS

Evaluate Understanding 

Have students work in groups to develop a short public service announcement on the other dangers facing areas that have experienced an earthquake.

Reteach 

Ask students to use the diagram in Figure 11 to explain how tsunamis are generated and how they move to shore.

Connecting Concepts

If there were some way to measure the amount of energy stored in rocks, this might lead to the prediction of earthquakes. If scientists could observe and measure the buildup of stress within rocks, they might be able to determine the amount of stress the rocks could withstand before the energy needed to be released. This could provide an estimate of time for an earthquake.

Download a worksheet on predicting earthquakes for students to complete, and find additional teacher support from NSTA SciLinks.

Figure 13 Effects of Subsidence Due to Liquefaction This tilted building rests on unconsolidated sediment that imitated quicksand during the 1985 earthquake in Mexico.

For: Links on predicting earthquakes
Visit: www.SciLinks.org
Web Code: cjn-3082

Predicting Earthquakes

The earthquake in Northridge, California, in 1994 caused 57 deaths and about $40 billion in damage. Scientists warn that quakes of similar or greater strength will occur. But can earthquakes be predicted?

Short-Range Predictions The goal of short-range prediction is to provide an early warning of the location and magnitude of a large earthquake. Researchers monitor possible precursors—things that precede and may warn of a future earthquake. They measure uplift, subsidence, and strain in the rocks near active faults. They measure water levels and pressures in wells. Radon gas emissions from fractures and small changes in the electromagnetic properties of rocks are also monitored. **So far, methods for short-range predictions of earthquakes have not been successful.**

Long-Range Forecasts Long-range forecasts give the probability of a certain magnitude earthquake occurring within 30 to 100-plus years. These data are important for updating building codes, which have standards for designing earthquake-resistant structures. Long-range forecasts are based on the idea that earthquakes are repetitive or cyclical. In other words, as soon as one earthquake is over, the forces in Earth will begin to build strain in the rocks again. Eventually the rocks will slip again, causing another earthquake. Scientists study historical records of earthquakes to see if there are any patterns of recurrence. They also study seismic gaps. A **seismic gap** is an area along a fault where there has not been any earthquake activity for a long period of time. There has been only limited success in long-term forecasting. **Scientists don't yet understand enough about how and where earthquakes will occur to make accurate long-term predictions.**

Section 8.3 Assessment

Reviewing Concepts

1. What destructive events can be triggered by an earthquake?
2. What physical changes have been used in the attempts to predict earthquakes?
3. What is a tsunami?
4. What is a seismic gap?

Critical Thinking

5. **Making Judgments** Do you think scientists are close to being able to accurately predict earthquakes? Explain your answer.
6. **Drawing Conclusions** Why is it incorrect to refer to tsunamis as tidal waves?

Connecting Concepts

Earthquakes In Section 8.1, you learned about the elastic energy stored in rocks before an earthquake and the elastic rebound hypothesis. How could this information be used to try to predict earthquakes?

Section 8.3 Assessment

1. Events such as landslides, tsunamis, and fires can be triggered by earthquakes.
2. Physical changes such as uplift, subsidence, strain in rocks along faults, water levels in wells, and radon gas emissions from fractures have been measured in hopes of predicting earthquakes.
3. A tsunami is a seismic sea wave created by an underwater earthquake or a landslide under the ocean floor generated by an earthquake.
4. A seismic gap is an area along a fault that has not had any earthquake activity for a long period of time.
5. Answers will vary. Sample answer: Scientists don't yet understand enough about how and where earthquakes occur to make accurate predictions.
6. Tidal waves are caused by the gravitational pull of the moon and sun. Tsunamis are large waves caused by earthquake movements.

8.4 Earth's Layered Structure

Reading Focus

Key Concepts

- What is Earth's internal structure?
- What is the composition of Earth's interior?

Vocabulary

- crust
- mantle
- lithosphere
- asthenosphere
- outer core
- inner core
- Moho

Reading Strategy

Sequencing Copy the flowchart. After you read, complete the sequence of layers in Earth's interior.

Earth's Internal Structure

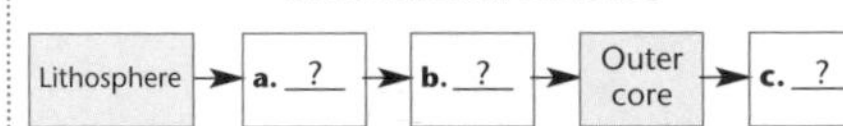

Earth's interior lies not very far beneath our feet, but we can't reach it. The deepest well has drilled only 12 kilometers into Earth's crust. With such limited access, how do we know what Earth's interior is like? Most knowledge of the interior comes from the study of earthquake waves that travel through Earth.

Layers Defined by Composition

If Earth were made of the same materials throughout, seismic waves would spread through it in straight lines at constant speed. However, this is not the case. Seismic waves reaching seismographs located farther from an earthquake travel at faster average speeds than those recorded at locations closer to the event. This general increase in speed with depth is due to increased pressure, which changes the elastic properties of deeply buried rock. As a result, the paths of seismic waves through Earth are refracted, or bent, as they travel. Figure 14 shows this bending. **Earth's interior consists of three major zones defined by its chemical composition—the crust, mantle, and core.**

Figure 14 The arrows show only a few of the many possible paths that seismic waves take through Earth.
Inferring ***What causes the wave paths to change?***

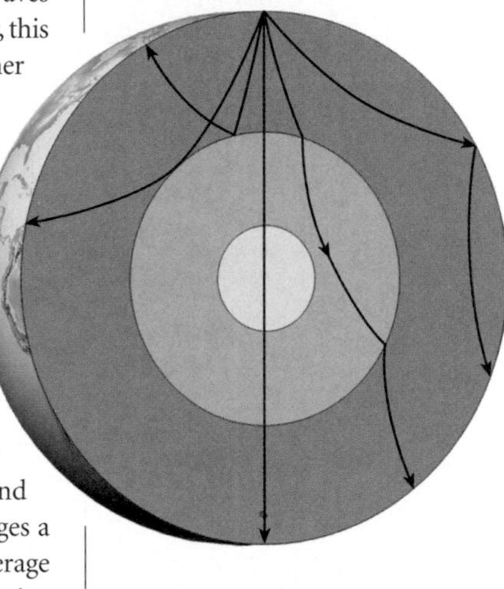

Crust The **crust,** the thin, rocky outer layer of Earth, is divided into oceanic and continental crust. The oceanic crust is roughly 7 kilometers thick and composed of the igneous rocks basalt and gabbro. The continental crust is 8–75 kilometers thick, but averages a thickness of 40 kilometers. It consists of many rock types. The average composition of the continental crust is granitic rock called granodiorite. Continental rocks have an average density of about 2.7 g/cm^3 and some are over 4 billion years old. The rocks of the oceanic crust are younger (180 million years or less) and have an average density of about 3.0 g/cm^3.

Section 8.4

1 FOCUS

Section Objectives

8.10 **List** the layers of Earth based on composition and physical properties.

8.11 **Describe** the composition of each layer of Earth.

Reading Focus

Build Vocabulary L2

LINCS Have students: **L**ist the parts of the vocabulary that they know, such as *core, sphere,* and *litho-*. **I**magine what the interior of Earth might look like and how the terms might fit together. **N**ote a reminding, sound-alike term, such as apple core or atmosphere. **C**onnect the terms, perhaps in a long sentence or as labels on a diagram. **S**elf-test.

Reading Strategy L2

a. asthenosphere
b. lower mantle
c. inner core

2 INSTRUCT

Layers Defined by Composition

Use Visuals L1

Figure 14 Have students look at the model of Earth and seismic waves in the diagram. Ask: **One seismic wave travels straight through the center of Earth. Would this be a P wave or an S wave?** *(P wave)*
Visual

Answer to . . .

Figure 14 *Seismic rays change direction because as pressure increases with depth, elastic properties of rocks change.*

Layers Defined by Physical Properties

Build Reading Literacy L2

Refer to **p. 502D** in **Chapter 18,** which provides the guidelines for using visualization.

Visualize Have students keep their books closed. Tell them to listen carefully while you read the paragraph about defining the layers of Earth based on physical properties. Ask students to describe how they visualize the interior of Earth. Then, ask students to work in pairs and discuss how they visualized the process.
Visual

Floating Crackers L2

Purpose To model for students the characteristics and behavior of the lithosphere and asthenosphere.

Materials shallow baking pan, package of chocolate pudding, 2 cups of milk, several animal crackers

Procedure Review with students the general characteristics and thicknesses of the lithosphere and asthenosphere. You may want to introduce the idea of the lithosphere being broken into smaller pieces called plates. These plates move about on top of the asthenosphere. Then make the pudding and pour it into the shallow baking pan. This will model the asthenosphere. Once the pudding has set, place the animal crackers on top of the asthenosphere to represent the lithosphere.

Expected Outcomes Students should see that the lithospheric plates are relatively thin compared to the asthenosphere. They also can see how the lithosphere "floats" on top of the asthenosphere, without sinking into it. The asthenosphere has a solid consistency yet has some ability to move.
Logical, Visual

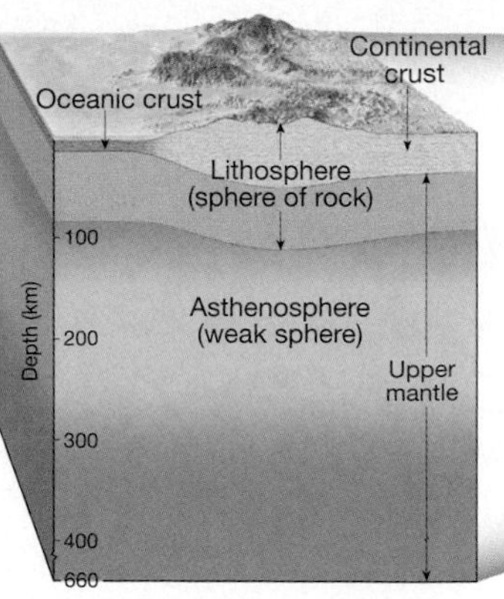

Figure 15 Earth's Layered Structure The left side of the globe shows that Earth's interior is divided into three different layers based on compositional differences—the crust, mantle, and core. The right side of the globe shows the five main layers of Earth's interior based on physical properties and mechanical strength—the lithosphere, asthenosphere, mesosphere, outer core, and inner core. The block diagram shows an enlarged view of the upper portion of Earth's interior.

Mantle Over 82 percent of Earth's volume is contained in the **mantle**—a solid, rocky shell that extends to a depth of 2890 kilometers. The boundary between the crust and mantle represents a change in chemical composition. The dominant rock type in the uppermost mantle is peridotite, which has a density of 3.4 g/cm^3.

Core The core is a sphere composed of an iron-nickel alloy. At the extreme pressures found in the center of the core, the iron-rich material has an average density of almost 13 g/cm^3 (13 times heavier than water).

What is the composition of the core?

Layers Defined by Physical Properties

Earth's interior has a gradual increase in temperature, pressure, and density with depth. When a substance is heated, the transfer of energy increases the vibrations of particles. If the temperature exceeds the melting point, the forces between particles are overcome and melting begins.

If temperature were the only factor that determined whether a substance melted, our planet would be a molten ball covered with a thin, solid outer shell. Fortunately, pressure also increases with depth and increases rock strength. Depending on the physical environment (temperature and pressure), a material may behave like a brittle solid, a putty, or a liquid. **Earth can be divided into layers based on physical properties—the lithosphere, asthenosphere, outer core, and inner core.**

Lithosphere and Asthenosphere Earth's outermost layer consists of the crust and uppermost mantle and forms a relatively cool, rigid shell called the **lithosphere.** This layer averages about 100 kilometers in thickness.

Customize for English Language Learners

Imagine that Earth was a ball. If you could cut it in half, you would see that Earth is made up of layers. The deepest layer is a solid core of metal, which is surrounded by a core of liquid metal. The liquid metal spins as Earth rotates. These two parts are thick and unbelievably hot. The next layer is called the mantle. The mantle is much cooler than the core, but it is still so hot that some of the rock is completely liquid.

A brittle crust of solid rock covers the mantle. All life on Earth exists on the top layer of this crust. Now imagine that you are taking a trip through Earth. Write and illustrate a journal entry for your trip. Share your journal entry with the class.

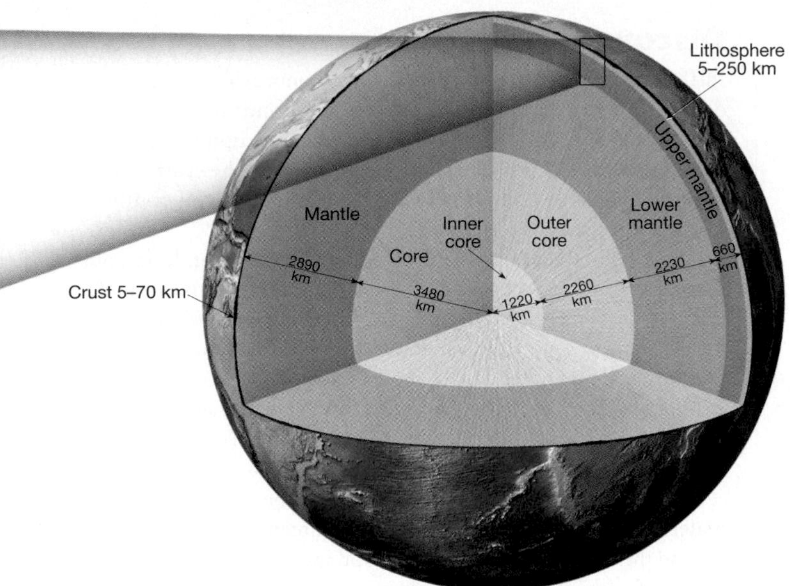

Beneath the lithosphere lies a soft, comparatively weak layer known as the **asthenosphere.** The asthenosphere has temperature/pressure conditions that may result in a small amount of melting. Within the asthenosphere, the rocks are close enough to their melting temperatures that they are easily deformed. Thus, the asthenosphere is weak because it is near its melting point, just as hot wax is weaker than cold wax. The lower lithosphere and asthenosphere are both part of the upper mantle.

Lower Mantle From a depth of about 660 kilometers down to near the base of the mantle lies a more rigid layer called the lower mantle. Despite their strength, the rocks of the lower mantle are still very hot and capable of gradual flow. The bottom few hundred kilometers of the mantle, laying on top of the hot core, contains softer, more flowing rock like that of the asthenosphere.

Inner and Outer Core The core, which is composed mostly of an iron-nickel alloy, is divided into two regions with different physical properties. The **outer core** is a liquid layer 2260 kilometers thick. The flow of metallic iron within this zone generates Earth's magnetic field. The **inner core** is a sphere having a radius of 1220 kilometers. Despite its higher temperature, the material in the inner core is compressed into a solid state by the immense pressure.

Why is the inner core solid?

Build Science Skills 

Calculating The mantle makes up roughly 82 percent of Earth. The mantle is composed of two different layers, the upper mantle and the lower mantle. The mantle reaches to a depth of approximately 2900 km. **Using the numbers given on Figure 15, what percent of the mantle is upper mantle?** *(660 km/2900 km = 23 percent)* **What percent is lower mantle?** *(2230 km/2900 km = 77 percent)*
Logical

Integrate Language Arts 

Word Parts Students can remember vocabulary by recognizing word parts in certain words. For example, the Greek suffix *litho-* means "rock, or stone." Ask: **What other word part is a clue to meaning of vocabulary terms such as lithosphere and asthenosphere?** *(–sphere)* **What do you think it means?** *(Sample answer: rounded)*

 *The core is composed of an iron-nickel alloy.*

 *because it is under extreme pressure and is compressed into a solid as a result*

Discovering Earth's Layers

Integrate Physics L2

Physical and Chemical Properties Have students read the caption for Figure 16. Then ask students for examples of physical and chemical properties. Make a two-column chart on the board and compile a list of physical and chemical properties. *(Examples of physical properties: conductivity, hardness, melting point, density, pressure. Examples of chemical properties: flammability, reactivity.)* Ask: **What physical properties change between the mantle and outer core?** *(hardness, density, pressure, state; outer core is liquid, mantle is solid)*

Build Reading Literacy L1

Refer to **p. 186D** in **Chapter 7**, which provides guidelines for relating text and visuals.

Relate Text and Visuals Instruct students to look at Figure 16. Refer them to the key and point out that P waves and S waves are different colors in the picture. Ask: **What happens when P waves hit the mantle-core boundary?** *(They bend around the core, or go through the core.)* **What sentences in the text support this observation?** *("It was observed that P waves were bent around the liquid outer core. . . P waves that travel through the core. . . ")* **What happens when S waves meet the boundary?** *(They stop travelling.)* **What sentence in the text supports this?** *("It was further shown that S waves could not travel through the outer core.")*

Discovering Earth's Layers

In 1909, a Croatian seismologist, Andrija Mohorovičić, presented evidence for layering within Earth. By studying seismic records, he found that the velocity of seismic waves increases abruptly below about 50 kilometers of depth. This boundary separates the crust from the underlying mantle and is known as the Mohorovičić discontinuity. The name is usually shortened to **Moho.**

Another boundary was discovered between the mantle and outer core. Seismic waves from even small earthquakes can travel around the world. This is why a seismograph in Antarctica can record earthquakes in California or Italy. However, it was observed that P waves were bent around the liquid outer core beyond about 100 degrees away from an earthquake. The outer core also causes P waves that travel through the core to arrive several minutes later than expected. This region, where bent P waves arrive, is sometimes called the shadow zone.

The bent wave paths can be explained if the core is composed of material that is different from the overlying mantle. The P waves bend around the core in a way similar to sound waves being bent around the corner of a building. For example, you can hear people talking from around the side of a building even if you cannot see them. In this way, rather than actually stopping the P waves in the shadow zone, the outer core bends them, as you can see modeled in Figure 16. It was further shown that S waves could not travel through the outer core. Therefore, geologists concluded that this region is liquid.

Reading Checkpoint *What is the Moho?*

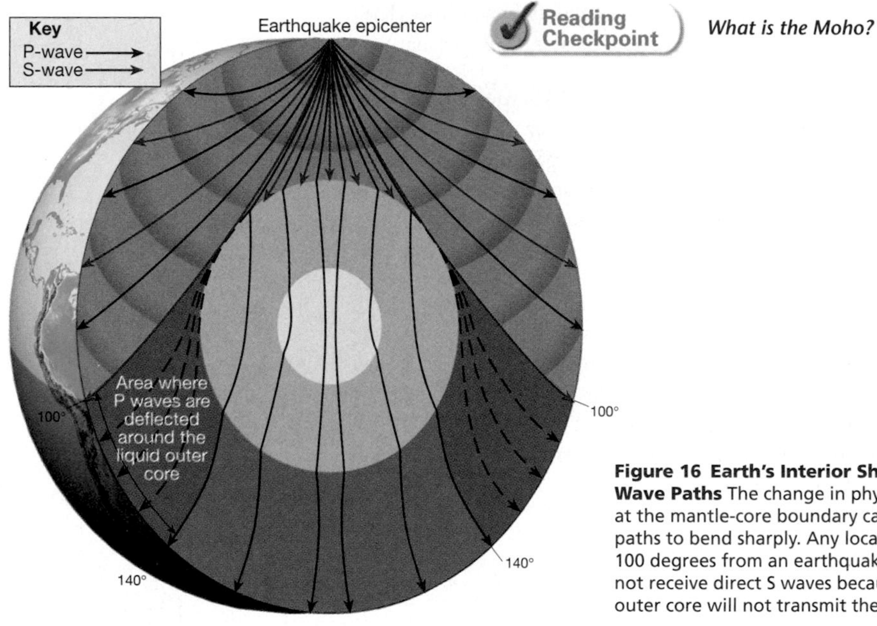

Figure 16 Earth's Interior Showing P and S Wave Paths The change in physical properties at the mantle-core boundary causes the wave paths to bend sharply. Any location more than 100 degrees from an earthquake epicenter will not receive direct S waves because the liquid outer core will not transmit them.

Facts and Figures

Andrija Mohorovičić was a Croatian scientist who lived from 1857 to 1936. Best known for his work as a seismologist, Mohorovičić also contributed to the sciences of meteorology and astronomy.

He established a station to follow thunderstorms, conducted climatic studies that lead to the conclusion that temperature in the atmosphere decreases with an increase in altitude, and published widely on clouds, rainstorms, and winds. After studying the seismic waves from the October 8, 1909, earthquake in the Kupa valley of Croatia, he made a very important discovery. At a depth of approximately 50 km, there was a dramatic change in material within Earth. This was based on his observation of a change in velocity of seismic waves at this depth. This inconsistency became known as the Moho, which is the boundary between the crust and the mantle.

Discovering Earth's Composition

We have examined Earth's structure, so now let's look at the composition of each layer. **Early seismic data and drilling technology indicate that the continental crust is mostly made of lighter, granitic rocks.** Until the late 1960s, scientists had only seismic evidence they could use to determine the composition of oceanic crust. The recovery of ocean-floor samples was made possible with the development of deep-sea drilling technology. **The crust of the ocean floor has a basaltic composition.**

The composition of the rocks of the mantle and core is known from more indirect data. Some of the lava that reaches Earth's surface comes from the partially melted asthenosphere within the mantle. In the laboratory, experiments show that partially melting the rock called peridotite produces a substance that is similar to the lava that erupts during volcanic activity of islands such as Hawaii.

Surprisingly, meteorites that collide with Earth provide evidence of Earth's inner composition. Meteorites are assumed to be composed of the original material from which Earth was formed. Their composition ranges from metallic meteorites made of iron and nickel to stony meteorites composed of dense rock similar to peridotite. Because Earth's crust contains a smaller percentage of iron than do meteorites, geologists believe that the dense iron, and other dense metals, sank toward Earth's center during the planet's formation. Lighter substances may have floated to the surface, creating the less-dense crust. **Earth's core is thought to be mainly dense iron and nickel, similar to metallic meteorites. The surrounding mantle is believed to be composed of rocks similar to stony meteorites.**

Section 8.4 Assessment

Reviewing Concepts

1. List the major layers of Earth's internal structure based on physical properties. List the layers in order from Earth's center to the surface.
2. What is the composition of Earth's core?
3. What evidence indicates that Earth's outer core is liquid?
4. What is the composition of the mantle?

Critical Thinking

5. **Comparing and Contrasting** Compare the physical properties of the asthenosphere and the lithosphere.
6. **Inferring** Why are meteorites considered important clues to the composition of Earth's interior?

Writing in Science

Creative Writing Write a short fictional story about a trip to Earth's core. Make sure the details about the layers of Earth's interior are scientifically accurate.

Discovering Earth's Composition

3 ASSESS

Evaluate Understanding L2

Ask students to draw two cross sections of Earth: one where the layers are defined by composition and one where the layers are defined by physical properties. Have students exchange papers and check each other's work.

Reteach 

Use Figure 15 to review the layers of Earth.

Stories will vary but students should include accurate information on the lithosphere, upper mantle, lower mantle, as well as the inner and outer core.

Section 8.4 Assessment

1. inner core, outer core, lower mantle, asthenosphere, lithosphere (upper mantle)
2. The core is made of an iron-nickel alloy.
3. the fact that S waves do not travel though this layer
4. The mantle is composed of peridotite.
5. The lithosphere is a cool, rigid shell formed from the crust and upper mantle. On average it is 100 km thick. The asthenosphere is a soft, weak layer that experiences the conditions needed to produce a small amount of melting.
6. Meteorites are thought to be made of the same material from which Earth was formed. Therefore, when they are found, they can give us an indication of the composition of the interior of Earth.

Answer to . . .

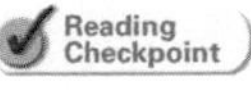

The Moho is the boundary between the crust and the mantle.

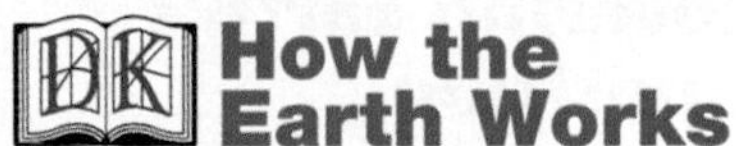

How the Earth Works

1 FOCUS

Objectives

In this feature, students will
- explain what causes an earthquake.
- describe the possible physical effects of an earthquake.

Reading Focus

Build Vocabulary L2

Key Terms Write the key terms on the board. Ask volunteers to write definitions beside them. Then have the class work together to use the words in sentences that describe the causes and effects of earthquakes.

2 INSTRUCT

Bellringer L1

Ask students what comes to mind when they think of earthquakes. Discuss earthquake experiences they may have had or heard about.
Verbal

Use Visuals L1

Have students read and examine the photographs on this page and the next. Ask: **What do you suppose people in these regions had to do after the earthquake?** *(They had to find people who were trapped under snow and rubble, rebuild buildings, and fix streets.)*
Visual

How the Earth Works

Effects of Earthquakes

An **earthquake** is a shaking of the ground caused by sudden movements in the Earth's crust. The biggest quakes are set off by the movement of tectonic plates. Some plates slide past one another gently. However, others get stuck, and the forces pushing the plates build up. The stress mounts until the plates suddenly shift their positions and cause the Earth to shake. Most earthquakes last less than one minute. Even so, the effects of an earthquake can be devastating and long-lasting.

TSUNAMI
In 1755, an earthquake in Lisbon, Portugal, caused a tsunami, as illustrated in this painting. A **tsunami** is a huge sea wave that is set off by an undersea earthquake or volcanic eruption. When tsunamis break on shore, they often devastate coastal areas. Tsunamis can race at speeds of about 450 miles per hour and may reach heights of about 100 feet (30.5 m).

LANDSLIDE
In January 2001, an earthquake struck El Salvador. It caused the landslide that left these Salvadoran women homeless. A **landslide** is a sudden drop of a mass of land down a mountainside or hillside. Emergency relief workers from around the world often rush to the site of an earthquake disaster like the one that occurred in El Salvador.

238 Chapter 8

Customize for Inclusion Students

Gifted Ask students to research a historic earthquake, like the one that hit Lisbon in 1755. Have them imagine that they survived it and are writing a story about it for a foreign newspaper. Encourage them to use factual details and fictional interviews in their stories. Before they begin, remind them that the first paragraph should answer these questions: *Who? What? Where? When?* and *Why?*

INFRASTRUCTURE DAMAGE
When an earthquake occurred in Los Angeles in 1994, underground gas and water lines burst, causing fires and floods. Earthquakes often cause tremendous damage to the **infrastructure**—the network of services that supports a community. Infrastructure includes power utilities, water supplies, and transportation and communication facilities.

AVALANCHE
Earthquakes may trigger an **avalanche**—a sudden fall of a mass of ice and snow. In 1970, a severe earthquake off the coast of Peru caused a disastrous slide of snow and rock that killed some 18,000 people in the valley below.

WHEN THE EARTH CRACKS
Most people killed or injured by an earthquake are hit by debris from buildings. Additional damage can be caused by **aftershocks**—tremors that can occur hours, days, or even months after an earthquake. The scene above shows the city of Anchorage, Alaska, after a major earthquake. Extensive ground tremors caused the street to break up as the soil below it collapsed. Buildings and cars were dropped more than 10 feet (3 m) below street level.

When two tectonic plates suddenly move past each other, waves of built-up energy are released.

Epicenter

As shock waves travel away from the epicenter, the destruction caused by the earthquake decreases.

Shock waves radiate outward and upward from the focus, or hypocenter.

Focus, or hypocenter

SEISMIC WAVES
As tectonic forces build, rock beneath the surface bends until it finally breaks. The tectonic plates suddenly move, causing **seismic waves,** or vibrations, to travel through the ground. The waves radiate outward from an underground area called the focus, or hypocenter. Damage is usually greatest near the **epicenter,** the point on the surface directly above the focus.

ASSESSMENT

1. **Key Terms** Define **(a)** earthquake, **(b)** tsunami, **(c)** landslide, **(d)** infrastructure, **(e)** avalanche, **(f)** aftershock, **(g)** seismic wave, **(h)** epicenter.
2. **Physical Processes** What physical processes cause an earthquake to occur?
3. **Environmental Change** How can an earthquake cause changes to the physical characteristics of a place?
4. **Natural Hazards** **(a)** How can an earthquake change the human characteristics of a place? **(b)** How does the international community respond to a devastating earthquake?
5. **Critical Thinking** **Solving Problems** What can a community do to reduce the amount of earthquake damage that might occur in the future?

239

3 ASSESS

Evaluate Understanding L2

Work with students to model how an earthquake happens. Encourage them to build models using everyday classroom materials, such as books for tectonic plates and paper strips for seismic waves.

Reteach L1

Group students in groups of four or five. Have each group create an earthquake safety pamphlet. Tell students to find out the recommended ways to protect themselves during an earthquake. Have them create a pamphlet that explains and illustrates safety instructions. Each group should have researchers, an editor to compile the instructions, and an illustrator to create the pictures. Post the completed pamphlets on a bulletin board.

Assessment

1. **(a)** a shaking of the ground caused by sudden movements in Earth's crust; **(b)** a huge sea wave that is set off by an undersea earthquake or volcanic eruption; **(c)** a sudden drop of a mass of land down a mountainside or hillside; **(d)** the network of services that supports a community; **(e)** a sudden fall of a mass of ice and snow; **(f)** tremors that can occur days, or even months, after an earthquake; **(g)** vibrations that travel through the ground; **(h)** the point on the surface directly above the focus
2. sudden movements in Earth's crust
3. Earthquakes can change the level of the land, cause fires and floods, and cover areas with snow and ice.
4. **(a)** Sample answer: Damage from an earthquake can destroy buildings and make a place uninhabitable; **(b)** Emergency relief workers from around the world may arrive to help with rescue and cleanup efforts. People around the world may donate money to help victims survive until they rebuild their lives.
5. Sample answers: Design buildings to withstand the shock of an earth quake. Build villages, towns, and cities far from fault lines.

Exploration Lab

Locating an Earthquake **L2**

Objective
Students should be able to determine the location of an earthquake epicenter.

Skills Focus Measuring, Interpreting maps, Interpreting Graphs

Prep Time 15 minutes

Advance Prep Photocopy the map on p. 241 for each student.

Class Time 45 minutes

Safety Students should use caution when using the drawing compasses. The ends are sharp.

Teaching Tips

- Encourage students to be very neat and precise in their measurements. It is important that the circles they draw be as accurate as possible in order to achieve the most accurate epicenter location. You may want to encourage them to place the map on top of their notebooks when they draw the circles with the compass, giving the tip of the compass something to dig into.
- Also, students should realize that they may not get an exact point for their epicenter location. It is possible that they will draw a small triangle at the junction of their circles. This is acceptable, but the triangle should be small.
- Too big an area indicates that either the calculations were incorrect or the circles were not precise enough.

Exploration Lab

Locating an Earthquake

The focus of an earthquake is the actual place within Earth where the earthquake originates. When locating an earthquake on a map, scientists plot the epicenter, the point on Earth's surface directly above the focus. To locate an epicenter, records from three different seismographs are needed.

New York, NY

(Time marks in minutes)

9:00 UTC

Problem How can you determine the location of an earthquake's epicenter?

Materials

- pencil
- drawing compass
- world map or atlas
- photocopy of map on page 241

Skills Measuring, Interpreting Maps, Interpreting Graphs

Procedure  

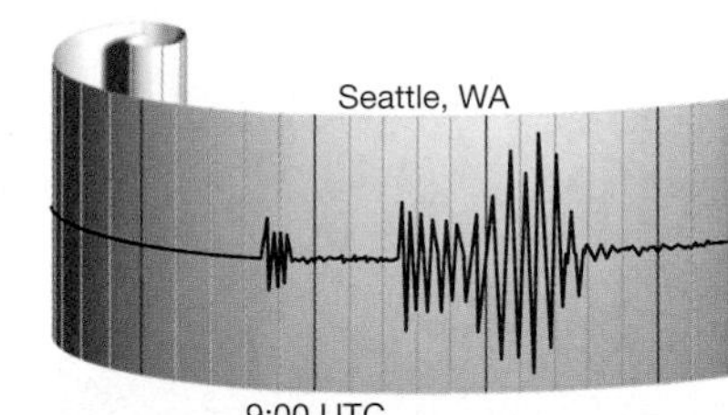

1. These three seismograms recorded the same earthquake, in New York City, Seattle, and Mexico City. Use the travel-time graph to determine the distance that each station is from the epicenter. Record your answers in a data table like the one shown.
2. Refer to a world map or atlas for the locations of the three seismic stations. Place a small dot showing the location of each of the three stations on the photocopy of the map on the next page. Neatly label each city on the map.

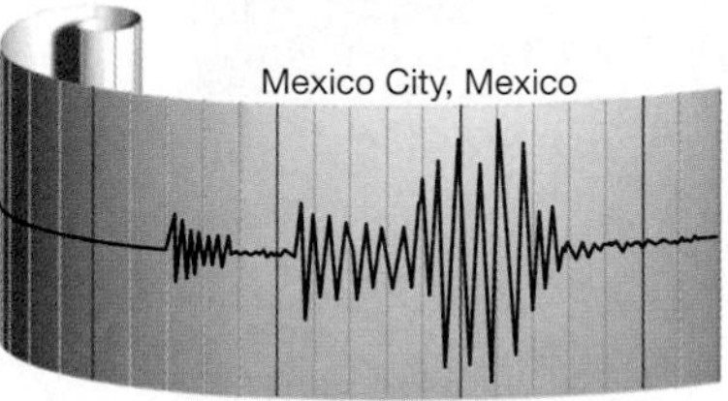

Data Table

	New York	Seattle	Mexico City
Elapsed time between first P and first S waves			
Distance from epicenter in miles			

3. On the map, use a drawing compass to draw a circle around each of the three stations. The radius of the circle, in miles, should be equal to each station's distance from the epicenter. Use the scale on the map to set the distance on the drawing compass for each station. **CAUTION** *Use care when handling the drawing compass.*

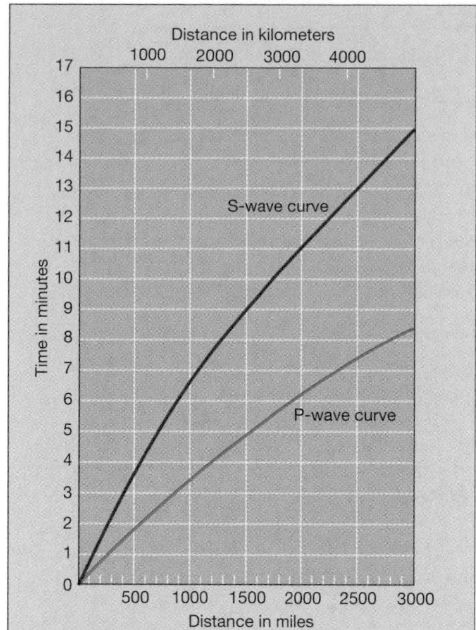

Analyze and Conclude

1. **Using Graphs** How far from the epicenter are the three cities located?
2. **Calculating** What would the distances from the epicenter to the cities be in kilometers?
3. **Interpreting Maps** What is the approximate latitude and longitude of the epicenter of the earthquake that was recorded by the three stations?
4. **Drawing Conclusions** On the New York seismogram the first P wave was recorded at 9:01 UTC. UTC is the international standard on which most countries base their time. At what time (UTC) did the earthquake actually occur? Explain.

Go Further Use the Internet or the library to find the locations of recent earthquake epicenters. Make a data table displaying the location, date, and magnitude of ten recent earthquakes. Report your findings to the class.

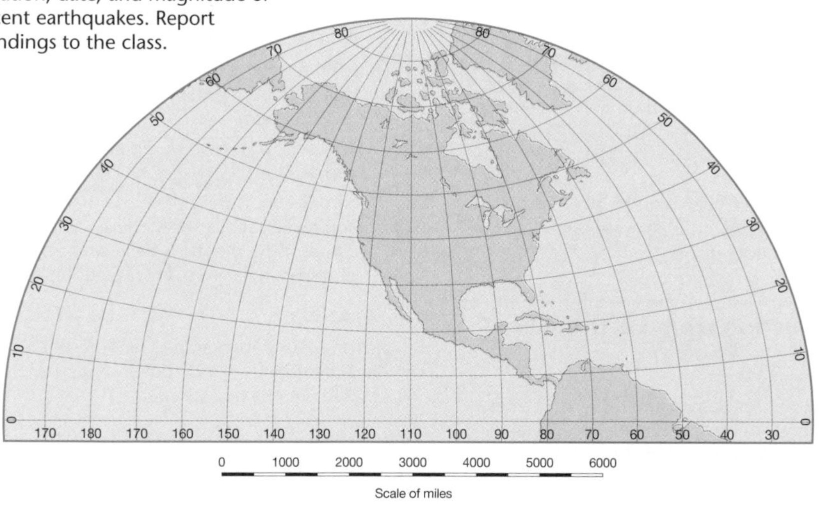

Expected Outcome Students should find a unique point or location for the epicenter of the earthquake.

Analyze and Conclude

1. NY—approximately 2400 miles; Seattle—approximately 1400 miles; Mexico City—approximately 1200 miles
2. NY—approximately 3864 km; Seattle—approximately 2254 km; Mexico City—approximately 1932 km
3. 28° latitude and 112°30'W longitude
4. 8:54 UTC; There is 7 minutes difference between the actual time of the earthquake and when it was recorded in New York.

Go Further

Answers will vary, but students' data tables should neatly show the dates, locations, and magnitudes of ten recent earthquakes.
Visual, Logical

Study Guide

Study Tip

Prioritize
Schedule your time realistically. Stick to your deadlines.

CHAPTER 8

Study Guide

8.1 What Is an Earthquake?

Key Concepts

- Faults are fractures in Earth along which movement has occurred.
- Most earthquakes are produced by the rapid release of elastic energy. This energy is stored in rock that has been subjected to great forces. When the strength of the rock is exceeded, it suddenly breaks, causing the vibrations of an earthquake.

Vocabulary

earthquake, *p. 218;* focus, *p. 218;* epicenter, *p. 219;* fault, *p. 219;* elastic rebound hypothesis, *p. 220;* aftershock, *p. 221;* foreshock, *p. 221*

8.2 Measuring Earthquakes

Key Concepts

- A seismogram shows the three main types of seismic waves—surface waves, P waves, and S waves.
- Travel-time graphs from three or more seismographs can be used to find the exact location of an earthquake epicenter.
- Historically, scientists have used two different measurement types to describe the size of an earthquake—intensity and magnitude.
- Moment magnitude is the most widely used measurement for earthquakes because it is the only magnitude scale that estimates the energy released by earthquakes.

Vocabulary

seismograph, *p. 222;* seismogram, *p. 222;* surface wave, *p. 223;* P wave, *p. 223;* S wave, *p. 223;* moment magnitude, *p. 227*

8.3 Destruction from Earthquakes

Key Concepts

- The damage to buildings and other structures from earthquake waves depends on several factors. These factors include the intensity and the duration of the vibrations, the nature of the material on which the structure is built, and the design of the structure.
- A tsunami triggered by an earthquake occurs where a slab of the ocean floor is displaced vertically along a fault. A tsunami also can occur when the vibration of a quake sets an underwater landslide into motion.
- With many earthquakes, the greatest damage to structures is from landslides and ground subsidence, or the sinking of the ground triggered by the vibrations.
- So far, methods for short-range predictions of earthquakes have not been successful.
- Scientists don't yet understand enough about how and where earthquakes will occur to make accurate long-term predictions.

Vocabulary

liquefaction, *p. 230;* tsunami, *p. 230;* seismic gap, *p. 232*

8.4 Earth's Layered Structure

Key Concepts

- Earth's interior consists of three major zones defined by its chemical composition—the crust, mantle, and core.
- Earth can be divided into layers based on physical properties—the lithosphere, asthenosphere, outer core, and inner core.
- Early seismic data and drilling technology indicate that the continental crust is mostly made of lighter, granitic rocks.
- The crust of the ocean floor has a basaltic composition.
- Earth's core is thought to be mainly dense iron and nickel, similar to metallic meteorites. The surrounding mantle is believed to be composed of rocks similar to stony meteorites.

Vocabulary

crust, *p. 233;* mantle, *p. 234;* lithosphere, *p. 234;* asthenosphere, *p. 235;* outer core, *p. 235;* inner core, *p. 235;* Moho, *p. 236*

Chapter Assessment Resources

Print
Chapter Test, Chapter 8
Test Prep Resources, Chapter 8

Technology
Computer Test Bank, Chapter 8 Test
Online Text, Chapter 8
Go Online, PHSchool.com, Chapter 8

CHAPTER 8

NY Regents Content Item

Assessment

Interactive textbook with assessment at PHSchool.com 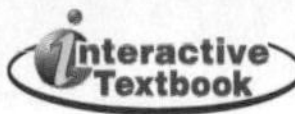

Reviewing Content

Choose the number that best answers the question or completes the statement.

1 Approximately how many earthquakes are strong enough to be felt each year worldwide?
(1) 500 (2) 1000
(3) 10,000 (4) 30,000

2 What is the location on the surface directly above the earthquake focus called? NY
(1) epicenter (2) fault
(3) magnitude (4) Moho

3 The rigid layer of Earth that includes the entire crust and the uppermost part of the mantle is called the NY
(1) asthenosphere (2) mesosphere
(3) lithosphere (4) Moho

4 The instrument that records earthquakes is called NY
(1) a seismogram (2) a seismologist
(3) seismology (4) a seismograph

5 Which of the following regions has the greatest amount of earthquake activity? NY
(1) central Europe
(2) the circum-Pacific belt or Ring of Fire
(3) the eastern United States
(4) central Africa

6 What material do scientists believe makes up a large part of the upper mantle?
(1) basalt (2) granite
(3) iron (4) peridotite

7 The point at which an earthquake begins is called NY
(1) a foreshock (2) the epicenter
(3) the focus (4) the Moho

8 In areas where loosely consolidated materials are saturated with water, earthquakes can turn stable soil into a liquid during a process called NY
(1) faulting (2) liquefaction
(3) tsunamis (4) subsidence

9 To find the epicenter of an earthquake, what is the minimum number of seismic stations that are needed? NY
(1) three (2) nine
(3) five (4) two

10 What scale is currently used to express the magnitude of an earthquake? NY
(1) Richter scale
(2) moment magnitude
(3) tsunami scale
(4) Moho scale

Understanding Concepts

Use the diagram below to answer questions 11 and 12.

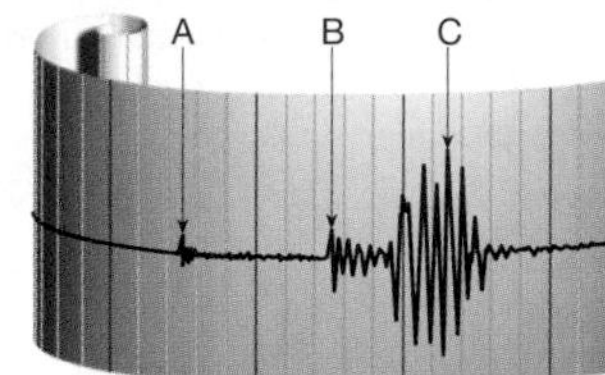

11 The diagram shows a typical recording of an earthquake. What is the record called? NY

12 Identify the waves recorded at A, B, and C on the diagram. NY

13 Does all motion along large faults occur in the form of destructive earthquakes? NY

14 What type of seismic wave causes the greatest destruction to buildings? NY

15 In addition to the damage caused directly by seismic vibrations, list three other types of destructive events that can be triggered by earthquakes. NY

16 Describe the composition and physical properties of both the continental and oceanic crusts. NY

17 What is liquefaction and how can earthquakes cause liquefaction to occur?

18 List the major differences between P waves and S waves. NY

19 How much does the amplitude of the waves increase between an earthquake that measures 4.2 on the Richter scale and an earthquake that measures 6.2 on the Richter scale?

20 What are two factors that can determine the amount of destruction that results from an earthquake? NY

Homework Guide

Section	Questions
1	1, 2, 7
2	4, 5, 9–12, 18, 19, 22, 24–29
3	8, 13–15, 17, 20, 21, 30
4	3, 6, 16, 23

Assessment

Reviewing Content

(1) 4 (2) 1 (3) 3
(4) 4 (5) 2 (6) 4
(7) 3 (8) 2 (9) 1
(10) 2

Understanding Concepts

(11) seismogram
(12) A: P waves
B: S waves
C: surface waves
(13) no
(14) surface waves
(15) fire, landslides, and tsunamis
(16) The crust is the thin, rocky outer layer of Earth. The oceanic crust is composed of basalt and gabbro. The continental crust is largely composed of granite.
(17) Liquefaction is when stable soil turns to a liquid that is unable to support buildings. This happens when soil saturated with water is shaken during an earthquake.
(18) P waves travel faster than S waves. P waves are push-and-pull waves while S waves shake the particles at right angles to the direction of travel.
(19) 100 times
(20) Answer should include two of the following: intensity and duration of earthquake, nature of material the structure is built on, and design of structure.

Critical Thinking

(21) if a moderate earthquake occurs in a more densely populated area than an earthquake with a higher magnitude; or if the moderate earthquake occurs in an area that lacks earthquake-safe building stands; or if the moderate earthquake triggers landslides, fires, or tsunamis
(22) The Richter scale is logarithmic and based on the amplitude of the largest seismic wave, and so depends on ground motion as recorded by a seismograph. Conversely, the moment magnitude scale estimates the amount of energy released by earthquakes; it is a calculation based on the average amount of movement along the fault, the area of the surface break, and the strength of the broken rock.
(23) by looking at the behavior of seismic waves as they travel through the different layers of Earth

Analyzing Data

(24) approximately 1500 km
(25) The first P wave will arrive 5 minutes after the earthquake. The first S wave will arrive 9 minutes after the earthquake.
(26) approximately 2 minutes

Concepts in Action

(27) The moment magnitude scale is the most frequently used because it is the only scale that measures the energy released by an earthquake.
(28) the Ring of Fire
(29) You will be able to receive surface waves only. P and S waves are body waves and travel out from the focus of an earthquake inside Earth. The "earthquake" created by the ship occurred on the surface and therefore did not produce P and S waves.
(30) Answers will vary. Accept reasonable answers.

CHAPTER 8

Assessment *continued*

Critical Thinking

21 **Applying Concepts** Give two reasons why an earthquake with a moderate magnitude might cause more extensive damage than an earthquake with a high magnitude.

22 **Comparing and Contrasting** How are the moment magnitude scale and the Richter scale different?

23 **Inferring** How did scientists determine the structure and composition of Earth's interior?

Analyzing Data

Use the diagram below to answer questions 24–26.

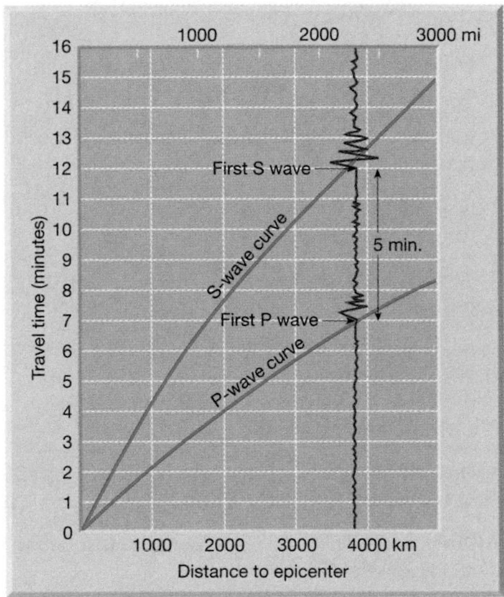

24 **Using Graphs** Determine the distance of a seismic station if the first S wave arrives three minutes after the first P wave.

25 **Using Graphs** If a seismic station is 2500 kilometers from the earthquake's epicenter, approximately when will the first P wave be received? When will the first S wave be received?

26 **Calculating** What is the difference in the travel-times of the first P wave and the first S wave if the seismic station is 1000 kilometers from the earthquake epicenter?

Concepts in Action

27 **Applying Concepts** Why is the moment magnitude the most commonly used scale by scientists for measuring earthquakes?

28 **Classifying** In what major earthquake zone would an earthquake in Indonesia be located?

29 **Hypothesizing** You are on a large ocean research ship. You have generated seismic waves by causing an explosion on a platform towed behind the ship. What seismic waves will be recorded by a seismograph located on the ocean floor beneath the ship? Explain your answer.

30 **Writing in Science** Research a recent earthquake and write about the earthquake damage in the style of a newspaper article.

Performance-Based Assessment

Designing an Experiment Design a model seismograph to record simulated earthquakes. When your model is completed, test it for the class. Then determine how your seismograph design could be improved or changed if it doesn't work well.

Regents Practice Exam

Test-Taking Tip

Narrowing the Choices
If, after reading all the answer choices, you are not sure which one is correct, eliminate those answers that you know are wrong. In the question below, first eliminate the choices you know are wrong. For example, answer choice 1 can be eliminated since the fact that earthquakes are destructive does not affect long-range forecasting. Then focus on the remaining choices.

Long-range earthquake forecasts are based on the assumption that earthquakes are
(1) destructive
(2) random
(3) fully understood
(4) repetitive

(Answer: 4)

For *each* statement or question, choose the *number* of the word or expression that, of those given, best completes the statement or answers the question. Some questions may require the use of the *Earth Science Reference Tables.*

1 If a P wave arrived at your station at 6:25 P.M., and an S wave arrived 5 minutes later, how far away is your station from the epicenter of the earthquake responsible for the waves?
(1) 2600 km
(2) 3.6 km
(3) 1300 km
(4) 3600 km

2 How far can a P wave travel in 7 minutes?
(1) 4000 km
(2) 1 km
(3) 7 km
(4) 1900 km

3 An earthquake on the ocean floor can cause a destructive sea wave called a
(1) P wave
(2) S wave
(3) high tide
(4) tsunami

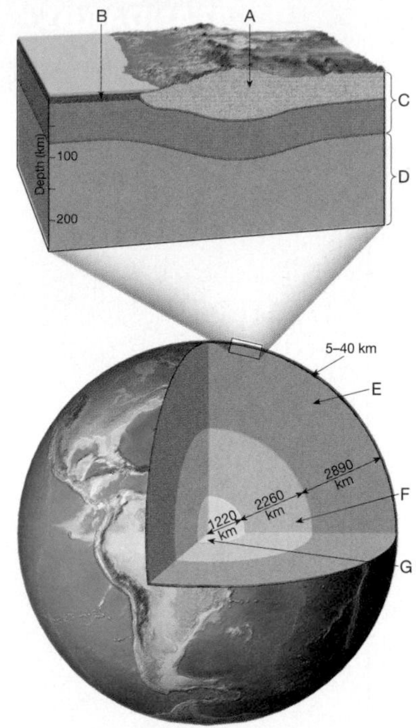

Answer the following questions in complete sentences. Some questions may require the use of the *Earth Science Reference Tables.* Base your answers to questions 4 through 6 on the diagram above, which shows Earth's Layered Structure.

4 What layer of Earth's interior is labeled *F* in the diagram? Describe this layer. How did geologists determine the phase of this layer?

5 What layer is labeled *A* in the diagram? Compare the densities of layer *A* and layer *B*.

6 Give the name for layer *G*. What phase of matter would you encounter in this layer?

7 What is the primary difference between the lithosphere and the asthenosphere?

8 What property of P waves and S waves allows scientists to determine the location of an epicenter?

Regents Practice Exam

(1) 4
(2) 1
(3) 4
(4) Layer *F* is the outer core, and it is made of liquid metal. Geologists determined that this layer is a liquid by observing that S waves do not travel through the outer core.
(5) Layer *A* is the continental crust. Layer *A* is less dense than layer *B* (oceanic crust).
(6) Layer *G* is the inner core. It is solid.
(7) The primary difference is that the lithosphere is hard, rigid, and rocky, while the asthenosphere is softer, and partially melted.
(8) P waves and S waves travel at different speeds.

Performance-Based Assessment

Sample answer: Students may design a seismograph with a pen hanging on a string above a paper towel roll.

Your students can independently test their knowledge of the chapter and print out their results.

CHAPTER 9

Planning Guide

Use these planning tools
Use Teacher Express for all your planning needs

SECTION OBJECTIVES	STANDARDS NATIONAL	STANDARDS STATE	ACTIVITIES and LABS
9.1 Continental Drift, pp. 248–253 1 block or 2 periods 9.1 **Describe** the hypothesis of continental drift. 9.2 **Evaluate** the evidence in support of continental drift. 9.3 **Identify** the main objections to Wegener's hypothesis of continental drift.	A-1, A-2, D-3, E-2, G-1, G-2, G-3		**SE** Inquiry Activity: How Do the Continents Fit Together? p. 247 **L2** **TE** Teacher Demo: Evidence: Matching Fossils, p. 249 **L2** **TE** Build Science Skills, p. 251 **L2** **SE** Quick Lab: Charting the Age of the Atlantic Ocean, p. 252 **L2**
9.2 Plate Tectonics, pp. 254–257 1/2 block or 1 period 9.4 **Explain** the theory of plate tectonics. 9.5 **Describe** lithospheric plates. 9.6 **Identify** the three types of plate boundaries.	D-1, D-3, G-3		**TE** Build Science Skills, p. 254 **L2** **TE** Teacher Demo: A Convergent Model, p. 256 **L2**
9.3 Actions at Plate Boundaries, pp. 258–264 2 blocks or 4 periods 9.7 **Explain** how seafloor spreading and continental rifting cause formation of new lithosphere. 9.8 **Describe** the process of lithosphere destruction that takes place at subduction zones. 9.9 **Differentiate** among subduction at oceanic-continental, oceanic-oceanic, and continental-continental convergent boundaries. 9.10 **Describe** the action of plates at a transform fault boundary.	D-1, D-3		**TE** Build Science Skills, p. 259 **L2** **TE** Teacher Demo: Creating a Continental Rift, p. 260 **L2** **LM** Modeling a Plate Boundary **L2**
9.4 Testing Plate Tectonics, pp. 265–268 1 block or 2 periods 9.11 **Explain** how paleomagnetism and magnetic reversals provide evidence that supports the theory of plate tectonics. 9.12 **Evaluate** how earthquakes, ocean drilling, and hot spots provide evidence that supports the theory of plate tectonics.	D-3, E-2, G-1, G-2, G-3		**TE** Teacher Demo: Testing Minerals for Magnetism, p. 266 **L1** **SE** Exploration Lab: Paleomagnetism and the Ocean Floor, pp. 272–273 **L2**
9.5 Mechanisms of Plate Motion, pp. 269–270 1/2 block or 1 period 9.13 **Compare** the mechanisms of slab-pull and ridge-push as contributing to plate motion. 9.14 **Relate** the unequal distribution of heat in Earth and the mechanism of mantle convection to the movement of tectonic plates.	A-1, A-2, D-1, G-1		**TE** Reteach, p. 270 **L1**

Ability Levels	
L1	For students who need additional help
L2	For all students
L3	For students who need to be challenged

Components

SE	Student Edition	**GRSW**	Guided Reading & Study Workbook	**TP**	Test Prep Resources	**GEO**	Geode CD-ROM
TE	Teacher's Edition			**onT**	onlineText	**T**	Transparencies
LM	Laboratory Manual	**TEX**	Teacher Express	**DC**	Discovery Channel Videos	**GO**	Internet Resources
CUT	Chapter Tests	**CTB**	Computer Test Bank				

RESOURCES PRINT and TECHNOLOGY	SECTION ASSESSMENT
GRSW Section 9.1 **T-95** Reconstruction of Pangaea **T-96** Best Fit of South America and Africa **T-97** Fossils of *Mesosaurus* as Evidence of Pangaea **T-98** Matching Mountain Ranges Across the North Atlantic **T-99** Supercontinent Pangaea and the Continents Today **TEX** Lesson Planning 9.1	**SE** Section 9.1 Assessment, p. 253 **onT** Section 9.1
GRSW Section 9.2 **T-100, T-101** World Maps—Plate Boundaries GEODe Forces Within ↳ Plate Tectonics **TEX** Lesson Planning 9.2	**SE** Section 9.2 Assessment, p. 255 **onT** Section 9.2
GRSW Section 9.3 **T-102** Location of Most Divergent Plate Boundaries **T-103** Sea-Floor Spreading **T-104** East African Rift Valleys **T-105** Three Types of Convergent Plate Boundaries **T-106** The World's Oceanic Trenches, Ridge System, and Transform Faults **T-107** India Colliding with Asia **T-108** Transform Faults **T-109** Role of Transform Faults **DC** Plate Tectonics **TEX** Lesson Planning 9.3	**SE** Section 9.3 Assessment, p. 264 **onT** Section 9.3
GRSW Section 9.4 **T-110** Apparent Polar Wandering Paths **T-111** Illus. of Paleomagnetism **T-112** Time Scale of Earth's Magnetic Field **T-113** Magnetic Reversals Record Sea-Floor Spreading **T-114** World Map **T-115** Dist. of Earthquake Foci **T-116** Hot Spots Trace Plate Movement **TEX** Lesson Planning 9.4	**SE** Section 9.4 Assessment, p. 268 **onT** Section 9.4
GRSW Section 9.5 **T-117** Directions and Rates of Plate Motion **T-118** Models of the Driving Force for Plate Tectonics **T-119** Breakup of Pangaea **T-120** Earth 50 Million Years from Now **TEX** Lesson Planning 9.5	**SE** Section 9.5 Assessment, p. 270 **onT** Section 9.5

Go Online

Go online for these Internet resources.

PHSchool.com
Web Code: cjk-9999

NSTA SCILINKS
Web Code: cjn-3091
Web Code: cjn-3093

Materials for Activities and Labs

Quantities for each group

STUDENT EDITION

Inquiry Activity, p. 247
atlas or world map, paper, scissors

Quick Lab, p. 252
calculator

Exploration Lab, pp. 272–273
pencil, metric ruler, calculator

TEACHER'S EDITION

Teacher Demo, p. 249
2 groups of photographs or samples of fossils, including at least one type of fossil found in both groups

Build Science Skills, p. 251
child's jigsaw puzzle, 2 pieces of cardboard the size of the puzzle or larger, pencil or marker

Build Science Skills, p. 254
hard-boiled egg

Teacher Demo, p. 256
two slabs of modeling clay, wax paper

Build Science Skills, p. 259
2 colors of modeling clay

Teacher Demo, p. 260
2 slices of individually wrapped American cheese, dull knife or fingernail, metric ruler

Teacher Demo, p. 266
magnet, minerals (include at least one sample of a mineral that contains iron or cobalt), compass

Reteach, 270
beaker, water, hot plate, ice cube, food coloring

Chapter Assessment

ASSESSMENT

SE Assessment, pp. 275–276
CUT Chapter 9 Test
CTB Chapter 9
onT Chapter 9

STANDARDIZED TEST PREP

SE Chapter 9, p. 277
TP Progress Monitoring Assessments

interactive textbook with assessment at PHSchool.com

CHAPTER 9

Before you teach

Michael Wysession
Washington University

Big Ideas

Earth's lithosphere is broken into about a dozen major pieces and many other smaller pieces. These "plates" move about Earth's surface in a process called plate tectonics, which is the unifying framework within which all of modern geology is understood. Plate tectonics explains the existence of earthquakes, volcanoes, mountains, oceans, and many other things.

Space and Time Earth's plates have been moving around, changing and reforming, for at least 4 billion years. The moving plates drag the continents around with them, sometimes bringing them together to form supercontinents, the last of which was Pangaea.

Forces and Motion Plates move slowly but steadily, and interesting geology occurs when they collide, separate, or move past each other. Plates that are subducting into the mantle tend to move fast, pulled by the slab-pull force and pushed by the ridge-push force. Plates that contain continents tend to move slowly.

Matter and Energy Plate tectonics is the surface expression of a global cycle of mantle convection. Oceanic plates form at mid-ocean ridges, cool, and sink back into the mantle at subduction zones. The decay of radioactive isotopes is the source of heat that drives mantle convection.

Earth as a System Plate tectonics has profoundly affected the history of Earth's life: volcanic eruptions affect the atmosphere, the positions of continents affect ocean circulation, and plate collisions have created the continents and their unique distributions of minerals, metals, and other resources.

Earth Science Refresher

Why do we have plate tectonics?

Plate tectonics, and all of the exciting geology associated with it, is the result of Earth's attempt to cool down. It is the result of the second law of thermodynamics, which implies that heat tends to flow from hotter regions to cooler regions. Earth, as well as all other planets, was very hot when it formed. Earth's center is still hotter than 5000 K. This heat will try to make its way to the surface and out into space in the fastest way possible. The situation is complicated because heat is still being generated by the decay of radioactive isotopes, the four most important of which are uranium-235, uranium-238, thorium-232, and potassium-40. There were many other short-lived radioactive isotopes providing heat early in Earth's history.

Address Misconceptions

Students often think that the movement of lithospheric plates causes Earth's surface area to become either larger or smaller (depending on which way the plates move.) Explain that if surface area decreased, the interior would become compressed and internal pressure would increase. If surface area increased, either the interior would expand or the lithosphere would separate from the mantle. For a strategy that helps to overcome this misconception, see **Address Misconceptions** on **p. 257.**

Planets cool down by a combination of radiation, conduction, and convection. Once the heat gets out to Earth's surface, it radiates out into space, but it gets to the surface by conduction and convection. When rock is stiff, like with the lithosphere, or where there are compositional boundaries, like between the core and mantle, heat must conduct. This is a slow process, which is why rock-like materials such as ceramic are used for coffee mugs. Throughout most of the Earth, however, heat moves by convection, by which it is carried along with the moving material. This occurs in the core and across most of the mantle. This cycle of convection, not unlike a pot of

Go Online NSTA PD LINKS

For: Chapter 9 Content Support
Visit: www.SciLinks.org/PDLinks
Web Code: cjn-0999

boiling soup, involves hot rock rising, forming oceanic plates, cooling off by heating the ocean, and sinking back down into the mantle. The cycle may take, on average, about a half-billion years. Because it moves slowly, the Earth is cooling slowly, and plate tectonics will continue throughout Earth's lifetime.

It is interesting to note that no other planets in our solar system have Earth-like plate tectonics. There are many factors needed for plate tectonics to occur. The existence of an asthenosphere layer is vital, as this soft layer allows the overlying plates to move horizontally more easily than they otherwise would. Water plays a vital role, as the existence of the asthenosphere is due to the large amount of water (perhaps more than five oceanfuls!) that exists in the mantle, making the mantle rock softer and lowering its melting point.

Address Misconceptions

Some students may think that the continents have remained in approximately the same positions since the breakup of Pangaea. In reality, the locations of continents have continued to shift. For a strategy that helps to overcome this misconception, see **Address Misconceptions** on **p. 250**.

Build Reading Literacy

Relate Cause and Effect

Understanding How and Why Things Occur

Strategy Help students read and understand relationships between events. Cause-effect relationships are integral to science, so it is very important that students understand the cause-effect relationships developed in the text. Before students begin, assign a passage in Chapter 9 for them to read, such as pp. 254–255 in Section 9.2.

Example

1. Remind students that a cause is what makes something happen and the effect is what happens as a result. Point out that in science, many actions cause other actions to occur.
2. Have students identify cause-effect relationships in the passage. Remind them that the text does not always directly state the cause-effect relationship, but in many cases clue words or phrases do point out such a connection: *because, so, since, results, therefore, cause, lead to*. For example, "Rain is always slightly acidic because carbon dioxide dissolves in water droplets and forms carbonic acid."
3. Then, explain that causes and effects often occur in chains, with effects becoming causes of later effects. Have students find a cause-effect chain and show it in the form of a flowchart. For example, insufficient oxygen for complete combustion → carbon monoxide produced → inhaled and absorbed by blood → hemoglobin cannot carry oxygen to cells.

See p. 251 for a script on how to use this strategy with students. For additional strategies, see pp. 255, 261, 263, and 268.

ASSESS PRIOR KNOWLEDGE

Use the Chapter Pretest below to assess students' prior knowledge. As needed, review these concepts.

Review Science Concepts

Section 9.1 Reviewing fossil formation and rock types ensures that students will understand the concepts of matching fossils and rock types and formations as evidence for continental drift. An understanding of erosion and deposition leads to an understanding of the gaps and overlaps between continents.

Section 9.2 and Section 9.3 A knowledge of Earth's structure will help students understand plate tectonics and how Earth's lithosphere is changing.

Section 9.4 Reviewing the causes of earthquakes and the structure of Earth's interior will help students understand the evidence supporting plate tectonics.

Section 9.5 A knowledge of the convection process and how radioactive decay produces heat is essential for an understanding of the causes of plate motion.

CHAPTER

Plate Tectonics

CONCEPTS in Action

Quick Lab
Charting the Age of the Atlantic Ocean

Exploration Lab
Paleomagnetism and the Ocean Floor

Understanding Earth
Plate Tectonics into the Future

Forces Within
↳ Plate Tectonics

Video Field Trip

Plate Tectonics

Take a plate tectonics field trip with Discovery Channel and see how the crust of Earth is in constant motion. Answer the following questions after watching the video.

1. What does the discovery of identical basalt rock in South America and Africa help to prove?
2. How was the Atlantic Ocean formed?

Go Online PHSchool.com

For: Chapter 9 Resources
Visit: PHSchool.com
Web Code: cjk-9999

This photograph is a composite satellite image of Europe, North Africa, and the Arabian Peninsula. ▶

Chapter Pretest

1. True or False: P waves are compressional waves that can travel through rock. *(True)*

2. What is the outer portion of solid Earth containing the crust and uppermost mantle? *(b)*
   a. outer core b. lithosphere
   c. hydrosphere d. atmosphere

3. Explain briefly how an earthquake can cause mass movement of material in Earth's crust. *(Earthquakes can dislodge large volumes of rock and soil by their vibrations. If this material moves downward in a landslide, the appearance of Earth's crust can change.)*

4. What term describes the total number of neutrons and protons in the nucleus of an atom? *(c)*
   a. isotope
   b. atomic weight
   c. mass number
   d. atomic number

5. Why is there such a large diversity in the chemical composition of igneous rocks? *(The chemical composition depends on the composition of the magma from which the rock crystallized. During stages of crystallization, the solid and liquid components of magma separate to form many different minerals.)*

6. Name two sources of sedimentary rocks. *(solid particles from weathered rocks and soluble material from chemical weathering)*

FORCES WITHIN

Chapter Preview

Inquiry Activity

How Do the Continents Fit Together?

Procedure

1. Get a copy of a world map from your teacher. Cut out the major continents along their coastlines. **CAUTION** *Be careful when using scissors.*
2. Try to fit together the pieces into one large landmass. Look for a "best-fit" configuration.
3. Compare your large landmass with those of other students. Did anyone come up with a landmass that was very different from the others?

Think About It

1. **Observing** From your continental reconstruction, where did the continents fit together well? Where did problems occur?
2. **Developing Hypotheses** Use your observations to develop a hypothesis on how to get a better fit of the continents. How could the overlaps and large gaps be explained? (*Hint:* What if the outline of the coasts was not the same as the boundaries of the continents themselves?)

Plate Tectonics **247**

DISCOVERY CHANNEL SCHOOL **Video Field Trip**

Plate Tectonics

Encourage students to view the Video Field Trip "Plate Tectonics."

ENGAGE/EXPLORE

How Do the Continents Fit Together? L2

Purpose In this activity, students begin to recognize the shapes of the continents and fit together cutouts of the continents to form one large landmass.

Address Misconceptions

Students may believe that some pieces of the continents have sunk into the oceans, causing them to not fit together well. Explain that overlaps occur because of sedimentation at river deltas and deformation of the plates.

Skills Focus **Observing, Developing Hypotheses**

Prep Time 5 minutes

Materials world map or atlas, paper, scissors

Advance Prep 20 minutes to copy maps

Class Time 10 minutes

Safety Remind students to handle scissors carefully.

Teaching Tips

You may want to paste the maps onto cardboard in advance of class. Maps will last longer and can be used repeatedly. The cardboard should not be so thick that students cannot easily cut it with scissors.

Expected Outcome Africa and South America fit together well. Other continents will fit together with areas of overlap and gaps.

Think About It

1. Students should find that Africa and South America fit together well. Other continental pieces will fit together with many areas of overlap and large gaps.
2. If the continental shelves are used as the outer edges of the continents, the fit will be better in many areas. Students may hypothesize that the outlines of the continents have been modified by depositional and stretching processes that make the reconstruction difficult. Students also may hypothesize (incorrectly) that some pieces of the continents have sunk into the oceans.

1 FOCUS

Section Objectives

9.1 **Describe** the hypothesis of continental drift.
9.2 **Evaluate** the evidence in support of continental drift.
9.3 **Identify** the main objections to Wegener's hypothesis of continental drift.

Reading Focus

Build Vocabulary L2

Word Forms Before students read this section, ask them to write a sentence or two describing the meaning of the word *drift*. Then have them write a prediction for what they think continental drift means. After students read the section, have them examine their predictions and discuss whether their predictions must be changed.

Reading Strategy L2

a. continental puzzle
b. matching fossils
c. matching rocks and structures
d. ancient climates

2 INSTRUCT

An Idea Before Its Time

Use Visuals L1

Figure 1 Point out the small areas of brown and light blue between Africa and South America. Ask: **What could cause the brown-shaded regions of overlap?** *(accumulation of sediments deposited by rivers and stretching of the plates)* **What do you think the light blue areas represent?** *(the continental shelf)*
Visual

9.1 Continental Drift

Reading Focus

Key Concepts
- What is the hypothesis of continental drift?
- What evidence supported continental drift?

Vocabulary
- continental drift
- Pangaea

Reading Strategy
Summarizing Copy the table. Fill it in as you read to summarize the evidence of continental drift.

Hypothesis	Evidence
Continental Drift	a. continental puzzle
	b. ____?____
	c. ____?____
	d. ____?____

Will California eventually slide into the ocean? Have continents really drifted apart over the centuries? Early in the twentieth century, most geologists thought that the positions of the ocean basins and continents were fixed. During the last few decades, however, new data have dramatically changed our understanding of how Earth works.

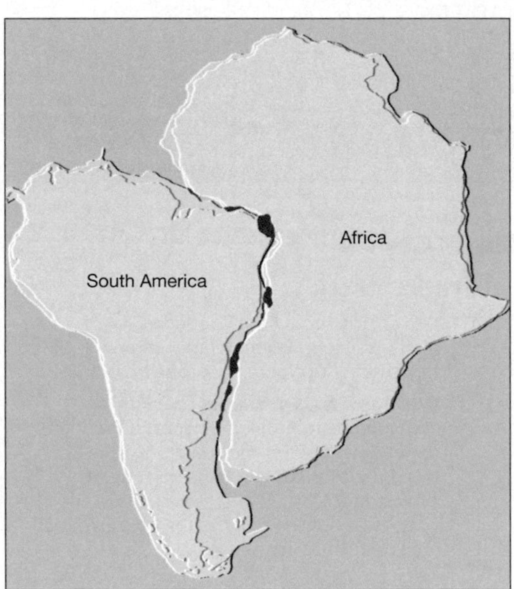

Figure 1 A Curious Fit This map shows the best fit of South America and Africa at a depth of about 900 meters. The areas where continents overlap appear in brown.
Inferring ***Why are there areas of overlap?***

An Idea Before Its Time

The idea that continents fit together like pieces of a jigsaw puzzle came about when better world maps became available. Figure 1 shows the two most obvious pieces of this jigsaw puzzle. However, little significance was given this idea until 1915, when Alfred Wegener, a German scientist, proposed his radical hypothesis of **continental drift.** **Wegener's continental drift hypothesis stated that the continents had once been joined to form a single supercontinent.** He called this supercontinent **Pangaea,** meaning *all land.*

Wegener also hypothesized that about 200 million years ago Pangaea began breaking into smaller continents. These continents then drifted to their present positions, as shown on page 250. Wegener and others collected much evidence to support these claims. Let's examine their evidence.

Evidence: The Continental Puzzle Wegener first thought that the continents might have been joined when he noticed the similarity between the coastlines on opposite sides of the South Atlantic Ocean. He used present-day shorelines to show how the continents fit together. However, his opponents correctly argued that erosion continually changes shorelines over time.

Evidence: Matching Fossils **Fossil evidence for continental drift includes several fossil organisms found on different landmasses.** Wegener reasoned that these organisms could not have crossed the vast oceans presently separating the continents. An example is *Mesosaurus,* an aquatic reptile whose fossil remains are limited to eastern South America and southern Africa, as shown in Figure 2. If *Mesosaurus* had been able to swim well enough to cross the vast South Atlantic Ocean, its fossils should be more widely distributed. This is not the case. Therefore, Wegener argued, South America and Africa must have been joined somehow.

The idea of land bridges was once the most widely accepted explanation for similar fossils being found on different landmasses. Most scientists believed that during a recent glacial period, the lowering of sea level allowed animals to cross the narrow Bering Strait between Asia and North America. However, if land bridges did exist between South America and Africa, their remnants should still lie below sea level. But no signs of such land bridges have ever been found in the Atlantic Ocean.

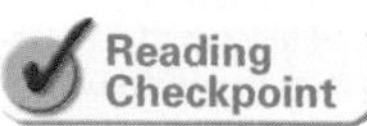

How does the distribution of Mesosaurus *fossils provide evidence for continental drift?*

Q *If all the continents were once joined as Pangaea, what did the rest of Earth look like?*

A When all the continents were together, there must also have been one huge ocean surrounding them. This ocean is called *Panthalassa* (*pan* = all, *thalassa* = sea). Today all that remains of Panthalassa is the Pacific Ocean, which has been decreasing in size since the breakup of Pangaea.

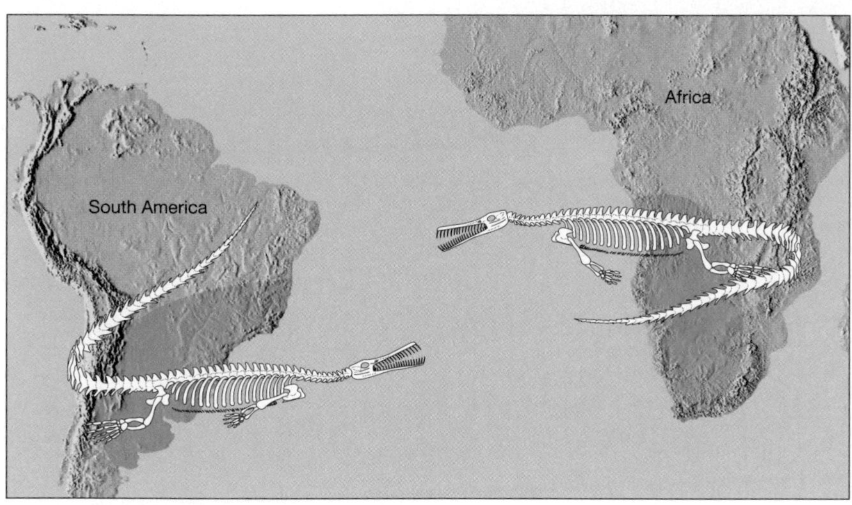

Figure 2 Location of Mesosaurus Fossils of *Mesosaurus* have been found on both sides of the South Atlantic and nowhere else in the world. Fossil remains of this and other organisms on the continents of Africa and South America appear to link these landmasses at some time in Earth's history.

Teacher Demo

Evidence: Matching Fossils L2

Purpose Students compare two groups of fossils from two continents to identify those fossils that are common to both continents.

Materials 2 groups of photographs or samples of fossils, including at least one type of fossil found in both groups

Procedure Have students examine the two groups of fossils. Tell them that the two groups were found on different continents. Ask them to identify any fossils that were found on both continents. Have students infer the implications of this observation.

Expected Outcome Students should infer that the two continents had to be connected at some point in the past when the organism in the fossil lived.
Visual, Logical

Customize for Inclusion Students

Visually Impaired Puzzle pieces of continents can be made out of sandpaper by gluing a map onto the back of a piece of sandpaper and cutting out the continents. This learning tool can be used by both visually impaired students and students who learn tactilely. Remind students who use these pieces that the piece must be held with the rough side down for correct geographical orientation of the continent.

Answer to . . .

Figure 1 *Areas where there are rivers or streams have deposited large amounts of sediments.*

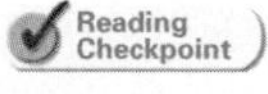
Mesosaurus *occurs only in eastern South America and southern Africa.*

Use Visuals L1

Figure 3 Have students study the maps showing the breakup of Pangaea. Ask: **In the breakup of Pangaea, what continents appear to have separated first?** *(North America and Africa)* **What ocean began to form when North America and Africa separated?** *(Atlantic Ocean)* **How was India formed?** *(India broke away from Gondwanaland. It moved north and eventually collided with Asia.)*
Visual, Logical

Address Misconceptions L2

Some students may think that the continents have remained in approximately the same positions since the breakup of Pangaea. Make transparencies of the five parts of Figure 3. Superimpose the transparencies two at a time to show students the changes. Ask students to come up to the projection to point out changes in the location of continents from one transparency to another.
Ask which continent has moved the farthest. *(Asia)*
Visual, Logical

Breakup of Pangaea

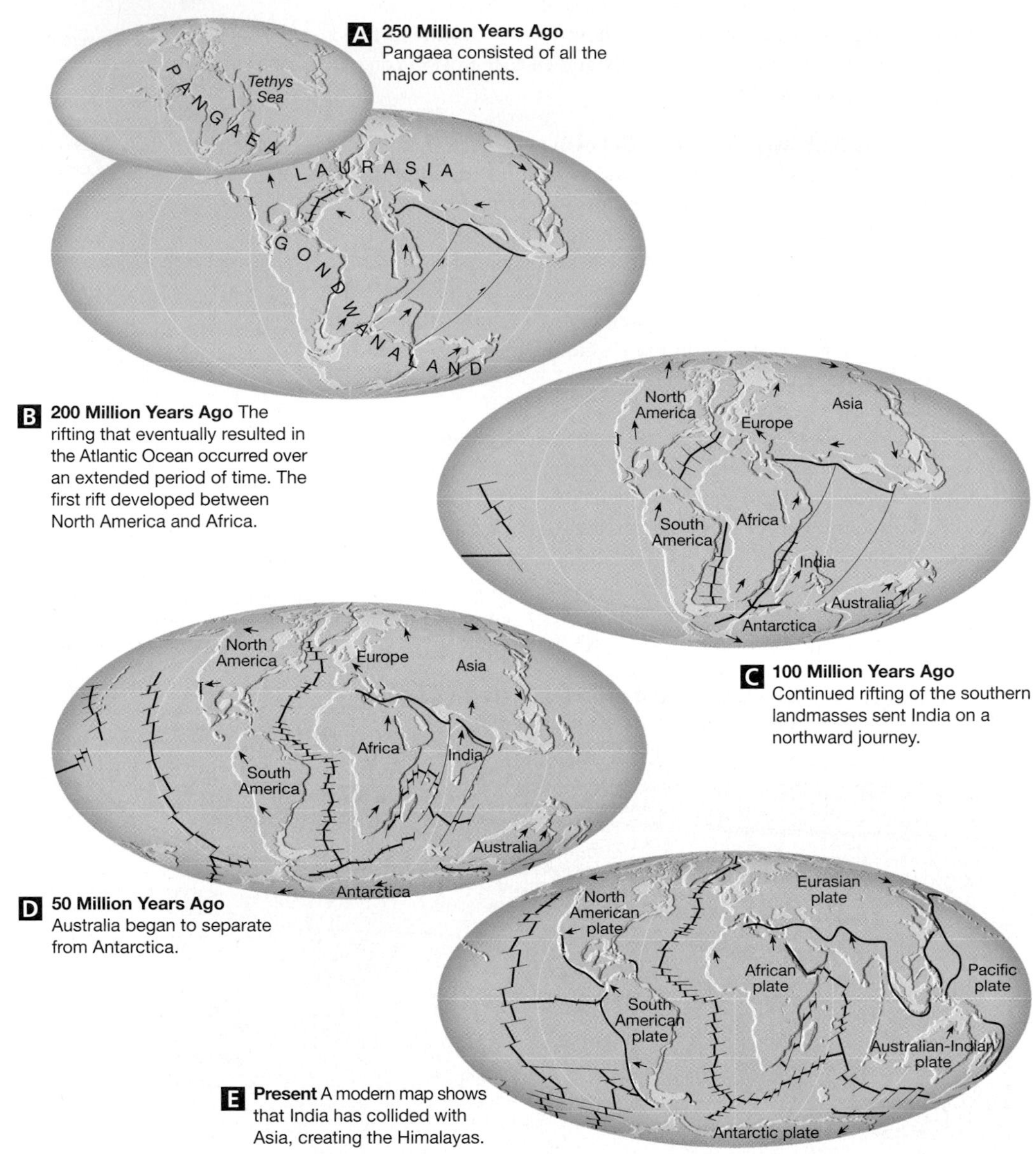

A **250 Million Years Ago** Pangaea consisted of all the major continents.

B **200 Million Years Ago** The rifting that eventually resulted in the Atlantic Ocean occurred over an extended period of time. The first rift developed between North America and Africa.

C **100 Million Years Ago** Continued rifting of the southern landmasses sent India on a northward journey.

D **50 Million Years Ago** Australia began to separate from Antarctica.

E **Present** A modern map shows that India has collided with Asia, creating the Himalayas.

Figure 3 Pangaea broke up gradually over a period of 200 million years.

Facts and Figures

Recently, a unique species of purple frog that lives underground was discovered in southwestern India. DNA analysis showed that the frog was related to a group of frogs that live only in the Seychelles Islands off the eastern coast of Africa and almost 3000 km across the Indian Ocean from India. Biologists think that the two frog populations are additional evidence for continental drift.

Matching Mountain Ranges

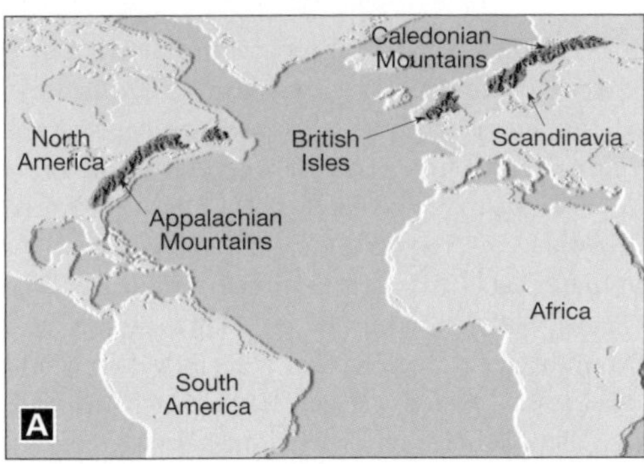

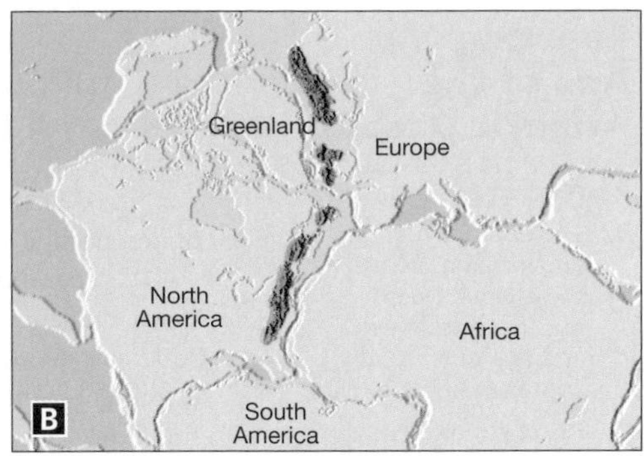

Figure 4 **A** The Appalachian Mountains run along the eastern side of North America and disappear off the coast of Newfoundland. Mountains that are similar in age and structure are found in the British Isles and Scandinavia. **B** When these landmasses are united as Pangaea, these ancient mountain chains form a nearly continuous belt.

Evidence: Rock Types and Structures Anyone who has worked a jigsaw puzzle knows that the pieces must fit together to form a clear picture. The clear picture in the continental drift puzzle is one of matching rock types and mountain belts. If the continents existed as Pangaea, the rocks found in a particular region on one continent should closely match in age and type those in adjacent positions on the adjoining continent.

Rock evidence for continental drift exists in the form of several mountain belts that end at one coastline, only to reappear on a landmass across the ocean. For example, the Appalachian mountain belt runs northeastward through the eastern United States, ending off the coast of Newfoundland, as shown in Figure 4A. Mountains of the same age with similar rocks and structures are found in the British Isles and Scandinavia. When these landmasses are fit together as in Figure 4B, the mountain chains form a nearly continuous belt.

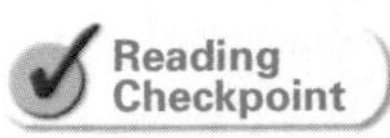

How does the location of mountain chains provide evidence of continental drift?

Evidence: Ancient Climates Wegener was a meteorologist, so he was interested in obtaining data about ancient climates to support continental drift. And he did find evidence for dramatic global climate changes. Wegener found glacial deposits showing that between 220 million and 300 million years ago, ice sheets covered large areas of the Southern Hemisphere. Layers of glacial till were found in southern Africa and South America, as well as in India and Australia. Below these beds of glacial debris lay scratched and grooved bedrock carved by the ice. In some locations, the scratches and grooves showed that the ice had moved from what is now the sea onto land. It is unusual for large continental glaciers to move from the sea

For: Links on continental drift
Visit: www.SciLinks.org
Web Code: cjn-3091

Build Science Skills L2

Using Models Have students use a child's jigsaw puzzle with several large pieces to demonstrate matching rock types and mountain belts as follows. Students should put the puzzle together on a piece of cardboard. After putting it together, the puzzle should be covered with another piece of cardboard and flipped over. On the back of the puzzle, students should draw lines representing a mountain belt that extends across several puzzle pieces. Students will understand when the puzzle is put together how mountain chains form continuous belts across land masses.
Kinesthetic, Visual

Build Reading Literacy L1

Refer to **p. 246D** which provides the guidelines for relating cause and effect.

Relate Cause and Effect Have students read the section on pp. 251–252 about ancient climates as evidence for continental drift. Ask: **Why did Wegener believe that the existence of glaciers in tropical regions of the Southern Hemisphere was evidence of continental drift rather than climatic change?** *(The Northern Hemisphere was once tropical, as evidenced by coal deposits that were formed from tropical plants. If the Northern Hemisphere had once been closer to the equator, the Southern Hemisphere probably had also been further south, closer to the South Pole. It was not likely that such a large change in climate could have taken place without continental drift.)*
Logical

Facts and Figures

Scientists think that 200 million years ago, what is now Pennsylvania was located farther south, near the equator. Fossils from coal fields in Pennsylvania show that the plants from which the coal formed had large leaf-like structures that are typical of tropical plants. The trunks of the plants had no growth rings, also typical of tropical plants because there is little seasonal temperature fluctuation to produce the rings. Scientists believe that these fossils are evidence that Pennsylvania once had a tropical climate and was located closer to the equator.

Download a worksheet on continental drift for students to complete, and find additional teacher support from NSTA SciLinks.

Answer to . . .

If mountain chains can be continued across present-day oceans, they provide evidence that the areas were once connected.

Charting the Age of the Atlantic Ocean L2

Objective
After completing this activity, students will be able to calculate the length of time it takes two land masses to separate, given the rate of spreading.

Skills Focus **Calculating, Inferring**

 **Prep Time** none

Class Time 10 minutes

Teaching Tips You might want to review conversion factors with students.

Expected Outcome The two continents took more than 130 million years to separate.

Analyze and Conclude
1. 130.3 million years
2. The rate would probably have varied over time because the driving mechanism was most likely not uniform. Few Earth processes are uniform over time.
Logical

For Enrichment L3

Have students research the following question: Pangaea began to break up and South America and Africa began to separate 200 million years ago. What types of living organisms were found on Earth when the two continents reached their current positions?

Quick Lab

Charting the Age of the Atlantic Ocean

Procedure

1. The distance between two locations across the Atlantic Ocean, one in South America and one in Africa, is approximately 4300 km.
2. Assume that these two locations were once joined as part of Pangaea.

Analyze and Conclude

1. **Calculating** If the two landmasses moved away from each other at a rate of 3.3 cm/y, how long did it take these two locations to move to their current positions?
2. **Inferring** Do you think the Atlantic Ocean would have formed at a constant rate or would that rate have varied over time? Why?

onto land. It is also interesting that much of the land area that shows evidence of this glaciation now lies near the equator in a subtropical or tropical climate.

Could Earth have been cold enough to allow the formation of continental glaciers in what is now a tropical region? Wegener rejected this idea because, during this same time period, large tropical swamps existed in the Northern Hemisphere. The lush vegetation of these swamps eventually became the major coal fields of the eastern United States, Europe, and Siberia.

Wegener thought there was a better explanation for the ancient climate evidence he observed. Thinking of the landmasses as a supercontinent, with South Africa centered over the South Pole, would create the conditions necessary to form large areas of glacial ice over much of the Southern Hemisphere. The supercontinent idea would also place the northern landmasses nearer the tropics and account for their vast coal deposits, as shown in Figure 5.

Summarize the climate evidence for continental drift.

Glacier Evidence

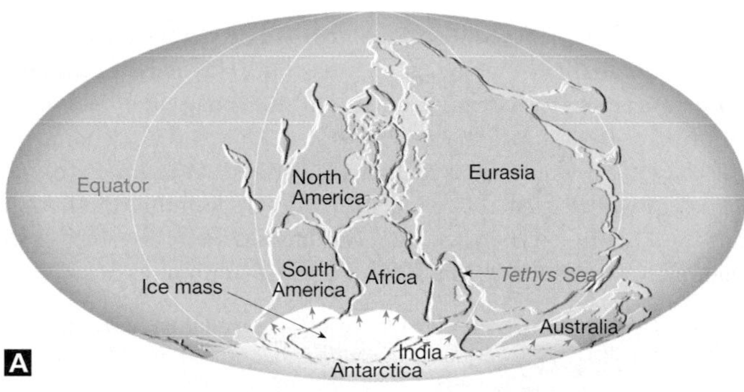

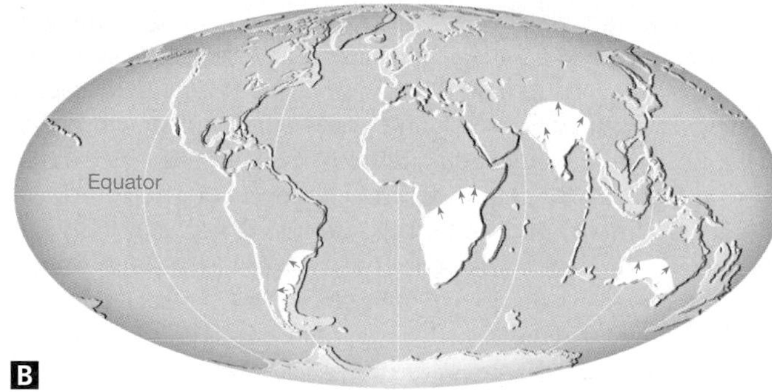

Figure 5 A The area of Pangaea covered by glacial ice 300 million years ago. **B** The continents as they are today. The white areas indicate where evidence of the old ice sheets exists. **Interpreting Diagrams** ***Where were the continents located when the glaciers formed?***

Rejecting a Hypothesis

Wegener's drift hypothesis faced a great deal of criticism from other scientists. One objection was that Wegener could not describe a mechanism that was capable of moving the continents across the globe. Wegener proposed that the tidal influence of the Moon was strong enough to give the continents a westward motion. However, physicists quickly responded that tidal friction of the size needed to move the continents would stop Earth's rotation.

Wegener also proposed that the larger and sturdier continents broke through the oceanic crust, much like ice breakers cut through ice. However, no evidence existed to suggest that the ocean floor was weak enough to permit passage of the continents without the ocean floors being broken and deformed in the process.

Most scientists in Wegener's day rejected his hypothesis. However, a few geologists continued to search for additional evidence of continents in motion.

Why was Wegener's hypothesis rejected?

A New Theory Emerges During the years that followed Wegener's hypothesis, major strides in technology enabled scientists to map the ocean floor. Extensive data on earthquake activity and Earth's magnetic field also became available. By 1968, these findings led to a new theory, known as plate tectonics. This theory provides the framework for understanding most geologic processes, such as the formation of the mountains shown in Figure 6.

Q *Some day will the continents come back together and form a single landmass?*

A Yes, but not anytime soon. Based on current plate motions, it appears that the continents may meet up again in the Pacific Ocean—in about 300 million years.

Figure 6 Mountain ranges are commonly formed at plate boundaries. This photograph shows part of the Canadian Rockies in Banff National Park, Alberta, Canada.

Section 9.1 Assessment

Reviewing Concepts

1. What is the hypothesis of continental drift?
2. List the evidence that supported the hypothesis of continental drift.
3. What was one of the main objections to Wegener's continental drift hypothesis?
4. What is Pangaea?

Critical Thinking

5. **Applying Concepts** Would the occurrence of the same plant fossils in South America and Africa support continental drift? Explain.
6. **Drawing Conclusions** How did Wegener explain the existence of glaciers in the southern landmasses, and the lush tropical swamps in North America, Europe, and Siberia?

Writing in Science

Descriptive Paragraph Write a paragraph describing Pangaea. Include the location and climate of Pangaea. Use the equator as your reference for position.

Rejecting a Hypothesis

Build Science Skills **L2**

Using Tables and Graphs Have students make a table listing the reasons why Wegener's hypothesis was criticized by some people and accepted by others.
Intrapersonal, Verbal

3 ASSESS

Evaluate Understanding **L2**

To assess students' knowledge of section content, have them write two or three sentences describing each of the four lines of evidence for Wegener's continental drift hypothesis.

Reteach **L1**

Have students explain in their own words why Figure 2 shows evidence for continental drift.

Pangaea was a supercontinent made up of all the major continents joined together. It began breaking into smaller continents about 200 million years ago. Pangaea was located near the South Pole. The southern part of Pangaea, made up of South America, Africa, India, Australia, and Antarctica, had a cold climate with large continental glaciers.

Section 9.1 Assessment

1. a hypothesis that proposes that the continents where once joined to form one supercontinent
2. matching continental outlines, matching fossils, matching rocks and structures, ancient climates
3. He could not provide a mechanism to explain the movement of the continents.
4. the supercontinent proposed by Wegener's hypothesis of continental drift
5. Yes, a land plant most likely could not travel across a large ocean such as the Atlantic. If the plant is found in both Africa and South America, those areas had to have been joined when the plant was growing.
6. It is difficult to imagine that Earth had cooled enough to form glaciers in tropical latitudes, so in order to explain the glaciers, those areas had to have been closer to the poles than in the present day. Also, the glacial grooves indicate the ice was coming from an area that at present is ocean. Large continental glaciers form only on land, so that area had to be land.

Answer to . . .

Figure 5 *The continents were near the South Pole when the glaciers formed.*

Glaciers in southern South America, southern Africa, India, and Australia are found in areas that now have tropical climates. There is also evidence for tropical climates and coal swamps in areas that are now at higher latitudes, such as northern Europe and the northeastern United States.

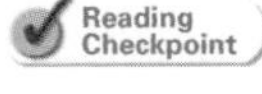

He could not provide a mechanism for the movement of the continents.

Section 9.2

1 FOCUS

Section Objectives

9.4 **Explain** the theory of plate tectonics.
9.5 **Describe** lithospheric plates.
9.6 **Identify** the three types of plate boundaries.

Reading Focus

Build Vocabulary L2

Concept Map Have students make a concept map using the term *plate tectonics* as the starting point. All the vocabulary terms in this section should be used.

Reading Strategy L2

a. plates move together
b. plates move apart
c. plates slide past each other

2 INSTRUCT

Earth's Major Plates

Build Science Skills L2

Using Analogies

Crack the shell of a hard-boiled egg. Ask students if the egg reminds them of anything. The egg can be seen as a tiny model of Earth. The thin eggshell is analogous to Earth's crust, divided into plates. Within the shell is the firm mantle. Have students move the pieces of shell around. They should notice how the shell buckles in some places and exposes "mantle" in other places. This movement is analogous to the movement of Earth's crust. However, Earth's movement results in the formation of mountains, earthquakes, and new ocean floor. **Kinesthetic, Visual**

9.2 Plate Tectonics

Reading Focus

Key Concepts
- What is the theory of plate tectonics?
- What are lithospheric plates?
- What are the three types of plate boundaries?

Vocabulary
- plate tectonics
- plate
- divergent boundary
- convergent boundary
- transform fault boundary

Reading Strategy

Comparing and Contrasting Copy the table. After you read, compare the three types of plate boundaries by completing the table.

Boundary Type	Relative Plate Motion
convergent	a. ____ ? ____
divergent	b. ____ ? ____
transform fault	c. ____ ? ____

Earth's Major Plates

According to the plate tectonics theory, the uppermost mantle, along with the overlying crust, behaves as a strong, rigid layer. This layer is known as the lithosphere. The outer shell lies over a weaker region in the mantle known as the asthenosphere. The lithosphere is divided into segments called **plates,** which move and continually change shape and size. Figure 8 on pages 256-257 shows the seven major plates. The largest is the Pacific plate, covering most of the Pacific Ocean. Notice that several of the large plates include an entire continent plus a large area of the seafloor. This is a major departure from Wegener's continental drift hypothesis, which proposed that the continents moved through the ocean floor, not with it. Note also that none of the plates is defined entirely by the margins of a continent.

The lithospheric plates move relative to each other at a very slow but continuous rate that averages about 5 centimeters per year—about as fast as your fingernails grow. This movement is driven by the unequal distribution of heat within Earth. Hot material found deep in the mantle moves slowly upward as part of Earth's internal convection system. At the same time, cooler, denser slabs of oceanic lithosphere descend into the mantle, setting Earth's rigid outer shell into motion. The grinding movements of Earth's lithospheric plates generate earthquakes, create volcanoes, and deform large masses of rock into mountains.

What is plate tectonics?

Types of Plate Boundaries

All major interactions among individual plates occur along their boundaries. **The three main types of boundaries are convergent, divergent, and transform fault boundaries.**

Divergent boundaries Divergent boundaries (also called spreading centers) occur when two plates move apart. This process results in upwelling of material from the mantle to create new seafloor, as shown in Figure 7A. A relatively new divergent boundary is located in Africa, in a region known as the East African Rift valley.

Convergent boundaries Convergent boundaries form where two plates move together. This process results in oceanic lithosphere plunging beneath an overriding plate, and descending into the mantle, as shown in Figure 7B. At other locations, plates carrying continental crust are presently moving toward each other. Eventually, these continents may collide and merge. Thus, the boundary that once separated two plates disappears as the plates become one.

Transform fault boundaries Transform fault boundaries are margins where two plates grind past each other without the production or destruction of lithosphere, as shown in Figure 7C. The San Andreas Fault zone in California is an example of a transform fault boundary.

Each plate contains a combination of these three types of boundaries. Although the total surface area of Earth does not change, plates may shrink or grow in area. This shrinking or growing depends on the locations of convergent and divergent boundaries. The Antarctic plate is growing larger. The Philippine plate is descending into the mantle along its margins and is becoming smaller. New plate boundaries can be created because of changes in the forces acting on these rigid slabs.

Figure 7 Three Types of Plate Boundaries

A

Divergent boundary

B

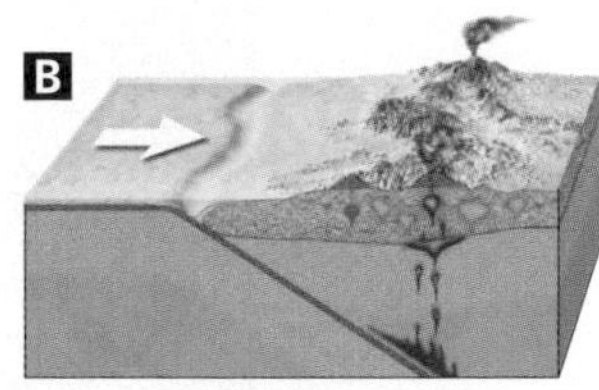

Convergent boundary

C

Transform fault boundary

Section 9.2 Assessment

Reviewing Concepts

1. Define the term *lithospheric plate.*
2. List the three types of plate boundaries.
3. What theory proposes that Earth's outer shell consist of a number of rigid slabs?

Critical Thinking

4. **Comparing and Contrasting** Compare the plate motions in the three types of boundaries.
5. **Drawing Conclusions** What is the major difference in the role of the ocean floor between the continental drift hypothesis and the theory of plate tectonics?

Connecting Concepts

Plate Boundaries Use what you have learned about plate tectonics to compare Wegener's continental drift hypothesis to the theory of plate tectonics.

Types of Plate Boundaries

Build Reading Literacy L1

Refer to **p. 502D** in **Chapter 18**, which provides the guidelines for this visualizing strategy.

Visualize Have students read the section on types of plate boundaries and then try to form a mental picture of each type of boundary. Ask: **In which type of boundary do the plates move without changing the lithosphere?** *(transform fault boundary)*
Visual, Verbal

3 ASSESS

Evaluate Understanding L2

To assess students' knowledge of section content, have them draw diagrams of the three types of plate boundaries. Each diagram should have a caption describing the movement of the plates.

Reteach L1

Have students use any materials they wish, such as blocks of wood, to illustrate the plate movements in the three types of boundaries.

Connecting Concepts

In Wegener's hypothesis, the continents moved through the ocean floor. The ocean floor did not move and was not part of the block of continental crust. The boundaries of the continents were defined by either the shorelines or continental shelves. In plate tectonics, the plates are divided by boundaries along which different types of motion and deformation occur. The ocean floors are part of the plates and move along with the continents.

Section 9.2 Assessment

1. a section of the crust and upper mantle (the lithosphere) that moves as a unit
2. convergent, divergent, and transform fault boundaries
3. the theory of plate tectonics
4. In convergent boundaries, the two plates move together. In divergent boundaries, the two plates move apart. In transform fault boundaries, the two plates grind past each other.
5. In the continental drift hypothesis, the continents plowed through the ocean floors; in the plate tectonics theory, the ocean floors are an integral part of the lithospheric plates and move with the continents.

Answer to . . .

Reading Checkpoint *A theory that states that Earth's rigid outer shell is broken into plates made up of the crust and upper mantle, also known as the lithosphere. A plate moves as a unit with respect to the surrounding plates.*

MAP MASTER Skills Activity

Answer

Locate South American plate. Divergent: Caribbean plate, Mid-Atlantic Ridge; Southeast Indian Ridge, Antarctic plate. Convergent: Nazca plate, South American plate; Australian-Indian plate, Eurasian plate. Transform fault: Antarctic plate, Pacific plate; Caribbean plate, North American plate

Use Visuals L1

Figure 8 Have students examine the figure. They may need help from an atlas or a globe to locate the features in the questions. Ask: **How do you think the Andes Mountains were formed?** *(The Nazca plate collided with the South American plate.)* **How do you think the Red Sea was formed?** *(The African plate and the Arabian plate moved apart, forming a rift that became the Red Sea.)* **Which plate is the largest? Where is it located?** *(The Pacific plate; it is mostly within the Pacific Ocean.)*
Visual

Teacher Demo

A Convergent Model 

Purpose Students will observe what happens when two plates collide in a model of a convergent boundary.

Materials two slabs of modeling clay, wax paper

Procedure Place the slabs of clay on the wax paper on a table so they will slide easily. Push the two slabs of clay together to model a collision of two plates.

Expected Outcome The clay slabs will buckle up to create folds and breaks that resemble mountains.
Kinesthetic, Visual

Earth's Tectonic Plates

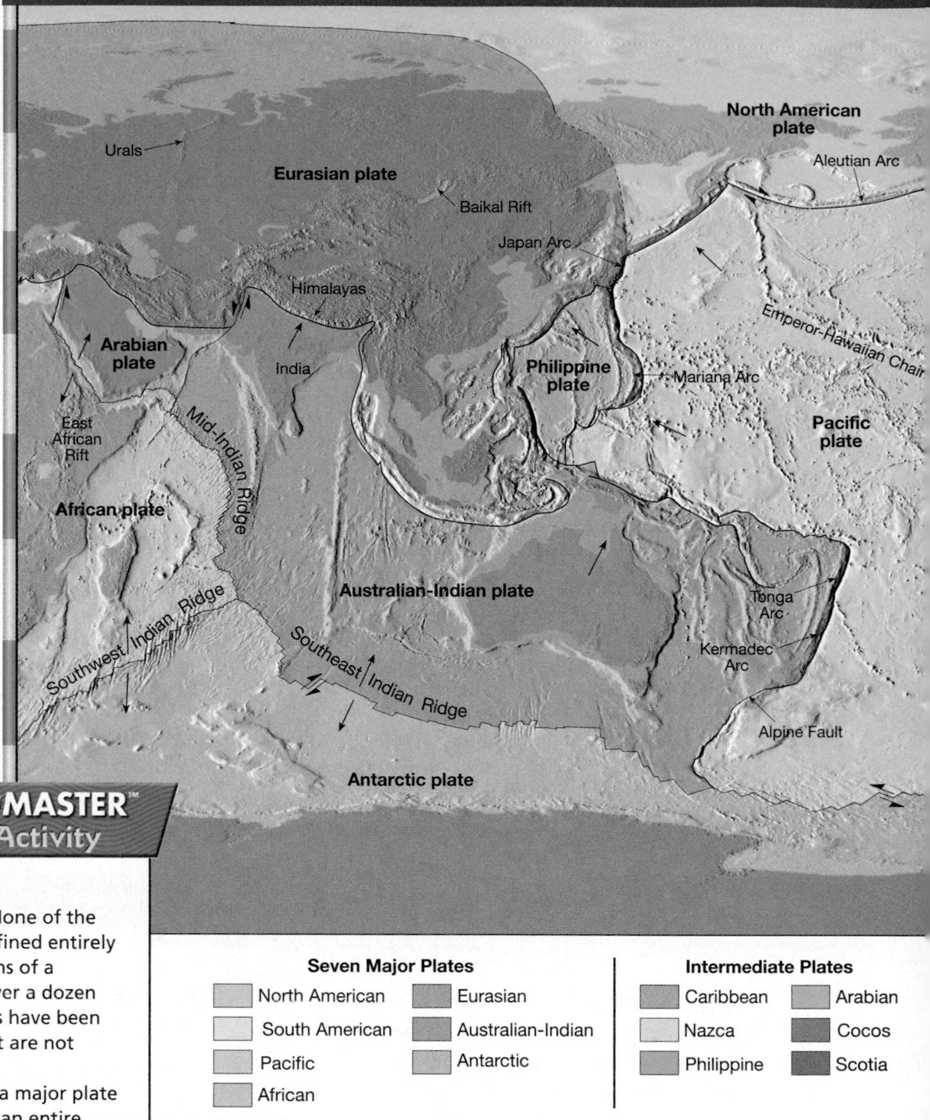

Seven Major Plates: North American, South American, Pacific, African, Eurasian, Australian-Indian, Antarctic

Intermediate Plates: Caribbean, Nazca, Philippine, Arabian, Cocos, Scotia

MAP MASTER Skills Activity

Figure 8

Location None of the plates are defined entirely by the margins of a continent. Over a dozen smaller plates have been identified but are not shown.

Locate Find a major plate that includes an entire continent plus a large area of seafloor. Name two other examples of a divergent boundary, a convergent boundary, and a transform fault boundary.

Customize for English Language Learners

Students who are learning disabled will benefit by having globes in the classroom. You might want to mark the major plates on a globe so students can better visualize how Earth's lithosphere is divided into tectonic plates.

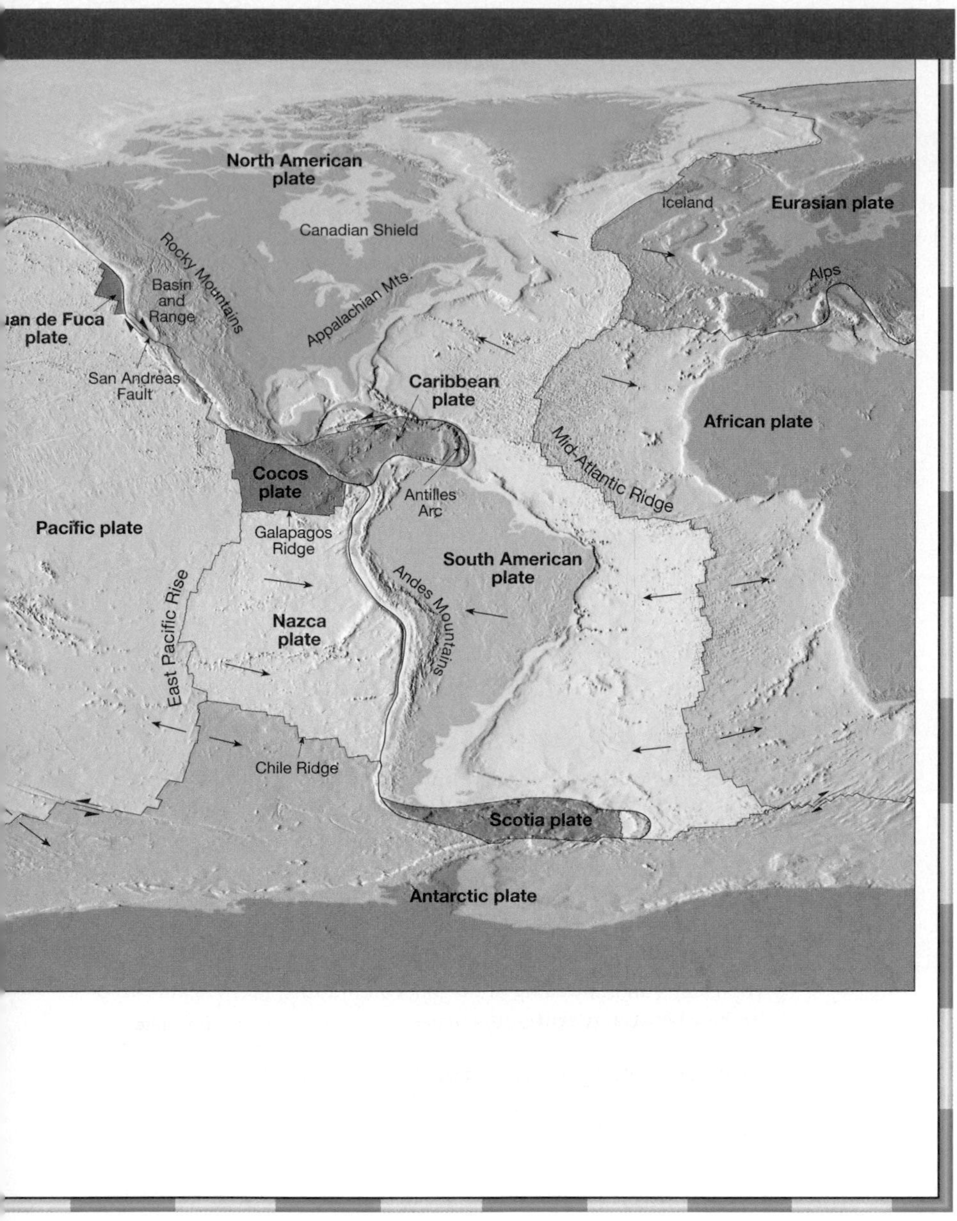

Address Misconceptions

L2

Students may think that the movement of lithospheric plates causes Earth's surface area to become either larger or smaller (depending on which way the plates move.) Explain that individual plates can become larger or smaller, but Earth's total surface area cannot change. Give students a basketball or soccer ball and ask them to imagine what will happen to the interior of the ball if the surface area changed. *(If surface area decreased, the interior would become compressed and internal pressure would increase. If surface area increased, either the interior would expand or the lithosphere would separate from the mantle.)*
Visual, Logical

Use Community Resources

L2

Invite a geologist or physicist in your community to talk to the class about global positioning systems (GPS), how they work, and what they are used for. Encourage students to think about and ask questions about how GPS can be used to measure the movements of landmasses.
Verbal, Interpersonal

Facts and Figures

The continents are still moving, and eventually they will probably collide to form a single landmass again. Earth scientists predict that the continents will probably merge again somewhere in the Pacific Ocean. When will this happen? Research suggests that, based on the current rate of plate movements, a single landmass is formed about once every 500 million years. Since it has been about 200 million years since Pangaea broke up, the next supercontinent may form in a few hundred million years.

Section 9.3

1 FOCUS

Objectives

9.7 **Explain** how seafloor spreading and continental rifting cause formation of new lithosphere.

9.8 **Describe** the process of lithosphere destruction that takes place at subduction zones.

9.9 **Differentiate** among subduction at oceanic-continental, oceanic-oceanic, and continental-continental convergent boundaries.

9.10 **Describe** the action of plates at a transform fault boundary.

Reading Focus

Build Vocabulary L2

Word Parts Have students break the word *subduction* into roots, prefixes, or suffixes. They may need to use a dictionary to find the meaning of some parts. *(Subduction comes from the Latin prefix* sub-, *meaning "below" and the Latin root word* ducere, *meaning "to draw or pull." Thus, subduction means to draw or pull below.)*

Reading Strategy L2

I. Divergent Boundaries
  A. Ocean Ridges and Seafloor Spreading
  B. Continental Rifts
II. Convergent Boundaries
  A. Oceanic-Continental
  B. Oceanic-Oceanic
  C. Continental-Continental
III. Transform Fault Boundaries

Download a worksheet on plate boundaries for students to complete, and find additional teacher support from NSTA SciLinks.

9.3 Actions at Plate Boundaries

Reading Focus

Key Concepts

- What is seafloor spreading?
- What is a subduction zone?

Vocabulary

- oceanic ridge
- rift valley
- seafloor spreading
- subduction zone
- trench
- continental volcanic arc
- volcanic island arc

Reading Strategy

Outlining Before you read, make an outline of this section. Use the green headings as the main topics and the blue headings as subtopics. As you read, add supporting details.

Actions at Boundaries
I. Divergent Boundaries
A. ___?___
B. ___?___
II. ___?___

Tremendous forces are at work where tectonic plates meet. Let's take a closer look at what happens at the three types of plate boundaries.

Divergent Boundaries

Most divergent plate boundaries are located along the crests of oceanic ridges. These plate boundaries can be thought of as *constructive plate margins* because this is where new oceanic lithosphere is generated. Look again at the divergent boundary in Figure 7A on page 255. As the plates move away from the ridge axis, fractures are created. These fractures are filled with molten rock that wells up from the hot mantle below. Gradually, this magma cools to produce new slivers of seafloor. Spreading and upwelling of magma continuously adds oceanic lithosphere between the diverging plates.

Oceanic Ridges and Seafloor Spreading Along well-developed divergent plate boundaries, the seafloor is elevated, forming the **oceanic ridge**. The system of ocean ridges is the longest physical feature on Earth's surface, stretching more than 70,000 kilometers in length. This system winds through all major ocean basins like the seam on a baseball. The term *ridge* may be misleading. These features are not narrow like a typical ridge. They are 1000 to 4000 kilometers wide. Deep faulted structures called **rift valleys** are found along the axes of some segments. As you can see in Figure 9, rift valleys and spreading centers can develop on land, too.

For: Links on plate boundaries
Visit: www.SciLinks.org
Web Code: cjn-3093

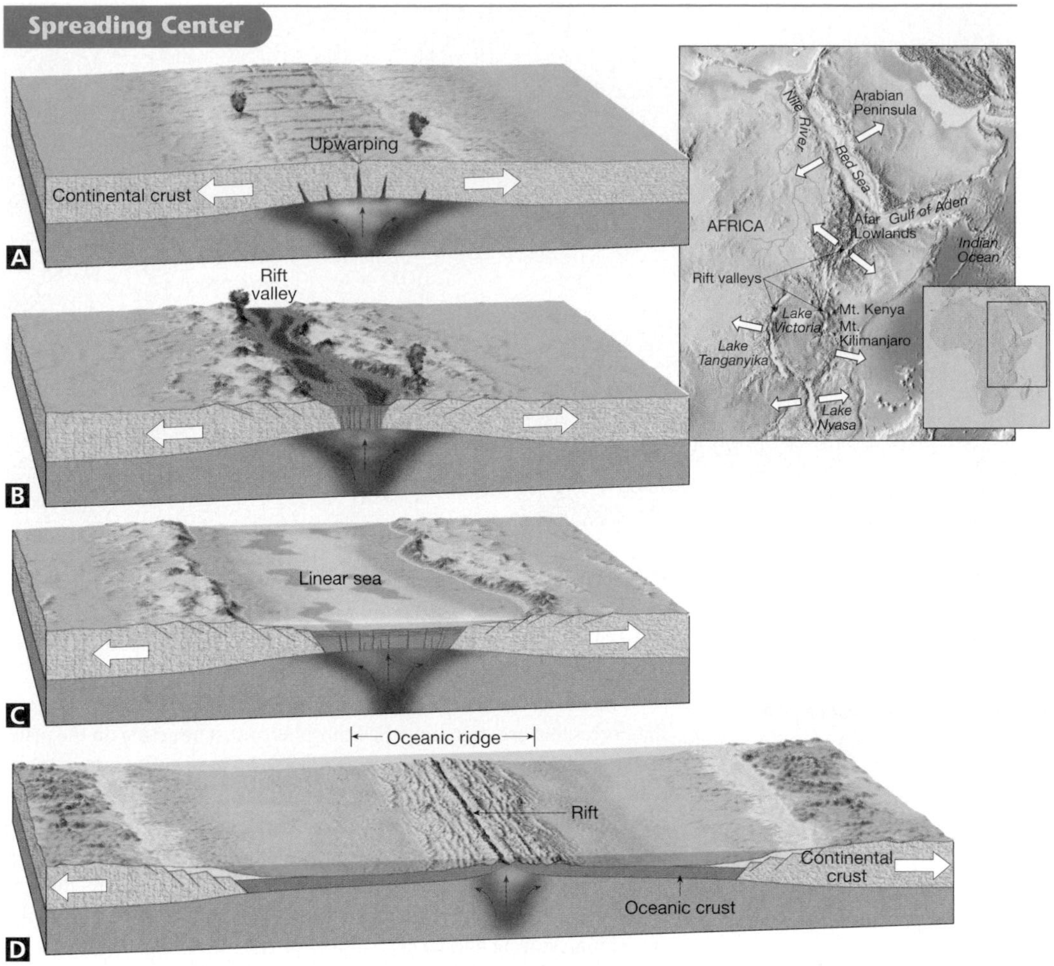

Spreading Center

A Continental crust Upwarping

B Rift valley

C Linear sea

D Oceanic ridge Rift Continental crust Oceanic crust

AFRICA Nile River Arabian Peninsula Red Sea Afar Lowlands Gulf of Aden Indian Ocean Rift valleys Lake Victoria Mt. Kenya Mt. Kilimanjaro Lake Tanganyika Lake Nyasa

Figure 9 The East African rift valleys may represent the initial stages of the breakup of a continent along a spreading center. **A** Rising magma forces the crust upward, causing numerous cracks in the rigid lithosphere. **B** As the crust is pulled apart, large slabs of rock sink, causing a rift zone. **C** Further spreading causes a narrow sea. **D** Eventually, an ocean basin and ridge system is created.
Relating Cause and Effect ***What causes the continental crust to stretch and break?***

Seafloor spreading is the process by which plate tectonics produces new oceanic lithosphere. Typical rates of spreading average around 5 centimeters per year. These rates are slow on a human time scale. However, they are rapid enough so that all of Earth's ocean basins could have been generated within the last 200 million years. In fact, none of the ocean floor that has been dated is older than 180 million years.

2 INSTRUCT

Divergent Boundaries

Build Math Skills L1

Conversion Factors Remind students to label the units of each factor when solving the following problem. Doing this ensures that all the conversion factors are included and the answer has the correct units. Tell students that seafloor spreading occurs at an average rate of 5 cm per year. At this rate, how long would it take for a narrow sea that is 1 km wide to form? *(about 20,000 years)*
Logical

Use Visuals L1

Figure 9 Point out the rising magma in each of the diagrams. Ask: **What happens to the rising magma in the diagram?** *(It fills the cracks formed by the diverging plates.)* **Why is this process called seafloor spreading? Does the seafloor actually get thinner and spread out?** *(The seafloor does not get thinner. Rather, the seafloor spreads apart and new rock is constantly added to the ridge.)*
Visual

Build Science Skills L2

ACTIVITY

Using Models Give students two colors of modeling clay (one color for the magma and the other color for the crust) and have them model the activity that occurs at a divergent boundary.
Kinesthetic, Visual

Customize for English Language Learners

Encourage students to work in groups to brainstorm different types of boundaries. Their types of boundaries can come from other sciences, such as cell membranes, or from everyday life, such as the boundary between a sidewalk and the strip of grass between the sidewalk and the curb. Ask students what all these boundaries have in common and how they are different.

Answer to . . .

Figure 9 *The continental crust is stretched and broken by the upwarping of the crust, caused by rising magma.*

Teacher Demo

Creating a Continental Rift L2

Purpose Students will observe how fractures grow to create a continental rift as a result of the stretching of the lithosphere.

Materials 2 slices of individually wrapped American cheese, dull knife or fingernail, metric ruler

Procedure Using your fingernail or a dull knife, make a small cut in the center of a cheese slice parallel to one edge. Pull on the two cheese edges parallel to the cut. You will be pulling perpendicular to the direction of the cut. Observe how the small defect (the cut) concentrates the tearing. Observe the shape of the fracture that forms, especially the pointed tips where the tearing is taking place, and how the fracture tips move faster as the fracture gets bigger.

Now, make a cut near the center of the second piece of cheese. Make a second parallel cut about 2 cm below and 2 cm to the right of the first cut. Pull on the cheese as before. Fractures will begin to form from each of the cuts. As the tips of these fractures begin to move past each other, they will begin to curve toward each other and eventually link up into a single fracture.

Safety Do not allow students to eat the cheese.

Expected Outcome Students should infer that the fractures in the cheese are analogous to the formation of faults that result in the development of a rift valley.
Visual, Logical

Figure 10 East African Rift Valley This valley may be where the African continent is splitting apart.
Interpreting Diagrams ***What stage in the drawings on page 259 does this photograph show?***

Continental Rifts When spreading centers develop within a continent, the landmass may split into two or more smaller segments. Examples of active continental rifts include the East African rift valley and the Rhine Valley in Northwest Europe.

The most widely accepted model for continental breakup suggests that forces that are stretching the lithosphere must be acting on the plate. These stretching forces by themselves are not large enough to actually tear the lithosphere apart. Rather, the rupture of the lithosphere is thought to begin in those areas where plumes of hot rock rise from the mantle. This hot-spot activity weakens the lithosphere and creates domes in the crust directly above the hot rising plume. Uplifting stretches the crust and makes it thinner, as shown in Figure 9A. Along with the stretching, faulting and volcanism form a rift valley, as in Figure 9B

The East African rift valley, shown in Figure 10, may represent the beginning stage in the breakup of a continent. Large mountains, such as Kilimanjaro and Mount Kenya, show the kind of volcanic activity that accompanies continental rifting. If the stretching forces continue, the rift valley will lengthen and deepen, until the continent splits in two. At this point, the rift becomes a narrow sea with an outlet to the ocean, similar to the Red Sea. The Red Sea formed when the Arabian Peninsula rifted from Africa about 20 million years ago. In this way, the Red Sea provides scientists with a view of how the Atlantic Ocean may have looked in its infancy.

How do rifts begin to form?

Facts and Figures

The first rift that developed as Pangaea began to break apart 200 million years ago resulted in the separation of North America and Africa. Large quantities of basalts were produced. These basalts can be found today as weathered rock beds along the eastern seaboard of the United States. They are buried beneath rocks that form the continental shelf and have been radiometrically dated as being between 200 million and 165 million years old. The rifting eventually formed the Atlantic Ocean basin.

Convergent Boundaries

Although new lithosphere is constantly being added at the oceanic ridges, our planet is not growing larger. Earth's total surface area remains the same. How can that be? To accommodate the newly created lithosphere, older portions of oceanic plates return to the mantle along convergent plate boundaries. Because lithosphere is "destroyed" at convergent boundaries, they are also called *destructive plate margins.* As two plates slowly converge, the leading edge of one is bent downward, allowing it to slide beneath the other. Destructive plate margins where oceanic crust is being pushed down into the mantle are called **subduction zones.** The surface feature produced by the descending plate is an ocean **trench,** as shown in Figure 11. **A subduction zone occurs when one oceanic plate is forced down into the mantle beneath a second plate.**

Convergent boundaries are controlled by the type of crust involved and the forces acting on the plate. Convergent boundaries can form between two oceanic plates, between one oceanic plate and one continental plate, or between two continental plates.

Oceanic-Continental When the leading edge of a continental plate converges with an oceanic plate, the less dense continental plate remains floating. The denser oceanic slab sinks into the asthenosphere. When a descending plate reaches a depth of about 100 to 150 kilometers, some of the asthenosphere above the descending plate melts. The newly formed magma, being less dense than the rocks of the mantle, rises. Eventually, some of this magma may reach the surface and cause volcanic eruptions.

The volcanoes of the Andes, located along western South America, are the product of magma generated as the Nazca plate descends beneath the continent. Figure 11 shows this process. The Andes are an example of a **continental volcanic arc.** Such mountains are produced in part by the volcanic activity that is caused by the subduction of oceanic lithosphere.

Figure 11 Oceanic-Continental Convergent Boundary Oceanic lithosphere is subducted beneath a continental plate.
Inferring *Why doesn't volcanic activity occur closer to the trench?*

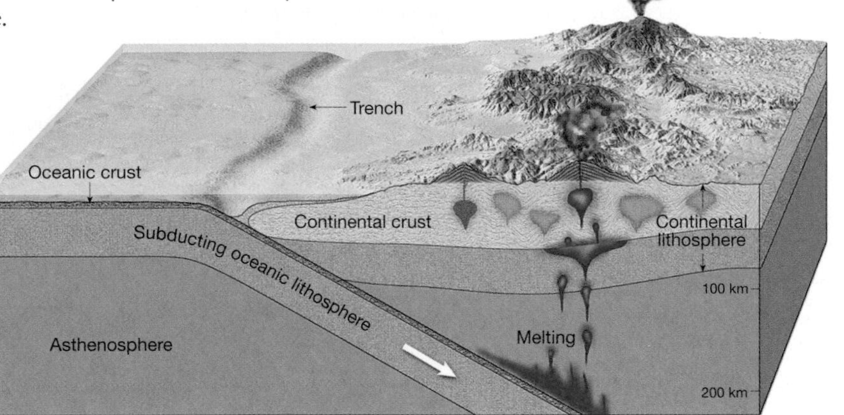

Convergent Boundaries

Build Reading Literacy **L1**

Refer to **p. 420D** in **Chapter 15,** which provides the guidelines for this predicting strategy.

Predict Have students read the section on p. 260 about continental rifts. Ask: **Predict what a rift valley might look like if it stopped developing.** *(The valley would probably be filled with ancient volcanic rocks that formed from the magma that rose to the surface.)*
Logical

Use Visuals **L1**

Figure 11 Have students study the diagram showing an oceanic-continental convergent boundary. Ask: **Which plate is subducted? Which plate floats?** *(The oceanic plate is subducted. The continental plate floats.)* **Why do the two plates in the diagram always move the way they do?** *(The oceanic plate is denser than the continental plate, so it slides under the continental plate and sinks into the asthenosphere.)*
Visual, Logical

Answer to . . .

Figure 10 *Large slabs of rock sink, causing a rift zone.*

Figure 11 *The plate doesn't get deep enough for melting to occur until farther from the trench.*

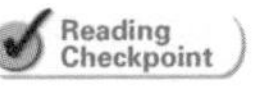

Rifts begin when the lithosphere is stretched and a plume of hot rock from the mantle weakens and then splits the lithosphere.

Address Misconceptions L2

A commonly held misconception is that the volcanoes in a volcanic island arc are interconnected and that an eruption of one volcano in the arc will trigger eruptions in all the volcanoes. Draw a cross-sectional diagram similar to Figure 12. Show a separate magma chamber for each volcano in the arc.
Visual

Use Visuals L1

Figure 12 Have students study the diagram showing an oceanic-oceanic convergent boundary. Ask: **How is an oceanic-oceanic convergent boundary different from an oceanic-continental convergent boundary?** *(Volcanoes form on the ocean floor in an oceanic-oceanic boundary rather than on Earth's surface.)* **What is formed by sustained volcanic activity at an oceanic-oceanic convergent boundary?** *(an island chain, called a volcanic island arc)*
Visual, Verbal

Use Visuals L1

Figure 13 Have students study the diagram showing a continental-continental convergent boundary. Ask: **Why isn't the continental lithosphere subducted far into the asthenosphere in this diagram?** *(The continental lithosphere is buoyant and does not sink into the asthenosphere to a great depth.)* **Why aren't volcanoes formed in a continental-continental convergent boundary?** *(Because molten magma that forms down deep is unable to rise all the way to the tops of the mountains. The magma cools within the cores of the mountains to form large granitic plutons.)*
Visual, Verbal

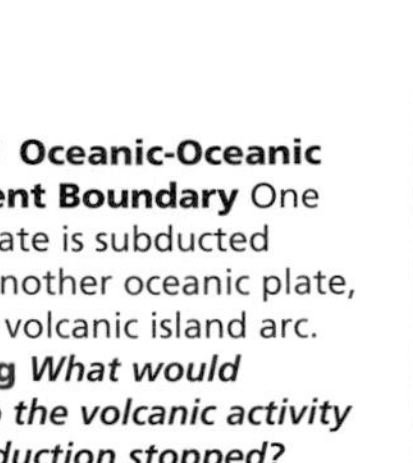

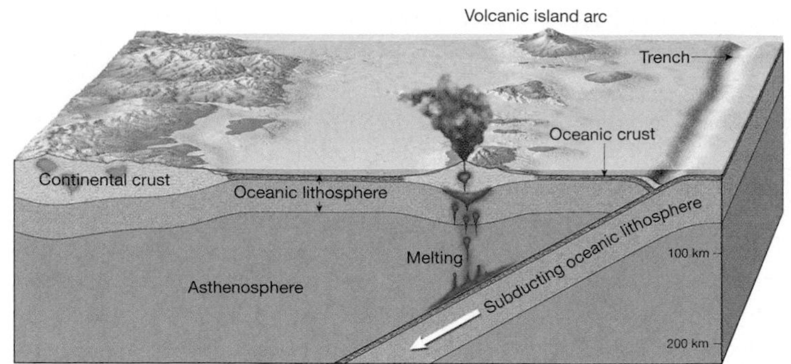

Figure 12 Oceanic-Oceanic Convergent Boundary One oceanic plate is subducted beneath another oceanic plate, forming a volcanic island arc. ***Predicting** What would happen to the volcanic activity if the subduction stopped?*

Oceanic-Oceanic When two oceanic slabs converge, one descends beneath the other. This causes volcanic activity similar to what occurs at an oceanic-continental boundary. However, the volcanoes form on the ocean floor instead of on a continent, as shown in Figure 12. If this activity continues, it will eventually build a chain of volcanic structures that become islands. This newly formed land consisting of an arc-shaped chain of small volcanic islands is called a **volcanic island arc.** The Aleutian Islands off the shore of Alaska are an example of a volcanic island arc. Next to the Aleutians is the Aleutian trench.

Continental-Continental When an oceanic plate is subducted beneath continental lithosphere, a continental volcanic arc develops along the margin of the continent. However, if the subducting plate also contains continental lithosphere, the subduction eventually brings the two continents together, as shown in Figure 13. Continental lithosphere is buoyant, which prevents it from being subducted to any great depth. The result is a collision between the two continents, which causes the formation of complex mountains such as the Himalayas in South Asia.

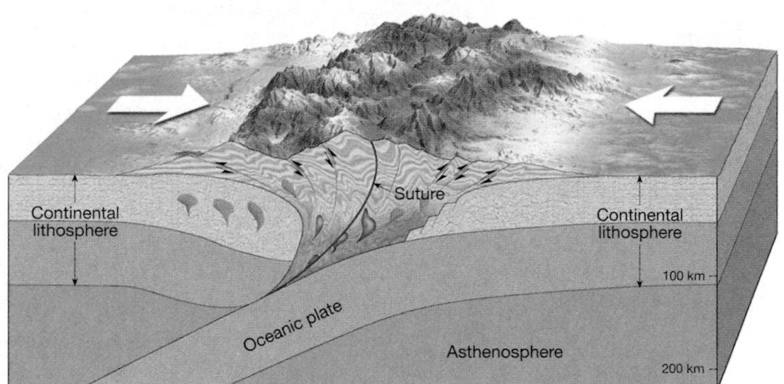

Figure 13 Continental-Continental Convergent Boundary Continental lithosphere cannot be subducted because it floats. The collision of two continental plates forms mountain ranges.

Facts and Figures

Only two volcanic island arcs are located in the Atlantic Ocean—the Lesser Antilles adjacent to the Caribbean Sea and the Sandwich Islands in the South Atlantic. There have been many volcanic eruptions in the Lesser Antilles. In 1902 on the island of Martinique, Mount Pelé erupted, killing 28,000 people and destroying the town of St. Pierre. More recently, the Soufriere Hills Volcano on the island of Montserrat erupted from 1995 until 1997. Although volcanic activity has since decreased, seismic activity has increased. There were several earthquakes on Montserrat in early 2004.

Before continents collide, the landmasses involved are separated by an ocean basin. As the continents move toward each other, the seafloor between them is subducted beneath one of the plates. When the continents collide, the collision folds and deforms the sediments along the margin as if they were placed in a giant vise. A new mountain range forms that is composed of deformed and metamorphosed sedimentary rocks, fragments of the volcanic arc, and possibly slivers of oceanic crust.

This kind of collision occurred when the subcontinent of India rammed into Asia and produced the Himalayas, as shown in Figure 14. During this collision, the continental crust buckled and fractured. Several other major mountain systems, including the Alps, Appalachians, and Urals, were also formed as a result of continental collisions.

Figure 14 **A** The leading edge of the plate carrying India is subducted beneath the Eurasian plate. **B** The landmasses collide and push up the crust. **C** India's collision with Asia continues today.

Collision of India and Asia

A

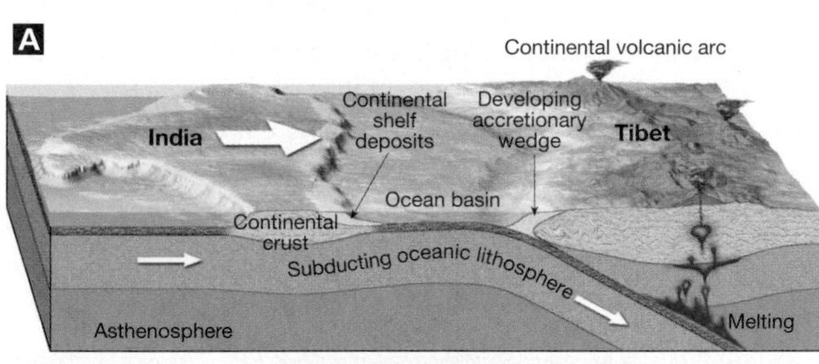

C

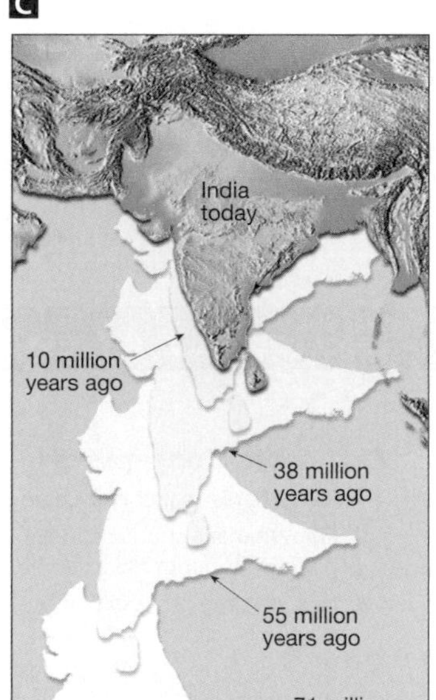

B

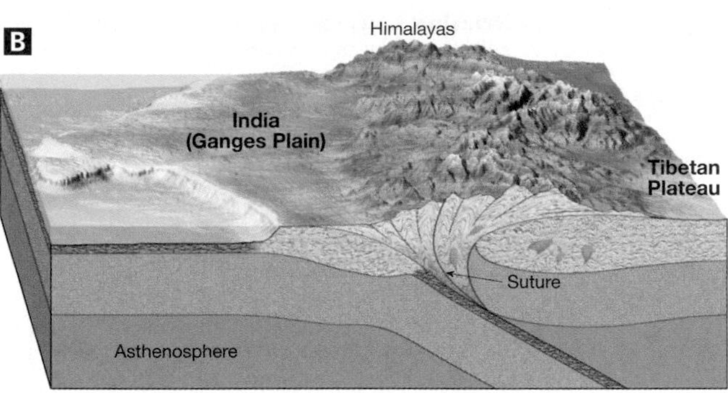

Build Science Skills L2

Using Analogies The discussion on this page uses an analogy of a giant vise to help students visualize and understand what happens to the lithosphere during a continental-continental collision. Be sure students understand what a vise is. *(a tool that holds an object by squeezing two plates together, usually by turning a large screw)* If they are not familiar with the term, have them look it up in a dictionary, or have another student describe it. Revisit the text and discuss why the analogy is useful. *(A squeezing vise could fold and deform material as colliding continents fold and deform rock)* Ask: **What other analogies might be used to describe continental-continental collisions?** *(Sample answers: small entry rug crumpling as it gets caught between an opening door and a wall, two cars colliding)*
Intrapersonal, Logical

Facts and Figures

The Himalayas include the highest mountains on Earth. When India and Asia collided, the leading edge of the Indian plate was forced partially under Asia, generating an unusually great thickness of continental lithosphere. This accumulation accounts in part for the high elevation of the Himalayas and may also explain the elevated Tibetan Plateau to the north.

Answer to . . .

Figure 12 *If the subduction stopped, the volcanic activity would probably also soon stop because the source of new magma is the continuing subduction of the oceanic plate.*

Section 9.3 (continued)

Transform Fault Boundaries

Build Science Skills L2

Relating Cause and Effect Remind students that plates in a transform fault boundary move past each other without production or destruction of lithosphere. Ask: **Why does this movement cause earthquakes?** *(The tremendous friction caused by two plates grinding past each other causes earthquakes.)*
Logical

3 ASSESS

Evaluate Understanding 

To assess students' knowledge of section content, have them write three short paragraphs describing the three convergent boundaries and what results when they converge.

Reteach 

Have students demonstrate the action of the three convergent boundaries by using their hands to represent the converging plates.

Answers should be accurate and show an understanding of the process of rifting at a divergent plate boundary.

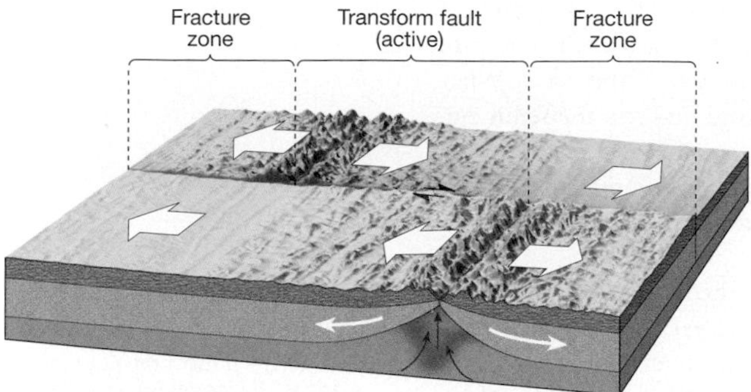

Figure 15 A transform fault boundary offsets segments of a divergent boundary at an oceanic ridge.

Transform Fault Boundaries

The third type of plate boundary is the transform fault boundary. **At a transform fault boundary, plates grind past each other without destroying the lithosphere.** Most transform faults join two segments of a mid-ocean ridge, as shown in Figure 15. These faults are present about every 100 kilometers along the ridge axis. Active transform faults lie between the two offset ridge segments. The seafloor produced at one ridge axis moves in the opposite direction as seafloor is produced at an opposing ridge segment. So between the ridge segments these slabs of oceanic crust are grinding past each other along a transform fault.

Although most transform faults are located within the ocean basins, a few cut through the continental crust. One example is the San Andreas Fault of California. Along the San Andreas, the Pacific plate is moving toward the northwest, past the North American plate. If this movement continues, that part of California west of the fault zone will become an island off the west coast of the United States and Canada. It could eventually reach Alaska. However, a more immediate concern is the earthquake activity triggered by movements along this fault system.

Section 9.3 Assessment

Reviewing Concepts

1. What is seafloor spreading?
2. What is a subduction zone? What types of plate boundaries have subduction zones?
3. Describe the process that occurs when continents converge.
4. What actions of plate boundaries cause the destruction of the lithosphere?

Critical Thinking

5. **Drawing Conclusions** What evidence supports the idea that the Earth is neither growing nor shrinking in size?
6. **Relating Cause and Effect** During the collision between two continents, why doesn't a subduction zone form?
7. **Predicting** How will the angle at which an oceanic plate is subducted affect the distance from the volcanic arc to the trench?

Writing in Science

Creative Writing Write a paragraph that describes the rifting apart of a continent to form a new ocean. The paragraph should be written from the point of view of a person witnessing the events.

Section 9.3 Assessment

1. Seafloor spreading is the creation of new seafloor at oceanic ridges.
2. Subduction zones occur at deep-ocean trenches where slabs of oceanic lithosphere are descending into the mantle. Subduction zones are associated with convergent boundaries, either oceanic-oceanic or oceanic-continental.
3. two continental plates collide with each other, forming a mountain range
4. Lithosphere is destroyed at convergent boundaries in subduction zones.
5. the evidence that the production and destruction of the lithosphere is going on at about the same rate.
6. Continental lithosphere floats and can't be forced down into the mantle at a subduction zone.
7. The higher the angle of subduction, the closer the volcanic arc will be to the trench. If the angle is shallow, the volcanic arc will be located farther behind the trench because the descending plate doesn't reach a depth where melting occurs until farther from the trench.

9.4 Testing Plate Tectonics

Reading Focus

Key Concepts

- What evidence supports the theory of plate tectonics?
- How does paleomagnetism support the theory of plate tectonics?

Vocabulary

- paleomagnetism
- normal polarity
- reverse polarity
- hot spot

Reading Strategy

Predicting Copy the table. Write a prediction of where earthquakes will occur. After you read, if your prediction was incorrect or incomplete, write where earthquakes actually occur.

Probable Locations	Actual Locations
a. ___?___	b. ___?___

Evidence for Plate Tectonics

With the birth of the plate tectonics model, researchers from all of the Earth sciences began testing it. You have already seen some of the evidence supporting continental drift and seafloor spreading. Additional evidence for plate tectonics came as new technologies developed.

Paleomagnetism If you have ever used a compass to find direction, you know that the magnetic field has a north pole and a south pole. These magnetic poles align closely, but not exactly, with the geographic poles.

In many ways, Earth's magnetic field is much like that produced by a simple bar magnet. Invisible lines of force pass through Earth and extend from one pole to the other. A compass needle is a small magnet that is free to move about. The needle aligns with these invisible lines of force and points toward the magnetic poles.

Certain rocks contain iron-rich minerals, such as magnetite. When heated above a certain temperature, these magnetic minerals lose their magnetism. However, when these iron-rich mineral grains cool down, they become magnetized in the direction parallel to the existing magnetic field. Once the minerals solidify, the magnetism they possess stays frozen in this position. So magnetized rocks behave much like a compass needle because they point toward the existing magnetic poles. If the rock is moved or if the magnetic pole changes position, the rock's magnetism retains its original alignment. Rocks formed millions of years ago thus show the location of the magnetic poles at the time of their formation, as shown in Figure 16. These rocks possess **paleomagnetism.**

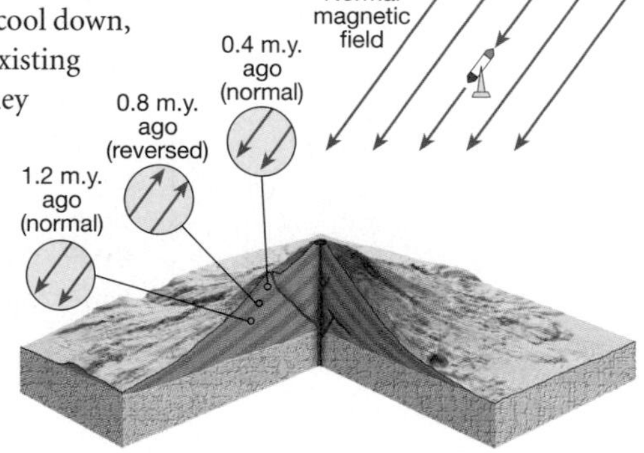

Figure 16 Paleomagnetism Preserved in Lava Flows As the lava cools, it becomes magnetized parallel to the magnetic field present at that time. When the polarity randomly reverses, a record of the paleomagnetism is preserved in the sequence of lava flows.

Section 9.4

1 FOCUS

Section Objectives

9.11 **Explain** how paleomagnetism and magnetic reversals provide evidence that supports the theory of plate tectonics.

9.12 **Evaluate** how earthquakes, ocean drilling, and hot spots provide evidence that supports the theory of plate tectonics.

Reading Focus

Build Vocabulary L2

Word Parts Have students break the vocabulary term paleomagnetism into roots, prefixes, or suffixes. Students may need to use a dictionary to find the meanings of some parts. (Paleo- *is a combination form of the Greek word palaios meaning "ancient." The word magnetism comes from the Greek root words* Magnes (lithos), *literally meaning a stone of Magnesia, an ancient city in Asia Minor.)*

Reading Strategy L2

a. at convergent plate boundaries
b. at all plate boundaries

2 INSTRUCT

Evidence for Plate Tectonics

Integrate Biology L2

Birds and Magnetism Tell students that birds use Earth's magnetic field to locate places to stop and eat along their migration route. In addition, the birds use Earth's magnetic field to navigate. They read the angle at which magnetic fields enter the ground and thus determine their latitude relative to the magnetic poles. Ask: **Why is it so important for birds to locate food sources?** *(The location of these places is critical because birds must have large quantities of food to provide energy during their long migrations.)*
Verbal, Logical

Teacher Demo

Testing Minerals for Magnetism 

Purpose Students test various minerals with a magnet to determine whether they have magnetic properties.

Materials magnet, minerals (include at least one sample of a mineral that contains iron or cobalt), compass

Procedure Have students test the mineral samples with the magnet to see if they are attracted by it. Have students place the compass near each mineral sample to see if the needle moves. If it does, the material is magnetic.

Expected Outcomes Minerals that contain iron or cobalt, such as lodestone, have magnetic properties. Meteorites also have magnetic properties.
Kinesthetic, Visual

Use Visuals 

Figure 17 Have students study the figure. Ask: **Could the rocks in a strip possessing reverse polarity ever possess normal polarity?** *(No, once the rocks solidify, their polarity is permanently set.)* **How do you think the width of a strip relates to the seafloor spreading rate?** *(The faster the spreading rate is, the wider the strip will be.)*
Visual, Logical

Polarity of Ocean Crust

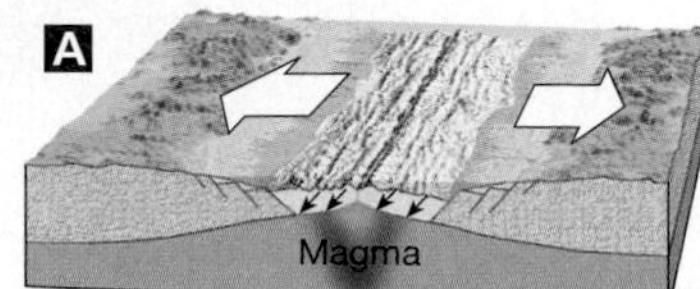

Period of normal magnetism

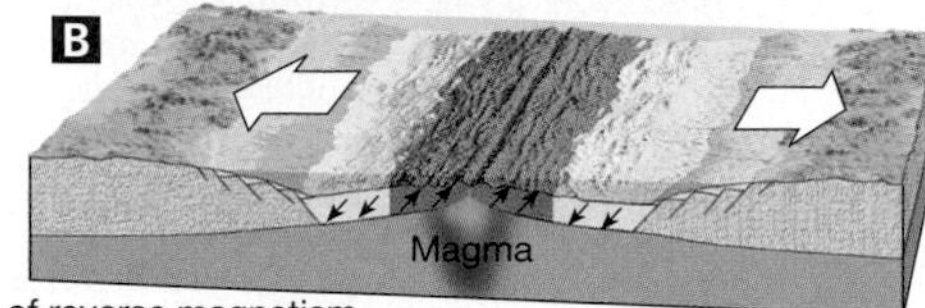

Period of reverse magnetism

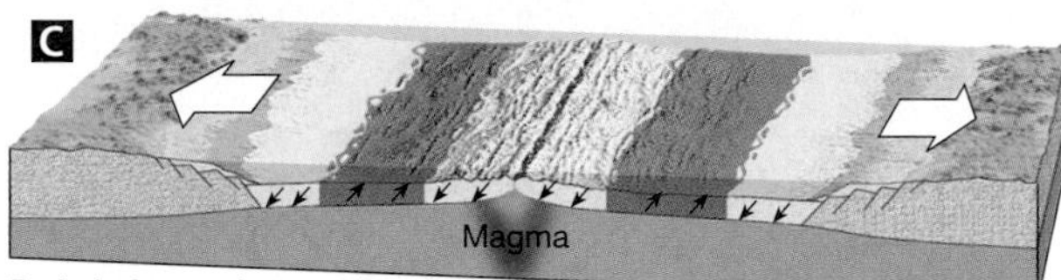

Period of normal magnetism

Figure 17 **A** As new material is added to the ocean floor at the oceanic ridges, it is magnetized according to Earth's existing magnetic field. **B** This process records each reversal of Earth's magnetic field. **C** Because new rock is added in approximately equal amounts to the trailing edges of both plates, strips of equal size and polarity parallel both sides of the ocean ridges. ***Applying Concepts*** ***Why are the magnetized strips about equal width on either side of the ridge?***

Geophysicists learned that Earth's magnetic field periodically reverses polarity. The north magnetic pole becomes the south magnetic pole, and vice versa. A rock solidifying during one of the periods of reverse polarity will be magnetized with the polarity opposite that of rocks being formed today.

When rocks show the same magnetism as the present magnetic field, they are described as having **normal polarity.** Rocks that show the opposite magnetism are said to have **reverse polarity.** A relationship was discovered between the magnetic reversals and the seafloor-spreading hypothesis. Ships towed instruments called magnetometers across segments of the ocean floor. This research revealed alternating strips of high- and low-intensity magnetism that ran parallel to the ridges. The strips of high-intensity magnetism are regions where the paleomagnetism of the ocean crust is of the normal type. These positively magnetized rocks enhance the existing magnetic field. The low-intensity strips represent regions where the ocean crust is polarized in the reverse direction and, therefore, weaken the existing magnetic field. As new basalt is added to the ocean floor at the oceanic ridges, it becomes magnetized according to the existing magnetic field, as shown in Figure 17. **The discovery of strips of alternating polarity, which lie as mirror images across the ocean ridges, is among the strongest evidence of seafloor spreading.**

Earthquake Patterns **Scientists found a close link between deep-focus earthquakes and ocean trenches. Also, the absence of deep-focus earthquakes along the oceanic ridge system was shown to be consistent with the new theory.**

Compare the distribution of earthquakes shown in Chapter 8 on page 226 with the map of plate boundaries on pages 256–257. The close link between plate boundaries and earthquakes is obvious. When the depths of earthquake foci and their locations within the trench systems are plotted, a pattern emerges.

Customize for English Language Learners

Explain to students that there are many uses of the term *polar*, both in science and in everyday usage. For example, in magnetism, polarity refers to the magnetic poles. In chemistry, polar molecules have partial charges. Polar also means diametrically opposite. Have students look up the various meanings of the term *polar* and use each meaning in a sentence.

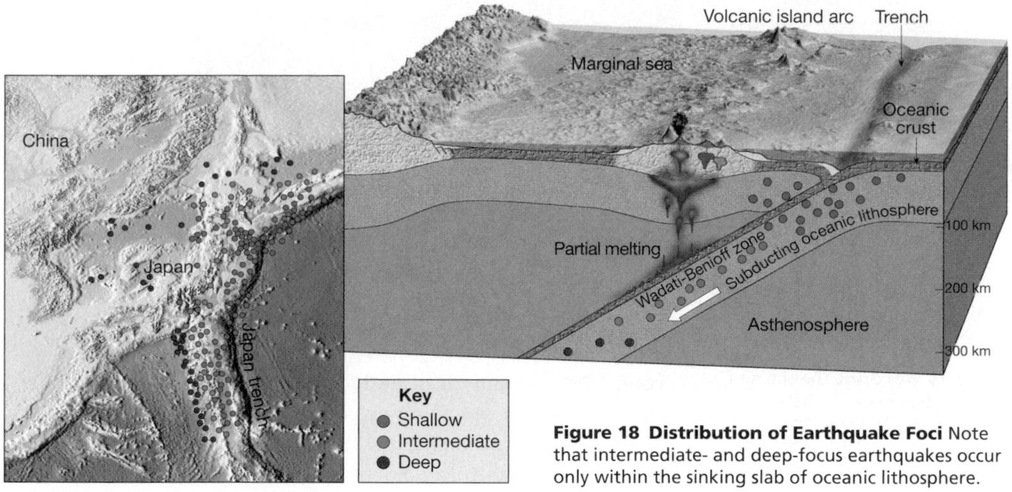

Figure 18 Distribution of Earthquake Foci Note that intermediate- and deep-focus earthquakes occur only within the sinking slab of oceanic lithosphere.

Look at Figure 18. It shows the distribution of earthquakes near the Japan trench. Here, most shallow-focus earthquakes occur within or adjacent to the trench. Intermediate- and deep-focus earthquakes occur toward the mainland.

In the plate tectonics model, deep-ocean trenches are produced where cool, dense slabs of oceanic lithosphere plunge into the mantle. Shallow-focus earthquakes are produced as the descending plate interacts with the lithosphere above it. As the slab descends farther into the mantle, deeper-focus earthquakes are produced. No earthquakes have been recorded below 700 kilometers. At this depth, the slab has been heated enough to soften.

Ocean Drilling Some of the most convincing evidence confirming the plate tectonics theory has come from drilling directly into ocean-floor sediment. The Deep Sea Drilling Project from 1968 to 1983 used the drilling ship *Glomar Challenger* to drill hundreds of meters into the sediments and underlying crust.

When the oldest sediment from each drill site was plotted against its distance from the ridge crest, it was revealed that the age of the sediment increased with increasing distance from the ridge. **The data on the ages of seafloor sediment confirmed what the seafloor-spreading hypothesis predicted. The youngest oceanic crust is at the ridge crest and the oldest oceanic crust is at the continental margins.**

The data also reinforced the idea that the ocean basins are geologically young. No sediment older than 180 million years was found. By comparison, some continental crust has been dated at 4.0 billion years.

Facts and Figures

During its 15 years of operation, the *Glomar Challenger* drilled 1092 holes and obtained more than 96 km of invaluable core samples. The Ocean Drilling Program has succeeded the Deep Sea Drilling Project and, like its predecessor, is a major international program. A more technologically advanced drilling ship, the *JOIDES Resolution*, now continues the work of the *Glomar Challenger*.

Build Science Skills

Interpreting Diagrams Have students study Figure 18. Ask:

- **From the map, identify the direction in which the sinking slab of oceanic lithosphere is moving.** *(from right to left)*
- **Locate Korea on the map. Why do you think Korea has relatively few earthquakes compared to Japan?** *(Korea is located far from ocean trenches; Japan is close to a trench.)*
- **What pattern does the map show?** *(Deeper earthquakes occur farther from the trench.)* Be sure students can distinguish the blue dots from the green dots.
- **What can geologists learn from this pattern?** *(They can use the plotted foci to track the plate's descent into the mantle.)*

Visual, Logical

Answer to . . .

Figure 17 *Both sides of the ocean plate are moving away from the ridge at equal rates, so the magnetized strips will be about equal in width.*

Build Reading Literacy L1

Refer to **p. 530D** in **Chapter 19,** which provides the guidelines for making inferences.

Making Inferences Have students read the section about hot spots on this page. Ask: **What can you infer about a hot spot from the description of how the islands in a volcanic island arc form at different times by the hot spot?** *(You can infer that the hot spot is relatively stationary with respect to the mantle, and so moves relative to the plate. If it moved along with the plate, a line of islands would not have formed.)*
Verbal, Intrapersonal

3 ASSESS

Evaluate Understanding L2

To assess students' knowledge of section content, have them make flashcards for the vocabulary terms and the four lines of evidence supporting the plate tectonic theory. For each vocabulary term, the card should include a definition and an example, where applicable. For each line of evidence, the card should give an explanation of why it supports the theory and include an example. Students can use the cards to quiz one another.

Reteach L1

Have students explain in their own words why data produced by drilling into ocean-floor sediment supports the tectonic plate theory.

The age of the seafloor increases with increasing distance from the spreading center at an ocean ridge. The theory of seafloor spreading states that new ocean lithosphere is created at ocean ridges, so the ocean floor should be younger closer to the ridges and older farther from the ridge.

Answer to . . .

Figure 19 *A new Hawaiian island will form to the southeast of the island of Hawaii.*

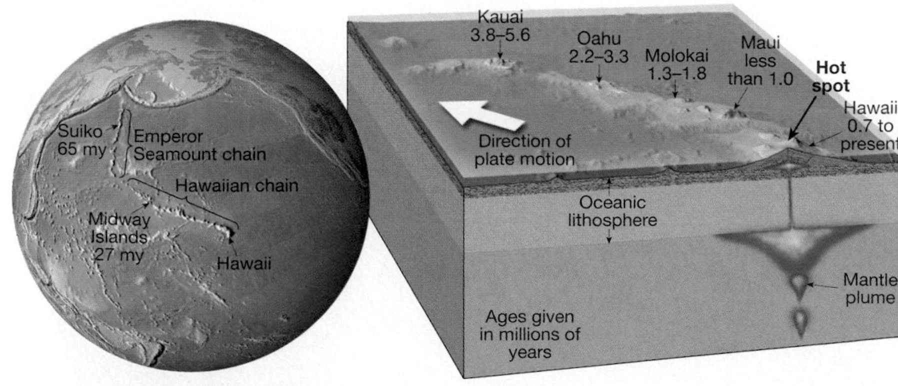

Figure 19 Hot Spot The chain of islands and seamounts that extends from Hawaii to the Aleutian trench results from the movement of the Pacific plate over a stationary hot spot. **Predicting** ***Where will a new Hawaiian island be located?***

Hot Spots Mapping of seafloor volcanoes in the Pacific revealed a chain of volcanic structures extending from the Hawaiian Islands to Midway Island and then north to the Aleutian trench, as shown in Figure 19. Dates of volcanoes in this chain showed that the volcanoes increase in age with increasing distance from Hawaii. Suiko Seamount is 65 million years old. Midway Island is 27 million years old. The island of Hawaii formed less than a million years ago and is still forming today.

A rising plume of mantle material is located below the island of Hawaii. Melting of this hot rock as it nears the surface creates a volcanic area, or **hot spot.** As the Pacific plate moves over the hot spot, successive volcanic mountains have been created. The age of each volcano indicates the time when it was situated over the hot spot. Kauai is the oldest of the large islands in the Hawaiian chain. Its volcanoes are extinct. The youthful island of Hawaii has two active volcanoes—Mauna Loa and Kilauea. **Hot spot evidence supports the idea that the plates move over Earth's surface.**

Section 9.4 Assessment

Reviewing Concepts

1. List and describe the evidence for the plate tectonics theory.
2. Define the term *paleomagnetism.*
3. What is the age of the oldest ocean crust? How do the ages of the ocean crust compare to the age of continental rocks?
4. What is a hot spot?

Critical Thinking

5. **Applying Concepts** How do hot spots and the plate tectonics theory account for the different ages of the Hawaiian Islands?
6. **Predicting** Would earthquakes occur at depths of over 700 kilometers? Why or why not?

Explanatory Paragraph Write a paragraph explaining why the age pattern of the ocean floor supports seafloor spreading.

Section 9.4 Assessment

1. paleomagnetism: iron-rich minerals in rocks line up with the magnetic field at the time they cool; earthquake patterns: earthquake foci are concentrated at plate boundaries; ocean drilling: the age of the ocean lithosphere was found from drilling; hot spots: the location of hot mantle plumes shows plate motion.
2. Paleomagnetism is the natural magnetism in rocks, which was acquired from Earth's magnetic field at the time the rock formed.
3. The oldest ocean crust is about 180 million years old. Some continental rocks are about 3.9 billion years old.
4. an area where a plume of hot mantle material rises up and causes volcanic activity
5. Hot spots are relatively stationary plumes of hot rock from the mantle. As a plate moves over a hot spot, the hot material causes volcanic activity. The previously formed volcanoes become extinct and increase in age as the distance from the hot spot (and the active volcanic activity) increases.
6. No, below 700 km the plates are no longer rigid enough.

9.5 Mechanisms of Plate Motion

Reading Focus

Key Concepts

- What are the mechanisms of plate motion?
- What causes plate motion?

Vocabulary

- convective flow
- slab-pull
- ridge-push
- mantle plume

Reading Strategy

Identifying Main Ideas Copy the table. As you read, write the main ideas for each topic.

Topic	Main Idea
Slab-pull	a. ___?___
Ridge-push	b. ___?___
Mantle convection	c. ___?___

Causes of Plate Motion

Scientists generally agree that convection occurring in the mantle is the basic driving force for plate movement. During convection, warm, less dense material rises and cooler, denser material sinks. The motion of matter resulting from convection is called **convective flow.** The slow movements of the plates and mantle are driven by the unequal distribution of Earth's heat. The heat is generated by the radioactive decay of elements, such as uranium, found within Earth's mantle and crust.

Slab-Pull and Ridge-Push Several mechanisms produce forces that cause plate motion. One mechanism, called **slab-pull,** occurs because old oceanic crust, which is relatively cool and dense, sinks into the asthenosphere and "pulls" the trailing lithosphere along. **Slab-pull is thought to be the primary downward arm of convective flow in the mantle.** By contrast, **ridge-push** results from the elevated position of the oceanic ridge system. **Ridge-push causes oceanic lithosphere to slide down the sides of the oceanic ridge.** The downward slide is the result of gravity acting on the oceanic lithosphere. Ridge-push, although active in some spreading centers, is probably less important than slab-pull.

Mantle Convection Most models suggest that hot plumes of rock are the upward flowing arms in mantle convection. These rising **mantle plumes** sometimes show themselves on Earth's surface as hot spots and volcanoes.

Section 9.5

1 FOCUS

Section Objectives

9.13 **Compare** the mechanisms of slab-pull and ridge-push as contributing to plate motion.

9.14 **Relate** the unequal distribution of heat in Earth and the mechanism of mantle convection to the movement of tectonic plates.

Reading Focus

Build Vocabulary L2

Paraphrase Have students explain, in their own words, the meaning of the new vocabulary terms in this section. Since each term contains an "action-type" word (*pull, push, plume, convection*), students should be able to form mental images to help with their explanations.

Reading Strategy L2

a. mechanism of plate motion in which the descending slab pulls on the plate
b. mechanism of plate motion in which the force of new crust formed at the high ridges pushes on the plate
c. the major mechanism of plate motion as the upward flow of hot, less dense mantle material and the downward flow of cold, dense material drives plate tectonics

2 INSTRUCT

Causes of Plate Motion

Build Science Skills L2

Using Models Challenge students to use their hands, phone books, or other objects to model slab-pull and ridge-push. Have them explain the processes as they manipulate the model.
Verbal, Kinesthetic

Section 9.5 (continued)

Use Visuals L1

Figure 20 Have students study the figure. Ask: **At what type of boundary does upward convective movement occur?** *(divergent)* **At what type of boundary does downward convective movement occur?** *(convergent)*

3 ASSESS

Evaluate Understanding L2

To assess students' knowledge of section content, have them write a short paragraph explaining convection. Paragraphs should include the cause of convection currents and the movements that occur.

Reteach L1

Demonstrate convection as follows: Heat a beaker of water on a hot plate. When the water is hot, add an ice cube to the water near the edge of the beaker. Drop a few drops of food coloring next to the ice cube. Students will be able to watch the food coloring move through the water by convection.

Connecting Concepts

It would provide the missing mechanism that causes the continents to move.

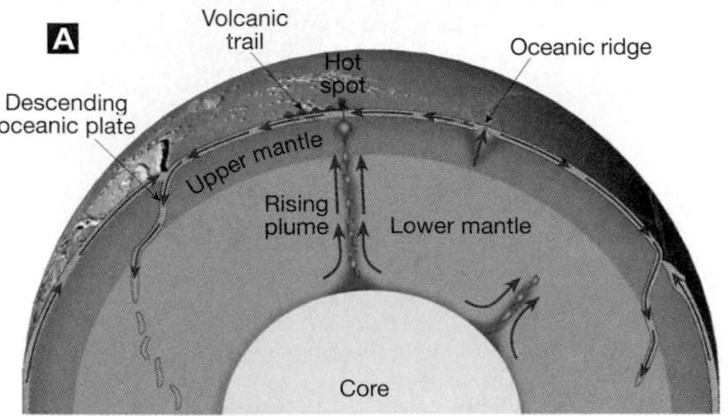

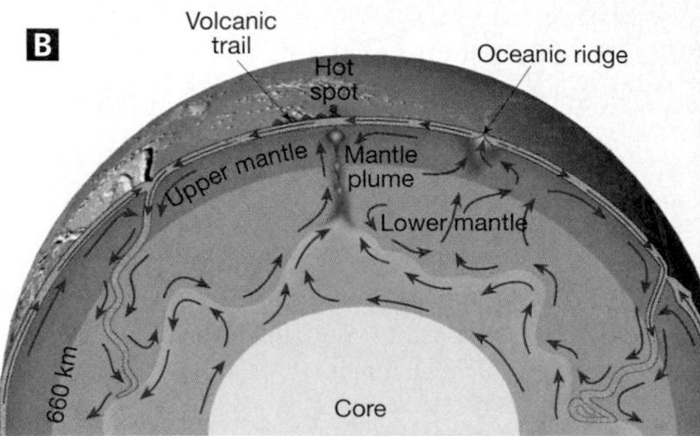

Figure 20 Mantle Convection Models A In the whole-mantle convection model, cold oceanic lithosphere descends into the mantle. Hot mantle plumes transport heat toward the surface. **B** The deep-layer model suggests that Earth's heat causes these layers of convection to slowly swell and shrink in complex patterns. Some material from the lower layer flows upward as mantle plumes.

One recent model is called whole-mantle convection. In this model, slabs of cold oceanic lithosphere descend into the lower mantle. This process provides the downward arm of convective flow, as shown in Figure 20A. At the same time, hot mantle plumes originating near the mantle-core boundary move heat toward the surface. Another model is the deep-layer model. You might compare this model to a lava lamp on a low setting. As shown in Figure 20B, the lower mantle is like the colored fluid in the bottom layer of a lava lamp. Like a lava lamp, heat from Earth's interior causes the two layers to slowly swell and shrink in complex patterns without much mixing. A small amount of material from the lower layer flows upward as mantle plumes, creating hot-spot volcanism at the surface.

There is still much to be learned about the mechanisms that cause plates to move. But one thing is clear. **The unequal distribution of heat within Earth causes the thermal convection in the mantle that ultimately drives plate motion.** Exactly how this convection operates is still being debated.

Section 9.5 Assessment

Reviewing Concepts

1. Describe the mechanisms of plate motion.
2. What drives the slow movement of the plates and the convection in the mantle?
3. What is the main source of heat in Earth's interior?

Critical Thinking

4. **Relating Cause and Effect** How is the theory of plate tectonics related to the radioactive decay of elements within Earth's interior?
5. **Calculating** If Africa and Australia are moving apart at a rate of 4.4 centimeters per year, approximately how long will it take for the ocean between the two continents to increase by 1000 kilometers?

Connecting Concepts

Heat Flow Review Section 9.1. How would the flow of heat generated by radioactive decay benefit the theory of continental drift?

Section 9.5 Assessment

1. slab-pull: force where the descending slab pulls on the plate; ridge-push: force of gravity causing the cold lithosphere to move away from the ridge by sliding down over the asthenosphere, which gets more elevated toward the ridge; mantle convection: motion caused by flow of hot, less-dense material upwards and cold, more-dense material downward
2. the unequal distribution of heat within Earth's interior drives plate motions
3. heat generated by radioactive decay of elements in Earth's interior
4. If radioactive decay stopped, no additional heat would be generated within Earth's interior. This heat drives the mantle convection that is the driving mechanism for plate tectonics, so plate motion would gradually stop.
5. approximately 23 million years

understanding
EARTH

Plate Tectonics into the Future

Two geologists, Robert Dietz and John Holden, used present-day plate movements to predict the locations of landmasses in the future. The map below shows where they predict Earth's landmasses will be 50 million years from now if plate movements remain at their present rates.

Future Continent Positions

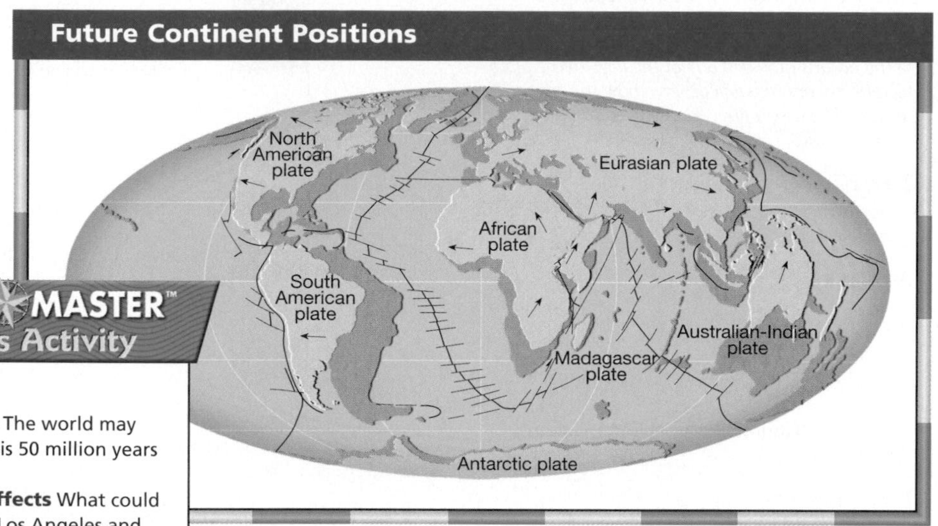

MAP MASTER™ Skills Activity

Figure 21

Location The world may look like this 50 million years from now.
Identify Effects What could happen to Los Angeles and San Francisco if this proposed movement occurs?

L.A. on the Move

In North America, the Baja Peninsula and the portion of southern California that lies west of the San Andreas Fault will have slid past the North American plate. If this northward motion takes place, Los Angeles and San Francisco will pass each other in about 10 million years. In about 60 million years Los Angeles will begin to descend into the Aleutian trench.

New Sea in Africa

Major changes are seen in Africa, where a new sea emerges as East Africa is ripped away from the mainland. In addition, Africa will have moved slowly into Europe, perhaps creating the next major mountain-building stage on Earth. Meanwhile, the Arabian Peninsula continues to move away from Africa, allowing the Red Sea to widen and close the Persian Gulf.

Atlantic Ocean Grows

In other parts of the world, Australia will be located across the equator and, along with New Guinea, will be on a collision course with Asia. Meanwhile, North and South America will begin to separate, while the Atlantic and Indian oceans will continue to grow as the Pacific Ocean shrinks.

These projections into the future, although interesting, must be viewed with caution because many assumptions must be correct for these events to occur. We can be sure that large changes in the shapes and positions of continents will occur for millions of years to come.

understanding
EARTH

Plate Tectonics into the Future **L2**

MAP MASTER™ Skills Activity

Answer
Identify Effects The cities could have a change in climate as they move north. They may also undergo damage from earthquakes associated with the movement.

Background
Robert Dietz began his career as a marine geologist. He was an early proponent of continental drift and of seafloor spreading, which he named. Much of his early work was conducted in submersibles off the coast of California. John Holden was Dietz's colleague and his illustrator.

Teaching Tip
Have students cut out outlines of the continents and place them on a piece of white poster paper in their current locations. As students read each paragraph of the feature, they should move the continents to their predicted location. When they finish reading the feature, ask students to write a short paragraph describing how plant and animal life would be different on the continents in their new positions.
For example, tropical vegetation in southern California would be replaced with plant life that could exist in an Arctic climate.
Verbal, Kinesthetic

Exploration Lab

Paleomagnetism and the Ocean Floor

L2

Objectives
In this activity, students will
- interpret diagrams of seafloor sections with respect to paleomagnetism.
- measure the distance that different ocean basins have opened.
- calculate the rate of seafloor spreading in different ocean basins based on magnetic polarity reversals.

Address Misconceptions

Students may think that the rocks on the ocean floor change their polarity every time Earth's polarity reverses. Remind students that magnetic polarity cannot be changed after rock material crystallizes. Ask: **What causes a substance to be magnetic?** *(The molecules in the substance are all aligned in the same direction.)* Tell students that once the substance solidifies, its molecules are held in a rigid lattice and cannot change their alignment.

Skills Focus Observing, Comparing and Contrasting, Inferring, Calculating, Measuring, Interpreting Diagrams

Prep Time 20 minutes to copy diagrams

Advance Prep Copy the diagrams on these two pages and distribute them to students.

Class Time 30 minutes

Teaching Tips
- Copying and handing out the diagrams in this lab will ensure that students will not write in their textbooks.
- Have students review the material on paleomagnetism before they begin the lab.

Expected Outcome Students will find that the left side of the Pacific basin has spread about 80 km in 2 million years, whereas the left side of the North Atlantic basin has spread only 37 km during the same time period. During this time period, the ocean basins opened by the following distances: Pacific—approximately 160 km; North Atlantic—approximately 74 km; South Atlantic—approximately 78 km

Exploration Lab

Paleomagnetism and the Ocean Floor

In the continental drift hypothesis, the ocean floors were not really involved. The continents were proposed to move through the oceans like icebreaking ships plowing through ice. Later studies of the oceans provided one of the keys to the plate tectonic theory. You will observe how the magnetic rocks on the ocean floor can be used to understand plate tectonics.

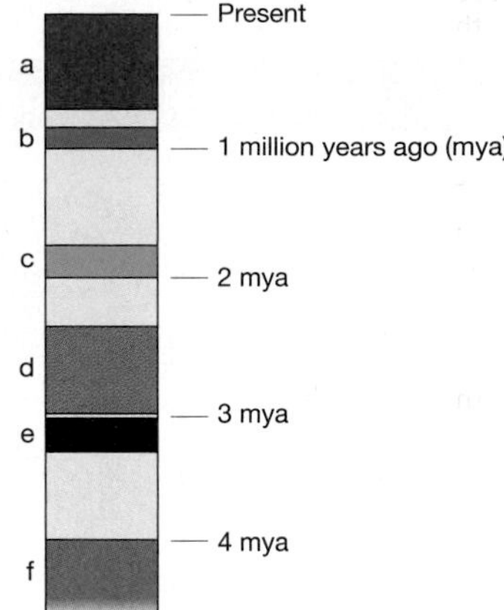

Problem
How are the paleomagnetic patterns on the ocean floor used to determine the rate of seafloor spreading?

Materials
- pencil
- metric ruler
- calculator
- photocopy of diagrams on page 273

Skills
Measuring, Interpreting Diagrams, Calculating

Procedure
1. Scientists have reconstructed Earth's magnetic polarity reversals over the past several million years. A record of these reversals is shown above. Periods of normal polarity, when a compass would have pointed north as it does today, are shown in color. Periods of reverse polarity are shown in white. Record the number of times Earth's magnetic field has had reversed polarity in the last 4 million years.
2. The three diagrams on the next page illustrate the magnetic polarity reversals across sections of the mid-ocean ridges in the Pacific, South Atlantic, and North Atlantic oceans. Periods of normal polarity are shown in color and match the colors in the illustration above. Observe that the patterns of polarity in the rock match on either side of the ridge for each ocean basin.
3. On the photocopy of the three ocean-floor diagrams, identify and mark the periods of normal polarity with the letters *a–f*. Begin at the ridge crest and label along both sides of each ridge. (*Hint:* The left side of the South Atlantic has already been done and can act as a guide.)
4. Using the South Atlantic as an example, label the beginning of the normal polarity period c, "2 million years ago," on the left sides of the Pacific and North Atlantic diagrams.
5. Using the distance scale shown with the ocean floor diagrams, determine which ocean basin has spread the greatest distance during the last 2 million years.
6. Refer to the distance scale. Notice that the left side of the South Atlantic basin has spread approximately 39 kilometers from the center of the ridge crest in 2 million years.

Analyze and Conclude

1. **Analyzing Data** How many kilometers has the left side of the Pacific basin spread in 2 million years?
2. **Analyzing Data** How many kilometers has the left side of the North Atlantic basin spread in 2 million years?
3. **Inferring** How many kilometers has each ocean basin opened in the past 2 million years?
4. **Calculating** If both the distance that each ocean basin has opened and the time it took to open that distance are known, the rate of seafloor spreading can be calculated. Determine the rate of seafloor spreading for the South Atlantic Ocean basin in centimeters per year. (*Hint:* To determine the rate of spreading in centimeters per year for each ocean basin, first convert the distance from kilometers to centimeters and then divide this distance by the time, 2 million years.)
5. **Calculating** Determine the rate of seafloor spreading for the North Atlantic and Pacific Ocean basins.
6. **Drawing Conclusions** Which ocean basin is spreading the fastest? The slowest?
7. **Inferring** Do ocean basins spread uniformly over the entire basin? Explain.

Go Further Use the library or the Internet to research the spreading rates for other divergent plate boundaries on Earth. Where is the fastest spreading rate? The slowest spreading rate?

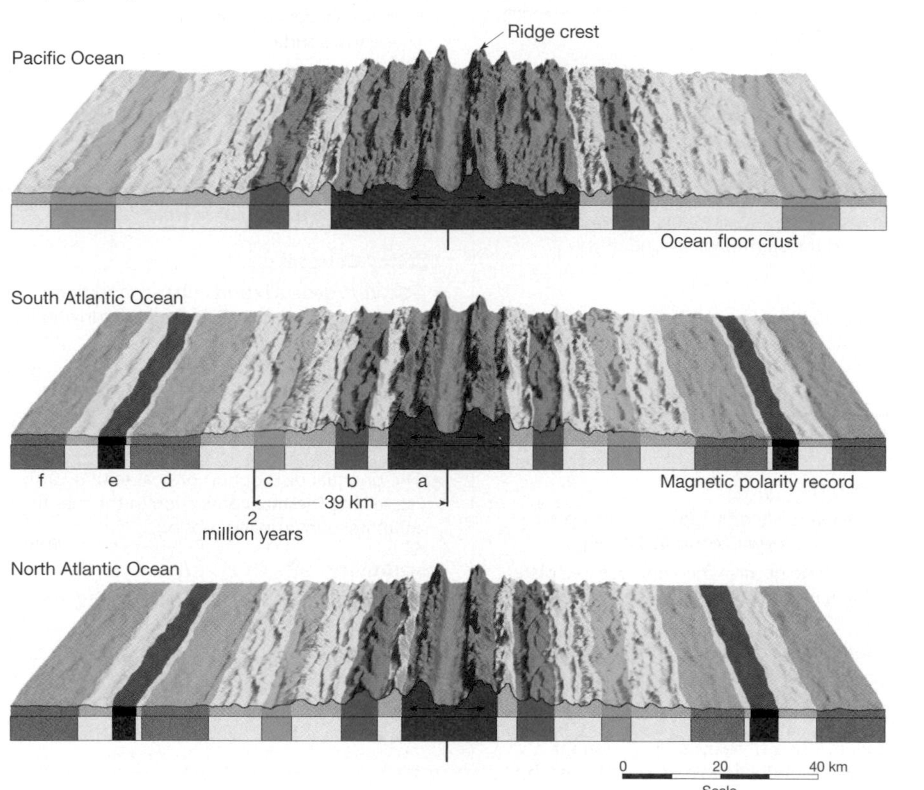

Answers to Procedure Questions
1. five times
5. The Pacific Ocean basin has spread the greatest distance.

Analyze and Conclude
1. approximately 80 km
2. approximately 37 km
3. Pacific: approximately 160 km; North Atlantic: approximately 74 km; South Atlantic: approximately 78 km
4. The South Atlantic Ocean basin's spreading rate is 3.9 cm/yr.
5. The Pacific Ocean basin's spreading rate is 8.0 cm/yr. The North Atlantic Ocean basin's spreading rate is 3.7 cm/yr.
6. Fastest: Pacific; slowest: North Atlantic
7. No, large basins such as the Pacific Ocean basin are spreading at various rates along their spreading ridges.

Go Further

The fastest spreading rate is the northern part of the Pacific plate, which is spreading at approximately 15.6 cm/yr. The slowest spreading rate is the Southwest Indian Ridge, between the African plate and the Antarctic plate, which is spreading at 1.4–1.5 cm/yr.
Visual, Logical

Study Guide

Study Tip

Organize New Information
Have students make vocabulary flashcards by writing a vocabulary word on one side of a card and its definition on the other side. Students can also give an example or draw a simple diagram of the term's meaning. Have students quiz each other by using the cards.

CHAPTER 9

Study Guide

9.1 Continental Drift

Key Concepts

- Wegener's continental drift hypothesis stated that the continents had once been joined to form a single supercontinent.
- Fossil evidence for continental drift includes several fossil organisms found on different landmasses.
- Rock evidence for continental drift exists in the form of several mountain belts that end at one coastline, only to reappear on a landmass across the ocean.

Vocabulary

continental drift, *p. 248;* Pangaea, *p. 248*

9.2 Plate Tectonics

Key Concepts

- According to the plate tectonics theory, the uppermost mantle, along with the overlying crust, behaves as a strong, rigid layer. This layer is known as the lithosphere.
- The three types of boundaries are convergent, divergent, and transform fault boundaries.

Vocabulary

plate tectonics, *p. 254;* plate, *p. 254;* divergent boundary, *p. 255;* convergent boundary, *p. 255;* transform fault boundary, *p. 255*

9.3 Actions at Plate Boundaries

Key Concepts

- Seafloor spreading is the process by which plate tectonics produces new oceanic lithosphere.
- A subduction zone occurs when one oceanic plate is forced down into the mantle beneath a second plate.
- At a transform fault boundary, plates grind past each other without destroying the lithosphere.

Vocabulary

oceanic ridge, *p. 258;* rift valley, *p. 258;* seafloor spreading, *p. 259;* subduction zone, *p. 261;* trench, *p. 261;* continental volcanic arc, *p. 261;* volcanic island arc, *p. 262*

9.4 Testing Plate Tectonics

Key Concepts

- The discovery of strips of alternating polarity, which lie as mirror images across the ocean ridges, is among the strongest evidence of seafloor spreading.
- Scientists found a close link between deep-focus earthquakes and ocean trenches. Also, the absence of deep-focus earthquakes along the oceanic ridge system was shown to be consistent with the new theory.
- The data on the ages of seafloor sediment confirmed what the seafloor-spreading hypothesis predicted. The youngest oceanic crust is at the ridge crest and the oldest oceanic crust is at the continental margins.
- Hot spot evidence supports that the plates move over Earth's surface.

Vocabulary

paleomagnetism, *p. 265;* normal polarity, *p. 266;* reverse polarity, *p. 266;* hot spot, *p. 268*

9.5 Mechanisms of Plate Motion

Key Concepts

- Scientists generally agree that convection occurring in the mantle is the basic driving force for plate movement.
- Slab-pull is thought to be the primary downward arm of convective flow in the mantle.
- Ridge-push causes oceanic lithosphere to slide down the sides of the oceanic ridge.
- The unequal distribution of heat within Earth causes the thermal convection in the mantle that ultimately drives plate motion.

Vocabulary

convective flow, *p. 269;* slab-pull, *p. 269;* ridge-push, *p. 269;* mantle plume, *p. 269*

274 *Chapter 9*

Chapter Assessment Resources

Print
Chapter Test, Chapter 9
Test Prep Resources, Chapter 9

Technology
Computer Test Bank, Chapter 9 Test
Online Text, Chapter 9
Go Online, PHSchool.com, Chapter 9

CHAPTER 9

NY Regents Content Item

Assessment

Interactive textbook with assessment at PHSchool.com 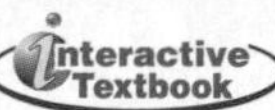

Reviewing Content

Choose the number that best answers the question or completes the statement.

1 What is the weaker, hotter zone beneath the lithosphere that allows for motion of Earth's rigid outer shell? NY
(1) crust (2) asthenosphere
(3) outer core (4) inner core

2 Most of Earth's earthquakes, volcanoes, and mountain building occur NY
(1) in the center of continents
(2) in the Himalayas
(3) at plate boundaries
(4) at volcanic island arcs

3 Alfred Wegener is best known for what hypothesis?
(1) plate tectonics (2) seafloor spreading
(3) continental drift (4) subduction

4 Complex mountain systems such as the Himalayas are the result of NY
(1) oceanic-oceanic convergence
(2) hot spots
(3) continental volcanic arcs
(4) continental-continental convergence

5 The best approximation of the true outer boundary of the continents is the seaward edge of NY
(1) continental shelf
(2) mid-ocean ridge
(3) present-day shorelines
(4) ocean trenches

6 What is the name given by Wegener to the supercontinent he proposed existed before the current continents? NY
(1) Euroamerica (2) Atlantis
(3) Pangaea (4) Panamerica

7 Which of the following mountain ranges was NOT the result of continental-continental convergence?
(1) Himalayas (2) Alps
(3) Appalachians (4) Andes

8 What is the type of plate boundary where two plates move together, causing one of the slabs of lithosphere to descend into the mantle beneath an overriding plate?
(1) oceanic-continental convergent
(2) divergent
(3) transform fault
(4) continental-continental convergent

9 Most deep-focus earthquakes are linked to
(1) hot spots
(2) ocean trenches
(3) ocean ridges
(4) transform fault boundaries

10 One of the main objections to Wegener's hypothesis of continental drift was that he was unable to provide an acceptable
(1) rate of continental drift
(2) date of continental drift
(3) mechanism of continental drift
(4) direction of continental drift

Understanding Concepts

11 What are the three types of convergent plate boundaries?

12 Briefly explain the theory of plate tectonics. Give three forms of evidence to support the theory. NY

13 How have earthquake patterns been used to support the theory of plate tectonics? NY

14 What type of plate boundary is shown? What types of lithosphere are involved? NY

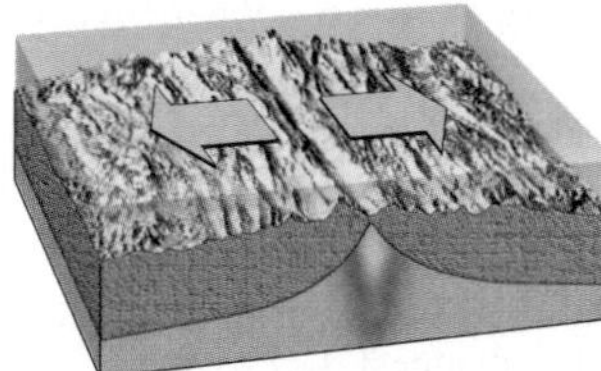

15 At what location is most lithosphere created? At what location is most lithosphere destroyed? NY

16 What feature produces volcanoes that do not occur at plate boundaries? NY

17 What boundaries produce subduction zones?

Homework Guide

Section	Questions
1	3, 6, 10, 18, 19, 21
2	1, 2, 4, 8, 11, 12, 15, 16, 20, 28, 29
3	5, 7, 14, 17, 22, 23, 25, 27, 31
4	9, 13, 26, 30
5	24

Assessment

Reviewing Content

(1) 2 (2) 3 (3) 3
(4) 4 (5) 1 (6) 3
(7) 4 (8) 1 (9) 2
(10) 3

Understanding Concepts

(11) oceanic-oceanic, oceanic-continental, and continental-continental
(12) The theory of plate tectonics states that Earth's rigid outer shell consists of rigid slabs called plates that are in continuous slow motion relative to each other. This interaction of plates causes volcanoes, earthquakes, and mountains.
(13) Earthquake patterns are used to show plate boundaries and to trace how the slabs descend into the mantle.
(14) divergent boundary, with oceanic lithosphere on both sides
(15) Lithosphere is created at divergent boundaries at ocean ridges. It is destroyed at convergent boundaries in subduction zones.
(16) a hot spot
(17) oceanic-oceanic convergent and oceanic-continental convergent boundaries

Critical Thinking

(18) at the continental margins
(19) The evidence that supported continental drift included the fact that the continents, especially South America and Africa, looked like they could fit together. Similar rock types and structures such as mountain ranges match up on different continents now separated by oceans. Similar fossils are found on different continents. Climate data supports continental drift because glacial deposits occur in areas that now have more tropical climates.
(20) No, California is formed by continental lithosphere, which can't sink. Continental lithosphere floats. If the current plate motion continues, California may collide with the Aleutian Islands at the Aleutian trench.
(21) If *Mesosaurus* were able to swim well enough to cross the Atlantic Ocean, its remains should be found over a wider area on other continents. Since its remains are not found, the two continents were together.

Critical Thinking (continued)

(22) The collision of an oceanic plate with a continental plate produces a subduction zone and the formation of a deep-ocean trench and a continental volcanic arc. No subduction zone, trench, or volcanic arc is produced during the collision of two continental plates. Instead, the collision produces a major mountain range.

Analyzing Data

(23) The boundary is an oceanic-continental convergent boundary. The plate on the left is made up of oceanic lithosphere, and the plate on the right is made up of continental lithosphere.
(24) As the slab descends, water leaves it and travels into the warm mantle rock above, where partial melting occurs. When the magma reaches the surface, volcanic activity results. The volcanoes that form are called a continental volcanic arc.
(25) The earthquake foci would be shallow along and within the slab as it begins to descend beneath the continental plate. As the plate descends deeper, the earthquake foci will also be deeper within the slab.

Concepts in Action

(26) The paleomagnetic strips would be wider because more ocean lithosphere is being created. The more lithosphere that is created at a particular polarity, the wider the paleomagnetic strip that will form.
(27) A transform fault boundary is formed. Examples include the San Andreas Fault in California and many faults along ocean ridges.
(28) If the motion of India changed to a southward direction, the boundary would change from a continental-continental convergent boundary to a divergent boundary. As India moved away from Asia, rifting would occur between them, and a new ocean might form.
(29) The Atlantic Ocean would grow 250 km in 10 million years at a spreading rate of 2.5 cm/yr.
(30) Hot spots are relatively stationary plumes of hot mantle rock. According to the plate tectonics theory, as a plate moves over a hot spot, volcanic activity often results. The Hawaiian Islands were formed as the Pacific plate moved over a hot spot. The Hawaiian Islands farthest from the current hot spot are oldest. The islands are younger closer to the hot spot. The island of Hawaii is currently over the hot spot and has active volcanoes.
(31) Student answers will vary but should emphasize that most earthquakes occur along plate boundaries, not in the middle of continents.

CHAPTER 9

Assessment *continued*

Critical Thinking

18 **Drawing Conclusions** In the Atlantic Ocean basin, where would the oldest oceanic lithosphere be found? NY

19 **Summarizing** Describe the evidence that supported the hypothesis of continental drift. NY

20 **Applying Concepts** Some people predict that California will sink into the ocean. Does this idea fit with the theory of plate tectonics? Explain. NY

21 **Inferring** Why did the discovery of *Mesosaurus*, in both South America and Africa but nowhere else, support the hypothesis of continental drift? NY

22 **Comparing and Contrasting** What is the difference between the collision of an oceanic plate with a continental plate and the collision of two continental plates?

Analyzing Data

Use the diagram below to answer questions 22–24.

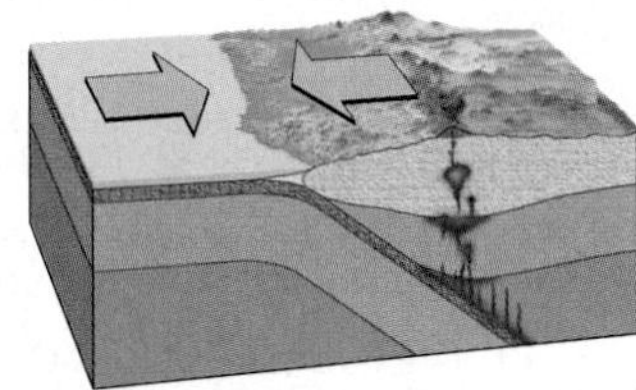

23 **Interpreting Diagrams** What type of boundary is shown? What types of lithosphere are involved? NY

24 **Inferring** What process is triggered as the slab descends beneath the other plate? NY

25 **Drawing Conclusions** How would the foci of earthquakes change if they were plotted in the diagram? NY

Concepts in Action

26 **Inferring** If an ocean ridge spreading rate increased, how would the width of paleomagnetic strips on the ocean floor be affected? Assume magnetic reversals occurred at original rate. NY

27 **Classifying** What type of plate boundary is formed when two plates grind past each other? Give an example of this type of boundary. NY

28 **Formulating Hypotheses** Form a hypothesis to explain what you think would happen if the direction of motion between India and Asia would change and India began to move in a southward direction. NY

29 **Calculating** How much wider would the Atlantic Ocean become in 10 million years if the spreading rate at the Mid-Atlantic Ridge was 2.5 cm/yr? Give your answer in kilometers.

30 **Connecting Concepts** What relationship exists between the ages of the Hawaiian Islands, hot spots, and plate tectonics?

31 **Writing in Science** Write a paragraph explaining why it is less likely that there will be a large earthquake in a location in the middle of North America, such as in Chicago, Illinois.

Performance-Based Assessment

Classifying Use a world map to choose ten different locations around the world. Then use Figure 8 on pages 256–257 to find the plate boundary nearest each location. Classify each boundary.

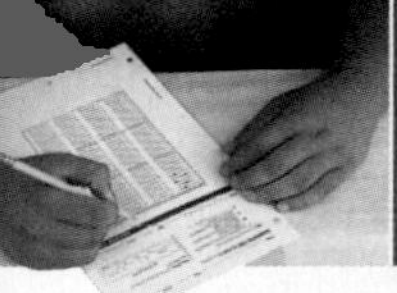

Regents Practice Exam

Test-Taking Tip

Eliminating Unreasonable Answers
When you answer a multiple-choice question, you can often eliminate at least one answer choice because it is clearly incorrect. If you eliminate one or more choices, you increase your odds of choosing the correct answer.

In the question below, you can immediately eliminate choice 2 because the outer core is located deep in Earth's interior. The mantle, answer choice 1, is another layer that is found in Earth's interior. So you can eliminate 1. You have narrowed your choices down to either 3, the lithosphere, or 4, the asthenosphere. The asthenosphere is not rigid. It is a weak layer over which the plates move. The remaining choice 3, must be the correct answer.

What is Earth's strong, rigid outer layer called?
(1) the mantle
(2) the outer core
(3) the lithosphere
(4) the asthenosphere

For *each* statement or question, choose the *number* of the word or expression that, of those given, best completes the statement or answers the question. Some questions may require the use of the *Earth Science Reference Tables.*

1 Which of the following was NOT used by Wegener to support his continental drift theory?
(1) fossil evidence (2) paleomagnetism
(3) the fit of South America and Africa (4) ancient climates

2 At which of the following plate boundaries do plates move apart, resulting in the upwelling of material from the mantle to create new seafloor?
(1) San Andreas Fault (2) Mariana Trench
(3) Peru-Chile Trench (4) Mid-Atlantic Ridge

Answer the following questions in complete sentences. Some questions may require the use of the *Earth Science Reference Tables.* Base your answers to questions 3 and 4 on the diagram at top right, which shows an Oceanic-Continental Convergent Boundary.

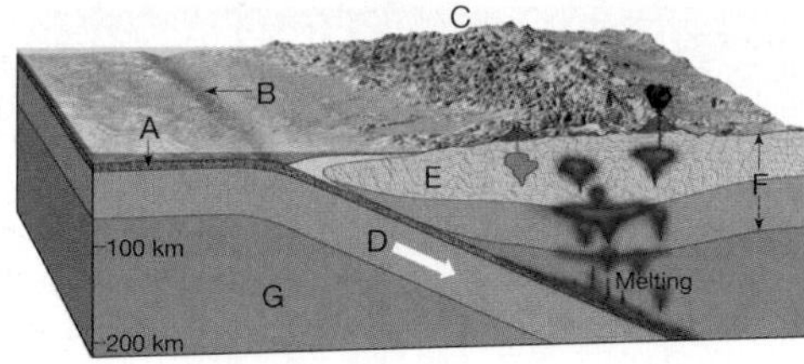

3 Which of the following statements is true?
(1) Layer *G* is the inner core.
(2) The crust at *A* is denser than the crust at *E*.
(3) The crust at *A* has the same density as the crust at *E*.
(4) The crust at *A* is less dense than the crust at *E*.

4 The process occurring at the location labeled *D* is
(1) oceanic lithosphere being created
(2) continental lithosphere being created
(3) a continental-continental collision occurring
(4) oceanic lithosphere being subducted

5 As you travel across the ocean floor from South America to Africa, crossing the Mid-Atlantic Ridge, what happens to the age of the oceanic crust?

6 Why is Earth's diameter not increasing, even though new lithosphere is constantly being created at the oceanic ridges?

7 Describe what happens when two oceanic plates collide, when two continental plates collide, and when an oceanic plate collides with a continental plate.

8 Explain how hot spots create volcanic mountain chains.

Regents Practice Exam

(1) 2
(2) 4
(3) 2
(4) 4
(5) As you travel from South America to the Mid-Atlantic Ridge, the crust gets younger, then, as you travel from the ridge to Africa, the crust gets older again.
(6) The Earth is not increasing in diameter because old lithosphere is constantly being melted back into the mantle at convergent boundaries.
(7) When two oceanic plates collide, the denser of the two subducts. When two continental plates collide, neither plate subducts, and mountains are created on the surface as the two plates fold upward together. When an oceanic plate meets a continental plate, the oceanic plate subducts.
(8) When a plate sits over a hot spot, a volcano is created, as the plate slowly moves, the volcano that was directly over the hot spot is carried off that spot and becomes inactive. At the same time, the part of the plate now over the hot spot gets a volcano. This creates volcanic island chains with younger, active volcanoes close to or directly over the hot spot while the older volcanoes sit in a line leading away from the hot spot.

Performance-Based Assessment

Student answers will vary but should accurately reflect the information presented in Figure 8. An example would be as follows: The boundary between India and Asia is a continental-continental convergent boundary.

Your students can independently test their knowledge of the chapter and print out their results.

CHAPTER 10

Planning Guide

Use these planning tools
Use Teacher Express for all your planning needs

SECTION OBJECTIVES	STANDARDS NATIONAL	STANDARDS STATE	ACTIVITIES and LABS
10.1 The Nature of Volcanic Eruptions, pp. 280–288 2 blocks or 4 periods **10.1** **Explain** the factors that determine the type of volcanic eruptions that occur. **10.2** **Describe** the various types of volcanic materials that are ejected from volcanoes. **10.3** **List** the three main types of volcanoes. **10.4** **Distinguish** how the different types of volcanic landforms form.	A-1, D-2, D-3, F-5		**SE** Inquiry Activity: Where Are Volcanoes Located? p. 279 L2 **SE** Quick Lab: Why are some volcanoes explosive? p. 281 L2 **TE** Teacher Demo: Observing Viscosity, p. 282 L2 **TE** Teacher Demo: Observing an Explosive Eruption, p. 285 L2
10.2 Intrusive Igneous Activity, pp. 289–292 1 block or 2 periods **10.5** **Classify** intrusive igneous features. **10.6** **Describe** the major intrusive igneous features. **10.7** **Describe** the origin of magma.	D-2, G-2		**TE** Build Science Skills, p. 291 L2
10.3 Plate Tectonics and Igneous Activity, pp. 293–295 1 block or 2 periods **10.8** **Explain** the relationship between plate tectonics and volcanism. **10.9** **Explain** where intraplate volcanism occurs.	A-1, A-2, D-1, D-2, G-3		**TE** Teacher Demo: Observing Plate Movement, p. 294 L2 **SE** Exploration Lab: Melting Temperatures of Rocks, pp. 300–301 L2

Ability Levels

- **L1** For students who need additional help
- **L2** For all students
- **L3** For students who need to be challenged

Components

SE	Student Edition	**GRSW**	Guided Reading & Study Workbook	**TP**	Test Prep Resources	**GEO**	Geode CD-ROM
TE	Teacher's Edition			**onT**	onlineText	**T**	Transparencies
LM	Laboratory Manual	**TEX**	Teacher Express	**DC**	Discovery Channel Videos	**GO**	Internet Resources
CUT	Chapter Tests	**CTB**	Computer Test Bank				

RESOURCES PRINT and TECHNOLOGY	SECTION ASSESSMENT
GRSW Section 10.1 **T-121** Magmas Have Different Compositions **T-122** Composite Cone **T-123** Profiles of Volcanic Landforms **T-124** Sequence of Events that Formed Crater Lake, Oregon **T-125** Volcanic Areas in the Northwestern U.S. GEODe Forces Within ↳ Igneous Activity **TEX** Lesson Planning 10.1	**SE** Section 10.1 Assessment, p. 288 **onT** Section 10.1
GRSW Section 10.2 **T-126** Basic Igneous Structures **T-127** Decompression Melting **T-128** Magma Formation at Subduction Zones **TEX** Lesson Planning 10.2	**SE** Section 10.2 Assessment, p. 292 **onT** Section 10.2
GRSW Section 10.3 **T-129** Location of Major Volcanoes **T-130** Three Zones of Volcanism **T-131** Three Zones of Volcanism **T-132** History of Cascade Range Volcanism **DC** Death and Destruction **TEX** Lesson Planning 10.3	**SE** Section 10.3 Assessment, p. 295 **onT** Section 10.3

Go Online

Go online for these Internet resources.

PHSchool.com
Web Code: cjk-9999

NSTA SCI LINKS
Web Code: cjn-3101
Web Code: cjn-3103

Materials for Activities and Labs

Quantities for each group

STUDENT EDITION

Inquiry Activity, p. 279
Internet and library resources, world map copy or overlay for world atlas, permanent marker

Quick Lab, p. 281
2 bottles of noncarbonated water, 2 bottles of club soda, paper towels

Exploration Lab, pp. 300–301
photocopy of Temperature Curves graph, colored pencils (3 different colors)

TEACHER'S EDITION

Teacher Demo, p. 282
2 large beakers, hot plate, water, 2 large test tubes, test-tube clamp, ice, corn syrup

Teacher Demo, p. 285
2-L soda bottle, rubber stopper, white vinegar, baking soda, paper towel, rubber band, thin bath or kitchen towel, scissors

Build Science Skills, p. 291
2 flat rocks, infrared thermometer (optional)

Teacher Demo, p. 294
9 student textbooks, 2 pieces of poster board, thin cardboard or 1-cm stack of notebook paper

Chapter Assessment

ASSESSMENT

SE Assessment, pp. 303–304
CTB Chapter 10
onT Chapter 10

STANDARDIZED TEST PREP

SE Chapter 10, p. 305
TP Progress Monitoring Assessments

interactive textbook with assessment at PHSchool.com

CHAPTER 10

Before you teach

Michael Wysession
Washington University

Big Ideas

Volcanic activity leads to the formation of igneous rock, and so is the foundation of the rock cycle. Volcanoes are a continual reminder of how geologically active Earth's interior is.

Space and Time Volcanoes come in many different forms, the most common of which are shield volcanoes, cinder cones, and composite cones. Magma comes up through a conduit which ends with a vent. The top of a volcano often forms a depression called a crater. Magma that cools underground produces a variety of forms that include sills, laccoliths, dikes, and batholiths.

Forces and Motion Volcanic eruptions take the form of lava flows, gases (mostly water vapor and carbon dioxide), and pyroclastic material (such as ash and bombs). Volcanic eruptions can pose significant hazards in the form of pyroclastic flows, ash falls, and lahars (mudflows). Volcanism occurs at divergent margins, such as mid-ocean ridges, through the mechanism of pressure release, and at convergent margins (subduction zones) through the subduction of water, which lowers the melting point of rock. Intraplate volcanism can occur from the eruption of hot plumes of mantle rock called hot spots.

Matter and Energy The style of volcanic eruption is determined by the magma's viscosity, which is due to factors that include the magma's temperature and composition (amount of silica and dissolved gases). Large amounts of dissolved gases often result in explosive eruptions.

Earth as a System Volcanoes are the most dramatic examples of the connection between Earth's surface and interior systems. Volcanic eruptions were largely responsible for forming Earth's early oceans, and still greatly affect global climate.

Earth Science Refresher

Not All Hot Spots Are Equal

An exciting new area of geophysical research involves the discovery of several different reasons why rock melts to cause intraplate volcanism. Three-dimensional images of Earth's interior structure made using seismic waves (a process called seismic tomography) have verified that there are indeed giant mantle plumes of hot rock that extend from the bottom to the top of the mantle and erupt as hot spot volcanoes. However, many more sites of intraplate volcanism that were traditionally considered hot spots are now found to originate closer to the surface and to occur for other reasons. Earth is a fascinating and complex planet, and it is often not possible to explain its geology with a single simple model.

Hawaii is the classic example of a hot spot mantle plume. Seismic tomography shows the presence of hot rock extending from the base of the mantle up to Hawaii. The rock is heated at the bottom of the mantle by heat from the outer core that conducts across the core-mantle boundary. The added heat makes the rock expand and become buoyant, and it pushes slowly upward, reaching the surface after tens of millions of years.

Address Misconceptions

Students may have the misconception that earthquakes shaking the region around the volcano are the only reason for volcanic eruptions. Earthquakes are common triggers of volcanic eruptions, but are not the only factors involved. For a strategy that helps to overcome this misconception, see **Address Misconceptions** on **p. 282.**

Go Online
NSTA PD Links
For: Chapter 10 Content Support
Visit: www.SciLinks.org/PDLinks
Web Code: cjn-1099

Iceland's large volume of lava, however, may have a different origin. When North America collided with Europe more than 400 million years ago, basaltic ocean crust of the Iapetus Ocean (the previous Atlantic Ocean) was subducted into the mantle. Now that North America and Europe are moving apart to form a new Atlantic Ocean, it seems some of this old basaltic crust is being pulled toward the mid-Atlantic ridge to fill the void created. Because the basalt melts more easily than mantle rock, it is creating a greater volume of magma that has become the island of Iceland, one of the few places where a mid-ocean ridge occurs above sea level. Another cause of volcanism at Iceland and other "hot spots" may be a larger amount of water in the mantle, which lowers the melting temperature of rock and so causes more melting. Such volcanoes would be the result of "wet spots" and not "hot spots."

The volcanism at Yellowstone has long been attributed to a hot spot, but here seismic tomography shows that the source of the magma is very shallow, so it clearly cannot be a true mantle plume hotspot. Several explanations are currently being examined for the cause of Yellowstone volcanism, including small-scale convection beneath the lithosphere and a propagating rift. Whatever the cause, it is worth noting that Yellowstone poses one of the greatest seismic hazards on this continent, and though it doesn't erupt often, it can do so dramatically. An eruption at Yellowstone 630,000 years ago covered the continent with ash, ejecting about 1000 cubic km of pyroclastic material. In comparison, Mt. St. Helens only erupted about 1 cubic km of ash in its big 1980 eruption. Many scientists are concerned that Yellowstone has shown a recent increase in thermal activity associated with rising temperatures, because when Yellowstone erupts, it does so extremely explosively.

Address Misconceptions

Some students may have the misconception that all mountains are volcanoes (either extinct, dormant, or active). Actually most mountains are the result of crustal deformation. Mountain building is discussed in the next chapter. For a strategy that helps to overcome this misconception, see **Address Misconceptions** on **p. 291**.

Build Reading Literacy

Identify Main Idea/Details

Locating Topic Sentences in Paragraphs

Strategy Help students understand and remember the most important information about a topic. This strategy can be applied to short segments of text, such as a single paragraph or a subsection, to find the main idea and details that support the topic. Assign students a short passage to read, such as Anatomy of a Volcano on pp. 283–284.

Example

1. Tell students that many paragraphs have a topic sentence that expresses the paragraph's main idea. Topic sentences are often the first or second sentence in the paragraph. Sometimes, however, they are the last sentence, or even a sentence in the middle of the paragraph.
2. Then, explain that the rest of the paragraph contains details, or additional facts and examples about the main idea.
3. Direct students' attention to a paragraph with a clearly stated topic sentence, and ask students which sentence best states the main idea of the paragraph.
4. Next, help students find sentences with details that explain more about the main idea.
5. Have students organize the main idea and details visually in a web format.
6. Have students work in pairs to identify the main idea and details in another passage and organize them in a web.

See p. 283 for a script on how to use this strategy with students. For additional strategies, see pp. 290 and 295.

CHAPTER 10 Volcanoes and Other Igneous Activity

ASSESS PRIOR KNOWLEDGE

Use the Chapter Pretest below to assess students' prior knowledge. As needed, review these concepts.

Review Science Concepts

Section 10.1 Review the composition and nature of the formation of basaltic, andesitic, and rhyolitic rocks with students.

Section 10.2 Review sedimentary rock composition and formation with students.

Section 10.3 Have students review the theory of plate tectonics.

CONCEPTS in Action

Quick Lab
Why are some volcanoes explosive?

Exploration Lab
Melting Temperatures of Rocks

How the Earth Works
Effects of Volcanoes

Forces Within
↳ Igneous Activity

Video Field Trip
Death and Destruction

Take a field trip to the ancient city of Pompeii with Discovery Channel and find out how the eruption of Mount Vesuvius destroyed a civilization. Answer the following questions after watching the video.

1. Judging from its eruption, what type of volcano is Vesuvius?
2. Are the cities near Vesuvius any safer today than they were in 79 A.D.? Why or why not?

Go Online PHSchool.com
For: Chapter 10 Resources
Visit: PHSchool.com
Web Code: cjk-9999

This photograph shows a recent eruption of Italy's Mount Etna. ▶

Chapter Pretest

1. Rhyolite is composed of which of the following? *(a)*
   a. light-colored silicates
   b. dark-colored silicates
   c. a high percentage of iron and magnesium
2. True or False: Basalt is the most common type of extrusive igneous rock. *(True)*
3. True or False: Andesitic rocks contain at least 75 percent dark silicate minerals. *(False)*
4. Identify the type of rock formed by the settling of solid material from a fluid. *(sedimentary rock)*
5. What is the name of the most recent supercontinent in the plate tectonics theory? *(Pangaea)*
6. How do scientists explain the evidence of glacial features in present-day Africa, Australia, South America, and India? *(These areas were once joined into a single continent and located at latitudes farther south than they are today.)*
7. What types of activity can be found along plate boundaries? *(volcanoes, earthquakes, mountain building)*

Chapter Preview

Inquiry Activity

Where Are Volcanoes Located?

Procedure

1. Use the Internet and library resources to locate at least 15 active volcanoes and 10 historical volcanic eruptions.
2. Plot the locations of these volcanoes on a copy of a world map or on an overlay for a world atlas.
3. Neatly label the volcanoes on the map or overlay.
4. Compare your volcano map with the map of earthquake epicenters in Figure 9 on page 226 and the map of plate boundaries in Figure 8 on pages 256 and 257.

Think About It

1. **Observing** What is the relationship between the locations of the volcanoes you plotted and the earthquake epicenters and plate boundaries on the maps?
2. **Inferring** If there have been numerous volcanic eruptions in an area, would the area be a likely place for earthquakes to occur? Explain your answer.
3. **Predicting** Use your volcano map to predict if a volcanic eruption would be likely or not likely in each of the following areas: eastern coast of North America, Spain, eastern coast of South America, Italy, and Japan.

ENGAGE/EXPLORE

Where Are Volcanoes Located?

Purpose In this activity, students will observe the locations of volcanic activity in the world.

Skills Focus **Observing, Inferring, Predicting, Interpreting Diagrams/Photographs**

Prep Time 5 minutes

Materials Internet access, library resource materials, world map copy or overlay for world atlas, permanent marker

Advance Prep Find Web sites and library sources in advance to reduce the time it takes for students to complete the lab. Have copies of world maps or overlays readily available for students to use.

Class Time 30 minutes

Teaching Tip Useful sites for this lab can be found at
http://volcano.und.nodak.edu/vw.html
http://hvo.wr.usgs.gov
http://volcanoes.usgus.gov

Expected Outcome Students will observe a pattern in the locations of volcanic activity, earthquake epicenters, and plate boundaries.

Think About It

1. Volcanoes and earthquake epicenters both occur along plate boundaries for the most part. Only a few volcanoes occur within plates, such as the Hawaiian volcanoes.
2. yes; both volcanoes and earthquake epicenters mostly occur along plate boundaries.
3. eastern coast of North America: no; Spain: no; eastern coast of South America: no; Italy: yes; Japan: yes.

Discovery Channel School — **Video Field Trip**
Death and Destruction

Encourage students to view the Video Field Trip "Death and Destruction."

Section 10.1

1 FOCUS

Section Objectives

10.1 **Explain** the factors that determine the type of volcanic eruptions that occur.

10.2 **Describe** the various types of volcanic materials that are ejected from volcanoes.

10.3 **List** the three main types of volcanoes.

10.4 **Distinguish** how the different types of volcanic landforms form.

Reading Focus

Build Vocabulary L2

Word Parts Explain to students that the prefix *pyro-* is Latin and Greek for "fire" or "heat." *Clastic* means "made from fragments of preexisting rocks." Pyroclastic materials are hot fragments of preexisting rocks that are blown from the vent of a volcano.

Reading Strategy L2

a. viscosity and dissolved gases
b. What are the types of volcanic materials? lava flows; pyroclastic material, such as ash; volcanic gases
c. What are the types of volcanoes? shield volcanoes, cinder cones, composite cones
d. What are some other volcanic landforms? calderas, pipes, lava plateaus

2 INSTRUCT

Use Visuals L1

Figure 1 During the eruption of Mount St. Helens, the height of the volcano was lowered by 400 meters. Ask: **What would have caused this damage?** *(Force built up within the volcano and blew the top off.)* **Infer where the debris from this blast went.** *(Some of the fine debris particles remained in the air for a time before settling; some of the material flowed down the side of the volcano in the form of mud; some of the material simply tumbled down the side of the volcano.)* **Verbal**

10.1 The Nature of Volcanic Eruptions

Reading Focus

Key Concepts

- What determines the type of volcanic eruption?
- What materials are ejected from volcanoes?
- What are the three main types of volcanoes?
- What other landforms are associated with volcanic eruptions?

Vocabulary

- viscosity
- vent
- pyroclastic material
- volcano
- crater
- shield volcano
- cinder cone
- composite cone
- caldera

Reading Strategy

Previewing Copy the table. Before you read the section, rewrite the green topic headings as questions. As you read, write the answers to the questions.

The Nature of Volcanic Eruptions	
What factors affect an eruption?	a. ___?___

Volcanic eruptions are more than spectacular sights. They are windows to Earth's interior. Because volcanoes eject molten rock that formed at great depth, they provide opportunities to observe the processes that occur deep beneath Earth's surface.

On May 18, 1980, one of the largest volcanic eruptions to occur in North America changed a scenic volcano into the smoldering wreck shown in Figure 1. On this date, Mount St. Helens erupted with tremendous force. The blast blew out the entire north flank of the volcano, leaving a gaping hole. The eruption ejected nearly a cubic kilometer of ash and rock debris. The air over Yakima, Washington, 130 kilometers to the east, was so filled with ash that noon became almost as dark as midnight. Why do volcanoes like Mount St. Helens erupt explosively, while others like Kilauea in Hawaii are relatively quiet?

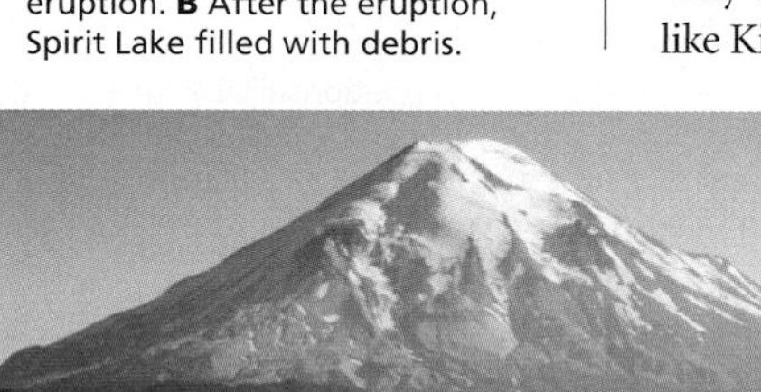

Figure 1 A Mount St. Helens before the May 18, 1980, eruption. **B** After the eruption, Spirit Lake filled with debris.

Table 1 Magma Composition

Composition	Silica Content	Viscosity	Gas Content	Tendency to Form Pyroclastics (ejected rock fragments)	Volcanic Landform
Basaltic	Least (~50%)	Least	Least (1–2%)	Least	Shield Volcanoes Basalt Plateaus Cinder Cones
Andesitic	Intermediate (~60%)	Intermediate	Intermediate (3–4%)	Intermediate	Composite Cones
Rhyolitic	Most (~70%)	Greatest	Most (4–6%)	Greatest	Pyroclastic Flows Volcanic Domes

Factors Affecting Eruptions

The primary factors that determine whether a volcano erupts violently or quietly include magma composition, magma temperature, and the amount of dissolved gases in the magma.

Viscosity Viscosity is a substance's resistance to flow. For example, maple syrup is more viscous than water and flows more slowly. Magma from an explosive eruption may be thousands of times more viscous than magma that is extruded quietly.

The effect of temperature on viscosity is easy to see. If you heat maple syrup, it becomes more fluid and less viscous. In the same way, the mobility of lava is strongly affected by temperature. As a lava flow cools and begins to harden, its viscosity increases, its mobility decreases, and eventually the flow halts.

The chemical composition of magmas has a more important effect on the type of eruption. The viscosity of magma is directly related to its silica content. In general, the more silica in magma, the greater is its viscosity. Because of their high silica content, rhyolitic lavas are very viscous and don't flow easily. Basaltic lavas, which contain less silica, tend to be more fluid.

Dissolved Gases During explosive eruptions, the gases trapped in magma provide the force to eject molten rock from the **vent,** an opening to the surface. These gases are mostly water vapor and carbon dioxide. As magma moves nearer the surface, the pressure in the upper part of the magma is greatly reduced. The reduced pressure allows dissolved gases to be released suddenly.

Very fluid basaltic magmas allow the expanding gases to bubble upward and escape relatively easily. Therefore, eruptions of fluid basaltic lavas, such as those that occur in Hawaii, are relatively quiet. At the other extreme, highly viscous magmas slow the upward movement of expanding gases. The gases collect in bubbles and pockets that increase in size until they explosively eject the molten rock from the volcano. The result is a Mount St. Helens.

Why are some volcanoes explosive?

Procedure  

1. Obtain two bottles of noncarbonated water and two bottles of club soda.
2. Open one bottle of the noncarbonated water and one bottle of the club soda. Record your observations.
3. Gently shake each of the remaining unopened bottles. **CAUTION:** *Wear safety goggles and point the bottles away from everyone.*
4. Carefully open each bottle over a sink or outside. Record your observations.

Analyze and Conclude

1. **Observing** What happened when the bottles were opened?
2. **Inferring** Which bottle represents lava with the most dissolved gas?

Customize for English Language Learners

Have students work in pairs to make a chart showing the facts about factors affecting eruptions, volcanic material, types of volcanoes, and other volcanic landforms. Students may want to illustrate their facts with drawings to further their understanding of the concepts. Students can use this chart as a study aid for quizzes and tests.

Factors Affecting Eruptions

Quick Lab

Why are some volcanoes explosive? L2

Objective
After completing this activity, students will be able to explain why trapped gases cause explosive reactions in volcanoes.

Skills Focus Observing, Inferring, Predicting

 **Prep Time** 5 minutes

Materials 2 bottles of noncarbonated water, 2 bottles of club soda, paper towels

Class Time 20 minutes

Safety Be sure that students point the open bottles away from everyone.

Teaching Tip Have paper towels available for students to use to clean up after the lab.

Expected Outcome Students will observe dissolved gases and fluid "explode" from the bottle of carbonated liquid.
Kinesthetic, Logical

Analyze and Conclude
1. Answers may vary but should state that the bottles with non-carbonated water opened without any escaping gases or fizzing. The bottles of club soda, when opened, fizzed with the escaping carbon dioxide. After the club soda was shaken, the gases escaped more explosively.
2. the shaken bottle of club soda

For Enrichment 

Have students research the violent eruption of Krakatau in 1883. Have students prepare a newspaper article detailing the events surrounding the eruption of this volcano. The article should be written as if the volcano had erupted recently.

Volcanic Material

Address Misconceptions 

Students may have the misconception that earthquakes shaking the region around the volcano are the only reason for volcanic eruptions. Earthquakes are common triggers of volcanic eruptions, but are not the only factors involved. Explain to students that volcanoes can erupt whenever magma builds up enough force to erupt from underground to the surface. The factors that determine the violence of the eruption are magma composition, magma temperature, and the amount of dissolved gases the magma contains.
Verbal

Use Visuals

L1

Figure 2 Have students look closely at these photographs. Ask: **How can you tell the aa flow is slow moving?** *(It is rough and jagged rather than smooth.)*
Visual

Observing Viscosity

Purpose Students will observe fluids that have different viscosities.

Materials 2 large beakers, hot plate, water, 2 large test tubes, test-tube clamp, ice, corn syrup

Procedure Pour corn syrup into the two large test tubes in advance. Put one test tube into a large beaker filled with ice. Put the other test tube into a large beaker half filled with water on a hot plate. Heat the syrup in a hot-water bath until it is very hot. Boiling the syrup is not necessary. Slowly pour the contents of each test tube into another beaker one at a time to demonstrate the nature of fluids with differing viscosities.

Expected Outcome Students will observe that the cold syrup is very viscous and flows very slowly—similar to silica-rich lava. The hot syrup is not viscous and flows very fast—similar to silica-poor lava.
Visual, Verbal

Figure 2 Lava Flows A Typical pahoehoe (ropy) lava flow, Kilauea Hawaii. **B** Example of a slow-moving aa flow.
Drawing Conclusions ***Which of the flows has more viscous lava?***

Volcanic Material

Lava may appear to be the main material extruded from a volcano, but this is not always the case. Just as often, explosive eruptions eject huge quantities of broken rock, lava bombs, fine ash, and dust. All volcanic eruptions also emit large amounts of gas.

Lava Flows Hot basaltic lavas are usually very fluid because of their low silica content. Flow rates of 10 to 300 meters per hour are common. In contrast, the movement of silica-rich (rhyolitic) lava is often too slow to be visible. When fluid basaltic lavas harden, they commonly form a relatively smooth skin that wrinkles as the still-molten subsurface lava continues to move. These are known as pahoehoe (pah HOH ee hoh ee) flows and resemble the twisted braids in ropes, as shown in Figure 2. Another common type of basaltic lava called aa (AH ah) has a surface of rough, jagged blocks with dangerously sharp edges and spiny projections.

Gases Magmas contain varied amounts of dissolved gases held in the molten rock by confining pressure, just as carbon dioxide is held in soft drinks. As with soft drinks, as soon as the pressure is reduced, the gases begin to escape. The gaseous portion of most magmas is only about 1 to 6 percent of the total weight. The percentage may be small, but the actual quantity of emitted gas can exceed thousands of tons each day. Samples taken during a Hawaiian eruption consisted of about 70 percent water vapor, 15 percent carbon dioxide, 5 percent nitrogen, 5 percent sulfur, and lesser amounts of chlorine, hydrogen, and argon. Sulfur compounds are easily recognized because they smell like rotten eggs and readily form sulfuric acid, a natural source of air pollution. The composition of volcanic gases is important because they have contributed greatly to the gases that make up the atmosphere.

Pyroclastic Materials When basaltic lava is extruded, dissolved gases propel blobs of lava to great heights. Some of this ejected material may land near the vent and build a cone-shaped structure. The wind will carry smaller particles great distances. Viscous rhyolitic magmas are highly charged with gases. As the gases expand, pulverized rock and lava fragments are blown from the vent. **Pyroclastic material** is the name give to particles produced in volcanic eruptions. **The fragments ejected during eruptions range in size from very fine dust and volcanic ash (less than 2 millimeters) to pieces that weigh several tons.**

Particles that range in size from small beads to walnuts (2–64 millimeters) are called lapilli or more commonly cinders. Particles larger than 64 millimeters in diameter are called blocks when they are made of hardened lava and bombs when they are ejected as glowing lava. Because bombs are semimolten upon ejection, they often take on a streamlined shape as they hurtle through the air.

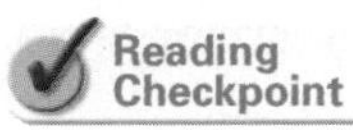

What is a volcanic bomb?

Types of Volcanoes

Volcanic landforms come in a wide variety of shapes and sizes. Each structure has a unique eruptive history. **The three main volcanic types are shield volcanoes, cinder cones, and composite cones.**

Anatomy of a Volcano Volcanic activity often begins when a fissure, or crack, develops in the crust as magma is forced toward the surface. The gas-rich magma moves up this fissure, through a circular pipe, ending at a vent, as shown in Figure 3. Repeated eruptions of lava or pyroclastic material often separated by long inactive periods eventually build the mountain called a **volcano.** Located at the summit of many volcanoes is a steep-walled depression called a **crater.**

Go Online SCiLINKS NSTA

For: Links on volcanic eruptions
Visit: www.SciLinks.org
Web Code: cjn-3101

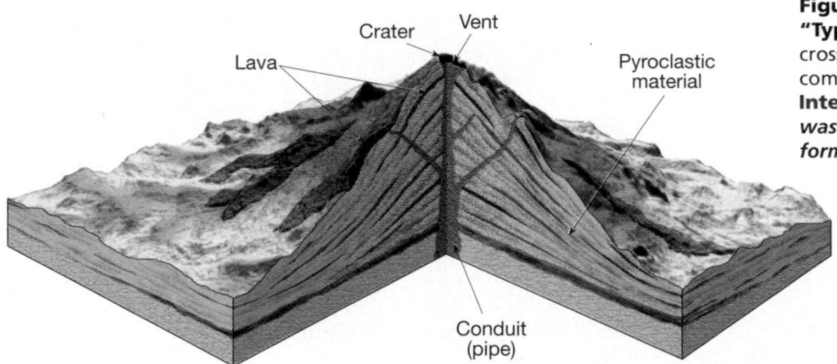

Figure 3 Anatomy of a "Typical" Volcano This cross section shows a typical composite cone. **Interpreting Diagrams** *How was the volcano in the diagram formed?*

Types of Volcanoes

Build Reading Literacy L1

Refer to **p. 278D** in this chapter, which provides the guidelines for identifying main ideas and details.

Identify Main Idea/Details Have students read Types of Volcanoes on pp. 283–286. Ask them to identify the main idea of each paragraph. Point out that the main idea is usually within the first or second sentence of a paragraph. Encourage students to include this exercise in the notes they use to study.
Verbal

Build Science Skills L2

Interpreting Diagrams/ Photographs Have students study Figure 3. Ask: **Why do you think the term *parasitic cone* is given to this feature in the diagram?** *(This cone does not have its own lava source but gets its lava from another conduit, or pipe.)*
Visual, Logical

Download a worksheet on volcanic eruptions for students to complete, and find additional teacher support from NSTA SciLinks.

Answer to . . .

Figure 2 *The lava in the aa lava flow is more viscous.*

Figure 3 *The volcano was formed as layers of pyroclastic material and lava flows were built up around the vent.*

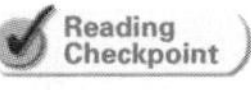

a large streamlined chunk of pyroclastic material that is larger than 64 mm in diameter

Integrate Physics L2

Geothermal Energy Hot magma near the surface of Earth can be beneficial. Geothermal energy takes advantage of Earth's internal energy and uses it as an energy source. Have students research this renewable source of energy. Students should prepare a short report about this natural energy source. The report should include an illustration showing an example of how geothermal energy can be used in a specific application.
Verbal

Use Visuals L1

Figure 4 Have students compare the photograph to the drawing. Ask: **Why might photographs of shield volcanoes make them look not as tall as they really are?** *(Because shield volcanoes are so broad, they often give the impression of being lower than they are.)* **How would you describe the viscosity of the lava at a shield volcano?** *(low viscosity)* **What is the origin of the other islands in the diagram? What do you think they would look like under the sea level?** *(They are shield volcanoes, or parts of shield volcanoes. Beneath the surface, the rocky formations likely flare outward either as individual shield volcanoes or as portions of a volcano shared by one or more of the other islands.)*

The form of a volcano is largely determined by the composition of the magma. As you will see, fluid lavas tend to produce broad structures with gentle slopes. More viscous silica-rich lavas generate cones with moderate to steep slopes.

Shield Volcanoes **Shield volcanoes** are produced by the accumulation of fluid basaltic lavas. Shield volcanoes have the shape of a broad, slightly domed structure that resembles a warrior's shield, as shown in Figure 4. Most shield volcanoes have grown up from the deep-ocean floor to form islands. Examples of shield volcanoes include the Hawaiian Islands and Iceland.

Cinder Cones Ejected lava fragments the size of cinders, which harden in the air, build a **cinder cone.** These fragments range in size from fine ash to bombs but consist mostly of lapilli, or cinders. Cinder cones are usually a product of relatively gas-rich basaltic magma. Although cinder cones are composed mostly of loose pyroclastic material, they sometimes extrude lava.

Cinder cones have a very simple shape as shown in Figure 5A. The shape is determined by the steep-sided slope that loose pyroclastic material maintains as it comes to rest. Cinder cones are usually the product of a single eruption that sometimes lasts only a few weeks and rarely more than a few years. Once the eruption ends, the magma in the pipe connecting the vent to the magma chamber solidifies, and the volcano never erupts again. Because of this short life span, cinder cones are small, usually between 30 meters and 300 meters and rarely exceed 700 meters in height.

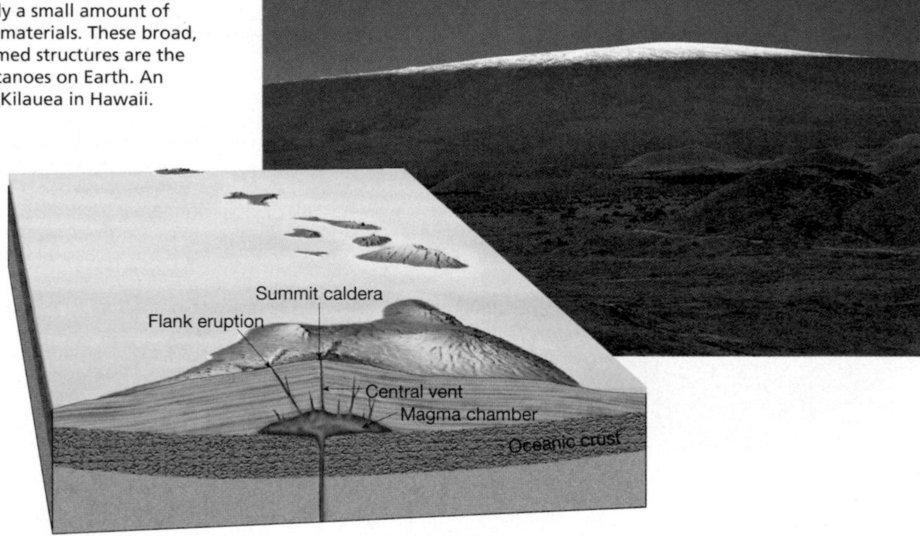

Figure 4 Shield Volcanoes Shield volcanoes are built mainly of fluid basaltic lava flows. They contain only a small amount of pyroclastic materials. These broad, slightly domed structures are the largest volcanoes on Earth. An example is Kilauea in Hawaii.

Facts and Figures

Parícutin is an active volcano in Mexico. It is one of the youngest volcanoes on Earth. On February 20, 1943, Parícutin began erupting from a fissure in a cornfield. By the end of the first year, the cone had reached an elevation of 450 m. Volcanic eruptions finally ended in 1952.

The resulting fire, ash, and lava destroyed two villages. In one of the villages, a local church is still standing at the edge of the lava flow. The top of the church and the bell tower are visible, but the lower portions of the church are buried in lava.

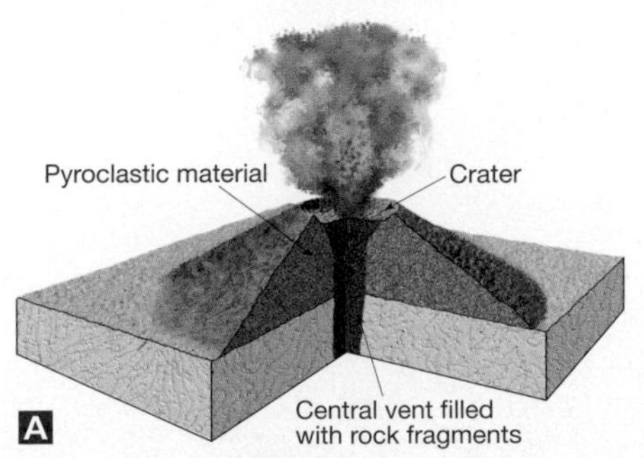

Figure 5 Cinder Cones
A A typical cinder cone has steep slopes of 30–40 degrees. **B** This photograph shows SP Crater, a cinder cone north of Flagstaff, Arizona.
Inferring ***What feature is shown in the lower part of the photograph?***

Cinder cones are found by the thousands all around Earth. Some, like the one shown in Figure 5B, near Flagstaff, Arizona, are located in volcanic fields. This field consists of about 600 cones. Others form on the sides of larger volcanoes. Mount Etna, for example, has dozens of cinder cones dotting its flanks.

Composite Cones Earth's most beautiful and potentially dangerous volcanoes are composite cones, or stratovolcanoes. Most are located in a relatively narrow zone that rims the Pacific Ocean, appropriately called the Ring of Fire. The Ring of Fire includes the large cones of the Andes in South America and the Cascade Range of the western United States and Canada. The Cascade Range includes Mount St. Helens, Mount Rainier, and Mount Garibaldi. The most active regions in the Ring of Fire are located along curved belts of volcanic islands next to the deep ocean trenches of the northern and western Pacific. This nearly continuous chain of volcanoes stretches from the Aleutian Islands to Japan, the Philippines, and New Zealand.

A **composite cone** is a large, nearly symmetrical structure composed of layers of both lava and pyroclastic deposits. For the most part, composite cones are the product of gas-rich magma having an andesitic composition. The silica-rich magmas typical of composite cones generate viscous lavas that can only travel short distances. Composite cones may generate the most explosive eruptions that eject huge quantities of pyroclastic material. Compare the shape and height of composite cones with other types of volcanoes in Figure 6.

Figure 6 Profiles of Volcanic Landforms A Profile of Mauna Loa, Hawaii, the largest shield volcano in the Hawaiian chain. **B** Profile of Mount Rainier, Washington, a large composite cone. **C** Profile of Sunset Crater, Arizona, a typical steep-sided cinder cone.

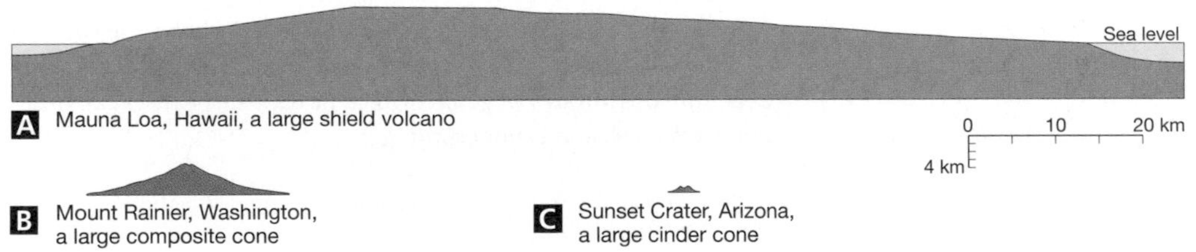

Teacher Demo

Observing an Explosive Eruption L2

Purpose Students will observe the explosive nature of gases trapped in an enclosed container.

Materials 2-L soda bottle, rubber stopper, white vinegar, baking soda, paper towel, rubber band, thin bath or kitchen towel, scissors

Procedure Pour 150 mL of vinegar into the empty soda bottle. For safety, fold the towel around the bottle. Secure the towel at the neck of the bottle with a rubber band. Cut an 8-cm square piece of paper towel. Put about 5 mL of baking soda in the center of the paper towel. Fold the paper towel around the baking soda to make a packet. Drop the packet into the bottle. Put the stopper into the bottle. Do not put the stopper in too tight. Have everyone stand a safe distance away from the bottle.

Expected Outcome Students will observe the explosive forces that are created when trapped gases are released. Point out to students that this is similar to gases trapped inside an active volcano. When enough force is built up, trapped gases can blow the top off of the volcano. Gases, magma, and pyroclastic materials then flow from the volcano through the new opening.
Visual

Answer to . . .

Figure 5 *a lava flow*

Section 10.1 (continued)

Integrate Social Studies L2

Mount Pelée Living in the shadow of a composite cone can be particularly dangerous. In 1902, Mount Pelée erupted in a fiery pyroclastic flow of hot gases infused with incandescent ash and larger rock fragments. The most destructive of pyroclastic flows, a nuée ardente (burning cloud), destroyed the port town of St. Pierre on the Caribbean island of Martinique. The destruction happened in moments. All of the 28,000 inhabitants of the town were killed with the exception of one person who was being held in a dungeon on the outskirts of town. A few people that were on ships in the harbor also were spared.

Shortly after this eruption, scientists arrived on the scene. They discovered masonry walls almost one meter thick knocked over like dominoes. Large trees were uprooted, and cannons were torn from their mounts. Have students use the Internet to research this volcanic eruption and prepare a short report on it. Ask: **What name is given to eruptions that are similar to the one that destroyed St. Pierre?** *(a peelean-type eruption, which is named after Mount Pelée)*
Verbal

Figure 7 Composite Cone Mount Shasta, California, is one of the largest composite cones in the Cascade Range. Shastina is the smaller cone that formed on the left flank of Mt. Shasta.

Fujiyama in Japan and Mount Shasta in California show the classic shape you would expect of a composite cone, with its steep summit and gently sloping flanks, as shown in Figure 7. About 50 such volcanoes have erupted in the United States in the past 200 years. On a global scale, numerous destructive eruptions of composite cones have occurred during the past few thousand years. A few of these have had a major influence on human civilization.

Dangers from Composite Cones One of the most devastating features associated with composite cones are pyroclastic flows. They consist of hot gases, glowing ash, and larger rock fragments. The most destructive of these fiery flows are capable of racing down steep volcanic slopes at speeds of nearly 200 kilometers per hour. Some pyroclastic flows result when a powerful eruption blasts material out the side of a volcano. Usually they form from the collapse of tall eruption columns that form over a volcano during an explosive event. Once gravity overcomes the upward thrust provided by the escaping gases, the material begins to fall. Massive amounts of hot fragments, ash, and gases begin to race downhill under the influence of gravity.

Large composite cones may also generate mudflows called lahars. These destructive mudflows occur when volcanic debris becomes saturated with water and rapidly moves down steep volcanic slopes, often following stream valleys. Some lahars are triggered when large volumes of ice and snow melt during an eruption. Others are generated when heavy rainfall saturates weathered volcanic deposits. Lahars can occur even when a volcano is not erupting.

What is a lahar?

Facts and Figures

The five deadliest volcanic eruptions known are (1) Tambora, Indonesia, which occurred in 1815. There were 92,000 deaths, primarily the result of starvation. (2) Krakatau, Indonesia, which occurred in 1883. There were 36,000 deaths, primarily the result of a tsunami. (3) Mount Pelée, Martinique, which occurred in 1902. There were 28,000 deaths, primarily the result of pyroclastic flows. (4) Nevado del Ruiz, Colombia, which occurred in 1985. There were 25,000 deaths, primarily the result of mudflows. (5) Unzen, Japan, which occurred in 1792. There were 14,000 deaths, primarily the result of a volcano collapse and a tsunami.

Caldera Formation

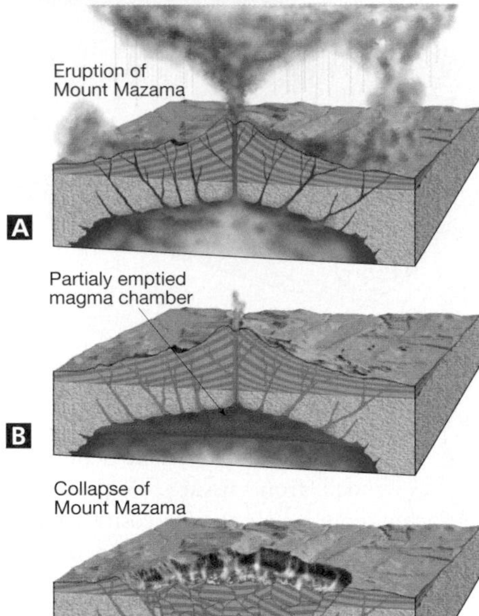

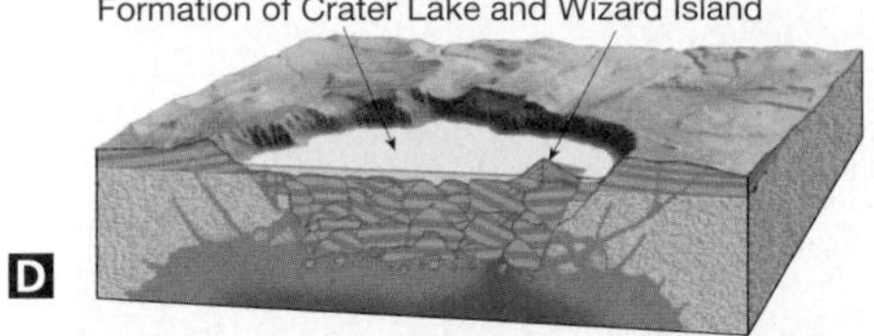

Figure 8 Crater Lake in Oregon occupies a caldera about 10 kilometers in diameter. About 7000 years ago, the summit of former Mount Mazama collapsed following a violent eruption that partly emptied the magma chamber. Rainwater then filled the caldera. Later eruptions produced the cinder cone called Wizard Island.

Other Volcanic Landforms

Calderas **A caldera is a large depression in a volcano.** Most calderas form in one of two ways: by the collapse of the top of a composite volcano after an explosive eruption, or from the collapse of the top of a shield volcano after the magma chamber is drained. Crater Lake, Oregon, is located in a caldera. This caldera formed about 7000 years ago when a composite cone, Mount Mazama, violently erupted and collapsed, as shown in Figure 8.

Necks and Pipes **Most volcanoes are fed magma through conduits, called pipes, connecting a magma chamber to the surface.** Volcanoes are always being weathered and eroded. Cinder cones are easily eroded because they are made up of loose materials. When the rock in the pipe is more resistant and remains standing above the surrounding terrain after most of the cone has been eroded, the structure is called a volcanic neck, as shown in Figure 9A on page 288.

The best-known volcanic pipes are the diamond-bearing pipes of South Africa. The rocks filling these pipes formed at depths of at least 150 kilometers, where pressure is high enough to form diamonds. The process of moving unaltered magma through 150 kilometers of solid rock is unusual, resulting in the rarity of diamonds.

Other Volcanic Landforms

Use Visuals L1

Figure 8 Have students study the diagrams in Figure 8. Tell students that the word *caldera* means "a cooking pot." Ask: **Why is an eruption that empties or partially empties the magma chamber an important first step for a caldera to form?** *(The magma chamber must be emptied or partially emptied to create a void. Then the volcano collapses into the newly created void to create a deep depression in the landscape.)* **Why is the name caldera a good description of this type of landform?** *(When the volcano collapses, a large well is created that resembles a cooking pot.)*
Verbal, Logical

Use Community Resources L2

Many U.S. Geological Survey (USGS) offices have educational outreach staff and programs. Contact your regional office and ask a USGS scientist to speak to your class about plate tectonics and volcanic activity.
Interpersonal

Answer to . . .

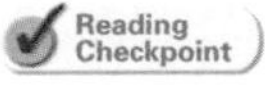

a mudflow down the slope of a volcano

Section 10.1 (continued)

Use Visuals

L1

Figure 9 Have students study Figure 9. Ask: **Infer why the volcanic neck is still in place while the surrounding terrain has eroded away.** *(The rock in the volcanic neck is more resistant to erosion than the surrounding terrain.)*
Verbal, Logical

3 ASSESS

Evaluate Understanding

L2

Have students play a quiz game to review the material in this section. Ask each student to write three questions on three separate sheets of paper. Collect the questions. Divide the class into two teams. To play the game, alternate giving a member of each team a question from the collected papers. Give each team a point for each correct response. The team with the most points wins the game.

Reteach

L1

Set aside any questions that are answered incorrectly from the quiz game above. After the game, give each team the stack of missed questions. Let the entire team work together to give the correct response to the questions.

Answers will vary, but should accurately classify the volcano and give a clear description of the eruption.

Figure 9 Other Volcanic Landforms A Ship Rock, New Mexico, is a volcanic neck. Ship Rock consists of igneous rock that crystallized in the pipe of a volcano that then was eroded away. **B** Lava erupting from a fissure forms fluid lava flows called flood basalts. **C** These dark-colored basalt flows are near Idaho Falls, Idaho.

Lava Plateaus You probably think of volcanic eruptions as building a mountain from a central vent. But the greatest volume of volcanic material is extruded from fissures. Rather than building a cone, low-viscosity basaltic lava flows from these fissures, covering a wide area, as shown in Figure 9B. The extensive Columbia Plateau in the northwestern United States was formed this way. Here, numerous fissure eruptions extruded very fluid basaltic lava, shown in Figure 9C. Successive flows, some 50 meters thick, buried the landscape, building a lava plateau nearly 1.6 kilometers thick.

Section 10.1 Assessment

Reviewing Concepts

1. What factors determine the type of volcanic eruption?
2. List the materials ejected from volcanoes.
3. Describe the three types of volcanoes.
4. What is a caldera?

Critical Thinking

5. **Comparing and Contrasting** Compare the formation of a lava plateau with the formation of a cinder cone.
6. **Applying Concepts** What type of eruption produces a viscous magma containing 53 percent silica and a gas content of 2 percent?
7. **Calculating** If a pyroclastic flow was traveling 145 kilometers per hour, how long would it take to reach a town 2.5 kilometers from the volcano's crater?

Writing in Science

Summary Research a volcanic eruption. Write a paragraph describing the eruption. Make sure to classify what type of volcano erupted.

Section 10.1 Assessment

1. The type of volcanic eruption is determined by the magma composition, magma temperature, and amount of dissolved gases.
2. The materials ejected from volcanoes include lava, gases, and pyroclastic materials, such as ash, dust, cinders, volcanic blocks, and volcanic bombs.
3. Cinder cones are small, steep cones, composed mainly of loose cinders. Shield volcanoes are large, gently sloping volcanoes composed of layers of mainly quiet lava flows. Composite cones are large, steep cones, composed of layers of lava flows and pyroclastic material from more explosive eruptions.
4. A caldera is a large, collapsed depression in a volcano.
5. A lava plateau is formed by repeated eruptions from a long, narrow fissure that can build up to form a thick deposit of volcanic rock over a large area. A cinder cone is a small volcanic cone that forms from cinders, usually from a single eruption.
6. The eruption would most likely be explosive.
7. The pyroclastic flow would reach the town in just over 1 minute (1.03 minutes).

10.2 Intrusive Igneous Activity

Reading Focus

Key Concepts

- How are intrusive igneous features classified?
- What are the major intrusive igneous features?
- What is the origin of magma?

Vocabulary

- pluton
- sill
- laccolith
- dike
- batholith
- geothermal gradient
- decompression melting

Reading Strategy

Comparing and Contrasting After you read the section, compare the types of plutons by completing the table.

Types of Plutons	Description
Sill	a. ___?___
Laccolith	b. ___?___
Dike	c. ___?___
Batholith	d. ___?___

Although volcanic eruptions are among the most violent and spectacular events in nature, most magma cools deep within Earth. The structures that result form the roots of mountain ranges and some of the most familiar features in the landscape.

Plutons

The structures that result from the cooling and hardening of magma at depth are called **plutons.** Because all plutons form beneath Earth's surface, they can be studied only after uplift and erosion have exposed them. Plutons occur in a great variety of sizes and shapes. **Intrusive igneous bodies, or plutons, are generally classified according to their shape, size, and relationship to the surrounding rock layers.**

Sills and Laccoliths **Sills and laccoliths are plutons that form when magma is intruded close to the surface.** Sills and laccoliths differ in shape and often differ in composition. A **sill** forms when magma is injected along sedimentary bedding surfaces, parallel to the bedding planes. Horizontal sills, like the one shown in Figure 10, are the most common.

For a sill to form, the overlying sedimentary rock must be lifted to a height equal to the thickness of the sill. Although this is a not an easy task, at shallow levels it often requires less energy than forcing the magma up to the surface. Because of this, sills form only at shallow depths, where the pressure exerted by the weight of overlying rock layers is low. As shown in Figure 11A on page 290, sills look like buried lava flows.

Figure 10 Sills This dark, horizontal band is a sill of basalt that intruded into horizontal layers of sedimentary rock in Salt River Canyon, Arizona.
Inferring ***How could you determine if a horizontal igneous rock layer was a lava flow or a sill?***

Section 10.2

1 FOCUS

Section Objectives

10.5 **Classify** intrusive igneous features.
10.6 **Describe** the major intrusive igneous features.
10.7 **Describe** the origin of magma.

Reading Focus

Build Vocabulary L2

Word Parts List on the board the following word parts and meanings: *lakkos*, "reservoir"; *lithos*, "stone"; *bathos*, "depth." Have students identify these word parts in the vocabulary terms. Discuss the terms' meanings with students.

Reading Strategy L2

a. pluton formed parallel with sedimentary rocks, commonly horizontal
b. similar to a sill, but forms a lens-shaped mass that pushes the overlying strata upward
c. pluton that cuts across the preexisting rocks
d. largest intrusive igneous body with a surface exposure of over 100 sq km

2 INSTRUCT

Plutons

Use Visuals L1

Figure 10 Have students study Figure 10. Ask: **Why do sills only form at shallow depths?** *(The overlying sedimentary rock must be lifted to a height equal to the height of the sill, so the weight of the rock cannot be more than the magma can lift.)* **Why does the sill form below the sedimentary rock instead of at the surface?** *(because it requires less force to raise the sedimentary rock than to force the magma to the surface)*
Verbal

Answer to . . .

Figure 10 *The upper surface of a lava flow would not show evidence of contact with another rock layer above it, while the upper surface of a sill shows evidence that it was intruded into preexisting layers of sedimentary rocks. The sedimentary rock layers above the sill could also show evidence of heating and contact metamorphism.*

Volcanoes and Other Igneous Activity 289

Build Reading Literacy L1

Refer to **p. 474D** in **Chapter 17,** which provides guidelines for monitoring your understanding.

Monitor Your Understanding Have students read the passages Plutons and Origin of Magma (pp. 289–292). When they reach the bottom of p. 289, have them stop and write down the main ideas in the passages. Have them ask themselves, "Did I have any trouble reading this passage? If so, why?" Then, have them come up with their own strategies to improve their understanding. Have students use this strategy as they continue reading. **Interpersonal, Verbal**

Integrate Social Studies L2

The Henry Mountains These mountains, located in southeastern Utah, are largely composed of several laccoliths believed to be fed by a much larger magma body nearby. The mountain range is named for Joseph Henry, an American scientist. Henry was the first secretary of the Smithsonian Institution. Have students find the Henry Mountains on a map or an atlas. **Verbal**

Types of Igneous Plutons

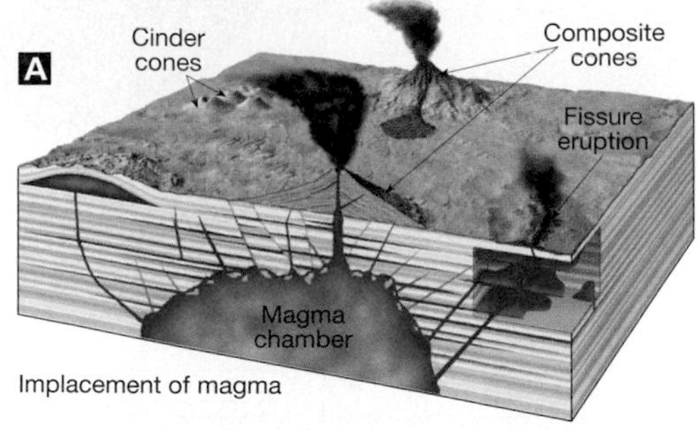

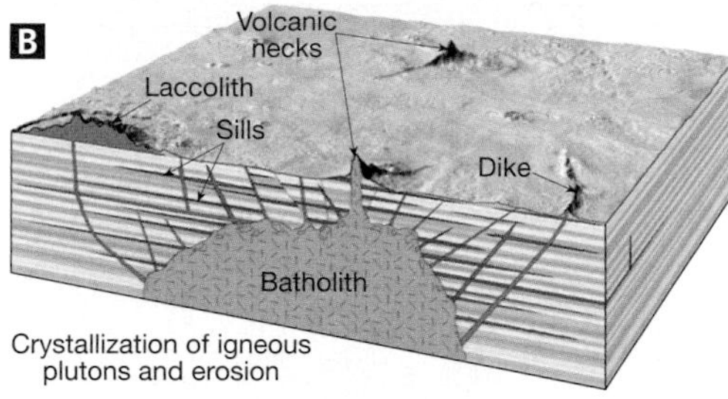

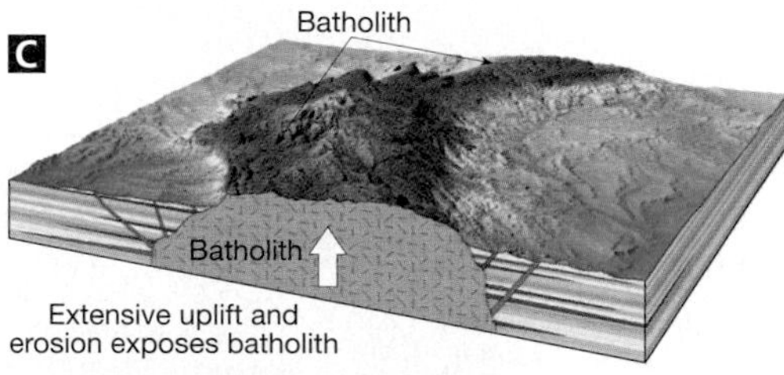

Figure 11 A This diagram shows the relationship between volcanism and intrusive igneous activity. **B** This view shows the basic intrusive igneous structures, some of which have been exposed by erosion long after their formation. **C** After millions of years of uplift and erosion, a batholith is exposed at the surface.

Laccoliths are similar to sills because they form when magma is intruded between sedimentary layers close to the surface. However, the magma that generates laccoliths is more viscous. This less-fluid magma collects as a lens-shaped mass that pushes the overlying strata upward. Most laccoliths are not much wider than a few kilometers.

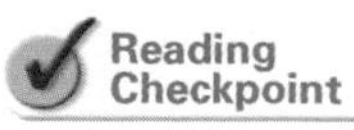

Compare and contrast sills and laccoliths.

Dikes Some plutons form when magma is injected into fractures, cutting across preexisting rock layers. Such plutons are called **dikes,** as in Figure 11B. These sheetlike structures have thicknesses ranging from less than a centimeter to more than a kilometer. Most dikes, however, are a few meters thick and extend laterally for no more than a few kilometers.

Some dikes radiate, like spokes on a wheel, from an eroded volcanic neck. The movement of magma probably formed fissures in the volcanic cone from which the magma flowed to form the dikes. **Many dikes form when magma from a large magma chamber invades fractures in the surrounding rocks.**

Batholiths The largest intrusive igneous bodies are **batholiths.** The Idaho batholith, for example, covers an area of more than 40,000 square kilometers and consists of many individual plutons. Indirect evidence from gravity and seismic studies indicates that batholiths are also very thick, possibly extending dozens of kilometers into the crust.

Customize for Inclusion Students

Learning Disabled Make concept maps for each section and cover them with clear contact paper. Then, cut the maps into puzzle pieces. Provide students with the pieces and have them put the puzzle together. After students complete the puzzle, have them make flashcards with concept connections and added notes. For example, students may have cards with the names of plutons on one side and a definition or example on the other. Students also may have key concept cards with an important word missing. For example, **A ________ is a pluton formed when magma is injected along sedimentary bedding surfaces, parallel to the bedding planes.** *(sill)*

An intrusive igneous body must have a surface exposure greater than 100 square kilometers to be considered a batholith. Smaller plutons are called stocks. Many stocks appear to be portions of batholiths that are not yet fully exposed. Batholiths may form the core of mountain ranges, as shown in Figure 12. In this case, uplift and erosion have removed the surrounding rock, exposing the batholith.

Figure 12 Batholiths Mount Whitney in California makes up just a tiny portion of the Sierra Nevada batholith, a huge structure that extends for approximately 400 kilometers.

Origin of Magma

The origin of magma has been controversial in geology for a long time. Based on available scientific evidence, Earth's crust and mantle are composed primarily of solid, not molten, rock. Although the outer core is a fluid, its iron-rich material is very dense and stays deep within Earth. What is the source of magma that produces igneous activity? **Geologists conclude that magma originates when essentially solid rock, located in the crust and upper mantle, partially melts. The most obvious way to generate magma from solid rock is to raise the temperature above the level at which the rock begins to melt.**

Role of Heat What source of heat is sufficient to melt rock? Workers in underground mines know that temperatures get higher as they go deeper. The rate of temperature change averages between 20°C and 30°C per kilometer in the upper crust. This change in temperature with depth is known as the **geothermal gradient.** Estimates indicate that the temperature at a depth of 100 kilometers ranges between 1400°C and 1600°C. At these high temperatures, rocks in the lower crust and upper mantle are near, but not quite at their melting point temperatures. So they are very hot but still essentially solid.

There are several ways that enough additional heat can be generated within the crust or upper mantle to produce some magma. First, at subduction zones, friction generates heat as huge slabs of crust slide past each other. Second, crustal rocks are heated as they descend into the mantle during subduction. Third, hotter mantle rocks can rise and intrude crustal rocks. All of these processes only form relatively small amounts of magma. As you'll see, the vast bulk of magma forms without an additional heat source.

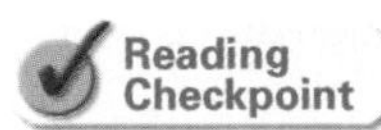

What is a geothermal gradient?

Origin of Magma

L2

Some students may have the misconception that all mountains are volcanoes (either extinct, dormant, or active). Explain to students that most mountains are the result of crustal deformation. Mountain building is discussed in the next chapter. Ask: **What clues could scientists use to determine if a mountain is the result of volcanic activity?** *(Scientists could look for signs of volcanic activity, such as the presence of igneous rock or plutons.)*
Verbal

Build Science Skills **L2**

Observing Friction and Heat Gather two flat rocks. Have students feel the temperature of the rocks before the following activity begins. If an infrared thermometer is available, take the temperature of the rocks. Simulate the motion of two plates at a subduction zone by rubbing and grinding two flat rocks together. After a few minutes, feel the rocks again or take the temperature of the rocks with the infrared thermometer. Students will observe a temperature increase in rocks due to the friction between the two rocks. This is similar to the activity that occurs at a subduction zone. However, the rocks at a subduction zone are much larger and are forced together with a great deal of force, resulting in a great deal of friction and heat. Friction is not a factor in the melting of magma beneath subduction zones.
Kinesthetic, Logical

Facts and Figures

American geologist Ferdinand Vandiveer Hayden lived from 1829 to 1887. Hayden explored and documented information about the American West for over 30 years. The "Hayden surveys" provided scientific information on the geology, botany, and zoology of the American West. In 1867, he was placed in charge of the newly established U.S. Geological and Geographical Survey of the Territories. This department was the precursor of the U.S. Geological Survey, which is now part of the United States Department of the Interior.

Answer to . . .

Both sills and laccoliths are plutons formed by magma intrusions close to the surface, but they differ in shape and usually differ in composition.

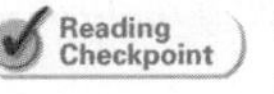

the change in temperature with depth

Section 10.2 (continued)

Integrate Physics L2

Kinetic Theory and Pressure The kinetic theory can help students visualize the role that pressure plays in the melting of rock. Have students recall that the particles in a solid are closely packed and are bonded to the particles surrounding them. When a substance is heated or gains thermal energy, the kinetic energy of the individual particles increases. Have students recall that temperature is the average kinetic energy of the individual particles in a substance. A substance melts when the particles have enough kinetic energy to overcome the bonds between the particles in a solid. If a substance is under pressure, the particles must gain more thermal energy to overcome the bonds between the particles and the force (pressure) holding the particles in place. Therefore, the substance, in this case the rock, must absorb more thermal energy to overcome the additional force. This gives the substance a higher melting temperature. Have students explain why reducing confining pressure lowers a rock's melting temperature. *(The particles no longer have to overcome the additional force.)*
Verbal, Logical

3 ASSESS

Evaluate Understanding L2

Have students write three review questions from the chapter. Then have students work with a partner to ask each other their questions.

Reteach L1

Use Figure 11 to review the different types of igneous plutons.

Connecting Concepts

Sample answer: Convection currents within the mantle bring hot mantle material closer to the surface.

Answer to . . .

Figure 13 *It appears to have a low viscosity because it is flowing relatively easily from a fissure.*

Figure 13 Basaltic Magma at the Surface Lava extruded along the East Rift Zone, Kilauea, Hawaii.
Observing *Does this lava appear to have a high viscosity or a low viscosity? Explain.*

Role of Pressure If temperature were the only factor that determined whether or not rock melts, Earth would be a molten ball covered with a thin, solid outer shell. This is not the case because pressure also increases with depth. Melting, which causes an increase in volume, occurs at higher temperatures at depth because of greater confining pressure. In this way, an increase in confining pressure causes an increase in the rock's melting temperature. The opposite is also true. Reducing confining pressure lowers a rock's melting temperature. When confining pressure drops enough, **decompression melting** is triggered. This process generates magma beneath Hawaii where plumes of hot rock melt as they rise toward the surface.

Role of Water Another important factor affecting the melting temperature of rock is its water content. Water causes rock to melt at lower temperatures. Because of this, "wet" rock buried at depth has a much lower melting temperature than does "dry" rock of the same composition and under the same pressure. Laboratory studies have shown that the melting point of basalt can be lowered by up to 100°C by adding only 0.1 percent water. In addition to a rock's composition, its temperature, depth (confining pressure), and water content determine if it is a solid or liquid.

In summary, magma can be formed in three ways. First, heat may be added when a magma body from a deeper source intrudes and melts crustal rock. Second, a decrease in pressure (without the addition of heat) can result in decompression melting. Third, water can lower the melting temperature of mantle rock enough to form magma.

Section 10.2 Assessment

Reviewing Concepts

1. How are intrusive features classified?
2. List the major intrusive igneous bodies.
3. What are the three major ways that magma forms?
4. What is a pluton?

Critical Thinking

5. **Comparing and Contrasting** Describe the difference between a sill and a dike.
6. **Relating Cause and Effect** What effect does a decrease in confining pressure have on the melting temperature of rocks in the upper mantle?

Connecting Concepts

Convection Currents Recall what you learned about convection currents in Chapter 9. Explain how convection currents could affect the depth at which molten rocks are found.

Section 10.2 Assessment

1. Intrusive features are classified by their shape, size, and relationship to the surrounding rock layers.
2. batholiths, laccoliths, sills, and dikes
3. Magma forms by (1) heat being added to crustal rocks when hotter, deeper mantle rocks rise into the crust; (2) by a decrease in pressure without an increase in temperature; (3) by the addition of water, which can lower the melting point enough to form magma.
4. the structure that results from the cooling and hardening of magma at depth
5. A sill is a pluton that forms when magma is injected along bedding surfaces and parallel to the bedding planes. A dike is a pluton that forms when magma is injected into fractures, cutting across preexisting rock layers.
6. A decrease in confining pressure will decrease the melting temperature, causing decompression melting to occur.

10.3 Plate Tectonics and Igneous Activity

Reading Focus

Key Concepts

- What is the relationship between plate boundaries and igneous activity?
- Where does intraplate volcanism occur?

Vocabulary

- intraplate volcanism

Reading Strategy

Outlining After you read, make an outline of the most important ideas in the section.

I. **Plate Tectonics and Igneous Activity**
   A. Convergent Plate Boundaries
      1. ___?___
      2. ___?___

More than 800 active volcanoes have been identified worldwide. Most of them are located along the margins of the ocean basins, mainly within the circum-Pacific belt known as the Ring of Fire. A second group of volcanoes is found in the deep-ocean basins, including on Hawaii and Iceland. A third group includes volcanic structures that are irregularly distributed in the interiors of the continents. Until the late 1960s, geologists had no explanation for the distribution of volcanoes. With the development of the theory of plate tectonics, the picture became clearer.

Convergent Plate Boundaries

The basic connection between plate tectonics and volcanism is that plate motions provide the mechanisms by which mantle rocks melt to generate magma. At convergent plate boundaries, slabs of oceanic crust are pushed down into the mantle. As a slab sinks deeper into the mantle, the increase in temperature and pressure drives water from the oceanic crust. Once the sinking slab reaches a depth of about 100 to 150 kilometers, the fluids reduce the melting point of hot mantle rock enough for melting to begin. The magma formed slowly migrates upward forming volcanoes such as Mount St. Helens shown here. As you read about the relationships between plate tectonics and igneous activity, refer to Figure 17 on pages 296–297, which summarizes the relationships.

Figure 14 Convergent Boundary Volcano Mount St. Helens emitting volcanic ash on July 22, 1980, two months after the huge May eruption. Mount St. Helens is located at a convergent boundary between the Juan de Fuca plate and the North American plate.

Section 10.3

1 FOCUS

Section Objectives

10.8 **Explain** the relationship between plate tectonics and volcanism.

10.9 **Explain** where intraplate volcanism occurs.

Reading Focus

Build Vocabulary L2

Definitions Have students write a definition for *continental volcanic arc* and *intraplate volcanism* in their own words. After students read the section, ask them to draw a diagram that illustrates the definitions.

Reading Strategy L2

1. Ocean-Ocean
2. Ocean-Continent

B. Divergent Boundaries
C. Intraplate Igneous Activity

2 INSTRUCT

Convergent Plate Boundaries

Build Science Skills L2

Interpreting Diagrams/Photographs In the caption for Figure 14, it states that Mount St. Helens is located on the convergent boundary of the Juan de Fuca plate and the North American plate. Have students find these plates on a map of Earth's plates. Ask: **How do the sizes of the two plates compare?** *(The Juan de Fuca plate is much smaller than the North American plate.)* **Which plate is subducting?** *(the Juan de Fuca plate)*
Verbal

Divergent Plate Boundaries

Observing Plate Movement

L2

Purpose Students will observe convergent plate movements.

Materials 9 student textbooks, 2 pieces of poster board, thin cardboard or 1-cm stack of notebook paper

Procedure Stack eight textbooks in two equal stacks. Leave about 5 cm between the textbook stacks. The remaining textbook will represent a continental crustal plate. The poster board will represent the subducting oceanic lithosphere. Give the poster board a slight curve so that it will subduct downward. Place the textbook on one of the stacks and the poster board on the other stack. Ask: **What do you predict will happen when these two plates collide?** *(The less rigid plate will subduct under the rigid plate.)* Start moving the "plates" toward each other. The oceanic lithosphere should subduct under the continental plate. Repeat this procedure using two pieces of poster board. Before moving the plates together, ask: **What do you predict will happen when these two plates collide?** *(The two slabs of crust will form a trench as they descend into the mantle.)* One piece of poster board needs to be curved so it will form a trench as it subducts.

Expected Outcomes Students will observe how the oceanic lithosphere subducts under the crustal plate and how two oceanic plates form a trench.
Visual, Kinesthetic

MAP MASTER™ Skills Activity

Answer

Inferring They occur at divergent boundaries for continental plates and at ocean ridges for oceanic plates.

Go Online NSTA SciLINKS

Download a worksheet on volcanic activity for students to complete, and find additional teacher support from NSTA SciLinks.

MAP MASTER™ Skills Activity

Major Volcanoes

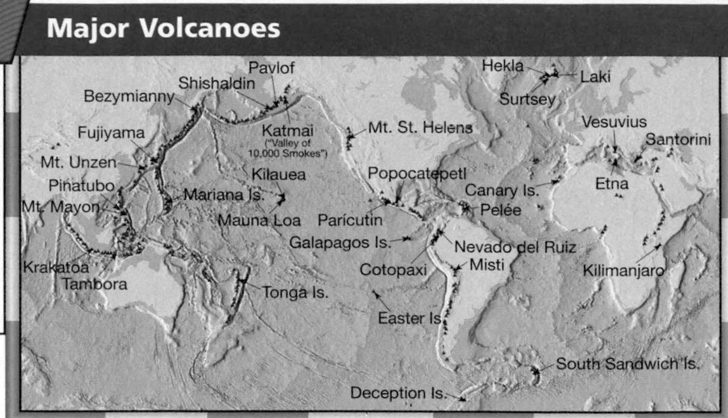

Figure 15
Location Note the concentration of volcanoes encircling the Pacific basin, known as the Ring of Fire.
Inferring How are the volcanoes in the middle of the Atlantic Ocean related to a plate boundary?

Ocean-Ocean Volcanism at a convergent plate where one oceanic slab descends beneath another results in the formation of a chain of volcanoes on the ocean floor. Eventually, these volcanic structures grow large enough to rise above the surface and are called volcanic island arcs. Several volcanic island arcs border the Pacific basin, including the Aleutians.

Ocean-Continent Volcanism associated with convergent plate boundaries may also develop where slabs of oceanic lithosphere are subducted under continental lithosphere to produce a continental volcanic arc. The mechanisms are basically the same as those at island arcs. The major difference is that continental crust is much thicker and is composed of rocks with a higher silica content than oceanic crust. As the silica-rich crustal rocks melt, the magma may change composition as it rises through continental crust. The volcanoes of the Andes Mountains along the western edge of South America are an example of a continental volcanic arc, as shown in Figure 15.

Divergent Plate Boundaries

Most magma is produced along the oceanic ridges during seafloor spreading. Below the ridge axis where the plates are being pulled apart, the solid yet mobile mantle rises upward to fill in the rift where the plates have separated. As rock rises, confining pressure decreases. The rock undergoes decompression melting, producing large amounts of magma. This newly formed basaltic magma is less dense than the mantle rock from which it was formed, so it buoyantly rises.

Partial melting of mantle rock at spreading centers produces basaltic magma. Although most spreading centers are located along the axis of an oceanic ridge, some are not. The East African Rift in Africa is a site where continental crust is being rifted apart.

Go Online SCI LINKS NSTA

For: Links on predicting volcanic activity
Visit: www.SciLinks.org
Web Code: cjn-3103

Customize for English Language Learners

Select and copy an appropriate paragraph from one of the sections, such as the last paragraph on p. 293. Leave the first and last sentences intact, since they are usually the introductory and concluding sentences. For the sentences in the middle, remove key words and replace them with a blank. For example, leave blanks for *convergent* in the second sentence of this paragraph, *mantle* in the third sentence, and the last use of *melting* in the fourth sentence. Have students read the paragraph and fill in the blanks with the appropriate words.

Intraplate Igneous Activity

Kilauea is Earth's most active volcano, but it is in the middle of the Pacific plate, thousands of kilometers from a plate boundary. **Intraplate volcanism** occurs within a plate, not at a plate boundary. Another site of intraplate volcanism is Yellowstone National Park.

Most intraplate volcanism occurs where a mass of hotter than normal mantle material called a mantle plume rises toward the surface. Most mantle plumes appear to form deep within Earth at the core-mantle boundary. These plumes of hot mantle rock rise toward the surface in a way similar to the blobs that form within a lava lamp. Once the plume nears the top of the mantle, decompression melting forms basaltic magma. The result may be a small volcanic region a few hundred kilometers across called a hot spot. More than 40 hot spots have been identified, and most have lasted for millions of years. By measuring the heat flow at hot spots, geologists found that the mantle beneath some hot spots may be 100–150°C hotter than normal.

The volcanic activity on the island of Hawaii, shown in Figure 16, is the result of a hot spot. Where a mantle plume has persisted for long periods of time, a chain of volcanoes may form as the overlying plate moves over it. Mantle plumes are also thought to cause the vast outpourings of lava that create large lava plateaus such as the Columbia Plateau in the northwestern United States.

Figure 16 Intraplate Volcano An eruption of Hawaii's Kilauea volcano. The Hawaiian hot spot activity is currently centered beneath Kilauea and is an example of intraplate volcanic activity.

Section 10.3 Assessment

Reviewing Concepts

1. How are the locations of volcanoes related to plate boundaries?
2. What causes intraplate volcanism?
3. Where is most of the magma produced on Earth on a yearly basis?
4. What is the Ring of Fire?

Critical Thinking

5. **Comparing and Contrasting** What are the differences between volcanic island arcs and continental volcanic arcs?
6. **Predicting** Would it be more likely for a major explosive eruption to occur at an ocean ridge or at a convergent ocean-continental boundary? Explain your answer.

Writing in Science

Explanatory Paragraph Write a paragraph to explain how magma is formed in the crust without adding heat.

Intraplate Igneous Activity

Build Reading Literacy L1

Refer to **p. 186D** in **Chapter 7**, which provides the guidelines for relating text and visuals.

Relate Text and Visuals Have students compare the drawings of the plates and volcanic activity in Figures 15 and 16 to the text explanations in this section.
Visual

3 ASSESS

Evaluate Understanding L2

Have students create a ten-question crossword puzzle or word scramble using the concepts from this section. Have students exchange papers and work the puzzles.

Reteach 

Use Figure 15 to reteach the concepts in this section.

Magma can form by decompression melting if the rock begins to rise and the pressure decreases. This causes the temperature at which melting occurs to decrease. If water is added, the temperature at which the rock melts decreases. A body of hotter rock may rise and trigger melting in the crust.

Section 10.3 Assessment

1. Most volcanoes are located at either divergent or convergent plate boundaries, where plate motions provide the mechanisms to form magma.
2. Intraplate volcanism is caused by hot mantle plumes rising up from the core-mantle boundary, causing decompression melting and forming small areas of volcanic activity on the surface.
3. Most of the magma produced each year on Earth is produced at ocean ridges during seafloor spreading.
4. The Ring of Fire is a chain of volcanoes that are located around the edge of the Pacific Basin.
5. A volcanic island arc is formed when two oceanic plates converge and form a subduction zone. The magma produced is of basaltic composition. A continental volcanic arc is formed by subduction of an ocean plate beneath a continental plate. The magma produced is more silica rich than that formed at a volcanic island arc.
6. An explosive eruption would be more likely at a convergent ocean-continental boundary, because the magma produced is more silica rich, more viscous, and contains more water.

MAP MASTER™ Skills Activity

Answer
Drawing Conclusions Volcanoes occur on both continental and oceanic plates in all the zones—convergent plate volcanism, divergent plate volcanism, and intraplate volcanism.

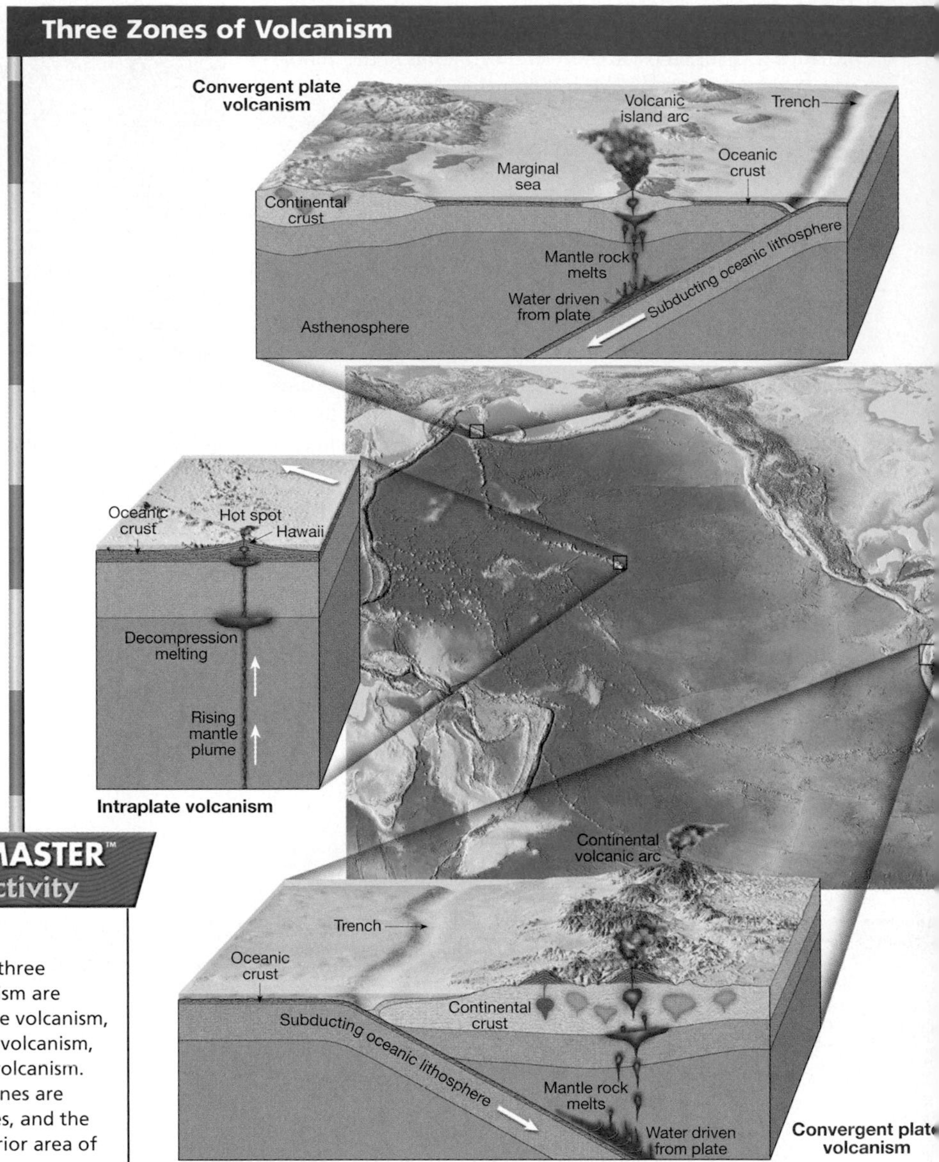

MAP MASTER™ Skills Activity

Figure 17

Regions The three zones of volcanism are convergent plate volcanism, divergent plate volcanism, and intraplate volcanism. Two of these zones are plate boundaries, and the third is the interior area of the plates.
Drawing Conclusions In which zones do volcanoes occur on both continental plates and oceanic plates?

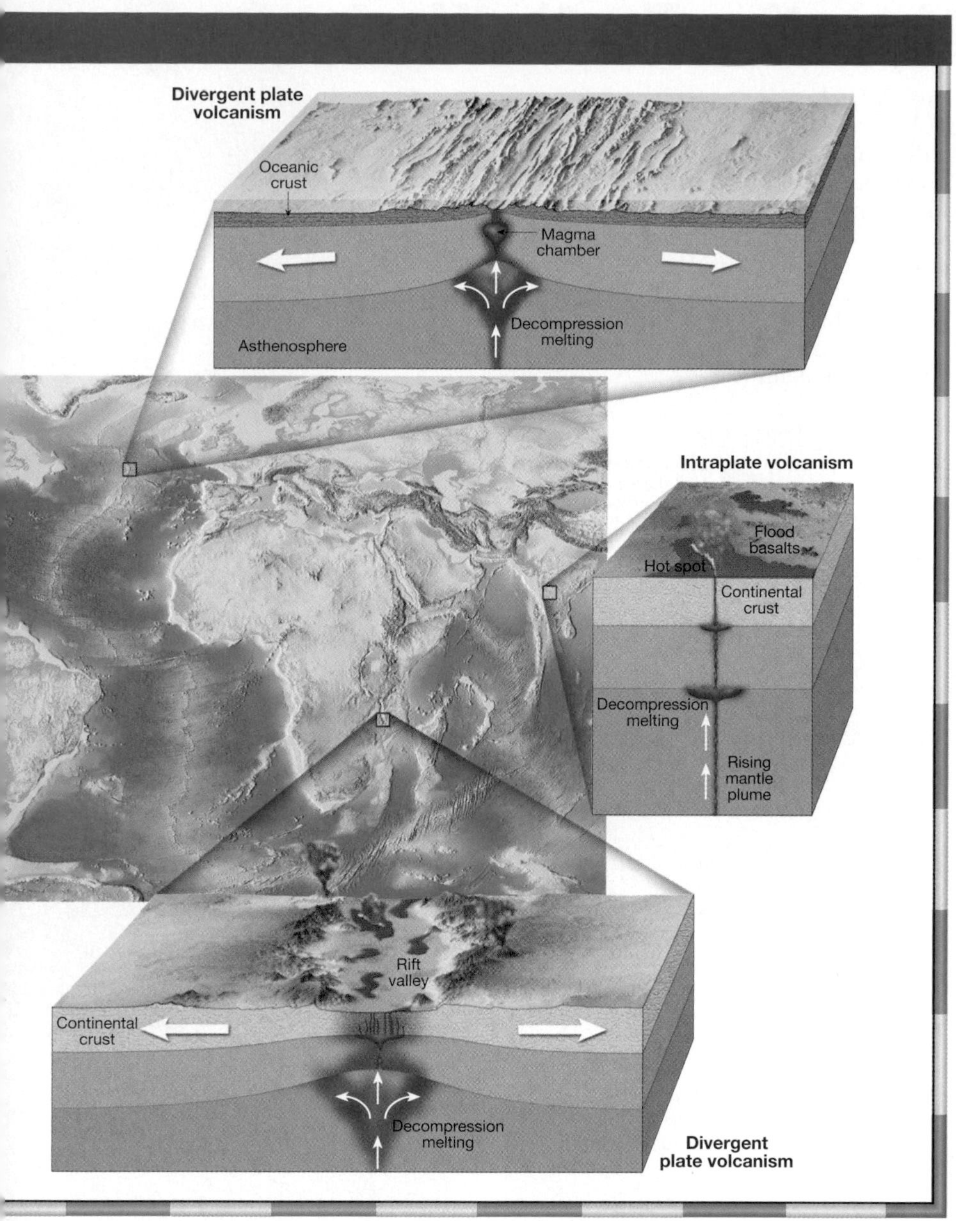

Volcanoes and Other Igneous Activity 297

How the Earth Works

1 FOCUS

Objectives

In this feature, students will
- explain what a volcano is.
- describe the immediate effects of a volcanic eruption.
- identify some long-term effects of a volcanic eruption.

Reading Focus

Build Vocabulary L2

Classify Terms Draw a four-column chart on the board. Label the columns as follows: *Volcanic Effect*, *Definition of Effect*, *Immediate or Long-Term Effect*, and *Local or Worldwide Effect*. Have students use information on these two pages to complete the chart.

2 INSTRUCT

Use Visuals L2

Ask students to read the captions on this page and the next. Have them make a list of places in the United States and in other countries where volcanoes are or have been active.
Visual

Bellringer L2

Have students list ten effects of a volcanic eruption. Examples may include clouds of smoke, lava trails, and a scorched landscape.
Logical

How the Earth Works

Effects of Volcanoes

A **volcano** is an opening in the Earth's crust from which **lava,** or molten rock, escapes to the surface. The impact of powerful volcanic eruptions is both immediate and long-lasting. Burning rocks are flung out in all directions. Huge clouds of scorching ash and fiery gases billow high into the sky. As a result, the landscape and even the weather can be changed. Soil may become more fertile when enriched with nutrients from volcanic ash. Islands, mountains, and other landforms may be created from the material emitted by volcanoes.

The Giant's Causeway in Northern Ireland

DRAMATIC ROCK FORMATIONS
Lava flows can form amazing rock formations. **Columnar rocks** are volcanic rocks that split into columns as the lava cools. The Devil's Tower in Wyoming (below) is one example of a columnar rock. Another example is the Giant's Causeway (left). This rock formation in Northern Ireland is the result of a lava flow that erupted millions of years ago.

The Devil's Tower in Wyoming

DUST AND GAS
Explosive volcanoes, like Mount St. Helens in Washington (right), spit clouds of ash and fumes into the sky. The debris can completely cover human communities. Another hazard is that volcanic gases may be deadly poisons.

ERUPTING LAVA
Red-hot lava is hurled into the air during an eruption of a volcano on Stromboli, an island off the coast of southern Italy. The Stromboli volcano is one of only a few volcanoes to display continuous eruptive activity over a period of more than a few years.

298 Chapter 10

Facts and Figures

The ancient Roman city of Pompeii was encased in lava when Mount Vesuvius erupted in A.D. 79. The volcano destroyed the city, and most people were buried in ash and lava. Rain hardened the ash, forming perfect molds of people and preserving articles of everyday life. Pompeii's ruins were first discovered in the late sixteenth century. Since 1748, archaeologists have excavated materials that provide a detailed picture of life in a busy Roman port town. In addition to houses, bakeries, restaurants, and factories, scholars have uncovered inscriptions on buildings, tombs, and statues. Even the graffiti on Pompeii's walls gives us clues about the values and concerns of this ancient society.

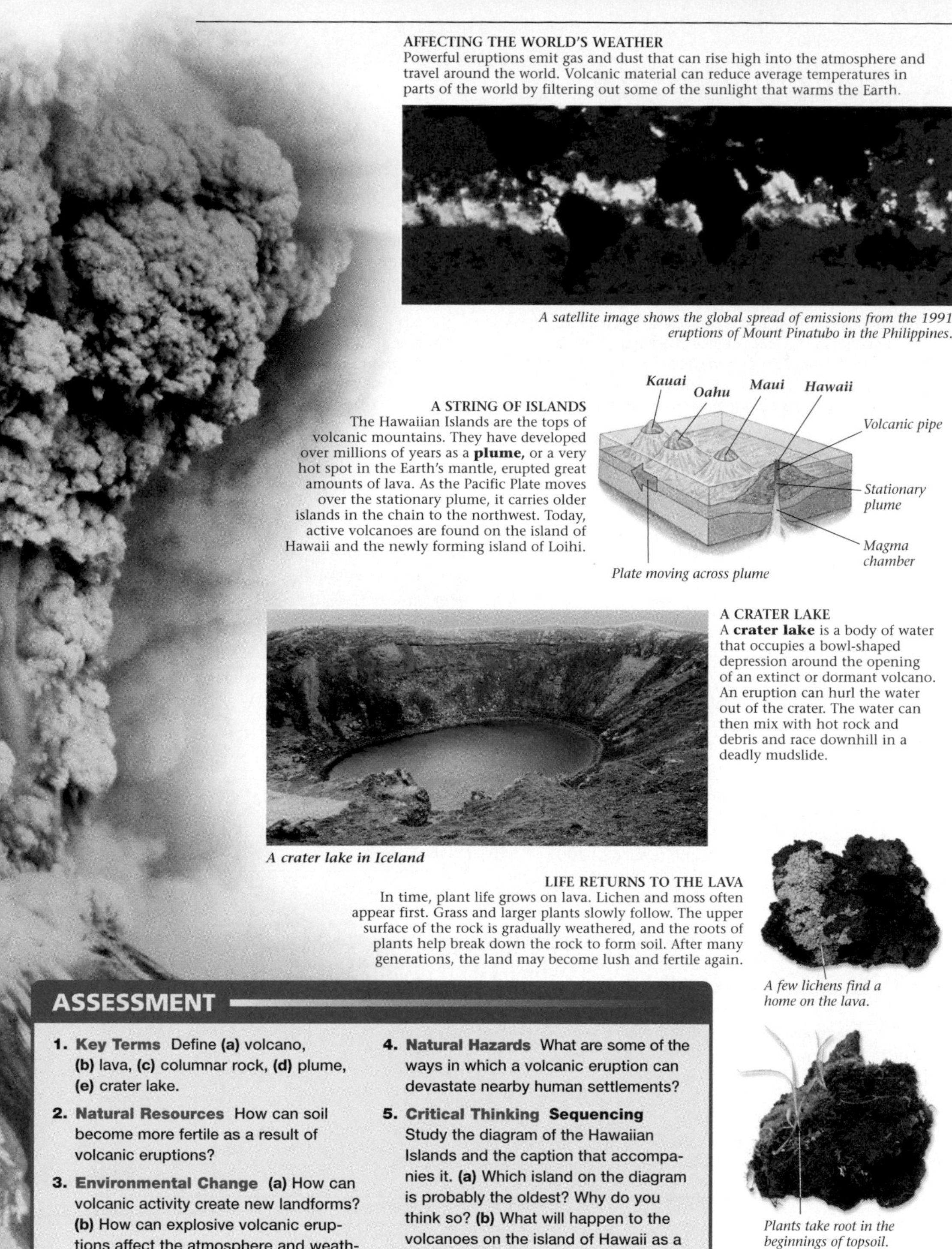

AFFECTING THE WORLD'S WEATHER
Powerful eruptions emit gas and dust that can rise high into the atmosphere and travel around the world. Volcanic material can reduce average temperatures in parts of the world by filtering out some of the sunlight that warms the Earth.

A satellite image shows the global spread of emissions from the 1991 eruptions of Mount Pinatubo in the Philippines.

A STRING OF ISLANDS
The Hawaiian Islands are the tops of volcanic mountains. They have developed over millions of years as a **plume,** or a very hot spot in the Earth's mantle, erupted great amounts of lava. As the Pacific Plate moves over the stationary plume, it carries older islands in the chain to the northwest. Today, active volcanoes are found on the island of Hawaii and the newly forming island of Loihi.

A CRATER LAKE
A **crater lake** is a body of water that occupies a bowl-shaped depression around the opening of an extinct or dormant volcano. An eruption can hurl the water out of the crater. The water can then mix with hot rock and debris and race downhill in a deadly mudslide.

A crater lake in Iceland

LIFE RETURNS TO THE LAVA
In time, plant life grows on lava. Lichen and moss often appear first. Grass and larger plants slowly follow. The upper surface of the rock is gradually weathered, and the roots of plants help break down the rock to form soil. After many generations, the land may become lush and fertile again.

A few lichens find a home on the lava.

Plants take root in the beginnings of topsoil.

ASSESSMENT

1. **Key Terms** Define **(a)** volcano, **(b)** lava, **(c)** columnar rock, **(d)** plume, **(e)** crater lake.
2. **Natural Resources** How can soil become more fertile as a result of volcanic eruptions?
3. **Environmental Change** **(a)** How can volcanic activity create new landforms? **(b)** How can explosive volcanic eruptions affect the atmosphere and weather around the world?
4. **Natural Hazards** What are some of the ways in which a volcanic eruption can devastate nearby human settlements?
5. **Critical Thinking** **Sequencing** Study the diagram of the Hawaiian Islands and the caption that accompanies it. **(a)** Which island on the diagram is probably the oldest? Why do you think so? **(b)** What will happen to the volcanoes on the island of Hawaii as a result of plate movement?

299

3 ASSESS

Evaluate Understanding L2

Have students review the information in the charts they have created. Ask: **What are some positive effects of volcanoes?** *(They create islands, fertilize soil, and create beautiful rock formations.)*

Reteach L1

Have students compare and contrast the formation and eruptions of Mount St. Helens shown in the photograph with the Hawaiian Islands shown in the diagram.

Assessment

1. (a) an opening in Earth's crust from which lava escapes to the surface; (b) molten rock; (c) volcanic rocks that split into columns as the lava cools; (d) a very hot spot in Earth's mantle; (e) a body of water that occupies a bowl-shaped depression around the opening of an extinct or dormant volcano
2. Soil becomes enriched with nutrients from volcanic ash.
3. (a) Underwater plumes erupt great amounts of lava over millions of years, building the tops of underwater volcanic mountains.
(b) Gas and dust from an eruption may rise high into the atmosphere, travel around the world, and filter out sunlight.
4. Volcanic debris can completely cover human communities, and volcanic gases are deadly poisons.
5. (a) Kauai is the oldest island because of the direction in which the plate is moving.
(b) The volcanoes on the island of Hawaii will become extinct as plate movement causes the island to move away from the stationary plume.

Exploration Lab

Melting Temperature of Rocks

L2

Objectives
After completing this activity, students will be able to
- describe the temperature gradient for Earth's interior.
- explain the relationship between depth and the melting temperatures of granite and basalt rocks.

Skills Focus **Using Tables and Graphs, Analyzing Data, Drawing Conclusions**

 **Prep Time** 5 minutes

Class Time 45 minutes

Teaching Tip Closely monitor students who may have difficulty constructing graphs or assign these students a partner to help them construct their graphs. These students may need extra time to complete this lab.

Expected Outcome Students will observe the relationships between depth and melting temperature of basalt and granite rocks. Students will observe that basalt rock melts at higher temperatures than granite at all depths.

Sample Data

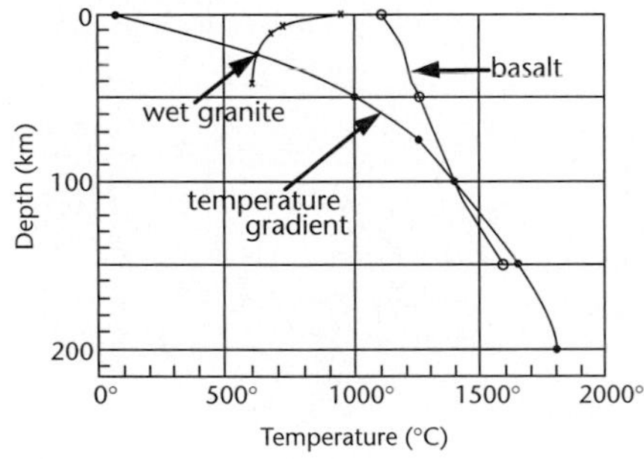

Exploration Lab

Melting Temperatures of Rocks

Measurements of temperatures in wells and mines have shown that Earth's internal temperatures increase with depth. Recall that this rate of temperature increase is called the geothermal gradient. Although the geothermal gradient varies from place to place, it is possible to calculate an average. In this lab, you will investigate Earth's internal temperatures and the temperatures at which rocks melt. You will also investigate the effect of water on the melting temperatures of rock.

Problem How can rocks melt to form magma in the crust and uppermost mantle?

Materials
- photocopy of Temperature Curves graph
- colored pencils (three different colors)
- ruler

Skills Analyzing Data, Graphing, Calculating

Procedure

1. Obtain a photocopy of the Temperature Curves graph on page 301. You will use it to plot the average temperature gradient for Earth's interior. Plot the temperature gradient on graph paper labeled like the graph shown.
2. Plot the temperature values from Table 1 on your graph. Then draw a single best-fit line through the points with a colored pencil. Extend your line from the surface to 200 kilometers. Label the line "Temperature Gradient."
3. The melting temperature of a rock changes as pressure increases deeper within Earth. The approximate melting points of the igneous rocks, granite and basalt, under various pressures (depths) have been determined in the laboratory and are shown in Table 2. Granite and basalt were used because they are common materials in the upper layer of Earth. Plot the melting temperatures from Table 2 on the same graph you made above. Use a different colored pencil to plot each set of points and draw the best-fit lines.
4. Label the two lines "Melting Curve for Wet Granite" and "Melting Curve for Basalt."

Table 1 Idealized Internal Temperatures of Earth

Depth (kilometers)	Temperature (°C)
0	20
25	600
50	1000
75	1250
100	1400
150	1700
200	1800

Table 2 Melting Temperatures of Granite (with water) and Basalt at Various Depths Within Earth

Granite (with water)		Basalt	
Depth (km)	Melting Temperature (°C)	Depth (km)	Melting Temperature (°C)
0	950	0	1100
5	700	25	1160
10	660	50	1250
20	625	100	1400
40	600	150	1600

Analyze and Conclude

1. **Using Graphs** Does the rate of increase of Earth's internal temperature stay the same or change with increasing depth?
2. **Using Graphs** Is the rate of temperature increase greater from the surface to 100 kilometers or below 100 kilometers?
3. **Interpreting Data** What is the temperature at 100 kilometers below the surface?
4. **Calculating** Use the data and your graph to calculate the average temperature gradient for the upper 100 kilometers of Earth in °C/100 kilometers and in °C/kilometer.
5. **Drawing Conclusions** Based on your data, at approximately what depth within Earth would wet granite reach its melting temperature and begin to form magma? Explain.
6. **Drawing Conclusions** Based on your data, at what depth will basalt have reached its melting temperature and begin to form magma?

Go Further What is the name of the layer within Earth's upper mantle that is below about 100 kilometers? Why do scientists theorize that this zone is capable of "flowing" more easily than other mantle rock, allowing the lithosphere to move across it?

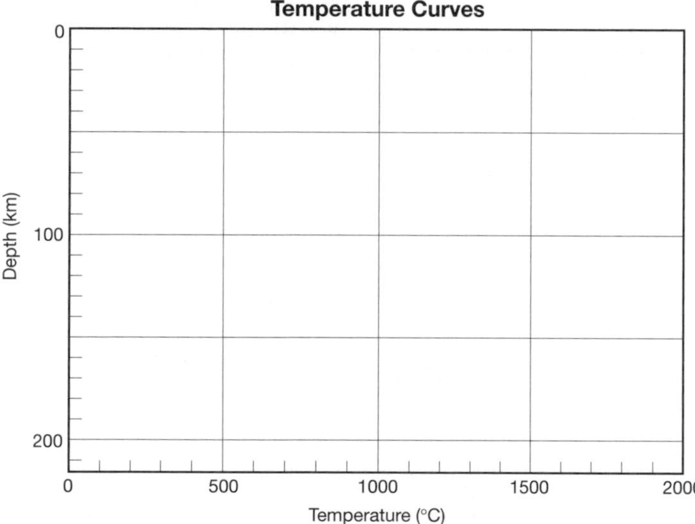

Analyze and Conclude

1. change with increasing depth
2. greater from the surface to 100 km
3. 1400°C
4. 1400°C/100 km; 14°C/km
5. approximately 25 km; at this depth, the internal temperature of Earth is approximately the same as the melting temperature for wet granite. (The two curves intersect.)
6. Basalt will reach its melting temperature at approximately 100 km in depth.

Go Further

asthenosphere; one model proposed by scientists states that because the asthenosphere is partially molten, heat from within Earth may cause convection currents to form more easily in this layer. These convection cells within the asthenosphere act like conveyor belts that allow the lithosphere to move horizontally.

Verbal, Logical

Study Guide

Study Tip

Flashcards

Making flashcards is a good way to organize new or hard-to-learn information. Encourage students to review their notes every evening and make flashcards for the material covered that day. Students can review the flashcards alone or with a study partner.

Thinking Visually

a. shield volcanoes
b. composite cones
c. divergent plate volcanism
d. intraplate volcanism
e. magma composition
f. gas content (or amount of dissolved gases)

CHAPTER 10

Study Guide

10.1 The Nature of Volcanic Eruptions

Key Concepts

- The primary factors that determine whether a volcano erupts violently or quietly include magma composition, magma temperature, and the amount of dissolved gases in the magma.
- The fragments ejected during eruptions range in size from very fine dust and volcanic ash (less than 2 millimeters) to pieces that weigh several tons.
- The three main volcanic types are shield volcanoes, cinder cones, and composite cones.
- A caldera is a large depression in a volcano.
- Most volcanoes are fed magma through conduits, called pipes, connecting a magma chamber to the surface.

Vocabulary

viscosity, *p. 281;* vent, *p. 281;* pyroclastic material, *p. 283;* volcano, *p. 283;* crater, *p. 283;* shield volcano, *p. 284;* cinder cone, *p. 284;* composite cone, *p. 285;* caldera, *p. 287*

10.2 Intrusive Igneous Activity

Key Concepts

- Intrusive igneous bodies, or plutons, are generally classified according to their shape, size and relationship to the surrounding rock layers.
- Sills and laccoliths are plutons that form when magma is intruded close to the surface.
- Many dikes form when magma from a large magma chamber invades fractures in the surrounding rocks.
- An intrusive igneous body must have a surface exposure greater than 100 square kilometers to be considered a batholith.
- Geologists conclude that magma originates when essentially solid rock, located in the crust and upper mantle, partially melts. The most obvious way to generate magma from solid rock is to raise the temperature above the level at which the rock begins to melt.

Vocabulary

pluton, *p. 289;* sill, *p. 289;* laccolith, *p. 290;* dike, *p. 290;* batholith, *p. 290;* geothermal gradient, *p. 291;* decompression melting, *p. 292*

10.3 Plate Tectonics and Igneous Activity

Key Concepts

- The basic connection between plate tectonics and volcanism is that plate motions provide the mechanisms by which mantle rocks melt to generate magma.
- Most intraplate volcanism occurs where a mass of hotter than normal mantle material called a mantle plume rises toward the surface.

Vocabulary

intraplate volcanism, *p. 295*

Thinking Visually

Web Diagram Copy the web diagram below and use information from the chapter to complete it.

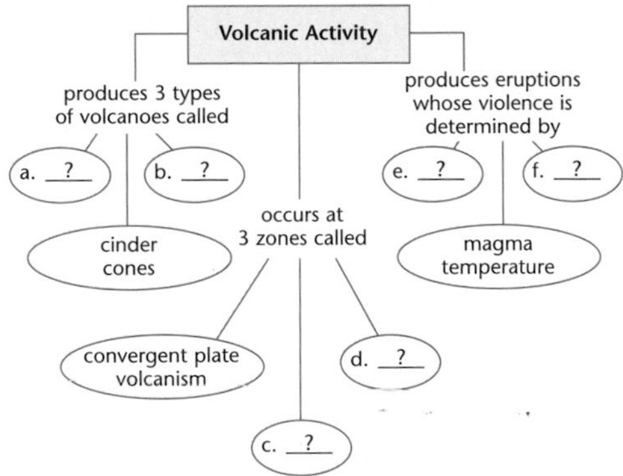

Chapter Assessment Resources

Print
Chapter Test, Chapter 10
Test Prep Resources, Chapter 10

Technology
Computer Test Bank, Chapter 10 Test
Online Text, Chapter 10
Go Online, PHSchool.com, Chapter 10

CHAPTER 10

NY Regents Content Item

Assessment

Interactive textbook with assessment at PHSchool.com 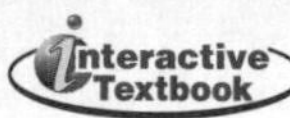

Reviewing Content

Choose the number that best answers the question or completes the statement.

1 Underground igneous rock bodies are called
(1) lava flows (2) plutons
(3) volcanoes (4) calderas

2 The greatest volume of volcanic material is produced by
(1) eruptions of cinder cones
(2) eruptions of composite cones
(3) eruptions along ocean ridges
(4) eruptions of shield volcanoes

3 The most violent type of volcanic activity is associated with
(1) cinder cones (2) sills
(3) composite cones (4) shield volcanoes

4 A magma's viscosity is directly related to its
(1) depth (2) age
(3) color (4) silica content

5 What are the pulverized rock, lava, ash, and other fragments ejected from the vent of a volcano called?
(1) sills (2) craters
(3) pahoehoes (4) pyroclastic material

6 Which type of volcano consists of layers of lava flows and pyroclastic material?
(1) composite cone (2) cinder cone
(3) shield volcano (4) laccolith

7 Fluid basaltic lavas, like those in Hawaii, commonly form
(1) aa flows (2) pahoehoe flows
(3) pyroclastic flows (4) lapilli flows

8 What is the very large depression at the top of some volcanoes called? NY
(1) a vent (2) a lava plateau
(3) a volcanic neck (4) a caldera

9 When silica-rich magma is extruded, ash, hot gases, and larger fragments may be propelled from the vent at high speeds and produce which of the following?
(1) a lava plateau (2) a lahar
(3) a pahoehoe flow (4) a pyroclastic flow

10 What feature may form in an intraplate area over a rising plume of hot mantle material?
(1) a hot spot (2) a dike
(3) a subduction zone (4) an ocean ridge

Understanding Concepts

11 What is a volcanic neck and how does it form?

12 Describe the Ring of Fire. NY

13 The Hawaiian Islands and Yellowstone National Park are associated with which of the three zones of volcanism?

14 What is the chain of volcanoes called that forms at a convergent boundary between a subducting oceanic plate and a continental plate? What type of volcano commonly forms?

15 Explain how most magma is theorized to originate. NY

Use the diagram below to answer questions 16 and 17.

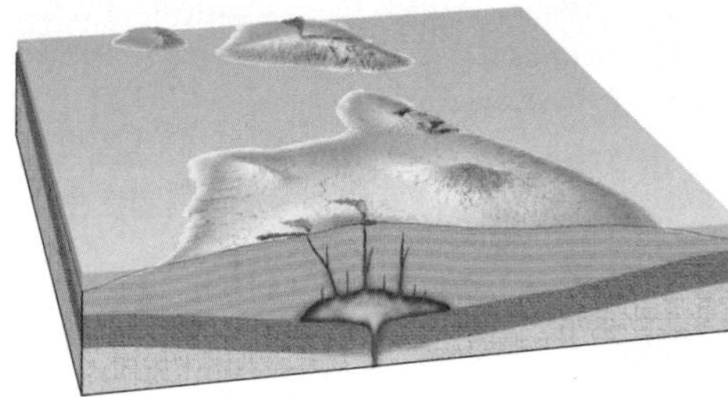

16 Identify the type of volcano shown in the diagram.

17 What types of eruptions are commonly associated with this type of volcano?

18 How do hot spots form?

19 How are pyroclastic materials classified?

20 What is viscosity and how does it affect volcanic eruptions?

21 Give an example of each of the three types of volcanoes.

22 How do dikes form?

Homework Guide

Section	Questions
1	2, 3, 5–9, 11, 16, 17, 19–23, 24–27, 30, 32–35
2	1, 4, 15, 22, 23
3	10, 12–14, 18, 25

Assessment

Reviewing Content

(1) 2 (2) 3 (3) 3
(4) 4 (5) 4 (6) 1
(7) 2 (8) 4 (9) 4
(10) 1

Understanding Concepts

(11) A volcanic neck is the rock in a volcanic pipe that is more resistant to erosion and remains standing after the surrounding volcanic cone has been eroded.
(12) It is the name for the volcanoes that are located around the margins of the Pacific basin.
(13) intraplate volcanism
(14) a continental volcanic arc; composite cone
(15) Most magma originates by the partial melting of rock in the crust and upper mantle, either when heat is added by hot, deeper mantle material intruding into the lithosphere, by a decrease in pressure as the rock rises into the crust, or by the addition of water to lower the melting point.
(16) shield volcano
(17) quiet eruptions of basaltic lava, forming mainly pahoehoe lava flows
(18) A plume of hot mantle material produced at the core-mantle boundary rises to the surface and causes volcanic activity at the surface.
(19) by size and shape
(20) Viscosity is resistance to flow of a substance. The more viscous the magma or lava, the more explosive the volcanic eruption will be.
(21) Answers will vary. Sample answer: cinder cone—small cones on the side of shield volcanoes, SP Crater in Arizona, Sunset Crater in Arizona, Parícutin; composite cones—Fujiyama, Mount St. Helens, Mount Rainier, Mount Shasta; shield volcanoes—Kilauea, Mauna Loa, Mauna Kea
(22) Dikes form when magma from a magma chamber intrudes into fractures in the surrounding rock and cuts across the preexisting rock layers.

Critical Thinking

(23) Laccoliths are intruded at shallow depths and often push up the overlying rock layers to form a lens-shaped structure. This structure may be detected before the laccolith itself is exposed by erosion.
(24) When magma moves close to the surface, the gases dissolved in the magma begin to rise and expand. The viscosity of the magma determines how easily the gases can escape. Highly viscous magma prevents the gases from escaping easily, so they can accumulate and cause a violent eruption.
(25) Pahoehoe lava flows have smooth, ropy surfaces and are formed from very fluid basaltic lava. Aa lava flows have sharp, jagged surfaces and are formed when more viscous lava cools.
(26) A lahar is a mudflow on the slopes of a volcano. Lahars can be triggered by heavy rainfall saturating the loose, weathered volcanic deposits on the steep slopes of a volcano without an eruption occurring.
(27) Cinder cones commonly erupt once for a short time. When the eruption ends, the magma in the pipe solidifies and the volcano doesn't erupt again. Because cinder cones erupt only once for a short time, they don't build large cones.

Analyzing Data

(28) Toba
(29) over 7 times greater (7.14 times)
(30) Vesuvius erupted in A.D. 79 before much was known about volcanic eruptions, while Pinatubo erupted more recently and people were warned and evacuated. Most likely more people were killed by the Vesuvius eruption because more people lived closer to Vesuvius than near Pinatubo.
(31) 44 km − 19 km = 25 km higher and 19/44 × 100 = 43.2% higher

CHAPTER 10

Assessment *continued*

Critical Thinking

23 **Applying Concepts** Why might a laccolith be detected at Earth's surface before being exposed by erosion?

24 **Inferring** Why is a volcano fed by a highly viscous magma likely to be a greater threat to people than a volcano fed by very fluid magma?

25 **Comparing and Contrasting** Compare pahoehoe lava flows and aa lava flows.

26 **Relating Cause and Effect** What is a lahar? Explain why a lahar can occur on a volcano without an eruption.

27 **Drawing Conclusions** Why are cinder cones usually small?

Analyzing Data

Use the data table below to answer questions 28–31.

Notable Volcanic Eruptions

Volcano	Date	Volume Ejected	Height of Plume
Toba	74,000 years ago	2800 km^3	50–80 km
Vesuvius	A.D. 79	4 km^3	32 km
Tambora	1815	150 km^3	44 km
Krakatau	1883	21 km^3	36 km
Mount St. Helens	1980	1 km^3	19 km
Mount Pinatubo	1991	5 km^3	35 km

28 **Interpreting Data** What volcanic eruption listed in the data table produced the most pyroclastic material? NY

29 **Calculating** The volume of material ejected by the eruption of Tambora in 1815 was how many times larger than the volume of material ejected in 1883 by the eruption of Krakatau?

30 **Forming Hypotheses** Develop a hypothesis to explain why the eruption of Mount Vesuvius in A.D. 79 was more deadly than the eruption of Mount Pinatubo in 1991, even though the eruptions were approximately the same size.

31 **Calculating** Calculate how much higher the plume of volcanic debris was during the eruption of Tambora in 1815 compared to the plume from the 1980 eruption of Mount St. Helens. Calculate the increase in kilometers and in percentage of increase.

Concepts in Action

32 **Hypothesizing** Large volcanic eruptions eject large amounts of gas, dust, and ash into the atmosphere. This volcanic material can affect the world's climate by blocking incoming solar radiation. An eruption from what type of volcano is most likely to cause global climate changes? Explain your answer.

33 **Classifying** On the side of a composite cone you see a large area where there are no trees and the ground surface looks disturbed. What possible volcanic feature or event could have caused this?

34 **Applying Concepts** Would you be safer from a violent, explosive eruption while vacationing in Arizona near a cinder cone or while skiing in the Andes Mountains of South America? Explain.

35 **Writing in Science** Write a paragraph describing what an eruption of a nearby composite cone might be like.

Performance-Based Assessment

Making a Poster Make a poster illustrating the internal and external features that are typical of a composite cone. Include on your poster copies of photographs of some classic composite cones. Also explain some of the possible dangers associated with living near a composite cone.

Concepts in Action

(32) An eruption of a composite cone is more likely to affect global climate because these volcanoes have the most explosive eruptions due to the amount of gases and high viscosity of their magmas.
(33) either a recent lava flow or a lahar (mudflow)
(34) You would probably be safer near a cinder cone in Arizona. Composite cones in the Andes Mountains erupt more violently, and the snow could melt to form a lahar.
(35) Answers will vary, but should be scientifically accurate as to the types of pyroclastic material ejected, and other possible features associated with eruptions of composite cones.

Regents Practice Exam

Test-Taking Tip

Paying Attention to the Details
Sometimes two or more answers to a question may seem correct. If you do not read the question and answer choices carefully, you may select an incorrect answer by mistake. In the question below, two answer choices, (1) dissolved gases and (2) gravity, would seem to be possible correct answers to the question. However, the question asks what force extrudes magma from the vent, not down the slopes of the volcano. So only the answer choice, (1) dissolved gases, is correct.

What is the force that extrudes magma from a volcanic vent?
(1) dissolved gases
(2) gravity
(3) the magma's heat
(4) the volcano's slope

(Answer: 1)

For *each* statement or question, choose the *number* of the word or expression that, of those given, best completes the statement or answers the question. Some questions may require the use of the *Earth Science Reference Tables.*

1 Which of the following creates magma?
(1) plate movements (2) gravity
(3) solar energy (4) meteorite impacts

2 Which statement about the Hawaiian Islands is true?
(1) They are an island arc formed as a result of subduction.
(2) They were created by a divergent plate boundary.
(3) They were created by a hot spot.
(4) They are all the same age.

Answer the following questions in complete sentences. Some questions may require the use of the *Earth Science Reference Tables.* Base your answers to questions 3 and 4 on the diagram at top right, which shows Basic Intrusive Igneous Structures.

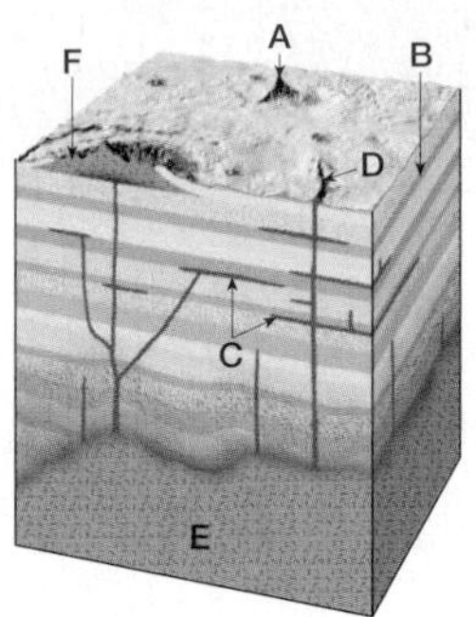

3 What intrusive igneous feature in the diagram is labeled C?
(1) a dike (2) a sill
(3) a batholith (4) a laccolith

4 Which is NOT shown in the diagram?
(1) a fault (2) layers of sediment
(3) a dike (4) a volcano

5 Where are most volcanoes found? Why?

6 Describe one benefit of volcanoes and one danger volcanoes pose.

7 Most volcanic eruptions occur at tectonic plate boundaries, but some occur within a tectonic plate, far from plate boundaries.

Part A Explain how volcanoes form at plate boundaries.

Part B Explain how volcanoes form in the middle of a plate.

Regents Practice Exam

(1) 1
(2) 3
(3) 2
(4) 1

Constructed Response

(5) Most volcanoes are found at plate boundaries because that is where most magma is produced.
(6) Benefits: The soil left behind when volcanic features weather, is very fertile. Hot magma near the surface can be used for geothermal energy, and early volcanic eruptions helped create Earth's atmosphere.
Dangers: Volcanoes release very hot molten rock, which can start fires, and create ash, which can bury crops, collapse buildings, and emit poisonous gases that can suffocate people. Volcanic eruptions can also trigger mudflows called lahars. Broken rock, lava bombs, dust, and other hazardous pyroclastic materials can also be released by volcanoes.
(7) **Part A** At convergent plate boundaries, the subducting plate melts, creating magma which rises to the surface and forms volcanoes. At divergent plate boundaries, partially melted mantle rock rises to the surface and melts further due to pressure decreases.
Part B When a mass of hotter than normal mantle material rises to the surface near the middle of a plate, a volcano can form.

Performance-Based Assessment

Posters should be scientifically accurate, neatly labeled, and clearly explain the potential dangers, such as pyroclastic flows and lahars.

Your students can independently test their knowledge of the chapter and print out their results.

CHAPTER 11

Planning Guide

Use these planning tools
Use Teacher Express for all your planning needs

SECTION OBJECTIVES	STANDARDS NATIONAL	STANDARDS STATE	ACTIVITIES and LABS
11.1 Rock Deformation, pp. 308–313 1 1/2 blocks or 3 periods **11.1** **Identify** the factors that determine the strength of a rock and how it will deform. **11.2** **Explain** how rocks permanently deform. **11.3** **Distinguish** among the types of stresses that affect rocks. **11.4** **List** the three main types of folds and **identify** the main types of faults.	A-1, A-2, D-3		**SE** Inquiry Activity: Can You Model How Rocks Deform? p. 307 L2 **TE** Build Science Skills, p. 309 L2 **TE** Teacher Demo: Making an Anticline, p. 310 L2 **TE** Build Science Skills, p. 311 L2 **SE** Exploration Lab: Investigating Anticlines and Synclines, pp. 326–327 L2
11.2 Types of Mountains, pp. 314–316 1/2 block or 1 period **11.5** **Explain** how mountains are classified. **11.6** **Explain** the difference between folded mountains and fault-block mountains. **11.7** **Describe** the formation of a dome.	D-3		**TE** Build Science Skills, p. 315 L2
11.3 Mountain Formation, pp. 317–324 1 1/2 blocks or 3 periods **11.8** **Identify** the type of mountains associated with convergent plate boundaries. **11.9** **Distinguish** between mountains formed by ocean-ocean convergence and mountains formed by ocean-continental convergence. **11.10** **Identify** the type of mountains associated with divergent plate boundaries. **11.11** **Explain** how isostatic adjustment is involved in mountain formation.	A-1, A-2, D-3, G-2, G-3		**SE** Problem-Solving Activity: Rates of Mountain Building, p. 319 L2 **TE** Teacher Demo: Partial Melting, p. 318 L2 **TE** Teacher Demo: Modeling Isostasy, p. 323 L2 **LM** Interpreting a Geologic Map L1

Ability Levels

- **L1** For students who need additional help
- **L2** For all students
- **L3** For students who need to be challenged

Components

SE	Student Edition	**GRSW**	Guided Reading & Study Workbook	**TP**	Test Prep Resources	**GEO**	Geode CD-ROM
TE	Teacher's Edition	**TEX**	Teacher Express	**onT**	onlineText	**T**	Transparencies
LM	Laboratory Manual	**CTB**	Computer Test Bank	**DC**	Discovery Channel Videos	**GO**	Internet Resources
CUT	Chapter Tests						

RESOURCES PRINT and TECHNOLOGY	SECTION ASSESSMENT
GRSW Section 11.1 **T-133** Principal Types of Folded Strata **T-134** Plunging Folds **T-135** Black Hills of South Dakota **T-136** Michigan Basin **T-137** Four Types of Faults **GEODe** Forces Within ↳ Igneous Activity **TEX** Lesson Planning 11.1	**SE** Section 11.1 Assessment, p. 313 **onT** Section 11.1
GRSW Section 11.2 **T-138** Downfaulted Block (Graben) and Upfaulted Block (Horst) **T-379** Major Physiographic Provinces of the U.S. **T-380** Shaded Relief Landform Map of U.S. **DC** Earthquake Zone **TEX** Lesson Planning 11.2	**SE** Section 11.2 Assessment, p. 316 **onT** Section 11.2
GRSW Section 11.3 **T-139** Development of a Mature Volcanic Island Arc **T-140** Mountain Building Along an Andean-Type Subduction Zone **T-141** Major Mountainous Landforms of the Western U.S. **T-142** Oceanic Plateaus and Submerged Crustal Fragments **T-143** Collision of Volcanic Island Arc and Andean-Type Plate Margin **T-144** Accreted Terranes **T-145** Wooden Blocks Illustrate Isostasy **T-146** Effect of Erosion and Isostatic Adjustment **T-147** Temperatures and Precipitation for Seattle and Spokane **T-148** San Andreas Fault System **T-149** Proposal for the Formation of the Basin and Range Province **TEX** Lesson Planning 11.3	**SE** Section 11.3 Assessment, p. 324 **onT** Section 11.3

Go Online

Go online for these Internet resources.

PHSchool.com
Web Code: cjk-9999

Web Code: cjn-3113

Materials for Activities and Labs

Quantities for each group

STUDENT EDITION

Inquiry Activity, p. 307
large, thick rubber band; plastic putty; straight, thin wooden stick about 25 cm long

Exploration Lab, pp. 326–327
pencil, protractor, tracing paper

TEACHER'S EDITION

Build Science Skills, p. 309
marshmallow or piece of foam rubber

Teacher Demo, p. 310
stack of construction paper sheets in several colors

Build Science Skills, p. 311
2 wooden blocks, small towel or piece of fabric

Build Science Skills, p. 315
3 wooden blocks

Teacher Demo, p. 318
can of frozen grape juice concentrate (inexpensive brands work best), can opener, plastic tub, rubber gloves, apron, water, plastic pitcher, paper towels for clean-up

Teacher Demo, p. 323
large plastic container, water, balance, metric ruler, several blocks of varying sizes and kinds of wood

Chapter Assessment

ASSESSMENT

SE Assessment, pp. 329–330
CUT Chapter 11 Test
CTB Chapter 11
onT Chapter 11

STANDARDIZED TEST PREP

SE Chapter 11, p. 331
TP Progress Monitoring Assessments

interactive textbook with assessment at PHSchool.com

CHAPTER 11

Before you teach

Michael Wysession
Washington University

Big Ideas

Mountains provide evidence of enormous tectonic forces within Earth, which are usually associated with the boundaries between lithospheric plates.

Space and Time Mountains primarily form by folding and faulting rock at compressional plate boundaries, by faulting rock at tensional plate boundaries, by uplifting the lithosphere, and through volcanism.

Forces and Motion Rock deforms in an elastic, brittle, or ductile manner, depending upon the type and amount of stress, the applied temperature and pressure, the type of rock, and the amount of time it is stressed. Stress can be tensional, compressional, or shear. Folds, such as anticlines and synclines, occur when rock strains in a ductile manner. Faults, in the form of normal, reverse, and strike-slip, occur when rock deforms in a brittle manner.

Matter and Energy The world's longest mountain chain is of volcanoes along the interconnected divergent plate boundaries of the mid-ocean ridges. At ocean-ocean convergent plate boundaries, volcanic mountains form an island arc. At an ocean-continent convergent boundary, mountains form from composite volcanoes and accreted sediments. At continent-continent boundaries, mountains form from folded continental crust and the accretion of sediments, island arcs, continental fragments, and slivers of ocean crust.

Earth as a System Because of isostasy, mountains have deep crustal roots, and buoy upward when the tops are eroded. Continents like North America have grown in size through the accretion of land at their edges during plate collisions.

Earth Science Refresher

How do Continents Grow?

There is currently a debate within geology as to how continents grow over time. One point of view is that continents began as small fragments of continental crust, and have grown to their current size over time as a result of major plate collisions. Continents now cover about 39 percent of Earth's surface (including the continental shelves that are under water). North America would seem to fit this model well. Our continent contains pieces of crust that are about 4 billion years old. Called cratons, or shields, or platforms, these pieces of old crust located in Canada seem to have been sutured together by younger rock when they collided about 2 billion years ago. As you go from Canada to Florida, however, you pass across terranes of successively younger ages that were added onto North America when it collided with other continents and island arcs. The rock of Missouri is about 1.7 billion years old, but the rock of Florida is only a few hundred million years old.

However, another point of view is that there has always been about the same amount of continental crust, but it has continually been altered and reworked, so there is very little in its original form. Continental crust is continually changing. Continents can grow by accretion of added terranes. They also grow by volcanism and platform deposition. Most volcanoes add rock to the edges of continents, but some add to the middle.

Address Misconceptions

Students may have the common misconception that southern California is going to slide into the Pacific Ocean due to movement of the San Andreas Fault. Explain that the San Andreas Fault is a strike-slip fault that runs northwest. The Pacific Ocean is due west. Movement of the crust is north and not west toward the ocean. For a strategy that helps to overcome this misconception, see **Address Misconceptions** on **p. 313.**

Go Online PD LINKS

For: Chapter 11 Content Support
Visit: www.SciLinks.org/PDLinks
Web Code: cjn-1199

Address Misconceptions

Students may have the misconception that mountain-building processes are no longer taking place on Earth. Using Mount Everest as an example, students will learn that recent data show that the Indian and Eurasian plates are still pushing against each other and causing movement. For a strategy that helps to overcome this misconception, see **Address Misconceptions** on **p. 319.**

Platform deposition is the addition of sedimentary rocks like limestone, shale, and sandstone, to the surface of continents when they are flooded by oceans.

At the same time, however, continents shrink by lateral accretion and erosion. Lateral accretion is the horizontal shortening of continents that occurs during plate collisions. The rock gets narrower but taller, as mountains form. Mountains erode quickly, however, so rock gets removed from continents quickly this way. The Appalachian Mountains used to be about 10 km taller than they are now. Much of that rock is now on the ocean seafloor.

This continental rock, in the form of ocean sediments, gets returned to continents, however. When the ocean seafloor subducts beneath a continent, much of the sediment get scraped off and added to the edge of the continent in the form of an accretionary wedge. And much of the sediment that does get subducted likely comes back up to the surface with the water-rich magma that erupts as volcanoes like Mt. St. Helens. This is the essence of part of the rock cycle. So it is possible that most of the continental rock has been around for 4 billion years, but has traveled through the rock cycle enough times that only a few pieces, like the Canadian cratons, are still in their original form.

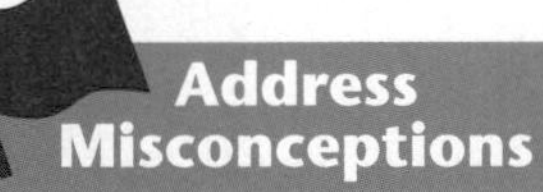

Address Misconceptions

Students may confuse the words terrane *and* terrain. Using a dictionary will help students distinguish between the two words. For a strategy that helps to overcome this misconception, see **Address Misconceptions** on **p. 322.**

Build Reading Literacy

KWL (Know-Want to Know-Learned)

What I Know/Want to Know/Learned

Strategy To help students access prior knowledge, set a purpose for reading, recall what has been read, and link new information to prior knowledge. The KWL strategy has students create and complete a three-column chart similar to the one below. As students read, they complete the Learned.

Know	Want to Know	Learned

Finally, students categorize information they learned in a box titled Information I Expect to Use.

Information I Expect to Use

Assign a section in Chapter 11, such as Folds, pp. 310–313, for students to read. Before they begin, have them create and complete the first two columns of the KWL chart.

Example

1. Draw a three-column KWL chart on the board for students to copy.
2. Have students complete the Know column with facts, examples, and other information they already know about the topic.
3. Tell students to complete the Want to Know column with questions about the topic that they want answers to. Students may scan the section to help them generate questions.
4. Have students read the section to learn more about the topic and determine answers to their questions. As they read, have them note answers in the Learned column, along with other facts, examples, and details they learned.
5. Below their KWL chart, have students draw an Information I Expect to Use box. Have them review the information in the Learned column and use it to complete the box with the useful categories of information.

See p. 309 for a script on how to use this strategy with students. For additional strategies, see pp. 312, 314, and 321.

ASSESS PRIOR KNOWLEDGE

Use the Chapter Pretest below to assess students' prior knowledge. As needed, review these concepts.

Review Science Concepts

Section 11.1 Review the structure of different types of rock and minerals to help students understand why different rock types deform in predictable ways. A review of faults and the movements that take place along faults will be necessary for students to learn how stress is involved in deformation.

Section 11.2 The material on mountain types in this section follows directly from the discussion of rock deformation in Section 11.1. Be sure students have mastered the concepts involved in rock folding and faulting in Section 11.1 before beginning Section 11.2.

Section 11.3 Review the theory of plate tectonics and the actions at plate boundaries to give students a starting point for understanding how mountains are formed at different boundaries.

CHAPTER

11 Mountain Building

CONCEPTS in Action

Exploration Lab
Investigating Anticlines and Synclines

Understanding Earth
Mountain Building away from Plate Margins

People and the Environment
The San Andreas Fault System

Problem Solving
Rates of Mountain Building

Forces Within
↳ Igneous Activity

Discovery CHANNEL SCHOOL **Video Field Trip**
Earthquake Zone

Take a field trip to the Himalayas with Discovery Channel and learn about the excitement and danger that surround the world's most dramatic mountain range. Answer the following questions after watching the video.

1. How were the Himalayas formed?
2. Why is the convergence of tectonic plates surrounding the Himalayas so dangerous?

For: Chapter 11 Resources
Visit: PHSchool.com
Web Code: cjk-9999

Mount Moran (on right) in Wyoming's Grand Teton National Park ▶

Chapter Pretest

1. Explain why granite is likely to fracture rather than bend when subjected to stress. *(Granite is composed of minerals that are held together by strong internal forces. When granite is subjected to stress, the mineral particles hold together until the external forces exceed the strength of the internal forces. Then the granite fractures.)*

2. What plate is subducted in an ocean-continental convergent boundary? *(The oceanic plate is subducted.)*

3. Which rock is formed when shale is subjected to stress? *(c)*
   a. granite b. sandstone c. slate

4. True or False: Most earthquakes occur along faults in Earth's crust and mantle. *(True)*

5. Which of the following is a result of ocean-continental convergence? *(b)*
   a. Volcanoes form on the ocean floor.
   b. Volcanoes form on a continent.
   c. A narrow linear sea forms.

6. When is a rift valley formed? *(It forms when two continental plates diverge.)*

7. Why does the oceanic plate sink during ocean-continental convergence? *(The oceanic plate is more dense than the continental plate, so it sinks.)*

Chapter Preview

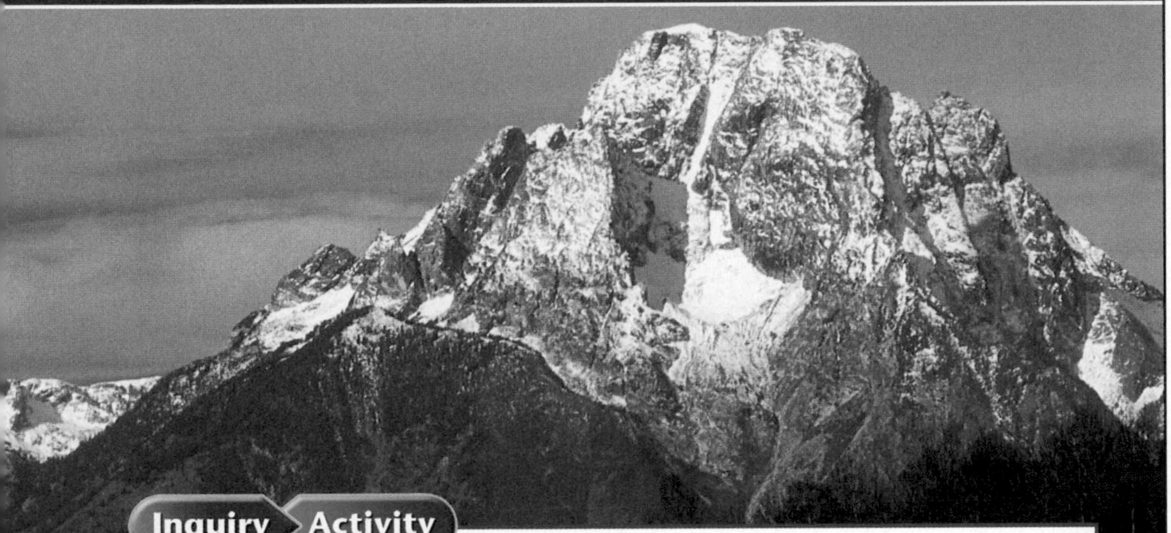

Inquiry Activity

Can You Model How Rocks Deform?

Procedure

1. Take a large, thick rubber band and stretch it out a few centimeters. Then let it relax. **CAUTION:** *Be sure to hold on to both ends of the rubber band so it does not snap your fingers. Record your observations.*
2. Take a chunk of plastic putty. Pull on the ends of the piece of putty rapidly. Record your observations.
3. Now take the chunk of plastic putty, and work it gently until it is warm and flexible. Slowly stretch it. Record your observations.
4. Take a straight, thin wooden stick about 25 centimeters long, and gently bend the ends of the stick until it breaks. **CAUTION:** *Be sure to wear safety goggles when bending the stick.* Record your observations.

Think About It

1. **Observing** Describe how the rubber band, plastic putty, and wooden stick behaved when you deformed them.
2. **Observing** Which item or items returned to the original shape and size after the force was removed?
3. **Drawing Conclusions** Which item was the easiest to deform? The hardest to deform?
4. **Inferring** Under what conditions do you think rocks are easier to bend? Under what conditions to you think rocks will break?

Video Field Trip

Earthquake Zone

Encourage students to view the Video Field Trip "Earthquake Zone."

ENGAGE/EXPLORE

Can You Model How Rocks Deform?

Purpose In this activity, students model the various ways rocks can deform.

Skills Focus Observing, Inferring, Drawing Conclusions

Prep Time 10 minutes

Materials large, thick rubber band; plastic putty; straight, thin wooden stick about 25 cm long

Advance Prep Purchase plastic putty. Gather sticks.

Class Time 10 minutes

Teaching Tips Use a thin, relatively flexible stick that is not too thick or dry and that will bend quite a bit before it breaks. Twigs from bushes work well.

Expected Outcome The rubber band stretches when pulled and then returns to the same size and shape when released. The cool putty stretches somewhat and then breaks into two pieces when stretched rapidly. The warm putty pulls into a long, thin strip when stretched, before pulling apart. The stick bends quite a bit before breaking.

Think About It

1. The rubber band stretched when pulled, then returned to the same size and shape when released. The cooler piece of plastic putty stretched a small amount, and then broke into two pieces when stretched rapidly. The warmer piece of putty slowly pulled into a long, thin strip before pulling apart. The stick bent quite a bit before breaking.
2. Only the rubber band returned to its original size and shape.
3. The warm plastic putty was the easiest to deform, and the stick was the hardest to deform.
4. Rocks probably will bend more easily when they are warmer and are deformed slowly. Rocks will probably break when they are cool and deform rapidly.

1 FOCUS

Section Objectives

11.1 **Identify** the factors that determine the strength of a rock and how it will deform.
11.2 **Explain** how rocks permanently deform.
11.3 **Distinguish** among the types of stresses that affect rocks.
11.4 **List** the three main types of folds and **identify** the main types of faults.

Reading Focus

Build Vocabulary L2

Word Parts The terms *anticline* and *syncline* have the same Greek root word, *klinein*, meaning "to lean." *Anti-* means "opposite" or "against." In an anticline, the layers bend downward in opposite directions from the crest. *Syn-* is a Greek prefix meaning "together with," so a syncline has layers that dip toward each other.

Reading Strategy L2

a. hanging wall block moves down relative to footwall block; high angle fault
b. Reverse fault
c. hanging wall block moves up relative to footwall block; high angle fault
d. Thrust fault
e. hanging wall block moves up and over the footwall block; low angle fault
f. Strike-slip fault
g. movement is horizontal and parallel to the trend of the fault surface; usually consists of a zone of roughly parallel fractures

2 INSTRUCT

Factors Affecting Deformation

Integrate Physics L2

Force Remind students that force is defined as a push or pull exerted on an object. A force has magnitude; for example, you can push hard or gently on an object. Force also has direction; you can push on an object to the left, to the right, up, or down.
Logical

11.1 Rock Deformation

Reading Focus

Key Concepts

- What determines the strength of a rock?
- What are the types of stresses that affect rocks?
- What are the three main types of folds?
- What are the main types of faults?

Vocabulary

- deformation
- stress
- strain
- anticline
- syncline
- monocline
- normal fault
- reverse fault
- thrust fault
- strike-slip fault

Reading Strategy

Comparing and Contrasting After you read the section, compare types of faults by completing the table below.

Types of Fault	Description
Normal fault	a. ?
b. ?	c. ?
d. ?	e. ?
f. ?	g. ?

Mountains, like those shown in Figure 1, provide some of the most spectacular scenery on our planet. It is theorized that all continents were once mountainous masses and grow by the addition of mountains to their edges. As geologists unravel the secrets of mountain formation, they also gain a deeper understanding of the evolution of Earth's continents. However, if continents do grow by adding mountains to their edges, then how do mountains exist in the interior of continents?

Figure 1 Mountain Ranges This peak is part of the Karakoram Range in Pakistan.

Factors Affecting Deformation

Every body of rock, no matter how strong, has a point at which it will bend or break. **Deformation** is a general term that refers to all changes in the original shape and/or size of a rock body. Most crustal deformation occurs along plate margins. Plate motions and interactions at plate boundaries create forces that cause rock to deform.

Stress is the force per unit area acting on a solid. When rocks are under stresses greater than their own strength, they begin to deform, usually by folding, flowing, or fracturing. The change in shape or volume of a body of rock as a result of stress is called **strain.** How can rock masses be bent into folds without being broken? When stress is gradually applied, rocks first respond by deforming elastically. Changes that result from elastic deformation are recoverable. Like a rubber band, the rock will return to almost its original size and shape once the force is removed. Once the elastic limit or strength of a rock is surpassed, it either flows or fractures. **The factors that influence the strength of a rock and how it will deform include temperature, confining pressure, rock type, and time.**

Temperature and Pressure **Rocks deform permanently in two ways: brittle deformation and ductile deformation.** Rocks near the surface, where temperatures and confining pressures are low, usually behave like brittle solids and fracture once their strength is exceeded. This type of deformation is called brittle failure or brittle deformation. You know that glass objects, wooden pencils, china plates, and even our bones show brittle failure once their strength is exceeded.

At depth, where temperatures and confining pressures are high, rocks show ductile behavior. Ductile deformation is a type of solid-state flow that produces a change in the size and shape of an object without fracturing the object. Objects that display ductile behavior include modeling clay, bee's wax, caramel candy, and most metals. For example, a copper penny placed on a railroad track will be flattened and deformed without breaking by the force applied by a passing train. Ductile deformation of a rock that is strongly aided by high temperature and high confining pressure is somewhat similar to the deformation of a penny flattened by a train.

Rock Type The mineral composition and texture of a rock also greatly affect how it will deform. Rocks like granite and basalt that are composed of minerals with strong internal molecular bonds usually fail by brittle fracture. Sedimentary rocks that are weakly cemented or metamorphic rocks that contain zones of weakness—such as foliation—are more likely to deform by ductile flow. Rocks that are weak and most likely behave in a ductile manner when under force include rock salt, gypsum, and shale. Limestone, schist, and marble are of intermediate strength and may also behave in a ductile manner.

Time In nature small stresses applied over long time spans play an important role in the deformation of rock. You can see the effects of time on deformation in everyday settings. For example, marble benches have been known to sag under their own weight over a span of a hundred years or so. **Forces that are unable to deform rock when first applied may cause rock to flow if the force is maintained over a long period of time.**

What is brittle deformation?

Types of Stress

Rocks are exposed to many different forces due to plate motions. **The three types of stresses that rocks commonly undergo are tensional stress, compressional stress, and shear stress.** Look at Figure 2. When rocks are squeezed or shortened the stress is compressional. Tensional stress is caused by rocks being pulled in opposite directions. Shear stress causes a body of rock to be distorted.

Figure 2 Undeformed material is changed as it undergoes different types of stress. The arrows show the direction of maximum stress. **A** Compressional stress causes a material to shorten. **B** Tensional stress causes a material to be stretched or to undergo extension. **C** Shear stress causes a material to be distorted with no change in volume.

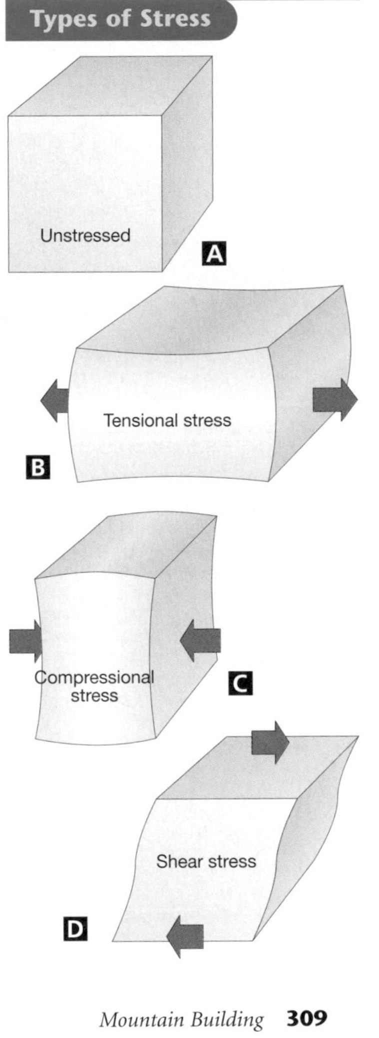

Build Reading Literacy L1

Refer to **p. 306D**, which provides the guidelines for KWL (Know-Want to Know-Learned).

KWL Have students make a KWL chart containing three columns entitled "What I Know," "What I Want to Know," and "What I Learned." Before reading this section, have students fill in the first column with what they know about the factors affecting deformation of rocks. They should have prior knowledge about rocks from Chapters 2 and 3. The second column should be filled out as students read pp. 308 and 309. Finally, students should fill in the third column after they have finished reading this section. The material in this column can take the form of an outline of the material under the head Factors Affecting Deformation.
Verbal, Logical

Types of Stress

Use Visuals L1

Figure 2 Have students examine the diagrams. Ask: **What happens to the shape of a rock that undergoes compressional stress?** *(It shortens.)* **What happens to the shape of a rock that undergoes tensional stress?** *(It stretches or extends.)* **What happens to the shape of a rock that undergoes shear stress?** *(The rock becomes distorted.)*
Visual

Build Science Skills L2

Using Models ACTIVITY Have students model the three kinds of stress by pulling or pushing on a marshmallow or piece of foam rubber. The material can be cut in half to model shear stress. Students will be able to observe how shape changes with tensional and compressional stress and how the shape becomes distorted with shear stress.
Visual, Kinesthetic

Customize for Inclusion Students

Visually Impaired Many of the concepts in this section can be modeled for visually impaired students. Faults can be represented by using blocks of wood. Folds can be modeled using construction paper or sheets of flexible foam rubber. Types of stress can be modeled using marshmallows or foam rubber, as in the Build Science Skills activity on this page. Rock deformation can be illustrated by using a stick of chewing gum. When a stick of gum is cold, an applied stress causes it to crack and break. When the gum is warm, it will bend easily.

Answer to . . .

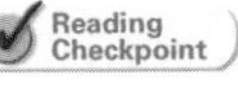

Brittle deformation is deformation where the strength of a material is exceeded, and the material breaks or fractures.

Folds

Use Visuals

L1

Figure 3 Have students examine the diagram of the types of folds. Ask: **Where would you expect to find the oldest rock layer in an anticline?** *(in the center of the fold)* **Where would you expect to find the oldest rock layer in a syncline?** *(on the outside of the fold)* **How would you describe a symmetrical fold?** *(a fold in which the two sides are mirror images)* **How would you describe an overturned fold?** *(a fold in which one limb is tilted beyond the vertical)*
Visual, Logical

Making an Anticline

L2

Purpose Students observe how an anticline is produced.

Materials stack of construction paper sheets in several colors

Procedure Make a stack containing several sheets of colored construction paper. Each colored sheet will represent a rock layer. Lay the stack on a table. Place your two hands on the stack, one at each end of the stack. Press down on the paper with your hands and slowly push them together.

Expected Outcomes The entire stack of paper will form an anticline. Rock layers will be visible when viewed from the side.
Kinesthetic, Visual

Address Misconceptions

L2

Students may have trouble remembering the direction in which an anticline and a syncline fold. The terms were named according to the direction of the limbs in relation to the axis of the fold. Remind students that *anti-* means "opposite" or "against." In an anticline, the layers bend downward in opposite directions from the crest. The prefix *syn-* means "together with," so a syncline has layers that dip toward each other. Students can remember the direction of these folds if they think of an ant climbing up a hill. The word *anticline* contains the word *ant*.

Folds

During mountain building, flat-lying sedimentary and volcanic rocks are often bent into a series of wavelike ripples called folds. Folds in sedimentary strata are much like those that would form if you were to hold the ends of a sheet of paper and then push them together. In nature, folds come in a wide variety of sizes and shapes. **The three main types of folds are anticlines, synclines, and monoclines.**

Anticlines The two most common types of folds are anticlines and synclines. An **anticline** is most commonly formed by the upfolding, or arching, of rock layers, as shown in Figure 3.

Synclines Often found in association with anticlines are downfolds, or troughs, called **synclines.** Notice in Figure 3 that the limb of an anticline is also a limb of the adjacent syncline. Folds do not continue forever. Instead their ends die out much like the wrinkles in cloth.

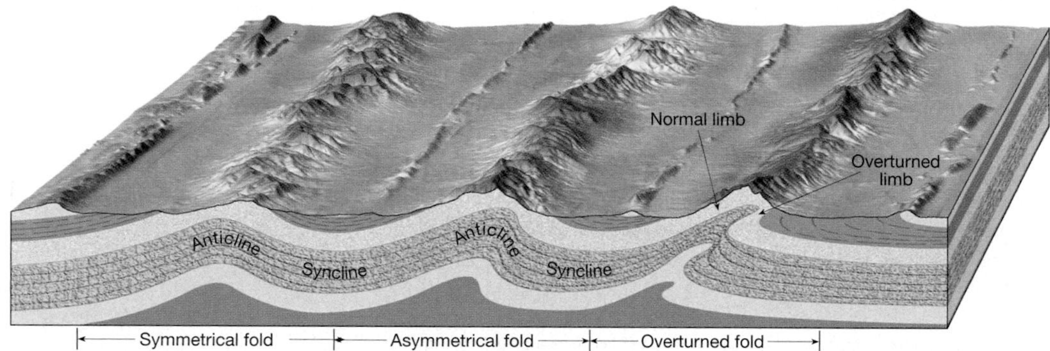

Figure 3 Anticlines and Synclines The upfolded or arched structures are anticlines. The downfolds or troughs are synclines. Notice that the limb of an anticline is also the limb of the adjacent syncline.

Monoclines Although we will discuss folds and faults separately, in the real world folds are generally closely associated with faults. Examples of this close association are broad, regional features called monoclines. **Monoclines** are large, step-like folds in otherwise horizontal sedimentary strata. Monoclines seem to occur as sedimentary layers have been folded over a large faulted block of underlying rock. Monoclines are prominent features of the Colorado Plateau area in Colorado, New Mexico, Utah, and Arizona, as shown in Figure 4 on the next page.

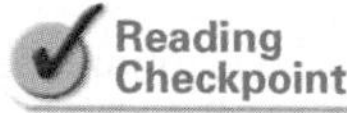

What is a syncline?

310 *Chapter 11*

Facts and Figures

The Colorado Plateau is a high, sparsely vegetated region of deep canyons, mesas, and plateaus. It encompasses almost 363,000 sq km at the four corners—the area where Utah, Colorado, Arizona, and New Mexico come together. The Colorado Plateau includes the Colorado River and its tributaries. The high Sierra Nevada mountain range located to the west of the Plateau prevents moisture-laden air masses from reaching the region. This rain shadow effect causes the region to be very dry; the average precipitation is about 25 cm per year. Because plant cover is so sparse, the area has been eroded by fast-moving streams, which has exposed the bare rocks that contribute to the area's beauty.

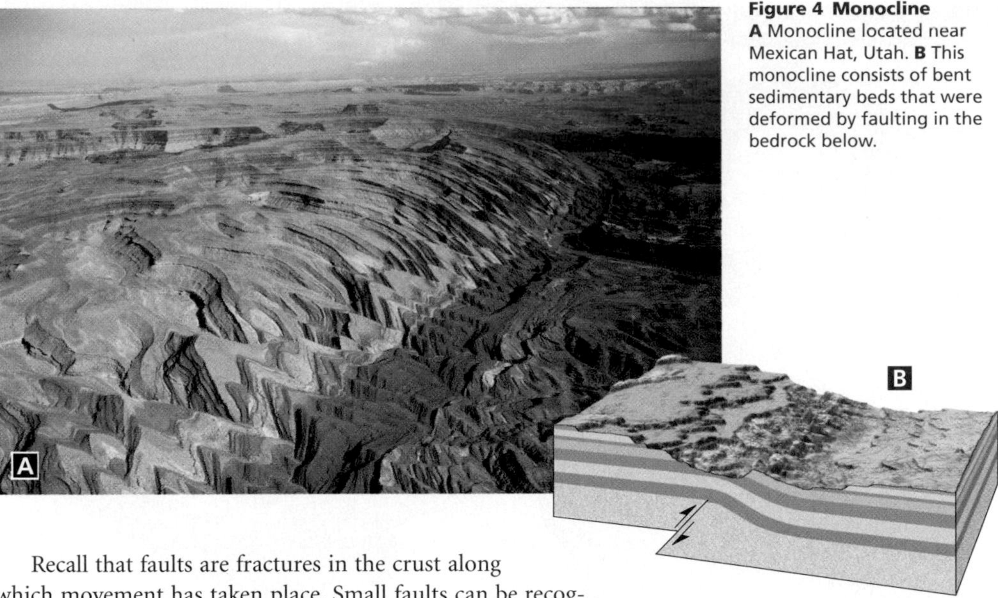

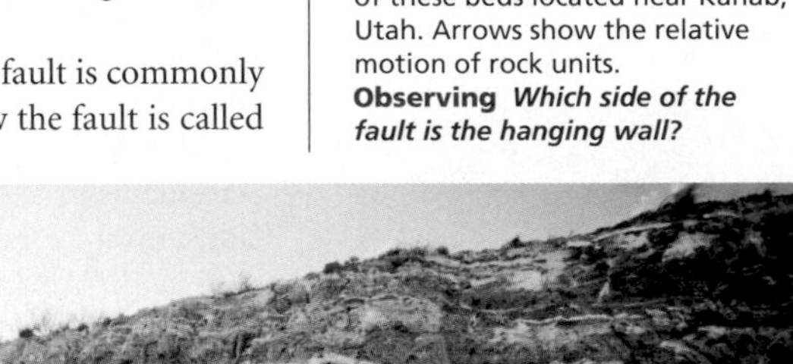

Figure 4 Monocline
A Monocline located near Mexican Hat, Utah. **B** This monocline consists of bent sedimentary beds that were deformed by faulting in the bedrock below.

Recall that faults are fractures in the crust along which movement has taken place. Small faults can be recognized in road cuts where sedimentary beds have been offset a few meters, as shown in Figure 5. Faults of this size usually occur as single breaks. By contrast, large faults, like the San Andreas fault in California, have displacements of hundreds of kilometers and consist of many interconnecting fault surfaces. These fault zones can be many kilometers wide and are often easier to identify from high-altitude photographs than at ground level.

The rock surface that is immediately above the fault is commonly called the hanging wall, and the rock surface below the fault is called the footwall. **The major types of faults are normal faults, reverse faults, thrust faults, and strike-slip faults.**

Normal Faults A **normal fault** occurs when the hanging wall block moves down relative to the footwall block. Most normal faults have steep dips of about 60°, as shown in Figure 6A on the next page. These dips often flatten out with depth. The movement in normal faults is mainly in a vertical direction, with some horizontal movement. Because of the downward motion of the hanging wall block, normal faults result in the lengthening, or extension, of the crust.

Figure 5 Normal Fault Faulting caused the vertical displacement of these beds located near Kanab, Utah. Arrows show the relative motion of rock units.
Observing *Which side of the fault is the hanging wall?*

Build Science Skills L2

Using Models Have students model the formation of a monocline by holding two wooden blocks together so the "fault" between them runs at 60° angle. Have another student carefully drape the towel or fabric over the wooden blocks. The student holding the blocks should slide them along the "fault" until the towel forms a fold. Ask: **What does the towel represent?** *(sedimentary rock layers)* **What do the wooden blocks represent?** *(rock blocks)*
Kinesthetic, Logical

Use Visuals L1

Figure 5 Have students examine the photograph of a normal fault. Ask: **Which side of the fault is the footwall?** *(the right side)* **How can you tell which side is the footwall?** *(A normal fault occurs when the hanging wall block moves down relative to the footwall. In the picture, the right side is higher than the left side, so it must be the footwall.)* **Can you tell from the photo which side of the fault has moved?** *(No, there is no way to tell. The two sides of the fault have moved relative to each other but it is impossible to know whether one side has moved up or the other side has moved down.)*
Visual, Logical

Facts and Figures

The terms *hanging wall* and *footwall* were coined by prospectors and miners who excavated shafts and tunnels along fault zones because these are frequent sites of ore deposits. In these tunnels, the miners would walk on the rocks below the mineralized fault zone (the footwall) and hang their lanterns on the rocks above (the hanging wall).

Answer to . . .

Figure 5 *The hanging wall is on the left side.*

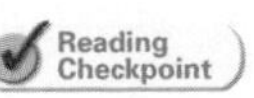 *A syncline is a down fold or trough.*

Use Visuals L1

Figure 6 Have students examine the diagrams. Tell them to imagine two houses located side by side. Ask: **Will the houses be closer together or farther apart if a normal fault forms between them? Why?** *(They will be farther apart because normal faults are tensional.)* **Will the houses be closer together or farther apart if a reverse fault forms between them? Why?** *(They will be closer together because reverse faults are compressional.)* **Will the houses be closer together or farther apart if a thrust fault forms between them? Why?** *(They'll be closer together because thrust faults are compressional.)* **What will be the relative location of the houses if a strike-slip fault forms between them?** *(The houses will move farther apart, but they will no longer be side by side. One house will be somewhat behind the other.)*
Visual, Logical

Build Reading Literacy L1

Refer to **p. 246D** in **Chapter 9**, which provides the guidelines for relating cause and effect.

Relate Cause and Effect Ask: **What type of faulting would you expect to find in an area where continental plates are diverging?** *(a normal fault)* **Why would you find this type of fault?** *(When continental plates diverge, the crust is pulled apart. This creates tensional forces that stretch or expand the crust.)* **What type of faulting would you expect to find in an area where plates are subducting or colliding? Why?** *(a reverse fault or a thrust fault because plate subduction and collision cause compressional forces, which cause the crust to shorten)*
Logical

Four Types of Faults

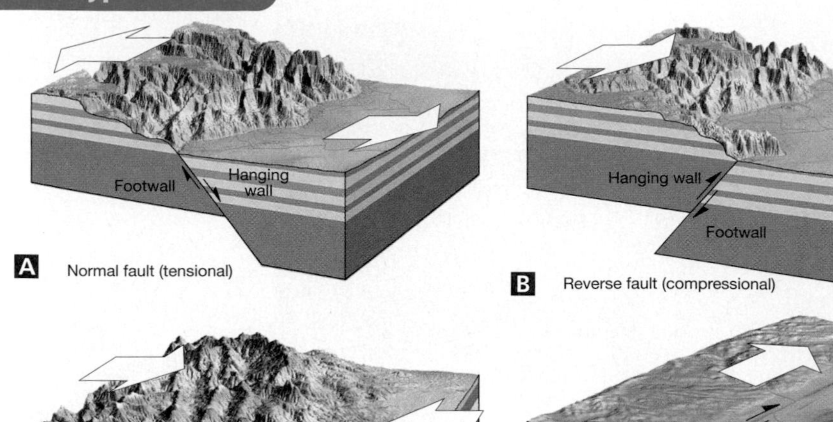

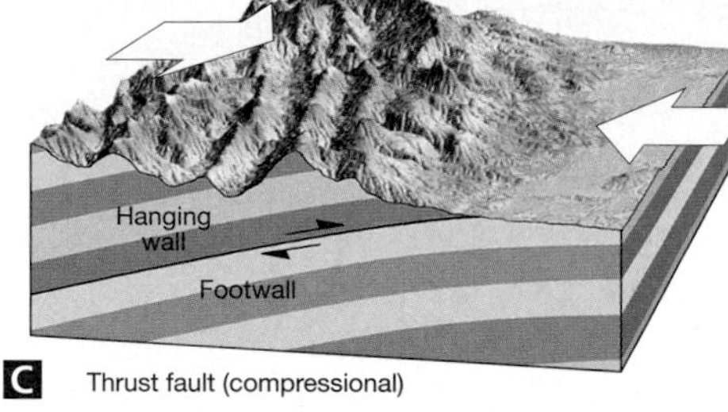

C Thrust fault (compressional)

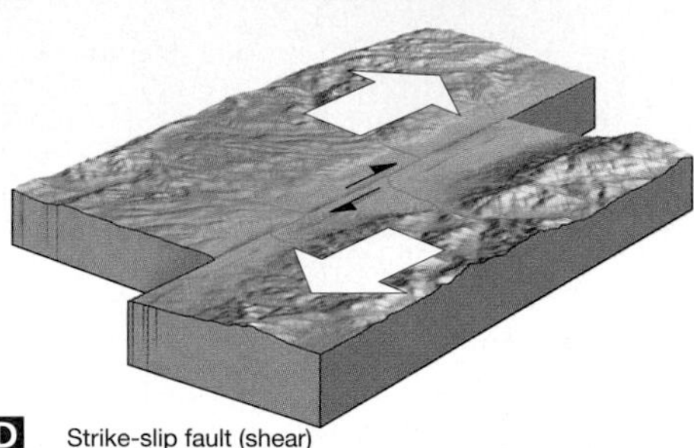

D Strike-slip fault (shear)

Figure 6 A Normal fault **B** Reverse fault **C** Thrust fault **D** Strike-slip fault
Interpreting Diagrams ***Which type of fault would cause extension in an area?***

Q *How do you determine which side of a fault has moved?*

A For the fault shown in Figure 5, did the left side move down, or did the right side move up? Since the surface at the top of the photo has been eroded flat, either side could have moved, or both sides could have moved, with one side moving more than the other. That's why geologists talk about *relative* motion across faults. In this case, the left side moved down *relative* to the right side, and the right side moved up *relative* to the left side.

Reverse Faults and Thrust Faults A **reverse fault** is a fault in which the hanging wall block moves up relative to the footwall block. Reverse faults are high-angle faults with dips greater than 45°. **Thrust faults** are reverse faults with dips of less than 45°. Because the hanging wall block moves up and over the footwall block, reverse and thrust faults result in a shortening of the crust, as shown in Figure 6B and 6C.

Most high-angle reverse faults are small. They cause only local displacements in regions dominated by other types of faulting. Thrust faults, on the other hand, exist at all scales. In mountainous regions such as the Alps, northern Rockies, Himalayas, and Appalachians, thrust faults have displaced rock layers as far as 50 kilometers over adjacent rocks. The result of this large-scale movement is that older rocks end up on top of younger rocks.

Normal faults occur due to tensional stresses, and reverse and thrust faults result from compressional stresses. Compressional forces generally produce folds as well as faults. These compressional forces result in a thickening and shortening of the rocks.

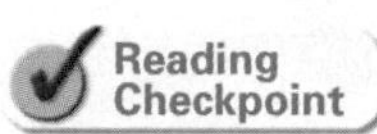

What are the major types of faults?

Strike-Slip Faults Faults in which the movement is horizontal and parallel to the trend, or strike, of the fault surface are called **strike-slip faults,** as shown in Figure 6D. Because of their large size and linear nature, many strike-slip faults produce a trace that is visible over a great distance. Rather than a single fracture, large strike-slip faults usually consist of a zone of roughly parallel fractures. The zone may be up to several kilometers wide. The most recent movement, however, is often along a section only a few meters wide, which may offset features such as stream channels. Crushed and broken rocks produced during faulting are more easily eroded, often producing linear valleys or troughs that mark the locations of strike-slip faults. Scientific records of strike-slip faulting were made following surface ruptures that produced large earthquakes. Strike-slip faults are commonly caused by shear stress. The San Andreas fault in California and the Great Glen fault in Scotland are well-known examples of strike-slip faults.

Figure 7 Joints These joints are found in Arches National Park, near Moab, Utah. The joints in the sandstone stand out because chemical weathering is enhanced along them.

Joints Among the most common rock structures are fractures called **joints.** Unlike faults, joints are fractures along which no appreciable movement has occurred. Although some joints have a random orientation, most occur in roughly parallel groups, as shown in Figure 7. Joints usually form as the result of large-scale regional stresses.

Section 11.1 Assessment

Reviewing Concepts

1. What factors determine the strength of a rock?
2. In what ways do rocks deform? Explain the differences in these deformations.
3. Describe the different types of stress.
4. List the three types of folds.
5. Explain the direction of movement in the four types of faults.

Critical Thinking

6. **Inferring** What type of deformation would a rock in the lower part of the mantle be more likely to undergo? Explain.
7. **Comparing and Contrasting** How is an anticline different from a syncline?
8. **Applying Concepts** What type of faults should be most common at a spreading ocean ridge? Explain.

Connecting Concepts

Compressional Stress Review the types of plate boundaries in Chapter 9. At which type of boundary would compressional stresses be the dominant force?

Address Misconceptions L2

It is commonly believed that California is in danger of sliding into the Pacific Ocean due to the movement of the San Andreas Fault. Have students examine the map on p. 325 and note the general direction of the fault. *(northwest)* Remind them that the San Andreas Fault is a strike-slip fault. Ask: **Is it possible that the San Andreas Fault will cause California to slide into the ocean? Explain.** *(No, the movement in strike-slip faults is horizontal and parallel to the trend, so the southern California coast is moving north, not west.)*
Visual, Logical

3 ASSESS

Evaluate Understanding L2

To assess students' knowledge of the section content, ask: **How does a joint differ from a fault?** *(A fault is a fracture along which movement has occurred. A joint is a fracture along which no movement has occurred.)* **How does a reverse fault differ from a thrust fault?** *(A thrust fault is a reverse fault with a dip of less than 45°. A reverse fault usually has a dip greater than 45°.)*

Reteach L1

Have students make a table listing the four factors that influence the strength of a rock. For each factor, students should write a brief description of how that factor influences rock deformation.

Connecting Concepts

Compressional forces are dominant at convergent plate boundaries.

Answer to . . .

Figure 6 *A normal fault causes extension or stretching in an area.*

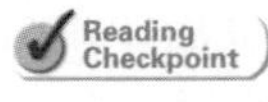

Reading Checkpoint *normal, reverse, thrust, and strike-slip faults*

Section 11.1 Assessment

1. temperature, confining pressure, rock type, and time
2. brittle deformation which causes an object to fracture, and ductile deformation, which changes the shape and size of the object without fracturing it
3. Compressional stress is a force that compresses, shortens, or squeezes a rock. Tensional stress is a force that pulls a rock apart, causing extension or lengthening of the rock. Shear stress is a force that causes a rock body to be distorted.
4. anticlines, synclines, and monoclines
5. In normal faults, the hanging wall moves down relative to the footwall and the movement is mainly vertical. In reverse and thrust faults, the hanging wall moves up relative to the footwall. In reverse faults the movement is mainly vertical; in thrust faults, the movement is mainly horizontal. Strike-slip faults move parallel to the trend of the fault, and the movement is mainly horizontal.
6. ductile deformation because of high temperatures and pressures in the lower mantle
7. Anticline: Rock layers are folded upwards to form an arch. Syncline: Rock layers are folded downwards to form a trough.
8. Normal faults; the plates at an ocean ridge are being pulled apart or are undergoing extension, which results in normal faults.

Section 11.2

1 FOCUS

Section Objectives

11.5 **Explain** how mountains are classified.

11.6 **Explain** the difference between folded mountains and fault-block mountains.

11.7 **Describe** the formation of a dome.

Reading Focus

Build Vocabulary L2

Concept Map Have students make a concept map using all the vocabulary terms. Maps should begin with the term *orogenesis.*

Reading Strategy L2

Sample answers:
What are folded mountains?
a. mountains formed primarily by folding
b. formed by compressional stress
c. formed also by thrust faulting
d. *What are fault-block mountains?*
e. formed from tensional stress
f. consist of elongated mountain ranges
g. separated by valleys formed by grabens
h. *What are domes and basins?*
i. formed by uplifting of basement rock
j. produce circular or elongated structures
k. usually found isolated, not as part of mountain range

2 INSTRUCT

Folded Mountains

Build Reading Literacy L1

Refer to **p. 362D** in **Chapter 13,** which provides the guidelines for using prior knowledge.

Use Prior Knowledge Have students review the material on folds in Section 1. Have them draw a diagram of an anticline and a syncline. Ask: **What are three types of folds?** *(anticlines, synclines, and monoclines)* **What types of folds can you see in the photograph in Figure 8?** *(anticlines and synclines)*
Logical, Visual

11.2 Types of Mountains

Reading Focus

Key Concepts
- How are mountains classified?
- What are the major types of mountains?

Vocabulary
- orogenesis
- folded mountain
- fault-block mountain
- graben
- horst
- uplifted mountain

Reading Strategy
Previewing Make a table like the one below. Before you read the section, rewrite the green topic headings as questions. As you read, write answers to the questions.

Types of Mountains
What are folded mountains?
a. ____ ? ____
b. ____ ? ____
c. ____ ? ____

Mountains are one of the most inspiring features on Earth. The collection of processes that produce a mountain belt is called **orogenesis.** The rocks in mountains provide striking evidence of the enormous compressional forces that have deformed and lifted Earth's crust. Folding is often the most obvious sign of these forces, but thrust faulting, metamorphism, and igneous activity are also important processes in mountain building. **Mountains are classified by the dominant processes that have formed them.**

Figure 8 Folded Mountains Folded sedimentary layers are exposed in the northern Rocky Mountains on the face of Mount Kidd, Alberta, Canada.

Folded Mountains

Many mountains contain huge spectacular folds of rocks, as shown in Figure 8. **Mountains that are formed primarily by folding are called folded mountains.** Compressional stresses are the major force that forms folded mountains.

Customize for English Language Learners

Encourage students to use a dictionary to find the origins of the term *orogenesis.* (*from the Greek word parts* oros- *meaning "mountain" and* genesis *meaning to "come into being"*) Inform students that the words *rise, arise,* and *rose* also come from the Greek word part *oros.* Have students look up these words and explain why they might come from a word meaning "mountain."

Thrust faulting is also important in the formation of folded mountains, which are often called fold-and-thrust belts. Folded mountains often contain numerous stacked thrust faults that have displaced the folded rock layers many kilometers horizontally. The Appalachian Mountains, the northern Rocky Mountains, and the Alps in Europe are examples of folded mountain ranges.

Fault-Block Mountains

Most normal faults are small and have displacements of only a meter or so. Others extend for tens of kilometers where they may outline the boundary of a mountain front. **Large-scale normal faults are associated with structures called fault-block mountains.** These mountains form as large blocks of crust are uplifted and tilted along normal faults.

In the western United States, examples of fault-block mountains include the Teton Range of Wyoming and the Sierra Nevada of California. Both are faulted along their eastern flanks, which were uplifted as the blocks tilted downward to the west. These steep mountain fronts were produced over a period of 5 million to 10 million years by many episodes of faulting. Each event produced just a few meters of displacement.

Normal faulting occurs where tensional stresses cause the crust to be stretched or extended. As the crust is stretched, a block called a **graben,** which is bounded by normal faults, drops down. *Graben* is the German word for ditch or trench. Grabens produce an elongated valley bordered by relatively uplifted structures called **horsts.** The Basin and Range Province of Nevada, Utah, and California, shown in Figure 9, is made of elongated grabens. Above the grabens, tilted fault-bound blocks or horsts produce linear fault-block mountains.

What is a horst?

A

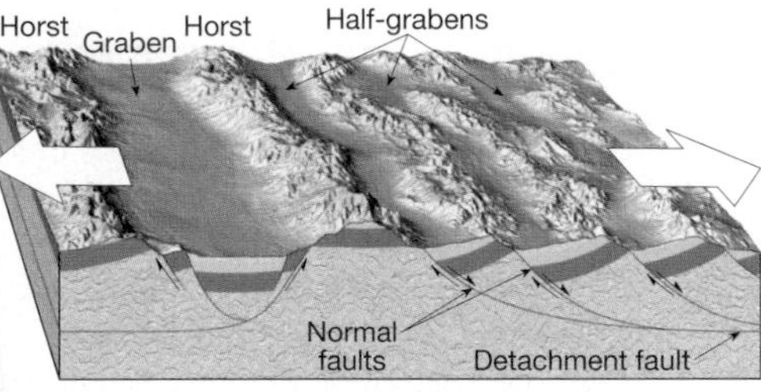

B

Figure 9 Fault-Block Mountains A Part of the Basin and Range Province of Nevada, California, and Utah **B** Here, tensional stresses have elongated and fractured the crust into numerous blocks. Movement along these fractures has tilted the blocks producing parallel mountain ranges called fault-block mountains.

Fault-Block Mountains

Use Visuals L1

Figure 9 Have students examine the diagram of fault-block mountains. Ask: **What type of faults bound a graben?** *(normal faults)* **What causes a graben to form, and what type of feature does it form?** *(The crust is stretched, and the graben block drops down, forming a valley.)* **What causes the formation of a horst?** *(Fault-bound rock blocks have become uplifted and tilted.)*
Visual, Logical

Build Science Skills L2

ACTIVITY

Using Models Have students model the formation of fault-block mountains and grabens by using three wooden blocks. If the blocks are rectangular rather than square, long narrow grabens will be formed. Suggest to students that they produce their "fault-block mountains" with several small movements rather than one large movement.
Kinesthetic, Visual

Integrate Biology L2

East Africa Rift Valley Tell students that the Rift Valley of East Africa is nearly 6000 km long and is made up of several large grabens, above which tilted horsts produce a linear mountainous topography. The Rift Valley contains the excavation sites of some of the earliest human fossils ever found. It has been hypothesized that humans (genus *Homo*) originated in this area from 2.5 to 1.6 million years ago. Further hypotheses suggest that humans left Africa about 100,000 years ago and that all modern humans *(Homo sapiens)* have evolved from this migration. This last hypothesis is known as the "out-of-Africa" model and is supported by DNA analysis of human fossils. Ask: **How do you think scientists have learned about human origins?** *(They have studied the fossil record and compared the DNA of various groups of humans.)* **What DNA evidence would support the out-of-Africa model?** *(DNA that showed similarities among different groups of humans in different parts of the world)*
Logical

Answer to . . .

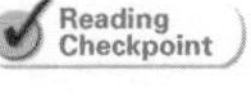

A horst is an uplifted block bounded by normal faults.

Domes and Basins

MAP MASTER™ Skills Activity

Identify The granite core, consisting of the oldest rocks, is found in the center or core of the Black Hills in the area labeled "Central crystalline area."

3 ASSESS

Evaluate Understanding L2

To assess students' knowledge of the section content, have each student draw a labeled diagram of one of the three types of mountains discussed in this section. Each student should then exchange his or her diagram with a classmate who diagramed a different type of mountain. Each student should label the type of mountain shown in one another's drawing. The student who made the diagram should be sure the label is correct.

Reteach L1

Have students make a table of mountain types. For each type of mountain listed, students should describe its features and explain how it was formed.

Answers will vary but should accurately reflect the structures and rocks commonly found in uplifted mountains. Uplifted mountains have sedimentary rocks around the outside, tilted away from the center of the mountains. The core of the mountains could be older sedimentary rocks, older igneous or metamorphic rocks, or an exposed intrusive igneous laccolith.

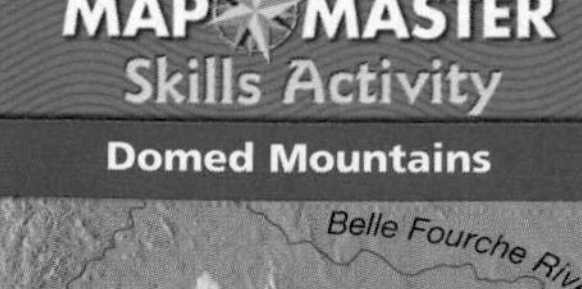

Domed Mountains

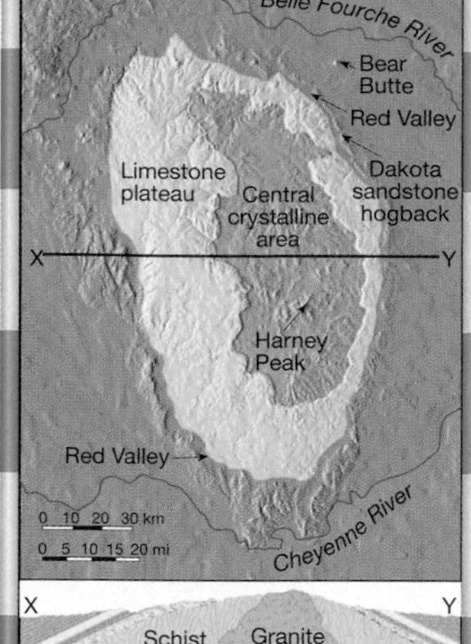

Figure 10

Regions The Black Hills of South Dakota is a large domed structure, exposing resistant igneous and metamorphic rocks in the center. **Identify** Locate the schist and granite core of the Black Hills, shown on the cross section.

Domes and Basins

The Black Hills of western South Dakota form a large domed structure thought to be formed by upwarping. Broad upwarping in basement rock may deform the overlying cover of sedimentary strata. This upwarping can generate large folds. **When upwarping produces a circular or elongated structure, the feature is called a dome.** Erosion has stripped away the highest portion of the sedimentary beds in the Black Hills, exposing older igneous and metamorphic rocks in the center. Look at the map in Figure 10. The remnants of the sedimentary layers surround the crystalline core of the mountains. The oldest rocks form the core.

Where are the oldest rocks found in a dome?

Downwarped structures having a circular shape are called basins. Several large basins exist in the United States. The basins of Michigan and Illinois have very gently sloping beds similar to saucers. These basins are thought to be the result of large accumulations of sediment, whose weight caused the crust to subside.

Because large basins usually contain sedimentary beds sloping at very low angles, the basins are usually identified by the age of the rocks composing them. The youngest rocks are found near the center. The oldest rocks are at the flanks. A geologic map of lower Michigan, for example, looks somewhat like a bull's-eye. The oldest rocks are near the center of the state. Progressively younger rocks ring the center. This is just the opposite order of a domed structure, such as the Black Hills, where the oldest rocks form the core.

Section 11.2 Assessment

Reviewing Concepts

1. Describe how mountains are classified.
2. List the major types of mountains.
3. What is a graben? In what type of mountains are grabens most commonly found?
4. What is the dominant type of stress associated with folded mountains?

Critical Thinking

5. **Applying Concepts** In a mountain range, you observe a series of anticlines and synclines and numerous thrust faults. How would you classify the type of mountains in this mountain range?
6. **Comparing and Contrasting** Compare uplifted mountains and fault-block mountains.

Descriptive Paragraph Write a paragraph describing a trip across an uplifted mountain. Describe the types of rocks and structures you might observe.

Section 11.2 Assessment

1. Mountains are classified by the processes that are involved in forming them.
2. folded mountains, fault-block mountains, and uplifted or domed mountains
3. A graben is a block that is bounded by normal faults that has been down-dropped. Grabens are most commonly found in fault-block mountains.
4. compressional stress
5. Most likely, it is a folded mountain range.
6. Uplifted mountains are formed when a large basement block or a laccolith uplifts the overlying rocks. Uplifted mountains commonly are isolated and are not part of a mountain range. Fault-block mountains are formed when tensional stresses cause an area to be stretched by normal faulting. The area is faulted to form elongated valleys or grabens, separated by horsts or uplifted blocks that form linear fault-block mountains.

Answer to . . .

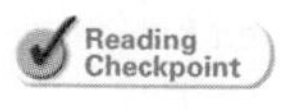

in the center or core of the dome

11.3 Mountain Formation

Reading Focus

Key Concepts

- What mountains are associated with convergent plate boundaries?
- What mountains are associated with divergent plate boundaries?
- How is isostatic adjustment involved in mountain formation?

Vocabulary

- accretionary wedge
- accretion
- terrane
- isostasy
- isostatic adjustment

Reading Strategy

Outlining As you read, make an outline of the important ideas in this section. Use the green topic headings as the main topics and the blue headings as subtopics.

I. Mountain Formation
   A. Mountain Building at Convergent Boundaries
      1. Ocean-Ocean Convergence
      2. a. ______?______
      3. b. ______?______
   B. Mountain Building at Divergent Boundaries

Mountain building still occurs in several places worldwide. For example, the Himalayas began to form 45 million years ago and are still rising. Older mountain ranges, such as the Appalachians in the eastern United States, are deeply eroded, but they have many features found in younger mountains.

Many hypotheses have been proposed to explain mountain formation. One early proposal suggested that mountains are wrinkles in Earth's crust, produced as the planet cooled from its early semi-molten state. People believed that as Earth cooled, it contracted and shrank. In this way, the crust was deformed the way an apple peel wrinkles as it dries out. However, this early hypothesis and many others were not able to withstand careful analysis and had to be discarded.

Figure 11 Young Mountains The Grand Tetons of Wyoming are an example of relatively young mountains.

Mountain Building at Convergent Boundaries

With the development of the theory of plate tectonics, a widely accepted model for orogenesis became available. **Most mountain building occurs at convergent plate boundaries. Colliding plates provide the compressional forces that fold, fault, and metamorphose the thick layers of sediments deposited at the edges of landmasses.** The partial melting of mantle rock also provides a source of magma that intrudes and further deforms these deposits.

Section 11.3

1 FOCUS

Section Objectives

11.8 **Identify** the type of mountains associated with convergent plate boundaries.

11.9 **Distinguish** between mountains formed by ocean-ocean convergence and mountains formed by ocean-continental convergence.

11.10 **Identify** the type of mountains associated with divergent plate boundaries.

11.11 **Explain** how isostatic adjustment is involved in mountain formation.

Reading Focus

Build Vocabulary L2

Paraphrase After students have read the definition of *accretionary wedge* on p. 319, but before they have learned the definition of accretion on p. 321, have them write a short paragraph describing in their own words the process of accretion. After they have read the definition of *accretion*, ask if they would change their definitions.

Reading Strategy L2

I. Mountain Formation
   A. Mountain Building at Convergent Boundaries
      1. Ocean-Ocean Convergence
      2. Ocean-Continental Convergence
      3. Continent-Continent Convergence
   B. Mountain Building at Divergent Boundaries
   C. Non-Boundary Mountains
   D. Continental Accretion
      1. Terranes
      2. Mountains from Accretion
   E. Principle of Isostasy
      1. Isostatic Adjustment for Mountains

2 INSTRUCT

Mountain Building at Convergent Boundaries

Use Visuals L1

Figure 12 Have students study the diagrams of ocean-ocean convergence. Ask: **What is the result of the convergence of two oceanic plates?** *(formation of a volcanic island arc)* **Why does the volume of the crust increase in this type of convergence?** *(Volcanic magma is added to the crust. Sediment that is scraped off the subducting plate accumulates to increase crustal volume.)* **Visual, Logical**

Partial Melting L2

Purpose Students observe the process that generates magma during boundary convergence.

Materials can of frozen grape juice concentrate (inexpensive brands work best), can opener, plastic tub, rubber gloves, apron, water, plastic pitcher, paper towels for clean-up

Procedure Allow the grape juice to thaw slightly, but do not let it liquefy. Use a can opener or pull tab to remove one end of the can. Squeeze the juice concentrate out of the can through your hands, letting it fall into the plastic tub. Tell students to look for evidence of partial melting in the concentrate. Be sure to wear an apron and rubber gloves. Use the water, pitcher, and paper towels for cleaning up.

Expected Outcomes The sugary juice has a melting point of about −40°C, whereas the ice crystals in the juice melt at 0°C. If the juice is thawed to a temperature of about −5°C, part of the mixture is liquid, but the ice crystals are still solid. Explain to students that when a plate is subducted, it experiences partial melting. Sometimes the mantle wedge above the subducting plate also can melt when magma coming up from a subducted slab doesn't get all the way to the surface immediately. This melting and migration generates magma and causes the formation of volcanic arcs. **Kinesthetic, Visual**

Ocean-Ocean Convergence

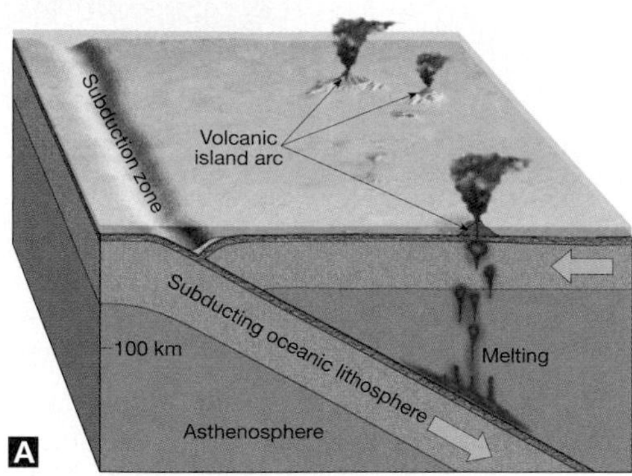

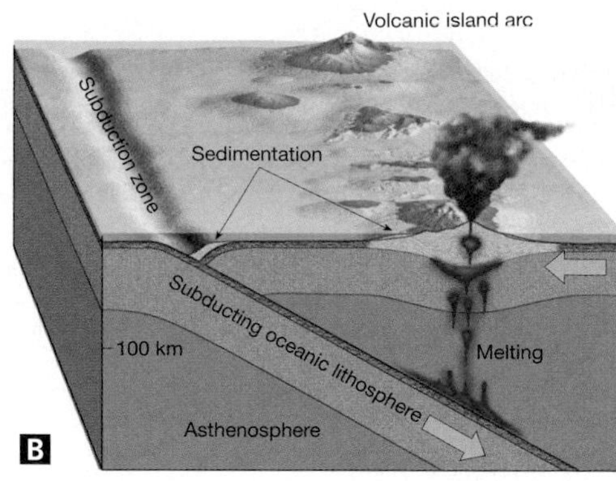

Figure 12 **A** A volcanic island arc develops due to the convergence of two oceanic plates. **B** Continued subduction along this type of convergent boundary results in the development of volcanic mountains.

Ocean-Ocean Convergence Ocean-ocean convergence occurs where two oceanic plates converge and one is subducted beneath the other, as shown in Figure 12. The converging plates result in partial melting of the mantle above the subducting plate and can lead to the growth of a volcanic island arc on the ocean floor. Because they are associated with subducting oceanic lithosphere, island arcs are typically found on the margins of a shrinking ocean basin, such as the Pacific. These features tend to be relatively long-lived. Here, somewhat sporadic volcanic activity, the depth of magma, as well as the accumulation of sediment that is scraped off the subducting plates, increases the volume of the crust. An example of an active island arc is the Aleutian arc, which forms the Aleutian Islands in Alaska. Some volcanic island arcs, such as Japan, appear to have been built up by two or three different periods of subduction. As shown by Japan, the continued development of a volcanic island arc can result in the formation of mountains made up of belts of igneous and metamorphic rocks. **Ocean-ocean convergence mainly produces volcanic mountains.**

Ocean-Continental Convergence Mountain building along continental margins involves the convergence of an oceanic plate and a plate whose leading edge contains continental crust. A good example is the west coast of South America. In this area, the Nazca plate is being subducted beneath the South American plate along the Peru-Chile trench. As shown by the Andes Mountains, ocean-continental convergence results in the formation of a continental volcanic arc inland of the continental margin.

Customize for English Language Learners

Have students use a dictionary to look up the origin of the term *isostasy.* (Iso- *means "equal" and* stasis *means "standing."*) Ask students to brainstorm words that begin with *iso-*. Ask them how the words are similar or different in meaning. (*Students may know the word* isobar *[equal air pressure] and* isotherm *[equal temperature] from meteorology,* isotonic *[equal concentration] from chemistry, and* isometric *and* isosceles *[equal sides] from geometry.*)

The convergence of the continental block and the subduction of the oceanic plate leads to deformation and metamorphism of the continental margin. Partial melting of mantle rock above the subducting slab generates magma that migrates upward. This melting and fluid migration occurs once the oceanic plate moves down to about 100 kilometers. During the development of this continental volcanic arc, sediment derived from the land and scraped from the subducting plate is stuck against the landward side of the trench. This accumulation of different sedimentary and metamorphic rocks with some scraps of ocean crust is called an **accretionary wedge.** A long period of subduction can build an accretionary wedge of rock that is large enough to stand above sea level, as shown in Figure 13.

Ocean-continental convergence produces mountain ranges composed of two roughly parallel belts. The continental volcanic arc develops on the continental block. The arc consists of volcanoes and large intrusive bodies mixed with high-temperature metamorphic rocks. The seaward belt is the accretionary wedge. It consists of folded, faulted sedimentary and metamorphic rocks. **The types of mountains formed by ocean-continental convergence are volcanic mountains and folded mountains.**

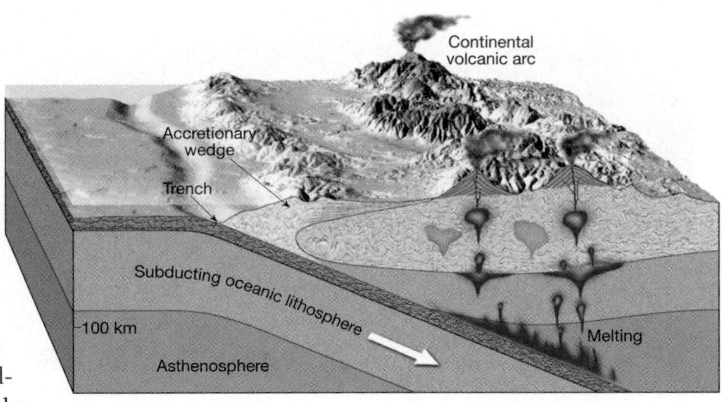

Figure 13 Ocean-Continental Convergence Plate convergence generates a subduction zone, and partial melting produces a continental volcanic arc. Continued convergence and igneous activity further deforms the crust and forms a roughly parallel folded mountain belt. **Observing** ***What type of mountains result from the partial melting?***

Problem-Solving Activity

Rates of Mountain Building

The mighty Himalayas between India and Tibet are the tallest mountains on Earth, rising to more than 8 kilometers. These mountains are still rising at about 1 centimeter per year. Mount Everest is the tallest peak with an elevation of 8848 meters above sea level. The Himalayas formed as a result of India colliding with the Eurasian plate.

1. **Calculating** If you assume that the Himalayas will continue to be uplifted at the current rate of 1 centimeter per year, how long will it take the mountains to rise another 500 meters?
2. **Calculating** Assuming a rate of uplift of 1 centimeter per year, how much higher could the Himalayas be in one million years?
3. **Applying Concepts** If the convergence of tectonic plates is causing the Himalayas to rise in elevation, what common surface processes are working to decrease their elevations?
4. **Inferring** Do you think it is reasonable for the Himalayas to continue to rise in elevation indefinitely? Explain your answer.

Problem-Solving Activity

Rates of Mountain Building L2

1. 1 cm/year = 0.01 m/year; 500 m ÷ 0.01 m/year = 50,000 years
2. 1,000,000 years × 0.01 m/year = 10,000 m or 10 km
3. the processes of weathering and erosion
4. Accept all reasonable answers. A possible answer could be as follows: No, the mountains probably can't keep growing taller forever. Erosion would occur at a faster pace than mountain building. In addition, Earth's mantle probably can support only a particular amount of lithospheric thickness. The area of the mountains may begin to spread out or the convergence will stop.
Logical

For Extra Help L1

Review conversion factors and dimensional analysis with students. Have students practice making conversions from centimeters to meters and from meters to centimeters by using dimensional analysis. Remind students to label units for each factor and to make sure all unwanted units cancel out to yield a final answer in the desired units.

Address Misconceptions L2

Ask students if Mount Everest will always be the highest mountain on Earth. If they say yes, they may think that mountain-building processes are no longer taking place and that mountains will remain the same size as they are now. Because the Indian and Eurasian plates continue to push against each other—at a rate of about 2 cm a year—the Himalayas are continuing to grow. According to data from recent GPS experiments, the Himalayas are growing at a rate of 5 mm a year. Ask: **What process could prevent the Himalayas from growing?** *(erosion)* **What would happen if the Indian and Eurasian plates stop moving?** *(The Himalayas will stop growing and will decrease in height due to erosion.)*
Logical

Facts and Figures

For years, scientists thought that the elevation of Mount Everest was 8848 m above sea level. A number of attempts over several years were made to set up Global Position System (GPS) equipment so the mountain could be measured using satellite-based technology. A team of seven climbers successfully measured the mountain from the summit on May 5, 1999. The data were collected from various GPS satellite receivers, one of which had to be placed in bedrock, at the top of Mount Everest. Using GPS technology, Mount Everest finally was re-measured and was found to be 8850 m above sea level.

Answer to . . .

Figure 13 *volcanic mountains*

Use Visuals **L1**

Figure 14 Have students examine the diagram of continent-continent convergence. Ask: **Why are there sedimentary rocks and oceanic crust high above sea level in the Himalayas?** *(They come from sediment and bits of crust that were scraped off an oceanic slab as it subducted under India. When India and Asia collided, this material was uplifted.)* **What caused the formation of a continental volcanic arc in the Himalayas?** *(partial melting of the overlying mantle rocks triggered by the subducting oceanic slab)*
Visual, Logical

Build Science Skills 

Inferring Have students infer how a mountain range can occur far inland. *(Two continental plates must have collided sometime in the past.)*
Logical

Use Community Resources 

Invite a civil engineer to your class, and have students interview him or her to find out what a civil engineer needs to know about local landforms when planning new roads. Have students prepare questions for the guest speaker in advance of his or her visit.
Verbal

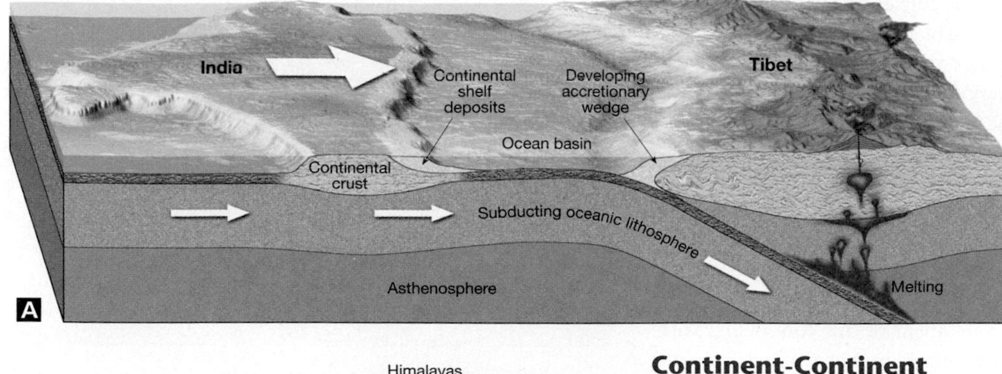

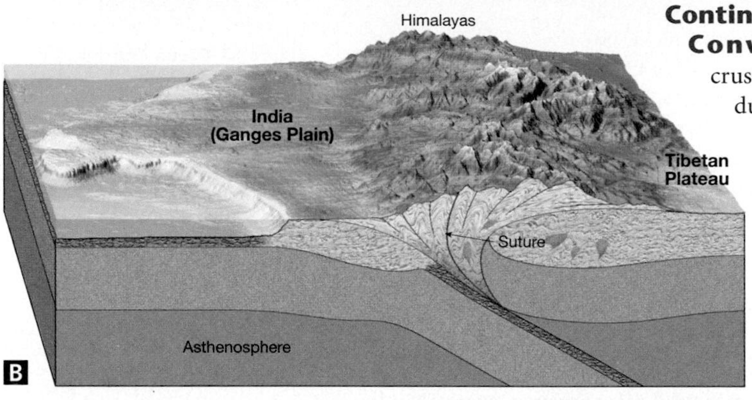

Figure 14 Continental-Continental Convergence The ongoing collision of India and Asia started about 45 million years ago and produced the majestic Himalayas. **A** Converging plates generated a subduction zone, producing a continental volcanic arc. **B** Eventually the two landmasses collided, which deformed and elevated the mountain range.

Continent-Continent Convergence Continental crust floats too much to be subducted. **At a convergent boundary between two plates carrying continental crust, a collision between the continental fragments will result and form folded mountains.**

An example of such a collision began about 45 million years ago when India collided with the Eurasian plate, as shown in Figure 14. Before this event, India was once part of Antarctica, and it had split from that continent over the course of millions of years. It slowly moved a few thousand kilometers due north. The result of the collision was the formation of the spectacular Himalaya Mountains and the Tibetan Plateau. Most of the oceanic crust that separated these landmasses before the collision was subducted, but some was caught up in the collision zone, along with the sediment along the shoreline. Today these sedimentary rocks and slivers of oceanic crust are elevated high above sea level.

A similar but much older collision is believed to have taken place when the European continent collided with the Asian continent to produce the Ural Mountains in Russia. Before the theory of plate tectonics, geologists had difficulty explaining mountain ranges such as the Urals, which are located far within continents.

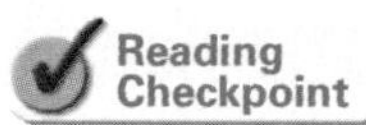

Why can't continental crust be subducted?

Facts and Figures

Numerous earthquakes recorded off the southern coast of India indicate that a new subduction zone may be forming. If formed, it would provide a subduction site for the floor of the Indian Ocean, which is continually being produced at a spreading center located to the southwest. Should this occur, India's northward journey, relative to Asia, would come to an end, and the growth of the Himalayas would cease.

Mountain Building by Continental Accretion

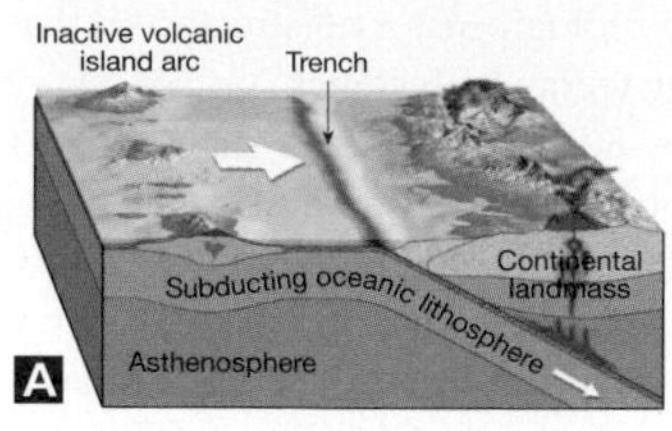

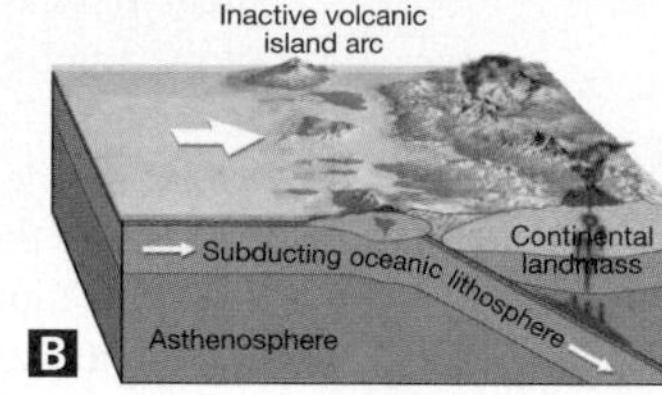

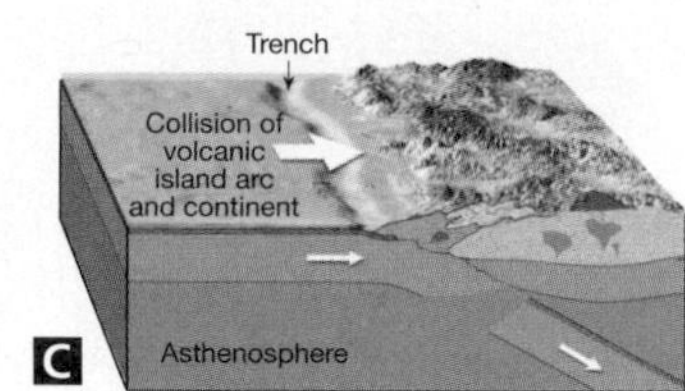

Figure 15 This sequence illustrates the collision of an inactive volcanic island arc with the margin of a continental plate. The island arc becomes embedded or accreted onto the continental plate.

Mountain Building at Divergent Boundaries

Most mountains are formed at convergent boundaries, but some are formed at divergent boundaries, usually on the ocean floor. These mountains form a chain that curves along the ocean floor at the ocean ridges. This mountain chain is over 65,000 kilometers long and rises to 2000 to 3000 meters above the ocean floor. **The mountains that form along ocean ridges at divergent plate boundaries are fault-block type mountains.** The mountain chain that makes up the Mid-Atlantic Ridge is an example.

Non-Boundary Mountains

Even though most mountains are formed at plate boundaries, some are found far from any boundaries. Some upwarped mountains, fault-block mountains, and volcanic mountains are not formed at plate boundaries. Volcanic mountains such as the Hawaiian Islands are formed at a hot spot, far from any plate boundary. Many fault-block mountains occur in areas that are undergoing regional extension or stretching. These areas may possibly become a plate boundary if the plate rifts apart.

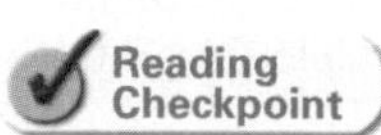

Where is the longest mountain range?

Continental Accretion

Plate tectonics theory originally suggested two major mechanisms for orogenesis at convergent boundaries: continental collisions and subduction of oceanic lithosphere to form volcanic arcs. Further studies have lead to another mechanism in which smaller crustal fragments collide and merge with continental margins. When the fragments collide with a continental plate they become stuck to or embedded into the continent in a process called **accretion**. Many of the mountainous regions rimming the Pacific have been produced through the process of collision and accretion.

For: Links on mountain building
Visit: www.SciLinks.org
Web Code: cjn-3113

Mountain Building at Divergent Boundaries

Build Science Skills **L2**

Problem Solving Have students describe a process whereby mountains can form at divergent boundaries. Students should draw a series of diagrams showing the formation of an ocean ridge and describe what is happening in each diagram.
Visual

Non-Boundary Mountains

Build Reading Literacy **L1**

Refer to **p. 124D** in **Chapter 5,** which provides the guidelines for summarizing.

Summarize Have students reread the description in Chapter 9 of how hot spots cause the formation of volcanic mountain arcs. Students should write a short summary of the process. Then they should write a paragraph about how the formation of hot spots relates to this section.
Verbal

Continental Accretion

Use Visuals **L1**

Figure 15 Have students examine the diagram of continental accretion. Ask: **What is the crustal fragment in these diagrams?** *(the volcanic island arc)* **Will the mountains that are formed by this process be as large as mountains formed by converging continental plates?** *(No, there is much less crustal material in the fragment.)*
Visual, Logical

Go Online NSTA SCiLINKS

Download a worksheet on mountain building for students to complete, and find additional teacher support from NSTA SciLinks.

Answer to . . .

It is too buoyant.

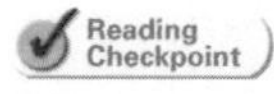

the Mid-Atlantic Ridge on the Atlantic Ocean floor

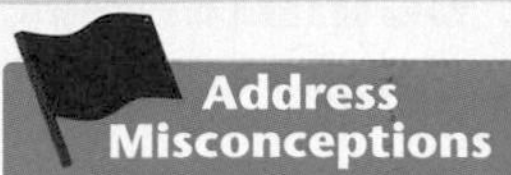

L2

Students often confuse a *terrane* with a *terrain.* The term *terrane* is used to designate a distinct and recognizable series of rock formations that has been transported by plate tectonic processes. Since geologists who mapped these rocks were unsure where they came from, these rocks were sometimes called "exotic," "suspect," "accreted," or "foreign" terranes. The term *terrain* describes the shape of the surface topography or "lay of the land." Have students use the two terms in sentences so that their meanings are clear.
Verbal

Use Visuals **L1**

Figure 16 Have students examine the map showing terranes added to western North America. Ask: **What mechanism of plate tectonics might have caused the addition of so many terranes to the West Coast?** *(The North American plate could have moved westward, overriding the Pacific Basin and picking up crustal fragments as it moved.)* **What was the origin of the Baja Peninsula?** *(It was originally an island arc.)* **What does this map imply about the number of times crustal material has been added to the West Coast?** *(Based on the many sources of crustal material, it is likely that material has been added many times.)*
Visual, Logical

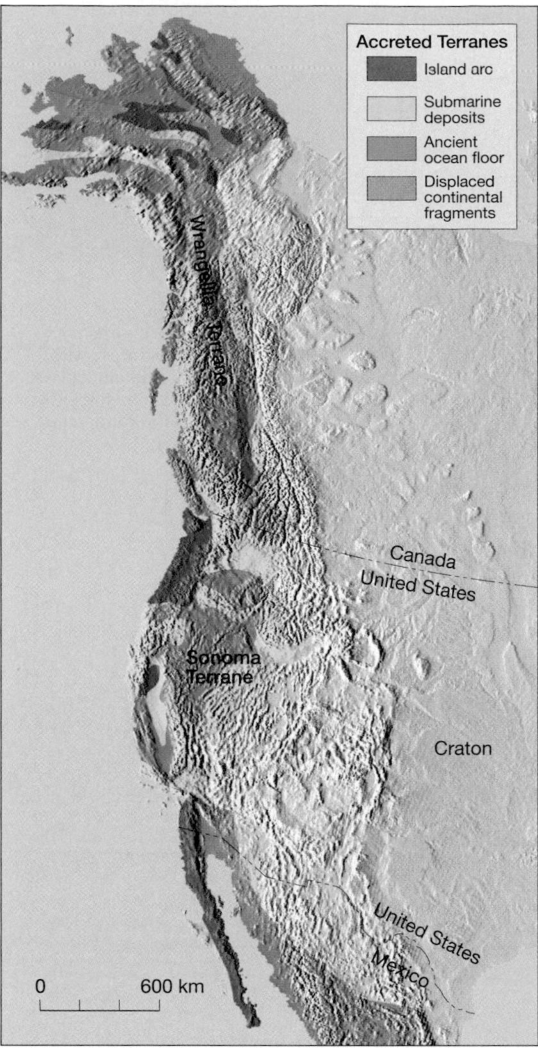

Figure 16 Accretion in Western North America These terranes are thought to have been added to western North America during the past 200 million years.
Interpreting Maps ***What do the areas in blue represent?***

Terranes Geologists refer to accreted crustal blocks as terranes. A **terrane** is any crustal fragment that has a geologic history distinct from that of the adjoining terranes. Terranes come in many shapes and sizes. Some are no larger than volcanic islands, while others are immense, such as the one making up the entire Indian subcontinent. Before their accretion to a continental block, some of the fragments may have been microcontinents similar to the present-day island of Madagascar, located in the Indian Ocean east of Africa. Many others were island arcs like Japan and the Philippines.

As oceanic plates move, they carry the embedded volcanic island arcs and microcontinents along with them. Eventually a collision between the crustal fragment and the continent occurs. Relatively small crustal pieces are peeled from the oceanic plate at a subduction zone, and thin sheets of the crustal fragment are thrust onto the continental block. This newly added material increases the width and thickness of the continental crust. The material may later be displaced farther inland by the addition of other fragments.

Mountains from Accretion The accretion of larger crustal fragments, such as a mature island arc, may result in a mountain range. These mountain ranges are much smaller than the ones that result from a continent–continent collision. Because of its buoyancy, or ability to float, an island arc will not subduct beneath the continental plate. Instead, it will plow into the continent and deform both blocks.

The idea that mountain building occurs in connection with the accretion of crustal fragments to a continental mass came mainly from studies in western North America. See Figure 16. Areas in the mountains of Alaska and western Canada were found to contain rocks, fossils, and structures that were different from those in surrounding areas. These areas have been accreted to the western margin of North America.

What is a terrane?

Facts and Figures

Imagine 45-million-year-old tree stumps of 50-m-tall trees existing next to glaciers. These trees resemble the remains of a redwood forest that once grew in northern California. Fossils of palm trees and tropical rain forest plants have all been found in Alaska within 800 km of the North Pole. Not only is the present climate too cold to support life of these organisms, but they would not be able to live in a region that has limited sunlight five months of the year. Either the climate of Earth was different when the palms grew 45 million years ago or else the rocks in which the fossils occur moved in from someplace else. Most paleontologists think the rocks were once part of terranes that were added to the Pacific coast of North America.

Principle of Isostasy

Figure 17 **Isostatic Adjustment** This drawing illustrates how wooden blocks of different thicknesses float in water. In a similar manner, thick sections of crustal material float higher than thinner crustal slabs. **Inferring** ***Would a denser wooden block float at a higher or lower level?***

In addition to the horizontal movements of lithospheric plates, gradual up-and-down motions of the crust are seen at many locations around the globe. Although much of this vertical movement occurs along plate margins and is linked to mountain building, some of it is not. The up-and-down motions also occur in the interiors of continents far from plate boundaries.

Earth's crust floats on top of the denser and more flexible rocks of the mantle. The concept of a floating crust in gravitational balance is called **isostasy** (*iso* = equal and *stasis* = standing). One way to understand the concept of isostasy is to think about a series of wooden blocks of different heights floating in water, as shown in Figure 17. Note that the thicker wooden blocks float higher than the thinner blocks. In a similar way, many mountain belts stand high above the surface because they have buoyant (less dense) crustal "roots" that extend deep into the denser mantle. The denser mantle supports the mountains from below.

What would happen if another small block of wood were placed on top of one of the blocks in Figure 17? The combined block would sink until a new isostatic balance was reached. However, the top of the combined block would actually be higher than before, and the bottom would be lower. This process of establishing a new level of gravitational equilibrium is called **isostatic adjustment.**

Isostatic Adjustment in Mountains

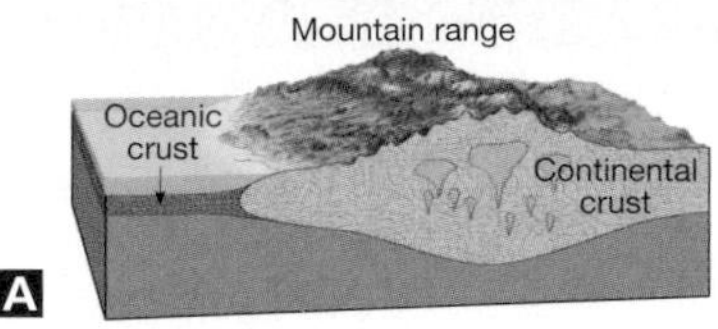

A When mountains are young, the continental crust is thickest.

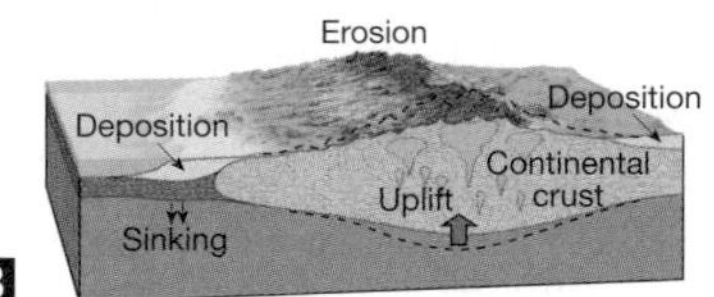

B As erosion lowers the mountains, the crust rises in response to the reduced load.

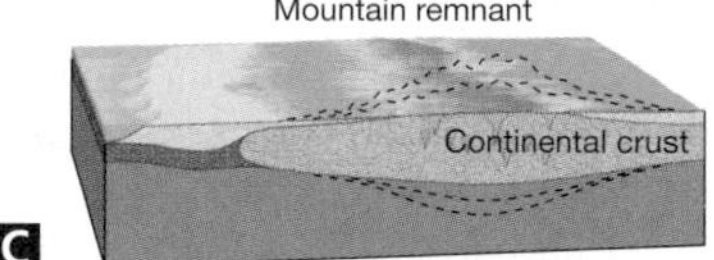

C Erosion and uplift continue until the mountains reach "normal" crustal thickness.

Figure 18 This sequence illustrates how the combined effect of erosion and isostatic adjustment results in a thinning of the crust in mountainous regions.

Principle of Isostasy

Modeling Isostasy **L2**

Purpose Students model the principle of isostasy by measuring how high blocks of varying density float in water.

Materials large plastic container, water, balance, metric ruler, several blocks of varying sizes and kinds of wood

Procedure Wear apron and goggles. Fill a large plastic container approximately half full with water. Determine the mass and volume of each of the wooden blocks. Calculate the density of each. Place each block in the water. Use a ruler to measure how much of each block is supported above the water. Stack two or more blocks on top of the other blocks in the water. Measure how much of the blocks are supported above the water.

Expected Outcomes The thicker blocks floated higher than the thinner blocks. The blocks that had lower densities also floated higher than the denser blocks.
Visual, Kinesthetic

Facts and Figures

Archimedes, born in Sicily in 287 B.C., is credited with discovering the principle of buoyancy. He was ordered by King Hiero to determine whether a crown was pure gold or whether the goldsmith who had made it had replaced some of the gold with cheaper silver. Archimedes realized while taking a bath that he could solve the puzzle using water displacement. After determining the volume of water displaced by the crown, a piece of pure gold could easily be made to match the volume of the displaced water, and thus the volume of the crown. In theory, if the volume of the crown and the volume of the gold block are the same, they should also have the same mass. The only reason they would not have the same mass is if one of them was not pure gold. Archimedes tested the crown and found that it, indeed, weighed less than the block of gold. The goldsmith confessed.

Answer to . . .

Figure 16 *ancient ocean floor deposits*

Figure 17 *at a lower level*

A terrane is an area that has a different geologic history from surrounding areas.

Build Science Skills 

Predicting When you place a block of wood in a pail of water, the block displaces some of the water, and the water level rises. Ask: **If you could measure the mass of the water that the block displaces, what would you find?** *(The mass of the water equals the mass of the block.)* **If 1 million kg of ice were added to a land mass, how much mantle would be displaced?** *(1 million kg)*
Logical

3 ASSESS

Evaluate Understanding 

Ask students to describe two events that would cause crust to subside. *(Accept any event that increases the mass of the crust, such as formation of large ice sheets, accumulation of large amounts of sediments, or formation of volcanic mountains.)*

Reteach 

Have students design an experiment that models the formation of an uplifted mountain. Students may use a bicycle pump, balloon, fabric, and any other materials they choose when designing their model.

Students' descriptions will vary. Be sure they correctly describe the volcanic arc and another mountain range inland of the continental margin.

Answer to . . .

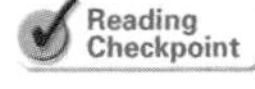

The weight of added ice causes crust to subside. When ice melts, and weight is removed, crust rebounds.

Isostatic Adjustment for Mountains Applying the concept of isostasy, we should expect that when weight is added to the crust, the crust responds by subsiding. Also when weight is removed, the crust will rebound. Evidence of crustal subsidence followed by crustal rebound is provided by the continental ice sheets that covered parts of North America during the Pleistocene epoch. The added weight of a 3-kilometer-thick mass of ice depressed Earth's crust by hundreds of meters. In the 8000 years since the last ice sheet melted, uplift of as much as 330 meters has occurred in Canada's Hudson Bay region, where the ice was thickest.

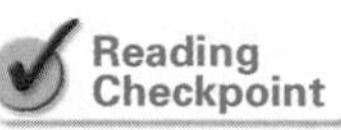

How are ice sheets related to isostatic adjustment?

Crustal buoyancy can account for considerable vertical movement. Most mountain building causes the crust to shorten and thicken. **Because of isostasy, deformed and thickened crust will undergo regional uplift both during mountain building and for a long period afterward.** As the crust rises, the processes of erosion increase, and the deformed rock layers are carved into a mountainous landscape.

As erosion lowers the summits of mountains, the crust will rise in response to the reduced load, as shown in Figure 18 on page 323. The processes of uplifting and erosion will continue until the mountain block reaches "normal" crustal thickness. When this occurs, the mountains will be eroded to near sea level, and the once deeply buried interior of the mountain will be exposed at the surface.

Section 11.3 Assessment

Reviewing Concepts

1. What types of mountains are associated with convergent plate boundaries?
2. What mountains are associated with divergent plate boundaries?
3. How is isostatic adjustment involved in mountain building?
4. How is accretion involved in mountain formation?

Critical Thinking

5. **Comparing and Contrasting** Compare mountain building along an ocean-continent convergent boundary and a continent-continent convergent boundary.
6. **Drawing Conclusions** How does the theory of plate tectonics help explain the existence of marine fossils in sedimentary rocks on top of the Himalayas?
7. **Applying Concepts** How would the accretion of a large microcontinent affect the isostatic adjustment of the region around a mountain range?

Creative Writing Describe a trip through a mountain range like the Andes that has formed at an ocean-continent convergent boundary.

Section 11.3 Assessment

1. mainly volcanic mountains
2. Fault-block mountains at ocean ridges are associated with divergent boundaries.
3. As the crust is thickened due to mountain building, the lithosphere will sink deeper into the mantle. But the lithosphere is less dense than the mantle, so the lithosphere will stand higher. To balance the added thickness, the crust will rise as a new level of gravitational equilibrium is reached.
4. At a subduction zone, if an oceanic plate is carrying any island arcs or small continental fragments, they will be stuck to or embedded into the margin of the continental plate. This process of accretion deforms the continental plate and can form mountains.
5. Ocean-continent convergent boundary: subduction of oceanic crust beneath continental crust, development of a continental volcanic arc, and formation of folded mountains as accretionary wedge is deformed and folded. Continent-continent convergent boundary: no subduction because the continental lithosphere is too buoyant, continental plates collide and form folded mountains with a lot of deformation, shortening, and thrust faulting, and little volcanism.
6. The ocean basin between India and the Eurasia was subducted before the collision of India with the Eurasian plate. The sedimentary rocks on the ocean floor and along the shoreline were scraped off and uplifted and folded up into the mountains.
7. The addition or accretion of a large fragment onto a mountain range would load the crust and cause the crust to subside.

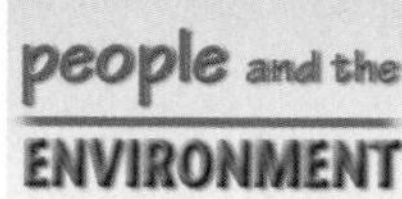

The San Andreas Fault System

The San Andreas, the largest fault system in North America, first attracted attention after the 1906 San Francisco earthquake. But this dramatic event is just one of many thousands of earthquakes that have resulted from movements along the San Andreas over the last 29 million years.

The San Andreas fault system, as shown in the map, trends in a northwesterly direction for nearly 1300 kilometers through much of western California. In many places, a linear trough marks the trace of the San Andreas fault. From the air, linear scars, offset stream channels, and elongated ponds mark the location of the fault. On the ground, however, evidence of the fault is harder to find. Some of the most distinctive landforms include long, straight cliffs, narrow ridges, and sag ponds formed by the settling of blocks within the fault zone.

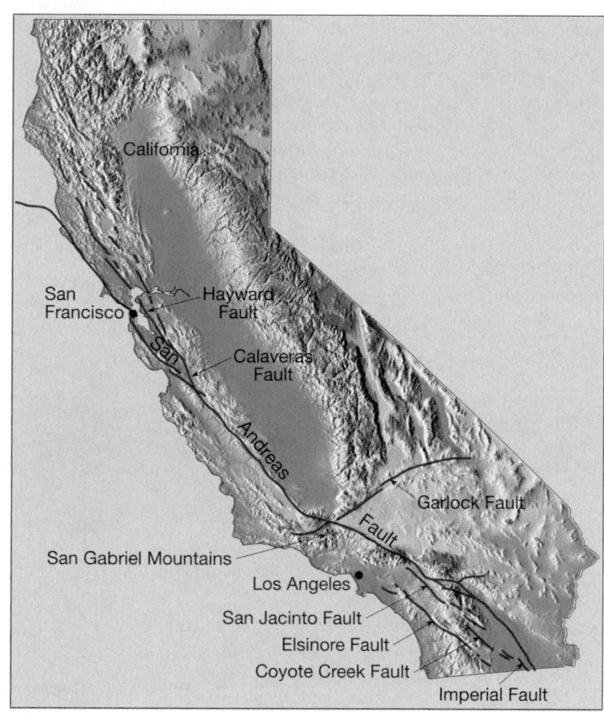

Transform Boundary Mountains

The San Andreas fault is a transform fault boundary separating two crustal plates that move very slowly. The Pacific plate, located to the west, moves northwestward in relation to the North American plate.

Some large blocks of crust within the fault zone are pushed up forming hills or mountains of various sizes. Other blocks are forced down and form depressions called sag ponds. The fault trace is not straight. It has many bends along its length. In one of these major bends, the force of the two sides of the fault moving past one another has caused the uplift of the San Gabriel Mountains north of Los Angeles.

Fault System

Different segments of the San Andreas behave differently. Some portions creep slowly with little noticeable seismic activity. Other segments regularly slip, producing small earthquakes. Still other segments seem to store elastic energy for hundreds of years and rupture in great earthquakes.

Because of the great length and complexity of the San Andreas fault, it is more appropriately referred to as a "fault system." This major fault system consists primarily of the San Andreas fault and several major branches, including the Hayward and Calaveras faults of central California and the San Jacinto and Elsinore faults. By matching rock units across the fault, geologists have determined that the total displacement from earthquakes and creep along the San Andreas is greater than 560 kilometers.

The San Andreas Fault System **L2**

Background

The 1906 San Francisco earthquake resulted from a 5-m displacement along the San Andreas Fault. The earthquake had a magnitude of 8.25, one of the two largest along this fault. The other 8.25-magnitude earthquake occurred in 1857 in Fort Tejon, near Los Angeles. As much as 80 percent of the damage in the San Francisco earthquake was caused by fire.

Teaching Tips

- Use an overhead projector to project the map of California. Use blocks of wood or rigid plastic foam to demonstrate the movement of the fault. Emphasize that the Pacific plate, along with the California coast, is moving northwest in relation to the North American plate.
- Have students think about what will eventually happen to southwestern California if present movements continue. Examining a globe and the map on this page will help them make predictions. Refer to Address Misconceptions on p. 313 about California's coast sliding into the Pacific Ocean. *(Los Angeles will move northward and become close to San Francisco. Eventually, the Baja Peninsula may become an island off the coast of Oregon or Washington.)*
- Tell students that each segment of the San Andreas Fault exhibits somewhat different behavior. Some portions exhibit a slow creep with little noticeable seismic activity. Other segments regularly slip, producing small earthquakes. Still other segments seem to store elastic energy for hundreds of years and then rupture in great earthquakes. Have students research how various segments of the fault system behave. Ask them to make predictions for future seismic activity around Los Angeles and San Francisco.

Verbal, Visual

Exploration Lab

Investigating Anticlines and Synclines L2

Objective In this activity, students will:

- measure the angles of rock layers in diagrams of an anticline and a syncline.
- determine whether a fold is an anticline or a syncline.
- visualize how rocks are oriented in anticlines and synclines.
- make a block diagram to show the appearance of an eroded fold.

Skills Focus Observing, Measuring, Classifying, Interpreting Diagrams

 **Prep Time** none

Class Time 30 minutes

Teaching Tips

- You may have to remind students how to measure angles with a protractor.
- Have students review the material about folds, domes, and basins in the text before doing this lab.
- Students may have trouble visualizing the three-dimensional structure of an eroded fold when drawing the diagram in step 5. Making a model of the fold out of different-colored layers of clay and then cutting off the top of the model to represent erosion will help them to draw the diagram.

Expected Outcome In Fold A, an anticline, the left limb dips at about 50°, and the right limb dips at 80°. In Fold B, a syncline, both limbs dip at about 45°.

Exploration Lab

Investigating Anticlines and Synclines

The axial plane of a fold is an imaginary plane drawn through the long axis of a fold. The axial plane divides the fold into two halves called limbs as shown in Figure 1. In a symmetrical fold, the limbs are mirror images of each other and move away at the same angle. In an asymmetrical fold, the limbs dip or tilt at different angles. Folds do not continue forever. Where the fold axis dips and is no longer horizontal, the fold is said to be plunging, as shown in Figure 2. A geologic principle known as the principle of superposition states that in most situations with layered rocks, the oldest rocks are at the bottom of the sequence.

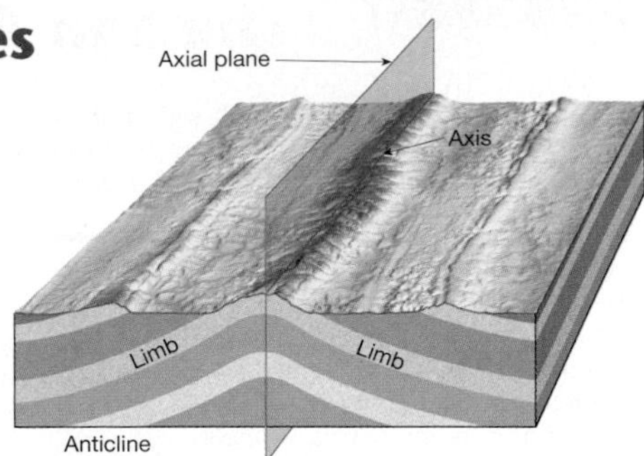

Figure 1 Horizontal Axis

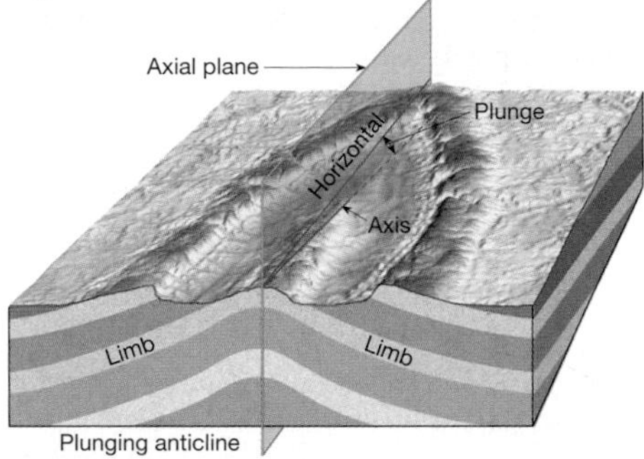

Figure 2 Plunging Axis

Problem

How are rocks oriented in anticlines and synclines?

Materials

- pencil
- protractor
- tracing paper

Skills

Observing, Measuring, Classifying, Interpreting Diagrams

Procedure

1. Study the two diagrams, labeled Fold A and Fold B in Figures 3 and 4.
2. Use a protractor to measure the angles of the rock layers in both limbs of Fold A. Repeat your measurements for both limbs of Fold B. For consistency, measure the angles on both folds at the surface between layers 3 and 4.
3. Use Figures 3 and 4 and Figure 3 on page 310 to determine what types of folds are shown by Fold A and Fold B.
4. Anticlines and synclines are linear features caused by compressional stresses. Two other types of folds—domes and basins—are often nearly circular and result from vertical displacement. Uplift produces domes like those shown in Figure 3. A basin is a downwarped structure, as shown in Figure 4.

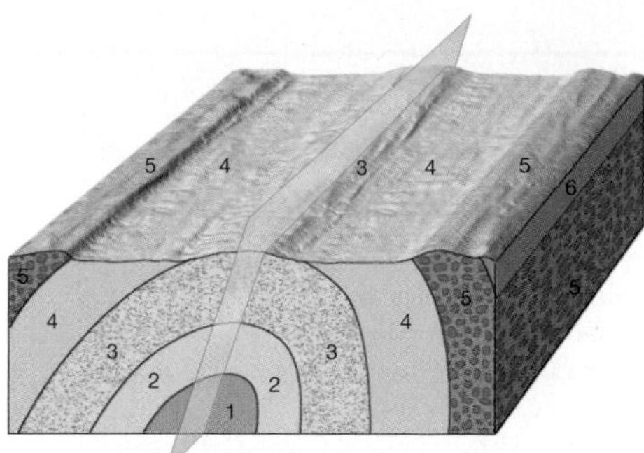

Figure 3 Fold A

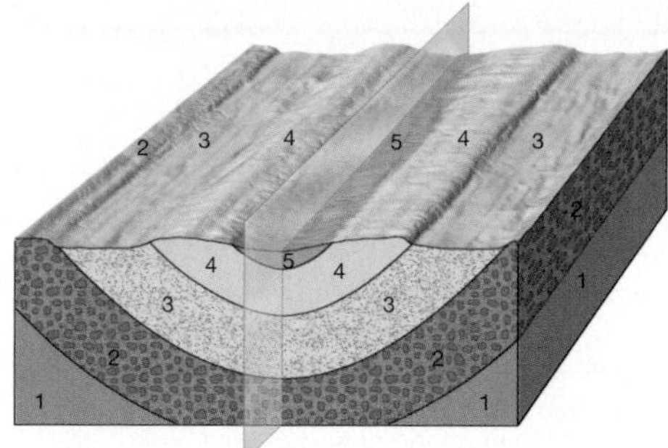

Figure 4 Fold B

5. Use tracing paper to make a copy of the blank block diagram shown below. Complete all three sides of the diagram to show an eroded fold consistent with the rock layer shown on the right side of the block.

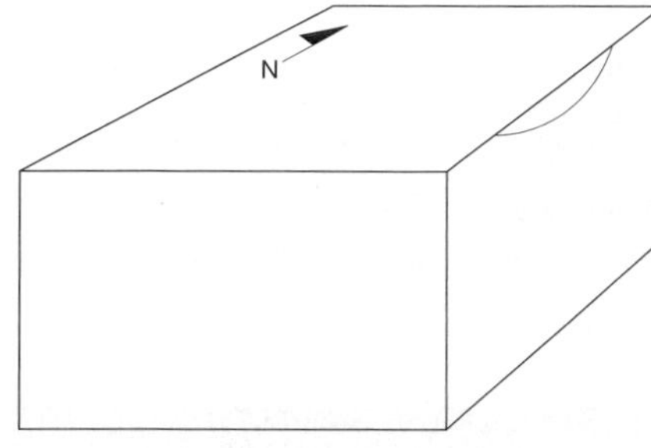

Analyze and Conclude

1. **Interpreting Diagrams** What type of fold is shown by Fold A? In what direction do the limbs dip or tilt from the axial plane?
2. **Interpreting Diagrams** What type of fold is shown by Fold B? In what direction do the limbs dip or tilt from the axial plane?
3. **Drawing Conclusions** In Fold A, which rock layer is the oldest shown? Which rock layer is the youngest shown?
4. **Measuring** In Fold A, at what angle are the rock layers in both limbs dipping or tilted?
5. **Drawing Conclusions** In Fold B, which rock layer is the oldest shown? Which rock layer is the youngest shown?
6. **Measuring** In Fold B, at what angle are the rock layers in both limbs dipping or tilted?
7. **Classifying** What type of fold did you draw in the blank block diagram on your tracing paper?
8. **Observing** Is Fold A symmetrical or asymmetrical? Is Fold B symmetrical or asymmetrical?
9. **Observing** Is Fold A plunging or nonplunging? Is Fold B plunging or nonplunging?
10. **Applying Concepts** If you walk away from the axis on an eroded anticline, do the rocks get older or younger? How do the ages of the rocks change as you walk away from the axis in a syncline?

Go Further Use library or Internet sources to research the geologic terms "strike" and "dip." Draw a block diagram showing rocks layers that illustrate these terms. Give a presentation to the class, and explain the terms using your diagram as a visual aid.

Analyze and Conclude

1. an anticline; away from the axial plane
2. a syncline; towards the axial plane
3. In Fold A, the oldest rock layer shown is #1; the youngest is #6.
4. In Fold A the left limb dips at about 50°, and the right limb dips at 80°.
5. In Fold B, the oldest rock layer shown is #1; the youngest is #5.
6. In Fold B, both limbs dip at about 45°.
7. The completed block diagram should show a basin with the rock layers dipping or tilted towards the center. The older rocks should be indicated as occurring toward the outside of the basin, with younger rocks in the center. Diagrams should show the basin from all three sides (top, front, and side)
8. Fold A is asymmetrical; Fold B is symmetrical.
9. Both Fold A and Fold B are nonplunging folds.
10. On an eroded anticline, the rock layers get younger as you walk away from the axial plane. On an eroded syncline, the rock layers get older as you walk away from the axial plane.

Go Further

Strike is the direction or trend of a bedding or fault plane as it intersects the horizontal. Dip is the angle that a bedding or fault plane makes with the horizontal, measured perpendicular to the strike of the planar surface. Student diagrams should clearly illustrate these concepts. Student presentations should clearly explain strike and dip and be organized and scientifically accurate.
Visual, Kinesthetic

Study Guide

Study Tip

Organize New Information
Have students make a glossary for the chapter vocabulary terms using their own words for the definitions. Many of the vocabulary terms can be described visually. Encourage students to use illustrations or mnemonics in their glossary to help them remember meanings.

Thinking Visually

a. ocean-ocean
b. continent-continent
c. volcanic island arc on the ocean floor and volcanic mountains
d. folded mountains

CHAPTER 11

Study Guide

11.1 Rock Deformation

Key Concepts

- The factors that influence the strength of a rock and how it will deform include temperature, confining pressure, rock type, and time.
- Rocks deform permanently in two ways: brittle deformation and ductile deformation.
- Forces that are unable to deform rock when first applied may cause rock to flow if the force is maintained over a long period of time.
- The three types of stresses that deform rocks are tensional stress, compressional stress, and shear stress.
- The three main types of folds are anticlines, synclines, and monoclines.
- The major types of faults are normal faults, reverse faults, thrust faults, and strike-slip faults.

Vocabulary

deformation, *p. 308;* stress, *p. 308;* strain, *p. 308;* anticline, *p. 310;* syncline, *p. 310;* monocline, *p. 310;* normal fault, *p. 311;* reverse fault, *p. 312;* thrust fault, *p. 312;* strike-slip fault, *p. 313*

11.2 Types of Mountains

Key Concepts

- Mountains are classified by the dominant processes that have formed them.
- Mountains that are formed primarily by folding are called folded mountains.
- Large-scale normal faults are associated with structures called fault-block mountains.
- Mountains formed by the upwarping of a large block of basement rock are called domed mountains. Downwarped structures having a circular shape are called basins.

Vocabulary

orogenesis, *p. 314;* folded mountain, *p. 314;* fault-block mountain, *p. 315;* graben, *p. 315;* horst, *p. 315;* uplifted mountain, *p. 316*

11.3 Mountain Formation

Key Concepts

- Most mountain building occurs at convergent plate boundaries. Colliding plates provide the compressional forces that fold, fault, and metamorphose the thick layers of sediments deposited at the edges of landmasses.
- Ocean-ocean convergence mainly produces volcanic mountains.
- The types of mountains formed by ocean-continental convergence are volcanic mountains and folded mountains.
- At a convergent boundary between two continental plates, a collision between the continental fragments will result and form folded mountains.
- The mountains that form along ocean ridges at divergent plate boundaries are fault-block mountains.
- Because of isostasy, deformed and thickened crust will undergo regional uplift both during mountain building and for a long period afterward.

Vocabulary

accretionary wedge, *p. 319;* accretion, *p. 321;* terrane, *p. 322;* isostasy, *p. 323;* isostatic adjustment, *p. 323*

Thinking Visually

Concept Map Copy the concept map onto a sheet of paper. Use information from the chapter to complete it.

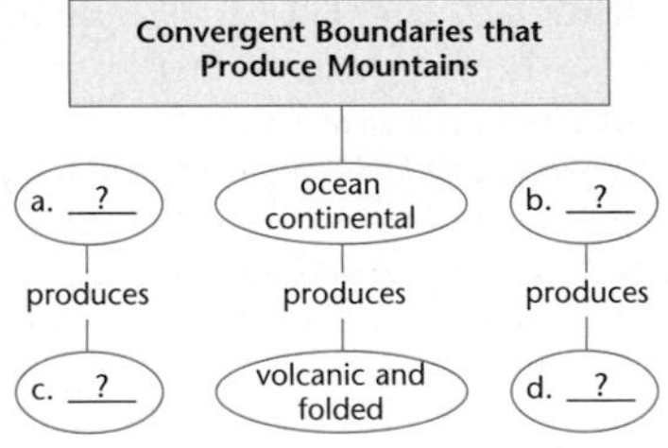

Chapter Assessment Resources

Print
Chapter Test, Chapter 11
Test Prep Resources, Chapter 11

Technology
Computer Test Bank, Chapter 11 Test
Online Text, Chapter 11
Go Online, PHSchool.com, Chapter 11

NY Regents Content Item

Assessment

Interactive textbook with assessment at PHSchool.com 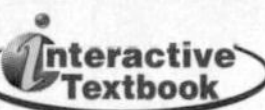

Reviewing Content

Choose the number that best answers the question or completes the statement.

1 Which one of the following is NOT a form of rock deformation?
(1) elastic deformation
(2) ductile deformation
(3) brittle deformation
(4) oblique deformation

2 The two most common types of linear folds are
(1) anticlines and synclines
(2) basins and monoclines
(3) domes and synclines
(4) thrusts and anticlines

3 Orogenesis or orogeny refers to those processes that produce NY
(1) spreading centers
(2) earthquakes
(3) mountains
(4) subduction zones

4 Which one of the following is NOT a factor that affects the strength of a rock?
(1) time
(2) age of the rock
(3) rock type
(4) temperature

5 The rock surface immediately above a fault surface is commonly called the
(1) anticline
(2) foot wall
(3) hanging wall
(4) syncline

6 Folding is usually the result of what type of stress?
(1) tensional stress
(2) compressional stress
(3) shear stress
(4) faulting

7 The collision and joining of crustal fragments to a continent is called
(1) subduction
(2) isostasy
(3) accretion
(4) extension

8 The San Andreas Fault is an example of what type of fault? NY
(1) normal fault
(2) strike-slip or transverse fault
(3) reverse fault
(4) thrust fault

9 What type of mountains form at convergent boundaries where two oceanic plates meet?
(1) volcanic mountains
(2) upwarped mountains
(3) folded mountains
(4) fault-block mountains

10 What is the most important difference between faults and joints?
(1) Joints occur along folds.
(2) Joints are often parallel.
(3) Joints have no displacement.
(4) Joints are always vertical.

Understanding Concepts

11 How does tensional stress deform a body of rock?

12 What is ductile deformation?

13 How is a syncline different from an anticline?

14 What types of faults are most commonly associated with fault-block mountains?

15 Define graben.

16 What types of faults are most commonly formed by compressional stresses?

Use the diagram below to answer questions 17–18.

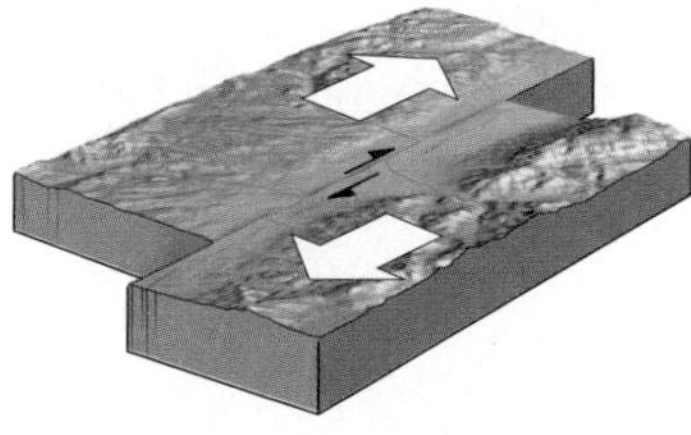

17 What type of fault is shown in the diagram?

18 What type of stress formed the fault shown in the diagram?

Homework Guide

Section	Questions
1	1, 2, 4–6, 8, 10–13, 16–18, 24, 25, 27, 29, 31–34
2	3, 14, 15, 22, 30
3	7, 9, 19–21, 23, 25, 26, 28, 35–37

Assessment

Reviewing Content

(1) 4	(2) 1	(3) 3
(4) 2	(5) 3	(6) 2
(7) 3	(8) 2	(9) 1
(10) 3		

Understanding Concepts

(11) Tensional stress pulls a body of rock apart or stretches it.
(12) It is a type of deformation that occurs in a solid state and produces a change in size and shape of an object without fracturing.
(13) Both are types of folds with two limbs. The limbs of an anticline dip or tilt in towards the fold axis. The limbs of a syncline dip or tilt away from the fold axis. The oldest rocks are in the axis of an anticline. A syncline has younger rocks in the axis.
(14) normal faults
(15) A graben is a fault-bounded block that has been down-dropped to form a valley or depression.
(16) reverse faults and thrusts faults
(17) a strike-slip fault
(18) shear stress
(19) Mountain building is most directly associated with convergent plate boundaries.
(20) As a subducting plate bends and begins to descend into the mantle, most sediments are scraped off the oceanic crust and from along the shoreline. These sediments are deposited in a wedge along the edge of the continental plate. This wedge of rock is deformed, faulted, and folded as subduction continues.
(21) A terrane refers to an area that has different rocks, fossils, and structures from the surrounding areas.
(22) Folded mountains are formed from compressional stresses. Folds and thrust faults are the primary structures found in folded mountains. The Alps, northern Rocky Mountains, and the Appalachians are examples of folded mountains.
(23) Volcanic mountains can form at mantle hot spots. The volcanoes in the Hawaiian Islands are examples.
(24) The rocks are oldest near the axis of the fold and get younger towards the outside of the fold.
(25) Tensional stress is most common at divergent boundaries. Fault-block mountains most commonly form at divergent boundaries. The Mid-Atlantic Ridge is an example.

Critical Thinking

(26) The erosion would remove rock from the mountain range, which would thin the crust. As the crust is thinned, it will rise because the load on the crust is reduced. In this way, the "roots" of the mountain range will rise to balance the crustal load lost to erosion.
(27) Normal faults and reverse faults are both relatively high-angle faults. Normal faults are caused by tensional stress, while reverse faults are caused by compressional stress. In a normal fault, the hanging wall moves down relative to the footwall. In a reverse fault, the hanging wall moves up relative to the footwall.
(28) The continental fragment would not be subducted because it is too buoyant. The fragment would be accreted onto the edge of the continent. The collision would probably cause deformation and mountain building.
(29) Over time, erosion often levels the surface expression of anticlines, leaving only the upfolded rock layers below the surface.
(30) Both a dome and basin are circular in shape and are caused by warping. A dome is caused by broad upwarping in basement rock. Basins are caused by downwarping. In basins, the youngest rocks are found near the center. In a dome, the oldest rocks form the core.

Analyzing Data

(31) the hanging wall
(32) The hanging wall has moved up relative to the footwall.
(33) a reverse fault
(34) compressional stress

Assessment *continued*

19 In the plate tectonics theory, what type of plate boundary is associated with the formation of the Himalayas and Appalachians? NY

20 What is an accretionary wedge? Briefly describe its formation.

21 Define terrane.

22 Describe folded mountains. Give an example of folded mountains.

23 How do volcanic mountains form at locations that are not near plate boundaries? Give an example.

24 How do the ages of rock layers change from the axial plane or center of an anticline or fold outwards towards the limbs or outer edges? NY

25 What type of stress is most common at divergent boundaries? What type of mountains are most often found at this type of boundary? Give an example. NY

Critical Thinking

26 **Applying Concepts** How would a period of major erosion affect the isostatic adjustment of a mountain range?

27 **Comparing and Contrasting** Compare normal faults and reverse faults.

28 **Predicting** What would most likely happen if a continental fragment the size of Greenland was carried by an oceanic plate into a subduction zone along the margin of a continental plate? NY

29 **Inferring** Why don't anticlines always appear as hills, even though the rocks beneath the surface are folded upward?

30 **Comparing and Contrasting** How are a dome and a basin similar? How are they different?

Analyzing Data

Use the diagram below to answer questions 31–34.

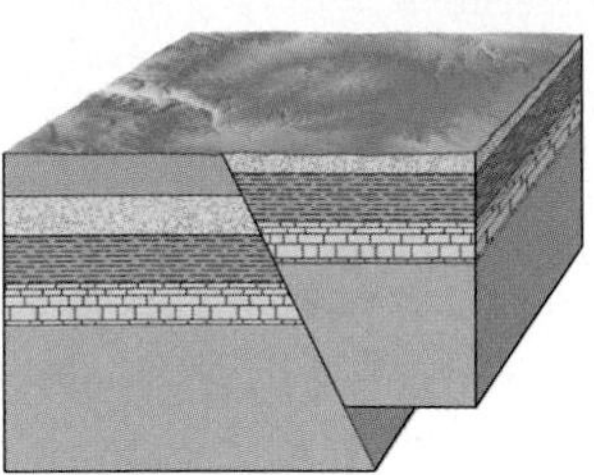

31 **Inferring** What is the block on the right side of the fault called?

32 **Observing** Describe the movement along the fault. NY

33 **Interpreting Diagrams** What type of fault is shown in the diagram? NY

34 **Drawing Conclusions** What type of stress was responsible for forming this fault?

Concepts in Action

35 **Designing an Experiment** Put together an experiment that models the isostatic adjustment that results from a continent-continent collision and the erosion that takes place on the resulting mountain range.

36 **Hypothesizing** Explain how a slice of ocean crust could be found on top of a peak in the Himalayas. NY

37 **Writing in Science** Write a paragraph briefly describing the development of volcanic mountains at an oceanic-oceanic convergent boundary.

Performance-Based Assessment

Classifying Use a world physiographic map or a world atlas and Figure 8 in Chapter 9 to classify the following mountains or mountain ranges: Mount Baker in Washington State, the Zagros Mountains in Iran, Mount Fuji in Japan, and the mountains in western Egypt.

Concepts in Action

(35) Students could use wooden blocks or books stacked on a surface that can be depressed by the weight, such as a blanket or rubber sheet stretched between tables. The surface must be able to "give" under the weight, but it cannot break or slide completely down, so it needs to be secured in some way.
(36) The Himalayas were formed by a collision between India and the Eurasian plate. A slice of ocean crust that occurred in the ocean between India and the Eurasian plate before the collision could have been incorporated into the accretionary wedge along the edge of the Eurasian plate and then become thrust-faulted, folded, or uplifted up onto the peaks of the mountains after the continental collision.
(37) A volcanic island arc occurs where two oceanic plates converge and one is subducted beneath the other. The interaction of the two plates results in partial melting of the mantle above the subducting plate. The magma slowly rises, creating volcanoes on the seafloor that eventually grow into volcanic mountains.

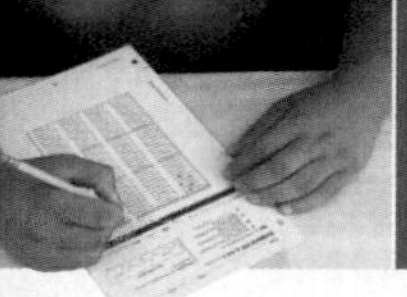

Regents Practice Exam

Test-Taking Tip

Avoiding Careless Mistakes
Students often make mistakes when they fail to examine a test question and possible answers thoroughly. Always read a question carefully and underline key words, such as NOT, EXCEPT, or EXCLUDING. After choosing an answer, reread the question to check your selection.

Which of the following is NOT caused by compressional stresses?

(1) thrust faults
(2) anticlines
(3) reverse faults
(4) normal faults

(Answer: 4)

For *each* statement or question, choose the *number* of the word or expression that, of those given, best completes the statement or answers the question. Some questions may require the use of the *Earth Science Reference Tables.*

1 What will most likely happen when two continental plates collide?
(1) subduction (2) a trench will form
(3) a ridge will form (4) folded mountains will form

2 Downwarping of the crust causes
(1) subsidence
(2) subduction
(3) basins
(4) kettle lakes

3 Deposition would be the most likely to occur at a(n)
(1) basin (2) plateau
(3) anticline (4) trench

4 Which of the following are NOT generally associated with convergent margins?
(1) volcanic mountains (2) folded mountains
(3) strike-slip faults (4) island arcs

Answer the following questions in complete sentences. Some questions may require the use of the Earth Science Reference Tables. Base your answers to questions 5 through 7 on the diagram at top right, which shows Ocean-Continental Convergence.

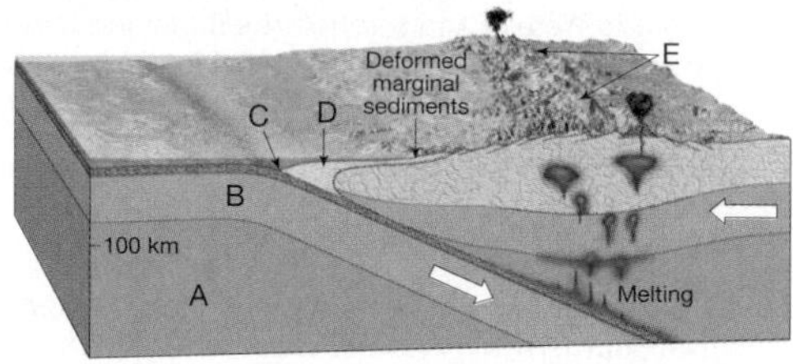
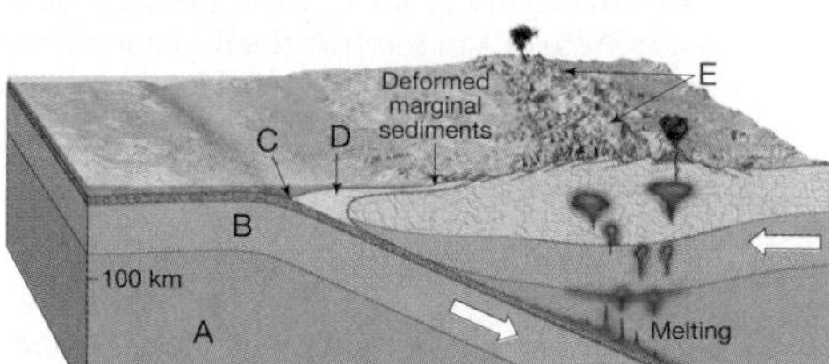

5 According to the diagram,
(1) oceanic crust is thicker than continental crust
(2) oceanic crust is thinner than continental crust
(3) divergence causes subduction
(4) upwarping occurs when oceanic and continental crust meet

6 What types of mountains can form at the type of plate boundary illustrated in the diagram?
(1) upwarped mountains and volcanic mountains
(2) volcanic mountains and fault-block mountains
(3) volcanic mountains and folded mountains
(4) folded mountains and upwarped mountains

7 At which of the following locations would you find a plate boundary like the one shown above?
(1) San Andreas Fault
(2) Mid-Atlantic Ridge
(3) East African Rift
(4) Peru-Chile Trench

8 Describe the relative motion of plates at the San Andreas Fault. What type of fault is the San Andreas Fault?

9 Explain how the Himalaya Mountains formed. What type of plate boundary exists at the Himalayas today?

10 Describe one observable surface feature that indicates plate movement.

Regents Practice Exam

(1) 4
(2) 3
(3) 1
(4) 3
(5) 2
(6) 3
(7) 4
(8) The Pacific Plate appears to be moving northwest while the North American Plate appears to be moving southeast. The San Andreas Fault is a strike-slip fault.
(9) The Himalayas formed when the Indian subcontinent collided with Asia, causing folded mountains. It is still a convergent boundary today.
(10) An accurate description of any feature associated with a plate boundary is acceptable. For example, folded mountains, evidence of lateral faulting, volcanoes, etc…

Performance-Based Assessment

volcanic mountain; folded mountains; volcanic mountain; fault-block mountains

Go Online PHSchool.com

Your students can independently test their knowledge of the chapter and print out their results.

understanding **EARTH**

Mountain Building away from Plate Margins L2

Background

The mountain ranges generated during the Laramide Orogeny include Colorado's Front Range, the Sangre de Cristo of New Mexico and Colorado, and Wyoming's Bighorns.

Teaching Tips

- Be sure students understand that the processes described and illustrated represent one possible mechanism for the uplift that led to the formation of the southern Rockies, Colorado Plateau, and Basin and Range Province. Other mechanisms may be possible.
- Refer students back to p. 315 for more on the formation of the fault-block mountains that make up the Basin and Range Province.
- Point out that the structural geology of a mountain range, or any other geologic feature, is not always evident from looking at the topography. For example, to the casual observer, a mountain range produced primarily by folding may look like a mountain range produced primarily by faulting. Ask students why this is the case. *(Erosion and deposition shape the landscape and often obscure the structural geology of the area.)* Discuss how geologists learn about the structural geology of an area. *(by making observations of the entire area; identifying and mapping the rock, faults, folds, and other geologic features in the area; correlating this information with that from adjacent areas; and putting all the information together to get an accurate picture of an area's geology)*

Logical

understanding **EARTH**

Mountain Building away from Plate Margins

In the American West, extending from the Front Range of the southern Rocky Mountains across the Colorado Plateau and through the Basin and Range Province, the topography consists of lofty peaks and elevated plateaus. According to the plate tectonics model, you would expect mountain belts to be produced along continental margins and convergent plate boundaries. But this mountainous region extends inland almost 1600 kilometers, far from the nearest plate boundary.

The Laramide Orogeny

The portion of the Rocky Mountains that extends from southern Montana to New Mexico was produced by a period of uplift known as the Laramide Orogeny. This event, which created some of the most picturesque scenery in the United States, peaked about 60 million years ago.

The event that may have triggered the Laramide Orogeny started with the nearly horizontal subduction of the Farallon plate eastward beneath North America. As the diagrams show, this plate extended inland as far as the Black Hills of South Dakota. As the subducted slab scraped beneath the continent, compressional forces started a period of tectonic activity. About 65 million years ago the Farallon plate began to sink into the mantle. As this relatively cool plate gradually separated from the lithosphere above, it was replaced by hot rock that upwelled from the mantle. Thus, according to this scenario, the hot mantle provided the buoyancy to raise the southern Rockies, as well as the Colorado Plateau and the Basin and Range Province.

Basin and Range

In the southern Rockies this event uplifted large blocks of ancient basement rocks along high-angle faults. This produced mountains separated by large basins that became filled with sediment as the mountains eroded. The upwelling that is associated with the Basin and Range Province started about 50 million years ago and remains active today. Here the buoyancy of the warm material caused upwarping and rifting that elongated the overlying crust by 200 to 300 kilometers. The lower crust is ductile and easily stretched. The upper crust, on the other hand, is brittle and deforms by faulting. The extension and faulting broke the uplifted crust, causing individual blocks to shift. The high portions of these tilted blocks make up the mountain ranges, whereas their low areas form the basins, now partially filled with sediment.

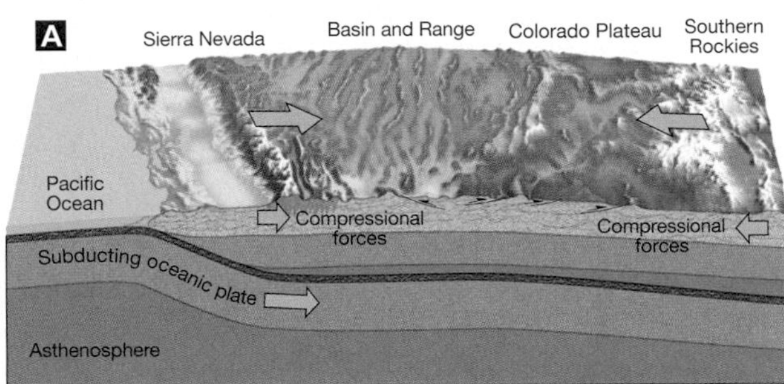

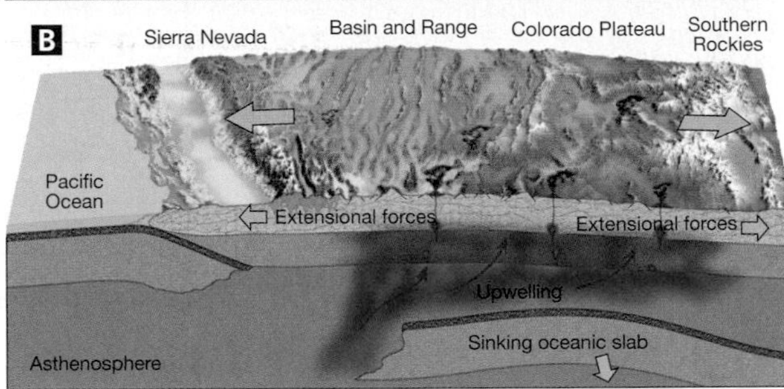

A Nearly horizontal subduction of an oceanic plate initiated a period of tectonic activity. **B** Sinking of this oceanic slab allowed for upwelling of hot mantle material that buoyantly raised the crust.

Contents

Landform Relief Map for New York

Objectives Overview

Standards that appear in more than one section are listed by code number only. Refer to the Core Curriculum listing at the front of this book for the full text of each Standard.

Growth and Economic Development
NY 7.1.
KEY IDEA 7.1. The knowledge and skills of mathematics, science, and technology are used together to make informed decisions and solve problems, especially those relating to issues of science/technology/society, consumer decision making, design, and inquiry into phenomena.

Geological History
NY 4.2.1.m., 4.2.1.n., 4.2.1.u., 6.5.
4.2.1.m. Many processes of the rock cycle are consequences of plate dynamics.
4.2.1.n. Many of Earth's surface features such as mid-ocean ridges / rifts, trenches / subduction zones/island arcs, mountain ranges, hot spots, and the magnetic and age patterns in surface bedrock are a consequence of forces associated with plate motion and interaction.
4.2.1.u. The natural agents of erosion include streams, glaciers, wave action, and wind.
KEY IDEA 6.5. Identifying patterns of change is necessary for making predictions about future behavior and conditions.

Physiographic Regions
NY 4.2.1.p., 4.2.1.r., 4.2.1.s., 4.2.1.u.,
4.2.1.p. Landforms are the result of the interaction of tectonic forces and the processes of weathering, erosion, and deposition.
4.2.1.r. Climate variations, structure, and characteristics of bedrock influence the development of landscape features including mountains, plateaus, plains, valleys, ridges, escarpments, and stream drainage patterns.
4.2.1.s. Weathering is the physical and chemical breakdown of rocks at or near Earth's surface. Soils are the result of weathering and biological activity over long periods of time.

Geology of Landforms
NY 4.2.1.p., 4.2.1.q., 4.2.1.v., 6.1.
4.2.1.q. Topographic maps represent landforms through the use of contour lines that are isolines connecting points of equal elevation. Gradients and profiles can be determined from changes in elevation over a given distance.

4.2.1.v. Patterns of deposition result from a loss of energy within the transporting system and are influenced by the size, shape, and density of the transported particles. Sediment deposits may be sorted or unsorted.
KEY IDEA 6.1. Through systems thinking, people can recognize the commonalities that exist among all systems and how parts of a system interrelate and combine to perform specific functions.

Natural Resources
NY 4.3.1.a., 4.3.1.c., 6.6., 7.1.
4.3.1.a. Minerals have physical properties determined by their chemical composition and crystal structure.
4.3.1.c. Rocks are usually composed of one or more minerals.
KEY IDEA 6.6. In order to arrive at the best solution that meets criteria within constraints, it is often necessary to make trade-offs

Ecosystems
NY 4.1.2.g., 4.2.1.c., 4.2.2.d., 7.1.
4.1.2.g. Earth has continuously been recycling water since the outgassing of water early in its history. This constant recirculation of water at and near Earth's surface is described by the hydrologic (water) cycle.
4.2.1.c. Weather patterns become evident when weather variables are observed, measured, and recorded. These variables include air temperature, air pressure, moisture (relative humidity and dewpoint), precipitation (rain, snow, hail, sleet, etc.), wind speed and direction, and cloud cover.
4.2.2.d. Temperature and precipitation patterns are altered by: natural events such as El Niño and volcanic eruptions and human influences including deforestation, urbanization, and the production of greenhouse gases such as carbon dioxide and methane.

Soil
NY 4.2.1.p., 4.2.1.s., 4.2.1.v., 4.2.1.w.
4.2.1.w. Sediments of inorganic and organic origin often accumulate in depositional environments. Sedimentary rocks form when sediments are compacted and/or cemented after burial or as the result of chemical precipitation from seawater.

Earth System Profile NEW YORK

CONCEPTS — in Action —

How do science concepts apply to your world? Here are some questions you'll be able to answer after you read this chapter.

- What are New York's natural resources?
- What ecosystems are found in your area of the state?
- How did the Finger Lakes form?
- What is being done to protect the coast of New York?
- What is the average precipitation your area of New York receives in a year?
- Why do some areas of New York get so much snow?

This chapter was prepared by Nanette Kalis, Renee Skelton, and Mary Dylewski.

Although New York is known for its bustling cities, the state is also home to many scenic natural wonders. One of these wonders, the Adirondack Mountains, is located in northeastern New York. Pictured here, the Ausable River cascades through these beautiful mountains. ▶

Fresh Water
NY 4.1.2.g., 6.1., 6.6.
KEY IDEA 6.6. In order to arrive at the best solution that meets criteria within constraints, it is often necessary to make trade-offs

Coastal Regions
NY 4.2.1.u., 6.6., 7.1.
4.2.1.u. The natural agents of erosion include streams, glaciers, wave action, and wind.

Climate
NY 4.2.1.c., 4.2.1.g., 4.2.2., 4.2.2.c.
4.2.1.g. Weather variables can be represented in a variety of formats including radar and satellite images, weather maps (including station models, isobars, and fronts), atmospheric cross-sections, and computer models.
INDICATOR 4.2.2. Explain how incoming solar radiation, ocean currents, and land masses affect weather and climate.

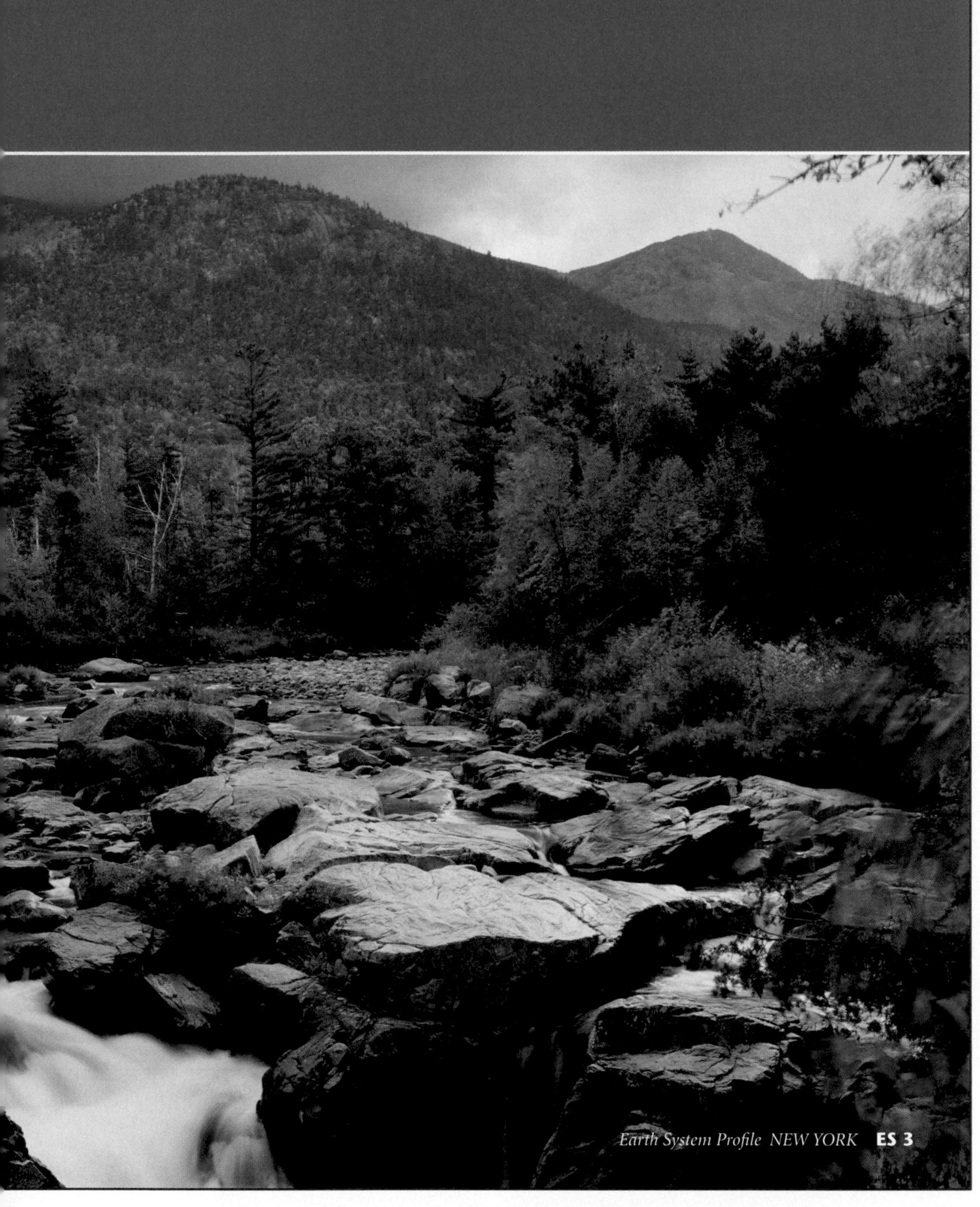

Weather Patterns
NY 4.2.1.c., 4.2.1.h., 4.2.1.i., 4.2.2.c.
4.2.2.c. A locations climate is influenced by latitude, proximity to large bodies of water, ocean currents, prevailing winds, vegetative cover, elevation, and mountain ranges.

Using the Internet to Research Disaster Safety
NY 2.1., 2.2., 4.2.1.h, 7.1.
KEY IDEA 2.1. Information technology is used to retrieve, process, and communicate information as a tool to enhance learning.
KEY IDEA 2.2. Knowledge of the impacts and limitations of information systems is essential to its effective and ethical use.
4.2.1.h. Atmospheric moisture, temperature and pressure distributions; jet streams, wind; air masses and frontal boundaries; and the movement of cyclonic systems and associated tornadoes, thunderstorms, and hurricanes occur in observable patterns. Loss of property, personal injury, and loss of life can be reduced by effective emergency preparedness.

How Could Global Warming Impact New York?
NY 4.2.1.c., 4.2.1.i., 4.2.2.d., 7.1.
4.2.1.i. Seasonal changes can be explained using concepts of density and heat energy. These changes include the shifting of global temperature zones, the shifting of planetary wind and ocean current patterns, the occurrence of monsoons, hurricanes, flooding, and severe weather.

INVESTIGATION
NY 7.2
Collect, collate, and process data concerning potential natural disasters; develop an emergency action plan.

Review Science Concepts

Chapter 11A
In this chapter students will apply many of the concepts they studied in Chapters 1–11. To prepare, students should review the process of plate tectonics and the interactions that occur at plate boundaries. There are a variety of features that can form as two plates interact. An understanding of these will provide students with the background necessary to fully comprehend the different landforms and regions in New York.

Students should be familiar with glaciers and the landforms glaciers create. New York has been heavily influenced by glaciations and students should be able to recognize glacially modified features in their area.

Reviewing information about natural and mineral resources will prepare students for a better understanding of the impact and importance of New York's natural resources. They should also be familiar with the idea that soil, water, and air are important resources that need to be conserved and protected.

ENGAGE/EXPLORE

The following websites are locations where more information on New York can be gathered.

Official Website for the State of New York
http://www.state.ny.us/

State University of New York website
www.suny.edu

New York State Department of Environmental Conservation
http://www.dec.state.ny.us/

New York State Climate Office
http://nysc.eas.cornell.edu/

Growth and Economic Development

1 FOCUS

Section Objective

KEY IDEA 7.1. The knowledge and skills of mathematics, science, and technology are used together to make informed decisions and solve problems, especially those relating to issues of science/technology/society, consumer decision making, design, and inquiry into phenomena.

Reading Focus

Build Vocabulary L2

Word Parts Ask students to define the word immigrant in their own words. *(Answers will vary but may include people who move to a country.)* Tell them that the term comes from the Latin *immigrat-* or to go into.

2 INSTRUCT

Bellringer L2

Ask students to name the governor of New York. Then see if they can name any of their state representatives or senators. Some students may have some knowledge of their county government. Ask them what role their county government plays in their every day lives. *(It oversees health, education, and welfare issues.)*

Growth and Economic Development

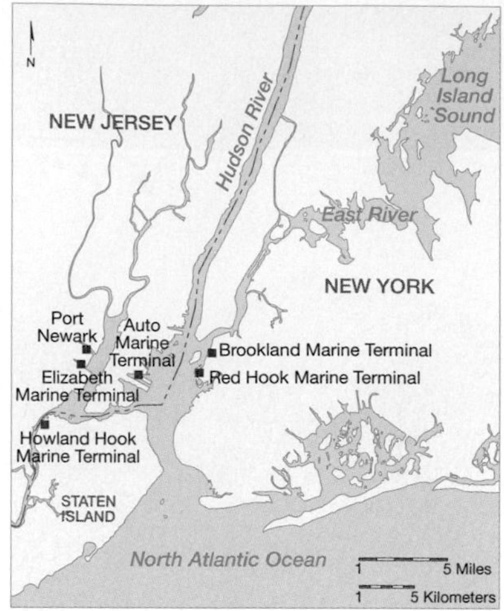

Figure 1 Ports of New York and New Jersey

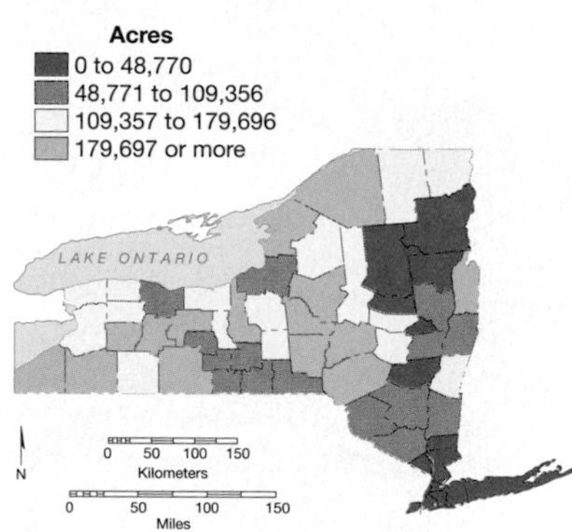

Figure 2 Agricultural Land Use in New York

New York ranks 27th in area compared with the rest of the United States. However, with nearly 19 million people, it is the third most populous state. About 84 percent of New York's residents live in urban areas. The state has always had a strong metropolitan history. During the first U.S. Census taken in 1790, New York City had a population of 33,000, making it the largest city in America. Today, more than 8 million people live in the city, and it retains the title of the largest city in the United States.

Economic Development

Led by New York City, New York state is the banking, financial, and communications center of the United States. It is the largest center for printing and publishing in the country. New York's fine natural harbor makes it a hub for trade, with the Port of New York ranking third in the United States in the amount of traffic it handles each year. See Figure 1. Manufacturing also plays a big role in the state's economy; its 24,000 industrial plants produce everything from chemicals to machinery, electronics, and baked goods. The state ranks 14th in the nation in mineral production with its 2500 mines. Although agriculture accounts for a relatively small portion of New York's total economy, the state's farms are among the nation's top dairy and fruit producers. See Figure 2.

In most of New York's 62 counties, county governments oversee local services, while state issues are addressed in Albany, the state capital.

Population Centers

Table 1 shows the populations of New York's five largest cities. **Using Tables** *Calculate the percentage change in population for each of New York's largest cities.*

Table 1 Population of New York's Largest Cities

City	2000 Census	1990 Census
New York City	8,008,278	7,322,564
Buffalo	292,648	328,123
Rochester	219,773	231,636
Yonkers	196,086	188,082
Syracuse	147,306	163,860

Source: U.S. Census

Facts and Figures

Welcome to... Gull Island? Oyster Island? When Manhattan was occupied by the Mohegan Indians in the 17th century, Ellis Island was just a small sandy island. The Mohegans named it Gull Island. The island was purchased by a Dutchman in the 1600's and he renamed it Oyster Island as it was used as a place to gather oysters. When the British took possession of the island in 1664 they renamed it Gull Island. Shortly thereafter the name was changed to Gibbet Island because pirates were hanged there. The island was ultimately named after Samuel Ellis who bought the island in the 1770's. He turned the island into a picnic spot before the US War Department bought it in 1808.

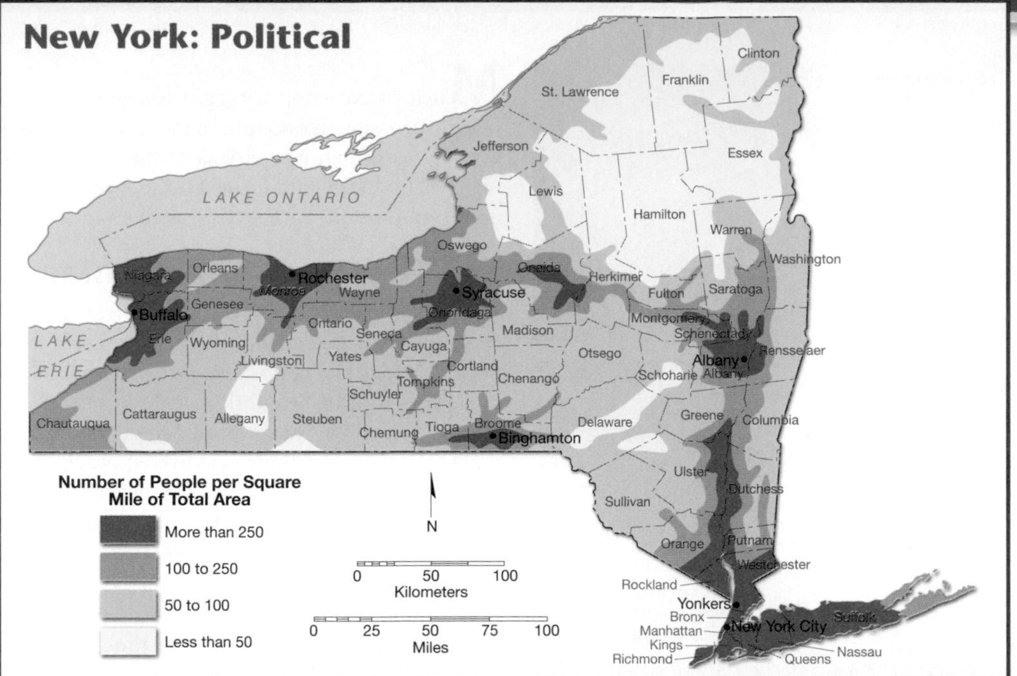

Figure 3 New York Counties, Major Cities, and Population Centers

Population Growth

Today, almost 20 percent of New York's population is non-native. After steady population growth for much of its history, New York lost more than 500,000 residents in the 1970s and 1980s. This decrease in population was largely due to an economic slump. In the 1990s, however, the economy recovered, unemployment fell, and people returned to the state to take advantage of new job opportunities. Between 1990 and 2003 New York's population grew by more than one million people. New York now has an average of 402 people per square mile—that's five times the national average. See Figure 3. This high population density creates challenges in transportation, affordable housing, and availability of urban resources, as shown in Figure 4.

Inferring *What other problems might New York face because of its high population density?*

What caused New York's population decrease in the 1970s and 1980s?

Figure 4 Building Up In New York City, high-rise buildings accommodate the population's need for space to live and work.

Map Study Extension **L2**

Have students locate the county they live in. What part of the state is it in? *(Answers will vary.)* Are there any major population centers in the county? *(Answers will vary.)* What do the citizens of the county do for a living? *(Answers will vary.)* How do people who live elsewhere in the state make a living? *(Answers will vary.)*

3 ASSESS

Evaluate Understanding **L2**

Have students write three review questions for this section. Collect the questions and read them aloud to the class, challenging students to answer them.

Answer to . . .

Using Tables

New York City	*+9.36%*
Buffalo	*−10.81%*
Rochester	*−5.12%*
Yonkers	*+4.26%*
Syracuse	*−10.10%*

Inferring *Answers may vary. Sample answer: increase in crime and pollution*

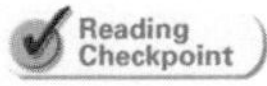

An economic slump occurred.

1 FOCUS

Section Objectives

4.2.1.m. Many processes of the rock cycle are consequences of plate dynamics. These include the production of magma (and subsequent igneous rock formation and contact metamorphism) at both subduction and rifting regions, regional metamorphism within subduction zones, and the creation of major depositional basins through down-warping of the crust.
4.2.1.n. Many of Earth's surface features such as mid-ocean ridges / rifts, trenches / subduction zones/island arcs, mountain ranges (folded, faulted, and volcanic), hot spots, and the magnetic and age patterns in surface bedrock are a consequence of forces associated with plate motion and interaction.
4.2.1.u. The natural agents of erosion include streams, glaciers, wave action, and wind.
KEY IDEA 6.5. Identifying patterns of change is necessary for making predictions about future behavior and conditions.

Reading Focus

Build Vocabulary L2

Flowchart Ask the students to create a flowchart of the geologic history of New York State and the Northern Appalachians. They should start at 600 million years ago.

2 INSTRUCT

Bellringer L2

Inform students that earthquakes do occasionally occur in New York. Ask students if they have experienced one. Ask students to think of ways that they should be prepared for an earthquake, if one was to hit their area. What precautions should they take before, during, and after an earthquake?

Geological History

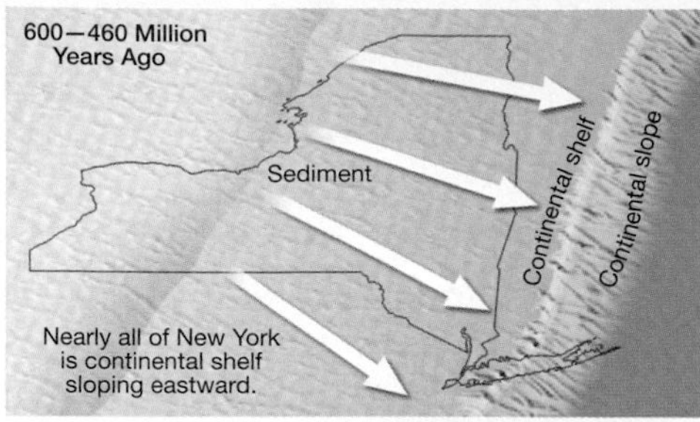

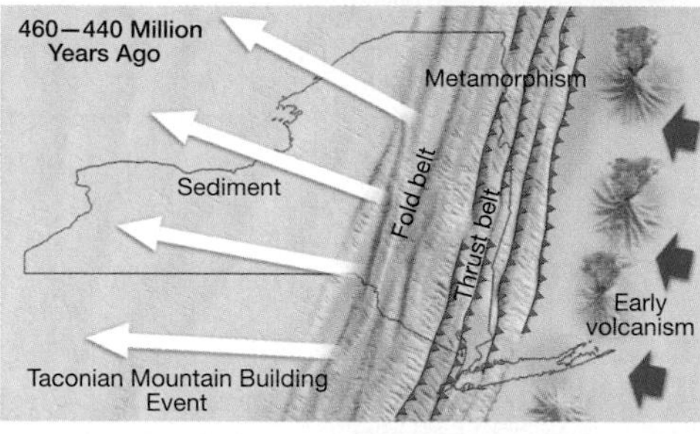

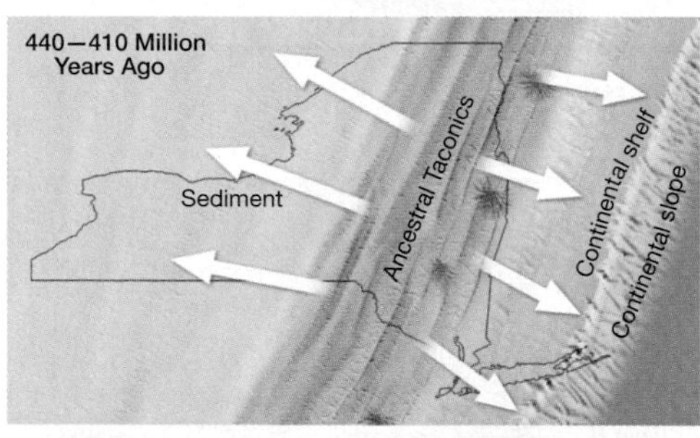

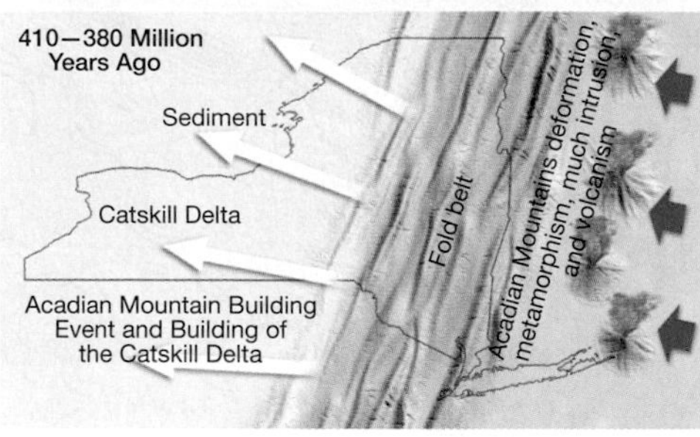

Figure 5 Formation of the Northern Appalachians

Much of New York's rugged topography is the result of processes that occurred hundreds of millions of years ago as tectonic plates collided. Other topographic highs in the state were formed more recently when uplift, erosion, and glaciers changed the land.

The Northern Appalachians

The Appalachian Mountains form a narrow band of deformed rocks that roughly parallel the eastern shore of North America. The northern part of this mountain range extends into New York state. Most of the sedimentary rocks in the range formed at least 600 million years ago when a shallow sea covered much of the eastern part of North America. As shown in Figure 5, this sea began to close about 460 million years ago as tectonic plates moved slowly toward one another. As the plates collided, one descended into the mantle and parts of it melted to form magma. This magma rose to form a chain of volcanoes. Over time, these volcanic rocks were thrust onto North America and, together with the sedimentary rocks, folded and faulted as the plates continued to collide. The mountains that formed as the result of these processes were the ancestral Taconic Mountains.

About 410 million years ago, another period of mountain building began. As the plates carrying North America and Europe continued to move toward each other, a microcontinent became wedged between the two plates. Folding, faulting, and uplift of the edges of the plates produced the Acadian Mountains. Further deformation of Acadian Mountains occurred when the North American plate collided with the African plate to form the present Appalachians.

Forces acting on the ancestral Taconic and Acadian Mountains produced many of New York's present-day mountains. The Catskills formed as the result of weathering and erosion of ancestral Taconic Mountains. The present-day Taconic Range consists of vast slices of rock that were thrust westward and then eroded millions of years ago.

Customize for English Language Learners

Orogeny is the process that occurs during mountain-building. The Appalachian orogeny of North America resulted from a collision between North America and Africa. This collision happened during a geologic time called the Paleozoic Era. The Appalachian Mountains were formed. Look up the word "Paleozoic" in an encyclopedia. Write down the definition in your notebook. These mountains span hundreds of miles from Alabama to New Jersey. With a partner, look at a map of the United States. Identify the start of this mountain range in the Southern states. Follow the mountain range North. Write the definition of "orogeny" in your notebook.

North American Ice Sheets

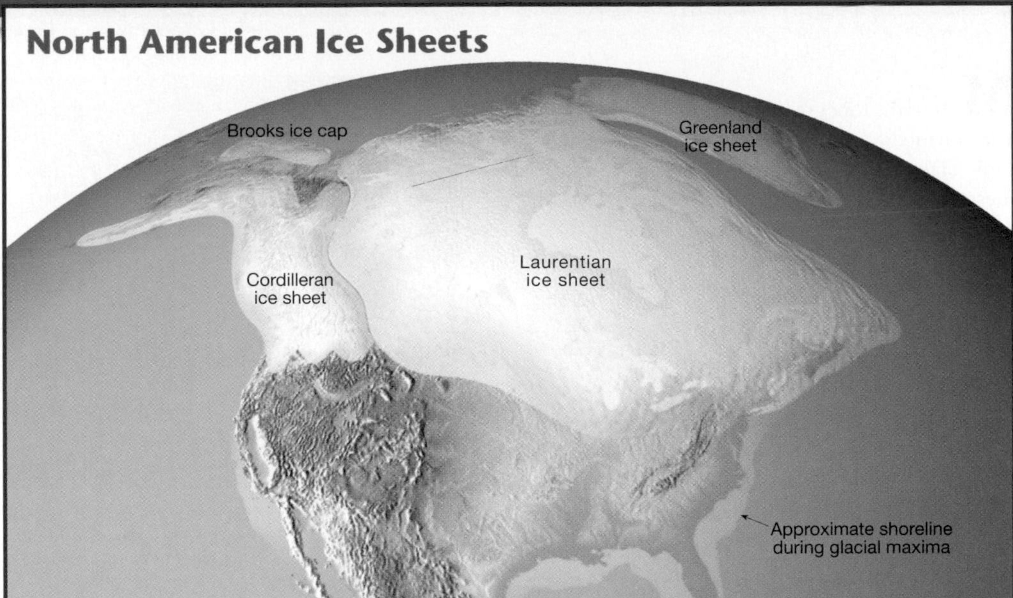

Figure 6 During the last ice age, which ended about 10,000 years ago, most of New York was covered by glaciers.

The Adirondack Mountains

Most of the rocks that make up the Adirondack Mountains are among the oldest rocks in the state. These rocks were once buried as much as 30 km beneath the surface. At such depths, intense heat and pressure changed the rocks into metamorphic rocks. Over the next several billion years, erosion removed much of the overlying material. The area also experienced intense deformation and faulting. Sometime between 40 and 60 million years ago, a dome-shaped area began to rise. This uplift may have been fueled by a hot spot deep beneath the crust. Erosion by both streams and glaciers then carved the individual peaks one sees today in the Adirondacks.

Glacial Activity

As Figure 6 shows, glaciers covered most of New York during the last ice age, which began about 3 million years ago. At its greatest extent, the Laurentian ice sheet reached as far south as Long Island. Many of New York's landforms were altered by the advance and retreat of glaciers.

Compare and contrast the formation of the northern Appalachian and the Adirondack mountains.

Map Study Extension **L2**

Have students examine the map of the ice sheets in North America. Direct them to the Laurentian ice sheet in particular. Ask them which New York state feature is at the front end of the glacier. *(Long Island)* Why is that feature located there? *(It represents the rocks and sediment the glacier was pushing in front of it. As the glacier retreated, the rocks were deposited in that location.)* How do we know that no other glacier traveled further south? *(If another glacier had pushed further south, the rocks deposited in that location would most likely have been picked up or scraped away by the passing glacier.)*

3 ASSESS

Evaluate Understanding **L2**

Have students create a timeline that shows the history and development of the northern Appalachian Mountains. They should choose their own scale to depict the changes in age.

Answer to . . .

The northern Appalachians formed from folding and uplifting associated with a series of continental collisions. The Adirondacks formed from uplifting associated with a hot spot.

Physiographic Regions

1 FOCUS

Section Objectives

4.2.1.p. Landforms are the result of the interaction of tectonic forces and the processes of weathering, erosion, and deposition.
4.2.1.r. Climate variations, structure, and characteristics of bedrock influence the development of landscape features including mountains, plateaus, plains, valleys, ridges, escarpments, and stream drainage patterns.
4.2.1.s. Weathering is the physical and chemical breakdown of rocks at or near Earth's surface. Soils are the result of weathering and biological activity over long periods of time.
4.2.1.u. The natural agents of erosion include streams, glaciers, wave action, and wind.

Reading Focus

Build Vocabulary L2

Paraphrase Ask students to write the following words on a sheet of paper: *drumlin, glaciated, eroded,* and *fertile.* Students should then come up with their own definition for these terms and relate them to the different regions of New York.

2 INSTRUCT

Bellringer L2

Ask students what images come to mind when they think of plateaus. Ask: **What type of industry might be found in the plateaus in New York?** *(farming)*

Physiographic Regions

Most of the topographic highlands in the state of New York formed as the result of uplift, movements of tectonic plates, and faulting. The landforms produced by these processes were often changed by the massive ice sheets that advanced and retreated over the state. New York can be divided into eight major physical regions, as shown in Figure 9.

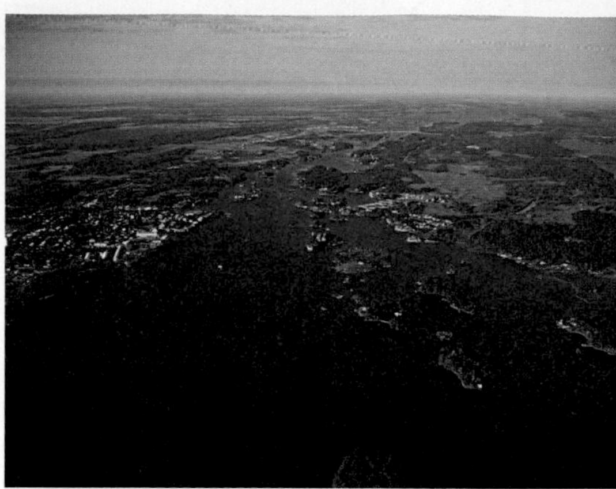

Figure 7 Thousand Islands in the St. Lawrence River Actually, 1864 islands make up this group of islands.

St. Lawrence Lowland and Great Lakes Lowland

The St. Lawrence Lowland borders the St. Lawrence River in the northern part of the state. Harder rocks were resistant to glacial erosion while softer rocks were removed. The more resistant rocks formed isolated hills. As the glaciers melted, water surrounded these hills to form the Thousand Islands, some of which are shown in Figure 7. The Great Lakes Lowland region borders the Great Lakes. This low-lying area is dotted with drumlins.

Figure 8 Finger Lakes Each of the eleven Finger Lakes is linear in shape. They stretch across the state in a 75-mile-wide path

Adirondack Upland and Tug Hill Plateau

South of the St. Lawrence Lowland is the Adirondack Upland. This region has the highest elevations in the state, with more than 40 peaks topping 1200 meters. Mount Marcy, the state's highest point at 1629 meters, is located here. The thin, glaciated soils in this region are poor for farming.

The Tug Hill Plateau lies to the southwest of the Adirondack Upland. Glaciers eroded this area and deposited much debris. This debris has weathered to form soils that are very poor for growing.

Appalachian Plateau and Hudson-Mohawk Lowland

The Appalachian Plateau is the largest region in New York, covering nearly half of the state. Long after it formed, glaciers moved over the plateau and deepened many of the river valleys in the western and central part of the plateau. As the glaciers melted, they deposited debris that dammed some of the rivers to form eleven Finger Lakes, which are shown in Figure 8.

The Hudson-Mohawk Lowland lies in the Hudson and Mohawk River valleys. This area of fertile soil is no more than 48 kilometers wide, but it forms the only navigable route through the Appalachian Mountains that was not created by people.

Facts and Figures

The St. Lawrence River connects the Great Lakes to the Atlantic Ocean. It is the world's longest deep-draft inland waterway and has the largest discharge of any river in North America.

MAP MASTER™ Skills Activity

New York: Physical

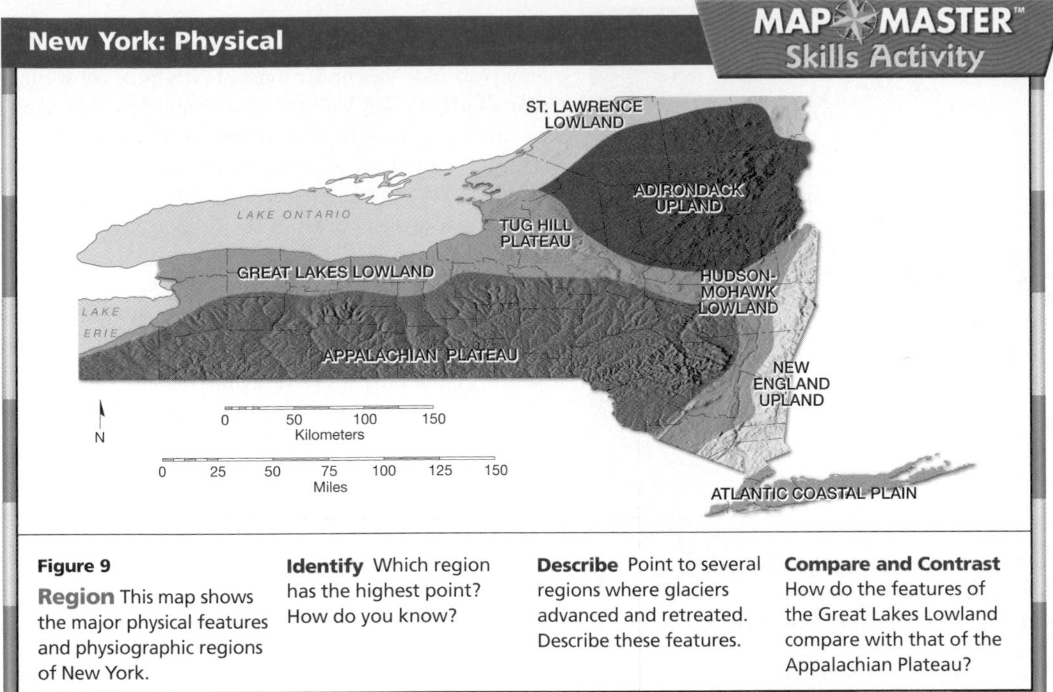

Figure 9
Region This map shows the major physical features and physiographic regions of New York.

Identify Which region has the highest point? How do you know?

Describe Point to several regions where glaciers advanced and retreated. Describe these features.

Compare and Contrast How do the features of the Great Lakes Lowland compare with that of the Appalachian Plateau?

New England Upland

The New England Upland is an area of hills and low mountains, such as the Taconic and Shawangunk ranges. The Palisades, shown in Figure 10, are steep, dark cliffs. They formed nearly 200 million years ago when magma flowed along cracks in the rocks. The magma cooled to form a sill that was exposed when the softer rock around the sill eroded.

Atlantic Coastal Plain

The Atlantic Coastal Plain includes Staten Island and Long Island. These islands are glacial ridges called moraines. As sea level rose at the end of the last glacial period, these moraines became cut off from the mainland to form islands.

How did Long Island form?

Figure 10 The Palisades on the Hudson River are one of the most striking features in the New England Upland.

MAP MASTER™ Skills Activity

Answers

Identify Adirondack Upland. The map shows mountainous regions in the Adirondack Upland and the Appalachian Plateau. The text points out the Adirondack Upland has the highest regions in the state. Also, uplifting has caused peaks to form on many mountains in this region.

Describe Sample answer: Glaciers carved many lakes (such as Finger Lakes) and rivers in the Appalachian Plateau. Glaciers also left behind the Thousand Islands in the St. Lawrence Lowland.

Compare and Contrast The Great Lakes Lowland appears as very flat terrain. The Appalachian Plateau is much higher with hills and valleys and a mountainous region near its Eastern border.

3 ASSESS

Evaluate Understanding

L2

Have students outline and summarize the different land features in NY State. Then, divide the class into groups and have students exchange papers and edit each other's outlines. Then, return the papers to the original owners to rewrite.

Answer to . . .

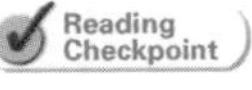

Long Island is part of a moraine, or ridge formed by glacial deposits of rock, clay, and sand. When the glaciers melted, sea level rose. The tip of the moraine was cut off from the mainland and transformed into Long Island.

Geology of Landforms

1 FOCUS

Section Objectives

4.2.1.p. Landforms are the result of the interaction of tectonic forces and the processes of weathering, erosion, and deposition.
4.2.1.q. Topographic maps represent landforms through the use of contour lines that are isolines connecting points of equal elevation. Gradients and profiles can be determined from changes in elevation over a given distance.
4.2.1.v. Patterns of deposition result from a loss of energy within the transporting system and are influenced by the size, shape, and density of the transported particles. Sediment deposits may be sorted or unsorted.
KEY IDEA 6.1. Through systems thinking, people can recognize the commonalities that exist among all systems and how parts of a system interrelate and combine to perform specific functions.

Reading Focus

Build Vocabulary L2

Compare-and-Contrast Table Ask students to create a compare-and-contrast table for different landforms discussed in this section: Niagara Falls, Howe Caverns, and Long Island

2 INSTRUCT

Bellringer L2

Ask students if they have ever visited Niagara Falls or a cave in central New York State. Ask them to describe what they saw and infer what the area might have looked 3 thousand years ago. Ask students to predict how this feature might change over the next few thousand years.

Geology of Landforms

Figure 11 Niagara Escarpment at Niagara Falls

Ancient Precambrian rock—between 800 million and 1.2 billion years old—lies under most of New York. Most surface landforms in New York are younger and were created or exposed by glaciers during the Paleozoic era. The glaciers changed river drainage patterns, scooped out lakes, sheared off tops of hills and mountains, and left behind ridges and hills of debris in their retreat, as shown in Figure 14.

Niagara Falls

Niagara Falls sits at the head of a gorge created as the Niagara River tumbles over the Niagara Escarpment as shown in Figure 11. The escarpment is made up of beds of shale, sandstone, and limestone, capped by harder Lockport dolostone. As water tumbles over the falls and pounds on the rock below, it carves out a plunge pool, or hollow, in the softer rock below and behind the falling water. This carving of the softer rock undercuts the hard dolostone cap rock, leaving a ledge that eventually falls in. This undercutting moves the falls gradually upstream by about 1 meter per year.

Howe Caverns

Between the Silurian and Devonian Periods of geologic time, about 395 to 435 million years ago, the land that is now New York was part of a large landmass near the equator. A warm, shallow sea covered this landmass. Over millions of years, calcium carbonate—the mineral calcite—was deposited from the water. Slowly, it became cemented and compressed to form a type of limestone called travertine. Outcrops of this limestone can be found at or very near the surface in several places around New York, including Schoharie and Albany Counties. As slightly acidic rainwater flows over the limestone, it dissolves the rock. Some of the water also seeps into the ground where it dissolves large volumes of rock to form huge caverns. Probably the most well known are Howe Caverns, just west of Albany.

In addition to its role in the formation of caves, the acidic water also deposits some of the dissolved calcite. Water that evaporates from the ceiling of a cave creates stalactites, as shown in Figure 12. When the water hits the cave floor and evaporates, the calcite crystals grow upward to form stalagmites.

Figure 12 Stalactites in Howe Caverns

Customize for English Language Learners

Students can work in pairs to explore the geology behind some of New York's famous landforms. First, have each pair of students study the four landforms mentioned in the text. Next, have them write down what they have learned about these landforms. Finally, encourage students to explain what they learned to the class.

Ronkonkoma Moraine

The Ronkonkoma moraine, which was deposited during the last episode of glaciation in New York, forms the backbone of Long Island. Figure 13 shows the Montauk Lighthouse at the eastern tip of the island. Here, and all along the moraine, wave energy is constantly removing material from the cliffs. At the same time, longshore currents are depositing sand along southern Long Island's beaches. At the lighthouse, the moraine dips beneath the ocean where it is continually being eroded by ocean currents.

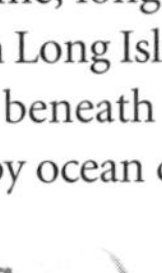

Reading Checkpoint *How were cavern systems formed and what do they look like?*

Figure 13 Montauk Lighthouse on Long Island

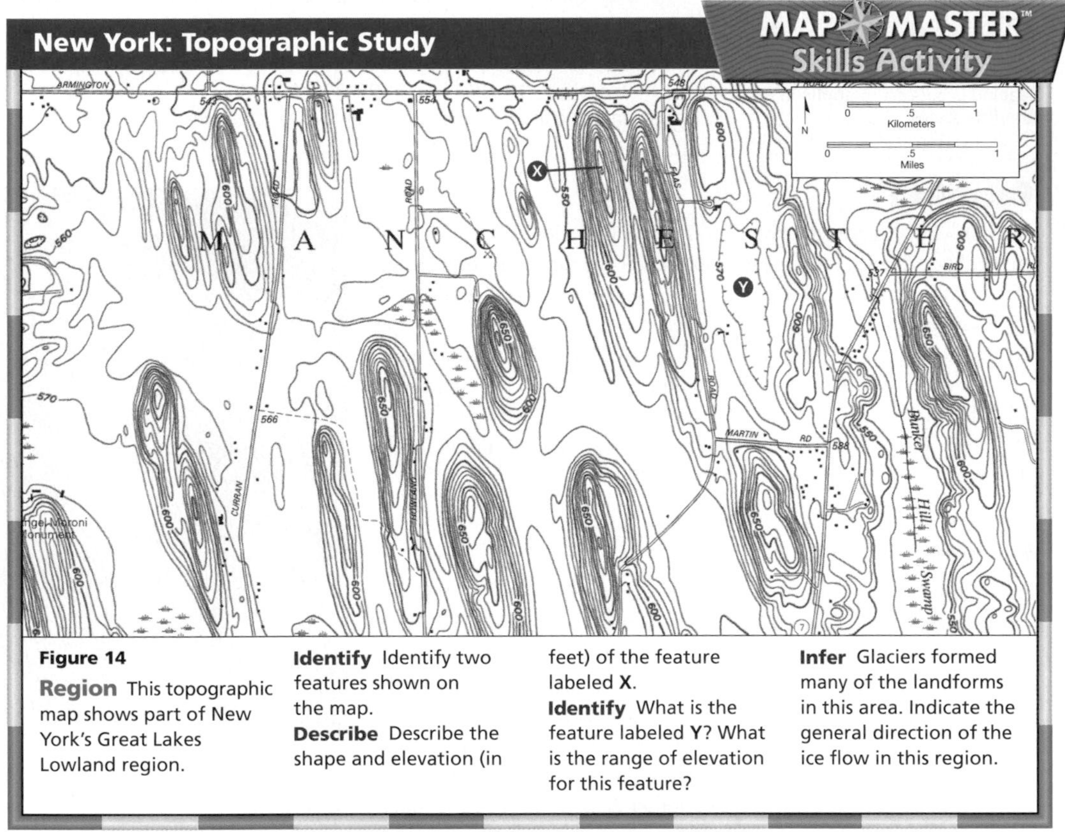

Figure 14
Region This topographic map shows part of New York's Great Lakes Lowland region.

Identify Identify two features shown on the map.
Describe Describe the shape and elevation (in feet) of the feature labeled **X**.
Identify What is the feature labeled **Y**? What is the range of elevation for this feature?

Infer Glaciers formed many of the landforms in this area. Indicate the general direction of the ice flow in this region.

MAP MASTER™ Skills Activity

Answers
Identify Possible answers: drumlin, depression, swamp, road
Describe The north side of the drumlin is steeper than the south side. The summit is 670 feet.
Identify a depression; 560–570 feet
Infer The ice flowed to the slight northwest.

3 ASSESS

Evaluate Understanding

Ask students to write paragraphs summarizing one of the landforms in the text: Niagara Falls, the cave region, or Long Island. The paragraph should include information on how the landform formed and the rock type that is responsible.

Answer to . . .

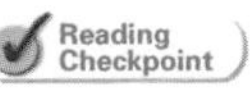

Reading Checkpoint *The water tumbling over falls pounds on the rock below and carves out a plunge pool. This undercuts the ledge, which eventually falls in and moves the falls upstream 1 meter per year.*

Natural Resources

1 FOCUS

Section Objectives

4.3.1.a. Minerals have physical properties determined by their chemical composition and crystal structure.
4.3.1.c. Rocks are usually composed of one or more minerals.
KEY IDEA 6.6. In order to arrive at the best solution that meets criteria within constraints, it is often necessary to make trade-offs
KEY IDEA 7.1. The knowledge and skills of mathematics, science, and technology are used together to make informed decisions and solve problems, especially those relating to issues of science/technology/society, consumer decision making, design, and inquiry into phenomena.

Reading Focus

Build Vocabulary L2

Word Parts Ask students to come up with words that have the prefix similar to *ager-(agriculture, agrarian, agronomy)*. Inform them that the prefix *ager-* comes from the Latin word for land. Then ask what they think the term *agrobiology* means. *(It is the science of plant and animal growth and nutrition as related to soil variation and crop yield.)*

2 INSTRUCT

Bellringer L2

Give students five minutes to list the reasons it is important for landowners to have guidance on issues such as reforestation and fire prevention. Lists will vary but should include information including the need to maintain ecosystems, renew the resource, and prevent devastating forest fires.

Natural Resources

Figure 15 New York's garnet mines yield industrial garnets and smaller stones for jewelry.

Figure 16 New York is one of the leading producers of apples in the fifty states.

New York has an abundance of natural resources, ranking 14th in the nation in the value of its minerals. Fertile soils support thousands of farms. Forests provide pulp for paper and lumber for furniture and construction. The state's waters are an important resource as well, providing hydroelectric power along the Niagara and St. Lawrence Rivers, as well as water for homes, farms, and industry. New York's 204-kilometer-long Atlantic coastline, more than 84,000 kilometers of streams and rivers, and 2000 lakes also support recreational and commercial fishing.

Rocks and Minerals

As Figure 18 shows, most of New York's mineral resources are nonmetals, such as crushed stone, sand, and gravel. These materials are used primarily for construction. The state is a producer of emery, salt, talc, soapstone, garnet (shown in Figure 15), pyrophyllite, and wollastonite. Most of these minerals are mined from the Adirondack Mountains, which are shown in Figure 17.

The state is the third largest producer of zinc in the country. Some other metallic minerals found in New York include lead, iron, and silver.

Farming

Almost 37,000 farms dot the New York countryside. The main agricultural occupation is dairy farming. New York is also a leading grower of several fruit and vegetable crops. It is the second largest producer of apples in the nation and the third largest producer of grapes and maple syrup. Most apple orchards are on the lowlands near Lake Ontario and the Hudson River. Figure 16 shows an apple orchard in Burnt Hills. The state produces more than 90 million kilograms of McIntosh apples each year. Vineyards are located near the Finger Lakes and along the shores of Lake Erie. Other important crops include potatoes, hay, corn, onions, garlic, and cabbage.

Forests

About 60 percent of New York's 141,089 square kilometers are forested. These forests provide recreational opportunities and supply raw materials for the state's thriving paper and pulp industries. Hardwoods as well as some softwood trees are used to produce furniture. Although the state's trees have many commercial uses, New York is a leader in forest conservation. The Adirondack Forest Preserve alone contains more than 2.5 million acres of forests. The Catskill Forest Preserve and ancient forests throughout New York cover another 700,000 acres of the state.

Figure 17 The metamorphic rocks of the Adirondacks are rich in mineral resources.

Facts and Figures

Herkimer Diamonds Herkimer, New York has a unique claim to fame. This is the home of the legendary Herkimer Diamond mines. Are there real diamonds to be found in central New York state? No. These "diamonds" are double-terminated quartz crystals. This gives them a diamond shape. Collectors and amateurs come from all over to rent rock hammers and discover their own "diamonds".

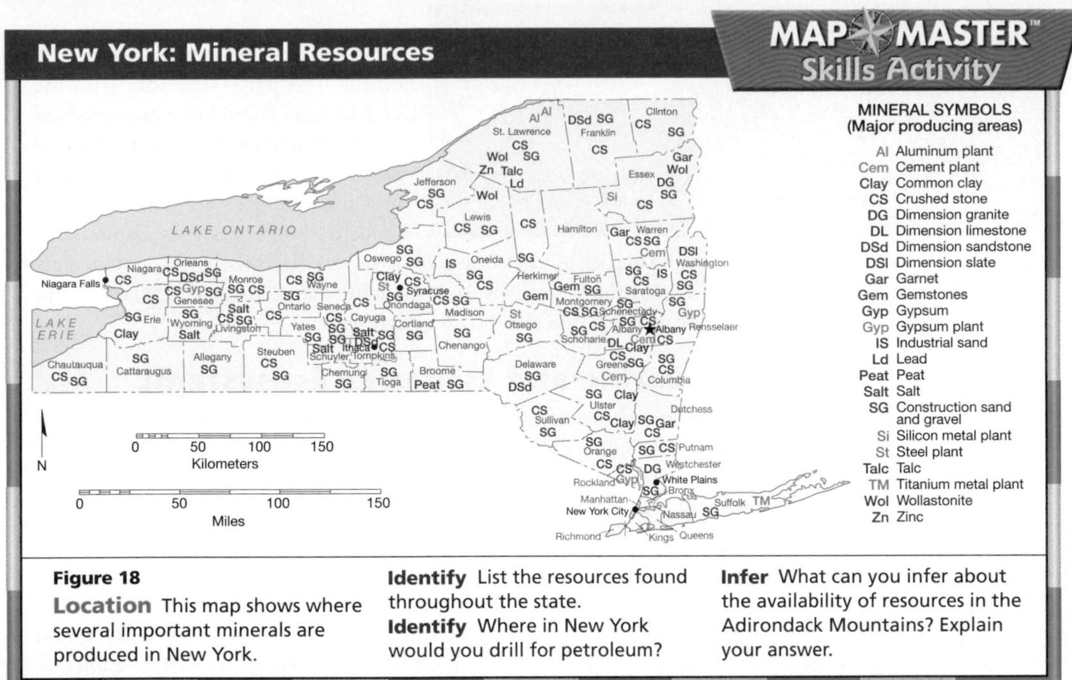

Figure 18
Location This map shows where several important minerals are produced in New York.

Identify List the resources found throughout the state.
Identify Where in New York would you drill for petroleum?

Infer What can you infer about the availability of resources in the Adirondack Mountains? Explain your answer.

Fisheries

Most commercial fishing in New York takes place in Long Island Sound and, to a lesser degree, the lower Great Lakes region. Oysters, clams, lobster, and flounder are caught in the salty waters surrounding Long Island. Trout, perch, pike, and eel are found in the freshwater Great Lakes. Problems with water pollution in the Sound and the Hudson have restricted the catching of fish and shellfish in recent years. In the late 1990s, disease killed 75 percent of the oysters in Long Island Sound, and the oyster fishery has still not recovered. Contamination from PCBs—a group of toxic chemicals—in the Hudson River had not only resulted in the decrease in some fish populations but in health advisories limiting the consumption of some fish species. With the implementation of environmental controls in recent decades, the water quality of the Hudson River has improved. Populations of striped bass and Atlantic sturgeon are on the rise. Figure 19 shows one way sturgeon are being protected.

Figure 19 Reintroducing Fish This scientist releases a captive sturgeon into the cleaner Hudson River.

Where does most commercial fishing take place in New York?

MAP MASTER™ Skills Activity

Answers
Identify stone, sand, and gravel
Identify in the southwest part of the state
Infer Sample answer: The Adirondack Mountains contain a wide variety of resources. This is evident from the map, which shows that garnet, anorthosite, lead, zinc, silver, and iron, among other resources, are found in the Adirondacks.

3 ASSESS

Evaluate Understanding

Choose students at random to list some of the natural resources found in New York State.

Answer to . . .

Applying Concepts *Answers may vary. Sample answer: Crushed stone, sand, and gravel are used in my home, school, and in our streets and parking lots. Salt is used in food, and silver is used in jewelry.*

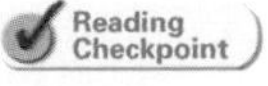

Long Island Sound and lower Great Lakes region

1 FOCUS

Section Objectives

4.1.2.g. Earth has continuously been recycling water since the outgassing of water early in its history. This constant recirculation of water at and near Earth's surface is described by the hydrologic (water) cycle.
4.2.1.c. Weather patterns become evident when weather variables are observed, measured, and recorded. These variables include air temperature, air pressure, moisture (relative humidity and dewpoint), precipitation (rain, snow, hail, sleet, etc.), wind speed and direction, and cloud cover.
4.2.2.d. Temperature and precipitation patterns are altered by: natural events such as El Niño and volcanic eruptions and human influences including deforestation, urbanization, and the production of greenhouse gases such as carbon dioxide and methane.
KEY IDEA 7.1. The knowledge and skills of mathematics, science, and technology are used together to make informed decisions and solve problems, especially those relating to issues of science/technology/society, consumer decision making, design, and inquiry into phenomena.

Reading Focus

Build Vocabulary L2

Compare-and-Contrast Table Invite students to create a compare-and-contrast table for four of the ecosystems found in New York State: marine and estuarine, freshwater ecosystem, grasslands and scrublands, and forests.

2 INSTRUCT

Bellringer L2

Ask students to make a list of the organisms that might live in a freshwater ecosystem. Point out that this ecosystem is actually fragile and is impacted by pollution and human practices. Ask students how they think the human impact on ecosystems will continue in the next few decades.

Ecosystems

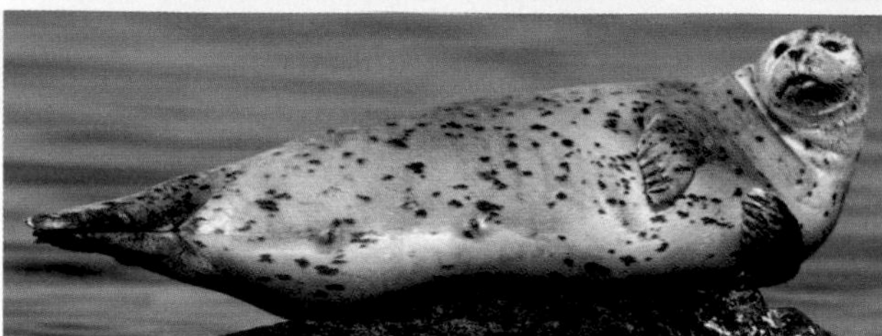

Figure 20 A harbor seal rests near Montauk, Long Island.

As you can see from the biome map on the next page, New York is in the mid-latitude mixed forest biome, which covers much of the eastern United States. This biome is characterized by moderate temperatures and abundant precipitation. Forests are habitats for animals such as black bears, white-tailed deer, owls, hawks, and the state animal, the beaver. New York has more than 200 ecosystems, which can be grouped into four broad categories.

Marine and Estuarine Ecosystems

Marine ecosystems are found off the southeast corner of New York in the Atlantic Ocean. Whales, dolphins, sea turtles, and seals, such as the one shown in Figure 20, migrate through these coastal waters. Estuaries are located where the freshwater of rivers meets the saltwater of the sea. In New York, the Hudson River estuary extends along the river for 246 kilometers, from Troy to where it empties into the Atlantic Ocean at New York harbor. These ecosystems, with their mixture of fresh water and salt water, serve as "nurseries" for many aquatic species that spend much of their youth in estuaries before braving the ocean as adults.

Freshwater Ecosystems

New York's freshwater rivers, streams, and lakes are home to numerous aquatic species, including trout, pickerel, bass, and herons like the one in Figure 21.

Many of the state's wetlands also fall into the category of freshwater ecosystems. Wetlands are land ecosystems that are covered by water all or part of the year. These ecosystems serve an important environmental function by filtering urban runoff before it enters streams or seeps into ground. New York's 2.4 million acres of freshwater wetlands are especially endangered. Since the 1700s, many original wetlands have been filled or drained to build roads and homes and to create farmland. Nearly 60 percent of the state's original wetlands have been lost.

Figure 21 Thousand Acre Swamp in Penfield is home for this great blue heron.

Grasslands and Shrublands

Grasses, herbs, mosses, sparse trees, and shrubs characterize these ecosystems, which are found in scattered pockets throughout the state. Clumps of beach grass, for example, grow in the dunes of the Great Lakes region. Other grasses and shrubs are found along riverbanks and clinging to cliffs.

Customize for English Language Learners

Use Narrative English language learners can better understand science content when it is framed in the context of a personal narrative. Have students use narrative to better understand the different ecosystems found in New York. Pair ELL students and encourage them to narrate the features they find in each ecosystem.

Biomes of North America

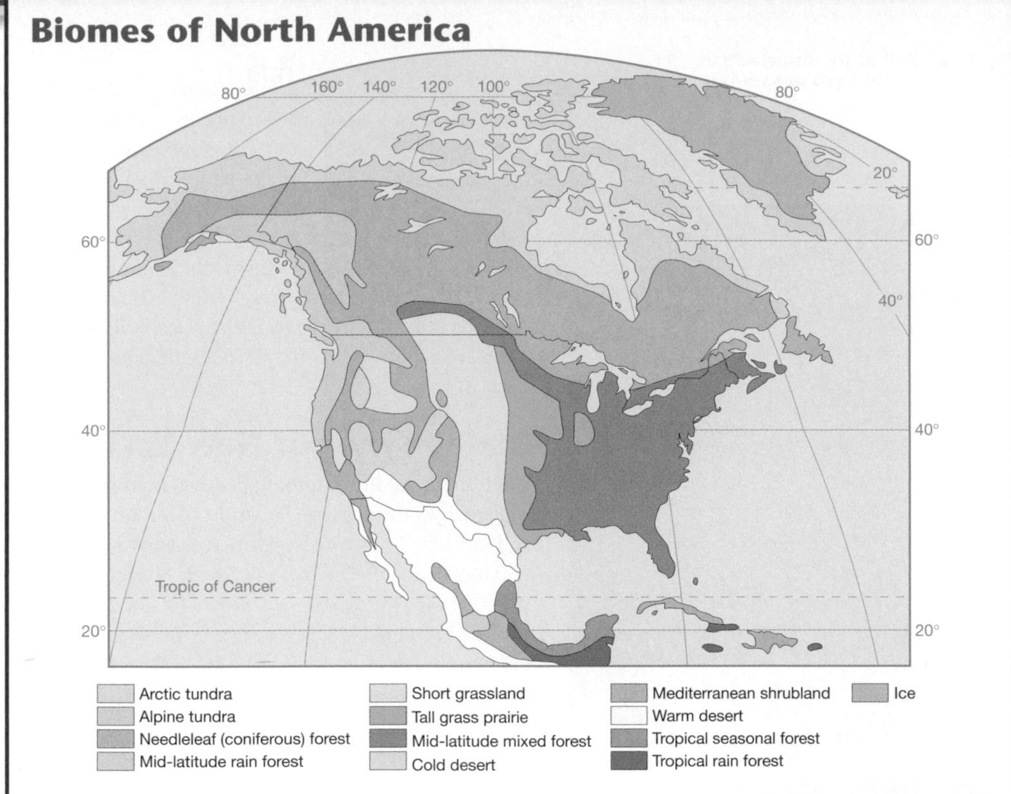

Figure 22 Each biome has a certain range of climate and vegetation.

Forests at Risk

Acid rain has been a major environmental problem for many of New York's sensitive forest ecosystems. The state is downwind of several large midwestern power plants that burn fossil fuels, such as coal. These plants emit sulfur dioxide and nitrogen oxides that are carried on high-level winds. They then mix with precipitation forming weak acids that fall on New York's forests. In the Adirondacks, acid rain has weakened trees like the sugar maple shown in Figure 23, and fish have disappeared from many of the region's lakes. The state's Acid Rain Monitoring Network keeps track of the levels of acid deposition across the state in order to track the effectiveness of clean-up efforts.

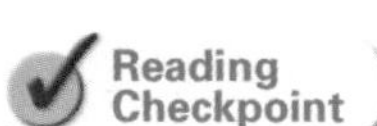

List one distinguishing characteristic of each New York ecosystem.

Figure 23 Sugar maples are vulnerable to disease when their soil becomes acidic due to acid rain.

Map Study Extension  L2

The text of this section indicates that New York is part of the midlatitude mixed forest biome. Ask students what features are attributed to this biome. *(moderate temperatures, abundant precipitation, black bears, hawks, and beavers)* What other places in the United States are part of this biome? *(most of the east coast of the US)*

3 ASSESS

Evaluate Understanding  L2

Ask students to write paragraphs summarizing one of the four broad categories of ecosystems found in New York State. The paragraph should include the general location of the ecosystems; dominate vegetation and animal life, as well as the importance the ecosystem may hold to the environment.

Answer to . . .

Answers may vary. Sample answer: Estuarine ecosystems have a mixture of fresh water and salt water and serve as "nurseries" for many aquatic species. Freshwater wetlands are covered by water all or part of the year. Grasses, herbs, mosses, sparse trees, and shrubs characterize grasslands and shrublands. New York forests are made up of both deciduous trees, such as maples, and coniferous trees, such as white pines.

1 FOCUS

Section Objectives

4.2.1.p. Landforms are the result of the interaction of tectonic forces and the processes of weathering, erosion, and deposition.

4.2.1.s. Weathering is the physical and chemical breakdown of rocks at or near Earth's surface. Soils are the result of weathering and biological activity over long periods of time.

4.2.1.v. Patterns of deposition result from a loss of energy within the transporting system and are influenced by the size, shape, and density of the transported particles. Sediment deposits may be sorted or unsorted.

4.2.1.w. Sediments of inorganic and organic origin often accumulate in depositional environments. Sedimentary rocks form when sediments are compacted and/or cemented after burial or as the result of chemical precipitation from seawater.

Reading Focus

Build Vocabulary L2

Compare-and-Contrast Table Ask students to create a compare-and-contrast table for the five different common New York soil types.

2 INSTRUCT

Bellringer L2

Ask students to predict what would happen if the soil that is in their area became contaminated. *(Since soil provides the nutrients to grow the food that we eat, our food supply would be greatly impacted.)*

Soil

Figure 24 Soil of the Appalachian Plateau in Saratoga

Figure 25 New York Honeoye Soil Profile

Much of the soil that covers New York formed from glacial till. Till is mixture of unsorted rocks and minerals that are deposited when a glacier melts. Some of New York's soils began to form after tectonic processes brought deeply buried igneous and metamorphic rocks to the surface. Still other soils form from the sedimentary rocks that blanket some parts of the state.

Major Types of New York Soils

There are five common soil types in New York, as shown in Figure 26 and Table 3. The most common is Honeoye soil, which is an alfisol. Honeoye soils cover about 500,000 acres of New York between Niagara Falls and the western Hudson River Valley. Honeoye soil, which is shown in Figure 25, is very fertile and is used to grow many of the crops around the state including soybeans, grapes, and apples. Honeoye soil also supports many of the state's deciduous forests.

Entisols are another common soil in New York. These young soils are very thin and lack distinct horizons. Entisols form in the highland regions of the state. Histosols, unlike entisols, are soils rich in organic matter. Most of the histosols in New York form in the Great Lakes region or other wet, inland areas. Many of the soils in the Catskill region of New York are inceptisols. Like entisols, most inceptisols lack distinct horizons. Most inceptisols in New York support woodlands and pastureland. The last of the common soils are the spodosols, which form in the Adirondack region. Spodosols are sandy, very acidic soils with little humus.

Drawing Conclusions *Look back at the agricultural land use map, Figure 2 on ES 4. Also consult the relief map on ES 1 and the soil orders map on ES 17. What conclusions can be drawn between types of soil and number of farms in a region? Use examples to explain your conclusions.*

Customize for English Language Learners

Learning Disabled There are many different materials and different sizes in the soil. This is sometimes difficult to realize since the soil that we see is mixed. Set up this simple demonstration to illustrate to students the different materials within soil. Fill a large plastic jar with a lid about half full of local soil. Be sure to obtain more than the surface layer of organic matter. Then add water so that the jar is full of water. Cap the jar and shake well. Place the jar on a desk or shelf and allow the students to observe the properties of the soil/water mixture as the soil settles out of the water. They should note that larger particles tend to drop to the bottom of the jar and the smaller materials remain in the water for longer and therefore settle on the top of the column. Organic material may actually float in the

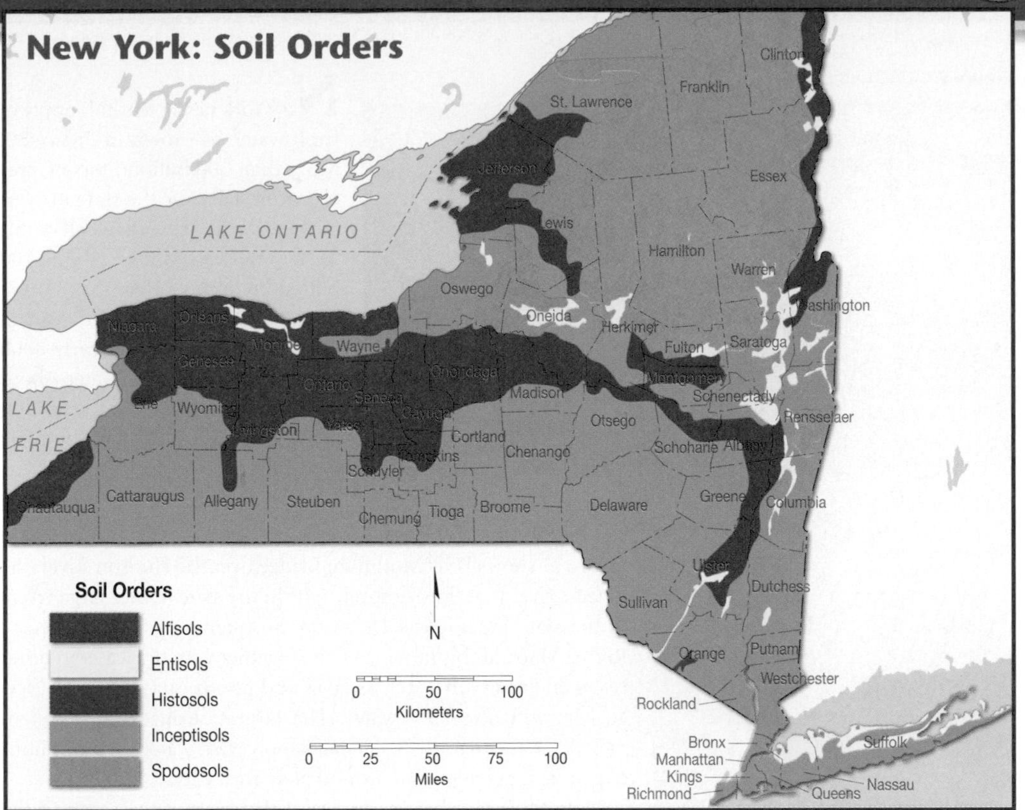

Figure 26

Table 3 Common New York Soil Orders*

Soil	Characteristics
Alfisols	Brown or yellowish topsoils with moderate organic matter and well-developed subsoils. Form in humid climates under forests or grasslands.
Entisols	Recently formed soils that are shallow and similar to the bedrock from which they developed.
Histosols	Soils with lots of organic matter that form in wet areas such as swamps or bogs.
Inceptisols	Slightly developed soils that are common on steep mountainsides or areas of the coastal plain where the land is easily eroded.
Spodosols	Infertile, acidic, sandy soils that are light in color and have subsoils that usually contain iron, aluminum, and organic material. Usually form in wet climates.

* Soil orders are broad categories that are divided into many smaller groupings by soil scientists. Soils of the same order have the same general physical characteristics, chemical makeup, natural vegetation, and common agricultural uses.

What factors control the type of soil that develops in an area?

Map Study Extension **L2**

In small groups, have the students examine the map of New York soils. Have them locate the soils in their area on the map. What type of soil is it? *(Answers will vary.)* According to the soil orders chart, what would this soil be made of? *(Answers will vary.)* What could this soil be used for? *(Answers will vary.)* Is this consistent with farming or industry in your area? *(Answers will vary.)*

3 ASSESS

Evaluate Understanding **L2**

Have students make flashcards of the different types of soils in New York. Write the soil type on one side of the card and a short description of the soil on the other side. Students can use these flashcards to quiz each other in class.

Answer to . . .

Drawing Conclusions *The land relief and soil profile maps show that most fertile soils (alfisols) good for agriculture are found in Great Lakes Lowland, the northern part of Appalachian Plateau, and the western parts of Hudson-Mohawk Lowland and New England Uplands. Figure 2 supports the idea that most agricultural land use is represented in these regions with fertile soil*

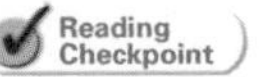

the natural vegetation that decays in the soil, the parent rock from which the soil develops, climate, local topography, and the age of the soil

1 FOCUS

Section Objectives

4.1.2.g. Earth has continuously been recycling water since the outgassing of water early in its history. This constant recirculation of water at and near Earth's surface is described by the hydrologic (water) cycle.
KEY IDEA 6.1. Through systems thinking, people can recognize the commonalities that exist among all systems and how parts of a system interrelate and combine to perform specific functions.
KEY IDEA 6.6. In order to arrive at the best solution that meets criteria within constraints, it is often necessary to make trade-offs

Reading Focus

Build Vocabulary L2

Paraphrase Ask students to write the following words on a sheet of paper: *hydroelectricity, reservoir, aqueduct.* Instruct students to write a definition, in their own words, for each term as they encounter it while going through the chapter. Ask students to identify how these terms relate to fresh water resources.

2 INSTRUCT

Bellringer L2

Tell students that there is an abundance of fresh water located under the surface of Earth. Ask students to guess where that water is stored underground. They do not have to volunteer their answer but they should write their answer in their notebook. Point out that they will learn the answer as the lesson progresses.

Fresh Water

Figure 27 The Hudson River is 195 kilometers long.

New York has a plentiful supply of fresh water, as shown in Figure 30. More than 300 billion liters of precipitation fall over the state of New York each year. More than half of this fresh water evaporates. About 100 billion liters enter New York's more than 84,000 kilometers of rivers and streams and the state's nearly 8000 bodies of standing fresh water. About 50 billion liters seep into the ground and get stored in the many aquifers below the surface.

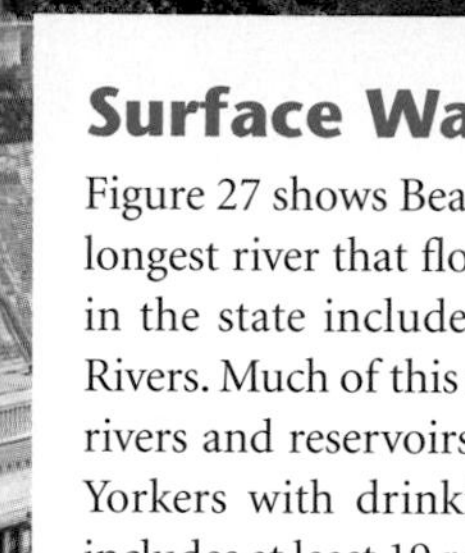

Figure 28 This plant produces hydroelectricity on the Niagara River.

Surface Water

Figure 27 shows Bear Mountain Bridge over the Hudson River, the longest river that flows entirely within the state. Other large rivers in the state include the Delaware, Susquehanna, and Allegheny Rivers. Much of this moving water, together with the water in other rivers and reservoirs such as lakes and ponds, supplies most New Yorkers with drinking water. The largest surface water system includes at least 19 reservoirs that supply fresh water to the millions of people that live in and around New York City.

In addition to being sources of drinking water, some of the rivers in New York are used to produce hydroelectricity. The power plants on the Niagara River, for example, can divert as much as 100,000 liters of water per second from the river and use this to produce low-cost electricity. The turbines and generators at power plants like the one shown in Figure 28 can generate enough electricity to light 24 million 100-watt light bulbs at the same time.

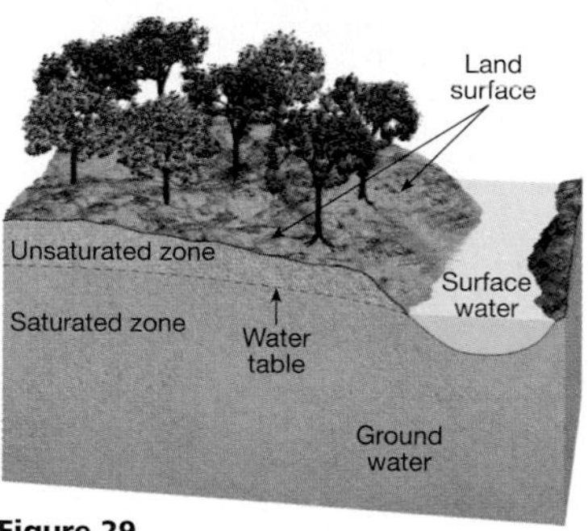

Figure 29

Groundwater

In addition to surface water, many New Yorkers depend on groundwater for nearly all of their freshwater needs. See Figure 29. Long Island's residents, for example, must use the fresh water that seeps into one of the island's three major aquifers—the Upper Glacial aquifer, the Magothy aquifer, or the Lloyd aquifer—to supply them with drinking water. If too much of this water is removed from the aquifers or if too little precipitation falls, many of the island's streams, lakes, and ponds dry up.

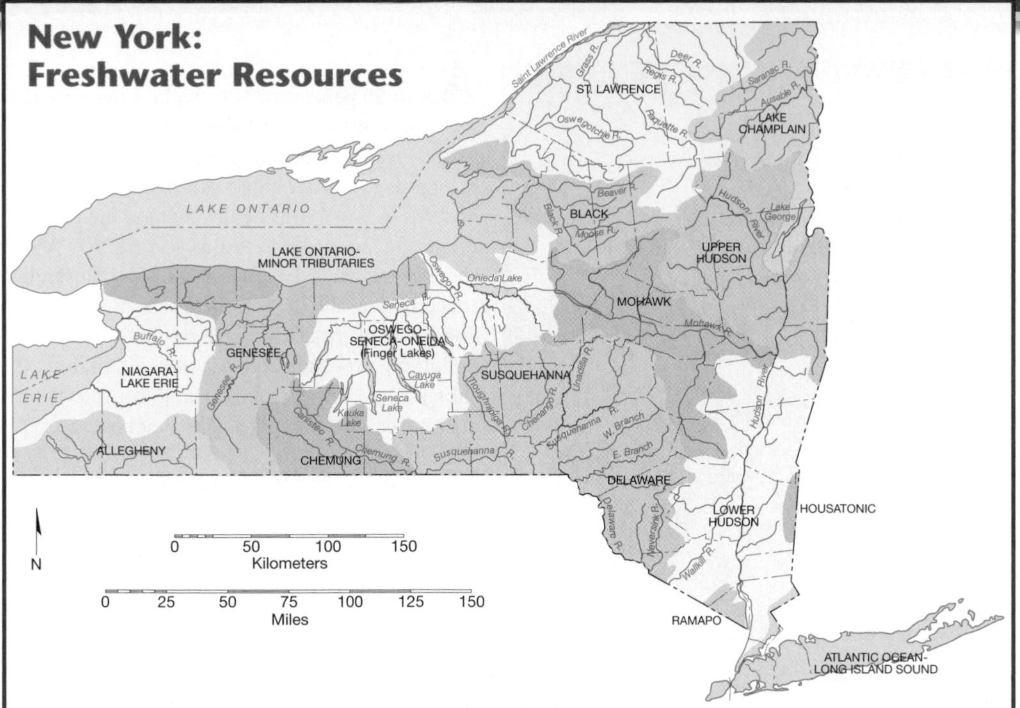

Figure 30 This map shows the river basins in New York and the major surface water features in each one.

Water Quality

To ensure that the fresh water consumed in New York is free of most harmful substances, laboratories around the state continually monitor and test many of New York's freshwater bodies. Municipal water supplies are treated with chlorine to destroy harmful bacteria. Other chemicals are added to the water prevent dangerous substances such as lead from entering the water supply. In some areas, including the Catskill/Delaware region, substances are added to the water to make it less acidic. In some areas of New York, chemicals are pumped into groundwater wells to prevent too much iron and manganese from entering drinking water supplies. In the future, some municipal water plants, including those that supply water to New York City, plan to treat water with ultraviolet light to destroy some of the harmful organisms often found in fresh water. Other plants will install special filters to remove impurities from New York's drinking water supplies.

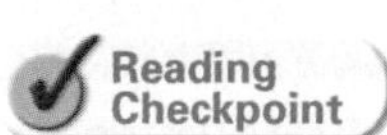

From which type of water body do most New Yorkers get their drinking water?

Map Study Extension **L2**

Hand out a piece of tracing paper to each student. They should overlay the paper onto Figure 31. Only writing on the paper, instruct them to trace out the river basin(s) closest to their home. Also included on their map should be the major surface water features. Students should then be able to discuss what impact the river basin and surface water feature has on the lifestyle and economy of their area.

3 ASSESS

Evaluate Understanding **L2**

Have students create a compare-and-contrast table that explores the similarities and differences between surface water and groundwater.

Facts and Figures

The Hudson River Problem The Hudson River is the thirty-third most polluted river in the United States. Contaminants such as PCB's (Polychlorinated biphenyl's) and DDT are present. The Hudson River is designated as a Superfund Site by the Environmental Protection Agency. Two General Electric facilities alone contaminated over 200 miles of the river from Hudson Falls to the New York Harbor. GE was found guilty of dumping more than one million pounds of PCB's for 30 years. In 1977, a ban on PCB dumping went into effect. Today, environmental dredging continues to remove PCBs from the river.

Answer to . . .

Most New Yorkers get drinking water from surface systems such as rivers and reservoirs.

Coastal Regions

1 FOCUS

Section Objectives

4.2.1.u. The natural agents of erosion include streams, glaciers, wave action, and wind.
KEY IDEA 6.6. In order to arrive at the best solution that meets criteria within constraints, it is often necessary to make trade-offs
KEY IDEA 7.1. The knowledge and skills of mathematics, science, and technology are used together to make informed decisions and solve problems, especially those relating to issues of science/technology/society, consumer decision making, design, and inquiry into phenomena.

Reading Focus

Build Vocabulary L2

Paraphrase Ask students to come up with their own, unique definition for a coastal ecosystem.

2 INSTRUCT

Bellringer L2

Ask students what type of organisms live in a coastal ecosystem. *(Answers may include fish, crabs, grasses, shrubs, birds.)* Then ask the students why it is important for all of us to preserve and protect these ecosystems. *(Answer will vary but may include the fact that we depend on the animals for food or recreation, that there is a delicate balance in nature, and the survival of these organisms impacts others in other areas, etc.)*

Coastal Regions

Figure 31 Fire Island National Seashore

About 90 percent of New Yorkers live on either the shores of the Great Lakes or the Atlantic coast. These coastal regions are shown on Maps A and B in Figure 33. Either shore can be breathtaking to observe as water continually changes the environments. In addition to being scenic, New York's shorelines provide the water needed for many industrial processes and the commercial transportation of goods. All of these uses have resulted in increased pollution, crowding, and loss of habitats along the shores. New Yorkers are working to protect these areas while continuing to enjoy their beauty.

The Atlantic Coast

New York has about 189 kilometers of Atlantic coastline. Day-to-day waves and currents, together with extreme weather conditions such as hurricanes and nor'easters, constantly change this coast. Longshore currents along Fire Island National Seashore, shown in Figure 31, for example, transport sediments along the beach in an east-west direction. Depending on the speed of the current and its direction, beaches at this seashore can change in size. Human activities such as development, recreation, and the construction of barriers also change New York's Atlantic coast. Fire Island National Seashore is one of the many areas set aside to preserve the coast.

Summarizing *What causes New York's Atlantic coast to change?*

The Great Lakes Coast

Western New York borders both Lake Erie and Lake Ontario. The dunes or bluffs, such as those shown in Figure 32, and beaches scattered along these freshwater shores absorb some of the impact of powerful storm waters. Dunes and beaches also help prevent severe flooding and erosion along the shore. Like the Atlantic coast, development along the Great Lakes has destroyed many of the dunes and reduced the size of many beaches. These changes not only increase erosion, but also destroy both aquatic and terrestrial habitats.

Explaining *How do beaches and dunes affect shorelines?*

Figure 32 Bluffs Along Lake Ontario

Customize for Inclusion Students

Visually Impaired If you live in a coastal area take the students for a field trip to that coastline. Visually impaired students may have had a difficult time imagining the coastal ecosystem. A walk along the coast will allow these students to experience the noise associated with the local wildlife, smell the damp soil and the plants associated with the water, and feel the dampness in the air. Be sure to leave the local fauna and flora in place but allow visually impaired students to touch some of the local plants.

New York: Coastal Regions

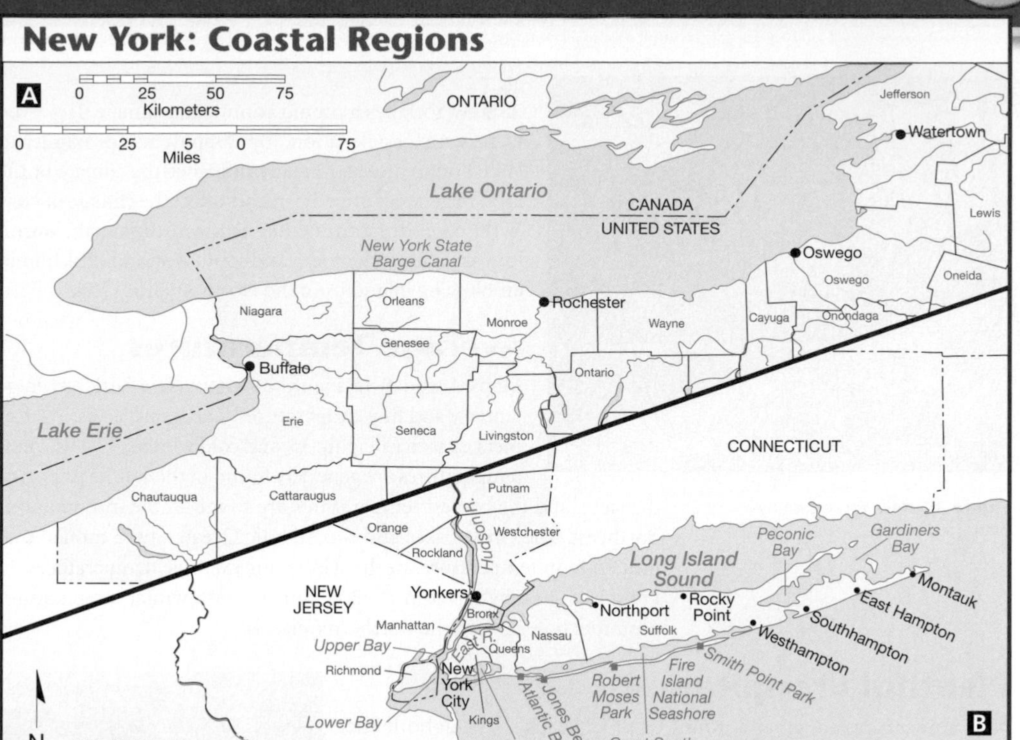

Figure 33 Map A shows New York's Great Lakes coastal region. Map B shows New York's Atlantic coastal region.

Protecting Coastal Regions

Several programs have been implemented to help revitalize and protect coastal areas. The Division of Coastal Resources works with other state and federal agencies to monitor development. The state also offers grants to communities to help them implement balanced coastal management plans. Some communities in Westchester County along Long Island Sound have done plantings along streams to help filter pollution from runoff. In other areas, dunes have been restored to stop coastal erosion. In addition, 250 ecosystems have been designated as Significant Coastal Fish and Wildlife Habitats. Development is limited in these areas to protect the uniqueness of coastal habitats and the species they contain. The piping plover in Figure 34 is one example of a protected species.

Identify one program implemented to protect New York's coastal regions.

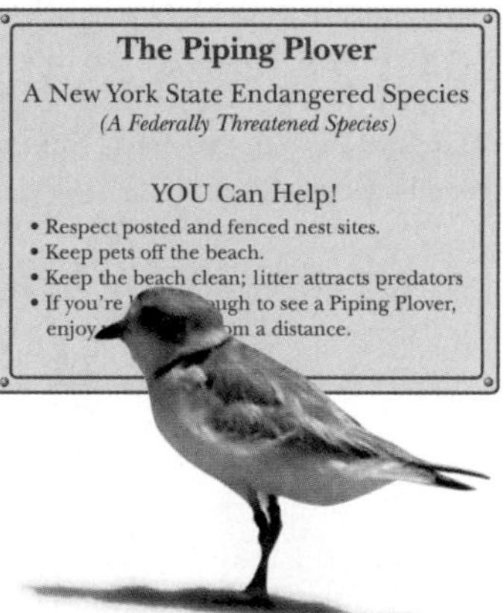

Figure 34 Recreation on beaches has attributed to the population decline of the piping plover.

Map Study Extension **L2**

Have teams of students study the map of the Great Lakes coastal region. Then they should create the text of a travel commercial that highlights the Great Lakes region as a wonderful place to visit. Allow class time for the students to present their commercial to the class.

3 ASSESS

Evaluate Understanding **L2**

Ask students to create a study guide to help them remember the characteristics of the different coastal regions found in New York.

Answer to . . .

Summarizing *Day-to-day waves and currents, as well as extreme weather conditions change New York's Atlantic coast.*

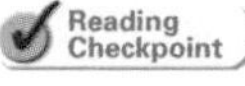

Grants are offered to communities to help them implement balanced coastal management plans.

Climate

1 FOCUS

Section Objectives

4.2.1.c. Weather patterns become evident when weather variables are observed, measured, and recorded. These variables include air temperature, air pressure, moisture (relative humidity and dewpoint), precipitation (rain, snow, hail, sleet, etc.), wind speed and direction, and cloud cover.
4.2.1.g. Weather variables can be represented in a variety of formats including radar and satellite images, weather maps (including station models, isobars, and fronts), atmospheric cross-sections, and computer models.
INDICATOR 4.2.2. Explain how incoming solar radiation, ocean currents, and land masses affect weather and climate.
4.2.2.c. A locations climate is influenced by latitude, proximity to large bodies of water, ocean currents, prevailing winds, vegetative cover, elevation, and mountain ranges.

Reading Focus

Build Vocabulary L2

Word Forms Ask students to define the word *climate.* Point out that there are other, non-meteorological meanings for the word *climate.* Ask students to write a sentence using *climate* in a few different contexts.

2 INSTRUCT

Bellringer L2

Ask students to describe the weather during the four seasons in their section of New York. Ask how they think this compares with the rest of the state.

Climate

Figure 35 New Yorkers enjoy a warm, sunny day.

New York has a humid continental climate. However, factors such as elevation, topography, and proximity to large bodies of water greatly influence the climate of the area. In general, three air masses affect the climate of New York: cool, dry continental air from the north; warm, humid air from the south and southwest; and cool, humid air blowing inland from the North Atlantic Ocean.

Average Temperatures

Maps A and B in Figure 38 show New York's average January and July temperatures. The state has warm summers, shown in Figure 35, and cold winters. The warmest temperatures are generally found in the southeast part of the state, and the coolest temperatures are found in the mountainous northeast. The Great Lakes and the Atlantic Ocean have a moderating influence on temperature. In the winter, for example, temperatures on Long Island rarely dip below −20°C. In contrast, winter temperatures plummet to −31°C in the northern uplands.

Plentiful Precipitation

New York receives a great amount of precipitation throughout the year. As Map C in Figure 38 shows, most areas receive between 89 and 115 centimeters of precipitation annually. Snowfall is abundant, particularly in the Great Lakes region and the Tug Hill Plateau. For more than 60 percent of the state, average snowfall amounts exceed 177 centimeters.

Calculating *Approximately what percentage of the year are the skies over Buffalo cloudy?*

Figure 36 Fog rises from Sagamore Lake.

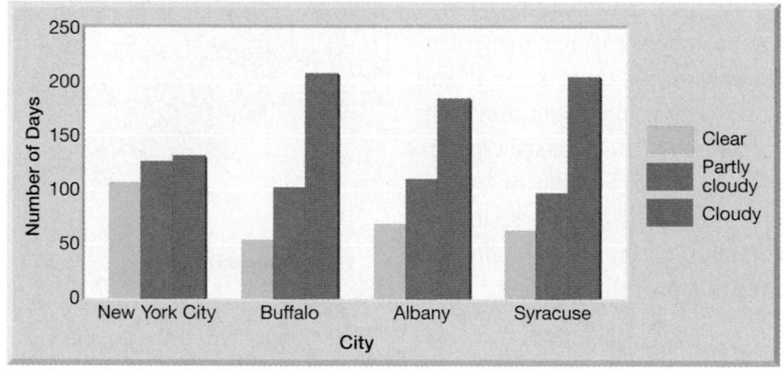

Figure 37 This bar graph shows the average number of days per year that New Yorkers in these four cities see sunshine or clouds.

Customize for English Language Learners

Simplify the Presentation The specific details about average temperatures and precipitation rates can be overwhelming. By simplifying your presentation of the data, the English language learners in your class will have a better comprehension of the important information in the section. Emphasize that the actual numbers are not the important take-away information. Help students use the chart to see general trends in the data.

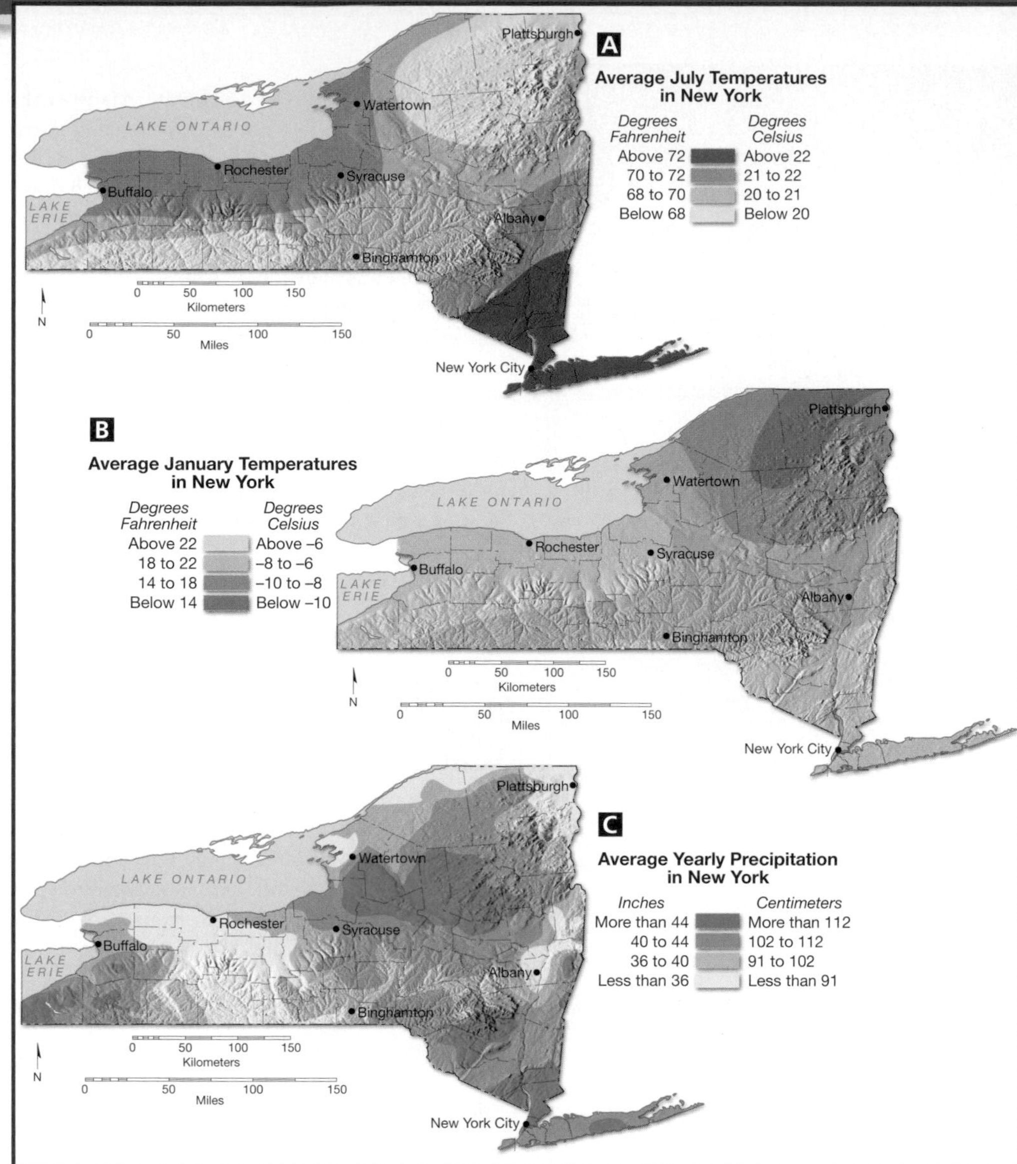

Figure 38 Average Temperature and Precipitation

What bodies of water influence New York's climate?

Map Study Extension **L2**

Students should examine the maps and look for patterns. Is there any connection between the precipitation highs and lows and the temperature extremes in June and January? What might be the cause for this? If there is no connection, could there be more data that could be examined that might have a connection between temperature and precipitation rates?

3 ASSESS

Evaluate Understanding **L2**

Ask students to construct a table listing the three air masses that affect the climate of New York. The tables should include information about the temperatures and precipitation associated with the air masses as well as the direction from which the air mass moves.

Answer to . . .

Calculating *about 57 percent of the year*

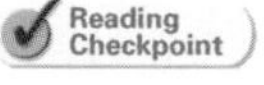 *the Great Lakes and the Atlantic Ocean*

1 FOCUS

Section Objectives

4.2.1.c. Weather patterns become evident when weather variables are observed, measured, and recorded. These variables include air temperature, air pressure, moisture (relative humidity and dewpoint), precipitation (rain, snow, hail, sleet, etc.), wind speed and direction, and cloud cover.
4.2.1.h. Atmospheric moisture, temperature and pressure distributions; jet streams, wind; air masses and frontal boundaries; and the movement of cyclonic systems and associated tornadoes, thunderstorms, and hurricanes occur in observable patterns. Loss of property, personal injury, and loss of life can be reduced by effective emergency preparedness.
4.2.1.i. Seasonal changes can be explained using concepts of density and heat energy. These changes include the shifting of global temperature zones, the shifting of planetary wind and ocean current patterns, the occurrence of monsoons, hurricanes, flooding, and severe weather.
4.2.2.c. A locations climate is influenced by latitude, proximity to large bodies of water, ocean currents, prevailing winds, vegetative cover, elevation, and mountain ranges.

Reading Focus

Build Vocabulary L2

Compare-and-Contrast Table Ask students to create a compare-and-contrast table for the two types of weather events discussed in this section: lake-effect storms and nor'easters.

2 INSTRUCT

Bellringer L2

Ask students to discuss an incident of severe weather they have experienced in the area of New York in which they live. What precautions did their family take to prepare for this event? How much warning did they have of the impending storm?

Weather Patterns

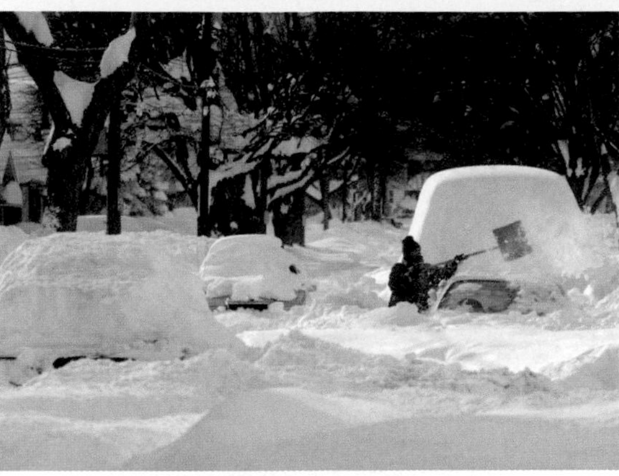

Figure 39 A single lake-effect snowfall can last for 48 hours and drop as much as 193 cm of snow in one day.

New York has a moderate climate. Many of the severe-weather events—such as tornadoes and hurricanes—that strike other states are infrequent events. Each year, three to four weak tornadoes touch down in various New York locales. While hurricanes sometimes hit Long Island, the last major hurricane New York suffered was in October 1954.

New York experiences an average of 30 days of thunderstorms each year. These storms and melting ice jams can cause damaging floods, particularly in the spring. As Figure 39 shows, the most prevalent weather condition in New York is snow—vast amounts of snow. Heavy snowstorms affect the largest land area and population centers in New York. See Table 4 for New York weather extremes.

Lake-Effect Snow

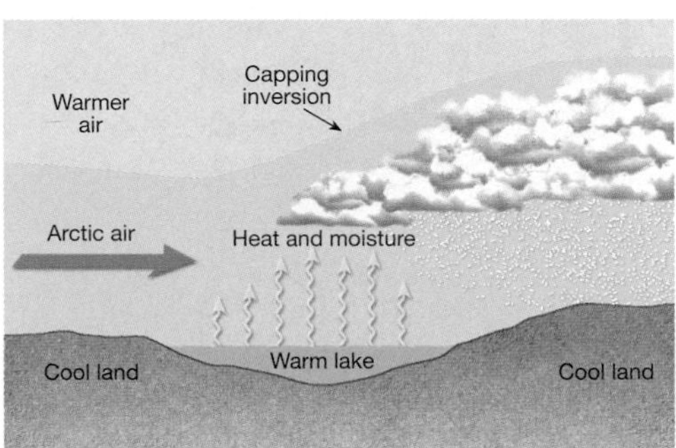

Figure 40 Lake-effect snow forms when arctic air moves over a relatively warm lake. As the air moves, it picks up moisture that eventually falls as snow.

Buffalo, Syracuse, and Rochester are a few of the cities in New York that experience lake-effect snow as a result of their proximity to the Great Lakes. As shown in Figure 40, lake-effect snow occurs when a cold air mass moves over a relatively warm body of water such as a lake. The difference in temperature between the air mass and the lake causes water from the lake to evaporate and rise. As it cools, the water vapor condenses to form clouds that drop large volumes of snow over the area. Up to 60 percent of the annual snowfall received in New York's Great Lakes region can be attributed to lake-effect snow. See Figure 41.

Table 4 Weather Extremes

Weather Event		Location	Date
Highest Temperature	42.2°C	Troy	July 22, 1926
Lowest Temperature	–46.7°C	Stillwater Reservoir	February 9, 1934
		Old Forge	February 18, 1979
Highest Monthly Rainfall	64 cm	West Shokan	October 1995
Greatest Snowfall in Single Storm	241 cm	Montague	January 1997

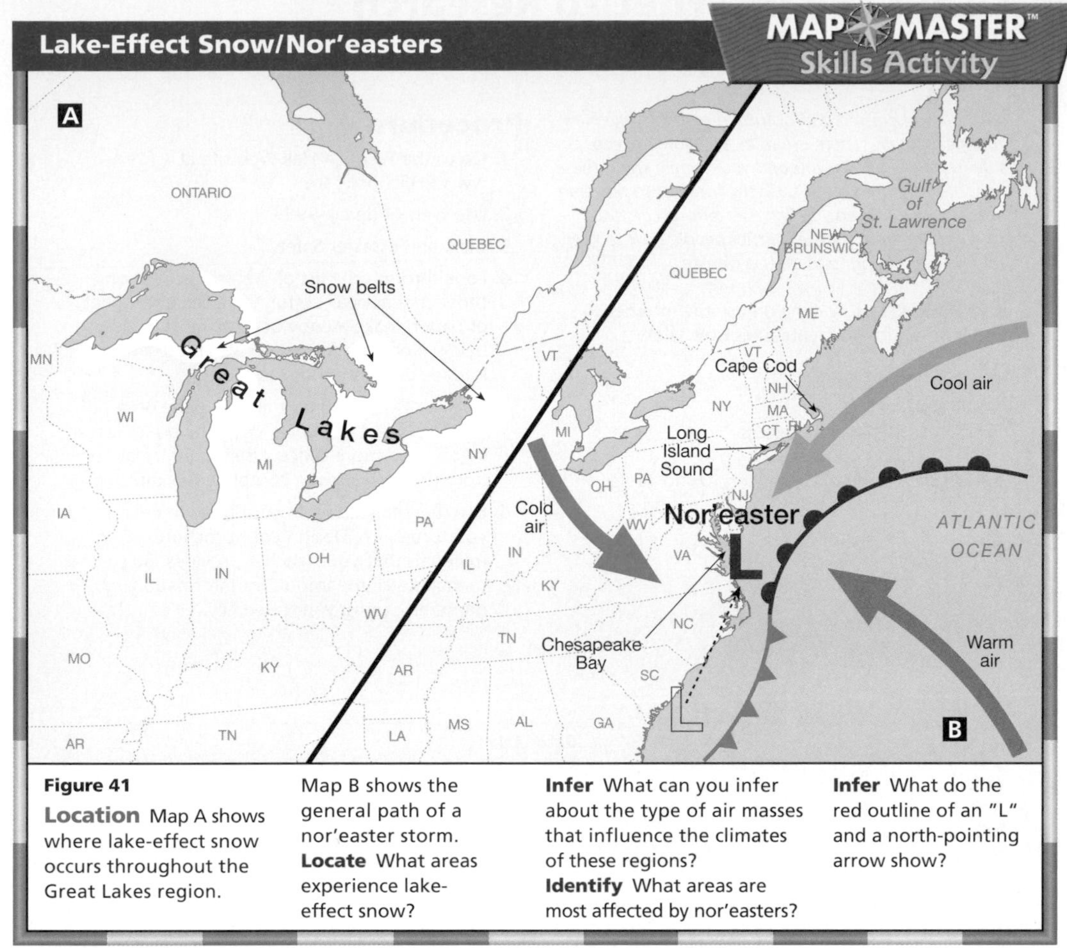

Figure 41
Location Map A shows where lake-effect snow occurs throughout the Great Lakes region. Map B shows the general path of a nor'easter storm.
Locate What areas experience lake-effect snow?
Infer What can you infer about the type of air masses that influence the climates of these regions?
Identify What areas are most affected by nor'easters?
Infer What do the red outline of an "L" and a north-pointing arrow show?

Nor'easters

In winter or early spring, coastal New York often experiences "nor'easters," which are low-pressure storms associated with violent winds and heavy precipitation in the form of rain, snow, or sleet. These mid-latitude storms usually develop off the east coast and then move in a northeasterly direction up the coast—hence, their name.

Reading Checkpoint *What is a nor'easter?*

Facts and Figures

Buffalo Snows On November 20–23, 2000, Buffalo, NY and the surrounding areas were hit with a 60-hour lake-effect snowstorm. During the period, the storm dumped up to 79 cm of snow. The November 2000 storm had frequent lightning as snow showers blossomed into heavy thunder snow pellet showers. Snow fell at the rate of 5–10 cm/h for several hours. It was the most disruptive storm in the Buffalo area since the Blizzard of 1977.

MAP MASTER™ Skills Activity

Answers

Locate northwest part of New York along Lake Ontario, parts of the following states that border the Great Lakes: Michigan, Indiana, Ohio, and Pennsylvania, parts of Ontario, Canada

Infer Their climates are influenced by dry, arctic air masses.

Identify areas along the coast that lie near water such as the Atlantic Ocean or a bay

Infer The low pressure system is moving north along the coast.

3 ASSESS

Evaluate Understanding

L2

State aloud facts about the dominate weather patterns across New York, such as "low-pressure storms associated with violent winds and heavy precipitation", and have students identify the type of weather pattern that matches each fact.

Answer to . . .

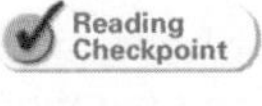
Reading Checkpoint *a low-pressure storm associated with violent winds and heavy precipitation in the form of rain, snow, or sleet*

Exploration Lab

Using the Internet to Research Disaster Safety

L2

Objective Students will use the Internet to gather information on hurricane safety.

Skills Focus **Observing, Classifying, Using Tables and Graphs, Drawing Conclusions, Evaluating**

Prep Time 10 minutes

Advance Prep Provide the following materials to students to make the brochures: white 8-1/2 × 11 paper, construction paper of various colors, colored pencils, markers, scissors, and glue

Class time 1 period

Teaching Tips

- Review a sample of a disaster preparedness web site with students. Examine and compare several sites, pointing out which organizations or individuals maintain the sites. Advise students that government and university organizations are usually the most reliable sources of disaster-related information.
- Have students review the questions in Table 2. Discuss if there are any other questions students might want to add.
- Point out that information that is included in only one site may not be reliable.

Sample Answers for Data Table 2

BEFORE A DISASTER

- types of disasters: winter storms, floods, blackouts, droughts, fires, heat waves, cold waves, terrorism, chemical emergencies
- disaster information: National Weather Service, Red Cross, the Disaster Center New York page, media outlets
- information on family disaster plans: National Weather Service, Red Cross, the Disaster Center New York page
- family disaster kit: first aid kit, battery-powered radio, canned food and can opener, bottled water, extra clothing and blankets
- An evacuation plan details where to go if told you must leave the area during a disaster. The plan should include escape routes, a safe destination, and a communication plan in case the family is separated.
- A family should leave their home and implement their evacuation plan when evacuation advisories are issued.
- A family can install smoke alarms and purchase a fire extinguisher. All family members should know how to turn off gas, electric, and water valves. A "house hazard hunt" should be conducted prior to a disaster. Potentially dangerous objects such as pictures hanging in glass frames can be taken down in the event of a disaster.

DURING A DISASTER

- The safest place to stay in a home would depend upon the disaster. Basements, for example, are safe during heavy storms, but not during chemical emergencies.
- Television and radio stations offer updated information on disasters.

AFTER A DISASTER

- You can return home when local or state authorities announce that it is safe to do so.
- Again, you can go outside when local or state authorities announce that it is safe to venture outdoors.

Exploration Lab

Using the Internet to Research Disaster Safety

Both human-caused and natural disasters strike New York periodically. There are rules to follow to keep safe from danger. Do you and your family know these rules? In this lab, you will use the Internet to research disaster safety. Then you will use your research to create a brochure that tells other people how to keep safe before, during, and after a disaster.

Problem How can you use the Internet to find information to create a disaster safety brochure?

Materials
computer with Internet access

Skills Observing, Classifying, Using Tables and Graphs, Drawing Conclusions, Evaluating

Procedure

1. Go to the Prentice-Hall Web site at www.PHSchool.com
2. Use Web Code cjk-9999
3. Click on "Disaster Safety."
4. Look through the list of Web sites. Click on those that appear useful. On a separate sheet of paper, make a copy of Data Table 1 shown below. Record information about the sites you intend to use for your brochure.
5. Copy Data Table 2 on the next page on a separate sheet of paper. Make the boxes larger if you need more space. Use the information from the Web sites to complete this table.
6. Use the information in your table to create your brochure. Design your brochure, using materials that your teacher provides. Be sure to include all the important information you gathered during your research.

Data Table 1

Name of Web Site	Web Site Address	Type of Information

Data Table 2	
Information Needed	Information for Brochure
BEFORE A DISASTER	
What types of disasters might your area face?	
Where can you get information about an impending natural or human-caused disaster?	
Where can you get information about family disaster plans?	
What should your family disaster kit contain?	
What is an evacuation plan, and what should yours contain?	
What should your family do if told to evacuate?	
How can your family prepare your home for a disaster?	
DURING A DISASTER	
Where is the safest place to stay in your home?	
How can you get updated information during a disaster?	
AFTER A DISASTER	
When can you return home if you have evacuated?	
When can you go outside if you are at home?	

Analyze and Conclude

1. **Using Graphs** The graph below shows average monthly snowfall amounts for Buffalo, New York. Use the graph to determine the best time of year to distribute a brochure on winter storm safety. Explain your answer.
2. **Classifying** What types of Web sites have the most useful information?
3. **Evaluating** Were you able to easily find all the data needed for your brochure? If not, how could you improve your research methods?

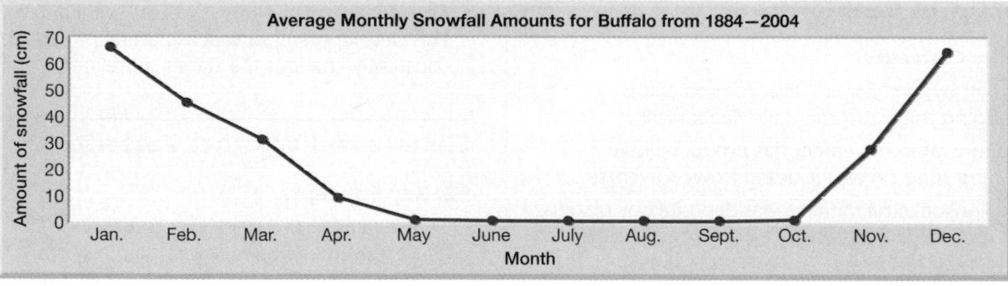

Analyze and Conclude

1. Sample answer: October might be a good month to distribute a brochure on winter storm safety because these types of storms occur from November through March, and a brochure published in October would give people time to prepare.
2. Sample answer: Government and university organizations have reliable, unbiased information.
3. Sample answer: Information was fairly easy to obtain. Research methods could be improved by using more specific key words.

NEW YORK
Earth System Profile

Study Guide

Study Tip

Study in Pairs
Recommend that students study in pairs. They can quiz each other, compare notes, and discuss discrepancies.

Study Guide

Growth and Economic Development

Key Concepts

- New York is the third most populous state. About 84 percent of its residents reside in urban areas.
- New York is an important manufacturing state and also serves as the nation's banking, financial, and communications center.

Geological History

Key Concepts

- Hundreds of millions of years ago, plate tectonics helped create the ancestral Taconic Mountains. The Acadian Mountains and the modern Appalachians were also formed by plate tectonics.
- The Adirondacks are mostly metamorphic rocks, some of which are 1.1 billion years old. These mountains began to rise about 40 to 60 million years ago.

Physiographic Regions

Key Concepts

- New York has eight major regions: the St. Lawrence Lowland, the Great Lakes Lowland, the Adirondack Upland, the Tug Hill Plateau, the Appalachian Plateau, the Hudson-Mohawk Lowland, the New England Upland, and the Atlantic Coastal Plain.
- Many of New York's landforms were formed as the result of uplift, plate tectonics, and faulting and were later changed by glacial activity.

Geology of Landforms

Key Concepts

- Erosion by the Niagara River formed and is changing the escarpment at Niagara Falls.
- Groundwater movement has produced many underground caves, including Howe Caverns.
- The Ronkonkoma moraine was deposited by glaciers but is changed today by ocean waves and currents.

Natural Resources

Key Concepts

- Most of New York's mineral resources are nonmetals that are used for construction purposes.
- Dairy, lumber, fruit, vegetables, and commercial fishing are important to New York's economy.

Ecosystems

Key Concepts

- Marine, estuarine, and freshwater ecosystems support many aquatic organisms.
- Grasslands, forest, and shrubs cover more than 2 million acres of New York State.

Soil

Key Concepts

- Most of New York's soils formed as the result of weathering and erosion of glacial debris.
- Five common soils blanket New York State: alfisols, entisols, histisols, inceptisols, and spodosols.

Fresh Water

Key Concepts

- Most New Yorkers obtain water from groundwater or surface sources, such as rivers and reservoirs.

Coastal Regions

Key Concepts

- About 90 percent of New Yorkers live along a coast. This development, as well as natural processes, constantly changes the state's shorelines.

Climate and Weather Patterns

Key Concepts

- Severe weather events in New York include lake-effect snow, nor'easters, severe thunderstorms, hail, and sleet. Tornadoes and tropical weather systems are rare occurrences.

Assessment

Interactive textbook with assessment at PHSchool.com 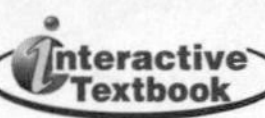

Reviewing Content

Choose the number that best answers the question or completes the statement.

1 Today, most people in New York live in
(1) villages
(2) mountain communities
(3) urban areas
(4) forests

2 The Appalachian, Taconic, and Catskill Mountains formed as the result of
(1) glacial activity
(2) tectonics
(3) groundwater erosion
(4) surface-water weathering

3 New York is the third largest producer of which of the following minerals?
(1) zinc (2) gold
(3) silver (4) lead

4 An important estuary in New York is located where the Hudson River empties into
(1) the Atlantic Ocean (2) Lake Erie
(3) Niagara Falls (4) Lake Ontario

5 About how much of New York is covered by water?
(1) 110 square kilometers
(2) 1100 square kilometers
(3) 11,000 square kilometers
(4) 110,000 square kilometers

6 Most of New York's soil formed from
(1) river sediments (2) humus
(3) clays (4) glacial till

7 Which of these is NOT true of the Ronkonkoma moraine?
(1) It was deposited by glaciers.
(2) It forms the backbone of Long Island.
(3) Tectonic collisions between two plates are changing it today.
(4) Ocean waves and currents are eroding parts of the moraine.

8 Most New Yorkers get their water from
(1) aquifers
(2) surface-water sources
(3) wells
(4) desalination plants

9 What percentage of New Yorkers live in coastal regions?
(1) 10 percent (2) 20 percent
(3) 50 percent (4) 90 percent

10 What type of climate does New York have?
(1) humid maritime
(2) dry maritime
(3) dry continental
(4) humid continental

Understanding Concepts

Use the map to answer questions 11 and 12.

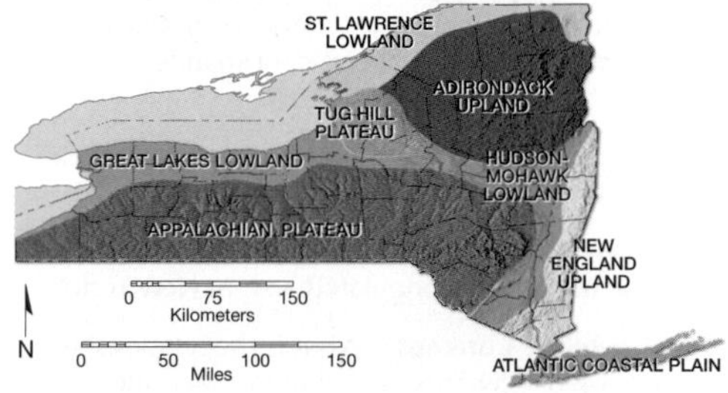

11 Which regions are affected by lake-effect snow? Explain why.

12 In which region did the glaciers of the last ice age reach their southernmost point? Cite evidence to support your answer

13 Describe New York's Honeoye soil.

14 What are the sources of fresh water in New York?

15 In which biome is New York located?

16 What important environmental function do wetlands serve?

17 How did the Catskill Mountains form?

18 What types of plants are found in New York's grasslands and shrublands?

19 What is a Significant Coastal Fish and Wildlife Habitat?

20 What air masses affect New York's climate?

21 Contrast extreme winter weather on New York's freshwater and saltwater shores.

Assessment

Reviewing Content

(1) 3 (2) 2 (3) 1
(4) 1 (5) 3 (6) 4
(7) 3 (8) 2 (9) 4
(10) 4

Understanding Concepts

(11) Area A is affected by lake-effect snow because it includes the Great Lakes region. Cold arctic air and the warm waters of the Great Lakes combine to form lake-effect snow.
(12) All of New York was covered by glaciers; thus, all areas were affected by glacial activity.
(13) Honeoye soil is well-drained and slightly acidic.
(14) The sources of fresh water in New York include rivers, streams, lakes, ponds, and aquifers.
(15) New York is located in the mid-latitude mixed forest biome.
(16) Wetlands filter pollutants from urban runoff before they enter streams or seep underground.
(17) Plate collisions and uplifted formed the Taconic Mountains. Weathering and erosion of the Taconic Mountains produced the Catskills.
(18) The ecosystems may include grasses, herbs, mosses, sparse trees, and shrubs.
(19) A Significant Coastal Fish and Wildlife Habitat is one of 250 coastal areas in New York in which development is limited in order to protect the uniqueness of these coastal habitats and the species they contain.
(20) The three air masses are cool, dry continental air from the north; warm, humid air from the south and southwest; and cool, humid air blowing inland from the North Atlantic Ocean.
(21) Lake-effect snow is common in winter in the Great Lakes region. Cold air blowing over the relatively warm lakes results in large amounts of snowfall. The Atlantic coast experiences blustery winds known as nor'easters that bring heavy precipitation to the coast.

NEW YORK Earth System Profile

Critical Thinking

(22) Glaciers eroded and deposited much of the land over which they moved. Erosion resulted in the features such as the Great Lakes, Thousand Islands, and the Finger Lakes. Deposition produced tills, which were eroded to form some of New York's soils. Deposition also resulted in some of New York's moraines.
(23) The rocks that make up the Adirondacks are very old; however, the mountains were uplifted in relatively recent geologic time.
(24) It helps protect unique habitats from development.
(25) Answers will vary depending upon students' location.
(26) Sample answer: In New York, coastal areas provide many job opportunities and recreational amenities.
(27) The Tug Hill Plateau has a harsh climate and poor soils.
(28) The forests provide the raw materials for New York's printing industry.

Assessment *continued*

Critical Thinking

22 **Relating Cause and Effect** Explain at least three effects of glaciers on the landscape of New York.

23 **Inferring** The Adirondacks have been described as both the oldest and youngest mountains in New York. What evidence supports this statement?

24 **Making Judgments** What is the advantage of creating Significant Coastal Fish and Wildlife Habitats?

25 **Observing** Based on what you know about the natural vegetation in your area, do you live in a forest, grassland, freshwater, or marine ecosystem?

26 **Making Generalizations** Why do you think most New Yorkers live in coastal areas?

27 **Drawing Conclusions** Why is the Tug Hill Plateau the least populated area in New York?

28 **Applying Concepts** What is the relationship between New York's printing industry and its forests?

Concepts in Action

29 **Inferring** Why do scientists' ideas sometimes differ about when a particular mountain-building event occurred?

30 **Applying Concepts** While working on your car, you spill some oil in your driveway. Describe how this oil may become a source of water pollution.

31 **Writing in Science** Write a short paragraph describing how the northern Appalachian Mountains formed.

Performance-Based Assessment

Making a Diagram Find out how hydroelectricity is produced in New York. Draw and label a diagram showing the energy transformations that take place in a hydroelectric plant.

Applying Concepts Create a topographic map for the area around your school. Note drainage patterns and propose solutions for any drainage problems.

Applying Concepts Investigate the use of Doppler radar in forecasting weather in your area. How does the use of Doppler radar help people deal with weather disasters?

Applying Concepts Obtain a topographic map covering your local area. Analyze the features of your area and report your findings to the class.

Applying Concepts Report on energy issues currently affecting your area. What are the sources of electric power for your area? What environmental concerns have been highlighted from the use of fossil fuels?

Concepts in Action

(29) It is difficult to place an exact date on events that occurred millions of years ago.
(30) The oil could be carried by rain and enter a river or stream as runoff, or it could seep into the ground and contaminate groundwater supplies.
(31) A series of mountain-building events between 460 million and 380 million years ago created the ancestral northern Appalachian Mountains. The modern northern Appalachians formed when the North American plate collided with the African plate between 330 and 250 million years ago, causing additional folding and uplifting.

Regents Practice Exam

Test-Taking Tip

Eliminating Unreasonable Answers
When you answer a multiple-choice question, you can often eliminate at least one answer because it is clearly incorrect. If you eliminate one or more choices, you increase your odds of choosing the correct answer. In the question below, you can immediately eliminate choice 1 because forests are not glacial deposits. Clearly, choices 2 and 3 cannot both be true because they relate to the same phenomenon. The remaining choice, 4, must be the correct answer.

A ridge formed by glacial deposits is called a
(1) forest
(2) drumlin
(3) moraine
(4) elongated mound

For each statement or question, choose the number *of the word or expression that, of those given, best completes the statement or answers the question. Some questions may require the use of the* Earth Science Reference Tables.

1 The Palisades are found in the
(1) Atlantic Coastal Plain
(2) southern United States
(3) New England Upland
(4) Great Lakes Lowland

2 Which of the following weather events are common in New York?
(1) hurricanes and tornadoes
(2) lake-effect snow and nor'easters
(3) hurricanes and blizzards
(4) tornadoes and floods

3 What happened to the population of New York during the 1970s and 1980s?
(1) It decreased.
(2) It doubled.
(3) It increased slightly.
(4) It remained steady.

Base your answers to questions 4–6 on the topographic map shown below. Points A, B, C, and D are reference points on the map. Elevations are measured in meters.

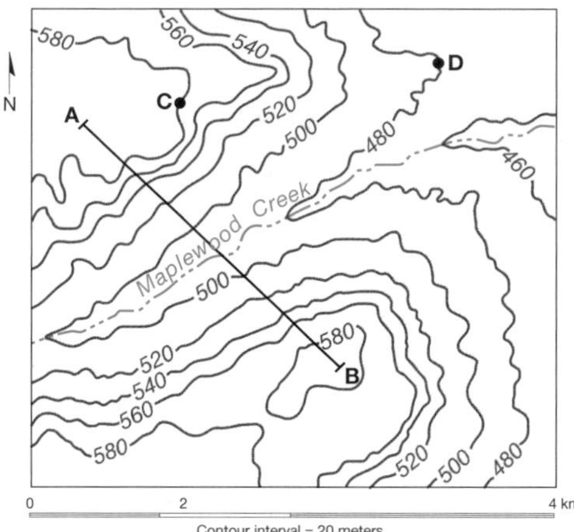

4 State the general direction in which Maplewood Creek is flowing.

5 Create a grid in your notebook and construct a topographic profile along line *AB*.

6 Calculate the gradient between points *C* and *D* on the map.

7 Describe the characteristics of an estuary. Why are estuaries important habitats?

Regents Practice Exam

(1) 3
(2) 2
(3) 1
(4) Maplewood Creek is flowing northeast. The map shows that the creek crosses contour lines at 500, 480, and 460 meters. Because the creek flows downhill, it must flow from near the point where it crosses the 500-m contour line toward the point where it crosses the 460-m contour line.
(5) Grid should look like this:

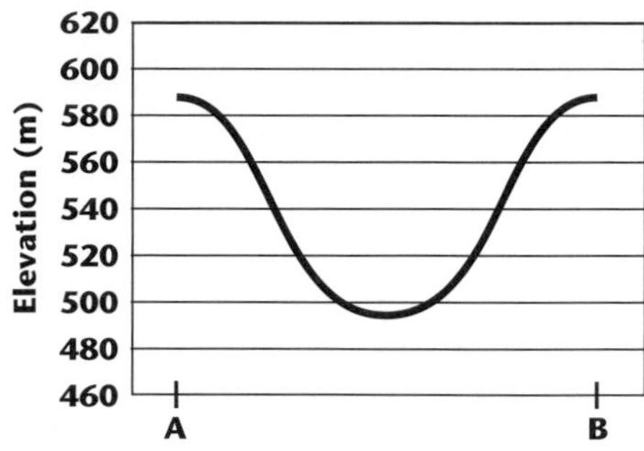

(6) Gradient = change in elevation/distance. The change in elevation is 580 m − 480 m = 100 m; the distance is 2 km. Gradient = 100 m/2 km = 50 m/km. Refer to first page of *Earth Science Reference Tables* for the equation for gradient.
(7) Estuaries contain a mixture of fresh water and salt water. They are important habitats because many aquatic species spend their youth there before migrating to the ocean as adults.

Performance-Based Assessment

Student diagrams will vary.

Your students can independently test their knowledge of the chapter and print out their results.

How will Global Warming Impact New York? L2

Teaching Tips

- Begin the discussion by comparing the greenhouse effect on Earth to the way that a car heats up in the hot summer sun. Greenhouse gases are much like the car's windows in that they trap in solar radiation, heating up the interior. A car may be warmed by the sun on winter days but can quickly become too hot in the summer. Earth has the potential to warm up if greenhouse gases in the atmosphere are increased.
- Discuss the fact that over the history of Earth, there have been changes in global temperatures. Earth has cycled through many warmer and colder periods creating phenomena such as ice ages for example. Natural causes for these variations are in debate but may include extreme volcanic eruptions or asteroid impacts. Recently, humans are thought to be the most significant factor increasing the greenhouse gases.
- Stress to the students that global temperatures do not have to rise to extremes to have a detrimental impact on the environment. A change as minor as several degrees Celsius could have grave effects.
- Stress that the predictions cited are based on models and patterns in nature. Both are subject to modification. Be sure students understand the difference between facts and predictions.

people and the ENVIRONMENT

How Could Global Warming Impact New York?

Global warming is an increase in Earth's average surface temperatures. Greenhouse gases, including water vapor and carbon dioxide, trap radiation from the sun, keeping temperatures on Earth at just the right levels to support life. The volumes of these greenhouse gases, as well as other gases in Earth's atmosphere fluctuate. When greenhouse gas levels are much higher than usual, Earth experiences of global warming. Earth is in a period of global warming now. How could global warming affect New York?

New York Climate

According to the United States Environmental Protection Agency, or EPA, Albany has experienced about a 0.5°C increase in temperature since the late 1800s. During this same period, the amount of precipitation falling over the state has increased by about 20 percent. Some studies project that by the year 2100, temperatures in the state may rise as much as −14.4 to −13.9°C in winter and as much as −13.9 to −13.3°C in the summer. These temperature changes could produce a drier climate overall for the state. But seasonal changes could produce wetter winters and drier summers.

Agriculture

The predicted changes in New York's temperatures and precipitation could affect agriculture in different ways. A warmer climate, for example, could lengthen the growing season. Such a change would probably have a positive affect on New York's agriculture. On the other hand, a warmer climate offers a more favorable environment for crop-damaging pests, which would be a negative effect of global warming. Likewise, a wetter climate would lessen the need for irrigation but could cause flooding that would damage crops, as shown in Figure 42.

Human Health

Some studies that analyze climate changes suggest that the number of heat-related deaths in New York City might double as the result of global warming. Also, to counter the heat, more air conditioners would be used, increasing the demand for electricity produced from fossil fuels. This increase in fossil fuel use would send more pollutants into the air, resulting in more smog in and around larger cities. Smog can pose problems for those with respiratory illnesses. Warmer temperatures might also increase the number of persons who contract diseases caused by mosquitoes and ticks.

New York's Forests

Climate changes might also affect the types of trees that would grow around the state. If the climate of New York were to become wetter and warmer, for example, pines might replace trees such as maples and beeches, which might not be able to adapt to the new climate. Some studies estimate that as much as 50–70 percent of New York's maple trees would disappear as the result of predicted changes in climate.

New York's Coastal Areas

Some studies suggest that global warming would result in a decrease in the Great Lakes' water levels. Increasing temperatures could lead to a greater rate of evaporation. Changes in water levels would also affect the hundreds of different populations that live in and around the lakes.

As global temperatures rise, ice caps are melting. New York's Atlantic coast has seen a 25-centimeter rise in sea level in the past 100 years. Some studies indicate that, by 2100, sea level might be as much as 56 centimeters higher than it is now. This rise will increase the flooding of low-lying areas, increase shoreline erosion, and destroy coastal wetlands.

Figure 42 Severe storms and floods caused by global warming could decrease crop productivity.

DATABANK
Earth Science Reference Tables

The University of the State of New York • THE STATE EDUCATION DEPARTMENT • Albany, New York 12234 • www.nysed.gov

PHYSICAL CONSTANTS

Radioactive Decay Data

RADIOACTIVE ISOTOPE	DISINTEGRATION	HALF-LIFE (years)
Carbon-14	$C^{14} \rightarrow N^{14}$	5.7×10^{3}
Potassium-40	$K^{40} \rightarrow Ar^{40}$, $K^{40} \rightarrow Ca^{40}$	1.3×10^{9}
Uranium-238	$U^{238} \rightarrow Pb^{206}$	4.5×10^{9}
Rubidium-87	$Rb^{87} \rightarrow Sr^{87}$	4.9×10^{10}

Concept Link Chapter 12

Specific Heats of Common Materials

MATERIAL	SPECIFIC HEAT (calories/gram • C°)
Water — solid	0.5
Water — liquid	1.0
Water — gas	0.5
Dry air	0.24
Basalt	0.20
Granite	0.19
Iron	0.11
Copper	0.09
Lead	0.03

Concept Link Chapter 2

Properties of Water

Energy gained during melting	80 calories/gram
Energy released during freezing	80 calories/gram
Energy gained during vaporization	540 calories/gram
Energy released during condensation	540 calories/gram
Density at 3.98°C	1.00 gram/milliliter

Concept Link Chapter 18

EQUATIONS

Percent deviation from accepted value	$\text{deviation (\%)} = \dfrac{\text{difference from accepted value}}{\text{accepted value}} \times 100$
Eccentricity of an ellipse	$\text{eccentricity} = \dfrac{\text{distance between foci}}{\text{length of major axis}}$
Gradient	$\text{gradient} = \dfrac{\text{change in field value}}{\text{distance}}$
Rate of change	$\text{rate of change} = \dfrac{\text{change in field value}}{\text{time}}$
Density of a substance	$\text{density} = \dfrac{\text{mass}}{\text{volume}}$

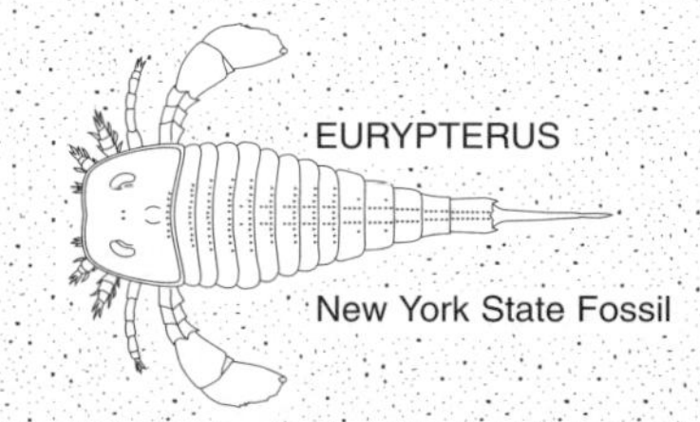

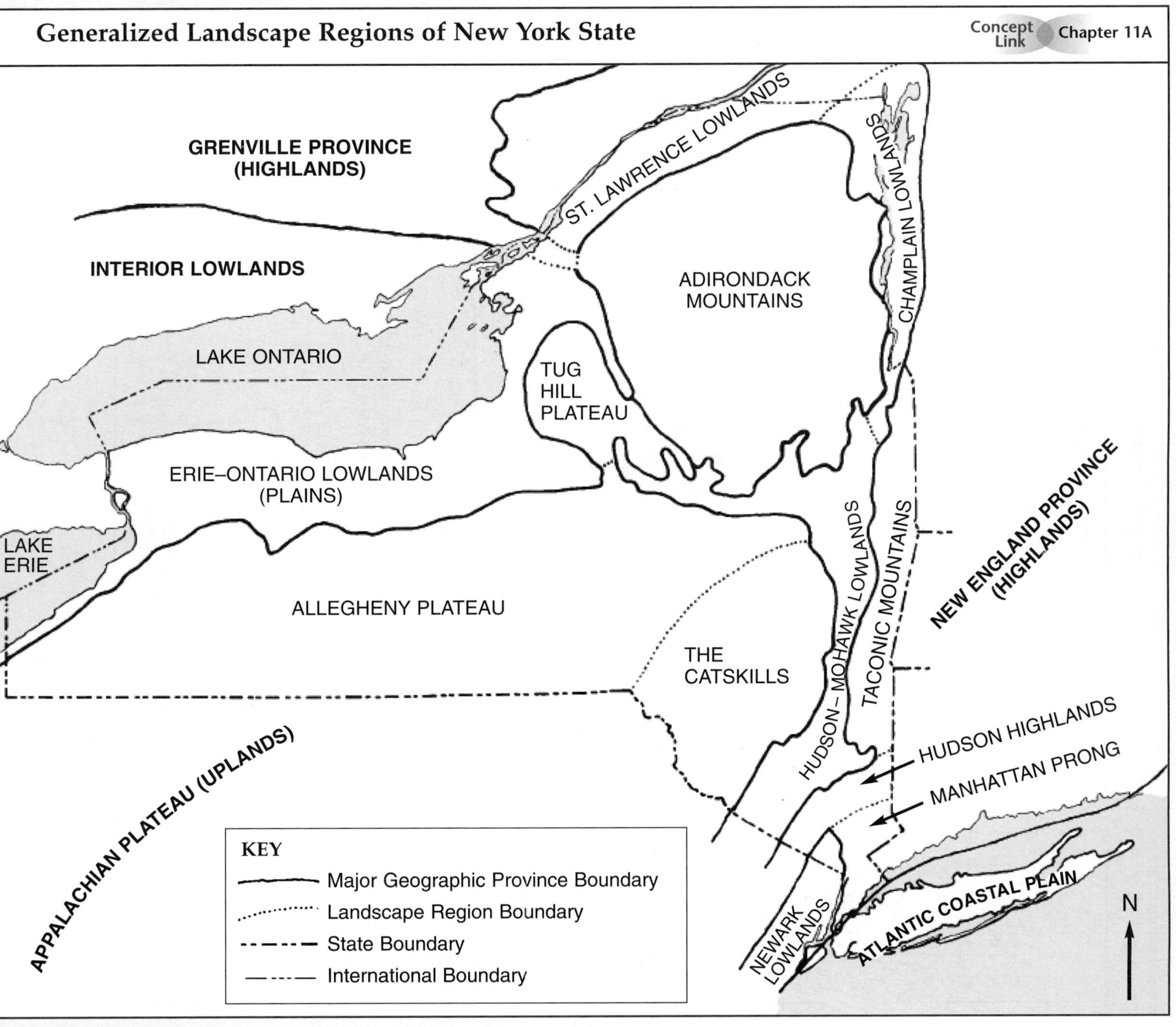
Generalized Landscape Regions of New York State
Concept Link
Chapter 11A
GRENVILLE PROVINCE (HIGHLANDS)
INTERIOR LOWLANDS
LAKE ONTARIO
ERIE–ONTARIO LOWLANDS (PLAINS)
LAKE ERIE
ALLEGHENY PLATEAU
APPALACHIAN PLATEAU (UPLANDS)
TUG HILL PLATEAU
ST. LAWRENCE LOWLANDS
ADIRONDACK MOUNTAINS
CHAMPLAIN LOWLANDS
THE CATSKILLS
HUDSON–MOHAWK LOWLANDS
TACONIC MOUNTAINS
NEW ENGLAND PROVINCE (HIGHLANDS)
HUDSON HIGHLANDS
MANHATTAN PRONG
NEWARK LOWLANDS
ATLANTIC COASTAL PLAIN
N
KEY
Major Geographic Province Boundary
Landscape Region Boundary
State Boundary
International Boundary

Generalized Bedrock Geology of New York State

modified from
GEOLOGICAL SURVEY
NEW YORK STATE MUSEUM
1989

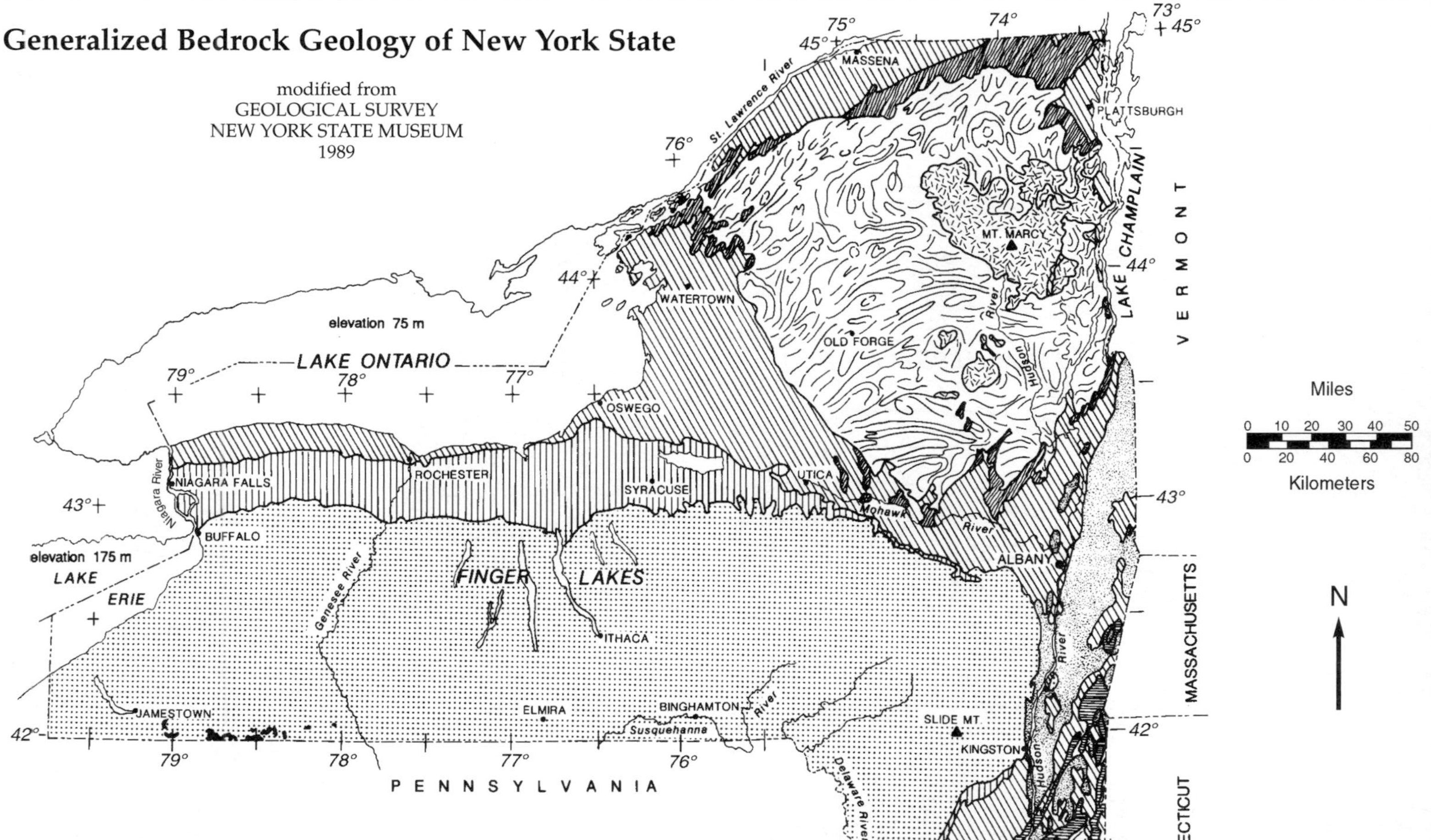

LAKE ONTARIO
elevation 75 m
LAKE ERIE
elevation 175 m
FINGER LAKES
PENNSYLVANIA
VERMONT
MASSACHUSETTS
CONNECTICUT
NEW JERSEY
LONG ISLAND SOUND
LONG ISLAND
ATLANTIC OCEAN
MASSENA
PLATTSBURGH
WATERTOWN
OLD FORGE
MT. MARCY
OSWEGO
ROCHESTER
NIAGARA FALLS
BUFFALO
SYRACUSE
UTICA
ALBANY
ITHACA
ELMIRA
BINGHAMTON
JAMESTOWN
SLIDE MT.
KINGSTON
NEW YORK CITY
RIVERHEAD
St. Lawrence River
Niagara River
Genesee River
Mohawk River
Hudson River
Susquehanna River
Delaware River
LAKE CHAMPLAIN

Miles
0 10 20 30 40 50
0 20 40 60 80
Kilometers

N

GEOLOGICAL PERIODS AND ERAS IN NEW YORK

Dominantly Sedimentary Origin

- CRETACEOUS, TERTIARY, PLEISTOCENE (Epoch) weakly consolidated to unconsolidated gravels, sands, and clays
- LATE TRIASSIC and EARLY JURASSIC conglomerates, red sandstones, red shales, and diabase (in Palisades Sill)
- PENNSYLVANIAN and MISSISSIPPIAN conglomerates, sandstones, and shales
- DEVONIAN, SILURIAN: limestones, shales, sandstones, and conglomerates. *Silurian also contains salt, gypsum, and hematite.*
- ORDOVICIAN, CAMBRIAN: limestones, shales, sandstones, and dolostones

Dominantly Metamorphosed Rocks

- CAMBRIAN and EARLY ORDOVICIAN sandstones and dolostones. *Moderately to intensely metamorphosed east of the Hudson River.*
- CAMBRIAN and ORDOVICIAN (undifferentiated) quartzites, dolostones, marbles, and schists. *Intensely metamorphosed; includes portions of the Taconic Sequence and Cortlandt Complex.*
- TACONIC SEQUENCE sandstones, shales, and slates. *Slightly to intensely metamorphosed rocks of* CAMBRIAN *through* MIDDLE ORDOVICIAN *ages.*

Intensely Metamorphosed Rocks (regional metamorphism about 1,000 m.y.a.)

- MIDDLE PROTEROZOIC gneisses, quartzites, and marbles. *Lines are generalized structure trends.*
- MIDDLE PROTEROZOIC anorthositic rocks

Concept Link Chapter 11A

Surface Ocean Currents

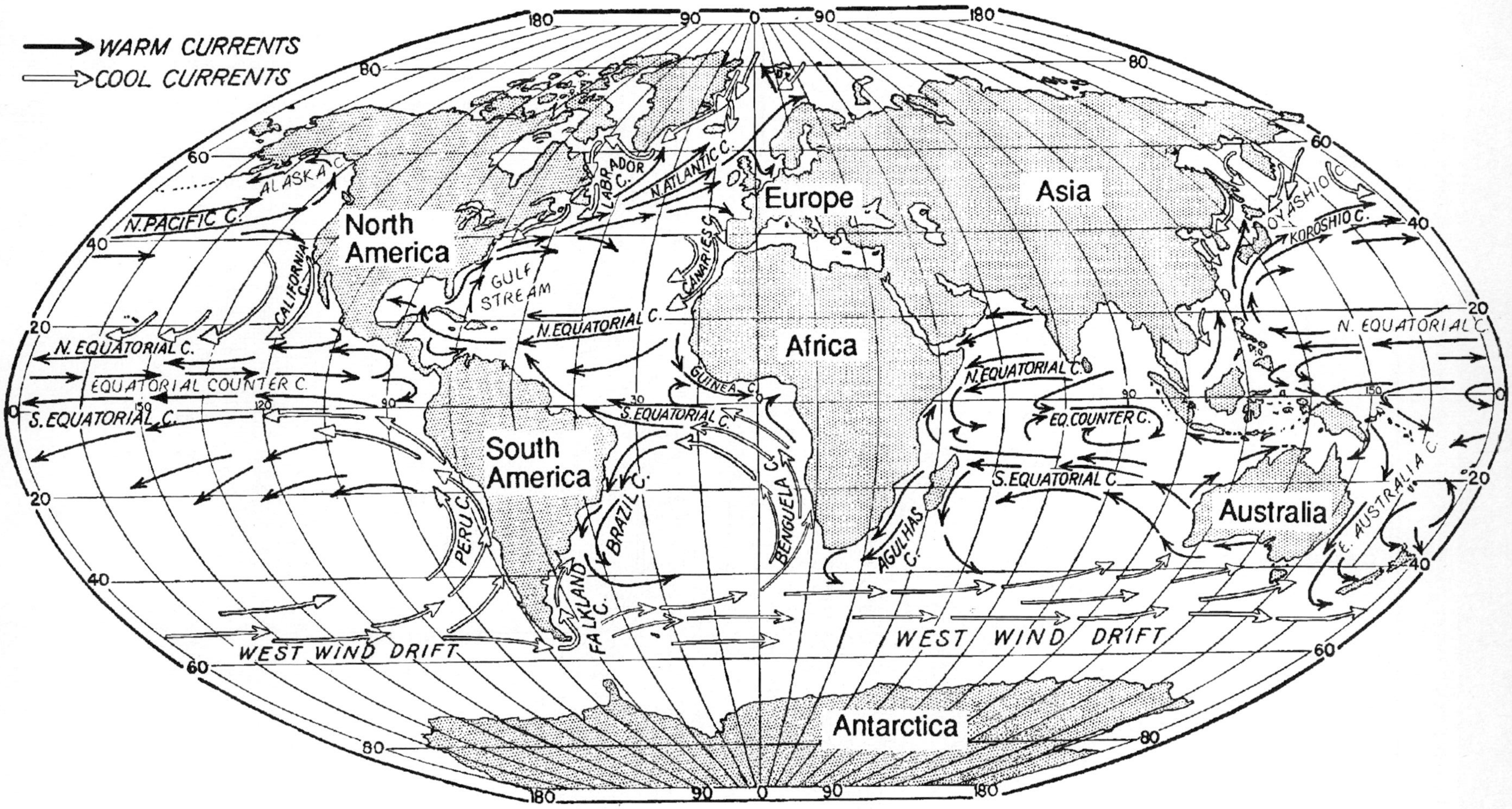

WARM CURRENTS
COOL CURRENTS

North America
South America
Europe
Africa
Asia
Australia
Antarctica

ALASKA C.
N. PACIFIC C.
CALIFORNIA C.
N. EQUATORIAL C.
EQUATORIAL COUNTER C.
S. EQUATORIAL C.
PERU C.
WEST WIND DRIFT
GULF STREAM
LABRADOR C.
N. ATLANTIC C.
CANARIES C.
N. EQUATORIAL C.
GUINEA C.
S. EQUATORIAL C.
BRAZIL C.
FALKLAND C.
BENGUELA C.
AGULHAS C.
N. EQUATORIAL C.
EQ. COUNTER C.
S. EQUATORIAL C.
WEST WIND DRIFT
OYASHIO C.
KOROSHIO C.
N. EQUATORIAL C.
E. AUSTRALIA C.

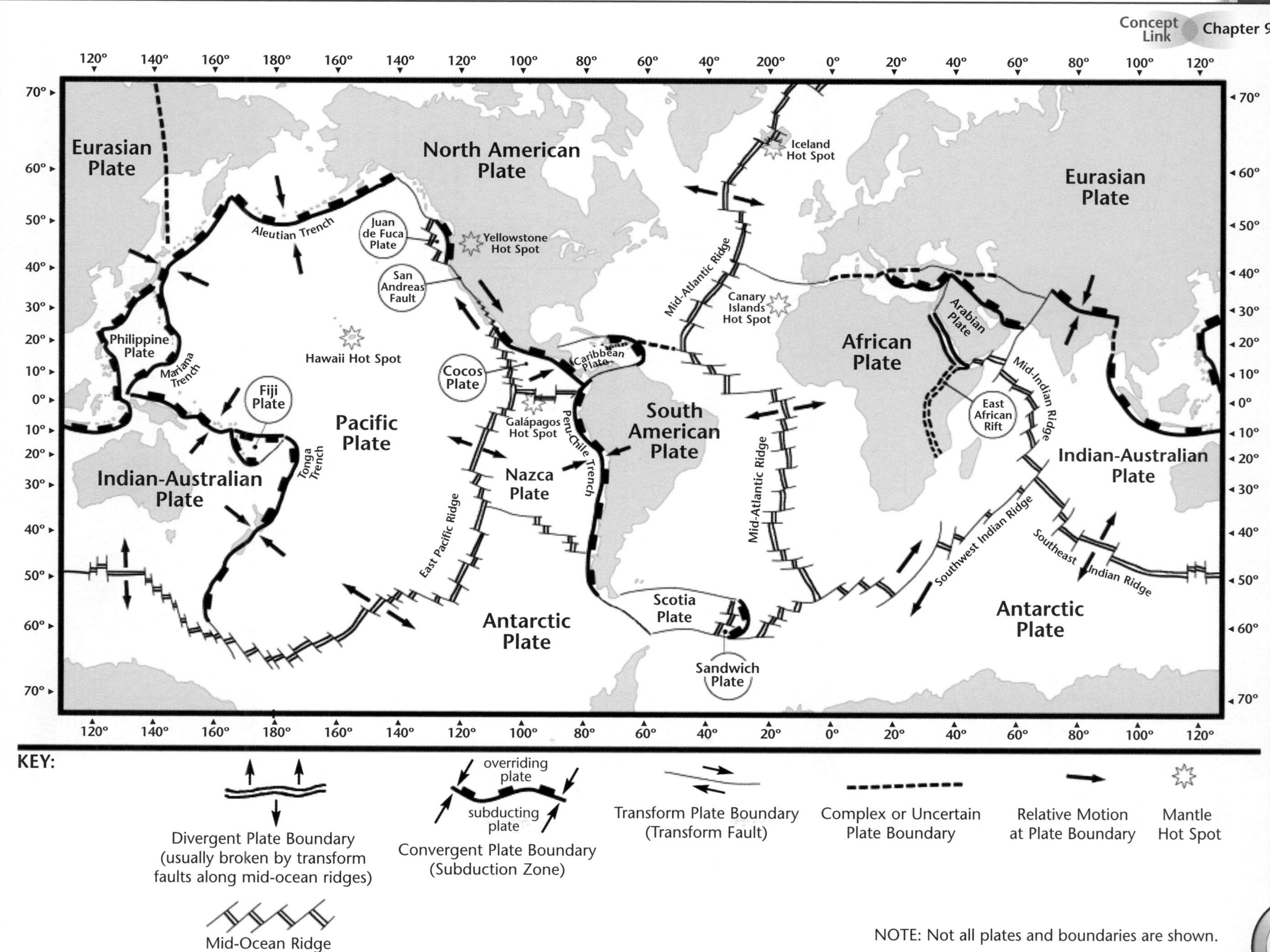

Eurasian Plate
North American Plate
Eurasian Plate
Iceland Hot Spot
Juan de Fuca Plate
Yellowstone Hot Spot
Aleutian Trench
San Andreas Fault
Mid-Atlantic Ridge
Canary Islands Hot Spot
Arabian Plate
Philippine Plate
Mariana Trench
Hawaii Hot Spot
Cocos Plate
Caribbean Plate
African Plate
Mid-Indian Ridge
Fiji Plate
Pacific Plate
Galápagos Hot Spot
South American Plate
East African Rift
Peru-Chile Trench
Tonga Trench
Indian-Australian Plate
Nazca Plate
Mid-Atlantic Ridge
Indian-Australian Plate
East Pacific Ridge
Southwest Indian Ridge
Southeast Indian Ridge
Scotia Plate
Antarctic Plate
Antarctic Plate
Sandwich Plate
120° 140° 160° 180° 160° 140° 120° 100° 80° 60° 40° 200° 0° 20° 40° 60° 80° 100° 120°
70° 60° 50° 40° 30° 20° 10° 0° 10° 20° 30° 40° 50° 60° 70°
120° 140° 160° 180° 160° 140° 120° 100° 80° 60° 40° 20° 0° 20° 40° 60° 80° 100° 120°
KEY:
Divergent Plate Boundary (usually broken by transform faults along mid-ocean ridges)
Mid-Ocean Ridge
overriding plate
subducting plate
Convergent Plate Boundary (Subduction Zone)
Transform Plate Boundary (Transform Fault)
Complex or Uncertain Plate Boundary
Relative Motion at Plate Boundary
Mantle Hot Spot
NOTE: Not all plates and boundaries are shown.

Rock Cycle in Earth's Crust

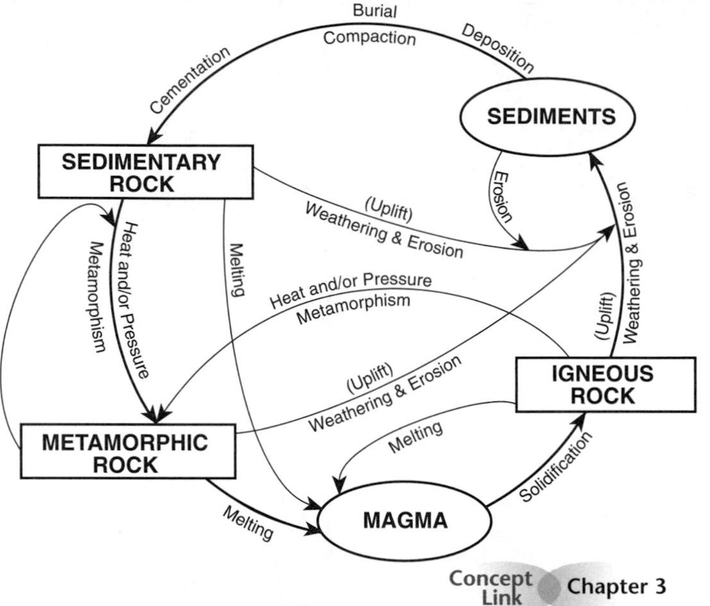

Concept Link Chapter 3

Relationship of Transported Particle Size to Water Velocity

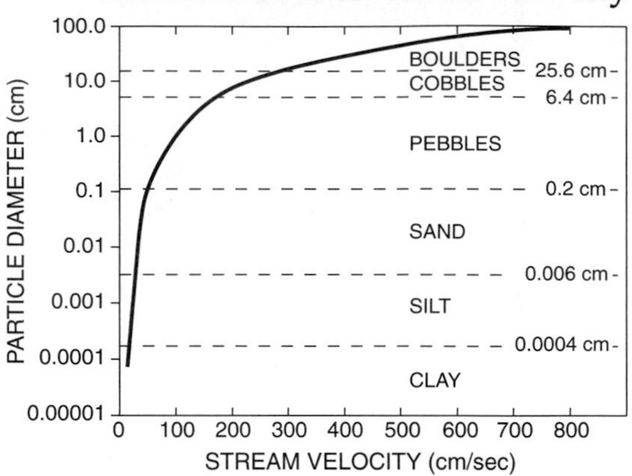

*This generalized graph shows the water velocity needed to maintain, but not start, movement. Variations occur due to differences in particle density and shape.

Concept Link Chapter 6

Scheme for Igneous Rock Identification

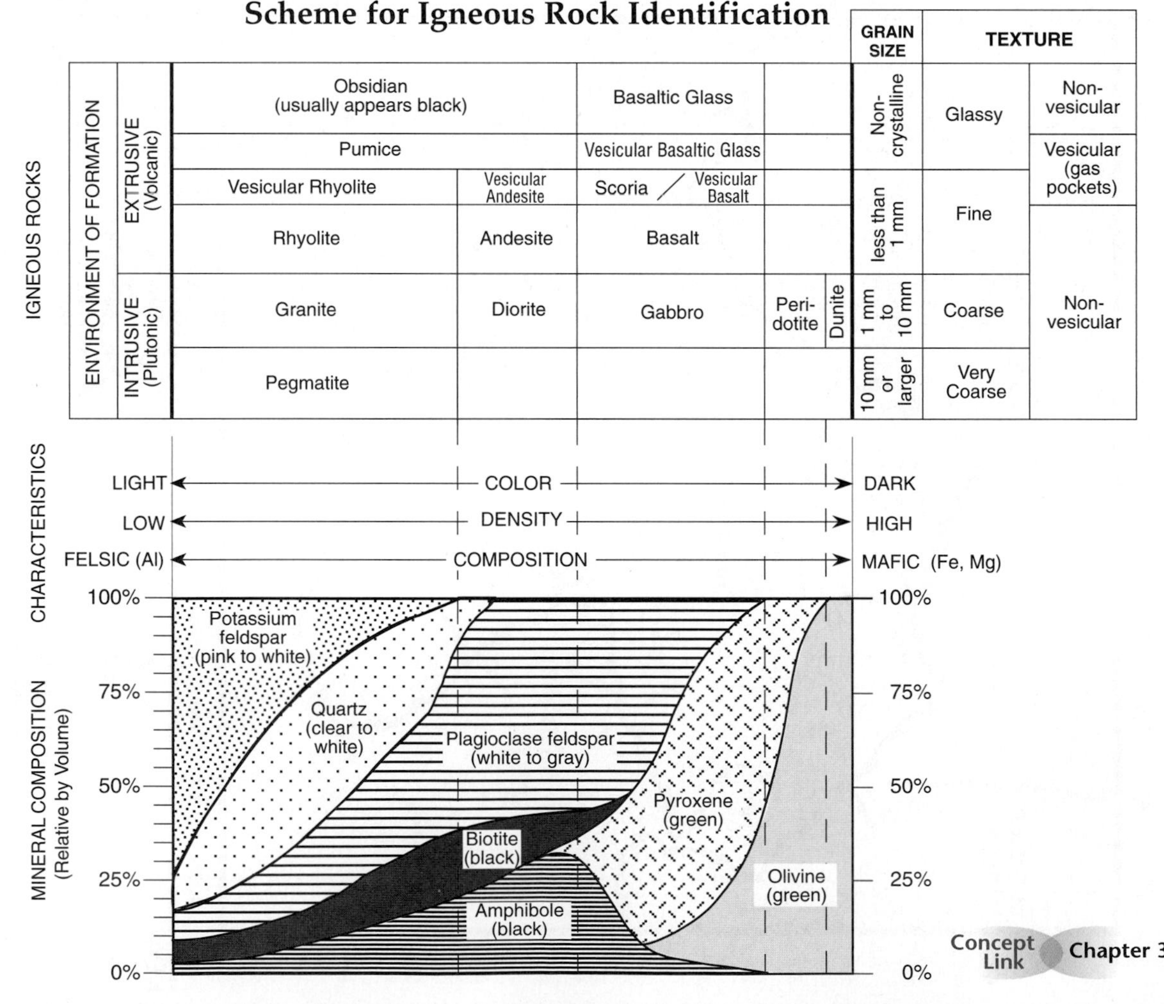

Concept Link Chapter 3

Scheme for Sedimentary Rock Identification

Concept Link Chapter 3

INORGANIC LAND-DERIVED SEDIMENTARY ROCKS					
TEXTURE	**GRAIN SIZE**	**COMPOSITION**	**COMMENTS**	**ROCK NAME**	**MAP SYMBOL**
Clastic (fragmental)	Pebbles, cobbles, and/or boulders embedded in sand, silt, and/or clay	Mostly quartz, feldspar, and clay minerals; may contain fragments of other rocks and minerals	Rounded fragments	Conglomerate	
			Angular fragments	Breccia	
	Sand (0.2 to 0.006 cm)		Fine to coarse	Sandstone	
	Silt (0.006 to 0.0004 cm)		Very fine grain	Siltstone	
	Clay (less than 0.0004 cm)		Compact; may split easily	Shale	

CHEMICALLY AND/OR ORGANICALLY FORMED SEDIMENTARY ROCKS					
TEXTURE	**GRAIN SIZE**	**COMPOSITION**	**COMMENTS**	**ROCK NAME**	**MAP SYMBOL**
Crystalline	Varied	Halite	Crystals from chemical precipitates and evaporites	Rock Salt	
	Varied	Gypsum		Rock Gypsum	
	Varied	Dolomite		Dolostone	
Bioclastic	Microscopic to coarse	Calcite	Cemented shell fragments or precipitates of biologic origin	Limestone	
	Varied	Carbon	From plant remains	Coal	

Scheme for Metamorphic Rock Identification

Concept Link Chapter 3

TEXTURE		GRAIN SIZE	COMPOSITION	TYPE OF METAMORPHISM	COMMENTS	ROCK NAME	MAP SYMBOL
FOLIATED	MINERAL ALIGNMENT	Fine	MICA	Regional	Low-grade metamorphism of shale	Slate	
		Fine to medium	MICA, QUARTZ, FELDSPAR, AMPHIBOLE, GARNET	(Heat and pressure increase with depth)	Foliation surfaces shiny from microscopic mica crystals	Phyllite	
			MICA, QUARTZ, FELDSPAR, AMPHIBOLE, GARNET, PYROXENE		Platy mica crystals visible from metamorphism of clay or feldspars	Schist	
	BAND-ING	Medium to coarse	MICA, QUARTZ, FELDSPAR, AMPHIBOLE, GARNET, PYROXENE		High-grade metamorphism; some mica changed to feldspar; segregated by mineral type into bands	Gneiss	
NONFOLIATED		Fine	Variable	Contact (Heat)	Various rocks changed by heat from nearby magma/lava	Hornfels	
		Fine to coarse	Quartz	Regional or Contact	Metamorphism of quartz sandstone	Quartzite	
			Calcite and/or dolomite		Metamorphism of limestone or dolostone	Marble	
		Coarse	Various minerals in particles and matrix		Pebbles may be distorted or stretched	Metaconglomerate	

Geologic History of New York State

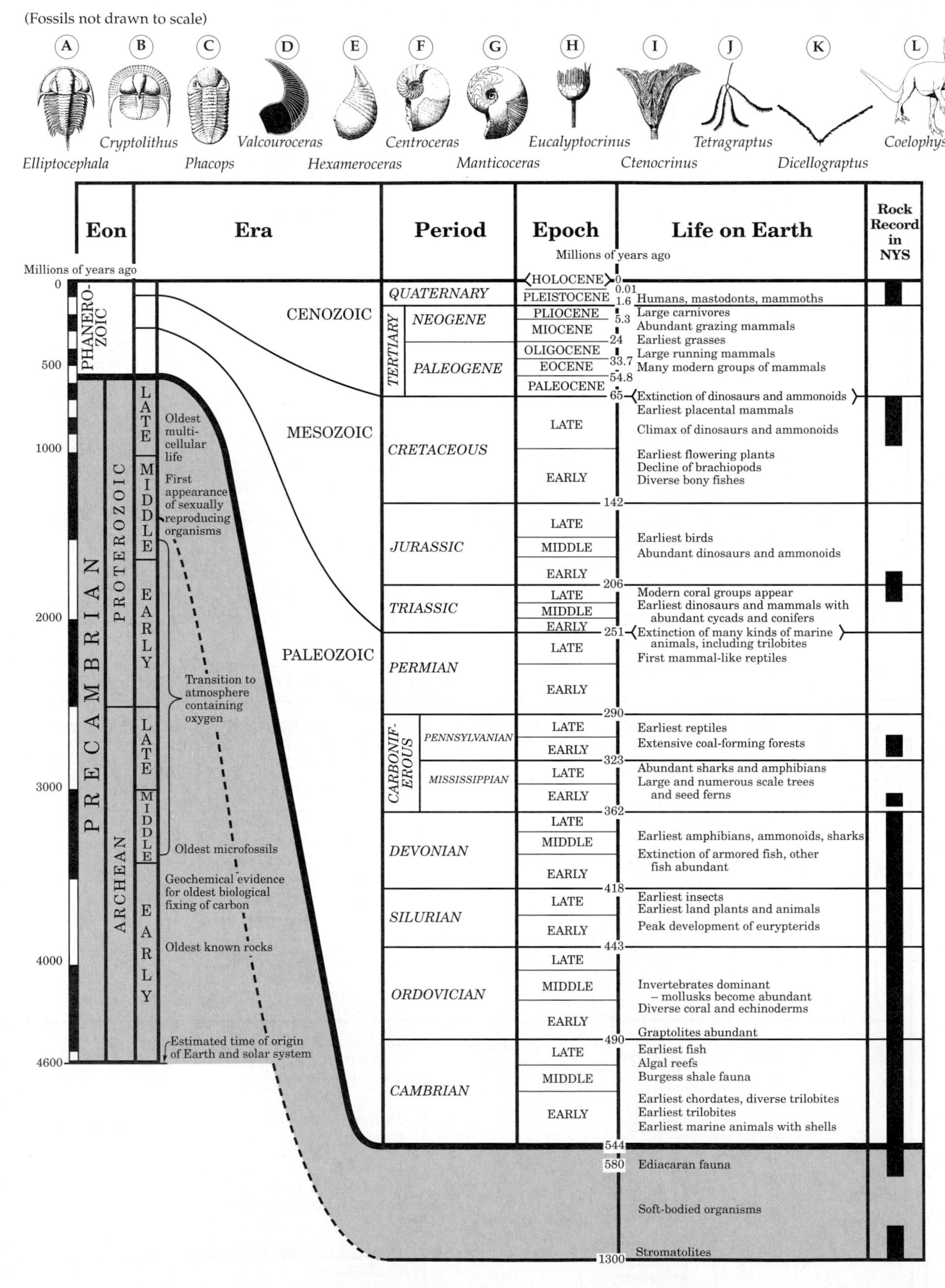

Concept Link Chapter 13

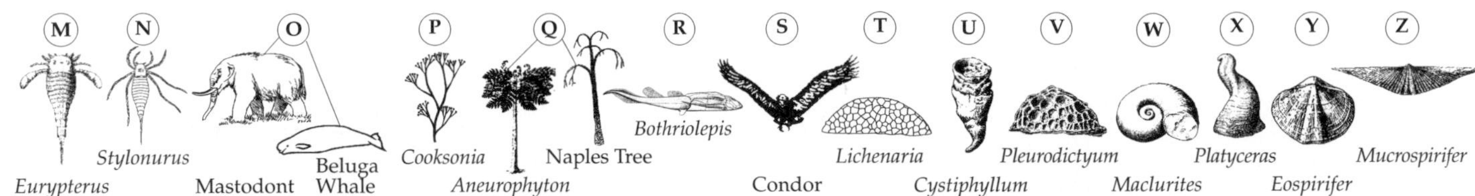

Time Distribution of Fossils (Including Important Fossils of New York)

Lettered circles indicate the approximate time of existence of a specific index fossil (e.g. Fossil (A) lived at the end of the Early Cambrian).

TRILOBITES (A, B, C); NAUTILOIDS (D, E, F); AMMONOIDS (G); CRINOIDS (H, I); GRAPTOLITES (J, K); DINOSAURS (L); EURYPTERIDS (M, N); MAMMALS (O); VASCULAR PLANTS (P, Q); PLACODERM FISH (R); BIRDS (S); CORALS (T, U, V); GASTROPODS (W, X); BRACHIOPODS (Y, Z)

Earth's first forest (Q)

Earth's first coral reef (T)

Tectonic Events Affecting Northeast North America

Rifting; Passive Margin; Subduction; Continental Collision; Transform Collision

Important Geologic Events in New York

Advance and retreat of last continental ice

Uplift of Adirondack region

Sands and shales underlying Long Island and Staten Island deposited on margin of Atlantic Ocean

Development of passive continental margin

Initial opening of Atlantic Ocean
North America and Africa separate

Intrusion of Palisades sill
Pangea begins to break up

Extensive erosion

Appalachian (Alleghanian) Orogeny caused by collision of North America and Africa along transform margin, forming Pangea

Catskill Delta forms
Erosion of Acadian Mountains

Acadian Orogeny caused by collision of North America and Avalon and closing of remaining part of Iapetus Ocean

Salt and gypsum deposited in evaporite basins

Erosion of Taconic Mountains; Queenston Delta forms

Taconian Orogeny caused by closing of western part of Iapetus Ocean and collision between North America and volcanic island arc

Iapetus passive margin forms

Rifting and initial opening of Iapetus Ocean
Erosion of Grenville Mountains

Grenville Orogeny: Ancestral Adirondack Mtns. and Hudson Highlands formed

Inferred Position of Earth's Landmasses

TERTIARY 59 million years ago

CRETACEOUS 119 million years ago

TRIASSIC 232 million years ago

DEVONIAN/MISSISSIPPIAN 362 million years ago

ORDOVICIAN 458 million years ago

99-098 CDK(rev) 8/2000

Inferred Properties of Earth's Interior

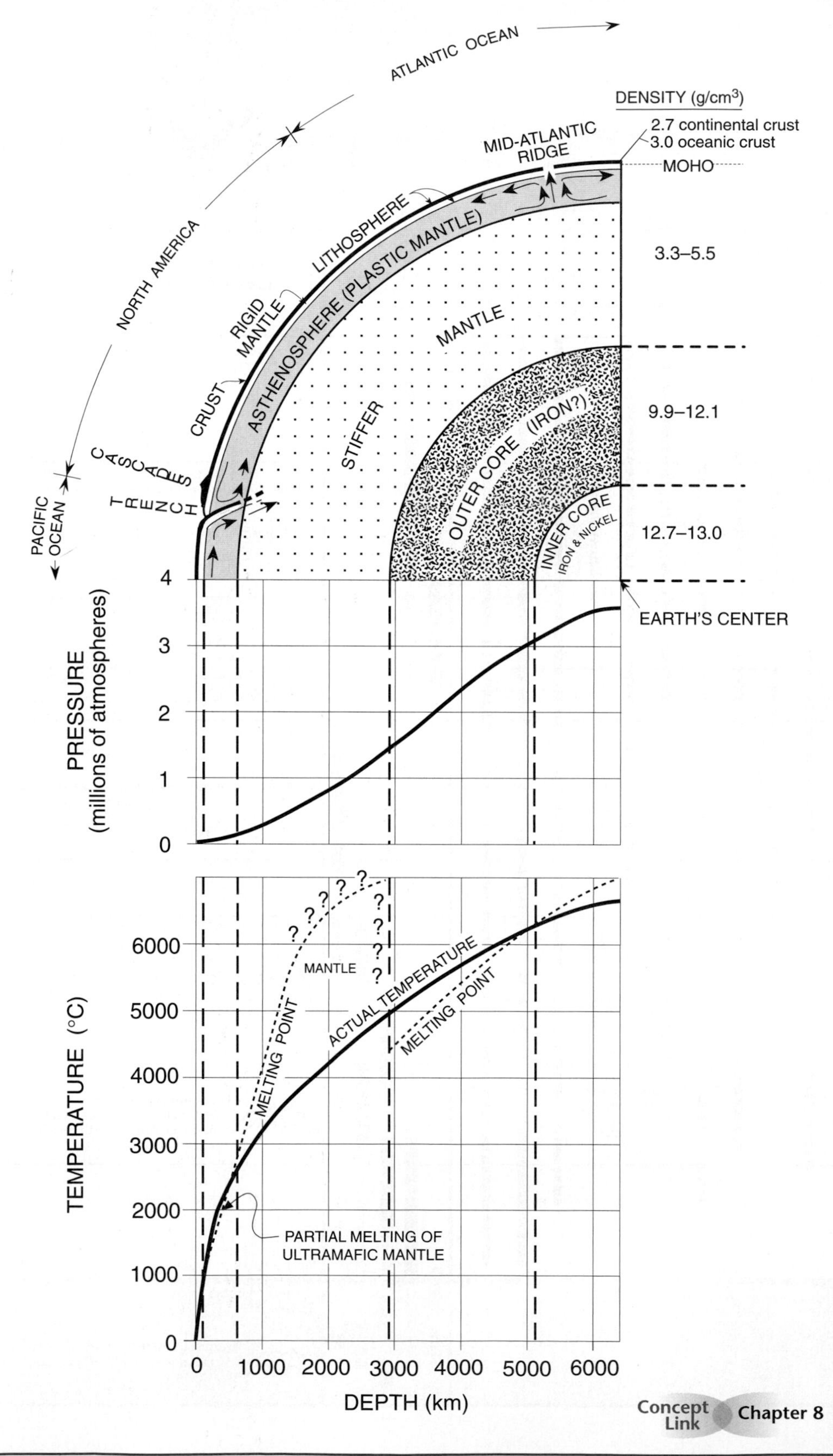

Concept Link Chapter 8

Average Chemical Composition of Earth's Crust, Hydrosphere, and Troposphere

ELEMENT (symbol)	CRUST		HYDROSPHERE	TROPOSPHERE
	Percent by Mass	Percent by Volume	Percent by Volume	Percent by Volume
Oxygen (O)	46.40	94.04	33.0	21.0
Silicon (Si)	28.15	0.88		
Aluminum (Al)	8.23	0.48		
Iron (Fe)	5.63	0.49		
Calcium (Ca)	4.15	1.18		
Sodium (Na)	2.36	1.11		
Magnesium (Mg)	2.33	0.33		
Potassium (K)	2.09	1.42		
Nitrogen (N)				78.0
Hydrogen (H)			66.0	
Other	0.66	0.07	1.0	1.0

Concept Link Chapter 2

Earthquake P-wave and S-wave Travel Time

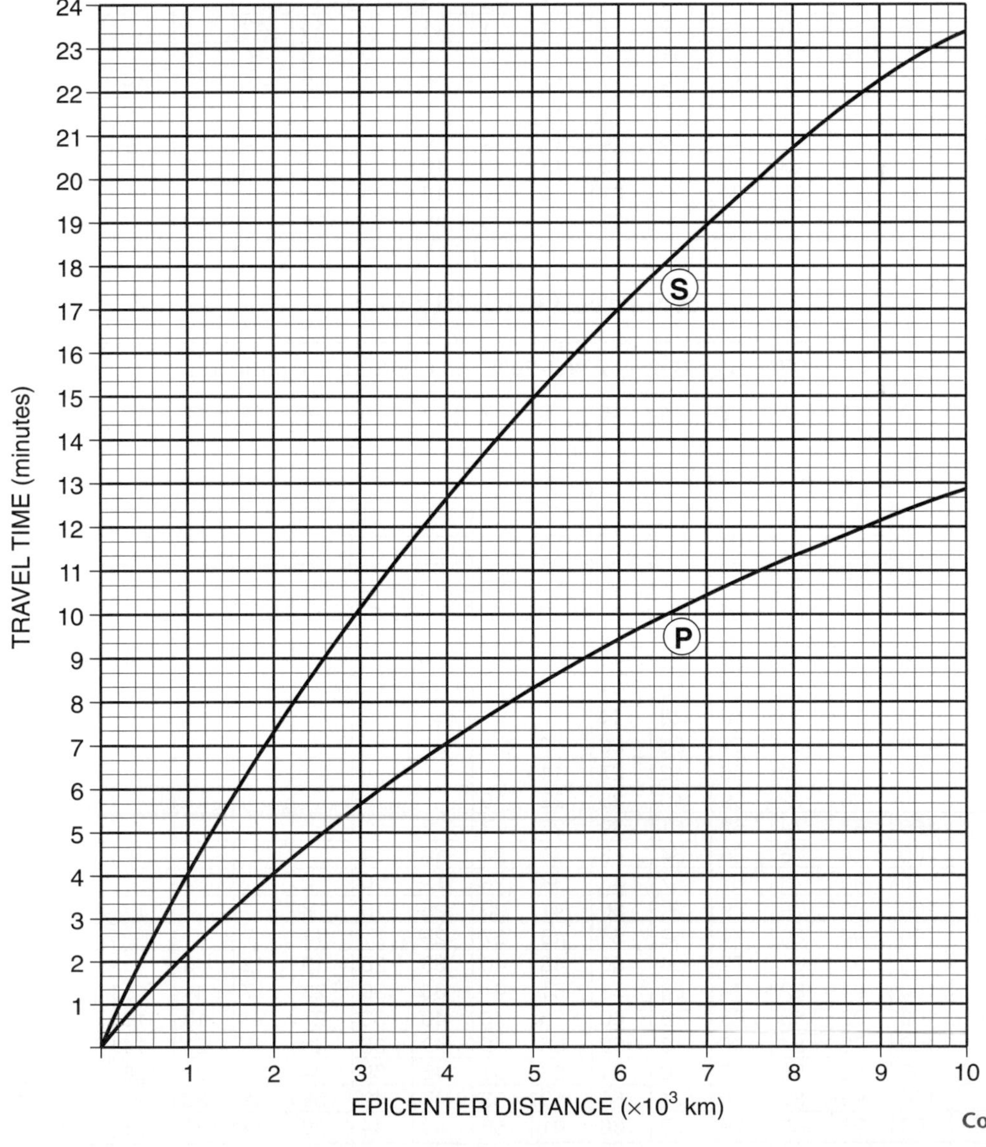

Concept Link Chapter 8

Dewpoint Temperatures (°C)

Concept Link Chapter 18

Dry-Bulb Tempera-ture (°C)	Difference Between Wet-Bulb and Dry-Bulb Temperatures (C°)															
	0	**1**	**2**	**3**	**4**	**5**	**6**	**7**	**8**	**9**	**10**	**11**	**12**	**13**	**14**	**15**
−20	−20	−33														
−18	−18	−28														
−16	−16	−24														
−14	−14	−21	−36													
−12	−12	−18	−28													
−10	−10	−14	−22													
−8	−8	−12	−18	−29												
−6	−6	−10	−14	−22												
−4	−4	−7	−12	−17	−29											
−2	−2	−5	−8	−13	−20											
0	0	−3	−6	−9	−15	−24										
2	2	−1	−3	−6	−11	−17										
4	4	1	−1	−4	−7	−11	−19									
6	6	4	1	−1	−4	−7	−13	−21								
8	8	6	3	1	−2	−5	−9	−14								
10	10	8	6	4	1	−2	−5	−9	−14	−28						
12	12	10	8	6	4	1	−2	−5	−9	−16						
14	14	12	11	9	6	4	1	−2	−5	−10	−17					
16	16	14	13	11	9	7	4	1	−1	−6	−10	−17				
18	18	16	15	13	11	9	7	4	2	−2	−5	−10	−19			
20	20	19	17	15	14	12	10	7	4	2	−2	−5	−10	−19		
22	22	21	19	17	16	14	12	10	8	5	3	−1	−5	−10	−19	
24	24	23	21	20	18	16	14	12	10	8	6	2	−1	−5	−10	−18
26	26	25	23	22	20	18	17	15	13	11	9	6	3	0	−4	−9
28	28	27	25	24	22	21	19	17	16	14	11	9	7	4	1	−3
30	30	29	27	26	24	23	21	19	18	16	14	12	10	8	5	1

Relative Humidity (%)

Concept Link Chapter 18

Dry-Bulb Tempera-ture (°C)	Difference Between Wet-Bulb and Dry-Bulb Temperatures (C°)															
	0	**1**	**2**	**3**	**4**	**5**	**6**	**7**	**8**	**9**	**10**	**11**	**12**	**13**	**14**	**15**
−20	100	28														
−18	100	40														
−16	100	48														
−14	100	55	11													
−12	100	61	23													
−10	100	66	33													
−8	100	71	41	13												
−6	100	73	48	20												
−4	100	77	54	32	11											
−2	100	79	58	37	20	1										
0	100	81	63	45	28	11										
2	100	83	67	51	36	20	6									
4	100	85	70	56	42	27	14									
6	100	86	72	59	46	35	22	10								
8	100	87	74	62	51	39	28	17	6							
10	100	88	76	65	54	43	33	24	13	4						
12	100	88	78	67	57	48	38	28	19	10	2					
14	100	89	79	69	60	50	41	33	25	16	8	1				
16	100	90	80	71	62	54	45	37	29	21	14	7	1			
18	100	91	81	72	64	56	48	40	33	26	19	12	6			
20	100	91	82	74	66	58	51	44	36	30	23	17	11	5		
22	100	92	83	75	68	60	53	46	40	33	27	21	15	10	4	
24	100	92	84	76	69	62	55	49	42	36	30	25	20	14	9	4
26	100	92	85	77	70	64	57	51	45	39	34	28	23	18	13	9
28	100	93	86	78	71	65	59	53	47	42	36	31	26	21	17	12
30	100	93	86	79	72	66	61	55	49	44	39	34	29	25	20	16

Temperature

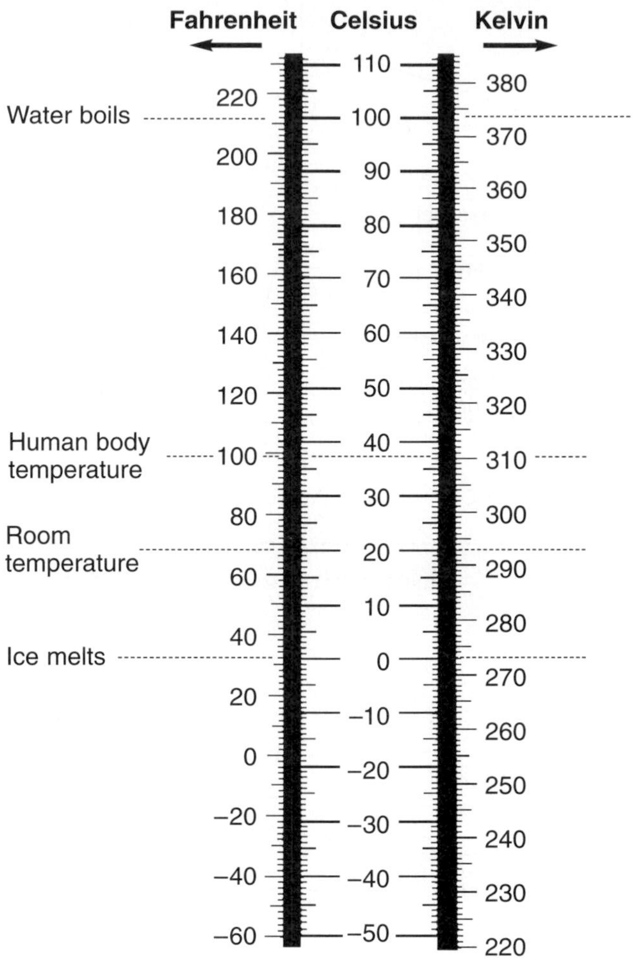

Fahrenheit ← Celsius → Kelvin

Fahrenheit: 220, 200, 180, 160, 140, 120, 100, 80, 60, 40, 20, 0, –20, –40, –60

Celsius: 110, 100, 90, 80, 70, 60, 50, 40, 30, 20, 10, 0, –10, –20, –30, –40, –50

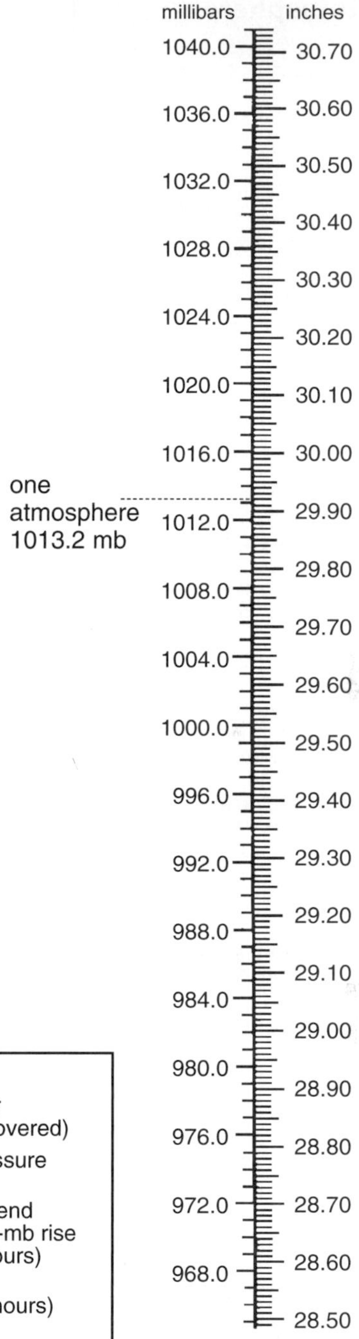

Kelvin: 380, 370, 360, 350, 340, 330, 320, 310, 300, 290, 280, 270, 260, 250, 240, 230, 220

Water boils

Human body temperature

Room temperature

Ice melts

Pressure

millibars: 1040.0, 1036.0, 1032.0, 1028.0, 1024.0, 1020.0, 1016.0, 1012.0, 1008.0, 1004.0, 1000.0, 996.0, 992.0, 988.0, 984.0, 980.0, 976.0, 972.0, 968.0

inches: 30.70, 30.60, 30.50, 30.40, 30.30, 30.20, 30.10, 30.00, 29.90, 29.80, 29.70, 29.60, 29.50, 29.40, 29.30, 29.20, 29.10, 29.00, 28.90, 28.80, 28.70, 28.60, 28.50

one atmosphere 1013.2 mb

Weather Map Symbols

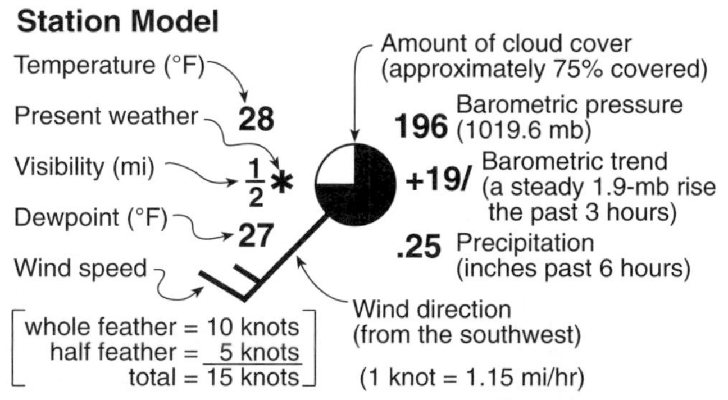

Station Model

Temperature (°F) 28

Present weather *

Visibility (mi) 1/2

Dewpoint (°F) 27

Wind speed

whole feather = 10 knots
half feather = 5 knots
total = 15 knots

Amount of cloud cover (approximately 75% covered)

196 Barometric pressure (1019.6 mb)

+19/ Barometric trend (a steady 1.9-mb rise the past 3 hours)

.25 Precipitation (inches past 6 hours)

Wind direction (from the southwest)

(1 knot = 1.15 mi/hr)

Concept Link Unit 6

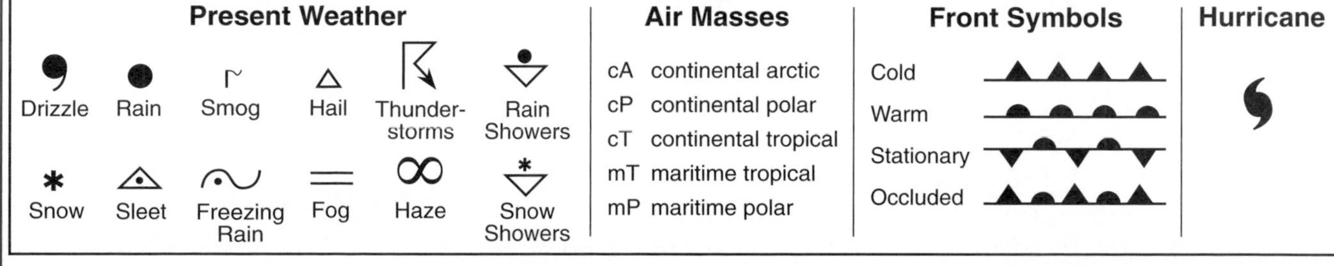

Selected Properties of Earth's Atmosphere

Concept Link Chapter 17

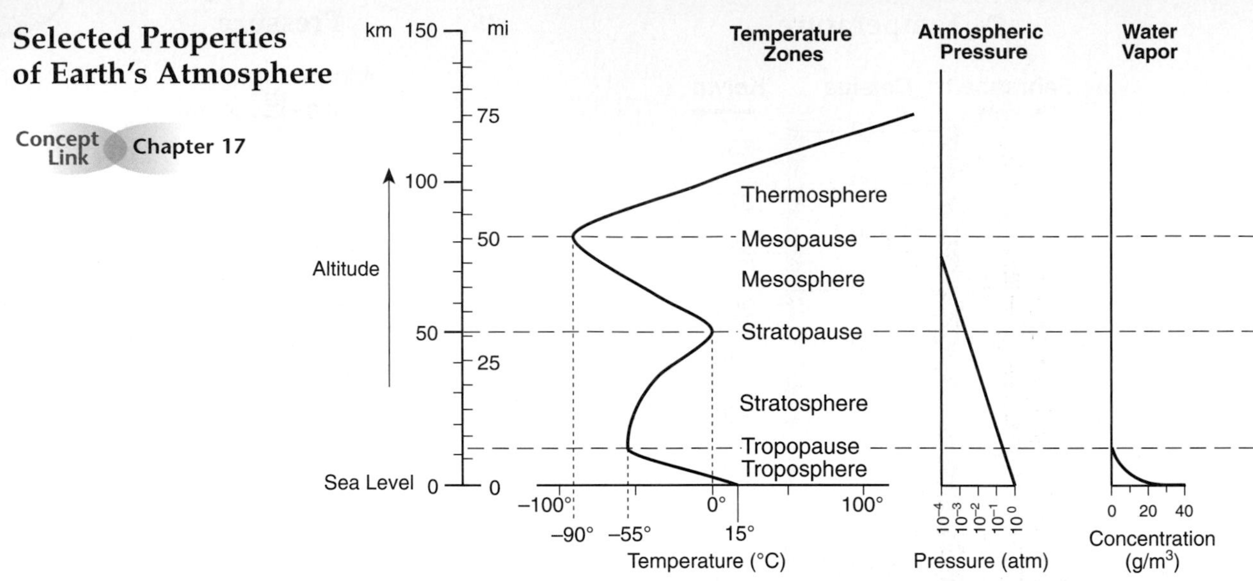

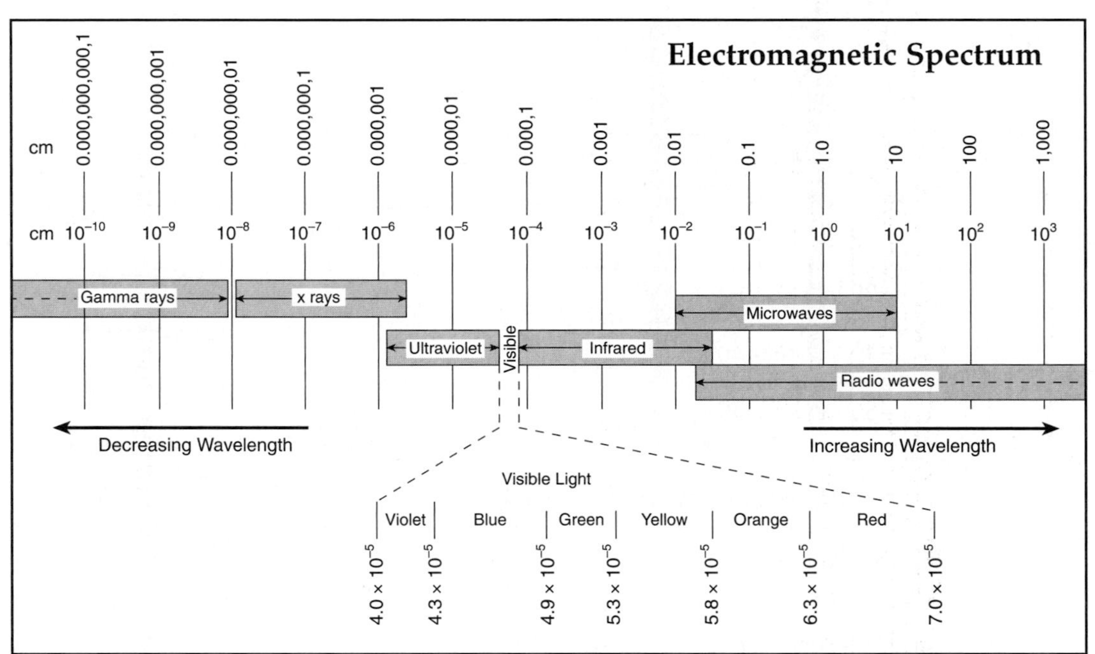

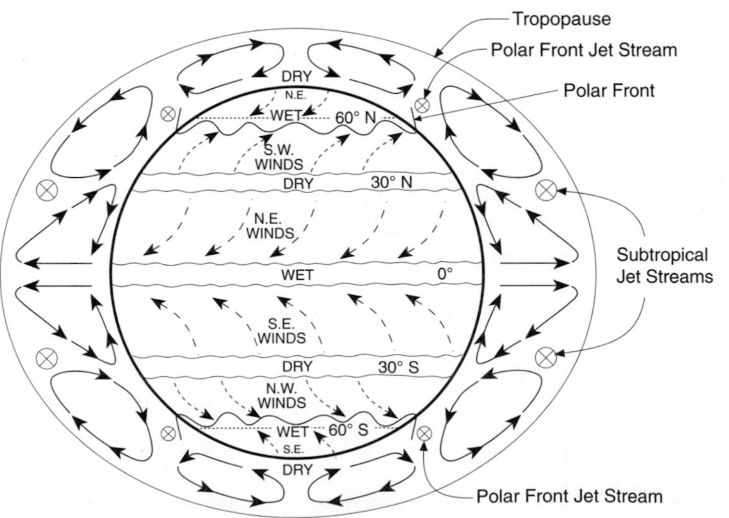

Planetary Wind and Moisture Belts in the Troposphere

The drawing to the left shows the locations of the belts near the time of an equinox. The locations shift somewhat with the changing latitude of the Sun's vertical ray. In the Northern Hemisphere, the belts shift northward in summer and southward in winter.

Concept Link Chapter 19

Luminosity and Temperature of Stars

(Name in italics refers to star shown by a ⊕)

Concept Link Chapter 25

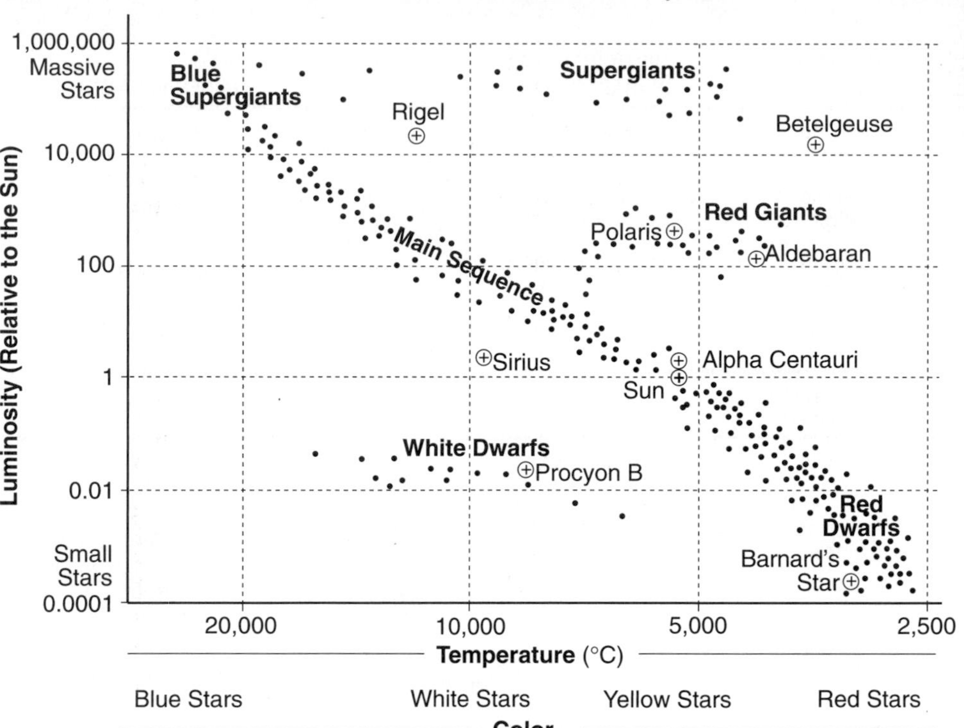

Luminosity is the brightness of stars compared to the brightness of our Sun as seen from the same distance from the observer.

Solar System Data

Concept Link Chapter 23

Object	Mean Distance from Sun (millions of km)	Period of Revolution	Period of Rotation	Eccentricity of Orbit	Equatorial Diameter (km)	Mass (Earth = 1)	Density (g/cm^3)	Number of Moons
SUN	—	—	27 days	—	1,392,000	333,000.00	1.4	–
MERCURY	57.9	88 days	59 days	0.206	4,880	0.553	5.4	0
VENUS	108.2	224.7 days	243 days	0.007	12,104	0.815	5.2	0
EARTH	149.6	365.26 days	23 hr 56 min 4 sec	0.017	12,756	1.00	5.5	1
MARS	227.9	687 days	24 hr 37 min 23 sec	0.093	6,787	0.1074	3.9	2
JUPITER	778.3	11.86 years	9 hr 50 min 30 sec	0.048	142,800	317.896	1.3	16
SATURN	1,427	29.46 years	10 hr 14 min	0.056	120,000	95.185	0.7	18
URANUS	2,869	84.0 years	17 hr 14 min	0.047	51,800	14.537	1.2	21
NEPTUNE	4,496	164.8 years	16 hr	0.009	49,500	17.151	1.7	8
PLUTO	5,900	247.7 years	6 days 9 hr	0.250	2,300	0.0025	2.0	1
EARTH'S MOON	149.6 (0.386 from Earth)	27.3 days	27 days 8 hr	0.055	3,476	0.0123	3.3	—

Properties of Common Minerals

LUSTER	HARD-NESS	CLEAVAGE	FRACTURE	COMMON COLORS	DISTINGUISHING CHARACTERISTICS	USE(S)	MINERAL NAME	COMPOSITION*
Metallic Luster	1–2	✔		silver to gray	black streak, greasy feel	pencil lead, lubricants	**Graphite**	C
Metallic Luster	2.5	✔		metallic silver	very dense (7.6 g/cm^3), gray-black streak	ore of lead	**Galena**	PbS
Metallic Luster	5.5–6.5		✔	black to silver	attracted by magnet, black streak	ore of iron	**Magnetite**	Fe_3O_4
Metallic Luster	6.5		✔	brassy yellow	green-black streak, cubic crystals	ore of sulfur	**Pyrite**	FeS_2
Either	1–6.5		✔	metallic silver or earthy red	red-brown streak	ore of iron	**Hematite**	Fe_2O_3
Nonmetallic Luster	1	✔		white to green	greasy feel	talcum powder, soapstone	**Talc**	$Mg_3Si_4O_{10}(OH)_2$
Nonmetallic Luster	2		✔	yellow to amber	easily melted, may smell	vulcanize rubber, sulfuric acid	**Sulfur**	S
Nonmetallic Luster	2	✔		white to pink or gray	easily scratched by fingernail	plaster of paris and drywall	**Gypsum** (Selenite)	$CaSO_4 \bullet 2H_2O$
Nonmetallic Luster	2–2.5	✔		colorless to yellow	flexible in thin sheets	electrical insulator	**Muscovite Mica**	$KAl_3Si_3O_{10}(OH)_2$
Nonmetallic Luster	2.5	✔		colorless to white	cubic cleavage, salty taste	food additive, melts ice	**Halite**	NaCl
Nonmetallic Luster	2.5–3	✔		black to dark brown	flexible in thin sheets	electrical insulator	**Biotite Mica**	$K(Mg,Fe)_3 AlSi_3O_{10}(OH)_2$
Nonmetallic Luster	3	✔		colorless or variable	bubbles with acid	cement, polarizing prisms	**Calcite**	$CaCO_3$
Nonmetallic Luster	3.5	✔		colorless or variable	bubbles with acid when powdered	source of magnesium	**Dolomite**	$CaMg(CO_3)_2$
Nonmetallic Luster	4	✔		colorless or variable	cleaves in 4 directions	hydrofluoric acid	**Fluorite**	CaF_2
Nonmetallic Luster	5–6	✔		black to dark green	cleaves in 2 directions at 90°	mineral collections	**Pyroxene** (commonly Augite)	$(Ca,Na)\ (Mg,Fe,Al)\ (Si,Al)_2O_6$
Nonmetallic Luster	5.5	✔		black to dark green	cleaves at 56° and 124°	mineral collections	**Amphiboles** (commonly Hornblende)	$CaNa(Mg,Fe)_4\ (Al,Fe,Ti)_3\ Si_6O_{22}(O,OH)_2$
Nonmetallic Luster	6	✔		white to pink	cleaves in 2 directions at 90°	ceramics and glass	**Potassium Feldspar** (Orthoclase)	$KAlSi_3O_8$
Nonmetallic Luster	6	✔		white to gray	cleaves in 2 directions, striations visible	ceramics and glass	**Plagioclase Feldspar** (Na-Ca Feldspar)	$(Na,Ca)AlSi_3O_8$
Nonmetallic Luster	6.5		✔	green to gray or brown	commonly light green and granular	furnace bricks and jewelry	**Olivine**	$(Fe,Mg)_2SiO_4$
Nonmetallic Luster	7		✔	colorless or variable	glassy luster, may form hexagonal crystals	glass, jewelry, and electronics	**Quartz**	SiO_2
Nonmetallic Luster	7		✔	dark red to green	glassy luster, often seen as red grains in NYS metamorphic rocks	jewelry and abrasives	**Garnet** (commonly Almandine)	$Fe_3Al_2Si_3O_{12}$

*Chemical Symbols: Al = aluminum, C = carbon, Ca = calcium, Cl = chlorine, F = fluorine, Fe = iron, H = hydrogen, K = potassium, Mg = magnesium, Na = sodium, O = oxygen, Pb = lead, S = sulfur, Si = silicon, Ti = titanium

✔ = dominant form of breakage

people and the ENVIRONMENT

Damaging Earthquakes East of the Rockies

When you think of earthquakes, you probably think of California and Japan. However, six major earthquakes have occurred in the central and eastern United States since colonial times. Three of these had estimated moment magnitudes of 7.3, 7.0, and 7.5, and they were centered near the Mississippi River Valley in southeastern Missouri. Occurring on December 16, 1811, January 23, 1812, and February 7, 1812, these earthquakes, plus numerous smaller tremors, destroyed the town of New Madrid, Missouri, triggered massive landslides, and caused damage over a six-state area. The course of the Mississippi River was altered, and Tennessee's Reelfoot Lake was enlarged. Chimneys toppled in Cincinnati, Ohio, and Richmond, Virginia, while Boston residents, located 1770 kilometers away, felt the tremor.

Damage to Charleston, South Carolina, caused by the August 31, 1886 earthquake.

Memphis, Tennessee, the largest population center in the New Madrid area today, is located on unconsolidated floodplain deposits. Therefore, buildings are more susceptible to damage than similar structures built on bedrock. It has been estimated that if earthquakes the size of New Madrid events were to strike in the next decade, they would result in casualties in the thousands and damages in tens of billions of dollars.

Damaging earthquakes that occurred in Aurora, Illinois (1909), and Valentine, Texas (1931), remind us that other areas in the central United States are vulnerable.

The greatest historical earthquake in the eastern states occurred August 31, 1886, in Charleston, South Carolina. The event, which spanned 1 minute, caused 60 deaths, numerous injuries, and great economic loss within 200 kilometers of Charleston. Within 8 minutes, effects were felt as far away as Chicago and St. Louis, where strong vibrations shook the upper floors of buildings, causing people to rush outdoors. In Charleston alone, over 100 buildings were destroyed, and 90 percent of the remaining structures were damaged. It was difficult to find a chimney still standing as the photograph shows.

Numerous other strong earthquakes have been recorded in the eastern United States. New England and adjacent areas have experienced sizable shocks since colonial times. The first reported earthquake in the Northeast took place in Plymouth, Massachusetts, in 1683, and was followed in 1755 by the destructive Cambridge, Massachusetts, earthquake. Moreover, ever since records have been kept, New York State alone has experienced over 300 earthquakes large enough to be felt.

Earthquakes in the central and eastern United States occur far less frequently than in California. Yet history indicates that the East is vulnerable. Further, these shocks east of the Rockies have generally produced structural damage over a larger area than counterparts of similar magnitude in California. The reason is that the underlying bedrock in the central and eastern United States is older and more rigid. As a result, seismic waves are able to travel greater distances with less weakening than in the western United States. It is estimated that for earthquakes of similar magnitude, the region of maximum ground motion in the East may be up to 10 times larger than in the West. Therefore, the higher rate of earthquake occurrence in the western United States is balanced somewhat by the fact that central and eastern U.S. quakes can damage larger areas.

people and the ENVIRONMENT

Damaging Earthquakes East of the Rockies L2

Background

The seismic zone around the New Madrid fault is very active. Between 1975 and 1995, 4600 earthquakes were recorded, though most were tremors too slight to be felt by people. Still, the probability of a moderate earthquake occurring in the New Madrid seismic zone in the future is high—90 percent probability within the next 50 years. In response to what scientists have learned about this seismic zone in the last 20 years, actions have been taken to reduce the loss of life and property in future quakes. Among them:

- In 1983 the states of Arkansas, Illinois, Indiana, Kentucky, Mississippi, Missouri, and Tennessee formed the Central United States Earthquake Consortium (CUSEC) to encourage research, coordinate planning, and promote public awareness.
- Several of the CUSEC states hold Earthquake Awareness Weeks.
- CUSEC state geologists have been mapping earthquake hazards. In 1995 they completed a soils map that can be used to identify areas prone to intense shaking during earthquakes.
- Most CUSEC states now have building codes that include earthquake design standards.
- Efforts have been made in many CUSEC states to strengthen dams, bridges, and highways to meet earthquake design standards.

Teaching Tips

- Use the Internet and keywords "New Madrid Earthquake" to find maps of the New Madrid seismic zone as well as maps showing current seismic activity in the central and eastern United States. Use these maps to supplement the discussion of this feature.
- Invite students to research the New Madrid quakes or other earthquakes east of the Mississippi River. Then they can use the information to write articles as if they were newspaper reporters at that time. Encourage students to use eyewitness accounts and to give information on the geology of the area in their articles.

Visual, Logical

CHAPTER 12

Planning Guide

Use these planning tools
Use Teacher Express for all your planning needs

SECTION OBJECTIVES	STANDARDS NATIONAL	STANDARDS STATE	ACTIVITIES and LABS
12.1 Discovering Earth's History, pp. 336–342 1 block or 2 periods **12.1** **Explain** how rocks allow geologists to interpret Earth's history. **12.2** **Recognize** how uniformitarianism helps explain Earth's features. **12.3** **List** the key principles of relative dating and **describe** how geologists use relative dating in their work. **12.4** **Describe** the importance of unconformities in unraveling Earth's history.	A-1, D-3, G-1, G-2, G-3		**SE** Inquiry Activity: What Can Become a Fossil? p. 335 **L2** **TE** Teacher Demo: Cross-Cutting Relationships, p. 339 **L2** **TE** Evaluate Understanding, p. 342 **L2**
12.2 Fossils: Evidence of Past Life, pp. 343–346 1 block or 2 periods **12.5** **Define** fossils and **explain** how fossils are made. **12.6** **Identify** the factors that determine if an organism will become a fossil. **12.7** **State** the principle of fossil succession.	D-2, D-3, G-1, G-2, G-3		**TE** Teacher Demo: Charcoal and Fossil Fuels, p. 344 **L2** **TE** Build Science Skills, p. 345 **L2**
12.3 Dating with Radioactivity, pp. 347–350 1 block or 2 periods **12.8** **Define** radioactivity and half-life. **12.9** **Explain** radiometric dating. **12.10** **Describe** how carbon-14 is used in radiometric dating.	A-2, B-2, D-2, D-3		**TE** Teacher Demo: Modeling Half-Lives, p. 350 **L2** **TE** Reteach, p. 350 **L1**
12.4 The Geologic Time Scale, pp. 352–355 1 block or 2 periods **12.11** **Describe** the geologic time scale. **12.12** **Explain** how the geologic time scale is organized. **12.13** **Identify** some complications in dating rocks.	A-1, A-2, D-1, D-3, G-1, G-2, G-3		**SE** Exploration Lab: Fossil Occurrence and the Age of Rocks, pp. 356–357 **L2** **LM** Modeling Radioactive Decay **L1**

Ability Levels
L1 For students who need additional help
L2 For all students
L3 For students who need to be challenged

Components

SE	Student Edition	**GRSW**	Guided Reading & Study Workbook	**TP**	Test Prep Resources	**GEO**	Geode CD-ROM
TE	Teacher's Edition	**TEX**	Teacher Express	**onT**	onlineText	**T**	Transparencies
LM	Laboratory Manual	**CTB**	Computer Test Bank	**DC**	Discovery Channel Videos	**GO**	Internet Resources
CUT	Chapter Tests						

RESOURCES PRINT and TECHNOLOGY	SECTION ASSESSMENT
GRSW Section 12.1 **T-150** Cross-cutting Relationships **T-151** Nonconformity **T-152** Cross-section Through the Grand Canyon **T-153** Cross-section of a Hypothetical Region GEODe Geologic Time ↳ Relative Dating **DC** Grand Canyon **TEX** Lesson Planning 12.1	**SE** Section 12.1 Assessment, p. 342 **onT** Section 12.1
GRSW Section 12.2 **T-154** Overlapping Ranges of Fossils **TEX** Lesson Planning 12.2	**SE** Section 12.2 Assessment, p. 346 **onT** Section 12.2
GRSW Section 12.3 **T-155** Common Types of Radioactive Decay **T-156** Decay of U-238 **T-157** Radioactive Decay Curve **T-158** Production and Decay of Carbon-14 GEODe Geologic Time ↳ Radiometric Dating **TEX** Lesson Planning 12.3	**SE** Section 12.3 Assessment, p. 350 **onT** Section 12.3
GRSW Section 12.4 **T-159** Geologic Time Scale **T-160** Absolute Dates for Sedimentary Layers **T-161** Cross Dating: Dendrochronology GEODe Geologic Time ↳ Geologic Time Scale **TEX** Lesson Planning 12.4	**SE** Section 12.4 Assessment, p. 355 **onT** Section 12.4

Go Online

Go online for these Internet resources.

PHSchool.com
Web Code: cjk-9999

NSTA SCILINKS
Web Code: cjn-4122
Web Code: cjn-4124
Web Code: cjn-4125

Materials for Activities and Labs

Quantities for each group

STUDENT EDITION

Inquiry Activity, p. 335
raisin, seashell, small bone, small tooth, insect wing, hair, leaf, stick, apple slice with seeds, peanut, orange seed, magnifying glass, microscope

Exploration Lab, pp. 356–357
geologic time scale, graph paper

TEACHER'S EDITION

Teacher Demo, p. 339
wooden stick, piece of foam

Evaluate Understanding, p. 342
clay

Teacher Demo, p. 344
wooden splints, Bunsen burner, test tube, test tube stand

Build Science Skills, p. 345
clay, plastic container, beaker, plaster of Paris, water

Teacher Demo, p. 350
scissors, adding machine tape, metric ruler

Reteach, p. 350
different-colored jelly beans

Chapter Assessment

ASSESSMENT

SE Assessment, pp. 359–360
CUT Chapter 12 Test
CTB Chapter 12
onT Chapter 12

STANDARDIZED TEST PREP

SE Chapter 12, p. 361
TP Progress Monitoring Assessments

interactive textbook with assessment at PHSchool.com

CHAPTER 12

Before you teach

Michael Wysession
Washington University

Big Ideas

Few aspects of geology have had a more profound impact than the discovery that the Earth is exceedingly old—4.56 billion years old. An important concept in geology is uniformitarianism—the idea that geologic processes operating today have been slowly at work through much of Earth's history.

Space and Time The geologic time scale was created in order to establish correlations in space and time between rocks layers found in different locations. Divisions in the geologic time scale were largely determined by periods of mass extinctions and major changes in the evolution of life.

Forces and Motion Relative geologic dating was determined through an understanding of the sequence of geologic events, and relies upon the principles of superposition, original horizontality, cross-cutting, index fossils, and the presence of unconformities between rock layers.

Matter and Energy Absolute dates were assigned to the time divisions of the geologic time scale using radiometric dating, which relies upon the radioactive decay of unstable isotopes. Because different radioactive isotopes have different half-lives, different parent-daughter pairs are used to date objects of different ages. For example, the short half-life of carbon-14 makes it useful for dating more recent objects.

Earth as a System A record of the history of biological evolution exists in the form of fossils, which can be found as unaltered remains, altered remains (like molds, casts, and carbonized remains), indirect evidence (like tracks, burrows, and dung), and conditions (hard parts, rapid burial). Fossils are also important indicators of the paleoenvironments in which they formed.

Earth Science Refresher

Determining the Age of Earth

In today's age it is hard to get a feeling for just how revolutionary the discovery of radioactivity was for the determination of Earth's age. Scientists and theologians had spent centuries trying to quantify the age of the planet through a variety of means. At times, the topic was at the center of a struggle between science and religion, and between the opposing philosophies of uniformitarianism and catastrophism. Radiometric dating, however, laid all of these debates to rest.

Some of the early attempts of determining Earth's age were very clever. The ancient Greek, Xenophanes of Colophon (570–470 B.C.), realized that fossils were the ancient remains of life and that Earth was therefore extremely old. Another Greek, Herodotus (about 450 B.C.) used sediments from the Nile River. The Nile floods each year, depositing an additional layer of sediment. Herodotus dug into the river bank and counted the layers, determining that Earth was at least many thousands of years old.

Address Misconceptions

Some students mistakenly think that when theories gain enough supporting evidence, they automatically become laws. In reality, a theory never becomes a law. A scientific law simply describes the behavior of an event or process in nature. A theory attempts to explain this behavior. For a strategy that helps to overcome this misconception, see **Address Misconceptions** on **p. 337**.

Go Online PD LINKS NSTA

For: Chapter 12 Content Support
Visit: www.SciLinks.org/PDLinks
Web Code: cjn-1299

In 1779, the Count de Buffon compared Earth to a ball of cooling iron, and came up with an age of 75,000 years. Several scientists tried to use the saltiness of the ocean to determine Earth's age. In 1899, John Joly compared the ocean's salinity to the amount of salt entering the ocean from rivers, and concluded that Earth was 90 million years old. His calculations were wrong because salt precipitates out when the ocean becomes supersaturated with it.

The most significant determination of Earth's age was by William Thompson, also known as Lord Kelvin, who held Newton's chair at the Royal Astronomical Society in London. Thompson used the best understanding of the physical property of heat conduction, combined with actual measurements of the rate of heat flow out of Earth's surface, and concluded, in 1897, that Earth was no older than 20 to 40 million years. As Thompson was considered the leading physicist in Europe, his calculation was a blow to geologists and evolutionary biologists, who were sure Earth had to be older in order to explain the rock and fossil records. Charles Darwin wrote that he would die an unhappy man if Thompson was right, because his work would then be wrong.

Radioactivity proved that Darwin was correct, of course. Radioactivity not only provides the means of determining Earth's age, but it provides the necessary heat to keep Earth warm and prevent if from cooling down. Thompson did the best job he could, but he did not know about radioactivity, which was first explained at the start of the twentieth century by Ernest Rutherford, and not fully understood until much later.

Build Reading Literacy

Outline

Understanding Text Structure

Strategy Help students focus on the text and not simply skim it. Outlining is a good strategy to apply to an entire section, if it is not excessively long, using the headings as major divisions. Outlining is best applied to sections in which the headings are parallel, and in which there are main headings and subheadings. Before you begin, choose a section for students to read and outline, such as Section 12.3, pp. 347–350.

Example

1. Before students read, have them preview the section's title and headings. Demonstrate and display how to make a skeleton outline for the section. Have students list the section title as the top level, the main headings as major divisions, and the subheadings as the next level.

I. Section Title
  A. Main Heading
    1. Subheading
      a. detail
      b. detail
      c. detail

2. Have students copy the skeleton outline as they read, filling in details under each subheading of the outline.

3. Tell students not to outline sections that focus on the details of cycles or processes. Students can represent these by diagrams and flowcharts rather than outlining.

4. After reading, have students review the entire section and their outlines to make sure they have included all vocabulary definitions and key concepts as main ideas or details under the appropriate levels of their outlines.

See p. 344 for a script on how to use this strategy with students. For additional strategies, see pp. 338, 340, 349, and 355.

ASSESS PRIOR KNOWLEDGE

Use the Chapter Pretest below to assess students' prior knowledge. As needed, review these concepts.

Review Science Concepts

Section 12.1, Section 12.2 Review how igneous, metamorphic, and sedimentary rocks form. Discuss igneous features, such as dikes and sills, and the process of deposition.

Section 12.3 Have students recall the basic structure and properties of an atom. They should be able to define nucleus, proton, neutron, electron, mass number, and atomic number. Briefly review the periodic table of elements.

Section 12.4 Remind students that Earth is 4.6 billion years old, and that the physical features and environmental conditions for any particular area have changed over time.

CHAPTER

12 Geologic Time

CONCEPTS in Action

Exploration Lab
Fossil Occurrence and the Age of Rocks

Understanding Earth
Using Tree Rings to Date and Study the Recent Past

Geologic Time
↳ Relative Dating
Radiometric Dating
Geologic Time Scale

Discovery Channel School **Video Field Trip**
Grand Canyon

Take a field trip to the Grand Canyon with Discovery Channel and get a scenic glimpse of Earth's history. Answer the following questions after watching the video.

1. How was the Grand Canyon formed?
2. What kinds of historic records are contained within the Canyon's walls?

For: Chapter 12 Resources
Visit: PHSchool.com
Web Code: cjk-9999

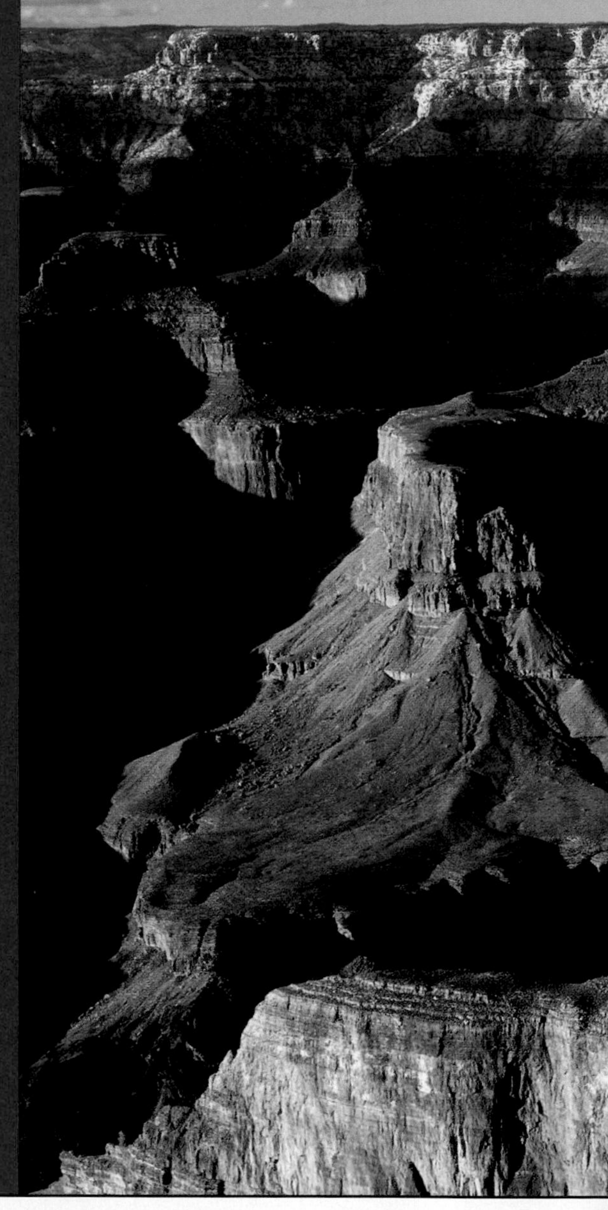

The rock layers exposed in Arizona's Grand Canyon contain clues to hundreds of millions of years of Earth history. ▶

334 *Chapter 12*

Chapter Pretest

1. Describe the formation of igneous, metamorphic, and sedimentary rocks. *(Igneous rocks form by melting and solidification. Metamorphic rocks form by heat and pressure. Sedimentary rocks form by compaction and cementation.)*
2. How is a dike formed? *(A dike is formed when magma is injected into fractures in rock.)*
3. True or False: Sediments are deposited through the process of weathering. *(False)*
4. Which atomic particles orbit the nucleus? *(c)*
   a. protons
   b. neutrons
   c. electrons
   d. elements
5. Which atomic particles have a positive electrical charge? *(a)*
   a. protons
   b. neutrons
   c. electrons
   d. all of the above
6. How old is Earth? *(4.6 billion years)*

HISTORICAL GEOLOGY

Chapter Preview

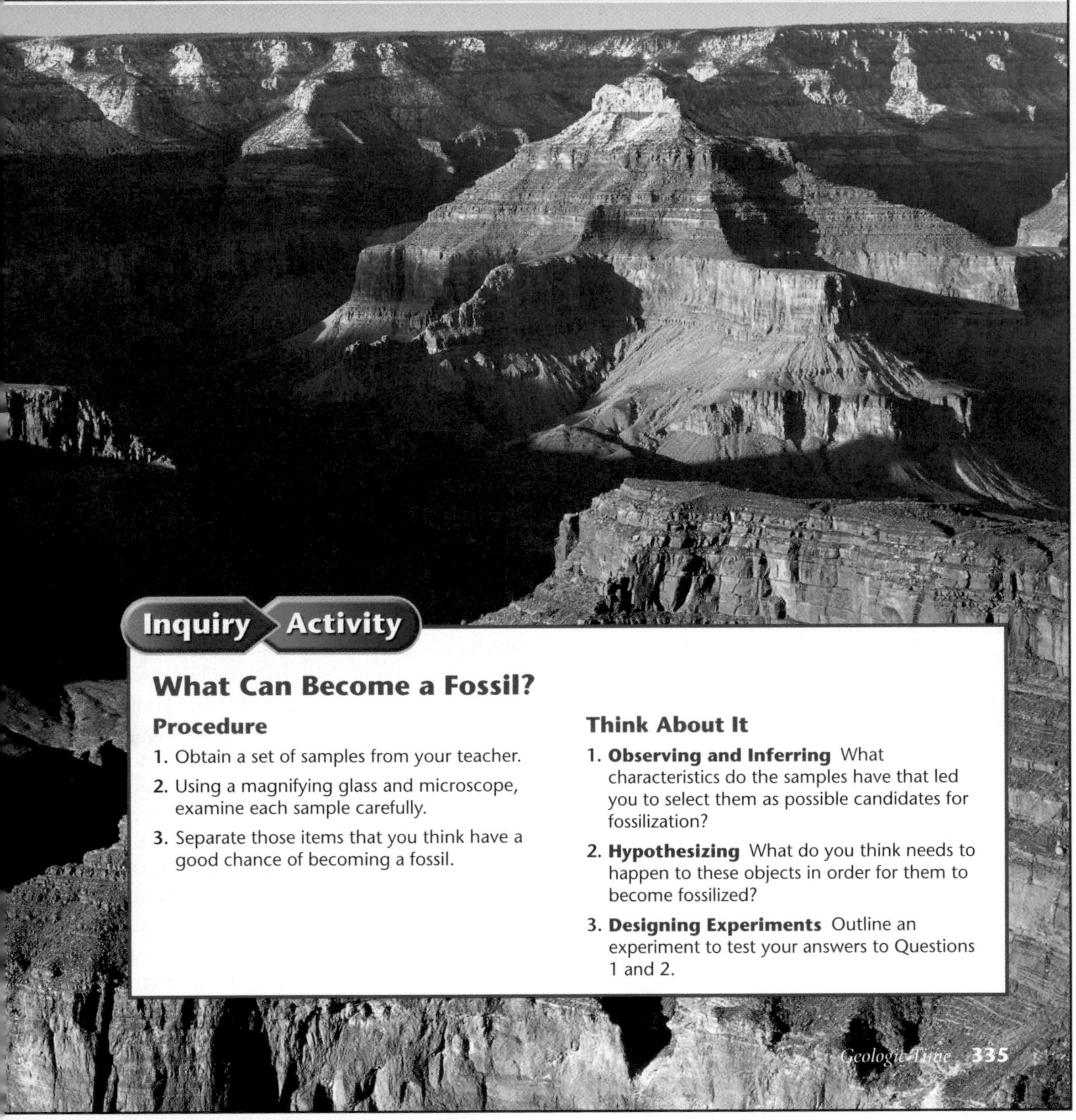

Inquiry Activity

What Can Become a Fossil?

Procedure

1. Obtain a set of samples from your teacher.
2. Using a magnifying glass and microscope, examine each sample carefully.
3. Separate those items that you think have a good chance of becoming a fossil.

Think About It

1. **Observing and Inferring** What characteristics do the samples have that led you to select them as possible candidates for fossilization?
2. **Hypothesizing** What do you think needs to happen to these objects in order for them to become fossilized?
3. **Designing Experiments** Outline an experiment to test your answers to Questions 1 and 2.

DISCOVERY CHANNEL SCHOOL **Video Field Trip**

Grand Canyon

Encourage students to view the Video Field Trip "Grand Canyon."

ENGAGE/EXPLORE

What Can Become a Fossil?

Purpose Students will infer what types of organic materials may become fossils.

Skills Focus Observing, Inferring, Hypothesizing, Designing Experiments

 **Prep Time** 10 minutes

Materials raisin, seashell, small bone, small tooth, insect wing, hair, leaf, stick, apple slice with seeds, peanut, orange seed, magnifying glass, microscope

Class Time 15 minutes

Teaching Tips

- Remind students that it takes a long time for fossils to form. Tell them to consider what might happen to organic matter such as apples and raisins over a long period of time. *(They decompose.)*
- Have students make a two-column table to classify the samples as "Potential Fossil" or "Non-Fossil."

Expected Outcome Students will recognize that hard materials, such as teeth, are more suitable to fossilization than soft materials, such as raisins.

Think About It

1. Sample answer: The presence of hard parts might help in fossilization.

2. Sample answer: They need to be buried quickly and protected from oxygen and predators.

3. Sample answer: Bury the items in dirt or sand, weigh down the dirt with a heavy object, then observe the materials after one month or more.

Section 12.1

1 FOCUS

Section Objectives

12.1 **Explain** how rocks allow geologists to interpret Earth's history.

12.2 **Recognize** how uniformitarianism helps explain Earth's features.

12.3 **List** the key principles of relative dating and **describe** how geologists use relative dating in their work.

12.4 **Describe** the importance of unconformities in unraveling Earth's history.

Reading Focus

Build Vocabulary L2

Word Forms Point out that the word *uniform* is closely tied to this section's vocabulary term *uniformitarianism*. Ask students to state the meaning of *uniform* in their own words. *(Sample answer: always the same)* Tell them that the meaning of *uniform* can help them to remember the meaning of *uniformitarianism*, which refers to processes that have operated in a similar manner throughout Earth's history.

Reading Strategy L2

Sample answers: **a.** rock record; **b.** clues to geological events and changing life forms; **c.** uniformitarianism; **d.** today's processes mimic those of the past; **e.** relative dating; **f.** the relative order of events

2 INSTRUCT

Rocks Record Earth History

Build Science Skills L2

Using Analogies Have students create analogies that describe the following key concept: "Rocks record geological events and changing life forms of the past." A sample analogy might be that rocks are like a long and complicated well-worn novel. Even though some of the pages might be missing or torn, enough of the book remains for the story to be understood.
Verbal

12.1 Discovering Earth's History

Reading Focus

Key Concepts

- How do rocks allow geologists to interpret Earth's history?
- How does uniformitarianism help explain Earth's features?
- How do geologists use relative dating in their work?
- What are the key principles of relative dating?
- What do unconformities represent?

Vocabulary

- uniformitarianism
- relative dating
- law of superposition
- principle of original horizontality
- principle of cross-cutting relationships
- unconformity
- correlation

Reading Strategy

Identifying Main Ideas Copy and expand the table below. As you read, fill in the first column with a main idea and add details that support it in the second column.

Main Idea	Details
1. a. ?	b. ?
2. c. ?	d. ?
3. e. ?	f. ?

A

B

Figure 1 Exploring the Grand Canyon A John Wesley Powell, pioneering geologist and the second director of the U.S. Geological Survey. **B** Start of the expedition from Green River station.

In the 18th and 19th centuries, scientists recognized that Earth had a very long history and that Earth's physical features must have taken a long time to form. But they had no way of knowing Earth's true age. A geologic time scale was developed that showed the sequence, or order, of events based on several principles of relative dating. What are these principles? What part do fossils play? In this chapter you will learn the answers to these questions.

Rocks Record Earth History

In 1869, Major John Wesley Powell, shown in Figure 1A, led an expedition down the Colorado River and through the Grand Canyon, shown in Figure 1B. Powell realized that the evidence for an ancient Earth was concealed in its rocks. Powell was impressed with the record of Earth's history contained in the rocks exposed along the walls of the Grand Canyon.

Rocks record geological events and changing life forms of the past. Erosion has removed a lot of Earth's rock record but enough of it remains to allow much of the story to be studied and interpreted.

Geological events by themselves, however, have little meaning until they are put into a time perspective. The geologic time scale revolutionized the way people think about time and how they perceive our planet. **We have learned that Earth is much older than anyone had previously imagined and that its surface and interior have been changed by the same geological processes that continue today.**

A Brief History of Geology

The primary goal of geologists is to interpret Earth's history. By studying rocks, especially sedimentary rocks, geologists can begin to understand and explain the past.

In the mid-1600s, Archbishop James Ussher constructed a chronology or time line of both human and Earth history in which he determined that Earth was more than five thousand years old. He believed Earth had been created in 4004 B.C. Ussher published his chronology, and his book earned widespread acceptance among Europe's scientific and religious leaders.

In the late 1700s, James Hutton, a Scottish physician and gentleman farmer, published his *Theory of the Earth.* In this work, Hutton put forth the fundamental principle of **uniformitarianism,** which simply states that the physical, chemical, and biological laws that operate today have also operated in the geologic past. **Uniformitarianism means that the forces and processes that we observe today have been at work for a very long time.** To understand the geologic past, we must first understand present-day processes and their results.

Today, scientists understand that these same processes may not always have had the same relative importance or operated at precisely the same rate. Moreover, some important geologic processes are not currently observable, but evidence that they occur is well established. For example, we know that Earth has been hit by large meteorites even though we have no human witnesses. Such events altered Earth's crust, modified its climate, and strongly influenced life on the planet.

The acceptance of uniformitarianism meant the acceptance of a very long history for Earth. It is important to remember that although many features of our physical landscape may seem to be unchanging over our lifetimes, they are still changing, but on time scales of hundreds, thousands, or even millions of years.

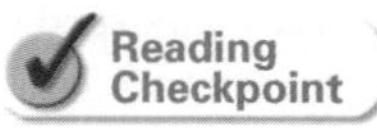

How do the laws that govern geological processes change through time?

Relative Dating—Key Principles

During the late 1800s and early 1900s, several attempts were made to determine the age of Earth. To establish a relative time scale, a few basic principles or rules had to be discovered and applied. These principles were major breakthroughs in thinking at the time, and their discovery and acceptance was an important scientific achievement.

Relative dating means identifying which rock units formed first, second, third, and so on. **Relative dating tells us the sequence in which events occurred, not how long ago they occurred.**

A Brief History of Geology

Use Community Resources **L2**

Arrange for students to visit a local museum or historical society to view artifacts that relate to important events in your community's geologic history.
Kinesthetic

Relative Dating—Key Principles

L2

As students read about the law of superposition, make sure they clearly distinguish between theories and laws. Some students mistakenly think that when theories gain enough supporting evidence, they automatically become laws. In reality, a theory never becomes a law. A scientific law simply describes the behavior of an event or process in nature. A theory attempts to explain this behavior.
Verbal

Customize for English Language Learners

Use a cloze strategy to extract information from the text about the key principles of relative time. For example, after reading pp. 336–337, have ELL students fill in the blanks in the following paragraph: **Rocks record _______ events and changing _______ of the past. Uniformitarianism means that the _______ and processes that operate _______ have been at work for a very long time.** *(geological, life forms, forces, today)* Use student answers to pinpoint misunderstandings and clarify key concepts.

Answer to . . .

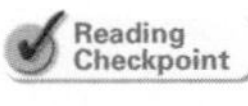

The same laws that operated in the past still operate today.

Use Visuals 

Figure 2 Have students state the law of superposition in their own words. *(Unless layers of sedimentary rock are disturbed, the oldest rocks will be on the bottom. The rocks get younger from bottom to top.)* Then have students sequence the layers of rock from oldest to youngest. *(Supai Group, Hermit Shale, Coconino Sandstone, Toroweap Formation, Kaibab Limestone)*
Visual

Build Reading Literacy 

Refer to the Build Reading Literacy strategy for **Chapter 1,** which provides the guidelines for an anticipation guide.

Anticipation Guide Before students read about the principle of cross-cutting relationships and unconformities, have them review the law of superposition. Point out that this law only pertains to an undisturbed sequence of sedimentary rocks. Ask: **What might happen if the rocks were disturbed?** *(Sample answer: The youngest rocks might not necessarily be on top.)* Have students read the text on pp. 339–342 to see if their predictions were correct.
Verbal, Logical

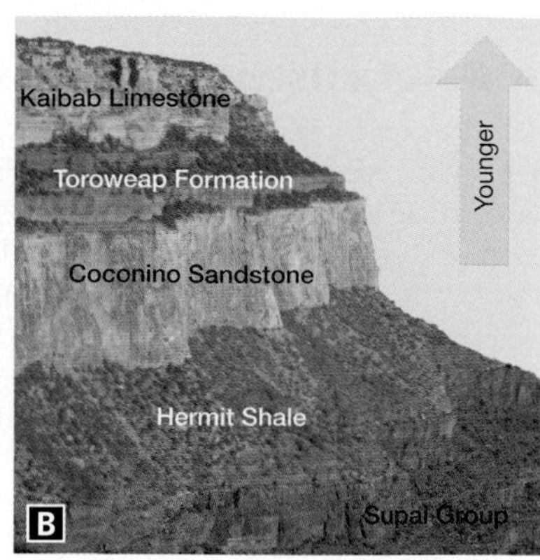

Figure 2 Ordering the Grand Canyon's History The law of superposition can be applied to the layers exposed in the Grand Canyon. **Interpreting Illustrations** *Which layer is the oldest? youngest?*

Law of Superposition Nicolaus Steno, a Danish anatomist, geologist, and priest (1636–1686), is credited with describing a set of geologic observations that are the basis of relative dating. The first observation is the **law of superposition.** **The law of superposition states that in an undeformed sequence of sedimentary rocks, each bed is older than the one above it and younger than the one below it.** Although it may seem obvious that a rock layer could not be deposited unless it had something older beneath it for support, it was not until 1669 that Steno stated the principle. This rule also applies to other surface-deposited materials, such as lava flows and beds of ash from volcanic eruptions. Applying the law of superposition to the beds exposed in the upper portion of the Grand Canyon, shown in Figure 2, you can easily place the layers in their proper order.

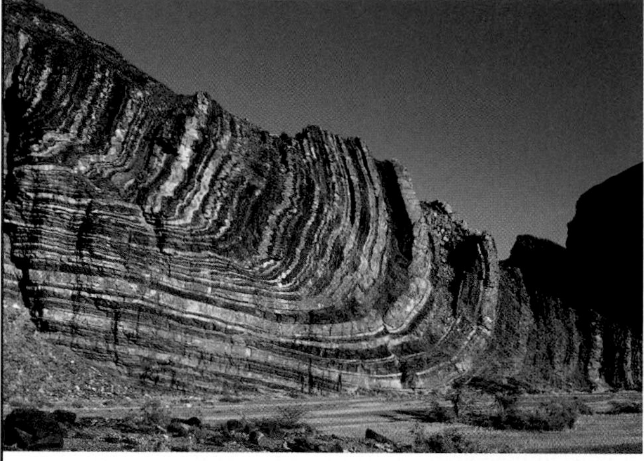

Figure 3 Disturbed Rock Layers Rock layers that are folded or tilted must have been moved into that position by crustal disturbances after their deposition. These folded layers are exposed in the Namib Desert (southwestern Africa).

Principle of Original Horizontality Another of Steno's observations is called the **principle of original horizontality.** **The principle of original horizontality means that layers of sediment are generally deposited in a horizontal position.** If you see rock layers that are flat, it means they haven't been disturbed and they still are in their original horizontal position. The layers in the Grand Canyon shown on pages 334–335 and in Figure 2 clearly demonstrate this. However, the rock layers shown in Figure 3 have been tilted and bent. This tilting means they must have been moved into this position sometime after their deposition.

Reading Checkpoint *To what rock type can the law of superposition and the principle of original horizontality be best applied?*

Facts and Figures

The work of Swiss scientist Louis Agassiz provides an excellent example of the application of the principle of uniformitarianism. In 1821, Agassiz heard another scientist present a paper stating that glacial features occurred in places that were far from existing glaciers in the Alps. The hypothesis implied that these glaciers had once been much larger in size. Agassiz doubted the hypothesis and set out to prove it wrong. Ironically, he was the one who was wrong. In the Alps, Agassiz found the same unique deposits and features that could be seen forming with active glaciers far beyond the limits of the ice in the Alps. Subsequent work led Agassiz to hypothesize that a great ice age had occurred in response to a period of worldwide climate change. Agassiz's ideas eventually developed into our present-day glacial theory.

Principle of Cross-Cutting Relationships

The principle of cross-cutting relationships is Steno's third observation. The **principle of cross-cutting relationships** states that when a fault cuts through, or when magma intrudes other rocks and crystallizes, we can assume that the fault or intrusion is younger than the rocks affected. For example, in Figure 4 you can see that fault A occurred after the sandstone layer was deposited because it "broke" the layer. However, fault A occurred before the conglomerate was laid down, because that layer is unbroken. Because they cut through the layers of sedimentary rock, the faults and dikes clearly must have occurred after the sedimentary layers were deposited.

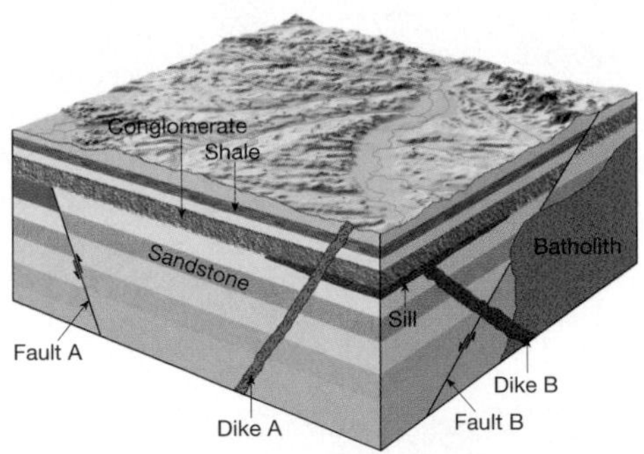

Figure 4 Applying Steno's Principles Cross-cutting relationships are an important principle used in relative dating. An intrusive rock body is younger than the rocks it intrudes. A fault is younger than the rock layers it cuts.
Interpreting Diagrams ***What is the age relationship between the batholith, dike B, dike A, and the sill?***

Inclusions Sometimes inclusions can help the relative dating process. Inclusions are pieces of one rock unit that are contained within another. The rock unit next to the one containing the inclusions must have been there first in order to provide the rock fragments. Therefore, the rock unit containing inclusions is the younger of the two. Figure 5 provides an example. The photograph in Figure 5C shows inclusions of igneous rock within a layer of sedimentary rock. How did they get there? The inclusions indicate that the sedimentary layer was deposited on top of the weathered igneous mass. The sedimentary layer must be younger than the igneous rock because the sedimentary layer contains pieces of the igneous rock. We know the layer was not intruded upon by magma from below that later crystallized because the sedimentary rock is still horizontal.

Formation of Inclusions

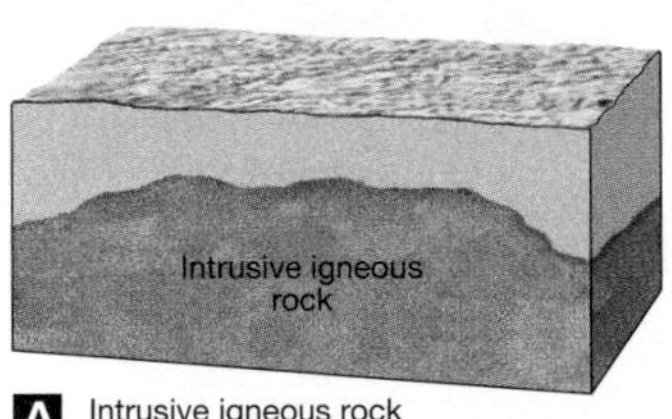

A Intrusive igneous rock

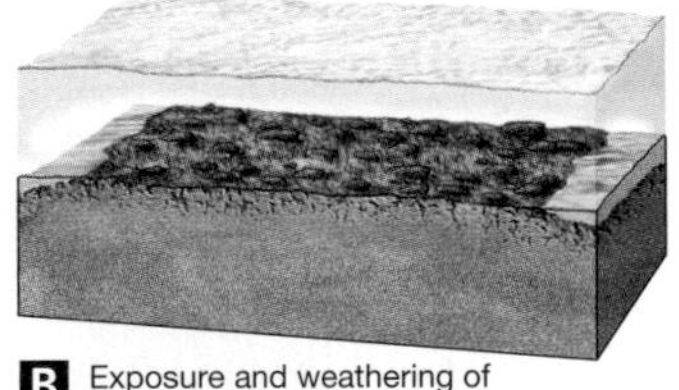

B Exposure and weathering of intrusive igneous rock

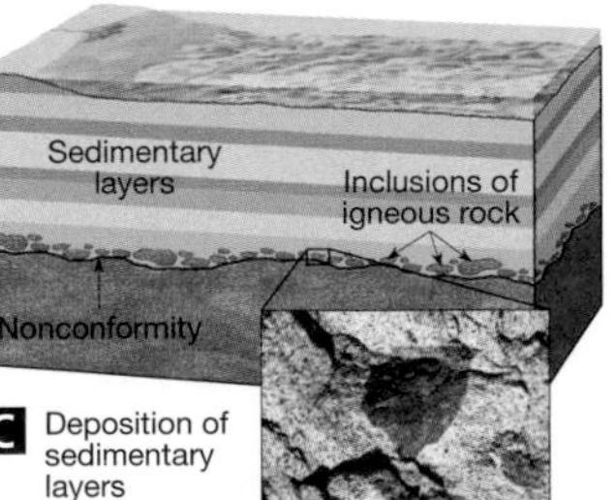

C Deposition of sedimentary layers

Figure 5 A A mass of igneous rock formed from magma that intruded an older rock body. **B** The older rock erodes and exposes the igneous rock to weathering. **C** Sedimentary rock layers form on top of the weathered igneous rock.

Teacher Demo

Cross-Cutting Relationships L2

Purpose Students will observe how cross-cutting relationships can be used in relative dating.

Materials wooden stick, piece of foam

Procedure To represent a dike, insert a wooden stick into a corner of the foam from underneath. Then break off that corner and realign the pieces so that the foam and stick are close to their original positions. Ask students to explain what each element represents, and the relative ages of those elements.

Expected Outcomes Students will recognize that the foam represents the oldest layer of rock. The wooden stick represents a younger intrusion. The broken foam represents a fault; it is the youngest element.
Visual

Answer to . . .

Figure 2 *The oldest layer is the Supai Group. The youngest layer is the Kaibab Limestone.*

Figure 4 *The batholith is oldest. The sill and dike B are the same unit. Dike A is the youngest.*

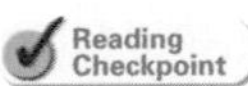
Reading Checkpoint *undisturbed sedimentary rocks*

Build Reading Literacy **L1**

Refer to **p. 530D** in **Chapter 19,** which provides the guidelines for making inferences.

Make Inferences Have students draw on their prior knowledge to infer why sedimentary rocks in particular help scientists learn about Earth's past.
Ask: **How would heat, pressure, and melting affect fossils?** *(They would destroy fossils.)* **What type of rock likely contains most fossils? Explain your answer.** *(Sedimentary rock likely contains most fossils because it has not been affected by melting, heat, or pressure.)*
Verbal, Logical

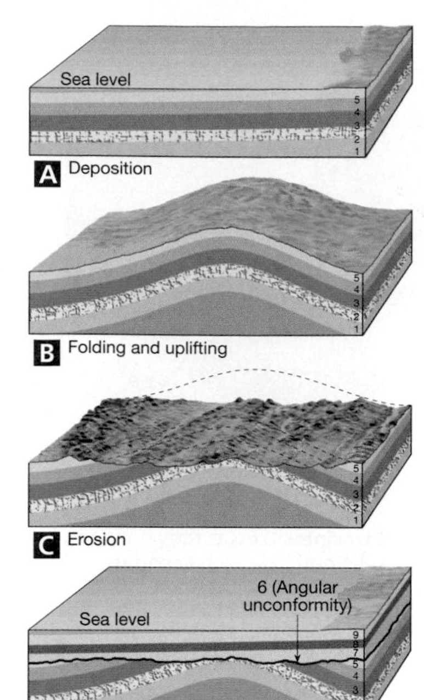

Figure 6 Formation of an Angular Conformity An angular unconformity represents an extended period during which deformation and erosion occurred.

Unconformities Casual observation of layers of rock may look like they represent a complete geologic history of an area. However, no place on Earth is geologically complete. Throughout Earth's history, the deposition of sediment has been interrupted again and again. All such breaks in the rock record are termed **unconformities.** **An unconformity represents a long period during which deposition stopped, erosion removed previously formed rocks, and then deposition resumed.** In each case uplift and erosion are followed by subsidence and renewed sedimentation, as shown in Figure 6. Unconformities are important features because they represent significant geologic events in Earth history. Moreover, their recognition helps us identify what intervals of time are not represented in the rock record.

A geologic cross section of the Grand Canyon is shown in Figure 7. It shows the three basic types of unconformities: angular unconformities, disconformities, and nonconformities. Perhaps the most easily recognized unconformity is an angular unconformity. It appears as tilted or folded sedimentary rocks that are overlain by younger, more flat-lying strata. **An angular unconformity indicates that during the pause in deposition, a period of deformation (folding or tilting) and erosion occurred.**

Two sedimentary rock layers that are separated by an erosional surface are called a disconformity. Disconformities are more common than angular unconformities, but they are more difficult to recognize. The third basic type of unconformity is a nonconformity. Nonconformities mean the erosional surface separates older metamorphic or intrusive igneous rocks from younger sedimentary rocks.

What are the three basic types of unconformities?

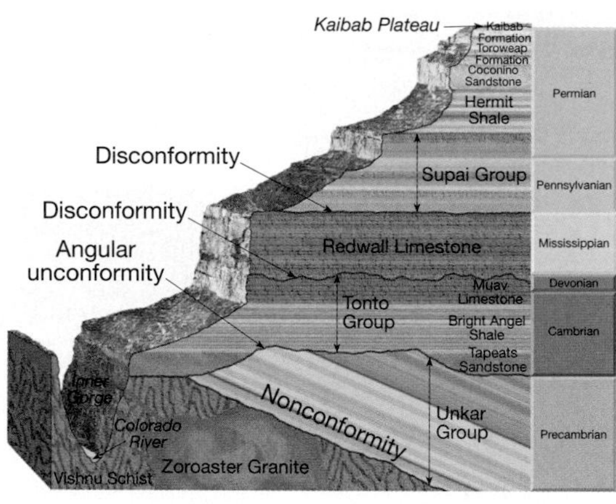

Figure 7 A Record of Uplift, Erosion, and Deposition This cross section through the Grand Canyon illustrates the three basic types of unconformities.

Facts and Figures

Although Earth processes vary in intensity, they still take a very long time to create or destroy major landscape features. For example, geologists have established that mountains once existed in portions of present-day Minnesota, Wisconsin, and Michigan. Today the region consists of low hills and plains. Erosion gradually wore down these peaks. Scientists estimate that the North American continent is eroding at a rate of about 3 cm every 1000 years.

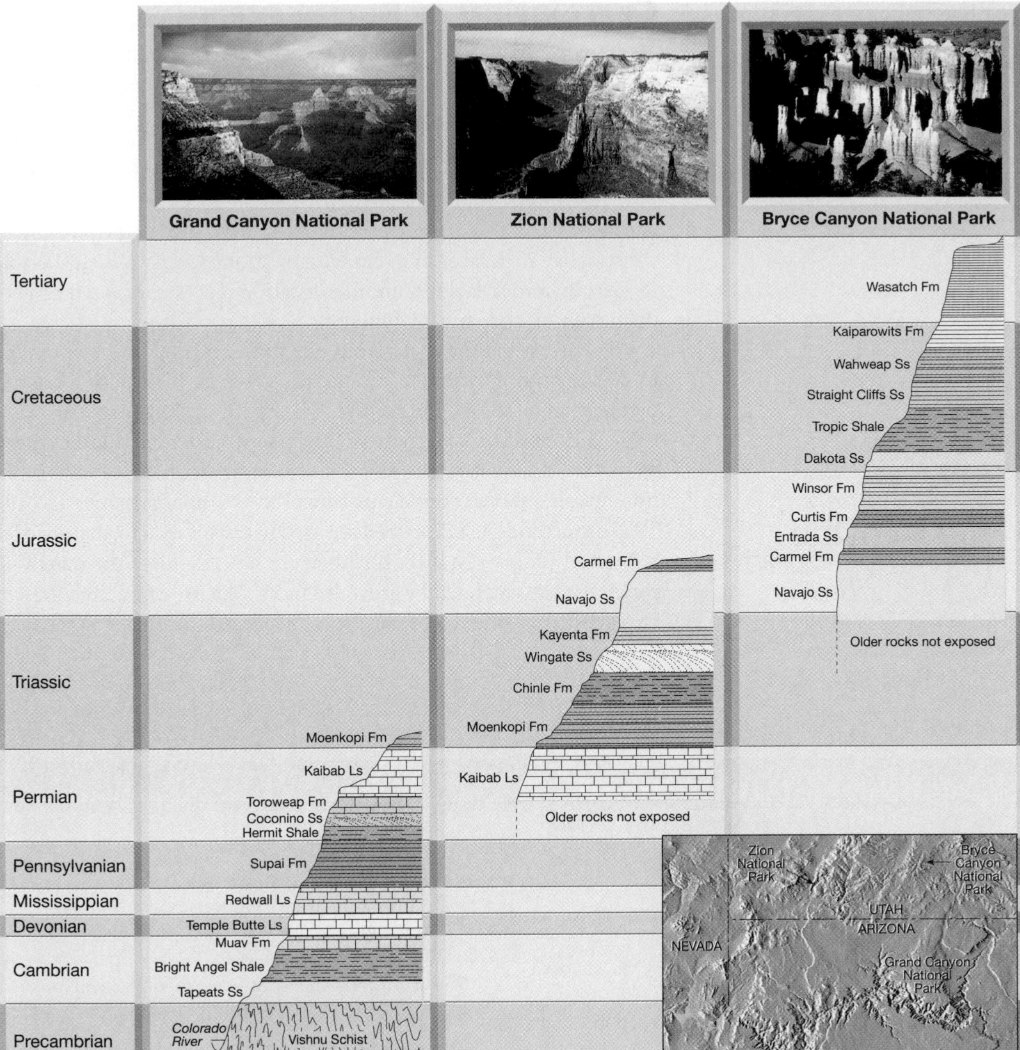

Figure 8 Correlation of strata at three locations on the Colorado Plateau reveals a more complete view of the extent of sedimentary rocks in the region.

Use Visuals L1

Figure 8 To fully understand this diagram, which includes geologic subdivisions, students will need to examine a copy of the geologic time scale. Either obtain a copy or refer students to Figure 17 on p. 353. Ask: **Which site has the oldest exposed rocks?** *(Grand Canyon National Park)*
Visual

Build Science Skills L2

Making Judgments Build on prior knowledge to ensure that students understand the concept of relative dating. Ask: **If you were told that a person has an older sister and a younger brother, what can you determine about their ages?** *(You can determine the relative ages of the three siblings. You would need additional information, however, to determine the actual ages.)*
Logical

Answer to . . .

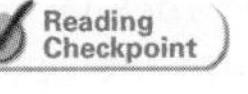

angular unconformity, disconformity, and nonconformity

Correlation of Rock Layers

Build Science Skills L2

Applying Concepts Review Steno's principles. Then ask: **Why must the rock layers be undisturbed in order to apply them?** *(Sample answer: Tectonism can cause entire sequences of rock to be overturned, in which case the oldest layers would be on the top.)*
Logical

3 ASSESS

Evaluate Understanding L2

Have students use clay to model the three basic types of unconformities.

Reteach 

Have students summarize how our views of Earth's age have changed over time. *(People once believed that Earth was only a few thousand years old. We now know that Earth is 4.6 billion years old.)*

Writing in Science

A sample paragraph might use the law of superposition to describe the layers from bottom to top; the principle of original horizontality to describe the rock layers on either side of the canyon and how they match up; and the principle of cross-cutting relationships to explain the relative ages of the dikes toward the bottom of the canyon.

Download a worksheet on relative dating for students to complete, and find additional teacher support from NSTA SciLinks.

Go Online SCiLINKS NSTA

For: Links on relative dating
Visit: www.SciLinks.org
Web Code: cjn-4122

Correlation of Rock Layers

To develop a geologic time scale that can be applied to the entire Earth, rocks of similar age in different regions must be matched up. This task is called **correlation.**

Within a small area, you can correlate the rocks of one locality with those of another by simply walking along the outcropping edges. However, this might not be possible when the rocks are covered by soil and vegetation. You can correct this problem by noting the position of a distinctive rock layer in a sequence of strata. Or, you might be able to identify a rock layer in another location if it is composed of very distinctive or uncommon minerals.

By correlating the rocks from one place to another, it is possible to create a more complete view of the geologic history of a region. Figure 8 on page 341, for example, shows the correlation of strata at three sites on the Colorado Plateau in southern Utah and northern Arizona. No single location contains the entire sequence. But correlation reveals a more complete picture of the sedimentary rock record.

The methods just described are used to trace a rock formation over a relatively short distance. But they are not adequate for matching rocks that are separated by great distances. The use of fossils comes in to play when trying to correlate rocks separated by great distances.

Section 12.1 Assessment

Reviewing Concepts

1. What information do rocks provide to geologists?
2. What does uniformitarianism tell us about processes at work on Earth's surface today?
3. How can relative dating be used in geology?
4. List and briefly describe Steno's principles.
5. What is an unconformity?
6. What is the name of the process in which rock layers in different regions are matched?

Critical Thinking

7. **Applying Concepts** How did the acceptance of uniformitarianism change the way scientists viewed Earth?
8. **Comparing and Contrasting** How does Archbishop Ussher's work compare to that of James Hutton? What did each do to back up their ideas?
9. **Summarizing** What features would you look for to correlate rocks from one area to another?

Writing in Science

Descriptive Paragraph Imagine that you are hiking down into the Grand Canyon. Use some of Steno's principles to write a paragraph describing what you see, how old it all is, and how it was deposited.

Section 12.1 Assessment

1. They provide information about geological events and changing life forms of the past.
2. The processes also operated in the geologic past.
3. It helps to identify the order of events, such as which rock layer was deposited first.
4. The law of superposition states that in a sequence of undisturbed rock layers, the oldest layer is on the bottom; the upper layers are progressively younger. The principle of original horizontality states that sedimentary rocks are generally deposited horizontally. The principle of cross-cutting relationships states that features such as faults and intrusions are younger than the features they cut across.
5. a break in the rock record
6. correlation
7. They learned that Earth was very old, that Earth's landscape is always changing, and that the processes they observed had also been at work in the past.
8. Ussher made a timeline of human history and Earth history. He did not consider Earth's physical features. Hutton's ideas came from direct observations of Earth and Earth processes.
9. same rock type, distinctive layers, uncommon minerals, specific fossils

12.2 Fossils: Evidence of Past Life

Reading Focus

Key Concepts
- What are fossils?
- What determines if an organism will become a fossil?
- What is the principle of fossil succession?

Vocabulary
- fossil
- index fossil

Reading Strategy
Monitoring Your Understanding Draw and complete a chart like the one below. After you finish this section, correct or add details as needed.

Fossils	How Fossils Form	How Fossils are Used
a. ?	b. ?	c. ?

Fossils are important tools for interpreting the geologic past. **Fossils are the remains or traces of prehistoric life. They are important components of sediment and sedimentary rocks.** Knowing the nature of the life forms that existed at a particular time helps researchers understand past environmental conditions. Further, fossils are important time indicators. They play a key role in correlating rocks of similar ages that are from different places.

Figure 9 Unaltered Remains Frozen animals are an extreme and unusual type of fossilization.

Fossil Formation

There are many types of fossils. **The type of fossil that is formed is determined by the conditions under which an organism died and how it was buried.**

Unaltered Remains Some remains of organisms—such as teeth, bones, and shells—may not have been altered, or changed, hardly at all over time. It is far less common to find the remains of an entire animal, including flesh. In Siberia, archaeologists recently found a fully preserved, frozen mammoth, shown in Figure 9. This is an excellent example of unaltered remains.

Altered Remains The remains of an organism are likely to be changed over time. Fossils often become petrified, or "turned into stone." When a fossil is petrified, mineral-rich water soaks into the small cavities and pores of the original organism. The minerals precipitate from the water and fill the spaces. The log of petrified wood in Figure 10E shows the result. In other instances, the cell walls or other solid material of an organism are replaced with mineral matter. Sometimes the microscopic details of the replaced structure are preserved.

Section 12.2

1 FOCUS

Section Objectives

12.5 **Define** fossils and **explain** how fossils are made.
12.6 **Identify** the factors that determine if an organism will become a fossil.
12.7 **State** the principle of fossil succession.

Reading Focus

Build Vocabulary 

Compare/Contrast Tables Have students make tables that compare and contrast the different types of fossils, such as unaltered remains, molds and casts, carbonization, and trace fossils. Students can list each type of fossil at the top of a column, and add supporting details in the rows below.

Reading Strategy 

Possible answers include:
a. Fossils are traces or remains of once-living prehistoric organisms. **b.** Fossils can form by freezing or drying, burial and replacement with minerals, carbonization, preservation in amber, and solidification of indirect evidence. **c.** Fossils are used to correlate rock layers, show changes in life forms through time, and provide information on ancient environments.

2 INSTRUCT

Fossil Formation

Integrate Biology 

Wooly Mammoth The remains of the mammoth found in Siberia are estimated to be about 20,000 years old. The mammoth itself died relatively young—no more than 49 years. Currently, a team of international scientists is studying the specimen. The scientists have discussed cloning the mammoth or using its frozen sperm to fertilize a living elephant when this phase is complete. Have students discuss the pros and cons of these proposals.
Verbal

Build Reading Literacy L1

Refer to **p. 334D**, which provides the guidelines for outlining.

Outline Have students create an outline of Section 12.2 (pp. 343–346). Outlines should follow the head structure used in the text. Major headings are shown in green and subheadings are shown in blue. Ask: **Based on your outlines, what are the two major concepts of this section?** *(Fossil Formation and Fossils and Correlation)*
Verbal

Teacher Demo

Charcoal and Fossil Fuels L2

Purpose Students will observe the formation of charcoal.

Materials wooden splints, Bunsen burner, test tube, test tube stand

Procedure Attach the test tube to the stand. Tilt the tube so that its mouth is slightly higher than its end. Place four wooden splints in the test tube. Heat the test tube until the splints turn black. At the same time, light a splint and hold it in the mouth of the test tube.

Expected Outcomes Students will observe that charcoal is formed in the bottom of the test tube. Explain that charcoal is a form of carbon; it is produced when an organic material, such as wood, does not have enough oxygen to burn completely. Also explain that the splint in the mouth of the test tube burns because gas is released by the reaction that changes burning wood into charcoal. This gas is similar to natural gas, a fossil fuel.
Visual

Figure 10 Types of Fossilization Six examples are shown here. **A** A fossil bee was preserved as a thin carbon film. **B** Impressions are common fossils and often show considerable detail. **C** An insect in amber **D** This dinosaur footprint was found in fine-grained limestone near Tuba City, Arizona. **E** Petrified wood in Petrified Forest National Park, Arizona **F** Natural casts of shelled organisms called ammonites

Molds and casts are another common type of fossil. A fossil mold is created when a shell or other structure is buried in sediment and then dissolved by underground water. The mold accurately reflects only the shape and surface markings of the organism. It doesn't reveal any information about its internal structure. Cast fossils (Figure 10F) are created if the hollow spaces of a mold are later filled with mineral matter.

A type of fossilization called carbonization is particularly effective in preserving leaves and delicate animal forms. Carbonization occurs when an organism is buried under fine sediment. As time passes, pressure squeezes out the liquid and gaseous components of an organism and leaves behind a thin residue of carbon, like that shown in Figure 10A. Black shale often contains abundant carbonized remains. If the carbon film is lost from a fossil preserved in fine-grain sediment, a replica of the surface, or an impression, may remain. The impression may still show considerable detail. An impression is shown in Figure 10B.

Delicate organisms, such as insects, are difficult to preserve, so they are relatively rare in the fossil record. For a fossil of an insect to form, the insect must be protected from any pressure that would crush it. Some insects have been preserved in amber—the hardened resin of ancient trees. The fly in Figure 10C was preserved after being trapped in a drop of the sticky resin.

Indirect Evidence

Trace fossils are indirect evidence of prehistoric life. Tracks, like those in Figure 10D, are animal footprints made in soft sediment that was later compacted and cemented. Burrows are holes made by an animal in sediment, wood, or rock that were later filled with mineral matter and preserved. Some of the oldest known fossils are believed to be worm burrows. Coprolites are fossils of dung and stomach contents. These can often provide useful information regarding the food habits of organisms. Gastroliths are highly polished stomach stones that were used in the grinding of food by some extinct reptiles.

What are three types of fossils?

Customize for Inclusion Students

Visually Impaired Whenever possible, use models or samples to help students with visual impairments conceptualize key concepts in the text. This section, for example, offers an excellent opportunity for students to handle various fossil samples. As students study each sample, be sure to tell them which type of fossil they are examining (i.e., mold, impression, or trace fossil). Encourage students to orally describe the textures of the fossils and to try to distinguish among fossil types.

Conditions Favoring Preservation **Two conditions are important for preservation: rapid burial and the possession of hard parts.** The soft parts of a dead animal are usually eaten by scavengers or decomposed by bacteria. However, if the remains are buried quickly by sediment, they are protected from the environment. Then there is a chance that the organism will become a fossil. In addition, organisms have a better chance of being preserved if they have hard parts such as shells, bones, and teeth. Fossils of hard parts dominate the fossil record even though fossils of soft-bodied animals such as jellyfish and worms do exist.

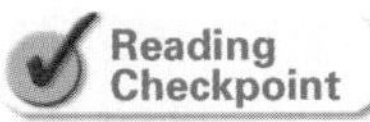
Why are soft parts of dead animals rarely preserved?

Fossils and Correlation

In the late 18th century, William Smith, an English engineer and canal builder, demonstrated the usefulness of fossils to geology. He found that fossils weren't randomly distributed throughout the rock layers he cut through. Instead, each layer contained a distinct assortment of fossils that did not occur in the layers above or below it. Smith also noted that sedimentary rock layers in distant areas could be identified and correlated by the distinct fossils they contained.

Based on Smith's observations and the findings of many geologists who followed, one of the most important principles in historical geology was formulated. **The principle of fossil succession states that fossil organisms succeed one another in a definite and determinable order. Therefore, any time period can be recognized by its fossil content.**

Based on the rock record from around the world, geologists have identified an order of fossils: an Age of Trilobites, an Age of Fishes, an Age of Coal Swamps, an Age of Reptiles, and an Age of Mammals. These "ages" correspond to particular time periods and are characterized by distinct and abundant fossils. This same order of dominant organisms is found on every continent.

Once fossils were recognized as time indicators, they became the most useful means of correlating rocks of similar age in different regions. Geologists pay particular attention to **index fossils.** **Index fossils are widespread geographically, are limited to a short span of geologic time, and occur in large numbers.** Their presence provides an important method of matching rocks of the same age. Rock formations, however, do not always contain a specific index fossil. Then groups of fossils are used to establish the age of a rock layer. Figure 11 shows how an assemblage of fossils can be used to date rocks more precisely than using only one kind of fossil.

Fossils and Correlation

Build Science Skills L2

Using Models Have students work in small groups to make model mold-and-cast fossils. Provide each group with clay, a plastic container, beaker, plaster of Paris, and water. Have students line the bottom of the plastic container with clay. They should then press the shell into the clay. After removing the shell, have students mix water and plaster of Paris in the beaker until it reaches a creamy consistency. Tell them to pour the plaster of Paris into the plastic container and let the mixture set overnight. The next morning, they should gently remove the model cast from its mold. **Kinesthetic, Interpersonal**

Facts and Figures

Early attempts at determining Earth's age included a method based on the deposition of sediment. Some scientists thought that if they could determine both the rate of sediment accumulation and the total thickness of sedimentary rock that had been deposited throughout Earth's history, they could estimate the length of geologic time. To do this, scientists divided the rate of sediment accumulation into the total thickness of the sedimentary rock. However, estimates of Earth's age varied each time the method was attempted. The calculated age of Earth ranged from 3 million to 1.5 billion years.

Answer to . . .

Sample answers: petrified remains, molds, casts, impressions, and trace fossils

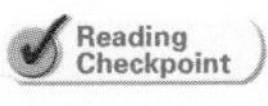
They are destroyed by decomposition.

Section 12.2 (continued)

Use Visuals **L1**

Figure 11 Ask: **Which time range represents the oldest period? How do you know?** *(Time 1 represents the oldest period. This is indicated by the arrow at the far right of the diagram.)* **Can you use this diagram to determine the actual ages of the rocks or fossils? Why or why not?** *(The diagram provides information about the relative ages of rocks and fossils; it cannot be used to determine actual ages.)*
Visual, Logical

3 ASSESS

Evaluate Understanding **L2**

Have students use their outlines of this section to quiz one another on key concepts.

Reteach **L1**

Use Figures 9 and 10 to review the different types of fossils and how they form.

Connecting Concepts

The law of superposition states that the oldest rocks are at the bottom of a sequence of rocks. The principle of fossil succession states that layers of rock contain specific fossils that change from layer to layer. Thus, the oldest fossils would be in the oldest layer of rock, which in turn would be at the bottom.

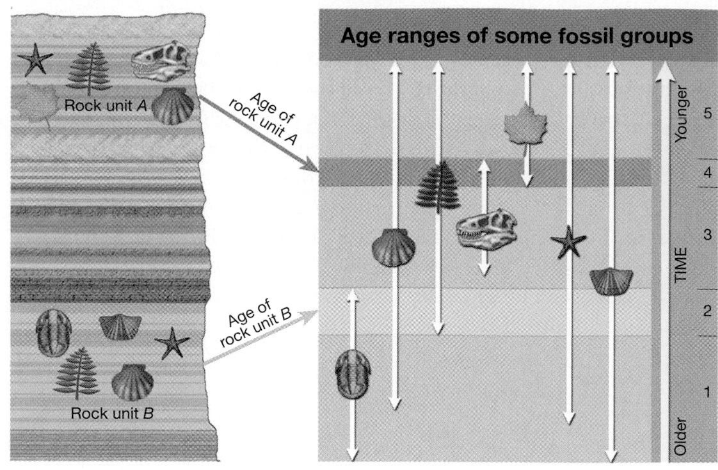

Figure 11 Overlapping ranges of fossils help date rocks more exactly than using a single fossil. The fossils contained in rock unit A all have overlapping age ranges in time 4. The fossils in rock unit B have overlapping age ranges in time 2.

Interpreting Environments **Fossils can also be used to interpret and describe ancient environments.** For example, geologists can conclude that a region was once covered by a shallow sea when the remains of certain clam shells are found in the limestone of that region. The geologists might also be able to conclude the approximate position of the ancient shoreline by observing the types and locations of fossils. For instance, fossil animals with thick shells capable of withstanding pounding waves must have lived near shorelines.

Fossils can also indicate the former temperature of the water. Certain present-day corals require warm and shallow tropical seas—like those around Florida and the Bahamas. When similar corals are found in ancient limestones, they indicate that a Florida-like marine environment must have existed when the corals were alive. These examples illustrate how fossils can help unravel the complex story of Earth history.

Section 12.2 Assessment

Reviewing Concepts

1. What are fossils?
2. What conditions are necessary to insure fossilization?
3. What is the principle of fossil succession?

Critical Thinking

4. **Sequencing** Describe how a clam might become a fossil.
5. **Inferring** The remains of a large animal are found in a cave along with a large pile of fossilized dung. How can you incorporate this dung into your studies of this unknown animal?

Connecting Concepts

Relating Ideas How are the law of superposition and the principle of fossil succession related?

Section 12.2 Assessment

1. remains or traces of once-living, prehistoric organisms
2. quick burial, possession of hard parts
3. Specific groups of fossils occur in particular rock layers. Each layer differs, and changes in life forms can be observed from layer to layer.
4. Sample answer: The shell falls to the bottom and is buried under mud and sediment. Mineral-rich water soaks into the pore spaces, leaving minerals behind. Over time, the shell becomes incorporated into the mud. As the mud turns to rock, the shell becomes a fossil.
5. Sample answer: You could analyze the dung for evidence of the food the animal ate. You could possibly determine if the animal was a carnivore or herbivore. You might be able to make inferences about the animal's jaw structure.

12.3 Dating with Radioactivity

Reading Focus

Key Concepts
- What is radioactivity?
- What is half-life?
- What is radiometric dating?
- How is carbon-14 used in radiometric dating?

Vocabulary
- radioactivity
- half-life
- radiometric dating
- radiocarbon dating

Reading Strategy

Monitoring Your Understanding Preview the key concepts, topics, headings, vocabulary, and figures in this section. Copy the chart below. List two things you expect to learn about each. After reading, state what you learned about each item you listed.

What I expect to learn	What I learned
1. a. ?	b. ?
2. c. ?	d. ?

Today, it is possible to obtain reliable numerical dates for events in the geologic past. For example, we know that Earth is about 4.56 billion years old and that the last dinosaurs became extinct about 65 million years ago. Although these great spans of time are hard to imagine, the vast expanse of geologic time is a reality. In this section you will learn how scientists measure time using radioactivity and radiometric dating.

Basic Atomic Structure

Recall from Chapter 2 that each atom has a nucleus containing protons and neutrons and that the nucleus is orbited by electrons. Electrons have a negative electrical charge and protons have a positive charge. A neutron has no charge. The atomic number of an element is the number of protons in its nucleus. Different elements have different atomic numbers, but atoms of the same element always have the same atomic number. An atom's mass number is the number of protons and neutrons in an atom's nucleus. The number of neutrons can vary, and these variants, or isotopes, have different mass numbers.

Radioactivity

The forces that bind protons and neutrons together in the nucleus are usually strong. However, in some isotopes, the forces binding the protons and neutrons together are not sufficiently strong and the nuclei are unstable. When nuclei are unstable, they spontaneously break apart, or decay, in a process called **radioactivity.** An unstable or radioactive isotope of an element is called the parent. The isotopes that result from the decay of the parent are called the daughter products.

Figure 12 Common Types of Radioactive Decay In each case, the number of protons (atomic number) in the nucleus changes, thus producing a different element.

Alpha Emission
Unstable parent nucleus
Daughter nucleus
Neutron
Proton
Alpha particle emission
Daughter nucleus- Atomic number: 2 fewer
Atomic mass: 4 fewer

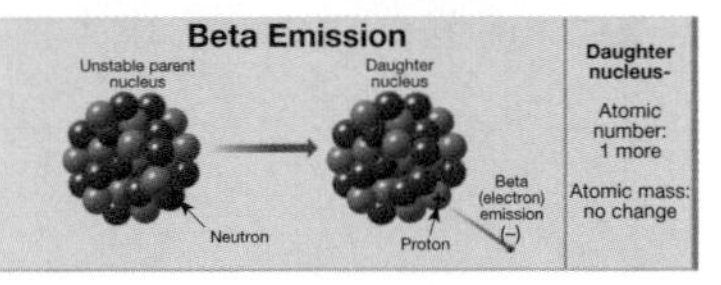

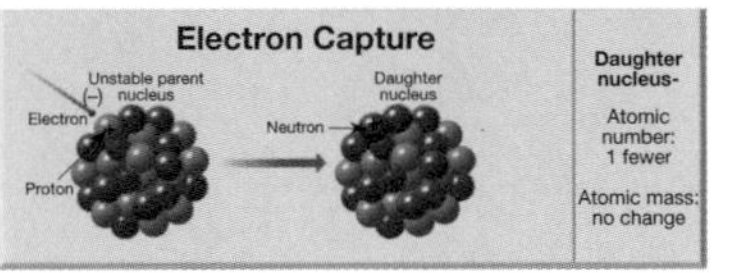

Section 12.3

1 FOCUS

Section Objectives

12.8 **Define** radioactivity and half-life.
12.9 **Explain** radiometric dating.
12.10 **Describe** how carbon-14 is used in radiometric dating.

Reading Focus

Build Vocabulary 

Vocabulary Rating Chart Have students make a four-column chart with the headings "Term," "Can Define or Use It," "Heard or Seen It," and "Don't Know." Have them write *radioactivity, half-life, radiometric dating,* and *radiocarbon dating* in the first column. Students should then rate their knowledge of each term by putting a checkmark in one of the other columns. Ask them to revise their charts after they have read the section.

Reading Strategy 

Sample answers include:
a. What is radioactivity? **b.** the breakdown of unstable nuclei; **c.** What is half-life? **d.** the time required for one half of the nuclei in a sample to decay to its stable isotope

2 INSTRUCT

Basic Atomic Structure

Build Science Skills L2

Using Models Have students draw models of atoms. Student models should show protons (positive charge) and neutrons (neutral charge) in the nucleus. Electrons (negative charge) should orbit outside the nucleus.
Kinesthetic, Logical

Radioactivity

Use Visuals 

Figure 12 Ask: **What happens to the number of protons in each case?** *(It either increases or decreases.)*
Visual

Half-Life

Use Visuals L1

Figure 13 Have students predict how much of the radioactive parent will remain after six half-lives. *(1/64)* Ask: **At which point is the parent/daughter ratio 1:1?** *(after one half-life)*
Visual

Radiometric Dating

Build Science Skills L2

Applying Concepts Have students review Figure 12 on p. 347. Tell them that the element thorium has an atomic number of 90 and a mass number of 232. Ask: **If a radioactive isotope of thorium emits six alpha particles and four beta particles during radioactive decay, what are the atomic number and mass number of the stable daughter product?** *(Each time beta decay occurs, the atomic number increases by one; mass number does not change. Each alpha decay decreases the atomic number by two and the mass number by four. Thus, for six alpha decays and four betas, the atomic number of the daughter would be 90 − (6 × 2) + 4 = 82. The mass number of the daughter would be 232 − (6 × 4) = 208).*
Logical

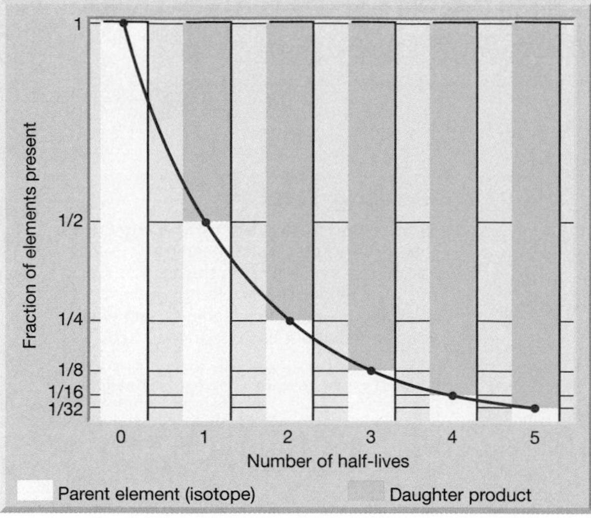

Figure 13 The Half-Life Decay Curve The radioactive decay curve shows change that is exponential. Half of the radioactive parent remains after one half-life. After a second half-life, one quarter of the parent remains, and so forth. **Interpreting Graphs** ***If $\frac{1}{32}$ of the parent material remains, how many half-lives have passed?***

What happens when unstable nuclei break apart? Radioactive decay continues until a stable or non-radioactive isotope is formed. A well-documented decay series is uranium-238, which decays over time to form the stable isotope lead-206. Three common types of radioactive decay are shown in Figure 12 on page 347.

Half-Life

A **half-life** is a common way of expressing the rate of radioactive decay. **A half-life is the amount of time necessary for one half of the nuclei in a sample to decay to its stable isotope.** Figure 13 illustrates what occurs when a radioactive parent decays directly into its stable daughter product. If the half-life of a radioactive isotope is known and the parent/daughter ratio can be measured, the age of the sample can be calculated. For example, if the half-life of an unstable isotope is 1 million years, and the parent/daughter ratio is 1:16, the ratio indicates that four half-lives have passed. The sample must be 4 million years old.

what is a half-life?

Radiometric Dating

One of the most important results of the discovery of radioactivity is that it provides a way to calculate the ages of rocks and minerals that contain certain radioactive isotopes. The procedure is called **radiometric dating.** The rates of decay for many isotopes have been precisely measured and do not vary under the physical conditions that exist in Earth's outer layers. **Each radioactive isotope has been decaying at a constant rate since the formation of the rocks in which it occurs.** The products of decay have also been accumulating at a constant rate. For example, when uranium is incorporated into a mineral that crystallizes from magma, lead isn't present from previous decay. The radiometric "clock" starts at this point. **As the uranium decays, atoms of the daughter product are formed, and measurable amounts of lead eventually accumulate.**

What is a radiometric dating?

Customize for English Language Learners

Give ELL students opportunities to interact verbally with non-ELL classmates. Place students in cooperative groups to discuss key concepts or chapter activities. Do not place all ELL students in one group—the goal is to help them improve their English skills in an informal setting. Encourage all students to be supportive during the discussions. For example, if a student easily grasps a difficult concept, he or she can attempt to simplify the concept for others in a relaxed manner.

Of the many radioactive isotopes that exist in nature, five have proved particularly useful in providing radiometric ages for ancient rocks. The five radioactive isotopes are listed in Table 1.

Table 1 Radioactive Isotopes Frequently Used in Radiometric Dating

Radioactive Parent	Stable Daughter Product	Currently Accepted Half-Life Values
Uranium-238	Lead-206	4.5 billion years
Uranium-235	Lead-207	713 million years
Thorium-232	Lead-208	14.1 billion years
Rubidium-87	Strontium-87	47.0 billion years
Potassium-40	Argon-40	1.3 billion years

An accurate radiometric date can be obtained only if the mineral remained in a closed system during the entire period since its formation. If the addition or loss of either parent or daughter isotopes occurs, then it is not possible to calculate a correct date. For example, an important limitation of the potassium-argon method stems from the fact that argon is a gas. Argon may leak from minerals and throw off measurements. Cross-checking of samples, using two different radiometric methods, is done where possible to ensure accuracy. Although the basic principle of radiometric dating is simple, the actual procedure is quite complex. The analysis that determines the quantities of parent and daughter must be painstakingly precise. In addition, some radioactive materials do not decay directly into the stable daughter product. Uranium-238, for example, produces thirteen intermediate unstable daughter products before the fourteenth and final daughter product, the stable isotope lead-206, is produced.

Why is a closed system necessary in radiometric dating?

Dating with Carbon-14

To date recent events, carbon-14 is used in a method called **radiocarbon dating.** Carbon-14 is the radioactive isotope of carbon. Carbon-14 is continuously produced in the upper atmosphere. It quickly becomes incorporated into carbon dioxide, which circulates in the atmosphere and is absorbed by living matter. As a result, all organisms—including you—contain a small amount of carbon-14.

Q *In radioactive decay, is there ever a time when all of the parent material is converted into the daughter product?*

A Theoretically, no. During a half-life, half of the parent material is converted into the daughter product. Then half of the remaining parent material is converted to the daughter product in another half life, and so on. By converting only half of the parent material with each half-life, there is never a time when all the parent material would be converted. However, after many half-lives, the parent material can exist in such small amounts that it is essentially undetectable.

For: Links on radioactive dating
Visit: www.SciLinks.org
Web Code: cjn-4124

Dating with Carbon-14

Build Reading Literacy L1

Refer to **p. 246D** in **Chapter 9**, which provides the guidelines for relating cause and effect.

Relate Cause and Effect Remind students that a cause makes something happen; the effect is what happens because of the cause. After students have read about dating with carbon-14, ask: **Why do all organisms contain a small amount of carbon-14?** *(It circulates in the atmosphere and is absorbed by living matter.)* **Why is the ratio of carbon-14 to carbon-12 constant during an organism's lifetime?** *(Carbon-14 is continually replaced.)* **At what point does the amount of carbon-14 in an organism began to decrease?** *(when the organism dies and starts to decay)*
Verbal, Logical

Download a worksheet on radioactive dating for students to complete, and find additional teacher support from NSTA SciLinks.

Facts and Figures

In a sample of uranium-238, unstable nuclei decay and produce a variety of daughter products, including radon—a colorless, odorless, invisible gas. Radon itself decays, having a half-life of only about four days. Its decay products are mainly radioactive solids that stick to dust particles, many of which are inhaled by people. During prolonged exposure to a radon-contaminated environment, some decay will occur while the gas is in the lungs, thereby placing the radioactive radon in direct contact with delicate lung tissue. Growing evidence indicates that radon is a significant cause of lung cancer, second only to smoking.

Answer to . . .

Figure 13 *Five half-lives have passed.*

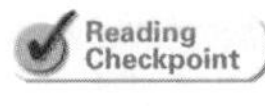

the amount of time necessary for one half of the nuclei in a sample to decay to its stable isotope

Reading Checkpoint *the process of using radioactivity to calculate the ages of rocks and minerals that contain certain radioactive isotopes*

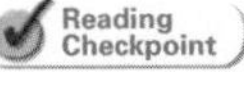

An accurate radiometric date can be obtained only if the mineral remained a closed system since its formation.

Section 12.3 (continued)

Importance of Radiometric Dating

Teacher Demo

Modeling Half-Lives **L2**

Purpose Students will recognize how a radioactive parent isotope decays into its daughter product.

Materials scissors, adding machine tape, metric ruler

Procedure Begin with a piece of adding machine tape approximately 1 m long. Cut the paper in half. Set the two equal pieces aside. Take another 1-m long piece of paper and fold it into four equal pieces. Cut off one-fourth of the paper and set the two pieces aside. Ask students which two pieces of paper represent the parent/daughter ratio after one half-life. Ask which two represent the ratio after two half-lives.

Expected Outcomes Students will recognize that the two equal pieces of paper represent one half-life. The unequal pieces of paper, cut to represent one-quarter of the remaining parent isotope, represent two half-lives.
Visual

3 ASSESS

Evaluate Understanding **L2**

Have students choose a radioactive isotope from Table 1 on p. 349 and make a graph showing its decay curve through several half-lives.

Reteach **L1**

Use different-colored jelly beans to represent protons, neutrons, and electrons. Then model the common types of radioactive decay, using Figure 12 as a guide.

Connecting Concepts

Sample answer: Carbon-14 could be used to radiometrically date artifacts, assuming they are younger than 75,000 years.

Answer to . . .

the ratio of carbon-14 to carbon-12

Figure 14 Carbon-14 is used to date recent events and objects.

While an organism is alive, the decaying radiocarbon is continually replaced. Thus, the ratio of carbon-14 to carbon-12—the stable isotope of carbon—remains constant. **When an organism dies, the amount of carbon-14 gradually decreases as it decays. By comparing the ratio of carbon-14 to carbon-12 in a sample, radiocarbon dates can be determined.**

Because the half-life of carbon-14 is only 5730 years, it can be used to date recent geologic events up to about 75,000 years ago. The age of the object shown in Figure 14 was determined using radiocarbon dating. Carbon-14 has become a valuable tool for anthropologists, archaeologists, and historians, as well as for geologists who study recent Earth history.

What is compared when dating with carbon-14?

Importance of Radiometric Dating

Radiometric dating methods have produced thousands of dates for events in Earth's history. Rocks formed on Earth have been dated to be as much as 4 billion years old. Meteorites have been dated at 4.6 billion years old.

Radiometric dating has supported the ideas of James Hutton, Charles Darwin, and others who inferred that geologic time must be immense. Modern dating methods have proved that there has been enough time for the processes we observe to have accomplished tremendous tasks.

Section 12.3 Assessment

Reviewing Concepts

1. What happens to atoms that are radioactive?
2. Explain the concept of half-life.
3. What is needed to do radiometric dating?
4. Describe radiocarbon dating.

Critical Thinking

5. **Explaining Data** A grain of zircon in a sandstone is dated at 3 billion years. But the sandstone is from a unit of rock dated at 250 million years old. Explain how this can be.
6. **Understanding Concepts** How do scientists use half-lives in radiometric dating?

Connecting Concepts

Comparing and Contrasting Discuss the use of radiocarbon dating in determining the age of an ancient civilization. How can these two methods be used together?

Section 12.3 Assessment

1. The nuclei decay or react by emitting alpha or beta particles.
2. Half-life is the amount of time required for half of the nuclei of a radioactive substance to decay to form nuclei of a stable isotope.
3. radioactive isotopes and known decay rates for the isotopes
4. Materials containing carbon-14 are used. C-14 maintains a constant level in living organisms but not in dead organisms. So the ratio of C-14 to the stable isotope C-12 can be measured and a date of death determined.
5. Sandstone and other sedimentary rocks are made from sediments of pre-existing rocks. Therefore, the sediments can be much older than the rock itself.
6. If the half-life of a radioactive isotope is known and the parent/daughter ratio can be measured, the scientist can calculate the age of the sample.

understanding **EARTH**

Using Tree Rings to Date and Study the Recent Past

If you look at the top of a tree stump or at the end of a log, you will see that it is made of a series of concentric rings, like those shown in Figure 15. Every year in temperate regions trees add a layer of new wood under the bark. Each of these tree rings becomes larger in diameter outward from the center. During favorable environmental conditions, a wide ring is produced. During unfavorable environmental conditions, a narrow ring is produced. Trees growing at the same time in the same region show similar tree-ring patterns.

Because a single growth ring is usually added each year, you can determine the age of the tree by counting the rings. Cutting down a tree to count the rings is not necessary anymore. Scientists can use small, non-destructive core samples from living trees. The dating and study of annual rings in trees is called dendrochronology.

To make the most effective use of tree rings, extended patterns known as ring chronologies are established. They are produced by comparing the patterns of rings among trees in an area. If the same pattern can be identified in two samples, one of which has been dated, the second sample can be dated from the first by matching the ring pattern common to both. This technique, called cross dating, is illustrated in Figure 16. Tree-ring chronologies extending back for thousands of years have been established for some regions. To date a timber sample of unknown age, its ring pattern is matched against the reference chronology.

Tree-ring chronologies have important applications in such disciplines as climate, geology, ecology, and archaeology. For example, tree rings are used to reconstruct long-term climate variations within a certain region. Knowledge of such variations is of great value in studying and understanding the recent record of climate change.

Dendrochronology provides useful numerical dates for events in the historic and recent prehistoric past. Because tree rings are a storehouse of data, they are a valuable tool in the reconstruction of past environments.

Figure 15 Each year's growth for a tree can be seen as a ring. Because the amount of growth (thickness of a ring) depends upon precipitation and temperature, tree rings are useful records of past climates.

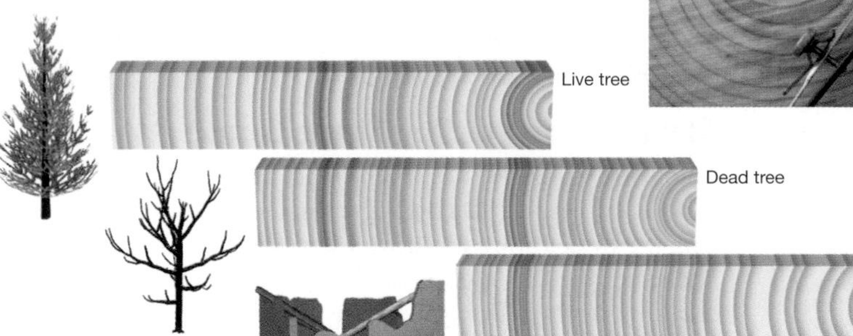

Figure 16 Using Tree Rings to Date Ancient Civilizations Cross dating is used to date an archaeological site by correlating tree-ring patterns using wood from trees of three different ages. First, a tree-ring chronology for the area is established using cores extracted from living trees. This chronology is extended further back in time by matching overlapping patterns from older, dead trees. Finally, cores taken from beams inside the ruin are dated using the chronology established from the other two sites.

Using Tree Rings to Date and Study the Recent Past L2

Background

One of the most basic principles of geology is also used in the study of dendrochronology—the principle of uniformitarianism, which states that the same processes at work today were also active in the past. The doctrine helps dendrochronologists to make inferences about ancient environmental conditions. It also allows them to predict future patterns based on evidence of past conditions. Other doctrines used by dendrochronologists include the principle of limiting factors, which states that life processes, such as growth, are constrained by the most limiting environmental factor of a particular area, such as precipitation. The principle of ecological amplitude states that trees located at the extremes of their species' geographic range will be most vulnerable to changing environmental factors. Other dendrochronologic principles cover site selection, cross-dating, and sampling techniques.

Teaching Tips

- Obtain several thin cross-sections of tree trunks. Allow students to examine the rings. Have them count the rings and try to establish the age of the tree.
- Tell students that clues to ancient environments can also be determined by examining ice cores. The cores are obtained by drilling through thick layers of ice, which are found in places such as Greenland and Siberia. By analyzing gases and other materials trapped in the layers of ice, scientists can reconstruct past climatic conditions.

Visual

Section 12.4

1 FOCUS

Section Objectives

12.11 **Describe** the geologic time scale.
12.12 **Explain** how use the geologic time scale is organized.
12.13 **Identify** some complications in dating rocks.

Reading Focus

Build Vocabulary

L2

Paraphrase Tell students to list the vocabulary terms on a sheet of paper, leaving enough space for definitions. As they read, students should write the definitions in their own words.

Reading Strategy

L2

Sample answers include:

The Geologic Time Scale
I. Structure of the Time Scale
  A. Divided into eons, eras, periods, and epochs
    1. *Phanerozoic* means "visible life."
    2. Three eras in the Phanerozoic: Paleozoic, Mesozoic, Cenozoic
    3. Cenozoic divided into epochs

12.4 The Geologic Time Scale

Reading Focus

Key Concepts

- What is the geologic time scale?
- How is the geologic time scale constructed?
- What are some complications in dating rocks?

Vocabulary

- geologic time scale
- eon
- era
- period
- epoch

Reading Strategy

Outlining As you read, make an outline of the important ideas in this section. Use the green headings as the main topics and fill in details from the remainder of the text.

The Geologic Time Scale
I. Structure of the Time Scale
A. ____?____
B. ____?____

Historians divide human history into certain periods, such as the Renaissance and the Industrial Revolution, based on human events. Thus you can produce a timeline of human history. Geologists have done something similar. **Based on their interpretations of the rock record, geologists have divided Earth's 4.56-billion-year history into units that represent specific amounts of time. Taken together, these time spans make up the geologic time scale.** The geologic time scale is shown in Figure 17. The major units of the time scale were described during the nineteenth century, principally by scientists working in Western Europe and Great Britain. Because radiometric dating was unavailable at that time, the entire time scale was created using methods of relative dating. It was only in the twentieth century that radiometric dating permitted numerical dates to be added.

Structure of the Time Scale

As shown in Figure 17, the geologic time scale is divided into eons, eras, periods, and epochs. **Eons represent the greatest expanses of time. Eons are divided into eras. Each era is subdivided into periods. Finally, periods are divided into still smaller units called epochs.** The eon that began about 540 million years ago is the **Phanerozoic,** a term derived from Greek words meaning "visible life." It is an appropriate description because the rocks and deposits of the Phanerozoic Eon contain abundant fossils that document major changes in life-forms over time.

What is the geologic time scale divided into?

There are three eras within the Phanerozoic. The Paleozoic, which means "ancient life," the Mesozoic, which means "middle life," and the Cenozoic, which means "recent life."** As the names imply, the eras are bounded by profound worldwide changes in life forms. **Each era is subdivided into periods, each of which is characterized by a somewhat less profound change in life forms as compared with the eras.**

What do each of the eras within the Phanerozoic Eon mean?

The periods of the Cenozoic are divided into still smaller units called epochs. The epochs of other periods, however, are not usually referred to by specific names. Instead, the terms early, middle, and late are generally applied to the epochs of these earlier periods.

Precambrian Time

Notice that the detail of the geologic time scale doesn't begin until the start of the Cambrian Period, about 540 million years ago. The more than 4 billion years prior to the Cambrian is divided into eons, as shown in Figure 17. The common name for this huge expanse of time is the Precambrian. The view of the time scale on page 357 gives you a better idea of the expanse of time represented by the Precambrian.

Although it represents about 88 percent of Earth history, the Precambrian is not divided into nearly as many smaller time units as is the Phanerozoic eon. The reason is simple. Precambrian history is not known in great enough detail. The amount of information that geologists have acquired about Earth's past decreases substantially the farther back in time you go. **During Precambrian time, there were fewer life forms. These life forms are more difficult to identify and the rocks have been disturbed often.**

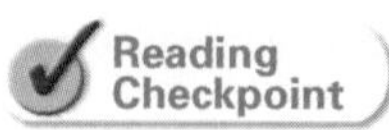

Why does detail in the geologic time scale begin at the Cambrian Period?

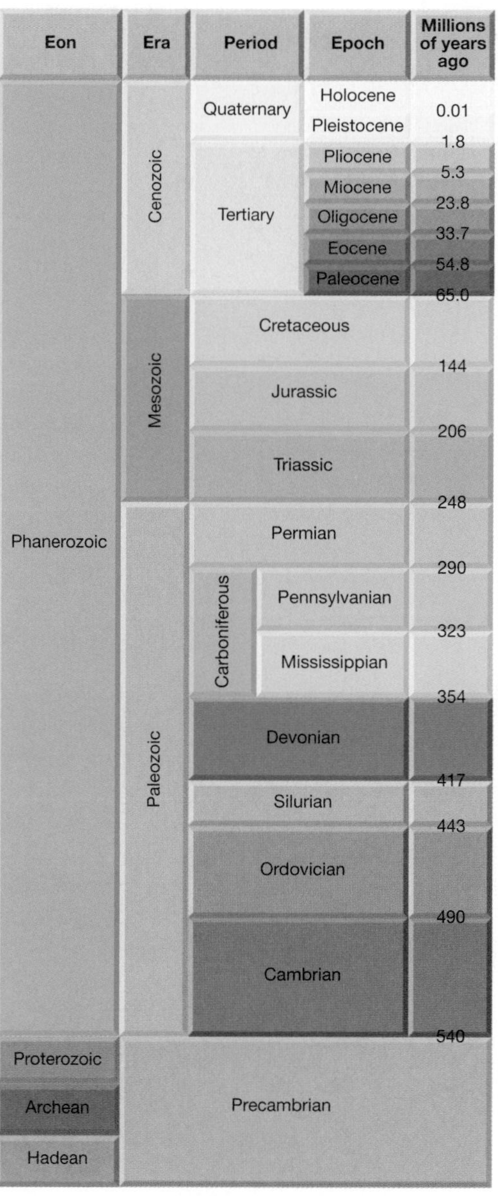

Eon
Era
Period
Epoch
Millions of years ago
Quaternary
Holocene
Pleistocene
0.01
1.8
Cenozoic
Tertiary
Pliocene
Miocene
Oligocene
Eocene
Paleocene
5.3
23.8
33.7
54.8
65.0
Mesozoic
Cretaceous
144
Jurassic
206
Triassic
248
Phanerozoic
Paleozoic
Permian
290
Carboniferous
Pennsylvanian
323
Mississippian
354
Devonian
417
Silurian
443
Ordovician
490
Cambrian
540
Proterozoic
Archean
Hadean
Precambrian

Figure 17 The Geologic Time Scale The numerical dates were added long after the time scale had been established using relative dating techniques.

2 INSTRUCT

Structure of the Time Scale

Use Visuals **L1**

Figure 17 Make enlarged copies of the time scale so that all students can easily read it. Ask students to identify the era, period, and epoch in which they live. *(era: Cenozoic; period: Quaternary; epoch: Holocene)* Ask: **When did the Holocene Epoch began?** *(0.01 million years ago)*
Visual

Precambrian Time

Build Science Skills

Classifying Have students use Figure 18 to classify the rock units according to the geologic period in which they belong. *(volcanic ash: Jurassic Period; Dakota sandstone, Mesaverde formation, and igneous dike: Cretaceous Period; Wasatch formation: Tertiary Period)*
Visual

Customize for Inclusion Students

Learning Disabled For students who have difficulty absorbing large blocks of text, use Figure 17 as a visual aid as you discuss the geologic time divisions. Consider adding benchmarks to the time scale to help students recall the various geologic divisions. For example, you could point out that mass extinctions mark the end of both the Paleozoic and Mesozoic eras. The first fish appear in the fossil record in the Ordovician Period; the first land plants appear in the Silurian Period.

Answer to . . .

eons, eras, periods, and epochs

Paleozoic means "ancient life," Mesozoic means "middle life," and Cenozoic means "recent life."

The time preceding the Cambrian is only divided into eons.

Difficulties With the Geologic Time Scale

Integrate Language Arts L2

Recorded history is generally thought to have begun with the Sumerians, who developed cuneiform writing some 5000 years ago. Ask: **Assuming that Earth is 4.6 billion years old, what percentage of geologic time is represented by recorded history?** *(approximately 0.000001 percent)* **Logical**

For: Links on the geologic time scale
Visit: www.SciLinks.org
Web Code: cjn-4125

Difficulties With the Geologic Time Scale

Although reasonably accurate numerical dates have been determined for the periods of the geologic time scale, the task is not easy. The basic problem comes from the fact that not all rocks can be dated by radiometric methods. For a radiometric date to be useful, all minerals in the rock must have formed at about the same time. For this reason, radioactive isotopes can be used to determine when minerals in an igneous rock crystallized and when pressure and heat made new minerals in a metamorphic rock.

However, samples of sedimentary rock can rarely be dated directly by radiometric means. **A sedimentary rock may contain particles that contain radioactive isotopes, but these particles are not the same age as the rock in which they occur.** The sediments that are eventually cemented together into a sedimentary rock have been weathered from older rocks. Radiometric dating would not be accurate since sedimentary rock forms from so many older rock particles.

Radiometric dating of metamorphic rocks may also be difficult. **The age of a particular mineral in a metamorphic rock does not necessarily represent the time when the rock first formed. Instead, the date may indicate when the rock was metamorphosed.**

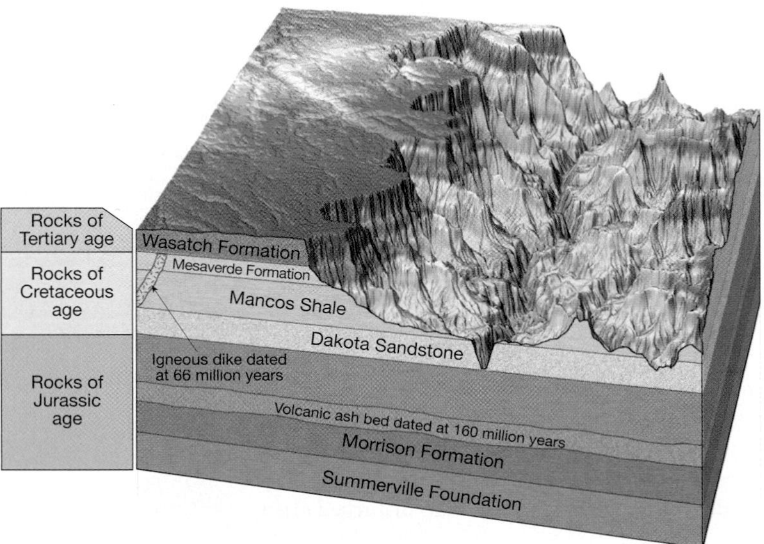

Figure 18 Using Radiometric Methods to Help Date Sedimentary Rocks Numerical dates for sedimentary layers are usually determined by examining their relationship to igneous rocks.
Interpreting Illustrations *Which of Steno's principles (pages 338–339) can you use to interpret the relative ages of these rock layers?*

Facts and Figures

With more research, scientists continue to refine the geologic time scale. Some may think that scientists would expect every date to be consistent with the current geologic time scale, but this is not true. In fact, the age of a particular sample and a particular geologic time scale only represent our current understanding. As more precise data are collected, scientists refine the time scale with smaller and smaller revisions. Who knows what the geologic time scale will look like one hundred years from now?

Go Online NSTA SciLinks

Download a worksheet on the geologic time scale for students to complete, and find additional teacher support from NSTA SciLinks.

If samples of sedimentary rocks rarely produce reliable radiometric ages, how can numerical dates be assigned to sedimentary layers? Usually geologists must relate sedimentary rocks to datable igneous masses, as shown in Figure 18. In this example, radiometric dating has determined the ages of the volcanic ash bed within the Morrison Formation and the dike cutting the Mancos Shale and Mesaverde Formation. Both formations are igneous rock. The area covered by the Morrison Formation includes the following states: Montana, North and South Dakota, Nebraska, Kansas, Oklahoma, Texas, New Mexico, Arizona, Colorado, Utah, Wyoming, and Idaho. Using the principle of superposition, you can tell that the sedimentary beds below the ash are older than the ash, and all the layers above the ash are younger. Using the principle of cross-cutting relationships, you can see that the dike is younger than the Mancos Shale and the Mesaverde Formation. But the dike is older than the Wasatch Formation because the dike does not intrude the Tertiary rocks.

How can geologists overcome the problem of sedimentary rocks and dating the time units of the geologic time scale?

The Morrison Formation is one example of literally thousands that illustrates how datable materials are used to bracket the various episodes in Earth history within specific time periods. It shows the necessity of combining laboratory methods with field observations of rocks.

Section 12.4 Assessment

Reviewing Concepts

1. What is the geologic time scale?
2. What subdivisions make up the geologic time scale?
3. What is the basis on which the subdivisions are made?
4. What is the geologic time scale used for?
5. Why can it be difficult to assign dates to the divisions of the geologic time scale?

Thinking Critically

6. **Connecting Ideas** Explain how igneous intrusions and Steno's laws help geologists get around the problem of dating sedimentary rock layers.
7. **Inferring** What might have happened at the end of the Precambrian Eon and the beginning of the Phanerozoic Eon to allow geologists to mark this boundary on the time scale?

Connecting Concepts

Hypothesizing The boundaries of the geologic time scale are based on significant geologic events, while the epochs of the Cenozoic are based on the percentage occurrence of different fossil animals. Explain why you think it is possible to do this.

Build Reading Literacy 

Refer to **p. 186D** in **Chapter 7,** which provides the guidelines for relating text and visuals.

Relate Text and Visuals Have students reexamine Figure 18 and give specific examples of how Steno's principles can be used to interpret the relative ages of rocks. For example, ask: **How might you tell if the igneous dike is older than the Wasatch formation?** *(If you could determine that the Mesaverde/Wasatch boundary is an unconformity.)*
Visual, Verbal

3 ASSESS

Evaluate Understanding L2

Have students brainstorm other ways to depict geologic time. For example, geologic time has been represented in calendars and on clocks.

Reteach L1

Have students list the three eras within the Phanerozic. *(Paleozoic, Mesozoic, Cenozoic)*

Connecting Concepts

The fossil record in the Cenozoic is more complete. Given this fact, it is possible to use changes in life forms to divide geologic time into epochs.

Section 12.4 Assessment

1. The geologic time scale divides Earth's history into units that each represent specific amounts of time.
2. eons, eras, periods, and epochs
3. Subdivisions are based on geologic events that are recorded in rocks and on changing life forms.
4. Geologists use the time scale to sequence important events in Earth's history. They also use it to assign relative ages to fossils and distinctive rock units.
5. Not all rocks can be dated by radiometric methods.
6. Sample answer: Geologists could date the intrusion using radiometric dating methods. They then could apply Steno's principles to assign relative ages to the units above and below the intrusion.
7. Sample answer: There was a huge change in the diversity and abundance of life forms at this boundary.

Answer to . . .

Figure 18 *law of superposition, principle of original horizontality, and principle of cross-cutting relationships*

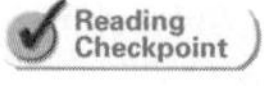

Geologists can date igneous rocks, then determine how the igneous rocks relate to nearby sedimentary rocks.

Exploration Lab

Fossil Occurrence and the Age of Rocks L2

Objective
After completing this activity, students will be able to use fossils to assign relative dates to rocks and rock sequences.

L2

Many people mistakenly think that "cavemen" and dinosaurs coexisted. Remind students that dinosaurs went extinct about 65 million years ago. Have them use the geologic time scale to pinpoint the period that marks the extinction of the dinosaurs. *(Cretaceous)* Humans belong to the species *Homo sapiens*, which in turn belongs to a group of primates called hominids. Hominids made their first appearance in the fossil record approximately 4.4 million years ago. Have students use the geologic time scale to determine which period marks the appearance of hominids. *(Tertiary)* Students should recognize that tens of millions of years separate the last of the dinosaurs from the earliest human ancestors.
Logical

Skills Focus Interpreting Diagrams, Graphing, Hypothesizing, Inferring

 **Prep Time** 5 minutes

Class Time 45 minutes

Teaching Tips
- Encourage students to work in pairs or small groups to complete this investigation.
- To save time, you can plot the data on a graph on the board. Have different volunteers plot the range data for different fossils.
- Have students refer back to Figure 11 on p. 346 for guidance in plotting the range data.

Questioning Strategies
Ask: **Which geologic principles are particularly useful for correlating fossils to rock units?** *(the law of superposition and the principle of fossil succession)* **Which type of fossils do geologists look for when attempting to date rock units?** *(index fossils)*

Expected Outcome Students should be able to use the graph to determine the relative age of a rock unit.

Exploration Lab

Fossil Occurrence and the Age of Rocks

Groups of fossil organisms occur throughout the geologic record for specific intervals of time. This time interval is called the fossil's range. Knowing the range of the fossils of specific organisms or groups of organisms can be used to relatively date rocks and sequences of rocks. In this laboratory exercise, you will use such information to assign a date to a hypothetical unit of rock.

Problem How can the occurrence of fossils and their known age ranges be used to date rocks?

Materials
- geologic time scale
- graph paper
- pencil

Skills Interpreting Diagrams, Graphing, Hypothesizing, Inferring

Procedure
1. A section of rock made up of layers of limestone and shale has been studied and samples have been taken. A large variety of fossils were collected from the rock samples. Use a sheet of graph paper to make a bar graph using the information shown in the Fossil Data Table. Begin by listing the individual fossils on the horizontal axis. Use Figure A to list the units of the geologic time scale on the vertical axis.
2. Transfer the range data of each fossil onto your graph. Draw an X in each box, beginning at the oldest occurrence of the organism up to the youngest occurrence. Shade in the marked boxes. You will end up with bars depicting the geologic ranges of each of the fossils listed.
3. Examine your graph. Are there any time units that contain all of the fossils listed? Write this time period at the bottom of the graph.

Fossil Data Table

	Type of Fossil	Oldest occurrence	Youngest occurrence
1	Foraminifera	Silurian	Quaternary
2	Bryozoan	Silurian	Permian
3	Gastropod	Devonian	Pennsylvanian
4	Brachiopod	Silurian	Mississippian
5	Bivalve	Silurian	Permian
6	Gastropod	Ordovician	Devonian
7	Trilobite	Silurian	Devonian
8	Ostracod	Devonian	Tertiary
9	Brachiopod	Cambrian	Devonian

Sample Data

Neogene/Quaternary	x								
Paleogene	x							x	
Cretaceous	x							x	
Jurassic	x							x	
Triassic	x							x	
Permian	x	x			x			x	
Pennsylvanian	x	x	x		x			x	
Mississippian	x	x	x	x	x			x	
Devonian	x	x	x	x	x	x	x	x	x
Silurian	x	x		x	x	x	x		x
Ordovician						x			x
Cambrian									x
	1	2	3	4	5	6	7	8	9

Analyze and Conclude

1. **Reading Graphs** What is the age of the hypothetical rock layer that these fossils were collected from?
2. **Inferring** Based on the age determined, do you think that this group of fossils could be considered index fossils? Why or why not?
3. **Inferring** A species of the trilobite listed in line 7 of the data table *(phacops logani)* is limited to rocks of lower Devonian age. Trilobite fossils are widespread throughout North America. Can this fossil be considered an index fossil? Why or why not?
4. **Connecting Concepts** These fossils were collected from limestone and shale rocks. Based on what you have learned about the formation of these rock types, what type of environment did these organisms live in?
5. **Understanding Concepts** Shale often contains fossils of leaves. If the gastropods listed in line 3 and line 6 were collected from shale containing leaf fossils, could you use radiocarbon dating to assign a numerical date to this rock unit? Explain.

Go Further Use the library or Internet to research these fossils. Find out how some of them are used in the oil industry or the cosmetics industry.

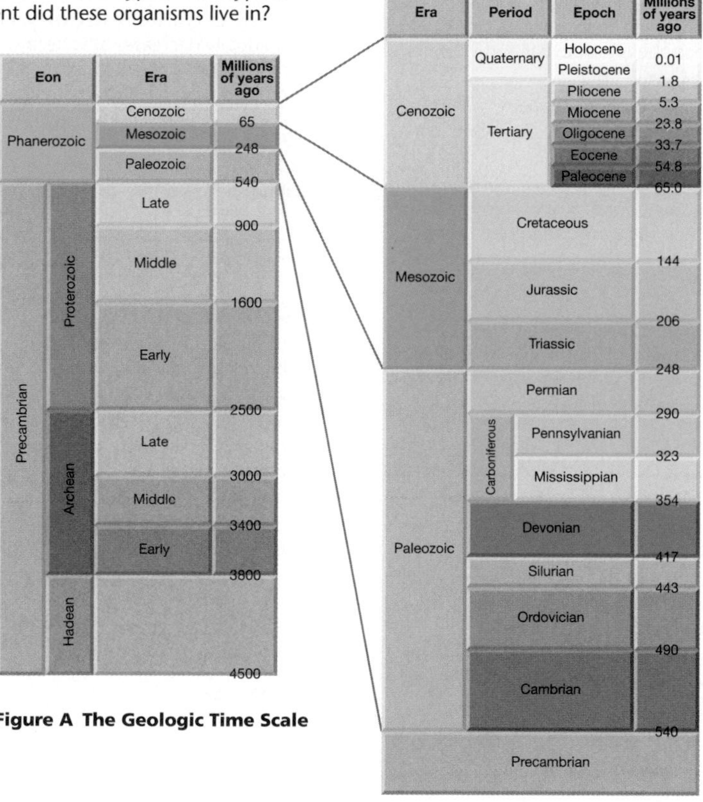

Figure A The Geologic Time Scale

Analyze and Conclude

1. The age of the rock unit is Devonian (354 to 417 million years ago).
2. No, because the age is Devonian which covers 31 million years. In terms of geologic time, this is too long to meet the requirements for an index fossil.
3. Yes, because it is widespread, which indicates that it was abundant, and it lived over a short geologic time span.
4. The environment was an ocean.
5. No, radiocarbon methods can only be used on materials that are less than 75,000 years old. The gastropods are much older than that.

Go Further

Sample answer: *Foraminifera* are used to aid oil exploration.
Kinesthetic, Portfolio

Study Guide

Study Tip

Choose a Quiet Place to Study
Tell students that they will absorb concepts better if they study in a quiet place. Stress that they should minimize distractions such as radios, CD players, cell phones, and televisions.

CHAPTER 12

Study Guide

12.1 Discovering Earth's History

Key Concepts

- Rocks record geological events and changing life of the past.
- We have learned that Earth is much older than anyone had previously imagined and that its surface and interior have been changed by the same geologic processes that continue today.
- Uniformitarianism means that the forces and processes that we observe today have been at work for a very long time.
- Relative dating can't tell us how long ago something took place. It can only tell us the sequence in which events occurred.
- The law of superposition states that in an undeformed sequence of sedimentary rocks, each bed is older than the one above it and younger than the one below it.
- The principle of original horizontality means that layers of sediment are generally deposited in a horizontal position.
- An unconformity represents a long period during which deposition stopped, erosion removed previously formed rocks, and then deposition resumed.

Vocabulary

uniformitarianism, *p. 337;* relative dating, *p. 339;* law of superposition, *p. 340;* principle of original horizontality, *p. 340;* principle of cross-cutting relationships, *p. 341;* unconformity, *p. 341;* correlation, *p. 342*

12.2 Fossils: Evidence of Past Life

Key Concepts

- Fossils are the remains or traces of prehistoric life, and they are important components of sediment and sedimentary rocks.
- The type of fossil that is formed is determined by the conditions under which an organism died and how it was buried.
- The principle of fossil succession combines the law of superposition and the study of the fossils the rock layers contain.

Vocabulary

fossil, *p. 343;* index fossil, *p. 346*

12.3 Dating with Radioactivity

Key Concepts

- A half-life is the amount of time necessary for one half of the nuclei in a sample to decay to its stable isotope.
- An accurate radiometric date can be obtained only if the mineral remained a closed system during the entire period since its formation.
- When an organism dies, the amount of carbon-14 gradually decreases at is decays. By comparing the ratio of carbon-14 to carbon-12 in a sample, radiocarbon dates can be determined.

Vocabulary

radioactivity, *p. 347;* half-life, *p. 348;* radiometric dating, *p. 348;* radiocarbon dating, *p. 349*

12.4 The Geologic Time Scale

Key Concepts

- Geologists have divided Earth's 4.56 billion year history into specific time units.
- Eons represent the greatest expanses of time. Eons are divided into eras. Each era is subdivided into periods. Finally periods are divided into still smaller units called epochs.
- A sedimentary rock may contain particles that contain radioactive isotopes, but these particles are not the same age as the rock in which they occur.
- The age of a particular mineral in a metamorphic rock does not necessarily represent the time when the rock first formed. Instead, the date may indicate when the rock was metamorphosed.

Vocabulary

geologic time scale, *p. 353;* eon, *p. 353;* era, *p. 353;* period, *p. 353;* epoch, *p. 353*

Chapter Assessment Resources

Print
Chapter Test, Chapter 12
Test Prep Resources, Chapter 12

Technology
Computer Test Bank, Chapter 12 Test
Online Text, Chapter 12
Go Online, PHSchool.com, Chapter 12

CHAPTER 12

NY Regents Content Item

Assessment

Interactive textbook with assessment at PHSchool.com 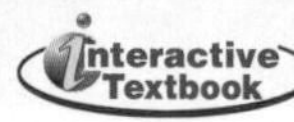

Reviewing Content

Choose the number that best answers the question or completes the statement.

1 What is the name of the doctrine or principle that states the physical, chemical and biological laws that operate today have also operated in the geologic past? NY
(1) uniformitarianism
(2) unity
(3) Earth science
(4) law of superposition

2 What is the name of the process that matches up rocks of similar ages in different regions? NY
(1) indexing (2) correlation
(3) succession (4) superposition

3 What name is given to fossils that are widespread geographically, are abundant in number, and are limited to a short span of time? NY
(1) key (2) succeeding
(3) relative (4) index

4 What is the name of the process during which atomic nuclei decay? NY
(1) fusion (2) fission
(3) nucleation (4) radioactivity

5 Which unit of geologic time is the greatest span of time?
(1) era (2) eon
(3) period (4) epoch

6 What are remains or traces of prehistoric life called? NY
(1) indicators (2) replicas
(3) fossils (4) fissures

7 What name is given to layers of tilted rocks that are overlain by younger, more flat-lying rock layers? NY
(1) disconformity
(2) angular unconformity
(3) nonconformity
(4) fault

8 What are atoms with the same atomic number but different mass numbers called? NY
(1) protons (2) isotopes
(3) ions (4) nucleotides

9 Which of Steno's principles states that most layers of sediments are deposited in a horizontal position? NY
(1) original horizontality
(2) cross-cutting relationships
(3) fossil succession
(4) superposition

10 What name is given to pieces of rock that are contained within another, younger rock? NY
(1) intrusions (2) interbeds
(3) hosts (4) inclusions

11 About how old is Earth? NY
(1) 4000 years (2) 4.0 million years
(3) 5.8 million years (4) 4.56 billion years

Understanding Concepts

12 How have the processes that affect Earth's surface changed through time? NY

13 Why does the law of superposition apply primarily to sedimentary rocks? NY

14 How are cross-cutting relationships used in relative dating? NY

15 How do unconformities form? NY

16 List and briefly describe three different types of fossils. NY

17 What two conditions increase an organism's chance of becoming a fossil?

18 Why can certain fossils, such as corals, be used to indicate former water temperature? NY

19 What is a half-life? NY

20 Explain how radioactivity and radiometric dating are related.

21 Why can't radiometric dating be used with accuracy on metamorphic rocks?

Homework Guide

Section	Questions
12.1	1, 2, 7, 9–10, 12–15
12.2	3, 6, 16–18, 25, 27, 28, 30, 31
12.3	4, 8, 19–24, 26, 29, 32, 33
12.4	5, 11

Assessment

Reviewing Content

(1) 1 (2) 2 (3) 4
(4) 4 (5) 2 (6) 3
(7) 2 (8) 2 (9) 1
(10) 4 (11) 4

Understanding Concepts

(12) The rate at which they occur and the size or scope of their occurrence have changed.
(13) These are the only rocks that are laid down horizontally, except for igneous rock extrusive lava flows, ash flows, and falls.
(14) The rock that is cut or broken by an intrusion or fault is older.
(15) Unconformities form when deposition stops and/or surfaces are eroded, thus leaving a gap in the rock record.
(16) Sample answer: Unaltered remains are mummified or frozen animals. Altered remains are shells that have been filled in with minerals such as quartz. Carbon films form when liquid and gaseous matter is driven off by pressure.
(17) the presence of hard parts and rapid burial after death
(18) Some corals live in warm waters today. Using the theory of uniformitarianism, scientists can infer that some fossil corals must have lived in warm waters, too.
(19) Half-life is the amount of time necessary for one half of the nuclei in a sample to decay to its stable isotope.
(20) Radiometric dating makes use of the known decay rates of some radioactive isotopes.
(21) Radioactive decay begins as soon as a radioactive mineral is formed. When such a mineral is metamorphosed, it can lose its daughter products. Dating this mineral would result in a younger date than actually is correct.

Chapter 12

Critical Thinking

(22) Relative dating correlates rock layers based on their positions. There is no computation involved; it is all based on observation in the field. Numerical dating uses radiometric methods that involve calculations. This is all done in a laboratory.
(23) The decay rate of carbon-14 is very short.
(24) The dates are calculated using the ratio of parent-to-daughter materials. If the system is open and some of the daughter material escapes or some parent material is added, the ratio will not accurately reflect the amount of time that has elapsed.
(25) These fossils would have thick, robust shells that could withstand the high energy of the breaking waves.
(26) Decay rates do not vary.

Analyzing Data

(27) Fault A is older because it does not reach all the way to the top layer) Fault B does reach the top so it formed after the final layers of rock were deposited.
(28) Dike B is older because additional sediments have deposited above it.
(29) Two half-lives have passed; the sample is 2.6 billion years old.

Concepts in Action

(30) You can use radiocarbon dating to assign an age to the bog body.
(31) Sample answer: A modern coastline has sand along the shore, with clams and other shelled organisms living in the sand. If the sequence of rock under study is made of sandstone or limestone with fossils, this may indicate that it once was a shoreline such as the one described above.
(32) Because the ship and clothing are younger than 75,000 years old, you can use radiocarbon dating to assign an age to these items. The coins can only be dated by comparing them to other coins of known age.
(33) We would need to wait 6 half-lives, or 27 billion years.

CHAPTER 12

Assessment *continued*

Critical Thinking

22 **Comparing and Contrasting** Compare the techniques of relative dating to those of numerical dating. NY

23 **Drawing Conclusions** Why can't carbon-14 be used to date material that is older than 75,000 years? NY

24 **Making Connections** Why is it important to have a closed system when using radiometric dating? NY

25 **Predicting** An analysis of some sedimentary rocks suggests the environment was close to the shoreline where high energy waves hit the shore. Corals and shelled organisms lived here. Describe what their fossils would be like.

26 **Applying Concepts** Why is radiometric dating the most reliable method of dating the geologic past? NY

Analyzing Data

Refer to the diagram to answer questions 27 and 28.

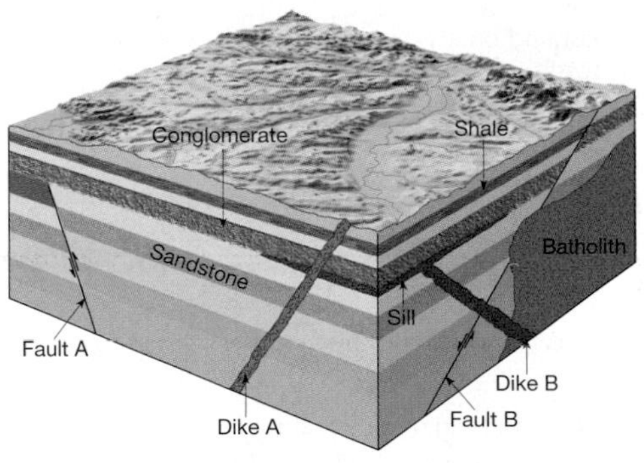

27 Which fault is older, A or B? Explain how you know. NY

28 Which dike is older, A or B? Explain how you know. NY

29 **Calculating** A sample of potassium-40 has a mass of 12.5 grams. If the sample originally had 50 grams of potassium-40 at the start of radioactive decay, how many half-lives have passed? The decay rate of potassium-40 is 1.3 billion years. How old is the sample?

Concepts in Action

30 **Applying Concepts** Fossilized human remains called bog bodies are often found in bogs, which are wet, low-oxygen areas that contain decaying plant material. By what method would you find the age of the fossil? NY

31 **Comparing and Contrasting** Apply the concept of uniformitarianism to explain how a particular sequence of rock layers could be interpreted as a former ocean coastline. (*Hint:* compare what you might see at a modern shoreline to what you would see in the rocks).

32 **Analyzing Data** A sunken Spanish ship containing a treasure in gold coins has recently been found at the bottom of the Atlantic Ocean. What types of dating techniques can be used to date the ship?

33 **Calculating** Nuclear power plants produce radioactive waste that must be stored properly until it is no longer harmful to life on Earth. Uranium-238 has a half-life of 4.5 billion years. If, in order to be safe, a uranium sample must decay to 1/64 of its original amount, how many years must we wait? NY

Performance-Based Assessment

Describing and Classifying Create a poster illustrating the different ways that fossils can form. Be sure to include altered and unaltered remains with examples of both. Include samples of fossils that are found in your area.

Geologic Time Scale

Eon	Era	Period	Epoch	Development of Plants and Animals
Phanerozoic	Cenozoic	Quaternary	Holocene 0.01	Humans develop
			Pleistocene 1.8	
		Tertiary	Pliocene 5.3	"Age of Mammals"
			Miocene 23.8	
			Oligocene 33.7	
			Eocene 54.8	
			Paleocene 65.0	Extinction of dinosaurs and many other species
	Mesozoic	Cretaceous 144	"Age of Reptiles"	First flowering plants
		Jurassic 206		First birds
		Triassic 248		Dinosaurs dominant
	Paleozoic	Permian 290	"Age of Amphibians"	Extinction of trilobites and many other marine animals
		Carboniferous: Pennsylvanian 323		First reptiles
		Carboniferous: Mississippian 354		Large coal swamps
				Amphibians abundant
		Devonian 417	"Age of Fishes"	First insect fossils
				Fishes dominant
		Silurian 443		First land plants
		Ordovician 490	"Age of Invertebrates"	First fishes
				Trilobites dominant
		Cambrian 540		First organisms with shells
Proterozoic	2500	Collectively called Precambrian, comprises about 88% of the geologic time scale		First multicelled organisms
Archean	3800			First one-celled organisms
Hadean	4500			Origin of Earth

Relative Time Span of Eras
Cenozoic
Mesozoic
Paleozoic
Precambrian

Figure 2 Numbers on the time scale represent time millions of years before the present.
Analyzing ***The Precambrian accounts for approximately what percentage of geologic time?***

2 INSTRUCT

Precambrian History

Use Visuals L1

Figure 2 Point out to students that this is a visual representation of Earth's history. Advise students that they should try to get a good understanding of how this figure works, and they should look back at it frequently as they go through the other sections of this chapter. Ask: **Name the eon, era, period, and epoch in which we live.** *(Phanerozoic, Cenozoic, Quaternary, Holocene)* **About how many years ago did the first land plants appear?** *(443 million years ago)* **During what period did the first organisms with shells appear?** *(Cambrian)* **How many years ago did Earth form?** *(4500 million years ago, or 4.5 billion years ago)* **Visual**

Customize for English Language Learners

Use Transparency 162 to make a photocopy of the geologic time scale on p. 365 for students. Encourage them to take notes in their primary language or in English on their copy. Have English language learners work together to understand the large amount of information presented in this chapter and organize it, using the geologic time scale.

Answer to . . .

Figure 2 *Precambrian time accounts for approximately 88 percent of geologic time.*

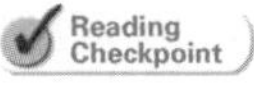

Most Precambrian rocks do not contain fossils, which makes correlating rock layers difficult. Many Precambrian rocks are metamorphosed and deformed, extremely eroded, or hidden by overlaying strata.

Build Reading Literacy L1

Refer to **p. 216D** in **Chapter 8,** which provides the guidelines for comparing and contrasting.

Compare and Contrast Have students compare and contrast Earth's original atmosphere to the atmosphere that exists on Earth today. Ask: **How is today's atmosphere similar to Earth's original atmosphere?** *(Both contain nitrogen, argon, carbon dioxide, and water vapor.)* **How is today's atmosphere different from Earth's original atmosphere?** *(Today's atmosphere contains oxygen, while the original atmosphere did not.)*
Verbal, Visual

Precambrian Rocks Looking at Earth from the space shuttle, astronauts see mostly ocean and much less land area. Over large expanses of the continents, the orbiting space scientists gaze upon many Paleozoic, Mesozoic, and Cenozoic rock surfaces, but few Precambrian surfaces. The lack of Precambrian rock illustrates the law of superposition—Precambrian rocks in these regions are buried from view underneath more recent rocks. Precambrian rocks do show through the surface where younger strata are extensively eroded, such as in the Grand Canyon and in some mountain ranges. However, large core areas of Precambrian rocks dominate the surface of some continents, mostly as deformed metamorphic rocks. These areas are called **shields** because they roughly resemble a warrior's shield in shape. For example, in North America, the Canadian Shield encompasses 7.2 million square kilometers, which is equal to about 10 states of Texas put together. See Figure 3.

Much of what we know about Precambrian rocks comes from ores mined from shields. The mining of iron, nickel, gold, silver, copper, chromium, uranium, and diamonds has provided Precambrian rock samples for study. Surveys to locate ore deposits also have revealed much about the rocks.

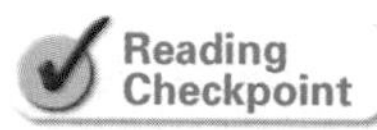

What are shields?

Earth's Atmosphere Evolves Earth's atmosphere is unlike that of any other body in the solar system. No other planet has the same life-sustaining mixture of gases as Earth.

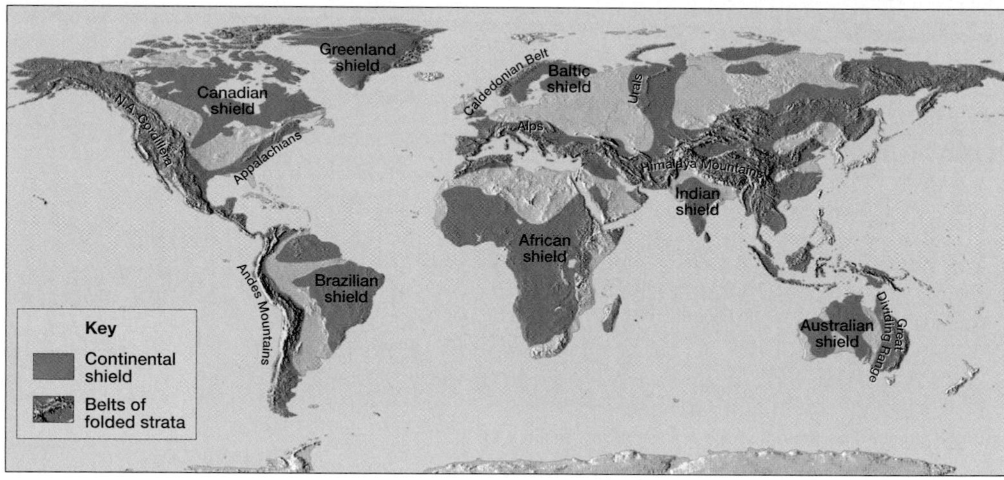

Figure 3 Remnants of Precambrian rocks are the continental shields. They are largely made up of metamorphosed igneous and sedimentary rocks.

Facts and Figures

Precambrian rocks are economically valuable due to their high concentration of valuable ores. However, fossil fuels (oil, natural gas, and coal) are notably absent in Precambrian rocks. This is probably because prior to 540 million years ago, there were no land plants to form coal swamps and no animals to form petroleum. Fossil fuels became much more common in rock layers formed after the "Cambrian explosion" of life on Earth.

366 Chapter 13

Today, the air you breathe is a stable mixture of nitrogen, oxygen, a small amount of argon, and trace gases like carbon dioxide and water vapor. But our planet's original atmosphere, several billion years ago, was far different.

Early in Earth's history, the high-velocity impact of nebular debris caused at least the outer shell of our planet to melt. After this period of bombardment subsided, Earth slowly cooled and the molten surface solidified into a crust. The gases that had been dissolved in the molten rock were gradually released. **Earth's original atmosphere was made up of gases similar to those released in volcanic eruptions today—water vapor, carbon dioxide, nitrogen, and several trace gases, but no oxygen.**

As the planet continued to cool, the water vapor condensed to form clouds, and great rains began. At first the rain water evaporated in the hot air before reaching the ground or quickly boiled or evaporated when it did reach the ground. This evaporation sped up the cooling of Earth's surface. Torrential rains continued and slowly filled low areas, forming the oceans. This rain and the forming of the oceans reduced not only the water vapor in the air but also the amount of carbon dioxide, which became dissolved in the water. A nitrogen-rich atmosphere remained.

The first life forms on Earth did not need oxygen. **Later, primitive organisms evolved that used photosynthesis and released oxygen.** These organisms, primarily cyanobacteria, did not adapt to Earth's atmosphere. They actually influenced it, dramatically changing the make up of Earth's atmosphere by using carbon dioxide and releasing oxygen. Slowly, the oxygen content of Earth's atmosphere increased. The influence the ancestors of plants had on the atmosphere is a good example of how Earth operates as a giant system in which living things interact. The Precambrian rock record suggests that much of the first free oxygen did not remain free because it combined with iron. Iron combines with oxygen to form iron oxides, or rust, at any opportunity.

Once the available iron finished reacting, oxygen began to accumulate in the atmosphere. By the beginning of the Paleozoic era—about 4 billion years into Earth's existence—the fossil record reveals abundant ocean-dwelling organisms that require oxygen to live. These fossils show that the composition of Earth's atmosphere has evolved together with its life forms, from an oxygen-free envelope to today's oxygen-rich environment. **Oxygen began to accumulate in the atmosphere about 2.5 billion years ago.**

How did Earth's oceans form?

Q *The era names refer to "ancient," "middle," and "recent" life. What is the origin of period names?*

A There is no overall scheme for naming the periods; rather, these names have diverse origins. Several names refer to places that have prominent strata of that age. For example, the Cambrian period is taken from the Roman name for Wales (Cambria). The Permian is named for the province of Perm in Russia, while the Jurassic period gets its name from the Jura Mountains located between France and Switzerland.

Build Reading Literacy L1

Refer to **p. 446D** in **Chapter 16,** which provides guidelines for sequencing.

Sequence As students read Earth's Atmosphere Evolves, ask them to create a flowchart showing the steps from the formation of Earth's early atmosphere to today's atmosphere. *(Sample answer: Earth's outer shell melts → Earth's crust cools and solidifies, releasing volcanic gases → water vapor condenses into clouds → torrential rainfall → oceans form → water vapor and carbon dioxide fill the oceans leaving less of those gases in the atmosphere → a nitrogen-rich atmosphere results)*

Visual, Verbal

Integrate Biology L2

Origin of Life on Earth The heterotroph hypothesis is one explanation of how life first evolved on Earth. It states that the first living things functioned like cells. These organisms obtained nutrition from their environment (were heterotrophic), because the early oceans were rich in minerals and dissolved gases. These primordial life-forms released carbon dioxide, which accumulated in the atmosphere until the development of autotrophs that made their own food by using carbon dioxide, water, and sunlight. As these autotrophs performed photosynthesis, they released more oxygen into the air, which created an environment where the earliest oxygen-breathing organisms could develop. Ask: **Where do you think the minerals and dissolved gases in the early oceans came from?** *(carried down from the atmosphere by the rain and out of undersea thermal vents at places such as mid-ocean ridges)* **How did early heterotrophs change the atmosphere?** *(released carbon dioxide)* **How did autotrophs change the atmosphere?** *(released oxygen)*

Verbal

Facts and Figures

Precambrian rocks contain a great deal of iron ore, mostly as the mineral hematite (Fe_2O_3). These iron-rich sedimentary rocks probably formed when Earth's oxygen levels became great enough to react with the iron dissolved in shallow lakes and seas. Because most of Earth's free oxygen results from plant photosynthesis, the formation of extensive Precambrian deposits of iron ore is linked to life in the sea. This connection led to much excitement over the discovery of extensive hematite deposits on Mars by NASA's rovers Spirit and Opportunity.

Answer to . . .

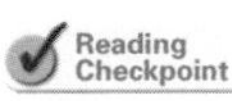
Shields are large areas of Precambrian rocks that resemble a warrior's shield in shape.

Earth's oceans formed from the water vapor that was released from molten rock. This water vapor then fell as rain into low areas, forming Earth's oceans.

Build Science Skills L2

Applying Concepts Students learned the law of uniformitarianism in Chapter 12. Activating this knowledge here will help them remember that law and help them retain more information about stromatolites. Ask: **What does the law of uniformitarianism state?** *(The present is the key to the past because the processes that occur today are the same as the processes that occurred long ago.)* **How did scientists use this law to determine that stromatolites were fossils?** *(Stromatolite fossils look like deposits made by modern algae.)*
Verbal, Logical

3 ASSESS

Evaluate Understanding L2

Have students create a five-question quiz for this section. Students should then trade quizzes, answer the questions, and grade each other's answers.

Reteach L1

Have students color-code and illustrate their own version of the geologic time scale. They can then add additional illustrations of life-forms or the positions of landmasses described in this section. Students should then keep this sheet and add to it as they read the rest of the chapter.

Solution
8. The circle graph should be similar to the bar portion that makes up Figure 2.

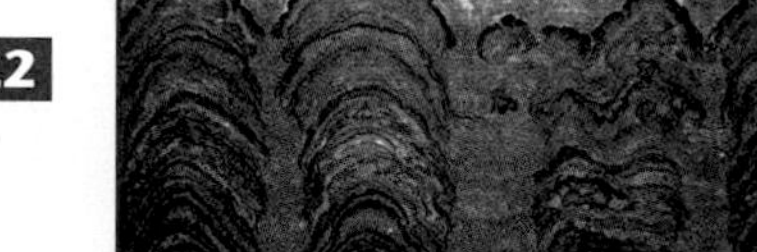

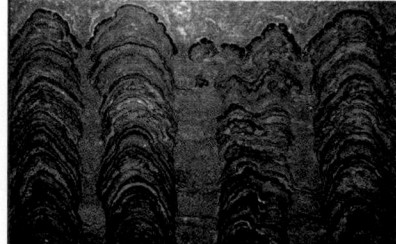

Figure 4 Stromatolites are among the most common Precambrian fossils. **Interpreting** ***What are stromatolites made of?***

Precambrian Fossils Precambrian fossils are disappointing if you are expecting to see fascinating plants and large animals, for these organisms had not yet evolved. **The most common Precambrian fossils are stromatolites.** Stromatolites are distinctively layered mounds or columns of calcium carbonate, as shown in Figure 4. They are not the remains of actual organisms but are material deposited by algae. Stromatolites are indirect evidence of algae because they closely resemble similar deposits made by modern algae.

Stromatolites did not become common until the middle Precambrian, around 2 billion years ago. Although stromatolites are large, most actual organisms preserved in Precambrian rocks are microscopic. Remains of bacteria and blue-green algae have been discovered, which extend the record of life back beyond 3.5 billion years.

Many of these ancient fossils are preserved in chert—a hard, dense chemical sedimentary rock. Chert must be sliced very thin and studied under a powerful microscope to see the bacteria and algae fossils within it. These fossils are the most primitive organisms, called prokaryotes. More advanced organisms called eukaryotes evolved later, and are among billion-year-old fossils discovered.

The development of eukaryotes may have dramatically increased the rate of evolutionary change. Plant fossils date from the middle Precambrian, but animal fossils date to the late Precambrian. Many are trace fossils. Trace fossils are not fossils of the animals themselves but rather impressions of their activities, such as trails and worm holes.

Section 13.1 Assessment

Reviewing Concepts

1. What time span is encompassed by Precambrian time?
2. Describe the components that made up Earth's first atmosphere.
3. Why did the amount of oxygen in Earth's atmosphere increase dramatically?
4. What kinds of fossils of Precambrian life have been found?
5. Describe how shields play an important role in providing information about Earth's formation.

Critical Thinking

6. **Comparing and Contrasting** Compare and contrast Earth's early atmosphere with today's atmosphere.
7. **Inferring** Why did life not develop on the other planets in our solar system?

Math Practice

8. Using Figure 2, create a circle graph that shows the percentages of relative time encompassed by the Cenozoic, Mesozoic, Paleozoic, and Precambrian eras. Then estimate the percentage of time in Earth's history that humans have existed.

Section 13.1 Assessment

1. Precambrian time encompasses 4.56 billion years.
2. Earth's first atmosphere was probably made up of nitrogen and small amounts of water vapor, carbon dioxide, and other trace gases.
3. The evolution of organisms that used photosynthesis caused the release of increasing amounts of oxygen into the atmosphere.
4. stromatolites, microscopic organisms, prokaryotes, trace fossils
5. Shields are large areas of Precambrian rocks that are on the surface. Shields contain large amounts of ore, which can be analyzed.
6. Earth's early atmosphere probably contained water vapor, carbon dioxide, nitrogen, and several trace gases, but no oxygen. Today the atmosphere contains oxygen.
7. Other planets did not develop an atmosphere that would be conducive to life. It is likely that the condensation of water vapor was an essential part.

Answer to . . .

Figure 4 *calcium carbonate*

13.2 Paleozoic Era: Life Explodes

Reading Focus

Key Concepts

- When was the Paleozoic era?
- How did tectonic movements affect the locations and formations of the continents during the Paleozoic era?
- What kind of life existed in the early Paleozoic?
- How did life evolve during the Paleozoic era?

Vocabulary

- Gondwana
- Laurasia

Reading Strategy

Identifying Details Copy the table below. As you read the section, fill out the table with notes.

	Continental positions	Plant life	Animal life
Early Paleozoic			
Middle Paleozoic			
Late Paleozoic			

As the Precambrian came to a close, the fossil record disclosed diverse and complete multicelled organisms. This set the stage for more complex plants and animals to evolve at the dawn of the Paleozoic era. **Following the long Precambrian, the most recent 540 million years of Earth's history are divided into three eras: Paleozoic, Mesozoic, and Cenozoic.** The Paleozoic era encompasses about 292 million years and is by far the longest of the three.

Before the Paleozoic, life forms possessed no hard parts, such as shells, scales, bones, or teeth. Hard parts greatly enhanced a life form's chance of being preserved as part of the fossil record. The Paleozoic era contains many more diverse fossils due to the emergence of life forms with hard parts.

Abundant Paleozoic fossils have allowed geologists to construct a far more detailed time scale for the last one-eighth of geologic time than for the preceding seven-eighths, the Precambrian. Moreover, because every organism is associated with a particular environment, the greatly improved fossil record provided invaluable information for learning about ancient environments. For our brief tour of the Paleozoic, we divide it into Early Paleozoic (Cambrian, Ordovician, Silurian periods) and Late Paleozoic (Devonian, Mississippian, Pennsylvanian, Permian periods).

Section 13.2

1 FOCUS

Section Objectives

13.4 **List** the periods that make up the Paleozoic era.

13.5 **Explain** how tectonic movements affected the locations of the continents during the Paleozoic era.

13.6 **Describe** some of the life-forms that existed in the early Paleozoic era.

13.7 **Explain** how life evolved during the Paleozoic era.

Reading Focus

Build Vocabulary 

Graphic Organizers As they read this section, have students create a concept map or flowchart that includes the vocabulary terms and major concepts for this section.

Reading Strategy 

Sample answers: Early Paleozoic—Gondwana at the South Pole, other landmasses near the equator; confined to the sea; marine invertebrates such as trilobites, cephalopods, and brachiopods developed and animals with hard shells; Late Paleozoic—Pangaea formed; land plants developed from leafless spikes to full trees; fish developed scales, and amphibians became dominant

2 INSTRUCT

Early Paleozoic

Build Reading Literacy L1

Refer to **p. 392D** in **Chapter 14,** which provides guidelines for previewing.

Preview Have students scan the boldfaced material, topic headings, and graphics in this section to get an idea of how it is organized and what it is about. This preview of the section will help students know where to find the information needed to complete the table for this section's reading strategy.
Visual, Verbal

Early Paleozoic

The early Paleozoic consists of a 123-million-year span that includes the Cambrian, Ordovician, and Silurian periods. Looking at Earth from space at this time, you would have seen the familiar blue planet with many clouds, but the arrangement of the continents would be very different from today.

Early Paleozoic History **During the Cambrian, Ordovician, and Silurian periods, the vast southern continent of Gondwana encompassed five continents (South America, Africa, Australia, Antarctica, India, and perhaps China).**

North America and several other landmasses were not part of Gondwana. Although the exact position of these northern continents is uncertain, they are thought to have been near the equator and separated by a narrow sea, as shown on the map in Figure 5.

At the beginning of the Paleozoic, North America was a land with no living things, plant or animal. Soon, a mountain-building event affected eastern North America. The final chapter in this story was the formation of the Appalachian Mountains, over 200 million years later.

During the Silurian period, much of North America was once again covered by shallow seas. This time, large barrier reefs restricted circulation between shallow marine basins and the open ocean. Water in these basins evaporated, depositing large quantities of rock salt and gypsum.

Why are more fossils found from the Paleozoic era than Precambrian time?

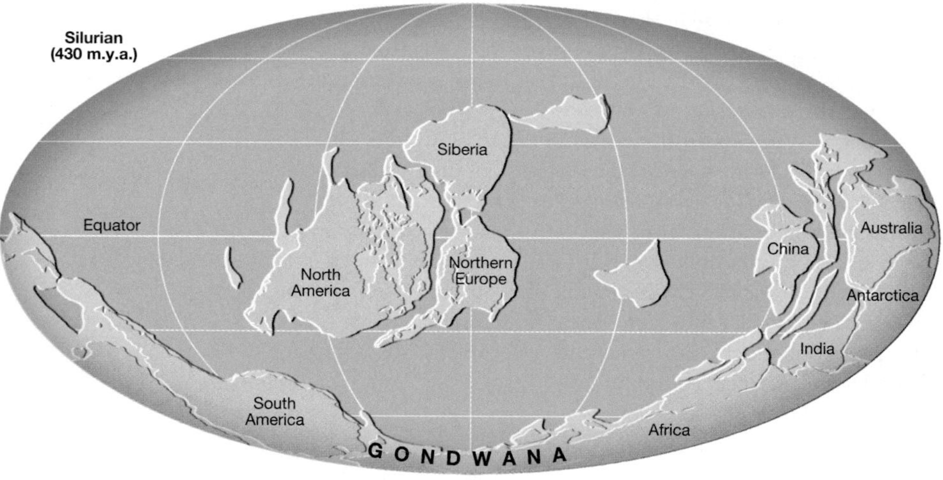

Figure 5 A landmass called Gondwana and the northern continental landmasses existed in early Paleozoic time.
Explaining ***What continents made up Gondwana?***

Customize for Inclusion Students

Learning Disabled Graphic organizers are essential to managing the large amount of information presented in this chapter. Help students who are learning disabled use the reading strategy for this section by having students complete this activity in heterogeneous cooperative groups. Also, remind students to refer back to the geologic time scale on p. 365 if they get lost in what they are reading. Tell students to add details to their own version of the scale as they read. (See Reteach in Section 13.1.)

Early Paleozoic Life

Life in early Paleozoic time was restricted to the seas. Vertebrates had not yet evolved, so life consisted of several invertebrate groups. The Cambrian period was the golden age of trilobites. More than 600 types of these mud-burrowing scavengers flourished worldwide. By Ordovician times, brachiopods outnumbered the trilobites. Brachiopods are among the most widespread Paleozoic fossils and, except for one modern group, are now extinct. The adult brachiopods lived attached to the seafloor, but the young larvae were free swimming. This mobility accounts for the group's wide geographic distribution.

The Ordovician also marked the appearance of cephalopods—mobile and highly developed mollusks that became the major predators of the time. Squid and octopus are descendents of these early cephalopods. Cephalopods were the first truly large organisms on Earth. Figure 6 shows some cephalopods and other organisms of the Ordovician.

The beginning of the Cambrian period marks an important event in animal evolution. For the first time, organisms appeared that secreted material that formed hard parts, such as shells. Hard parts clearly served many useful purposes and aided adaptations to new ways of life. Mollusks, such as clams and snails, secreted external shells that protected them and allowed body organs to function in a more controlled environment. The successful trilobites developed an exoskeleton of a protein called chitin, which permitted them to burrow through soft sediment in search of food. The fossil in Figure 7 shows the exoskeleton of a trilobite.

How did the formation of hard parts benefit animals?

Figure 6 Cephalopods, trilobites, brachiopods, snails, and corals inhabited the waters of the Ordovician period.

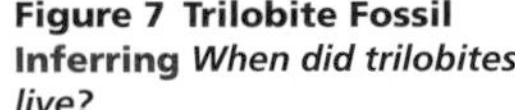

Figure 7 Trilobite Fossil
Inferring *When did trilobites live?*

Facts and Figures

The thick layers of rock salt and gypsum deposited during the early Paleozoic are called evaporite beds because they form as a result of water evaporating and leaving previously dissolved materials behind. These beds are an important resource for the chemical, rubber, plasterboard, and photographic industries in Ohio, Michigan, and western New York State.

Integrate Biology **L2**

Trilobites Have students research the different varieties of trilobites. Students should then present their findings to the class, including pictures and a comparison of sizes and structures of the different varieties.
Verbal

Use Community Resources **L2**

If possible, bring students to a nearby museum to observe fossils and recreations of ancient environments.
Visual, Kinesthetic

Answer to . . .

Figure 5 *South America, Africa, Australia, Antarctica, India, and perhaps China*

Figure 7 *Trilobites lived during the Cambrian period.*

There were more organisms with hard parts, which greatly enhanced a life-form's chance of being preserved in the fossil record.

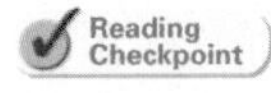
Hard parts allowed animals to venture into different environments.

Late Paleozoic

Build Reading Literacy L1

Refer to **p. 362D** in **Chapter 13**, which provides guidelines for using prior knowledge.

Use Prior Knowledge Review the law of superposition with students. (The oldest rock layers will always be found on the bottom of an outcrop unless that outcrop has been overturned or intruded.) Ask students to apply this law during the Quick Lab.

Relative Dating 

Objective After completing this activity, students will be able to apply the law of superposition to put layers in a sequence.

Skills Focus **Observing, Inferring**

 **Prep Time** none

Class Time 10 minutes

Teaching Tip Give students about 5 minutes to complete the activity, then spend a few minutes discussing the results with the class.

Expected Outcome Students will correctly apply the law of superposition to determine the sequence in which the cards were laid down.

Analyze and Conclude

1. 8 of hearts, 6 of diamonds, 3 of diamonds, 7 of spades, 10 of hearts, 5 of spades, ace of clubs, 4 of hearts, 9 of clubs

2. All the cards, except the 2 of clubs, could be put in sequence. The 2 of clubs was not in the stack, so it was not possible to determine where it would have gone in the sequence.

3. An intrusion would be like slipping a card in from the side.

Visual, Logical

Quick Lab

Relative Dating

Geologists can relatively date the fossils they uncover with respect to their positions in the ground. Assume the playing cards shown are layers of rocks viewed from above. Using the cards, answer the questions below.

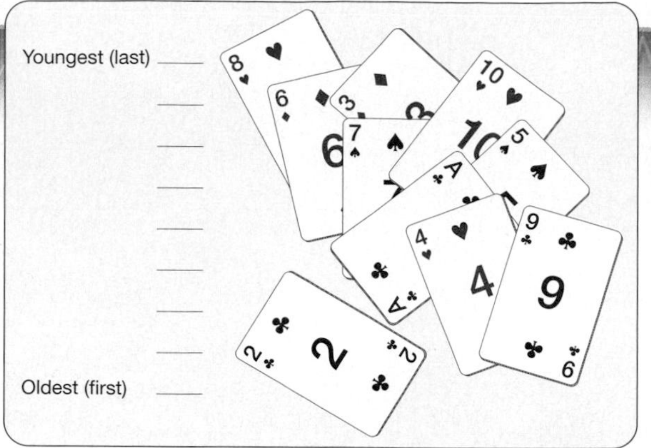

Analyze and Conclude

1. **Observing** List the order, first (oldest) to last (youngest), that the cards were laid down.
2. **Inferring** Were you able to place all of the cards in sequence? If not, which one(s) could not be "relatively" dated and why not?
3. **Applying** What geologic process would be represented by slipping a card in from the side?

Late Paleozoic

The late Paleozoic consists of four periods—the Devonian, Mississippian, Pennsylvanian, and Permian—that span about 160 million years. Tectonic forces reorganized Earth's landmasses during this time, creating the supercontinent Pangaea.

Late Paleozoic History As ancestral North America collided with Africa, the narrow sea that separated these landmasses began to close slowly, as compared in Figure 8B and 8C. Strong forces of compression from this collision deformed the rocks to produce the Appalachian Mountains of eastern North America.

During the union of North America and Africa, the other northern continents began to join, as shown in Figure 8. By the Permian period, this newly formed landmass had collided with western Asia and the Siberian landmass along the line of the Ural Mountains. Through this union, the northern continent of **Laurasia** was born, made up of present-day North America, Europe, western Asia.

As Laurasia was forming, Gondwana moved northward. By the Pennsylvanian period, Gondwana collided with Laurasia, forming a mountainous belt through central Europe. **By the end of the Paleozoic, all the continents had fused into the supercontinent of Pangaea.** With only a single vast continent, the world's climate changed dramatically. The interior of this large continent, located far from a source of moisture became quite arid. In addition, these regions became very seasonal, having extremes far greater than those we experience today.

Facts and Figures

In the early Paleozoic, a mountain-building event affected eastern North America from the present-day Appalachians to Newfoundland. These mountains have since eroded away, leaving behind deformed strata and a large volume of sedimentary rocks from the weathering of these mountains.

Late Paleozoic Plate Movements

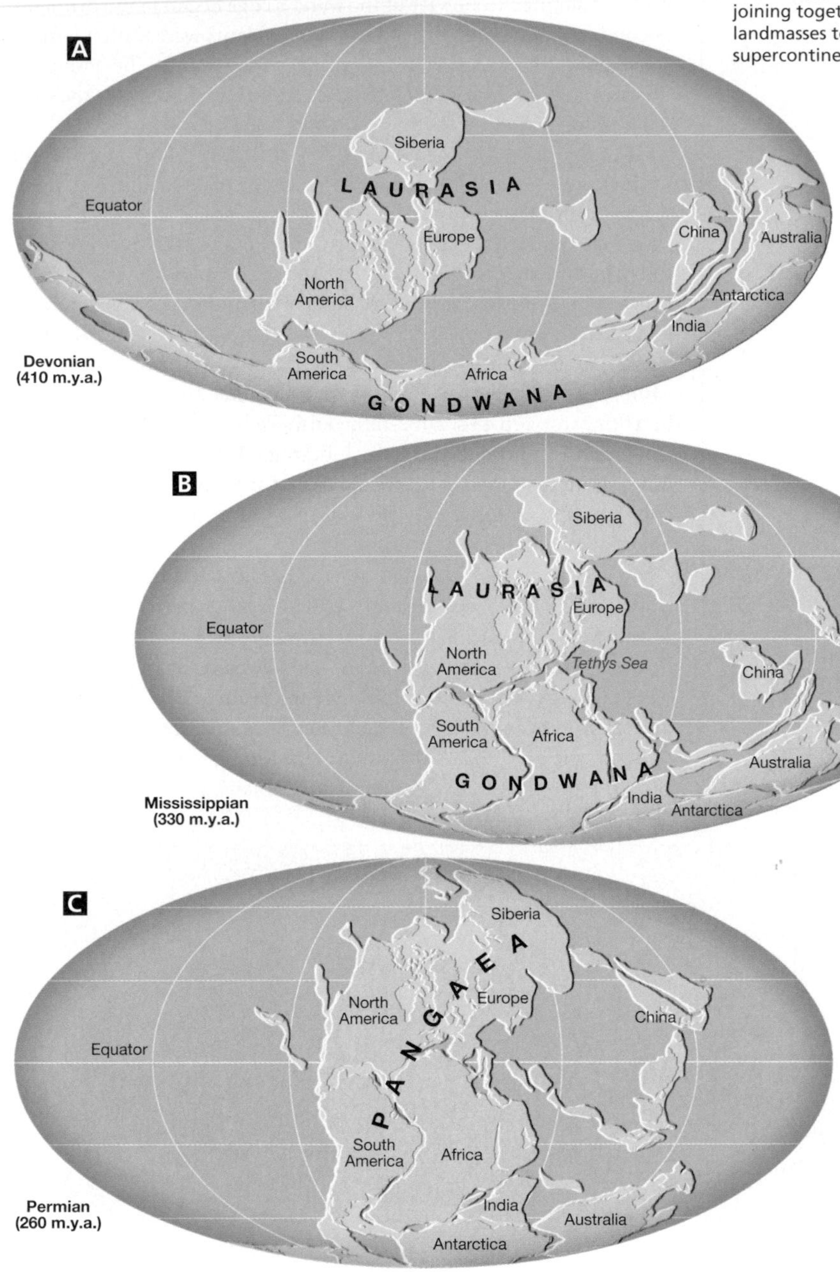

Figure 8 During the late Paleozoic, plate movements were joining together the major landmasses to produce the supercontinent of Pangaea.

A

Devonian (410 m.y.a.)

Siberia, LAURASIA, Equator, Europe, North America, China, Australia, Antarctica, India, South America, Africa, GONDWANA

B

Mississippian (330 m.y.a.)

Siberia, LAURASIA, Europe, Equator, North America, Tethys Sea, China, South America, Africa, Australia, GONDWANA, India, Antarctica

C

Permian (260 m.y.a.)

Siberia, PANGAEA, North America, Europe, China, Equator, South America, Africa, India, Australia, Antarctica

Build Reading Literacy L1

Refer to p. **186D** in **Chapter 7**, which provides guidelines for relating text and visuals.

Relate Text and Visuals Remind students to look back at the geologic time scale on p. 365 as they read to see when the major events happened and to review the sequence of epochs and periods.
Visual

Use Visuals L1

Figure 8 This diagram shows the movement of landmasses during the late Paleozoic. Ask: **During the late Paleozoic, how did Gondwana move relative to the equator?** *(toward the equator)* **How would this movement have affected the climate of Gondwana?** (*It would have gotten warmer.)* **During the late Paleozoic, how did Siberia move relative to the equator?** *(away from the equator)* **How would this movement have affected the climate of Siberia?** *(It would have gotten colder.)*
Visual

Facts and Figures

In the Mississippian period, when Laurasia and Gondwana were forming, ancestral North America and Africa collided, creating strong compressional forces that deformed rocks, producing the northern Appalachian Mountains of eastern North America. As Pangaea was forming in the Pennsylvanian period, the African fragment of Gondwana and the southeastern edge of North America collided, creating the southern Appalachian Mountains.

Integrate Biology L2

Survival of the Fittest Evolution is largely based on the idea of natural selection, or survival of the fittest. This idea states that any mutation that increases the chance of an organism's survival, and therefore reproductive success, would be passed along to future generations, making each successive generation more fit than the last. Have students consider why the following adaptations would be passed on. Ask: **Why would a fish with specialized organs for lungs be more fit than fish with gills?** *(The fish with lung structures could obtain oxygen from air. It could survive if the water dried up or the tide went out, leaving it on dry land.)* **Why would organisms able to reproduce on land be more fit than other organisms?** *(Organisms able to reproduce on land could survive in a more arid environment.)*
Verbal, Logical

Late Paleozoic Life During most of the late Paleozoic, organisms diversified dramatically. **Some 400 million years ago, plants that had adapted to survive at the water's edge began to move inland, becoming land plants.** These earliest land plants were leafless vertical spikes about the size of your index finger. However, by the end of the Devonian, 40 million years later, the fossil record indicates the existence of forests with trees tens of meters high.

In the oceans, armor-plated fishes that had evolved during the Ordovician continued to adapt. Their armor plates thinned to lightweight scales that increased the organisms' speed and mobility, as shown in Figure 9. Other fishes evolved during the Devonian, including primitive sharks that had a skeleton made of cartilage and bony fishes—the groups to which virtually all modern fishes belong. Because of this, the Devonian period is often called the "age of fishes."

By late Devonian time, several fish became adapted to land environments. The fishes had primitive lungs that supplemented their breathing through gills. Lobe-finned fish likely occupied tidal flats and small ponds. Through time, the lobe-finned fish began to use their lungs more than their gills. By the end of the Devonian period, they had developed lungs and eventually evolved into true air-breathing amphibians with fishlike heads and tails.

Modern amphibians, like frogs, toads, and salamanders, are small and occupy limited biological niches. However, conditions during the remainder of the Paleozoic were ideal for these newcomers to the land. Plants and insects, which were their main diet, already were very abundant and large. **The amphibians rapidly diversified because they had minimal competition from other land dwellers.** Some groups took on roles and forms that were more similar to modern reptiles, such as crocodiles, than to modern amphibians.

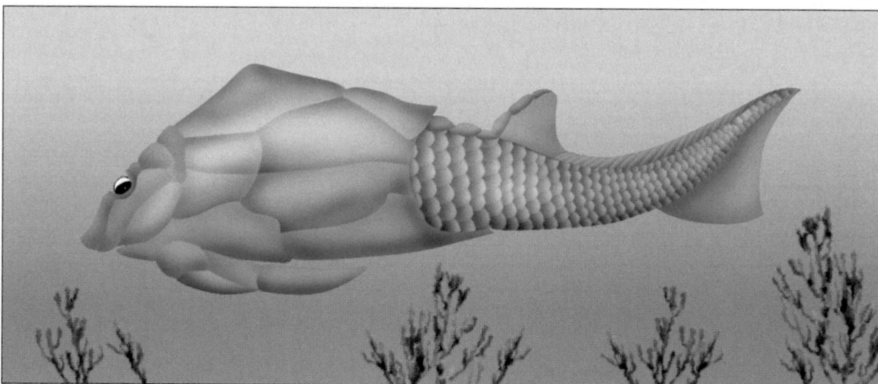

Figure 9 Armor-plated fish were common during the Devonian period.
Inferring *What steps were involved in the evolution of armor-plated fish into modern day fish?*

Facts and Figures

The lobe-finned fish that developed during the late Devonian may have used their bony fins to "walk" from dried-up pools in search of other ponds. As they moved farther across arid Pangaea to find water, a lobe-finned fish with an evolved lung structure would be more likely to survive the trek. Eventually, these hardy survivors evolved into true amphibians. Some lobe-finned fish with only primitive lungs did manage to survive this difficult time, and these became today's fish. Today's fish still have primitive lungs in addition to gills.

By the Pennsylvanian period, large tropical swamps extended across North America, Europe, and Siberia. Trees approached 30 meters, with trunks over a meter across. The coal deposits that we use today for fuel originated in these swamps. See Figure 10. These lush swamps allowed the amphibians to evolve quickly into a variety of species.

Figure 10 Model of a Pennsylvanian Coal Swamp Shown are scale trees (left), seed ferns (lower left), and scouring rushes (right). Note the large dragonfly.

The Great Paleozoic Extinction

The Paleozoic ended with the Permian period, a time when Earth's major landmasses joined to form the supercontinent Pangaea. This redistribution of land and water and changes in the elevations of landmasses brought pronounced changes in world climates. Broad areas of the northern continents became elevated above sea level, and the climate became drier. These climate changes are believed to have triggered extinctions of many species on land and sea.

By the close of the Permian, 75 percent of the amphibian families had disappeared, and plants had declined in number and variety. Although many amphibian groups became extinct, their descendants, the reptiles, would become the most successful and advanced animals on Earth. Much of the marine life did not adapt and survive. At least 80 percent, and perhaps as much as 95 percent, of marine life disappeared. Many marine invertebrates that had been dominant during the Paleozoic, including all the remaining trilobites as well as some types of corals and brachiopods, could not adapt to the widespread environmental changes.

The Great Paleozoic Extinction

Build Reading Literacy L1

Refer to **p. 446D** in **Chapter 16,** which provides guidelines for sequencing.

Sequence As students read Late Paleozoic Life, ask them to create a flowchart showing how the "age of fishes" became the "age of amphibians." *(Sample answer: fish, the dominant life-form, developed primitive lungs and could stay on land longer → lobe-finned fish spent more and more time on land, so lobe-finned fish with stronger lungs were more likely to survive → lobe-finned fish lungs developed further, making them true air-breathing amphibians → with very little competition on land, amphibians took off as the dominant life-forms)*
Visual, Verbal

Facts and Figures

Large bodies of water moderate the climate of nearby land areas. Since water heats and cools slower than land does, coastal areas that benefit from sea breezes are warmer in the winter and cooler in the summer. When all the continents merged to form Pangaea, many areas that had been coastal became landlocked in the continent's interior. Interior regions do not benefit from the moderating effects of large bodies of water. So these areas had much hotter summers and much colder winters.

Answer to . . .

Figure 9 *The armor plates thinned and became light-weight scales, which increased the speed and mobility of the fish.*

3 ASSESS

Evaluate Understanding L2

Have students review with the class by putting them in cooperative groups to share the tables they created for the Reading Strategy in this section. Encourage students to modify their tables as needed based on discussion with their group.

Reteach L1

Review the essential content of this section with students by using the geologic time scale on p. 365. This figure clearly shows the order of periods in the Paleozoic as well as the life-forms present during each period. Then use Figure 8 to review how landmasses moved during the late Paleozoic and how these movements would have affected life at that time.

Writing in Science

Answers should follow the logical progression of life described in the chapter, but should begin with late Paleozoic life (closer to the surface) and end with early Paleozoic life (deeper). Recommend that students use the geologic time scale on p. 365 or the table they created in this section to help them.

The late Paleozoic extinction was the greatest of at least five mass extinctions to occur over the past 500 million years. Each of the mass extinctions drastically changed the existing biosphere and wiped out large numbers of species. In each case, however, the survivors formed new biological communities that were more diverse than their predecessors. Thus, mass extinctions actually allowed life on Earth to flourish, as the few hardy survivors eventually filled more niches than the ones left by the victims.

The cause of the great Paleozoic extinction is uncertain. The climate changes from the formation of Pangaea and the associated drop in sea level undoubtedly stressed many species. In addition, at least 2 million cubic kilometers of lava flowed across Siberia to produce what is called the Siberian Traps. Perhaps debris from these volcanic eruptions blocked incoming sunlight, or perhaps enough sulfuric acid was emitted to make the seas virtually unfit to live in. Some recent research suggests that an impact with an extraterrestrial body may have contributed to the mass extinction. Whatever caused the late Paleozoic extinction, it is clear that without it a very different population of organisms would exist today.

Section 13.2 Assessment

Reviewing Concepts

1. What are the seven periods that make up the Paleozoic era?
2. Which present-day continents made up Gondwana, Laurasia, and Pangaea?
3. Which life forms dominated the early, middle, and late parts of the Paleozoic era?
4. What allowed amphibians to flourish on land?

Critical Thinking

5. **Comparing and Contrasting** Compare and contrast the life that existed at the beginning of the Paleozoic era with the life that existed at the end of the era.
6. **Applying Concepts** Explain how life made the transition from water to land.

Writing in Science

Descriptive Paragraph Imagine you are uncovering rocks and fossils from a site that was formed during the Paleozoic era. Write a paragraph describing what kinds of fossils you would expect to find as you dug from the surface and moved downward.

Section 13.2 Assessment

1. Cambrian, Ordovician, Silurian, Devonian, Mississippian, Pennsylvanian, Permian
2. Gondwana—South America, Africa, Australia, Antarctica, India, and perhaps China; Laurasia—North America, Europe, western Asia; Pangaea—all the present-day continents
3. early—invertebrates; late—amphibians
4. Amphibians were able to colonize areas that other animals were not. The lack of competition for resources allowed amphibians to be successful.
5. Life at the beginning of the Paleozoic was mostly restricted to water. By the end of the Paleozoic, life had begun to inhabit land at a rapid pace.
6. Life moved onto land as plants developed seeds and other characteristics that allowed them to live without depending on water. Animals developed hard parts and ways to reproduce without standing water. Once some plants and animals were able to live on land, the lack of competition allowed them to grow and diversify rapidly.

13.3 Mesozoic Era: Age of Reptiles

Reading Focus

Key Concepts

- What continental movements occurred during the Mesozoic era?
- What plant and animal life dominated the Mesozoic?
- What caused the extinction that marks the end of the Mesozoic?

Vocabulary

- dinosaur
- gymnosperm

Reading Strategy

Summarizing List the blue headings from the section, leaving space to write after each heading. Use a bulleted list to write a brief summary of the text for each heading.

I. Mesozoic History
- Begins with most areas above sea level.
- Shallow seas invade most continents.
- ______?______

Mesozoic Era

The Mesozoic era spanned about 183 million years, and it is divided into three periods: the Triassic, Jurassic, and Cretaceous. The Mesozoic era marked the beginning of the breakup of the supercontinent Pangaea. During this era, organisms that survived the great Permian extinction began to diversify in amazing ways. On land, **dinosaurs** became dominant and remained unchallenged for over 100 million years.

Mesozoic History The Mesozoic era began with much of the world's land above sea level. In fact, very few marine fossils are found in North America from the Triassic period.

As the Jurassic period gave way to the Cretaceous, shallow seas invaded much of western North America, the Atlantic, and Gulf coastal regions. These shallow seas created great swamps like those of the Paleozoic era, forming Cretaceous coal deposits that are very important economically to the western United States and Canada.

A major event of the Mesozoic era was the breakup of Pangaea. Follow this breakup in Figure 11. A rift developed between what is now the eastern United States and western Africa, marking the birth of the Atlantic Ocean and the beginning of the breakup of Pangaea, a process that continued for 200 million years, through the Mesozoic and into the Cenozoic.

For: Links on CAT scanning fossils
Visit: www.SciLinks.org
Web Code: cjn-4133

Section 13.3

1 FOCUS

Section Objectives

13.8 **Explain** how continental positions changed during the Mesozoic era.
13.9 **Describe** the plant life and animal life that dominated during the Mesozoic era.
13.10 **State** the cause of the mass extinction at the end of the Mesozoic era.

Reading Focus

Build Vocabulary

Using Context Clues Encourage students to keep a list of unfamiliar words they encounter while reading. For each word, they should write a definition based on the context and then verify their definition in a dictionary.

Reading Strategy

Mountains form in western North America.

2 INSTRUCT

Mesozoic Era

Build Reading Literacy L1

Refer to **p. 362D** which provides guidelines for using prior knowledge.

Use Prior Knowledge Students learned about plate tectonics and the causes of plate movements in Chapter 9. Ask: **What is happening to the Atlantic Ocean today because of plate tectonics?** *(It continues to widen because of seafloor spreading.)* **What causes seafloor spreading and plate movements?** *(convection currents in the mantle)* **What Earth activity caused the breakup of Pangaea?** *(Tectonic activity/convection currents drove the breakup of Pangaea.)* **Verbal**

Download a worksheet on scanning fossils for students to complete, and find additional teacher support from NSTA SciLinks.

MAP MASTER™ Skills Activity

Answer
Predicting Sample answer: Asia's east coast and North America's west coast will be touching since they are moving toward each other, and Australia will be farther north into Asia.

Teacher Demo

Forming the Rocky Mountains L2

Purpose Students see how deformation of the North American plate could have formed the mountains of western North America.

Materials student textbook, towel slightly wider than the textbook

Procedure Lay the towel flat and slide the textbook just under the short edge of the towel. Then slowly push the textbook toward the towel so that the towel bunches up in front of the book.

Expected Outcome The towel will form ripples in front of the book, demonstrating the wave of deformation that created the mountains of western North America.
Visual, Kinesthetic

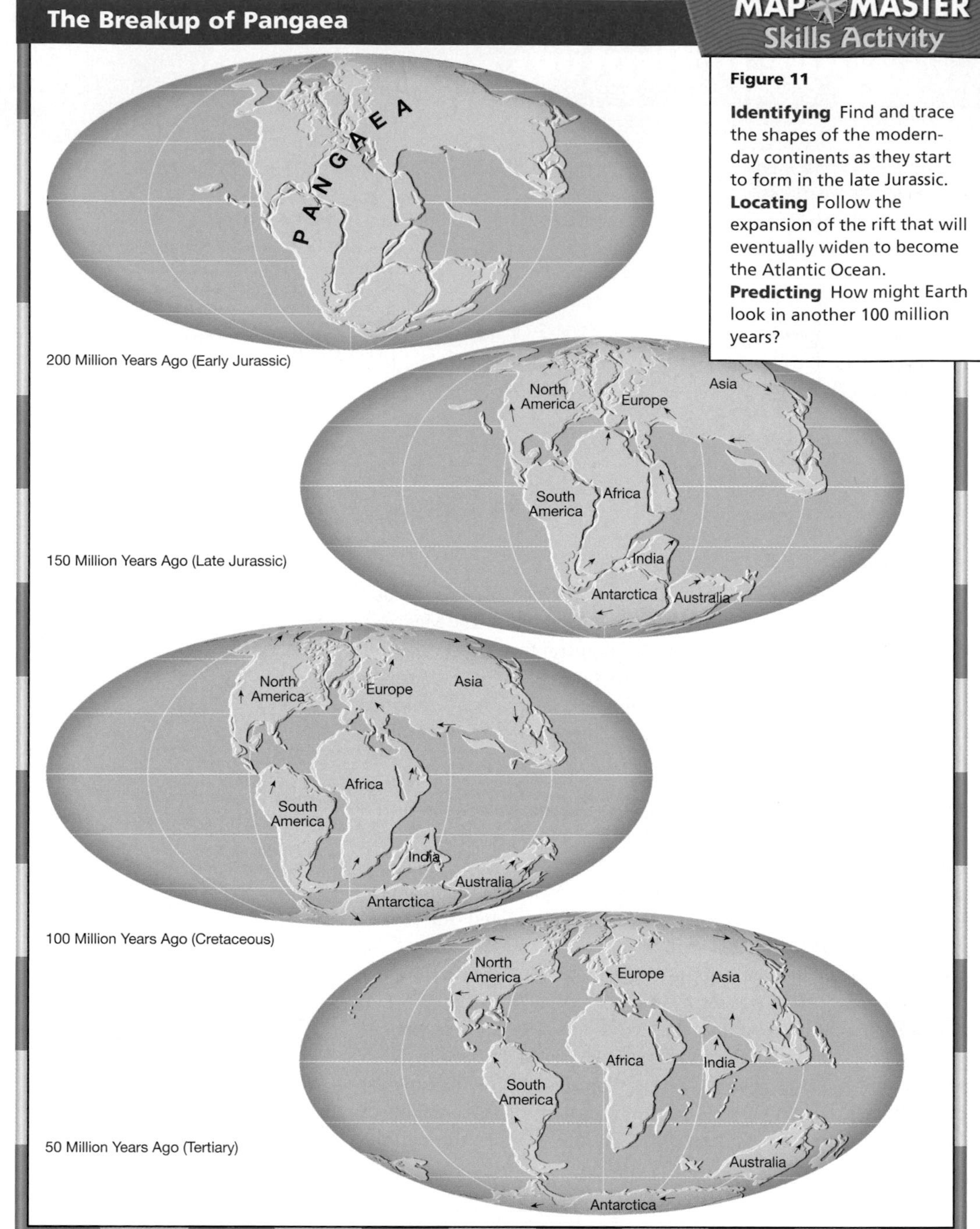

MAP MASTER™ Skills Activity

Figure 11

Identifying Find and trace the shapes of the modern-day continents as they start to form in the late Jurassic.
Locating Follow the expansion of the rift that will eventually widen to become the Atlantic Ocean.
Predicting How might Earth look in another 100 million years?

378 *Chapter 13*

Customize for English Language Learners

In addition to keeping a list of unfamiliar words and defining them based on context, students may also want to write the meaning of the new word in their primary language. Recommend that students list synonyms for their words instead of dictionary definitions. This will allow students to get a general concept of a word's meaning.

As Pangaea broke apart, the westward-moving North American plate began to override the Pacific plate. Tectonic activity began a continual wave of deformation that moved inland along the entire western part of the continent. The tectonic activity that began in the Jurassic continued throughout the Cretaceous. This activity formed the vast mountains of western North America, like those in Figure 12. Toward the end of the Mesozoic, the ranges of the Rocky Mountains located in Colorado and surrounding states began to form.

Explain how the Atlantic Ocean was formed.

Mesozoic Life When the Mesozoic era began, its life forms were the survivors of the great Paleozoic extinction. These survivors were diversified in many ways and filled the biological emptiness created at the end of the Paleozoic. On land, conditions favored life that could adapt to drier climates. Among plants, the **gymnosperms** were a group of seed-bearing plants that did not depend on free-standing water for fertilization. Unlike the first plants to invade the land, gymnosperms were not restricted to living near the water's edge, and they could take advantage of nutrients and space available in dry areas.

The gymnosperms quickly became the dominant plants of the Mesozoic. Gymnosperm trees included the cycads, the conifers, and the ginkgoes. The cycads resembled a large pineapple plant. The ginkgoes had fan-shaped leaves, much like their modern relatives. The largest plants were the conifers, whose modern descendants include the pines, firs, and junipers.

Figure 12 Mountain ranges such as the Canadian Rockies were formed throughout the Cretaceous.
Relating Cause and Effect ***What forces created the mountains?***

Build Science Skills L2

Using Models After completing the Teacher Demo above, explain to students that this model represents the deformation of the North American plate that occurred as it overrode the Pacific plate when Pangaea broke up. Ask: **What do the ripples in the towel represent?** *(mountains forming on North America)* **What does the book represent?** *(the Pacific plate)* **How is this model an accurate representation of the interaction between these two plates?** *(Sample answer: The towel is deformed the way land would be and shows the North American plate on top.)* **How is this model inaccurate?** *(Sample answer: Subduction of the Pacific plate would have caused volcanic activity not shown by the model. The actual process took much longer.)* **What would make this model better?** *(Sample answer: The towel should be stiffer, and the top of the book should have a rougher surface to grab the towel as it slides.)*
Visual, Kinesthetic

Facts and Figures

Some geologists believe there is a supercontinent cycle that repeats itself about every 500 million years. They believe that during this cycle a supercontinent is created by all of Earth's landmasses coming together, and then the supercontinent is broken apart and the landmasses move away from each other again. Their theory is supported by evidence that a supercontinent called Rodinia broke apart at the end of the Precambrian. Rodinia formed 750 million years ago and broke apart during the late Precambrian and early Proterozoic.

Answer to . . .

Figure 12 *the tectonic activity that began in the Jurassic and continued throughout the Cretaceous*

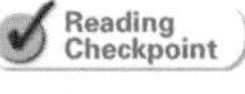

A rift developed during the breakup of Pangaea that widened and eventually became the Atlantic Ocean.

Address Misconceptions L2

Many students think that all large reptiles were dinosaurs. However, dinosaurs are just one particular group of reptiles that share certain characteristics. Use the Build Science Skills activity below to correct this misconception.

Build Science Skills L2

Classifying Before reading this page, have students write down their definitions of a dinosaur. Then, give each student a set of pictures of large reptiles and dinosaurs such as pterosaurs, crocodilians, iguanas, plesiosaurs, raptors, stegosaurs, sauropods, and mosasaurs. Ask students to determine which pictures are of dinosaurs. After students have made their initial classifications, tell them that all dinosaurs were terrestrial (lived on land) and that none could fly. Also tell students that dinosaurs walked with their legs positioned directly under them, like a dog, bird, or human. Other reptiles walked with their legs sprawled out to the side, like a crocodile. Then, have students reclassify their pictures and determine which are dinosaurs. **Visual, Verbal**

The Shelled Egg Among the animals, reptiles readily adapted to the drier Mesozoic environment. They were the first true land animals. Unlike amphibians, reptiles have shell-covered eggs that can be laid on land. The elimination of a water-dwelling stage (like the tadpole stage in frogs) was an important evolutionary step.

Reptiles Dominate **With the perfection of the shelled egg, reptiles quickly became the dominant land animals.** They continued this dominance for more than 160 million years. The dinosaurs were the most awesome of the Mesozoic reptiles. Some of the huge dinosaurs were carnivorous—meat eaters—while others were herbivorous—plant eaters. For example, *Tyrannosaurus* was a carnivorous dinosaur. *Apatosaurus* (formerly *Brontosaurus*) was an herbivore. However, not all dinosaurs were large. Some small dinosaurs resembled the fleet-footed lizards that exist today.

The reptiles made a spectacular adaptation that had already occurred for insects. One group, the pterosaurs, began to fly. These "dragons of the sky" possessed huge membranous wings that allowed them basic flight, as shown in Figure 13. Another group of reptiles, demonstrated by the fossil *Archaeopteryx,* led to more successful flyers—the birds. Whereas some reptiles took to the skies, others returned to the sea, including the fish-eating plesiosaurs and ichthyosaurs. These reptiles became proficient swimmers but retained their reptilian teeth and breathed by means of lungs.

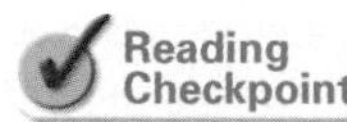

Reading Checkpoint *How did reptiles become the dominant land animals?*

Figure 13 The flying reptile Pteranodon had a wingspan of 7 meters.

Facts and Figures

There is a great deal of evidence that a meteorite impact on Mexico's Yucatan Peninsula caused the mass extinction at the end of the Mesozoic. However, there is controversy over this theory partly because tropical plants were barely affected by this extinction event, while plants adapted to a temperate climate were largely destroyed. This does not support the impact theory, which suggests a large ash cloud blocked the sun, creating an extended winter. If this was the case, then tropical plants should have been more affected since they do not have the dormancy adaptations that temperate plants have. Temperate plants should have had the advantage during this extended winter by being able to go dormant and then come back to life after the crisis.

At the end of the Mesozoic, many reptile groups became extinct. Only a few types of reptiles survived to recent times, including the turtles, snakes, crocodiles, and lizards. The huge land-dwelling dinosaurs, the marine plesiosaurs, and the flying pterosaurs are known only through the fossil record. Most scientists believe that the extinction of these reptiles was caused by a large meteorite that collided with Earth. They believe this collision created huge quantities of dust that blocked out the sun, causing plants to die because they could not turn sunlight into food. Without plants, the huge herbivores could not find enough to eat and eventually could not survive. Then, the carnivores who ate the herbivores could no longer find food. The smaller animals probably survived because they needed less food than the huge dinosaurs.

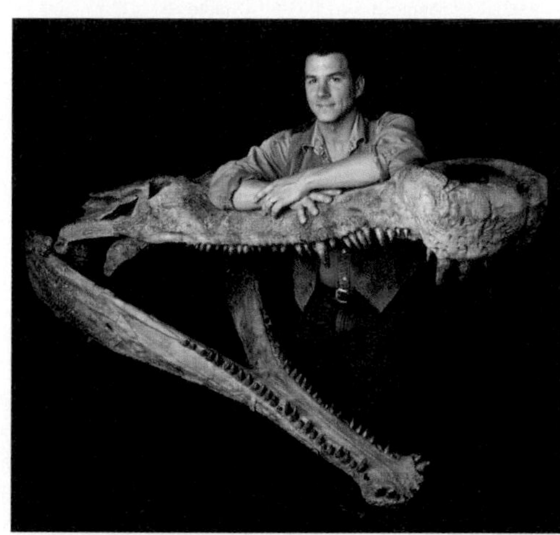

Figure 14 A fossil skull of a large crocodile—*Sarcosuchus imperator*

Q *Many dinosaurs were very large. Were they the only large reptiles?*

A No. One well-publicized example is a crocodile known as *Sarcosuchus imperator,* shown in Figure 14. This huge river dweller lived in Africa about 110 million years ago during the Cretaceous period. By age 50 or 60, the animal weighed 8 metric tons and was about 12 meters long—as long as *Tyrannosaurus rex* and much heavier. Its jaws were roughly as long as an adult human. This animal has appropriately been dubbed "supercroc." Paleontologists indicate that the teeth and jaw suggest a diet of large vertebrates, including fish and dinosaurs.

Section 13.3 Assessment

Reviewing Concepts

1. How did plate tectonics create dramatic changes in the continental land mass during the Mesozoic?
2. What advantage allowed both reptiles and gymnosperms to dominate as life forms in the Mesozoic?
3. What caused the extinction of so many of the reptile groups that had flourished?

Critical Thinking

4. **Comparing and Contrasting** Compare and contrast the physical environment of the Mesozoic era with the Paleozoic.
5. **Predicting** Why do scientists find so many more fossils from the Mesozoic era than from the Paleozoic?

Connecting Concepts

Hypothesizing The fluid in many eggs is similar to seawater, causing some scientists to refer to shelled eggs as "private aquariums." Propose a hypothesis on how environmental conditions might cause shelled eggs to develop and allow animals to move onto land.

Build Reading Literacy

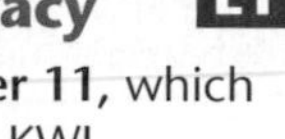

Refer to **p. 306D** in **Chapter 11,** which provides guidelines for this KWL strategy.

KWL (Know-Want to Know-Learned) Have students create a KWL chart on the extinction of the dinosaurs. Before reading this page, have students list what they already know about the extinction of the dinosaurs and some things they would like to know. After reading this section, have students complete the last column with what they learned.
Visual, Verbal

3 ASSESS

Evaluate Understanding — L2

Put students in cooperative groups and have them answer the Key Concepts questions at the beginning of this section.

Reteach — L1

Review content by referring to the summary that each student created for this section's Reading Strategy. Help students expand on their summaries as needed to make them complete.

Connecting Concepts

Sample answer: As the waters dried up, reptiles needed a way to keep their developing young in a moist environment.

Section 13.3 Assessment

1. Tectonic activity caused the supercontinent of Pangaea to break up during the Mesozoic.
2. The advantage of being able to live on land allowed both dinosaurs and gymnosperms to exploit new resources and diversify.
3. Scientists think the mass extinction at the end of the Mesozoic was caused by a meteorite impact.
4. Paleozoic—mostly land, continents move together to eventually form Pangaea, marked by severe climate change; Mesozoic—the breakup of Pangaea into several separate continents, much more ocean and water
5. There are more organisms with hard parts, there are more organisms in general, and the rock layers are less disturbed, weathered, and metamorphosed.

Answer to . . .

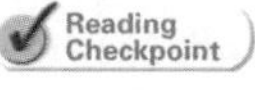

The development of shelled eggs allowed dinosaurs and other reptiles to dominate the land.

Section 13.4

1 FOCUS

Section Objectives

13.11 **List** the periods that make up the Cenozoic era.
13.12 **Describe** the land formations created during the Cenozoic era.
13.13 **Describe** the plant life and animal life that became prominent in the Cenozoic era.
13.14 **Describe** the conditions that helped mammals become dominant in the Cenozoic era.

Reading Focus

Build Vocabulary L2

Flowcharts Have students create flowcharts showing how early plants eventually developed into angiosperms and how mammals changed over time. Recommend that students use this section, as well as previous sections in this chapter. *(Sample answer: aquatic plants that can only survive in water → gymnosperms that must live near a large body of water → angiosperms that do not need to live near a large body of water.)*

Reading Strategy L2

Angiosperms: developed flowers and covered seeds
Mammals: warm-blooded, insulating body hair, more efficient heart and lungs, increase in size and brain capacity, specialized teeth and limbs

2 INSTRUCT

Cenozoic North America

Build Reading Literacy L1

Refer to **p. 216D** in **Chapter 8**, which provides the guidelines for comparing and contrasting.

Compare and Contrast After students have read Cenozoic North America, ask: **How were the landscapes of the east and west coasts of North America similar?** *(Both were above sea level.)* **How were the landscapes of the east and west coast of North America different?** *(The west coast was tectonically active. The east coast was not tectonically active.)*
Verbal

13.4 Cenozoic Era: Age of Mammals

Reading Focus

Key Concepts

- What time period is defined by the Cenozoic era?
- Which land formations were created during the Cenozoic era?
- What types of life forms became prominent in the Cenozoic?
- What adaptations enabled mammals to diversify?

Vocabulary

- mammal
- angiosperm

Reading Strategy

Identifying Details Copy the table below. As you read, list the adaptations of each life form.

Angiosperms	Mammals

The Cenozoic era, or "era of recent life," encompasses the past 65 million years of Earth history. It is the "post-dinosaur" era, the time of mammals, including humans. It is during this span that the physical landscapes and life forms of our modern world came into being. The Cenozoic era represents a much smaller fraction of geologic time than either the Paleozoic or the Mesozoic. The Cenozoic era is shorter than the other eras, but it possesses a rich history because the completeness of the geologic record improves as time approaches the present. The rock formations of this time span are more widespread and less disturbed than those of any preceding time.

The Cenozoic era is divided into two periods of very unequal duration, the Tertiary period and the Quaternary period. The Tertiary period embraces about 63 million years, practically all of the Cenozoic era. The Quaternary period represents only the last 2 million years of geologic time.

Cenozoic North America

Most of North America was above sea level throughout the Cenozoic era. However, the eastern and western margins of the continent experienced contrasting events because of their different relationships with plate boundaries. The Atlantic and Gulf coastal regions were far removed from an active plate boundary, so they were tectonically stable. In contrast, western North America was the leading edge of the North American plate. **Plate interactions during the Cenozoic caused many events of mountain building, volcanism, and earthquakes in the West.**

Cenozoic Life

Mammals replaced reptiles as the dominant land animals in the Cenozoic. The Cenozoic is often called the "age of mammals" because land animals came to dominate land life. It could also be called the "age of flowering plants" because the angiosperms enjoyed a similar status in the plant world. **Angiosperms—flowering plants with covered seeds—replaced gymnosperms as the dominant land plants.** Marine invertebrates took on a modern look.

The advances in seed fertilization and dispersal allowed angiosperms to experience a rapid development and expansion as the Mesozoic drew to a close. As the Cenozoic era began, angiosperms were already the dominant land plants.

Development of the flowering plants strongly influenced the evolution of both birds and mammals. Birds that feed on seeds and fruits, for example, evolved rapidly during the Cenozoic in close association with the flowering plants. During the middle Tertiary, grasses developed rapidly and spread over the plains. This fostered the emergence of herbivorous mammals that were mainly grazers. In turn, the development and spread of grazing animals established the setting for the evolution of the carnivorous mammals that preyed upon them.

Q *What are the La Brea tar pits?*

A The La Brea tar pits, located in downtown Los Angeles, are famous because they contain rich and very well preserved fossils, as shown in Figure 15. These organisms roamed southern California from 40,000 to 8000 years ago. The collection of fossils includes 59 species of mammals and more than 130 species of birds. Hundreds of invertebrate and plant fossils are also preserved.

Mammals Replace Reptiles Back in the Mesozoic, an important evolutionary event was the appearance of primitive mammals in the late Triassic, about the same time the dinosaurs emerged. Yet throughout the period of dinosaur dominance, mammals remained as small and primitive. By the close of the Mesozoic era, dinosaurs and other reptiles no longer dominated the land. It was only after these large reptiles became extinct that mammals became the dominant land animals. The transition is a major example in the fossil record of the replacement of one large group by another.

Mammals are distinct from reptiles in important ways. Mammalian young are born alive rather than in eggs, and mammals maintain a steady body temperature—they are "warm-blooded." Because mammals are warm-blooded, they could survive in cold regions and search for food during any season or time of day. Other adaptations included the development of insulating body hair and more efficient heart and lungs. **These adaptations allow mammals to lead more active lives than reptiles.**

Figure 15 Fossils being excavated from the La Brea tar pits in 1914. **Inferring** ***What kinds of fossils were found in the La Brea tar pits?***

Cenozoic Life

Build Science Skills L2

Relating Cause and Effect During the Cenozoic, evolutionary developments of one group quickly led to developments in other groups. Ask: **How did the development of angiosperms and grasses cause changes in other forms of life?** *(Development of plants with fruits and flowers led to the development of groups of birds and mammals that ate them. The increasing abundance of grasses resulted in the development of grazing mammals that ate the grasses, and this led to the development of carnivores that ate the grazing mammals.)* **Verbal, Logical**

Integrate Biology L2

Seed Dispersal Ask: **What do the following fruits have in common: peach, apple, orange, pumpkin, and strawberry?** *(Many answers are acceptable, but emphasize that they all contain one or more seeds. Point out that strawberry seeds are on the outside.)* Plants make fruits to protect and disperse their seeds, and many animals eat fruits. However, few animals actually eat and digest the seeds. Many animals simply eat around the seeds, leaving the seeds on the ground when they finish their meal. However, even animals that eat the fruit whole will then excrete the seeds intact. This is because the digestive systems of most animals are incapable of digesting seeds. Whether an animal never eats the seed or eats the seeds but cannot digest them, the end result is that the seeds are dropped in a new location, usually far from the parent plant. **Verbal**

Customize for Inclusion Students

Learning Disabled Have students create their own version of the information in the geologic time scale, using a format that is comfortable for them. This format could be similar to Figure 2 on p. 365, in the form of a concept map, in a single straight line, or in any other orientation the student chooses. Help students put the information they need to know about each geologic time period on their graphic organizer, and let them use what they create during their exam.

Answer to . . .

Figure 15 *A wide variety of fossils, including mammals, birds, invertebrates, and plants were found.*

3 ASSESS

Evaluate Understanding 

Have students work in small groups to determine the answers to the Section Assessment questions.

Reteach 

Use Figure 2 on p.365 to reteach the main ideas of this section. Have students add information to their version of the geologic time scale about angiosperms and major continental events during the Cenozoic era.

Connecting Concepts

Plants and animals are tied to each other for food and reproductive purposes. Angiosperms became a prominent source of food for animals. Animals became a means to disperse seeds more efficiently for plants.

Download a worksheet on environmental disruptions for students to complete, and find additional teacher support from NSTA SciLinks.

Answer to . . .

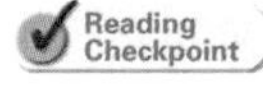

Mammals are warm-blooded, so they could survive in cold regions. They also developed insulating body hair and more efficient hearts and lungs.

For: Links on environmental disruptions
Visit: www.SciLinks.org
Web Code: cjn-4134

With the demise of most Mesozoic reptiles, Cenozoic mammals diversified rapidly. The many forms that exist today evolved from small primitive mammals that were characterized by short legs, flat five-toed feet, and small brains. Their development and specialization took four principal directions: (1) increase in size, (2) increase in brain capacity, (3) specialization of teeth to better accommodate a particular diet, and (4) specialization of limbs to better equip the animal for life in a particular environment.

What adaptations caused mammals to be successful?

Large Mammals and Extinction Some groups of mammals became very large. For example, by the Oligocene epoch a hornless rhinoceros that stood nearly 5 meters high had evolved. It is the largest land mammal known to have existed. Many large forms of mammals were common as recently as 11,000 years ago. However, a wave of late Pleistocene extinctions rapidly eliminated these animals from the landscape.

In North America, the mastodon and mammoth, both huge relatives of the elephant, became extinct. In addition, saber-toothed cats, giant beavers, large ground sloths, horses, camels, giant bison, and others died out. The reason for this recent wave of extinctions puzzles scientists. These animals had survived several major glacial advances and interglacial periods, so it is difficult to say that climatic change caused the extinctions. Some scientists believe that early humans hurried the decline of these mammals by selectively hunting large forms. Although this hypothesis is preferred by many, it is not yet accepted by all.

Section 13.4 Assessment

Reviewing Concepts

1. What proportion of the Cenozoic era do each of the two periods make up?
2. How were the mountains of western North America created?
3. What adaptations caused angiosperms to surpass the success of gymnosperms?
4. How did the extinctions at the end of the Mesozoic era allow mammals to be successful?

Critical Thinking

5. **Making Generalizations** How did mobility play a role in the evolutionary success of plants and animals?
6. **Inferring** Although the Quaternary period encompasses much less time than any of the other periods you've studied, a vast majority of fossils and remains found are from this period. Why?

Connecting Concepts

Evolutionary Development In what ways were the evolutionary development of plants and animals tied to each other?

Section 13.4 Assessment

1. The Tertiary period makes up about 63 million years of the Cenozoic, while the Quaternary period makes up only about 2 million years of the Cenozoic.
2. Western North America was on the edge of a tectonic plate, causing mountain-building activities when the plate overrode the Pacific plate.
3. Angiosperms developed flowering plants with covered seeds. These advances allowed better seed fertilization and dispersal and improved reproduction by integrating animals into the angiosperms' life cycles.
4. The extinctions of dinosaurs and other reptiles made room for mammals to exploit the resources available and become successful.
5. Mobility allowed some plants and animals to find and use resources that other plants and animals could not reach.
6. There are many more animals populating this period, so there are more fossils. The animals that lived in this period were generally larger and had hard parts that fossilized more easily. In addition, less time has passed since the fossils were created, so they are less likely to be weathered away.

understanding

EARTH Demise of the Dinosaurs

The boundary between the Mesozoic era—"middle life"—and Cenozoic era—"recent life"—about 65 million years ago is of special interest. Around this time, more than half of all plant and animal species died out in a mass extinction. This boundary marks the end of the era in which dinosaurs and other reptiles dominated the landscape and the beginning of the era when mammals become very important.

The extinction of the dinosaurs is generally attributed to the group's inability to adapt to some radical change in the environment's conditions. What event could have caused the rapid extinction of the dinosaurs—one of the most successful groups of land animals ever to have lived?

The most strongly supported hypothesis about the extinction of the dinosaurs states that about 65 million years ago a large meteorite about 10 kilometers in diameter collided with Earth, see Figure 16. The speed of the meteorite impact was believed to be 70,000 kilometers per hour. The force of the impact vaporized the meteorite and trillions of tons of Earth's crust. Huge quantities of dust and other metamorphosed debris were blasted high into the atmosphere.

For months the encircling dust cloud would have greatly restricted the sunlight reaching Earth's surface. Without sunlight for photosynthesis, delicate food chains would have collapsed. By the time the sunlight returned, more than half of the species on Earth, including numerous marine organisms, had become extinct.

What evidence points to such a catastrophic collision 65 million years ago? First, a thin layer of sediment nearly 1 centimeter thick has been discovered worldwide. This sediment contains a high level of the element iridium, which is rare in Earth's crust but is found in high proportions in stony meteorites. Could this layer be the scattered remains of the meteorite that was responsible for the environmental changes that led to the demise of many reptile groups?

Despite its growing support, some scientists disagree with the impact hypothesis. These scientists suggest that huge volcanic eruptions led to the breakdown in the food chain. They cite enormous outpourings of lavas in the Deccan Plateau of northern India about 65 million years ago as support for their thesis. It could be that both volcanism and a catastrophic impact played a role.

Whatever caused the extinction, we now have a greater appreciation of the role of catastrophic events in shaping the history of our planet and the life that occupies it. Could a catastrophic event having similar results occur today? This possibility may explain why an event that occurred 65 million years ago has captured the interest of so many.

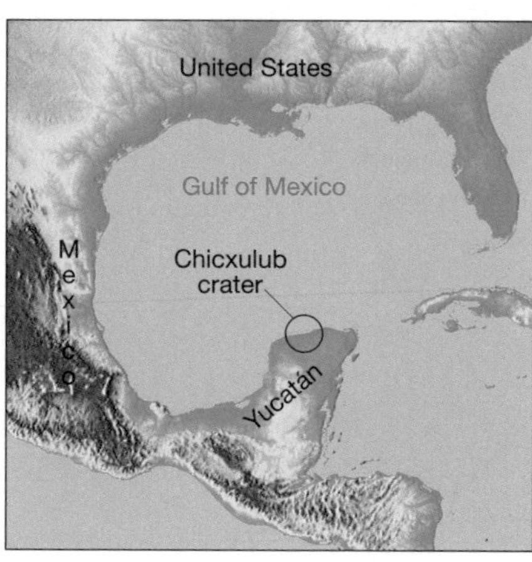

Figure 16 Some researchers believe that the Chicxulub crater is the impact site that resulted in the demise of the dinosaurs.

Facts and Figures

Other support for the impact hypothesis comes from evidence of the largest wave in history, which was 914.4 m tall. Evidence of this wave, a layer of chaotically distributed plant material mixed with deep-sea sediments, exists around the Gulf of Mexico, and dates to 65 million years ago. A type of glass spherules that form only during high velocity impacts and a round crater shape exist on the Yucatán.

understanding

EARTH

Demise of the Dinosaur

L2

Teaching Tips

- Take students to their local public or college library to do additional research on this event. Tell students that the time of this mass extinction is called the Cretaceous-Tertiary, or KT boundary. (K is used for Cretaceous to avoid confusion with the other periods beginning with the letter C.)
- It may be helpful for students to know that in 1980 Luis and Walter Alvarez first suggested the impact hypothesis for the extinction of the dinosaurs. Students should be able to find a great deal of information about past meteorite impacts and new ideas to protect Earth from future impacts. Invite students to present what they learn to the rest of the class.

Verbal

Modeling the Geologic Time Scale L2

Objective In this activity, students will represent the geologic time scale in a way that allows a clear visual understanding of the time scales involved.

Address Misconceptions

Some students think that early life was primarily plants and animals. However, the first life consisted of simple single-celled organisms called prokarytes, which evolved into two forms: bacteria and archaea. The first algaea, called cyanobacteria, began making stromatolites as early as 3.5 billion years ago.This lab will help students see that plants and animals developed rather late in Earth's history.

Skills Focus Measuring, Calculating, Interpreting Diagrams

Prep Time 5 minutes

Advance Prep You may want to have students do this lab in the hallway, or classroom furniture may need to be rearranged.

Class Time 60 minutes (2 class periods)

Teaching Tip Show students how to use the scale given to plot the first event or two on their timelines. For example, the whole class could start by plotting the end of the Mesozoic and extinction of the dinosaurs 65 mm away from the line they marked as Present, because the scale has 1 mm = 1 million years, and dinosaurs became extinct 65 million years ago.

Expected Outcomes Students will create a roughly 5-m long representation of the geologic time scale and will see that the length of time humans have existed is not even 1 mm on this scale. Students will gain a sense of how long the Precambrian really was and how short the other eras and periods were in comparison.

Application Lab

Modeling the Geologic Time Scale

Applying the techniques of geologic dating, the history of Earth has been subdivided into several different units that provide a meaningful time frame. The events that make up Earth's history can be arranged within this time frame to provide a clearer picture of the past. The span of a human life is like the blink of an eye compared to the age of Earth. Because of this, it can be difficult comprehending the magnitude of geologic time.

Problem How can the geologic time scale be represented in a way that allows a clearer visual understanding?

Materials

- strip of adding machine paper measuring 5 meters or longer
- meterstick or metric measuring tape
- pencil

Skills Measuring, Calculating, Interpreting Diagrams

Procedure

1. Obtain a piece of adding machine paper slightly longer than 5 meters in length. Draw a line at one end of the paper and label it "Present."
2. Using the following scale, construct a timeline by completing Steps 3 and 4.

   Scale

   1 meter = 1 billion years

   10 centimeters = 100 million years

   1 centimeter = 10 million years

   1 millimeter = 1 million years
3. Using the geologic time scale on page 387 as a reference, divide your timeline into the eons and eras of geologic time. Label each division with its name and indicate its absolute age.
4. Using the scale, plot and label the plant and animal events on your timeline that are listed on the geologic time scale.

Analyze and Conclude

1. **Calculating** What fraction or percent of geologic time is represented by the Precambrian eon?
2. **Explaining** Using your text and class notes as references, explain why the approximate time of 540 million years ago was selected to mark the end of the Precambrian eon and the beginning of Phanerozoic eon.
3. **Inferring** Suggest one reason why the periods of the Cenozoic era have been further subdivided into several epochs with reasonably reliable accuracy.
4. **Analyzing Data** How many times longer is the whole of geologic time than the time represented by the 5000 years of recorded history?
5. **Calculating** For what fraction or percent of geologic time have land plants been present on Earth?

Geologic Time Scale

Eon		Era	Millions of years ago
Phanerozoic		Cenozoic	65
Phanerozoic		Mesozoic	248
Phanerozoic		Paleozoic	540
Precambrian	Proterozoic	Late	900
Precambrian	Proterozoic	Middle	1600
Precambrian	Proterozoic	Early	2500
Precambrian	Archean	Late	3000
Precambrian	Archean	Middle	3400
Precambrian	Archean	Early	3800
Precambrian	Hadean		4500
Origin of Earth			

Era	Period	Epoch	Development of Plants and Animals
Cenozoic	Quaternary	Holocene 0.01	Humans develop
		Pleistocene 1.8	
	Tertiary	Pliocene 5.3	"Age of Mammals"
		Miocene 23.8	
		Oligocene 33.7	
		Eocene 54.8	
		Paleocene 65.0	Extinction of dinosaurs and many other species
Mesozoic	Cretaceous 144	"Age of Reptiles"	First flowering plants
	Jurassic 206		First birds
	Triassic 248		Dinosaurs dominant
Paleozoic	Permian 290	"Age of Amphibians"	Extinction of trilobites and many other marine animals
	Carboniferous: Pennsylvanian 323		First reptiles
			Large coal swamps
	Carboniferous: Mississippian 354		Amphibians abundant
	Devonian 417	"Age of Fishes"	First insect fossils
			Fishes dominant
	Silurian 443		First land plants
	Ordovician 490	"Age of Invertebrates"	First fishes
			Trilobites dominant
	Cambrian 540		First organisms with shells
Precambrian			First multicelled organisms

Analyze and Conclude

1. 3960/4560, or 88%, is Precambrian
2. appearance of the first organisms with shells and other hard parts
3. The Cenozoic is the most recent era, so the fossils from this time period are the best preserved. This allows scientists to study the fossils in detail and observe even small changes over time.
4. 4,500,000,000/5000 = 900,000 times longer
5. 443,000,000/4,500,000,000 = 0.098 × 100 = 9.8% of the time

Visual, Logical

Study Guide

Study Tip

Use Graphic Organizers
Have students create and modify graphic organizers in a format they are comfortable with. Encourage students to create their own version of the geologic time scale that includes major events for each time period. Students can then use this graphic organizer to prepare for tests.

CHAPTER 13

Study Guide

13.1 Precambrian Time: Vast and Puzzling

Key Concepts

- The Precambrian encompasses immense geological time, from Earth's distant beginning 4.56 billion years ago until the start of the Cambrian period, over 4 billion years later.
- Much of what we know about Precambrian rocks comes from data gathered in exploring the mineral resources in shields.
- Earth's original atmosphere was made up of gases similar to those released in volcanic emissions today—water vapor, carbon dioxide, nitrogen, and several trace gases.
- Primitive organisms evolved that used photosynthesis and released oxygen.
- Oxygen began to accumulate in the atmosphere about 2.5 billion years ago.
- The most common Precambrian fossils are stromatolites.

Vocabulary
shields, *p. 366;* stromatolites, *p. 368*

13.2 Paleozoic Era: Life Explodes

Key Concepts

- Following the long Precambrian, the most recent 540 million years of Earth history are divided into three eras: Paleozoic, Mesozoic, and Cenozoic.
- During the Cambrian, Ordovician, and Silurian periods, the vast southern continent of Gondwana encompassed five continents (South America, Africa, Australia, Antarctica, India, and perhaps China).
- Life in early Paleozoic time was restricted to the seas.
- By the end of the Paleozoic, all the continents had fused into the supercontinent of Pangaea.
- Some 400 million years ago, plants that had adapted to survive at the water's edge began to move inland, becoming land plants.
- The amphibians rapidly diversified because they had minimal competition from other land dwellers.

Vocabulary
Gondwana, *p. 370;* Pangaea, *p. 372;* Laurasia, *p. 372*

13.3 Mesozoic Era: Age of Reptiles

Key Concepts

- A major event of the Mesozoic era was the breakup of Pangaea.
- Gymnosperms quickly became the dominant plants of the Mesozoic.
- With the perfection of the shelled egg, reptiles quickly became the dominant land animals of the Mesozoic era.
- At the end of the Mesozoic, many reptile groups became extinct.

Vocabulary
dinosaur, *p. 377;* gymnosperm, *p. 379*

13.4 Cenozoic Era: Age of Mammals

Key Concepts

- The Cenozoic era is divided into two periods of very unequal duration, the Tertiary period and the Quaternary period.
- Plate interaction during the Cenozoic caused many events of mountain building, volcanism, and earthquakes in the West.
- Mammals replaced reptiles as the dominant land animals in the Cenozoic.
- Angiosperms—flowering plants with covered seeds—replaced gymnosperms as the dominant land plants.
- With the extinction of the dinosaurs, mammals diversified forming many new groups including bats and whales.

Vocabulary
mammal, *p. 383;* angiosperm, *p. 383*

388 *Chapter 13*

Chapter Assessment Resources

Print
Chapter Test, Chapter 13
Test Prep Resources, Chapter 13

Technology
Computer Test Bank, Chapter 13 Test
Online Text, Chapter 13
Go Online, PHSchool.com, Chapter 13

CHAPTER 13

NY Regents Content Item

Assessment

Interactive textbook with assessment at PHSchool.com 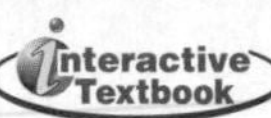

Reviewing Content

Choose the number that best answers the question or completes the statement.

1 Which era spans the least amount of time on the geologic scale? NY
(1) Cenozoic (2) Mesozoic
(3) Paleozoic (4) Precambrian

2 The most common Precambrian fossils are NY
(1) fish
(2) stromatolites
(3) trilobites
(4) ferns

3 Which era is known as the "age of reptiles"? NY
(1) Cenozoic (2) Mesozoic
(3) Paleozoic (4) Proterozoic

4 Modern squids descended from what type of early Paleozoic organisms? NY
(1) cephalopods (2) trilobites
(3) brachiopods (4) amphibians

5 The Devonian period is known as the NY
(1) "age of reptiles"
(2) "age of amphibians"
(3) "age of fishes"
(4) "age of invertebrates"

6 Which adaptation allowed gymnosperm plants to colonize and dominate land?
(1) stems (2) seeds
(3) leaves (4) flowers

7 Reptiles that were adapted to fly included the
(1) plesiosaurs (2) pterosaurs
(3) ichthyosaurs (4) tyrannosaurs

8 Humans first appeared during the NY
(1) Cretaceous period
(2) Jurassic period
(3) Quaternary period
(4) Tertiary period

9 Insulating body hair is a characteristic of NY
(1) mammals
(2) amphibian
(3) reptiles
(4) invertebrates

10 What development caused the emergence of animals that were grazing herbivores?
(1) seed plants
(2) grasses
(3) fruits
(4) carnivorous mammals

Understanding Concepts

11 How did plants help change Earth's early atmosphere? NY

12 What are shields? What kind of information is gained from shields?

Use the photograph below to answer question 13.

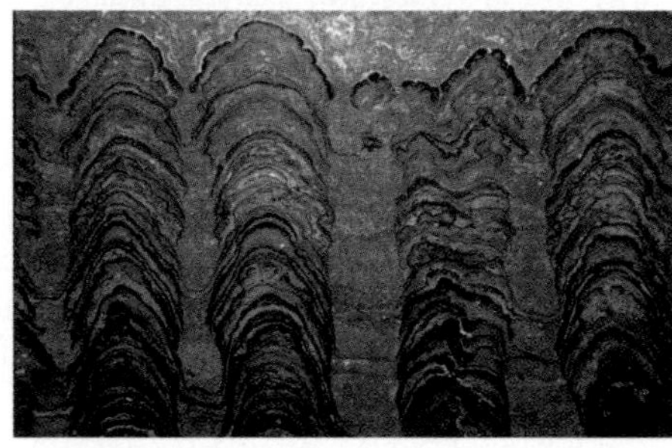

13 This photograph shows evidence of what kind of organism?

14 What significant tectonic activity occurred during the Mesozoic? NY

15 What present-day continents made up Gondwana? NY

16 Which kind of animals are trilobites and cephalopods?

17 Modern fishes and sharks both evolved from what type of ancient animals?

18 What development allowed mammals to adapt to different environments successfully?

Homework Guide

Section	Questions
1	2, 11–13, 20–24
2	4, 5, 15–17
3	3, 6, 7, 14, 19, 25
4	1, 8–10, 18, 26, 27

Assessment

Reviewing Content

(1) 1 (2) 3 (3) 2
(4) 1 (5) 3 (6) 2
(7) 2 (8) 3 (9) 1
(10) 2

Understanding Concepts

(11) Primitive plants used photosynthesis and released oxygen. Plants dramatically changed the makeup of Earth's atmosphere by using carbon dioxide and releasing oxygen. The oxygen content of Earth's atmosphere increased.
(12) Shields are areas of Precambrian rock that reach the surface. Metal ores from shields provide information about Precambrian time.
(13) stromatolites
(14) Pangaea broke up.
(15) South America, Africa, Australia, Antarctica, India, and perhaps China
(16) They are both invertebrates.
(17) armor-plated fishes
(18) Mammals are warm-blooded, which allows them to inhabit colder regions and remain active at different seasons and times of day.

Critical Thinking

(19) plesiosaurs, pterosaurs, lizards, crocodilians
(20) Coal swamps were characterized by lush tropical-like vegetation such as large trees with scales, seed ferns, scouring rushes, as well as large insects.
(21) North America was located near the equator. Due to plate movement, North America had moved away from the equatorial location to where it exists today.
(22) The early rock record has been obscured by Earth processes such as plate tectonics, erosion, and deposition.
(23) Earth's original atmosphere was made of water vapor, carbon dioxide, nitrogen, and several trace gases that were released by outgassing from molten rock from the interior (geosphere). Eventually carbon dioxide became mixed in the primitive oceans (hydrosphere) as they formed on the cooling surface. Photosynthetic organisms (biosphere), began releasing oxygen. Once the available iron was oxidized, substantial quantities of free oxygen accumulated in the atmosphere.
(24) Plants provide the majority of free oxygen in Earth's atmosphere.
(25) Some examples could include: Reptiles reproduce by laying eggs with shells. Amphibians do not have shelled eggs. Amphibians spend time in water and land environments. Reptiles can inhabit water, land, or air.

CHAPTER 13 Assessment *continued*

Critical Thinking

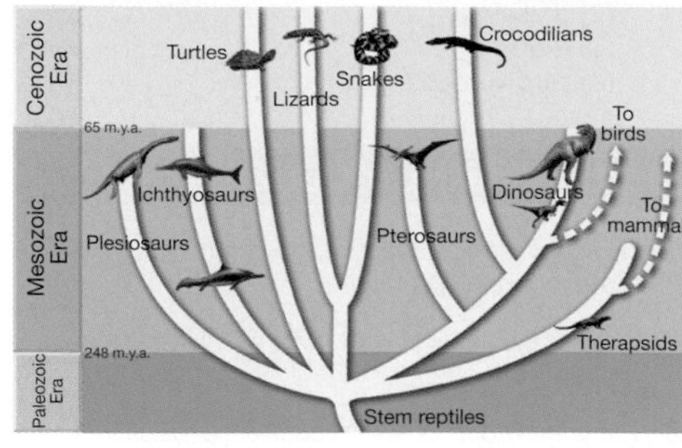

19 **Interpreting Diagrams** Examine the figure above, which shows the origin and development of reptile groups. Arrange these groups in relative chronological order from first appearance: crocodilians, lizards, plesiosaurs, and pterosaurs.

20 **Interpreting Photographs** Most of the vast North American coal resources located from Pennsylvania to Illinois began forming during the Pennsylvanian and Mississippian periods. Using Figure 10 on page 375, describe the climatic and biological conditions associated with this environment.

21 **Interpreting Diagrams** Examine Figure 8B and C. Where, relative to the equator, was North America located during the time of coal formation? What role did plate tectonics play in determining the conditions that produced North America's coal reserves? NY

22 **Making Generalizations** Why is so little known about the Precambrian time? NY

23 **Relating Cause and Effect** Describe the role of the biosphere, hydrosphere, and solid Earth in forming the current level of atmospheric oxygen. NY

24 **Inferring** What is the major source of free oxygen in Earth's atmosphere? NY

25 **Comparing and Contrasting** Make a list of differences between amphibians and reptiles.

Concepts in Action

26 **Classifying** Match the following words and phrases to the most appropriate time span. Select among the following: Precambrian, early Paleozoic, late Paleozoic, Mesozoic, and Cenozoic. NY

a Pangaea came into existence
b Encompasses the least amount of time
c Shields
d Age of dinosaurs
e Triassic, Jurassic, and Cretaceous
f Formation of most of the world's major iron-ore deposits
g Age of fishes
h Cambrian, Ordovician, and Silurian
i Golden age of trilobites
j Gymnosperms were dominant

27 **Writing in Science** Write a paragraph explaining the relationship between the development and movement of plants, herbivore animals, and carnivore animals.

Performance-Based Assessment

Researching Research and select several different types of gymnosperm and angiosperm plants that are mentioned in the chapter. Also, research more primitive plants that existed before gymnosperms. Write a paragraph describing each plant, including information on its physical structure, reproduction, and characteristics that might cause it to be more successful in some eras than others.

Concepts in Action

(26) (a) Paleozoic, (b) Cenozoic, (c) Precambrian, (d) Mesozoic, (e) Mesozoic, (f) Precambrian, (g) Paleozoic, (h) Paleozoic, (i) Paleozoic, (j) Mesozoic,
(27) Paragraphs should provide information about how these organisms interact, especially in obtaining food, and how these interactions helped organisms evolve and occupy a variety of niches throughout history. For example, birds that feed on seeds and fruits evolved rapidly during the Cenozoic in close association with the development and spread of flowering plants.

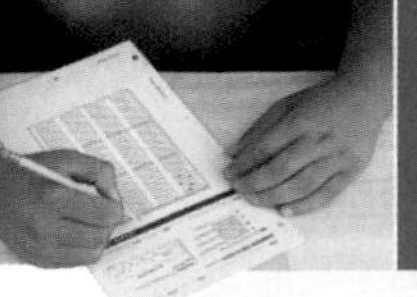

Regents Practice Exam

Test-Taking Tip

Anticipate the Answer
When answering multiple-choice questions, a useful strategy is to cover up the given answers and supply your own answer. Then compare your answer with those listed and select the one that most closely matches.

Practice anticipating the answer in this question.

Early in Earth's history, which gas was largely removed from the atmosphere and became more concentrated in seawater?
(1) oxygen
(2) carbon dioxide
(3) argon
(4) hydrogen

(Answer: 2)

For *each* statement or question, choose the *number* of the word or expression that, of those given, best completes the statement or answers the question. Some questions may require the use of the *Earth Science Reference Tables.*

1 During which geologic time period did the earliest dinosaurs live?
 (1) Cretaceous
 (2) Jurassic
 (3) Devonian
 (4) Triassic

2 Where did the water that makes up Earth's oceans originally come from?
 (1) water vapor that was present in the original atmosphere
 (2) water vapor dissolved in molten rock
 (3) liquid water from beneath Earth's surface
 (4) liquid water from the moon

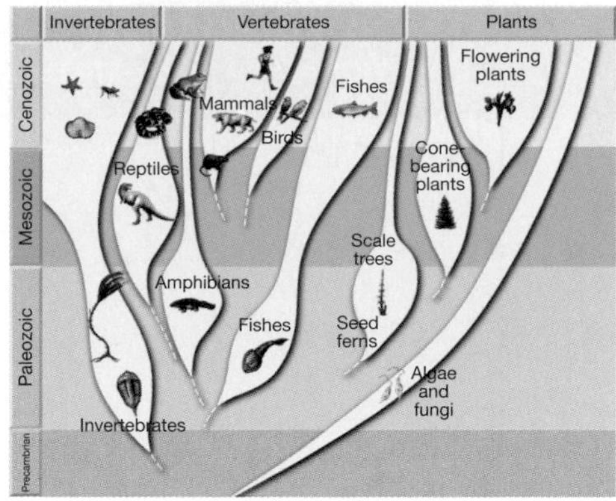

Answer the following questions in complete sentences. Some questions may require the use of the *Earth Science Reference Tables.* Base your answer to questions 3 and 4 on the diagram above, which shows the Origin and Development of Reptile Groups.

3 According to the diagram, which group of organisms appeared first?
 (1) invertebrates
 (2) flowering plants
 (3) algae and fungi
 (4) fishes

4 According to the diagram, when did the first mammals appear?
 (1) Precambrian
 (2) Paleozoic
 (3) Mesozoic
 (4) Cenozoic

5 On what basis is Earth's history divided into geologic time periods?

6 Why is so little known about the Precambrian era?

7 Select two cities in New York State that are likely to have similar fossils. State the names of the two cities and explain how you determined they would contain similar fossils.

Regents Practice Exam

(1) 4
(2) 2
(3) 3
(4) 3
(5) Earth's history is divided into geologic time periods based on fossil evidence.
(6) Very few fossils have been found from the Precambrian. Also, Precambrian rocks have been intensely metamorphosed, deformed, and eroded to the point that their original form often cannot be determined.
(7) Answers will vary, but all should include two cities that contain bedrock from the same geologic period, as show on the *Generalized Bedrock Geology of New York State* map found in the *Earth Science Reference Tables.*

Performance-Based Assessment

Research should focus on such gymnosperms as cycads, conifers, and ginkgoes. Angiosperms should include monocots such as irises, lilies, and grasses and dicots such as legumes, mustards, and fruit trees. Students might also research specific plants of the coal swamps of the Pennsylvania period such as scale trees, seed ferns, and scouring rushes.

Your students can independently test their knowledge of the chapter and print out their results.

CHAPTER 14

Planning Guide

Use these planning tools
Use Teacher Express for all your planning needs

SECTION OBJECTIVES	STANDARDS NATIONAL	STANDARDS STATE	ACTIVITIES and LABS
14.1 The Vast World Ocean, pp. 394–400 1 block or 2 periods **14.1** **Recognize** that most of Earth's surface is covered by water. **14.2** **List** Earth's four main ocean basins and **identify** their locations. **14.3** **Describe** the topography of the ocean floor and **compare** it to land. **14.4** **Identify** and **describe** three major technologies used to study the ocean floor.	A-1, A-2, E-2, G-1		**SE** Inquiry Activity: How Does Particle Size Affect Settling Rates? p. 393 L2 **TE** Teacher Demo: One Ocean, p. 394 L2
14.2 Ocean Floor Features, pp. 401–405 1 block or 2 periods **14.5** **List** the three main regions of the ocean floor. **14.6** **Differentiate** between the continental margins of the Atlantic and Pacific Oceans. **14.7** **Explain** the formation of new ocean floor at deep-ocean trenches, abyssal plains, and mid-ocean ridges.	A-2, B-3, D-2, F-3, G-1		**TE** Teacher Demo: Sediment Buildup, p. 404 L2 **SE** Exploration Lab: Modeling Seafloor Depth Transects, pp. 414–415 L2 **LM** Modeling the Ocean Floor L1
14.3 Seafloor Sediments, pp. 407–409 1 block or 2 periods **14.8** **List** the three types of ocean floor sediments. **14.9** **Describe** the formation of terrigenous, biogenous, and hydrogenous sediments.	D-2		**TE** Build Science Skills, p. 408 L2 **TE** Teacher Demo: Biogenous Deposits, p. 409 L2
14.4 Resources from the Seafloor, pp. 410–413 1 block or 2 periods **14.10** **Identify** ocean resources used for energy production. **14.11** **Explain** how gas hydrates are formed. **14.12** **List** other types of ocean resources.	A-1, A-2, D-2, E-2, F-3		**SE** Quick Lab: Evaporative Salts, p. 412 L2

Ability Levels

- **L1** For students who need additional help
- **L2** For all students
- **L3** For students who need to be challenged

Components

SE	Student Edition	**GRSW**	Guided Reading & Study Workbook	**TP**	Test Prep Resources	**GEO**	Geode CD-ROM
TE	Teacher's Edition	**TEX**	Teacher Express	**onT**	onlineText	**T**	Transparencies
LM	Laboratory Manual	**CTB**	Computer Test Bank	**DC**	Discovery Channel Videos	**GO**	Internet Resources
CUT	Chapter Tests						

RESOURCES PRINT and TECHNOLOGY	SECTION ASSESSMENT
GRSW Section 14.1 **T-173** Uneven Distribution of Land and Water Between Hemispheres **T-174** Distribution of Land and Water **T-175** Echo Sounders **T-176** Decay of U-238 **T-187** IJOIDES Resolution **DC** Seafloor Maps **TEX** Lesson Planning 14.1	**SE** Section 14.1 Assessment, p. 400 **onT** Section 4.1
GRSW Section 14.2 GEODe Oceans → Floor of the Ocean **T-177** Topography of Earth Map, Part 1 **T-178** Topography of Earth Map, Part 2 **T-179** Map and Profile of the North Atlantic **T-180** Passive Continental Margin **T-181** Submarine Canyons **T-182** Active Continental Margin **T-183** Seismic Cross-section of an Abyssal Plain **TEX** Lesson Planning 14.2	**SE** Section 14.2 Assessment, p. 405 **onT** Section 4.2
GRSW Section 14.3 **T-184** Distribution of Marine Sediment **T-185** Newfoundland Earthquake **T-186** Formation of Coral Atoll **TEX** Lesson Planning 14.3	**SE** Section 14.3 Assessment, p. 409 **onT** Section 4.3
GRSW Section 14.4 **TEX** Lesson Planning 14.4	**SE** Section 14.4 Assessment, p. 413 **onT** Section 4.4

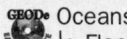

Go Online

Go online for these Internet resources.

PHSchool.com
Web Code: cjk-9999

Web Code: cjn-5141
Web Code: cjn-5142
Web Code: cjn-5144

Materials for Activities and Labs

Quantities for each group

STUDENT EDITION

Inquiry Activity, p. 393
2 large transparent containers, water, clay, sand, 2 sheets of white paper, hand lens, stopwatch

Quick Lab, p. 412
400 mL beaker, table salt, tablespoon, balance, glass stirrer

Exploration Lab, pp. 414–415
shoe box, modeling clay, aluminum foil, pencil, scalpel, graph paper

TEACHER'S EDITION

Teacher Demo, p. 394
world globe

Teacher Demo, p. 404
small glass aquarium tank, rocks, pebbles, coarse gravel, coarse and fine aquarium sand, bone meal or other fine material that settles out but does not dissolve quickly in water

Teacher Demo, p. 409
prepared microscope slides of diatoms, foraminifera, and radiolaria; or photographic slides of photomicrographs of these organisms and a slide projector

Chapter Assessment

ASSESSMENT

SE	Assessment, pp. 417–418
CUT	Chapter 14 Test
CTB	Chapter 14
onT	Chapter 14

STANDARDIZED TEST PREP

SE	Chapter 14, p. 419
TP	Progress Monitoring Assessments

interactive textbook with assessment at PHSchool.com

CHAPTER 14

Before you teach

Michael Wysession
Washington University

Big Ideas

Seventy-one percent of Earth's surface is covered by ocean water. There are four main ocean basins: the Pacific, Atlantic, Indian, and Arctic. The bathymetry of the ocean seafloor is very varied, a result of many different geological processes.

Space and Time The margins of continents (including the continental shelf, slope, and rise) are often under sea water. The ocean floor is deepest at trenches, where oceanic lithosphere sinks back into the mantle. The seafloor bathymetry also varies with the presence of seamounts, fracture zones, and mid-ocean ridges. Ocean sediments (formed chemically, biologically, or carried in from the continents) cover most of the ocean floor. These sediments are shallowest at mid-ocean ridges, and often thickest along continental margins.

Forces and Motion The ocean seafloor forms at mid-ocean ridges, which rest higher than the surrounding basin seafloor because the new rock is hot and buoyant. Hot water circulating through the mid-ocean ridge system removes metals and minerals from the crust out of hydrothermal vents.

Matter and Energy A variety of technologies are used to investigate the ocean. Sonar is used to map seafloor bathymetry. Microwaves transmitted from satellites are used to map the ocean surface and seafloor features. Underwater submersibles directly investigate the seafloor.

Earth as a System The ocean is the source of many important natural resources such as oil, natural gas, gas hydrates (as of yet untapped), sand, gravel, salts, and metals.

Earth Science Refresher

Guyots, Parabolas, and Sea Level

When new ocean lithosphere forms at mid-ocean ridges, the rock is very hot, so it is less dense than surrounding rock. As a result, the ridges rise higher than the average seafloor depth. As the ocean plate cools, it becomes denser and therefore sinks. The result is that the ocean floor continues to sink after it forms at a ridge (until it reaches equilibrium, after about 80 million years). This is why guyots, flat-topped seamounts, are so common. Oceanic islands are continuously sinking along with the entire seafloor.

Interestingly, the bathymetry of the cooling, sinking seafloor has a particular shape. It turns out that the cooling of the ocean plate occurs most rapidly right after it forms, and then gradually cools more slowly. The result is that the distance away from the ridge is proportional to the square of the temperature of the ocean plate, and therefore the depth to the seafloor. Any curve with an equation such as $y = x^2$ is a parabola, so the bathymetry of the seafloor makes the shape of a parabola as it moves away from the ridge.

One very important result of the sinking of cooling ocean lithosphere concerns global sea levels. During the Cretaceous Period, sea levels were about 300 m higher than the present time, flooding major portions of the continents. However, if all of Earth's glacial ice were melted today, sea level would only rise

Address Misconceptions

Many students may think that features such as seamounts and mid-ocean ridges formed exclusively in the past, and fail to recognize the ongoing processes that continue to shape the ocean floor. Explain that tectonic activity continues to cause changes in ocean topography. For a strategy that helps to overcome this misconception, see **Address Misconceptions** of **p. 404.**

Go Online PD LINKS NSTA

For: Chapter 14 Content Support
Visit: www.SciLinks.org/PDLinks
Web Code: cjn-1499

about 80 m. How, then, is it possible to flood the continents? It turns out that during the Cretaceous Period there were many ridge systems, and plate velocities were relatively fast. This meant that there was a lot of warm ocean lithosphere, so the average level of the seafloor was much higher than today. If you lift up the seafloor, the water gets pushed up onto the continents. This has happened several times in Earth's history, with the result that many parts of the continents that are now far from the ocean are covered with horizontal layers of sedimentary rock like shale, sandstone, and limestone, all of which formed under water.

The Ocean Seafloor Mineral Factory

The theory of plate tectonics explains many things about Earth's geology, but one of the most relevant has to do with the global distribution of resources of metals and ores. It turns out that high concentrations of metals and ores are often found at subduction zones or ancient subduction zones. Why is this? The answer, interestingly, begins at mid-ocean ridges. The high volumes of water circulating through the mid-ocean ridge act like a chemical factory, removing metals and ores from the ocean crust. Cold water is pulled into the crust, and as it heats up, it begins to dissolve out incompatible elements like metals. This can be seen at mid-ocean ridge thermal vents, which are so rich in metals that the water is black. When the hot water rises up into the ocean, however, the metals precipitate out onto the seafloor. Then, these metals are carried toward an ocean trench along the ocean floor, like a slow conveyor belt. Upon reaching the trench of the subduction zone, some of the metals are scraped off into accretionary wedges. Others are subducted, but rise back up as part of the magma that forms subduction zone volcanoes. In either case, the process of plate tectonics removes metals and ores from ocean crust and concentrates it at subduction zones.

Build Reading Literacy

Preview

Skim Ahead to Understand Text Organization

Strategy Get an advance idea of how the text is organized and activate prior knowledge. This prereading strategy involves skimming the titles, headings, visuals, and boldfaced text. Like checking a roadmap before beginning a trip, previewing helps the reader to recall familiar material and to prepare to learn new material. Before students begin to read, select a portion of Chapter 14 for them to preview, such as pp. 394–400.

Example

1. Ask students to look at the chapter title, section titles, and heads. Tell them to notice whether the terms and concepts mentioned are familiar or unfamiliar.
2. Have students look at the Reading Focus for the specific section to be previewed.
3. Ask students to compare the key concepts and the boldfaced statements in the section.
4. Have students look at the visuals in the section and (where possible) relate each to a specific heading.
5. You may wish to have students prepare a study guide using the headings, key concept questions, and vocabulary as categories in a chart showing the section organization. Have students read the selected pages in depth, filling in the chart with details as they read.

See p. 402 for a script on how to use this strategy with students. For additional strategies, see pp. 399 and 408.

ASSESS PRIOR KNOWLEDGE

Use the Chapter Pretest below to assess students' prior knowledge. As needed, review these concepts.

Review Science Concepts

Section 14.1 Reviewing the size and geography of the ocean basins will help students recognize the importance of Earth's oceans as a component of Earth Science. Learning about methods used to map the ocean floor leads to an understanding of the multidisciplinary nature of oceanography.

Section 14.2 Knowledge of the features of the ocean floor and how they are formed allows students to compare the geology of the ocean floor with the geology of land features.

Section 14.3 Understanding how ocean sediments are formed gives students an opportunity to explore how geology, biology, and chemistry contribute to the study of oceanography.

Section 14.4 Knowledge of how energy and mineral resources form on and under the ocean floor helps ensure that students understand the economic importance of ocean resources and the technological challenges involved in recovering those resources.

Review Math Skills

Calculating; Line Graphs Students need to calculate rates of speed and graph data.

Direct students to the **Math Skills** in the **Skill Handbook** at the end of the student text.

CHAPTER

14 The Ocean Floor

CONCEPTS in Action

Quick Lab
Evaporative Salts

Exploration Lab
Modeling Seafloor Depth Transects

Understanding Earth
Explaining Coral Atolls—Darwin's Hypothesis

Oceans
↳ Floor of the Ocean

Video Field Trip
Seafloor Maps

Take a field trip to the bottom of the sea with Discovery Channel and learn how the ocean floor can be measured. Answer the following questions after watching the video.

1. Describe how sonar technology can help scientists map an area of sea floor.
2. Does sonar technology provide realistic measurements for the entire ocean floor? Why or why not?

Go Online
PHSchool.com

For: Chapter 14 Resources
Visit: PHSchool.com
Web Code: cjk-9999

This photograph shows a view of the Atlantic Ocean near Cape Canaveral, Florida. ▶

Chapter Pretest

1. Approximately how much of Earth's surface is covered by ocean? *(c)*
   a. 60% b. 66%
   c. 71% d. 78%
2. Which of the following is not a major topographic region of the ocean floor? *(c)*
   a. mid-ocean ridge
   b. continental margin
   c. coral atoll
   d. ocean basin floor
3. Which of the following is not a feature found on the ocean floor? *(b)*
   a. abyssal plain
   b. coral atoll
   c. submarine canyon
   d. guyot
4. Sediments that cover the ocean floor come from which of the following? *(d)*
   a. life forms **b.** land
   c. water **d.** all of the above
4. Name the Earth's four main ocean basins. *(Pacific, Atlantic, Indian, Arctic)*
5. Name three kinds of technologies used to study the ocean floor. *(sonar, satellite, submersibles)*
6. Name at least five natural resources that are mined from the ocean floor. *(oil, natural gas, gas hydrates, sand and gravel, evaporative salts, manganese nodules)*

Chapter Preview

Inquiry Activity

How Does Particle Size Affect Settling Rates?

Procedure

1. Fill two large transparent containers with water. Place two samples of sediment, one clay and one sand, on separate sheets of white paper. Examine the sediments with a hand lens. Determine which sediment sample has larger-sized particles. Record your observations.
2. Carefully measure 1 tbsp of the clay sample. Hold the spoon directly above the first container and pour the clay into the water. Using a stopwatch, time how long it takes for the entire clay sample to reach the bottom of the container and settle. Record the time.
3. Repeat Step 2 using the second container and the sand sample. Be sure to hold the spoon the same distance from the container as you did in the clay sample.

Think About It

1. **Drawing Conclusions** Which sample had smaller particles? Which sample took longer to settle in the water? Explain the general relationship between sediment size and settling rates.
2. **Predicting** Both of these sediments enter ocean water from rivers. Predict which type of sediment would be found closest to the coast. Which will be found father away? Explain.

Discovery Channel School **Video Field Trip**
Seafloor Maps

Encourage students to view the Video Field Trip "Seafloor Maps."

ENGAGE/EXPLORE

How Does Particle Size Affect Settling Rates?

Purpose In this activity, students will begin to

- recognize that sediment particle size affects settling rate.
- understand that settling rates affect how far sediments can be carried by river water that enters the ocean.

Skills Focus **Measuring, Inferring**

Prep Time 15 minutes

Materials 2 large transparent containers, water, clay, sand, 2 sheets of white paper, hand lens, stopwatch

Class Time 15–20 minutes

Expected Outcome Clay sample has smaller particles and takes longer to settle. Sand has larger particles and takes less time to settle.

Think About It

1. The clay sample has smaller particles and takes longer to settle. The smaller and finer the sediment, the longer it will take to settle.
2. Sand, which is larger, will settle first and will be found closer to the coast. Clay takes longer to settle, will be carried farther by ocean currents, and will reach areas further from the coast.

Section 14.1

1 FOCUS

Section Objectives

14.1 **Recognize** that most of Earth's surface is covered by water.

14.2 **List** Earth's four main ocean basins and **identify** their locations.

14.3 **Describe** the topography of the ocean floor and **compare** it to land.

14.4 **Identify** and **describe** three major technologies used to study the ocean floor.

Reading Focus

Build Vocabulary L2

Word Parts Before students read this section, ask them to write the meanings of the prefix *bathy-* and the suffix *-metry*. Then have them write what they think the word *bathymetry* means. After students read the section, have them discuss whether their prediction was correct.

Reading Strategy L2

a. science that studies all aspects of the world's ocean
b. measurement of ocean depths and charting the shape of the ocean floor
c. echo sounding to measure ocean depth
d. small underwater craft used for deep-sea research

2 INSTRUCT

The Blue Planet

One Ocean L2

Purpose Students see how Earth's ocean basins are connected.

Materials world globe

Procedure Have students point out the regions on the globe where oceans connect.

Expected Outcome Students will see that the Atlantic, Pacific, and Indian Oceans connect in the region surrounding Antarctica. The Atlantic and Pacific Oceans connect with the Arctic Ocean.
Visual, Logical

14.1 The Vast World Ocean

Reading Focus

Key Concepts

- How much of Earth's surface is covered by water?
- How can the world ocean be divided?
- How does the topography of the ocean floor compare to that on land?
- What types of technology are used to study the ocean floor?

Vocabulary

- oceanography
- bathymetry
- sonar
- submersible

Reading Strategy

Building Vocabulary Draw a table similar to the one below that includes all the vocabulary terms listed for the section. As you read the section, define each term in your own words.

Vocabulary Term	Definition
oceanography	a. ?
bathymetry	b. ?
sonar	c. ?
submersible	d. ?

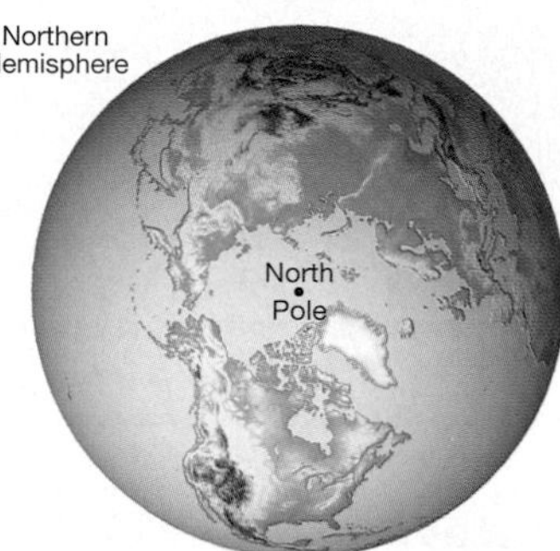

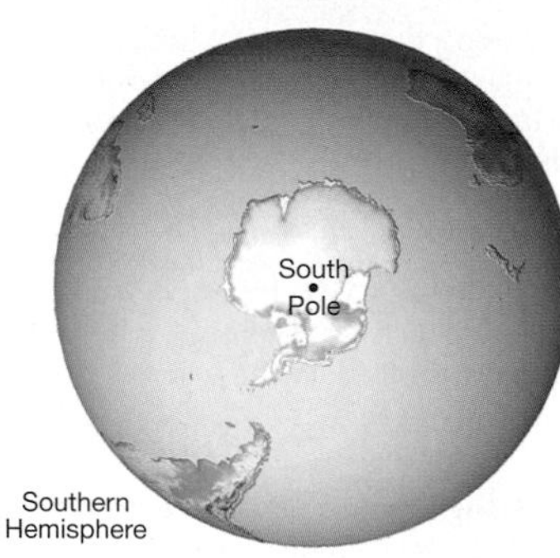

Figure 1 The World Ocean These views of Earth show the planet is dominated by a single interconnected world ocean.

How deep is the ocean? How much of Earth is covered by the global ocean? What does the ocean floor look like? Humans have long been interested in finding answers to these questions. However, it was not until relatively recently that these simple questions could be answered. Suppose, for example, that all of the water were drained from the ocean. What would we see? Plains? Mountains? Canyons? Plateaus? You may be surprised to find that the ocean conceals all of these features, and more.

The Blue Planet

Look at Figure 1. You can see why the "blue planet" or the "water planet" are appropriate nicknames for Earth. **Nearly 71 percent of Earth's surface is covered by the global ocean.** Although the ocean makes up a much greater percentage of Earth's surface than the continents, it has only been since the late 1800s that the ocean became an important focus of study. New technologies have allowed scientists to collect large amounts of data about the oceans. As technology has advanced, the field of oceanography has grown. **Oceanography** is a science that draws on the methods and knowledge of geology, chemistry, physics, and biology to study all aspects of the world ocean.

Distribution of Land and Water

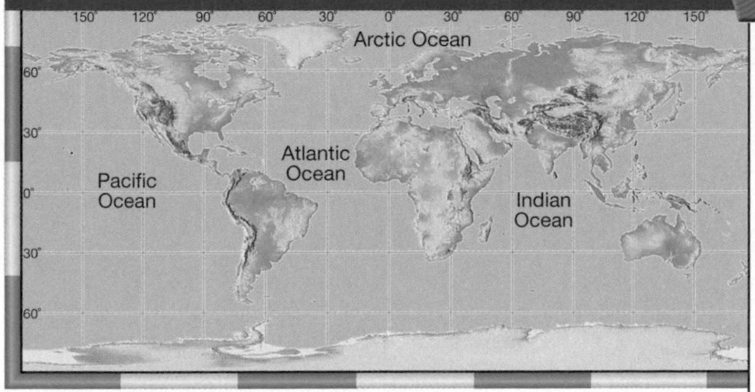

Arctic Ocean

Pacific Ocean

Atlantic Ocean

Indian Ocean

MAP MASTER™ Skills Activity

Figure 2

Human-Environment Interaction The four main ocean basins are the Pacific Ocean, the Atlantic Ocean, the Indian Ocean, and the Arctic Ocean.

Predicting What is the longitude of the easternmost point of the Pacific Ocean? What is the longitude of the westernmost point of the Atlantic Ocean?

Geography of the Oceans

The area of Earth is about 510 million square kilometers. Of this total, approximately 360 million square kilometers, or 71 percent, is represented by oceans and smaller seas such as the Mediterranean Sea and the Caribbean Sea. Continents and islands comprise the remaining 29 percent, or 150 million square kilometers. **The world ocean can be divided into four main ocean basins—the Pacific Ocean, the Atlantic Ocean, the Indian Ocean, and the Arctic Ocean.** These ocean basins are shown in Figure 2.

The Pacific Ocean is the largest ocean. In fact, it is the largest single geographic feature on Earth. It covers more than half of the ocean surface area on Earth. It is also the world's deepest ocean, with an average depth of 3940 meters.

The Atlantic Ocean is about half the size of the Pacific Ocean, and is not quite as deep. It is a relatively narrow ocean compared to the Pacific. The Atlantic and Pacific Oceans are bounded to the east and west by continents.

The Indian Ocean is slightly smaller than the Atlantic Ocean, but it has about the same average depth. Unlike the Pacific and Atlantic oceans, the Indian Ocean is located almost entirely in the southern hemisphere.

The Arctic Ocean is about 7 percent of the size of the Pacific Ocean. It is only a little more than one-quarter as deep as the rest of the oceans.

What are the four main ocean basins?

MAP MASTER™ Skills Activity

Answer

Predicting easternmost point of Pacific: approximately 70°W; westernmost point of Atlantic: approximately 100°W

Geography of the Oceans

Integrate Math

L2

Geometry and Projections Explain to students that the map pictured on this page is a Mercator projection. Because Earth is a sphere, two-dimensional representations of Earth invariably have some distortion. On projections such as this, the degree of distortion increases with distance from the equator. Ask: **Where on this projection is distortion greatest?** *(the northern and southern extremes, or the poles)* **What landmasses do you think are the most distorted?** *(Greenland and Antarctica)* **Explain in geometric terms why these landmasses are so distorted.** *(Since Earth is a sphere, lines of longitude come closer together as distance from the equator increases. These lines meet at the poles. To represent a spherical body as a two-dimensional grid, the lines run parallel rather than meeting at the poles, and the features between them become stretched.)*
Visual, Logical

Customize for Inclusion Students

Visually Impaired Provide students with a relief world map or globe. Allow students to experience the interconnected nature of the world's oceans by helping them trace the outlines of the oceans with their fingers. Students can also compare the sizes of Earth's four main ocean basins. This learning tool can be used by both visually impaired students and tactile learners. (A relief map of the ocean floor can be used in a similar way to allow students to experience deep ocean trenches, ridges, seamounts, and guyots.)

Answer to . . .

Pacific Ocean, Atlantic Ocean, Indian Ocean, Arctic Ocean

Mapping the Ocean Floor

Use Visuals L1

Figure 3 Have students examine the map showing the topographic features of the ocean floor. Ask: **In which ocean basin are most of the oceanic trenches located?** *(Pacific)* **Which ocean basins contain oceanic ridges?** *(Atlantic, Indian)* **What is the major undersea geological feature in the Atlantic Ocean?** *(Mid-Atlantic Ridge)* **What kind of geological feature is the Hawaiian islands a part of?** *(a linear chain of undersea volcanoes)*

Build Science Skills 

Posing Questions Have students write one or more questions they have about the characteristics of the ocean floor. Ask them to formulate each question so that it could be used as the basis for scientific research. *(Sample questions:* **Does the chemical composition of seawater vary from place to place around the world? What methods can be used to accurately measure the speed of ocean currents?***)* After students have written their questions, ask them to describe how they might go about answering their questions. *(Sample answers: Collect and analyze seawater samples from a variety of locations. Design an experiment or field study to test different devices used to measure water speed.)* If necessary, assist students in phrasing their questions so that they can serve as the basis for a scientific inquiry.
Verbal, Logical

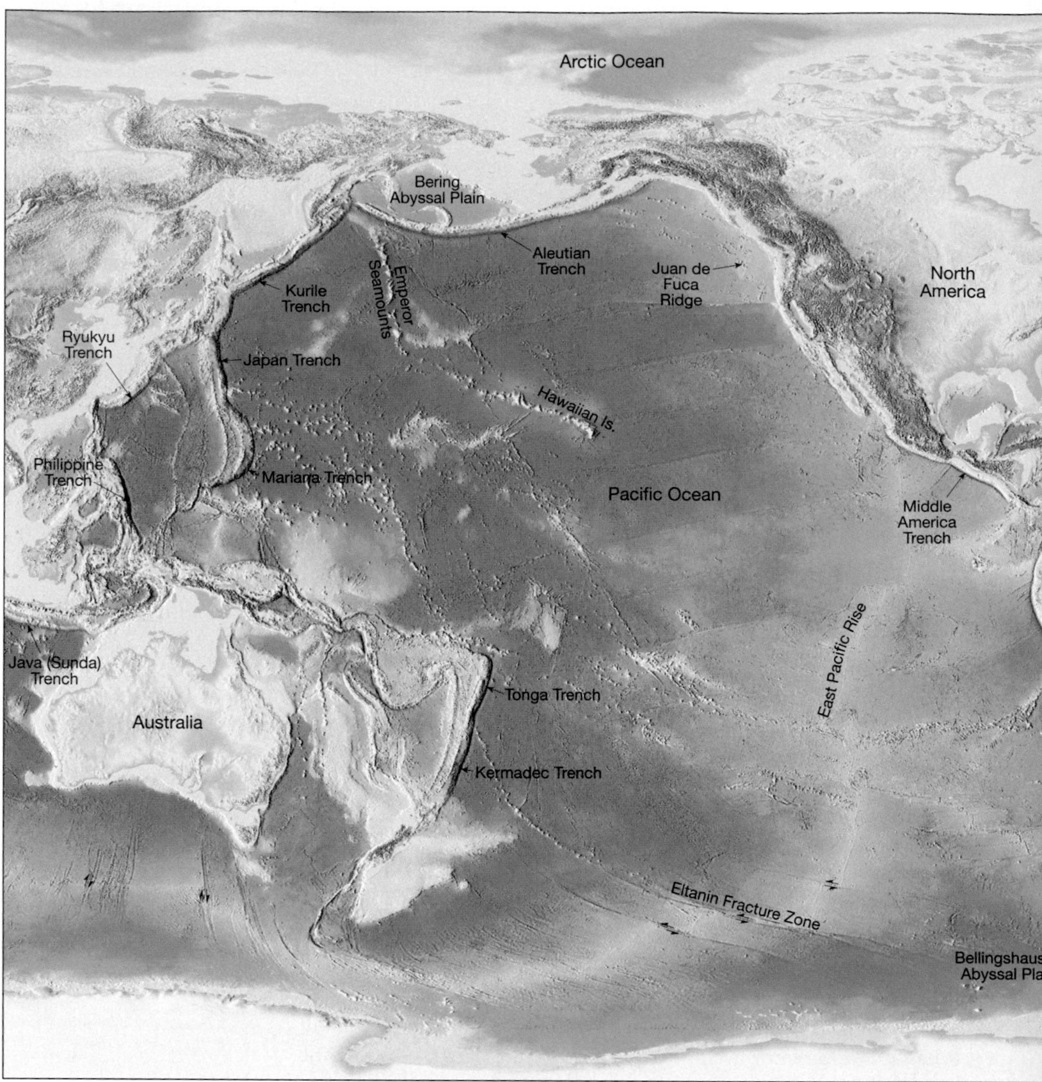

Figure 3 The topography of the ocean floor is as varied as the topography of the continents. The ocean floor contains mountain ranges, trenches, and flat regions called abyssal plains.
Interpreting Diagrams ***List all of the features you can identify in the figure.***

Mapping the Ocean Floor

If all the water were drained from the ocean basins, a variety of features would be seen. These features include chains of volcanoes, tall mountain ranges, trenches, and large submarine plateaus. **The topography of the ocean floor is as diverse as that of continents.** The topographic features of the ocean floor are shown in Figure 3.

An understanding of ocean-floor features came with the development of techniques to measure the depth of the oceans. **Bathymetry**

Facts and Figures

On average, the depth of the oceans is more than four times the elevation of the continents. The average elevation of the continents is about 840 m above sea level. The average depth of the oceans is 3729 m. If Earth's solid mass were perfectly smooth and spherical, ocean water would cover it all to a depth of more than 2000 m.

(*bathos* = depth, *metry* = measurement) is the measurement of ocean depths and the charting of the shape or topography of the ocean floor.

The first understanding of the ocean floor's varied topography did not unfold until the historic three-and-a-half-year voyage of the HMS *Challenger*. From December 1872 to May 1876, the *Challenger* expedition made the first—and perhaps still the most comprehensive—study of the global ocean ever attempted by one agency. The 127,500 kilometer trip took the ship and its crew of scientists to every ocean

For: Links on oceans
Visit: www.SciLinks.org
Web Code: cjn-5141

Integrate Social Studies L2

Challenger Expedition Explain to students that the journey of the *HMS Challenger* is considered by many to be the birth of the science of oceanography. Before the Challenger Expedition, enough information about Earth's oceans had been collected to make scientists and sailors alike realize that an extensive ocean survey would be of great benefit. The success of the expedition inspired the launching of many subsequent ocean research surveys. Point out to students that the expedition took place during a time when most ships used wind and sail for propulsion, and submarine cables carried most transoceanic communications. Ask: **In what ways would data on ocean currents, prevailing winds, and weather patterns collected by *Challenger* scientists have been useful to others?** *(added to knowledge about the oceans; provided help to sailors and ship captains trying to chart the best course for a journey)* **In what ways would depth measurements and other data about the nature of the ocean bottom have been helpful to others?** *(assist companies in making decisions about where and how to lay submarine cables)*
Verbal

Download a worksheet on oceans for students to complete, and find additional teacher support from NSTA SciLinks.

Facts and Figures

The Challenger Expedition took data from 362 locations scattered throughout the Atlantic, Pacific, and Indian Oceans. Scientists traveling with the expedition took charge of different research aspects. Matthew Maury (1806–1873), an American naval officer, was in charge of charts and instruments. Edward Forbes (1815–1854) was a British biologist who had already done extensive research in shallower waters around Britain and in the Aegean Sea. Forbes led the expedition's collection and analysis of biological specimens. Before the expedition, Forbes had predicted that life would not be found below about 2000 m in the deep sea. Challenger Expedition findings proved that life existed at least as deep as 6000 m; it is now known that life exists even at the bottom of the deepest ocean trenches.

Answer to . . .

Figure 3 *mid-ocean ridges, trenches, abyssal plains, seamounts*

Build Math Skills L1

Line Graphs Have students graph sonar results for a hypothetical transect of the ocean bottom. Provide students with the following time intervals for four sonar data points, each taken 10 km apart. Sample data: 3.2 s, 5.5 s, 7.2 s, 6.4 s. First, have students calculate the depth for each data point (time/2 × 1500 m/s). *(3.2 s: 2400 m; 5.5 s: 4125 m; 7.2 s: 5400 m; 6.4 s: 4800 m)* Second, invite students to graph their results, placing distance (km) between data points on the *x*-axis and depth (m) on the *y*-axis. Have students connect their data points to create a line on the graph. Ask students what the line represents. *(a rough profile of part of the ocean floor)*

Logical, Visual

Build Science Skills 

Inferring Remind students of the difference between sound waves and microwaves. Sound waves are produced by vibrating matter. Microwaves are a form of electromagnetic energy. Ask: **Which type of wave has more energy?** *(microwaves)* **Why can't sound waves be used to gather ocean height data from satellites?** *(Sound waves must have a medium to travel through. Satellites orbit high in Earth's atmosphere, where there are too few molecules to transmit sound.)*

Logical, Verbal

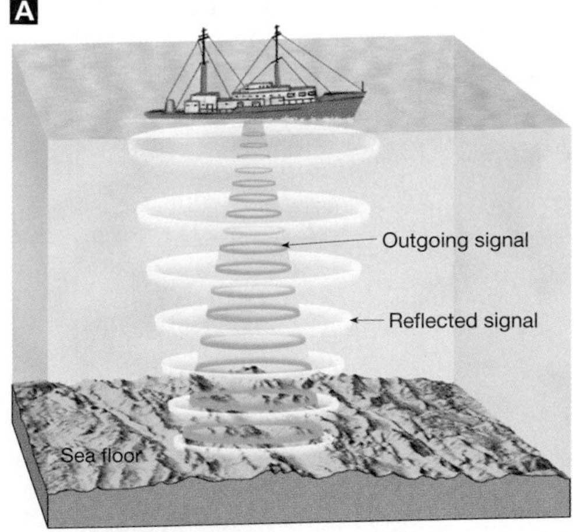

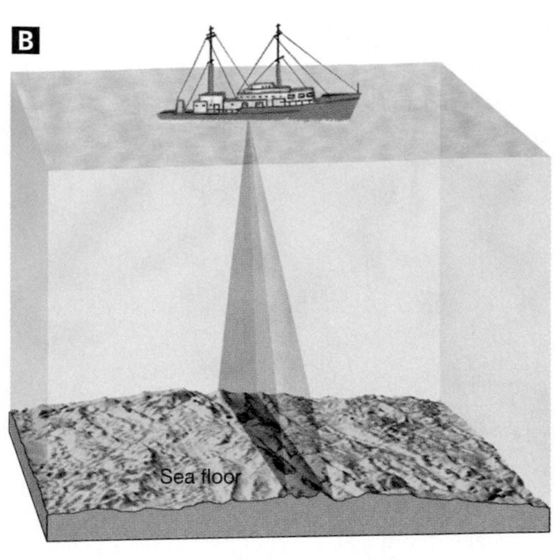

Figure 4 Sonar Methods
A By using sonar, oceanographers can determine the depth of the ocean floor in a particular area.
B Modern multibeam sonar obtains a profile of a narrow swath of seafloor every few seconds.

except the Arctic. Throughout the voyage, they sampled various ocean properties. They measured water depth by lowering a long, weighted line overboard. **Today's technology—particularly sonar, satellites, and submersibles—allows scientists to study the ocean floor in a more efficient and precise manner than ever before.**

Sonar In the 1920s, a technological breakthrough occurred with the invention of sonar, a type of electronic depth-sounding equipment. Sonar is an acronym for **so**und **na**vigation **a**nd **r**anging. It is also referred to as echo sounding. Sonar works by transmitting sound waves toward the ocean bottom, as shown in Figure 4A. With simple sonar, a sensitive receiver intercepts the echo reflected from the bottom. Then a clock precisely measures the time interval to fractions of a second. Depth can be calculated from the speed of sound waves in water—about 1500 meters per second—and the time required for the energy pulse to reach the ocean floor and return. The depths determined from continuous monitoring of these echoes are plotted. In this way a profile of the ocean floor is obtained. A chart of the seafloor can be produced by combining these profiles.

In the last few decades, researchers have designed even more sophisticated sonar to map the ocean floor. In contrast to simple sonar, multibeam sonar uses more than one sound source and listening device. As you can see from Figure 4B, this technique obtains a profile of a narrow strip of ocean floor rather than obtaining the depth of a single point every few seconds. These profiles are recorded every few seconds as the research vessel advances. When a ship uses multibeam sonar to make a map of a section of ocean floor, the ship travels through the area in a regularly spaced back-and-forth pattern. Not surprisingly, this method is known as "mowing the lawn."

Satellites Measuring the shape of the ocean surface from space is another technological breakthrough that has led to a better understanding of the ocean floor. After compensating for waves, tides, currents, and atmospheric effects, scientists discovered that the ocean surface is not perfectly flat. This is because gravity attracts water toward regions where massive ocean floor features occur. Therefore, mountains and ridges produce elevated areas on the ocean surface. Features such as canyons and trenches cause slight depressions.

The differences in ocean-surface height caused by ocean floor features are not visible to the human eye. However, satellites are able to measure these small differences by bouncing microwaves off the ocean surface. Figure 5 shows how the outgoing radar pulses are reflected back to a satellite. The height of the ocean surface can be calculated by knowing the satellite's exact position. Devices on satellites can measure variations in sea-surface height as small as 3 to 6 centimeters. This type of data has added greatly to the knowledge of ocean-floor topography. Cross-checked with traditional sonar depth measurements, the data are used to produce detailed ocean-floor maps, such as the one previously shown in Figure 3.

How do satellites help us learn about the shape of the seafloor?

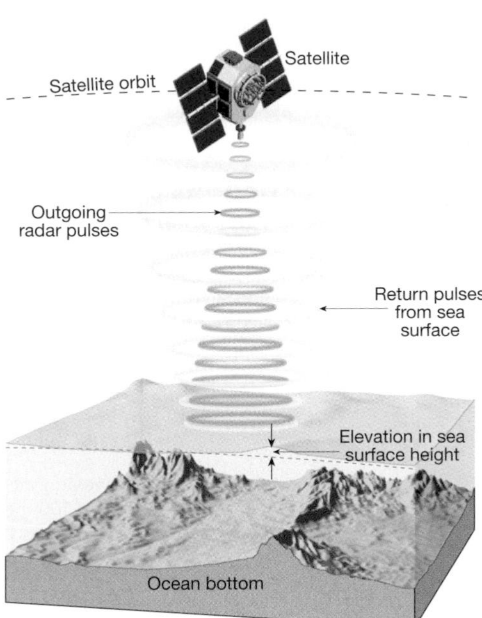

Figure 5 Satellite Method
Satellites can be used to measure sea-surface height. The data collected by satellites can be used to predict the location of large features on the seafloor. This method of data collection is much faster than using sonar.

Build Reading Literacy 

Refer to **p. 216D** in **Chapter 8,** which provides guidelines for this compare and contrast strategy.

Compare and Contrast After students have read the sections on bathymetric methods, have them create a table that compares simple sonar, multibeam sonar, and satellite bathymetry technologies in terms of data collection method used and the type of data obtained. Ask students to summarize advantages or disadvantages of each technology with respect to the others.

	Simple sonar	Multibeam sonar	Satellite
Method	Sound waves	Sound waves	Microwaves
Type of data	Ocean floor depth	Ocean floor depth	Ocean surface height, correlated to ocean depth
Advantages	Simple to use	More detailed	Most detailed of all
Disadvantages	Time-consuming	Time-consuming	Must be cross-checked with sonar measurements

Verbal, Visual

Answer to . . .

 *Satellites bounce microwaves off the ocean surface. Outgoing radar pulses are reflected back to the satellite and can be used to detect differences in sea surface height that can be correlated to seafloor features.*

Section 14.1 (continued)

Build Science Skills 

Communicating Results Have students work in small groups to research information about submersibles and the scientists who use them. Have each group investigate a different submersible. Possibilities include William Beebe's sphere, *Trieste*, *Alvin*, *Sea Cliff II*, and *Jason*. Have the groups orally present their findings to the class.

3 ASSESS

Evaluate Understanding 

To assess students' knowledge of section content, have them write a short paragraph comparing the ocean floor to Earth's landmasses. Have them write another paragraph describing how sonar, satellites, and submersibles can be used to gather data about the deep ocean.

Reteach 

Have students create a timeline that describes how bathymetric techniques have changed over the years since the *Challenger* expedition. Invite students to explain their timelines and each of the methods shown on their timelines to the class.

Solution

8. 4.5 s/2 × 1500 m/s = 3375 m

Submersibles A **submersible** is a small underwater craft used for deep-sea research. Submersibles are used to collect data about areas of the ocean that were previously unreachable by humans. Submersibles are equipped with a number of instruments ranging from thermometers to cameras to pressure gauges. The operators of submersibles can record video and photos of previously unknown creatures that live in the abyss. They can collect water samples and sediment samples for analysis.

The first submersible was used in 1934 by William Beebe. He descended to a depth of 923 meters off of Bermuda in a steel sphere that was tethered to a ship. Since that time, submersibles have become more sophisticated. In 1960, Jacques Piccard descended in the untethered submersible *Trieste* to 10,912 meters below the ocean surface into the Mariana Trench. *Alvin* and *Sea Cliff II* are two other manned submersibles used for deep-sea research. *Alvin* can reach depths of 4000 meters, and *Sea Cliff II* can reach 6000 meters.

Today, many submersibles are unmanned and operated remotely by computers. These remotely operated vehicles (ROVs) can remain under water for long periods. They collect data, record video, use sonar, and collect sample organisms with remotely operated arms. Another type of submersible, the autonomous underwater vehicle (AUV), is under development. Its goal is to collect long-term data without interruption.

Section 14.1 Assessment

Reviewing Concepts

1. How does the area of Earth's surface covered by the oceans compare with the area covered by land?
2. Name the four ocean basins. Which of the four ocean basins is the largest? Which is located almost entirely in the southern hemisphere?
3. How does the topography of the ocean floor compare to that on land? Name three topographic features found on the ocean floor.
4. What types of technology are used to study the ocean floor?
5. Describe how sonar is used to determine seafloor depth.

Critical Thinking

6. **Comparing and Contrasting** Compare and contrast the use of satellites and submersibles to collect data about the topography of the seafloor.
7. **Inferring** Why is deep-sea exploration and data collection difficult?

Math Practice

8. Assuming the average speed of sound waves in water is 1500 meters per second, determine the water depth in meters if a sonar signal requires 4.5 seconds to hit the bottom and return to the recorder.

Section 14.1 Assessment

1. Nearly 71 percent of Earth's surface is covered by oceans, 29 percent is covered by land.
2. Pacific Ocean, Atlantic Ocean, Indian Ocean, Arctic Ocean; Pacific Ocean; Indian Ocean
3. The topography of the ocean floor is as diverse as that of continents. Three topographic features: mid-ocean ridges, trenches, abyssal plains.
4. sonar, satellites, submersibles
5. Sonar works by transmitting sound waves to the ocean bottom. A receiver intercepts the echo reflected from the ocean bottom and a clock measures the time it takes for the sound wave to travel to the ocean bottom and back.
6. Both are used to find out more about the seafloor's topography. Satellites use remote sensing to bounce microwaves off the sea surface to determine differences in height. Submersibles can be manned or unmanned, travel to deep areas, and record data with video and other instruments.
7. The deep ocean is a harsh environment for humans—cold, dark, and under high pressure. It is difficult to supply submersibles with power for continuous use.

400 Chapter 14

14.2 Ocean Floor Features

Reading Focus

Key Concepts

- What are the three main regions of the ocean floor?
- How do continental margins in the Atlantic Ocean differ from those in the Pacific Ocean?
- How are deep-ocean trenches formed?
- How are abyssal plains formed?
- What is formed at mid-ocean ridges?

Vocabulary

- continental margin
- continental shelf
- continental slope
- submarine canyon
- turbidity current
- continental rise
- ocean basin floor
- abyssal plains
- seamounts
- mid-ocean ridge
- seafloor spreading

Reading Strategy

Outlining Before you read, make an outline of this section. Use the green headings as the main topics and the blue headings as subtopics. As you read, add supporting details.

I. Continental Margins
  A. Continental Shelf
  B. Continental Slope
  C. ____?____
II. ____?____
  A. ____?____

Oceanographers studying the topography of the ocean floor have divided it into three major regions. **The ocean floor regions are the continental margins, the ocean basin floor, and the mid-ocean ridge.** The map in Figure 6 outlines these regions for the North Atlantic Ocean. The profile at the bottom of the illustration shows the varied topography. Scientists have discovered that each of these regions has its own unique characteristics and features.

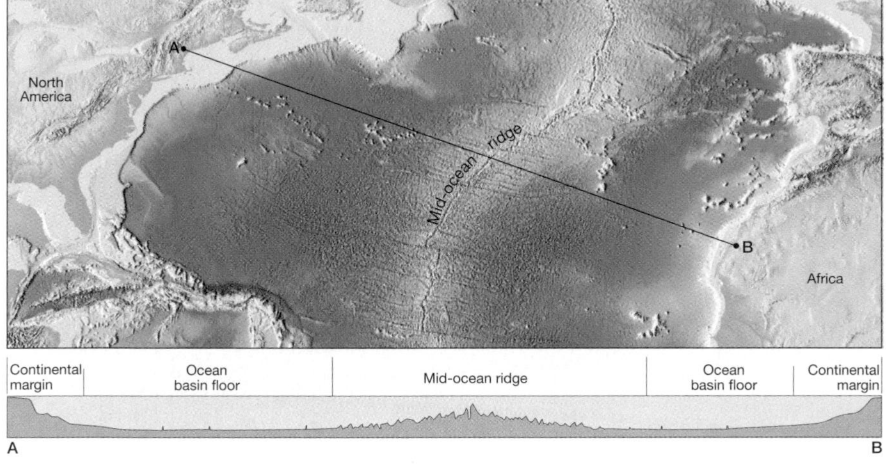

Figure 6 Topography of the North Atlantic Ocean Basin Beneath the map is a profile of the area between points A and B. The profile has been exaggerated 40 times to make the topographic features more distinct.

Section 14.2

1 FOCUS

Section Objectives

14.5 **List** the three main regions of the ocean floor.
14.6 **Differentiate** between the continental margins of the Atlantic and Pacific Oceans.
14.7 **Explain** the formation of new ocean floor at deep-ocean trenches, abyssal plains, and mid-ocean ridges.

Reading Focus

Build Vocabulary L2

Concept Map Have students make a concept map using the term *ocean floor features* as the starting point. All the vocabulary terms in this section should be used.

Reading Strategy L2

  C. Continental Rise
II. Ocean Basin Floor
  A. Deep-Ocean Trenches
  B. Abyssal Plains
  C. Seamounts and Guyots
III. Mid-Ocean Ridges
  A. Seafloor Spreading
  B. Hydrothermal Vents

2 INSTRUCT

Use Visuals L1

Figure 6 Point out to students that the profile shown below the map is a side view of the ocean floor along the line between points A and B on the map. Ask: **Why do the topographic features have to be exaggerated to make them more distinct?** *(The scale of the map is so large that the elevation differences between ocean floor, continental margin, and mid-ocean ridge would not be visible. If the map were 40 times larger, the exaggeration wouldn't be necessary, but the map would be too large to print.)* **Look back at the map of the ocean floor shown in Figure 3. How would a profile of the Pacific Ocean basin differ from this profile of the Atlantic Ocean?** *(The profile of the Pacific Ocean basin would not show a central mid-ocean ridge. Instead, depending on how the transect line is drawn, it would show trenches, chains of volcanic islands, or coral atolls.)*
Visual, Logical

Build Reading Literacy L1

Refer to p. 392D, which provides the guidelines for this previewing strategy.

Preview Have students skim headings, titles of visuals, and boldfaced text for Section 14.2 Ocean Floor Features. Invite them to think in broad terms about what they will read. Ask: **What do the green section heads have in common?** *(They are all parts of the ocean floor.)* **What do the blue section heads have in common?** *(Most are terms for smaller features of the ocean, usually associated with one of the three parts of the ocean.)*
Visual, Logical

Continental Margins

Integrate Biology L2

Sunlight and Ocean Life Explain that the ocean bottom along the continental margins supports a greater variety of living organisms than other regions of the ocean floor. Tell students that sunlight penetrates ocean water to an average depth of about 300 meters. Ask: **What kinds of organisms form the basis of almost every food chain?** *(organisms capable of photosynthesis)* **Why does the continental shelf support a greater amount and variety of life than deeper parts of the ocean floor?** *(Sunlight can penetrate to the bottom of at least some parts of the continental shelf; algae and other photosynthetic organisms can live on the bottom and serve as the basis for ocean food chains along the continental shelf. Deeper regions of the ocean floor do not receive sunlight and so do not support photosynthetic organisms that would form the basis of food chains.)*
Logical, Verbal

Continental Margins

The zone of transition between a continent and the adjacent ocean basin floor is known as the **continental margin.** **In the Atlantic Ocean, thick layers of undisturbed sediment cover the continental margin. This region has very little volcanic or earthquake activity.** This is because the continental margins in the Atlantic Ocean are not associated with plate boundaries, unlike the continental margins of the Pacific Ocean. **In the Pacific Ocean, oceanic crust is plunging beneath continental crust. This force results in a narrow continental margin that experiences both volcanic activity and earthquakes.** Figure 7 shows the features of a continental margin found along the Atlantic coast.

Continental Shelf What if you were to begin an underwater journey eastward across the Atlantic Ocean? The first area of ocean floor you would encounter is the continental shelf. The **continental shelf** is the gently sloping submerged surface extending from the shoreline. The shelf is almost nonexistent along some coastlines. However, the shelf may extend seaward as far as 1500 kilometers along other coastlines. On average, the continental shelf is about 80 kilometers wide and 130 meters deep at its seaward edge. The average steepness of the shelf is equal to a drop of only about 2 meters per kilometer. The slope is so slight that to the human eye it appears to be a horizontal surface.

Continental shelves have economic and political significance. **Continental shelves contain important mineral deposits, large reservoirs of oil and natural gas, and huge sand and gravel deposits.** The waters of the continental shelf also contain important fishing grounds, which are significant sources of food.

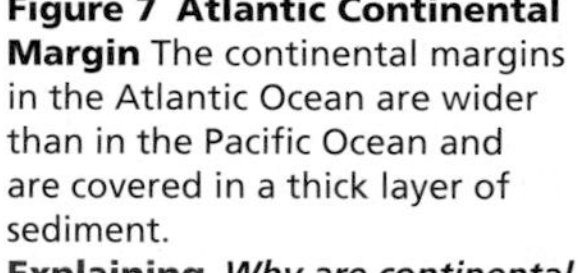

Figure 7 Atlantic Continental Margin The continental margins in the Atlantic Ocean are wider than in the Pacific Ocean and are covered in a thick layer of sediment.
Explaining ***Why are continental margins in the Pacific Ocean narrower and associated with earthquakes and volcanic activity?***

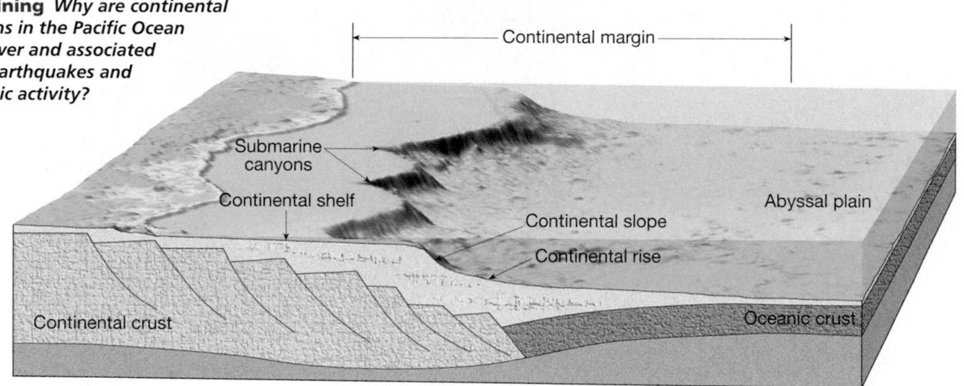

Customize for English Language Learners

Tell students that the words *abyss* and *floor* are used as synonyms with reference to the deep ocean bottom. Explain that the word *abyss* means a "bottomless depth" and historically has been used to describe the unknown. Before humans discovered technologies for deep sea exploration, the bottom of the ocean was considered by many to be the abyss referred to in many myths—a bottomless pit that humans could not know or understand. The word *floor* means "the ground surface." Its use as a descriptor of the ocean bottom is more recent, and does not imply a sense of the unknown.

Continental Slope Marking the seaward edge of the continental shelf is the **continental slope.** This slope is steeper than the shelf, and it marks the boundary between continental crust and oceanic crust. The continental slope can be seen in Figure 7 on page 402. Although the steepness of the continental slope varies greatly from place to place, it averages about 5 degrees. In some places the slope may exceed 25 degrees. The continental slope is a relatively narrow feature, averaging only about 20 kilometers in width.

Deep, steep-sided valleys known as **submarine canyons** are cut into the continental slope. These canyons may extend to the ocean basin floor. Figure 8 shows how submarine canyons are formed. Most information suggests that submarine canyons have been eroded, at least in part, by turbidity currents. **Turbidity currents** are occasional movements of dense, sediment-rich water down the continental slope. They are created when sand and mud on the continental shelf and slope are disturbed—perhaps by an earthquake—and become suspended in the water. Because such muddy water is denser than normal seawater, it flows down the slope. As it flows down, it erodes and accumulates more sediment. Erosion from these muddy torrents is believed to be the major force in the formation of most submarine canyons. Narrow continental margins, such as the one located along the California coast, are marked with numerous submarine canyons.

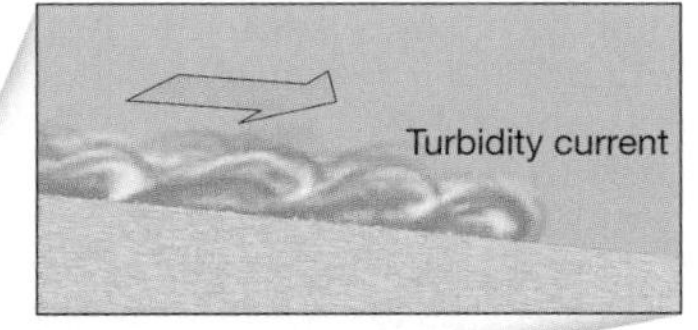

Figure 8 Submarine Canyons Most evidence suggests that submarine canyons probably formed as river valleys during periods of low sea level during recent ice ages. Turbidity currents continue to change the canyons.

Turbidity currents are known to be an important mechanism of sediment transport in the ocean. Turbidity currents erode submarine canyons and deposit sediments on the deep-ocean floor.

Continental Rise In regions where trenches do not exist, the steep continental slope merges into a more gradual incline known as the **continental rise.** Here the steepness of the slope drops to about 6 meters per kilometer. Whereas the width of the continental slope averages about 20 kilometers, the continental rise may be hundreds of kilometers wide.

Compare and contrast the continental slope and continental rise.

For: Links on ocean floor features
Visit: www.SciLinks.org
Web Code: cjn-5142

Use Visuals L1

Figure 8 Have students examine the figure. Explain to students that turbidity currents are made up of water that contains suspended particles of rock, sand, and mud, which increase the density of the water. Ask: **How is density important to the action of turbidity currents?** *(Gravity causes the denser, heavier water to fall to the bottom and flow down the slope.)* **What happens to the sediment once it reaches the bottom of the slope?** *(The sediment forms fan-shaped deposits.)*
Visual, Logical

Build Science Skills L2

Inferring Explain to students that there are probably many kinds of events that could set a turbidity current flowing down a continental slope. Scientists do not yet completely understand the complex workings of turbidity currents. Ask: **What kinds of events, besides earthquakes, might set off turbidity currents?** *(Accept all reasonable answers. Possible answers: A heavy accumulation of sediment particles that builds up over time along an existing steep edge could reach the point where it becomes too heavy to be supported by the underlying sediments and begins to flow down slope. Human activities, such as underwater explosions or mining activities, could create sediment-laden water that then flows down slope.)*
Logical, Verbal

Download a worksheet on ocean floor features for students to complete, and find additional teacher support from NSTA SciLinks.

Facts and Figures

When a turbidity current loses its momentum, it gradually slows down and deposits its load of sediment in a fan-shaped bed. Beds of sediment deposited by turbidity currents are called *turbidites*. Heavier sediments settle out first and lighter sediments settle out on top of them, creating a layered feature known as a *graded bed*. Each turbidity current event creates a separate graded bed that decreases in sediment size from bottom to top. Layers of graded beds build up over time, leaving a record of turbidity current activity.

Answer to . . .

Figure 7 *In the Pacific Ocean, oceanic crust is being pushed beneath continental crust.*

Continental slope marks the steep boundary between continental crust and oceanic crust. The continental rise occurs at the end of the continental slope and has a more gradual decline.

Teacher Demo

Sediment Buildup **L2**

Purpose Demonstrate to students how layers of sediment build up over time on the ocean floor, covering irregular rock to form a flat abyssal plain.

Materials small glass aquarium tank, rocks, pebbles, coarse gravel, coarse and fine aquarium sand, bone meal or other fine material that settles out but does not dissolve quickly in water

Procedure Use rocks, pebbles, and gravel to create a model of an irregular ocean floor in the bottom of the aquarium tank. Fill tank 2/3 full of water. As students watch, sprinkle the top of the water with coarse sand and let it settle to the bottom. After it has settled, add a layer of fine sand and let it settle. Repeat alternating layers of sand and other materials.

Expected Outcome As the layers build up, the bottom of the tank will slowly be covered with a smooth layer that models the appearance of an abyssal plain.

Visual, Kinesthetic

Ocean Basin Floor

Address Misconceptions **L2**

Many students think that Earth's features, including the ocean floor, are unchanging or formed only in the past. To help students realize that tectonic activity and plate motions continue to alter Earth's surface, have them investigate rates of seafloor spreading. Explain to students that new crust is created at spreading centers. You may choose to limit the scope of their research to the Mid-Atlantic Ridge. *(According to the United States Geological Survey, the Mid-Atlantic Ridge is spreading at a rate of about 2.5 cm per year.)*

Logical

Q *Have humans ever explored the deepest ocean trenches? Could anything live there?*

A Humans have indeed visited the deepest part of the oceans—where there is crushing high pressure, complete darkness, and near-freezing water temperatures. In January 1960, U.S. Navy Lt. Don Walsh and explorer Jacques Piccard descended to the bottom of the Challenger Deep region of the Mariana Trench in the deep-diving submersible *Trieste.* It took more than five hours to reach the bottom at 10,912 meters—a record depth of human descent that has not been broken since. They did see some organisms that are adapted to life in the deep: a small flatfish, a shrimp, and some jellyfish.

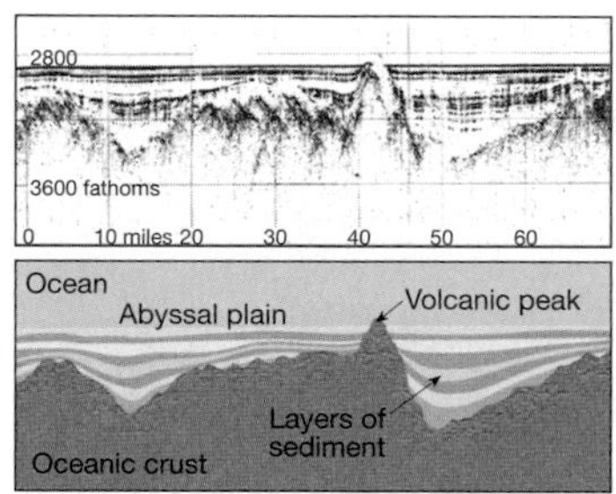

Figure 9 Abyssal Plain Cross Section This seismic cross section and matching sketch of a portion of the Madeira abyssal plain in the eastern Atlantic Ocean shows how the irregular oceanic crust is buried by sediments.

Ocean Basin Floor

Between the continental margin and mid-ocean ridge lies the **ocean basin floor.** The size of this region—almost 30 percent of Earth's surface—is comparable to the percentage of land above sea level. This region includes deep-ocean trenches, very flat areas known as abyssal plains, and tall volcanic peaks called seamounts and guyots.

Deep-Ocean Trenches Deep-ocean trenches are long, narrow creases in the ocean floor that form the deepest parts of the ocean. Most trenches are located along the margins of the Pacific Ocean, and many exceed 10,000 meters in depth. A portion of one trench—the Challenger Deep in the Mariana Trench—has been measured at a record 11,022 meters below sea level. It is the deepest known place on Earth.

Trenches form at sites of plate convergence where one moving plate descends beneath another and plunges back into the mantle. Earthquakes and volcanic activity are associated with these regions. The large number of trenches and the volcanic activity along the margins of the Pacific Ocean give the region its nickname as the *Ring of Fire.*

Abyssal Plains **Abyssal plains** are deep, extremely flat features. In fact, these regions are possibly the most level places on Earth. Abyssal plains have thick accumulations of fine sediment that have buried an otherwise rugged ocean floor, as shown in Figure 9. **The sediments that make up abyssal plains are carried there by turbidity currents or deposited as a result of suspended sediments settling.** Abyssal plains are found in all oceans of the world. However, the Atlantic Ocean has the most extensive abyssal plains because it has few trenches to catch sediment carried down the continental slope.

Seamounts and Guyots The submerged volcanic peaks that dot the ocean floor are called **seamounts.** They are volcanoes that have not reached the ocean surface. These steep-sided cone-shaped peaks are found on the floors of all the oceans. However, the greatest number have been identified in the Pacific. Some seamounts form at volcanic hot spots. An example is the Hawaiian-Emperor Seamount chain, shown in Figure 3 on page 396. This chain stretches from the Hawaiian Islands to the Aleutian trench.

Once underwater volcanoes reach the surface, they form islands. Over time, running water and wave action erode these volcanic islands to near sea level. Over millions of years, the islands gradually sink and may disappear below the water surface. This process occurs as the moving plate slowly carries the islands away from the elevated oceanic ridge or hot spot where they originated. These once-active, now-submerged, flat-topped structures are called guyots.

What are abyssal plains?

Customize for Inclusion Students

Visually Impaired Have students use modeling clay to create a model of the Atlantic Ocean floor, from the continental margin of Africa to the continental margin of North America. Allow students to base their models on Figure 6. After students have completed their models, help them to cut apart the model along a transect line. Show them the cut side and explain that it is a profile view of their ocean floor model.

Mid-Ocean Ridges

The **mid-ocean ridge** is found near the center of most ocean basins. It is an interconnected system of underwater mountains that have developed on newly formed ocean crust. This system is the longest topographic feature on Earth's surface. It exceeds 70,000 kilometers in length. The mid-ocean ridge winds through all major oceans similar to the way a seam winds over the surface of a baseball.

The term *ridge* may be misleading because the mid-ocean ridge is not narrow. It has widths from 1000 to 4000 kilometers and may occupy as much as one half of the total area of the ocean floor. Another look at Figure 3 shows that the mid-ocean ridge is broken into segments. These are offset by large transform faults where plates slide past each other horizontally, resulting in shallow earthquakes.

Seafloor Spreading A high amount of volcanic activity takes place along the crest of the mid-ocean ridge. This activity is associated with seafloor spreading. **Seafloor spreading** occurs at divergent plate boundaries where two lithospheric plates are moving apart. **New ocean floor is formed at mid-ocean ridges as magma rises between the diverging plates and cools.**

Hydrothermal Vents Hydrothermal vents form along mid-ocean ridges. These are zones where mineral-rich water, heated by the hot, newly-formed oceanic crust, escapes through cracks in oceanic crust into surrounding water. As the super-heated, mineral-rich water comes in contact with the surrounding cold water, minerals and metals such as sulfur, iron, copper, and zinc precipitate out and are deposited.

Section 14.2 Assessment

Reviewing Concepts

1. What are the three main regions of the ocean floor?
2. How do continental margins in the Atlantic Ocean differ from those in the Pacific Ocean?
3. What are trenches? How are deep-ocean trenches formed?
4. What are abyssal plains? How are abyssal plains formed?
5. What is formed at mid-ocean ridges?

Critical Thinking

6. **Comparing and Contrasting** Compare and contrast seamounts and guyots.
7. **Applying Concepts** Explain how turbidity currents are related to submarine canyons.

Writing in Science

Descriptive Paragraph Imagine you are about to take an underwater journey in a submersible across the Atlantic Ocean. Your journey begins at the coast, and you travel out toward the mid-ocean ridge. Write a paragraph describing the ocean floor features you will likely see on your journey.

Mid-Ocean Ridges

Build Science Skills L2

Relating Cause and Effect Remind students that seafloor spreading and hydrothermal vents occur where two crustal plates are moving apart. Ask: **Why don't these features occur in regions where crustal plates are moving together?** *(Both seafloor spreading and hydrothermal vents occur where magma rises up from below the Earth's crust. Plates that are moving apart create a thin place in the crust between them, through which magma can rise. Crustal plates that are moving together may form deep trenches where one plate slides beneath another, and sometimes creates a thin region in the crust through which magma can rise.)*
Logical, Verbal

3 ASSESS

Evaluate Understanding L2

Have students draw and label a profile of the ocean floor that includes examples of the following: continental margin, continental slope, continental rise, ocean floor, mid-ocean ridge, abyssal plain, submarine trench, seamount, and guyot.

Reteach

Have students work in pairs to produce a set of flashcards for each of the section's vocabulary terms. Students can use the cards to quiz each other.

Writing in Science

Student responses may vary but should include the continental shelf and continental rise, the ocean basin floor with abyssal plains and possibly seamounts, trenches, or a mid-ocean ridge.

Answer to . . .

deep, extremely flat regions of the ocean floor

Section 14.2 Assessment

1. continental margin, ocean basin floor, mid-ocean ridge
2. Continental margins in the Atlantic Ocean consist of thick layers of undisturbed sediment and there is little volcanic or earthquake activity. In Pacific Ocean margins, oceanic crust is being pushed beneath continental crust, leaving narrow margins with volcanic and earthquake activity.
3. Trenches are long, narrow creases in the seafloor. They are formed at convergence sites where one plate descends beneath another and plunges back into the mantle.
4. Abyssal plains are deep, extremely flat features of the ocean floor. They are formed as sediments from coastal regions are transported far out to sea and settle to the ocean floor, and as materials from the water column above settle to the bottom.
5. new ocean floor
6. A seamount is an underwater volcano that has not reached the surface of the water yet. A guyot is a volcanic island that has been eroded and sunk back under the water's surface.
7. Turbidity currents consist of dense, mud-choked water that flows down the continental slope. As the currents flow, they erode and accumulate more sediment, creating submarine canyons.

understanding **EARTH**

Explaining Coral Atolls—Darwin's Hypothesis L2

Have students use an atlas to identify the locations of coral atolls worldwide. Ask: **At what latitudes are the majority of Earth's coral reefs found?** *(tropical latitudes)* **What does Darwin's hypothesis of atoll formation imply about the relationship between the rate of growth of coral reefs and the rate of subsidence of volcanoes?** *(In regions where atolls form, corals are able to build reefs at the same rate that the volcano beneath them subsides.)* **According to the theory of plate tectonics, what would cause a volcano to sink below the ocean surface?** *(Over time, hot ocean seafloor moves away from mid-ocean ridges, cooling and sinking as it becomes more dense. Volcanic islands thus are gradually lowered below the water surface.)*
Visual, Verbal

understanding **EARTH**

Explaining Coral Atolls—Darwin's Hypothesis

Coral atolls are ring-shaped structures that often extend several thousand meters below sea level. Corals are colonial animals about the size of an ant. They are related to jellyfish and feed with stinging tentacles. Most corals protect themselves by precipitating a hard external skeleton made of calcium carbonate. Coral reefs occur where corals reproduce and grow over many centuries. Their skeletons fuse into large structures called coral reefs.

The Problem with Corals

Corals require specific environmental conditions to grow. For example, reef-building corals grow best in waters with an average annual temperature of about 24°C. They cannot survive prolonged exposure to temperatures below 18°C or above 30°C. Reef-building corals also need clear sunlit water. As a result, the limiting depth of most active reef growth is only about 45 meters.

Gathering Data

How can corals—which require warm, shallow, sunlit water no deeper than a few dozen meters to live—create thick structures like coral atolls that extend into deep water? The naturalist Charles Darwin was one of the first to formulate a hypothesis on the origin of atolls. From 1831 to 1836, he sailed aboard the British ship HMS *Beagle* during its famous voyage around the world. In various places Darwin noticed a series of stages in coral-reef development. Development begins with a fringing reef, like the one shown in Figure 10A. The fringing reef forms along the sides of a volcanic island. As the volcanic island slowly sinks, the fringing reef becomes a barrier reef, as shown in Figure 10B. Figure 10C shows the final stage of development of the atoll. The volcano sinks completely underwater but the coral reef remains near the surface.

Darwin's Hypothesis

Figure 10 is a drawing that summarizes Darwin's hypothesis about atoll formation. As a volcanic island slowly sinks, the corals continue to build the reef upward. This explained how living coral reefs, which are restricted to shallow water, can build structures that now exist in much deeper water. The theory of plate tectonics supports Darwin's hypothesis.Plate tectonics explains how a volcanic island can become extinct and experience a change in elevation over long periods of time. As the hot ocean seafloor moves away from the mid-ocean ridge, it becomes denser and sinks. This is why islands also sink. Darwin's hypothesis is also supported by evidence from drilling that shows volcanic rock is beneath the oldest and deepest coral reef structures. Atolls owe their existence to the gradual sinking of volcanic islands containing coral reefs that build upward through time.

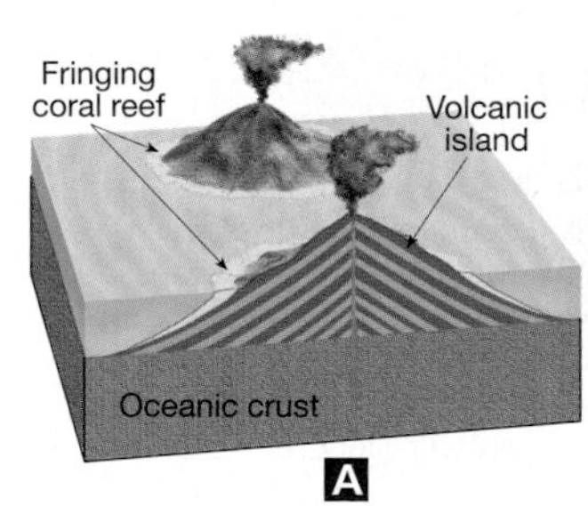

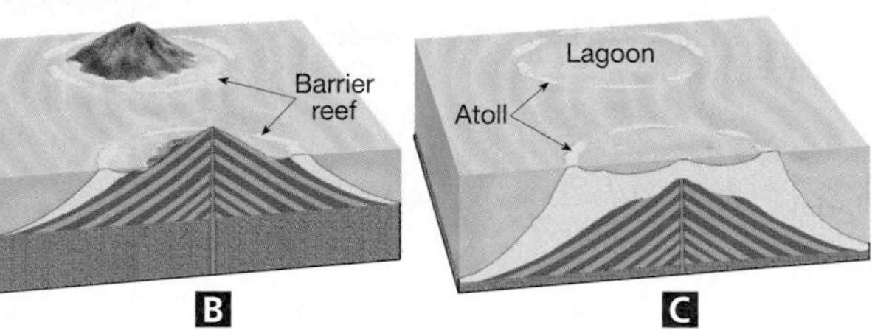

Figure 10 Formation of a Coral Atoll A A fringing coral reef forms around a volcanic island. **B** As the volcanic island sinks, the fringing reef slowly becomes a barrier reef. **C** Eventually, the volcano is completely underwater and a coral atoll remains.

14.3 Seafloor Sediments

Reading Focus

Key Concepts

- What are the three types of ocean-floor sediments?
- What does terrigenous sediment consist of?
- What is the composition of biogenous sediment?
- How is hydrogenous sediment formed?

Vocabulary

- terrigenous sediment
- biogenous sediment
- calcareous ooze
- siliceous ooze
- hydrogenous sediment

Reading Strategy

Summarizing Make a table like the one below that includes all the headings for the section. Write a brief summary of the text for each heading.

Actions at Boundaries
I. Types of Seafloor Sediments • Terrigenous sediments originated on land. • Biogenous sediments are biological in origin. • ________ ?

Except for steep areas of the continental slope and the crest of the mid-ocean ridge, most of the ocean floor is covered with sediment. Some of this sediment has been deposited by turbidity currents. The rest has slowly settled onto the seafloor from above. The thickness of ocean-floor sediments varies. Some trenches act as traps for sediment originating on the continental margin. The accumulation may approach 10 kilometers in thickness. In general, however, accumulations of sediment are much less—about 500 to 1000 meters.

Generally, coarser sediments, such as sand, cover the continental shelf and slope while finer sediments, such as clay, cover the deep-ocean floor. Figure 11 shows the distribution of the different types of ocean-floor sediments. Various types of sediment accumulate on nearly all areas of the ocean floor in the same way dust accumulates in all parts of your home. Even the deep-ocean floor, far from land, receives small amounts of windblown material and microscopic parts of organisms.

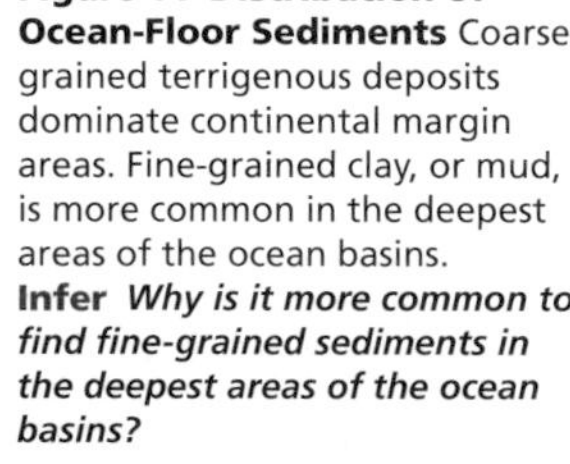

Figure 11 Distribution of Ocean-Floor Sediments Coarse-grained terrigenous deposits dominate continental margin areas. Fine-grained clay, or mud, is more common in the deepest areas of the ocean basins.
Infer ***Why is it more common to find fine-grained sediments in the deepest areas of the ocean basins?***

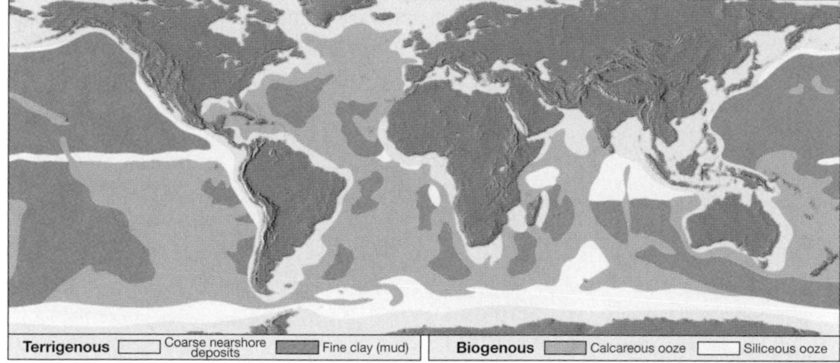

Facts and Figures

Most seafloor sediments contain the remains of microscopic organisms that once lived near the ocean surface. When these organisms die, their hard parts can settle onto the ocean floor, where they may become buried and preserved over time. The deep ocean floor has become a repository for sediments representing millions of years of Earth's history. They are useful recorders of climate change because the numbers and types of organisms living near the surface change with the climate.

Section 14.3

1 FOCUS

Section Objectives

14.8 **List** the three types of ocean floor sediments.

14.9 **Describe** the formation of terrigenous, biogenous, and hydrogenous sediments.

Reading Focus

Build Vocabulary L2

Word Parts Have students break the words *terrigenous*, *biogenous*, and *hydrogenous* into parts, using a dictionary to find the meaning of each part. (*terri-* is from *terra* which means "earth" or "ground"; *bio-* means "life"; *hydro-* means "water"; *-genous* means "producing", "yielding", "origin.")

Reading Strategy L2

Actions at Boundaries
I. Types of Seafloor Sediments • Terrigenous sediments originated on land. They come from minerals of continental rocks. These sediments are composed of sand and gravel. • Biogenous sediments are biological in origin. They come from shells and skeletons of marine animals and algae. These sediments are composed of calcareous ooze, siliceous ooze, and phosphate-rich material. • Hydrogenous sediments originated in ocean water. They are crystallized through chemical reactions. These sediments are composed of manganese nodules, calcium carbonates, and evaporites.

2 INSTRUCT

Build Science Skills L2

Predicting After students have read the introduction, ask: **Why do sediment deposits near the continental margins tend to be thicker than those on floor of the open ocean, far from land?** *(Water from rivers and runoff from coastal land transports land sediments to margins. This sediment source does not exist in the open ocean.)*
Logical, Verbal

Answer to . . .

Figure 11 *They are less dense and transported further than coarser sediments that settle closer to shore.*

Use Visuals

Figure 11 Have students examine the map showing the distribution of marine sediments in the world's oceans. Ask: **What kinds of terrigenous sediments are shown on the map?** *(coarse nearshore deposits and fine abyssal clay)* **How do the locations of two types of terrigenous deposits differ?** *(Fine-grained clays are found farther from landmasses; coarser deposits are closer to landmasses.)* **According to the map, which type of biogenous sediment appears to be more common?** *(biogenous calcareous ooze)* **Which type of sediment is found along the west coast of North America? The east coast of North America?** *(biogenous siliceous ooze; terrigenous coarse nearshore deposits)*
Visual, Logical

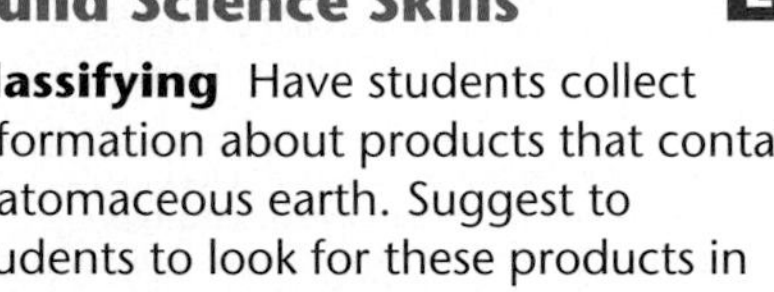

Types of Seafloor Sediments

Build Science Skills

L2

Classifying Have students collect information about products that contain diatomaceous earth. Suggest to students to look for these products in local grocery, hardware, auto supply, pool supply, and garden supply stores. By reading the labels, students can collect data about the uses for each product. Challenge students to identify the general applications diatomaceous earth is used for *(filters, abrasives, absorbents)* and classify each product they investigated according to its general application. *(Sample answers: filters: pool cleaning equipment; abrasives: toothpaste, garden insect control; absorbents: materials for cleaning chemical spills)*
Logical, Interpersonal

Build Reading Literacy

Refer to **p. 362D** in **Chapter 13,** which provides the guidelines for this Use Prior Knowledge strategy.

Use Prior Knowledge Before students read this section, have them make a list of the kinds of materials they think make up the sediment deposits on the ocean floor. After they have read the section, have students revise their lists.
Logical, Intrapersonal

Q *Do we use diatoms in any products?*

A Diatoms are used in filters for refining sugar, straining yeast from beer, and cleaning swimming pool water. They also are mild abrasives in household cleaning and polishing products and facial scrubs; and absorbents for chemical spills. You use diatoms in a variety of household products such as toothpaste, facial scrubs, and cleaning solutions.

Types of Seafloor Sediments

Ocean-floor sediments can be classified according to their origin into three broad categories: terrigenous sediments, biogenous sediments, and hydrogenous sediments. Ocean-floor sediments are usually mixtures of the various sediment types.

Terrigenous Sediment **Terrigenous sediment** is sediment that originates on land. **Terrigenous sediments consist primarily of mineral grains that were eroded from continental rocks and transported to the ocean.** Larger particles such as gravel and sand usually settle rapidly near shore. Finer particles such as clay can take years to settle to the ocean floor and may be carried thousands of kilometers by ocean currents. Clay accumulates very slowly on the deep-ocean floor. To form a 1-centimeter abyssal clay layer, for example, requires as much as 50,000 years. In contrast, on the continental margins near the mouths of large rivers, terrigenous sediment accumulates rapidly and forms thick deposits. In the Gulf of Mexico, for instance, the sediment is many kilometers thick.

Biogenous Sediment **Biogenous sediment** is sediment that is biological in origin. **Biogenous sediments consist of shells and skeletons of marine animals and algae.** This debris is produced mostly by microscopic organisms living in surface waters. Once these organisms die, their hard shells sink, accumulating on the seafloor.

The most common biogenous sediment is calcareous ooze. **Calcareous ooze** is produced from the calcium carbonate shells of organisms. Calcareous ooze has the consistency of thick mud. When calcium carbonate shells slowly sink into deeper parts of the ocean, they begin to dissolve. In ocean water deeper than about 4500 meters, these shells completely dissolve before they reach the bottom. As a result, calcareous ooze does not accumulate in the deeper areas of ocean basins.

Other biogenous sediments include siliceous ooze and phosphate-rich material. **Siliceous ooze** is composed primarily of the shells of diatoms—single-celled algae—and radiolarians—single-celled animals that have shells made out of silica. The shells of these organisms are shown in Figure 12. Phosphate-rich biogenous sediments come from the bones, teeth, and scales of fish and other marine organisms.

Name two types of biogenous sediments.

Customize for English Language Learners

Help students understand chemical terms in this section by explaining their derivations. Tell students that *sulfides* are substances that contain the element sulfur. *Carbonates* are substances that contain the element carbon. The term *evaporites* is derived from the word evaporation.

Hydrogenous Sediment **Hydrogenous sediment consists of minerals that crystallize directly from ocean water through various chemical reactions.** Hydrogenous sediments make up only a small portion of the overall sediment in the ocean. They do, however, have many different compositions and are distributed in many different environments. Some of the most common types of hydrogenous sediment are listed below.

- Manganese nodules are rounded, hard lumps of manganese, iron, and other metals. These metals precipitate around an object such as a grain of sand. The nodules can be up to 20 centimeters in diameter and are often scattered across large areas of the deep ocean floor.
- Calcium carbonates form by precipitation directly from ocean water in warm climates. If this material is buried and hardens, a type of limestone forms. Most limestone, however, is composed of biogenous sediment.
- Evaporites form where evaporation rates are high and there is restricted open-ocean circulation. As water evaporates from such areas, the remaining ocean water becomes saturated with dissolved minerals that then begin to precipitate. Collectively termed "salts," some evaporite minerals do taste salty, such as halite, or common table salt. Other salts do not taste salty, such as the calcium sulfate minerals anhydrite ($CaSO_4$) and gypsum.

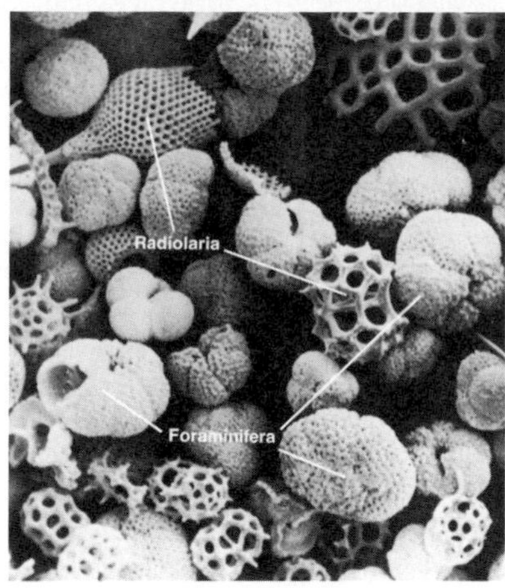

Figure 12 Biogenous Sediments The microscopic shells of radiolarians and foraminifers are examples of biogenous sediments. This photomicrograph has been enlarged hundreds of times.

Section 14.3 Assessment

Reviewing Concepts

1. What are the three types of ocean floor sediments?
2. What does terrigenous sediment consist of?
3. What is the composition of biogenous sediment?
4. How is hydrogenous sediment formed?

Critical Thinking

5. **Comparing and Contrasting** Compare and contrast calcareous ooze and siliceous ooze.
6. **Predicting** Would you expect to find more evaporites in an area of warm water that receives large amounts of sunlight such as the Red Sea or in an area of cold water that receives less sunlight such as the Greenland Sea?

Connecting Concepts

Origin of Sediments An oceanographer is studying sediment samples from the Bahama Banks. The sediments have a high amount of calcium carbonate. They are labeled biogenous but are later found to contain no shells from organisms that typically make up calcareous ooze. What other explanation is there for the origin of these sediments?

Section 14.3 Assessment

1. terrigenous, biogenous, hydrogenous
2. mineral grains weathered from continental rocks
3. shells and skeletons of marine animals and algae
4. minerals crystallize directly from the water through chemical reactions
5. Calcareous ooze and siliceous ooze both have the consistency of thick mud and are examples of biogenous sediments. Calcareous ooze is formed from the calcium carbonate tests, or hard parts, of organisms. Siliceous ooze is formed from the siliceous tests of organisms. Calcareous ooze is not found below depths of 4500 m.
6. area of warm water with lots of sunlight because these conditions are more favorable for evaporation

Teacher Demo

Biogenous Deposits L2

Purpose Students observe similarities and differences among the types of organisms that form biogenous sediment deposits.

Materials prepared microscope slides of diatoms, foraminifera, and radiolaria; or photographic slides of photomicrographs of these organisms and a slide projector

Procedure Have students examine prepared slides under the microscope or view projected photographic slides. Inform students that these organisms are single-celled members of the phylum protista. Diatoms are algae (plant-like protists) that make their own food through photosynthesis. Foraminifera and radiolaria are animal-like protists that feed on other microscopic organisms. Have students observe similarities and differences among the organisms shown.

Expected Outcome Students will observe that these organisms all have hard structures that vary in shape from species to species and can be preserved after the organisms' soft tissues decay.

Visual

3 ASSESS

Evaluate Understanding L2

Present students with a blank table that lists the three major categories of seafloor sediments down the left column. The center column should be titled Origin. The right column should be labeled Composition. Have students fill in the Origin and Composition columns.

Reteach L1

Have each student write ten questions that cover the content of this section. Invite students to use their questions to quiz each other.

Connecting Concepts

They are hydrogenous, formed from calcium carbonate precipitating directly from seawater.

Answer to . . .

calcareous ooze, siliceous ooze

Section 14.4

1 FOCUS

Section Objectives

14.10 **Identify** ocean resources used for energy production.

14.11 **Explain** how gas hydrates are formed.

14.12 **List** other types of ocean resources.

Reading Focus

Build Vocabulary L2

Paraphrase Have students explain, in their own words, the meanings of the new vocabulary terms in this section, plus the terms *evaporative salts* and *halite*. Have students write their definitions and share them.

Reading Strategy L2

a. rock fragments and shells of marine organisms
b. landfill, recreational beaches, concrete
c. diamonds, tin, platinum, gold, titanium

2 INSTRUCT

Energy Resources

Address Misconceptions L2

Students may have the misconception that sand contains only the mineral silicon. However, the term sand refers more to particle size (smaller than gravel but larger than silt) than to mineral content. Ask students to explain how they think sand is formed. Guide them to understand that sand particles are made up of minerals that come primarily from pulverized rocks, which have varying compositions. Sand particles can also come from pulverized shells of marine organisms.
Logical

14.4 Resources from the Seafloor

Reading Focus

Key Concepts

- Which ocean resources are used for energy production?
- How are gas hydrates formed?
- What other resources are derived from the ocean?

Vocabulary

- gas hydrates
- manganese nodule

Reading Strategy

Identifying Details Copy the concept map below. As you read, complete it to identify details about resources from the ocean.

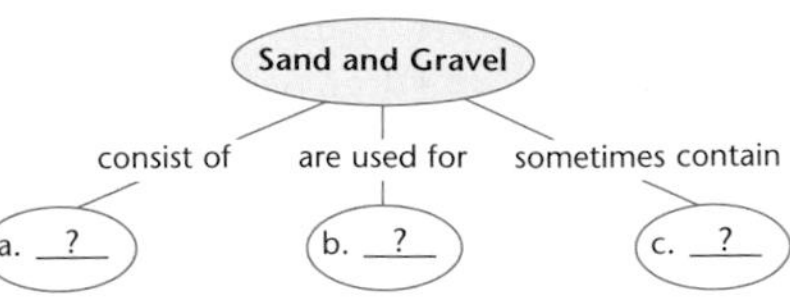

The ocean floor is rich in mineral and organic resources. Recovering them, however, involves technological challenges and high costs. As technology improves we are able to access some of these resources more efficiently. However, other resources, such as manganese nodules, remain untouched.

Energy Resources

Most of the value of nonliving resources in the ocean comes from their use as energy products. **Oil and natural gas are the main energy products currently being obtained from the ocean floor.** Other resources have the potential to be used as a source of energy in the future.

Oil and Natural Gas The ancient remains of microscopic organisms are the source of today's deposits of oil and natural gas. These organisms were buried within marine sediments before they could decompose. After millions of years of exposure to heat from Earth's interior and pressure from overlying rock, the remains were transformed into oil and natural gas. The percentage of world oil produced from offshore regions has increased from trace amounts in the 1930s to more than 30 percent today. Most of this increase is due to the continual update of the technology used by offshore drilling platforms such as the one shown in Figure 13.

Major offshore reserves exist in the Persian Gulf, in the Gulf of Mexico, off the coast of southern California, in the North Sea, and in the East Indies. Additional reserves are probably located off the north coast of Alaska and in the Canadian Arctic, Asian seas, Africa, and Brazil. One

Figure 13 Offshore drilling rigs tap the oil and natural gas reserves of the continental shelf. These platforms are near Santa Barbara, California.
Inferring ***What changes to the marine environment may occur as a result of drilling for oil?***

410 Chapter 14

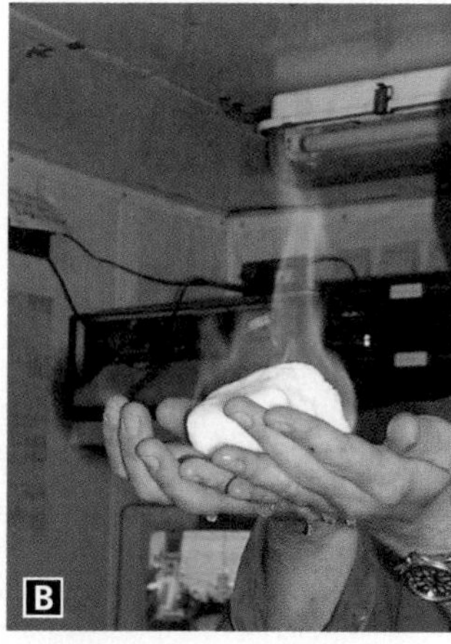

environmental concern about offshore petroleum exploration is the possibility of oil spills caused by accidental leaks during the drilling process.

Gas Hydrates **Gas hydrates** are compact chemical structures made of water and natural gas. The most common type of natural gas is methane, which produces methane hydrate. Gas hydrates occur beneath permafrost areas on land and under the ocean floor at depths below 525 meters.

Most oceanic gas hydrates are created when bacteria break down organic matter trapped in ocean-floor sediments. The bacteria produce methane gas along with small amounts of ethane and propane. These gases combine with water in deep-ocean sediments in such a way that the gas is trapped inside a lattice-like cage of water molecules.

Vessels that have drilled into gas hydrates have brought up samples of mud mixed with chunks of gas hydrates like the one shown in Figure 14A. These chunks evaporate quickly when they are exposed to the relatively warm, low-pressure conditions at the ocean surface. Gas hydrates resemble chunks of ice but ignite when lit by a flame, as shown in Figure 14B. The hydrates burn because methane and other flammable gases are released as gas hydrates evaporate.

An estimated 20 quadrillion cubic meters of methane are locked up in sediments containing gas hydrates. This amount is double the amount of Earth's known coal, oil, and natural gas reserves combined. One drawback to using gas hydrates as an energy source is that they rapidly break down at surface temperatures and pressures. In the future, however, these ocean-floor reserves of energy may help provide our energy needs.

What happens when gas hydrates are brought to the surface?

Figure 14 Gas Hydrates
A A sample from the ocean floor has layers of white, ice-like gas hydrate mixed with mud.
B Gas hydrates evaporate when exposed to surface conditions, releasing natural gas that can be burned.

For: Links on ocean resources
Visit: www.SciLinks.org
Web Code: cjn-5144

Use Visuals L1

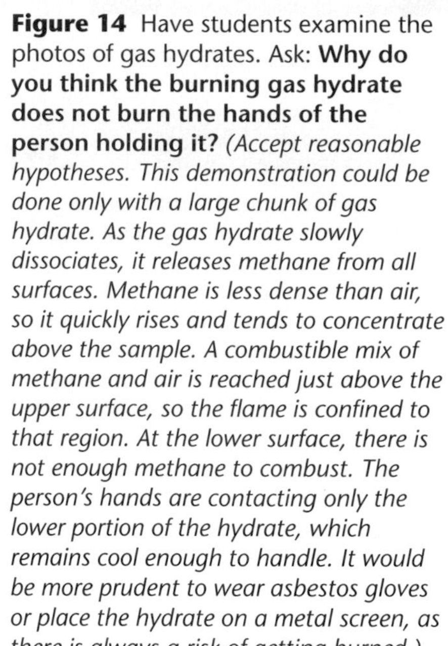

Figure 14 Have students examine the photos of gas hydrates. Ask: **Why do you think the burning gas hydrate does not burn the hands of the person holding it?** *(Accept reasonable hypotheses. This demonstration could be done only with a large chunk of gas hydrate. As the gas hydrate slowly dissociates, it releases methane from all surfaces. Methane is less dense than air, so it quickly rises and tends to concentrate above the sample. A combustible mix of methane and air is reached just above the upper surface, so the flame is confined to that region. At the lower surface, there is not enough methane to combust. The person's hands are contacting only the lower portion of the hydrate, which remains cool enough to handle. It would be more prudent to wear asbestos gloves or place the hydrate on a metal screen, as there is always a risk of getting burned.)*
Logical, Verbal

Build Science Skills L2

Inferring Remind students that when water freezes, the molecules arrange themselves in a lattice structure that takes up more space than liquid water. This lattice contains open spaces that are large enough to hold methane molecules. If methane molecules enter those spaces during lattice formation, a hydrate may be produced. The presence of methane molecules inside the cavities helps hold the hydrate crystal together. Point out to students that methane is produced by bacteria involved in the decomposition of organic matter. Ask: **Why do gas hydrates form only where there is plenty of decaying organic matter?** *(Bacteria involved in decomposition produce methane, which is required for gas hydrate formation.)*
Logical, Verbal

Download a worksheet on ocean resources for students to complete, and find additional teacher support from NSTA SciLinks.

Answer to . . .

Figure 13 *Drilling platforms may provide structure for some marine organisms to live on; drilling may disturb some organisms or destroy habitats; an oil spill could be harmful to organisms in the immediate area*

Gas hydrates evaporate quickly at surface temperature and pressure.

Other Resources

Address Misconceptions L2

Students may not think that ordinary tap water contains minerals that would precipitate out during evaporation. Guide students to understand that, because water is the universal solvent, there is virtually always something dissolved in it. Heat tap water in a pan with a black Teflon© coating. When the water boils off, a white residue remains of mineral salts. Explain that there are a number of physical and chemical processes that can be used to remove non-water molecules and ions from a sample of water. Have students look up information about the effectiveness of various water purification methods, such as distillation, active carbon filtration, and ozone treatment systems.
Logical, Verbal

Evaporative Salts L2

Objective Students observe that any salt dissolved in water is left behind when the water evaporates.

Skills Focus Observing, Measuring, Comparing, Drawing Conclusions, Predicting

Prep time 10 minutes

Class Time 10–15 minutes to set up; 5 minutes to make final measurements

Expected Outcome Students find that all of the salt they put into the water is left behind when the water evaporates.

Analyze and Conclude
1. The masses should be equal.
2. It is left behind (precipitates out).
3. Certain areas with proper conditions could be used to evaporate water and collect solid salt.

Kinesthetic, Logical

For Enrichment L3

Have students evaporate water taken from a variety of sources (tap water, rainwater, bottled water) to determine if an evaporite is left behind. Students could test any evaporite they obtain for the presence of minerals.

Other Resources

Other major resources from the ocean floor include sand and gravel, evaporative salts, and manganese nodules.

Sand and Gravel The offshore sand-and-gravel industry is second in economic value only to the petroleum industry. Sand and gravel, which include rock fragments that are washed out to sea and shells of marine organisms, are mined by offshore barges using suction devices. Sand and gravel are used for landfill, to fill in recreational beaches, and to make concrete.

In some cases, materials of high economic value are associated with offshore sand and gravel deposits. Gem-quality diamonds, for example, are recovered from gravels on the continental shelf offshore of South Africa and Australia. Sediments rich in tin have been mined from some offshore areas of Southeast Asia. Platinum and gold have been found in deposits in gold-mining areas throughout the world. Some Florida beach sands are rich in titanium.

Figure 15 These manganese nodules lie 5323 meters on the Pacific Ocean floor south of the island of Tahiti.
***Applying Concepts** How do manganese nodules form?*

Manganese Nodules As described earlier, **manganese nodules** are hard lumps of manganese and other metals that precipitate around a smaller object. Figure 15 shows manganese nodules on the deep-ocean floor. They contain high concentrations of manganese, iron, and smaller concentrations of copper,

Quick Lab: Evaporative Salts

Materials

400 mL beaker, table salt, tablespoon, balance, glass stirrer

Procedure

1. Place the empty beaker on the balance and add between 3 and 5 tablespoons of the salt. Measure the combined mass of the balance and the salt. Record the measurement and remove the beaker from the balance.
2. Add 100 mL of water to the beaker and stir until the salt is dissolved.
3. Place the beaker in a warm, sunny area and allow the water to evaporate.
4. When all of the water has evaporated, place the beaker and its remaining contents on the balance and record the measurement.

Analyze and Conclude

1. **Comparing** How did the mass of the beaker and salt before the water was added compare to the mass of the beaker and salt after the water evaporated?
2. **Drawing Conclusions** What happened to the salt when the water evaporated?
3. **Predicting** How could the oceans be used as a source of salt?

Facts and Figures

In Earth's geologic history, there have been incidents in which an entire body of salt water evaporated away. The evidence for this includes extensive deposits of evaporite minerals, including one in the Mediterranean Sea. Evidence suggests that, about 6 million years ago, the Mediterranean Sea was cut off from the Atlantic Ocean at the Strait of Gibraltar. The Mediterranean Sea almost completely evaporated within a few thousand years, leaving a thick deposit of evaporites on the hot, dry basin floor. A half million years later, water re-entered the Mediterranean Sea, filling it with seawater again.

nickel, and cobalt, all of which have a variety of economic uses. Cobalt, for example, is important because it is required to produce strong alloys with other metals. These alloys are used in high-speed cutting tools, powerful permanent magnets, and jet engine parts. With current technology, mining the deep-ocean floor for manganese nodules is possible but not economically profitable.

Manganese nodules are widely distributed along the ocean floor, but not all regions have the same potential for mining. Good locations for mining must have a large amount of nodules that contain an optimal mix of copper, nickel, and cobalt. Sites like this are limited. In addition, it is difficult to establish mining rights far from land. Also, there are environmental concerns about disturbing large portions of the deep-ocean floor.

Figure 16 Common table salt, or halite, is harvested from the salt left behind when ocean water evaporates. About 30 percent of the world's salt is produced by evaporating seawater.

Evaporative Salts When seawater evaporates, the salts increase in concentration until they can no longer remain dissolved. When the concentration becomes high enough, the salts precipitate out of solution and form salt deposits. These deposits can then be harvested, as shown in Figure 16. The most economically important salt is halite—common table salt. Halite is widely used for seasoning, curing, and preserving foods. It is also used in agriculture, in the clothing industry for dying fabric, and to de-ice roads.

Section 14.4 Assessment

Reviewing Concepts

1. What are the main energy resources from the ocean?
2. How are gas hydrates formed?
3. What drawbacks are associated with harvesting ocean resources for energy use?
4. What other resources are derived from the ocean?
5. What are the uses of evaporative salts?
6. What are manganese nodules? Why is it difficult to recover them from the ocean?

Critical Thinking

7. **Making Generalizations** How does technology influence the availability of resources from the ocean?
8. **Inferring** Near-shore mining of sand and gravel can result in large amounts of sediments being suspended in water. How might this affect marine organisms living in the area?

Connecting Concepts

Sand and Gravel Why are most sand and gravel deposits found on the continental shelf? What type of sediment is sand and gravel?

Use Community Resources L2

Ask the owner or manager of a local quarry to explain to the class how gravel and sand are mined, their uses, and their economic value. If possible, have the presenter bring samples of different types of sand and gravel for students to examine. Ask the presenter to discuss the differences between sand and gravel from marine and terrestrial sources.
Interpersonal, Visual

3 ASSESS

Evaluate Understanding L2

Have students explain how gas hydrates and evaporative salts are formed. Ask students to write a short paragraph on each.

Reteach L1

On the board, write a skeleton of an outline for the content of this section, with Energy Resources as Roman numeral I and Other Resources as Roman numeral II. Have students copy the skeleton and complete the outline by adding the ocean resources discussed in this section, along with details about their uses and how they form.

Connecting Concepts

Sand and gravel are coarse sediments that settle out more quickly than fine-grained sediments. Sand and gravel are terrigenous sediments.

Answer to . . .

Figure 15 *Manganese nodules form when metals such as manganese and iron precipitate around an object, such as a grain of sand.*

Section 14.4 Assessment

1. oil and natural gas
2. Most oceanic gas hydrates are formed when bacteria break down organic matter trapped in seafloor sediments. The bacteria produce methane gas along with small amounts of ethane and propane. These gases combine with water in deep-ocean sediments in such a way that the gas is trapped inside a lattice-like cage of water molecules.
3. possibility of oil spills, possible effects on marine habitats, gas hydrates break down quickly when brought to the surface
4. sand and gravel, evaporative salts, manganese nodules
5. used to season, cure, and preserve foods; used in agriculture, to dye fabric, and to de-ice roads
6. Manganese nodules are round, hard lumps of manganese, iron, and other metals that precipitate around an object, such as a grain of sand.
7. As technology improves, people may be able to retrieve resources more efficiently.
8. Suspended sediments can make water cloudy, interfering with the amount of light that penetrates water. This can affect organisms that need light for photosynthesis. Suspended sediments can also affect filter-feeding organisms, preventing them from feeding properly.

Exploration Lab

Modeling Seafloor Depth Transects L2

Objectives

In this activity, students will
- create a model of a portion of the seafloor.
- simulate depth measurements made by depth sounding.
- infer from depth measurements the region of the ocean floor their model represents.

Skills Focus Measuring, Graphing, Inferring, Drawing Conclusions

Prep Time 15 minutes to assemble materials

Class Time 30 minutes for Part A; 30 minutes for Part B

Teaching Tips
- Instruct students to limit their model to a continental margin, an ocean basin floor, or a mid-ocean ridge.
- Supervise students' model-making and make suggestions about ensuring their models will be decipherable by others during Part B.
- Make sure the size of the rulers used in this activity will enable students to make measurements precise enough to allow them to reach a conclusion.
- Encourage students to take measurements along two or more transect lines.

Exploration Lab

Modeling Seafloor Depth Transects

Oceanographers use a number of methods to determine the depth and topography of the ocean floor. Technology, such as sonar, satellites, and submersibles, have allowed scientists to produce detailed maps of the ocean floor in each ocean basin. In this lab, you will model a seafloor depth transect to determine the topography of an ocean basin created by your classmates.

Problem How can the topography of an ocean basin be determined?

Materials
- shoe box
- modeling clay
- aluminum foil
- pencil
- scalpel
- graph paper
- ruler

Skills Measuring, Graphing, Inferring, Drawing Conclusions

Procedure

Part A: Making a Model of the Seafloor

1. Reexamine Figure 3, Figure 7, and the figure below to determine which area of the ocean floor you will model. Be sure to identify the specific features that would be found in the area you choose to model. For example, if you were to model the continental margin you would want to include the continental shelf, continental slope, continental rise, and maybe some submarine canyons in your model. If you were to model the ocean basin floor you would want to include abyssal plains, trenches, seamounts, and guyots. Do not discuss the plan for your model with students outside your group.
2. Once you have determined which area of the ocean floor you will model, use the clay to make a contoured model of the seafloor inside the shoebox.

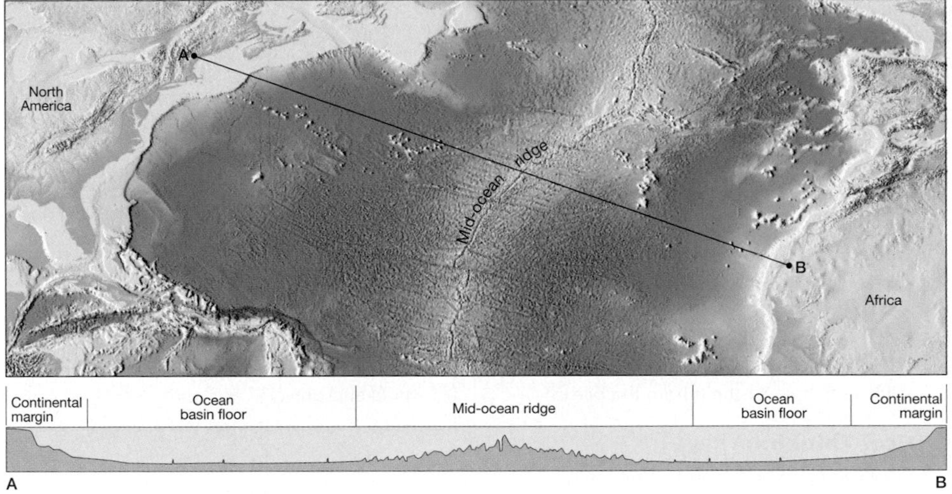

414 Chapter 14

3. Cover the box with its top and exchange boxes with another group from your class. Do not remove the top of the box that you receive from another group.

Part B: Completing a Depth Transect

4. Obtain a piece of aluminum foil that is large enough to cover the top of the shoebox and fold over the sides of the box about an inch all the way around.
5. Spread the foil flat on your lab table. Place the ruler lengthwise on the foil, parallel to the edge of the foil. The ruler can be in the middle of the foil or off to the side. The line formed by the edge of the ruler will be your transect line.
6. Use a pencil to make tick marks on the foil piece every centimeter along the entire length of the foil.
7. Hold the foil in place over the top of the box. Quickly and carefully remove the top of the box and set the foil piece down in place of the top. Do not look in the box. Secure the foil in place on top of the box by turning down the foil over the sides of the box. Be sure the foil is taut across the top.
8. Label your graph paper. The *x*-axis will be "Distance along Transect Line" in centimeters, and the *y*-axis will be "Depth" in centimeters. Make tick marks along the *x*-axis once every centimeter. Make tick marks along the *y*-axis every half of a centimeter.
9. Use the scalpel to carefully make a slit in the foil along the first centimeter mark. **CAUTION** *The scalpel is extremely sharp. Handle it carefully.* After cutting the foil, gently place the ruler through the slit until it makes contact with the clay in the box. Be sure to hold the ruler straight and take the depth measurement. Record your data on the graph.
10. Repeat Step 9 for each point along the foil. When you are done, you should have a depth profile for the entire length of the box along your transect line.
11. Remove the foil from the box and examine the contour of the model.

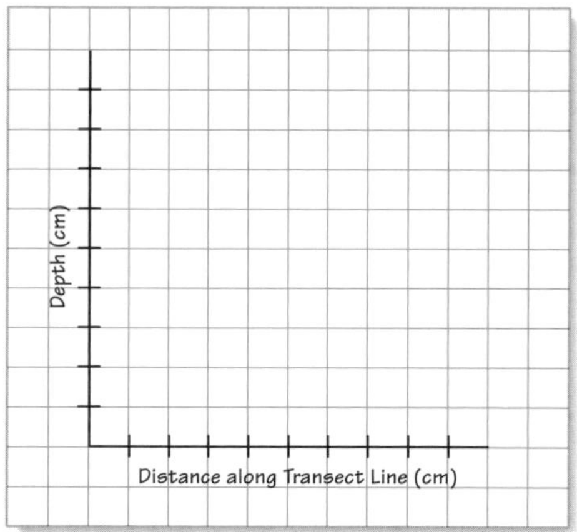

Analyze and Conclude

1. **Inferring** Based on your contour profile, what part of the ocean floor was being modeled? Check your answer with the group that created the model. Were you correct? Why or why not?
2. **Comparing** How does the profile on your graph compare with the contour of the model? Are there any major features in the model that did not appear on your graph? Why or why not?
3. **Analyzing Data** What could you have done to make your profile match the contour more accurately?
4. **Explaining** Before sonar was used to measure ocean depth, a less sophisticated method was used. A long line of rope with a lead weight on the end was tossed over the side of a ship and lowered until the weight hit the bottom. How is this method similar to what you did in the lab? How can the rope method lead to inaccuracies when trying to build an ocean floor profile?

Expected Outcome Students should be able to infer from their measurements whether the model they are examining corresponds to a continental margin, an ocean basin floor, or a mid-ocean ridge.

Analyze and Conclude

1. continental margin, ocean basin floor, or mid-ocean ridge
2. Student responses will depend on which area of the ocean floor was contoured and what area of the model they choose to measure. If major features are missing from the measurements, it might be because only one transect line was measured. The larger the number of transects, the more accurate the results.
3. Collect data along additional transect lines.
4. The methods are similar in that no technology was used to collect data. A ruler was extended into the model until it reached the bottom, then a measurement was taken. The data collected gives information about only a very small area of the model. Large topographic features could be missed due to low sampling ratios.
Kinesthetic, Visual

Study Guide

Study Tip

Get Into the Habit of Actively Studying Each Day Encourage students to schedule a specific time each day to study. Suggest that they allot part of that time to outline information from their text or class notes, in addition to completing assignments.

CHAPTER 14

Study Guide

14.1 The Vast World Ocean

Key Concepts

- Nearly 71 percent of Earth's surface is covered by the global ocean.
- The world ocean can be divided into four main ocean basins—the Pacific Ocean, the Atlantic Ocean, the Indian Ocean, and the Arctic Ocean.
- The topography of the ocean floor is as diverse as that of continents.
- Today, technology—particularly sonar, satellites, and submersibles—allows scientists to study the ocean floor in a more efficient and precise manner.

Vocabulary

oceanography, *p. 394*; bathymetry, *p. 396*; sonar, *p. 398*; submersible, *p. 400*

14.2 Ocean Floor Features

Key Concepts

- The ocean floor regions are the continental margins, the ocean basin floor, and the mid-ocean ridge.
- In the Atlantic Ocean thick layers of undisturbed sediment cover the continental margin. This region has very little volcanic or earthquake activity.
- In the Pacific Ocean oceanic crust is plunging beneath continental crust. This force results in a narrow continental margin that experiences both volcanic activity and earthquakes.
- Continental shelves contain important mineral deposits, large reservoirs of oil and natural gas, and huge sand and gravel deposits.
- Trenches form at sites of plate convergence where one moving plate descends beneath another and plunges back into the mantle.
- The sediments that make up abyssal plains are carried there by turbidity currents or are deposited as a result of suspended sediments settling.
- New ocean floor is formed at mid-ocean ridges as magma rises between the diverging plates and cools.

Vocabulary

continental margin, *p. 402*; continental shelf, *p. 402*; continental slope, *p. 403* submarine canyon, *p. 403*; turbidity current, *p. 403*; continental rise, *p. 403*; ocean basin floor, *p. 404*; abyssal plains, *p. 404*; seamounts, *p. 404*; mid-ocean ridge, *p. 405*; seafloor spreading, *p. 405*

14.3 Seafloor Sediments

Key Concepts

- Ocean-floor sediments can be classified according to their origin into three broad categories: terrigenous sediments, biogenous sediments, and hydrogenous sediments.
- Terrigenous sediments consist primarily of mineral grains that were eroded from continental rocks and transported to the ocean.
- Biogenous sediments consist of shells and skeletons of marine animals and algae.
- Hydrogenous sediments consist of minerals that crystallize directly from ocean water through various chemical reactions.

Vocabulary

terrigenous sediment, *p. 408*; biogenous sediment, *p. 408*; calcareous ooze, *p. 408*; siliceous ooze, *p. 408*; hydrogenous sediment, *p. 409*

14.4 Resources from the Seafloor

Key Concepts

- Oil and natural gas are the main energy products currently being obtained from the ocean floor.
- Most oceanic gas hydrates are created when bacteria break down organic matter trapped in ocean-floor sediments.
- Other major resources from the seafloor include sand and gravel, evaporative salts, and manganese nodules.

Vocabulary

gas hydrates, *p. 411*; manganese nodule, *p. 412*

Chapter Assessment Resources

Print

Chapter Test, Chapter 14
Test Prep Resources, Chapter 14

Technology

Computer Test Bank, Chapter 14 Test
Online Text, Chapter 14
Go Online, PHSchool.com, Chapter 14

CHAPTER 14

NY Regents Content Item

Assessment

Interactive textbook with assessment at PHSchool.com 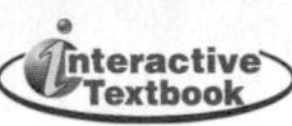

Reviewing Content

Choose the number that best answers the question or completes the statement.

1 Approximately what percentage of Earth's surface is covered by oceans? NY
(1) 40 (2) 50
(3) 60 (4) 70

2 Which ocean basin is the largest? NY
(1) the Atlantic (2) the Indian
(3) the Pacific (4) the Arctic

3 The use of sound waves to determine the depth of the ocean is called
(1) submarine sounding
(2) sonar
(3) satellite altimetry
(4) submersible sounding

4 The gently sloping submerged surface that extends from the shoreline toward the ocean basin floor is the continental NY
(1) shelf (2) slope
(3) rise (4) margin

5 Submarine canyons are believed to have been created by
(1) rivers during the ice age
(2) earthquakes
(3) lost ships
(4) subduction

6 Important mineral deposits, including large reservoirs of oil and natural gas, are associated with
(1) the ocean basin floor
(2) the continental shelf
(3) abyssal plains
(4) the continental rise

7 Calcareous ooze is an example of
(1) terrigenous sediment
(2) biogenous sediment
(3) hydrogenous sediment
(4) a combination of hydrogenous and terrigenous sediment

8 Sediments that consist of mineral grains that were eroded from continental rocks are called
(1) terrigenous (2) biogenous
(3) hydrogenous (4) hydrates

9 What could gas hydrates be used for? NY
(1) as landfill
(2) to make concrete
(3) as a source of energy
(4) as a source of cobalt and copper

10 Economically valuable materials such as diamonds, tin, and platinum are associated with which ocean floor resource?
(1) oil and natural gas
(2) sand and gravel
(3) evaporative salts
(4) manganese nodules

Understanding Concepts

11 Why is Earth called the "blue planet"?

12 What is bathymetry? What techniques do scientists use to discover more about the bathymetry of ocean basins?

13 Why is multibeam sonar more efficient than simple sonar at collecting data from the ocean floor?

14 Compare and contrast the size and topography of the Atlantic Ocean basin to that of the Pacific Ocean basin.

15 What is a continental shelf? What economic significance do continental shelves have?

16 Compare and contrast deep-ocean trenches and mid-oceanic ridges. NY

17 In which ocean basin are most trenches found? Why? NY

18 What is the difference between terrigenous sediments and biogenous sediments?

19 Explain the process by which hydrogenous sediments are formed.

20 Why is it uncommon to find calcareous ooze in deep-ocean basins?

21 From which area of the ocean basin are the resources of oil and natural gas harvested?

22 What current disadvantages exist to using gas hydrates as a form of energy? NY

23 What are the uses for sand and gravel harvested from the continental shelf?

Homework Guide

Section	Questions
1	1–3, 11–14, 24, 25, 29
2	4–6, 15–18, 26, 27, 30, 33
3	7, 8, 20, 21, 28, 31
4	9, 10, 22, 23

Assessment

Reviewing Content

(1) 4 (2) 3 (3) 2 (4) 1
(5) 2 (6) 1 (7) 2 (8) 1
(9) 3 (10) 2

Understanding Concepts

(11) Earth is called the "blue planet" because nearly 71 percent of Earth's surface is covered by oceans.
(12) Bathymetry is the measurement of ocean depths and charting the shape or topography of the ocean floor; sonar, satellites, submersibles
(13) Multibeam sonar uses more than one sound source and listening device. This allows scientists to obtain a profile of a narrow strip of floor and from that build a swath of detailed coverage.
(14) The Pacific Ocean basin is about twice the size of the Atlantic Ocean basin. Both have a variety of topographic features including mid-ocean ridges, abyssal plains, and seamounts. Trenches are more prevalent in the Pacific Ocean than the Atlantic Ocean. The continental margins of the Pacific Ocean are narrow and have more volcanic and earthquake activity than Atlantic Ocean margins. Plates in the Pacific Ocean are converging.
(15) The continental shelf is the gently sloping submerged surface extending from shoreline to the ocean basin floor. Continental shelves contain mineral deposits, large reservoirs of oil and natural gas, as well as huge sand and gravel deposits.
(16) Deep-ocean trenches are formed at convergence sites where one plate is being pushed beneath another, descending into Earth's mantle. Mid-ocean ridges are areas of divergence where new ocean floor is formed.
(17) The Pacific Ocean; plates in the Pacific Ocean are converging
(18) Terrigenous sediments are formed from weathered continental rocks. Biogenous sediments are formed from the remains of marine animals and algae.
(19) Hydrogenous sediments are formed when minerals crystallize directly from seawater through various chemical reactions.
(20) As the calcium carbonate tests of organisms sink into deeper parts of the ocean they dissolve. In seawater deeper than 4500 m, the tests dissolve completely before they reach the bottom.
(21) the continental shelf

Assessment (continued)

(22) Gas hydrates evaporate quickly when brought to the surface.
(23) Sand and gravel are used to make concrete, for landfill, and to fill recreational beaches.

Critical Thinking

(24) A large portion of the Southern Hemisphere is covered by ocean water. In the Northern Hemisphere, there are more continents that separate ocean basins.
(25) Gravity attracts water toward regions in the ocean where massive seafloor features occur. This creates elevations or depressions in sea surface height that can be measured using satellites.
(26) Passive continental margins are not areas of convergence. There is little volcanic and earthquake activity on passive margins. Active margins are areas of convergence where one plate is descending beneath another. They are associated with volcanic and earthquake activity.
(27) Mid-ocean ridges are far from coastal areas so there is less sediment reaching these areas. Also mid-ocean ridges are the site of new seafloor formation where sediments have not had a chance to settle.
(28) Student responses will vary but should show an understanding that manganese nodules have to be collected from great depths in the ocean where it is dark. The nodules are spread apart and would need to be located with accuracy. Accept all answers with reasonable supporting arguments.

Math Skills

(29) 1500 m/s · 10s = 15,000 m
15,000 m/1500 m/s = 10 s
(30) 2.5 cm/yr × 7 yr = 17.5 cm
(31) 4 km = 4000 m
4000 m ÷ 360m/day = 11.11 days

Concepts in Action

(32) Student graphs should reflect the data given in the table with the *x*-axis being the station number and the *y*-axis being depth.
(33) seamount or guyot

CHAPTER 14

Assessment *continued*

Critical Thinking

24 **Interpreting Diagrams** Reexamine Figure 1. Why do you think that the Northern Hemisphere is called the "land hemisphere" and the Southern Hemisphere is called the "water hemisphere"? NY

25 **Making Generalizations** A friend says that because of gravity we can learn about the topography of the ocean floor. Explain why this is true.

26 **Inferring** The continental margin of the Atlantic Ocean is often referred to as a "passive" continental margin whereas Pacific Ocean continental margins are referred to as "active." Infer what the characteristics of passive and active continental margins would be. NY

27 **Inferring** There is usually very little sediment accumulation found at mid-ocean ridges. Why do you think this is true? NY

28 **Applying Concepts** Imagine you have been asked to invent a device that would be used to retrieve manganese nodules. What characteristics would the device have in order to successfully achieve this goal?

Math Skills

29 **Calculating** Assuming the average speed of sound waves in water is 1500 meters per second, determine, in seconds, how long it would take a sonar signal to hit the bottom and return to the recorder if the water depth is 7500 meters.

30 **Calculating** The rate of seafloor spreading in the Atlantic Ocean has been estimated to be about 2.5 centimeters per year. By how many centimeters will the Atlantic Ocean basin increase over a period of 7 years? NY

31 **Calculating** If the settling rate of very fine sand in the open ocean is 360 meters per day, how many days will it take for the sediment to reach the ocean floor at a depth of 4 kilometers?

Concepts in Action

Use the table below to answer questions 32 and 33.

The table shows the kind of data that a simple sonar echo sounder would provide. The sonar is taken along a transect line in the Pacific Ocean. The stations are approximately 500 meters apart from each other.

Sonar Data

Station Number	Depth (in meters)	Station Number	Depth (in meters)
1	5500	7	3110
2	5550	8	3285
3	4540	9	3490
4	4000	10	4000
5	3675	11	4675
6	3355	12	5000

32 **Making Graphs** Plot these points on a sheet of graph paper.

33 **Interpreting Data** The data recorded in the table was taken over a portion of the ocean basin floor in the Pacific Ocean. What ocean basin feature could be between stations 2 and 12?

Performance-Based Assessment

Researching Choose a resource that is harvested from the ocean. Research information about how the resource is formed, where in the ocean it is harvested, what methods and equipment are used in the harvesting of the resource, what it is used for, and if there are any negative impacts on the marine environment as a result of harvesting the resource. Present the results of your research to your class in the form of an oral presentation.

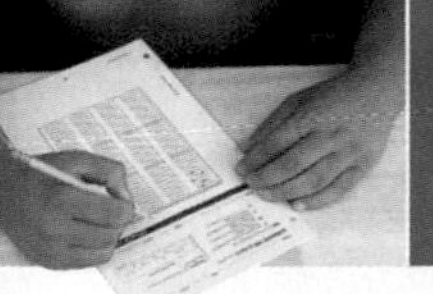

Regents Practice Exam

Test-Taking Tip

Avoiding Careless Mistakes
Students often make mistakes when they fail to examine a test question and possible answers thoroughly. Read the question carefully and underline key words that may change the meaning of the question, such as *not, except, excluding,* and so on. After choosing an answer, reread the question to check your selection.

Which of the following is NOT one of the four major topographic features of the ocean basin floor?
(1) deep-ocean trench
(2) abyssal plain
(3) submarine canyon
(4) seamount

(Answer: 3)

For *each* statement or question, choose the *number* of the word or expression that, of those given, best completes the statement or answers the question. Some questions may require the use of the *Earth Science Reference Tables.*

1 Which of the following is NOT true of deep ocean trenches?
(1) They are long and narrow depressions in the ocean floor.
(2) They are sites where plates plunge back into the mantle.
(3) They are geologically very stable.
(4) They may act as sediment traps.

2 Movements of sediment-rich water down the continental slope are know as
(1) streaming currents (2) longshore currents
(3) turbidity currents (4) avalanches

Answer the following questions in complete sentences. Some questions may require the use of the *Earth Science Reference Tables.* Base your answer to questions 3 and 4 on the diagram at top right, which shows the Atlantic Continental Margin.

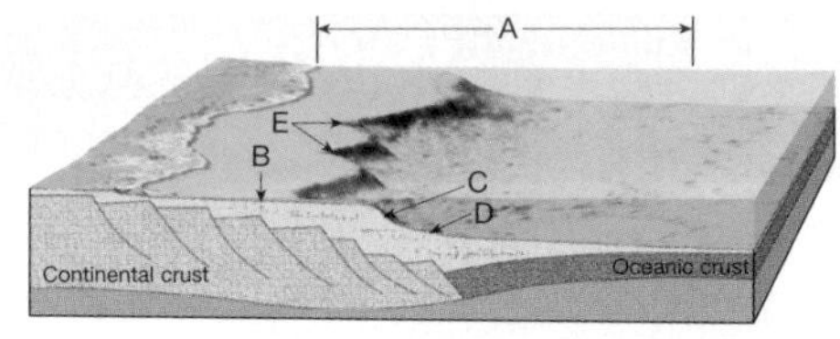

3 Which type of sediment would be carried the farthest from shore into area *A*?
(1) pebble (2) sand
(3) silt (4) clay

4 Sediments found at location *B* would most likely be
(1) sorted and rounded
(2) unsorted and angular
(3) sorted and angular
(4) unsorted and rounded

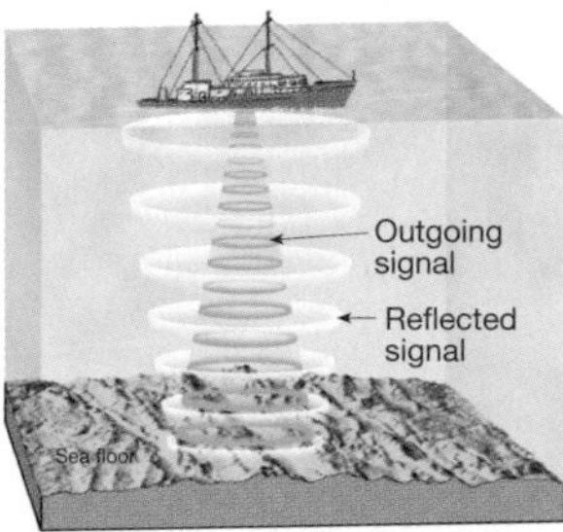

Base your answer to question 5 on the diagram above, which shows Sonar Methods.

5 How is sonar used to determine the topography of ocean basins?

6 Explain the process of sea floor spreading. Be sure to include both cause(s) and effect(s).

7 Explain how deep ocean trenches form.

8 The ocean and the ocean floor contain many valuable resources. Discuss one of these resources and explain why it is harvested or not harvested.

Regents Practice Exam

(1) 3
(2) 3
(3) 4
(4) 1
(5) Sonar works by transmitting sound waves toward the ocean bottom. A sensitive receiver intercepts the echo reflected from the bottom, and a clock precisely measures the time interval to fractions of a second. By knowing the speed of sound waves in water and the time required for the energy pulse to reach the ocean floor and return, depth can be calculated.
(6) When two plates move apart at a divergent boundary magma wells up to the surface, emerges, and cools at mid-ocean ridges forming new oceanic crust.
(7) At convergent plate boundaries where a denser plate subducts under a less dense plate and back into the mantle, a trench is formed.
(8) Answers will vary, but all should include relevant information. For example, salt present in the oceans is harvested because it is easy to collect water and evaporate it to get the salts out. Or, gas hydrates on the ocean floor would be a great source for methane, but the hydrates evaporate too quickly once brought to the surface. Perhaps future technologies will allow us to harvest the gas hydrates.

Performance-Based Assessment

Students' research and presentations on an ocean resource will vary but should accurately reflect proper and thorough research of the topic.

Your students can independently test their knowledge of the chapter and print out their results.

CHAPTER 15

Planning Guide

Use these planning tools
Use Teacher Express for all your planning needs

SECTION OBJECTIVES	STANDARDS		ACTIVITIES and LABS
	NATIONAL	STATE	
15.1 The Composition of Seawater, pp. 422–427 1 block or 2 periods **15.1** **Identify** the units used to express the salinity of ocean water. **15.2** **List** the sources of salt in ocean water. **15.3** **Recognize** the factors that affect the density of ocean water. **15.4** **Compare and contrast** the three main zones of the open ocean.	A-1, C-5, D-1, D-2		**SE** Inquiry Activity: How Does Salinity Affect the Density of Water? p. 421 L2 **TE** Teacher Demo: Synthetic Seawater, p. 423 L1 **TE** Teacher Demo: Solar Incidence Angles, p. 424 L2
15.2 The Diversity of Ocean Life, pp. 428–432 1 block or 2 periods **15.5** **Recognize** how marine organisms can be classified. **15.6** **Differentiate** between plankton and nekton. **15.7** **Describe** the area of the ocean in which most benthic organisms live. **15.8** **List** the factors used to divide the ocean into marine zones.	C-4, C-5, C-6		
15.3 Oceanic Productivity, pp. 433–437 1 block or 2 periods **15.9** **List** the factors that influence a region's photosynthetic productivity. **15.10** **Describe** the transfer of energy from one trophic level to another. **15.11** **Compare and contrast** food webs and food chains.	A-1, A-2, C-1, C-4, C-5		**TE** Teacher Demo: Creating an Energy Pyramid, p. 436 L2 **SE** Exploration Lab: How Does Temperature Affect Water Density? pp. 440–441 L2

Ability Levels		Components							
L1	For students who need additional help	SE	Student Edition	GRSW	Guided Reading and Study Workbook	TP	Test Prep Resources	GEO	Geode CD-ROM
L2	For all students	TE	Teacher's Edition	TEX	Teacher Express	onT	onlineText	T	Transparencies
L3	For students who need to be challenged	LM	Laboratory Manual	CTB	Computer Test Bank	DC	Discovery Channel Videos	GO	Internet Resources
		CUT	Chapter Tests						

RESOURCES PRINT and TECHNOLOGY	SECTION ASSESSMENT
GRSW Section 15.1 **T-188** Proportions of Water and Dissolved Salts in Seawater **T-189** Variations in Ocean Surface Temperature and Salinity **T-190** Recipe for Artificial Seawater **T-191** Variations in Ocean Water Temperature with Depth **T-192** Variations in Ocean Water Density with Depth **T-193** Three Layers of the Ocean **TEX** Lesson Planning 15.1	**SE** Section 15.1 Assessment, p. 427 **onT** Section 15.1
GRSW Section 15.2 **T-194** Marine Life Zones **T-195** Marine Life Zones **DC** Ocean Water and Ocean Life **TEX** Lesson Planning 15.2	**SE** Section 15.2 Assessment, p. 432 **onT** Section 15.2
GRSW Section 15.3 **T-196** Productivity in Polar Oceans **T-197** Productivity in Tropical Oceans **T-198** Productivity in Temperate Oceans **T-199** Comparing Productivities **T-200** Ecosystem Energy Flow **T-201** Food Chain and Food Web **TEX** Lesson Planning 15.3	**SE** Section 15.3 Assessment, p. 437 **onT** Section 15.3

Go Online

Go online for these Internet resources.

PHSchool.com
Web Code: cjk-9999

Web Code: cjn-5152

Materials for Activities and Labs

Quantities for each group

STUDENT EDITION

Inquiry Activity, p. 421
2 500-mL graduated cylinders, fresh water, salt water, small rubber ball or stopper small enough to fit inside the graduated cylinders

Exploration Lab, pp. 440–441
2 100-mL graduated cylinders, 2 test tubes, 2 beakers, food coloring or dye, stirrer, ice, tap water, graph paper, colored pencils

TEACHER'S EDITION

Teacher Demo, p. 423
samples of some or all of the chemical salts found in seawater: sodium chloride (NaCl), magnesium chloride (MgCl), sodium sulfate (Na_2SO_4), calcium chloride ($CaCl_2$), potassium chloride (KCl), sodium bicarbonate ($NaHCO_3$), potassium bromide (KBr), hydrogen borate (H_3BO_3), strontium chloride ($SrCl_2$), sodium fluoride (NaF), scale, 10 small beakers, 1 large beaker, stirring rod

Teacher Demo, p. 424
flashlight or slide/filmstrip projector

Teacher Demo, p. 436
classroom chalkboard, optional drawings or cutouts of ocean producers and consumers shown in Figure 16

Chapter Assessment

ASSESSMENT

SE Assessment, pp. 443–444
CUT Chapter 15 Test
CTB Chapter 15
onT Chapter 15

STANDARDIZED TEST PREP

SE Chapter 15, p. 445
TP Progress Monitoring Assessments

interactive textbook with assessment at PHSchool.com

CHAPTER 15

Before you teach

Michael Wysession
Washington University

Big Ideas

The oceans are rich and diverse with life, with a photosynthetic productivity that of the same order as life on land. Life has existed in the oceans for roughly 4 billion years, and has adapted to many different ocean environments.

Space and Time The ocean is effectively layered due to vertical differences in temperature, salinity, and the amount of sunlight received. Marine organisms are classified by where within the ocean they exist and how they move: plankton float near the surface, nekton swim (at a variety of depths), and benthos live at the seafloor. The first life on Earth may have evolved at undersea mid-ocean ridges.

Forces and Motion The factors that affect ocean life include the availability of sunlight, distance from shore, and water depth. Different zones of ocean life (photic, aphotic, intertidal, neritic, oceanic, pelagic, and benthic) are determined based on these factors.

Matter and Energy Salts comprise about 3.5 percent of the composition of seawater, with most of this being sodium chloride (NaCl). Variations in salinity, which are relatively small, occur largely because of geographic changes in evaporation rates and the influx of fresh water.

The temperature of deep seawater is about 2°C everywhere, but surface temperatures vary, largely according to latitude.

Earth as a System Primary productivity of life occurs primarily through photosynthesis, and varies according to latitude. Chemical energy within life passes through a food chain from one trophic level to the next.

Earth Science Refresher

Seawater and Life

The beginning of this chapter says that our own body chemistry is close to that of seawater. The same holds for all other living organisms as well. In fact, we cannot conceive of a life form that is not based upon salt water. Our own bodies are like small oceans, to the point that, poetically speaking, we could be seen as the ocean's attempt to finally conquer the land of the continents.

The oceans certainly contained large numbers of organic molecules early on in their history. These organic molecules occur naturally—they are even found within meteorites. It is not until these molecules developed into cell membranes that enclosed self-replicating "genetic" molecules that we consider the beginning of life. However, even in the simple one-celled organisms (usually divided into two classes—archaea and bacteria), the fluid inside the cell membrane remained remarkably close to the composition of seawater, and it has been this way with all cells since.

Address Misconceptions

Students may think that the salt in ocean water is composed simply of sodium chloride, common table salt. Show students samples of several of the following chemical salts found in ocean water, to give them an idea of the variety of salts in the ocean: sodium chloride (NaCl), magnesium chloride (MgCl), sodium sulfate (Na_2SO_4), calcium chloride ($CaCl_2$), potassium chloride (KCl), sodium bicarbonate ($NaHCO_3$), potassium bromide (KBr), hydrogen borate (H_3BO_3), strontium chloride ($SrCl_2$), sodium fluoride (NaF). For a strategy that helps to overcome this misconception, see **Address Misconceptions** on **p. 423.**

Go Online PDLINKS NSTA
For: Chapter 15 Content Support
Visit: www.SciLinks.org/PDLinks
Web Code: cjn-1599

Evolutionary Survival Techniques

Life in the oceans is much more diverse than it was several billion years ago. Part of the reason for this is the wide variety of survival techniques that life-forms have adapted in order to survive. For example, the mitochondria in animal cells and the chloroplasts in plant cells are separate simple one-celled organisms that exist in a symbiotic relationship with their host cells. At some point in the evolution of life, mitochondria invaded other one-celled ocean organisms, and the arrangement was of benefit to both. The mitochondria provided energy to the host cell, and the host provided a safe, comfortable place for the mitochondria. These were the first animals, in the form of complex one-celled organisms, called eukarya.

A wide variety of symbiotic relationships now exists among ocean life-forms. For instance, the tentacles of the sea anemone are poisonous and are used to trap fish for food. However, the clownfish has evolved to be immune to the toxin as part of a symbiotic relationship with the anemones. The clownfish cleans the anemone's tentacles, and the anemone protects the clownfish from predators. Both survive better with each other than without.

One of the most important factors driving the evolution of ocean species is the interaction of predators and prey. In fact, the sudden burst in ocean life diversity at the start of the Cambrian period is likely a result of this. New species of life kept evolving to do a better job of avoiding being eaten as prey (hard shells, speed, camouflage, size, multiple offspring), so predators kept evolving to do a better job of catching prey (teeth, claws, fins, eyes, taste). Over time, most ocean life-forms have gone extinct, replaced by organisms that did a better job in whatever niche they occupied. However, a few life-forms, like the shark and nautilus, did their jobs extremely efficiently, and so have changed very little over hundreds of millions of years.

Address Misconceptions

Students may think that higher trophic levels actually contain more energy than lower trophic levels because they may reason that energy accumulates as you move up a food chain. Emphasize that the solar energy absorbed by producers is the only energy available to all the succeeding levels of the food chain. For a strategy that helps to overcome the misconception, see **Address Misconceptions** on **p. 436.**

Build Reading Literacy

Predict

Previewing to Predict Content

Strategy Help students activate their prior knowledge about a topic and become actively engaged in reading. The process of making and confirming predictions also helps students correct their own misconceptions. Before the students begin, have them focus on one topic in Chapter 15, such as the introductory paragraph on p. 422.

Example

1. Introduce students to the topic by having them read the heading and subheadings.

2. Ask students what they think they will learn about the topic.

3. Have a student read aloud the first Key Concept under Reading Focus at the top of the page.

4. Have another student read aloud the Previewing instructions in the Reading Strategy.

5. Based on what they've read so far, ask students to predict the content of the section. Write their predictions on the board.

6. Have a student read aloud the boldfaced key statement on p. 424. Then, have other students read aloud the boldfaced terms on p. 426.

7. Discuss with students the predictions on the board. Allow them to revise the predictions if they wish.

8. Have students read through the section independently. Afterwards, ask which of their predictions were confirmed. Point out that there's nothing wrong with making an incorrect prediction. Predicting can help readers learn more about a topic.

See p. 425 for a script on how to use this strategy with students. For additional strategies, see pp. 428 and 435.

ASSESS PRIOR KNOWLEDGE

Use the Chapter Pretest below to assess students' prior knowledge. As needed, review these concepts.

Review Science Concepts

Section 15.1 A knowledge of the effects of salinity and density on ocean water leads to an understanding of the major characteristics of the world ocean and how those characteristics vary from one part of the globe to another.

Section 15.2 A knowledge of the classification of ocean life and the marine zones in which they live helps students recognize the diversity and importance of ocean dwelling organisms.

Section 15.3 A knowledge of how energy moves from one trophic level to another in ocean environments is essential for an understanding of how ocean organisms survive.

CHAPTER 15 Ocean Water and Ocean Life

CONCEPTS in Action

Exploration Lab
How Does Temperature Affect Water Density?

How the Earth Works
Ocean Life

Discovery Channel School **Video Field Trip**
Ocean Water and Ocean Life

Take an underwater field trip with the Discovery Channel and learn about the feeding relationships among sea creatures. Answer the following questions after watching the video.

1. How do sardines ingest plankton?
2. Why do dolphins need to pin their prey close to the ocean surface?

For: Chapter 15 Resources
Visit: PHSchool.com
Web Code: cjk-9999

The marine environment is a habitat for ▶ thousands of species of organisms, including the damselfish and corals shown here in the south Pacific near Fiji.

420 *Chapter 15*

Chapter Pretest

1. What units are used to measure the salinity of ocean water? *(c)*
   a. percent
   b. parts per billion
   c. parts per thousand
   d. parts per million

2. Which of the following samples of seawater has the greatest density? *(d)*
   a. A at 35°C b. B at 25°C
   c. C at 15°C d. D at 5°C

3. The top layer of ocean water through which sunlight penetrates is the ________. *(b)*
   a. aphotic zone b. photic zone
   c. benthos d. oceanic zone

4. What is the difference between plankton and nekton? *(Plankton are moved about by ocean currents; nekton can swim about independent of ocean currents.)*

5. True or False: All producer organisms living in the ocean are capable of photosynthesis. *(False)*

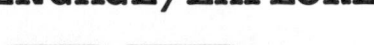

OCEANOGRAPHY

Chapter Preview

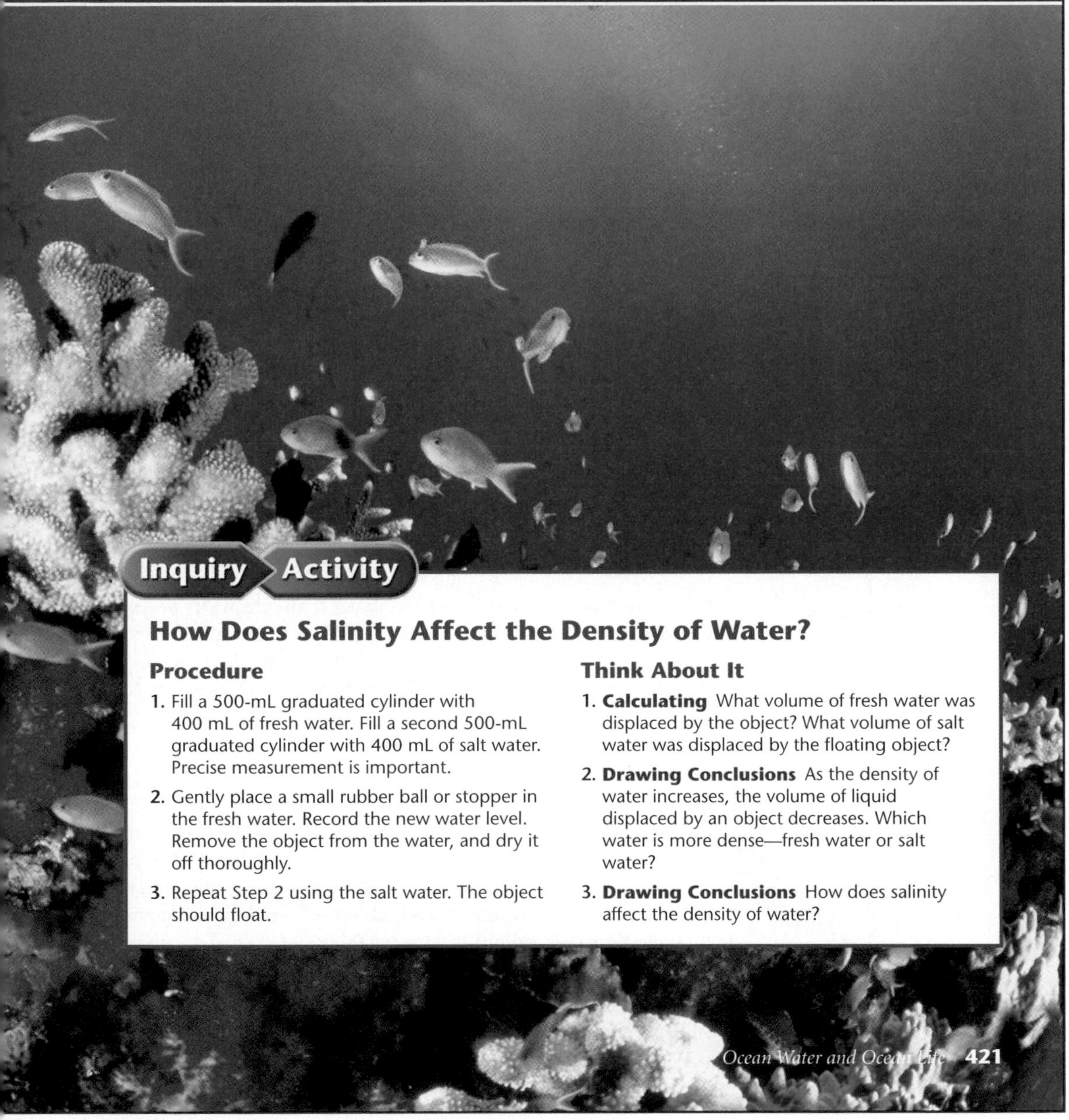

Inquiry Activity

How Does Salinity Affect the Density of Water?

Procedure

1. Fill a 500-mL graduated cylinder with 400 mL of fresh water. Fill a second 500-mL graduated cylinder with 400 mL of salt water. Precise measurement is important.
2. Gently place a small rubber ball or stopper in the fresh water. Record the new water level. Remove the object from the water, and dry it off thoroughly.
3. Repeat Step 2 using the salt water. The object should float.

Think About It

1. **Calculating** What volume of fresh water was displaced by the object? What volume of salt water was displaced by the floating object?
2. **Drawing Conclusions** As the density of water increases, the volume of liquid displaced by an object decreases. Which water is more dense—fresh water or salt water?
3. **Drawing Conclusions** How does salinity affect the density of water?

Video Field Trip

Ocean Water and Ocean Life

Encourage students to view the Video Field Trip "Ocean Water and Ocean Life."

ENGAGE/EXPLORE

How Does Salinity Affect the Density of Water? L2

Purpose In this activity, students begin to recognize the relationship between the salinity and density of water and understand that higher salinity correlates with higher density.

Skills Focus Measuring, Inferring

 **Prep Time** 10 minutes

Materials 2 500-mL graduated cylinders, fresh water, salt water, small rubber ball or stopper small enough to fit inside the graduated cylinders

Class Time 15 minutes

Teaching Tip The floating object could be a "superball" (small, very bouncy ball), a rubber stopper, the screw cap from a glass vial, or anything from the laboratory that will fit in the mouth of the graduated cylinder but has enough mass and density to displace a measurable amount of water and stay afloat. A cork is too light and a marble too heavy.

Expected Outcome Floating object will displace more fresh water, indicating that fresh water has a lower density.

Think About It

1. Student answers will vary depending on the floating object used in the experiment, but the volume of salt water displaced should be less than the volume of fresh water displaced.
2. salt water
3. The addition of salt increases the density of water.

1 FOCUS

Section Objectives

15.1 **Identify** the units used to express the salinity of ocean water.

15.2 **List** the sources of salt in ocean water.

15.3 **Recognize** the factors that affect the density of ocean water.

15.4 **Compare and contrast** the three main zones of the open ocean.

Reading Focus

Build Vocabulary L2

Word Parts Before students read this section, ask them to write the meanings of the prefix *thermo-* (*"temperature"*) and the suffix *-cline* (*"slope"*). Then have students write a definition for what they think the word *thermocline* means. After students read the section, have them examine their definition and discuss whether or not it needs to be changed.

Reading Strategy L2

a. evaporation, runoff, ice formation, melting of ice

Sample additional questions and answers for **b.** to **g.**: **What are the sources of sea salts?** *(weathered rocks, volcanic eruptions)* **What factors affect seawater temperature?** *(sunlight, depth)* **What factors affect seawater density?** *(salinity, temperature)*

2 INSTRUCT

Salinity

Use Visuals L1

Figure 1 Have students examine the graph. Ask: **Which of these two types of measures—weight or volume—is used to determine the percentages of salts and water in a sample of seawater?** *(weight)* **What unit of measure is used?** *(grams)* **Why do you suppose salinity is usually expressed as "parts per thousand" instead of "percent" or "parts per hundred"?** *(easier to use in calculations, because fewer decimal places are required)* **Visual**

15.1 The Composition of Seawater

Reading Focus

Key Concepts

- What units are used to express the salinity of ocean water?
- What are the sources of salt in ocean water?
- What factors affect the density of ocean water?
- What are the three main zones of the open ocean?

Vocabulary

- salinity
- thermocline
- density
- pycnocline
- mixed zone

Reading Strategy

Previewing Copy the table below. Before you read, preview the figures in this section and add three more questions to the table. As you read, write answers to your questions.

Questions About Seawater	Answers
What processes affect seawater salinity?	a. ?
b. ? ?	c. ?
d. ? ?	e. ?
f. ? ?	g. ?

Figure 1 Salts in Seawater This circle graph shows that 1000 grams of seawater with a salinity of 35‰ consists of 965 grams of water and 35 grams of various salts and other solids dissolved in the water.

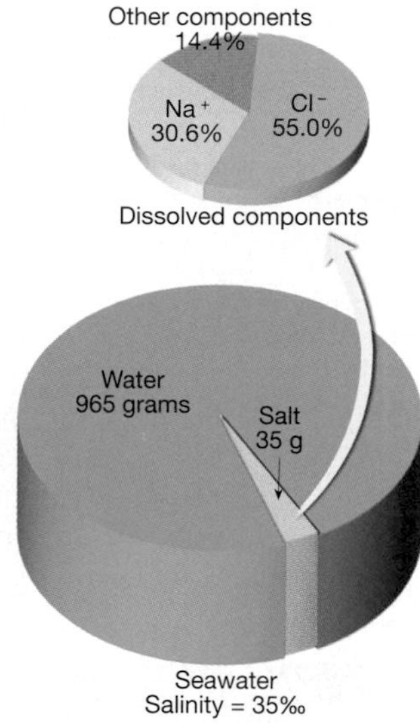

What is the difference between pure water and seawater? One of the most obvious differences is that seawater contains dissolved substances that give it a salty taste. These dissolved substances include sodium chloride, other salts, metals, and even dissolved gases. In fact, every known naturally occurring element is found dissolved in at least trace amounts in seawater. The salt content of seawater makes it unsuitable for drinking or for irrigating most crops and causes it to be highly corrosive to many materials. However, many parts of the ocean are full of life adapted to this environment.

Water is the major component of nearly every life form on Earth. Our own body fluid chemistry is similar to the chemistry of seawater. Seawater consists of about 3.5 percent dissolved mineral substances that are collectively termed "salts." Although the percentage of dissolved components may seem small, the actual quantity is huge because the ocean is so vast.

Salinity

Salinity (*salinus* = salt) is the total amount of solid material dissolved in water. It is the ratio of the mass of dissolved substances to the mass of the water sample. Many common quantities are expressed in percent (%), which is parts per hundred. **Because the proportion of dissolved substances in seawater is such a small number, oceanographers typically express salinity in parts per thousand (‰).** The average salinity of seawater is 3.5% or 35‰. Figure 1 shows the principal elements that contribute to the ocean's salinity. **Most of the salt in seawater is sodium chloride, common table salt.**

Sources of Sea Salts What are the primary sources of dissolved substances in the ocean? **Chemical weathering of rocks on the continents is one source of elements found in seawater.** These dissolved materials reach oceans through runoff from rivers and streams at an estimated rate of more than 2.3 billion metric tons per year. **The second major source of elements found in seawater is from Earth's interior.** Through volcanic eruptions, large quantities of water vapor and other gases have been emitted into the atmosphere during much of geologic time. Scientists believe that this is the principal source of water in the oceans. About 4 billion years ago, as Earth's temperature cooled, the water vapor condensed and torrential rains filled the ocean basins with water. Certain elements—particularly chlorine, bromine, sulfur, and boron—were emitted along with the water. These elements exist in the ocean in much greater quantities than could be explained by weathering of rocks alone.

Processes Affecting Salinity Because the ocean is well mixed, the relative concentrations of the major components in seawater are essentially constant, no matter where the ocean is sampled. Surface salinity variation in the open ocean normally ranges from 33‰ to 38‰. Variations in salinity result from changes in the water content of the solution.

Figure 2 shows some of the different processes that affect the amount of water in seawater, thereby affecting salinity. Some processes add large amounts of fresh water to seawater, decreasing salinity. These processes include precipitation, runoff from land, icebergs melting, and sea ice melting.

Q *Is the ocean getting saltier?*

A Evidence suggests that the composition of seawater has been relatively stable for millions of years. Material is being removed just as rapidly as it is added by rivers and volcanic activity. Some dissolved components are removed from sea water by organisms as they build hard structures. Other components are lost when they chemically precipitate out of the water as sediment. Still others are exchanged at the oceanic ridge at hydrothermal vents. The net effect is that the overall makeup of seawater has remained relatively constant for a long time.

Figure 2 Natural processes affect the salinity of seawater. ***Applying Concepts** Which processes decrease the salinity of seawater? Which processes increase it?*

Customize for English Language Learners

Explain to students that *pycno* is from the Greek word *pyknos*, which means "dense" or "compact." *Cline* can mean "slope" or "gradient." (*Gradient* means "incline" or "a change in the value of a quantity.") Have students use this information to write the meaning of the term *pycnocline* in their own words. *(Possible answers: density slope or density gradient)* Have students find and look up the meanings of other words that include one of these two word elements. *(Possible answers: pycnometer—device used to measure water density; inclined plane—sloping surface)*

Address Misconceptions L2

Students may think that the salt in ocean water is composed simply of sodium chloride, common table salt. Show students samples of several of the following chemical salts found in ocean water, to give them an idea of the variety of salts in the ocean: sodium chloride (NaCl), magnesium chloride (MgCl), sodium sulfate (Na_2SO_4), calcium chloride ($CaCl_2$), potassium chloride (KCl), sodium bicarbonate ($NaHCO_3$), potassium bromide (KBr), hydrogen borate (H_3BO_3), strontium chloride ($SrCl_2$), sodium fluoride (NaF). Have students make a list of all the elements represented.
Visual, Logical

Synthetic Seawater L2

Purpose Students work together as a class to make artificial seawater.

Materials 10 salts listed in the table below, scale, 10 small beakers, 1 large beaker, stirrer

Procedure Assign each of ten groups one salt and have them measure out the grams of that salt according to the table below. After all groups have added their salts to the same container, add enough water to make 1000 g of solution.

Safety Students should wear goggles and take care not to ingest the salts.

Expected Outcome Students create a solution of synthetic seawater.
Kinesthetic

Recipe for Artificial Seawater

Salt	Amount (grams)
NaCl	23.48
MgCl	4.98
Na_2SO_4	3.92
$CaCl_2$	1.10
KCl	0.66
$NaHCO_3$	0.192
KBr	0.096
H_3BO_3	0.026
$SrCl_2$	0.024
NaF	0.003

Kinesthetic, Visual

Answer to . . .

Figure 2 *decrease: precipitation, runoff from land, icebergs melting, sea ice melting; increase: evaporation, formation of sea ice*

Ocean Temperature Variation

Build Science Skills L2

Inferring Ask students to refer to the line graph in Figure 3 and a world map or globe to answer the following questions. Ask: **At which latitude is sea surface salinity the lowest?** *(60°N)* **Where on the globe is this region located?** *(near the Arctic circle)* **During what season(s) of the year were salinity data for latitude 60°N probably taken?** *(spring or summer)* **How do you know?** *(Ice probably was melting, which increases salinity.)* **In what ways can temperature affect salinity?** *(Above-freezing temperatures allow polar ice to melt, adding fresh water to the ocean surface and decreasing salinity. Ice formation in below-freezing temperatures removes fresh water, increasing salinity.)* **Visual, Logical**

Teacher Demo

Solar Incidence Angles L2

Purpose Students observe the difference in the angle of incidence of the sun's rays at the equator and the poles.

Materials flashlight or slide/filmstrip projector

Procedure Darken the room. Aim the light perpendicular to the ceiling, and have students measure or estimate the area illuminated. Explain to students that this is similar to the angle at which the sun's light reaches equatorial regions of Earth. Next, slant the light so that it covers a much larger area. Encourage students to estimate or measure the illuminated area. Explain to students that this is more like the angle at which the sun's light reaches the polar regions of Earth. Point out to students that, since the energy of the light source is unchanged, a smaller amount of light energy is reaching each unit of illuminated area.

Expected Outcome Students observe that light energy from the sun is more concentrated in equatorial regions, which explains why temperatures are warmer at the equator than at the poles. **Visual, Logical**

Other processes remove large amounts of fresh water from seawater, increasing salinity. These processes include evaporation and the formation of sea ice. High salinities, for example, are found where evaporation rates are high, as is the case in the dry subtropical regions. In areas where large amounts of precipitation dilute ocean waters, as in the mid-latitudes and near the equator, salinity is lower. Both of these examples are shown on the graph in Figure 3.

Surface salinity in polar regions varies seasonally due to the formation and melting of sea ice. When seawater freezes in winter, salts do not become part of the ice. Therefore, the salinity of the remaining seawater increases. In summer when sea ice melts, the addition of relatively fresh water dilutes the solution and salinity decreases.

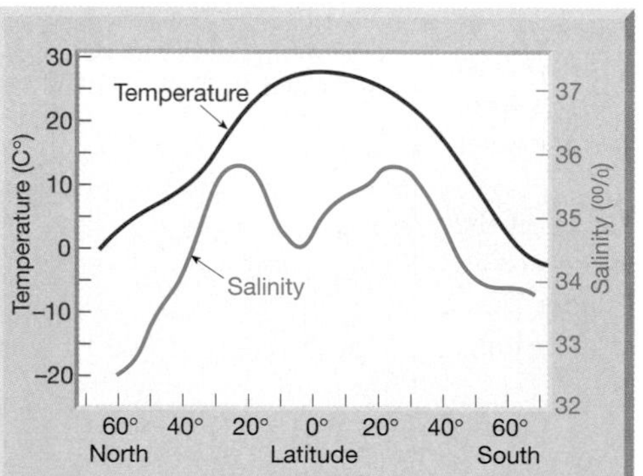

Figure 3 This graph shows the variations in ocean surface temperature (top curve) and surface salinity (lower curve). ***Interpreting Diagrams*** *At which latitudes is sea surface temperature highest? Why?*

Ocean Temperature Variation

The ocean's surface water temperature varies with the amount of solar radiation received, which is primarily a function of latitude. The graph in Figure 3 shows this relationship. The intensity of solar radiation in high latitudes is much less than the intensity of solar radiation received in tropical latitudes. Therefore, lower sea surface temperatures are found in high-latitude regions. Higher sea surface temperatures are found in low-latitude regions.

Temperature Variation with Depth If you lowered a thermometer from the surface of the ocean into deeper water, what temperature pattern do you think you would find? Surface waters are warmed by the sun, so they generally have higher temperatures than deeper waters. However, the observed temperature pattern depends on the latitude.

Figure 4 on page 425 shows two graphs of temperature versus depth: one for low-latitude regions and one for high-latitude regions. The low-latitude curve begins with high temperature at the surface. However, the temperature decreases rapidly with depth because of the inability of the sun's rays to penetrate very far into the ocean. At a depth of about 1000 meters, the temperature remains just a few degrees above freezing and is relatively constant from this level down to the ocean floor. The **thermocline** (*thermo* = heat, *cline* = slope) is the layer of ocean water between about 300 meters and 1000 meters, where there is a rapid change of temperature with depth. The thermocline is a very important structure in the ocean because it creates a vertical barrier to many types of marine life.

Facts and Figures

The salinity of seawater is about four times greater than the salinity of body fluids. If seawater enters the digestive system, it causes internal membranes to lose water through osmosis, which transports water molecules from higher concentrations to lower concentrations. Drinking seawater would cause water from one's body fluids to move into the digestive tract and eventually be expelled from the body, causing dehydration. This can be a problem if seawater is consumed in large amounts, but an occasional swallow when swimming or snorkeling is nothing to worry about.

The high-latitude curve in Figure 4 shows a very different pattern from the low-latitude curve. Surface water temperatures in high latitudes are much cooler than in low latitudes, so the curve begins at the surface with a low temperature. Deeper in the ocean, the temperature of the water is similar to that at the surface, so the curve remains vertical. There is no rapid change of temperature with depth. A thermocline is not present in high latitudes. Instead, the water column is isothermal (*iso* = same, *thermo* = heat).

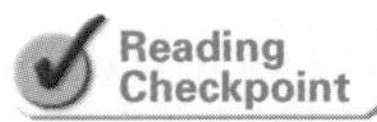

What is the thermocline?

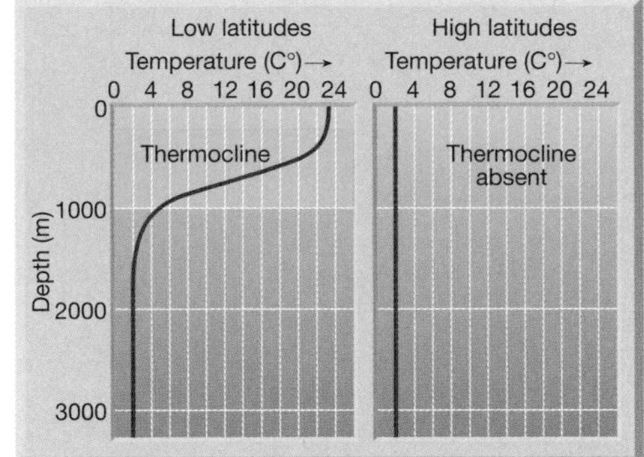

Figure 4 These graphs show the variations in ocean water temperature with depth for low-latitude and high-latitude regions. **Applying Concepts** ***Why is the thermocline absent in the high latitudes?***

Ocean Density Variation

Density is defined as mass per unit volume. It can be thought of as a measure of how heavy something is for its size. For example, an object that has low density is lightweight for its size, such as a dry sponge, foam packing, or a surfboard. An object that has high density is heavy for its size, such as cement, most metals, or a large container full of water.

Density is an important property of ocean water because it determines the water's vertical position in the ocean. Density differences cause large areas of ocean water to sink or float. When high-density seawater is added to low-density fresh water, the denser seawater sinks below the fresh water.

Factors Affecting Seawater Density **Seawater density is influenced by two main factors: salinity and temperature.** An increase in salinity adds dissolved substances and results in an increase in seawater density. An increase in temperature results in a decrease in seawater density. Temperature has the greatest influence on surface seawater density because variations in surface seawater temperature are greater than salinity variations. In fact, only in the extreme polar areas of the ocean—where temperatures are low and remain relatively constant—does salinity significantly affect density. Cold water that also has high salinity is some of the highest-density water in the world.

Ocean Density Variation

Build Reading Literacy L1

Refer to **p. 420D**, which provides the guidelines for this preview strategy.

Predict Have students preview the remainder of this section by looking over the headings, figures, figure captions, and boldfaced terms. Ask students to write their predictions of how seawater density is affected by salinity and by temperature. After students have read the section, have them evaluate their predictions and make changes, if necessary.
Verbal, Logical

Integrate Physics L2

Weight and Density Remind students that the weight of a given volume of material increases as its density increases. Ask: **What physical force causes water of a higher density to sink below water of a lower density?** *(gravity)*
Logical

Use Visuals L1

Figure 4 Have students examine the two graphs. Ask: **What is the temperature range within the thermocline at low latitudes?** *(approximately 24°C to 4°C)* **What is the lowest water temperature shown on the graph?** *(approximately 2°C)* **What is the range of depths at which water of this temperature is found at low latitudes?** *(from approximately 1500 m to below 3000 m)* **At high latitudes?** *(from the surface to below 3000 m)*
Visual, Verbal

Facts and Figures

Seawater has unique thermal properties that make it resistant to changes in temperature. Many marine species cannot withstand rapid temperature changes. Researchers have concluded that the ocean's stability as a habitat has been instrumental in the development of life on Earth. Scientists who study the effects of global warming indicate that atmospheric warming would eventually be transferred to the ocean, potentially affecting marine organisms. A research project conducted by scientists at the Scripps Institute of Oceanography in the 1990s used sound waves transmitted across an ocean basin to measure ocean temperature. The speed of sound in seawater increases as the water temperature increases, so in the future, if the oceans are getting warmer, the sound would take less time to travel the same distance.

Answer to . . .

Figure 3 *Sea surface temperature is highest at the equator and low latitudes because these areas receive the most solar radiation at the highest angle of incidence.*

Figure 4 *The thermocline is absent in the high latitudes because the temperature of surface water is closer to the temperature of deeper water.*

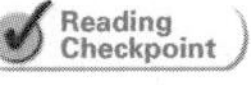

The thermocline is the layer of ocean water between about 300 m and 1000 m, where there is a rapid change of temperature with depth.

Build Science Skills L2

Compare and Contrast Have students compare the graph showing a thermocline in Figure 4 with the graph showing a pycnocline in Figure 5. Ask: **In what way are the data plot lines in these two graphs similar?** *(Both show variations that occur from the ocean surface down to depths of close to 1000 m.)* **In what way are the data plot lines in these two graphs different?** *(Temperature decreases within the thermocline; density increases within the pycnocline.)*
Visual, Logical

Build Science Skills 

Inferring Have students examine the two graphs shown in Figure 5. Ask: **What can you infer about temperature by looking at these two graphs? Why?** *(Since the density of ocean water is affected more by temperature than by salinity, it follows that the density gradient shown in the low latitude graph reflects variations in temperature with changes in depth, and the lack of a density gradient in the high latitude graph reflects little or no variation in temperature with changes in depth.)* **Under what circumstances might a pycnocline occur in high latitude waters?** *(During warmer seasons of the year, ice melt could add fresh water to the upper layer of seawater, creating a variation in density with respect to water at greater depths.)*
Visual, Logical

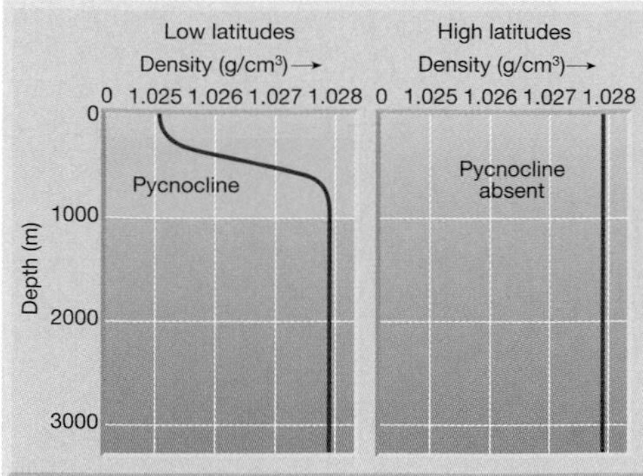

Figure 5 The graphs show variations in ocean water density with depth for low-latitude and high-latitude regions.
Interpreting Diagrams
What is the difference between the low-latitude graph and the high-latitude graph? Why does this difference occur?

Density Variation with Depth By sampling ocean waters, oceanographers have learned that temperature and salinity—and the water's resulting density—vary with depth. Figure 5 shows two graphs of density versus depth. One graph shows the density for low-latitude regions and the other for high-latitude regions. Compare the density curves in Figure 5 to the temperature curves in Figure 4. They are similar. This similarity demonstrates that temperature is the most important factor affecting seawater density. It also shows that temperature is inversely proportional to density. When two quantities are inversely proportional, they can be multiplied together to equal a constant. Therefore, if the value of one quantity increases, the value of the other quantity decreases proportionately. When water temperature increases, its density decreases.

Reading Checkpoint *How does temperature affect the density of seawater?*

The **pycnocline** (*pycno* = density, *cline* = slope) is the layer of ocean water between about 300 meters and 1000 meters where there is a rapid change of density with depth. A pycnocline presents a significant barrier to mixing between low-density water above and high-density water below. A pycnocline is not present in high latitudes; instead, the water column is about the same density throughout.

Ocean Layering

The ocean, like Earth's interior, is layered according to density. Low-density water exists near the surface, and higher-density water occurs below. Except for some shallow inland seas with a high rate of evaporation, the highest-density water is found at the greatest ocean depths. **Oceanographers generally recognize a three-layered structure in most parts of the open ocean: a shallow surface mixed zone, a transition zone, and a deep zone.** These zones are shown in Figure 6.

Surface Zone Because solar energy is received at the ocean surface, it is here that water temperatures are warmest. The **mixed zone** is the area of the surface created by the mixing of water by waves, currents, and tides. The mixed zone has nearly uniform temperatures. The depth and temperature of this layer vary, depending on latitude and season. The zone usually extends to about 300 meters, but it may extend to a depth of 450 meters. The surface mixed zone accounts for only about 2 percent of ocean water.

426 Chapter 15

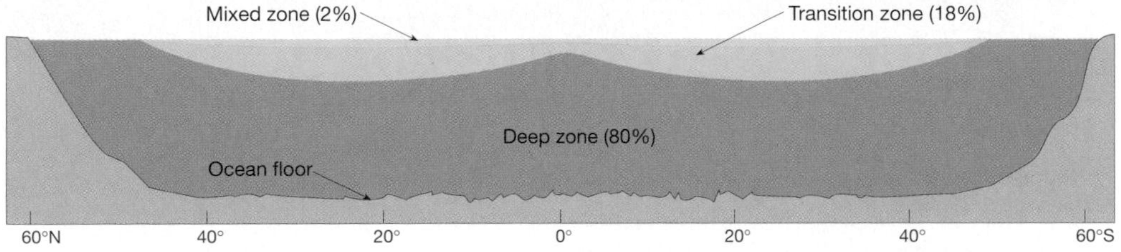

Figure 6 Ocean Zones Oceanographers recognize three main zones of the ocean based on water density, which varies with temperature and salinity.

Transition Zone Below the sun-warmed zone of mixing, the temperature falls abruptly with depth as was seen in Figure 4. Here, a distinct layer called the transition zone exists between the warm surface layer above and the deep zone of cold water below. The transition zone includes a thermocline and associated pycnocline. This zone accounts for about 18 percent of ocean water.

Deep Zone Below the transition zone is the deep zone. Sunlight never reaches this zone, and water temperatures are just a few degrees above freezing. As a result, water density remains constant and high. The deep zone includes about 80 percent of ocean water.

In high latitudes, this three-layered structure of the open ocean does not exist as seen in Figure 6. The three layers do not exist because there is no rapid change in temperature or density with depth. Therefore, good vertical mixing between surface and deep waters can occur in high-latitude regions. Here, cold high-density water forms at the surface, sinks, and initiates deep-ocean currents, which are discussed in Chapter 16.

Section 15.1 Assessment

Reviewing Concepts

1. What is salinity? What units are used to express the salinity of ocean water?
2. What are the six most abundant elements in seawater?
3. What are the sources of salt in ocean water?
4. Explain the relationship between latitude and sea surface temperature.
5. What factors affect the density of ocean water?
6. What are the three main zones of the open ocean?

Critical Thinking

7. **Inferring** Why does the salinity of seawater remain relatively constant over time?
8. **Summarizing** Explain the general pattern of temperature variation with depth in low-latitude oceans.

Writing in Science

Descriptive Paragraph Write a paragraph that describes the different characteristics of the three zones of the open ocean. Include an explanation of why polar regions do not exhibit the same pattern of water stratification.

Ocean Layering

Use Visuals

Figure 5 After students have read the description of the transition zone, have them look back at Figure 5. Ask: **What is the depth range of the transition zone as shown in this graph?** *(region of most abrupt temperature change, from about 500–1000 m)*
Visual

3 ASSESS

Evaluate Understanding L2

To assess students' understanding of section content, present them with an unlabeled diagram showing an ocean profile similar to the one shown in Figure 5. Have students label the three ocean zones, or layers, and use arrows to indicate the direction in which water temperature increases at lower latitudes, and the direction in which density increases at lower latitudes.

Reteach L1

Have students work in pairs to create a set of flash cards for all the vocabulary terms in this section. Have students use the flash cards to quiz each other on the definitions.

Writing in Science

The surface mixed zone has the warmest temperatures and the most light. Water is well mixed by waves, currents, and tides. The water temperature is nearly uniform. The transition zone includes the thermocline and pycnocline in which both temperature and density change rapidly with depth. Sunlight does not reach the deep zone where water is near freezing in temperature. This pattern does not exist at polar latitudes because water is isothermal and of uniform density, so there is good vertical mixing in the water column.

Section 15.1 Assessment

1. Salinity is the total amount of solid material dissolved in water; parts per thousand
2. sodium, chlorine, sulfur, oxygen, magnesium, calcium
3. chemical weathering of rocks on continents; Earth's interior
4. Sea surface temperature is higher at the equator and low latitudes. Sea surface temperature decreases as latitude increases.
5. temperature and salinity
6. surface mixed zone, transition zone, deep zone
7. Dissolved components are being removed as rapidly as they are being added.
8. Temperature decreases with increasing depth; a thermocline is present between 300 m and 1000 m.

Answer to . . .

Figure 5 *Pycnocline is not present in high latitude waters. This occurs because density and temperature do not vary with depth.*

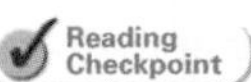
As the temperature of seawater decreases, its density increases.

Section 15.2

1 FOCUS

Section Objectives

15.5 **Recognize** how marine organisms can be classified.
15.6 **Differentiate** between plankton and nekton.
15.7 **Describe** the area of the ocean in which most benthic organisms live.
15.8 **List** the factors used to divide the ocean into marine zones.

Reading Focus

Build Vocabulary L2

Concept Map Have students make a concept map using the term *marine life zones* as the starting point that connects to the following three terms: *availability of sunlight, distance from shore,* and *depth.* Students should use the following terms to complete their concept map: *pelagic zone, photic zone, oceanic zone, benthic zone, abyssal zone, intertidal zone,* and *neritic zone.*

Reading Strategy L2

a. plankton capable of photosynthesis
b. microscopic algae
c. animal plankton
d. larval fish
e. organisms capable of moving independently of ocean currents
f. fish
g. organisms living on or near the ocean bottom
h. marine worms

2 INSTRUCT

Classification of Marine Animals

Build Reading Literacy L2

Refer to **p. 362D** in **Chapter 13**, which provides the guidelines for this reading strategy.

Use Prior Knowledge Have students write the names of several ocean organisms they know about or have heard about. Next to each name, have students write a description of the organism, where it lives, and how it obtains food. After students have read the section, have them review their lists and make corrections, if necessary.
Logical

15.2 The Diversity of Ocean Life

Reading Focus

Key Concepts

- How can marine organisms be classified?
- What is the difference between plankton and nekton?
- In which area of the ocean can most benthos organisms be found living?
- What factors are used to divide the ocean into marine life zones?

Vocabulary

- plankton
- phytoplankton
- zooplankton
- nekton
- benthos
- photic zone
- intertidal zone
- neritic zone
- oceanic zone
- pelagic zone
- benthic zone
- abyssal zone

Reading Strategy

Building Vocabulary Copy the table below. As you read, add definitions and examples to complete the table.

Definitions	Examples
Plankton: organisms that drift with ocean currents	bacteria
Phytoplankton: a. ___?___	b. ___?___
Zooplankton: c. ___?___	d. ___?___
Nekton: e. ___?___	f. ___?___
Benthos: g. ___?___	h. ___?___

A wide variety of organisms inhabit the marine environment. These organisms range in size from microscopic bacteria and algae to the largest organisms alive today—blue whales, which are as long as three buses lined up end to end. Marine biologists have identified over 250,000 marine species. This number is constantly increasing as new organisms are discovered.

Most marine organisms live within the sunlit surface waters. Strong sunlight supports photosynthesis by marine algae. Algae either directly or indirectly provide food for the majority of organisms. All marine algae live near the surface because they need sunlight to survive. Most marine animals also live near the surface because this is where they can find food.

Figure 7 Plankton are organisms that drift with ocean currents. **A** This photo shows a variety of phytoplankton from the Atlantic Ocean. **B** The zooplankton shown here include copepods and the larval stages of other common marine organisms.

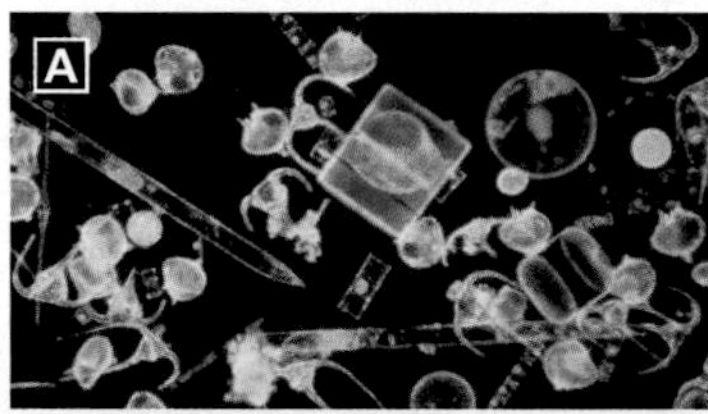

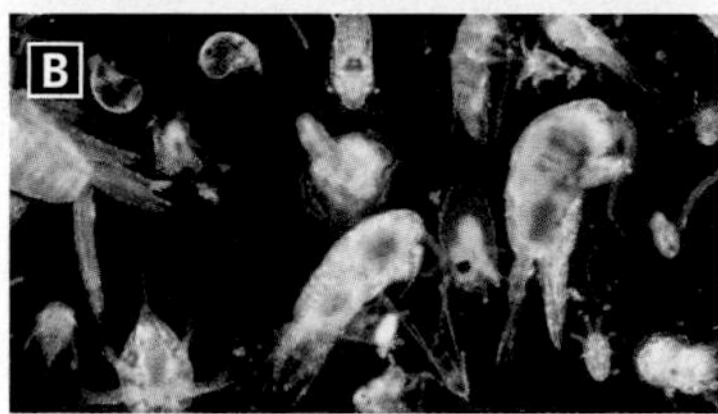

Classification of Marine Organisms

Marine organisms can be classified according to where they live and how they move. They can be classified as either plankton (floaters) or nekton (swimmers). All other organisms are benthos, or bottom dwellers.

Plankton **Plankton** (*planktos* = wandering) **include all organisms—algae, animals, and bacteria—that drift with ocean currents.** Just because plankton drift does not mean they are unable to swim. Many plankton can swim but either move very weakly or move only vertically.

Among plankton, the algae that undergo photosynthesis are called **phytoplankton.** Most phytoplankton, such as diatoms, are microscopic. Animal plankton, are called **zooplankton.** Zooplankton include the larval stages of many marine organisms such as fish, sea stars, lobsters, and crabs. Figure 7 shows members of each group.

Nekton **Nekton (*nektos* = swimming) include all animals capable of moving independently of the ocean currents, by swimming or other means of propulsion.** Nekton are able to determine their position within the ocean and in many cases complete long migrations. Nekton include most adult fish and squid, marine mammals, and marine reptiles. Figure 8 shows examples of nekton.

Fish may appear to exist everywhere in the oceans, but they are more abundant near continents and islands and in colder waters. Some fish, such as salmon, swim upstream in fresh water rivers to spawn. Many eels do just the reverse, growing to maturity in fresh water and then swimming out of the streams to breed in the depths of the ocean.

Benthos **The term *benthos* (*benthos* = bottom) describes organisms living on or in the ocean bottom.** Figure 9 shows some examples of benthos organisms. The shallow coastal ocean floor contains a wide variety of physical conditions and nutrient levels. Most benthos organisms can be found living in this area. Shallow coastal areas are the only locations where large marine algae, often called seaweeds, are found attached to the bottom. These are the only areas of the seafloor that receive enough sunlight for the algae to survive.

Throughout most of the deeper parts of the seafloor, animals live in perpetual darkness, where photosynthesis cannot occur. They must feed on each other or on whatever nutrients fall from the productive surface waters. The deep-sea bottom is an environment of coldness, stillness, and darkness. Under these conditions, life progresses slowly. Organisms that live in the deep sea usually are widely distributed because physical conditions vary little on the deep-ocean floor.

Figure 8 Nekton includes all animals capable of moving independently of ocean currents. **A** This squid can use propulsion to move through the water. **B** This school of grunts swims through the water with ease.
Inferring *Why do you think some organisms, such as fish, are classified as plankton during some stages of their lives and nekton during other stages?*

Figure 9 Benthos describes organisms living on or in the ocean bottom. **A** Sea star **B** Coral crab

Use Visuals L1

Figure 7 Have students examine the two photographs. Explain that the phytoplankton organisms shown in photograph A include dinoflagellates and diatoms. Explain that long narrow projections and other distinctive shapes contribute to the ability of these organisms to stay afloat. Remind students that diatoms have shell-like tests. Ask: **What may happen to these hard parts after these organisms die?** *(decay, or fall to the bottom and contribute to the sediment layer)* Explain that the zooplankton shown in photograph B are larval and adult copepods. Inform students that copepods are small crustaceans (related to crab and shrimp) on which many larger organisms depend for food. Ask: **What are the likely functions of the appendages on the larger specimens shown in the photograph?** *(feeding and swimming)*
Visual, Logical

Build Science Skills

Classifying Show students photographs or dried or preserved specimens of organisms to classify as plankton, nekton, or benthos. Ask students to explain the reasoning behind their classification decisions. *(Possible answers: Plankton are microscopic or very small. Phytoplankton have green pigment and show the ability to photosynthesize. Zooplankton have small swimming appendages; examples include diatoms, dinoflagellates, copepods, jellyfish, larval fish. Nekton have swimming appendages, are large and strong enough to swim against ocean currents; examples include adult fish, dolphins, whales, squid. Benthos live on the ocean bottom; examples include sea stars, most crabs, sea anemones, sea snails, clams, mussels.)*
Visual, Logical

Customize for Inclusion Students

Behaviorally Disordered Have students work together to create a two-dimensional model of ocean life zones on the classroom bulletin board. Students can use Figure 10 as a starting point. Challenge students to draw or paint and label continental shelf, continental slope, ocean basin, photic zone, aphotic zone, and benthic zone on a large piece of poster board or butcher paper. Have students add labeled organisms to appropriate areas of their model. Students can make their own drawings of organisms, cut out photographs from old magazines, or photocopy illustrations from books.

Answer to . . .

Figure 8 *As larvae, fish are not able to move against ocean currents, they drift with the current. As adults, fish are able to swim and move independently of ocean currents.*

Marine Life Zones

Use Community Resources **L2**

Aquarium Field Trip Take students on a field trip to a local public aquarium or museum with ocean life exhibits. Alternatively, students could visit a pet store that specializes in saltwater aquariums. Have students select one or more organisms they observe during their visit and write a short paper describing it. Encourage students to classify each of their organisms as belonging to plankton, nekton, or benthos; to identify the ocean zone in which the organism lives; and to explain how the organism obtains food.
Kinesthetic, Logical

Use Visuals **L1**

Figure 10 Have students examine the drawing of the ocean basin. Ask: **What marine life zones are found on or above the continental shelf?** *(intertidal, neritic, photic)* **Where does photosynthesis take place?** *(euphotic zone)*
Visual, Logical

Build Science Skills **L2**

Inferring After students have examined Figure 10, ask: **Should all intertidal and neritic organisms be classified as benthos? Why?** *(No. Not all of the organisms in these zones live on the ocean bottom. Some of these organisms, including many fish species, jellyfish, and plankton, live above bottom in the water column.)*
Logical, Verbal

Download a worksheet on marine ecosystems for students to complete, and find additional teacher support from NSTA SciLinks.

For: Links on marine ecosystems
Visit: www.SciLinks.org
Web Code: cjn-5152

Marine Life Zones

The distribution of marine organisms is affected by the chemistry, physics, and geology of the oceans. Marine organisms are influenced by a variety of physical factors. **Three factors are used to divide the ocean into distinct marine life zones: the availability of sunlight, the distance from shore, and the water depth.** Figure 10 shows the different zones in which marine life can be found.

Availability of Sunlight The upper part of the ocean into which sunlight penetrates is called the **photic zone** (*photos* = light). The clarity of seawater is affected by many factors, such as the amount of plankton, suspended sediment, and decaying organic particles in the water. In addition, the amount of sunlight varies with atmospheric conditions, time of day, season of the year, and latitude.

The euphotic zone is the portion of the photic zone near the surface where light is strong enough for photosynthesis to occur. In the open ocean, this zone can reach a depth of 100 meters, but the zone will be much shallower close to shore where water clarity is typically reduced. In the euphotic zone, phytoplankton use sunlight to produce food and become the basis of most oceanic food webs.

Although photosynthesis cannot occur much below 100 meters, there is enough light in the lower photic zone for marine animals to avoid predators, find food, recognize their species, and locate mates. Below this zone is the aphotic zone, where there is no sunlight.

What is the difference between the photic zone and the aphotic zone?

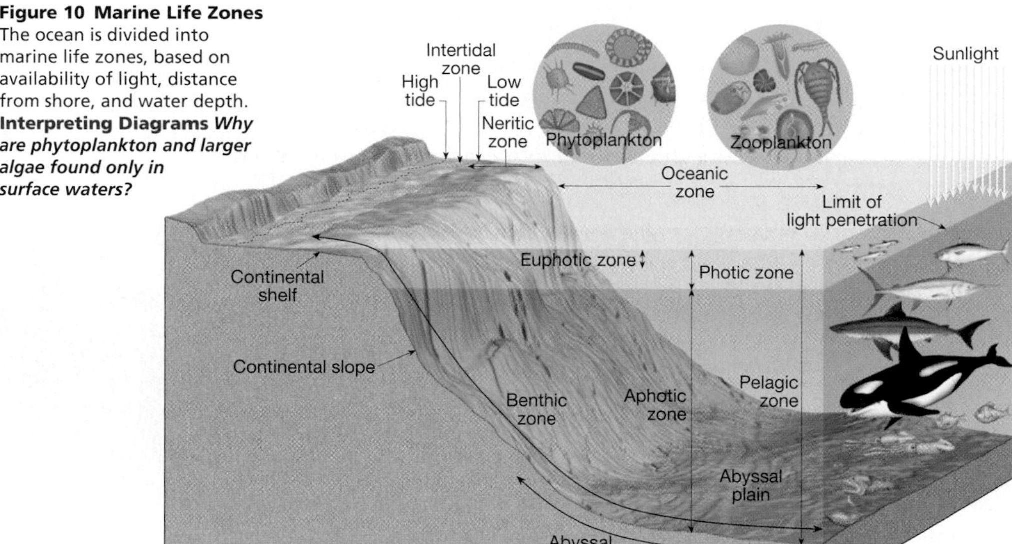

Figure 10 Marine Life Zones The ocean is divided into marine life zones, based on availability of light, distance from shore, and water depth. **Interpreting Diagrams** ***Why are phytoplankton and larger algae found only in surface waters?***

430 *Chapter 15*

Facts and Figures

Of the more than 300 shark species, about 80 percent are unable to harm people or rarely encounter people. The largest shark—also the largest fish in the world—is the whale shark *(Rhincodon typus)*. It reaches lengths of up to 15 m but eats only plankton and is therefore not considered dangerous. The great white shark *(Carcharodon carcharias)* is a predator that feeds preferentially on pinnipeds (seals and sea lions) and has attacked humans swimming or surfing in pinniped habitat areas. A great white can grow to 7 m long and weigh up to 2250 kg. Sharks are classified as nekton.

Distance from Shore Marine life zones can also be subdivided based on distance from shore. The area where the land and ocean meet and overlap is the **intertidal zone.** This narrow strip of land between high and low tides is alternately covered and uncovered by seawater with each tidal change. It appears to be a harsh place to live with crashing waves, periodic drying out, and rapid changes in temperature, salinity, and oxygen concentrations. However, the species that live here are well adapted to the constant environmental changes.

Seaward from the low-tide line is the **neritic zone.** This zone covers the gently sloping continental shelf. The neritic zone can be very narrow or may extend hundreds of kilometers from shore. It is often shallow enough for sunlight to reach all the way to the ocean floor, putting it entirely within the photic zone.

Although the neritic zone covers only about 5 percent of the world ocean, it is rich in both biomass and number of species. Many organisms find the conditions here ideal because photosynthesis occurs readily, nutrients wash in from the land, and the bottom provides shelter and habitat. This zone is so rich that it supports 90 percent of the world's commercial fisheries.

Beyond the continental shelf is the **oceanic zone.** The open ocean reaches great depths. As a result, surface waters typically have lower nutrient concentrations because nutrients tend to sink out of the photic zone to the deep-ocean floor. This low nutrient concentration usually results in smaller populations than the more productive neritic zone.

Water Depth A third method of classifying marine habitats is based on water depth. Open ocean of any depth is called the **pelagic zone.** Animals in this zone swim or float freely. The photic part of the pelagic zone is home to phytoplankton, zooplankton, and nekton, such as tuna, sea turtles, and dolphins. The aphotic part of this zone has giant squid and other species that are adapted to life in deep water.

Benthos organisms such as giant kelp, sponges, crabs, sea anemones, sea stars, and marine worms that attach to, crawl upon, or burrow into the seafloor occupy parts of the benthic zone. The **benthic zone** includes any sea-bottom surface regardless of its distance from shore and is mostly inhabited by benthos organisms.

The **abyssal zone** is a subdivision of the benthic zone. The abyssal zone includes the deep-ocean floor, such as abyssal plains. This zone is characterized by extremely high water pressure, consistently low temperature, no sunlight, and sparse life. Food sources at abyssal depths typically come from the surface. Some food is in the form of tiny decaying particles that steadily "rain" down from the surface. These particles provide food for filter-feeders, brittle stars, and burrowing worms. Other food arrives as large fragments or entire carcasses of organisms that sink from the surface. These pieces supply meals for actively searching fish, such as the grenadier, tripodfish, and hagfish.

Q *Do any deep-sea organisms produce light themselves?*

A Over half of deep-sea organisms—including fish, jellies, crustaceans, and deep-sea squid—can bioluminesce, which means they can produce light organically. These organisms produce light through a chemical reaction in specially designed structures or cells called photophores. Some of these cells contain luminescent bacteria that live symbiotically within the organism. In a world of darkness, the ability to produce light can be used to attract prey, define territory, communicate with others, or avoid predators.

Build Science Skills L2

Classifying After students have finished reading about marine life zones, have them create a table with two columns. Have students label the left column Photic Zone and the right column Aphotic Zone. Ask students to place each of the following marine life zones in the correct column: intertidal, neritic, oceanic, benthic, abyssal. If necessary, offer students the hint that some marine life zones may exist in both photic and aphotic zones. *Photic: intertidal, neritic, oceanic (partly), pelagic (partly) benthic (partly); Aphotic: benthic (partly), oceanic (partly), pelagic (partly), abyssal*
Logical

Customize for Inclusion Students

Gifted Invite interested students to create classroom exhibits describing an ecosystem from one of the marine life zones. For example, students could put together a labeled photo collage of intertidal benthos organisms or a poster depicting a pelagic food web.

Answer to . . .

Figure 10 *Both types of organisms need sunlight for photosynthesis.*

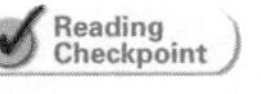

Sunlight penetrates the photic zone; no sunlight reaches the aphotic zone.

Hydrothermal Vents

Integrate Biology L2

Explain to students that the giant tubeworms living in hydrothermal vent communities do not have digestive systems. Even so, they can grow up to 3 m long. When scientists first discovered these organisms, they were baffled as to how they could grow so large with no obvious means of obtaining energy. Eventually, scientists learned that the worms get all the nutrition they need from bacteria growing inside their body cavities. Encourage students to look up more information about hydrothermal vents and the biological communities they support.
Verbal, Logical

3 ASSESS

Evaluate Understanding L2

To assess students' understanding of section content, present a profile of the ocean floor and have them label the locations of the following marine life zones: intertidal, neritic, oceanic, benthic, abyssal, photic, aphotic, and euphotic.

Reteach L1

Help students review the marine life zones by asking them to identify similarities and differences in pairs of terms, such as *intertidal* zone and *neritic* zone *(both in photic zone, continental shelf region, include benthos, nekton, and plankton; interidal is between tides, neritic is below tides)*; *phytoplankton* and *zooplankton (float with ocean currents, found in oceanic and intertidal zones, phytoplankton photosynthesize, zooplankton do not)*; *benthic* zone and *abyssal* zone *(both involve ocean bottom, abyssal is deep ocean bottom only)*

Writing in Science

Student tables should reflect the material presented in this section.

Figure 11 When super-heated water meets cold seawater, minerals and metals precipitate out of the water to form this black smoker.

Hydrothermal Vents

Among the most unusual seafloor discoveries of the past 30 years have been the hydrothermal vents along the oceanic ridge. Here seawater seeps into the ocean floor through cracks in the crust.

The water becomes super-heated and saturated with minerals. Eventually the heated water escapes back into the ocean. When the hot water comes in contact with the surrounding cold water, the minerals precipitate out, giving the water the appearance of black smoke. These geysers of hot water are referred to as black smokers, like the one shown in Figure 11.

At some vents water temperatures of 100°C or lower support communities of organisms found nowhere else in the world. In fact, hundreds of new species have been discovered surrounding these deep-sea habitats since scientists found some vents along the Galápagos Rift in 1977. Chemicals from the vents become food for bacteria. The bacteria produce sugars and other foods that enable them and many other organisms to live in this very unusual and extreme environment. Look at Figure 12 for another example of organisms found along hydrothermal vents.

Figure 12 Tube worms up to 3 meters in length are among the organisms found along hydrothermal vents.

Section 15.2 Assessment

Reviewing Concepts

1. How can marine organisms be classified?
2. What is the difference between plankton and nekton?
3. In which area of the ocean do most benthos organisms live?
4. What factors are used to divide the ocean into marine life zones?
5. Why is the neritic zone rich in life?

Critical Thinking

6. **Inferring** Why do many fish in the abyssal zone locate food through chemical sensing?
7. **Inferring** Organisms that live in the intertidal zone must deal with harsh and changing conditions. What types of adaptations would benefit organisms living in this zone?

Writing in Science

Making Tables Make a table to organize the information about marine life zones presented in this section. Include the basis by which the zone is classified, any subdivisions of the zone, and the characteristics of each zone within the table.

Section 15.2 Assessment

1. by where they live and how they move
2. Nekton are able to move independently of ocean currents. Plankton are not.
3. on the shallow coastal ocean floor
4. availability of sunlight, distance from shore, water depth
5. Conditions are ideal for photosynthesis because there is light and nutrients from runoff; the bottom provides shelter and habitat.
6. The abyssal zone is vast and there is no light, so fish cannot depend on being able to find food by sight.
7. Students' answers will vary but should show that they understand the factors an organism living in the intertidal zone has to deal with. Answers may include having a shell that can be sealed to prevent drying out, having a way to attach firmly to rocks, having a shell to protect against wave action, being able to live in an area with a wide temperature and salinity range.

15.3 Oceanic Productivity

Reading Focus

Key Concepts

- What factors influence a region's photosynthetic productivity?
- Describe the transfer efficiency between trophic levels.
- What advantage do organisms in a food web have over those in a food chain?

Vocabulary

- primary productivity
- photosynthesis
- chemosynthesis
- trophic level
- food chain
- food web

Reading Strategy

Identifying Main Ideas Copy the table below. As you read, write the main idea of each topic.

Topic	Main Idea
Productivity in polar oceans	a. ?
Productivity in tropical oceans	b. ?
Productivity in temperate oceans	c. ?

Like other ecosystems on Earth, organisms in the marine environment are interconnected through the web of food production and consumption. Marine producers include phytoplankton, larger algae such as seaweeds, and bacteria. Consumers include crabs, clams, sea stars, fish, dolphins, and whales. Why are some regions of the ocean teeming with life, while other areas seem barren? The answer is related to the amount of primary productivity in various parts of the ocean.

Primary Productivity

Primary productivity is the production of organic compounds from inorganic substances through photosynthesis or chemosynthesis. **Photosynthesis** is the use of light energy to convert water and carbon dioxide into energy-rich glucose molecules. **Chemosynthesis** is the process by which certain microorganisms create organic molecules from inorganic nutrients using chemical energy. Bacteria in hydrothermal vents use hydrogen sulfide as an energy source. Acting as producers, these bacteria support the hydrothermal vent communities.

Two factors influence a region's photosynthetic productivity: the availability of nutrients and the amount of solar radiation, or sunlight. Primary producers need nutrients such as nitrogen, phosphorus, and iron. Lack of nutrients can be a limiting factor in productivity. Thus, the most abundant marine life exists where there are ample nutrients and good sunlight. Oceanic productivity, however, varies dramatically because of the uneven distribution of nutrients throughout the photosynthetic zone and the availability of solar energy due to seasonal changes.

Section 15.3

1 FOCUS

Section Objectives

15.9 **List** the factors that influence a region's photosynthetic productivity.

15.10 **Describe** the transfer of energy from one trophic level to another.

15. 11 **Compare and contrast** food webs and food chains.

Reading Focus

Build Vocabulary L2

Paraphrase Help students understand the terms *primary productivity* and *trophic level* by explaining their meanings using words students are already familiar with. *Primary productivity* can be described as the amount of light (or chemical) energy that is turned into food by producer organisms. The term *trophic* refers to nutrition, and *trophic level* refers to the amount of food energy available to organisms at each step in a food chain.

Reading Strategy L2

a. Phytoplankton peaks in May, and zooplankton peaks in July and August; limited by availability of solar energy.
b. limited by lack of nutrients because of permanent thermocline that prevents mixing of warm surface water with colder, deeper water
c. lowest in winter and summer, higher in fall, highest in summer; limited by solar energy in winter and fall, by nutrients in summer and spring

2 INSTRUCT

Primary Productivity

Build Science Skills L2

Compare and Contrast Have students describe the similarities and differences of photosynthesis and chemosynthesis. *(Similarities: Both produce energy-rich glucose molecules. Differences: Photosynthesis uses light and is used by most producer organisms; chemosynthesis uses inorganic molecules from the environment and is limited to bacteria in hydrothermal vent communities.)*
Logical, Verbal

Use Visuals **L1**

Figure 13 Explain to students that this graph shows the relative numbers of phytoplankton and zooplankton biomass over time. Inform students that biomass data represents the total mass of the organisms sampled. Ask: **Biomass data on what phytoplankton organism is given in this graph?** *(diatoms)* **During what season does the phytoplankton biomass reach its peak?** *(spring)* **During what season does the zooplankton biomass reach its peak?** *(summer)*
Visual

Build Science Skills 

Infer After students examine Figure 13, ask: **Why is there a lag time between the peak biomass of phytoplankton and the peak biomass of zooplankton?** *(Zooplankton feed on phytoplankton. Zooplankton that are able to obtain plenty of food will reproduce, creating more zooplankton. As long as there are plenty of phytoplankton, the zooplankton will continue to increase in numbers.)*
Visual, Logical

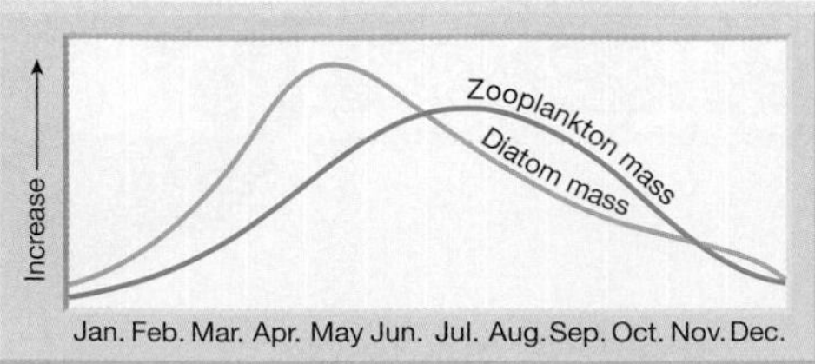

Figure 13 One example of productivity in polar oceans is illustrated by the Barents Sea. **Interpreting Diagrams** ***Describe the relationship between the zooplankton and phytoplankton populations.***

Productivity in Polar Oceans Polar regions such as the Arctic Ocean's Barents Sea, off the northern coast of Europe, experience continuous darkness for about three months of winter and continuous illumination for about three months during summer. Productivity of phytoplankton, mostly single-celled algae called diatoms, peaks there during May. This trend is shown in the graph in Figure 13. During May the sun rises high enough in the sky so that sunlight penetrates deep into the water. As soon as the diatoms develop, zooplankton begin feeding on them. As Figure 13 shows, the zooplankton biomass peaks in June and continues at a relatively high level until winter darkness begins in October.

Recall that density and temperature change very little with depth in polar regions and mixing occurs between surface waters and deeper, nutrient-rich waters. In the summer, however, melting ice creates a thin, low-salinity layer that does not readily mix with the deeper waters. This lack of mixing between water masses is crucial to summer production, because it helps prevent phytoplankton from being carried into deeper, darker waters. Instead, they are concentrated in the sunlit surface waters where they reproduce continuously.

Because of the constant supply of nutrients rising from deeper waters below, high-latitude surface waters typically have high nutrient concentrations. **The availability of solar energy, however, is what limits photosynthetic productivity in polar areas.**

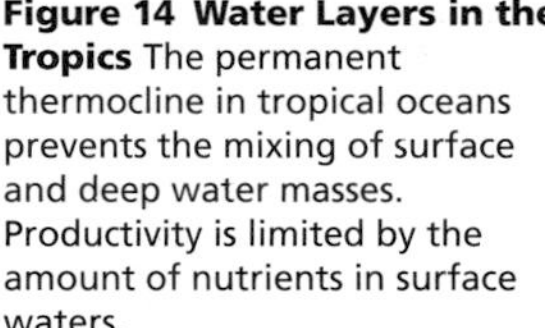

Productivity in Tropical Oceans You may be surprised to learn that productivity is low in tropical regions of the open ocean. Because the sun is more directly overhead, light penetrates much deeper into tropical oceans than in temperate and polar waters. Solar energy also is available year-round. However, productivity is low because a permanent thermocline prevents mixing between surface waters and nutrient-rich deeper waters. Figure 14 shows how water masses are separated in the tropics. The thermocline is a barrier that cuts off the supply of nutrients from deeper waters below. **Productivity in tropical regions is limited by the lack of nutrients.** These areas have so few organisms that they are considered biological deserts.

Figure 14 Water Layers in the Tropics The permanent thermocline in tropical oceans prevents the mixing of surface and deep water masses. Productivity is limited by the amount of nutrients in surface waters.

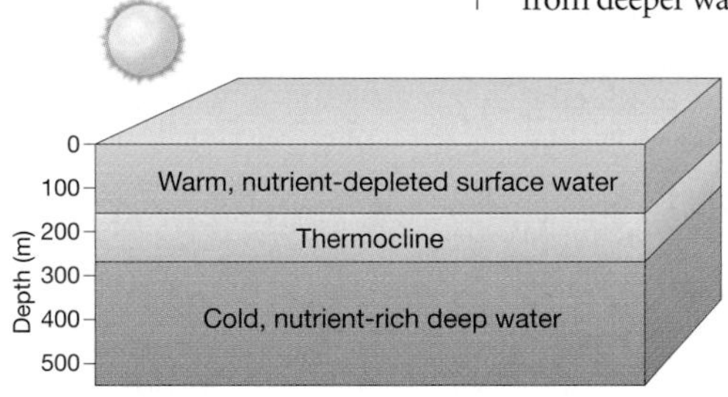

Customize for English Language Learners

Help students understand the biological terms in this section by having them explore word parts and word roots. Explain that the term *productivity* is related to the word "produce." Have students look up the definitions of *product, producer,* and *produce.* Explain to students that the suffix *-synthesis* is a word that implies the meaning "to put together." *Trophic* means "of or relating to nutrition."

Productivity in Temperate Oceans Productivity is limited by available sunlight in polar regions and by nutrient supply in the tropics. **In temperate regions, which are found at mid-latitudes, a combination of these two limiting factors, sunlight and nutrient supply, controls productivity.** These relationships are shown in Figure 15.

- **Winter** Productivity in temperate oceans is very low during winter, even though nutrient concentration is highest at this time. The reason is that solar energy is limited because days are short, and the sun angle is low. As a result, the depth at which photosynthesis can occur is so shallow that phytoplankton do not grow much.
- **Spring** The sun rises higher in the sky during spring, creating a greater depth at which photosynthesis can occur. A spring bloom of phytoplankton occurs because solar energy and nutrients are available, and a seasonal thermocline develops. The thermocline traps algae in the euphotic zone. This creates a tremendous demand for nutrients in the euphotic zone, so the supply is quickly depleted, causing productivity to decrease sharply. Even though the days are lengthening and sunlight is increasing, productivity during the spring bloom is limited by the lack of nutrients.
- **Summer** The sun rises even higher in the summer, so surface waters in temperate parts of the ocean continue to warm. A strong seasonal thermocline is created that prevents the mixing of surface and deeper waters. So nutrients depleted from surface waters cannot be replaced by those from deeper waters. Throughout summer, the phytoplankton population remains relatively low.
- **Fall** Solar radiation decreases in the fall as the sun moves lower in the sky. Surface temperatures drop and the summer thermocline breaks down. Nutrients return to the surface layer as increased wind strength mixes surface waters with deeper waters. These conditions create a fall bloom of phytoplankton, which is much less dramatic than the spring bloom. The fall bloom is very short-lived because sunlight becomes the limiting factor as winter approaches to repeat the seasonal cycle.

Figure 15 Productivity in Northern Hemisphere, Temperate Oceans The graph shows the relationship among phytoplankton, zooplankton, amount of sunshine, and nutrient levels for surface waters.
Analyzing ***What happens to phytoplankton in the spring and in the fall?***

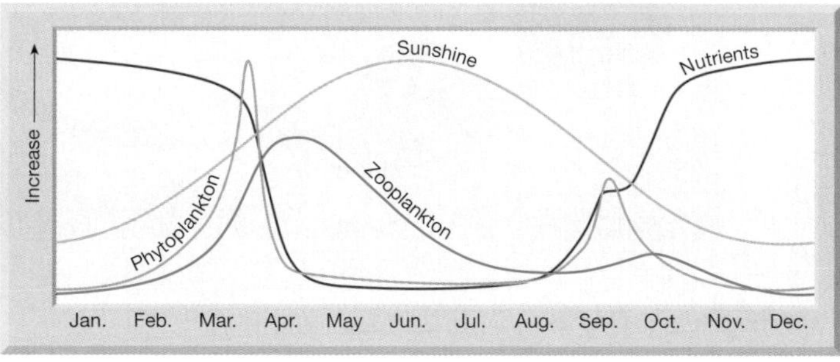

Build Reading Literacy L1

Refer to **p. 186D** in **Chapter 7**, which provides the guidelines for this reading strategy.

Relate Text and Visuals As students read each bulleted text section on this page, have them relate the information to the data plotted on the graph in Figure 15. First, ask students to identify which months on the *y*-axis of the graph represent the season under discussion. *(Example: winter, approximately November–February)* Then ask students to explain how the lines on the graph correspond to the information in the text. *(winter: Nutrient levels are higher than all other seasons, productivity lower than all other seasons.)* Finally, ask students to describe how they could use the graph to explain whether productivity is limited by nutrients or by sunlight. *(winter: Plenty of nutrients are available, so sunshine must be the limiting factor.)*
Verbal, Visual

Build Science Skills L2

Using Tables Have students use the information on this page to create a table that shows whether sunlight or nutrient availability is the principle limit of productivity at each season of the year in temperate oceans.

Season	Productivity Limited by
spring	nutrients
summer	nutrients
fall	sunlight
winter	sunlight

Logical

Facts and Figures

Earth's average surface temperature has been increasing over the past 130 years, likely as a result of human activities that increase carbon dioxide (CO_2) in the atmosphere. Stimulating a rise in ocean productivity has been suggested as a way of removing CO_2 from the atmosphere, because phytoplankton convert CO_2 to carbohydrates and oxygen. Increasing the number of photosynthetic ocean organisms would increase the amount of CO_2 removed from the atmosphere.

Iron has been identified as the nutrient that limits productivity in some ocean regions. Tests conducted in the Pacific Ocean showed that adding finely ground iron increases productivity up to 30 times. Some scientists fear that fertilizing with iron could upset the ocean's natural chemical balance and alter the global marine ecosystem. Others claim that stimulating productivity is a promising solution for helping to reduce atmospheric CO_2.

Answer to . . .

Figure 13 *As phytoplankton biomass increases, zooplankton biomass also increases, but only after a time lag.*

Figure 15 *The population of phytoplankton blooms in both the spring and fall, with the spring bloom being more pronounced.*

Oceanic Feeding Relationships

Address Misconceptions L2

Students may think that higher trophic levels actually contain more energy than lower trophic levels because they may reason that energy accumulates as you move up a food chain. Emphasize that the solar energy absorbed by producers is the only energy available to all the succeeding levels of the food chain. Ask students to think about what happens to the solar energy that the producers of a food chain convert into food molecules. *(Part of the food energy is used by the plant to make more food, absorb water and nutrients from the soil, transport materials from one part of a plant to another, and so on. Part of the food energy is consumed by organisms on the next level of the food chain.)* Challenge students to describe how this process could result in an increase in net energy as you move up the levels of a food chain. *(It cannot. Energy is used to make new cells and conduct other life processes, but no energy is added.)*

Teacher Demo

Creating an Energy Pyramid L2

Purpose Students will observe how total available energy decreases at succeeding levels of a food chain.

Procedure Draw a large pyramid shape on the board. Draw four horizontal lines across the pyramid to create five trophic levels. In each level, write the number of units of energy available as given in Figure 16. Write names of the organisms that make up each trophic level. Ask for students input as you create an energy pyramid for the organisms as shown in the food web in Figure 17. Instead of numbers, each level of this pyramid should contain the names of organisms belonging to that level.

Expected Outcome Students should see that the shape of the pyramid is a visual representation of the decrease in available energy at higher levels of a food chain or food web.
Visual, Logical

Oceanic Feeding Relationships

Marine algae, plants, bacteria, and bacteria-like organisms are the main oceanic producers. As producers make food available to the consuming animals of the ocean, energy passes from one feeding population to the next. Only a small percentage of the energy taken in at any level is passed on to the next because energy is consumed and lost at each level. As a result, the producers' biomass in the ocean is many times greater than the mass of top consumers, such as sharks or whales.

Trophic Levels Chemical energy stored in the mass of the ocean's algae is transferred to the animal community mostly through feeding. Zooplankton are herbivores (*herba* = grass, *vora* = eat), so they eat algae. Larger herbivores feed on the larger algae and marine plants that grow attached to the ocean bottom near shore. The herbivores are then eaten by carnivores (*carni* = meat, *vora* = eat). Smaller carnivores are eaten by another population of larger carnivores, and so on. Each of these feeding stages is called a **trophic level.**

Transfer Efficiency **The transfer of energy between trophic levels is very inefficient.** The efficiencies of different algal species vary, but the average is only about 2 percent. This means that 2 percent of the light energy absorbed by algae is ultimately changed into food and made available to herbivores. Figure 16 shows the passage of energy between trophic levels through an entire ecosystem—from the solar energy used by phytoplankton to a top-level carnivore, humans.

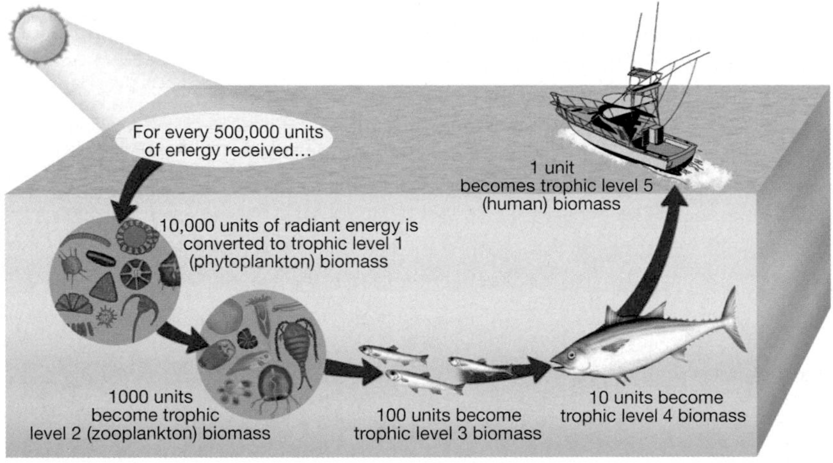

For every 500,000 units of energy received...
1 unit becomes trophic level 5 (human) biomass
10,000 units of radiant energy is converted to trophic level 1 (phytoplankton) biomass
1000 units become trophic level 2 (zooplankton) biomass
100 units become trophic level 3 biomass
10 units become trophic level 4 biomass

Figure 16 Energy Flow and Transfer Efficiency in an Ecosystem For every 500,000 units of radiant energy input available to the producers, only one unit of mass is added to the fifth trophic level.
***Analyzing** What is the average transfer efficiency for phytoplankton? What is it for all of the other trophic levels?*

Facts and Figures

Generally, individual members of a feeding population are larger, but not too much larger, that the organisms they eat. There are conspicuous exceptions, however, such as the blue whale. Up to 30 m long, the blue whale is possibly the largest animal that has ever existed on Earth. Yet it feeds mostly on krill—shrimp-like crustaceans—that have a maximum length of only 6 cm.

Food Chains and Food Webs A **food chain** is a sequence of organisms through which energy is transferred, starting with the primary producer. A herbivore eats the producer, then one or more carnivores eats the herbivore. The chain finally culminates with the "top carnivore," which is not usually preyed upon by any other organism.

Figure 17A shows a simple food chain. Feeding relationships are rarely as simple as this food chain suggests. More often, top carnivores in a food chain feed on a number of different animals, each of which feeds on a variety of organisms. These feeding relationships form a **food web,** as shown in Figure 17B for North Sea herring.

Animals that feed through a food web rather than a food chain are more likely to survive because they have alternative foods to eat should one of their food sources diminish or disappear. Newfoundland herring, on the other hand, eat only copepods, so the disappearance of copepods would greatly affect their population.

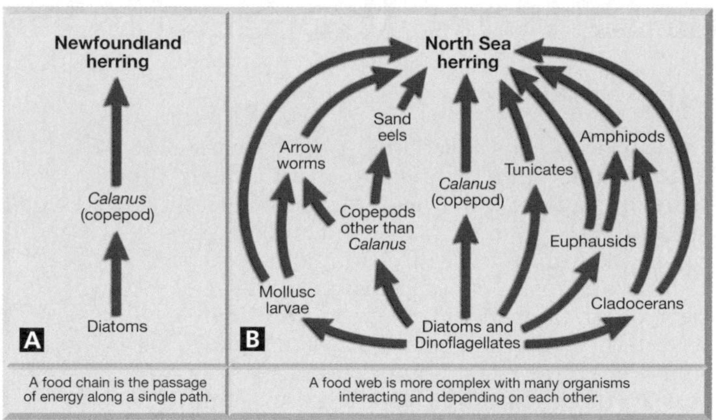

Figure 17 **A** A food chain is the passage of energy along a single path. **B** A food web is a complex series of feeding relationships with many organisms interacting and depending on each other.

Section 15.3 Assessment

Reviewing Concepts

1. What factors influence a region's photosynthetic productivity?
2. Describe the transfer efficiency between trophic levels.
3. What advantage do organisms in a food web have over those in a food chain?
4. What limits primary productivity in tropical oceans? Why?

Critical Thinking

5. **Comparing and Contrasting** Compare and contrast photosynthesis and chemosynthesis. Give examples of organisms that undergo each process.
6. **Drawing Conclusions** Explain why producers are always the first tropic level in a food chain or food web.

Math Practice

7. If 700,000 energy units are received by phytoplankton in the ocean surface, how many energy units will reach a consumer that is on the fourth trophic level of a food chain?

Build Science Skills 

Using Models Have students work individually to research and draw a food chain from the same intertidal or coral reef ecosystem. Then have students work as a class to see how their food chains fit together to form a food web.
Logical, Visual

3 ASSESS

Evaluate Understanding

L2

To assess students' knowledge of section content, have them write a paragraph explaining how energy is transferred from one level of a food web to another.

Reteach 

Ask each student to write ten questions about the content of this section and create a separate answer key. Encourage students to use their questions to quiz each other.

Solution
7. 14 energy units

Section 15.3 Assessment

1. sunlight and nutrient availability
2. very inefficient, as little as 2 percent
3. Organisms in a food web have alternative foods to eat if one of their food sources diminishes or disappears.
4. the availability of nutrients; solar energy is available year-round but nutrients are trapped in deeper waters because the permanent thermocline prevents mixing between surface water and deeper water.
5. Both are examples of primary production. Energy-rich chemical compounds are the energy source for chemosynthesis. Light is the energy source for photosynthesis. Diatoms undergo photosynthesis, bacteria at hydrothermal vents undergo chemosynthesis.
6. Producers are organisms that are able to use light or chemical energy to produce glucose. Consumers cannot produce their own food and rely on producers as a food source.

Answer to . . .

Figure 16 *2 percent, 10 percent*

1 FOCUS

Objectives

In this feature, students will
- describe the conditions in each of the ocean's vertical zones.
- identify the special features and phenomena that allow organisms to survive in the different vertical zones.
- explain how atolls are formed.

Reading Focus

Build Vocabulary L2

Define Terms Write *bioluminescence, eyespots, hydrothermal vents,* and *coral reef* on the board. Have students review the material on this page and the next to define each term. Then discuss how each feature or phenomenon supports ocean life.

2 INSTRUCT

Bellringer L2

Ask students to name as many organisms as they can that live in the ocean. Make a list of all of these organisms on the board.
Logical

Use Visuals L1

Have students examine the chart of vertical zones on this page. Ask: **How many of those organisms did you name in the Bellringer activity?** Then have them list the animals they do not know. Discuss with the class the possible reasons certain animals are less familiar than others. *(Sample answer: Animals that live deeper in the ocean are not seen in aquariums or zoos.)*
Visual

How the Earth Works

Ocean Life

The world's oceans cover almost three quarters of the Earth's surface and are home to a vast array of life. Below the surface, the oceans become increasingly cold and dark. Even so, plants and animals, ranging in size from giant whales to microscopic floating organisms called **plankton,** thrive at every depth. Some jellyfish and turtles float or swim near the surface. Whales and squid often live in the ocean's middepths. A whole host of strange-looking creatures swim or crawl around the darkest ocean depths.

Distribution of world's major oceans

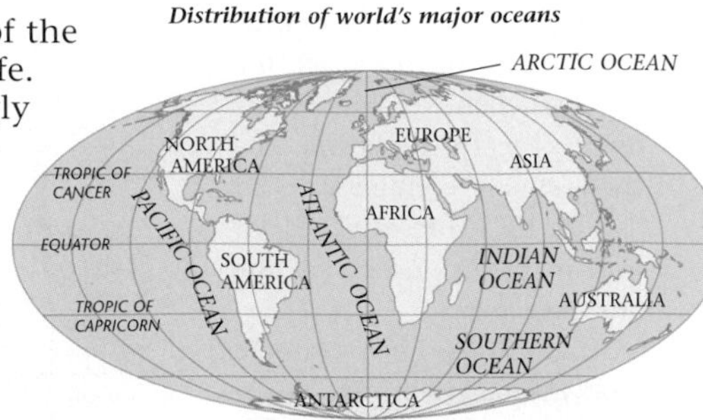

BIOLUMINESCENCE
Some fish have special organs called photophores that give off a glow. In this process, called **bioluminescence,** fish use the light to recognize members of their own species or as lures for attracting prey.

Black snaggletooth fish

VERTICAL ZONES
Oceanographers divide the oceans into zones based on depth. Each zone is home to living things that are adapted to survive at that depth. For example, deep-water animals cope with darkness, very cold temperatures, and pressures that would crush a human. Some creatures can survive in more than one zone.

Life in the ocean zones

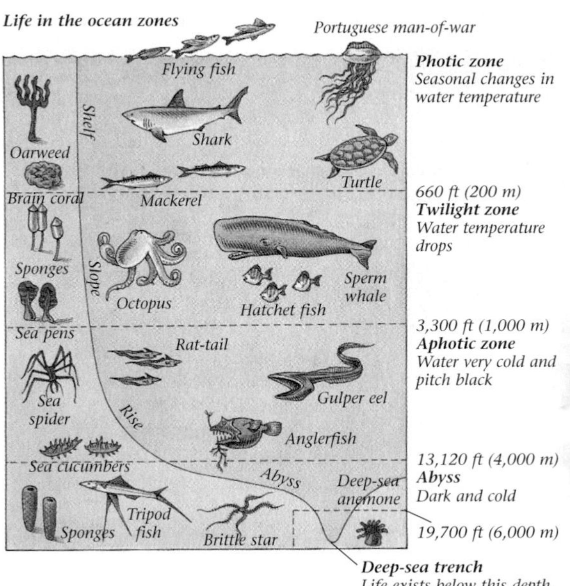

A school of chromis swims among the coral in Australia's Great Barrier Reef.

Facts and Figures

To study the deepest regions of the sea, scientists at Woods Hole Oceanographic Institute in Woods Hole, Massachusetts, use a deep submergence vehicle, or deep-sea sub, called *Alvin. Alvin* is approximately 7 m long and 3.6 m high. It can carry three scientists to a depth of 4000 m—the top of the abyss. The submersible's video equipment records life in deep ocean regions, and its manipulators, or long arms, collect specimens. In recent years, *Alvin* has helped scientists explore hydrothermal vents.

CORAL REEFS
A coral is a tubular animal with tentacles. Most corals attach to a surface and build reefs that can rise above sea level around islands and continents. Other reefs are ring-shaped **atolls** around a lagoon of shallow water. Atolls grow over millions of years.

Growth of a coral atoll

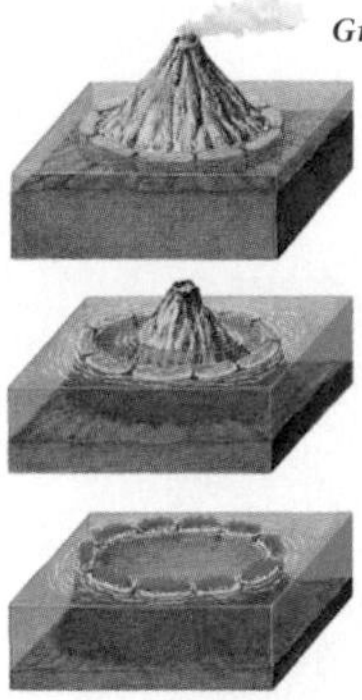

1. Coral starts to grow around a volcanic island.

2. The island sinks. Sand collects on the growing coral reef and forms land.

3. The island disappears. Vegetation grows on the atoll that remains.

Australian sea lions are marine mammals that breathe air, feed at sea, and breed on land.

PHOTIC ZONE
Sunlight supports the growth of algae, sea grasses, and other plants on which some sea creatures feed. Marine mammals, squid, fish, and other animals have to be strong swimmers to move in the surface currents. Sea grasses and coral reefs provide food, shelter, and breeding sites for a variety of creatures.

HYDROTHERMAL VENTS
On the deep ocean floor, hot, mineral-rich water gushes from cracks, called **hydrothermal vents.** Bacteria feed on chemicals in this water, forming the basis of a food chain that does not rely on sunlight and plants. Giant tube worms, clams, and blind white crabs live around these vents.

Worms and crabs live near a hydrothermal vent.

Jellyfish can swim, but they are also influenced by ocean currents.

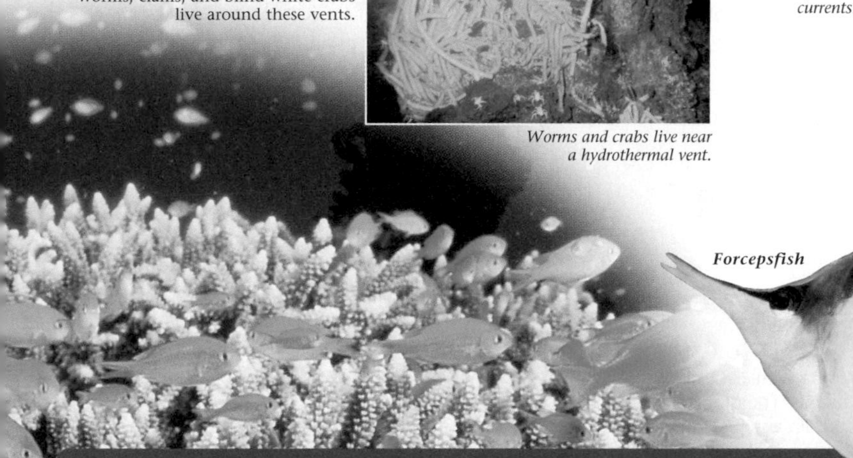

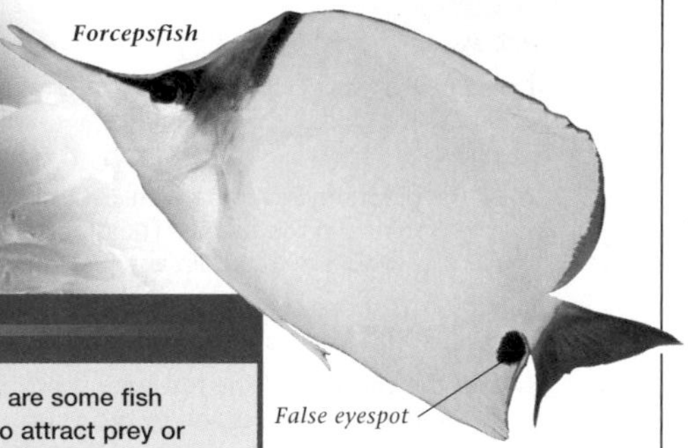

Forcepsfish

False eyespot

BRIGHT COLORS
Many fish have bright colors that attract mates and confuse predators. Complex coloration makes it hard to detect the outline of a fish. Some fish have eyespots, or false eyes. As a predator attacks the false head, the fish darts off in the opposite direction.

ASSESSMENT

1. **Key Terms** Define **(a)** plankton, **(b)** bioluminescence, **(c)** atoll, **(d)** hydrothermal vent.
2. **Ecosystems** Why does plant life grow near the ocean surface but not on the deep ocean floor?
3. **Physical Processes** How can the emergence of a volcano lead to the growth of coral and the formation of an atoll?
4. **Ecosystems** How are some fish specially adapted to attract prey or to escape predators?
5. **Critical Thinking Analyzing Processes** Suppose that changes in the environment cause a decline in the population of ocean plants and corals. How might that environmental change also cause damage to populations of fish, marine mammals, and other sea creatures?

439

 ASSESS

Evaluate Understanding L2

Have students choose one of the organisms in the vertical zone chart to learn more about. Ask them to do research in the library or on the Internet to find out about the organism's features and adaptations. Have them summarize why the organism lives in its particular part of the ocean.

Reteach L1

Have students identify the world's major coral reefs and find out what steps have been taken to protect them. Have each student write a pamphlet that describes rules and regulations that visitors to reefs must obey. Post the pamphlets on a bulletin board. Discuss what students learned.

Assessment

1. (a) microscopic floating organisms; **(b)** glow given off by special fish organs called photophores; **(c)** ring-shaped coral reef around a lagoon of shallow water; **(d)** crack on deep ocean floor through which hot, mineral-rich water gushes

2. Most plant life requires sunlight for growth.

3. Coral grows around a volcanic island and as the island sinks, sand collects on the coral reef and forms land. Then vegetation grows on the atoll that remains.

4. Some fish use bioluminescence to attract prey, and many fish have eyespots or bright colors that confuse predators.

5. Such a change in the environment would disrupt the food chain and would cause fish, mammals, and other sea creatures to starve.

Exploration Lab

How Does Temperature Affect Water Density? 

Objectives
After completing this activity, students will be able to
- create a model of how temperature affects water density.
- plot density data on a line graph.
- infer how environmental conditions in different ocean regions affect, and are affected by, temperature-related differences in water density.

Skills Focus **Observing, Graphing, Inferring, Drawing Conclusions**

 **Prep Time** 15 minutes to assemble materials

Advance Prep Photocopy the graph on page 441 for each student.

Class Time 20 minutes for Part A; 20 minutes for Part B

Teaching Tip Instruct students to pour the colored water into the graduated cylinders slowly, to limit the effect of mechanical mixing on their experiment.

Expected Outcome Students will infer from their measurements that cold water is denser than warmer water, and that colder water tends to sink beneath warmer water.

Exploration Lab

How Does Temperature Affect Water Density?

Ocean water temperatures vary from equator to pole and change with depth. Temperature, like salinity, affects the density of seawater. However, the density of seawater is more sensitive to temperature fluctuations than salinity. Cool surface water, which has a greater density than warm surface water, forms in the polar regions, sinks, and moves toward the tropics.

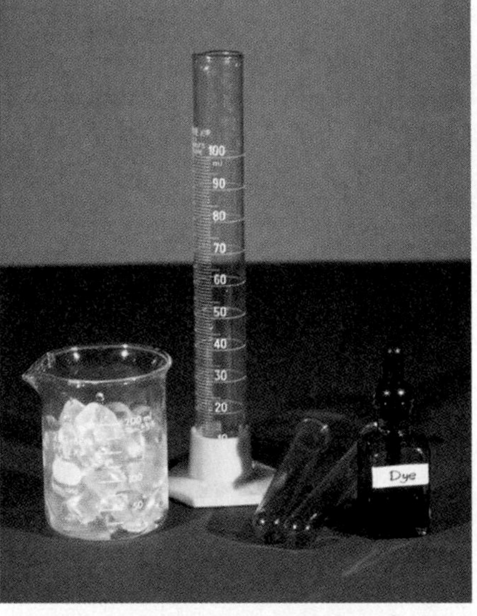

Problem How can you determine the effects of temperature on water density?

Materials
- 100 mL graduated cylinders (2)
- test tubes (2)
- beakers (2)
- food coloring or dye
- stirrer
- ice
- tap water
- graph paper
- colored pencils

Skills Observing, Graphing, Inferring, Drawing Conclusions

Procedure   

Part A
1. In a beaker, mix cold tap water with several ice cubes. Stir until the water and ice are well mixed.
2. Fill the graduated cylinder with 100 mL of the cold water from the beaker. The graduated cylinder should not contain any pieces of ice.
3. Put 2 to 3 drops of dye in a test tube and fill it 1/2 full with hot tap water.
4. Pour the contents of the test tube slowly into the graduated cylinder and record your observations.
5. Add a test tube full of cold tap water to a beaker. Mix in 2 to 3 drops of dye and a handful of ice to the beaker. Stir the solution thoroughly.
6. Fill the test tube 1/2 full of the solution from Step 5. Do not allow any ice into the test tube.
7. Fill the second graduated cylinder with 100 mL of hot tap water.
8. Pour the test tube of cold liquid slowly into the cylinder of hot water. Record your observations.
9. Clean the glassware and return it along with other materials to your teacher.

Part B
1. Photocopy the graph on the next page or copy it onto a separate sheet of graph paper.
2. Using the data in Table 1, plot a line on your graph for temperature. Using a different colored pencil, plot a line for density on the same graph.

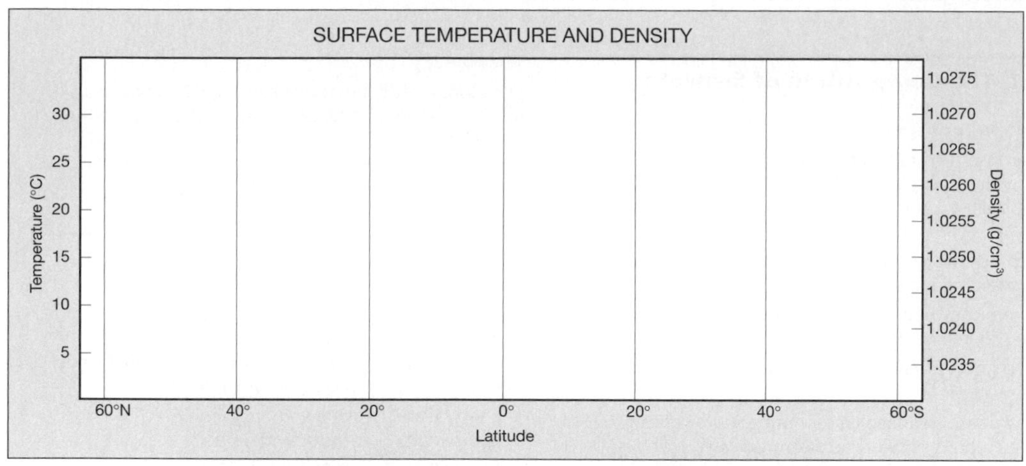

Table 1 Idealized Ocean Surface Water Temperatures and Densities at Various Latitudes

Latitude	Surface Temperature (C°)	Surface Density (g/cm³)
60°N	5	1.0258
40°N	13	1.0259
20°N	24	1.0237
0°	27	1.0238
20°S	24	1.0241
40°S	15	1.0261
60°S	2	1.0272

Analyze and Conclude

1. **Observing** What differences did you observe in the behavior of the water samples from Part A and Part B? Which water sample was the most dense in each experiment?
2. **Inferring** How does temperature affect the density of water?
3. **Drawing Conclusions** If two water samples of equal mass had equal salinities, which sample would be more dense: Water Sample A, which has a temperature of 25°C or water Sample B, which has a temperature of 14°C?
4. **Interpreting Diagrams** Describe the density and temperature characteristics of water in equatorial regions. Compare these characteristics to water found in polar regions.
5. **Inferring** What is the reason that higher average surface densities are found in the Southern Hemisphere?

Analyze and Conclude

1. The hot water remained on the surface of the cooler water. The cold water sank beneath the warmer water in the cylinder. The cold water has the highest density in both experiments.
2. As temperature decreases, water density increases.
3. Water Mass B
4. The water in equatorial regions is warm and the density is low. The water in polar regions is cold and the density is high.
5. The temperature of surface waters is cooler.

Go Further

Have students repeat this lab and include temperature measurements in their data collection. Students can determine how much of a temperature difference is required to create density differences that result in layering.
Kinesthetic, Interpersonal

Study Guide

Study Tip

Organize New Information

Have students make vocabulary flashcards by writing a vocabulary term on one side of a card and the definition on the other. Along with the definitions, students can include examples or simple diagrams. Have students quiz each other using the cards.

Thinking Visually

a. pelagic zone
b. benthic zone
c. intertidal zone
d. oceanic zone

CHAPTER 15

Study Guide

15.1 The Composition of Seawater

Key Concepts

- Because the proportion of dissolved substances in seawater is such a small number, oceanographers typically express salinity in parts per thousand (‰).
- Most of the salt in seawater is sodium chloride—common table salt.
- Chemical weathering of rocks on the continents is one source of elements found in seawater.
- The second major source of elements found in seawater is from Earth's interior.
- The ocean's surface water temperature varies with the amount of solar radiation received, which is primarily a function of latitude.
- Seawater density is influenced by two main factors: salinity and temperature.
- Oceanographers generally recognize a three-layered structure in most parts of the open ocean: a shallow surface mixed zone, a transition zone, and a deep zone.

Vocabulary

salinity, *p. 422*; thermocline, *p. 424*; density, *p. 425*; pycnocline, *p. 426*; mixed zone, *p. 426*

15.2 The Diversity of Ocean Life

Key Concepts

- Marine organisms can be classified according to where they live and how they move.
- Plankton include all organisms—algae, animals, and bacteria—that drift with ocean currents.
- Nekton include all animals capable of moving independently of the ocean currents, by swimming or other means of propulsion.
- The term *benthos* describes organisms living on or in the ocean bottom.
- Three factors are used to divide the ocean into distinct marine life zones: the availability of sunlight, the distance from shore, and the water depth.

Vocabulary

plankton, *p. 428*; phytoplankton, *p. 429*; zooplankton, *p. 429*; nekton, *p. 429*; benthos, *p. 429*; photic zone, *p. 430*; intertidal zone, *p. 431*; neritic zone, *p. 431*; oceanic zone, *p. 431*; pelagic zone, *p. 431*; benthic zone, *p. 431*; abyssal zone, *p. 431*

15.3 Oceanic Productivity

Key Concepts

- Two factors influence a region's photosynthetic productivity: the availability of nutrients and the amount of solar radiation, or sunlight.
- The availability of solar energy limits photosynthetic productivity in polar areas.
- Productivity in tropical regions is limited by the lack of nutrients.
- In temperate regions, which are found at mid-latitudes, a combination of these two limiting factors, sunlight and nutrient supply, controls productivity.
- The transfer of energy between trophic levels is very inefficient.
- Animals that feed through a food web rather than a food chain are more likely to survive because they have alternative foods to eat should one of their food sources diminish in quantity or even disappear.

Vocabulary

primary productivity, *p. 433*, photosynthesis, *p. 433*, chemosynthesis, *p. 433*, trophic level, *p. 436*, food chain, *p. 437*, food web, *p. 437*

Thinking Visually

Web Diagram Use the information in the chapter to complete the web diagram on marine life zones.

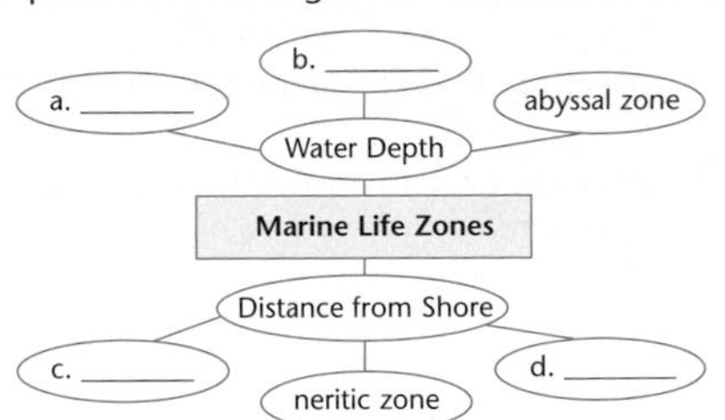

Chapter Assessment Resources

Print

Chapter Test, Chapter 15
Test Prep Resources, Chapter 15

Technology

Computer Test Bank, Chapter 15 Test
Online Text, Chapter 15
Go Online, PHSchool.com, Chapter 15

CHAPTER 15

NY Regents Content Item

Assessment

Interactive textbook with assessment at PHSchool.com

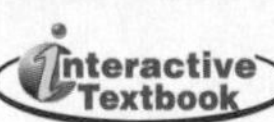

Reviewing Content

Choose the number that best answers the question or completes the statement.

1 The most abundant salt in seawater is
(1) calcium chloride (2) magnesium chloride
(3) sodium chloride (4) sodium fluoride

2 Which process does NOT lead to a decrease in the salinity of seawater?
(1) runoff from land (2) precipitation
(3) evaporation (4) sea ice melting

3 Which term refers to the layer of water in which there is a rapid change of temperature with depth in the ocean?
(1) pycnocline (2) abyssal zone
(3) thermocline (4) isothermal line

4 Which is NOT a zone in the three-layered structure of the ocean according to density?
(1) mixed zone (2) deep zone
(3) transition zone (4) intertidal zone

5 Organisms that drift with ocean currents are
(1) nekton (2) plankton
(3) neritic (4) pelagic

6 Which term describes the upper part of the ocean into which sunlight penetrates?
(1) neritic zone (2) intertidal zone
(3) oceanic zone (4) photic zone

7 Phytoplankton are usually found in the
(1) benthic zone (2) photic zone
(3) abyssal zone (4) aphotic zone

8 The use of light energy by organisms to convert water and carbon dioxide into organic molecules is
(1) chemosynthesis (2) decomposition
(3) photosynthesis (4) consumption

9 During which season does primary productivity reach its peak in polar oceans?
(1) spring (2) summer
(3) fall (4) winter

10 In temperate oceans, primary productivity is limited by
(1) nutrients and oxygen concentration
(2) nutrients and water temperature
(3) sunlight and oxygen concentration
(4) sunlight and nutrients

Understanding Concepts

11 Why is salinity expressed in parts per thousand instead of percent?

12 What is the principal source of water in oceans? Why do scientists reach this conclusion? NY

13 Explain how the salinity of water in polar regions varies seasonally.

14 What is the range of salinity for surface waters in the open ocean?

15 Is there a thermocline present in high-latitude ocean waters? Why or why not?

16 Compare and contrast phytoplankton and zooplankton.

17 What factors may affect the depth of the photic zone in any given area of the ocean?

18 What is the oceanic zone? What limits the amount of production in the oceanic zone?

19 What is the difference between the pelagic zone and the benthic zone?

20 How does the permanent thermocline in tropical oceans affect primary productivity in those areas?

Copy the diagram onto a separate sheet of paper and use it to answer questions 21 and 22.

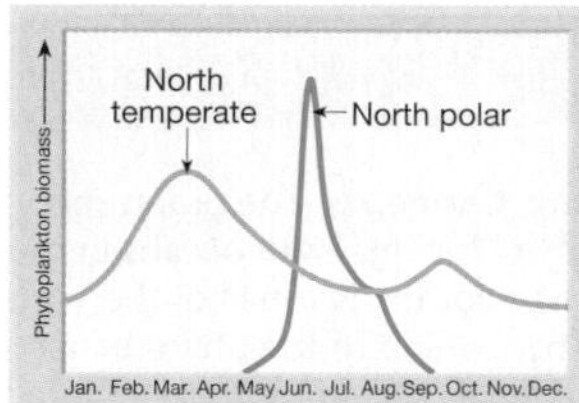

21 Draw a line on the graph that correctly represents the productivity of tropical oceans year-round.

22 Draw a line on the graph that represents the changes in zooplankton population in north temperate oceans throughout the course of a year.

23 What is the difference between a food chain and a food web?

Homework Guide

Section	Questions
1	1–4, 11–15, 24, 25, 30, 31
2	5–8, 16–19, 32
3	9–10, 20–23, 26–29

Assessment

Reviewing Content

(1) 3 (2) 3 (3) 3 (4) 4
(5) 2 (6) 4 (7) 2 (8) 3
(9) 2 (10) 4

Understanding Concepts

(11) because the proportion of dissolved substances in seawater is such a small number
(12) water vapor that originated in Earth's interior; as Earth cooled, the water vapor condensed and torrential rains filled ocean basins. Certain elements exist in ocean water in much greater abundance than can be explained by weathering from rocks alone.
(13) Seasonal variation exists because of the melting and formation of sea ice. In summer, when ice melts, salinity decreases. In winter, when ice forms, salinity increases.
(14) from 33 percent to 38 percent
(15) No, because surface waters in high latitudes are cooler and similar in temperature to deeper waters, so there is no rapid change in temperature with depth.
(16) Both drift with ocean currents. Phytoplankton are producers capable of photosynthesis in surface waters. Zooplankton are consumers.
(17) amount of plankton, suspended sediment, and decaying organic particles present in the water; the amount of sunlight available
(18) ocean area beyond the continental shelf; low nutrient concentrations
(19) pelagic: open ocean of any depth; benthic: any ocean bottom regardless of distance from shore
(20) limits mixing of nutrient-rich deeper waters with nutrient-poor surface waters; so productivity is limited by low-nutrient availability.
(21) The graph should include an increase in productivity beginning in February with a bloom in mid-March to April. Productivity steadily decreases from there with a slight increase and small bloom again in September–October, after which productivity decreases again.
(22) The zooplankton population should reflect the increases and decreases in productivity with a month's lag time.
(23) A food chain is a simple model that shows how energy is transferred from one species to another. A food web is a more complex model that shows interrelationships among several species.

Critical Thinking

(24) higher; amount of evaporation that is taking place exceeds the amount of freshwater input from precipitation and runoff. Evaporation leaves salt behind, leading to increased salinity levels.
(25) B (lowest density), A, C (highest density); B; C
(26) Because there is no thermocline or pycnocline in polar waters, there is good vertical mixing between surface water and deeper nutrient-rich water. This allows nutrients to reach surface waters, where photosynthesis takes place, which allows for increased productivity.
(27) The phytoplankton population increases in productivity and undergoes a bloom during the spring, when solar energy and nutrients are available. After this productivity drops off due to lack of available nutrients. The zooplankton population follows the curve of the phytoplankton biomass with about a month's lag time.
(28) Productivity begins to increase again in August leading to a small bloom of phytoplankton in September, after which productivity declines again. The zooplankton population stays relatively low with a small increase in biomass in October following the phytoplankton bloom. The fall bloom is much smaller than the spring bloom.
(29) The fall bloom would occur in March and April and the spring bloom would occur during September.

Concepts in Action

(30) a thermocline
(31) Temperature variation with depth is present in temperate and tropical oceans. This occurs because solar radiation heats surface waters so that they have higher temperatures than the deeper layers beneath them. As temperature increases, the density of water decreases. The layer of warm surface water sits on top of the colder, higher density water with little mixing.
(32) The zooplankton are feeding on phytoplankton at night, when numbers are highest after a full day of photosynthesis. Zooplankton also avoid predation by spending daylight hours at depth.

Assessment *continued*

Critical Thinking

24 **Analyzing** In the Red Sea, evaporation values are higher than the values of precipitation and river runoff, particularly in summer months. Do you think that the salinity of the water here is higher or lower than average ocean water salinity? Why?

25 **Drawing Conclusions** Water Mass A is 2°C with a salinity of 34.50‰. Water Mass B is 2°C with a salinity of 34.00‰. Water Mass C is 2°C with a salinity of 34.78‰. Order the water masses from lowest density to highest density. Which water mass will be nearest the surface? Which will be closest to the bottom?

26 **Relating Cause and Effect** Explain how the phytoplankton productivity in polar waters is related to the fact that density and temperature change very little with depth in polar waters.

Use the figure below to answer questions 27–29.

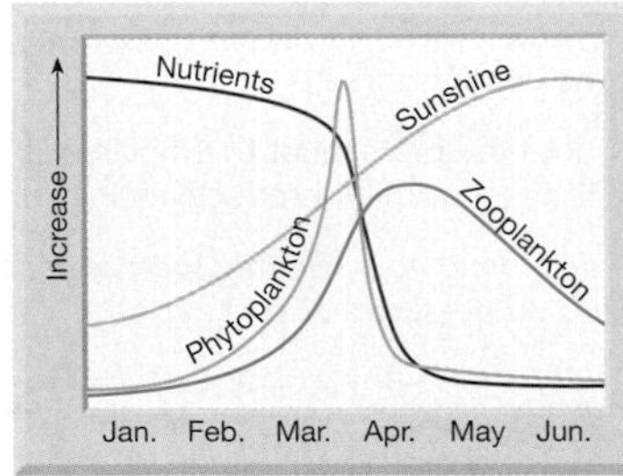

27 **Applying Concepts** The graph shows the productivity in temperate oceans in the northern hemisphere for the first half of the year. Describe what is happening to the phytoplankton and zooplankton populations in the graph. Explain what factors are affecting productivity.

28 **Inferring** Describe what the graph would look like if it were extended through December. How is it different than the January through June portion?

29 **Drawing Conclusions** How would this graph be different if it were for a temperate ocean in the southern hemisphere?

Concepts in Action

Use the table below to answer questions 30 and 31.

Depth (m)	Temperature (°C)
0	23
200	22.5
400	20
600	14
800	8
1000	5
1200	4.5
1400	4.5
1600	4

30 **Interpreting Data** An oceanographer records the following temperature data for an area of ocean water. Graph the data on a sheet of graph paper. What feature exists between 400 and 1200 meters?

31 **Applying Concepts** For which area of the world oceans would this temperature variation with depth be present? What processes cause this to occur?

32 **Formulating Hypotheses** It has been observed that some species of zooplankton migrate vertically in ocean water. They spend the daylight hours at deeper depths of about 200 meters and at night move to the surface. Formulate a hypothesis that might explain this behavior.

Performance-Based Assessment

Designing Equipment Imagine you have been asked to collect marine plankton samples from surface waters near the coast. Recall that many plankton are microscopic or nearly so and that by definition, plankton drift with currents. Design a piece of equipment that will allow you to collect the plankton so that they can be brought to the lab and examined under a microscope. Include the materials you will use to construct the equipment, a drawing of it, and an explanation of how it should be used in the field.

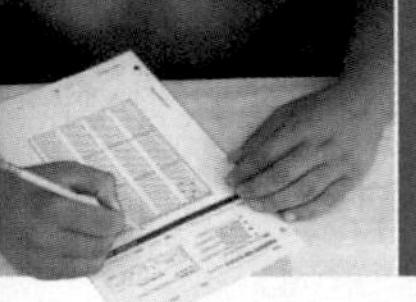

Regents Practice Exam

Test-Taking Tip

Watch for Qualifiers

The words *best*, *least*, and *greatest* are examples of qualifiers. If a question contains a qualifier, more than one answer will contain correct information. However, only one answer will be complete and correct for the question asked. Look at the question below. Eliminate any answers that are clearly incorrect. Then choose the remaining answer that offers the best explanation for the question asked.

Which factor has the *greatest* influence on the density of surface water in the ocean?

(1) temperature
(2) pressure
(3) salinity
(4) oxygen

(Answer: 1)

For *each* statement or question, choose the *number* of the word or expression that, of those given, best completes the statement or answers the question. Some questions may require the use of the *Earth Science Reference Tables.*

1 Which of the following processes would increase ocean salinity?
(1) evaporation (2) precipitation
(3) sea ice melting (4) seismic activity

2 Using light energy and carbon dioxide to build carbohydrate molecules is called
(1) chemosynthesis (2) carbonation
(3) photosynthesis (4) decomposition

3 Plankton living off the east coast of Florida would most likely
(1) drift southeast toward Africa
(2) remain off the coast of Florida
(3) drift toward South America
(4) drift northeast toward Europe

Answer the following questions in complete sentences. Some questions may require the use of the *Earth Science Reference Tables.* Base your answer to questions 6 and 7 on the diagram at top right, which shows Variations in Ocean Water Density.

4 What are the main factors affecting the density of ocean water?

5 Explain why vast quantities of ocean water sink at high latitudes.

6 Below 1000 meters, how does the density at high latitudes compare with the density at low latitudes? What do you think explains this relationship?

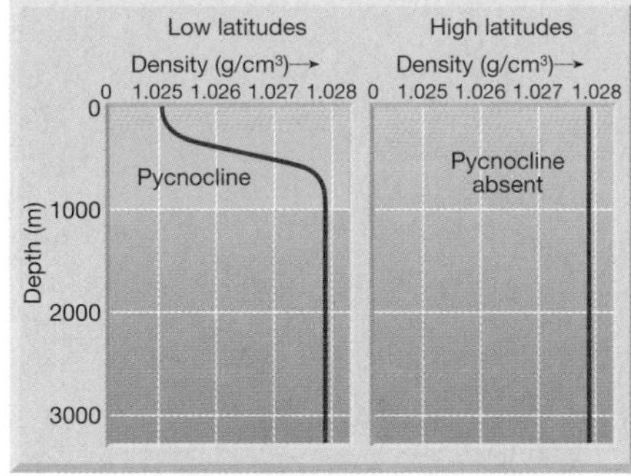

7 What relationship exists between density and depth at high latitudes?

Base your answer to question 8 on the diagram below, which shows a Food Web.

8 What changes would occur to the food web below if the population of copepods was killed by a bacterial disease?

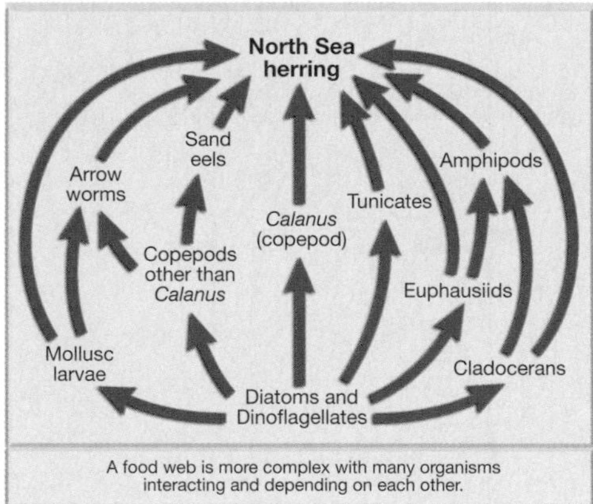

A food web is more complex with many organisms interacting and depending on each other.

Regents Practice Exam

(1) 1
(2) 3
(3) 4
(4) The main factors affecting ocean water density are temperature and salinity.
(5) Ocean water sinks at high latitudes because it is very cold (due to latitude) and very salty (due to sea ice formation). Since both low temperature and high salinity increase density, the water is very dense, so it will sink.
(6) Below 1000 m the density at high and low latitudes is equal. This is because surface conditions have a negligible effect on the density of water below 1000 m.
(7) At high latitudes, density does not change with depth.
(8) The sand eels would be greatly affected as copepods are their only food source. The arrow worms would also be affected and would have to eat more mollusk larvae to survive. The North Sea herring would be affected the least as they have many other food sources. There would be a greater number of diatoms and dinoflagellates for other organisms to eat.

Performance-Based Assessment

Student answers will vary but their designs should indicate that they have considered the size of phytoplankton and the motion of ocean currents.

Your students can independently test their knowledge of the chapter and print out their results.

CHAPTER 16

Planning Guide

Use these planning tools
Use Teacher Express for all your planning needs

SECTION OBJECTIVES	STANDARDS NATIONAL	STANDARDS STATE	ACTIVITIES and LABS
16.1 Ocean Circulation, pp. 448–454 1 block or 2 periods **16.1** **Explain** how surface currents develop. **16.2** **Describe** how ocean currents affect climate. **16.3** **State** the importance of upwelling. **16.4** **Describe** the formation of density currents.	A-1, C-4, D-1, D-2		**SE** Inquiry Activity: How Do Ocean Waves Form? p. 447 **L2** **TE** Teacher Demo: Creating Density Currents, p. 451 **L2**
16.2 Waves and Tides, pp. 455–460 1 block or 2 periods **16.5** **Describe** how ocean waves get their energy. **16.6** **State** three factors that determine the characteristics of a wave. **16.7** **Describe** how energy moves through a wave. **16.8** **Explain** the forces that produce tides.	B-4, B-6, D-1, G-3		**TE** Teacher Demo: Wave Motion, p. 455 **L2** **SE** Exploration Lab: Graphing Tidal Cycles, pp. 468–469 **L2**
16.3 Shoreline Processes and Features, pp. 461–467 1 block or 2 periods **16.9** **List** the agents responsible for the movement of sediments along the shoreline. **16.10** **Explain** how refraction affects wave action along the shore. **16.11** **Describe** the processes that form shoreline features. **16.12** **List** the structures that can be built to protect a shoreline.	A-1, A-2, B-4, B-6, C-4, D-1, D-3, F-6		**TE** Build Science Skills, p. 465 **L2** **TE** Build Science Skills, p. 466 **L2** **LM** Shoreline Features **L1**

Ability Levels

- **L1** For students who need additional help
- **L2** For all students
- **L3** For students who need to be challenged

Components

SE	Student Edition	**GRSW**	Guided Reading & Study Workbook	**TP**	Test Prep Resources	**GEO**	Geode CD-ROM
TE	Teacher's Edition	**TEX**	Teacher Express	**onT**	onlineText	**T**	Transparencies
LM	Laboratory Manual	**CTB**	Computer Test Bank	**DC**	Discovery Channel Videos	**GO**	Internet Resources
CUT	Chapter Tests						

RESOURCES PRINT and TECHNOLOGY	SECTION ASSESSMENT
GRSW Section 16.1 **T-202** Surface Ocean Currents **T-203** Conveyor Belt Model **TEX** Lesson Planning 16.1	**SE** Section 16.1 Assessment, p. 453 **onT** Section 16.1
GRSW Section 16.2 **T-204** Idealized Ocean Wave **T-205** Toy Boat Model **T-206** Wave Moves onto Shore **T-213** Tides on Earth **T-214** Spring Tide and Neap Tide **T-215** Tidal Patterns **DC** Waves and Tides **TEX** Lesson Planning 16.2	**SE** Section 16.2 Assessment, p. 460 **onT** Section 16.2
GRSW Section 16.3 **T-207** Wave Refraction **T-208** Beach Drift and Longshore Currents **T-209** Barrier Islands **T-210** Changes to an Initially Irregular Coastline **T-211** Changes to an Initially Irregular Coastline **T-212** Estuaries Along the East Coast **T-216** Flood Delta 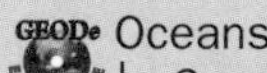 Oceans ↳ Coastal Processes **TEX** Lesson Planning 16.3	**SE** Section 16.3 Assessment, p. 467 **onT** Section 16.3

Go Online

Go online for these Internet resources.

PHSchool.com
Web Code: cjk-9999

Web Code: cjn-5161
Web Code: cjn-5162
Web Code: cjn-5163

Materials for Activities and Labs

Quantities for each group

STUDENT EDITION

Inquiry Activity, p. 447
rectangular clear plastic container, water, fan with high and low settings, ruler

Exploration Lab, pp. 468–469
graph paper, pencil

TEACHER'S EDITION

Teacher Demo, p. 451
2 deep and clear containers, ice water, salt, tap water, food coloring, 2 smaller and clear containers

Teacher Demo, p. 455
Slinky™ toy

Build Science Skills, p. 465
materials for building models of erosional and depositional features

Chapter Assessment

ASSESSMENT

SE Assessment, pp. 471–472
CUT Chapter 16 Test
CTB Chapter 16
onT Chapter 16

STANDARDIZED TEST PREP

SE Chapter 16, p. 473
TP Progress Monitoring Assessments

interactive textbook with assessment at PHSchool.com

CHAPTER 16

Before you teach

Michael Wysession
Washington University

Big Ideas

Ocean water is constantly in motion. Ocean currents, controlled by the outlines of the continents, move water through a global set of interconnected cycles.

Space and Time The gravitational attraction of the moon and sun causes tides. The patterns of tides and tidal currents vary according to location, and change with the relative positions of the moon, sun, and Earth.

Forces and Motion Surface currents follow the general pattern of wind belts, and often form gyres as a result of the Coriolis effect. Upwelling, induced by wind, involves the rising of cold, nutrient-rich water. Deep-ocean currents are driven by density differences due to variations in temperature and salinity.

Matter and Energy Ocean waves are transfer of energy, originating from the wind, across the ocean surface. The height, wavelength, and period of the waves are influenced by wind speed and duration. Waves erode shorelines through wave impact and abrasion. Near-shore waves also transport sediment and are responsible for deposition of sedimentary features like spits and barrier islands. Shoreline erosion and deposition tend to straighten out coastlines that may be irregular due to changes in sea level.

Earth as a System Erosion along a shoreline can be reduced through the construction of breakwaters and seawalls, and through the addition of beach sand.

Earth Science Refresher

Geologic Battle Over Coastlines

Geologic processes operating within shore environments tend to make jagged coastlines straight. Any promontories of rock that stick out away from the shore become eroded more quickly due to the process of wave refraction, which bends waves toward them. Any bays and inlets tend to be filled in quickly because water moves more slowly there, allowing sediment to deposit out. Why, then, aren't all coastlines perfectly straight? The reason is that sea levels, both locally and globally, are constantly changing, creating new jagged coastlines.

Sometimes sea level seems to change because of local tectonics. For example, in regions where ocean plate subduction is occurring, such as off the coast of Oregon and Washington, the edge of the continent goes up and down over relatively short time periods. As the ocean plate slowly subducts, it pulls down the overriding continental edge. Then when a large earthquake occurs, the continental plate detaches from the ocean plate and snaps back up suddenly. Over a cycle of hundreds of years, the coastline may be pulled down and snapped back up many meters or tens of meters. Shoreline processes of erosion and deposition seem to therefore be constantly trying to catch up with the changing shoreline.

With the recent rise in global sea level due to the melting of glacial ice from the recent Ice Age, many coastlines around the world have been submerged. The new coastlines are jagged because they show the contours of flooded former river valleys, like the Pamlico and Albemarle Sounds in Figure 21, or glacial valleys, like the fjords of Norway. If sea level stays constant for awhile, these coastlines will again begin to straighten, but as soon as the sea level changes again, new coastlines will be exposed.

Why the Mediterranean Sea Doesn't Overflow

If you ever go to Gibraltar, you will notice a strange thing: water from the Atlantic Ocean is constantly pouring eastward into the Mediterranean Sea. There is always an eastward current. This is strange because many rivers like the Nile and Danube eventually flow into the Mediterranean. Why doesn't the Mediterranean Sea overflow? What happens to the water?

These questions have two answers. First, more water evaporates from the surface of the sea than is replenished by rivers that flow into it, so water must be added from the Atlantic. Second, the salinity of the Mediterranean water increases greatly due to all of the evaporation (which leaves the salts behind), and some water actually flows back out into the Atlantic. However, because this water is dense, it flows westward underneath the incoming water, and isn't seen at the surface.

Address Misconceptions

Salt added to water does not change the density of the water. Actually, salty water is much denser than water without salt, and the more salt that is added, the denser the water becomes. For a strategy that helps to overcome this misconception, see **Address Misconceptions** on **p. 451.**

Build Reading Literacy

Sequence

Ordering Events

Strategy Help students understand and visualize the steps in a process, or the order in which events occur. Sequences frequently involve cause-effect relationships. Readers can construct graphic organizers to help themselves visualize and comprehend a sequence. For most sequences, flowcharts are the graphic of choice. However, cycle diagrams are more appropriate for cycles. Before students begin, locate a description or figure in the text of a several-step process or a chain of causes and effects, such as Evolution of Shoreline Features in Section 16.3.

Example

1. Have students read the passage or study the figure, thinking about what takes place first, second, third, and so on. Point out that the text will not always use order words such as *first*, *next*, *then*, and *finally*.

2. Ask students to list the steps or events in order.

3. If the passage or figure describes a chain of steps or events, draw a flowchart on the board, having students tell the sequence of events, steps, or causes and effects, and writing each part of the process in a separate box.

4. If the passage describes a cycle, use a cycle diagram to show the sequence.

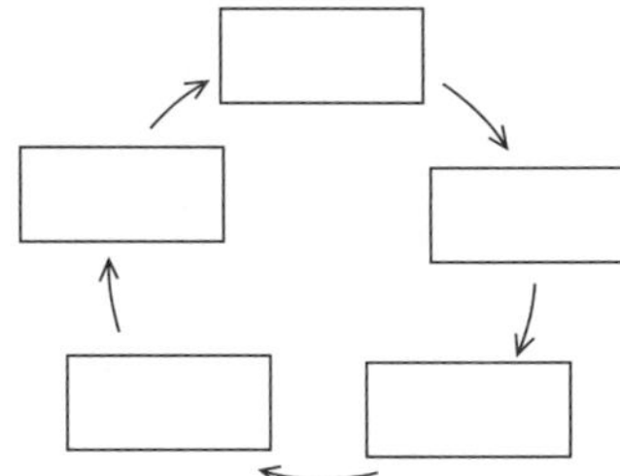

5. Have students locate additional examples of sequential relationships in the text or visuals of the chapter. Students can depict the steps or events using graphic organizers.

See p. 453 for a script on how to use this strategy with students. For additional strategies, see pp. 452, 456, 458, 464, and 465.

ASSESS PRIOR KNOWLEDGE

Use the Chapter Pretest below to assess students' prior knowledge. As needed, review these concepts.

Review Science Concepts

Section 16.1 Review with students that denser objects sink and less dense objects float. Also review how temperature affects density. These concepts will help students understand deep-ocean circulation.

Section 16.2 Have students recall a time when they swam in the ocean or saw ocean waves in a movie. These memories will help students understand how waves move.

Section 16.3 Have students recall a trip to the beach to help them understand the processes affecting shorelines. Review with students that agents of erosion are the most powerful when they are moving the fastest. Remind them that deposition tends to occur when the agents slow down.

CHAPTER

16 The Dynamic Ocean

CONCEPTS in Action

Exploration Lab
Graphing Tidal Cycles

Understanding Earth
Shoes and Toys as Drift Meters

Oceans
↳ Coastal Processes

Discovery Channel School

Video Field Trip

Waves and Tides

Take a surfing field trip with Discovery Channel and learn about waves, swells, and tides. Answer the following questions after watching the video.

1. How are waves created?
2. Describe the way in which the moon influences the tides.

For: Chapter 16 Resources
Visit: PHSchool.com
Web Code: cjk-9999

Waves break along California's rocky Big Sur coast. ▶

Chapter Pretest

1. How does heating water affect the water's density? *(b)*
   a. It increases. b. It decreases.
   c. It remains the same.
2. What does cold water tend to do when it comes in contact with warm water? *(a)*
   a. sink b. rise c. stay in place
3. As you are standing in the ocean, what do passing waves usually do? *(c)*
   a. carry you in to shore
   b. carry you out to sea
   c. move you up and down
4. If you enter the ocean directly in front of your beach blanket and swim for about an hour, where will you most likely be when you come out of the water? *(b)*
   a. directly in front of your beach blanket
   b. further up the beach in the direction the waves are moving
   c. further down the beach, opposite to the direction the waves are moving
5. At point A on the beach the waves come in rapidly, and hit with great force. At point B on the same beach, the waves come in slowly with very little force. At which location(s) would you expect to see the most erosion? *(a)*
   a. point A b. point B
   c. Points A and B would have the same amount of erosion.

Chapter Preview

Inquiry Activity

How Do Ocean Waves Form?

Procedure

1. Fill a rectangular, clear, plastic container with water to within about 3 cm of the top of the container.
2. Place a fan next to the container, aiming the flow of air toward the water. **CAUTION:** *Make sure the cord and the fan do not come in contact with the water in the container.*
3. Turn the fan on low power for 2–3 minutes. Observe what effect this has on the water in the container. Using a ruler, measure the size of the waves produced. Record your observations and data.
4. Turn the fan off and allow the water in the container to settle. Repeat Step 3 with the fan on high power.

Think About It

1. **Inferring** Where does the energy to produce most ocean waves come from?
2. **Drawing Conclusions** What is the relationship between the speed of the wind and the size of a wave?

Video Field Trip

Waves and Tides

Encourage students to view the video field trip "Waves and Tides."

ENGAGE/EXPLORE

How Do Ocean Waves Form?

Purpose In this activity, students will discover how wind causes waves and observe that stronger winds result in taller waves.

Skills Focus Observing

 **Prep Time** 10 minutes

Materials rectangular clear plastic container, water, fan with high and low settings, ruler

Advance Prep You may want to set up the containers and fans ahead of time. You may also want to test how much water can be put in the container, and how far away the fan needs to be to not splash water out of the container.

Class Time 10 minutes

Safety Make sure that students do not let the cord or fan touch the water.

Teaching Tip Waves can be created simply by blowing on the water, and the waves can be shown to the class by putting the clear container on an overhead projector.

Expected Outcome Students will discover that wind causes waves, and stronger wind results in taller waves.

Think About It

1. wind

2. As wind speed increases, wave height increases.

Section 16.1

1 FOCUS

Section Objectives

16.1 **Explain** how surface currents develop.
16.2 **Describe** how ocean currents affect climate.
16.3 **State** the importance of upwelling.
16.4 **Describe** the formation of density currents.

Reading Focus

Build Vocabulary L2

Paraphrase Have students define the words in this section using their own words. For example, students may define *gyre* as "flow of water in a large circle."

Reading Strategy L2

Possible responses are as follows:
a. caused by wind
b. circular movement of water
c. Currents transfer heat from hotter regions to cooler regions and modify climate.
d. cold water exposed at the surface
e. vertical currents caused by density differences; denser water sinks
f. Cold surface water sinks at the poles because it is dense.
g. causes increased salinity and increased density
h. Ocean water moves around Earth because of density differences.

16.1 Ocean Circulation

Reading Focus

Key Concepts

- How do surface currents develop?
- How do ocean currents affect climate?
- Why is upwelling important?
- How are density currents formed?

Vocabulary

- ocean current
- surface current
- gyre
- Coriolis effect
- upwelling
- density current

Reading Strategy

Identifying Main Ideas Copy and expand the table below. As you read, write the main idea of each topic.

Topic	Main Idea
Surface currents	a. ____?____
Gyres	b. ____?____
Ocean currents and climate	c. ____?____
Upwelling	d. ____?____

Figure 1 Wind not only creates waves, but it also provides the force that drives the ocean's surface circulation.

Ocean water is constantly in motion, powered by many different forces. Winds, for example, generate surface currents, which influence coastal climate. Winds also produce waves like the ones shown in Figure 1. Some waves carry energy from powerful storms to distant shores, where their impact erodes the land. In some areas, density differences create deep-ocean circulation. This circulation is important for ocean mixing and recycling nutrients.

Surface Circulation

Ocean currents are masses of ocean water that flow from one place to another. The amount of water can be large or small. Ocean currents can be at the surface or deep below. The creation of these currents can be simple or complex. In all cases, however, the currents that are generated involve water masses in motion.

Surface Currents **Surface currents** are movements of water that flow horizontally in the upper part of the ocean's surface. **Surface currents develop from friction between the ocean and the wind that blows across its surface.** Some of these currents do not last long, and they affect only small areas. Such water movements are responses to local or seasonal influences. Other surface currents are more permanent and extend over large portions of the oceans. These major horizontal movements of surface waters are closely related to the general circulation pattern of the atmosphere.

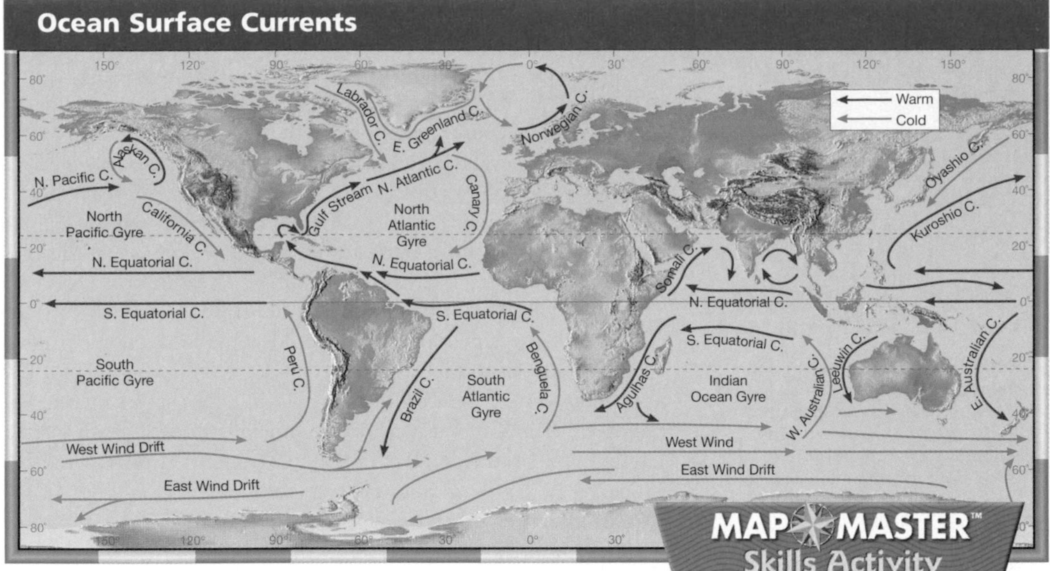

Figure 2
The ocean's circulation is organized into five major gyres, or circular current systems. The West Wind Drift flows around the continent of Antarctica.

Movement
Locate Which currents make up the North Atlantic Gyre?
Locate Find the West Wind Drift on the map. Explain why the West Wind Drift is the only current that completely encircles Earth.
Drawing Conclusions Why is there not another comparable current that encircles Earth at the same latitude in the Northern Hemisphere?

Gyres Huge circular-moving current systems dominate the surfaces of the oceans. These large whirls of water within an ocean basin are called **gyres** (*gyros* = a circle). There are five main ocean gyres: the North Pacific Gyre, the South Pacific Gyre, the North Atlantic Gyre, the South Atlantic Gyre, and the Indian Ocean Gyre. Find these gyres in Figure 2.

Although wind is the force that generates surface currents, other factors also influence the movement of ocean waters. The most significant of these is the Coriolis effect. The **Coriolis effect** is the deflection of currents away from their original course as a result of Earth's rotation. **Because of Earth's rotation, currents are deflected to the right in the Northern Hemisphere and to the left in the Southern Hemisphere.** As a consequence, gyres flow in opposite directions in the two different hemispheres.

Four main currents generally exist within each gyre. For example, the North Pacific Gyre consists of the North Equatorial Current, the Kuroshio Current, the North Pacific Current, and the California Current. The tracking of floating objects that are released into the ocean reveals that it takes about six years for the objects to go all the way around the loop.

Why do gyres in the Northern Hemisphere flow in the opposite direction of gyres in the Southern Hemisphere?

2 INSTRUCT

Surface Circulation

MAP MASTER Skills Activity

Locate *North Atlantic Gyre consists of the North Equatorial Current, the Gulf Stream, the North Atlantic Current, the Canary Current.*

Locate *The West Wind Drift can encircle Earth because there are no land masses/continents obstructing its path.*

Drawing Conclusions *In the Northern Hemisphere at the same latitude, there are landmasses and continents that block the path of a circumpolar current.*

Use Visuals

Figure 2 This diagram shows ocean surface currents all over the world. Ask: **What happens to ocean currents when they hit a landmass?** *(They are deflected parallel to the shore.)* **Why do gyres in the northern Atlantic and Pacific oceans mostly rotate clockwise?** *(The Coriolis effect causes currents to be deflected to the right in the Northern Hemisphere.)* **Why do gyres in the southern Atlantic and Pacific oceans mostly rotate counterclockwise?** *(The Coriolis effect causes currents to be deflected to the left in the Southern Hemisphere.)*
Visual

Customize for English Language Learners

Teach students that *gyre* comes from the word *gyros*, which means "circle." List several other words containing this root, and have students look up their definitions. Have students explain what all the words have in common. For example: *gyre, gyroscope, gyrate, gyration,* and *gyroscopic* all have to do with moving in a circle. Also introduce students to the Greek food, the gyro, which is meat that rotates on a spit and is served in a pita. Show students a picture of a gyro, and if possible let them taste one.

Answer to . . .

because currents are deflected to the right in the Northern Hemisphere and to the left in the Southern Hemisphere due to Earth's rotation

Section 16.1 (continued)

Integrate Social Studies 

Early Settlers Early settlers of the 13 original colonies were quite surprised by, and unprepared for, the bitter cold winters they encountered in the New World. Since America was farther south than England, they assumed the climate here would be warmer. However, they did not know that the powerful, warm Gulf Stream current kept England at a warmer temperature than would be expected based on latitude alone. Direct students to use Figure 2, the reading, and their own knowledge to answer the following questions. Ask: **What parts of North America are at the same latitude as England?** *(Alaska, northern Canada)* **Why is northeastern Canada so much colder than England?** *(England is warmed by the Gulf Stream Current, while northeastern Canada is cooled by the Labrador Current.)* **If the English knew America was colder than England, how might this have changed their expeditions?** *(Sample answers: They would have brought warmer clothes or more food, or they might not have settled in the northern colonies.)*
Visual, Logical

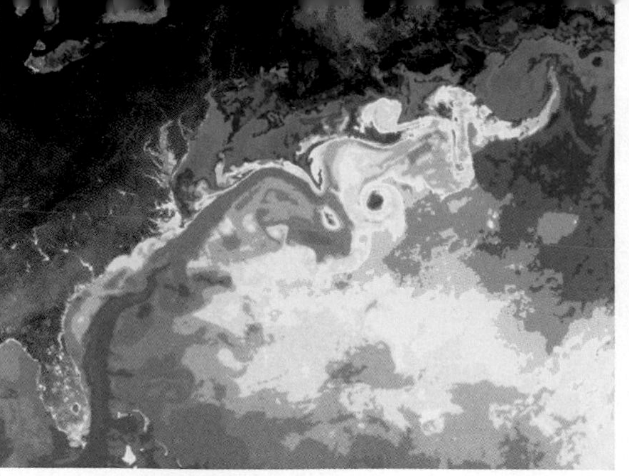

Figure 3 Gulf Stream This false-color satellite image of sea surface temperatures shows the course of the Gulf Stream. The warm waters of the Gulf Stream are shown in red and orange along the east coast of Florida and the Carolinas. The surrounding colder waters are shown in green, blue, and purple. Compare this image to the map of the Gulf Stream in Figure 2.

Ocean Currents and Climate Ocean currents have an important effect on climates. **When currents from low-latitude regions move into higher latitudes, they transfer heat from warmer to cooler areas on Earth.** The Gulf Stream, a warm water current shown in Figure 3, is an excellent example of this phenomenon. The Gulf Stream brings warm water from the equator up to the North Atlantic Current, which is an extension of the Gulf Stream. This current allows Great Britain and much of northwestern Europe to be warmer during the winter than one would expect for their latitudes, which are similar to the latitudes of Alaska and Newfoundland. The prevailing westerly winds carry this warming effect far inland. For example, Berlin, Germany (52 degrees north latitude), has an average January temperature similar to that experienced at New York City, which lies 12 degrees latitude farther south.

The effects of these warm ocean currents are felt mostly in the middle latitudes in winter. In contrast, the influence of cold currents is most felt in the tropics or during summer months in the middle latitudes. Cold currents begin in cold high-latitude regions. **As cold water currents travel toward the equator, they help moderate the warm temperatures of adjacent land areas.** Such is the case for the Benguela Current along western Africa, the Peru Current along the west coast of South America, and the California Current. These currents are shown in Figure 2.

Ocean currents also play a major role in maintaining Earth's heat balance. They do this by transferring heat from the tropics, where there is an excess of heat, to the polar regions, where less heat exists. Ocean water movement accounts for about a quarter of this heat transport. Winds transport the remaining three-quarters.

Upwelling In addition to producing surface currents, winds can also cause vertical water movements. **Upwelling** is the rising of cold water from deeper layers to replace warmer surface water. Upwelling is a common wind-induced vertical movement. One type of upwelling, called coastal upwelling, is most characteristic along the west coasts of continents, most notably along California, western South America, and West Africa.

Coastal upwelling occurs in these areas when winds blow toward the equator and parallel to the coast. Coastal winds combined with the Coriolis effect cause surface water to move away from shore. As the surface layer moves away from the coast, it is replaced by water that "upwells" from below the surface. This slow upward movement of water from depths of 50 to 300 meters brings water that is cooler than

For: Links on ocean currents
Visit: www.SciLinks.org
Web Code: cjn-5161

Facts and Figures

During upwelling, cold water is exposed at the surface when the warm surface layer of water is removed by strong winds. Upwelling of nutrient rich cold water is critical to fishing industries all over the world, but it is especially important off the coast of Peru. Unfortunately, El Niño events often disrupt upwelling by reducing surface wind speeds, which causes terrible consequences for fishes.

Download a worksheet on ocean currents for students to complete, and find additional teacher support from NSTA SciLinks.

the original surface water and results in lower surface water temperatures near the shore.

Upwelling brings greater concentrations of dissolved nutrients, such as nitrates and phosphates, to the ocean surface. These nutrient-enriched waters from below promote the growth of microscopic plankton, which in turn support extensive populations of fish and other marine organisms. Figure 4 is a satellite image that shows high productivity due to coastal upwelling off the southwest coast of Africa.

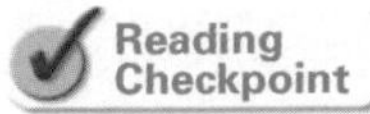

What is upwelling?

Deep-Ocean Circulation

In contrast to the largely horizontal movements of surface currents, deep-ocean circulation has a significant vertical component. It accounts for the thorough mixing of deep-water masses.

Density Currents **Density currents** are vertical currents of ocean water that result from density differences among water masses. Denser water sinks and slowly spreads out beneath the surface. **An increase in seawater density can be caused by a decrease in temperature or an increase in salinity.** Processes that increase the salinity of water include evaporation and the formation of sea ice. Processes that decrease the salinity of water include precipitation, runoff from land, icebergs melting, and sea ice melting. Density changes due to salinity variations are important in very high latitudes, where water temperature remains low and relatively constant.

High Latitudes Most water involved in deep-ocean density currents begins in high latitudes at the surface. In these regions, surface water becomes cold, and its salinity increases as sea ice forms. When this water becomes dense enough, it sinks, initiating deep-ocean density currents. Once this water sinks, it is removed from the physical processes that increased its density in the first place. Its temperature and salinity remain largely unchanged during the time it is in the deep ocean. Because of this, oceanographers can track the movements of density currents in the deep ocean. By knowing the temperature, salinity, and density of a water mass, scientists are able to map the slow circulation of the water mass through the ocean.

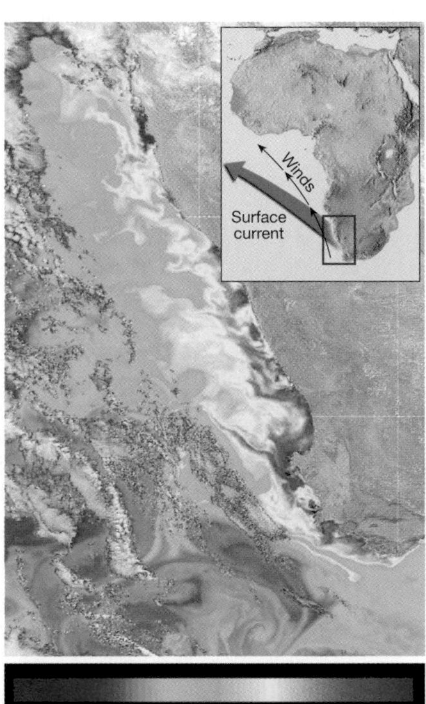

Figure 4 Effects of Upwelling This image from the SeaStar satellite shows chlorophyll concentration along the southwest coast of Africa. High chlorophyll concentrations, in red, indicate high amounts of photosynthesis, which is linked to upwelling nutrients.

Deep-Ocean Circulation

L2

Many students think that salinity has no effect on the density of water. During the Teacher Demo described below, students will see that saltwater sinks beneath fresh water. Therefore, saltwater is denser than fresh water.
Visual

Teacher Demo

Creating Density Currents

L2

Purpose Students will see how temperature and salinity create density currents.

Materials 2 deep and clear containers, ice water, salt, tap water, food coloring, 2 smaller and clear containers

Procedure Partly fill each deep container with tap water, and add red food coloring. Add blue food coloring to ice water in a small container. Add salt and green food coloring to tap water in another small container. Slowly pour the blue ice water into one deep container that is already partly filled with red tap water. Slowly pour the green saltwater into the other deep container that is partly filled with red tap water.

Safety Food coloring may stain skin or clothing.

Expected Outcomes Students will see that both cold water and saltwater sink to the bottom and spread out in the warmer fresh water. Repeat this demonstration as needed until students are convinced that saltwater and cold water are denser than warmer, fresh water. Students may ask you to try putting the cold or salty water in first, or they may ask you to try heating the tap water before adding the cold or salty water. You can also allow students to try this activity themselves or in small groups.
Visual, Kinesthetic

Facts and Figures

Before large ocean currents like the Gulf Stream were understood, people wondered why a boat trip west across the Atlantic Ocean took nearly two weeks longer than the trip back east. Ben Franklin's cousin, Timothy Folger, advised Franklin that this was because the captains of many ships were not aware of the Gulf Stream Current that flowed west to east across the Atlantic. Franklin then shared this information with the mariners by creating a map showing the Gulf Stream. This map allowed sailors attempting to go from east to west to avoid being slowed down by this powerful current.

Answer to . . .

Upwelling is the rising of cold water from deeper layers to replace warmer surface water.

Build Reading Literacy L1

Refer to page **246D** in **Chapter 9**, which provides guidelines for relating cause and effect.

Relate Cause and Effect Once students have read this section, ask: **What are the possible causes for an increase in density?** *(temperature decrease and salinity increase)* **How does temperature affect density?** *(Higher temperatures result in lower density, while colder temperatures result in higher density.)* **How does salinity affect density?** *(Higher salinity results in higher density.)* **How does evaporation affect density?** *(Evaporation leads to higher salinity and thus higher density.)*
Verbal, Logical

Use Visuals L1

Figure 6 Be sure students understand the orientation of this cross section by comparing it geographically to the map in Figure 2. The cross section would be represented by a north-south line through the Atlantic Ocean. Ask: **Why don't the arrows on the two figures match?** *(Figure 2 shows surface currents; Figure 6 shows density currents.)* **Describe the probable temperature and salinity characteristics and general movements of the Antarctic Bottom Water.** *(cold and highly saline; forms in the Antarctic, sinks, and flows northward along the ocean floor as far as 20oN latitude)* **Describe the probable temperature and salinity characteristics and general movements of the water from the Mediterranean.** *(warm and highly saline; flows westward into the Atlantic, cools, and sinks slightly as most of it heads toward the equator)*

Figure 5 Sea Ice in the Arctic Ocean When seawater freezes, sea salts do not become part of the ice, leading to an increase in the salinity of the surrounding water.
Drawing Conclusions ***How does this process lead to the formation of a density current?***

Near Antarctica, surface conditions create the highest density water in the world. This cold, salty water slowly sinks to the sea floor, where it moves throughout the ocean basins in slow currents. After sinking from the surface of the ocean, deep waters will not reappear at the surface for an average of 500 to 2000 years.

Evaporation Density currents can also result from increased salinity of ocean water due to evaporation. In the Mediterranean Sea conditions exist that lead to the formation of a dense water mass at the surface that sinks and eventually flows into the Atlantic Ocean. Climate conditions in the eastern Mediterranean include a dry northwest wind and sunny days. These conditions lead to an annual excess of evaporation compared to the amount of precipitation. When seawater evaporates, salt is left behind, and the salinity of the remaining water increases. The surface waters of the eastern Mediterranean Sea have a salinity of about 38‰ (parts per thousand). In the winter months, this water flows out of the Mediterranean Sea into the Atlantic

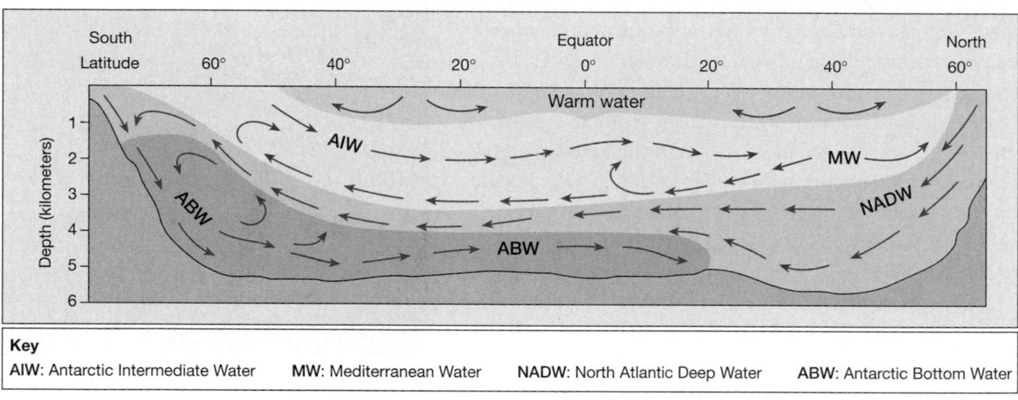

Figure 6 This cross section of the Atlantic Ocean shows the deep-water circulation of water masses formed by density currents.

Ocean. At 38‰, this water is more dense than the Atlantic Ocean surface water at 35‰, so it sinks. This Mediterranean water mass can be tracked as far south as Antarctica. Figure 6 shows some of the different water masses created by density currents in the Atlantic Ocean.

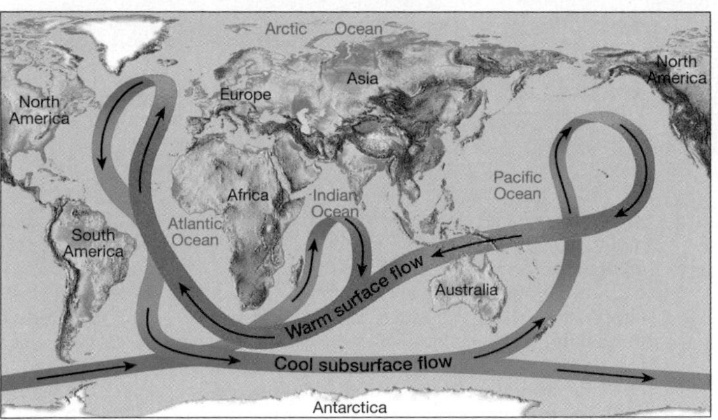

Figure 7 This "conveyor belt" model of ocean circulation shows a warm surface current with an underlying cool current.

A Conveyor Belt A simplified model of ocean circulation is similar to a conveyor belt that travels from the Atlantic Ocean through the Indian and Pacific oceans and back again. Figure 7 shows this conveyor belt model. In this model, warm water in the ocean's upper layers flows toward the poles. When the water reaches the poles, its temperature drops and salinity increases, making it more dense. Because the water is dense, it sinks and moves toward the equator. It returns to the equator as cold, deep water that eventually upwells to complete the circuit. As this "conveyor belt" moves around the globe, it influences global climate by converting warm water to cold water and releasing heat to the atmosphere.

Section 16.1 Assessment

Reviewing Concepts

1. How do surface currents develop?
2. What is the Coriolis effect? How does it influence the direction of surface currents flowing in the ocean?
3. How do ocean currents affect climate?
4. Why is upwelling important?
5. How are density currents formed?

Thinking Critically

6. **Applying Concepts** The average surface water temperature off of the coast of Ecuador is 21°C. The average surface water temperature off of the coast of Brazil at the same latitude is about 27°C. Explain why there is such a difference in water temperature between these areas at the same latitude.
7. **Inferring** During an El Niño event, the upwelling of cold, nutrient-rich water stops in areas off the coast of Peru. How might this affect the food web in this area?

Writing in Science

Explanatory Paragraph During the 1700s, mail ships sailed back and forth between England and America. It was noted that it took the ships two weeks longer to go from England to America than to travel the same route from America to England. It was determined that the Gulf Stream was delaying the ships. Write a paragraph explaining why this is true. Use Figure 2 to explain how sailors could avoid the Gulf Stream when sailing to America.

Build Reading Literacy L1

Refer to p. **446D**, which provides guidelines for sequencing.

Sequence As students read the section *A Conveyor Belt*, ask them to create a flowchart showing the movement of water starting with the phrase "warm water flows toward poles" and ending with the phrase "the cycle repeats." *(For example: warm water flows toward poles → temperature drops and salinity increases → density increases → dense water moves toward equator → cold, deep water upwells → upwelled water warms → the cycle repeats)*
Visual, Verbal

3 ASSESS

Evaluate Understanding L2

Ask students to use Figure 2 to predict the movement of an abandoned boat left adrift in the Atlantic Ocean off the coast of Florida (the Bermuda Triangle).

Reteach L1

Have students write a short story describing the voyage of a droplet of water through the ocean. The droplet should start and end near the north pole.

Writing in Science

Sample answer: When ships traveled from England to America they had to move against the direction of the Gulf Stream, thus delaying their arrival. Ships could cross the Gulf Stream at its northern end and travel near the coast between the current and land to avoid having to move against the current.

Answer to . . .

Figure 5 *As salinity increases, the density of water increases. As surface water becomes denser than underlying water, it sinks, forming a density current.*

Section 16.1 Assessment

1. Surface currents develop from friction between the ocean and the wind that blows across its surface.
2. The deflection of currents away from their original course as a result of Earth's rotation is the Coriolis effect. It causes currents in the Northern Hemisphere to turn to the right and currents in the Southern Hemisphere to turn to the left.
3. Warm water currents that come from equatorial regions transfer heat to cooler areas of Earth; for example, the Gulf Stream and North Atlantic currents warm northwestern Europe in the winter months. Cold water currents from the poles moderate warm temperatures of adjacent land areas.
4. Upwelling brings dissolved nutrients to the ocean surface, providing the necessary nutrients for phytoplankton to undergo photosynthesis. This productivity supports extensive populations of fish and other organisms.
5. They are formed when the density of water changes due to a change in salinity or temperature.
6. The current off of the coast of Ecuador is a cold-water current that comes from high latitudes. The current off of the coast of Brazil is a warm-water current that comes from the equator.
7. The food web in this area is dependent upon the high levels of productivity that result from it having nutrient-rich water. Without the nutrients, productivity significantly declines, leaving many organisms with too little food or no food source. Organisms will either starve or must seek out another food source.

understanding EARTH

Shoes and Toys as Drift Meters **L2**

Teaching Tips

- Have students read this feature in groups and then share their feelings about what they read. Students may wonder about the environmental impact of ships spilling their cargo, or how scientists were able to find out when and where cargo was lost and then found.
- Discuss what this feature reveals about the stories of people setting adrift a message in a bottle. *(The message could travel great distances as the bottle drifts on ocean currents. Quite possibly the bottle will be washed onshore in a distant land.)*

Interpersonal, Verbal

understanding EARTH

Shoes and Toys as Drift Meters

Any floating object can serve as a makeshift drift meter, as long as it is known where the object entered the ocean and where it was retrieved. The path of the object can then be inferred, providing information about the movement of surface currents. If the times of release and retrieval are known, the speed of currents can also be determined. Oceanographers have long used drift bottles—a radio-transmitting device set adrift in the ocean—to track the movement of currents and, more recently, to refine computer models of ocean circulation.

Many objects have accidentally become drift meters when ships have lost some (or all) of their cargo at sea. In this way, athletic shoes have helped oceanographers advance the understanding of surface circulation in the North Pacific Ocean. In May 1990, the container vessel *Hansa Carrier* was traveling from Korea to Seattle, Washington, when it encountered a severe North Pacific storm. During the storm the ship lost 21 deck containers overboard, including five that held athletic shoes. The shoes that were released from their containers floated and were carried east by the North Pacific Current. Within six months, thousands of the shoes began to wash up along the beaches of Alaska, Canada, Washington, and Oregon—over 2400 kilometers from the site of the spill. The inferred course of the shoes is shown in Figure 8. A few shoes were found on beaches in northern California, and over two years later shoes from the spill were even recovered from the north end of the main island of Hawaii.

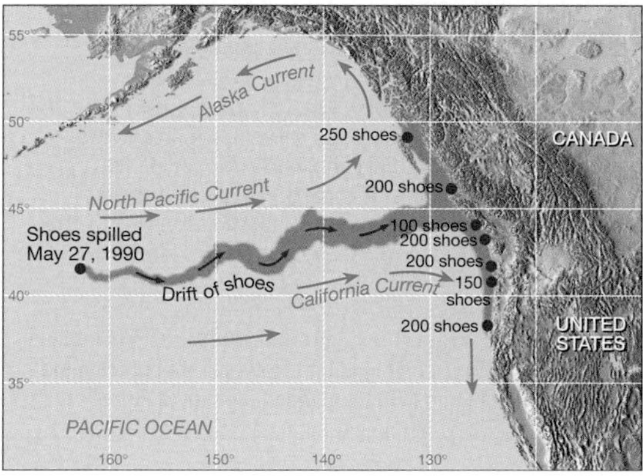

Figure 8 The map shows the path of drifting shoes and recovery locations from a spill in 1990.

With help from the beachcombing public and remotely based lighthouse operators, information on the location and number of shoes collected was compiled during the months following the spill. Serial numbers inside the shoes were traced to individual containers, which indicated that only four of the five containers had released their shoes. Most likely, one entire container sank without opening. A maximum of 30,910 pairs of shoes (61,820 individual shoes) were released. Before the shoe spill, the largest number of drift bottles purposefully released at one time by oceanographers was about 30,000. Although only 2.6 percent of the shoes were recovered, this compares favorably with the 2.4 percent recovery rate of drift bottles released by oceanographers conducting research.

In January 1992, another cargo ship lost 12 containers overboard during a storm to the north of where the shoes had previously spilled. One of these containers held 29,000 packages of small, floatable, colorful plastic bathtub toys in the shapes of blue turtles, yellow ducks, red beavers, and green frogs. Even though the toys were housed in plastic packaging glued to a cardboard backing, studies showed that after 24 hours in seawater, the glue deteriorated, thereby releasing over 100,000 individual floating toys.

The floating bathtub toys began to come ashore in southeast Alaska 10 months later, which verified computer models of North Pacific circulation. The models indicate that many of the bathtub toys will continue to be carried by the Alaska Current and will eventually disperse throughout the North Pacific Ocean.

Since 1992, oceanographers have continued to study ocean currents by tracking other floating items spilled from cargo ships, including 34,000 hockey gloves, 5 million plastic Lego pieces, and an unidentified number of small plastic doll parts.

16.2 Waves and Tides

Reading Focus

Key Concepts

- From where do ocean waves obtain their energy?
- What three factors affect the characteristics of a wave?
- How does energy move through a wave?
- What force produces tides?

Vocabulary

- wave height
- wavelength
- wave period
- fetch
- tide
- tidal range
- spring tide
- neap tide

Reading Strategy

Building Vocabulary Copy the table below. As you read the section, define in your own words each vocabulary word listed in the table.

Vocabulary Term	Definition
Wave height	a. ___?___
Wavelength	b. ___?___
Wave period	c. ___?___
Fetch	d. ___?___

The movement of ocean water is a powerful thing. Waves created by storms release energy when they crash along the shoreline. Sometimes the energy of water movement can be harnessed and used to generate electricity.

Waves

Ocean waves are energy traveling along the boundary between ocean and atmosphere. Waves often transfer energy from a storm far out at sea over distances of several thousand kilometers. That's why even on calm days the ocean still has waves that travel across its surface. The power of waves is most noticeable along the shore, the area between land and sea where waves are constantly rolling in and breaking. Sometimes the waves are low and gentle. Other times waves, like the ones shown in Figure 9, are powerful as they pound the shore. If you make waves by tossing a pebble into a pond, or by splashing in a pool, or by blowing across the surface of a cup of coffee, you are giving energy to the water. The waves you see are just the visible evidence of the energy passing through the water. When observing ocean waves, remember that you are watching energy travel through a medium, in this case, water. In Chapter 24, you will study waves of the electromagnetic spectrum (which includes light). These waves transfer energy without matter as a medium.

Figure 9 The Force of Breaking Waves These waves are slamming into a seawall that has been built at Sea Bright, New Jersey, to protect the nearby electrical lines and houses from the force of the waves.

Section 16.2

1 FOCUS

Section Objectives

16.5 **Describe** how ocean waves get their energy.

16.6 **State** three factors that determine the characteristics of a wave.

16.7 **Describe** how energy moves through a wave.

16.8 **Explain** the forces that produce tides.

Reading Focus

Build Vocabulary **L2**

Concept Map As they read this section, have students create a concept map that includes all the vocabulary terms for this section.

Reading Strategy **L2**

Sample Answers:
a. height of wave
b. length of wave
c. time between waves
d. distance wind blows before starting a wave

Waves

Wave Motion **L2**

Purpose Students will see that wave energy travels without causing individual particles of the medium to move very much.

Materials Slinky™ toy

Procedure Have a student hold one end of a slinky without moving it. Stretch the slinky out, gather a few rings together, and then release them all at once while still holding the end of the slinky in your hand.

Expected Outcomes Students will notice that the energy of the wave will move from one end of the slinky to the other, even though individual rings only move a small amount back and forth.
Visual, Kinesthetic

2 INSTRUCT

Build Reading Literacy L1

Refer to **p. 278D** in **Chapter 10,** which provides guidelines for identifying main ideas and details.

Identify Main Idea/Details Have students use the section called Wave Characteristics to determine the characteristics of a wave *(height, length, and period)*, and the factors that dictate a wave's characteristics *(wind speed, length of time wind has blown, and fetch).*
Verbal

Build Science Skills L2

Using Models Have students create a simple wave diagram showing the general shape of a wave. Have them label wave height, wavelength, crest, and trough.
Visual

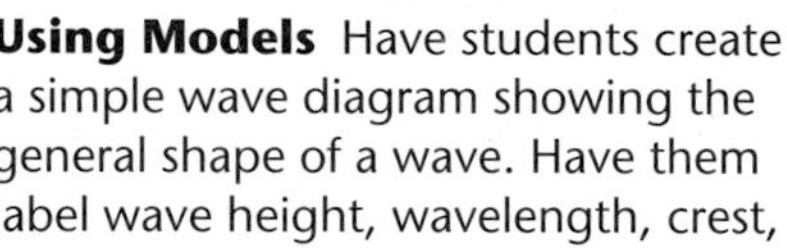

Build Reading Literacy L1

Refer to **p. 92D** in **Chapter 4,** which provides guidelines for using context clues.

Use Context Clues Have students read the section called Wave Motion, and study Figure 10 to determine the meaning of *waveform (shape of the wave).*
Visual, Verbal

Q *Do waves always travel in the same directions as currents?*

A Not in all cases. Most surface waves travel in the same direction as the wind blows, but waves radiate outward in all directions from the disturbance that creates them. In addition, as waves move away from the sea area where they were generated, they enter areas where other currents exist. As a result, the direction of wave movement is often unrelated to that of currents. In fact, waves can even travel in a direction completely opposite to that of a current. A rip current, for example, moves away from the shoreline, opposite to the direction of incoming waves.

Wave Characteristics **Most ocean waves obtain their energy and motion from the wind.** When a breeze is less than 3 kilometers per hour, only small waves appear. At greater wind speeds, more stable waves gradually form and advance with the wind.

Characteristics of ocean waves are illustrated in Figure 10. The tops of the waves are the crests, which are separated by troughs. Halfway between the crests and troughs is the still water level, which is the level that the water would occupy if there were no waves. The vertical distance between trough and crest is called the **wave height.** The horizontal distance between two successive crests or two successive troughs is the **wavelength.** The time it takes one full wave—one wavelength—to pass a fixed position is the **wave period.**

The height, length, and period that are eventually achieved by a wave depend on three factors: (1) wind speed; (2) length of time the wind has blown; and (3) fetch. Fetch is the distance that the wind has traveled across open water. As the quantity of energy transferred from the wind to the water increases, both the height and steepness of the waves also increase. Eventually, a critical point is reached where waves grow so tall that they topple over, forming ocean breakers called whitecaps.

Wave Motion Waves can travel great distances across ocean basins. In one study, waves generated near Antarctica were tracked as they traveled through the Pacific Ocean basin. After more than 10,000 kilometers, the waves finally expended their energy a week later along the shoreline of the Aleutian Islands of Alaska. The water itself does not travel the entire distance, but the wave does. As a wave travels, the water particles pass the energy along by moving in a circle. This movement, shown in Figure 10, is called circular orbital motion.

Observations of a floating object reveals that it moves not only up and down but also slightly forward and backward with each successive wave.

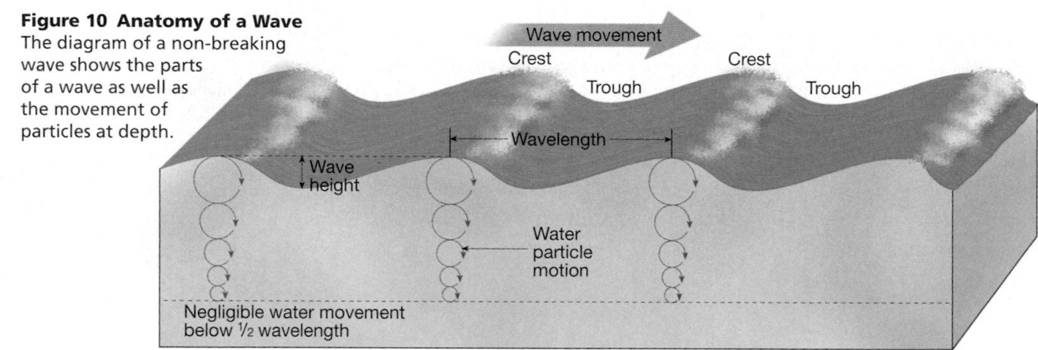

Figure 10 Anatomy of a Wave The diagram of a non-breaking wave shows the parts of a wave as well as the movement of particles at depth.

Customize for Inclusion Students

Learning Disabled Students often have difficulty understanding how a wave can appear to move from one place to another while the actual wave particles simply move in a circle. Help students understand this with a physical example. Have students in your class do "the wave" that is done at sporting events. Ask: **Did the wave travel across the room?** *(yes)* **Did any students have to travel across the room to produce this result?** *(no)* **How did each student move to pass the wave along?** *(up and down, in place)*
Kinesthetic, Visual

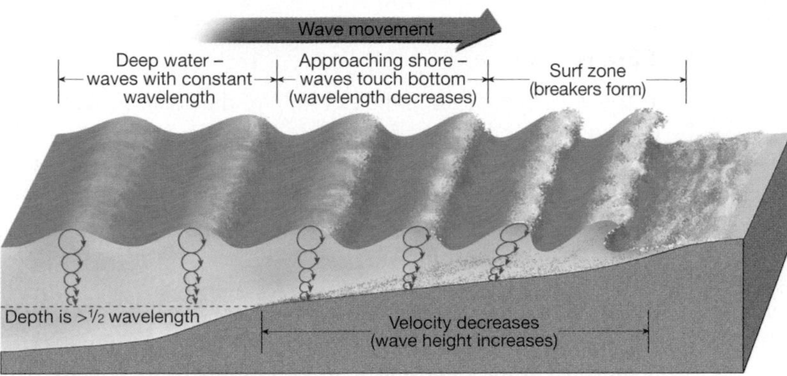

Figure 11 Breaking Waves Changes occur as a wave moves onto shore. As the waves touch bottom, wave speed decreases. The decrease in wave speed results in a decrease in wavelength and an increase in wave height.

This movement results in a circle that returns the object to essentially the same place in the water. **Circular orbital motion allows energy to move forward through the water while the individual water particles that transmit the wave move around in a circle.**

The energy contributed by the wind to the water is transmitted not only along the surface of the sea but also downward. However, beneath the surface, the circular motion rapidly diminishes until—at a depth equal to one-half the wavelength measured from still water level—the movement of water particles becomes negligible. The dramatic decrease of wave energy with depth is shown by the rapidly decreasing diameters of water-particle orbits in Figure 10.

Breaking Waves As long as a wave is in deep water, it is unaffected by water depth. However, when a wave approaches the shore, the water becomes shallower and influences wave behavior. The wave begins to "feel bottom" at a water depth equal to half of its wavelength. Such depths interfere with water movement at the base of the wave and slow its advance. Figure 11 shows the changes that occur as a wave moves onto shore.

As a wave advances toward the shore, the slightly faster waves farther out to sea catch up and decrease the wavelength. As the speed and length of the wave decrease, the wave steadily grows higher. Finally, a critical point is reached when the wave is too steep to support itself, and the wave front collapses, or breaks, causing water to advance up the shore.

The turbulent water created by breaking waves is called surf. On the landward margin of the surf zone, the turbulent sheet of water from collapsing breakers, called swash, moves up the slope of the beach. When the energy of the swash has been expended, the water flows back down the beach toward the surf zone as backwash.

At what depth do the characteristics of a wave begin to change as it approaches the shore?

For: Links on ocean waves
Visit: www.SciLinks.org
Web Code: cjn-5162

Build Science Skills

Using Analogies Ask students if they have ever attempted to stand still in the ocean. If they have, tell them that the way their body moved each time a waved passed by is like the way a particle of water moves in circular orbital motion. Model this motion with your body and have students do the same. A good synopsis of this motion is given in the last sentence on page 456.
Visual, Kinesthetic

Integrate Physics

Friction and Breakers Explain to students that waves break because when waves feel the bottom, they are affected by friction with the ocean floor. The friction forces the waves to slow down so other waves catch up, making the original wave taller. The friction also causes the wave's base to lag behind the wave's crest, causing the wave to eventually fall over and break on the shore.
Verbal, Logical

Download a worksheet on ocean waves for students to complete, and find additional teacher support from NSTA SciLinks.

Facts and Figures

Strong backwash may result in a rip current. Rip currents are strong but narrow currents that move rapidly out to sea. If severe rip currents are present, beaches may be closed or swimming may be forbidden. This is because rip currents can be dangerous to swimmers, carrying them quickly out to very deep water.

Anyone caught in a rip current should immediately swim parallel to shore (perpendicular to the rip current) to get out of the narrow rip current. Attempts to swim directly back to shore while still in the rip current may result in death.

Answer to . . .

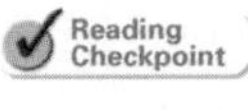

at a water depth equal to half of the wave's wavelength

Tides

Build Reading Literacy L1

Refer to **p. 306D** in **Chapter 11,** which provides guidelines for the KWL strategy (Know-Want to Know-Learned).

KWL Have students create a KWL chart on tides. Before reading this section, have students list what they already know about tides and some things they would like to know. After reading this section, have students complete the last column with what they learned. Check students' charts to make sure they understood the section. Remediate as needed.
Visual, Verbal

Use Visuals L1

Figure 12 Direct students' attention to Figure 12. Ask: **Which direction does the Earth rotate?** *(west to east)* **What kind of tide would the east and gulf coasts of North America be experiencing in the position shown in the figure?** *(low tide)* **What kind of tide would the west coast of South America experience in about 5 hours?** *(high tide)*

Q *Where is the world's largest tidal range?*

A The world's largest tidal range is found in the northern end of Nova Scotia's 258-kilometer-long Bay of Fundy. During maximum spring tide conditions, the tidal range at the mouth of the bay is only about 2 meters. However, the tidal range progressively increases from the mouth of the bay inward because the natural geometry of the bay concentrates tidal energy. In the northern end of Minas Basin, the maximum spring tidal range is about 17 meters. This extreme tidal range leaves boats high and dry during low tide.

Tides

Tides are daily changes in the elevation of the ocean surface. Their rhythmic rise and fall along coastlines have been noted throughout history. Other than waves, they are the easiest ocean movements to observe. Although known for centuries, tides were not well explained until Sir Isaac Newton applied the law of gravitation to them. Newton showed that there is a mutual attractive force between two bodies, as between Earth and the moon. Because both the atmosphere and the ocean are fluids and are free to move, both are changed by this force. **Ocean tides result from the gravitational attraction exerted upon Earth by the moon and, to a lesser extent, by the sun.**

Tide-Causing Force The primary body that influences the tides is the moon, which makes one complete revolution around Earth every 29 and a half days. The sun, however, also influences the tides. It is far larger than the moon, but because it is much farther away, its effect is considerably less. In fact, the sun's tide-generating effect is only about 46 percent that of the moon's.

To illustrate how tides are produced, consider the Earth as a rotating sphere covered to a uniform depth with water. Think about the tide-generating forces that result from the Earth-moon system, ignoring the influence of the sun for now. **The force that produces tides is gravity.** Gravity is the force that attracts Earth and the moon to each other. On the side of Earth closest to the moon, the force of the moon's gravity is greater. At this time, water is pulled in the direction of the moon and produces a tidal bulge. On the side of Earth furthest from the moon, water is pulled away from the direction of the moon and produces an equally large tidal bulge on the side of Earth directly opposite the moon. These idealized tidal bulges are shown in Figure 12.

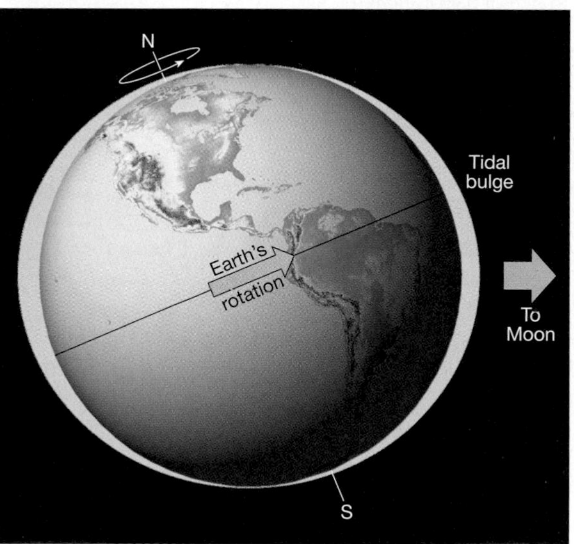

Figure 12 Tidal Bulges on Earth Caused by the Moon Analyzing ***What force is involved in causing the tidal bulges?***

Facts and Figures

The moon's gravitational pull does not just affect the oceans. It also causes a *solid body tide* of the Earth, stretching the solid Earth slightly and causing the land to pull back from the ocean water on the side of Earth far from the moon. Earth's solid tides are about 1/2 m in amplitude. On the side of Earth closer to the moon, the ocean is pulled toward the moon more than the solid Earth is pulled because the mass of the water is so much less than the mass of Earth. The moon's gravitational pull creates tidal bulges on opposite sides of Earth.

Because the position of the moon changes only moderately in a single day, the tidal bulges remain in place while Earth rotates "through" them. For this reason, if you stand on the seashore for 24 hours, Earth will rotate you through alternating areas of higher and lower water. As you are carried into each tidal bulge, the tide rises. As you are carried into the intervening troughs between the tidal bulges, the tide falls. Therefore, most places on Earth experience two high tides and two low tides each day.

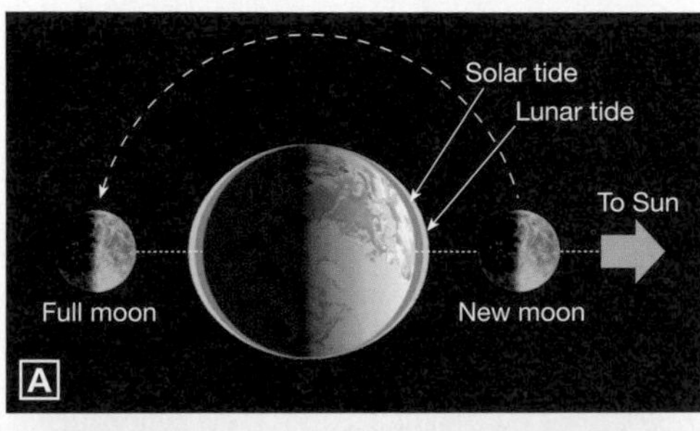

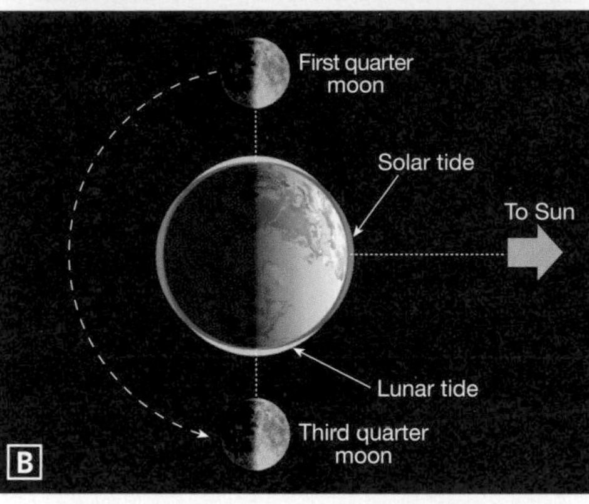

Figure 13 Earth-Moon-Sun Positions and the Tides
A When Earth, moon, and sun are aligned, spring tides are experienced. **B** When Earth, moon, and sun are at right angles to each other, neap tides are experienced.
Describing ***How does the sun influence the formation of spring and neap tides?***

Tidal Cycle Although the sun is farther away from Earth than the moon, the gravitational attraction between the sun and Earth does play a role in producing tides. The sun's influence produces smaller tidal bulges on Earth. These tidal bulges are the result of the same forces involved in the bulges created by the moon. The influence of the sun on tides is most noticeable near the times of new and full moons. During these times, the sun and moon are aligned, and their forces are added together, as shown in Figure 13A. The combined gravity of these two tide-producing bodies causes larger tidal bulges (higher high tides) and larger tidal troughs (lower low tides). This combined gravity produces a large tidal range. The **tidal range** is the difference in height between successive high and low tides. **Spring tides** are tides that have the greatest tidal range due to the alignment of the Earth–moon–sun system. They are experienced during new and full moons. Conversely, at about the time of the first and third quarters of the moon, the gravitational forces of the moon and sun act on Earth at right angles. The sun and moon partially offset the influence of the other, as shown in Figure 13B. As a result, the daily tidal range is less. These tides are called **neap tides.** Each month there are two spring tides and two neap tides, each about one week apart.

What is the tidal range?

Use Visuals L1

Figure 13 This diagram shows the positions of the sun, moon, and Earth during spring and neap tides. Ask: **How are the Earth, sun, and moon aligned for a spring tide?** *(in a straight line)* **How does this alignment cause an extra high high tide?** *(The sun and moon are pulling on the ocean in the same direction.)* **How are the Earth, sun, and moon aligned for a neap tide?** *(at right angles to each other)* **How does this alignment cause an extra low high tide?** *(The pull of the sun and moon nearly cancel each other out.)* **Visual**

Answer to . . .

Figure 12 *gravity and inertia*

Figure 13 *When the sun is aligned with Earth and the moon, the lunar and solar bulges are combined, producing spring tides. When the sun, Earth, and moon are at right angles to each other, the forces of the sun and the moon are offset, creating neap tides.*

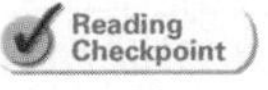

the difference in height between successive high and low tides

Build Science Skills L2

Using Tables and Graphs Have students study Figure 14. Ask: **How many hours apart are the high tides in a mixed tidal pattern?** *(12)* **In a diurnal tidal pattern?** *(24)* **In a semidiurnal pattern?** *(12)*
Visual

3 ASSESS

Evaluate Understanding L2

Review vocabulary with the class by putting students in groups to share the concept maps they created of the vocabulary words in this section. Encourage students to modify their concept maps as needed based on the discussion with their group.

Reteach L1

Have students make colored and labeled sketches of a wave, spring tides, and neap tides, showing the positions of Earth, sun, moon, and tidal bulges.

Math Practice

Solutions
11. 187 m ÷ 16.8 m/s = 11.13 s
The period is 11.13 seconds.

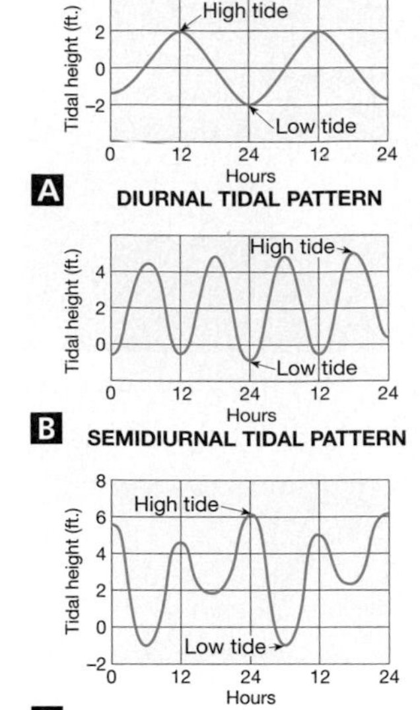

Figure 14 Tidal patterns

Tidal Patterns You now know the basic causes and types of tides. However, many factors—including the shape of the coastline, the configuration of ocean basins, and water depth—greatly influence the tides. Consequently, tides at various locations respond differently to the tide-producing forces. This being the case, the nature of the tide at any coastal location can be determined most accurately by actual observation. The predictions in tidal tables and tidal data on nautical charts are based on such observations.

Three main tidal patterns exist worldwide: diurnal tides, semidiurnal tides, and mixed tides. A diurnal tidal pattern is characterized by a single high tide and a single low tide each tidal day, as shown in the graph in Figure 14A. Tides of this type occur along the northern shore of the Gulf of Mexico.

A semidiurnal tidal pattern exhibits two high tides and two low tides each tidal day. The two highs are about the same height, and the two lows are about the same height. Figure 14B shows a semidiurnal tide pattern. This type of tidal pattern is common along the Atlantic Coast of the United States.

A mixed tidal pattern, shown in Figure 14C, is similar to a semidiurnal pattern except that it is characterized by a large inequality in high water heights, low water heights, or both. In this case, there are usually two high and two low tides each day. However, the high tides are of different heights, and the low tides are of different heights. Such tides are found along the Pacific Coast of the United States and in many other parts of the world.

Section 16.2 Assessment

Reviewing Concepts

1. From where do ocean waves obtain their energy?
2. What three quantities are used to describe a wave?
3. How does energy move by means of a wave?
4. What changes occur in a wave as it approaches shore?
5. Which celestial bodies influence Earth tides?
6. What force produces tides?
7. What are the three types of tidal patterns?

Thinking Critically

8. **Inferring** Two waves have the same fetch and were created by winds of equal speed. Why might one wave be higher than the other?
9. **Relating Cause and Effect** Explain how the forces of gravity and inertia lead to tides in Earth's oceans.
10. **Comparing and Contrasting** Compare and contrast spring tides and neap tides.

Math Practice

11. **Calculating** Wavelength, wave period, and wave speed can be related to each other in the equation:

$$\frac{\text{wavelength}}{\text{wave period}} = \text{wave speed.}$$

If wavelength = 187 meters, and wave speed = 16.8 meters per second, what is the period of this wave?

Section 16.2 Assessment

1. wind
2. wind speed, the length of time the wind has blown, fetch
3. Circular orbital motion allows energy to move forward through a wave, while the individual water particles that transmit the wave move around in a circle.
4. As a wave approaches the shore, its speed and wavelength decrease. This causes the wave height to increase. The wave becomes too steep to support itself, and it breaks, causing water to advance up the shore.
5. the sun and the moon
6. gravity
7. diurnal, semidiurnal, mixed
8. The wind blew for a longer time to create the larger wave.
9. Gravity and inertia are two of the forces involved as Earth rotates around the moon and the sun. On the side of Earth closest to the moon, the force of gravity is larger than that of inertia, which creates a tidal bulge. On the side of Earth opposite the moon, the force of inertia is greater than that of gravity, creating a similar tidal bulge.
10. Both are tides produced as a result of the Earth–moon–sun system and the position of each body relative to the other. When the Earth, moon, and sun are aligned, spring tides, which have the largest tidal range, are produced. When the Earth, moon, and sun are at right angles to each other, neap tides, which have the smallest tidal range, are produced.

16.3 Shoreline Processes and Features

Reading Focus

Key Concepts

- How are sediments along the shoreline moved?
- How does refraction affect wave action along the shore?
- What do longshore currents do?
- By which processes do shoreline features form?
- What structures can be built to protect a shoreline?
- What is beach nourishment?

Vocabulary

- beach
- wave refraction
- longshore current
- barrier islands

Reading Strategy

Summarizing Read the section on wave refraction. Then copy and complete the concept map below to organize what you know about refraction.

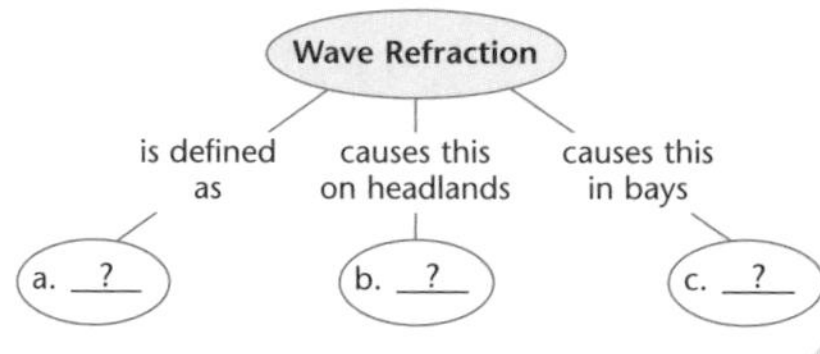

Beaches and shorelines are constantly undergoing changes as the force of waves and currents act on them. A **beach** is the accumulation of sediment found along the shore of a lake or ocean. Beaches are composed of whatever sediment is locally available. They may be made of mineral particles from the erosion of beach cliffs or nearby coastal mountains. This sediment may be relatively coarse in texture. Some beaches have a significant biological component. For example, most beaches in southern Florida are composed of shell fragments and the remains of organisms that live in coastal waters. Regardless of the composition, the sediment that makes up the beach does not stay in one place. The waves that crash along the shoreline are constantly moving it. Beaches can be thought of as material in transit along the shoreline.

Figure 15 Erosion has undercut this sandstone cliff at Gabriola Island, British Columbia, Canada.

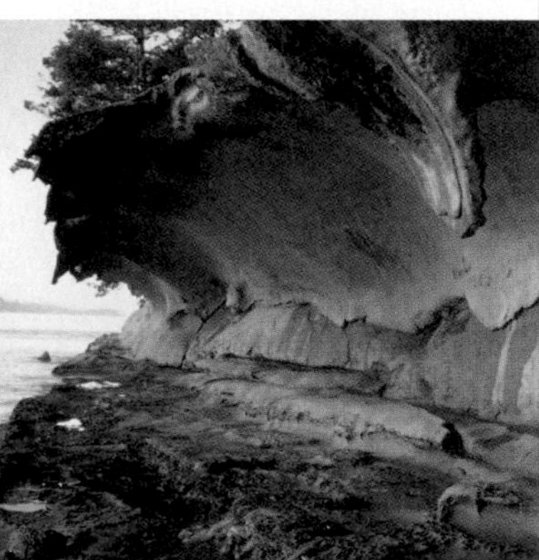

Forces Acting on the Shoreline

Waves along the shoreline are constantly eroding, transporting, and depositing sediment. Many types of shoreline features can result from this activity.

Wave Impact During calm weather, wave action is minimal. During storms, however, waves are capable of causing much erosion. The impact of large, high-energy waves against the shore can be awesome in its violence. Each breaking wave may hurl thousands of tons of water against the land, sometimes causing the ground to tremble.

Section 16.3

1 FOCUS

Section Objectives

16.9 **List** the agents responsible for the movement of sediments along the shoreline.

16.10 **Explain** how refraction affects wave action along the shore.

16.11 **Describe** the processes that form shoreline features.

16.12 **List** the structures that can be built to protect a shoreline.

Reading Focus

Build Vocabulary L2

Using Context Clues Encourage students to keep a list of unfamiliar words they encounter while reading. For each word they should write a definition based on the context, and then have them verify their definition with a dictionary.

Reading Strategy L2

a. bending of waves
b. erosion
c. deposition

2 INSTRUCT

Forces Acting on the Shoreline

Use Visuals L1

Figure 15 Have students observe the shape and texture of the feature shown in this figure. Ask: **What could have caused this?** *(waves crashing into the cliff)* **Why is it so smooth?** *(The sand carried by crashing waves acts like sandpaper on the cliff.)* **What will most likely happen to the trees on top of this cliff?** *(They will eventually fall into the ocean.)*
Visual

Build Science Skills L2

Predicting Have students look at Figure 16 and the reading passage to see that erosion is concentrated on the headlands and deposition is concentrated in the bays. Based on this observation, have students predict how the coastline in Figure 16 will eventually look. *(Eventually, the headlands will erode back and the bays will fill forward until the two meet, forming a smooth coastline without headlands or bays.)*
Visual, Logical

Use Community Resources 

If possible, bring students to a nearby beach to observe wave motion and the shoreline features created by waves. If it is warm enough, let students go into the water to feel the wave motion, as well.
Visual, Kinesthetic

Use Visuals  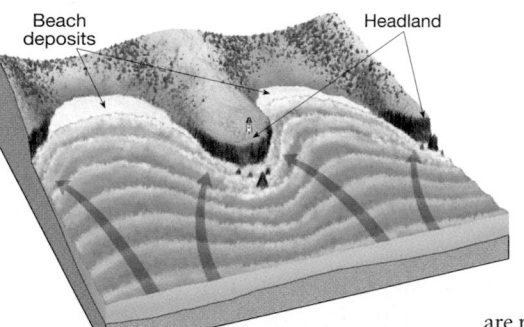

Figure 16 Direct students' attention to Figure 16. Ask: **Where is most erosion occurring in this diagram?** *(headland in the middle)* **What evidence suggests the headland once extended further into the sea?** *(Rocky remnants are offshore from the headland)* **How will wave refraction affect the lighthouse?** *(Energy from refracted waves will cause erosion of the headland to the point where the lighthouse might fall into the sea or have to be moved.)*

It is no wonder that cracks and crevices are quickly opened in cliffs, coastal structures, and anything else that is subjected to these enormous impacts. Water is forced into every opening, causing air in the cracks to become highly compressed by the thrust of crashing waves. When the wave subsides, the air expands rapidly. This expanding air dislodges rock fragments and enlarges and extends preexisting fractures.

Abrasion In addition to the erosion caused by wave impact and pressure, erosion caused by abrasion is also important. In fact, abrasion is probably more intense in the surf zone than in any other environment. Abrasion is the sawing and grinding action of rock fragments in the water. Smooth, rounded stones and pebbles along the shore are evidence of the continual grinding action of rock against rock in the surf zone. Such fragments are also used as "tools" by the waves as they cut horizontally into the land, like the sandstone shown in Figure 15. Waves are also very effective at breaking down rock material and supplying sand to beaches.

Figure 16 Wave Refraction Waves are refracted as they come into shore. Wave energy is concentrated at the headlands and dispersed in the bays. **Inferring** ***What processes occur as a result of wave refraction on this shoreline?***

Wave Refraction **Wave refraction** is the bending of waves, and it plays an important part in shoreline processes. Wave refraction affects the distribution of energy along the shore. It strongly influences where and to what degree erosion, sediment transport, and deposition will take place.

Waves seldom approach the shore straight on. Rather, most waves move toward the shore at a slight angle. However, when they reach the shallow water of a smoothly sloping bottom, the wave crests are refracted, or bent, and tend to line up nearly parallel to the shore. Such bending occurs because the part of the wave nearest the shore touches bottom and slows first, whereas the part of the wave that is still in deep water continues forward at its full speed. The change in speed causes wave crests to become nearly parallel to the shore regardless of their original orientation.

Because of refraction, wave energy is concentrated against the sides and ends of headlands that project into the water, whereas wave action is weakened in bays. This type of wave action along irregular coastlines is illustrated in Figure 16. Waves reach the shallow water in front of the headland sooner than they do in adjacent bays. Therefore, wave energy is concentrated in this area, leading to erosion. By contrast, refraction in the bays causes waves to spread out and expend less energy. This refraction leads to deposition of sediments and the formation of sandy beaches.

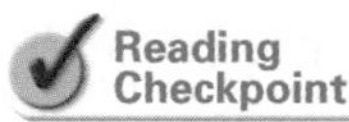

What is wave refraction?

Customize for English Language Learners

Show English Language Learners pictures of beaches that show some natural features, and what people do there. Teach students that beaches are a type of shore. Have students infer the meaning of *beach towel, beach umbrella, beach bum, beached whale, beach buggy,* and *beachcomber.* Allow students to use a dictionary. Check students' answers, and clarify their answers as needed.

Longshore Transport Although waves are refracted, most still reach the shore at a slight angle. As a result, the uprush of water, or swash, from each breaking wave is at an oblique angle to the shoreline. These angled waves produce currents within the surf zone. The currents flow parallel to the shore and move large amounts of sediment along the shore. This type of current is called a **longshore current,** shown in Figure 17.

The water in the surf zone is turbulent. **Turbulence allows longshore currents to easily move the fine suspended sand and to roll larger sand and gravel particles along the bottom.** At Sandy Hook, New Jersey, for example, the quantity of sand transported along the shore over a 48-year period averaged almost 680,000 metric tons annually. For a 10-year period at Oxnard, California, more than 1.4 million metric tons of sediment moved along the shore each year. Longshore currents can change direction because the direction that waves approach the beach changes with the seasons. Nevertheless, longshore currents generally flow southward along both the Atlantic and Pacific shores of the United States.

What causes longshore currents?

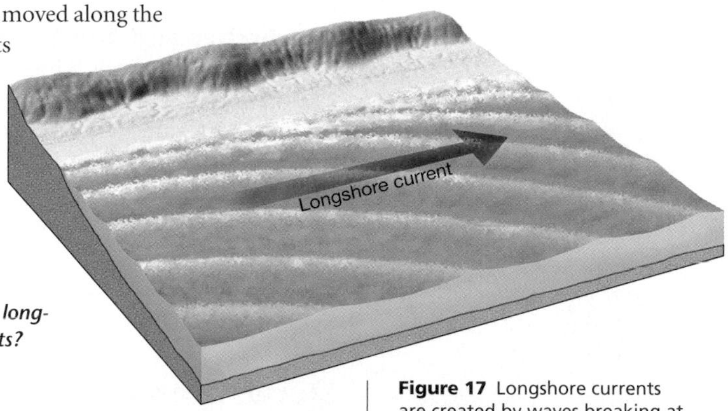

Figure 17 Longshore currents are created by waves breaking at an angle.
Applying Concepts *Explain how longshore currents can change direction.*

Erosional Features

A fascinating assortment of shoreline features can be observed along the world's coastal regions. These shoreline features vary depending on the type of rocks exposed along the shore, the intensity of waves, the nature of coastal currents, and whether the coast is stable, sinking, or rising. **Shoreline features that originate primarily from the work of erosion are called erosional features. Sediment that is transported along the shore and deposited in areas where energy is low produce depositional features.**

Many coastal landforms owe their origin to erosional processes. Such erosional features are common along the rugged and irregular New England coast and along the steep shorelines of the West Coast of the United States.

Erosional Features

Use Visuals L1

Figure 17 Have students place a finger on the left side of the diagram in the water and trace the motion of a wave's swash, or uprush of water, as the wave strikes the shore at an angle. Then tell them to trace the backwash of that wave, which is straight down the slope of the beach back toward the water. Have them continue this pattern of swash and backwash unbroken until they run their finger off the right side of the diagram. Ask: **How would you describe the pattern made with your finger?** *(zigzag)* **What do you think this pattern does to sand and pebbles on the beach?** *(moves them along the beach)* Tell students that this movement is called beach drift. Typically, beach drift moves sediment along the beach 5 to 10 meters per day. Though not as significant a transporter as longshore currents, the combination of beach drift and longshore currents moves tremendous amounts of sediment annually. The quantities given for Sandy Hook and Oxnard represent sediments moved through a combination of combination of beach drift and longshore currents.

Build Science Skills L2

Observing Have students observe large scale maps of the Maine and New England coast and portions of the Washington, Oregon, and California coast. Challenge them to find erosional features and to mark them on the maps using self-sticking notes. Or, if you can laminate the maps, students can use washable markers. Discuss how the features that students have marked show erosion. As students read the next few pages, have them revisit their maps to find and discuss other erosional features.
Visual

Answer to . . .

Figure 16 *Erosion occurs on the headlands, and deposition occurs in the bays.*

Figure 17 *Longshore currents can change direction because the direction that waves approach the beach changes seasonally.*

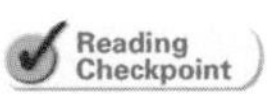

the bending of waves; the angling of waves in the surf zone

Depositional Features

Build Science Skills L2

Comparing and Contrasting Students should make flashcards of each feature described in this chapter. The sketch and feature's name should be on one side of the card, and how the feature forms and if it is erosional or depositional should be on the other side. The sketches can be done on full-size paper or on flashcards. Features include the following: wave-cut cliff, wave-cut platform, sea arch, sea stack, spit, baymouth bar, tombolo, and barrier islands. Sketches of the following would also be useful, along with a description of why they are used: groin, breakwater, and seawall. Ask students to compare and contrast various features.
Visual, Kinesthetic

Build Reading Literacy L1

Refer to **p. 556D** in **Chapter 20**, which provides guidelines for active comprehension.

Active Comprehension Ask students to write down some things they would like to know about shoreline features. Have some students share their responses with the class, and record these responses on the board where they can be referred to at the end of the section.
Verbal

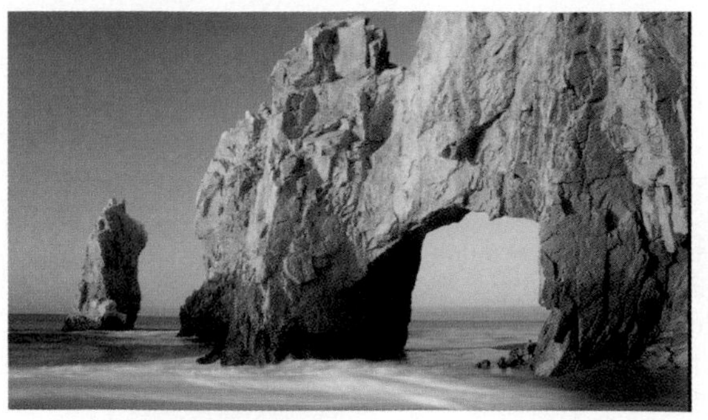

Figure 18 In time, the sea arch will collapse and form a sea stack like the one on the left.

Wave-Cut Cliffs and Platforms Wave-cut cliffs, like the one shown in Figure 20C, result from the cutting action of the surf against the base of coastal land. As erosion progresses, rocks that overhang the notch at the base of the cliff crumble into the surf, and the cliff retreats. A relatively flat, benchlike surface, called a wave-cut platform, is left behind by the receding cliff. The platform broadens as the wave attack continues. Some debris produced by the breaking waves remains along the water's edge as sediment on the beach. The rest of the sediment is transported farther seaward.

Sea Arches and Sea Stacks Headlands that extend into the sea are vigorously attacked by waves because of refraction. The surf erodes the rock selectively and wears away the softer or more highly fractured rock at the fastest rate. At first, sea caves may form. When two caves on opposite sides of a headland unite, a sea arch like the one in Figure 18 results. Eventually, the arch falls in, leaving an isolated remnant, or sea stack, on the wave-cut platform.

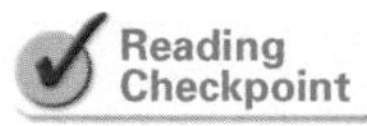

How does a sea arch form?

Depositional Features

Recall that a beach is the shore of a body of water that is covered in sand, gravel, or other larger sediments. Sediment eroded from the beach is transported along the shore and deposited in areas where wave energy is low. Such processes produce a variety of depositional features.

Spits, Bars, and Tombolos Where longshore currents and other surf zone currents are active, several features related to the movement of sediment along the shore may develop. As shown in Figure 20B and C, a spit is an elongated ridge of sand that projects from the land into the mouth of an adjacent bay. Often the end in the water hooks landward in response to the dominant direction of the longshore current. The term baymouth bar is applied to a sandbar that completely crosses a bay, sealing it off from the open ocean. Find the baymouth bar in Figure 19. Such a feature tends to form across bays where currents are weak. The weak currents allow a spit to extend to the other side and form a baymouth bar. A tombolo is a ridge of sand that connects an island to the mainland or to another island. A tombolo forms in much the same way as a spit. Follow the formation of tombolos and other shoreline features in Figure 20.

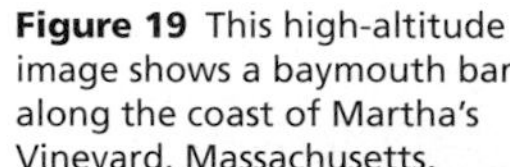

Figure 19 This high-altitude image shows a baymouth bar along the coast of Martha's Vineyard, Massachusetts.

Facts and Figures

Wave deposition can create dramatic land features. The long, curving arm of Cape Cod, Massachusetts is a prime example. Cape Cod was originally a moraine—a pile of till deposited at the leading edge of a glacier that covered the Northeast during the most recent ice age. At that time, about 20,000 years ago, the sea level was low, and the moraine was deposited on dry land. Since that time, the sea level has risen and the moraine has become subjected to wave erosion. Sediment from the loose pile of till has been carried northward along the shore, continually extending the arm of land in that direction.

464 Chapter 16

Evolution of Shoreline Features

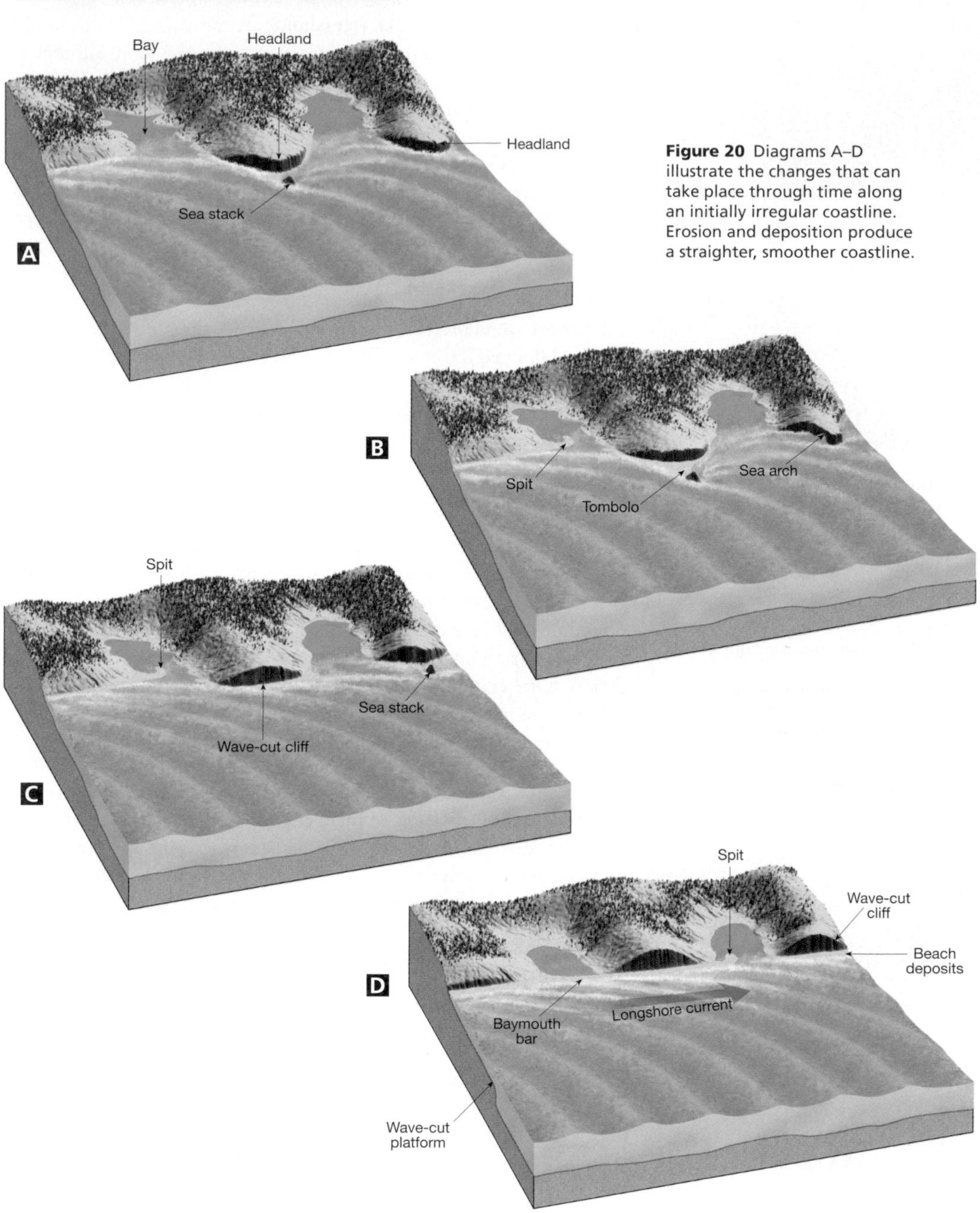

A
Bay
Headland
Headland
Sea stack
B
Spit
Tombolo
Sea arch
C
Spit
Sea stack
Wave-cut cliff
D
Spit
Wave-cut
cliff
Beach
deposits
Baymouth
bar
Longshore current
Wave-cut
platform

Figure 20 Diagrams A–D illustrate the changes that can take place through time along an initially irregular coastline. Erosion and deposition produce a straighter, smoother coastline.

Depositional Features

Build Reading Literacy **L1**

Refer to **p. 216D** in **Chapter 8,** which provides the guidelines for comparing and contrasting.

Compare and Contrast Advise students to create a compare and contrast table about erosional and depositional features. Similarities may include the following: caused by waves and constantly changing. Differences may include the following: erosional features are caused by fast moving waves while depositional features are caused by slower moving waves, and erosional features tend to shrink over time while depositional features tend to grow over time.
Verbal, Visual

Build Science Skills **L2**

Using Models Have students create three dimensional models of the erosional and depositional features described in this section. Individual models of each feature can be created, or one large model of an erosional coastline and another of a depositional coastline can be put together.
Visual, Kinesthetic

Answer to . . .

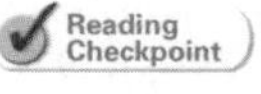

Reading Checkpoint *Sea arches form when two caves (eroded by surf) on opposite sides of a headland unite.*

The Dynamic Ocean 465

Stabilizing the Shore

Use Visuals L1

Figure 21 Tell students that the thin, nearly continuous stretch of land just offshore in this figure is a chain of barrier islands. After they have finished reading the section, arrange students in cooperative groups. Ask: **How might barrier islands benefit coastal areas on the other side of the sound?** *(Barrier islands absorb much of the energy from incoming waves, protecting the sound from rough seas and the coasts further inland from intense erosion. Barrier islands are like natural breakwaters.)* **What do you think would happen on a barrier island during a storm?** *(The island might flood or suffer severe erosion.)* **Do you think people should live on barrier islands? Why or why not?** *(Sample answer: No, because barrier islands will suffer terrible damage in storms.)*
Interpersonal

Build Science Skills L2

Making Judgments Suggest that students prepare for a mock town meeting. Assign one group of students to speak out against beach nourishment and another group to speak in favor of this intervention.
Group, Interpersonal

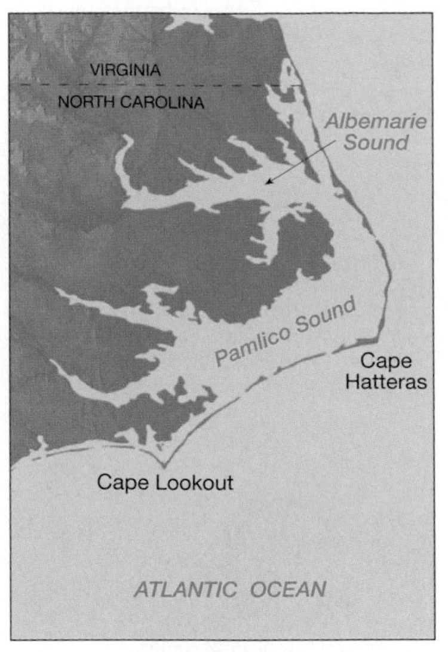

Figure 21 The islands along the coast of North Carolina are examples of barrier islands.

Barrier Islands The Atlantic and Gulf Coastal Plains are relatively flat and slope gently seaward. The shore zone in these areas is characterized by barrier islands. **Barrier islands** are narrow sandbars parallel to, but separated from, the coast at distances from 3 to 30 kilometers offshore. From Cape Cod, Massachusetts, to Padre Island, Texas, nearly 300 barrier islands rim the coast. The barrier islands along the coast of North Carolina are shown in Figure 21.

Barrier islands probably formed in several ways. Some began as spits that were later cut off from the mainland by wave erosion or by the general rise in sea level following the last glacial period. Others were created when turbulent waters in the line of breakers heaped up sand that had been scoured from the bottom. Finally, some barrier islands may be former sand-dune ridges that began along the shore during the last glacial period, when sea level was lower. As the ice sheets melted, sea level rose and flooded the area behind the beach-dune complex.

What is a barrier island?

Stabilizing the Shore

Shorelines are among Earth's most dynamic places. They change rapidly in response to natural forces. Storms are capable of eroding beaches and cliffs at rates that far exceed the long-term average erosion. Such bursts of accelerated erosion not only affect the natural evolution of a coast but can also have a profound impact on people who reside in the coastal zone. Erosion along the coast causes significant property damage. Huge sums of money are spent annually not only to repair damage but also to prevent or control erosion.

Figure 22 A series of groins traps sand along the shore in Sussex, England.
Inferring *In which direction does the sand move along the coast in this photo? How do you know?*

Protective Structures  **Groins, breakwaters, and seawalls are some structures built to protect a coast from erosion or to prevent the movement of sand along a beach.** Groins are sometimes constructed to maintain or widen beaches that are losing sand. A groin is a barrier built at a right angle to the beach to trap sand that is moving parallel to the shore. Notice how a series of groins has trapped sand along the shore in Figure 22.

Protective structures can also be built parallel to the shoreline. A breakwater is one such structure. Its purpose is to protect boats from the force of large breaking waves by creating a quiet water zone near the shore. A seawall is another protective structure built parallel to the shore. A seawall is designed to shield the coast and defend property from the force of breaking waves. Waves expend much of their energy as they move across an open beach. Seawalls reduce this process by reflecting the force of unspent waves seaward.

For: Links on coastal changes
Visit: www.SciLinks.org
Web Code: cjn-5163

Facts and Figures

At 21 stories high, the Cape Hatteras lighthouse in North Carolina is the tallest one in the United States, and is one of our nation's most prominent landmarks. The lighthouse was built in 1870 on a barrier island, 457 m from the shoreline, to warn sailors of dangerous waters. Waves gradually eroded at the barrier island, bringing the ocean as close as 37 m from the lighthouse. In 1970 the U.S. Navy started building groins and adding sand to the beach to protect the lighthouse from further erosion, but their attempts failed. Ultimately, in 1999, the National Park Service decided to move the entire lighthouse 884 m further inland for protection.

Download a worksheet on coastal changes for students to complete, and find additional teacher support from NSTA SciLinks.

Protective structures often only offer temporary solutions to shoreline problems. The structures themselves interfere with the natural processes of erosion and deposition. Then more structures often need to be built in order to counteract the new problems that arise. Many scientists feel that using protective structures to divert the ocean's energy causes more harm than good.

Beach Nourishment **Beach nourishment is the addition of large quantities of sand to the beach system.** It is an attempt to stabilize shoreline sands without building protective structures. Examine the before and after photos shown in Figure 23. By building the beaches seaward, both beach quality and storm protection are improved. However, the same processes that removed the sand in the first place will eventually wash away the replacement sand as well.

Beach nourishment can be very expensive because huge volumes of sand must be transported to the beach from offshore areas, nearby rivers, or other source areas for sand. Beach nourishment can also have detrimental effects on local marine life. For example, beach nourishment at Waikiki Beach, Hawaii, involved replacing the natural coarse beach sand with softer, muddier sand. Destruction of the softer sand by breaking waves increased the water's turbidity, or "cloudiness," and killed offshore coral reefs.

Figure 23 Miami Beach
A Before beach nourishment
B After beach nourishment
Analyzing ***What are the advantages and disadvantages of beach nourishment?***

Section 16.3 Assessment

Reviewing Concepts

1. How are sediments along the shoreline moved?
2. What effect does wave impact have on shorelines?
3. How does refraction affect wave action along the shore?
4. What do longshore currents do?
5. By which processes do shoreline features form?
6. Name three examples of shoreline features formed by erosion.
7. How do barrier islands form?
8. What structures can be built to protect a shoreline?
9. What is beach nourishment?

Thinking Critically

10. **Analyzing** How can beach nourishment be helpful? How can it be harmful?
11. **Comparing and Contrasting** Compare and contrast a tombolo and a barrier island.
12. **Relating Cause and Effect** A breakwater is built to reduce wave action in near-shore areas. How might the reduced wave action along the shore behind the breakwater affect sediment deposition? What problems might this cause?

Connecting Concepts

Wave Refraction Relate the concept of wave refraction to the changes that occur as a wave enters shallow water and goes into shore.

3 ASSESS

Evaluate Understanding L2

Have students use their flashcards to quiz each other on their ability to recognize erosional and depositional structures. As a class, revisit the questions students had at the beginning of the chapter to see if students can now answer their original questions.

Reteach L1

Use the sketches and descriptions of each term that students created as they read, or use the three dimensional models created in this section, to review the main concepts.

Connecting Concepts

As a wave approaches shore and touches the shallow bottom (at a depth of one half the wavelength of the wave) the part of the wave nearest shore slows, whereas the part of the wave that is still in deep water continues forward at its full speed. This causes the wave crests to become nearly parallel to shore regardless of their original orientation.

Answer to . . .

Figure 22 *Groins are built at right angles to the beach to trap sand that is moving parallel to the shore.*

Figure 23 *Protective structures do not have to be built to stabilize shorelines. It can be expensive and the natural processes that eroded away the original sand will eventually erode away the replacement sand. It can have negative effects on marine life. It can only be used successfully in a few areas.*

Reading Checkpoint *A barrier island is a narrow sandbar parallel to, but separate from, the coast at distances from 3 to 30 km offshore.*

Section 16.3 Assessment

1. erosion and deposition
2. Wave impact leads to shoreline erosion.
3. Wave energy is concentrated against the sides of headlands, and it is weakened in bays.
4. They move fine suspended sand and roll larger sand and gravel along the bottom and along the shore.
5. Waves erode, transport, and deposit sediment, forming many shoreline features.
6. Any three: wave-cut cliff, wave-cut platform, sea arches, sea stacks
7. Some may have originated as spits that were severed from the mainland, others were created when turbulent waters in the line of breakers heaped up sand scoured from the bottom, some may be former sand-dune ridges that are no longer attached to the mainland due to ice melting.
8. groins, breakwaters, seawalls
9. an approach to stabilizing the shoreline by adding large quantities of sand to the beach system
10. Beach quality and storm protection are improved. The process is expensive and can harm local marine life.
11. Both can be formed by deposition. A tombolo is a ridge of sand that connects an island to the mainland or to another island. A barrier island is a narrow sandbar parallel to, but separated from, the coast.
12. The reduced wave action behind the breakwater allows sand to accumulate. This means that the protected area will eventually fill with sand, while the downstream beach erodes.

Exploration Lab

Graphing Tidal Cycles **L2**

Objective
After completing this activity, students will be able to use tidal data to determine the tidal pattern an area experiences.

Skills Focus **Graphing, Interpreting Data, Inferring, Drawing Conclusions**

 **Prep Time** 15 minutes

Advanced Prep You may want to plot the data yourself before students begin so you can more easily help them set up their axes, and can tell quickly if students are graphing correctly.

Class Time 1 block or 2 periods

Teaching Tip Show students how to divide each day into 6-hour intervals on the *x*-axis in order to plot correctly. Then plot the first few points with the class on the board or on an overhead projector. Figure 14 on page 460 will help students answer question #1.

Expected Outcome Students will create a graph showing the regular rise and fall of tides to determine the tidal pattern for an area.

Exploration Lab

Graphing Tidal Cycles

Tides are the cyclical rise and fall of sea level caused by the gravitational attraction of Earth to the moon and, to a lesser extent, to the sun. Gravitational pull creates a bulge in the ocean on the side of Earth nearest the moon. This inertia creates a similar bulge on the opposite side of Earth from the moon. Tides develop as the rotating Earth moves through these bulges causing periods of high and low water. In this lab, you will make a graph of tidal data to determine whether an area has diurnal, semidiurnal, or mixed tides.

High tide in Nova Scotia's Bay of Fundy

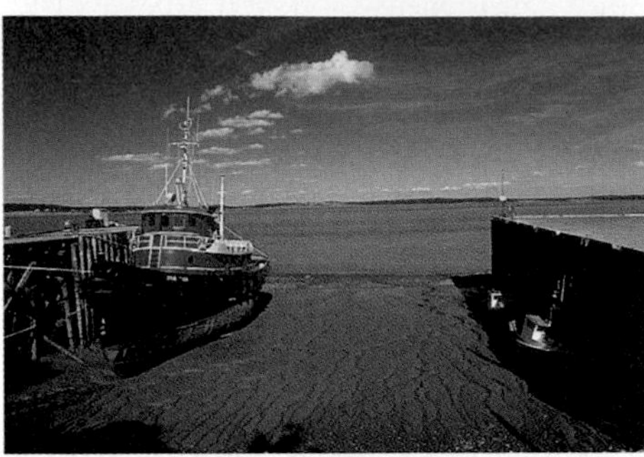

Low tide in the same area

Problem
How can you determine the tidal pattern an area experiences?

Materials
- graph paper
- pencil

Skills
Graphing, Interpreting Data, Inferring, Drawing Conclusions

Procedure
1. Label the graph paper as below to make a graph of the tidal cycle. The *x*-axis should be in days, and the *y*-axis should be in feet. It is often easier to place the *x*-axis at the top of the graph, rather than at the bottom, when graphing a tidal cycle.
2. Use the data in Table 1 to make a graph of the tidal cycle.

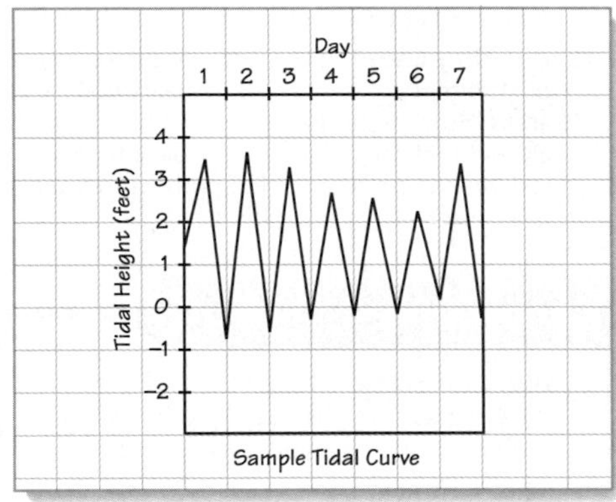

Analyze and Conclude
1. **Applying Concepts** What tidal pattern does this area experience? Explain how you determined this.
2. **Calculating** What is the greatest tidal range for the data you graphed? What is the least tidal range? What types of tides correspond to each of these tidal ranges?
3. **Draw Conclusions** Based on your graph, identify the days when each moon phase could have occurred: new moon, first quarter moon, full moon, last quarter moon. How do you know this?
4. **Applying Concepts** On January 5th (Day 5 on the table) at 9:00 A.M., Jarred anchored his boat in about 4 feet of water at the beach. When he returned to his boat at 3:30 that afternoon, the boat was completely in the sand. What had happened? How long did Jarred have to wait to leave the area in his boat?

Table 1 Tidal Data for Long Beach, New York, January 2003

All times are listed in Local Standard Time (LST). All heights are in feet.

Day	Time	Height	Time	Height	Time	Height	Time	Height
1	05:45 A.M.	5.5	12:16 P.M.	−0.7	06:12 P.M.	4.4	——	—
2	12:18 A.M.	−0.5	06:35 A.M.	5.6	01:07 P.M.	−0.8	07:03 P.M.	4.4
3	01:10 A.M.	−0.5	07:23 A.M.	5.5	01:56 P.M.	−0.8	07:53 P.M.	4.4
4	01:59 A.M.	−0.4	08:11 A.M.	5.4	02:42 P.M.	−0.7	08:42 P.M.	4.3
5	02:45 A.M.	−0.2	08:59 A.M.	5.1	03:25 P.M.	−0.5	09:32 P.M.	4.2
6	03:30 A.M.	0.0	09:47 A.M.	4.8	04:07 P.M.	−0.3	10:23 P.M.	4.0
7	04:14 A.M.	0.3	10:35 A.M.	4.6	04:49 P.M.	−0.1	11:12 P.M.	3.9
8	05:01 A.M.	0.6	11:22 A.M.	4.3	05:32 P.M.	0.2	11:59 P.M.	3.9
9	05:54 A.M.	0.8	12:09 P.M.	4.0	06:18 P.M.	0.4	——	—
10	12:45 A.M.	3.9	06:56 A.M.	0.9	12:57 P.M.	3.7	07:10 P.M.	0.5
11	01:31 A.M.	3.9	07:59 A.M.	0.9	01:47 P.M.	3.5	08:02 P.M.	0.5
12	02:19 A.M.	4.0	08:57 A.M.	0.8	02:41 P.M.	3.4	08:53 P.M.	0.5
13	03:10 A.M.	4.1	09:50 A.M.	0.6	03:39 P.M.	3.5	09:41 P.M.	0.4
14	04:02 A.M.	4.3	10:38 A.M.	0.3	04:34 P.M.	3.6	10:28 P.M.	0.2
15	04:51 A.M.	4.6	11:26 A.M.	0.1	05:23 P.M.	3.7	11:15 P.M.	0.1
16	05:36 A.M.	4.8	12:12 P.M.	−0.1	06:08 P.M.	3.9	——	—
17	12:02 A.M.	−0.1	06:17 A.M.	5.0	12:57 P.M.	−0.3	06:51 P.M.	4.1
18	12:49 A.M.	−0.2	06:58 A.M.	5.1	01:40 P.M.	−0.5	07:32 P.M.	4.2
19	01:35 A.M.	−0.4	07:38 A.M.	5.2	02:22 P.M.	−0.6	08:15 P.M.	4.3
20	02:20 A.M.	−0.4	08:21 A.M.	5.2	03:30 P.M.	−0.7	09:01 P.M.	4.4
21	03:05 A.M.	−0.4	09:07 A.M.	5.1	03:44 P.M.	−0.7	09:51 P.M.	4.5
22	03:52 A.M.	−0.3	09:58 A.M.	4.9	04:27 P.M.	−0.6	10:44 P.M.	4.6
23	04:43 A.M.	−0.1	10:52 A.M.	4.7	05:13 P.M.	−0.4	11:37 P.M.	4.7
24	05:43 A.M.	0.1	11:48 A.M.	4.4	06:08 P.M.	−0.2	——	—
25	12:32 A.M.	4.7	06:53 A.M.	0.2	12:47 P.M.	4.2	07:11 P.M.	−0.1
26	01:30 A.M.	4.8	08:06 A.M.	0.2	01:50 P.M.	3.9	08:17 P.M.	0.0
27	02:31 A.M.	4.8	09:12 A.M.	0.1	02:57 P.M.	3.8	09:19 P.M.	0.0
28	03:35 A.M.	4.8	10:13 A.M.	−0.1	04:05 P.M.	3.9	10:17 P.M.	−0.1
29	04:37 A.M.	5.0	11:09 A.M.	−0.3	05:07 P.M.	4.0	11:13 P.M.	−0.2
30	05:33 A.M.	5.1	12:01 P.M.	−0.5	06:01 P.M.	4.2	——	—
31	12:06 A.M.	−0.3	06:22 A.M.	5.2	12:51 P.M.	−0.6	06:50 P.M.	4.3

Source: Center for Operational Oceanographic Products and Services, National Oceanographic and Atmospheric Association, National Ocean Service.

Analyze and Conclude

1. Semidiurnal; this can be determined by studying the graph produced from the data. The area has two high tides and two low tides in approximately a 24-hour period, with the high tides being similar height and the low tides being similar height.

2. 6.4 feet; 2.6 feet; spring tides and neap tides respectively

3. A new moon or a full moon could have occurred on Day 2. A new moon or a full moon could have occurred on Day 20. These days correspond with the highest tidal range, or spring tides. A first or third quarter moon could have occurred on Day 11. A first or third quarter moon could have occurred on Day 26. These days correspond with the lowest tidal range, or neap tides.

4. The tide went out while Jarred was gone. At 3:25 P.M. low tide occurred. He would have to wait until the tide came in again, so there would be enough water for him to move his boat. The longest he would have had to wait is about six hours, until high tide occurred at 9:32 P.M.

Visual, Logical

Study Guide

Study Tip

Make Flashcards
Teach students to make flashcards of the vocabulary, sketches, and processes they need to know for each chapter. Students can use the flashcards to quiz themselves or others. Advise students to keep their flashcards even after the chapter test is over, so the same cards can be used to study for their final exams or standardized tests.

Assessment

Reviewing Content

(1) 2 (2) 1 (3) 4
(4) 3 (5) 4 (6) 2
(7) 1 (8) 3 (9) 4
(10) 2

Understanding Concepts

(11) Coriolis effect deflects currents from their original course due to the rotation of Earth. In the Northern Hemisphere, currents are deflected to the right. In the Southern Hemisphere, currents are deflected to the left.
(12) Cold ocean currents travel from the poles toward the equator and moderate warm temperatures on adjacent landforms.
(13) They transfer heat from the tropics, where there is an excess of heat, to the polar regions, where there is a heat deficit. Ocean water movements account for about one quarter of this heat transport.
(14) Coastal upwelling is vertical circulation that brings cool, nutrient-rich water from depth to the surface to replace warm surface waters moved by wind. The nutrient-rich water supports high productivity and a large population of phytoplankton and subsequently fish and other marine consumers.

CHAPTER 16 Study Guide

16.1 Ocean Circulation

Key Concepts

- Surface currents develop from friction between the ocean and the wind that blows across its surface.
- Because of Earth's rotation, currents are deflected to the right in the Northern Hemisphere and to the left in the Southern Hemisphere.
- When currents from low-latitude regions move into higher latitudes, they transfer heat from warmer to cooler areas on Earth.
- As cold water currents travel toward the equator, they help moderate the warm temperatures of adjacent land areas.
- Upwelling brings greater concentrations of dissolved nutrients, such as nitrates and phosphates, to the ocean surface.
- An increase in seawater density can be caused by a decrease in temperature or an increase in salinity.

Vocabulary
ocean current, *p. 448;* surface current, *p. 448;* gyre, *p. 449;* Coriolis effect, *p. 449;* upwelling, *p. 450;* density current, *451*

16.2 Waves and Tides

Key Concepts

- Most ocean waves obtain their energy and motion from the wind.
- The height, length, and period that are eventually achieved by a wave depend on three factors: (1) wind speed; (2) length of time the wind has blown; and (3) fetch.
- Circular orbital motion allows energy to move forward through the water while the individual water particles that transmit the wave move around in a circle.
- Ocean tides result from the gravitational attraction exerted upon Earth by the moon and, to a lesser extent, by the sun.
- The force that produces tides is gravity.
- Three main tidal patterns exist worldwide: diurnal tides, semidiurnal tides, and mixed tides.

Vocabulary
wave height, *p. 456;* wavelength, *p. 456;* wave period, *p. 456;* fetch, *p. 456;* tide, *p. 458;* tidal range, *p. 459;* spring tide, *p. 459;* neap tide, *p. 459*

16.3 Shoreline Processes and Features

Key Concepts

- Waves are responsible for the movement of sediment along the shoreline.
- Because of refraction, wave energy is concentrated against the sides and ends of headlands that project into the water, whereas wave action is weakened in bays.
- Turbulence allows longshore currents to easily move the fine suspended sand and to roll larger sand and gravel particles along the bottom.
- Shoreline features that originate primarily from the work of erosion are called erosional features. Sediment is transported along the shore and deposited in areas where energy is low produce depositional features.
- Groins, breakwaters, and seawalls are some structures built to protect a coast from erosion or to prevent the movement of sand along a beach.
- Beach nourishment is the addition of large quantities of sand to the beach system.

Vocabulary
beach, *p. 461;* wave refraction, *p. 462;* longshore current, *p. 463;* barrier island, *p. 466*

Chapter Assessment Resources

Print
Chapter Test, Chapter 16
Test Prep Resources, Chapter 16

Technology
Computer Test Bank, Chapter 16 Test
Online Text, Chapter 16
Go Online, PHSchool.com, Chapter 16

CHAPTER 16

NY Regents Content Item

Assessment

Interactive textbook with assessment at PHSchool.com 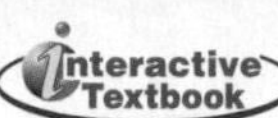

Reviewing Content

Choose the number that best answers the questions or completes the statement.

1 An ocean current moving from the equator toward a pole is NY
(1) cold
(2) warm
(3) cold in the Northern Hemisphere and warm in the Southern Hemisphere
(4) warm in the Northern Hemisphere and cold in the Northern Hemisphere

2 Because of the Coriolos effect, surface currents in the Southern Hemisphere are deflected NY
(1) to the left (2) to the right
(3) north (4) south

3 Which term describes the rising of cold water from deeper layers to replace warmer surface water?
(1) density current (2) downwelling
(3) surface current (4) upwelling

4 The energy and motion of most waves is derived from NY
(1) currents (2) tides
(3) wind (4) gravity

5 The five huge circular-moving systems of ocean surface currents are called
(1) density currents (2) fetches
(3) drifts (4) gyres

6 Daily changes in the elevation of the ocean surface are called NY
(1) surface currents (2) tides
(3) waves (4) density currents

7 Which of the following results from wave refraction?
(1) Wave energy is concentrated on headlands projecting into the water.
(2) Wave energy is concentrated in the recessed areas between headlands.
(3) Wave energy is largely dissipated before waves reach the shore.
(4) Headlands are enlarged because sediment is deposited on their seaward side.

8 The movement of water within the surf zone that parallels the shore is called NY
(1) tidal current (2) density current
(3) longshore current (4) surface current

9 Which describes a ridge of sand that connects an island to the mainland or another island?
(1) baymouth bar (2) sea arch
(3) sea stack (4) tombolo

10 Which is created through the process of erosion?
(1) baymouth bar (2) sea arch
(3) spit (4) tombolo

Understanding Concepts

11 Describe the influence that the Coriolis effect has on the movement of ocean waters. NY

12 Describe the effect that cold ocean currents have on the climates of adjacent land areas. NY

13 What role do ocean currents play in maintaining Earth's heat balance? NY

14 Describe coastal upwelling and the effect it has on fish populations.

15 Where and how is the densest water in all the oceans formed?

Use the figure below to answer questions 16–18.

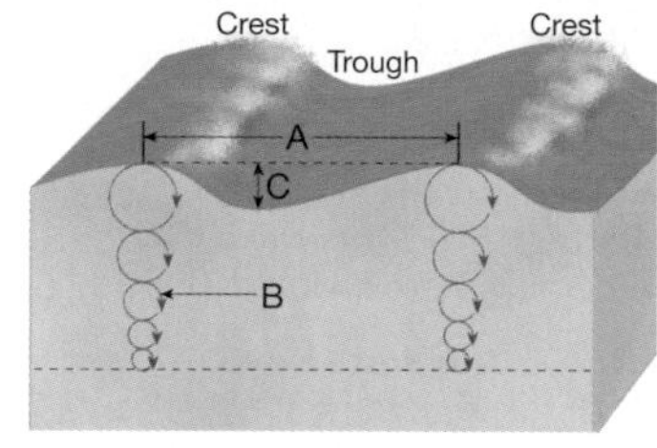

16 Identify which wave characteristics are represented by *A* and *C*.

17 Explain what *B* represents. What happens to a floating object as a wave passes through the water?

18 What factors can lead to an increase in the height of this wave? NY

Homework Guide

Section	Questions
1	1–5, 11–15, 23, 28, 29
2	6, 16–19, 24, 26, 27, 30
3	7–10, 20–22, 25

(15) The densest water is formed in the near Antarctica. As sea ice forms, the already cold surface water becomes more dense and sinks to the bottom.
(16) A is the wavelength; C is the wave height.
(17) B represents the circular orbital motion a water particle undergoes as a wave passes through the water. A floating object moves up and backward as the crest approaches, then down and forward after the crest passes. As the trough approaches, the object continues to move, down and backward, then rises and moves backward again as the next crest advances.
(18) an increase in wind speed, length of time the wind has blown, and/or the fetch
(19) A diurnal tidal pattern is characterized by a single high tide and a single low tide each tidal day. Tides of this type occur along the northern shore of the Gulf of Mexico. A semidiurnal tidal pattern exhibits two high tides and two low tides each tidal day, with the two highs about the same height and the two lows about the same height. This type of tidal pattern is common along the Atlantic Coast of the United States.
(20) Refraction in bays causes waves to diverge and expend less energy, leading to deposition of sediments and the formation of sandy beaches.
(21) Wave-cut cliffs result from the cutting action of the surf against the base of coastal land. As erosion progresses, rocks overhanging the notch at the base of the cliff crumble into the surf and the cliff retreats. A relatively flat, benchlike surface, called a wave-cut platform, is left behind by the receding cliff.
(22) Any two: groin, breakwater, seawall

Critical Thinking

(23) Student responses will vary but should indicate an understanding of the processes that create upwelling. Winds and moving water under the influence of the Coriolis effect cause surface water to move away from shore. As the surface layer moves away from the coast, it is replaced by water that "upwells" from below the surface.
(24) spring tide; new moon
(25) Rivers contain sediments weathered from continental rocks, some of which is deposited on beaches and shorelines when the rivers reach the sea. If a river is dammed, sediment input is reduced and the beach can be narrowed by erosion when existing sediment is carried away and not replaced.
(26) Tides are created as a result of the gravitational attraction between Earth and the moon and Earth and the sun. On the side of Earth closest to the moon, the force of gravity is greater than inertia, and water is pulled in the direction of the moon, producing a tidal bulge. On the side of Earth furthest from the moon, inertia is greater than gravity, and water is pulled away from the direction of the moon, producing an equally large tidal bulge on the side of Earth directly opposite the moon. Although the sun is more massive than the moon it is much farther away from Earth. This accounts for the fact that the sun's influence on tides is only 46 percent of that of the moon.

Math Skills

(27) $\frac{1}{7} = \frac{\text{wave height } (x)}{50 \text{ m}}$

$7x = 50 \text{ m}$

$7x = \frac{50 \text{ m}}{7}$

$x = 7.14 \text{ m}$

Assessment *continued*

19 Compare and contrast a diurnal tidal pattern with a semidiurnal tidal pattern.

20 How does wave refraction result in sediment deposition in some shoreline areas? NY

21 How are a wave-cut cliff and wave-cut platforms related? NY

22 What are two types of protective structures used to stop erosion on beaches? NY

Critical Thinking

23 **Creating Models** Create a diagram that models the steps involved in the process of upwelling.

24 **Applying Concepts** The figure below shows the Earth–moon–sun system. What type of tide is experienced when Earth, the moon, and the sun are in these positions? What is the phase of the moon in the diagram? NY

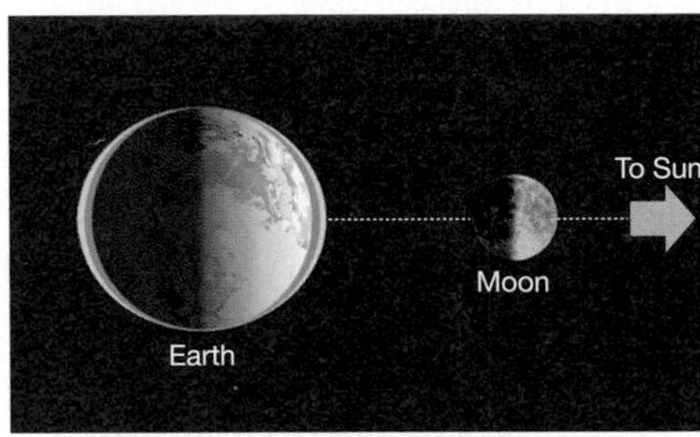

25 **Predicting** Predict the effect that the damming of rivers would have on beaches.

26 **Relating Cause and Effect** Discuss the origin of tides. Explain why the sun's influence on Earth's tides is only about half that of the moon's, even though the sun is much more massive than the moon. NY

Math Skills

27 **Calculating** As waves enter shallow water and decrease in speed, wave height increases and eventually a wave will break. The point at which a wave will break can be calculated using the formula for wave steepness: steepness = wave height/wavelength. When the steepness of a wave reaches 1/7, the wave will break. If the wavelength of a wave is 50 m, at what height will the wave break?

Concepts in Action

28 **Applying Concepts** Reexamine Figure 6. Describe the probable temperature and salinity characteristics for each water mass: Antarctic Bottom Water, North Atlantic Deep Water, and Mediterranean Water.

29 **Inferring** How do you think an increase in Earth's surface temperature would affect the "conveyor belt" model of currents in the ocean? NY

30 **Interpreting Diagrams** The graph below shows a tidal curve for Seattle, Washington. What type of tidal pattern does Honolulu experience?

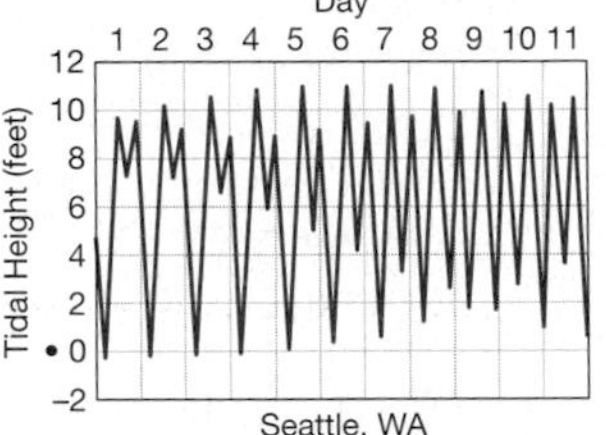

Performance-Based Assessment

Synthesizing Investigate the problems associated with shoreline development. Choose a coastal area that is experiencing problems with shoreline erosion. What actions have been taken to try to resolve the problems? Have the actions been effective? Why or why not? What are the advantages and disadvantages to different methods of preventing shoreline erosion? Offer a solution for the area you investigated.

Concepts in Action

(28) Antarctica Bottom Water (ABW) is very cold and salty, and it is the densest water of the three. North Atlantic Deep Water (NADW) is also cold and salty, and it is formed through the same process as ABW. It is not as dense as ABW. Mediterranean Water (MW) is warmer, but very salty, as it is formed when high rates of evaporation occur in the Mediterranean Sea. This is why it is more dense that the surface water.
(29) If Earth's surface temperature warmed, the conveyor belt may stop. The conveyor belt is driven by the formation of deep water in the North Atlantic. If temperatures warm, the temperature of ocean surface water would increase, making water less dense. Also, sea ice will melt, decreasing the salinity of ocean water in this area, and sea ice may not form, both of which would lead to water being less dense. If the surface water in the North Atlantic does not sink, the conveyor belt does not run.
(30) mixed

Regents Practice Exam

Test-Taking Tip

Anticipate the Answer
When answering a multiple-choice question, a useful strategy is to cover up the given answers and supply your own answer. Then compare your answer with those listed and select the one that most closely matches your answer.

Practice anticipating the answer in this question.

When waves reach shallow water, they are often bent and tend to become parallel to shore. This process is referred to as
(1) oscillation
(2) refraction
(3) reflection
(4) abrasion

(Answer: 2)

For *each* statement or question, choose the *number* of the word or expression that, of those given, best completes the statement or answers the question. Some questions may require the use of the *Earth Science Reference Tables.*

1 Which of the following statements best describes the behavior of ocean waves?
(1) Water particles move in a circular path.
(2) Waves continue to move without change, regardless of depth.
(3) The waveform moves forward, and the water particles also advance.
(4) A floating object does not move at all as a wave passes through the water.

2 Why does a wave tend to break as it gets close to shore?
(1) The bottom of the wave moves faster than the top.
(2) Friction slows the bottom of the wave.
(3) The entire wave speeds up as it approaches the shore.
(4) Rip currents interact with incoming waves.

3 What is the primary source for energy for ocean surface waves?
(1) the sun (2) the moon
(3) Earth's rotation (4) the wind

4 What causes longshore drift?
(1) waves crashing parallel to shore
(2) waves hitting the shore head on
(3) waves crashing at an angle to the shore
(4) plate movements

5 Which of the following conditions would most likely result in a spring tide?
(1) warm weather
(2) the sun and moon pulling on Earth at right angles
(3) a third quarter moon
(4) the sun and moon arranged in a horizontal line with Earth

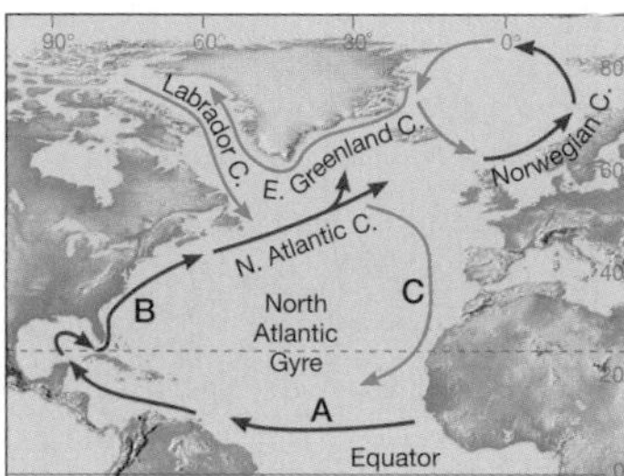

Answer the following questions in complete sentences. Some questions may require the use of the *Earth Science Reference Tables.* Base your answer to question 7 on the diagram above, which shows Ocean Surface Currents.

6 What is the primary driving force of surface currents in the ocean? How do the distribution of continents on Earth and the Coriolis effect influence these currents?

7 Identify the currents in the North Atlantic Gyre represented by *A, B,* and *C.* Specify whether each current is a warm water current or a cold water current. How does the North Atlantic Current affect weather in northwestern Europe?

Regents Practice Exam

(1) 1
(2) 2
(3) 4
(4) 3
(5) 4
(6) Wind drives surface currents. Due to the Coriolis effect, currents are deflected to the right in the Northern Hemisphere and to the left in the Southern Hemisphere; landmasses also deflect currents. The West Wind Drift is the only current that flows uninterrupted by a landmass. It encircles Earth near Antarctica.
(7) *A* is the North Equatorial Current, and it is warm. *B* is the Gulf Stream which is warm. *C* is the cold Canaries Current. The North Atlantic Current keeps much of northwestern Europe warmer during the winter than would be expected for its latitude, which is similar to the latitude of Alaska and Labrador.

Performance-Based Assessment
Student responses will vary but should indicate an understanding of the scope of the problem they investigated.

Your students can independently test their knowledge of the chapter and print out their results.

CHAPTER 17

Planning Guide

Use these planning tools
Use Teacher Express for all your planning needs

SECTION OBJECTIVES	STANDARDS NATIONAL	STANDARDS STATE	ACTIVITIES and LABS
17.1 Atmosphere Characteristics, pp. 476–482 1 block or 2 periods **17.1** **Compare and contrast** weather and climate. **17.2** **Explain** why seasonal changes occur.	A-1, C-4, D-1, D-3, F-4		**SE** Inquiry Activity: Modeling the Angle of the Sun, p. 475 L2 **TE** Build Science Skills, p. 479 L2 **TE** Teacher Demo: Angles and Seasons, p. 481 L2
17.2 Heating the Atmosphere, pp. 483–487 1 block or 2 periods **17.3** **Explain** how heat and temperature are related. **17.4** **List** the three major mechanisms of heat transfer. **17.5** **Describe** how the atmosphere is affected by heat transfer mechanisms.	B-5, B-6, D-1, D-2		**TE** Teacher Demo: Heat Conducting, p. 484 L2 **TE** Build Science Skills, p. 484 L2 **TE** Build Science Skills, p. 486 L2 **LM** Determining How Temperature Changes with Altitude L1
17.3 Temperature Controls, pp. 488–493 1 block or 2 periods **17.6** **Explain** what a temperature control is. **17.7** **Compare and contrast** the heating of land and water. **17.8** **Explain** why some clouds reflect a portion of sunlight back to space.	A-1, A-2, B-5, D-1		**TE** Teacher Demo: Heating of Land and Water, p. 490 L2 **SE** Exploration Lab: Heating Land and Water, pp. 496–497 L2 **LM** Investigating Factors That Control Temperature L2

Ability Levels	Components			
L1 For students who need additional help	**SE** Student Edition	**GRSW** Guided Reading & Study Workbook	**TP** Test Prep Resources	**GEO** Geode CD-ROM
L2 For all students	**TE** Teacher's Edition	**TEX** Teacher Express	**onT** onlineText	**T** Transparencies
L3 For students who need to be challenged	**LM** Laboratory Manual	**CTB** Computer Test Bank	**DC** Discovery Channel Videos	**GO** Internet Resources
	CUT Chapter Tests			

RESOURCES PRINT and TECHNOLOGY	SECTION ASSESSMENT
GRSW Section 17.1 **T-217** Gases Composing Dry Air **T-218** Atmospheric Pressure Variation With Altitude **T-219** Thermal Structure of the Atmosphere **T-220** Daily Paths of Sun **T-221** Changes in Sun Angle **T-222** Sun Rays Striking Earth **T-223** Earth-Sun Relationships **T-224** Characteristics of the Solstices and Equinoxes **T-225** Length of Daylight **DC** About Weather **TEX** Lesson Planning 17.1	**SE** Section 17.1 Assessment, p. 482 **onT** Section 17.1
GRSW Section 17.2 **T-226** Three Mechanisms of Heat Transfer **T-227** Electromagnetic Spectrum **T-228** Distribution of Incoming Solar Radiation **T-230** Reflection and Scattering **T-231** Heating of the Atmosphere **GEODe** The Atmosphere → Heating the Atmosphere **TEX** Lesson Planning 17.2	**SE** Section 17.2 Assessment, p. 487 **onT** Section 17.2
GRSW Section 17.3 **T-229** Albedo of Various Surfaces **T-232** Variation in Annual Mean Temperature Range with Latitude **T-233** Monthly Temperatures for Vancouver, BC, and Winnipeg, Manitoba **T-234** Monthly Temperatures for Quito and Guayaquil **T-235** Monthly Temperatures for Eureka, CA, and New York City **T-236** Monthly Temperatures for Seattle and Spokane, WA **T-237** Clouds Reduce Daily Temperature **T-238** World Distribution of Mean Temperatures for January **T-239** World Distribution of Mean Temperatures for July **T-240** Primary Pollutants **T-241** Ozone Distribution of the Southern Hemisphere—October 1995 **T-242** Isothermal Map **TEX** Lesson Planning 17.3	**SE** Section 17.3 Assessment, p. 493 **onT** Section 17.3

Go Online

Go online for these Internet resources.

PHSchool.com
Web Code: cjk-9999

Web Code: cjn-6171
Web Code: cjn-6172

Materials for Activities and Labs

Quantities for each group

STUDENT EDITION

Inquiry Activity, p. 475
dark construction paper, flashlight, pencil

Exploration Lab, pp. 496–497
2 250-mL beakers, dry sand, tap water, ring stand, light source, 2 flat wooden sticks, 2 thermometers, graph paper, 3 colored pencils

TEACHER'S EDITION

Build Science Skills, p. 479
6 identical heavy books, 6 sheets of scrap paper

Teacher Demo, p. 481
narrow-beam flashlight, globe on stand

Teacher Demo, p. 484
red candle, wood, metal, and plastic rods of the same length (at least 15 cm), 500-mL beaker, water, hot plate

Build Science Skills, p. 484
crumpled-up piece of scrap paper

Build Science Skills, p. 486
flashlight or other strong light source

Teacher Demo, p. 490
2 500-mL beakers, water, sand or dry soil, 2 thermometers, sunny window or lamp with 100-W bulb

Chapter Assessment

ASSESSMENT

SE Assessment, pp. 499–500
CUT Chapter 17 Test
CTB Chapter 17
onT Chapter 17

STANDARDIZED TEST PREP

SE Chapter 17, p. 501
TP Progress Monitoring Assessments

interactive textbook with assessment at PHSchool.com

CHAPTER 17

Before you teach

Michael Wysession
Washington University

Big Ideas

Weather is the state of the atmosphere at a particular place for a short period of time. Climate is a generalization of the weather conditions at a particular place over a long period of time. The major components of weather and climate are air temperature, humidity, cloudiness, precipitation, air pressure, and wind.

Space and Time The atmosphere is 99 percent nitrogen (N_2) and oxygen (O_2). Though existing only in trace amounts, gases like carbon dioxide (CO_2), water vapor (H_2O), and ozone (O_3) play important roles for weather and climate. Air pressure decreases dramatically with height above ground, though the temperature profile is more complicated. The atmosphere is described as having four layers: troposphere, stratosphere, mesosphere, and thermosphere.

Forces and Motion The atmosphere is heated by solar radiation, which can be scattered, reflected, or absorbed by air molecules and the ground. The greenhouse effect is a result of the atmosphere's absorption of long-wavelength radiation radiated by Earth's ground after it has been heated by the sun.

Matter and Energy Heat is transferred by three mechanisms: conduction, convection, and radiation. All three of these processes operate in the atmosphere. The atmosphere's temperature is affected by differential heating of land and water, altitude, geographic position, cloud cover, and the patterns of ocean currents.

Earth as a System Humans exert a tremendous influence on the atmosphere through changes in ground cover and the emission of different gases.

Earth Science Refresher

Water in the Atmosphere

If all of the water in the atmosphere was removed, it would make a liquid layer only 2 mm thick. This is remarkable, given that all of the water of the hydrologic cycle must pass through the atmosphere. The solution to this paradox is that water has a very short residence time in the atmosphere, usually less than a day. As soon as it gets evaporated, it precipitates out. So even though there is not a lot of water in the atmosphere at any given moment, a vast amount of water is continually moving through the atmosphere. About 1100 km^3 of water is evaporated every day—about 400,000 km^3 every year. This is equal to a cube of water about 75 km on a side.

When this water precipitates out of the atmosphere, it converts its gravitational potential energy into work. The result is that water is the primary mechanism for shaping the surface of the continents. The amount of work done by water returning to the oceans is equal to about 90 Mississippi Rivers flowing over a 1-km cliff. No wonder mountains get eroded away so quickly (geologically speaking). All of this water must flow through the atmosphere, which contains only 0.001 percent of Earth's surface water at any given moment.

Address Misconceptions

Students often think that when liquid water turns into water vapor, it breaks apart into hydrogen and oxygen. Students also sometimes have trouble distinguishing between water vapor and liquid water in the atmosphere. Actually, water vapor is a gas made up of individual water molecules that are too small to see. Different amounts of water vapor in the air make the air feel dry or humid. Liquid water in the atmosphere is usually in the form of tiny droplets. For a strategy that helps to overcome this misconception, see **Address Misconceptions** on **p. 477.**

Go Online PD LINKS NSTA

For: Chapter 17 Content Support
Visit: www.SciLinks.org/PDLinks
Web Code: cjn-1799

Radiation

The atmosphere responds in many different ways to the different sources of radiation that affect it. Most important, of course, is the radiation from the sun. But also important is the radiation from objects on Earth's surface (rock, plants, water, ice), as well as gases in the atmosphere itself. It is sometimes hard for students to understand that all objects are constantly absorbing and re-radiating electromagnetic radiation, because we can't see most of it. The sun's radiation is peaked in the visible range, which is why the eyes of animals have evolved to see "visible" light. But if you use infrared goggles, you can see the radiation that we emit, even at nighttime. Colder objects emit longer wavelength radiation—the U.S. Navy can track icebergs in the North Atlantic Ocean by looking for microwave signals.

Trade-Off Between Altitude and Latitude

The drop-off of atmospheric pressure with altitude is dramatic. Even though some air exists many hundreds of kilometers above Earth's surface, half of the air is found below an altitude of 5.6 km. Any student who has ever climbed very tall mountains will understand this. The air becomes so thin that breathing becomes difficult. Also, the risk of sunburn becomes very great—there is much less air to filter out the sun's radiation. Sleeping at high altitudes can also be difficult, as it is not uncommon to wake up repeatedly, gasping for air. Understandably, this atmospheric change also has a tremendous effect on ecosystems. You can be in a region that has a temperate forest climate, but if you climb up a local mountain, you might find plants and animals that are common to tundra climates.

Build Reading Literacy

Monitor Your Understanding

Self-Questioning and Self-Adjusting While Reading

Strategy Help students read and understand difficult technical material. This strategy enables students to focus on their own thought processes as they actively question and apply fix-up strategies to improve comprehension. First, present the three steps in the example below, reviewing the fix-up strategies in Step 2. Then, before students begin, assign a section in Chapter 17, such as Section 17.1, pp. 476–482, for them to read. You might want to model the strategy with a paragraph or two before having students practice it on their own.

Example

1. Self-Question Have students read and think about the paragraphs under each heading, stopping often to ask themselves questions such as, "Do I understand this?" "Is this clear?" and "Does this answer my questions about __________?"

2. Identify Trouble Spots and Apply Fix-up Strategies

- **Reread/Adjust Reading Pace** When students do not understand a paragraph, have them reread it slowly, making sure they understand each sentence before continuing.
- **Clarify** When students encounter a difficult paragraph, suggest they state what they do understand, talk through confusing points or steps in a process, or relate new information to concepts and examples that are already familiar to them.
- **Read Ahead/Use Visuals and Captions** Show students how to use visuals and captions to help clarify a process or a concept. Suggest that they can also read ahead to see whether a process or concept is discussed further as part of another concept.
- **Use Outside Resources** Point out, too, that students should seek assistance from friends, teachers, or other resources. Hearing additional examples or more than one person's explanation often aids comprehension.

3. Self-Check After students read, have them check their understanding by summarizing or retelling the main idea of a paragraph or section.

See p. 485 for a script on how to use this strategy with students. For additional strategies, see pp. 480 and 491.

ASSESS PRIOR KNOWLEDGE

Use the Chapter Pretest below to assess students' prior knowledge. As needed, review these concepts.

Review Science Concepts

Section 17.1 Review what a gas is and the concept of a mixture to help students understand Earth's atmosphere and how the mixture of these gases are essential to our existence. Reviewing the concept of pressure will ensure that students understand how air pressure changes with altitude.

Section 17.2 Reviewing the nature of electromagnetic radiation and how it travels will help students understand the energy that comes from the sun and how that energy creates our weather.

Section 17.3 Review the concept of specific heat capacity.

Review Math Skills

Calculating with Significant Figures Remind students that when multiplying, the measurement with the smallest number of significant figures determines the number of significant figures in the answer. Direct students to the Math Skills section in the Skills Handbook at the end of the student text.

CHAPTER 17

The Atmosphere: Structure and Temperature

CONCEPTS in Action

Exploration Lab
Heating Land and Water

How the Earth Works
Earth's Atmosphere

The Atmosphere
↳ Heating the Atmosphere

Discovery CHANNEL SCHOOL

Video Field Trip
About Weather

Take a weather field trip with Discovery Channel and learn about Earth's atmosphere. Answer the following questions after watching the video.

1. What protects Earth from the hot and cold extremes of space?
2. How do clouds form?

For: Chapter 17 Resources
Visit: PHSchool.com
Web Code: cjk-9999

A bald eagle, found only in North America, soars over Mount Rainier National Park in Washington State. ▶

Chapter Pretest

1. What are the main components of the atmosphere? *(b)*
   a. oxygen and carbon dioxide
   b. oxygen and nitrogen
   c. nitrogen and carbon dioxide
   d. oxygen and water vapor
2. True or False: The seasons are caused by changes in Earth's distance from the sun. *(False)*
3. True or False: Heat is energy transferred between objects (matter) that are at different temperatures. *(True)*
4. What are three mechanisms of heat transfer? *(c)*
   a. conduction, emission, and radiation
   b. conduction, convection, and reflection
   c. conduction, convection, and radiation
   d. scattering, convection, and radiation
5. Does land or water heat more rapidly? *(Land heats more rapidly.)*
6. If you move from sea level to a location in the mountains, how will the temperature change? *(It will get colder.)*

Chapter Preview

Inquiry Activity

Modeling the Angle of the Sun

Procedure

1. Place a sheet of dark construction paper on a desk or table top. Hold a flashlight approximately 10 cm above the paper. The flashlight should be held at a 90° angle and pointed toward the paper.
2. Darken the room, and turn on the flashlight. Have a partner trace the perimeter of the light on the paper.
3. Repeat step 2, but this time, tilt the flashlight so that it is at 45 degrees to the paper. The end of the light should be 10 cm above the paper. Have a partner trace the perimeter of the light on the paper.

Think About It

1. **Observing** Describe the sizes and shapes of the light on the paper for steps 2 and 3.
2. **Modeling** Suppose the flashlight represents the sun, and the paper represents Earth's surface. Which angle gives more energy, per unit area, on the surface of Earth?

Video Field Trip

About Weather

Encourage students to view the Video Field Trip "About Weather."

ENGAGE/EXPLORE

Modeling the Angle of the Sun L2

Purpose In this activity, students compare a model of two angles of the sun in relation to Earth's surface. They conclude which angle concentrates the most energy from the sun.

Skills Focus Observing, Modeling

 **Prep Time** 5 minutes

Materials sheet of dark construction paper, flashlight, pencil

Class Time 10 minutes

Expected Outcome Students will conclude that when the sun is directly overhead, its energy is more concentrated than when the sun moves to one side.

Think About It

1. When the flashlight is held at a 90° angle to the paper, the bright spot is smaller and circular in shape; when the light is held at a 45° angle, the spot is larger, its brightness is less intense, and the shape is stretched out, or more oblong.
2. More energy per unit area would be concentrated on Earth's surface with the sun directly overhead, than when the sun is located to one side.

Section 17.1

1 FOCUS

Section Objectives

17.1 **Compare and contrast** weather and climate.

17.2 **Explain** why seasonal changes occur.

Reading Focus

Build Vocabulary L2

Word Part Analysis Ask students what the word *sphere* means. Tell them it's a three-dimensional object in which all points are equidistant from a fixed point, like a ball or globe. Tell them that *atmos-* comes from the Latin word meaning "vapor." The word *atmosphere* thus refers to the spherical layer of gases, or "vapors," around Earth. Have students try to figure out what the words on the vocabulary list that end in *sphere* mean, based on their prefixes. If they cannot figure a word out, have them look it up. (*tropo-* means "change"; *strato-* means "layer"; *meso-* means "middle"; *thermo-* means "heat")

Reading Strategy L2

Venn Diagram

a. Northern Hemisphere: June 21 or 22; Southern Hemisphere: December 21 or 22. For the summer solstice in the Northern Hemisphere, the sun's rays are directly over the Tropic of Cancer; for the summer solstice in the Southern Hemisphere, the sun's rays are directly over the Tropic of Capricorn.

b. Both summer and winter solstices represent extremes in the solar energy received by Earth. Both result from Earth's 23 1/2 degree axis tilt toward the North Star.

c. Northern Hemisphere: December 21 or 22; Southern Hemisphere: June 21 or 22. For the winter solstice in the Northern Hemisphere, the sun's rays are directly over the Tropic of Capricorn; for the winter solstice in the Southern Hemisphere, the sun's rays are directly over the Tropic of Cancer.

17.1 Atmosphere Characteristics

Reading Focus

Key Concepts

- How does weather differ from climate?
- Why do seasonal changes occur?

Vocabulary

- ozone
- troposphere
- stratosphere
- mesosphere
- thermosphere
- summer solstice
- winter solstice
- autumnal equinox
- spring equinox

Reading Strategy

Comparing and Contrasting Copy the Venn diagram below. As you read, complete the diagram by comparing and contrasting summer and winter solstices.

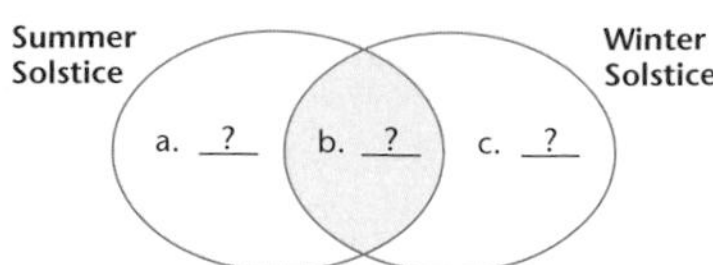

Earth's atmosphere is unique. No other planet in our solar system has an atmosphere with the exact mixture of gases or the moisture conditions and heat needed to sustain life as we know it. The gases that make up Earth's atmosphere and the controls to which they are subject are vital to our existence. In this chapter, you will begin to examine the ocean of air in which we live.

The state of the atmosphere at a given time and place is known as weather. The combination of Earth's motions and energy from the sun produce a variety of weather. As shown in Figure 1, weather strongly influences our everyday activities. **Weather is constantly changing, and it refers to the state of the atmosphere at any given time and place. Climate, however, is based on observations of weather that have been collected over many years. Climate helps describe a place or region.** Climate often is defined simply as "average weather," but this is not a complete description. For example, farmers need to know not only the average rainfall during a growing season, but they also need to know the frequency of extremely wet and extremely dry years. The most important measurable properties of weather and climate are air temperature, humidity, type and amount of precipitation, air pressure, and the speed and direction of the wind.

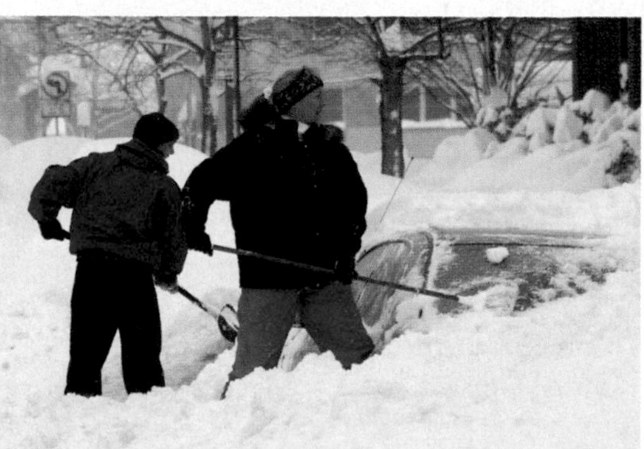

Figure 1 Buffalo, New York, was under a state of emergency in late December 2001 after receiving almost 2 meters of snow.

How does weather differ from climate?

Composition of the Atmosphere

The composition of the atmosphere has changed dramatically over Earth's nearly 4.6 billion year history. The atmosphere is thought to have started as gases that were emitted during volcanic eruptions. Evidence indicates that oxygen did not start to accumulate in the atmosphere until about 2.5 billion years ago. The atmosphere continues to exchange material with the oceans and life on Earth's surface.

Major Components Sometimes the term *air* is used as if it were a specific gas, which it is not. Air is a mixture of different gases and particles, each with its own physical properties. The composition of air varies from time to time and from place to place. However, if the water vapor, dust, and other variable components were removed from the atmosphere, its makeup would be very stable worldwide up to an altitude of about 80 kilometers.

Look at Figure 2. Two gases—nitrogen and oxygen—make up 99 percent of the volume of clean, dry air. Although these gases are the most common components of air, they don't affect the weather much. The remaining 1 percent of dry air is mostly the inert gas argon (0.93 percent) plus tiny quantities of a number of other gases. Carbon dioxide is present in only small amounts (approximately 0.039 percent), but it is an important component of air. Carbon dioxide is an active absorber of energy given off by Earth. Therefore, it plays a significant role in heating the atmosphere.

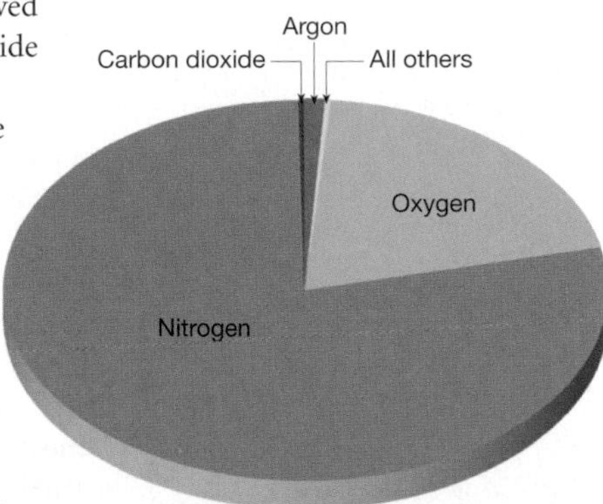

Figure 2 Volume of Clean, Dry Air Nitrogen and oxygen dominate the volume of gases composing dry air.

Variable Components Important materials that vary in the air from time to time and place to place include water vapor, dust particles, and ozone. These components also can have significant effects on weather and climate.

The amount of water vapor varies from almost none to about 4 percent by volume. Why is such a small quantity so significant? **Water vapor is the source of all clouds and precipitation. Like carbon dioxide, water vapor absorbs heat given off by Earth. It also absorbs some solar energy.**

Movements of the atmosphere allow a large quantity of solid and liquid particles to be suspended within it. Although visible dust sometimes clouds the sky, these relatively large particles are too heavy to stay in the air for very long. Still, many particles are microscopic and remain suspended for longer periods of time. These particles include sea salts from breaking waves, fine soil blown into the air, smoke and soot from fires, pollen and microorganisms lifted by the wind, and ash and dust from volcanic eruptions.

2 INSTRUCT

Composition of the Atmosphere

L2

Students often think that when liquid water turns into water vapor, it breaks apart into hydrogen and oxygen. Students also sometimes have trouble distinguishing between water vapor and liquid water in the atmosphere. Explain that water vapor is a gas made up of individual water molecules that are too small to see. Different amounts of water vapor in the air make the air feel dry or humid. Liquid water in the atmosphere is usually in the form of tiny droplets. Ask students to give examples of this. *(clouds, fog, mist, rain, drizzle)*
Logical

Build Science Skills L2

Analyzing Data Give students a brief historical background of the *Farmer's Almanac,* a publication that predicts long-term weather forecasts in North America by using a complex formula that considers sunspots, moon phases, and other astronomical and atmospheric conditions. Farmers have used it since early in the nineteenth century as a primary source for weather forecasts.

Instruct students to visit *www.farmersalmanac.com* to obtain local weather forecasts as predicted by the *Farmer's Almanac.* Then review newspapers or local media records for your area. Distribute your findings to students and discuss with them how accurate the almanac's forecasts are.

If Web resources are not available, use printed almanacs of previous years. You could build a bar graph plotting yearly weather predictions by the almanac, and compare it to a bar graph of actual weather conditions for the same year as recorded by local weather stations.

Customize for English Language Learners

Adapt your content presentation to the less proficient ELL students. Use visual examples as much as possible to explain important concepts. For example, when discussing the components of air, emphasize the pie chart in Figure 2. When discussing how pressure varies with altitude, emphasize the graph in Figure 4. When discussing the structure of the atmosphere, refer to Figure 6. When discussing the seasons, use Figures 7 and 8.

Answer to . . .

Weather changes constantly, but climate is based on patterns of weather that have been observed over years. Climate helps describe a place or region.

Address Misconceptions L2

Students sometimes think that global warming is caused by the ozone hole. Dispel this misconception by explaining that although both phenomena occur in the atmosphere, they are otherwise not related. The depletion of ozone may lead to increases in UV radiation, which may be harmful to living things. Global warming is an increase in the temperature of the atmosphere that may be partly caused by increases in carbon dioxide.
Logical

Use Visuals

Figure 3 Use this diagram to discuss primary pollutants and where they come from. Ask: **What is the main primary pollutant?** *(carbon monoxide)* **What is the main source of primary pollutants?** *(transportation)* **What does the term "transportation" refer to?** *(cars, trucks, trains, ships, and airplanes)* **What do you think the term "stationary source fuel combustion" refers to?** *(power plants, furnaces in homes, and businesses)*
Visual, Logical

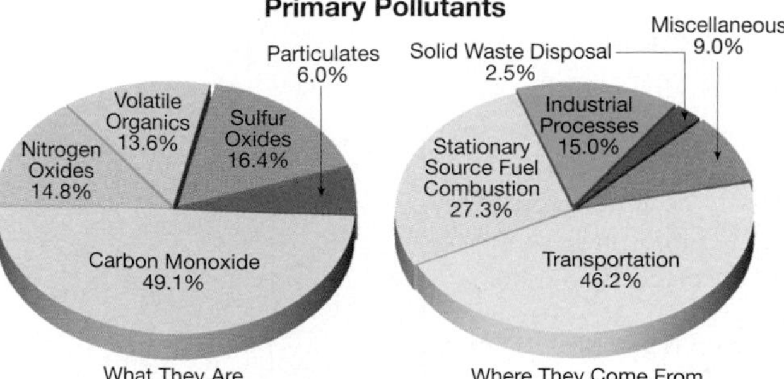

Figure 3 Primary Pollutants These circle graphs show major primary pollutants and their sources. Percentages are calculated by weight.

Source: U.S. Environmental Protection Agency.

Another important variable component of the atmosphere is ozone. **Ozone** is a form of oxygen that combines three oxygen atoms into each molecule (O_3). Ozone is not the same as the oxygen we breathe, which has two atoms per molecule (O_2). There is very little ozone in the atmosphere, and it is not distributed evenly. It is concentrated in a layer located between 10 and 50 kilometers above Earth's surface.

In this altitude range, oxygen molecules (O_2) are split into single atoms of oxygen (O) when they absorb ultraviolet (UV) radiation emitted by the sun. Ozone is then produced when a single atom of oxygen (O) and a molecule of oxygen (O_2) collide. This collision must happen in the presence of a third, neutral molecule that acts as a catalyst. A catalyst allows a reaction to take place without being consumed in the process. Ozone is concentrated 10 to 50 kilometers above Earth because the UV radiation from the sun is sufficient to produce single atoms of oxygen. In addition, there are enough gas molecules to bring about the required collisions.

The ozone layer is crucial to life on Earth. Ozone absorbs potentially harmful UV radiation from the Sun. **If ozone did not filter most UV radiation and all of the sun's UV rays reached the surface of Earth, our planet would be uninhabitable for many living organisms.**

Human Influence Air pollutants are airborne particles and gases that occur in concentrations large enough to endanger the health of organisms. Primary pollutants, shown in Figure 3, are emitted directly from identifiable sources. Emissions from transportation vehicles account for nearly half the primary pollutants by weight.

Secondary pollutants are not emitted directly into air. They form in the atmosphere when reactions take place among primary pollutants and other substances. For example, after the primary pollutant sulfur dioxide enters the atmosphere, it combines with oxygen to produce sulfur trioxide. Then the sulfur trioxide combines with water to create sulfuric acid, an irritating and corrosive substance.

Reactions triggered by strong sunlight are called photochemical reactions. For instance, when nitrogen oxides absorb solar radiation, a chain of complex reactions begins. If certain volatile organic compounds are present, secondary products form that are reactive, irritating, and toxic. This noxious mixture of gases and particles is called photochemical smog.

What are secondary pollutants?

Facts and Figures

Significant improvements in air quality have occurred since the U.S. Environmental Protection Agency initiated air-pollution control programs. Between 1970 and 2000, national total emissions of primary pollutants declined by about one third. This occurred during a period when the U.S. population increased by about one third, and vehicle miles traveled rose nearly 130 percent. Despite continued improvements in air quality, standards have not yet been met in large numbers of places. In 2000, more than 100 million people lived in countries with unhealthy air.

Height and Structure of the Atmosphere

Where does the atmosphere end and outer space begin? There is no sharp boundary. **The atmosphere thins as you travel away from Earth until there are too few gas molecules to detect.**

Pressure Changes To understand the vertical extent of the atmosphere, examine Figure 4, which shows changes in atmospheric pressure with height. Atmospheric pressure is simply the weight of the air above. At sea level, the average pressure is slightly more than 1000 millibars, or slightly more than 1 kilogram per square centimeter. One half of the atmosphere lies below an altitude of 5.6 kilometers. Above 100 kilometers, only 0.00003 percent of all the gases making up the atmosphere exist.

Temperature Changes The pictures of snow-capped mountains rising above snow-free valleys shown in Figure 5 might remind you that Earth's atmosphere becomes colder as you climb higher. But not all layers of the atmosphere show this temperature pattern.

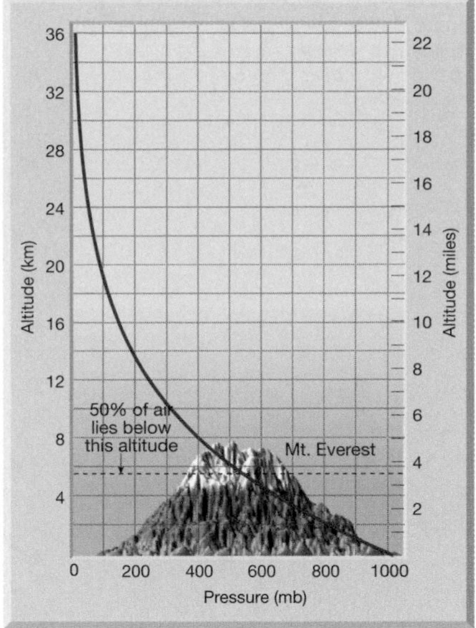

Figure 4 Atmospheric Pressure vs. Altitude This graph shows how atmospheric pressure varies with altitude.
Comparing ***How do changes in air pressure at low altitudes compare with air pressure changes at high altitudes?***

Figure 5 In Jasper National Park in Alberta, Canada, snowy mountaintops contrast with warmer, snow-free lowlands below.

Height and Structure of the Atmosphere

Build Science Skills L2

Using Models To help students understand how and why air pressure decreases as you go up through the atmosphere, have them work in groups to build models of the atmosphere. Have each group make a stack of at least 6 identical heavy books. Have them place a sheet of scrap paper between each layer, with part of the paper sticking out the same amount. Have students then try to pull out each sheet of paper from between the layers. Ask: **Which sheet was the hardest to pull out?** *(the one on the bottom)* **Why was it so hard to pull out?** *(It had the most layers of books piled on it, and thus the most weight.)* **Which sheet was the easiest to pull out?** *(the one on the top)* **Why was it so easy to pull out?** *(It had only one book piled on it, and thus the least weight.)*
Visual, Logical

Integrate Physics L2

Units of Air Pressure Students may be confused by the many different units used to measure air pressure. Newspaper and television weather reports often use the non-metric unit inches of mercury, which is related to the height of a column of mercury in a mercury barometer. The average air pressure at sea level is about 29.92 inches of mercury. The metric (SI) unit for air pressure is the pascal (Pa), the equivalent of one newton per square meter (N/m^2), which is force per unit area. Meteorologists use the unit millibar (mb), which equals 100 Pa. The average air pressure at sea level is about 101,325 Pa. Ask: **How many millibars would 101,325 Pa be?** *(1013.25 mb)*
Logical

Answer to . . .

Figure 4 *Air pressure decreases rapidly near Earth's surface and more gradually at greater heights.*

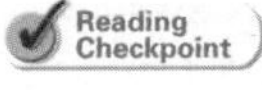 *Secondary pollutants are pollutants that form when reactions take place among primary pollutants and other substances.*

Build Reading Literacy L1

Refer to **p. 186D** in **Chapter 7,** which provides the guidelines for relating text and visuals.

Relate Text and Visuals Have students read the text on p. 480 that describes the features of the layers of the atmosphere. Have students use Figure 6 to describe how temperature changes as you go up through the atmosphere. *(It decreases with altitude in the troposphere; it remains constant in the lower part of the stratosphere and then gradually increases until 50 km above Earth; it decreases with height in the mesosphere; and it increases again in the thermosphere.)*
Visual

Use Visuals L1

Figure 6 Use this diagram to discuss layers of the atmosphere. Ask: **What is the lowest level of the atmosphere, and what happens there?** *(troposphere; essentially all important weather phenomenon occur)* **What is the second-lowest level of the atmosphere, and what important gas is found there?** *(stratosphere; ozone)* **What are the third and upper levels of the atmosphere?** *(mesosphere; thermosphere)*
Visual, Logical

Go Online NSTA SciLinks

Download a worksheet on layers of the atmosphere for students to complete, and find additional teacher support from NSTA SciLinks.

Figure 6 This diagram illustrates the thermal structure of the atmosphere. **Interpret** ***How do air temperatures change with height in the mesosphere?***

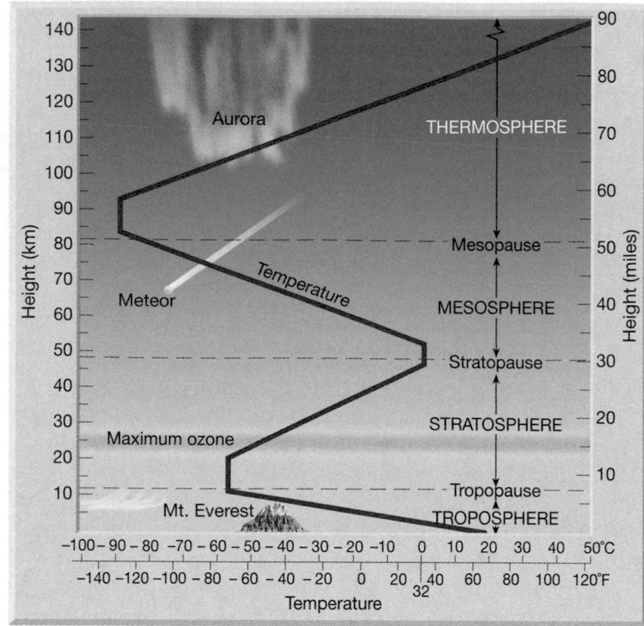

For: Links on the layers of the atmosphere
Visit: www.SciLinks.org
Web Code: cjn-6171

The atmosphere can be divided vertically into four layers based on temperature. Figure 6 illustrates these layers. The bottom layer, where temperature decreases with an increase in altitude, is the **troposphere.** It is in this layer that essentially all important weather phenomena occur. The thickness of the troposphere is not the same everywhere. It varies with latitude and the season. On average, the temperature drop continues to a height of about 12 kilometers, where the outer boundary of the troposphere, called the tropopause, is located.

Beyond the tropopause is the **stratosphere.** In the stratosphere, the temperature remains constant to a height of about 20 kilometers. It then begins a gradual increase in temperature that continues until the stratopause, at a height of nearly 50 kilometers above Earth's surface. Temperatures increase in the stratosphere because the atmosphere's ozone is concentrated here. Recall that ozone absorbs ultraviolet radiation from the sun. As a result, the stratosphere is heated.

In the third layer, the **mesosphere,** temperatures again decrease with height until the mesopause. The mesopause is more than 80 kilometers above the surface and the temperatures approach −90°C. The fourth layer extends outward from the mesopause and has no well-defined upper limit. It is the **thermosphere,** a layer that contains only a tiny fraction of the atmosphere's mass. Temperatures increase in the thermosphere because oxygen and nitrogen absorb short-wave, high-energy solar radiation.

Facts and Figures

The rate of temperature decrease in the troposphere is called the environmental lapse rate. Its average value is 6.5°C/km. This figure is known as the normal lapse rate. The environmental lapse rate is not a constant but can be highly variable. To determine the actual environmental lapse rate, as well as gather information about vertical changes in pressure, wind, and humidity, meteorologists use radiosondes. A radiosonde is an instrument package that is attached to a balloon, and it transmits data by radio as it ascends through the atmosphere.

Earth-Sun Relationships

Nearly all of the energy that drives Earth's variable weather and climate comes from the sun. Earth absorbs only a tiny percentage of the energy given off by the sun—less than one two-billionth. This may seem insignificant, but the amount is several hundred thousand times the electrical-generating capacity of the United States.

Solar energy is not distributed evenly over Earth's surface. The amount of energy received varies with latitude, time of day, and season of the year. As you will see, the variations in solar heating are caused by the motions of Earth relative to the sun and by variations in Earth's land and ocean surface. It is the unequal heating of Earth that creates winds and drives the ocean's currents. These movements transport heat from the tropics toward the poles in an attempt to balance energy differences. The results of these processes are the phenomena we call weather.

Earth's Motions Earth has two principal motions—rotation and revolution. Rotation is the spinning of Earth about its axis. The axis is an imaginary line running through the north and south poles. Our planet rotates once every 24 hours, producing the daily cycle of daylight and darkness. Revolution is the movement of Earth in its orbit around the sun. Earth travels at nearly 113,000 kilometers per hour in an elliptical orbit about the sun.

Earth's Orientation We know that it is colder in the winter than in the summer. But why? Length of day and a gradual change in the angle of the noon sun above the horizon affect the amount of energy Earth receives. **Seasonal changes occur because Earth's position relative to the sun continually changes as it travels along its orbit.** Earth's axis is not perpendicular to the plane of its orbit around the sun. Instead it is tilted 23.5 degrees from the perpendicular, as shown in Figure 7. Because the axis remains pointed toward the North Star as Earth moves around the sun, the position of Earth's axis to the sun's rays is constantly changing. If the axis were not tilted, we would not have seasonal changes.

The orientation of Earth relative to the sun and the constant movement of Earth cause the angle of the noon sun to vary by up to 47 degrees (−23.5 degrees to +23.5 degrees) for many locations during the year. For example, a mid-latitude city like New York, located about 40 degrees north latitude, has a maximum noon sun angle of 73.5 degrees when the sun's vertical rays reach their farthest northward location in June. Six months later, New York has a minimum noon sun angle of 26.5 degrees.

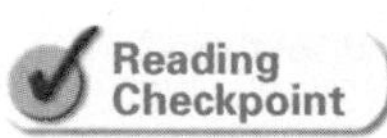
In which direction does Earth's axis point?

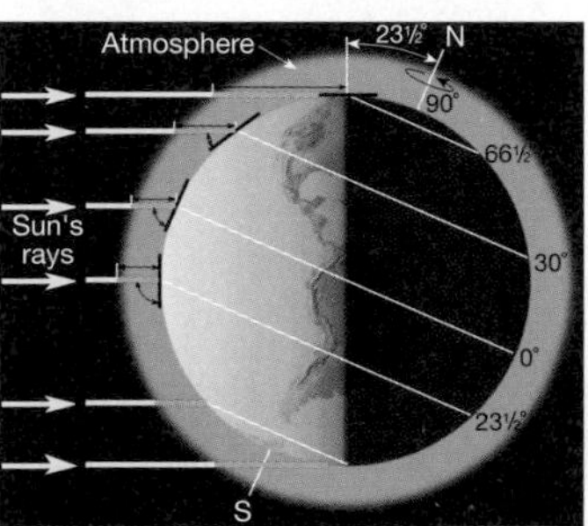

Figure 7 Tilt of Earth's Axis
Earth's axis always points toward the North Star as it revolves around the sun.

Earth-Sun Relationships

Angles and Seasons L2

Purpose Students observe how differences in the angle of the sun's rays affect heating of Earth's surface.

Materials narrow-beam flashlight, globe on stand

Procedure Dim the room lights. Position the globe similarly to how Earth is shown in Figure 7. First, shine the light around 23 degrees S so it makes a tight circle. Explain that this represents summer in the Southern Hemisphere. Then move the flashlight and beam up to about 23 degrees N (keeping the flashlight horizontal). Ask students to describe how the area covered by the light changed, and what season this represents in the Northern Hemisphere.

Expected Outcome The light spreads out to cover a greater area, which represents winter in the Northern Hemisphere. Make sure students understand that the light from the flashlight represents a fixed amount of energy. When it spreads out, it may look as if more energy is hitting the surface of the globe. Actually, the same amount of energy is being spread out over a larger area.

Visual, Logical

Answer to . . .

Figure 6 *Air temperatures decrease with height in the mesosphere.*

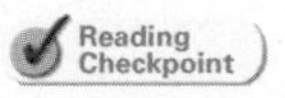 *Earth's axis points toward the North Star.*

L2

Students may think that summer begins before June 21, and winter begins before December 21. Explain that the seasons are officially defined by astronomers using the dates of the solstices and equinoxes as the first day of each season. Meteorologists sometimes prefer to refer to summer as June, July, and August, and winter as December, January, and February. These definitions match the actual weather conditions associated with the seasons more closely.
Logical

3 ASSESS

Evaluate Understanding

L2

Ask students to explain what causes the seasons. Suggest that they can draw diagrams to help them understand the seasons.

Reteach

Use Figure 6 to review the layers of the atmosphere and their characteristics.

Connecting Concepts

The combination of Earth's tilt and its revolution around the sun cause the solstices and equinoxes to be opposite in the Northern Hemisphere and Southern Hemisphere. In the Northern Hemisphere, the maximum energy from the sun is received on the summer solstice, June 21 or 22; in the Southern Hemisphere, the maximum energy is received on the winter solstice, December 21 or 22.

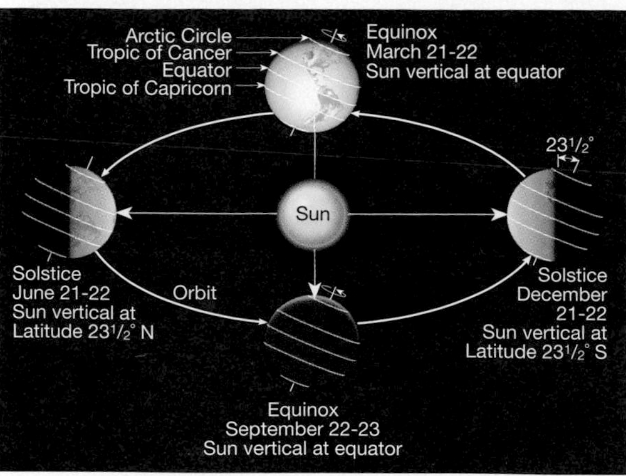

Figure 8 Solstices and equinoxes are important events in Earth's yearly weather cycle.

Solstices and Equinoxes On June 21 or 22 each year the axis is such that the Northern Hemisphere is "leaning" 23.5 degrees toward the sun. This date, shown on the left side of Figure 8, is known as the **summer solstice,** or the first "official" day of summer. Six months later, in December, when Earth has moved to the opposite side of its orbit, the Northern Hemisphere "leans" 23.5 degrees away from the sun. December 21 or 22 is the **winter solstice,** the first day of winter. On days between these extremes, Earth's axis is leaning at amounts less than 23.5 degrees to the rays of the sun.

The equinoxes occur midway between the solstices. September 22 or 23 is the date of the **autumnal equinox** in the Northern Hemisphere. March 21 or 22 is the date of the **spring equinox** for the Northern Hemisphere. On these dates, the vertical rays of the sun strike the equator (0 degrees latitude) because Earth is in a position in its orbit so that the axis is tilted neither toward nor away from the sun.

Length of Daylight The length of daylight compared to darkness also is determined by Earth's position in orbit. All latitudes receive 12 hours of daylight during the vernal and autumnal equinoxes (equal night). The length of daylight on the summer solstice in the Northern Hemisphere is greater than the length of darkness. The farther you are north of the equator on the summer solstice, the longer the period of daylight. When you reach the Arctic Circle, at 66.5 degrees N latitude, the length of daylight is 24 hours.

Section 17.1 Assessment

Reviewing Concepts

1. Compare and contrast weather and climate.
2. Why do seasonal changes occur?
3. How much of Earth's atmosphere is located below about 5.6 kilometers?
4. How do ozone molecules form in the stratosphere?
5. In which layers of the atmosphere does temperature increase with increasing height?

Critical Thinking

6. **Applying Concepts** Explain what would happen to air temperatures in the troposphere if carbon dioxide were removed from air.

Connecting Concepts

Connecting Concepts Using Figure 8, explain why solstices and equinoxes are opposite for the Northern and Southern hemispheres.

Section 17.1 Assessment

1. Climate is a description of aggregate weather conditions for an area, and weather is the state of the atmosphere at a given moment in time.
2. Seasonal changes occur because Earth's axis is tilted. Earth's orientation to the sun continually changes as it travels along its orbit.
3. About 50 percent of Earth's atmosphere is below about 5.6 km.
4. Ozone forms when a single atom of oxygen (O) collides with a diatomic molecule of oxygen (O_2).
5. Temperature increases with height in the stratosphere and thermosphere.
6. Because carbon dioxide absorbs heat from Earth efficiently, air temperatures would decrease if it were removed from the troposphere.

17.2 Heating the Atmosphere

Reading Focus

Key Concepts

- How are heat and temperature related?
- What are the three major mechanisms of heat transfer?
- How is the atmosphere affected by each of the heat transfer mechanisms?

Vocabulary

- heat
- temperature
- conduction
- convection
- radiation
- reflection
- scattering
- greenhouse effect

Reading Strategy

Using Prior Knowledge Before you read, copy the table below and write your definition for each vocabulary term. After you read, write the scientific definition of each term and compare it with your original definition.

Term	Your Definition	Scientific Definition
Heat	a. ?	b. ?
Temperature	c. ?	d. ?

The concepts of heat and temperature often are confused. The phrase "in the heat of the day" is one common expression in which the word "heat" is misused to describe the concept of temperature. **Heat is the energy transferred from one object to another because of a difference in their temperatures.** Recall that all matter is composed of atoms or molecules that possess kinetic energy, or the energy of motion. **Temperature** is a measure of the average kinetic energy of the individual atoms or molecules in a substance. When energy is transferred to the gas atoms and molecules in air, those particles move faster and air temperature rises. When air transfers energy to a cooler object, its particles move slower, and air temperature drops.

Energy Transfer as Heat

Three mechanisms of energy transfer as heat are conduction, convection, and radiation. All three processes, illustrated in Figure 9, happen simultaneously in the atmosphere. These mechanisms operate to transfer energy between Earth's surface (both land and water) and the atmosphere.

Conduction Anyone who has touched a metal spoon that was left in a hot pan has experienced the result of heat conducted through the spoon. **Conduction** is the transfer of heat through matter by molecular activity. The energy of molecules is transferred by collisions from one molecule to another. Heat flows from the higher temperature matter to the lower temperature matter.

Figure 9 Energy Transfer as Heat A pot of water on the campfire illustrates the three mechanisms of heat transfer.

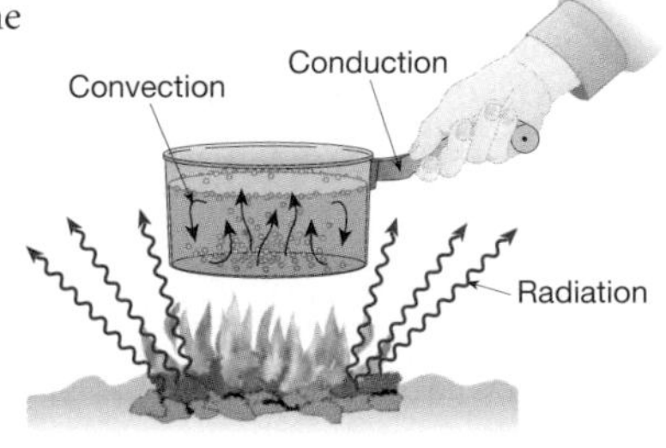

Section 17.2

1 FOCUS

Section Objectives

17.3 **Explain** how heat and temperature are related.

17.4 **List** the three major mechanisms of heat transfer.

17.5 **Describe** how the atmosphere is affected by heat transfer mechanisms.

Reading Focus

Build Vocabulary L2

Concept Map Have students construct a concept map using the terms *heat*, *conduction*, *convection*, and *radiation*. The main concept (heat) should be at the top. Tell students to place the terms in ovals and connect the ovals with lines on which linking words are placed. For each mechanism of heat transfer, they should include a brief description and some examples.

Reading Strategy L2

a. Sample answer: a source of warmth
b. the energy transferred from one object to another because of a difference in their temperatures
c. Sample answer: a measure of how hot or cold it is
d. a measure of the average kinetic energy of individual atoms or molecules in a substance

2 INSTRUCT

Energy Transfer as Heat

Use Visuals L1

Figure 9 After they have read the accompanying text, have students describe each mechanism of energy transfer in terms of what is pictured in the diagram. *(Conduction: Heat energy is transferred from warmer to cooler objects through collisions of molecules, i.e., through direct contact, from the pot, to the handle, to person's hand. Convection: Warmer water expands and becomes less dense, rising through cooler water above, creating transfer of heat by circulation within a liquid. Radiation: The fire is the hottest thing pictured; it emits the most radiant energy.)*
Visual

Teacher Demo

Heat Conduction

L2

Purpose Students observe differences in the ability of different substances to conduct heat.

Materials red candle, wood, metal, and plastic rods of the same length (at least 15 cm), 500-mL beaker, water, hot plate

Procedure Before doing the demo, use the candle to drip spots of wax at about 1-cm intervals onto all of the rods. Then, place the rods in about 1 cm of water in the beaker. Put the beaker on the hot plate and turn it on. Ask students to predict what they think will happen. Have them observe what actually happens. Then ask them to explain their observations.

Expected Outcome The wax dots will melt in order from the bottom up. The dots on the metal rod will melt the fastest (since metal conducts heat the best), followed by the plastic and then the wood.
Visual, Logical

Build Science Skills

L2

Using Models Have students work in pairs to develop ways to model the three methods of heat transfer. Give each pair a crumpled-up piece of scrap paper and tell them it represents heat. Each student represents a molecule. Tell students to use physical movements to model each method of transfer. For example, to demonstrate conduction, students can pass the ball directly to the partner; for convection, students can carry the ball to the partner; and for radiation, students can throw the ball to the partner.
Kinesthetic, Logical

The ability of substances to conduct heat varies greatly. Metals are good conductors, as those of us who have touched hot metal have quickly learned. Air, however, is a very poor conductor of heat. Because air is a poor conductor, conduction is important only between Earth's surface and the air directly in contact with the surface. For the atmosphere as a whole, conduction is the least important mechanism of heat transfer.

Convection Much of the heat transfer that occurs in the atmosphere is carried on by convection. **Convection** is the transfer of heat by mass movement or circulation within a substance. It takes place in fluids, like the ocean and air, where the atoms and molecules are free to move about. Convection also takes place in solids, such as Earth's mantle, that behave like fluids over long periods of time.

The pan of water in Figure 9 shows circulation by convection. Radiation from the fire warms the bottom of the pan, which conducts heat to the water near the bottom of the container. As the water is heated, it expands and becomes less dense than the water above. The warmer water rises because of its buoyancy. At the same time, cooler, denser water near the top of the pan sinks to the bottom, where it becomes heated. As long as the water is heated unequally, it will continue to circulate. In much the same way, most of the heat acquired by radiation and conduction in the lowest layer of the atmosphere is transferred by convective flow.

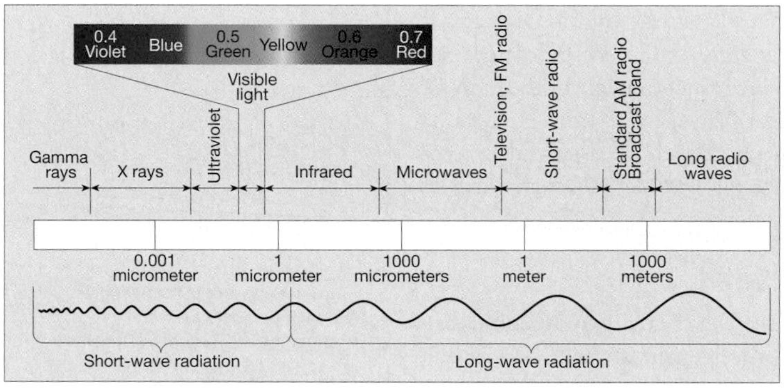

0.4 Violet, Blue, 0.5 Green, Yellow, 0.6 Orange, 0.7 Red
Visible light
Gamma rays, X rays, Ultraviolet, Infrared, Microwaves, Television, FM radio, Short-wave radio, Standard AM radio Broadcast band, Long radio waves
0.001 micrometer, 1 micrometer, 1000 micrometers, 1 meter, 1000 meters
Short-wave radiation, Long-wave radiation

Figure 10 Electromagnetic Spectrum Electromagnetic energy is classified according to wavelength in the electromagnetic spectrum.

Electromagnetic Waves The sun is the ultimate source of energy that creates our weather. You know that the sun emits light and heat as well as the ultraviolet rays that cause a suntan. These forms of energy are only part of a large array of energy called the electromagnetic spectrum. This spectrum of electromagnetic energy is shown in Figure 10. All radiation, whether X-rays, radio waves, or heat waves, travel through the vacuum of space at 300,000 kilometers per second. They travel only slightly slower through our atmosphere.

What is convection?

Customize for Inclusion Students

Gifted Have students create a computer graphics presentation that compares the different mechanisms of heat transfer. The presentations should include both diagrams and photographs.

Imagine what happens when you toss a pebble into a pond. Ripples are made and move away from the location where the pebble hit the water's surface. Much like these ripples, electromagnetic waves move out from their source and come in various sizes. The most important difference among electromagnetic waves is their wavelength, or the distance from one crest to the next. Radio waves have the longest wavelengths, ranging to tens of kilometers. Gamma waves are the shortest, and are less than a billionth of a centimeter long.

Visible light is the only portion of the spectrum you can see. White light is really a mixture of colors. Each color corresponds to a specific wavelength, as shown in Figure 11. By using a prism, white light can be divided into the colors of the rainbow, from violet with the shortest wavelength—0.4 micrometer (1 micrometer is 0.0001 centimeter)—to red with the longest wavelength—0.7 micrometer.

Figure 11 Visible light consists of an array of colors commonly called the colors of the rainbow.

Radiation The third mechanism of heat transfer is radiation. As shown in Figure 9, **radiation** travels out in all directions from its source. **Unlike conduction and convection, which need material to travel through, radiant energy can travel through the vacuum of space.** Solar energy reaches Earth by radiation.

To understand how the atmosphere is heated, it is useful to think about four laws governing radiation.

1. **All objects, at any temperature, emit radiant energy.** Not only hot objects like the sun but also Earth—including its polar ice caps—continually emit energy.
2. **Hotter objects radiate more total energy per unit area than colder objects do.**
3. **The hottest radiating bodies produce the shortest wavelengths of maximum radiation.** For example, the sun, with a surface temperature of nearly 6000°C radiates maximum energy at 0.5 micrometers, which is in the visible range. The maximum radiation for Earth occurs at a wavelength of 10 micrometers, well within the infrared range.
4. **Objects that are good absorbers of radiation are good emitters as well.** Gases are selective absorbers and radiators. The atmosphere does not absorb certain wavelengths of radiation, but it is a good absorber of other wavelengths.

For: Links on conduction and convection
Visit: www.SciLinks.org
Web Code: cjn-6172

Build Reading Literacy L1

Refer to **p. 474D**, which provides the guidelines for monitoring understanding.

Monitor Your Understanding Have students read the passage Radiation on pp. 484–485. When they reach the bottom of p. 485, have them stop and write down the main ideas of the passage. They should have two main groups of ideas: the different types of electromagnetic waves, and the laws that govern radiation. Have students ask themselves, "Did I have any trouble reading this passage? If so, why?" Lead a class discussion of strategies that can be used to improve understanding, such as looking up difficult words and discussing difficult concepts with a partner. Have students use these strategies as they continue reading.
Logical, Verbal

Integrate Physics L2

Rainbows Tell students that a rainbow occurs when white light passes through tiny drops of water in the air. Each water drop acts like a tiny prism. When light enters a drop, it slows down and refracts, or bends. Red light slows down and bends the least, whereas violet light slows down and bends the most. The light then reflects off the far inner surface of the drop and passes back through the drop, refracting again. Have students use prisms to separate light into a spectrum and project it onto a sheet of white paper.
Logical

Download a worksheet on conduction and convection for students to complete, and find additional teacher support from NSTA SciLinks.

Answer to . . .

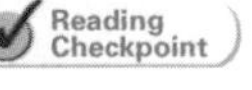

Convection is the transfer of heat by mass movement or circulation within a substance.

What Happens to Solar Radiation?

Use Visuals L1

Figure 12 Use the diagram to discuss what happens to solar radiation. Ask: **What percentage of radiation is reflected from clouds?** *(20 percent)* **What percentage of radiation is lost to space by reflection and scattering?** *(30 percent)* **What types of radiation are absorbed by land and sea?** *(direct and diffused radiation)*
Visual

Build Science Skills L2

Applying Concepts ACTIVITY
Dim the room lights and shine a beam of light through the air from a large flashlight or other strong light source. Have students look at the beam and describe what they see. *(tiny particles)* Ask students what phenomenon allows them to see these particles. *(scattering)*
Logical

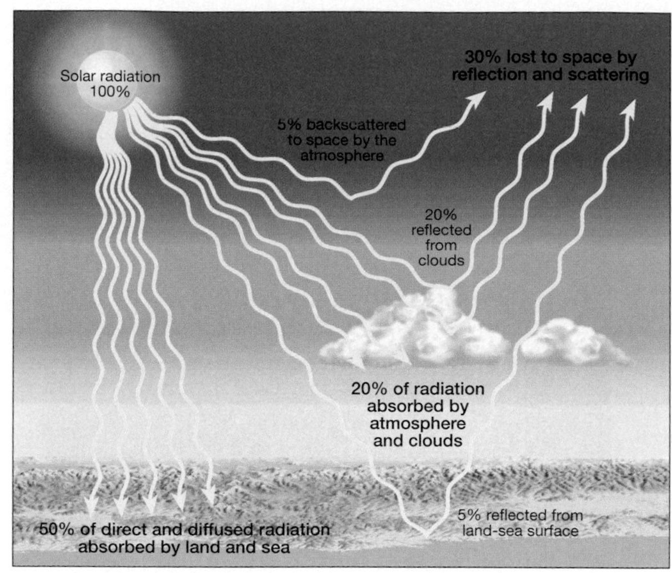

Figure 12 Solar Radiation This diagram shows what happens, on average, to incoming solar radiation by percentage.

What Happens to Solar Radiation?

When radiation strikes an object, there usually are three different results.

1. **Some energy is absorbed by the object.** When radiant energy is absorbed, it is converted to heat and causes a temperature increase.
2. **Substances such as water and air are transparent to certain wavelengths of radiation.** These substances transmit the radiant energy. Radiation that is transmitted does not contribute energy to the object.
3. **Some radiation may bounce off the object without being absorbed or transmitted.** Figure 12 shows what happens to incoming solar radiation, averaged for the entire globe.

Reflection and Scattering **Reflection** occurs when light bounces off an object. The reflected radiation has the same intensity as the incident radiation. In contrast, **scattering** produces a larger number of weaker rays that travel in different directions. See Figure 13. Scattering disperses light both forward and backward. However, more energy is dispersed in the forward direction. About 30 percent of the solar energy reaching the outer atmosphere is reflected back to space. This 30 percent also includes the amount of energy sent skyward by scattering. This energy is lost and does not play a role in heating Earth's atmosphere.

Small dust particles and gas molecules in the atmosphere scatter some incoming radiation in all directions. This explains how light reaches into the area beneath a shade tree, and how a room is lit in the absence of direct sunlight. Scattering also accounts for the brightness and even the blue color of the daytime sky. In contrast, bodies like the moon and Mercury—which are without atmospheres—have dark skies and "pitch-black" shadows even during daylight hours. About half of the solar radiation that is absorbed at Earth's surface arrives as scattered light.

Figure 13 Reflection vs. Scattering
A Reflected light bounces back with the same intensity.
B Scattering produces more light rays with a weaker intensity.

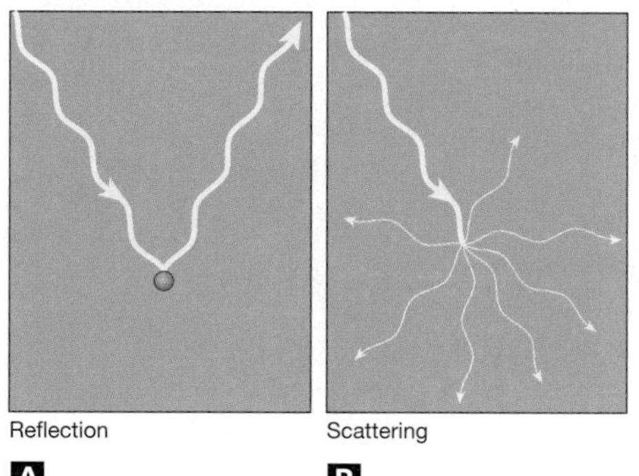

What causes the blue color of the daytime sky?

Facts and Figures

The fraction of the total radiation that is reflected by a surface is called its albedo. The albedo for Earth as a whole (the planetary albedo) is 30 percent. The albedo varies considerably from place to place and time to time in the same location. Albedo can vary with amount of cloud cover and particles in the air, as well as the nature of the surface and the angle of the sun's rays. A lower sun angle means that the rays pass through more of the atmosphere, and more solar radiation is lost. Albedo can be as low as 5 percent for a forest and as high as 90 percent for fresh snow.

Absorption About 50 percent of the solar energy that strikes the top of the atmosphere reaches Earth's surface and is absorbed, as shown in Figure 12. Most of this energy is then reradiated skyward. Because Earth has a much lower surface temperature than the sun, the radiation that it emits has longer wavelengths than solar radiation does.

The atmosphere efficiently absorbs the longer wavelengths emitted by Earth. Water vapor and carbon dioxide are the major absorbing gases. When a gas molecule absorbs light waves, this energy is transformed into molecular motion that can be detected as a rise in temperature. Gases in the atmosphere eventually radiate some of this energy away. Some energy travels skyward, where it may be reabsorbed by other gas molecules. The remainder travels Earthward and is again absorbed by Earth. In this way, Earth's surface is continually being supplied with heat from the atmosphere as well as from the sun.

Without these absorbing gases in our atmosphere, Earth would not be a suitable habitat for humans and other life forms. This important phenomenon has been termed the **greenhouse effect** because it was once thought that greenhouses were heated in a similar manner. A more important factor in keeping a greenhouse warm is the fact that the greenhouse itself prevents the mixing of air inside with cooler air outside. Nevertheless, the term greenhouse effect is still used.

Q *Isn't the greenhouse effect responsible for global warming?*

A It is important to note that the greenhouse effect and global warming *are not* the same thing. Without the greenhouse effect, Earth would be uninhabitable. We do have mounting evidence that human activity (particularly the release of carbon dioxide into the atmosphere) is responsible for a rise in global temperatures. Thus, human activities seem to be enhancing an otherwise natural process (the greenhouse effect) to increase Earth's temperature. Nevertheless, to equate the greenhouse effect, which makes life possible, with undesirable changes to our atmosphere caused by human activity is incorrect.

L2

Students often think that the greenhouse effect and global warming are the same phenomenon. Emphasize that the greenhouse effect occurs naturally and is essential to keeping the atmosphere warm enough for living things to survive on Earth. Global warming, on the other hand, is an increase in the temperature of Earth's atmosphere that may be caused or influenced by human activities.
Logical

3 ASSESS

Evaluate Understanding **L2**

Ask students to list and describe the three ways heat can be transferred. Have them give an example of each process in the atmosphere.

Reteach **L1**

Use Figure 12 to review what happens to incoming solar radiation.

Student paragraphs should clearly state the fundamental principles of radiation, and they should include examples to reinforce the principles.

The four laws are: All objects emit radiant energy, hotter objects radiate more energy than colder objects, the hottest radiating bodies produce the shortest wavelengths of maximum radiation, objects that are good absorbers are also good emitters.

Answer to . . .

Reading Checkpoint *The blue color is caused by gas molecules in the atmosphere that scatter incoming solar radiation.*

Section 17.2 Assessment

Reviewing Concepts

1. How are heat and temperature related?
2. List and describe the three major mechanisms of heat transfer in the atmosphere.
3. How is the atmosphere affected by
   a. convection?
   b. conduction?
   c. radiation?
4. Describe what happens to solar radiation when it strikes an object.
5. Contrast reflection and scattering.

Critical Thinking

6. **Applying Concepts** Dark objects tend to absorb more radiation than light-colored objects. Explain whether dark objects or light objects on Earth's surface would be better radiators of heat.

Writing in Science

Descriptive Paragraph Write a paragraph that describes the four laws governing radiation discussed in this chapter. Make sure to use your own words. Use examples to reinforce concepts wherever possible.

Section 17.2 Assessment

1. Both heat and temperature arise from thermal vibrations in atoms and molecules. Heat is energy transferred between objects (matter) that are at different temperatures. Temperature is the average kinetic energy of individual atoms and molecules in the substance.
2. Conduction: heat transfer through matter by particle activity. Convection: heat transfer by mass movement within a substance. Radiation: energy transfer by electromagnetic waves.
3. Convection: Much of the heat transfer in the atmosphere is carried by convection. Most of the heat acquired by radiation and conduction in the lowest layer of the atmosphere is transferred by convective flow; Conduction: Air is a poor conductor of heat, so conduction is most important between Earth's surface and the air directly in contact with the surface. Conduction is the least important mechanism of heat transfer in the atmosphere; Radiation: Solar energy reaches Earth by radiation. The radiation can be absorbed, transmitted, or reflected. The radiant energy that is absorbed is converted to heat and causes an increase in temperature.
4. When solar radiation strikes an object, it can absorb, reflect, or scatter the radiation.
5. Reflection: radiation bouncing off an object at the same angle and intensity as the incident radiation. Scattering: radiation bouncing off in all directions with intensities that are weaker than the incident radiation.
6. Because good absorbers also tend to be good radiators of heat, dark-colored objects are expected to be better radiators than light-colored objects.

Section 17.3

1 FOCUS

Section Objectives

17.6 **Explain** what a temperature control is.
17.7 **Compare and contrast** the heating of land and water.
17.8 **Explain** why some clouds reflect a portion of sunlight back to space.

Reading Focus

Build Vocabulary L2

LINCS Have students use the LINCS strategy to learn and review the terms *albedo, windward, leeward,* and *isotherm.* In LINCS exercises, students **L**ist what they know about each term, **I**magine a picture that describes the word, **N**ote a "sound-alike" word, **C**onnect the terms to the sound-alike word by making up a short story, and then perform a brief **S**elf-test.

Reading Strategy L2

a. slight temperature variation
b. more extreme temperature variation

2 INSTRUCT

Why Temperatures Vary

Build Science Skills L2

Interpreting Photographs Have students look at Figure 14 carefully. Ask: **What is inside this shelter?** *(an electrical thermometer called a thermistor)* **Why does the thermistor need to be protected by a shelter?** *(Direct sunlight would spoil the temperature readings, and it needs to be protected from breaking.)* **What does the shelter need to have vents for air flow?** *(The air inside the shelter cannot get hotter than the outside air.)*
Logical, Visual

17.3 Temperature Controls

Reading Focus

Key Concepts
- What is a temperature control?
- How do the heating of land and water differ?
- Why do some clouds reflect a portion of sunlight back to space?

Vocabulary
- albedo
- isotherm

Reading Strategy
Previewing Copy the table below. Before you read, use Figure 15 to describe the temperature variations for Vancouver and Winnipeg.

Temperature Variations	
Vancouver	a. ?
Winnipeg	b. ?

Figure 14 This modern instrument shelter contains an electrical thermometer called a thermistor.

Temperature is one of the basic elements of weather and climate. When someone asks what it is like outside, air temperature is often the first element we mention. At a weather station, the temperature is read on a regular basis from instruments mounted in an instrument shelter like the one in Figure 14. The shelter protects the instruments from direct sunlight and allows a free flow of air.

Why Temperatures Vary

A temperature control is any factor that causes temperature to vary from place to place and from time to time. Earlier in this chapter you examined the most important cause for temperature variations—differences in the receipt of solar radiation. Because variations in the angle of the sun's rays and length of daylight depend on latitude, they are responsible for warmer temperatures in the tropics and colder temperatures toward the poles. Seasonal temperature changes happen as the sun's vertical rays move toward and away from a particular latitude during the year. **Factors other than latitude that exert a strong influence on temperature include heating of land and water, altitude, geographic position, cloud cover, and ocean currents.**

List three factors that influence temperature.

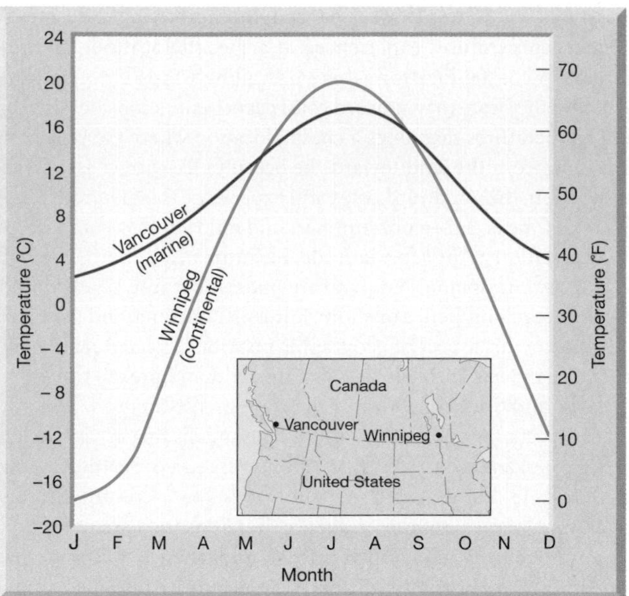

Figure 15 Mean Monthly Temperatures for Vancouver and Winnipeg Winnipeg illustrates the greater extremes associated with an interior location.
Calculating ***How much lower is Winnipeg's January mean temperature than Vancouver's? Calculate the temperature to the nearest degree.***

Land and Water The heating of Earth's surface controls the temperature of the air above it. To understand variations in air temperature, we consider the characteristics of the surface. Different land surfaces absorb varying amounts of incoming solar energy. The largest contrast, however, is between land and water. **Land heats more rapidly and to higher temperatures than water. Land also cools more rapidly and to lower temperatures than water.** Temperature variations, therefore, are considerably greater over land than over water.

Monthly temperature data for two cities, shown in Figure 15, show the influence of a large body of water. Vancouver, British Columbia, is located along the windward Pacific coast. Winnipeg, Manitoba, is far from the influence of water. Both cities are at about the same latitude, so they experience similar lengths of daylight and angles of the sun's rays. Winnipeg, however, has much greater temperature extremes than Vancouver does. Vancouver's moderate year-round climate is due to its location by the Pacific Ocean.

Temperature variations in the Northern and Southern hemispheres are compared in Table 1. Water accounts for 61 percent of the Northern Hemisphere, and land accounts for the remaining 39 percent. In the Southern Hemisphere, 81 percent of the surface is water and only 19 percent of the surface is land. The Southern Hemisphere shows smaller annual temperature variations.

Table 1 Variation in Annual Mean Temperature Range (°C) with Latitude

Latitude	Northern Hemisphere	Southern Hemisphere
0	0	0
15	3	4
30	13	7
45	23	6
60	30	11
75	32	26
90	40	31

Integrating Physics L2

Specific Heat Water requires a great deal more heat to raise its temperature the same amount as an equal quantity of land. The amount of energy needed to raise the temperature of 1 g of a substance 1°C is its specific heat. The higher a substance's specific heat, the more heat it takes to raise its temperature a certain amount. Ask: **When you go to the beach on a sunny day, why does the sand feel hot?** *(The sand has a low specific heat, so its temperature rises quickly.)* **Why does the water feel cold even though it is sunny?** *(The water has a high specific heat, so its temperature rises slowly.)*
Logical

Use Visuals L1

Figure 15 Use this graph to help students understand how data are presented on climate graphs. Ask: **What does the left axis indicate?** *(temperature in degrees Celsius)* **What does the right axis indicate?** *(temperature in degrees Fahrenheit)* **What does the bottom axis indicate?** *(month)* **What do the curves for Vancouver and Winnipeg indicate about their climates?** *(They have similar summer climates but Winnipeg has a much colder winter climate.)*
Visual, Logical

Customize for English Language Learners

ELL students can benefit from relating examples from their lives to material in the section. Encourage students to think about the climate where they were born or grew up. Have them explain that climate in terms of the factors that influence temperature.

Answer to . . .

Figure 15 *It is 21°C lower.*

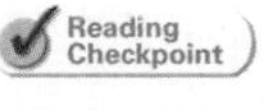

Accept any three of the following: latitude, differential heating of land and water, altitude, geographic position, cloud cover, ocean currents

Teacher Demo

Heating of Land and Water

L2

Purpose Students observe how land and water heat up at different rates.

Materials 2 500-mL beakers, water, sand or dry soil, 2 thermometers, sunny window or lamp with 100-W bulb

Procedure Before the demo, half-fill one beaker with water and the other with sand or dry soil. Put a thermometer into each (well below the surface of the soil), and set them aside until they both reach room temperature. Show students the beakers and that both are at the same temperature. Place them in a sunny spot or under a hot lamp. As students what they think will happen. Check the thermometers regularly until you see a noticeable difference. Ask students to explain the results.

Expected Outcome The temperature of the soil will increase much faster than the temperature of the water.
Visual, Logical

Geographic Position The geographic setting can greatly influence temperatures experienced at a specific location. Examine Figure 16. A coastal location where prevailing winds blow from the ocean onto the shore (a windward coast) experiences considerably different temperatures than does a coastal location where the prevailing winds blow from the land toward the ocean (a leeward coast). In the first situation, the windward coast will experience the full moderating influence of the ocean—cool summers and mild winters, compared to an inland station at the same latitude. In contrast, a leeward coast will have a more continental temperature pattern because winds do not carry the ocean's influence onshore. Eureka, California, and New York City illustrate this aspect of geographic position. The annual temperature range in New York City is 19°C greater than Eureka's range.

Seattle and Spokane, both in the state of Washington, illustrate another aspect of geographic position—mountains that act as barriers. Although Spokane is only about 360 kilometers east of Seattle, the towering Cascade Range separates the cities. As a result, Seattle's temperatures show a marine influence, but Spokane's are more typically continental, as shown in Figure 17. Spokane is 7°C cooler than Seattle in January and 4°C warmer than Seattle in July. The annual range in Spokane is 11°C greater than in Seattle. The Cascade Range cuts Spokane off from the moderating influence of the Pacific Ocean.

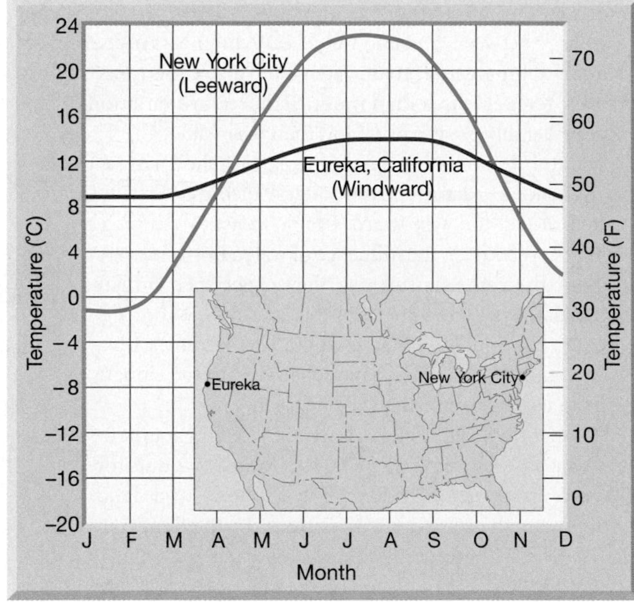

Figure 16 Monthly Mean Temperatures for Eureka and New York City Eureka is strongly influenced by prevailing ocean winds, and New York City is not.

Facts and Figures

There are many reasons why land and water heat up differently. First, water has a much higher specific heat capacity than land, so it heats up more slowly. Second, land surfaces are opaque, so energy is absorbed only at the surface. Water absorbs energy to a depth of several meters. Third, when surface water is heated, it often mixes with water below it, distributing the heat through a larger mass of water. Fourth, evaporation, which is a cooling process, is greater from water surfaces than from land.

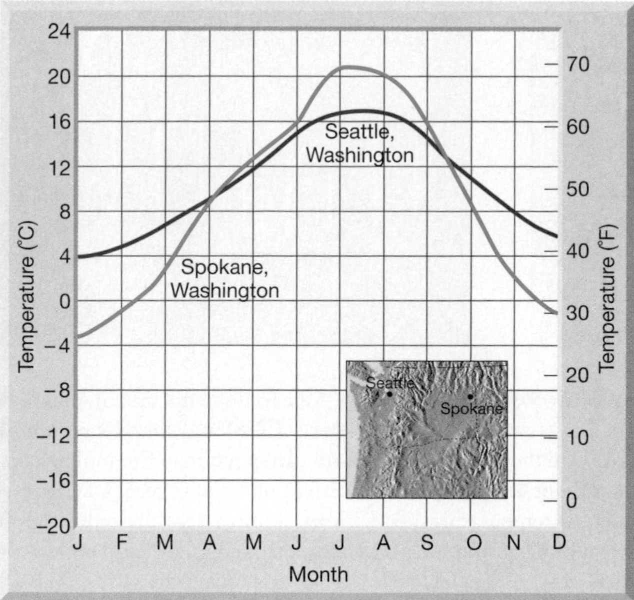

Figure 17 Monthly Mean Temperatures for Seattle and Spokane The Cascade Mountains cut off Spokane from the moderating influence of the Pacific Ocean. **Relating Cause and Effect** ***How does this affect Spokane's annual temperature range?***

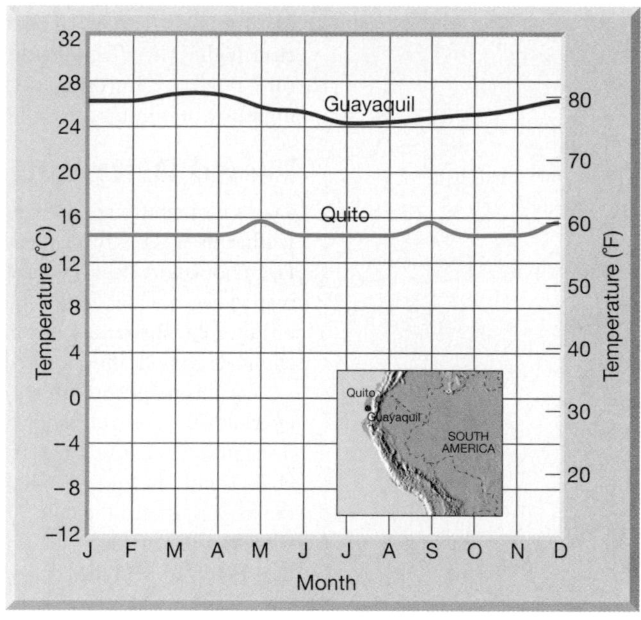

Figure 18 Altitude Affects Temperature Quito's altitude is much higher than Guayaquil's, causing Quito to experience cooler temperatures than Guayaquil.

Altitude Two cities in Ecuador, Quito and Guayaquil, demonstrate the influence of altitude on mean temperature. Both cities are near the equator and relatively close to one another, as shown in Figure 18. The annual mean temperature at Guayaquil is 25°C, compared to Quito's mean of 13°C. If you note these cities' elevations, you can understand the temperature difference. Guayaquil is only 12 meters above sea level, whereas Quito is high in the Andes Mountains at 2800 meters.

Build Reading Literacy **L1**

Refer to **p. 246D** in **Chapter 9,** which provides the guidelines for relating cause and effect.

Relate Cause and Effect Have students read the passage Geographic Position on pp. 490–491. Explain that the temperature of water changes less throughout the year than the temperature of land. The more constant temperature of water causes the air passing over water to also have less temperature change throughout the year. If the air blows from water onto land, then the effect will be to moderate the climate of the land. Ask: **What cause and effect relationship explains climates where the wind blows from land to ocean?** *(The temperature of the air over land changes much more throughout the year than the temperature of air over water. The effect is that areas affected by air blowing off land have climates with a wider range of temperatures.)*
Logical

Build Science Skills **L2**

Inferring Tell students that San Francisco is on the Pacific coast. Denver is at a similar latitude, but it is high in the Rocky Mountains and far inland. Ask students to infer what differences in climate they would expect to see between these two cites, and to explain why. *(San Francisco will have a much more moderate climate than Denver because San Francisco is on a windward coast, and Denver is inland. Denver will have a much colder climate overall because it is at high elevation.)*
Logical

Answer to . . .

Figure 17 *Spokane's annual temperature range is greater because it is cut off from the influence of the Pacific Ocean.*

Use Visuals L1

Figure 19 Use the diagrams to help students understand the effect cloud cover has on temperature. Ask: **What is happening to the solar radiation in Figure A?** *(The clouds are reflecting the solar energy back into space.)* **How do the clouds during the day affect the temperature?** *(Because they reflect the solar radiation, less radiation reaches Earth, so the temperatures are lower.)* **What is happening in Figure B?** *(The clouds are absorbing radiation from land and reradiating some of it to Earth.)* **How do the clouds affect the temperature?** *(The clouds increase the temperature because they are re-radiating the radiation from the land, increasing the temperature.)* **Why do clouds during the day and night affect temperature differently?** *(They block the radiation in different ways. During the day, they block the sun's radiation, and during the night they block the radiation from land.)*
Visual, Logical

World Distribution of Temperature

Use Community Resources L2

Invite a climatologist from a local college to visit the classroom and discuss factors that affect climate and worldwide temperature patterns. Ask students to prepare questions for the climatologist in advance. Remind them to use *Who, What, Where, When, Why,* and *How* questions.
Interpersonal

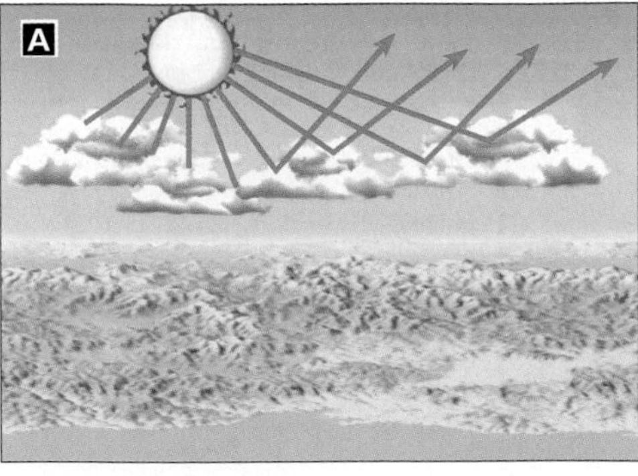

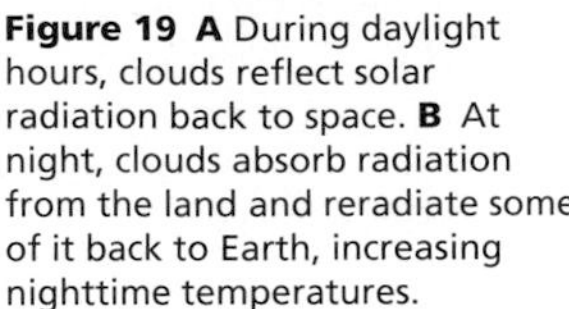

Figure 19 A During daylight hours, clouds reflect solar radiation back to space. **B** At night, clouds absorb radiation from the land and reradiate some of it back to Earth, increasing nighttime temperatures.

Cloud Cover and Albedo **Albedo** is the fraction of total radiation that is reflected by any surface. **Many clouds have a high albedo, and therefore reflect a significant portion of the sunlight that strikes them back to space.** The extent of cloud cover is a factor that influences temperatures in the lower atmosphere. By reducing the amount of incoming solar radiation, the maximum temperatures on a cloud-covered day will be lower than on a day when the clouds are absent and the sky is clear, as shown in Figure 19A.

At night, clouds have the opposite effect, as shown in Figure 19B. Clouds act as a blanket by absorbing outgoing radiation emitted by Earth and reradiating a portion of it back to the surface. Thus, cloudy nighttime air temperatures do not drop as low as they would on a clear night. The effect of cloud cover is to reduce the daily temperature range by lowering the daytime maximum and raising the nighttime minimum.

World Distribution of Temperature

Take a moment to study Figure 20, which is a world isothermal map. **Isotherms** are lines that connect points that have the same temperature. From hot colors near the equator to cool colors toward the poles, this map shows mean sea-level temperatures in the seasonally extreme month of July. All temperatures on this map have been reduced to sea level to eliminate complications caused by differences in altitude.

On this map, you can study global temperature patterns and the effects of the controlling factors of temperature, especially latitude, distribution of land and water, and ocean currents. The isotherms generally trend east and west and show a decrease in temperatures from the tropics toward the poles. This map emphasizes the importance of latitude as a control on incoming solar radiation, which in turn heats Earth's surface and the atmosphere above it.

Facts and Figures

The highest temperature ever recorded at Earth's surface is nearly 59°C. It was recorded on September 13, 1922, at Azizia, Libya, in North Africa's Sahara Desert. Not surprisingly, the lowest temperature was measured in Antarctica. It was –89°C. This temperature was recorded at the Russian Vostok Station on August 24, 1960. The greatest annual range of temperatures is in Siberia (eastern Russia). Temperatures in Verkhoyansk, Siberia have gone from −68°C to 37°C, a span of 105°C.

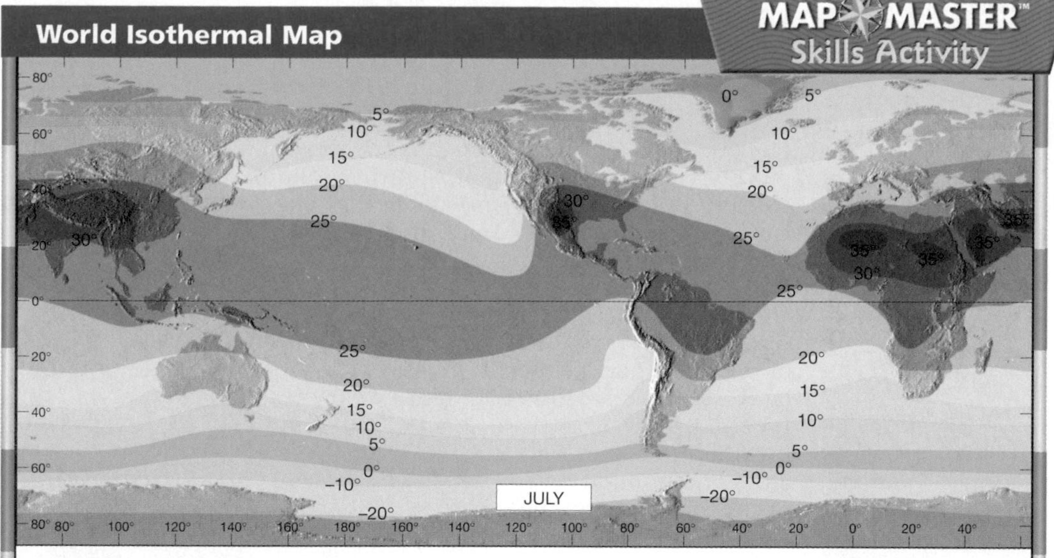

Figure 20

Regions The map shows the distribution of world mean sea-level temperatures averaged for the month of July.
Locating Estimate the latitude range for temperatures between 20 and 25 degrees Celsius in the Northern Hemisphere. Approximate to the nearest 5 degrees latitude for each extreme.
Predicting Do you expect the color of the temperature band to change near the equator for the month of January? Explain your prediction.

Section 17.3 Assessment

Reviewing Concepts

1. What is a temperature control?
2. How do the heating of land and water differ?
3. Why do many clouds reflect a significant amount of sunlight back to space?
4. Why do some coastal cities experience a moderation of temperature from water, while others do not?
5. List four specific controls of atmospheric temperature.

Critical Thinking

6. **Inferring** Look back at the graph in Figure 18. Why do the temperatures of these two cities stay within a limited range throughout the year?

Math Practice

7. Using the data in Table 1, determine the latitude that shows the greatest variation in average mean temperature between the Northern and Southern Hemispheres.

MAP MASTER™ Skills Activity

Answers
Locating The range is approximately 10°N latitude to 55°N latitude.
Predicting No; regions near the equator receive about the same amount of solar radiation all year long.

3 ASSESS

Evaluate Understanding

Ask students to describe and explain three factors that have a strong influence on temperature.

Reteach

Use Figure 19 to review how clouds affect surface temperatures during the day and night.

Solution
7. 60°

Section 17.3 Assessment

1. A temperature control is any factor that causes temperature to vary from place to place and from time to time.
2. Land heats and cools more rapidly and to greater temperature extremes than water does.
3. Clouds reflect a significant amount of sunlight back to space because of their high albedos.
4. Some coastal cities are influenced more strongly from prevailing ocean winds than others are.
5. Accept any of the following: latitude, altitude, geographic position, continental versus marine positions, ocean currents.
6. because they are both located near the equator and receive about the same amount of solar radiation all year long

1 FOCUS

Objectives

In this feature, students will be able to
- name the layers of Earth's atmosphere and the gases it contains.
- describe how the atmosphere supports human and plant life on Earth.
- explain how the atmosphere was formed and how the ozone layer is in danger of being destroyed.

Reading Focus

Build Vocabulary L2

Understand Terms Have students explain how the stratosphere differs from the troposphere. Then have them use the terms to write sentences.

2 INSTRUCT

Bellringer L1

Ask students what images come to mind when they think of Earth's atmosphere. Ask: **Do you usually think about the atmosphere as just containing the bottom layer where weather occurs?** *(Answers will vary.)* **Do you know what that layer is called?** *(troposphere)* **Do you know how many other layers there are?** *(three other layers)* **Logical**

Build Science Skills L2

Using a Chart Discuss the role of oxygen and carbon dioxide in Earth's atmosphere. Then have volunteers draw a cause-and-effect chart on the board to show the cycle of how gases are created and used by humans and plants. **Visual**

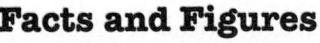

How the Earth Works

Earth's Atmosphere

The outermost part of the Earth is the atmosphere, a multilayered mixture of gases, water vapor, and tiny solid particles. It extends at least 600 miles (1,000 km) above the solid surface of the Earth, but about half the mass of these gases is in the lowest (5.6 kilometers). The atmosphere's gases support plant and animal life. They also protect the Earth from the sun's harmful rays. The layer of the atmosphere closest to land is the **troposphere.** It contains the air that we breathe. Here, temperature and humidity change rapidly, and the air is turbulent, creating weather patterns.

OXYGEN FROM PHOTOSYNTHESIS
Oxygen is a relative newcomer in the Earth's atmosphere. It has come from plants that, during **photosynthesis,** use carbon dioxide to make their food, while giving out oxygen. The earliest photosynthesizing plants, which probably looked like these algae, evolved about 3,500 million years ago.

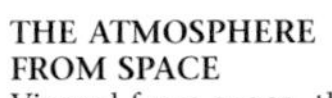

Viewed from space, the Earth looks totally unlike other planets of our solar system. It is partly shrouded in white clouds, which swirl in patterns, making weather. **Clouds** are masses of tiny particles of water and dust floating in the atmosphere. A very low cloud is called fog.

OXYGEN CYCLE
A vast store of oxygen exists in oceans, rocks, and the atmosphere. Oxygen created by plant photosynthesis balances oxygen used by people and animals.

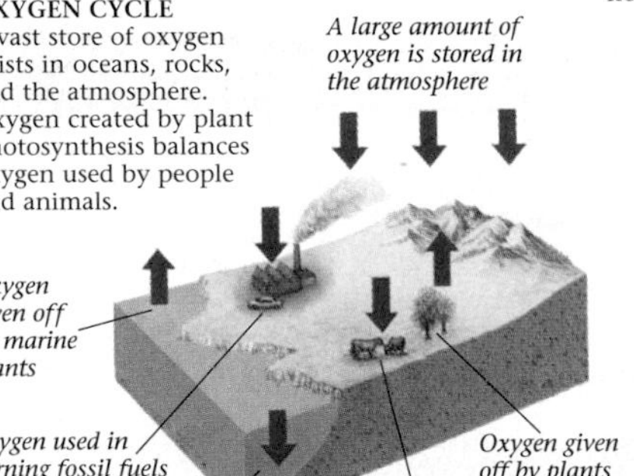

FERTILE LAND
The atmosphere helps life to flourish on the Earth. It offers protection from harmful radiations and provides nourishment for both plants and animals. Winds in the troposphere moderate daily and seasonal temperatures by distributing heat around the world.

494 *Chapter 17*

Facts and Figures

Although the entire troposphere contains oxygen, the amount of oxygen varies at different altitudes. The summit of Mount Everest is the highest point on Earth, measuring about 8.8 km high. At that level, oxygen levels are extremely low, which makes climbing Everest very dangerous. If climbers do not get enough oxygen, they become dizzy and disoriented. Today, climbing teams carry tanks of oxygen with them in their efforts to reach the summit.

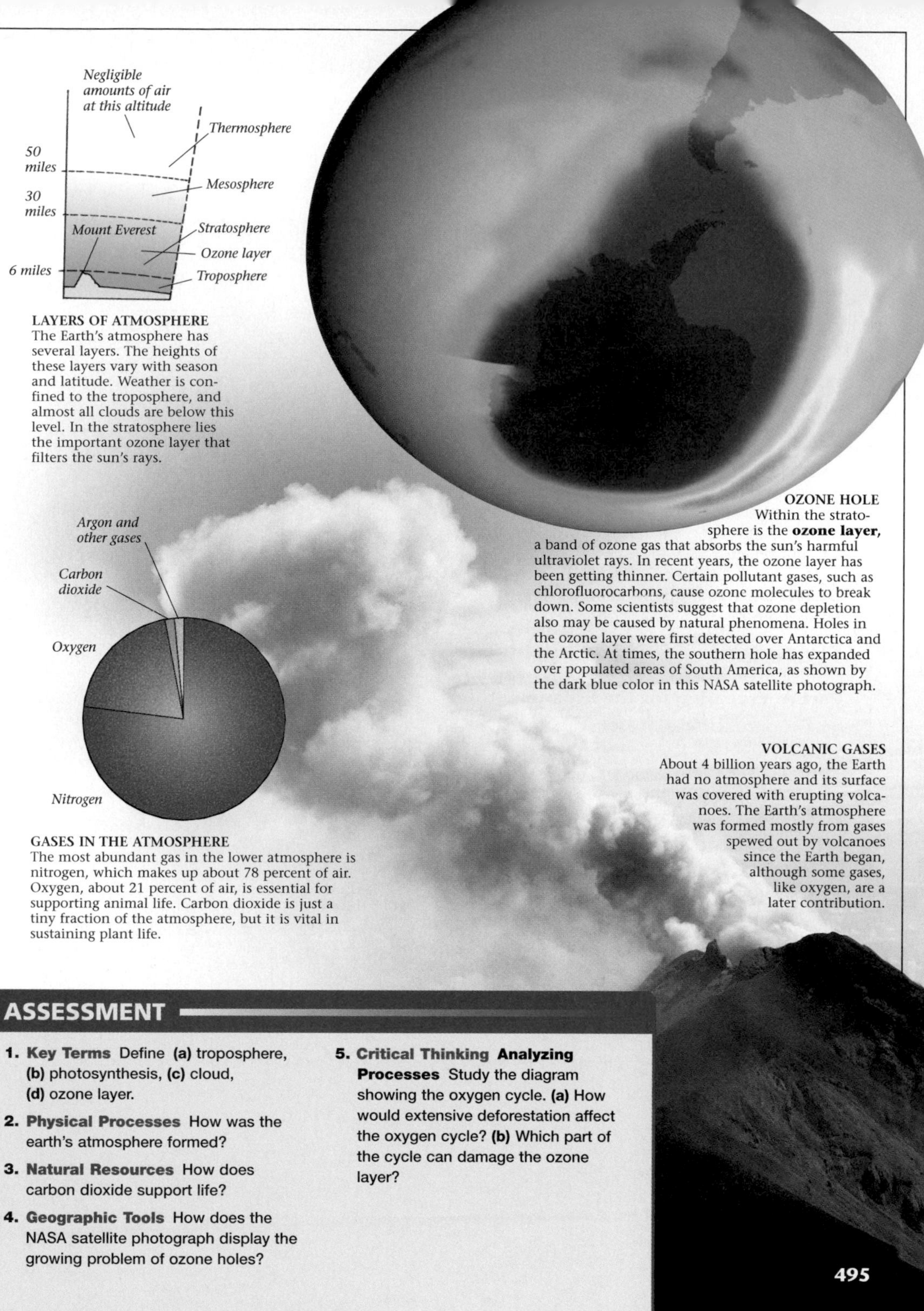

LAYERS OF ATMOSPHERE
The Earth's atmosphere has several layers. The heights of these layers vary with season and latitude. Weather is confined to the troposphere, and almost all clouds are below this level. In the stratosphere lies the important ozone layer that filters the sun's rays.

OZONE HOLE
Within the stratosphere is the **ozone layer,** a band of ozone gas that absorbs the sun's harmful ultraviolet rays. In recent years, the ozone layer has been getting thinner. Certain pollutant gases, such as chlorofluorocarbons, cause ozone molecules to break down. Some scientists suggest that ozone depletion also may be caused by natural phenomena. Holes in the ozone layer were first detected over Antarctica and the Arctic. At times, the southern hole has expanded over populated areas of South America, as shown by the dark blue color in this NASA satellite photograph.

GASES IN THE ATMOSPHERE
The most abundant gas in the lower atmosphere is nitrogen, which makes up about 78 percent of air. Oxygen, about 21 percent of air, is essential for supporting animal life. Carbon dioxide is just a tiny fraction of the atmosphere, but it is vital in sustaining plant life.

VOLCANIC GASES
About 4 billion years ago, the Earth had no atmosphere and its surface was covered with erupting volcanoes. The Earth's atmosphere was formed mostly from gases spewed out by volcanoes since the Earth began, although some gases, like oxygen, are a later contribution.

ASSESSMENT

1. **Key Terms** Define **(a)** troposphere, **(b)** photosynthesis, **(c)** cloud, **(d)** ozone layer.
2. **Physical Processes** How was the earth's atmosphere formed?
3. **Natural Resources** How does carbon dioxide support life?
4. **Geographic Tools** How does the NASA satellite photograph display the growing problem of ozone holes?
5. **Critical Thinking Analyzing Processes** Study the diagram showing the oxygen cycle. **(a)** How would extensive deforestation affect the oxygen cycle? **(b)** Which part of the cycle can damage the ozone layer?

495

Integrate Chemistry L2

Troposphere's Gases After students read the paragraph labeled Earth's Atmosphere, tell them that the troposphere includes the air they breathe. Have students brainstorm to create a list of gases that exist in the troposphere.
Logical

3 ASSESS

Evaluate Understanding L2

Have students examine the hole in the ozone layer shown on the next page. Have students predict some of the problems South America might be experiencing because of the hole.

Reteach L1

Refer students to the diagram of the layers of atmosphere. Have students summarize the feature's sections and main topics by describing them in terms of what layer they are associated with most. *(Accept all reasonable and accurate answers. Sample answers—Oxygen from Photosynthesis: Troposphere, since photosynthesis is a process in plants at the surface. The Atmosphere from Space: Troposphere, since most weather patterns and cloud masses that can be seen from space take shape here, due to rapid changes in temperature and humidity. Oxygen Cycle and Fertile Land: Troposphere, since these sections describe conditions and processes at the surface, such as photosynthesis and consuming fossil fuels. Gases in the Atmosphere: Troposphere, since about half of the mass of gases is in lowest 3.8 miles (5.6 km) of atmosphere. Ozone Hole: Stratosphere, since this zone is where ozone reactions occur. Volcanic Gases: Troposphere, since volcanoes erupt at Earth's surface.)*

Assessment

1. (a) layer of the atmosphere closest to land; **(b)** the process during which plants use carbon dioxide to make their food, while giving out oxygen; **(c)** a mass of tiny particles of water and dust floating in the atmosphere; **(d)** a band of ozone gas that absorbs the sun's harmful ultraviolet rays
2. It was formed mainly from gases spewed out by volcanoes. Some gases, such as oxygen, formed later.
3. Plants use carbon dioxide to complete the process of photosynthesis.
4. It uses color to show how the ozone hole over Antarctica has spread.
5. (a) It would reduce the number of oxygen-producing plants. **(b)** burning fossil fuels

Exploration Lab

Heating Land and Water L2

Objectives
In this activity, students will
- conduct an experiment investigating the differential heating of dry sand, water, and damp sand.
- measure temperature changes in these materials with time as they are exposed to radiation from a light source.
- interpret time/temperature data obtained from irradiating the materials with a light source.

Skills Focus Modeling, Observing, Measuring, Analyzing Data

 **Prep Time** 10 minutes

Alternative Materials pencils and tape (for suspending thermometers), beakers could be 200-mL

Advance Prep Copy and distribute the data table and graph sheet so students don't have to copy each themselves. Set up each beaker and mount thermometers to save classtime for students' observations and discussion of Analyze and Conclude questions.

Class Time 40 minutes

Teaching Tip Copying and handing out the sample graph in this lab will ensure that students will not write in their textbooks.

Expected Outcome Students will observe that dry sand, which represents land, heats up faster than water does. Damp sand does not heat up as fast as dry sand. Dry sand achieves a higher temperature when irradiated than damp sand and water do.

Exploration Lab

Heating Land and Water

In this lab you will model the difference in the heating of land and water when it is subjected to a source of radiation. You first will assemble simple tools. Then you will observe and record temperature data. Finally, you will explain the results of the experiment and how they relate to the moderating influence of water on air temperatures near Earth's surface.

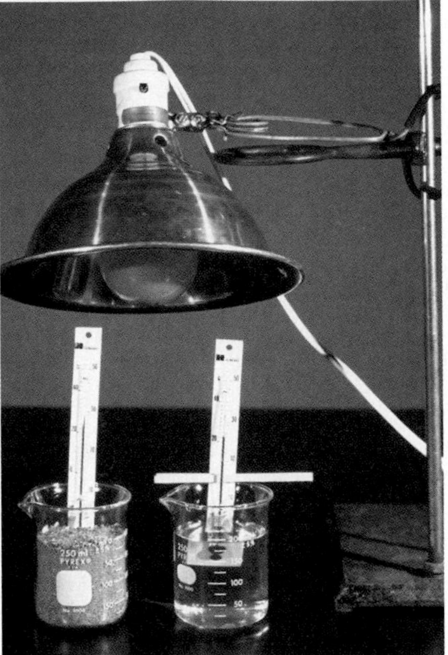

Problem How do the heating of land and water compare?

Materials
- 2 250-mL beakers
- dry sand
- tap water
- ring stand
- light source
- 2 flat wooden sticks
- 2 thermometers
- graph paper
- 3 colored pencils

Skills Modeling, Observing, Measuring, Analyzing Data

Procedure 

Part A: Preparing for the Experiment

1. On a separate sheet of paper, copy the data table shown.
2. Pour 200 mL of dry sand into one of the beakers. Pour 200 mL of water into the other beaker.

Land and Water Heating Data Table

	Starting Temperature	1 min	2 min	3 min	4 min	5 min	6 min	7 min	8 min	9 min	10 min
Water											
Dry sand											
Damp sand											

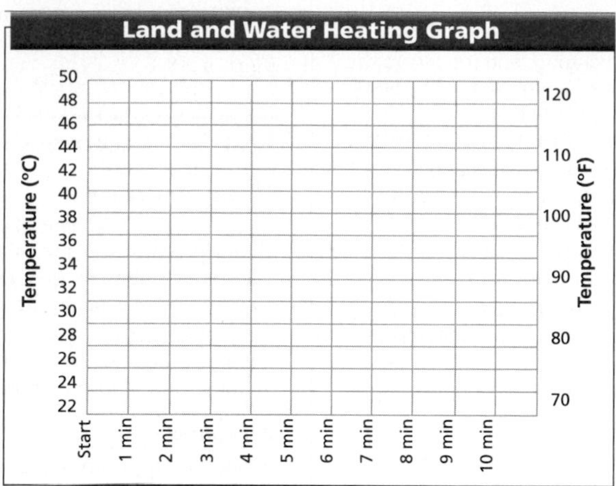

3. Hang a light source from a ring stand so that it is about 5 inches above the beaker of sand and the beaker of water. The light should be situated so that it is at the same height above both beakers.
4. Using the wooden sticks, suspend a thermometer in each beaker. The thermometer bulbs should be just barely below the surfaces of the sand and the water.
5. Record the starting temperatures for both the dry sand and the water in the data table.

Part B: Heating the Beakers

CAUTION *Do not touch the light source or the beakers without using thermal mitts.*

6. Turn on the light. Observe and record the temperatures in the data table at one-minute intervals for 10 minutes.
7. Turn off the light for several minutes. Dampen the sand with water and record the starting temperature for damp sand. Repeat step 6 for the damp sand.

Analyze and Conclude

1. **Using Tables and Graphs** Copy the sample land and water heating graph sheet onto a separate piece of graph paper. Use the data you collected to plot the temperatures for the water, dry sand, and damp sand. Use a different color line to connect the points for each material.
2. **Comparing and Contrasting** How does the changing temperature differ for dry sand and water when they are exposed to equal amounts of radiation?
3. **Comparing and Contrasting** How does the changing temperature differ for dry sand and damp sand when they are exposed to equal amounts of radiation?
4. **Applying** Locate Eureka, California, and Lafayette, Indiana, on a map. Infer which city would show the greatest annual temperature range. Explain your answer.

Analyze and Conclude

1. Student graphs should have three different-colored lines on them: one representing water, another representing dry sand, and the last line representing damp sand. The graphs should indicate that dry sand heats up faster and hotter than water and damp sand.
2. Dry sand heats up and gets hotter faster than water does.
3. Dry sand heats up faster and gets hotter faster than damp sand does.
4. Lafayette, Indiana, would show the greater annual temperature range because of its continental location.
Visual, Logical

Study Guide

Study Tip

Organize New Information
Tell students that learning detail-oriented information is easier when using strategies such as making outlines of a section, making charts of details, making graphic organizers, and making flashcards. Tell students that by using these techniques and reviewing them daily, they can avoid "cramming" for a test.

Thinking Visually

a. altitude changes
b. troposphere (or mesosphere)
c. mesosphere (or troposphere)

CHAPTER 17

Study Guide

17.1 Atmosphere Characteristics

Key Concepts

- Weather is constantly changing, and it refers to the state of the atmosphere at any given time or place. Climate is the sum of all statistical weather information that helps describe a place or region.
- Water vapor is the source of all clouds and precipitation. Like carbon dioxide, it absorbs heat given off by Earth as well as some solar energy.
- If ozone did not filter most UV radiation, Earth would be uninhabitable for many living organisms.
- The atmosphere thins as you travel away from Earth, until there are too few gas molecules to detect.
- The atmosphere can be divided vertically into four layers based on temperature.
- Seasonal changes occur because Earth's position relative to the sun continually changes as it travels along its orbit.

Vocabulary

ozone, *p. 478;* troposphere, *p. 480;* stratosphere, *p. 480;* mesosphere, *p. 480;* thermosphere, *p. 480;* summer solstice, *p. 482;* winter solstice, *p. 482;* autumnal equinox, *p. 482;* spring equinox, *p. 482*

17.2 Heating the Atmosphere

Key Concepts

- Heat is the transfer of energy between two objects resulting from differences in their temperatures. Temperature is a measure of the average kinetic energy of individual particles.
- Three mechanisms of heat transfer are conduction, convection, and radiation. Unlike conduction and convection, radiant energy can travel through the vacuum of space.
- All objects, at any temperature, emit radiant energy. Hotter objects radiate more total energy per unit area than colder objects do. The hottest radiating bodies produce the shortest wavelengths of maximum radiation. Objects that are good absorbers of radiation are good emitters as well.
- Objects can absorb, transmit, scatter, or reflect radiation that strikes them.

Vocabulary

heat, *p. 483;* temperature, *p. 483;* conduction, *p. 483;* convection, *p. 484;* radiation, *p. 485;* reflection, *p. 486;* scattering, *p. 486;* greenhouse effect, *p. 487*

17.3 Temperature Controls

Key Concepts

- Factors other than latitude that exert a strong influence on temperature include heating of land and water, altitude, geographic position, cloud cover, and ocean currents.
- Land heats more rapidly and to higher temperatures than water. Land also cools more rapidly and to lower temperatures than water.

Vocabulary

albedo, *p. 492;* isotherm, *p. 492*

Thinking Visually

Concept Map Copy the concept map below onto a sheet of paper. Use information from the chapter to complete the concept map.

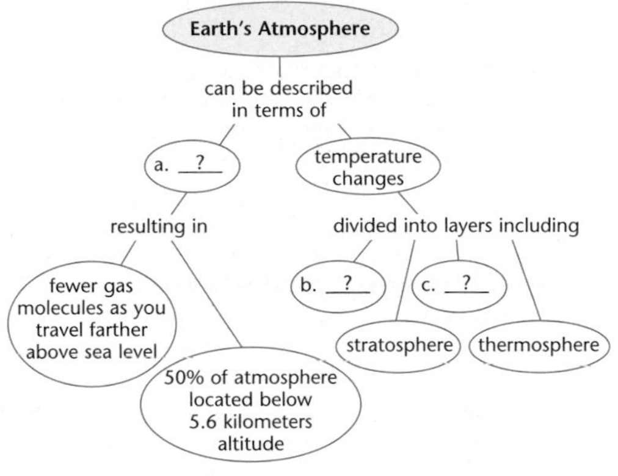

Chapter Assessment Resources

Print
Chapter Test, Chapter 17
Test Prep Resources, Chapter 17

Technology
Computer Test Bank, Chapter 17 Test
Online Text, Chapter 17
Go Online, PHSchool.com, Chapter 17

CHAPTER 17

NY Regents Content Item

Assessment

Interactive textbook with assessment at PHSchool.com

Reviewing Content

Choose the number that best answers the question or completes the statement.

1 What is a description of atmospheric conditions over a long period of time? NY
(1) climate (2) meteorology
(3) precipitation (4) weather

2 The bottom layer of the atmosphere in which we live is called the NY
(1) mesosphere (2) stratosphere
(3) thermosphere (4) troposphere

3 Which form of radiation has the longest wavelength? NY
(1) blue light (2) infrared
(3) radio waves (4) ultraviolet

4 This layer of atmosphere contains ozone that filters UV radiation. NY
(1) mesosphere (2) stratosphere
(3) thermosphere (4) troposphere

5 The average kinetic energy of all the atoms and molecules that make up a substance is referred to as NY
(1) radiation (2) greenhouse effect
(3) temperature (4) heat

6 The two principle absorbers of radiation emitted by Earth's surface are carbon dioxide and NY
(1) nitrogen (2) oxygen
(3) ozone (4) water vapor

7 On a map showing temperature distributions, what are the lines connecting points of equal temperature? NY
(1) isobars (2) isotemps
(3) isotherms (4) equigrads

8 Which gas is most abundant in clean, dry air? NY
(1) argon (2) carbon dioxide
(3) nitrogen (4) oxygen

9 Select the best description of air. NY
(1) It is a compound.
(2) It is an element.
(3) It is a mixture.
(4) It is mainly oxygen and carbon dioxide.

10 Earth's atmosphere is thought to have become enriched in which gas about 2.5 billion years ago? NY
(1) argon (2) carbon dioxide
(3) nitrogen (4) oxygen

Understanding Concepts

11 Why are temperature variations greater over dry land than they are over water? NY

12 Describe how the ozone in the stratosphere forms. NY

13 Describe the three types of heat transfer in the atmosphere. NY

14 In what ways can geographic position be considered a temperature control?

15 Describe the two principle motions of Earth. NY

16 Explain why Earth's atmosphere is mainly heated from the ground up. NY

17 Describe the effects of cloud cover on air temperature. NY

18 Why do temperatures increase in the stratosphere? NY

19 What causes the position of the noon sun to vary by up to 47 degrees over a year's time? NY

Use the figure below to answer question 20.

20 The illustration below shows two ways that radiation bounces off objects. Identify the process shown in each diagram. What clues in the illustration helped you identify these processes?

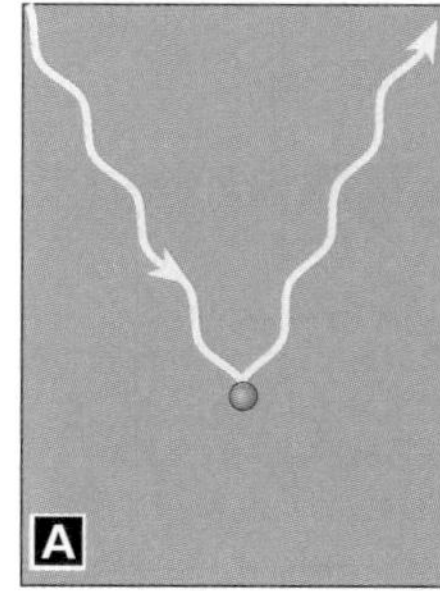

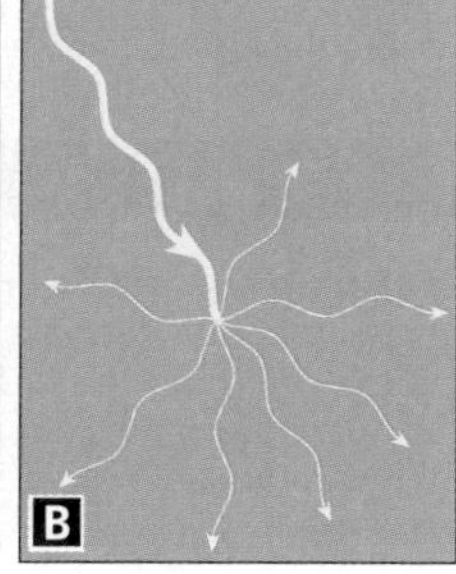

Homework Guide

Section	Questions
1	1–4, 8–10, 12, 15, 18, 19, 23, 24, 29
2	5, 6, 13, 16, 20, 30
3	7, 11, 14, 17, 21, 22, 25–28

Assessment

Reviewing Content

(1) 1 (2) 4 (3) 3
(4) 2 (5) 3 (6) 4
(7) 3 (8) 3 (9) 3
(10) 4

Understanding Concepts

(11) Dry land heats and cools faster and to greater temperature extremes than water does.
(12) In the stratosphere, UV radiation is absorbed by diatomic oxygen (O_2) molecules, causing some to split and produce monatomic (O) oxygen. In the presence of a catalyst, O and O_2 collide to form ozone (O_3).
(13) Air in direct contact with Earth's surface is heated by energy transfer as molecules collide with each other (conduction). Lower layers of atmosphere are warmed, become less dense and are forced upward, where they cool and sink (convection). Earth's surface receives radiation from the sun. Earth's surface, in turn, re-radiates longer-wavelength radiation that is absorbed by atmospheric gases (radiation).
(14) When a location is near a source of water, cut off from prevailing winds over water or in a continental interior location, it is a geographic position that also is a temperature control.
(15) Rotation: Earth spins about its axis; one rotation occurs every 24 hours. Revolution: Earth completes one elliptical orbit about the sun each year.
(16) Radiation emitted by Earth is absorbed by atmospheric gases, resulting in the atmosphere being heated from the ground up.
(17) During daylight, clouds reflect solar radiation back to space. At night, clouds slow the loss of heat. The net effect of these processes is that the daily temperature range is reduced.
(18) Ozone is concentrated in this layer. Ozone molecules absorb UV radiation from the sun and heat up.
(19) The variation is caused by a combination of Earth's 23 1/2 degree axis tilt and its annual revolution around the sun.
(20) Diagram A is reflection and diagram B is scattering. Diagram A: The incoming ray and the reflected ray encounter and bounce off the object at the same angle, and the thicknesses of both rays are the same, indicating the same intensity for both. Diagram B: The thicknesses of the rays bouncing off are less than the incident ray and the rays are bouncing off in different directions.

Chapter 17

Critical Thinking

(21) Snow, clouds, white sand, and light-colored soil have high albedos compared to other surfaces.
(22) September 22–23 (autumnal equinox): From September to December, the Earth is tilted so that the Southern Hemisphere receives more sunlight.
(23) The altitude of the noon sun and length of day would remain the same at each latitude throughout the year and no seasonal variations would occur.

Math Skills

(24) The temperature would decrease by 13°C (6.5°C/km × 2 km = 13°C). The air temperature would be 23°C − 13°C = 10°C.

Concepts in Action

(25) Yakutsk is located at a high latitude and in the center of a large landmass, far from any marine influence.
(26) Less ocean area would lead to much larger temperature extremes on Earth. Many organisms that exist on Earth today might not be able to survive such extremes.
(27) Water vapor is the source of all clouds and precipitation. Both water vapor and carbon dioxide are efficient absorbers of heat in the troposphere. Without these gases most life forms on Earth could not exist.
(28) The higher the temperature of a radiating body, the shorter the wavelengths of the radiation that it emits.
(29) In regions where isotherms are closely spaced, the temperature changes more rapidly over a given distance on Earth's surface.
(30) Student paragraphs should include environments that have good reflecting surfaces, such as clouds, snow, light-colored soil, and water.

CHAPTER 17

Assessment *continued*

Critical Thinking

Use the table below to answer questions 21 and 22.

Albedo of Various Surfaces

Surface	Percent Reflected
Clouds, stratus	
<meters thick	25–63
150–300 meters thick	45–75
300–600 meters thick	59–84
Average of all types and thicknesses	50–55
Concrete	17–27
Crops, green	5–25
Forest, green	5–10
Meadows, green	5–25
Ploughed field, moist	14–17
Road, blacktop	5–10
Sand, white	30–60
Snow, fresh-fallen	80–90
Snow, old	45–70
Soil, dark	5–15
Soil, light (or desert)	25–30
Water	8*

*Typical albedo value for a water surface. The albedo of a water surface varies greatly depending upon the sun angle.

21 **Analyzing Data** Using the data in the table, determine which types of surfaces have the highest average albedos. NY

22 **Applying Concepts** Determine the date after which the length of daylight gets progressively longer going south from the equator. Use Figure 8 to explain your answer.

23 **Inferring** Give an example of how the Earth system might be affected if Earth's axis were perpendicular to the plane of its orbit instead of being tilted 23.5 degrees. NY

Math Skills

24 **Calculating** Assume that the average rate of temperature decrease in the troposphere is 6.5°C/km. Using this rate, determine the air temperature at a height of 2 kilometers if the temperature at sea level were 23°C.

Concepts in Action

25 **Inferring** Yakutsk is located in Siberia at about 60 degrees north latitude. This Russian city has one of the highest average annual temperature ranges in the world: 62.2°C. Explain the reasons for the very high annual temperature range.

26 **Making Generalizations** Speculate on the changes in global temperatures that might occur if Earth had substantially more land area and less ocean area than it does at present. How might such changes influence the biosphere? NY

27 **Applying Concepts** Why are carbon dioxide and water vapor such important components in Earth's atmosphere? What would happen to life forms on Earth if these gases were no longer present in the atmosphere? NY

28 **Generalizing** State the relationship between the temperature of a radiating body and the wavelengths of radiation that it emits.

29 **Interpreting Illustrations** Refer to Figure 20. What can you determine about temperatures in regions where isotherms are closely spaced, compared with regions where isotherms are farther apart? NY

30 **Writing in Science** Write a paragraph that describes two environmental settings where you would expect the albedo of surfaces to be high. Your scenarios can describe any reasonable area on Earth's surface. Be sure to include as much detail as possible in your paragraph.

Performance-Based Assessment

Designing an Experiment Design and conduct an experiment that models how variations in color of an object can affect the amount of radiation it absorbs. As a first step, write a clear hypothesis statement. Then plan the materials you will need to design the experiment. Have your teacher approve your plan before you begin.

Regents Practice Exam

Test-Taking Tip

Sometimes all the response choices to a test question look similar. For example, they might have the same prefix or suffix. When all of the answer choices are similar, try answering the question BEFORE looking at the answers. Once you have answered the test item yourself, then look for the answer choice that agrees with your answer. Look for words that are correct words, but do not belong with the others.

The transfer of heat through matter by molecular activity occurs in
(1) convection
(2) conduction
(3) radiation
(4) reflection

(Answer: 2)

For *each* statement or question, choose the *number* of the word or expression that, of those given, best completes the statement or answers the question. Some questions may require the use of the *Earth Science Reference Tables.*

1 What is the most abundant gas in Earth's atmosphere?
(1) oxygen (2) argon
(3) water vapor (4) nitrogen

2 Which layer of the Earth's atmosphere experiences the highest temperatures?
(1) troposphere (2) mesosphere
(3) thermosphere (4) stratosphere

3 The primary wavelengths of radiation emitted by Earth's surface are
(1) longer than those emitted by the sun
(2) shorter than those emitted by the sun
(3) about the same as those emitted by the sun
(4) about the same as UV radiation

4 Which of the following statements is the best example of heat transfer by convection as a pot of water is heated over an open flame? Heat is transferred from
(1) the flame to the bottom of the pot
(2) the bottom of the water to the top of the water
(3) the pot's handle to your hand
(4) the hot water to a metal spoon used for stirring

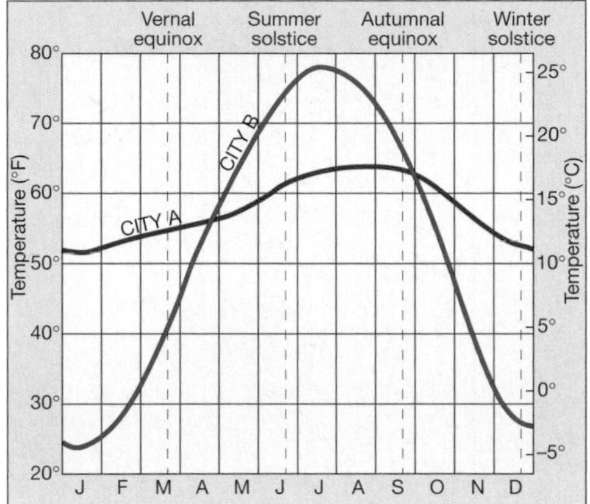

Answer the following questions in complete sentences. Some questions may require the use of the *Earth Science Reference Tables.* Base your answers to questions 5 and 6 on the diagram above, which shows Monthly Mean Temperatures for City *A* and City *B.*

5 Determine the difference in December mean temperatures for cities *A* and *B*. Express your answer to the nearest degree Celsius. Explain one possible reason why city *B* experiences a much greater temperature range than city *A*.

6 Determine the hemisphere in which city *A* and city *B* are located. Explain your answer using the information given in the graph.

7 Explain why temperature ranges in coastal and inland locations differ.

Regents Practice Exam

(1) 4
(2) 3
(3) 1
(4) 2
(5) The difference is approximately 14 C. City *A* is probably located in a coastal and/or equatorial area, while city *B* is most likely inland and/or at a higher latitude.
(6) Both cities are located in the Northern Hemisphere because their maximum temperatures occur during June, July, and August, which are summer months in the northern hemisphere.
(7) Since water heats and cools slower than land, coastal areas that experience onshore flow due to prevailing winds tend to have smaller temperature ranges than inland locations. Cities near a large body of water often experience cooler summers and warmer winters as onshore winds moderate their temperatures.

Performance-Based Assessment

Experimental designs will vary. Students should be careful to control all dependent variables other than the one they are testing (color of object).

Your students can independently test their knowledge of the chapter and print out their results.

The Atmosphere: Structure and Temperature 501

CHAPTER 18

Planning Guide

Use these planning tools
Use Teacher Express for all your planning needs

SECTION OBJECTIVES	STANDARDS NATIONAL	STANDARDS STATE	ACTIVITIES and LABS
18.1 Water in the Atmosphere, pp. 504–509 1 block or 2 periods **18.1** **Identify** the gas that is most important for understanding atmospheric processes. **18.2** **Describe** what happens during a change of state. **18.3** **Compare and contrast** the abilities of cold air and warm air to hold water vapor. **18.4** **Define** relative humidity. **18.5** **Describe** the factors that affect the relative humidity of air.	A-1, B-2, B-5, D-2		**SE** Inquiry Activity: What Causes Condensation? p. 503 L2 **TE** Teacher Demo: Water From Plants, p. 507 L2 **TE** Build Science Skills, p. 508 L2 **SE** Exploration Lab: Measuring Humidity, pp. 524–525 L2
18.2 Cloud Formation, pp. 510–516 1 block or 2 periods **18.6** **Describe** what happens to air when it is compressed or allowed to expand. **18.7** **List** four mechanisms that cause air to rise. **18.8** **Compare and contrast** movements of stable and unstable air. **18.9** **Describe** the conditions in air that favor condensation of water.	B-5, D-1		**TE** Teacher Demo: Compression and Expansion, p. 511 L2 **TE** Build Science Skills, p. 514 L2 **TE** Teacher Demo: Making a Cloud, p. 515 L2 **LM** Recipe for a Cloud L2
18.3 Cloud Types and Precipitation, pp. 517–522 1 block or 2 periods **18.10** **Describe** how clouds are classified. **18.11** **Compare and contrast** clouds and fogs. **18.12** **Explain** what must happen for precipitation to form. **18.13** **Identify** what controls the type of precipitation that reaches Earth's surface.	A-1, A-2, B-2, D-1		**TE** Build Science Skills, p. 519 L2 **TE** Teacher Demo: Making Hail, p. 522 L2

Ability Levels

L1 For students who need additional help
L2 For all students
L3 For students who need to be challenged

Components

SE Student Edition	**GRSW** Guided Reading & Study Workbook	**TP** Test Prep Resources	**GEO** Geode CD-ROM
TE Teacher's Edition	**TEX** Teacher Express	**onT** onlineText	**T** Transparencies
LM Laboratory Manual	**CTB** Computer Test Bank	**DC** Discovery Channel Videos	**GO** Internet Resources
CUT Chapter Tests			

RESOURCES PRINT and TECHNOLOGY	SECTION ASSESSMENT
GRSW Section 18.1 **T-243** Changes of State **T-245** Changing Relative Humidity by Changing Specific Humidity **T-246** Changing Relative Humidity by Changing Temperature **T-247** Variations in Temperature and Humidity in Washington, D.C. **T-248** Relative Humidity of Ice When Relative Humidity of Water is 100% **T-377** Relative Humidity (Percent) **T-378** Dew Point Temperature **DC** Rain **TEX** Lesson Planning 18.1	**SE** Section 18.1 Assessment, p. 509 **onT** Section 18.1
GRSW Section 18.2 **T-244** Cloud Types and Characteristics **T-250** Adiabatic Rate **T-251** Four Processes that Lift Air **T-252** Stable Atmosphere and Adiabatic Rate **T-253** Absolute Stability **T-254** Absolute Instability **T-255** Conditional Instability **T-256** Classification of Clouds **T-257** Comparative Diameters 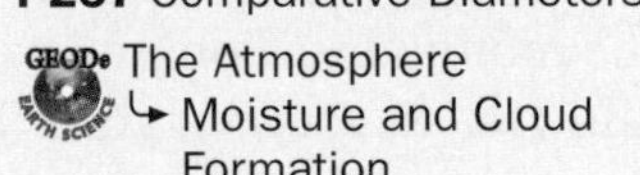 The Atmosphere → Moisture and Cloud Formation **TEX** Lesson Planning 18.2	**SE** Section 18.2 Assessment, p. 516 **onT** Section 18.2
GRSW Section 18.3 **T-249** Forms of Precipitation **T-258** The Bergeron Process **T-259** The Collision-Coalescence Process **T-260** Precipitation Measurement **T-261** Weather Radar Display **T-262** Temperature Profile for a Surface Inversion **T-263** Inversion Conditions **T-264** Distribution of Fog **TEX** Lesson Planning 18.3	**SE** Section 18.3 Assessment, p. 522 **onT** Section 18.3

Go Online

Go online for these Internet resources.

PHSchool.com
Web Code: cjk-9999

Web Code: cjn-6181
Web Code: cjn-6183
Web Code: cjn-6184

Materials for Activities and Labs

Quantities for each group

STUDENT EDITION

Inquiry Activity, p. 503
250-mL beaker, tap water, ice, thermometer

Exploration Lab, pp. 524–525
calculator, water at room temperature, psychrometer (alternative materials for psychrometer: 2 thermometers, cotton gauze, paper fan, string)

TEACHER'S EDITION

Teacher Demo, p. 507
small potted house plant, clear plastic bag

Build Science Skills, p. 508
long human hair, tape, ring stand or other support, small washer or button, toothpick, index card, small cardboard box

Teacher Demo, p. 511
bicycle tire, bicycle pump, can of compressed air duster

Build Science Skills, p. 514
helium balloon, hot water, cold water, thermometer, meter stick, stopwatch or clock with second hand, other materials of the students' choosing

Teacher Demo, p. 515
valve stem from a car or bicycle, 2-hole rubber stopper, glass tubing, rubber tubing, hose clamp, warm water, Erlenmeyer flask, match, bicycle pump, sheet of black paper, flashlight

Build Science Skills, p. 519
log book

Teacher Demo, p. 522
salt, water, 600-mL beaker, stirring rod, large test tube, ice chip

Chapter Assessment

ASSESSMENT

SE Assessment, pp. 527–528
CUT Chapter 18 Test
CTB Chapter 18
onT Chapter 18

STANDARDIZED TEST PREP

SE Chapter 18, p. 529
TP Progress Monitoring Assessments

interactive textbook with assessment at PHSchool.com

CHAPTER 18

Before you teach

Michael Wysession
Washington University

Big Ideas

Water plays a dominant role in atmospheric processes, even though it is a tiny component of it. This is partly due to water's unique ability to exist in three states—solid, liquid, and vapor—at Earth's surface. Clouds form from the condensation of water vapor.

Space and Time In the troposphere, there are three main types of clouds: cirrus, cumulus, and stratus. However, the forms that these clouds take also depend upon whether they are at high, middle, or low altitudes within the troposphere. Clouds at Earth's surface are known as fog.

Forces and Motion Water vapor condenses when it gets cold, and temperature gets higher with altitude, so clouds form when moist air is lifted. Air gets lifted by several different mechanisms including orographic lifting (over mountains), frontal wedging, convergence, and localized convective lifting (due to regional warming). Stable air masses, such as those that occur with temperature inversions, resist lifting, so clouds don't form.

Matter and Energy There are two ways to describe humidity, or the amount of water vapor in the atmosphere. One description is the relative humidity, which is the amount of water vapor in air compared to the maximum amount of water vapor that could occur in the air at the current temperature and pressure. The other is the dew point, which is the temperature at which the water vapor of a given parcel of air would begin to condense.

Earth as a System Precipitation, in the form of rain, snow, sleet, glaze, and hail, occurs when cloud droplets become too large to stay suspended in air. Precipitation forms the basis of the erosion of continental surfaces.

Earth Science Refresher

Temperature Inversions and Smog in Los Angeles

When people think of urban smog, Los Angeles often comes to mind. However, it turns out that the smog in Los Angeles is variable depending upon the time of year. Smog tends to be much worse in summer than in winter. The reason for this has to do with the effect of temperature inversions on convection.

During the winter time, the average temperature in Los Angeles is about 12°C. Bordering Los Angeles on the east are the San Gabriel Mountains, and on the other side of these mountains there is a plateau that includes the Mojave Desert. While we usually think of deserts as being hot places, this is not true in the winter if they are at high elevation and far from water. While the low elevation and proximity of the Pacific Ocean keep Los Angeles warm in winter, this is not the case for the desert plateau, where temperatures drop to about 7°C in the winter. The result is that it is hard for smog to stay over Los Angeles for extended periods of time. The warm Los Angeles air rises, and is replaced by cold air from the desert that comes down over the mountains. Convection is allowed to occur, and the smog gets swept away.

Students may have many misconceptions about what clouds are made of and how they form. They may think that clouds are made of smoke or water vapor. They may think that clouds form when bodies of water boil. For a strategy that helps to overcome these misconceptions, see **Address Misconceptions** on **p. 517**.

Go Online NSTA PDLinks

For: Chapter 18 Content Support
Visit: www.SciLinks.org/PDLinks
Web Code: cjn-1899

This is not what usually happens during the summer, however. During summer months, the average temperature in Los Angeles is about 24°C, but the temperature up in the desert is even warmer—about 29°C. Instead of being 5° colder, it is now 5°warmer. That means that the warm, smog-filled air in Los Angeles has nowhere to go, because the air over the mountains is even warmer. If air comes over the mountains from the desert, it is even warmer than the city air, so it rests on top of it. This is called a temperature inversion. Cold, heavy air rests below warm, more buoyant air, so there is no convection. Ironically, temperature inversions in many parts of the world are often associated with clear, cloud-free skies at night, when the ground cools efficiently, but radiates energy that heats the atmosphere. This is not the case for Los Angeles, where summertime smog can get trapped against the mountains for extended periods of time.

Address Misconceptions

Students may think that condensation occurs when air turns into a liquid. In fact, condensation consists of water droplets, and water vapor is only a small part of air. The remaining components of air remain as gases. For a strategy that helps to overcome these misconceptions, see **Address Misconceptions** on **p. 506.**

Build Reading Literacy

Visualize

Forming Mental Pictures

Strategy Help students understand and recall complex text by forming mental pictures as they read. In some cases, visual elements of the text can aid students in visualizing; in other cases students must rely solely on text descriptions. Choose several paragraphs from Chapter 18, such as the four on pp. 512–513. If possible, include at least one paragraph that has an accompanying figure and at least one other paragraph that refers to concepts or events that are not illustrated in visual elements, such as diagrams, charts, graphs, or photographs.

Example

1. Have students keep their books closed. Tell them to listen while you read and visualize, or form mental pictures of, each object or action you read about.

2. Then, read a paragraph or so aloud, pausing frequently to demonstrate, by thinking aloud, how to visualize each thing described. When reading complex or technical text, pausing after reading each phrase will often be appropriate.

3. Tell students to continue visualizing. Slowly and clearly, read on. Then, select a logical stopping point and discuss with students the images they visualized.

4. If there is an accompanying figure, have students open to it and see how it compares with their visualizing. Point out that visuals in the text help readers picture what they are reading.

5. Have students work with partners to practice by taking turns reading and visualizing aloud. Tell them to expand on visuals that appear in the text and to describe their own mental images of ideas or events that are not shown in visuals.

See p. 507 for a script on how to use this strategy with students. For additional strategies, see pp. 512 and 518.

ASSESS PRIOR KNOWLEDGE

Use the Chapter Pretest below to assess students' prior knowledge. As needed, review these concepts.

Review Science Concepts

Section 18.1 Review the different states of matter and transitions among them.

Section 18.2 Review how air behaves when it is compressed and when it expands.

Section 18.3 Review the basic types of clouds and precipitation.

Review Math Skills

Data Tables Review with students how data tables are organized and how units of measurement are shown. Direct students to the Math Skills in the Skills Handbook at the end of the student text.

CHAPTER 18 Moisture, Clouds, and Precipitation

CONCEPTS in Action

Exploration Lab
Measuring Humidity

People and the Environment
Atmospheric Stability and Air Pollution

The Atmosphere
↳ Moisture and Cloud Formation

Video Field Trip
Rain

Take a rainy-day field trip with Discovery Channel and learn how precipitation forms. Answer the following questions after watching the video.

1. Why do cold fronts cause the heaviest rains?
2. The top of the Grand Canyon gets twenty times as much rain as the bottom. Why?

Go Online PHSchool.com
For: Chapter 18 Resources
Visit: PHSchool.com
Web Code: cjk-9999

Towering cumulonimbus cloud develops over San Carlos, Mexico. ▶

Chapter Pretest

1. What are the three states of matter? *(b)*
   a. gas, liquid, and vapor
   b. gas, liquid, and solid
   c. vapor, liquid, and solid
   d. gas, vapor, and solid

2. True or False: Heat is released when water evaporates. *(False)*

3. What is the change from a gas to a liquid state called? *(condensation)*

4. What will happen if air is heated by the ground below it? *(The air will rise.)*

5. On what basis are clouds classified? *(c)*
   a. form and thickness
   b. color and height
   c. form and height
   d. form and precipitation

6. True or False: Small particles of ice are called sleet. *(True)*

Chapter Preview

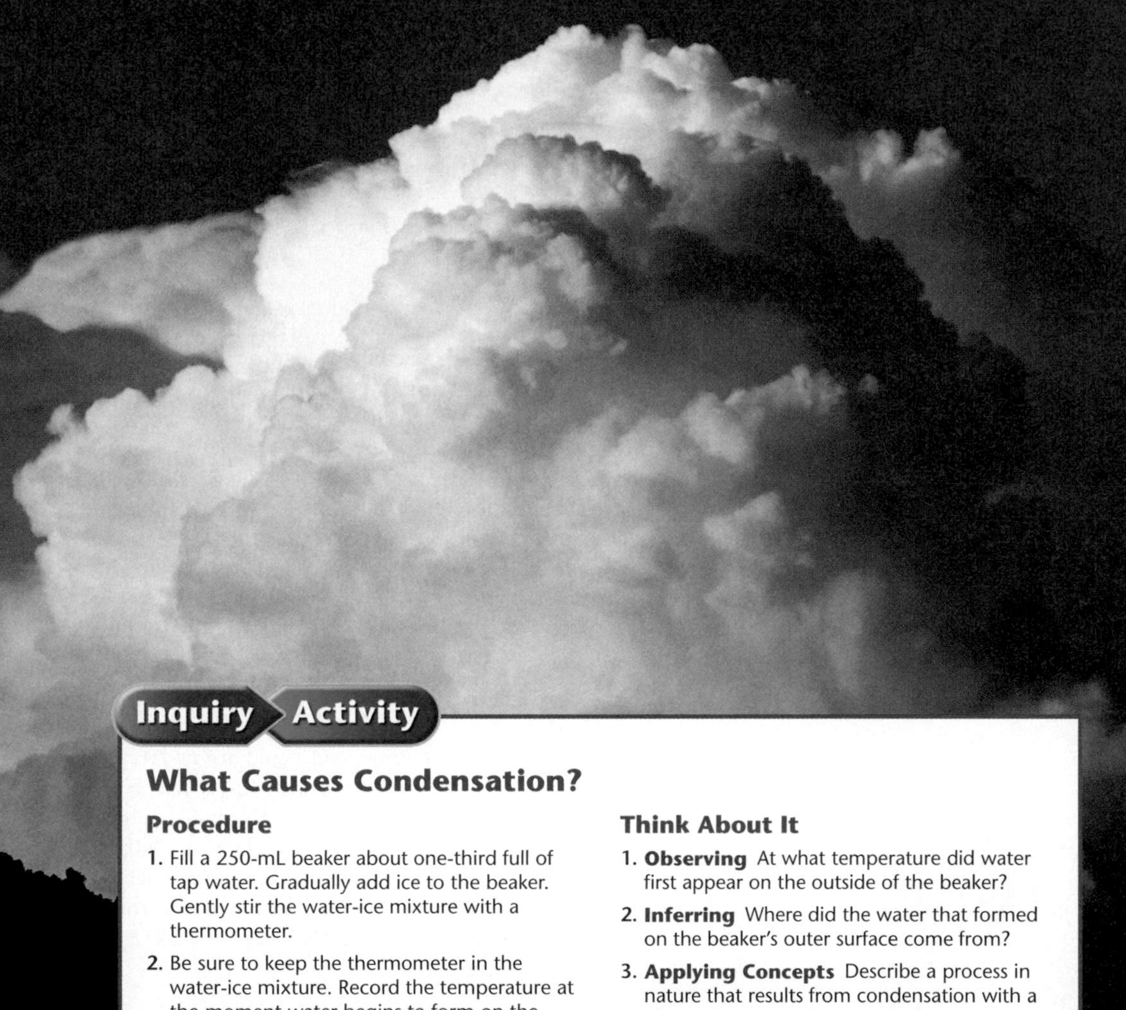

Inquiry Activity

What Causes Condensation?

Procedure

1. Fill a 250-mL beaker about one-third full of tap water. Gradually add ice to the beaker. Gently stir the water-ice mixture with a thermometer.
2. Be sure to keep the thermometer in the water-ice mixture. Record the temperature at the moment water begins to form on the outside surface of the beaker.

Think About It

1. **Observing** At what temperature did water first appear on the outside of the beaker?
2. **Inferring** Where did the water that formed on the beaker's outer surface come from?
3. **Applying Concepts** Describe a process in nature that results from condensation with a change in temperature.

ENGAGE/EXPLORE

What Causes Condensation?

L2

Purpose In this activity, students think about the cause of condensation.

Skills Focus **Observing, Inferring**

Prep Time 5 minutes

Materials 250-mL beaker, tap water, ice, thermometer

Class Time 10 minutes

Safety Remind students to handle glass thermometers carefully.

Expected Outcome Condensation forms on the outside of the beaker.

Think About It

1. Temperatures should agree with dew-point temperature of air where the experiment is carried out. Students could check online meteorological resources for local dew-point temperatures for the day of the experiment. They also could measure the dew point if a psychrometer is available or can be constructed. Determinative tables for dew-point temperature also would be needed. See the Laboratory Manual for a dew-point table.

2. The water came from water vapor in the air.

3. Processes include dew, fog, or cloud formation.

Discovery Channel School

Video Field Trip

Rain

Encourage students to view the Video Field Trip "Rain."

Section 18.1

1 FOCUS

Section Objectives

18.1 **Identify** the gas that is most important for understanding atmospheric processes.
18.2 **Describe** what happens during a change of state.
18.3 **Compare and contrast** the abilities of cold air and warm air to hold water vapor.
18.4 **Define** relative humidity.
18.5 **Describe** the factors that affect the relative humidity of air.

Reading Focus

Build Vocabulary L2

Word Forms Point out that the words *evaporation*, *vapor*, and *vaporization* are related. Water vapor is a gas. The words *evaporation* and *vaporization* both contain the word *vapor*, and both essentially mean the same thing: the process by which a liquid changes into a gas, or vapor.

Reading Strategy L2

Sample answers:
a. Water is important for cloud formation.
b. how clouds form
c. Clouds form when air rises, expands, and cools to the dew point.
d. Water is important for precipitation.
e. how precipitation forms
f. Precipitation forms by Bergeron or collision-coalescence processes.

18.1 Water in the Atmosphere

Reading Focus

Key Concepts

- Which gas is most important for understanding atmospheric processes?
- What happens during a change of state?
- How do warm and cold air compare in their ability to hold water vapor?
- What is relative humidity?
- What can change the relative humidity of air?

Vocabulary

- precipitation
- latent heat
- evaporation
- condensation
- sublimation
- deposition
- humidity
- saturated
- relative humidity
- dew point
- hygrometer

Reading Strategy

Monitoring Your Understanding Before you read, copy the table. List what you know about water in the atmosphere and what you would like to learn. After you read, list what you have learned.

What I Know	What I Would Like to Learn	What I Have Learned
a. ?	b. ?	c. ?
d. ?	e. ?	f. ?

As you observe day-to-day weather changes, you can see the powerful role of water in the air. Water vapor is the source of all condensation and **precipitation,** which is any form of water that falls from a cloud. Look at Figure 1. Clouds and fog, as well as rain, snow, sleet, and hail, are examples of some of the more noticeable weather conditions. **When it comes to understanding atmospheric processes, water vapor is the most important gas in the atmosphere.** Water vapor makes up only a small fraction of the gases in the atmosphere, varying from nearly 0 to about 4 percent by volume. But the importance of water in the air greatly exceeds what these small percentages would indicate.

Figure 1 This downpour shows how precipitation can affect daily activities.

Water's Changes of State

The three states of matter are solid, liquid, and gas. Water can change from one state of matter to another—at temperatures and pressures experienced on Earth. This unique property allows water to freely leave the oceans as a gas and return again as a liquid, producing the water cycle. All water in the cycle must pass through the atmosphere as water vapor, even though the atmosphere only holds enough to make a global layer about 2 mm deep.

What is the range in volume percent of water in the atmosphere?

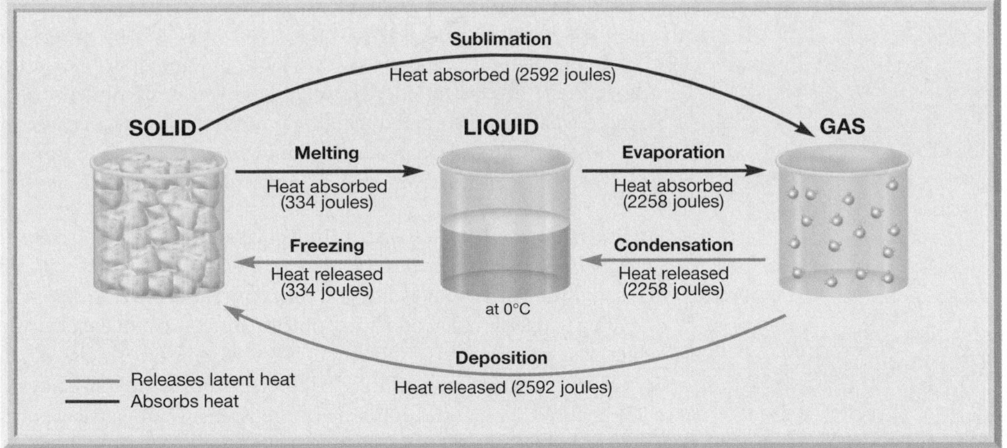

Figure 2 Changes of State The heat energy, in joules, is indicated for 1 gram of water.

Solid to Liquid **The process of changing state requires that energy is transferred in the form of heat.** When heat is transferred to a glass of ice water, the temperature of the ice water remains a constant 0°C until all the ice has melted. If adding heat does not raise the temperature, then where does this energy go? In this case, the added heat breaks apart the crystal structure of the ice cubes. The bonds between water molecules in the ice crystals are broken forming the noncrystalline substance liquid water. You know this process as melting.

The heat used to melt ice does not produce a temperature change, so it is referred to as **latent heat.** *Latent* means "hidden," like the latent fingerprints hidden at a crime scene. This energy, measured in joules or calories, becomes stored in the liquid water and is not released as heat until the liquid returns to the solid state.

Latent heat plays a crucial role in many atmospheric processes. For example, the release of latent heat aids in forming the towering clouds often seen on warm summer days. It is the major source of energy for thunderstorms, tornadoes, and hurricanes.

Liquid to Gas The process of changing a liquid to a gas is called **evaporation.** You see in Figure 2 that it takes approximately 2258 joules of energy to convert 1 gram of liquid water to water vapor. The energy absorbed by the water molecules during evaporation gives them the motion needed to escape the surface of the liquid and become a gas. This energy is referred to as latent heat of vaporization.

You might have experienced a cooling effect when stepping dripping wet from a swimming pool or bathtub. This cooling results because it takes considerable energy to evaporate water. In this situation, the energy comes from your skin—hence the expression that "evaporation is a cooling process."

Customize for English Language Learners

Use a Cloze strategy for students with very limited English proficiency. Have students fill in the blanks in the following sentences while reading Water's Changes of State. **The three states of matter are ________, liquid, and ________. Changing state requires that ________ be absorbed or ________. The heat used to melt ice is ________ heat. The process of changing from liquid to gas is ________. The change from water vapor to liquid is ________. The conversion of a solid directly to a gas is ________.** *(gas, solid, energy, released, latent, evaporation, condensation, sublimation)*

2 INSTRUCT

Water's Changes of State

Integrate Biology L2

The Water Cycle Tell students that the water cycle is essential to life on land. Water evaporates from the oceans and from the leaves of plants. Some of the water vapor condenses and falls as precipitation over land. As the precipitation runs over the land back to the oceans, it is drunk by animals and absorbed by plants through their roots. Ask: **What would happen if water evaporated and condensed at temperatures not found on Earth's surface?** *(The water cycle would not exist.)* **What effect would this have on life on Earth?** *(Life would not be able to survive on land.)*
Logical

Use Visuals L1

Figure 2 Review the meaning of joules with students. Use this diagram to explain how water changes from one state to another. Ask: **Which processes absorb heat?** *(melting, evaporation, and sublimation)* **Which processes release heat?** *(freezing, condensation, and deposition)* **Give an everyday example of one of the processes shown.** *(Sample answers include ice cubes freezing in a freezer and water boiling in a pot on the stove.)*
Visual, Logical

Integrate Biology L2

Perspiration Tell students that the body cools itself by producing perspiration, or sweat. Sweat is mostly water. Ask: **How does perspiration cool the body?** *(As water evaporates, it absorbs heat from the skin.)* **Why do you think perspiration cools the body more effectively when the air is dry?** *(The water evaporates more easily when there is less water vapor already in the air.)*
Logical

Answer to . . .

Reading Checkpoint *Atmosphere is nearly 0 to about 4 percent water by volume.*

Humidity

Address Misconceptions L2

Students may think that condensation occurs when air turns into a liquid. Emphasize that condensation consists of water droplets, and that water vapor is only a small part of air. The remaining components of air remain as gases. Have students draw diagrams of molecules to represent the main gases in air and draw an arrow from a water molecule to a drawing of a water droplet.
Logical, Visual

Address Misconceptions L2

Students may be somewhat mislead by the phrases "air has as much water as it can hold" and "filled to capacity" in the text. Explain that while these are convenient phrases, air does not actually "hold" water the way a sponge does. Water vapor evaporates and condenses in response to changes in temperature independently of the gases in air. In fact, it would do so even if those other gases were not present.
Logical

The opposite process where water vapor changes to the liquid state is called **condensation.** In the atmosphere, condensation generates clouds and fog. For condensation to occur, water molecules must release their stored heat energy, called latent heat of condensation, equal to what was absorbed during evaporation. This released energy plays an important role in producing violent weather and can transfer great quantities of heat from tropical oceans toward the poles.

Solid to Gas Water also can be transformed from a solid to a vapor state. **Sublimation** is the conversion of a solid directly to a gas, without passing through the liquid state. You may have observed this change in watching the sublimation of dry ice, which is frozen carbon dioxide, into white, wispy vapor. Dry ice sometimes is used to generate smoke in theatrical productions. **Deposition** is the reverse process, the conversion of a vapor directly to a solid. This change happens when water vapor is deposited as frost on cold objects such as grass or windows.

Humidity

The general term for the amount of water vapor in air is **humidity.** Meteorologists use several methods to express the water-vapor content of the air. These include relative humidity and dew-point temperature.

Table 1 Water Vapor Needed for Saturation

Temperature		Water Vapor Content at Saturation (g/kg)
°C	(°F)	
−40	(−40)	0.1
−30	(−22)	0.3
−20	(−4)	0.75
−10	(14)	2
0	(32)	3.5
5	(41)	5
10	(50)	7
15	(59)	10
20	(68)	14
25	(77)	20
30	(86)	26.5
35	(95)	35
40	(104)	47

Saturation Imagine a closed jar half full of water and half full of dry air. As the water begins to evaporate from the water surface, a small increase in pressure can be detected in the air above. This increase is the result of the motion of the water-vapor molecules that were added to the air through evaporation. As more and more molecules escape from the water surface, the pressure in the air above increases steadily. This forces more and more water molecules to return to the liquid. Eventually, the number of vapor molecules returning to the surface will balance the number leaving. At that point, the air is said to be **saturated.** The amount of water vapor required for saturation depends on temperature as shown in Table 1. **When saturated, warm air contains more water vapor than cold air.**

Relative Humidity The most familiar and most misunderstood term used to describe the moisture content of air is relative humidity. **Relative humidity is a ratio of the air's actual water-vapor content compared with the amount of water vapor air can hold at that temperature and pressure.** Relative humidity indicates how near the air is to saturation, rather than the actual quantity of water vapor in the air.

Facts and Figures

Freezer burn is a term used to describe the dried-out appearance of food that has been left in a frost-free freezer for long periods of time. Frost-free freezers circulate fairly dry air. This causes ice on the freezer walls to sublimate and be removed by the circulating air. This process, however, also removes moisture from frozen foods that are not in airtight containers. Over a few months, these foods dry out rather than actually burn.

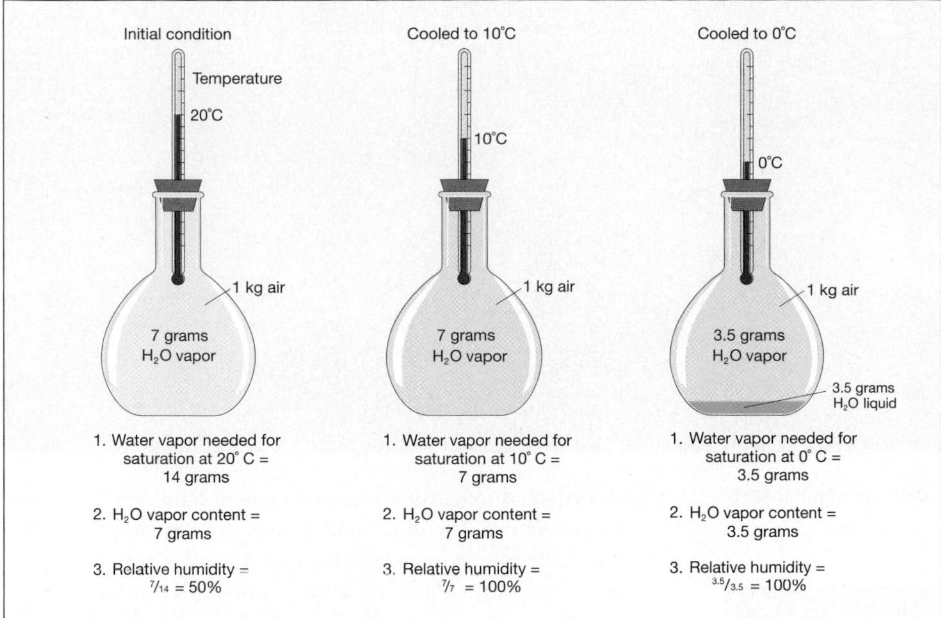

Figure 3 Relative humidity varies with temperature.

Relative humidity can be changed in two ways. First, it can be changed by adding or removing water vapor. In nature, moisture is added to air mainly by evaporation from the oceans and smaller bodies of water.

Second, because the amount of moisture needed for saturation depends on temperature, relative humidity varies with temperature. Notice in Figure 3 that when the flask is cooled from 20°C to 10°C, the relative humidity increases from 50 to 100 percent. However, once the air is saturated, further cooling does not change the relative humidity. Further cooling causes condensation, which keeps the air at its saturation level for the temperature. When air far above Earth's surface is cooled below its saturation level, some of the water vapor condenses to form clouds. Because clouds are made of liquid droplets, this moisture is no longer part of the water-vapor content of the air. **To summarize, when the water-vapor content of air remains constant, lowering air temperature causes an increase in relative humidity, and raising air temperature causes a decrease in relative humidity.**

For: Links on atmospheric moisture
Visit: www.SciLinks.org
Web Code: cjn-6181

Build Reading Literacy 

Refer to **p. 502D,** which provides the guidelines for visualizing.

Visualize Tell students that forming a mental image of concepts they are learning helps them remember new concepts. After students have read about saturation and relative humidity, have them visualize the individual water molecules moving from the surface of the water into the air and back into the water. Then encourage students to draw diagrams that demonstrate the differences among these three types of bonds.
Visual

Water From Plants L2

Purpose Students will observe transpiration from plants and condensation of water.

Materials small potted house plant, clear plastic bag

Procedure Cover the plant with the plastic bag, and leave it in a sunny spot for about 15 minutes. Then have students observe the inside of the bag. Ask students what they see on the inside of the bag. *(droplets of water)* Then ask where the water came from. *(It came from the plant's leaves.)* Explain that the release of water by plants is called transpiration. Ask what process formed the droplets on the inside of the bag. *(condensation)*

Expected Outcome Droplets of water will form on the inside of the bag.
Visual, Logical

Download a worksheet on atmospheric moisture for students to complete, and find additional teacher support from NSTA SciLinks.

Build Science Skills

L2

Measuring Have students work in small groups to build hair hygrometers as follows.

Wash a long human hair. Tie or tape one end of the hair to a ring stand or other support. Tie or tape a small washer or button to the other end of the hair so it hangs about 4 cm off the table. Tape or glue a toothpick vertically to the washer or button. Tape an index card to the side of a small cardboard box and place it behind the toothpick. As humidity changes, the hair will stretch or contract. Students can calibrate the hair hygrometer according to weather reports or readings from a psychrometer.

Visual, Logical

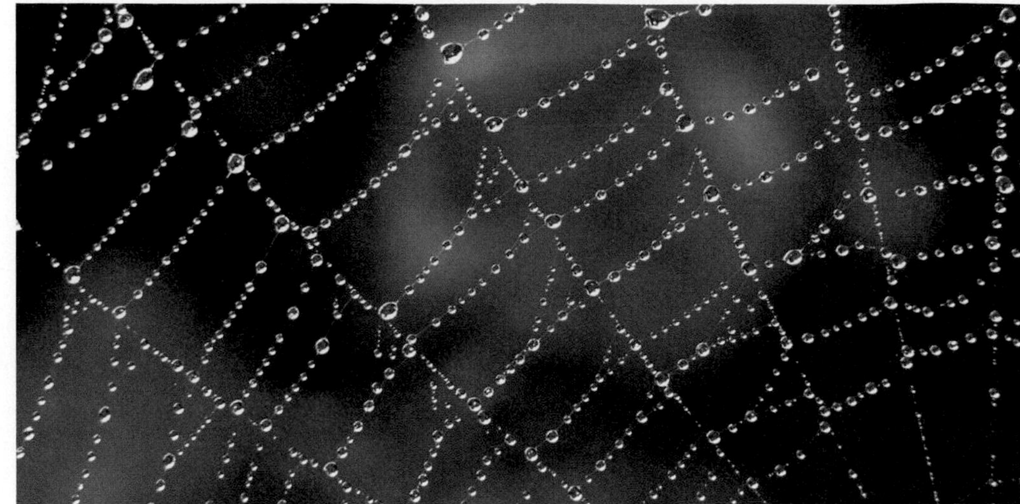

Figure 4 Dew on a Spider Web

Dew Point Another important measure of humidity is the dew-point temperature. The dew-point temperature or simply the **dew point** is the temperature to which a parcel of air would need to be cooled to reach saturation. If the same air was cooled further, the air's excess water vapor would condense, typically as dew, fog, or clouds. During evening hours, objects near the ground often cool below the dew-point temperature and become coated with water. This is known as dew, shown on the spider web in Figure 4.

For every 10°C increase in temperature, the amount of water vapor needed for saturation doubles. Therefore, relatively cold saturated air at 0°C contains about half the water vapor of saturated air at a temperature of 10°C, and roughly one-fourth that of hot saturated air with a temperature of 20°C as shown in Table 1 on page 506. Because the dew point is the temperature at which saturation occurs, high dew-point temperatures indicate moist air, and low dew-point temperatures indicate dry air.

Figure 5 Sling Psychrometer This psychrometer is used to measure both relative humidity and dew point.
Interpreting Photographs ***Identify the wet bulb and the dry bulb in this photograph.***

Measuring Humidity Relative humidity is commonly measured by using a **hygrometer.** One type of hygrometer, called a psychrometer, consists of two identical thermometers mounted side by side. See Figure 5. One thermometer, the dry-bulb thermometer, gives the present air temperature. The other, called the wet-bulb thermometer, has a thin cloth wick tied around the end.

To use the psychrometer, the cloth wick is saturated with water and air is continuously passed over the wick. This is done either by swinging the instrument freely in the air or by fanning air past it. Water evaporates from the wick, and the heat absorbed by the evaporating water makes the temperature of the wet bulb drop. The loss of heat that was required to evaporate water from the wet bulb lowers the thermometer reading. This temperature is referred to as the wet-bulb temperature.

Facts and Figures

You may have noticed that dew often forms on grass. The reason for this is that grass releases water vapor in a process called transpiration. On calm nights, this causes the relative humidity of the air near the grass to be much higher than the relative humidity of the air even a few inches above the surface. As a result, dew forms on grass before it does on most other objects.

The amount of cooling that takes place is directly proportional to the dryness of the air. The drier the air, the more moisture evaporates, and the lower is the temperature of the wet bulb. The larger the difference is between temperatures observed on the thermometers, the lower the relative humidity. If the air is saturated, no evaporation will occur, and the two thermometers will have identical readings. To determine the precise relative humidity and to calculate the dew point, standard tables are used.

A sling psychrometer would not be all that useful in a weather balloon used to monitor conditions in the upper atmosphere. A different type of hygrometer is used in instrument packages that transmit data back to a station on the ground. The electric hygrometer contains an electrical conductor coated with a chemical that absorbs moisture. The passage of current varies with the amount of moisture absorbed.

Q *Why is the air in buildings so dry in the winter?*

A If the water-vapor content of air stays constant, an increase in temperature lowers the relative humidity, and a drop in temperature raises the relative humidity. During winter months, outside air is comparatively cold. When this air is drawn into a building, it is heated to room temperature. This causes the relative humidity to drop, often to uncomfortably low levels of 10 percent or lower. Living with dry air can mean static electrical shocks, dry skin, sinus headaches, or even nosebleeds.

Section 18.1 Assessment

Reviewing Concepts

1. What is the most important gas for understanding atmospheric processes?
2. What happens to heat during a change of state?
3. How does the temperature of air influence its ability to hold water?
4. What does relative humidity describe about air?
5. List two ways that relative humidity can be changed.
6. What does a low dew point indicate about the moisture content of air?

Critical Thinking

7. **Interpreting Illustrations** Study Figure 2. For 1 gram of water, how do the energy requirements for melting and evaporation compare?

Math Practice

8. The air over Fort Myers, Florida, has a dew point of 25°C. Fort Myers has twice the water vapor content of the air over St. Louis, Missouri, and four times the water vapor content as air over Tucson, Arizona. Determine the dew points for St. Louis and Tucson.

Use Community Resources **L2**

Invite a meteorologist to the class to discuss relative humidity and other weather factors. Ask students to prepare questions in advance to ask the visitor. **Interpersonal**

3 ASSESS

Evaluate Understanding **L2**

Ask students to describe at least three changes of state and explain whether heat is absorbed or released during each change. For each change of state, students should name the process and describe the type of change. For example, for sublimation, students would indicate that the phase change is from solid to gas.

Reteach **L1**

Use Figure 3 to review the concept of relative humidity. Make sure to emphasize the difference between humidity and relative humidity. Ask: **How does lowering air temperature affect relative humidity?** *(It increases relative humidity.)* **How does raising air temperature affect relative humidity?** *(It decreases relative humidity.)*

Math Practice

Solutions

8. St. Louis dew point: 15°C; Tucson dew point: 5°C

Section 18.1 Assessment

1. Water vapor is the most important.
2. Heat is absorbed or released, depending on the change of state.
3. When saturated, warm air contains more water vapor than cold air.
4. Relative humidity describes how near the air is to being saturated.
5. Relative humidity can be changed by adding or removing water vapor or by changing temperature.
6. The air is dry.
7. More energy is required for evaporation to occur than for melting to occur. About 7.5 times more energy is required for evaporation.

Answer to . . .

Figure 5 *The wet-bulb thermometer is on the left. The dry-bulb thermometer is on the right.*

Section 18.2

1 FOCUS

Section Objectives

18.6 **Describe** what happens to air when it is compressed or allowed to expand.
18.7 **List** four mechanisms that cause air to rise.
18.8 **Compare and contrast** movements of stable and unstable air.
18.9 **Describe** the conditions in air that favor condensation of water.

Reading Focus

Build Vocabulary L2

LINCS Have students use the LINCS strategy to learn and review the terms *adiabatic, orographic,* and *inversion.* In LINCS exercises, students **L**ist what they know about each term, **I**magine a picture that describes the word, **N**ote a "sound-alike" word, **C**onnect the terms to the sound-alike word by making up a short story, and then perform a brief **S**elf-test.

Reading Strategy L2

a. Adiabatic temperature changes are those that occur without the addition or subtraction of heat.
b. Stability measurements are made using meteorological instruments that measure the temperature profile of the atmosphere.
c. Degrees of stability relate to the tendency of air to resist vertical movement (stable) ranging to air that tends to rise (unstable).

18.2 Cloud Formation

Reading Focus

Key Concepts

- What happens to air when it is compressed or allowed to expand?
- List four mechanisms that can cause air to rise.
- Contrast movements of stable and unstable air.
- What conditions in air favor condensation of water?

Vocabulary

- dry adiabatic rate
- wet adiabatic rate
- orographic lifting
- front
- temperature inversion
- condensation nuclei

Reading Strategy

Identifying Main Ideas Copy the table. As you read, write the main idea for each topic.

Topic	Main Idea
Adiabatic temperature changes	a. ?
Stability measurements	b. ?
Degrees of stability	c. ?

Figure 6 Clouds form when air is cooled to its dew point.

Recall that condensation occurs when water vapor changes to a liquid. Condensation may form dew, fog, or clouds. Although these three forms are different, all require saturated air to develop. Saturation occurs either when enough water vapor is added to air or, more commonly, when air is cooled to its dew point.

Near Earth's surface, heat is quickly exchanged between the ground and the air above. During evening hours, the surface radiates heat away, causing the surface and adjacent air to cool rapidly. This radiational cooling causes the formation of dew and some types of fog. In contrast, clouds, like those shown in Figure 6, often form during the warmest part of the day. Clearly, some other process must cool air enough to generate clouds.

Air Compression and Expansion

If you have pumped up a bicycle tire, you might have noticed that the pump barrel became warm. The increase in temperature you felt resulted from the work you did on the air to compress it. When air is compressed, the motion of gas molecules increases and the air temperature rises. The opposite happens when air is allowed to escape from a bicycle tire. The air expands and cools. The expanding air pushes on the surrounding air and cools by an amount equal to the energy used up.

Adiabatic Temperature Changes Temperature changes that happen even though heat isn't added or subtracted are called *adiabatic temperature changes.* They result when air is compressed or allowed to expand. **When air is allowed to expand, it cools, and when it is compressed, it warms.**

Expansion and Cooling As you travel from Earth's surface upward through the atmosphere, the atmospheric pressure decreases. This happens because there are fewer and fewer gas molecules. Any time a volume of air moves upward, it passes through regions of successively lower pressure. As a result, the ascending air expands and cools. Unsaturated air cools at the constant rate of 10°C for every 1000 meters of ascent. In contrast, descending air encounters higher pressures, compresses, and is heated 10°C for every 1000 meters it moves downward. This rate of cooling or heating applies only to unsaturated air and is called the **dry adiabatic rate.**

If a parcel of air rises high enough, it will eventually cool to its dew point. Here the process of condensation begins. From this point on as the air rises, latent heat of condensation stored in the water vapor will be released. Although the air will continue to cool after condensation begins, the released latent heat works against the adiabatic cooling process. This slower rate of cooling caused by the addition of latent heat is called the **wet adiabatic rate.** Because the amount of latent heat released depends on the quantity of moisture present in the air, the wet adiabatic rate varies from 5–9°C per 1000 meters.

Figure 7 shows the role of adiabatic cooling in the formation of clouds. Note that from the surface up to the condensation level the air cools at the dry adiabatic rate. The wet adiabatic rate begins at the condensation level.

Reading Checkpoint

What happens to heat stored in water vapor when it is cooled to its dew point?

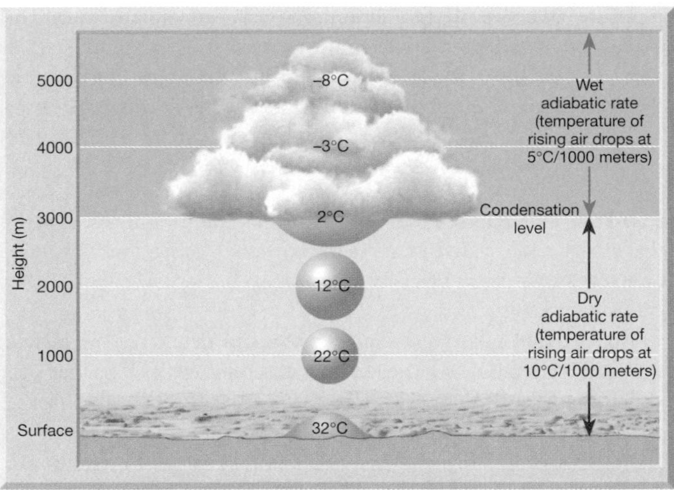

Figure 7 Cloud Formation by Adiabatic Cooling Rising air cools at the dry adiabatic rate of 10°C per 1000 meters, until the air reaches the dew point and condensation (cloud formation) begins. As air continues to rise, the latent heat released by condensation reduces the rate of cooling.
Interpreting Diagrams ***Use this diagram to determine the approximate air temperature at 3500 m.***

Customize for English Language Learners

Students who are learning English can benefit from real-life examples that relate to science content. Encourage students to think of observations they have made about rising objects or processes that cause objects to rise. For example, they likely have seen a helium balloon rising. They may also have seen wedges such as those used as doorstops. Encourage students to share their observations with the class.

2 INSTRUCT

Teacher Demo

Air Compression and Expansion

Compression and Expansion L2

Purpose Students observe how compression and expansion of air cause temperature changes.

Materials bicycle tire, bicycle pump, can of compressed air duster

Procedure Ask students what they think will happen to the bicycle pump when you use it to add air to the tire. Pump up the tire a bit, then let the student feel the barrel of the pump. Ask them why the pump got warm. *(Energy was used to compress the air.)* Now ask students what they think will happen to the can of compressed air duster when you release some air from it. Release some air, then let students feel the can. Ask them why the can became cold. *(Energy was absorbed by the expanding air.)*

Expected Outcomes The bicycle pump will get warm, and the can will get cold.
Kinesthetic, Logical

Build Science Skills L2

Relating Cause and Effect Go through each step in what happens as a parcel of air rises through the atmosphere. Ask: **Why does air cool as it rises?** *(It expands, a process that absorbs heat.)* **Why does air cool more slowly after it reaches its dew point?** *(Above the dew point, condensation begins. Condensation releases heat, which somewhat counteracts the cooling effect of expansion.)* **Why does the wet adiabatic rate vary?** *(The amount of heat released varies with the amount of moisture. The more moisture, the more heat is released and the slower the cooling is.)*
Logical

Answer to . . .

Figure 7 *The temperature is −0.5°C.*

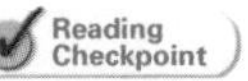
Reading Checkpoint *Latent heat is released.*

Section 18.2 (continued)

Processes That Lift Air

Use Visuals L1

Figure 8: A and B Use this diagram to explain how air can be lifted by mountains or cooler air masses. Ask: **What happens as air rises up the side of a mountain?** *(It cools, often creating clouds and precipitation.)* **What happens when warm and cold air masses collide?** *(The colder, denser air forces the warmer air up.)* **How are the processes in A and B similar?** *(In both cases, air is forced to rise by a barrier, often resulting in clouds and precipitation.)*
Visual, Logical

Build Reading Literacy L1

Refer to **p. 306D** in **Chapter 11,** which provides the guidelines for KWL (Know/Want to Know/Learned).

KWL Teach this independent study skill as a whole-class exercise. 1. Draw a three-column KWL chart on the board for students to copy. 2. Have students complete the Know column with facts, examples, and other information that they already know about processes that lift air. Have students use one row for each of the four processes. 3. Tell students to complete the Want to Know column with questions about these processes. 4. Have students read pp. 512–513 to learn more about these processes. As they read, have them note answers in the Learned column, along with other facts, examples, and details they learned. 5. Have students draw an Information I Expect to Use box below their KWL chart. Have them review the information in the Learned column and categorize the useful information in the box.
Verbal

Processes that Lift Air

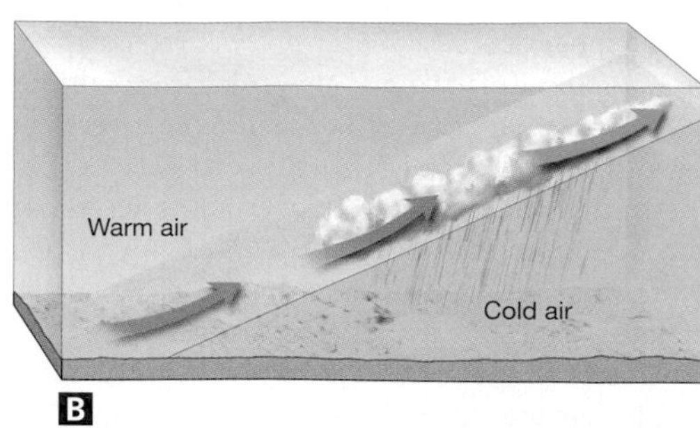

Figure 8 A Orographic Lifting B Frontal Wedging
Relating Cause and Effect ***Why does the warm air mass move upward over the cold air mass?***

Processes That Lift Air

In general, air resists vertical movement. Air located near the surface tends to stay near the surface. Air far above the surface tends to remain far above the surface. Some exceptions to this happen when conditions in the atmosphere make air buoyant enough to rise without the aid of outside forces. In other situations, clouds form because there is some mechanical process that forces air to rise. **Four mechanisms that can cause air to rise are orographic lifting, frontal wedging, convergence, and localized convective lifting.**

Orographic Lifting When elevated terrains, such as mountains, act as barriers to air flow, **orographic lifting** of air occurs. Look at Figure 8A. As air goes up a mountain slope, adiabatic cooling often generates clouds and precipitation. Many of the rainiest places on Earth are located on these windward mountain slopes.

By the time air reaches the leeward side of a mountain, much of its moisture has been lost. If the air descends, it warms adiabatically. This makes condensation and precipitation even less likely. A rain shadow desert can occur on the leeward side of the mountain. For example, the Great Basin Desert of the western United States lies only a few hundred kilometers from the Pacific Ocean, cut off from the ocean's moisture by the Sierra Nevada Mountains.

Frontal Wedging If orographic lifting was the only mechanism that lifted air, the relatively flat central portion of North America would be an expansive desert instead of the nation's breadbasket. Fortunately, this is not the case.

In central North America, masses of warm air and cold air collide, producing a **front.** Here the cooler, denser air acts as a barrier over which the warmer, less dense air rises. This process, called frontal wedging, is shown in Figure 8B. Weather-producing fronts are associated with specific storm systems called middle-latitude cyclones. You will study these in Chapter 20.

Facts and Figures

The phrase *parcel of air* is often used in meteorology to help understand and simplify discussion of principles. It refers to an imaginary volume of air isolated from other air by, for example, a thin elastic cover. (Picture a hot-air balloon.) A parcel is typically considered to be a few hundred cubic meters in volume. It is assumed to act independently of the surrounding air. It is also assumed that no heat is transferred into or out of the parcel. Although parcels are imaginary, over short time periods, a parcel is a good model for the actual behavior of a volume of air moving vertically through the atmosphere.

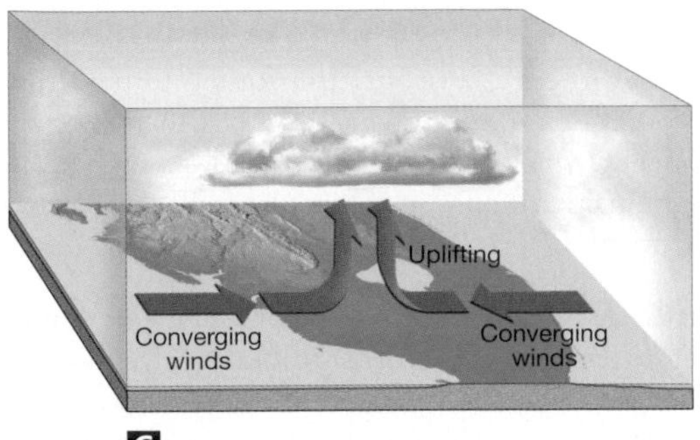

C

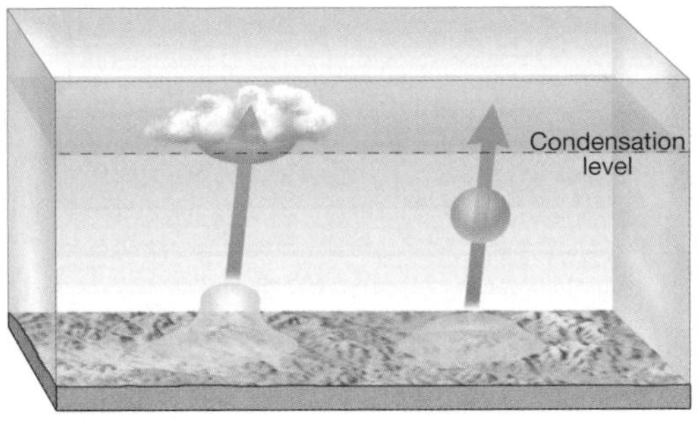

D

Figure 8 C Convergence D Localized Convective Lifting

Convergence Recall that the collision of contrasting air masses forces air to rise. In a more general sense, whenever air in the lower atmosphere flows together, lifting results. This is called convergence. When air flows in from more than one direction, it must go somewhere. Because it cannot go down, it goes up, as shown in Figure 8C. This leads to adiabatic cooling and possibly cloud formation.

The Florida peninsula provides an example of how convergence can cause cloud development and precipitation. On warm days, the airflow is from the ocean to the land along both coasts of Florida. This leads to a pileup of air along the coasts and general convergence over the peninsula. This pattern of air movement and the uplift that results is helped along by intense solar heating of the land. The result is that the peninsula of Florida experiences the greatest number of mid-afternoon thunderstorms in the United States.

Localized Convective Lifting On warm summer days, unequal heating of Earth's surface may cause pockets of air to be warmed more than the surrounding air. For example, air above a paved parking lot will be warmed more than the air above an adjacent wooded park. Consequently, the parcel of air above the parking lot, which is warmer and less dense than the surrounding air, will move upward, as shown in Figure 8D. These rising parcels of warmer air are called thermals. The process that produces rising thermals is localized convective lifting. Birds such as hawks and eagles use these thermals to carry them to great heights where they can gaze down on unsuspecting prey. People have learned to use these warm parcels effectively for hang gliding. When warm parcels of air rise above the condensation level, clouds form. These clouds may produce mid-afternoon rain showers.

What are thermals?

Use Visuals

Figure 8: C and D Use this diagram to explain convergence and convective lifting. Ask: **What happens when two similar air masses converge and collide?** *(Air is forced up at the center, possibly causing cloud formation.)* **How does local convective lifting occur?** *(A pocket of air may be warmed more than surrounding air, causing it to rise.)* **What happens when such a parcel rises above the condensation level?** *(Water vapor condenses, forming clouds.)*
Visual, Logical

Integrate Biology

L2

Birds and Thermals Tell students that using thermals is important to many birds of prey, such as hawks and vultures. Ask: **How do birds of prey use thermals?** *(Birds use thermals to be carried up to great heights, where they can look for prey.)* **What would happen if the birds could not use thermals? What problem would this cause?** *(Birds would have to flap their wings to gain altitude. Doing so would waste a lot of energy.)*
Logical

Answer to . . .

Figure 8 *Warm air is less dense, and therefore more buoyant, than the cold air mass is.*

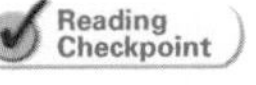

Thermals are rising parcels of air that are warmer than surrounding air.

Stability

Build Science Skills

L2

Designing Experiments Ask students to design experiments to determine the effects of temperature on the buoyancy of a helium balloon. They should compare buoyancy for at least two different temperatures. Students may use materials of their choosing, with the exception of open flames. They should write a hypothesis, develop an experimental plan, submit the plan to you for approval, do the experiment, draw conclusions, and report their results. *(One approach is to heat the balloon, using hot water, and/or cool it, using cold water or ice. Buoyancy can be tested by releasing the balloon at a fixed distance above the floor and using a meter stick and stopwatch to measure how fast the balloon rises or falls.)*
Logical, Visual

Stability

If a volume of air was forced to rise, its temperature would drop because of expansion. If this volume of air was cooler than the surrounding environment, it would be denser, and if allowed to do so, it would sink to its original position. Air of this type, called stable air, resists vertical movement.

Density Differences If this imaginary volume of rising air was warmer and therefore less dense than the surrounding air, it would continue to rise until it reached an altitude where its temperature equaled that of its surroundings. This is exactly how a hot-air balloon works. The balloon rises as long as it is warmer and less dense than the surrounding air, as shown in Figure 9. This type of air is classified as unstable air. **Stable air tends to remain in its original position, while unstable air tends to rise.**

Stability Measurements Air stability is determined by measuring the temperature of the atmosphere at various heights. The rate of change of air temperature with height is called the environmental lapse rate. This rate is determined from observations made by aircraft and by radiosondes. A radiosonde is an instrument designed to collect weather data high in the atmosphere. Radiosondes are often carried into the air by balloons. It is important not to confuse the environmental lapse rate with adiabatic temperature changes.

Figure 9 Hot-air balloons will rise as long as the air inside them is warmer than the air in the atmosphere surrounding them.

Degrees of Stability Air is stable when the temperature decreases gradually with increasing altitude. The most stable conditions happen when air temperature actually increases with height, called a **temperature inversion.** Temperature inversions frequently happen on clear nights as a result of radiation cooling off Earth's surface. The inversion is created because the ground and the air immediately above the ground will cool more rapidly than air higher above the ground. Under these conditions, there is very little vertical air movement. In contrast, air is considered unstable when the air close to the surface of Earth is significantly warmer than the air higher above the surface, indicating a large environmental lapse rate. Under these conditions, the air actually turns over, as the warm air below rises and is displaced by the colder air higher above the ground.

Facts and Figures

A hot-air balloon has three main parts: the basket, the envelope, and the burner. The basket holds the balloonist, passengers, propane tanks, navigation equipment, and other needed supplies. The basket is often made out of wicker because it is fairly lightweight but also strong and flexible enough to absorb some of the energy of landings. The envelope, which is essentially a large nylon bag, holds the hot air. The burner is somewhat like a giant Bunsen burner. It burns propane that is stored as a liquid in large tanks. When the balloonist fires the burner, it heats the air inside the balloon and increases its buoyancy, lifting the balloon. To lower the balloon, the balloonist pulls a cord that opens a parachute valve at the top of the balloon and lets some of the hot air out.

Figure 10 These clouds provide evidence of unstable conditions in the atmosphere.

Stability and Daily Weather Recall that stable air resists vertical movement and that unstable air rises freely. But how do these facts apply to the daily weather?

Because stable air resists upward movement, you might conclude that clouds won't form when stable conditions are present in the atmosphere. Although this seems reasonable, remember that there are processes that force air above Earth's surface. These include orographic lifting, frontal wedging, and convergence. When stable air is forced above Earth's surface, the clouds that form are widespread and have little vertical thickness when compared to their horizontal dimension. Precipitation, if any, is light to moderate.

In contrast, clouds associated with the lifting of unstable air are towering and often generate thunderstorms and occasionally even a tornado. For this reason, on a dreary, overcast day with light drizzle, stable air has been forced above Earth's surface. During a day when cauliflower-shaped clouds appear to be growing as if bubbles of hot air are surging upward, the air moving up is unstable. Figure 10 shows cauliflower-shaped clouds caused by the rising of unstable air.

What types of weather can result when stable air rises?

Build Science Skills L2

Comparing and Contrasting
Compare the behavior of stable and unstable air parcels. Ask: **What factors cause stable air to rise?** *(orographic lifting, frontal wedging, and convergence)* **Why are clouds formed from stable air widespread and thin?** *(Because the air is stable, it all stays at roughly the same altitude.)* **What factors cause unstable air to rise?** *(localized convective lifting)* **Why are clouds formed from unstable air often towering?** *(Strong convection lifts and spreads out the clouds.)*
Logical

Condensation

Teacher Demo

Making a Cloud L2

Purpose Students observe how a cloud forms.

Materials valve stem from a car or bicycle, 2-hole rubber stopper, glass tubing, rubber tubing, hose clamp, warm water, Erlenmeyer flask, match, bicycle pump, sheet of black paper, flashlight

Procedure In advance, insert a valve stem from a car or bicycle into one hole of a 2-hole rubber stopper. Insert a piece of glass tubing into the other hole and attach a piece of rubber tubing to the glass tubing, Clamp off the rubber tubing. Pour a small amount of warm water into an Erlenmeyer flask. In front of students, light a match and hold it inside the flask for a few seconds. Insert the stopper into the flask and use a bicycle pump to increase the pressure of the flask. Stand up a sheet of black paper behind the flask and shine a flashlight through it. Now open the clamp. Ask students what they observed. *(A cloud forms.)* Ask why it formed. *(The sudden drop in pressure cooled the air, causing water vapor to condense and form a cloud of droplets.)* Ask what the role of the smoke was. *(It provided condensation nuclei on which the droplets could form.)*

Expected Outcome A small cloud will form inside the flask.
Visual, Logical

Answer to . . .

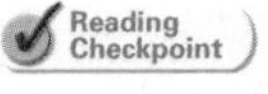

Clear weather may occur or light-to-moderate precipitation.

3 ASSESS

Evaluate Understanding L2

Ask students in turn to explain one process that lifts air. Encourage them to draw diagrams on the board to help explain the process.

Reteach L1

Use Figure 7 to review adiabatic cooling and its role in cloud formation. Explain why the moist adiabatic rate is slower than the dry adiabatic rate.

Connecting Concepts

The general cooling trend with height in the troposphere is called the environmental lapse rate. This is different from parcels of air that rise, expand, and cool adiabatically.

Condensation

Recall that condensation happens when water vapor in the air changes to a liquid. This may be in the form of dew, fog, or clouds. **For any of these forms of condensation to occur, the air must be saturated.** Saturation occurs most commonly when air is cooled to its dew point, or less often when water vapor is added to the air.

Types of Surfaces Generally, there must be a surface for water vapor to condense on. When dew forms, objects at or near the ground, such as grass and car windows, serve this purpose. But when condensation occurs in the air above the ground, tiny bits of particulate matter, called **condensation nuclei,** serve as surfaces for water-vapor condensation. These nuclei are important because if they are absent, a relative humidity much above 100 percent is needed to produce clouds.

Condensation nuclei such as microscopic dust, smoke, and salt particles from the ocean are abundant in the lower atmosphere. Because of these plentiful particles, relative humidity rarely exceeds 100 percent. Some particles, such as ocean salt, are especially good nuclei because they absorb water. When condensation takes place, the initial growth rate of cloud droplets is rapid. It diminishes quickly because the excess water vapor is quickly absorbed by the numerous competing particles. This results in the formation of a cloud consisting of millions upon millions of tiny water droplets. These droplets are all so fine that they remain suspended in air. In the next section, you will examine types of clouds and the precipitation that forms from them.

Section 18.2 Assessment

Reviewing Concepts

1. Describe what happens to air temperature when work is done on the air to compress it.
2. What does stability mean in terms of air movement?
3. List four mechanisms that cause air to rise.
4. Describe conditions that cause condensation of liquid water in air.
5. What is a temperature inversion?
6. Which types of condensation nuclei are especially good for condensation to form?

Critical Thinking

7. **Hypothesizing** Study a world map. Hypothesize about other regions on Earth, other than the Florida peninsula, where convergence might cause cloud development and precipitation.

Connecting Concepts

Air Temperature Review the description of atmospheric temperature changes in Section 17.1. Then write a paragraph explaining how these differ from adiabatic temperature changes in parcels of air.

516 *Chapter 18*

Section 18.2 Assessment

1. Air temperature rises when work is done on the air to compress it.
2. Stable air tends to remain in its original position, while unstable air tends to rise.
3. The mechanisms are frontal wedging, orographic lifting, convergence, and localized convective lifting.
4. Condensation of liquid water in air occurs when the air is saturated.
5. A temperature inversion is a stable-air situation in which air temperature increases with height.
6. Good condensation nuclei are those that absorb water, such as ocean salt.
7. Sample answer: Yucatan Peninsula; peninsulas in Northern Australia; New Zealand; Indonesia; tropical islands in general

18.3 Cloud Types and Precipitation

Reading Focus

Key Concepts

- How are clouds classified?
- How are clouds and fogs similar and different?
- What must happen in order for precipitation to form?
- What controls the type of precipitation that reaches Earth's surface?

Vocabulary

- cirrus
- cumulus
- stratus
- Bergeron process
- supercooled water
- supersaturated air
- collision-coalescence process

Reading Strategy

Building Vocabulary Copy the table. As you read, add definitions.

Vocabulary Term	Definition
Cirrus	a. ?
Cumulus	b. ?
Stratus	c. ?
Coalescence	d. ?

Clouds are among the most striking and noticeable effects of the atmosphere and its weather. Clouds are a form of condensation best described as visible mixtures of tiny droplets of water or tiny crystals of ice. Clouds are of interest to meteorologists because clouds show what is going on in the atmosphere. If you try to recognize different types of clouds, you might find it hard to do. But, if you learn the basic classification scheme for clouds, recognizing cloud types will be easy.

Types of Clouds

Clouds are classified on the basis of their form and height. The three basic forms are: cirrus, cumulus, and stratus. All other clouds reflect one of these three basic forms or are combinations or modifications of them.

Cirrus (*cirrus* = a curl of hair) clouds are high, white, and thin. They can occur as patches or as delicate veil-like sheets or extended wispy fibers that often have a feathery appearance. An example of cirrus clouds is shown in Figure 11.

Cumulus (*cumulus* = a pile) clouds consist of rounded individual cloud masses. Refer to Figure 10 on page 515. Normally, they have a flat base and the appearance of rising domes or towers. These clouds are frequently described as having a cauliflower structure.

Figure 11 Cirrus Clouds

Section 18.3

1 FOCUS

Section Objectives

18.10 **Describe** how clouds are classified.

18.11 **Compare and contrast** clouds and fogs.

18.12 **Explain** what must happen for precipitation to form.

18.13 **Identify** what controls the type of precipitation that reaches Earth's surface.

Reading Focus

Build Vocabulary

L2

Concept Map Have students create concept maps of the types of clouds. Have them start with Clouds at the top and put the three families of clouds classified by height on the next level. Below that, they should put the types of clouds within each family, and on the last row, some details about each one.

Reading Strategy

L2

a. clouds that are high, white, and thin
b. clouds that consist of rounded individual cloud masses
c. clouds that occur as sheets or layers that cover much or all of the sky
d. the process in which larger drops fall through clouds, collide, and join together with smaller, slower droplets

2 INSTRUCT

Types of Clouds

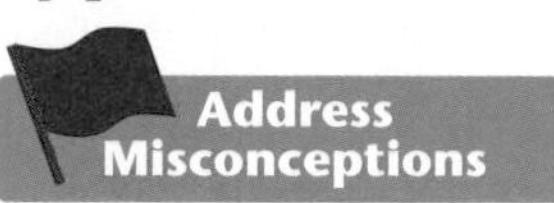

L2

Students may have many misconceptions about what clouds are made of and how they form. They may think that clouds are made of smoke or water vapor. They may think that clouds form when bodies of water boil. Have students make flowcharts with diagrams to show that clouds are made of tiny water droplets, and form when air containing water vapor is cooled.
Logical, Visual

Build Reading Literacy L1

Refer to **p. 278D** in **Chapter 10,** which provides the guidelines for identifying main ideas and details.

Identify Main Idea/Details Have students read Types of Clouds on pp. 517–520. Ask them to identify the main idea of each subheading. Point out that the main idea is usually in the first or second sentence of a subheading. Encourage students to use this exercise in the notes they use to study.
Verbal

Use Visuals 

Figure 12 Use this diagram to explain the different types of clouds and their names. Ask: **To what does "stratus" refer?** *(clouds that cover much of the sky)* **What can you tell about altocumulus clouds from their name?** *(They are mid-level clouds made up of individual cloud masses.)* **What can you tell about cirrocumulus clouds from their name?** *(They are high-level clouds made up of individual cloud masses.)* **Are you likely to see all of these kinds of clouds in the sky at the same time? Explain your answer.** *(No, because many of the clouds form under different atmospheric conditions.)*
Visual, Verbal

Stratus (*stratum* = a layer) clouds are best described as sheets or layers that cover much or all of the sky. While there may be minor breaks, there are no distinct individual cloud units.

There are three levels of cloud heights: high, middle, and low, as shown in Figure 12. High clouds normally have bases above 6000 meters. Middle clouds generally occupy heights from 2000 to 6000 meters. Low clouds form below 2000 meters. The altitudes listed for each height category are not hard and fast. There is some seasonal and latitudinal variation. For example, at high latitudes or during cold winter months in the mid-latitudes, high clouds often are found at lower altitudes.

High Clouds Three cloud types make up the family of high clouds: cirrus, cirrostratus, and cirrocumulus. Look at Figure 12. Cirrocumulus clouds consist of fluffy masses, while cirrostratus clouds are flat layers. All high clouds are thin and white and are often made up of ice crystals. This is because of the low temperatures and small quantities of water vapor present at high altitudes. These clouds are not considered precipitation makers. However, when cirrus clouds are followed by cirrocumulus or cirrostratus clouds and increased sky coverage, they may warn of approaching stormy weather.

Middle Clouds Clouds that appear in the middle range, from about 2000 to 6000 meters, have the prefix *alto-* as part of their name. Altocumulus clouds are composed of rounded masses that differ from

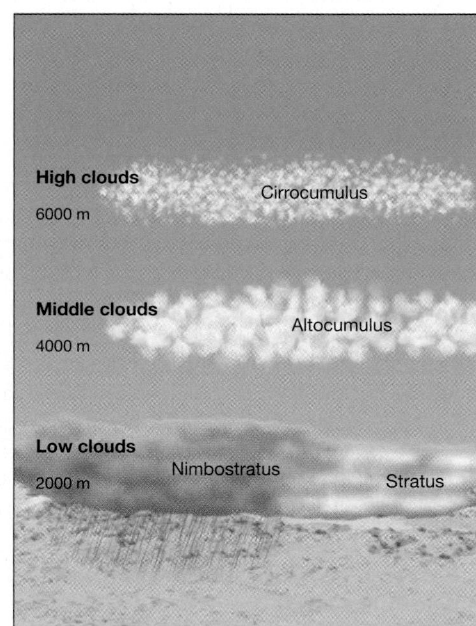

Figure 12 Cloud Classification Clouds are classified according to form and height.
Interpreting Diagrams ***Which cloud types are the chief precipitation makers?***

Customize for Inclusion Students

Behaviorally Disordered Have students work in groups to create a set of flashcards. Each card should contain information about a different type of cloud. One side of the card should have the name of the cloud (for example, altostratus) and three categories of color-keyed questions: Form of cloud, Height of cloud, Typical weather. Color key the answers on the other side of the card. *(flat layers, middle height, infrequent light snow or drizzle)* Students can use the cards to support one another in small study groups.

cirrocumulus clouds in that altocumulus clouds are larger and denser, as shown in Figure 12. Altostratus clouds create a uniform white to grayish sheet covering the sky with the sun or moon visible as a bright spot. Infrequent light snow or drizzle may accompany these clouds.

Low Clouds There are three members in the family of low clouds: stratus, stratocumulus, and nimbostratus. As illustrated in Figure 12, stratus clouds are a uniform, fog-like layer of clouds that frequently covers much of the sky. Occasionally, these clouds may produce light precipitation. When stratus clouds develop a scalloped bottom that appears as long parallel rolls or broken rounded patches, they are called stratocumulus clouds.

Nimbostratus clouds derive their name from the Latin word *nimbus,* which means "rainy cloud," and *stratus,* which means "to cover with a layer." As the name suggests, nimbostratus clouds are one of the main precipitation makers. Nimbostratus clouds form during stable conditions. You might not expect clouds to develop in stable air. But cloud growth of this type is common when air is forced upward, as occurs along a mountain range, a front, or where converging winds cause air to rise. Such a forced upward movement of stable air can result in a cloud layer that is largely horizontal compared to its depth.

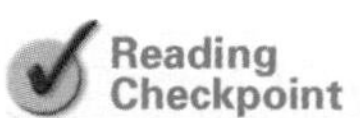

What does the Latin word* stratus *mean?

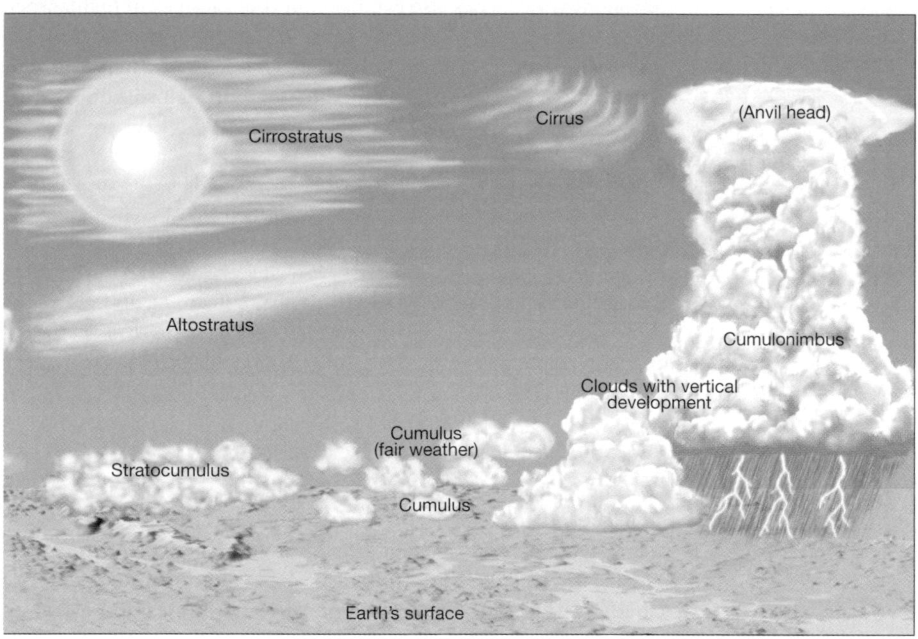

Build Science Skills L2

Classifying Show students photographs of a variety of clouds. Have students classify the clouds according to Figure 12.
Visual

Build Science Skills L2

ACTIVITY

Observing Ask students if they have ever wondered how some people can look out the window and predict the weather. Explain that learning to observe and identify clouds will help develop the ability to predict weather. Have students keep a log of cloud and weather observations for a least one month. For each page of their logs, have students record the date and time of observation; a description and drawing of the cloud cover, including the general altitude (high, middle, low), percent of sky coverage, and the thickness or relative height of clouds; a general description of any weather phenomena, such as wind or precipitation; and the temperature (either specific readings or general terms). After a period of time, students should analyze their observations and look for patterns between clouds and weather.
Visual, Logical

Answer to . . .

Figure 12 *The chief precipitation makers are nimbostratus and cumulonimbus clouds.*

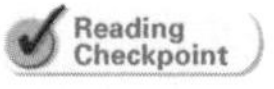 Stratus *means "to cover with a layer."*

Fog

Build Science Skills 

Comparing and Contrasting Make sure that students understand the similarities and differences between fog and other types of clouds. Ask: **What is a fog?** *(It is a cloud with its base at or very near the ground.)* **How are fog and other clouds similar?** *(They are the same physically.)* **How are fog and other clouds different?** *(Clouds result from air rising and cooling adiabatically. Fogs form as a result of radiation cooling, movement of air over a cold surface, or evaporation of water vapor.)*
Logical

Download a worksheet on clouds and fog for students to complete, and find additional teacher support from NSTA SciLinks.

For: Links on clouds and fog
Visit: www.SciLinks.org
Web Code: cjn-6183

Clouds of Vertical Development Some clouds do not fit into any one of the three height categories mentioned. Such clouds have their bases in the low height range but often extend upward into the middle or high altitudes. They all are related to one another and are associated with unstable air. Although cumulus clouds are often connected with fair weather, they may grow dramatically under the proper circumstances. Once upward movement is triggered, acceleration is powerful, and clouds with great vertical range form. The end result often is a cumulonimbus cloud that may produce rain showers or a thunderstorm.

Fog

Physically, there is no difference between a fog and a cloud. Their appearance and structure are the same. The difference is the method and place of formation. Clouds result when air rises and cools adiabatically. Most fogs are the result of radiation cooling or the movement of air over a cold surface. Fogs also can form when enough water vapor is added to the air to bring about saturation. **Fog is defined as a cloud with its base at or very near the ground.** When fog is dense, visibility may be only a few dozen meters or less, making travel not only difficult but often dangerous.

Figure 13 This steam fog rose from upper St. Regis Lake, Adirondack Mountains, New York.

Fogs Caused by Cooling A blanket of fog is produced in some West Coast locations when warm, moist air from the Pacific Ocean moves over the cold California Current and then is carried onshore by prevailing winds. Fogs also can form on cool, clear, calm nights when Earth's surface cools rapidly by radiation. As the night progresses, a thin layer of air in contact with the ground is cooled below its dew point. As the air cools, it becomes denser and drains into low areas such as river valleys, where thick fog accumulations may occur.

Fogs Caused by Evaporation When cool air moves over warm water, enough moisture may evaporate from the water surface to produce saturation. As the rising water vapor meets the cold air, it immediately condenses and rises with the air that is being warmed from below. This type of fog over water has a steaming appearance, as shown in Figure 13. It is fairly common over lakes and rivers in the fall and early winter, when the water may still be relatively warm and the air is rather crisp.

How Precipitation Forms

Cloud droplets are very tiny, averaging less than 20 micrometers in diameter. Because of their small size, the rate at which cloud droplets fall is incredibly slow. Most cloud droplets would evaporate before falling a few meters into unsaturated air below. **For precipitation to form, cloud droplets must grow in volume by roughly one million times.**

Cold Cloud Precipitation

The **Bergeron process,** shown in Figure 14, relies on two physical processes: supercooling and supersaturation. Cloud droplets do not freeze at 0°C as expected. In fact, pure water suspended in air does not freeze until it reaches a temperature of nearly −40°C. Water in the liquid state below 0°C is said to be **supercooled.** Supercooled water will readily freeze if it impacts a solid object. Freezing nuclei are materials that have a crystal form that closely matches that of ice. Freezing nuclei can cause supercooled water to freeze.

When air is saturated (100% relative humidity) with respect to water, it is **supersaturated** with respect to ice (greater than 100% humidity). Ice crystals cannot coexist with water droplets in the air because the air "appears" supersaturated to the ice crystals. Any excess water vapor becomes ice that lowers the relative humidity near the surrounding droplets. Water droplets then evaporate to provide a continual source of water vapor for the growth of ice crystals.

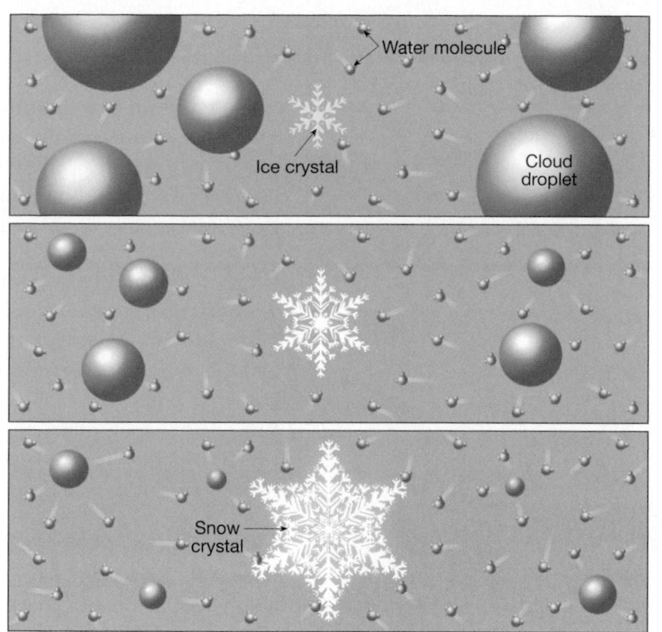

Figure 14 The Bergeron Process Ice crystals grow at the expense of cloud droplets until they are large enough to fall. The size of these particles has been greatly exaggerated.

Because the level of supersaturation with respect to ice can be quite high, the growth of ice crystals is rapid enough to produce crystals that are large enough to fall. As they fall the ice crystals contact cloud drops causing them to freeze. A chain reaction can occur and large crystals, called snowflakes form. When the surface temperature is above 4°C, snowflakes usually melt before they reach the ground. Even on a hot summer day, a heavy downpour may have started as a snowstorm high in the clouds.

Warm Cloud Precipitation Much rainfall can be associated with clouds located well below the freezing level, especially in the tropics. In warm clouds, the mechanism that forms raindrops is the **collision-coalescence process.** Some water-absorbing particles, such as salt, can remove water vapor from the air at relative humidities less than 100 percent, forming drops that are quite large. As these large droplets move through the cloud, they collide and coalesce (join together) with smaller, slower droplets.

For: Links on precipitation
Visit: www.SciLinks.org
Web Code: cjn-6184

How Precipitation Forms

Use Visuals L1

Figure 14 Use this diagram to explain one way ice crystals form. Ask: **How do ice crystals grow?** *(They use water vapor from the atmosphere.)* **How is the water vapor replenished?** *(It evaporates from water droplets.)* **What happens to the water droplets?** *(They get smaller and smaller.)*
Visual, Logical

L2

Many students think that raindrops have a teardrop shape because that is how they are usually shown in artists' drawings. Explain that small water droplets, which are less than 1 millimeter in diameter, are shaped like spheres, as shown in Figure 14. Larger droplets form a shape more like that of a hamburger bun as they fall through the air. Very large droplets, which are more than 5 millimeters in diameter, will break up into smaller droplets.
Logical, Visual

Facts and Figures

The highest average annual rainfall on Earth was recorded at a station on Mount Waialeule, Hawaii. The station is on a windward mountain slope and gets an average of 1234 cm of rain a year. The record for most rainfall in a 12-month period occurred at Cherrapunji, India, where 2647 cm fell. Over one third of this rainfall—930 cm—fell in the month of July alone. This is 10 times more rain than Chicago receives in an average year.

Download a worksheet on precipitation for students to complete, and find additional teacher support from NSTA SciLinks.

Forms of Precipitation

Making Hail L2

Purpose Students will observe the process by which hailstones form.

Materials salt, water, 600-mL beaker, stirring rod, large test tube, ice chip

Procedure Put 15 g of salt and 50 mL of water into a 600-mL beaker. Stir the water until most of the salt dissolves. Clean a large test tube thoroughly and put 15 mL of cold water in it. Place the test tube in the beaker. Add crushed ice to the beaker until it is almost full. Tell students to watch the next step closely. Take the test tube out of the beaker and drop a small chip of ice into it. Ask students what they observed. *(A layer of ice formed on the ice chip.)* Tell students that hailstones form by a similar process.

Expected Outcome A layer of ice will quickly form around the ice chip.
Visual

3 ASSESS

Evaluate Understanding L2

Ask students to draw flowcharts showing the major steps in the Bergeron process of precipitation formation. Their charts should show at least three steps and be consistent with the text and Figure 14.

Reteach L1

Use Figure 12 to review different types of clouds. Ask students to explain the name of a cloud and describe the type of weather associated with it.

Both processes are mechanisms that produce precipitation. The Bergeron process occurs in cold clouds and can result in any form of precipitation. The collision-coalescence process occurs in warm clouds and generally produces rain. Paragraphs should include a clear topic statement and several minor sentences that provide detail.

Forms of Precipitation

The type of precipitation that reaches Earth's surface depends on the temperature profile in the lowest few kilometers of the atmosphere. Temperature profile is the way the air temperature changes with altitude. Even on a hot summer day, a heavy downpour may have begun as a snowstorm high in the clouds overhead.

Rain and Snow In meteorology, the term *rain* means drops of water that fall from a cloud and have a diameter of at least 0.5 mm. When the surface temperature is above 4°C, snowflakes usually melt and continue their descent as rain before they reach the ground. At very low temperatures (when the moisture content of air is small) light, fluffy snow made up of individual six-sided ice crystals forms. At temperatures warmer than −5°C, ice crystals join into larger clumps. Snowfalls of these snowflakes are heavy and have high moisture contents.

Sleet, Glaze, and Hail Sleet is the fall of small particles of clear-to-translucent ice. For sleet to form, a layer of air with temperatures above freezing must overlie a subfreezing layer near the ground. Glaze, also known as freezing rain, results when raindrops become supercooled (below 0°C) as they fall through subfreezing air near the ground and turn to ice when they impact objects.

Hail is produced in cumulonimbus clouds. Hailstones begin as small ice pellets that grow by collecting supercooled water droplets as they fall through a cloud. If the ice pellets encounter a strong updraft, they may be carried upward and begin the downward journey once more. Each trip through the supercooled portion of the cloud may be represented by another layer of ice, as shown in Figure 15.

Figure 15 This largest recorded hailstone fell over Kansas in 1970 and weighed 766 grams.

Section 18.3 Assessment

Reviewing Concepts

1. How are clouds classified?
2. Compare and contrast clouds and fogs.
3. What must happen in order for precipitation to form?
4. Describe how the temperature profile of air near Earth's surface controls the type of precipitation that falls to the ground.

Critical Thinking

5. **Predicting** What type of precipitation would fall to Earth's surface if a thick layer of air near the ground was −8°C?
6. **Classifying** Identify the following cloud types as producers of heavy, light, or generally no precipitation.
   a. cirrocumulus b. cumulonimbus
   c. stratus d. nimbostratus

Writing in Science

Compare-Contrast Paragraph Write a paragraph comparing the Bergeron and collision-coalescence processes. Relate each to the type(s) of precipitation that can result.

Section 18.3 Assessment

1. Clouds are classified according to form and height.
2. Clouds and fogs are physically the same. Fogs are clouds with their bases at or very near the ground.
3. Cloud droplets must increase in volume by about one million times.
4. Ice crystals formed at higher layers in the atmosphere become liquid and fall as rain if temperatures are warm enough near the ground. The thickness of layers at certain temperatures must also be thick enough to impart a change in the type of precipitation.
5. Light, fluffy snow would fall.
6. a. generally no precipitation **b.** heavy precipitation **c.** light or no precipitation **d.** light-to-heavy precipitation

people and the ENVIRONMENT

Atmospheric Stability and Air Pollution

Air quality is closely linked to the atmosphere's ability to scatter pollutants. Perhaps you've heard "Dilution is the solution to pollution." To a large degree, this is true. If the air into which pollution is released is not dispersed, the air will become more toxic. Two of the most important atmospheric conditions affecting the distribution of pollutants are wind strength and air stability.

When winds are weak or calm, the concentration of pollutants is higher than when winds are strong. High wind speeds mix polluted air into a larger volume of surrounding air, causing the pollution to be more diluted. When winds are light, there is less turbulence and mixing, so the concentration of pollutants is higher.

Atmospheric stability affects vertical movements of air. In general, the larger the extent of vertical mixing, the better the air quality is. During a temperature inversion, the atmosphere is very stable and it does not move much vertically. Warm air overlying cooler air acts as a lid and prevents upward movement, which leaves pollutants trapped near the ground, as shown in Figure 16.

Some inversions form near the ground, while others form higher above the ground. A surface inversion develops close to the ground on clear and relatively calm nights because the ground is a better radiator of heat than the air above it. Radiation from the ground to the clear night sky causes more rapid cooling at the surface than higher in the atmosphere. The result is that the air close to the ground is cooled more than the air above, yielding a temperature profile similar to the one shown in Figure 17. After sunrise, the ground is heated and the inversion disappears.

Although surface inversions usually are shallow, they may be thick in regions where the land surface is uneven. Because cold air is denser than warm air, the chilled air near the surface gradually drains from slopes into adjacent lowlands and valleys. As might be expected, these thicker surface inversions will not spread out as quickly after sunrise.

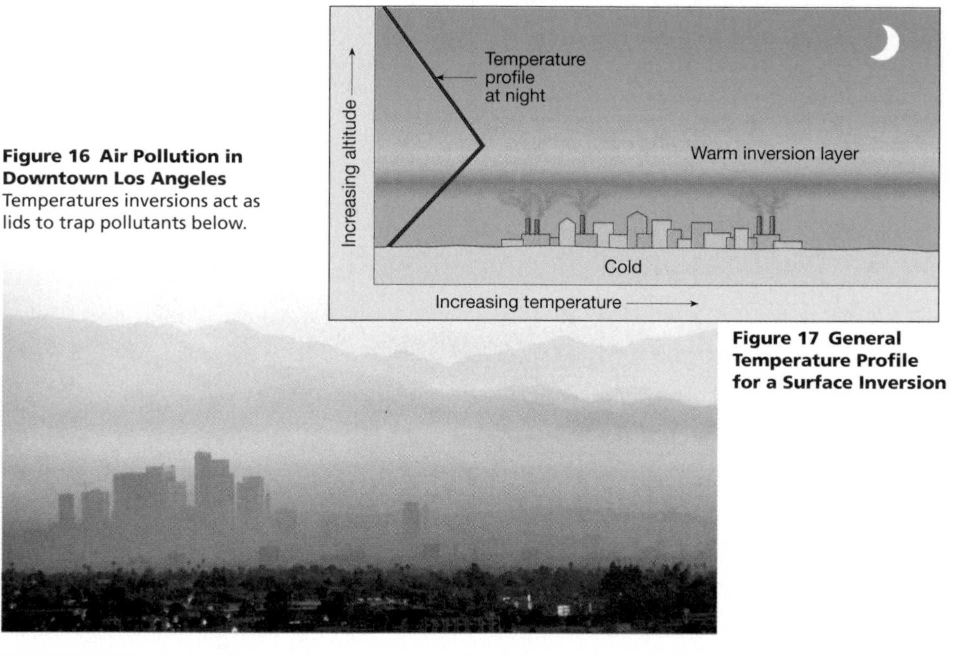

Figure 16 Air Pollution in Downtown Los Angeles Temperatures inversions act as lids to trap pollutants below.

Figure 17 General Temperature Profile for a Surface Inversion

Atmospheric Stability and Air Pollution

L2

Background

- The strength of the wind and the stability of the air are critical because they determine how rapidly pollutants are diluted by mixing with the surrounding air after leaving the source.
- The distance between Earth's surface and the height to which vertical air movements extend is termed the *mixing depth*. Generally, the greater the mixing depth, the better the air quality. When the mixing depth is several kilometers, pollutants are mixed through a large volume of cleaner air and dilute rapidly. When the mixing depth is shallow, pollutants are confined to a much smaller volume of air and concentrations can reach unhealthy levels.
- Because heating of Earth's surface by the sun enhances convectional movements, mixing depths are usually greater during the afternoon hours. For the same reason, mixing depths during the summer months are typically greater than during the winter months.
- Many extensive and long-lived air-pollution episodes are linked to temperature inversions that develop in association with the sinking air that characterizes slow-moving centers of high pressure. As the air sinks to lower altitudes, it is compressed and so its temperature rises. Because turbulence is almost always present near the ground, this lowermost portion of the atmosphere is generally prevented from participating in the general subsidence. Thus, an inversion develops aloft between the lower turbulent zone and the subsiding warmed layers above.

Teaching Tip

Ask students to research various methods that meteorologists use to define atmospheric stability. Have them explain each method and cite the pros and cons of each use.

Exploration Lab

Measuring Humidity

L2

Objectives

In this activity, students will

- calculate relative humidity from air moisture content data.
- determine the relative humidity inside and outside using a psychrometer.

Skills Focus Observing, Measuring, Analyzing Data, Calculating

 **Prep Time** 10 minutes

Alternative Materials (if a psychrometer is not available) 2 thermometers, cotton gauze, paper fan, string

Class Time 30 minutes

Teaching Tip To save time, construct the wet-bulb thermometer before the lab.

Expected Outcomes Students will practice calculating relative humidity from the moisture content of air. They also will experience using a psychrometer and determinative tables to determine the relative humidity in the classroom and outside. Relative humidity will vary widely with location; students can compare outside measurements with local meteorological data if they are available.

Sample Data

Procedure 3.

Data Table 1 Relative Humidity Determination Based on Water Vapor Content

Air Temperature (°C)	Water Vapor Content (g/kg)	Water Vapor Capacity (g/kg)	Relative Humidity (%)
25	5	20	25
25	12	[20]	[60]
25	18	[20]	[90]

Procedure 4. 51 percent

Exploration Lab

Measuring Humidity

Relative humidity is a measurement used to describe water vapor in the air. In general, it expresses how close the air is to saturation. In this lab, you will use a psychrometer and a data table to determine the relative humidity of air.

Problem

How can relative humidity be determined?

Materials

- calculator
- water at room temperature
- psychrometer

Alternative materials for psychrometer:

- 2 thermometers
- cotton gauze
- paper fan
- string

Skills

Observing, Measuring, Analyzing Data, Calculating

Procedure  

Part A: Calculating Relative Humidity From Water Vapor Content

1. On a sheet of paper, make a copy of Data Table 1.
2. Relative humidity is the ratio of the air's water vapor content to its water vapor capacity at a given temperature. Relative humidity is expressed as a percent.

   Relative humidity (%) =

   $$\frac{\text{Water vapor content}}{\text{Water vapor capacity}} \times 100$$

3. At 25°C, the water vapor capacity is 20 g/kg. Use this information to complete Data Table 1.

Part B: Determining Relative Humidity Using a Psychrometer

4. A psychrometer consists of two thermometers. The wet-bulb thermometer has a cloth wick that is wet with water and spun for about 1 minute. Relative humidity is determined by the difference in temperature reading between the dry-bulb temperature and the wet-bulb temperature, and using Data Table 2. For example, suppose a dry-bulb temperature is measured as 20°C, and a wet-bulb temperature is 14°C. Read the relative humidity from Data Table 2.
5. If a psychrometer is not available, construct a wet-bulb thermometer by tying a piece of cotton gauze around the end of a thermometer. Wet it with room-temperature water and fan it until the temperature stops changing.
6. Make wet-bulb and dry-bulb temperature measurements for air in your classroom and air outside. On a separate sheet of paper, make a copy of Data Table 3. Record your measurements. Use your measurements and Data Table 2 to determine the relative humidity inside and outside.

Data Table 1 Relative Humidity Determination Based on Water Vapor Content

Air Temperature (°C)	Water Vapor Content (g/kg)	Water Vapor Capacity (g/kg)	Relative Humidity (%)
25	5	20	25
25	12		
25	18		

Data Table 2 Relative Humidity (percent)

Depression of Wet-bulb Temperature
(Dry-bulb Temperature − Wet-bulb Temperature = Depression of the Wet Bulb)

Dry-bulb Temperature (°C)	1	2	3	4	5	6	7	8	9	10	11	12	13	14	15	16	17	18	19	20	21	22
−20	28																					
−18	40																					
−16	48	0																				
−14	55	11																				
−12	61	23																				
−10	66	33	0																			
−8	71	41	13																			
−6	73	48	20	0																		
−4	77	54	43	11																		
−2	79	58	37	20	1																	
0	81	63	45	28	11																	
2	83	67	51	36	20	6																
4	85	70	56	42	27	14																
6	86	72	59	46	35	22	10	0														
8	87	74	62	51	39	28	17	6														
10	88	76	65	54	43	33	24	13	4													
12	88	78	67	57	48	38	28	19	10	2												
14	89	79	69	60	50	41	33	25	16	8	1											
16	90	80	71	62	54	45	37	29	21	14	7	1										
18	91	81	72	64	56	48	40	33	26	19	12	6	0									
20	91	82	74	66	58	51	44	36	30	23	17	11	5	0								
22	92	83	75	68	60	53	46	40	33	27	21	15	10	4	0							
24	92	84	76	69	62	55	49	42	36	30	25	20	14	9	4	0						
26	92	85	77	70	64	57	51	45	39	34	28	23	18	13	9	5						
28	93	86	78	71	65	59	53	47	42	36	31	26	21	17	12	8	2					
30	93	86	79	72	66	61	55	49	44	39	34	29	25	20	16	12	8	4				
32	93	86	80	73	68	62	56	51	46	41	36	32	27	22	19	14	11	8	4			
34	93	86	81	74	69	63	58	52	48	43	38	34	30	26	22	18	14	11	8	5		
36	94	87	81	75	69	64	59	54	50	44	40	36	32	28	24	21	17	13	10	7	4	
38	94	87	82	76	70	66	60	55	51	46	42	38	34	30	26	23	20	16	13	10	7	5
40	94	89	82	76	71	67	61	57	52	48	44	40	36	33	29	25	22	19	16	13	10	7

Relative Humidity Values

Data Table 3 Relative Humidity Determinations Using Dry- and Wet-Bulb Thermometers

	Inside	Outside
Dry-bulb temperature (°C)		
Wet-bulb temperature (°C)		
Difference between dry-bulb and wet-bulb temperatures (°C)		
Relative humidity (%)		

Analyze and Conclude

1. **Comparing and Contrasting** How do the relative humidity measurements for inside and outside compare? Why are your determinations similar or different?
2. **Applying Concepts** Explain the principle behind using a psychrometer to determine relative humidity.
3. **Applying Concepts** Suppose you hear on the radio that the relative humidity is 90 percent on a winter day. Can you conclude that this air contains more moisture than air on a summer day with a 40 percent relative humidity? Explain why or why not.
4. **Applying Concepts** Why is a cool basement often damp in the summer?

Analyze and Conclude

1. Outdoor relative humidity determinations can be compared to meteorological reports for the day. Indoor relative humidity will vary widely depending on whether classrooms are air-conditioned, what season it is, or other variables.

2. Relative humidity determinations with the psychrometer depend on the evaporation rate of the wick on the wet bulb. The drier the air, the larger the wet-bulb temperature will be depressed, and the lower the relative humidity.

3. No; relative humidity depends on the capacity of air to hold water, which varies with temperature. The actual water content of winter air with 90 percent relative humidity can be less than summer air with 40 percent relative humidity.

4. The relative humidity will increase as air is cooled in the basement.

Kinesthetic, Logical

Study Guide

Study Tip

Change Subjects and Take Breaks
Tell students that when they feel that they are losing their ability to focus, they should change the task they are working on, the subject they are studying, or even the room they are in. Suggest that students organize all their subjects into manageable blocks. When students have finished one block, they should switch to another block in another part of the subject or to a different subject. Encourage students to take five-minute breaks every 30–40 minutes to refresh themselves.

Thinking Visually

a. form
b. cumulus (or stratus)
c. stratus (or cumulus)
d. high (or low)
e. low (or high)

CHAPTER 18

Study Guide

18.1 Water in the Atmosphere

Key Concepts

- Water vapor is the most important gas in the atmosphere for understanding atmospheric processes.
- The process of changing state requires that energy is transferred in the form of heat.
- When saturated, warm air contains more water vapor than cold air.
- Relative humidity is a ratio of the air's actual water-vapor content compared with the amount of water vapor needed for saturation at that temperature and pressure.
- When the water-vapor content of air remains constant, lowering air temperature causes an increase in relative humidity, and raising air temperature causes a decrease in relative humidity.

Vocabulary

precipitation, *p. 504;* latent heat, *p. 505;* evaporation, *p. 505;* condensation, *p. 506;* sublimation, *p. 506;* deposition, *p. 506;* humidity, *p. 506;* saturated, *p. 506;* relative humidity, *p. 506;* dew point, *p. 508;* hygrometer, *p. 508*

18.2 Cloud Formation

Key Concepts

- When air is allowed to expand, it cools, and when it is compressed, it warms.
- Four mechanisms that can cause air to rise are orographic lifting, frontal wedging, convergence, and localized convective lifting.
- Stable air tends to remain in its original position, while unstable air tends to rise.
- For condensation of water to occur, the air must be saturated.

Vocabulary

dry adiabatic rate, *p. 511;* wet adiabatic rate, *p. 511;* orographic lifting, *p. 512;* front, *p. 512;* temperature inversion, *p. 514;* condensation nuclei, *p. 516*

18.3 Cloud Types and Precipitation

Key Concepts

- Clouds are classified on the basis of their form and height.
- Fog is a cloud with its base at or very near the ground.
- In order for precipitation to form, cloud droplets must grow in volume by roughly one million times.
- The type of precipitation that reaches Earth's surface depends on the temperature profile in the lowest few kilometers of the atmosphere.

Vocabulary

cirrus, *p. 517;* cumulus, *p. 517;* stratus, *p. 518;* Bergeron process, *p. 521;* supercooled water, *p. 521;* supersaturated air, *p. 521;* collision-coalescence process, *p. 521*

Thinking Visually

Concept Map Copy the concept map below onto a sheet of paper. Use information from the chapter to complete the concept map.

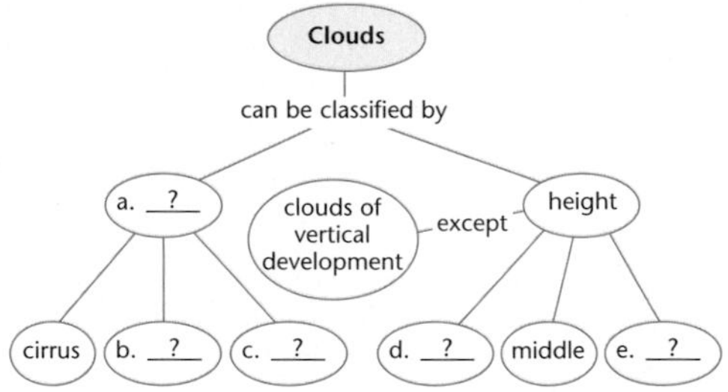

Chapter Assessment Resources

Print
Chapter Test, Chapter 18
Test Prep Resources, Chapter 18

Technology
Computer Test Bank, Chapter 18 Test
Online Text, Chapter 18
Go Online, PHSchool.com, Chapter 18

CHAPTER 18

NY Regents Content Item

Assessment

Interactive textbook with assessment at PHSchool.com

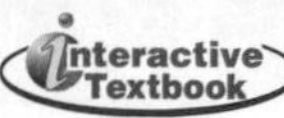

Reviewing Content

Choose the number that best answers the question or completes the statement.

1 What is the general term for water vapor in air? NY
(1) capacity (2) condensation
(3) humidity (4) saturation

2 During which process does water vapor change to the liquid state? NY
(1) condensation (2) deposition
(3) melting (4) sublimation

3 The ratio of air's actual water-vapor content to the amount of water needed for saturation is the NY
(1) adiabatic rate (2) dew point
(3) relative humidity (4) water capacity

4 What are visible mixtures of tiny water droplets or ice crystals suspended in air? NY
(1) clouds (2) dew
(3) hail (4) sleet

5 Air that has a 100 percent relative humidity is said to be NY
(1) dry (2) saturated
(3) stable (4) unstable

6 Compared to clouds, fogs are NY
(1) a different composition
(2) at lower altitudes
(3) colder
(4) thicker

7 Which of the following clouds are high, white, and thin?
(1) cirrus (2) cumulus
(3) nimbostratus (4) stratus

8 Which of the following words means "rainy cloud"?
(1) cirrus (2) cumulus
(3) nimbus (4) stratus

9 Which of the following substances changes from one state of matter to another at temperatures and pressures experienced at Earth's surface? NY
(1) carbon dioxide (2) nitrogen
(3) oxygen (4) water

10 Which of the following forms when supercooled raindrops freeze on contact with solid objects near Earth's surface?
(1) glaze (2) hail
(3) sleet (4) snow

Understanding Concepts

11 What happens when unstable air is forced to rise? NY

12 Describe the conditions that might cause convergence.

13 As you drink an ice-cold beverage on a hot day, the outside of the glass becomes wet. Explain why this happens. NY

14 What is the difference between condensation and precipitation? NY

15 Why does air cool when it rises through the atmosphere? What is this type of cooling known as? NY

16 Write a general statement relating air temperature and the amount of water vapor needed to saturate the air. NY

17 Describe the difference between clouds and water vapor. NY

18 List two changes of state for water that cause latent heat to be released. NY

Use the figure below to answer questions 19 and 20.

19 Which air-lifting mechanism is shown? NY

20 Use the dry adiabatic rate of 10°C per kilometer to determine the air temperature on the windward side of the mountains at an altitude of 500 meters. NY

Homework Guide

Section	Questions
1	1–3, 5, 9, 13, 16, 18, 25–27, 30
2	4, 11, 12, 15, 17, 19–23, 28, 29
3	6–8, 10, 14, 24

Assessment

Reviewing Content

(1) 3 (2) 1 (3) 3
(4) 1 (5) 2 (6) 2
(7) 1 (8) 3 (9) 4
(10) 1

Understanding Concepts

(11) Towering clouds form that often produce heavy thunderstorms or other severe weather.
(12) When air in the lower atmosphere flows together, lifting occurs, often causing clouds and precipitation.
(13) The cold glass cools the air in contact with it below the air's dew point, and water vapor condenses on the glass.
(14) Condensation is the process of changing water vapor to the liquid state. Precipitation is any form of water that falls from a cloud.
(15) Air expands as it rises, which causes it to cool. This type of cooling is known as adiabatic cooling.
(16) The warmer the air temperature, the more water vapor is needed to saturate the air.
(17) Clouds are composed of liquid water droplets or ice particles. Water vapor is water in the gaseous state.
(18) Two changes of state are water vapor changing to liquid water (condensation) and liquid water changing to ice (freezing).
(19) The mechanism is orographic lifting.
(20) The temperature is 20°C.

Critical Thinking

(21) Thermals are warm air parcels that are less dense than surrounding air. Their buoyancy gives birds lift as they glide above them.
(22) Some types of pavement, such as blacktop, in urban areas have low reflecting capabilities, and therefore low albedos. When these areas absorb sunlight and radiate heat, hot pockets of air can form that rise by localized convective uplift.
(23) In general, when unstable air rises it produces towering clouds and heavy precipitation. In contrast, a stable air mass resists movement vertically (does not turn over), which may stagnate weather patterns.
(24) Low lying areas such as river valleys should be avoided because thick fog accumulations may form in them.

Math Skills

(25) a. 47 g/kg
b. 3.5 g/kg
c. 2 g/kg
(26) It decreases by 3.5 g/kg. This is a 50% decrease.
(27) 7 g/kg ÷ 10 g/kg × 100 = 70%

Concepts in Action

(28) Moist air from the Pacific Ocean is forced up the windward slope by orographic lifting, causing cloud formation and heavy precipitation.
(29) Heat is absorbed when ice changes to water (melting), when water changes to water vapor (evaporation), and when ice turns directly to water vapor without passing through the liquid state (sublimation). Heat is liberated during condensation, freezing, and deposition.
(30) Student paragraphs should reflect the following concepts: An increase in elevation often brings more precipitation, especially on windward slopes. A decrease in the area covered by forests and other types of vegetation would reduce precipitation because less moisture would be added to the atmosphere from plants. Winds blowing more frequently from an adjacent body of water would increase the amount of precipitation as more moisture is brought to the area.

Assessment *continued*

Critical Thinking

21 **Applying Concepts** What is the physical property of thermals that helps birds of prey? Describe how this physical property helps these birds. NY

22 **Applying Concepts** Explain how urban areas contribute to localized convective lifting. NY

23 **Identifying Cause and Effect** Describe how atmospheric stability affects daily weather. Include specific examples.

24 **Applying Concepts** In general, when traveling in foggy conditions, what types of topography should you be most cautious of? NY

Math Skills

Use the table below to answer questions 25–27.

Water Vapor Needed for Saturation

Temperature		Mass of water vapor per kg of air (g/kg)
°C	(°F)	
−40	(−40)	0.1
−30	(−22)	0.3
−20	(−4)	0.75
−10	(14)	2
0	(32)	3.5
5	(41)	5
10	(50)	7
15	(59)	10
20	(68)	14
25	(77)	20
30	(86)	26.5
35	(95)	35
40	(104)	47

25 **Analyzing Data** According to the table, how much water vapor is required to saturate a kilogram of air at each of the following temperatures?
(1) 40°C
(2) 0°C
(3) −10°C

26 **Calculating** How does the amount of water vapor required to saturate 1 kilogram of air change when it is cooled from 10°C to 0°C? NY

27 **Calculating** Use the table to determine the relative humidity of air at 15°C when its water vapor content is 7 g/kg.

Concepts in Action

28 **Inferring** Mount Waialeale, Hawaii, is located on a windward mountain slope. A weather station there records the highest average annual rainfall at 1234 cm. Explain what processes could contribute to this extreme rainfall. NY

29 **Interpreting Illustrations** After studying Figure 2, summarize the processes by which water changes from one state of matter to another. For each case, point out whether heat energy is absorbed or released. NY

30 **Writing in Science** The amount of precipitation that falls at any particular place and time is controlled by the quantity of moisture in the air and many other factors, which may include (1) an increase in the elevation of the land, (2) a decrease in the area covered by forests and other types of vegetation, and (3) an increase in the percentage of time that the winds blow from an adjacent body of water. Write a paragraph explaining how each of these factors might change the precipitation at a particular location. NY

Performance-Based Assessment

Designing an Experiment Design and conduct an experiment that explores daily variations in temperature and relative humidity. As a first step, write a clear hypothesis statement. Then plan and design the experiment. Include sample data tables in your plan. Have your teacher approve your plan before you begin.

Regents Practice Exam

Test-Taking Tip

When answering a question with a graph, keep these tips in mind:

- Read the question thoroughly to identify what the question is asking.
- Study the title of the graph. This may help you identify what information is available from the graph.
- Examine the graph and note the axes labels.
- Identify the scale of the axes.
- Recall information, equations, definitions, relationship, and so forth that may be required to interpret the graph.
- Once you have chosen your answer, check it against the graph.

Graph 1 Temperature and Relative Humidity

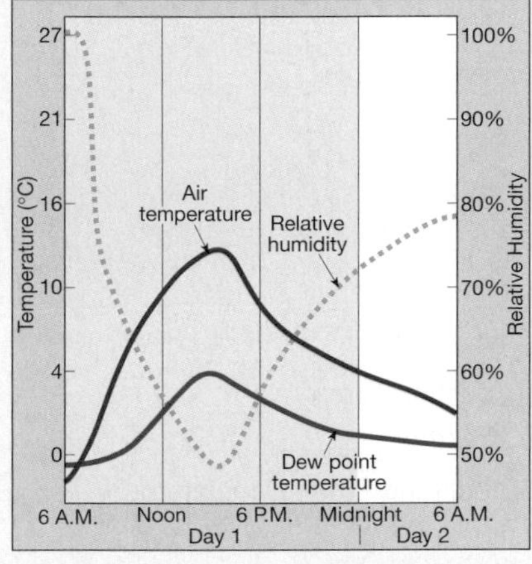

The graph above depicts variations in temperature and relative humidity on a spring day. Which of the following statements is true?

(1) When temperature increases, relative humidity increases.
(2) When temperature decreases, relative humidity decreases.
(3) When temperature increases, relative humidity decreases.
(4) Temperature and relative humidity are not related.

(Answer: 3)

For *each* statement or question, choose the *number* of the word or expression that, of those given, best completes the statement or answers the question. Some questions may require the use of the *Earth Science Reference Tables.*

1 The dew point is the temperature at which
  (1) cumulus clouds change to cirrus clouds
  (2) hailstones are formed
  (3) liquid water changes to vapor
  (4) water vapor condenses to liquid

2 Which process is most important for cloud formation?
  (1) cooling by compression of air
  (2) cooling by contact with a cold surface
  (3) cooling by expansion of air
  (4) cooling by radiation from Earth's surface

3 Which choice best lists the steps necessary for cloud formation?
  (1) Air rises, expands, and cools to its dew point.
  (2) Air rises, compresses and warms to its dew point.
  (3) Air sinks, expands, and cools to its dew point.
  (4) Air sinks, compresses, and warms to its dew point.

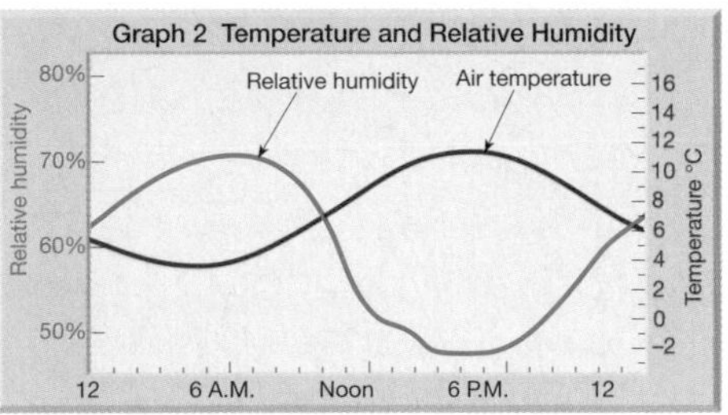

Answer the following questions in complete sentences. Some questions may require the use of the *Earth Science Reference Tables.* Base your answers to questions 4 through 6 on the diagram above, which shows Temperature and Relative Humidity.

4 According to the graph, at approximately what time was the relative humidity at its maximum?

5 What is the relationship between relative humidity and temperature? Explain why this is the case even when the absolute humidity of the air remains constant.

Regents Practice Exam

(1) 4
(2) 3
(3) 1
(4) The relative humidity was greatest at approximately 6 A.M.
(5) At temperature increases, relative humidity decreases because expansion of the air allows warmer air to hold more moisture than cooler air.

Performance-Based Assessment

Student hypotheses should state that relative humidity decreases as daytime temperatures increase. Students should plan times to make relative humidity measurements that are spaced throughout the day. Equipment needed is the same as that used in the Exploration Lab.

Your students can independently test their knowledge of the chapter and print out their results.

CHAPTER 19

Planning Guide

Use these planning tools
Use Teacher Express for all your planning needs

SECTION OBJECTIVES	STANDARDS NATIONAL	STANDARDS STATE	ACTIVITIES and LABS
19.1 Understanding Air Pressure, pp. 532–536 1 block or 2 periods **19.1** **Describe** how air pressure is exerted on objects. **19.2** **Explain** how changes in air pressure affect the mercury column of a barometer. **19.3** **Identify** the ultimate energy source for wind. **19.4** **Describe** how the Coriolis effect influences freely moving objects.	A-1, A-2, B-4, D-1		**SE** Inquiry Activity: How Do Gradients Influence Speed? p. 531 L2 **TE** Teacher Demo: Measuring the Mass of Air, p. 532 L2 **TE** Teacher Demo: Air Pressure, p. 533 L2
19.2 Pressure Centers and Winds, pp. 537–542 1 block or 2 periods **19.5** **Explain** how winds blow around pressure centers in the Northern and Southern Hemispheres. **19.6** **Describe** the air pressure patterns within cyclones and anticyclones. **19.7** **Describe** how friction controls the net flow of air around a cyclone and an anticyclone. **19.8** **Explain** how the unequal heating of Earth's surface affects the atmosphere.	B-4, D-1		**TE** Build Science Skills, p. 537 L2 **TE** Teacher Demo: Warm Air Rises, p. 538 L2 **LM** Analyzing Pressure Systems L2
19.3 Regional Wind Systems, pp. 543–548 1 block or 2 periods **19.9** **Identify** the causes of local winds. **19.10** **Describe** the general movement of weather in the United States. **19.11** **Compare and contrast** weather patterns characteristic of El Niño and La Niña events.	A-1, A-2, D-1, G-1		**TE** Teacher Demo: Differential Heating, p. 544 L2 **SE** Exploration Lab: Observing Wind Patterns, pp. 550–551 L2

Ability Levels

L1 For students who need additional help
L2 For all students
L3 For students who need to be challenged

Components

SE	Student Edition	**GRSW**	Guided Reading & Study Workbook	**TP**	Test Prep Resources	**GEO**	Geode CD-ROM
TE	Teacher's Edition	**TEX**	Teacher Express	**onT**	onlineText	**T**	Transparencies
LM	Laboratory Manual	**CTB**	Computer Test Bank	**DC**	Discovery Channel Videos	**GO**	Internet Resources
CUT	Chapter Tests						

RESOURCES PRINT and TECHNOLOGY	SECTION ASSESSMENT
GRSW Section 19.1 **T-265** Mercury Barometer and Aneroid Barograph **T-266** Weather Map of U.S. **T-267** Coriolis Effect **T-268** The Geostrophic Wind **T-269** Upper-Air Winds **T-270** Comparison: Upper-Level Winds and Surface Winds **GEODe** The Atmosphere ↳ Air Pressure and Wind **TEX** Lesson Planning 19.1	**SE** Section 19.1 Assessment, p. 536 **onT** Section 19.1
GRSW Section 19.2 **T-271** Cyclonic and Anticyclonic Winds **T-272** Airflow Associated with Surface Cyclones and Anticyclones **T-273** Global Circulation on Non-Rotating Earth **T-274** Idealized Global Circulation **T-275** Average Surface Barometric Pressure in Millibars **T-276** Sea and Land Breezes **T-277** Valley and Mountain Breezes **T-278** Wind Roses **TEX** Lesson Planning 19.2	**SE** Section 19.2 Assessment, p. 542 **onT** Section 19.2
GRSW Section 19.3 **T-279** Relationship Between the Southern Oscillation and El Niño **T-280** Southern Oscillation **T-281** Average Annual Precipitation in Millimeters **T-282** Wind Power **T-283** Tracking El Niño From Space **TEX** Lesson Planning 19.3	**SE** Section 19.3 Assessment, p. 548 **onT** Section 19.3

Go Online

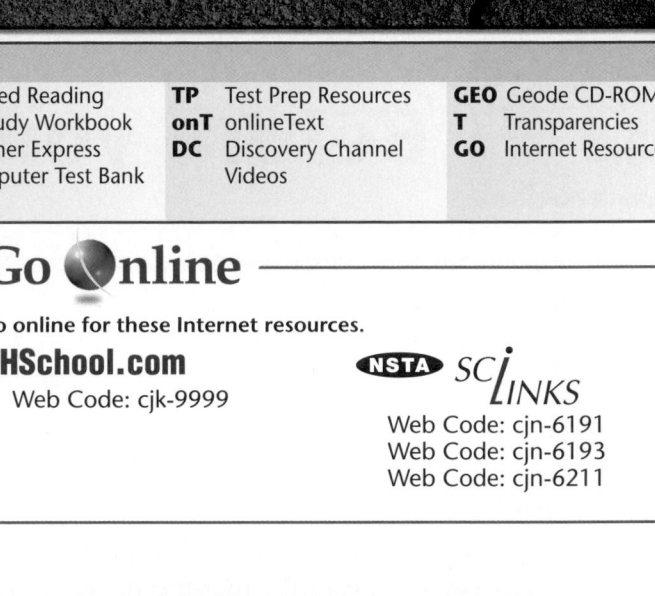

Go online for these Internet resources.

PHSchool.com
Web Code: cjk-9999

Web Code: cjn-6191
Web Code: cjn-6193
Web Code: cjn-6211

Materials for Activities and Labs

Quantities for each group

STUDENT EDITION

Inquiry Activity, p. 531
textbooks, wood blocks, or other items to raise one end of ramp; wood plank to use as ramp; tennis ball; stopwatch

Exploration Lab, pp. 550–551
1 copy each of Figure 1 and Figure 2 from the Earth Science Laboratory Manual, paper, pencil

TEACHER'S EDITION

Teacher Demo, p. 532
balloon, balance scale

Teacher Demo, p. 533
glass, water, cardboard, sink or basin

Build Science Skills, p. 537
globe, pointer

Teacher Demo, p. 538
2 meter sticks, 2 large paper grocery bags, string, tape, lamp with incandescent bulb

Teacher Demo, p. 544
2 containers, soil, water, 2 thermometers

Chapter Assessment

ASSESSMENT

SE Assessment, pp. 553–554
CUT Chapter 19 Test
CTB Chapter 19
onT Chapter 19

STANDARDIZED TEST PREP

SE Chapter 19, p. 555
TP Progress Monitoring Assessments

interactive textbook with assessment at PHSchool.com

CHAPTER 19

Before you teach

Michael Wysession
Washington University

Big Ideas

Weather is a complicated and hard-to-predict result of interactions between atmospheric pressure, ocean temperatures, and land conditions.

Space and Time The atmosphere applies air pressure, which is exerted in all directions, and can be measured with a barometer. Wind is the result of air flowing from areas of high pressure to areas of low pressure.

Forces and Motion Wind patterns are controlled by atmospheric pressure differences, the Coriolis effect, and friction. Steep pressure gradients cause strong winds. The Coriolis effect is a result of Earth's rotation. In the Northern Hemisphere, winds blow inward and counterclockwise around an area of low pressure, forming a cyclone; winds blow outward and clockwise around an area of high pressure, forming an anticyclone. Bad weather is often associated with cyclones.

Matter and Energy Global wind patterns result from the atmospheric heat transfer system, which moves warm air toward the poles and cool air toward the equator, as well as from the Coriolis effect and the locations of continents. Local winds often result from daily changes in temperature that result from topographic variations (like between mountains and valleys) or changes in surface composition (like between land and ocean).

Earth as a System Changes in ocean currents, like with the El Niño and La Niña conditions, can have significant effects on weather patterns.

Earth Science Refresher

The Coriolis Effect

The Coriolis effect often seems very mysterious to students. Contrary to popular myth, the Coriolis effect is too small to make your sink drain in a clockwise direction (try it—about half the time it will drain clockwise; the other half, counterclockwise). However, the Coriolis effect is noticeable in some everyday applications. As you will see on p. 535 (Facts and Figures), the Coriolis effect can have a measurable change in the path of a hard-hit baseball. One of the most famous results of the Coriolis effect occurred in 1915 in a sea battle between the British and German navies near the Falkland Islands, off the coast of South America. To the surprise of the gunners of the British ships, their usually accurate shots were landing almost 100 m to the left of their targets (the German ships). While the British engineers certainly knew about the Coriolis effect, they had calibrated their guns for the Northern Hemisphere, where the Coriolis effect made their shots veer to the right. Here in the Southern Hemisphere, the Coriolis effect made the shots veer to the left. As a result of their mistaken calibration, they actually doubled the Coriolis effect's change in their cannon targets.

Address Misconceptions

Students may have the misconception that no outside factor except heat is required to cause masses of warm air to rotate as they rise upward in the atmosphere. Point out that the cyclonic motion in low-pressure cells is primarily a result of the Coriolis effect. For a strategy that helps to overcome this misconception, see **Address Misconceptions** on **p. 538.**

The Coriolis effect is also important in another, less observable, way. It is the Coriolis effect on the flow of liquid iron in Earth's outer core that is responsible for Earth's magnetic field. The outer core's liquid iron is vigorously convecting as it cools off, losing its heat to the surrounding mantle. As this liquid flows, the Coriolis effect causes it to move in a spiraling motion, just like flowing air in the atmosphere. Because the core's liquid iron is electrically charged, the spiraling motion creates a magnetic field, which we can measure at the surface. We not only use the magnetic field for navigation (as do some migratory birds, which have been found to have magnetite mineral grains in their brains!), but the magnetic field protects Earth from the ionized particles of the solar wind, which would otherwise be harmful for life.

The Worst Wind Ever

Doppler radar has clocked wind speeds in some tornadoes at over 500 km per hour. However, the world's record for the greatest wind speed recorded on land is 372 km/h, recorded during a storm at the top of Mt. Washington in New Hampshire. This record wind, the strongest ever recorded on an anemometer, occurred on April 12, 1934. Mt. Washington is the tallest mountain in New England, and because of its height and location, is often subject to some incredibly bad storms, which is why it has had weather observatories on its summit dating back to 1870. The mountain's summit now has a state-of-the-art weather station and museum. In 1934, however, the meteorologists' ability to survive and maintain the station's operation during the record storm was as remarkable as the wind speeds themselves.

Go Online NSTA PD LINKS

For: Chapter 19 Content Support
Visit: www.SciLinks.org/PDLinks
Web Code: cjn-1999

Build Reading Literacy

Make Inferences

Reading Between the Lines

Strategy Help students fill in information not found in the text by drawing on prior knowledge and using context clues. To use this strategy, students must identify their prior knowledge, recognize clues in the text, and make connections between their prior knowledge and text clues to make an inference. The passage Non-Rotating Earth Model on p. 540 in Section 19.2 provides a sample.

Example

1. Read aloud or have students read aloud a portion of the chosen text. Point out an example of the author's referring to something without explaining it completely. Tell students that texts often do not explain every detail because they assume that the reader has a certain amount of background knowledge.
2. Model this strategy by thinking aloud. First, mention facts you already know that are directly related to the subject, either from your own experience or from what you have read about it previously in the text.
3. Next, read text clues aloud and point out what those clues tell about the concept.
4. Then, explain what you understand about the text by combining your prior knowledge and text clues.
5. Have students read the next paragraph or two silently, applying the strategies to make an inference. Discuss their inferences.
6. Repeat this process, having students work with partners to find other opportunities to make inferences in the chapter.

See pp. 534 and 539 for a script on how to use this strategy with students. For additional strategies, see p. 546.

ASSESS PRIOR KNOWLEDGE

Use the Chapter Pretest below to assess students' prior knowledge. As needed, review these concepts.

Review Science Concepts

Section 19.1 Reviewing the definition of air pressure and learning how friction, the Coriolis effect, and air pressure differences affect winds will help students begin to understand the mechanisms that drive Earth's weather.

Section 19.2 Knowledge of cyclonic and anticyclonic pressure centers and Earth's global winds gives students further understanding of how air pressure patterns affect weather.

Section 19.3 Learning how locally generated pressure gradients produce small-scale winds further enhances student understanding of weather. Learning how El Niño and La Niña events affect air movement, locally as well as globally, helps students recognize the complexity of Earth's weather patterns.

Review Math Skills

Analyzing Data, Measuring, Calculating Students need to analyze data shown on a weather map and calculate how often winds blow from different directions in the mapped area.

Direct students to the Math Skills in the Skills Handbook at the end of the student text.

CHAPTER

19 Air Pressure and Wind

CONCEPTS in Action

Exploration Lab
Observing Wind Patterns

Understanding Earth
Tracking El Niño from Space

The Atmosphere
↳ Air Pressure and Wind

For: Chapter 19 Resources
Visit: PHSchool.com
Web Code: cjk-9999

Sailboats in this Norwegian fjord get their power from the wind. ▶

Chapter Pretest

1. What source of energy fuels the wind? *(sunlight)*

2. Which of the following statements about air pressure is NOT true? *(d)*
   - a. Air pressure is exerted in all directions.
   - b. Air pressure equals weight of air.
   - c. Air pressure is measured using the element mercury.
   - d. Air pressure is not associated with weather.

3. What instrument is used to measure air pressure? *(a)*
   - a. barometer
   - b. anemometer
   - c. hygrometer
   - d. thermometer

4. Which of the following is influenced by the Coriolis effect? *(b)*
   - a. wind speed
   - b. wind direction
   - c. air pressure
   - d. pressure gradients

5. Which of the following causes wind? *(c)*
   - a. ocean currents
   - b. land masses
   - c. pressure gradients
   - d. weather patterns

6. Which of the following best describes weather near the center of a region of high pressure? *(b)*
   - a. cloudy with rain
   - b. clear and fair
   - c. hurricane
   - d. fog

Chapter Preview

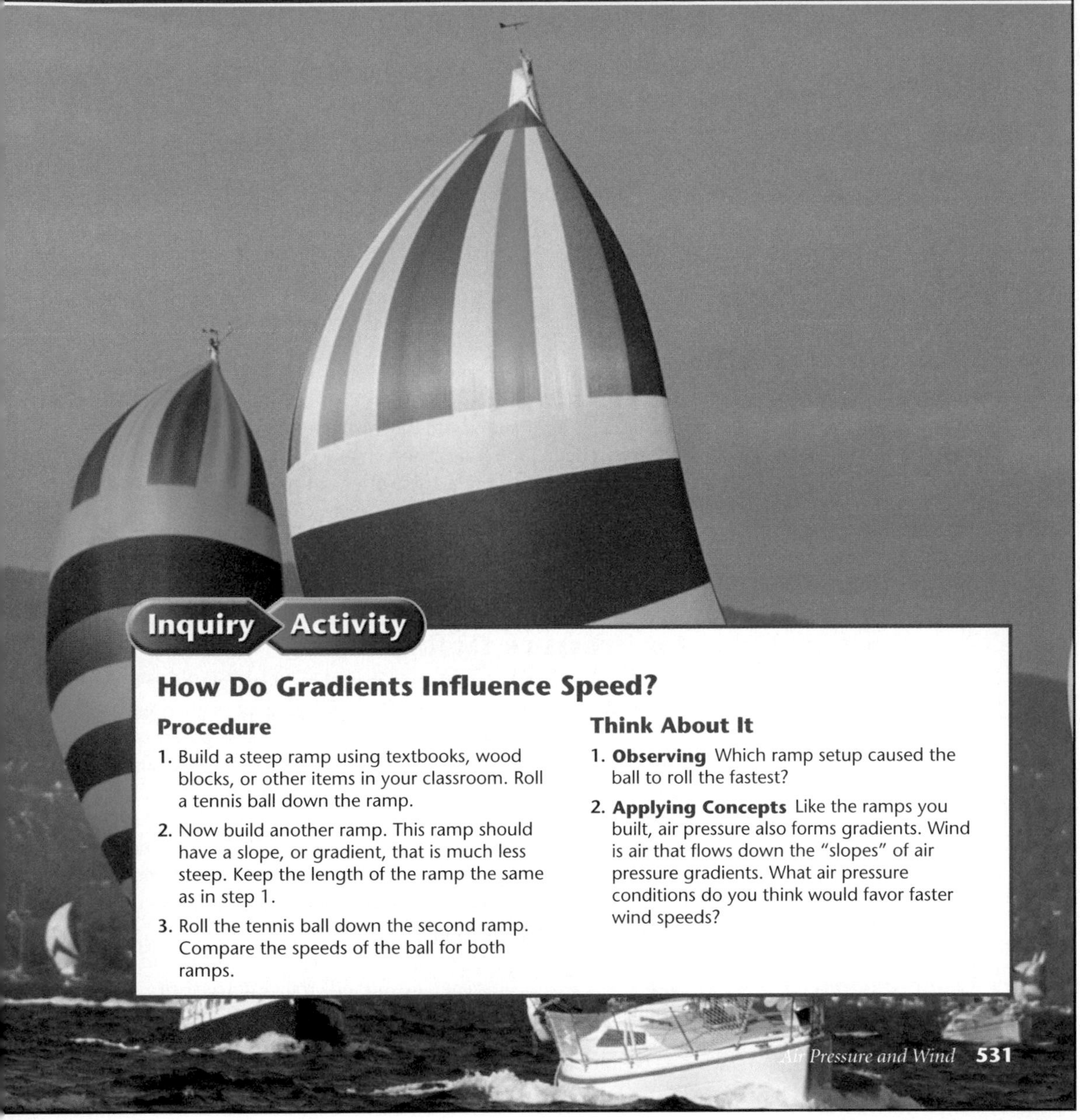

Inquiry Activity

How Do Gradients Influence Speed?

Procedure

1. Build a steep ramp using textbooks, wood blocks, or other items in your classroom. Roll a tennis ball down the ramp.
2. Now build another ramp. This ramp should have a slope, or gradient, that is much less steep. Keep the length of the ramp the same as in step 1.
3. Roll the tennis ball down the second ramp. Compare the speeds of the ball for both ramps.

Think About It

1. **Observing** Which ramp setup caused the ball to roll the fastest?
2. **Applying Concepts** Like the ramps you built, air pressure also forms gradients. Wind is air that flows down the "slopes" of air pressure gradients. What air pressure conditions do you think would favor faster wind speeds?

ENGAGE/EXPLORE

How Do Gradients Influence Speed? L2

Purpose In this activity, students begin to recognize that the steepness of a gradient affects the speed of matter falling, or flowing, down that gradient, and understand that an increase in the steepness of an air pressure gradient will increase wind speed.

Skills Focus **Observing, Applying Concepts**

 **Prep Time** 15 minutes

Materials textbooks; wood blocks, or other items to raise one end of ramp; wood plank to use as a ramp; tennis ball; stopwatch

Class Time 15–20 minutes

Expected Outcome The speed of the tennis ball increases with the steepness of the ramp.

Think About It

1. Students will note faster speeds for steeper ramps made from the same materials.
2. Students will infer that large changes in air pressure, or "steeper" air pressure gradients, would cause faster wind speeds.

Section 19.1

1 FOCUS

Section Objectives

- **19.1** **Describe** how air pressure is exerted on objects.
- **19.2** **Explain** how changes in air pressure affect the mercury column of a barometer.
- **19.3** **Identify** the ultimate energy source for wind.
- **19.4** **Describe** how the Coriolis effect influences freely moving objects.

Reading Focus

Build Vocabulary L2

Visualize Explain to students that the Coriolis effect is named after French mathematician Gaspard Gustave de Coriolis, who described the effect of Earth's rotation on the direction of winds and ocean currents in 1835. Tell students that they may remember the term more easily if they create a mental picture. Have them imagine looking down at Earth from a high-altitude aircraft traveling down a line of longitude, watching the globe rotate beneath them as they move from one pole to the other.

Reading Strategy L2

a. Air pressure is measured with barometers, using the principle that fluids will deform if the weight of air is exerted on them. **b.** the pressure gradient, Coriolis effect, and friction

2 INSTRUCT

Air Pressure Defined

Measuring the Mass of Air L2

Purpose Students prove air has mass by comparing the mass of a balloon when empty and when filled with air.

Materials balloon, balance

Procedure Blow up a balloon and determine its mass using a balance. Remove the balloon, release the air, and replace the balloon on the balance. Find the mass again.

Expected Outcome Students will see that the empty balloon is lighter than the air-filled balloon.
Visual, Logical

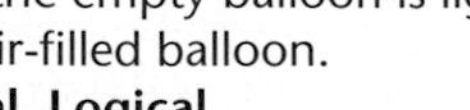

19.1 Understanding Air Pressure

Reading Focus

Key Concepts

- Describe how air pressure is exerted on objects.
- What happens to the mercury column of a barometer when air pressure changes?
- What is the ultimate energy source for wind?
- How does the Coriolis effect influence free-moving objects?

Vocabulary

- air pressure
- barometer
- pressure gradient
- Coriolis effect
- jet stream

Reading Strategy

Identifying Main Ideas Copy the table below. As you read, write the main ideas for each topic.

Topic	Main Ideas
Air Pressure Defined	Air pressure is the weight of air above. It is exerted in all directions.
Measuring Air Pressure	a. ?
Factors Affecting Wind	b. ?

Figure 1 These palm trees in Corpus Christi, Texas, are buffeted by hurricane-force winds.

Of the various elements of weather and climate, changes in air pressure are the least noticeable. When you listen to a weather report, you probably focus on precipitation, temperature, and humidity. Most people don't wonder about air pressure. Although you might not perceive hour-to-hour and day-to-day variations in air pressure, they are very important in producing changes in our weather. For example, variations in air pressure from place to place can generate winds like those shown in Figure 1. The winds, in turn, bring change in temperature and humidity. Air pressure is one of the basic weather elements and is an important factor in weather forecasting. Air pressure is closely tied to the other elements of weather in a cause-and-effect relationship.

Air Pressure Defined

Air pressure is simply the pressure exerted by the weight of air above. Average air pressure at sea level is about 1 kilogram per square centimeter. This pressure is roughly the same pressure that is produced by a column of water 10 meters in height. You can calculate that the air pressure exerted on the top of a 50-centimeter-by-100-centimeter school desk exceeds 5000 kilograms, which is about the mass of a 50-passenger school bus. Why doesn't the desk collapse under the weight of the air above it? **Air pressure is exerted in all directions—down, up, and sideways. The air pressure pushing down on an object exactly balances the air pressure pushing up on the object.**

What is average air pressure at sea level?

Imagine a tall aquarium that has the same dimensions as the desktop in the previous example. When this aquarium is filled to a height of 10 meters, the water pressure at the bottom equals 1 atmosphere, or 1 kilogram per square centimeter. Now imagine what will happen if this aquarium is placed on top of a student desk so that all the force is directed downward. The desk collapses because the pressure downward is greater than the pressure exerted in the other directions. When the desk is placed inside the aquarium and allowed to sink to the bottom, however, the desk does not collapse in the water because the water pressure is exerted in all directions, not just downward. The desk, like your body, is built to withstand the pressure of 1 atmosphere.

Measuring Air Pressure

When meteorologists measure atmospheric pressure, they use a unit called the millibar. Standard sea-level pressure is 1013.2 millibars. You might have heard the phrase "inches of mercury," which is used by the media to describe atmospheric pressure. This expression dates from 1643, when Torricelli, a student of the famous Italian scientist Galileo, invented the mercury barometer. A **barometer** is a device used for measuring air pressure (*bar* = pressure, *metron* = measuring instrument).

Torricelli correctly described the atmosphere as a vast ocean of air that exerts pressure on us and all objects around us. To measure this force, he filled a glass tube, closed at one end, with mercury. He then put the tube upside down into a dish of mercury, as shown in Figure 2A. The mercury flowed out of the tube until the weight of the column was balanced by the pressure that the atmosphere exerted on the surface of the mercury in the dish. In other words, the weight of mercury in the column (tube) equaled the weight of the same size column of air that extended from the ground to the top of the atmosphere.

When air pressure increases, the mercury in the tube rises. When air pressure decreases, so does the height of the mercury column. With some improvements, the mercury barometer is still the standard instrument used today for measuring air pressure.

The need for a smaller and more portable instrument for measuring air pressure led to the development of the aneroid barometer. The aneroid barometer uses a metal chamber with some air removed. This partially emptied chamber is extremely sensitive to variations in air pressure. It changes shape and compresses as the air pressure increases, and it expands as the pressure decreases. One advantage of the aneroid barometer is that it can be easily connected to a recording device, shown in Figure 2B. The device provides a continuous record of pressure changes with the passage of time.

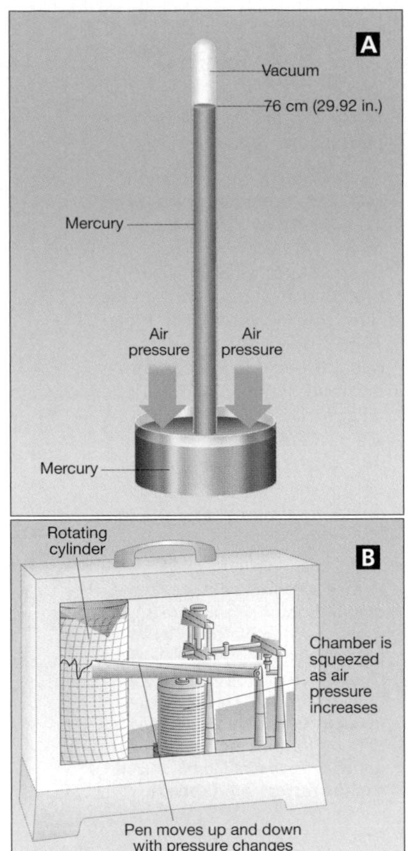

Figure 2 A Mercury Barometer Standard atmospheric pressure at sea level is 29.92 inches of mercury. **B Aneroid Barometer** The recording mechanism provides a continuous record of pressure changes over time. ***Applying Concepts*** ***Why would a continuous record help weather forecasters?***

For: Links on atmospheric pressure
Visit: www.SciLinks.org
Web Code: cjn-6191

Measuring Air Pressure

Use Visuals L1

Figure 2 After students have examined both illustrations, have them explain in their own words how each type of barometer works. *(Mercury barometer: Air pressure pushes down on pool of mercury, forcing the fluid to rise in the tube. Aneroid barometer: Chamber with air removed is made of a flexible material that changes shape as air pressure changes. Change in shape is transferred to graph paper by a pen attached to the outside of the chamber.)*
Visual, Verbal

Teacher Demo

Air Pressure L2

Purpose Students show that air pressure is exerted in all directions—down, up, and sideways.

Materials glass, water, cardboard, sink or basin

Procedure Fill the glass with water to the brim. Place a piece of cardboard on top of the glass. Working over a sink or basin, hold the cardboard in place and invert the glass. Then, remove your hand from the cardboard.

Expected Outcome The pressure of air pushing up on the cardboard holds it against the full glass of water, preventing it from spilling.
Visual, Logical

Download a worksheet on atmospheric pressure for students to complete, and find additional teacher support from NSTA SciLinks.

Customize for English Language Learners

Explain to students that *gradient* comes from the word *grade*. Have students discuss the various definitions of the word *grade* and write a sentence using each meaning. *(to arrange in a scale or series, as in to assign a grade; to level off to a smooth surface, as in grading a building site prior to construction; the degree of slope in a road or other surface)*

Answer to . . .

Figure 2 *A continuous record would show that patterns of pressure change over time. This would help in correlating pressure changes with weather.*

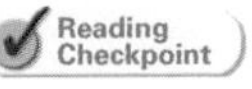
Average air pressure at sea level is about 1 kilogram per square centimeter.

Factors Affecting Wind

Use Visuals **L1**

Figure 3 Have students examine the isobar lines on the weather map. Ask: **What symbol signifies calm air? Where is this symbol located on this map?** *(two concentric circles; away from the high and low pressure cells)* **How do the wind flag symbols signify wind speed?** (*The number and length of lines on the flag increase with wind speed; pennant shapes are used in place of multiple lines at speeds of 55 mph and greater.*) **What does the circle at the base of each wind flag indicate?** *(the location where the wind measurement was taken)*
Visual, Logical

Build Reading Literacy **L1**

Refer to **p. 530D**, which provides the guidelines for making inferences.

Make Inferences Review the kinetic theory of matter, which states that the particles of a gas are always in motion. Ask: **How does the kinetic theory of matter explain why atmospheric gases move from areas of higher pressure to areas of lower pressure?** *(The higher the pressure, the more dense the gas, which means the particles of the gas are closer together and collide with one another more often. Collisions add to the motion of the particles, gradually moving them out into areas of lower pressure and density, where collisions become less frequent.)*
Verbal, Logical

Q&A

Q *What is the lowest barometric pressure ever recorded?*

A All of the lowest recorded barometric pressures have been associated with strong hurricanes. The record for the United States is 888 millibars (26.20 inches) measured during Hurricane Gilbert in September 1988. The world's record, 870 millibars (25.70 inches), occurred during Typhoon Tip, a Pacific hurricane, in October 1979. Although tornadoes undoubtedly have produced even lower pressures, they have not been accurately measured.

Factors Affecting Wind

As important as vertical motion is, far more air moves horizontally, the phenomenon we call wind. What causes wind?

Wind is the result of horizontal differences in air pressure. Air flows from areas of higher pressure to areas of lower pressure. You may have experienced this flow of air when opening a vacuum-packed can of coffee or tennis balls. The noise you hear is caused by air rushing from the higher pressure outside the can to the lower pressure inside. Wind is nature's way of balancing such inequalities in air pressure. **The unequal heating of Earth's surface generates pressure differences. Solar radiation is the ultimate energy source for most wind.**

If Earth did not rotate, and if there were no friction between moving air and Earth's surface, air would flow in a straight line from areas of higher pressure to areas of lower pressure. But both factors do exist so the flow of air is not that simple. **Three factors combine to control wind: pressure differences, the Coriolis effect, and friction.**

Pressure Differences Wind is created from differences in pressure—the greater these differences are, the greater the wind speed is. Over Earth's surface, variations in air pressure are determined from barometric readings taken at hundreds of weather stations. These pressure data are shown on a weather map, like the one in Figure 3, using isobars. Isobars are lines on a map that connect places of equal air pressure. The spacing of isobars indicates the amount of pressure change occurring over a given distance. These pressure changes are expressed as the **pressure gradient.**

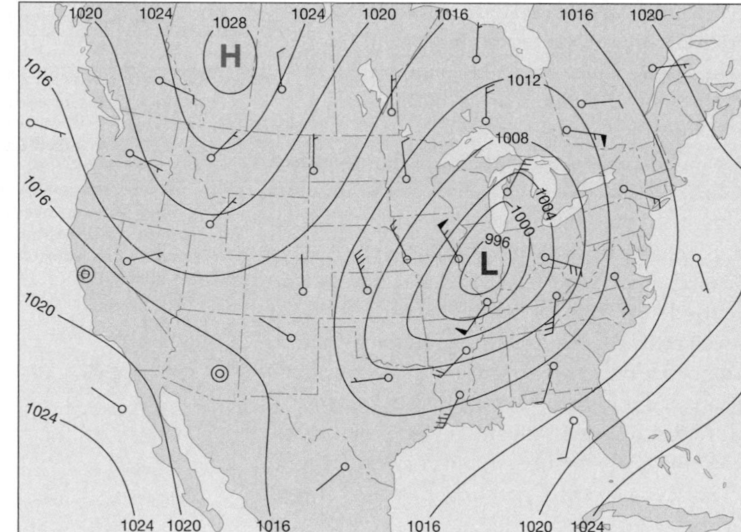

ff	Miles per hour
◎	Calm
	1–2
	3–8
	9–14
	15–20
	21–25
	26–31
	32–37
	38–43
	44–49
	50–54
	55–60
	61–66
	67–71
	72–77
	78–83
	84–89
	119–123

Figure 3 Isobars The distribution of air pressure is shown on weather maps using isobar lines. Wind flags indicate wind speed and direction. Winds blow toward the station circles. ***Interpreting Visuals*** ***Use the data on this map to explain which pressure cell, high or low, has the fastest wind speeds.***

Facts and Figures

The only force acting on a stationary parcel of air is the pressure-gradient force. Once the air begins to accelerate, the Coriolis effect deflects it—to the right in the Northern Hemisphere, to the left in the Southern Hemisphere. Greater wind speeds result in a stronger Coriolis effect, therefore a stronger deflection, until the pressure-gradient force is equal and opposite to the force of the Coriolis effect. At this point the wind direction is parallel to the isobars and the flow is called a geostrophic wind. Geostrophic winds occur only where isobars are straight and evenly spaced, and where there are no frictional forces. They are rare in nature, though airflow in the upper troposphere can sometimes closely approach geostrophic winds.

A steep pressure gradient, like a steep hill, causes greater acceleration of a parcel of air. A less steep pressure gradient causes a slower acceleration. **Closely spaced isobars indicate a steep pressure gradient and high winds. Widely spaced isobars indicate a weak pressure gradient and light winds.** The pressure gradient is the driving force of wind. The pressure gradient has both magnitude and direction. Its magnitude is reflected in the spacing of isobars. The direction of force is always from areas of higher pressure to areas of lower pressure and at right angles to the isobars. Friction affects wind speed and direction. The Coriolis effect affects wind direction only.

Coriolis Effect The weather map in Figure 3 shows typical air movements associated with high- and low-pressure systems. Air moves out of the regions of higher pressure and into the regions of lower pressure. However, the wind does not cross the isobars at right angles as you would expect based solely on the pressure gradient. This change in movement results from Earth's rotation and has been named the **Coriolis effect.**

The Coriolis effect describes how Earth's rotation affects moving objects. All free-moving objects or fluids, including the wind, are deflected to the right of their path of motion in the Northern Hemisphere. In the Southern Hemisphere, they are deflected to the left. The reason for this deflection is illustrated in Figure 4. Imagine the path of a rocket launched from the North Pole toward a target located on the equator. The true path of this rocket is straight, and the path would appear to be straight to someone out in space looking down at Earth. However, to someone standing on Earth, it would look as if the rocket swerved off its path and landed 15 degrees to the west of its target.

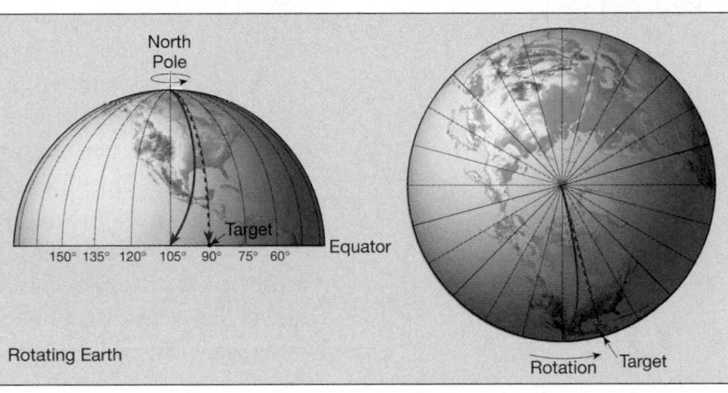

Figure 4 The Coriolis Effect Because Earth rotates 15° each hour, the rocket's path is curved and veers to the right from the North Pole to the equator. **Calculating** ***How many degrees does Earth rotate in one day?***

This slight change in direction happens because Earth would have rotated 15 degrees to the east under the rocket during a one-hour flight. The counterclockwise rotation of the Northern Hemisphere causes path deflection to the right. In the Southern Hemisphere, the clockwise rotation produces a similar deflection, but to the left of the path of motion.

The apparent shift in wind direction is attributed to the Coriolis effect. This deflection: 1) is always directed at right angles to the direction of airflow; 2) affects only wind direction and not wind speed; 3) is affected by wind speed—the stronger the wind, the greater the deflection; and 4) is strongest at the poles and weakens toward the equator, becoming nonexistent at the equator.

Integrate Physics L2

Gas Laws Review with students the laws that govern the behavior of enclosed gases. Charles's law states that the volume of a gas is directly proportional to its temperature, assuming constant pressure and density. Boyle's law states that the volume of a gas is inversely proportional to the pressure, assuming constant temperature and density. The combined gas law describes the interrelationships of temperature, pressure, volume, and density in gases. Ask: **In what way do the gas laws, which are stated in terms of enclosed gases, apply to gases in the atmosphere?** *(Gases in the atmosphere are not in a closed system. However, the relationship between temperature and pressure, as described by the gas laws, still applies. As temperature increases, pressure decreases. A decrease in pressure also decreases the density of the gases. Density differences help explain the movement of air masses. The direction of motion of a mass of atmospheric gas at one temperature and pressure is influenced by other, nearby masses of different temperatures and pressures. For example, a mass of high-pressure, dense air will tend to move into an area of lower-pressure, less dense air—either up into the less dense regions of the atmosphere or into a neighboring area of low pressure.)* **Verbal, Logical**

Facts and Figures

Over very short distances, the Coriolis effect is too small to be noticed. Nevertheless, in the middle latitudes the Coriolis effect is great enough to potentially affect the outcome of a baseball game. A ball hit a horizontal distance of 100 m in 4 s down the right field line will be deflected 1.5 cm to the right by the Coriolis effect. This could be just enough to turn a potential home run into a foul ball.

Answer to . . .

Figure 3 *For this particular map, isobar lines are most closely spaced in the low-pressure cell, which indicates fastest wind speeds in this cell.*

Figure 4 *360°*

Section 19.1 (continued)

Build Science Skills L2

Comparing and Contrasting Help students distinguish the effects of friction from the effects of the Coriolis force on wind direction. Point out that in the upper atmosphere, only the Coriolis effect and pressure gradients determine wind direction. At altitudes up to about 600 m, wind speed and direction are affected by those two factors plus friction. Ask: **How does friction interact with the Coriolis effect?** *(The Coriolis effect increases with wind speed. Friction decreases wind speed, which in turn decreases the directional influence of the Coriolis effect at lower altitudes.)*
Verbal, Logical

3 ASSESS

Evaluate Understanding 

Have students write a paragraph describing how air pressure gradients create wind and how the Coriolis effect and friction influence wind speed and/or direction. *(Dense air in areas of higher pressure move toward less dense air in areas of lower pressure. This flow of air is the wind. The Coriolis effect deflects wind motion relative to the ground because of Earth's rotation, but does not affect wind speed. Friction between air and the ground reduces wind speed at low altitudes.)*

Reteach 

Have students work in pairs or small groups to explain to each other how air pressure gradients form and how they create wind. Students should also explain how the Coriolis effect influences wind direction and how friction influences wind speed and direction. Listen to student explanations and offer corrections as needed.

Connecting Concepts

Unequal heating of Earth's surface by solar radiation results from differences in angles of incident radiation and differential heating of land and water. Unequal heating produces air pressure differences that in turn drive global circulation of air.

Effect of Friction

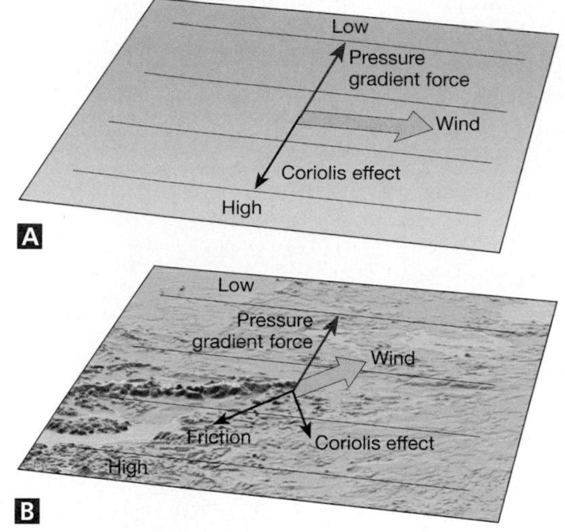

Figure 5 A Upper-level wind flow is balanced by the Coriolis effect and pressure gradient forces. **B** Friction causes surface winds to cross isobars and move toward lower pressure areas.

Friction The effect of friction on wind is important only within a few kilometers of Earth's surface. Friction acts to slow air movement, which changes wind direction. To illustrate friction's effect on wind direction, first think about a situation in which friction does not play a role in wind's direction.

When air is above the friction layer, the pressure gradient causes air to move across the isobars. As soon as air starts to move, the Coriolis effect acts at right angles to this motion. The faster the wind speed, the greater the deflection is. The pressure gradient and Coriolis effect balance in high-altitude air, and wind generally flows parallel to isobars, as shown in Figure 5A. The most prominent features of airflow high above the friction layer are the jet streams. **Jet streams** are fast-moving rivers of air that travel between 120 and 240 kilometers per hour in a west-to-east direction. One such jet stream is situated over the polar front, which is the zone separating the cool polar air from warm subtropical air. Jet streams originally were encountered by high-flying bombers during World War II.

For air close to Earth's surface, the roughness of the terrain determines the angle of airflow across the isobars. Over the smooth ocean surface, friction is low, and the angle of airflow is small. Over rugged terrain, where the friction is higher, winds move more slowly and cross the isobars at greater angles. As shown in Figure 5B, friction causes wind to flow across the isobars at angles as great as 45 degrees. Slower wind speeds caused by friction decrease the Coriolis effect.

Section 19.1 Assessment

Reviewing Concepts

1. Why don't objects such as a table collapse under the weight of air above them?
2. Suppose the height of a column in a mercury barometer is decreasing. What is happening?
3. What is the ultimate energy source for most wind?
4. How does the Coriolis effect influence motion of free-moving objects?
5. Why do jet streams flow parallel to isobars?

Critical Thinking

6. **Interpreting illustrations** Study Figures 5A and 5B. Why are the wind arrows drawn to different lengths in these figures?

Connecting Concepts

Solar Radiation Review section 17.3. Describe examples of unequal heating of Earth's atmosphere that could lead to air pressure differences that ultimately influence wind.

Section 19.1 Assessment

1. because air pressure is exerted in all directions
2. Air pressure is decreasing.
3. the sun
4. The Coriolis effect deflects free-moving objects to the right (in the Northern Hemisphere) or to the left (in the Southern Hemisphere).
5. Because jet streams are generally above the friction layer, the effect of friction is negligible. Jet stream wind direction is balanced by the pressure gradient and the Coriolis effect. The net effect of the balance is for winds to flow parallel to isobars.
6. Different lengths represent different magnitudes; the longer the arrow, the faster the wind speed.

19.2 Pressure Centers and Winds

Reading Focus

Key Concepts

- Describe how winds blow around pressure centers in the Northern and Southern Hemispheres.
- What are the air pressure patterns within cyclones and anticyclones?
- How does friction control net flow of air around a cyclone and an anticylone?
- How does the atmosphere attempt to balance the unequal heating of Earth's surface?

Vocabulary

- cyclone
- anticyclone
- trade winds
- westerlies
- polar easterlies
- polar front
- monsoon

Reading Strategy

Comparing and Contrasting Copy the table below. As you read about pressure centers and winds, fill in the table indicating to which hemisphere the concept applies. Use N for Northern Hemisphere, S for Southern Hemisphere, and B for both.

Cyclones rotate counterclockwise.	a. ?
Net flow of air is inward around a cyclone.	b. ?
Anticyclones rotate counterclockwise.	c. ?
Coriolis effect deflects winds to the right.	d. ?

Pressure centers are among the most common features on any weather map. By knowing just a few basic facts about centers of high and low pressure, you can increase your understanding of present and forthcoming weather. You can make some weather generalizations based on pressure centers. For example, centers of low pressure are frequently associated with cloudy conditions and precipitation. By contrast, clear skies and fair weather may be expected when an area is under the influence of high pressure, as shown in Figure 6.

Highs and Lows

Lows, or **cyclones** (*kyklon* = moving in a circle) are centers of low pressure. Highs, or **anticyclones,** are centers of high pressure. **In cyclones, the pressure decreases from the outer isobars toward the center. In anticyclones, just the opposite is the case—the values of the isobars increase from the outside toward the center.**

Figure 6 These sunbathers at Cape Henlopen, Delaware, are enjoying weather associated with a high-pressure center.

Section 19.2

1 FOCUS

Section Objectives

19.5 **Explain** how winds blow around pressure centers in the Northern and Southern Hemispheres.

19.6 **Describe** the air pressure patterns within cyclones and anticyclones.

19.7 **Describe** how friction controls the net flow of air around a cyclone and an anticyclone.

19.8 **Explain** how the unequal heating of Earth's surface affects the atmosphere.

Reading Focus

Build Vocabulary L2

Concept Map Have students make a concept map using the term *global winds* as the starting point. All the vocabulary terms in this section except *cyclone* and *anticyclone* should be used. Have students include the definitions of the vocabulary terms in their concept maps.

Reading Strategy L2

a. N **b.** B
c. S **d.** N

2 INSTRUCT

Highs and Lows

Build Science Skills L2

Use Models Have students use a globe to review and demonstrate the Coriolis effect. One student can rotate the globe while the other uses a pointer to show a flow of air moving straight down from a pole to the equator. Students can also use the model to compare the direction in which airflow is deflected in the Northern and Southern Hemispheres. Ask: **Seen from Earth's orbit, what is the relationship between Earth's surface and the line along which the air is flowing?** *(Earth rotates beneath the line of airflow.)* **Seen from Earth's surface, what appears to be happening?** (*Earth's rotation makes it appear that the airflow is deflected to one side—to the right in the Northern Hemisphere, to the left in the Southern Hemisphere.)*
Visual, Verbal

Teacher Demo

Warm Air Rises L2

Purpose Students see that air rises upward as it is warmed by a heat source.

Materials 2 meter sticks, 2 large paper grocery bags, string, tape, lamp with incandescent bulb

Procedure Tape string to the bottom of each bag. Tie the two strings to a meter stick, as far apart as possible. The bags should be hanging upside down. Use more string to hang this meter stick at its balance point from another meter stick that rests between two student desks. Place the lamp beneath one of the bags and switch it on.

Expected Outcomes The lamp heats the air inside the bag, causing it to rise above the other bag and showing that warm air rises.
Visual, Logical

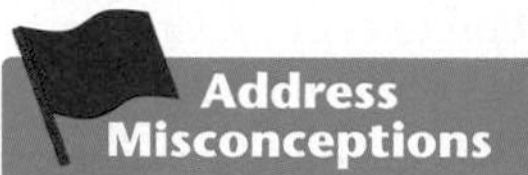

Address Misconceptions L2

Students may have the misconception that no outside factor except heat is required to cause masses of warm air to rotate as they rise upward in the atmosphere. Point out that the cyclonic motion in low-pressure cells is primarily a result of the Coriolis effect. As a follow-up, ask: **What is the primary cause of the anticyclonic motion of high-pressure cells?** *(Coriolis effect)*
Verbal, Logical

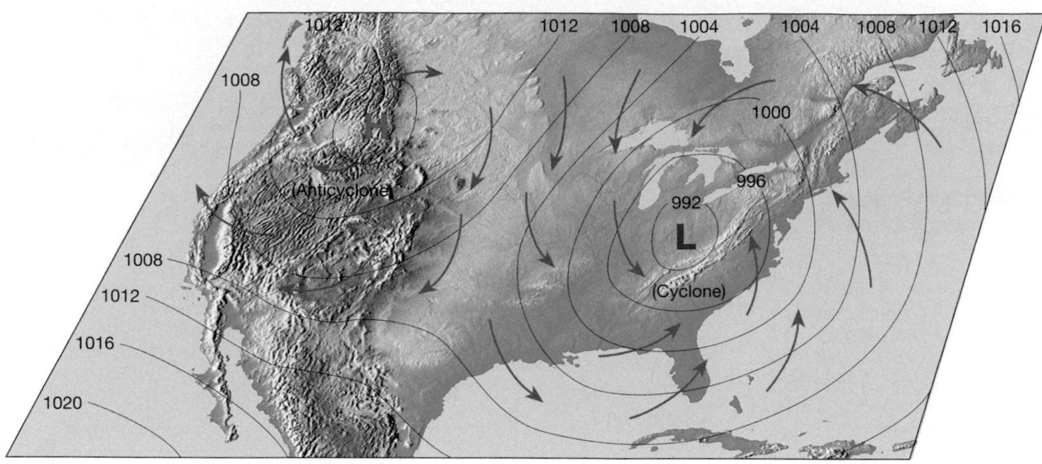

Figure 7 This map shows cyclonic and anticyclonic winds in the Northern Hemisphere.

Cyclonic and Anticyclonic Winds You learned that the two most significant factors that affect wind are the pressure gradient and the Coriolis effect. Winds move from higher pressure to lower pressure and are deflected to the right or left by Earth's rotation. **When the pressure gradient and the Coriolis effect are applied to pressure centers in the Northern Hemisphere, winds blow counterclockwise around a low. Around a high, they blow clockwise.** Notice the wind directions in Figure 7.

In the Southern Hemisphere, the Coriolis effect deflects the winds to the left. Therefore, winds around a low move clockwise. Winds around a high move counterclockwise. **In either hemisphere, friction causes a net flow of air inward around a cyclone and a net flow of air outward around an anticyclone.**

Weather and Air Pressure Rising air is associated with cloud formation and precipitation, whereas sinking air produces clear skies.

Imagine a surface low-pressure system where the air is spiraling inward. Here the net inward movement of air causes the area occupied by the air mass to shrink—a process called horizontal convergence. Whenever air converges (or comes together) horizontally, it must increase in height to allow for the decreased area it now occupies. This increase in height produces a taller and heavier air column. A surface low can exist only as long as the column of air above it exerts less pressure than does the air in surrounding regions. This seems to be a paradox—a low-pressure center causes a net accumulation of air, which increases its pressure.

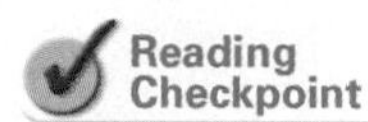

Reading Checkpoint *With what type of weather is rising air associated?*

Customize for Inclusion Students

Visually Impaired Help visually impaired students compare cyclones and anticyclones by using their hands to model the motions of these phenomena. Explain that, in the Northern Hemisphere, cyclonic winds blow inward and counterclockwise around a low-pressure center. Have students use one hand to represent Earth's surface. This hand remains stationary. They can use the other hand to make the counterclockwise, inward motion of a cyclonic wind. Then have students use the same hand to make the clockwise, outward motion of an anticyclonic wind in the Northern Hemisphere.

Airflow Patterns, Surface and Aloft

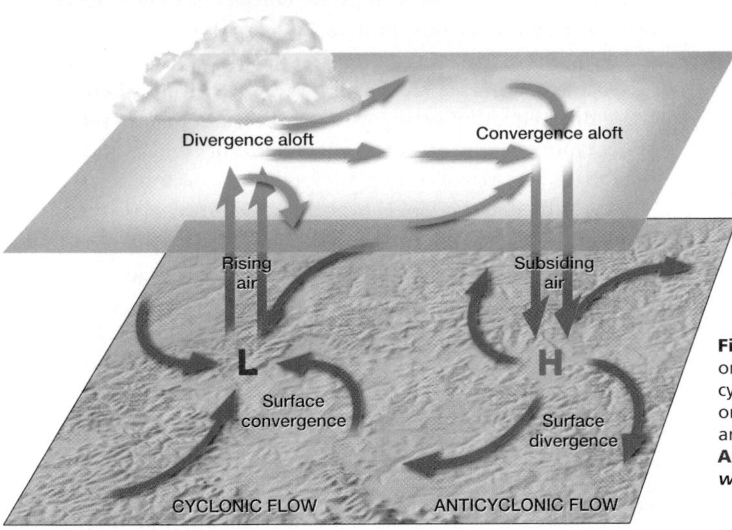

Figure 8 Air spreads out, or diverges, above surface cyclones, and comes together, or converges, above surface anticyclones.
Applying Concepts ***Why is fair weather associated with a high?***

In order for a surface low to exist for very long, converging air at the surface must be balanced by outflows aloft. For example, surface convergence could be maintained if divergence, or the spreading out of air, occurred above the low at a rate equal to the inflow below. Figure 8 shows the relationship between surface convergence (inflow) and divergence (outflow) needed to maintain a low-pressure center. Surface convergence around a cyclone causes a net upward movement. Because rising air often results in cloud formation and precipitation, a low-pressure center is generally related to unstable conditions and stormy weather.

Like cyclones, anticyclones also must be maintained from above. Outflow near the surface is accompanied by convergence in the air above and a general sinking of the air column, as shown in Figure 8.

Weather Forecasting Now you can see why weather reports emphasize the locations and possible paths of cyclones and anticyclones. The villain in these reports is always the low-pressure center, which can produce bad weather in any season. Lows move in roughly a west-to-east direction across the United States, and they require a few days, and sometimes more than a week, for the journey. Their paths can be somewhat unpredictable, making accurate estimation of their movement difficult. Because surface conditions are linked to the conditions of the air above, it is important to understand total atmospheric circulation.

Build Reading Literacy L1

Refer to **p. 530D**, which provides the guidelines for making inferences.

Make Inferences After students have finished reading this section, ask: **What does sunlight have to do with the occurrence of rainy weather?** *(Sunlight warms the atmosphere. Differential warming creates pressure gradients, which result in the formation of high- and low-pressure centers. Winds blow toward low-pressure centers, bringing moist air in which clouds can form.)*
Verbal, Logical

Use Visuals L1

Figure 8 After students have examined the illustration, ask: **Where does air enter a cyclonic flow?** *(at Earth's surface)* **Where does air leave a cyclonic flow?** *(aloft)* **Where does air enter an anticyclonic flow?** *(aloft)* **Where does air leave an anticyclonic flow?** *(at Earth's surface)*
Visual, Verbal

Facts and Figures

Accurate forecasts require that meteorologists not only predict the movement of low-pressure centers, but also determine if the airflow aloft will intensify an embryo storm or act to suppress its development. Surface cyclones would quickly eradicate themselves—not unlike the incoming rush of air that occurs when a vacuum-packed can is opened—without divergence in the air above. As a result, meteorologists must base their forecasts on data from upper and lower atmospheric conditions. Because of the close relationship between conditions at the surface and aloft, understanding of total atmospheric circulation, particularly in the mid-latitudes, is very important.

Answer to . . .

Figure 8 *Convergence aloft causes a column of air to sink, creating a zone of high pressure and fair weather. Sinking air is compressed and warmed as it nears Earth's surface, which discourages cloud formation.*

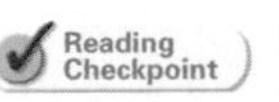

cloud formation and precipitation

Global Winds

Use Visuals

L1

Figure 9 After students have examined the illustration, ask: **What happens to surface air at the equator?** *(It rises upward as it is warmed by the sun.)* **Why does air flow from the poles to the equator?** *(Air at the equator receives more heat from the sun, thus making the area lower in density and pressure than colder air at the poles. Since higher pressure air moves toward lower pressure air, the net flow is toward the equator.)*
Visual, Logical

Build Science Skills

L2

Relating Cause and Effect Explain to students that, as warm air rises from the surface at the equator, cooler air coming from the poles moves in to fill the space. Ask: **Why is the warm air in the upper atmosphere above the equator drawn toward the poles?** *(The tropopause prevents the air from rising any higher. The only possible direction of motion is toward the poles.)*
Verbal, Logical

Global Winds

The underlying cause of wind is the unequal heating of Earth's surface. In tropical regions, more solar radiation is received than is radiated back to space. In regions near the poles the opposite is true—less solar energy is received than is lost. **The atmosphere balances these differences by acting as a giant heat-transfer system. This system moves warm air toward high latitudes and cool air toward the equator.** On a smaller scale, but for the same reason, ocean currents also contribute to this global heat transfer. Global circulation is very complex, but you can begin to understand it by first thinking about circulation that would occur on a non-rotating Earth.

Reading Checkpoint *How does the atmosphere balance the unequal heating of Earth's surface?*

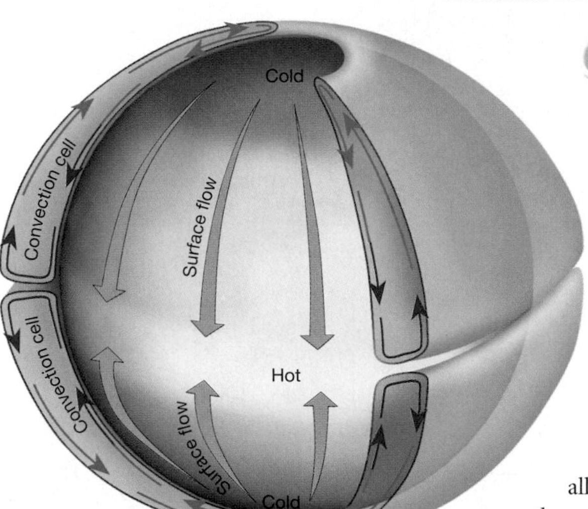

Figure 9 Circulation on a Non-Rotating Earth A simple convection system is produced by unequal heating of the atmosphere.
Relating Cause and Effect *Why would air sink after reaching the poles?*

Non-Rotating Earth Model On a hypothetical non-rotating planet with a smooth surface of either all land or all water, two large thermally produced cells would form, as shown in Figure 9. The heated air at the equator would rise until it reached the tropopause—the boundary between the troposphere and the stratosphere. The tropopause, acting like a lid, would deflect this air toward the poles. Eventually, the upper-level airflow would reach the poles, sink, spread out in all directions at the surface, and move back toward the equator. Once at the equator, it would be reheated and begin its journey over again. This hypothetical circulation system has upper-level air flowing toward the pole and surface air flowing toward the equator.

Rotating Earth Model If the effect of rotation were added to the global circulation model, the two-cell convection system would break down into smaller cells. Figure 10 illustrates the three pairs of cells that would carry on the task of redistributing heat on Earth. The polar and tropical cells retain the characteristics of the thermally generated convection described earlier. The nature of circulation at the middle latitudes, however, is more complex.

Near the equator, rising air produces a pressure zone known as the equatorial low—a region characterized by abundant precipitation. As shown in Figure 10, the upper-level flow from the equatorial low reaches 20 to 30 degrees, north or south latitude, and then sinks back toward the surface. This sinking of air and its associated heating due

Facts and Figures

George Hadley, an English meteorologist of the eighteenth century, first proposed the simple convection system pictured in Figure 9. Because Earth rotates, however, meteorologists had to develop a more complex global circulation model. This model is pictured in Figure 10 and has three cells on each side of the equator. The Hadley cells, named after George Hadley and also called tropical cells, are shown north and south of the equator. The next cell, which is unlabeled on the diagram, is the mid-latitude cell. It is also called a Ferrel cell after William Ferrel, a nineteenth century American meteorologist who helped explain atmospheric circulation at mid-latitudes. The third type of cell, also unlabeled, is the polar cell.

to compression produce hot, arid conditions. The center of this zone of sinking dry air is the subtropical high, which encircles the globe near 30 degrees north and south latitude. The great deserts of Australia, Arabia, and the Sahara in North Africa exist because of the stable dry conditions associated with the subtropical highs.

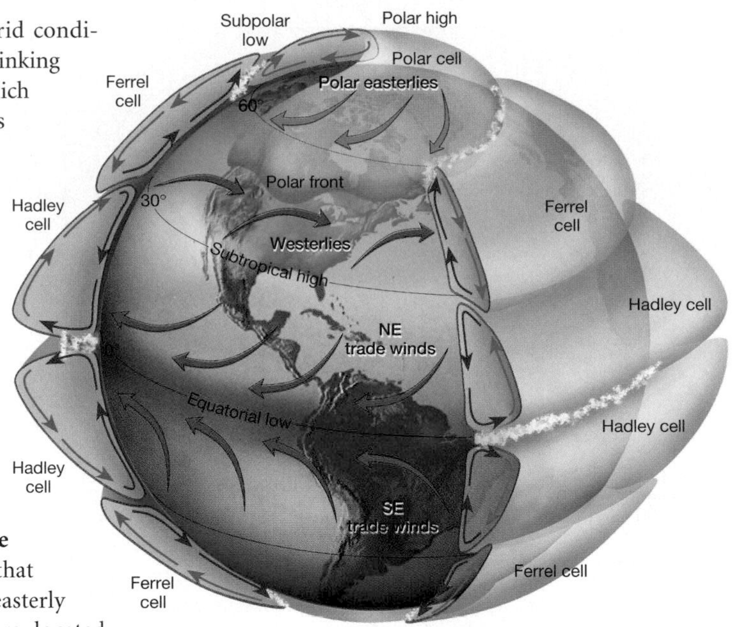

Figure 10 Circulation on a Rotating Earth This model of global air circulation proposes three pairs of cells. **Interpreting Diagrams** ***Describe the patterns of air circulation at the equatorial and subpolar lows.***

At the surface, airflow moves outward from the center of the subtropical high. Some of the air travels toward the equator and is deflected by the Coriolis effect, producing the trade winds. **Trade winds** are two belts of winds that blow almost constantly from easterly directions. The trade winds are located between the subtropical highs and the equator. The remainder of the air travels toward the poles and is deflected, generating the prevailing **westerlies** of the middle latitudes. The westerlies make up the dominant west-to-east motion of the atmosphere that characterizes the regions on the poleward side of the subtropical highs. As the westerlies move toward the poles, they encounter the cool polar easterlies in the region of the subpolar low. The **polar easterlies** are winds that blow from the polar high toward the subpolar low. These winds are not constant winds like the trade winds. In the polar region, cold polar air sinks and spreads toward the equator. The interaction of these warm and cool air masses produces the stormy belt known as the **polar front.**

This simplified global circulation is dominated by four pressure zones. The subtropical and polar highs are areas of dry subsiding (sinking) air that flows outward at the surface, producing the prevailing winds. The low-pressure zones of the equatorial and subpolar regions are associated with inward and upward airflow accompanied by clouds and precipitation.

What is the polar front?

Use Visuals

L1

Figure 10 After students have read Rotating Earth Model and examined the illustration, ask: **What happens to warm equatorial air that has risen into the upper atmosphere?** *(It moves toward the poles until it reaches latitudes of 20 or 30 degrees, then sinks downward.)* **What kind of weather is characteristic of regions around 20 to 30 degrees latitude?** *(dry, hot)* **What factor is primarily responsible for the trade winds?** *(Coriolis effect)* **What factors create the polar front?** *(meeting of the warmer, subpolar westerlies with the colder polar easterlies)* **What kind of weather is characteristic of the polar front?** *(stormy)*
Visual, Logical

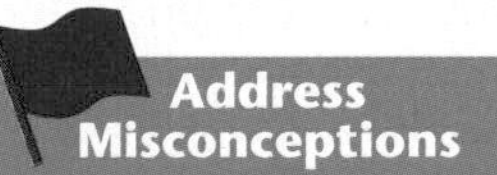

L2

Students may think that heat is "lost" from air as it sinks toward Earth's surface in a high-pressure center. Explain to students that the term *adiabatic* refers to the cooling or warming of air caused when air is allowed to expand or is compressed, not because heat is added to or subtracted from the system. In other words, no heat enters or leaves the system. Compression of air as it sinks creates adiabatic heating. Expansion of air as it rises creates adiabatic cooling. The air continues to cool as it rises until it reaches its dew point. Then condensation takes place and clouds begin to form. Ask: **How does adiabatic cooling help explain why precipitation is associated with low-pressure centers but not high-pressure centers?** *(Rising air in a low-pressure center becomes cool enough for condensation. Sinking air in a high-pressure system is heated adiabatically, preventing condensation.)*
Verbal

Answer to . . .

Figure 9 *Air becomes more dense as it cools, causing it to sink.*

Figure 10 *Both are zones where two cells, or air masses, converge and air rises, forming zones of low pressure.*

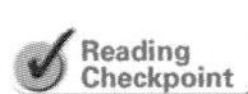

The atmosphere transfers heat by moving warm air toward high latitudes and cool air toward the equator.

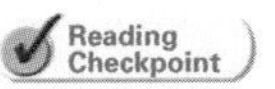

the stormy belt where subpolar westerlies and polar easterlies meet

Build Science Skills L2

Applying Concepts Use a world map to help students visualize the movement of monsoons in south Asia. Have them picture a high-pressure system above the land that pushes air out to sea. Then have them picture how heat from the land during summer causes air to rise, producing a low-pressure system that pulls in moist air from the ocean. **Visual, Logical**

3 ASSESS

Evaluate Understanding L2

Have students write a paragraph comparing and contrasting cyclonic and anticyclonic winds. Have students write a second paragraph explaining how each of the following global winds is formed: trade winds, westerlies, and polar easterlies.

Reteach L1

Draw a globe on the board or use a laminated world map. On the map, draw in each type of global wind while explaining its formation to students. Use Figure 10 as a reference.

Solutions

8. 992 (−) to 1020 (+) millibars. In other words, the map includes pressures a bit less than 992 millibars and a bit more than 1020 millibars. Isobar interval equals 4 millibars.

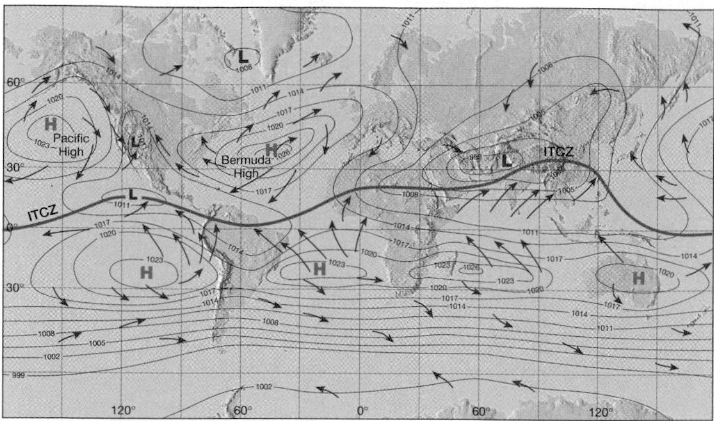

Figure 11 Average Surface Pressure and Associated Global Circulation for July. The ITCZ line stands for the Intertropical Convergence Zone.

Influence of Continents

The only truly continuous pressure belt is the subpolar low in the Southern Hemisphere. Here the ocean is uninterrupted by landmasses. At other latitudes, particularly in the Northern Hemisphere where landmasses break up the ocean surface, large seasonal temperature differences disrupt the pressure pattern. Large landmasses, particularly Asia, become cold in the winter when a seasonal high-pressure system develops. From this high-pressure system, surface airflow is directed off the land. In the summer, landmasses are heated and develop low-pressure cells, which permit air to flow onto the land as shown in Figure 11. These seasonal changes in wind direction are known as the **monsoons.** During warm months, areas such as India experience a flow of warm, water-laden air from the Indian Ocean, which produces the rainy summer monsoon. The winter monsoon is dominated by dry continental air. A similar situation exists to a lesser extent over North America.

Section 19.2 Assessment

Reviewing Concepts

1. Describe how winds blow around pressure centers in the Northern Hemisphere.
2. Compare the air pressure for a cyclone with an anticyclone.
3. How does friction control the net flow of air around a cyclone and an anticyclone?
4. Describe how the atmosphere balances the unequal heating of Earth's surface.
5. What is the only truly continuous pressure belt? Why is it continuous?
6. In general, what type of weather can you expect if a low-pressure system is moving into your area?

Critical Thinking

7. **Identifying Cause and Effect** What must happen in the air above for divergence at the surface to be maintained? What type of pressure center accompanies surface divergence?

Math Practice

8. Examine Figure 7. What is the approximate range of barometric pressure indicated by the isobars on the map? What is the pressure interval between adjacent isobars?

Section 19.2 Assessment

1. In the Northern Hemisphere, winds blow counterclockwise and inward around a low, and clockwise and outward around a high.
2. In cyclones, air pressure decreases toward the center of the cell. In anticyclones, air pressure increases toward the center of the cell.
3. The effect of friction is to cause a net flow of air inward around a cyclone and a net flow outward about an anticyclone.
4. The atmosphere acts like a huge heat-transfer system, transporting warm air from the equator toward the poles and cold air from the poles toward the equator.
5. The subpolar low in the Southern Hemisphere; no landmasses break up the pressure system.
6. cloud formation and precipitation
7. Convergence must occur aloft in order for a surface divergence to be maintained. A surface divergence is associated with a high-pressure center.

19.3 Regional Wind Systems

Reading Focus

Key Concepts

- What causes local winds?
- Describe the general movement of weather in the United States.
- What happens when unusually strong, warm ocean currents flow along the coasts of Ecuador and Peru?
- How is a La Niña event triggered?

Vocabulary

- prevailing wind
- anemometer
- El Niño

Reading Strategy

Previewing Copy the table below. Before you read, use Figure 17 to locate examples of the driest and wettest regions on Earth. After you read, identify the dominant wind system for each location.

Precipitation	Location	Dominant Wind System
Extremely low	a. ?	b. ?
Extremely high	c. ?	d. ?

Circulation in the middle latitudes is complex and does not fit the convection system described for the tropics. Between about 30 and 60 degrees latitude, the general west-to-east flow, known as the westerlies, is interrupted by migrating cyclones and anticyclones. In the Northern Hemisphere, these pressure cells move from west to east around the globe.

Local Winds

Small-scale winds produced by a locally generated pressure gradient are known as local winds. **The local winds are caused either by topographic effects or by variations in surface composition—land and water—in the immediate area.**

Land and Sea Breezes In coastal areas during the warm summer months, the land surface is heated more intensely during the daylight hours than an adjacent body of water is heated. As a result, the air above the land surface heats, expands, and rises, creating an area of lower pressure. As shown in Figure 12, a sea breeze then develops because cooler air over the water at higher pressure moves toward the warmer land and low pressure air. The breeze starts developing shortly before noon and generally reaches its greatest intensity during the mid- to late afternoon. These relatively cool winds can be a moderating influence on afternoon temperatures in coastal areas.

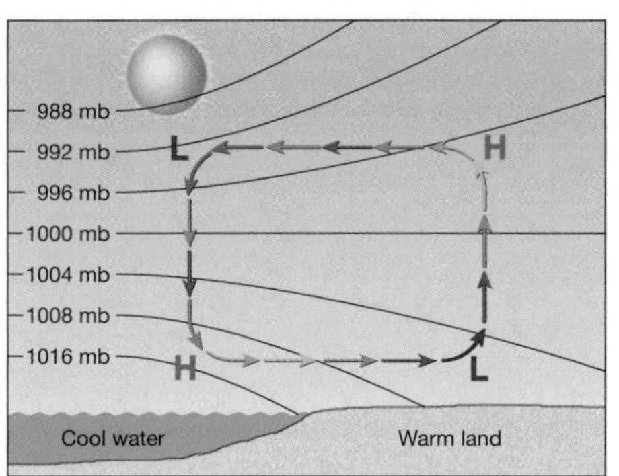

Figure 12 Sea Breeze During daylight hours, the air above land heats and rises, creating a local zone of lower air pressure.

Section 19.3

1 FOCUS

Section Objectives

19.9 **Identify** the causes of local winds.

19.10 **Describe** the general movement of weather in the United States.

19.11 **Compare and contrast** weather patterns characteristic of El Niño and La Niña events.

Reading Focus

Build Vocabulary L2

Word Parts Explain to students that the word *anemometer* is a combination of the Greek word *anemos,* meaning "wind," and the Latin *meter.* Have students use this information to predict the definition of *anemometer.* After they have studied the section, have them correct their predictions if necessary.

Reading Strategy L2

Sample answers:
a. Arabian Desert
b. sinking trade winds produce tropical high
c. Amazon rain forest
d. rising trade winds produce equatorial low

Local Winds

Use Visuals L1

Figure 12 After students have examined the illustration, ask: **Does a sea breeze move toward the sea or away from the sea?** *(away from the sea)* **Why does a sea breeze usually reach its highest speeds in the late afternoon?** (*The heat differential between land and water increases with the number of hours the sun has been shining.)*
Visual, Logical

Use Visuals L1

Figure 13 After students have examined the illustration, ask: **Does a land breeze move toward the land or away from the land?** *(away from the land)* **Why do land breezes usually take place at night?** *(After sunset, both land and water begin to cool, but land cools more rapidly.)*
Visual, Logical

Build Science Skills L2

Comparing and Contrasting Have students create a table that contrasts sea, land, valley, and mountain breezes.

	Direction	Day/ Night	Cause
sea	toward land	day	sun heats land faster than water; air above land rises, creating low pressure zone
land	toward sea	night	land cools faster than water; air above land sinks, creating high pressure zone relative to air above water
valley	upslope	day	air along slopes heats faster than air above valley, glides up slope because it is less dense
mountain	downslope	night	air along slopes cools faster than air above valley, sinks down slope into valley

Verbal, Logical

Differential Heating L2

Purpose Students observe that soil heats faster than water.

Materials 2 containers, soil, water, 2 thermometers

Procedure Fill the two containers 2/3 full, one with water and the other with soil. Place a thermometer in each container and place both in a hot, sunny location. Read temperature measurements at the beginning of the experiment and after about 25 minutes.

Expected Outcome Soil heats faster than water.
Visual, Kinesthetic

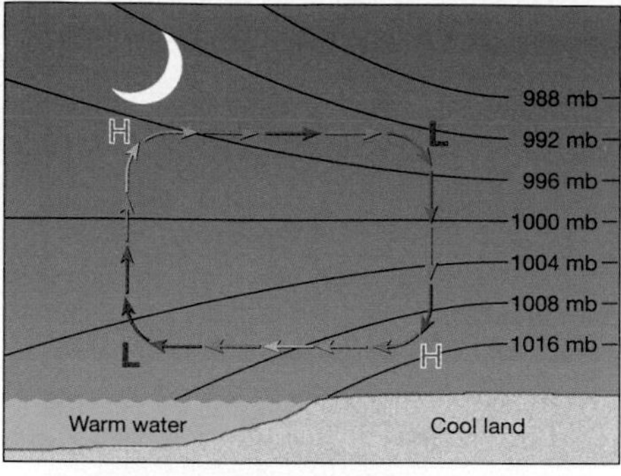

Figure 13 Land Breeze At night, the land cools more rapidly than the sea, generating an offshore flow called a land breeze. ***Inferring** How would the isobar lines be oriented if there was no air pressure change across the land–water boundary?*

At night, the reverse may take place. The land cools more rapidly than the sea, and a land breeze develops, as shown in Figure 13. The cooler air at higher pressures over the land moves to the sea, where the air is warmer and at lower pressures. Small-scale sea breezes also can develop along the shores of large lakes. People who live in a city near the Great Lakes, such as Chicago, recognize this lake effect, especially in the summer. They are reminded daily by weather reports of the cool temperatures near the lake as compared to warmer outlying areas.

Valley and Mountain Breezes A daily wind similar to land and sea breezes occurs in many mountainous regions. During daylight hours, the air along the slopes of the mountains is heated more intensely than the air at the same elevation over the valley floor. Because this warmer air on the mountain slopes is less dense, it glides up along the slope and generates a valley breeze, as shown in Figure 14A. The occurrence of these daytime upslope breezes can often be identified by the cumulus clouds that develop on adjacent mountain peaks.

Figure 14 A Valley Breeze Heating during the day generates warm air that rises from the valley floor. **B Mountain Breeze** After sunset, cooling of the air near mountain slopes can result in cool air moving into the valley.

After sunset, the pattern may reverse. The rapid cooling of the air along the mountain slopes produces a layer of cooler air next to the ground. Because cool air is denser than warm air, it moves downslope into the valley. Such a movement of air, illustrated in Figure 14B, is called a mountain breeze. In the Grand Canyon at night, the sound of cold air rushing down the sides of the canyon can be louder than the sound of the Colorado River below.

The same type of cool air drainage can occur in places that have very modest slopes. The result is that the coldest pockets of air are usually found in the lowest spots. Like many other winds, mountain and valley breezes have seasonal preferences. Although valley breezes are most common during the warm season when solar heating is most intense, mountain breezes tend to be more dominant in the cold season.

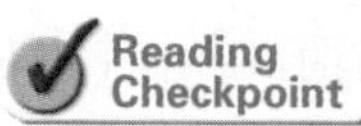

What type of local wind can form in the Grand Canyon at night?

Customize for English Language Learners

Explain that the terms *prevailing* and *predominant* are synonyms. They are adjectives that mean "having superior strength, influence, or authority." Have students look up the definitions of verb forms of these words and use each in a sentence. Then ask students to look up definitions for the related verb *dominate* and the related adjective *dominant*. Students also could be asked to compare and contrast the meanings of all six words, as well as the suffix *pre-*.

How Wind Is Measured

Two basic wind measurements—direction and speed—are particularly important to the weather observer. Winds are always labeled by the direction from which they blow. A north wind blows from the north toward the south. An east wind blows from the east toward the west. The instrument most commonly used to determine wind direction is the wind vane, shown in the upper right of Figure 15. Wind vanes commonly are located on buildings, and they always point into the wind. The wind direction is often shown on a dial connected to the wind vane. The dial indicates wind direction, either by points of the compass—N, NE, E, SE, etc.—or by a scale of 0° to 360°. On the degree scale, 0° or 360° are north, 90° is east, 180° is south, and 270° is west.

Figure 15 Wind Vane and Cup Anemometer
Interpreting Photographs *How can you tell which direction the wind is blowing?*

Reading Checkpoint *Toward which direction does a SE wind blow?*

Wind Direction When the wind consistently blows more often from one direction than from any other, it is called a **prevailing wind.** Recall the prevailing westerlies that dominate circulation in the middle latitudes. **In the United States, the westerlies consistently move weather from west to east across the continent.** Along within this general eastward flow are cells of high and low pressure with the characteristic clockwise and counterclockwise flows. As a result, the winds associated with the westerlies, as measured at the surface, often vary considerably from day to day and from place to place. In contrast, the direction of airflow associated with the trade winds is much more consistent.

Wind Speed Shown in the upper left of Figure 15, a cup **anemometer** (*anemo* = wind, *metron* = measuring instrument) is commonly used to measure wind speed. The wind speed is read from a dial much like the speedometer of an automobile. Places where winds are steady and speeds are relatively high are potential sites for tapping wind energy.

For: Links on winds
Visit: www.SciLinks.org
Web Code: cjn-6193

How Wind Is Measured

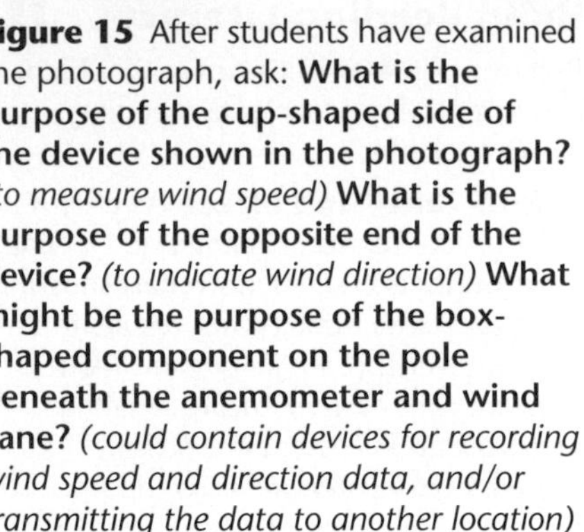

Use Visuals L1

Figure 15 After students have examined the photograph, ask: **What is the purpose of the cup-shaped side of the device shown in the photograph?** *(to measure wind speed)* **What is the purpose of the opposite end of the device?** *(to indicate wind direction)* **What might be the purpose of the box-shaped component on the pole beneath the anemometer and wind vane?** *(could contain devices for recording wind speed and direction data, and/or transmitting the data to another location)*
Visual, Logical

Use Community Resources L2

Take students on a field trip to visit a weather station maintained by a community member or local or government organization. Ask the person in charge to show students how wind direction and speed are measured at the station, how records are kept, and how the information is used.
Interpersonal, Kinesthetic

Download a worksheet on winds for students to complete, and find additional teacher support from NSTA SciLinks.

Answer to . . .

Figure 13 *Isobars would be horizontal.*

Figure 15 *Wind vanes point into the wind.*

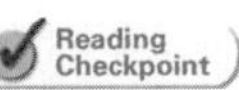

mountain breeze

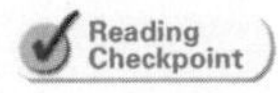

NW

El Niño and La Niña

Build Reading Literacy L1

Refer to **p. 246D** in **Chapter 9,** which provides the guidelines for relating cause and effect.

Relate Cause and Effect As they read through the text on El Niño and La Niña, have students create a flowchart showing the cause-effect chain that results in an El Niño event. *(Sample answer: high pressure over eastern Pacific → warm water pileup in eastern Pacific that prevents cold water upwelling and promotes formation of low air pressure zone → inland areas receive abnormal amounts of rain → trade winds weaken or may reverse direction → subtropical and mid-latitude jet streams are displaced → abnormal rainfall in Florida/southern United States and mild winter temperatures west of the Rocky Mountains)*
Verbal, Logical

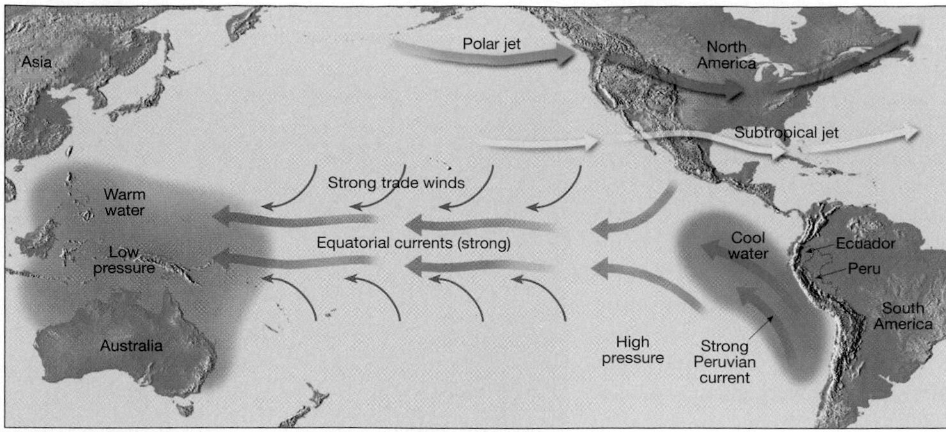

Figure 16 Normal Conditions Trade winds and strong equatorial ocean currents flow toward the west.

El Niño and La Niña

Look at Figure 16. The cold Peruvian current flows toward the equator along the coasts of Ecuador and Peru. This flow encourages upwelling of cold nutrient-filled waters that are the primary food source for millions of fish, particularly anchovies. Near the end of the year, however, a warm current that flows southward along the coasts of Ecuador and Peru replaces the cold Peruvian current. During the nineteenth century, the local residents named this warm current El Niño ("the child") after the Christ child because it usually appeared during the Christmas season. Normally, these warm countercurrents last for a few weeks and then give way to the cold Peruvian flow again.

El Niño **At irregular intervals of three to seven years, these warm countercurrents become unusually strong and replace normally cold offshore waters with warm equatorial waters.** Scientists use the term **El Niño** for these episodes of ocean warming that affect the eastern tropical Pacific.

The onset of El Niño is marked by abnormal weather patterns that drastically affect the economies of Ecuador and Peru. As shown in Figure 17, these unusually strong undercurrents accumulate large quantities of warm water that block the upwelling of colder, nutrient-filled water. As a result, the anchovies starve, devastating the local fishing industry. At the same time, some inland areas that are normally arid receive an abnormal amount of rain. Here, pastures and cotton fields have yields far above the average. These climatic fluctuations have been known for years, but they were originally considered local phenomena. It now is understood that El Niño is part of the global circulation and that it affects the weather at great distances from Peru and Ecuador.

When an El Niño began in the summer of 1997, forecasters predicted that the pool of warm water over the Pacific would displace the

Facts and Figures

The seesaw pattern of atmospheric pressure changes between the eastern and western Pacific is called the Southern Oscillation. During average years, high pressure over the eastern Pacific causes surface winds and warm equatorial waters to flow westward. The result is a pileup of warm water in the western Pacific, which promotes the lowering of air pressure. An El Niño event begins as surface pressure increases in the western Pacific and decreases in the eastern Pacific. This air pressure reversal weakens or may even reverse the trade winds, and results in an eastward movement of the warm waters that had accumulated in the western Pacific.

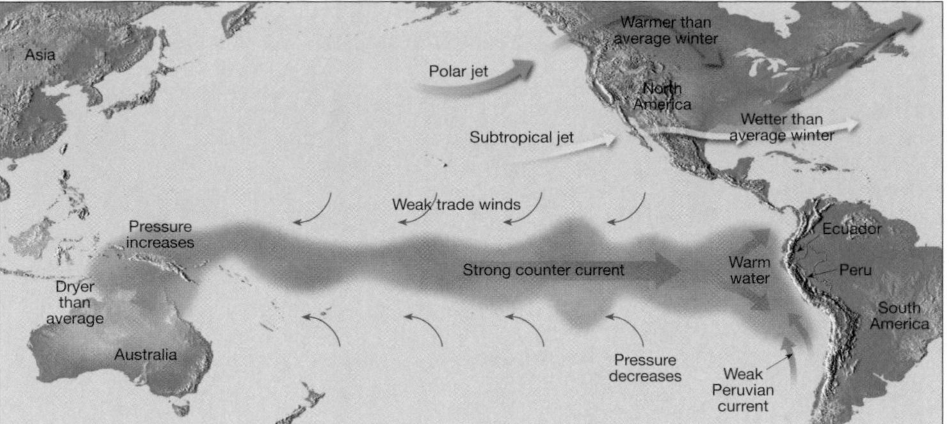

Figure 17 El Niño Warm countercurrents cause reversal of pressure patterns in the western and eastern Pacific.

paths of both the subtropical and midlatitude jet streams, as shown in Figure 17. The jet streams steer weather systems across North America. As predicted, the subtropical jet brought rain to the Gulf Coast. Tampa, Florida, received more than three times its normal winter precipitation. The mid-latitude jet pumped warm air far north into the continent. As a result, winter temperatures west of the Rocky Mountains were significantly above normal.

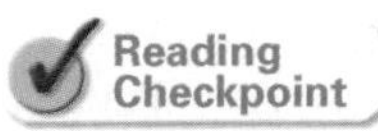

What is an El Niño and what effect does it have on weather?

La Niña The opposite of El Niño is an atmospheric phenomenon known as La Niña. Once thought to be the normal conditions that occur between two El Niño events, meteorologists now consider La Niña an important atmospheric phenomenon in its own right. **Researchers have come to recognize that when surface temperatures in the eastern Pacific are colder than average, a La Niña event is triggered that has a distinctive set of weather patterns.** A typical La Niña winter blows colder than normal air over the Pacific Northwest and the northern Great Plains. At the same time, it warms much of the rest of the United States. The Northwest also experiences greater precipitation during this time. During the La Niña winter of 1998–99, a world-record snowfall for one season occurred in Washington State. La Niña impact can also increase hurricane activity. A recent study concluded that the cost of hurricane damages in the United States is 20 times greater in La Niña years as compared to El Niño years.

The effects of both El Niño and La Niña on world climate are widespread and vary greatly. These phenomena remind us that the air and ocean conditions of the tropical Pacific influence the state of weather almost everywhere.

For: Links on La Niña and El Niño
Visit: www.SciLinks.org
Web Code: cjn-6211

Integrate Physics

L2

Thermal Energy Transfer Remind students that heat is the transfer of energy between two objects of different temperatures. Heat can be transferred directly, when the objects are in contact. It also can be transferred indirectly, by radiation and convection. Radiation is the transfer of energy via electromagnetic waves. Convection is the transfer of energy by fluid motion. In a fluid, convection works when colder, denser fluid sinks below warmer, less dense fluid. Ask: **Which of these three types of heat transfer is involved in El Niño formation and the weather patterns that result?** *(All three; direct transfer takes place between ocean water and air. Radiation transfers heat from sun to land and atmosphere. Convection is the airflow that occurs between high- and low-pressure regions.)*
Verbal, Logical

Download a worksheet on La Niña and El Niño for students to complete, and find additional teacher support from NSTA SciLinks.

Facts and Figures

When winds blow along the surface of the ocean, the water is not pushed along directly in front of the wind. Instead, it is deflected by about 45 degrees as a result of the Coriolis effect. When surface waters are deflected, colder, deeper water rises to take its place. This cold water is richer in nutrients than warmer surface water and promotes highly productive coastal fisheries. In years when coastal upwelling does not occur, coastal fish populations may be reduced or absent.

Answer to . . .

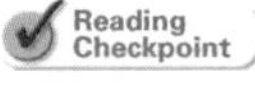

An episode—occurring every three to seven years—of ocean warming that affects the eastern tropical Pacific; warm countercurrents become unusually strong and replace normally cold offshore waters with warm equatorial waters.

Section 19.3 (continued)

Global Distribution of Precipitation

Answers
Using the Map Key less than 400 mm
Identify Causes subtropical high pressure cells

3 ASSESS

Evaluate Understanding — L2

To assess students' knowledge of section content, have them write a short description of each of the four types of local winds. Then have students write two or three sentences describing the events that give rise to an El Niño event.

Reteach

Have students draw and label their own diagrams illustrating sea, land, valley, and mountain breezes. Allow students to use Figures 12, 13, and 14 as references, if needed.

Writing in Science

Student paragraphs should contrast the ocean water temperature conditions that trigger each phenomenon and describe how these in turn influence air pressure. Specific examples of weather associated with El Niño and La Niña also should be included in the paragraph.

MAP MASTER™ Skills Activity

Figure 18

Regions The map shows average annual precipitation in millimeters. **Using the Map Key** Determine the range of precipitation that dominates Northern Africa. **Identify Causes** Which weather pattern influences precipitation in this area?

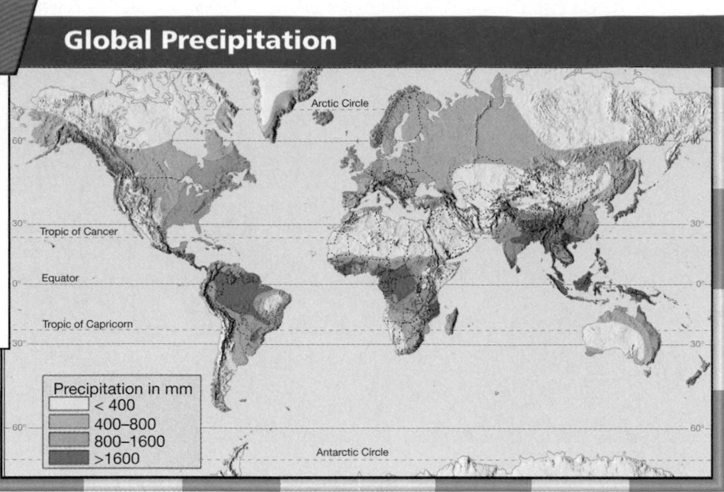

Global Distribution of Precipitation

Figure 18 shows that the tropical region dominated by the equatorial low is the rainiest region on Earth. It includes the rain forests of the Amazon basin in South America and the Congo basin in Africa. In these areas, the warm, humid trade winds converge to yield abundant rainfall throughout the year. In contrast, areas dominated by the subtropical high-pressure cells are regions of extensive deserts. Variables other than pressure and wind complicate the pattern. For example, the interiors of large land masses commonly experience decreased precipitation. However, you can explain a lot about global precipitation if you apply your knowledge of global winds and pressure systems.

Section 19.3 Assessment

Reviewing Concepts

1. What are local winds, and how are they caused?
2. Describe the general movement of weather in the United States.
3. What happens when strong, warm countercurrents flow along the coasts of Ecuador and Peru?
4. How is a La Niña event recognized?
5. What two factors mainly influence global precipitation?

Critical Thinking

6. **Interpreting illustrations** Study Figure 17. How could air pressure changes influence weather patterns in this region?

Compare-Contrast Paragraph Write a paragraph comparing the features and effects of El Niño and La Niña. Include specific weather patterns associated with each phenomenon.

Section 19.3 Assessment

1. Local winds are small-scale winds caused by local variations in air pressure, which are caused by topography and unequal heating of land and water, or unequal heating of air above slopes and valleys.
2. from west to east
3. An El Niño event blocks normal upwelling of cold, nutrient-laden waters off the shores of these countries, and causes heavy precipitation inland. El Niño can have far-reaching effects on weather patterns of regions that are great distances from Ecuador and Peru.
4. La Niña is triggered when surface temperatures in the eastern Pacific are colder than average.
5. moisture content of air and distribution of land and water
6. Warm water near Ecuador and Peru would heat air and cause it to rise, producing lower pressure and precipitation. Regions north of Australia that normally receive more warm water would experience higher pressure, possibly leading to drought.

understanding
EARTH Tracking El Niño from Space

The images in Figure 19 show the progression of the 1997–98 El Niño. They were derived from data collected by the satellite TOPEX/Poseidon.* This satellite bounces radar signals off the ocean surface to precisely measure the distance between the satellite and the sea surface. When combined with high-precision data from the Global Positioning System (GPS) of satellites, maps of sea-surface topography like these can be produced. These maps show the topography of the sea surface. The presence of hills indicates warmer-than-average water, and the areas of low topography, or valleys, indicate cooler-than-normal water. Using water topography, scientists can determine the speed and direction of surface ocean currents.

The colors in these images show sea-level height relative to the average. When you focus on the images, remember that hills are warm colors and valleys are cool colors. The white and red areas indicate places of higher-than-normal sea-surface heights. In the white areas, the sea surface is between 14 and 32 centimeters above normal. In the red areas, sea level is elevated by about 10 centimeters. Green areas indicate average conditions, whereas purple shows zones that are at least 18 centimeters below average sea level.

The images show the progression of the large warm-water mass from west to east across the equatorial Pacific Ocean. At its peak in November 1997, the surface area covered by the warm water mass was about one and one half times the size of the 48 contiguous United States. The amount of warm water added to the eastern Pacific with a temperature between 21°C and 30°C was about 30 times the combined volume of the water in all of the United States Great Lakes.

**Source: NASA's Goddard Space Flight Center*

April 25, 1997

July 25, 1997

November 10, 1997

March 14, 1998

Figure 19 Progression of the 1997–98 El Niño

understanding
EARTH

Tracking El Niño from Space L2

Background

The image for April 25, 1997, shows the Pacific Ocean on the eve of the 1997–1998 El Niño event. By examining the images for July 25 and November 10, you can see the dramatic buildup of warm water (white and red areas) in the eastern Pacific and the enlarging region of cooler water (purple) in the western Pacific. By the time of the March 14, 1998, image, the area of warm water in the eastern Pacific was much smaller.

Teaching Tips

- The directional terms *eastern Pacific* and *western Pacific* may give some students trouble, since the eastern Pacific Ocean borders the western coast of the United States. Ask: **What continents are bordered by the eastern Pacific Ocean?** *(North America, South America, and Central America)*
- As students examine each of the four images in Figure 19, ask: **What colors indicate warmer than average water temperatures?** *(white and red)* **What colors indicate cooler than average water temperatures?** *(purple)* **Where is the warm water mass located on April 25, 1997?** *(warm water mass not yet evident)* **Where is the warm water mass located on July 25 and November 10?** *(eastern Pacific)* **What does the map indicate about the warm water mass on March 14?** *(It is dissipating.)*

Exploration Lab

Observing Wind Patterns L2

Objective
After completing this activity, students will be able to:
- interpret diagrams of surface barometric pressure and high- and low-pressure cells.
- summarize basic characteristics of air movement in high- and low-pressure cells.
- compare and contrast air movement in pressure cells in the Northern and Southern Hemispheres.

Skills Focus Observing, Analyzing Data, Calculating

Prep Time Use the diagrams provided in the Earth Science Laboratory Manual or copy the diagrams in the manual for students. 15 minutes to copy the diagrams on these two pages if needed.

Class Time 30 minutes

Teaching Tip Using copies of these diagrams from the lab manual will ensure that students will not write in their textbooks.

Expected Outcome Students will become familiar with air pressure data plotted on maps. They will learn to interpret how air moves in a given region as indicated by isobar lines.

Exploration Lab

Observing Wind Patterns

Atmospheric pressure and wind are two elements of weather that are closely interrelated. Most people don't usually pay close attention to the pressure given in a weather report. However, pressure differences in the atmosphere drive the winds that often bring changes in temperature and moisture.

Problem How can surface barometric pressure maps be interpreted?

Materials
- 1 copy each of Figure 1 and Figure 2
- paper
- pencil

Skills Observing, Analyzing Data, Calculating

Procedure
1. Look at Figure 2. This map shows global wind patterns and average global barometric pressure for the month of January.
2. Examine the individual pressure cells in Figure 2. Then complete the diagrams in your copy of Figure 1. Label the isobars with appropriate pressures, and use arrows to indicate the surface air movement in each pressure cell.
3. Copy the data table below. Indicate the movements of air in high and low pressure cells by completing the table.

Northern Hemisphere

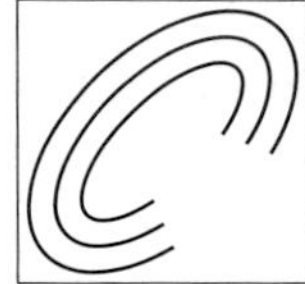

Southern Hemisphere

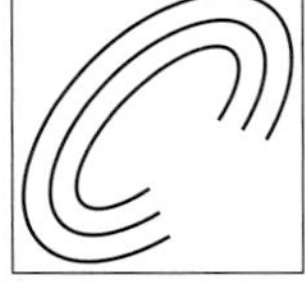
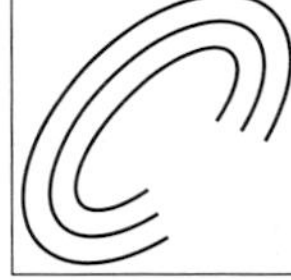

Figure 1

Air Movement in Pressure Cells Data Table				
Air Movement	N. Hem. High	N. Hem. Low	S. Hem High	S. Hem. Low
into/out of				
rises/sinks				
rotates CW/CCW*				

* CW = clockwise; CCW = counterclockwise

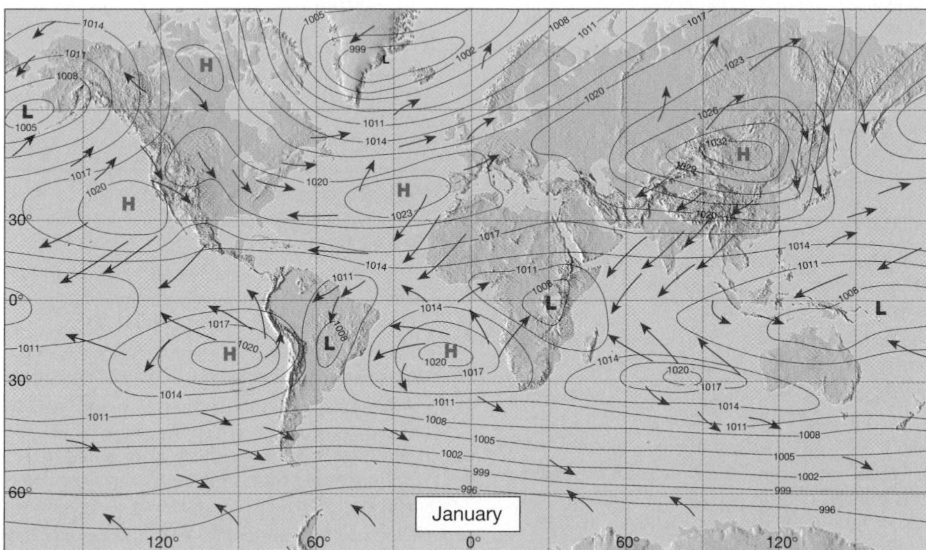

Figure 2

Analyze and Conclude

1. **Comparing and Contrasting** Summarize the differences and similarities in surface air movement between a Northern Hemisphere cyclone and a Southern Hemisphere cyclone.
2. **Interpreting Illustrations** Use your textbook as a reference to locate and write the name of each global wind belt at the appropriate location on your copy of the map in Figure 2. Also indicate the region of the polar front.
3. **Applying** Label areas on your copy of Figure 2 where you would expect high wind speeds to occur.
4. **Applying** Label areas on your copy of Figure 2 where circulation is most like the idealized global wind model for a rotating Earth. Explain why this region on Earth is so much like the model.

Answers to Procedure Questions

2. Northern Hemisphere

High (Anticyclone)

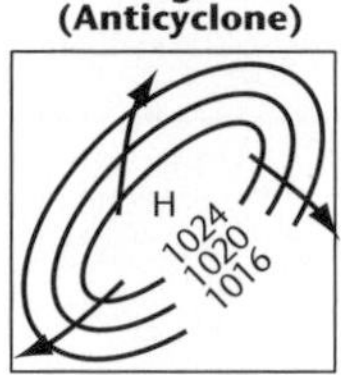

Low (Cyclone)

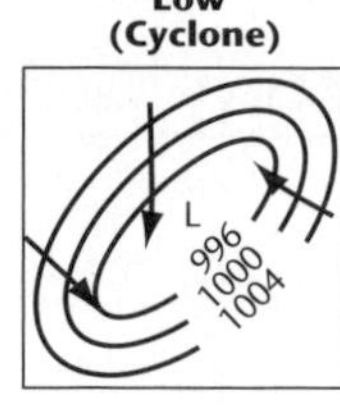

Southern Hemisphere

High (Anticyclone)

H 1024 1020 1016

Low (Cyclone)

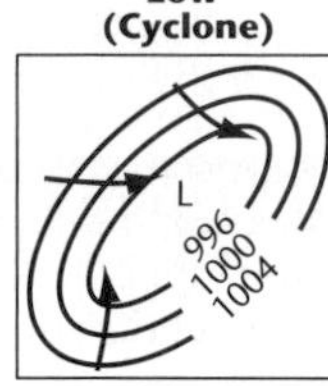

3. Table 1 Air Movement in Pressure Cells

Air Movement	N. Hem. High	N. Hem. Low	S. Hem. High	S. Hem. Low
into/out of	out of	into	out of	into
rises/sinks	sinks	rises	sinks	rises
rotates CW/ CCW*	CW	CCW	CCW	CW

*CW = clockwise; CCW = counterclockwise

Analyze and Conclude

1. In a Northern Hemisphere cyclone, air rotates counterclockwise, whereas air rotates clockwise in an anticyclone. These rotation directions result from the Coriolis effect and so they are reversed for cyclones and anticyclones in the Southern Hemisphere. In either hemisphere, the net flow of air is inward for a cyclone and outward for an anticyclone. This net effect inward and outward is due to friction. Also, air sinks in an anticyclone and rises in a cyclone in both hemispheres.

2. Student locations of wind belts, pressure zones, and fronts should be like those in Figure 10 on p. 541 of the textbook. Use latitudes for these zones as indicated in Figure 10.

3. Areas of high wind speed correlate to closely spaced isobars on the map.

4. Students should locate the subpolar low in the Southern Hemisphere, at approximately 60 degrees south latitude. There are no landmasses in the region of this subpolar low to create seasonal temperature differences. Therefore, the air circulation pattern is not disrupted.

Visual, Logical

Study Guide

Study Tip

Prioritize

Tell students to make a list of all the study tasks they need to accomplish. Tell them to schedule study time realistically and stick to their deadlines.

Thinking Visually

a. wind speed
b. North Pole
c. South Pole

CHAPTER 19

Study Guide

19.1 Understanding Air Pressure

Key Concepts

- Air pressure is exerted in all directions—down, up, and sideways. The air pressure pushing down on an object exactly balances the air pressure pushing up on the object.
- When air pressure increases, the mercury in the tube rises. When air pressure decreases, so does the height of the mercury column.
- Wind is the result of horizontal differences in air pressure. Air flows from areas of higher pressure to areas of lower pressure.
- The unequal heating of Earth's surface generates pressure differences. Solar radiation is the ultimate energy source for most wind.
- Three factors combine to control wind: pressure differences, the Coriolis effect, and friction.
- Closely spaced isobars indicate a steep pressure gradient and high winds. Widely spaced isobars indicate a weak pressure gradient and light winds.
- The Coriolis effect describes how Earth's rotation affects moving objects. All free-moving objects or fluids, including the wind, are deflected to the right of their path of motion in the Northern Hemisphere. In the Southern Hemisphere, they are deflected to the left.

Vocabulary

air pressure, *p. 532;* barometer *p. 533;* pressure gradient, *p. 534;* Coriolis effect, *p. 535;* jet stream, *p. 536*

19.2 Pressure Centers and Winds

Key Concepts

- In the Northern Hemisphere, winds blow inward and counterclockwise around a low. Around a high, they blow outward and clockwise.
- In cyclones, the pressure decreases from the outer isobars toward the center. In anticyclones, just the opposite is the case—the values of the isobars increase from the outside toward the center.
- In either hemisphere, pressure difference, the Coriolis effect, and friction causes a net flow of air inward around a cyclone and a net flow of air outward around an anticyclone.
- The atmosphere balances differences in solar radiation in the tropics and the poles by acting as a giant heat-transfer system. This system moves warm air toward high latitudes and cool air toward the equator.

Vocabulary

cyclone, *p. 538;* anticyclone, *p. 538;* trade winds, *p. 541;* westerlies, *p. 541;* polar easterlies, *p. 541;* polar front, *p. 541;* monsoon, *p. 542*

19.3 Regional Wind Systems

Key Concepts

- The local winds are caused either by topographic effects or by variations in surface composition—land and water—in the immediate area.
- In the United States, the westerlies consistently move weather from west to east across the continent.
- At irregular intervals of three to seven years, warm equatorial currents along the coasts of Ecuador and Peru become unusually strong and replace normally cold offshore waters with warm waters. This occurrence is referred to as an El Niño event.
- When surface temperatures in the eastern Pacific are colder than average, a La Niña event is triggered that has a distinctive set of weather patterns.

Vocabulary

prevailing wind, *p. 545;* anemometer, *p. 545;* El Niño, *p. 546;* La Niña, *p. 547*

Thinking Visually

Concept Map Copy the concept map below onto a sheet of paper. Use information from the chapter to complete the concept map.

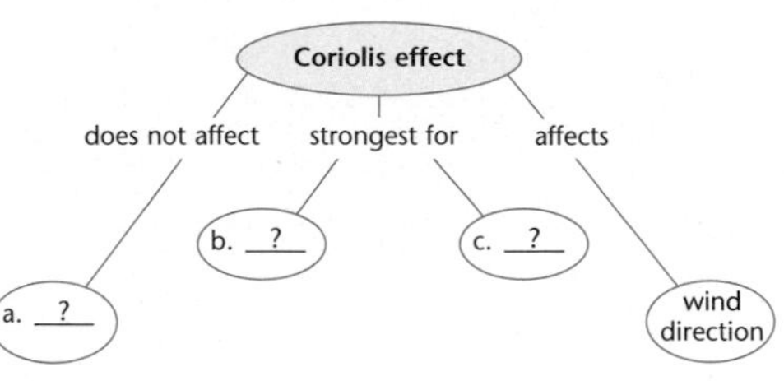

Chapter Assessment Resources

Print
Chapter Test, Chapter 19
Test Prep Resources, Chapter 19

Technology
Computer Test Bank, Chapter 19 Test
Online Text, Chapter 19
Go Online, PHSchool.com, Chapter 19

CHAPTER 19

NY Regents Content Item

Assessment

Interactive textbook with assessment at PHSchool.com 

Reviewing Content

Choose the number that best answers the question or completes the statement.

1 The mercurial barometer was invented by
(1) Galileo (2) Newton
(3) Torricelli (4) Watt

2 The force exerted by the air above is called NY
(1) air pressure (2) convergence
(3) divergence (4) the Coriolis effect

3 What are centers of low pressure called? NY
(1) air masses (2) anticyclones
(3) cyclones (4) jet streams

4 Variations in air pressure from place to place are the principal cause of NY
(1) clouds (2) lows
(3) hail (4) wind

5 In the winter, large landmasses often develop a seasonal NY
(1) high-pressure system
(2) low-pressure system
(3) typhoon
(4) trade wind

6 A sea breeze is most intense NY
(1) during mid- to late afternoon
(2) in the late morning
(3) late in the evening
(4) at sunrise

7 What is the pressure zone that is associated with rising air near the equator? NY
(1) equatorial low (2) equatorial high
(3) subtropical low (4) subtropical high

8 What are high-altitude, high-velocity winds? NY
(1) cyclonic currents (2) isobars
(3) jet streams (4) pressure gradients

9 Where is deflection of wind due to the Coriolis effect the strongest? NY
(1) near the equator (2) in the midlatitudes
(3) near the poles (4) near the westerlies

10 In what stormy region do the westerlies and polar easterlies converge? NY
(1) equatorial low (2) subpolar high
(3) polar front (4) subtropical front

Understanding Concepts

11 Describe how an aneroid barometer works. NY

12 Write a general statement relating the spacing of isobars to wind speed. NY

13 Describe the weather that usually accompanies a
a drop in barometric pressure.
b rise in barometric pressure. NY

14 How does the Coriolis effect modify air movement in the Southern Hemisphere? NY

15 The trade winds originate from which pressure zone?

16 List and briefly describe three examples of local winds.

17 On a wind vane with a degree scale, which type of wind is indicated by 90 degrees?

Use the figure below to answer questions 18–20.

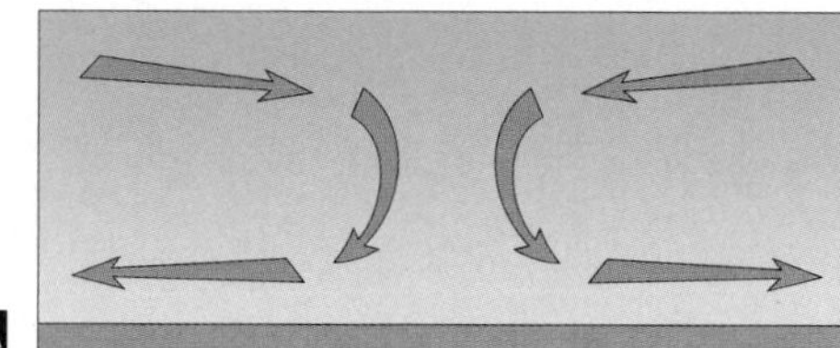
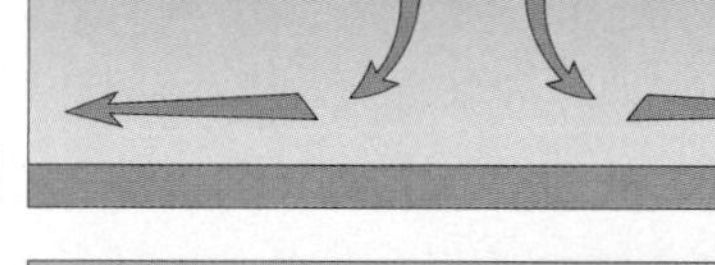

A

B

18 In diagram A, what type of surface air flow is shown? NY

19 What type of surface pressure system is illustrated in diagram B? NY

20 Select the diagram in which air at the surface first begins to pile up.

Homework Guide

Section	Questions
1	1, 2, 8, 9, 11–13, 22, 28
2	3–5, 7, 10, 14, 15, 18–21, 23
3	6, 16, 17, 24–27, 29

Assessment

Reviewing Content

(1) 3 (2) 1 (3) 3
(4) 4 (5) 1 (6) 1
(7) 1 (8) 3 (9) 3
(10) 3

Understanding Concepts

(11) An aneroid barometer consists of evacuated metal chambers that compress as air pressure increases and expand when air pressure decreases.
(12) Closely spaced isobars indicate a strong wind; widely spaced isobars indicate a light wind.
(13) A drop in barometric pressure is associated with converging winds and ascending air; therefore it is often associated with clouds and precipitation. In contrast, a rise in air pressure is associated with fair weather.
(14) The deflective force of Earth's rotation (Coriolis effect) causes air to be deflected to the left of its path of motion in the Southern Hemisphere.
(15) Trades winds originate from the equatorial low.
(16) Three examples of local winds are sea breezes, land breezes, and mountain breezes. Sea and land breezes result from pressure changes associated with differential heating of land and water. Mountain breezes result when air near mountain slopes cools at night by rapid radiation cooling and descends down mountain slopes.
(17) an east wind
(18) surface divergence
(19) low (cyclone)
(20) diagram B

Critical Thinking

(21) The winds west of a cyclone in the Northern Hemisphere would be northwest or west-northwest; winds west of an anticyclone would be south to southeast.
(22) Because wind turbines would be used in regions with high sustained winds, you would look for a place marked by closely spaced isobars.
(23) Regions dominated by low-pressure systems are expected to be cloudy with abundant precipitation, which would support abundant vegetation. Clear skies and desert conditions with sparse vegetation are expected for regions with sustained high-pressure centers.

Math Skills

(24) NW/SW/W, or westerlies
(25) about 6 percent
(26) about 37 percent

CHAPTER 19

Assessment *continued*

Critical Thinking

21 **Predicting** If you are in the Northern Hemisphere and are directly west of the center of a cyclone, what most likely will be the wind direction? What will the wind direction be if you are west of an anticyclone in the Northern Hemisphere? NY

22 **Applying Concepts** If you were looking for a location to place a wind turbine to generate electricity, how would you use the spacing of isobars in making your decision? NY

23 **Hypothesizing** What differences in the biosphere would you predict for areas dominated by low-pressure systems compared to those dominated by high-pressure systems? NY

Math Skills

Use the illustration below to answer questions 24–26.

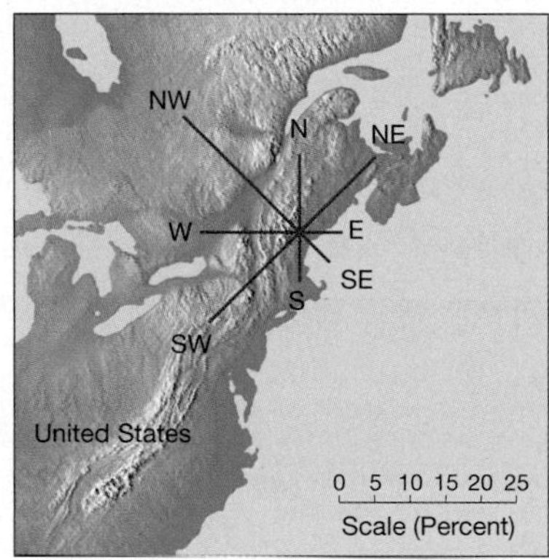

24 **Analyzing Data** According to the map, which winds dominate this region? NY

25 **Measuring** About what percent of the time do winds blow from the east? NY

26 **Calculating** Determine the approximate percent of time that winds blow from either the west or the northwest in this area.

Concepts in Action

27 **Predicting** How might a La Niña event impact the weather in your area? NY

28 **Applying Concepts** Mercury is 13 times heavier than water. If you built a barometer using water rather than mercury, how tall would it have to be to record standard sea-level pressure? Express your answer in centimeters. (Hint: How many centimeters of mercury represent standard sea-level pressure?)

29 **Interpreting Illustrations** After studying Figure 16, explain the relationship between water temperature and the type of air pressure system that develops.

Performance-Based Assessment

Observing For two weeks, keep a daily air pressure, wind, and precipitation log in your science notebook. Be sure to note any changes, and note if any of the changes occur over the course of a single day. At the end of two weeks, organize your information into a data table. Prepare a short summary that includes any patterns you determine among these variables. Report the results orally to your class.

Concepts in Action

(27) Students' answers obviously will depend on their locations, but reasonable answers should indicate colder and wetter conditions in the Pacific Northwest, and warming trends for most of the rest of the United States. In addition, Southeastern and Gulf Coast states could see increasing hurricane activity.
(28) Standard sea level pressure in centimeters equals 76 cm of mercury. The height of standard sea level pressure if a water barometer is used would need to be 13 times higher than 76 cm, or 988 cm.
(29) In general, low-pressure regions form over warm water, and high-pressure regions form over cold water.

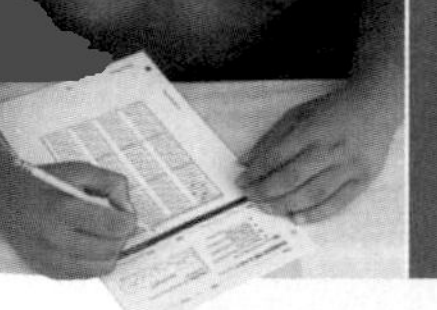

Regents Practice Exam

Test-Taking Tip

Anticipate the Answer
When answering multiple choice questions, a useful strategy is to cover up the given answers and supply your own answer. Then compare your answer with those listed and select the one that most closely matches.

Practice anticipating the answer in questions 1–4.

For *each* statement or question, choose the *number* of the word or expression that, of those given, best completes the statement or answers the question. Some questions may require the use of the *Earth Science Reference Tables.*

1 Prevailing winds cause most of New York State's weather to come from the
  (1) northeast
  (2) east
  (3) south
  (4) west

2 Air in a high pressure system generally circulates
  (1) clockwise and into the center
  (2) counterclockwise and into the center
  (3) clockwise and out from the center
  (4) counterclockwise and out from the center

4 What effect does the Coriolis force have on wind?
  (1) Winds in the northern hemisphere are deflected to their left.
  (2) Winds in the northern hemisphere are deflected to their right.
  (3) Winds in the southern hemisphere are deflected to their right.
  (4) Winds in the southern hemisphere are deflected to their south.

5 A sea breeze usually originates during the
  (1) evening and flows toward the land
  (2) day and flows toward the land
  (3) evening and flows toward the water
  (4) day and flows toward the water

Answer the following questions in complete sentences. Some questions may require the use of the *Earth Science Reference Tables.*

6 What is the relationship between pressure gradient and wind speed?

7 Use the scale below. What is the standard sea level pressure in millibars and inches? Express your answer to the nearest tenth of a millibar, and the nearest hundredth of an inch.

8 Predict the sky conditions for a city where the pressure has been dropping for a few hours.

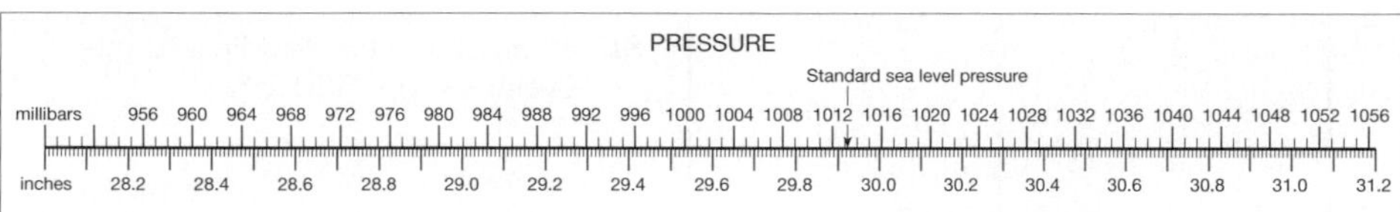

3 During an El Niño event, thunderstorms form in the eastern Pacific Ocean because the warm, moist air is
  (1) less dense, rising, expanding, and cooling
  (2) less dense, sinking, compressing, and warming
  (3) more dense, sinking, compressing, and warming
  (4) more dense, rising, expanding, and cooling

Regents Practice Exam

(1) 4
(2) 3
(3) 1
(4) 2
(5) 2
(6) As pressure gradient increases, wind speed increases.
(7) Standard sea level pressure is 1013.2 mb or 29.92 in of mercury.
(8) A good prediction would be increasing clouds, and possibly precipitation.

Performance-Based Assessment

Student reports should include observations in an organized table or spreadsheet format. They should express relationships observed among air pressure, wind, and precipitation

Your students can independently test their knowledge of the chapter and print out their results.

Air Pressure and Wind 555

CHAPTER 20

Planning Guide

Use these planning tools
Use Teacher Express for all your planning needs

SECTION OBJECTIVES	STANDARDS NATIONAL	STANDARDS STATE	ACTIVITIES and LABS
20.1 Air Masses, pp. 558–563 2 blocks or 4 periods **20.1** **Define** air mass. **20.2** **Explain** how air masses are classified. **20.3** **Explain** the characteristic features of each air mass class. **20.4** **Explain** the influence of continental polar and maritime tropical air masses on the majority of North America.	A-1, D-1, F-5		**SE** Inquiry Activity: How Can You Model the Movement of Air in a Tornado? p. 557 L2 **TE** Teacher Demo: Air Masses in a Bottle, p. 559 L2
20.2 Fronts, pp. 564–570 1 block or 2 periods **20.5** **Describe** the formation of a front. **20.6** **Differentiate** among the formation of a warm front, cold front, stationary front, and occluded front. **20.7** **Describe** the weather patterns associated with each type of front.	B-5		**TE** Build Science Skills, p. 566 L2 **TE** Teacher Demo: Getting to the Point of Fronts, p. 568 L2 **SE** Application Lab: Middle-Latitude Cyclones, pp. 580–581 L2
20.3 Severe Storms, pp. 571–577 2 blocks or 4 periods **20.8** **Explain** the formation of a thunderstorm. **20.9** **Describe** the conditions needed for a tornado to form. **20.10** **Identify** the conditions that must exist for a hurricane to form.	A-1, A-2, F-5, F-6		**TE** Teacher Demo: Homemade Tornado, p. 573 L2 **LM** Analyzing Severe Weather Data L2 **LM** Interpreting Weather Diagrams L2 **LM** Creating a Weather Station L2

Ability Levels	Components			
L1 For students who need additional help	**SE** Student Edition	**GRSW** Guided Reading & Study Workbook	**TP** Test Prep Resources	**GEO** Geode CD-ROM
L2 For all students	**TE** Teacher's Edition	**TEX** Teacher Express	**onT** onlineText	**T** Transparencies
L3 For students who need to be challenged	**LM** Laboratory Manual	**CTB** Computer Test Bank	**DC** Discovery Channel Videos	**GO** Internet Resources
	CUT Chapter Tests			

RESOURCES PRINT and TECHNOLOGY	SECTION ASSESSMENT
GRSW Section 20.1 **T-284** Influence of Canadian Air Mass **T-285** Air Mass Source Regions **T-286** Continental Polar and Maritime Polar Air Masses GEODe The Atmosphere → Basic Weather Patterns **TEX** Lesson Planning 20.1	**SE** Section 20.1 Assessment, p. 563 **onT** Section 20.1
GRSW Section 20.2 **T-287** Warm Front **T-288** Cold Front and Cumulonimbus Clouds **T-289** Formation of an Occluded Front **T-290** Life Cycle of a Middle-Latitude Cyclone **T-291** Cloud Patterns Associated with Middle-Latitude Cyclones **T-292** Role of Airflow Aloft in Cyclonic Activity **TEX** Lesson Planning 20.2	**SE** Section 20.2 Assessment, p. 570 **onT** Section 20.2
GRSW Section 20.3 **T-293** U.S. Map—Distribution of Thunderstorms **T-294** Development of a Thunderstorm **T-295** Tornadoes Have Multiple Suction Vortices **T-296** Formation of a Mesocyclone **T-297** Tornado Incidence **T-298** Paths of Illinois Tornadoes **T-299** Fujita Intensity Scale **T-300** Hurricane Cross Section **T-301** Safir–Simpson Hurricane Scale **DC** Violent Weather **TEX** Lesson Planning 20.3	**SE** Section 20.3 Assessment, p. 577 **onT** Section 20.3

Go Online

Go online for these Internet resources.

PHSchool.com
Web Code: cjk-9999

NSTA SCILINKS
Web Code: cjn-6201
Web Code: cjn-6203

Materials for Activities and Labs

Quantities for each group

STUDENT EDITION

Inquiry Activity, p. 557
2 1-L transparent plastic soda bottles from which the labels have been removed, flat rubber washer with a 3/8" hole in the center, duct tape, scissors, tap water, 30-mL liquid dishwashing soap, paper towels to wipe up spills, 1/4 teaspoon glitter or plastic confetti

Application Lab, pp. 580–581
tracing paper, sharp pencil, paper clips or removable tape, metric ruler, colored pencils

TEACHER'S EDITION

Teacher Demo, p. 559
2 wide-mouthed jars of the same size, matches, small pan, hot water, ice cubes, flashlight

Build Science Skills, p. 566
red and blue clay

Teacher Demo, p. 568
pencil

Teacher Demo, p. 573
piece of sturdy cardboard; glue; 2 transparency sheets; small hand-held, battery-operated fan; small plastic bowl; clear plastic plant dish, approximately 7" in diameter with a hole cut in the middle; water; dry ice

Chapter Assessment

ASSESSMENT

SE	Assessment, pp. 583–584
CUT	Chapter 20 Test
CTB	Chapter 20
onT	Chapter 20

STANDARDIZED TEST PREP

SE	Chapter 20, p. 585
TP	Progress Monitoring Assessments

interactive textbook with assessment at PHSchool.com

CHAPTER 20

Before you teach

Michael Wysession
Washington University

Big Ideas

Weather is a result of the movement of different air masses. Storms result from interactions between these air masses.

Space and Time Air masses are classified by temperature (tropical or polar) and place of origin (continental or maritime).

Fronts are boundaries between two air masses, and are often the location of storms and precipitation. Warm fronts involve warm air moving into cooler air. Cold fronts involve cold air moving into warmer air. Occluded fronts occur when a cold front overtakes a warm front, lifting warm air away from surface.

Forces and Motion Most weather in the United States is produced by middle-latitude cyclones, traveling west to east. A cyclone at the ground involves convergence of air toward a low pressure zone, and is accompanied by divergence of air high in the jet stream.

Matter and Energy About 100,000 thunderstorms associated with cumulonimbus clouds occur in the United States each year. Thunderstorms form when warm humid air rises and moisture precipitates out. They can be the sites of tornadoes, areas of rotating wind and intense low pressure, which can extend down from a cumulonimbus cloud during a thunderstorm.

Earth as a System Hurricanes are large tropical cyclones involving an interaction of ocean, atmosphere, and land systems that begin over the ocean, but can move onto land. Hurricanes can be very destructive, involving tremendous winds and flooding.

Earth Science Refresher

Lightning and Thunder

Lightning and thunder are some of the most dramatic aspects of thunderstorms. They occur when electrical current is transferred between locations within the clouds, or between the clouds and the ground. Differences in electrical charge at the top and bottom of cumulonimbus clouds build up during the repeated vertical motions of rain and ice within the clouds. The transfer of current is visible, and this is the lightning. If the current reaches the ground, a return stroke of current occurs, and this is usually brighter then the down stroke.

There is a tremendous amount of energy in a lightning stroke—about 1–10 billion joules, enough to supply the electricity for a home for more than a month. Along the path of the lightning, the air gets heated to temperatures on the order of 25,000°C—hotter than the surface of the sun! This sudden increase in temperature causes the air to rapidly expand as a shock wave, which then converts into a booming sound wave we hear as thunder. We see the lightning almost instantaneously because of the great speed of light, with the sound of the thunder arriving later. Because the speed of sound in air is about 335 m/s (depending upon the temperature of the air), if you divide the number of seconds between the lightning and thunder by 3, you will get the distance of the lightning in kilometers.

Address Misconceptions

Students may think that the terms warm front *and* cold front *are actually referring to masses of warm air and cold air.* This is not true. A warm front brings an air mass with warmer air into an area, and a cold front brings cooler air into an area. For a strategy that helps to overcome this misconception, see **Address Misconceptions** on **p. 566**.

Go Online PD LINKS
NSTA

For: Chapter 20 Content Support
Visit: www.SciLinks.org/PDLinks
Web Code: cjn-2099

The United States National Lightning Detection Network identifies about 22 million cloud-to-ground flashes every year. In the United States, about 100 people are killed and 500 injured by lightning each year. It is estimated that you therefore have a 1 in 600,000 chance of being killed or injured by lightning each year. Most lightning occurs in the direct region of a storm, but some strikes are more than 100 km long, and have been known to hit the ground far from a storm, in areas of blue sky.

Lightning plays an important geological role because it can often cause forest fires. These fires reduce ground cover, and therefore increase the susceptibility of the land to erosion and mass wasting. Vegetation has evolved , which can adapt to forest fires that occur from lightning strikes. In fact, there are some plants that have seeds that are only released following a fire. These are the first plants to regenerate, followed by successions of other kinds of vegetation. Ironically, putting out the small fires that repeatedly occur from lightning strikes can cause a buildup of undergrowth, which can result in a catastrophic fire when it does burn.

Build Reading Literacy

Active Comprehension

Engaging Interest in a Topic

Strategy Stimulate students' interest in a topic prior to reading. As with the KWL strategy, students generate questions based on their curiosity. Interest is thus translated into a purpose for reading. Looking for answers to the questions during reading helps keep students engaged in what they are reading. Before students begin reading, choose an opening paragraph from one of the sections in Chapter 20, for example, the first paragraph on p. 558.

Example

1. Have a student read the opening paragraph.

2. Ask the group, "What more would you like to know about storms and weather?" Make a list of student responses.

3. Tell students to read the remainder of the section, keeping the questions in mind as they read.

4. After reading, you may discuss the extent to which each question was answered by the text. Ask students also to comment on any new information they learned that was surprising.

5. Have students work in small groups, applying the active comprehension strategy to the reading of each section of the chapter.

See p. 567 for a script on how to use this strategy with students. For additional strategies, see pp. 561 and 576.

ASSESS PRIOR KNOWLEDGE

Use the Chapter Pretest below to assess students' prior knowledge. As needed, review these concepts.

Review Science Concepts

Section 20.1 An understanding of how water is a part of the atmosphere and the conditions that dictate how much water vapor can exist in the atmosphere will help students understand how polar and tropical air masses are different.

Section 20.2 Reviewing air pressure and the movement of air from areas of high pressure to areas of low pressure will help explain the movement of air masses along fronts.

Section 20.3 Reviewing the different types of clouds and their formation is essential for an understanding of the formation of severe storms in the atmosphere.

CHAPTER 20 Weather Patterns and Severe Storms

CONCEPTS in Action

Application Lab
Middle-Latitude Cyclones

How the Earth Works
Winds and Storms

The Atmosphere
↳ Basic Weather Patterns

Discovery Channel School **Video Field Trip**

Violent Weather

Take a stormy field trip with Discovery Channel and find out how hurricanes and tornadoes occur. Answer the following questions after watching the video.

1. What is the biggest danger in a hurricane?
2. How does the funnel of a tornado form?

For: Chapter 20 Resources
Visit: PHSchool.com
Web Code: cjk-9999

Lightning forms suddenly when negative charges near the bottom of a cloud flow toward the positively charged ground. ▶

556 *Chapter 20*

Chapter Pretest

1. True or False: More water vapor can exist in warm air than in cold air. *(True)*
2. When water vapor in air condenses, what must occur in order for clouds to form? *(c)*
   a. The air is heated.
   b. Snow falls.
   c. The air is cooled.
   d. The air is superheated.
3. Explain briefly how wind forms. *(Wind is the result of the movement of air from an area of high pressure to an area of low pressure.)*
4. What are low, sheetlike clouds called? *(c)*
   a. cirrus clouds
   b. cumulus clouds
   c. stratus clouds
   d. cirrocumulus clouds
5. Where would the air contain the most moisture—over Kenya or over Antarctica? Why? *(over Kenya because the air is warmer there)*

Chapter Preview

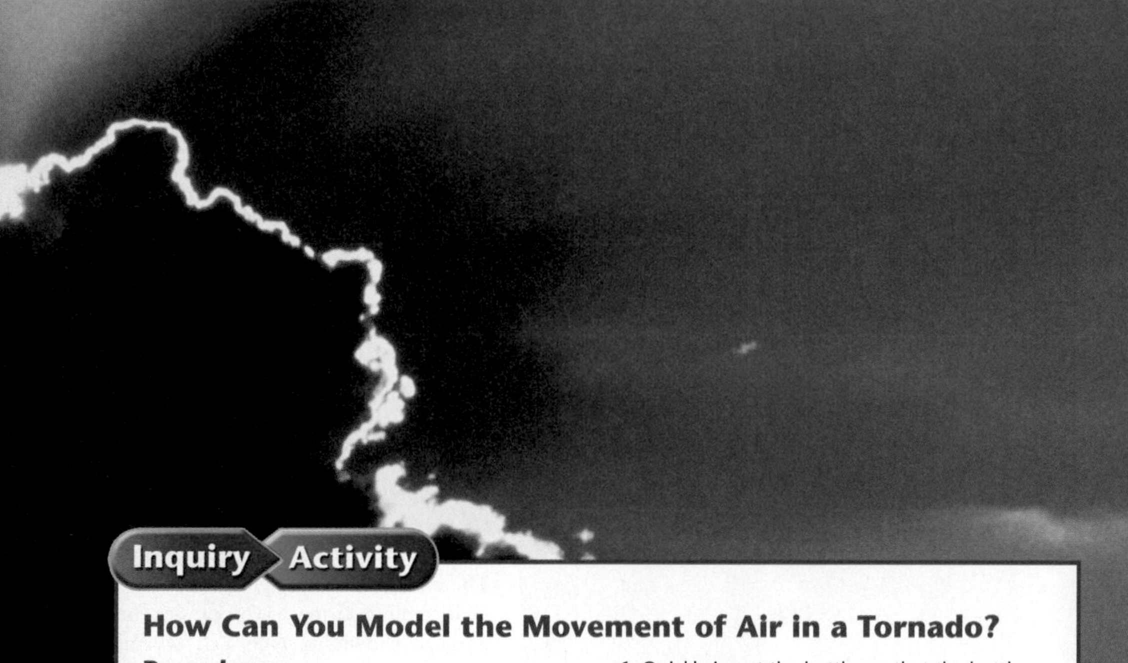

Inquiry Activity

How Can You Model the Movement of Air in a Tornado?

Procedure

1. Pour tap water into a 1-L plastic bottle until it is about two-thirds full. Wipe off any water from the outside of the bottle as well as from the opening.
2. Without getting any of either substance on the outside of the bottle, add about 30 mL of liquid dishwashing soap and a spoonful of glitter to the water in the bottle.
3. Center a washer on the mouth of the bottle.
4. Invert another 1-L empty bottle and place its mouth over the washer.
5. Wrap about 10 cm of duct tape around the mouths of the bottles to seal them. Be careful not to move the washer as you do this.
6. Quickly invert the bottles so that the bottle holding the water is on top. Then, while holding the top bottle, swirl the bottles in a counterclockwise direction.
7. Observe your mini-tornado.

Think About It

1. **Observing** How did the water move in the bottle?
2. **Modeling** What might the glitter represent?
3. **Formulating Hypotheses** What kinds of forces do you think acted on the water to make it move as it did?

Video Field Trip

Violent Weather

Encourage students to view the Video Field Trip "Violent Weather."

ENGAGE/EXPLORE

How Can You Model the Movement of Air in a Tornado?

Purpose In this activity, students will use water to model the movement of air in a tornado.

Skills Focus Observing, Modeling, Formulating Hypotheses

Prep Time 10 minutes to gather materials

Materials (per pair of students) 2 1-L transparent plastic soda bottles from which the labels have been removed, flat rubber washer with a 3/8" hole in the center, duct tape, scissors, tap water, 30-mL liquid dishwashing soap, paper towels to wipe up spills, 1/4 teaspoon glitter or plastic confetti

Advance Prep Have each student bring from home one 1-L transparent plastic soda bottle from which the label has been removed.

Class Time 15–20 minutes

Safety Students should wipe up any spills immediately to avoid slips and falls.

Teaching Tip Remind students to keep the outsides of the bottles—including the necks—dry.

Expected Outcome Students will observe the formation of a vortex that forms as centripetal force on the water causes the water to spin.

Think About It

1. The swirling water (vortex) moved in a counterclockwise direction within the top bottle and down into the bottom bottle.
2. The glitter represents debris carried by the swirling winds of a tornado.
3. Centripetal forces caused the water to swirl. Gravity caused the water to move into the lower bottle.

Section 20.1

1 FOCUS

Section Objectives

20.1 **Define** air mass.
20.2 **Explain** how air masses are classified.
20.3 **Explain** the characteristic features of each air mass class.
20.4 **Explain** the influence of continental polar and maritime tropical air masses on the majority of North America.

Reading Focus

Build Vocabulary L2

Paraphrase Ask students to write the vocabulary words on a sheet of paper. Instruct students to write a definition, in their own words, for each term as they encounter the term while going through the chapter. After writing their own definition, they should also write a complete sentence using the term.

Reading Strategy L2

a. an immense body of air characterized by similar temperatures and amounts of moisture at any given altitude
b. area over which an air mass gets its characteristic properties of temperature and moisture
c. cold air mass that forms at high latitudes toward Earth's poles
d. warm air mass that forms at low latitudes
e. dry air mass that forms over land
f. humid air mass that forms over water

20.1 Air Masses

Reading Focus

Key Concepts

- What is an air mass?
- What happens as an air mass moves over an area?
- How are air masses classified?
- Which air masses influence much of the weather in North America?
- Why do continental tropical air masses have little effect on weather in North America?

Vocabulary

- air mass

Reading Strategy

Building Vocabulary Copy the table. As you read this section, write a definition for each of the terms in the table. Refer to the table as you read the rest of the chapter.

Term	Definition
Air mass	a. ?
Source region	b. ?
Polar air mass	c. ?
Tropical air mass	d. ?
Continental air mass	e. ?
Maritime air mass	f. ?

Figure 1 Tornado Damage in Kansas The force of the wind during a tornado was strong enough to drive a piece of metal into the utility pole.

Severe storms are among nature's most destructive forces. Every spring, for example, newspapers and newscasts report the damage caused by tornadoes, which are short but violent windstorms that move quickly over land. The forces associated with these storms can be incredibly strong, as you can see from the damage shown in Figure 1. During late summer and early fall, you have probably heard reports about severe storms known as hurricanes. Unlike tornadoes, hurricanes form over Earth's tropical oceans. As they move toward land, the strong winds and heavy rains produced by these storms can destroy anything in their paths. You are probably most familiar with a type of severe storm known as a thunderstorm. Thunderstorms are a type of severe weather that produces heavy rains, loud noises you know as thunder, and flashes of light called lightning. Before learning more about these different types of violent weather, you will learn about the atmospheric conditions that most often affect the day-to-day weather.

Air Masses and Weather

For the many people who live in the middle latitudes, which include much of the United States, summer heat waves and winter cold spells are familiar experiences. During summer heat waves, several days of high temperatures and high humidity often end when a series of storms pass through the area. This stormy weather is followed by a few days of relatively cool weather. By contrast, winter cold spells are often characterized by periods of frigid temperatures under clear skies. These bitter cold periods are usually followed by cloudy, snowy, relatively warm days that seem mild when compared to those just a day earlier. In both of these situations, periods of fairly constant weather conditions are followed by a short period of changes in the weather. What do you think causes these changes?

Air Masses The weather patterns just described result from movements of large bodies of air called air masses. **An air mass is an immense body of air that is characterized by similar temperatures and amounts of moisture at any given altitude.** An air mass can be 1600 kilometers or more across and several kilometers thick. Because of its size, it may take several days for an air mass to move over an area. This causes the area to experience fairly constant weather, a situation often called air-mass weather. Some day-to-day variations may occur, but the events will be very unlike those in an adjacent air mass.

Movement of Air Masses When an air mass moves out of the region over which it formed, it carries its temperature and moisture conditions with it. An example of the influence of a moving air mass is shown in Figure 2. A cold, dry air mass from northern Canada is shown moving southward. The initial temperature of the air mass is −46°C. It warms 13 degrees by the time it reaches Winnipeg. The air mass continues to warm as it moves southward through the Great Plains and into Mexico. Throughout its southward journey, the air mass becomes warmer. But it also brings some of the coldest weather of the winter to the places in its path. **As it moves, the characteristics of an air mass change and so does the weather in the area over which the air mass moves.**

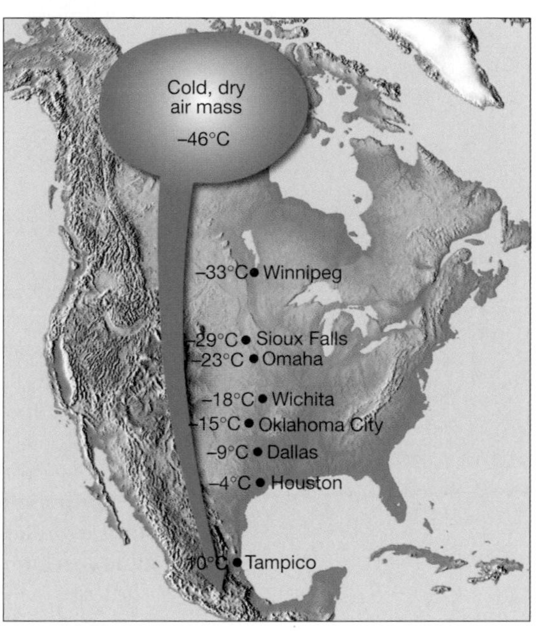

Figure 2 As a frigid Canadian air mass moves southward, it brings colder weather to the area over which it moves.
Computing *How much warmer was the air mass when it reached Tampico, Mexico, than when it formed?*

What is an air mass, and what happens as it moves over an area?

2 INSTRUCT

Air Masses and Weather

Air Masses in a Bottle **L2**

Purpose Students will observe what occurs when hot and cold air masses collide.

Materials 2 wide-mouthed jars of the same size, matches, small pan, hot water, ice cubes, flashlight

Procedure Place the hot water in the pan. Place one of the jars in the pan. Using the matches, fill both jars with smoke. Place the second jar on top of the one in the pan. Place the ice cubes on top of the second jar. Darken the classroom and use the flashlight to observe the movement of the smoke within the jars.

Expected Outcomes The hot air will rise in the first jar; the cold air will sink in the second jar
Kinesthetic, Visual

Customize for English Language Learners

Direct students to Figure 3 on p. 560. Before they read, have them use the figure to make a list of the four types of air masses impacting North America. Students should add definitions for the terms to the glossary as they read the section.

Answer to . . .

Figure 2 *56°C warmer*

An air mass is an immense body of air characterized by similar temperatures and amounts of moisture at any given altitude. As it moves, the characteristics of an air mass change and the weather in the area over which the air mass moves also changes.

Classifying Air Masses

Use Visuals L1

Figure 3 Direct students' attention to the map in Figure 3. Ask: **What type of air mass influence the weather in the northeast?** *(maritime polar)* **The southeast?** *(maritime tropical)*
Visual

Use Community Resources L2

Invite a meteorologist to speak to the class about the role that air masses play in the weather in North America. Have students ask about the dominant air masses that influence your local area.
Interpersonal

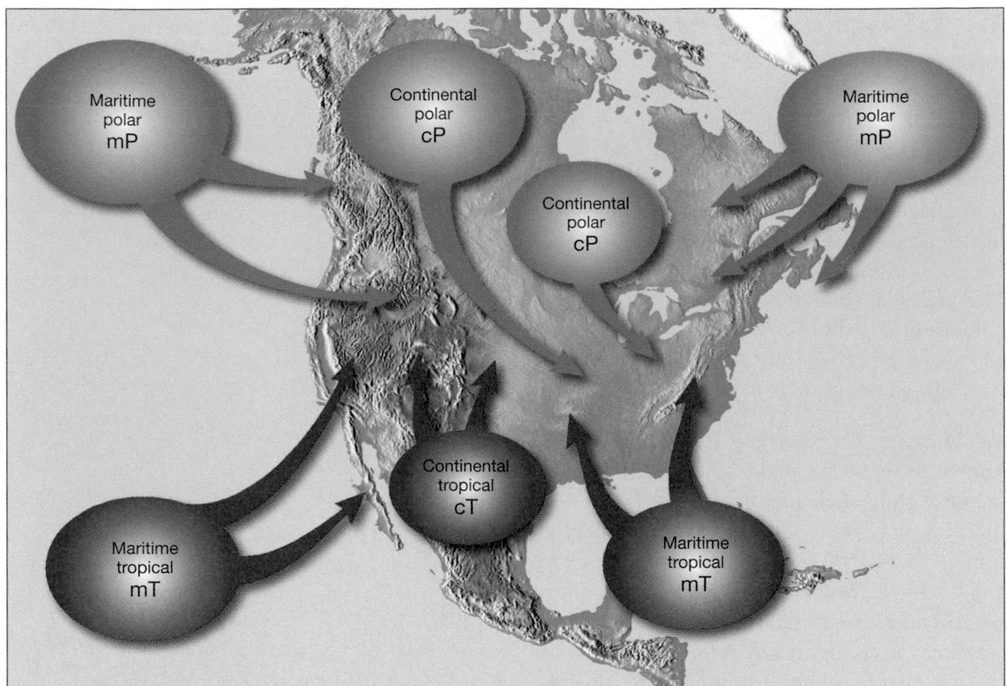

Figure 3 Air masses are classified by the region over which they form. **Interpreting Maps** ***What kinds of air masses influence the weather patterns along the west coast of the United States?***

Classifying Air Masses

The area over which an air mass gets its characteristic properties of temperature and moisture is called its source region. The source regions that produce air masses that influence the weather in North America are shown in Figure 3. Air masses are named according to their source region. Polar (P) air masses form at high latitudes toward Earth's poles. Air masses that form at low latitudes are tropical (T) air masses. The terms *polar* and *tropical* describe the temperature characteristics of an air mass. Polar air masses are cold, while tropical air masses are warm.

In addition to their overall temperature, air masses are classified according to the surface over which they form. Continental (c) air masses form over land. Maritime (m) air masses form over water. The terms *continental* and *maritime* describe the moisture characteristics of the air mass. Continental air masses are likely to be dry. Maritime air masses are humid.

Using this classification scheme, there are four basic types of air masses. A continental polar (cP) air mass is dry and cool. A continental tropical (cT) air mass is dry and warm or hot. Maritime polar (mP) and maritime tropical (mT) air masses both form over water. But a maritime polar air mass is much colder than a maritime tropical air mass.

For: Links on air masses
Visit: www.SciLinks.org
Web Code: cjn-6201

Facts and Figures

Maritime polar air originates over cold ocean currents or high-latitude ocean waters. This air does not have as much moisture content as mT air, yet it can produce widespread rain or snow. This air mass is notorious for producing fog, drizzle, cloudy weather, and long-lasting light-to-moderate rain. Maritime polar air changes as it moves over elevated terrain. On the windward side of mountain ranges, mP air can produce an abundance of rain and snow. Once on the lee side of mountains, the mP air mass modifies into a continental air mass. These air masses produce cold fronts, but the air is not as cold as polar or arctic fronts. They are often referred to as "Pacific fronts" or "back-door cold fronts." Maritime polar air occurs frequently in the Pacific Northwest and to a lesser degree in New England.

Download a worksheet on air masses for students to complete, and find additional teacher support from NSTA SciLinks.

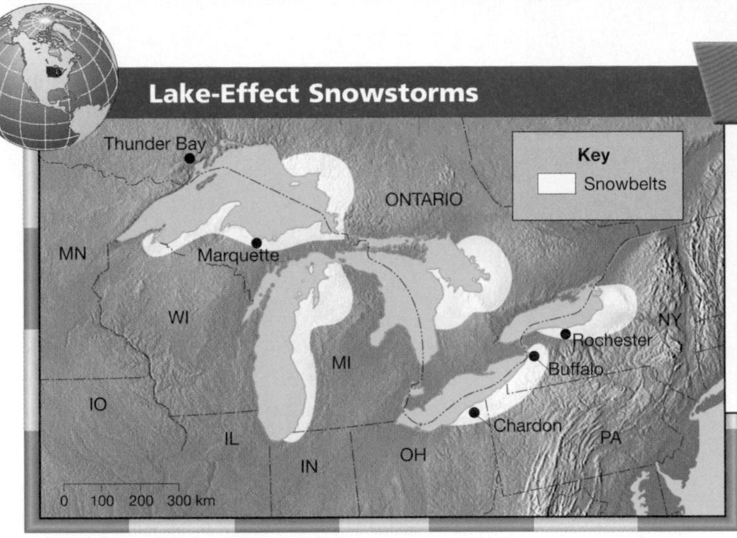

MAP MASTER™ Skills Activity

Figure 4

Location Marquette, Michigan, is southeast of Thunder Bay, Ontario. **Identify** What type of air mass influences the weather of these two cities? **Infer** Which of these cities receives more snow in an average winter? Why?

Weather in North America

Much of the weather in North America, especially weather east of the Rocky Mountains, is influenced by continental polar (cP) and maritime tropical (mT) air masses. The cP air masses begin in northern Canada, the interior of Alaska, and the Arctic areas. The mT air masses most often begin over the warm waters of the Gulf of Mexico, the Caribbean Sea, or the adjacent Atlantic Ocean.

Continental Polar Air Masses Continental polar air masses are uniformly cold and dry in winter and cool and dry in summer. In summer, cP air masses may bring a few days of relatively cooler weather. In winter, this continental polar air brings the clear skies and cold temperatures you associate with a cold wave.

Continental polar air masses are not, as a rule, associated with heavy precipitation. However, those that cross the Great Lakes during late autumn and winter sometimes bring snow to the leeward shores, as shown in Figure 4. These localized storms, which are known as lake-effect snows, make Buffalo and Rochester, New York, among the snowiest cities in the United States. What causes lake-effect snow? During late autumn and early winter, the difference in temperature between the lakes and adjacent land areas can be large. The temperature contrast can be especially great when a very cold cP air mass pushes southward across the lakes. When this occurs, the air gets large quantities of heat and moisture from the relatively warm lake surface. By the time it reaches the opposite shore, the air mass is humid and unstable. Heavy snow, like that shown in Figure 5, is possible.

What causes large amounts of snow to fall on the southern and eastern shores of the Great Lakes?

Figure 5 A six-day lake-effect snowstorm in November 1996 dropped a record 175 cm (69 in.) of snow on Chardon, Ohio.

Weather in North America

Build Reading Literacy L1

Refer to **p. 334D** in **Chapter 12,** which provides the guidelines for outlining.

Outline Have students read the section. Then, have students use the headings as major divisions in an outline. Allow students to refer to their outlines when answering the questions in Section 20.1 Assessment.
Visual

MAP MASTER™ Skills Activity

Answers
Identify Continental polar air masses influence the weather in this region.

Infer Because it is on the downwind side of Lake Superior, Marquette receives more snow than Thunder Bay does.

Facts and Figures

On November 20–23, 2000, Buffalo, NY, and the surrounding area were hit with a 60-hour lake-effect snowstorm. During the period, the storm dumped up to 79 cm of snow and was the most widespread and significant November lake-effect storm since 1996, when a longer lasting storm dropped about a meter of snow.

The November 2000 storm had frequent lightning as snow showers grew heavy. Snow fell at the rate of 5–10 cm per hour for several hours. The timing of the most intense snowfall could not have been worse. It hit just before the evening commute. Thousands were reported to have spent the night in their cars or to have taken shelter in stores and hotels. Many schoolchildren and school buses became trapped. It was the most disruptive storm in the Buffalo area since the blizzard of 1977.

Answer to . . .

Figure 3 *maritime polar (mP) and maritime tropical (mT) air masses*

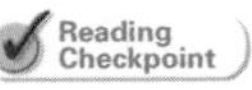

Continental polar air masses, crossing the Great Lakes, cause heavy lake-effect snows.

Build Science Skills L2

Using Tables and Graphs Have students create a table to compare and contrast the four basic types of air masses.
Intrapersonal, Verbal

Build Reading Literacy 

Refer to **p. 124D** in **Chapter 5,** which provides the guidelines for this strategy.

Summarize Have students summarize what they have learned in this section by listing the characteristics of each type of air mass. Ask them to create a two-column chart with the column headings "Air mass type" and "Characteristics." (You may alternatively create a chart on the board to make this an interactive class activity.) Make sure students describe four air masses: cP, cT, mP, and mT.
Portfolio, Group

Use Community Resources 

Invite students to find out what types of air masses commonly affect their region. Encourage them to consult periodicals at their local library. If their sources do not explicitly mention a specific type of air mass, have them record temperature and precipitation data. Then lead a discussion about what air masses are likely to cause such conditions.
Verbal, Group

Figure 6 Rain Storm over Florida Bay in the Florida Keys

Maritime Tropical Air Masses Maritime tropical air masses also play a dominant role in the weather of North America. These air masses are warm, loaded with moisture, and usually unstable. Maritime tropical air is the source of much, if not most, of the precipitation received in the eastern two thirds of the United States. The heavy precipitation shown in Figure 6 is the result of maritime tropical air masses moving through the area. In summer, when an mT air mass invades the central and eastern United States, it brings the high temperatures and oppressive humidity typically associated with its source region.

Maritime Polar Air Masses During the winter, maritime polar air masses that affect weather in North America come from the North Pacific. Such air masses often begin as cP air masses in Siberia. The cold, dry continental polar air changes into relatively mild, humid, unstable maritime polar air during its long journey across the North Pacific, as shown in Figure 7. As this maritime polar air arrives at the western shore of North America, it is often accompanied by low clouds and showers. When this maritime polar air advances inland against the western mountains, uplift of the air produces heavy rain or snow on the windward slopes of the mountains.

Maritime polar air masses also originate in the North Atlantic off the coast of eastern Canada. These air masses influence the weather of the northeastern United States. In winter, when New England is on the northern or northwestern side of a passing low-pressure center, the counterclockwise winds draw in maritime polar air. The result is a storm characterized by snow and cold temperatures, known locally as a nor'easter.

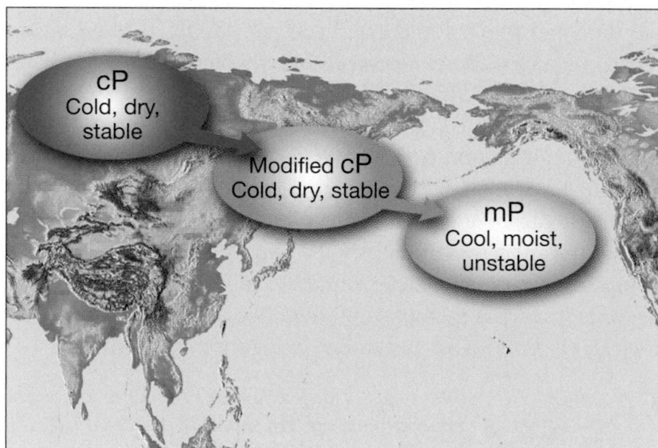

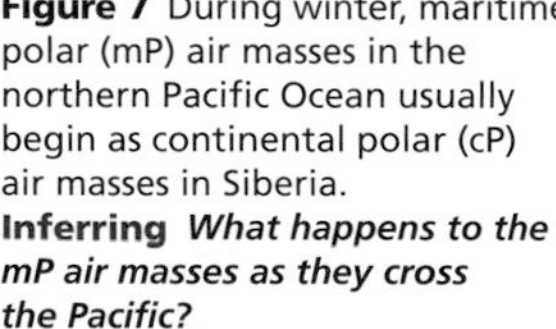

Figure 7 During winter, maritime polar (mP) air masses in the northern Pacific Ocean usually begin as continental polar (cP) air masses in Siberia.
Inferring ***What happens to the mP air masses as they cross the Pacific?***

Continental Tropical Air Masses Continental tropical air masses have the least influence on the weather of North America. These hot, dry air masses begin in the southwestern United States and Mexico during the summer. **Only occasionally do cT air masses affect the weather outside their source regions.** However, when a cT air mass does move from its source region, it can cause extremely hot, droughtlike conditions in the Great Plains in the summer. Movement of such air masses in the fall results in mild weather in the Great Lakes region, often called Indian summer. Conditions during Indian summer are unseasonably warm and mild, as shown in Figure 8.

Figure 8 A cT air mass produces a few days of warm weather amid the cool days of fall in the Great Lakes region.

Section 20.1 Assessment

Reviewing Concepts

1. What is an air mass?
2. What happens as an air mass moves over an area?
3. How are air masses classified?
4. Which types of air masses have the greatest effect on weather in North America?
5. Why do continental tropical air masses have little effect on weather in North America?

Critical Thinking

6. **Comparing and Contrasting** Compare and contrast the four types of air masses.
7. **Explaining** Explain which type of air mass could offer relief from a scorching summer to the Midwestern United States. Justify your choice.
8. **Applying Concepts** How can continental polar air be responsible for lake-effect snowstorms in the Great Lakes region?
9. **Identifying** Look again at Figure 3. What kinds of air masses influence the weather patterns over Florida?
10. **Synthesizing** What kind of weather could be expected in southern Canada if an mT air mass was to invade the region in mid-July?

Writing in Science

Explanatory Paragraph Pick one of the air masses shown in Figure 3 that affects the weather in your area. Write a paragraph that explains the weather typically associated with the air mass in both the summer and the winter.

3 ASSESS

Evaluate Understanding

L2

Have each student write a paragraph explaining the term *air-mass weather.* *(Answers should include the fact that weather is a result of moving air masses. Because air masses are so huge it usually takes several days for them to move over an area. This causes fairly constant weather, known as* air mass weather.*)*

Reteach

L1

Use Figure 3 to review the classification of air masses.

Writing in Science

Answers will depend on students' choices of air masses. Continental polar air masses bring clear skies and cold temperatures in winter and relatively cool, dry days in summer. Maritime tropical air masses bring high temperatures and much humidity in summer and much precipitation year round. Continental tropical air masses affect only the southwestern United States and result in dry, warm weather in their source region. Maritime polar masses often bring low clouds and showers in summer and snow and cold temperatures in winter.

Answer to . . .

Figure 7 *The cP air mass acquires moisture as it slowly moves over the ocean to become an mP air mass.*

Section 20.1 Assessment

1. An air mass is an immense body of air characterized by similar temperatures and amounts of moisture at any given altitude.
2. The air mass changes the weather in the area over which it moves.
3. Air masses are classified by temperature (polar or tropical) and the surface (continental or maritime) over which they form.
4. continental polar and maritime tropical air masses
5. Such air masses rarely move from their source regions.
6. They are similar in that each influences weather in North America. They differ in that continental air masses form over land and thus are dry. Maritime air masses form over water and thus are wet. Polar air masses are cold, while tropical air masses are warm.
7. A continental polar (cP) air mass is cool and dry and is usually associated with high pressure and clear skies. Such an air mass would offer relief from hot summer weather.
8. Although cP air masses are cold and dry, they acquire moisture as they cross the relatively warm lakes. The addition of moisture and the increase in temperature make the air masses unstable, causing snow to fall downwind of the lakes.
9. maritime tropical
10. Oppressively hot and humid weather typical of the source region of the air mass would occur in southern Canada.

Section 20.2

1 FOCUS

Section Objectives

20.5 **Describe** the formation of a front.

20.6 **Differentiate** among the formation of a warm front, cold front, stationary front, and occluded front.

20.7 **Describe** the weather patterns associated with each type of front.

Reading Focus

Build Vocabulary L2

Web Diagram Have students construct a web diagram of the vocabulary words in this section. The main concept (fronts) should be at the top of the diagram. Ask students to provide one descriptive statement for each of the other vocabulary words.

Reading Strategy L2

I. A. warm air moves into an area formerly covered by cooler air
   B. light-to-moderate precipitation over wide area for extended time

II. A. cold air moves into region occupied by warmer air
   B. heavy downpours and winds followed by drop in temperature

III. Stationary front
   A. flow of air parallel along front
   B. gentle-to-moderate precipitation

IV. Occluded front
   A. an active cold front overtakes an active warm front
   B. light precipitation

2 INSTRUCT

Formation of Fronts

Use Visuals L1

Figure 9 Direct students' attention to the photograph in the figure. Ask: **What type of precipitation is falling?** *(a light rain)* **What do you know about the general weather conditions in this area based on the photograph?** *(The temperature is above freezing.)* **Visual**

20.2 Fronts

Reading Focus

Key Concepts

- What happens when two air masses meet?
- How is a warm front produced?
- What is a cold front?
- What is a stationary front?
- What are the stages in the formation of an occluded front?
- What is a middle-latitude cyclone?
- What fuels a middle-latitude cyclone?

Vocabulary

- front
- warm front
- cold front
- stationary front
- occluded front

Reading Strategy

Outlining As you read, make an outline like the one below. Include information about how each of the weather fronts discussed in this section forms and the weather associated with each.

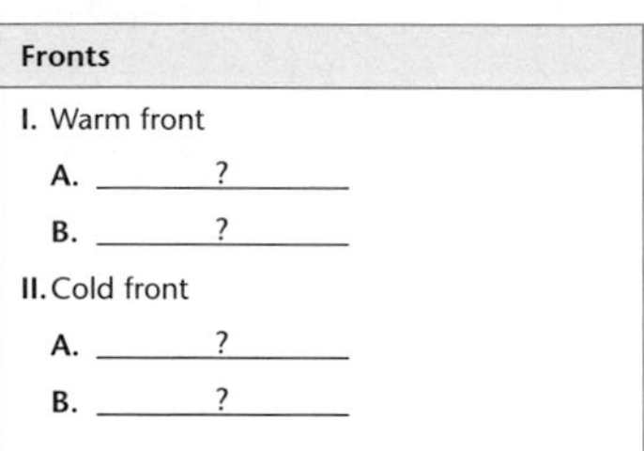
Fronts

I. Warm front
   A. ___?___
   B. ___?___

II. Cold front
   A. ___?___
   B. ___?___

Formation of Fronts

Recall that air masses have different temperatures and amounts of moisture, depending on their source regions. Recall also that these properties can change as an air mass moves over a region. What do you think happens when two air masses meet? **When two air masses meet, they form a front, which is a boundary that separates two air masses.** Fronts can form between any two contrasting air masses. Fronts are often associated with some form of precipitation, such as that shown in Figure 9.

Figure 9 Precipitation from a Storm in South Africa

In contrast to the vast sizes of air masses, fronts are narrow. Most weather fronts are between about 15 and 200 km wide. Above Earth's surface, the frontal surface slopes at a low angle so that warmer, less dense air overlies cooler, denser air. In the ideal case, the air masses on both sides of a front move in the same direction and at the same speed. When this happens, the front acts simply as a barrier that travels with the air masses. In most cases, however, the distribution of pressure across a front causes one air mass to move faster than the other. When this happens, one air mass advances into another, and some mixing of air occurs.

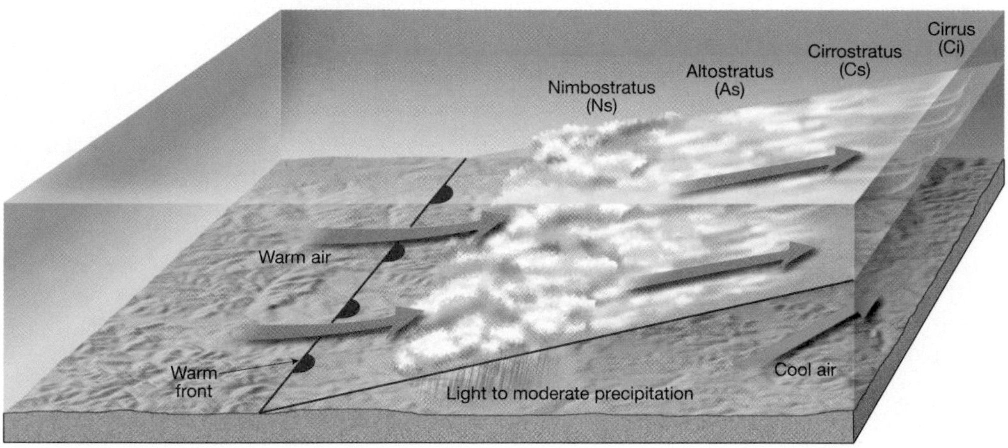

Types of Fronts

Fronts are often classified according to the temperature of the advancing front. There are four types of fronts: warm fronts, cold fronts, stationary fronts, and occluded fronts.

Warm Fronts **A warm front forms when warm air moves into an area formerly covered by cooler air.** On a weather map, the surface position of a warm front is shown by a red line with red semicircles that point toward the cooler air.

The slope of the warm front is very gradual, as shown in Figure 10. As warm air rises, it cools to produce clouds, and frequently precipitation. The sequence of clouds shown in Figure 10 typically comes before a warm front. The first sign of the approaching warm front is the appearance of cirrus clouds. As the front nears, cirrus clouds change into cirrostratus clouds, which blend into denser sheets of altostratus clouds. About 300 kilometers ahead of the front, thicker stratus and nimbostratus clouds appear, and rain or snow begins.

Because of their slow rate of movement and very low slope, warm fronts usually produce light-to-moderate precipitation over a large area for an extended period. A gradual increase in temperature occurs with the passage of a warm front. The increase is most apparent when a large temperature difference exists between adjacent air masses. Also, a wind shift from the east to the southwest is associated with a warm front.

What causes a warm front to form?

Figure 10 Formation of a Warm Front A warm front forms when warm air glides up over a cold, dense air mass. The affected area has warmer temperatures, and light to moderate precipitation.

Types of Fronts

Use Visuals

Figure 10 Have students examine the diagram of a warm front in the figure. Ask: **As a warm front approaches, what type of weather can you expect?** *(rainy weather)* **Describe how the sky conditions change as a warm front approaches.** *(It becomes increasingly cloudy.)*
Visual

Build Science Skills

L2

Applying Concepts Students will process and remember information about fronts if they can connect this information to their daily experiences. First, gather and display current weather maps. (Many national newspapers have maps that show notable air masses and fronts. Online resources, such as accuweather.com, also have current national and regional weather maps.) Next, ask students to describe local weather conditions. Then discuss how their observations relate to the data presented in the maps.
Verbal, Visual

Customize for English Language Learners

Students who are learning English can benefit from real-life examples that relate to science content. Encourage students to think of observations they have made about the weather. For example, ask students if they notice that after a severe, rather fast-moving thunderstorm, things become cooler the next few days. Explain that this is because a cold front moved into the area, bringing thunderstorms and cooler weather.

Answer to . . .

When warm air moves into an area formerly covered by cooler air, a warm front forms.

Build Science Skills

Using Models Provide students with red and blue clay. The red clay will represent a warm air mass, and the blue clay will represent a colder air mass. Ask students to use the clay to model one of the four air masses discussed in the text. They should then present their model to the class, explaining the motion of each air mass.
Kinesthetic, Interpersonal

Students may think that the terms *warm front* and *cold front* are actually referring to masses of warm air and cold air. It is important that they realize that warm and cold are comparative terms. For example, a warm front may pass though Iowa in the middle of February. This warm air mass may have a temperature of −26°C when the air mass already in place has a temperature of −32°C. Death Valley in the middle of July may have a cold front move through that brings temperatures of 46°C, while the air in place may have a temperature of 49°C. Emphasize to students that a warm front brings warmer air to an area and a cold front brings cooler air.
Verbal

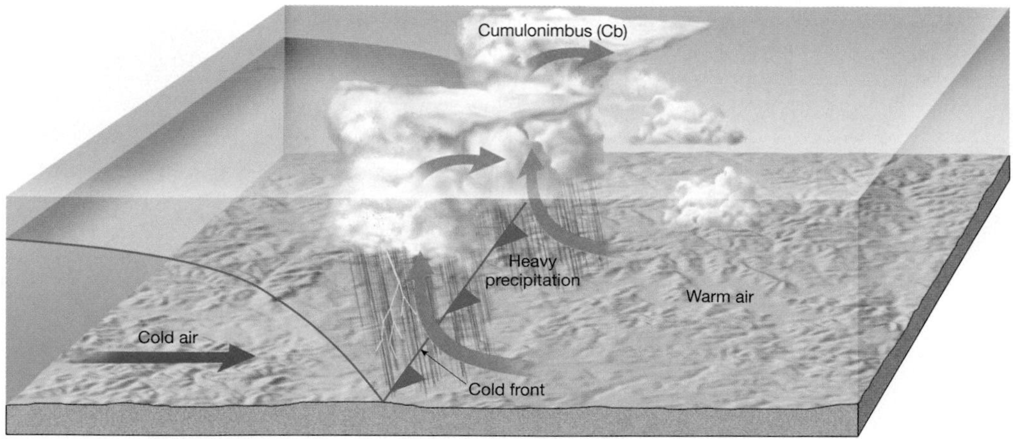

Figure 11 Formation of a Cold Front A cold front forms when cold air moves into an area occupied by warmer air. The affected area experiences thunderstorms if the warm air is unstable.

Cold Fronts

A cold front forms when cold, dense air moves into a region occupied by warmer air. On a weather map, the surface position of a cold front is shown by a blue line edged with blue triangles that point toward the warmer air mass.

Figure 11 shows how a cold front develops. As this cold front moves, it becomes steeper. On average, cold fronts are about twice as steep as warm fronts and advance more rapidly than warm fronts do. These two differences—rate of movement and steepness of slope—account for the more violent weather associated with a cold front.

The forceful lifting of air along a cold front can lead to heavy downpours and gusty winds. As a cold front approaches, towering clouds often can be seen in the distance. Once the cold front has passed, temperatures drop and wind shifts. The weather behind a cold front is dominated by a cold air mass. So, weather clears soon after a cold front passes. When a cold front moves over a warm area, low cumulus or stratocumulus clouds may form behind the front.

Stationary Fronts

Occasionally, the flow of air on either side of a front is neither toward the cold air mass nor toward the warm air mass, but almost parallel to the line of the front. **In such cases, the surface position of the front does not move, and a stationary front forms.** On a weather map, stationary fronts are shown by blue triangles on one side of the front and red semicircles on the other. Sometimes, gentle to moderate precipitation occurs along a stationary front.

How are cold fronts different from warm fronts?

Occluded Fronts When an active cold front overtakes a warm front, an occluded front forms. As you can see in Figure 12, an occluded front develops as the advancing cold air wedges the warm front upward. The weather associated with an occluded front is generally complex. Most precipitation is associated with the warm air's being forced upward. When conditions are suitable, however, the newly formed front is capable of making light precipitation of its own.

It is important to note that the descriptions of weather associated with fronts are general descriptions. The weather along any individual front may or may not conform to the idealized descriptions you've read about. Fronts, like all aspects of nature, do not always behave as we would expect.

Middle-Latitude Cyclones

Now that you know about air masses and what happens when they meet, you're ready to apply this information to understanding weather patterns in the United States. The main weather producers in the country are middle-latitude cyclones. On weather maps, these low-pressure areas are shown by the letter L.

Middle-latitude cyclones are large centers of low pressure that generally travel from west to east and cause stormy weather. The air in these weather systems moves in a counterclockwise direction and in toward the center of the low. Most middle-latitude cyclones have a cold front, and frequently a warm front, extending from the central area. Forceful lifting causes the formation of clouds that drop abundant precipitation.

How do cyclones develop and form? The first stage is the development of a front, which is shown in Figure 14A on page 569. The front forms as two air masses with different temperatures move in opposite directions. Over time, the front takes on a wave shape, as shown in Figure 14B. The wave is usually hundreds of kilometers long.

Formation of an Occluded Front

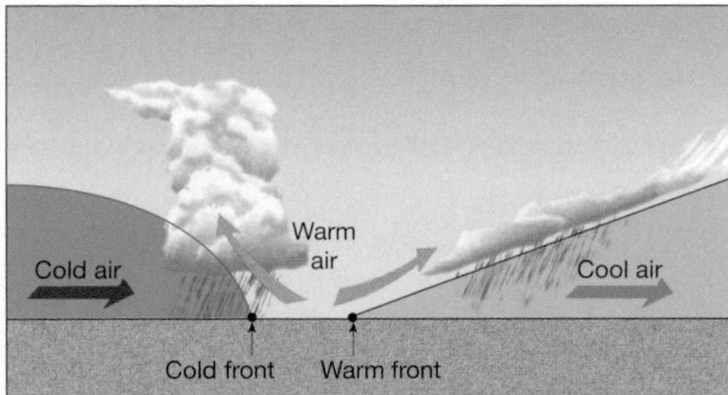

A A cold front moves toward a warm front, forcing warm air aloft.

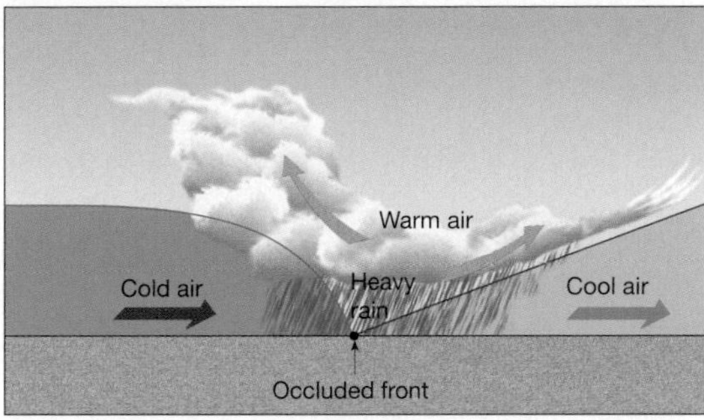

B A cold front merges with the warm front to form an occluded front that drops heavy rains.

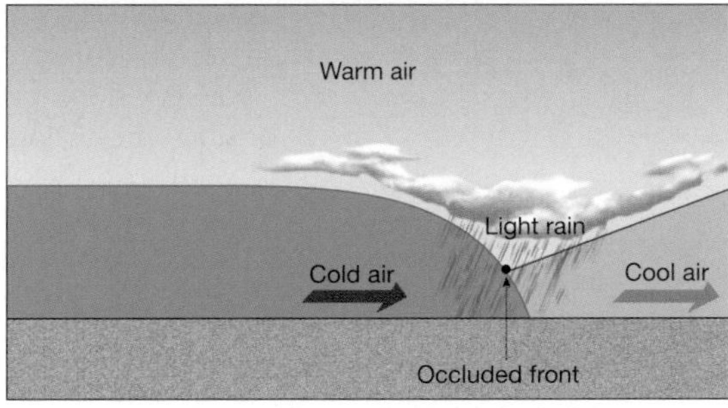

C Because occluded fronts often move slowly, light precipitation can fall for several days.

Figure 12 An occluded front forms when a cold front overtakes a warm front, producing a complex weather pattern.

Middle-Latitude Cyclones

Build Reading Literacy L1

Refer to **p. 556D,** which provides the guidelines for active comprehension.

Active Comprehension Instruct students to read the first two paragraphs of Middle-Latitude Cyclones on p. 567. Ask: **What more would you like to know about middle-latitude cyclones** or **Where does the weather in your area come from?** You will need to make connections for students between the weather and their lives. For example, students may notice from weather reports on television or on the Internet that stormy weather seems to move from the west to the east. Write down several students' responses on the board. Have students continue reading the section and examine Figure 14 on p. 569. While reading, have students consider the questions they had about the material. Have students discuss the section content, making sure that each question raised at the beginning is answered or that students know where to look for the answer.
Verbal

Facts and Figures

One-Eyed Storms Have students consider the word *Cyclops*. These giants of Greek mythology had a single eye in the middle of their foreheads. This word comes from the Greek word *Kyklōps*, which means "round-eyed." The word *cyclone* has a similar meaning. It comes from the Greek word *kykloein*, which means "to circle around." Students can think of cyclones as one-eyed monsters.

Answer to . . .

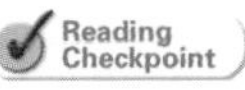

Cold fronts are much steeper than warm fronts and advance more rapidly than warm fronts do, causing more violent weather to form.

Getting to the Point of Fronts

L2

Purpose Students will observe the motion of mid-latitude cyclones.

Materials pencil

Procedure This activity may be performed as a demonstration or each student can participate individually. Place a pencil between your hands. Explain that your hands represent two different air masses and the gap between them is the front. Slowly move your right hand forward and your left hand backward. This models the movement of the wind in a stationary front. Direct students' attention to the movement of the pencil.

Expected Outcome The pencil should move in a counterclockwise direction. This models the movement of a mid-latitude cyclone.
Kinesthetic, Visual

Build Reading Literacy

Refer to **p. 186D** in **Chapter 7,** which provides the guidelines for this strategy.

Relate Text and Visuals The text describes Figure 13 as a "mature cyclone." Ask students to describe what has happened to form this mature cyclone. *(A cold front has overtaken and lifted up a warm front to form an occluded front.)* Now ask students to compare Figures 13 and 14. Ask: **Which phase of Figure 14 is most representative of Figure 13?** *(Both D and E are acceptable answers, although the occluded front in Figure 13 seems to be well-developed, making E the better answer.)* Ask: **What weather conditions would this phase of a cyclone produce?** *(high wind speeds and heavy precipitation)*
Verbal, Visual

As the wave develops, warm air moves towards Earth's poles. There it invades the area formerly occupied by colder air. Meanwhile, cold air moves toward the equator. This change in airflow near the surface is accompanied by a change in pressure. The result is airflow in a counterclockwise direction, as Figure 14C shows.

Figure 13 This is a satellite view of a mature cyclone over the eastern United States.

Recall that a cold front advances faster than a warm front. When this occurs in the development of a middle-latitude cyclone, the cold front closes in and eventually lifts the warm front, as Figure 14D shows. This process, which is known as occlusion, forms the occluded front shown in Figure 14E. As occlusion begins, the storm often gets stronger. Pressure at the storm's center falls, and wind speeds increase. In the winter, heavy snowfalls and blizzard-like conditions are possible during this phase of the storm's evolution. A satellite view of this phase of a mature cyclone is shown in Figure 13.

As more of the warm air is forced to rise, the amount of pressure change weakens. In a day or two, the entire warm area is displaced. Only cold air surrounds the cyclone at low levels. The horizontal temperature difference that existed between the two air masses is gone. At this point, the cyclone has exhausted its source of energy. Friction slows the airflow near the surface, and the once highly organized counterclockwise flow ceases to exist (Figure 14F).

The Role of Airflow Aloft

Airflow aloft plays an important role in maintaining cyclonic and anticyclonic circulation. In fact, these rotating surface wind systems are actually generated by upper-level flow.

Cyclones often exist for a week or longer. For this to happen, surface convergence must be offset by outflow somewhere higher in the atmosphere. As long as the spreading out of air high up is equal to or greater than the surface inflow, the low-pressure system can be sustained. **More often than not, air high up in the atmosphere fuels a middle-latitude cyclone.**

How do middle-latitude cyclones form and develop?

Middle-Latitude Cyclone Model

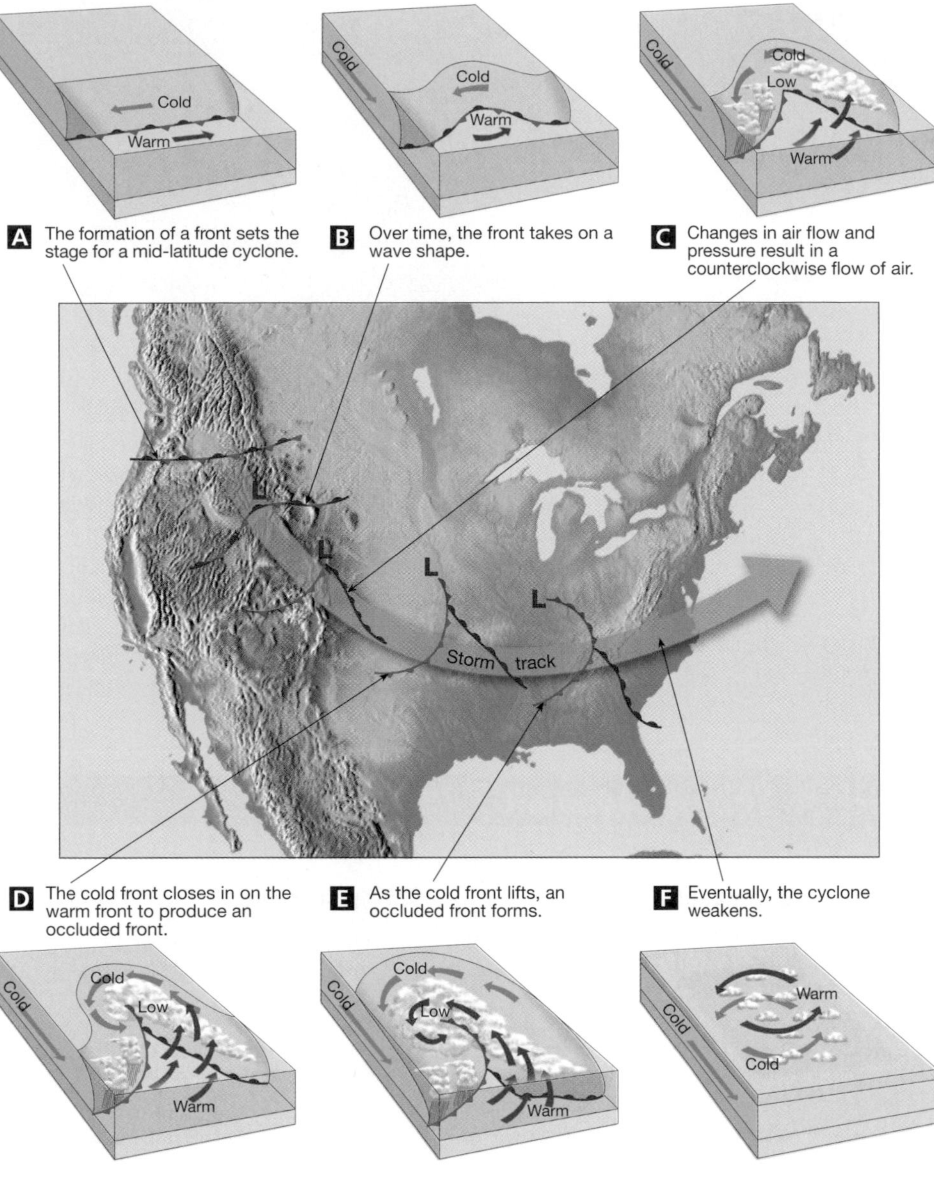

Cold
Warm
A The formation of a front sets the stage for a mid-latitude cyclone.
Cold
Cold
Warm
B Over time, the front takes on a wave shape.
Cold
Cold
Low
Warm
C Changes in air flow and pressure result in a counterclockwise flow of air.
L
L
L
L
Storm track
D The cold front closes in on the warm front to produce an occluded front.
E As the cold front lifts, an occluded front forms.
F Eventually, the cyclone weakens.
Cold
Cold
Low
Warm
Cold
Cold
Low
Warm
Cold
Warm
Cold

Figure 14 Cyclones have a fairly predictable life cycle.

The Role of Airflow Aloft

Use Visuals L1

Figure 14 Instruct students to study the details of the cyclone in the figure. Ask: **In what direction is the air moving in this cyclone?** *(counterclockwise)*
Visual

Integrate Language Arts L2

Cyclones Ask students to study Figure 14. The development of a middle-latitude cyclone is complex. Engage students in a discussion about the complexity of this diagram. So much information is conveyed here that often students may feel that they have not gathered all the information they need from it. Challenge them to write a descriptive narrative, explaining the formation of a middle-latitude cyclone in their own words. Students should share their narratives with small groups to make sure that all the steps have been covered.
Verbal, Interpersonal

Answer to . . .

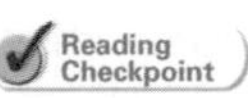

Reading Checkpoint

The first stage is the development of a front. Over time, the front takes on a wave shape. Changes in air flow and pressure result in a counterclockwise flow of air. The cold front eventually closes in on the warm front to produce an occluded front. As the cold front lifts, an occluded front forms. Eventually, the cyclone weakens.

Section 20.2 (continued)

3 ASSESS

Evaluate Understanding L2

Have each student write a paragraph explaining the relationship between fronts and precipitation. *(Answers will vary, but students should mention that precipitation is often associated with fronts.)*

Reteach L1

Review the fact that the main weather producers in the United States are middle-latitude cyclones. Use Figure 14 as a visual aid to discuss how middle-latitude cyclones work.

An occluded front forms in the late stage of development of a middle-latitude cyclone as fast-moving cold air catches up to a warm front. The warmer air then is forced aloft and eventually dissipates. When this warmer air is gone, there is little condensation and therefore little precipitation.

Answer to . . .

Figure 15 *Both result from changes in surface pressure. Both systems depend on the flow of air high in the atmosphere to maintain their circulation. Cyclones are fueled by upward air movement and reduced surface pressure. Anticyclones form as the result of the downward movement of air and increased surface pressure.*

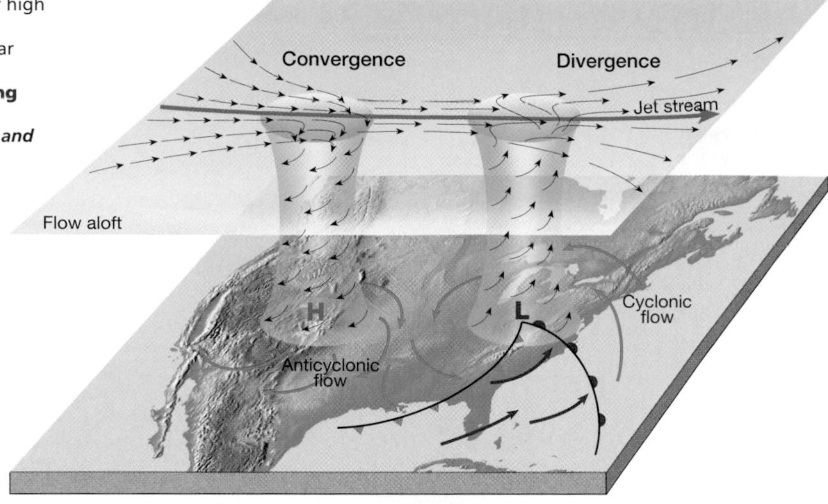

Figure 15 Movements of air high in the atmosphere fuel the cyclones and anticyclones near Earth's surface.
***Comparing and Contrasting** Compare and contrast the movement of air in cyclones and anticyclones.*

Because cyclones bring stormy weather, they have received far more attention than anticyclones. However, a close relationship exists between these two pressure systems. As shown in Figure 15, the surface air that feeds a cyclone generally originates as air flowing out of an anticyclone. As a result, cyclones and anticyclones typically are found next to each other. Like a cyclone, an anticyclone depends on the flow of air high in the atmosphere to maintain its circulation. In an anticyclone, air spreading out at the surface is balanced by air coming together from high up.

Section 20.2 Assessment

Reviewing Concepts

1. What happens when two air masses meet?
2. How does a warm front form?
3. What is a cold front?
4. What is a stationary front?
5. What are the stages in the formation of an occluded front?
6. What is a middle-latitude cyclone?
7. What causes a middle-latitude cyclone to sustain itself?

Critical Thinking

8. **Comparing and Contrasting** Compare and contrast warm fronts and cold fronts.
9. **Synthesizing** Use Figure 15 and what you know about Earth's atmosphere to describe the air movement and pressure conditions associated with both cyclones and anticyclones.

Writing in Science

Explanatory Paragraph Write a paragraph to explain this statement: The formation of an occluded front marks the beginning of the end of a middle-latitude cyclone.

Section 20.2 Assessment

1. When two air masses meet, they form a front, which is a boundary that separates two air masses.
2. A warm front forms when warmer air moves into an area formerly covered by cooler air.
3. A cold front forms when colder, denser air moves into a region occupied by warmer air.
4. Occasionally, the flow of air on either side of a front is neither toward the cold air mass nor toward the warm air mass, but almost parallel to the line of the front. The surface position of the front does not move, and a stationary front forms.
5. A cold front moves toward a warm front, forcing warmer air aloft. The cold front merges with the warm front to form an occluded front that drops heavy rains. The heavy rains are followed by periods of light precipitation.
6. A middle-latitude cyclone is a large center of low pressure that generally travels from west to east in the United States and causes stormy weather.
7. Airflow aloft plays an important role in sustaining a middle-latitude cyclone.
8. Both fronts form when two air masses meet. Warm fronts form when warmer air moves into a region formerly occupied by cold air. Cold fronts form when colder air actively moves into a region occupied by warmer air. Warm fronts move more slowly than cold fronts and have more gradual slopes than cold fronts have.
9. Cyclones are fueled by upward air movement and reduced surface pressure. Anticyclones form as the result of the downward movement of air and increased surface pressure.

20.3 Severe Storms

Reading Focus

Key Concepts
- What is a thunderstorm?
- What causes a thunderstorm to form?
- What is a tornado?
- How does a tornado form?
- What is a hurricane?
- How does a hurricane form?

Vocabulary
- thunderstorm
- tornado
- hurricane
- eye wall
- eye
- storm surge

Reading Strategy
Identifying Cause and Effect Copy the table and complete it as you read this section.

Severe Storms		
	Causes	Effects
Thunderstorms	a. ?	b. ?
Tornadoes	c. ?	d. ?
Hurricanes	e. ?	f. ?

Severe weather has a fascination that everyday weather does not provide. For example, a thunderstorm with its jagged lightning and booming thunder can be an awesome sight. The damage and destruction caused by these storms, as well as other severe weather, can also be frightening. A single severe storm can cause billions of dollars in property damage as well as many deaths. This section discusses three types of severe storms and their causes.

Thunderstorms

Have you ever seen a small whirlwind carry dust or leaves upward on a hot day? Have you observed a bird glide effortlessly skyward on an invisible updraft of hot air? If so, you have observed the effects of the vertical movements of relatively warm, unstable air. These examples are caused by a similar thermal instability that occurs during the development of a thunderstorm. **A thunderstorm is a storm that generates lightning and thunder. Thunderstorms frequently produce gusty winds, heavy rain, and hail.** A thunderstorm may be produced by a single cumulonimbus cloud and influence only a small area. Or it may be associated with clusters of cumulonimbus clouds that stretch for kilometers along a cold front.

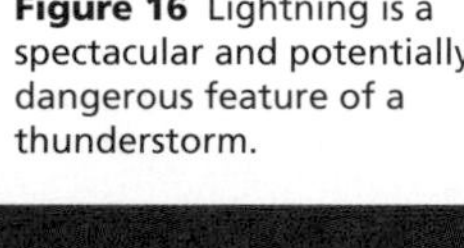

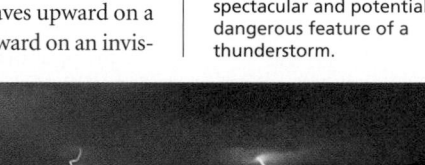

Figure 16 Lightning is a spectacular and potentially dangerous feature of a thunderstorm.

Section 20.3

1 FOCUS

Section Objectives

20.8 **Explain** the formation of a thunderstorm.

20.9 **Describe** the conditions needed for a tornado to form.

20.10 **Identify** the conditions that must exist for a hurricane to form.

Reading Focus

Build Vocabulary L2

Venn Diagram Have students create a Venn diagram of hurricanes and tornadoes.

Reading Strategy L2

a. warm, humid air rising in an unstable environment
b. gusty winds, heavy rain, hail
c. associated with thunderstorms and the development of a mesocyclone
d. violent windstorm, isolated path
e. water temperatures warm enough to provide heat and moisture to air
f. widespread damage as winds can reach 300 km/h

2 INSTRUCT

Thunderstorms

Use Visuals L1

Figure 16 Ask students to look at the photograph in Figure 16. Ask: **What type of clouds is probably in the area in this photograph?** *(cumulonimbus clouds)*
Visual

Address Misconceptions

L2

Students may have heard or noticed in media photographs that many tornadoes seem to hit trailer parks. It may even seem that trailers attract tornadoes. In reality, there are possibly hundreds of very small tornadoes that touch down in the United States every year, but are not recorded because they do no damage. However, since a trailer flips over so easily in even the weakest tornado, trailers probably act as "mini tornado detectors." This makes it seem like tornadoes are attracted to trailers, but that is because trailers are some of the only things that reveal the presence of what would otherwise be an unrecorded event.
Logical

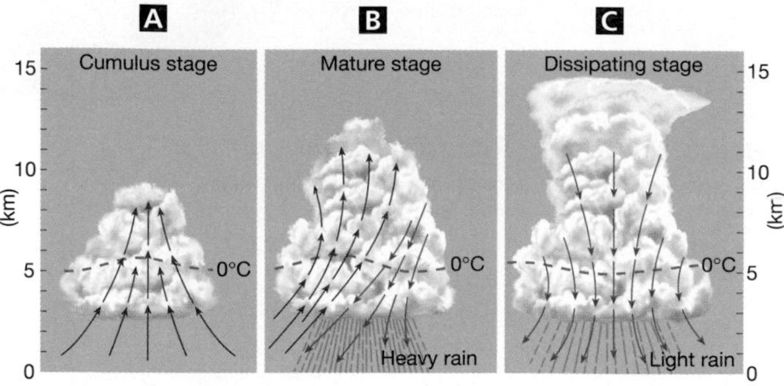

Figure 17 A During the cumulus stage, warm, moist air is supplied to the cloud. **B** Heavy precipitation falls during the mature stage. **C** The cloud begins to evaporate during the dissipating stage. **Observing** ***How do the clouds involved in the development of a thunderstorm vary?***

Occurrence of Thunderstorms How common are thunderstorms? Consider these numbers. At any given time, there are an estimated 2000 thunderstorms in progress on Earth. As you might expect, the greatest number occurs in the tropics where warmth, plentiful moisture, and instability are common atmospheric conditions. About 45,000 thunderstorms take place each day. More than 16 million occur annually around the world. The United States experiences about 100,000 thunderstorms each year, most frequently in Florida and the eastern Gulf Coast region. Most parts of the country have from 30 to 100 storms each year. The western margin of the United States has little thunderstorm activity because warm, moist, unstable maritime tropical air seldom penetrates this region.

Development of Thunderstorms

Thunderstorms form when warm, humid air rises in an unstable environment. The development of a thunderstorm generally involves three stages. During the cumulus stage, shown in Figure 17A, strong updrafts, or upward movements of air, supply moist air. Each new surge of warm air rises higher than the last and causes the cloud to grow vertically.

Usually within an hour of the initial updraft, the mature stage begins, as shown in Figure 17B. At this point in the development of the thunderstorm, the amount and size of the precipitation is too great for the updrafts to support. So, heavy precipitation is released from the cloud. The mature stage is the most active stage of a thunderstorm. Gusty winds, lightning, heavy precipitation, and sometimes hail are produced during this stage.

Eventually, downdrafts, or downward movements of air, dominate throughout the cloud, as shown in Figure 17C. This final stage is called the dissipating stage. During this stage, the cooling effect of the falling precipitation and the flowing in of colder air from high above cause the storm to die down.

The life span of a single cumulonimbus cell within a thunderstorm is only about an hour or two. As the storm moves, however, fresh supplies of warm, humid air generate new cells to replace those that are scattering.

Describe the stages in the development of a thunderstorm.

Customize for Inclusion Students

Behaviorally Disordered Have students work in pairs and use index cards to create a set of flashcards. Students can use the cards to support each other in small study groups. Each card should contain information about a characteristic of one of the three types of storms in this section. One side of the card should contain the term *thunderstorm, tornado,* or *hurricane*. The other side should have some fact about the formation of each storm, some factors contributing to each storm, or damage done by each storm.

Tornadoes

Tornadoes are violent windstorms that take the form of a rotating column of air called a vortex. The vortex extends downward from a cumulonimbus cloud. Some tornadoes consist of a single vortex. But within many stronger tornadoes, smaller vortexes rotate within the main funnel. These smaller vortexes have diameters of only about 10 meters and rotate very rapidly. Smaller vortexes explain occasional observations of tornado damage in which one building is totally destroyed, while another one, just 10 or 20 meters away, suffers little damage.

Occurrence and Development of Tornadoes In the United States, about 770 tornadoes are reported each year. These severe storms can occur at any time during the year. However, the frequency of tornadoes is greatest from April through June. In December and January, tornadoes are far less frequent.

Most tornadoes form in association with severe thunderstorms. An important process in the formation of many tornadoes is the development of a mesocyclone. A mesocyclone is a vertical cylinder of rotating air that develops in the updraft of a thunderstorm. The formation of this large vortex begins as strong winds high up in the atmosphere cause winds lower in the atmosphere to roll, as shown in Figure 18A. In Figure 18B, you can see that strong thunderstorm updrafts cause this rolling air to tilt. Once the air is completely vertical (Figure 18C), the mesocyclone is well established. The formation of a mesocyclone does not necessarily mean that a tornado will follow. Few mesocyclones produce tornadoes like the one shown in Figure 19 on page 574.

For: Links on fronts and severe weather
Visit: www.SciLinks.org
Web Code: cjn-6203

Q *What is the most destructive tornado on record?*

A The Tri-State Tornado, which occurred on March 18, 1925, started in southeastern Missouri and remained on the ground over a distance of 352 kilometers, until it reached Indiana. Casualties included 695 people dead and 2027 injured. Property losses were also great, with several small towns almost totally destroyed.

Formation of a Mesocyclone

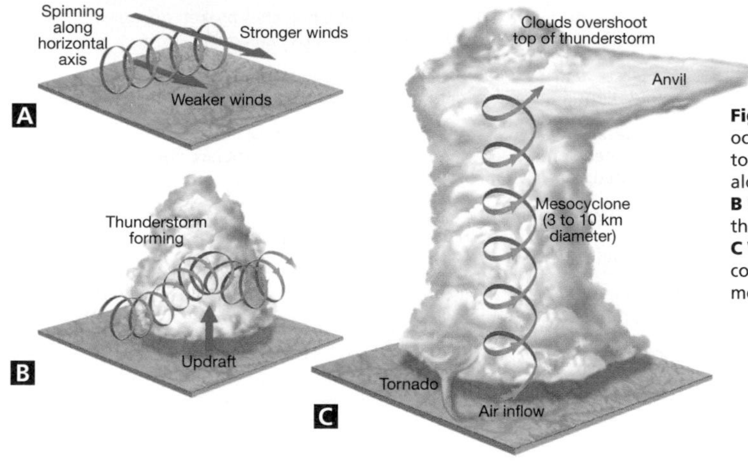

Figure 18 A mesocyclone can occur before the formation of a tornado. **A** First, stronger winds aloft cause lower winds to roll. **B** Updrafts tilt the rolling air so that it becomes nearly vertical. **C** When the rotating air is completely vertical, the mesocyclone is established.

Tornadoes

Homemade Tornado **L2**

Purpose Students will observe a visual model of a tornado.

Materials piece of sturdy cardboard; glue; 2 transparency sheets; small hand-held, battery-operated fan; small plastic bowl; clear plastic plant dish, approximately 7" in diameter with a hole cut in the middle; water; dry ice

Procedure Glue the plastic bowl to the center of the cardboard. Glue half of one of the transparency sheets to one side of the bowl. Glue the rest of the sheet in a half circle around the bowl without touching the bowl. Glue the second sheet to the opposite side of the cup in the same manner. The two sheets must overlap but not touch. Pour about half a cup of water in the cup. Using gloves, add a few small pieces of dry ice to the water. Place the plant dish upside down on top of the transparencies. Turn on the fan and place it in the hole, facing up to draw air up.

Expected Outcome Students should see the "smoke" from the dry ice form in a tornado pattern as it flows past the transparency sheets with the air being drawn up.
Kinesthetic, Visual

Download a worksheet on fronts and severe weather for students to complete, and find additional teacher support from NSTA SciLinks.

Answer to . . .

Figure 17 *The clouds vary in height, the smallest being the cloud that initiates the storm.*

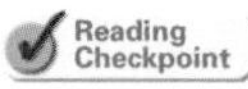

During the cumulus stage, strong updrafts supply moist air that causes the cloud to grow vertically. Usually within about an hour of the initial updraft, heavy precipitation is released from the cloud. Gusty winds, lightning, and sometimes hail also are experienced during this stage. Eventually, downdrafts dominate throughout the cloud and the storm dies down.

Facts and Figures

The largest recorded tornado was in the high plains of the Texas panhandle near the town of Gruver on June 9, 1971. At times, the tornado was nearly 4 km wide, with an average width of about 2 km. This is probably close to the maximum size for tornadoes, but it is possible that larger, unrecorded tornadoes have occurred.

Integrate Social Studies L2

Storm Warnings Accurate storm predictions and warnings can help to minimize the loss of property and of life. The National Weather Service has created a system to inform the public of the likelihood of a storm event in their area. They use the terms *watch* and *warning* to relay the imminent danger. A hurricane watch means that hurricanes are possible in the area within 36 hours. A hurricane warning means that hurricanes are expected in the area within 24 hours. Also a tornado watch means that conditions are favorable for a tornado in the area. A tornado warning means that a tornado has been sighted or has been seen on radar. Challenge students to devise a plan of action that should be taken during a hurricane watch and warning or a tornado watch and warning. Ask them to present their findings to the class in the form of a poster or an emergency bulletin.
Interpersonal

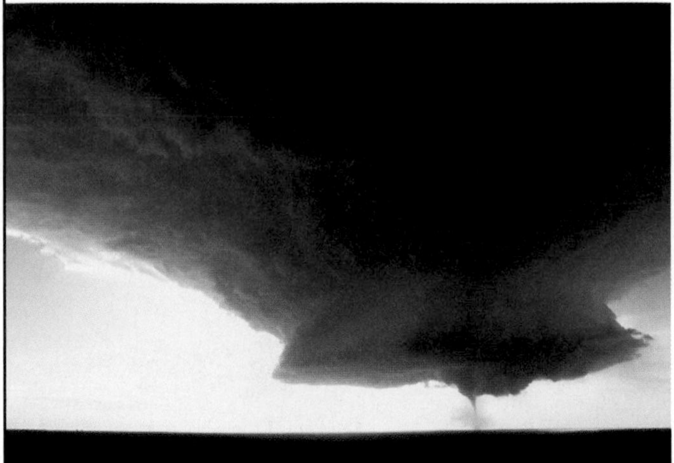

Figure 19 The tornado shown here descended from the lower portion of a mesocyclone in the Texas Panhandle in May, 1996.

Tornado Intensity Pressures within some tornadoes have been estimated to be as much as 10 percent lower than pressures immediately outside the storm. The low pressure within a tornado causes air near the ground to rush into a tornado from all directions. As the air streams inward, it spirals upward around the core. Eventually, the air merges with the airflow of the cumulonimbus cloud that formed the storm. Because of the tremendous amount of pressure change associated with a strong tornado, maximum winds can sometimes approach 480 kilometers per hour. One scale used to estimate tornado intensity is the Fujita tornado intensity scale, shown in Table 1. Because tornado winds cannot be measured directly, a rating on this scale is determined by assessing the worst damage produced by a storm.

Tornado Safety The Storm Prediction Center (SPC) located in Norman, Oklahoma, monitors different kinds of severe weather. The SPC's mission is to provide timely and accurate forecasts and watches for severe thunderstorms and tornadoes. Tornado watches alert people to the possibility of tornadoes in a specified area for a particular time period. A tornado warning is issued when a tornado has actually been sighted in an area or is indicated by weather radar.

Table 1 Fujita Tornado Intensity Scale

Intensity	Wind Speed Estimates (kph)	Typical Damage
F0	< 116	Light damage. Some damage to chimneys; branches broken off trees; shallow-rooted trees pushed over; sign boards damaged.
F1	116–180	Moderate damage. Peels surface off roofs; mobile homes pushed off foundations or overturned; moving cars blown off roads.
F2	181–253	Considerable damage. Roofs torn off frame houses; mobile homes demolished; large trees snapped or uprooted; light-object missiles generated; cars lifted off ground.
F3	254–332	Severe damage. Roofs and some walls torn off well-constructed houses; trains overturned; most trees in forest uprooted; heavy cars lifted off the ground and thrown.
F4	333–419	Devastating damage. Well-constructed houses leveled; structures with weak foundations blown some distance; cars thrown; large missiles generated.
F5	> 419	Incredible damage. Strong frame houses lifted off foundations and carried away; automobile-sized missiles fly through the air in excess of 100 m; bark torn off trees.

Facts and Figures

The deadliest tornado in the United States occurred on March 18, 1925. The so-called Tri-State Tornado killed 695 people as it raced along at 96–117 km/h in a 352 km-long track across parts of Missouri, Illinois, and Indiana, producing F5 damage. This event also holds the known record for most tornado fatalities in a single city or town: at least 234 at Murphysboro, IL.

Hurricanes

If you've ever been to the tropics or seen photographs of these regions, you know that warm breezes, steady temperatures, and heavy but brief tropical showers are the norm. It is ironic that these tranquil regions sometimes produce the most violent storms on Earth. **Whirling tropical cyclones that produce winds of at least 119 kilometers per hour are known in the United States as hurricanes.** In other parts of the world, these severe tropical storms are called typhoons, cyclones, and tropical cyclones.

Regardless of the name used to describe them, hurricanes are the most powerful storms on Earth. At sea, they can generate 15-meter waves capable of destruction hundreds of kilometers away. Should a hurricane hit land, strong winds and extensive flooding can cause billions of dollars in damage and great loss of life. Hurricane Floyd, which is shown in a satellite image in Figure 20, was one such storm. In September 1999, Floyd brought flooding rains, high winds, and rough seas to a large portion of the Atlantic coast. More than 2.5 million people evacuated their homes. Torrential rains caused devastating inland flooding. Floyd was the deadliest hurricane to strike the U.S. mainland since Hurricane Agnes in 1972. Most of the deaths caused by Hurricane Floyd were the result of drowning from floods.

Hurricanes are becoming a growing threat because more and more people are living and working near coasts. At the close of the twentieth century, more than 50 percent of the U.S. population lived within 75 kilometers of a coast. This number is expected to increase even more in the early decades of this century. High population density near shorelines means that hurricanes and other large storms place millions of people at risk.

Q *Why are hurricanes given names, and who picks the names?*

A Actually, the names are given once the storms reach tropical-storm status (winds between 61–119 kilometers per hour). Tropical storms are named to provide ease of communication between forecasters and the general public regarding forecasts, watches, and warnings. Tropical storms and hurricanes can last a week or longer, and two or more storms can be occurring in the same region at the same time. Thus, names can reduce the confusion about what storm is being described.

The World Meteorological Organization creates the lists of names. The names for Atlantic storms are used again at the end of a six-year cycle unless a hurricane was particularly destructive or otherwise noteworthy. Such names are retired to prevent confusion when the storms are discussed in future years.

Figure 20 This satellite image of Hurricane Floyd shows its position off the coast of Florida a few days before the hurricane moved onto land. Floyd eventually made landfall near Cape Fear, North Carolina.

Hurricanes

Use Visuals **L1**

Figure 20 Direct students' attention to the satellite image in the figure. Ask: **What is the direction of air flow in Hurricane Floyd?** *(counterclockwise)* **Visual**

Use Community Resources **L2**

Invite students to gather first-hand reports of any significant tornadoes or hurricanes in their area. Help them identify good people to interview, and prepare questions in advance. For example: Have there been any especially severe storms in this area? When did this event occur? What damage did it do? Then have students look for quantitative records of the event's intensity, in terms of the Fujita Scale for tornadoes and the Saffir-Simpson Scale for hurricanes. **Interpersonal**

Facts and Figures

Of all the hurricane-prone areas of the United States, Tampa Bay, FL, is considered one of the most vulnerable to severe flooding, damage, and loss of life in a major hurricane. There are several reasons for this. Tampa Bay is located on a peninsula with long stretches of waterfront. This makes the area one of the most densely populated in Florida, and leads to limited evacuation routes. There is also a large population of elderly people in the area. The evacuation of this segment of the population could prove to be difficult for emergency workers. Tampa Bay's geography could also increase the effects of a storm surge; the Gulf of Mexico has a broad, shallow continental shelf on which a storm surge could build to heights great enough to destroy or damage thousands of homes and businesses. The Tampa Bay area has not received a direct hit from a major hurricane in several decades.

Build Science Skills L2

Comparing and Contrasting Ask students to explore the similarities and differences of tornadoes and hurricanes by making a chart. They should include in their chart information on location, associated storms, pressures associated with the storm, impact on society, and maximum wind strength.
Logical

Build Reading Literacy L1

Refer to **p. 502D** in **Chapter 18,** which provides the guidelines for visualizing.

Visualize Ask students to read the section under Development of Hurricanes on p. 576. After the first reading, instruct students to close their eyes and think of a hurricane. Have them suppose they are flying through the clouds of a hurricane and note the changes in wind velocity and pressure as they travel from one side to the other. Have students refer to Figure 21 to help them visualize their trip.
Intrapersonal

Occurrence of Hurricanes Most hurricanes form between about 5 and 20 degrees north and south latitude. The North Pacific has the greatest number of storms, averaging 20 per year. The coastal regions of the southern and eastern United States experience fewer than five hurricanes, on average, per year. Although many tropical disturbances develop each year, only a few reach hurricane status. A storm is a hurricane if the spiraling air has winds blowing at speeds of at least 119 kilometers per hour.

Development of Hurricanes A hurricane is a heat engine that is fueled by the energy given off when huge quantities of water vapor condense. **Hurricanes develop most often in the late summer when water temperatures are warm enough to provide the necessary heat and moisture to the air.** A hurricane begins as a tropical disturbance that consists of disorganized clouds and thunderstorms. Low pressures and little or no rotation are characteristic of these storms.

Occasionally, tropical disturbances become hurricanes. Figure 21 shows a cross section of a well-developed hurricane. An inward rush of warm, moist surface air moves toward the core of the storm. The air then turns upward and rises in a ring of cumulonimbus clouds. This doughnut-shaped wall that surrounds the center of the storm is the **eye wall.** Here the greatest wind speeds and heaviest rainfall occur. Surrounding the eye wall are curved bands of clouds that trail away from the center of the storm. Notice that near the top of the hurricane, the rising air is carried away from the storm center. This outflow provides room for more inward flow at the surface.

At the very center of the storm is the **eye** of the hurricane. This well-known feature is a zone where precipitation ceases and winds subside. The air within the eye gradually descends and heats by compression, making it the warmest part of the storm.

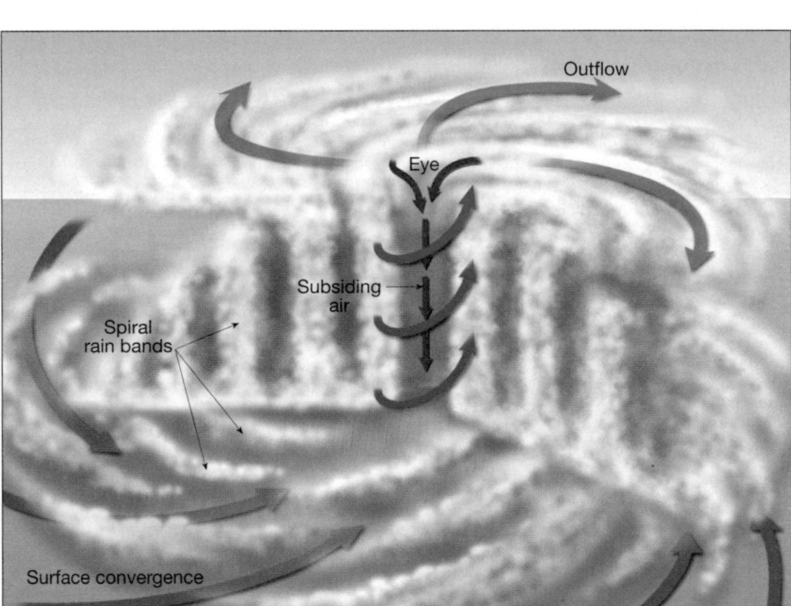

Figure 21 Cross Section of a Hurricane The eye of the hurricane is a zone of relative calm, unlike the eye wall region where winds and rain are most intense.
Describing ***Describe the airflow in different parts of a hurricane.***

Facts and Figures

Hurricanes in the past were identified using awkward latitude/longitude methods. It became clear that the use of short, distinctive names would be quicker and less subject to error. These advantages are especially important in exchanging detailed storm information between hundreds of widely scattered stations, coastal bases, and ships at sea. Since 1953, Atlantic tropical storms have been named from lists originated by the National Hurricane Center. The lists featured only women's names until 1979, when men's and women's names were alternated. If a storm is deadly or very costly, the name is never used again.

Hurricane Intensity The intensity of a hurricane is described using the Saffir-Simpson scale shown in Table 2. The most devastating damage from a hurricane is caused by storm surges. A **storm surge** is a dome of water about 65 to 80 kilometers wide that sweeps across the coast where a hurricane's eye moves onto land.

A hurricane weakens when it moves over cool ocean waters that cannot supply adequate heat and moisture. Intensity also drops when storms move over land because there is not sufficient moisture. In addition, friction with the rough land surface causes winds to subside. Finally, if a hurricane reaches a location where the airflow aloft is unfavorable, it will die out.

Table 2 Saffir-Simpson Hurricane Scale

Category	Sustained Wind Speeds (kph)	Typical Damage
1	119–153	Storm surge 1.2–1.5 meters; some damage to unanchored mobile homes, shrubbery, and trees; some coastal flooding; minor pier damage.
2	154–177	Storm surge 1.6–2.4 meters; some damage to buildings' roofs, doors, and windows; considerable damage to mobile homes and piers; moderate coastal flooding.
3	178–209	Storm surge 2.5–3.6 meters; some structural damage to small buildings; some large trees blown over; mobile homes destroyed; some coastal and inland flooding.
4	210–249	Storm surge 3.7–5.4 meters; severe damage to trees and signs; complete destruction of mobile homes; extensive damage to doors and windows; severe flooding inland.
5	> 249	Storm surge >5.4 meters; complete roof failure on many buildings; some complete building failure; all treees and signs blown away; major inland flooding.

Section 20.3 Assessment

Reviewing Concepts

1. What is a thunderstorm?
2. What causes a thunderstorm?
3. What is a tornado?
4. How does a tornado form?
5. What is a hurricane?
6. How does a hurricane form?

Critical Thinking

7. **Formulating Hypotheses** What kind of front is associated with the formation of tornadoes? Explain.
8. **Synthesizing** Explain why a hurricane quickly loses its strength as the storm moves onto land.

Writing in Science

Explanatory Paragraph Examine Tables 1 and 2 to contrast the damage caused by tornadoes and hurricanes. Use the data to explain why even though hurricanes have lower wind speeds, they often cause more damage than tornadoes do.

3 ASSESS

Evaluate Understanding

Have students make a game of concentration using the terms in the chapter and their definitions. Have groups of students write each term on separate index cards and the definition of each term on a second set of index cards. To play the game, students should shuffle all the cards together and then lay them face down in a grid. Each student takes turns flipping over two index cards. If the cards match (definition matches the term), the student can remove the cards from the grid. If the cards do not match, the student places the cards face down. After all of the cards are gone, the student who has removed the most cards wins the match.

Reteach

L1

Use Figures 17, 18, and 21 as visual aids to summarize the development of severe storms.

Hurricanes generally inflict more damage because they are larger and last longer than tornadoes do.

Section 20.3 Assessment

1. A thunderstorm is a severe storm that generates lightning, thunder, gusty winds, heavy rain, and hail.
2. A thunderstorm forms when relatively warm, humid air rises in an unstable environment.
3. A tornado is a violent rotating column of air that extends downward from cumulonimbus clouds.
4. Most tornadoes form in association with severe thunderstorms.
5. A hurricane is a whirling tropical cyclone that produces wind that can reach 300 km/h.
6. A hurricane develops when water temperatures are warm enough to provide the necessary heat and moisture to the air.
7. Tornadoes often form in thunderstorms that develop along cold fronts because air masses on either side of the front have very different temperature and moisture conditions.
8. There is not sufficient moisture. The rough land surface causes winds to subside.

Answer to . . .

Figure 21 *Air entering the storm from the surface is moving counterclockwise. Air within the eye region is also moving counterclockwise. Outflow, however, is moving in a clockwise direction.*

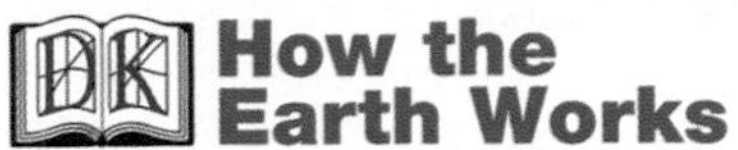

How the Earth Works

1 FOCUS

Objectives

In this feature, students will
- explain what causes wind and what factors affect wind speed.
- describe the development of the different types of storms.
- summarize the impact of storms.

Reading Focus

Build Vocabulary L2

Key Terms Write these key terms on the board: *wind, tornado, blizzard, tropical cyclone, typhoon, storm surge.* Ask students to define them. Then have students explain what causes wind and what factors affect wind speed.

2 INSTRUCT

Bellringer L2

Have students read the feature caption heads that name different types of storms. Ask: **Do any of these kinds of storms occur in your region?** If so, have students estimate how frequently the storms occur. Discuss how location and regional climate account for the frequency of storms.
Verbal, Logical

How the Earth Works

Winds and Storms

The world's atmosphere is forever on the move. **Wind,** or air in motion, occurs because solar radiation heats up some parts of the sea and land more than others. Air above these hot spots becomes warmer and lighter than the surrounding air and therefore rises. Elsewhere, cool air sinks because it is heavier. Winds blow because air squeezed out by sinking, cold air is sucked in under rising, warm air. Wind may move slowly as in a gentle breeze. In extreme weather, wind moves rapidly, creating terrifyingly destructive storms.

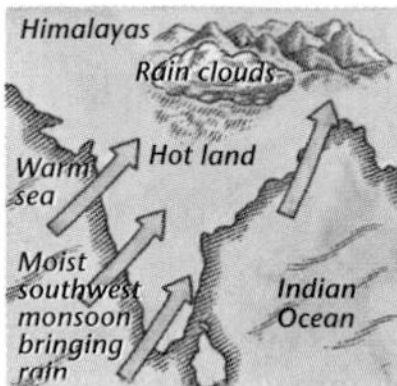

Southwest Monsoon
During the early summer, the hot, dry lands of Asia draw in cooler, moist air from the Indian Ocean.

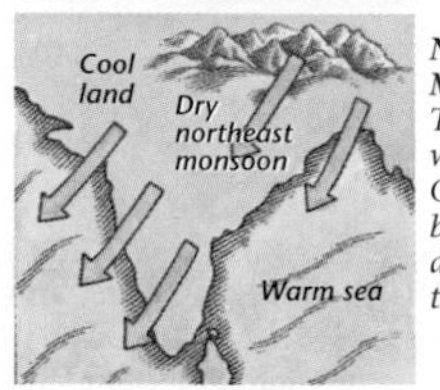

Northeast Monsoon
The cold, dry winter air from Central Asia brings chilly, dusty conditions to South Asia.

MONSOONS
Seasonal winds called monsoons affect large areas of the tropics and subtropics. They occur in South Asia, southern North America, eastern Australia, and other regions of the world. In South Asia, southwest monsoons generally bring desperately needed rain from May until October.

THUNDERSTORMS
Thunderclouds are formed by powerful updrafts of air that occur along cold fronts or over ground heated very strongly by the sun. Ice crystals and water droplets high in the cloud are torn apart and smashed together with such ferocity that they become charged with electricity. Thunderstorms can unleash thunder, lightning, wind, rain, and hail.

LIGHTNING AND THUNDER
Electricity is discharged from a thundercloud in the form of lightning. A bolt of lightning can heat the air around it to a temperature four times as hot as the sun. The heated air expands violently and sends out a rumbling shock wave that we hear as thunder.

Customize for Inclusion Students

Gifted Explain to students that the term *tropical cyclones* is used to refer to certain hurricanes and typhoons. Have students find out how many tropical cyclones occurred last year and make a chart with the name, dates, and location (ocean) of each storm. Post the chart in your classroom and discuss whether or not there is a pattern in the chart.

TORNADOES
Tornadoes may strike wherever thunderstorms occur. A **tornado** begins when a column of strongly rising warm air is set spinning by high winds at a cloud's top. A funnel is formed and may touch the ground. With winds that can rise above 419 kph, tornadoes can lift people, cars, and buildings high into the air and then smash them back to the ground.

BLIZZARDS
In a **blizzard,** heavy snowfall and strong winds often make it impossible to see. Winds pile up huge drifts of snow. Travel and communication can grind to a halt.

HOW TROPICAL STORMS DEVELOP
Tropical storms begin when water evaporates over an ocean in a hot tropical region to produce huge clouds and thunderstorms. When the storms cluster together and whirl around a low-pressure center, they form a **tropical cyclone.** Tropical cyclones with winds of at least 119 kph are called hurricanes in some regions and **typhoons** in other regions. The sequence below shows satellite images of an Atlantic hurricane.

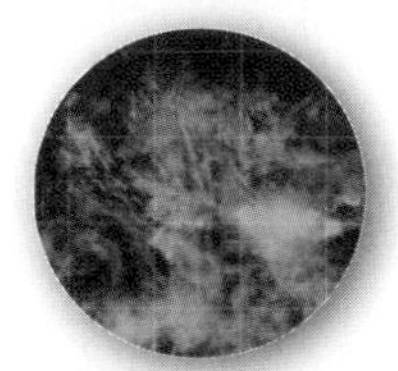

Stage 1: Thunderstorms develop over the ocean.

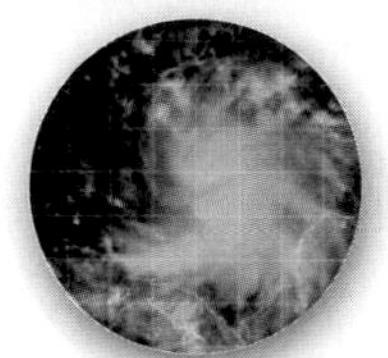

Stage 2: Storms group to form a swirl of cloud.

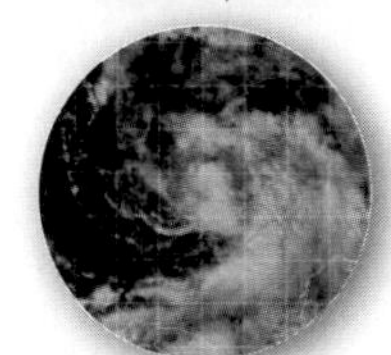

Stage 3: Winds grow and a distinct center forms in the cloud swirl.

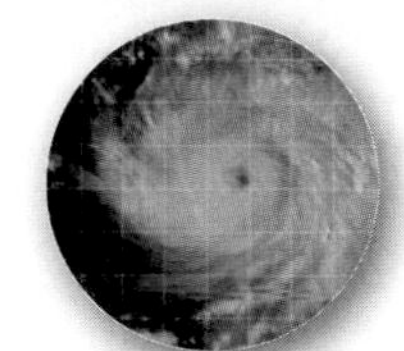

Stage 4: Eye forms. The hurricane is now at its most dangerous.

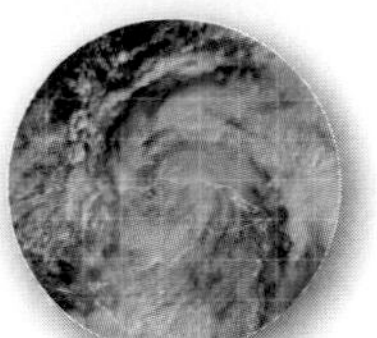

Stage 5: Eye passes over land. The hurricane starts to weaken.

IMPACT OF TROPICAL STORMS
Tropical storms are often devastating. The strongest winds, with gusts sometimes more than 249 kph, occur at the storm's center, or eye. When a tropical storm strikes land, raging winds can uproot trees and destroy buildings. Vast areas may be swamped by torrential rain, and coastal regions may be overwhelmed by a **storm surge,** a wall of water some 8 m high sucked up by the storm's eye.

These women wade through the streets of Dhaka, Bangladesh, flooded by a tropical cyclone. In 1991, a cyclone killed more than 130,000 Bangladeshis.

A Pacific typhoon struck this ship off the coast of Taiwan in November 2000. Many of the crew members fell victim to the raging sea.

ASSESSMENT

1. **Key Terms** Define **(a)** wind, **(b)** tornado, **(c)** blizzard, **(d)** tropical cyclone, **(e)** typhoon, **(f)** storm surge.
2. **Physical Processes** How do thunderstorms come into being?
3. **Economic Activities** **(a)** How can storms have a negative impact on economic activities? **(b)** How can monsoons benefit economic activities?
4. **Natural Hazards** How can a tropical cyclone result in the loss of thousands of lives?
5. **Critical Thinking** **Developing a Hypothesis** Since 1991, the Bangladeshi government has constructed hundreds of concrete storm shelters in coastal regions of the country. **(a)** Why do you think the government decided on this policy? **(b)** How do you think the policy has benefited the country?

Integrate Social Studies 

Ask students to discuss which kind of storm seems most threatening to their community and why. Then discuss the kinds of emergency services that are in place to help in case of a storm.
Logical

3 ASSESS

Evaluate Understanding 

Have students compare and contrast the development of the different types of storms described in the feature (monsoons, thunderstorms, tornadoes, blizzards, and tropical cyclones). Then have students draw diagrams on the board that show how these storms form.

Reteach L1

Have students create flash cards for the key terms *wind, tornado, blizzard, tropical cyclone, typhoon,* and *storm surge.* Encourage them to use their flash cards to review the definitions of different types of storms.

Assessment

1. (a) air in motion; **(b)** a spinning column of air with high winds; **(c)** a storm with heavy snowfall and strong winds; **(d)** a cluster of tropical thunderstorms that whirl around a low-pressure center; **(e)** a tropical cyclone that has winds moving at least 74 mph **(f)** a wall of water sucked up by a storm's eye
2. Thunderstorms are formed by powerful updrafts of air that occur along cold fronts or over heated ground. Ice crystals and water droplets high in the cloud are torn apart and smashed together so energetically that they become charged with electricity.
3. (a) During a severe storm, economic activities may come to a halt. When property is destroyed, people spend money to replace or rebuild it. **(b)** Monsoons bring rain to South Asia, and rain is needed to grow crops.
4. Extremely strong winds can destroy buildings, bring torrential rain that results in floods, or cause a storm surge. Any of these can result in loss of life.
5. (a) Bangladesh is located in a region that is subject to tropical storms. The government hopes to offer shelter to the people who are most likely to be affected by the storms. **(b)** Sample answer: It has provided shelter for people who live in coastal areas.

Application Lab

Middle-Latitude Cyclones

L2

Objectives

In this activity, students will

- explain how middle-latitude cyclones affect the weather of the area over which they form.
- predict how middle-latitude cyclones change weather patterns as they move through an area.

Skills Focus Observing, Comparing and Contrasting, Predicting

Prep Time 10 minutes

Advance Prep If time is limited, provide students with light photocopies of the map on the facing page and have students color and mark the copies.

Class Time 40 minutes

Teaching Tips

- If necessary, review the steps in the formation of a middle-latitude cyclone with students prior to their beginning the activity. Also review the information in Chapters 18 and 19 on humidity, precipitation, wind, and air pressure if needed.
- Walk around the room as students work on this activity and monitor students' progress. Should anyone have problems getting started or answering the questions, prompt him or her with appropriate questions.

Expected Outcome Students should be able to correctly label the map and answer the questions. Note that the cold front is the front designated by the blue line with the triangular notches. The warm front is the red line with the semicircular notches. The occluded front is the front shown by the line with both the red and blue notches. Precipitation is falling at the center of the system and along the eastern boundaries of both the cold and warm fronts.

Application Lab

Middle-Latitude Cyclones

You've learned that much of the day-to-day weather in the United States is caused by middle-latitude cyclones. In this lab, you will identify some of the atmospheric conditions associated with a middle-latitude cyclone. Then you will use what you know about Earth's atmosphere and weather to predict how the movement of the low-pressure system affects weather in the area.

Problem How do middle-latitude cyclones affect weather patterns?

Materials

- tracing paper
- sharp pencil
- paper clips or removable tape
- metric ruler
- colored pencils

Skills Observing, Comparing and Contrasting, Predicting

Procedure

1. Use the paper clips or removable tape to secure the tracing paper over the map on the facing page.
2. Carefully trace all of the features and boundaries on the map. Be sure to include the isobars—the lines that show atmospheric pressure. Use the ruler to trace lines EA and GF.
3. Remove the tracing paper. Place it next to the map.
4. Transfer all of the letters and numbers on the map to your tracing.
5. Use the colored pencils to color the land and water areas on the tracing. Also color the symbols used to designate the fronts.
6. Identify and label the cold front, warm front, and occluded front on your tracing.
7. Draw arrows that show the direction of surface winds at points A, C, E, F, and G.

Analyze and Conclude

1. **Describing** In which direction are the surface winds moving?
2. **Identifying** At which stage of formation is the cyclone? Explain your answer. Refer to Figure 14 if necessary.
3. **Explaining** Is the air in the center of the cyclone rising or falling? What effect does this have on the potential for condensation and precipitation?
4. **Inferring** Find the center of the low, which is marked with the letter L. What type of front has formed here? What happens to the maritime tropical air in this type of front?

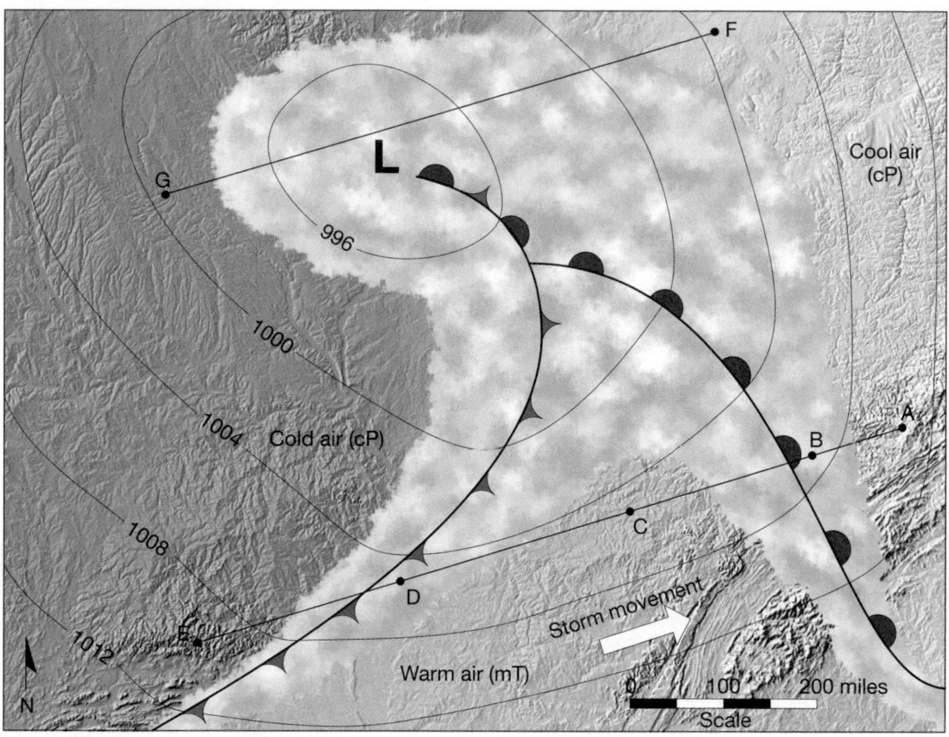

5. **Predicting** Once the warm front passes, in which direction will the wind at point B blow?
6. **Synthesizing** Describe the changes in wind direction and moisture in the air that will likely occur at point D after the cold front passes.
7. **Synthesizing** Describe the wind directions, humidity, and precipitation expected for a city as the cyclone moves and the city's relative position changes from point A to B, point C, point D, and finally from point D to E.

Go Further Find out and explain how subpolar lows affect middle-latitude cyclones over the United States in winter.

Analyze and Conclude

1. The winds at point A are blowing toward north-northwest. At point C, they are blowing almost directly north. At point E, the winds are moving almost directly east. At point F, the winds are blowing from the southeast toward the northwest. At point G, the winds are blowing from the northwest to the southeast.
2. The middle-latitude cyclone shown is at the mature stage as indicated by the occluded front.
3. The air at the center of the cyclone is rising. The potential for condensation and precipitation will be good because as the air rises, cooling will occur and the dew-point temperature may be reached.
4. An occluded front has formed at the center of the low pressure system. The warm mT air is lifted above the cooler air.
5. After the warm front passes, the wind at point B will be from the south.
6. The wind will blow from the northwest and the moisture content will decrease.
7. point A to point B: low stratus clouds, possible precipitation, wind from the southeast, moisture should increase, point C: wind from the south, warm and perhaps humid air; point D: vertical clouds, possible thunderstorms; point D to point E: wind from the northwest, cool or cold temperatures, clearing sky, moisture should decrease

Go Further

During the winter, subpolar lows and the polar front are farthest south in North America. Thus, the central United States will experience a greater frequency of passing middle-latitude cyclones.
Kinesthetic, Visual

Study Guide

Study Tip

Organize New Information
Tell students to create outlines, charts, flashcards, timelines, and concept maps to help them visualize relationships.

Thinking Visually

Two air masses meet to form a front, which can be a warm front, cold front, stationary front, or an occluded front.

Assessment

Reviewing Content

(1) 1 (2) 4 (3) 2
(4) 2 (5) 2 (6) 4
(7) 3 (8) 4 (9) 2

Understanding Concepts

(10) Its temperature and moisture conditions change. Also, the air mass changes the weather in the area over which it moves.
(11) In summer, cP air masses may bring a few days of relatively cool weather. In winter, this air brings the clear skies and cold temperatures you associate with a cold wave. Continental polar air masses can also cause lake-effect snow. Maritime tropical air masses are warm, moisture-laden, and usually unstable and the sources of most of the precipitation in the eastern two-thirds of the United States. In summer, when an mT air mass invades the central and eastern United States, it brings high temperatures and high humidity.
(12) Rain or snow begins and often continues for a long time. A gradual increase in temperature occurs with the passage of a warm front as well as a wind shift from the east to the southwest.
(13) Weather along a cold front consists of heavy downpours and gusty winds. Once the front has passed, temperatures drop and wind shifts. The weather behind a cold front is dominated by a relatively cold air mass. Thus, weather clears soon after a cold front passes.
(14) A stationary front forms when the flow of air on either side of a front is almost parallel to the line of the front.

CHAPTER 20

Study Guide

20.1 Air Masses

Key Concepts

- An air mass is an immense body of air that is characterized by similar temperatures and amounts of moisture at any given altitude.
- As an air mass moves, its characteristics can change and so does the weather in the area over which the air mass moves.
- Air masses are classified according to their source region, the place where they form.
- Much of the weather in North America is influenced by continental polar (cP) and maritime tropical (mT) air masses.
- Polar (P) or tropical (T) indicates the temperature of an air mass. Continental (c) or maritime (m) indicates whether the air mass is dry or humid.

Vocabulary
air mass, *p. 559*

20.2 Fronts

Key Concepts

- When two air masses meet, they form a front, which is a boundary that separates two contrasting air masses.
- A warm front forms when warm air moves into an area formerly covered by cooler air.
- A cold front forms when cold, dense air moves into a region occupied by warmer air.
- A stationary front forms when the surface position between two air masses does not move.
- An occluded front forms when a cold front overtakes a warm front, producing a complex weather pattern.
- A middle-latitude cyclone is a large center of low pressure that generally travels from west to east and causes stormy weather.

Vocabulary
front, *p. 564;* warm front, *p. 565;* cold front, *p. 566;* stationary front, *p. 566;* occluded front, *p. 567*

20.3 Severe Storms

Key Concepts

- A thunderstorm generates thunder and lightning and frequently produces gusty winds, heavy rain, and hail. Thunderstorms form when warm, humid air rises in an unstable environment.
- Tornadoes are violent windstorms that take the form of a rotating column of air called a vortex, which extends downward from a cumulonimbus cloud. Most tornadoes are associated with severe thunderstorms.
- Hurricanes are whirling tropical cyclones with high winds that sometimes develop over the ocean when water temperatures are warm enough to provide the necessary heat and moisture to fuel the storms.

Vocabulary
thunderstorm, *p. 571;* tornado, *p. 573;* hurricane, *p. 575;* eye wall, *p. 576;* eye, *p. 576;* storm surge, *p. 577*

Thinking Visually

Concept Map Use what you know about fronts and air masses to complete this concept map.

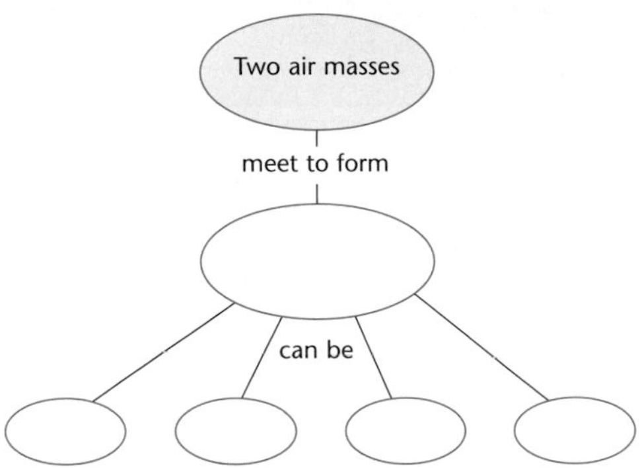

Chapter Assessment Resources

Print
Chapter Test, Chapter 20
Test Prep Resources, Chapter 20

Technology
Computer Test Bank, Chapter 20 Test
Online Text, Chapter 20
Go Online, PHSchool.com, Chapter 20

CHAPTER 20

NY Regents Content Item

Assessment

Interactive textbook with assessment at PHSchool.com

Reviewing Content

Choose the number that best answers the question or completes the statement.

1 If an area is experiencing consecutive days of constant weather, this weather is called NY
(1) air-mass weather
(2) warm-front weather
(3) cold-front weather
(4) occluded-front weather

2 An air mass that forms over the Gulf of Mexico is a(n) NY
(1) cP air mass (2) mP air mass
(3) cT air mass (4) mT air mass

3 Air masses that have the greatest influence on weather in the midwestern United States are NY
(1) mT and cT air masses
(2) cP and mT air masses
(3) mP and cP air masses
(4) cT and cP air masses

4 Lake-effect snow is associated with a(n) NY
(1) mP air mass (2) mT air mass
(3) cP air mass (4) cT air mass

5 "Rain long foretold, long last; short notice, soon past." The first five words of this weather proverb refer to a(n) NY
(1) warm front (2) cold front
(3) anticyclone (4) tornado

6 Which front often produces hours of moderate-to-light precipitation over a large area? NY
(1) polar (2) maritime
(3) cold (4) warm

7 A thunderstorm is most intense during its
(1) cumulus stage (2) wave stage
(3) mature stage (4) dissipating stage

8 When a hurricane reaches land, its intensity decreases as the result of NY
(1) increase in pressure and temperature
(2) lack of cold, dry air to fuel the storm
(3) successive updrafts into the eye wall
(4) friction and the lack of warm, moist air

9 The eye of a hurricane NY
(1) has the greatest wind speeds
(2) is warmer than the rest of the storm
(3) experiences high pressures
(4) is responsible for heavy precipitation

Understanding Concepts

10 What kinds of changes occur to an air mass as it moves over an area? NY

11 Describe the effects of cP and mT air masses on much of the weather in the United States. NY

12 Describe weather associated with a warm front. NY

13 What kind of weather is associated with a cold front while it is over an area and once it passes? NY

14 What is a stationary front? NY

15 Sequence the steps that lead to the formation of an occluded front. NY

16 Describe the stages involved in the development of a middle-latitude cyclone. NY

17 How are cyclones and anticyclones related? NY

18 Describe the formation of a thunderstorm. NY

19 What is a mesocyclone and how does it form? NY

20 Describe the different parts of a hurricane. NY

Use this map to answer questions 21–24.

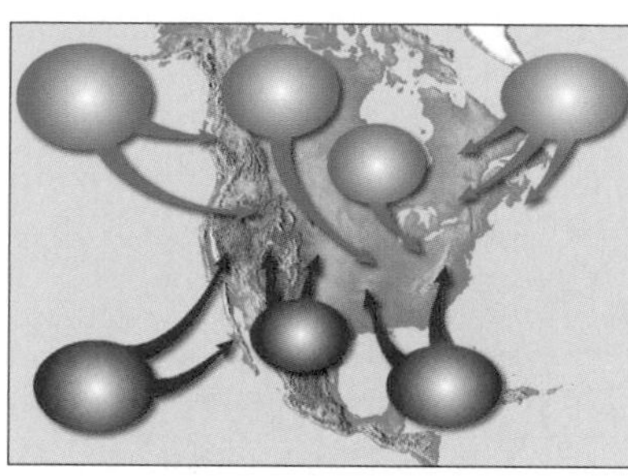

21 Name the three red air masses and identify the source region of each. NY

22 Identify the cold air masses, starting with the air mass farthest west and moving eastward. NY

23 Which air masses would supply the largest amount of precipitation to the area east of the Rocky Mountains? NY

24 Which of the air masses has the greatest influence on weather along the northwest coast? NY

Homework Guide

Section	Questions
1	1–4, 10, 11, 21–25
2	5, 6, 12–15, 26, 27, 37
3	7–9, 16–20, 28–36

(15) A cold front moves toward a warm front, forcing warm air aloft. The cold front merges with the warm front to form an occluded front that drops heavy rains. The heavy rains are followed by periods of light precipitation.
(16) The formation of a front sets the stage for the development of a middle-latitude cyclone. Over time, the front takes on a wave shape. Changes in air flow and pressure result in a counter-clockwise flow of air. The rapidly moving cold front closes in on the warm front. As the cold front lifts, an occluded front forms. Eventually, the cyclone weakens.
(17) The surface air that feeds a cyclone generally originates as air flowing out of an anticyclone. Thus, cyclones and anticyclones typically are found next to each other. Both systems depend on the flow of air high in the atmosphere to maintain their circulation.
(18) Strong updrafts supply the initial volume of moist air. Each new surge of warm air causes the cloud to grow vertically. Usually within an hour of the initial updraft, the amount and size of the precipitation is too great for the updrafts to support. So, heavy precipitation is released from the cloud. Gusty winds, lightning, heavy precipitation, and sometimes hail are produced.
(19) A mesocyclone is a vertical cylinder of rotating air that develops in the updraft of a thunderstorm. The formation of this large vortex begins as strong winds aloft cause winds lower in the atmosphere to roll. Strong thunderstorm updrafts cause this rolling air to tilt. Once the air is completely vertical, the mesocyclone is established.
(20) Warm, moist surface air moves toward the center of a tropical storm, turns upward, and rises in a ring of cumulonimbus clouds. This doughnut-shaped wall that surrounds the center of the storm is the eye wall. Here the greatest wind speeds and heaviest rainfall occur. Surrounding the eye wall are curved bands of clouds that trail away from the center of the storm. At the very center of the storm is the eye of the hurricane. At the eye, which is the warmest part of a hurricane, precipitation ceases and winds subside.
(21) Farthest west is the mT air mass, which forms over the Pacific Ocean. The cT air mass forms over the southwestern United Sates and Mexico. The mT mass, which is farthest east, has the Gulf of Mexico as its source region.
(22) From west to east, the cold masses are mP, cP, cP, and mP.
(23) cP and mT
(24) mP

Chapter 20

Critical Thinking

(25) Polar and tropical air masses are the same in that both are enormous bodies of air, each with similar temperatures and moisture conditions at any given altitude. Polar air masses, because of their high-latitude source regions, are colder than tropical air masses, which have source regions at low latitudes.
(26) an mT air mass
(27) North of the low pressure system, the storm reaches its greatest intensity. Temperatures would remain cold as the system passes, and heavy precipitation in the form of snow, sleet, and freezing rain would fall.
(28) Both are severe storms that can cause much damage. Tornadoes are small, quickly whirling vortices of air that form and move over land. Tornadoes last for only a short period of time—less than a few hours. Hurricanes are much larger than tornadoes and form and move over water. Hurricanes generally last for about a week. When they make landfall, hurricanes will die out.
(29) Although the hurricane has diminished, heavy rains and inland flooding due to storm surges can last for several days, causing much damage and loss of life.

Map Skills

(30) the Atlantic Ocean
(31) As indicated by the differences in line patterns, Floyd was a tropical storm on September 8 and 9 and after September 16.
(32) Hurricane Floyd moved east-northeast toward the eastern coastline of the United States during this time period.
(33) Hurricanes are fueled by warm, wet air. Floyd was most intense from September 10 until it made landfall. At landfall, friction with the land and the lack of warm, wet air caused the hurricane to die out.
(34) Hurricane Floyd moved onto land on September 16 when it crashed into the North Carolina coast.

CHAPTER 20

Assessment *continued*

Critical Thinking

25 **Comparing and Contrasting** Compare and contrast polar and tropical air masses. NY

26 **Synthesizing** What type of air mass is responsible for most of the warm fronts east of the Rocky Mountains? NY

27 **Inferring** What kinds of weather conditions would you expect in regions north of a middle-latitude cyclone during winter? NY

28 **Comparing and Contrasting** Compare and contrast tornadoes and hurricanes. NY

29 **Identifying Cause and Effect** Great damage and significant loss of life can take place a day or more after a hurricane has moved ashore and weakened. Explain why this might happen. NY

Map Skills

Use the map to answer questions 30–34.

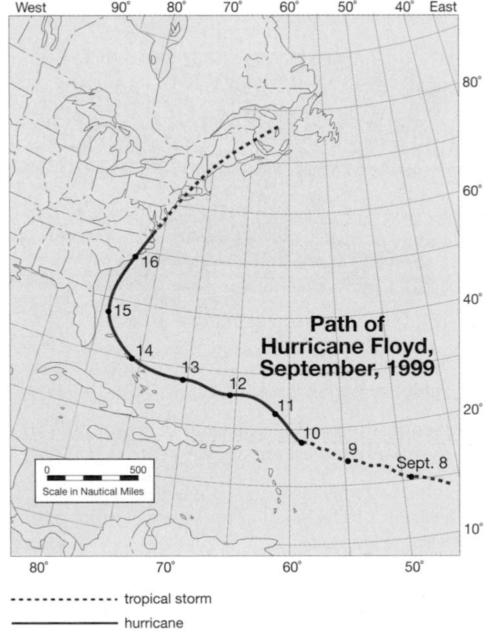

30 **Reading Maps** Over which ocean did Hurricane Floyd develop and move? NY

31 **Interpreting Graphs** On which days was Floyd a tropical storm? NY

32 **Describing** Describe the path of Hurricane Floyd from September 10 through September 16. NY

33 **Inferring** When was Hurricane Floyd most intense? Explain. NY

34 **Reading Maps** When and where did Hurricane Floyd move onto land? NY

Concepts in Action

35 **Synthesizing** Describe weather conditions that you would observe if the center of a middle-latitude cyclone passed north of you.

36 **Applying Concepts** What kinds of negative effects might a hurricane have on coastal ecosystems? NY

37 **Writing in Science** Use what you know about weather patterns to write a paragraph to explain which parts of the Earth system interact to produce the high snowfall in the Great Lakes region of North America. NY

Performance-Based Assessment

Applying Concepts Find out about precautions people should take during any of the three types of severe storms discussed in this chapter. Summarize your findings in three separate posters.

Concepts in Action

(35) As the low approached, one would experience cool temperatures because the warm part of the cyclone would be farther south. Air pressure would drop and clouds would form. Snow or rain would fall. As the occluded front passed, winds would shift and blow from the north or northeast. Skies would eventually clear and pressures would rise, but temperatures would remain cool.
(36) Flooding, the mixing of salt water and fresh water, increased erosion, removal of low-lying vegetation, and the uprooting of trees are some of the changes that might affect coastal ecosystems.
(37) High snowfall on the leeward sides of the Great Lakes occurs when the atmosphere, hydrosphere, and lithosphere interact. The lake-effect snow develops as cold cP air travels over the warmer water and acquires moisture. This warming and increase in moisture causes the air mass to become unstable. The result is often heavy snow over the cooler land on the downwind shores of the lakes.

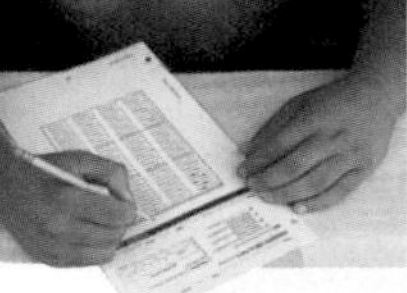

Regents Practice Exam

Test-Taking Tip

Using Maps
Most maps in Earth science are used to show geographic features such as mountains and bodies of water, tectonic features such as plate boundaries, and different types of rocks. Maps, like those shown below, can also be used to show statistical information. When using such maps to answer questions, be sure you understand what each map is showing before you try to answer the questions.

For *each* statement or question, choose the *number* of the word or expression that, of those given, best completes the statement or answers the question. Some questions may require the use of the *Earth Science Reference Tables.*

1 Maritime tropical air masses generally originate over
(1) cold ocean waters
(2) warm land masses
(3) warm ocean waters
(4) cold land masses

Base your answers to questions 2 and 3 on the diagrams below, which show Average Number of Days/Year with Thunderstorms, and Average Annual Tornadoes per 26,000 km^2.

2 Which of the following colors represents the greatest average number of tornadoes per 26,000 km^2?
(1) tan (2) green (3) yellow (4) orange

3 How many tornadoes on average are experienced in the area referred to in question 2?
(1) 1.0 – 2.0
(2) 2.0 – 3.0
(3) 5.0 – 7.0
(4) 7.0 – 9.0

4 If a tornado warning is issued for your area, what should you do to protect yourself?

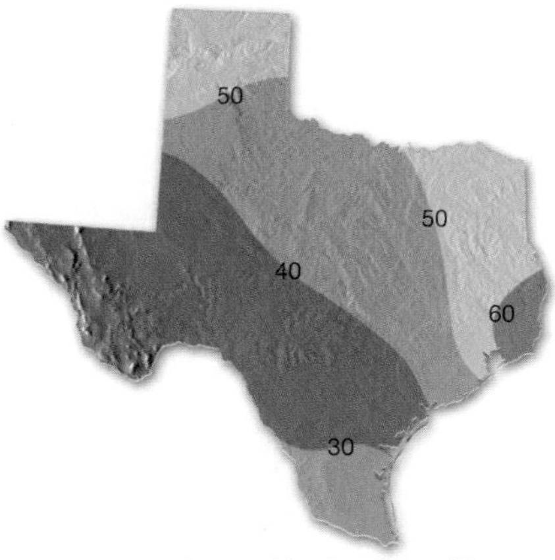

Average Number of Days/Year with Thunderstorms

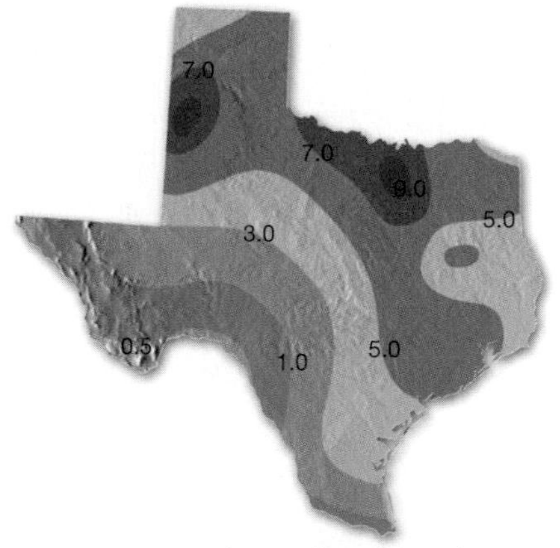

Average Annual Tornadoes per 26,000 km^2

Regents Practice Exam

(1) 3
(2) 4
(3) 3
(4) Go into a sturdy building and stay in an interior room on the first floor, basement, or storm shelter. Be sure to have a battery powered radio or TV with you to listen for weather updates and find out when it is safe to go outside again.

Performance-Based Assessment

Students' findings should include what should be done before, during, and after each type of storm strikes, as well as what should be done should storm watches and warnings be issued. This is probably a good time to review your school's or community's storm safety procedures.

Your students can independently test their knowledge of the chapter and print out their results.

CHAPTER 21

Planning Guide

Use these planning tools
Use Teacher Express for all your planning needs

SECTION OBJECTIVES	STANDARDS NATIONAL	STANDARDS STATE	ACTIVITIES and LABS
21.1 Factors That Affect Climate, pp. 588–591 1 block or 2 periods **21.1** **Describe** how latitude affects climate. **21.2** **Describe** how elevation and mountain ranges affect climate. **21.3** **Describe** how large bodies of water affect climate. **21.4** **Describe** how global winds affect climate. **21.5** **Describe** how vegetation affects climate.	A-1, A-2, D-1		**SE** Inquiry Activity: Global Warming: Fact or Fiction? p. 587 **L2** **TE** Teacher Demo: Heating and Angles, p. 589 **L2** **SE** Quick Lab: Observing How Land and Water Absorb and Release Energy, p. 590 **L2** **LM** Modeling the Greenhouse Effect **L2**
21.2 World Climates, pp. 592–599 1 block or 2 periods **21.6** **Explain** the Köppen climate classification system. **21.7** **Describe** humid tropical climates. **21.8** **Compare and contrast** humid mid-latitude climates. **21.9** **List** the characteristics of dry climates. **21.10** **List** the characteristics of polar climates. **21.11** **Compare and contrast** highland climates with nearby lowland climates.	D-1		**TE** Teacher Demo: Modeling Humid Climates, p. 596 **L2**
21.3 Climate Changes, pp. 600–603 1 block or 2 periods **21.12** **Describe** natural processes that can cause changes in climate. **21.13** **Explain** the greenhouse effect. **21.14** **Define** global warming. **21.15** **List** some of the consequences of global warming.	A-2, B-3, C-4, D-1, D-3, E-2, F-5, F-6, G-1		**TE** Teacher Demo: Earth's Motions and Climate, p. 601 **L2** **SE** Exploration Lab: Human Impact on Climate and Weather, pp. 606–607 **L2**

Ability Levels

L1 For students who need additional help
L2 For all students
L3 For students who need to be challenged

Components

SE	Student Edition	**GRSW**	Guided Reading & Study Workbook	**TP**	Test Prep Resources	**GEO**	Geode CD-ROM
TE	Teacher's Edition			**onT**	onlineText	**T**	Transparencies
LM	Laboratory Manual	**TEX**	Teacher Express	**DC**	Discovery Channel Videos	**GO**	Internet Resources
CUT	Chapter Tests	**CTB**	Computer Test Bank				

RESOURCES PRINT and TECHNOLOGY	SECTION ASSESSMENT
GRSW Section 21.1 **T-303** Climates of the World **T-304** Climates of the World **T-311** Influence of Elevation on Climate **TEX** Lesson Planning 21.1	**SE** Section 21.1 Assessment, p. 591 **onT** Section 21.1
GRSW Section 21.2 **T-302** Köppen System of Climatic Classification **T-305** Three Climactic Diagrams **T-306** Arid and Semiarid Climates **T-307** Climactic Diagrams for Arid and Semiarid Stations **T-308** Three Main Types of C Climates **T-309** D Climates **T-310** Two Basic Types of Polar Climates **DC** Polar Weather **TEX** Lesson Planning 21.2	**SE** Section 21.2 Assessment, p. 599 **onT** Section 21.2
GRSW Section 21.3 **T-312** Energy Consumption in the U.S. **T-313** Carbon Dioxide Concentrations **T-314** Global Temperature Variations GEODe Heating the Atmosphere ↳ The Greenhouse Effect **TEX** Lesson Planning 21.3	**SE** Section 21.3 Assessment, p. 603 **onT** Section 21.3

Go Online

Go online for these Internet resources.

PHSchool.com
Web Code: cjk-9999

NSTA SCiLINKS
Web Code: cjn-6212
Web Code: cjn-6213

Materials for Activities and Labs

Quantities for each group

STUDENT EDITION

Inquiry Activity, p. 587
computer with Internet access, paper, pen, colored markers or highlighters

Quick Lab, p. 590
2 small, identical containers; 2 laboratory thermometers; water; dry sand; masking tape; watch or clock; book; paper towels or rags for spills

TEACHER'S EDITION

Teacher Demo, p. 589
black construction paper, metric ruler, scissors, tape, 3 thermometers, 100-W incandescent lamp

Teacher Demo, p. 596
water, 2 small plastic bowls, transparent plastic wrap, rubber band

Teacher Demo, p. 601
globe, lamp

Chapter Assessment

ASSESSMENT

SE Assessment, pp. 609–610
CUT Chapter 21 Test
CTB Chapter 21
onT Chapter 21

STANDARDIZED TEST PREP

SE Chapter 21, p. 611
TP Progress Monitoring Assessments

interactive textbook with assessment at PHSchool.com

CHAPTER 21

Before you teach

Michael Wysession
Washington University

Big Ideas

Earth's lands display a remarkable diversity of climates. The major factors that affect climate include latitude, elevation, topography, the nearness of large bodies of water, the patterns of global winds, and the type and amount of vegetation.

Space and Time Climate classifications, such as the Köppen classification system, are used to recognize how climate responds to the different factors such as latitude and elevation. The major climate types are humid tropical, dry, middle latitude (with mild or severe winters), and polar.

Forces and Motion Earth's climate changes significantly over time, sometimes very rapidly. The driving mechanism for climate change is the variation in the amount and distribution of solar radiation due to changes in Earth's revolution and rotation (Milankovitch cycles).

Matter and Energy Climate change, however, has many other natural factors. Volcanic eruptions can change climate by adding gases and dust into the atmosphere. Changes in global ocean currents greatly affect how heat from the sun is distributed. It is even possible that changes in solar activity, perhaps associated with sunspots, affects climate as well.

Earth as a System Human activity affects climate both locally, with the development of cities, and globally. We are in a period of global warming due to an increase in carbon dioxide emissions and the reduction in forest land. This global warming involves an increase in global temperatures as well as a change in patterns of precipitation.

Earth Science Refresher

The History of Climate

The history of life is intimately connected with the history of climate. This is seen in the overall evolution of life, as well as the recent history of human culture and society.

When climates are warm, glacial ice melts, shorelines transgress, and large parts of the continents are covered with shallow seas, which are ideal environments for ocean life. The remarkable diversity of ocean life during the Cambrian period occurred during one of these times. The Cretaceous period, during the proliferation of the giant dinosaurs, was also extremely warm, and, on average, global climate has been cooling ever since.

Roughly 5 million years ago a major cooling trend began, and many forest habitats began to disappear, developing into plains. It has been proposed that this provided the selective force that caused our ancestors to evolve into bipedal hominids, leaving our hands free to develop tools. Many other important events, such as the emergence and dominance of *Homo sapiens* about 100,000 years ago, and the significant cultural expansion involving tools and jewelry about 50,000 to 40,000 years ago, are directly correlated with large climate changes.

Students may think that Earth's climate was exactly the same for millions of years, and only changed recently as a result of human activity. In reality, there have been many major natural changes in Earth's history. For a strategy that helps to overcome this misconception, see **Address Misconceptions** on **p. 600**.

Go Online PDLINKS NSTA

For: Chapter 21 Content Support
Visit: www.SciLinks.org/PDLinks
Web Code: cjn-2199

During the major ice age of about 20,000 years ago, sea level was low enough due to large land glaciers that all of the continents except for Antarctica were connected. This allowed northeast Asian people to cross the Bering Strait and settle in the Americas, and allowed Southeast Asian people to cross into Australia.

The rise of civilization began about 10,000 years ago, at the start of a stable global warm period. This allowed for the development of agriculture and the formation of cities. Most of the major migrations of peoples, including the movements of ancient tribes throughout the Middle East, the Greek and Roman conquests, the fall of Rome at the hands of the Goths and Huns, and many others, can be directly related to climate changes that either created prosperity or starvation.

On short time scales, volcanic eruptions have also been responsible for cultural change. For example, during the 1780s, volcanoes in Iceland and Japan significantly altered the global climates, and Europe suffered very cold temperatures and large-scale crop failures. Massive starvation lead to political unrest, and about a dozen European governments collapsed, including the French monarchy. Volcanoes caused the French Revolution!

The past 10,000 years have been remarkable not only in their unusually high temperatures, but also in the relatively small changes in temperature. While it seems that climate changes during this time were large, these changes were very small compared to previous times. If global climate patterns returned to the former level of large and rapid changes, the consequences for humanity would be severe.

Build Reading Literacy

SQ3R

Survey, Question, Read, Recite, and Review

Strategy Help students read material that contains technical information, diagrams, and figures. This strategy helps students focus on the main points in a section, making it easier for them to remember what they have read. Before students begin, assign a section in the textbook for them to read such as Factors That Affect Climate, pp. 588–591.

Example

1. S Have students survey the entire assignment and look at the heading, material in boldface and italics, and chapter summary. Have them write a short explanation of what they see in each diagram, photograph, or chart.

2. Q Have students write questions they will answer when they complete their survey. They should turn each heading into a question and leave room below it for the answer.

3. R Have students read the section and look for the answers to their questions.

4. R When students finish reading, tell them to think about what they read. They should recite the questions they wrote and—using their own words—give the answers they found. If students can't answer a question, have them reread the material for the related heading, looking more carefully to find the answer.

5. R Have students review the section by writing the answers they recited. Finally, refer students to the key concepts questions on the first page of the section. Have students answer each of these questions.

See p. 593 for a script on how to use this strategy with students. For additional strategies, see pp. 588 and 601.

ASSESS PRIOR KNOWLEDGE

Use the Chapter Pretest below to assess students' prior knowledge. As needed, review these concepts.

Review Science Concepts

Section 21.1 Review, from Section 17.3, factors that influence temperature.

Section 21.2 Review the idea of classification and why scientists classify things.

Section 21.3 Review, from Section 17.2, how the atmosphere is heated. Also review the concepts of El Niño and the greenhouse effect.

CHAPTER 21 Climate

CONCEPTS in Action

Quick Lab
Observing How Land and Water Absorb and Release Energy

Exploration Lab
Human Impact on Climate and Weather

How the Earth Works
Coniferous Forests

Heating the Atmosphere
↳ The Greenhouse Effect

Discovery Channel School **Video Field Trip**
Polar Weather

Take a field trip to the North and South Poles with Discovery Channel and learn about the coldest places on Earth. Answer the following questions after watching the video.

1. Why is Antarctica, which holds 80 percent of the world's ice, technically called a desert?
2. What would happen to the ocean if the ice shelves around Antarctica melted?

For: Chapter 21 Resources
Visit: PHSchool.com
Web Code: cjk-9999

Climate determines the types of vegetation that grow in an area. This forest in Denali Park, Alaska, includes a mix of coniferous forest and tundra vegetation. ▶

Chapter Pretest

1. As latitude increases, what happens to rays from the sun that strike Earth's surface? *(They spread out.)*
2. Why do large bodies of water moderate nearby land climates? *(c)*
   a. Land heats and cools more slowly than water.
   b. Land heats more rapidly than water, but cools more slowly.
   c. Land heats and cools more rapidly than water.
   d. Land heats more slowly than water, but cools more rapidly.
3. True or False: As altitude increases, temperature also increases. *(False)*
4. What are the major factors that determine climate? *(temperature and precipitation)*
5. True or False: El Niño is a change in ocean circulation that causes parts of the eastern tropical Pacific Ocean to become warmer than usual. *(True)*
6. What is the natural warming of Earth's atmosphere called? *(b)*
   a. El Niño
   b. the greenhouse effect
   c. global warming
   d. volcanism

Chapter Preview

Inquiry Activity

Global Warming: Fact or Fiction?

Global warming is perhaps one of the most hotly debated environmental issues. Is the world getting warmer? Do we need to worry about it? What are the economic and political issues behind the debate? In this activity, you will gather the evidence to decide for yourself.

Procedure

1. Gather information on the topic using the Internet. Focus your search to answer questions 1 through 4 under Think About It.
2. Now evaluate opposing points of view on this topic from credible sources. Search the Internet to find three articles that present the view that the damaging consequences of global warming are real. Find three articles that suggest that concerns about global warming are overstated.
3. Print each article and analyze the information you've collected by completing items 5 and 6. If your analysis shows that you don't have enough information, search for some additional articles.
4. Formulate your own opinion on the global warming issue based on your research. Complete items 7 and 8.

Think About It

1. What is the greenhouse effect?
2. List three greenhouse gases.
3. List three facts about global warming.
4. List three uncertainties about global warming.
5. Use a marker to highlight the facts in each article that are supported by data.
6. Use a marker of another color to highlight the claims in each article that are not well supported.
7. What did you decide? Is global warming a real threat, or are there more important environmental issues to resolve?
8. Write a letter in which you attempt to persuade your state senator to agree with your position. Support your stance with facts based on your research.

Video Field Trip

Polar Weather

Encourage students to view the Video Field Trip "Polar Weather."

ENGAGE/EXPLORE

Global Warming: Fact or Fiction? L2

Purpose In this activity, students will research global warming to form their own opinion on this environmental issue.

Skills Focus Researching, Analyzing, Formulating Opinions, Persuasive Writing

 **Prep Time** 10–15 minutes

Materials computer with Internet access, paper, pen, colored markers or highlighters

Class Time 30 minutes

Teaching Tip Review with students how to research using the Internet and how to focus their searches. List some Web sites on the board that may be helpful, such as environmental sites, government sites, news sites, and educational sites.

Expected Outcomes Students will better understand the issue of global warming, analyze the information they find, and formulate their opinion. Students will also learn how to write a persuasive letter and support their articles with facts from their research.

Think About It

1. The greenhouse effect is a natural warming of both Earth's lower atmosphere and Earth's surface.
2. carbon dioxide, methane, nitrous oxide, water vapor
3. Students should list three facts that they found in their research. Accept all reasonable answers.
4. Students should list three uncertainties about global warming they found in their research. Accept all reasonable answers.
5. See articles. Make sure students highlight only those facts with supporting data.
6. Check articles. Make sure students highlight only claims that are not well supported.
7. Students should formulate an opinion based on their research.
8. Students should write a persuasive letter with supporting facts from their research.

Section 21.1

1 FOCUS

Section Objectives

21.1 **Describe** how latitude affects climate.
21.2 **Describe** how elevation and mountain ranges affect climate.
21.3 **Describe** how large bodies of water affect climate.
21.4 **Describe** how global winds affect climate.
21.5 **Describe** how vegetation affects climate.

Reading Focus

Build Vocabulary L2

LINCS Have students use the LINCS strategy to learn and review the terms *tropical*, *temperate*, and *polar*. In LINCS exercises, students **L**ist what they know about each term, **I**magine a picture that describes the word, **N**ote a "sound-alike" word, **C**onnect the terms to the sound-alike word by making up a short story, and then perform a brief **S**elf test.

Reading Strategy L2

a. Climates get cooler as latitude increases.
b. Climates get cooler as elevation increases.
c. Windward sides of mountains are wet; leeward sides are dry.
d. Places downwind of large water bodies have cooler summers and milder winters.
e. Global winds influence climate by distributing heat and moisture.
f. Vegetation can moderate temperature and increase precipitation.

2 INSTRUCT

Factors That Affect Climate

Build Reading Literacy L2

Refer to **p. 420D** in **Chapter 15**, which provides the guidelines for predicting.

Predict Before students read Factors That Affect Climate, ask: **Why do you think some areas of the world are very hot, and others are very cold?** Once students have a list of predictions, have them read pp. 589–590 and evaluate whether their predictions were correct.
Logical, Interpersonal

21.1 Factors That Affect Climate

Reading Focus

Key Concepts

- How does latitude affect climate?
- How does elevation affect climate?
- What effect does a mountain range have on climate?
- How do large bodies of water affect climate?
- What effect do global winds have on climate?
- How does vegetation affect climate?

Vocabulary

- tropical zone
- temperate zone
- polar zone

Reading Strategy

Summarizing Information Copy the table. As you read, summarize the effect(s) each factor has on climate.

Factor	Effect(s) on Climate
1. Latitude	a. ?
2. Elevation	b. ?
3. Topography	c. ?
4. Water bodies	d. ?
5. Global wind	e. ?
6. Vegetation	f. ?

Figure 1 Maroon Bells Area, Colorado All of Earth's spheres interact to affect climate.
Identifying ***In the photograph, identify at least two components of each of the spheres shown.***

Recall from Chapter 17 that climate includes not only the average weather conditions of an area, but also any variations from those norms. In this section, you will learn that climate involves more than just the atmosphere. Powered by the sun, the climate system is a complex exchange of energy and moisture among Earth's different spheres, all of which are shown in Figure 1.

Factors That Affect Climate

The varied nature of Earth's surface and the many interactions that occur among Earth's spheres give every location a distinctive climate. You will now find out how latitude, elevation, topography, large bodies of water, global winds, and vegetation affect the two most important elements of climate—temperature and precipitation.

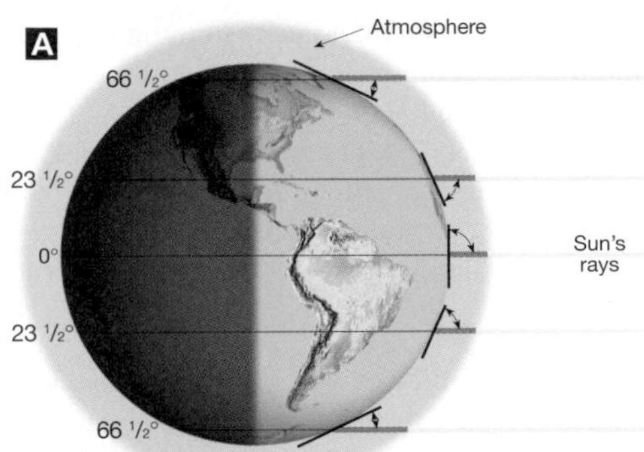

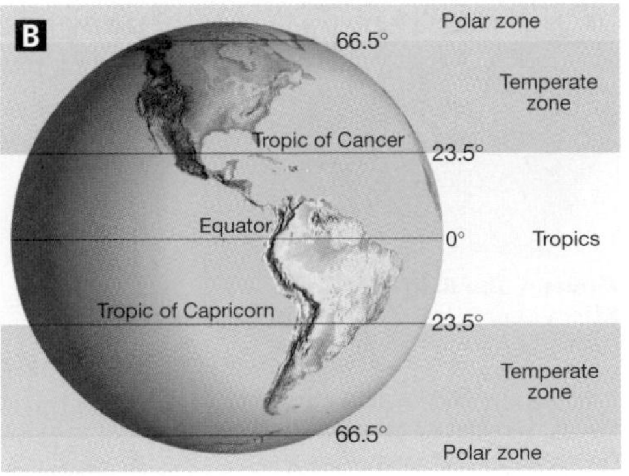

Latitude Latitude is the distance north or south of the equator. **As latitude increases, the intensity of solar energy decreases.** Can you explain why? Study Figures 2A and 2B. Notice that near the equator, the sun's energy strikes the planet at nearly right angles. Therefore, in this region, between about 23.5° north (Tropic of Cancer) and 23.5° south (Tropic of Capricorn) of the equator, the sun's rays are most intense. This region is called the tropics, or the **tropical zones.** Temperatures in the tropical zones are generally warm year-round. In the **temperate zones,** which are between about 23.5° and 66.5° north and south of the equator, the sun's energy strikes Earth at a smaller angle than near the equator. This causes solar energy to be spread out over a larger area. In addition, the length of daylight in the summer is much greater than in the winter. As a result, temperate zones have hot summers and rather cold winters. In the **polar zones,** which are between 66.5° north and south latitudes and the poles, the energy strikes at an even smaller angle, causing the light and heat to spread out over an even larger area. Therefore, the polar regions experience very cold temperatures, even in the summer.

Figure 2 Earth's Major Climate Zones A Solar energy striking Earth's surface near the poles is less intense than radiation striking near the equator. **B** Earth can be divided into three zones based on these differences in incoming solar radiation.

Elevation Elevation, or height above sea level, is another factor that affects the climate of an area. Recall from Chapter 17 that air temperature decreases with elevation by an average of about 6.5°C Celsius every 1000 meters. **The higher the elevation is, the colder the climate.** The elevation of an area also determines the amount of precipitation it receives. Examine the graph in Figure 3 to see how the climates of two cities at roughly the same latitude are affected by their height above sea level.

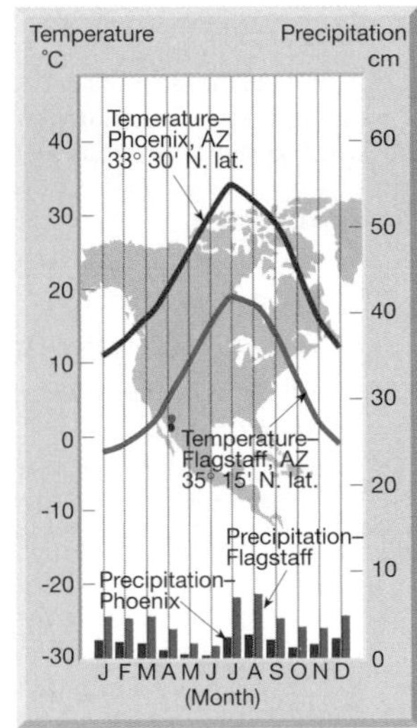

Figure 3 Climate Data for Two Cities This climate graph shows data for two cities in Arizona. Phoenix has an elevation of 338 m. Flagstaff has an elevation of 2134 m.
Interpreting Graphs *How does elevation affect annual temperatures and precipitation?*

How does the intensity of solar radiation vary at different parts of Earth?

Teacher Demo

Heating and Angles L2

Purpose Students observe how the angle at which light rays strike a surface affects temperature.

Materials black construction paper, metric ruler, scissors, tape, 3 thermometers, 100-W incandescent lamp

Procedure Before the demo, cut three 5 cm × 10 cm rectangles out of black construction paper. Fold them in half and tape them to make pockets. In front of the students, insert the bulb of a thermometer into each pocket. Use books or other props to arrange the thermometers so that one is in a pocket that is flat on the table, one is in a pocket that is at a 45° angle, and the last is in a pocket that is vertical. Make sure the pockets are close together. Have students observe and record the temperature on the thermometers. Place a 100-W incandescent lamp about 30 cm above the pockets and turn it on. Ask students to predict which pocket will heat up fastest. *(Most will say "the flat one.")* Have students observe and record the temperature on the thermometers every 15 minutes. Ask them why they got the results they did. *(The flat pocket heated up the fastest because it was exposed to the most direct rays. The vertical pocket heated up the slowest because it was exposed to the least direct rays.)*

Expected Outcomes The flat pocket will heat up the fastest. The vertical pocket will heat up the slowest.
Logical, Visual

Customize for English Language Learners

Using a cause/effect chart can ensure that students understand the concepts, as well as the word meanings, in this section. Have students work independently or in groups to make a two-column chart. The left column should be labeled "Cause" and the right column "Effect." As students read the section, encourage them to write on their charts different cause/effect relationships about climate. For example, one cause is increasing altitude, and the effect is decreasing temperature.

Answer to . . .

Figure 1 *atmosphere: air and clouds; hydrosphere: lake, ice, and snow; lithosphere: rocks, soil, land, and mountain peaks; biosphere: trees and other vegetation*

Figure 3 *Elevation provides for more precipitation and lower temperatures at least for this comparison.*

It decreases as latitude increases. Near the equator, the sun strikes the planet most directly. Farther from the equator, the energy spreads out over larger areas.

Use Visuals

Figure 4 Use this diagram to explain how topography affects precipitation. Ask: **What happens to humid air as it is blown up the windward side of the mountains?** *(It cools, forming clouds.)* **What often falls from these clouds?** *(heavy precipitation)* **What is the air like when it reaches the other side of the leeward side of the mountain?** *(very dry)* **What does the term "rain shadow" mean?** *(It refers to an area that rain cannot reach.)*
Visual, Logical

Observing How Land and Water Absorb and Release Energy

Objective
After completing this activity, students will be able to state that land and water absorb and release heat differently.

Skills Focus Using Models, Comparing and Contrasting, Measuring, Analyzing Data

Prep Time 10 minutes

Class Time 25–30 minutes

Materials 2 small, identical containers; 2 laboratory thermometers; water; dry sand; masking tape; watch or clock; book; paper towels or rags for spills

Safety Remind students to report any breakage of thermometers immediately. Wipe up any spills at once.

Expected Outcome Students will observe that water warms up and cools down more slowly than land.

Analyze and Conclude
1. The water heated faster than the sand, and the sand cooled more quickly than the water.
2. A large body of water moderates temperatures of an area near that water body, so these areas' temperatures vary less than those over land.
Kinesthetic, Logical

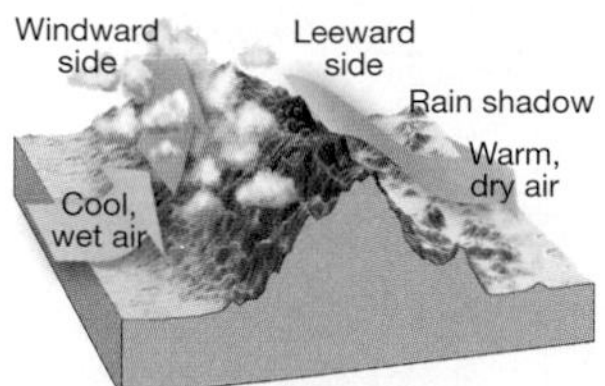

Figure 4 The Rain Shadow Effect Mountains influence the amount of precipitation that falls over an area.
Comparing and Contrasting ***Compare and contrast the climates on either side of a mountain.***

Topography **Topographic features such as mountains play an important role in the amount of precipitation that falls over an area.** As shown in Figure 4, humid air on the windward side of a mountain moves up the mountain's slopes and eventually cools to form clouds. Heavy precipitation often falls from these clouds. By the time air reaches the leeward side of a mountain, much of the moisture is lost. This dry area is called a rain shadow. Rain shadows can extend for hundreds of kilometers downwind of a mountain range.

Water Bodies **Large bodies of water such as lakes and oceans have an important effect on the temperature of an area because the temperature of the water body influences the temperature of the air above it.** Places downwind of a large body of water generally have cooler summers and milder winters than places at the same latitude that are farther inland. In the Quick Lab below, you can observe how a body of water can influence climate.

Quick Lab

Observing How Land and Water Absorb and Release Energy

Materials

2 small, identical containers; 2 laboratory thermometers; water; dry sand; masking tape; watch or clock; book; paper towels or rags for spills

Procedure

1. On a separate sheet of paper, make a copy of the data table shown.
2. Fill one container three-quarters full of dry sand.
3. Fill the other container three-quarters full of water.
4. Place the containers in a sunny area on a flat surface such as a tabletop or a lab bench.
5. Place the bulb of one of the thermometers into the sand. Prop up the thermometer with a book. Tape the thermometer in place so that only the bulb is covered with sand.
6. Repeat Step 5 with the water.
7. Record the initial temperature of each substance in your data table.
8. Record the temperature of each thermometer every 5 minutes for about 20 minutes.
9. Remove the containers from the sunny area.
10. Record the temperature of each thermometer for another 20 minutes.

Analyze and Conclude

1. **Comparing and Contrasting** Which substance heated faster? Which substance cooled faster?
2. **Drawing Conclusions** How does a large body of water affect the temperature of nearby areas?

Heat Absorption and Retention of Water and Sand

	Time	Temp H_2O	Temp Sand		Time	Temp H_2O	Temp Sand
Sunny Area	0			Shady Area	0		
	5				5		
	10				10		
	15				15		
	20				20		

Facts and Figures

Ocean currents also have important effects on climates. Currents moving from low-latitude to high-latitude regions transfer heat from warmer to cooler areas on Earth. For example, the North Atlantic Current is an extension of the Gulf Stream, the warm current that runs up the eastern shore of North America. The North Atlantic Current keeps Great Britain and much of northwestern Europe much warmer during the winter than areas such as Labrador and Alaska that are at similar latitudes.
Cold currents originate in cold high-latitude regions. As they travel towards the equator, they tend to moderate the warm temperatures of adjacent land areas. An example of this is the California Current, which moderates temperatures along the west coast of North America.

Atmospheric Circulation

Global winds are another factor that influences climate because they distribute heat and moisture around Earth. Recall from Chapter 19 that winds constantly move warm air toward the poles and cool air toward the equator. The low-pressure zones at the equator and in the subpolar regions lead to the formation of clouds that drop precipitation as rain or snow.

Figure 5 Arizona Vegetation **A** Cacti and scrub are common types of vegetation in the hot, dry climate of Phoenix, Arizona. **B** The vegetation in the highlands of Flagstaff, Arizona, is much different.
Formulating Hypotheses ***Which of these areas would receive more precipitation? Why?***

Vegetation You probably already know that the types of plants that grow in a region depend on climate, as shown in Figures 5A and 5B. But did you know that vegetation affects climate? **Vegetation can affect both temperature and the precipitation patterns in an area.** Vegetation influences how much of the sun's energy is absorbed and how quickly this energy is released. This affects temperature. During a process called transpiration, plants release water vapor from their leaves into the air. So, transpiration influences precipitation. Studies also indicate that some vegetation releases particles that act as cloud seeds. This increase in particles promotes the formation of clouds, which also influences regional precipitation patterns.

Integrate Biology L2

Biomes Tell students that biologists use the concept of biomes to classify and organize ecosystems. A biome is a particular physical environment that contains a characteristic assemblage of plants and animals. So biomes are defined according to the organisms that live in an area, whereas climates are defined according to temperature and precipitation. Biomes and climates, however, are closely related. Ask: **How do you think temperature affects which types of organisms can live in an area?** *(Some organisms, such as reptiles, cannot survive in cold areas, whereas others are not well adapted to hot areas.)*
Logical

3 ASSESS

Evaluate Understanding L2

Ask students to name a factor that affects climate and describe what effect it has.

Reteach L1

Use Figure 2 to review how solar energy strikes different parts of Earth' surface and how this results in different major climate zones.

Answers will vary depending on your area.

Section 21.1 Assessment

Reviewing Concepts

1. How does latitude affect climate?
2. How does elevation affect climate?
3. How does a mountain range affect climate?
4. How do large bodies of water affect climate?
5. What effect do global winds have on climate?
6. Describe different ways in which vegetation affects climate.

Critical Thinking

7. **Comparing and Contrasting** Compare and contrast tropical zones, temperate zones, and polar zones in terms of location and the intensity of solar radiation that each receives.
8. **Explaining** Explain why deserts are common on the leeward sides of mountain ranges.
9. **Applying Concepts** Look again at Figures 3 and 5. What two factors contribute to the average annual temperature in both areas?

Writing in Science

Explanatory Paragraph Write a paragraph to explain how three of the factors discussed in this section affect the climate of your area.

Answer to . . .

Figure 4 *windward side: wet and cool; leeward side: dry and warm*

Figure 5 *The area around Flagstaff would receive more precipitation because its vegetative cover is greater than that in the area around Phoenix.*

Section 21.1 Assessment

1. As latitude increases, the intensity of the solar energy that strikes an area decreases, and climates become cooler.
2. The higher the elevation, the colder the air and therefore, the colder the climate.
3. windward side: humid air moves up the mountain's slopes and cools to form clouds that produce precipitation; leeward side: the air is warm and very dry
4. Places downwind of a large body of water generally have milder seasons than places farther inland at the same latitude.
5. They move heat and moisture around Earth.
6. It influences how much of the sun's energy is absorbed and released, thereby affecting temperature. Plants release water vapor and influence regional precipitation patterns.
7. All are divisions of Earth based on the intensity of solar energy received. Tropical zones: near equator, the sun's energy strikes Earth at almost 90° angles, causing temperatures to be warm all year round. Temperate zones: north and south of the tropics, the sun's energy strikes Earth at a smaller angle, energy spreads out over a larger area, and yearly temperatures moderate. Polar regions: lie between 66 1/2° north and south latitudes and the poles, solar energy strikes at a more acute angle, spreading it over even a larger area. Polar regions experience very low temperatures year-round due to even smaller angles of sunlight.
8. On the leeward side of a mountain, the air is warm and very dry because moisture condenses on the windward side. This can cause desert conditions for hundreds of kilometers downwind of the mountain.
9. elevation and vegetation

1 FOCUS

Section Objectives

21.6 **Explain** the Köppen climate classification system.
21.7 **Describe** humid tropical climates.
21.8 **Compare and contrast** humid mid-latitude climates.
21.9 **List** the characteristics of dry climates.
21.10 **List** the characteristics of polar climates.
21.11 **Compare and contrast** highland climates with nearby lowland climates.

Reading Focus

Build Vocabulary L2

Concept Map Have students create concept maps of the Köppen system. Have them start with "Köppen system" at the top, and put the five principal groups of climates on the next level. Below that, they should put the subgroups within each group and, on the last row, details about each climate.

Reading Strategy L2

Students' outlines should be consistent with the information in the chapter and include the temperature and precipitation for each climate type and one location for each climate type.
A2. Tropical Wet and Dry
B1. Humid Mid-Latitude/Mild Winters
B2. Humid Mid-Latitude/Severe Winters
C1. Steppe (semiarid)
C2. Desert (arid)
(Others: Polar Climates, Tundra and Ice Cap; Highland Climates)

2 INSTRUCT

The Köppen Climate Classification System

Build Science Skills L2

Classifying Ask students to classify the five Köppen climate groups into two main groups. Invite several students to give their classifications; then point out that several different answers are possible. Ask students if they think the Köppen system is the only possible way to classify climates. *(no)* Point out that although classification systems are based on facts, they are invented by humans.
Visual, Logical

21.2 World Climates

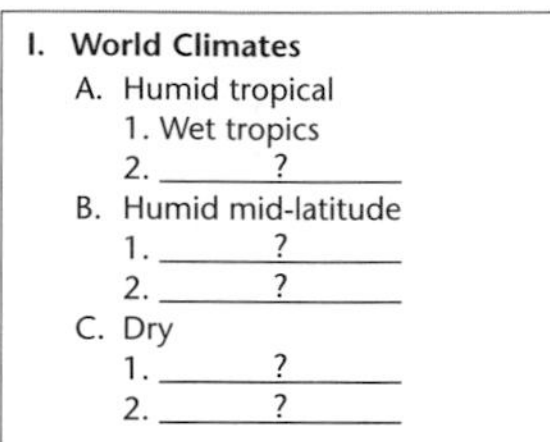

Reading Focus

Key Concepts

- What is the Köppen climate classification system?
- What are humid tropical climates?
- Contrast the different types of humid mid-latitude climates.
- What are the characteristics of dry climates?
- What are the characteristics of polar climates?
- How do highland climates compare with nearby lowlands?

Vocabulary

- Köppen climate classification system
- wet tropical climate
- tropical wet and dry climate
- humid subtropical climate
- marine west coast climate
- dry-summer subtropical climate
- subarctic climate

Reading Strategy

Outlining Copy and continue the outline for each climate type discussed in this section. Include temperature and precipitation information for each climate type, as well as at least one location with that climate type.

I. World Climates
  A. Humid tropical
    1. Wet tropics
    2. ___?___
  B. Humid mid-latitude
    1. ___?___
    2. ___?___
  C. Dry
    1. ___?___
    2. ___?___

If you were to travel around the world, you would find an incredible variety of climates. So many, in fact, that it might be hard to believe they could all occur on the same planet! Despite the diversity, climates can be classified according to average temperatures and amount of precipitation. In this section, you will learn about the Köppen climate classification system, which is commonly used to group climates.

Figure 6 An ice cap climate is a polar climate in which the average monthly temperature is always below freezing.

The Köppen Climate Classification System

Many classification systems have been used to group climates. Perhaps the best-known and most commonly used system is the Köppen climate classification system. **The Köppen climate classification system uses mean monthly and annual values of temperature and precipitation to classify climates.** This system is often used because it classifies the world into climatic regions in a realistic way.

The Köppen system has five principal groups: humid tropical climates, dry climates, humid mid-latitude climates, polar climates, and highland climates. An example of a polar climate is shown in Figure 6. Note that all of these groups, except climates classified as dry, are defined on the basis of temperature. Dry climates are classified according to the amount of precipitation that falls over an area. Each of the five major groups is further subdivided. See Figure 9 on page 594.

Figure 7 Rain Forest in Malaysia The vegetation in the tropical rain forest is the most luxuriant found anywhere on Earth.

Humid Tropical Climates

Humid tropical climates are climates without winters. Every month in such a climate has a mean temperature above 18°C. The amount of precipitation can exceed 200 cm. There are two types of humid tropical climates: wet tropical climates and tropical wet and dry climates.

Wet Tropical The tropical rain forest shown in Figure 7 is typical of a **wet tropical climate.** Wet tropical climates have high temperatures and much annual precipitation. Why? Recall what you've learned about how latitude affects climate. The intensity of the sun's rays in the tropics is consistently high. Because the sun is directly overhead much of the time, changes in the length of daylight throughout the year are slight. The winds that blow over the tropics cause the warm, humid, unstable air to rise, cool, condense, and fall as precipitation. Look at Figure 9 on pages 594 and 595. Notice that regions with humid tropical climates form a belt on either side of the equator.

Tropical Wet and Dry Refer again to Figure 9. Bordering the wet tropics are climates classified as tropical wet and dry climates. **Tropical wet and dry climates** have temperatures and total precipitation similar to those in the wet tropics, but experience distinct periods of low precipitation. Savannas, which are tropical grasslands with drought-resistant trees, are typical of tropical wet and dry climates. A savanna in Africa is shown in Figure 8.

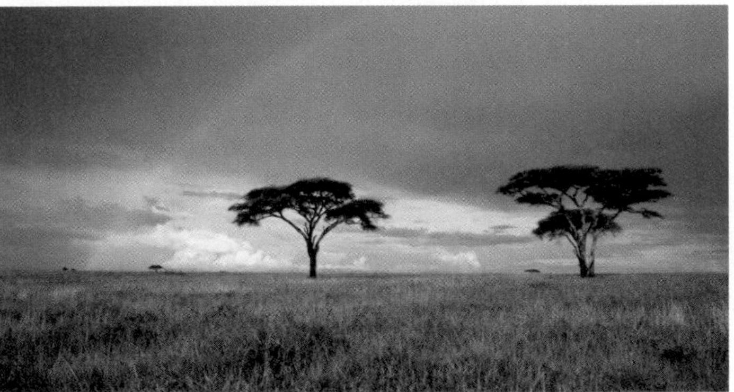

Figure 8 African Savanna Drought-resistant trees and tall grasses are typical vegetation of a savanna.

Humid Tropical Climates

Build Reading Literacy L1

Refer to **p. 586D,** which provides the guidelines for SQ3R (Study, Question, Read, Recite, Review).

SQ3R Teach this independent study skill as a whole-class exercise. Direct students to skim the section and have them write headings for each section, such as "Humid Tropical Climates." As they skim the section, ask students to write one question for each heading, such as "Why are rain forests so wet?" Then have students write answers to the questions as they read the section. After students finish reading, demonstrate how to recite the questions and answers, explaining that vocalizing concepts in their own words helps them retain what they have learned. Finally, have students review their notes the next day.
Verbal, Interpersonal

Build Science Skills L2

Comparing and Contrasting
To help students understand all the information on this page and pp. 596–599, suggest that they focus on a single factor at a time across all the climate regions. For example, first have students compare the climate regions' temperature ranges and sequence them from lowest temperature to highest temperature. Then have students compare the climate regions' precipitation and sequence these amounts from lowest to highest. Discuss any climate region features that are unfamiliar to students. Encourage students who have visited different climate regions to share their experiences.
Logical, Visual

Customize for English Language Learners

As students who are learning English read through the climate region descriptions, encourage them to make a glossary of any unfamiliar terms they encounter. Have them write the English term first, followed by the equivalent word in the student's first language. Encourage students to use the glossary as a reference tool rather than a list to be memorized.

Use Visuals

L1

Figure 9 Use this map to explain global climates and how they are related. First, orient students to the map by pointing out the equator and lines of latitude. Ask: **How are savannas and rainforests related?** *(Savannas are usually found north and south of rain forests.)* **How are steppes and deserts related?** *(Steppes are usually found north and south of deserts.)* Explain that savannas and steppes are transition zones between rainforests and deserts, respectively, and the next climate zones. **What pattern do you see as you go from south to north in eastern North America?** *(Climates go from subtropical to continental to polar.)*
Visual, Logical

Integrate Biology

L2

Biomes and Climate Regions
Remind students that biomes are defined according to the organisms that live in an area, whereas climates are defined according to temperature and precipitation. Tell them that Köppen used the distribution of plants to determine climate regions. As a result, many biomes cover the same area as a climate region, and they often have the same names. Ask: **What climate regions seem to be named based on what types of plants are present there?** *(rainforest, desert, tundra, ice cap)* **What is the typical vegetation in a savanna?** *(tropical grasslands with drought-resistant trees)* **What are the typical climate conditions in a rain forest?** *(high temperatures and large amounts of precipitation year-round)*
Logical

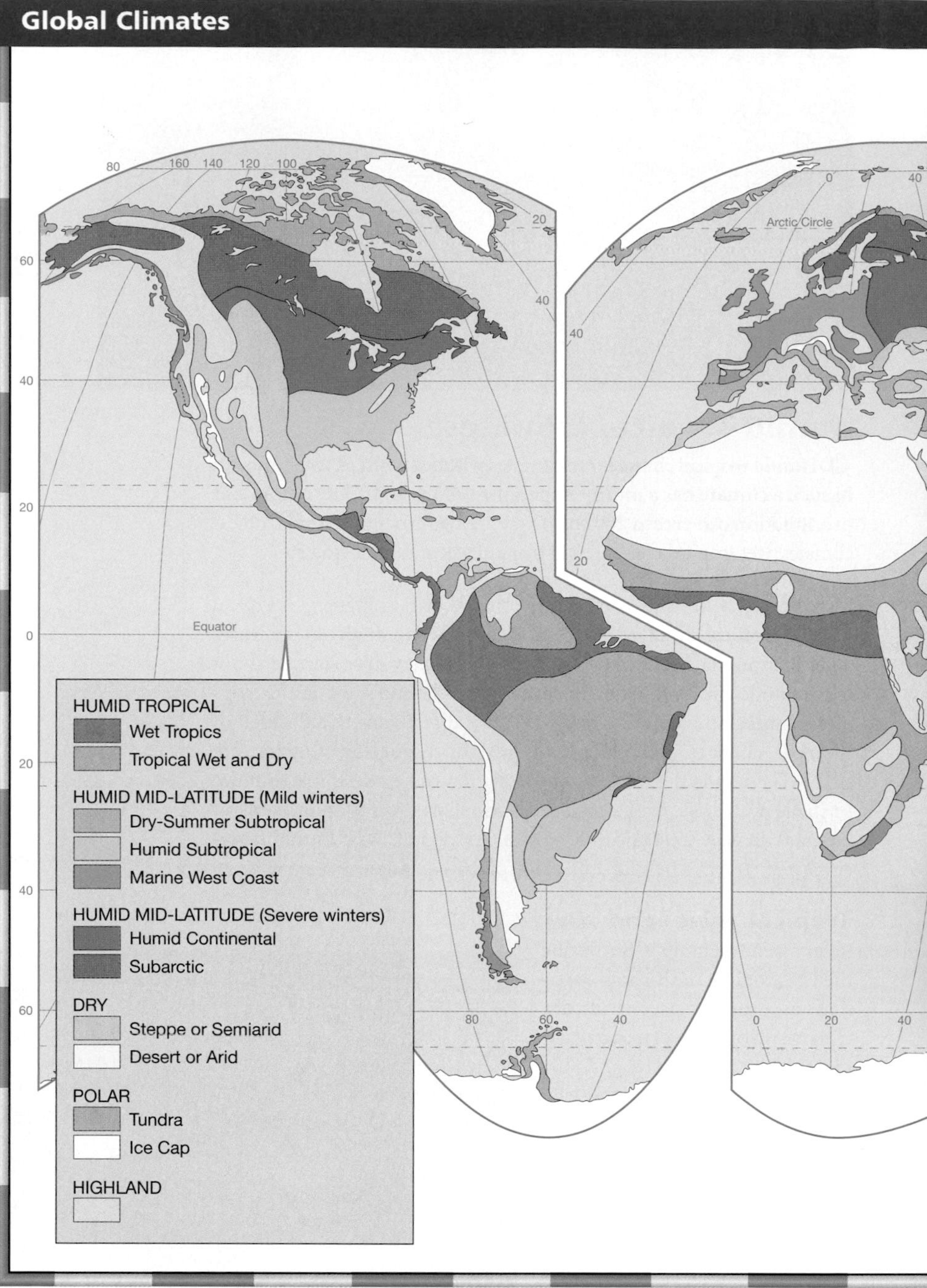

594 *Chapter 21*

Facts and Figures

Here is an overview of the major groups in the Köppen system:
A. Humid tropical: winterless climates; all months have a mean temperature above 18°C.
B. Dry: climates where evaporation exceeds precipitation; there is a constant water deficiency.
C. Humid mid-latitude: mild winters; average temperature of the coldest month is below 18°C but above −3°C.
D. Humid mid-latitude: severe winters; average temperature of the coldest month is below −3°C; warmest monthly mean exceeds 10°C.
E. Polar: summerless climates; average temperature of the warmest month is below 10°C.

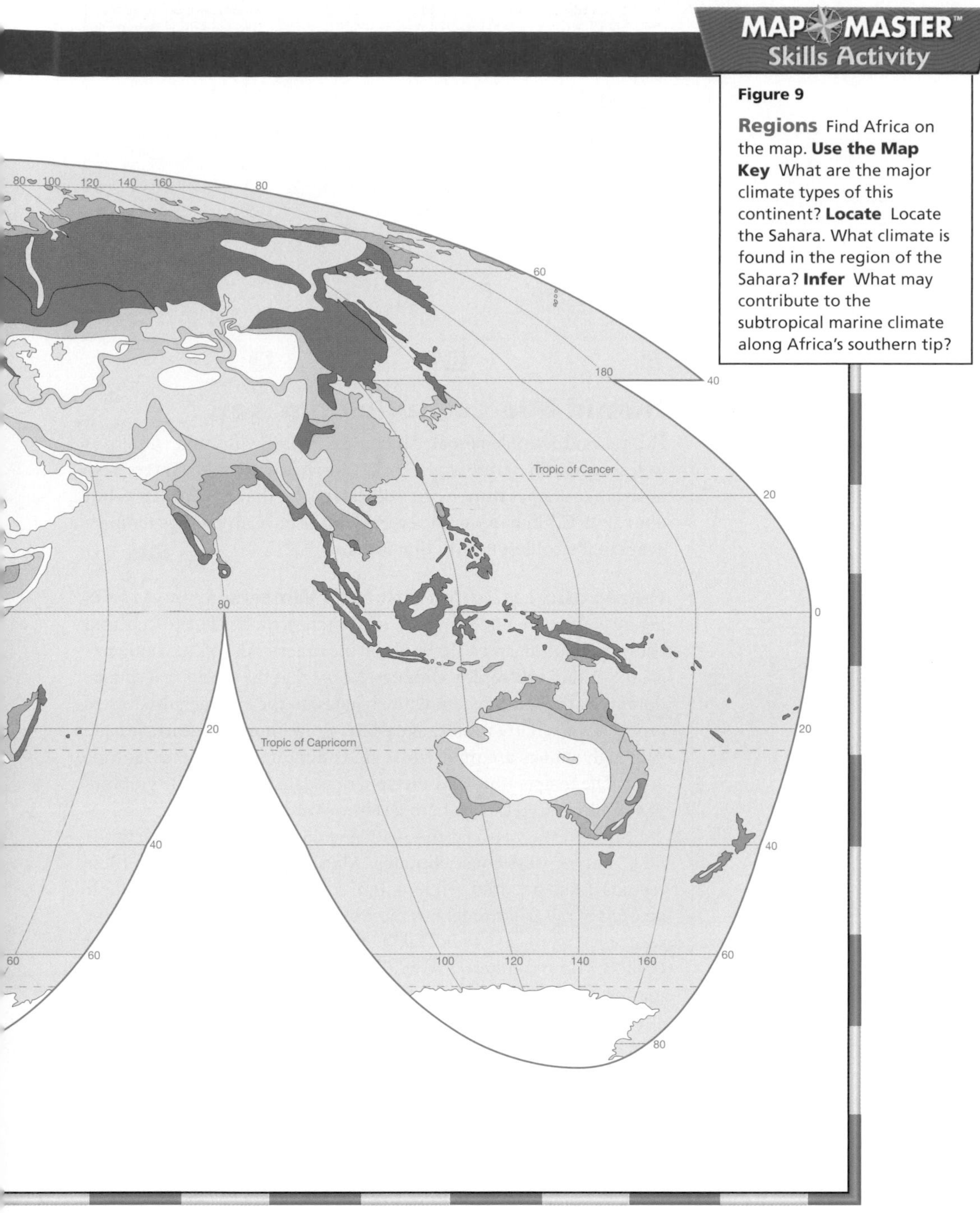

MAP MASTER™ Skills Activity

Figure 9

Regions Find Africa on the map. **Use the Map Key** What are the major climate types of this continent? **Locate** Locate the Sahara. What climate is found in the region of the Sahara? **Infer** What may contribute to the subtropical marine climate along Africa's southern tip?

MAP MASTER™ Skills Activity

Answers

Use the Map Key The major climate types are tropical and dry. A tiny portion of the cape has a subtropical climate. **Locate** The Sahara covers much of the northern part of Africa. The climate in the region of the Sahara is dry desert. **Infer** The subtropical climate at the cape is the result of the onshore flow of warm, ocean air.

Build Science Skills L2

Inferring Invite students to look back at Figure 2 on p. 589 and compare it with Figure 9. Ask: **Since there are only three main zones in Figure 2, why are there so many climate regions in Figure 9?** *(The three zones in Figure 2 are general temperature zones; the climate zones in Figure 9 are based on precipitation as well.)* **Which climate region(s) in Figure 9 span more than one of the zones in Figure 2?** *(dry climates)*
Logical, Visual

Humid Mid-Latitude Climates

Use Visuals **L1**

Figure 10 Use this diagram to explain the format of climate graphs. Go over what each axis represents. Make sure students understand that temperature is shown using a line with units on the left axis. Precipitation is shown using bars with units on the right axis. Ask: **In which month does Capetown have the lowest temperature?** *(July)* **The highest temperature?** *(January)* **In which month does Guangzhou have the least precipitation?** *(December)* **The most precipitation?** *(June)*
Visual, Logical

Modeling Humid Climates **L2**

Purpose Students observe how temperature affects the humidity of a climate.

Materials water, 2 small plastic bowls, transparent plastic wrap, rubber band

Procedure Place equal amounts of water into each of two small plastic bowls. Cover each bowl with transparent plastic wrap and use a rubber band to hold each piece of wrap in place. Place one bowl in a warm location such as a sunny windowsill or near a radiator. Place the other bowl in a cool location. Ask students to predict in which bowl more evaporation will occur. *(Most students will say "the warm one.")* The next day, have students observe the two bowls. Ask them what they observed. *(The warmer bowl had more condensation on the underside of the plastic wrap.)* Ask students how they think this relates to the differences between humid tropical climates and humid mid-latitude climates. *(The higher temperatures in the tropics lead to greater evaporation and greater rainfall than in the mid-latitudes.)*

Expected Outcome The warmer bowl will have more condensation on the underside of the plastic wrap.
Logical, Visual

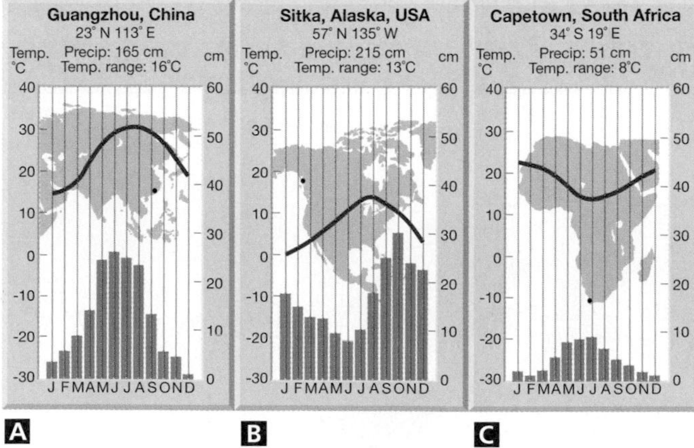

Figure 10 Each of these graphs shows typical climate data of the mid-latitude climates with mild winters. Graph **A** shows a humid subtropical climate. Graph **B** shows a marine west coast climate. Graph **C** shows a dry-summer subtropical climate.

Humid Mid-Latitude Climates

Humid mid-latitude climates include climates with mild winters as well as those with severe winters. **Climates with mild winters have an average temperature in the coldest month that is below 18°C but above −3°C. Climates with severe winters have an average temperature in the coldest month that is below −3°C.**

Humid Mid-Latitude With Mild Winters As you can see in Figure 9, there are three types of humid mid-latitude climates. Located between about 25° and 40° latitude on the eastern sides of the continents are the **humid subtropical climates.** Notice that the subtropical climate dominates the southeastern United States. In the summer, these areas experience hot, sultry weather as daytime temperatures are generally high. Although winters are mild, frosts are common in the higher-latitude areas. The temperature and precipitation data shown in the graph in Figure 10A are typical of a humid subtropical climate.

Coastal areas between about 40° and 65° north and south latitude have **marine west coast climates.** Maritime air masses over these regions result in mild winters and cool summers with an ample amount of rainfall throughout the year. In North America, the marine west coast climate extends as a narrow belt from northernmost California into southern Alaska. The data in Figure 10B are typical of marine west coast climates.

As you can see in Figure 9, regions with **dry-summer subtropical climates** are located between about 30° and 45° latitude. These climatic regions are unique because they are the only humid climate that has a strong winter rainfall maximum, as shown in Figure 10C. In the United States, dry-summer subtropical climate is found only in California. It is sometimes referred to as a mediterranean climate.

Describe the conditions typical of a humid subtropical climate.

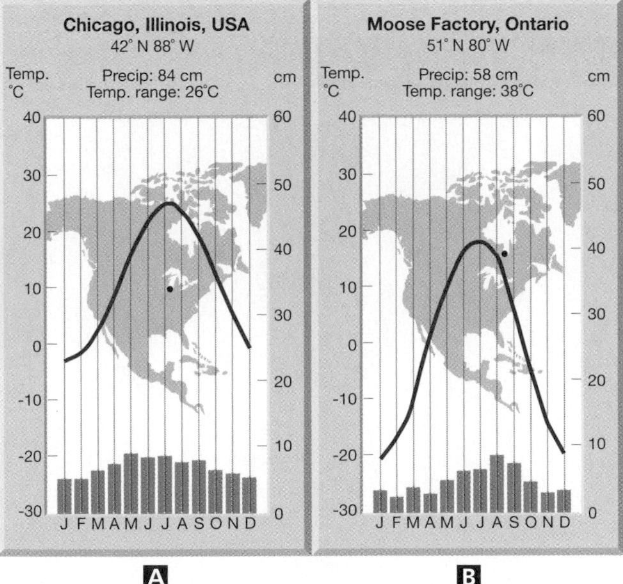

Figure 11 Graph **A** displays data typical of a humid continental climate. The trends shown in graph **B** are typical of a subarctic climate.
Interpreting Graphs *What are the typical temperatures and amounts of precipitation for Chicago, Illinois, in May and June?*

Humid Mid-Latitude With Severe Winters There are two types of humid mid-latitude climates with severe winters: the humid continental climates and the subarctic climates. Continental landmasses strongly influence both of these climates. As a result, such climates are absent in the Southern Hemisphere. There, oceans dominate the middle-latitude zone. Locate the regions having a humid continental climate, which are shown in blue, on Figure 9. Note that areas with such climates lie between approximately 40° and 50° north latitude. As you can see in Figure 11A the winters are severe, while the summers are typically quite warm. Note, too, that precipitation is generally greater in summer than in winter.

North of the humid continental climate and south of the tundra is an extensive **subarctic climate** region. From Figure 9, you can see that this climate zone covers a broad expanse. Such climates stretch from western Alaska to Newfoundland in North America, and from Norway to the Pacific coast of Russia in Eurasia. Winters in these regions are long and bitterly cold. By contrast, summers in the subarctic are remarkably warm but very short. The extremely cold winters and relatively warm summers combine to produce the highest annual temperature ranges on Earth.

Compare and contrast two types of humid mid-latitude climates with severe winters.

Facts and Figures

Winters in the subarctic region are nearly as cold as those in polar regions. Winter minimum temperatures are among the lowest ever recorded outside the ice sheets of Greenland and Antarctica. In fact, for many years the world's lowest temperature was attributed to Verkhoyansk in east central Siberia, where the temperature dropped to −68°C on February 5 and 7, 1892. Over a 23-year period, this same station had an average monthly minimum of −62°C during January. Although exceptional, these temperatures illustrate the extreme cold that envelops the subarctic region in winter.

L2

Students may think that the term *taiga* refers to the entire coniferous forest of the Northern Hemisphere. Explain that although some books use the term that way, the *taiga* is really only the northern part of the coniferous forest. The word *taiga* is Russian, and it refers to the forests just south of the tundra. The term *boreal forest* is also often used for this region.
Logical, Verbal

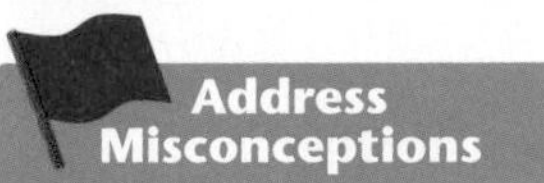

L2

Students may think that it never gets very hot in subarctic areas such as Alaska. Dispel this misconception by pointing out that summer temperatures in southern Alaska are usually between 15°–25° C). Also tell students that the record high temperature in Alaska is 38°C. This record was set on June 27, 1915, in Fort Yukon, a town along the Arctic Circle in the interior of Alaska.
Logical

Use Community Resources

L2

Invite a climatologist from a local college into the classroom to discuss climate regions and the factors that cause each one. Ask students to prepare questions in advance to ask the visitor.
Interpersonal

Answer to . . .

Figure 11 *Temperatures range from about 10°C to 20°C. Precipitation is nearly 10 cm.*

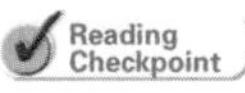
Hot, sultry summers with high daytime temperatures and afternoon or evening thunderstorms are common. Winters are mild, and the precipitation that falls then is in the form of snow.

Both are strongly influenced by continental landmasses. Humid continental climates experience severe temperatures, and precipitation is generally greater in summer than in winter. Subarctic climates have winters that are long and bitterly cold and summers that are remarkably warm but short. These differences combine to produce the highest annual temperature ranges on Earth.

Dry Climates

MAP MASTER™ Skills Activity

Answers

Locate 1. Atacama Desert; 2. Sonoran Desert; 3. Simpson Desert; 4. Great Indian Desert; 5. Namib Desert and Kalahari Desert

Describe About 40 percent of Australia is desert.

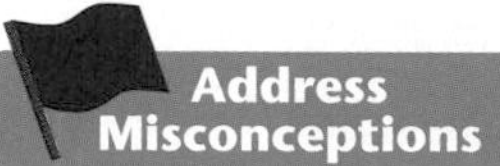

Address Misconceptions **L2**

Students may think that the terms *arid* and *drought* have roughly the same meaning. Explain that droughts occur temporarily as a result of atmospheric conditions. In contrast, arid regions are those where low rainfall is a permanent feature of the climate.
Logical, Verbal

Extent of Dry Climate Zones — MAP MASTER™ Skills Activity

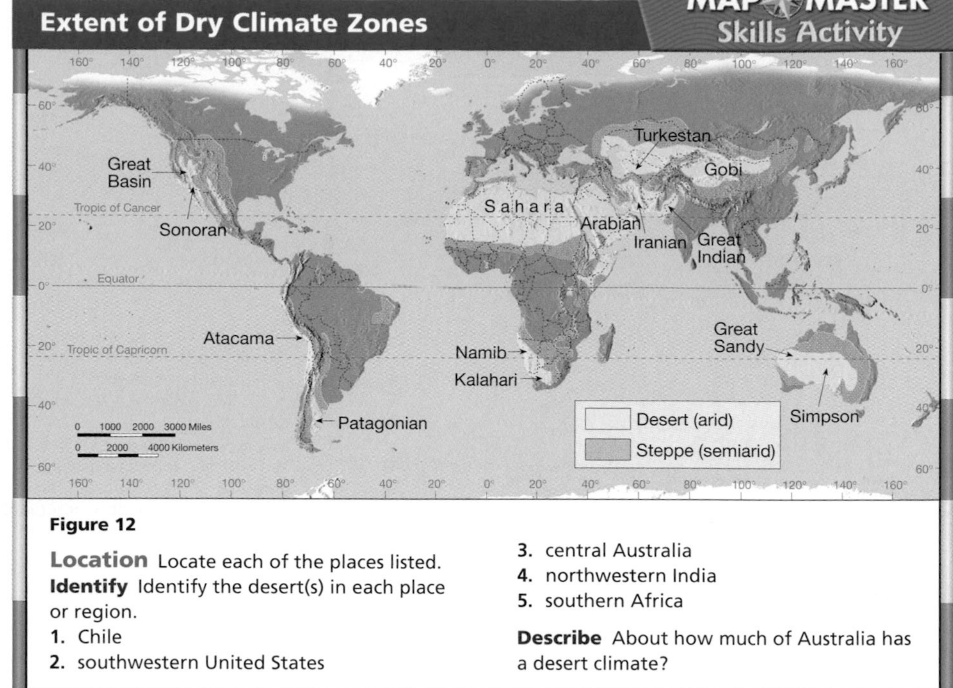

Figure 12

Location Locate each of the places listed.
Identify Identify the desert(s) in each place or region.
1. Chile
2. southwestern United States
3. central Australia
4. northwestern India
5. southern Africa

Describe About how much of Australia has a desert climate?

Q *Are deserts always hot?*

A Deserts can certainly be hot places. The record high temperature for the United States, 57°C, was set at Death Valley, California. However, deserts also experience very cold temperatures. The average daily minimum in January in Phoenix, Arizona, is 1.7°C, a temperature just barely above freezing. At Ulan Bator in Mongolia's Gobi Desert, the average high temperature in January is only −19°C!

Dry Climates

A dry climate is one in which the yearly precipitation is not as great as the potential loss of water by evaporation. In other words, dryness is not only related to annual rainfall, but is also a function of evaporation. Evaporation, in turn, is closely dependent upon temperature. There are two types of dry climates: arid or desert and semi-arid or steppe, as shown in Figure 12. These two climate types are classified as BW and BS, respectively, in the Köppen classification system. Arid and semi-arid climates have many features in common. In fact, the difference between them is slight. The steppe is a marginal and more humid variant of the desert. The steppe represents a transition zone that surrounds the desert and separates it from humid climates.

Dry climates exist as the result of the global distribution of air pressure and winds. In regions near the tropics of Cancer and Capricorn, air is subsiding. When air sinks, it is compressed and warmed. Such conditions are opposite of those needed for clouds to form precipitation. As a result, regions with dry climates experience mostly clear, sunny skies and dry climates. Other dry areas including the Great Basin in North America and the Gobi Desert of Eurasia occur where prevailing winds meet mountain barriers. These arid regions are called rain shadow deserts.

Polar Climates

Polar climates are those in which the mean temperature of the warmest month is below 10°C. Winters in these regions are periods of perpetual night, or nearly so, making temperatures at most polar locations extremely cold. During the summer months, temperatures remain cool despite the long days. Very little precipitation falls in polar regions. Evaporation, too, in these areas is limited.

There are two types of polar climates. The tundra climate, like that shown in Figure 13, is a treeless region found almost exclusively in the Northern Hemisphere. The ice cap climate does not have a single monthly mean above 0°C. Little vegetation grows and the landscape in these regions is covered by permanent ice and snow. Ice cap climates occur in scattered high mountain areas and in Greenland and Antarctica.

Figure 13 Tundra North of Nome, Alaska Tundra plant life includes mostly mosses, shrubs, and flowering herbs.

Highland Climates

The climate types discussed so far are very similar from place to place and extend over large areas. Some climates, however, are localized, which means that they are much different from climates in surrounding areas. One such climate is a highland climate. Conditions of highland climates often vary from one place to another. For example, south-facing slopes are warmer than north-facing slopes, and air on the windward sides of mountains is wetter than air on the leeward sides. **In general, highland climates are cooler and wetter than nearby areas at lower elevations.** Locate the highland climate regions on Figure 9. What do they all have in common?

For: Links on climates of the world
Visit: www.SciLinks.org
Web Code: cjn-6212

Section 21.2 Assessment

Reviewing Concepts

1. What is the Köppen climate classification system?
2. Describe the characteristics of humid tropical climates.
3. What are some characteristics of humid mid-latitude climates?
4. What defines a dry climate?
5. What are the characteristics of polar climates?
6. How do highland climates compare with nearby lowlands?

Critical Thinking

7. **Identifying** Use Figure 9 to identify the climate type of your city. Describe some characteristics of your city's climate type.
8. **Formulating Conclusions** Can tundra climates exist at low latitudes? Explain.

Writing in Science

Explanatory Paragraph Write a paragraph in which you explain why Antarctica can be classified as a desert.

Polar Climates

Build Science Skills L2

Inferring Have students refer back to Figure 9 on pp. 594–595. Discuss why polar climates occur where they do. Ask: **Why are tundra climates found almost exclusively in the Northern Hemisphere?** *(There is very little land in the Southern Hemisphere that is at the same latitude as tundra climates in the Northern Hemisphere.)*
Visual, Logical

Highland Climates

Build Science Skills L2

Applying Concepts Have students refer back to Section 21.1 to help them understand what causes highland climates. Ask: **What two main factors cause highland climates?** *(elevation and topography)* **What effect does elevation have on highland climates?** *(Temperature decreases with elevation, so highland climates are cooler than nearby climates at lower elevations.)*
Visual, Logical

3 ASSESS

Evaluate Understanding L2

Describe characteristics of various climate regions, and call on students to identify them. For example, if you say "very cold with no plants," students should respond "ice cap."

Reteach L1

Use Figure 9 to review the characteristics of each climate region and subregion.

Deserts are dry climates that are defined primarily by the amount of precipitation that falls rather than temperature. Antarctica and other areas in Earth's polar regions are deserts because they receive very little precipitation that does not evaporate much annually.

Section 21.2 Assessment

1. The Köppen system uses mean monthly and annual values of temperature and precipitation to classify climates.
2. Humid tropical climates have no winters. Every month has a mean temperature above 18°C and has a lot of precipitation.
3. Humid mid-latitude climates with mild winters have an average temperature in the coldest month that is below 18°C but above −3°C. Humid mid-latitude climates with severe winters have an average temperature in the coldest month that is below −3°C.
4. both the amount of precipitation that falls and the amount that can be lost as the result of evaporation
5. Polar climates are extremely cold, even in the summer months. Very little precipitation falls in polar regions, and evaporation is limited.
6. Highland climates generally are cooler and wetter than nearby places at lower elevations.
7. Answers will vary depending on your location. If necessary, have students use a map.
8. yes, at high elevations where temperatures are very low

Download a worksheet on climates of the world for students to complete, and find additional teacher support from NSTA SciLinks.

Section 21.3

1 FOCUS

Section Objectives

21.12 **Describe** natural processes that can cause changes in climate.
21.13 **Explain** the greenhouse effect.
21.14 **Define** global warming.
21.15 **List** some of the consequences of global warming.

Reading Focus

Build Vocabulary L2

Paraphrase Explain the meaning of the vocabulary words by using terms that are familiar to students. For example, tell students that *global* can be though of as "globe-like." Point out a classroom globe as an example.

Reading Strategy L2

a. Volcanic Eruptions
b. Possible increase in the amount of solar radiation reflected back to space can cause lower temperatures.
c. Ocean Circulation
d. Changes can result in short-term climate fluctuations.
e. Earth Motions
f. Geographic changes in Earth's land and water due to Earth motion cause changes in climate.

2 INSTRUCT

Natural Processes That Change Climate

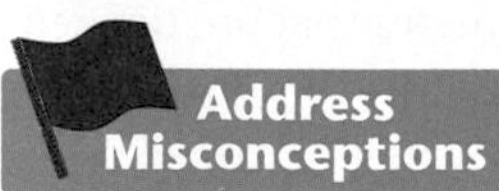

L2

Students may think that Earth's climate was exactly the same for millions of years, and only changed recently as a result of human activity. Point out that there have been many major natural changes in Earth's history. For example, during the Ice Ages that began 2 to 3 million years ago Earth's climate was much colder. At other times Earth's climate has been much warmer than it is now. Emphasize that there are many different causes of climate change, and that human action is just one of them. **Logical**

21.3 Climate Changes

Reading Focus

Key Concepts

- Describe natural processes that can cause changes in climate.
- What is the greenhouse effect?
- What is global warming?
- What are some of the consequences of global warming?

Vocabulary

- greenhouse effect
- global warming

Reading Strategy

Identifying Cause and Effect Copy the table. Identify the causes and effects of climate change presented in this section.

Climate Changes	
Causes	**Effects**
a. ?	b. ?
c. ?	d. ?
e. ?	f. ?

Like most conditions on Earth, climate is always changing. Some of these changes are short-term. Others occur over long periods of geologic time. Some climate changes are the result of natural processes, such as the volcanic eruption shown in Figure 14. Others are related to human activities. In this section, you will learn about some of the ways in which climate changes.

Natural Processes That Change Climate

Many different natural processes can cause a climate to change. Some of the climate-changing processes that you will learn about include volcanic eruptions as well as changes in ocean circulation, solar activity, and Earth motions.

Figure 14 Eruption of Mount Pinatubo

Volcanic Eruptions As you can see in Figure 14, volcanic eruptions can emit large volumes of ash and dust into Earth's atmosphere. What you can't see in the photograph is that volcanic eruptions also send minute particles containing sulfur, into the air. If the volume of these very fine particles called aerosols, is great enough, it can cause short-term changes in Earth's surface temperature. Can you hypothesize why? **The presence of aerosols (volcanic ash, dust, and sulfur-based aerosols) in the air increases the amount of solar radiation that is reflected back into space. This causes Earth's lower atmosphere to cool.**

Ocean Circulation Recall from Chapter 19 that El Niño is a change in ocean circulation that causes parts of the eastern tropical Pacific Ocean to become warmer than usual. **These changes in ocean circulation also can result in short-term climate fluctuations.** For example, some areas that are normally arid receive large amounts of rain during El Niño. Refer to Figure 15. Also, some regions that receive abundant precipitation may experience dry periods when ocean circulation patterns change.

Figure 15 Effect of El Niño In 1998, bad weather conditions and flooding in Alabama were attributed to El Niño.

Solar Activity The most studied hypotheses for the causes of climate change are based on changes in the output of solar energy. When the sun is most active, it contains dark blemishes called sunspots. The formation of sunspots appears to correspond with warm periods in Europe and North America. Although variations in solar output may cause short-term climatic change, no evidence for long-term variations due to solar activity exist.

Earth Motions A number of Earth motions are thought to cause changes in climate. Most of these changes are long-term changes. Tectonic plate movements, for example, cause the crust and upper mantle to move slowly over Earth's surface. These movements cause ocean basins to open and close. Plate movements also cause changes in the positions of landmasses. **These geographic changes in Earth's land and water bodies cause changes in climate.**

Changes in the shape of Earth's orbit and the tilt of Earth on its axis are other Earth motions that affect global climates. Earth's orbit, or path around the sun, is always elliptical. But over a 100,000-year period, the path becomes more and then less elliptical. This change in shape brings Earth closer to and then farther from the sun. This affects global climates. Like its orbit, the tilt of Earth on its axis changes about 2 degrees over a 41,000-year period. Because the angle of tilt varies, the severity of the seasons also changes. The smaller the tilt, the smaller the temperature difference between summer and winter.

Identify four natural processes that can result in climate changes.

Build Reading Literacy L1

Refer to **p. 334D** in **Chapter 12,** which provides the guidelines for outlining.

Outline Have students read the text in this section about climate change. Then, have students use the headings as major divisions in an outline. Have students refer to their outlines when answering the questions in the Section 21.3 Assessment.
Verbal, Logical

Teacher Demo

Earth's Motions and Climate L2

Purpose Students observe how changes in Earth's motions affect Earth's climate.

Materials globe, lamp

Procedure If necessary, review what causes the seasons on pp. 481–482 in Chapter 17. Use a globe and a lamp to demonstrate how changes in the shape of Earth's orbit and tilt of Earth's axis can affect global climate. First, set the lamp in the middle of a table and turn it on. Move the globe around the lamp in a circular motion. Then move the globe around the lamp in a more elliptical (oval) motion. Ask students how they think this movement would affect climates. *(It could increase the differences between the seasons.)* Next, increase the tilt of the globe's axis and again move the globe around the lamp. Ask students how they think this would affect climates. *(It would decrease the total amount of sunlight Earth would receive, and therefore lower global temperatures.)*

Expected Outcome Students will understand how changes in Earth's motions affect Earth's climate.
Logical, Visual

Customize for Inclusion Students

Gifted Many scientists think that global warming is not entirely caused by carbon dioxide emissions. They predict that global warming will have positive consequences for some parts of the world. There is also debate over the relative benefits of various attempts to slow global warming. Invite gifted students to research different views of global warming and report back to the class. Some Web sites where they can begin their research include:
http://www.cato.org/current/global-warming/index.html
http://www.marshall.org/subcategory.php?id=9
http://cfa-www.harvard.edu/press/pr0310.html

Answer to . . .

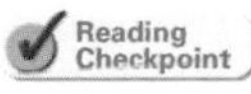

Volcanic eruptions, changes in global ocean circulation, solar activity, and certain Earth motions can cause changes in climate.

Human Impact on Climate Changes

Address Misconceptions

L2

Students may be misled by the term *greenhouse effect*. The term may make them think that the atmosphere is heated in exactly the same way as a greenhouse. The term was coined to describe the process that heats the atmosphere because it was once thought that greenhouses were heated in a similar way. One factor in heating a greenhouse is the blocking of heat radiation. However, a more important factor is that the glass of the greenhouse prevents warm air from escaping by convection.
Logical

Use Visuals

L1

Figure 16 Use these graphs to explain how carbon dioxide emissions affect carbon dioxide concentrations in the atmosphere. Make sure that students understand that the emissions amounts and atmospheric concentrations in graph B are shown in different units. Ask: **What unit is used for carbon dioxide emissions?** *(gigatons of carbon/yr)* **What unit is used for carbon dioxide concentrations in the atmosphere?** *(ppm, or parts per million)* **What does graph C show?** *(carbon dioxide concentrations in the atmosphere)*
Visual, Logical

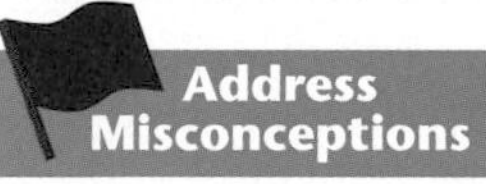

Address Misconceptions

L2

Students often think that the greenhouse effect and global warming are the same phenomenon. Emphasize that the greenhouse effect occurs naturally and is essential to keeping the atmosphere warm enough for living things to survive on Earth. Global warming, on the other hand, is an increase in the temperature of Earth's atmosphere that may be caused or influenced by human activities.
Logical

Human Impact on Climate Changes

Natural processes have certainly contributed to many climatic changes throughout Earth's 4.6-billion year history. These processes will also be responsible for some of the future shifts in Earth's climates. Besides these processes of nature, human activities have contributed and will contribute to global climatic change.

The Greenhouse Effect

The greenhouse effect is a natural warming of both Earth's lower atmosphere and Earth's surface. The major gases involved in the greenhouse effect are water vapor and carbon dioxide. These greenhouse gases, as they are often called, are transparent to incoming solar radiation and therefore much of this energy reaches Earth's surface. Most of this energy is then reradiated skyward. The greenhouse gases are good absorbers of Earth's radiation, which accounts for the warm temperatures of the lower atmosphere.

The greenhouse effect is very important because it makes life as we know it possible on Earth. Without this effect, Earth would be much too cold to support any kind of complex life forms. However, an increase in the greenhouse effect could also prove devastating to Earth's billions of organisms.

Studies indicate that human activities for the past 200 or so years have had a huge impact on the greenhouse effect. As you can see in Figure 16, carbon dioxide levels in the air have risen at a rapid pace since about 1850. Much of this greenhouse gas has been added by the burning of fossil fuels such as coal, petroleum, and natural gas. The clearing of forests also contributes to an increase in carbon dioxide because this gas is released when vegetation is burned or when it decays.

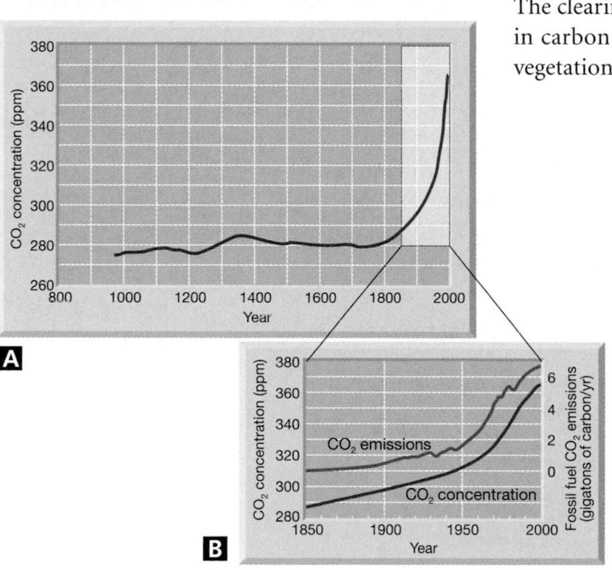

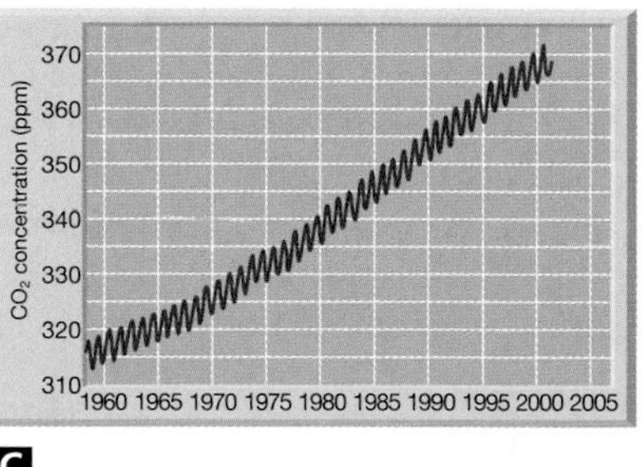

Figure 16 The rapid increase in carbon dioxide concentration since 1850 has closely followed the increase in carbon dioxide emissions from burning fossil fuels. **Inferring** ***What do you think initiated this increase in carbon dioxide levels?***

Facts and Figures

Human influence on regional and global climates likely began long before the beginning of the modern industrial period. There is evidence that humans have been modifying the environment over extensive areas for thousands of years. The use of fire and the overgrazing of marginal lands by domestic animals have reduced the abundance and distribution of plants. Altering ground cover has affected important climate factors such as surface albedo, evaporation rates, and surface winds.

Global Warming **As a result of increases in carbon dioxide levels, as well as other greenhouse gases, global temperatures have increased. This increase is called global warming.** Refer to Figure 17. Note that during the twentieth century, Earth's average surface temperatures increased about 0.6°C. Scientists predict that by the year 2100, temperatures will increase by 1.4°C to 5.8°C. How will these temperature increases affect Earth?

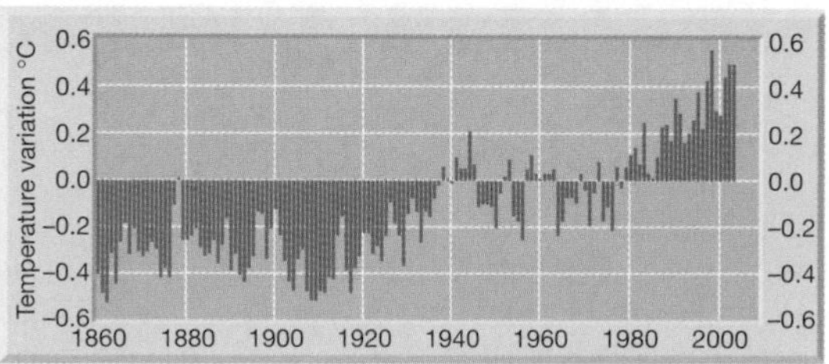

Figure 17 Increases in the levels of greenhouse gases have caused changes in Earth's average surface temperatures.
Interpreting Graphs ***What year was the warmest to date?***

Warmer surface temperatures increase evaporation rates. This, in turn, increases the amount of water vapor in the atmosphere. Water vapor is an even more powerful absorber of radiation emitted by Earth than is carbon dioxide. Therefore, more water vapor in the air will magnify the effect of carbon dioxide and other gases.

Temperature increases will also cause sea ice to melt. Ice reflects more incoming solar radiation than liquid water does. The melting of the ice will cause a substantial increase in the solar energy absorbed at the surface. This, in turn, will magnify the temperature increase created by higher levels of greenhouse gases. The melting of sea ice and ice sheets will also cause a global rise in sea level. This will lead to shoreline erosion and coastal flooding.

Scientists also expect that weather patterns will change as a result of the projected global warming. More intense heat waves and droughts in some regions and fewer such events in other places are also predicted. What other consequences of global warming do you think might occur?

For: Links on the carbon cycle/global warming
Visit: www.SciLinks.org
Web Code: cjn-6213

Section 21.3 Assessment

Reviewing Concepts

1. Describe four natural processes that can cause climate change.
2. What is the greenhouse effect?
3. What is global warming?
4. What are some of the possible effects of global warming?

Critical Thinking

5. **Formulating Hypotheses** Which would have a longer effect on climate changes—volcanic ash and dust or the same volume of sulfur-based aerosols? Why?
6. **Formulating Conclusions** How do you think cloud cover might change as the result of global warming?
7. **Synthesizing** How might global warming affect Earth's inhabitants, including humans?

Writing in Science

Persuasive Paragraphs Write at least two paragraphs to persuade your friends and family to reduce their consumption of fossil fuels. Be sure to explain why the usage of such energy sources should be reduced.

3 ASSESS

Evaluate Understanding L2

Ask students to describe three natural processes that change climate. Have them describe how each process works.

Reteach L2

Have students write several sentences that briefly explain what the greenhouse effect is.

Answers will vary but should include an explanation of how burning fossil fuels is thought to be increasing global temperatures and why reducing the usage of fossil fuels will slow this increase.

Go Online NSTA SCILINKS

Download a worksheet on the carbon cycle/global warming for students to complete, and find additional teacher support from NSTA SciLinks.

Answer to . . .

Figure 16 *Industrialization has greatly contributed to the rise in carbon dioxide levels in Earth's atmosphere.*

Figure 17 *1998*

Section 21.3 Assessment

1. volcanic eruptions (gases and solids trap and radiate solar energy back to space); ocean circulation patterns cause changes in atmospheric circulation that can result in drought and flooding; changes in solar activity coincide with global changes in temperature; Earth motions, including tectonism and revolution, also cause climates to change.
2. The greenhouse effect is a natural warming of both Earth's lower atmosphere and its surface that is caused by complex reactions between gases and particles in the air.
3. the term for an increase in global temperatures, due to increased levels of greenhouse gases
4. short-term and long-term changes in temperature and precipitation patterns that can result in both wetter-than-normal periods and drier-than-normal periods; a rise in sea level; an increase in shoreline erosion
5. sulfur-based aerosols tend to remain suspended in the air longer than their solid counterparts.
6. Global warming would probably produce an increase in cloud cover due to the higher moisture content of the air. Clouds would also produce opposite effects: they could diminish the amount of solar energy available to heat the atmosphere, and they could absorb and emit radiation that would otherwise be lost from the troposphere.
7. It could harm or kill ocean organisms; cause both land and water habitats to shift or be destroyed; increase the spread of diseases; and increase drought, heat waves, and flooding.

How the Earth Works

1 FOCUS

Objectives

In this feature, students will
- describe where the world's coniferous forests are located.
- recognize the features that enable conifers to withstand long, cold winters.
- identify the behaviors and adaptations that enable animals to survive in northern coniferous forests.

Reading Focus

Build Vocabulary L2

Word Origins Point out to students that *coniferous* sounds very much like another scientific term, *carnivorous.* Have them contrast the origins of these words. *(*Coniferous *comes from Latin and Greek roots that mean "cone-bearing."* Carnivorous *comes from the Latin words* caro, *which means "flesh," and* vorare, *which means "to swallow up.")* Encourage students to use both words correctly in sentences.

2 INSTRUCT

Bellringer L2

Have students list three features that make evergreen trees different from other trees. *(Lists might include pointy leaves or needles, pine cones, and staying green all year.)* Have students list types of trees found in their region. Then ask: **Are the trees you listed conifers or deciduous trees? How do you know?** **Verbal, Logical**

How the Earth Works

Coniferous Forests

The world's largest forests extend across the far north, where winters can last for eight months. These dense **coniferous forests** consist of spruces, pines, and other trees that carry their seeds in cones. They are particularly suited for coping with cold conditions. Animals in northern forests find plentiful food during the long days of summer, but the season is brief and cold weather soon returns. To survive the harsh winter, many animals migrate south, while others hibernate.

Distribution of northern coniferous forests

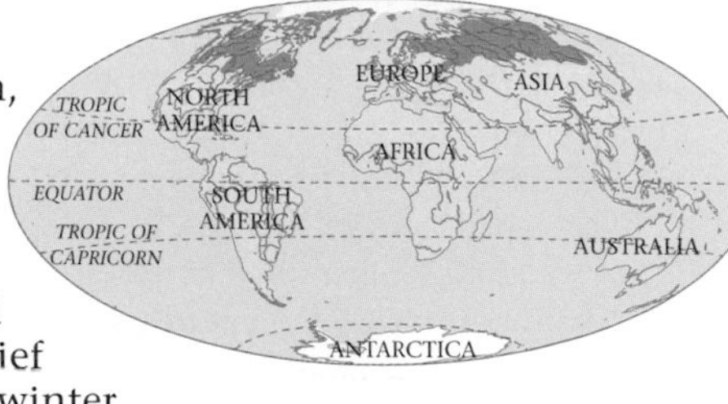

FORESTS AND LAKES
Coniferous forests often grow on land once covered by ice age glaciers. These glaciers scoured the ground, scraping away soil and creating rounded hills and hollows. When the glaciers melted, the hills became covered with trees and the hollows turned into lakes.

CONIFER LEAVES
Most conifers have small evergreen leaves that are tough enough to withstand the coldest winters. A narrow shape helps the leaves to cope with strong winds.

White spruce

Waterlogged soil beneath trees is acidic and infertile.

Bobcat

PREDATORS
Mammals are relatively scarce in northern forests, so the **predators** that feed upon other animals sometimes have to cover vast distances to find food. Bobcats may roam many miles searching for small prey. Wolves hunt in packs for deer and other large mammals.

604 Chapter 21

Customize for Inclusion Students

Gifted Mammals are not the only animals that hibernate in winter. Many fish, amphibians, and reptiles are also hibernators. Divide students into groups and have each find out how one type of animal hibernates. Have each group explain how that type of hibernation differs from mammal hibernation.

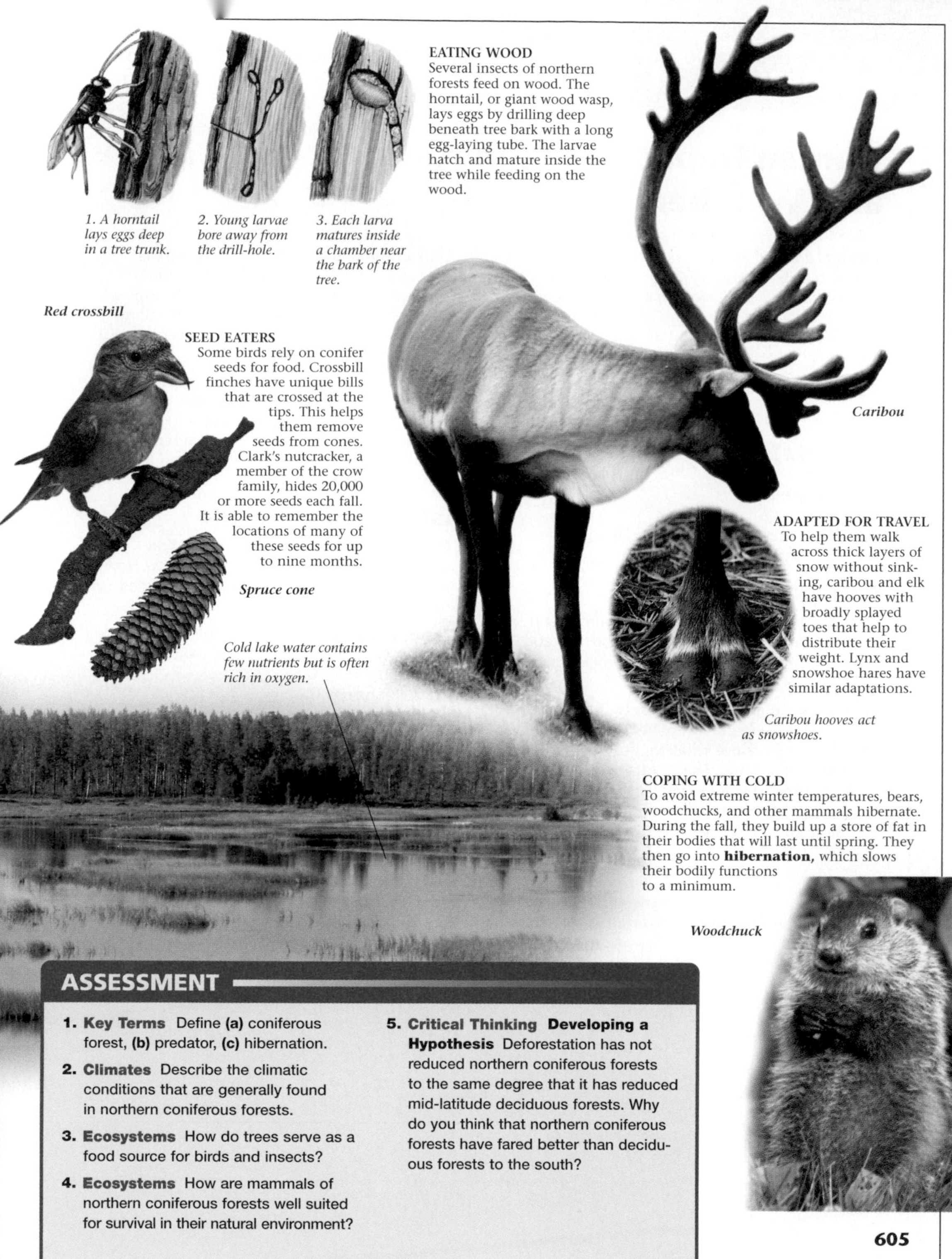

EATING WOOD
Several insects of northern forests feed on wood. The horntail, or giant wood wasp, lays eggs by drilling deep beneath tree bark with a long egg-laying tube. The larvae hatch and mature inside the tree while feeding on the wood.
1. A horntail lays eggs deep in a tree trunk.
2. Young larvae bore away from the drill-hole.
3. Each larva matures inside a chamber near the bark of the tree.
Red crossbill
SEED EATERS
Some birds rely on conifer seeds for food. Crossbill finches have unique bills that are crossed at the tips. This helps them remove seeds from cones. Clark's nutcracker, a member of the crow family, hides 20,000 or more seeds each fall. It is able to remember the locations of many of these seeds for up to nine months.
Spruce cone
Cold lake water contains few nutrients but is often rich in oxygen.
Caribou
ADAPTED FOR TRAVEL
To help them walk across thick layers of snow without sinking, caribou and elk have hooves with broadly splayed toes that help to distribute their weight. Lynx and snowshoe hares have similar adaptations.
Caribou hooves act as snowshoes.
COPING WITH COLD
To avoid extreme winter temperatures, bears, woodchucks, and other mammals hibernate. During the fall, they build up a store of fat in their bodies that will last until spring. They then go into **hibernation,** which slows their bodily functions to a minimum.
Woodchuck

ASSESSMENT

1. **Key Terms** Define **(a)** coniferous forest, **(b)** predator, **(c)** hibernation.
2. **Climates** Describe the climatic conditions that are generally found in northern coniferous forests.
3. **Ecosystems** How do trees serve as a food source for birds and insects?
4. **Ecosystems** How are mammals of northern coniferous forests well suited for survival in their natural environment?
5. **Critical Thinking Developing a Hypothesis** Deforestation has not reduced northern coniferous forests to the same degree that it has reduced mid-latitude deciduous forests. Why do you think that northern coniferous forests have fared better than deciduous forests to the south?

605

Build Science Skills L2

Have students read the introductory paragraph. Ask: **What is the feature that all conifers share?** *(They carry their seeds in cones.)* Then make a list on the board of all the conifers they can name. *(Possible answers: spruce, pine, juniper, cedar, sequoia, redwood, fir, and cypress)* **Logical**

3 ASSESS

Evaluate Understanding L2

Have students create a three-column chart about the types of animals that live in coniferous forests. The columns should be labeled: "Type of Animal," "Feature or Habit," and "How It Promotes Survival." Have students complete the chart using information from the feature. Ask them to write a paragraph describing the plant and animal life in a coniferous forest.

Reteach L1

Have students collect or draw the needles of different kinds of conifers. Then have them write a paragraph that explains how the leaves are well adapted for cold climates. Display collections and paragraphs in the classroom.

Assessment

1. (a) large, dense forests made of trees that carry their seeds in cones; **(b)** animals that feed on other animals; **(c)** a state in which an animal's body functions slow to a minimum for a season
2. Winters are long and cold; summers are brief.
3. Some insects eat wood. Some birds eat conifer seeds.
4. Some mammals, such as elk, have splayed toes that help them walk on snow. Other mammals build up stores of fat during the fall that will last until spring. In winter they hibernate.
5. Sample answer: Fewer people have wanted to settle in cold, northern areas. The land is not suited to farming, so humans have not cut these forests to clear land.

Exploration Lab

Human Impact on Climate and Weather L2

Objective
After completing this activity, students will be able to understand how human activity changes Earth's climates.

Skills Focus Calculating, Measuring, Using Tables, Analyzing Data

Class Time 30 minutes

Teaching Tip Review the tables and figures in this lab. Make sure students understand how to read the information properly. Ask: **What units are used for Table 1?** *(millions of metric tons/year)* **What information does Table 2 provide?** *(Average Climatic Changes Produced by Cities)* **What effect does this data represent?** *(the urban heat island effect)* **What data does Figure A provide?** *(emissions of three pollutants each year)* **What data does Figure B provide?** *(carbon dioxide concentration per year)*

Expected Outcome Students will use data to understand some of the ways that human activities change the atmosphere and Earth's climates.

Exploration Lab

Human Impact on Climate and Weather

Scientists are now closely monitoring how daily human activity is changing microclimates. There is concern that changing microclimates can have an effect on global climates. In this investigation, you will explore some of the ways that human activities are changing the atmosphere.

Problem How do we know that human activity is changing Earth's climates?

Materials
- paper
- pen or pencil

Skills Calculating, Measuring, Using Tables, Analyzing Data

Procedure
1. Table 1 lists many of the types, sources, and amounts of primary pollutants. Use this table to answer items 1, 2, 3, and 4 under Analyze and Conclude.
2. Look at Figure A. The pollutants listed are linked to a wide variety of negative health effects such as eye irritation, heart damage, and lung damage. The pollutants shown are also linked to reduced visibility, reduced crop yields, and damage to ecosystems. Study the figure and answer items 5, 6, and 7.
3. Look at Figure B. Scientists have noted the increasing levels of carbon dioxide in the atmosphere. Research continues to determine whether these increasing levels are affecting global climates. Use Figure B to answer item 8.
4. Look at Table 2. This table presents data on the effects of large cities on their surrounding microclimates. Temperatures in cities can be higher than the surrounding countryside. Meteorologists call this effect "the urban heat island". Study the data in the table and answer items 9, 10, and 11.

Analyze and Conclude
1. **Interpreting Data** What is the leading source (by weight) of primary pollutants? How many metric tons of this pollutant are added to the atmosphere each year?
2. **Interpreting Data** Which of the following is the most abundant primary pollutant?
   a. carbon monoxide
   b. sulfur oxides
3. **Calculating** Your answer for item 2 is what percentage of all primary pollutants?
   a. 25% b. 50% c. 75%
4. **Calculating** What is the approximate total weight (in million metric tons) of all primary pollutants added to the atmosphere?

Table 1 Estimated Nationwide Emissions (millions of metric tons/year)

Source	Carbon Monoxide	Partic-ulates	Sulfur Oxides	Volatile Organics	Nitrogen Oxides	Total
Transportation	43.5	1.6	1.0	5.1	7.3	58.5
Stationary Source Fuel Combustion	4.7	1.9	16.6	0.7	10.6	34.5
Industrial Processes	4.7	2.6	3.2	7.9	0.6	19.0
Solid Waste Disposal	2.1	0.3	0.0	0.7	0.1	3.2
Miscellaneous	7.2	1.2	0.0	2.8	0.2	11.4
Total	62.2	7.6	20.8	17.2	18.8	126.6

Source: U.S. Environmental Protection Agency

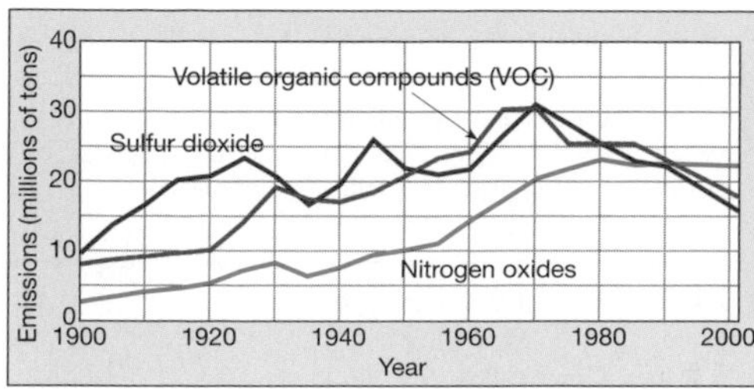

Figure A

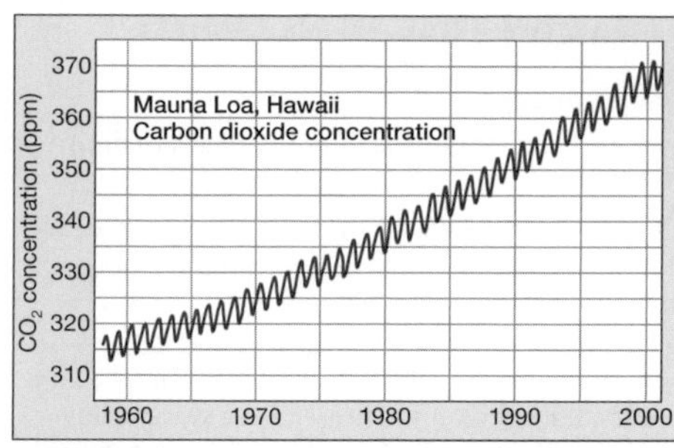

Figure B

5. **Interpreting Data** Describe the trend you see in the data for atmospheric pollutants prior to 1970.
6. **Interpreting Data** Describe the trend you see in the data for atmospheric pollutants since 1970.
7. **Inferring** Suggest a reason for the changing trend.
8. **Calculating** What has been the approximate percentage increase in atmospheric carbon dioxide near Mauna Loa since 1958?
9. **Interpreting Data** Compared to rural areas, which factors are increased by urbanization? Which factors are decreased?
10. **Interpreting Data** Of all of the factors shown, which shows the greatest increase due to urbanization?
11. **Predicting** Suggest a possible reason for each of the following effects on the weather that is influenced by a city.
    a. increased frequency of thunderstorms
    b. lower wind speed
    c. increased precipitation

Go Further Use the internet to search for climate data for your region. What trends do you see in the data since 1970? Suggest a hypothesis that could be used to test your conclusions.

Table 2 Average Climatic Changes Produced by Cities

Element	Comparison with Rural Areas
Particulate matter	10 times more
Temperature	
Annual mean	0.5–1.5°C higher
Winter	1–2°C higher
Solar radiation	15–30% less
Ultraviolet, winter	30% less
Ultraviolet, summer	5% less
Precipitation	5–15% more
Thunderstorm frequency	16% more
Winter	5% more
Summer	29% more
Relative humidity	6% lower
Winter	2% lower
Summer	8% lower
Cloudiness (frequency)	5–10% more
Fog (frequency)	60% more
Winter	100% more
Summer	30% more
Wind speed	25% lower
Calms	5–20% more

Source: After Landsberg, Changnon, and others.

Analyze and Conclude

1. transportation; 58.5 million metric tons
2. a
3. b
4. 126.6 million metric tons
5. Emissions of atmospheric pollutants were generally on the rise prior to 1970.
6. Atmospheric pollutant emissions have generally decreased since 1970.
7. Industrialization and increased transportation using fossil fuels increased CO_2 concentrations until 1970, when government regulations took effect and began lowering CO_2 concentrations.
8. net change: 370 ppm − 315 ppm = 55 ppm; 55 ppm ÷ 370 ppm = approximately 15 percent increase in atmospheric carbon dioxide
9. Increased: particulate matter, temperature, precipitation, thunderstorm frequency, cloudiness, fog, calms. Decreased: solar radiation, relative humidity, wind speed
10. fog in winter
11. a. Urban heating reduces the stability of the atmosphere.
b. Buildings impede the flow of air.
c. Urban heating reduces the stability of the atmosphere; there are more condensation nuclei from industrial pollution; buildings impede the movement of weather systems causing rain producing weather to linger.

Go Further

Accept all reasonable answers.
Logical

Chapter 21

Study Guide

Study Tip

Study With a Partner
Once in a while, study with a partner. Quiz each other, compare notes from class lectures, and go over homework answers. Also, discuss concepts that you need help understanding.

Thinking Visually

1. Colder climate
2. High elevation/mountains
3. Global warming
4. Rise in sea level
5. Short-term lower temperatures
6. More moderate climate

Assessment

Reviewing Content

(1) 3 (2) 4 (3) 1
(4) 2 (5) 3 (6) 1
(7) 1

Understanding Concepts

(8) arid or desert
(9) semiarid or steppe, marine west coast, humid subtropical, tropical wet and dry
(10) lower latitude and the effect of a large body of water
(11) Powered by the sun, the climate system is a complex exchange of energy and moisture among Earth's atmosphere, biosphere, hydrosphere, and lithosphere.
(12) The three major zones are the tropical, the temperate zones, and the polar regions. They differ in the intensity at which sunlight strikes the surface in the region. In the tropics, the sun's rays strike at almost 90° angles, causing this region to be warm all year round. In the temperature zones, the sun's energy strikes Earth at a smaller angle. This causes solar energy to be spread out over a larger area, causing these regions to experience moderate yearly temperatures. In the polar regions, solar energy strikes at a more acute angle, causing the light and heat to spread out over even a larger area. Therefore, the polar regions experience very low temperatures year-round.

CHAPTER 21

Study Guide

21.1 Factors That Affect Climate

Key Concepts

- As latitude increases, the intensity of solar energy decreases.
- The higher the elevation is, the colder the climate.
- Mountains play an important role in the amount of precipitation that falls over an area.
- Large bodies of water such as lakes and oceans have an important effect on the temperature of an area because the temperature of the water body influences the temperature of the air above it.
- Global winds affect climate because they distribute heat and moisture around Earth.
- Vegetation can affect both temperature and the precipitation patterns in an area.

Vocabulary

tropical zone, *p. 589;* temperate zone, *p. 589;* polar zone, *p. 589*

21.2 World Climates

Key Concepts

- The Köppen climate classification system uses mean values of temperature and precipitation to classify climates.
- Humid tropical climates have no winters.
- Humid mid-latitude climates with mild winters have an average temperature in the coldest month that is below 18°C but above −3°C. Humid mid-latitude climates with severe winters have an average temperature in the coldest month that is below −3°C.
- A dry climate is one in which the yearly precipitation is not as great as the potential loss of water by evaporation.
- Polar climates have a mean temperature in the warmest month that is below 10°C.
- Highland climates are generally cooler and wetter than nearby areas at lower elevations.

Vocabulary

Köppen climate classification system, *p. 592;* wet tropical climate, *p. 593;* tropical wet and dry climate, *p. 593;* humid subtropical climate, *p. 596;* marine west coast climate, *p. 596;* dry-summer subtropical climate, *p. 596;* subarctic climate, *p. 597*

21.3 Climate Changes

Key Concepts

- Aerosols, volcanic ash, dust, and sulfur-based aerosols in the air can cause a short-term cooling of the lower atmosphere.
- Changes in ocean circulation can result in short-term climate fluctuations.
- Changes in the shape of Earth's orbit and the tilt of Earth's axis affect global climates.
- The greenhouse effect is a natural warming of Earth's lower atmosphere and Earth's surface.
- As a result of increases in carbon dioxide levels, as well as other greenhouse gases, global temperatures have increased to cause global warming.
- Global warming causes changes in sea level.

Vocabulary

greenhouse effect, *p. 602;* global warming, *p. 603*

Thinking Visually

Identifying Causes and Effects Copy the table below onto a sheet of paper. Use the information in the chapter to complete the table.

Some Factors That Influence Climate	
Causes	**Effects**
1. Increase in latitude	1. ___?___
2. ___?___	2. Highland climate
3. Increase in greenhouse gases	3. ___?___
4. ___?___	4. More coastal erosion
5. Large volcanic eruption	5. ___?___
6. Nearby lake	6. ___?___

Chapter Assessment Resources

Print
Chapter Test, Chapter 21
Test Prep Resources, Chapter 21

Technology
Computer Test Bank, Chapter 21 Test
Online Text, Chapter 21
Go Online, PHSchool.com, Chapter 21

CHAPTER 21

NY Regents Content Item

Assessment

Interactive textbook with assessment at PHSchool.com

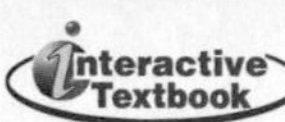

Reviewing Content

Choose the number that best answers the question or completes the statement.

1 Which of the following is true? NY
(1) Climates at high latitudes are very warm.
(2) A nearby lake causes a climate to be colder.
(3) Vegetation can increase the amount of precipitation that falls over an area.
(4) Places at lower elevations generally have lower temperatures.

2 Humid tropical climates always experience NY
(1) severe winters (2) dry summers
(3) low humidity (4) warm temperatures

3 In a dry climate, yearly precipitation is NY
(1) less than the rate of evaporation
(2) greater than the rate of evaporation
(3) greater in a desert than a steppe
(4) less than that in a polar climate

4 The greenhouse effect is best described as NY
(1) an increase in Earth's surface temperature
(2) a natural warming effect of the atmosphere
(3) a result of global warming
(4) any short-term change in climate

5 Recent global warming appears to be the result of NY
(1) changes in global wind patterns
(2) a decrease in the greenhouse effect
(3) increases in greenhouse gases in the air
(4) changes in Earth's revolution around the sun

6 Melting ice caps can result in which of the following? NY
(1) a rise in sea level
(2) a fall in sea level
(3) colder temperatures
(4) less precipitation

7 An increase in ocean temperatures can cause NY
(1) melting of sea ice
(2) most forms of ocean life to flourish
(3) a decrease in sea level
(4) global wind patterns to stabilize

Understanding Concepts

Use this map to answer questions 8–10.

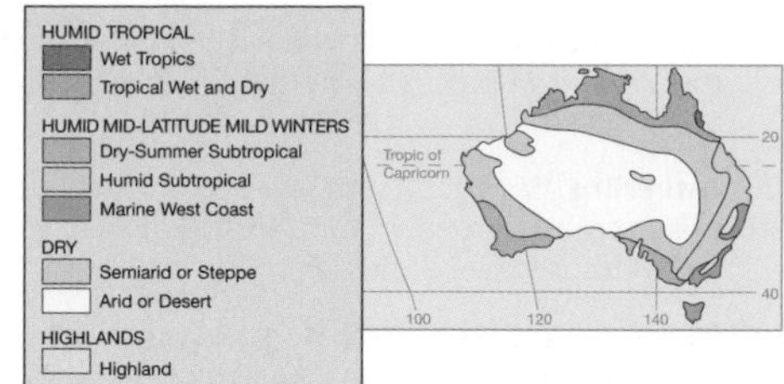

8 Describe the dominant climate in Australia. NY

9 Identify the type of climate found on the other parts of the continent. NY

10 What causes much of the east-southeastern part of the country to experience warm, humid, and marine west coast climates? NY

11 What powers Earth's climate system, and which of Earth's spheres are involved in this system? NY

12 Name the three major climate zones, and explain why their overall temperatures differ. NY

13 Why can two places at the same latitude have different climates? NY

14 What climate data are needed in order to classify a climate using the Köppen climate classification system? NY

15 Describe the characteristics of a wet tropical climate. NY

16 Describe the characteristics of a humid continental climate, and give one example of a place with such a climate. NY

17 Explain the greenhouse effect caused by Earth's atmosphere. NY

18 How have humans contributed to the increase in the levels of carbon dioxide in the atmosphere? NY

19 What is global warming? NY

20 How might global warming affect global precipitation? NY

Homework Guide

Section	Questions
1	1, 6, 7, 11–13, 21, 22
2	2, 3, 8–10, 14–16, 23–29
3	4, 5, 17–20, 30–32

(13) Latitude is only one factor that affects a climate. The places may be at different elevations and may have different topographies and different kinds and amounts of vegetative cover. Proximity to a body of water can also influence climate.
(14) Mean monthly and annual values of temperature and precipitation are used to classify climates in the Köppen scheme.
(15) Wet tropical climates have high temperatures and year-round precipitation because of the angle at which the sun strikes the area and because the winds that blow over these regions cause the warm, humid, unstable air to rise, cool, condense, and fall as precipitation.
(16) Areas with humid continental climates lie between approximately 40° and 50° north latitude. Both winter and summer temperatures in such climates are relatively severe and precipitation is generally greater in summer than in winter. One example is Chicago, Illinois.
(17) The greenhouse effect is a natural warming of Earth's lower atmosphere and its surface. This effect is caused by complex reactions between gases and particles in the air. Certain gases, including carbon dioxide and water vapor, absorb solar energy and are heated. As the gases cool, they send some of the energy back into space. Some of the energy radiates back toward Earth and warms it.
(18) Burning fossil fuels and clearing forests have contributed to increased levels in carbon dioxide in the air.
(19) Global warming is an increase in Earth's average surface temperature over time.
(20) Warmer surface temperatures will increase evaporation rates, which will put more water vapor into the atmosphere. Water vapor is a powerful absorber of radiation emitted by Earth and will magnify the effect of carbon dioxide and other gases. Temperature increases will also cause sea ice to melt, causing a substantial increase in the solar energy absorbed at the surface. This, in turn, will magnify the initial temperature increase created by higher levels of greenhouse gases.

Critical Thinking

(21) Yes, if the region is at a high enough elevation, it can be cold enough to experience snow.
(22) Because it is cooler, air at higher elevations generally contains less moisture than air at lower elevations. Thus, regions at higher elevations often experience less precipitation than areas at lower elevations.
(23) Marine west coast climates are dominated by the onshore flow of oceanic air. Only a narrow region of such climates exists in North America because mountains block the oceanic air and prevent it from flowing over land. In western Europe, there are no mountainous regions to block this flow of air. Thus, such climates dominate this part of Europe.
(24) Most fogs form when enough water vapor is added to air to bring about saturation. Deserts regions lack enough water to produce fog. The arid regions called the rain shadow deserts occur because prevailing winds meet mountain barriers.

Using Graphs

(25) The highest annual temperature of 26°C occurred in July.
(26) The lowest annual temperature of 0°C occurred in January.
(27) The range is 0°C to 26°C , or 26°C.
(28) The wettest season of the year in St. Louis is late winter or early spring.
(29) The climate is humid subtropical.

CHAPTER 21

Assessment *continued*

Critical Thinking

21 **Synthesizing** Can a region at low latitudes have snow? Explain.

22 **Applying Concepts** How does elevation affect the amount of precipitation that falls over an area?

23 **Inferring** Why do marine west coast climates exist only as narrow strips in North America, yet are widespread in western Europe?

24 **Formulating Hypotheses** Hypothesize why rain shadow deserts rarely experience fog.

Using Graphs

Use the graph below to answer questions 25–29.

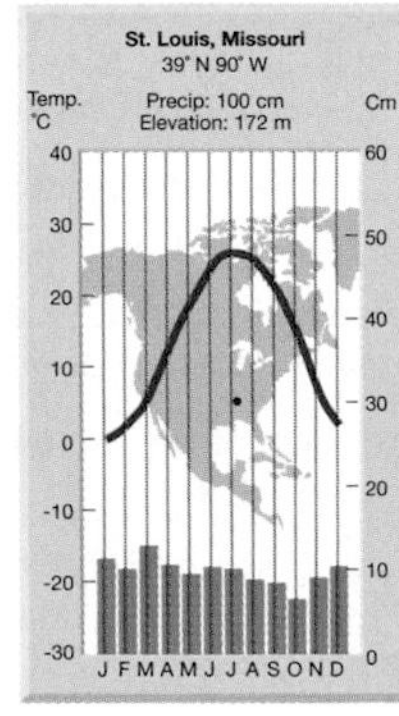

25 **Reading Graphs** What is the highest average annual temperature, and during which month does it occur?

26 **Reading Graphs** What is the lowest annual temperature, and during which month does it occur?

27 **Calculating** What is the average annual temperature range for St. Louis?

28 **Inferring** What is the wettest season of the year in St. Louis?

29 **Classifying** Classify the climate of St. Louis using the Köppen climate classification system.

Concepts in Action

30 **Synthesizing** Cities are referred to as urban heat islands. Use what you know about factors that affect climate to explain this statement.

31 **Applying Concepts** What do you think can be done to reduce the steady increase in global carbon dioxide levels?

32 **Writing in Science** Suppose you're a writer for the school newspaper. You are doing a story on how global warming might affect your area. Write an article that explains at least three effects that an increase in Earth's surface temperature might have on the climate of your area.

Performance-Based Assessment

Applying Concepts Make flyers with catchy slogans to suggest ways to reduce your community's use of fossil fuels. Get permission to post the flyers in grocery stores, community halls, shopping malls, and other common areas.

Concepts in Action

(30) Cities are warmer than nearby undeveloped areas because sidewalks, buildings, streets, and roads radiate heat, causing urban temperatures to be higher than areas with more vegetation or nearby bodies of water. Cities also contribute to local climate regimes by producing greater amounts of heat and pollutants than undeveloped areas, and causing areas downwind of them to be cloudier and wetter than areas upwind of them.
(31) Answers will vary, but should include alternatives to burning fossil fuels and a reduction in the clearing of forests, other vegetated areas, and the development of wetlands.
(32) Answers will vary, but students' stories should include at least three effects on temperature and precipitation patterns. Depending on your location, the effects on sea levels might also be included.

Regents Practice Exam

Test-Taking Tip

Using More Than One Visual
Sometimes an answer to a test question requires that you use or interpret more than one visual. When this occurs, carefully study the visuals before you read the questions pertaining to them. Look for similarities and differences between the visuals. Refer to the visuals again as you read each of the questions associated with the visuals. Use the graphs to answer the questions on this page.

For *each* statement or question, choose the *number* of the word or expression that, of those given, best completes the statement or answers the question. Some questions may require the use of the *Earth Science Reference Tables.* Base your answers to questions 1 through 4 on the diagram below, which shows the Changes in Temperature and Carbon Dioxide Levels in the Air Over the Past 160,000 Years.

1 Earth's temperatures were similar to the temperatures on our planet today
(1) about 150,000 years ago
(2) about 135,000 years ago
(3) about 50,000 years ago
(4) about 25,000 years ago

2 When do you think Earth was covered with more ice than is on our planet today?
(1) between 15,000 and 140,000 years ago
(2) between 140,000 and 120,000 years ago
(3) between 135,000 and 20,000 years ago
(4) between 20,000 and 10,000 years ago

3 What is the relationship between carbon dioxide concentration and Antarctic temperatures?
(1) As carbon dioxide concentration increases, temperature decreases.
(2) As carbon dioxide concentration decreases, temperature increases.
(3) As carbon dioxide concentration increases, temperature increases.
(4) There is no relationship.

4 Which of the following factors does NOT affect climate?
(1) atmospheric carbon dioxide concentration
(2) longitude
(3) latitude
(4) proximity to large bodies of water

5 Which area of New York State is likely to have the smallest annual temperature range?
(1) the Allegheny Plateau
(2) the Catskills
(3) the Hudson highlands
(4) Long Island

Answer the following questions in complete questions. Some questions may require the use of the *Earth Science Reference Tables.*

6 Explain how ocean currents and global winds can affect the climate of a region.

7 Describe how mountains affect both the temperature and precipitation of a region.

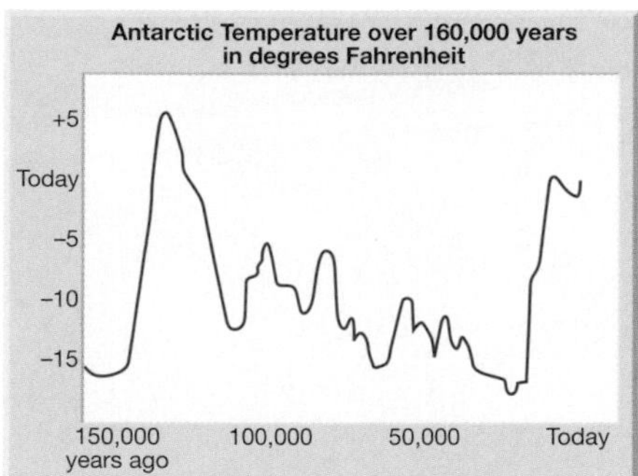

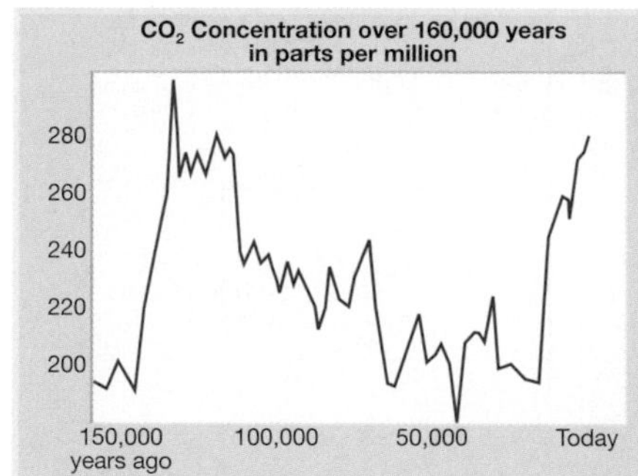

Regents Practice Exam

(1) 2
(2) 3
(3) 3
(4) 2
(5) 4
(6) Warm ocean currents warm the climate, while cold ocean currents cool the climate. Global winds determine where air masses come from and thus if a climate is generally hot, cold, dry, or wet. Global winds also determine if a coastal area will have a more marine climate, or a more continental climate.
(7) As elevation increases, temperatures decrease. Mountains cause lifting of air resulting in increased precipitation on the windward side of mountain ranges and dry conditions on the leeward side.

Performance-Based Assessment
Encourage students to be creative in generating their slogans. Assist them with posting the flyers, if necessary.

Your students can independently test their knowledge of the chapter and print out their results.

CHAPTER 22

Planning Guide

Use these planning tools
Use Teacher Express for all your planning needs

SECTION OBJECTIVES	STANDARDS NATIONAL	STANDARDS STATE	ACTIVITIES and LABS
22.1 Early Astronomy, pp. 614–621 1 block or 2 periods 22.1 **Describe** the contributions of ancient Greeks to astronomy. 22.2 **Compare and contrast** the geocentric and heliocentric models of the solar system. 22.3 **Explain** the contributions to astronomy of Copernicus, Brahe, Kepler, Galileo, and Newton.	A-1, A-2, B-4, D-3, E-2, G-1, G-2, G-3		**SE** Inquiry Activity: How Do Impact Craters Form? p. 613 L2 **TE** Teacher Demo: Visualizing an Astronomical Unit, p. 618 L2 **TE** Teacher Demo: A Simple Mirror Telescope, p. 620 L2
22.2 The Earth-Moon-Sun System, pp. 622–629 1 block or 2 periods 22.4 **Describe** the movements of Earth known as rotation, revolution, and precession. 22.5 **Explain** how the moon goes through phases. 22.6 **Explain** how eclipses occur.	D-3		**TE** Teacher Demo: Observing Precession, p. 625 L2 **SE** Exploration Lab: Modeling Synodic and Sidereal Months, pp. 636–637 L2 **LM** Measuring the Angle of the Sun at Noon L2
22.3 Earth's Moon, pp. 630–634 1 block or 2 periods 22.7 **Describe** how the physical features of the lunar surface were created. 22.8 **Explain** the history of the moon.	A-1, A-2, B-4, D-3, E-2		**TE** Build Science Skills, p. 632 L2

Ability Levels

L1 For students who need additional help
L2 For all students
L3 For students who need to be challenged

Components

SE	Student Edition	**GRSW**	Guided Reading & Study Workbook	**TP**	Test Prep Resources	**GEO**	Geode CD-ROM
TE	Teacher's Edition	**TEX**	Teacher Express	**onT**	onlineText	**T**	Transparencies
LM	Laboratory Manual	**CTB**	Computer Test Bank	**DC**	Discovery Channel Videos	**GO**	Internet Resources
CUT	Chapter Tests						

RESOURCES PRINT and TECHNOLOGY	SECTION ASSESSMENT
GRSW Section 22.1 **T-315** Eratosthene's Experiment **T-316** Ptolemy's Model **T-317** Retrograde Motion of Mars **T-318** Drawing Ellipses **T-319** Period of Revolution and Solar Distances on Planets **T-320** Kepler's Law **DC** Introduction to Space Exploration **TEX** Lesson Planning 22.1	**SE** Section 22.1 Assessment, p. 621 **onT** Section 22.1
GRSW Section 22.2 **T-321** Orbital Motion of Earth and Other Planets **T-322** Astronomical Coordinate System **T-323** Locating the North Star **T-324** Solar Day vs Sidereal Day **T-325** Earth's Orbital Motion **T-326** Apparent Position of the Sun **T-327** Precession **TEX** Lesson Planning 22.2	**SE** Section 22.2 Assessment, p. 629 **onT** Section 22.2
GRSW Section 22.3 **T-328** Sidereal Month vs. Synodic Month **T-329** Solar Eclipse **T-330** Lunar Eclipse **T-331** Moon Phases **T-332** Proof of Earth's Rotation **T-333** Twelve Constellations of the Zodiac GEODe Astronomy ↳ Earth's Moon **TEX** Lesson Planning 22.3	**SE** Section 22.3 Assessment, p. 634 **onT** Section 22.3

Go Online

Go online for these Internet resources.

PHSchool.com
Web Code: cjk-9999

NSTA SCiLINKS
Web Code: cjn-7221
Web Code: cjn-7222

Materials for Activities and Labs

Quantities for each group

STUDENT EDITION

Inquiry Activity, p. 613
plastic container, sand, wooden ruler, 3 different-sized balls, meter stick

Exploration Lab, pp. 636–637
pencil, paper, lamp, basketball, softball

TEACHER'S EDITION

Teacher Demo, p. 618
several rolls of adding machine tape, meter sticks, tape, Table 1 from p. 618 of student text

Teacher Demo, p. 620
lightbulb in a lamp base, magnifying lens, mirror with concave surface (magnifying mirror with 2 sides—used for makeup and shaving)

Teacher Demo, p. 625
toy top

Build Science Skills, p. 632
foam poster board, soft modeling clay, toothpicks, narrow paper strips, tape, marker (or pencil or pen)

Chapter Assessment

ASSESSMENT

SE Assessment, pp. 639–640
CUT Chapter 22 Test
CTB Chapter 22
onT Chapter 22

STANDARDIZED TEST PREP

SE Chapter 22, p. 641
TP Progress Monitoring Assessments

interactive textbook with assessment at PHSchool.com

CHAPTER 22

Before you teach

Michael Wysession
Washington University

Big Ideas

Satellites, moons, planets, and stars travel along predictable paths that are determined by the mass of the objects and the laws of gravity.

Space and Time Many early people believed in a geocentric model of the universe, where all objects revolved around Earth. The Ptolemaic system adapted the geocentric model to include explanations of the apparent retrograde motions of planets. Copernicus showed that the heliocentric model, with Earth revolving around the sun, was simpler. Planets, moons, and satellites follow elliptical orbits when they revolve around another body, as shown by Kepler.

Forces and Motion Earth rotates once per day. This day is 24 hours with respect to the sun, but 23 hours and 56 minutes with respect to the stars. Earth revolves around the sun once every 365.25 days, or one year. The seasons are a result of the tilt of Earth's axis of rotation, which is 23.5° with respect to the solar ecliptic. The direction that Earth's axis points to changes, or precesses, over a period of 26,000 years. The phases of the moon are a result of the relative positions of the sun, moon, and Earth. Solar and lunar eclipses occur when these three bodies are lined up.

Matter and Energy The Apollo missions, during which astronauts visited the moon, revealed a great deal about our nearest neighbor. The moon formed from the ejected debris of an enormous impact of a Mars-sized planetesimal with Earth early in our planet's history. Because the moon has so little mass, it lacks an atmosphere, hydrosphere, or biosphere, and so its structure and surface are very different from Earth's.

Earth Science Refresher

General Relativity and Motions in Space

As with many things in science, simple explanations can give you 99 percent of the story, but the full picture is somewhat more complicated. This certainly holds true for gravity and the motions of objects in space. Most all orbital motions can be nicely explained by the simple laws discovered by Kepler and Newton. However, some could not, and the most famous was the precession of the orbit of Mercury. It took Einstein and his theory of general relativity to explain these motions.

The problem with Mercury had to do with the precession, or rotational shift of its elliptical orbit. Newton's laws of gravity predicted a certain continual shift in the orbit, but not enough. Einstein's theory of general relativity exactly predicted this orbital precession, which was considered to be proof of his theory.

Einstein predicted that all mass actually distorts the fabric of space and time. For larger masses, the effect is more noticeable. This has some interesting implications, the most important of which for astronomy is that light does not always go in a straight line. For example, light will be bent around a massive object, like a galaxy. Einstein would say that the light is not actually bent, but that space itself is warped. The result, however, is that the galaxy acts like a refracting lens, and light from the distant object is focused together and therefore more visible. This phenomenon, called a gravitational lens, allows astronomers to see very distant objects that would otherwise be too faint to see.

Go Online NSTA PD LINKS

For: Chapter 22 Content Support
Visit: www.SciLinks.org/PDLinks
Web Code: cjn-2299

Another interesting result of general relativity is that time slows down the closer you are to a large object. A clock running at the bottom of a tower, closer to Earth, actually runs slower than a clock at the top of a tower. All clocks on Earth run slower when Earth is closest to the sun, at around January 5, and run faster in August, even though the accumulated difference is only a fraction of a second. These gravitational time effects also need to be taken into account with global positioning systems (GPS), which rely upon time signals sent through satellites. So, this effect won't make you late to any appointments, and your wristwatch will do for most applications. But if you want to know the time exactly, or use GPS to know your location exactly, you need to use general relativity.

Address Misconceptions

Some students may think that modern astronomy was developed recently by a small number of scientists. The body of astronomical knowledge is an accumulation of work by many scientists over many centuries of time. Modern astronomers study the works of earlier scientists and build on the foundation of knowledge that they have laid. In fact, Sir Isaac Newton has been quoted as saying, "If I have seen further, it is by standing on the shoulders of giants." For a strategy that helps to overcome this misconception, see **Address Misconceptions** on **p. 617**.

Build Reading Literacy

Think Aloud

Verbalize Thought Processes While Reading

Strategy Model cognitive and metacognitive processes that students can use to build meaning, self-correct, and monitor their own comprehension. Choose part of a section from Chapter 22, such as Ancient Greeks on pp. 614–616, and preview it. As you do so, imagine that you are reading these paragraphs for the first time, just as your students will be. Make a copy of the section, and on it write comments and questions that you can use as "think-aloud" models.

Example

1. Read several paragraphs aloud and have your students follow along silently. Have them listen to how you pause to check your own comprehension and to determine meaning at trouble spots. You might model some of the following strategies aloud as you read:

- Make a prediction, then revise or verify it.
- Describe mental pictures as they form.
- Connect new information with prior knowledge or related ideas; share an analogy.
- Verbalize confusing points and work out steps to clarify their meanings; adjust your reading pace if needed.

2. Select a logical stopping point. Then, have students read the next paragraph silently and apply similar strategies internally. Afterward, ask students to share the strategies they used. Repeat this step several times.

3. Have students work in pairs, taking turns applying think-aloud strategies to the next several paragraphs.

See p. 619 for a script on how to use this strategy with students. For additional strategies, see pp. 624 and 631.

ASSESS PRIOR KNOWLEDGE

Use the Chapter Pretest below to assess students' prior knowledge. As needed, review these concepts.

Review Science Concepts

Section 22.1 Review the relationships between the orbits of the planets in our solar system to be sure that students fully understand the misconceptions of early astronomers.

Section 22.2 Have students review the concept of rotational motion.

Section 22.3 A knowledge of the Apollo moon missions will give students a greater appreciation and understanding of their study of the moon.

CHAPTER 22 Origin of Modern Astronomy

CONCEPTS in Action

Exploration Lab
Modeling Synodic and Sidereal Months

Understanding Earth
Foucault's Experiment

Astronomy
↳ Earth's Moon

Discovery Channel School **Video Field Trip**

Introduction to Space Exploration

Take a historical field trip with the Discovery Channel and find out about the history of space exploration. Answer the following questions after watching the video.

1. What was Galileo's major astronomical invention, and what theory did it enable him to confirm?
2. How was Pluto discovered?

For: Chapter 22 Resources
Visit: PHSchool.com
Web Code: cjk-9999

This photograph shows the moon ▶ over Mount Humphreys, in California's eastern Sierras.

Chapter Pretest

1. True or False: Early Greek astronomers (600 B.C.–A.D. 150) used telescopes to observe the stars. *(False)*

2. What lies at the center of our solar system? *(a)*
   a. the sun b. Mars
   c. Earth d. the moon

3. What is rotation? *(the turning, or spinning, of a body on its axis)*

4. What is the approximate time that it takes Earth to rotate on its axis? *(a)*
   a. 24 hours b. 12 hours
   c. 30 days d. 365 days

5. What was the most important accomplishment of the Apollo moon missions? *(landing on the moon and collecting data and samples from the moon's surface)*

6. Approximately how long does it take for the moon to go through all of its phases? *(c)*
   a. 24 hours b. 12 hours
   c. 30 days d. 365 days

7. How would geometry and trigonometry have been useful to early astronomers? *(These would have provided a method of approximating sizes and distances.)*

Chapter Preview

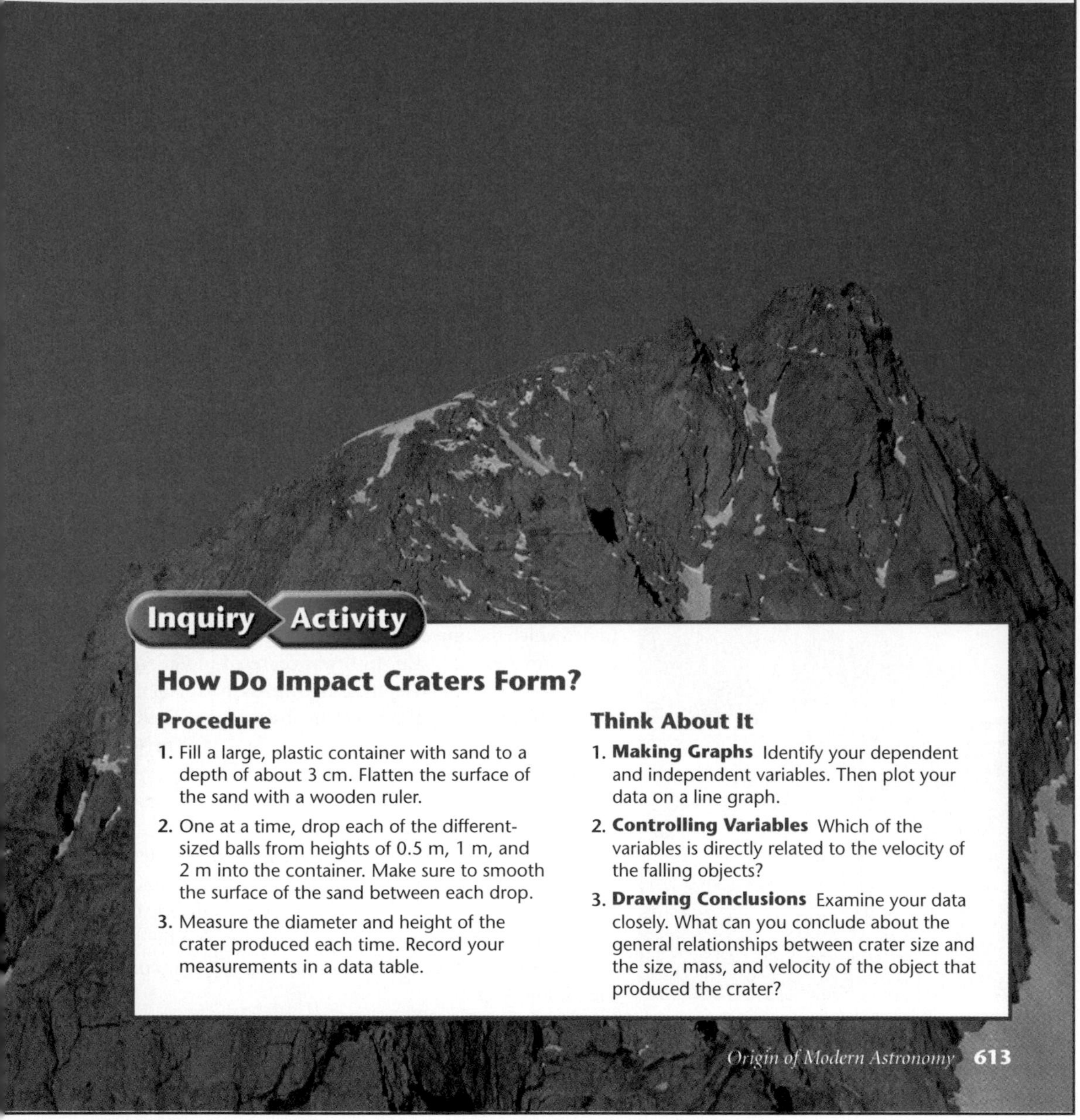

Inquiry Activity

How Do Impact Craters Form?

Procedure

1. Fill a large, plastic container with sand to a depth of about 3 cm. Flatten the surface of the sand with a wooden ruler.
2. One at a time, drop each of the different-sized balls from heights of 0.5 m, 1 m, and 2 m into the container. Make sure to smooth the surface of the sand between each drop.
3. Measure the diameter and height of the crater produced each time. Record your measurements in a data table.

Think About It

1. **Making Graphs** Identify your dependent and independent variables. Then plot your data on a line graph.
2. **Controlling Variables** Which of the variables is directly related to the velocity of the falling objects?
3. **Drawing Conclusions** Examine your data closely. What can you conclude about the general relationships between crater size and the size, mass, and velocity of the object that produced the crater?

Video Field Trip

Introduction to Space Exploration

Encourage students to view the Video Field Trip "Introduction to Space Exploration."

ENGAGE/EXPLORE

How Do Impact Craters Form?

Purpose In this activity, students will observe the relationship between crater size and the size, mass, and velocity of the object that produced the crater.

Skills Focus Observing, Measuring, Using Tables and Graphs, Drawing Conclusions

Prep Time 5 minutes

Materials plastic container, sand, wooden ruler, 3 different-sized balls, meter stick

Advance Prep Sand and large plastic containers can be purchased inexpensively from hardware stores or home improvement centers.

Class Time 10 minutes

Safety Students should wear safety goggles.

Teaching Tip The balls should vary in mass so that students will see the mass and crater depth relationship.

Expected Outcome If two or more balls are dropped from the same height, the ball with the greater mass will produce a deeper crater. A ball dropped from a greater height will have greater velocity upon impact and will produce a deeper crater.

Think About It

1. Dependent variable: size of ball; independent variable: height from which ball is dropped

2. the height from which the ball is dropped

3. Mass and velocity have the greatest influence on the size and depth of the craters.

1 FOCUS

Section Objectives

22.1 **Describe** the contributions of ancient Greeks to astronomy.
22.2 **Compare and contrast** the geocentric and heliocentric models of the solar system.
22.3 **Explain** the contributions to astronomy of Copernicus, Brahe, Kepler, Galileo, and Newton.

Reading Focus

Build Vocabulary L2

Word Origins Explain to students that the prefix *geo-* is a Latin and Greek prefix that means "Earth." *Centric* is from the Greek word *kentrikos,* which means "located in the center." So the word *geocentric* means "having Earth as the center." *Helio-* is a Latin and Greek prefix that means "sun." So the word *heliocentric* means "having the sun as the center."

Reading Strategy L2

a. orbits Earth
b. Aristotle, Ptolemy
c. orbits sun
d. center of universe
e. Aristarchus, Copernicus

2 INSTRUCT

Ancient Greeks

Integrate Social Studies L2

Aristotle was an ancient Greek philosopher and scientist who had a broad range of capabilities. He worked in many areas including physics, chemistry, biology, zoology, botany, psychology, political theory, logic, metaphysics, and philosophy. Have students research the life and works of Aristotle. Encourage students to make an oral presentation to the class.
Verbal

22.1 Early Astronomy

Reading Focus

Key Concepts

- How does the geocentric model of the solar system differ from the heliocentric model?
- What were the accomplishments of early astronomers?

Vocabulary

- astronomy
- geocentric
- heliocentric
- retrograde motion
- ellipse
- astronomical unit (AU)

Reading Strategy

Comparing and Contrasting Copy the table below. As you read about the geocentric and heliocentric models of the solar system, fill in the table.

	Location of Earth	Location of Sun	Supporters of Model
Geocentric Model	center of universe	a. ?	b. ?
Heliocentric Model	c. ?	d. ?	e. ?

Earth is one of nine planets and many smaller bodies that orbit the sun. The sun is part of a much larger family of perhaps 100 billion stars that make up our galaxy, the Milky Way. There are billions of galaxies in the universe. A few hundred years ago scientists thought that Earth was the center of the universe. In this chapter, you will explore some events that changed the view of Earth's place in space. You will also examine Earth's moon.

Figure 1 Early astronomers often used instruments called astrolabes to track the positions of the sun and stars.

Ancient Greeks

Astronomy is the science that studies the universe. Astronomy deals with the properties of objects in space and the laws under which the universe operates. The "Golden Age" of early astronomy (600 B.C.–A.D. 150) was centered in Greece. The early Greeks used philosophical arguments to explain natural events. However, they also relied on observations. The Greeks used instruments such as the one in Figure 1. The Greeks developed the basics of geometry and trigonometry. Using these branches of mathematics, they measured the sizes and distances of the sun and the moon.

The Greeks made many astronomical discoveries. The famous Greek philosopher Aristotle (384–322 B.C.) concluded that Earth is round because it always casts a curved shadow on the moon when it passes between the sun and the moon. Aristotle's belief that Earth is round was largely abandoned in the Middle Ages.

The first successful attempt to establish the size of Earth is credited to Eratosthenes (276–194 B.C.). As shown in Figure 2, Eratosthenes observed the angles of the noonday sun in two Egyptian cities that were roughly north and south of each other—Syene (presently Aswan) and Alexandria. Finding that the angles differed by 7 degrees, or 1/50 of a complete circle, he concluded that the circumference of Earth must be 50 times the distance between these two cities. The cities were 5000 stadia apart, giving him a measurement of 250,000 stadia. Many historians believe the stadia was 157.6 meters. This would make Eratosthenes' calculation of Earth's circumference—39,400 kilometers—a measurement very close to the modern circumference of 40,075 kilometers.

Calculating Earth's Circumference

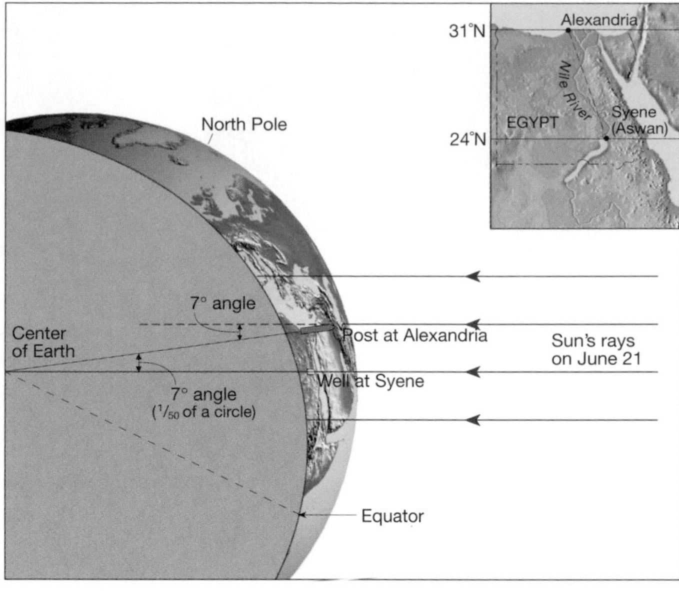

Figure 2 This diagram shows the orientation of the sun's rays at Syene (Aswan) and Alexandria in Egypt on June 21 when Eratosthenes calculated Earth's circumference.

Probably the greatest of the early Greek astronomers was Hipparchus (second century B.C.), best known for his star catalog. Hipparchus determined the location of almost 850 stars, which he divided into six groups according to their brightness. He measured the length of the year to within minutes of the modern year and developed a method for predicting the times of lunar eclipses to within a few hours.

Geocentric Model The Greeks believed in the **geocentric** view. They thought that Earth was a sphere that stayed motionless at the center of the universe. **In the geocentric model, the moon, sun, and the known planets—Mercury, Venus, Mars, and Jupiter—orbit Earth.** Beyond the planets was a transparent, hollow sphere on which the stars traveled daily around Earth. This was called the celestial sphere. To the Greeks, all of the heavenly bodies, except seven, appeared to remain in the same relative position to one another. These seven wanderers included the sun, the moon, Mercury, Venus, Mars, Jupiter, and Saturn. Each was thought to have a circular orbit around Earth. The Greeks were able to explain the apparent movements of all celestial bodies in space by using this model. This model, however, was not correct. Figure 3A on page 616 illustrates the geocentric model.

Go Online SciLinks NSTA

For: Links on early astronomers
Visit: www.SciLinks.org
Web Code: cjn-7221

Address Misconceptions L2

Some students may confuse astrology and astronomy to the point of thinking that they are the same. *Astronomy* is a scientific probing of the universe to derive the properties of celestial objects and the laws under which the universe operates. *Astrology* is based on ancient superstitions, which explain that an individual's actions and personality are determined by the positions of the planets and stars at the present time, and at the time of the person's birth. Scientists do not accept astrology as a true science. Ask: **Why don't scientists accept astrological beliefs as scientific fact?** *(Astrology is not based on scientific facts or principles. It is based on superstition.)*
Verbal

Build Science Skills L2

Calculating Have students confirm Eratosthenes's calculations of the circumference of Earth and calculate the percent error of the calculation.

$$\frac{7}{360} = \frac{1}{50}$$

5000 stadia × 50 = 250,000 stadia; if 1 stadia = 157.6 m, then,

$$250{,}000 \text{ stadia} \times \frac{157.6 \text{ m}}{1 \text{ stadia}} =$$

39,400,000 m = 39,400 km;

percent error =

$$\frac{39{,}400 \text{ km} - 40{,}075 \text{ km}}{40{,}075 \text{ km}} \times 100$$

= 1.7%

Eratosthenes's calculation of Earth's circumference is amazing considering this was calculated before 194 B.C.
Logical

Download a worksheet on early astronomers for students to complete, and find additional teacher support from NSTA SciLinks.

Customize for English Language Learners

Encourage English language learners to make a science glossary as they read the section. Students should start with the vocabulary terms and add any other new words they encounter. Have students write brief definitions of each term or draw an illustration that helps them understand the term. Students may want to include definitions in both English and their native language in their glossary.

Use Visuals L1

Figure 3 Have students compare the geocentric and heliocentric models represented in the figure. Ask: **What is the main difference in these two models of the solar system?** *(In the geocentric model, Earth is at the center. In the heliocentric model, the sun is at the center.)* **How do the changing models of the solar system demonstrate the self-correcting nature of science?** *(As new information was discovered about the solar system, the models were changed to incorporate the new information. As more and more information was collected and as technology improved, the model of the solar system became more accurate.)*
Verbal, Portfolio

A

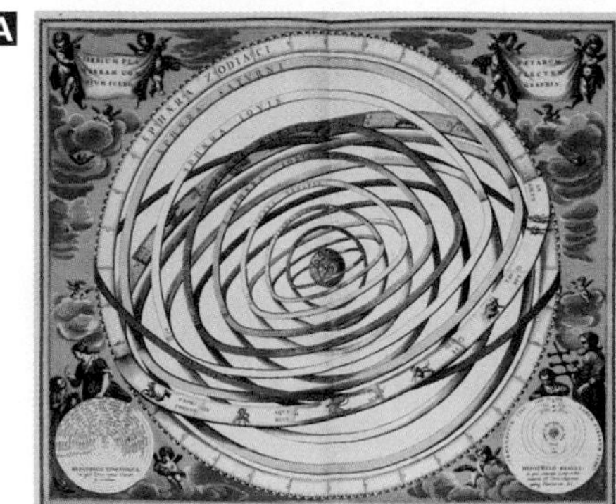

B

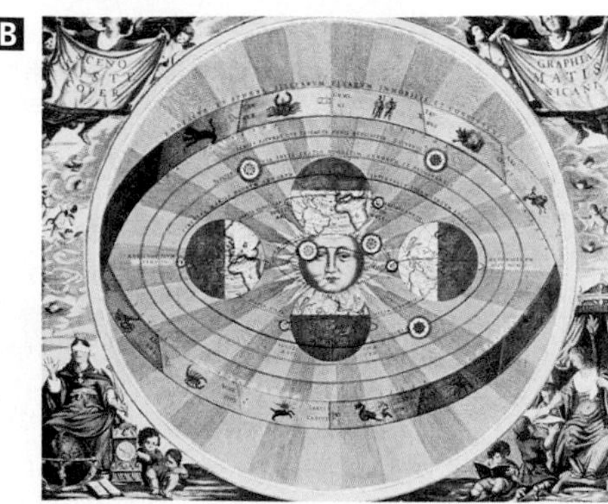

Figure 3 A Geocentric Model of the Universe
B Heliocentric Model of the Universe

Heliocentric Model Aristarchus (312–230 B.C.) was the first Greek to believe in a sun-centered, or **heliocentric,** universe. **In the heliocentric model, Earth and the other planets orbit the sun.** Aristarchus used geometry to calculate the relative distances from Earth to the sun and from Earth to the moon. He later used these distances to calculate the size of the sun and the moon. But Aristarchus came up with measurements that were much too small. However, he did learn that the sun was many times more distant than the moon and many times larger than Earth. Though there was evidence to support the heliocentric model, as shown in Figure 3B, the Earth-centered view, shown in Figure 3A, dominated Western thought for nearly 2000 years.

Ptolemaic System Much of our knowledge of Greek astronomy comes from Claudius Ptolemy. In a 13-volume work published in A.D. 141, Ptolemy presented a model of the universe that was called the Ptolemaic system. It accounted for the movements of the planets. The precision with which his model was able to predict the motion of the planets allowed it to go unchallenged for nearly 13 centuries.

Just like the Greeks, Ptolemy's model had the planets moving in circular orbits around a motionless Earth. However, the motion of the planets against the background of stars seemed odd. Each planet, if watched night after night, moves slightly eastward among the stars. Periodically, each planet appears to stop, reverse direction for a time, and then resume an eastward motion. The apparent westward drift is called **retrograde motion** and is diagrammed in Figure 4 on page 617. This rather odd apparent motion results from the combination of the motion of Earth and the planet's own motion around the sun, as shown in Figure 4.

It is difficult to accurately represent retrograde motion by using the Earth-centered model. Even though Ptolemy used the wrong model, he was able to account for the planets' motions.

What is retrograde motion?

Facts and Figures

Ptolemy's most famous work was a 13-volume text written in Greek called *He mathematike syntaxis*, or *The Mathematical Collection*. This great work was translated into Arabic by Arab scholars and renamed *al-Majisti,* or *Great Work*. The book is now known as the *Almagest*. In this work, Ptolemy used mathematical terms to explain the motions of the heavenly bodies. Ptolemy's explanations of the planets' movements were widely accepted.

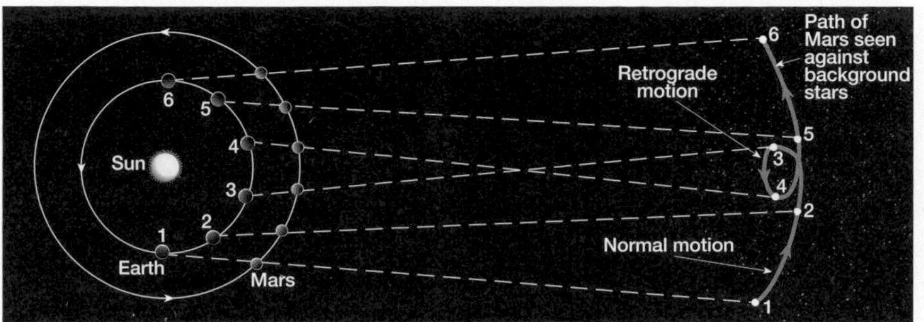

Figure 4 **Retrograde Motion** When viewed from Earth, Mars moves eastward among the stars each day. Then periodically it appears to stop and reverse direction. This apparent movement, called retrograde motion, occurs because Earth has a faster orbital speed than Mars and overtakes it.

The Birth of Modern Astronomy

The development of modern astronomy involved a break from previous philosophical and religious views. Scientists began to discover a universe governed by natural laws. We will examine the work of five noted scientists: Nicolaus Copernicus, Tycho Brahe, Johannes Kepler, Galileo Galilei, and Sir Isaac Newton.

Nicolaus Copernicus For almost 13 centuries after the time of Ptolemy, very few astronomical advances were made in Europe. The first great astronomer to emerge after the Middle Ages was Nicolaus Copernicus (1473–1543) from Poland. Copernicus became convinced that Earth is a planet, just like the other five planets that were known. The daily motions of the heavens, he reasoned, could be better explained by a rotating Earth.

Copernicus concluded that Earth is a planet. He proposed a model of the solar system with the sun at the center. This was a major break from the ancient idea that a motionless Earth lies at the center. Copernicus used circles, which were considered to be the perfect geometric shape, to represent the orbits of the planets. However, the planets seemed to stray from their predicted positions.

Tycho Brahe Tycho Brahe (1546–1601) was born of Danish nobility three years after the death of Copernicus. Brahe became interested in astronomy while viewing a solar eclipse that had been predicted by astronomers. He persuaded King Frederick II to build an observatory near Copenhagen. The telescope had not yet been invented. At the observatory, Brahe designed and built instruments, such as the angle-measuring device shown in Figure 5. He used these instruments for 20 years to measure the locations of the heavenly bodies. **Brahe's observations, especially of Mars, were far more precise than any made previously.** In the last year of his life, Brahe found an able assistant, Johannes Kepler. Kepler kept most of Brahe's observations and put them to exceptional use.

Figure 5 Tycho Brahe in His Observatory Brahe (central figure) is painted on the wall within the arc of a sighting instrument called a quadrant.

The Birth of Modern Astronomy

Use Visuals L1

Figure 4 To help students understand the concept of retrograde motion, have them trace the eye's line of sight with their finger. Tell students to find the number 1 in the left part of the diagram and follow the dotted line to the position of Mars. Then have students repeat this process for each numbered position.

Ask: **Why does Mars appear to have retrograde motion?** *(Earth has a faster orbital speed than Mars has and overtakes it.)* **Using Newton's laws of motion, explain why retrograde motion is impossible.** *(Mars would not reverse its direction of motion unless it was acted upon by an outside force that would change its direction. Inertia and gravity will keep it moving in a forward direction.)* **Visual**

L2

Some students may think that modern astronomy was developed recently by a small number of scientists. The body of astronomical knowledge is an accumulation of work by many scientists over many centuries of time. Modern astronomers study the works of earlier scientists and build on the foundation of knowledge that they have laid. In fact, Sir Isaac Newton has been quoted as saying, "If I have seen further, it is by standing on the shoulders of giants." Ask: **What is an example of a field of science that does not contain an accumulation of knowledge that was acquired over many years?** *(There is no such field of science. All fields of science are accumulations of knowledge.)* **Verbal**

Facts and Figures

The Copernican explanation of the solar system challenged the belief that Earth was the center of the universe and was considered heretical by the Roman Catholic Church. Copernicus's text, *De Revolutionibus, Orbium Coelestium (On the Revolution of the Heavenly Spheres)*, was published as he lay on his deathbed in 1543. One of Copernicus's followers, Giordano Bruno, was seized in 1600 during the Inquisition, a Roman Catholic tribunal for the discovery and punishment for heresy. He refused to denounce the Copernican theory and was burned at the stake.

Answer to . . .

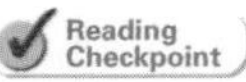

Retrograde motion is the apparent westward drift of a planet resulting from the combination of the motion of Earth and the planet's own motion around the sun.

Visualizing an Astronomical Unit L2

Purpose Students will make a model showing the distances between the planets.

Materials several rolls of adding machine tape, meter sticks, tape, Table 1 from p. 618 of the student text

Procedure Have students mark off the distance each planet is from the sun using adding machine tape. Tell students to use one meter to represent ten astronomical units. Students may have to stretch the tape down a long hallway to view the entire tape at once.

Expected Outcome Students will observe the distance relationships between the planets by making a model.
Kinesthetic, Logical

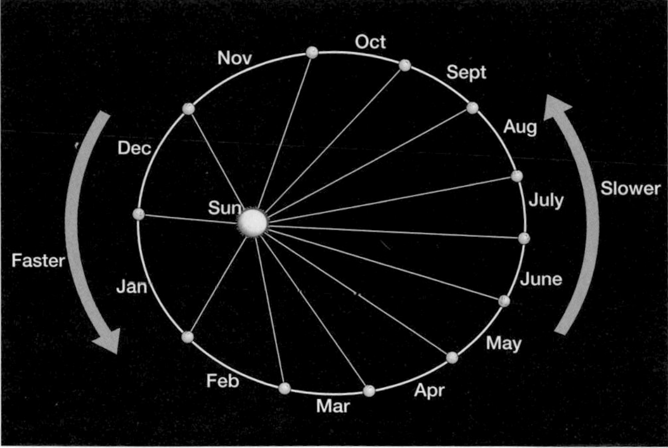

Figure 6 Planet Revolution A line connecting a planet to the sun would move in such a manner that equal areas are swept out in equal times. Thus, planets revolve slower when they are farther from the sun and faster when they are closer.

Johannes Kepler Copernicus ushered out the old astronomy, and Johannes Kepler (1571–1630) ushered in the new. Kepler had a good mathematical mind and a strong faith in the accuracy of Brahe's work. **Kepler discovered three laws of planetary motion.** The first two laws resulted from his inability to fit Brahe's observations of Mars to a circular orbit. Kepler discovered that the orbit of Mars around the sun is not a perfect circle. Instead, it is an oval-shaped path called an **ellipse.** About the same time, he realized that the speed of Mars in its orbit changes in a predictable way. As Mars approaches the sun, it speeds up. As it moves away from the sun, it slows down.

After decades of work, Kepler summarized three laws of planetary motion:

1. The path of each planet around the sun is an ellipse, with the sun at one focus. The other focus is symmetrically located at the opposite end of the ellipse.
2. Each planet revolves so that an imaginary line connecting it to the sun sweeps over equal areas in equal time intervals, as shown in Figure 6. If a planet is to sweep equal areas in the same amount of time, it must travel more rapidly when it is nearer the sun and more slowly when it is farther from the sun.
3. The square of the length of time it takes a planet to orbit the sun (orbital period) is proportional to the cube of its mean distance to the sun.

Table 1 Period of Revolution and Solar Distances of Planets

Planet	Solar Distance (AU)*	Period (Earth years)
Mercury	0.39	0.24
Venus	0.72	0.62
Earth	1.00	1.00
Mars	1.52	1.88
Jupiter	5.20	11.86
Saturn	9.54	29.46
Uranus	19.18	84.01
Neptune	30.06	164.80
Pluto	39.44	247.70

*AU = astronomical unit.

In its simplest form, the orbital period of revolution is measured in Earth years. The planet's distance to the sun is expressed in astronomical units. The **astronomical unit (AU)** is the average distance between Earth and the sun. It is about 150 million kilometers.

Using these units, Kepler's third law states that the planet's orbital period squared is equal to its mean solar distance cubed ($P^2 = a^3$). Therefore, the solar distances of the planets can be calculated when their periods of revolution are known. For example, Mars has a period of 1.88 years, which squared equals 3.54. The cube root of 3.54 is 1.52, and that is the distance to Mars in astronomical units shown in Table 1.

Galileo Galilei Galileo Galilei (1564–1642) was the greatest Italian scientist of the Renaissance. **Galileo's most important contributions were his descriptions of the behavior of moving objects.** All astronomical discoveries before his time were made without the aid of a telescope. In 1609, Galileo heard that a Dutch lens maker had devised a system of lenses that magnified objects. Apparently without ever seeing a telescope, Galileo constructed his own. It magnified distant objects to three times the size seen by the unaided eye.

Using the telescope, Galileo was able to view the universe in a new way. He made many important discoveries that supported Copernicus's view of the universe, such as the following:

1. *The discovery of four satellites, or moons, orbiting Jupiter.* This proved that the old idea of Earth being the only center of motion in the universe was wrong. Here, plainly visible, was another center of motion—Jupiter. People who opposed the sun-centered system said that the moon would be left behind if Earth really revolved around the sun. Galileo's discovery disproved this argument.
2. *The discovery that the planets are circular disks, not just points of light, as was previously thought.* This showed that the planets must be Earth-like.
3. *The discovery that Venus has phases just like the moon.* So Venus orbits its source of light—the sun. Galileo saw that Venus appears smallest when it is in full phase and therefore farthest from Earth, as shown in Figure 7.
4. *The discovery that the moon's surface was not smooth.* Galileo saw mountains, craters, and plains. He thought the plains might be bodies of water. This idea was also believed by others, as we can tell from the names given to these features (Sea of Tranquility, Sea of Storms, and so forth).
5. *The discovery that the sun had sunspots, or dark regions.* Galileo tracked the movement of these spots and estimated the rotational period of the sun as just under a month.

The Solar System Model Evolves

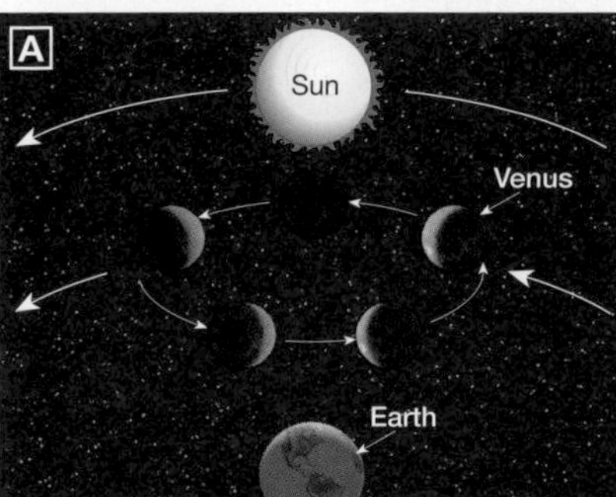

In the Ptolemaic system, the orbit of Venus lies between the sun and Earth.

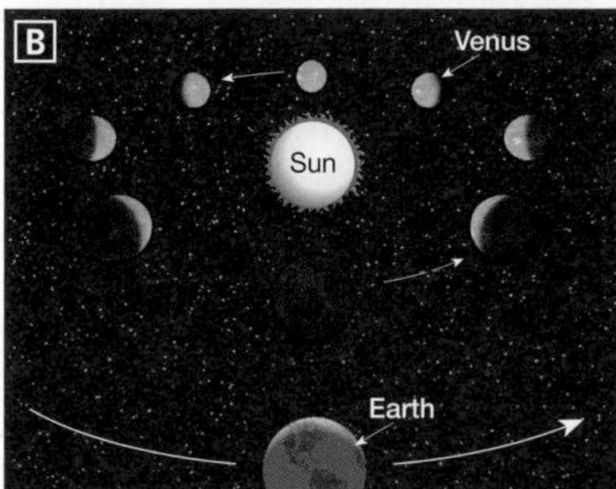

In the Copernican system, Venus orbits the sun and all its phases are visible from Earth.

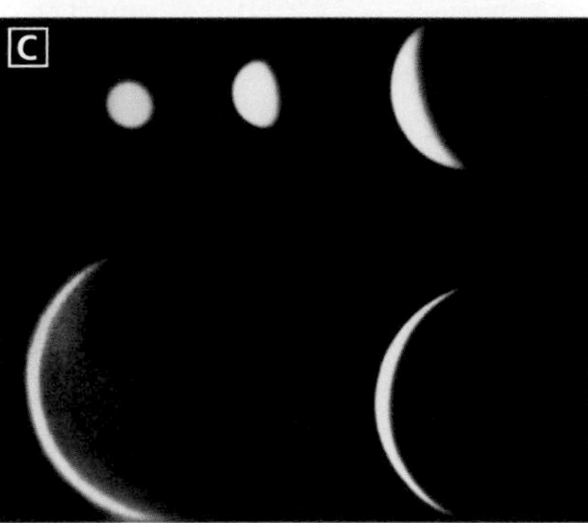

As Galileo observed, Venus goes through phases similar to the moon.

Figure 7
Relating Cause and Effect ***In the geocentric model, which phase of Venus would be visible from Earth?***

Build Reading Literacy L1

Refer to **p. 612D**, which provides the guidelines for thinking aloud.

Think Aloud Set the example for this strategy by verbalizing your own thought processes while reading about "Galileo Galilei." Encourage students to read "Sir Isaac Newton" while quietly verbalizing their thought processes. Then have a class discussion about the advantages students found in staying focused on a logical thought process when reading in this manner.
Intrapersonal, Auditory

Facts and Figures

The Roman Catholic Church continued to try to control the work of scientists during Galileo's time. In 1616, the Church condemned the Copernican theory and told Galileo to abandon it. Galileo refused and wrote his most famous work, *Dialogue of the Great World Systems*. After it was published, critics pointed out that Galileo was promoting the Copernican view of the solar system. Galileo was called before the Inquisition. He was tried and convicted of proclaiming doctrines contrary to religious doctrine and was sentenced to permanent house arrest. He lived the last ten years of his life under house arrest.

Answer to . . .

Figure 7 *only the crescent phase*

Teacher Demo

A Simple Mirror Telescope 

Purpose Students will observe how a mirror telescope works.

Materials lightbulb in a lamp base, magnifying lens, mirror with concave surface (magnifying mirror with 2 sides—used for makeup and shaving)

Procedure Place the light on a table in a darkened room. Turn the light on and use the concave surface of the mirror to reflect the lightbulb on the wall. Move the mirror until you get a sharp image on the wall. Observe the image of the bulb on the wall through the magnifying glass. Move the magnifying glass to get the largest and clearest image.

Expected Outcome Students will observe how a mirror telescope enlarges an image to make it easier to study. **Kinesthetic, Visual**

Figure 8 Sir Isaac Newton

Sir Isaac Newton Sir Isaac Newton (1642–1727) was born in the year of Galileo's death. See Figure 8. Many scientists had attempted to explain the forces involved in planetary motion. Kepler believed that some force pushed the planets along in their orbits. Galileo correctly reasoned that no force is required to keep an object in motion. And he proposed that a moving object will continue to move at a constant speed and in a straight line. This concept is called inertia.

The problem, then, was not to explain the force that keeps the planets moving but rather to determine the force that keeps them from going in a straight line out into space. At the age of 23, Newton described a force that extends from Earth into space and holds the moon in orbit around Earth. **Although others had theorized the existence of such a force, Newton was the first to formulate and test the law of universal gravitation.**

Universal Gravitation According to Newton, every body in the universe attracts every other body with a force that is directly proportional to their masses and inversely proportional to the square of the distance between their centers of mass.

The gravitational force decreases with distance, so that two objects 3 kilometers apart have 3^2, or 9, times less gravitational attraction than if the same objects were 1 kilometer apart.

The law of universal gravitation also states that the greater the mass of the object, the greater is its gravitational force. For example, the mass of the moon creates a gravitational force strong enough to cause ocean tides on Earth. But the tiny mass of a satellite has no measurable effect on Earth. The mass of an object is a measure of the total amount of matter it contains. But more often mass is measured by finding how much an object resists any effort to change its state of motion.

Often we confuse the concept of mass with weight. Weight is the force of gravity acting upon an object. Weight is properly expressed in newtons (N). Therefore, weight varies when gravitational forces change. See Figure 9.

Figure 9 Weight is the force of gravity acting on an object. **A** An astronaut with a mass of 88 kg weighs 863 N on Earth. **B** An astronaut with a mass of 88 kg weighs 141 N on the moon. **Calculating** ***If the same astronaut stood on Mars where the acceleration due to gravity is about 3.7 m/s^2, how much would the astronaut weigh?***

A Astronaut on Earth
Mass = 88.0 kg; Weight = 863 N

B Astronaut on Moon
Mass = 88.0 kg; Weight = 141 N

Newton proved that the force of gravity, combined with the tendency of a planet to remain in straight-line motion, results in the elliptical orbits that Kepler discovered. Earth, for example, moves forward in its orbit about 30 kilometers each second. During the same second, the force of gravity pulls it toward the sun about 0.5 centimeter. Newton concluded that it is the combination of Earth's forward motion and its "falling" motion that defines its orbit. As Figure 10 shows, if gravity were somehow eliminated, Earth would move in a straight line out into space. If Earth's forward motion suddenly stopped, gravity would pull it directly toward the sun.

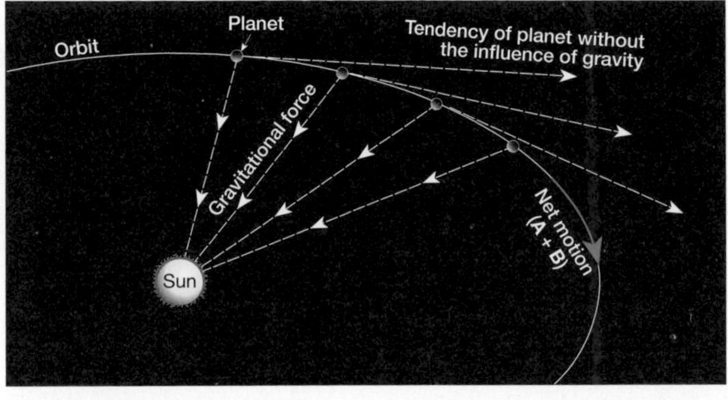

Figure 10 Without the influence of gravity, planets would move in a straight line out into space.

Newton used the law of universal gravitation to redefine Kepler's third law, which states the relationship between the orbital periods of the planets and their solar distances. When restated, Kepler's third law takes into account the masses of the bodies involved and provides a method for determining the mass of a body when the orbit of one of its satellites is known.

Section 22.1 Assessment

Reviewing Concepts

1. Compare and contrast the geocentric and heliocentric models of the universe.
2. What produces the retrograde motion of Mars?
3. What geometric arrangements did Ptolemy use to explain retrograde motion?
4. What major change did Copernicus make in the Ptolemaic system? Why was this change significant?

Critical Thinking

5. **Applying Concepts** What role did the telescope play in Galileo's contributions to science?
6. **Summarizing** In your own words, summarize Kepler's three laws of planetary motion.

Math Practice

7. Use Kepler's third law to show that the distance of a planet whose period is 5 years is 2.9 AU from the sun. Do the same for a planet with a period of 10 years at 4.6 AU from the sun, and a planet with a period of 10 days at 0.09 AU from the sun.

3 ASSESS

Evaluate Understanding **L2**

Have students write three review questions for this section. Students should then work in small groups and ask one another their questions.

Reteach **L1**

Use Figures 3 and 4 to review geocentric and heliocentric models of the solar system.

Solutions

7. $P^2 = a^3$

$5^2 = 2.9^3$

$10^2 = 4.6^3$

$\left(\frac{10}{365}\right)^2 = 0.09^3$

Section 22.1 Assessment

1. In the geocentric model, the sun and planets revolve around Earth. In the heliocentric model, Earth and the other planets revolve around the sun.
2. Retrograde motion occurs when Earth, which travels faster than Mars, passes Mars. This makes Mars appear to go westward.
3. Ptolemy showed planets moving in circular orbits around Earth.
4. Copernicus placed the sun at the center of the solar system. This was a major break from the ancient idea that Earth lies at the center.
5. Sample answer: The telescope allowed Galileo to view the universe in a new way, leading to many discoveries on his part.
6. The path of a planet around the sun is an ellipse. Each planet revolves so that an imaginary line connecting it to the sun sweeps over equal areas at equal time intervals. The squares of the orbital periods of the planets to the cubes of their average distances from the sun.

Answer to . . .

Figure 9 *325.6 N*

Section 22.2

1 FOCUS

Section Objectives

22.4 **Describe** the movements of Earth known as rotation, revolution, and precession.

22.5 **Explain** how the moon goes through phases.

22.6 **Explain** how eclipses occur.

Reading Focus

Build Vocabulary L2

Word-Part Analysis List on the board the following word parts and meanings: *helios*, "sun"; *ge* or *gee*, "earth"; *peri-*, "around or near"; *ap-* or *apo-*, "away from." Have students identify these word parts in the vocabulary terms. Discuss the terms' meanings with students.

Reading Strategy L2

a. Earth comes between the moon and sun.
b. solar eclipse.
c. lunar eclipse.

2 INSTRUCT

Motions of Earth

Integrate Language Arts L2

Archaeologists believe that Stonehenge was built in three stages between about 3000 to 1000 B.C. Stonehenge was probably used as a religious center or a type of astronomical clock or calendar. Have students research information on the construction and possible purposes for Stonehenge. Students should prepare a short report and make a visual aid showing the layout of Stonehenge.
Verbal, Portfolio

22.2 The Earth-Moon-Sun System

Reading Focus

Key Concepts

- In what ways does Earth move?
- What causes the phases of the moon?
- Why are eclipses relatively rare events?

Vocabulary

- rotation
- revolution
- precession
- perihelion
- aphelion
- perigee
- apogee
- phases of the moon
- solar eclipse
- lunar eclipse

Reading Strategy

Monitoring Your Understanding Copy the flowchart below. As you read, complete it to show how eclipses occur.

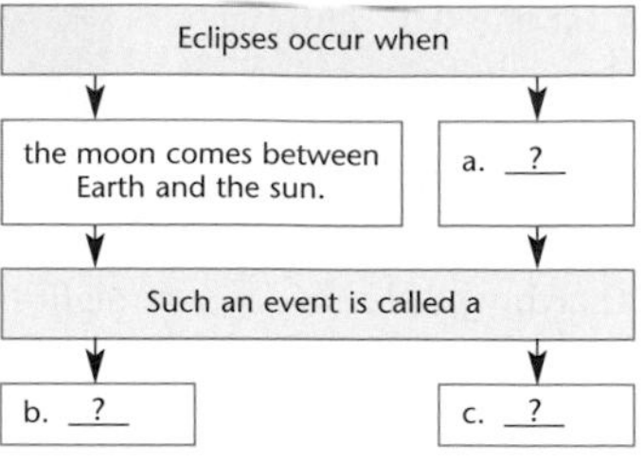

If you gaze away from the city lights on a clear night, it will seem that the stars produce a spherical shell surrounding Earth. This impression seems so real that it is easy to understand why many early Greeks regarded the stars as being fixed to a solid, celestial sphere. People have always been fascinated by the changing positions of the sun and moon in the sky. Prehistoric people, for example, built observatories. The structure known as Stonehenge, shown in Figure 11, was probably an attempt at better solar predictions. At the beginning of summer in the Northern Hemisphere (the summer solstice on June 21 or 22), the rising sun comes up directly above the heel stone of Stonehenge. Besides keeping this calendar, Stonehenge may also have provided a method of determining eclipses. In this section, you'll learn more about the movements of bodies in space that cause events such as eclipses.

Figure 11 On the summer solstice, the sun can be observed rising above the heel stone of Stonehenge, an ancient observatory in England.

Motions of Earth

The two main motions of Earth are rotation and revolution. **Rotation** is the turning, or spinning, of a body on its axis. **Revolution** is the motion of a body, such as a planet or moon, along a path around some point in space. For example, Earth revolves around the sun, and the moon revolves around Earth. Earth also has another very slow motion known as **precession,** which is the slight movement, over a period of 26,000 years, of Earth's axis.

622 Chapter 22

Rotation The main results of Earth's rotation are day and night. Earth's rotation has become a standard method of measuring time because it is so dependable and easy to use. Each rotation equals about 24 hours. You may be surprised to learn that we can measure Earth's rotation in two ways, making two kinds of days. Most familiar is the mean solar day, the time interval from one noon to the next, which averages about 24 hours. Noon is when the sun has reached its zenith, or highest point in the sky.

The sidereal day, on the other hand, is the time it takes for Earth to make one complete rotation (360 degrees) with respect to a star other than our sun. The sidereal day is measured by the time required for a star to reappear at the identical position in the sky where it was observed the day before. The sidereal day has a period of 23 hours, 56 minutes, and 4 seconds (measured in solar time), which is almost 4 minutes shorter than the mean solar day. This difference results because the direction to distant stars barely changes because of Earth's slow revolution along its orbit. The direction to the sun, on the other hand, changes by almost 1 degree each day. This difference is shown in Figure 12.

Why do we use the mean solar day instead of the sidereal day as a measurement of our day? In sidereal time, "noon" occurs four minutes earlier each day. Therefore, after six months, "noon" occurs at "midnight." Astronomers use sidereal time because the stars appear in the same position in the sky every 24 sidereal hours. Usually, an observatory will begin its sidereal day when the position of the spring equinox is directly overhead.

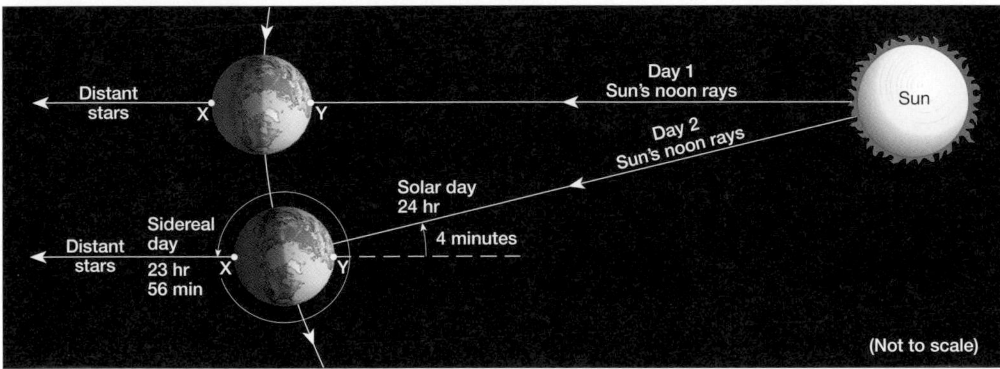

Figure 12 Sidereal Day It takes Earth 23 hours and 56 minutes to make one rotation with respect to the stars (sidereal day). However, after Earth has completed one sidereal day, point Y has not yet returned to the "noon position" with respect to the sun. Earth has to rotate another 4 minutes to complete the solar day.

Use Visuals **L1**

Figure 12 Have students examine the movement of Earth and the locations of points X and Y carefully. Ask: **What are the reference points for a mean solar day and a sidereal day?** *(A mean solar day is measured using the sun as a reference point. A sidereal day is measured using a star other than the sun as a reference point.)* **Why do these two reference points give two different results?** *(The direction from Earth to a distant star barely changes, but the distance from Earth to the sun changes by almost one degree each day.)* **Why do astronomers choose to use the sidereal day instead of the mean solar day?** *(The stars appear in the same position in the sky every 24 sidereal hours.)*
Visual, Logical

Customize for English Language Learners

Have students draw simple illustrations for the motions of Earth, the motions of the Earth-moon-sun system, and eclipses. Have them explain each illustration to a partner. Then have each pair of students discuss why the motions occur as they do.

Build Reading Literacy L1

Refer to **p. 334D** in **Chapter 12,** which provides the guidelines for outlining.

Outline Have students read the text on pp. 622–629 relating to the Earth-moon-sun system. Then ask students to use the headings as major divisions in an outline. Suggest that students refer to their outlines when answering the questions in the Section 22.2 Assessment.
Verbal

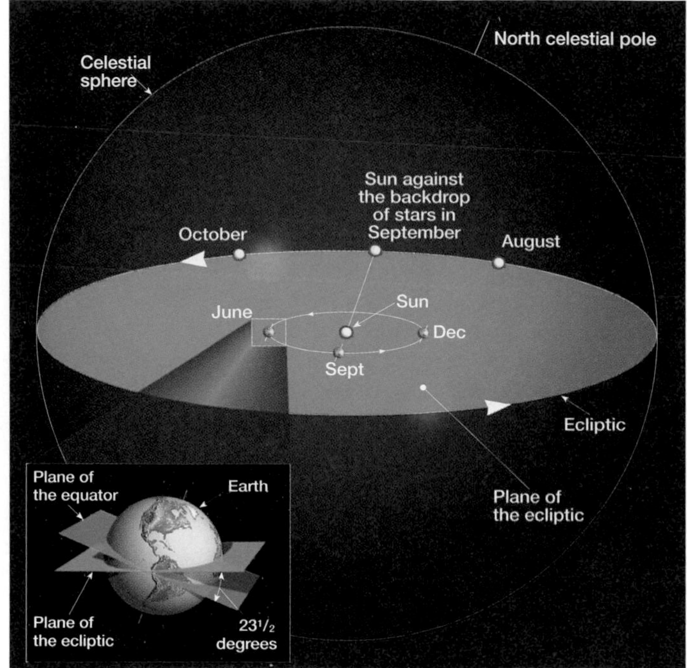

Figure 13 The Ecliptic Earth's orbital motion causes the apparent position of the sun to shift about 1 degree each day on the celestial sphere.

Revolution Earth revolves around the sun in an elliptical orbit at an average speed of 107,000 kilometers per hour. Its average distance from the sun is 150 million kilometers. But because its orbit is an ellipse, Earth's distance from the sun varies. At **perihelion,** Earth is closet to the sun—about 147 million kilometers away. Perihelion occurs about January 3 each year. At **aphelion,** Earth is farthest from the sun—about 152 million kilometers away. Aphelion occurs about July 4. So Earth is farthest from the sun in July and closest to the sun in January.

Because of Earth's annual movement around the sun, each day the sun appears to be displaced among the constellations at a distance equal to about twice its width, or 1 degree. The apparent annual path of the sun against the backdrop of the celestial sphere is called the ecliptic, as shown in Figure 13. Generally, the planets and the moon travel in nearly the same plane as Earth. So their paths on the celestial sphere lie near the ecliptic.

Earth's Axis and Seasons The imaginary plane that connects Earth's orbit with the celestial sphere is called the plane of the ecliptic. From the reference plane, Earth's axis of rotation is tilted about 23.5 degrees. Because of Earth's tilt, the apparent path of the sun and the celestial equator intersect each other at an angle of 23.5 degrees. This angle is very important to Earth's inhabitants. Because of the inclination of Earth's axis to the plane of the ecliptic, Earth has its yearly cycle of seasons.

When the apparent position of the sun is plotted on the celestial sphere over a period of a year's time, its path intersects the celestial equator at two points. From a Northern Hemisphere point of view, these intersections are called the spring equinox (March 20 or 21) and autumn equinox (September 22 or 23). On June 21 or 22, the date of the summer solstice, the sun appears 23.5 degrees north of the celestial equator. Six months later, on December 21–22, the date of the winter solstice, the sun appears 23.5 degrees south of the celestial equator.

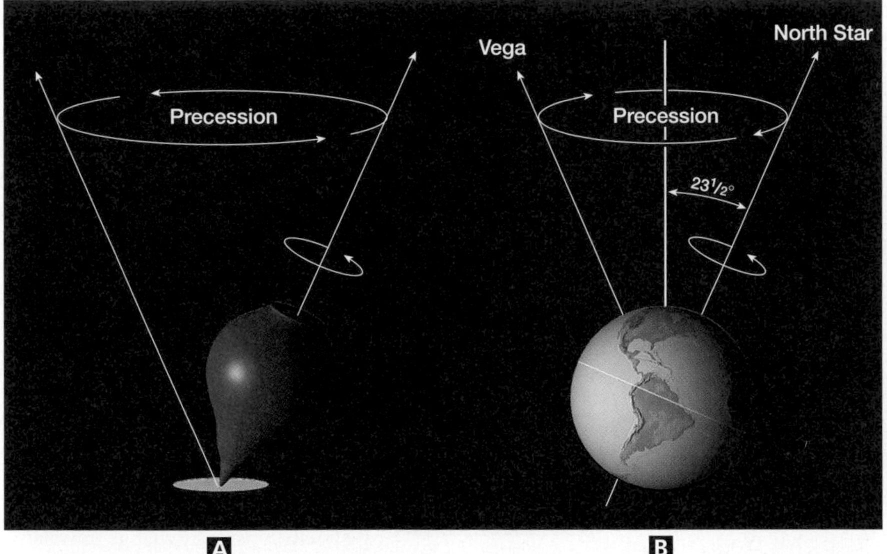

Precession A third and very slow movement of Earth is called precession. Earth's axis maintains approximately the same angle of tilt. But the direction in which the axis points continually changes. As a result, the axis traces a circle on the sky. This movement is very similar to the wobble of a spinning top, as shown in Figure 14A. At the present time, the axis points toward the bright star Polaris. In the year 14,000, it will point toward the bright star Vega, which will then become the North Star, as shown in Figure 14B. The period of precession is 26,000 years. By the year 28,000, Polaris will once again be the North Star.

Precession has only a minor effect on the seasons, because the angle of tilt changes only slightly. It does, however, cause the positions of the seasons (equinox and solstice) to move slightly each year among the stars.

Earth-Sun Motion In addition to its own movements, Earth accompanies the sun as the entire solar system speeds in the direction of the bright star Vega at 20 kilometers per second. Also, the sun, like other nearby stars, revolves around the galaxy. This trip takes 230 million years to traverse at speeds approaching 250 kilometers per second. The galaxies themselves are also in motion. Earth is presently approaching one of its nearest galactic neighbors, the Great Galaxy in Andromeda. The motions of Earth are many and complex, and its speed in space is very great.

What is precession?

Figure 14 Precession
A Precession is similar to a spinning top. It causes the North Pole to point at different parts of the sky during a 26,000-year cycle. **B** Today, the North Pole points to Polaris.
Interpreting Illustrations ***What star will the North Pole point to in 13,000 years?***

Observing Precession **L2**

Purpose Students will observe the precession of a toy top.

Materials a toy top similar to the one shown in Figure 14

Procedure Put a distinctive mark on the top of the top where the axis of rotation is located. This will give students a specific point to observe. Put the top in motion. Have students observe the precession of the top.

Expected Outcome Students will observe an object in precession, which is similar to Earth's motion.
Visual

Answer to . . .

Figure 14 *Vega*

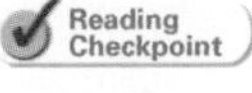
Precession is the slow movement of Earth's axis over a period of 26,000 years.

Motions of the Earth-Moon System

Build Science Skills L2

Interpreting Diagrams/ Photographs Compare the photographs at the bottom of the page, Figure 15B, with those in Figure 15A. Ask students to label the photographs with the phase of the moon that is shown from left to right. *(Crescent, waning; Third quarter; Gibbous, waning; and Full.)* Challenge students to recognize the patterns for a waxing and waning moon. *(When the right side of the moon is lit, the moon is in its waxing phase. When the left side is lit, the moon is waning.)*
Visual, Logical

L2

Students may have four different misconceptions of why the moon goes through phases. (1) Clouds cover part of the moon. (2) Planets cast a shadow on the moon. (3) The shadow of the sun falls on the moon. (4) The shadow of Earth falls on the moon. Help students realize that lunar phases are a result of the motion of the moon and the sunlight that is reflected from its surface.
Logical

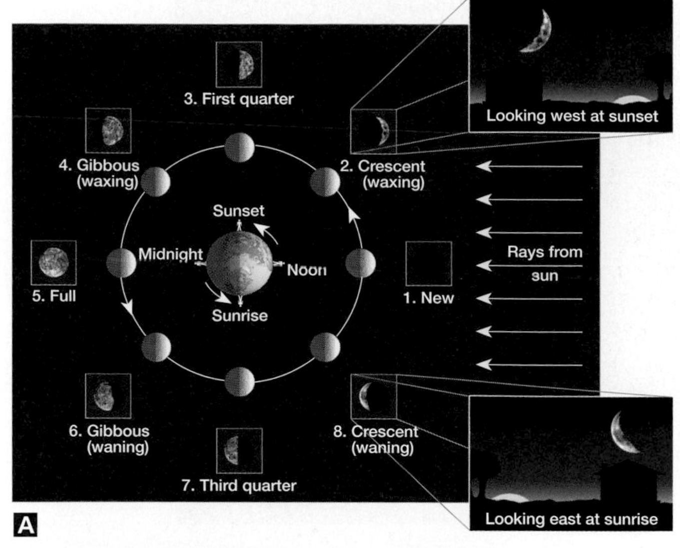

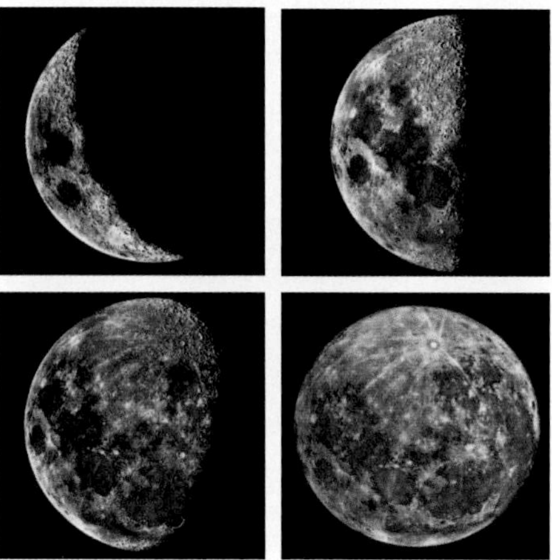

Figure 15 Phases of the Moon
A The outer figures show the phases as seen from Earth.
B Compare these photographs with the diagram.

Motions of the Earth-Moon System

Earth has one natural satellite, the moon. In addition to accompanying Earth in its annual trip around the sun, our moon orbits Earth within a period of about one month. When viewed from above the North Pole, the direction of this motion is counterclockwise. Because the moon's orbit is elliptical, its distance to Earth varies by about 6 percent, averaging 384,401 kilometers. At a point known as **perigee,** the moon is closest to Earth. At a point known as **apogee,** the moon is farthest from Earth.

The motions of the Earth-moon system constantly change the relative positions of the sun, Earth, and moon. This results in changes in the appearance of the moon, as you'll read about next.

Phases of the Moon The first astronomical event to be understood was the regular cycle of the phases of the moon. On a monthly basis, we observe the **phases of the moon** as a change in the amount of the moon that appears lit. Look at the new moon shown in Figure 15A. About two days after the new moon, a thin sliver (crescent phase) appears low in the western sky just after sunset. During the following week, the lighted portion of the moon visible from Earth increases (waxing) to a half circle (first-quarter phase) and can be seen from about noon to midnight. In another week, the complete disk (full-moon phase) can be seen rising in the east as the sun is sinking in the west. During the next two weeks, the percentage of the moon that can be seen steadily declines (waning), until the moon disappears altogether (new-moon phase). The cycle soon begins again with the reappearance of the crescent moon.

Lunar phases are a result of the motion of the moon and the sunlight that is reflected from its surface. See Figure 15B. Half of the moon is illuminated at all times. But to an observer on Earth, the percentage of the bright side that is visible depends on the location of the moon with respect to the sun and Earth. When the moon lies between the sun and Earth, none of its bright side faces Earth.

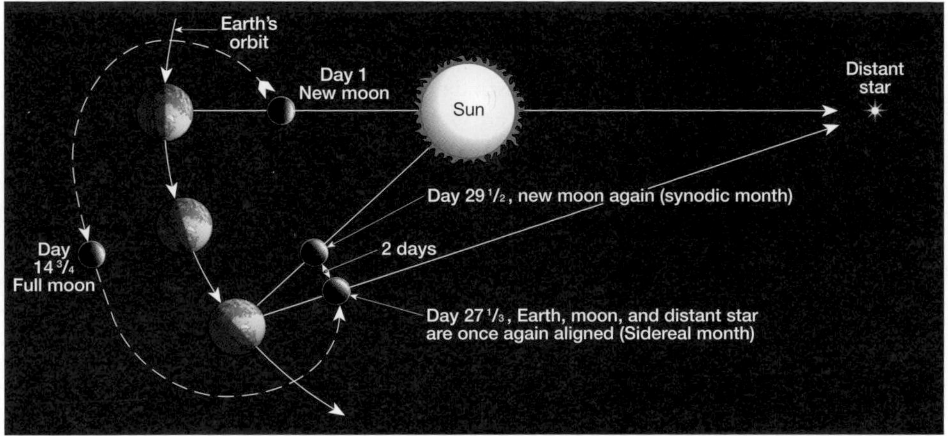

Figure 16 Lunar Motion As the moon orbits Earth, the Earth-moon system also moves in orbit around the sun. Thus, even after the moon makes one revolution around Earth, it has not yet reached its starting point in relation to the stars.

When the moon lies on the side of Earth opposite the sun, all of its lighted side faces Earth. So we see the full moon. At all positions between the new moon and the full moon, a part of the moon's lit side is visible from Earth.

Lunar Motions The cycle of the moon through its phases requires 29 1/2 days, a time span called the synodic month. This cycle was the basis for the first Roman calendar. However, this is the apparent period of the moon's revolution around Earth and not the true period, which takes only 27 1/3 days and is known as the sidereal month. The reason for the difference of nearly two days each cycle is shown in Figure 16. Note that as the moon orbits Earth, the Earth-moon system also moves in an orbit around the sun. Even after the moon has made a complete revolution around Earth, it has not yet reached its starting position, which was directly between the sun and Earth (new-moon phase). The additional motion to reach the starting point takes another two days.

An interesting fact about the motions of the moon is that the moon's period of rotation about its axis and its revolution around Earth are the same. They are both 27 1/3 days. Because of this, the same side of the moon always faces Earth. All of the crewed Apollo missions took place on the side of the moon facing Earth. Only orbiting satellites and astronauts have seen the "back" side of the moon.

Because the moon rotates on its axis only once every 27 1/3 days, any location on its surface experiences periods of daylight and darkness lasting about two weeks. This, along with the absence of an atmosphere, accounts for the high surface temperature of 127°C on the day side of the moon and the low surface temperature of −173°C on its night side.

Why does the same side of the moon always face Earth?

Q *Why do we sometimes see the moon in daytime?*

A During phases of the lunar cycle other than the full moon, the moon and sun are not directly opposite each other. This makes it possible to see the moon during daylight hours.

Use Visuals 

Figure 16 Have students examine this figure. Ask: Why do the synodic and sidereal month differ? *(The moon makes a complete orbit around Earth in 27 1/3 days, as viewed from a distant star. It takes the moon 29 1/2 days to go through its phases.)* **What is the reference point for the sidereal month?** *(A distant star)* **For the synodic month?** *(The sun)*
Visual

Integrate Social Studies L2

The calendar that we use today was devised in 45–44 B.C. by Julius Caesar and is known as the Julian calendar. Have students research to find the basis of the modern calendar. Ask students to define a year, month, week, and day. Encourage students to find out the traditions that were adopted when devising this calendar. Have students prepare a report on the history of the modern calendar.
Verbal, Portfolio

Facts and Figures

Ancient calendars were based on phases of the moon. The month was originally defined as the time between two full moons, or 29 1/2 days. The lunar calendar year was 354 days, which is 11 1/4 days short of a solar year. An additional month was occasionally added to lunar calendars to align the calendar with the seasons. Ancient Egyptians were the first to devise a calendar based on a solar year.

Answer to . . .

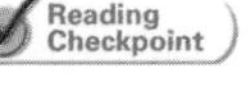

The moon's period of rotation about its axis and its revolution around Earth are the same.

Eclipses

Use Community Resources **L2**

Arrange for your class to visit a planetarium. Have students prepare questions regarding the topics in this chapter in advance.
Interpersonal

Use Visuals **L1**

Figure 17A Have students examine this figure. Ask: **During a solar eclipse, why do observers in the umbra see a total solar eclipse?** *(The moon completely blocks the sun from the viewer.)* **Why do observers in the penumbra see a partial eclipse?** *(The moon only partially blocks the sun from the viewer.)*

Figure 17B Have students examine this figure. Ask: **When does a total lunar eclipse occur?** *(A total lunar eclipse occurs when Earth completely blocks the moon from the sun and the moon is completely in Earth's shadow.)* **When does a partial lunar eclipse occur?** *(A partial lunar eclipse occurs when Earth partially blocks the moon from the sun and only a portion of the moon is in Earth's shadow.)*
Visual, Logical

Download a worksheet on eclipses for students to complete, and find additional teacher support from NSTA SciLinks.

For: Links on eclipses
Visit: www.SciLinks.org
Web Code: cjn-7222

Eclipses

Along with understanding the moon's phases, the early Greeks also realized that eclipses are simply shadow effects. When the moon moves in a line directly between Earth and the sun, it casts a dark shadow on Earth. This produces a **solar eclipse.** This situation occurs during new-moon phases. The moon is eclipsed when it moves within Earth's shadow, producing a **lunar eclipse.** This situation occurs during full-moon phases. Figure 17 illustrates solar and lunar eclipses.

Why doesn't a solar eclipse occur with every new moon and a lunar eclipse with every full moon? They would if the orbit of the moon lay exactly along the plane of Earth's orbit. However, the moon's orbit is inclined about 5 degrees to the plane that contains Earth and the sun. During most new-moon phases, the shadow of the moon misses Earth (passes above or below). During most full-moon phases, the shadow of Earth misses the moon. **During a new-moon or full-moon phase, the moon's orbit must cross the plane of the ecliptic for an eclipse to take place.** Because these conditions are normally met only twice a year, the usual number of eclipses is four. These occur as a set of one solar and one lunar eclipse, followed six months later with another set. Occasionally, the alignment can result in additional eclipses. However, the total number of eclipses in one year isn't more than seven.

Solar and Lunar Eclipse

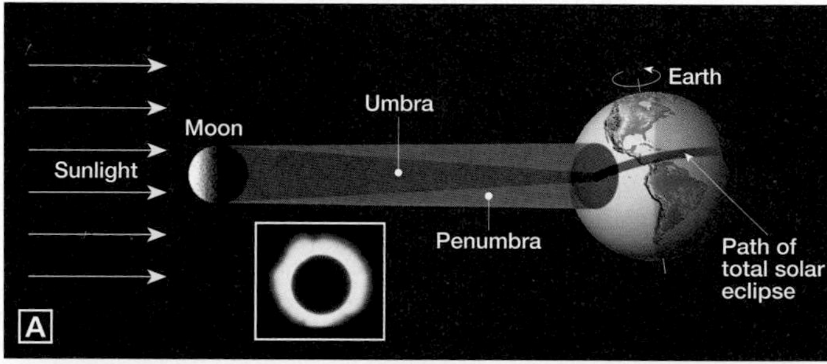

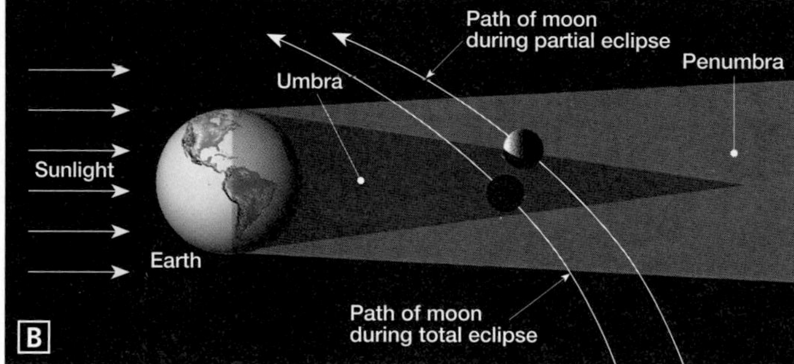

Figure 17 A Observers in the umbra see a total solar eclipse. Those in the penumbra see a partial eclipse. The path of the solar eclipse moves eastward across the globe. The figure shows a total solar eclipse. **B** During a total lunar eclipse, the moon's orbit carries it into Earth's umbra. During a partial eclipse, only a portion of the moon enters the umbra.

Facts and Figures

One of the earliest surviving records of eclipse observations is from ancient China. Astronomers recorded their observations from 722 to 481 B.C. in a chronicle called *Ch'un-ch'iu (Spring and Autumn Annals)*. As many as 32 of the eclipses recorded in the *Ch'un-ch'iu* can be identified by modern calculations.

During a total lunar eclipse, Earth's circular shadow can be seen moving slowly across the disk of the full moon. When totally eclipsed, the moon is completely within Earth's shadow, but it is still visible as a coppery disk. This happens because Earth's atmosphere bends and transmits some long-wavelength light (red) into its shadow. A total eclipse of the moon can last up to four hours and is visible to anyone on the side of Earth facing the moon.

During a total solar eclipse, the moon casts a circular shadow that is never wider than 275 kilometers, about the size of South Carolina. Anyone observing in this region will see the moon slowly block the sun from view and the sky darken. When the eclipse is almost complete, the temperature sharply drops a few degrees. The solar disk is completely blocked for seven minutes at the most. This happens because the moon's shadow is so small. Then one edge reappears.

When the eclipse is complete, the dark moon is seen covering the complete solar disk. Only the sun's brilliant white outer atmosphere is visible. Total solar eclipses are visible only to people in the dark part of the moon's shadow known as the umbra. A partial eclipse is seen by those in the light portion of the shadow, known as the penumbra.

Partial solar eclipses are more common in the polar regions. In this zone, the penumbra covers the dark umbra of the moon's shadow, just missing Earth. A total solar eclipse is a rare event at any location. The next one that will be visible from the United States will take place on August 21, 2017.

Section 22.2. Assessment

Reviewing Concepts

1. In what ways does Earth move?
2. What phenomena result from Earth's rotation and revolution?
3. What causes the phases of the moon?
4. How does the crescent phase that precedes the new moon differ from the crescent phase that follows the new moon?
5. Why don't eclipses occur during every full-moon or new-moon phase?
6. Describe the locations of the sun, moon, and Earth during a solar eclipse and during a lunar eclipse.

Critical Thinking

7. **Predicting** Currently, Earth is closest to the sun in January (perihelion) and farthest from the sun in July (aphelion). However, 13,000 years from now, precession will cause perihelion to occur in July and aphelion to occur in January. Assuming no other changes, how might this affect average summer temperatures for your location? What about average winter temperatures?

Writing in Science

Firsthand Account Imagine you are an assistant for one of the ancient astronomers. You are present when the astronomer makes an important discovery. Write a firsthand account describing the discovery and its impact on science.

3 ASSESS

Evaluate Understanding

Call out different phases of the moon. Have students draw the phases on the board or in their notebooks.

Reteach

Write *rotation, revolution,* and *precession* on the board. Have students quiz each other on these motions of Earth.

Writing in Science

Students should choose one of the astronomers and include factual details in their paragraphs. An example might be Copernicus, whose heliocentric view changed the way people viewed the universe. Paragraphs should be written from the first-person point of view.

Section 22.2 Assessment

1. Earth revolves around the sun, rotates on its axis, and moves slightly on its axis. It also revolves with the solar system around the Milky Way.
2. rotation: day and night; revolution: seasons
3. the motion of the moon and the amount of sunlight reflected from its surface that can be seen from Earth
4. The left edge of the moon is visible during the crescent phase that precedes the new moon, while the right side of the moon is visible during the crescent phase that follows the new moon.
5. The moon's orbit must cross the plane of the ecliptic for an eclipse to take place.
6. During a solar eclipse, the moon is between the sun and Earth. During a lunar eclipse, Earth is between the sun and moon.
7. Sample answer: The difference between perihelion and aphelion has little influence on the quantity of radiation received by Earth. The primary cause of seasons is Earth's tilted axis, not its distance from the sun. So any changes in summer or winter temperatures would be small. The overall impact on the biosphere and hydrosphere would also be small.

Section 22.3

1 FOCUS

Section Objectives

22.7 **Describe** how the physical features of the lunar surface were created.

22.8 **Explain** the history of the moon.

Reading Focus

Build Vocabulary L2

Vocabulary Rating Chart Have students construct a chart with four columns labeled Term, Can Define or Use It, Heard or Seen It, and Don't Know. Have students copy the terms *crater*, *ray*, *mare*, *rille*, and *lunar regolith* into the first column and rate their term knowledge by putting a check in one of the other columns. Ask how many students actually know each term. Have them share their knowledge. Ask focused questions to help students predict text content based on the term, thus enabling them to have a purpose for reading. After students have read the section, have them rate their knowledge again.

Reading Strategy L2

a. Huge quantities of crust and mantle were ejected into space.
b. The debris began orbiting Earth.
c. Debris united to form the moon.

22.3 Earth's Moon

Reading Focus

Key Concepts

- What processes create surface features on the moon?
- How did the moon form?

Vocabulary

- crater
- ray
- mare
- rille
- lunar regolith

Reading Strategy

Sequencing Copy Copy the flowchart below. As you read, fill in the stages leading to the formation of the moon.

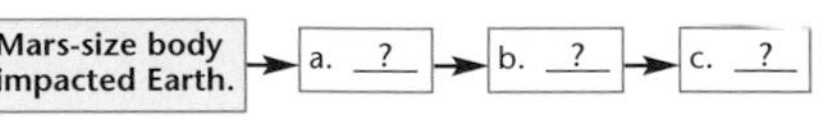

Earth now has hundreds of satellites. Only one natural satellite, the moon, accompanies us on our annual journey around the sun. Other planets have moons. But our planet-satellite system is unusual in the solar system, because Earth's moon is unusually large compared to its parent planet. The diameter of the moon is 3475 kilometers, about one-fourth of Earth's 12,756 kilometers.

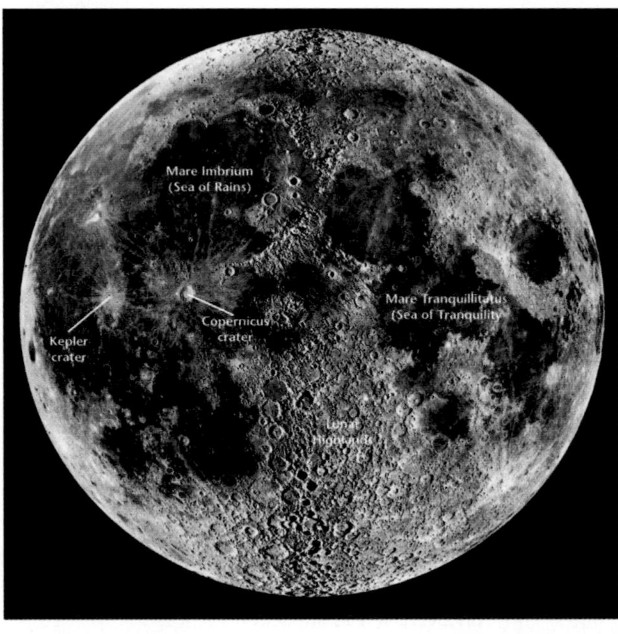

Figure 18 This is what the moon's surface looks like from Earth when viewed through a telescope.

Much of what we know about the moon, shown in Figure 18, comes from data gathered by the *Apollo* moon missions. Six *Apollo* spacecraft landed on the moon between 1969 and 1972. Uncrewed spacecraft such as the *Lunar Prospector* have also explored the moon's surface. From calculation of the moon's mass, we know that its density is 3.3 times that of water. This density is comparable to that of mantle rocks on Earth. But it is considerably less than Earth's average density, which is 5.5 times that of water. Geologists have suggested that this difference can be accounted for if the moon's iron core is small. The gravitational attraction at the lunar surface is one-sixth of that experienced on Earth's surface. (A 150-pound person on Earth weighs only 25 pounds on the moon). This difference allows an astronaut to carry a heavy life-support system easily. An astronaut on the moon could jump six times higher than on Earth.

The Lunar Surface

When Galileo first pointed his telescope toward the moon, he saw two different types of landscape—dark lowlands and bright highlands. Because the dark regions resembled seas on Earth, they were later named maria, which comes from the Latin word for *sea.* Today we know that the moon has no atmosphere or water. Therefore, the moon doesn't have the weathering and erosion that continually change Earth's surface. Also, tectonic forces aren't active on the moon, therefore volcanic eruptions no longer occur. However, because the moon is unprotected by an atmosphere, a different kind of erosion occurs. Tiny particles from space continually bombard its surface and gradually smooth out the landscape. Moon rocks become slightly rounded on top after a long time at the lunar surface. Even so, it is unlikely that the moon has changed very much in the last 3 billion years, except for a few craters.

Craters The most obvious features of the lunar surface are **craters,** which are round depressions in the surface of the moon. There are many craters on the moon. The moon even has craters within craters! The larger craters are about 250 kilometers in diameter, about the width of Indiana. **Most craters were produced by the impact of rapidly moving debris.**

By contrast, Earth has only about a dozen easily recognized impact craters. Friction with Earth's atmosphere burns up small debris before it reaches the ground. Evidence for most of the craters that formed in Earth's history has been destroyed by erosion or tectonic processes.

The formation of an impact crater is modeled in Figure 19. Upon impact, the colliding object compresses the material it strikes. This process is similar to the splash that occurs when a rock is dropped into water. A central peak forms after the impact.

Most of the ejected material lands near the crater, building a rim around it. The heat generated by the impact is enough to melt rock. Astronauts have brought back samples of glass and rock formed when fragments and dust were welded together by the impact.

Formation of a Crater

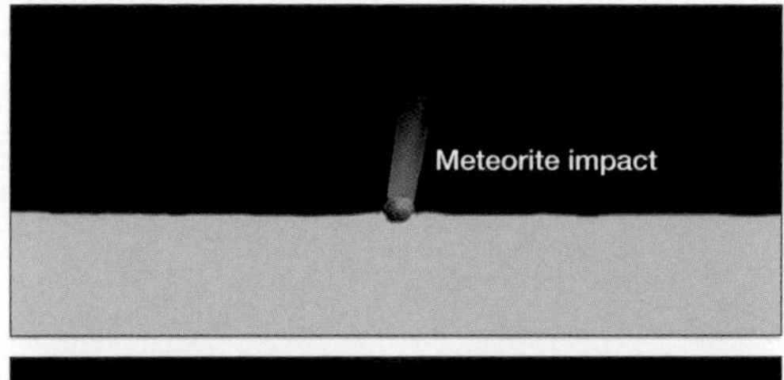

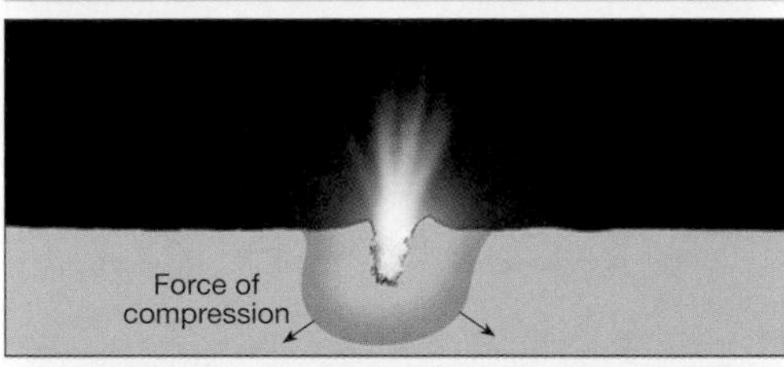

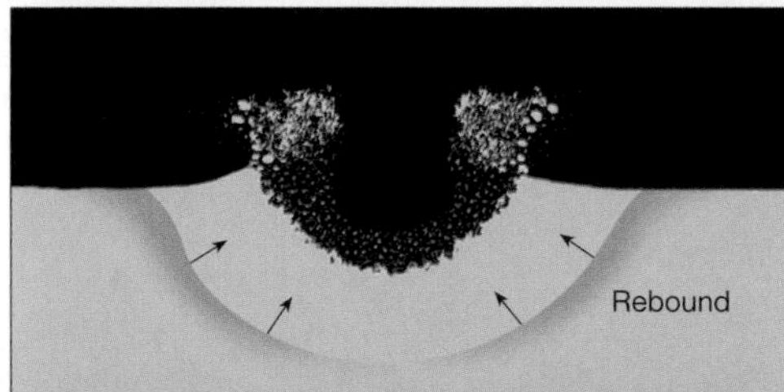

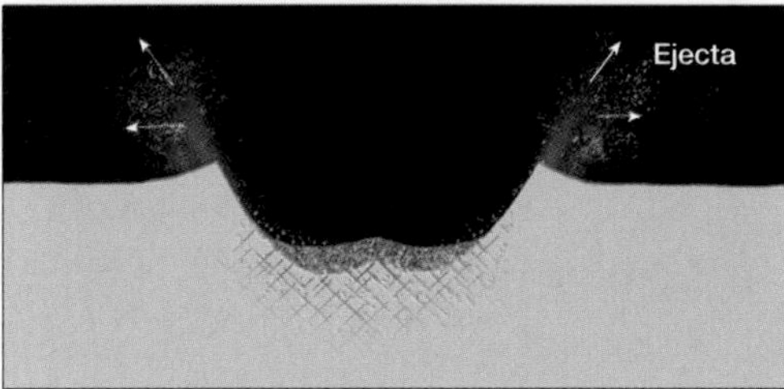

Figure 19 The energy of the rapidly moving meteoroid is transformed into heat energy. Rock compresses, then quickly rebounds. The rebounding rock causes debris to be ejected from the crater.

2 INSTRUCT

The Lunar Surface

Build Reading Literacy L1

Refer to **p. 306D** in **Chapter 11,** which provides the guidelines for KWL (Know/Want to Know/Learned) charts.

KWL Teach this independent study skill as a whole-class exercise.

1. Draw a three-column KWL chart on the board for students to copy.
2. Have students complete the Know column with facts, examples, and other information that they already know about the lunar surface.
3. Tell students to complete the Want to Know column with questions about the moon's surface.
4. Have students read pp. 631 and 632 about the moon. As they read, have them note answers to their questions in the Learned column, along with facts, examples, and details they learned.
5. Have students draw an Information I Expect to Use box below their KWL chart. Have them review the information in the Learned column and categorize the useful information in the box.

Verbal

Customize for Inclusion Students

Visually Impaired Have students with visual impairments feel the topography of the moon, using a relief globe or map of the moon. Assign visually-impaired students a partner to guide their fingers and to read the map or globe for them. Discuss with students what they have discovered about the surface of the moon.

Build Science Skills

L2

Using Models

Purpose Students will model the surface features of the lunar surface.

Materials foam poster board; soft modeling clay; toothpicks; narrow paper strips; tape; pencil, pen, or marker

Class Time 30 minutes

Procedure Have students use Figure 20 as a guide for their topographic map. First, instruct students to draw the physical features on the foam poster board. Next, have students use the soft modeling clay to build the surface features. Then students should create flag-type labels for the physical features, using narrow strips of paper, toothpicks, and tape. Finally, have students use the markers to identify the physical features on the surface of their topographical map.

Expected Outcome Students learn the major topographical surface features on the lunar surface.
Visual, Kinesthetic

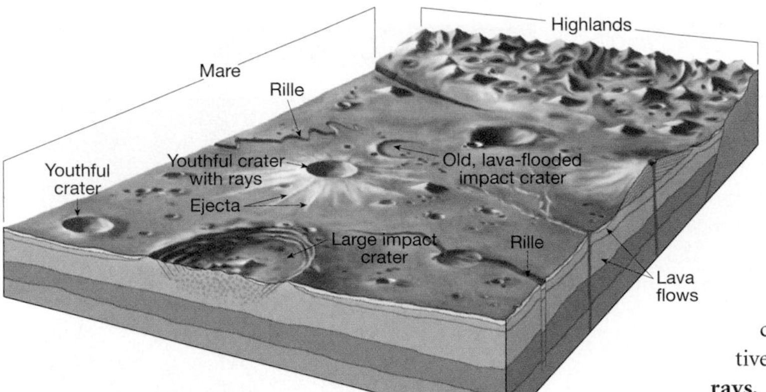

Figure 20 Major topographic features on the moon's surface include craters, maria, and highlands.
Identifying *Where are rilles located?*

A meteoroid only 3 meters in diameter can blast out a 150-meter-wide crater. A few of the large craters, such as those named Kepler and Copernicus, formed from the impact of bodies 1 kilometer or more in diameter. These two large craters are thought to be relatively young because of the bright **rays,** or splash marks that radiate outward for hundreds of kilometers.

Highlands Most of the lunar surface is made up of densely pitted, light-colored areas known as highlands. In fact, highlands cover the surface of the far side of the moon. The same side of the moon always faces Earth. Within the highland regions are mountain ranges. The highest lunar peaks reach elevations of almost 8 kilometers. This is only 1 kilometer lower than Mount Everest. Figure 20 shows highlands and other features of the moon.

Maria The dark, relatively smooth area on the moon's surface is called a **mare** (plural: maria). **Maria, ancient beds of basaltic lava, originated when asteroids punctured the lunar surface, letting magma bleed out.** Apparently the craters were flooded with layer upon layer of very fluid basaltic lava somewhat resembling the Columbia Plateau in the northwestern United States. The lava flows are often over 30 meters thick. The total thickness of the material that fills the maria could reach thousands of meters.

Long channels called **rilles** are associated with maria. Rilles look somewhat similar to valleys or trenches. Rilles may be the remnants of ancient lava flows.

Regolith All lunar terrains are mantled with a layer of gray debris derived from a few billion years of bombardment from meteorites. This soil-like layer, called **lunar regolith,** is composed of igneous rocks, glass beads, and fine lunar dust. In the maria that have been explored by *Apollo* astronauts, the lunar regolith is just over 3 meters thick.

What is lunar regolith?

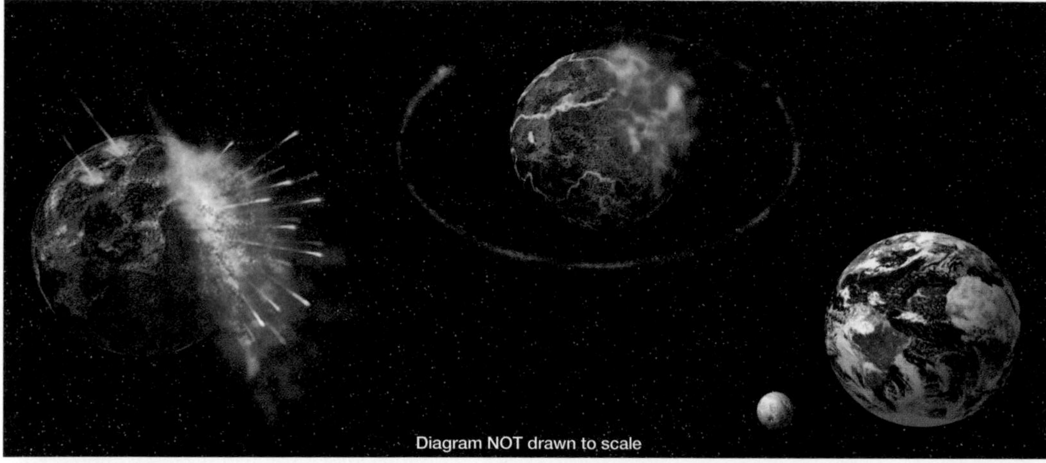

Figure 21 The moon may have formed when a large object collided with Earth. The resulting debris was ejected into space. The debris began orbiting around Earth and eventually united to form the moon.

Lunar History

The moon is our nearest planetary neighbor. Although astronauts have walked on its surface, much is still unknown about its origin. **The most widely accepted model for the origin of the moon is that when the solar system was forming, a body the size of Mars impacted Earth.** The impact, shown in Figure 21, would have liquefied Earth's surface and ejected huge quantities of crustal and mantle rock from an infant Earth. A portion of this ejected debris would have entered an orbit around Earth where it combined to form the moon.

The giant-impact hypothesis is consistent with other facts known about the moon. The ejected material would have been mostly iron-poor mantle and crustal rocks. These would account for the lack of a sizable iron core on the moon. The ejected material would have remained in orbit long enough to have lost the water that the moon lacks. Despite this supporting evidence, some questions remain unanswered.

Geologists have worked out the basic details of the moon's later history. One of their methods is to observe variations in crater density (the number of craters per unit area). The greater the crater density, the older the surface must be. From such evidence, scientists concluded that the moon evolved in three phases—the original crust (highlands), maria basins, and rayed craters.

During its early history, the moon was continually impacted as it swept up debris. This continuous attack, combined with radioactive decay, generated enough heat to melt the moon's outer shell and possibly the interior as well. Remnants of this original crust occupy the densely cratered highlands. These highlands have been estimated to be as much as 4.5 billion years old, about the same age as Earth.

Lunar History

Integrate Language Arts

Much of the scientific information that is known about the composition of the lunar surface is due to the Apollo Space Program. Have students research the scientific discoveries that were made as a result of this program. Students should prepare a presentation about the information they have learned. If possible, encourage students to make a computer presentation that includes actual photographs from the various missions.
Verbal, Portfolio

Use Visuals L1

Figure 21 Have students study this figure. Ask: **What evidence suggests that the moon came from mostly iron-poor mantle and crustal rocks from Earth?** *(The lack of a sizeable iron core on the moon)* **Why doesn't this ejected material contain water?** *(The material has been in orbit long enough to have lost any water that it may have had.)*
Verbal

Facts and Figures

The United States was not the only country with a space program. The former Union of Soviet Socialist Republics also had one. In fact, the U.S.S.R. was the first country to launch an artificial Earth satellite, *Sputnik 1*, in 1957. In early 1959, the Soviet spacecraft, *Luna 1*, became the first artificial object to orbit the sun. Later in 1959, *Luna 2* crashed into the moon to become the first artificial object on the lunar surface. Also in 1959, *Luna 3* took the first pictures of the moon's far side. The Soviet goal to send the first crewed spacecraft to the moon was never realized. In 1969, the United States became the first country that safely landed a person on the moon.

Answer to . . .

Figure 20 *Rilles are associated with maria.*

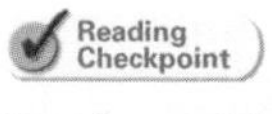

a soil-like layer of igneous rocks, glass beads, and fine lunar dust

Section 22.3 (continued)

3 ASSESS

Evaluate Understanding L2

Have students make flashcards on the details found in this section. Tell students to write a question on one side of the card and the answer on the other. Students can use these flashcards to quiz each other in class.

Reteach L1

Write the headings *Lunar Surface* and *Lunar History* on the board. Ask students to give you facts from the section about each topic. Write the information under the appropriate heading. Students can copy this information from the board and use it as a study aid.

Connecting Concepts

Scientists observe variations in crater density. They also analyze material gathered from space missions.

Figure 22 Rayed craters such as Copernicus were the last major features to form on the moon.

One important event in the moon's evolution was the formation of maria basins. Radiometric dating of the maria basalts puts their age between 3.2 billion and 3.8 billion years, about a billion years younger than the initial crust. In places, the lava flows overlap the highlands, which also explains the younger age of the maria deposits.

The last prominent features to form were the rayed craters. Material ejected from these young depressions is clearly seen covering the surface of the maria and many older rayless craters. Even a relatively young crater like Copernicus, shown in Figure 22, must be millions of years old. If it had formed on Earth, erosional forces would have erased it long ago. If photographs of the moon taken several hundreds of millions of years ago were available, they would show that the moon has changed little. The moon is an inactive body wandering through space and time.

Section 22.3 Assessment

Reviewing Concepts

1. How do craters form?
2. How did maria originate?
3. What are the stages that formed the moon.

Critical Thinking

4. **Identifying** On Earth, the four major spheres (atmosphere, hydrosphere, solid Earth, and biosphere) interact as a system. Which of these spheres are absent, or nearly absent, on the moon? Based on your answer, identify at least five processes that operate on Earth but not on the moon.
5. **Inferring** Why are craters more common on the moon than on Earth, even though the moon is a much smaller target?

Connecting Concepts

Scientific Evidence Write a paragraph explaining what evidence scientists use to reconstruct the history of the moon.

Section 22.3 Assessment

1. Craters form from the impact of rapidly moving debris.
2. when asteroids punctuated the lunar surface, letting magma bleed out
3. A Mars-sized object collided with Earth. Huge quantities of crust and mantle were ejected into space. The debris began orbiting Earth and eventually united to form the moon.
4. Of the four spheres, the atmosphere, hydrosphere, and biosphere are absent, or nearly absent, on the moon. Because the moon lacks these spheres, processes such as chemical weathering, erosion, soil formation, weather in general, and sedimentation are all absent.
5. Erosion and subduction have removed most craters from Earth's surface.

understanding **EARTH**

Foucault's Experiment

Earth rotates on its axis once each day to produce periods of daylight and darkness. However, day and night and the apparent motions of the stars can be accounted for equally well by a sun and celestial sphere that revolve around a stationary Earth. Copernicus realized that a rotating Earth greatly simplified the existing model of the universe. He was unable, however, to prove that Earth rotates. The first real proof was presented 300 years after his death by the French physicist Jean Foucault.

The Swinging Pendulum

In 1851, Foucault used a free-swinging pendulum to demonstrate that Earth does, in fact, turn on its axis. To picture Foucault's experiment, imagine a large pendulum swinging over the North Pole, as shown in the illustration on this page. Keep in mind that once a pendulum is put into motion, it continues swinging in the same plane unless acted upon by some outside force. Assume that a sharp point is attached to the bottom of this pendulum, marking the snow as it swings. If we were to observe the marks made by the point, we would see that the pendulum is slowly but continually changing position. At the end of 24 hours, the pendulum would have returned to its starting position.

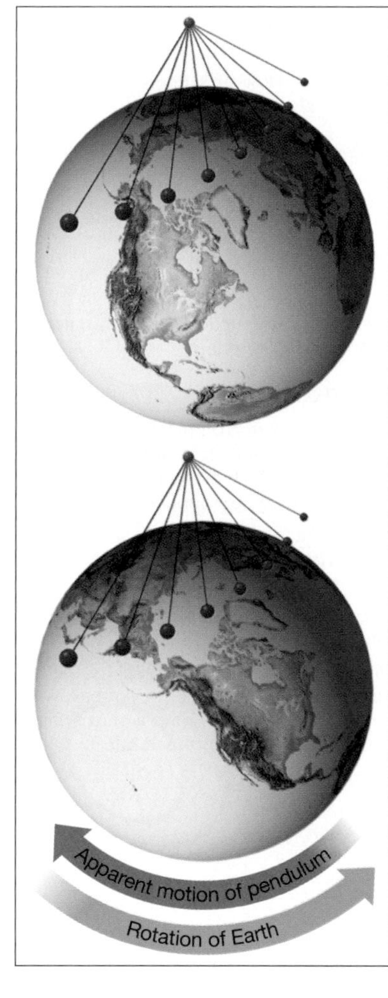

Evidence of Earth's Rotation

No outside force acted on the pendulum to change its position. So what we observed must have been Earth rotating beneath the pendulum. Foucault conducted a similar experiment when he suspended a long pendulum from the dome of the Pantheon in Paris. Today, Foucault pendulums can be found in some museums to re-create this famous scientific experiment.

understanding **EARTH**

Foucault's Experiment **L2**

Background
The Foucault pendulum was constructed in 1851 by Jean Bernard Foucault and was demonstrated for the first time at the world's fair in Paris. The pendulum consisted of a 28-kg iron ball suspended from the dome of the Pantheon by a 67-m long steel wire.

Teaching Tips
After students have read p. 635, ask: **Once the pendulum is set in motion, it will continue to swing in the same direction unless it is pushed or pulled by a force. Why is this true?** *(The pendulum's motion will obey Newton's first law of motion.)*

What outside force is acting on the pendulum? *(There is no outside force acting on the pendulum.)*

Why does the pendulum change position over time? *(The pendulum did not change position, Earth moved beneath the pendulum.)*

How does this prove that Earth is rotating? *(The pendulum continued moving in the same direction because no outside force acted upon it. Since the pendulum did not change its motion, Earth beneath it must be moving.)*
Verbal

Exploration Lab

Modeling Synodic and Sidereal Months 

Objective
After completing this activity, students will be able to explain the difference between synodic and sidereal months.

Students might think that the time it takes for the moon to go through its phases, 29 1/2 days, is the same as the time it takes the moon to make one revolution around the Earth, 27 1/3 days. After performing this lab, ask students to explain the difference between these two cycles.

Skills Focus **Observing, Using Models, Interpreting Diagrams/Photographs**

 **Prep Time** 5 minutes

Advanced Prep Obtain lamps, basketballs, and softballs for each lab group.

Class Time 30 minutes

Safety Position the electrical cords for the lamps so that they are not near a water source.

Teaching Tips
- Borrow softballs and basketballs from the athletic department at your school.
- Encourage students to repeat Step 5 until they get the movements synchronized correctly.

Exploration Lab

Modeling Synodic and Sidereal Months

The time interval required for the moon to complete a full cycle of phases is 29.5 days, or one synodic month. The true period of the moon's revolution around Earth, however, takes only 27.3 days and is known as the sidereal month. In this lab, you will model the differences between synodic and sidereal months.

Problem How do synodic and sidereal months differ?

Materials
- pencil
- paper
- lamp
- basketball
- softball

Skills Observing, Using Models, Analyzing Data, Drawing Conclusions

Procedure
1. Copy the diagram on the next page on a piece of paper. In Month 1, indicate the dark half of the moon on each of the eight lunar positions by shading the appropriate area with a pencil.
2. On the diagram of Month 1, label the position of the new moon. Do the same for the other lunar phases.
3. Repeat Steps 1 and 2 for the diagram of Month 2.
4. Place the lamp on a desk or table. The lamp represents the sun. Hold the softball, which represents the moon. Have a partner hold the basketball, which represents Earth.
5. Stand so that the "moon" is in the position of the new-moon phase in Month 1, relative to "Earth" and the "sun." Revolve the moon around Earth while at the same time moving both Earth and the moon to Month 2. Stop at the same numbered position at which you began. Use the diagrams to guide your movements.

Analyze and Conclude
1. **Using Models** After one complete revolution beginning at the new-moon phase in Month 1, in what position is the moon located in Month 2?
2. **Interpreting Data** Based on your answer to the previous question, does this position occur before or after the moon has completed one full cycle of phases?
3. **Identifying** In Month 2, what position represents the new-moon phase? When the moon reaches this position, will it have completed a synodic or sidereal month?
4. **Summarizing** In your own words, explain the difference between a sidereal and synodic month.

Go Further With your partner's help, use the lamp, softball, and basketball to model the positions of the sun, Earth, and moon during a lunar eclipse and a solar eclipse. On your diagram, label the position of the moon during each eclipse.

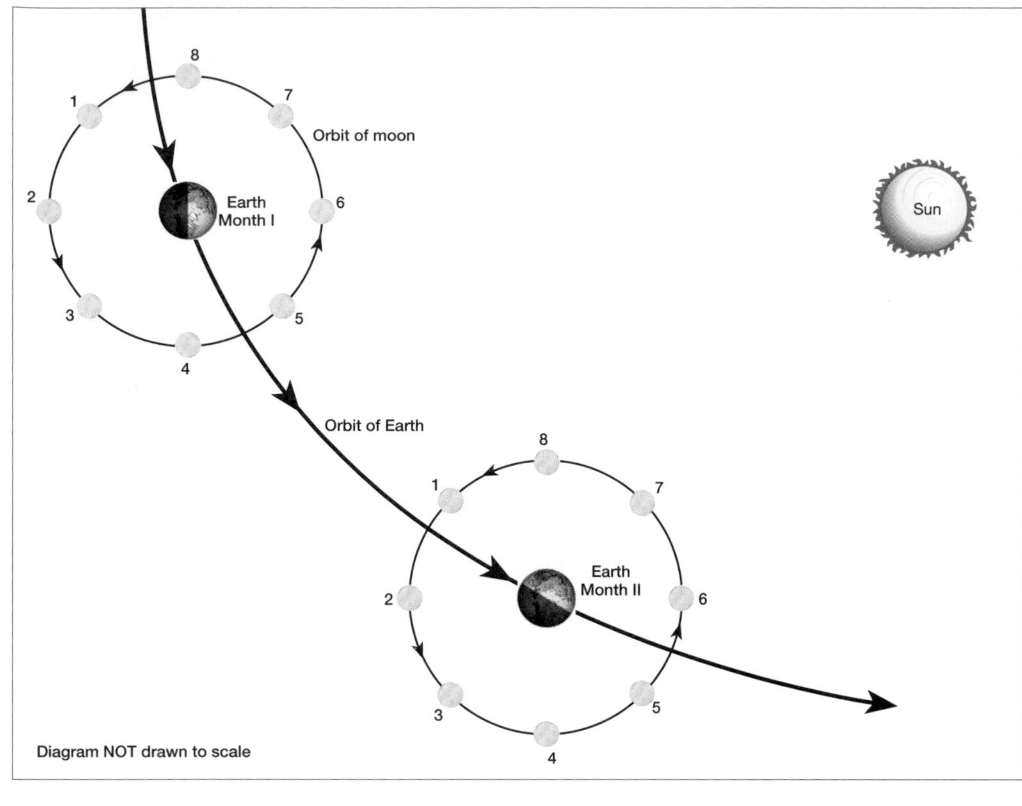

Expected Outcome By modeling the movements of the sun-Earth-moon system, students should observe the difference between synodic and sidereal months.

Analyze and Conclude

1. Position 6

2. before

3. Position 7; a synodic month

4. A sidereal month is one complete revolution of the moon around Earth. During a synodic month, the moon completes one cycle of phases. The synodic month is about two days longer than the sidereal month because of the motion of the Earth-moon system around the sun.

Go Further

During a lunar eclipse, Earth should be between the sun and moon. During a solar eclipse, the moon should be between Earth and the sun. Lunar eclipses can only occur during full moons (position 2 in Month 1 and position 3 in Month I2). Solar eclipses can only occur during new moons (position 6 in Month 1 and position 7 in Month 2).

Kinesthetic, Verbal

Chapter 22

Study Guide

Study Tip

Study With a Partner
On occasion, study with a friend. Quiz each other, compare notes from class lectures, go over homework answers, and discuss concepts that you need help with understanding.

Thinking Visually

a. Brahe
b. Galilei
c. Newton
d. heliocentric model
e. astronomical observations
f. laws of planetary motion
g. discovery of Venus's phases

CHAPTER 22

Study Guide

22.1 Early Astronomy

Key Concepts

- In the geocentric model, the moon, sun, and the known planets—Mercury, Venus, Mars, and Jupiter—orbit Earth.
- In the heliocentric model, Earth and the other planets orbit the sun.
- Copernicus placed the sun at the center of the solar system, with the planets orbiting around it.
- Brahe's observations, especially of Mars, were far more precise than any made previously.
- Using Brahe's precise observations, Kepler discovered three laws of planetary motion.
- Galileo described the behavior of moving objects.
- Newton was the first to formulate and test the law of universal gravitation.

Vocabulary

astronomy, *p. 614;* geocentric, *p. 615;* heliocentric, *p. 616;* retrograde motion, *p. 616;* ellipse, *p. 618;* astronomical unit (AU), *p. 618*

22.2 The Earth-Moon-Sun System

Key Concepts

- The two main motions of Earth are rotation and revolution.
- Lunar phases are a result of the motion of the moon and the sunlight that is reflected from its surface.
- An eclipse can only occur during a new moon or full moon when the moon's orbit crosses the plane of the ecliptic.

Vocabulary

rotation, *p. 622;* revolution, *p. 622;* precession, *p. 622;* perihelion, *p. 624;* aphelion, *p. 624;* perigee, *p. 626;* apogee, *p. 626;* phases of the moon, *p. 626;* solar eclipse, *p. 628;* lunar eclipse, *p. 628*

22.3 Earth's Moon

Key Concepts

- Most craters were produced by the impact of rapidly moving debris.
- Mare, an ancient bed of basaltic lava, originated when asteroids punctured the lunar surface, letting the magma bleed out.
- The most widely accepted model for the origin of the moon is that when solar system was forming, a body the size of Mars impacted Earth.

Vocabulary

crater, *p. 631;* ray, *p. 632;* mare, *p. 632;* rille, *p. 632;* lunar regolith, *p. 632*

Thinking Visually

Use the information from the chapter to complete the concept map below.

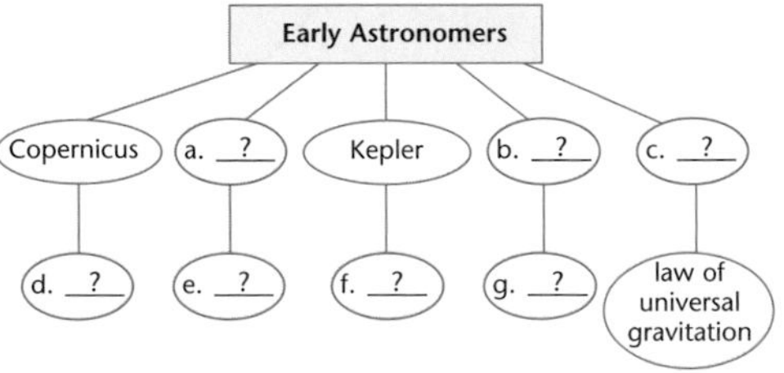

Chapter Assessment Resources

Print
Chapter Test, Chapter 22
Test Prep Resources, Chapter 22

Technology
Computer Test Bank, Chapter 22 Test
Online Text, Chapter 22
Go Online, PHSchool.com, Chapter 22

CHAPTER 22

NY Regents Content Item

Assessment

Interactive textbook with assessment at PHSchool.com 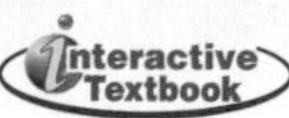

Reviewing Content

Choose the number that best answers the question or completes the statement.

1 Which Greek first proposed that the sun was the center of the universe?
(1) Aristotle
(2) Aristarchus
(3) Anaxogoras
(4) Hipparchus

2 One astronomical unit averages about NY
(1) 93 million kilometers
(2) 150 million kilometers
(3) 210 million kilometers
(4) 300 million kilometers

3 During which month is Earth farthest from the sun? NY
(1) January
(2) April
(3) July
(4) October

4 In the year 14,000, Earth's axis will point toward NY
(1) Polaris
(2) Vega
(3) the sun
(4) the moon

5 When is the moon nearest to Earth during its orbit? NY
(1) at apogee
(2) at perihelion
(3) during an eclipse
(4) at perigee

6 What type of eclipse occurs when the moon casts its shadow on Earth? NY
(1) lunar
(2) sidereal
(3) solar
(4) synodic

7 During the period that the moon's phases are changing from new to full, the moon is
(1) waning
(2) approaching Earth
(3) waxing
(4) receding from Earth

8 The large, dark regions on the moon are called
(1) highlands
(2) craters
(3) mountains
(4) maria

9 Rilles are associated with which of the following lunar features?
(1) craters
(2) maria
(3) rays
(4) highlands

10 The oldest lunar features are
(1) highlands
(2) rayed craters
(3) rilles
(4) maria

Understanding Concepts

11 List three accomplishments of Hipparchus.

12 Describe how Eratosthenes measured the size of Earth.

13 What was Tycho Brahe's contribution to science?

14 Use Kepler's third law ($p^2 = d^3$) to determine the period of a planet whose solar distance is 10 AU.

15 What is an astronomical unit? NY

16 Newton learned that the orbits of planets are the results of what two forces? NY

17 Explain the difference between the mean solar day and the sidereal day. NY

18 What is the approximate length of the cycle of the phases of the moon? NY

19 What phase of the moon occurs approximately one week after the new moon?

20 How many eclipses normally occur each year?

21 How long can a total eclipse of the moon last? A total eclipse of the sun?

22 Describe three features found on the moon's surface.

23 Briefly outline the history of the moon.

Homework Guide

Section	Questions
1	1, 2, 11–16, 31, 32
2	3–7, 17–21, 24–27, 33
3	8–10, 22, 23, 28–30, 34

Assessment

Reviewing Content

(1) 2 (2) 2 (3) 3
(4) 2 (5) 4 (6) 3
(7) 3 (8) 4 (9) 2
(10) 1

Understanding Concepts

(11) Star catalog, measured length of year, developed method for predicting lunar eclipses
(12) He observed and calculated the difference between the angles of the noonday sun in two cities.
(13) His contribution was his accurate observations of Mars that were later used by Kepler to determine the three laws of planetary motion.
(14) 31.6 years
(15) The average distance between Earth and the sun, or about 150 million kilometers
(16) Gravity and inertia
(17) Earth takes 23 hours and 56 minutes to make one rotation with respect to a star, a period known as a sidereal day. Earth must rotate another 4 minutes to return to the noon position with respect to the sun, a period known as a mean solar day.
(18) 29 1/2 days, or one synodic month
(19) First-quarter phase
(20) Four
(21) A total eclipse of the moon can last up to four hours. A total eclipse of the sun lasts only about seven minutes.
(22) Sample answer: depressions called craters, light-colored highlands, dark regions called maria
(23) Accumulation of debris formed the moon; heat may have melted the moon's outer layer, remnants of which exist in lunar highlands; maria basins formed, which are later filled in by basaltic lava; large rayed craters formed last.

Chapter 22

Critical Thinking

(24) Earth moves faster in January. Therefore, the longest solar day occurs in January.
(25) The slow lunar rotation, along with the absence of an atmosphere, cause high surface temperatures on the side of the moon facing the sun and low surface temperatures on the side of the moon facing away from the sun.
(26) A lunar eclipse is visible to anyone on the side of Earth facing the moon. A solar eclipse is visible only by those in the narrow region covered by the moon's shadow.
(27) Sample answer: The two most obvious interactions may be gravity and the light cast on Earth during the brighter phases of the moon. Without gravity, there would be no tides. Without tides, heat exchange between ocean and atmosphere would be altered, and ocean life would be affected. Without moonlight, lives of nocturnal animals would be affected, as well as the migratory habits of some species.

Analyzing Data

(28) Mare; when layer upon layer of basaltic lava flooded the moon's surface
(29) Point D is a rayed crater; point C shows highlands.
(30) Point C is oldest.

Concepts in Action

(31) Venus is full when it is on the opposite side of the sun from Earth, an alignment that could only happen in the Copernican view of the universe.
(32) It showed that the sun was not perfect and rotated, just like other bodies in space.
(33) The same side of the moon always faces Earth.
(34) The greater the crater density, the longer the topographic feature must have existed.

Assessment *continued*

Critical Thinking

24 **Drawing Conclusions** Does Earth move faster in its orbit near perihelion (January) or near aphelion (July)? Based on your answer, is the solar day longest in January or July?

25 **Predicting** The moon rotates very slowly on its axis. Predict how this affects the lunar surface temperature. NY

26 **Applying Concepts** Solar eclipses are slightly more common than lunar eclipses. Why then is it more likely that your region of the country will experience a lunar eclipse? NY

27 **Making Generalizations** In what ways do the interactions between Earth and its moon influence the Earth-moon system? If Earth did not have a moon, would the atmosphere, hydrosphere, solid Earth, and biosphere be any different? Explain.

Analyzing Data

Use the photograph below to answer questions 28–30.

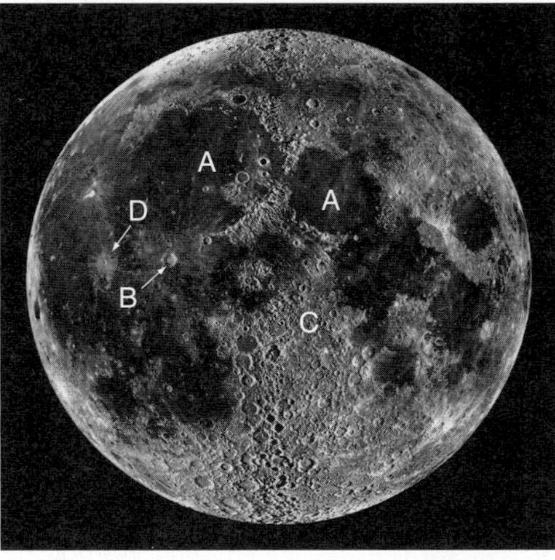

28 **Interpreting Data** What feature exists at point A? How did this feature likely form?

29 **Identifying** Which point represents a ray? Which point represents highlands?

30 **Inferring** What is the oldest feature in the photograph? How do you know?

Concepts in Action

31 **Relating Cause and Effect** How does the fact that Venus appears full when it is smallest support Copernicus's view rather than the Ptolemaic system?

32 **Explaining** Explain how Galileo's discovery of a rotating sun supported the heliocentric model.

33 **Identifying** What is the result of the moon's period of rotation and revolution being the same? NY

34 **Applying Concepts** How is crater density used in the relative dating of features on the moon?

Performance-Based Assessment

Observing Record at least four observations of the moon over the next two weeks. Sketch the moon at each observation. Use shading to show the phase you see. Note the date and time of each observation. Afterwards, write a paragraph describing how the size and shape of the lit portion of the moon changed over the length of your observations.

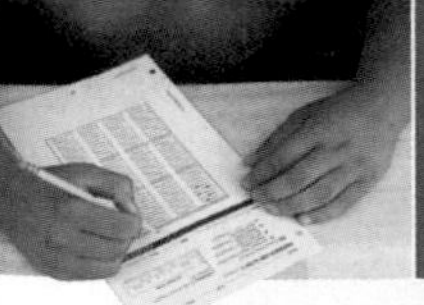

Regents Practice Exam

Test-Taking Tip

Eliminating Unreasonable Answers
When you answer a multiple-choice question, you can often eliminate at least one answer because it is clearly incorrect. If you eliminate one or more choices, you increase your odds of choosing the correct answer. In the question below, you can immediately eliminate choice 1 because the moon does not have rivers on its surface. Clearly, choices 2 and 4 cannot both be true because they relate to the same phenomenon. You can eliminate both of these choices because volcanic activity is not currently occurring on the moon. The remaining choice, 3, must be the correct answer.

The most important forces currently modifying the moon's surface are
(1) rivers
(2) lava flows
(3) tiny particles from space
(4) volcanoes

For *each* statement or question, choose the *number* of the word or expression that, of those given, best completes the statement or answers the question. Some questions may require the use of the *Earth Science Reference Tables.*

1 The movement of a Foucault pendulum is evidence that
(1) Earth rotates around it axis
(2) Earth is tilted on its axis
(3) Earth revolves around the sun
(4) The sun revolves around Earth

2 During which of the following months is Earth the farthest from the sun?
(1) December
(2) March
(3) June
(4) September

Answer the following questions in complete sentences. Some questions may require the use of the *Earth Science Reference Tables.* Base your answers to questions 6 and 7 on the diagram at top right, which shows Motion of the Earth-Moon System.

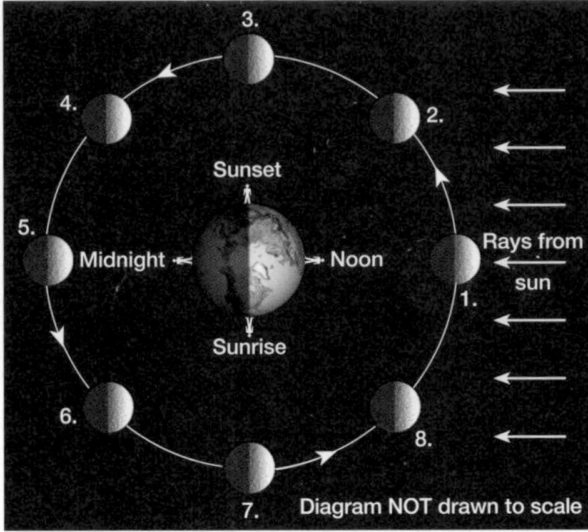

3 Explain why the planets sometimes exhibit retrograde motion.

4 Explain why the Earth does not orbit at the same speed all year.

5 Compare and contrast an umbra and a penumbra.

6 Select the number that illustrates the moon's position in its orbit for each of the following phases: full moon, third quarter, waxing crescent, new moon, waning crescent.

7 Which number represents the position of the moon during a lunar eclipse? A solar eclipse?

8 Why do we not experience lunar eclipses and solar eclipses every month?

Regents Practice Exam

(1) 1
(2) 3
(3) Retrograde motion results from the combination of the motion of Earth and the planet's own motion around the sun. Periodically, Earth overtakes a planet in its orbit, which makes it appear for a time as though the planet were moving westward across the sky (retrograde motion).
(4) Since the sun's gravitational pull on Earth is stronger when the Earth is closer to the sun, the Earth moves more quickly when it is closer to the sun.
(5) The darker, inner part of a shadow is known as the umbra. The lighter, outer portion of a shadow is called the penumbra. Both are parts of a shadow, but the penumbra is wider than the umbra.
(6) The full moon occurs at position 5, the third quarter is at position 7, waxing crescent is at position 2, new moon is at position 1, and waning crescent occurs at position 6.
(7) During a lunar eclipse the moon is at position 5, and during a solar eclipse the moon is at position 1.
(8) The moon's orbit is inclined 5° to the plane containing Earth's orbit and the sun. Therefore, the Earth, moon, and sun only line up perfectly four times each year, when the planes cross.

Performance-Based Assessment

Students should choose a safe location from which to view the moon. Have them begin their observations on a clear night. They should take along a notebook to record the observations and make sketches.

CHAPTER 23

Planning Guide

Use these planning tools
Use Teacher Express for all your planning needs

SECTION OBJECTIVES	STANDARDS NATIONAL	STANDARDS STATE	ACTIVITIES and LABS
23.1 The Solar System pp. 644–648 1 block or 2 periods **23.1** **List** the major differences between the terrestrial and Jovian planets. **23.2** **Explain** how the solar system formed.	A-1, B-4, D-3		**SE** Inquiry Activity: What Is the Shape of a Planetary Orbit? p. 643 L2 **TE** Teacher Demo: Speeding Up a Spinning Nebula, p. 647 L2
23.2 The Terrestrial Planets pp. 649–653 1.5 blocks or 3 periods **23.3** **Describe** the distinguishing characteristics of each terrestrial planet.	A-2, D-1, E-2		
23.3 The Outer Planets pp. 654–659 1.5 blocks or 3 periods **23.4** **Describe** the distinguishing characteristics of each Jovian planet.	A-2, E-2		**TE** Teacher Demo: Discovering the Rings of Uranus, p. 658 L2 **LM** Exploring Orbits L2
23.4 Minor Members of the Solar System pp. 660–664 1 block or 2 periods **23.5** **Identify** the location within our solar system where most asteroids are found. **23.6** **Describe** the structure of a comet. **23.7** **Explain** the possible origins for a meteoroid.	A-1, A-2, E-2		**TE** Teacher Demo: Modeling a Comet's Tail, p. 662 L2 **SE** Exploration Lab: Modeling the Solar System, pp. 666–667 L2

Ability Levels	
L1	For students who need additional help
L2	For all students
L3	For students who need to be challenged

Components

SE	Student Edition	**GRSW**	Guided Reading & Study Workbook	**TP**	Test Prep Resources	**GEO**	Geode CD-ROM
TE	Teacher's Edition	**TEX**	Teacher Express	**onT**	onlineText	**T**	Transparencies
LM	Laboratory Manual	**CTB**	Computer Test Bank	**DC**	Discovery Channel Videos	**GO**	Internet Resources

RESOURCES PRINT and TECHNOLOGY	SECTION ASSESSMENT
GRSW Section 23.1 **T-334** Orbits of the Planets **T-335** Planetary Data **T-336** Planets Drawn to Scale **T-337** Topographic Features on the Lunar Surface **T-338** Formation of an Impact Crater **T-339** Formation of Lunar Maria GEODe Astronomy ↳ The Planets: An Overview Earth's Moon **DC** Heavenly Bodies **TEX** Lesson Planning Section 23.1	**SE** Section 23.1 Assessment, p. 648 **onT** Section 23.1
GRSW Section 23.2 GEODe Astronomy ↳ Calculating Your Age and Weight on Other Planets **TEX** Lesson Planning Section 23.2	**SE** Section 23.2 Assessment, p. 653 **onT** Section 23.2
GRSW Section 23.3 **T-340** Jupiter with Great Red Spot **T-341** Structure of Jupiter's Atmosphere **T-342** Ring System of Saturn **T-346** Pluto and Its Moon **TEX** Lesson Planning Section 23.3	**SE** Section 23.3 Assessment, p. 659 **onT** Section 23.3
GRSW Section 23.4 **T-343** Orbit of Asteroids **T-344** Orientation of a Comet's Tail in Orbit **T-345** Major Meteor Showers **T-347** World Map of Major Impact Structures GEODe Astronomy ↳ A Brief Tour of the Planets **TEX** Lesson Planning Section 23.4	**SE** Section 23.4 Assessment, p. 664 **onT** Section 23.4

Go Online

Go online for these Internet resources.

PHSchool.com
Web Code: cjk-9999

NSTA SCiLINKS
Web Code: cjn-7232
Web Code: cjn-7233

Materials for Activities and Labs

Quantities for each group

STUDENT EDITION

Inquiry Activity, p. 643
cardboard (about 20 cm^2), 2 pushpins, ruler, piece of string, pencil, tape, unlined paper

Exploration Lab, p. 666–667
meter stick, colored pencils, calculator, 6-m length of adding machine paper

TEACHER'S EDITION

Teacher Demo, p. 647
chair that spins in place

Teacher Demo, p. 658
meter stick, flashlight

Teacher Demo, p. 662
table-top fan, light-weight paper, tape

Chapter Assessment

ASSESSMENT

SE Assessment, pp. 669–670
CTB Chapter 23
onT Chapter 23

STANDARDIZED TEST PREP

SE Chapter 23, p. 671
TP Progress Monitoring Assessments

interactive textbook with assessment at PHSchool.com

CHAPTER 23

Before you teach

Michael Wysession
Washington University

Big Ideas

Earth is part of a solar system, which consists of the sun, nine (but possibly ten) planets and their moons, asteroids, meteoroids, and comets.

Space and Time The solar system is enormous, extending outward from the sun more than 10,000 times the Earth-sun distance (10,000 AU). The solar system formed from the contraction of a pre-solar nebula, a vast cloud of gas and dust. The center of the nebula became the sun, and the outer parts accreted to form millions of planetesimals, which eventually collided and coalesced to form the planets.

Forces and Motion All of the planets revolve around the sun in the same direction, and most rotate around their axes in the same direction. Planets further from the sun take longer to revolve around it.

Matter and Energy The sun makes up 99.85 percent of the mass of the solar system. The terrestrial planets (Mercury, Venus, Earth, Mars) are relatively small, and are mostly made of a rocky mantle and metal core. The gas giants (Jupiter, Saturn, Uranus, Neptune) are relatively large, have thick layers of gas and liquid above a rock/metal interior, and are orbited by moons and rings. The Kuiper belt objects, like Pluto, extend 100 AU out from the sun, and are mostly rock and ice. Small icy comets also orbit the sun, though most are found in the Oort cloud, which extends to edge of the solar system.

Earth as a System Earth is constantly bombarded by tiny meteoroids, which streak across the sky as meteors, and by cometary debris, which has been a source of Earth's water. Some meteoroids originate in the Asteroid belt.

Earth Science Refresher

Astrobiology

Are we alone in the universe? This is perhaps the most culturally significant question that planetary science is addressing. Much of the current efforts of NASA involve the search for life on other planets. Some of these efforts involve direct investigations of other planetary bodies. Mars is very important in this respect, because it appears likely that this neighbor once had plentiful water on its surface, and as we have found on Earth, where there is water there is life. Another important target for robotic missions is the moon of Jupiter, Europa, which likely has a salt-water ocean beneath an outer layer of ice. Life on Earth began in a salt-water ocean, and scientists are excited to investigate the possibility that there may currently be life on Europa.

Some of NASA's investigations, however, are of a more theoretical nature. Using what we have learned from the planets and moons in our solar system, can we determine what kind of a planet would be needed to develop intelligent life? Life on Earth took 4 billion years before it learned to play the piano. That is a long time to require the presence of liquid water on the surface. If Earth was twice as big, would this still have happened? If Earth was twice as far from the sun, or if the sun was twice as big, would life still have evolved?

Address Misconceptions

The solar system and outer space in general are very crowded. Actually, the planets and stars are very far apart. For a strategy that helps to overcome this misconception, see **Address Misconceptions** on **p. 646.**

It is beginning to look like the conditions needed for intelligent life to evolve on a planet are very narrow. If Earth were a little different in size, a little different in distance from the sun, or the sun a little different in size, water would not be continuously liquid. Earth has the right composition and amount of water to allow plate tectonics to occur, which is the reason that we

Go Online PDLINKS

NSTA

For: Chapter 23 Content Support
Visit: www.SciLinks.org/PDLinks
Web Code: cjn-2399

Address Misconceptions

Scientific knowledge is gathered solely through controlled experiments. Many advances in science actually come from fieldwork and careful observations. For a strategy that helps to overcome this misconception, see **Address Misconceptions** on **p. 649.**

have land (and there is some debate as to whether civilizations could have developed if life never left the oceans). Earth also benefits from a nearly circular orbit, which keeps annual temperatures nearly constant; the presence of a large moon, which helps to stabilize its axis of rotation; and the presence of large outer planets such as Jupiter, which have the right size and orbit to stabilize the asteroid belt and to gravitationally hurl out of the solar system rogue asteroids that might collide with Earth. Our sun is small enough to last for a long time (large suns burn out quickly), but large enough to keep us warm. Our solar system is also in the right location within the right kind of galaxy—go too close to the center of the Milky Way and the radiation is too intense and the impacts too frequent; go too far out, and stars are too small and metal-poor. There are whole galaxies that seem to be too poor in metals to allow for planets such as Earth.

A couple of decades ago a formula was developed called the Drake equation, which took into account many aspects of planetary, galactic, and cultural evolution, to predict how many other planets in our galaxy might have sufficiently advanced societies that would be trying to contact us. Some early predictions put the number in the millions. However, with what we are now learning about the stringent conditions required to support life on a planet for billions of years, Earth might be the only one.

Build Reading Literacy

Compare and Contrast

Identify Similarities and Differences

Strategy Help students read and understand material that discusses two or more related topics or concepts. This strategy helps students identify similarities and differences, thus enabling them to link prior knowledge with new information. Before students begin, assign a section in Chapter 23 for them to read, such as Section 23.1, pp. 644–648.

Example

1. Have students compare two or more topics or concepts under a section heading. Tell them that when they compare, they should focus on both similarities and differences. Remind them to look for these signal words:

- Similarities: similar, similarly, also, just as, like, likewise, in the same way
- Differences: but, however, although, whereas, on the other hand, different, unlike

2. Have students contrast two or more topics or concepts. Remind students that when they contrast, they should focus only on differences.

3. Have students create a chart or diagram comparing or contrasting two or more topics or concepts they read about in the section. Suggest that they create either a compare/contrast table or a Venn diagram to present their information.

See p. 645 for a script on how to use this strategy with students. For additional strategies, see pp. 650, 652, 656, 661, 663, and 664.

ASSESS PRIOR KNOWLEDGE

Use the Chapter Pretest below to assess students' prior knowledge. As needed, review these concepts.

Review Science Concepts

Section 23.1 Review with students that the density of water is 1.0 g/cm^3. Objects with a density greater than water will sink, and those with a density less than water will float. Reviewing density will help students comprehend the densities of the planets.

Section 23.2 Reviewing characteristics of Earth will help provide students with a reference point to compare the other planets. Students may need to review the meaning of revolve (move around the sun) and rotate (spin on an axis). Reviewing the structure of shield volcanoes and the dynamics of a hot spot will help students imagine volcanism and volcanic structures on Mars and Venus.

Section 23.3 Remind students that convection currents can occur in any heated fluid (gas or liquid). Remind them that in convection currents hot, less dense fluid rises while cooler, denser fluid sinks. Also, review with students that solar energy causes convection currents in our atmosphere, while the heat from Earth's core and the decay of radiometric isotopes in the mantle power the convection currents in the mantle. Reviewing convection will help students understand the information about convection currents in the atmospheres of some outer planets.

Section 23.4 Talking with students about "shooting stars" will help prepare them to learn about meteor showers.

CHAPTER 23 Touring Our Solar System

CONCEPTS in Action

Exploration Lab
Modeling the Solar System

Earth as A System
Is Earth on a Collision Course?

Astronomy
↳ The Planets: An Overview
Calculating Your Age and Weight on Other Planets
Earth's Moon
A Brief Tour of the Planets

Video Field Trip
Heavenly Bodies

Take a field trip through our solar system with Discovery Channel and learn about some of our neighboring planets.

1. Name one reason scientists think it is possible that life has existed on Mars.
2. Why are scientists certain that no life can exist on Saturn, Jupiter, Neptune, and Uranus?

Go Online
PHSchool.com

For: Chapter 23 Resources
Visit: PHSchool.com
Web Code: cjk-9999

Meteor Crater, near Winslow, Arizona, is about 1.2 kilometers across and 170 meters deep. The solar system is cluttered with meteoroids and other objects that can strike Earth with explosive force.

642 *Chapter 23*

Chapter Pretest

1. An object with a density of 1.2 g/cm^3 placed in a cup filled with water, will *(a)*
   a. sink to the bottom.
   b. float on top of the water.
   c. float in the middle of the water.
2. Earth's atmosphere is mostly made of *(c)*
   a. water vapor.
   b. carbon dioxide.
   c. nitrogen.
3. It takes Earth about ______ to rotate once. *(b)*
   a. 1 year
   b. 24 hours
   c. 30 days
4. Convection currents can occur in *(d)*
   a. solids only.
   b. liquids only.
   c. gases only.
   d. liquids, gases, and solids.
5. True or False: In a convection current, the warmer, less dense fluid rises. *(True)*
6. Convection currents in Earth's atmosphere are caused by (a)
   a. solar energy.
   b. heat from Earth's interior.
   c. gravity.
   d. plate movements.
7. True or False: A shooting star is actually a star that is falling from the sky. *(False)*

Chapter Preview

Inquiry Activity

What Is the Shape of a Planetary Orbit?

Procedure

1. Place a piece of cardboard about 20 cm square on a flat surface. Place two push pins into the cardboard about 3 cm apart.
2. Tie the ends of a piece of string together. Loop the string around the pushpins.
3. Using a pencil to keep the string taut, trace around the pins.
4. Repeat steps 1 through 3, varying the distance between the two pins.

Think About It

1. **Observing** What type of shape did you draw?
2. **Observing** What happened when the pins were moved farther apart?
3. **Comparing** How do your drawings compare with the shapes you see in Figure 1 on the next page?

Touring Our Solar System 643

Video Field Trip
Heavenly Bodies

Encourage students to view the Video Field Trip "Heavenly Bodies."

ENGAGE/EXPLORE

What Is the Shape of a Planetary Orbit? 

Purpose In this activity, students will discover how ellipses are made and observe that changing the foci of an ellipse changes its eccentricity.

Skills Focus **Observing**

 **Prep Time** 10 minutes

Materials cardboard (about 20 cm^2), 2 pushpins, ruler, piece of string, pencil, tape, unlined paper

Advance Prep Precut the pieces of string, making each piece about 30–35 cm long.

Class Time 25 minutes

Teaching Tips

- Have students tape a piece of unlined paper onto their cardboard before putting the pins in. If students draw on the paper, rather than directly on the cardboard, the cardboard may be reused for multiple classes or multiple years.
- This activity will have more meaning if you explain that ellipses have two foci that are used to draw the shape. The pins students use in this activity serve as the foci for each ellipse they draw.

Expected Outcome Students will discover that ellipses can be drawn by using two foci. They will learn that all planets orbit the sun in ellipses of varying eccentricities.

Think About It

1. Students should have drawn three different shapes that are slightly elliptical
2. Students should find that the farther the pins were moved apart, the more flattened the ellipse became.
3. Student answers may vary, but their drawings should be elliptical.

Section 23.1

1 FOCUS

Section Objectives

23.1 **List** the major differences between the terrestrial and Jovian planets.

23.2 **Explain** how the solar system formed.

Reading Focus

Build Vocabulary L2

Word Part Analysis Teach students that *terr-* means "Earth," and *-ial* and *-ian* mean "of, or related to" so *terrestrial* means "Earthly" or "Earth-like." Terrestrial planets are those similar to Earth while Jovian planets are those similar to Jupiter.

Advise students that *nebula* is related to the word *nebulous*, which means "hazy" or "unclear." The word *nebula* is used to describe a "hazy mass of gases and dust seen among the stars." Tell students that *infinitesimal* means "infinitely small," and have them predict the meaning of *planetesimal*. *(Planetesimals are small solid bodies that combine to form planets.)*

Reading Strategy L2

a. The sun formed at the center of a disk.
b. Matter collided to form planetesimals.
c. Planetesimals eventually grow into planets.

2 INSTRUCT

Use Visuals L1

Figure 1 This diagram shows the orbits of all 9 planets around the sun. Ask: **Which planet is the closest to the sun?** *(Mercury)* **The asteroid belt is found between which two planets?** *(Mars and Jupiter)*

Direct students to observe the scale along the bottom of the figure that shows the scale distances from planet to planet. Tell students that the inner planets are those found before the asteroid belt, and the outer planets are found after the asteroid belt. Ask: **How does the distance between the inner planets differ from the distance between the outer planets?** *(The inner planets are much closer together than the outer planets.)*
Visual

23.1 The Solar System

Reading Focus

Key Concepts

- How do terrestrial planets differ from Jovian planets?
- How did the solar system form?

Vocabulary

- terrestrial planet
- Jovian planet
- nebula
- planetesimal

Reading Strategy

Relating Text and Diagrams As you read, refer to Figure 3 to complete the flowchart on the formation of the solar system.

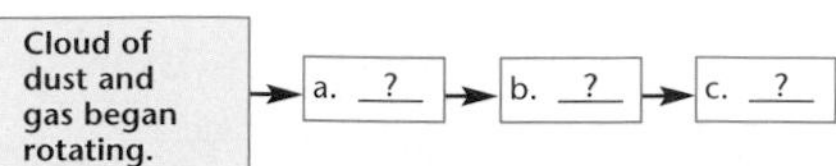

The sun is the hub of a huge rotating system of nine planets, their satellites, and numerous smaller bodies. An estimated 99.85 percent of the mass of our solar system is contained within the sun. The planets collectively make up most of the remaining 0.15 percent. As Figure 1 shows, the planets, traveling outward from the sun, are Mercury, Venus, Earth, Mars, Jupiter, Saturn, Uranus, Neptune, and Pluto.

Guided by the sun's gravitational force, each planet moves in an elliptical orbit, and all travel in the same direction. The nearest planet to the sun—Mercury—has the fastest orbital motion at 48 kilometers per second, and it has the shortest period of revolution. By contrast, the most distant planet, Pluto, has an orbital speed of 5 kilometers per second, and it requires 248 Earth-years to complete one revolution.

Imagine a planet's orbit drawn on a flat sheet of paper. The paper represents the planet's orbital plane. The orbital planes of seven planets lie within 3 degrees of the plane of the sun's equator. The other two, Mercury and Pluto, are inclined 7 and 17 degrees, respectively.

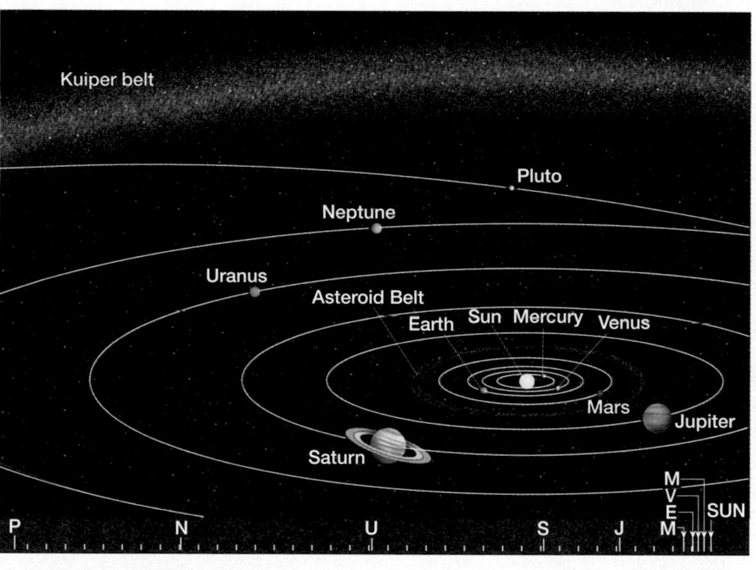

Figure 1 Orbits of the Planets The positions of the planets are shown to scale along the bottom of the diagram.

644 Chapter 23

The Planets: An Overview

Careful examination of Table 1 shows that the planets fall quite nicely into two groups. The **terrestrial planets**—Mercury, Venus, Earth, and Mars—are relatively small and rocky. (*Terrestrial* = Earth-like.)The **Jovian planets**—Jupiter, Saturn, Uranus, and Neptune—are huge gas giants. (*Jovian* = Jupiter-like.) Small, cold Pluto does not fit neatly into either category.

Size is the most obvious difference between the terrestrial and the Jovian planets. The diameter of the largest terrestrial planet, Earth, is only one-quarter the diameter of the smallest Jovian planet, Neptune. Also, Earth's mass is only 1/17 as great as Neptune's. Hence, the Jovian planets are often called giants. Because of their distant locations from the sun, the four Jovian planets and Pluto are also called the outer planets. The terrestrial planets are closer to the sun and are called the inner planets. As we shall see, there appears to be a correlation between the positions of these planets and their sizes.

Density, chemical makeup, and rate of rotation are other ways in which the two groups of planets differ. The densities of the terrestrial planets average about five times the density of water. The Jovian planets, however, have densities that average only 1.5 times the density of water. One of the outer planets, Saturn, has a density only 0.7 times that of water, which means that Saturn would float if placed in a large enough water tank. The different chemical compositions of the planets are largely responsible for these density differences.

Compare the densities of terrestrial planets and Jovian planets.

Table 1 Planetary Data

Planet	Average Distance from Sun AU	Average Distance from Sun Millions of km	Period of Revolution	Orbital Velocity km/s	Period of Rotation	Diameter (km)	Relative Mass (Earth = 1)	Average Density (g/cm^3)	Number of Known Satellites*
Mercury	0.39	58	88^d	47.5	59^d	4878	0.06	5.4	0
Venus	0.72	108	225^d	35.0	244^d	12,104	0.82	5.2	0
Earth	1.00	150	365.25^d	29.8	$23^h 56^m 04^s$	12,756	1.00	5.5	1
Mars	1.52	228	687^d	24.1	$24^h 37^m 23^s$	6794	0.11	3.9	2
Jupiter	5.20	778	12^{yr}	13.1	$9^h 50^m$	143,884	317.87	1.3	63
Saturn	9.54	1427	29.5^{yr}	9.6	$10^h 14^m$	120,536	95.14	0.7	31
Uranus	19.18	2870	84^{yr}	6.8	$17^h 14^m$	51,118	14.56	1.2	25
Neptune	30.06	4497	165^{yr}	5.3	$16^h 03^m$	50,530	17.21	1.7	13
Pluto	39.44	5900	248^{yr}	4.7	6.4^d	approx. 2300	0.002	1.8	1

*Includes all satellites discovered as of March 2004.

The Planets: An Overview

Build Reading Literacy **L1**

Refer to **p. 642D**, which provides guidelines for this reading strategy.

Compare and Contrast Have students create a chart comparing the characteristics of the terrestrial planets and the Jovian planets. Have them start with what they observed about the distances between planets in the **Use Visuals** activity on p. 644, and use the reading, tables, and figures on pp. 645–647. For example:

Terrestrial Planets	Jovian Planets
Orbits are close together	Orbits are far apart
Smaller diameter	Larger diameter
More dense	Less dense
Rotate slower	Rotate faster
Thin or no atmosphere	Thick atmosphere
Composed mostly of rocky and metallic substances, with few gases and ices	Mostly made of gases and ices, but with rocky and metallic materials in their cores

Visual, Verbal

Customize for Inclusion Students

Learning Disabled Help students complete Compare and Contrast activities by providing them with scaffolding. Give them a chart to fill in that lists the categories they should be comparing. For example, these students could be given a chart such as the one below to use for the Compare and Contrast activity on this page.

Characteristic	Terrestrial Planets	Jovian Planets
Distance from one planet to the next		
Diameter		
Density		
Rotation rate		
Atmosphere		
Composition		

Answer to . . .

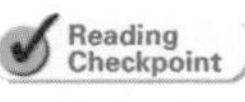

The terrestrial planets have greater densities than the Jovian planets.

Use Visuals

Figure 2 Have students study Figure 2 and answer the caption question. Ask: **Which planet is the smallest?** *(Pluto)* **Which planet is the largest?** *(Jupiter)* **How does the size of the largest planet compare to the size of the sun?** *(Jupiter is much smaller than the sun.)*
Visual

Many students think that the solar system and outer space are very crowded. Help students overcome this misconception by using Table 1 Planetary Data. Have students look at the column describing the distance from the sun. Point out to them that the distances are given in *millions* of kilometers. Tell students that if they chose a point in the solar system at random, it is unlikely it would be near a planet.
Visual, Verbal

Figure 2 The planets are drawn to scale.
Interpreting Diagrams ***How do the sizes of the terrestrial planets compare with the sizes of the Jovian planets?***

The Interiors of the Planets The planets are shown to scale in Figure 2. The substances that make up the planets are divided into three groups: gases, rocks, and ices. The classification of these substances is based on their melting points.

1. The gases—hydrogen and helium—are those with melting points near absolute zero (−273°C or 0 kelvin).
2. The rocks are mainly silicate minerals and metallic iron, which have melting points above 700°C.
3. The ices include ammonia (NH_3), methane (CH_4), carbon dioxide (CO_2), and water (H_2O). They have intermediate melting points. For example, H_2O has a melting point of 0°C.

The terrestrial planets are dense, consisting mostly of rocky and metallic substances, and only minor amounts of gases and ices. The Jovian planets, on the other hand, contain large amounts of gases (hydrogen and helium) and ices (mostly water, ammonia, and methane). This accounts for their low densities. The outer planets also contain substantial amounts of rocky and metallic materials, which are concentrated in their cores.

The Atmospheres of the Planets The Jovian planets have very thick atmospheres of hydrogen, helium, methane, and ammonia. By contrast, the terrestrial planets, including Earth, have meager atmospheres at best. A planet's ability to retain an atmosphere depends on its mass and temperature, which accounts for the difference between Jovian and terrestrial planets.

Simply stated, a gas molecule can escape from a planet if it reaches a speed known as the escape velocity. For Earth, this velocity is 11 kilometers per second. Any material, including a rocket, must reach this speed before it can escape Earth's gravity and go into space.

A comparatively warm body with a small surface gravity, such as our moon, cannot hold even heavy gases, like carbon dioxide and radon. Thus, the moon lacks an atmosphere. The more massive terrestrial planets of Earth, Venus, and Mars retain some heavy gases. Still, their atmospheres make up only a very small portion of their total mass.

Facts and Figures

Why are the Jovian planets so much larger than the terrestrial planets? According to the nebular hypothesis, the planets formed from a rotating disk of dust and gases that surrounded the sun. The growth of planets began as solid bits of matter began to collide and clump together. In the inner solar system, the temperatures were so high that only the metals and silicate materials could form solid grains. It was too hot for ices of water, carbon dioxide, and methane to form. Thus, the innermost (terrestrial) planets grew mainly from the high melting point substances found in the solar nebula. By contrast, in the frigid out reaches of the solar system, it was cold enough for ices of water and other substances to form. Consequently, the outer planets are thought to have grown not only from accumulations of solid bits of metals and silicate minerals but also from large quantities of ices. Eventually, the outer planets became large enough to gravitationally capture the lightest gases (hydrogen and helium), and thus grow to become "giant" planets.

In contrast, the Jovian planets have much greater surface gravities. This gives them escape velocities of 21 to 60 kilometers per second—much higher than the terrestrial planets. Consequently, it is more difficult for gases to escape from their gravitational pulls. Also, because the molecular motion of a gas depends upon temperature, at the low temperatures of the Jovian planets even the lightest gases are unlikely to acquire the speed needed to escape.

Formation of the Solar System

Between existing stars is "the vacuum of space." However, it is far from being a pure vacuum because it is populated with clouds of dust and gases. A cloud of dust and gas in space is called a **nebula** (*nebula* = cloud; plural: *nebulae*). A nebula, shown in Figure 3A, often consists of 92 percent hydrogen, 7 percent helium, and less than 1 percent of the remaining heavier elements. For some reason not yet fully understood, these thin gaseous clouds begin to rotate slowly and contract gravitationally. As the clouds contract, they spin faster. For an analogy, think of ice skaters—their speed increases as they bring their arms near their bodies.

Nebular Theory Scientific studies of nebulae have led to a theory concerning the origin of our solar system. **According to the nebular theory, the sun and planets formed from a rotating disk of dust and gases.** As the speed of rotation increased, the center of the disk began to flatten out, as shown in Figure 3B. Matter became more concentrated in this center, where the sun eventually formed.

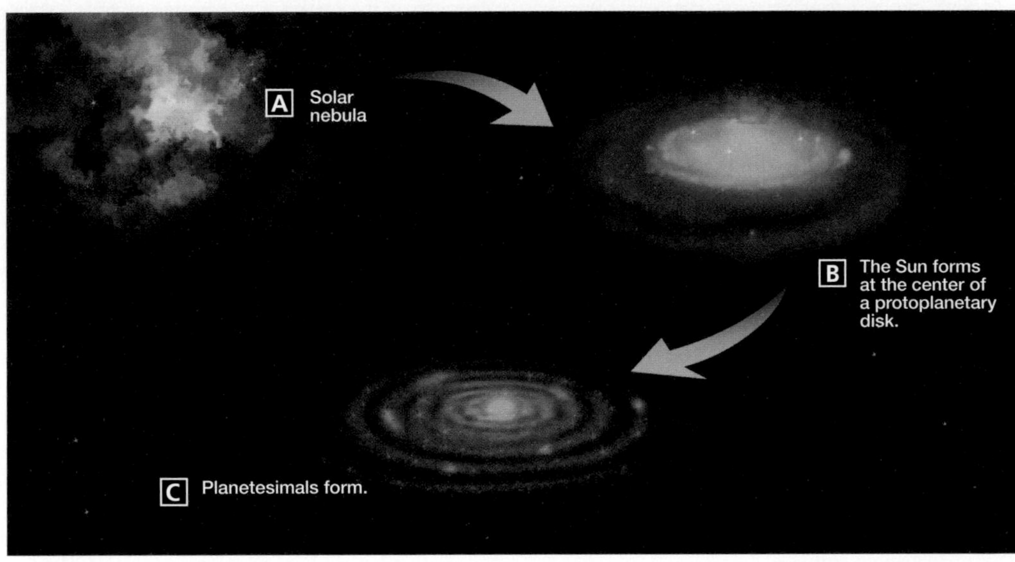
A Solar nebula
B The Sun forms at the center of a protoplanetary disk.
C Planetesimals form.

Figure 3 Formation of the Universe A According to the nebular theory, the solar system formed from a rotating cloud of dust and gas. **B** The sun formed at the center of the rotating disk. **C** Planetesimals collided, eventually gaining enough mass to be planets.

Formation of the Solar System

Speeding Up a Spinning Nebula

Purpose Students will see how rotational speed would have increased as the nebula contracted early in the formation of our solar system.

Materials a chair that can be spun in place

Procedure One person sits in the chair, and the chair is spun. The seated person extends his or her arms out to the sides, which will cause the spinning to slow. Then the seated person pulls his or her arms in, causing the spinning rate to increase. This activity can be repeated with multiple students.

Safety A lighter student will be easier to spin, however, you may prefer to be the person in the chair. The person in the chair should not move in any way other than to put his or her arms in and out.

Expected Outcomes Students will see that extended arms (representing the early, wider nebula) results in a slower spin. Pulling in the arms (representing the contracting nebula) causes an increase in spinning rate.
Visual, Kinesthetic

Answer to . . .

Figure 2 *The terrestrial planets are much smaller than the Jovian planets.*

Section 23.1 (continued)

3 ASSESS

Evaluate Understanding 

Have students create quiz questions from this section and put them on flashcards. Then put the students in small groups where they will compete to see who can answer the most questions correctly. Put the cards in the center of the table, and have students take turns selecting a card and trying to answer it. If a student cannot answer the question on the card he or she selects, it is returned to the bottom of the pile. Students earn the card of each question they answer correctly. The winner is the one with the most cards at the end of the game.

Reteach L1

Have students summarize the differences between the terrestrial and Jovian planets by using the figures and tables in this section.

Math Practice

8. Show students how to use the equation: distance = rate / time to answer these questions. Since they are asked to find time, the equation can be rearranged as time = distance / rate.

Solutions

(1) 6.3×10^8 km ÷ 100 km/h = 6,300,000 h ÷ 24 h/day = 262,500 days ÷ 365 days/yr = 719 yrs
(2) 6.3×10^8 km ÷ 1000 km/h = 630,000 h ÷ 24 h/day = 26,250 days ÷ 365 days/yr = 72 yrs
(3) 6.3×10^8 km ÷ 40,000 km/h = 15,750 h ÷ 24 h/day = 656 days ÷ 365 days/yr = 1.8 yrs
(4) 6.3×10^8 km ÷ 300,000 km/s = 2100 s ÷ 60 s/ 1 min = 35 minutes

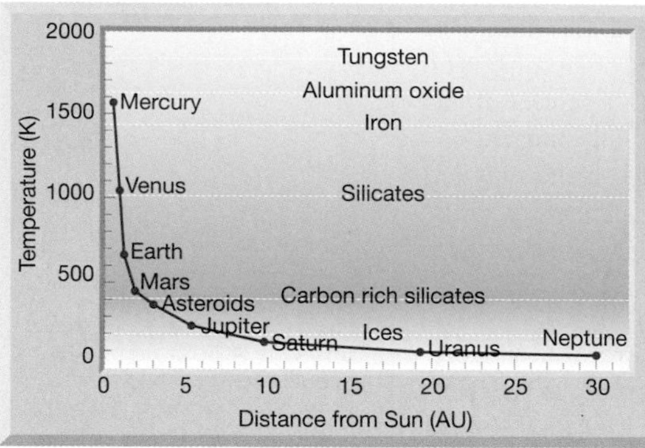

Figure 4 The terrestrial planets formed mainly from silicate minerals and metallic iron that have high melting points. The Jovian planets formed from large quantities of gases and ices.

Planetesimals The growth of planets began as solid bits of matter began to collide and clump together through a process known as accretion. The colliding matter formed small, irregularly shaped bodies called **planetesimals.** As the collisions continued, the planetesimals grew larger, as shown in Figure 3C on page 647. They acquired enough mass to exert a gravitational pull on surrounding objects. In this way, they added still more mass and grew into true planets.

In the inner solar system, close to the sun, temperatures were so high that only metals and silicate minerals could form solid grains. It was too hot for ices of water, carbon dioxide, and methane to form. As shown in Figure 4, the inner planets grew mainly from substances with high melting points.

In the frigid outer reaches of the solar system, on the other hand, it was cold enough for ices of water and other substances to form. Consequently, the Jovian planets grew not only from accumulations of solid bits of material but also from large quantities of ices. Eventually, the Jovian planets became large enough to gravitationally capture even the lightest gases, such as hydrogen and helium. This enabled them to grow into giants.

Section 23.1 Assessment

Reviewing Concepts

1. Which planets are classified as terrestrial? Which planets are classified as Jovian?
2. Sequence the nine planets in order, beginning with the planet closest to the sun.
3. How do the terrestrial planets differ from the Jovian planets?
4. What is a nebula?
5. How did distance from the sun affect the size and composition of the planets?

Critical Thinking

6. **Summarizing** Summarize the nebular theory of the formation of the solar system.
7. **Inferring** Among the planets in our solar system, Earth is unique because water exists in all three states—solid, liquid, and gas—on its surface. How would Earth's water cycle be different if its orbit was outside the orbit of Mars?

Math Practice

8. Jupiter is 6.3×10^8 (630 million kilometers) from Earth. Calculate how long it would take to reach Jupiter if you traveled at
1) 100 km/h (freeway speed);
2) 1,000 km/h (jetliner speed);
3) 40,000 km/h (rocket speed); and
4) 3.0×10^8 km/s (speed of light).

Section 23.1 Assessment

1. Terrestrial: Mercury, Venus, Earth, and Mars; Jovian: Jupiter, Saturn, and Neptune
2. Mercury, Venus, Earth, Mars, Jupiter, Saturn, Uranus, Neptune, Pluto
3. The terrestrial planets are small and rocky. The Jovian planets are gas giants.
4. A nebula is a cloud of dust and gas in space.
5. In the inner solar system, close to the sun, temperatures were so high that only metals and silicate minerals could form solid grains. Thus, the inner planets grew mainly from substances with high melting points. In the outer reaches of the solar system, it was cold enough for ices of water and other substances to form. Consequently, the Jovian planets grew not only from accumulations of solid bits of material but also from large quantities of gases and ices.
6. According to the nebular theory, the sun and planets formed from a rotating disk of dust and gases.
7. Sample answer: If Earth's orbit were outside the orbit of Mars, the extreme cold would freeze all water and only ice would exist. With only frozen water, there would be no precipitation, runoff, or infiltration—the water cycle and life itself would not exist.

23.2 The Terrestrial Planets

Reading Focus

Key Concepts

- What are the distinguishing characteristics of each terrestrial planet?

Reading Strategy

Using Prior Knowledge Copy the web diagram below. Before you read, add properties that you already know about Mars. Then add details about each property as you read. Make a similar web diagram for the other terrestrial planets.

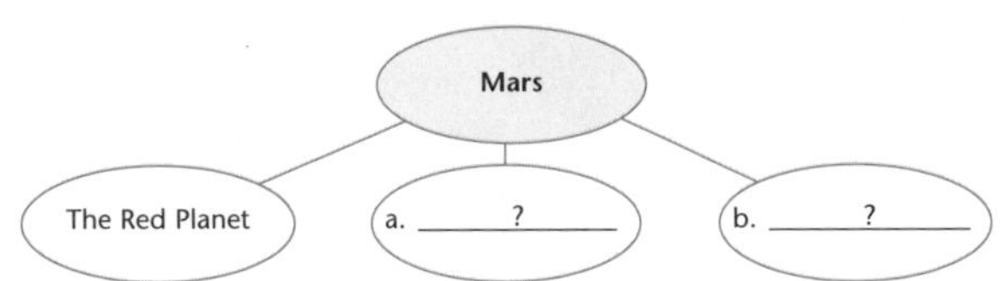

In January 2004, the space rover, *Spirit*, bounced onto the rock-littered surface of Mars, known as the Red Planet. Shown in Figure 5, *Spirit* and its companion rover, *Opportunity*, were on the Red Planet to study minerals and geological processes, both past and present. They also searched for signs of the liquid water—such as eroded rocks or dry stream channels on Mars's surface. For the next few months, the rovers sent back to Earth numerous images and chemical analysis of Mars's surface. Much of what we learn about the planets has been gathered by rovers, such as *Spirit*, or space probes that travel to the far reaches of the solar system, such as *Voyager*. In this section, we'll explore three terrestrial planets—Mercury, Venus, and Mars—and see how they compare with the fourth terrestrial planet, Earth.

Figure 5 *Spirit* roved the surface of Mars and gathered data about the Red Planet's geologic past and present.

Mercury: The Innermost Planet

Mercury, the innermost and second smallest planet, is hardly larger than Earth's moon and is smaller than three other moons in the solar system. Like our own moon, it absorbs most of the sunlight that strikes it and reflects only 6 percent of sunlight back into space. This low percentage of reflection is characteristic of terrestrial bodies that have no atmosphere. Earth, on the other hand, reflects about 30 percent of the light that strikes it. Most of this reflection is from clouds.

Section 23.2

1 FOCUS

Section Objective

23.3 **Describe** the distinguishing characteristics of each terrestrial planet.

Reading Focus

Build Vocabulary L2

Vocabulary List Encourage students to keep a list of new terms they encounter as they read this chapter. Have them use the context of each term to predict its definition. Go over the terms with the class. Some terms they may select are *rover, nonexistent, penetrate, veiled, summit, flank, advent,* and *prominent*.

Reading Strategy L2

Sample answers:
a. explored by rovers
b. numerous large volcanoes

Address Misconceptions L2

Some students may think that scientific knowledge is only acquired from controlled experiments. However, a great deal of scientific knowledge is a result of fieldwork and careful observations. In fact, a great deal of what we know about the universe and our solar system, we learned strictly from observation. To help students realize this, ask these questions as you teach this section. Ask: **What did we learn about Venus from the Magellan spacecraft?** *(Venus has varied topography like Earth.)* **What did we learn about Mars from the orbiting spacecraft Mariner 9?** *(Mars has volcanoes and canyons.)* **What did we learn about Mars from the rovers Spirit and Opportunity?** *(Mars has evaporite minerals and evidence of geological processes caused by liquid water; Mars has sand dunes and impact craters.)* **What did we learn from Mars Global Surveyor?** *(Underground springs may have existed on Mars.)* **Could we have learned these things simply from controlled experiments on Earth?** *(no)* **Verbal**

2 INSTRUCT

Mercury: The Innermost Planet

Build Reading Literacy L1

Refer to **p. 362D** in **Chapter 13**, which provides guidelines for this reading strategy.

Use Prior Knowledge Have students make a web diagram for Mercury that includes information they already know about it. Have them add new information to their web as they read. Possible characteristics for web include: small, hot, closest to sun, has craters, very dense, revolves around sun quickly, rotates slowly, three months of night and three months of day, greatest temperature extremes of any planet.
Visual, Verbal

Venus: The Veiled Planet

Build Science Skills 

Comparing and Contrasting Have students write a list of the similarities between Earth and Venus. *(size, density, mass, location in solar system, clouds, plateaus and mountains, volcanoes, have few impact craters)* Then have students create a chart contrasting Venus and Earth. For example:

Venus	Earth
One year is 255 Earth-days	One year is 365 Earth-days
Covered in thick clouds	Thin atmosphere
Very hot surface temperature	Surface temperature allows liquid water
97 percent of atmosphere is carbon dioxide	Very little of the atmosphere is carbon dioxide
Very little water vapor and nitrogen	Lots of water vapor and nitrogen
Atmospheric pressure is 90 times Earth's surface pressure	

Verbal, Visual

Download a worksheet on extra-terrestrial volcanoes for students to complete, and find additional teacher support from NSTA SciLinks.

Figure 6 Mercury's surface looks somewhat similar to the far side of Earth's moon.

Surface Features Mercury has cratered highlands, much like the moon, and some smooth terrains that resemble maria. Unlike the moon, however, Mercury is a very dense planet, which implies that it contains a large iron core for its size. Also, Mercury has very long scarps (deep slopes) that cut across the plains and craters alike. These scarps may have resulted from crustal changes as the planet cooled and shrank.

Surface Temperature Mercury, shown in Figure 6, revolves around the sun quickly, but it rotates slowly. One full day-night cycle on Earth takes 24 hours. On Mercury, one rotation requires 59 Earth-days. Thus, a night on Mercury lasts for about three months and is followed by three months of daylight. Nighttime temperatures drop as low as –173°C, and noontime temperatures exceed 427°C—hot enough to melt lead. **Mercury has the greatest temperature extremes of any planet.** The odds of life as we know it existing on Mercury are almost nonexistent.

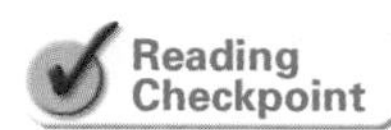

How does Mercury's period of rotation compare with Earth's?

Venus: The Veiled Planet

Venus, second only to the moon in brilliance in the night sky, is named for the goddess of love and beauty. It orbits the sun in a nearly perfect circle once every 255 Earth-days. Venus is similar to Earth in size, density, mass, and location in the solar system. Thus, it has been referred to as "Earth's twin." Because of these similarities, it is hoped that a detailed study of Venus will provide geologists with a better understanding of Earth's history.

Figure 7 Venus This global view of the surface of Venus is computer generated from two years of Magellan Project radar mapping. The twisting bright features that cross the planet are highly fractured mountains and canyons of the eastern Aphrodite highland.

Surface Features Venus is covered in thick clouds that visible light cannot penetrate. Nevertheless, radar mapping by the uncrewed *Magellan* spacecraft and by instruments on Earth have revealed a varied topography with features somewhat between those of Earth and Mars, as shown in Figure 7. To map Venus, radar pulses are sent toward the planet's surface, and the heights of plateaus and mountains are measured by timing the return of the radar echo. **These data have confirmed that basaltic volcanism and tectonic activity shape Venus's surface. Based on the low density of impact craters, these forces must have been very active during the recent geologic past.**

For: Links on extraterrestrial volcanoes
Visit: www.SciLinks.org
Web Code: cjn-7232

Customize for English Language Learners

Have students use a thesaurus rather than a dictionary to look up unfamiliar words. This will help them learn the meaning of multiple words simultaneously. It is likely that at least one synonym listed is a word they know.

About 80 percent of Venus's surface consists of plains covered by volcanic flows. Some lava channels extend hundreds of kilometers—one is 6800 kilometers long. Scientists have identified thousands of volcanic structures. Most are small shield volcanoes, although more than 1500 volcanoes greater than 20 kilometers across have been mapped. Figure 8 shows two of these volcanoes—one is Sapas Mons, 400 kilometers across and 1.5 kilometers high. Flows from this volcano mostly erupted from its flanks rather than its summit, in the manner of Hawaiian shield volcanoes.

Only 8 percent of Venus's surface consists of highlands that may be similar to continental areas on Earth. Tectonic activity on Venus seems to be driven by upwelling and downwelling of material in the planet's interior.

Figure 8 Sapas Mons and Maat Mons In this computer-generated image from Venus, Maat Mons, a large volcano, is near the horizon. Sapas Mons is the bright feature in the foreground.
Comparing and Contrasting *What features on Venus are similar to those on Earth? What features are different?*

Surface Temperature Before the advent of spacecraft, Venus was considered to be a possible habitat for living things. However, evidence from space probes indicates otherwise. The surface temperature of Venus reaches 475°C, and its atmosphere is 97 percent carbon dioxide. Only small amounts of water vapor and nitrogen have been detected. Venus's atmosphere contains a cloud layer about 25 kilometers thick. The atmospheric pressure is 90 times that at Earth's surface. This hostile environment makes it unlikely that life as we know it exists on Venus.

Describe the composition of Venus's atmosphere.

Mars: The Red Planet

Mars has evoked greater interest than any other planet. When one imagines intelligent life on other worlds, little green Martians may come to mind. Mars is easy to observe, which may explain why so many people are fascinated by it. The surfaces of all other planets within telescopic range are hidden by clouds—except for Mercury, whose nearness to the sun makes viewing it difficult. Mars is known as the Red Planet because it appears as a reddish ball when viewed through a telescope. Mars also has some dark regions that change intensity during the Martian year. The most prominent telescopic features of Mars are its brilliant white polar caps.

Mars: The Red Planet

Use Community Resources **L2**

If possible, invite an astronomer or geologist in your community to talk to students about the findings of the rovers *Spirit* and *Opportunity* on Mars. Encourage students to list questions they have about Mars before the speaker comes to visit.
Verbal, Interpersonal

Integrate Chemistry **L3**

Polar Ice Caps Inform students that Mars has polar ice caps that are made mostly of frozen carbon dioxide, with some frozen water. Have advanced students brainstorm how these ice caps could be used to help make Mars habitable for humans.
Verbal, Logical

Facts and Figures

Mars has two natural satellites (moons), Phobos and Deimos. Although Mars is easy to observe from Earth, these moons were not discovered until 1977. Perhaps this is because they are only 24 and 15 km in diameter. Phobos is closer to Mars than any other natural satellite in the solar system, and it requires just 7 hours and 39 minutes for one revolution. *Mariner 9* found that both moons are irregularly shaped and have numerous impact craters.

Answer to . . .

Figure 8 *Features on Venus that are similar to those on Earth include plains, highlands, mountains, and volcanoes. Features on Venus that are different than those on Earth include thick clouds that can't be penetrated by visible light, volcanic flows covering most plains, thousands of volcanoes, no process of plate tectonics, and an atmosphere that can't sustain life.*

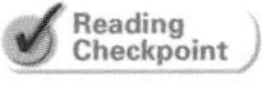

One full day-night cycle on Earth takes 24 hours. On Mercury, it requires 179 Earth-days.

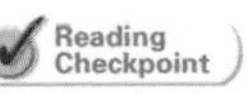

Venus's atmosphere is mainly made of carbon dioxide with traces of water vapor and nitrogen.

Build Reading Literacy L1

Refer to **p. 1D** in **Chapter 1**, which provides guidelines for this reading strategy.

Anticipation Guide
Ask students to respond to the following questions in writing before they read the section on Mars. Have the students check over their answers and make changes as needed after they finish reading the section. Students should answer True or False to the following series of statements: **Mars's polar ice caps are mostly made of water.** *(False)* **There are active volcanoes on Mars.** *(False)* **Mars often has dust storms with hurricane force winds.** *(True)* **Mars has canyons that are much larger than Earth's Grand Canyon.** *(True)* **There is evidence that liquid water once flowed on Mars.** *(True)* **Liquid water currently flows on the Martian surface.** *(False)*
Verbal

Figure 9 Many parts of Mars's landscape resemble desert areas on Earth.

The Martian Atmosphere

The Martian atmosphere has only 1 percent the density of Earth's. It is made up primarily of carbon dioxide with tiny amounts of water vapor. Data from Mars probes confirm that the polar caps of Mars are made of water ice, covered by a thin layer of frozen carbon dioxide. As winter nears in either hemisphere, temperatures drop to −125°C, and additional carbon dioxide is deposited.

Although the atmosphere of Mars is very thin, extensive dust storms occur and may cause the color changes observed from Earth. Hurricane-force winds up to 270 kilometers per hour can persist for weeks. As shown in Figure 9, images from *Spirit* reveal a Martian landscape remarkably similar to a rocky desert on Earth, with abundant sand dunes and impact craters partially filled with dust.

Figure 10 Valles Marineris Mars's Valles Marineris canyon system is more than 5000 kilometers long and up to 8 kilometers deep. The dark spots on the left edge of the image are huge volcanoes.

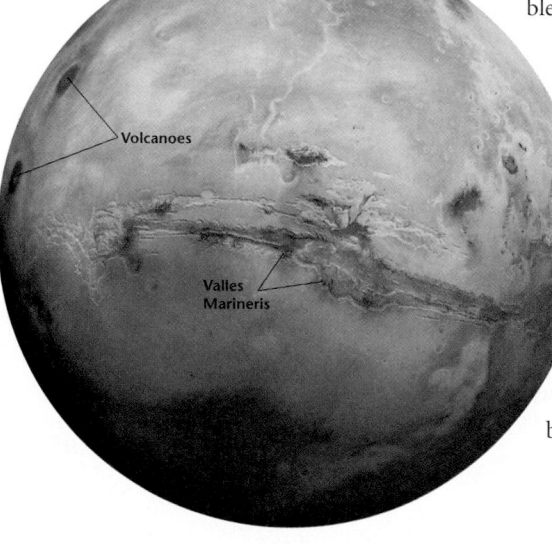

Surface Features *Mariner 9*, the first spacecraft to orbit another planet, reached Mars in 1971 amid a raging dust storm. When the dust cleared, images of Mars' northern hemisphere revealed numerous large volcanoes. The biggest, Olympus Mons, is the size of Ohio and is 23 kilometers high—over two and a half times higher than Mount Everest. This gigantic volcano and others resemble Hawaiian shield volcanoes on Earth.

Most Martian surface features are old by Earth standards. The highly cratered southern hemisphere is probably 3.5 billion to 4.5 billion years old. Even the relatively "fresh" volcanic features of the northern hemisphere may be older than 1 billion years.

Another surprising find made by *Mariner 9* was the existence of several canyons that are much larger than Earth's Grand Canyon. The largest, Valles Marineris, is shown in Figure 10. It is thought to have formed by slippage of material along huge faults in the crustal layer. In this respect, it would be comparable to the rift valleys of Africa.

Facts and Figures

Students may ask why the volcanoes on Earth are so much smaller than volcanoes on Mars. The reason is that Earth's crust is tectonically active, so the crust over a mantle plume is constantly moving. This motion creates a series of smaller volcanoes. Since Mars does not have plates that move, a volcano was able to grow larger and larger each time it erupted.

Water on Mars Some areas of Mars exhibit drainage patterns similar to those created by streams on Earth. The rover *Opportunity*, for example, found evidence of evaporite minerals and geologic formations associated with liquid water, as shown in Figure 11. In addition, *Viking* images have revealed ancient islands in what is now a dry streambed. When these streamlike channels were first discovered, some observers speculated that a thick water-laden atmosphere capable of generating torrential downpours once existed on Mars. If so, what happened to this water? The present Martian atmosphere contains only traces of water.

Images from the *Mars Global Surveyor* indicate that groundwater has recently migrated to the surface. These spring-like seeps have created gullies where they emerge from valley and crater walls. Some of the escaping water may have initially frozen due to the average Martian temperatures that range between −70°C and −100°C. Eventually, however, it seeped out as a slurry of sediment, ice, and liquid that formed the gullies.

Many scientists do not accept the theory that Mars once had an active water cycle similar to Earth's. Rather, they believe that most of the large stream-like valleys were created by the collapse of surface material caused by the slow melting of subsurface ice. Data from *Opportunity*, however, indicate that some areas were "drenched" in water. It will take scientists many months, if not years, to analyze the data gathered by the latest Mars mission. Because water is an essential ingredient for life, scientists and nonscientists alike are enthusiastic about exploring this phenomenon.

Figure 11 The composition and markings of some Martian rocks indicate that liquid water was once present on Mars's surface. The marking shown in the center of the rock, however, was created by a NASA rover during chemical analysis.

Section 23.2 Assessment

Reviewing Concepts

1. Which inner planet is smallest?
2. How does Venus compare with Earth?
3. Identify one distinguishing characteristic of each inner planet.
4. What surface features does Mars have that are also common on Earth?

Critical Thinking

5. **Making Judgments** Besides Earth, which inner planet may have been most able to support life? Explain your answer.
6. **Relating Cause and Effect** Why are surface temperatures so high on Venus?

Writing in Science

Editorial A space mission to the moon or Mars often costs millions of dollars. Yet, it is hoped that space exploration can give us valuable knowledge about the solar system. Consider the pros and cons of space exploration. Then write an editorial stating whether or not you believe the costs are worth the potential benefits.

3 ASSESS

Evaluate Understanding L2

Review with the class by stating a characteristic of one of the planets. Have students respond with the name of the planet having that characteristic.

Reteach L1

Have students make a colored sketch of each planet. They should list each planet's characteristics next to their sketch. Then have students put their sketches in order (Mercury out to Pluto) and display their work.

Writing in Science

Remind students that writing an editorial means stating a position and backing up that statement with factual evidence.

Student editorials should discuss both the costs and benefits of space exploration. Student opinions should be supported by facts.

Section 23.2 Assessment

1. Mercury
2. Venus is similar to Earth in size, density, mass, and location in the solar system.
3. Sample answer: Mercury has the greatest temperature extremes of any planet. Venus shows evidence of recent volcanic and tectonic activity. Earth is the only place where water exists in all three states. Mars experiences extensive dust storms and high winds.
4. volcanoes, sand dunes, and large canyons
5. Sample answer: Mars may have been the most able to support life because it may have had liquid water on its surface.
6. Venus's atmosphere is mainly made up of carbon dioxide, which traps radiation so the heat cannot escape.

Section 23.3

1 FOCUS

Section Objective

23.4 **Describe** the distinguishing characteristics of each Jovian planet.

Reading Focus

Build Vocabulary L2

Vocabulary Rating Chart Have students construct a chart with four columns labeled Word, Can Define or Use It, Heard or Seen It, and Don't Know. Have students copy words as they read the section into the first column and rate their word knowledge by putting a check in one of the other columns. Ask how many students actually know each word. Have them share their knowledge. Ask focused questions to help students predict text content based on the word, thus enabling them to have a purpose for reading. After students have read the section, have them rate their knowledge again.

Reading Strategy L2

Sample answers:
a. Saturn
b. largest ring system
c. Uranus
d. axis tilted more than 90°
e. Neptune
f. winds exceed 1000 km per hour
g. Pluto
h. orbit is highly eccentric

2 INSTRUCT

Jupiter: Giant Among Planets

Build Reading Literacy L1

Refer to **p. 392D** in **Chapter 14**, which provides guidelines for this reading strategy.

Preview Have students preview this section by skimming the headings and visuals. This will help students to activate their previous knowledge about the outer planets and will likely make them interested to read more about each planet.
Visual, Verbal

23.3 The Outer Planets

Reading Focus

Key Concepts

What characteristics distinguish each outer planet?

Reading Strategy

Summarizing Make a table like the one on the right that includes a row for each outer planet. Write a brief summary of the characteristics of each planet.

Outer Planets	Characteristics
Jupiter	largest; most mass, Great Red Spot
a. ___?___	b. ___?___
c. ___?___	d. ___?___

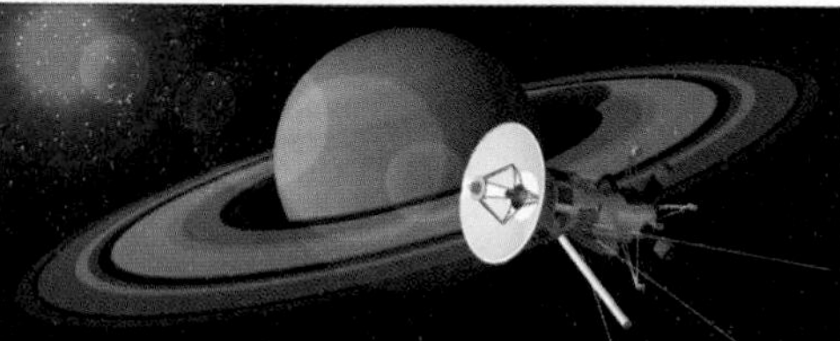

Figure 12 This artist's rendition shows *Cassini* approaching Saturn.

In 2004, the space probe *Cassini,* launched seven years earlier, finally reached the planet Saturn. The mission of *Cassini,* shown in Figure 12, is to explore Saturn's stunning ring system and its moons, including the unique moon Titan. During its four-year tour, *Cassini* is expected to orbit the ringed giant 74 times and make nearly four dozen flybys of Titan. The *Hugyens* probe, carried into space by the *Cassini* orbiter, will descend to Titan's surface for further studies. In this section, we'll take a clue from *Cassini* and explore the outer planets—Jupiter, Saturn, Neptune, Uranus, and Pluto.

Figure 13 **A** When photographed by *Voyager 2,* the Great Red Spot was the size of two Earth-size circles placed side by side. **B** The light clouds are regions where gases are sinking and cooling. The convection currents and the rapid rotation of the planet generate high-speed winds.

Jupiter: Giant Among Planets

Jupiter is only 1/800 as massive as the sun. Still, it is the largest planet by far. **Jupiter has a mass that is 2 1/2 times greater than the mass of all the other planets and moons combined.** In fact, had Jupiter been about 10 times larger, it would have evolved into a small star. Jupiter rotates more rapidly than any other planet, completing one rotation in slightly less than 10 Earth-hours. The effect of this fast spin is to make its equatorial region bulge and its poles flatten slightly.

When viewed through a telescope or binoculars, Jupiter appears to be covered with alternating bands of multicolored clouds that run parallel to its equator. The most striking feature is the Great Red Spot in the southern hemisphere, shown in Figure 13A. The Great Red Spot was first discovered more than three centuries ago. However, when *Pioneer 11* moved within 42,000 kilometers of Jupiter's cloud tops, images from the orbiter indicated that the Great Red Spot is a cyclonic storm.

Structure of Jupiter Jupiter's hydrogen-helium atmosphere also contains small amounts of methane, ammonia, water, and sulfur compounds. The wind systems, shown in Figure 13B, generate the light- and dark-colored bands that encircle this giant. Unlike the winds on Earth, which are driven by solar energy, Jupiter itself gives off nearly twice as much heat as it receives from the sun. Thus, the interior heat from Jupiter produces huge convection currents in the atmosphere.

Atmospheric pressure at the top of the clouds is equal to sea-level pressure on Earth. Because of Jupiter's immense gravity, the pressure increases rapidly toward its surface. At 1000 kilometers below the clouds, the pressure is great enough to compress hydrogen gas into a liquid. Consequently, Jupiter is thought to be a gigantic ocean of liquid hydrogen. Less than halfway into Jupiter's interior, extreme pressures cause the liquid hydrogen to turn into liquid metallic hydrogen. Jupiter is also believed to have a rocky and metallic central core.

Jupiter's Moons Jupiter's satellite system, consisting of 28 moons discovered so far, resembles a miniature solar system. The four largest moons were discovered by Galileo. They travel in nearly circular orbits around the planet. To the surprise of almost everyone images from *Voyagers 1* and *2* in 1979 revealed that each of the four Galilean satellites is a unique geological world. The moons are shown in Figure 14. The innermost of the Galilean moons, Io, is one of three known volcanically active bodies in our solar system. The other volcanically active bodies are Earth—and Neptune's moon Triton. The heat source for volcanic activity on Io is thought to be tidal energy generated by a relentless "tug of war" between Jupiter and the other Galilean moons. The gravitational power of Jupiter and nearby moons pulls and pushes on Io's tidal bulge as its orbit takes it alternately closer to and farther from Jupiter. This gravitational flexing of Io is transformed into heat energy and results in Io's volcanic eruptions.

For: Links on the outer planets
Visit: www.SciLinks.org
Web Code: cjn-7233

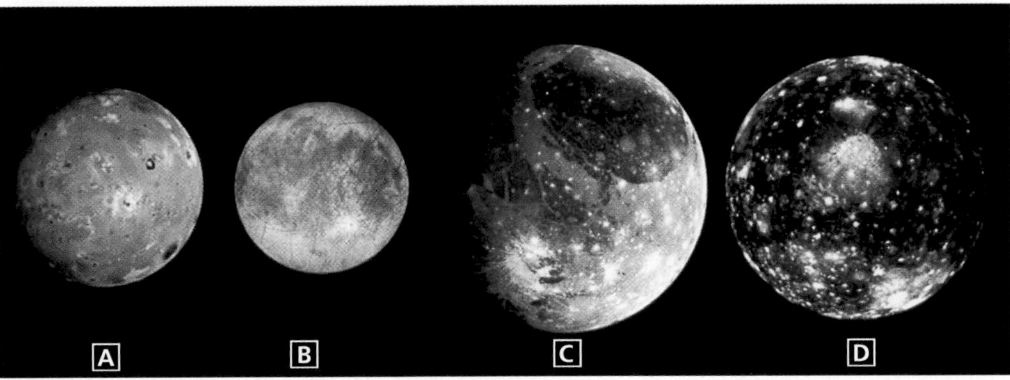

Figure 14 Jupiter's Moons
A Io is the innermost moon and is one of only three volcanically active bodies in the solar system. **B** Europa—the smallest of the Galilean moons—has an icy surface that is crossed by many linear features. **C** Ganymede is the largest Jovian moon, and it contains cratered areas, smooth regions, and areas covered by numerous parallel grooves. **D** Callisto—the outermost of the Galilean moons—is densely cratered, much like Earth's moon.

Use Visuals L1

Figure 14 This diagram shows Jupiter's four largest moons. Ask: **What do these moons have in common with each other?** *(They are all round, and they orbit around Jupiter.)* **Which of these moons have craters?** *(Europa, Callisto, and Io)* **Could Europa have craters?** *(Yes, but its surface is covered in ice.)* **Which of these moons has volcanoes?** *(Io)*
Visual

Integrate Language Arts L2

Mythological Characters All of the planets in our solar system, except for Earth, are named for characters or gods in Greek or Roman mythology. Have students work in groups. Each group should select the name of one planet to research. They should find out which mythological character or god the planet was named after, learn about the character, and determine why the name may have been given to the planet. For example, Mercury was named after the Roman messenger god because it is the planet with the fastest revolution rate around the sun. Each group should present their findings to the class.
Verbal, Interpersonal

Customize for English Language Learners

Have students create a concept map to organize what they will learn about the outer planets. Have them start with the main concept of the outer planets. Then have branches for Jupiter, Saturn, Uranus, Neptune, and Pluto, which they will expand on by filling in characteristics of each planet as they read.

Download a worksheet on the outer planets for students to complete, and find additional teacher support from NSTA SciLinks.

Saturn: The Elegant Planet

Build Reading Literacy L1

Refer to **p. 124D** in **Chapter 5**, which provides the guidelines for this Reading Strategy.

Summarize Have students summarize the major characteristics of Saturn as they read. For example, Saturn has wind, storms, many moons, and rings. **Verbal**

Use Visuals L1

Figure 15 This diagram shows the rings of Saturn. Ask: **How are rings A and B different from ring C?** *(Ring C is a darker color.)* **What do you think is the cause of this difference?** *(They have different compositions.)* **How are the outer rings different from the inner rings?** *(The outer rings are much thinner than the inner rings.)* **How is ring E different from the other rings?** *(Ring E looks green, and is more diffuse.)* **Visual**

Jupiter's Rings Jupiter's ring system was one of the most unexpected discoveries made by *Voyager 1.* By analyzing how these rings scatter light, researchers concluded that the rings are composed of fine, dark particles, similar in size to smoke particles. The faint nature of the rings also indicates that these minute fragments are widely dispersed. The particles are thought to be fragments blasted by meteorite impacts from the surfaces of Metis and Adrastea, two small moons of Jupiter.

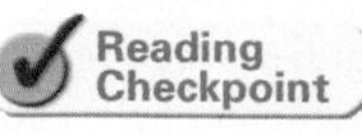

Which Galilean moon is volcanically active?

Saturn: The Elegant Planet

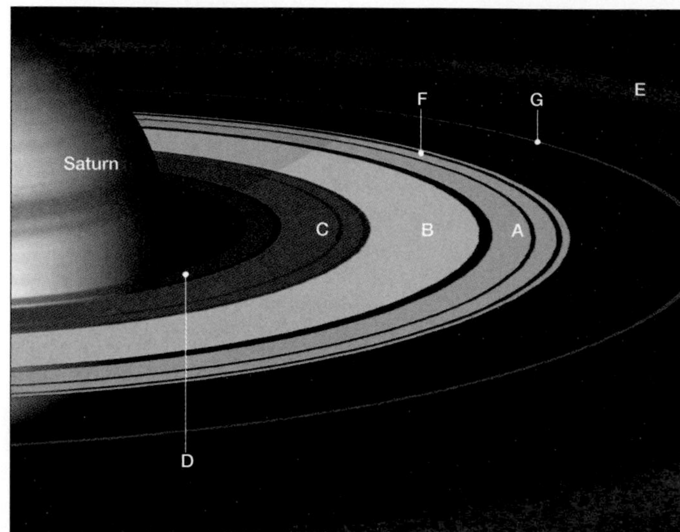

Figure 15 Saturn's Rings Saturn's rings fall into two categories based on particle density. The main rings (A and B) are densely packed. In contrast, the outer rings are composed of widely dispersed particles.

Requiring 29.46 Earth-years to make one revolution, Saturn is almost twice as far from the sun as Jupiter. However, its atmosphere, composition, and internal structure are thought to be remarkably similar to Jupiter's. **The most prominent feature of Saturn is its system of rings, shown in Figure 15.** In 1610, Galileo used a primitive telescope and first saw the structures that were later found to be the rings. They appeared as two small bodies adjacent to the planet. Their ring nature was explained 50 years later by the Dutch astronomer Christian Huygens.

Features of Saturn In 1980 and 1981, flyby missions of the nuclear-powered *Voyagers 1* and *2* spacecraft came within 100,000 kilometers of Saturn. More information was gained in a few days than had been acquired since Galileo first viewed this elegant planet.

1. Saturn's atmosphere is very active, with winds roaring at up to 1500 kilometers per hour.
2. Large cyclonic "storms" similar to Jupiter's Great Red Spot, although smaller, occur in Saturn's atmosphere.
3. Eleven additional moons were discovered.
4. The rings of Saturn were found to be more complex than expected.

More recently, observations from ground-based telescopes, the Hubble Space Telescope, and *Cassini* have added to our knowledge of Saturn's ring and moon system. When the positions of Earth and Saturn allowed the rings to be viewed edge-on—thereby reducing the glare from the main rings—Saturn's faintest rings and satellites became visible.

Facts and Figures

Scientists believe that liquid water is the key to the development of life, so they carefully search other planets and moons for this key ingredient. Studies of Jupiter's moon, Europa, have revealed that it is covered with a thick layer of ice, and scientists have inferred that there may be liquid water beneath this layer. This makes Europa a prime target for future space probes to look for evidence of life on this moon.

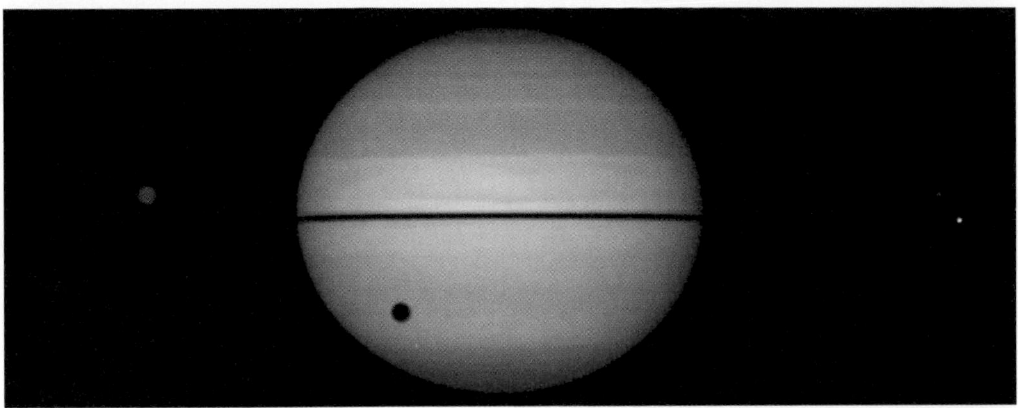

Figure 16 **Saturn's Moons** This image of Saturn shows several of its moons.

Saturn's Rings Until the discovery that Jupiter, Uranus, and Neptune also have ring systems, this phenomenon was thought to be unique to Saturn. Although the four known ring systems differ in detail, they share many attributes. They all consist of multiple concentric rings separated by gaps of various widths. In addition, each ring is composed of individual particles—"moonlets" of ice and rock—that circle the planet while regularly impacting one another.

Most rings fall into one of two categories based on particle density. Saturn's main rings, designated A and B in Figure 15, and the bright rings of Uranus are tightly packed and contain "moonlets" that range in size from a few centimeters to several meters. These particles are thought to collide frequently as they orbit the parent planet. Despite the fact that Saturn's dense rings stretch across several hundred kilometers, they are very thin, perhaps less than 100 meters from top to bottom.

At the other extreme, the faintest rings, such as Jupiter's ring system and Saturn's outermost rings, are composed of very fine particles that are widely dispersed. Saturn's outermost rings are designated E in Figure 15. In addition to having very low particle densities, these rings tend to be thicker than Saturn's bright rings.

Saturn's Moons Saturn's satellite system consists of 31 moons, some of which are shown in Figure 16. Titan is the largest moon and is bigger than Mercury. It is the second-largest moon in the solar system. Titan and Neptune's Triton are the only moons in the solar system known to have substantial atmospheres. Because of its dense gaseous cover, the atmospheric pressure at Titan's surface is about 1.5 times that at Earth's surface. Another moon, Phoebe, exhibits retrograde motion. It, like other moons with retrograde orbits, is most likely a captured asteroid or large planetesimal left over from the formation of the planets.

How many moons of Saturn have been discovered thus far?

Build Science Skills L2

Inferring After reading the section on Saturn's rings, have students take another look at the image of Saturn's rings in Figure 15. Ask students to use what they read and observed, in addition to their prior knowledge of how the solar system formed, to infer how Saturn's rings might have formed. Have students share their ideas with the class. Then share the information in the Facts and Figures box below with the class.
Visual, Logical

Facts and Figures

There are several theories regarding the origin of ring particles. Some scientists believe the rings formed out of a cloud of gas and dust from which the planet formed. Others believe the rings formed later when a moon or asteroid was pulled apart by the planet's gravity. Still others believe a crash with a foreign body blasted apart one of the planet's moon. Scientists hope that future missions to Saturn will help them resolve this controversy.

Answer to . . .

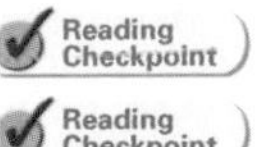

Io is volcanically active.

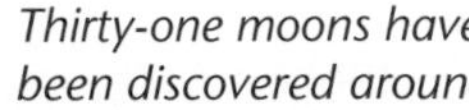

Thirty-one moons have been discovered around Saturn.

Uranus: The Sideways Planet

Teacher Demo

Discovering the Rings of Uranus

L2

Purpose Students will experience a simulation of how the rings of Uranus were discovered.

Materials meter stick, flashlight

Procedure Darken the classroom, and have one student hold the flashlight at the front of the room. Hold the meter stick horizontally to represent the rings of Uranus. While the student holds the flashlight steadily, pass the meter stick slowly up and down in front of the flashlight so it appears to blink on and off to the class. Explain to students that the flashlight represents the distant star which was blocked by Uranus in 1977. Help students understand that the rings would have caused the light of the star to blink on and off a few times as Uranus and its rings passed in front of the distant star.

Expected Outcome Students will see that Uranus's rings would have caused the occluded star to blink on and off a few times before and after the passing of Uranus's body in front of the star.
Visual, Kinesthetic

Figure 17 This image of Titania, one of Uranus's moons, was taken by *Voyager 2* from a distance of 1 million kilometers.

Uranus: The Sideways Planet

A unique feature of Uranus is that it rotates "on its side." **Instead of being generally perpendicular to the plane of its orbit like the other planets, Uranus's axis of rotation lies nearly parallel with the plane of its orbit.** Its rotational motion, therefore, has the appearance of rolling, rather than the top-like spinning of the other planets. Uranus's spin may have been altered by a giant impact.

A surprise discovery in 1977 revealed that Uranus has a ring system. This find occurred as Uranus passed in front of a distant star and blocked its view. Observers saw the star "wink" briefly both before and after Uranus passed by. Later studies indicate that Uranus has at least nine distinct ring belts.

Spectacular views from *Voyager 2,* such as seen in Figure 17, show the varied terrains of the five largest moons of Uranus. Some have long, deep canyons and linear scars, whereas others possess large, smooth areas on otherwise crater-riddled surfaces. Miranda, the innermost of the five largest moons, has a greater variety of landforms than any body yet examined in the solar system.

What is unique about Uranus's axis of rotation?

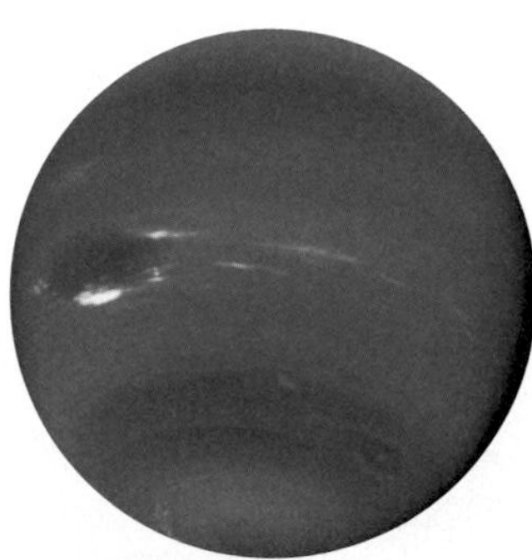

Figure 18 The Great Dark Spot of Neptune is visible in the center of the left of the image. Bright cirrus-like clouds that travel at high speeds around the planet are also visible.
Identifying ***What is the Great Dark Spot?***

Neptune: The Windy Planet

As shown in Figure 18, Neptune has a dynamic atmosphere, much like those of Jupiter and Saturn. **Winds exceeding 1000 kilometers per hour encircle Neptune, making it one of the windiest places in the solar system.** It also has an Earth-size blemish called the Great Dark Spot that is reminiscent of Jupiter's Great Red Spot. The Great Dark Spot is assumed to be a large rotating storm. About five years after the Great Dark Spot was discovered, it vanished, only to be replaced by another dark spot in the planet's northern hemisphere.

Perhaps most surprising are the white, cirrus-like clouds that occupy a layer about 50 kilometers above the main cloud deck. The clouds are most likely frozen methane. Neptune has 13 known moons. *Voyager* images revealed that the bluish planet also has a ring system.

Triton, Neptune's largest moon, is nearly the size of Earth's moon. Triton is the only large moon in the solar system that exhibits retrograde motion. This motion indicates that Triton formed independently of Neptune and was gravitationally captured.

Triton also has the lowest surface temperature yet measured on any body in the solar system at −200°C. Its atmosphere is mostly nitrogen with a little methane. Despite low surface temperatures, Triton displays volcanic-like activity.

Facts and Figures

The existence of Neptune was predicted before it was discovered. This prediction was based on irregularities in the orbit of Uranus and Newton's Universal Law of Gravitation. Scientists were ecstatic, in 1846, when Neptune was discovered exactly where it had been predicted. This discovery is an excellent example of a hypothesis being tested not in a lab, but in outer space itself.

Pluto: Planet X

Pluto lies on the fringe of the solar system, almost 40 times farther from the sun than Earth. It is 10,000 times too dim to be visible to the unaided eye. Because of its great distance and slow orbital speed, it takes Pluto 248 Earth-years to orbit the sun. Since its discovery in 1930, it has completed about one-fourth of a revolution. **Pluto's orbit is highly eccentric, causing it to occasionally travel inside the orbit of Neptune, where it resided from 1979 through February 1999.**

In 1978 the moon Charon was discovered orbiting Pluto. Because of its close proximity to the planet, the best ground-based images of Charon show it only as an elongated bulge. In 1990 the Hubble Space Telescope produced a clearer image of the two icy worlds, shown in Figure 19. Charon orbits Pluto once every 6.4 Earth-days at a distance 20 times closer to Pluto than our moon is to Earth.

Current data indicate that Pluto has a diameter of approximately 2300 kilometers, making it the smallest planet in the solar system. Charon is about 1300 kilometers across, exceptionally large in proportion to its parent.

The average temperature of Pluto is estimated at −210°C, which is cold enough to solidify most gases that might be present. Thus, Pluto might best be described as a dirty iceball of frozen gases with lesser amounts of rocky substances.

A growing number of astronomers assert that Pluto's small size and location within a swarm of similar icy objects means that it should be reclassified as a minor planet. Other astronomers insist that demoting Pluto to a minor planet would dishonor astronomical history and confuse the public.

Figure 19 This Hubble image shows Pluto and its moon Charon.

Section 23.3 Assessment

Reviewing Concepts

1. What is the largest planet? What is the smallest?
2. What is Jupiter's Great Red Spot?
3. Identify one distinguishing characteristic of each outer planet.
4. How are Saturn's moon, Titan, and Neptune's Triton similar?
5. In what way is Io similar to Earth? What other body shows this similarity?

Critical Thinking

6. **Relating Cause and Effect** What may have caused Uranus's unique axis of rotation?
7. **Making Judgments** Should Pluto be reclassified as a minor planet? Explain your answer.

Connecting Concepts

Convection Currents Write a brief paragraph comparing and contrasting atmospheric convection currents on Jupiter and Earth.

Pluto: Planet X

Build Science Skills L2

Comparing and Contrasting Challenge students to find similarities and differences between Pluto and the other planets (both terrestrial and Jovian). They may also want to compare Pluto to some of the moons in our solar system.
Verbal

3 ASSESS

Evaluate Understanding L2

Put students in cooperative groups, and have them compare the summaries of this section that they made in response to this section's first Reading Strategy.

Reteach L1

Have students make concept maps for each outer planet that list its major characteristics.

Connecting Concepts

Before students begin writing, review with them how convection currents in Earth's atmosphere work. Describe their cause *(solar energy)*, what they look like *(hot, less dense air rises while cooler, denser air sinks)*, and some results of convection currents *(wind)*.

Sample answer: On Earth, atmospheric convection currents are driven by solar energy. Jupiter, however, gives off nearly twice as much heat as it receives from the sun. The interior heat from Jupiter produces huge convection currents in the atmosphere.

Section 23.3 Assessment

1. Jupiter is the largest planet. Pluto is the smallest.
2. a cyclonic storm
3. Sample answer: Jupiter is the largest planet. Saturn has an amazing ring system. Uranus's axis of rotation is nearly parallel with the plane of its orbit. Neptune is one of the windiest places in the solar system. Pluto is small and cold with a very eccentric orbit.
4. Titan and Triton are the only moons in the solar system with significant atmospheres.
5. Io is volcanically active, just like Earth. Neptune's moon Triton is also volcanically active.
6. A giant impact may have changed Uranus's spin.
7. Sample answer: Further study is likely required to determine if our definition of a planet still applies to Pluto.

Answer to . . .

Figure 18 *The Great Dark Spot is assumed to be a large rotating storm, much like Jupiter's Great Red Spot.*

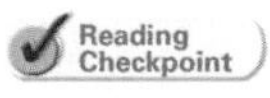

Uranus's axis lies nearly parallel with the plane of its orbit.

Section 23.4

1 FOCUS

Section Objectives

23.5 **Identify** the location within our solar system where most asteroids are found.

23.6 **Describe** the structure of a comet.

23.7 **Explain** the possible origins for a meteoroid.

Reading Focus

Build Vocabulary L2

Concept Map Have students make a concept map for the vocabulary terms in this section. The center of the map should be "Minor members of the solar system," the terms *asteroid*, *comet*, and *meteoroid* should branch off of this topic, and students should expand their map with the other vocabulary terms as they learn about each term.

Reading Strategy L2

a. small rocky body
b. comet
c. body made up of rocky and metallic materials held together by frozen gases
d. coma
e. glowing head of a comet
f. meteoroid
g. small solid particle that travels through space
h. meteor
i. meteoroid that enters Earth's atmosphere and burns up
j. meteorite
k. meteoroid that reaches Earth's surface

23.4 Minor Members of the Solar System

Reading Focus

Key Concepts

- Where are most asteroids located?
- What is the structure of a comet?
- What is the origin of most meteoroids?

Vocabulary

- asteroid
- comet
- coma
- meteoroid
- meteor
- meteorite

Reading Strategy

Building Vocabulary Copy the table below. Then as you read the section, write a definition for each vocabulary term in your own words.

Vocabulary	Definition
asteroid	a. ?
b. ?	c. ?
d. ?	e. ?

Figure 20 This artist's rendition shows *NEAR Shoemaker* touching down on the asteroid Eros.

In February 2001 an American spacecraft, *NEAR Shoemaker,* finished its mission in spectacular fashion—it became the first visitor to an asteroid. This historic accomplishment was not part of *NEAR Shoemaker's* original goal, which was to orbit the asteroid, taking images and gathering data about these objects in space. With this mission accomplished, however, NASA engineers wanted to see if they could actually land a spacecraft on an asteroid. The data they would gather would be priceless. As an added benefit, NASA would gain valuable experience that might help in the future to deflect an asteroid on a collision course with Earth.

Although it was not designed for landing, *NEAR Shoemaker*—shown in Figure 20—successfully touched down on the asteroid, Eros. It generated information that has planetary geologists both intrigued and perplexed. The spacecraft drifted toward the surface of Eros at the rate of 6 kilometers per hour. The images obtained revealed a barren, rocky surface composed of particles ranging in size from fine dust to boulders up to 8 meters across. Researchers unexpectedly discovered that fine debris is concentrated in the low areas that form flat deposits resembling ponds. Surrounding the low areas, the landscape is marked by an abundance of large boulders.

Seismic shaking is one of several hypotheses being considered as an explanation for the boulder-laden topography. This shaking would move the boulders upward. The larger materials rise to the top while the smaller materials settle to the bottom, which is similar to what happens when a can of mixed nuts is shaken.

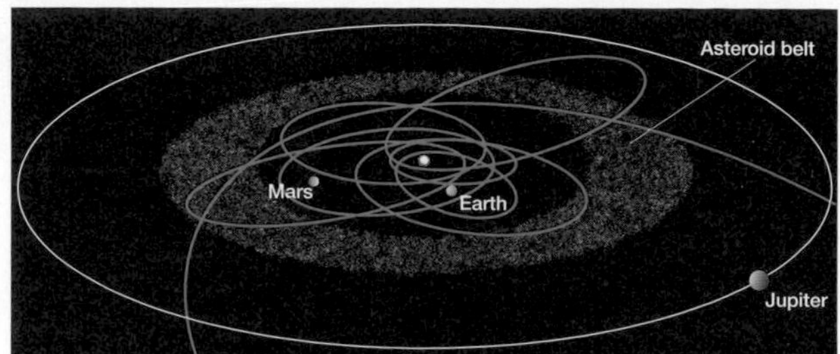

Figure 21 The orbits of most asteroids lie between Mars and Jupiter. Also shown are the orbits of a few near-Earth asteroids. Perhaps a thousand or more asteroids pass close to Earth. Luckily, only a few dozen are thought to be larger than 1 kilometer in diameter.

Asteroids: Microplanets

What exactly is an asteroid? **Asteroids** are small rocky bodies that have been likened to "flying mountains." The largest, Ceres, is about 1000 kilometers in diameter, but most are only about 1 kilometer across. The smallest asteroids are assumed to be no larger than grains of sand. **Most asteroids lie between the orbits of Mars and Jupiter. They have orbital periods of three to six years.** Some asteroids have very eccentric orbits and travel very near the sun, and a few larger ones regularly pass close to Earth and the moon as shown by the diagram in Figure 21. Many of the most recent impact craters on the moon and Earth were probably caused by collisions with asteroids. Inevitably, future Earth–asteroid collisions will occur, as discussed in this chapter's feature on page 665.

Many asteroids have irregular shapes, as shown in Figure 22. Because of this, planetary geologists first speculated that they might be fragments of a broken planet that once orbited between Mars and Jupiter. However, the total mass of the asteroids is estimated to be only 1/1000 that of Earth, which itself is not a large planet. What happened to the remainder of the original planet? Others have hypothesized that several larger bodies once coexisted in close proximity, and their collisions produced numerous smaller ones. The existence of several families of asteroids has been used to support this explanation. However, no conclusive evidence has been found for either hypothesis.

Figure 22 Asteroid 951, also called Gaspra, is probably the fragment of a larger body that was torn apart by a collision.

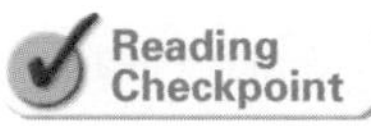

What is an asteroid?

Comets

Comets are among the most interesting and unpredictable bodies in the solar system. **Comets** are pieces of rocky and metallic materials held together by frozen gases, such as water, ammonia, methane, carbon dioxide, and carbon monoxide. Many comets travel in very elongated orbits that carry them far beyond Pluto. These comets take hundreds of thousands of years to complete a single orbit around the sun. However, a few have orbital periods of less than 200 years and make regular encounters with the inner solar system.

2 INSTRUCT

Asteroids: Microplanets

Use Visuals

Figure 21 This image shows the orbital paths of several asteroids in our solar system. Have students look carefully at the figure and read the caption. Ask: **Where are most asteroids found?** *(between Mars and Jupiter, in the asteroid belt)* **Are most of the asteroids near Earth found in the asteroid belt?** *(no)* **What is the shape of all of the asteroid orbits?** *(elliptical)*
Visual

Comets

Build Reading Literacy L1

Refer to **p. 306D** in **Chapter 11**, which provides guidelines for this reading strategy.

KWL Create a KWL chart with students before reading the section on comets. Students will probably already know that comets are "dirty snowballs," and will be able to name at least one comet. What students want to know will vary. After teaching the section on comets, have students complete the chart on what they learned. Clarify learning as needed.
Verbal

Customize for English Language Learners

Put beginning English language learners in groups with native English speakers of average to below-average ability. These groups will allow the conversations to be at appropriate levels. Have students work together over a few class periods to complete their concept maps for this section's vocabulary words. Once ELL students reach the intermediate level, they can work with average to above-average students.

Answer to . . .

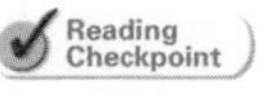

An asteroid is a small, irregularly shaped body in space.

Modeling a Comet's Tail L2

Purpose The demonstration will help students understand why a comet's tail always points away from the sun.

Materials tabletop fan, light-weight paper, tape

Procedure Have students create simple models of comets using a ball of paper or an actual ball as the coma with light-weight paper streamers as the tail. Turn on the fan, and have students hold their models in the breeze. The streamers will always point away from the fan's breeze.

Expected Outcome Students will see how radiation pressure and solar wind will cause a comet's tail to always point away from the sun.
Visual, Kinesthetic

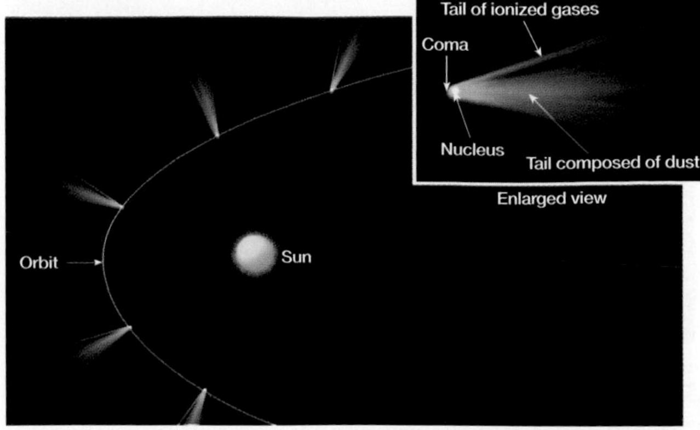

Figure 23 A comet's tail always points away from the sun.

Coma When first observed, a comet appears very small. But as it approaches the sun, solar energy begins to vaporize the frozen gases. This produces a glowing head called the **coma,** shown in Figure 23. **A small glowing nucleus with a diameter of only a few kilometers can sometimes be detected within a coma. As comets approach the sun, some, but not all, develop a tail that extends for millions of kilometers.**

The fact that the tail of a comet points away from the sun in a slightly curved manner led early astronomers to propose that the sun has a repulsive force that pushes the particles of the coma away, thus forming the tail. Today, two solar forces are known to contribute to this formation. One, radiation pressure, pushes dust particles away from the coma. The second, known as solar wind, is responsible for moving the ionized gases, particularly carbon monoxide. You'll learn more about solar wind in the next chapter. Sometimes a single tail composed of both dust and ionized gases is produced, but often two tails are observed.

As a comet moves away from the sun, the gases forming the coma recondense, the tail disappears, and the comet returns to cold storage. Material that was blown from the coma to form the tail is lost from the comet forever. Therefore it is believed that most comets cannot survive more than a few hundred close orbits of the sun. Once all the gases are expelled, the remaining material—a swarm of tiny metallic and stony particles—continues the orbit without a coma or a tail.

Kuiper Belt Comets apparently originate in two regions of the outer solar system. Those with short orbital periods are thought to orbit beyond Neptune in a region called the Kuiper belt. Like the asteroids in the inner solar system, most Kuiper belt comets move in nearly circular orbits that lie roughly in the same plane as the planets. A chance collision between two Kuiper belt comets, or the gravitational influence of one of the Jovian planets, may occasionally alter the orbit of a comet enough to send it to the inner solar system, and into our view.

In which direction does the tail of a comet point?

Facts and Figures

Many of the scientists who want to declassify Pluto as a planet consider it a Kuiper belt object. The highly eccentric orbit of Pluto, its size, and its icy and rocky composition, give it the characteristics of many other objects orbiting the sun in the Kuiper belt.

Oort Cloud Unlike Kuiper belt comets, comets with long orbital periods aren't confined to the plane of the solar system. These comets appear to be distributed in all directions from the sun, forming a spherical shell around the solar system called the Oort cloud. See Figure 24. Millions of comets are believed to orbit the sun at distances greater than 100,000 times the Earth-sun distance. The gravitational effect of another object in space is thought to send an occasional Oort cloud comet into a highly eccentric orbit that carries it toward the sun. However, only a tiny portion of the Oort cloud comets pass into the inner solar system.

Halley's Comet The most famous short-period comet is Halley's comet. Its orbital period averages 76 years, and every one of its 29 appearances since 240 B.C. has been recorded by Chinese astronomers. When seen in 1910, Halley's comet had developed a tail nearly 1.6 million kilometers long and was visible during the daylight hours.

In 1986, the European probe *Giotto* approached to within 600 kilometers of the nucleus of Halley's comet and obtained the first images of this elusive structure. We now know that the nucleus is potato-shaped, 16 kilometers by 8 kilometers. The surface is irregular and full of craterlike pits. Gases and dust that vaporize from the nucleus to form the coma and tail appear to gush from its surface as bright jets or streams. Only about 10 percent of the comet's total surface was emitting these jets at the time of the rendezvous. The remaining surface area of the comet appeared to be covered with a dark layer that may consist of organic material.

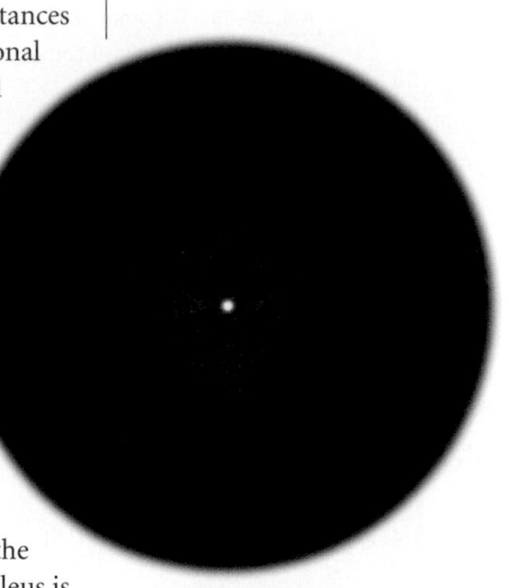

Figure 24 The Oort cloud is a sphere of comets surrounding the sun and planets.

Meteoroids

Nearly everyone has seen a "shooting star." This streak of light occurs when a meteoroid enters Earth's atmosphere. A **meteoroid** is a small solid particle that travels through space. **Most meteoroids originate from any one of the following three sources: (1) interplanetary debris that was not gravitationally swept up by the planets during the formation of the solar system, (2) material from the asteroid belt, or (3) the solid remains of comets that once traveled near Earth's orbit.** A few meteoroids are believed to be fragments of the moon, or possibly Mars, that were ejected when an asteroid impacted these bodies.

Some meteoroids are as large as asteroids. Most, however, are the size of sand grains. Consequently, they vaporize before reaching Earth's surface. Those that do enter Earth's atmosphere and burn up are called **meteors.** The light that we see is caused by friction between the particle and the air, which produces heat.

Meteoroids

Build Reading Literacy L1

Refer to **p. 612D** in **Chapter 22**, which provides the guidelines for this reading strategy.

Think Aloud The first paragraph of the Meteoroids section is very important, but it contains many words that may confuse students. Read this paragraph out loud, and stop at the end of each sentence to ask yourself (and the class) a question to check for comprehension. For example, after the first sentence you can ask, "Have I ever seen a shooting star?" The third sentence is completely in bold, meaning it is really important so you may want to ask multiple questions about that one, such as "What is interplanetary debris? Where's the asteroid belt? What would the remains of a comet look like?" If your students are not able to answer your questions, encourage them to go back in the chapter to find the answers. For example, students may need to reread the section on comets to figure out what the remains of a comet are.
Verbal, Intrapersonal

Facts and Figures

Scientists have hypothesized that comets may contain organic material, and the Giotto probe observed what appeared to be organic material on the surface of Halley's comet. Since comets occasionally come close the Earth, or even crash into Earth's surface, some people believe that life on Earth originated from organic material carried to our planet by a comet.

Answer to . . .

away from the sun

Section 23.4 (continued)

Build Reading Literacy L1

Refer to **p. 474D** in **Chapter 17**, which provides the guidelines for this reading strategy.

Monitor Your Understanding After students have read the paragraphs on meteoroids, advise students to make sure they understand the difference between meteoroids, meteors, and meteorites. Also, have them verify that they recognize the relationship between meteor showers and comets. Recommend to students that they reread the passage if they did not understand these ideas.
Verbal, Intrapersonal

3 ASSESS

Evaluate Understanding L2

Check for understanding by putting the students in groups and having the groups write an answer for each Key Concept question in the chapter.

Reteach L1

Review the content in this chapter with a series of Venn diagrams or concept maps.

Solution
7. 1×10^{11} tons of mass $\div$ 1×10^{8} tons of mass lost/orbit $= 1 \times 10^{3}$ or 1000 orbits remaining; 76 years/orbital period $\times$ 1,000 orbits $=$ 76,000 years of life remaining

Table 2 Major Meteor Showers

Shower	Approximate Dates	Associated Comet
Quadrantids	Jan. 4–6	
Lyrids	Apr. 20–23	Comet 1861 I
Eta Aquarids	May 3–5	Halley's comet
Delta Aquarids	July 30	
Perseids	Aug. 12	Comet 1862 III
Draconids	Oct. 7–10	Comet Giacobini-Zinner
Orionids	Oct. 20	Halley's comet
Taurids	Nov. 3–13	Comet Encke
Andromedids	Nov. 14	Comet Biela
Leonids	Nov. 18	Comet 1866 I
Geminids	Dec. 4–16	

Occasionally, meteor sightings can reach 60 or more per hour. These displays, called meteor showers, result when Earth encounters a swarm of meteoroids traveling in the same direction and at nearly the same speed as Earth. As shown in Table 2, the close association of these swarms to the orbits of some comets strongly suggests that they are material lost by these comets. The notable Perseid meteor shower occurs each year around August 12 and is believed to be the remains of the Comet 1862 III.

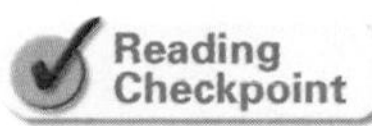
What is a meteor shower?

A meteoroid that actually reaches Earth's surface is called a **meteorite.** A few very large meteorites have blasted out craters on Earth's surface, similar to those on the moon. The most famous is Meteor Crater in Arizona. (See pages 642–643.) This huge cavity is about 1.2 kilometers across, 170 meters deep, and has an upturned rim that rises 50 meters above the surrounding countryside. Over 30 tons of iron fragments have been found in the immediate area, but attempts to locate the main body have been unsuccessful. Based on erosion, the impact likely occurred within the last 20,000 years.

Figure 25 This meteorite, made up of mostly iron, was found in the desert sands.

Prior to moon rocks brought back by astronauts, meteorites such as the one in Figure 25 were the only extraterrestrial materials that could be directly examined. Meteorite dating indicates that our solar system's age exceeds 4.5 billion years. This "old age" has been confirmed by data from lunar samples.

Section 23.4 Assessment

Reviewing Concepts

1. Where are most asteroids located?
2. Describe the structure of a comet.
3. Where do short-period comets come from? What about long-period comets?
4. Meteoroids originate from what three sources?

Critical Thinking

5. **Comparing and Contrasting** Compare and contrast a meteoroid, meteor, and meteorite.
6. **Predicting** What do you think would happen if Earth passed through the tail of a comet?

Math Practice

7. It has been estimated that Halley's comet has a mass of 1×10^{11} tons. This comet is estimated to lose 1×10^{8} tons of material each time its orbit brings it close to the sun. With an orbital period of 76 years, what is the maximum remaining life span of Halley's comet?

Section 23.4 Assessment

1. Most asteroids lie between the orbits of Mars and Jupiter.
2. A comet is made up of frozen gases and pieces of rocky and metallic materials. As the comet approaches the sun, vaporizing gases produce a glowing head called a coma. Within the coma, a small glowing nucleus is sometimes present. Most comets have long tails.
3. Short-period comets come from the Kuiper belt. Long-period comets come from the Oort cloud.
4. Most meteoroids originate from: (1) interplanetary debris that was not gravitationally swept up by the planets during the formation of the solar system, (2) material form the asteroid belt, or (3) the solid remains of comets that once traveled near Earth's orbit.
5. Meteoroids are small solid particles traveling through space. Meteors are meteoroids that enter Earth's atmosphere and burn up. Meteorites are meteoroids that strike Earth's surface.
6. Sample answer: There would be a huge meteor shower.

Is Earth on a Collision Course?

The solar system is cluttered with meteoroids, asteroids, active comets, and extinct comets. These fragments travel at great speeds and can strike Earth with the explosive force of a powerful nuclear weapon.

Ancient Collisions

During the last few decades, it has become increasingly clear that comets and asteroids have collided with Earth far more frequently than was previously known. The evidence for these collisions is giant impact structures. See Figure 26. More than 100 impact structures have been identified as shown on the map in Figure 27. Most are so old that they no longer resemble impact craters. However, evidence of their intense impact remains. One notable exception is a very fresh-looking crater near Winslow, Arizona, known as Meteor Crater.

Evidence is mounting that about 65 million years ago a large asteroid about 10 kilometers in diameter collided with Earth. This impact may have caused the extinction of the dinosaurs, as well as nearly 50 percent of all plant and animal species.

Figure 26 Manicouagan, Quebec, is a 200-million-year-old eroded impact structure. The lake outlines the crater remnant.

Close Calls

More recently, a spectacular explosion has been linked to the collision of our planet with a comet or asteroid. In 1908, in a remote region of Siberia, a "fireball" that appeared more brilliant than the sun exploded with a violent force. The shock waves rattled windows and triggered reverberations heard up to 1000 kilometers away. The "Tunguska event," as it is called, scorched, de-limbed, and flattened trees up to 30 kilometers from the epicenter. However, expeditions to the area did not find any evidence of an impact crater or metallic fragments. It is believed that the explosion—which equaled at least a 10-megaton nuclear bomb—occurred a few kilometers above the surface. It was most likely the end of a comet or perhaps a stony asteroid. The reason it exploded prior to impact remains unclear.

A reminder of the dangers of living with these small but deadly objects from space came in 1989 when an asteroid—nearly 1 kilometer across—shot past Earth. The asteroid came close to Earth, passing it by only twice the distance to the moon. It traveled at a speed of 70,000 kilometers per hour, and it could have made an impact crater 10 kilometers in diameter and perhaps 2 kilometers deep.

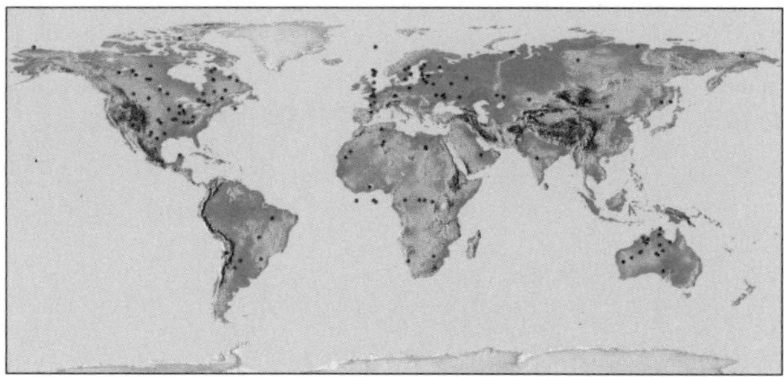

Figure 27 World Map of Major Impact Structures

Is Earth on a Collision Course? L2

Background
The solar system is cluttered with meteoroids, asteroids, active comets, and extinct comets. These fragments travel at great speeds and can strike Earth with the explosive force of a powerful nuclear weapon.

Teaching Tip
Tell students to imagine they were close enough to the Tunguska event to see it. Have them write what they experienced—saw, heard, or smelled—during the event, how they felt, and what they thought it was. This can be written in the format of a newspaper article or diary entry.
Verbal

Answer to . . .

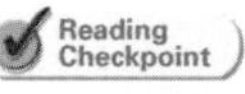

a display of numerous meteors burning up in Earth's atmosphere

Exploration  Lab

Modeling the Solar System **L2**

Objective After completing this activity, students will be able to model the distances among the plants and their distances from the sun

Address Misconceptions

Emphasize that students are creating a scale model of the solar system. The actual distances are proportional, though they are much greater than what they create here.

Skills Focus **Calculating, Using Models**

 **Prep Time** less than 5 minutes

Class Time 40 minutes

Teaching Tip
You may want to calculate the proper scale distances as a class to make sure students are doing it correctly.

Expected Outcome Students will realize that the outer planets have much greater distances between them than the inner planets have.

Exploration Lab

Modeling the Solar System

An examination of any scale model of the solar system reveals that the distances from the sun and the spacing between the planets appear to follow a regular pattern. The best way to examine this pattern is to build an actual scale model of the solar system.

Problem How can you model distances among the planets and their distances from the sun?

Materials

- meter stick
- colored pencils
- calculator
- 6-meter length of adding machine paper

Skills Calculating, Using Models

Procedure

Note: Figure A on page 667 may help you model the solar system.

1. Place the 6-meter length of adding machine paper on the floor.
2. Draw an "X" about 10 centimeters from one end of the adding machine paper. Label this mark "sun."

Table 3

Planet	Distance from Sun		Diameter (km)
	AU	Millions of km	
Mercury	0.39	58	4878
Venus	0.72	108	12,104
Earth	1.00	150	12,756
Mars	1.52	228	6794
Jupiter	5.20	778	143,884
Saturn	9.54	1427	120,536
Uranus	9.18	2870	51,118
Neptune	30.06	4497	50,530
Pluto	39.44	5900	2300

3. Table 3 shows the mean distances of the planets from the sun, as well as their diameters. Use the table and the following scale to calculate the proper scale distance of each planet from the sun:

   1 millimeter = 1 million kilometers

   1 centimeter = 10 million kilometers

   1 meter = 1000 million kilometers
4. After calculating the scale distances, draw a small circle for each planet at its proper scale distance from the sun. Use a different-colored pencil for the inner and outer planets. Write the name of each planet next to its position.

666 Chapter 23

Analyze and Conclude

1. **Using Models** Where is Earth located on your model? Where are the rest of the planets located?
2. **Observing** What pattern of spacing do you observe? Summarize the pattern for both the inner and outer planets.
3. **Interpreting Data** Which planet or planets vary most from the general pattern of spacing?

Go Further Determine how to expand your model to include the scale sizes of the planets. Refer to the table for the diameters of each planet (Table 3). Develop a scale, and then calculate the proper scale size of the planets. Draw the planets to scale on your model.

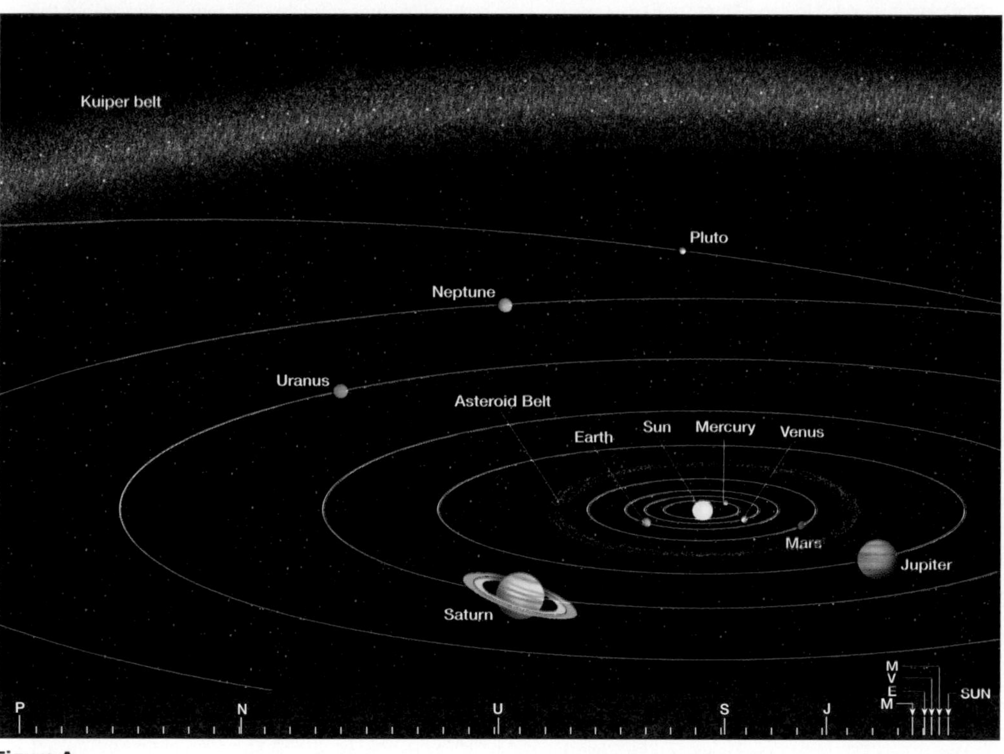

Figure A

Analyze and Conclude

1. Earth: 15 cm; Mercury: 5.8 cm; Venus: 10.8 cm; Mars: 22.8 cm; Jupiter: 77.8 cm; Saturn: 1.4 m; Uranus: 2.9 m; Neptune: 4.5 m; Pluto: 5.9 m
2. The inner planets are closely spaced together. The largest space exists between Earth and Mars. The outer planets are widely spaced apart. The smallest space is between Jupiter and Saturn.
3. The space between Neptune and Pluto varies the most from the general pattern.

Go Further

Using a scale of 1 cm = 4000 km, the scale model diameter of each planet would be: Mercury: 1.2 cm; Venus: 3 cm; Earth: 3.2 cm; Mars: 1.7 cm; Jupiter: 36 cm; Saturn: 30.3 cm; Uranus: 11.8 cm; Neptune: 11.7 cm; Pluto: 0.6 cm
Logical

Study Guide

Study Tip

Write Questions
Encourage students to create their own chapter test by writing and answering questions based on the key concepts and vocabulary words for the chapter. Suggest that students write at least one short answer question for each key concept and at least one fill-in-the-blank or multiple choice question for every vocabulary word. Encourage students to review the chapter by quizzing each other using the tests they created.

Thinking Visually

a. Venus; 12,104 km (diameter); 0.72 AU (distance from sun)
b. Earth; 12,756 km (diameter); 1.00 AU (distance from sun)
c. Mars; 6794 km (diameter); 1.52 AU (distance from sun)
d. Saturn; 120,536 km (diameter); 9.54 AU (distance from sun)
e. Uranus; 51,118 km (diameter); 19.18 AU (distance from sun)
f. Neptune; 50,530 km (diameter); 30.06 AU (distance from sun)
g. Pluto; 2300 km (approx. diameter); 39.44 AU (distance from sun)

CHAPTER 23

Study Guide

23.1 The Solar System

Key Concepts

- Size is the most obvious difference between the terrestrial and the Jovian planets.
- Density, chemical makeup, and rate of rotation are other ways in which the two groups of planets differ.
- According to the nebular theory, the sun and planets formed from a rotating disk of dust and gases.

Vocabulary

terrestrial planet, *p. 645;* Jovian planet, *p. 645;* nebula, *p. 647;* planetesimal, *p. 648*

23.2 The Terrestrial Planets

Key Concepts

- Mercury has the greatest temperature extremes of any planet.
- The surface temperature of Venus reaches 475°C, and its atmosphere is 97 percent carbon dioxide.
- Some areas of Mars exhibit drainage patterns similar to those created by streams on Earth.

23.3 The Outer Planets

Key Concepts

- Jupiter has a mass that is 2 1/2 times greater than the mass of all the other planets and moons combined.
- The most prominent feature of Saturn is its system of rings.
- Instead of being generally perpendicular to the plane of its orbit like the other planets, Uranus's axis of rotation lies nearly parallel with the plane of its orbit.
- Winds exceeding 1000 kilometers per hour encircle Neptune, making it one of the windiest places in the solar system.
- Pluto's orbit is highly eccentric, causing it to occasionally travel inside the orbit of Neptune, where it resided from 1979 through February 1999.

23.4 Minor Members of the Solar System

Key Concepts

- Most asteroids lie between the orbits of Mars and Jupiter. They have orbital periods of three to six years.
- A small glowing nucleus with a diameter of only a few kilometers can sometimes be detected within a coma. As comets approach the sun, some, but not all, develop a tail that extends for millions of kilometers.
- Most meteoroids originate from any one of the following three sources: (1) interplanetary debris that was not gravitationally swept up by the planets during the formation of the solar system, (2) material from the asteroid belt, or (3) the solid remains of comets that once traveled near Earth's orbit.

Vocabulary

asteroid, *p. 661;* comet, *p. 661;* coma, *p. 662;* meteoroid, *p. 663;* meteor, *p. 663;* meteorite, *p. 664*

Thinking Visually

Copy and complete the table below comparing and contrasting the inner and outer planets. Include information about each planet's diameter, distance from the sun, composition, and number of moons.

Inner and Outer Planets		
Inner Planets		
	Diameter	**Distance from Sun**
Mercury	4878 km	0.39 AU
a. ___?___		
b. ___?___		
c. ___?___		
Outer Planets		
	Diameter	**Distance from Sun**
Jupiter	143,884 km	5.3 AU
d. ___?___		
e. ___?___		
f. ___?___		
g. ___?___		

Chapter Assessment Resources

Print
Chapter Test, Chapter 23
Test Prep Resources, Chapter 23

Technology
Computer Test Bank, Chapter 23 Test
Online Text, Chapter 23
Go Online, PHSchool.com, Chapter 23

CHAPTER 23

NY Regents Content Item

Assessment

Interactive textbook with assessment at PHSchool.com 

Reviewing Content

Choose the number that best answers the question or completes the statement.

1 Which of these planets is not a terrestrial planet? NY
(1) Earth (2) Mercury
(3) Venus (4) Uranus

2 What theory describes the formation of the solar system from a huge cloud of dust and gases? NY
(1) protoplanet theory
(2) nebular theory
(3) planetesimal theory
(4) solar theory

3 Which of the following is NOT a characteristic of Jovian planets? NY
(1) large size
(2) composed mostly of gases and ice
(3) lack of moons
(4) located beyond the orbit of Mars

4 Which planet was explored by the rovers *Spirit* and *Opportunity?*
(1) Mercury (2) Pluto
(3) Mars (4) Venus

5 Which two planets are most alike? NY
(1) Jupiter and Pluto
(2) Earth and Neptune
(3) Mars and Uranus
(4) Uranus and Saturn

6 Which of the following is NOT true of Jupiter?
(1) It is more massive than all the other planets and moons combined
(2) It has huge rotating storms
(3) It has a thin ring system
(4) It has a solid surface

7 Which moon is known to have active volcanism?
(1) Io (2) Phobos
(3) Europa (4) Titan

8 What bodies in the solar system orbit between Mars and Jupiter? NY
(1) comets
(2) stars
(3) asteroids
(4) meteorites

9 A comet's tail always points NY
(1) away from the sun
(2) toward the sun
(3) up
(4) down

10 Meteoroids that strike Earth are called
(1) asteroids
(2) comets
(3) meteors
(4) meteorites

Understanding Concepts

11 List the objects that are found in the solar system. NY

12 What substances make up most of the solar system? Classify them as gas, rock, or ice.

13 Describe general characteristics and location of the terrestrial planets. NY

14 What is Olympus Mons? Where is it found?

15 Why has Mars been the planet most studied by telescopes?

16 Why is life unlikely to exist on Venus?

17 Which planets have ring systems?

18 What three bodies in the solar system exhibit volcanic activity?

19 What are moonlets?

20 How are Uranus and Neptune similar? NY

21 Why isn't Pluto classified as either a terrestrial planet or a Jovian planet?

22 How big is the largest asteroid?

23 Which minor members of the solar system are thought to have formed beyond the orbit of Pluto? NY

24 What is the bright glowing head of a comet called?

25 What evidence indicates that our solar system is about 4.5 billion years old? NY

Homework Guide

Section	Questions
1	1–3, 11, 12, 35, 36
2	4, 5, 13–16, 26, 27, 31–34
3	6, 7, 17–21, 28–30
4	8–10, 22–25, 37

Assessment

Reviewing Content

(1) 4 (2) 2 (3) 3
(4) 3 (5) 4 (6) 4
(7) 1 (8) 3 (9) 1
(10) 4

Understanding Concepts

(11) The solar system includes the sun, the major planets and their moons, asteroids, comets, and meteoroids.
(12) Most of the solar system is made up of the gases hydrogen and helium, the rocky substances silicate minerals and metallic iron, and the icy substances ammonia, methane, carbon dioxide, and water.
(13) In general, the terrestrial planets are small and rocky. They are closer to the sun than the Jovian planets.
(14) Olympus Mons is a volcano. It is found on Mars.
(15) Mars is the only planet whose surface can be viewed using a telescope.
(16) Atmospheric pressure and surface temperatures are very high on Venus.
(17) Jupiter, Saturn, Uranus, and Neptune have ring systems.
(18) The three bodies in the solar system that exhibit volcanic activity are Earth, Io, and Triton.
(19) Moonlets are individual particles of ice and rock that make up planetary rings.
(20) They are about the same size and have a similar composition and structure.
(21) Pluto is located in the outer solar system, so it cannot be considered a terrestrial planet. The Jovian planets are also located in the outer solar system. However, unlike the Jovian planets, Pluto is small and rocky. It has more in common with the icy bodies found beyond Neptune's orbit than with the other major planets.
(22) The largest asteroid is about 1000 km in diameter.
(23) Comets are thought to have formed beyond the orbit of Pluto.
(24) The bright, glowing head of a comet is called a coma.
(25) Meteorite dating and lunar rocks indicate that the solar system is 4.5 billion years old.

Critical Thinking

(26) Mars has drainage patterns and geologic structures associated with liquid water. The Martian atmosphere contains very little water vapor.
(27) Venus's atmosphere traps heat on its surface.
(28) The moon formed independently of its parent planet and was captured by the planet's gravity.
(29) The Jovian planets are more massive and have greater escape velocities. They are also colder.
(30) Uranus does not have a solid surface so no evidence of the impact remains.

Analyzing Data

(31) Venus and Mars have similar atmospheric compositions.
(32) Venus has a much greater surface atmospheric pressure.
(33) Oxygen is present in Earth's atmosphere. Earth's oxygen-rich atmosphere reflects the presence of life.
(34) Greater atmospheric pressure leads to less variation in surface temperature.

Concepts in Action

(35) A person would weigh the least on Pluto because it is the least massive planet and thus has the smallest gravitational pull.
(36) A year on Jupiter is equivalent to 12 Earth-years. A 15-year-old student would be 1.4 years old in Jupiter-years.
(37) impact craters

Assessment *continued*

Critical Thinking

26 **Analyzing Data** What evidence supports the theory that liquid water may have existed on Mars? What evidence refutes the possibility of a wet Martian climate? NY

27 **Drawing Conclusions** Mercury is closer to the sun than Venus. Venus, however, is hotter. Why? NY

28 **Inferring** What can you infer about a moon that exhibits retrograde motion?

29 **Making Generalizations** Why is it more difficult for gases to escape from the Jovian planets than from the terrestrial planets? NY

30 **Applying Concepts** Why would it be difficult to verify that an impact may have altered Uranus's axis of rotation?

Analyzing Data

Use the table in the right column to answer questions 31–34.

31 **Identifying** Which two planets have similar atmospheric compositions? NY

32 **Interpreting Data** What makes these two planets' atmospheres very different? NY

33 **Inferring** What gas is present in Earth's atmosphere, but nearly absent in the atmospheres of Venus and Mars? What do you think explains its presence on Earth? (*Hint:* What does Earth have that Venus and Mars both lack?) NY

34 **Analyzing Data** Based on the data in the table, how would you describe the effect of increasing atmospheric pressure on surface temperature? NY

Concepts in Action

35 **Relating Cause and Effect** Weight is a function of the gravitational attraction of an object on your mass. On which planet would you weigh the least? Explain your answer.

36 **Calculating** Refer to Table 1 on page 645. Using the table, determine how old you are in Jupiter-years.

37 **Identifying** Which features on Earth offer clear evidence that comets and asteroids have struck its surface?

Performance-Based Assessment

Using Models Use a fan, a Styrofoam ball, several pushpins, and several pieces of ribbon to create a model of a comet. Explain what each part of the model represents. Work with a partner to demonstrate the orbit of your model. Make sure that the "tail" points in the proper direction.

Comparison of the Atmospheres and Surface Temperatures of Mercury, Venus, Earth, Mars

Planet or Body	Gases (% by volume)			Surface Temperature (range)	Surface Atmospheric Pressure (bars)
	N_2	O_2	CO_2		
Mercury	0	trace	0	−173° to 427°C	10^{-15}
Venus	3.5	< 0.01	96.5	475°C (small range)	92
Earth	78.01	20.95	0.03	−40° to 75°C	1.014
Mars	2.7	1.3	95.32	−120° to 25°C	0.008

Regents Practice Exam

Test-Taking Tip

Questions with NOT
Questions containing absolute negative qualifiers, such as NOT, can be tricky. If the question lists statements, it helps to look at each statement and add NOT just before the verb. For example, rephrase statement A below as "Mars does NOT have moons." Then try to think of one example that disproves this statement. Mars and Earth are the only two terrestrial planets that have moons. Thus, the statement is not true. Repeat this process for each choice until you find one that is true in all cases.

Which of the following is NOT true of Mars?
(1) Mars has moons.
(2) Mars has rings.
(3) Mars is often called the Red Planet.
(4) Mars has volcanoes.

(Answer: 2)

For *each* statement or question, choose the *number* of the word or expression that, of those given, best completes the statement or answers the question. Some questions may require the use of the *Earth Science Reference Tables.*

1 Which of the following is NOT an obvious difference between the terrestrial and Jovian planets?
(1) size
(2) color
(3) density
(4) chemical composition

2 Which planet does NOT have a density that is greater than water?
(1) Jupiter
(2) Pluto
(3) Venus
(4) Saturn

3 Which of the following planets orbits the fastest around the sun?
(1) Uranus
(2) Mars
(3) Jupiter
(4) Saturn

Answer the following questions in complete sentences. Some questions may require the use of the Earth Science Reference Tables. Base your answers to question 7 on the diagram below, which shows a comet.

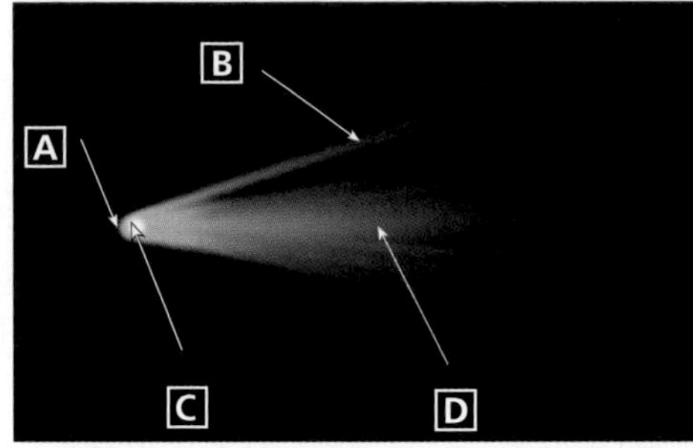

4 Explain the nebular theory.

5 Why did Earth and the other planets in our solar system develop layered structures?

6 Many scientists believe meteorite impacts have caused mass extinctions in Earth's past. Explain how an impact event could lead to a mass extinction.

7 What features do labels *B* and *D* represent? How do these features form?

Regents Practice Exam

(1) 2
(2) 4
(3) 2
(4) The nebular theory says that the sun and planets of our solar system formed from a rotating disk of gas and dust called a nebula. As the nebula contracted gravitationally and started spinning faster, the sun and planets formed.
(5) As the planets were forming from the original nebula, they were spinning, and the spinning caused the denser materials to concentrate in the center of each planet. The dense material collected in the center of each planet could form a core, while the less dense material could form the planet's outer layers and atmosphere.
(6) An impact could release a large quantity of debris into the atmosphere. This debris could decrease the amount of insulation reaching Earth's surface by so much that plants could not perform photosynthesis. If this occurred, the plants would start to die, followed by the animals that ate the plants (herbivores), followed by the carnivores.
(7) Features *B* and *D* represent comet tails. Comet tails form when the sun's energy vaporizes frozen gases from the comet's nucleus, creating a glowing coma, and then radiation pressure pushes dust particles, and solar wind pushes ionized gases, causing the particles to stream away from the comet's head, and away from the sun.

Performance-Based Assessment

Students should explain that the fan represents the sun, the ball represents the nucleus of the comet, and the ribbons represent the tail. The push pins are used to attach the ribbons to the ball. Students should make sure that the "tail" always points away from the sun. While one partner holds the comet, the other partner can rotate the fan so that the air blows the tail away from the sun.

Your students can independently test their knowledge of the chapter and print out their results.

CHAPTER 24

Planning Guide

Use these planning tools
Use Teacher Express for all your planning needs

SECTION OBJECTIVES	STANDARDS NATIONAL	STANDARDS STATE	ACTIVITIES and LABS
24.1 The Study of Light, pp. 674–677 1 block or 2 periods **24.1** **Describe** the waves that compose the electromagnetic spectrum. **24.2** **Describe** what the different types of spectra reveal about stars. **24.3** **Explain** how the Doppler effect is applied to the motion of stars in relation to Earth.	A-1, A-2, B-6, E-2, G-1, G-2, G-3		**SE** Inquiry Lab: How Does the Position of the Setting Sun Change? p. 673 L2 **TE** Teacher Demo: Making a Simple Spectrometer, p. 676 L2
24.2 Tools for Studying Space, pp. 678–683 1 block or 2 periods **24.4** **Explain** how refracting, reflecting, and radio telescopes work. **24.5** **Describe** the advantages and disadvantages of each type of telescope. **24.6** **Explain** the advantages that a space telescope has over an Earth-based telescope.	B-6, E-2, G-1, G-3		**TE** Teacher Demo: Making a Simple Refracting Telescope, p. 679 L2
24.3 The Sun, pp. 684–690 1 block or 2 periods **24.7** **Explain** the structure of the sun. **24.8** **Describe** the physical features on the surface of the sun. **24.9** **Explain** how the sun produces energy.	A-1, A-2, B-1, B-5, B-6, D-1, D-3, D-4, E-2, G-3		**TE** Teacher Demo: Earth and Solar Winds, p. 686 L2 **TE** Build Science Skills, p. 687 L2 **SE** Exploration Lab: Tracking Sunspots, pp. 692–693 L2 **LM** Measuring the Diameter of the Sun L2

Ability Levels

- **L1** For students who need additional help
- **L2** For all students
- **L3** For students who need to be challenged

Components

SE	Student Edition	**GRSW**	Guided Reading & Study Workbook	**TP**	Test Prep Resources	**GEO**	Geode CD-ROM
TE	Teacher's Edition			**onT**	onlineText	**T**	Transparencies
LM	Laboratory Manual	**TEX**	Teacher Express	**DC**	Discovery Channel Videos	**GO**	Internet Resources
CUT	Chapter Tests	**CTB**	Computer Test Bank				

RESOURCES PRINT and TECHNOLOGY	SECTION ASSESSMENT
GRSW Section 24.1 **T-348** Spectrum of Light **T-349** Colors and Corresponding Wavelengths **T-350** Formation of Three Types of Spectra **T-351** The Doppler Effect **T-352** Measurement of Doppler Shifts **TEX** Lesson Planning 24.1	**SE** Section 24.1 Assessment, p. 677 **onT** Section 24.1
GRSW Section 24.2 **T-353** Simple Refracting Telescope **T-354** Viewing Methods **T-355** Light Gathering Ability of Two Lenses **TEX** Lesson Planning 24.2	**SE** Section 24.2 Assessment, p. 683 **onT** Section 24.2
GRSW Section 24.3 **T-356** Solar Structure **T-357** Mean Annual Sunspot Numbers **DC** Fireball **TEX** Lesson Planning 24.3	**SE** Section 24.3 Assessment, p. 690 **onT** Section 24.3

Go Online

Go online for these Internet resources.

PHSchool.com
Web Code: cjk-9999

NSTA SCI LINKS
Web Code: cjn-7241
Web Code: cjn-7242
Web Code: cjn-7243

Materials for Activities and Labs

Quantities for each group

STUDENT EDITION

Inquiry Activity, p. 673
paper, pencil

Exploration Lab, pp. 692–693
telescope, small cardboard box, large cardboard box, piece of white paper, metric ruler, pencil, tape

TEACHER'S EDITION

Teacher Demo, p. 676
empty paper towel cardboard tube, diffracting grating (about 5 cm × 5 cm), piece of black paper (about 9 cm × 9 cm), tape, rubber band, razor blade, bright light

Teacher Demo, p. 679
2 magnifying lenses

Teacher Demo, p. 686
bar magnet, 2 sheets of notebook paper, iron filings, drinking straw

Build Science Skills, p. 687
2 empty 2-L plastic soda bottles, water, colored glitter, duct tape, paper towel, washer (same diameter as the mouth of the plastic soda bottle)

Chapter Assessment

ASSESSMENT

SE	Assessment, pp. 695–696
CUT	Chapter 24 Test
CTB	Chapter 24
onT	Chapter 24

STANDARDIZED TEST PREP

SE	Chapter 24, p. 697
TP	Progress Monitoring Assessments

interactive textbook with assessment at PHSchool.com

CHAPTER 24

Before you teach

Michael Wysession
Washington University

Big Ideas

Space and Time Reflecting telescopes are usually used to collect visible light because they can be built larger and more inexpensively than refractors. Radio telescopes can "see" objects not viewable with visible light because of intervening interstellar dust. The Doppler shift of light is used to determine if objects are moving away or toward us. The sun can be divided into four layers: the interior, photosphere, chromosphere, and corona. The photosphere is the visible surface of the sun.

Forces and Motion The solar wind consists of protons and electrons generated from the sun's corona. Sunspots, cooler regions of the photosphere, come and go in an 11-year cycle. The sun's surface is turbulent, occasionally erupting in prominences and generating solar flares.

Matter and Energy All luminous objects emit electromagnetic radiation, which takes the form of gamma rays, X-rays, ultraviolet and visible light, infrared radiation, microwaves, and radio waves. Light behaves as both a particle and a wave in different situations. The spectroscopic emission and absorption spectra are used to determine the composition of stars and the matter of interstellar space. The sun generates light through the fusion of hydrogen to form helium, and is about 15 million degrees K in its interior.

Earth as a System Telescopes in space like the Hubble telescope produce the clearest images because they are not distorted by Earth's atmosphere.

Earth Science Refresher

Chance and the Sun's Chromosphere

Science tends to be suspicious of chance and coincidence. However, statistically, that is just how things are bound to happen sometimes. One example has been our ability to view the outer structure of the sun, which has been best observed during total solar eclipses. The solar corona is very observable because the usually overwhelming light from the photosphere has been entirely blocked by the moon. By total coincidence, both the sun and moon appear to be the same size when viewed from Earth, about 0.5°. This led people in ancient times to think that there was some special reason they were created this way. There isn't. By coincidence, the sun's diameter is about 400 times wider than the moon's, but the sun is also about 400 times further from Earth than the moon.

Interestingly, the sun and moon haven't always appeared the same size when viewed from Earth. The moon used to be much closer to Earth, which would have meant not only that the moon would have appeared much larger, but that the size of the tides along shorelines would have been much greater. At that time Earth also rotated much faster, so that there were fewer hours in the day and more days in the year. We know this

Address Misconceptions

Many students may think that since the sun is an enormous ball of gas it does not have a surface. The visible surface of the sun, the photosphere, is a layer of gas about 500 km thick. For a strategy that helps to overcome this misconception, see **Address Misconceptions** on **p. 685**.

Go Online NSTA PD LINKS

For: Chapter 24 Content Support
Visit: www.SciLinks.org/PDLinks
Web Code: cjn-2499

from the layers of calcium carbonate in fossil marine shells. Over time, the moon has spiraled further away from Earth, and in the future, it will appear smaller than the sun. So, if we had evolved a billion years from now, we would not have been able to use solar eclipses to study the chromosphere.

Of course, the sun and moon do not appear to be the exact same size. The sun's average size appears to be 0.015° larger than the moon's. What's more, because the orbits of the moon and Earth are both elliptical this changes over the course of the year. Because Earth is closer to the sun in January, the sun appears to be 0.54° in diameter. In the summer time, it is only 0.52°. The moon's orbit around Earth is even more elliptical, and its apparent size varies between 0.49° and 0.56°. When the moon appears as large or larger than the sun, solar eclipses are total, and the sun's photosphere is totally blocked, allowing good viewing of the outer corona. When the orbital distances are such that the moon appears smaller than the sun, then solar eclipses are annular, and there is still a ring of the sun's bright outer corona visible.

Build Reading Literacy

Summarize

Briefly Restating the Main Ideas

Strategy Help students understand a topic by restating the main ideas. Students read a section of the text and then identify main ideas and supporting details. They summarize what they have read by briefly restating the main concepts in a sentence or two. Summarizing can be employed to review brief subsections as well as entire sections and chapters. Have students read the beginning of Section 24.2, pp. 678–679.

Example

1. Ask students to carefully read the selected passage. Then, have them review the passage and identify the main ideas. Demonstrate this process by using the bold headings, Key Concept statements, and vocabulary as aids in determining what the passage is mostly about. List the main ideas on the board.

2. Direct students to write brief summaries of the passage by restating each of the main ideas in one or two sentences, using their own words. Remind students to focus on the most important concepts, omitting details and examples. Students should check to be sure that their summary covers the terms mentioned in the bold headings.

3. Assign the next passage for students to read and summarize. You may want to have students work in small groups to compare their summaries.

4. Have students read and summarize the rest of Section 24.2.

See p. 675 for a script on how to use this strategy with students. For additional strategies, see pp. 678 and 684.

ASSESS PRIOR KNOWLEDGE

Use the Chapter Pretest below to assess students' prior knowledge. As needed, review these concepts.

Review Science Concepts

Section 24.1 Encourage students to recall what they have learned about electromagnetic waves and the Doppler effect in previous science courses.

Section 24.2 Review the wave properties of refraction and reflection to help students understand how refracting and reflecting telescopes work.

Section 24.3 Encourage students to recall what they have learned about nuclear fusion in previous science courses.

CHAPTER 24 Studying the Sun

CONCEPTS in Action

Exploration Lab
Tracking Sunspots

Earth as a System
Solar Activity and Climatic Change

Video Field Trip
Fireball

Take a solar field trip with Discovery Channel and learn about the inner core and the outer surface of our sun. Answer the following questions after watching the video.

1. How did scientists discover the activity of the sun's core?
2. How do auroras occur?

Go Online PHSchool.com

For: Chapter 24 Resources
Visit: PHSchool.com
Web Code: cjk-9999

This photograph shows Kitt Peak National Observatory near Tucson, Arizona. ▶

Chapter Pretest

1. What is an electromagnetic wave? *(a transverse wave consisting of changing electric and magnetic fields)*
2. What do all waves transport from one place to another? *(energy)*
3. In which of the following scenarios would the Doppler effect be present? *(a)*
   a. A police car, with its siren sounding, speeds past you as you sit in your car at a stop light.
   b. A firefighter turns on the siren in a parked fire truck as a demonstration for the crowd of young children.
   c. The coach blows his whistle in the gym during basketball practice.
   d. You shout to a friend while inside a cave.
4. True or False: As light travels from one medium into another, such as from air to water, it will refract. *(True)*
5. Which wave property is demonstrated when you look into a mirror and see yourself? *(reflection)*
6. What is nuclear fusion? *(a nuclear reaction in which the nuclei of two atoms combine to form a larger nucleus)*

Chapter Preview

Inquiry Activity

How Does the Position of the Setting Sun Change?

Procedure

1. Several minutes before sunset, estimate where the sun will set on the western horizon. Draw prominent features, such as buildings and trees, to the north and south of the sun's setting position.
2. As the sun sets, draw its position relative to the fixed features on the horizon. **CAUTION** *Never look directly at the sun; eye damage may result.*
3. Note the date and time of your observation.
4. Return to the same position several days later. Repeat the activity and record the results. Wait several more days then do the activity one more time.

Think About It

1. **Observing** How did the sun's position at sunset change over the course of your observations?
2. **Predicting** Based on your observations, predict where the sun might set in several weeks time. Sketch the sun on your drawing relative to the fixed features on the horizon.

Video Field Trip

Fireball

Encourage students to view the Video Field Trip "Fireball."

ENGAGE/EXPLORE

How Does the Position of the Setting Sun Change? L2

Purpose In this activity, students will realize that the sun does not set in the same location every day.

Skills Focus Observing, Predicting

 **Prep Time** 5 minutes

Materials paper and pencil

Class Time none; 60 minutes outside class time over several days

Safety Remind students to never look directly at the sun.

Expected Outcome Students will observe the sun's setting position change over time.

Think About It

1. In general, observations made between June 21 and December 22 will show the sun setting farther south with each successive observation. Observations made between December 21 and June 21 will show the sun setting farther north with each successive observation. The opposite occurs in the southern hemisphere.
2. If the observations were made between June 21 and December 22, drawings should show the sun setting farther south along the horizon. If the observations were made between December 22 and June 21, drawings will show the sun setting farther north along the horizon.

Section 24.1

1 FOCUS

Section Objectives

24.1 **Describe** the waves that compose the electromagnetic spectrum.

24.2 **Describe** what the different types of spectra reveal about stars.

24.3 **Explain** how the Doppler effect is applied to the motion of stars in relation to Earth.

Reading Focus

Build Vocabulary L2

Vocabulary Rating Chart Have students make a chart with four columns with the headings Term, Can Define or Use It, Heard or Seen It, and Don't Know. Have students copy the seven vocabulary terms into the first column and rate their knowledge by putting a checkmark in one of the other columns. Ask how many students actually know each term. Then, give students a purpose for reading by asking focused questions to help students predict text content based on each term. After students have read the section, have them rate themselves again.

Reading Strategy L2

a. Answers will vary.
b. The electromagnetic spectrum is the arrangement of electromagnetic radiation including gamma rays, X-rays, ultraviolet light, visible light, infrared radiation, microwaves, and radio waves according to their wavelengths and frequencies.

24.1 The Study of Light

Reading Focus

Key Concepts

- What types of radiation make up the electromagnetic spectrum?
- What can scientists learn about a star by studying its spectrum?
- How can astronomers determine whether a star is moving toward or away from Earth?

Vocabulary

- electromagnetic spectrum
- photon
- spectroscopy
- continuous spectrum
- absorption spectrum
- emission spectrum
- Doppler effect

Reading Strategy

Predicting Copy the table. Before you read, predict the meaning of the term *electromagnetic spectrum*. After you read, revise your definition if it was incorrect.

Vocabulary Term	Before You Read	After You Read
electromagnetic spectrum	a. ?	b. ?

Astronomers are in the business of gathering and studying light. Almost everything that is known about the universe beyond Earth comes by analyzing light from distant sources. Consequently, an understanding of the nature of light is basic to modern astronomy. This chapter deals with the study of light and the tools used by astronomers to gather light in order to probe the universe. In addition, we will examine the nearest source of light, our sun. By understanding how the sun works, astronomers can better grasp the nature of more distant objects in space.

Electromagnetic Radiation

The vast majority of our information about the universe is obtained from the study of the light emitted from stars and other bodies in space. Although visible light is most familiar to us, it makes up only a small part of the different types of energy known as electromagnetic radiation. **Electromagnetic radiation includes gamma rays, X-rays, ultraviolet light, visible light, infrared radiation, microwaves, and radio waves.** The arrangement of these waves according to their wavelengths and frequencies is called the **electromagnetic spectrum.** Figure 1 shows the electromagnetic spectrum. All energy, regardless of wavelength, travels through the vacuum of space at the speed of light, or 300,000 kilometers per second. Over a 24-hour day, this equals a staggering 26 billion kilometers.

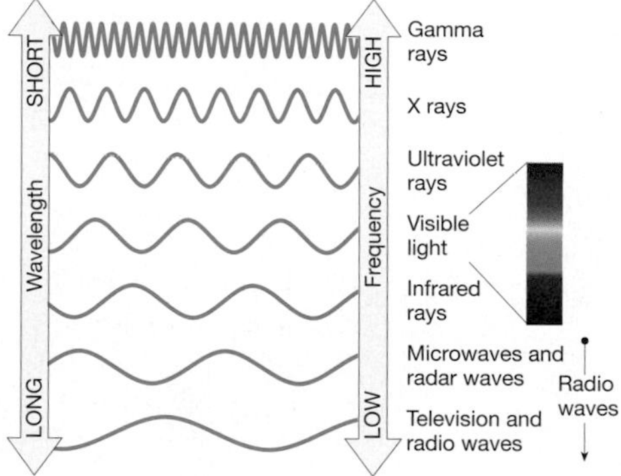

Figure 1 Electromagnetic Spectrum The electromagnetic spectrum classifies radiation according to wavelength and frequency.
Interpreting Diagrams *Which type of radiation has the shortest wavelength?*

Nature of Light Experiments have shown that light can be described in two ways. In some instances light behaves like waves, and in others like particles. In the wave sense, light can be thought of as swells in the ocean. This motion is characterized by a property known as wavelength, which is the distance from one wave crest to the next. Wavelengths vary from several kilometers for radio waves to less than a billionth of a centimeter for gamma rays, as shown in Figure 1. Most of these waves are either too long or too short for our eyes to see.

The narrow band of electromagnetic radiation we can see is sometimes called visible light. However, visible light consists of a range of waves with various wavelengths. This fact is easily demonstrated with a prism, as shown in Figure 2. As visible light passes through a prism, the color with the shortest wavelength, violet, is bent more than blue, which is bent more than green, and so forth. Thus, visible light can be separated into its component colors in the order of their wavelengths, producing the familiar rainbow of colors.

Table 1 Colors and Corresponding Wavelengths

Color	Wavelength (nanometers*)
Violet	380–440
Blue	440–500
Green	500–560
Yellow	560–590
Orange	590–640
Red	640–750

*One nanometer is 10^{-9} meter.

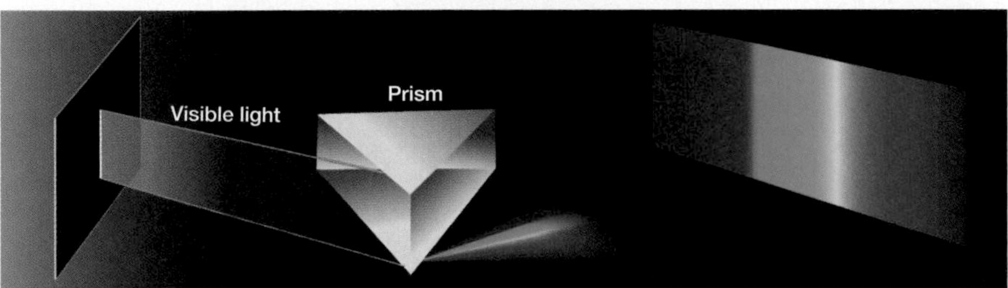

Figure 2 Spectrum A spectrum is produced when sunlight or visible light is passed through a prism, which bends each wavelength at different angles.

Photons Wave theory, however, cannot explain some effects of light. In some cases, light acts like a stream of particles called **photons.** Photons can be thought of as extremely small bullets fired from a machine gun. They can push on matter. The force they exert is called radiation pressure. Photons from the sun are responsible for pushing material away from a comet to produce its tail. Each photon has a specific amount of energy, which is related to its wavelength in a simple way: Shorter wavelengths have more energetic photons. Thus, blue light has more energetic photons than does red light.

Which theory of light—the wave theory or the particle theory—is correct? Both, because each will predict the behavior of light for certain phenomena. As George Abell, a well-known astronomer, stated about all scientific laws, "The mistake is only to apply them to situations that are outside their range of validity."

What are photons?

For: Links on the electromagnetic spectrum
Visit: www.SciLinks.org
Web Code: cjn-7441

2 INSTRUCT

Electromagnetic Radiation

Use Visuals **L1**

Figure 1 Point out to students that although these waves have different frequencies and wavelengths, they travel at the same speed in a vacuum, which is 3.00×10^8 m/s. Ask: **What is the product of any electromagnetic frequency and its wavelength?** *(the speed of light, 3.00×10^8 m/s)* **What happens to the wavelength of an electromagnetic wave as the frequency decreases?** *(The wavelength increases.)*
Verbal, Logical

Build Science Skills **L2**

Calculating Have students use the data in Table 1 to find the frequencies of violet and red light. Tell students to use the lower value for the wavelength in their calculations. *(violet: 7.9×10^{14} 1/s or Hz; red: 4.7×10^{14} Hz)* Ask: **Which color has the longer wavelength?** *(red)* **Which color has the highest frequency?** *(violet)*
Visual, Logical

Build Reading Literacy **L1**

Refer to **p. 672D**, which provides the guidelines for summarizing.

Summarize Summarizing the information presented in the text will help students focus on main ideas and remember what they read. Have students read the paragraphs about electromagnetic radiation and summarize them by restating the main idea in their own words.
Verbal

Download a worksheet on the electromagnetic spectrum for students to complete, and find additional teacher support from NSTA SciLinks.

Customize for English Language Learners

The details of electromagnetic radiation, spectroscopy, and the Doppler effect may be difficult for students that are learning English. Simplify your presentation so they will have better comprehension of the material. Speak clearly, use simple words and short sentences, and make frequent use of diagrams to clarify the material in this section.

Answer to . . .

Figure 1 *gamma rays*

Photons are streams of particles of light that exert radiation pressure.

Spectroscopy

Making a Simple Spectrometer L2

Purpose Students will observe how a spectrometer breaks light into the wavelengths that compose it.

Materials empty paper towel cardboard tube, diffracting grating (about 5 cm × 5 cm), piece of black paper (about 9 cm × 9 cm), tape, rubber band, razor blade, bright light

Procedure Tape the diffracting grating over one end of the cardboard tube. Cover the opposite end of the tube with black paper. Secure the black paper over the end of the tube with a rubber band. Carefully cut a narrow slit in the center of the black paper. The slit should be about two-thirds the width of the opening. Point the slit toward a bright light and slowly rotate the tube until you see the spectrum. Allow students to use the spectrometer to view the spectrum.

Safety Do not allow students to use this spectrometer to directly view the sun.

Expected Outcome The diffraction grating works like a prism and breaks visible light into its basic colors. Students will be able to use this simple spectrometer to see bright light broken into its component colors or wavelengths.
Visual, Kinesthetic

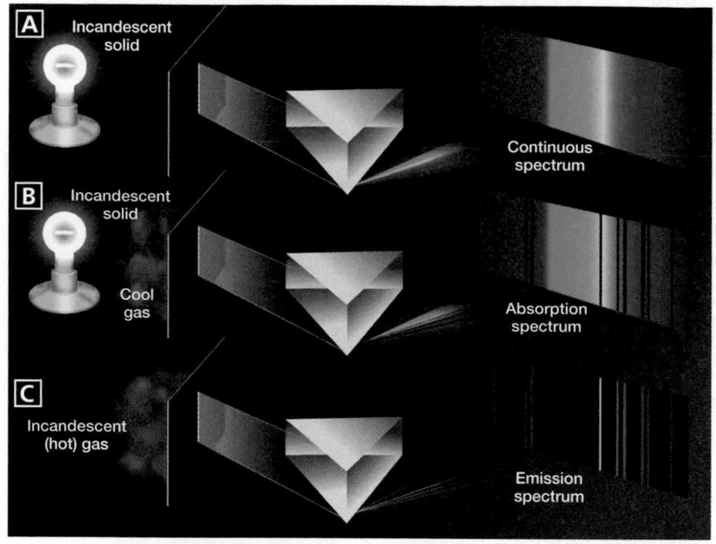

Figure 3 Formation of Spectra
A A continuous spectrum consists of a band of uninterrupted color. **B** An absorption spectrum contains dark lines. **C** An emission spectrum contains bright lines.

Spectroscopy

When Sir Isaac Newton used a prism to disperse visible light into its component colors, he unknowingly introduced the field of spectroscopy. **Spectroscopy** is the study of the properties of light that depend on wavelength. The rainbow of colors Newton produced included all wavelengths of light. It was later learned that two other types of spectra exist. Each is generated under somewhat different conditions.

Continuous Spectrum A **continuous spectrum** is produced by an incandescent solid, liquid, or gas under high pressure. (*Incandescent* means "to emit light when hot.") The spectrum consists of an uninterrupted band of color, as shown in Figure 3A. One example would be light generated by a common light bulb. This is the type of spectrum Newton produced.

Absorption Spectrum An **absorption spectrum** is produced when visible light is passed through a relatively cool gas under low pressure. The gas absorbs selected wavelengths of light. So the spectrum appears continuous, but with a series of dark lines running through it, as shown in Figure 3B.

Emission Spectrum An **emission spectrum** is produced by a hot gas under low pressure. It is a series of bright lines of particular wavelengths, depending on the gas that produces them. As shown in Figure 3C, these bright lines appear in the exact location as the dark lines that are produced by the same gas in an absorption spectrum.

The spectra of most stars are of the dark-line, or absorption, type. The importance of these spectra is that each element or compound in its gaseous form produces a unique set of spectral lines. **When the spectrum of a star is studied, the spectral lines act as "fingerprints." These lines identify the elements present and thus the star's chemical composition.** The spectrum of the sun contains thousands of dark lines. More than 60 elements have been identified by matching these lines with those of elements known on Earth.

What is spectroscopy?

The Doppler Effect

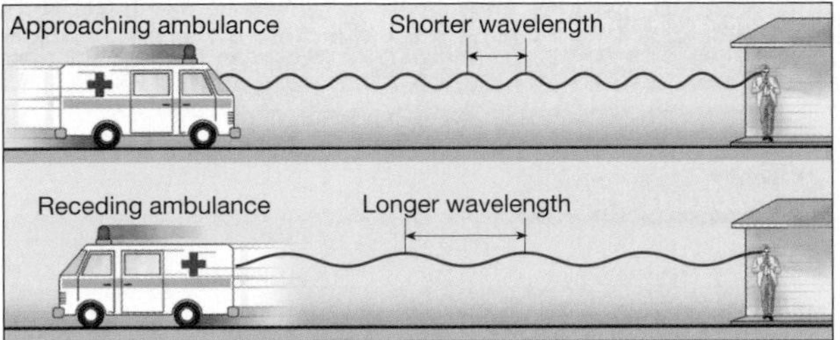

When an ambulance approaches, the siren seems to have a higher-than-normal pitch. When it is moving away, the pitch sounds lower than normal. This effect, which occurs for both sound and light waves, is called the Doppler effect. The **Doppler effect** refers to the perceived change in wavelength of a wave that is emitted from a source that is moving away or toward an object. It takes time for the wave to be emitted. If the source is moving away from you, the beginning of the wave is emitted nearer to you than the end. From the listener's perspective the wave appears to be stretched, as shown in the model for Figure 4. The opposite is true for a wave moving toward you.

The light from a source that is moving away from an observer appears redder than it actually is because its waves are lengthened. This effect is only noticeable to the human eye at velocities approaching the speed of light. Objects moving toward an object have their light waves shifted toward the blue, or shorter wavelength. In addition, the amount of shift is related to the rate of movement. Thus, if a source of red light moved toward you, it could actually appear blue. The same effect would be produced if you moved and the light source was stationary.

In astronomy, the Doppler effect is used to determine whether a star or other body in space is moving away from or toward Earth. Larger Doppler shifts indicate higher speeds; smaller Doppler shifts indicate slower speeds. Doppler shifts are generally measured from the dark lines in the spectra of stars by comparing them with a standard spectrum produced in the laboratory.

Figure 4 The Doppler Effect The wavelength of the sound of an approaching ambulance is compressed as it approaches an observer. For a receding ambulance, the wavelength is stretched out and the observer notes a lower-pitched sound. When this effect is applied to light, a shorter wavelength is noted for an approaching object and is seen as blue light. A longer wavelength is noted for a receding object, which is seen as red light.

Section 24.1 Assessment

Reviewing Concepts

1. What types of radiation make up the electromagnetic spectrum?
2. Compare and contrast the three different types of spectra.
3. How do scientists determine the elements present in a star?
4. How can scientists determine whether a star is moving toward or away from Earth?

Critical Thinking

5. **Sequencing** Sequence the components of visible light according to wavelength, beginning with the shortest wavelength.
6. **Applying Concepts** Based on what you know about visible light, how do rainbows form in Earth's atmosphere?

Writing in Science

List of Questions Make a list of questions that you would like to ask a scientist about the nature of light. Your questions should cover both the wave theory and the particle theory of light.

The Doppler Effect

Integrate Physics L2

A Sonic Boom The Doppler effect and a sonic boom are similar phenomena. When an object such as an airplane is traveling near the speed of sound, the compression waves bunch up near the nose of the aircraft. When the aircraft exceeds the speed of sound, a loud explosion is heard known as a sonic boom. The sonic boom occurs because some of the sound wavefronts arrive at the same instant. Have students research how a sonic boom and a Mach cone are created. Have students make posters showing how each of these phenomena occurs.
Verbal

3 ASSESS

Evaluate Understanding L2

Have students write one question on each of the following topics: electromagnetic radiation, spectroscopy, and the Doppler effect. Have groups of students ask one another their questions.

Reteach L1

Use Figure 3 on p. 676 to review the different types of spectrums.

Writing in Science

Sample questions: In which circumstances does light behave like a wave? When does it behave like a stream of particles? Who developed the theories? If time permits, have students research the answers to their questions.

Answer to . . .

Reading Checkpoint *Spectroscopy is the study of the properties of light that depend on wavelength.*

Section 24.1 Assessment

1. Electromagnetic radiation includes gamma rays, X-rays, ultraviolet light, visible light, infrared radiation, microwaves, and radio waves.
2. A continuous spectrum is produced by an incandescent solid, liquid, or gas under high pressure. It consists of an uninterrupted band of color. An absorption spectrum is produced when white light is passed through a relatively cool gas under low pressure. The spectrum appears continuous, but with a series of dark lines running through it. An emission spectrum is produced by a hot gas under low pressure. It is a series of bright lines of particular wavelengths, depending on the gas that produces them.
3. Scientists study the star's spectrum. The spectral lines act as "fingerprints," which identify the elements present and thus the star's chemical composition.
4. Scientists study Doppler shifts. A red shift indicates that a star is moving away from Earth. A blue shift indicates that a star is moving toward Earth.
5. violet, blue, green, yellow, orange, and red
6. Visible light is bent when it encounters water droplets in the atmosphere and is separated into its component colors.

Section 24.2

1 FOCUS

Section Objectives

24.4 **Explain** how refracting, reflecting, and radio telescopes work.

24.5 **Describe** the advantages and disadvantages of each type of telescope.

24.6 **Explain** the advantages that a space telescope has over an Earth-based telescope.

Reading Focus

Build Vocabulary L2

Concept Map Have students make a concept map using the term *telescopes* as the starting point. All the vocabulary terms in this section should be used.

Reading Strategy L2

a. uses a lens to bend and redirect light to a focal point behind a mirror
b. uses a concave mirror to focus light to a point in front of a mirror

2 INSTRUCT

Refracting Telescopes

Build Reading Literacy L1

Refer to **p. 642D** in **Chapter 23**, which provides the guidelines for comparing and contrasting.

Compare and Contrast Have students read the section. As they read, they should create lists of how the various types of telescopes are similar and different.
Verbal

24.2 Tools for Studying Space

Reading Focus

Key Concepts

- How does a refracting telescope produce an image?
- Why are most large telescopes reflecting telescopes?
- How does a radio telescope gather data?
- What advantages do space telescopes have over Earth-based telescopes?

Vocabulary

- refracting telescope
- chromatic aberration
- reflecting telescope
- radio telescope

Reading Strategy

Comparing and Contrasting Copy the Venn diagram. As you read, complete it to show the differences between refracting and reflecting telescopes.

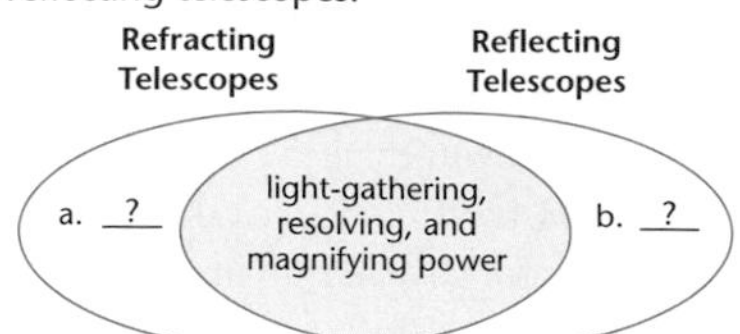

Now that we've examined the nature of light, let's turn our attention to the tools astronomers use to intercept and study the energy emitted by distant objects in the universe. Because the basic principles of detecting radiation were originally developed through visual observations, the astronomical tools we'll explore first will be optical telescopes. An example is shown in Figure 5. The 10-meter Keck Telescope, located on Mauna Kea in Hawaii, uses a mosaic of 36 six-sided, 1.8-meter mirrors. The mirrors are carefully positioned by a computer to give the optical effect of a 10-meter mirror. The Keck Telescope is a type of optical telescope. To create an image that is a great distance away, a telescope must collect as much light as possible. Optical telescopes contain mirrors, lenses, or both to accomplish this task.

Figure 5 Keck Telescope This optical telescope is located at the summit of Hawaii's Mauna Kea volcano.

Refracting Telescopes

Galileo is considered to be the first person to have used telescopes for astronomical observations. Having learned about the newly invented instrument, Galileo built one of his own that was capable of magnifying objects 30 times. Because this early instrument, as well as its modern counterparts, used a lens to bend or refract light, it is known as a **refracting telescope.**

Focus The most important lens in a refracting telescope, the objective lens, produces an image by bending light from a distant object so that the light converges at an area called the focus (*focus* = central point). For an object such as a star, the image appears as a point of light. For nearby objects it appears as an inverted replica of the original.

You can easily demonstrate the latter case by holding a lens in one hand and, with the other hand, placing a white card behind the lens. Now vary the distance between them until an image appears on the card. The distance between the focus (where the image appears) and the lens is called the focal length of the lens.

Astronomers usually study an image from a telescope by first photographing the image. However, if a telescope is used to examine an image directly, a second lens, called an eyepiece, is required. The eyepiece magnifies the image produced by the objective lens. In this respect, it is similar to a magnifying glass. The objective lens produces a very small, bright image of an object, and the eyepiece enlarges the image so that details can be seen. Figure 6 shows the parts of a refracting telescope.

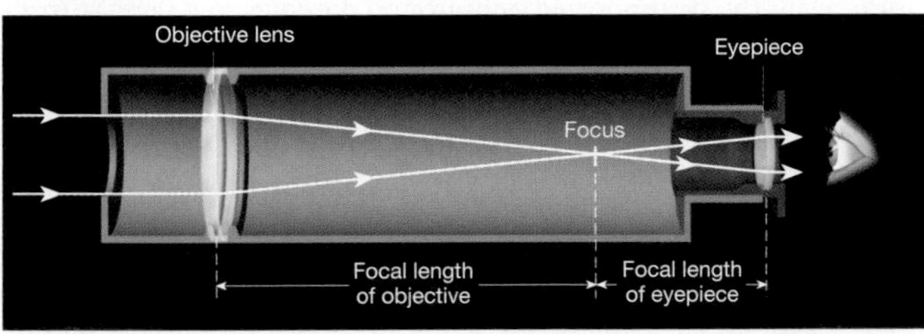

Figure 6 Simple Refracting Telescope A refracting telescope uses a lens to bend light.

Chromatic Aberration Although used extensively in the nineteenth century, refracting telescopes suffer a major optical defect. As light passes through any lens, the shorter wavelengths of light are bent more than the longer wavelengths. Consequently, when a refracting telescope is in focus for red light, blue and violet light are out of focus. The troublesome effect, known as **chromatic** (*chroma* = color) **aberration** (*aberrare* = to go astray), weakens the image and produces a halo of color around it. When blue light is in focus, a reddish halo appears. When red light is in focus, a bluish halo appears. Although this effect cannot be eliminated completely, it is reduced by using a second lens made of a different type of glass.

Reading Checkpoint *What is chromatic aberration?*

Use Community Resources L2

Invite an astronomer to talk to your class about telescopes. Ask if he or she could bring small telescopes to use for demonstrations. If possible, see if the astronomer could come at night and have a moon-gazing or star-gazing party.
Verbal, Interpersonal

Teacher Demo

Making a Simple Refracting Telescope L2

Purpose Students will observe the simple concepts behind a refracting telescope.

Materials 2 magnifying lenses

Procedure Observe an object in the distance with one of the magnifying lenses. Move the lens back and forth until you get a sharp image. Place the second magnifying lens in front of your eye. Move the second lens back and forth until you get a clear image. The image should appear larger. Pass the lenses around the classroom to give students an opportunity to view an image.

Expected Outcome Students will see that a simple refracting telescope consists of two lenses. In this example, it consists of two convex lenses. A convex lens is thicker in the middle and thinner around the edges.
Visual, Kinesthetic

Customize for Inclusion Students

Learning Disabled For students with difficulty absorbing concepts by reading, use Figures 6, 7, and 8 as a visual aid as you describe how each of these telescopes work. Be sure students understand the differences in these telescopes.

Answer to . . .

Reading Checkpoint *Chromatic aberration is a troublesome effect associated with refracting telescopes that weakens an image and produces a halo of color around it.*

Reflecting Telescopes

Use Visuals L1

Figure 7 Have students examine the figure. Ask: **Where is the viewer positioned for each type of reflecting telescope?** *(In A, the viewer is in a viewing cage inside the telescope, positioned at the focal point. In B, the viewer is seated below the telescope at the focal point. In C, the viewer is at the side of the telescope, viewing the image at an angle.)* **Infer why the prime focus method is used only for large telescopes.** *(The telescope has to be large for a person to sit inside the telescope to view the image.)*
Verbal, Logical

L2

Students may think that increasing the magnification of a reflecting telescope will improve the clarity of an image. This is not necessarily true. What can be viewed telescopically is limited by atmospheric conditions and the resolving power of the telescope. Any part of an image that is not clear at low magnification will appear only as a larger blur at higher magnification. Increasing magnification spreads out the light and decreases the brightness of the object. Astronomers describe telescopes not in terms of their magnification, but by the diameter of the objective mirror or lens, because it is this factor that determines both the light-gathering power and the resolving power of a telescope.
A good rule of thumb for amateur astronomers is that for every inch of aperture you can use up to 60 power. A three inch telescope would have a useful magnification of 180×.
Verbal

Download a worksheet on telescopes for students to complete, and find additional teacher support from NSTA SciLinks.

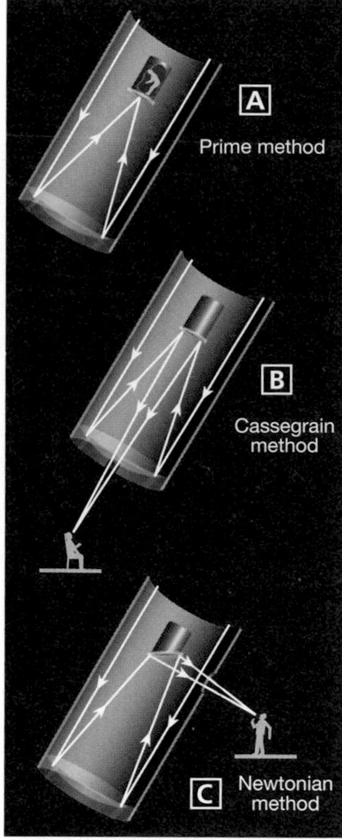

Figure 7 Viewing Methods with Reflecting Telescopes
A The prime method is only used with very large telescopes.
B The Cassegrain method is most commonly used. Note that a small hole in the center of the mirror allows light to pass through.
C This figure shows the Newtonian method.

For: Links on telescopes
Visit: www.SciLinks.org
Web Code: cjn-7242

Reflecting Telescopes

Newton was bothered by chromatic aberration so he built telescopes that reflected light from a shiny surface—a mirror. Because reflected light is not dispersed into its component colors, the chromatic aberration is avoided. **Reflecting telescopes** use a concave mirror that focuses the light in front of a mirror, rather than behind it, like a lens. The mirror is generally made of glass that is finely ground and coated with a highly reflective material, usually an aluminum compound.

Because the focus of a reflecting telescope is in front of the mirror, an observer must be able to view the image without blocking too much incoming light. Figure 7A shows a viewing cage for the observer within the telescope. Figures 7B and 7C show that the observer can remain indoors. Most large telescopes employ more than one type.

Advantages of Reflecting Telescopes As you might guess, it's a huge task to produce a large piece of high-quality, bubble-free glass for refracting telescopes. **Most large optical telescopes are reflectors. Light does not pass through a mirror so the glass for a reflecting telescope does not have to be of optical quality.** In addition, a lens can be supported only around the edge, so it sags. Mirrors, on the other hand, can be supported fully from behind. One disadvantage of reflecting telescopes is that the secondary mirror blocks some light entering the telescope. Thus, a reflecting telescope with a 10-inch opening will not collect as much light as a 10-inch refractor.

Properties of Optical Telescopes Both refracting and reflecting telescopes have three properties that aid astronomers in their work: 1) light-gathering power, 2) resolving power, and 3) magnifying power. Light-gathering power refers to the telescope's ability to intercept more light from distant objects, thereby producing brighter images. Telescopes with large lenses or mirrors "see" farther into space than do those with small ones.

Another advantage of telescopes with large objectives is their greater resolving power, which allows for sharper images and finer detail. For example, with the naked eye, the Milky Way appears as a vague band of light in the night sky. But even a small telescope is capable of resolving, or separating it into, individual stars. Lastly, telescopes have magnifying power, which is the ability to make an object larger. Magnification is calculated by dividing the focal length of the objective by the focal length of the eyepiece. Thus, the magnification of a telescope can be changed by simply changing the eyepiece.

What is light-gathering power?

Radio Telescopes

A

B

Figure 8 A The 43-meter Radio Telescope at Green Bank, West Virginia The dish acts like the mirror of a reflecting telescope, focusing radio waves onto the antenna. **B The Very Large Array Near Socorro, New Mexico** Twenty-seven identical antennas operate together to form this radio network. **Identifying** *What is a network of radio telescopes called?*

Detecting Invisible Radiation

As you learned earlier, sunlight is made up of more than just the radiation that is visible to our eyes. Gamma rays, X-rays, ultraviolet radiation, infrared radiation, and radio waves are also produced by stars. Photographic film that is sensitive to ultraviolet and infrared radiation has been developed. This extends the limits of our vision. However, most of this radiation cannot penetrate our atmosphere, so balloons, rockets, and satellites must transport cameras "above" the atmosphere to record it.

A narrow band of radio waves is able to penetrate the atmosphere. Measurement of this radiation is important because we can map the galactic distribution of hydrogen. Hydrogen is the main material from which stars are made.

Radio Telescopes The detection of radio waves is accomplished by big dishes called **radio telescopes,** shown in Figure 8A. In principle, the dish of one of these telescopes operates in the same manner as the mirror of an optical telescope. **A radio telescope focuses the incoming radio waves on an antenna, which absorbs and transmits these waves to an amplifier, just like a radio antenna.**

Because radio waves are about 100,000 times longer than visible radiation, the surface of the dish doesn't need to be as smooth as a mirror. Except for the shortest radio waves, a wire mesh is a good reflector. However, because radio signals from celestial sources are very weak, large dishes are necessary to intercept an adequate signal.

Radio telescopes have poor resolution, making it difficult to pinpoint the radio source. Pairs or groups of telescopes reduce this problem. When several radio telescopes are wired together, as shown in Figure 8B, the resulting network is called a radio interferometer.

Facts and Figures

The Very Large Array consists of 27 radio antennas set up in a Y-shaped configuration. The site is located on the Plains of San Augustin 50 miles west of Socorro, New Mexico. Each antenna measures 25 m in diameter. When the antennas are combined electronically, they give an equivalent resolution of an antenna 36 km in diameter. The combination of the antennas has the sensitivity of a dish that is 130 m in diameter.

Detecting Invisible Radiation

Build Science Skills

L2

Inferring Explain to students that radio waves are able to penetrate Earth's atmosphere and are used to map the distribution of hydrogen in the galaxy. Ask: **The largest radio telescope is 300 m (1,000 ft) in diameter. Why is a radio telescope this large an advantage?** *(Radio signals from celestial sources are very weak. This telescope is able to collect a larger number of signals because of its size.)* **This radio telescope was built in a depression in the landscape. Why was this location chosen?** *(This depression blocks human-made radio signals from the telescope.)* **Verbal, Logical**

Answer to . . .

Figure 8 *a radio interferometer*

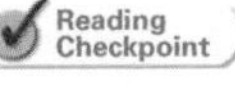

Light-gathering power refers to the telescope's ability to intercept more light from distant objects, thereby producing brighter images.

Space Telescopes

Integrate Language Arts L2

The Hubble Space Telescope The Hubble Space Telescope has provided spectacular images of the universe. This program also has experienced failures. Have students in groups research the Hubble Space Telescope project and create a computer presentation to share with their classmates. The Internet contains many photographs that can be included in the presentation. **Verbal, Interpersonal**

Q *Why do astronomers build observatories on mountaintops?*

A Observatories are most often located on mountaintops because sites above the densest part of the atmosphere provide better conditions for "seeing."

Advantages of Radio Telescopes Radio telescopes have some advantages over optical telescopes. They are much less affected by turbulence in the atmosphere, clouds, and the weather. No protective dome is required, which reduces the cost of construction. "Viewing" is possible 24 hours a day. More important, radio telescopes can "see" through interstellar dust clouds that obscure visible wavelengths. Radio signals from distant points in the universe pass unhindered through the dust, giving us an unobstructed view. Furthermore, radio telescopes can detect clouds of gases too cool to emit visible light. These cold gas clouds are important because they are the sites of star formation.

Radio telescopes are, however, hindered by human-made radio interference. While optical telescopes are placed on remote mountaintops to reduce interference from city lights, radio telescopes are often hidden in valleys to block human-made radio interference.

Radio telescopes have revealed such spectacular events as the collision of two galaxies. They led to the important discovery of quasars and pulsars.

Reading Checkpoint *Why can radio telescopes be used 24 hours a day?*

Space Telescopes

Have you ever seen a blurring effect caused by the movement of air on a hot summer day? That blurring effect also distorts the images produced by most telescopes on Earth. On a night when the stars twinkle, viewing is difficult because the air is moving rapidly. This causes the image to move about and blur.

Observatories are most often located on mountaintops. This is because sites above the densest part of the atmosphere provide better conditions for "seeing." At high elevations, there is less air to scatter and dim the incoming light. Also, there is less water vapor to absorb infrared radiation. Further, the thin air on mountaintops causes less distortion of the images being observed.

There is one other way to get around the distorting effects of Earth's atmosphere—send telescopes into space. **Space telescopes orbit above Earth's atmosphere and thus produce clearer images than Earth-based telescopes.**

Figure 9 Hubble Space Telescope Hubble was deployed into Earth orbit by the space shuttle *Discovery*.

Hubble Space Telescope The first space telescope, built by NASA, was the Hubble Space Telescope, shown in Figure 9. Hubble was put into orbit around Earth in April 1990. This 2.4-meter space telescope has 10 billion times more light-gathering power than the human eye. Hubble has given us many spectacular images. For example, the

682 Chapter 24

Hubble Space Telescope has provided images that clearly resolve the separation between Pluto and its moon, Charon. It has also provided data about planets that orbit other stars, the birth of stars, black holes, the age of the universe, and the expansion of the universe.

Other Space Telescopes Other types of radiation are also affected by Earth's atmosphere. To study X-rays, NASA uses the Chandra X-Ray Observatory. This space telescope was launched in 1999. One of its main missions is to gather data about black holes—objects whose gravity is so strong that visible light cannot escape them. Another space telescope, the Compton Gamma-Ray Observatory, was used to study both visible light and gamma rays. In 2011, NASA plans to launch the James Webb Space Telescope to study infrared radiation. As Figure 10 shows, images obtained by different telescopes offer different information about the same object in space—in this case, the Milky Way galaxy. By studying all the images together, astronomers obtain a more thorough understanding of the galaxy.

Figure 10 Images of the Milky Way Galaxy These images were taken by different types of telescopes, including visible light, X-ray, gamma ray, and infrared.

Section 24.2 Assessment

Reviewing Concepts

1. How does a refracting telescope work?
2. How does a reflecting telescope differ from a refracting telescope?
3. Why are most large telescopes reflecting telescopes?
4. How do radio telescopes gather data?
5. Why do space telescopes obtain clearer images than Earth-based telescopes?

Critical Thinking

6. **Calculating** If a telescope has an objective with a focal length of 50 centimeters and an eyepiece with a focal length of 25 millimeter, what will be the magnification?
7. **Applying Concepts** Using the numbers from the previous question, would an eyepiece with a greater focal length increase or decrease magnification? Explain.

Connecting Concepts

Electromagnetic Radiation Recall the different types of electromagnetic radiation. Based on what you've learned in this section, would you recommend sending a telescope into space to study radio waves? Why or why not?

3 ASSESS

Evaluate Understanding

L2

Have students write down the following types of telescopes: refracting, reflecting, and radio. Then, have students write down three facts about each telescope. Have students share their facts with the class.

Reteach

L1

Use Figures 6, 7, and 8 to review how each of the these telescopes works.

Connecting Concepts

Sample answer: Radio waves can easily pass through Earth's atmosphere. Therefore, there is little advantage in sending a radio telescope into space.

Answer to . . .

They do not need visible light to obtain images.

Section 24.2 Assessment

1. The objective lens produces an image by bending light from a distant object so that the light converges at an area called the focus.
2. A reflecting telescope uses a concave mirror to produce an image. A refracting telescope uses a lens to bend or refract light.
3. Because light does not pass through a mirror, the glass for a reflecting telescope does not have to be of optical quality. In addition, a lens can be supported only around the edge, so it sags. Mirrors, on the other hand, can be supported fully from behind.
4. A radio telescope focuses the incoming radio waves on an antenna, which absorbs and transmits the waves to an amplifier.
5. Space telescopes orbit above Earth's atmosphere and thus produce clearer images than Earth-based telescopes.
6. Magnification is calculated by dividing the focal length of the objective by the focal length of the eyepiece. In this example, 500 mm ÷ 25 mm = 20; magnification would be 20 times.
7. An eyepiece with a greater focal length, such as 50 mm, would decrease magnification because 500 mm ÷ 50 mm = 10 times magnification.

Section 24.3

1 FOCUS

Section Objectives

24.7 **Explain** the structure of the sun.

24.8 **Describe** the physical features on the surface of the sun.

24.9 **Explain** how the sun produces energy.

Reading Focus

Build Vocabulary L2

LINCS There are several words in the vocabulary list that sound like other words students may be familiar with. Have students: **L**ist the parts that they know; **I**magine a picture; **N**ote a reminding sound-alike word; **C**onnect the terms; and **S**elf-test.

Reading Strategy L2

a. Answers will vary.
b. Answers will vary.
c. Answers will vary.
d. Answers will vary.

2 INSTRUCT

Build Reading Literacy L1

Refer to **p. 392D** in **Chapter 14,** which provides the guidelines for previewing.

Preview Before they read the section, have students skim the titles, headings, visual elements, and boldfaced type to preview how the text is organized.
Visual

24.3 The Sun

Reading Focus

Key Concepts

- What is the structure of the sun?
- What are the characteristics of features on the sun?
- How does the sun produce energy?

Vocabulary

- photosphere
- chromosphere
- corona
- solar wind
- sunspot
- prominence
- solar flare
- aurora
- nuclear fusion

Reading Strategy

Monitoring Your Understanding Preview the Key Concepts, topic headings, vocabulary, and figures in this section. Copy the table below, listing two things you expect to learn. After reading, fill in the table below, stating what you have learned about each item you listed.

What I Expect to Learn	What I Learned
a. ?	b. ?
c. ?	d. ?

The sun is one of the 100 billion stars that make up the Milky Way galaxy. Although the sun is of no significance to the universe as a whole, it is Earth's primary source of energy. Everything—from the fossil fuels we burn in our automobiles to the food that we eat—is ultimately derived from solar energy. The sun is also important to astronomers, since it is the only star whose surface we can study. Even with the largest telescopes, other stars appear only as points of light.

Because of the sun's brightness and its damaging radiation, it is not safe to observe it directly. However, a telescope can project its image on a piece of cardboard held behind the telescope's eyepiece. In this manner, the sun can be studied safely. This basic method is used in several telescopes around the world, which keep a constant watch of the sun. One of the finest is at the Kitt Peak National Observatory in southern Arizona, shown in Figure 11. It consists of an enclosure with moving mirrors that directs sunlight to an underground mirror. From the mirror, an image of the sun is projected to an observing room, where it is studied.

Figure 11 The McMath-Pierce Solar Telescope at Kitt Peak Near Tucson, Arizona Movable mirrors at the top follow the sun, reflecting its light down the sloping tunnel.

Compared to other stars, the sun is an "average star." However, on the scale of our solar system, it is truly gigantic. Its diameter is equal to 109 Earth diameters, or 1.35 million kilometers. Its volume is 1.25 million times as great as Earth's. Its mass is 332,000 times the mass of Earth and its density is only one quarter that of solid Earth.

Structure of the Sun

Because the sun is made of gas, no sharp boundaries exist between its various layers. **Keeping this in mind, we can divide the sun into four parts: the solar interior; the visible surface, or photosphere; and two atmospheric layers, the chromosphere and corona.** These parts are shown in Figure 12. The sun's interior makes up all but a tiny fraction of the solar mass. Unlike the outer three layers, the solar interior cannot be directly observed. Let's discuss the visible layers first.

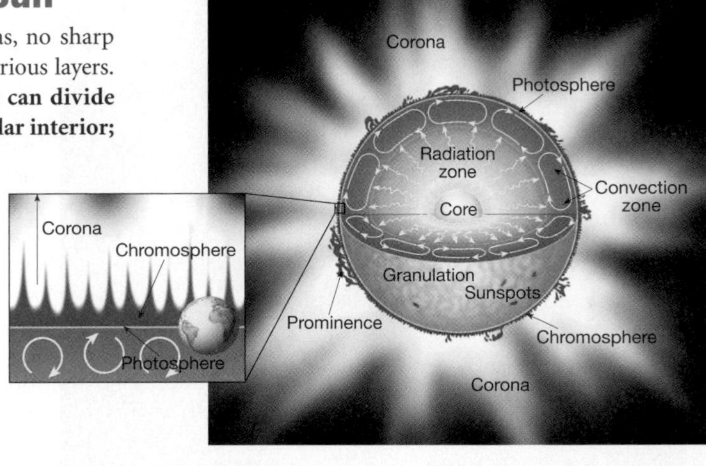

Figure 12 Structure of the Sun The sun can be divided into four parts: the solar interior, the photosphere, the chromosphere, and the corona.

Photosphere The **photosphere** (*photos* = light, *sphere* = a ball) radiates most of the sunlight we see and can be thought of as the visible "surface" of the sun. The photosphere consists of a layer of gas less than 500 kilometers thick. It is neither smooth nor uniformly bright, as the ancients had imagined.

When viewed through a telescope, the photosphere's grainy texture is apparent. This is the result of numerous relatively small, bright markings called granules, which are surrounded by narrow, dark regions, as shown in Figure 13. Granules are typically the size of Texas, and they owe their brightness to hotter gases that are rising from below. As this gas spreads, cooling causes it to darken and sink back into the interior. Each granule survives only 10 to 20 minutes. The combined motion of new granules replacing old ones gives the photosphere the appearance of boiling. This up-and-down movement of gas is called convection. Besides producing the grainy appearance of the photosphere, convection is believed to be responsible for the transfer of energy in the uppermost part of the sun's interior.

The composition of the photosphere is revealed by the dark lines of its absorption spectrum. Studies reveal that 90 percent of the sun's surface atoms are hydrogen, almost 10 percent are helium, and only minor amounts of the other detectable elements are present. Other stars also have high proportions of these two lightest elements, a fact we shall discuss later.

Figure 13 Granules Granules are the yellowish-orange patches on the photosphere. **Describing** ***Describe the movement of gases in the convection zone.***

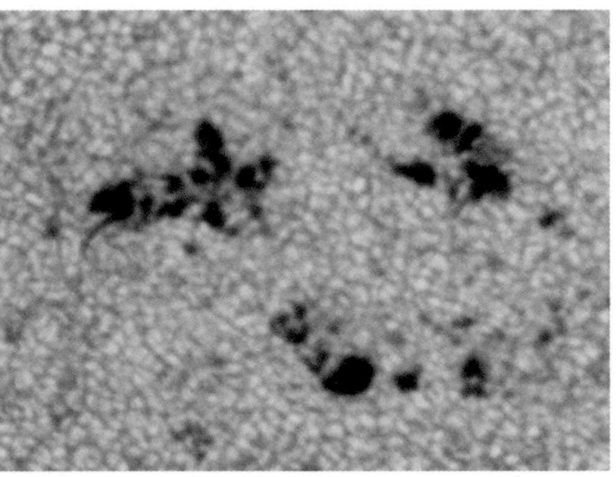

Structure of the Sun

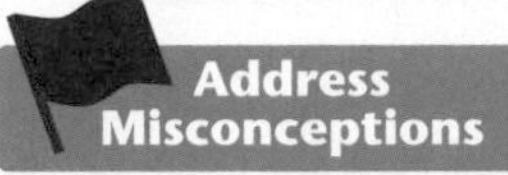

L2

Many students may think that since the sun is an enormous ball of gas it does not have a surface. The visible surface of the sun, the photosphere, is a layer of gas about 500 km thick. Most of the sunlight that we receive is from this layer. Although more light is emitted from the layer below the photosphere, that light is absorbed in the overlying layers of gas. Above the photosphere, the gas is less dense and thus unable to radiate much light. The photosphere is the layer that is dense enough to emit ample light yet has a density low enough to allow light to escape. Since the photosphere emits most of the light we see, it appears as the outermost surface of the sun.
Verbal

Customize for English Language Learners

Encourage English language learners to make a science glossary as they read the section. Suggest that they start with the vocabulary terms and then add any other new words they encounter. Encourage students to write brief definitions of each term and draw an illustration that helps them understand the term.

Answer to . . .

Figure 13 *Gases rise to the surface of the sun, cool, then sink back into the interior.*

Teacher Demo

Earth and Solar Winds L2

Purpose Students will observe how Earth is protected from solar winds.

Materials bar magnet, 2 sheets of notebook paper, iron filings, drinking straw

Procedure Cover the magnet with a sheet of paper. Fold the other sheet of paper in half. Sprinkle iron filings in the fold. Hold the paper about 15 cm from the magnet. Blow through the straw, directing the stream of air at the iron filings. The iron filings should be attracted to the magnet.

Expected Outcome Students will observe how a magnetic field attracts charged particles. The solar wind is composed of ionized or charged particles. Just as the iron filings are drawn to the magnet, the solar wind is attracted to Earth's magnetic field. Earth's magnetic field prevents the solar wind from reaching Earth's surface and bombarding it.
Visual, Logical

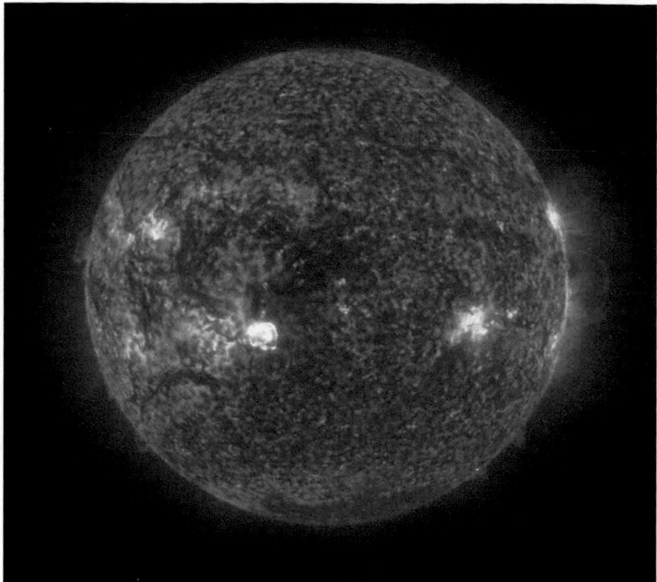

Figure 14 Chromosphere The chromosphere is a thin layer of hot gases that appears as a red rim around the sun.

Chromosphere Just above the photosphere lies the **chromosphere,** a relatively thin layer of hot gases a few thousand kilometers thick. The chromosphere is observable for a few moments during a total solar eclipse or by using a special instrument that blocks out the light from the photosphere. Under such conditions, it appears as a thin red rim around the sun. Because the chromosphere consists of hot, incandescent gases under low pressure, it produces an emission spectrum that is nearly the reverse of the absorption spectrum of the photosphere. One of the bright lines of hydrogen contributes a good portion of its total light and accounts for this sphere's red color.

Corona The outermost portion of the solar atmosphere, the **corona** (*corona* = crown) is very weak and, as with the chromosphere, is visible only when the brilliant photosphere is covered. This envelope of ionized gases normally extends a million kilometers from the sun and produces a glow about half as bright as the full moon.

At the outer fringe of the corona, the ionized gases have speeds great enough to escape the gravitational pull of the sun. The streams of protons and electrons that boil from the corona constitute the **solar wind.** This wind travels outward through the solar system at speeds up to 800 kilometers per second and eventually is lost to space. During its journey, the solar wind interacts with the bodies of the solar system, continually bombarding lunar rocks and altering their appearance. Although Earth's magnetic field prevents the solar winds from reaching our surface, these winds do affect our atmosphere, as we'll discuss later.

Studies of the energy emitted from the photosphere indicate that its temperature averages about 6000 K. Upward from the photosphere, the temperature unexpectedly increases, exceeding 1 million K at the top of the corona. Although the corona temperature is much higher than that of the photosphere, it radiates much less energy because of its very low density.

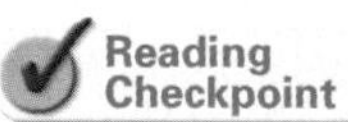

What is the solar wind?

Facts and Figures

The high temperature of the corona is probably caused by sound waves generated by the convection motion of the photosphere. Just as boiling water makes noise, the energetic sound waves generated in the photosphere are believed to be absorbed by the gases of the corona and thereby raise their temperatures.

The Active Sun

The most conspicuous features on the surface of the sun are the dark regions. They were occasionally observed before the advent of the telescope, but were generally regarded as objects located somewhere between the sun and Earth. In 1610, Galileo concluded that these regions were part of the solar surface. From their motion, he deduced that the sun rotates on its axis about once a month. Later observations indicated that not all parts of the sun rotate at the same speed. The sun's equator rotates once in 25 days, while a location 70 degrees from the solar equator, whether north or south, requires 33 days for one rotation. Imagine if Earth rotated in a similar manner! The sun's nonuniform rotation is evidence of its gaseous nature.

Sunspots What are those dark areas Galileo observed? The dark regions on the surface of the photosphere are called **sunspots.** As Figure 15 shows, an individual spot contains a black center rimmed by a lighter region. **Sunspots appear dark because of their temperature, which is about 1500 K less than that of the surrounding solar surface.** If these dark spots could be observed away from the sun, they would appear many times brighter than the full moon.

During the early nineteenth century, it was believed that a tiny planet named Vulcan orbited between Mercury and the sun. In the search for Vulcan an accurate record of sunspot occurrences was kept. Although the planet was never found, the sunspot data revealed that the number of sunspots observable varies in an 11-year cycle.

First, the number of sunspots increases to a maximum, with perhaps a hundred or more visible at a given time. Then their numbers gradually decline to a minimum, when only a few or even none are visible.

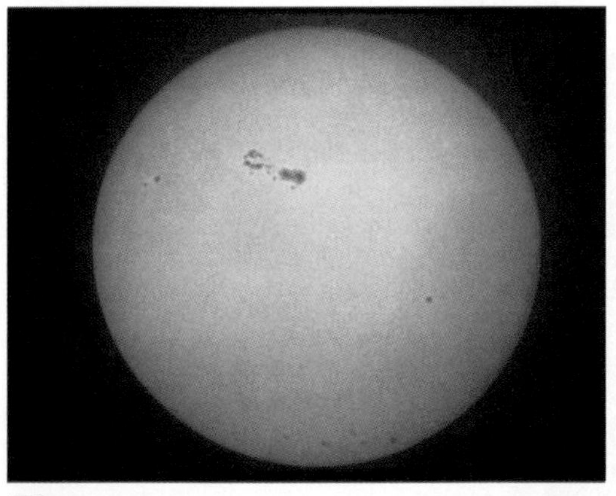
A

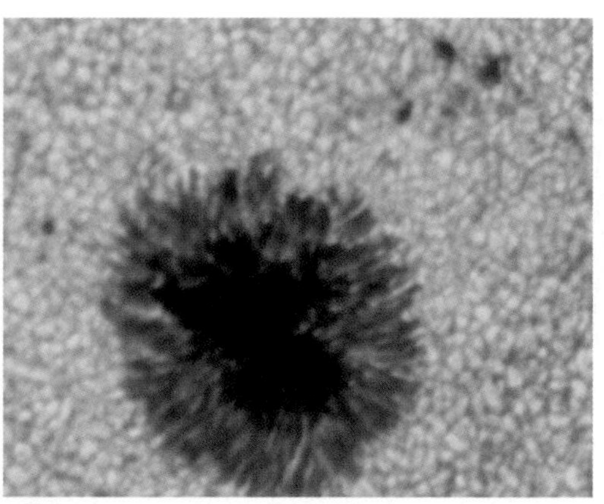
B

Figure 15 Sunspots A Sunspots often appear as groups of dark areas on the sun. **B** A close-up of an individual sunspot shows a black center surrounded by a lighter region.

The Active Sun

Build Science Skills

Using Models Have students complete the following activity. Fill one of the empty soda bottles half full with water. Add 5 mL of glitter to the bottle of water. Place the washer on the mouth of the bottle. Dry the mouths of both bottles with a paper towel to be sure that the tape sticks. Place the mouth of the second bottle on top of the washer. Tape the two bottles together securely with duct tape. Swirl the two bottles several times. Then, turn the bottles upside down, placing the empty bottle on the table. The glitter demonstrates how fluids travel at different rates as the fluid moves through the funnel. Since the sun is not a solid body, the fluids are free to rotate at various speeds. So different parts of the sun rotate at different rates, just as they do in the bottles.
Kinesthetic, Visual

Facts and Figures

An interesting characteristic of sunspots was discovered by astronomer George Hale, for whom the Hale telescope is named. Hale found that the large sunspots are strongly magnetized, and when they occur in pairs, they have opposite magnetic poles. Also, every pair located in the same hemisphere is magnetized in the same manner. However, all pairs in the other hemisphere are magnetized in the opposite manner. At the beginning of each sunspot cycle, the polarity reverses. The cause of this change in polarity is not fully understood.

Answer to . . .

streams of protons and electrons that boil from the corona

Use Visuals L1

Figure 17 Have students examine the photograph. Ask: **Why do auroras occur near the polar regions instead of other locations on Earth?** *(The ionized particles in the solar flares are attracted to the north and south magnetic poles of Earth's magnetic field. The ions follow the magnetic field lines because a force is generated when they move with some component perpendicular to the lines, and the field lines mostly reach Earth at the magnetic poles.)* **Why do the auroral displays vary with the 11-year sunspot cycle?** *(Auroral displays are caused by sunspot activity.)*
Verbal, Logical

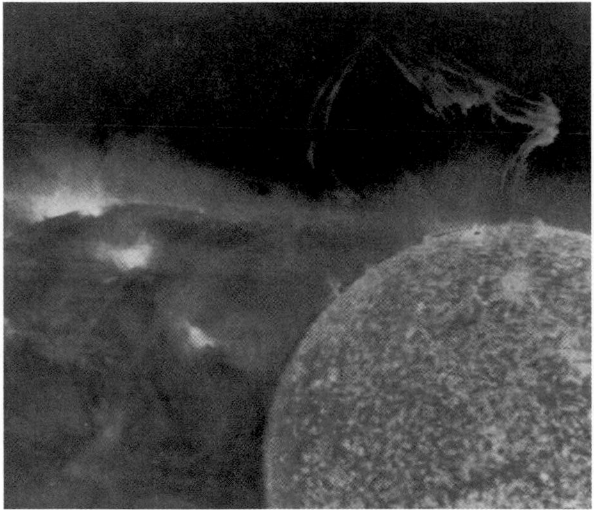

Figure 16 Solar Prominence Solar prominences are huge, arched structures, best observed when they are on the edge of the sun.

Prominences Among the more spectacular features of the active sun are prominences (*prominere* = to jut out). **Prominences** are huge cloudlike structures consisting of chromospheric gases. They often appear as great arches that extend well into the corona. Many prominences have the appearance of a fine tapestry and seem to hang motionless for days at a time. Others rise almost explosively away from the sun. These eruptive prominences reach speeds up to 1000 kilometers per second and may leave the sun entirely. **Prominences are ionized gases trapped by magnetic fields that extend from regions of intense solar activity.** Refer to Figure 16.

Solar Flares The most explosive events associated with sunspots are solar flares. **Solar flares** are brief outbursts that normally last about an hour and appear as a sudden brightening of the region above a sunspot cluster. **During their existence, solar flares release enormous amounts of energy, much of it in the form of ultraviolet, radio, and X-ray radiation.** At the same time, fast-moving atomic particles are ejected, causing the solar wind to intensify. Although a major flare could conceivably endanger the crew of a space flight, they are relatively rare. About a day after a large outburst, the ejected particles reach Earth, where they can affect long-distance radio communications.

The most spectacular effects of solar flares, however, are the **auroras,** also called the northern and southern lights. Following a strong solar flare, Earth's upper atmosphere near its magnetic poles is set aglow for several nights. The auroras appear in a wide variety of forms, one of which is shown in Figure 17. Sometimes the display looks like colorful ribbons moving with the breeze. At other times, the auroras appear as a series of luminous arcs or as a foglike glow. Auroral displays, like other solar activities, vary in intensity with the 11-year sunspot cycle.

Figure 17 Aurora Borealis or Northern Lights in Alaska The same phenomenon occurs toward the south pole, where it is called the aurora australis or southern lights.

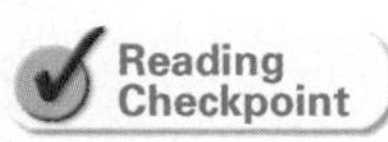

What are solar flares?

688 Chapter 24

The Solar Interior

The interior of the sun cannot be observed directly. For that reason, all we know about it is based on information acquired from the energy it radiates and from theoretical studies. The source of the sun's energy was not discovered until the late 1930s.

Nuclear Fusion Deep in its interior, the sun produces energy by a process known as **nuclear fusion.** This nuclear reaction converts four hydrogen nuclei into the nucleus of a helium atom. Tremendous energy is released. **During nuclear fusion, energy is released because some matter is actually converted to energy, as shown in Figure 18.** How does this process work? Consider that four hydrogen atoms have a combined atomic mass of 4.032 atomic mass units (4 × 1.008) whereas the atomic mass of helium is 4.003 atomic mass units, or 0.029 less than the combined mass of the hydrogen. The tiny missing mass is emitted as energy according to Einstein's equation:

$$E = mc^2$$

E equals energy, m equals mass, and c equals the speed of light. Because the speed of light is very great (300,000 km/s), the amount of energy released from even a small amount of mass is enormous.

The conversion of just one pinhead's worth of hydrogen to helium generates more energy than burning thousands of tons of coal. Most of this energy is in the form of high-energy photons that work their way toward the solar surface. The photons are absorbed and reemitted many times until they reach a layer just below the photosphere. Here, convection currents help transport this energy to the solar surface, where it radiates through the transparent chromosphere and corona.

Only a small percentage of the hydrogen in the nuclear reaction is actually converted to energy. Nevertheless, the sun is consuming an estimated 600 million tons of hydrogen each second; about 4 million tons are converted to energy. As hydrogen is consumed, the product of this reaction—helium—forms the solar core, which continually grows in size.

What happens during the process of nuclear fusion?

For: Links on nuclear fusion in the sun
Visit: www.SciLinks.org
Web Code: cjn-7243

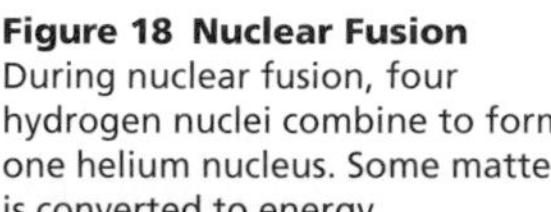

Figure 18 Nuclear Fusion During nuclear fusion, four hydrogen nuclei combine to form one helium nucleus. Some matter is converted to energy.

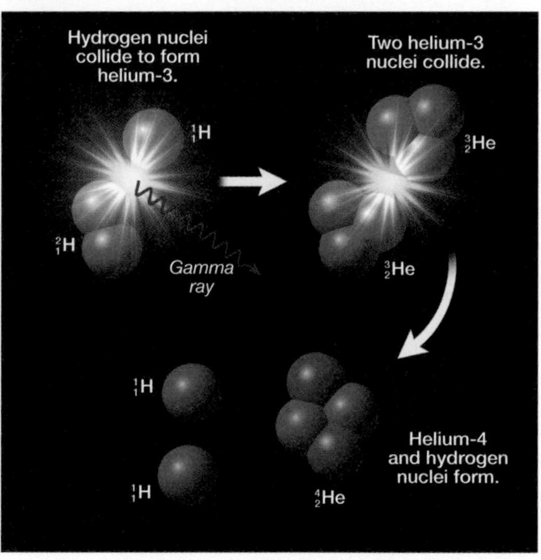

The Solar Interior

Use Visuals L1

Figure 18 Explain to students that the equation for nuclear fusion is:

$^2_1H + ^1_1H \rightarrow ^3_2He$ + gamma ray photon
$^3_2He + ^3_2He \rightarrow ^4_2He + 2^1_1H$

The superscripts in these equations represent the mass numbers (number of protons plus neutrons), and the subscripts represent the atomic number (number of protons). Ask: **What is the next step in this reaction?** *(The hydrogen atoms, ^1_1H, continue the chain reaction by striking two additional ^2_1H atoms.)*
Verbal, Logical

Integrate Physics L2

Nuclear Fusion as an Energy Source Using nuclear fusion as an electrical energy source could provide a limitless supply of electrical power. Constructing practical fusion reactors has proven to be difficult. Have students research nuclear fusion as a renewable energy source and prepare a report to present to the class. The report should contain promising techniques that scientists are currently investigating.
Verbal

Download a worksheet on nuclear fusion in the sun for students to complete, and find additional teacher support from NSTA SciLinks.

Answer to . . .

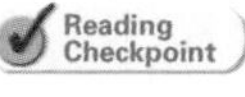
Solar flares are brief outbursts that normally last an hour or so, and appear as a sudden brightening of the region above a sunspot cluster.

Reading Checkpoint *Some matter is converted to energy, and energy is released.*

Section 24.3 (continued)

3 ASSESS

Evaluate Understanding L2

Have students draw and label a diagram of the sun. Have students include all of the applicable vocabulary words in the diagram. Then, have students explain how the sun gets its energy and what an aurora is.

Reteach L1

Use Figure 12 to review the structure of the sun.

Solution

9. 4×10^6 tons $\div$ 6×10^8 tons = $0.0066 \times 100 = 0.7$ percent

Figure 19 The sun is the source of more than 99 percent of all energy on Earth.

Just how long can the sun produce energy at its present rate before all of its hydrogen fuel is consumed? Even at the enormous rate of consumption, the sun, shown in Figure 19, has enough fuel to last easily another 100 billion years. However, evidence from other stars indicates that the sun will grow dramatically and engulf Earth long before all of its hydrogen is gone. It is thought that a star the size of the sun can exist in its present stable state for 10 billion years. As the sun is already 4.5 billion years old, it is "middle-aged."

To initiate nuclear fusion, the sun's internal temperature must have reached several million degrees. But what was the source of this heat? The solar system is believed to have formed from an enormous compressed cloud of dust and gases—mostly hydrogen. When gases are compressed, their temperature increases. All of the bodies in the solar system were compressed. However, the sun was the only one, because of its size, that became hot enough to trigger nuclear fusion. Astronomers currently estimate its internal temperature at 15 million K.

The planet Jupiter is basically a hydrogen-rich gas ball; if it were about 10 times more massive, it too might have become a star. The idea of one star orbiting another may seem odd, but recent evidence indicates that about 50 percent of the stars in the universe probably occur in pairs or multiples!

Section 24.3 Assessment

Reviewing Concepts

1. What is the structure of the sun?
2. Which layer of the sun can be thought of as its surface?
3. Describe some characteristics of features on the sun.
4. Are the same number of sunspots always present on the sun? Explain.
5. How does the sun produce energy?
6. How much longer will the sun likely exist in its present state?

Critical Thinking

7. **Relating Cause and Effect** Why do sunspots appear dark?
8. **Applying Concepts** What is the effect on Earth's atmosphere of a strong solar flare?

Math Practice

9. Of the 6×10^8 tons of hydrogen the sun consumes each second, about 4×10^6 tons are converted to energy. What percentage of the total energy consumed per second is converted to energy?

Section 24.3 Assessment

1. The sun contains the following parts: the solar interior, the photosphere, the chromosphere, and the corona.
2. the photosphere
3. Sunspots appear dark because of their temperature, which is about 1500 K less than that of the surrounding solar surface. Prominences are huge cloudlike structures of chromospheric gases. Solar flares release enormous amounts of energy.
4. No, because the number of sunspots varies in an 11-year cycle.
5. Deep in its interior, the sun produces energy by a process known as nuclear fusion, wherein four hydrogen nuclei are converted into the nucleus of a helium atom and tremendous energy is released.
6. The sun is estimated to last easily another 5 billion years.
7. Sunspots are somewhat cooler than the surrounding surface.
8. During a solar flare, fast-moving particles are ejected from the sun, increasing the solar wind. The ejected particles reach Earth and disturb long-distance radio communication. They also produce auroras.

Solar Activity and Climatic Change

Some people believe that changes in solar activity relate to climatic change. The effect of such changes would seem direct and easily understood: Increases in solar output would cause the atmosphere to warm, and reductions would result in cooling. This notion is appealing because it can be used to explain climatic changes of any length or intensity.

Still, there is at least one major drawback: No major long-term variations in the total intensity of solar radiation have yet been measured. Such measurements were not even possible until satellite technology became available. Now that it is possible, we will need many years of records before we begin to sense how variable the sun really is.

Sunspot Cycles

Several theories for climatic change based on a variable sun relate to sunspot cycles. The most recognizable features on the surface of the sun are the dark regions called sunspots. See Figure 20. The number of sunspots seems to increase and decrease over a cycle of about 11 years. The graph in Figure 21 below shows the annual number of sunspots, beginning in the early 1700s. However, this pattern is not always regular.

There have been long periods when sunspots have been absent or nearly absent. These events correspond closely with cold periods in Europe and North America. In contrast, periods of high sunspot activity have been associated with warmer times in these regions.

Conflicting Evidence

Because of these data, some scientists have suggested that changes in solar activity are an important cause of climatic change. But other scientists seriously question this notion. Their hesitation stems in part from investigations using different climatic records from around the world that failed to find a significant relationship between solar activity and climate. Even more troubling is that there is no way to test the relationship.

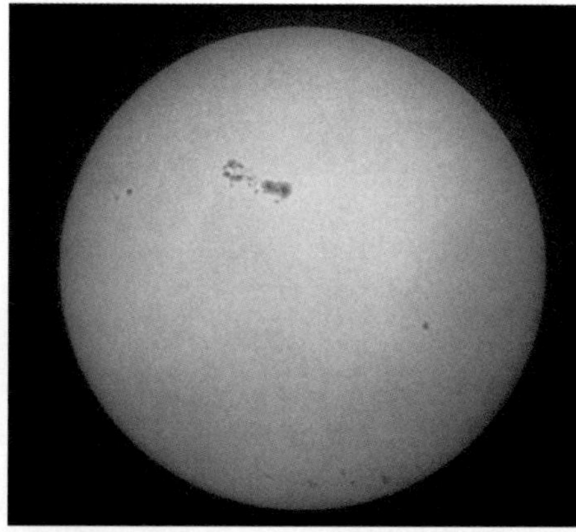

Figure 20 Dark regions on the surface of the sun are called sunspots.

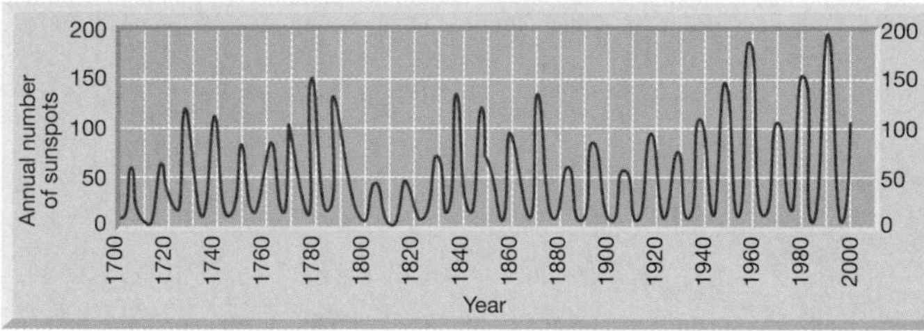

Figure 21 Mean Annual Sunspot Numbers

Solar Activity and Climatic Change **L2**

Background

A National Aeronautics and Space Administration (NASA) computer climate model suggests that low solar activity from the 1400s to the 1700s could have triggered the "Little Ice Age" in North America and Europe. Changes in the sun's energy were one of the biggest factors influencing climatic changes during this time period. While solar activity primarily influenced temperature variations during the Middle Ages, this is not true today. The accumulation of greenhouse gases in the atmosphere, caused by human activities, is the primary catalyst for temperature changes today.

Teaching Tip

Have students research information available from NASA, National Oceanic and Atmospheric Administration (NOAA), and other reliable sources on the relationship between Earth temperature and solar activity. Students should write a short report detailing the information they have found.
Verbal

Exploration Lab

Tracking Sunspots **L2**

Objective
Students will observe sunspots and their movement over several days.

Skills Focus **Observing, Interpreting Data, Making and Using Graphs**

 **Prep Time** 20 minutes for setup

Class Time 150 minutes total viewing time, 30 minutes for 5 sessions

Safety Remind students to never look directly at the sun.

Teaching Tips
- Have students take turns tracing the sunspots each day.
- Make copies of the drawings so each lab group can do the calculations.

Expected Outcome
Students will observe the sunspots move over time.

Exploration Lab

Tracking Sunspots

Sunspots begin as small areas about 1600 kilometers in diameter. Most last for only a few hours. However, some grow into dark regions many times larger than Earth and last for a month or more. In this lab you will count the number of sunspots over the course of several days.

Problem How can you use a telescope to safely view and count the number of sunspots on the sun's surface?

Materials
- telescope
- small cardboard box
- large cardboard box
- piece of white paper
- metric ruler
- pencil
- tape

Skills Observing, Interpreting Data, Making and Using Graphs

Procedure  

1. Position a telescope on a tripod outside in a sunny spot away from trees and other obstacles. The eyepiece should face away from the sun. **CAUTION** *Never look at the sun directly. Do not view the sun through the telescope. These actions could cause eye damage.*
2. Place the large cardboard box on the ground about 15 centimeters in front of the telescope's eyepiece.
3. Use the pencil to punch a hole in one side of the small cardboard box. Tape a sheet of white paper inside the opposite end of the box, as shown in the illustration on this page.
4. Place the small box on top of the large box so that its front is open for viewing. The hole in the small box should face the eyepiece of the telescope. Adjust the telescope so that the eyepiece, the hole, and the white paper are aligned.

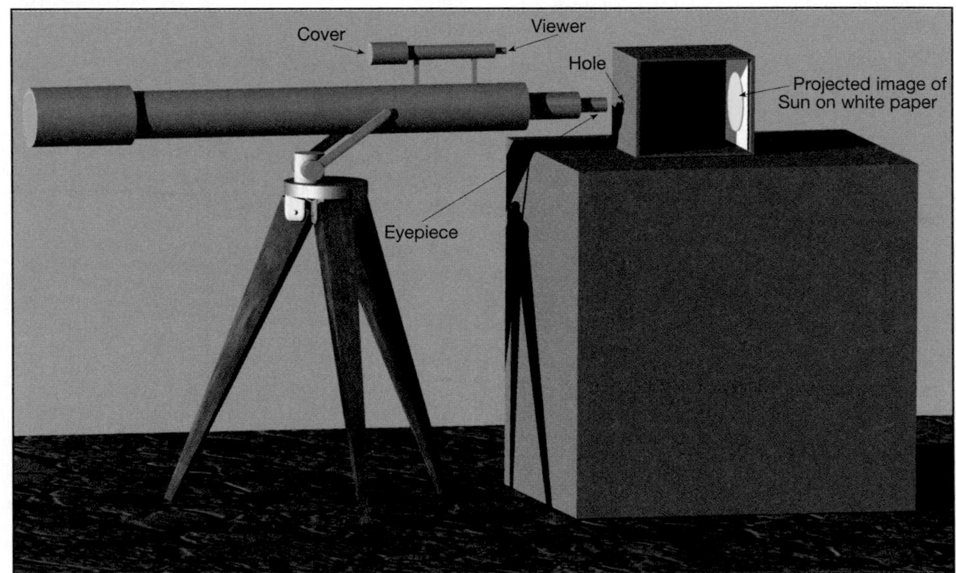

5. Adjust the small box until you see an image of the sun projected onto the paper. You may adjust the telescope to obtain a clearer image, but do not look through the viewer to accomplish this. You may also vary the distance between the box and the telescope to obtain better images.
6. Record the number of sunspots that you observe in a data table similar to the one below. Trace the outlines of sunspots on the paper. Shade in the sunspots and use the ruler to measure their size.
7. As weather permits, make several more viewings of sunspots over the course of the next few days. During each viewing, repeat steps 1–6. Be sure to note the movement of the sunspots.

Analyze and Conclude

1. **Making Graphs** How many sunspots did you observe? Make a line graph of your data using your data table.
2. **Observing** How did the number of sunspots vary over the course of your observations?
3. **Interpreting Data** Why did the sunspots move?

Go Further The diameter of the sun is approximately 1.35 million kilometers. Use this number to develop a scale to estimate the sizes of the sunspots.

Sample Data Table

Day	Number of Sunspots	Movement?
1		
2		
3		
4		
5		

Analyze and Conclude

1. Sample answer: about 15 large sunspots; check students' graphs.
2. Sample answer: The number of sunspots remained fairly steady over the course of the observations.
3. The sunspots moved because the sun rotates on its axis.

Go Further

Sample answer: A possible scale might be 1 mm = 10,000 km. The estimated size of a large sunspot might be 60,000 km.
Visual, Logical

Study Guide

Study Tip

Choose a Quiet Place to Study
Tell students that they will absorb concepts better if they study in a quiet place. Stress that they should minimize distractions, such as radios, CD players, and televisions.

Thinking Visually

a. reflecting
b. lens

CHAPTER 24

Study Guide

24.1 The Study of Light

Key Concepts

- Electromagnetic radiation includes gamma rays, X-rays, ultraviolet light, visible light, infrared radiation, microwaves, and radio waves.
- When the spectrum of a star is studied, the spectral lines act as "fingerprints." These lines identify the elements present and thus the star's chemical composition.
- In astronomy, the Doppler effect is used to determine whether a star or other body in space is moving away from or toward Earth.

Vocabulary

electromagnetic spectrum, *p. 674;* photon, *p. 675;* spectroscopy, *p. 676;* continuous spectrum, *p. 676;* absorption spectrum, *p. 676;* emission spectrum, *p. 676;* Doppler effect, *p. 677*

24.2 Tools for Studying Space

Key Concepts

- In a refracting telescope, the objective lens produces an image by bending light from a distant object in such a way that the light converges at an area called the focus.
- Most large optical telescopes are reflectors. Light does not pass through a mirror so the glass for a reflecting telescope does not have to be of optical quality. This means chromatic aberration is not a problem.
- A radio telescope focuses the incoming radio waves on an antenna, which absorbs and transmits these waves to an amplifier, just like any radio antenna.
- Space telescopes orbit above Earth's atmosphere and thus produce clearer images than Earth-based telescopes.

Vocabulary

refracting telescope, *p. 678;* chromatic aberration, *p. 679;* reflecting telescope, *p. 680;* radio telescope, *p. 681*

24.3 The Sun

Key Concepts

- The sun can be divided into four parts: the solar interior; the visible surface, or photosphere; and two atmospheric layers, the chromosphere and corona.
- Sunspots appear dark because of their temperature, which is about 1500 K less than that of the surrounding solar surface.
- Prominences are ionized gases trapped by magnetic fields that extend from regions of intense solar activity.
- Solar flares release enormous amounts of energy, much of it in the form of ultraviolet, radio, and X-ray radiation.
- During nuclear fusion, energy is released because some matter is converted to energy.

Vocabulary

photosphere, *p. 685;* chromosphere, *p. 686;* corona, *p. 686;* solar wind, *p. 686;* sunspot, *p. 687;* prominence, *p. 688;* solar flare, *p. 688;* aurora, *p. 688;* nuclear fusion, *p. 689*

Thinking Visually

Concept Map Use information from the chapter to complete the concept map below.

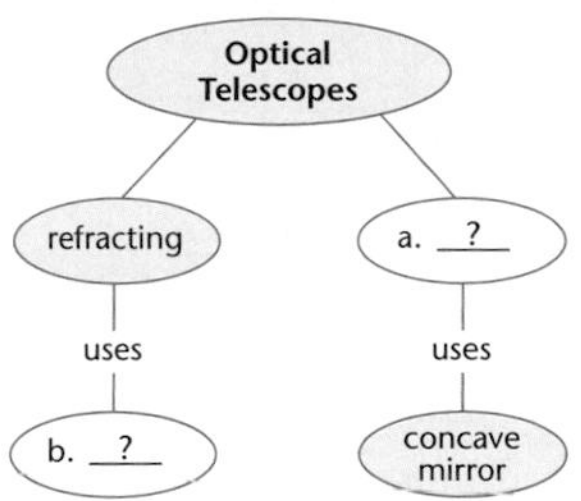

Chapter Assessment Resources

Print
Chapter Test, Chapter 24
Test Prep Resources, Chapter 24

Technology
Computer Test Bank, Chapter 24 Test
Online Text, Chapter 24
Go Online, PHSchool.com, Chapter 24

CHAPTER 24

NY Regents Content Item

Assessment

Interactive textbook with assessment at PHSchool.com 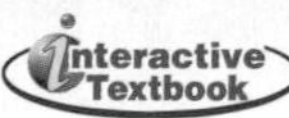

Reviewing Content

Choose the number that best answers the question or completes the statement.

1 Which type of radiation has the shortest wavelength? NY
(1) gamma rays (2) X-rays
(3) visible light (4) radio waves

2 The energy of a photon is related to its NY
(1) size (2) mass
(3) density (4) wavelength

3 As light passes through a prism, which color will bend the most?
(1) red (2) violet
(3) yellow (4) blue

4 Which type of telescope uses a concave mirror?
(1) refracting (2) reflecting
(3) ultraviolet (4) infrared

5 Which of the following is not a property of optical telescopes?
(1) resolving power
(2) magnifying power
(3) reflecting power
(4) light-gathering power

6 When several radio telescopes are wired together, the resulting network is called a radio
(1) receiver
(2) interferometer
(3) tuner
(4) antenna

7 The numerous, relatively small bright markings on the sun's photosphere are called
(1) auroras (2) sunspots
(3) granules (4) prominences

8 The thin, red rim seen around the sun during a total solar eclipse is the
(1) chromosphere (2) corona
(3) solar wind (4) photosphere

9 Which features of the sun look like huge cloudlike arches?
(1) solar flares (2) sunspots
(3) auroras (4) prominences

10 What is the source of the sun's energy? NY
(1) magnetism
(2) nuclear fission
(3) nuclear fusion
(4) radiation pressure

Understanding Concepts

11 What two factors determine how radiation is arranged on the electromagnetic spectrum?

12 Which color has the longest wavelength? The shortest? NY

13 Compare and contrast the wave theory and the particle theory of light.

14 Describe a continuous spectrum. Give an example of a natural phenomenon that exhibits a continuous spectrum.

15 Which type of spectrum do most stars have?

16 What optical defect is associated with refracting telescopes?

17 What three properties do optical telescopes have that aid astronomers?

18 What are some advantages of radio telescopes over optical telescopes?

19 List three space telescopes and describe the type of radiation studied by each.

20 Compare the diameter of the sun to that of Earth. NY

21 What is solar wind? NY

22 What "fuel" does the sun consume? NY

23 What happens to the matter that is consumed in nuclear fusion? NY

Homework Guide

Section	Questions
1	1–3, 11–15, 24, 32
2	4–6, 16–19, 25, 33
3	7–10, 20–23, 26–31, 34

Assessment

Reviewing Content

(1) 1 (2) 4 (3) 2
(4) 2 (5) 3 (6) 2
(7) 3 (8) 1 (9) 4
(10) 3

Understanding Concepts

(11) wavelength and frequency
(12) red; violet
(13) The wave theory states that light can be thought of as swells in the ocean. This motion is characterized by a property known as wavelength, which is the distance from one wave crest to the next. The particle theory states that light sometimes acts like a stream of particles, called photons, that push on matter, exerting radiation pressure.
(14) A continuous spectrum is produced by an incandescent solid, liquid, or gas under high pressure. One example would be light generated by a common light bulb.
(15) Most stars have an absorption, or dark-line, spectrum.
(16) chromatic aberration
(17) light-gathering power, resolving power, and magnifying power
(18) Radio telescopes can operate 24 hours a day, are generally cheaper to construct, and can "see" through interstellar dust clouds.
(19) The Hubble Space Telescope studies visible and ultraviolet light. The Chandra X-Ray Observatory studies X-rays. The Compton Gamma-Ray Observatory studied both gamma rays and visible light. The James Webb Space telescope will study infrared radiation.
(20) The diameter of the sun is equal to 109 Earth diameters.
(21) Streams of protons and electrons that boil from the corona and travel outward through the solar system at high speeds constitute the solar wind.
(22) hydrogen
(23) The hydrogen nuclei are converted to helium nuclei with a small percentage of the matter converted to energy.

Chapter 24

Critical Thinking

(24) Larger Doppler shifts indicate higher speeds; smaller Doppler shifts indicate slower speeds.
(25) The absence of an atmosphere on the moon would greatly increase the resolving power of a telescope.
(26) Hot gases rise to the photosphere, forming granules. Granules cool, darken, and sink back into the sun's interior. Each granule lasts only 10 to 20 minutes. New granules constantly replace old ones. The up-and-down motion gives the photosphere a boiling appearance.
(27) The solar wind is made up of photons, or streams of particles, that travel outward from the corona. Thus, it supports the particle theory of light.

Analyzing Data

(28) The lowest sunspot activity occurred around 1712 and 1811. The highest sunspot activity occurred around 1990.
(29) Sunspot activity peaks about every 11 years. Some peak years have relatively few sunspots, while others have many.
(30) The last peak occurred in 2001. The next peak will occur about 11 years later, or in 2012.
(31) No, it is not possible to predict how many sunspots will occur in a given peak year because the number of sunspots changes with every cycle. Some peak years have close to 200 sunspots, while other peak years have less than 50.

Concepts in Action

(32) The star is moving away from Earth.
(33) Telescopes with large lenses or mirrors intercept more light and produce brighter images. Consequently, large telescopes can view very dim objects, which are often located at great distances. Also, large telescopes have greater resolving powers than do telescopes with smaller objectives.
(34) A strong solar flare has occurred on the sun.

CHAPTER 24

Assessment *continued*

Critical Thinking

24 **Summarizing** Briefly summarize the relationship between Doppler shift and the speed of a moving object. NY

25 **Inferring** Why would the moon make a good site for an observatory? NY

26 **Relating Cause and Effect** The photosphere has a boiling appearance. Why?

27 **Drawing Conclusions** The solar wind can be thought of as evidence for which theory of light? Explain your answer.

Analyzing Data

Use the graph to answer questions 28–31.

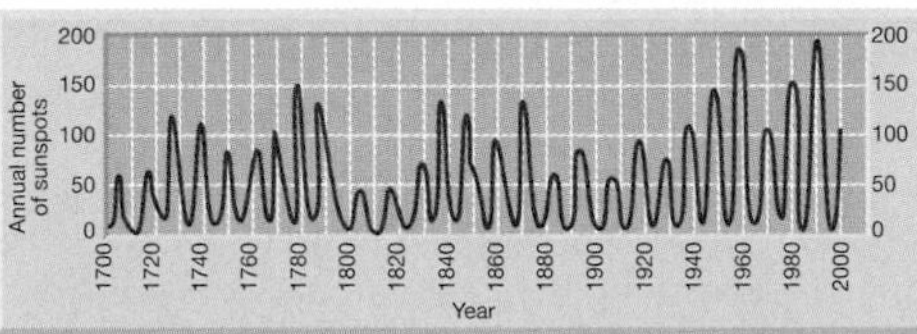

28 **Identifying** Which years had the lowest number of sunspots? The highest? NY

29 **Interpreting Data** Describe any patterns in the data. NY

30 **Predicting** When will the next period of maximum sunspot activity occur? NY

31 **Analyzing Data** Based on the data alone, is it possible to predict how many sunspots will occur during the next peak? Why or why not? NY

Concepts in Action

32 **Inferring** What can you infer about a star that exhibits a red shift in its spectra? NY

33 **Explaining** Why do astronomers seek to design telescopes with larger and larger objectives?

34 **Relating Cause and Effect** What could you infer about solar activity if you spotted an aurora that lasted several nights?

Performance-Based Assessment

Oral Presentation The sun is Earth's main source of energy. Work in a group to develop a presentation describing what might happen if the sun's energy increased by 10 percent. Discuss the effects on global temperatures, ocean shorelines, and polar caps. Be sure to consider changes in the amount of surface vegetation, and the impact of these changes on levels of atmospheric carbon dioxide.

Regents Practice Exam

Test-Taking Tip

Scientific Drawings

Some test questions may include a drawing of a scientific instrument, such as a telescope, or an object studied by scientists, such as the sun. It is important that you carefully study the information presented in the question, as well as the picture provided. Keep these tips in mind when answering a question with drawings of objects or scientific instruments.

- Identify the item shown so you can determine what information the drawing can provide.
- Think of similar drawings or questions you have seen. These may help you determine information available from the drawing.
- The illustrations may not be drawn to scale. You must read and interpret the scales carefully.
- Carefully read the question. You may not need all the information. You may need more information than is presented in the drawing.

Practice using these tips in questions 7 and 8.

For *each* statement or question, choose the *number* of the word or expression that, of those given, best completes the statement or answers the question. Some questions may require the use of the *Earth Science Reference Tables.*

1 Which of the following is NOT considered a form of electromagnetic radiation?
(1) radio waves
(2) gravity
(3) gamma rays
(4) visible light

2 Which color has the longest wavelength?
(1) blue (2) green (3) violet (4) red

3 The sun produces energy by
(1) nuclear fusion of oxygen nuclei into carbon dioxide
(2) converting oxygen nuclei into nitrogen nuclei
(3) nuclear fusion of hydrogen nuclei into helium nuclei
(4) nuclear fission of helium nuclei into hydrogen nuclei

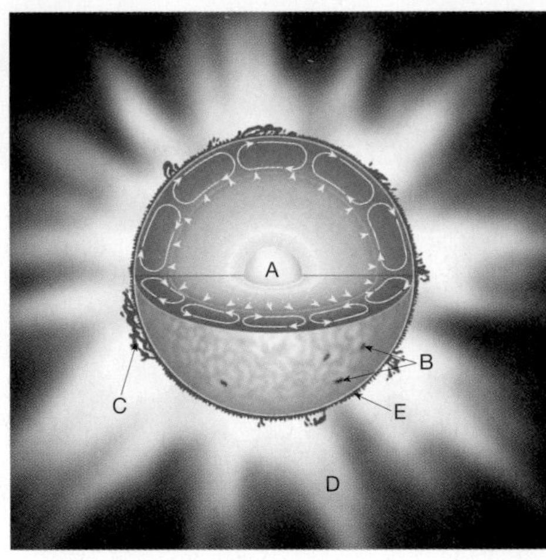

4 Why does the sun appear to rise in the east and set in the west?
(1) The sun rotates on its axis.
(2) The sun moves around the Earth.
(3) Earth revolves around the sun.
(4) Earth rotates on its axis.

5 Distant galaxies exhibit a red shift in their bright line spectra because
(1) they are moving toward Earth
(2) they are moving away from Earth
(3) they are very far away
(4) they are exploding

Answer the following questions in complete sentences. Some questions may require the use of the *Earth Science Reference Tables.* Base your answers to questions 7 and 8 on the diagram above, which shows the Structure of the Sun.

6 Explain why the Doppler effect causes objects moving away from Earth to appear more red.

7 What is the innermost layer of the sun called? What is the outermost layer called? How does the temperature change as you move from the innermost to the outermost layer of the sun?

8 Which letters represent features found on the sun's surface? Identify each feature.

Regents Practice Exam

(1) 2
(2) 4
(3) 3
(4) 4
(5) 2
(6) From our perspective on Earth, objects moving away from Earth have their wavelengths stretched out. Since the red end of the spectrum contains the longer wavelengths, objects moving away from the observer appear more red.
(7) The innermost layer of the sun is called the core. The outmost layer of the sun is called the corona. As you move from the core to the corona the temperature decreases.
(8) *B* is sunspots, and *C* is a prominence.

Performance-Based Assessment

Students should note that if the sun's energy increased by 10 percent, global temperatures would increase. Polar caps would melt and sea level would rise. Shorelines would move inland. Warmer temperatures would also produce an increase in vegetation, which, in turn, would remove more carbon dioxide from the air during photosynthesis. Because carbon dioxide is a greenhouse gas, a reduction in the amount of carbon dioxide would decrease global temperatures.

Your students can independently test their knowledge of the chapter and print out their results.

CHAPTER 25

Planning Guide

Use these planning tools
Use Teacher Express for all your planning needs

SECTION OBJECTIVES	STANDARDS NATIONAL	STANDARDS STATE	ACTIVITIES and LABS
25.1 Properties of Stars, pp. 700–706 1 block or 2 periods **25.1** **Describe** what astronomers can learn by studying star properties. **25.2** **Explain** how distance affects parallax. **25.3** **List** the factors that determine a star's apparent magnitude. **25.4** **Describe** the relationship shown on a Hertzprung-Russell diagram.	A-1, A-2, B-5, D-4, G-3		**SE** Inquiry Activity: How Do Astronomers Measure Distance to Nearby Stars? p. 699 L2 **TE** Teacher Demo: Binary Star Motion, p. 701 L2 **TE** Teacher Demo: Apparent and Absolute Magnitude, p. 703 L2 **SE** SE Exploration Lab: Observing Stars, p. 723 L2
25.2 Stellar Evolution, pp. 707–714 1 block or 2 periods **25.5** **Identify** which stage marks the birth of a star. **25.6** **Explain** why all stars eventually die. **25.7** **List** the stages of the sun's life cycle.	A-2, B-1, B-3, B-4, B-6, D-4 G-2, G-3		**TE** Build Science Skills, p. 707 L2 **TE** Teacher Demo: Modeling a Pulsar, p. 713 L2 **LM** Modeling the Rotation of Neutron Stars L3
25.3 The Universe, pp. 715–721 1 block or 2 periods **25.8** **Describe** the size and structure of the Milky Way Galaxy. **25.9** **List** the ways in which galaxies differ from one another. **25.10** **Cite** the evidence that indicates that the universe is expanding. **25.11** **Describe** how the universe began according to the big bang theory.	A-1, A-2, D-4 E-2, G-1, G-3		**TE** Build Science Skills, p. 716 L2 **TE** Build Science Skills, p. 717 L2 **TE** Teacher Demo: "Stretching" Light Waves, p. 718 L2 **TE** Build Science Skills, p. 719 L2

Ability Levels

- **L1** For students who need additional help
- **L2** For all students
- **L3** For students who need to be challenged

Components

SE	Student Edition	**GRSW**	Guided Reading & Study Workbook	**TP**	Test Prep Resources	**GEO**	Geode CD-ROM
TE	Teacher's Edition	**TEX**	Teacher Express	**onT**	onlineText	**T**	Transparencies
LM	Laboratory Manual	**CTB**	Computer Test Bank	**DC**	Discovery Channel Videos	**GO**	Internet Resources
CUT	Chapter Tests						

RESOURCES PRINT and TECHNOLOGY	SECTION ASSESSMENT
GRSW Section 25.1 **T-358** Geometry of Stellar Parallax **T-359** Ratios of Star Brightness **T-360** Distance, Apparent Magnitude, and Absolute Magnitude of Some Stars **T-361** Orbit of Binary Stars **T-362** Hertzsprung-Russell Diagram **TEX** Lesson Planning 25.1	**SE** Section 25.1 Assessment, p. 706 **onT** Section 25.1
GRSW Section 25.2 **T-363** Stellar Evolution **T-364** Summary of Evolution of Stars of Various Masses **T-365** Evolutionary Stages of Stars **DC** Stars: Life and Death **TEX** Lesson Planning 25.2	**SE** Section 25.2 Assessment, p. 714 **onT** Section 25.2
GRSW Section 25.3 **T-366** Possible Function of a Binary Pair **T-367** Partial Structure of the Milky Way Galaxy **T-368** Raisin Bread Analogy **T-369** Light Period and Absolute Magnitude **TEX** Lesson Planning 25.3	**SE** Section 25.3 Assessment, p. 721 **onT** Section 25.3

Go Online

Go online for these Internet resources.

PHSchool.com
Web Code: cjk-9999

NSTA SCiLINKS
Web Code: cjn-7252
Web Code: cjn-7253

Materials for Activities and Labs

Quantities for each group

STUDENT EDITION

Exploration Lab, p. 723
star charts (in the Appendix), penlight, notebook

TEACHER'S EDITION

Teacher Demo, p. 701
string, tape, 2 tennis balls, pencil, table tennis ball

Teacher Demo, p. 703
2 equally bright flashlights, 1 dimmer flashlight

Build Science Skills, p. 707
series of photographs of people of different ages, series of photographs of the life cycle of an insect such as a butterfly that undergoes complete metamorphosis

Integrate Physics, p. 713
balloon

Teacher Demo, p. 713
string; long, thin flashlight

Build Science Skills, p. 716
sharp pencil, sheet of paper, tape, cardboard

Build Science Skills, p. 717
cotton balls, coat hangers, and other materials of students' choice

Teacher Demo, p. 718
old bicycle inner tube, scissors, chalk

Build Science Skills, p. 719
Slinky™ toy

Chapter Assessment

ASSESSMENT

SE Assessment, pp. 725–726
CUT Chapter 25 Test
CTB Chapter 25
onT Chapter 25

STANDARDIZED TEST PREP

SE Chapter 25, p. 727
TP Progress Monitoring Assessments

interactive textbook with assessment at PHSchool.com

CHAPTER 25

Before you teach

Michael Wysession
Washington University

Big Ideas

Our sun is one of about 100 billion stars in the Milky Way galaxy, which may be one of about 125 billion galaxies in the universe. The universe formed about 13.7 billion years ago from the big bang, and is still rapidly expanding.

Space and Time Galaxies exist in spiral, elliptical, or irregular forms. The Milky Way is about 100,000 light years across and contains about 100 billion stars. Galaxies are often found in groups called galaxy clusters.

Forces and Motion Stars form from the dust and gas of interstellar matter that gets pulled together by the force of gravity. For about 90 percent of its life, a star will fuse hydrogen to make helium during its main-sequence stage. During a supergiant phase, some stars expand to enormous size because their outer layers are forced outward from radiation emitted by a contracting core. For some stars, a final supernova phase follows the completion of fusion reactions, resulting in an implosion that creates a shock wave and ejects heavier elements into space.

Matter and Energy The color of stars is an indication of their temperature. Binary star orbits can be used to find the mass of the stars. The mass of a star determines its evolution. Low-mass stars last a long time, but massive stars have short lives. Low-mass and medium-mass stars end as white dwarves. Massive stars go through supergiant and supernova phases, and end as neutron stars or black holes.

Earth Science Refresher

The Birth of the Universe

Using the laws of physics, scientists have been able to reconstruct the infancy of our universe, starting a fraction of a second after the big bang. What happened at the instant of the big bang remains a mystery, because the laws of physics break down when all of space and time collapse to a single point. But once our universe got its start, we have a fairly good idea of what might have happened.

Our universe began extremely small and extremely hot—so hot, in fact that there was no matter, only radiated energy. As the universe expanded, it cooled, and the radiation began to convert into matter. By 10^{-32} seconds after the big bang, there were particles like electrons and quarks, but the quarks had not yet come together to form protons and neutrons. At this time, the temperature of the universe was 3×10^{26} K, and it was about 30 cm across—the size of a beach ball!

By 10^{-5} seconds after the big bang (1/100,000 of a second), the sub-atomic particles called quarks were able to combine to make protons and neutrons. At this time, the temperature of the universe was 10^{13} K, and it was about 0.002 light-years across (this is about 100 times the current distance from Earth to the sun).

Address Misconceptions

Students are often confused by the term light-year *and think that it is a unit of time. Explain that the "year" refers to the time that bit takes for light to travel the distance known as a* light-year. For a strategy that helps to overcome this misconception, see **Address Misconceptions** on **p. 702.**

Go Online PDLINKS NSTA
For: Chapter 25 Content Support
Visit: www.SciLinks.org/PDLinks
Web Code: cjn-2599

By three minutes after the big bang, the universe had cooled enough that the neutrons and protons could combine to make atomic nuclei, of which were about 75 percent hydrogen nuclei and 25 percent helium nuclei. At this point in time, the temperature of the universe was 10^9 K (1 trillion degrees), and it was about 50 light-years across.

By 10,000 years after the big bang, the universe had cooled to the point that the energy of the radiation was less than the energy of matter (atomic particles). At this time, the temperature of the universe was 30,000 K, and it was about 2 million light-years across.

By 300,000 years after the big bang, the atomic nuclei were able to combine with electrons to make the first true atoms. This stage is called decoupling, because the radiation was separated from the atomic particles, allowing light to travel unhindered by the free-flying electrons. This is as far back in time as a telescope like the Hubble telescope could ever see. At this point in time, the temperature of the radiation within the universe was only 5000 K, and the universe was already 15 million light-years across.

The first stars and protogalaxies formed after about a billion years, and the first galactic disks formed about 3 billion years after the big bang. Now, 13.7 billion years after the big bang, the universe has expanded so much that radiation left over from the big bang is in the form of microwaves traveling through space with a very low temperature of only 2.7° above absolute zero.

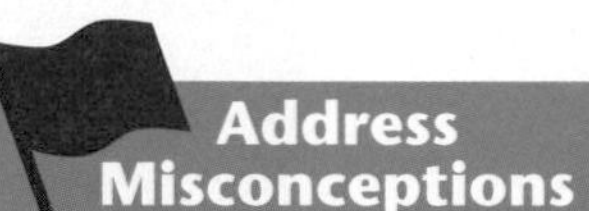

Address Misconceptions

Students may think that the big bang occurred at a certain point at the center of the universe. They may also think that material from the big bang exploded into already existing space. For a strategy that helps to overcome this misconception, see **Address Misconceptions** on **p. 720.**

Build Reading Literacy

Sequence

Ordering Events

Strategy Help students understand and visualize the steps in a process, or the order in which events occur. Sequences frequently involve cause-effect relationships. Readers can construct graphic organizers to help them visualize and comprehend a sequence. For most sequences, flowcharts are the graphic of choice. However, cycle diagrams are more appropriate for cycles. Before students begin, locate in the text a several-step process or a chain of causes and effects, such as the passage, Star Birth, on pp. 707–709 and the figure, Life Cycle of Sunlike Star, on p. 709.

Example

1. Have students read the passage, thinking about what takes place first, second, third, and so on. Point out that the text will not always use order words such as *first*, *next*, *then*, and *finally*.

2. Review the passage, listing the steps or events in order.

3. If the passage describes a chain of steps or events, draw a flowchart on the board, having students tell the sequence of events, steps, or causes and effects, and writing each part of the process in a separate box.

4. If the passage describes a cycle, use a cycle diagram to show the sequence.

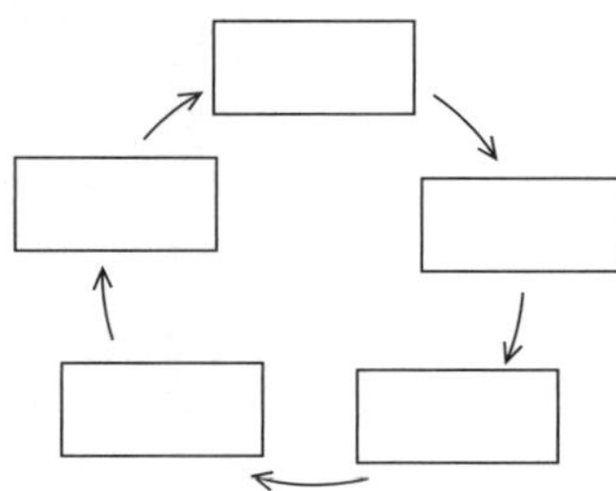

5. Have students locate additional examples of sequential relationships in the text or visuals of the chapter. Students can depict the steps or events using graphic organizers.

See p. 720 for a script on how to use this strategy with students. For additional strategies, see pp. 703 and 708.

ASTRONOMY

Chapter 25

ASSESS PRIOR KNOWLEDGE

Use the Chapter Pretest below to assess students' prior knowledge. As needed, review these concepts.

Review Science Concepts

Section 25.1 Review temperature scales and how the Kelvin scale is related to the Celsius and Fahrenheit scales.

Section 25.2 Review the concept of fusion from physics. Also review the structure of the atom and what protons, neutrons, and electrons are.

Section 25.3 Review electromagnetic radiation and the Doppler effect.

CHAPTER 25 Beyond Our Solar System

CONCEPTS in Action

Exploration Lab
Observing Stars

Understanding Earth
Astrology—Forerunner of Astronomy

Video Field Trip
Stars: Life and Death

Take a field trip through outer space with Discovery Channel and find out how stars are born, and why they die. Answer the following questions after watching the video.

1. What happens when a star runs out of hydrogen fuel?
2. Describe what will happen to the sun when it dies.

Go Online PHSchool.com

For: Chapter 25 Resources
Visit: PHSchool.com
Web Code: cjk-9999

Stars embedded in clouds of dust and gases produce colorful nebulae. ▶

698 *Chapter 25*

Chapter Pretest

1. To what Celsius temperature is 400 K equivalent? *(d)*
   a. 400°C
   b. 800°C
   c. 273°C
   d. 127°C
2. What happens during nuclear fusion? *(Less massive nuclei are forced together to form a more massive nucleus.)*
3. What is the nucleus of a helium atom made up of? *(b)*
   a. protons and electrons
   b. protons and neutrons
   c. neutrons and electrons
   d. protons only
4. True or False: Electrons are small positively charged particles. *(False)*
5. If a light source is moving toward you at a very high speed, how will the light from it be affected? *(It will be shifted toward the blue.)*
6. True or False: Visible light is a form of electromagnetic radiation. *(True)*

Chapter Preview

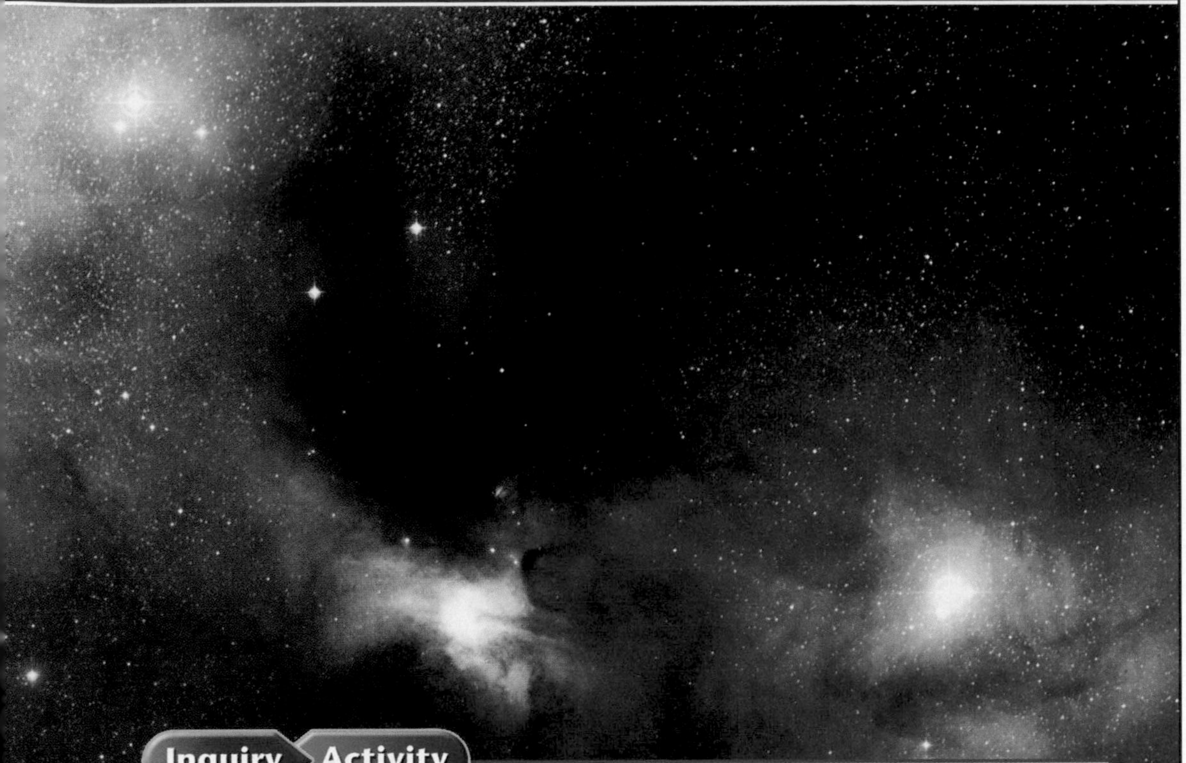

Inquiry Activity

How Do Astronomers Measure Distances to Nearby Stars?

Procedure

1. Close your left eye. With your index finger in a vertical position, use your right eye to line up your finger with a distant object, such as a tree.
2. Without moving your finger, view the object with your left eye opened and your right eye closed.

Think About It

1. **Observing** What happened to the position of your finger when you observed it with your left eye?
2. **Predicting** What might happen if you repeated the activity, holding your finger farther from your eyes? Test your prediction.

Video Field Trip

Stars: Life and Death

Encourage students to view the Video Field Trip "Stars: Life and Death."

ENGAGE/EXPLORE

How Do Astronomers Measure Distances to Nearby Stars? L2

Purpose Students will infer the considerations astronomers must make when measuring distances to nearby stars.

Skills Focus **Observing, Predicting, Inferring**

Class Time 5–10 minutes

Teaching Tip Assist visually impaired students by describing what occurs when doing the activity.

Expected Outcome Students' fingers will appear to shift.

Think About It

1. The finger appeared to shift to the right.
2. The farther away you hold your finger, the less its position seems to shift.

Section 25.1

1 FOCUS

Section Objectives

25.1 **Describe** what astronomers can learn by studying star properties.

25.2 **Explain** how distance affects parallax.

25.3 **List** the factors that determine a star's apparent magnitude.

25.4 **Describe** the relationship shown on a Hertzprung-Russell diagram.

Reading Focus

Build Vocabulary L2

Word Parts and Roots Have students look up the prefix *bi-* to help them understand what *binary* means. (*"two," "having two distinct parts"*) Have them look up the origin of *nova* and relate it to its meaning. (*from the Latin* novus, *meaning "new"; refers to a bright star that suddenly appears in the sky*) Also have them look up the meaning of *nebulous* and relate it to the meaning of *nebula*. (*"lacking definite form or limits"; describes the appearance of a nebula*)

Reading Strategy L2

Possible answers:
a. What information does the H-R diagram show?
b. absolute magnitude and temperature
c. What is the largest group of stars on the H-R diagram?
d. the main sequence

2 INSTRUCT

Integrate Language Arts L2

Greek Mythology Tell students that many of the constellations were named by the ancient Greeks after characters in stories. Other peoples, such as Native Americans, had different names and stories associated with various star patterns. Ask students to each research a different constellation and write a paragraph describing the story associated with it. Students can also make up their own patterns and stories if they wish.
Verbal

25.1 Properties of Stars

Reading Focus

Key Concepts

- What can we learn by studying star properties?
- How does distance affect parallax?
- What factors determine a star's apparent magnitude?
- What relationship is shown on a Hertzsprung-Russell diagram?

Vocabulary

- constellation
- binary star
- light-year
- apparent magnitude
- absolute magnitude
- main-sequence star
- red giant
- supergiant
- Cepheid variable
- nova
- nebulae

Reading Strategy

Previewing Copy the table below. Before you read, write two questions about the Hertzsprung-Russell diagram on page 704. As you read, write answers to your questions.

Questions about the Hertzsprung-Russell Diagram	
Question	Answer
a. ?	b. ?
c. ?	d. ?

The star Proxima Centauri is about 100 million times farther away from Earth than the moon. Yet, besides the sun, it is the closest star to Earth. The universe is incomprehensibly large. What is the nature of this vast universe? Do stars move, or do they remain in one place? Does the universe extend infinitely in all directions, or does it have boundaries? This chapter will answer these questions by examining the universe and the most numerous objects in the night sky—the stars.

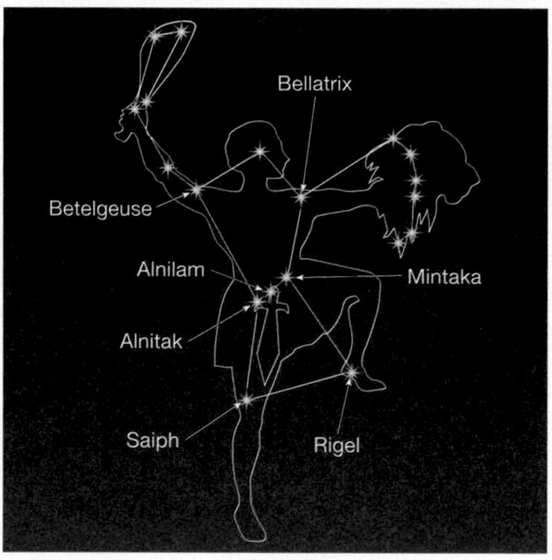

Figure 1 Orion The constellation Orion was named for a hunter.

As early as 5000 years ago, people became fascinated with the star-studded skies and began to name the patterns they saw. These patterns of stars, called **constellations,** were named in honor of mythological characters or great heroes, such as Orion, shown in Figure 1.

Although the stars that make up a constellation all appear to be the same distance from Earth, some are many times farther away than others. So, the stars in a particular constellation are not associated with one another in any physical way.

Today 88 constellations are recognized. They are used to divide the sky into units, just as state boundaries divide the United States. Every star in the sky is in, but is not necessarily part of, one of these constellations. Therefore, constellations can be used as a "map" of the night sky.

Characteristics of Stars

A great deal is known about the universe beyond our solar system. This knowledge hinges on the fact that stars, and even gases in the "empty" space between stars, radiate energy in all directions into space. The key to understanding the universe is to collect this radiation and unravel the secrets it holds. Astronomers have devised many ways to do just that. We will begin by examining some properties of stars, such as color, temperature, and mass.

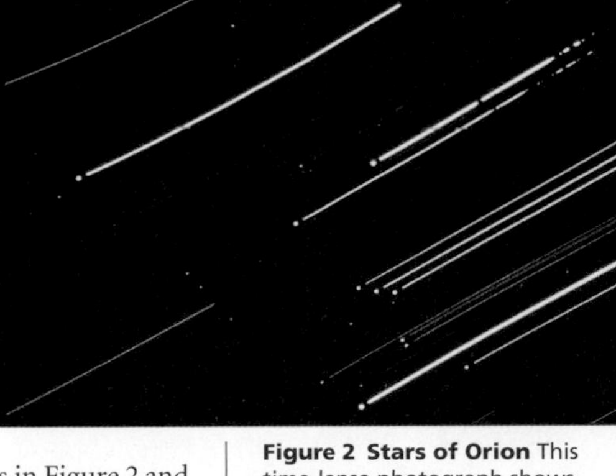

Figure 2 Stars of Orion This time-lapse photograph shows stars as streaks across the night sky as Earth rotates. The streaks clearly show different star colors.

Star Color and Temperature Study the stars in Figure 2 and note their color. **Color is a clue to a star's temperature.** Very hot stars with surface temperatures above 30,000 K emit most of their energy in the form of short-wavelength light and therefore appear blue. Red stars are much cooler, and most of their energy is emitted as longer-wavelength red light. Stars with temperatures between 5000 and 6000 K appear yellow, like the sun.

Binary Stars and Stellar Mass In the early nineteenth century, astronomers discovered that many stars orbit each other. These pairs of stars, pulled toward each other by gravity, are called **binary stars.** More than 50 percent of the stars in the universe may occur in pairs or multiples.

Binary stars are used to determine the star property most difficult to calculate—its mass. The mass of a body can be calculated if it is attached by gravity to a partner. This is the case for any binary star system. As shown in Figure 3, binary stars orbit each other around a common point called the center of mass. For stars of equal mass, the center of mass lies exactly halfway between them. If one star is more massive than its partner, their common center will be closer to the more massive one. If the sizes of their orbits are known, the stars' masses can be determined.

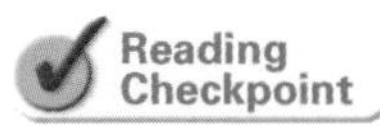

What is a binary star system?

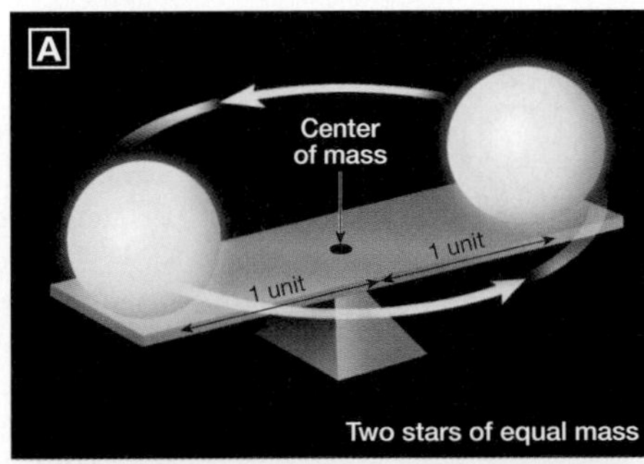

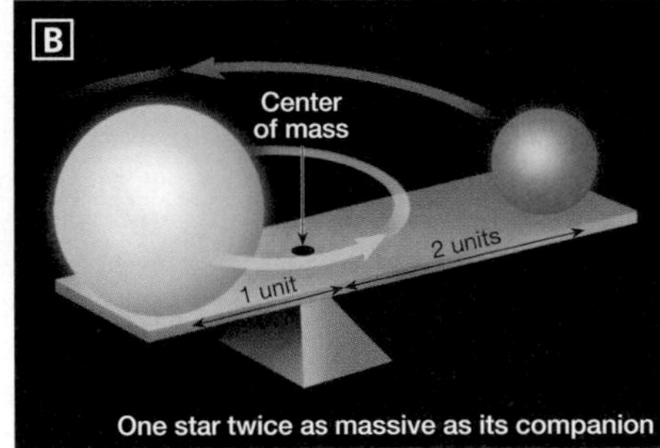

Figure 3 Common Center of Mass
A For stars of equal mass, the center of mass lies in the middle. **B** A star twice as massive as its partner is twice as close to the center of mass. It therefore has a smaller orbit than its less massive partner.

Customize for English Language Learners

Write each of the vocabulary words at the top of an index card and post them on a word wall. As students read the section, discuss the definitions of each term and add them to the index cards. Work with students to help them organize the words into groups based on their scientific meanings. Revisit the word wall and use it as an interactive tool to help students learn the terms. Refer to the words as often as you can and incorporate them into homework or other assignments.

Characteristics of Stars

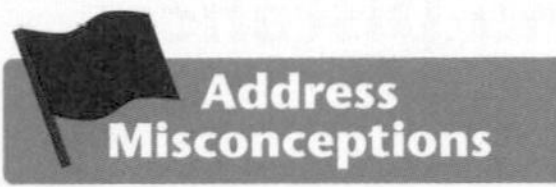

L2

Students often think that all stars are found alone in space, as the sun is. Explain that most stars are actually in pairs or larger groups. Fewer than half are single stars. Many familiar stars in the sky are actually multiple star systems. For example, the very bright star Sirius A has a dimmer companion, Sirius B. Alpha Centauri is actually a double star and forms a triple system along with Proxima Centauri.
Verbal

Teacher Demo

Binary Star Motion **L2**

Purpose Students observe how stars of equal and different masses revolve around a common center of mass.

Materials string, tape, 2 tennis balls, pencil, table tennis ball

Procedure Use string and tape to hang a tennis ball from one end of a pencil. Hang another tennis ball from the other end of the pencil. Tell students that the balls represent stars and the pencil represents gravity holding them together. Tie another string to the center of the pencil so that the pencil is balanced when hung from the string. Twist the string so that the balls rotate around each other. Ask students what figure in the text this represents. *(Figure 3A)* Ask them to predict what will happen if one of the balls is replaced with a smaller one. *(The center of mass will be closer to the large ball, and it will move less.)* Replace one tennis ball with a table tennis ball. Adjust the string on the pencil until it balances and sets the system rotating. Ask students what figure in the text this represents. *(Figure 3B)*

Expected Outcome The tennis balls will revolve around an equidistant center of mass. The tennis ball and table tennis ball will revolve around a center of mass close to the tennis ball.
Visual, Logical

Answer to . . .

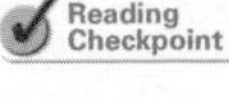

A binary star system is made up of two stars that orbit each other.

Section 25.1 (continued)

Measuring Distances to Stars

Use Visuals L1

Figure 4 Use this figure to explain how parallax works. Emphasize that the drawing is not to scale; the star would actually be much farther away and the parallax angle very small. Ask: **What does the simulated photograph at the top left show?** *(It shows the star as seen from Earth's original position.)* **What does the simulated photograph at the bottom left show?** *(It shows the star as seen from Earth 6 months later.)* **How is the parallax angle related to the distance between the star and Earth?** *(The farther away the star is, the smaller the angle.)*
Visual, Logical

L2

Students are often confused by the term *light-year* and think that it is a unit of time. Explain again that the "year" refers to the time it takes for light to travel the distance known as a *light-year*. Have students calculate the distance to Proxima Centauri in kilometers.
(4.3 light-years × 9.5×10^{12} km = ≈ 41×10^{12} km)
Logical

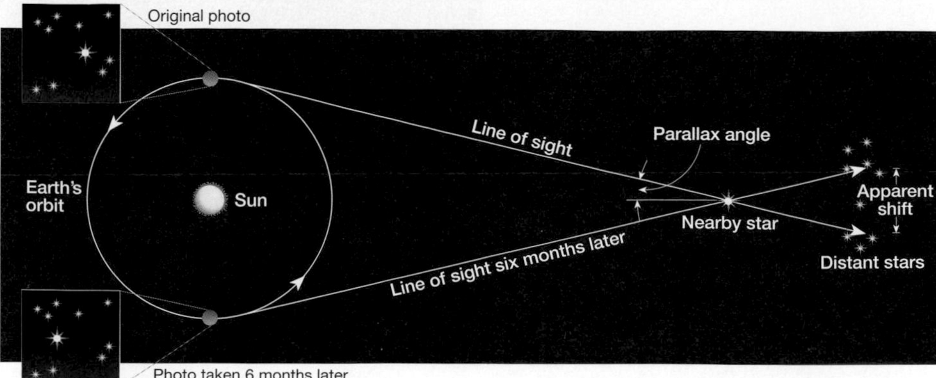

Figure 4 Parallax The parallax angle shown here is exaggerated to illustrate the principle. Because the distances to even the nearest stars are huge, astronomers work with very small angles.
Relating Cause and Effect ***What caused the star to appear to shift?***

Measuring Distances to Stars

Although measuring the distance to a star is very difficult, astronomers have developed some methods of determining stellar distances.

Parallax The most basic way to measure star distance is parallax. Parallax is the slight shifting in the apparent position of a nearby star due to the orbital motion of Earth. Parallax is determined by photographing a nearby star against the background of distant stars. Then, six months later, when Earth has moved halfway around its orbit, a second photograph is taken. When these photographs are compared, the position of the nearby star appears to have shifted with respect to the background stars. Figure 4 shows this shift and the resulting parallax angle.

The nearest stars have the largest parallax angles, while those of distant stars are too small to measure. In fact, all parallax angles are very small. The parallax angle to the nearest star (besides the sun), Proxima Centauri, is less than 1 second of arc, which equals 1/3600 of a degree. To put this in perspective, fully extend your arm and raise your little finger. Your finger is roughly 1 degree wide. Now imagine tracking a movement that is only 1/3600 as wide as your finger.

In principle, the method used to measure stellar distances may seem simple. But in practice, measurements are greatly complicated because of the tiny angles involved and because the sun, as well as the star being measured, also move through space. Even with today's technology, parallax angles for only a few thousand of the nearest stars are known with certainty.

Light-Year Distances to stars are so large that units such as kilometers or astronomical units are often too hard to use. A better unit to express stellar distance is the **light-year,** which is the distance light travels in one year—about 9.5×10^{12} or 9.5 trillion kilometers. Proxima Centauri is about 4.3 light-years away from the sun.

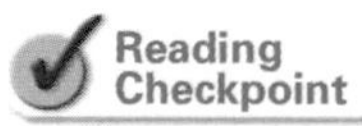

What is a light-year?

Stellar Brightness

The measure of a star's brightness is its magnitude. The stars in the night sky have an assortment of sizes, temperatures, and distances, so their brightnesses vary widely.

Apparent Magnitude Some stars may appear dimmer than others only because they are farther away. A star's brightness as it appears from Earth is called its **apparent magnitude.** **Three factors control the apparent brightness of a star as seen from Earth: how big it is, how hot it is, and how far away it is.**

Astronomers use numbers to rank apparent magnitude. The larger the number is, the dimmer the star. Just as we can compare the brightness of a 50-watt bulb to that of a 100-watt bulb, we can compare the brightness of stars having different magnitudes. A first-magnitude star is about 100 times brighter than a sixth-magnitude star. Therefore, two stars that differ by 5 magnitudes have a ratio in brightness of 100 to 1. It follows, then, that the brightness ratio of two stars differing by only one magnitude is about 2.5. A star of the first magnitude is about 2.5 times brighter than a star of the second magnitude.

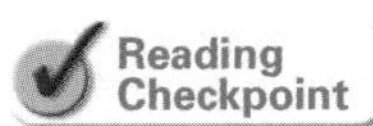

What is apparent magnitude?

Absolute Magnitude Astronomers are also interested in how bright a star actually is, or its **absolute magnitude.** Two stars of the same absolute magnitude usually do not have the same apparent magnitude because one may be much farther from us than the other. The one that is farther away will appear dimmer. To compare their absolute brightness, astronomers determine what magnitude the stars would have if they were at a standard distance of about 32.6 light-years. For example, the sun, which has an apparent magnitude of −26.7, would, if located at a distance of 32.6 light-years, have an absolute magnitude of about 5. Stars with absolute magnitude values lower than 5 are actually brighter than the sun. Because of their distance, however, they appear much dimmer. Table 1 lists the absolute and apparent magnitudes of some stars as well as their distances from Earth.

Table 1 Distance, Apparent Magnitude, and Absolute Magnitude of Some Stars

Name	Distance (light-years)	Apparent Magnitude*	Absolute Magnitude*
Sun	NA	−26.7	5.0
Alpha Centauri	4.27	0.0	4.4
Sirius	8.70	−1.4	1.5
Arcturus	36	−0.1	−0.3
Betelgeuse	520	0.8	−5.5
Deneb	1600	1.3	−6.9

*The more negative, the brighter; the more positive, the dimmer.

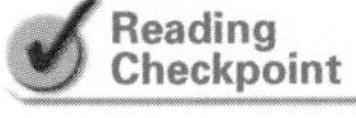

What is absolute magnitude?

Stellar Brightness

Build Reading Literacy L1

Refer to **p. 216D** in **Chapter 8,** which provides guidelines for comparing and contrasting.

Compare and Contrast Have students create and fill in a table to compare and contrast apparent and absolute magnitude. They should consider what determines the value of apparent and absolute magnitude and whether each one is a relative value or an absolute value.
Visual

Teacher Demo

Apparent and Absolute Magnitude L2

Purpose Students observe the difference between apparent and absolute magnitude.

Materials 2 equally bright flashlights, 1 dimmer flashlight

Procedure Place two equally bright flashlights near the front of the class, one as close to the students as possible and one as far away as possible. Dim the lights and turn the flashlights on. Ask: **Which flashlight has the greater apparent magnitude?***(the closer one)* **Which flashlight has the lower apparent magnitude?** *(the more distant one)* Place the two flashlights side by side. Ask: **How do the flashlights' apparent magnitudes compare?** *(They are the same.)* **How do the flashlights' absolute magnitudes compare?** *(They are the same.)* Replace one flashlight with a dimmer one. Ask: **Which flashlight has the greater apparent magnitude?** *(the brighter one)* **Which flashlight has the greater absolute magnitude?** *(the brighter one)*

Expected Outcome Students will observe how distance and brightness affect apparent and absolute magnitude.
Visual

Facts and Figures

Stars were first classified according to their brightness around the second century B.C., when the Greek astronomer Hipparchus classified about 1000 stars into six categories. In 1989, the European Space Agency launched the satellite Hipparcos (High Precision Parallax Collecting Satellite). Hipparcos used parallax to measure the distances to all visible stars within about 150 light-years of the sun. The accuracy of the measurements was about 2 milliarcseconds, or within 10 percent.

Answer to . . .

Figure 4 *Earth moved in its orbit.*

the distance light travels in one year—about 9.5 trillion km

the brightness of a star as seen from Earth

how bright a star actually is

Hertzsprung-Russell Diagram

Address Misconceptions L2

Students often think that the H-R diagram is a star chart that shows the locations of stars in the sky. Emphasize that the H-R diagram is a graph that shows the characteristics of stars. Go over the units shown on the axes so that students understand why it is a graph. Explain that the stars are shown different sizes on the graph for illustration only. Also explain that an H-R diagram can be used to plot any sample of stars.
Visual

Use Visuals L1

Figure 5 Use this diagram to explain the main groups of stars on the H-R diagram. Ask: **To what group of stars does the sun belong?** *(It belongs to the main sequence.)* **How are absolute magnitude and temperature related within the main sequence?** *(As absolute magnitude increases, so does temperature.)* **What types of stars have high absolute magnitude but low temperature?** *(giants and supergiants)* **What types of stars have low absolute magnitudes and medium temperatures?** *(white dwarfs)*
Visual, Logical

Hertzsprung-Russell Diagram

Early in the twentieth century, Einar Hertzsprung and Henry Russell independently developed a graph used to study stars. It is now called a Hertzsprung-Russell diagram (H-R diagram). **A Hertzsprung-Russell diagram shows the relationship between the absolute magnitude and temperature of stars.** By studying H-R diagrams, we learn a great deal about the sizes, colors, and temperatures of stars.

In the H-R diagram shown in Figure 5, notice that the stars are not uniformly distributed. About 90 percent are **main-sequence stars** that fall along a band that runs from the upper-left corner to the lower-right corner of the diagram. As you can see, the hottest main-sequence stars are the brightest, and the coolest main-sequence stars are the dimmest.

The brightness of the main-sequence stars is also related to their mass. The hottest blue stars are about 50 times more massive than the sun, while the coolest red stars are only 1/10 as massive. Therefore, on the H-R diagram, the main-sequence stars appear in decreasing order, from hotter, more massive blue stars to cooler, less massive red stars.

Above and to the right of the main sequence in the H-R diagram lies a group of very bright stars called **red giants.** The size of these giants can be estimated by comparing them with stars of known size that have the same surface temperature. Objects with equal surface temperatures radiate the same amount of energy per unit area. Therefore, any difference in the brightness of two stars having the same surface temperature is due to their relative sizes. Some stars are so large that they are called **supergiants.** Betelgeuse, a bright red supergiant in the constellation Orion, has a radius about 800 times that of the sun.

Stars in the lower-central part of the H-R diagram are much fainter than main-sequence stars of the same temperature. Some probably are no bigger than Earth. This group is called white dwarfs, although not all are white.

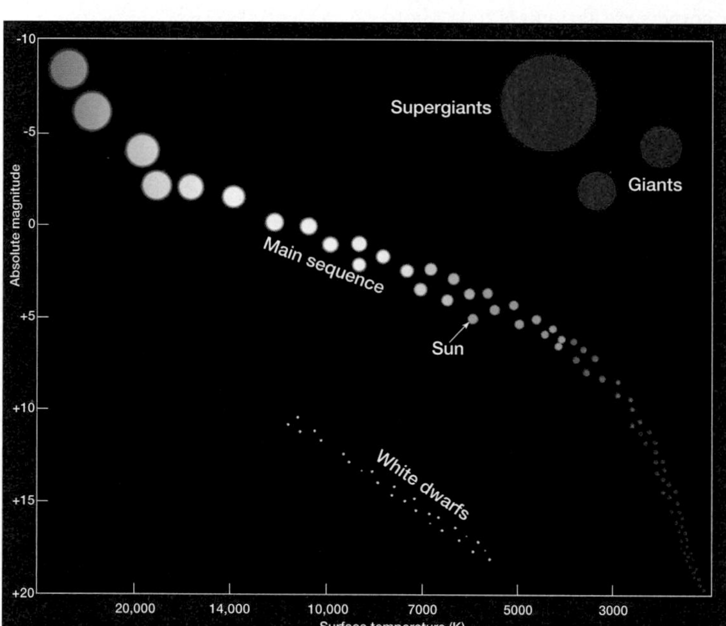

Figure 5 Hertzsprung-Russell Diagram In this idealized chart, stars are plotted according to temperature and absolute magnitude.

Facts and Figures

Einar Hertzsprung was born in 1873 in Denmark. He worked as a chemist before switching to studying astronomy. In 1912, he discovered that for most stars temperature is closely related to absolute magnitude. Before this discovery, astronomers had thought that stars could have any combination of temperature and absolute magnitude.

Henry Norris Russell was born in 1877 in the United States. While working in England in 1921, Russell independently found the same relationship that Hertzsprung had. Hertzsprung continued to work into his nineties. Russell spent six decades at Princeton University.

Soon after the first H-R diagrams were developed, astronomers realized their importance in interpreting stellar evolution. Just as with living things, a star is born, ages, and dies. After considering some variable stars and the nature of interstellar matter, we'll return to the topic of stellar evolution.

Variable Stars Stars may fluctuate in brightness. Some stars, called **Cepheid variables,** get brighter and fainter in a regular pattern. The interval between two successive occurrences of maximum brightness is called a light period. In general, the longer the light period of a Cepheid, the greater its absolute magnitude is. Once the absolute magnitude is known, it can be compared to the apparent magnitude of the Cepheid. Measuring Cepheid variable periods is an important means of determining distances within our universe.

A different type of variable is associated with a **nova,** or sudden brightening of a star. During a nova eruption, the outer layer of the star is ejected at high speed. A nova, shown in Figure 6, generally reaches maximum brightness in a few days, remains bright for only a few weeks, then slowly returns in a year or so to its original brightness. Only a small amount of its mass is lost during the flare-up. Some stars have experienced more than one such event. In fact, the process probably occurs repeatedly.

Scientists think that novas occur in binary systems consisting of an expanding red giant and a nearby hot white dwarf. Hydrogen-rich gas from the oversized giant is transferred by gravity to the white dwarf. Eventually, the added gas causes the dwarf to ignite explosively. Such a reaction rapidly heats and expands the outer layer of the hot dwarf to produce a nova. In a relatively short time, the white dwarf returns to its prenova state, where it remains inactive until the next buildup occurs.

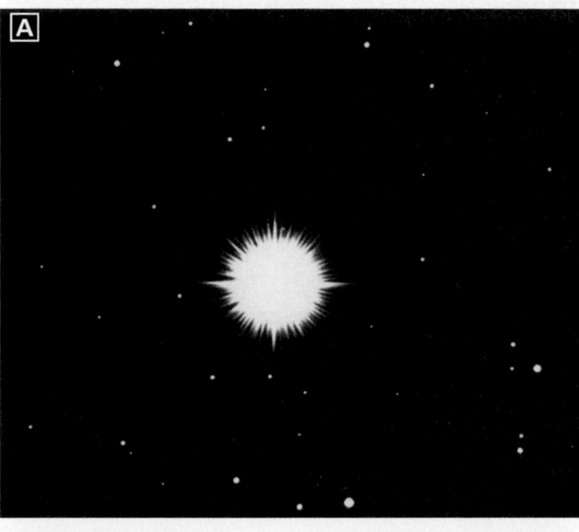

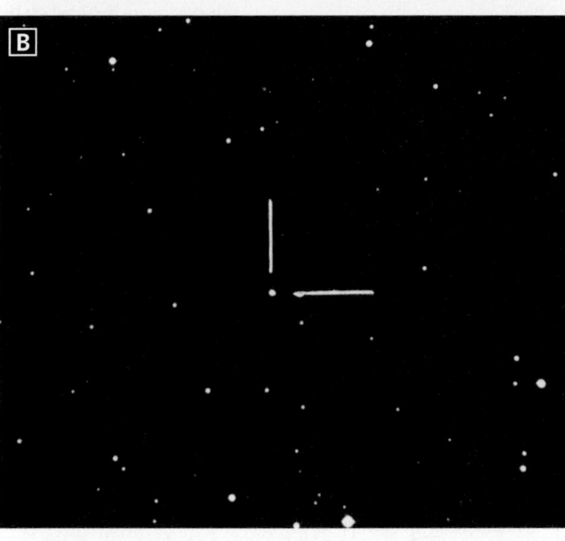

Figure 6 Nova These photographs, taken two months apart, show the decrease in brightness that follows a nova flare-up.

Build Science Skills

Relating Cause and Effect
Go through the cyclical process that may cause some novas to flare up repeatedly. Ask: **What is the first step in the process?** *(Hydrogen-rich gas is transferred from a red giant to a white dwarf.)* **What effect does this have on the white dwarf?** *(The gas eventually causes the dwarf to ignite explosively.)* **What effect does this reaction have on the white dwarf?** *(The outer layer is heated and expands, producing a nova.)* Have students draw cycle diagrams of the entire process.
Logical

Build Reading Literacy

L1

Refer to **p. 92D** in **Chapter 4,** which provides guidelines for this using context clues strategy.

Using Context Clues Tell students that the term *nova* derives from the Latin word *novus,* meaning new. Ask students to explain why the term nova got this name. *(The sudden brightening of an existing star may have been interpreted as the creation of a new star.)* Encourage students to look up words and consider their roots as they encounter new vocabulary.
Verbal

3 ASSESS

Evaluate Understanding L2

Ask students to write a summary paragraph explaining how scientists use parallax to determine the difference to nearby stars.

Reteach L1

Use Figure 5 to review how different types of stars are plotted on an H-R diagram.

Student Web sites should explain how stars are plotted on the H-R diagram according to absolute magnitude and temperature. Web sites should also include definitions of key terms and a color key explaining the relationship between star color and temperature.

Figure 7 Dark Nebula The Horsehead Nebula is found in the constellation Orion.

Interstellar Matter Between existing stars is "the vacuum of space." However, it is not a pure vacuum, for there are clouds of dust and gases known as **nebulae.** If this interstellar matter is close to a very hot star, it will glow and is called a bright nebula. The two main types of bright nebulae are emission nebulae and reflection nebulae.

Emission nebulae consist largely of hydrogen. They absorb ultraviolet radiation emitted by a nearby hot star. Because these gases are under very low pressure, they emit this energy as visible light. This conversion of ultraviolet light to visible light is known as fluorescence. You can see this effect in fluorescent lights. Reflection nebulae, as the name implies, merely reflect the light of nearby stars. Reflection nebulae are thought to be composed of dense clouds of large particles called interstellar dust.

Some nebulae are not close enough to a bright star to be lit up. They are called dark nebulae. Dark nebulae, such as the one shown in Figure 7, can easily be seen as starless regions when viewing the Milky Way.

Although nebulae appear very dense, they actually consist of thinly scattered matter. Because of their enormous size, however, their total mass may be many times that of the sun. Astronomers study nebulae because stars and planets form from this interstellar matter.

Section 25.1 Assessment

Reviewing Concepts

1. What can astronomers learn by studying a star's color?
2. Binary stars can be used to establish what property of stars?
3. How does distance affect parallax?
4. What factors determine a star's apparent magnitude?
5. The H-R diagram shows the relationship between what two factors?

Critical Thinking

6. **Problem Solving** How many times brighter is a star with a magnitude of 7 than a star with a magnitude of 12?
7. **Inferring** Scientists think that only a small amount of a star's mass is lost during a nova. Based on what you have learned about novas, infer what evidence scientists use to support this theory.

Writing in Science

Web Site Make an educational Web site about the H-R diagram for younger students. Use Figure 5 as a guide. Include a color key and other elements to help clarify concepts such as star temperature, the Kelvin scale, and absolute magnitude.

Section 25.1 Assessment

1. Astronomers can learn about a star's temperature by studying its color.
2. Binary stars can be used to establish a star's mass.
3. The nearest stars have the largest parallax angles, while the parallax angles of distant stars are too small to measure.
4. Three factors determine the apparent magnitude of a star: how big it is, how hot it is, and how far away it is.
5. absolute magnitude and the temperature of stars
6. The magnitude 7 star is 100 times brighter.
7. Following the nova flare-up, the star returns to its prenova state. If a great amount of mass had been lost, this would not be possible, nor would it be possible for the star to experience more than one nova eruption.

25.2 Stellar Evolution

Reading Focus

Key Concepts

- What stage marks the birth of a star?
- Why do all stars eventually die?
- What stages make up the sun's life cycle?

Vocabulary

- protostar
- supernova
- white dwarf
- neutron star
- pulsar
- black hole

Reading Strategy

Sequencing Copy the flowchart below. As you read, complete it to show how the sun evolves. Expand the chart to show the evolution of low-mass and high-mass stars.

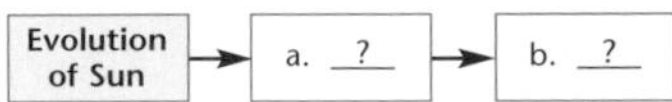

Determining how stars are born, age, and then die was difficult because the life of a star can span billions of years. However, by studying stars of different ages, astronomers have been able to piece together the evolution of a star. Imagine that an alien from outer space lands on Earth. This alien wants to study the stages of human life. By examining a large number of humans, the alien observes the birth of babies, the activities of children and adults, and the death of elderly people. From this information, the alien then attempts to put the stages of human development into proper sequence. Based on the number of humans in each stage of development, the alien would conclude that humans spend more of their lives as adults than as children. In a similar way, astronomers have pieced together the story of stars.

Star Birth

The birthplaces of stars are dark, cool interstellar clouds, such as the one in Figure 8. These nebulae are made up of dust and gases. In the Milky Way, nebulae consist of 92 percent hydrogen, 7 percent helium, and less than 1 percent of the remaining heavier elements. For some reason not yet fully understood, some nebulae become dense enough to begin to contract. A shock wave from an explosion of a nearby star may trigger the contraction. Once the process begins, gravity squeezes particles in the nebula, pulling every particle toward the center. As the nebula shrinks, gravitational energy is converted into heat energy.

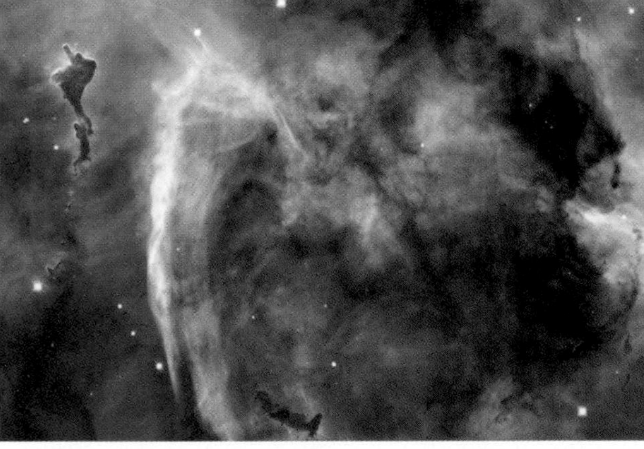

Figure 8 Nebula Dark, cool clouds full of interstellar matter are the birthplace of stars.

Section 25.2

1 FOCUS

Section Objectives

25.5 **Identify** which stage marks the birth of a star.
25.6 **Explain** why all stars eventually die.
25.7 **List** the stages of the sun's life cycle.

Reading Focus

Build Vocabulary L2

Concept Map As students read the section, have them make a concept map showing how the vocabulary terms are related. The concept map should show how a star changes during its lifetime.

Reading Strategy L2

a. cloud of dust and gases (nebula stage)
b. protostar stage

2 INSTRUCT

Star Birth

Build Science Skills L2

Using Analogies ACTIVITY
Show students a series of photographs of people of different ages. Ask them to put the photos in order by age. Then, show students a series of photographs of the life cycle of an insect, such as a butterfly, that undergoes complete metamorphosis. Ask them to put the photos in order by age. Ask: **Why was the second series was harder to sequence than the first one?** *(You can't easily tell by looking at the photos which stage comes in what order.)* Point out that astronomers have the same problem with stars. It's not obvious just from looking at various stages of stars how old they are.
Logical, Visual

Integrate Physics L2

Fission and Fusion Review the concepts of fission and fusion with students. During fission, atomic nuclei are split apart to make smaller nuclei. This is the process used in nuclear power plants. During fusion, atomic nuclei combine to make larger nuclei. Sustained fusion occurs only within stars. Main-sequence stars fuse four hydrogen nuclei to form a helium nucleus. The helium nucleus has slightly less mass than the hydrogen nuclei. The remaining mass is converted into energy. Hotter stars can produce carbon and other elements by fusion.
Logical, Verbal

Build Reading Literacy L1

Refer to **p. 392D** in **Chapter 14,** which provides guidelines for previewing.

Preview Before they read the section, have students skim the headings, visuals, and boldfaced words to preview how the text is organized.
Verbal, Visual

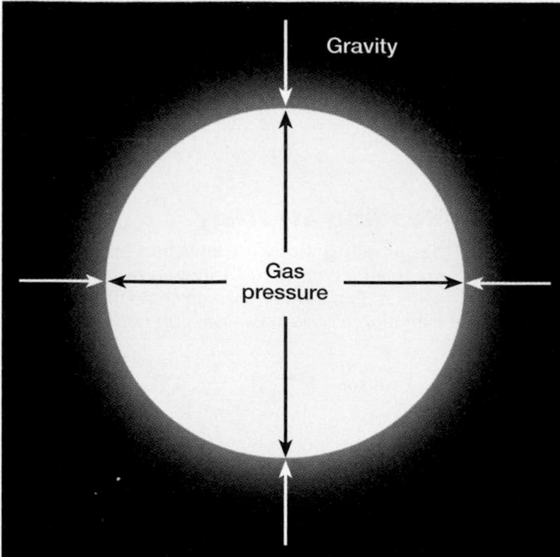

Figure 9 Balanced Forces A main-sequence star is balanced between gravity, which is trying to squeeze it, and gas pressure, which is trying to expand it.

Protostar Stage The initial contraction spans a million years or so. As time passes, the temperature of this gaseous body slowly rises until it is hot enough to radiate energy from its surface in the form of long-wavelength red light. This large red object is called a protostar. A **protostar** is a developing star not yet hot enough to engage in nuclear fusion.

During the protostar stage, gravitational contraction continues—slowly at first, then much more rapidly. This collapse causes the core of the protostar to heat much more intensely than the outer layer. **When the core of a protostar has reached about 10 million K, pressure within is so great that nuclear fusion of hydrogen begins, and a star is born.**

Heat from hydrogen fusion causes the gases to increase their motion. This in turn causes an increase in the outward gas pressure. At some point, this outward pressure exactly balances the inward force of gravity, as shown in Figure 9. When this balance is reached, the star becomes a stable main-sequence star. Stated another way, a stable main-sequence star is balanced between two forces: gravity, which is trying to squeeze it into a smaller sphere, and gas pressure, which is trying to expand it.

Main-Sequence Stage From this point in the evolution of a main-sequence star until its death, the internal gas pressure struggles to offset the unyielding force of gravity. Typically, hydrogen fusion continues for a few billion years and provides the outward pressure required to support the star from gravitational collapse.

Different stars age at different rates. Hot, massive blue stars radiate energy at such an enormous rate that they deplete their hydrogen fuel in only a few million years. By contrast, the least massive main-sequence stars may remain stable for hundreds of billions of years. A yellow star, such as the sun, remains a main-sequence star for about 10 billion years.

An average star spends 90 percent of its life as a hydrogen-burning, main-sequence star. Once the hydrogen fuel in the star's core is depleted, it evolves rapidly and dies. However, with the exception of the least-massive red stars, a star can delay its death by fusing heavier elements and becoming a giant.

Customize for Inclusion Students

Gifted Have students create a computer graphic presentation that compares the life cycles of different masses of stars. The presentations should include scale diagrams of each stage along with labels and a brief caption. Invite students to share their presentations with the class.

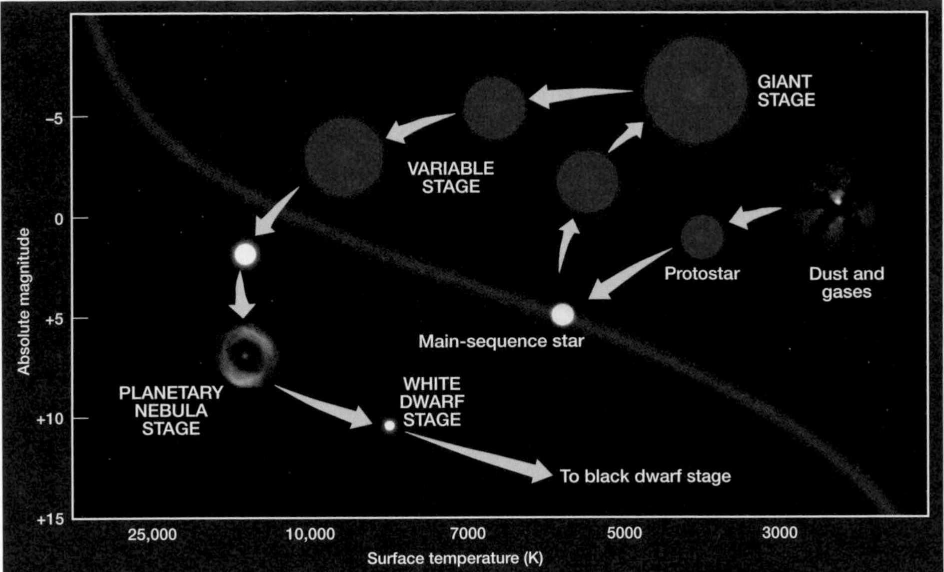

Figure 10 Life Cycle of a Sunlike Star A medium-mass star, similar to the sun, will evolve along the path shown here. **Interpreting Diagrams** ***What is the first stage in the formation of the star? What is the last stage?***

Red-Giant Stage The red-giant stage occurs because the zone of hydrogen fusion continually moves outward, leaving behind a helium core. Eventually, all the hydrogen in the star's core is consumed. While hydrogen fusion is still progressing in the star's outer shell, no fusion is taking place in the core. Without a source of energy, the core no longer has enough pressure to support itself against the inward force of gravity. As a result, the core begins to contract.

As the core contracts, it grows hotter by converting gravitational energy into heat energy. Some of this energy is radiated outward, increasing hydrogen fusion in the star's outer shell. This energy in turn heats and expands the star's outer layer. The result is a giant body hundreds to thousands of times its main-sequence size, as shown in Figure 10.

As the star expands, its surface cools, which explains the star's reddish appearance. During expansion, the core continues to collapse and heat until it reaches 100 million K. At this temperature, it is hot enough to convert helium to carbon. So, a red giant consumes both hydrogen and helium to produce energy.

Eventually, all the usable nuclear fuel in these giants will be consumed. The sun, for example, will spend less than a billion years as a giant. More massive stars will pass through this stage even more rapidly. The force of gravity will again control the star's destiny as it squeezes the star into the smallest, most dense piece of matter possible.

Why do red giants have a reddish appearance?

Use Visuals L1

Figure 10 Use this figure to explain how a star like the sun evolves. Emphasize that the drawing shows changes in the characteristics of the star, not movement in the sky. Also explain that the main sequence is shown for reference. Ask: **What happens to the star after it leaves the main sequence?** *(It becomes a red giant.)* **How do the characteristics of the star change as it changes from a red giant to a planetary nebula?** *(It becomes hotter but less bright.)* **Where would the black dwarf stage be on the drawing? Why?** *(It would be in the bottom right corner or past it. A black dwarf is cold and dark.)*
Visual, Logical

Build Reading Literacy L1

Refer to **p. 446D** in **Chapter 16,** which provides guidelines for this sequence strategy.

Sequence Some students may be confused by the lifecycle of a sunlike star as pictured in Figure 10. To bypass the complexity of criteria such as surface temperature and absolute magnitude, have students write each step or phase on a separate flashcard. Then have them mix up the cards and practice placing them in the proper sequence.
Verbal, Kinesthetic

Answer to . . .

Figure 10 *The first stage is a nebula, or cloud of dust and gases. The last stage is a black dwarf.*

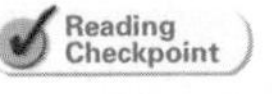

As they expand, their surfaces cool, which explains the red appearance.

Burnout and Death

Use Visuals L1

Figure 11 Use this figure to explain how the evolution of stars depends on their mass. Ask: **What stages do all stars go through?** *(nebula, protostar, main-sequence star)* **Which stars become red giants?** *(medium-mass and massive stars)* **Which stars become white dwarfs?** *(low-mass and medium-mass stars)* **What are two possible results of the death of a massive star?** *(It can become a neutron star or a black hole.)*
Visual, Logical

L2

Students may be confused by the term *planetary nebula* and think that planets form from planetary nebulae. Explain that a planetary nebula is a stage in the evolution of a star and has nothing to do with planets. The name is a result of historical accident. When planetary nebulae were discovered 200 years ago, they looked like small greenish disks similar to the planet Uranus. Even though they are not related to planets, the name stuck.
Verbal

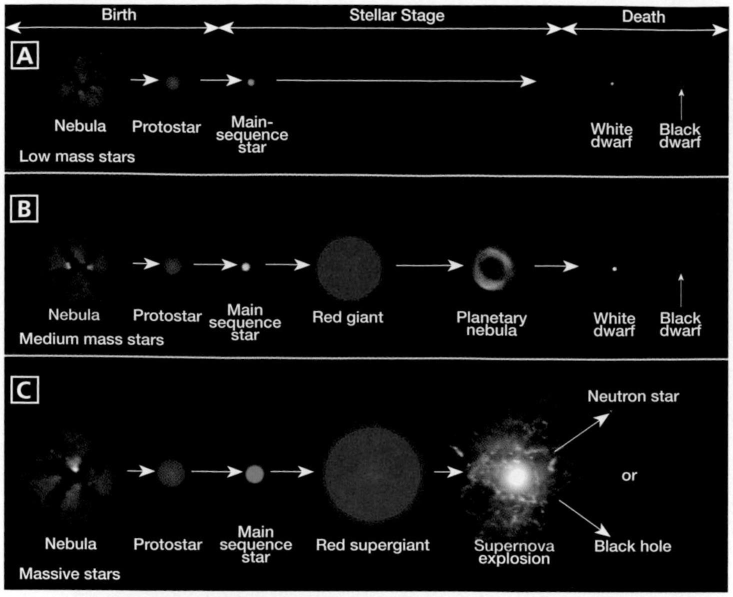

Birth | Stellar Stage | Death

A: Nebula → Protostar → Main-sequence star → White dwarf → Black dwarf (Low mass stars)

B: Nebula → Protostar → Main sequence star → Red giant → Planetary nebula → White dwarf → Black dwarf (Medium mass stars)

C: Nebula → Protostar → Main sequence star → Red supergiant → Supernova explosion → Neutron star or Black hole (Massive stars)

Figure 11 Stellar Evolution
A A low-mass star uses fuel at a low rate and has a long life span. **B** Like a low-mass star, a medium-mass star ends as a black dwarf. **C** Massive stars end in huge explosions, then become either neutron stars or black holes.

Burnout and Death

Most of the events of stellar evolution discussed so far are well documented. What happens next is based more on theory. **We do know that all stars, regardless of their size, eventually run out of fuel and collapse due to gravity.** With this in mind, let's consider the final stages of stars of different masses.

Death of Low-Mass Stars As shown in Figure 11A, stars less than one half the mass of the sun consume their fuel at a fairly slow rate. Consequently, these small, cool red stars may remain on the main sequence for up to 100 billion years. Because the interior of a low-mass star never reaches high enough temperatures and pressures to fuse helium, its only energy source is hydrogen. So, low-mass stars never evolve into red giants. Instead, they remain as stable main-sequence stars until they consume their hydrogen fuel and collapse into a white dwarf, which you will learn more about later.

Figure 12 Planetary Nebula
During its collapse from a red giant to a white dwarf, a medium-mass star ejects its outer layer, forming a round cloud of gas.

Death of Medium-Mass Stars As shown in Figure 11B, stars with masses similar to the sun evolve in essentially the same way. During their giant phase, sunlike stars fuse hydrogen and helium fuel at a fast rate. Once this fuel is exhausted, these stars also collapse into white dwarfs.

During their collapse from red giants to white dwarfs, medium-mass stars are thought to cast off their bloated outer layer, creating an expanding round cloud of gas. The remaining hot, central white dwarf heats the gas cloud, causing it to glow. These often beautiful, gleaming spherical clouds are called planetary nebulae. An example of a planetary nebula is shown in Figure 12.

Facts and Figures

In a few billion years, the sun's core will run out of hydrogen fuel, triggering hydrogen fusion in the surrounding shell. As a result, the sun's outer envelope will expand, producing a red giant hundreds of times larger and brighter. Intense solar radiation will boil Earth's oceans, and solar winds will drive away Earth's atmosphere. Another billion years later, the sun will expel its outermost layer, producing a planetary nebula. The interior will collapse to produce a small, dense white dwarf. Gradually the sun will emit its remaining energy and become a cold black dwarf.

Death of Massive Stars

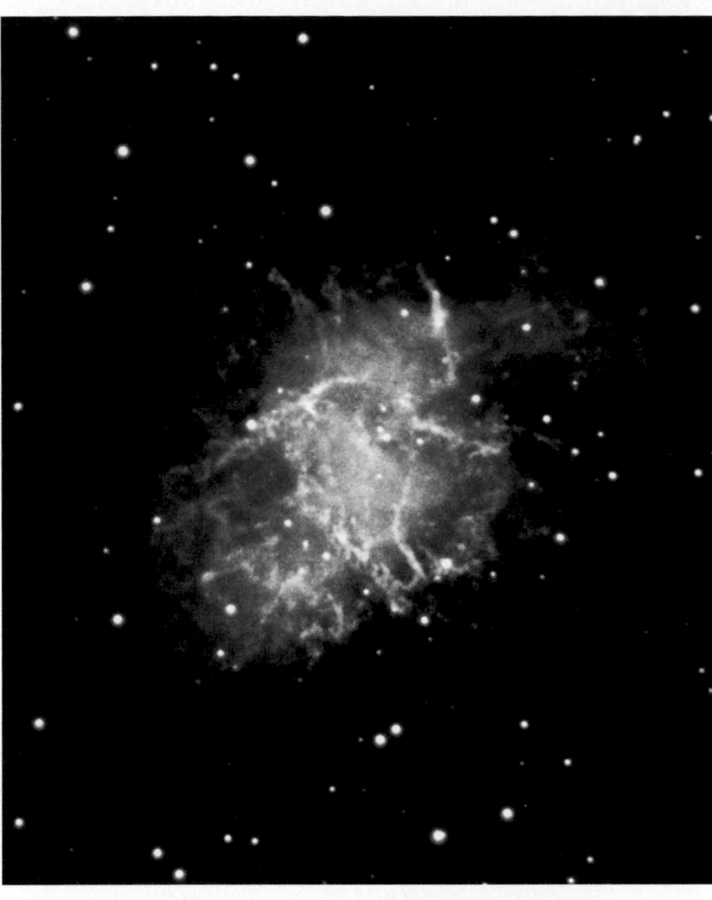

Figure 13 Crab Nebula This nebula, found in the constellation Taurus, is the remains of a supernova that took place in 1054.

In contrast to sunlike stars, which die gracefully, stars with masses three times that of the sun have relatively short life spans, as shown in Figure 11C. These stars end their lives in a brilliant explosion called a **supernova.** During a supernova, a star becomes millions of times brighter than its prenova stage. If one of the nearest stars to Earth produced such an outburst, it would be brighter than the sun. Supernovae are rare. None have been observed in our galaxy since the invention of the telescope, although Tycho Brahe and Galileo each recorded one about 30 years apart. An even larger supernova was recorded in 1054 by the Chinese. Today, the remnant of this great outburst is the Crab Nebula, shown in Figure 13.

A supernova event is thought to be triggered when a massive star consumes most of its nuclear fuel. Without a heat engine to generate the gas pressure required to balance its immense gravitational field, the star collapses. This implosion, or bursting inward, is huge, resulting in a shock wave that moves out from the star's interior. This energetic shock wave destroys the star and blasts the outer shell into space, generating the supernova event.

H-R Diagrams and Stellar Evolution Hertzsprung-Russell diagrams have been helpful in formulating and testing models of stellar evolution. They are also useful for illustrating the changes that take place in an individual star during its life span. Refer back to Figure 10, which shows the evolution of a star about the size of the sun. Keep in mind that the star does not physically move along this path. Its position on the H-R diagram represents the color and absolute magnitude of the star at various stages in its evolution.

What is a supernova?

Integrate Chemistry **L2**

Formation of Heavy Elements Tell students that all of the heavy (high atomic mass) atoms on Earth were formed inside stars. Initially the universe contained almost entirely hydrogen and helium. Biologically important elements such as carbon, nitrogen, and oxygen form inside many stars. However, very heavy elements such as lead and gold form only in the incredible explosions of supernovas. When the supernova fades, the elements are scattered throughout the area and may become part of a new solar system such as our own. Have students research the chain reactions inside stars and supernovas that produce heavy elements.
Logical

Use Community Resources **L2**

Invite an astronomer or astrophysicist from a local college or university to the classroom to discuss astronomy and research. Ask students to prepare questions in advance to ask the visitor.
Interpersonal

Answer to . . .

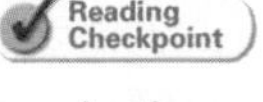

A supernova is the brilliant explosion that marks the end of a massive star.

Stellar Remnants

Build Science Skills L2

Using Analogies Use an analogy of a star to a charcoal briquette in a barbecue grill to describe the life of a low-mass star. When the briquette is first lit, it begins to consume its fuel and glows red-hot (main sequence). As it runs out of fuel, it becomes cooler and dimmer (white dwarf). Eventually it runs out of fuel and becomes a cold cinder (black dwarf). Ask students how the briquette is different from an actual star. *(The briquette burns because of chemical reactions, not fusion. It doesn't get hotter in the "white dwarf" stage.)*
Logical, Visual

Stellar Remnants

Eventually, all stars consume their nuclear fuel and collapse into one of three documented states—white dwarf, neutron star, or black hole. Although different in some ways, these small, compact objects are all composed of incomprehensibly dense material and all have extreme surface gravity.

White Dwarfs **White dwarfs** are the remains of low-mass and medium-mass stars. They are extremely small stars with densities greater than any known material on Earth. Although some white dwarfs are no larger than Earth, the mass of such a dwarf can equal 1.4 times that of the sun. So, their densities may be a million times greater than water. A spoonful of such matter would weigh several tons. Densities this great are possible only when electrons are displaced inward from their regular orbits, around an atom's nucleus, allowing the atoms to take up less than the "normal" amount of space. Material in this state is called degenerate matter.

In degenerate matter, the atoms have been squeezed together so tightly that the electrons are displaced much nearer to the nucleus. Degenerate matter uses electrical repulsion instead of molecular motion to support itself from total collapse. Although atomic particles in degenerate matter are much closer together than in normal Earth matter, they still are not packed as tightly as possible. Stars made of matter that has an even greater density are thought to exist.

As a star contracts into a white dwarf, its surface becomes very hot, sometimes exceeding 25,000 K. Even so, without a source of energy, it can only become cooler and dimmer. Although none have been observed, the last stage of a white dwarf must be a small, cold body called a black dwarf. Table 2 summarizes the evolution of stars of various masses. **As you can see, the sun begins as a nebula, spends much of its life as a main-sequence star, becomes a red giant, planetary nebula, white dwarf, and finally, black dwarf.**

Table 2 Summary of Evolution for Stars of Various Masses

Initial Mass of Interstellar Cloud (Sun = 1)	Main-Sequence Stage	Giant Phase	Evolution After Giant Phase	Final Stage
1–3	Yellow	Yes	Planetary nebula	White dwarf
6	White	Yes	Supernova	Neutron star
20	Blue	Yes (Supergiant)	Supernova	Black hole

Neutron Stars After studying white dwarfs, scientists made what might at first appear to be a surprising conclusion. The smallest white dwarfs are the most massive, and the largest are the least massive. The explanation for this is that a more massive star, because of its greater gravitational force, is able to squeeze itself into a smaller, more densely packed object than can a less massive star. So, the smaller white dwarfs were produced from the collapse of larger, more massive stars than were the larger white dwarfs.

This conclusion led to the prediction that stars smaller and more massive than white dwarfs must exist. These objects, called **neutron stars,** are thought to be the remnants of supernova events. In a white dwarf, the electrons are pushed close to the nucleus, while in a neutron star, the electrons are forced to combine with protons to produce neutrons. If Earth were to collapse to the density of a neutron star, it would have a diameter equal to the length of a football field. A pea-size sample of this matter would weigh 100 million tons. This is approximately the density of an atomic nucleus. Neutron stars can be thought of as large atomic nuclei.

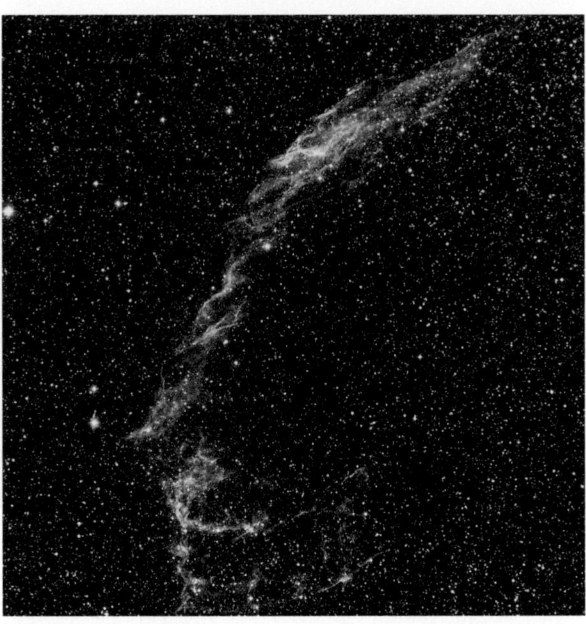

Figure 14 Veil Nebula Located in the constellation Cygnus, this nebula is the remnant of an ancient supernova.

Supernovae During a supernova, the outer layer of the star is ejected, while the core collapses into a very hot neutron star about 20 kilometers in diameter. Although neutron stars have high surface temperatures, their small size would greatly limit their brightness. Finding one with a telescope would be extremely difficult.

However, astronomers think that a neutron star would have a very strong magnetic field. Further, as a star collapses, it will rotate faster, for the same reason ice skaters rotate faster as they pull in their arms. Radio waves generated by these rotating stars would be concentrated into two narrow zones that would align with the star's magnetic poles. Consequently, these stars would resemble a rapidly rotating beacon emitting strong radio waves. If Earth happened to be in the path of these beacons, the star would appear to blink on and off, or pulsate, as the waves swept past.

In the early 1970s, a source that radiates short bursts or pulses of radio energy, called a **pulsar**, was discovered in the Crab Nebula. Studies of this radio source revealed it to be a small spinning star centered in the nebula. The pulsar found in the Crab Nebula is undoubtedly the remains of the supernova of 1054.

Teacher Demo

Modeling a Pulsar **L2**

Purpose Students observe a model of how a pulsar appears from Earth.

Materials string; long, thin flashlight

Procedure Tie a string to the middle of a long, thin flashlight. Twist the string a few times. Turn on the flashlight, turn off the room lights, and let the flashlight spin around. Ask: **What does the flashlight look like from your perspective?** *(It looks as if it is flashing on and off.)* **Is the flashlight actually flashing? If not, ask what it is doing.** *(No, it is producing a continuous beam.)* **Why does the flashlight appears to be flashing?** *(The beam is only visible when it points toward the observer.)* Twist the string more tightly and let the flashlight spin again. Ask: **What is different this time, and why?** *(The flashing is more frequent because the flashlight is rotating more rapidly.)*

Expected Outcome The flashlight will appear to be flashing and will appear to flash more rapidly as it rotates faster.
Visual, Logical

Facts and Figures

Pulsars were discovered by Jocelyn Bell Burnell in 1967. Burnell was a graduate student working on her advisor Anthony Hewish's project to study rapid fluctuations in radio waves received from stars. One day she noticed some strong, rapid, and regular pulses coming from fixed points on the sky. Some people thought the pulses might by signals sent by an alien civilization, or "little green men," so the sources were at first called LGM 1, LGM 2, LGM 3, and LGM 4. However, astronomers soon concluded that the signals had natural sources, which were named pulsars.

Use Visuals L1

Figure 15 Use this figure to explain how black holes can be detected. Ask: **Can a black hole be detected directly? Why or why not?** *(no, because its gravity is so strong that not even light can escape)* **What may happen if a black hole has a companion star?** *(The black hole may pull material out of the star and into itself.)* **What happens to material as it falls into a black hole?** *(It becomes very hot and emits X-rays.)* **What would be good evidence for a black hole?** *(stellar material being heated and then apparently disappearing into nothingness)*
Visual, Logical

3 ASSESS

Evaluate Understanding L2

Call on students to describe the stages that stars of different masses go through during their life cycles.

Reteach 

Use Figure 10 to review the life cycle of a sunlike star and to emphasize that the H-R diagram is a graph, not a star chart.

Connecting Concepts

Sample answer: The effect on Earth would likely be devastating. Depending on the intensity of the radiation, living organisms would either be destroyed or genetically and physically damaged. Because the biosphere interacts with the remaining Earth systems, the entire Earth would be altered eventually.

Download a worksheet on black holes for students to complete, and find additional teacher support from NSTA SciLinks.

Black Holes Are neutron stars made of the most dense materials possible? No. During a supernova event, remnants of stars three times more massive than the sun apparently collapse into objects even smaller and denser than neutron stars. Even though these objects, called **black holes,** are very hot, their gravity is so strong that not even light can escape their surface. So they disappear from sight. Anything that moves too near a black hole would be swept in by its gravity and lost forever.

How can astronomers find an object whose gravitational field prevents the escape of all matter and energy? One strategy is to find evidence of matter being rapidly swept into a region of apparent nothingness. Scientists think that as matter is pulled into a black hole, it should become very hot and emit a flood of X-rays before being pulled in. Because isolated black holes would not have a source of matter to swallow up, astronomers first looked at binary-star systems.

A likely candidate for a black hole is Cygnus X-1, a strong X-ray source in the constellation Cygnus. In this case, the X-ray source can be observed orbiting a supergiant companion with a period of 5.6 days. It appears that gases are pulled from this companion and spiral into the disk-shaped structure around the black hole, as shown in Figure 15.

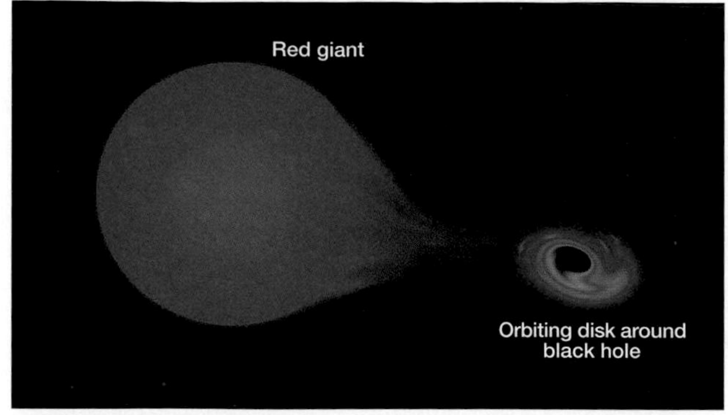

Figure 15 Black Hole Gases from the red giant spiral into the black hole.

Go Online SCI LINKS NSTA

For: Links on black holes
Visit: www.SciLinks.org
Web Code: cjn-7252

Section 25.2 Assessment

Reviewing Concepts

1. What is a protostar?
2. At what point is a star born?
3. What causes a star to die?
4. Describe the life cycle of the sun.

Critical Thinking

5. **Inferring** Why are less massive stars thought to age more slowly than more massive stars, even though less massive stars have much less "fuel"?
6. **Relating Cause and Effect** Why is interstellar matter important to stellar evolution?

Connecting Concepts

Supernova If a supernova explosion were to occur near our solar system, what might be some possible consequences of the intense X-ray radiation that would reach Earth?

Section 25.2 Assessment

1. A protostar is a developing star not yet hot enough to engage in nuclear fusion.
2. When the core of a protostar has reached about 10 million K, pressure within it is so great that nuclear fusion of hydrogen begins, and a star is born.
3. A star runs out of fuel and collapses due to gravity.
4. The sun began as a nebula, became a protostar and then a main-sequence star. It will become a red giant, planetary nebula, white dwarf, and finally a black dwarf.
5. A less massive star will live longer because it consumes fuel at a slower rate than do more massive stars.
6. Stars are born out of clouds of interstellar matter.

25.3 The Universe

Reading Focus

Key Concepts

- What is the size and structure of the Milky Way Galaxy?
- In what ways do galaxies differ from one another?
- What evidence indicates that the universe is expanding?
- According to the big bang theory, how did the universe begin?

Vocabulary

- galaxy
- galaxy cluster
- Hubble's law
- big bang theory

Reading Strategy

Outlining As you read, make an outline of the most important ideas in this section.

I. The Universe
  A. Milky Way Galaxy
    1. ___?___
    2. ___?___
  B. ___?___
    1. Spiral Galaxy
    2. Elliptical Galaxy
    3. ___?___

On a clear and moonless night away from city lights, you can see a truly marvelous sight—our own Milky Way Galaxy, as shown in Figure 16. **Galaxies** are groups of stars, dust, and gases held together by gravity. There may be more than 100 billion stars in the Milky Way Galaxy alone. Our galaxy looks milky because the solar system is located within a flat disk —the galactic disk. We view it from the inside and see stars in every direction.

For: Links on galaxies
Visit: www.SciLinks.org
Web Code: cjn-7253

The Milky Way Galaxy

When astronomers began to survey the stars located along the plane of the Milky Way, it appeared that equal numbers lay in every direction. Could Earth actually be at the center of the galaxy? Scientists came up with a better explanation. Imagine that the trees in an enormous forest represent the stars in the galaxy. After hiking into this forest, you look around. You see an equal number of trees in every direction. Are you in the center of the forest? Not necessarily. Anywhere in the forest will seem to be the center, except at the very edge.

Figure 16 Milky Way Galaxy Notice the dark band caused by interstellar dark nebulae.

Section 25.3

1 FOCUS

Section Objectives

25.8 **Describe** the size and structure of the Milky Way Galaxy.
25.9 **List** the ways in which galaxies differ from one another.
25.10 **Cite** the evidence that indicates that the universe is expanding.
25.11 **Describe** how the universe began according to the big bang theory.

Reading Focus

Build Vocabulary L2

LINCS Have students use the LINCS strategy to learn and review the terms *galaxy*, *galactic cluster*, and *elliptical galaxy*. In LINCS exercises, students **L**ist what they know about each term, **I**magine a picture that describes the word, **N**ote a sound-alike word, **C**onnect the terms to the sound-alike word by making up a short story, and then perform a brief **S**elf-test.

Reading Strategy L2

A. Milky Way Galaxy
  1. Size—100,000 light-years wide and 10,000 light-years thick
  2. Structure—at least three spiral arms, nearly round halo
B. Types of Galaxies
  1. Spiral galaxy—disk-shaped, large
  2. Elliptical galaxy–round to oval, mostly small
  3. Irregular galaxy—Only 10 percent of galaxies have irregular shapes.
  4. Galactic clusters—groups of galaxies
C. Expanding Universe
  1. Red shifts—Light from distant galaxies is "stretched."
  2. Hubble's law—The universe is expanding.

Download a worksheet on galaxies for students to complete, and find additional teacher support from NSTA SciLinks.

2 INSTRUCT

The Milky Way Galaxy

Build Science Skills L2

Inferring ACTIVITY Tell groups of students to use a sharp pencil to carefully poke several dozen holes in a sheet of paper. Have them tape the sheets to a piece of cardboard and then look at them from the other side of the room. Ask students whether they can see the individual holes. *(no)* Ask students to compare the sheets to the photographs of the Milky Way on p. 715 and explain why both the Milky Way and the holes look fuzzy in both cases. *(The holes and stars are too small compared to their distances to be clearly visible.)*
Logical, Visual

Use Visuals L1

Figure 17 Use this figure to discuss the structure of the Milky Way Galaxy. Ask: **How wide is the Milky Way Galaxy?** *(about 100,000 light-years)* **What is at the center of the Milky Way Galaxy?** *(the nucleus)* **What part of the Milky Way Galaxy lies outside the main disk? What is it made up of?** *(the halo; thin gas and globular clusters)* **Where is the sun in the Milky Way Galaxy?** *(It is about two thirds of the way from the center on one of the spiral arms.)*
Visual, Logical

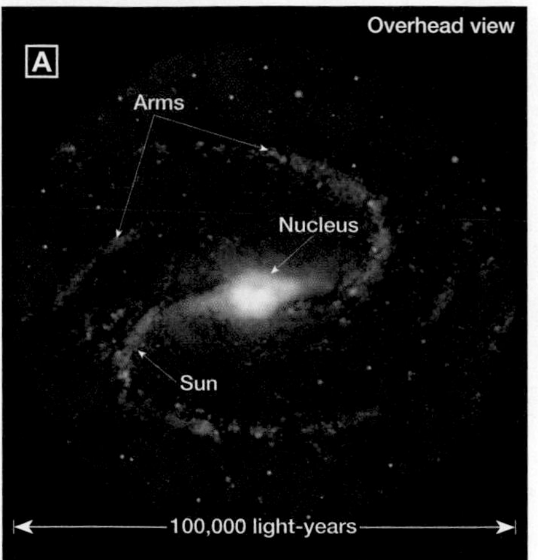

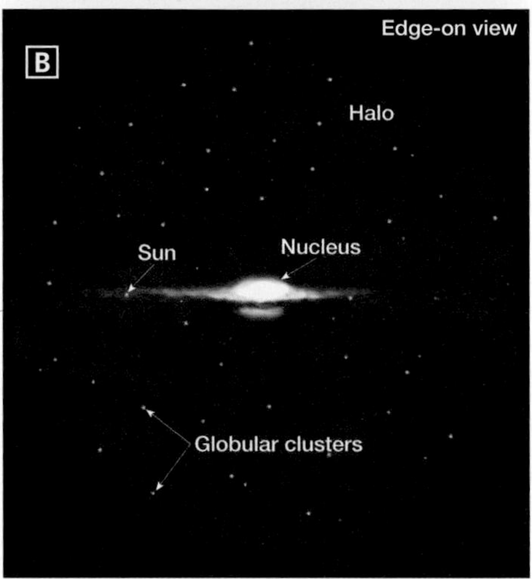

Figure 17 Structure of the Milky Way A The spiral arms are clearly visible in the overhead view of our galaxy. **B** Our solar system is located about 30,000 light-years from the galactic nucleus.

Size of the Milky Way It's hard to study the Milky Way Galaxy with optical telescopes because large quantities of interstellar matter block our vision. With the aid of radio telescopes, scientists have determined the structure of our galaxy. **The Milky Way is a large spiral galaxy whose disk is about 100,000 light-years wide and about 10,000 light-years thick at the nucleus, as shown in Figure 17A.** As viewed from Earth, the center of the galaxy lies beyond the constellation Sagittarius. Figure 17B shows an edge-on view of the Milky Way.

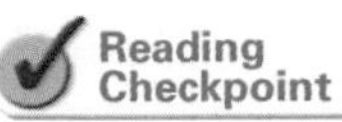

How big is the Milky Way Galaxy?

Structure of the Milky Way Radio telescopes reveal that the Milky Way has at least three distinct spiral arms, with some signs of splintering. The sun is positioned in one of these arms about two thirds of the way from the center, or galactic nucleus, at a distance of about 30,000 light-years. The stars in the arms of the Milky Way rotate around the galactic nucleus. The most outward arms move the slowest, and the ends of the arms appear to trail. Our solar system orbits the galactic nucleus about every 200 million years.

Surrounding the galactic disk is a nearly round halo made of thin gas and numerous clusters of stars. These star clusters do not participate in the rotating motion of the arms but have their own orbits that carry them through the disk. Although some clusters are very dense, they pass among the stars of the arms with plenty of room to spare.

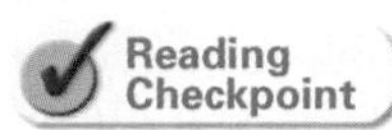

Where is our solar system located within the Milky Way Galaxy?

Types of Galaxies

In the mid-1700s, German philosopher Immanuel Kant proposed that the fuzzy patches of light scattered among the stars were actually distant galaxies like the Milky Way. Today we know that the universe includes hundreds of billions of galaxies, each containing hundreds of billions of stars. From these hundreds of billions of galaxies, scientists have identified several basic types.

Customize for English Language Learners

Concepts such as galaxies, redshift, Hubble's law, and the big bang theory can be difficult to understand. Help English language learners understand these concepts by having them construct a Reading/Learning log. Have students write what they understand in the left column and what they still have questions about in the right column.

Spiral Galaxies As shown in Figure 18A, spiral galaxies are usually disk-shaped, with a somewhat greater concentration of stars near their centers. There are numerous variations, though. Viewed broadside, the arms are often seen extending from the central nucleus and sweeping gracefully away. The outermost stars of these arms rotate most slowly, giving the galaxy the appearance of a pinwheel.

One type of spiral galaxy, however, has its stars arranged in the shape of a bar, which rotates as a rigid system. Attached to each end of these bars are curved spiral arms. These have become known as barred spiral galaxies, as shown in Figure 18B. Recent evidence indicates that the Milky Way may be a barred spiral galaxy. Spiral galaxies are generally quite large. About 10 percent of all galaxies are thought to be barred spirals, and another 20 percent are regular spiral galaxies.

Figure 18 Spiral Galaxies
A A spiral galaxy looks somewhat like a pinwheel. **B** A barred spiral galaxy has a bar through its center, with arms extending outward from the bar.

Elliptical Galaxies About 60 percent of galaxies are classified as elliptical galaxies. Elliptical galaxies range in shape from round to oval. Although most are small, the very largest known galaxies—200,000 light-years in diameter—are elliptical. This type of galaxy, shown in Figure 19, does not have spiral arms.

Irregular Galaxies Only 10 percent of the known galaxies have irregular shapes and are classified as irregular galaxies. The best-known irregular galaxies, the Large and Small Magellanic Clouds, are easily visible with the unaided eye. These galaxies were named after the explorer Ferdinand Magellan, who observed them when he sailed around Earth in 1520. They are our nearest galactic neighbors—only 150,000 light-years away. An irregular galaxy is shown in Figure 20.

In addition to shape and size, one of the major differences among different types of galaxies is the age of their stars. Irregular galaxies are composed mostly of young stars, while elliptical galaxies contain old stars. The Milky Way and other spiral galaxies have both young and old stars, with the youngest located in the arms.

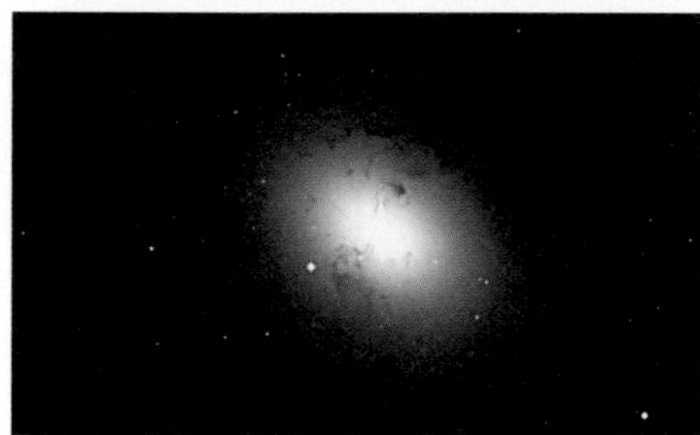

Figure 19 Elliptical Galaxy Most galaxies are classified as elliptical with shapes ranging from round to oval.

Figure 20 Irregular Galaxy Irregular galaxies have irregular shapes.
Describing ***What type of stars would you find in an irregular galaxy?***

Types of Galaxies

Build Science Skills **L2**

Using Models Invite students to make models of different types of galaxies, using cotton balls, coat hangers, and other materials of their choice. Each student should model at least two different types of galaxies. Students should write paragraphs on index cards explaining each galaxy and its characteristics. Have students calculate and include the approximate scale of their models. Have students view some of the models of spiral galaxies from the side and close up so they see why it is so hard for us to see the structure of our own galaxy.
Logical, Visual

Use Visuals **L1**

Figures 18–20 Use these figures to compare and contrast the different types of galaxies. Ask: **How is a spiral galaxy different from an elliptical galaxy?** *(A spiral galaxy has arms; an elliptical galaxy doesn't.)* **How is an irregular galaxy different from other galaxies?** *(An irregular galaxy does not have a regular shape.)* **How are all galaxies similar?** *(They are all made up of stars and have a denser region at their center.)*
Visual, Logical

Answer to . . .

Figure 20 *Irregular galaxies are composed mostly of young stars.*

The Milky Way Galaxy is about 100,000 light-years wide and 10,000 light-years thick at the nucleus.

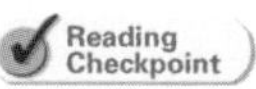
Our solar system is about two thirds of the way from the center on one of the spiral arms of the galaxy.

The Expanding Universe

Integrate Physics

L2

Doppler Effect Review the electromagnetic spectrum and the Doppler effect. Ask: **What is the electromagnetic spectrum?** *(the full range of frequencies of electromagnetic radiation)* **What is visible light?** *(the part of the spectrum that the human eye can see)* **What is wavelength?** *(the distance from the peak of one wave to the peak of the next)* **How does the Doppler effect affect wavelength if the source of the waves is moving toward the observer?** *(The waves will seem to be closer together. They will have a smaller wavelength.)* **Logical**

Teacher Demo

"Stretching" Light Waves

L2

Purpose Students observe a model of how light is redshifted.

Materials old bicycle inner tube, scissors, chalk

Procedure Before the demo, cut an old bicycle inner tube on both sides of the valve to form a long tube. Cut the tube lengthwise to form a long narrow band of rubber. In front of the students, use white chalk to draw a galaxy at one end of the tube to represent the Milky Way. Draw another galaxy at the other end. Draw a wavy line to represent light coming from the other galaxy toward the Milky Way. Then, hold both ends of the strip and stretch them apart. Ask students what happens to the "wave." *(It gets stretched out.)* Ask how this affects the color of the light. *(The wavelength increases, so the light is shifted toward the red end of the spectrum.)* Tell students that light from distant galaxies is redshifted by a similar process.

Expected Outcome Students will observe the "wave" being "redshifted." **Visual, Logical**

Figure 21 Galaxy Cluster This cluster of galaxies is located about 1 million light-years from Earth.

Galaxy Clusters Once astronomers discovered that stars were found in groups, they wondered whether galaxies also were grouped or just randomly distributed throughout the universe. They found that, like stars, galaxies are grouped in **clusters.** One such cluster is shown in Figure 21. Some clusters may contain thousands of galaxies. Our own cluster, called the Local Group, contains at least 28 galaxies. Of these, three are spirals, 11 are irregulars, and 14 are ellipticals. Galaxy clusters also make up huge groups called superclusters. Studies indicate that superclusters may be the largest entities in the universe.

Reading Checkpoint *Describe the shape of elliptical galaxies.*

The Expanding Universe

Recall the Doppler effect that you read about in Chapter 24. Remember that when a source is moving away, its light appears redder than it actually is, because its waves appear lengthened. Objects approaching have their light waves shifted toward the blue or shorter wavelengths. Therefore, the Doppler effect reveals whether a star or other body in space is moving away from Earth or toward Earth. The amount of shift allows us to calculate the rate at which the relative movement is occurring. Large Doppler shifts indicate higher speeds; smaller Doppler shifts indicate lower speeds.

Red Shifts One of the most important discoveries of modern astronomy was made in 1929 by Edwin Hubble. Observations completed several years earlier revealed that most galaxies have Doppler shifts toward the red end of the spectrum. The red shift occurs because the light waves are "stretched," which shows that Earth and the source are moving away from each other. Hubble set out to explain this red shift phenomenon.

Hubble realized that dimmer galaxies were probably farther away than were brighter galaxies. He tried to determine whether a relationship existed between the distances to galaxies and their red shifts. Hubble used estimated distances based on relative brightness and Doppler red shifts to discover that galaxies that exhibit the greatest red shifts are the most distant.

Reading Checkpoint *What relationship did Hubble discover between red shifts and the distances of galaxies from Earth?*

Hubble's Law A consequence of the universal red shift is that it predicts that most galaxies—except for a few nearby—are moving away from us. Recall that the amount of Doppler red shift depends on the speed at which the object is moving away. Greater red shifts indicate faster speeds. Because more distant galaxies have greater red shifts, Hubble concluded that they must be retreating from us at greater speeds. This idea is currently termed **Hubble's law.** It states that galaxies are retreating from us at a speed that is proportional to their distance.

Hubble was surprised at this discovery because it implied that the most distant galaxies are moving away from us many times faster than those nearby. What does this mean? **The red shifts of distant galaxies indicate that the universe is expanding.**

To help visualize the nature of this expanding universe, imagine a loaf of raisin bread dough that has been set out to rise for a few hours. As shown in Figure 22 , as the dough doubles in size, so does the distance between all of the raisins. However, the raisins that were originally farther apart traveled a greater distance in the same time span than those located closer together. We therefore conclude that in an expanding universe, as in the raisin bread dough analogy, those objects located farther apart move away from each other more rapidly.

Another feature of the expanding universe can be demonstrated. No matter which raisin you select, it will move away from all the other raisins. Likewise, no matter where one is located in the universe, every other galaxy—again, except those in the same cluster—will be moving away. Hubble had indeed advanced our understanding of the universe. The Hubble Space Telescope is named in his honor.

What is Hubble's law?

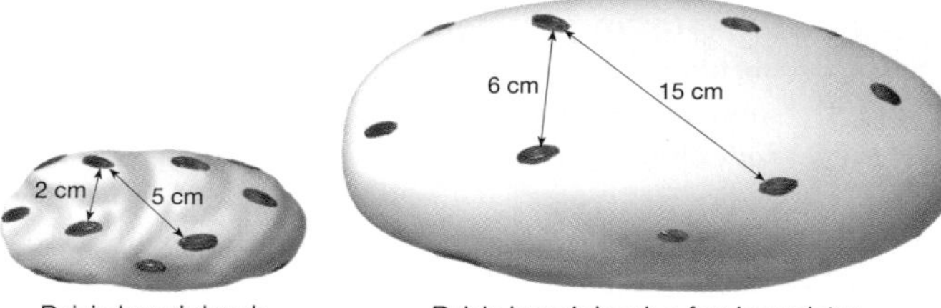

Raisin bread dough before it rises.

A

Raisin bread dough a few hours later.

B

Figure 22 Raisin Dough Analogy As the dough rises, raisins that were farther apart travel a greater distance in the same time as those that were closer together. Like galaxies in an expanding universe, the distant raisins move away from one another more rapidly than those that are near one another.

Use Visuals

L1

Figure 22 Use this figure to explain how the universe is expanding. Tell students to imagine that the galaxy at the top left is our galaxy. Ask: **If the raisin that is 2 cm from us becomes 6 cm away 2 hours later, how fast is it moving relative to us?** *([6 cm − 2 cm] / 2 hr = 2 cm/hr)* **If the raisin that is 5 cm from us becomes 15 cm away 2 hours later, how fast is it moving relative to us?** *([15 cm − 5 cm] / 2 hr = 5 cm/hr)* **How do your answers relate to Hubble's law?** *(The farther away a galaxy is, the faster it is moving.)*
Visual, Logical

Build Science Skills

L2

Use Analogies The text cites the raisin dough analogy as a way of explaining the expansion of the universe. Model a Slinky as an analogy for red shifts. Have groups of two grip each side of a Slinky. Instruct one student to stay in place, and another to slowly back away. Ask students to discuss the following: **Which of you represents our galaxy?** *(the stationary student)* **Which of you represents a galaxy that is moving away?** *(the student who is backing up)* **How does the Slinky represent a red shift?** *(As the coils stretch, the distance between each one grows, modeling the lengthening of wavelengths over distance.)*
Kinesthetic, Interpersonal

ACTIVITY

Facts and Figures

Edwin Hubble was born in 1889 in Marshfield, Missouri. He initially studied law and only later decided to go into astronomy. In the early 1920s, astronomers did not know whether some "spiral nebulae" were small clouds of stars within our galaxy or separate galaxies entirely. Hubble measured the distance to the Andromeda nebula in 1924 and showed that it was about 100,000 times as far away as nearby stars. He concluded that it was a separate galaxy. In 1929, Hubble established that the red shift of galaxies was proportional to their distance, and thus that the universe is expanding. Much of Hubble's work was done using what at the time was the world's best telescope—the 100-in. telescope on Mt. Wilson in California. Hubble died in 1953.

Answer to . . .

Elliptical galaxies range in shape from round to oval.

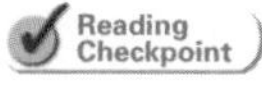

Galaxies that have the greatest red shifts are the most distant.

Hubble's law states that galaxies are receding from Earth at a speed that is proportional to their distance.

The Big Bang

Build Reading Literacy L1

Refer to **p. 698D,** which provides guidelines for sequencing.

Sequence While reading about the big bang, have students create a flowchart showing the chain of events starting with the big bang and ending with the formation of stars and galaxies. *(big bang → atoms form → gases cool and condense → stars and galaxies form)*
Visual, Verbal

Address
Misconceptions

L2

Students may think that the big bang occurred at a certain point at the center of the universe. They may also think that material from the big bang exploded into already existing space. Tell students that space itself expanded as a result of the big bang. Space is within the universe rather than the universe being within space. There is no center from which the universe is expanding. The big bang essentially occurred everywhere at once. Evidence for this is that the cosmic background radiation comes from every direction, not just from a specific location.
Verbal

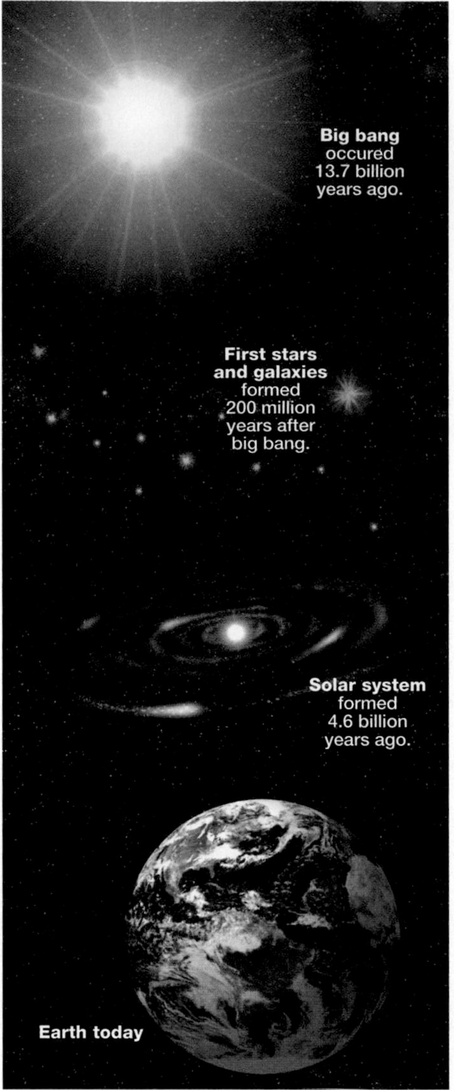
Big bang occured 13.7 billion years ago.
First stars and galaxies formed 200 million years after big bang.
Solar system formed 4.6 billion years ago.
Earth today

Figure 23 The Big Bang According to the big bang theory, the universe began 13.7 billion years ago. Two hundred million years later, the first stars and galaxies began to form.

The Big Bang

Did the universe have a beginning? Will it have an end? Scientists are trying to answer these questions.

Any theory about the origin of the universe must account for the fact that all distant galaxies are moving away from us. Because all galaxies appear to be moving away from Earth, is our planet in the center of the universe? Probably not, because if we are not even in the center of our own solar system, and our solar system is not even in the center of the galaxy, it seems unlikely that we could be in the center of the universe.

A more probable explanation exists. Imagine a balloon with paper-punch dots glued to its surface. When the balloon is inflated, each dot spreads apart from every other dot. Similarly, if the universe is expanding, every galaxy would be moving away from every other galaxy.

This concept of an expanding universe led to the widely accepted big bang theory. According to the **big bang theory,** the universe began as a violent explosion from which the universe continues to expand, evolve, and cool. **The big bang theory states that at one time, the entire universe was confined to a dense, hot, supermassive ball. Then, about 13.7 billion years ago, a violent explosion occurred, hurling this material in all directions.** The big bang, as shown in Figure 23, marks the beginning of the universe. All matter and space were created at that instant. After several hundred thousand years, the universe became cool enough for atoms to form. Gases in the universe continued to cool and condense. They eventually formed the stars that make up the galaxies we now observe moving away from us.

Supporting Evidence Through decades of experimentation and observation, scientists have gathered substantial evidence that supports the big bang theory. For example, the red shift of galaxies that you read about earlier indicates that the universe is still expanding. Scientists discovered a type of energy called cosmic background radiation. This energy was detected as faint radio signals coming from every direction in space. Scientists think that this radiation was produced during the big bang.

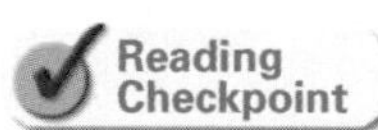
Reading Checkpoint

What evidence supports the big bang?

The Big Crunch? If the universe began with a big bang, how will it end? One view is that the universe will last forever. In this scenario, the stars will slowly burn out, being replaced by invisible degenerate matter and black holes that will travel outward through an endless, dark, cold universe. The other possibility is that the outward flight of the galaxies will slow and eventually stop. Gravitational contraction would follow, causing the galaxies to collide and combine into the high-energy, high-density mass from which the universe began. This fiery death of the universe, the big bang operating in reverse, has been called the "big crunch."

Whether or not the universe will expand forever or eventually collapse upon itself depends on its average density. If the average density of the universe is more than its critical density—about one atom for every cubic meter—the gravitational field is enough to stop the outward expansion and cause the universe to contract. On the other hand, if the density of the universe is less than the critical value, it will expand forever. Current estimates of the density of the universe place it below the critical density, which predicts an ever-expanding, or open, universe. Additional support for an open universe comes from studies that indicate the universe is expanding faster now than in the past. The view currently favored by most scientists is an expanding universe with no ending point.

It should be noted, however, that the methods used to determine the ultimate fate of the universe have substantial uncertainties. It is possible that previously undetected matter exists in great quantities in the universe. If this is so, the galaxies could, in fact, collapse in the "big crunch."

3 ASSESS

Evaluate Understanding L2

Write "The Expanding Universe" on the board. Ask students to contribute ideas that indicate that the universe is expanding.

Reteach L1

Have students use Figures 18–20 to review the basic types of galaxies.

Medium-mass stars, like our sun, may be the most likely candidates to have planets that support life. In our own galaxy, there are millions of sun-like stars. If these stars are orbited by planets, the existence of life would depend on the planets' composition and temperature, among other factors.

Section 25.3 Assessment

Reviewing Concepts

1. What is a galaxy?
2. Describe the size and structure of the Milky Way Galaxy.
3. How do galaxies differ?
4. What evidence indicates that the universe is expanding?
5. What is the big bang theory?

Critical Thinking

6. **Comparing and Contrasting** Compare and contrast the three types of galaxies.
7. **Inferring** If the universe is an open universe, what can you infer about its average density?

Writing in Science

Descriptive Paragraph Scientists are continuously searching the Milky Way Galaxy for other stars that may have planets. What types of stars would most likely have a planet or planets suitable for life as we know it? Write a paragraph describing these stars.

Answer to . . .

The red shift of distant galaxies and cosmic background radiation support the big bang.

Section 25.3 Assessment

1. A galaxy is a group of stars, dust, and gases held together by gravity.
2. The Milky Way is a large spiral galaxy whose disk is about 100,000 light-years wide and about 10,000 light-years thick at the nucleus.
3. Galaxies differ in size, shape, and the ages of their stars.
4. The red shifts of distant galaxies indicate that the universe is expanding.
5. The big bang theory states that about 13.7 billion years ago, the universe began at one point and has been expanding at close to the speed of light ever since.
6. The most obvious difference is their shape: spiral galaxies have arms; elliptical galaxies range in shape from round to oval; irregular galaxies have no regular shape. Irregular galaxies are composed mostly of young stars, while elliptical galaxies contain mostly older stars. Spiral galaxies are composed of stars of various ages, with the youngest stars in the arms.
7. Its average density must be less than its critical density.

understanding EARTH

Astrology—Forerunner of Astronomy L2

Background

Until about 400 years ago, science was not a separate field of study as it is today. It was rare for anyone to study the natural world merely out of curiosity. Belief in what we would now call unscientific superstitions was quite common even among well-educated people. Kepler, for example, believed that observations of the stars could be used to predict future events. Part of his job as an astronomy professor was to make such predictions.

Teaching Tips

- Have students make a table with the headings Astronomy and Astrology. As student read the feature, have them note the features of each. When they are finished, have them use their tables to make a Venn diagram showing the differences and similarities between astronomy and astrology.
- Have students research early astronomers and the connections between astronomy and the rest of society at that time. Ask them to present a brief report to the class.

Visual, Logical

understanding EARTH

Astrology—Forerunner of Astronomy

Many people confuse astrology and astronomy to the point of believing these terms to be synonymous. Nothing can be further from the truth. Astronomy is a scientific investigation of the universe to discover the properties of celestial objects and the laws under which the universe operates. Astrology, on the other hand, is based on ancient superstitions that a person's actions and personality are based on the positions of the planets and stars now, and at the person's birth. Scientists do not accept astrology, regarding it as a pseudoscience ("false science"). Most people who read horoscopes do so only as a pastime and do not let them influence their daily living.

Figure 24 The Constellations of the Zodiac Earth is shown in its autumn (September) position in orbit, from which the sun is seen against the background of the constellation Virgo.

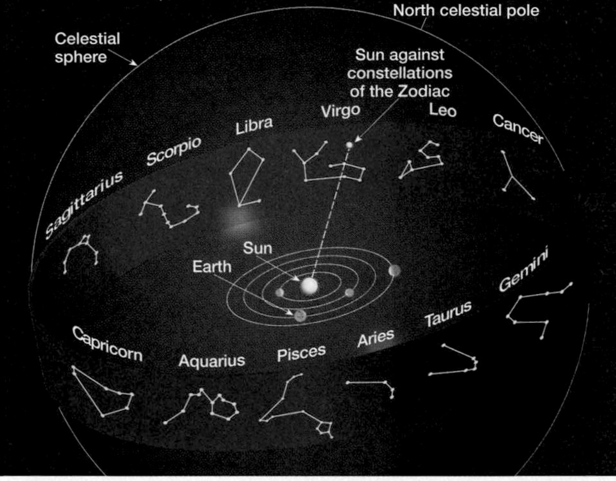

Astrology began more than 3000 years ago when the positions of the planets were plotted as they regularly migrated against the background of the "fixed" stars. Because the solar system is "flat," like a whirling Frisbee, the planets orbit the sun along nearly the same plane. Therefore, the planets, sun, and moon all appear to move along a band around the sky known as the zodiac. Because Earth's moon cycles through its phases about 12 times each year, the Babylonians divided the zodiac into 12 constellations, as shown in Figure 24. Thus, each successive full moon can be seen against the backdrop of the next constellation.

When the zodiac was first established, the vernal equinox (first day of spring) occurred when the sun was viewed against the constellation Aries. However, during each succeeding vernal equinox, the position of the sun shifts very slightly against the background of stars. Now, over 2000 years later, the vernal equinox occurs when the sun is in Pisces. In several years, the vernal equinox will occur when the sun appears against Aquarius.

Although astrology is not a science and has no basis in fact, it did contribute to the science of astronomy. The positions of the moon, sun, and planets at the time of a person's birth (sign of the zodiac) were considered to have great influence on that person's life. Even the great astronomer Kepler was required to make horoscopes part of his duties. To make horoscopes for the future, astrologers tried to predict the future positions of the celestial bodies. Thus, some of the improvements in astronomical instruments were made because of the desire for more accurate predictions of events such as eclipses, which were considered highly significant in a person's life.

Exploration Lab

Observing Stars

Throughout history, people have been recording the nightly movement of stars that results from Earth's rotation, as well as the seasonal changes in the constellations as Earth revolves around the sun. Early astronomers offered many explanations for the changes before the true nature of the motions was understood in the seventeenth century. In this lab, you'll observe and identify stars.

Problem How can you use star charts to identify constellations and track star movements?

Materials

- star charts (in the Appendix)
- penlight
- notebook

Skills Observing, Summarizing, Interpreting Data

Procedure

1. On a clear, moonless night far from street lights, go outside and observe the stars.
2. In a data table like the one below, make a list of the different colors of stars that you see.
3. Select one star that is overhead or nearly so. Observe and record its movement over a period of one hour. Also note the direction of its movement (eastward, westward).
4. Select a star chart suitable for your location and season. Locate several constellations. Sketch and label the constellations in your notebook.
5. Locate the North Star (Polaris) in the night sky. Observe the motion of stars that surround the North Star.
6. Repeat your observations several weeks later at the exact location.

Analyze and Conclude

1. **Observing** How many different colors of stars did you observe? How do these colors relate to star temperature?
2. **Interpreting Data** In which direction did the star that you observed appear to move? How is this movement related to the direction of Earth's rotation?
3. **Summarizing** Write a brief summary of the motion of the stars that surround the North Star. Be sure to include any changes you observed during your second viewing.

Go Further Find the Big Dipper, which is part of the constellation Ursa Minor. A binary star system makes up the stars of the Big Dipper. Locate the star pair and sketch them in their proper location in the Big Dipper.

Data Table

Date	Star Colors	Star Movement	Constellations	Motions of Stars Around North Star

Exploration Lab

Observing Stars L2

Objective
In this activity, students will observe and identify stars by using star charts.

Skills Focus Observing, Summarizing, Interpreting Data

Advance Prep Allow 5–10 minutes to copy star charts, if desired.

Class Time 20–30 minutes for after-lab discussion

Teaching Tip Because students will be observing stars at night from home, you may wish to help them choose the appropriate nights for viewing.

Expected Outcome Students will observe different colors of stars. They will also observe that the stars appeared to move.

Analyze and Conclude

1. Observed colors were blue, blue-white, red, and yellow. Blue and blue-white stars are hot, red stars are cool, and yellow stars are of medium temperature.
2. The star appeared to move westward. The rotation of Earth from west to east (eastward) makes the position of the star appear to move east to west (westward) throughout the night.
3. The stars surrounding the North Star appear to move in circles around the North Star, with the circles becoming larger the farther a star appears to be from the North Star.

Go Further

The binary star system is the second star in the handle of the Big Dipper.
Kinesthetic, Visual

Study Guide

Study Tip

Reviewing Notes
Tell students to make reviewing their notes part of their homework plan. By reviewing their notes for a few minutes each day, students will need to spend less time studying for tests.

Thinking Visually

a. Irregular
b. Elliptical
c. has round to oval shape
d. usually disk-shaped
e. contains young stars
f. contains both old and young stars

CHAPTER 25

Study Guide

25.1 Properties of Stars

Key Concepts

- Color is a clue to a star's temperature.
- Binary stars can be used to determine stellar mass.
- The nearest stars have the largest parallax angles, while those of distant stars are too small to measure.
- Three factors control the apparent brightness of a star as seen from Earth: how big it is, how hot it is, and how far away it is.
- A Hertzsprung-Russell diagram shows the relationship between the absolute magnitude and temperature of stars.

Vocabulary

constellation, *p. 700;* binary star, *p. 701;* light-year, *p. 702;* apparent magnitude, *p. 703;* absolute magnitude, *p. 703;* main-sequence star, *p. 704;* red giant, *p. 704;* supergiant, *p. 704;* cepheid variable, *p. 705;* nova, *p. 705;* nebulae, *p. 706*

25.2 Stellar Evolution

Key Concepts

- When the core of a protostar has reached at least 10 million K, pressure within is so great that nuclear fusion of hydrogen begins, and a star is born.
- All stars, regardless of their size, eventually run out of fuel and collapse due to gravity.
- Stars like the sun begin as a nebula, spend much of their lives as main-sequence stars, become red giants, planetary nebulae, white dwarfs, and finally, black dwarfs.

Vocabulary

protostar, *p. 708;* supernova, *p. 711;* white dwarf, *p. 712;* neutron star, *p. 713;* pulsar, *p. 713;* black hole, *p. 714*

25.3 The Universe

Key Concepts

- The Milky Way is a large spiral galaxy whose disk is about 100,000 light-years wide and about 10,000 light-years thick at the nucleus.
- In addition to shape and size, one of the major differences among different types of galaxies is the age of their stars.
- The red shifts of distant galaxies indicate that the universe is expanding.
- The big bang theory states that at one time, the entire universe was confined to a dense, hot, supermassive ball. Then, about 13.7 billion years ago, a violent explosion occurred, hurling this material in all directions.

Vocabulary

galaxy, *p. 715;* galaxy cluster, *p. 718;* Hubble's law, *p. 719;* big bang theory, *p. 720*

Thinking Visually

Concept Map Use information from the chapter to complete the concept map below.

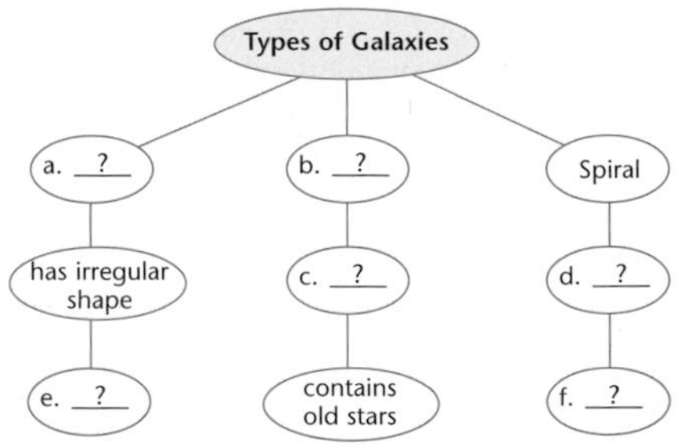

Chapter Assessment Resources

Print
Chapter Test, Chapter 25
Test Prep Resources, Chapter 25

Technology
Computer Test Bank, Chapter 25 Test
Online Text, Chapter 25
Go Online, PHSchool.com, Chapter 25

CHAPTER 25

NY Regents Content Item

Assessment

Interactive textbook with assessment at PHSchool.com 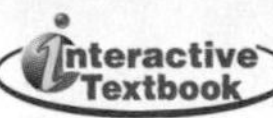

Reviewing Content

Choose the number that best answers the question or completes the statement.

1 Distances to stars are usually expressed in units called NY
(1) miles (2) kilometers
(3) light-years (4) astronomical units

2 The measure of a star's brightness is called its NY
(1) parallax
(2) color index
(3) visual binary
(4) magnitude

3 Distances to nearby stars can be determined from
(1) fluorescence
(2) stellar parallax
(3) stellar mass
(4) emission nebulae

4 Which color stars have the highest surface temperature? NY
(1) red (2) orange
(3) yellow (4) blue

5 Which type of star is the sun? NY
(1) black hole
(2) black dwarf
(3) main sequence
(4) red giant

6 What happens to a sun-like star after it has used up all the hydrogen in its core? NY
(1) supernova (2) neutron star
(3) red giant (4) nebula

7 Which object has such a strong surface gravity that light cannot escape it? NY
(1) black hole
(2) black dwarf
(3) red giant
(4) white dwarf

8 Stars that are composed of matter in which electrons have combined with protons are called NY
(1) black holes
(2) neutron stars
(3) red giants
(4) white dwarfs

9 Hubble's law states that galaxies are retreating from Earth at a speed that is proportional to their NY
(1) distance
(2) volume
(3) mass
(4) temperature

10 What theory states that the universe began in a violent explosion? NY
(1) the big crunch
(2) the Doppler effect
(3) Hubble's law
(4) the big bang

Understanding Concepts

11 Which property of a star can be determined by its color? NY

12 About how many stars are estimated to occur in pairs or multiples?

13 What is parallax?

14 Compare and contrast apparent magnitude and absolute magnitude. NY

15 What color is the most massive type of main-sequence star? The least massive? NY

16 At what temperature does nuclear fusion begin? NY

17 A stable main-sequence star is balanced between which two forces? NY

18 What element is the main fuel for main-sequence stars? For red giants? NY

19 What type of stars end their lives as supernovae? NY

20 What is a pulsar? NY

21 How long does it take our solar system to orbit the Milky Way Galaxy?

22 More distant galaxies have greater red shifts. What does this indicate about the universe? NY

23 What is cosmic background radiation? NY

Homework Guide

Section	Questions
1	1–5, 11–15, 26–31
2	6–8, 16–20
3	9, 10, 21–25

Assessment

Reviewing Content

(1) 3 (2) 4 (3) 2
(4) 4 (5) 3 (6) 3
(7) 1 (8) 2 (9) 1
(10) 4

Understanding Concepts

(11) A star's temperature can be determined by its color.
(12) About 50 percent of stars are estimated to occur in pairs or multiples.
(13) Parallax is the slight shifting in the apparent position of a nearby star due to the orbital motion of Earth.
(14) Apparent magnitude is how bright a star appears from Earth. Absolute magnitude is how bright a star actually is.
(15) The most massive type of main-sequence stars are hot, blue stars. The least massive are cool, red stars.
(16) 10 million K
(17) A stable main-sequence star is balanced between the forces of gravity and gas pressure.
(18) Hydrogen is the main fuel for main-sequence stars. Red giants consume hydrogen in their outer shells and eventually helium in their cores.
(19) massive stars
(20) A pulsar is a pulsating source of radio energy.
(21) It takes about 200 million years for our solar system to orbit the Milky Way Galaxy.
(22) It indicates that the universe is expanding.
(23) Cosmic background radiation is energy produced during the big bang. It can be detected coming from space in all directions.

Chapter 25

Critical Thinking

(24) Large quantities of interstellar matter block much of the visible light.
(25) You would study the arms of the spiral galaxy because most young stars are located in the arms.

Analyzing Data

(26) Rigel is the brightest star. Sirius B is the hottest star.
(27) White dwarfs have low absolute brightnesses compared with supergiants.
(28) The greater the absolute brightness of a main-sequence star, the higher its temperature is.

Assessment *continued*

Critical Thinking

24 **Explaining** Why are radio telescopes instead of optical telescopes used to determine the structure of the Milky Way Galaxy?

25 **Drawing Conclusions** Imagine that you are a scientist studying the birth of stars in a spiral galaxy. Which part of the galaxy would you study? Explain your answer. NY

Analyzing Data

Use the diagram below to answer questions 28–30.

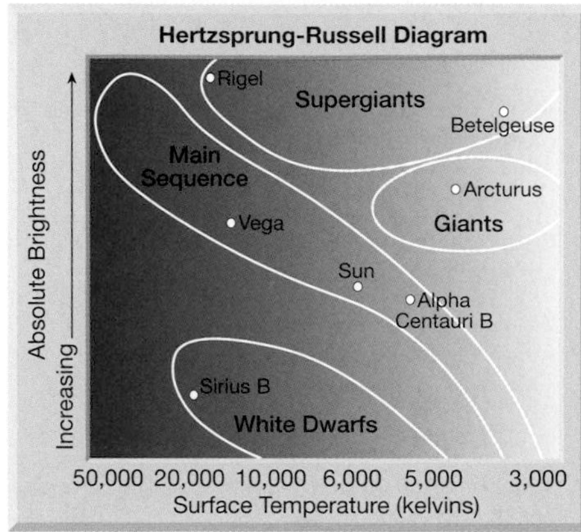

26 **Interpreting Graphs** What is the brightest star in the diagram? The hottest? NY

27 **Analyzing Data** How does the absolute brightness of white dwarfs compare with that of supergiants? NY

28 **Summarizing** What is the relationship between absolute brightness and temperature for a main-sequence star? NY

Concepts in Action

29 **Explaining** How can a binary star system be used to determine a star's mass?

30 **Inferring** Would you use parallax to determine the distance to a faraway star? Why or why not?

31 **Calculating** The closest star to the sun, Proxima Centauri, is 4.3 light-years away. How many kilometers from the sun is Proxima Centauri?

Performance-Based Assessment

Using Models Use materials provided by your teacher to construct a scale model of the Milky Way Galaxy. Before you begin, be sure to develop a workable scale for your model.

Concepts in Action

(29) The mass of a body can be calculated if it is gravitationally attached to a partner, which is the case for any binary star system. Binary stars orbit each other around a common point called the center of mass. For stars of equal mass, the center of mass lies exactly halfway between them. If one star is more massive than its partner, their common center will be closer to the more massive one.
(30) No, because the parallax angle of distant stars is too small to measure.
(31) One light-year equals about 9.5×10^{12} km; 9.5×10^{12} km / light-year $\times$ 4.3 light-years = 40.9×10^{12} km.

Regents Practice Exam

Test-Taking Tip

Sequencing a Series of Events
When a test question requires you to sequence a series of events, first try to predict the correct sequence before looking at the answer choices. Then compare your sequence to those listed. Be sure to pay attention to qualifiers in the question, such as *first, earliest, increasing,* or *decreasing,* as these may help you eliminate choices.

Which sequence of events describes the big bang theory? Begin with the earliest event.
(1) explosion; atoms form; stars form; all matter concentrated at a single point
(2) all matter concentrated at a single point; explosion; atoms form; stars form
(3) explosion; stars form; all matter concentrated at a single point; atoms form
(4) stars form; atoms form; all matter concentrated at a single point; explosion

(Answer: 2)

For *each* statement or question, choose the *number* of the word or expression that, of those given, best completes the statement or answers the question. Some questions may require the use of the *Earth Science Reference Tables.*

1 The hottest stars are
(1) red (2) blue (3) yellow (4) white

2 Based on the red shifts of distant galaxies, astronomers conclude that
(1) Earth is in the center of the universe
(2) the universe is contracting
(3) the universe is expanding
(4) new galaxies are continually being added to the universe

3 Which term encompasses the other three?
(1) galaxy
(2) solar system
(3) star
(4) universe

Answer the following questions in complete sentences. Some questions may require the use of the *Earth Science Reference Tables.* Base your answers to questions 6 and 7 on the diagram below, which shows Life Cycle of a Sun-like Star.

4 Explain how two stars with the same absolute magnitude could have different apparent magnitudes.

5 How do the lives of the most massive stars end? What are the two possible products of this event?

6 Sequence the steps in the evolution of a medium-mass star, such as the sun.

7 At which stage in its evolution is the star the hottest? The brightest?

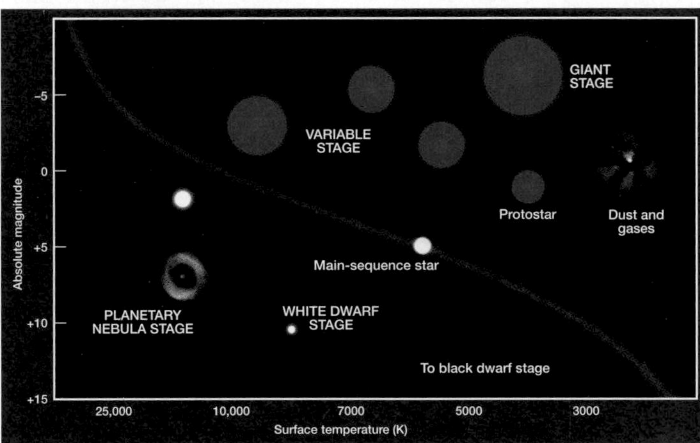

Regents Practice Exam

(1) 2
(2) 3
(3) 4
(4) A star that is farther away will have a lower apparent magnitude.
(5) A massive star ends as a supernova. The two possible products of this event are a neutron star and a black hole.
(6) In sequence, the stages in the evolution of a medium-mass star are: dust and gases, protostar, main-sequence star, giant, planetary nebula, white dwarf, black dwarf.
(7) The star is hottest during the planetary nebula stage; it is brightest during its giant stage.

Performance-Based Assessment

Provide students with clay, paper, paint, and other materials to construct their models. A workable scale might be 1 cm = 10,000 light-years. Models should reflect that the Milky Way is about 100,000 light-years wide and 10,000 light-years thick at its nucleus.

Your students can independently test their knowledge of the chapter and print out their results.

Science Skills

Basic Process Skills

During a science course, you often carry out some short lab activities as well as more detailed experiments. Here are some skills that you will use as you work.

Observing

In every science activity, you make a variety of observations. **Observing** is using one or more of the five senses to gather information. Many observations involve the senses of sight, hearing, touch, and smell.

Sometimes you will use tools that increase the power of your senses or make observations more precise. For example, hand lenses enable you to see things in greater detail. Tools may help you eliminate personal opinions or preferences.

In science it is customary to record your observations at the time they are made, usually by writing or drawing in a notebook. You may occasionally make records by using computers, cameras, videotapes, and other tools. As a rule, scientists keep complete accounts of their observations, often using tables to help organize their observations in a regular way.

Inferring

In science as in everyday life, observations are usually followed by inferences. **Inferring** is interpreting an observation or statement based on prior knowledge. For example, you can make several observations using the strobe photograph below. You can observe that the

ball is moving. Based on the motion of the ball, you might infer that the ball was thrown downward at an angle by an experimenter. In making that inference, you would use your knowledge about the motion of projectiles. Someone who knew more about projectile motion might infer that the ball loses energy with each bounce. That is why the height decreases with each bounce.

Notice that an inference is an act of reasoning, not a fact. That means an inference may be logical but not true. It is often necessary to gather further information before you can be confident that an inference is correct. For scientists, that information may come from further observations or from research into the work done by others.

Comparing Observations and Inferences

Sample Observation	Sample Inference
The ball moves less and less vertical distance in the time between each flash of the strobe light.	Gravity is slowing down the ball's upward motion.
The ball moves the same distance to the right in the time between each flash of the strobe light.	Air resistance is so small that it does not slow down the ball's horizontal motion.

Predicting

People often make predictions, but their statements about the future could be either guesses or inferences. In science, a **prediction** is an inference about a future event based on evidence, experience, or knowledge. For example, you can say, *On the first day next month, it will be sunny all day.* If your statement is based on evidence of weather patterns in the area, then the prediction is scientific. If the statement was made without considering any evidence, it's just a guess.

Predictions play a major role in science because they offer scientists a way to test ideas. If scientists understand an event or the properties of a particular object, they should be able to make accurate predictions about that event or object. Some predictions can be tested simply by making observations. For others, carefully designed experiments are needed.

Measuring

Measurements are important in science because they provide specific information and help observers avoid bias. **Measuring** is comparing an object or process to a standard. Scientists use a common set of standards, called the International System of Units, abbreviated as SI (for its French name, *Système International d'Unités*).

What distance does the ball travel in each time interval in the strobe photograph? You can make measurements on the photograph to make more precise statements about the ball's motion.

Calculating

Once scientists have made measurements, calculations are a very important part of analyzing data. How fast is a ball moving? You could directly measure the speed of a ball using probeware such as a motion sensor. But you can also calculate the speed using distance and time measurements. **Calculating** is a process in which a person uses mathematical operations to manipulate numbers and symbols.

Classifying

Classifying is grouping items according to some organizing idea or system. Classifying occurs in every branch of science but it's especially important in chemistry because there are so many different ways that elements can combine to form compounds.

Sometimes you place objects into groups using an established system. Other times you create a system by observing a variety of objects and identifying their properties. For example, you could group household cleaners into those that are abrasive and those that are not. Or you could categorize cleaners as toxic or nontoxic. Ammonia is toxic, whereas vinegar is not.

Using Tables and Graphs

Scientists represent and organize data in tables and graphs as part of experiments and other activities. Organizing data in tables and graphs makes it easier to see patterns in data. Scientists analyze and interpret data tables and graphs to determine the relationship of one variable to another and to make predictions based on the data.

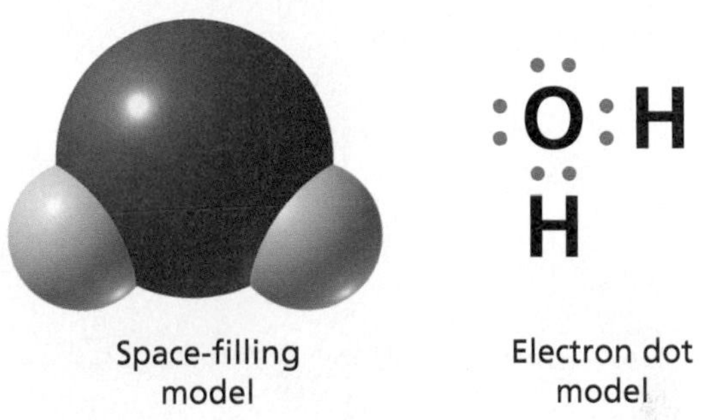

Using Models

Some cities refuse to approve new tall buildings if they would cast shadows on existing parks. As architects plan buildings in such locations, they use models to show where a proposed building's shadow will fall at any time of day at any season of the year. A **model** is a mental or physical representation of an object, process, or event. In science, models are usually made to help people understand natural objects and the processes that affect these objects.

Models can be varied. Mental models, such as mathematical equations, can represent some kinds of ideas or processes. For example, the equation for the surface area of a sphere can model the surface of Earth, enabling scientists to determine its size. Models can be two-dimensional (flat) or three-dimensional (having depth). In chemistry, for example, there are several ways to model the arrangement of atoms in a molecule. Two models for a water molecule are shown above. The electron dot model is two-dimensional. It has the advantage of clearly showing how electrons are shared among atoms in the molecule. The space-filling model cannot show the number of electrons inside the atoms or between atoms, but it does show the arrangement of atoms in space.

Experimental Methods

A science experiment is a procedure designed so that there is only one logical explanation for the results. Some types of experiments are fairly simple to design. Others may require ingenious problem solving.

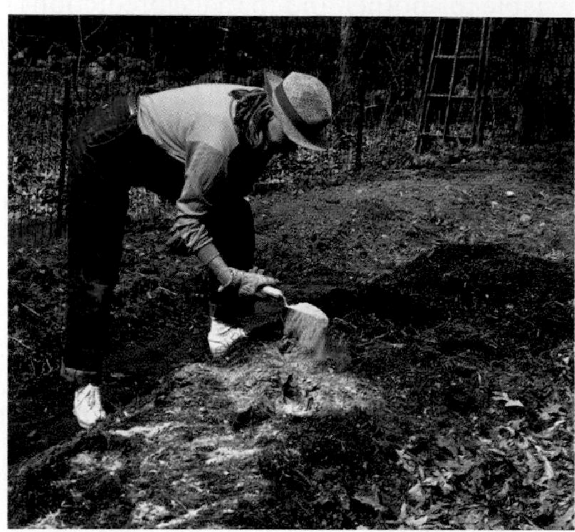

Posing Questions

As a gardener harvested corn in her vegetable garden, she noticed that on one side of the garden the plants produced very few ears of corn. The gardener wondered, *Why didn't the plants on one side of the garden produce as much corn?*

An experiment may begin when someone like the gardener asks a specific question or wants to solve a particular problem. Sometimes the original question leads directly to an experiment, but often researchers need to restate the problem before they can design an appropriate experiment. The gardener's question about the corn, for example, is too broad to be tested by an experiment, since there are so many possible different answers. To narrow the topic, the gardener might think about several related questions: *Were the seeds the same on both sides of the garden? Was the sunlight the same? Is there something different about the soil?*

Formulating Hypotheses

In science, a question about an event is answered by developing a possible explanation called a **hypothesis**. The hypothesis may be developed after long thought and research or come to a scientist "in a flash." To be useful, a hypothesis must lead to predictions that can be tested.

In this case, the gardener decided to focus on the quality of the soil on each side of her garden. She did some tests and discovered that the soil had a lower pH on the side where the plants did not produce well. That led her to propose this hypothesis: *If the pH of the soil is too low, the plants will produce less corn.* The next step is to make a prediction based on the hypothesis, for example, *If the pH of the soil is increased using lime, the plants will yield more corn.* Notice that the prediction suggests the basic idea for an experiment.

Designing Experiments

A carefully designed experiment can test a prediction in a reliable way, ruling out other possible explanations. As scientists plan their experimental procedures, they pay particular attention to the variables that must be controlled and the procedures that must be defined.

The gardener decided to study three groups of plants:

Group 1—20 plants on the side of the garden with a low pH;

Group 2—20 plants on the side of the garden with a low pH, but with lime added; and

Group 3—20 plants on the side of the garden with a high pH.

Controlling Variables

As researchers design an experiment, they identify the **variables**, factors that can change. Some common variables include mass, volume, time, temperature, light, and the presence or absence of specific materials. An experiment involves three categories of variables. The factor that scientists purposely change is called the **manipulated variable**. The factor that may change because of the manipulated variable and that scientists want to observe is called the **responding variable**. And the factors that scientists purposely keep the same are called the **controlled variables**. Controlling variables helps make researchers confident that the observed changes in the responding variable are due to changes in the manipulated variable.

For the gardener, the manipulated variable is the pH of the soil. The responding variable is the number of ears of corn produced by the plants. Among the variables that must be controlled are the amount of sunlight received each day, the time of year when seeds are planted, and the amount of water the plants receive.

What Is a "Control Group"?

When you read about certain experiments, you may come across references to a control group (or "a control") and the experimental groups. All of the groups in an experiment are treated exactly the same except for the manipulated variable. In an experimental group, the manipulated variable is being changed. The control group is used as a standard of comparison. It may consist of objects that are not changed in any way or objects that are being treated in the usual way. For example, in the gardener's experiment, Group 1 is the control group, because for these plants nothing is done to change the low pH of the soil.

Forming Operational Definitions

In an experiment, it is often necessary to define one or more variables explicitly so that any researcher could measure or control the variable in exactly the same way. An **operational definition** describes how a particular variable is to be measured or how a term is to be defined. In this context, the term *operational* means "describing what to do."

The gardener, for example, has to decide exactly how much lime to add to the soil. Can lime be added after the seeds are planted or only before planting? At what pH should no more lime be added to the soil? In this case, the gardener decided to add lime only before planting, and to add enough lime to make the pH equal in Groups 2 and 3.

Analyzing Data

The observations and measurements that are made in an experiment are called **data**. Scientists customarily record data in an orderly way. When an experiment is done, the researcher analyzes the data for trends or patterns, often by doing calculations or making graphs, to determine whether the results support the hypothesis.

For example, the gardener regularly measured and recorded data such as the soil moisture, daily sunlight, and pH of the soil. She found that the soil pH in Groups 2 and 3 started the same, but after two months the soil pH for Group 3 was a little higher than the soil pH for Group 2.

After harvesting the corn, the gardener recorded the numbers of ears of corn produced by each plant. She totaled the number of ears for each group. Her results were the following.

Group 1: 67 ears of corn
Group 2: 102 ears of corn
Group 3: 126 ears of corn

The overall trend was clear: The gardener's prediction was correct.

Drawing Conclusions

Based on whether the results confirm or refute the hypothesis, researchers make a final statement that summarizes the experiment. That final statement is called the **conclusion**. For example, the gardener's conclusion was, *Adding lime to soil with a low pH will improve the production of corn plants.*

Communicating Results

When an experiment has been completed, one or more events may follow. Researchers may repeat the experiment to verify the results. They may publish the experiment so that others can evaluate and replicate their procedures. They may compare their conclusion with the discoveries made by other scientists. And they may raise new questions that lead to new experiments. For example, *Why does the pH level decrease over time when soil is treated with lime?*

Evaluating and Revising

Scientists must be flexible about the conclusions drawn from an experiment. Further research may help confirm the results of the experiment or make it necessary to revise the initial conclusions. For example, a new experiment may show that lime can be effective only when certain microbes are present in the soil. Scientists continuously evaluate and revise experiments based on the findings in new research.

Science Safety

Laboratory work can be exciting, but it can be dangerous if you don't follow safety rules. Ask your teacher to explain any rules you don't understand. Always pay attention to safety symbols and **CAUTION** statements.

General Safety Rules and First Aid

1. Read all directions for an experiment several times. Follow the directions exactly as they are written. If you are in doubt, ask your teacher for assistance.
2. Never perform unauthorized or unsupervised labs, or handle equipment without specific permission.
3. When you design an experiment, do not start until your teacher has approved your plan.
4. If a lab includes physical activity, use caution to avoid injuring yourself or others. Tell your teacher if there is a reason that you should not participate.
5. Never eat, drink, or bring food into the laboratory.
6. Report all accidents to your teacher immediately.
7. Learn the correct ways to deal with a burn, a cut, and acid splashed in your eyes or on your skin.
8. Be aware of the location of the first-aid kit. Your teacher should administer any required first aid.
9. Report any fire to your teacher immediately. Find out the location of the fire extinguisher, the fire alarm, and the phone where emergency numbers are listed.

Dress Code

10. Always wear safety goggles to protect your eyes when working in the lab. Avoid wearing contact lenses. If you must wear contact lenses, ask your teacher what precautions you should take.
11. Wear a laboratory apron to protect your skin and clothing from harmful chemicals or hot materials.
12. Wear disposable plastic gloves to protect yourself from contact with chemicals that can be harmful. Keep your hands away from your face. Dispose of gloves according to your teacher's instructions.
13. Tie back long hair and loose clothing. Remove any jewelry that could contact chemicals or flames.

Heating and Fire Safety

14. Hot plates, hot water, and hot glassware can cause burns. Never touch hot objects with your bare hands. Use an oven mitt or other hand protection.
15. Use a clamp or tongs to hold hot objects. Test an object by first holding the back of your hand near it. If you feel heat on the back of your hand, the object may be too hot to handle.
16. Tie back long hair and loose clothing, and put on safety goggles before using a burner. Follow instructions from your teacher for lighting and extinguishing burners. If the flame leaps out of a burner as you are lighting it, turn the gas off. Never leave a flame unattended or reach across a flame. Make sure your work area is not cluttered with materials.
17. If flammable materials are present, make sure there are no flames, sparks, or exposed sources of heat.
18. Never heat a chemical without your teacher's permission. Chemicals that are harmless when cool can be dangerous when heated. When heating a test tube, point the opening away from you and others in case the contents splash or boil out of the test tube.
19. Never heat a closed container. Expanding hot gases may cause the container to explode.

Using Electricity Safely

20. To avoid an electric shock, never use electrical equipment near water, or when the equipment or your hands are wet. Use ground fault circuit interrupter (GFCI) outlets if you or your equipment may come into contact with moisture.
21. Use only sockets that accept a three-prong plug. Never use two-prong extension cords or adapters. When removing an electrical plug from a socket or extension cord, grasp the plug, not the cord.
22. Disconnect equipment that is not in use. Be sure cords are untangled and cannot trip anyone.
23. Do not use damaged electrical equipment. Look for dangerous conditions such as bare wires or frayed cords. Report damaged equipment immediately.

Using Glassware Safely

24. Handle fragile glassware, such as thermometers, test tubes, and beakers, with care. Do not touch broken glass. Notify your teacher if glassware breaks. Never use chipped or cracked glassware.
25. Never force glass tubing into a stopper. Your teacher will demonstrate the proper methods.
26. Never heat glassware that is not thoroughly dry. Use a wire screen to protect glassware from flames.
27. Hot glassware may not appear hot. Never pick up glassware without first checking to see if it is hot.
28. Never eat or drink from laboratory glassware.

Using Chemicals Safely

29. Do not let any corrosive or poisonous chemicals get on your skin or clothing, or in your eyes. When working with poisonous or irritating vapors, work in a well-ventilated area and wash your hands thoroughly after completing the activity.
30. Never test for an odor unless instructed by your teacher. Avoid inhaling a vapor directly. Use a wafting motion to direct vapor toward your nose.
31. Never mix chemicals "for the fun of it." You might produce a dangerous, possibly explosive substance.
32. Never touch, taste, or smell a chemical that you do not know for certain to be harmless.
33. Use only those chemicals listed in an investigation. Keep the lids on the containers when chemicals are not being used. To avoid contamination, never return chemicals to their original containers.
34. Take extreme care not to spill any chemicals. If a spill occurs, immediately ask your teacher about the proper cleanup procedure. Dispose of all chemicals as instructed by your teacher.
35. Be careful when working with acids or bases. Pour these chemicals over the sink, not over your workbench. If an acid or base gets on your skin or clothing, rinse it off with plenty of cold water. Immediately notify your teacher about an acid or base spill.
36. When diluting an acid, pour the acid into water. Never pour water into the acid.

Using Sharp Instruments

37. Use sharp instruments only as directed. Scissors, scalpels, pins, and knives are sharp and can cut or puncture your skin. Always direct sharp edges and points away from yourself and others.
38. Notify your teacher immediately if you cut yourself when in the laboratory.

End-of-Experiment Rules

39. All chemicals and any other materials used in the laboratory must be disposed of safely. Follow your teacher's instructions.
40. Clean up your work area and return all equipment to its proper place. Thoroughly clean glassware before putting it away.
41. Wash your hands thoroughly with soap, or detergent, and warm water. Lather both sides of your hands and between your fingers. Rinse well.
42. Check that all burners are off and the gas supply for the burners is turned off.

Safety Symbols

General Safety Awareness
Follow all safety instructions.

Physical Safety
Use caution in physical activities.

Safety Goggles
Always wear goggles in the laboratory.

Lab Apron
Always wear a lab apron in the laboratory.

Plastic Gloves
Protect your hands from unsafe chemicals.

Heating
Be careful using sources of heat.

Heat-Resistant Gloves
Do not touch hot objects with bare hands.

Flames
Work carefully around open flames.

No Flames
Flammable materials may be present.

Electric Shock
Take precautions to avoid electric shock.

Fragile Glassware
Handle glassware carefully.

Corrosive Chemical
Work carefully with corrosive chemicals.

Poison
Avoid contact with poisonous chemicals.

Fumes
Avoid inhaling dangerous vapors.

Sharp Object
Use caution with sharp or pointed tools.

Disposal
Follow instructions for disposal.

Hand Washing
Wash your hands before leaving the lab.

Reading and Study Skills

At the beginning of each section, you will find a reading strategy to help you study. Each strategy uses a graphic organizer to help you stay organized. The following strategies and graphic organizers are used throughout the text.

Reading Strategies

Using Prior Knowledge

This strategy helps you think about your own experience before you read a section. Research has shown that you learn new material better if you can relate it to something you already know.

Previewing

Previewing a lesson can give you a sense of how the textbook is organized and what lies ahead. One technique is to look at the section topics (in green and blue type). You also can preview by reading captions. Sometimes previewing helps you simply because you find out a topic isn't as hard as you thought it might be.

Predicting

You can preview a section and then make a prediction. For example, you might predict the meaning of an important concept. Then, as you read, check to see if your prediction was correct. Often you find out that you knew more about a topic than you realized.

Building Vocabulary

Start building new vocabulary by previewing a section and listing boldface terms you don't recognize. Then look for each term as you read. Writing a sentence with a term, and defining a term in your own words are two techniques that will help you remember definitions.

Identifying the Main Idea

The key symbols next to boldface sentences identify the main ideas in a section. You can use topic sentences to find the main idea in a paragraph. Often, a topic sentence is the first or second sentence in a paragraph.

Identifying Cause and Effect

Cause-and-effect relationships are very important in science. A flowchart will help you identify cause-and-effect relationships as you read about a process.

Comparing and Contrasting

Comparing and contrasting can help you understand how concepts are related. Comparing is identifying both similarities and differences, while contrasting focuses on the differences. Compare-and-contrast tables and Venn diagrams work best with this strategy.

Sequencing

When you sequence events, it helps you to visualize the steps in a process and to remember the order in which they occur. Sequences often involve cause-and-effect relationships. Use flowcharts for linear sequences and cycle diagrams for repeating sequences.

Relating Text and Figures

You can use diagrams and photographs to focus on the essential concepts in a section. Then find text that extends the information in the figures. You can also reinforce concepts by comparing different figures.

Summarizing

Summarizing requires you to identify key ideas and state them briefly in your own words. You will remember the content of an entire section better even if you summarize only a portion of the section.

Outlining

You can quickly organize an outline by writing down the green and blue headings in a section. Then add phrases or sentences from the boldface sentences to expand the outline with the most important concepts.

Monitoring Your Understanding

You can evaluate your progress with graphic organizers such as a Know-Write-Learn (KWL) table. To make a KWL table, construct a table with three columns, labeled K, W, and L. Before you read, write what you already know in the first column (K). In the middle column, write what you want to learn (W). After you read, write what you learned (L).

Graphic Organizers

Concept Maps and Web Diagrams

A **concept map** is a diagram that contains concept words in ovals and connects the ovals with linking words. Often the most general concept is placed at the top of the map. The content of the other ovals becomes more specific as you move away from the main concept. Linking words are written on a line between two ovals.

A **web diagram** is a type of concept map that shows how several ideas relate to one central idea. Each subtopic may also link to subtopics, creating the visual effect of a spider web. Linking words are usually not included.

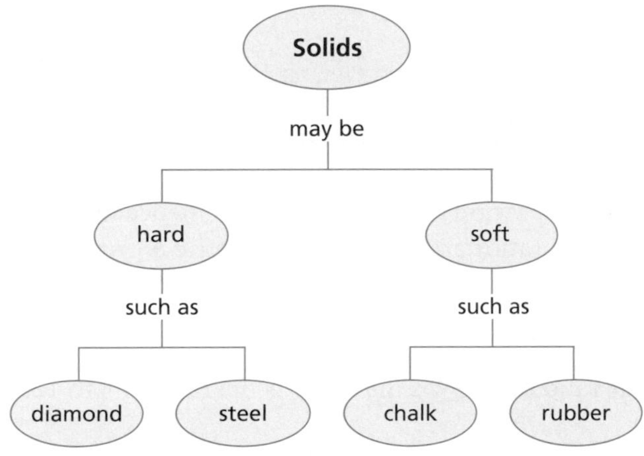

Compare-and-Contrast Tables

A **compare-and-contrast table** is a way of showing the similarities and differences between two or more objects or processes. The table provides an organized framework for making comparisons based on specific characteristics.

The items to be compared are usually column headings across the top of the table. Characteristics for comparison are listed in the first column. You complete the table by filling in information for each item.

Compare-and-Contrast Table

Contents	Book	CD-ROM
Paper pages	Yes	No
Photographs	Yes	Yes
Videos	No	Yes

Venn Diagrams

A **Venn diagram** consists of two or more ovals that overlap. Each oval represents a particular object or idea. Unique characteristics are shown in the part of each oval that does not overlap. Shared characteristics are shown in the area of overlap.

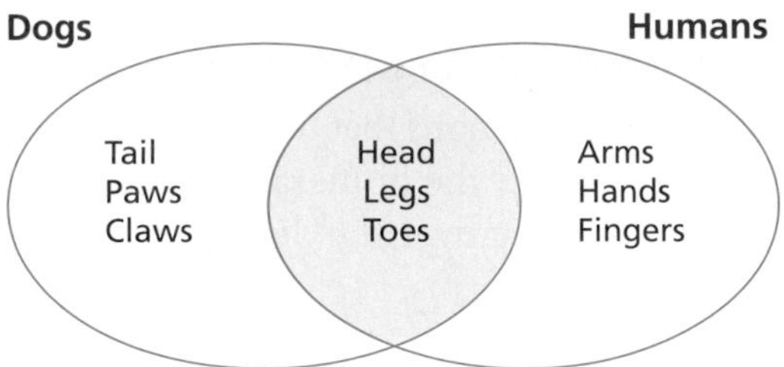

Flowcharts

A **flowchart** is used to represent the order in which a set of events occurs. Each step in the sequence is described in a box. Each box is linked to the next box with an arrow. The flowchart shows a sequence from beginning to end.

Preparing Pasta

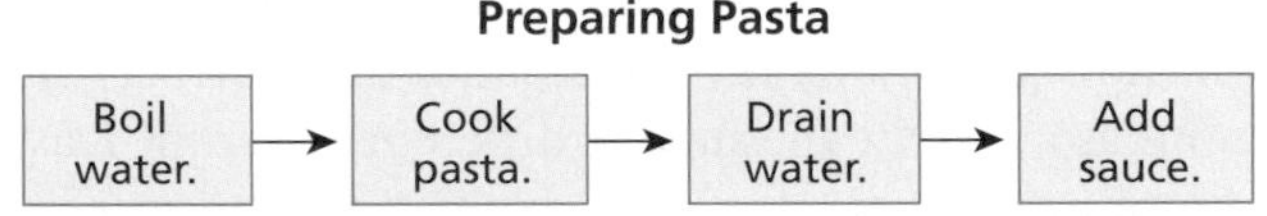

Cycle Diagrams

A **cycle diagram** shows boxes representing a cyclical sequence of events. As in a flowchart, boxes are linked with arrows, but the sequence does not have a beginning or end. The boxes are usually arranged in a clockwise circle.

The Moon as Seen From Earth

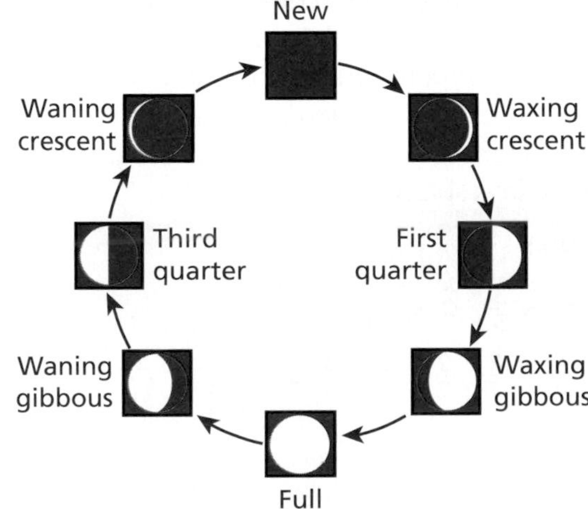

Skills Handbook

Math Skills

Throughout your study of science, you will often need to solve math problems. This appendix is designed to help you quickly review the basic math skills you will use most often.

Fractions

Adding and Subtracting Fractions

To add or subtract fractions that have the same denominator, add or subtract the numerators, and then write the sum or difference over the denominator. Express the answer in lowest terms.

Examples

$$\frac{3}{10} + \frac{1}{10} = \frac{3+1}{10} = \frac{4}{10} = \frac{2}{5}$$

$$\frac{5}{7} - \frac{2}{7} = \frac{5-2}{7} = \frac{3}{7}$$

To add or subtract fractions with different denominators, find the least common denominator. Write an equivalent fraction for each fraction using the least common denominator. Then add or subtract the numerators. Write the sum or difference over the least common denominator and express the answer in lowest terms.

Examples

$$\frac{1}{3} + \frac{3}{5} = \frac{5}{15} + \frac{9}{15} = \frac{5+9}{15} = \frac{14}{15}$$

$$\frac{7}{8} - \frac{1}{4} = \frac{7}{8} - \frac{2}{8} = \frac{7-2}{8} = \frac{5}{8}$$

Multiplying Fractions

When multiplying two fractions, multiply the numerators to find the product's numerator. Then multiply the denominators to find the product's denominator. It helps to divide any numerator or denominator by the greatest common factor before multiplying. Express the answer in lowest terms.

Examples

$$\frac{3}{5} \times \frac{2}{7} = \frac{3 \times 2}{5 \times 7} = \frac{6}{35}$$

$$\frac{4}{14} \times \frac{6}{9} = \frac{2 \times 2}{7 \times 2} \times \frac{2 \times 3}{3 \times 3} = \frac{2 \times 2}{7 \times 3} = \frac{4}{21}$$

Dividing Fractions

To divide one fraction by another, invert and multiply. Express the answer in lowest terms.

Examples

$$\frac{2}{5} \div \frac{3}{4} = \frac{2}{5} \times \frac{4}{3} = \frac{2 \times 4}{5 \times 3} = \frac{8}{15}$$

$$\frac{9}{16} \div \frac{5}{8} = \frac{9}{16} \times \frac{8}{5} = \frac{9 \times 1}{2 \times 5} = \frac{9}{10}$$

Ratios and Proportions

A ratio compares two numbers or quantities. A ratio is often written as a fraction expressed in lowest terms. A ratio also may be written with a colon.

Examples

The ratio of 3 to 4 is written as 3 to 4, $\frac{3}{4}$, or 3 : 4.

The ratio of 10 to 5 is written as $\frac{10}{5} = \frac{2}{1}$, or 2 : 1.

A proportion is a mathematical sentence that states that two ratios are equivalent. To write a proportion, place an equal sign between the two equivalent ratios.

Examples

The ratio of 6 to 9 is the same as the ratio of 8 to 12.

$$\frac{6}{9} = \frac{8}{12}$$

The ratio of 2 to 4 is the same as the ratio of 7 to 14.

$$\frac{2}{4} = \frac{7}{14}$$

You can set up a proportion to determine an unknown quantity. Use x to represent the unknown. To find the value of x, cross multiply and then divide both sides of the equation by the number that comes before x.

Example

Two out of five students have blue notebooks. If this same ratio exists in a class of twenty students, how many students in the class have blue notebooks?

$\frac{2}{5} = \frac{x}{20}$ ← **Cross multiply.**

$2 \times 20 = 5x$ ← **Divide.**

$8 = x$

Percents and Decimals

To convert a percent to a decimal value, write the number without the percent sign and move the decimal point two places to the left. Add a zero before the decimal point.

Examples

38% = 0.38
13.92% = 0.1392

You can convert a decimal value to a percent value by moving the decimal point two places to the right and adding the percent sign.

Examples

0.46 = 46%
0.8215 = 82.15%

Exponents

A base is a number that is used as a factor. An exponent is a number that tells how many times the base is to be used as a factor.

Example

$2^5 = 2 \times 2 \times 2 \times 2 \times 2 = 32$

A power is any number that can be expressed as a product in which all of the factors are the same. Any number raised to the zero power is 1. Any number raised to the first power is that number. The only exception is the number 0, which is zero regardless of the power it is raised to.

Exponents	
Powers of 2	**Powers of 10**
$2^2 = 4$	$10^2 = 100$
$2^1 = 2$	$10^1 = 10$
$2^0 = 1$	$10^0 = 1$
$2^{-1} = \frac{1}{2}$	$10^{-1} = \frac{1}{10}$
$2^{-2} = \frac{1}{4}$	$10^{-2} = \frac{1}{100}$

Multiplying Exponents

To multiply exponential expressions with the same base, add the exponents. The general expression for exponents with the same base is $x^a \times x^b = x^{a+b}$.

Example

$3^2 \times 3^4 = (3 \times 3) \times (3 \times 3 \times 3 \times 3) = 3^6 = 729$

To raise a power to a power, keep the base and multiply the exponents. The general expression is $(x^a)^b = x^{ab}$.

Example

$(3^2)^3 = (3^2) \times (3^2) \times (3^2) = 3^6 = 729$

To raise a product to a power, raise each factor to the power. The general expression is $(xy)^n = x^n y^n$.

Example

$(3 \times 9)^2 = 3^2 \times 9^2 = 9 \times 81 = 729$

Dividing Exponents

To divide exponential expressions with the same base, keep the base and subtract the exponents. The general expression is:

$\frac{x^a}{x^b} = x^{a-b}$

Example

$\frac{5^6}{5^4} = 5^{6-4} = 5^2 = 25$

When the exponent of the denominator is greater than the exponent of the numerator, the exponent of the result is negative. A negative exponent follows the general expression:

$x^{-n} = \frac{1}{x^n}$

Example

$2^3 \div 2^5 = 2^{3-5} = 2^{-2} = \frac{1}{2^2} = \frac{1}{4}$

Math Skills

Scientific Notation

Scientific notation is used to express very large numbers or very small numbers. To convert a large number to scientific notation, move the decimal point to the left until it is located to the right of the first nonzero number. The number of places that you move the decimal point becomes the positive exponent of 10.

Example

$18{,}930{,}000 = 1.893 \times 10^7$

To write a number less than 1 in scientific notation, move the decimal point to the right of the first nonzero number. Use the number of places you moved the decimal point as the negative exponent of 10.

Example

$$0.0027 = \frac{2.7}{10 \times 10 \times 10} = 2.7 \times 10^{-3}$$

Adding and Subtracting

To add or subtract numbers in scientific notation, the exponents must be the same. If they are different, rewrite one of the numbers to make the exponents the same. Then write the answer so that only one number is to the left of the decimal point.

Example

$$\begin{aligned} &3.20 \times 10^3 + 5.1 \times 10^2 \\ &= 32.0 \times 10^2 + 5.1 \times 10^2 \\ &= 37.1 \times 10^2 \\ &= 3.71 \times 10^3 \end{aligned}$$

Multiplying and Dividing

To multiply or divide numbers in scientific notation, the exponents are added or subtracted.

Examples

$$\begin{aligned} (1.2 \times 10^3) \times (3.4 \times 10^4) &= (4.1 \times 10^{3+4}) \\ &= 4.1 \times 10^7 \end{aligned}$$

$$\begin{aligned} (5.0 \times 10^9) \div (2.5 \times 10^6) &= (2.0 \times 10^{9-6}) \\ &= 2.0 \times 10^3 \end{aligned}$$

Significant Figures

When measurements are combined in calculations, the uncertainty of each measurement must be correctly reflected in the final result. The digits that are accurate in the answer are called significant figures. When the result of a calculation has more significant figures than needed, the result must be rounded off. If the first digit after the last significant digit is less than 5, round down. If the first digit after the last significant digit is 5 or more, round up.

Examples

1577 rounded to three significant figures is 1580.
1574 rounded to three significant figures is 1570.
2.458462 rounded to three significant figures is 2.46.
2.458462 rounded to four significant figures is 2.458.

Adding and Subtracting

In addition and subtraction, the number of significant figures in the answer depends on the number with the largest uncertainty.

Example

$$\begin{array}{lr} & 25.34\text{ g} \\ & 152\text{ g} \\ + & 4.009\text{ g} \\ \hline & 181\text{ g} \end{array}$$

The measurement with the largest uncertainty is 152 g and it is measured to the nearest gram. Therefore, the answer is given to the nearest gram.

Multiplying and Dividing

In multiplication and division, the measurement with the smallest number of significant figures determines the number of significant figures in the answer.

Example

$$\begin{aligned} \text{Density} &= \frac{\text{Mass}}{\text{Volume}} \\ &= \frac{20.79\text{ g}}{5.5\text{ mL}} \\ &= 3.8\text{ g/mL} \end{aligned}$$

Because 5.5 mL has only two significant figures, the answer must be rounded to two significant figures.

Formulas and Equations

An equation is a mathematical sentence that contains one or more variables and one or more mathematical operators (such as $+$, $-$, $\div$, $\times$, and $=$). An equation expresses a relationship between two or more quantities.

A formula is a special kind of equation. A formula such as $V = l \times w \times h$ states the relationship between unknown quantities represented by the variables V, l, w, and h. The formula means that volume (of a rectangular solid) equals length times width times height. Some formulas have numbers that do not vary, such as the formula for the perimeter of a square: $P = 4s$. In this formula, the number 4 is a constant.

To solve for a quantity in an equation or formula, substitute known values for the variables. Be sure to include units.

Example

An airplane travels in a straight line at a speed of 600 km/h. How far does it fly in 3.5 hours?

Write the formula that relates speed, distance, and time.

$$\text{Speed} = \frac{\text{Distance}}{\text{Time}}$$

$$v = \frac{d}{t}$$

To solve for distance, multiply both sides of the equation by t.

$$v = \frac{d}{t}$$

$$v \times t = \frac{d}{t} \times t$$

$$v \times t = d$$

Substitute in the known values.

$$600 \text{ km/h} \times 3.5 \text{ h} = d$$

$$d = 2100 \text{ km}$$

Conversion Factors

Many problems involve converting measurements from one unit to another. You can convert units by using an equation that shows how units are related. For example, 1 in. $=$ 2.54 cm relates inches and centimeters.

To write a conversion factor, divide both sides of the equation by 1 in.

$$\frac{1 \text{ in.}}{1 \text{ in.}} = \frac{2.54 \text{ cm}}{1 \text{ in.}}$$

$$1 = 2.54 \text{ cm/in.}$$

Because the conversion factor is equal to 1, you can multiply one side of an equation by it and preserve equality. You can make a second conversion factor by dividing both sides of the equation by 2.54 cm.

$$\frac{1 \text{ in.}}{2.54 \text{ cm}} = \frac{2.54 \text{ cm}}{2.54 \text{ cm}} = 1$$

One conversion factor converts inches to centimeters and the other converts centimeters to inches. Choose the conversion factor that cancels out the unit that you have a measurement for.

Example

Convert 25 inches to centimeters. Use d to represent the unknown number of centimeters.

$$d = 25 \text{ in.} \times \frac{2.54 \text{ cm}}{1 \text{ in.}}$$

$$= 64 \text{ cm}$$

Some conversions are more complicated and require multiple steps.

Example

Convert 23°F to a Celsius temperature.

The conversion formula is

$$°\text{F} = (\tfrac{9}{5} \times °\text{C}) + 32°\text{F}$$

Substitute in 23°F:

$$23°\text{F} = (\tfrac{9}{5} \times °\text{C}) + 32°\text{F}$$

$$23°\text{F} - 32°\text{F} = \tfrac{9}{5} \times °\text{C}$$

$$-9°\text{F} = \tfrac{9}{5} \times °\text{C}$$

$$-9°\text{F} \times \tfrac{5}{9} = -5°\text{C}$$

Math Skills

Data Tables

Data tables help to organize data and make it easier to see patterns in data. If you plan data tables before doing an experiment, they will help you record observations in an orderly fashion.

The data table below shows United States immigration data for the year 2001. Always include units of measurement so people can understand the data.

Immigration to the United States, 2001

Place of Origin	Number of Legal Immigrants
Africa	53,948
Asia	349,776
Europe	175,371
North America	407,888
South America	68,888

Bar Graphs

To make a bar graph, begin by placing category labels along the bottom axis. Add an overall label for the axis *Place of Origin.* Decide on a scale for the vertical axis. An appropriate scale for the data in the table is 0 to 500,000. Label the vertical axis *Number of People.* For each continent, draw a bar whose height corresponds to the number of immigrants. You will need to round off the values. For example, the bar for Africa should correspond to 54,000 people. Add a graph title to make it clear what the graph shows.

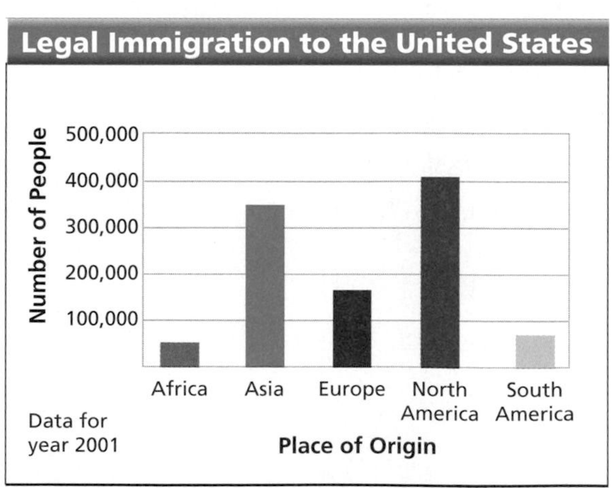

Circle Graphs

Use the total number to calculate percentages. For example, the percentage of immigrants from Africa in 2001 was $53{,}948 \div 1{,}061{,}984 = 0.051 \approx 5\%$. Multiply each percent by 360° to find the central angle of each wedge. For Africa, the central angle is 18°. Use a protractor to draw each central angle. Color and label the wedges and finish your graph with a title.

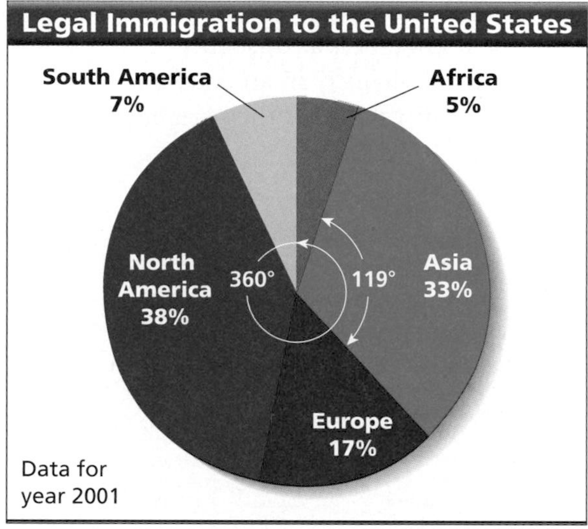

Line Graphs

The slope of a straight-line graph equals the "rise over the run." The rise is the change in the y values and the run is the change in the x values. Using points A and B on the graph below gives

$$\text{Slope} = \frac{\text{Rise}}{\text{Run}} = \frac{5-3}{9-3} = \frac{2}{6} = 0.33$$

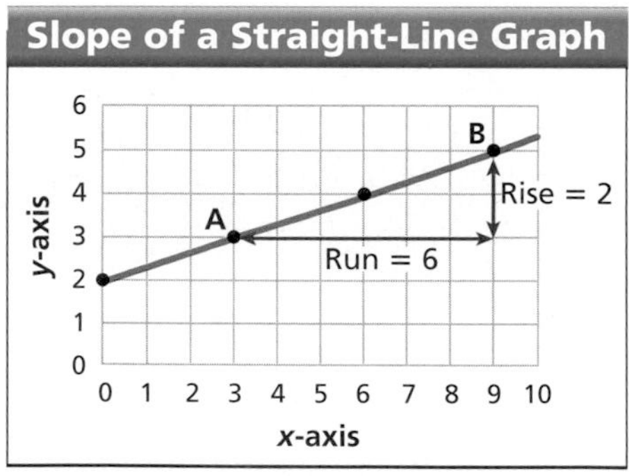

Appendix A SI Units

SI *(Système International d'Unités)* is a revised version of the metric system, which was originally developed in France in 1791. SI units of measurement are used by scientists throughout the world. The system is based on multiples of ten. Each unit is ten times larger or ten times smaller than the next unit. The most commonly used SI units are given below.

You can use conversion factors to convert between SI and non-SI units. Try the following conversions. How tall are you in meters? What is your weight in newtons? What is your normal body temperature in degrees Celsius?

Commonly Used Metric Units

Length	The distance from one point to another
meter (m)	A meter is slightly longer than a yard. 1 meter = 1000 millimeters (mm) 1 meter = 100 centimeters (cm) 1000 meters = 1 kilometer (km)

Volume	The amount of space an object takes up
liter (L)	A liter is slightly more than a quart. 1 liter = 1000 milliliters (mL)

Mass	The amount of matter in an object
gram (g)	A gram has a mass equal to about one paper clip. 1000 grams = 1 kilogram (kg)

Temperature	The measure of hotness or coldness
degrees Celsius (°C)	0°C = freezing point of water at sea level 100°C = boiling point of water at sea level

Metric–Customary Equivalents

2.54 centimeters (cm) = 1 inch (in.)
1 meter (m) = 39.37 inches (in.)
1 kilometer (km) = 0.62 miles (mi)
1 liter (L) = 1.06 quarts (qt)
250 milliliters (mL) = 1 cup (c)
9.8 newtons (N) = 2.2 pounds (lb)
$°C = 5/9 \times (°F - 32)$

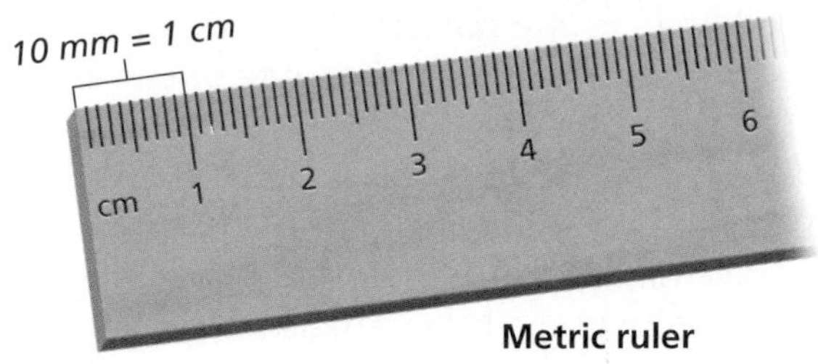

Metric ruler

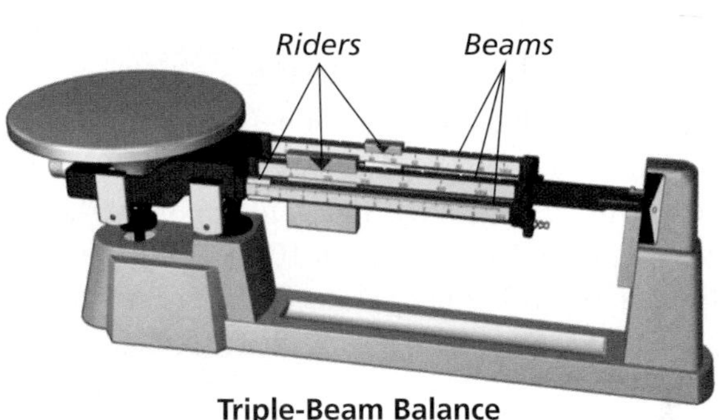

Triple-Beam Balance

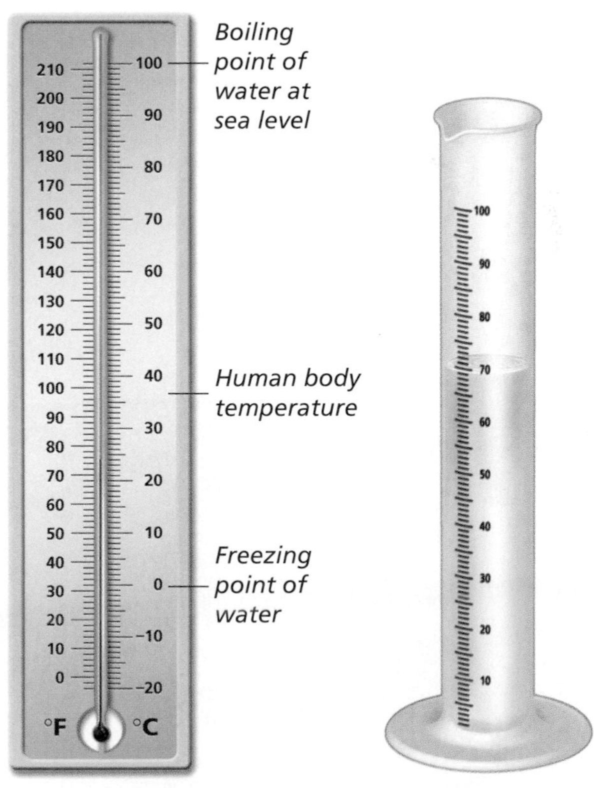

Thermometer

Graduated cylinder

Appendix B Using a Laboratory Balance

The laboratory balance is an important tool in scientific investigations. You can use a balance to determine the masses of materials that you study or experiment with in the laboratory.

Different kinds of balances are used in the laboratory. One kind of balance is the triple-beam balance. The balance that you may use in your science class is probably similar to the balance illustrated. To use the balance properly, you should learn the name, location, and function of each part of the balance you are using.

The Triple-Beam Balance

The triple-beam balance is a single-pan balance with three beams The back, or 100-gram, beam is divided into ten units of 10 grams. The middle, or 500-gram, beam is divided into five units of 100 grams. The front, or 10-gram, beam is divided into ten major units, each of which is 1 gram. Each 1-gram unit is further divided into units of 0.1 gram. What is the largest mass you could measure with a triple-beam balance?

The following procedure can be used to find the mass of an object with a triple-beam balance.

1. When no object is on the pan, and the riders are at zero, make sure the pointer is at zero. If it is not, use the adjustment screw to zero the balance.
2. Place the object on the pan.
3. Move the rider on the middle beam notch by notch until the horizontal pointer drops below zero. Move the rider back one notch.
4. Move the rider on the back beam notch by notch until the pointer again drops below zero. Move the rider back one notch.
5. Slowly slide the rider along the front beam until the pointer stops at zero. The mass of the object is the sum of the readings on the three beams.

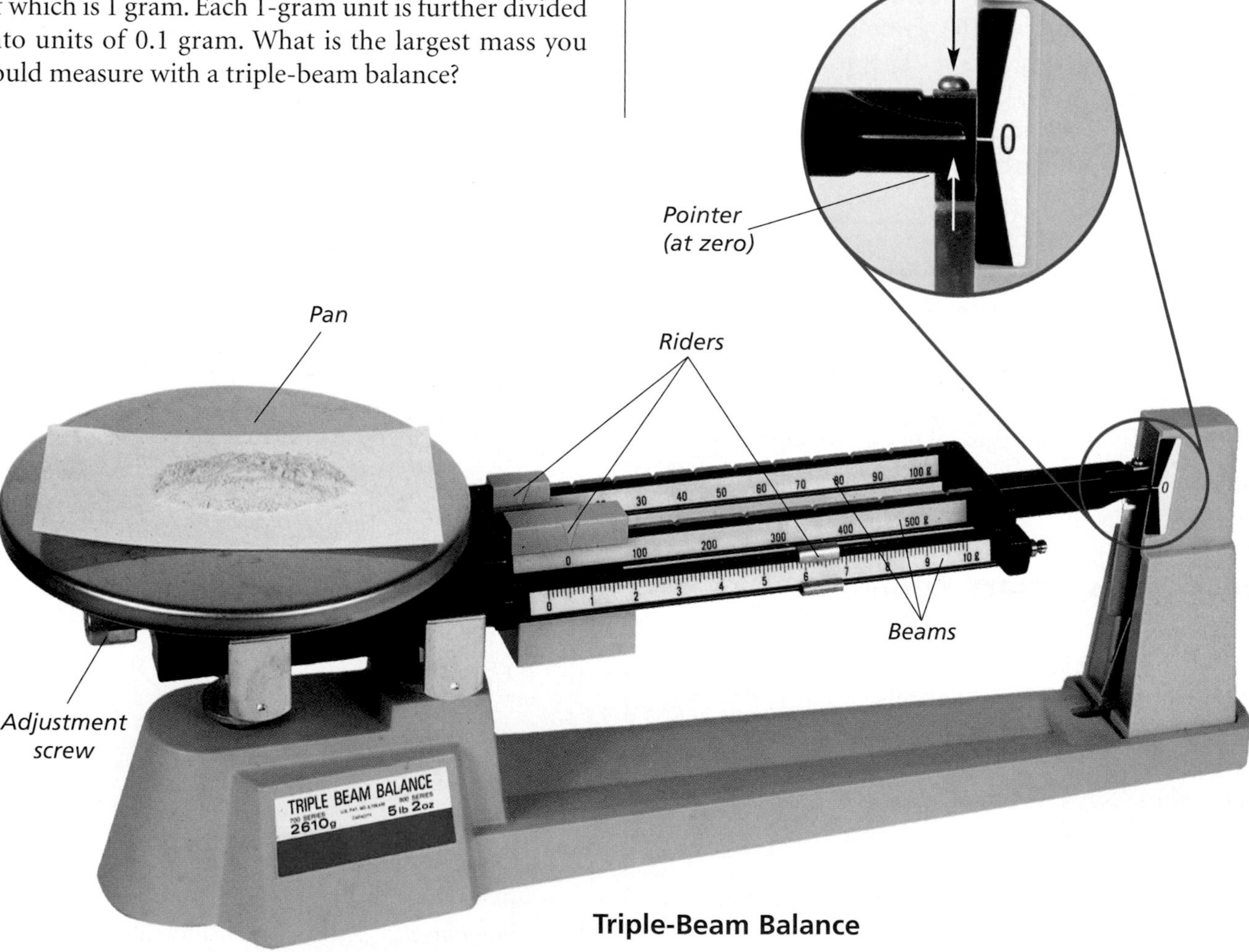

Triple-Beam Balance

Appendix C The Chemical Elements

Element	Symbol	Atomic Number	Atomic Mass†
Actinium	Ac	89	(277)
Aluminum	Al	13	26.982
Americium	Am	95	(243)
Antimony	Sb	51	121.75
Argon	Ar	18	39.948
Arsenic	As	33	74.922
Astatine	At	85	(210)
Barium	Ba	56	137.33
Berkelium	Bk	97	(247)
Beryllium	Be	4	9.0122
Bismuth	Bi	83	208.98
Bohrium	Bh	107	(264)
Boron	B	5	10.81
Bromine	Br	35	79.904
Cadmium	Cd	48	112.41
Calcium	Ca	20	40.08
Californium	Cf	98	(251)
Carbon	C	6	12.011
Cerium	Ce	58	140.12
Cesium	Cs	55	132.91
Chlorine	Cl	17	35.453
Chromium	Cr	24	51.996
Cobalt	Co	27	58.933
Copper	Cu	29	63.546
Curium	Cm	96	(247)
Dubnium	Db	105	(262)
Dysprosium	Dy	66	162.50
Einsteinium	Es	99	(252)
Erbium	Er	68	167.26
Europium	Eu	63	151.96
Fermium	Fm	100	(257)
Fluorine	F	9	18.998
Francium	Fr	87	(223)
Gadolinium	Gd	64	157.25
Gallium	Ga	31	69.72
Germanium	Ge	32	72.59
Gold	Au	79	196.97
Hafnium	Hf	72	178.49
Hassium	Hs	108	(265)
Helium	He	2	4.0026
Holmium	Ho	67	164.93
Hydrogen	H	1	1.0079
Indium	In	49	114.82
Iodine	I	53	126.90
Iridium	Ir	77	192.22
Iron	Fe	26	55.847
Krypton	Kr	36	83.80
Lanthanum	La	57	138.91
Lawrencium	Lr	103	(262)
Lead	Pb	82	207.2
Lithium	Li	3	6.941
Lutetium	Lu	71	174.97
Magnesium	Mg	12	24.305
Manganese	Mn	25	54.938
Meitnerium	Mt	109	(268)
Mendelevium	Md	101	(258)
Mercury	Hg	80	200.59
Molybdenum	Mo	42	95.94
Neodymium	Nd	60	144.24
Neon	Ne	10	20.179
Neptunium	Np	93	(237)
Nickel	Ni	28	58.71
Niobium	Nb	41	92.906
Nitrogen	N	7	14.007
Nobelium	No	102	(259)
Osmium	Os	76	190.2
Oxygen	O	8	15.999
Palladium	Pd	46	106.4
Phosphorus	P	15	30.974
Platinum	Pt	78	195.09
Plutonium	Pu	94	(244)
Polonium	Po	84	(209)
Potassium	K	19	39.098
Praseodymium	Pr	59	140.91
Promethium	Pm	61	(145)
Protactinium	Pa	91	231.04
Radium	Ra	88	(226)
Radon	Rn	86	(222)
Rhenium	Re	75	186.21
Rhodium	Rh	45	102.91
Rubidium	Rb	37	85.468
Ruthenium	Ru	44	101.07
Rutherfordium	Rf	104	(261)
Samarium	Sm	62	150.4
Scandium	Sc	21	44.956
Seaborgium	Sg	106	(263)
Selenium	Se	34	78.96
Silicon	Si	14	28.086
Silver	Ag	47	107.87
Sodium	Na	11	22.990
Strontium	Sr	38	87.62
Sulfur	S	16	32.06
Tantalum	Ta	73	180.95
Technetium	Tc	43	(98)
Tellurium	Te	52	127.60
Terbium	Tb	65	158.93
Thallium	Tl	81	204.37
Thorium	Th	90	232.04
Thulium	Tm	69	168.93
Tin	Sn	50	118.69
Titanium	Ti	22	47.90
Tungsten	W	74	183.85
Ununbium	Uub*	112	(277)
Ununnilium	Uun*	110	(269)
Ununquadium	Uuq*	114	—
Unununium	Uuu*	111	(272)
Uranium	U	92	238.03
Vanadium	V	23	50.941
Xenon	Xe	54	131.30
Ytterbium	Yb	70	173.04
Yttrium	Y	39	88.906
Zinc	Zn	30	65.38
Zirconium	Zr	40	91.22

† Number in parentheses gives the mass number of the most stable isotope.

* Name not officially assigned

Appendices

Appendix D United States Physical Map

95° W
90° W
85° W
80° W
75° W
70° W
65° W
A D A
Lake of the Woods
Namakan Lake
Red R.
James R.
MINNESOTA
Lake Superior
MICHIGAN
Lake Huron
VERMONT
MAINE
Mount Katahdin 5,265ft
Augusta
Gulf of Maine
45° N
Montpelier
NEW HAMPSHIRE
Concord
Adirondack Mountains
Saint Paul
WISCONSIN
Lake Michigan
Mississippi R.
Lake Ontario
Albany
Boston
MASSACHUSETTS
Providence
NEW YORK
Hartford
RHODE ISLAND
40° N
Madison
Lansing
Detroit
Lake Erie
Long Island
CONNECTICUT
IOWA
Missouri R.
Chicago
Cleveland
PENNSYLVANIA
New York
Trenton
Des Moines
Omaha
Davenport
ILLINOIS
Harrisburg
NEW JERSEY
Philadelphia
Des Moines R.
Wabash R.
OHIO
Columbus
Dover
DELAWARE
Lincoln
Illinois R.
INDIANA
Indianapolis
WEST VIRGINIA
Annapolis
WASHINGTON DC
MARYLAND
Springfield
Ohio R.
Spruce Knob 4,862ft
Appalachian Mountains
Kansas City
Topeka
Missouri R.
Lake of the Ozarks
Jefferson City
Charleston
Richmond
Chesapeake Bay
Frankfort
VIRGINIA
Ohio R.
KENTUCKY
Cumberland Plateau
Blue Ridge
Roanoke R.
35° N
Wichita
MISSOURI
Ozark Plateau
Raleigh
Nashville
NORTH CAROLINA
Pamlico Sound
Tulsa
Kentucky Lake
TENNESSEE
Mount Mitchell 6,682ft
Piedmont
Onslow Bay
Boston Mountains
ARKANSAS
Memphis
Columbia
Oklahoma City
Ouachita Mountains
Little Rock
Arkansas R.
Tennessee R.
Atlanta
SOUTH CAROLINA
Savannah R.
Red R.
Mississippi R.
MISSISSIPPI
ALABAMA
GEORGIA
Dallas
Chattahoochee R.
Montgomery
30° N
Jackson
LOUISIANA
Alabama R.
Okefenokee Swamp
ATLANTIC OCEAN
Brazos R.
Tallahassee
Austin
Baton Rouge
FLORIDA
Houston
New Orleans
Apalachee Bay
Cape Canaveral
Colorado R.
Mississippi River Delta
Tampa Bay
Lake Okeechobee
Charlotte Harbor
25° N
Padre Island
The Everglades
Miami
Gulf of Mexico
Straits of Florida
Florida Keys
TROPIC OF CANCER
CUBA
N
W
E
S
20° N
0 km
500
0 miles
500
95° W
90° W
85° W
80° W
75° W

Appendix E Weather Map

This weather map shows data collected from many weather stations. Below the map is an explanation of what the symbols mean.

Weather Map

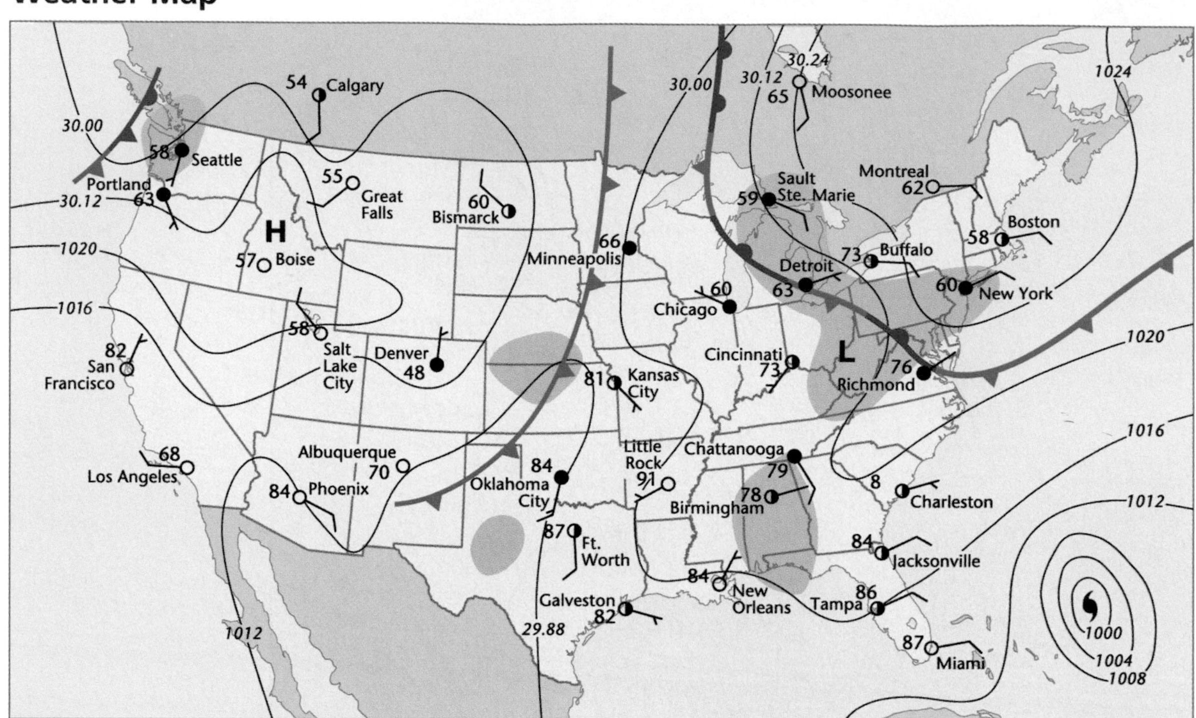

Explanation of Fronts

Cold Front
Boundary between a cold air mass and a warm air mass. Brings brief storms and cooler weather.

Warm Front
Boundary between a warm air mass and a cold air mass. Usually accompanied by precipitation.

Stationary Front
Boundary between warm and cold air masses when no movement occurs. Long periods of precipitation.

Occluded Front
Boundary on which a warm front has been overtaken by a cold front. Brings precipitation.

Weather	Symbol
Drizzle	
Fog	≡
Hail	△
Haze	∞
Rain	•
Shower	▽
Sleet	
Smoke	
Snow	*
Thunderstorm	
Hurricane	

Wind Speed (mph)	Symbol
1–2	
3–8	
9–14	
15–20	
21–25	
26–31	
32–37	
38–43	
44–49	
50–54	
55–60	
61–66	
67–71	
72–77	

Cloud Cover (%)	Symbol
0	○
10	
20–30	
40	
50	◑
60	
70–80	
90	
100	●

How Symbols Are Used on a Weather Map

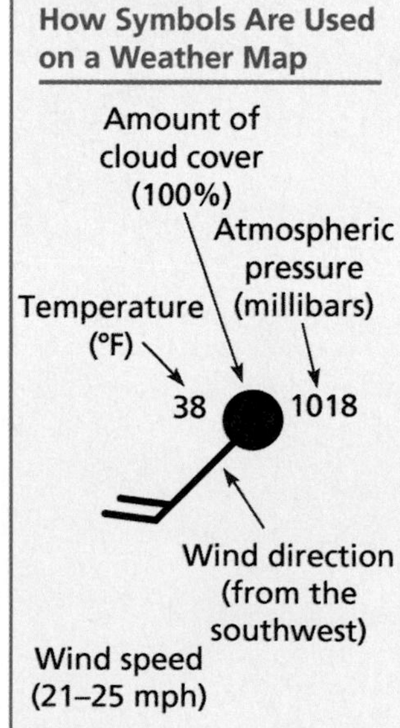

Appendix F Relative Humidity Chart

To find the relative humidity, measure the wet-bulb and dry-bulb temperatures with a sling psychrometer. Find the dry-bulb reading in the left column and the difference between readings at the top of the table. The number where these readings intersect is the relative humidity in percent.

Relative Humidity (percent)

Dry-Bulb Reading (°C)	Difference Between Wet-Bulb and Dry-Bulb Readings (°C)													
	1	2	3	4	5	6	7	8	9	10	11	12	13	14
5	86	72	58	45	33	20	7							
6	86	73	60	48	35	24	11							
7	87	74	62	50	38	26	15							
8	87	75	63	51	40	29	19	8						
9	88	76	64	53	42	32	22	12						
10	88	77	66	55	44	34	24	15	6					
11	89	78	67	56	46	36	27	18	9					
12	89	78	68	58	48	39	29	21	12					
13	89	79	69	59	50	41	32	23	15	7				
14	90	79	70	60	51	42	34	26	18	10				
15	90	80	71	61	53	44	36	27	20	13	6			
16	90	81	71	63	54	46	38	30	23	15	8			
17	90	81	72	64	55	47	40	32	25	18	11			
18	91	82	73	65	57	49	41	34	27	20	14	7		
19	91	82	74	65	58	50	43	36	29	22	16	10		
20	91	83	74	66	59	51	44	37	31	24	18	12	6	
21	91	83	75	67	60	53	46	39	32	26	20	14	9	
22	92	83	76	68	61	54	47	40	34	28	22	17	11	6
23	92	84	76	69	62	55	48	42	36	30	24	19	13	8
24	92	84	77	69	62	56	49	43	37	31	26	20	15	10
25	92	84	77	70	63	57	50	44	39	33	28	22	17	12
26	92	85	78	71	64	58	51	46	40	34	29	24	19	14
27	92	85	78	71	65	58	52	47	41	36	31	26	21	16
28	93	85	78	72	65	59	53	48	42	37	32	27	22	18
29	93	86	79	72	66	60	54	49	43	38	33	28	24	19
30	93	86	79	73	67	61	55	50	44	39	35	30	25	21

Appendix G Star Charts

Autumn Sky

To use this chart, hold it up in front of you and turn it so the direction you are facing is at the bottom of the chart. The chart works best at 35° N latitude, but it can be used at other latitudes. It works best at the following dates and times: September 1 at 10:00 P.M., October 1 at 8 P.M., and November 1 at 6 P.M.

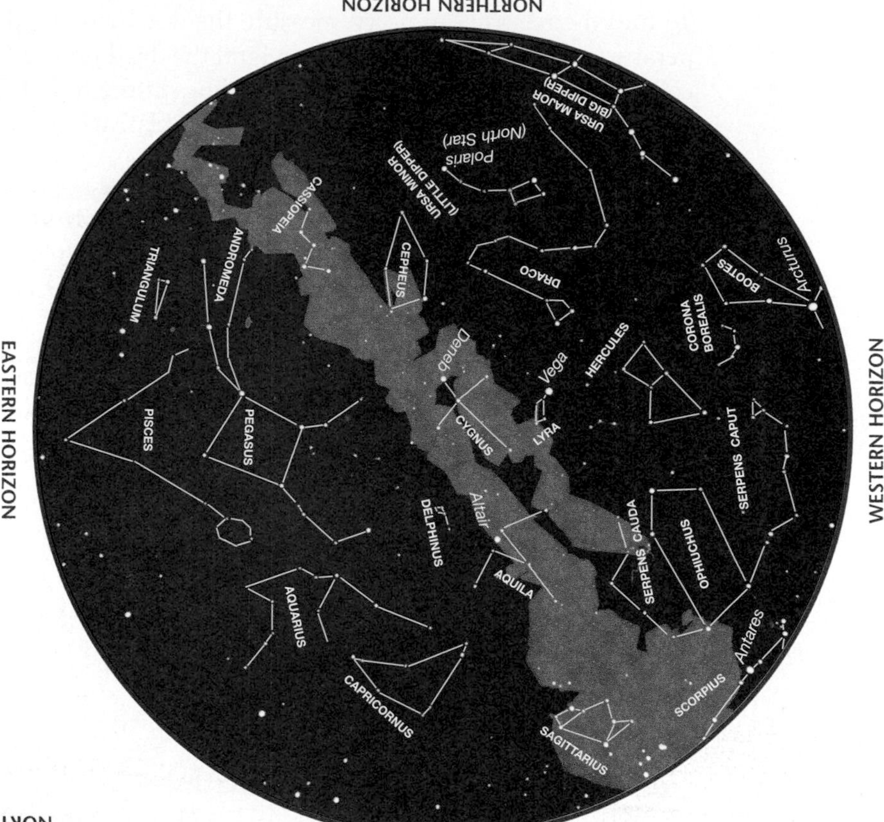

SOUTHERN HORIZON

Winter Sky

To use this chart, hold it up in front of you and turn it so the direction you are facing is at the bottom of the chart. The chart works best at 35° N latitude, but it can be used at other latitudes. It works best at the following dates and times: December 1 at 10:00 P.M., January 1 at 8 P.M., and February 1 at 6 P.M.

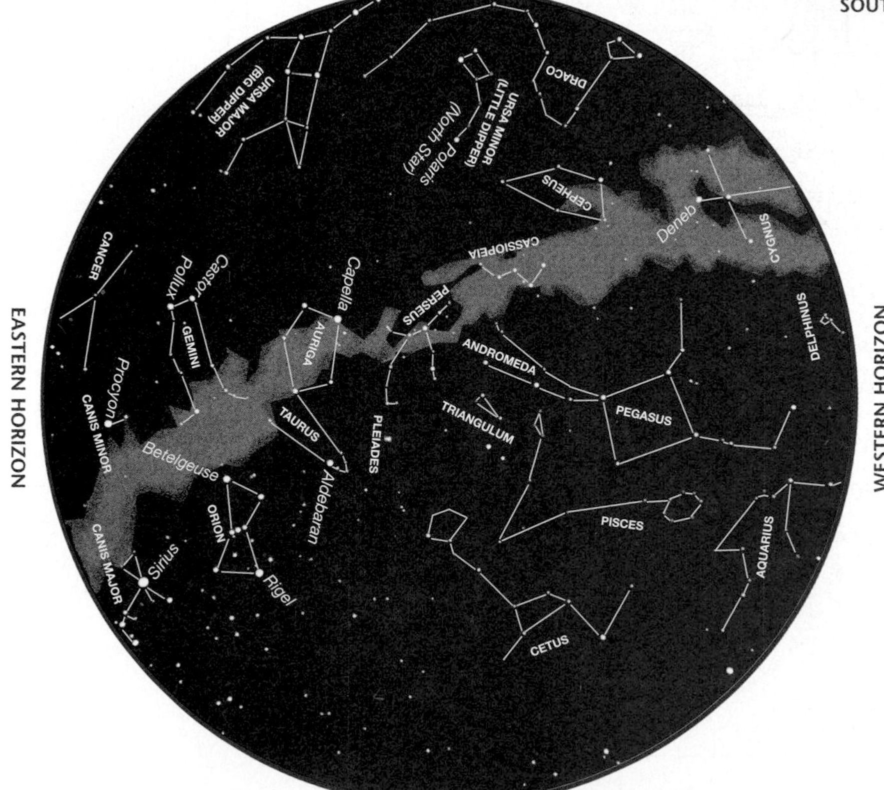

Spring Sky

To use this chart, hold it up in front of you and turn it so the direction you are facing is at the bottom of the chart. The chart works best at 35° N latitude, but it can be used at other latitudes. It works best at the following dates and times: March 1 at 10:00 P.M. and April 1 at 8 P.M.

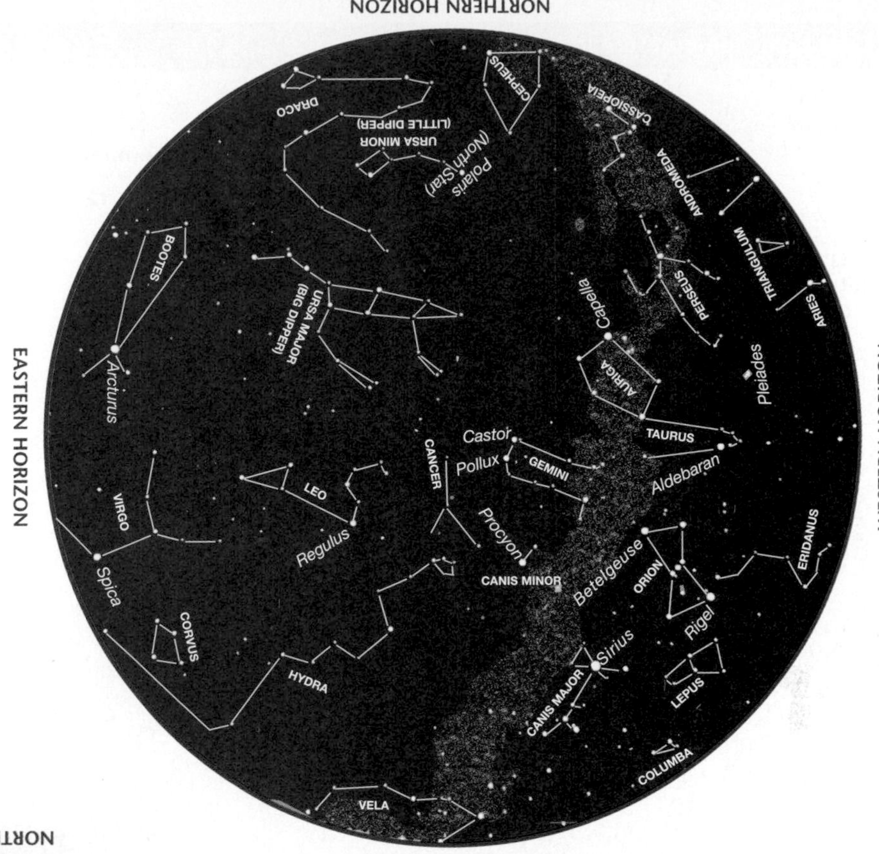

Summer Sky

To use this chart, hold it up in front of you and turn it so the direction you are facing is at the bottom of the chart. The chart works best at 35° N latitude, but it can be used at other latitudes. It works best at the following dates and times: May 15 at 11:00 P.M. and June 15 at 9 P.M.

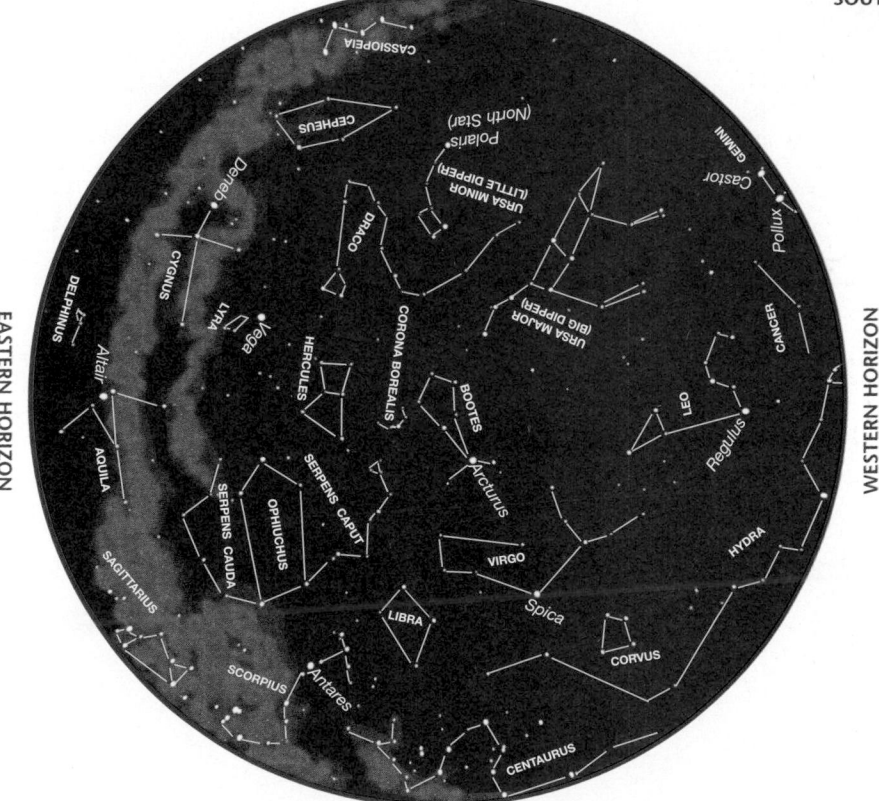

NORTHERN HORIZON
EASTERN HORIZON
WESTERN HORIZON
SOUTHERN HORIZON
CASSIOPEIA
CEPHEUS
Polaris (North Star)
URSA MINOR (LITTLE DIPPER)
GEMINI
Castor
Pollux
Deneb
CYGNUS
DRACO
DELPHINUS
LYRA
Vega
URSA MAJOR (BIG DIPPER)
CANCER
Altair
HERCULES
CORONA BOREALIS
BOOTES
LEO
Regulus
AQUILA
SERPENS CAPUT
Arcturus
SERPENS CAUDA
OPHIUCHUS
HYDRA
SAGITTARIUS
VIRGO
LIBRA
Spica
SCORPIUS
Antares
CORVUS
CENTAURUS

Appendices

Appendix H Dew Point

Dew-point temperature (°C)

Dry bulb (°C)	(Dry-Bulb Temperature Minus Wet-Bulb Temperature = Depression of the Wet Bulb)																				
	1	2	3	4	5	6	7	8	9	10	11	12	13	14	15	16	17	18	19	20	21	22
−20	−33																					
−18	−28																					
−16	−24																					
−14	−21	−36																				
−12	−18	−28																				
−10	−14	−22																				
−8	−12	−18	−29																			
−6	−10	−14	−22																			
−4	−7	−12	−17	−29																		
−2	−5	−8	−13	−20																		
0	−3	−6	−9	−15	−24																	
2	−1	−3	−6	−11	−17																	
4	1	−1	−4	−7	−11	−19																
6	4	1	−1	−4	−7	−13	−21															
8	6	3	1	2	−5	−9	−14															
10	8	6	4	1	−2	−5	−9	−14	−18													
12	10	8	6	4	1	−2	−5	−9	−16													
14	12	11	9	6	4	1	−2	−5	−10	−17												
16	14	13	11	9	7	4	1	−1	−6	−10	−17											
18	16	15	13	11	9	7	4	2	−2	5	10	−19										
20	19	17	15	14	12	10	7	4	2	−2	−5	−10	−19									
22	21	19	17	16	74	12	10	8	5	3	−1	−5	−10	−19								
24	23	21	20	18	16	14	12	10	8	6	2	−1	−5	−10	−18							
26	25	23	22	20	18	17	15	13	11	9	6	3	0	−4	−9	−18						
28	27	25	24	22	27	19	17	16	14	11	9	7	4	1	−3	−9	16					
30	29	27	26	24	23	21	19	18	16	14	12	70	8	5	1	−2	−8	−15				
32	31	29	28	27	25	24	22	21	19	17	15	13	11	8	5	2	−2	−7	−14			
34	33	31	30	29	27	26	24	23	21	20	18	16	14	12	9	6	3	−1	−5	−12	−29	
36	35	33	32	31	29	28	27	25	24	22	20	19	17	15	13	10	7	4	0	−4	−10	
38	37	35	34	33	32	30	29	28	26	25	23	21	19	17	15	13	11	8	5	1	−3	9
40	39	37	36	35	34	32	31	30	28	27	25	24	22	20	18	16	14	12	9	6	2	−2

Dry-Bulb (Air) Temperature

Dew-Point Values

Appendix I World Soils

The map on the next page shows the generalized pattern of global soil orders according to the *Comprehensive Soil Classification System* (CSCS). It should be examined in conjunction with the table below, which briefly describes each of the soil orders depicted on the map. To avoid subjective decisions as to classification (a problem that plagued earlier systems), the CSCS defined its classes strictly in terms of soil characterisitics. That is, it is based on features that can be observed or inferred.

The CSCS uses a hierarchy of six categories, or levels. The system recognizes 10 major global *orders* that can be further subdivided into *suborders, great groups, subgroups, families*, and *series*. Note, however, that on the scale of a world map, only the largest units (soil orders) can be shown and then only in an extremely generalized way. Although the distribution pattern of major soil orders is more complex than can be shown, the major distinguishing regional properties of world soils are depicted.

World Soil Orders	
Entisols	Youngest soils on the Earth. Just beginning to develop in response to the weathering phenomena in the environment. Do not display natural horizons. Found in all climates. They weather slowly over thousands of years; consequently, volcanic ash deposits or sand deposits form the basis for entisols.
Vertisols	Soils containing large amounts of clay, which shrink upon drying and swell with the addition of water. Found in subhumid to arid climates, provided that adequate supplies of water are available to saturate the soil after periods of drought. Soil expansion and contraction exert stresses on human structures.
Inceptisols	Young soils that reveal developmental characteristics (horizons) in response to climate and vegetation. Exist from the Arctic to the tropics on young land surfaces. Common in alpine areas, on river floodplains, in stables and dune areas, and in areas once glaciated.
Aridsols	Soils that develop in dry places, such as the desert, where water—precipitation and groundwater—is insufficient to remove soluble minerals. Frequently irrigated for intensive agricultural production, although salt accumulation poses a problem.
Mollisols	Dark, soft soils that have developed under grass vegetation, generally found in prairie areas. Soil fertility is excellent because potential evaporation generally exceeds precipitation. Also found in hardwood forests with significant earthworm activity. Climatic range is boreal or alpine to tropical. Dry seasons are normal.
Spodosols	Soils found only in humid regions on sandy material. Range from the boreal coniferous forests into tropical forests. Beneath the dark upper horizon of weathered organic material lies a light-colored horizon of leached material, the distinctive property of this soil.
Alfisols	Mineral soils that form under boreal forests or broadleaf deciduous forests, rich in iron and aluminum. Clay particles accumulate in a subsurface layer in response to leaching in moist environments. Fertile, productive soils, because they are neither too wet nor too dry.
Ultisols	Soils that represent the products of long periods of weathering. Water percolating through the soil concentrates clay particles in the lower horizons (argillic horizons). Restricted to humid climates in the temperate regions and the tropics where the growing season is long. Abundant water and a long frost-free period contribute to extensive leaching, hence poorer soil quality.
Oxisols	Soils that occur on old land surfaces unless parent materials were strongly weathered before they were deposited. Generally found in the tropics and subtropical regions. Rich in iron and aluminum oxides, oxisols are heavily leached; hence are poor soils for agricultural activity. Few, if any, exist in the United States.
Histosols	Organic soils with little or no climatic implications. Can be found in any climate where organic debris can accumulate to form a bog soil. Dark, partially decomposed organic material commonly referred to as *peat*.

Source: Robert E. Norris et al., *Geography: An Introductory Perspective*, Columbus, Ohio: Merrill, 1982.

Appendices

Appendix I World Soils

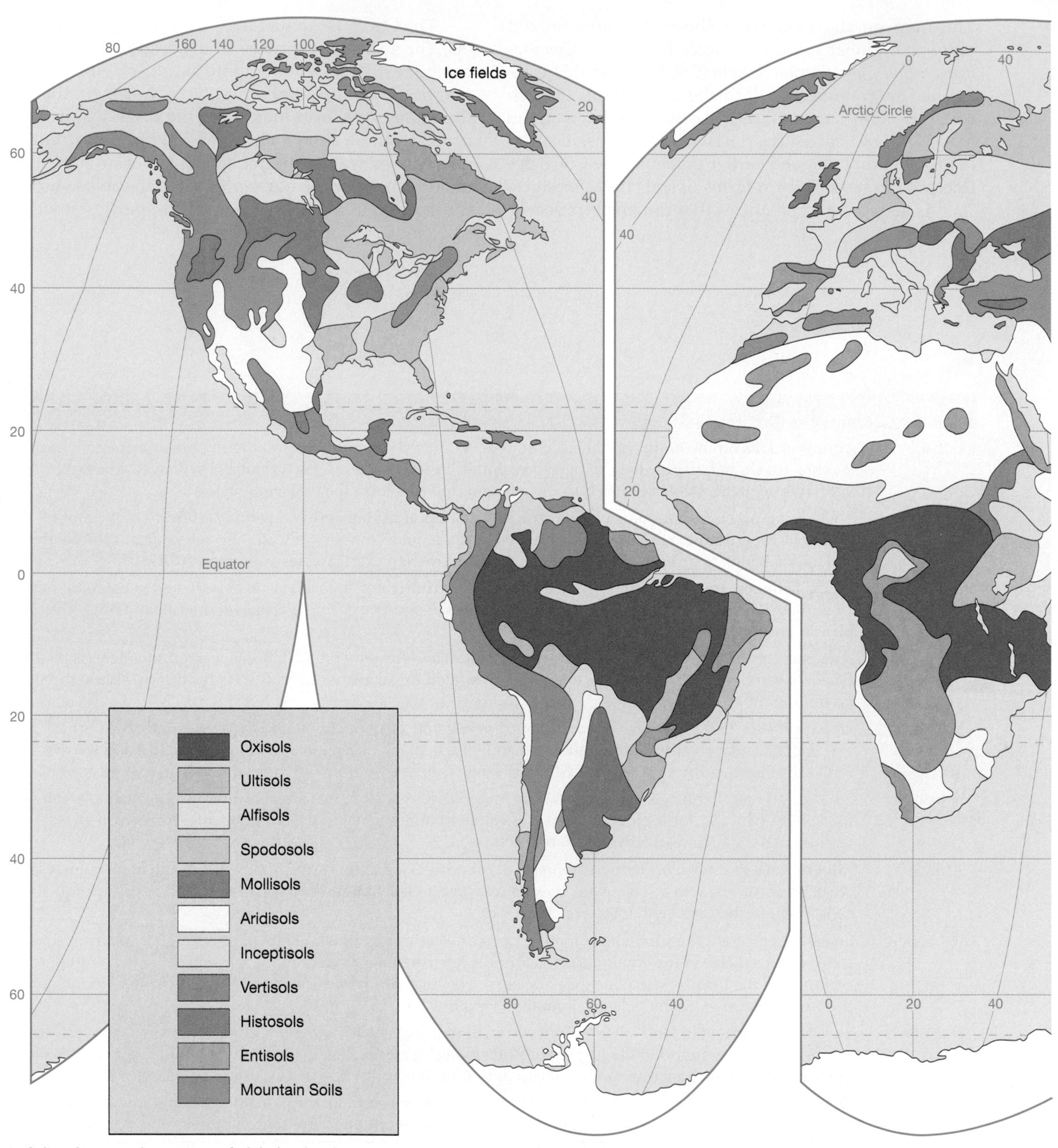

Soil distribution. The pattern of global soil orders is remarkably similar to the pattern of major climates. Soil classification is from the *Comprehensive Soil Classification System.*

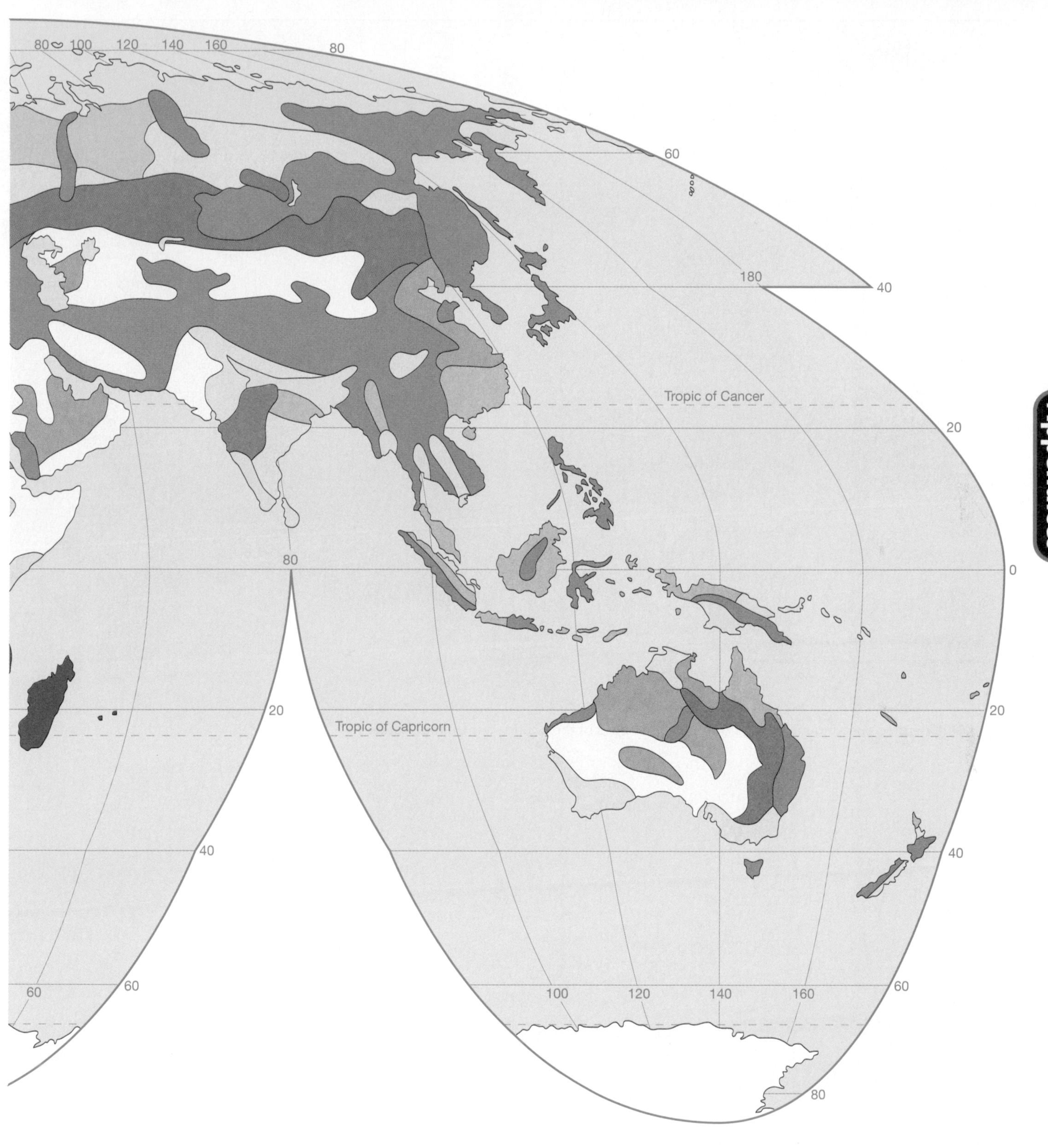

80
100
120
140
160
80
60
180
40
Tropic of Cancer
20
0
80
20
Tropic of Capricorn
20
40
40
60
60
100
120
140
160
60
80

Appendix J Contiguous United States Landforms

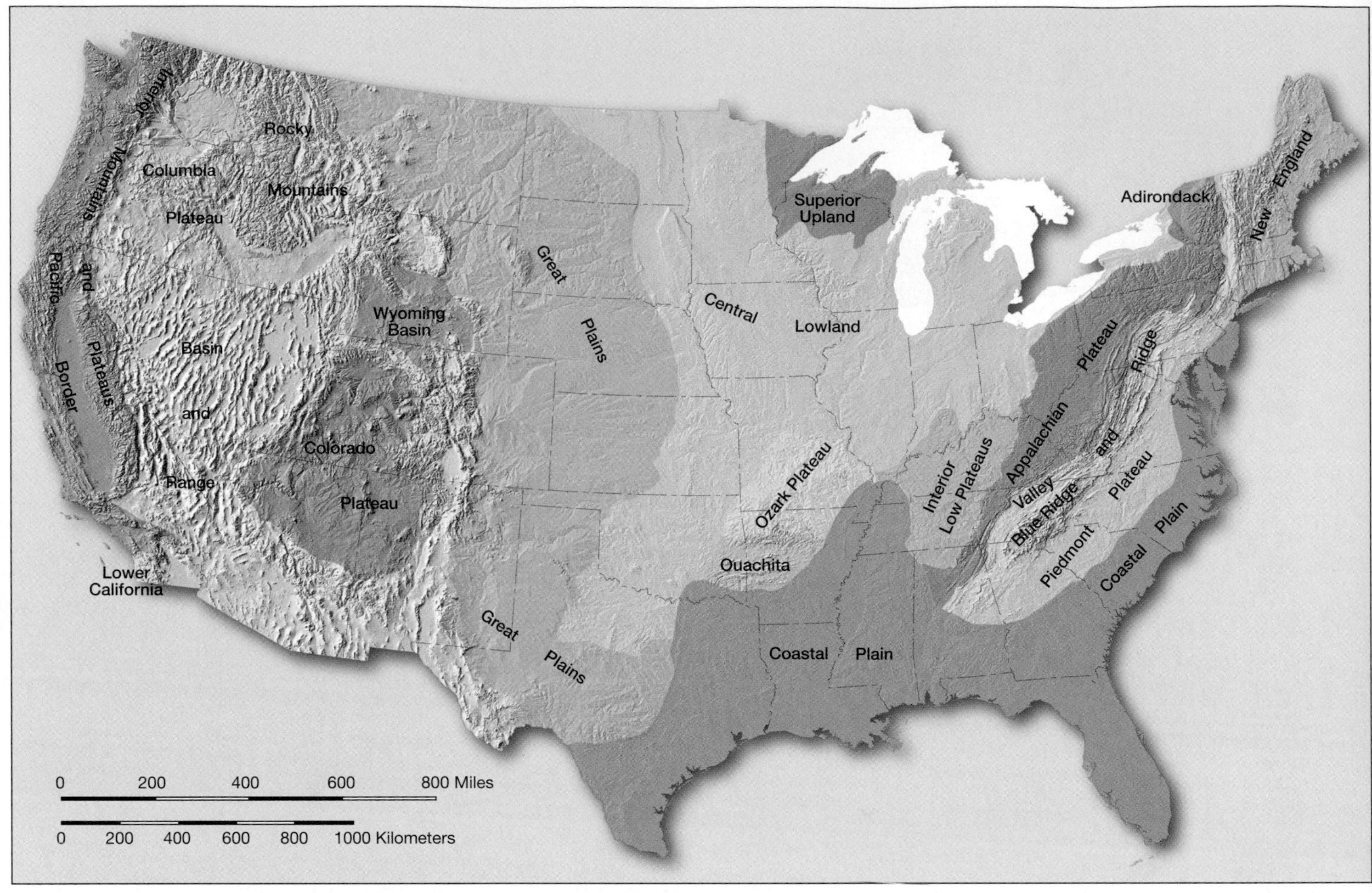

Outline map showing major physiographic provinces of the contiguous United States.

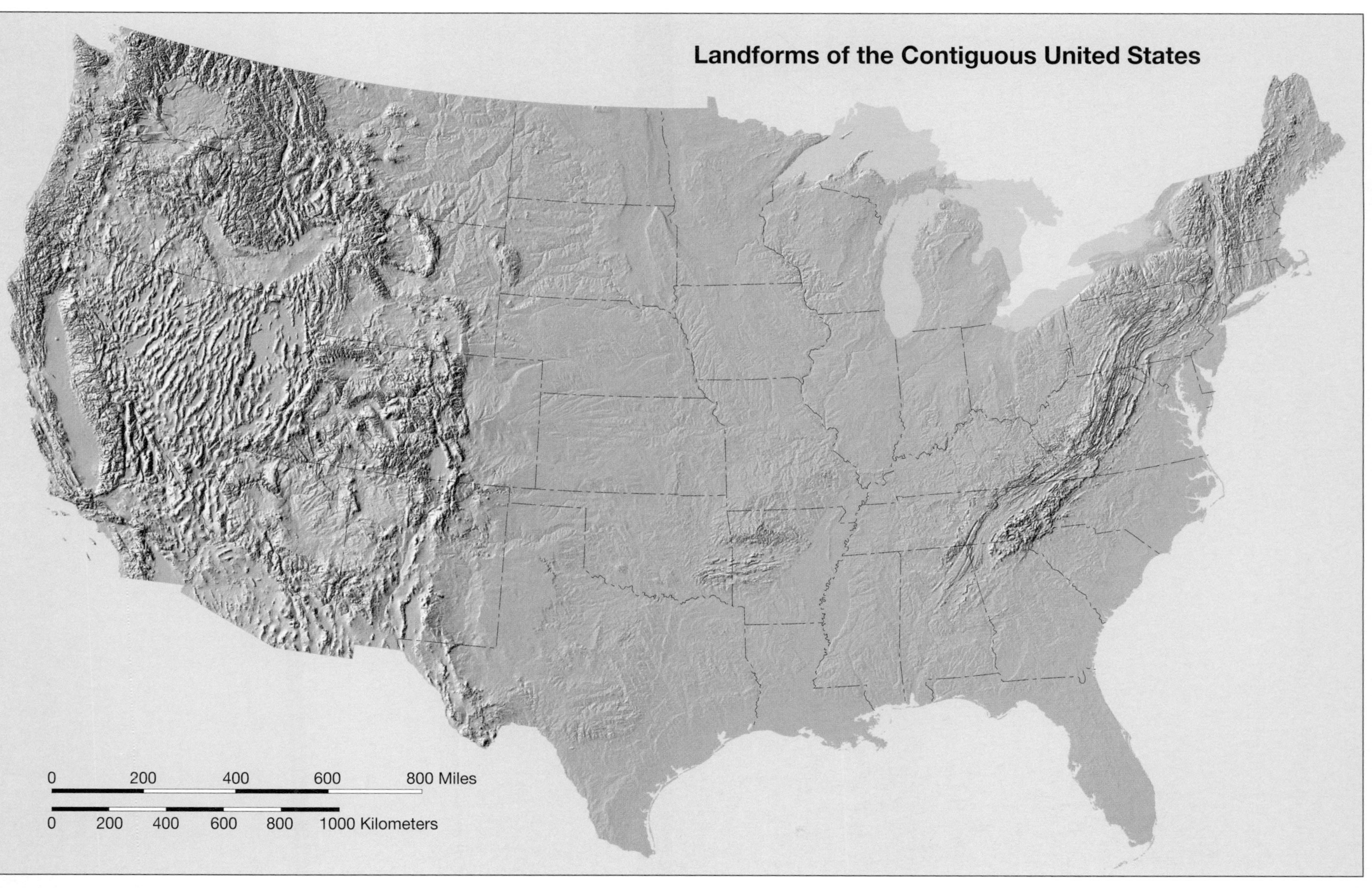

Digital shaded relief landform map of the United States. (Data provided by the U.S. Geological Survey)

Appendix K Physical Constants and Other Useful Measurements

Speed of light in a vacuum	3.00×10^{8} m/s
Free fall acceleration of Earth's surface	9.81 m/s^{2}
Moment of inertia for Earth	8.03×10^{31} kg•m^{2}
Mass of Earth	5.98×10^{24} kg
Radius of Earth	6.37×10^{6} m
Mass of the Moon	7.35×10^{22} kg
Radius of the Moon	1.74×10^{6} m
Mass of the Sun	1.99×10^{30} kg
Radius of the Sun	6.96×10^{5} km
Earth-Sun distance (mean)	1.496×10^{8} km
Earth-Moon distance (mean)	3.84×10^{5} km
Earth's gravitational constant	6.67×10^{11} N•m^{2}/kg^{2}

Some SI Derived Units

Quantity	Unit name	Abbreviation
Force	newton	N
Energy and work	joule	J
Power	watt	W
Pressure	pascal	Pa

A

absolute magnitude the apparent brightness of a star if it were viewed from a distance of 32.6 light-years; used to compare the true brightness of stars (p. 703)

absolute magnitude/magnitud absoluta luminosidad aparente de una estrella si se observara a una distancia de 32.6 años luz; usada para comparar la luminosidad real de las estrellas (pág. 703)

absorption spectrum a continuous spectrum produced when white light is passed through a cool gas under low pressure; The gas absorbs selected wavelengths of light, and the spectrum looks like it has dark lines superimposed. (p. 676)

absorption spectrum/espectro de absorción espectro continuo producido cuando pasa luz blanca a través de un gas frío a presión baja; el gas absorbe determinadas longitudes de onda de luz y el espectro pareciera tener líneas oscuras superpuestas (pág. 676)

abyssal plain very level area of the deep-ocean floor, usually lying at the foot of the continental rise (p. 404)

abyssal plain/planicie abisal área muy nivelada del fondo oceánico profundo, que se encuentra por lo general en la base del pie continental (pág. 404)

abyssal zone a subdivision of the benthic zone characterized by extremely high pressures, low temperatures, low oxygen, few nutrients, and no sunlight (p. 431)

abyssal zone/zona abisal subdivisión de la zona bentónica caracterizada por tener presiones extremadamente altas, bajas temperaturas, poco oxígeno, pocas sustancias nutrientes y ausencia de luz solar (pág. 431)

accretion process that occurs when crustal fragments collide with and stay connected to a continental plate (p. 321)

accretion/acreción proceso que ocurre cuando los fragmentos corticales chocan con una placa continental y permanecen conectados a ella (pág. 321)

accretionary wedge a large wedge-shaped mass of sediment that accumulates in subduction zones; Here sediment is scraped from the subducting oceanic plate and accreted to the overriding crustal block. (p. 319)

accretionary wedge/prisma acrecionario masa grande de sedimento en forma de prisma que se acumula en las zonas de subducción; el sedimento es raspado de la placa oceánica de subducción y acrecentado al bloque cortical preponderante (pág. 319)

aftershock a small earthquake that follows the main earthquake (p. 221)

aftershock/replica terremoto pequeño que sigue al terremoto mayor (pág. 221)

air mass a large body of air that is characterized by similar temperatures and amounts of moisture at any given altitude (p. 559)

air mass/masa de aire cuerpo grande de aire que se caracteriza por tener temperatura y humedad similares a cualquier altitud dada (pág. 559)

air pressure the force exerted by the weight of a column of air above a given point (p. 532)

air pressure/ presión de aire fuerza ejercida por el peso de una columna de aire sobre un punto dado (pág. 532)

albedo the fraction of total radiation that is reflected back by a surface (p. 492)

albedo/albedo fracción de la radiación total que es reflejada por una superficie (pág. 492)

alluvial fan a fan-shaped deposit of sediment formed when a stream's slope is abruptly reduced (p. 201)

alluvial fan/abanico alluvial depósito de sedimentos en forma de abanico, formado cuando la vertiente de una corriente de agua se reduce abruptamente (pág. 201)

andesitic composition the composition of igneous rocks lying between felsic and mafic (p. 73)

andesitic composition/composición andesítica composición de rocas ígneas que se encuentra entre las rocas félsicas y máficas (pág. 73)

anemometer an instrument used to determine wind speed (p. 545)

anemometer/anemómetro instrumento usado para determinar la velocidad del viento (pág. 545)

Glossary

angiosperm flowering plant that produces seeds within a fruit (p. 383)

angiosperm/angiosperma planta que da flores y produce semillas dentro de una fruta (pág. 383)

anticline a fold in sedimentary strata resembling an arch (p. 310)

anticline/anticlinal pliegue en el estrato sedimentario que parece un arco (pág. 310)

anticyclone a high-pressure center characterized by a clockwise flow of air in the Northern Hemisphere (p. 538)

anticyclon/anticiclón centro de alta presión en el hemisferio norte que se caracteriza por una masa de aire que se mueve en dirección de las agujas del reloj (pág. 538)

aphelion the place in the orbit of a planet where the planet is farthest from the sun (p. 624)

aphelion/afelio punto en la órbita de un planeta en el que éste se encuentra más alejado del Sol (pág. 624)

apogee the point where the moon is farthest from Earth (p. 626)

apogee/apogeo punto donde la Luna se encuentra más alejada de la Tierra (pág. 626)

apparent magnitude the brightness of a star when viewed from Earth (p. 703)

apparent magnitude/magnitud aparente luminosidad de una estrella vista desde la Tierra (pág. 703)

aquifer rock or soil through which groundwater moves easily (p. 171)

aquifer/acuífero roca o tierra a través de la cual el agua subterránea se mueve fácilmente (pág. 171)

artesian well a well in which the water naturally rises above the level of the water table (p. 173)

artesian well/pozo artesiano pozo en el cual el agua sube naturalmente por encima del nivel freático (pág. 173)

asteroid a small, rocky body, which can range in size from a few hundred kilometers to less than a kilometer; The asteroids' orbits lie mainly between those of Mars and Jupiter. (p. 661)

asteroid/asteroide cuerpo rocoso y pequeño, cuyo tamaño puede variar entre cientos de kilómetros a menos de un kilómetro; las órbitas de los asteroides se encuentran principalmente entre las órbitas de Marte y Júpiter (pág. 661)

asthenosphere a weak plastic layer of the mantle situated below the lithosphere; The rock within this zone is easily deformed. (p. 235)

asthenosphere/astenosfera capa plástica y débil del manto situada debajo de la litosfera; la roca en esta zona se deforma fácilmente (pág. 235)

astronomical unit (AU) average distance from Earth to the sun; 1.5×10^8, or 150 million kilometers (p. 618)

astronomical unit (AU)/unidad astronómica (UA) distancia promedio de la Tierra al Sol; 1.5×10^8, ó 150 millones de kilómetros (pág. 618)

astronomy the scientific study of the universe; It includes the observation and interpretation of celestial bodies and phenomena. (p. 3)

astronomy/astronomía estudio científico del universo; incluye la observación y la interpretación de cuerpos y fenómenos celestes (pág. 3)

atmosphere the gaseous portion of a planet; the planet's envelope of air; one of the traditional subdivisions of Earth's physical environment (p. 7)

atmosphere/atmósfera porción gaseosa de un planeta; envoltura de aire del planeta; una de las subdivisiones tradicionales del medio ambiente físico de la Tierra (pág. 7)

atomic number the number of protons in the nucleus of an atom (p. 35)

atomic number/número atómico número de protones en el núcleo de un átomo (pág. 35)

aurora a bright display of ever-changing light caused by solar radiation interacting with the upper atmosphere in the region of the poles (p. 688)

aurora/aurora polar luz brillante en constante movimiento causada por la radiación solar que interactúa con la parte superior de la atmósfera en la región de los polos (pág. 688)

autumnal equinox the equinox that occurs on September 22 or 23 in the Northern Hemisphere and on March 21 or 22 in the Southern Hemisphere (p. 482)

autummal equinox/equinoccio de otoño equinoccio que ocurre el 22 ó 23 de septiembre en el hemisferio norte y el 21 ó 22 de marzo en el hemisferio sur (pág. 482)

B

barometer an instrument that measures atmospheric pressure (p. 533)

barometer/barómetro instrumento que mide la presión atmosférica (pág. 533)

barrier island a low, elongated ridge of sand that parallels the coast (p. 466)

barrier island/isla barrera lomo de arena bajo y alargado que se encuentra paralelo a la costa (pág. 466)

basaltic composition a compositional group of igneous rocks indicating that the rock contains substantial dark silicate minerals and calcium-rich plagioclase feldspar (p. 73)

basaltic composition/composición basáltica grupo composicional de rocas ígneas que indica que la roca contiene cantidades sustanciales de minerales de silicato oscuros y feldespato de plagioclasa rico en calcio (pág. 73)

batholith a large mass of igneous rock that formed when magma intruded at depth, became crystallized, and subsequently was exposed by erosion; Batholiths have a surface exposure greater than 100 square kilometers. (p. 290)

batholith/batolito masa grande de roca ígnea que se forma cuando el magma penetra en la profundidad, se cristaliza y luego queda expuesta debido a la erosión; los batolitos tienen una superficie expuesta mayor a los 100 kilómetros cuadrados (pág. 290)

bathymetry the measurement of ocean depths and the charting of the shape or topography of the ocean floor (p. 396)

bathymetry/batimetría medición de las profundidades marinas y trazado de la forma o topografía del fondo marino (pág. 396)

beach the accumulation of sediment found along the shore of a lake or an ocean (p. 461)

beach/playa acumulación de sedimento que se encuentra a lo largo de la costa de un lago u océano (pág. 461)

bed load sediment that is carried by a stream along the bottom of its channel (p. 165)

bed load/carga del lecho sedimento arrastrado por una corriente de agua a lo largo del fondo de su canal (pág. 165)

benthic zone 0the marine-life zone that includes any sea-bottom surface regardless of its distance from shore (p. 431)

benthic zone/zona béntica zona de vida marina que incluye cualquier superficie del fondo del mar sin importar su distancia de la costa (pág. 431)

benthos the forms of marine life that live on or in the ocean bottom; includes marine algae, sea stars, and crabs (p. 429)

benthos/bentos organismos marinos que viven en el fondo marino; incluyen algas marinas, estrellas de mar y cangrejos (pág. 429)

Bergeron process a theory that relates the formation of precipitation to supercooled clouds, freezing nuclei, and the different saturation levels of ice and liquid water (p. 521)

Bergeron process/proceso de Bergeron teoría que relaciona la formación de precipitación con nubes sobreenfriadas, núcleos congelados y los diferentes niveles de saturación del agua helada y el agua líquida (pág. 521)

big bang theory the theory that proposes that the universe originated as a single mass, which subsequently exploded (p. 720)

big bang theory/teoría del Big Bang teoría que propone que el universo se originó como una masa única, la cual estalló posteriormente (pág. 720)

binary star one of two stars revolving around a common center of mass under their mutual gravitational attraction (p. 701)

binary star/estrella binaria una de dos estrellas que giran alrededor de un centro de masa común atraídas por su fuerza gravitacional mutua (pág. 701)

biogenous sediment seafloor sediment of biological origin, such as shells and skeletons of marine life (p. 408)

biogenous sediment/sedimento biogénico sedimento del fondo marino de origen biológico, como conchas y esqueletos de organismos marinos (pág. 408)

biosphere all life on Earth; the parts of the solid Earth, hydrosphere, and atmosphere in which living organisms can be found (p. 7)

biosphere/biosfera toda la vida en la Tierra; partes de la Tierra sólida, la hidrosfera y la atmósfera en las que se encuentran los organismos vivos (pág. 7)

black hole a massive star that has collapsed to such a small volume that its gravity prevents the escape of everything, including light (p. 714)

black hole/agujero negro estrella masiva que se ha reducido a un volumen tan pequeño que su fuerza de gravedad no permite que nada se escape, incluyendo la luz (pág. 714)

C

calcerous ooze thick, common biogenous sediment produced by dissolving calcium carbonate shells (p. 408)

calcerous ooze/fango calcáreo sedimento biógeno común y grueso, producido por la disolución de conchas de carbonato de calcio (pág. 408)

caldera a large depression typically caused by collapse or ejection of the summit area of a volcano (p. 287)

caldera/caldera depresión grande causada típicamente por el colapso o la expulsión de la cima de un volcán (pág. 287)

capacity the total amount of sediment a stream is able to transport (p. 165)

capacity/capacidad cantidad total de sedimento que puede transportar una corriente de agua (pág. 165)

cavern a naturally formed underground chamber or series of chambers most commonly produced by solution activity in limestone (p. 176)

cavern/caverna cámara subterráneas o serie de cámaras subterráneas formadas naturalmente y producidas comúnmente por actividad de solución sobre piedra caliza (pág. 176)

cementation solidification of sediments by the deposition of dissolved minerals in the tiny spaces between the sedimentary particles (p. 76)

cementation/cementación solidificación de sedimentos por el depósito de minerales disueltos en los espacios diminutos entre las partículas sedimentarias (pág. 76)

cepheid variable a star whose brightness varies periodically because it expands and contracts; a type of pulsating star (p. 705)

cepheid variable/variable cefeida estrella cuya luminosidad varía periódicamente porque se expande y se contrae; tipo de estrella púlsar (pág. 705)

chemical bond a force that holds together atoms that form a compound (p. 38)

chemical bond/enlace químico fuerza que une los átomos que forman un compuesto (pág. 38)

chemical sedimentary rock sedimentary rock consisting of material that was precipitated from water by either inorganic or organic means (p. 77)

chemical sedimentary rock/roca sedimentaria química roca sedimentaria formada de material precipitado del agua por medios inorgánicos u orgánicos (pág. 77)

chemical weathering the processes by which the internal structure of a mineral is altered by the removal and/or addition of elements (p. 129)

chemical weathering/meteorización química proceso mediante el cual la estructura interna de un mineral es alterada por la extracción y/o la suma de elementos (pág. 129)

chemosynthesis the process by which certain microorganisms use chemical energy to produce food (p. 433)

chemosynthesis/quimiosíntesis proceso por el cual ciertos microorganismos usan energía química para producir alimento (pág. 433)

chromatic aberration the property of a lens whereby light of different colors is focused at different places (p. 679)

chromatic aberration/aberración cromática propiedad de una lente en la cual se enfoca luz de diferentes colores en distintos lugares (pág. 679)

chromosphere the first layer of the solar atmosphere found directly above the photosphere (p. 686)

chromosphere/cromosfera primera capa de la atmósfera solar que se encuentra directamente por encima de la fotosfera (pág. 686)

cinder cone a small volcano built primarily of pyroclastic material ejected from a single vent (p. 284)

cinder cone/cono de escoria volcán pequeño formado principalmente de material piroclástico expulsado por una sola abertura (pág. 284)

cirque an amphitheater-shaped basin at the head of a glaciated valley produced by frost wedging and plucking (p. 193)

cirque/circo cuenca en forma de anfiteatro en la cabecera de un valle glaciar producida por la erosión de hielo (pág. 193)

cirrus one of three basic cloud forms; also one of the three high cloud types; They are thin, delicate ice-crystal clouds often appearing as veil-like patches or thin, wispy fibers. (p. 517)

cirrus/cirro una de las tres formaciones básicas de las nubes; también uno de los tres tipos de nubes altas; son nubes cristalinas delicadas que parecen retazos de velo o fibras tenues y finas (pág. 517)

clastic sedimentary rock a sedimentary rock made of broken fragments of preexisting rock (p. 77)

clastic sedimentary rock/roca sedimentaria clástica roca sedimentaria hecha de fragmentos rotos de roca preexistente (pág. 77)

cleavage the tendency of a mineral to break along planes of weak bonding (p. 52)

cleavage/clivaje tendencia de un mineral a fracturarse a lo largo de planos de enlace débiles (pág. 52)

cold front a front along which a cold air mass thrusts beneath a warmer air mass (p. 566)

cold front/frente frío frente en el que una masa de aire frío avanza bajo una masa de aire caliente (pág. 566)

collision-coalescence process a theory of raindrop formation in warm clouds (above 0°C) in which large cloud droplets collide and join together with smaller droplets to form a raindrop; Opposite electrical charges may bind the cloud droplets together. (p. 521)

collision-coalescence process/proceso de coalescencia y colisión teoría sobre la formación de gotas de agua en nubes cálidas (por encima de los 0 °C), en la cual las gotas grandes de agua en una nube chocan y se unen con gotitas más pequeñas para formar una gota de mayor tamaño; las corrientes eléctricas opuestas pueden unir las gotitas (pág. 521)

coma the fuzzy, gaseous component of a comet's head (p. 662)

coma/coma componente gaseoso y difuso que rodea el núcleo de un cometa (pág. 662)

comet a small body made of rocky and metallic pieces held together by frozen gases; Comets generally revolve about the sun in an elongated orbit. (p. 661)

comet/cometa cuerpo pequeño formado por materiales rocosos y metálicos unidos por medio de gases congelados; los cometas generalmente giran alrededor del Sol en una órbita alargada (pág. 661)

compaction process by which sediments are squeezed together by the weight of overlying materials driving out water (p. 76)

compaction/compactación proceso por el cual los sedimentos se unen y expulsan agua debido al peso de los materiales que los cubren (pág. 76)

composite cone a volcano composed of both lava flows and pyroclastic material (p. 285)

composite cone/estratovolcán volcán compuesto de flujos de lava y material piroclástico (pág. 285)

compost partly decomposed organic material that is used as fertilizer (p. 115)

compost/compost material orgánico parcialmente descompuesto que se usa como fertilizante (pág. 115)

compound a substance formed by the chemical combination of two or more elements in definite proportions and usually having properties different from those of its constituent elements (p. 37)

compound/compuesto sustancia formada por la combinación química de dos o más elementos en proporciones definidas y que tiene usualmente propiedades diferentes a las de los elementos que la componen (pág. 37)

condensation the change of state from a gas to a liquid (p. 506)

condensation/condensación cambio de estado de un gas a un líquido (pág. 506)

condensation nuclei tiny bits of particulate matter that serve as surfaces on which water vapor condenses (p. 516)

condensation nuclei/núcleos de condensación partículas muy pequeñas de materia que sirven como superficies para que se condense el vapor (pág. 516)

Glossary

Glossary

conduction the transfer of heat through matter by molecular activity; Energy is transferred through collisions from one molecule to another. (p. 483)

conduction/conducción transferencia de calor a través de la materia por actividad molecular; la energía se transfiere a través de choques de una molécula contra otra (pág. 483)

conservation the careful use of resources (p. 113)

conservation/conservación uso cuidadoso de los recursos (pág. 113)

constellation an apparent group of stars originally named for mythical characters; The sky is presently divided into 88 constellations. (p. 700)

constellation/constelación grupo aparente de estrellas nombrado originalmente a partir de personajes míticos; el cielo se encuentra en la actualidad dividido en 88 constelaciones (pág. 700)

contact metamorphism changes in rock caused by the heat from a nearby magma body (p. 81)

contact metamorphism/metamorfismo de contacto cambios en una roca causados por el calor de una masa de magma cercano (pág. 81)

continental drift a hypothesis that originally proposed that the continents had once been joined to form a single supercontinent; The supercontinent broke into pieces, which drifted into their present-day positions. (p. 248)

continental drift/deriva continental hipótesis que propuso originalmente que los continentes estuvieron unidos formando un solo supercontinente; el supercontinente se quebró en pedazos, los cuales se desplazaron hasta sus posiciones actuales (pág. 248)

continental glacier a very large, thick mass of glacial ice that covers a large region and flows outward in all directions from one or more accumulation centers; also called a continental ice sheet (p. 189)

continental glacier/glaciar continental masa muy grande y gruesa de hielo glacial que cubre una región grande y fluye hacia afuera en todas direcciones desde uno o más centros de acumulación; también se le llama capa de hielo continental (pág. 189)

continental margin that portion of the seafloor adjacent to the continents; It may include the continental shelf, continental slope, and continental rise. (p. 402)

continental margin/margen continental porción del suelo marino adyacente a los continentes; puede incluir la plataforma continental, el talud continental y el pie continental (pág. 402)

continental rise the gently sloping surface at the base of the continental slope (p. 403)

continental rise/pie continental superficie que se encuentra levemente en declive en la base del talud continental (pág. 403)

continental shelf the gently sloping submerged portion of the continental margin, extending from the shoreline to the continental slope (p. 402)

continental shelf/plataforma continental porción sumergida y levemente en declive del margen continental, que se extiende desde la costa hasta el talud continental (pág. 402)

continental slope the steep gradient that leads to the deep-ocean floor and marks the seaward edge of the continental shelf (p. 403)

continental slope/talud continental pendiente empinada que conduce al suelo marino profundo y marca el límite de la plataforma continental que da al mar (pág. 403)

continental volcanic arc mountains formed in part by volcanic activity caused by the subduction of oceanic lithosphere beneath a continent (p. 261)

continental volcanic arc/arco volcánico continental montañas formadas en parte por actividad volcánica causada por la subducción de la litosfera volcánica debajo de un continente (pág. 261)

continuous spectrum an uninterrupted band of light emitted by an incandescent solid, liquid, or gas under pressure (p. 676)

continuos spectrum/espectro continuo banda de luz continua emitida por un sólido, un líquido o un gas incandescente bajo presión (pág. 676)

contour interval on a topographic map, tells the distance in elevation between adjacent contour lines (p. 14)

contour interval/intervalo entre curvas de nivel en un mapa topográfico, indica la diferencia de altitud entre dos curvas de nivel adyacentes (pág. 14)

contour line line on a topographic map that indicates an elevation; Every point along a contour line has the same elevation. (p. 14)

contour line/curva de nivel línea en un mapa topográfico que indica una altitud; todos los puntos a lo largo de una curva de nivel tienen la misma altitud (pág. 14)

convection the transfer of heat by the movement of a mass or substance; It can take place only in fluids. (p. 484)

convection/convección transferencia de calor por el movimiento de una masa o sustancia; puede ocurrir sólo en líquidos (pág. 484)

convective flow the motion of matter resulting from changes in temperature; The convective flow of material in the mantle is due to Earth's unequal heating and causes the tectonic plates to move. (p. 269)

convective flow/flujo convectivo movimiento de materia resultante de cambios en la temperatura; el flujo convectivo de material en el manto se debe al calentamiento desigual de la tierra y hace que las placas tectónicas se muevan (pág. 269)

convergent boundary a boundary in which two plates move together (p. 255)

convergent boundary/límite convergente límite en el cual dos placas se muevan juntas (pág. 255)

core the innermost layer of Earth, located beneath the mantle; The core is divided into an outer core and an inner core. (p. 8)

core/núcleo capa más interna de la tierra, ubicada debajo del manto; el núcleo está dividido en un núcleo exterior y un núcleo interior (pág. 8)

Coriolis effect the apparent deflective force of Earth's rotation on all free-moving objects, including the atmosphere and oceans; Deflection is to the right in the Northern Hemisphere and to the left in the Southern Hemisphere. (p. 449)

Coriolis effect/efecto de Coriolis aparente fuerza desviadora que la rotación de la Tierra ejerce sobre todos los objetos que están en movimiento libre, incluyendo la atmósfera y los océanos; el desvío es hacia la derecha en el hemisferio norte y hacia la izquierda en el hemisferio sur (pág. 449)

corona the outer weak layer of the solar atmosphere (p. 686)

corona/corona solar débil capa exterior de la atmósfera solar (pág. 686)

correlation establishing the equivalence of rocks of similar age in different areas (p. 342)

correlation/correlación establecimiento de la equivalencia de rocas de edades similares en diferentes áreas (pág. 342)

covalent bond a bond that forms when atoms share electrons (p. 39)

covalent bond/enlace covalente enlace que se forma cuando los átomos comparten electrones (pág. 39)

crater the depression at the summit of a volcano or that which is produced by a meteorite impact (p. 283)

crater/cráter depresión en la cumbre de un volcán o la que se produce por el impacto de un meteorito (pág. 283)

creep the slow downhill movement of soil and regolith (p. 147)

creep/reptación movimiento lento cuesta abajo de tierra y regolitos (pág. 147)

crevasse a deep crack in the brittle surface of a glacier (p. 190)

crevasse/hendidura grieta profunda en la superficie frágil de un glaciar (pág. 190)

cross-cutting relationships, principle of a principle of relative dating; A rock or fault is younger than any rock or fault through which it cuts. (p. 341)

cross-cutting relationships, principle of/relaciones de corte transversal, principio de principio de datación relativa; una roca o falla es más joven que cualquier roca o falla que atraviesa (pág. 341)

crust the thin, rocky outer layer of Earth (p. 8)

crust/corteza capa exterior fina y rocosa de la tierra (pág. 8)

crystal form the external appearance of a mineral as determined by its internal arrangement of atoms (p. 49)

crystal form/forma cristalina apariencia externa de un mineral determinada según la distribución interna de los átomos (pág. 49)

cumulus one of three basic cloud forms; also the name given to one of the clouds of vertical development; They are billowy individual cloud masses that often have flat bases. (p. 517)

cumulus/cúmulo una de las tres formas básicas de las nubes; nombre dado también a una de las nubes de desarrollo vertical; son masas de nubes individuales ondulantes que tienen a menudo bases planas (pág. 517)

cyclone a low-pressure center characterized by a counterclockwise flow of air in the Northern Hemisphere (p. 538)

cyclone/ciclón centro de baja presión en el hemisferio norte caracterizado por una corriente de aire que corre en sentido contrario a las manecillas del reloj (pág. 538)

D

decompression melting melting due to a drop in confining pressure that occurs as rock rises (p. 292)

decompression melting/fusión por descompresión fusión debida a una disminución de la presión restrictiva que ocurre a medida que una roca va subiendo (pág. 292)

deflation the lifting and removal of loose material by wind (p. 203)

deflation/deflación levantamiento y remoción de material suelto por el viento (pág. 203)

deformation general term for the processes of folding, faulting, shearing, compression, or extension of rocks as the result of various natural forces (p. 308)

deformation/deformación término general para los procesos de plegamiento, formación de fallas, partición, comprensión o extensión en rocas, como resultado de diferentes fuerzas naturales (pág. 308)

delta an accumulation of sediment formed where a stream enters a lake or an ocean (p. 166)

delta/delta acumulación de sedimento que se forma donde una corriente de agua entra a un lago u océano (pág. 166)

density mass per unit volume of a substance, usually expressed as grams per cubic centimeter (p. 53)

density/densidad masa por unidad de volumen de una sustancia, expresada por lo general en gramos por centímetro cúbico (pág. 53)

density current current of ocean water that results from density differences among water masses (p. 451)

density current/corriente de densidad corriente de agua oceánica que resulta de las diferencias de densidad entre las masas de agua (pág. 451)

deposition the process by which an agent of erosion loses energy and drops the sediment it is carrying; also the process by which water vapor is changed directly to a solid without passing through the liquid state (p. 76, p. 506)

desposition/deposición proceso por el cual un agente de erosión pierde energía y deja caer el sedimento que arrastra; también es el proceso por el cual el vapor de agua pasa al estado sólido sin pasar por el estado líquido (pág. 76, pág. 506)

desert pavement a layer of coarse pebbles and gravel created when wind removed the finer material (p. 204)

desert pavement/pavimento desértico capa de guijarros gruesos y grava que se forma cuando el viento remueve el material más fino (pág. 204)

dew point the temperature to which air has to be cooled in order to reach saturation (p. 508)

dew point/punto de condensación temperatura a la cual se tiene que enfriar el aire para que alcance la saturación (pág. 508)

dike a tabular-shaped intrusive igneous feature that occurs when magma is injected into fractures in the surrounding rock, cutting across preexisting rock layers (p. 290)

dike/dique masa intrusiva de magma solidificado de forma tabular que se forma cuando el magma es inyectado en las fracturas de la roca circundante, penetrando transversalmente las capas de rocas preexistentes (pág. 290)

dinosaur land-dwelling reptile of the Mesozoic era (p. 377)

dinosaur/dinosaurio reptil de tierra de la era Mesozoica (pág. 377)

discharge the quantity of water in a stream that passes a given point in a period of time (p. 161)

discharge/caudal cantidad de agua en una corriente que pasa por un punto determinado en un período (pág. 161)

divergent boundary a region where the rigid plates are moving apart, typified by the oceanic ridges (p. 255)

divergent boundary/límite divergente zona donde las placas tectónicas se separan, tipificada por las dorsales oceánicas (pág. 255)

divide an imaginary line that separates the drainage of two streams; often found along a ridge (p. 169)

divide/divisoria de aguas línea imaginaria que separa el drenaje de dos corrientes de agua; frecuentemente se encuentra a lo largo de una elevación (pág. 169)

Doppler effect the apparent change in frequency of electromagnetic or sound waves caused by the relative motions of the source and the observer (p. 677)

Doppler effect/efecto Doppler variación aparente en la frecuencia de una onda sonora o electromagnética debido al movimiento relativo entre la fuente de la onda y el observador (pág. 677)

drainage basin the land area that contributes water to a stream (p. 169)

drainage basin/cuenca de avenamiento área de tierra que aporta agua a un arroyo (pág. 169)

drumlin a streamlined asymmetrical hill composed of glacial till; The steep side of the hill faces the direction from which the ice advanced. (p. 196)

drumlin/drumlin colina asimétrica compuesta de tilita glacial; el lado empinado de la colina mira hacia la dirección desde la cual avanzó el hielo (pág. 196)

dry adiabatic rate the rate of adiabatic cooling or warming in unsaturated air; The rate of temperature change is 1°C per 100 meters. (p. 511)

dry adiabatic rate/tasa adiabática seca tasa de enfriamiento o calentamiento adiabático en el aire no saturado; la tasa de cambio en la temperatura es de 1 °C por cada 100 metros (pág. 511)

dry-summer subtropical climate a climate located on the west sides of continents between 30° and 45° latitude; It is the only humid climate with a strong winter precipitation maximum. (p. 596)

dry-summer subtropical climate/clima subtropical de veranos secos clima que se encuentra en el occidente de los continentes entre los 30° y 45° de latitud; es el único clima húmedo que tiene una precipitación máxima elevada en invierno (pág. 596)

dune a hill or ridge of wind-deposited sand (p. 204)

dune/duna colina o elevación formada por arena depositada por el viento (pág. 204)

E

earthflow slow-moving downslope movement of water-saturated, clay-rich sediment, most characteristic of humid regions (p. 146)

earthflow/deslizamiento de tierra movimiento lento y descendente de sedimento saturado con agua, rico en arcilla, muy característico de las regiones húmedas (pág. 146)

earthquake the vibration of Earth produced by the rapid release of energy (p. 218)

earthquake/terremoto vibración de la Tierra producida por una liberación rápida de energía (pág. 218)

Earth science the name for all the sciences that collectively seek to understand Earth; It includes geology, oceanography, meteorology, and astronomy. (p. 2)

Earth science/ciencias de la Tierra nombre dado a todas las ciencias que colectivamente estudian la Tierra; incluye la geología, la oceanografía, la meteorología y la astronomía (pág. 2)

elastic rebound hypothesis the explanation stating that when rocks are deformed, they break, releasing the stored energy that results in the vibrations of an earthquake (p. 220)

elastic rebound hypothesis/teoría del rebote elástico explicación que dice que al deformarse las rocas, éstas se rompen, liberando energía que causa las vibraciones de un terremoto (pág. 220)

Glossary

electromagnetic spectrum the arrangement of electromagnetic radiation according to wavelength (p. 674)

electromagnetic spectrum/espectro electromagnético orden de la radiación electromagnética según la longitud de onda (pág. 674)

element a substance that cannot be broken down into simpler substances by ordinary chemical or physical means (p. 34)

element/elemento sustancia que no puede ser descompuesta en sustancias más sencillas a través de métodos químicos o físicos comunes (pág. 34)

ellipse an oval (p. 618)

ellipse/elipse óvalo (pág. 618)

El Niño the name given to the periodic warming of the ocean that occurs in the central and eastern Pacific; A major El Niño episode can cause extreme weather in many parts of the world. (p. 546)

El Niño/El Niño nombre dado al calentamiento periódico que ocurre en las regiones central y oriental del océano Pacífico; un episodio intenso de El Niño puede causar fenómenos climáticos extremos en muchas partes del mundo (pág. 546)

emission spectrum a series of bright lines of particular wavelengths produced by a hot gas under low pressure (p. 676)

emission spectrum/espectro de emisión serie de luces brillantes con longitudes de onda específicas, producidas por un gas caliente sometido a bajas presiones (pág. 676)

energy level one of several distinct regions around the nucleus of an atom where electrons are located (p. 35)

energy level/nivel de energía una de varias regiones específicas que rodea el núcleo de un átomo y en donde se ubican los electrones (pág. 35)

eon the largest time unit on the geologic time scale, next in order of magnitude above era (p. 353)

eon/eón unidad de mayor intervalo en la escala geocronológica, mayor que una era (pág. 353)

epicenter the location on Earth's surface directly above the focus, or origin, of an earthquake (p. 219)

epicenter/epicentro punto en la superficie de la Tierra que está justo sobre el foco, u origen, de un terremoto (pág. 219)

epoch a unit of the geologic time scale that is a subdivision of a period (p. 353)

epoch/época unidad de la escala geocronológica, que es una subdivisión de un período (pág. 353)

era a major division on the geologic time scale; Eras are divided into shorter units called periods. (p. 353)

era/era una de las grandes divisiones de la escala geocronológica; las eras se dividen en unidades más pequeñas llamadas períodos (pág. 353)

erosion the incorporation and transportation of material by a mobile agent, such as water, wind, or ice (p. 76)

erosion/erosión incorporación y transporte de un material por un agente móvil, como el agua, el viento o el hielo (pág. 76)

esker sinuous ridge composed largely of sand and gravel deposited by a stream flowing in a tunnel beneath a glacier near its terminus (p. 197)

esker/esker elevación alargada y sinuosa, compuesta por arena y grava que han sido depositadas por un arroyo que fluye por el túnel de un glaciar, cerca de su punta. (pág. 197)

evaporation the process of converting a liquid to a gas (p. 505)

evaporation/evaporación proceso mediante el cual un líquido se convierte en gas (pág. 505)

exfoliation type of weathering caused by reducing pressure on a rock surface, allowing slabs of outer rock to break off in layers (p. 128)

exfoliation/exfoliación tipo de meteorización causada por la disminución de la presión en una superficie rocosa, lo que permite que los estratos externos de la roca se desprendan en láminas (pág. 128)

extrusive igneous rock igneous rock that has formed on Earth's surface (p. 71)

extrusive igneous rock/roca ígnea extrusiva roca ígnea que ha sido formada en la superficie de la Tierra (pág. 71)

eye a zone of scattered clouds and calm averaging about 20 kilometers in diameter at the center of a hurricane (p. 576)

eye/ojo zona de calma, con pocas nubes, que en promedio mide 20 kilómetros de diámetro y que se encuentra en el centro de un huracán (pág. 576)

eye wall the doughnut-shaped area of intense cumulonimbus development and very strong winds that surrounds the eye of a hurricane (p. 576)

eye wall/pared del ojo zona en forma de rosquilla con gran intensidad de cumulonimbos y fuertes vientos, que rodea el ojo de un huracán (pág. 576)

F

fault a fracture in Earth along which movement has occurred (p. 219)

fault/falla fractura en la Tierra en la cual ha habido movimiento (pág. 219)

fault-block mountain a mountain formed when large blocks of crust are tilted, uplifted, or dropped between large normal faults (p. 315)

fault block mountain/montaña de bloque de falla montaña formada cuando los bloques grandes de corteza terrestre se inclinan, se elevan o caen entre fallas grandes (pág. 315)

fetch the distance that the wind has traveled across open water (p. 456)

fetch/alcance del viento distancia que ha recorrido el viento sobre aguas abiertas (pág. 456)

firn coarse grains of ice resulting from recrystallization of compressed snow (p. 189)

firn/neviza granos gruesos de hielo formados cuando la nieve comprimida se vuelve a cristalizar (pág. 189)

flood occurs when the discharge of a stream becomes so great that it exceeds the carrying capacity of its channel and overflows its banks (p. 168)

flood/inundación ocurre cuando el caudal de una corriente de agua es tan grande que sobrepasa la capacidad de su canal y se desborda por sus riberas (pág. 168)

floodplain the flat, low-lying portion of a stream valley subject to periodic flooding (p. 167)

floodplain/planicie aluvial parte plana y baja del valle de un arroyo que está expuesta a inundaciones periódicas (pág. 167)

focus the point within Earth where an earthquake originates (p. 218)

focus/foco punto dentro de la Tierra en el cual se origina un terremoto (pág. 218)

folded mountain a mountain created primarily by compressional stresses, which create folds in the rock layers (p. 314)

folded mountain/montaña de pligues montaña que ha sido creada principalmente por esfuerzos de compresión, los caules causan pliegues en los estratos de roca (pág. 314)

foliated metamorphic rock a metamorphic rock with a texture that gives the rock a layered appearance (p. 83)

foliated metamorphic rock/roca metamórfica esquistosa roca metamórfica que tiene una textura que le da una apariencia de capas (pág. 83)

food chain a succession of organisms through which food energy is transferred, starting with primary producers (p. 437)

food chain/cadena alimentaria serie de organismos a través de los cuales se transfiere la energía de los alimentos y que empieza por los productores primarios (pág. 437)

food web a group of interrelated food chains (p. 437)

food web/red alimentaria grupo de cadenas alimentarias interrelacionadas (pág. 437)

foreshock a small earthquake that often precedes a major earthquake (p. 221)

foreshock/sismo premonitor pequeño terremoto que generalmente precede a un terremoto mayor (pág. 221)

fossil the remains or traces of an organism preserved from the geologic past (p. 343)

fossil/fósil remanentes o vestigios de un organismo que ha sido preservado del pasado geológico (pág. 343)

fossil fuel general term for any hydrocarbon that may be used as a fuel, including coal, oil, and natural gas (p. 95)

fossil fuel/combustible fósil término general usado para describir los hidrocarburos que se utilizan como combustible, entre los cuales están el carbón mineral, el petróleo y el gas natural (pág. 95)
fracture any break or rupture in rock along which no appreciable movement has taken place (p. 53)
fracture/fractura discontinuidad en una roca en la cual no se manifiesta que haya ocurrido movimiento alguno (pág. 53)
front the boundary between two adjoining air masses having contrasting characteristics (p. 512)
front/frente límite entre dos masas de aire adyacentes que tienen características que contrastan (pág. 512)
frost wedging the mechanical breakup of rock caused by the expansion of freezing water in cracks and crevices (p. 127)
frost wedging/gelifracción fragmentación mecánica de una roca, causada por la expansión tras la congelación del agua en sus grietas y poros (pág. 127)

G

galaxy a group of stars, dust, and gases held together by gravity (p. 715)
galaxy/galaxia grupo de estrellas, polvo y gas unidos por la gravedad (pág. 715)
galaxy cluster a system of galaxies containing from several to thousands of member galaxies (p. 718)
galaxy cluster/cúmulo de galaxias sistema que puede contener hasta miles de galaxias (pág. 718)
gas hydrate a gas, such as methane, trapped in a lattice-like structure of water molecules (p. 411)
gas hydrate/hidrato de gas un gas, por ejemplo el metano, que queda atrapado en una red de moléculas de agua (pág. 411)
geocentric describes the concept of an Earth-centered universe (p. 615)
geocentric/geocéntrico describe un universo cuyo centro es la Tierra (pág. 615)
geologic time scale the division of Earth history into blocks of time—eons, eras, periods, and epochs; The time scale was created using relative dating principles. (p. 353)
geologic time scale/escala geocronológica división de la historia de la Tierra en bloques de tiempo: eones, eras, períodos y épocas; la escala cronológica fue creada usando los principios de datación relativa (pág. 353)
geology the science that examines Earth, its form and composition, and the changes it has undergone and is undergoing (p. 2)
geology/geología ciencia que estudia la Tierra, su forma, su composición y los cambios que ha tenido y que continúa teniendo (pág. 2)
geosphere layer of Earth under both the atmosphere and the oceans; It is composed of the core, the mantle, and the crust. (p. 7)
geosphere/geosfera estrato de la Tierra que se encuentra bajo la atmósfera y los océanos; está compuesta por el núcleo, el manto y la corteza (pág. 7)
geothermal energy energy that can be extracted from Earth's internal heat, for example, natural steam used for power generation (p. 105)
geothermal energy/energía geotérmica energía que puede extraerse del calor interno de la Tierra; por ejemplo, el vapor natural que se usa para generar electricidad (pág. 105)
geothermal gradient the gradual increase in temperature with depth in the crust; The average is 30°C per kilometer in the upper crust. (p. 291)
geothermal gradient/gradiente geotérmico aumento gradual de la temperatura a medida que se penetra en la corteza; la media es 30 °C por kilómetro en la corteza superior (pág. 291)
geyser a hot spring or fountain that ejects water at various intervals (p. 172)
geyser/géiser manantial o fuente de agua caliente que expele agua a intervalos (pág. 172)
glacial erratic an ice-transported boulder that was not derived from bedrock near its present site (p. 194)
glacial erratic/bloque errático roca transportada por el hielo y que no se originó del lecho rocoso donde se encuentra (pág. 194)
glacier a thick mass of ice originating on land

from the compaction and recrystallization of snow that shows evidence of past or present flow (p. 188)

glacier/glaciar masa gruesa de hielo que se origina en la superficie terrestre por compactación y recristalización de la nieve, mostrando evidencias de flujo en el pasado o en la actualidad (pág. 188)

global warming the increase in average temperatures of Earth and the atmosphere due in part to increased carbon dioxide levels (p. 110)

global warming/calentamiento global aumento de la temperatura media de la Tierra y de la atmósfera causado en parte por el aumento en los niveles de dióxido de carbono (pág. 110)

Gondwana late Paleozoic continent that formed the southern portion of Pangaea, consisting of all or parts of present-day South America, Africa, Australia, India, and Antarctica (p. 370)

Gondwana/Gondwana continente de finales del paleozoico, que formaba la porción austral de Pangea y que abarcaba lo que hoy en día son América del Sur, África, Australia, India y la Antártida (pág. 370)

graben a valley formed by the downward displacement of a fault-bounded block (p. 315)

graben/fosa tectónica valle formado por el desplazamiento descendente de un bloque rodeado de fallas (pág. 315)

gradient the slope of a stream over a certain distance (p. 161)

gradient/gradiente pendiente de un arroyo a lo largo de una distancia determinada (pág. 161)

granitic composition a compositional group of igneous rocks that indicate a rock is composed almost entirely of light-colored silicates, mainly quartz and feldspar (p. 73)

granitic composition/composición de granito grupo estructural de rocas ígneas que indica que una roca está compuesta casi enteramente de silicatos de color claro, principalmente cuarzo y feldespato (pág. 73)

greenhouse effect the heating of Earth's surface and atmosphere from solar radiation being absorbed and emitted by the atmosphere, mainly by water vapor and carbon dioxide (p. 487)

greenhouse effect/efecto invernadero calentamiento de la superficie y la atmósfera de la Tierra debido a la absorción y emisión de radiación solar por la atmósfera, principalmente por el vapor de agua y el dióxido de carbono (pág. 487)

groundwater water underground in the zone of saturation (p. 171)

groundwater/agua subterránea agua que se encuentra bajo la tierra, en las zonas de saturación (pág. 171)

gymnosperm seed-bearing plant that bears its seeds on the surfaces of cones (p. 379)

gymnosperm/gimnosperma planta cuyas semillas se encuentran en las superficies de los conos (pág. 379)

gyre the large circular surface current pattern found in each ocean (p. 449)

gyre/giro patrón de corriente circular grande que se encuentra en todos los océanos (pág. 449)

H

half-life the time required for one half of the atoms of a radioactive substance to decay (p. 348)

half-life/vida media tiempo requerido para que se desintegre la mitad de los átomos de una sustancia radiactiva (pág. 348)

hardness the resistance a mineral offers to scratching (p. 52)

hardness/dureza resistencia que ofrece un mineral a ser rayado (pág. 52)

heliocentric describes the view that the sun is at the center of the solar system (p. 616)

heliocentric/heliocéntrico describe la idea de que el Sol es el centro del sistema solar (pág. 616)

heat thermal energy transferred from one object to another (p. 483)

heat/calor energía térmica que se transfiere de un objeto a otro (pág. 483)

Hertzsprung-Russell diagram *See* H-R diagram

Hertzsprung-Russell diagram/diagrama Hertzprung-Russell *ver* diagrama HR

horst an elongated, uplifted block of crust bounded by faults (p. 315)

horst/pilar tectónico bloque de corteza alargado que ha sido empujado hacia arriba y se encuentra rodeado de fallas (pág. 315)

hot spot a concentration of heat in the mantle capable of producing magma, which rises to Earth's surface; The Pacific plate moves over a hot spot, producing the Hawaiian Islands. (p. 268)

hot spot/punto caliente concentración de calor en el manto capaz de producir magma, la cual sube a la superficie terrestre; la placa tectónica del Pacífico se mueve sobre un punto caliente que formó las islas hawaianas (pág. 268)

H-R diagram a plot of stars according to their absolute magnitudes and temperatures (p. 704)

H-R diagram/diagrama HR diagrama de estrellas basado en las temperaturas y magnitudes absolutas de las mismas (pág. 704)

Hubble's law a law that states that the galaxies are retreating from the Milky Way at a speed that is proportional to their distance (p. 719)

Hubble's law/ley de Hubble ley que establece que las galaxias se alejan de la vía láctea a una velocidad proporcional a sus distancias (pág. 719)

humidity a general term referring to water vapor in the air but not to liquid droplets of fog, cloud, or rain (p. 506)

humidity/humedad término general que se refiere al vapor de agua en el aire, excluyendo las gotas líquidas de niebla, nubes o lluvia (pág. 506)

humid subtropical climate a climate generally located on the eastern side of a continent and characterized by hot, sultry summers and cool winters (p. 596)

humid subtropical climate/clima subtropical húmedo clima que generalmente se encuentra en la parte oriental de un continente y que se caracteriza por tener veranos calientes y sofocantes, e inviernos templados (pág. 596)

hurricane a tropical cyclonic storm having winds in excess of 119 kilometers per hour (p. 575)

hurricane/huracán tormenta tropical ciclónica con vientos cuyas velocidades exceden los 119 kilómetros por hora (pág. 575)

hydroelectric power the power generated by falling water (p. 105)

hydroelectric power/energía hidroeléctrica energía generada por el agua en movimiento (pág. 105)

hydrogenous sediment seafloor sediment consisting of minerals that crystallize from seawater; An important example is manganese nodules. (p. 409)

hydrogenous sediment/sedimento hidrogenado sedimento del fondo oceánico, formado por minerales que se han cristalizado a partir del agua marina; un ejemplo importante son los nódulos de manganeso (pág. 409)

hydrosphere the water portion of Earth; one of the traditional subdivisions of Earth's physical environment (p. 7)

hydrosphere/hidrosfera parte acuática de la Tierra; una de las divisiones tradicionales del medio ambiente físico de la Tierra (pág. 7)

hydrothermal solution the hot, watery solution that escapes from a mass of magma during the later stages of crystallization; Such solutions may alter the surrounding rock. (p. 83)

hydrothermal solution/solución hidrotérmica solución acuosa y caliente que sale del magma durante las últimas fases de la cristalización; estas soluciones pueden alterar las rocas que las rodean (pág. 83)

hygrometer an instrument designed to measure relative humidity (p. 508)

hygrometer/higrómetro instrumento diseñado para medir la humedad relativa (pág. 508)

hypothesis a tentative explanation that is tested to determine if it is valid (p. 23)

hypothesis/hipótesis explicación tentativa cuya validez es sometida a prueba (pág. 23)

I

ice age a period of time when much of Earth's land is covered by glaciers (p. 88)

ice age/era glacial período en el que gran parte de la Tierra estaba cubierta por glaciares (pág. 88)

igneous rock a rock formed by the crystallization of molten magma (p. 66)

igneous rock/roca ígnea roca formada por la cristalización de magma líquido (pág. 66)

index fossil a fossil that is associated with a particular span of geologic time (p. 346)
index fossil/fósil índice fósil asociado a un período específico en la escala geocronológica (pág. 346)
infiltration the movement of surface water into rock or soil through cracks and pore spaces (p. 159)
infiltration/infiltración movimiento del agua desde la superficie hacia las rocas o la tierra a través de grietas y aperturas porosas (pág. 159)
inner core the solid innermost layer of Earth, about 1220 kilometers in radius (p. 235)
inner core/núcleo interno estrato sólido más profundo de la Tierra; tiene un radio de 1220 kilómetros (pág. 235)
intertidal zone the area where land and sea meet and overlap; the zone between high and low tides (p. 431)
intertidal zone/zona intermareal área donde se encuentran y se solapan la tierra y el mar; zona entre la marea alta y la marea baja (pág. 431)
intraplate volcanism igneous activity that occurs within a tectonic plate away from plate boundaries (p. 295)
intraplate volcanism/vulcanismo de placa actividad ígnea que ocurre en una placa tectónica lejos de sus límites (pág. 295)
intrusive igneous rock igneous rock that formed below Earth's surface (p. 71)
intrusive igneous rock/roca ígnea intrusiva roca ígnea formada bajo la superficie de la Tierra (pág. 71)
ion an atom or a molecule that possesses an electrical charge (p. 37)
ion/ion átomo o molécula que tiene una carga eléctrica (pág. 37)
ionic bond a bond that forms between negative and positive ions (p. 38)
ionic bond/enlace iónico enlace que se forma entre iones negativos e iones positivos (pág. 38)
isostasy the concept that Earth's crust is floating in gravitational balance upon the material of the mantle (p. 323)
isostasy/isostasia concepto que explica que la corteza terrestre está flotando sobre el material del manto gracias a un equilibrio gravitacional (pág. 323)
isostatic adjustment process of establishing a new level of gravitational equilibrium (p. 323)
isostatic adjustment/ajuste isostático proceso en el cual se establece un nuevo nivel de equilibrio gravitacional (pág. 323)
isotherm a line connecting points of equal temperature (p. 492)
isotherm/isoterma línea que conecta puntos que tienen temperaturas idénticas (pág. 492)
isotope an atom with the same number of protons but different numbers of neutrons for a given element; An isotope's mass number is different from that of the given element. (p. 36)
isotope/isótopo para cualquier elemento, es un átomo con igual número de protones pero distinto número de neutrones; el número de masa de un isótopo es distinto al de ese elemento (pág. 36)

J

jet stream swift (120–240 kilometers per hour), high-altitude winds (p. 536)
jet stream/corriente de chorro vientos de alta velocidad (120–240 kilómetros por hora) que se encuentran a grandes altitudes (pág. 536)
Jovian planet the Jupiter-like planets: Jupiter, Saturn, Uranus, and Neptune; These planets have relatively low densities and are huge gas giants. (p. 645)
Jovian planet/planeta joviano cualquier planeta de la familia de Júpiter: Júpiter, Saturno, Urano y Neptuno; estos planetas tienen densidades relativamente bajas y están compuestos principalmente de gas (pág. 645)

K

karst topography an area that has a land surface or topography with numerous depressions called sinkholes (p. 178)
karst topography/relieve kárstico zona cuya superficie o topografía presenta numerosas depresiones llamadas dolinas (pág. 178)
kettle depression created when a block of ice

became lodged in glacial deposits and subsequently melted (p. 196)

kettle/marmita depresión creada cuando se derrite un bloque de hielo que se había alojado en un depósito glacial (pág. 196)

Köppen climate classification system a system for classifying climates that is based on mean monthly and annual values of temperature and precipitation (p. 592)

Köppen climate classification system/sistema de clasificación de climas de Köppen sistema para clasificar los climas en base a los valores promedio de las temperaturas y de las precipitaciones mensuales y anuales (pág. 592)

L

laccolith a massive igneous body intruded between preexisting strata (p. 290)

laccolith/lacolito cuerpo ígneo gigantesco que ha penetrado entre dos estratos preexistentes (pág. 290)

latent heat the energy absorbed or released during a change in state (p. 505)

latent heat/calor latente energía absorbida o desprendida durante un cambio de estado físico (pág. 505)

laterite a red, highly leached soil type found in the tropics that is rich in oxides of iron and aluminum (p. 139)

laterite/laterita suelo rojizo y altamente lixiviado de las regiones tropicales, rico en óxidos de hierro y aluminio (pág. 139)

latitude the distance north or south of the equator, measured in degrees (p. 11)

latitude/latitud distancia al norte o al sur del ecuador, que se mide en grados (pág. 11)

Laurasia the continental mass that formed the northern portion of Pangaea, consisting of present-day North America and Eurasia (p. 372)

Laurasia/Laurasia masa continental que se formó en la parte norte de Pangea, y que abarcaba lo que hoy en día son América del Norte y Eurasia (pág. 372)

lava magma that reaches Earth's surface (p. 67)

lava/lava magma que ha llegado a la superficie de la Tierra (pág. 67)

light-year the distance light travels in a year, about 9.5 trillion kilometers (p. 702)

light-year/año luz distancia recorrida por la luz en un año o aproximadamente 9.5 billones de kilómetros (pág. 702)

liquefaction a phenomenon, sometimes associated with earthquakes, in which soils and other unconsolidated materials saturated with water are turned into a liquid that is not able to support buildings (p. 230)

liquefaction/licuefacción fenómeno, a veces asociado con los terremotos, en el cual la tierra, junto con otros materiales no consolidados saturados con agua, se convierten en un líquido que no es capaz de sostener los edificios (pág. 230)

lithosphere the rigid outer layer of Earth, including the crust and upper mantle (p. 234)

lithosphere/litosfera capa externa y rígida de la Tierra, que incluye la corteza y el manto superior (pág. 234)

loess deposits of windblown silt, lacking visible layers, generally light yellow, and capable of maintaining a nearly vertical cliff (p. 204)

loess/loes depósitos de limo transportado por el viento, generalmente amarillos y sin estratos visibles, y que son capaces de crear precipicios casi verticales (pág. 204)

longitude the distance east or west of the prime meridian, measure in degrees (p. 11)

longitude/longitud distancia hacia el este o el oeste del Primer meridiano; se mide en grados (pág. 11)

longshore current a near-shore current that flows parallel to the shore (p. 463)

longshore current/corriente litoral corriente que está cerca de la costa y que fluye paralela a la misma (pág. 463)

lunar eclipse an eclipse of the moon; A lunar eclipse occurs when the moon passes through Earth's shadow. (p. 628)

lunar eclipse/eclipse lunar eclipse de la Luna; ocurre cuando la Luna pasa a través de la sombra de la Tierra (pág. 628)

lunar regolith a thin, gray layer on the surface of

the moon, consisting of loosely compacted, fragmented material believed to have been formed by repeated impacts of meteorites (p. 632)

lunar regolith/regolito lunar capa gris y delgada sobre la superficie lunar compuesta de material fragmentado y ligeramente compactado, el cual se cree que fue formado por los impactos repetidos de meteoritos (pág. 632)

luster the appearance or quality of light reflected from the surface of a mineral (p. 49)

luster/brillo apariencia o calidad de la luz que es reflejada por la superficie de un mineral (pág. 49)

M

magma a body of molten rock found at depth, including any dissolved gases and crystals (p. 67)

magma/magma roca fundida que se encuentra en las profundidades de la Tierra; puede contener gas y cristales disueltos (pág. 67)

main-sequence star a star that falls into the main sequence category on the H-R diagram; This category contains the majority of stars and runs diagonally from the upper left to the lower right on the H-R diagram. (p. 704)

main-sequence star/estrella de secuencia principal estrella que pertenece a la categoría de Secuencia Principal en el diagrama HR; esta categoría contiene la mayoría de las estrellas y pasa diagonalmente de la esquina superior izquierda a la esquina inferior derecha en el diagrama HR (pág. 704)

mammal animal that bears live young and maintains a steady body temperature (p. 383)

mammal/mamífero animal que da a luz y es capaz de regular su temperatura corporal (pág. 383)

manganese nodule rounded lump of hydrogenous sediment scattered on the ocean floor, consisting mainly of manganese and iron and usually containing small amounts of copper, nickel, and cobalt (p. 412)

manganese nodule/nódulo de manganeso masa redonda de sedimento hidrogenado que se encuentra esparcida por el fondo oceánico; está formado principalmente por manganeso y hierro, y generalmente tiene pequeñas cantidades de cobre, níquel y cobalto (pág. 412)

mantle the 2890-kilometer-thick layer of Earth located below the crust (p. 8)

mantle/manto estrato de la Tierra que se encuentra justo por debajo de la corteza; tiene 2890 kilómetros de profundidad (pág. 8)

mantle plume a mass of hotter-than-normal mantle material that ascends toward the surface, where it may lead to igneous activity (p. 269)

mantle plume/pluma eruptiva masa de material del manto caliente que sube hacia la superficie, donde puede desencadenar una actividad ígnea (pág. 269)

mare (*plural* maria) the Latin name for the smooth areas of the moon formerly thought to be seas (p. 632)

mare/mare (plural: maria) nombre en Latín para las zonas lisas de la Luna que antiguamente se pensaba eran mares (pág. 632)

marine west coast climate a climate found on windward coasts from latitudes 40° to 65° and dominated by maritime air masses; Winters are mild, and summers are cool. (p. 596)

marine west coast climate/clima marítimo de la costa oeste clima de las costas expuestas al viento que se encuentran entre las latitudes 40° y 65°; en este clima predominan los aires marinos, los inviernos son templados y los veranos son frescos (pág. 596)

mass movement the downslope movement of rock, regolith, and soil under the direct influence of gravity (p. 143)

mass movement/movimiento de masas movimiento descendente de rocas, regolito y tierra por influencia directa de la gravedad (pág. 143)

mass number the number of neutrons and protons in the nucleus of an atom (p. 36)

mass number/número de masa número de neutrones y protones en el núcleo de un átomo (pág. 36)

meander a looplike bend in the course of a stream (p. 163)

meander/meandro sinuosidad en el recorrido de un arroyo (pág. 163)

mechanical weathering the physical disintegration of rock, resulting in smaller fragments (p. 126)
mechanical weathering/meteorización mecánica desintegración física de las rocas que produce fragmentos más pequeños (pág. 126)
mesosphere the layer of the atmosphere immediately above the stratosphere and characterized by decreasing temperatures with height (p. 480)
mesosphere/mesosfera estrato de la atmósfera que se encuentra inmediatamente por encima de la estratosfera y está caracterizada por el descenso de la temperatura con el aumento de la altura (pág. 480)
metallic bond a bond that forms when electrons are shared by metal ions (p. 39)
metallic bond/enlace metálico enlace que se forma cuando los iones metálicos comparten electrones (pág. 39)
metamorphic rock rock formed by the alteration of preexisting rock deep within Earth (but still in the solid state) by heat, pressure, and/or chemically active fluids (p. 66)
metamorphic rock/roca metamórfica roca formada por la alteración de una roca preexistente en las profundidades de la Tierra (pero todavía en estado sólido) debido al calor, la presión o líquidos químicamente activos (pág. 66)
metamorphism the changes in mineral composition and texture of a rock subjected to high temperature and pressure within Earth (p. 80)
metamorphism/metamorfismo cambios en la composición mineral y la textura de una roca sometida a temperaturas y presiones elevadas dentro de la Tierra (pág. 80)
meteor the luminous phenomenon observed when a meteoroid enters Earth's atmosphere and burns up, popularly called a shooting star (p. 663)
meteor/meteoro fenómeno luminoso que se observa cuando un meteoroide entra a la atmósfera de la Tierra y se desintegra, conocido popularmente como estrella fugaz (pág. 663)
meteorite any portion of a meteoroid that reaches Earth's surface (p. 664)
meteorite/meteorito cualquier fragmento de un meteoroide que llega a la superficie terrestre (pág. 664)
meteoroid a small, solid particle that travels through space (p. 663)
meteoroid/meteoroide partícula sólida y pequeña que viaja a través del espacio (pág. 663)
meteorology the scientific study of the atmosphere and atmospheric phenomena; the study of weather and climate (p. 3)
meteorology/meteorología estudio científico de la atmósfera y los fenómenos que ocurren en ella; estudio del estado del tiempo y el clima (pág. 3)
mid-ocean ridge *See* oceanic ridge
mid-ocean ridge/dorsal mesooceánica *ver* dorsal oceánica
mineral a naturally occurring, inorganic crystalline material with a unique chemical composition (p. 43)
mineral/mineral material cristalino inorgánico que ocurre de manera natural y que tiene una composición química única (pág. 43)
mixed zone an area of the ocean surface with uniform temperatures created by the mixing of water by waves, currents, and tides (p. 426)
mixed zone/zona mixta área de la superficie del océano que tiene una temperatura uniforme mantenida por la mezcla de aguas por el viento, las corrientes y las mareas (pág. 426)
Moho the Mohorovičić discontinuity, which is shortened to Moho; It is the boundary separating the crust from the mantle, discernible by an increase in the velocity of seismic waves. (p. 236)
Moho/Moho la discontinuidad de Mohorovičić, abreviada Moho; es el límite que separa la corteza del manto y que se distingue por un aumento en la velocidad de las ondas sísmicas (pág. 236)
Mohs scale a series of 10 minerals used as a standard in determining hardness (p. 52)
Mohs scale/escala de Mohs serie de 10 minerales usados como guía para determinar la dureza (pág. 52)
moment magnitude a more precise measure of earthquake magnitude than the Richter

scale, which is derived from the amount of displacement that occurs along a fault zone and estimates the energy released by an earthquake (p. 227)

moment magnitude/magnitud de momento medida más exacta para la magnitud de un terremoto que la escala de Richter, que se deriva del desplazamiento que ocurre a lo largo de una zona de falla y estima la energía que libera un terremoto (pág. 227)

monocline a large steplike fold in otherwise horizontal sedimentary strata (p. 310)

monocline/pliegue monoclinal pliegue grande en forma de escalón en un estrato horizontal de sedimento (pág. 310)

monsoon seasonal reversal of wind direction associated with large continents, especially Asia; In winter, the wind blows from land to sea. In summer, the wind blows from sea to land. (p. 542)

monsoon/monzón cambio estacional en la dirección del viento asociado con los grandes continentes, particularmente Asia; en invierno, el viento sopla de la tierra al mar y en verano, sopla del mar a la tierra (pág. 542)

moraine a ridge of unsorted sediment left by a glacier (p. 194)

moraine/morrena loma de sedimento mixto depositado por un glaciar (pág. 194)

mudflow quickly moving downhill flow of soil and rock fragments containing a large amount of water (p. 146)

mudflow/corriente de barro movimiento descendente y rápido de tierra y fragmentos de roca que contienen gran cantidad de agua (pág. 146)

N

natural levee an elevated landform that parallels a stream and acts to confine its waters, except during floodstage (p. 167)

natural levee/terraplén natural formación de tierra elevada paralela a un arroyo y que sirve para contener sus aguas, excepto durante una etapa de inundación (pág. 167)

neap tide lowest tidal range, occurring near the times of the first-quarter and third-quarter phases of the moon (p. 459)

neap tide/marea muerta menor rango entre mareas, que ocurre aproximadamente cuando la Luna está en cuarto creciente y en cuarto menguante (pág. 459)

nebula a cloud of gas and/or dust in space (p. 647)

nebula/nébula nube de gas y/o polvo en el espacio (pág. 647)

nekton organisms that can move independently of ocean currents by swimming or other means of propulsion; includes most adult fish and squid, marine mammals, and marine reptiles (p. 429)

nekton/necton grupo de organismos que pueden moverse independientemente de las corrientes del océano, nadando o mediante otros medios de propulsión; incluye la mayoría de los peces y calamares adultos, y los mamíferos y reptiles marinos (pág. 429)

neritic zone the marine-life zone that extends from the low-tide line out to the shelf break (p. 431)

neritic zone/zona nerítica zona con vida marítima que se extiende desde la línea de marea baja hasta el talud continental (pág. 431)

neutron star a star of extremely high density composed entirely of neutrons (p. 713)

neutron star/estrella de neutrones estrella de gran densidad, compuesta enteramente de neutrones (pág. 713)

nonfoliated metamorphic rock metamorphic rock that does not exhibit a banded or layered appearance (p. 83)

nonfoliated metamorphic rock/roca metamórfica no esquistosa roca metamórfica que no tiene una apariencia estratificada (pág. 83)

nonpoint source pollution water pollution that does not have a specific point of origin (p. 109)

nonpoint source pollution/contaminación no localizada contaminación del agua que no tiene un origen determinado (pág. 109)

nonrenewable resource resource that takes millions of years to form (p. 94)

nonrenewable resource/recurso no renovable recurso que toma millones de años en formarse (pág. 94)

normal fault a fault in which the rock above the fault plane has moved down relative to the rock below (p. 311)

normal fault/falla normal falla en la que la roca que está por encima del plano de la falla se desplaza hacia abajo, en relación a la roca que está por debajo (pág. 311)

normal polarity a magnetic field that is the same as that which exists at present (p. 266)

normal polarity/polaridad normal campo magnético igual al que existe en el presente (pág. 266)

nova a star that explosively increases in brightness (p. 705)

nova/nova estrella cuyo brillo aumenta repentinamente (pág. 705)

nuclear fusion the way in which the sun produces energy; Nuclear fusion occurs when less massive nuclei combine into more massive nuclei, releasing tremendous amounts of energy. (p. 689)

nuclear fusion/fusión nuclear proceso mediante el cual el Sol genera energía; la fusión nuclear ocurre cuando los núcleos menos masivos se unen para formar núcleos más masivos y desprenden enormes cantidades de energía en el proceso (pág. 689)

O

occluded front a front formed when a cold front overtakes a warm front; It marks the beginning of the end of a middle-latitude cyclone. (p. 567)

occluded front/frente ocluido frente que se forma cuando un frente frío alcanza a un frente cálido; indica el principio del fin de un ciclón de las latitudes medias (pág. 567)

ocean basin floor area of the deep-ocean floor between the continental margin and the oceanic ridge (p. 404)

ocean basin floor/cuenca del fondo oceánico zona del fondo de los océanos profundos, ubicada entre el margen continental y la elevación oceánica (pág. 404)

ocean current mass of ocean water that flows from one place to another (p. 448)

ocean current/corriente oceánica masa de agua oceánica que fluye de un lugar a otro (pág. 448)

oceanic ridge a continuous elevated zone on the floor of all the major ocean basins and varying in width from 1000 to 4000 kilometers; The rifts at the crests of ridges represent divergent plate boundaries. (p. 258)

oceanic ridge/dorsal oceánica zona de elevación continua en el fondo de todas las cuencas de los océanos, cuya anchura varía entre 1000 y 4000 kilómetros; las grietas en las cimas de las elevaciones representan límites divergentes de las placas tectónicas (pág. 258)

oceanic zone the marine-life zone beyond the continental shelf (p. 431)

oceanic zone/zona oceánica zona con vida marina que se encuentra más allá de la plataforma continental (pág. 431)

oceanography the scientific study of the oceans and oceanic phenomena (p. 3)

oceanography/oceanografía estudio científico de los océanos y sus fenómenos (pág. 3)

ore a material from which a useful mineral or minerals can be mined at a profit (p. 98)

ore/mena material a partir del cual se pueden explotar minerales útiles para obtener un beneficio económico (pág. 98)

original horizontality, principle of a principle of relative dating; Layers of sediments are generally deposited in a horizontal or nearly horizontal position. (p. 340)

original horizontality, principle of/horizontalidad original, principio de la principio de la datación relativa; los estratos de sedimentos generalmente son depositadas en posición horizontal o casi horizontal (pág. 340)

orogenesis the processes that collectively result in the formation of mountains (p. 314)

orogenesis/orogénesis aquellos procesos que en colectivo resultan en la formación de las montañas (pág. 314)

orographic lifting mountains acting as barriers to the flow of air, forcing the air to ascend; The air cools adiabatically, and clouds and precipitation may result. (p. 512)

orographic lifting/elevación orográfica montaña o montañas que forman una barrera para el flujo del aire, empujando el aire hacia arriba; el aire se enfría de manera adiabática, lo cual causa la formación de nubes y precipitación (pág. 512)

outer core a layer beneath the mantle about 2260 kilometers thick; The outer core contains liquid iron and generates Earth's magnetic field. (p. 235)

outer core/núcleo exterior estrato que se encuentra por debajo del manto, con un grosor de aproximadamente 2260 kilómetros; el núcleo exterior contiene hierro líquido y genera el campo magnético de la Tierra (pág. 235)

outwash plain a relatively flat, gently sloping plain consisting of materials deposited by meltwater streams in front of the margin of an ice sheet (p. 196)

outwash plain/llanura aluvial llanura relativamente plana y con leves inclinaciones formada por materiales depositados por los arroyos de aguanieve al borde de un helero (pág. 196)

ozone a molecule of oxygen containing three oxygen atoms (p. 478)

ozone/ozono molécula de oxígeno que contiene tres átomos de oxígeno (pág. 478)

P

P wave earthquake wave that pushes and pulls rocks in the direction of the wave; also known as a compression wave (p. 223)

P wave/onda P onda sísmica que empuja y atrae las rocas; también se llama onda de compresión (pág. 223)

paleomagnetism the natural remnant magnetism in rock bodies; the permanent magnetization acquired by rock that can be used to determine the location of the magnetic poles at the time it became magnetized (p. 265)

paleomagnetism/paleomagnetismo restos de magnetismo natural en cuerpos rocosos; magnetización permanente que adquieren las rocas, que se puede usar para determinar la localización de los polos magnéticos en el momento en que se magnetizaron (pág. 265)

Pangaea the proposed supercontinent that 200 million years ago began to break apart and form the present landmasses (p. 248)

Pangaea/Pangea supercontinente que hace 200 millones de años comenzó a fragmentarse y a formar las masas de tierra actuales (pág. 248)

pedalfer soil of humid regions characterized by the accumulation of iron oxides and aluminum-rich clays in the B horizon (p. 139)

pedalfer/pedalfer suelo de las regiones húmedas que se caracteriza por la acumulación de óxidos de hierro y de arcillas ricas en aluminio en el horizonte B (pág. 139)

pedocal soil associated with drier regions and characterized by an accumulation of calcium carbonate in the upper horizons (p. 139)

pedocal/pedocal suelo asociado con las regiones más secas y que se caracteriza por una acumulación de carbonato de calcio en los horizontes superiores (pág. 139)

pelagic zone open ocean of any depth; Animals in this zone swim or float freely. (p. 431)

pelagic zone/zona pelágica océano abierto de cualquier profundidad; los animales de esta zona nadan o flotan libremente (pág. 431)

perigee the point at which the moon is closest to Earth (p. 626)

perigee/perigeo el punto en el que la Luna está más cerca de la Tierra (pág. 626)

perihelion the point in the orbit of a planet where it is closest to the sun (p. 624)

perihelion/perihelio el punto en la órbita de un planeta en el que éste está más cerca del Sol (pág. 624)

period a basic unit of the geologic time scale that is a subdivision of an era; Periods may be divided into smaller units called epochs. (p. 353)

period/período unidad básica de la escala geocronológica que es una subdivisión de una era; los períodos pueden dividirse en unidades más pequeñas llamadas épocas (pág. 353)

permeability a measure of a material's ability to transmit fluids (p. 171)

permeability/permeabilidad la capacidad de un material para transmitir fluidos (pág. 171)

phases of the moon the progression of changes in the moon's appearance during the month (p. 626)

phases of the moon/fases de la Luna la progresión de los cambios de la apariencia de la Luna a lo largo del mes (pág. 626)

photic zone the upper part of the ocean into which sunlight penetrates (p. 430)

photic zone/zona fótica parte superior del océano en la que penetra la luz solar (pág. 430)

photon a small packet of light energy (p. 675)

photon/fotón partícula de energía luminosa (pág. 675)

photosphere the region of the sun that radiates energy to space; visible surface of the sun (p. 685)

photosphere/fotosfera región del Sol que irradia energía al espacio; la superficie visible del Sol (pág. 685)

photosynthesis the process by which plants, algae, and certain prokaryotes use light energy to convert water and carbon dioxide into energy-rich glucose molecules (p. 433)

photosynthesis/fotosíntesis proceso mediante el cual plantas, algas y ciertos procariotas usan la energía luminosa para convertir agua y dióxido de carbono en moléculas de glucosa ricas en energía (pág. 433)

phytoplankton algal plankton, which are the most important community of primary producers in the ocean (p. 429)

phytoplankton/fitoplancton plancton algal, que es la comunidad más importante de productores primarios del océano (pág. 429)

planetesimal small, irregularly shaped body formed by colliding matter (p. 648)

planetesimal/planetésimo cuerpo pequeño, de forma irregular, formado por materia en colisión (pág. 648)

plankton passively drifting or weakly swimming organisms that cannot move independently of ocean currents; includes microscopic algae, protozoa, jellyfish, and larval forms of many animals (p. 428)

plankton/plancton organismos que flotan pasivamente o nadan débilmente, que no se pueden mover independientemente de corrientes oceánicas; incluyen algas microscópicas, protozoos, medusas y formas larvales de muchos animales (pág. 428)

plate one of numerous rigid sections of the lithosphere that moves as a unit over the material of the asthenosphere (p. 254)

plate/placa una de las numerosas secciones rígidas de la litosfera que se mueve como unidad sobre la materia de la astenosfera (pág. 254)

plate tectonics the theory that proposes that Earth's outer shell consists of individual plates that interact in various ways and thereby produce earthquakes, volcanoes, mountains, and the crust itself (p. 254)

plate tectonics/tectónica de placas teoría que propone que la capa exterior de la Tierra se compone de placas individuales que interactúan de varias maneras y producen como resultado terremotos, volcanes, montañas y la corteza en sí (pág. 254)

playa lake a flat area on the floor of an undrained desert basin (playa) that fills and becomes a lake after heavy rain (p. 201)

playa lake/salar superficie plana en el suelo de una cuenca desértica sin drenaje que se llena y se convierte en un lago tras lluvias fuertes (pág. 201)

pluton an intrusive igneous structure that results from the cooling and hardening of magma beneath the surface of Earth (p. 289)

pluton/plutón estructura intrusiva ígnea que resulta del enfriamiento y endurecimiento del magma bajo la superficie de la Tierra (pág. 289)

point source pollution water pollution that comes from a known and specific location (p. 108)

point source pollution/contaminación de fuentes localizadas contaminación acuática que procede de una fuente conocida y específica (pág. 108)

polar easterlies in the global pattern of prevailing winds, winds that blow from the polar high toward the subpolar low; These winds, however, should not be thought of as persistent winds, such as the trade winds. (p. 541)

polar easterlies/vientos polares del este en el patrón global de vientos dominantes, los vientos que soplan desde la zona polar de alta presión a la zona subpolar de baja presión; sin embargo, estos vientos no deben considerarse como vientos persistentes, como por ejemplo los vientos alisios (pág. 541)

polar front the stormy frontal zone separating cold air masses of polar origin from warm air masses of tropical origin (p. 541)

polar front/frente polar la zona frontal tormentosa que separa masas de aire frío de origen polar de masas de aire cálido de origen tropical (pág. 541)

polar zone the region between 66.5° north and south latitudes and the poles; The sun's rays strike at a very small angle in the polar zone. (p. 589)

polar zone/zona polar la región entre los 66.5° de latitud y los polos; los rayos del Sol llegan a la zona polar en un ángulo muy pequeño (pág. 589)

porosity the volume of open spaces in rock or soil (p. 171)

porosity/porosidad el volumen de espacios abiertos en una roca o suelo (pág. 171)

porphyritic texture an igneous texture consisting of large crystals embedded in a matrix of much smaller crystals (p. 72)

porphyritic texture/textura porfirítica textura ígnea formada por grandes cristales incrustados en una matriz de cristales mucho más pequeños (pág. 72)

precession a slow motion of Earth's axis that traces out a cone over a period of 26,000 years (p. 622)

precession/precesión movimiento lento del eje de la Tierra que traza un cono a lo largo de un período de 26,000 años (pág. 622)

precipitation any form of water that falls from a cloud (p. 504)

precipitation/precipitación cualquier forma de agua que cae de una nube (pág. 504)

pressure gradient the amount of pressure change occurring over a given distance (p. 534)

pressure gradient/gradiente de presión medida del cambio de presión que ocurre a lo largo de una distancia dada (pág. 534)

prevailing wind a wind that consistently blows from one direction more than from another (p. 545)

prevailing wind/viento dominante un viento que sopla constantemente de una dirección más que de otra (pág. 545)

primary productivity the production of organic matter from inorganic substances through photosynthesis or chemosynthesis (p. 433)

primary productivity/productividad primaria la producción de materia orgánica a partir de sustancias inorgánicas a través de la fotosíntesis o quimiosíntesis (pág. 433)

prominence a concentration of gases above the solar surface that appears as a bright archlike structure (p. 688)

prominence/prominencia concentración de gases sobre la superficie solar que aparece como una estructura brillante en forma de arco (pág. 688)

protostar a collapsing cloud of gas and dust destined to become a star; a developing star not yet hot enough to engage in nuclear fusion (p. 708)

protostar/protoestrella nube de gas y polvo en colapso destinada a convertirse en una estrella; una estrella en desarrollo que todavía no está lo suficientemente caliente para iniciar la fusión nuclear (pág. 708)

pulsar a variable radio source of small size that emits radio pulses in very regular periods (p. 713)

pulsar/púlsar fuente de radio variable de tamaño pequeño que emite pulsaciones de radio en períodos muy regulares (pág. 713)

pycnocline a layer of water in which there is a rapid change of density with depth (p. 426)

pycnocline/picnoclina capa de agua en la que se produce un rápido cambio de densidad con la profundidad (pág. 426)

pyroclastic material the volcanic rock ejected during an eruption, including ash, bombs, and blocks (p. 283)

pyroclastic material/material piroclástico roca volcánica expulsada durante una erupción, incluyendo cenizas, bombas y bloques (pág. 283)

R

radiation the transfer of energy (heat) through space by electromagnetic waves (p. 485)

radiation/radiación transferencia de energía (calor) a través del espacio mediante ondas electromagnéticas (pág. 485)

radioactivity the spontaneous decay of certain unstable atomic nuclei (p. 347)

radioactivity/radiactividad desintegración espontánea de ciertos núcleos atómicos inestables (pág. 347)

radiocarbon (carbon-14) dating method for determining age by comparing the amount of carbon-14 to the amount of carbon-12 in a sample (p. 349)

radiocarbon (carbon-14) dating/datación por radiocarbono (carbono-14) método para determinar la edad mediante la comparación de la cantidad de carbono-14 con la cantidad de carbono-12 en una muestra (pág. 349)

radiometric dating the procedure of calculating the absolute ages of rocks and minerals that contain radioactive isotopes (p. 348)

radiometric dating/datación radiométrica procedimiento para calcular las edades absolutas de rocas y minerales que contienen isótopos radiactivos (pág. 348)

radio telescope a telescope designed to make observations in radio wavelengths (p. 681)

radio telescope/radiotelescopio telescopio diseñado para hacer observaciones en longitud de ondas de radio (pág. 681)

ray any of a system of bright elongated streaks, sometimes associated with a crater on the moon (p. 632)

ray/rayo cualquiera de los sistemas de haces alargados luminosos, a veces asociados con un cráter en la Luna (pág. 632)

recycling the collecting and processing of used items so they can be made into new products (p. 116)

recycling/reciclaje recolección y procesamiento de objetos usados para que puedan convertirse en nuevos productos (pág. 116)

red giant a large, cool star of high luminosity; a star occupying the upper-right portion of the H-R diagram (p. 704)

red giant/gigante roja estrella grande, fría, de gran luminosidad; estrella que ocupa la parte superior derecha del diagrama HR (pág. 704)

reflecting telescope a telescope that concentrates light from distant objects by using a concave mirror (p. 680)

reflecting telescope/telescopio reflector telescopio que concentra la luz de objetos distantes usando un espejo cóncavo (pág. 680)

reflection the process whereby light bounces back from an object at the same angle at which it encounters a surface and with the same intensity (p. 486)

reflection/reflexión proceso por el cual la luz rebota de un objeto en el mismo ángulo en el que llega a su superficie y con la misma intensidad (pág. 486)

refracting telescope a telescope that uses a lens to bend and concentrate the light from distant objects (p. 678)

refracting telescope/telescopio refractor telescopio que usa una lente para doblar y concentrar la luz de objetos distantes (pág. 678)

refraction *See* wave refraction.

refraction/refracción *ver* onda de refracción

regional metamorphism metamorphism associated with large-scale mountain-building processes (p. 81)

regional metamorphism/metamorfismo regional metamorfismo asociado con procesos de formación de montañas a gran escala (pág. 81)

regolith the layer of rock and mineral fragments that nearly everywhere covers Earth's surface (p. 133)

regolith/regolito manto de fragmentos de rocas y minerales que cubre casi toda la superficie de la Tierra (pág. 133)

rejuvenation a change in the base level of a stream, often caused by regional uplift (p. 163)

rejuvenation/rejuvenecimiento cambio en el nivel bajo de un arroyo, a menudo causado por levantamiento regional (pág. 163)

relative dating process by which rocks are placed in their proper sequence or order; Only the chronological order of events is determined, not the absolute age in years. (p. 339)

relative dating/datación relativa proceso por el que las rocas se colocan en su propia secuencia u orden; sólo se determina el orden cronológico de los sucesos, no la edad absoluta en años (pág. 339)

relative humidity the ratio of the air's water-vapor content to its water-vapor capacity (p. 506)

relative humidity/humedad relativa la proporción del contenido de vapor de agua en el aire y su capacidad de vapor de agua (pág. 506)

renewable resource a resource that is virtually inexhaustible or that can be replenished over relatively short time spans (p. 94)

renewable resource/recurso renovable recurso que virtualmente no se puede agotar o que se puede renovar en un lapso relativamente corto (pág. 94)

retrograde motion the apparent westward motion of the planets with respect to the stars (p. 616)

retrograde motion/movimiento retrógrado el aparente movimiento hacia el oeste de los planetas con respecto a las estrellas (pág. 616)

reverse fault a fault in which the material above the fault plane moves up in relation to the material below (p. 312)

reverse fault/falla inversa falla en la que el material sobre el plano de la falla se desliza hacia arriba en relación con el material de abajo (pág. 312)

reverse polarity a magnetic field opposite to that which exists at present (p. 266)

reverse polarity/polaridad inversa campo magnético opuesto al que existe en el momento (pág. 266)

revolution the motion of one body about another, as Earth about the sun (p. 622)

revolution/revolución o traslación movimiento de un cuerpo alrededor de otro, como el de la Tierra alrededor del Sol (pág. 622)

ridge-push a mechanism that may contribute to plate motion; It involves the oceanic lithosphere sliding down the oceanic ridge under the pull of gravity. (p.269)

ridge-push/empuje de dorsal mecanismo que puede contribuir al movimiento de placas; implica que la litosfera oceánica se desliza hacia abajo por la dorsal oceánica bajo la atracción de la gravedad (pág. 269)

rift valley deep faulted structure found along the axes of divergent plate boundaries; Rift valleys can develop on the seafloor or on land. (p. 258)

rift valley/valle de rift estructura de fallas profundas que se encuentra a lo largo de los ejes de los límites de placas divergentes; los valles de rift pueden formarse en el suelo marino o en la tierra (pág. 258)

rille long channel associated with lunar maria; A rille looks similar to a valley or a trench. (p. 632)

rille/rille canal alargado asociado con los maria lunares; un rille es parecido a un valle o una fosa (pág. 632)

rock a consolidated mixture of minerals (p. 66)

rock/roca mezcla de minerales consolidados (pág. 66)

rock cycle a model that illustrates the origin of the three basic rock types and the interrelatedness of Earth materials and processes (p. 67)

rock cycle/ciclo de la roca modelo que ilustra el origen de los tres tipos básicos de rocas y la interrelación de materiales y procesos de la Tierra (pág. 67)

rockfall occurs when rocks or rock fragments fall freely through the air; common on steep slopes (p. 145)

rockfall/desprendimiento de rocas ocurre cuando rocas o fragmentos de roca caen libremente por el aire; son comunes en pendientes pronunciadas (pág. 145)

rockslide occurs when a mass of rock slides rapidly downslope along planes of weakness (p. 145)

rockslide/deslizamiento de rocas ocurre cuando una masa de rocas se desliza rápidamente pendiente a lo largo de taludes inestables (pág. 145)

rotation the spinning of a body, such as Earth, about its axis (p. 622)

rotation/rotación el giro de un cuerpo, como la Tierra, alrededor de su eje (pág. 622)

runoff water that flows over the land surface rather than seeping into the ground (p. 109)

runoff/escorrentía agua que fluye sobre la superficie del suelo, en lugar de filtrarse en ella (pág. 109)

S

S wave a seismic wave that shakes particles perpendicular to the direction the wave is traveling (p. 223)

S wave/onda S onda sísmica que sacude partículas perpendiculares a la dirección en que viaja la onda (pág. 223)

salinity the proportion of dissolved salts to pure water, usually expressed in parts per thousand (‰) (p. 422)

salinity/salinidad la proporción de sales disueltas en agua pura, generalmente expresada en partes por miles (‰) (pág. 422)

saturated the state of air that contains the maximum quantity of water vapor that it can hold at any given temperature and pressure (p. 506)

saturated/saturado el estado del aire que contiene la máxima cantidad de vapor de agua que puede retener a una temperatura y presión determinadas (pág. 506)

scattering the redirecting (in all directions) of light by small particles and gas molecules in the atmosphere; The result is more light rays with weaker intensity. (p. 486)

scattering/dispersión la redirección (en todas direcciones) de luz por pequeñas partículas y moléculas de gas en la atmósfera; el resultado es más rayos de luz con menos intensidad (pág. 486)

seafloor spreading the process by which plate tectonics produces new oceanic lithosphere at ocean ridges (p. 259)

seafloor spreading/expansión de los suelos oceánicos proceso por el cual la tectónica de placas produce una nueva litosfera oceánica en las dorsales oceánicas (pág. 259)

seamount an isolated volcanic peak that rises at least 1000 meters above the deep-ocean floor (p. 404)

seamount/monte marino pico volcánico aislado que se eleva al menos 1000 metros sobre el suelo oceánico (pág. 404)

sediment loose particles created by the weathering and erosion of rock, by chemical precipitation from solution in water, or from the secretions of organisms and transported by water, wind, or glaciers (p. 68)

sediment/sedimento partículas sueltas formadas por la meteorización y la erosión de una roca, por la precipitación química de una solución en agua o por las secreciones de organismos, y transportadas por el agua, el viento o los glaciares (pág. 68)

sedimentary rock rock formed from the weathered products of preexisting rocks that have been transported, deposited, compacted, and cemented (p. 66)

sedimentary rock/roca sedimentaria roca formada a partir de productos erosionados de rocas anteriores que han sido transportados, depositados, endurecidos y cimentados (pág. 66)

seismic gap an area along a fault where there has not been any earthquake activity for a long period of time (p. 232)

seismic gap/brecha sísmica área a lo largo de una falla donde no ha habido actividad sísmica durante un largo período (pág. 232)

seismogram the record made by a seismograph (p. 222)

seismogram/sismograma registro hecho por un sismógrafo (pág. 222)

seismograph an instrument that records earthquake waves (p. 222)

seismograph/sismógrafo instrumento que registra ondas sísmicas (pág. 222)

shield A large, relatively flat expanse of ancient metamorphic rock within the stable continental interior (p. 365)

shield/escudo extensión grande y relativamente plana de roca metamórfica antigua dentro del interior continental estable (pág. 365)

shield volcano a broad, gently sloping volcano built from fluid basaltic lavas (p. 284)

shield volcano/volcán en escudo volcán ancho, de laderas poco inclinadas, formado por el fluido de lavas basálticas (pág. 284)

silicate any one of numerous minerals that have the oxygen and silicon tetrahedron as their basic structure (p. 45)

silicate/silicato cualquiera de los numerosos

minerales que tienen como su estructura básica el tetraedro de oxígeno y silicio (pág. 45)

siliceous ooze biogenous sediment composed of the silica-based shells of single-celled animals and algae (p. 408)

siliceous ooze/fango silíceo sedimento biógeno compuesto de esqueletos de sílice de animales unicelulares y algas (pág. 408)

silicon-oxygen tetrahedron a structure composed of four oxygen atoms surrounding a silicon atom, which constitutes the basic building block of silicate minerals (p. 45)

silicon-oxygen tetrahedron/tetraedro de oxígeno y silicio estructura compuesta de cuatro átomos de oxígeno que rodean un átomo de silicio, que constituye la pieza clave para formar los silicatos (pág. 45)

sill a tabular igneous body formed when magma is injected along sedimentary bedding surfaces (p. 298)

sill/sill cuerpo tabular ígneo que se forma cuando el magma es inyectado a lo largo de superficies de lechos sedimentarios (pág. 298)

sinkhole a depression produced in a region where soluble rock has been removed by groundwater (p. 178)

sinkhole/dolina depresión que se produce en una región cuando el agua subterránea disuelve la roca soluble (pág. 178)

slab-pull a mechanism that contributes to plate motion in which cool, dense oceanic crust sinks into the mantle and "pulls" the trailing lithosphere along (p. 269)

slab-pull/subducción de placa mecanismo que contribuye al movimiento de placas en el cual la corteza oceánica, densa y fría se hunde en el manto, arrastrando consigo la listosfera (pág. 269)

slump the downward slipping of a mass of rock or unconsolidated material moving as a unit along a curved surface (p. 146)

slump/desprendimienro el movimiento hacia abajo de una masa de rocas o material no consolidado que se mueve como unidad a lo largo de una superficie curva (pág. 146)

snowline lowest elevation in a particular area that remains covered in snow all year (p. 188)

snowline/línea de nieve elevación más baja en un área concreta que queda cubierta por la nieve todo el año (pág. 188)

soil a combination of mineral and organic matter, water, and air; that portion of the regolith that supports plant growth (p. 133)

soil/suelo combinación de materia mineral y orgánica, agua y aire; parte del regolito que permite el crecimiento de plantas (pág. 138)

soil horizon a layer of soil that has identifiable characteristics produced by chemical weathering and other soil-forming processes (p. 138)

soil horizon/horizonte capa del suelo que tiene unas características identificables producidas por alteraciones químicas y otros procesos de formación del suelo (p. 138)

soil profile a vertical section through a soil showing its succession of horizons and the underlying parent material (p. 138)

soil profile/perfil del suelo sección vertical de un suelo que muestra la sucesión de horizontes y los materiales litológicos subyacentes (pág. 138)

solar eclipse an eclipse of the sun; A solar eclipse occurs when the moon moves in a line directly between Earth and the sun, casting a shadow on Earth. (p. 628)

solar eclipse/eclipse solar eclipse del Sol; un eclipse solar ocurre cuando la Luna se mueve en línea directa entre la Tierra y el Sol, formando una sombra sobre la Tierra (pág. 268)

solar flare a sudden and tremendous eruption in the solar chromosphere (p. 688)

solar flare/destello solar gran erupción de energía repentina en la cromosfera solar (pág. 688)

solar wind streams of protons and electrons ejected at high speed from the solar corona (p. 686)

solar wind/viento solar ráfagas de protones y electrones lanzadas a alta velocidad desde la corona solar (pág. 686)

sonar An electronic depth-sounding mechanism; Sonar is an acronym for sound navigation and ranging. Sonar calculates ocean depth by recording the time it takes for an energy pulse to reach the ocean floor and return. (p. 398)

sonar/sonar mecanismo electrónico de sonido de profundidad; *sonar* es un acrónimo en inglés para *Sound Navigation and Ranging* (navegación y rango de sonido); un sonar calcula la profundidad del océano al registrar el tiempo que tarda una pulsación de energía en llegar al suelo oceánico y volver (pág. 398)

spectroscopy the study of the properties of light that depend on wavelength (p. 676)

spectroscopy/espectroscopia estudio de las propiedades de la luz que depende de la longitud de onda (pág. 676)

spring a flow of groundwater that emerges naturally at the ground surface (p. 171)

spring/manantial fuente de agua subterránea que emerge de forma natural en la superficie de la tierra (pág. 171)

spring equinox the equinox that occurs on March 21 or 22 in the Northern Hemisphere (p. 482)

spring equinox/equinoccio de primavera el equinoccio que tiene lugar el 21 ó 22 de marzo en el hemisferio norte (pág. 482)

spring tide highest tidal range that occurs due to the alignment of Earth, the moon, and the sun (p. 459)

spring tide/marea viva rango de marea más alto que ocurre debido a la alineación de la Tierra, la Luna y el Sol (pág. 459)

stalactite an icicle-like structure that hangs from the ceiling of a cavern (p. 177)

stalactite/estalactita estructura en forma de carámbano que cuelga del techo de una caverna (pág. 177)

stalagmite a columnlike form that grows upward from the floor of a cavern (p. 177)

stalagmite/estalagmita estructura en forma de columna que crece hacia arriba desde el suelo de una caverna (pág. 177)

stationary front a situation in which the surface position of a front does not move; The flow on either side of such a boundary is nearly parallel to the position of the front. (p. 566)

stationary front/frente estacionario situación en la que la posición de la superficie de un frente no se mueve; el movimiento a cada lado de ese límite es casi paralelo a la posición del frente (pág. 566)

storm surge the abnormal rise of the sea along a shore as a result of strong winds (p. 577)

storm surge/marea de tempestad la subida anormal del mar a lo largo de la costa como resultado de fuertes vientos (p. 577)

strain the change in shape or volume of a body of rock as a result of stress (p. 308)

strain/deformación el cambio en la forma o el volumen de un cuerpo rocoso como resultado del esfuerzo (pág. 308)

stratosphere the layer of the atmosphere immediately above the troposphere, characterized by increasing temperatures with height, due to the concentration of ozone (p. 480)

stratosphere/estratosfera la capa de la atmósfera inmediantamente por encima de la troposfera, que se caracteriza por el aumento de la temperatura con la altura, debido a la concentración de ozono (pág. 480)

stratus one of three basic cloud forms; They are sheets or layers that cover much or all of the sky. (p. 518)

stratus/estrato una de las tres formas básicas de las nubes; son como sábanas o capas que cubren todo o casi todo el cielo (pág. 518)

streak the color of a mineral in powdered form (p. 51)

streak/raya el color de un mineral en forma pulverizada (pág. 51)

stream channel the course that the water in a stream follows (p. 161)

stream channel/cauce el curso que sigue el agua de una corriente (pág. 161)

stress the force per unit area acting on a solid (p. 308)

stress/esfuerzo la fuerza por unidad de área que actúa sobre un sólido (pág. 308)

strike-slip fault a fault along which the movement is horizontal and parallel to the trend of the fault (p. 313)

strike-slip fault/falla de desgarre falla a lo largo de la cual el movimiento es horizontal y paralelo a la tendencia de la falla (pág. 313)

stromatolite structure produced by algae trapping

sediment and forming layered mounds of calcium carbonate (p. 368)

stromatolite/estromatolito estructura producida por algas atrapadas en sedimento que forma pilas estratificadas de carbonato de calcio (pág. 368)

subarctic climate A climate found north of the humid continental climate and south of the polar climate; characterized by bitterly cold winters and short cool summers; Places within this climatic realm experience the highest annual temperature ranges on Earth. (p. 597)

subartic climate/clima subártico clima que prevalece al norte del clima húmedo continental y al sur del clima polar; se caracteriza por inviernos fríos rigurosos y veranos frescos y cortos; los lugares que se hallan en este ambiente tienen el rango de temperaturas más elevado de la Tierra (pág. 597)

subduction zone a destructive plate margin where oceanic crust is being pushed down into the mantle beneath a second plate (p. 261)

subduction zone/zona de subducción margen de placa destructivo donde la corteza oceánica es empujada hacia abajo, al manto, bajo una segunda placa (pág. 261)

sublimation the conversion of a solid directly to a gas without passing through the liquid state (p. 506)

sublimation/sublimación conversión de un sólido directamente a gas sin pasar por estado líquido (pág. 506)

submarine canyon a seaward extension of a valley that was cut on the continental shelf during a time when sea level was lower; a canyon carved into the outer continental shelf, slope, and rise by turbidity currents (p. 403)

submarine canyon/cañón submarino extensión de un valle hacia el mar que se cortó en la plataforma continental durante una era en la que el nivel del mar era más bajo; un cañón cavado en la parte exterior de la plataforma continental, el talud continental y el pie continental por corrientes de turbidez (pág. 403)

submersible a small underwater craft used for deep-sea research (p. 400)

submersible/sumergible nave submarina pequeña que se usa en la investigación oceánica (pág. 400)

summer solstice the solstice that occurs on June 21 or 22 in the Northern Hemisphere and on December 21 or 22 in the Southern Hemisphere (p. 482)

summer solstice/solsticio de verano solsticio que tiene lugar el 21 ó 22 de junio en el hemisferio norte y el 21 ó 22 de diciembre en el hemisferio sur (pág. 482)

sunspot a dark spot on the sun, which is cool by contrast to the surrounding photosphere (p. 687)

sunspot/mancha solar área oscura del Sol que está más fría que la fotosfera que la rodea (pág. 687)

supercooled water the condition of water droplets that remain in the liquid state at temperatures well below 0°C (p. 521)

supercooled water/agua subenfriada condición en que las gotas de agua permanecen en estado líquido a temperaturas inferiores a 0 °C (pág. 521)

supergiant a very large, very bright red giant star (p. 704)

supergiant/supergigante estrella roja muy grande y muy brillante (pág. 704)

supernova an exploding star that increases in brightness many thousands of times (p. 711)

supernova/supernova estrella en explosión que aumenta su brillo muchos miles de veces (pág. 711)

superposition, law of a law that states that in any undeformed sequence of sedimentary rocks, each bed is older than the layers above and younger than the layers below. (p. 340)

superposition, law of/ley de superposición ley que enuncia que en cualquier secuencia no deformada de rocas sedimentarias, cada capa es más antigua que los estratos de arriba y más joven que los estratos de abajo (pág. 340)

supersaturated air the condition of air that is more highly concentrated than is normally possible under given temperature and pressure conditions; When describing humidity, it refers to a relative humidity that is greater than 100 percent. (p. 521)

supersaturated air/aire sobresaturado condición del aire con un nivel de concentración mucho más alto de lo que es normalmente posible bajo ciertas condiciones de temperatura y presión; al describir la humedad, se refiere a una humedad relativa que es mayor que el 100 por ciento (pág. 521)

surface current movement of water that flows horizontally in the upper part of the ocean's surface (p. 448)

surface current/corriente superficial movimiento de agua que fluye horizontalmente en la parte superior de la superficie oceánica (pág. 448)

surface wave a seismic wave that travels along the surface of Earth (p. 223)

surface wave/onda superficial onda sísmica que viaja a lo largo de la superficie de la Tierra (pág. 223)

syncline a linear downfold in sedimentary strata; the opposite of anticline (p. 310)

syncline/sinclinal pliegue lineal en el estrato sedimentario; lo opuesto de anticlinal (pág. 310)

system any size group of interacting parts that form a complex whole (p. 18)

system/sistema grupo de cualquier tamaño de partes relacionadas que forman un conjunto complejo (pág. 18)

T

talus an accumulation of rock debris at the base of a cliff (p. 127)

talus/talud acumulación de restos de roca al pie de un acantilado (pág. 127)

temperate zone region located between 23.5° and 66.5° north and south of the equator; The sun's rays strike Earth at a smaller angle in the temperate zone than near the equator. (p. 589)

temperate zone/zona templada región situada entre 23.5° y 66.5° norte y sur del ecuador; los rayos de Sol llegan a la Tierra formando un ángulo más pequeño en la zona templada que en el ecuador. (pág. 589)

temperature a measure of the average kinetic energy of individual atoms or molecules in a substance (p. 483)

temperature/temperatura medición de la energía cinética promedio de los átomos o moléculas individuales en una sustancia (pág. 483)

temperature inversion a layer of limited depth in the atmosphere of limited depth where the temperature increases rather than decreases with height (p. 514)

temperature inversion/inversión de temperatura capa de poca densidad en la atmósfera de poca densidad donde la temperatura aumenta con la altura en vez de descender (pág. 514)

terrane a crustal block bounded by faults, whose geologic history is distinct from the histories of adjoining crustal blocks (p. 322)

terrane/terreno formación de rocas de la corteza rodeada de fallas, cuya historia geológica es distinta a la historias de las formaciones de rocas lindantes (pág. 322)

terrestrial planet any of the Earth-like planets, including Mercury, Venus, Mars, and Earth (p. 645)

terrestrial planet/planeta terrestre cualquiera de los planetas similares a la Tierra, como Mercurio, Venus, Marte y Tierra (pág. 645)

terrigenous sediment seafloor sediment derived from eroded rocks on land (p. 408)

terrigenous sediment/sedimento terrígeno sedimento en el fondo oceánico que se deriva de la erosión de rocas en la tierra (pág. 408)

theory a well-tested and widely accepted view that explains certain observable facts (p. 24)

theory/teoría perspectiva comprobada y generalmente aceptada que explica ciertos hechos observables (pág. 24)

thermocline a layer of water in which there is a rapid change in temperature with depth (p. 424)

thermocline/termoclina capa de agua en la cual se observa un rápido cambio de temperatura con la profundidad (pág. 424)

thermosphere the region of the atmosphere immediately above the mesosphere and characterized by increasing temperatures due to absorption of very short-wave solar energy by oxygen (p. 480)

thermosphere/termosfera capa de la atmósfera inmediatamente superior a la mesosfera y que se caracteriza por un aumento de temperatura causado por la absorción de energía solar de ondas muy cortas por el oxígeno (pág. 480)

thrust fault a reverse fault with a dip less than 45°, normally about 10–15° (p. 312)

thrust fault/falla de empuje falla inversa con una depresión de menos de 45°, normalmente entre 10°y 15° (pág. 312)

thunderstorm a storm produced by a cumulonimbus cloud and always accompanied by lightning and thunder; It is of relatively short duration and usually accompanied by strong wind gusts, heavy rain, and sometimes hail. (p. 571)

thunderstorm/tormenta eléctrica tormenta causada por una nube cumulonimbo y siempre acompañada de relámpagos y truenos; es de duración relativamente corta y va generalmente acompañada de fuertes ráfagas de viento, precipitaciones y a veces granizo (pág. 571)

tidal range the difference in height between successive high and low tides (p. 459)

tidal range/rango de marea diferencia en altura entre sucesivas mareas altas y bajas (pág. 459)

tide daily change in the elevation of the ocean surface (p. 458)

tide/marea cambios diarios en el ascenso de la superficie oceánica (pág. 458)

till sediment of different sizes deposited directly by a glacier (p. 194)

till/tillita sedimentos de diferentes tamaños depositados directamente por un glaciar (pág. 194)

topographic map a map that represents Earth's surface in three dimensions; It shows elevation, distance, directions, and slope angles. (p. 14)

topographic map/mapa topográfico mapa que representa la superficie de la Tierra en tres dimensiones; muestra elevación, distancia, direcciones y ángulos de inclinación (pág. 14)

tornado a small, very intense cyclonic storm with exceedingly high winds, most often produced along cold fronts in conjunction with severe thunderstorms (p. 573)

tornado/tornado pequeña tormenta ciclónica pero sumamente intensa, con vientos de gran velocidad, que a menudo ocurre a lo largo de frentes fríos acompañados de poderosas tormentas eléctricas (pág. 573)

trade winds two belts of winds that blow almost constantly from easterly directions and are located on the north and south sides of the subtropical highs (p. 541)

trade winds/vientos alisios dos cinturones de viento que soplan casi constantemente desde la dirección del este y que se encuentran al norte y al sur de los centros de las altas presiones subtropicales (pág. 541)

transform fault boundary a boundary in which two plates slide past each other without creating or destroying lithosphere (p. 255)

transform fault boundary/límite de falla de transformación límite en el que dos placas se deslizan a lo largo de la falla sin generar o destruir litosfera (pág. 255)

travertine a form of limestone that is deposited by hot springs or as a cave deposit (p. 177)

travertine/travertino tipo de piedra caliza que es depositada por fuentes termales o que forma parte del depósito de cuevas (pág. 177)

trench a surface feature in the seafloor produced by the descending plate during subduction (p. 261)

trench/fosa depresión en el fondo oceánico causada por la placa descediente durante la subducción (pág. 261)

tributary a stream that empties itself into another stream (p. 162)

tributary/afluente corriente de agua que desemboca en otra corriente (pág. 162)

trophic level a nourishment level in a food chain; Plant and algae producers constitute the lowest level, followed by herbivores and a series of carnivores at progressively higher levels. (p. 436)

trophic level/nivel trófico nivel de alimentación en la cadena alimenticia; los productores como las plantas y las algas forman parte del nivel más bajo, seguidos de herbívoros y una serie de carnívoros en los niveles superiores progresivos (pág. 436)

tropical wet and dry climate a climate that is transitional between the wet tropics and the subtropical steppes (p. 593)

tropical wet and dry climate/clima tropical seco y húmedo clima de transición entre los húmedos trópicos y las estepas subtropicales (pág. 593)

tropical zone region between 23.5° north (the tropic of Cancer) and 23.5° south (the tropic of Capricorn) of the equator; The sun's rays are most intense and the temperatures are always warm. (p. 589)

tropical zone/zona tropical región entre 23.5° norte (trópico de Cáncer) y 23.5° sur (trópico de Capricornio) del ecuador; los rayos solares son de mayor intensidad y la temperatura es siempre cálida (pág. 589)

troposphere the lowermost layer of the atmosphere; It is generally characterized by a decrease in temperature with height. (p. 480)

troposphere/troposfera capa más inferior de la atmósfera; generalmente se caracteriza por un decrecimiento de la temperatura con la altura (pág. 480)

tsunami the Japanese word for a seismic sea wave (p. 230)

tsunami/tsunami palabra japonesa con la que se denomina a una ola sísmica marina (pág. 230)

turbidity current a downslope movement of dense, sediment-laden water created when sand and mud on the continental shelf and slope are dislodged and thrown into suspension (p. 403)

turbidity current/corriente de turbidez movimiento descendente de una densa masa de agua cargada de sedimentos que ocurre cuando la arena y el barro de la plataforma y el talud continental se desplazan y quedan en suspensión (pág. 403)

U

ultramafic igneous rock composed mainly of iron and magnesium-rich minerals (p. 73)

ultramafic/ultramáfica roca ígnea compuesta principalmente de hierro y minerales ricos en magnesio (pág. 73)

unconformity a surface that represents a break in the rock record, caused by erosion or lack of deposition (p. 341)

unconformity/discordancia superficie que representa una interrupción en la evolución de la roca, causada por erosión o por falta de deposición (pág. 341)

uniformitarianism the concept that processes that have shaped Earth in the past are essentially the same as those operating today (p. 337)

uniformitarianism/uniformismo principio que dice que los procesos que dieron forma a la Tierra en el pasado geológico son esencialmente los mismos que ocurren en la actualidad (pág. 337)

uplifted mountain a circular or an elongated structure formed by uplifting of the underlying basement rock (p. 316)

uplifted mountain/montaña formada por elevación estructura circular o elongada formada por el levantamiento de rocas subyacentes del basamento (pág. 316)

upwelling the rising of cold water from deeper layers to replace warmer surface water that has been moved away (p. 450)

upwelling/afloramiento movimiento ascendente de aguas frías desde las profundidades del mar para reemplazar las aguas más calidas de la superficie que han sido desplazadas (pág. 450)

V

valley glacier a glacier confined to a mountain valley, which in most instances had previously been a stream valley; also known as an alpine glacier (p. 189)

valley glacier/glaciar de valle glaciar localizado en un valle de montaña, que en varias etapas anteriores había sido un valle fluvial; también conocido como glaciar alpino (pág. 189)

vent an opening in the surface of Earth through which molten rock and gases are released (p. 281)

vent/chimenea abertura en la superficie de la Tierra a través de la cual salen roca derretida y gases (pág. 281)

ventifact a cobble or pebble polished and shaped by the sandblasting effect of wind (p. 204)

ventifact/ventifacto canto o guijarro pulido y esculpido por el efecto abrasivo del viento (pág. 204)

viscosity a measure of a fluid's resistance to flow (p. 281)

viscosity/viscosidad una medida que indica la resistencia de un líquido al fluir (pág. 281)
volcanic island arc a chain of volcanic islands generally located a few hundred kilometers from a trench where subduction of one oceanic slab beneath another is occurring (p. 262)
volcanic island arc/arco de islas volcánicas una cadena de islas volcánicas generalmente ubicada a unos cientos de kilómetros de una fosa donde está ocurriendo la subducción de una placa océanica debajo de otra (pág. 262)
volcano a mountain formed of lava and/or pyroclastic material (p. 283)
volcano/volcán montaña formada de lava y/o material piroclástico (pág. 283)

W

warm front a front along which a warm air mass overrides a retreating mass of cooler air (p. 565)
warm front/frente cálido zona frontal de una masa de aire cálido que avanza para reemplazar una masa de aire frío que retrocede (pág. 656)
water cycle the constant movement of water among the oceans, the atmosphere, geosphere, and the biosphere (p. 158)
water cycle/ciclo del agua movimiento constante del agua en los océanos, la atmósfera, la geosfera y la biosfera (pág. 283)
water table the upper level of the saturated zone of groundwater (p. 171)
water table/nivel freático nivel superior de la zona de saturación de las aguas subterráneas (pág. 171)
wave height the vertical distance between the trough and crest of a wave (p. 456)
wave height/altura de la ola distancia vertical entre el valle y la cresta de una ola (pág. 456)
wavelength the horizontal distance separating successive crests or troughs (p. 456)
wavelength/longitud de la ola distancia horizontal que separa crestas o valles sucesivos (pág. 456)
wave period the time interval between the passage of successive crests at a stationary point (p. 456)
wave period/período de la ola el intervalo entre el paso de crestas sucesivas por un mismo punto (pág. 462)
wave refraction the process by which the portion of a wave in shallow water slows, causing the wave to bend and tend to align itself with the underwater contours (p. 462)
wave refraction/refracción de la ola proceso en que la porción de una ola en aguas poco profundas disminuye su velocidad, lo cual causa que la ola se rompa y tienda a alinearse con las curvas de la superficie submarina (pág. 462)
weathering the disintegration and decomposition of rock at or near Earth's surface (p. 68)
weathering/meteorización la desintegración y descomposición de una roca en o cerca de la superficie de la Tierra (pág. 68)
well an opening bored into the zone of saturation (p. 173)
well/pozo abertura excavada dentro de la zona de saturación (pág. 173)
westerlies the dominant west-to-east motion of the atmosphere that characterizes the regions on the poleward side of the subtropical highs (p. 541)
westerlies/vientos del oeste el movimiento dominante de oeste a este de la atmósfera que caracteriza las regiones en el lado polar de las zonas de alta presión subtropicales (pág. 541)
wet adiabatic rate the rate of adiabatic temperature change in saturated air; The rate of temperature change is variable, but it is always less than the dry adiabatic rate. (p. 511)
wet adiabatic rate/tasa adiabática húmeda la tasa del cambio de temperatura adiabática en el aire saturado; la tasa de cambio de temperatura es variable, pero siempre es menor que la tasa adiabática seca (pág. 511)
wet tropical climate a climate with high temperatures and high annual precipitation (p. 593)
wet tropical climate/clima tropical húmedo clima de altas temperaturas y alta precipitación anual (pág. 593)
white dwarf a star that has exhausted most or all of its nuclear fuel and has collapsed to a very small size, believed to be near its final stage of evolution (p. 712)
white dwarf/enana blanca estrella que ha agotado todo o casi todo su combustible nuclear y que se desvanece hasta alcanzar un tamaño pequeño,

que se considera el estado final de su evolución (pág. 712)

winter solstice the solstice that occurs on December 21 or 22 in the Northern Hemisphere and on June 21 or 22 in the Southern Hemisphere (p. 482)

winter solstice/solsticio de invierno el solsticio que tiene lugar el 21 ó 22 de diciembre en el hemisferio norte, y el 21 ó 22 de junio en el hemisferio sur (pág. 482)

Z

zone of saturation zone where all open spaces in sediment and rock are completely filled with water (p. 171)

zone of saturation/zona de saturación zona donde todos los espacios abiertos en el sedimento y la roca están completamente llenos de agua (pág. 171)

zooplankton animal plankton (p. 429)

zooplankton/zooplancton plancton animal (pág. 429)

Index

Index

Index

Index

Index

Index

Index

Acknowledgments

Editorial development, design, and production
Navta Associates, Inc.

DK Pages 148–149, **Soil** Taken from *Dictionary of the Earth,* published by Dorling Kindersley Limited. © Dorling Kindersley Limited, 1994, pp. 130–132; *Ecology* published by Dorling Kindersley Limited. © Dorling Kindersley Limited, 2000, pp. 22–23; *Earth,* published by Dorling Kindersley Limited. © Dorling Kindersley Limited, 2000, pp. 52–53. Pages 208–209, **Erosion** Taken from *Earth,* published by Dorling Kindersley Limited. © Dorling Kindersley Limited, 2000, pp. 54–55; *Dictionary of the Earth,* published by Dorling Kindersley Limited. © Dorling Kindersley Limited, 1994, pp. 112–113, 123. Pages 238–239, **Effects of Earthquakes** Taken from *Volcano & Earthquake,* published by Dorling Kindersley Limited. © Dorling Kindersley Limited, 2000, pp.46–47, 56–57. Pages 298–299, **Effects of Volcanoes** Taken from *Volcano & Earthquake,* published by Dorling Kindersley Limited. © Dorling Kindersley Limited, 2000, pp. 14–15, 22, 34–35, 39, 40–41. Pages 438–439, **Ocean Life** Taken from *Nature Encyclopedia,* published by Dorling Kindersley Limited. © Dorling Kindersley Limited, 1998, pp. 68–69, 72–73, 188. Pages 494–495, **Earth's Atmosphere** Taken from *Earth,* published by Dorling Kindersley Limited. © Dorling Kindersley Limited, 2000, pp. 10–11. Pages 578–579, **Winds and Storms** Taken from *Weather,* published by Dorling Kindersley Limited. © Dorling Kindersley Limited, 2000, pp. 38–39, 44–45. Pages 604–605, **Coniferous Forests** Taken from *Nature Encyclopedia,* published by Dorling Kindersley Limited. © Dorling Kindersley Limited, 1998, pp. 78–79.

Illustration
All illustrations by Dennis Tasa

Cover design Jan Calek/Navta Associates, Inc.

Cover photo Carr Clifton Photography

Photo research Navta Associates, Inc.

Front matter
Page iv, Art Wolfe, Inc.; **vi tl,** GeoScience Resources/American Geological Institute (AGI); **vi ml, vi bl,** Edward J. Tarbuck; **vi r,** Dennis Tasa; **vii,** Carl Purcell/Photo Researchers, Inc.; **viii,** Tom & Susan Bean, Inc./DRK Photo; **ix t,** Greg Vaughn Photography; **ix b,** Ira Block/National Geographic Image Collection; **x,** Gary Bell/Seapics.com/Innerspace Visions; **xi,** Kent Wood/Science Source/Photo Researchers, Inc.; **xiii,** Royal Observatory, Edinburgh/AATB/Science Photo Library/Photo Researchers, Inc.; **xv t,** Bettmann/Corbis; **xv m,** Ted Spiegel/Black Star; **xv b,** Science Photo Library; **xviii tl,** Reuters/Corbis; **xviii tr,** David Parker/Science Photo Library/Photo Researchers, Inc.; **xviii b,** David Frazier/Photo Researchers, Inc.; **xix tl,** Owen Franken/Stock Boston; **xix tm,** Bill & Sally Fletcher/Tom Stack & Associates, Inc.; **xix tr,** Bojan Breceli/Corbis; **xix galaxy,** Pat Lanza-Field/Bruce Coleman, Inc.; **xix scientist,** James King-Holmes/Science Photo Library/Photo Researchers, Inc.

Chapter 1
Pages **x–1, 2 t,** Art Wolfe, Inc.; **2 b,** James L. Amos/Corbis; **3,** Randy M. Ury/Corbis; **6, 7 t,** Art Wolfe, Inc.; **7 bl,** NASA; **7 br,** NASA/Science Source/Photo Researchers, Inc.; **11,** Art Wolfe, Inc.; **16,** NASA; **18,** Art Wolfe, Inc.; **19,** Jack Dykinga Photography; **20,** Roger Wood/Corbis; **22 t,** Mike Yamashita/Woodfin Camp & Associates; **22 b,** Reuters/STR/Getty Images; **23, 25 t,** Art Wolfe, Inc.; **25 b,** NASA.

Chapter 2
Pages 32–33, 34, Jeffrey A. Scovil; **41,** Tom Pantages; **42 both,** Dennis Tasa; **43,** Corbis; **44 t,** Jeffrey A. Scovil; **44 bl,** Mark Schneider/Visuals Unlimited; **44 br,** Corbis; **45 t,** GeoScience Resources/American Geological Institute (AGI); **45 mt, 45 mb,** Edward J. Tarbuck; **45 b,** GeoScience Resources/American Geological Institute (AGI); **46 tl,** Tom & Susan Bean, Inc.; **46 tr,** GeoScience Resources/American Geological Institute (AGI); **46 b,** Dennis Tasa; **47,** Breck P. Kent; **49 both,** GeoScience Resources/American Geological Institute (AGI); **50 t,** Jeffrey A. Scovil; **50 b,** Fred Ward/Black Star; **51 tl, 51 tr,** Edward J. Tarbuck; **51 m,** G. Tompkinson/Photo Researchers, Inc.; **51 b,** Herve Berthoule/Photo Researchers, Inc.; **53 t,** Chip Clark; **53 b,** Edward J. Tarbuck; **54,** Paul Silverman/Fundamental Photographs; **56 t,** Jeffrey A. Scovil; **56 bl,** Science Photo Library; **56 br,** Dorling Kindersley; **57 t,** Jeffrey A. Scovil; **57 bl,** Ken Lucas/Visuals Unlimited; **57 br,** Stone/Getty Images; **58, 60,** Dennis Tasa.

Chapter 3
Pages 64–65, Carr Clifton Photography; **66 tl, 66 bl,** GeoScience Resources; **66 r,** Carr Clifton Photography; **68,** Jeff Gnass/Corbis; **69,** Edward J. Tarbuck; **70 t,** Carr Clifton Photography; **70 b,** G. Brad Lewis/Getty Images; **71 both, 72,** Edward J. Tarbuck; **73,** Hubert Stadler/Corbis; **75 t,** Carr Clifton Photography; **75 b,** Jeff Gnass Photography; **76 both, 77 both, 78 t,** Edward J. Tarbuck; **78 bl,** Stephen Trimble; **78 br,** Gary Yeowell/Getty Images; **80 t,** Carr Clifton Photography; **80 b,** Michael Collier; **81,** Andrew Ward/Getty Images; **82,** Phil Dombrowski; **83 t,** Edward J. Tarbuck; **83 b,** Breck P. Kent; **85,** Carr Clifton Photography; **86, 87 all, 91 all,** Edward J. Tarbuck.

Chapter 4
Pages 92–93, 94 t, Bettmann/Corbis; **94 b,** Kim Heacox/DRK Photo; **99,** James E. Patterson; **100,** Seaver Center for Western History Research/Natural History Museum of Los Angeles County; **102 t,** Bettmann/Corbis; **102 b,** Thomas Braise/Corbis; **103 t,** Martin Bond/Science Photo Library/Photo Researchers, Inc.; **103 b,** Comstock Images; **104,** John Mead/Science Photo Library/Photo Researchers, Inc.; **105,** Michael Collier; **106,** Pacific Gas & Electric Company; **108 t,** Bettmann/Corbis; **108 b,** Stocktrek/Corbis; **109,** Janis Burger/Bruce Coleman, Inc.; **110,** Stefan Zaklin/Getty Images; **111,** R. Ian Lloyd/Masterfile; **113 t,** Bettmann/Corbis; **113 b,** Steve Starr/Corbis; **114,** SuperStock, Inc.; **116,** Phil Degginger/Bruce Coleman, Inc.; **117 t,** Bettmann/Corbis; **117 b,** Michael Collier.

Chapter 5
Pages 124–125, 126 t, David Muench/Muench Photography, Inc.; **126 b,** Tom & Susan Bean, Inc.; **127,** Photo Researchers, Inc.; **128,** Breck P. Kent; **129 t,** Tom & Susan Bean, Inc./DRK Photo; **129 bl,** Stephen J. Krasemann/DRK Photo; **129 bm, 129 br,** Edward J. Tarbuck; **130,** Doug Plummer/Photo Researchers, Inc.; **131 l,** Edward J. Tarbuck; **131 r,** Martin Schmidt, Jr.; **132,** Art Wolfe, Inc.; **133,** David Muench/Muench Photography, Inc.; **137 l,** Corbis; **137 r,** Dan Richter/Visuals Unlimited; **138,** Dick Roberts/Visuals Unlimited; **139,** R. Ian Lloyd/Corbis; **140 t,** Wayne Lawler/Photo Researchers, Inc.; **140 b,** U.S. Department of Agriculture; **141,** Carl Purcell/Photo Researchers, Inc.; **143 t,** David Muench/Muench Photography, Inc.; **143 b,** ChromoSohm/Sohm/Corbis; **144,** Noel Quidu/Getty Images; **145,** Stephen Trimble; **146 t,** Chuck Place Photography; **146 b,** Edward J. Tarbuck; **147,** Science VU/Visuals Unlimited; **148–149,** Dorling Kindersley.

Chapter 6
Pages 156–157, 158, Carr Clifton Photography; **163 both,** Michael Collier; **164,** Carr Clifton Photography; **165,** Mark Lyons/Getty Images; **167,** Art Wolfe, Inc.; **168,** Space Imaging; **171,** Carr Clifton Photography; **172,** Ken Hamblin; **175,** U.S. Geological Survey, Denver; **176 t,** Roy Morsch/Corbis; **176 b,** F. Rossotto/Corbis; **177,** Harris Photographic/Tom Stack & Associates, Inc.; **178,** Tom & Susan Bean, Inc.; **179,** St. Petersburg Times/Getty Images; **180,** Carr Clifton Photography.

Chapter 7
Pages 186–187, 188 t, Tom & Susan Bean, Inc.; **188 b,** Carr Clifton Photography; **190,** Galen Rowell/Mountain Light Photography, Inc.; **191,** Tom & Susan Bean, Inc.; **192,** Carr Clifton Photography; **194 t,** Martin G. Miller; **194 b,** Edward J. Tarbuck; **195, 199 t,** Tom & Susan Bean, Inc.; **199 b,** David Muench/Muench Photography, Inc.; **200 both,** Edward J. Tarbuck; **201,** Michael Collier; **203 t,** Tom & Susan Bean, Inc.; **203 b,** State Historical Society of North Dakota; **204 t,** David Muench/Muench Photography, Inc.; **204 b,** James E. Patterson; **205 l,** Michael Collier; **205 r,** Muench Photography, Inc.; **208–209,** Dorling Kindersley.

Chapter 8
Pages 216–217, 218 t, Yann Arthus-Bertrand "Earth From Above"/Altitude/Peter Arnold, Inc.; **218 b,** David Weintraub/Photo Researchers, Inc.; **219,** Edward J. Tarbuck; **222, 229 t,** Yann Arthus-Bertrand "Earth From Above"/Altitude/Peter Arnold, Inc.; **229 b,** National Oceanic and Atmospheric Administration/Seattle; 231, James L. Beck; 232, U.S. Geological Survey, Denver; **233,** Yann Arthus-Bertrand "Earth From Above"/Altitude/Peter Arnold, Inc.; **238–239,** Dorling Kindersley.

Chapter 9
Pages 246–247, 248, WorldSat International Inc., 2001. www.worldsat.ca. All Rights Reserved.; **253,** Carr Clifton Photography; **254, 258,** WorldSat International Inc., 2001. www.worldsat.ca. All Rights Reserved.; **260,** M. Timothy O'Keefe/Bruce Coleman, Inc.; **265, 269, 271,** WorldSat International Inc., 2001. www.worldsat.ca. All Rights Reserved.

Chapter 10
Pages 278–279, 280 t, Art Wolfe, Inc.; **280 all,** U.S. Geological Survey, Denver; **282 l,** Doug Perrine/DRK Photo; **282 r,** J.D. Griggs/U.S. Geological Survey,

Denver; **284,** Greg Vaughn Photography; **285,** Michael Collier; **286,** David Muench/Muench Photography, Inc.; **287,** Greg Vaughn/Tom Stack & Associates, Inc.; **288 l,** Tom & Susan Bean, Inc./DRK Photo; **288 r,** John S. Shelton; **289 t,** Art Wolfe, Inc.; **289 b,** Edward J. Tarbuck; **291,** Art Wolfe, Inc.; **292,** Greg Vaughn Photography; **293 t,** Art Wolfe, Inc.; **293 b,** David Weintraub/Photo Researchers, Inc.; **295,** Arthur Roy/National Audubon Society/Photo Researchers, Inc.; **298–299,** Dorling Kindersley.

Chapter 11
Pages 306–307, 308 both, Art Wolfe, Inc.; **311 both,** Tom & Susan Bean, Inc./DRK Photo; **313,** Michael Collier; **314 t,** Art Wolfe, Inc.; **314 b,** Peter French/DRK Photo; **315,** Michael Collier; **317 t,** Art Wolfe, Inc.; **317 b,** David Muench/Muench Photography, Inc.; **325, 332,** Art Wolfe, Inc.; **333 t,** Art Wolfe, Inc.; **333 b,** U.S. Geological Survey, Denver.

Chapter 12
Pages 334–335, 336 t, Carr Clifton Photography; **336 m, 336 b,** U.S. Geological Survey, Denver; **338 t,** Edward J. Tarbuck; **338 b,** Michael Fogden/DRK Photo; **341 all,** Edward J. Tarbuck; **343 t,** Carr Clifton Photography; **343 b,** Reuters/Corbis; **344 tl,** Florissant Fossil Beds National Monument; **344 tr,** Edward J. Tarbuck; **344 ml,** Breck P. Kent; **344 mr,** Edward J. Tarbuck; **344 bl,** Muench Photography, Inc.; **344 br,** Edward J. Tarbuck; **347,** Carr Clifton Photography; **350,** Reuters/Corbis; **351 t,** Carr Clifton Photography; **351 b,** Stephen J. Krasemann/DRK Photo; **352,** Carr Clifton Photography.

Chapter 13
Pages 362–363, 364 t, David Muench/Muench Photography, Inc.; **364 b,** Ira Block/National Geographic Image Collection; **368,** Sinclair Stammers/Science Photo Library/Photo Researchers, Inc.; **369,** David Muench/Muench Photography, Inc.; **371 t,** The Field Museum, Neg #GEO 80820C, Chicago.; **371 b,** GeoScience Resources/American Geological Institute (AGI); **375,** The Field Museum, Neg #GEO85637C, Chicago. Photographer: John Weinstein.; **377,** David Muench/Muench Photography, Inc.; **379,** Carr Clifton/Minden Pictures; **381,** Project Exploration P.A.S.T.; **382,** David Muench/Muench Photography, Inc.; **383,** Courtesy of the George C. Page Museum; **385,** David Muench/Muench Photography, Inc.; **389,** Sinclair Stammers/Science Photo Library/Photo Researchers, Inc.

Chapter 14
Pages 392–393, 394, 401, Mark Muench/Muench Photography, Inc.; **406,** Douglas Peebles Photography; **406, 407,** Mark Muench/Muench Photography, Inc.; **409,** Deep Sea Drilling Project, Scripps Institution of Oceanography; **410 t,** Mark Muench/Muench Photography, Inc.; **410 b,** Gregory Ochocki/Photo Researchers, Inc.; **411 both,** GEOMAR Research Center; **412,** Lawrence Sullivan/Lamont Doherty Earth Observatory/Columbia University; **413,** William E. Townsend, Jr./Photo Researchers, Inc.

Chapter 15
Pages 420–421, 422, Gary Bell/Seapics.com/Innerspace Visions; **423 tl,** Tom & Susan Bean, Inc.; **423 tr,** Wolfgang Kaehler Photography; **423 bl,** NASA; **423 br,** Paul Steel/Corbis; **428 t,** Gary Bell/Seapics.com/Innerspace Visions; **428 m, 428 b,** Norman T. Nicoll; **429 t,** Tom McHugh/Photo Researchers, Inc.; **429 m,** Larry Lisky/DRK Photo; **429 bl,** David Hall/Photo Researchers, Inc.; **429 br,** Fred Bavendam/Peter Arnold, Inc.; **432 t,** Dudley Foster/Woods Hole Oceanographic Institution; **432 b,** Al Giddings Images, Inc.; **433,** Gary Bell/Seapics.com/Innerspace Visions; **438–439,** Dorling Kindersley; **440,** Edward J. Tarbuck.

Chapter 16
Pages 446–447, 448 t, Carr Clifton Photography; **448 b,** Marc Muench/Muench Photography, Inc.; **450,** O. Brown, R. Evans, and M. Carle, University of Miami Rosenstiel School of Marine and Atmospheric Science, Miami, Florida; **451,** Provided by the SeaWiFS Project, NASA/Goddard Space Flight Center and ORBIMAGE; **452,** Wayne Lynch/DRK Photo; **454, 455 t,** Carr Clifton Photography; **455 b,** Rafael Macia/Photo Researchers, Inc.; **461 t,** Carr Clifton Photography; **461 b,** Fletcher & Baylis/Photo Researchers, Inc.; **464 t,** Mark A. Johnson/Corbis; **464 b,** U.S. Department of Agriculture; **466,** Sandy Stockwell/London Aerial Photo Library/Bettmann/Corbis; **467 both,** U.S. Army Corps of Engineers, Headquarters; **468 both,** Nova Scotia Department of Tourism and Culture.

Chapter 17
Pages 474–475, 476 t, Stone/Getty Images; **476 b,** Mike Groll/Getty Images; **479,** Carr Clifton/Minden Pictures; **482,** Brian Stablyk/Getty Images; **483,** Stone/Getty Images; **485,** Carr Clifton Photography; **488 t,** Stone/Getty Images; **488 b,** Bobbe Z. Christopherson; **494–495,** Dorling Kindersley; **496,** Edward J. Tarbuck.

Chapter 18
Pages 502–503, 504 t, Gary Gray/DRK Photo; **504 b,** Mary Fulton/Getty Images; **508 t,** Wolfgang Kaehler Photography; **508 b,** Edward J. Tarbuck; **510 t,** Gary Gray/DRK Photo; **510 b,** Edward J. Tarbuck; **514,** Barbara Cushman Rowell/Mountain Light Photography, Inc.; **515,** Dick Canby/DRK Photo; **517 t,** Gary Gray/DRK Photo; **517 b,** Edward J. Tarbuck; **520,** Jim Brown/Corbis; **522,** Visual Communications/National Center for Atmospheric Research/University Corporation for Atmospheric Research/National Science Foundation; **523 t,** Gary Gray/DRK Photo; **523 b,** Ted Spiegel/Black Star.

Chapter 19
Pages 530–531, 532 t, The Image Bank/Getty Images; **532 b,** National Geographic Image Collection/Getty Images; **537 t,** The Image Bank/Getty Images; **537 b,** Mark E. Gibson/DRK Photo; **543,** The Image Bank/Getty Images; **545,** Belfort Instrument Company; **549 t,** The Image Bank/Getty Images; **549 b,** Courtesy of NASA Goddard Space Flight Center.

Chapter 20
Pages 556–557, 558 t, Kent Wood/Science Source/Photo Researchers, Inc.; **558 b,** John Sokich/National Oceanic and Atmospheric Administration/Seattle; **561,** AP/Wide World Photos; **562,** Tony Arruza/Corbis; **563,** Layne Kennedy/Corbis; **564 t,** Kent Wood/Science Source/Photo Researchers, Inc.; **564 b,** Kenneth Garrett/National Geographic Image Collection; **568,** John Jensenius/National Weather Service; **571 t,** Kent Wood/Science Source/Photo Researchers, Inc.; **571 b,** T.A. Wiewandt/DRK Photo; **574,** Warren Faidley/Weatherstock; **575,** AP/Wide World Photos; **578–579,** Dorling Kindersley.

Chapter 21
Pages 586–587, 588 t, Yva Momatiuk & John Eastcott/Photo Researchers, Inc.; **588 b,** Pete Saloutos/Corbis; **591 l,** Charlie Ott Photography/Photo Researchers, Inc.; **591 r,** Larry Ulrich/DRK Photo; **592 t,** Yva Momatiuk & John Eastcott/Photo Researchers, Inc.; **592 b,** David Keaton/Corbis; **593 t,** Art Wolfe/Photo Researchers, Inc.; **593 b,** Stan Osolinski/Dembinsky Photo Associates; **599,** Fred Bruemmer/DRK Photo; **600 t,** Yva Momatiuk & John Eastcott/Photo Researchers, Inc.; **600 b,** Getty Images; **601,** Michey Welsh/Montgomery Advisor/Corbis Sygma; **604–605,** Dorling Kindersley.

Chapter 22
Pages 612–613, 614 t, Galen Rowell/Mountain Light Photography, Inc.; **614 b,** David Lees/Corbis; **616 l,** Stapleton Collection/Corbis; **616 r,** Bettmann/Corbis; **617, 619,** With permission of the Royal Ontario Museum ©ROM.; **620 t,** Yerkes Observatory Photograph/University of Chicago; **620 bl,** AP/Wide World Photos; **620 br,** NASA; **622 t,** Galen Rowell/Mountain Light Photography, Inc.; **622 b,** Robin Scagell/Science Photo Library/Photo Researchers, Inc.; **626 all,** UC Regents/Lick Observatory; **628,** From Foundations of Astronomy, 3rd Edition, p. 54, by Michael Seeds. ©1992. Reprinted with permission of Brooks/Cole Publishing, a division of Thomson Learning.; **630 t,** Galen Rowell/Mountain Light Photography, Inc.; **630 b,** UC Regents/Lick Observatory; **634,** NASA; **635 t,** Galen Rowell/Mountain Light Photography, Inc.; **635 b,** Museum of Science and Industry; **640,** UC Regents/Lick Observatory.

Chapter 23
Pages 642–643, 644, 649 t, Michael Collier; **649 b, 650 t,** NASA; **650 b,** NASA/Jet Propulsion Laboratory; **651,** David P. Anderson, SMU/NASA/Science Photo Library/Photo Researchers, Inc.; **652 t,** NASA; **652 b,** U.S. Geological Survey, Denver; **653,** NASA; **654,** Michael Collier; **655, 657, 658 both, 659,** NASA; **660,** Michael Collier; **661,** NASA; **664,** Jon Mandaville/Aramco World Magazine; **665 t,** Michael Collier; **665 b,** U.S. Geological Survey, Denver.

Chapter 24
Pages **672–673, 674, 678 t,** David Parker/Science Photo Library/Photo Researchers, Inc.; **678 b,** Roger Ressmeyer/Bettmann/Corbis; **681 l,** National Astronomy and Ionosphere Center's Arecibo Observatory, operated by Cornell University under contract with the National Science Foundation. Photo courtesy of David Parker, 1997/Science Photo Library; **681 r,** National Radio Astronomy Observatory; **682, 683,** NASA; **684 t,** David Parker/Science Photo Library/Photo Researchers, Inc.; **684 b,** Kent Wood/Photo Researchers, Inc.; **685,** National Optical Astronomy Observatories; **686,** NASA; **687 l,** Celestron International; **687 r,** National Optical Astronomy Observatories; **688 t,** Photri/Corbis; **688 b,** Michio Hoshino/Minden Pictures; **690,** Thomas Dimock/Corbis; **691 t,** David Parker/Science Photo Library/Photo Researchers, Inc.; **691 b,** Celestron International.

Chapter 25
Pages 698–699, 700, Royal Observatory, Edinburgh/AATB/Science Photo Library/Photo Researchers, Inc.; **701,** National Optical Astronomy Observatories;

705 both, UC Regents/Lick Observatory; **706,** Anglo-Australian Observatory/ Royal Observatory, Edinburgh. Photograph from UK Schmidt plates by David Malin.; **707 t,** Royal Observatory, Edinburgh/AATB/Science Photo Library/Photo Researchers, Inc.; **707 b,** NASA; **710,** Anglo-Australian Observatory. Photography by David Malin.; **711,** UC Regents/Lick Observatory; **713,** California Inst. of Technology/Palomar/Hale Observatory; **715 t,** Royal Observatory, Edinburgh/ AATB/Science Photo Library/Photo Researchers, Inc.; **715 b,** Dr. Axel Mellinger; **717 t,** Anglo-Australian Observatory. Photography by David Malin.; **717 m,** Palomar Observatories/California Institute of Technology (Caltech); **717 bl,** ESO Education & Public Relations; **717 br, 718,** NASA; **722,** Royal Observatory, Edinburgh/AATB/Science Photo Library/Photo Researchers, Inc.

Skills and Reference Handbook

Page 728, Richard Megna/Fundamental Photographs; **729,** Russ Lappa; **730,** Jerry Howard; **731,** David Young-Wolff/PhotoEdit, Inc.; **742,** Russ Lappa.

Form and Space

sculpture of the twentieth century

EDUARD TRIER

with 213 illustrations

FREDERICK A. PRAEGER, *Publisher*
NEW YORK

BOOKS THAT MATTER

PUBLISHED IN THE UNITED STATES OF AMERICA IN 1962
BY FREDERICK A. PRAEGER, INC., PUBLISHER
64 UNIVERSITY PLACE, NEW YORK 3, N. Y.

LIBRARY OF CONGRESS CATALOG CARD NUMBER: 62-8371

TRANSLATED FROM THE GERMAN BY C. LIGOTA

PRINTED IN GERMANY

CO

BOOKS THAT MATTER

PUBLISHED IN THE UNITED STATES OF AMERICA IN 1962
BY FREDERICK A. PRAEGER, INC., PUBLISHER
64 UNIVERSITY PLACE, NEW YORK 3, N. Y.

LIBRARY OF CONGRESS CATALOG CARD NUMBER: 62-8371

TRANSLATED FROM THE GERMAN BY C. LIGOTA

PRINTED IN GERMANY

Form and Space

sculpture of the twentieth century

EDUARD TRIER

with 213 illustrations

FREDERICK A. PRAEGER, *Publisher*
NEW YORK

I do not, however, intend to repeat the well-worn comparisons between sculpture past and present or draw analogies from the world of nature. To treat of the works themselves and confront them one with another is in itself sufficiently exciting so that no other, extra-artistic stimuli are needed.

KERNEL SCULPTURE

It seems desirable to begin my formal analysis with the compact, entirely solid mass of material which the artist shapes but does not attempt to open up; this approach might be described as kernel sculpture; it is the simplest and perhaps the oldest variety of the art. In the 20th century the artist who has concerned himself most intensively with the shapes of compact volume is Constantin Brancusi. An early work of his, *The New-Born* (fig. 1), made in 1915, may serve, with its radical simplicity and single-minded concentration on mass and volume, as the first of my formal examples. What we have here is sculpture in its embryonic form. This marble piece is an embryo also in what it conveys: by shaping it as an egg Brancusi is making it signify emergent life. But the problem of meaning, though especially relevant in the case of Brancusi whose sculpture has always something to "say," will not be investigated here; I reserve it for later treatment in a broader context. *The New-Born,* smooth and rounded, is artistically effective simply as a three-dimensional object, quite apart from the associations it evokes. Brancusi's aim was the absolutely pure, universally valid, perfectly produced compact body of volume. He sought the extreme in simplicity and completeness. One of his favourite observations was that a piece of sculpture must have no holes; and the form realised after long years of patient work with chisel and file has all the rigour and immaculateness of the ideal vision with nothing left to add or subtract. It is perfect in itself and presents an optimum of formal maturity. Of course the artist could have equally well achieved this formal perfection with a sphere or a simple egg but the specific reference would have been lost: the tapering ridge rising out of the body of the egg, the oblique flattening at one end with its privative effect mitigated by the rounded swelling at the bottom—these formal inventions attest the artist's aim to produce an individual, unique figure. The coarse-grained stone of the base, rough-planed at the edges, is also an integral part of the work. It enhances by contrast the smoothness and high polish of the marble which not only invites the hand to touch but feasts the eye with the play of light and shadow and the richness of reflexion on the surface. Thus have Brancusi's hands wakened the dead stone to a life of its own—the life of forms.

As it is not my intention to discuss the influence of Brancusi's style on his contemporaries or younger artists, I have selected for comparison with his figured solids only

I THE PROBLEM OF FORM

In every work of art we are confronted first of all by the problem of form. It is form that conveys the artist's message and realises his intention. Thus the elucidation of the formal aspect of a work of art is the necessary preliminary to any knowledge or interpretation of its content. I shall, therefore, concern myself in the first instance with modes of appearance in modern sculpture. The criteria for this formal inquiry are supplied by basic distinctions which take no account as yet of stylistic differences arising out of individual handwriting, technique, or time and place of origin. They can be reduced to the category of plastic volume which implies both the mass of a work of art and the areas of shaped void annexed to it, as well as the relationship between the two. The modes of appearance include further the space surrounding a work of art whether delimited, touched or filled by it, either statically or through movement. Finally my formal analysis will extend to relief with its transitions to painting. On the other hand the artist's manipulation of his material is excluded from the discussion. Whether he carves in stone, solders and welds metals, or models for a bronze cast—these differences, of great moment for the content and significance of modern works of sculpture will, with a few exceptions, be discussed later.

These fundamental concepts of form do not, of course, apply solely to modern sculpture. The problems they involve are partly as old as the art itself. But mobile and constructive sculpture offers formal possibilities which the 20th century in particular has recognised and developed, though even here historical precedents could be cited.

art content cannot exist except as form; hence the results obtained in treating the first will often be drawn upon. Finally the third problem, that of purpose, will be concerned solely with sculpture as a public art. The reader is requested to consider the book as a unity in spite of this threefold division.

I have written this book as an *hommage* to modern sculpture and thus the threefold division and the resulting order in which the works are considered cannot possibly imply any judgment of value. It is by the inclusion of their works that I pay my tribute to the various artists concerned, and to this must be added my gratitude for the invaluable help that many of them have given me.

I wish, further, to thank directors of museums, private collectors, art galleries and the photographers named in the captions, and ask their forgiveness if I mention by name only a few whose help has been particularly valuable. My special thanks are due to my friend the painter Günther-Ferdinand Ris who undertook the laborious task of laying out the illustrations. I gratefully acknowledge the assistance and suggestions of Dr. Bernhard Sprengel in Hanover, Herr Gustav Stein in Cologne and Dr. Ferdinand Ziersch in Wuppertal, M. René Pandelaers, of the Middelheim Museum in Antwerp, who has again, on the occasion of this my second book on modern sculpture, been untiring in his readiness to help, Herr Adler of the Galerie Änne Abels in Cologne, Signor Claudio A. Bruni, Director of the Studio d'Arte "La Medusa" in Rome, Mme Iris Clert in Paris, Dr. Gioacchino Fraenkel in Cologne, Dr. Karlheinz Goerres in Aix-la-Chapelle, Dr. Robert Goldwater in New York, Professor Ludwig Grote in Nuremberg, M. Fernand C. Graindorge in Liège, Dr. H. L. C. Jaffé in Amsterdam, Dr. E. Joosten, curator at the Rijksmuseum Kröller-Müller in Otterloo, Herr Viktor Langen in Meererbusch, Dr. Hanspeter Landolt of the Kunstmuseum at Basle, Mr. Jules Langsner in Los Angeles, Herr Guido Lehmbruck in Stuttgart, Dr. Peter Leo of the Städtische Kunstgalerie in Bochum, M. R. Lipchitz in Paris, Monsignore Otto Mauer in Vienna, Vicomte Pierre de Montbas of the Galerie Cordier in Frankfurt-am-Main, Dr. G. Paolozzi of the Galleria Blu in Milan, Miss Frances Pernas of the Museum of Modern Art in New York, Frau A. Pinner in Cologne, Herr Werner Ruhnau in Gelsenkirchen, Mynheer W. Sandberg, Director of the Stedelijk Museum in Amsterdam, Dr. Bruno Schneider in Bad Godesberg, Mr. Herman Stein of the Amerika-Dienst in Bad Godesberg, Mynheer H. L. Swart, Director of De Nederlandse Kunststichting in Amsterdam, Mrs. June Wayne in Los Angeles, Dr. Paul Wember, Director of the Museum in Krefeld, and the following Galleries: Gimpel (London), Il Milione (Milan), Denise René (Paris), Claude Bernard (Paris), Stadler (Paris), Maeght (Paris), Louise Leiris (Paris), Studio Facchetti (Paris), and Hanover (London). To all these I extend my sincere thanks, which are also due to Frau Rosel Zimmer and, last but not least, to my wife who were my two closest collaborators.

FOREWORD

This book is not a history of style, nor a lexicon whose main advantage would be completeness from A to Z. Its purpose is rather to plot in word and image the typical features of 20th-century sculpture, bringing out connections and oppositions. Chronology, nationality and membership of this or that school play a subordinate role. Attention is directed to the *problems* of modern sculpture and an attempt is made to lend speech to this silent art.

Descriptions of individual pieces from many countries serve as so many approaches to the theme of form and space. The two terms are to be taken in the widest sense and as including their usual synonyms. This applies in particular to "form" which is not restricted in a classicizing spirit to the human figure. As to "space," it need hardly be pointed out that it is to be understood in the artistic not the scientific sense.

Regarding method and arrangement the following may be observed: using the examples assembled I consider successively the problems of form, of meaning and of purpose. The reader may suspect collusion in this game of question and answer; I hope, none the less, he will not reject the procedure as rhetorical or theorising. Its sole aim is to bring him into the closest possible contact with the works themselves.

The treatment of the first problem, which is concerned with typical manifestations of sculpture, is also an exercise in method serving to elaborate the framework for the treatment of the two other problems. The second one, that of meaning or theme, suggesting a kind of iconography, cannot, of course be divorced from the first since in

1. CONSTANTIN BRANCUSI The New-born, 1915 Marble Height 6″, Length 8½″ Philadelphia Museum of Art Photo: Museum

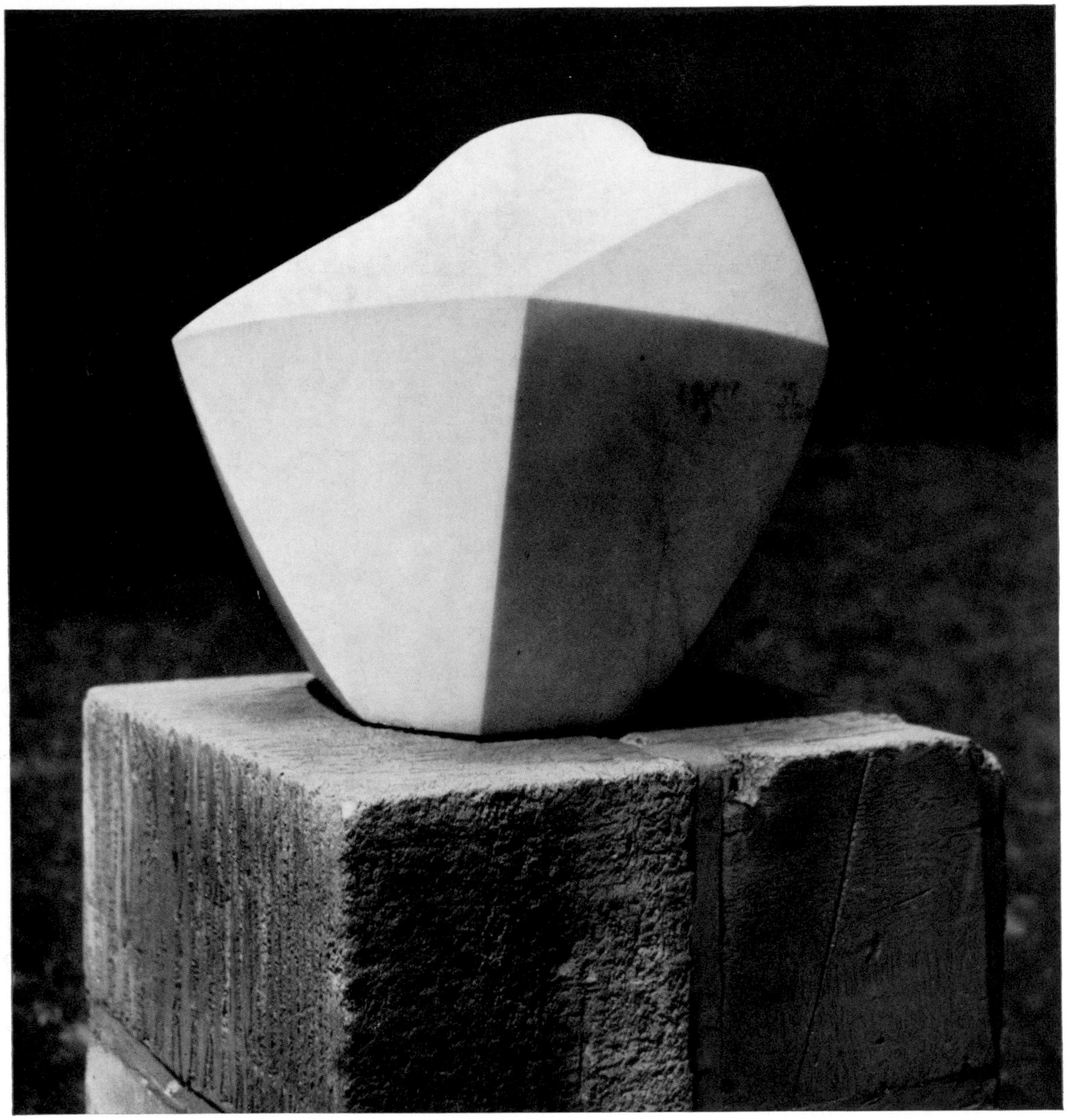

2. Emile Gilioli   Caravan, 1955   Carrara marble Height 18 1/8″   Galerie Louis Carré, Paris   Photo: Author

3. Henri-Georges Adam

The Couple, 1946
Plaster for marble
Height 78 3/4″
Photo-Malec, Levallois-Perret

4. Jacques Lipchitz Woman Standing with Guitar, 1926 Gilt bronze Height 10 1/4"
Formerly Curt Valentin collection, New York Photo: Marc Vaux, Paris

such works by other sculptors as spring from the same formal assumptions. The marble piece by the Parisian Emile Gilioli, *Caravan* (fig. 2) and the plaster cast *The Couple* (fig. 3) by his older fellow-countryman, Henri-Georges Adam, are based on the same conception of a solid, compact body shut in on all sides—a block expressing weight and stability. These later works likewise show a tendency towards neatly cut, smooth surfaces that clearly define the volume of the work and set it off sharply against the surrounding space. Only the facet-like character of the surfaces abruptly opposing each other distinguishes the younger artists from the older one. The growth of Brancusi's figures is a process of reduction while Gilioli and Adam construct with planes or spherical surfaces. The titles are no more than recognition marks for newly invented objects.

OPENING UP OF VOLUME

In opposition to the type of compact volume illustrated by examples from the work of Brancusi, Gilioli and Adam, and particularly congenial to the Latin spirit in art with its emphasis on clarity and the objective result to be achieved, we may set, in terms of a formal postulate, the disintegration of mass and opening-up of solid volume. As against representation in one—material—medium alone, appearing as a self-contained whole, we now have figures made up of solid *and* space, of mass *and* void, of outer *and* inner volume. Sculpture becomes more complicated, it is no longer "of a piece" as are Brancusi's and Gilioli's monoliths. The treatment of empty space as "sculptural material," as certain sculptors in fact treat it, implies the use of two different media of which the allegedly real one serves to make significant the otherness of its imagined companion. Concomitantly there appears a hierarchy of forms; subordinate and superordinate elements come to the fore.

Of course, we find such piercing and opening-up of solid volume in older sculpture as well; in the fundamental forms of art it is almost impossible to invent something radically new, something that has never before existed. But it is in the 20th century that the idea of combining positive and negative forms has been systematically exploited. The name given to this trend, *hole sculpture,* apposite if somewhat derogatory, shows that it has struck home.

I cannot consider here the misguided contention that this kind of sculpture tends towards nihilism, my purpose being neither exegesis nor apology but the elaboration of formal criteria. Similarly, since my approach is not an historical one, the question of original authorship as regards "transparent sculpture" is of secondary interest. There are earlier instances than the ones to be mentioned, e.g. the work of Alexander Archipenko.

My earliest example is the gilded bronze *Woman Standing with Guitar* (fig. 4) by Jacques Lipchitz. It is intended and executed as a *transparent* piece. The bodily substance of the various parts, swaying delicately or else twisting into spirals, appears less in volume than the space it enmeshes.

The piece, whose historical lineage could be traced to Cubism and Surrealism, documents a new artistic intention. The sculptor abandons the primacy of the compact solid, neglects the emphasis on weight and loosens up the composition to allow light and air to circulate inside it. The forms within and at the back, which can be grasped at a glance in their spatial relatedness, are just as important as the front and the allusively indicated internal space. Its transparence frees the sculpture from the static perspective: the single impression yields to the experience of spatial simultaneity.

The formal postulate discernible in Lipchitz' sculpture was taken by Henry Moore as the title for one of his bronzes (fig. 5): it is called *Internal-External Forms*—an explicit indication of the artistic purpose realised in it. Here too the specific assumptions and the symbolism involved will be left out of account, and only the formal principle considered. While Lipchitz reduces the mass of the body to a few thin, almost linear, elements, Moore's figure, in spite of the side opening, remains blocklike and heavy. The piece is not transparent and allows only glimpses into the interior whose partial exposure does not break the over-all cohesion of outline. The outer shell encompasses in hollow space the forms inside; these in turn are made up of positive (=solid) and negative (=spatial) elements. The reciprocal relationship between inner and outer, mass and void remains even.

The Spaniard Pablo Gargallo, a contemporary of Picasso, also uses positive and negative forms. The skeleton of his bronze *Prophet* (fig. 6), made up of concave and convex surfaces, curved contours and cut-out forms, is intended as a silhouette and should, therefore, be seen from the front. The actual volume of the body is slight and it is up to the spectator to establish its extension in space by imagining continuous surfaces from the outline indications that are supplied.

A later work, the cement *Great Mask* (fig. 7) by the Italian Mirko, shows the same formal intention. Its transparence suggests not so much a private sculptural space as permeation by the free surrounding space. Mirko's composition is even more open than Gargallo's; it draws into its spatial existence the whole environment.

SIGN IN SPACE

Mirko goes so far in reducing bodily substance that his work can be taken as a transition to the next formal type in which the opening-up and attenuation of solid volume create a new sculptural function, that of a sign in space. Here, if there is shrinking

5. Henry Moore

Internal-External Forms
1951 Bronze Height 24$^{3}/_{8}$″
Kunstmuseum, Basle

6. Pablo Gargallo

Prophet, 1933
Bronze Height 93¾″
Middelheim Museum
Antwerp
Photo: Author

7. Mirko

The Great Mask
Cement Height $59^{3}/_{8}''$
Photo: Author

8. Henri Matisse

Serpentine, 1909
Bronze Height 22 1/4″
Museum of Art, Baltimore
Photo: Museum

9. Wilhelm Lehmbruck

Attacking Figure, 1914/15
Bronze Height 17 3/8″
Dr. Berhard Sprengel
collection, Hanover
Photo: Hans Wagner
Hanover

10. Alberto Giacometti

Venice VII, 1957 Bronze Height 46 1/8"
Private collection

11. Julio Gonzalez

Dancer with Flowing Hair, 1934
Iron Height $24^{3}/_{8}$"
Private collection, Paris
Photo: Author

12. Herbert Ferber

The Bow, 1950
Lead Height 48″
Photo: Author

in one sense there is expansion in another. The figures of this type are not confined to a space of their own which they either fill bodily or at least somehow annex; their activity reaches beyond their own limits, spills over into infinite space which it seeks to inform. In strong contrast to the stillness, isolation and self-sufficiency of the sculptured blocks considered at the beginning of this chapter, their whole tendency is outwards. Formal concentration characteristic of kernel sculpture is replaced by eccentricity. The figure, as it were, parts with itself by projecting itself into space. It is no accident that this formal vocabulary has found particular favour with expressionist artists.

This tendency to disembodiment is already beginning to operate in the early bronzes of the painter and sculptor Henri Matisse. What has been said about the formal type applies fully to his *Serpentine* (fig. 8), dating from 1909. The title of the work, which recalls the Mannerists, is also a description of the form—a thin, elongated, serpent-like nude whose members traverse space in many directions so that the figure, though static, is not still; and its precarious balance is made even less secure by the complicated stance and the pronounced inclination of the chest.

Compared with Matisse's figure, whose strenuous composure could be that of a tight-rope walker, the *Attacking Figure* by Wilhelm Lehmbruck (fig. 9), dating from 1914–15, is more solidly built even though the subject involves movement. But Lehmbruck's youth shows on the one hand the characteristic diminution of solid volume, and on the other the outward, expansive striking force of the individual parts of the body, which are here no longer carefully balanced against each other but strive vehemently upwards. The artist charges the high stretched-out trunk and the arms crossed in open space with his will to overcome the weight of the body, to make the figure issue like a cry.

Yet more rigorous in the attenuation of his figures is Alberto Giacometti, though he does not attempt Lehmbruck's expansive gestures. *Venice VII* (*1957*; fig. 10), is like Lot's wife stiff as a pillar of salt. But this apparently motionless figure has many contacts with the space round it. The rough surface is tense with inner forces which seek to burst out. The thin, emaciated body is in constant communication with infinite space of which it occupies so little. It is almost an anthropomorphic signal tower —if this departure from formal analysis into interpretation of meaning may be permitted. The scabby, torn, almost dangling skin is more than merely an exposed surface offsetting the body against the surrounding space: its deep dents and craggy botches have dematerialised it to such an extent that it becomes an intermediate zone between the two.

The small iron figure of the *Dancer with Flowing Hair* (fig. 11) by Julio Gonzalez, though earlier in date—historical sequence is not relevant to my present purpose,—

represents the further transition from volume, already reduced to the status of an instrument for performing gestures in space, to the immaterial sign. The iron rods that give the dancer her shape are, from an artistic point of view, no more than lines which Gonzalez uses for marking space. The result is a diagram, unaffected by the sculptural problems of statics and gravity, displaying its weightlessness in the free space round it which it can serve to measure. The figure projects its form in every direction, upwards and downwards—as photographed, against a background of an airy, weightless trellis of branches whose wild growth both harmonises with and contradicts the rigid form disciplined by the hand of man.

Gonzalez' momentous invention of the "sign in space" spurred on many younger artists working after World War II to new discoveries in the language of space. *The Bow* (fig. 12; lead) by the American, Herbert Ferber, shows one of the many possibilities of building in space with bold, airy, seemingly self-supporting and loosely combined elements. The bronze *Eclipse* (fig. 13) by the Italian, Carmelo Cappello, intensifies this tendency and the result is a theatrical flight of sculptured form through space with the clouds in the sky, and not the earth, acting as backcloth.

CONSTRUCTIONS

The opening-up of solid volume or the elaboration of expressive sign figures in space are not the only possibilities to have been tackled by modern sculptors in their formal explorations. Artists with a constructional bent have also responded to the challenge. As early as 1920 Antoine Pevsner and Naum Gabo laid down in the "Realist Manifesto" of Constructivism that "(1) to be adequate to real life art must be based on two fundamentals, space and time; (2) volume is not the only means of expression in space; (3) kinetic and dynamic elements are needed to express real time, static rhythm is not sufficient; (4) art must cease to be imitative and discover new forms."

Naum Gabo's *Column* (fig. 14) made of wood, metal and artificial materials is still, it is true, entirely static in its structure. The spatial effect is obtained by the transparence of some of the materials used which, though they preserve some slight volume, all but abolish its function as a boundary by letting through light. In this way Gabo obtains free, flowing transitions between sculptural and external space, while the effect is strengthened by actual openings and breaks in the structure. The *Column* not only rises in rhythmical stages but—with the circular steps of its base, the obliquely set hoop and the projecting platforms—spreads out on all sides, communicating with free space, taking it in and releasing it.

A construction static in itself but entering into multiple relationships with the space round it is also what Nicolas Schöffer aims at in his *Lux 8* (fig. 15). Here the move-

13. CARMELO CAPPELLO

Eclipse, 1959
Bronze Height 88 5/8"
Photo: Allegri, Brescia

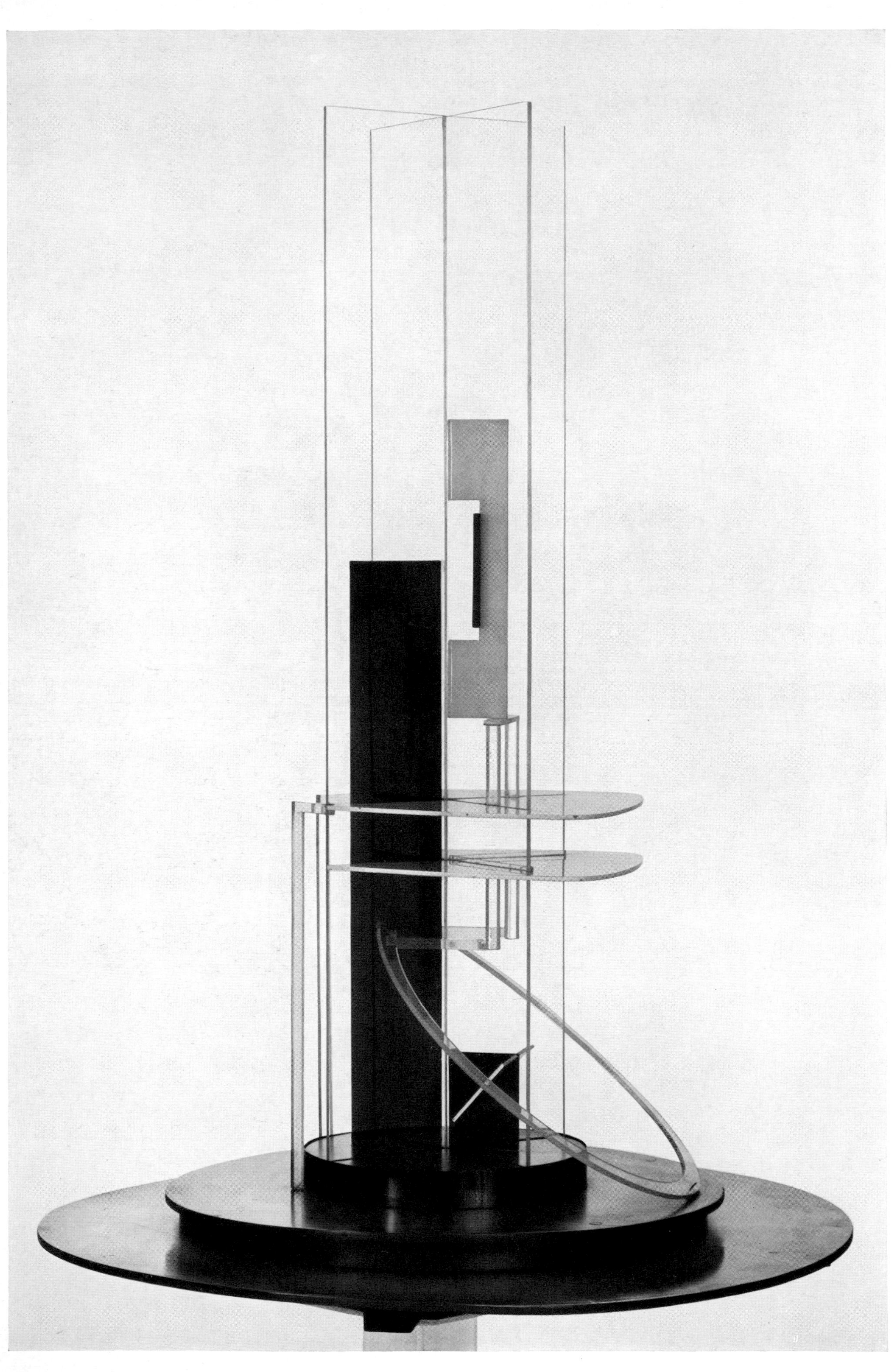

14. NAUM GABO

Column, 1923
Plastic, wood and metal
Height $41^1/_2$"
Solomon R. Guggenheim
Museum, New York
Photo: Museum
(left)

15. NICOLAS SCHÖFFER

Lux 8, Sculpture
spatiodynamique, 1959
Copperplated steel
Height 101"
Photo: Yves Hervochon
Paris
(right)

16. ANTOINE PEVSNER Construction in Space, 1929 Brass sheet and glass Height 27 1/8" Kunstmuseum, Basle Emanuel Hoffmann Foundation

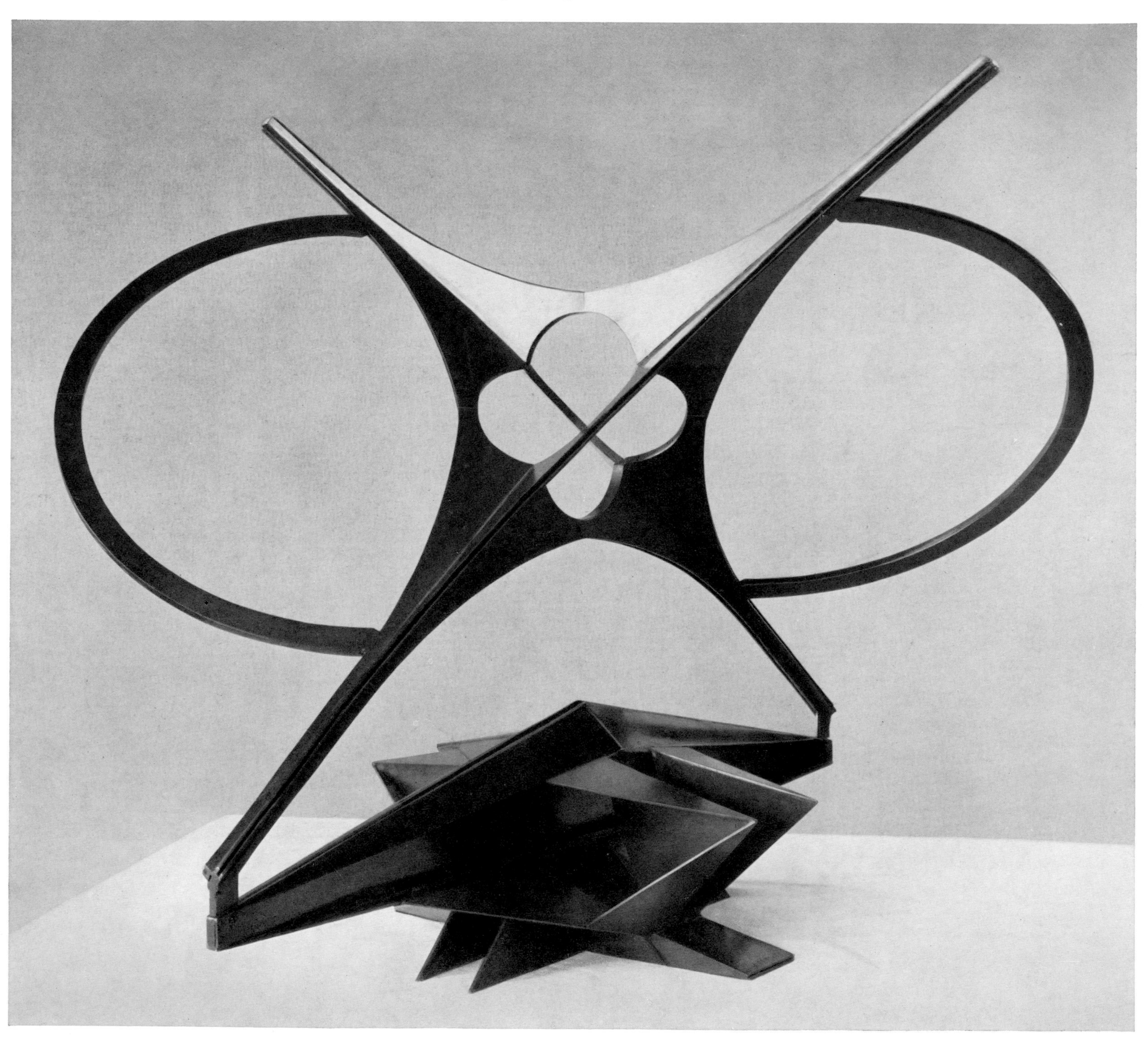

17. Richard Lippold Variations within a Sphere No. 10: The Sun, 1953–56 Gold wire Length $131^7/_8$", Height $263^3/_4$", Depth $65^7/_8$"
The Metropolitan Museum of Art, New York Fletcher Fund, 1956 Photo: Author

18. Georges Vantongerloo

Sculpture in Space
(y = ax³ – bx³ + cx), 1935
Argentine Height 15 1/8″
Kunstmuseum, Basle
Emanuel Hoffmann Foundation

19. Marino di Teana

Architectonic Conception
No. 1, 1959
Steel Height 27 3/8″
Galerie Denis René, Paris
Photo: Yves Hervochon
Paris

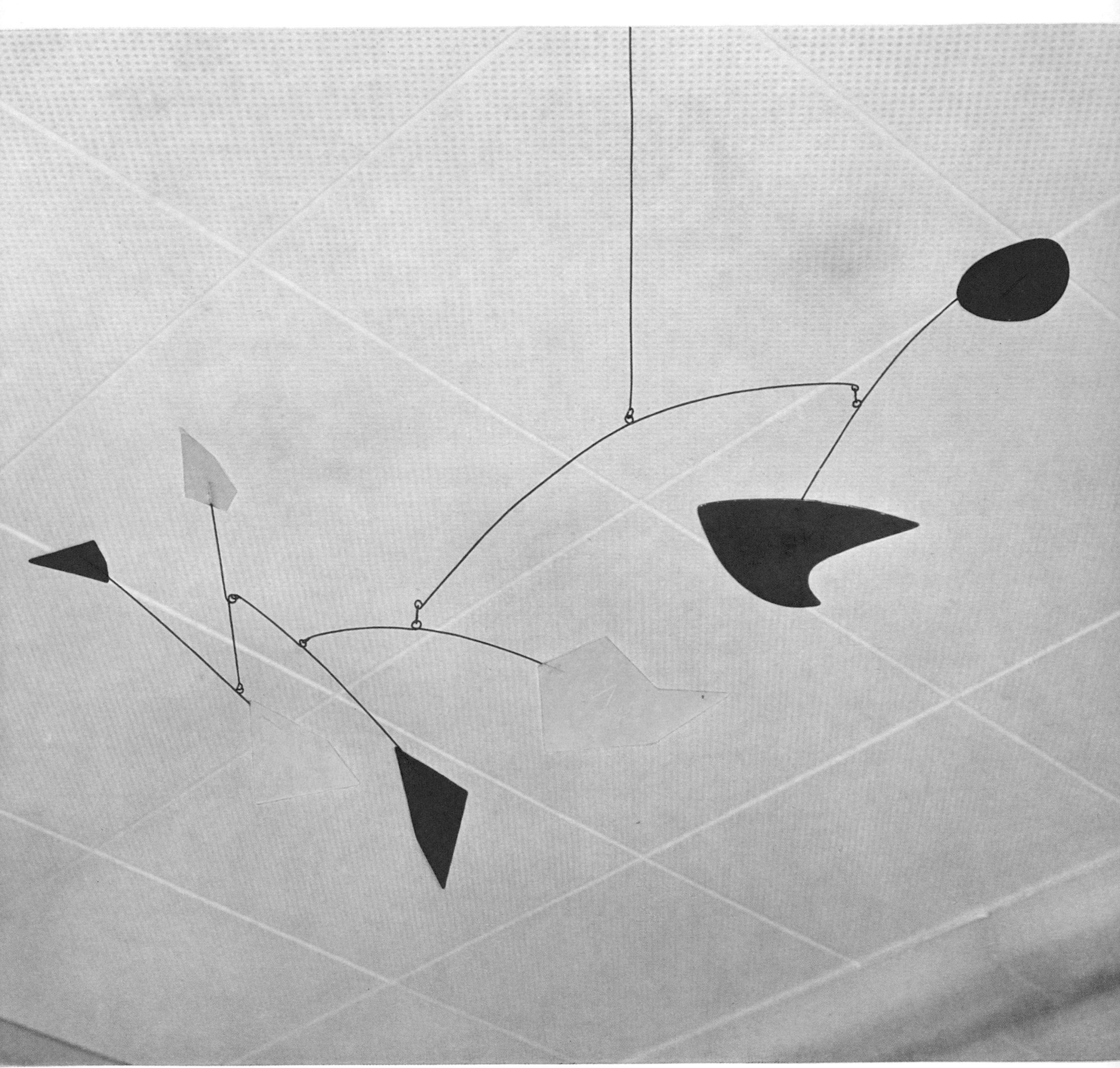

20. Alexander Calder Small Mobile of Seven Elements, 1958 Steel Dr. Bernhard Sprengel collection, Hanover

ment of light adds another dynamic element so that the rigid skeleton of iron beams and punched metal plates is taken up in a weightless play of solid and projected forms in space.

Gabo prefers translucid artificial materials while his brother, Antoine Pevsner, uses mainly metal. There are also stylistic differences between the two but these need not concern us; of prime relevance is the formal type elaborated by Pevsner, of which his *Construction in Space* (fig. 16) is an example. The piece consists of plane surfaces and curved lines which have no "body" or at least do not function artistically as volumes. They are put together to form an open unit with the circumambient air as, in Pevsner's words, an "integral part" of it. The *Construction in Space* carves out distinct polygonal figures in infinite space to which it declares itself to belong. It appears as entirely weightless and is in this respect opposed even more radically than Gonzalez' iron figures to the massive forms of Brancusi.

The dissolution of mass has been taken to an extreme by the American, Richard Lippold, in his *Variations within a Sphere No. 10: The Sun* (fig. 17). Lippold's sun is a luminous, apparently weightless, transparent constellation of golden lines and points. It is made of fine threads of pure gold soldered together and spun out on wires of stainless steel. As against the spatial dynamism of Pevsner the piece, constructed symmetrically and according to simple proportions, remains still. It flutters passively in space which invades its indistinct outline and absorbs its disembodied scintillations.

However, the negation of mass in favour of space is not the only resource of constructivist sculpture. Georges Vantongerloo, a Belgian living in Paris, at one time an adherent of the "Stijl" movement, adopts the opposite solution in his *Sculpture in Space* ($y=ax^3-bx^3+cx$) (fig. 18). But his cubical forms stand freely in space unaffected by the laws of statics. They create an architectural space though their structure is architecturally improbable.

Marino di Teana, an Argentinian living in Paris, seems at first sight to be a follower of "Stijl"; he uses right angles a great deal. But his *Architectonic Conception No. 1* (fig. 19) in forged steel is built, unlike Vantongerloo's composition, from the ground upwards. It involves no suspended or supported elements which Vantongerloo presents in a remarkable balancing act. The heavy steel beams standing upright, with only a few horizontal connections, are so arranged that the inner space is entirely shut off. Only the sharply projecting triangle breaks the motionless phalanx and sallies forth outwards.

So far my subject has been static volume in space with only occasional hints at movement. But this aspect deserves separate treatment and I now pass to sculpture in motion. My first example is from the work of the American, Alexander Calder. He was the first to think, in sculptural terms, of a "floating, not carried object," of "freedom from the earth." His *Small Mobile of Seven Elements* (fig. 20; coloured steel) recalls Lippold's *Sun* in the flimsiness of its material components. But it does not stand motionless like a taut sail; it moves in complex rhythm with every current of air that disturbs its balance and then slowly comes to rest. As for its relation to space, no one system of data defines it. Volume, extension and position vary according to the degree and kind of movement, entailing a succession of spatial patterns.

A somewhat different kind of mobile sculpture is offered by the Swiss, Walter Linck, who uses compressed steel bands and vibrating aerials (fig. 21). Movement here is both tenser and more restricted: it is produced by the gradual release of pressure and operates in fixed directions, the steel coils unwinding themselves like clock springs. The slow swinging of Calder's *Mobile* and the nervous trembling of Linck's steel constructions are both outdone by the young Basle sculptor, Jean Tinguely, who introduces clockwork and electric motors to generate motive power. This he uses as the very principle of his art: his compositions—the one illustrated here (fig. 22) consists of twenty-six mobile and two stationary parts—first come into existence when their solid (metal) elements are set in motion. Rotating about their axes at speeds that can vary from the dizzying to the imperceptibly slow, they create entities whose permanence resides in the constant change of pattern. Tinguely, no doubt, approaches the limit of sculptural possibilities beyond which lies not painting but the non-artistic representation of physical phenomena.

Physical, more particularly magnetic, forces are brought into artistic play by another sculptor interested in technical experiment. In his *Telemagnetic Sculpture* (fig. 23), Takis, a Greek living in Paris, shows the result of a movement produced in pieces of metal by a powerful magnet. The trajectory has not been completed: the spheroid and the cone are held back from actual contact with the magnet by almost invisible wires or nylon threads, and remain suspended in mid air. Their relationship to one another in space has been carefully calculated. The composition exists by virtue of the magnetic force, collapsing when this is withdrawn and re-forming when it is applied again. Both Tinguely's moving patterns and Takis' telemagnetic objects involve the use of technical devices. With the former it is velocity that constitutes the work of art, while the latter, with comparable extremism, sets up a temporary "sculptural situation" by means of an equilibrium of force and resistance.

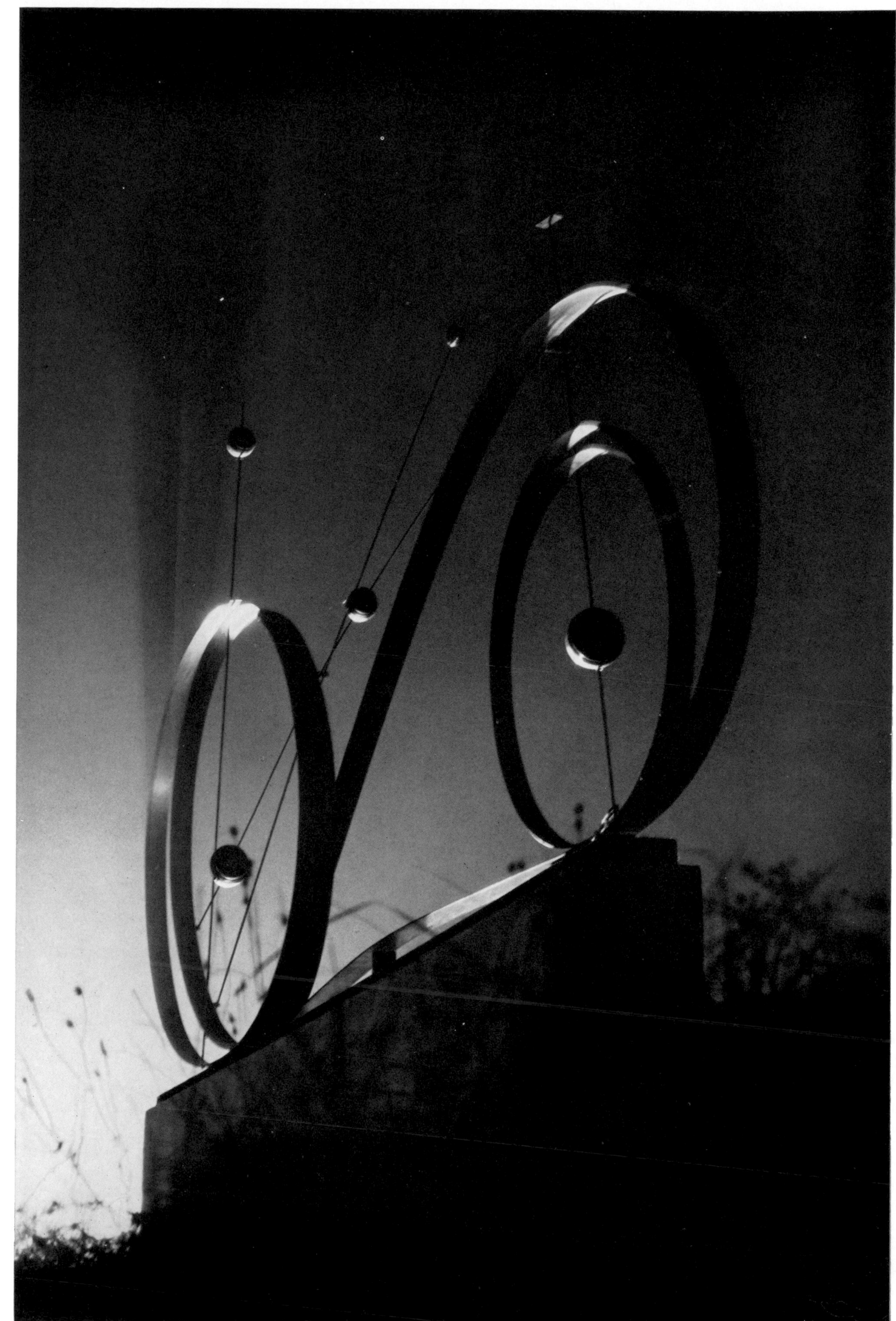

21. Walter Linck

Sculpture Mobile, 1959
Steel and Iron
Height 59″, Length 157 1/8″
Photo: Mario Tschabold
Steffisburg

22. Jean Tinguely Yokohama, in Metamorphosis, 1956 Oil paint on mechanisms Height 56¼", Length 49¼"
Galerie Denis René, Paris Photo: H. Stoecklin, Paris

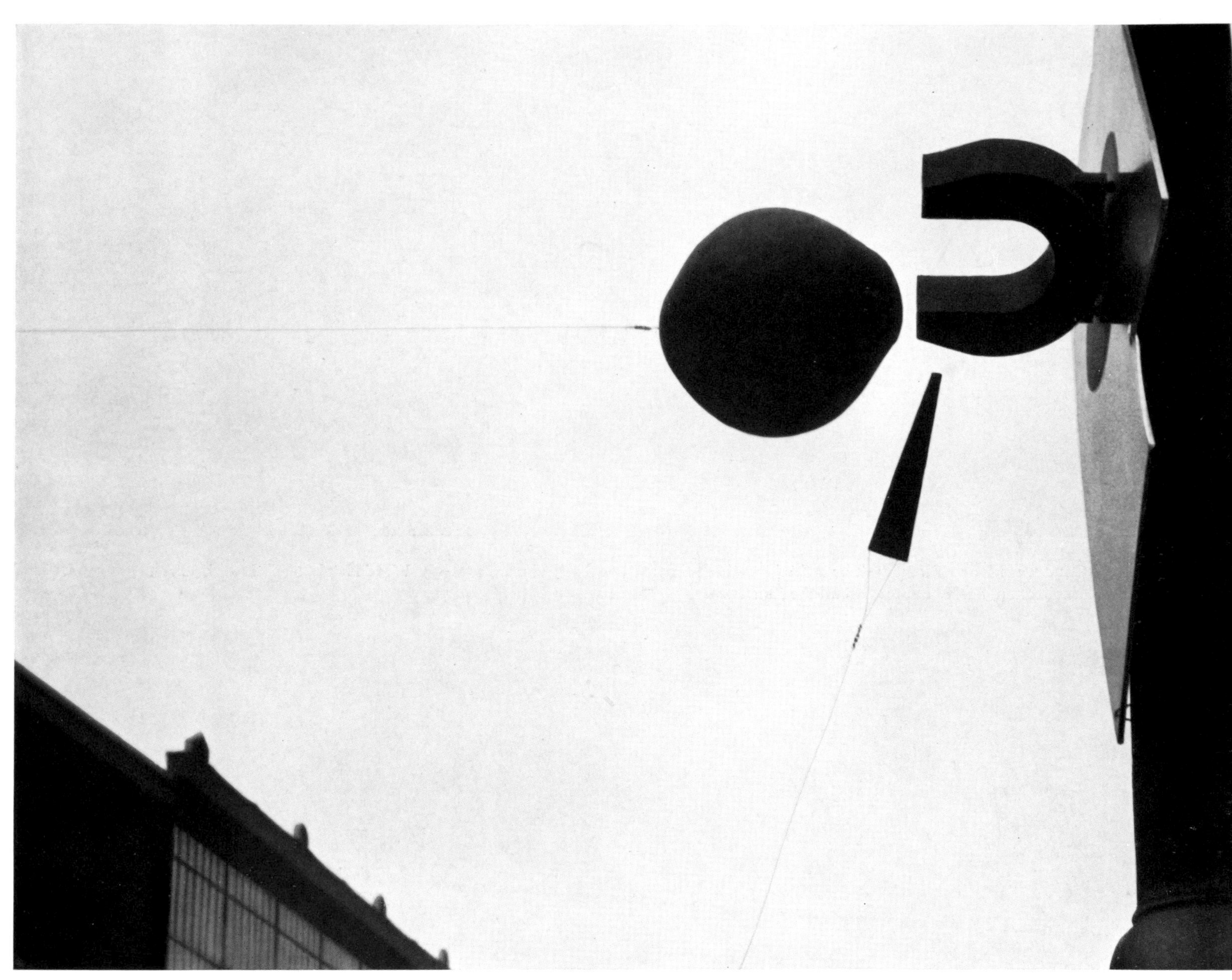

23. TAKIS Telemagnetic Sculpture, 1959 Magnet and iron Height 19 5/8", Length 13 3/4" Galerie Iris Clert, Paris

24. PAUL GAUGUIN Manao Tupapau – She is thinking about the spirit of the dead man, 1891–93 Wood Height 8 7/8", Length 20 5/8". Private collection, Basle Photo: Öffentliche Kunstsammlung, Basle

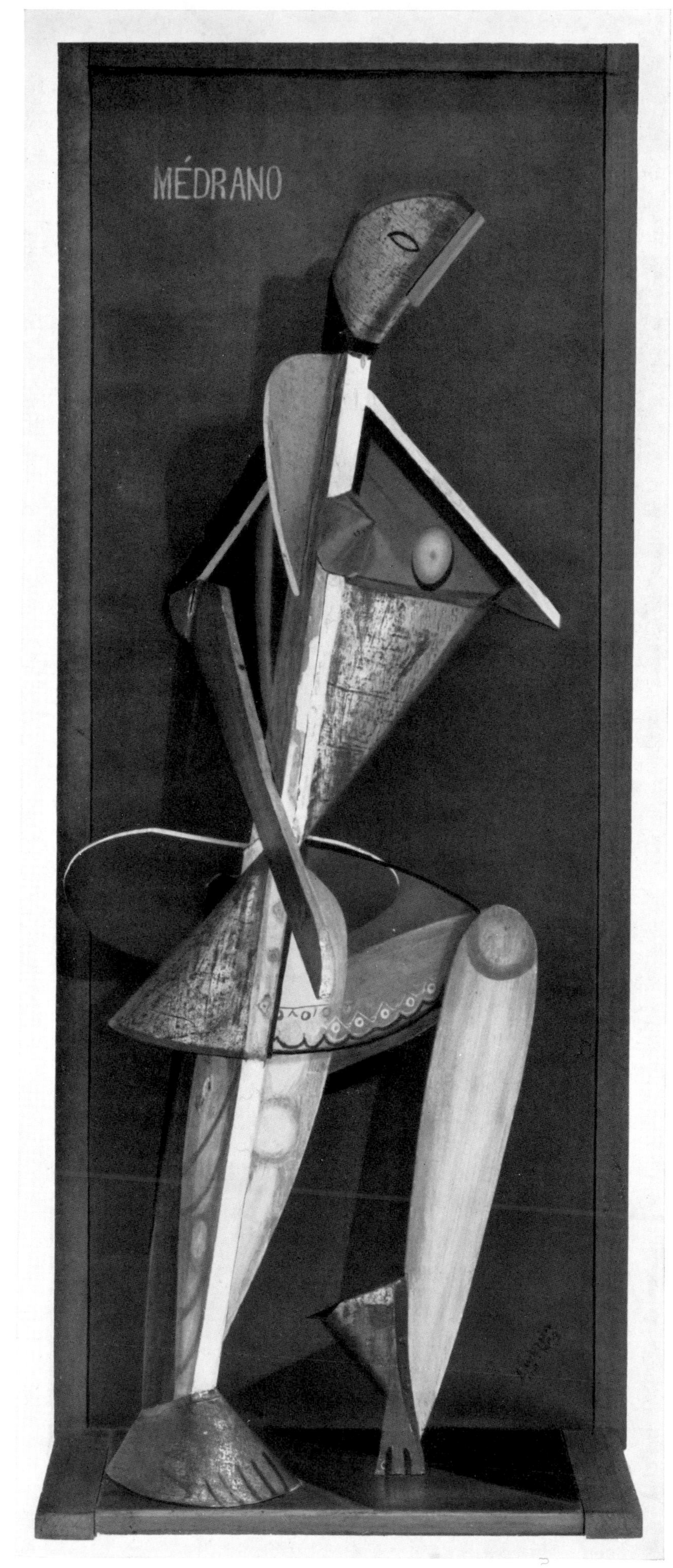

25. ALEXANDER ARCHIPENKO

Médrano, 1915
Painted tin, glass, wood and oilcloth Height 50″
Solomon R. Guggenheim Museum, New York
Photo: Museum

26. Manuel Rivera

Metamorphosis, 1959
Iron-wire and metal-netting
Height $35^{3}/_{8}''$, Length $23^{5}/_{8}''$
Galerie René Drouin, Paris
Photo: R. Bonache, Madrid
(left)

27. Pietro Consagra

Human Colloquium, 1958
Wood with burnt-in design
Height 52″, Length $45^{3}/_{16}''$
(right)

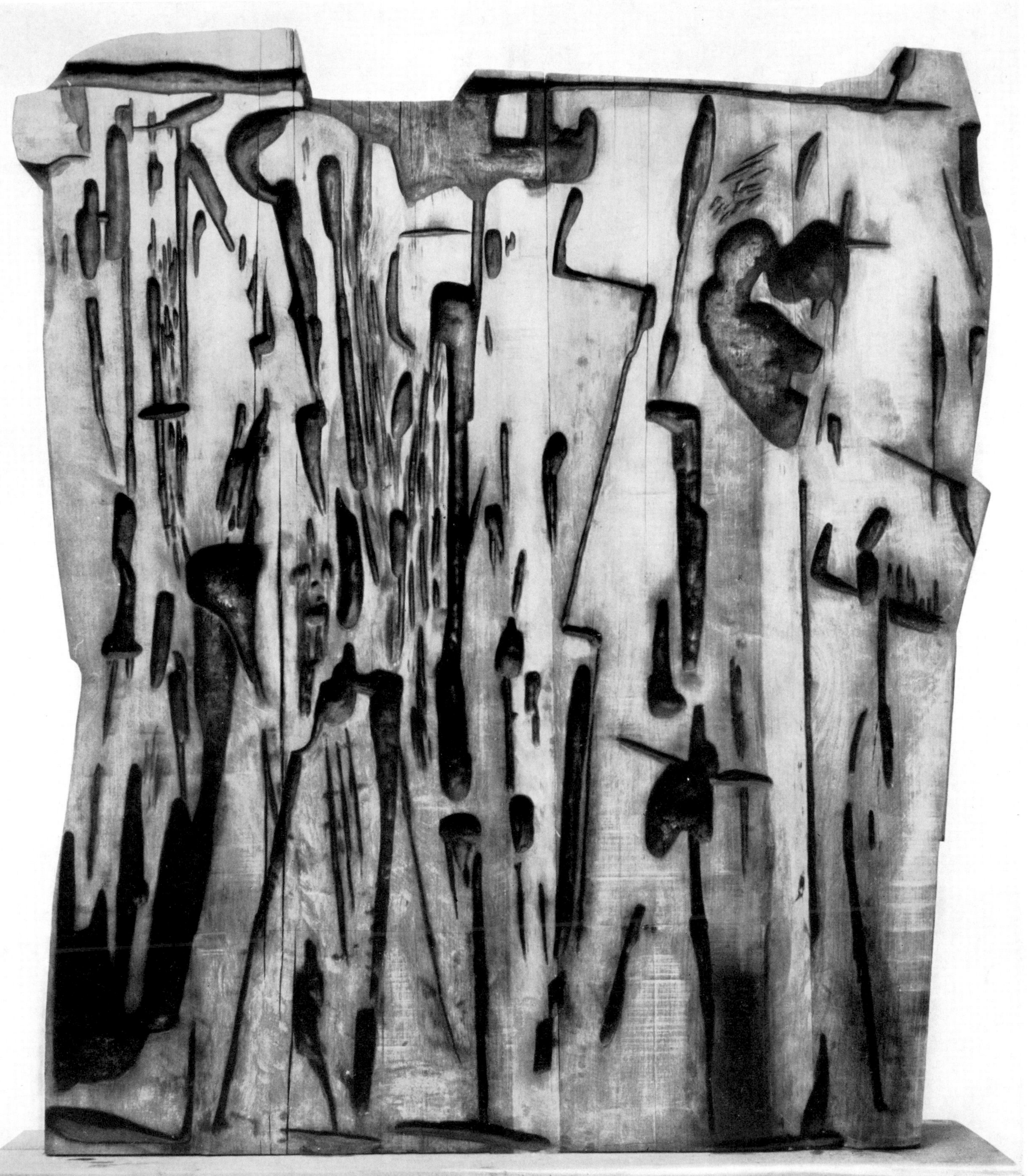

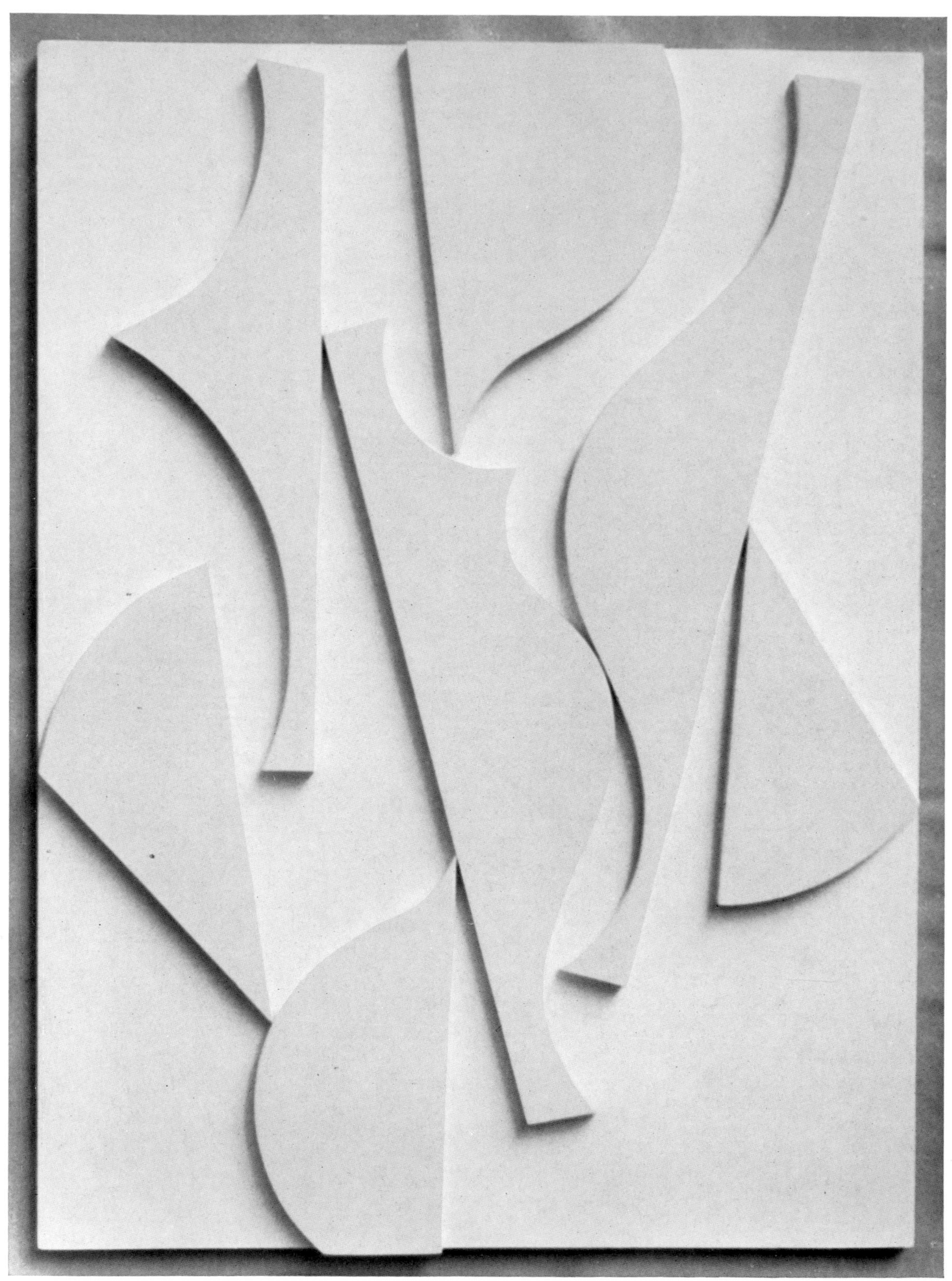

28. Sophie Täuber-Arp Parasols, 1938 Wood and white oil-paint Height 34⅝", Length 24⅞"
Rijksmuseum Kröller-Müller, Otterlo Photo: Museum

The last two examples have brought us to the frontier zone of sculpture. To this zone belongs relief as the accepted transition to painting. In the 20th century initiative has come in the first instance from the other side: painters have been attracted by the possibility of breaking away from the illusionism of the two-dimensional surface towards effects in real space, and also of introducing new materials. Numerous examples could be cited here, especially from the period of Cubism, though even today there are many painters who paste colours on the canvas in thick relief, or "paint" with other things. Suffice it to mention Jean Dubuffet and Alberto Burri, Jean Fautrier and Rolf Nesch, Antonio Tapies and Carl Buchheister, Emil Schumacher and Karlfred Dahmen, Bernhard Schultze, Claude Viseux and Robert Rauschenberg, finally also Ben Nicholson, Victor Pasmore and Otto Piene—to indicate how wide is the interest and how numerous are the variations, ranging as they do from incrustation to modelling by light and shadow.

However, apart from the application of relief in painting, the more properly sculptural use of it seems to be bound by tradition much more than is sculpture in the round. Paul Gauguin, who can be considered as the father of the modern painter-sculptor, consistently translates his style as a painter into three-dimensional terms in his wood relief *Manao Tupapau—She is thinking about the spirit of the dead man* (fig. 24); but the effect is one of flatness. It is noticeable that the piece was originally intended as a simple woodcut and only subsequently recut as a relief. Surfaces and lines play a dominant role to the detriment of spatial and plastic elements.

Not very different in this respect is Pietro Consagra's *Human Colloquium* (fig. 27) with its forms burnt into the flat surface of wooden planks. Although the incisions vary in depth to give the composition a certain spatial quality, the dominant effect comes from the linearism of the forms which adhere to the surface like a frieze. As against these attempts to use relief as a means of importing the third dimension into painting, Alexander Archipenko's sculpture-painting—a combination of solid and flat forms, involving the use of manufactured materials, with colour—was intended to open up new possibilities for sculpture. In his celebrated *Médrano* (fig. 25) of 1915, composed of painted tin, glass, wool and oilcloth, and mounted in full relief against a background, he sets out not only to reproduce the basic geometrical forms of the human figure but also to bring out its three-dimensional character, which he does by using solid and hollow volumes to obtain effects of light and shadow. "My sculpture-painting," says Archipenko, "is really nothing new; I have learnt it from the Egyptians. Only the new kind of forms is mine."

While Archipenko seeks to make relief more concrete, to "realise" it as a sculptural type, the aim of the Spaniard Manuel Rivera is dematerialisation. His compositions of iron wires and metal nets (fig. 26) are intended not as sculpture but as painting realised with sculptural materials. Consequently, the *pinturas metalicas* are not easy to define in spatial terms even though the wires and nets appear in varying depths. The transparent reticulations, disintegrating at the edges, do not range themselves in spatial relationships but act as flat patches of colour. The absence of background to give them relief completes the painterly effect.

The examples discussed so far have shown that relief, though at times very close to painting, can yet maintain its autonomy as a sculptural type. But, apart from Archipenko's high relief *Médrano*, a rare exception, relief today is gradually giving up this autonomy and returning to the flat surface out of which it emerged in the classical period of Greek art. The background is no longer the matrix of independent forms but merely the carrier of hardly projecting patterns. A wood composition by Sophie Täuber-Arp, *Parasols* (fig. 28), is a typical example. Executed in 1938 after an earlier drawing, it presents a rhythmic play of simple, melodiously shaped pieces of wood. They move in a flat foreground and even the recessed, "negative" forms are drawn into it.

The work of Zoltan Kemeny, a Swiss of Hungarian origin, presents a more difficult border-line case. Are his metal reliefs paintings with a special emphasis on the materiality of the medium or should the collection of miniature blocks and the interstices between them (fig. 29) be considered as a sculptural composition? Kemeny uses copper and brass, a typical sculptor's choice. The open cubes of various sizes with a fixed profile are organised in a loose diagonal formation resembling a mosaic or an air-view of a city that has grown without plan. The varying depth of the relief and the alternation of cavities and projecting sides could be interpreted in sculptural terms. On the other hand the serial repetition and "pointillist" bestrewing of a surface are more a painter's effects; and the scales are definitely weighted in favour of painting by the fact that the forms are deployed against a flat surface and not in depth, the third dimension being thus reduced to insignificance.

The ground plays an important role in the copper and aluminium reliefs of Étienne Hajdu (fig. 30). He does not treat it as a datum to be accepted as it is but meets its challenge as a matrix of forms. He uses the embossing technique and thus the forms he shapes are not "arranged" but grow out of the ground in continuous volumes and uninterrupted transitions. Modelled from inside out, the originally flat surface acquires a breathing, swelling movement which not only presses against the contours of the relief but advances and recedes in other directions. Yet this multiple commotion does not break the surface anywhere nor does the gentle play of light and shadow impair the firmness of sculptural form.

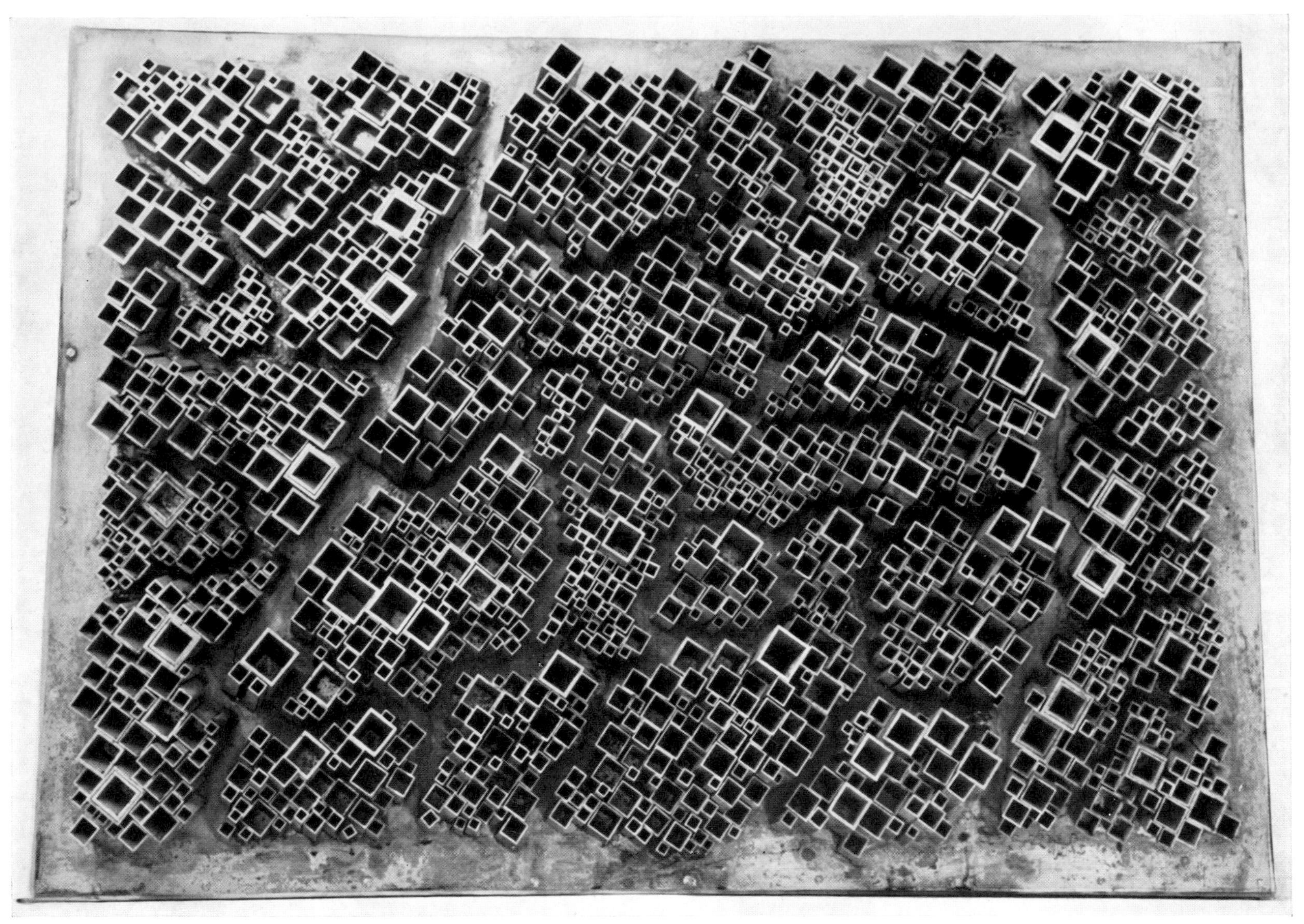

29. Zoltan Kemeny Banlieu des Anges, 1958 Copper Height 26 3/4", Length 37 3/8" Galerie Paul Facchetti, Paris

30. Étienne Hajdu The Wolves, 1953 Chased copper Height 66⁷/₈", Length 82⁵/₈" Photo: Claude Michaelides, Paris

31. Henri Laurens

Bottle and Newspaper, 1919
Wood and metal, painted
Height 20 1/8", Length 15 3/4"
Depth 8 5/8"
Stedelijk Museum
Amsterdam
Photo: Author

32. JEAN DUBUFFET

The Sorcerer, 1954
Lava slag and wood-roots
Height 43¼″
Galerie Daniel Cordier
Frankfurt/Main

By way of conclusion to this typology of modern sculpture may be added examples of conglomerates constructed with heterogeneous materials and of assemblages of *objets trouvés*. The problems involved here are not only formal but technical as well and can, therefore, be fitted into the terms of reference of this chapter only as an excursus. Henri Laurens' still-life of 1919, *Bottle and newspaper* (fig. 31), in painted wood and metal, is an early attempt to go beyond the Cubist conception of relief as painting with sculptural means, and construct, with fragments of ready-made objects, a new type of sculptural entity in space. Laurens dispenses with background but props his construction, an interplay of mass and void, against a wall. His *collage* is thus a cross between relief and sculpture; its spatial possibilities were developed by the Constructivists who did away with the aperspectivist overlapping.

Laurens uses artifacts which he dismantles and re-composes in different relationships. Jean Dubuffet, who has already been mentioned as a practitioner of relief in painting, adopts the opposite procedure. He takes insignificant, accidentally found objects like roots, pieces of slag or sponge, and puts them together with a minimum of working-over (fig. 32). Dubuffet's sculptures are no more than assemblages: the artist simply decrees that the formless is in fact informed because he has recognised it as such; by putting together the components he expounds this recognition.

The pieces of slag and the root growth "explain" one another as parts of a fantastic, yet archetypal figure. There is a distant resemblance to the 16th- and 17th-century device whereby fragments of minerals as *objets trouvés* were combined with decorative goldsmith's work. But Dubuffet excludes artifacts and uses accidental shapes as he finds them. This example of creating form by an act of recognition brings me to the end of the first part of my inquiry.

II THE PROBLEM OF MEANING

The analysis of selected formal types attempted in the first chapter involved no more than describing what is or occurs before our eyes. This objective and "public" orientation will be a useful check when interpretating meaning in which systems of reference—presuppositions, theories and associations—are necessarily more personal and difficult to control. The interpretation of meaning cannot, in any case, be divorced from the analysis of form; and by remaining close to that analysis it will remain close to the work of art itself. Its specific task will be to consider the formal choices of the artist not in themselves but as vehicles of a message.

The approach will, again, not be historical but more in the nature of an iconography, with the consequent arrangement of the illustrations by subject and not chronologically. It is hoped that the unity in multiplicity of modern sculpture will thereby become apparent. Within the various iconographic groups the same formal categories will be applied as in the first chapter.

In contrast to painting where non-objectivity is in the ascendant, 20th-century sculpture has preserved an interest in the appearance of the outside world, in so-called reality. More specifically, it continues to concern itself with the traditional but still valid task of representing the human figure, and the inquiry into meaning may fittingly begin with examples of this artistic preoccupation with man. I turn first to the statue; that is, to the representation of the motionless human figure, both naturalistic and abstract in varying degrees.

The years before World War I, so important for modern art, are characterised in sculpture by a tendency towards heavy, block-like figures. The determining influence here is not only the newly discovered art of archaic and "primitive" cultures but also a movement for reform designed to restore sculpture to its aesthetic autonomy which it had surrendered to painting. This alienation from itself had led to an alienation from the public and in 1899 August Schmarsow could say that "no art is so foreign to modern man as sculpture."

Thus the closed-in, angular and compact forms that we find in the works of Ernst Barlach (fig. 33), André Derain (fig. 35) at the beginning of the century and, not least, in those of Constantin Brancusi (figs. 1, 34), are to be understood as a reaction against the influence of painting, as a meditation on one of the age-old fundamentals of sculpture, the rendering not of the transient, momentary visual stimulation but of enduring and supra-personal values. Barlach's *Man Alone* (fig. 33), heavy, simplified forms carved in wood, portrays solitude not as a passing mood but as the lot of man. The sturdy mass of the body leaning to one side, imprisoned in its cloak, is a translation into sculptural terms of a statement concerning the nature of human existence. The need for formal clarity and firmness begins to preoccupy painters as well, many of whom turn for a time to sculpture. André Derain who in 1906, under Gauguin's influence, turned his attention to the so-called Negro sculpture, shuts up his *Squatter* (fig. 35) in the isolation of a rough-hewn block of stone. The solid block not only constitutes a formal postulate; it is also intended as an expression of the primeval and the original. Adapting Gauguin's words, one could say that in those years the compact hard volume was for many sculptors a "means of rejuvenation," the way back to human origins.

A similar tendency towards a naive expression of human life is to be found in Brancusi's almost contemporaneous *Kiss* (fig. 34), intended as a tombstone. The union of the man and the pregnant woman in the rectangular block is a union tense with contrary forces: the heaviness of the stone and the tenderness of the subject, symbols of life and death, the "primitive" form and the graceful composition. Brancusi gives full value to these polarities and yet fuses them into a whole.

While Derain and Brancusi equate the elementary human form to an object, a thing, Ewald Mataré's *Female Torso* (fig. 36), a headless statue in smooth, polished wood, is an attempt to conjure up a human presence and, at the same time, to transmute it into a "sign." The spare, almost sexless body, rigid under a taut surface, is charged with a heraldic meaning, becomes an emblem. The American Raoul Hague stresses, in a similar formal idiom, the magical aspect of metamorphosis. His torso (fig. 37) is a tree-trunk woken to life.

Marino Marini seeks an archaic, not a "primeval," effect in his lifesize *Dancer* (fig. 59),

33. Ernst Barlach

Man Alone, 1911
Wood Height 34 5/8″
Kunsthalle Hamburg
Photo: Dr. Wolfgang Salchow
Cologne

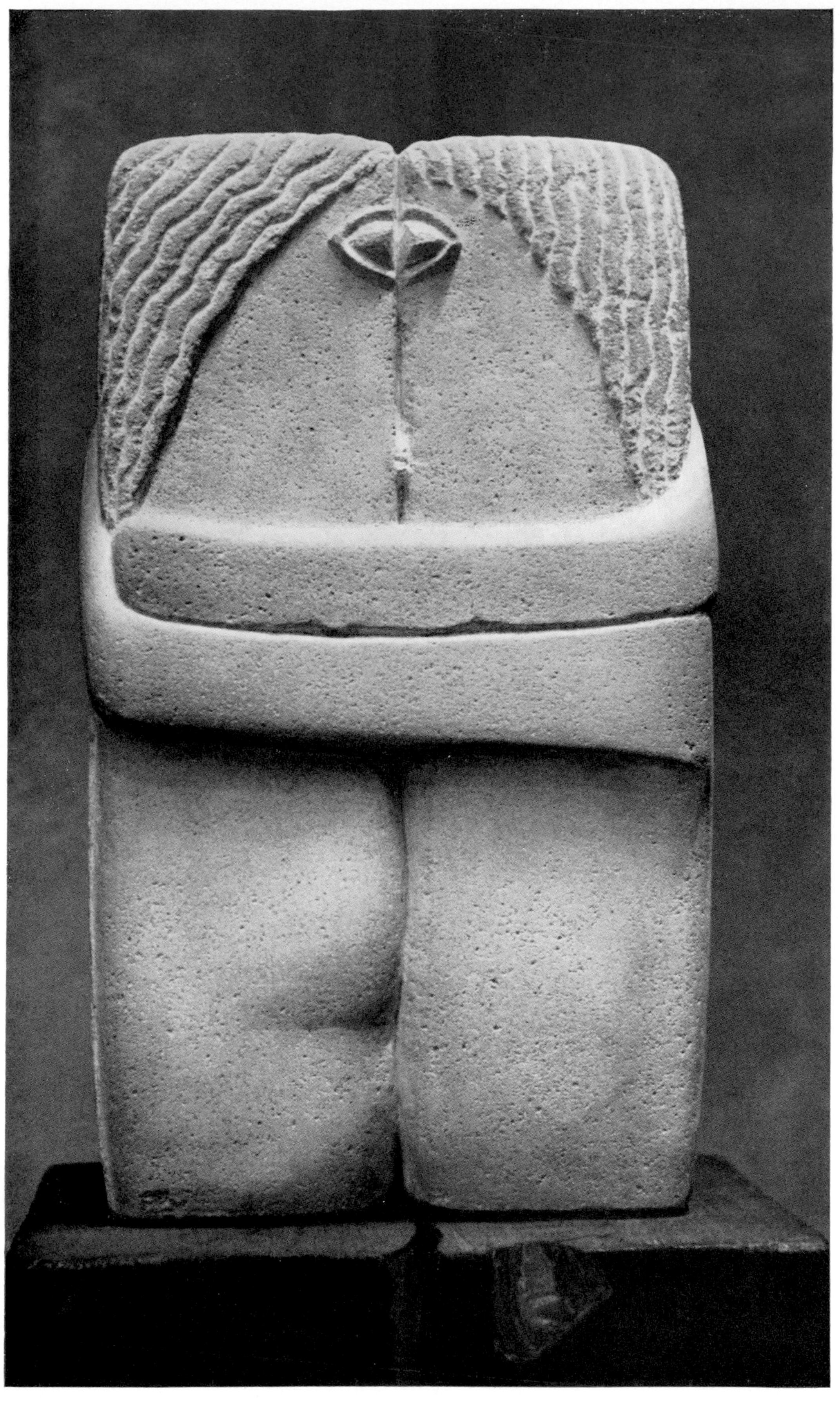

34. CONSTANTIN BRANCUSI The Kiss, 1908 Limestone Height 23″, Length 13″, Depth 10″
Philadelphia Museum of Art, Arensburg collection Photo: Author

35. André Derain Squatter, 1907 Stone Height 13″ D. H. Kahnweiler collection, Paris Photo: Author

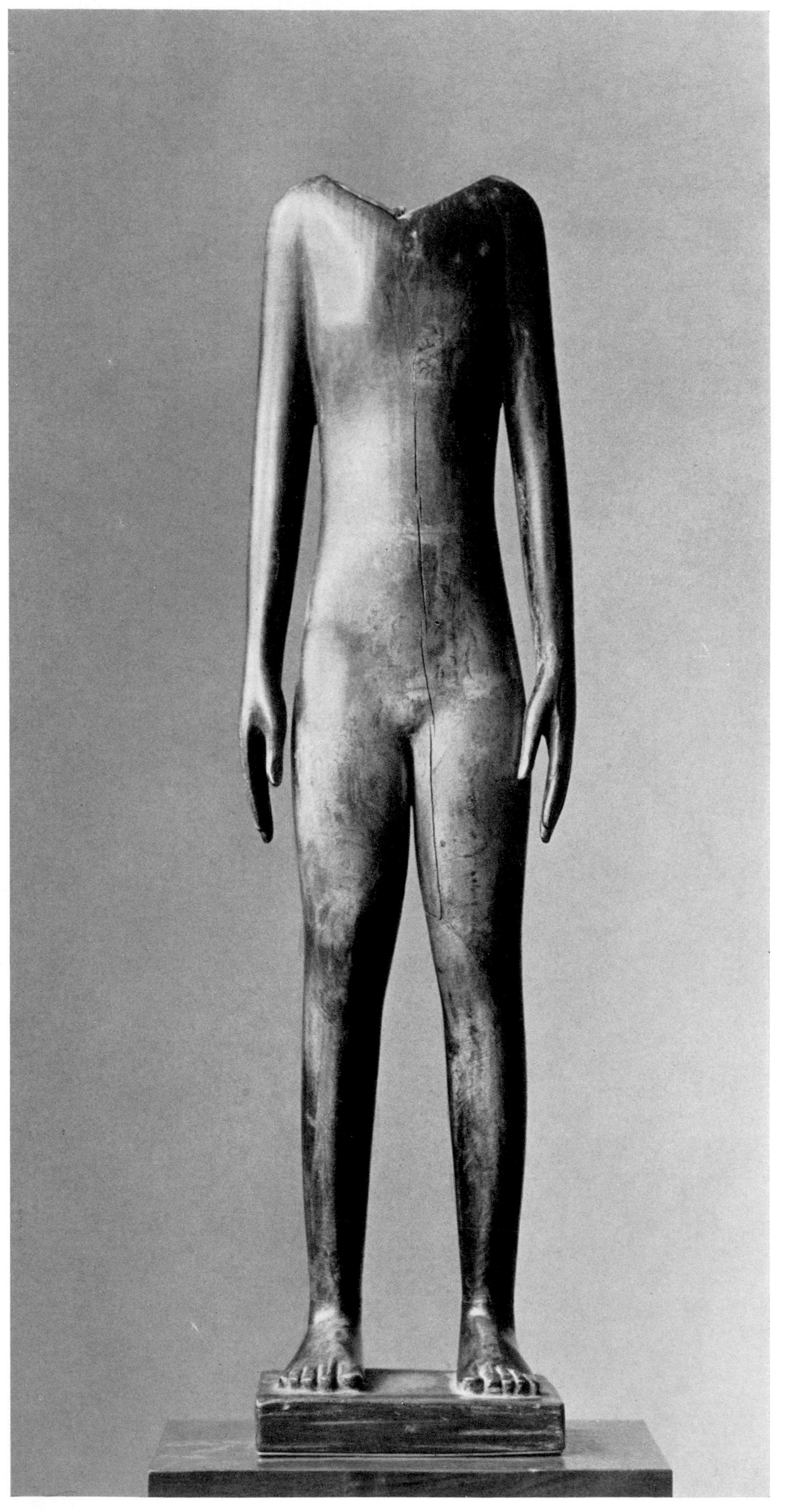

36. Ewald Mataré

Female Torso, c. 1926–28
Wood Height 22 1/4"
Lehmbruck Foundation, through the "Kulturkreis" Duisburg Museum
Photo: F. Hewicker, Kaldenkirchen

which might equally well be called Pomona. The artist sees woman as magna mater, as the embodiment of the fullness of life and the mystery of generation. The well-rounded, warm shapes of the body are maternal fertility itself. The stable stance is challenged by the dynamic pattern of colour.

Compared with Marini's elemental force, the nudes of his fellow countrymen, Marcello Mascherini (fig. 38) and Giacomo Manzù (fig. 39), are products of refined artificiality. However, Mascherini's figures with their thin joints, resilient limbs and sharply drawn outline have a certain inner energy which manifests itself in the mannered grace of their attitudes, while Manzù's girl, more reserved, displays a leisurely elegance in her arrested dance step. Quite different from these statues, each masterly in its kind, is Toni Stadler's *Eos* (fig. 40), a figure almost painterly in the fluidity of its forms, kneeling on both knees as though in the act of becoming conscious of its limbs.

Similarly relaxed, soft shapes, notwithstanding the clear modelling and articulation of the body, are to be found in the nudes of Edwin Scharff and Gustav Seitz. In Seitz' *Rosa in Bed* (fig. 41), the solemnity of the archetypal female becomes a humorous genre portrayal, without rendering the sculptural form in the least trivial.

The human bodies modelled by the young English sculptor, Anthony Caro, are likewise heavy, bulky masses; but they are in decay. Flabby flesh is ruthlessly exposed; its rank decomposition is to lead to new contacts with reality. The enterprise, intentionally abnormal and obviously absurd, deserves our attention: it is the experiences of Dada, Surrealism, abstract art and *art brut* that have brought Caro and his contemporaries to this anti-aesthetic extremism.

It would, however, be a mistake to take this attitude of protest as typical of the post-war generation of sculptors. For instance, the Italian Mario Negri rejects the softening-up of the body and all its implications, and gives his figures a more vigorous texture. The formal idiom of Lynn Chadwick's *Two Watchers* (fig. 42) expresses a comparable toughness and resolution: the two figures, a tense, crystal-hard phalanx, challenge the surrounding space and maintain themselves in it.

The possibilities of portraying the man of our time in sculpture are inexhaustible. This must be the reason, it seems to me, why the human figure continues to preoccupy the modern sculptor, whether his approach be constructive or destructive, in spite of the weight of tradition that, with his historical sense, he has to carry. It seems that the modern sculptor, in an arresting contrast to the modern painter, is each time confronted with the task of "creating the first man."

That the architecture of the human body can be portrayed as an abstraction may be illustrated by the works of two sculptors pursuing similar aims though their methods are distinct. The Swiss Hans Aeschbacher constructs his *Figure I* (fig. 44), of 1958, as a piece of ashlar masonry. Yet the figure is a monolith whose resistance the artist has to overcome without denying its strength. Red sandstone hardly lends itself to the carving of sweet nudes. The material imposes the form and determines what a stone figure is to look like: as an enduring monument and not an improvisation. On the other hand the force of the sculptor's informing will can be gauged from the bold diagonal across the middle. Here the ashlars could have slipped. But they are firmly knit together and held in position by a system of counter-weights, so that the figure stands immovable, a tower of rock fashioned by human hand.

Monumentality and architectural effects characterise also Fritz Wotruba's limestone figure (fig. 43) of 1959, more abstract than the Austrian artist's earlier works. The various parts, ascending in a powerful rhythm, are carved as a single block. Wotruba yields as little as Aeschbacher to the intractability of the material though, again as Aeschbacher, he recognises its nature. The stone must obey the sculptor, even swerve from the vertical when the intended form involves a challenge to tectonics. Thus even in the most solid piece of sculptured stone there is a point where the tension between form and material comes to a head, where the stability of the whole is jeopardised by a risk which the artist runs, even when as Wotruba and Aeschbacher he carves, as it were, for eternity. This readiness to take a risk is not least responsible for endowing Wotruba's stone figure with the quality of a living being.

Joannis Avramidis, a pupil of Wotruba, constructs his group of figures (fig. 45) with rigorous symmetry as a baluster-like shaft, a multiple unity. There may be an echo here of the rigidities of Byzantine art, perhaps also of the figures of Oskar Schlemmer, but the originality of plastic invention—a human group as a sheaf of columns—remains entire.

Étienne Hajdu's *Small Figure* (fig. 46) is also conceived as an anthropomorphic column, though with a more strongly emphasised rhythm of recesses which articulate the shaft. There is thus more openness than in Avramidis' introverted group, and the well-proportioned figure, like a caryatid freed from architectonic service, though it owes nothing to classical Greece, plays up with enchanting lightness to the anthropomorphic hints in the capital.

Wilhelm Loth's *Relief V/1959* (fig. 47), produced in Rome as one of a series of variations on the theme of the torso has no classical antecedents; nor is it a fragment. Loth has no antiquarian or archaeological interests and, as Ulrich Gertz has noted, his torsos are not synecdochal but wholes in their own right. Preserving at best distant memories of their derivation—vestigial hands or breasts—they have become artefacts to which anatomical criteria no longer apply. Neither fetish, nor idol nor sign—each of these has been a stage in the many metamorphoses that the human figure has undergone in our century—*Relief V/1959* interprets man in the widest, "romantic"

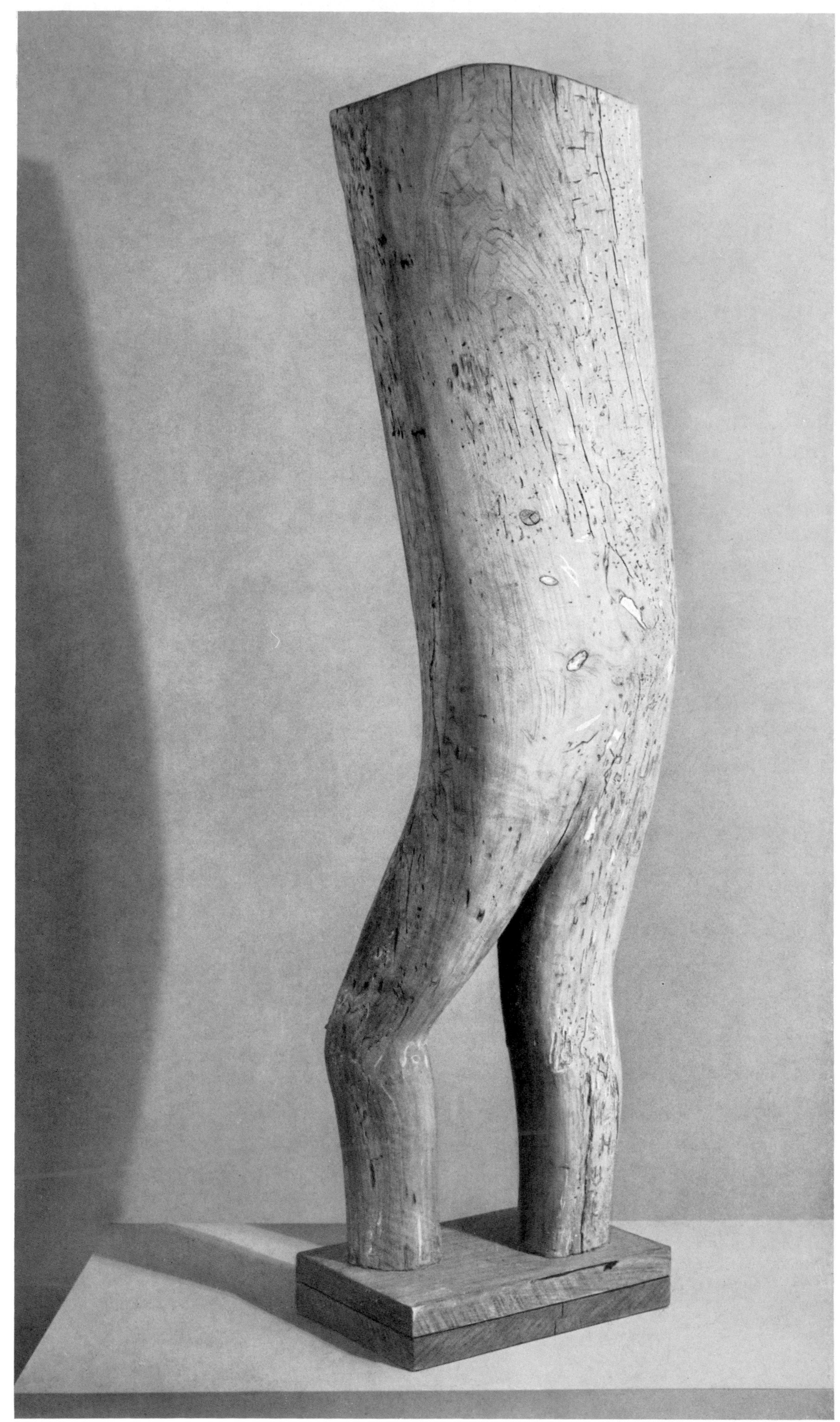

37. Raoul Hague

Ohayo Wormy Butternut
1947/48
Wood Height 66 1/2"
The Museum of Modern Art
New York
Photo: Museum

39. Giacomo Manzù The Dance Step, 1950 Bronze Height 63″
Middelheim Museum, Antwerp Photo: Jean de Maeyer, Antwerp

38. Marcello Mascherini

Heroic Torso, 1959 Bronze Height 63″
behind: Awakening Spring, 1954 Bronze Length 75″
Photo: Author

40. Toni Stadler

Kneeling Figure EOS, 1958 Bronze Height 59″
Lehmbruck Foundation, through the "Kulturkreis"
Duisburg Museum
Photo: J. Schmitz-Fabri, Cologne

41. Gustav Seitz Rosa in Bed, 1956 Bronze Height $7^{5}/_{8}$″, Length 15″ National Gallery, Berlin Photo: F. Hewicker, Kaldenkirchen

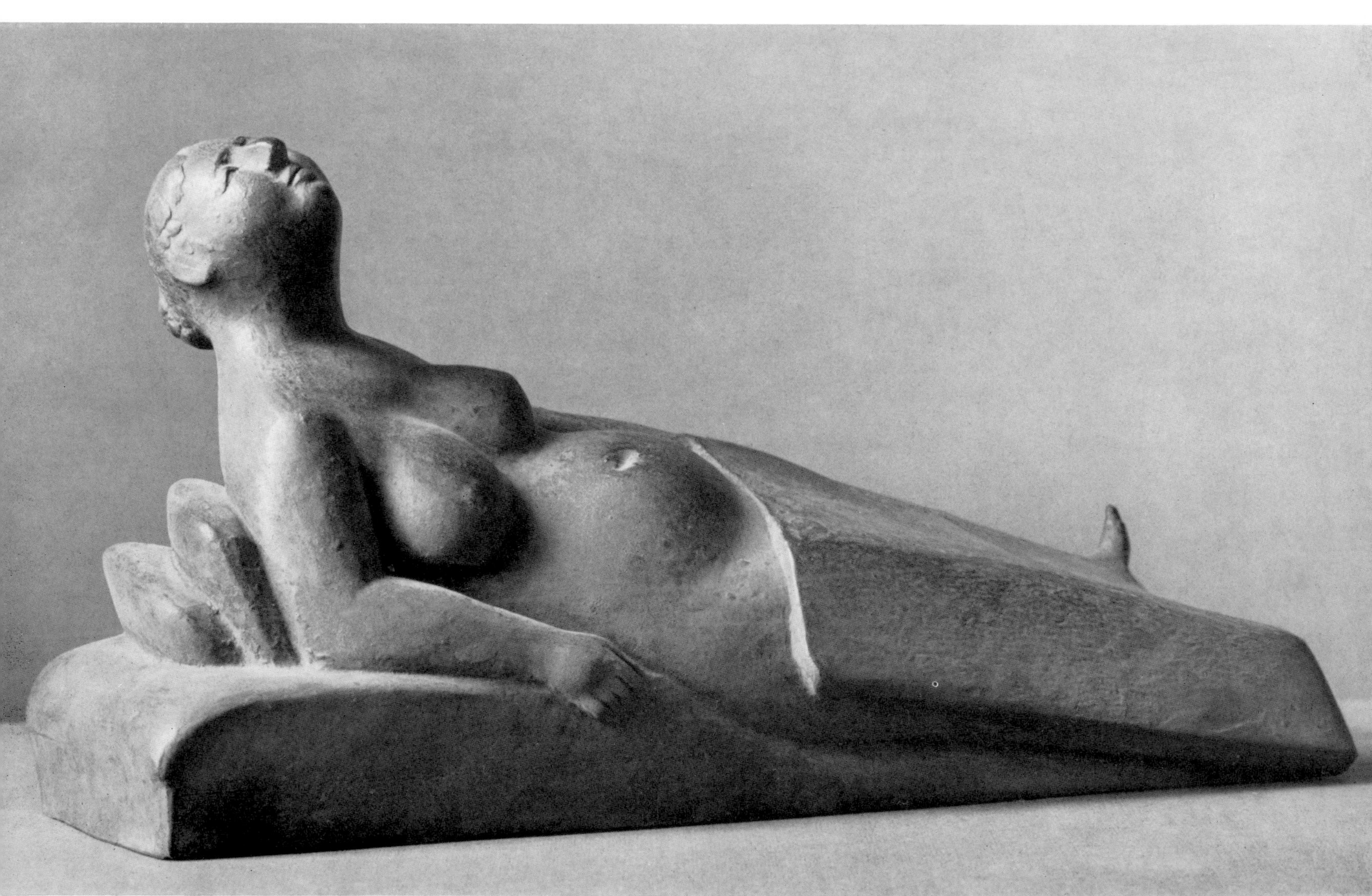

42. Lynn Chadwick

Two Watchers, 1958
Iron and plaster with iron chips
Height 19 5/8″
Dr. Ferdinand Ziersch collection, Wuppertal
Photo: Abisag Tüllmann, Frankfurt/Main

43. Fritz Wotruba Figure, 1959 Limestone Height 39 3/8", Length 26 3/4", Depth 19 5/8"
Photo: Elisabeth Speidel, Hamburg-Blankenese

44. Hans Aeschbacher Figure I (dedicated to Otto Müller), 1958 Red Sandstone Height 57 1/2″
Dr. Walter Bechtler collection, Zurich Photo: Author

sense as part of nature, identifying him with the earth and making him function as landscape.

Alberto Giacometti's *Leg* (fig. 48) in gilt bronze, planted on a high socle, surprises as, according to the artist, every authentic work of art should. It too is a torso, a theme which has long pre-occupied Giacometti. In his earlier work, beside heads and busts there are also arms and hands, and now (1959) this over-lifesize, long, thin leg with the already familiar active, tingling surface. What does the artist "mean"? Is it a macabre joke of the ex-Surrealist deriding monumental statuary?

We have Giacometti's own remarks on the problem of the autonomous fragment. As Pierre Courthion tells us, already as a student at the academy, the artist had confined himself to drawing models' feet. His contention is that a figure cannot be grasped in its totality; the living whole is not a sum of details. Hence the concentration on a part whose function is to evoke the whole. "I cannot see simultaneously the eyes, hands and feet of a person standing two or three metres away from me, but the individual part that I look at brings home the existence of the whole." And so too the spectator proceeds from the initial astonishment to recreate the figure that the fragment suggests. Inviting others to participate in his creativity Giacometti, it has been said, is more a poet than a sculptor.

The examples discussed so far have been characterised by compactness of volume clearly set off against the surrounding space. Those to follow will be considered from the standpoint of communication with space or of the participation of space in their existence. The first, Aristide Maillol's early work, *La Méditerranée* (fig. 49), can only be admitted on certain terms. Maillol's figures are solid and compact, a reaction, at the turn of the century, against the debilitating influence of painting. Yet the seated woman with her strong, rounded limbs can be described as an open composition. The clear articulation of weight and support recalls a Greek temple, as does the system of closed and open "plastic areas." The side view brings this out particularly well: the figure seems to be contained in an imaginary cube. In her classical proportions and her self-assured calm *La Méditerranée* embodies an antique principle of order. As André Gide has put it, "No thought disturbs her; no passion stirs in these strong breasts." Balanced and impersonal, this-worldly and monumental, she is the perfect woman adequately objectified in a form that is at once solid and open.

Hans Mettel's cast for his large *Seated Man* (fig. 50) is a piece of architecture in space. The symbolism professed by his contemporary, Maillol, does not apply to this rigorous composition whose figurativeness is abstract to a degree. Mettel's prime concern is proportion, the rhythmical structure of the whole, both the mass of the body and the areas of void enclosed by the limbs and intended to communicate with external space. Anatomical detail is reduced to a minimum. As I said in my *Moderne Plastik*, in connection with another work of the artist, Mettel seeks to portray man not as an individual but as a position in a system of co-ordinates—a metaphor for the reduction of the individual to an anonymous cipher in the order of our world, perhaps also a challenge to it.

In the elaborately articulated structure of *Prometheus Bound,* a bronze by Gerhard Marcks, now at the Wallraf-Richartz Museum in Cologne, an architectural conception is also apparent. Arms, legs and the trunk bending forward make up a composition characterized by a lively rhythm and with numerous overlappings. In contrast to Mettel's figure, integrated in a static order, the *Prometheus* struggles to break out. Adolf Rieth has accurately described it as a "spatial image of distress."

Karl Hartung's over-lifesize *Thronoi* (fig. 51) is both figure enthroned and throne. The gnarled beams and buttresses form an open, grotto-like structure, a kind of human tabernacle enshrining the hopes and fears, memories and premonitions of man. The ambiguity and the iconographic filiations of this monumental figure have been acutely analysed by Carl Linfert in his monograph on Hartung (in *Junge Künstler* 1959/60): "It is a throne. The sculptor (in conversation with me) has hinted at the thrones in the biblical hierarchy of angels as a possible source. I would elaborate this hint and cite the thrones with a book lying on them (in Early Byzantine mosaics which attest a highly developed angeology). The idea can be illustrated by other examples—the Renaissance allegories of the *trionfi,* Baroque scrolls of the most varied kind, any triumphal arch; a central space is left empty in expectation of a venerable or sacred presence which can either manifest itself or remain hidden. In Hartung's throne it remains hidden."

Similar archetypal and monumental elements appear in the seated *King and Queen* by Henry Moore (fig. 52), a work on the borderline between the figurative and the abstract. The artist's intention, as he himself has stressed, is not to portray a specific royal couple but to evoke the archaic idea of kingship as such. Moore adds: "The 'clue' to the group is perhaps the head of the King which is a head and crown, face and beard combined into one form and in my mind has some slight Pan-like suggestion, almost animal, and yet, I think, something Kingly."

Anonymous, mythical beings confront us in the large *Diarchy* by Kenneth Armitage (fig. 53). The two figures are fused into one body or, more exactly, into one upright plate with illegible signs scratched in it. Summary indications of breasts, and stumps of arms and legs protrude with surprising plasticity; the high held heads are merely hinted at. As a whole the composition takes almost no account of space; the body of the figures is a façade and their physiognomic expression has to be read from it, from its wrinkled skin grooved like the die of a stamp block. Primeval and hieratic, *Diarchy* appears as a monument of a primitive culture long since lost.

45. Joannis Avramidis

Group of Figures, 1959
Bronze Height $33^7/_8$"

46. Étienne Hajdu

Small Figure, 1957
Pentelic marble Height $20^{1}/_{2}$"
Width $7^{1}/_{8}$"
Photo: Rogi-André, Paris

47. Wilhelm Loth

Relief V, 1959
Bronze Height $17^{3}/_{4}$"
Length $23^{5}/_{8}$"
Dr. H. J. Imiela collection
Darmstadt

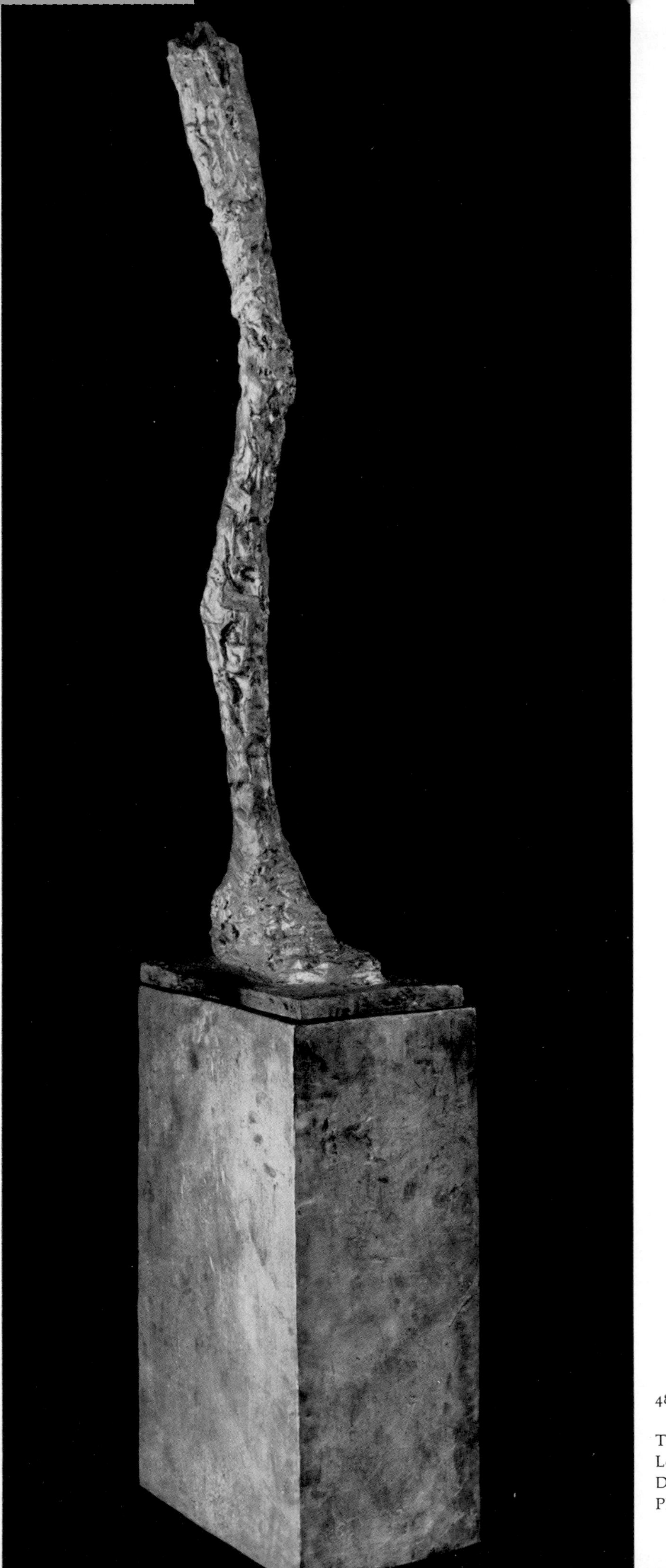

48. Alberto Giacometti

The Leg, 1959 Gilt bronze Height (with base) 86 1/4"
Lehmbruck Foundation, through the "Kulturkreis"
Duisburg Museum
Photo: Dr. Wolfgang Salchow, Cologne

The conception of the human body as an architecture of limbs is represented in German sculpture chiefly by Wilhelm Lehmbruck *(Youth Ascending; Fallen Man)*. Moving in Lehmbruck's wake, Hermann Blumenthal attempts to apply this abstract formula to the portrayal of men as he sees them in his environment. As against Lehmbruck's bolder conception, which I have described as "constructive expressionism," there is in his *Meditating Youth* (fig. 54) a definite emphasis on the solid body. Lehmbruck strives to rise to the transcendental through disembodiment; the creations of Blumenthal, a student of the industrial worker as a human type, remain on the ground.

The peculiarly Latin elements in the modern attitude to plastic form are well exemplified in the bronzes of Emilio Greco (fig. 55). To the soft, full modelling of the main parts of the body are opposed the tense, boldly stretched-out limbs, especially the pointed arms turned outwards, with an almost linear sharpness of outline. The tension is heightened by the twist of the trunk which propels the figure with centrifugal force into the surrounding space. Like Mascherini, Greco invites comparison with Mannerism not only in regard to formal idiom but also to spiritual attitude. His statues, at once formalist and natural, diagnose a dichotomy in the existence of modern man.

Henri Laurens, one of whose Cubist compositions has already been discussed (fig. 31), turned in his later work to stable solid shapes. However, in the *Great Amphion* (fig. 56) he boldly combines the powerful mass of the body with areas of shaped void. Amphion, son of Zeus and Antiope, built the walls of Thebes by the music of his lyre whose beauty moved the stones into place. Thus the theme of the composition is architecture born of music or, as Henri Focillon puts it in his *Éloge de la main*, the "effortlessness of work performed according to musical rhythm." The declamatory play of the hands reaching out into space and the stable architecture of the body are the determining "motifs"; they reappear, ambivalently combined, in the centre of the figure which is at once string instrument and fluted column shaft.

Ossip Zadkine's *Small Orpheus* (fig. 57) comes from a kindred world. But the restrained expression observable in the last few examples yields here to dramatic gesticulation and baroque overstatement. In a Surrealist conflation Orpheus' body becomes his instrument, opens up into a lyre (Zadkine calls his piece *personnage-instrument*). Music, song, plaint and the hero's tragic fate are simultaneously conveyed. The broken-up solid is thus not only formally significant but carries a representational, mimetic value.

Henry Moore's *Internal and External Forms* (compare fig. 5) have already been mentioned in the first chapter. The artist applies them not only in his abstract works but in his naturalist pieces as well, e.g. the *Draped Reclining Woman* (fig. 58). To quote

Moore's own words: "When the sculptor understands his material, has a knowledge of its possibilities and its constructive build, it is possible to keep within its limitations and yet turn an inert block into a composition which has a full form-existence, with masses of varied size and section conceived in their air-surrounded entirety, stressing and straining, thrusting and opposing each other in spatial relationship—being static, in the sense that the centre of gravity lies within the base (and does not seem to be falling or moving off its base)—yet having an alert dynamic tension between its parts."

This profession of the artist makes it clear to what extent even a representational work is for him a question of form. Whether he is portraying a naturalist female figure of classical monumentality or shaping "internal and external forms," Moore's theme is plastic form, the information of matter.

There are no holes in the body of the *Reclining Woman* as there are, for instance, in the large UNESCO figure (fig. 210), but the theme of the shaped void is not absent. The function of the drapery is formal, not decorative. It enhances what Moore calls the "forces pressing from inside," the movement of its folds, large and small, sweeps the heavy mass of the body upwards, and, where it adheres to the body, it emphasises the protruding parts.

Moore's reclining female figures with their calm flow of monumental form have an epic quality about them. Marino Marini on the other hand—his dancers (fig. 59) and Pomonas apart—explores the dramatic possibilities offered by horses and horsemen. In the *Miracolo* (fig. 60), the collapsing horse and the falling rider are caught in an architectonic formula of tense concision. Along the drawn-out downward line from the head of the man to the muzzle of the animal—the highest and the lowest point in the composition—the drama of both is being played out. According to Marini the rider must succumb, a symbol of humanity nearing its doom. But in his last despairing effort to hold himself up he is also perhaps defying that doom.

The search for primeval idioms of expression has taken modern sculptors far afield. Not only have they explored the archaic and prehistoric cultures of Europe and Asia in pursuit of the origins of sculpture, they have also discovered the primitive art of "unhistorical" peoples, those of Africa, the South Sea Islands and the two Americas—hitherto the exclusive domain of ethnographers.

The "Negro style" as a historical phenomenon, originating with the Cubists and the Expressionists, need not be discussed here. What is relevant is its influence on the work of individual artists. How liberating and fructifying it could be appears in a relatively late Cubist work, Jacques Lipchitz' *Figure* (fig. 61), dating from the years 1926 to 1930. In this monumental bronze totem, made up of positive and negative, convex and concave forms, the artist has attempted to preserve for our disenchanted

49. ARISTIDE MAILLOL La Méditerranée, 1902 Marble Height 40½″ Tuileries, Paris Photo: Author

50. HANS METTEL Seated Man, 1954 Plaster for bronze Height $25^{1}/_{4}''$, Length $10^{5}/_{8}''$, Depth $16^{1}/_{2}''$
Photo: G. Hauck, Frankfurt/Main

51. Karl Hartung

Thronoi, 1958–59
Plaster for bronze
Height 94 1/2"
Lehmbruck Foundation
through the "Kulturkreis"
Duisburg Museum
Photo: Gnilka, Berlin

53. Kenneth Armitage

Diarchy, 1957 Bronze Height $68^1/_2$″
Arnold H. Maremont collection, Chicago Photo: Author

52. Henry Moore King and Queen, 1952/53 Bronze Height $64^5/_8$″ Photo: Author

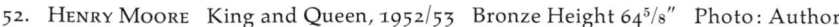

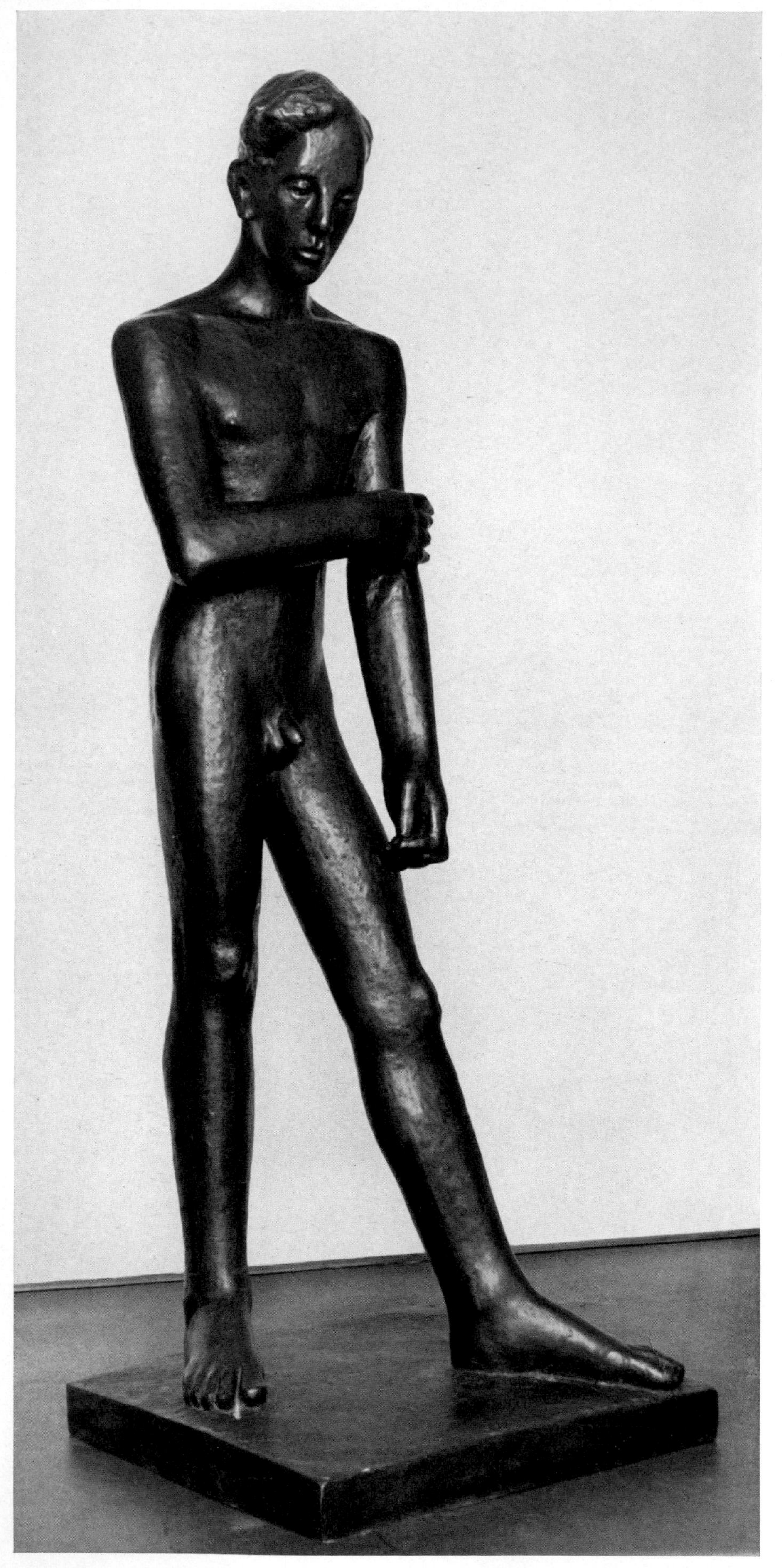

54. Hermann Blumenthal

Meditating Youth, 1929 Bronze Height $68^1/_2$"
Lehmbruck Foundation, through the "Kulturkreis"
Duisburg Museum

55. Emilio Greco

Large Female Bather No. 2
1957
Plaster for bronze
Height $89^{1}/_{2}$″

56. Henri Laurens

Great Amphion, 1952 Bronze Height 86 5/8"
Lehmbruck Foundation, through the "Kulturkreis"
Duisburg Museum Photo: Galerie Louise Leiris, Paris

57. Ossip Zadkine

Small Orpheus, 1948 Bronze Height $82^{5}/_{8}$"
Lehmbruck Foundation, through the "Kulturkreis"
Duisburg Museum Photo: Marc Vaux, Paris

58. Henry Moore Draped Reclining Woman, 1957 Bronze Height 53 1/8", Length 81 1/8" Bayrische Staatsgemäldesammlungen, Munich Photo: Author

and rationalist world the "solemn" quality that Nietzsche discerned in African art, its magic and incantatory power.

Archaism as a mode of expression, not as borrowed form, characterises the figures of the Austrian Rudolf Hoflehner (fig. 62). In contrast to other sculptors working in iron, Hoflehner does not treat his medium as infinitely ductile and malleable, does not forge and weld it but seeks to respect its "ironness." He composes cyclopic figures by piling massive blocks of raw iron on top of one another (they are secured by soldering), and it is the weight and thickness of the material, not an imposed shape, that he brings into play. Recently Hoflehner has taken to splitting his blocks into pairs of slender volumes with a recess or opening between them; this brings out the massiveness of the iron even more forcefully. Hoflehner's aim is the statue in the strict sense, as firm and immovable as ever there was one. His figures, colossal and stable, which are meant to be viewed from all angles, are designed to contradict the fleetingness of appearances in space, to attest the permanence of the spiritual act.

To Hoflehner's figures, motionless yet active, may be opposed the contemplative passivity of *The Self* (fig. 63), an iron piece by the American Isamu Noguchi. Its simple forms express spiritual self-sufficiency, inner concentration and calm—values for which, it can safely be surmised, Far Eastern art could offer many parallels. That Noguchi's *Self* speaks in an abstract idiom needs no particular explanation.

The portrayal of the human figure in plastic form interests sculptors of all persuasions, not only those who incline to figurative art. Hans Steinbrenner pursues the theme in his wood compositions (fig. 64) with their paired voids enclosed by gesticulating limbs, as does Étienne-Martin in his *Large Couple* (fig. 65), also in wood, an accumulation of heavy, massive shapes, partly figurative, designed to convey human vitality.

But the condition of man can also be seen as one of lyrical detachment, removed from all dramatic action, magic incantation or speculative thought. *In the Morning Wind* (fig. 66) by the Milanese Carlo Ramous may serve as an example. Yet another interpretation appears in the "beautiful" pose elaborated by Alberto Viani, though the effect is often endangered by an unintentional suggestion of decay.

The extent of this danger is revealed when the veil of flesh falls away leaving a fragile, unstable skeleton, as for instance in the visionary figures of Germaine Richier, exposed to every external power. Her *Don Quixote with the Sail of a Windmill* (fig. 67) is a hero of solitude. Pushed to the edge of his world (here the plate of the pedestal), he wages his hopeless struggle against a ghost beyond his reach because it is a projection of himself. In a hard world only the untragical, self-assured *Hero* (fig. 68) of Seymour Lipton can maintain himself as a non-conformist. Hammered and forged out of metal plates, its forms recalling shields and viziers, the statue is composed of several dovetailing pairs of volumes sharply demarcated from the outside world by the scaly armour.

Something of the aggressivity of this "hero" can also be seen in an aluminium composition by Wander Bertoni (settled in Vienna), *Icarus* (fig. 69), with its pointed thrusts in every direction, or in the sharp edges and projecting angles of the marble rider (fig. 70) by Umberto Mastroianni, though this latter piece, of an obviously Futurist descent, seems to expend its energy inwards rather than outwards. The ebb and flow of the forms evokes a movement in battle.

The subject of figure in motion has been incidentally touched upon; it deserves consideration in its own right. The rendering of motion in a plastic medium makes greater demands on the artist's sense of mass and rhythm than the seated or standing figure. Edgar Degas possessed this sense in an eminent degree when, threatened with blindness and misunderstood as a sculptor, he was modelling his wax statuettes of dancers. Neglecting physiognomic and anatomical detail, Degas strove to capture the climax of a dance movement; the moment, that is, when the figure becomes a construction in space.

This moment does not occur in Ernst Ludwig Kirchner's *Dancer with Raised Leg* (fig. 71). The figure, an early work of Kirchner's (1912), from the best years of *Die Brücke*, moves only in verticals and within the spatial limits of the tree trunk out of which it has been carved. A stiff rhythm, set by the firmly planted right foot, rises along the intersecting diagonals of the limbs. Not only the formal idiom, to be accounted for partly by the hardness of the material (oak) and the technique of carving, but the whole conception suggest a primitive ritual dance, diametrically opposed in its contraction to the artistic equilibrations of a Degas.

The lead figure by Germaine Richier, called *The Top* (fig. 120) from its small and unimportant attribute which appears on the pedestal, advances with measured and solemn step towards an undetermined goal. Emaciated, with cracks in its skin, it emerges from the relative protection of its spatial home, defined by the backdrop (painted over by Hans Hartung) and the pedestal, to expose itself to the perils of the infinite. In this highly expressive and surrealistically disquieting work the tension between figure and space—solid form and unformed void—appears as one of the basic experiences of the modern sculptor who has found in space a new and absorbing challenge.

Germaine Richier has been called "sculptor of the terrible" and her fantastical art does seem to belong less to the Mediterranean which is her home ground than to some dark region of storms, monsters and forest demons. The metamorphoses and hybrids that she imagines occur also, for instance, in the forest representations of

59. MARINO MARINI

Dancer, 1949–58 Polychromed bronze Height 67¾"
Lehmbruck Foundation, through the "Kulturkreis"
Duisburg Museum
Photo: Dr. Wolfgang Salchow, Cologne

Max Ernst while recalling the figure style of Alberto Giacometti. In her conception of man and space Germaine Richier conveys a tragic outlook.

Detachment from the ground, apparent weightlessness achieved by converting mass into energy—these problems, after having preoccupied the Baroque sculptors, fascinate those of the 20th century. We encounter them particularly often in the work of Jacques Lipchitz, for whom the expressiveness of form is closely linked with symbolic meaning. The theme of Prometheus which Lipchitz has repeatedly treated since 1933 is thus to be understood as much in terms of the contemporary situation—dictatorship, atmosphere of crisis, danger of war—as in those of the artist's formal and compositional postulates.

Prometheus Overcoming the Vulture (fig. 72), a study by Lipchitz for the monument in front of the Ministry of Health and Education in Rio de Janeiro, is a composition of solid volumes and shaped voids in turbulent movement flying, or on the point of flying, above ground—and as such a very topical allusion in mythological language. Floating in the air like passing clouds are also the *Genii* by the Swiss Arnold d'Altri (fig. 73). Their heavy cement bodies, though unsymmetrically arranged, are so skilfully balanced against one another that the slender support, planted in an undressed stone, is hardly noticed. There is here, as in Lipchitz' composition, an attempt to translate a Baroque allegory into modern terms.

Reg Butler, on the other hand, makes no attempt to conceal the rods supporting his flying *Figure in Space* (fig. 74). Indeed he gives them an aesthetic significance in that they repeat in an abstract version the gyrating movement of the stretched-out figure. The open construction and the compact female body could be taken as a compendious exposition of the general theme of this book, form and space.

The problem of the sculptural rendering of motion is tackled by Gerhard Marcks in an early work, the *Pair of Runners* (fig. 75), and by the American Peter Grippe in an abstract composition, *Figure in Movement* (fig. 76). Marcks presents two men in full career. His main concern is with the rhythm of the moving limbs which are observed and "captured" in a characteristic moment. The serial repetition of the pattern—long running steps and steering arms—is left to the imagination of the spectator, not without guidance from the artist who gives in full the first alternation. This could indeed suggest that not two courses but successive stages of one are represented—an impression that is strengthened by the anonymity of the runners' faces.

If this interpretation of Marcks' work is accepted, we may consider as parallel Peter Grippe's attempt to render simultaneously what occurs in succession (fig. 76). The appearance in different positions of certain defined forms whose identity is consistently maintained fixes the consecutive stages of a movement. The simultaneity aimed at is not only spatial but—a Futurist trait—temporal as well in that the successiveness

60. Marino Marini Miracolo, 1954 Bronze Height 51 1/8", Length 66 7/8" Photo: Author

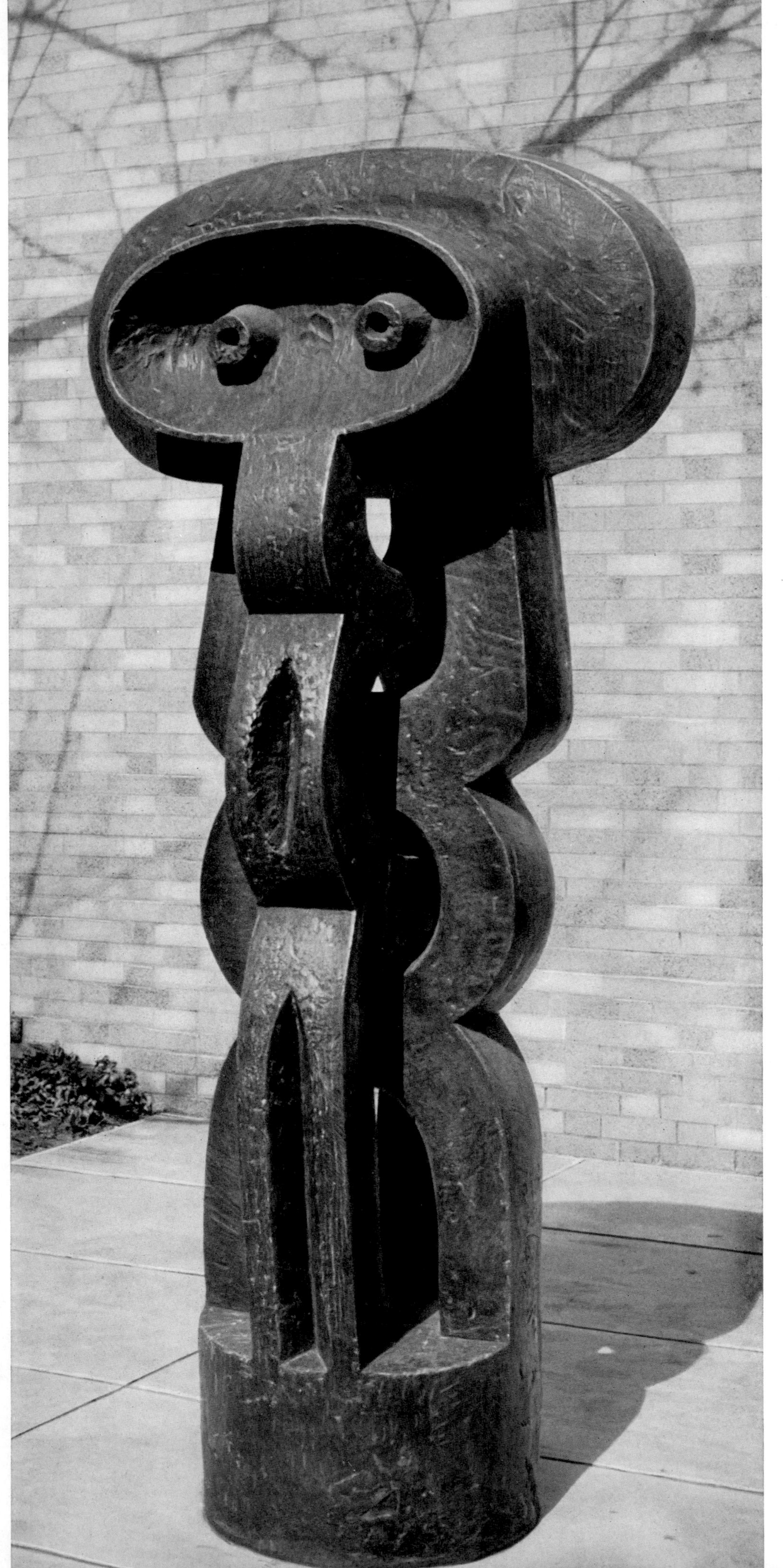

61. Jacques Lipchitz

Figure, 1926–30 Bronze Height 84⅝″
Museum of Modern Art, New York
Photo: Author

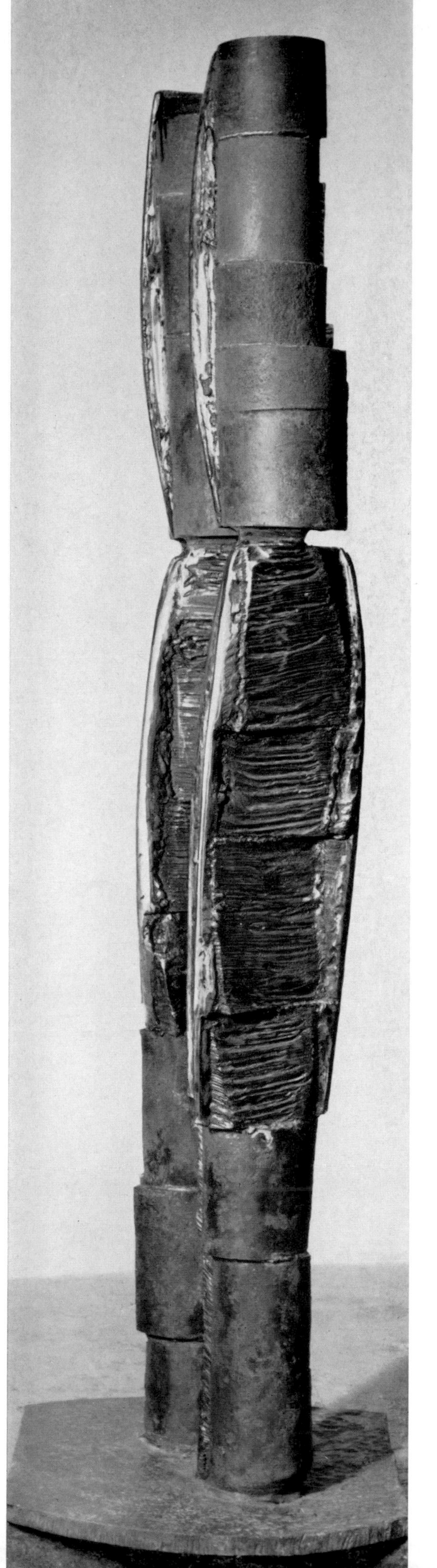

62. Rudolf Hoflehner

Doric Figure, 1958
Iron (solid) Height $73\frac{5}{8}''$
Zürich Museum

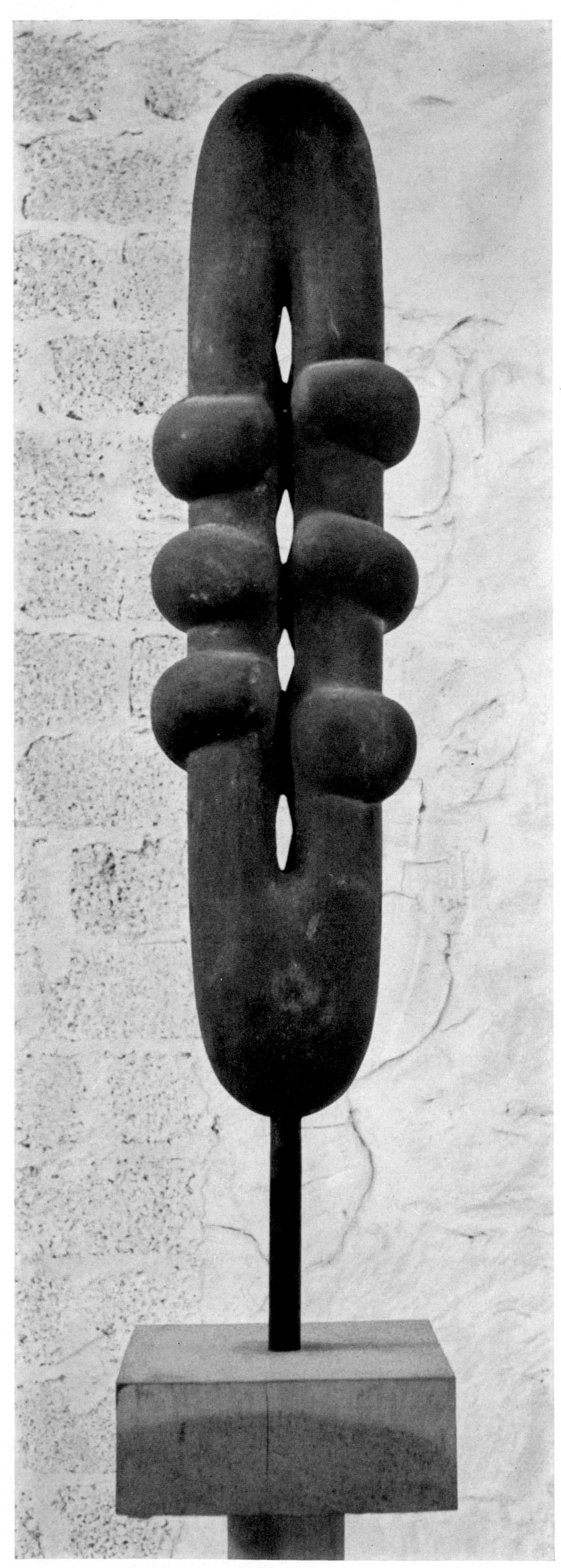

63. Isamu Noguchi

The Self, 1957
Iron Height 34″
Stable Gallery, New York
Photo: Author

64. HANS STEINBRENNER Composition, 1956 Elm wood Height 68⅞″
Middelheim Museum, Antwerp Photo: Author

65. ETIENNE-MARTIN

Large Couple, 1947
Elm wood Height $78^{3}/_{4}$″
Private collection, Paris

66. CARLO RAMOUS

In the Morning Wind, 1959
Bronze Height $37^{1}/_{4}$″
Photo: Paolo Monti, Milan

67. GERMAINE RICHIER

Don Quixote with the Sail of a Windmill, 1949
Gilt bronze Height 22 7/8″
Private collection Photo: Author

68. SEYMOUR LIPTON

The Hero, 1957 Nickeled silver on steel
Inland Steel Building, Chicago
Photo: Oliver Baker, New York

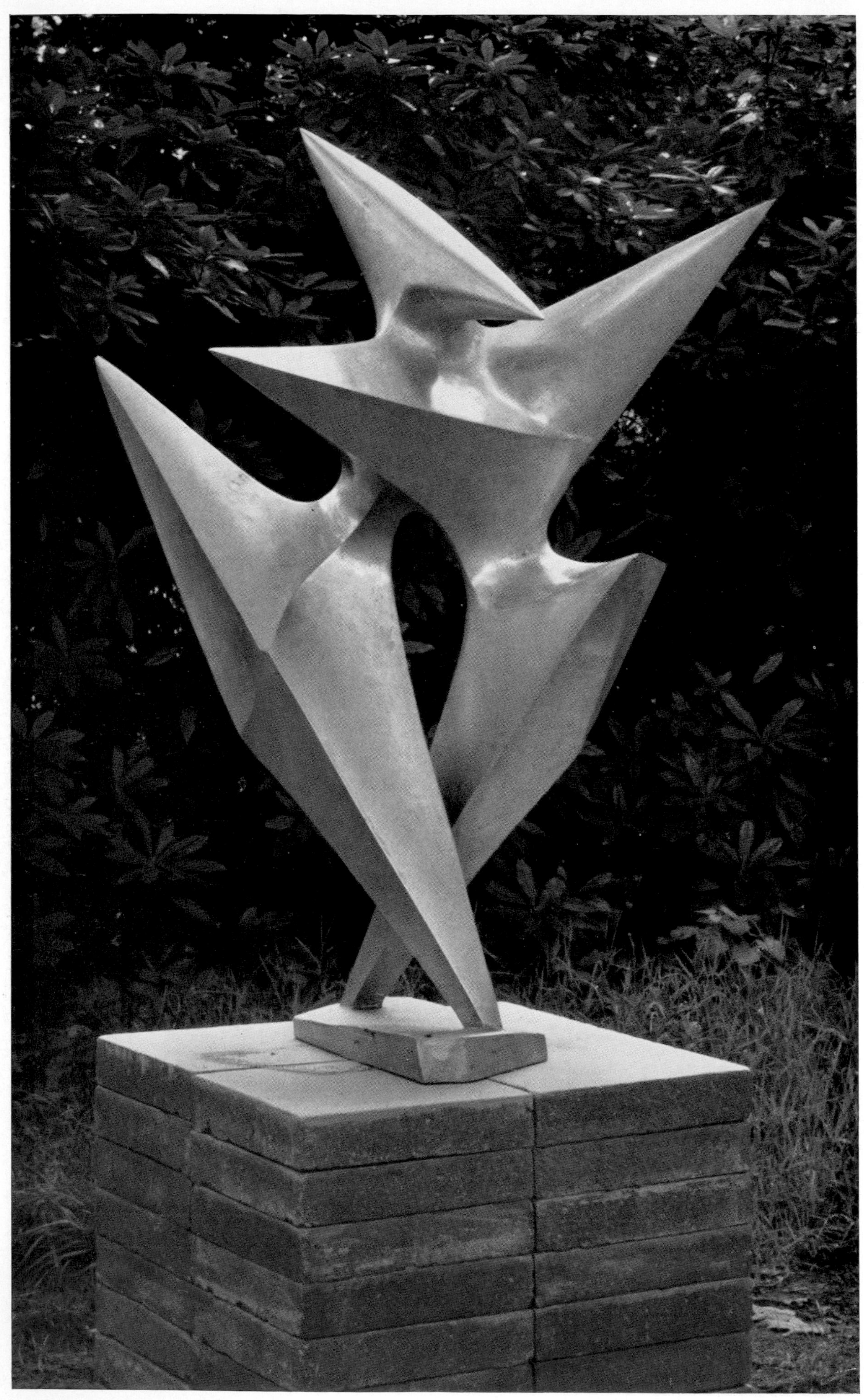

69. Wander Bertoni

Icarus, 1953
Aluminium Height 47 1/4″
Middelheim Museum, Antwerp
Photo: Author

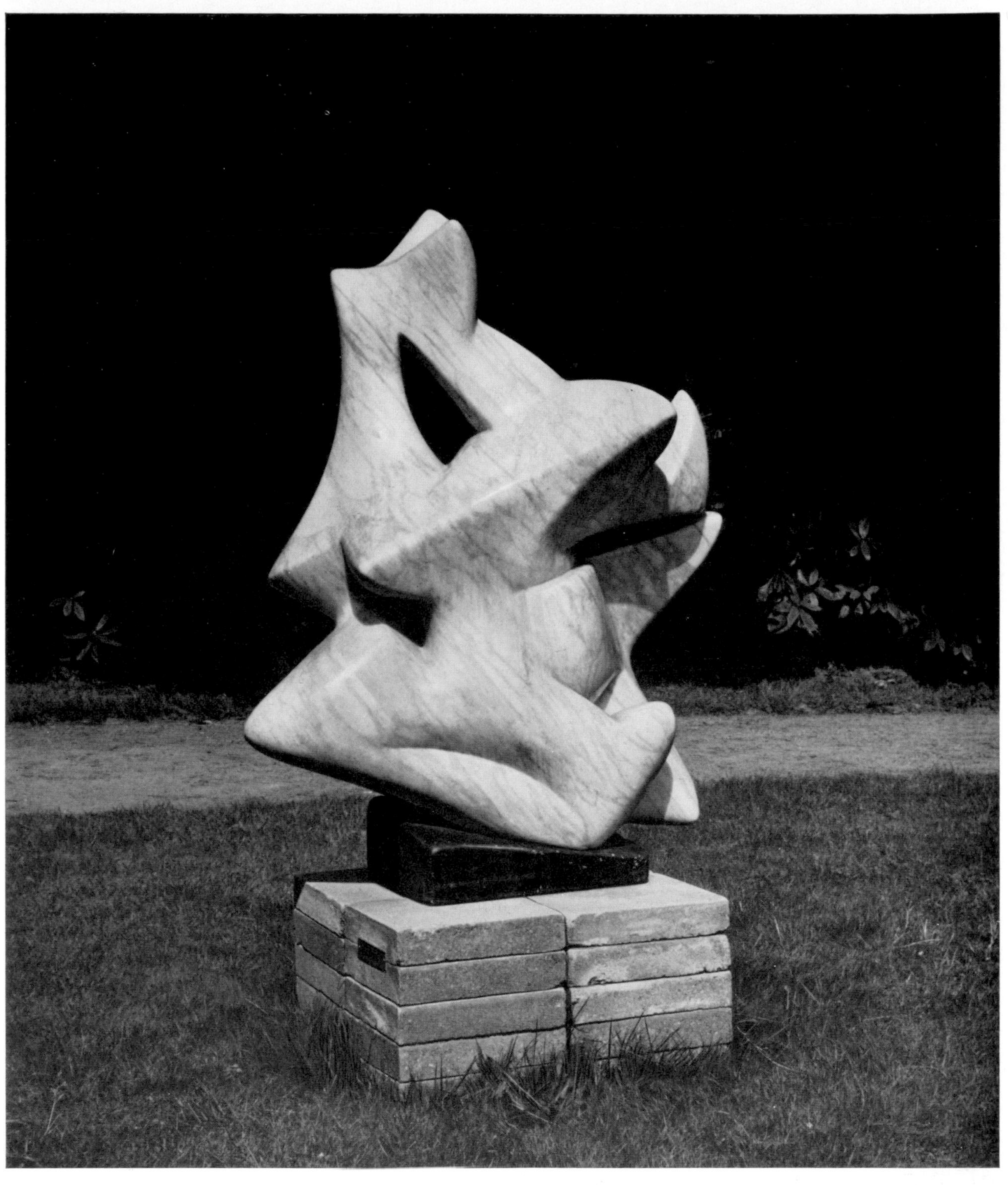

70. UMBERTO MASTROIANNI The Rider, 1953 White marble Height $53^{1}/_{8}$" Middelheim Museum, Antwerp Photo: Author

72. Jacques Lipchitz

Prometheus Overcoming
the Vulture, 1943
Bronze study Height *c.* 13¾″
Photo: Adolph Studly, New York

71. Ernst Ludwig Kirchner

Dancer with Raised Leg, 1912 Bog oak (painted) Height 26⅛″
Private collection By permission of the Stuttgarter Kunstkabinett
Photo: Author

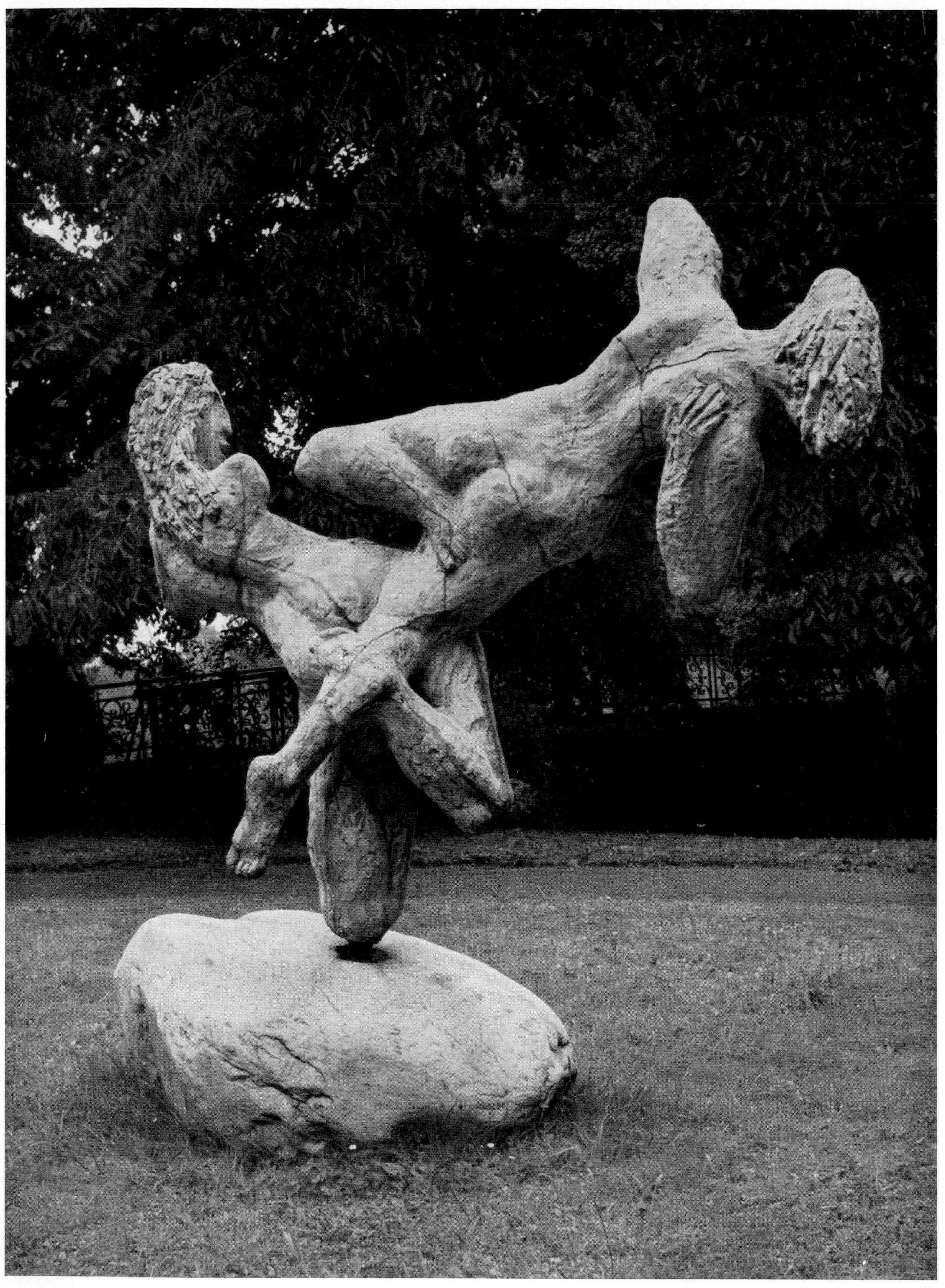

73. ARNOLD D'ALTRI Genii, 1949 Cement Height 86⅝″, Length 110¼″ Leverkusen Municipal Museum Photo: Author

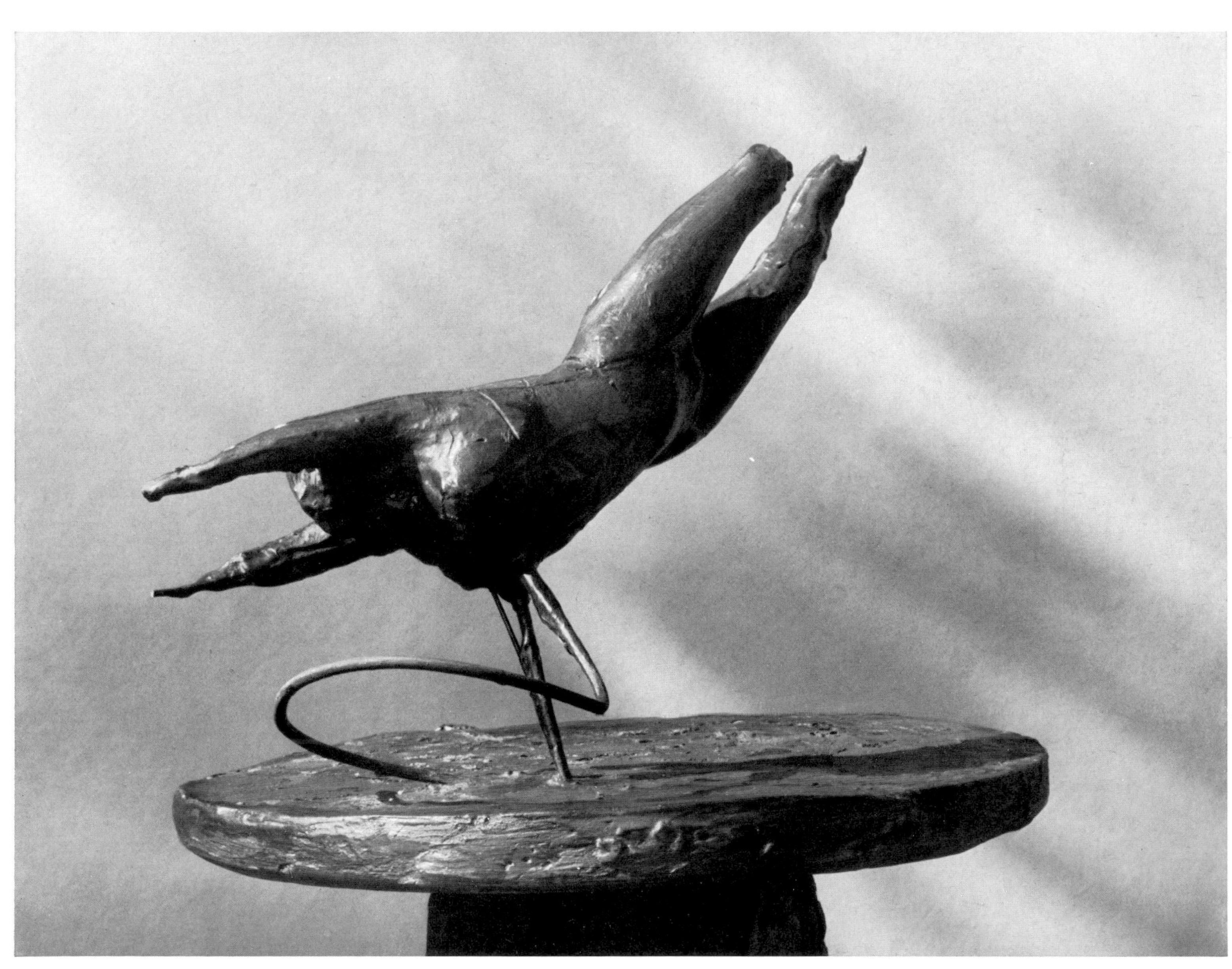

74. Reg Butler Figure in Space, 1959 Bronze Height $13^{7}/_{8}''$

75. GERHARD MARCKS Pair of Runners, 1923 Bronze Height 7⁵/₈", Length 7¹/₂" Dr. Walter Neuerburg collection, Hennef Photo: Author

76. Peter Grippe Figure in Movement, 1944 Bronze Height 12″, Length 13⁷/₈″, Depth 10″
Addison Gallery of American Art, Philips Academy, Andover, Mass., USA Photo: Andover Art Studio

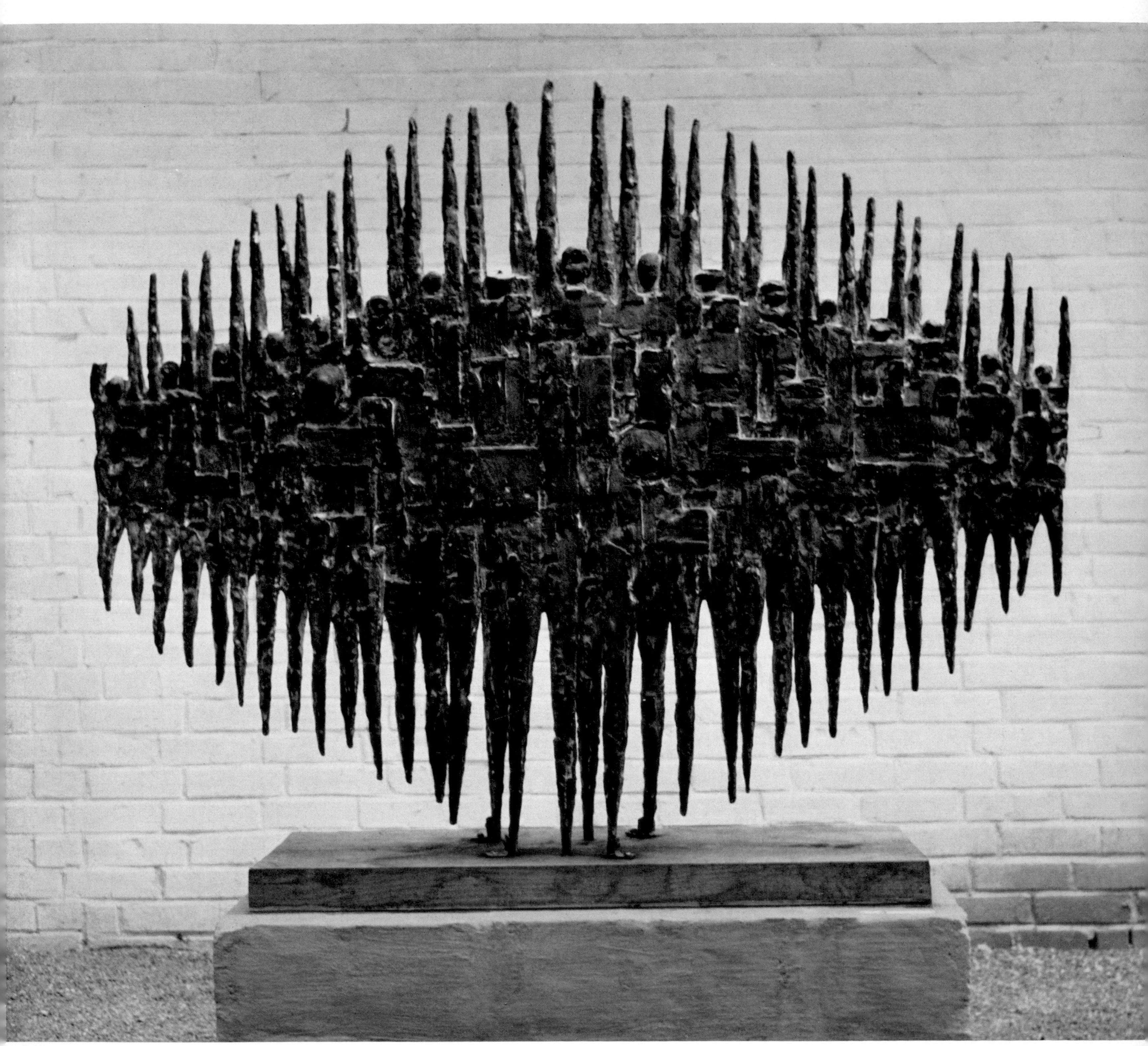

77. Drago Tršar The Demonstrators II, 1957 Bronze Height 53⅞", Length 66⅞" Photo: Author

represented relates both to the structure of the movement and to its duration. Thus the element of time, normally introduced in mobile constructions, is here rendered by static rhythms.

In its concern with modern man contemporary sculpture can hardly ignore the fact that it is dealing not only with the unique individual but also with the anonymous, fungible member of a mass society. Representations of crowds are not unknown in older sculpture, but it is only in the 20th century that the shapeless mass of human beings has claimed the artist's attention as a principal subject. Take for instance *The Demonstrators II* (fig. 77) by the Yugoslav sculptor, Drago Tršar. Tršar, with whom the motif is a recurrent one, has, however, integrated his crowd as a "sign," has given it a collective individuality.

What Tršar constructs as a relief, Fritz Koenig arranges in depth (fig. 79). With Koenig the several figures are also more distinct. The *Demonstrators* have one will which they proclaim in unison by one gesture. Koenig's *Group of Riders,* on the other hand, is a collection of individuals who, though all alike and, in one instance, grown together as Siamese twins, yet each preserve their autonomy, structurally articulated and defined in space by the rhythmical echelon deployment sideways and in depth.

Alberto Giacometti's fantastic painted bronze *Seven Figures—One Head* (fig. 78) is an even more individualised, indeed disparate assemblage. The tall and lanky human figures stand apart like trees in a thin wood—each on its own and without contact with the others. Here if anywhere is the sculptural simile for the existential situation of modern man, his isolation, his inability to communicate, his despair. Exposed to infinite space, passive and, in the strict sense of the word, vegetating, the seven figures and the solitary head are an epitome of human society—a futile nightmare in which the individual is condemned to suffer alone the common lot of solitude.

Groups of men engaged in discussion or negotiation, bathers, revolutionaries, spectators and listeners, or simply scenes of movement—this has been, for many years the repertory of the Nestor of contemporary German sculpture, Alfred Lörcher. Long unacknowledged, or not sufficiently well known, the work of the eighty-six-year-old artist is only now achieving the recognition that it deserves. The liveliness and directness of Lörcher's art are well exemplified by his *tachiste* relief *Troy in Ruins* (fig. 80) in which the wooden horse is the centre of a tumultuous scene enacted among the collapsing city walls.

Emil Cimiotti had a *Group of Figures* (fig. 81) in mind when he developed his open composition from the centre outwards—a cluster of human forms with pairs of legs standing closely spaced in a circle while bodies and arms open out in agitated gesticulation and, in an astonishing metamorphosis, begin to breathe as *one* body. It is hardly necessary to point out that in group compositions of this kind the inner logic of human forms is not binding. The artist's purpose is not to imitate his "subject" but to operate freely with what it has to offer.

This approach makes for, or brings out, a certain ambivalence in the interpretation of reality. Cimiotti's group of figures could equally well be seen as a plant, and the same applies to *One and Others* (fig. 82), a composition in painted wood by the American Louise Bourgeois. One could take it for a colony of mushrooms. The artist, however, knows better than to push the ambivalence in the direction of the excluded middle and thus deprive the work of the gay and serious poetry of strange and yet familiar objects standing close together, large and small, some in one colour, some striped or spotted, all similar to each other—except the One. This puzzling and witty invention can hardly have a sociological significance; it is much more like a fable—perhaps the fable of the white raven.

F. E. McWilliam remains closer to conventional reality, even though he translates the human figure into spatial schemata with radically altered proportions, as does the American artist Mary Callery whose group of *bozzetti* in the *Study for a Ballet* (fig. 83) and other group compositions embody various kinds of movement brought together in a choreographic conception.

It is a far cry from these scenes to the idyll of Pablo Picasso's *Bathers* (fig. 84) and an even farther one from that composition with its equivocations between satire, pastoral and drama to the *Petrified Crowd* of Claude Viseux (fig. 85). Yet an intelligible, if discontinuous, line of development in technique can be traced from the sketchy modelling of Lörcher to Picasso's lath figures stuck together in a rough-and-ready way, and from these again to Viseux' fantastic group made of straw wisps and, like the *Bathers*, cast in bronze for preservation. These sculptural essays in the problem of the human mass or crowd end inevitably in a surrealist masquerade or in the antithesis of the normal stability of sculpture, in its near dissolution.

The theme of the torso has already been touched upon. One of the most important and most frequent types is the bust or head; that is, in a narrower sense, portrait sculpture. However, the portrayal of a man's head or face alone has never been found as irritating as that of a limbless trunk or some other part of the body. The head is conventionally accepted as a synecdoche, for in it spirit, soul and character are supposed to be reflected. Thus this particular fragmentation of the human figure has been extensively practised in the past, and the examples that follow do no more than illustrate new ways of tackling an old problem.

Medardo Rosso tackles it as an Impressionist and elaborates a corresponding technique, modelling his *Lady with a Veil* (fig. 86) in wax. The face is a transitory appearance, schematic, evoked rather than present. Its plastic substance is slight; but how rich and subtle are the painterly effects extracted out of the soft material.

78. ALBERTO GIACOMETTI Seven Figures – One Head, 1950 Painted bronze Height 22 7/8", Length 22 1/2", Depth 18 1/8"

79. Fritz Koenig Group of Riders, 1956 Bronze Height 11 3/8", Length 21 5/8", Depth 11 3/4" On permanent loan from the "Kulturkreis" Brunswick Municipal Museum Photo: K. H. Steppe, Landshut

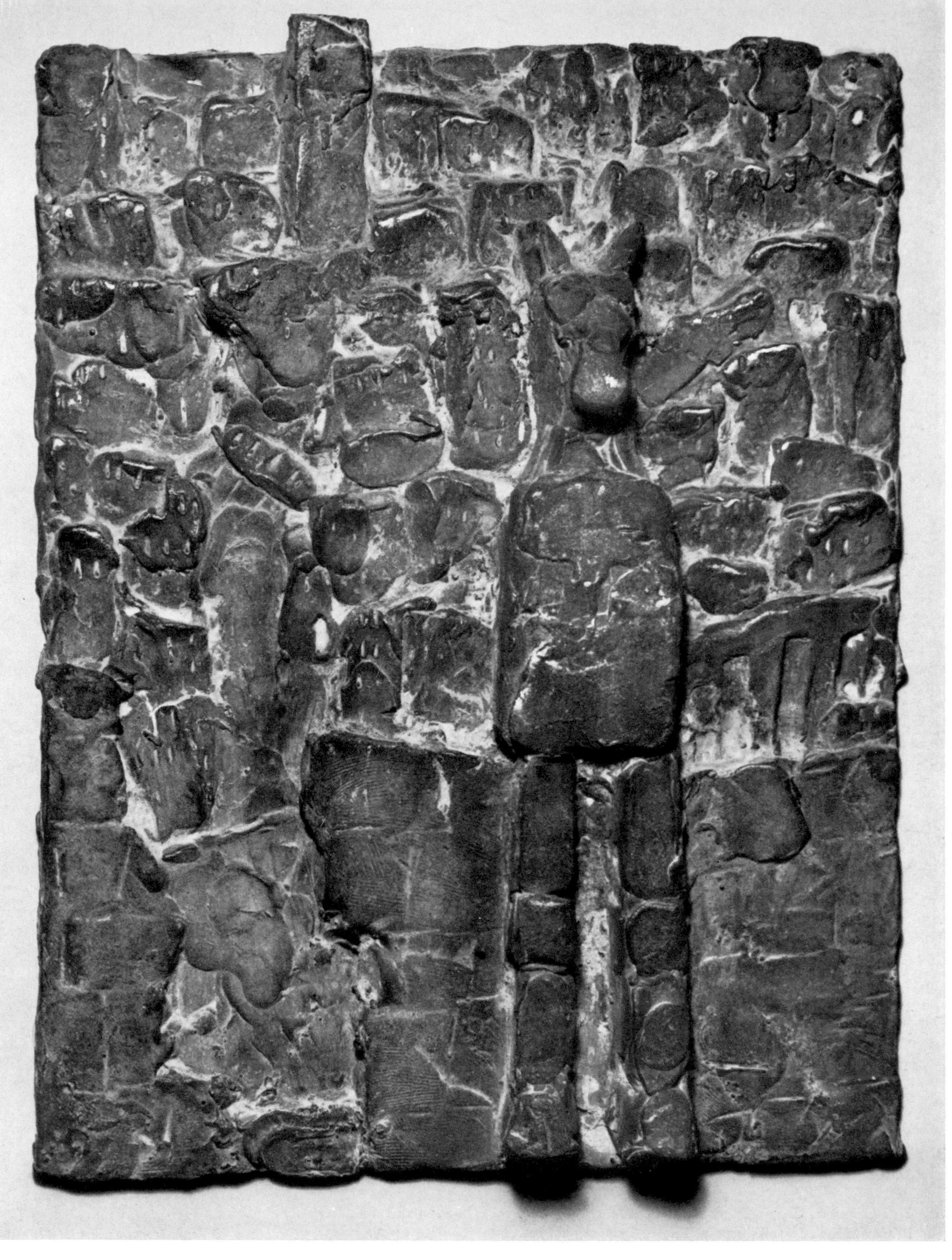

80. Alfred Lörcher Troy in Ruins, 1958 Bronze Height 11¾″, Length 9⅞″ On permanent loan from the "Kulturkreis" Bochum Municipal Museum Photo: J. Schmitz-Fabri, Cologne

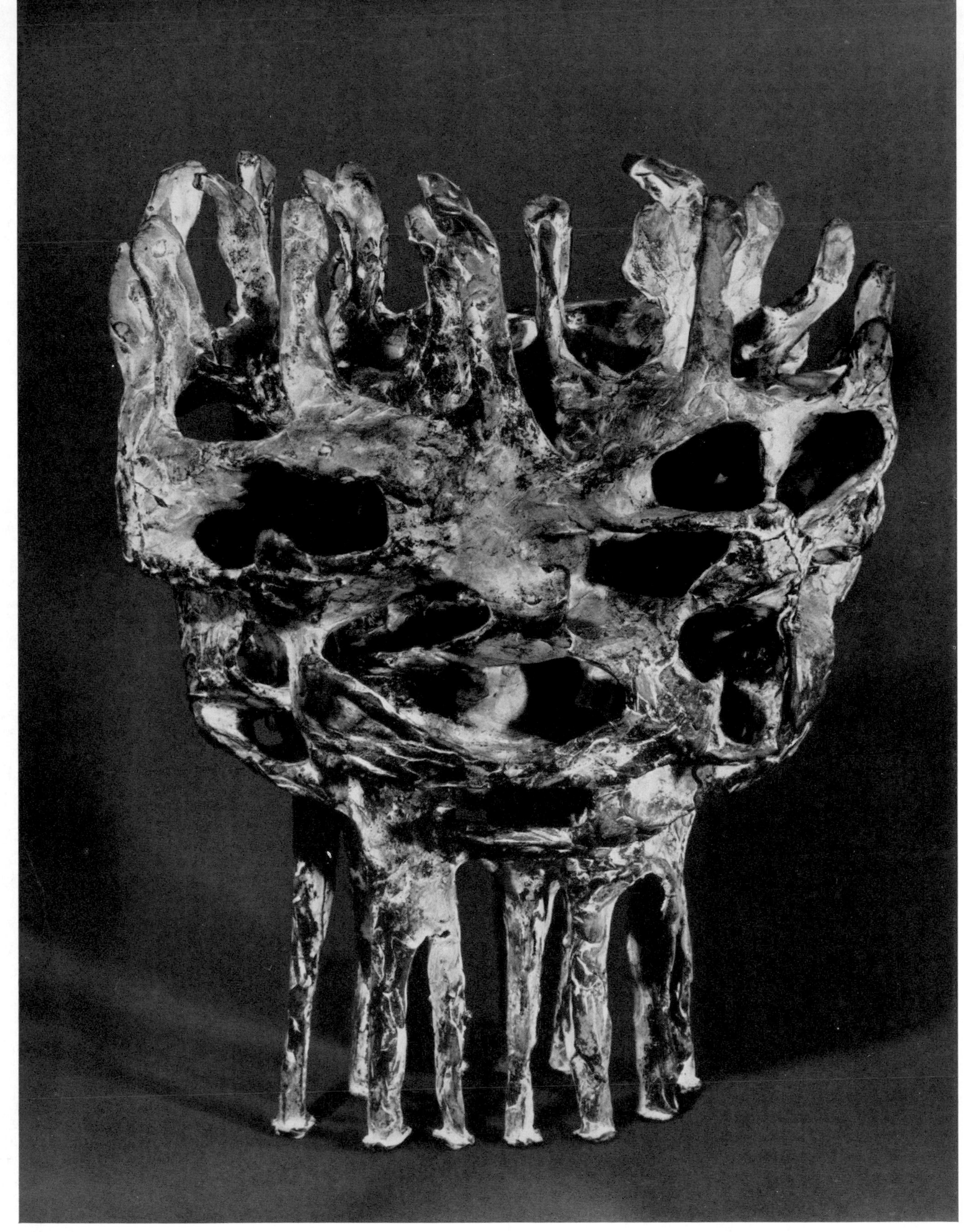

81. Emil Cimiotti Group of Figures, 1958 Bronze Height $15^3/_8$" On permanent loan from the "Kulturkreis" Brunswick Municipal Museum Photo: Dr. Wolfgang Salchow, Cologne

Painterly effects of light and shadow are also to be observed in the *Female Head* (fig. 87) by Picasso, but otherwise this Cubist piece with an objective, geometrical structure is the antithesis of the accidental, indistinct appearance of the *Lady with a Veil.* Amedeo Modigliani was even more radical in the reduction of his stone heads to elementary objective forms with a sharp emphasis on certain parts such as nose and eyes. In his stylisation he moved away furthest from the possibility of the individual portrait. He was harking back to the anonymity of Byzantine art.

But if Picasso's and Modigliani's heads have little to do with the individual portrait, it is not their Constructivist or Abstract tendencies that are responsible; for these are even more consistent in a relief of Antoine Pevsner's which he has called, none the less, *Portrait of Marcel Duchamp* (fig. 88), though we are not supposed to look for more than an ideal portrait with no claims to a striking likeness. Pevsner offers, as it were, a geometrical equation for the image of the great ironist and prince of Dada.

Alberto Giacometti also produced in his Surrealist period an abstract head. The thin, rectangular marble plate (now at the Stedelijk Museum, Amsterdam) represents an "absolute" profile which, like Jawlensky's heads *en face,* can be interpreted as a sign—here a sign of meditation. While Giacometti reduces his head to a quasi-geometrical form with only slight indications of a profile, Sergio Signori attempts in his *Portrait for Madame X* (fig. 92) a formal simile for the liveliness of a face. Drawing on the beauty of the costly material, he translates the features of his model into elegant, playful movements, the diastole and systole of volume endowed with breath.

Other sculptors have reverted to the orthodox portrait in search for a common denominator between autonomous form and likeness. Bernhard Heiliger finds it in his *Portrait of Ernst Reuter* (fig. 89), a solid volume activated from within. Three-dimensionality is characteristic of the model but it is no less a plastic phenomenon, a combination of moving surfaces. Heiliger, says Kurt Martin, translates the personal energy of the model into a plastic reality. Emy Roeder's *Self-Portrait* (fig. 90) is tauter than the rises and hollows softly flowing into one another of Heiliger's modelling. The skin adheres closely to the skull revealing its shape. The rigid construction and the incisive chiselling not only result in a particular formal type but convey something of the human quality of the model, here identical with the artist.

A careful balance of the "will to form" and receptivity to the medium can be discerned in the *Head* (fig. 91), carved in desert stone by the American Cornelia Runyon. Her work as an artist begins already with the choice of the stone. She picks the hardest specimens, even large half-precious stones common in her native parts, and observes them for a long time until they disclose their inner, exemplary form which she then, with patience and sympathy, proceeds to disengage. What emerges is the "archetype of the idea she set out with." (Jules Langsner)

By contrast, Claire Falkenstein's open, nest-like wire composition (fig. 93) is specifically identified as the *Portrait of the Painter Karel Appel* in spite of its abstract idiom. However, to understand the nature of this identification it is necessary to know that the model is a painter and that the portrait is intended as a three-dimensional correlative of his handwriting.

Before turning from the human figure to other themes of modern sculpture, it is worth glancing at the marginal but relevant sector of fantastical figurations with their implicit irony and deeper meaning. A master of these real-unreal creations is Jean Dubuffet; witness his *Madame j'ordonne* (fig. 94) which is made of blocks of lava picked up at random. The same black humour appears in the bronze *Anxious Friend* (fig. 95) by Max Ernst which shows as little artistic "skill" as Dubuffet's figure, appealing to our imagination by its buffoonery and its unexpected correlations.

Lynn Chadwick embodies his visions of the fantastic in chimaeras (fig. 98), angular, winged beings of iron and conglomerates, half bird, half man, in whose compact shapes Herbert Read has read the "geometry of fear"—an apposite reminder that the fear of demons and fear in general are among the primeval sources of artistic inspiration, and that the inhuman too is human.

César conjures up fabulous beings from the dark zone between nature and technology; he has also incarnated *The Devil* (fig. 96) out of industrial refuse. Hostility towards perfection and dislike of "beautiful" materials, so beloved of Signori and Hajdu—these are the driving forces of the artist from southern France whose inventions are theatrical figurines which he casts in a vast human tragi-comedy.

Akin to César's *Devil* are the abstruse fetishes that the Scotsman Eduardo Paolozzi fashions out of bronze clippings (fig. 97); but they have a ruthless outspokenness which César, with a devil's courtesy and obviously enjoying the game, avoids. The Dutchman Jaap Mooy (fig. 99) works from postulates which he shares with many young sculptors today, for example Robert Stankiewicz in the United States. Why should whole figures be welded out of clippings and shavings, out of refuse and waste? It seems that the activity of free re-composition or re-integration is all-important here, in the service of a new poetic of objects.

The American David Hare, whose *Man with Drum* (fig. 101) is of Surrealist lineage, declares the need to "break up reality and recombine it." He achieves this without allusions to the daemonic in things, showing humour and formal inventiveness in the way he integrates solid volume with shaped void. "Sculptors should present reality not as an object which might exist by itself in the closet, but as the relations between the object and the observer,"—this is how Hare sums up his conception of reality and of the relationship between subject and object, problems that today preoccupy sculptors all over the world.

82. Louise Bourgeois One and Others, 1955 Painted wood Height $20^{1}/_{4}$″ Whitney Museum of American Art, New York Photo: Oliver Baker, New York

83. MARY CALLERY Study for a Ballet Bronze M. Knoedler and Co., Inc., New York

84. Pablo Picasso The Bathers, 1957 Bronze Height 53 1/8"–103 7/8" Galerie Louise Leiris, Paris Photo: Author

86. Medardo Rosso

Lady with a Veil, 1896
Wax Height $29^{1}/_{2}$″
Middelheim Museum, Antwerp
Photo: Jean de Maeyer, Antwerp

85. Claude Viseux Petrified Crowd, 1959 Bronze Height $27^{5}/_{8}$″, Length $29^{1}/_{2}$″ Galerie Daniel Cordier, Paris and Frankfurt/Main

88. Antoine Pevsner Portrait of Marcel Duchamp, 1926 Celluloid on zinc Height 37", Breadth 25⁵/₈"
Yale University Art Gallery, Collection Societé Anonyme, New Haven Photo: Museum

87. Pablo Picasso

Female Head, 1910
Bronze Height 16¹/₂"
Photo: Brassai, Paris

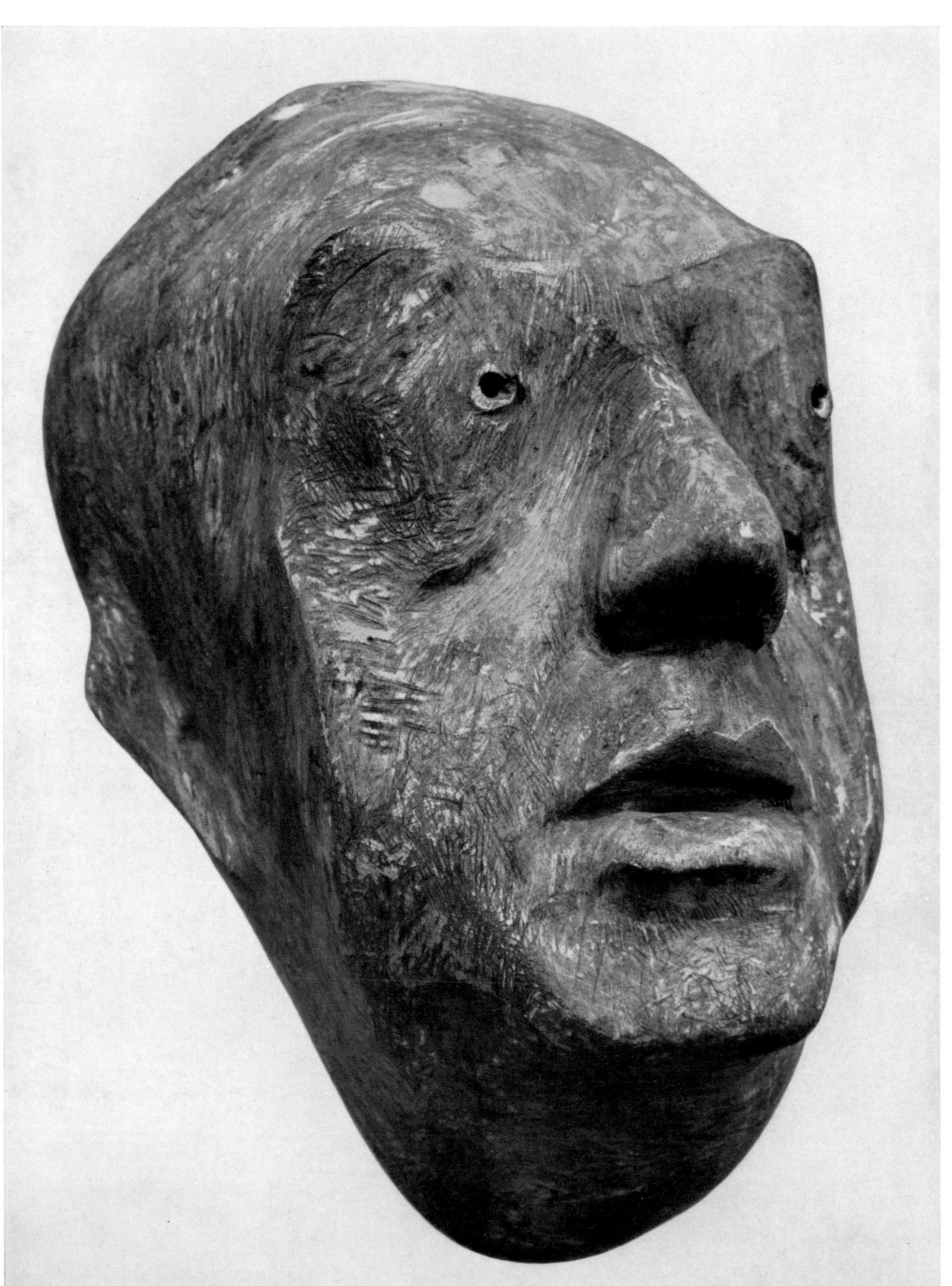

89. Bernhard Heiliger

Portrait of Ernst Reuter
1954
Cement Height 15¾″
Photo: Dr. Wolfgang Salchow
Cologne

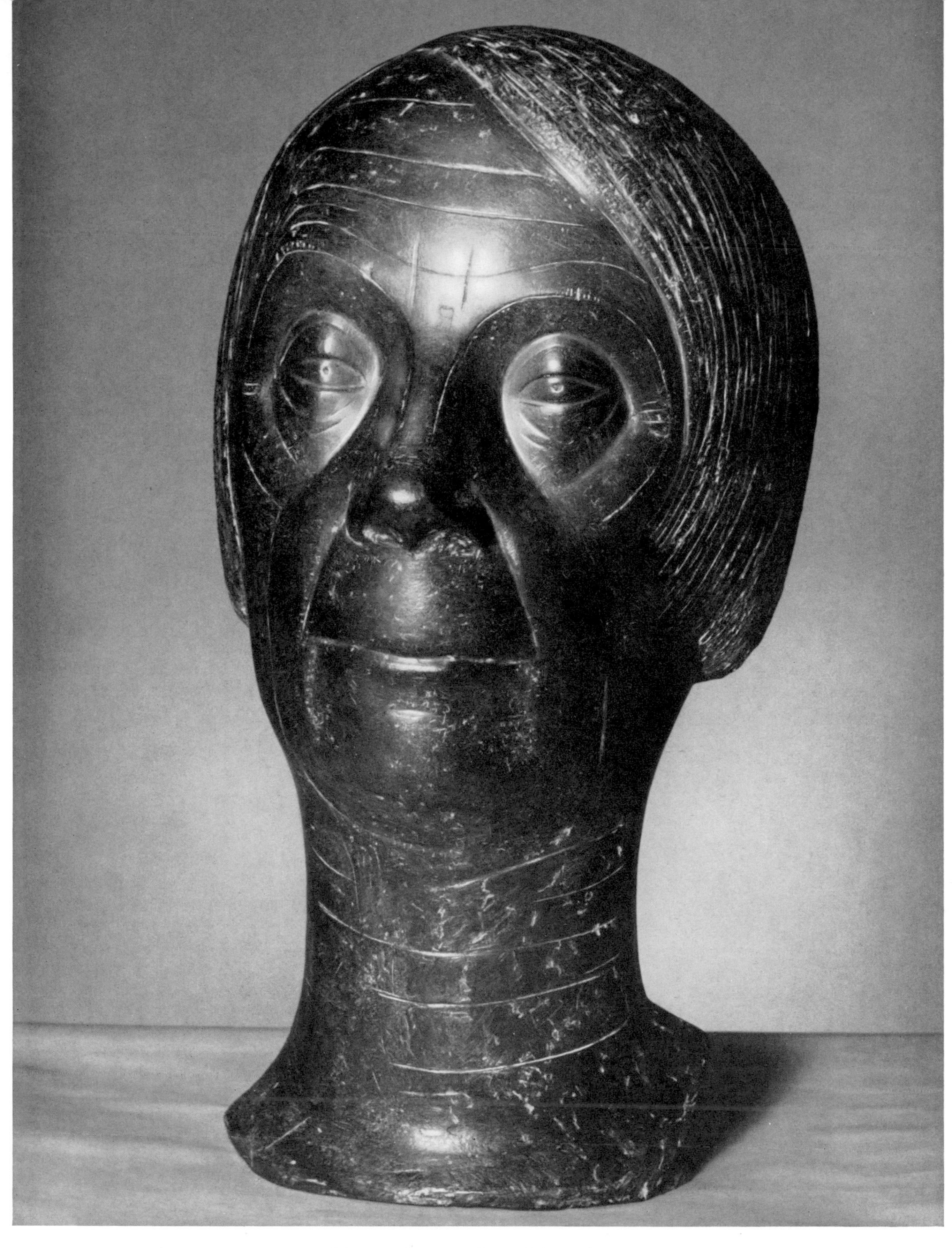

90. Emy Roeder Self-portrait, 1958 Bronze life-size Photo: J. Schmitz-Fabri, Cologne

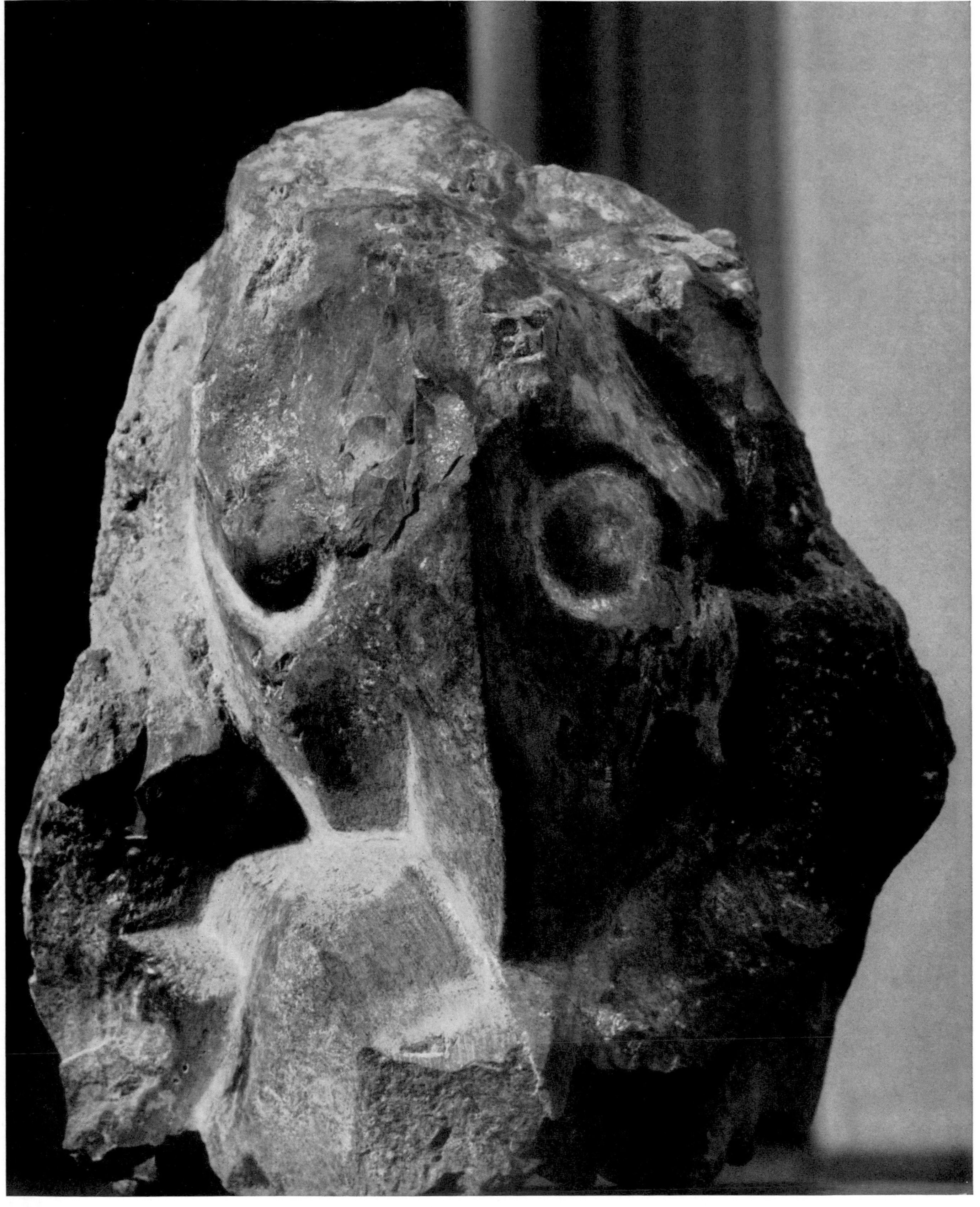

91. Cornelia Runyon Head, 1953 Greenish-brown desert stone Height 13″ Dr. and Mrs. George J. Wayne collection, Los Angeles
Photo: Russ Halford

Finally, the inexorable consequences of the sculptural exploration of the human figure are to be seen in the *Indifferent Man* (fig. 100), a bronze piece by Roël D'Haese. Its monstrous, puffed-up and shrivelled forms are plastic equivalents for the polarities of human existence.

Among the traditional themes of sculpture is the representation of animals. Only distant memories have, however, remained of its original connection with magic or its apotropaic functions. The 19th-century love of, and sentimentality over, animals is also out of fashion, if one disregards the popular baby animals of Renée Sintenis which, both on account of their formal idiom and as animal portraits, belong to late Impressionism. The sculptors of the 20th century are not interested in the characteristic form, bearing or movement of individual animals; their object is the animal as such, just as, in the human sphere, it is man as such; they are concerned with creatureliness and animality in the scheme of Creation. The animal is not primarily a companion, a zoological phenomenon or a parody of man. To generalise somewhat, it could be said that, besides the traditional symbolism (lion=strength; dove=peace) which is still accepted, the animal embodies for the 20th-century artist in the first place vitality and proximity to origins. The lions of August Gaul, Franz Marc's horses, the birds of Max Ernst, the exotic animal statuettes of Gerhard Marcks, Toni Stadler's *Dog*, Picasso's celebrated *She-Goat*, the animal reliefs of Philipp Harth, Chadwick's *Beasts* and, not least, Marino Marini's horses—all these indicate the prevailing trend of which a few notable stages will be discussed here, without its being suggested that the artists involved are in any sense specialised "animal sculptors."

The first radical transformation of the animal in modern sculpture occurs at the hands of Raymond Duchamp-Villon. His *Horse* (fig. 102), a horse-machine or a machine-horse, combines in semi-abstract forms the static and the dynamic aspects of the universal horse. The partly organic, partly mechanical elements find themselves in a peculiar state of vibrant suspension between rest and headlong movement. Up to the 19th century, and with extensions into the 20th, the horse was a symbol of sovereign power to be placed on a pedestal or else itself serving as one. Duchamp-Villon, anticipating the onset of technology, transfers it to the realm of mechanics. His piece embodies, as it were, the horse's horse-power or its dynamic potentiality.

Constantin Brancusi's *Bird in Space* (fig. 103) is a noble and radiant symbol. The highly polished bronze and the arrow-like shape shooting upwards declare the artist's intention to liberate form from matter. This bird in space is vital force and spiritual discipline, movement and rest, action and contemplation, the breath of life and abstraction. Perfectly conceived and adequately executed, it has been refined until it is no more than a gleaming surface and it glides away from the world of things.

The attraction of archaic forms is particularly noticeable in animal sculpture. The

Dutchman Toon Kelder who, besides producing wood pieces like the *Bird* (fig. 104), composes in metal and iron wire, seeks to recapture the simplicity of the Primitives and, while doing so, develops a rhythm of asymmetrical solids in space that is all his own. In the *Flying Figure* (fig. 105) by his fellow-countryman, Wessel Couzijn, the emphasis is on flight as such, not a specifically animal phenomenon, and here more in the nature of a poetic baroque image of a heavy and powerful wing-stroke.

Ewald Mataré's *Lying Cow* (fig. 106, wood) is stylised into a three-dimensional emblem. The artist has not copied any particular cow resting on the ground that he may have seen in the countryside of the Lower Rhineland; he has composed a heraldic cipher which, like mediaeval zoomorphic symbols, has a magical function. On the other hand, in Paul Dierkes' stone piece, *Sheep's Head* (fig. 107) the heraldic element yields to the Surrealist idea of transmuting the animal torso into a new plastic object existing in its own right and signifying nothing but itself. Dierkes is given to experimenting, and he combines great manual skill with an inventive imagination.

The structure of the animal body, its muscles and ligaments interest the young Parisian sculptor, Jacques Delahaye—but not from an anatomical point of view. His *Cat* (fig. 108) is a study in the self-propulsion and speed of a body which, apparently not subject to the laws of gravity, maintains itself in an arrested spring. The handling of the material is also in the service of this "new naturalism"; in remarkable contrast to the dynamic content it shrivels up and develops a fossil-like texture.

Excited movement and sudden arrest are brought together in a similar, contradictory, unsettling manner in the *Crowing Cock* (fig. 109) by Bernard Meadows. Meadows professes, in common with Delahaye and many other French sculptors, a symbolic realism which, with him in particular, has its roots in the fears and horrors of our time. In the monsters of Agenore Fabbri, akin to Germaine Richier's *mantis*, the obsession with fear acquires a theatrical quality.

Man and animal do not exhaust the repertory that modern sculpture draws from nature. The two themes have been treated in a wide sense so as to include forms in which the human or the animal is the starting point for free invention. What remains to be considered is the portrayal of organic growth whether in its human, animal or plant variety.

Growth can mean the slowly rising or gradually developing movement of a body generated from within, as we see in the rolling, cloud-like masses of Otto Freundlich's *Ascent* (fig. 110) or in the forms inspired by the human body characterizing Hans Arp's marble *Growth* (fig. 111); it can also have vegetal associations as in Bernhard Heiliger's explicit *Vegetative Sculpture* (fig. 112). Even Alicia Penalba's *Homage to Vallejo* (fig. 113) appears as a product of organic energy; its cactiform structure conforms to a law of nature.

Guido Jendritzko's *Composition II/1959* (fig. 114) and Francesco Somaini's *Iron 5925* (fig. 115) carry no vegetal allusions either explicitly in the title or in the artist's intention. Yet their structure, their articulation into leaf-like forms, and, not least, their contours evoke associations of that kind. General notions of organic growth are, no doubt, at work in these as in other compositions of the two young sculptors. In Theodore Roszak's *Thorn Blossom* (fig. 116) they lead to baroque inventions of an exotic splendour, while in *Space Knot 64* (fig. 117) by Otto Herbert Hajek they inspire forms that make up a thorny bush or a closely knit lattice work. These forms hark back to the Tree of Jesse and Late Gothic altar tabernacles; with such echoes Hajek's work finds its appropriate place in a church.

The interest in forms of organic growth for their own sake as distinguished from borrowings of fragments, usually for a technical rather than an aesthetic purpose (i.e. tree stumps as disguised props), is peculiar to modern sculpture. It leads to plastic invention of the most varied kind, for instance the artificial stone compositions of Ernst Hermanns (fig. 118) or the imaginative, half animal, half vegetable forms devised by Shinkichi Tajiri (fig. 119) and Theo Bechteler (fig. 121). The delicately membered metal compositions by the American Harold B. Cousins (fig. 122) with their roots and branches have both blossoming and growing as their theme. As in Hajek's space knots, solid forms and space intertwine in one indissoluble whole.

The last few examples have led us away from the representation of natural forms towards the creation of autonomous plastic objects. From here it is only a short step to forms that are entirely independent of human, animal or plant models—to artefacts or, more precisely, to objects invented by the human mind, fashioned by the human hand, and set over against the products of nature.

To survey this type of sculpture the scheme applied in the first chapter can be of service seeing that in plastic objects with no external referents the question of form must precede that of meaning. I shall, therefore, deal first with compact solids then with open constructions; but I shall also consider what any given work has to "say" and what the artist's intention may have been. The development from compact solids to spatial schemata, or from the realisation of order to the expression of vitality that can be observed in the sequence of illustrations should not, however, be understood as an evolution in a historical or a qualitative sense. It arises solely out of the method employed, whose scope and value have been discussed at the beginning of this book.

One of the earliest of these "independent" plastic objects, dating from 1912, is the bronze *Development of a Bottle in Space* (fig. 123) by the Futurist Umberto Boccioni. The problem is again the relation between solid volume and surrounding space: the forms develop outwards from a solid kernel in expanding, overlapping layers. In a centrifugal movement a phased occupation of space is effected.

With the less substantial solidity of his *Developed Form* (fig. 124) Vojn Bakić today pursues similar ends. With him too the spatial evolution of form, the fusion of solid volume with free space, is the basic motif. Both works bring to mind a sentence from the Futurist manifesto of 1912: "A Futurist sculptural composition will possess the wonderful mathematical elements of modern objects."

The intention realised by Robert Adams in the pattern of contraries offered by his rectangular, compact *Iron Sculpture* (fig. 125) is best explained by the words of the artist himself: "As an abstract and non-objective sculptor, I aim at creating formal compositions that owe everything to themselves, that are completely independent of external influences. My models are not derived by a process of abstraction from nature. My problem is ... to *objectify* each work." Adams' purpose is to produce "things" whose proportions work and whose forms are in harmony with the material used. In other words the artist sets up objective relationships between things that are valid in themselves. It is no accident that his compositions are instinct with the spirit of a rigorous architecture in whose service he has erected for the Theatre at Gelsenkirchen a similarly articulated wall of concrete.

Adams is a dialectician and an intellectual who keeps abreast of developments in modern science. The Belgian, Willy Anthoons, whose stone piece *Being* (fig. 126) offers an interesting comparison with Adams' iron composition, is, on the other hand, a meditative artist who chisels stone or carves wood with patience and devotion to obtain forms that embody a collected calm. The reclining block with long, drawn-out contours but with an energetic sign impressed into it in low relief, expresses both contemplation and action thus justifying its philosophical title.

"Moon-like, hollowed out, ghostly"—these are the epithets that Hans Arp applies to his composition in white marble (fig. 127). The title refers both to the formal and the expressive aspect, to the latter twice over but in the same vein. The artist has captured the essence of the work in this description, and other comment may seem inappropriate. It will not be amiss, however, to stress on the one hand how artistic in itself is this very fitness of name to object; on the other, the magnificent vitality of the work which, as it were, turns its inside out and yet preserves its kernel in a solid shell, which both grows and is at rest, which embodies breathing, sensuous life, and spiritual being. In this multiplicity of meaning lies the great poetical force of the work.

Similar swelling forms, forged in iron, are to be seen in *Sheba* (fig. 128) by the Swiss Robert Müller. Overflowing with vitality, she lies like a ripe, full-bodied but unknown fruit. Müller has linked up the rounded blades in a system of incapsulations. He leaves open narrow chinks where the cap-like forms overlap, so that one sees not only the life of what is exposed to view but divines the shape of what lies hidden inside.

92. Sergio Signori

Portrait for Madame X, 1958
Pakistan onyx Height 15 3/4″
Length 11 3/4″
Galerie Creuzevault, Paris
Photo: Cav. L. Bessi, Carrara

93. Claire Falkenstein

Portrait of the Painter Karel Appel, 1956–59
Iron wire Height 27⁵/₈″
Galerie Stadler, Paris

94. Jean Dubuffet

Madame j'ordonne, 1954
Lava Height 36¹/₄″
Galerie Daniel Cordier, Paris–Frankfurt/Main

95. MAX ERNST Eager Friend, 1943 Bronze Height *c.* 36¼″

96. César The Devil, 1956 Bronze Height 137¾″ Galerie Claude Bernard, Paris Photo: Author

97. Eduardo Paolozzi

St. Sebastian IV, 1957
Bronze Height $90^{1}/_{2}$″
D. Gomme collection, London
Photo: Author

98. LYNN CHADWICK The Stranger II, 1956 Iron and conglomerate Height $43^{3}/_{8}''$ Photo: Author

99. Jaap Mooy

Icarus
Iron Height 29 1/2″
Städtische
Kunsthalle
Recklinghausen

100. ROËL D'HAESE

The Indifferent Man, 1959
Bronze (cire perdue) Height 26³/₄"
Claude Bernard Haim
collection, Paris
Photo: Luc Joubert, Paris

102. Raymond Duchamp-Villon

The Horse, 1914 Bronze Height 40 1/8″
Museum of Modern Art, New York
Photo: Author

101. David Hare

Man with Drum, 1948
Bronze Height 23 5/8″
Photo: Amerika-Dienst

103. Constantin Brancusi

Bird in Space, 1925
Polished bronze on base of marble and oak Height 49 2/3″
Philadelphia Museum of Art
Arensberg collection Photo: Author

104. Toon Kelder

Bird
Wood Height $37^{3}/_{8}''$

105. Wessel Couzijn

Flying Figure, 1958
Bronze $22^{1}/_{2}'' \times 12^{5}/_{8}'' \times 5^{1}/_{2}''$
Stedelijk Museum, Amsterdam
Photo: Museum

106. Ewald Mataré Lying Cow, 1946 Ebony Length $8^{5}/_{8}''$ Photo: Dr. Wolfgang Salchow, Cologne

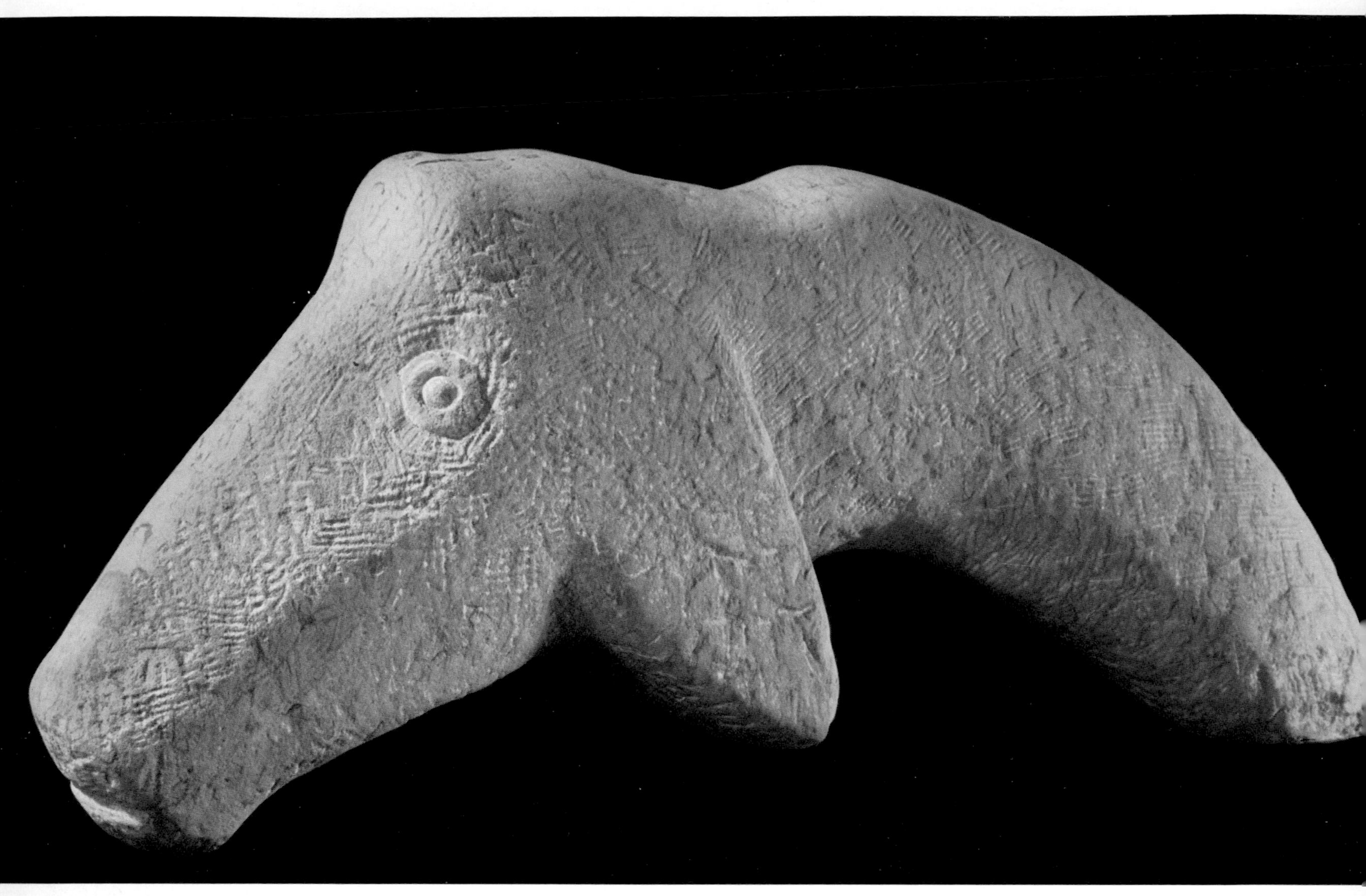

107. PAUL DIERKES Sheep's Head, 1952 Sandstone $11^3/_4'' \times 26^3/_4'' \times 4''$ On permanent loan from the "Kulturkreis" Museum am Ostwall, Dortmund
Photo: Gnilka, Berlin

108. JACQUES CHARLES DELAHAYE The Cat, 1952 Bronze $19^{5}/_{8}'' \times 63'' \times 14^{5}/_{8}''$ Galerie Stadler, Paris Photo: Augustin Dumage, Paris

109. Bernard Meadows Crowing Cock, 1955 Bronze Height $29^{7}/_{8}''$ Photo: British Council

110. Otto Freundlich Ascent, 1929 Plaster original Height $78^3/_4$″
Mme Jeanne Kosnickloss-Freundlich, Paris

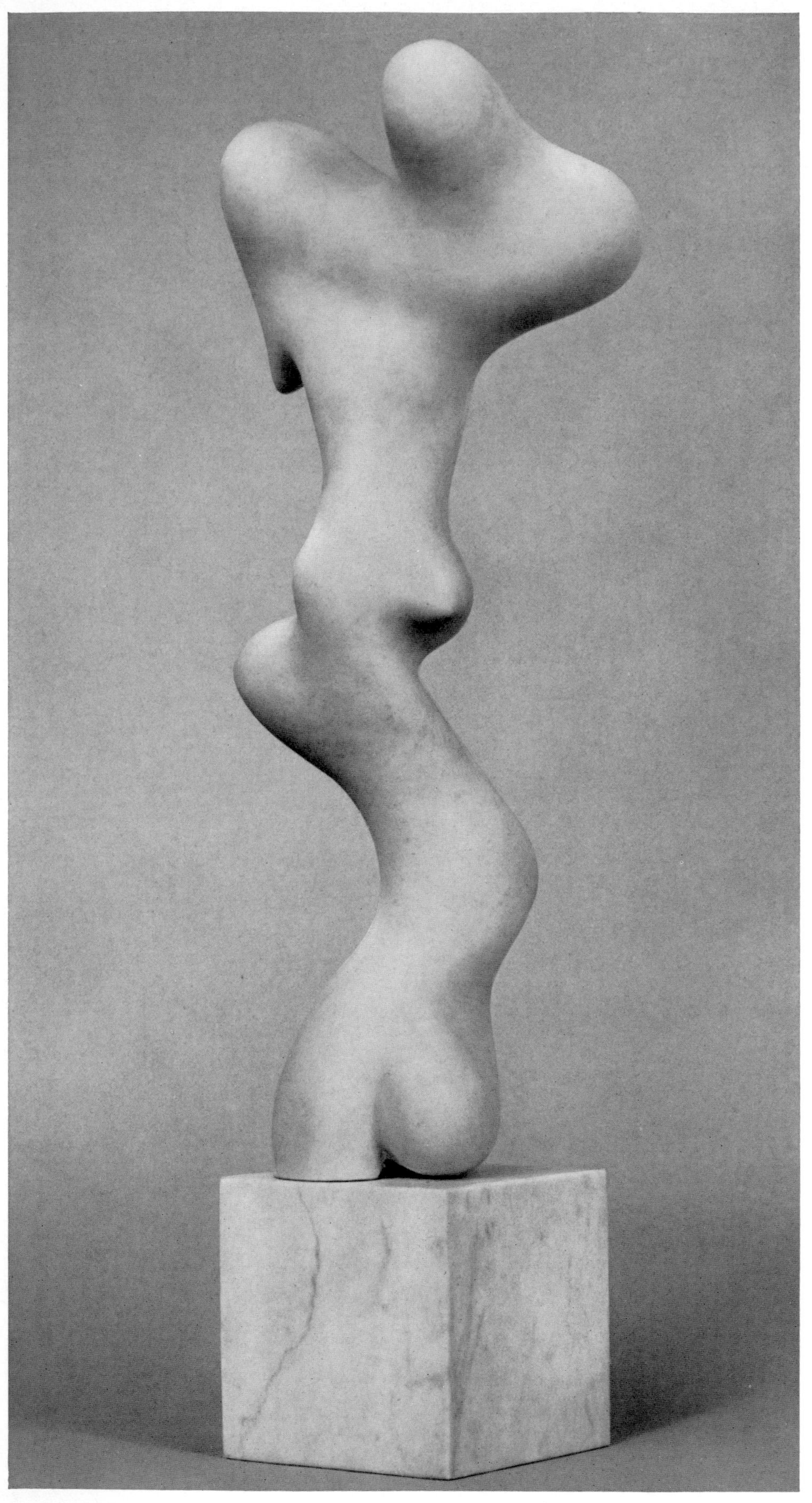

111. HANS ARP Growth, 1938 Marble Height $39^{3}/_{8}''$
Solomon R. Guggenheim Museum, New York Photo: Museum

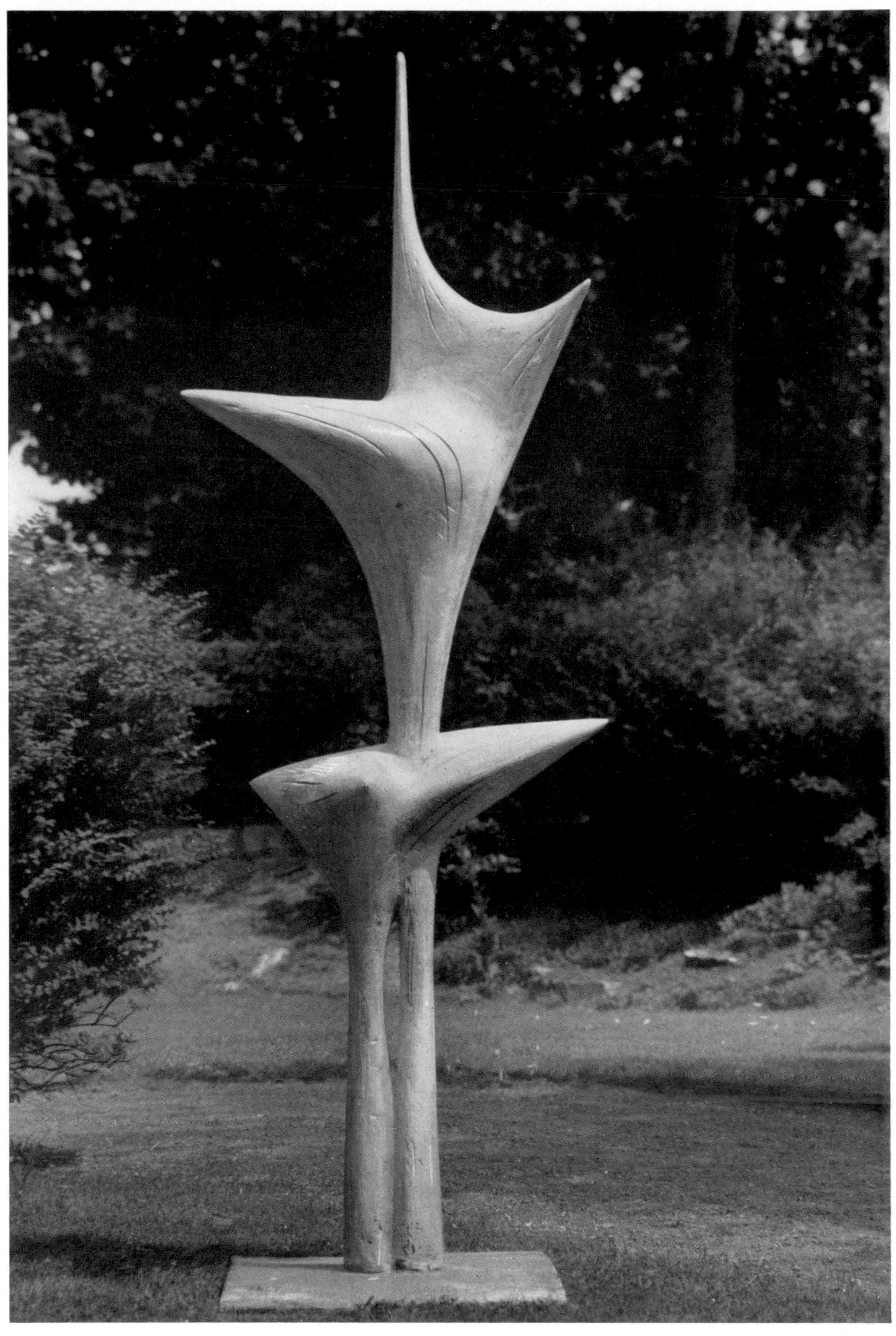

112. BERNHARD HEILIGER Vegetative Sculpture, 1955 Bronze Height 78¾″ Karl-Ernst-Osthaus Museum, Hagen
Photo: Gnilka, Berlin

113. Alicia Penalba Homage to Vallejo, 1957 Bronze Height $118^{1}/_{8}''$
Galerie Claude Bernard, Paris Photo: Author

114. GUIDO JENDRITZKO Composition II, 1959 Plaster for bronze 25 5/8″ × 17 3/8″ Photo: Gnilka, Berlin

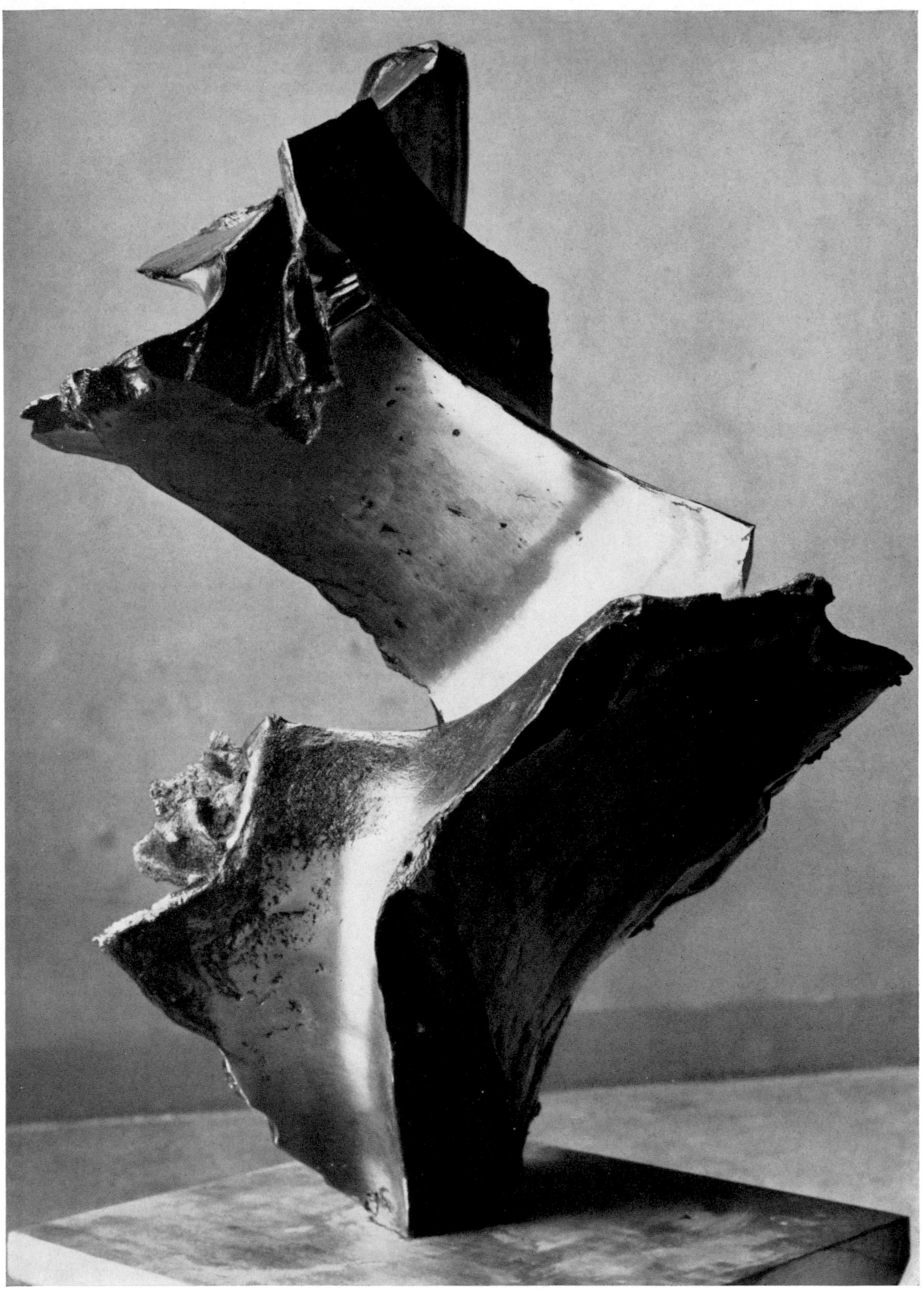

115. Francesco Somaini Iron 5925, 1959 Iron Height 38$^{5}/_{8}$" La Medusa, Rome

116. Theodore Roszak

Thorn Blossom, 1947
Steel with nickeled silver Height 33$^{1}/_{2}$"
Whitney Museum of American Art, New York
Photo: Oliver Baker, New York

117. Otto Herbert Hajek Space Knot 64, 1958 Bronze $27^{5}/_{8}'' \times 15'' \times 3^{7}/_{8}''$ Ravensburg church
Photo: Galerie Änne Abels, Cologne

118. Ernst Hermanns Relief, 1956 Artificial stone $31^{7}/_{8}'' \times 42^{1}/_{2}''$ Photo: Author

Gio Pomodoro attempts to give plastic expression to a very abstract concept, that of *Co-existence* (fig. 130). A direct political reference is probably not intended though such an interpretation is not impossible: two areas roughly equal in size but differing in configuration; a deep furrow separates them but it is visibly interrupted by a series of transversal seams. In this composition contours are secondary; what matters is the moving, breathing surface with its delicate yet forceful modulations.

By contrast, in Lucio Fontana's two-face relief *Conversation* (fig. 131) the surface does not bound a volume but functions as a lively, lambent silhouette. A calm, long-drawn-out line is engraved in it while the "conversing" back side is covered with rapid restless strokes. Both Pomodoro and Fontana attempt to convey a complex message in an abstract idiom. Maurice Lipsi's *Volvic Stone* (fig. 132), on the other hand, is a sturdy mass whose three-dimensionality can be inferred—without an all-round view—from the sharply cut contours which are so devised as to lead the eye continuously from one side to the next. The rhythmically articulated block has no perforations or hollows, only shallow caverns which draw external space into them but immediately thrust it out again by their changing configuration. This creates an over-all movement of advance and withdrawal which appears compatible with the static and monumental character of the piece. The *Stone* is a bulwark in space setting up a system of flexible resistance to it.

Shamaï Haber's works (fig. 133) seem at first closely akin to Lipsi's: sturdy, compact blocks with simple outlines which attest the artist's architectural turn of mind. But there are important divergences: the two sculptors, though both born in Lodz, have spent their formative years in different environments—Lipsi in Paris, Haber in Israel. While Lipsi inclines to monoliths, Haber builds up his compositions out of several stones. The example illustrated comprises only three blocks of granite but others have six or seven components, dressed in the same precise manner and balanced against each other without recourse to symmetry. This strong and sober art recalls Aeschbacher's stone figure (fig. 44), not in the sense of any direct filiation but in the general context of contemporary trends. With Aeschbacher, however, the joints are no more than depressions in the surface whereas Haber piles up a veritably Cyclopean structure, a unity of distinct parts monumental and primeval.

François Stahly opens up the compact solid to a greater degree but he proceeds with moderation and allows himself to be guided by the natural configuration of his material, the wood of a thick root. He reads meaning into what he finds and calls his piece *Medusa* (fig. 129). Eugène Dodeigne could have thought of similar correspondences but he has left his powerful composition in Belgian blue stone (fig. 134) without a descriptive title so as not to mediatise its monumental character or muffle the echoes of the heavy struggle between stone and chisel.

119. SHINKICHI TAJIRI

Plant, 1959
Bronze Height 27 5/8"
Photo: Paul Huf
Amsterdam

While Dodeigne's stone has only narrow perforations, Lorenzo Guerrini opens up his *Scultura forte* (fig. 135) into a gate-like structure whose massiveness, rugged outline and rough surface constitute an abstract variation on the theme of archaism. Peter H. Voulkos, an American of Greek descent, is similarly inspired by architectural notions. He builds up his large terracottas (fig. 136) with heavy blocks combining regular and rock-like formations.

Internal and external forms, which appeared as one of the main formal categories in chapter 1, are the theme of *Figure in Landscape* (fig. 137), an alabaster piece by Barbara Hepworth. The double perforation of the stone serves to open up the interior like a nutshell while allowing the eye that sees through it to annex the "back and beyond" to the composition. The relations between landscape and the human figure have for long been the artist's interest (she works mainly in the open air; her materials are stone and wood). They are interpreted in terms not of Romantic correspondences but of solid and spatial forms harmoniously balanced.

Day Schnabel, an American of Austrian extraction living in Paris, seems at first sight to work from similar postulates. For instance, the idea of a composition in two separate parts, as in her *In Memoriam* (fig. 138), is familiar from the work of both Hepworth and Henry Moore. The difference between the two sculptresses is largely one of theme: while Hepworth seeks equivalents of structure and rhythm for the subjective and emotional experience of landscape, Schnabel works out, with free concave and convex forms, an architectonic idea. *In Memoriam,* which calls to mind fantastical ruins, could be a monumental Requiem for some destroyed city of Europe.

While similar in structure—compact forms and open composition—the works of Jean Chauvin and Marta Pan carry no ostensive symbolic meaning. In his bronze *Wind of Life* (fig. 139) Chauvin goes beyond even Brancusi's abstractions and invents an object that is neither derived from reality nor has any parallel in it. The artifact creates its own significance of which the poetic title, the softly undulating forms and the opening into space are the elements. Marta Pan calls her piece simply *Equilibrium* (fig. 140). It is a beautiful object—harmonious and made of noble material—and nothing more; a complete, fully articulated form to be turned this way and that, with a smooth, convex surface for the hand to explore. As the title suggests, its sense is in its skilfully contrived balance, a favourite theme with Marta Pan whose work includes sketches for ballet—one even called *Equilibrium.*

The sculptures of her fellow Hungarian, Étienne Béothy, who also lives in Paris, have a similar elegance. The literary and atmospheric, but not very informative title, *Nocturno* (fig. 141) may be safely ignored; Eva Friedrich's periphrasis serves the purpose better: "tall and slim, light in make, projecting, collected, sharply cut, profiled." Partaking both of mathematical abstraction and of the sensuous immediacy of ob-

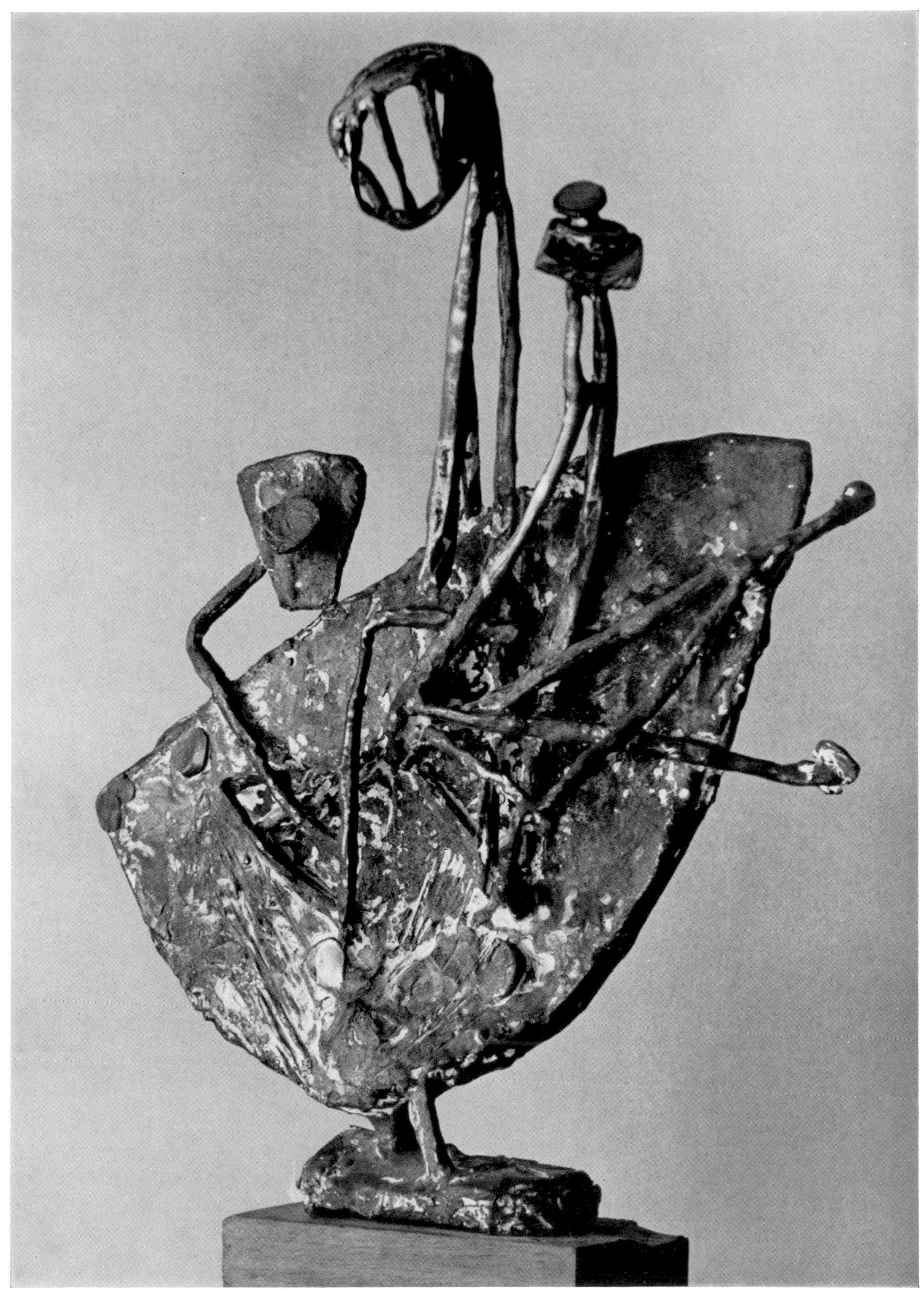

121. Theo Bechteler

Night Plant, 1957
Bronze
$15^3/_4'' \times 10^5/_8'' \times 3^1/_2''$
Photo: A. Beisser
Augsburg

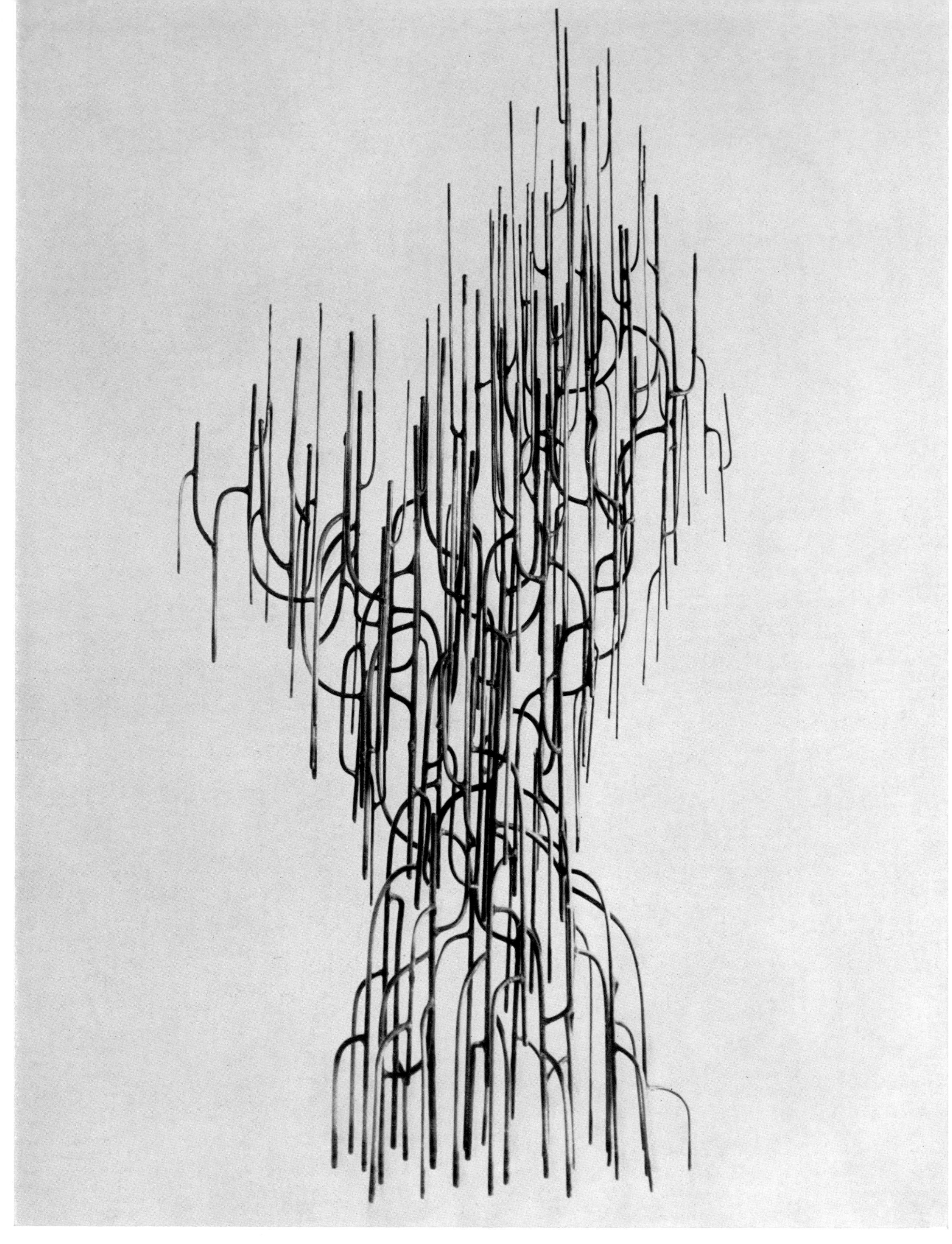

122. Harold B. Cousins Sculpture 1959 Iron $55^{1}/_{8}'' \times 26^{3}/_{8}'' \times 10^{5}/_{8}''$ Photo: Author

123. UMBERTO BOCCIONI Development of a Bottle in Space, 1912 Bronze Height 15″ Museum of Modern Art, New York
Photo: Museum (Soichi Sunami)

125. Robert Adams

Iron Sculpture, 1956
Height 16 1/8"
R. Jährling, Wuppertal
Photo: M. Abel-Menne, Wuppertal

124. Vojn Bakić

Developed Form, 1958 Plaster for bronze Height 27 5/8"
Galerie Denise René, Paris Photo: Tośo Dabac, Zagreb

127. Hans Arp

Moon-like, hollowed out, ghostly, 1950
White marble Height 16 1/2″
Dr. Bernhard Sprengel collection, Hanover
Photo: Hans Wagner, Hanover

126. Willy Anthoons Being, 1952–56 Stone from Poullenay 17 3/4″ × 35 3/8″ × 15 3/4″

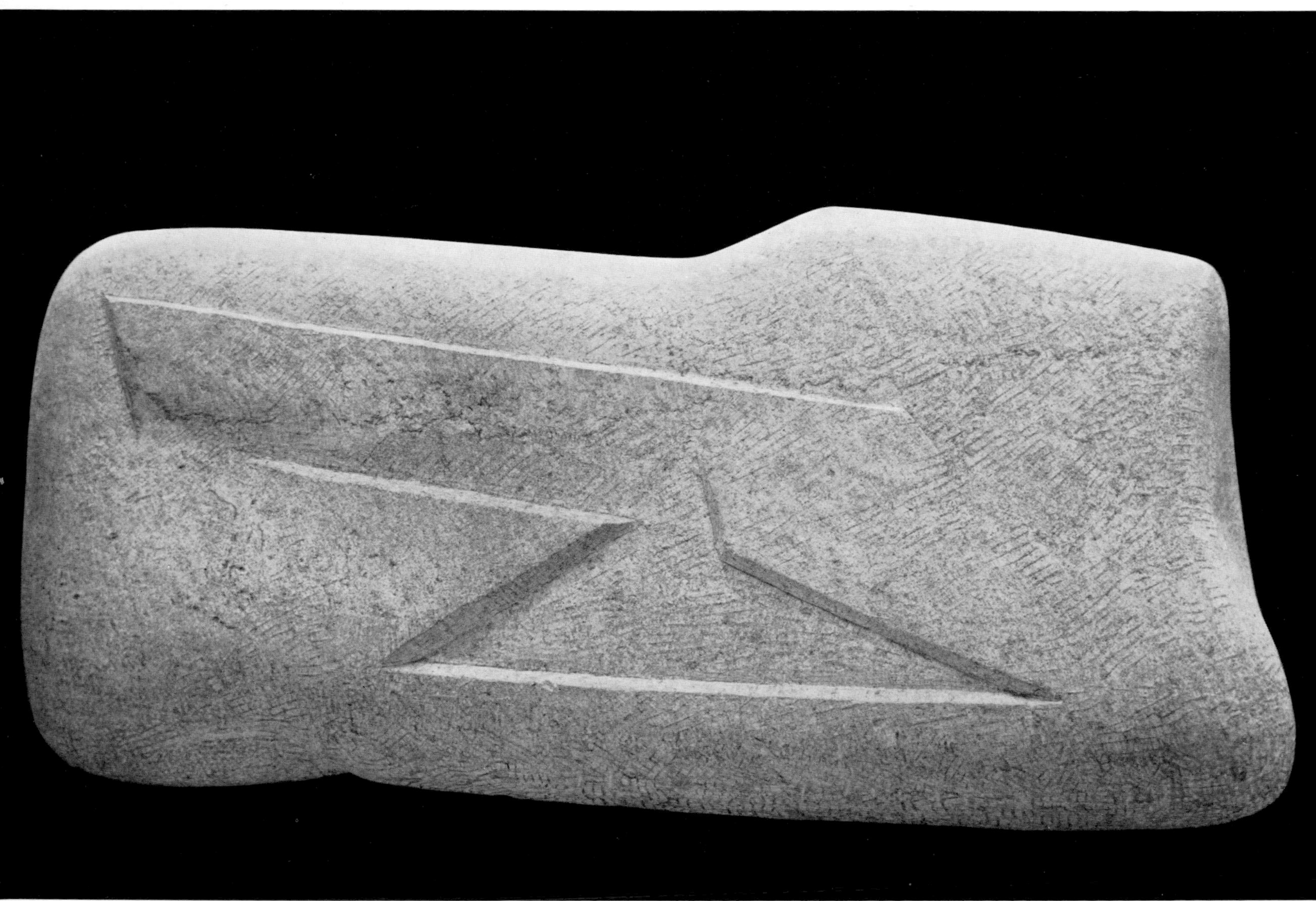

128. Robert Müller Sheba, 1958 Iron Breadth 30¼″ Elie de Rothschild collection Photo: Author

129. François Stahly

Medusa, 1959
Olive wood Height *c.* 23⅝″
Photo: Pe Willi, Zürich

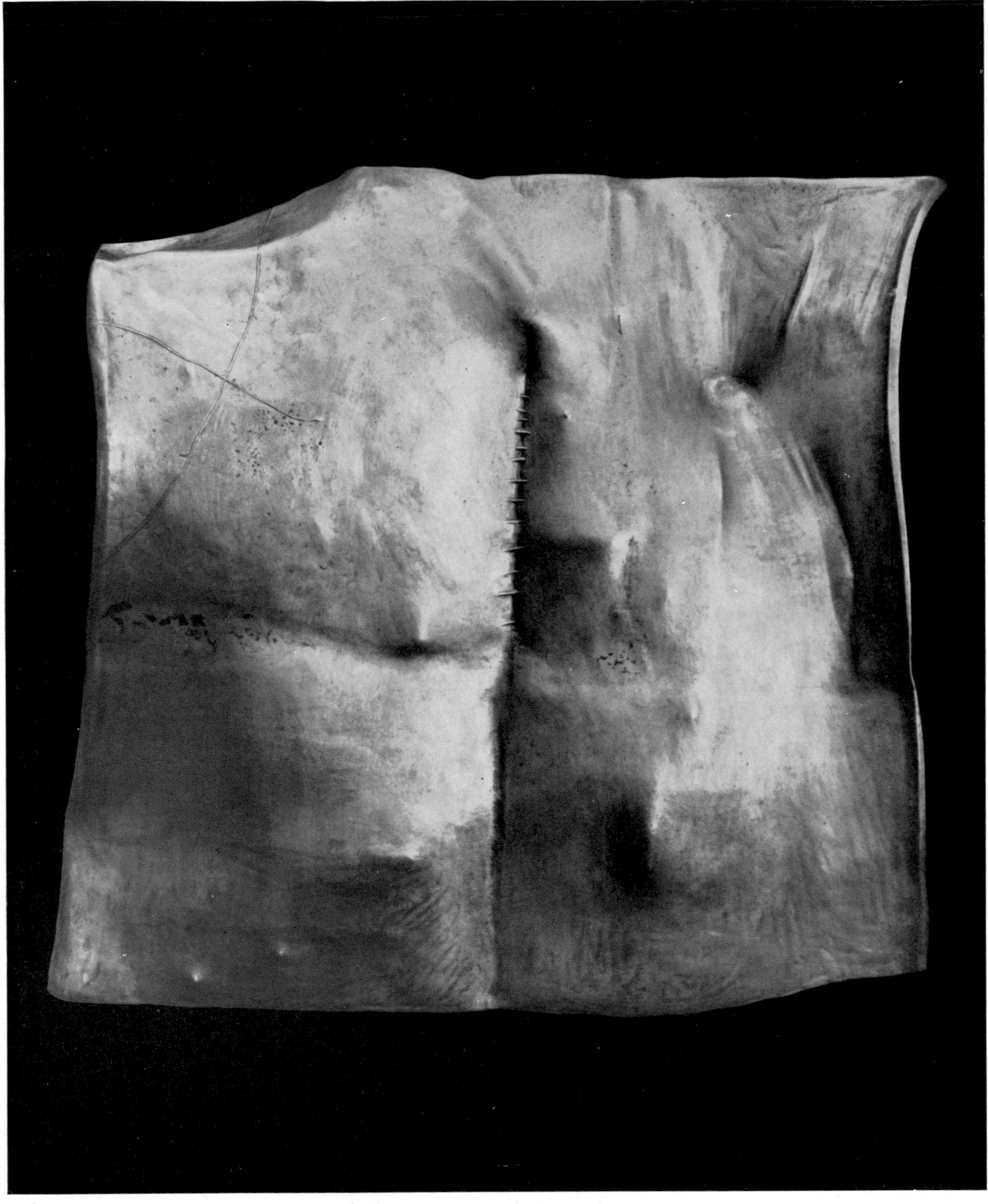

130. Gio Pomodoro Co-existence, 1958 Bronze 59″ × 63″

131. Lucio Fontana

Conversation, 1934
Bronze gilt Height $27^{5}/_{8}$″

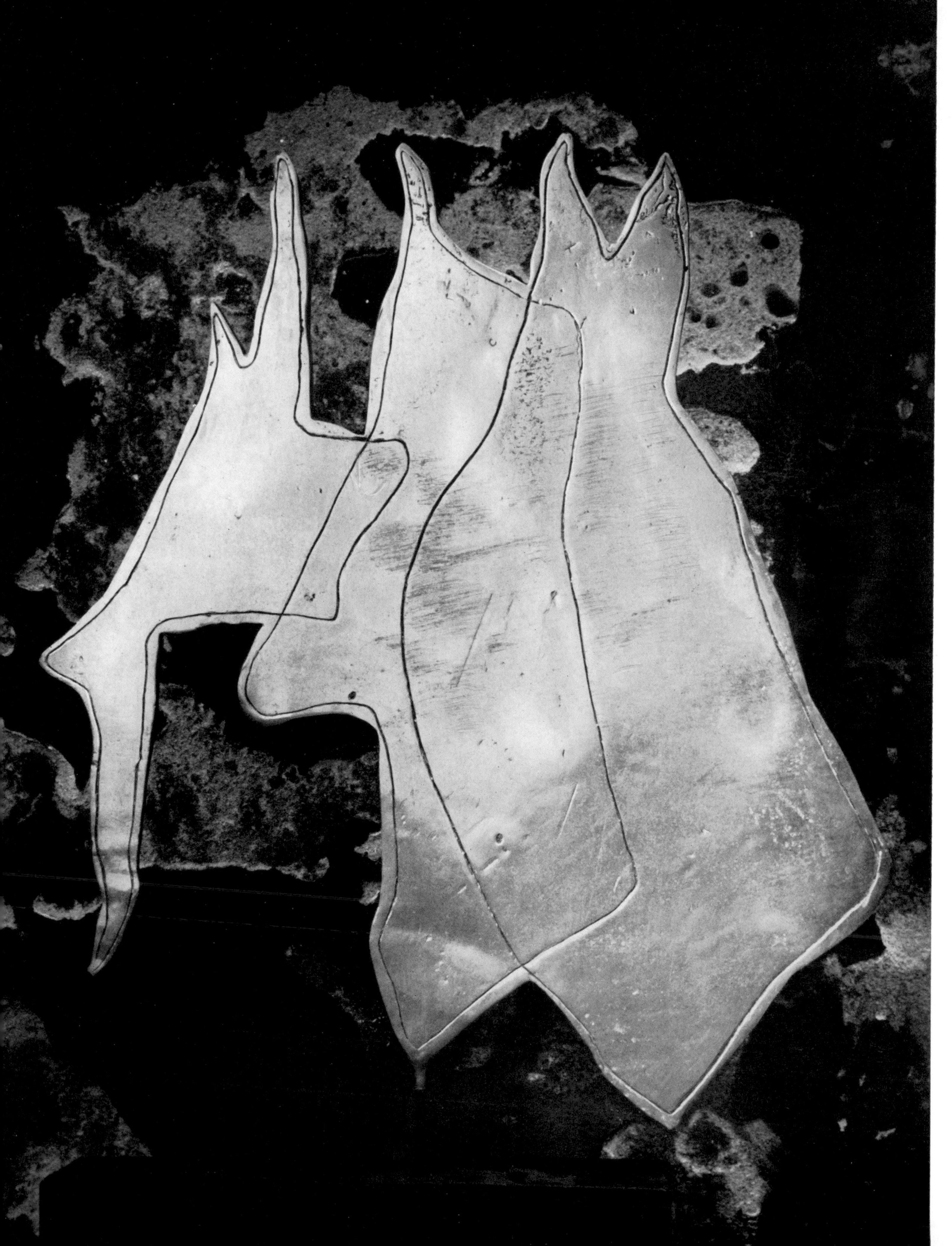

132. MAURICE LIPSI Volvic Stone, 1958 Height 45 1/4" Galerie Denise René, Paris Photo: Author

133. SHAMAÏ HABER Composition with 3 Stones, 1957–58 Breton granite Height $35^{3}/_{8}$" O. Le Corneur collection

134. Eugène Dodeigne Sculpture, 1958 Bluestone Height 74¾″ Photo: Author

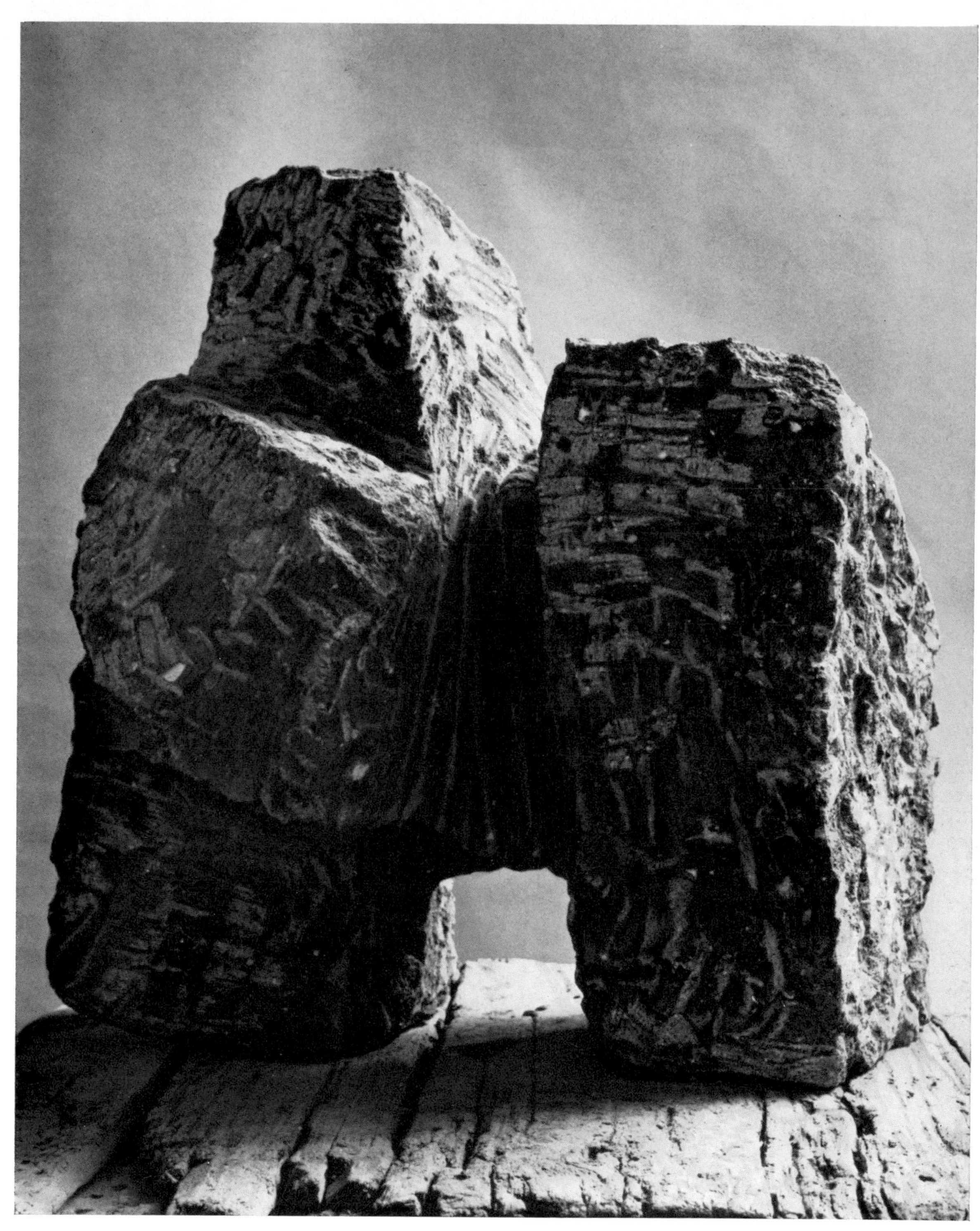

135. Lorenzo Guerrini Scultura forte, 1958 Stone Height 25 5/8″ Photo: Alfredo L. Ferretti

136. Peter H. Voulkos

Terracotta Sculpture
Height $29^{7}/_{8}$″

137. Barbara Hepworth Figure in Landscape, 1952 Alabaster Length 10″ Smith College of Art, Northampton, Mass., USA

138. Day Schnabel In Memoriam, 1952 Stone Height 31½″

to the earth though its awkward members, planted far apart, in the stance of a "Spanish rider," prop themselves up in a tense, haughty gesture to challenge the surrounding space. At the same time *Terrosa* has the sober adequacy of a peasant tool left lying in the field and—as the title suggests—belonging to it.

Alexander Calder, the father of mobile sculpture (see fig. 20), produces static compositions as well. The sinuous, smooth contours of his metal plates reach out into space often a considerable distance from a central shaft and, in overlapping, create spatial compartments bounded on two, at most on three sides. The *Whale* (fig. 147), a monumental "stabile" of black sheet steel thus appears as a silhouette but also as a powerful solid developing in space with an imposing rhythm. The associative title and the invented form seem to go well together.

"The problem of sculpture is conditioned by space," says Berto Lardera, one of the most forceful representatives of recent trends in iron sculpture; and he adds: "Conception and technique are intimately linked with one another... I use the materials of my time." Lardera's *Cathedral of Pain V* (fig. 148) is flat, without any artistically effective volume, a sculptural paradox mitigated by the fact that the metal plates, cut in various patterns, are soldered at such angles as to delimit compositions in space that are open on all sides. Lardera's compositions are both spatial constructions and signs in space, airy fabrics of metal surfaces that carry and are carried, intersect and thrust out in enveloping movements; they are often perforated to allow a free flow of space and to establish communications with the environment whether natural or architectural. There is, however, as little non-objectivity here as in the work of Gonzalez. The titles themselves are pointers; as in the example illustrated, they endow what they describe with a high emotional charge.

In conception Nino Franchina's *Nike* (fig. 149) derives from Gonzalez' sign in space and it is executed with the technique of the American metal sculptors. Placed on an archaistic socle, it shoots high into the air like a signalling beacon. Brigitte Meier-Denninghoff, on the other hand, in a modified application of the technique of her teacher, Antoine Pevsner, uses straight brass rods soldered together to construct her *Wings* (fig. 151) as surfaces moving in space. The shaft which carries the larger part of the composition and hoists it in the air is so slender that as a support it is hardly perceptible. The wings thus appear almost weightless; spreading out in a powerful beat they carve out portions in space while the undulation of their surfaces directs the eye to the central shaft as the axis of the figure.

These formal effects of outspread sails occur also in Luciano Minguzzi's *Dragons* (fig. 150) though its multiform, weightlessly fluttering silhouette is more open to space and maintains a more dynamic relationship with it. *Space Sculpture* (fig. 152), a steel composition by Norbert Kricke, has the same openness with bundles of intersecting rays that point in every direction and thus set up a vehement, stormy yet carefully planned and controlled movement. While Kricke's piece is pronouncedly excentric, the iron rods of Walter Bodmer's calmer construction (fig. 153) return towards each other without, however, forming a clear centre. Neither Bodmer nor Kricke relate their work conceptually to anything outside it. With its static, space-exploring rhythm, it exists for itself.

The American David Smith, on the other hand, intends his *Australia* (fig. 154), a robust steel composition, to carry associations which, if accepted, entail a specific way of looking at it, however vague and general the terms of the definition. Basically, *Australia* is not different from Bodmer's abstract piece. Why, then, should its forms do more than set up a certain rhythm and movement, why should they signify or *re*-present as well? There are elements in this composition that can be considered as figurative, allusions to instruments perhaps, levers or springs. These technological allusions the spectator is free to develop further, though whether he will find guidance in the title is a different matter. A parallel signifying intention might be discerned in the enveloping sweep of the work, a hieroglyph for the wide open spaces of the Fifth Continent. But the forms are not univocal and the scope for interpretation is limited.

Max Bill's 22 (fig. 155) does not, strictly speaking, fit into the series of works discussed so far. But it would be just as much out of place anywhere else in my selection, so pronounced is its "otherness." It is not merely that the relatively thin white marble plate with twenty-two perforations disposed in a meander sets itself off in its mathematical conception from the world of nature (which, incidentally, does not prevent it from having a more convincing presence than many a naturalist figure); it is different also in its execution, in the extreme simplicity of form and the complete absence of any individual "handwriting." The contrast is particularly telling if one compares Bill's 22 with, say, Arp's *Moon-like, hollowed out, ghostly* (fig. 127). Both are abstract, but Arp's composition "belongs" to nature; whereas Bill's square plate with the carefully plotted holes is a foreign body in it. This is not meant to be in the least derogatory, only to bring out the specific character of this artistic enterprise in which calculating invention replaces the free play of the imagination and in which formal order achieves aesthetically satisfying results, indeed creates symbols for our time. Max Bill himself points out that a mathematical way of thinking has, in spite of its apparent rationality, a certain ideological colouring which cannot be made fully explicit.

Bill's composition is slight in volume, its twenty-two holes serving neither to reveal an interior nor to communicate with external space. The perforations are points in a rhythmic pattern developed two-dimensionally on the surface and the overall impression is also one of flatness in spite of the fact that the work is clearly a plastic

139. JEAN CHAUVIN Wind of Life, 1949 Bronze $7^{1}/_{8}'' \times 26''$ Fernand C. Graindorge collection, Liège Photo: G. Jacoby, Liège

141. Étienne Béothy

Nocturno, 1956
Avodivé wood Height 47 1/4″
Photo: Author

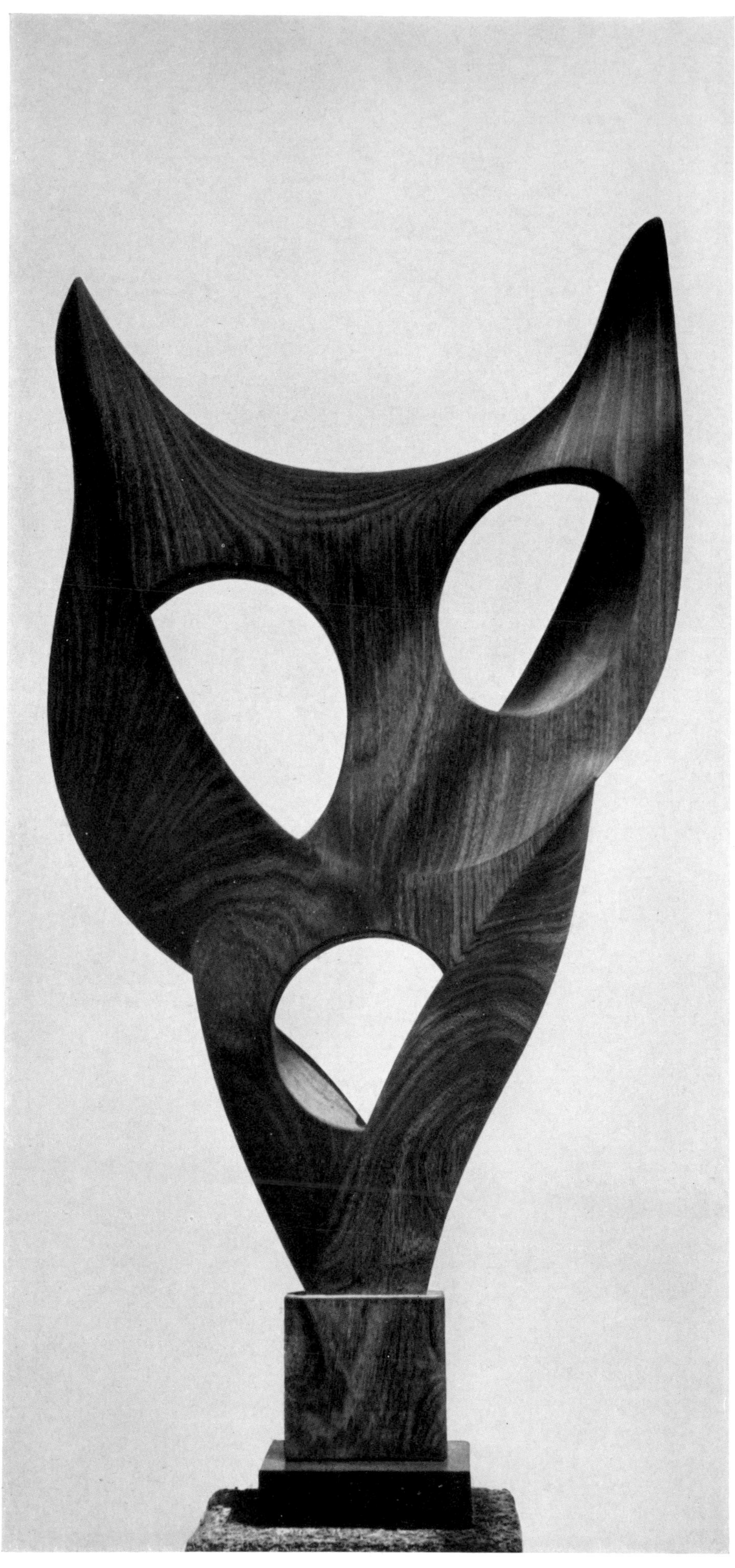

140. Marta Pan

Sculpture 53: Equilibrium, 1958
Ebony Height 13″
H. Wise collection,
Cleveland, Ohio, USA
Photo: Ifert

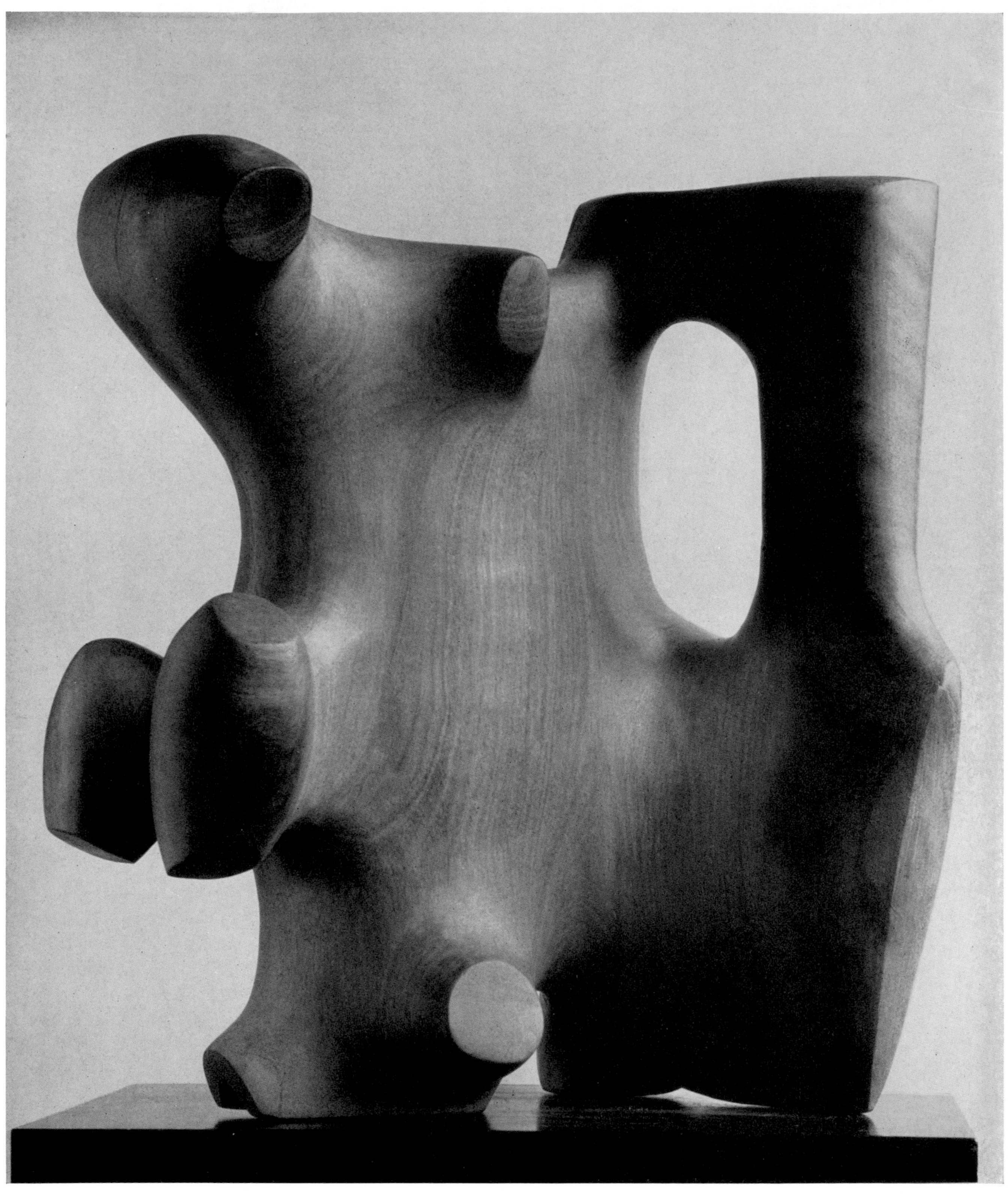

142. Karl Hartung Sculpture, 1947 Mahogany Height 14⁵/₈" Photo: Gnilka, Berlin

object. The constructive sculptor can, like Bill, express himself in precisely calculated and perfectly executed forms; he can also use what he finds ready formed to integrate it in a new order. This is the case with Ettore Colla, who constructs figures and reliefs out of clippings. The fantastical, the bizarre and the surprising, all characteristic of the works of other sculptors in this medium and conjuring up their Dada forebears, are of less interest to Colla; his aim is to bring out the formal harmonies that he discerns in what he finds. He does not, therefore, impose new shapes on the objects he assembles but studies their formal properties in order to elicit the elements of a significant pattern which he then proceeds to realise. The cooling tubes, winches, telephone insulators or simply rusty iron plate remain what they are. Only, by virtue of what the artist has discovered them to be, they acquire a new function—usually without any figurative reference—which removes them from the domain of technology to that of form—constructive form, as details like the use of screws and screw nuts attest. Colla's compositions embody the paradox of non-objective sculpture made up of objects.

The last few examples have taken me into the territory of constructivist sculpture. I have entered it without mentioning the fathers of the movement, Antoine Pevsner and Naum Gabo, as my ahistorical approach entitles me to do: the works selected for discussion are intended neither to illustrate a process of evolution nor to be representative in any way of the *oeuvre* of any given artist. My concern is with the individual work of art as an entity that creates its own norms. Thus I turn first to a younger constructivist, the Dane Robert Jacobsen who forges frame-like shapes out of massive iron plate; in the example illustrated (fig. 156) the frames can be made to rotate about their axis and assume various positions in relation to each other. Stability and static rhythm characterise also André Volten's *Construction with Crystal* (fig. 157) and Bernhard Luginbühl's *Composition 1959* (fig. 158), of which the first projects itself into general space while the second encompasses a private space allowing only the intervals to communicate with the exterior.

Ibram Lassaw, an American sculptor working in metal, creates sculptural space by composing transparent architectonic patterns with variations in the concentration and thickness of the solid parts which produce correlative variations in the depth of the space enclosed and filled by the composition (fig. 159). The natural colour of the metals and alloys used has a part to play in translating "internal and external reality" —of which Lassaw is a keen observer—into the language of sculpture.

Pevsner, two of whose earlier works have already been mentioned (figs. 16 and 88), rejects as passive static rhythms, flat surfaces and the simple order of horizontals and verticals. He postulates instead spatially active, that is curved surfaces (fig. 160) which both annex space and shape it. He produces them by ranging linear elements in rapid succession—brass rods which he welds together. His compositions, whose dynamic rhythm is supposed to contain time as "emotional factor" or "ideal substance," are far more complex than those of his followers. They present a varied play of light and shadow which—in opposition to Rodin—does not take place on the surface of the work but penetrates to the interior. However, Pevsner's purpose is not an exclusively artistic one as the refined perfection of his technique might suggest. His ultimate concern is with the function of sculpture in human society; I shall deal with this aspect of the matter when I come to speak of the tasks of sculpture as a public art.

Hans Uhlmann's *Rondo* (fig. 161) is conceived in a similar spirit, though it differs in theme and technique: two dancing movements, one effected by the close "steps" and the torsion of the bundle of brass rods in the centre, the other, wider and more sweeping, by curved brass bands.

Pevsner's brother, Naum Gabo, has pursued a parallel line which leads to spatially active constructions. He prefers transparent media to metal, so that his compositions appear almost immaterial, surfaces and volumes carved out in space and consisting of it. His *Spiral Theme* (fig. 162), in plastic, with its skilfully contrived, multi-directional movement is a variation on the general theme of constructivism: spatial forms active in time. But for Gabo this postulate is as little an end in itself as for Pevsner. Neither wants *l'art pour l'art* but realistic symbols of "progress." They look upon their spatial constructions as artistic equivalents of changes in science and society or, to use Gabo's words, as "essences of a world that is being striven for." Gabo's contention that constructivism is four-dimensional, because it introduces the element of time into sculpture, should also be understood in the light of these preoccupations. However, Gabo takes time to be both real and illusionist movement as well as rhythm so that what he calls four-dimensional sculpture is not the exclusive domain of the constructivists.

The followers are less ambitious than the initiators but use a similar vocabulary. Constructivist ideas have caught on particularly in South America where the rankness of nature seems like a hubristic challenge to man, to answer which he has recourse to art. Gyula Kosice, living in Buenos Aires, has systematically developed Gabo's teaching and explores in transparent compositions of plexiglass (fig. 166) the possibilities inherent in his spatial structures. Ideologically too the *Madi* group to which Kosice belongs goes beyond the aesthetic function of the work of art and envisages the integration of the arts in a new social order that is to find its fullest expression in architecture and town-planning. Such a programme is not without precedent, but in South America its realisation seems to have been undertaken with the greatest vigour (e.g. Brasilia).

Also constructivist is the aluminium piece *Sphère-Tension* (fig. 163) by the young

143. UMBERTO MILANI Two-Front Sculpture No. 2, 1958 Bronze $24^{3}/_{8}'' \times 26^{3}/_{4}''$ Galleria del Milione, Milan Photo: Paolo Monti, Milan

144. Friederich Werthmann

Struktur Remanit, 1959
Steel Height 98 3/8″

145. Franco Garelli

Figure Ema, 1958
Iron Height 61″

147. Alexander Calder

The Whale, 1937
Stabile of sheet steel Height 87″
Museum of Modern Art, New York
Donated by the artist
Photo: Museum (Soichi Sunami)

146. Eduardo Chillida Terrosa, 1957 Iron Breadth 22 1/2″ Dr. Bernhard Sprengel collection, Hanover Photo: Hans Wagner, Hanover

148. BERTO LARDERA Cathedral of Pain V, 1956 Iron and mosaic 52″ × 53 1/8″ Photo: Author

149. NINO FRANCHINA

Nike, 1958
Iron and brass Height 106¼″
Photo: Oscar Savio, Rome

150. Luciano Minguzzi The Dragons, 1958 Iron and bronze Height 157 1/2" Photo: Author

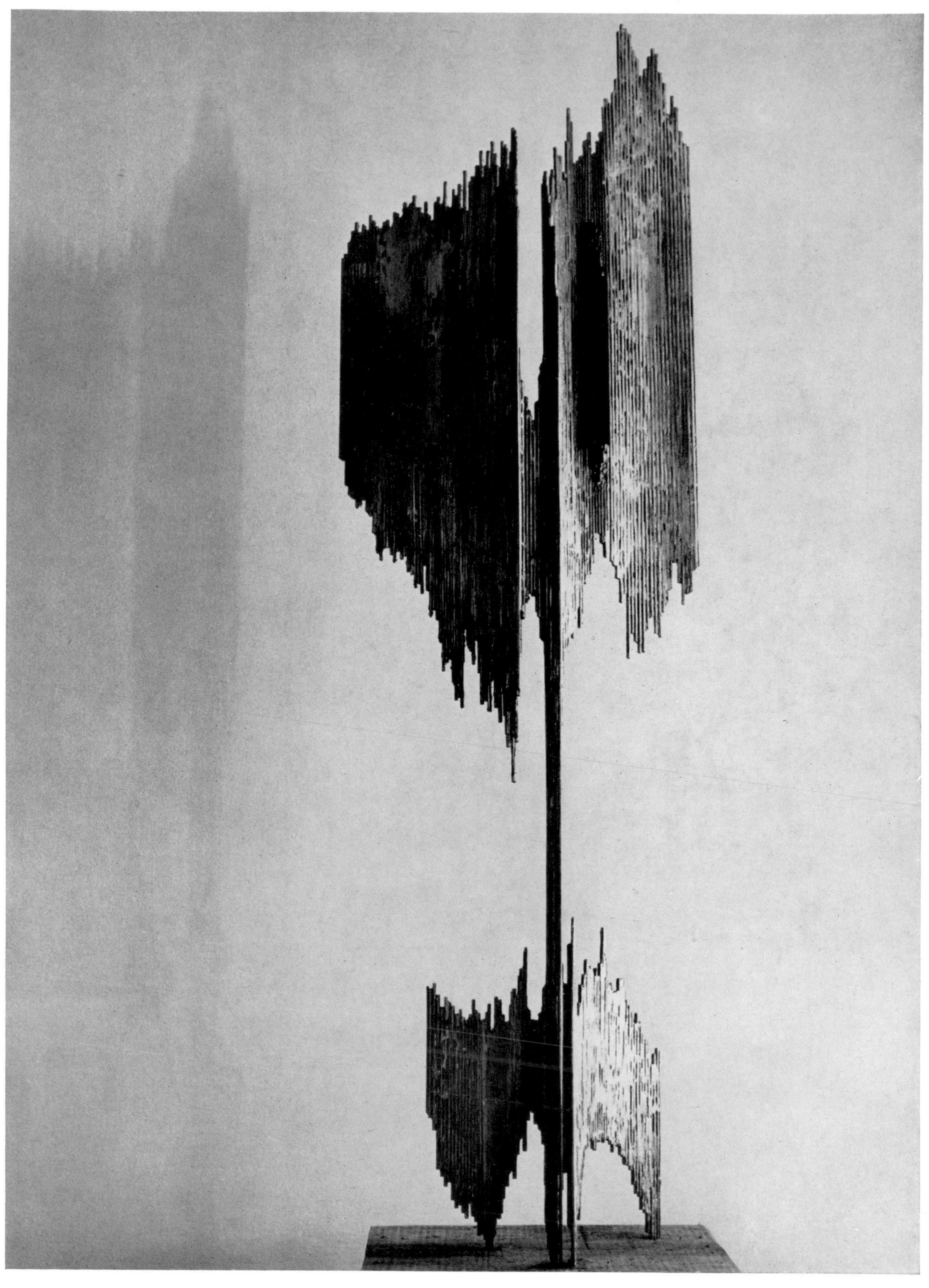

151. BRIGITTE MEIER-DENNINGHOFF Wings, 1958 Height 70 1/8" On permanent loan from the "Kulturkreis" Leverkusen Municipal Museum Photo: Martin Matschinsky

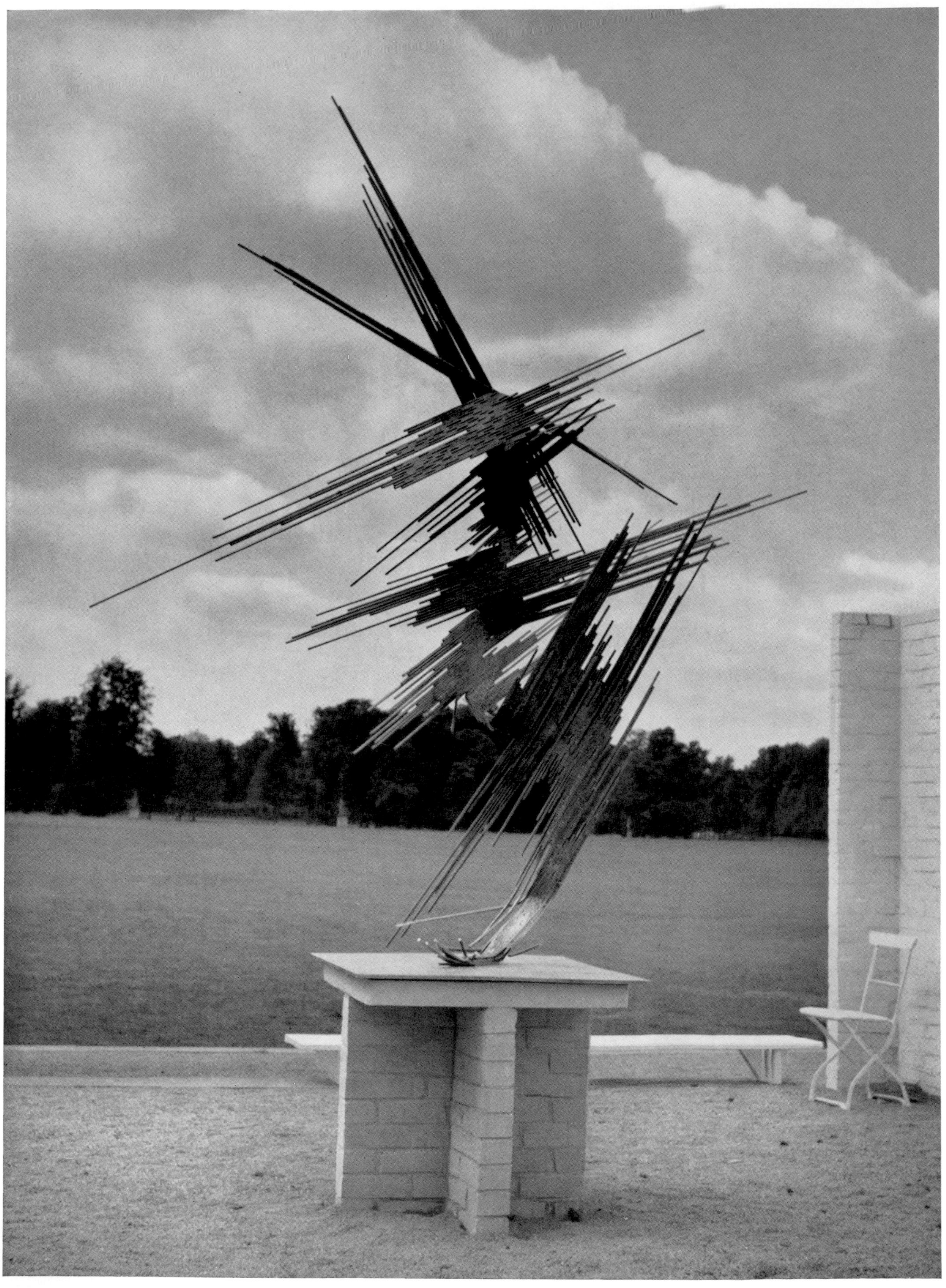

152. Norbert Kricke

Space Sculpture, 1958
Stainless steel
$112^{1}/_{4}'' \times 78^{3}/_{4}'' \times 70^{7}/_{8}''$
Leverkusen Municipality
Photo: Author

153. Walter Bodmer Sculpture, 1957–58 Iron $24^{3}/_{4}'' \times 58^{1}/_{4}''$ Photo: Author

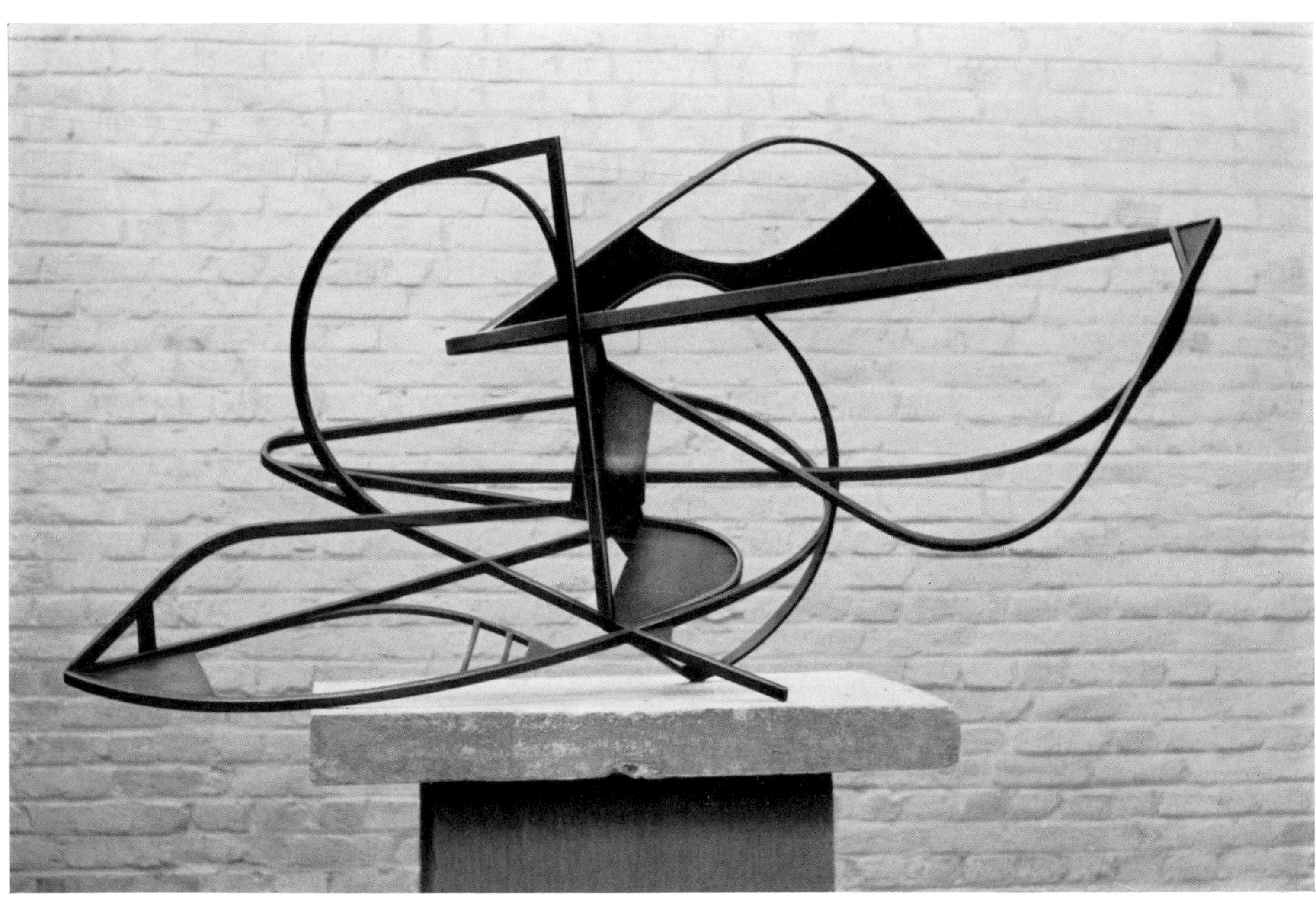

154. DAVID SMITH Australia, 1951 Steel Breadth 108 3/8″ Photo: Author

155. MAX BILL 22, 1953–57 Marble Height $58^{1}/_{4}$″ Photo: Author

156. Robert Jacobsen Construction, 1950–54 Iron 18 1/8" × 20 1/2" × 20 1/2" Stedelijk Museum, Amsterdam Photo: Author

157. André Volten Construction with Crystal, 1956 Steel Height 63″ Photo: Peter Marcuse

158. BERNHARD LUGINBÜHL

Composition, 1959
Iron 17 3/4" × 13 3/8" × 13 3/8"
Kunstmuseum Berne
Photo: Leonardo Bezzola, Berne

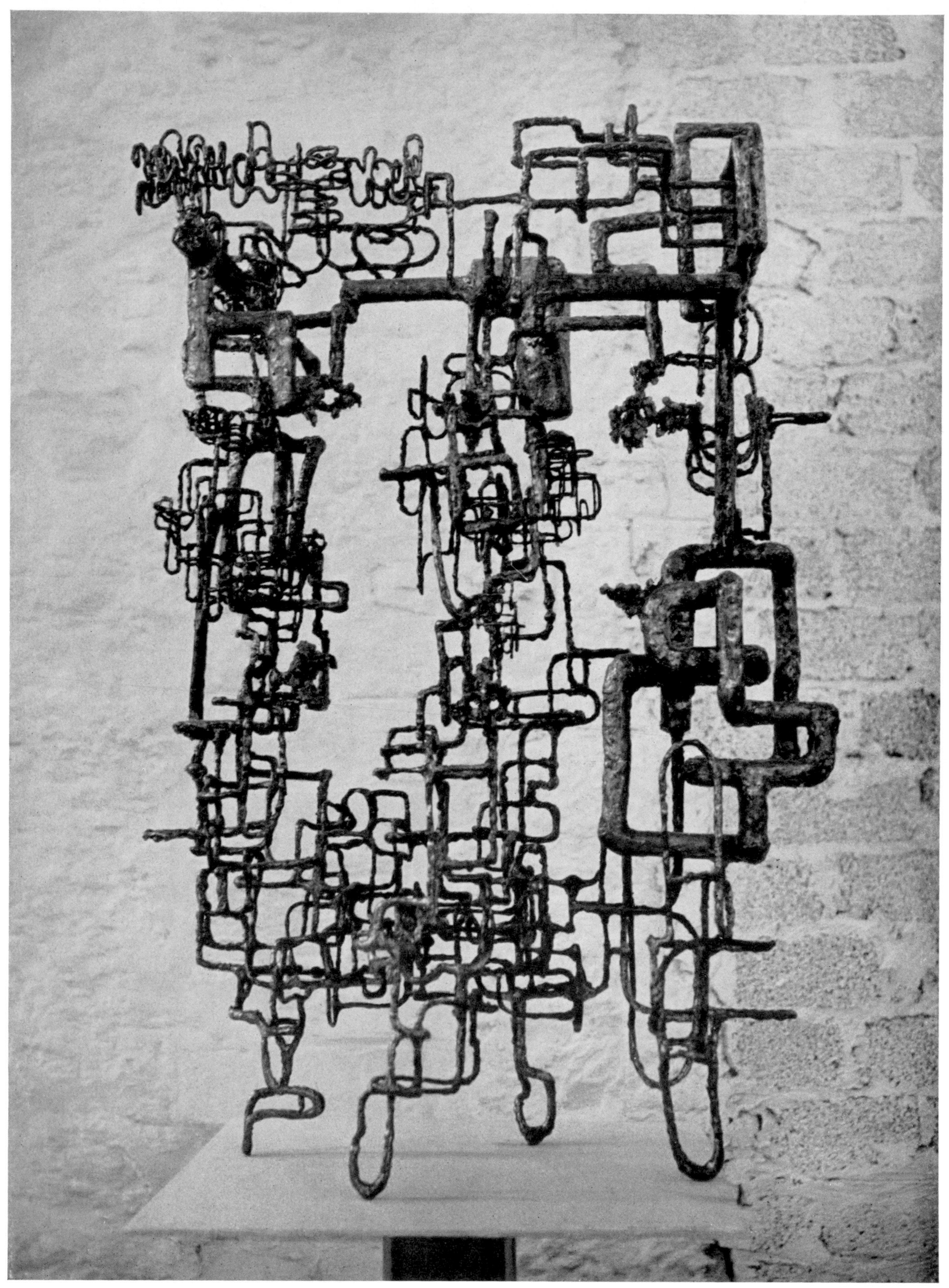

159. IBRAM LASSAW Counterpoint Castle, 1957 Bronze and copper Height 39″ Kootz Gallery, New York Photo: Author

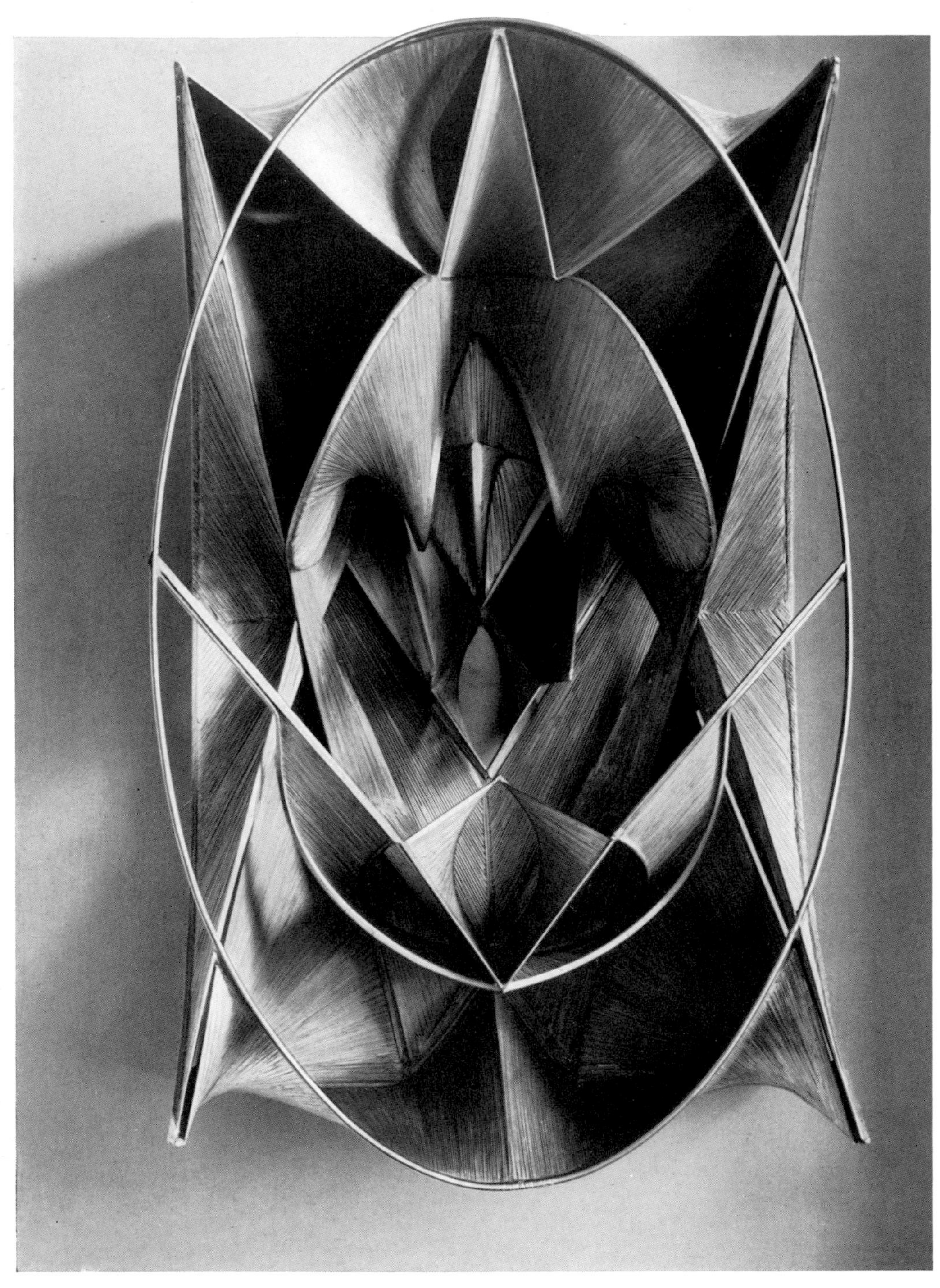

160. Antoine Pevsner Oval Fresco, 1945 Brass $51^{1}/_{8}'' \times 34^{1}/_{4}'' \times 13''$
Stedelijk Museum, Amsterdam Photo: Author

161. Hans Uhlmann

Rondo, 1958–59
Brass 59″ × 35³/₈″ × 31¹/₂″
Photo: Gnilka, Berlin

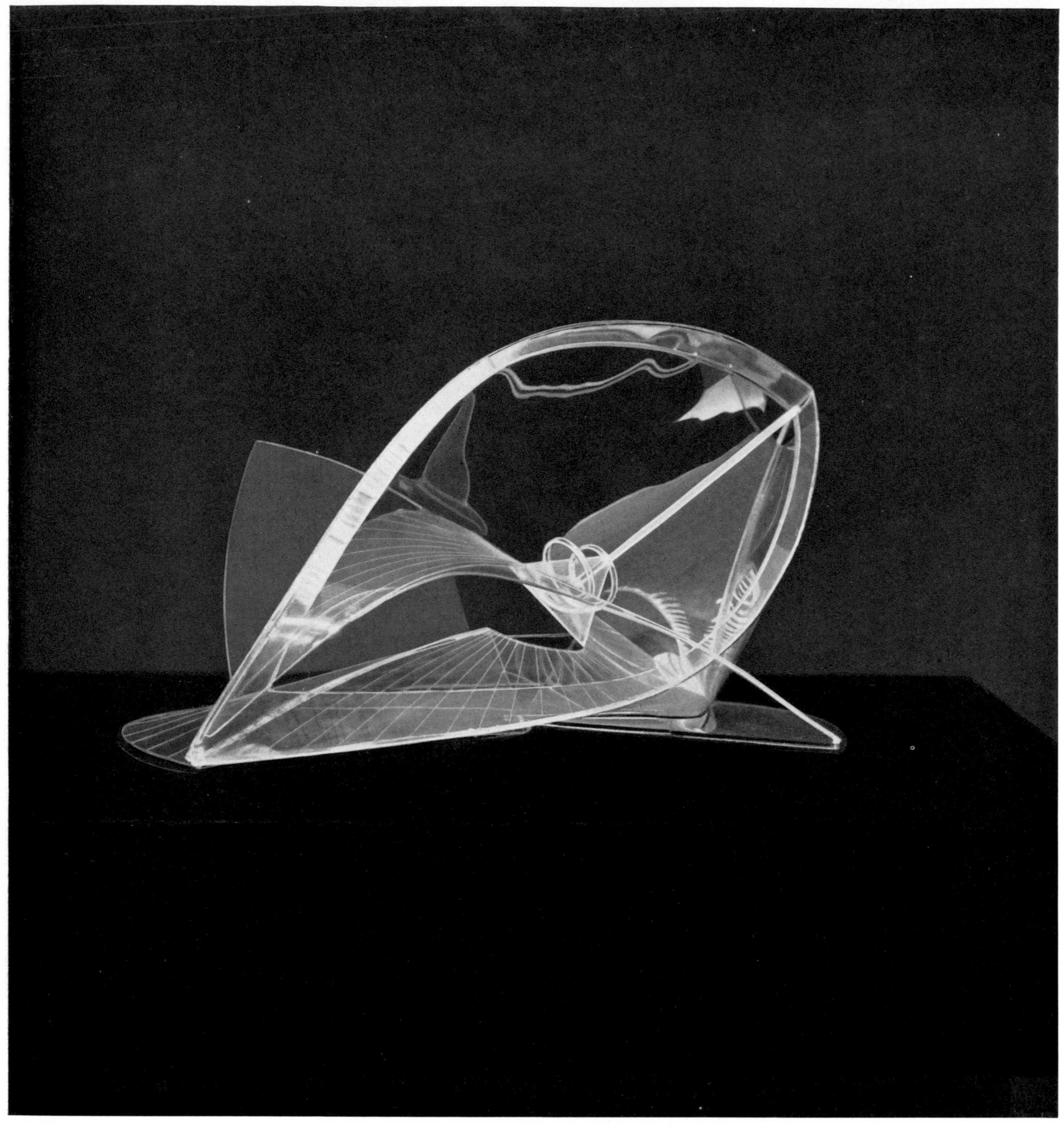

162. NAUM GABO Spiral Theme, 1941 Plastic Height 7 1/2" Museum of Modern Art, New York Photo: Museum

163. MARY VIEIRA Sphère-Tension, 1956–58 Aluminium 12 5/8" × 25 1/4" Floersheim collection, Chicago
Photo: Galerie d'Art Moderne, Basle

165. André Bloc

Brass Sculpture, 1959
Height $27^{5}/_{8}$"
Photo: Gilles Ehrmann
Bois-Colombes/Seine

164. José de Rivera Construction 8, 1954 Wrought chrome-nickel steel Height $9^{1}/_{2}$" Museum of Modern Art, New York, donated by Mrs. Heinz Schulz
Photo: Museum (Soichi Sunami)

166. Gyula Kosice

Sculpture, 1959 Plexiglass Height 23⅝″
Galerie Denise René, Paris

167. Kenneth Martin

Screw Mobile, 1959
Phosphor-bronze
Height 24⅞″
Photo: Adrian Flowers

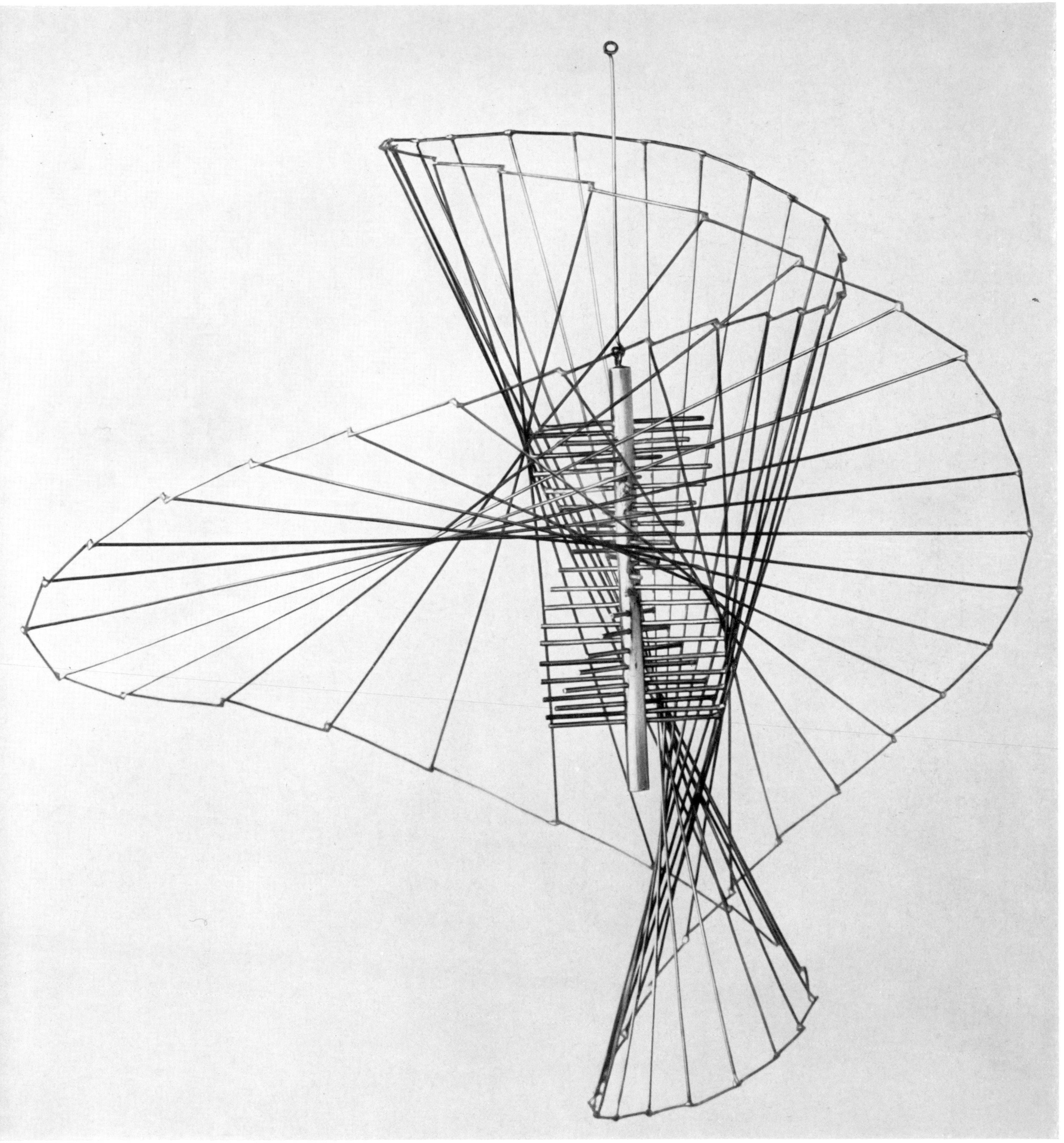

168. HANS VERHULST Natural Disaster, 1959 Bronze $9^{7}/_{8}'' \times 23^{5}/_{8}''$ Photo: Bram Wisman, Amsterdam

169. Raoul Ubac
Slate Relief, 1954

170. EMIL CIMIOTTI Rocks and Clouds, 1959 Bronze $17^{3}/_{4}'' \times 19^{5}/_{8}'' \times 11^{3}/_{4}''$ Private collection
Photo: Dr. Wolfgang Salchow, Cologne

171. Jochen Hiltmann Crazy Vegetation, 1959 Refined steel Diameter 55 1/8″ Schniewind collection, Neviges

172. ISAMU NOGUCHI Night Voyage, 1948 York marble Length 45 1/4" Stable Gallery, New York Photo: Author

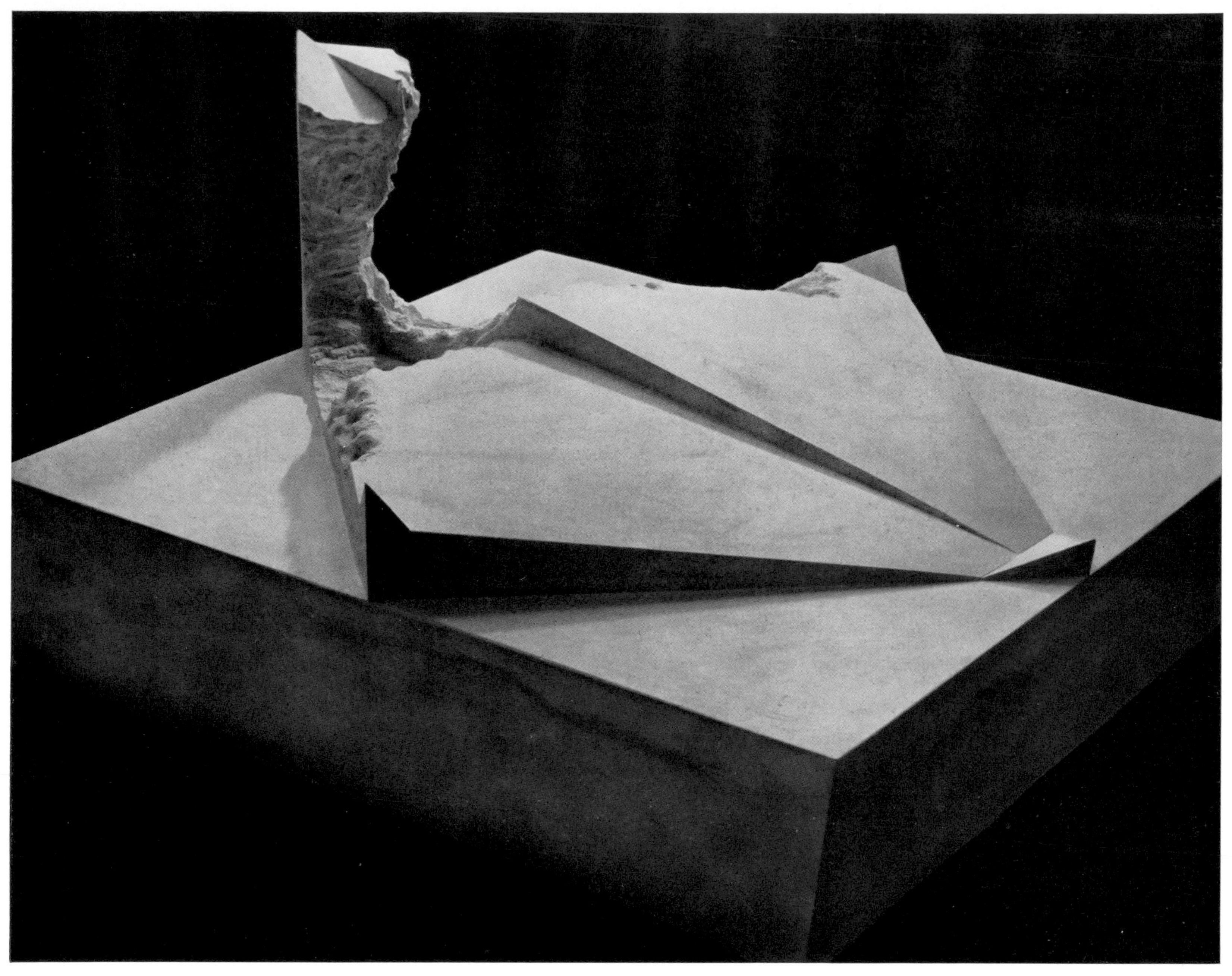

173. Günter Neusel Sculpture, 1956 Plaster for bronze $19^{5}/_{8}'' \times 19^{5}/_{8}''$ Beatefoto, Kassel

174. E. R. Nele

Relief, 1958 Iron *c.* 47¹/₄″ × 27⁵/₈″
Dr. Bechtler collection, Zürich

Brazilian Mary Vieira in which circular and spherical forms are held in a tense equilibrium between movement and rest. This harmony of movement in space, non-utilitarian technics and perfect execution characterises likewise *Construction 8* (fig. 164) in chromium-plated steel by the North American sculptor José de Rivera who makes infinite lines glide through space in a simple rhythm. In his own words: "The prime function is the total experience of the production. The social function, the communication of that experience."*

The integration of the arts, which I shall discuss further on with examples, has been taken up as a vocation by André Bloc who, apart from theoretical pronouncements and his work as a publicist, elaborates his own artistic solutions (fig. 165). Bloc's original preference was for solid, compact volume; he has abandoned it for airy constructions of metal rods, transparent honeycombs built into space. The systems of basic geometrical forms thus created Bloc regards as programmatic statements for the larger task of a world-transforming synthesis of the arts.

Though the works I have just discussed may have involved the use of technical procedures, they are intended as protests against the domination of the machine. Kenneth Martin, for instance, whose *Screw Mobile* is shown here (fig. 167), took part in an exhibition called *Artist against Machine*. Equilibrium and movement in space are the chief concern of the *plasticien-technicien*. He experiments with contemporary materials and technical procedures in order to harness them to his purpose, which is not only to create symbols for our time but also to exercise a direct influence by the use that can be made of his work. Martin has expounded this in his lectures on the connection between mobile sculpture and scientific research; he has also put it into practice by making mobiles for a children's hospital.

After discussing spatial construction in sculpture it would seem logical to turn to the relation between sculpture and architecture. However, I am reserving this problem for the last chapter where it will be treated in a larger context, and turn first to what is a somewhat unusual subject in the history of the art: *landscape in sculpture* or—to avoid the misapprehension that a parallel to naturalist landscape painting is intended —*sculpture as landscape*. While the converse, the articulation of a landscape or a garden in sculptural terms is known from the past, the introduction into sculpture of landscape and the surface of the earth in a general sense as motifs in their own right is a new and recent phenomenon.

Not that analogies with landscape could not be found in some of the works already treated (e.g. Henry Moore's and Barbara Hepworth's "landscape figures," the compositions of A. Giacometti or the early works of Brigitte Meier-Denninghoff). But the

* *Twelve Americans*, ed. Dorothy C. Miller, New York 1956.

significance of the theme will be more effectively brought out if it is illustrated from clear-cut cases such as *Sculpture* (fig. 173) by Günter Neusel which as an architectural model presupposes landscape as its environment, or the bronze *Natural Disaster* (fig. 168) by the Dutchman Hans Verhulst, a symbol of the struggle of man against the unleashed elements. The landscape theme is even more explicit in Emil Cimiotti's *Rocks and Clouds* (fig. 170). Rocks and clouds occur as properties in Baroque sculpture—e.g. in church pulpits in the Low Countries or in Bernini's *Ecstasy of St. Teresa* —but here for the first time they are made the chief and only subject of a sculptural composition. Cimiotti's idiom is Baroque, which explains perhaps why he was attracted by this theme when he worked in Rome for a few months. While some of his wax models are still in the process of changing from a group of figures (compare fig. 81) to a landscape, the bronze piece has definitely emerged from this metamorphosis. The light, broken clouds and the mass of rock are set out in effective contrasts of the compact and the open, of stability and motion.

While Cimiotti discovers extraordinary landscapes in Rome, Raoul Ubac, who grew up in the forests of the Ardennes, remains wholly attached as an artist to the spectacle of nature. His reliefs carved in slate (fig. 169) transform, as K. H. Goerres puts it, tree and rock, the archetypal experiences of his childhood, into heraldic signs.

Jochen Hiltmann's *Crazy Vegetation* (fig. 171; steel) appears like a landscape from the first days of Creation. Against the uniform pattern of the millstone, ready made and thus providing a welcome contrast, the mass of steel, still liquid from the heat of the welding burner, is beginning to set into hilly formations. Evolution of the earth—that is the theme of the piece in which "dry" land is born out of primeval chaos by the double process of solidifying into shape and emerging from an infinite expanse of waving spirals.

Compared with the cosmic event portrayed by Hiltmann, Isamu Noguchi's *Night Voyage* (fig. 172) strikes one as a piece of cultivated nature. Ever since his *Model for Contoured Playground* of 1940, Noguchi, modelling eminences and depressions, gentle valleys and precipitous conical mountains, has striven to unite solid volume with open space in the way that in nature the earth unites with the sky to form a landscape. For Noguchi, who is of Japanese extraction and familiar with Far Eastern art, nature is always ordered nature, with a complex system of relationships as it appears in the Japanese garden of which the marble composition is an epitome.

Apart from "geological" preoccupations present also in the relief painting of Jean Dubuffet, K. F. Dahmen, Emil Schumacher and others, the predominant tendency in modern "landscape sculpture" is a Surrealist one. There is an affinity between Surrealism and Romantic landscape art which can be observed, for instance, in the *Forests* of Max Ernst. Another aspect is illustrated in *Nightscape* (fig. 176), a wood compo-

175. BERNARD ROSENTHAL

Riverrun, 1959
Black aluminium 87" × 57 5/8"

176. LOUISE NEVELSON

Nightscape II
Wood $65^{3}/_{8}'' \times 61''$
Galerie Daniel Cordier, Paris
Photo: Henri Glaeser

177. Arnaldo Pomodoro

The Land Surveyor's Table, 1958
Zinc, brass, copper and tin
$94^{1/2}" \times 53^{1/8}"$
Photo: Ferruzzi, Venice

178. Berto Lardera The Hours and the Days No. 1, 1958–59 Stainless steel and iron 11′6″ × 11″6′ Private collection

sition by Louise Nevelson who has devised plastic symbols for expressing the irrational emotion aroused by the experience of what in her case is a townscape.

On the other hand Arnaldo Pomodoro's metal relief *The Land Surveyor's Table* (fig. 177) is not inspired by the dark side of art. It presents an analysis of soil structure, calling to mind geological cross-sections, mineral deposits and landmarks. But these associations are just as optional for the spectator as those evoked by the nocturnal scene of Nevelson; the richness of the artist's invention, though expressed in objects is not confined to them and can suggest other, non-objective correspondences as well. This applies also to Nele's *Relief* (fig. 174) with its structured surface and plastic thickets, and to Bernard Rosenthal's *Riverrun* (fig. 175)—at once a bird's-eye view of fertile or parched earth and invented objects with a reality of their own; not representations of the earth but metaphorical equivalents for it.

These sculptural paraphrases of landscape may be followed, in conclusion, by Berto Lardera's ground composition *The Hours and the Days* (fig. 178). It is part of a landscape garden, its flat layers fitting into the pattern but maintaining the contrast between artifact and nature. Lardera's piece shows that sculpture can not only represent landscape but enter into landscape to become, through its otherness, an organon of interpretation, while at the same time the fact of its being set in landscape adds to its own artistic strength. "The composition," says Lardera, "can be arranged in various ways, and thus it belongs to the seasons, in the best sense to the 'moods' of the seasons and their effects."

III THE PROBLEM OF PURPOSE

One more problem remains to be tackled, that of the purpose of modern sculpture. To pose it is not necessarily a reflection on sculpture that finds its place in the museum or the private house—after all the majority of the examples discussed in this book belong to that category. But sculpture is by tradition a public art and, after a period of alienation, the problem of its function in society has again become relevant.

Sculpture appears in the public realm in one of two ways: either as a monument or in combination with architecture. Let us consider first the monument; here of course, we can provide only a small selection of examples. Moreover, the discussion must clearly be limited to works either commissioned as monuments or intended as such by the artist, excluding, that is, works which owe their monumental status to an improvisation. There is nothing in the 20th century to compare with the vogue for monuments that characterised the 19th. Nor can the tendency of that century to eclectic "revivals" blind us to the merits of such works as Auguste Rodin's *Balzac* and *The Burghers of Calais* (both, it is true, erected as monuments only after the artist's death), Constantin Meunier's *Monument to Labour*, H. Lederer's Bismarck in Hamburg and Adolf von Hildebrand's Wittelsbach Fountain—or, conversely, to the monstrosities of our own time. Both centuries have aberrations to show in this domain. They cannot be chronicled here, any more than we can attempt to sketch the history of the monument from the obelisk to the *Atomium.* The subject, especially the 19th-century "national monument," would repay detailed investigation.

It has been said that our century, having tired of the type of symbolism traditionally associated with public monuments has turned its back on the genre altogether. But the rejection of the old has gone hand in hand with the emergence of the new: examples like the project for an abstract monument by H. Obrist, the models and ideas of Tatlin or Van Doesburg or Picasso's *projets pour un monument* are enough to show that a new symbolic idiom has been in process of elaboration. However, the public monument of our time can no longer imitate Renaissance fountains and Baroque apotheoses or serve to glorify deserving individuals. Its sense must be wider and more spiritual. This new tendency, already apparent in compositions like *Parents in Mourning* by Käthe Kollwitz, Barlach's Güstrow Memorial (second cast in Cologne), and Rodin's *Balzac*, becomes fully explicit in the attempts of the younger generation of sculptors to express through abstract signs the meaning and destiny of our time—witness Le Corbusier's Monument of the Open Hand for Chandigarh or the international competitions for a monument of the unknown political prisoner and for a memorial at Auschwitz.

The most celebrated public monument of the post-war years is, no doubt, Ossip Zadkine's *Destroyed City* (fig. 179), erected as a warning memorial of the bombing of Rotterdam. A cry made palpable in bronze, it rises in the midst of a wide square surrounded by the sluices, basins and new buildings of the resurrected city. In a powerful gesture, at once prayer and defence, the figure, pierced through in the middle, stretches its arms towards the sky from which in 1940 came death and destruction, and which it now entreats for a better future. The profoundly moving message of this monument can leave no one indifferent: the thrust into space, fully in view from every angle, is an appeal to humanity, all the more telling because free of resentment. *Destroyed City* has thus become an adequate symbol of the new Rotterdam.

Henry Moore's *Upright Motives* (fig. 180) which include the Glenkiln Cross are temporarily monuments without a site. But while these lines are being written negotiations are in progress to acquire either the Glenkiln Cross alone or the whole group for erection in some German town. They were photographed in their temporary surroundings during an open air exhibition. The monumental intention is obvious and so is the essential character of the relation to space. *Upright Motives* will come fully into their own on a public site in the open.

They have been interpreted as modern variations of ancient symbols; in particular the Glenkiln Cross has been compared to the Anglo-Saxon high crosses of the early Middle Ages. Analogies of this kind are undoubtedly present; they could even put one in mind of the three Crosses on Golgotha. But *Upright Motives* can be seen with equal cogency as primeval plastic forms. As with all great works of art no one interpretation exhausts the variety of possible meanings.

179. Ossip Zadkine The Destroyed City, 1951–53 Monument for Rotterdam Bronze Height 21′ 4″ Photo: Author

180. HENRY MOORE Upright Motives No. 1, 2 and 7, 1955–56 Bronze Height *c.* 10′—11′ Photo: Author

181. MARINO MARINI

Equestrian Monument, 1958–59
The Hague, Bouwgelust settlement
Bronze Height (without base) 16′ 5″
Photo: Dienst voor Schone Kunsten
der Gemeente 's Gravenhage

184. Helmut Wolff Design for an Auschwitz Monument, 1958 Wood Height 35 3/8″, Length 51 1/8″, Depth 22″ Intended for concrete (60′ × 85′ 4″ × 36′ 1″)

185. Mathias Goeritz

The Square of the Five Towers, 1957
Entrance to the satellite town
Mexico City Reinforced concrete
Height 121′, Length 164′
Photo: Marianne Goeritz

183. Reg Butler

Design for a Monument of an Unknown Political Prisoner, 1952
Bronze wire, sheet metal and plaster
Height 17 7/8″
Photo: F. L. Kenett, London

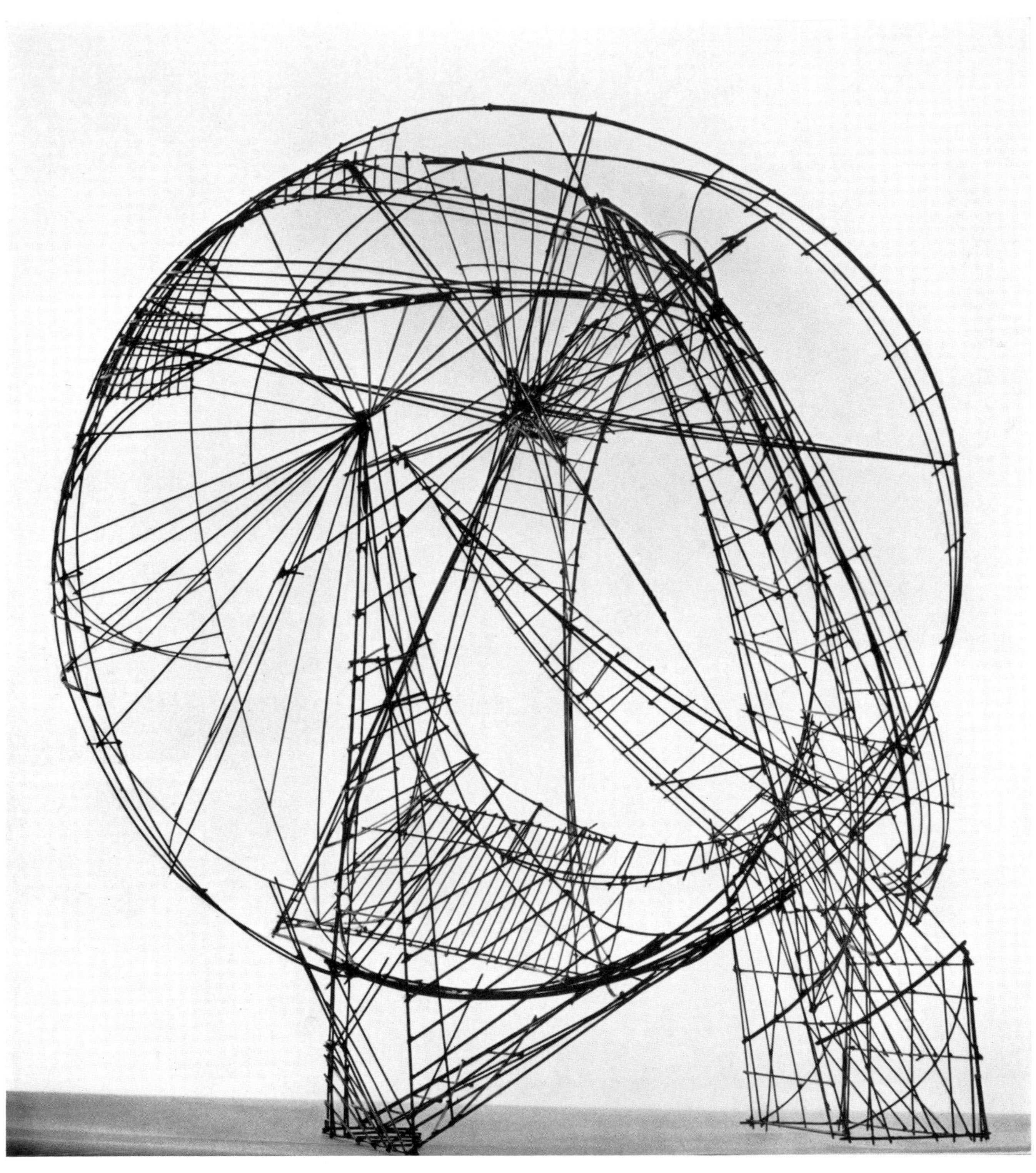

182. CONSTANT Projected Monument for Amsterdam, 1955 Iron wire Height 28 3/8″ Scale of model 1:25
Photo: Jan Versnel, Amsterdam

186. RUDOLF STEINER Goetheanum, Dornach near Basle, 1925–28 Reinforced concrete Height 121′, Length 295′, Breadth 276′
Photo: Author

187. LE CORBUSIER The Pilgrim Church of Notre-Dame du Haut, Ronchamp, 1950–55 North front with side towers Height 49′ Photo: Author

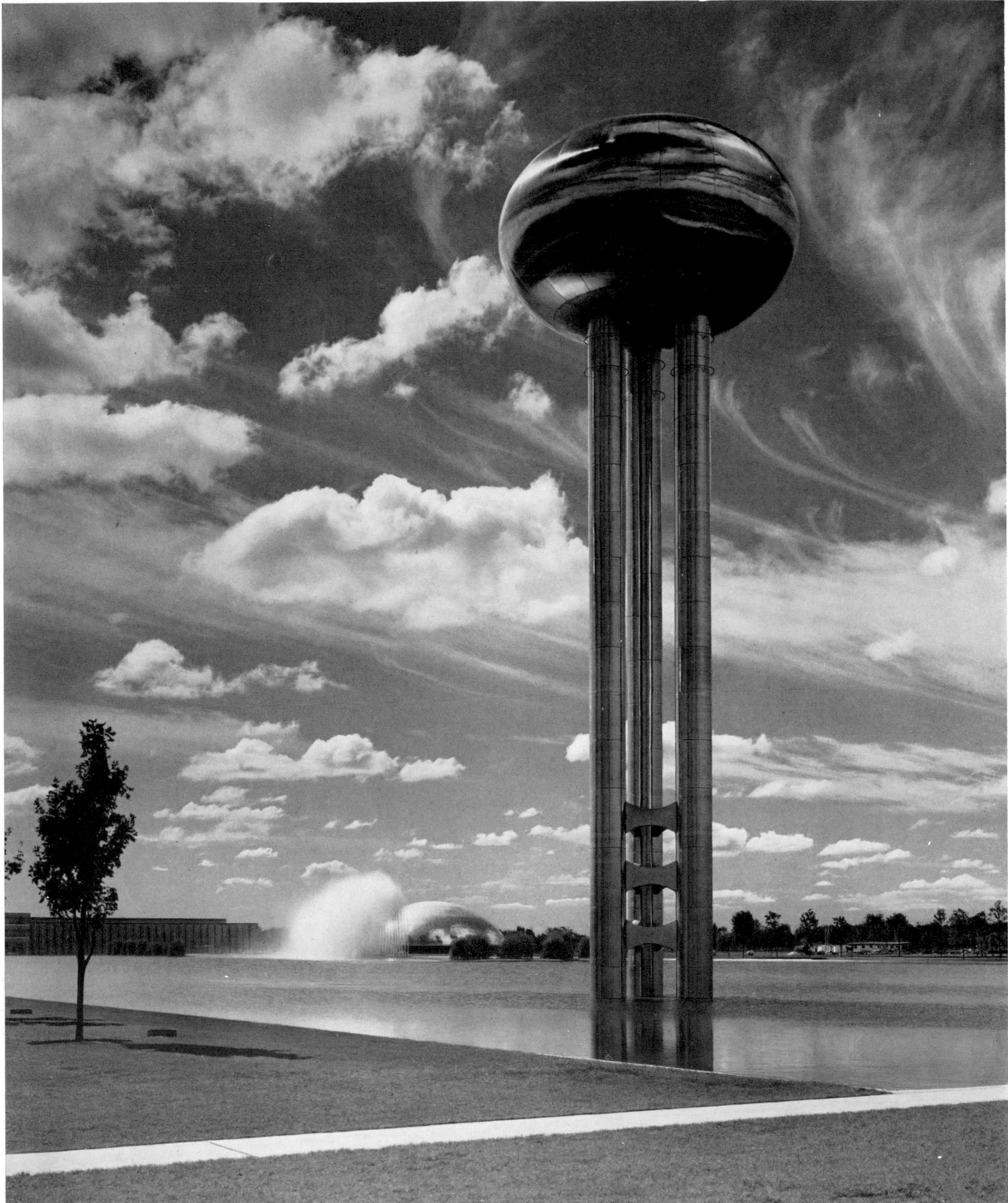

188. Eero Saarinen

General Motors Co. Technical Centre, Detroit, 1951–56
Water Tower of stainless steel Height *c.* 131′
Foto: Ezra Stoller

189. Isamu Noguchi Japanese Garden, 1958 UNESCO Building, Paris Photo: Author

190. Henry Moore Wall Relief at the Bouwcentrum, Rotterdam, 1955 (Arch. C. W. Boks) Brick Height *c.* 28′ 3″, Length 63′ Photo: Author

Marino Marini has so far had only one commission for an over-life-size rider to be erected as a monument on a specified site. His creation for the Bouwgelust settlement at the Hague (fig. 181) can be considered as the sum of his explorations of what is a central theme in his art. The work is a synthesis of abstract architecture and figural expression with a particular emphasis on the structural and tectonic element—more pronounced than in other compositions—so as to provide a clear and convincing relationship with the surrounding space and buildings.

Many modern monuments, especially those designed by the Constructivists, remain utopias. Vladimir Tatlin's design for a memorial to the Revolution, Pevsner's sketches for large sculptural complexes such as town centres, as well as the more recent *Projected Monument for Amsterdam* (fig. 182) by Constant, have not or not yet progressed beyond the model stage and have had no direct social impact. Constant said in 1958: "The artist's task is to invent new techniques, and to use light, tone, movement and, in general, every device that will influence the environment"; and he added in 1960, in connection with an exhibition of his work at the Van de Loo Gallery at Essen: "A universal work of art is related to life in all its aspects. In a unitary society, town life as we know it will no longer exist. Town planning will mean: interrelatedness of all forms of life in every respect." While Constant's work, as he is himself aware ("our game is the science fiction of social life and urban architecture"), embodies no more than a preliminary outline of his ideas, another bold venture in the same direction, Reg Butler's *Monument of an Unknown Political Prisoner* (fig. 183), to be erected in Berlin, seems much nearer to the projected final version. Admitting of many levels of meaning, this abstract structure combined with a naturalist group of figures has become a symbol of the overcoming of persecution and the fear of it.

The models of Constant and Butler postulate that the dimensions of the actual construction shall be huge. In other words, sculpture must itself become architecture, something one can step into and walk through. A similarly monumental scale is envisaged by the young Berlin sculptor, Helmut Wolff, for the memorial at Auschwitz (fig. 184). It calls for a composition of heavy, partly overhanging cubes of concrete with entrances between them which are reduced, as they penetrate into the "architectural" mass, to the size of the human body—a reconstruction arresting in its immediacy of what befell the millions of victims.

Also architectural in design are the five coloured towers in reinforced concrete (fig. 185), erected by Matthias Goeritz to mark the entrance of the satellite town outside Mexico City. However, they do not create any inner space between them and their function is a purely plastic one. Serving no practical purpose they can be entirely devoted to signalising the presence of a new town. They thrust boldly into the countryside setting up a system of axes that relates settlement and landscape.

The last two examples of sculpture as architecture prompt one to consider the converse: architecture as sculpture. It is a relatively widespread modern development: not only the Eiffel Tower, the earliest piece of constructivist sculpture as Pevsner has called it, but the work of Frank Lloyd Wright, Charles R. Makintosh, Henry Van den Velde, Bernhard Hoetger, Joseph Olbrich, Antonio Gaudi and Erich Mendelsohn as well as the very recent buildings of Hugh H. Stubbins, Pier Luigi Nervi and Konrad Wachsmann, all belong to this category. It is worth noting, though, that plasticity in architecture is not an entirely new invention. Since the subject is too vast to be tackled here, a few examples must suffice. One of the most significant, to my mind, is the Goetheanum at Dornach (fig. 186), designed by Rudolf Steiner, an amateur and "outsider" in architecture steadily ignored by the historians of the art. Steiner, the founder of anthroposophy, advocated "organic architecture" for which he elaborated a formal idiom evidently akin to the so-called organic abstraction in modern sculpture. When the first, wooden Goetheanum was burned down, Steiner had another one erected in reinforced concrete (1925–1928). This second edifice is in effect a gigantic piece of abstract sculpture: it was not built like a house, from inside out, so to speak, but enlarged from a model made by Steiner and cast in concrete. What is more, the visually sturdy walls offer little hint of the lightness of structure that can be achieved by this technique. The Goetheanum was clearly conceived as an organic sculptural solid to be carved in wood, the original medium being replaced by concrete for entirely practical reasons. The structure is at its most impressive seen from the outside, the magnificent mountain setting, in the midst of the Jura, enhancing the effect.

Le Corbusier's church at Ronchamp (fig. 187) is in many respects akin to the Goetheanum. Certain features in other buildings by Le Corbusier, such as the organic form of functional parts (e.g. chimneys), also recall Steiner's work. The emphasis at Ronchamp is on the body of the structure both in a geometrical and an organic sense, and sculptural values are in evidence in the articulation of individual parts as well as in the over-all conception which includes, no doubt, the integration of the edifice in the mountain scenery of the Jura.

Finally, one may classify as sculpture the water tower (fig. 188) in stainless steel, 40 metres high, standing in an artificial lake which belongs to the Technical Center built for General Motors at Detroit by Eero Saarinen. One expects water towers to be aesthetically among the least satisfactory features of an industrial plant. Against this expectation the effect of Saarinen's piece is all the more striking: a combination of bold design, sensitiveness to plastic form and a high standard of artistic excellence have resulted in a remarkable memorial to our technological age. Its full, rounded shape stands out against the flat façades of glass, steel and earthenware, while its

191. GÜNTER-FERDINAND RIS

Relief in Concrete (detail), 1959
Hildegardis Gymnasium
Cologne
(Arch. Berner and Jacobs)
27′3″ × 37′9″
Photo:
Dr. Wolfgang Salchow
Cologne

192. Karl Ehlers Buttressing Wall, 1957 LVA Clinic, Bad Salzuflen (Arch. Deilmann) Concrete Length 98′ 6″ Photo: Author

193. OTTO HERBERT HAJEK Spatial Wall, 1959 Revenue Office, Villingen (Arch. Carlfred Mutschler, Mannheim) Moulded concrete 6′ 10 5/8″ × 17′ 1″ × 2′ 11 3/8″

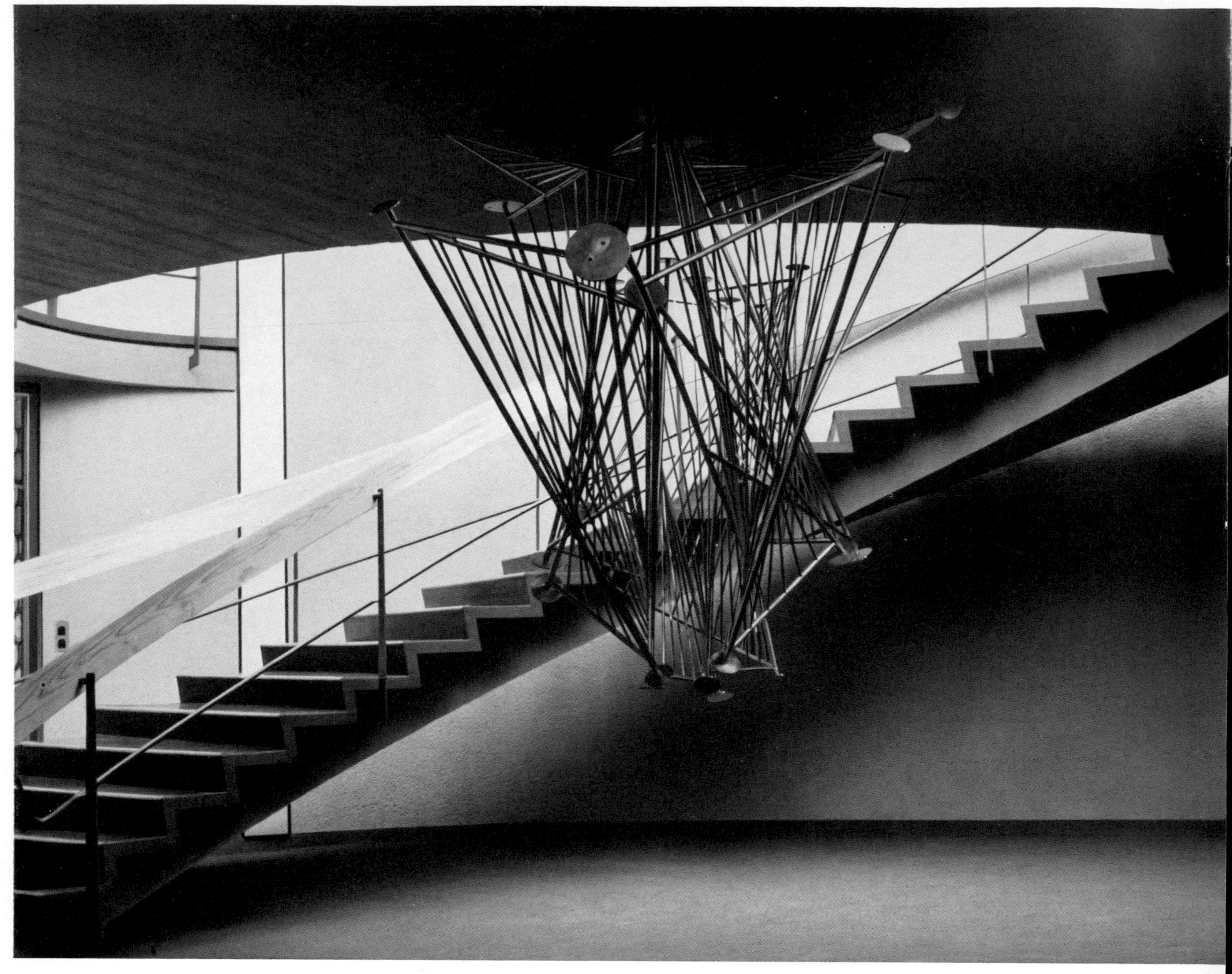

194. Hans Uhlmann Suspended Sculpture, 1957 Staircase for the University Library, Freiburg (Arch. Horst Linde and Hornschuh) Brass and chrome steel *c.* 5′ 3″ × 9′ 10″ × 4′ 11″ Photo: Author

195. Herbert Ferber Relief on the B'nai Israel Synagogue, 1952 Millburn, New York, USA (Arch. P. Goodman) Lead on copper $12' \times 8'$

196. August Endell Relief on the photographic studio Elvira, Munich, 1898 (executed by Joseph Hartwig) Stucco 23′ × 42′8″
Photo: Marburg picture archive

197. Norbert Kricke Surface Way in Two Planes, 1957–59 Theatre at Gelsenkirchen (Arch. W. Ruhnau, O. Rave, M. v. Hansen)
Steel Length 111′7″ Photo: Alfred Nagel, Gelsenkirchen

198. Harry Bertoia Screen Wall Manufacturers Trust Company, New York (Arch. Skidmore, Owings and Merrill) Steel and alloys Height 16′ Length 70′ Photo: Ezra Stoller

stability offers another contrast to the foaming water spray devised by Calder at the opposite end of the lake. When the wind blows through this wall of water, space and movement combine to create plastic forms that are aesthetically valid.

In quite a different border territory of sculpture lies the Japanese Garden (fig. 189) designed by Isamu Noguchi for the UNESCO headquarters in Paris. Its natural and carved stones together with watercourses, artificial escarpments and depressions, paths and plants form an artistic whole, a model of which we have already seen in Noguchi's marble piece *Night Voyage* (fig. 172). The lightness and variety of the forms and movements strikes a contrast to the strict pattern of the architecture. The spectator is drawn into the work of art, experiences it both as sculptural form and as organised space. Noguchi's Garden is sculpture in the widest sense, conceived as the environment of man.

The instances of contemporary public monuments, of sculpture as architecture and of the sculptural articulation of landscape we have so far discussed are extreme and, therefore, ideal cases without any direct bearing on the practical problem of the relationship between sculpture and architecture. The call for a synthesis of the two arts has been voiced with growing vigour over the years but, in fact, little progress has been made beyond the stage of makeshift solutions and mutual misunderstandings. Modern architecture tends to be self-sufficient—a heritage of its impassioned and purist youth, while modern sculpture seems at times totally oblivious of the tasks and requirements of the senior art. Thus, apart from a few early essays of *Jugendstil* inspiration, the rigorous, functional surfaces devised by modern architects have been innocent of all embellishment, sculptural or otherwise. Attempts to reverse this trend are of very recent date: the integration of the arts has been tackled at a practical level and, in certain instances, sculpture originally autonomous has been incorporated in an architectural setting.

When dealing with the encounter between modern sculpture and modern architecture we can establish certain general categories. In defining these it is important to remember that the two partners are autonomous and meet as equals—a radically new departure in the history of their relationship for which the term "architectural sculpture," implying as it does the subordination of sculpture to architecture, is no longer adequate. The categories I shall use in discussing the instances to follow are integration (or incorporation), application (or addition) and confrontation (whether by separation or by combination). This is only a very rudimentary system and it could easily be amplified. In the case of integration, for example, one could distinguish between the question of purely material or physical aspect and that of form and general conception; application could be either decorative or "signifying"; and confrontation either antithetical or harmonising.

One of the most important achievements in integrated sculpture is, to my mind, Henry Moore's relief for the Bouwcentrum Wall in Rotterdam (fig. 190). Here the architect, while himself remaining severely functional, thought of the sculptor and provided bulges in the fabric of the wall which Moore could work as though he had a monolith under his chisel. The tense composition, evoking the walls of burnt-out houses and ruined cities, is more than mere ornament; it shows what artistic and symbolic potentialities can be realised in a simple brick wall when a great sculptor intervenes.

Relief in Concrete (fig. 191), made by Günter-Ferdinand Ris for a school in Cologne, shows likewise that the integration of sculpture and architecture is possible only when the joint undertaking is coordinated from the start. For Ris the wall is not a background or a passive support carrying the relief but the very fabric of it. Exploiting the technique of concrete casting, he has produced wall and relief in one operation; the sculptural part consists in an "unfolding" of the wall surface which thus becomes a spatial structure of solid volumes and shaped voids. The sturdy, rigorously geometrical projections and recessions seem to waken the wall to life: it is their rhythm that makes explicit its architectural function. The same interplay of surfaces can be observed in the reliefs that Ris makes from welded sectional steel.

Function and ornament are also combined in the buttressing wall designed by Karl Ehlers for a clinic in Bald Salzuflen (fig. 192). The purpose of the wall is to shore up the garden laid out on a higher level and to provide a transition to the terrain below. A plain structure would have served this functional purpose equally well. But Ehlers discerned a sculptural element in the clear, plastic articulation of the building and composed a free variation on it, using concrete blocks with a red ground. His wall, made up of a few basic shapes, is thus in harmony with the building both formally and materially. It transposes the main architectural motif from the vertical into the horizontal and inserts it in the landscape.

By contrast, *Spatial Wall* (fig. 193), designed by Otto Herbert Hajek for the Revenue Office at Villingen, is both unfunctional and in formal opposition to the architecture. Though it fences in an area behind it, the artist intends it to be taken primarily as an autonomous piece of sculpture.

Hans Uhlmann's suspended construction of steel and brass (fig. 194) in the University Library at Freiburg has a complex spatial articulation. The transparence of the surfaces formed by the widely spaced rods has a somewhat constricting effect but, at the same time, it enhances the spiral movement of the stairs. The work presents itself as a sculptural paraphrase of the architecture whose rhythm it transposes into a highly refined idiom of its own.

The integration of disparate forms into one artistic whole is convincingly exemplified

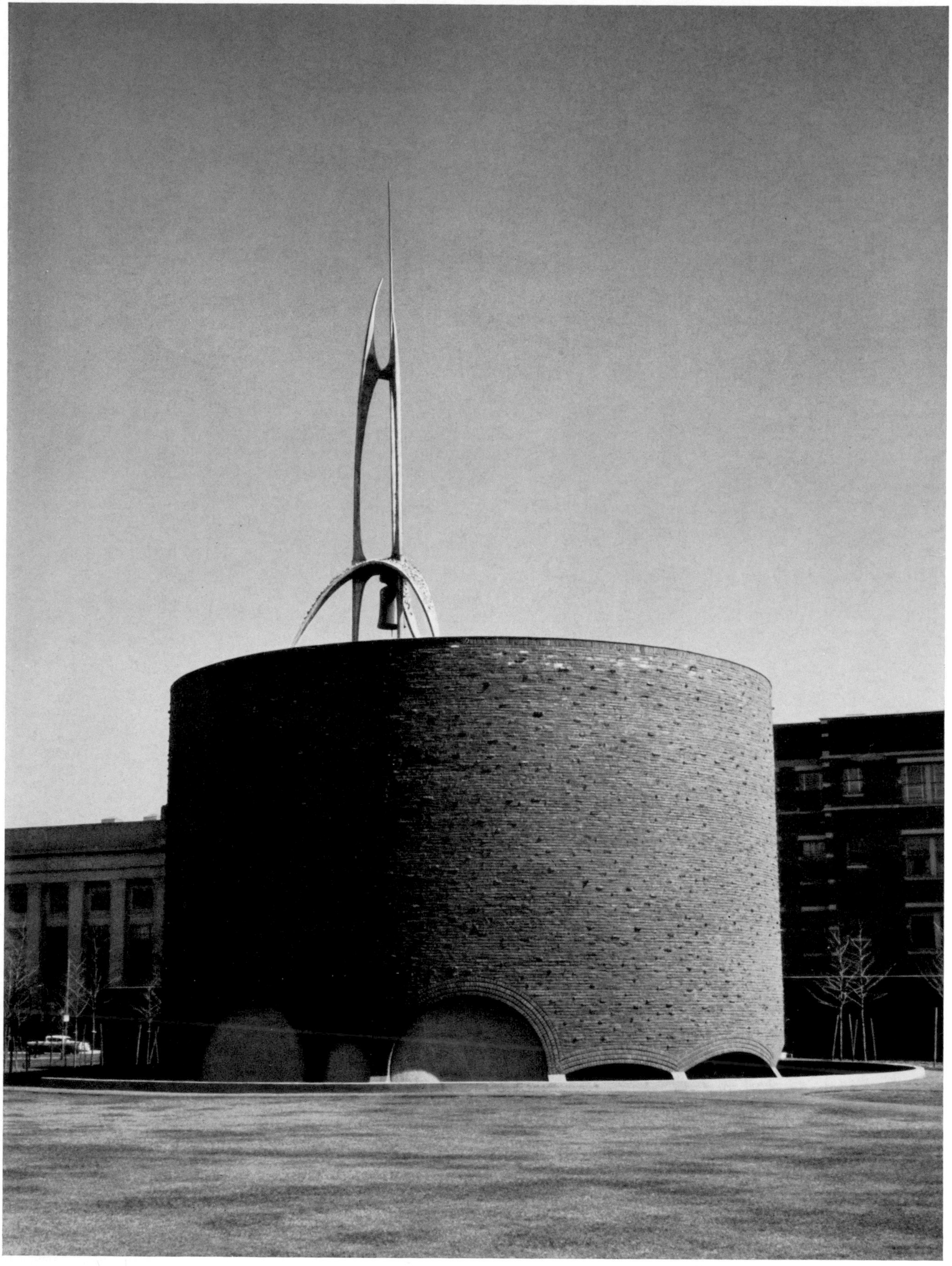

202. THEODORE ROSZAK Turret and belfry, 1955 Chapel of the Massachusetts Institute of Technology, Boston, USA (Arch. Eero Saarinen) Aluminium Photo: Author

200. Kurt Schwitters

MERZ Building, begun 1920 Hanover
(destroyed 1943)
Photo: Landesgalerie Hanover

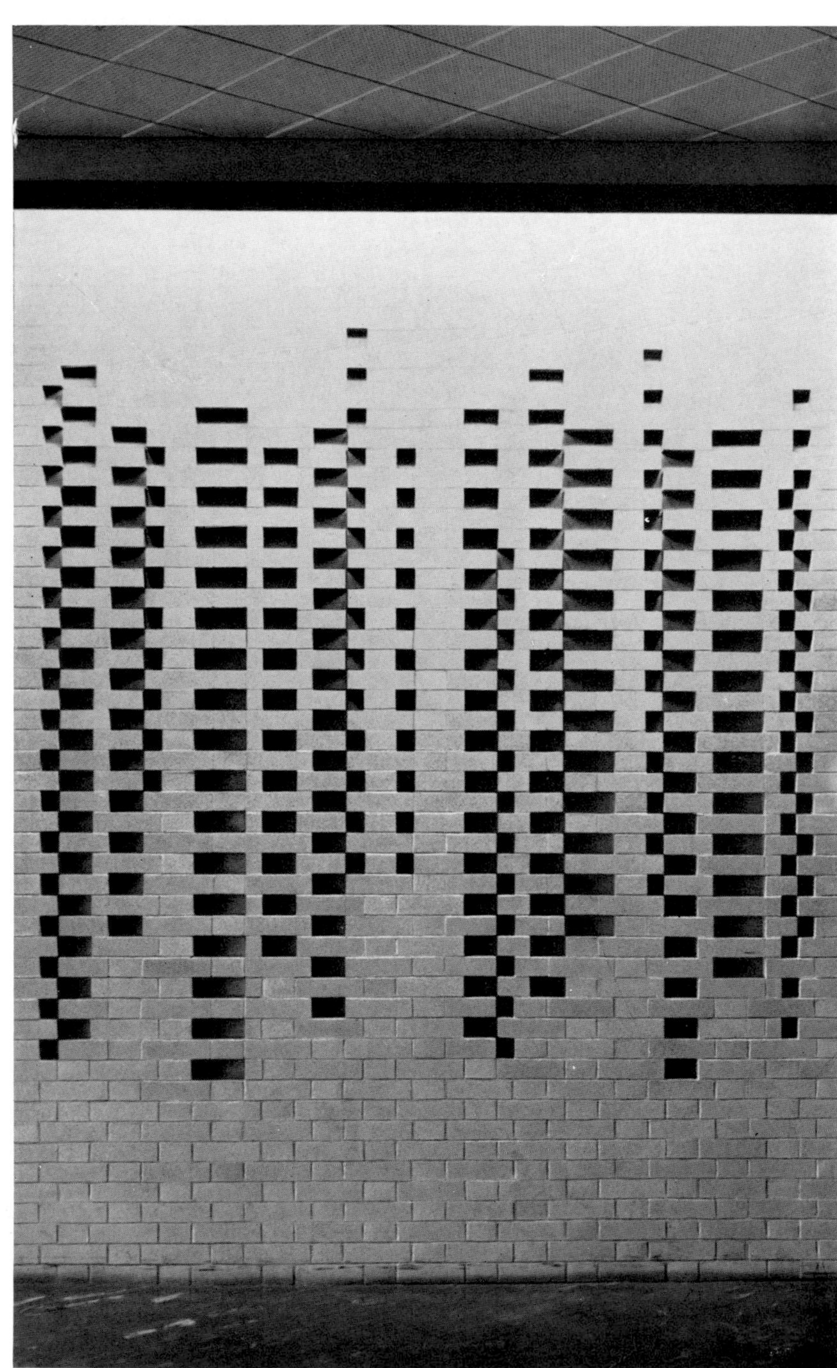

201. Josef Albers

Partition Wall, 1950
Harvard University Graduate Center
(Arch. Walter Gropius and
The Architects Collaborative)
Cambridge, Mass., USA Brick
Photo: Walter R. Fleischer

199. HANS ARP Wall Relief, 1950 Harvard University Graduate Center (Arch. Walter Gropius and The Architects Collaborative), Cambridge, Mass., USA Redwood Photo: Fred Stone

Fritz Wotruba

ront of the Municipal Hall, Vienna
·ch. Roland Rainer) Figure, 1959
ırble Height 118″

205. Hans Kock Granite Stele, 1957/58 Primary School at Hamburg-Niendorf Height 128″ Photo: Kay, Hamburg

206. Max Bill Construction, 1937 In front of the Park-Theater Grenchen, Switzerland Carved from Baveno granite, 1957/58 Diameter 71″

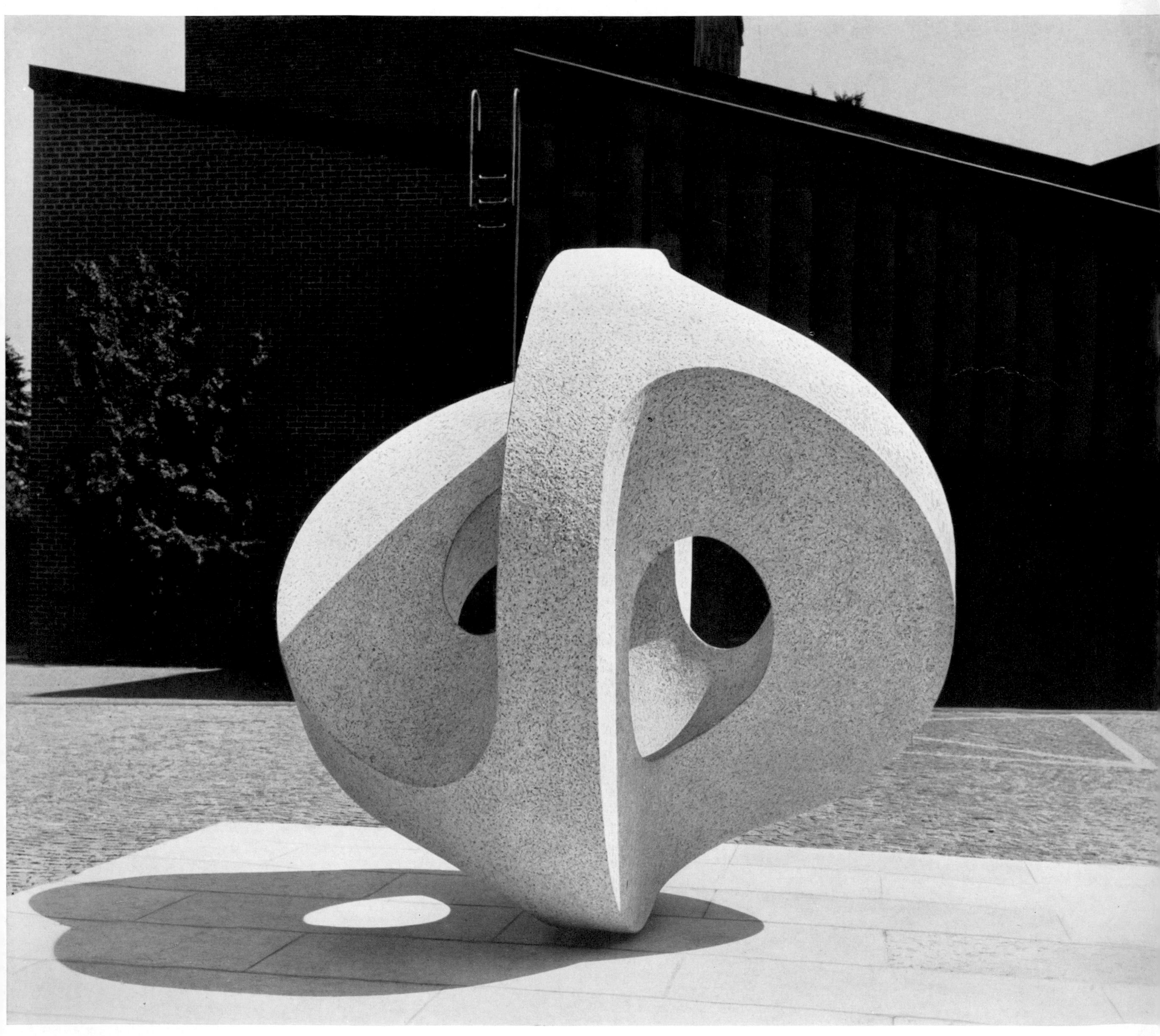

in the non-denominational chapel built by Eero Saarinen for the Massachussetts Institute of Technology, with a turret and belfry by Theodore Roszak (fig. 202). Standing directly above the excentric lantern which illuminates the altar, Roszak's spatial composition has both a "signifying" and a functional role: it identifies the sober, almost nondescript round structure as a House of God while at the same time serving as a belfry. Though fully integrated in the architecture, it preserves its sculptural autonomy, its transparence and differentiated articulation standing out against the compact mass of the edifice.

It is the Constructivists more than any other artistic movement in this century who have laid down for themselves as a cardinal postulate the unification of the arts in a comprehensive work of art *(Gesamtkunstwerk)*. This was also the aim, though pursued along entirely different, irrational lines, of Kurt Schwitters in his MERZ *Building* (fig. 200), a fantastic interior filling the artist's entire house. The remarkable and unique feature of this composition—at once sculpture, painting and architecture—is that the space contained in it "puts out" sculptural forms which develop from outside in and reduce the usual spatial schema of verticals and horizontals to a wild congeries of shapes set at all kinds of angles. Schwitters continued on his composition over a number of years adding more scrap of various sorts. A photograph cannot do it justice; it must be experienced *in situ*.

One could hardly imagine a stronger contrast to Schwitter's work than Josef Albers' composition in the Graduate Center built for Harvard University by Gropius (fig. 201). Albers maintains that any design organically linked with architecture must itself be architectural in structure, and he has used here the same materials and methods as the builder. His wall is in brick, flat and without any additional colouring. The bonding is a simple alternation of headers and stretchers; the specifically sculptural effect consists in a pattern of defined voids obtained by omitting a number of bricks in the facing courses. Against the horizontal emphasis of the brickwork the composition sets up a vertical accent. "For me the composition represents growth," says the artist, "perhaps structural growth. I have called it 'America'."

Two large reliefs in Brazil wood have been produced for the same establishment by Hans Arp (fig. 199). Instead of Albers' architectural structure we have here a constellation of organic forms which the artist patiently varied until he obtained perfect compositional harmony. The intrinsic perfection of the two reliefs, their balanced, as it were natural, rhythm communicate themselves to the space in front.

In designing a screen wall to stand behind the counter of a New York bank (fig. 198), Harry Bertoia took into account various possibilities offered by sculpture when it is linked with architecture. The wall, also called space-divider, was put up in close collaboration with the architects, Skidmore, Owings and Merrill. It consists of roughly rectangular steel plates ranged in six tiers above and behind each other, the whole carried by a steel framework. The regular pattern so obtained is interrupted by discoid shapes and projecting solids. Alloys have been soldered to the plates to give them colour. The light gold and darker bronze tones contribute to the over-all spatial effect: the wall becomes itself sculptural space.

The function of the wall is to divide the interior. But while it separates one part for a special purpose, it implies the whole. Moreover, its colour makes it conspicuous so that, clearly visible from the street, it acts as an instrument of publicity. Thus it fulfils at least two practical tasks without surrendering anything of its artistic integrity. Bertoia's screening wall is an essential component of the architectural ordinance of the interior and, at the same time, a piece of sculpture in its own right.

Far more numerous than attempts to unite sculpture and architecture, whether materially or formally, are instances of carved works being applied on buildings, not necessarily in a subordinate role, indeed as often as not in a dominant one. A good example is August Endell's stucco relief, no longer extant, for the photographic studio Elvira in Munich (fig. 196). A huge, overpowering *Jugendstil* arabesque sweeps across the low façade. It has no organic connection with the building, makes no concession to it and proclaims arbitrarily the primacy of ornament. No wonder that modern architects, repelled by the *Jugendstil,* turned against ornament and finally against any collaboration with painters or sculptors, unmindful of what they had learnt from these.

It is still exceptional today for a piece of sculpture to be intended from the start for a specific building. An example is the large steel relief *Flächenbahn in zwei Ebenen (Surface Way in Two Planes)* (fig. 197) designed by Norbert Kricke for the new theatre at Gelsenkirchen (architects: W. Ruhnau, Ortwin Rave and Max von Hausen), to the decoration of which R. Adams, P. Dierkes, Y. Klein and J. Tinguely have also contributed. Though added to the building as an autonomous work of art, the relief serves a purpose in the general conception: by its double movement to the right, it stresses the link between the projecting studio and the main structure while counteracting the weight of the large, dark wall to which it is attached. In spite of its vast dimensions the composition effect has an of lightness and gentle movement. As against the restless thrustings of his free-standing pieces (cf. fig. 152), Kricke has restrained his dynamism here to avoid aggressiveness. Seen from a distance, the rails are a distinctive sign; at close quarters they offer a genuine plastic experience. Conceived in an architectural spirit, the relief interprets and articulates the various parts of the structure as one artistic whole. Kricke is to enrich it further in the near future by providing static fountain effects.

Herbert Ferber's relief for the Synagogue in Millburn, New Jersey (fig. 195) also takes into account the architectural setting. But it is primarily a symbol and its reference is to the religious significance of the building. With the architecture it is enough for it to achieve a modus vivendi.

In the examples discussed so far sculpture applied on buildings was positively related either to their architectural character or to their purpose. Costantino Nivola does something different: the whole point of his monochrome relief covering the entire surface of a wall in the Olivetti showroom in New York (fig. 203) is to provide a contrast. It is also its purpose to "persuade" people to buy. This is unusual and seems to offend against the exaltedness of art. But surely there need be no offence if a work of art is useful as well as beautiful provided that its usefulness does not impair the truth of its beauty.

Nivola has the Italian's unerring sense for good decoration. Here it consists of recurring patterns, technological symbols and free vegetal forms which together make up a rich and varied but compact and clearly demarcated composition. The compactness is due not least to the fact that Nivola forgoes strong plastic effects and gives his relief little depth. The composition with its "intimate" forms and discreet allusions is reserved in tone. It must not distract; the coarse grain of its texture, and suggestions of the primeval and the hand-made, refer the onlooker to the opposite—the neat, precise forms of industrial products.

The confrontation of sculpture and architecture, which I have suggested as the third main category for considering the relationship between the two arts, is the one to be most frequently exemplified. In this type of relationship, sculpture is not linked to architecture either materially or structurally but merely accompanies it as a sign of identification or as ornament. A piece of sculpture can also act as a measure of comparison or mediate in establishing contact with space and with man. Its relative position may, but need not, be subordinate: it may serve to set off its architectural partner to advantage but it may equally well find itself in the main role, particularly if it itself combines sculptural with architectural forms—witness the well-known screening wall carved by Henry Moore for the Time and Life building in London.

In the case of Wotruba's marble figure (fig. 204) standing over against Roland Rainer's Municipal Hall in Vienna, the balance is even. The bold, open structure and the compact column shaft complete and define one another by their opposition. *Granite Stele* (fig. 205) by the Hamburg sculptor, Hans Kock, has likewise an architectural vis-à-vis whose horizontal ordinance it counterpoints by a vertical accent. Moreover, it opposes a free plastic variability to the uniform series of gridded surfaces in the wall facing it: the manifold alternation of projections and depressions, inclinations and breaks gives full scope to the operation of light which makes manifest the stele's positive and negative forms. The same principle, applied to the interpenetration of solid forms and shaped voids, can be observed in Max Bill's granite *Construction* (fig. 206) in front of the park theatre at Grenchen. On the other hand, the composition (fig. 207) designed by Henri-Georges Adam for the square in front of the new museum in Le Havre challenges the architecture by its vast dimensions. Its massive, even though perforated, bulk underlines the light, pavilion-like character of the building while its determined orientation and the dynamism of its front wedge thrusting forward like a ship's prow, mark a sharp contrast to the calm, flat ordinance of the museum.

Apart from the university town of Caracas, the most comprehensive, and the most interesting, example of an attempted synthesis of art and architecture is undoubtedly the one to be seen at the UNESCO headquarters in Paris. Noguchi's garden in this ensemble has already been mentioned (fig. 189). As regards sculpture *stricto sensu*, apart from the badly placed reliefs by Hans Arp resembling in composition those at the Harvard University Graduate Center (fig. 199), the contributions by Henry Moore and Alexander Calder must be singled out as being especially noteworthy.

Moore has carved for the wide square in front of the façade in the avenue Suffren a monumental *Reclining Figure* (fig. 210) in travertine. It is sometimes calles *Reclining Silhouette*, a reference on the one hand to its formal motif and on the other to the way it should be seen. For the figure, in spite of its enormous mass, is conceived in terms of transparence and hence as negating gravity. It has a view to offer from every side. The spectator looks through the perforations and catches a glimpse of the lively filigree of the UNESCO façade whose horizontal lines accord with the main emphasis of the figure, or sees the trees in the park with the bizarre contours of the old houses behind them; or he explores the interior and observes the life of forms within the sculptured edifice. This twofold penetrability is a constituent element in the meaning of the figure. Moore has here again tackled his theme of mass and void, internal and external forms, and composed a magnificent variation. Relaxed calm and powerful movement, rhythm and static balance are brought into play in a masterly fashion—truly an uninterrupted sequence of what Henri Laurens calls "plastic events" relating the autonomous work to the architecture behind it.

Alexander Calder's *Mobile* (fig. 209) stands in front of a travertine-faced wall of the UNESCO conference hall. It requires this calm background as it is itself perpetually in motion. Carried on a tripod—a typical Calder "stabile"—the black rods and sails strike out far into space forming delightful intersections and overlappings at constantly changing angles with the steeply rising skyline of Nervi's concrete structure conceived in a kindred contemporary spirit.

Wander Bertoni's steel composition (fig. 208), erected in the forecourt of the Municipal Hall in Vienna, stands on equal terms with the architecture. Its various parts

207. Henri-Georges Adam Sculpture in the square in front of the Museum of Le Havre, 1954/55 Height 23′ Length 72′ Photo: Jean Biaugeaud, Arceuil/Seine

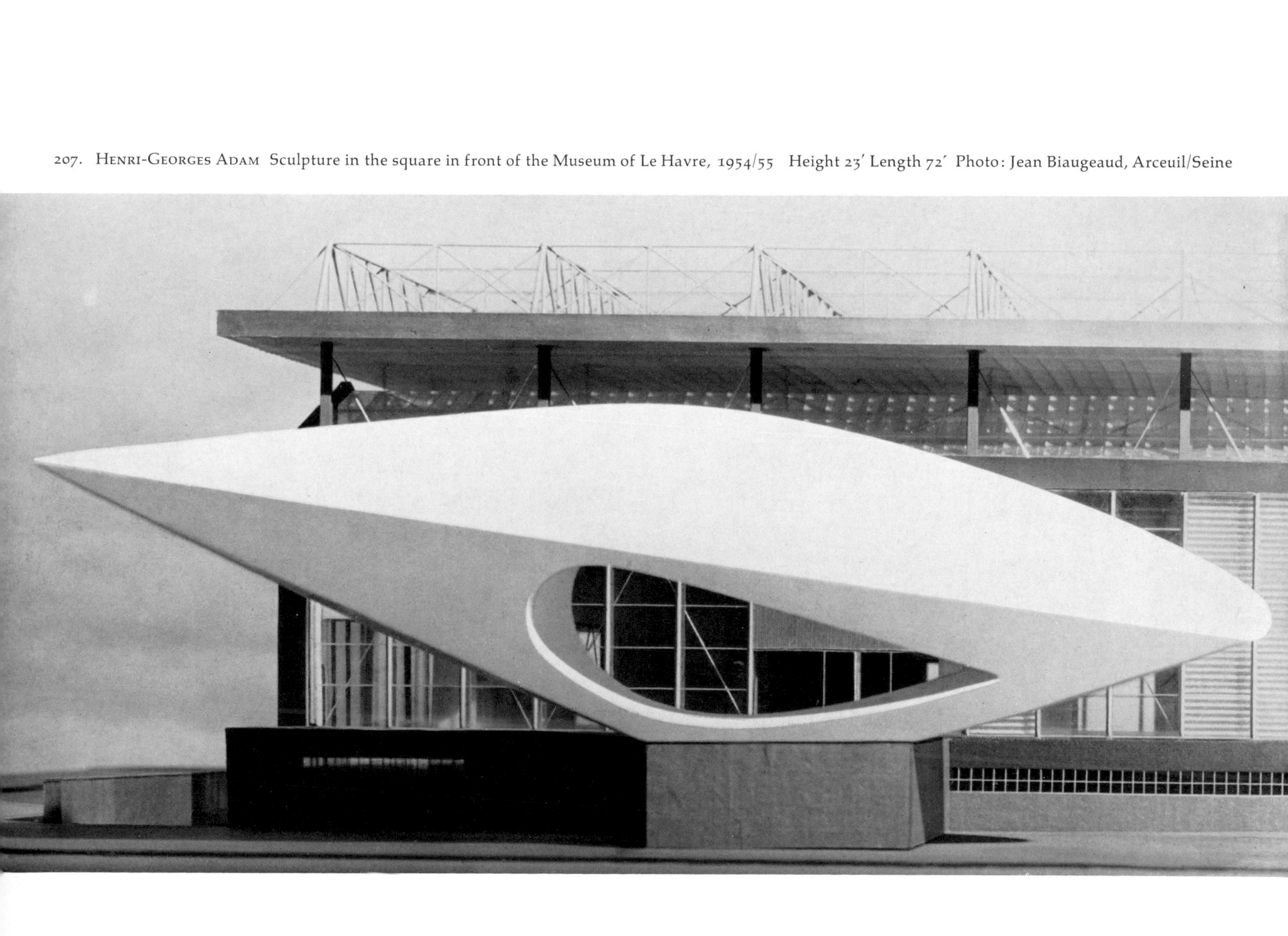

208. WANDER BERTONI Movement, 1955–58 Sculpture in front of the Vienna Municipal Hall (Arch. Roland Rainer) Stainless steel Height 177″, Length 98″, Depth 79″ Photo: Foreign Travel Agency, Vienna

209. ALEXANDER CALDER Mobile, 1959 By the UNESCO Conference Building, Paris (Arch. Pier Luigi Nervi)
Black steel Height 32′ 10″ Photo: Author

210. Henry Moore

Reclining Figure, 1957–58
In front of the UNESCO General Secretariat building
Paris (Arch. Marcel Breuer, Pier Luigi Nervi
Bernard Zehrfuss)
Roman travertine Length 16′ 5″

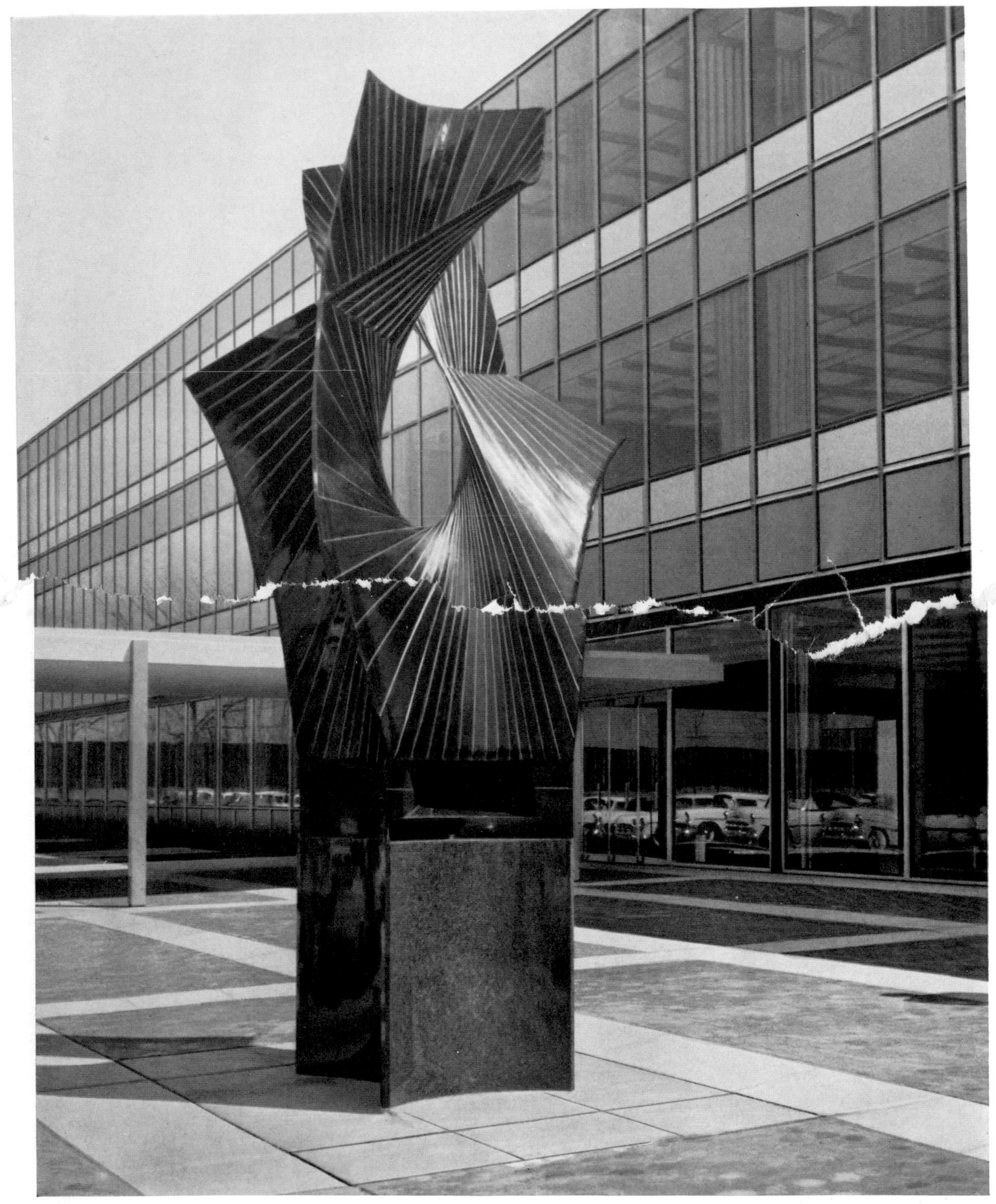

211. Antoine Pevsner Bird Soaring, 1956 General Motors Co. Technical Center, Detroit (Arch. Eero Saarinen) Bronze Height *c.* 16′ 5″ (Enlarged version of the "Column of Victory" of 1946)

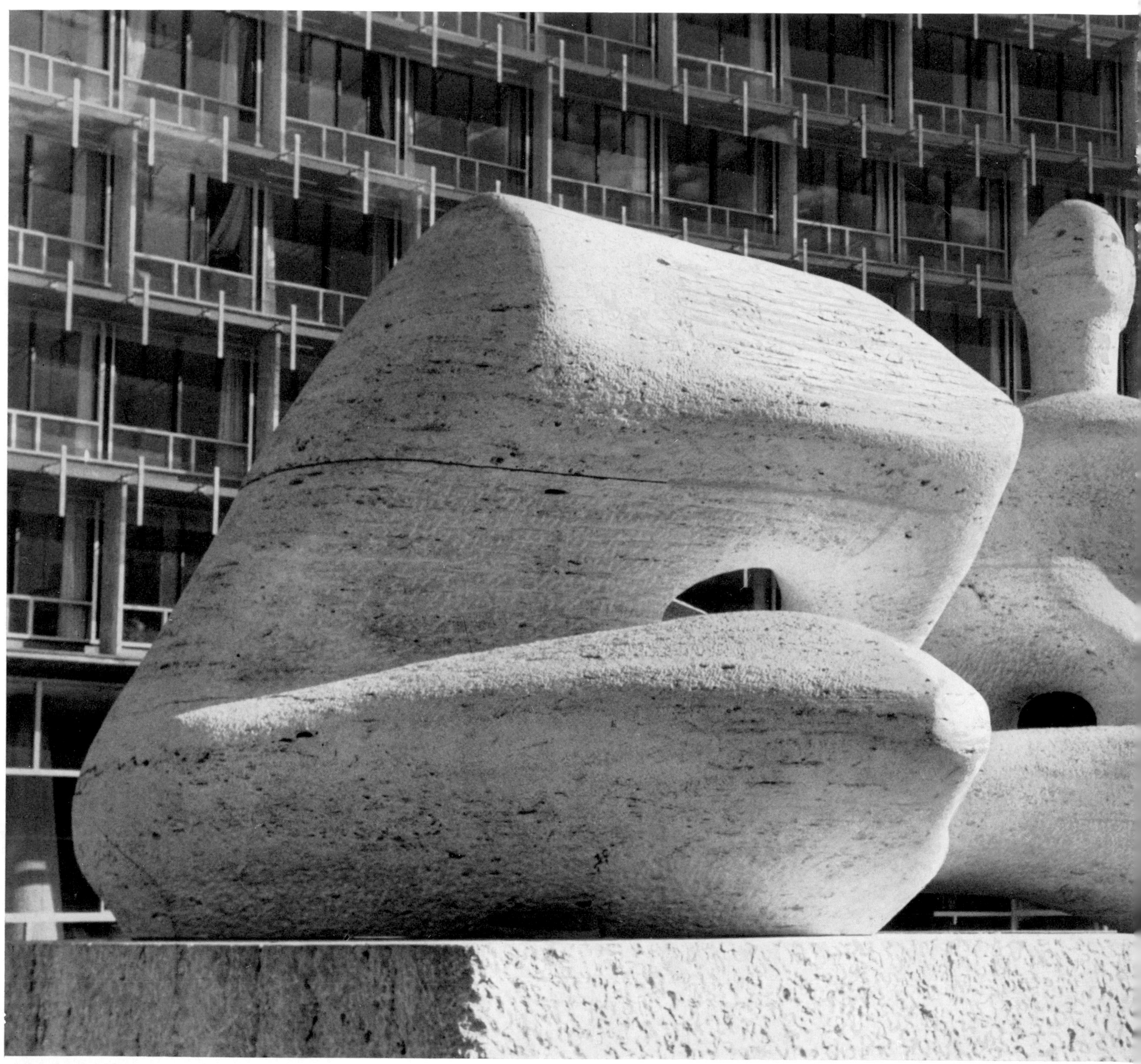

209. ALEXANDER CALDER Mobile, 1959 By the UNESCO Conference Building, Paris (Arch. Pier Luigi Nervi) Black steel Height 32′ 10″ Photo: Author

212. Naum Gabo Rotterdam Construction, 1954–57 In front of the "De Bijenkorf" store in Rotterdam (Arch. Marcel Breuer) Concrete, Steel and bronze wire Height 85′ Photo: Author

INDEX OF ARTISTS WITH BIOGRAPHICAL NOTES

The biographical notes are confined to the most important dates. For further information the reader is referred to the literature cited; this lays no claim to completeness; preference has been given to monographs.

Abbreviations for frequently cited general works:

Giedion-Welcker	*Carola Giedion-Welcker.* Plastik des XX. Jahrhunderts: Volumen und Raumgestaltung. Stuttgart, Hatje, 1955
Trier	*Eduard Trier.* Moderne Plastik. Berlin, Gebr. Mann, 1954
Ritchie	*Andrew C. Ritchie.* Sculpture of the Twentieth Century. New York. The Museum of Modern Art, 1952
Seuphor	*Michel Seuphor.* Die Plastik unseres Jahrhunderts: Wörterbuch der modernen Plastik. Cologne, DuMont Schauberg, 1959
II. documenta	*II. documenta 1959, Kassel.* Band Skulptur. Einführung und Texte von Eduard Trier. Cologne, DuMont Schauberg, 1959

ADAM, HENRI-GEORGES

Born 1904, Paris. At first painter and designer, since 1940 also sculptor. Lives in La Ville-du-Bois, Seine-et-Oise.

Lit.: *Stedelijk Museum, Amsterdam.* Catalogus der tentoonstelling no. 132. May–June 1950

ADAMS, ROBERT

Born 1917, Northampton. Teaches at the Central School of Arts and Crafts in London. Lives in Hampstead.

Lit.: *Galerie Parnass, Wuppertal.* Folio for the exhibition with foreword by John A. Thwaites and text by the artist. April 1957

AESCHBACHER, HANS

Born 1906, Zürich. Began as self-taught sculptor in 1936. Lives in Zürich.

Lit.: *Hans Aeschbacher.* Einleitung von Hans Fischli, Vorwort von Michel Seuphor. Neuchâtel, Éditions du Griffon, 1959

ALBERS, JOSEF

Born 1888, Bottrop, Westphalia. 1920–1923 studied at the Bauhaus in Weimar. 1933–1939 taught at the Blackmountain College in North Carolina, USA. Since 1950 Director of the Department of Design at Yale University, New Haven, Connecticut. Lives in New Haven. Better known as painter and designer.

Lit.: *Galerie Denise René, Paris.* Exhibition Catalogue with texts by Josef Albers, Hans Arp, Will Grohmann and Franz Roh. October–November 1957

ANTHOONS, WILLY

Born 1911, Malines, Belgium. Studied architecture and sculpture in Brussels. Has been living in Paris since 1948.

Lit.: *Michel Seuphor.* Willy Anthoons. Antwerp, De Sikkel, 1954 (Monographies de l'Art Belge)

ARCHIPENKO, ALEXANDER

Born 1887, Kiev. 1902–1905 studied painting and sculpture in Kiev, 1906–1908 in Moscow. 1908 settled in Paris. 1910 first one-man exhibition in Germany. 1912 started an art school in Paris. 1914 first "sculpture-paintings." 1921–1931 in Berlin then emigrated to USA. 1935–1936 taught at Washington State University. 1937 founded an art school in Chicago. 1939 in New York. Lives in Woodstock.

Lit.: *Erich Wiese.* Alexander Archipenko. Leipzig, Klinkhardt und Biermann, 1923 (Junge Kunst Bd. 40)
Landesmuseum Darmstadt u. a. Ausstellungskatalog mit Einführung von Erich Wiese und Texten des Künstlers. 1955
Alexander Archipenko. Fifty Creative Years. 1960

ARMITAGE, KENNETH

Born 1916, Leeds. 1937–1939 studied at the Slade School in London. 1946–1955 taught at the Bath Academy of Art. Lives in London.

Lit.: *Wallraf-Richartz Museum, Cologne.* Ausstellungskatalog Kenneth Armitage u. a. Einführung von Herbert Read. Jan.–Feb. 1959
Peter Selz, New Images of Man, New York, The Museum of Modern Art, 1959

ARP, HANS (JEAN)

Born 1887, Strasbourg. 1905–1907 studied at the Kunstschule in Weimar. 1908 brief stay in Paris, 1909 in Weggis, Switzerland. From 1911 connected with the Blaue Reiter group, from 1913 with the *Sturm* gallery in Berlin. 1914 meets Max Ernst in Cologne. 1914–1915 in Paris. 1915 settles in Zürich. 1916 Dada period begins. 1919–1920 in Cologne. 1922 marries Sophie Täuber. 1926 settles in Meudon near Paris. 1940–1941 in Southern France. 1942 flees to Switzerland. Has been living since 1946 mainly in Meudon.

Lit.: *Carola Giedion-Welcker.* Hans Arp. Stuttgart, Hatje 1958
James Thrall Soby (ed.), Arp. With texts by Jean Arp, Richard Huelsenbeck, Robert Melville, Carola Giedion-Welcker. New York, The Museum of Modern Art, 1958

AVRAMIDIS, JOANNIS

Born 1922, Batum USSR. 1937–1939 studied in Batum. 1939–1943 in Athens. Since 1943 has been living in Vienna, where he has studied mainly under Fritz Wotruba.

Lit.: *Seuphor*

BAKIĆ, VOJN

Born 1915, Bjelovar, Croatia. Studied in Zagreb. 1956 took part in the Venice Biennale. Lives in Zagreb.

Lit.: *Gradska Galerija Suvremene Umjetnosti, Zagreb.* Exhibition Catalogue. May 1958 Fig. 124; p. 130

BARLACH, ERNST

Born 1870, Wedel, Holstein. 1888–1891 studied in Hamburg, 1891–1895 at the Dresden Academy, 1895–1896 at the Académie Julian in Paris. 1897–1901 sojourns in Paris, Hamburg and Berlin. 1901–1904 in Wedel. 1904–1905 taught pottery-making in Höhr, Westerwald then, till 1906, in Berlin. 1906 trip to Russia. 1907 in Berlin. 1909 at the Villa Romana, Florence. 1910 settled in Güstrow, Mecklenburg. 1919 elected to the Akademie der Künste, Berlin. 1924 Kleist Prize. 1925 honorary member of the Munich Akademie der Künste. 1933 decorated with the Order *Pour le mérite.* 1936 honorary member of the Vienna Secession. 1938 381 works by Barlach, classified as "decadent art," are confiscated or destroyed. 1938 dies in Rostock.

Lit.: *Wolf Stubbe,* Ernst Barlach: Plastik. Munich, Piper, 1959
Friedrich Schult, Ernst Barlach: Das plastische Werk, Werkverzeichnis Bd. I, Hamburg, Hauswedell 1960

Fig. 33; pp. 54, 230

BECHTELER, THEO

Born 1903, Immenstadt, Allgäu. Studied in Berlin. 1959 at the Villa Romana, Florence. Lives in Augsburg.

Lit.: *Deutscher Künstlerbund.* Exhibition Catalogues 1959 ff.

Fig. 121; p. 129

BÉOTHY, ÉTIENNE

Born 1906, Heves, Hungary. 1918 began to study art in Budapest. 1920–1924 studied architecture. 1925 settled in Paris after extensive travel across Europe. One of the founders of the Abstraction-Création group (1932) and of the Salon des réalités nouvelles (1946). Lives at Montrouge, Seine.

Lit.: *Michel Seuphor,* Béothy. German text by Eva Friedrich. Paris, Collection Prisme, 1956 Fig. 141; p. 160 f.

BERTOIA, HARRY

Born 1915, San Lorenzo, Italy. Studied at the Cranbrook Academy near Detroit then taught metalwork there. Works for the furniture firm of Knoll Associates as designer of chairs and other "applied sculpture." Lives in Barto, Pennsylvania, USA.

Lit.: *Smithsonian Institution, Washington.* Exhibition Catalogue: Recent Work by Harry Bertoia, 1957
Eduard Trier, Angewandte Plastik: Zu den Arbeiten von Harry Bertoia und Costantino Nivola. form 1, 1957 Fig. 198; p. 263 f.

BERTONI, WANDER

Born 1925, Codisotto, Emilia, Italy. 1943 deported to Vienna. After the war, studied under Fritz Wotruba. Co-founder of the Art Club. Lives in Vienna.

Lit.: *Wander Bertoni: Plastiken 1945–1959.* Einleitung von Ulrich Baumgartner. Ed. Kulturreferat der Stadtgemeinde Kapfenberg, 1959 Figs. 69, 208; pp. 88, 266 f.

BILL, MAX

Born 1908, Winterthur, Switzerland. 1924–1927 studied at the Kunstgewerbeschule in Zürich. 1927–1929 at the Bauhaus in Dessau. 1930 settled in Zürich. Active as painter, sculptor, designer, publicist and teacher. Co-founder of the Hochschule für Gestaltung in Ulm; Rector there 1951–1956. 1951 First Prize for Sculpture at the Sao Paolo Biennale.

Lit.: *Eugen Gomringer, Hg.* Max Bill. Teufen, Niggli, 1958
Städtisches Museum Leverkusen, Schloss Morsbroich. Ausstellungskatalog. June–July 1959 Figs. 155, 206; pp. 182, 266

BLOC, ANDRÉ

Born 1896, Algiers. Architect. 1930 founded the periodical *L'architecture d'aujourd'hui.* 1940 turned to sculpture. 1949 founded the periodical *Art d'aujourd'hui,* followed in 1955 by *Aujourd'hui.* Lives in Boulogne-Billancourt, Seine.

Lit.: *Pierre Guéguen,* André Bloc. Boulogne, Seine, Coll. Espace, 1954
Charles Delloye, André Bloc. Paris, Coll. Prisme, 1959

Fig. 165; p. 221

BLUMENTHAL, HERMANN

Born 1905, Essen. 1920–1924 studied stone sculpture in Essen, then till 1931 at the Vereinigten Staatsschulen in Berlin. Pupil of Edwin Scharff. 1931–1932 in Rome, then till 1936 in Berlin. 1937 in Rome and Florence. 1942 killed in Russia.

Lit.: *Christoph-Adolph Isermeyer:* Der Bildhauer Hermann Blumenthal. Berlin, Gebr. Mann, 1947 Fig. 54; p. 75

BOCCIONI, UMBERTO

Born 1882, Reggio, Calabria. 1898–1902 worked under Giacomo Balla in Rome. 1902–1904 in Paris; visited St Petersburg. 1909 met Marinetti and launched into Futurism. 1911 met the Cubists in Paris. 1912 published the Technical Manifesto of Futurist Sculpture. Active as painter and sculptor. 1915 enrolled as volunteer. 1916 died in Verona after an accident.

Lit.: *Marco Valsecchi,* Boccioni. Venice, Cavallino, 1950

Fig. 123; p. 129

BODMER, WALTER

Born 1903, Basle; studied painting there. 1933 turned to abstract art. Has been teaching since 1939 at the Allgemeine Gewerbeschule in Basle. Lives in Basle.

Lit.: *Walter J. Moeschlin,* Walter Bodmer. Basle 1952
Marcel Joray, Schweizer Plastik der Gegenwart I und II. Neuchâtel, Éditions du Griffon, 1955 & 1959 Fig. 153; p. 182

BOURGEOIS, LOUISE

Born 1911, Paris. Studied with Bissière and Léger. Has been living in New York since 1938.

Lit.: *Giedion-Welcker; Seuphor.* Fig. 82; p. 110

BRANCUSI, CONSTANTIN

Born 1876, Pestisani Gorji near Turgu-Jui, Rumania. Trained as carpenter. 1898–1902 studied at the Academy in Bucharest. 1902–1904 on foot from Bucharest to Munich and Paris. 1904 at the École des Beaux-Arts. 1913 took part in the Armory Show in New York. 1937 in India. 1957 died in Paris.

Lit.: *Carola Giedion-Welcker,* Constantin Brancusi. Basle, Schwab, 1958 Figs. 1, 34, 103; pp. 10 f., 35, 127, 160

BUTLER, REG

Born 1913, Buntingford. Studied architecture. 1950 took up sculpture. 1953 First Prize in the international competition for a Monument to the Unknown Political Prisoner. Lives in Berkhamstead, Herts.

Lit.: *The Hanover Gallery.* Exhibition Catalogue with an introduction by Robert Melville. London, May–June 1957
Peter Selz, New Images of Man. New York, The Museum of Modern Art, 1959

Figs. 74, 183; pp. 90, 243

CALDER, ALEXANDER

Born 1896, Philadelphia, Pa US. 1915–1919 studied in New York. Till 1926 engineer and press designer. 1926–1927 and 1931 in Paris. 1932 first "mobiles." Has been living since 1933 in Roxbury, Conn., and intermittently in France.

Lit.: *James J. Sweeney,* Alexander Calder. New York, The Museum of Modern Art, 1951
Galerie Maeght, Paris. Derrière le miroir No. 31 (1950), 69–70 (1954), 113 (1959)

Figs. 20, 174, 209; pp. 36, 181, 253, 266

CALLERY, MARY

Born 1903, New York. Studied in New York and Paris. Numerous exhibitions at Curt Valentin's. Lives in New York and Paris.

Lit.: *Ritchie; Giedion-Welcker; Seuphor*
Mary Callery. Sculpture. Bibliography by Bernard Karpel. New York, 1959

Fig. 83; p. 110

CAPPELLO, CARMELO

Born 1912 in Ragusa, Sicily. Educated in Rome, Milan and Monza. 1937 took up sculpture. Lives in Milan.

Lit.: *Herta Wescher,* Carmelo Cappello. Milan, Schwarz, 1958

Fig. 13; p. 26

CARO, ANTHONY

Born 1924, London. 1951–1953 worked with Henry Moore. Teaches at St Martin's School of Art in London.

Lit.: *5de Biennale Beeldhouwkunst.* Catalogus der tentoonstelling. Middelheim Museum, Antwerp. May–Sept. 1959
Seuphor

P. 59

CÉSAR (BALDACCHINI)

Born 1921, Marseilles. Studied in Marseilles and Paris. Lives in Paris.

Lit.: *Peter Selz,* New Images of Man. New York, The Museum of Modern Art, 1959
Douglas Cooper. César. Amriswil, Bodensee-Verlag 1960

Fig. 96; p. 116

CHADWICK, LYNN

Born 1914, London. Studied architecture. 1945 first mobile composition. 1956 International Prize for Sculpture at the 28th Venice Biennale. Lives in Stroud, Glos.

Lit.: *Herbert Read.* Lynn Chadwick. Amriswil, Bodensee-Verlag, 1958

Figs. 42, 98; pp. 59, 116

CHAUVIN, JEAN

Born 1889, Rochefort, Charente-Inférieure. Lives in Malakoff, Seine.

Lit.: *Galerie Maeght.* Derrière le miroir no. 18, Paris 1949
Kunsthaus Zürich. Begründer der modernen Plastik. Ausstellungskatalog. Nov.–Dec. 1954

Fig. 139; p. 160

CHILLIDA, EDUARDO

Born 1924, San Sebastian, Spain. Studied architecture until 1947, then turned to sculpture. Lives in San Sebastian.

Lit.: *Galerie Maeght.* Derrière le miroir no. 90–91, Paris 1956
Seuphor; II. documenta

Fig. 146; p. 162 f.

CIMIOTTI, EMIL

Born 1927, Göttingen. Studied with Otto Baum, Karl Hartung and Ossip Zadkine. 1959 at the Villa Massimo, Rome. Lives in Stuttgart.

Lit.: *Kölnischer Kunstverein.* Ausstellungskatalog mit Einführung von Albert Schulze Vellinghausen. Cologne, Jan.–Feb. 1960
Eduard Trier, "Emil Cimiotti" in Junge Künstler 61/62. Hrsg. vom Kulturkreis im Bundesverband der Deutschen Industrie. Cologne, DuMont Schauberg, 1961

Figs. 81, 170; pp. 109, 222

COLLA, ETTORE

Born 1889, Parma. Studied in Parma, Paris, Brussels and Munich. 1949 founded the *Gruppo Origine* with Burri, Capograssi and others. 1953 teaching post (sculpture) at the Istituto statale d'arte in Rome. Lives in Rome.

Lit.: *Hatton Gallery, Durham University.* Folio with texts by Laurence Alloway and Charles Delloye. Newcastle, Dec. 1959

P. 187

CONSAGRA, PIETRO

Born 1920, Mazaro di Trapani, Italy. 1947 founded the group *Forma.* 1952 published *Necessità della scultura.* Has been living in Rome since 1944.

Lit.: *Umbro Apollonio.* Pietro Consagra. Rome 1957
Giulio Carlo Argan. Consagra. Brussels, Connaissance, 1958

Fig. 17; p. 45

CONSTANT (NIEUWENHUYS)

Born 1920, Amsterdam. Began as painter. 1949 co-founder of COBRA. 1950 in Paris. 1951 in London; experiments with spatial constructions. 1958 programme of *Urbanisme unitaire* (with G. E. Debord). Lives in Amsterdam.

Lit.: *Constant.* Paris, Bibliothèque d'Alexandrie, 1959
Galerie van de Loo. Constant: Konstruktionen und Modelle. Essen, Jan.–Febr. 1960

Fig. 182; p. 243

COUSINS, HAROLD B.

Born 1916, Washington, D. C. Studied in Washington, New York and Paris. Has been living in Paris since 1949.

Lit.: *II. documenta*
Museum Haus Lange, Krefeld. 3 Bildhauer aus Paris. Ausstellungskatalog mit Vorwort von Paul Wember, Krefeld, Nov. to Dec. 1959

Fig. 122; p. 129

COUZIJN, WESSEL

Born 1912 in Amsterdam. Studied in Amsterdam, New York, Rome and Paris. Lives in Amsterdam.

Lit.: *Seuphor*
Stedelijk Museum, Amsterdam. Catalogus der tentoonstelling: Beelden in het Heden. Inleiding van H. C. L. Jaffé. Amsterdam, Dec. 1959–Jan. 1960

Fig. 105; p. 128

D'ALTRI, ARNOLD

Born 1904, Zürich. Studied in Zürich, Munich, Paris, Florence, Rome and Pisa. Lives in Zürich.

Lit.: *Städtisches Museum Leverkusen.* Ausstellungskatalog mit Einführung von Fritz Laufer. April–May 1957
Kunsthalle Mannheim. Ausstellungskatalog mit Einführung von Heinz Fuchs. May 1958

Fig. 73; p. 90

DEGAS, EDGAR

Born 1834, Paris. Impressionist painter. 1866 first wax models. From 1893 onwards, mainly sculptural work on account of failing eyesight. 1917 died in Paris.

Lit.: *John Rewald,* Degas: Works in Sculpture. New York, Pantheon, 1944
Pierre Borel, Les sculptures inédites de Degas. Geneva, Cailler, 1949

P. 88

DELAHAYE, JACQUES CHARLES

Born 1928, Paris. Short course at the École des Beaux-Arts; otherwise self-taught. Lives in Paris.

Lit.: *Julien Alvard,* "J. C. Delahaye" in Quadrum ii, Nov. 1956
II. documenta

Fig. 108; p. 128

DERAIN, ANDRÉ

Born 1880, Chatou. 1899 met Vlaminck. 1901 met Matisse. 1905 exhibited first Fauve painting in the Salon. 1906 studied Negro sculpture, first sculptures. 1909–1911 pottery. From 1912 so-called "Gothic period." 1914 with Braque and Picasso in Montlavet. 1920 in Cahors. 1921 in Rome and Castelgandolfo. 1935 settled down in Chambourcy. Died in 1954.

Lit.: *Musée national d'art moderne, Paris.* Catalogue de l'exposition. Introduction par Jean Cassou. Paris, Éditions des musées nationaux, Dec. 1954–Jan. 1955
Georges Hilaire, André Derain. Geneva, Cailler, 1959

Fig. 35; p. 54

DE RIVERA, JOSÉ

Born 1904, West Baton Rouge, Louisiana. 1920–1930 worked in industry. 1928–1931 studied art in Chicago. Lives in New York.

Lit.: *The Museum of Modern Art, New York.* 12 Americans. Ed. by Dorothy C. Miller. May 1956

Fig. 164; p. 221

D'HAESE, ROËL

Born 1921, Grammont, Belgium. 1938–1942 studied with Oscar Jespers. Lives in Rhode-St. Genèse.

Lit.: *F. C. Legrand,* "Roël D'Haese" in Quadrum ii, Nov. 1956
II. documenta
Jan Walravens, "Dessins de Roël D'Haese" Quadrum viii, 1960

Fig. 100; p. 127

DIERKES, PAUL

Born 1904, Cloppenburg/Oldenburg. Trained as stone mason. 1948 teaching post at the Hochschule für Bildende Künste, Berlin.

Lit.: *Kunsthalle Baden-Baden.* Ausstellungskatalog: Deutsche Kunst I. Baden-Baden, 1959

Fig. 107; pp. 128, 264

DI TEANA, MARINO

Born 1920, Teana, Italy. Grew up in Italy and the Argentine. Since 1953 in Paris.

Lit.: *Seuphor.*

Fig. 19; p. 35

DODEIGNE, EUGÈNE

Born 1923, Rouvreux, Belgium. 1943 and 1946 in Paris. 1948 in Vézelay. 1959 took part in the symposium of European sculptors held at St. Margarethen, Austria. Lives in Les Bois Blancs near Lille.

Lit.: *Quadrum* iii

Fig. 134; p. 159

DUBUFFET, JEAN

Born 1901, Le Havre. 1918 in Paris to study painting. Abandoned the Academy after a few months and turned to literature, music and languages. 1924 abandoned work as artist and went into business. 1930–1931 started in the wholesale wine trade. 1934–1937 went back to painting, then resumed as wine merchant. 1942 third beginning as painter. Also sculpture in waste materials. 1947 sold wine business. Lives in Vence and Paris.

Lit.: *Georges Limbour,* L'art brut de Jean Dubuffet. Paris, Drouin, 1953
James Fitzsimmons, Jean Dubuffet: brève introduction à son œuvre. Brussels, Connaissance, 1958

Figs. 32, 94; pp. 45, 51, 116, 222

DUCHAMP-VILLON, RAYMOND

Born 1876, Damville, Eure. First studied medicine. 1898 turned to sculpture (self-taught). 1910 first exhibition with the Cubists. 1918 died in Cannes of war injuries.

Lit.: *The Solomon R. Guggenheim Museum.* Exhibition Catalogue: Jacques Villon, Raymond Duchamp-Villon, Marcel Duchamp. Foreword by James J. Sweeney. New York, Jan.–Feb. 1957

Fig. 102; p. 127

EHLERS, KARL

Born 1904, Hollenbeck near Ratzeburg. Studied in Essen and Düsseldorf. 1929 in Istanbul. Numerous works of sculpture in an architectural setting. 1958 teaching post in Münster i. W. Lives in Detmold.

Fig. 192; p. 254

ENDELL, AUGUST

Born 1871, Berlin. Practised architecture and the applied arts. Studied in Tübingen and Munich. Friend of Obrist, with whom he took part in the *Jugendstil.* 1918 director of the Academy in Breslau. 1925 died in Breslau.

Lit.: *Friedrich Ahlers-Hestermann,* Stilwende (2nd ed.). Berlin, Gebr. Mann, 1956
August Endell, "Formenschönheit und dekorative Kunst" in Dekorative Kunst ii, 1899. *Ibid.,* "Möglichkeiten und Ziele einer neuen Architektur" in Deutsche Kunst und Dekoration i, 1897–1898

Fig. 196; p. 264

ERNST, MAX

Born 1891, Brühl near Cologne. 1913 took part in the Erste Deutsche Herbstsalon in Berlin. 1914 met Hans Arp. 1919–1921 Dada period in Cologne. 1922 took up Surrealist painting and settled in Paris. Was already doing sculpture during the Dada period. Large stone compositions in A. Giacometti's garden in Maloja. 1938–1939 sculpture and murals for own house in St. Martin d'Ardèche. 1941–1945 in US. Since 1954, again resides in Paris or Huismes, Indre-et-Loire.

Lit.: *Patrick Waldberg,* Max Ernst. Paris, Pauvert 1958
Eduard Trier, Max Ernst. Recklinghausen, Bongers, 1959

Fig. 95; pp. 88 f., 116, 222

ÉTIENNE-MARTIN

Born 1913, Loriol, Drôme. Studied in Lyons and Paris. Lives in Paris.

Lit.: *Centro internazionale delle arti e del costume.* Catalogo della mostra. Vitalità nell'arte. Venice, Aug.–Oct. 1959
Seuphor

Fig. 65; p. 87

FABBRI, AGENORE

Born 1911, Barba (Pistoia). Studied in Pistoia. Lives in Milan.

P. 128

FALKENSTEIN, CLAIRE

Born 1909, Coos Bay, Oregon USA. University in California. Taught in San Francisco and at Mills College in Oakland. 1950 settled in Paris.

Lit.: *Michel Tapié*, Claire Falkenstein. Paris 1959

Fig. 93; p. 116

FERBER, HERBERT

Born 1906, New York. Studied dentistry and acquired an artistic education in New York. 1937 first exhibition of sculpture. Has also painted. Lives in New York.

Lit.: *Ritchie; Seuphor*
E. C. Goossen, "Herbert Ferber" in Three American Sculptors. Evergreen Gallery Book no. 2. New York, Grove Press, 1959

Figs. 12, 195; pp. 26, 264 f.

FONTANA, LUCIO

Born 1899, Rosario, Santa Fé, Argentina, of Italian parentage. Grew up in Italy. 1930 took up abstract art both in painting and in sculpture. 1939–1946 in Argentina. 1946 manifesto proclaiming *Spacialismo.* Lives in Milan.

Lit.: *II. documenta* (Catalogue of paintings)

Fig. 131; p. 159

FRANCHINA, NINO

Born 1912, Palermo. 1936 moved to Milan. Has been living alternately in Paris and Rome since 1939. 1947 took part in the first exhibition of the Fronte nuovo.

Lit.: *Giuseppe Marchiori*, Nino Franchina. Rome, de Luca 1954

Fig. 149; p. 181

FREUNDLICH, OTTO

Born 1878, Stolp, Pomerania. 1909 settled in Paris; contact with Cubists. Active as painter and sculptor. After World War I, in Germany for a time. 1924 return to Paris. Took part in the early phases of abstract art in Paris. 1943 deported to Poland and killed in a concentration camp.

Lit.: *Günter Aust*, Otto Freundlich. Cologne, DuMont Schauberg, 1960

Fig. 110; p. 128

GABO, NAUM

Born 1890, Briansk, Russia. Brother of Antoine Pevsner. 1909–1914 studied natural science and art in Munich. 1914–1917 in Oslo. 1917–1921 in Russia. 1921 published the Realist Manifesto with A. Pevsner in Moscow. 1921 moved to Berlin. 1932–1935 in Paris. 1936 moved to London. 1939–1945 in St. Ives, Cornwall. Since 1946 in Middlebury, Conn., USA.

Lit.: *Ruth Ohlsen and Abraham Chanin*, Gabo–Pevsner. Introduction by Herbert Read. New York, The Museum of Modern Art, 1948

Figs. 14, 162, 212, 213; pp. 26, 188, 275 f.

GARELLI, FRANCO

Born 1909, Diana d'Alba, Piedmont. Physician and surgeon. Teaches at the Accademia Albertina di Belle Arti, Turin.

Lit.: *Galleria Blu.* Sculture di Garelli. Introduzione di Michel Tapié. Milan, April–May, 1959

Fig. 145; p. 162

GARGALLO, PABLO

Born 1881, Maelia, Aragon. Studied at the Barcelona Academy. 1906 scholarship for Paris. 1907 teaching post in Barcelona. 1924 return to Paris. 1936 died in Spain during the Civil War.

Lit.: *Pierre Courthion*, Pablo Gargallo, Paris 1937

Fig. 6; p. 16

GAUGUIN, PAUL

Born 1848 in Paris. 1851–1855 in Lima, Peru, then at school in Orléans. 1865 joined the Navy, went to Rio de Janeiro. 1871 went into banking and stockbroking. 1874 befriended the Impressionist painters. 1883 gave up business career and took to painting. Stayed in Rouen, Paris and Bretagne till 1887, then visited Martinique. 1887 return to Paris. 1888 at Pont Aven in Bretagne, with Van Gogh in Arles, and in Paris. 1891–1893 first visited Tahiti. 1893–1895 in Paris and in Bretagne. 1895–1901 second stay in Tahiti. 1901–1903 on the island of La Dominique in the Marquesas. 1903 died on Atuana.

Lit.: *Maurice Malingue*, Gauguin: le peintre et son œuvre. Paris, Presses de la Cité 1948

Fig. 24; pp. 45, 54

GIACOMETTI, ALBERTO

Born 1901, Stampa, Switzerland. 1919–1920 in Geneva, then till 1922 in Italy. 1922–1925 worked with A. Bourdelle in Paris. About 1930, established contact with the Paris Surrealists. Took up painting after the war. Lives in Paris.

Lit.: *Galerie Maeght, Paris.* Derrière le miroir 39–40 (1951), 65 (1954), 98 (1957)
Alberto Giacometti: Schriften, Fotos, Zeichnungen. Hrsg. von Ernst Scheidegger. Zürich, Die Arche, 1958

Figs. 10, 48, 78; pp. 25, 69, 90

GILIOLI, ÉMILE

Born 1911, Paris. Studied in Nice and from 1931 in Paris. Lives in Paris.

Lit.: *Michel Ragon*, "Gilioli" in L'Oeil 16, April 1956

Fig. 2; p. 15

GOERITZ, MATTHIAS

Born 1915 in Danzig. 1937–1938 at the Kunstgewerbeschule in Berlin-Charlottenburg. 1940 studied philosophy and art history. 1941–1945 in Spanish Morocco. 1945–1947 in Granada. 1947–1949 in Madrid. 1948 founded the School of Altamira; first sculptural works. In Mexico since 1949, practising sculpture and architecture and teaching at the National University in Mexico City.

Lit.: *Eduardo Westerdahl*, Mathias Goeritz. Barcelona, Edic. Cobalto, 1949
Mauricio Gomez Mayorga, "Sobre la libertad de la creacíon" in Arquitectura (Mexico 1954)

Fig. 185; p. 243

GONZALEZ, JULIO

Born 1876, Barcelona. Trained there as goldsmith and painter. Moved to Paris about 1900. 1910 began engraving metal figures but, until 1927, remained primarily a painter. 1930–1932 worked with Picasso who was an important influence. 1942 died in Arceuil, Seine.

Lit.: *Stedelijk Museum, Amsterdam.* Catalogus der tentoonstelling 131, April–May 1955
The Museum of Modern Art, New York. Julio Gonzalez. Exhibition Catalogue. Introduction by Andrew C. Ritchie. 1956
Léon Degand, Julio Gonzalez. Cologne, Kiepenheuer & Witsch, 1956
Fig. 11; p. 25 f., 181

GRECO, EMILIO

Born 1913, Catania. Trained in marble cutting. 1943 went to Rome. Teaches at the Naples Academy. Lives in Rome.

Lit.: *Städtische Galerie Munich.* Ausstellungskatalog mit Einführung von Bernhard Degenhart. Jan.–Febr. 1959
Fig. 55; p. 75

GRIPPE, PETER

Born 1912, Buffalo, New York. Since 1939 has been living in New York.

Lit.: *Andrew C. Ritchie,* Abstract Painting and Sculpture in America. New York, The Museum of Modern Art 1951
Fig. 76; p. 90

GUERRINI, LORENZO

Born 1914, Milan. Studied in Rome, Milan, Berlin and Paris. Lives in Rome.

Lit.: *"Incontro con Lorenzo Guerrini"* in Illustrazione Nazionale, Rome, Dec. 1958
Fig. 135; p. 160

HABER, SHAMAÏ

Born 1922, Lodz. Grew up in Israel. Has been living in Paris since 1949. 1960 Prix Bourdelle.

Lit.: *Luce Hoctin,* "Trois jeunes sculpteurs: Penalba, Müller, Haber" in L'Oeil 63, March 1960
Fig. 133; p. 159

HAGUE, RAOUL

Born 1905, Constantinople, of Armenian parents. 1921 emigrated to the USA. 1925 in New York. 1950–1951 in London. Lives in Woodstock, N. Y.

Lit.: *The Museum of Modern Art, New York.* 12 Americans, ed. by Dorothy C. Miller, New York, May 1956
Fig. 37; p. 54

HAJDU, ÉTIENNE

Born 1907, Turda, Rumania, of Hungarian parents. 1927 moved to Paris. 1930 French subject; met F. Léger. Has been living in Bagneux near Paris since 1951.

Lit.: *Roberto Ganzo,* Hajdu. Paris, Musée de Poche, 1957
Michel Conil Lacoste, "Hajdu" in L'Oeil 41, May 1958
Figs. 30, 46; pp. 46, 60, 116

HAJEK, OTTO HERBERT

Born 1927, Kaltenbach, Czechoslovakia. Studied in Stuttgart. 1958 scholarship from the Kulturkreis. Lives in Stuttgart.

Lit.: *Galerie 22.* Ausstellungskatalog 3/1958. Texte von Albert Schulze Vellinghausen und Eduard Trier. Düsseldorf, April 1958
Franz Mon, Otto Herbert Hajek. Cologne, Änne Abels, 1960
Figs. 117, 193; pp. 129, 254

HARE, DAVID

Born 1917, New York. Began as a photographer. 1942 turned to sculpture. Lives in New York.

Lit.: *The Museum of Modern Art, New York.* 14 Americans, ed. Dorothy C. Miller, New York, 1946
Fig. 101; p. 116

HARTUNG, KARL

Born 1908, Hamburg. 1929–1931 in Paris. 1932–1933 in Florence. 1933–1936 in Hamburg. 1935 first abstract sculptures. Has been living in Berlin since 1936. Numerous works combining sculpture with architecture.

Lit.: *Carl Linfert,* "Karl Hartung" in Junge Künstler 59–60. Hrsg. vom Kulturkreis im Bundesverband der Deutschen Industrie. Cologne, DuMont Schauberg
Figs. 51, 142; pp. 70, 88, 162

HEILIGER, BERNHARD

Born 1915, Stettin. 1938–1939 in Paris. Has been living and teaching in Berlin since 1945.

Lit.: *Bernhard Heiliger:* Skulpturen, Zeichnungen seit 1945. Ausstellungskatalog mit Texten von Kurt Martin und Umbro Apollonio, hrsg. von der Stadt Wolfsburg, 1959
Figs. 89, 112; pp. 115, 128

HEPWORTH, BARBARA

Born 1903, Wakefield, Yorkshire. 1927–1959 in London. Since then, has been living in St. Ives, Cornwall. 1933–1935 belonged to the Abstraction-Création group.

Lit.: *A. M. Hammacher,* Barbara Hepworth. Cologne, Kiepenheuer & Witsch 1958; *J. P. Hodin,* "Barbara Hepworth, a classic artist" in Quadrum viii (1960)
Fig. 137; pp. 160, 221

HERMANNS, ERNST

Born 1914, Münster i. W. Co-founder of the *Junger Westen.* Lives in Münster.

Lit.: *Galerie 22.* Ausstellungskatalog 1/1958 mit Text von Albert Schulze Vellinghausen. Düsseldorf, Jan. 1958
Fig. 118; p. 129

HILTMANN, JOCHEN

Born 1935, Hamburg. Trained as farmer. Studied painting in Hamburg and Düsseldorf. Assisted Joseph Fassbender in the execution of murals. 1958 scholarship from the Kulturkreis. 1960 at the Villa Romana, Florence. Self-taught sculptor. Lives in Düsseldorf-Kaiserswerth.
Fig. 171; p. 222

HOFLEHNER, RUDOLF

Born 1916, Linz an der Donau. Studied mechanical engineering, and art at the Vienna Kunstakademie. 1945–1951 taught at the Kunstgewerbeschule, Linz. 1945 took up abstract wood sculpture. 1951 turned to iron and steel; on figurative work from 1954. Has been living in Vienna since 1951. 1959 exhibition at the 5th Biennale in Sao Paolo.

Lit.: *Werner Hofmann,* "Zum Werk Rudolf Hoflehners" in Alte und moderne Kunst 10, Vienna, 1959
Ibid., "Rudolf Hoflehner" in Quadrum viii, 1960
Fig. 42; p. 87

JACOBSEN, ROBERT

Born 1912, Copenhagen. 1930 first wood sculptures. Has done mainly metal work with constructivist forms since 1949, also figurative pieces in iron. Has been living in Paris since 1947.

Lit.: *Stedelijk Museum, Amsterdam.* Catalogus der tentoonstelling 140 met inleiding van Léon Degand. Nov.–Dec. 1955
Ibid., Catalogus der tentoonstelling 228 met inleiding van Eugène Jonescu. March 1960
Fig. 156; p. 187

JENDRITZKO, GUIDO

Born 1925, Kirchhain, Niederlausitz. 1950–1956 studied at the Hochschule für bildende Künste in Berlin. Karl Hartung's star pupil. Scholarship from the Kulturkreis. 1960 at the Villa Romana, Florence. Lives in Berlin-Friedenau.

Lit.: *Will Grohmann*, "Guido Jendritzko" in Junge Künstler 58–59, hrsg. vom Kulturkreis im Bundesverband der Deutschen Industrie. Cologne, DuMont Schauberg, 1958

Fig. 114; p. 129

KELDER, TOON

Born 1894, Rotterdam. Studied in Rotterdam and at the Hague. Began as a painter. 1949–1950 came to sculpture through the intermediate stage of linear iron wire compositions. Lives at the Hague.

Lit.: *Stedelijk Museum, Amsterdam.* Catalogus der tentoonstelling 110 (Nov. 1953) en 233 (March–April 1960) met inleidingen van Frank Elgar en Jos. de Gruyter
Frank Elgar, "Kelder" in XXe siècle, Paris, June 1957

Fig. 104; p. 128

KEMENY, ZOLTAN

Born 1907, Banica, Transylvania, Rumania. Studied in Budapest. 1930–1940 in Paris. Has been living in Switzerland since 1942; became a Swiss subject in 1957.

Lit.: *II. documenta* (Vol. Painting); *Quadrum vii*, 1959

Fig. 29; p. 46

KIRCHNER, ERNST LUDWIG

Born 1907, Aschaffenburg. 1901–1905 studied architecture in Dresden. 1903–1904 painting in Munich. Co-founder of the Künstlergemeinschaft Brücke. 1911–1916 in Berlin. 1917 moved to Davos where, in 1938, he committed suicide.

Lit.: *Max Sauerlandt*, "Holzbildwerke von Kirchner, Heckel und Schmidt-Rottluff im Hamburgischen Museum für Kunst und Gewerbe" in Museum der Gegenwart i, 3, 1930
Will Grohmann, Ernst Ludwig Kirchner. Stuttgart, Kohlhammer, 1958

Fig. 71; p. 88

KOCK, HANS

Born 1920, Kiel, grew up in Hamburg. 1945–1947 studied architecture in Brunswick. 1948–1952 at the Landeskunstschule in Hamburg under Gerhard Marcks. 1955 scholarship from the Kulturkreis. Lives in Hamburg.

Lit.: *Martin Urban*, "Hans Kock" in Junge Künstler 60–61, hrsg. vom Kulturkreis im Bundesverband der Deutschen Industrie. Cologne, DuMont Schauberg, 1960

Fig. 205; p. 265

KOENIG, FRITZ

Born 1924, Würzburg. 1946–1952 studied at the Munich Academy; A. Hiller's star pupil. Lives in Landshut, Bavaria.

Lit.: *Juliane Roh*, "Fritz Koenig" in Junge Künstler 58–59, hrsg. vom Kulturkreis im Bundesverband der Deutschen Industrie. Cologne, DuMont Schauberg, 1958

Fig. 79; p. 109

KOSICE, GYULA

Born 1924 on the Czechoslovak-Hungarian border. 1928 emigrated to Argentina. Wide literary and publicist activity in Argentina since 1939. 1946 founded the *Madi* group. Lives in Buenos Aires.

Lit.: *Gyula Kosice.* Géoculture de l'Europe d'aujourd'hui. Avant-propos de Herbert Read. Buenos Aires, Ediciones Losange, 1959
Galerie Denise René, Paris. Catalogue de l'exposition, introduction par Michel Seuphor, April 1960

Fig. 116; p. 188

KRICKE, NORBERT

Born 1922, Düsseldorf. 1946–1947 pupil of R. Scheibe in Berlin. 1952 first spatial compositions. 1955 in England. 1958 in USA. on a scholarship from the Graham Foundation. Lives in Düsseldorf.

Lit.: *Kunstverein Freiburg i. Br.* Ausstellungskatalog mit Einführung von S. B. Nov. 1957
Hanns Theodor Flemming, "Norbert Kricke" in Quadrum vii, 1959

Figs. 152, 197; pp. 181 f., 264

LARDERA, BERTO

Born 1911, La Spezia. Studied at Florence University; taught himself sculpture. Has been living in Paris since 1948. 1958 teaching post at the Hochschule für bildende Kunst in Hamburg.

Lit.: *Michel Seuphor*, Lardera. Milan, La Bibliofilia, 1953
Museum Haus Lange, Krefeld. Ausstellungskatalog mit Einleitung von Paul Wember, Sept.–Dec. 1956
Moderne Galerie Otto Stangl. Ausstellungskatalog mit Einleitung von Werner Haftmann. Munich, June–July 1958
Michel Conil-Lacoste, "Lardera, découpeur d'espace" in L'Oeil 37, January 1958

Figs. 148, 178; pp. 181, 237

LASSAW, IBRAM

Born 1913, Alexandria, Egypt, of Russian extraction. 1921 emigrated to USA. Studied in New York. 1950 teaching post at the American University, Washington D. C. Lives in New York and East Hampton, N. Y.

Lit.: *The Museum of Modern Art, New York.* 12 Americans, ed. by Dorothy C. Miller, May 1956

Fig. 159; p. 187

LAURENS, HENRI

Born 1885, Paris. Trained in sculptural decoration and stone masonry. 1911 introduced to Cubist painting by Braque. Practised Cubism till 1925, then turned to organic forms. 1937 commissions combining sculpture with architecture for the Paris World Exhibition. Apart from sculpture also book illustration, artistic typography and gouaches. 1954 died in Paris.

Lit.: *Le Point* xxxiii. Numéro spécial consacré à Henri Laurens. Lanzac, July 1946
Wallraf-Richartz-Museum, Cologne. Ausstellungskatalog mit Vorwort von Leopold Reidemeister, 1955
Cécile Goldscheider, Laurens. Cologne, Kiepenheuer & Witsch, 1956
Galerie Louise Leiris. Henri Laurens: sculptures en pierre de 1919 à 1943. Texte d'Y. Taillandier. Paris, Oct.–Nov. 1958
Galerie Claude Bernard. Laurens. Introduction par A. Giacometti. Paris, 1960

Figs. 31, 56; pp. 51, 75, 275, 277

LE CORBUSIER

Charles Edouard Jeanneret, born 1887, La Chaux-de-Fonds, Switzerland. Trained as engraver. 1908 in Paris, worked in the office of the architect Perret. 1910–1911 study travel in Germany. 1917 settled in Paris. Apart from working as architect, townplanner and publicist, also paints and carves. 1920 edited the periodical *Esprit nouveau.* Wide artistic activity in various parts of the world.

Lit.: *Oeuvres de Le Corbusier et P. Jeanneret.* 8 vols. Paris, Morancé
Anton Henze, Ronchamp. Recklinghausen, Paulus-Verlag, 1956

Fig. 187; pp. 230, 244

LEHMBRUCK, WILHELM

Born 1881, Meiderich near Duisburg. 1895–1899 studied at the Kunstgewerbeschule in Düsseldorf. 1906 and 1912 travelled to Italy. 1910 moved to Paris where he came into contact with avant-garde artists (Brancusi, Modigliani, Matisse and others). 1914 returned to Germany, in Berlin till 1917, then temporary stay in Zürich. 1919 died in Berlin.

Lit.: *Paul Westheim*, Wilhelm Lehmbruck (2nd ed.). Potsdam, Kiepenheuer, 1922
August Hoff, Wilhelm Lehmbruck. Berlin, Klinkhardt und Biermann, 1933 (Junge Kunst Bd. 61–62)
Ibid., Wilhelm Lehmbruck. Berlin, Rembrandt, 1936
Eduard Trier, Wilhelm Lehmbruck: Zeichnungen und Radierungen. Munich, Piper-Bücherei, 1955
Ibid., Wilhelm Lehmbruck: Die Kniende. Stuttgart, Reclam-Werkmonographien, 1958
Fig. 9; pp. 25, 75

LINCK, WALTER

Born 1903, Berne. 1916–1920 studied in Berne and Zürich. 1921–1926 in Berlin. 1930–1932 in Paris. 1932–1939 alternated between Berne and Paris. 1956–1957 taught at the Werkakademie in Kassel. Lives in Reichenbach-Zollikofen near Berne.

Lit.: *Kestner-Gesellschaft Hannover.* Ausstellungskatalog Theo Eble –Walter Linck. Einleitung von Albert Schulze Vellinghausen. Feb.–March 1958
Marcel Joray, Schweizer Plastik der Gegenwart i & ii. Neuchâtel, Éditions du Griffon, 1955 & 1959
Fig. 21; p. 36

LIPCHITZ, JACQUES

Born 1891, Druskieniki, Lithuania, at that time Russian. 1909–1912 in Paris. 1912 briefly in Russia. 1913 returned to Paris. 1914 trip to Madrid. 1925 settled down in Boulogne-sur-Seine. 1940 fled to Toulouse. 1941 emigrated to USA. 1945 returned for a time to Paris. Has been living in Hastings-on-Hudson, N.Y., USA., since 1947.

Lit.: *Maurice Raynal*, Jacques Lipchitz. Paris, Jeanne Bucher, 1947
Henry R. Hope, The Sculpture of Jacques Lipchitz. New York, The Museum of Modern Art, 1954
Robert Goldwater, Jacques Lipchitz. Cologne, Kiepenheuer & Witsch, 1954
Fine Arts Associates. Exhibition Catalogue: Jacques Lipchitz, Thirty Three Semi-Automatics. Text by the artist. New York, March 1957
Fine Arts Associates. Exhibition Catalogue of recent work, 1958–1959, with text "À la limite du possible" by the artist, New York, Nov.–Dec. 1959
Figs. 4, 61, 72; pp. 16, 76 f., 90, 275

LIPPOLD, RICHARD

Born 1915, Milwaukee, Wisconsin. 1933–1937 studied industrial design in Chicago. 1942 took up sculpture. Lives in New York.

Lit.: *The Museum of Modern Art, New York.* 15 Americans, ed. by Dorothy C. Miller, 1952
Eduard Trier, "Lippolds plastische Sonne" in form ii, 1958
Rosamonde Bernier, "Richard Lippold" in L'Oeil 64, April 1960
Fig. 17; p. 35

LIPSI, MAURICE

Born 1898, Lodz, Poland. In Paris since 1912. 1933 French naturalisation. 1942–1943 in South of France, then till 1945 in Switzerland. Now lives in Chevilly-Larue near Paris.

Lit.: *R. V. Gindertael*, Lipsi. Paris, Coll. Prisme, 1959
Fig. 132; p. 159

LIPTON, SEYMOUR

Born 1903, New York. Studied dentistry. 1932 took up sculpture (self-taught). Since 1943 various teaching posts. Lives in New York.

Lit.: *The Museum of Modern Art, New York.* 12 Americans, ed. by Dorothy C. Miller, 1956
Andrew C. Ritchie, "Seymour Lipton" in Art in America. Winter 1956–1957
Fig. 68; p. 87 f.

LÖRCHER, ALFRED

Born 1875, Stuttgart. 1892–1898 studied at schools of applied art in Stuttgart, Karlsruhe and Kaiserslautern. 1898–1902 at the Munich Academy. 1903 in Rome. 1904–1908 in Stuttgart. 1908–1915 in Berlin. 1919–1945 teaching post in Stuttgart. Lives in Stuttgart. Awarded the Grosse Kunstpreis by Nordrhein-Westfalen.

Lit.: *Festschrift Alfred Lörcher*, hrsg. von E. Petermann. Stuttgart, Kohlhammer, 1955
Fig. 80; p. 109

LOTH, WILHELM

Born 1920, Darmstadt. 1938 encouraged by Käthe Kollwitz to take up sculpture. Has been teaching since 1948 in Darmstadt and Karlsruhe. 1959 at the Villa Massimo, Rome. Lives in Karlsruhe.

Lit.: *Ulrich Gertz*, "Wilhelm Loth" in Junge Künstler 59–60, hrsg. vom Kulturkreis im Bundesverband der Deutschen Industrie. Cologne, DuMont Schauberg, 1959
Fig. 47; p. 60 f.

LUGINBÜHL, BERNHARD

Born 1929, Berne. Educated at the Kunstgewerbeschule in Berne. Lives in Moosseedorf near Berne.

Lit.: *Du*, August 1959
Marcel Joray, Schweizer Plastik der Gegenwart I & II. Neuchâtel, Éditions du Griffon, 1955 & 1959
Fig. 158; p. 187

MAILLOL, ARISTIDE

Born 1861, Banyuls, Roussillon. 1882–1886 studied painting and sculpture at the École des Beaux-Arts. 1887–1889 in Banyuls made carpets from own designs, also sculpture. 1901 sculpture becomes main pursuit. 1902 Vollard organizes first exhibition. 1906 trip to Greece. 1944 died in Banyuls.

Lit.: *John Rewald*, Maillol. London etc., Hyperion, 1939
Rolf Linnenkamp, Aristide Maillol. Die grossen Plastiken. Munich, Bruckmann, 1960
Fig. 49; p. 69

MANZÙ, GIACOMO

Born 1908, Bergamo, Italy. Studied at the Academy in Verona. Teaches at the Brera Academy and lives in Milan.

Lit.: *Carlo Ragghianti*, Giacomo Manzù. Milan, Edizioni del Milione, 1957
Bernhard Degenhart, Giacomo Manzù: Mädchen und Frauen. Munich, Piper-Bücherei, 1958
Fig. 39; p. 59

MARCKS, GERHARD

Born 1889, Berlin. 1919 appointment at the Bauhaus, in charge of the pottery kilns in Dornburg. 1925–1933 at the Kunstgewerbeschule in Halle-Giebichenstein. From 1933 onwards in Ahrenshoop/Ostsee. 1946–1950 at the Landeskunstschule in Hamburg. Has been living in Cologne since 1950.

Lit.: *Adolf Rieth*, Gerhard Marcks, Recklinghausen, Bongers, 1959
Fig. 75; pp. 70, 90, 127

MARINI, MARINO

Born 1901, Pistoia. Studied painting and sculpture at the Florence Academy. 1929–1940 taught at the art school Villa Reale in Monza. Since 1940, at the Brera Academy in Milan. 1942–1946 in Switzerland. Lives alternately in Milan and Forte dei Marmi.

Lit.: *Umbro Apollonio*, Marino Marini (3rd ed.). Milano, Edizioni del Milione, 1958
Eduard Trier, Marino Marini. Cologne, Der Spiegel, 1954
Emile Langui, Marino Marini. Cologne, Kiepenheuer & Witsch, 1954
Helmut Lederer–Eduard Trier, Marino Marini. London, Thames and Hudson, 1961 Figs. 59, 60, 181; pp. 54 f., 76, 127, 243

MARTIN, KENNETH

Born 1905, Sheffield. 1929–1932 studied at the Royal College of Art in London. 1948 taught at London University. 1953 first screw mobiles. 1955 lectures at the Slade School in London, at King's College, Newcastle-on-Tyne, and at the Institute of Contemporary Arts in London. Lives in Hampstead, London.

Lit.: *Andrew Forge*, "Notes on the Mobiles of Kenneth Martin" in Quadrum iii, 1957 Fig. 167; p. 221

MASCHERINI, MARCELLO

Born 1906, Udine. Has been living since 1910 in Trieste. Member since 1949 of the Accademia S. Luca in Rome.

Lit.: *Städtische Galerie Munich.* Marcello Mascherini. Einleitung von Bernhard Degenhart. 1957 Fig. 38; pp. 59, 75

MASTROIANNI, UMBERTO

Born 1910, Fontana Liri, Italy. Has been living since 1926 in Turin.

Lit.: *Giulio Carlo Argan*, Umberto Mastroianni. Venice, Cavallino, 1958 Fig. 70; p. 88

MATARÉ, EWALD

Born 1887, Aachen. 1907–1914 studied painting in Berlin. 1920 took up sculpture. 1932–1933 at the Düsseldorf Academy (re-appointed in 1945). Has been living since 1932 in Büderich bei Neuss.

Lit.: *Hans Th. Flemming*, Ewald Mataré. Munich, Prestel, 1955
Eduard Trier, Ewald Mataré. Recklinghausen, Bongers, 1958
Heinz Peters, Ewald Mataré: Das graphische Werk I–II. Cologne, Czwiklitzer, 1957 & 1958 Figs. 36, 106; pp. 54, 128

MATISSE, HENRI

Born 1869, Le Cateau. 1892 began studies in Paris. 1899 took up sculpture. 1900 worked for a time with A. Bourdelle. Sculpture remained his second pursuit throughout his career as a painter. 1917 settled down in Nice. 1939 moved to Vence. 1954 died in Nice.

Lit.: *Alfred H. Barr*, Matisse: His Art and His Public. New York, The Museum of Modern Art, 1951
Curt Valentin Gallery. The Sculpture of Henri Matisse. Introduction by Alfred H. Barr. New York, Feb. 1953
Fine Arts Associates. Henri Matisse: Sculpture. Introduction by Jean Cassou. New York, Nov.–Dec. 1958
Gaston Diehl, Henri Matisse. Paris, Tisné, 1958 Fig. 8; p. 25

McWILLIAM, F. E.

Born 1909, Banbridge. 1928–1931 studied at the Slade School in London. 1931–1932 in Paris. Lives in London.

Lit.: *The Hanover Gallery.* F. E. McWilliam Exhibition Catalogue. London, 1956 P. 110

MEADOWS, BERNARD

Born 1915, Norwich. 1936–1940 worked with Henry Moore. Lives in London.

Lit.: *J. P. Hodin*, "Bernard Meadows" in Quadrum vi, 1959

Fig. 109; p. 128

MEIER-DENNINGHOFF, BRIGITTE

Born 1923, Berlin. Trained under Henry Moore and A. Pevsner. 1959 awarded the Prix Bourdelle. Lives in Paris.

Lit.: *Udo Kultermann*, "Brigitte Meier-Denninghoff" in Junge Künstler 60–61, hrsg. vom Kulturkreis im Bundesverband der Deutschen Industrie. Cologne, DuMont Schauberg, 1960

Fig. 151; pp. 181, 221

METTEL, HANS

Born 1903, Salzwedel. 1921–1923 studied stone sculpture in Dresden. 1924 at the Vereinigte Staatsschule Berlin-Charlottenburg (under Scharff). 1925–1929 Prize scholar of the Preussische Akademie der Künste (under Lederer). 1930 on a scholarship at the Villa Massimo in Rome. 1931 settled down in Berlin. 1936 forbidden to exhibit, works confiscated. 1947 moved to Frankfurt-on-Main to teach sculpture at the Städelschule. 1950–1956 director of the Staatliche Hochschule für bildende Künste in Frankfurt. 1958 settled down in Falkenstein, Taunus.

Lit.: *Eduard Trier*, "Hans Mettel" in Junge Künstler 60–61, hrsg. vom Kulturkreis im Bundesverband der Deutschen Industrie. Cologne, DuMont Schauberg, 1960 Fig. 50; p. 69 f.

MILANI, UMBERTO

Born 1912, Milan. Began as painter. Studied at the Accademia di Brera. Lives in Milan.

Lit.: *Franco Russoli*, "Umberto Milani" in Il Milione 44 nuova serie, Milan, April–May 1959 Fig. 143; p. 162

MINGUZZI, LUCIANO

Born 1911, Bologna. Teaches at the Accademia di Brera and lives in Milan.

Lit.: *The Museum of Modern Art, New York.* The New Decade, ed. by Andrew C. Ritchie, New York, 1955
Giedion-Welcker; II. documenta; Seuphor Fig. 150; p. 181

MIRKO (BALSADELLA)

Born 1910, Udine, Italy. Studied in Venice, Rome, Florence and Monza. In Rome from 1934. At present in USA. as director of the Harvard University Workshop.

Lit.: *The Museum of Modern Art, New York.* The New Decade, ed. by Andrew C. Ritchie, New York, 1955
Giedion-Welcker; II. documenta; Seuphor Fig. 7; p. 16

MODIGLIANI, AMEDEO

Born 1884, Leghorn. Studied in Venice and Florence. 1906 moved to Paris. 1909 met Brancusi and took up sculpture under his influence. 1915 switched over to painting. 1920 died in Paris.

Lit.: *James T. Soby*, Modigliani: Paintings, Drawings, Sculpture. New York, The Museum of Modern Art, 1951
G. Scheiwiller, Amedeo Modigliani. Zürich, Die Arche, 1958
C. Roy, Modigliani. Geneva, Skira, 1958 P. 115

MOORE, HENRY

Born 1898, Castleford, Yorks. 1919–1921 Leeds School of Art, then till 1925 at the Royal College of Art in London. 1925 in Italy and Paris. Taught till 1939 at the Chelsea Art School. Numerous public works and distinctions. Lives in Much Hadham, Herts.

Lit.: *Herbert Read,* Henry Moore: Sculpture and Drawings (4th ed.). London, Lund Humphries, 1957
Ibid., Henry Moore, vol. ii: Sculpture and Drawings since 1948. London, Lund Humphries, 1955
Henry Moore, Schriften und Skulpturen, hrsg. von Werner Hofmann. Frankfurt-on-Main, Fischer, 1959
Will Grohmann, Henry Moore. London, Thames & Hudson, 1960

Figs. 5, 52, 58, 180, 190, 210; pp. 16, 70, 75 f., 160, 221, 230, 254, 265

MOOY, JAAP

Born 1905, Bergen-op-Zoom. Trained as a naval mechanic, taught himself sculpture. 1939–1956 painter. 1956 first sculpture in iron. Lives in Bergen-op-Zoom.

Lit.: *Kunsthalle Recklinghausen.* Ausstellungskatalog: Monteure: Jaap Mooy–Jaap Wagemaker. Texte von Lucebert und Grochowiak. Aug.–Sep. 1959 Fig. 99; p. 116

MÜLLER, ROBERT

Born 1920, Zürich. 1939–1944 Studied in Switzerland (with Germaine Richier). 1947–1950 in Italy. Has been living in Paris since 1950.

Lit.: *Maria Netter,* "Der Eisenschmied Robert Müller" in Quadrum vii, 1959
Luce Hoctin, "Trois jeunes sculpteurs: Penalba, Müller, Haber" in L'Oeil 63, March 1960 Fig. 128; p. 130

NEGRI, MARIO

Born 1906, Tirano. Studied in Milan. 1946 took up sculpture (self-taught). Lives in Milan.

Lit.: *Cesare Gnudi,* "Sculture di Mario Negri" in Il Milione 26 nuova serie, Milan, April 1957 P. 59

NELE, E. R.

Born 1932, Berlin. Trained as a goldsmith. Studied in London, Berlin (with H. Uhlmann) and Paris. 1958 scholarship from the Kulturkreis. Lives in Munich.

Lit.: *Galerie van de Loo.* Ausstellungskatalog mit Text der Künstlerin. München, Feb.–March 1960
Molton Gallery. Exhibition Catalogue, London, 1960

Fig. 174; p. 237

NEUSEL, GÜNTER

Born 1930, Kassel. Trained as stone mason. 1949–1950 studied in Düsseldorf (E. Mataré), then until 1953 in Berlin (P. Dierkes). 1953 worked with Mattern. 1955 scholarship from the Kulturkreis. Lives in Stuttgart. Fig. 173; p. 222

NEVELSON, LOUISE

Born 1900, Kiev, Russia. 1905 emigrated to USA. 1929–1930 studied in New York. 1931 with Hans Hofmann in Munich. Studied archaeology in Mexico and Central America. Lives in New York.

Lit.: *The Museum of Modern Art, New York.* Sixteen Americans, ed. by Dorothy C. Miller, New York, 1959
Hilton Kramer, "The Sculpture of Louise Nevelson" in Arts, June 1958 Fig. 176; p. 222 f.

NIVOLA, COSTANTINO

Born 1911, Orani, Sardinia. Studied in Italy with Marino Marini. Since 1939 in USA. Teaches at the Graduate School of Design, Harvard University. Lives in East Hampton, Long Island, New York.

Lit.: *Giedion-Welcker*
Eduard Trier, "Angewandte Plastik. Zu den Arbeiten von Harry Bertoia und Costantino Nivola" in form i, 1957 Fig. 203; p. 265

NOGUCHI, ISAMU

Born 1904, Los Angeles, California, of Japanese father and American mother. Grew up in Japan. 1918 in USA. 1924 trained as sculptor in New York. 1927–1929 Brancusi's assistant in Paris. 1929 returned to USA. then, until 1931, in China and Japan. 1949–1950 the Mediterranean and the Far East. Now living in Paris.

Lit.: *The Museum of Modern Art, New York.* Fourteen Americans, ed. by Dorothy C. Miller, New York, 1946
Noguchi. Text by Shuzo Takiguchi, Saburo Hasegawa, Isamu Noguchi. Tokio, Bijutsu Shuppan-Sha, 1953

Figs. 63, 172, 189; pp. 87, 222, 253, 266

PAN, MARTA

Born 1923, Budapest. Studied in Budapest. 1947 emigrated to Paris. 1952 French subject. Lives in Paris.

Lit.: *Michel Ragon,* "Marta Pan" in Quadrum ii, Nov. 1956
Seuphor

Fig. 140; p. 160

PAOLOZZI, EDUARDO

Born 1924, Edinburgh, of Italian parents. Studied in London. 1947–1950 in Paris. Has been living in London since 1955.

Lit.: *J. P. Hodin,* "Eduardo Paolozzi" in Quadrum i, May 1956
The Hanover Gallery. Exhibition Catalogue. London, Nov.–Dec. 1958
Peter Selz, New Images of Man. The Museum of Modern Art, New York, 1959
Robert Melville, "Eduardo Paolozzi" in L'Oeil 65, May 1960

Fig. 97; p. 116

PENALBA, ALICIA

Born 1918, Buenos Aires. 1948 moved to Paris where she took up sculpture and studied under Zadkine. Lives in Montrouge, Seine.

Lit.: *Patrick Waldberg,* Penalba. Paris, Galerie Éditions, 1957
Luce Hoctin, "Trois jeunes sculpteurs: Penalba, Müller, Haber" in L'Oeil 63, March 1960 Fig. 113; p. 128

PEVSNER, ANTOINE

Born 1886, Orel, Russia. 1902–1909 studied painting at the Kiev Academy. From 1909, at the Academy in St. Petersburg. 1911 and 1913–1914 in Paris. 1914–1917 in Norway, then, till 1921, in Russia. 1920 published with his brother, Naum Gabo, the Realist Manifesto in Moscow. 1922 in Berlin. Has been living in Paris since 1923.

Lit.: *Ruth Olsen and Abraham Chanin,* Gabo–Pevsner. Introduction by Herbert Read. New York, The Museum of Modern Art, 1948
Réne Massat, "Antoine Pevsner" in Cahiers d'art ii, 1950
Antoine Pevsner, "Propos d'un sculpteur" interview with Rosamonde Bernier in L'Oeil 23, Nov. 1956
René Massat, Antoine Pevsner et le constructivisme. Paris, Éditions Caractères, 1956
Musée national d'art moderne. Catalogue de l'exposition Antoine Pevsner. Paris, Éditions des Musées nationaux, 1956–1957

Figs. 16, 88, 160, 211; pp. 26 f., 115, 181, 187 f., 243, 275

PICASSO, PABLO

Born 1881, Malaga, Spain. Educated in Barcelona. 1901 first stay in Paris. 1904 moved to Paris. 1906 met Matisse and Derain. 1907 met Braque. 1909 in Horta de Ebro. 1910 in Cadaquès. 1911 and 1913 in Céret. 1917 in Rome. 1919 in London and St. Raphael. 1928 in Dinard. 1934 in Spain. 1940–1945 in Antibes and Royan. 1945 returned to Paris. Has been living since 1947 in the South of France. 1899–1914 first sculptural works. From 1929, again interested in sculpture which has since been the constant companion of his painting.

Lit.: *Daniel Henry Kahnweiler*, The Sculptures of Picasso. London, Rodney Phillips, 1949
Giulio Carlo Argan, Scultura di Picasso. Venezia, Alfieri 1953
Wilhelm Boeck, Pablo Picasso. Stuttgart, Kohlhammer, 1955
Anton Henze, "Neue Plastiken von Picasso" in Das Kunstwerk 9/XIII, March 1960
Figs. 84, 87; pp. 16, 110 f., 127, 230

(Permission to reprint given by SPADEM, Paris and Cosmopress, Geneva.)

POMODORO, ARNALDO

Born 1926, Orciano di Romagna, Italy. Studied architecture. Lives in Milan.

Lit.: *Gillo Dorfles*. "A. e G. Pomodoro" in La Biennale 34. Venice, Jan.–March 1959
Fig. 177; p. 237

POMODORO, GIO

Born 1930, Orciano di Pesaro, Italy. Studied architecture. Lives in Milan.

Lit.: *Gillo Dorfles*. "A. e G. Pomodoro" in La Biennale 34. Venice, Jan.–March 1959
Fig. 130; p. 159

RAMOUS, CARLO

Born 1926, Milan. Studied at the Liceo artistico in Bologna and at the Accademia di Brera in Milan (with Marino Marini). Lives in Milan.

Lit.: *Mario Valsecchi*, Carlo Ramous. Bologna, Cappelli, 1960
Fig. 66; p. 87

RICHIER, GERMAINE

Born 1904, Grasse (Alpes-Maritimes). 1925–1929 worked with A. Bourdelle. 1939–1949 in Switzerland, then again in Paris. 1959 died in Montpellier.

Lit.: *Jean Grenier*, "Germaine Richier, sculpteur du terrible" in L'Oeil 9, Sept. 1955
The Museum of Modern Art, New York. The New Decade, ed. by Andrew C. Ritchie. New York 1955
Musée national d'art moderne. Catalogue de l'exposition Germaine Richier. Avant-propos de Jean Cassou. Paris, Éditions des Musées nationaux, 1956
Peter Selz, New Images of Man. New York, The Museum of Modern Art, 1959
Figs. 69, 120; pp. 87, 88 f.

RIS, GÜNTER-FERDINAND

Born 1928, Manfort. Studied painting in Karlsruhe, Düsseldorf and Freiburg. 1957 scholarship from the Kulturkreis. Practises painting, sculpture, typography and architecture. Composes steel reliefs from pre-formed sections. Lives in Schlebusch.

Lit.: *Museum der Stadt Leverkusen*. Faltblatt zur Ausstellung mit Einleitung von Curt Schweicher. June–July 1955
Museum der Stadt Leverkusen. Ausstellungskatalog: Denise René expose. Einführung von Michel Seuphor. March–May 1959
Galerie Denise René, Paris. Jeune art constructif allemand. 1958
II. documenta (Grafik)
Carl Linfert, "Günter-Ferdinand Ris" in Junge Künstler 61/62. Hrsg. vom Kulturkreis im Bundesverband der Deutschen Industrie. Cologne, DuMont Schauberg, 1961
Fig. 191; p. 254

RIVERA, MANUEL

Born 1927, Granada. Studied at Seville. Since 1951 has been living in Madrid.

Lit.: *C. L. Popovici*, Las pinturas metalicas de Rivera. Madrid, Colleccion del art de hoy, 1958
Fig. 26; p. 46

RODIN, AUGUSTE

Born 1840, Paris. 1854 at the École des arts décoratifs. Pupil of Barye and Carrier-Belleuse. 1870–1877 in Brussels, where he met C. Meunier. Travelled in Italy and Germany. 1877 first important work, The Bronze Age. 1889 joint exhibition with Monet. 1900 special pavilion for his sculpture at the Paris World Exhibition. 1894 settled in Meudon; died there in 1917.

Lit.: *Franz Roh*, Rodin. Bern, Scherz, 1949
Rodin. Met inleiding van Sommerville Story, Utrecht, W. de Haan, 1951
Pp. 188, 229, 230

ROEDER, EMY

Born 1890, Würzburg. 1912–1914 pupil of B. Hoetger in Darmstadt. 1915–1930 in Berlin. 1933–1935 in Rome, then, till 1944, in Florence. 1937 forbidden to exhibit and proscribed. 1945–1949 in Rome. 1950 returned to Germany to teach in Mainz. Lives in Mainz.

Lit.: *Alfred Kuhn*, Emy Roeder. Leipzig, Klinkhardt & Biermann, 1921 (Junge Kunst, Bd. 18)
H. Siebenhüner, Emy Roeder: Bildwerke und Zeichnungen aus den Jahren 1919–1949. Bonn, 1950
Fig. 90; p. 115

ROSENTHAL, BERNARD

Born 1914, Highland Park, Illinois. Studied at the University of Michigan. Lives in Malibu, California.

Lit.: *Catherine Viviano, New York*. Exhibition Catalogue with foreword by Frederick S. Wight. Jan.–Feb. 1958
Catherine Viviano, New York. Exhibition Catalogue, Feb. 1960
Fig. 175; p. 237

ROSSO, MEDARDO

Born 1858, Turin. First active as painter. 1881–1883 at the Accademia di Brera in Milan. 1884–1885 in Paris, met A. Rodin; took up Impressionist sculpture. From 1889 lived mainly in Paris. 1928 died in Milan.

Lit.: *Giovanni Papini*, Medardo Rosso. Milan, Hoepli, 1945
Fig. 86; p. 110

ROSZAK, THEODORE

Born 1907, Poznan, Poland. 1909 moved to Chicago, USA. 1922 to 1928 studied in Chicago and New York. 1929–1930 in Europe. Began painting. 1931 took up sculpture in New York. 1940–1945 worked in aircraft industry. 1945 first steel sculptures. Lives in New York.

Lit.: *H. H. Arnason*, Theodor Roszak. Minneapolis, The Walker Art Center, 1956
Theodore Roszak, "The pursuit of an image" in Quadrum ii, Nov. 1956
Peter Selz, New Images of Man. New York, The Museum of Modern Art, 1959
Figs. 116, 202; pp. 129, 263

RUNYON, CORNELIA

Born 1887, USA. 1910 studied at the Art Students League, New York. Has been living since 1940 in Malibu, California.

Lit.: *Pasadena Art Museum.* Exhibition Catalogue with texts by Jules Langsner, Pegot Waring and Rico Lebrun. Pasadena, March–April 1956

Fig. 91; p. 115

SAARINEN, EERO

Born 1910, Helsinki. Architect. Lives in Bloomfield Hills, Michigan, USA.

Fig. 188; pp. 244 f., 263, 275

SCHARFF, EDWIN

Born 1887, Neu-Ulm. 1904–1907 studied painting in Munich. 1911–1913 in France. 1922–1932 in Berlin. 1932–1934 in Düsseldorf. Taught in Hamburg from 1946 and died there in 1955.

Lit.: *Gottfried Sello,* Edwin Scharff. Hamburg, 1956

P. 59

SCHNABEL, DAY

Born 1905, Vienna. Studied in Vienna and Holland. Emigrated to the USA. during the Second World War. 1947 moved to France. Lives in New York and Paris.

Lit.: *Giedion-Welcker; Seuphor*

Fig. 138; p. 160

SCHOEFFER, NICOLAS

Born 1912, Kalocsa, Hungary. Studied in Budapest. 1937 moved to Paris. 1950 turned to abstract sculpture. Lives in Paris.

Lit.: *II. documenta; Seuphor*

Fig. 15; p. 35

SCHWITTERS, KURT

Born 1897, Hanover. 1908–1914 studied in Hanover, Dresden and Berlin. 1915 settled in Hanover. 1918 first abstract compositions and beginning of MERZ-art. 1920 MERZ-Bau. From 1934 onwards, prolonged stays in Norway. 1937 settled down in Lysaker near Oslo. 1940 fled to England. 1941 after internment, settled in London. 1945 moved to Little Langdale, near Ambleside, Westmorland; died there in 1948.

Lit.: *Kestner-Gesellschaft, Hannover.* Katalog Kurt Schwitters. Einführung von Werner Schmalenbach. Feb.–March 1956

Fig. 200; p. 263

SEITZ, GUSTAV

Born 1906, Mannheim-Neckarau. 1924–1925 studied in Karlsruhe. 1925–1932 in Berlin. 1933–1938 ran a *Meisteratelier* at the Preussische Akademie der Künste. 1946–1958 taught in Berlin. Lives and teaches in Hamburg.

Lit.: *Galerie Rudolf Hoffmann, Hamburg.* Ausstellungskatalog Gustav Seitz. Einführung von Alfred Hentzen. Dec. 1957–Jan. 1958

Fig. 41; p. 59

SIGNORI, SERGIO

Born 1906, Milan. Has been living in Paris since 1924.

Lit.: *The Hanover Gallery.* Exhibition Catalogue. London, April–May 1959

Fig. 92; p. 115

SMITH, DAVID

Born 1906, Decatur, Indiana, USA. Educated in Ohio and New York. Employed for a time as metal worker. 1933 first steel sculpture. Has been living since 1941 in Bolton Landing, N. Y.

Lit.: *The Museum of Modern Art, New York.* David Smith Exhibition Catalogue. Introduction by Sam Hunter, 1957
Arts. Special number on David Smith. February 1960

Fig. 154; p. 182

SOMAINI, FRANCESCO

Born 1926, Comazzo, Como. Studied at the Accademia di Brera, Milan. 1948–1949 turned to abstract sculpture. Lives in Comazzo.

Lit.: *Galleria Odyssia, Rome.* Catalogo con testi di Enrico Crispoli e Michel Tapié, 1959

Fig. 115; p. 129

STADLER, TONI

Born 1888, Munich. 1925–1927 in Paris. 1928–1938 in Munich. 1939–1945 in Frankfurt-on-Main. Since 1946 has been living and teaching in Munich.

Lit.: *II. documenta*
Werner Haftmann, "Der Bildhauer Toni Stadler". Munich, Piper Bücherei, 1961

Fig. 40; pp. 59, 127

STAHLY, FRANÇOIS

Born 1911 in Constance. Grew up in Switzerland. 1931 began studies in Paris. 1939 French Subject. Lives in Meudon-Bellevue (Seine-et-Oise).

Lit.: François Stahly. Présenté par *Jean Arp* et *Henri-Pierre Rocher.* Paris, Collection Art naissant, Facchetti, 1953

Fig. 129; p. 159

STEINBRENNER, HANS

Born 1928, Frankfurt-on-Main. 1946–1954 studied in Offenbach, Frankfurt (H. Mettel), and Munich (T. Stadler). 1954 scholarship from the Kulturkreis. Lives in Frankfurt.

Lit.: *Kuratorium Kulturelles Frankfurt.* K-Hefte. Nov. 1959

Fig. 64; p. 87

STEINER, RUDOLF

Born 1861, Kraljevic, Croatia. Studied at the Technische Hochschule in Vienna. 1889–1896 worked on the Weimar edition of Goethe. 1898–1900 taught at the Arbeiter-Bildungsschule in Berlin. Founder of anthroposophy. 1913 erection of the first Goetheanum in Dornach as a *Hochschule der Geisteswissenschaften.* 1922 Goetheanum burnt down. 1925 rebuilding began from designs by Steiner. 1925 died in Dornach.

Lit.: *Rudolf Steiner,* Wege zu einem neuen Baustil, 1914
Ibid, Mein Lebensgang, 1924

Fig. 186; p. 244

TÄUBER-ARP, SOPHIE

Born 1889, Davos, Switzerland. 1908–1913 studied in St. Gallen, Munich and Hamburg. 1916–1926 taught at the Kunstgewerbeschule in Zürich. 1916–1920 Dada period in Zürich. 1921 married Hans Arp. 1928–1940 in Meudon near Paris. 1941–1943 in Grasse. 1943 died in Zürich.

Lit.: *Sophie Täuber-Arp.* Hrsg. von Georg Schmidt. Basle, Holbein, 1948

Fig. 28; p. 46

TAJIRI, SHINKICHI

Born 1923 in Los Angeles, California. Studied in Chicago and Paris. Lives in Amsterdam.

Lit.: *II. documenta; Seuphor*

Fig. 119; p. 129

TAKIS

Born 1925, Athens. Self-taught. 1954 moved to Paris. After a period of archaising figure sculpture, turned to iron mobiles. 1959 telemagnetic composition at Iris Clert's.

Lit.: *The Hanover Gallery*. Exhibition Catalogue, London (n. d.)

Fig. 23; p. 36

TINGUELY, JEAN

Born 1925, Basle. First active as a painter. 1950 took up sculpture. Interested primarily in compositions involving movement generated by motor devices.

Lit.: *Seuphor* Fig. 22; pp. 36, 264

TRŠAR, DRAGO

Born 1927, Planina, Yugoslavia. Lives in Ljublana.

Lit.: *II. documenta* Fig. 77; p. 109

UBAC, RAOUL

Born 1910, Malmédy. From 1929 in Paris. 1942 took up painting and slate reliefs.

Lit.: *Galerie Maeght, Paris.* Derrière le miroir 34 (1950), 74/76 (1955), 105/106 (1958)
Georges Limbour, "Raoul Ubac" in L'Oeil 29, May 1957
Galerie Parnass, Wuppertal. Ausstellungskatalog mit Einführung von Karlheinz Görres. Oct.–Nov. 1959 Fig. 169; p. 222

UHLMANN, HANS

Born 1900, Berlin. Began as engineer. 1925 turned to sculpture. Numerous commissions for modern buildings. Lives in Berlin.

Lit.: *The Museum of Modern Art, New York.* The New Decade, ed. by Andrew C. Ritchie, 1955
Galerie Der Spiegel. Geh durch den Spiegel Nr. 6. Texte von Will Grohmann und E. W. Nay. Cologne, July–August 1956
Kunst und Museumsverein Wuppertal. Katalog Plastik und Zeichnungen der Jahre 1935–1960. Einleitung von Harald Seiler, 1960 Figs. 161, 194; pp. 188, 254

VANTONGERLOO, GEORGES

Born 1886, Antwerp. Studied at the Brussels and Antwerp Academies. Took part in the Stijl movement and the group Abstraction-Création. Lives in Paris.

Lit.: *Georges Vantongerloo*, Paintings, Sculptures, Reflections. New York, Wittenborn, Schultz, 1948 Fig. 18; p. 35

VERHULST, HANS

Born 1921, Steenbergen, Noord Brabant, Netherlands. Studied in Antwerp and Brussels. Lives in Amsterdam.

Lit.: *Stedelijk Museum, Amsterdam.* Catalogus der tentoonstelling Beelden in het Heden. Inleiding van H. L. C. Jaffé. Dec. 1959–Feb. 1960 Fig. 168; p. 222

VIANI, ALBERTO

Born 1906, Quistello, Prov. Mantua. Studied in Venice. Worked as assistant with Arturo Marini. 1948 teaching post at the Liceo Artistico in Venice. Lives in Venice.

Lit.: *Umbro Apollonio*, "Lavoro di Viani" in La Biennale 31. Venice, April–June 1958 P. 87

VIEIRA, MARY

Born 1927, Sao Paolo, Brazil. 1952 in Zürich, pupil of Max Bill. Lives in Basle.

Lit.: *Módulo No. 16.* Esculturas de Mary Vieira. Rio de Janeiro, Dec. 1959 Fig. 163; pp. 188, 221

VISEUX, CLAUDE

Born 1927, Champagne-sur-Oise. 1944 first compositions. 1950 turned non-figurative. Both paints and carves. Lives in Paris.

Fig. 85; pp. 45, 110

VOLTEN, ANDRÉ

Born 1920, Andijk, Holland. Self-taught. Lives in Amsterdam.

Lit.: *A. M. Hammacher*, "André Volten" in Quadrum i, May 1956

Fig. 157; p. 187

VOULKOS, PETER H.

Born 1924, Bozeman, Montana, USA. Of Greek extraction. Trained as a pottery thrower. 1946–1952 studied in Montana and California. Has been teaching since 1954 at the Los Angeles County Art Institute, Ceramics Department. Lives in Los Angeles. Fig. 136; p. 160

WERTHMANN, FRIEDERICH

Born 1927, Wuppertal. Self-taught. 1948 took up sculpture. 1959 awarded the Deutscher Kunstpreis der Jugend. Lives in Düsseldorf-Kaiserswerth.

Lit.: *Galerie 22*, Düsseldorf. Ausstellungskatalog mit Einführung von René Deroudille, March 1960 Fig. 144; p. 162

WOLFF, HELMUT

Born 1932, Laubenheim near Mainz. 1951–1957 studied in Berlin with H. Uhlmann. 1959 scholarship from the Kulturkreis; at the Villa Massimo in Rome. Lives in Berlin.

Lit.: *Bauwelt 25.* Berlin, June 1958 Fig. 184; p. 243

WOTRUBA, FRITZ

Born 1907, Vienna. 1925–1927 studied in Vienna with Hanak. 1928 first stone composition. 1938–1945 in Switzerland. Since 1945 has been living in Vienna and teaching in the sculpture department of the Academy.

Lit.: *Elias Canetti*, Fritz Wotruba. Wien, Rosenbaum, 1955
Peter Selz, New Images of Man. New York, The Museum of Modern Art, 1959 Figs. 43, 204; pp. 60, 265

ZADKINE, OSSIP

Born 1890, Smolensk. 1906 at school in England. 1909 moved to Paris. 1911 set up as independent sculptor. 1940–1945 in the USA. 1945 returned to France. 1950 awarded the Grand Prix at the Venice Biennale. Lives in Paris.

Lit.: *Raymond Cogniat*, Zadkine. Paris, Éditions Hautefeuille, 1958
Kölnischer Kunstverein. Ausstellungskatalog: Ossip Zadkine, Plastiken, 1910–1959. Vorwort von Jean Cassou. Cologne, March–May 1960 Figs. 57, 179; pp. 75, 230